Current Law

YEAR BOOK
2000

VOLUME ONE

Maxwell
A THOMSON COMPANY

AUSTRALIA
LBC Information Services
Sydney

CANADA & USA
Carswell
Toronto

NEW ZEALAND
Brooker's
Auckland

SINGAPORE and MALAYSIA
Sweet & Maxwell Asia
Singapore and Kuala Lumpur

Current Law

YEAR BOOK 2000

Being a Comprehensive Statement of the Law of 2000

The Mode of Citation
of the Current Law Year Book is
[2000] C.L.Y. 1282
The 2000 Year Book is published in two volumes.

Published in 2001 by
Sweet & Maxwell Limited of
100 Avenue Road, Swiss Cottage, London NW3 3PF
Typeset by Sweet & Maxwell Limited,
Mytholmroyd, Hebden Bridge
Printed by The Bath Press, Bath, Avon.

A CIP catalogue record for this book is available
from the British Library

ISBN: 2000 Yearbook: 0-421-75190-8
2000 Yearbook with Case and Legislation Citators: 0-421-82690-8

No forests were destroyed to make this product;
farmed timber was used and then replanted.

ISBN 0-421-75190-8
9 780421 751903

PREFACE

The 2000 Current Law Year Book supersedes the issues of *Current Law Monthly Digest* for 2000 and covers the law from January 1 to December 31 of that year.

Jurisdiction

The text of the 2000 Current Law Year Book is divided into three sections respectively: UK, England and Wales and EU, Northern Ireland and Scotland. The European material comprises: cases appearing before the Court of First Instance and European Court of Justice which are published in the reports series and newspapers, and a selection of books.

Cases

The 2000 Current Law Year Book includes digests of 3,811 cases published in over 90 reports series, journals, *The Times* and *Independent* newspapers, transcripts and ex relatione contributions from barristers and solicitors. A number of reports edited by David Kemp Q.C. concerning damages awards in personal injury cases in England and Wales appears under the subject heading DAMAGES and is collated in tabular form together with Scottish personal injuries cases at the beginning of Vol. 1.

An alphabetical Table of Cases digested in the 2000 Year Book appears at the beginning of Volume 1. The Current Law Case Citator 2000 appears as a separate bound volume and forms part of the permanent bound volume series for the years 1947-76, 1977-1997, with separate volumes for 1998 and 1999 and for Scotland for the years 1948-76.

The editor thanks those barristers and solicitors who have submitted case reports, many of which demonstrate developments in county court litigation. Whilst all reasonable care is taken in the preparation of the digests it is not possible to guarantee the accuracy of each digest, particularly those cases ex relatione which are not taken from an authorised judgment.

Legislation

All public and private Acts of Parliament published in 2000 are abstracted and indexed. All Statutory Instruments, Scottish Statutory Instruments and Statutory Rules of Northern Ireland are abstracted. Cumulative tables of Statutory Instruments, arranged alphabetically, numerically and by subject are published in Vol. 1. Cumulative tables of Statutory Rules of Northern Ireland arranged alphabetically, numerically and by subject are also published in Vol. 1.

The Current Law Legislation Citators for 2000 appear as a separate bound volume and form part of the series of permanent bound volumes for the years 1989-1995 and 1996-1999.

Books

The full title, reference and author of books of interest to the legal profession published in 1999/2000 are arranged by subject heading. A separate list, arranged by author is included in Volume 2.

Index

The subject-matter index is closely associated with a Legal Thesaurus published by Sweet & Maxwell. The 30-year Index from 1947-76 may be found in the 1976 *Current Law Year Book*. The Scottish Index for the years 1972-86 may be found in the Scottish 1986 *Year Book*. Scottish material prior to 1972 can be found in the *Scottish Current Law Year Book Master Volumes*, published in 1956, 1961, 1966 and 1971.

July 2001

CONTENTS

VOLUME 1

THE LAW OF 2000 DIGESTED UNDER TITLES:
Note: Italicised entries refer to Scotland only.

CONTENTS

DIGEST HEADINGS IN USE

Accountancy
Administration of Justice
Administrative Law
Agency
Agriculture
Animals
Arbitration
Armed Forces
Banking
Charities
Civil Evidence
Civil Procedure
Commercial Law
Company Law
Competition Law
Conflict of Laws
Constitutional Law
Construction Law
Consumer Law
Contracts
Criminal Evidence
Criminal Law
Criminal Procedure
Criminal Sentencing
Culture
Damages
Defamation
Dispute Resolution
Ecclesiastical Law
Economics
Education
Electoral Process
Electricity Industry
Employment
Environment
Environmental Health
Equity
European Union
Extradition
Family Law
Finance
Financial Services
Fisheries
Food
Forestry
Government Administration
Health and Safety at Work
Health
Heritable Property and Conveyancing (Scotland)
Highway Control
Housing

Human Rights
Immigration
Industry
Information Technology
Insolvency
Insurance
Intellectual Property
International Law
International Trade
Jurisprudence
Landlord and Tenant
Legal Aid
Legal Methodology
Legal Profession
Legal Systems
Leisure Industry
Libraries
Licensing
Local Government
Media
Mental Health
Mining
Negligence
Nuisance
Oil and Gas Industry
Partnerships
Penology
Pensions
Personal Property
Planning
Police
Postal Services
Prescription (Scotland)
Rates
Real Property
Reparation (Scotland)
Rights In Security (Scotland)
Sale of Goods
Shipping
Social Security
Social Welfare
Succession
Taxation
Telecommunications
Torts
Transport
Trusts
Utilities
VAT
Water Industry

TABLE OF CASES

TABLE OF CASES

TABLE OF CASES

QUANTUM OF DAMAGES
PERSONAL INJURIES OR DEATH

The table below is a cumulative guide to quantum of damages cases reported in Current Law in 2000. (FIA = Fatal injuries awards).

Injury	Age (at time of injury unless otherwise stated)	Case	Award		Reference
			General £	Loss of Earnings Capacity, Family Care £	
Paraplegia	23	Thornton v. Kingston Upon Hull City Council	135,000	132,372	C.L.Y. 1494
Multiple injuries	32	Jones (CICA: Quantum: 2000: Multiple Injuries), Re	50,000		C.L.Y. 1495
	61	L (CICB: Quantum: 2000), Re	22,500		C.L.Y. 1496
	21	Ata v. Hellen	8,500		C.L.Y. 1497
Multiple injuries; psychiatric damage	18	Small v. Somerville Roberts	40,000		C.L.Y. 1498
Multiple injuries; leg	12	H (A Child) v. Reed	6,500		C.L.Y. 1499
Multiple injuries; foot	17	Chambers v. Flynn	26,250		C.L.Y. 1500
	63	Patterson v. Bunclark	25,000		C.L.Y. 1501
Very severe brain damage	Birth	O (A Minor) v. King's Healthcare NHS Trust	425,000		C.L.Y. 1506
	Birth	L (A Child) v. Berkshire HA	145,000	380,000	C.L.Y. 1502
	14	Dashiell v. Luttit	130,000		C.L.Y. 1505
	Birth	S (A Minor) v. Portsmouth and South East Hampshire HA	125,500		C.L.Y. 1503
	Birth	P (A Child) v. Hammersmith and Queen Charlotte's Special HA	120,000		C.L.Y. 1504
Very severe brain damage; epilepsy	Birth	H (A Child) v. Hillingdon HA	132,000		C.L.Y. 1507
Severe brain damage	8	T (A Child) v. Page	100,000		C.L.Y. 1508
	24	Jones (CICA: Quantum: 2000: Head Injuries), Re	100,000		C.L.Y. 1509
Severe brain damage; epilepsy	39	C (A Patient: Head Injuries) v. Ewin	85,000		C.L.Y. 1510
Severe brain damage; sight	25	Smith (CICB: Quantum: 2000), Re	145,000		C.L.Y. 1511
Less severe brain damage; multiple injuries	86	Stennett v. Hook	27,500		C.L.Y. 1518
Moderate brain damage	22	Rushton v. Jervis	80,000		C.L.Y. 1512
	56	Gasson v. OCS Group Ltd	80,000		C.L.Y. 1513
	Birth	K (A Child) v. Portsmouth and South East Hampshire HA	80,000		C.L.Y. 1514

Injury	Age (at time of injury unless otherwise stated)	Case	Award		Reference
			General £	Loss of Earnings Capacity, Family Care £	
Moderate brain damage -cont.	44	S v. Methodist Homes For The Aged	60,000		C.L.Y. 1515
	65	K v. Hickman	60,000		C.L.Y. 1516
	5	S (A Child) v. Forrester	40,000		C.L.Y. 1517
Psychiatric damage	27	B (CICB: Quantum: 2000), Re	45,000		C.L.Y. 1519
	10	C (A Patient: Dependency) v. Ewin	11,000		C.L.Y. 1520
	47	Crolla (CICB: Quantum: 1999), Re	7,500		C.L.Y. 1521
Psychiatric damage; whiplash type injury	18	Walker v. Miricki	3,115		C.L.Y. 1522
Psychiatric damage after sexual abuse	12 to 18	W (CICB: Quantum: 1999), Re	20,000		C.L.Y. 1523
	9 to 13	F (CICB: Quantum: 2000), Re	17,500		C.L.Y. 1524
	11 to 14	A (CICA: Quantum: 2000), Re	15,000		C.L.Y. 1525
	23	L (CICB: Quantum: 1999), Re	7,500		C.L.Y. 1527
	12	S (CICB: Quantum: 1999) (Sexual Abuse), Re	7,300		C.L.Y. 1528
	7 to 12	N (CICB: Quantum: 2000), Re	6,400		C.L.Y. 1526
Post traumatic stress disorder	43	H (CICB: Quantum: 2000), Re	50,000		C.L.Y. 1529
	25	Long (CICB: Quantum: 1999), Re	25,000		C.L.Y. 1530
	21 months	M (A Child) (CICB: Quantum: 1999), Re	15,000		C.L.Y. 1531
Post traumatic stress disorder; psychiatric damage	43	B (Francis) (CICA: Quantum: 2000), Re	145,000		C.L.Y. 1533
	16	DB and YB (Children) (CICA: Quantum: 2000), Re	20,000		C.L.Y. 1532
	14	DB and YB (Children) (CICA: Quantum: 2000), Re	17,500		C.L.Y. 1532
Post traumatic stress disorder; nose	32	S (CICB: Quantum: 2000), Re	16,500		C.L.Y. 1534
Head	5	W (A Child) v. Kerry	4,500		C.L.Y. 1535
Head; multiple injuries	39	Perkins (CICB: Quantum: 1999), Re	50,000		C.L.Y. 1536
Head; psychiatric damage	27	Hulme (CICB: Quantum: 2000), Re	40,000		C.L.Y. 1537
Head; neck	35	Dowle v. Graham	8,500		C.L.Y. 1538
Cheekbone; psychiatric damage	41	Calvert (CICB: Quantum: 2000), Re	37,500		C.L.Y. 1539

Injury	Age (at time of injury unless otherwise stated)	Case	Award		Reference
			General £	Loss of Earnings Capacity, Family Care £	
Cheekbone; teeth	23	Jackson (CICB: Quantum: 1999), Re	3,500		C.L.Y. 1540
Teeth	12	F (A Child) v. Bedford BC	4,000		C.L.Y. 1541
	8	G (A Child) v. Grindal	3,000		C.L.Y. 1542
	30	Finnegan v. Wiltshire	3,000		C.L.Y. 1543
Facial scars	29	Martin (CICB: Quantum: 2000), Re	11,000		C.L.Y. 1544
	4	C (A Child) v. Taylor	7,000		C.L.Y. 1545
	29	Hussain v. Nawaz	5,850		C.L.Y. 1546
	4	B (A Child) v. Littlewoods Plc	4,750		C.L.Y. 1547
	27	King v. Britannia Hotels Ltd	4,500		C.L.Y. 1548
Facial scars; psychiatric damage	30	Carrington (CICB: Quantum: 2000), Re	23,500		C.L.Y. 1549
	20	Penfold v. Da Silva	22,500		C.L.Y. 1550
	8	S (A Child) v. Bloomfield	6,750		C.L.Y. 1551
Ear	11	W (A Child) v. Classic Cuts	4,850		C.L.Y. 1552
Ear; facial scars	27	Holloway (CICB: Quantum: 2000), Re	22,500		C.L.Y. 1553
Sight	16	Avgerinos (CICB: Quantum: 1999), Re	27,500		C.L.Y. 1554
Hearing and speech		Neil v. UEC Industries	7,000		C.L.Y. 1555
	Birth	M (A Child) v. North & Mid Hamptonshire HA	50,000		C.L.Y. 1556
Neck	47	Mamczynski v. GM Buses (North) Ltd	3,000		C.L.Y. 1557
Neck; pre-existing disability or condition: aggravated by whiplash	41	Wesley v. Cobb (Deceased)	8,500		C.L.Y. 1558
	30	Calford v. Campbell	8,000		C.L.Y. 1559
	57	Diamond v. Wylie	7,000		C.L.Y. 1560
Neck; back	24	Gimblett v. Swansea City Council	6,750		C.L.Y. 1561
Neck; whiplash type injury	15	C (A Child) v. Kitchen	16,500		C.L.Y. 1562
	45	Giles v. Goss	13,500 (7,500 for whiplash)		C.L.Y. 1563
	22	Stevens v. London & County Ltd	12,750 (12,000 for whiplash)		C.L.Y. 1564
	48	Corner v. Osment	11,250 (7,250 for neck)		C.L.Y. 1565
	57	Parslow v. British Waterways Board	7,500		C.L.Y. 1566
	24	Gudge v. Milroy	7,250		C.L.Y. 1567
	20	Fryers v. Hirst	7,000		C.L.Y. 1568
	54	Palfrey v. Stagecoach Ltd	6,750		C.L.Y. 1569
	41	Davies v. Hayter	6,500		C.L.Y. 1570

Injury	Age (at time of injury unless otherwise stated)	Case	Award		Reference
			General £	Loss of Earnings Capacity, Family Care £	
Neck; whiplash type injury -cont.	25	Leach v. Pro Delta Systems Ltd	6,000		C.L.Y. 1571
	34	Goudie v. Night Freight (East) Ltd	6,000		C.L.Y. 1572
	61	Dorsett v. Grant (Quantum)	6,000		C.L.Y. 1577
	41	Kempster v. Ashfield	5,500		C.L.Y. 1574
	42	Utley v. Parker	5,500		C.L.Y. 1573
	19	Fallon v. Bateman	5,000		C.L.Y. 1576
	33	Harvey v. Blount	5,000		C.L.Y. 1575
	65	Dorsett v. Grant (Quantum)	4,800		C.L.Y. 1577
	27	Harbige v. Earl	4,500		C.L.Y. 1578
	51	Newton v. Whittaker	2,750		C.L.Y. 1579
	54	Morley v. Sussex Coastline Buses Ltd	600		C.L.Y. 1580
Spine	38	Aoudia (CICB: Quantum: 2000), Re	50,000		C.L.Y. 1581
Spine; neck	27	O'Regan v. Bedford Hospital NHS Trust	17,500		C.L.Y. 1582
Spine below neck	33	Goodall (CICB: Quantum: 1999), Re	40,000		C.L.Y. 1583
	40	Bhavsar (CICB: Quantum: 2000), Re	37,500		C.L.Y. 1584
	33	Griffiths v. Richard Medlins Contracts	15,000		C.L.Y. 1585
	34	Chappell v. TDC Motor Factors	14,000		C.L.Y. 1586
Spine below neck; whiplash type injury	32	Oliver v. Burton	8,000	4,000	C.L.Y. 1587
	53	McPherson v. Shiasson	5,500		C.L.Y. 1588
Back	23	Stone v. Commissioner of Police of the Metropolis	25,000		C.L.Y. 1589
	29	McHugh v. Carlisle City Council	14,500		C.L.Y. 1590
	53	McKerchar v. Campbell	9,000		C.L.Y. 1591
	38	Lloyd-Davies v. Lyth	8,500		C.L.Y. 1592
	40	Coots v. Stead McAlpine & Co Ltd	7,500		C.L.Y. 1593
	50	Wells v. West Hertfordshire HA (Quantum)	5,000		C.L.Y. 1594
Back; pre-existing disability or condition: aggravated by whiplash	70	Brown v. Owen	6,750		C.L.Y. 1595
Back; whiplash type injury	27	Rushton v. Gee	10,000		C.L.Y. 1596
	19	Brook v. Falkner	7,000		C.L.Y. 1597
Back; excretory organs	41	Wale v. London Underground Ltd	15,500 (6,500 back; 9,000 bladder)		C.L.Y. 1598

Injury	Age (at time of injury unless otherwise stated)	Case	Award		Reference
			General £	Loss of Earnings Capacity, Family Care £	
Whiplash type injury; other conditions	19	Bickley v. Bradley	2,750		C.L.Y. 1599
Shoulder	60	Fletcher (CICB: Quantum: 2000), Re	12,500		C.L.Y. 1600
	31	M (CICB: Quantum: 2000), Re	8,500		C.L.Y. 1601
	52	Morrissey v. Home Office	6,000		C.L.Y. 1602
Shoulder; psychiatric damage	51	Hutchinson v. Cunningham	14,500		C.L.Y. 1603
Arm	27	Kirkpatrick v. Todd	21,000	15,000	C.L.Y. 1604
Work related upper limb disorders	41	Molvaer v. Whirly Bird Services Ltd	7,000		C.L.Y. 1605
	35	Williams v. Kaye Presteigne Ltd	3,500		C.L.Y. 1606
Elbow	45	Plume v. Mason Bros (Butchers) Ltd	10,000		C.L.Y. 1607
Wrist	63	Hobson v. NTL Teeside Ltd	7,500		C.L.Y. 1611
	27	Havill v. Wilson	6,750		C.L.Y. 1608
	36	Hammant v. Stockport MBC	5,250		C.L.Y. 1609
	35	Richards v. Hampshire CC	5,000		C.L.Y. 1610
Fingers	2	C (A Child) v. London Underground Ltd	28,000		C.L.Y. 1612
	59	Harding v. Basingstoke & Deane BC	4,500		C.L.Y. 1613
	6	W (A Minor) v. Gloucestershire CC	3,500		C.L.Y. 1614
Sacrum, pelvis and hips	34	Rattray v. Hinds	45,000		C.L.Y. 1615
Sacrum, pelvis and hips; respiratory organs and chest	58	Uter v. Williams	7,000		C.L.Y. 1616
Leg	14	B (A Minor) v. Pleasure & Leisure Corporation	5,250		C.L.Y. 1617
Leg; arm; non facial scars	10	H (A Child) v. Cooper	33,500		C.L.Y. 1618
Leg; non facial scars	10	E (A Child) v. Calderdale MBC	2,000		C.L.Y. 1619
Loss of leg below knee	17	McFarlane v. Clifford Smith & Buchanan	55,000		C.L.Y. 1620
Severe leg injuries	44	Schembri (CICB: Quantum: 1999), Re	75,000		C.L.Y. 1621
Severe leg injuries; psychiatric damage	32	Currie (CICB: Quantum: 1999), Re	37,500		C.L.Y. 1622
Less severe leg injuries	18	Davies v. Gravelle Plant Ltd	8,000		C.L.Y. 1623
Knee	38	Grace v. Stagecoach Ltd	33,000		C.L.Y. 1624
	14	L (A Child) v. Bacon	26,000		C.L.Y. 1625

Injury	Age (at time of injury unless otherwise stated)	Case	Award		Reference
			General £	Loss of Earnings Capacity, Family Care £	
Knee -cont.	39	Morton (CICA: Quantum: 2000), Re	8,500		C.L.Y. 1626
	22	Carnell v. A-B Aegon	8,000		C.L.Y. 1627
	52	Patterson v. Midland Bank Plc	2,250		C.L.Y. 1628
Knee; neck	59	Rees v. Palmer	22,000		C.L.Y. 1629
Knee; spine below neck	28	Harvey v. Beck & Pollitzer	11,750		C.L.Y. 1630
Knee; shoulder	63	Dingley v. Bromley LBC (Quantum)	7,250		C.L.Y. 1631
Ankle	67	McClean v. Boult	7,500		C.L.Y. 1634
	67	Davies v. Shropshire CC	6,000		C.L.Y. 1632
	38	Hanrahan v. Home Office	4,000		C.L.Y. 1633
Foot	34	Paton v. Fekade	22,500		C.L.Y. 1635
	29	George v. Ministry of Defence	16,000		C.L.Y. 1636
	31	Goodwin v. GKN Sheepbridge Stokes Ltd	4,300		C.L.Y. 1637
	69	Jones v. Management Trustees of Pontesbury Public Hall	4,000		C.L.Y. 1638
	26	Short v. Trustees of Yeovil Agricultural Society	4,000		C.L.Y. 1639
Facial and non facial scars	2	F (A Minor) v. Slater	9,000		C.L.Y. 1640
Burns	55	Mizon v. Comcon International Ltd	55,000		C.L.Y. 1641
	27	Lindsay v. Taylor	5,000		C.L.Y. 1642
Burns; psychiatric damage	32	Terry v. Sands Farm Country House Hotel	7,500		C.L.Y. 1643
Burns; post traumatic stress disorder	44	S (CICB: Quantum: 2000) (Burns), Re	86,250		C.L.Y. 1644
Skin conditions	21	Puttock v. Kodak Ltd	8,500	15,000	C.L.Y. 1645
Respiratory organs and chest	34	Drabble v. Demolition Services Ltd	7,250		C.L.Y. 1646
	33	McCarthy v. Davis	6,500		C.L.Y. 1647
Respiratory organs and chest; asthma	54	Brobbey v. North Manchester Healthcare NHS Trust (Quantum)	15,000		C.L.Y. 1648
	7	C (A Child) v. Great Universal Stores Plc	5,000		C.L.Y. 1649
Respiratory organs and chest; asbestos related injury and disease	56	Sandford v. British Railways Board	58,000		C.L.Y. 1650
	50	O'Loughlin v. Cape Distribution Ltd	46,719		C.L.Y. 1651
	16 to 26	Elderbrant v. Cape Darlington Ltd	20,000		C.L.Y. 1652
	66 at trial	Meachen v. Harwich Dock Co Ltd	10,000		C.L.Y. 1653

Injury	Age (at time of injury unless otherwise stated)	Case	Award		Reference
			General £	Loss of Earnings Capacity, Family Care £	
Excretory organs; psychiatric damage after sexual abuse	45	W (CICB: Quantum: 2000), Re	50,000		C.L.Y. 1654
Reproductive organs: male	12	H (A Child) v. Parsons	14,500		C.L.Y. 1655
Other conditions	36	R. v. Gardner	6,800		C.L.Y. 1656
Toxicosis; food poisoning	48	Middlege v. Thomson Holidays	2,000		C.L.Y. 1657
	23	Duffy v. First Choice Holidays & Flights Ltd	1,500		C.L.Y. 1658
	7 months	A (A Child) v. Milupa Ltd	1,300		C.L.Y. 1659
Minor injuries	60	Lord v. Taymix Transport Ltd	4,000		C.L.Y. 1660
	37	Morris v. Coal Product Holdings Ltd	3,300		C.L.Y. 1661
	34	Mirtha v. Seriwala	2,500		C.L.Y. 1662
	22	Summerfield v. Mr Goostry (A Firm)	2,500		C.L.Y. 1663
	49	Graham v. Morini	2,000		C.L.Y. 1664
	14	E (A Child) v. Anderson	2,000		C.L.Y. 1665
	41	Greig v. South Wales Fire Service	1,500		C.L.Y. 1666
	16	A (A Child) v. Westminster Society for People with Learning Disabilities	1,500		C.L.Y. 1667
	9	Z (A Child) v. Greater Manchester Police Authority	1,250		C.L.Y. 1668
	14	J (A Child) v. Jones	1,000		C.L.Y. 1669
	7	K (A Child) v. Tesco Stores Ltd	500		C.L.Y. 1670
Minor injuries; psychiatric damage	19	Gibbens v. Wood	5,250		C.L.Y. 1671
	22	Watkinson v. Chief Constable of Police for the West Midlands	3,000		C.L.Y. 1672
	6	L (A Child) v. Anderson	1,275		C.L.Y. 1673
Minor injuries; head	22	Kelly v. Hemming	5,000		C.L.Y. 1674
	7	M (A Minor) v. Debenhams Plc	4,000		C.L.Y. 1675
	31	Williams v. Caterpillar (Peterlee) Ltd	3,750		C.L.Y. 1676
	53	Perkins v. Wakelin	2,000		C.L.Y. 1677
	36	Farrelly v. Courtaulds Chemicals	1,250		C.L.Y. 1678
Minor injuries; cheekbone	43	Rall v. Wallage	2,850		C.L.Y. 1679
Minor injuries; sight	52	Morgan v. Ford Motor Co Ltd	1,850		C.L.Y. 1680
Minor injuries; neck	51	Shanahan v. Willmott	4,000		C.L.Y. 1681
	24	Downie v. Williams	3,750		C.L.Y. 1682

Injury	Age (at time of injury unless otherwise stated)	Case	Award		Reference
			General £	Loss of Earnings Capacity, Family Care £	
Minor injuries; spine below neck	60	Burgess v. Electricity Sports & Social Club	30,000		C.L.Y. 1683
Minor injuries; back	43	Bleakley v. Home Office	4,000		C.L.Y. 1684
Minor injuries; back	20	Pearce v. Humpit Removals Ltd	3,500		C.L.Y. 1685
	28	Chambers v. Cardiff Community Housing Association Ltd	3,000		C.L.Y. 1686
Minor injuries; whiplash type injury	24	Dimelow v. Gradwell	5,700		C.L.Y. 1687
	49	Standing v. Werrett	5,000		C.L.Y. 1688
	31	Standing v. Werrett	4,750		C.L.Y. 1688
	43	Twycross v. Hilton	4,750		C.L.Y. 1689
	50	Hinde v. Cocksedge	4,500		C.L.Y. 1698
	46	Hill v. Holmes	4,250		C.L.Y. 1690
	35	Screeton v. East Riding DC	4,000		C.L.Y. 1691
	25	Fitzpatrick v. Royal Taxis	3,750		C.L.Y. 1692
	41	Towler v. Ali	3,750		C.L.Y. 1693
	29	Evans v. Lewis	3,300		C.L.Y. 1695
	27	Walton v. Magna Carta Polo	3,300		C.L.Y. 1694
	19	Appleton v. JB Taxis	3,200		C.L.Y. 1696
	54	Hinde v. Cocksedge	3,000		C.L.Y. 1698
	22	Shaw v. Divers	3,000		C.L.Y. 1697
	20	Singh v. M&N Contractors Ltd	2,900		C.L.Y. 1699
	19	Vanneck v. Sluggett	2,800		C.L.Y. 1700
	28	Gaddie v. Mitie Group Plc	2,750		C.L.Y. 1701
	27	Faulkner v. Shamji	2,500		C.L.Y. 1703
	36	Pawson v. Neil	2,500		C.L.Y. 1702
	12	M (A Child) v. Bukhari	2,500		C.L.Y. 1704
	34	Bunyan v. Vassor	2,500		C.L.Y. 1705
	17	Bevington v. Doyle	2,250		C.L.Y. 1706
	25	Hughes v. Bloor	2,200		C.L.Y. 1707
	22	Butland v. O'Connor	2,000		C.L.Y. 1708
	12	N (A Child) v. Smith & Whiteinch Group	2,000		C.L.Y. 1710
	64	Williams v. Thompson	2,000		C.L.Y. 1709
	11	M (A Child) v. Oraha	2,000		C.L.Y. 1712
	14	K (A Child) v Gobbi	1,800		C.L.Y. 1726
	29	Rowe v. Rogers	1,700		C.L.Y. 1711
	26	Bevington v. Doyle	1,750		C.L.Y. 1706
	7	M (A Child) v. Oraha	1,625		C.L.Y. 1712
	18	Edwards v. Pryce	1,600		C.L.Y. 1713
	41	Simpson v. Grant	1,500		C.L.Y. 1714
	14	C (A Child) v. Peers	1,500		C.L.Y. 1715
	34	Cave v. Crome	1,400		C.L.Y. 1716
	27	Simms v. Walls	1,400		C.L.Y. 1717
	25	James v. Johnson	1,350		C.L.Y. 1718
	12	H (A Child) v. Gray	1,300		C.L.Y. 1719
	33	Donegan v. Dunnigan	1,000		C.L.Y. 1720
	23	Bold v. Noon	1,000		C.L.Y. 1725
	23	Kalam v. Khan (Quantum)	900		C.L.Y. 1721
	36	Ashouri v. Penfold	850		C.L.Y. 1722
	30	Hughes v. Hunt	600		C.L.Y. 1723
	69	Nickless v. Osborne	580		C.L.Y. 1724

Injury	Age (at time of injury unless otherwise stated)	Case	Award		Reference
			General £	Loss of Earnings Capacity, Family Care £	
Minor injuries; shoulder	36	Brown v. Eom Construction Ltd	3,500		C.L.Y. 1727
	17	R (A Child) v. Taylor	3,000		C.L.Y. 1728
	25	Schnoor v. Cage	1,750		C.L.Y. 1729
Minor injuries; arm	21 months	C (A Child) v. Leeds NHS Teaching National Health Trust	600		C.L.Y. 1730
Minor injuries; hand	52	Bennett v. Hewitt	3,750		C.L.Y. 1731
	42	Green v. Leicester CC	3,000		C.L.Y. 1732
	42	Yates v. John Smedley Ltd	1,688		C.L.Y. 1733
	11	M (A Minor) v. De Koning	1,400		C.L.Y. 1734
	24	Pepperall v. Memory Lane Cakes Ltd	750		C.L.Y. 1735
	46	Ritter v. British Steel Plc	750		C.L.Y. 1736
Minor injuries; fingers	45	Duffy v. Carnaby	1,500		C.L.Y. 1737
	22	Burrows v. Kingston upon Hull City Council	1100		C.L.Y. 1738
Minor injuries; leg	2	G (A Child) v. Pitt (T/A KP Group)	4,000		C.L.Y. 1740
	22	Dean v. Wundpets Ltd	3,600		C.L.Y. 1739
Minor injuries; knee	11	J (A Child) v. Urdd Gobaith Cymru	3,500		C.L.Y. 1741
	16	M (A Child) v. Khan	2,000		C.L.Y. 1742
Minor injuries; ankle	40	Coles v. Lewis	3,500		C.L.Y. 1743
	32	Ahmed v. Cardiff CC	3,250		C.L.Y. 1744
Minor injuries; foot	27	Bevan v. South Wales Fire Service	800		C.L.Y. 1745
Minor injuries; toe	35	McBride v. Basildon & Thurrock Hospital NHS Trust	3,000		C.L.Y. 1746
Minor injuries; disease	Children	D (A Child) v. Sefton MBC	2,000		C.L.Y. 1747
Minor injuries; toxicosis	5	D (A Child) v. J Sainsbury Plc	1,250		C.L.Y. 1748
Claims for death of husband	27	Jones (CICB: Quantum: 1999), Re		Total award 311,592	C.L.Y. 1749
	26	McMillan (CICB: Quantum: 1999), Re		Total award 277,715	C.L.Y. 1750
Claims for death of parent	9 months	E (A Child) v. North Middlesex Hospital NHS Trust		Total award 275,000	C.L.Y. 1751
	4	W (A Child) (CICB: Quantum: 1999), Re	26,000		C.L.Y. 1752

SCOTTISH CASES

| Injury | Age (at time of injury unless otherwise stated) | Case | Award | | Reference |
			Solatium £	Total £	
Brain damage	–	McDonald v. Chambers	115,000		C.L.Y. 6163
Head	48	Wilson v. Pyeroy Ltd	166,400		C.L.Y. 6164
Sight	–	Duthie v. Macfish Ltd	75,000		C.L.Y. 6165
Neck	–	Wardlaw v. Fife Health Board	8,500	3,000	C.L.Y. 6166
Back	38	Leebody v. Liddle	15,000		C.L.Y. 6168
		Callaghan v. Southern General Hospital NHS Trust	12,000		C.L.Y. 6169
	8	Gibson v. Pickfords Removals Ltd	1,750		C.L.Y. 6167
Shoulder	–	Crowe v. French	12,000		C.L.Y. 6170
Leg		Oliver v. Brown & Root McDermott Fabricators Ltd (T/A Barmac)	10,000		C.L.Y. 6171
Knee		Cawkwell v. East Calder District Homing Society Social Club	9,000		C.L.Y. 6172
Ankle		Nimmo v. Secretary of State for Scotland	6,000		C.L.Y. 6173
Burns	12	McLeod v. British Rail	200,000		C.L.Y. 6174
Reproductive organs	26	Adamson v. Lothian Health Board	100,000		C.L.Y. 6175

RETAIL PRICE INDEX

The table below consists of the general index of retail prices (RPI) for 1999/2000 (January 1987 = 100).

1999

JAN	163.4 (up 2.4 per cent on Jan 1998)
FEB	163.7 (up 2.1 per cent on Feb 1998)
MAR	164.1 (up 2.1 per cent on Mar 1998)
APR	165.2 (up 1.6 per cent on Apr 1998)
MAY	165.6 (up 1.3 per cent on May 1998)
JUN	165.6 (up 1.3 per cent on Jun 1998)
JUL	165.1 (up 1.3 per cent on Jul 1998)
AUG	165.5 (up 1.1 per cent on Aug 1998)
SEP	166.2 (up 1.1 per cent on Sep 1998)
OCT	166.2 (up 1.2 per cent on Oct 1998)
NOV	166.7 (up 1.4 per cent on Nov 1998)
DEC	167.3 (up 1.8 per cent on Dec 1998)

2000

JAN	166.6 (up 2.0 per cent on Jan 1999)
FEB	167.5 (up 2.3 per cent on Feb 1999)
MAR	168.4 (up 2.6 per cent on Mar 1999)
APR	170.1 (up 3.0 per cent on Apr 1999)
MAY	170.7 (up 3.1 per cent on May 1999)
JUN	171.1 (up 3.3 per cent on Jun 1999)
JUL	170.5 (up 3.3 per cent on Jul 1999)
AUG	170.5 (up 3.0 per cent on Aug 1999)
SEP	171.7 (up 3.3 per cent on Sep 1999)
OCT	171.6 (up 3.1 per cent on Oct 1999)
NOV	172.1 (up 3.2 per cent on Nov 1999)
DEC	172.2 (up 2.9 per cent on Dec 1999)

TAX AND PRICE INDEX

The table below consists of the tax and price index (TPI) for 1999/2000 (January 1987 = 100).

1999

JAN	150.5 (up 2.3 per cent on Jan 1998)
FEB	150.8 (up 2.0 per cent on Feb 1998)
MAR	151.2 (up 1.9 per cent on Mar 1998)
APR	151.2 (up 1.0 per cent on Apr 1998)
MAY	151.7 (up 0.7 per cent on May 1998)
JUN	151.7 (up 0.8 per cent on Jun 1998)
JUL	151.1 (up 0.7 per cent on Jul 1998)
AUG	151.5 (up 0.5 per cent on Aug 1998)
SEP	152.3 (up 0.5 per cent on Sep 1998)
OCT	152.6 (up 0.7 per cent on Oct 1998)
NOV	152.8 (up 0.9 per cent on Nov 1998)
DEC	153.4 (up 1.3 per cent on Dec 1998)

2000

JAN	152.7 (up 1.5 per cent on Jan 1999)
FEB	153.7 (up 1.9 per cent on Feb 1999)
MAR	154.6 (up 2.2 per cent on Mar 1999)
APR	155.7 (up 3.0 per cent on Apr 1999)
MAY	156.3 (up 3.0 per cent on May 1999)
JUN	156.7 (up 3.3 per cent on Jun 1999)
JUL	156.1 (up 3.3 per cent on Jul 1999)
AUG	156.1 (up 3.0 per cent on Aug 1999)
SEP	157.3 (up 3.3 per cent on Sep 1999)
OCT	157.2 (up 3.0 per cent on Oct 1999)
NOV	157.7 (up 3.2 per cent on Nov 1999)
DEC	157.8 (up 2.9 per cent on Dec 1999)

ALPHABETICAL TABLE OF STATUTORY INSTRUMENTS 2000

The table below contains a list, in alphabetical order, of the Statutory Instruments digested by Current Law in 2000.

C.L.Y.

C.L.Y.

C.L.Y.

C.L.Y.

ALPHABETICAL TABLE OF STATUTORY INSTRUMENTS 2000

ADMINISTRATION OF JUSTICE

HEALTH AND SAFETY AT WORK

HIGHWAY CONTROL

MEDIA

SOCIAL SECURITY–*cont*

VAT

WATER INDUSTRY

NUMERICAL TABLE OF
STATUTORY INSTRUMENTS 2000

2000	C.L.Y.	2000	C.L.Y.
1	3150	206	3406
2	2998	207	2273
3	6454	208	2012
4	4823	209	2931
5	4563	210	2950
6	5216	211	2922
7	212	212	2840
8	3014	213	4125
10	2497	214	4126
11	4893	215	5259
12	5140	216 (C.5)	5266
22	167	217 (C.6)	2903
38	3067	218	2919
51	2641	219	2940
52 (C.1)	2438	220	2820
54	4166	221 (L.1)	379
55	4752	222 (C.7)	1755
57	1995	223	2937
58	2309	224	2682
62	4716	225	2686
63	4143	226	2933
89	2910	227	2269
90	2833	237	2866
92 (C.2)	2691	238	2850
107	1894	239	4848
108	4401	240	62
109	3857	241	2770
119	4757	242	2771
121	2830	243	2772
122	2810	244 (W.2)	4141
123	2827	245	4304
124	2826	246	3096
127	4873	247	3089
128	2974	250	2704
136	3797	251	2769
137	3798	252	4340
138	3708	253 (W.5)	796
155	5406	254	2936
157	5072	255	2946
162	5096	256	2947
163	5097	257	2953
168 (C.3)	3374	258	5363
174	5030	259	4085
175	4799	260	711
176	5719	261	708
177	965	262	701
179	2753	263	698
180	1900	265	3349
181	2651	266	5340
182	5220	267	2751
183 (C.4)	3420	283	2944
184	3416	284	2952
185	3418	285	2956
186	3404	286	2925
187	3407	287	2924
188	3403	288	5057
189	3405	289	5258
190	3408	290	834
191	3409	291	2591
192	2284	292	2792
205	162	293	712

2000	C.L.Y.	2000	C.L.Y.
294	1927	442	4013
297	1896	443	1837
298	2994	451	3954
299 (W.6)	4612	452	5445
300	956	464 (C.12)	3375
301	4406	476	5205
307	2954	477	5375
308	2011	478	1903
309	699	479 (W.20)	2712
310	700	480	207
311	705	481	2669
312	2019	482	4735
313	2040	483	4731
314	2063	484	4734
315	2082	485	3478
316	2039	486	4315
317	2043	501 (W.21)	4569
318	2052	502	4390
319	2048	503	5342
333	2017	516	3986
334	2030	519	5377
335	2062	520	4601
336	2081	521	4596
339	4080	522	2865
340 (C.8)	2265	523	2835
342	4362	524	5221
343	4123	525	4560
344 (C.9)	706	526	4778
346	5727	527	4779
349 (W.7)	3158	528	4769
350 (W.8)	169	529	3095
352 (W.10)	4595	530	3091
353	2699	531	3119
354	1817	532	4602
355	1850	533	4830
375	2693	534	4564
387	856	535	2862
388	855	536	2847
396 (C.10)	5453	537	4567
402	1779	538	3117
406	2873	539	4411
407	2854	540	4604
408	3097	541	3269
409	85	542	4379
410	2875	554	3102
411	2848	555 (W.22)	4594
412	4076	576	1858
413	3414	587	146
414	3411	588	151
415	3415	589	4129
416	3410	590	4833
417	3419	591	5098
418	3401	592	2784
419	3412	593	2831
420 (C.11)	2137	594	2899
421	4759	595	2814
422	1798	596	2806
423	1800	597	4060
424	4565	598	4572
425	4361	599	5138
426	4973	600	5009
427	2013	601	2816
428	5230	602	2824
429	4652	603	2748
430	4648	604	2743
431	3966	605	4373
432	2014	606	2822
433	2107	607	2884
434	2106	608	2888
435	2647	609	2887
440	4777	610	2894
441	3987	611	2898

2000	C.L.Y.	2000	C.L.Y.
612	2893	698	135
613	2891	699	3011
614	2889	700	4336
615	2896	701	3137
616	2895	702	3151
617	2882	703	1829
618	2750	704	3333
619	4372	705	6499
620	2812	706	3136
621	2836	707	5149
622	4101	717 (W.24)	4124
623	4102	718 (W.25)	4134
626	4877	719 (W.26)	178
627	3989	720	3123
629 (C.13)	4901	721	4760
630	4152	722	3015
631	5023	723	4806
632 (C.14)	4979	724	4763
633	4961	726	3545
634	5297	727	4804
635	273	728	5724
636	4750	729	4862
637	4829	730	5075
638	4825	731	5071
639 (L.2)	23	732	2876
640 (L.3)	41	733	2852
641 (L.4)	81	735 (C.15)	3020
642 (L.5)	78	736	4809
643	4014	737	5729
644	4029	738	2409
645	4975	739	106
646	195	740	4160
655	5405	741	5450
656	2679	743	3804
657	2711	744	91
658	2886	745	6387
660	2742	746	6381
661	2749	747	4805
662	2801	748	5725
664	1971	749	4378
665	4386	750	4354
666	4403	755	4854
667	5691	756	4161
668	2614	757	5731
669	2622	758	5726
670	3527	759	4991
671	6618	760	4855
672	4398	761	4807
673	2623	768	2680
674	2619	769	3107
675	67	770	5217
676	61	774 (C.16)	4
677	55	776	211
678	4749	777	3106
679	4377	778	3103
681	4771	779 (C.17)	2737
682	5166	780	2016
683	2992	781	2028
684	3338	782	2034
685	3340	783	2037
686	2230	784	2045
687	6395	785	2046
688	4852	786	2076
689	854	787	2080
690	5755	788	2026
691	4853	789	2009
692	4004	790	2667
693	3	791	3013
694	2834	792 (W.29)	4573
695	2832	793 (W.30)	4581
696	2745	794	5349
697	4843	795	4871

2000	C.L.Y.	2000	C.L.Y.
796	5767	899	4058
797	2800	900	4005
798	4896	906	1783
799	4772	907	4389
800 (C.18)	2293	908 (W.39)	4608
801 (C.19)	4094	909	2823
802	5292	910	3120
803	5027	911 (W.40)	1905
804	5328	912	3341
805	5367	913	3339
806	5001	914	832
807	5014	921	4996
808	4918	922 (C.22)	4976
809	5005	923	1844
810	4990	924 (C.24)	954
811	5296	928	2252
822	3991	929	2215
823	4006	930	2311
824	3988	931	4874
825 (W.31)	4086	932	857
826	2008	933	4052
827	2645	934	3007
828	173	935 (S.2)	6391
830	3090	936	4578
831	2279	937 (L.6)	628
832	4841	938 (L.7)	2512
833	4380	939 (L.8)	474
834 (W.32)	1832	940 (L.9)	381
835	1008	941	511
836	4737	942	4130
837	2837	943	3076
838	1828	944	1970
840	2092	945	5020
841	2855	946	4575
842	2874	947	4585
843	4381	948 (W.41)	4584
844	291	949	4593
845	2687	950	4611
846	2853	951	4583
847	2844	952	4610
848	4857	960	2690
849	5235	961	2871
854	3002	964	109
859	2892	965	5783
860	2897	966	6702
861	2890	967	5025
862	4131	968	2628
863	1799	969	5383
864	1793	970 (C.24)	1998
865	1792	971 (C.25)	3553
866	1797	972 (W.42)	137
867	1795	973 (W.43)	3121
868	2214	974 (W.44)	1816
869	5190	975 (W.45)	4571
870	2825	976 (W.46)	2648
871	3093	977 (W.47)	2807
872	3092	978 (W.48)	2902
873	3094	979	4765
874	2643	980	3114
875 (C.20)	2138	981	3065
876	2951	990 (W.51)	4133
877	2943	991	801
878	174	992 (W.52)	4084
879	3180	993	2859
880 (C.21)	3181	994	3850
891	293	995	3398
892	4941	999 (W.56)	2815
893	4945	1000	1991
895	5142	1001	1981
896	4081	1005	4368
897	4783	1012	4156
898	4756	1013	4154

2000	C.L.Y.	2000	C.L.Y.
1014	4155	1105	3814
1015 (W.57)	2802	1106	3822
1017	99	1107	3805
1022	1801	1108	970
1024	4568	1109	972
1025 (W.61)	4566	1111	5147
1026 (C.26; W.62)	2735	1112	4182
1027	4144	1113	5965
1029 (W.64)	4079	1114	3596
1030 (W.65)	4078	1115	3588
1031	5384	1116 (C.35)	4879
1032	4135	1117	3024
1033	4128	1118	4844
1034 (C.27)	946	1119	4019
1035 (W.66)	2741	1120	1968
1036 (W.67)	3155	1121	1842
1037	2775	1122	4301
1038	2774	1123	4349
1039 (W.68)	2262	1136	3085
1040	2010	1137	2999
1041 (C.28)	2738	1138	3074
1042	4089	1139	1087
1043	2270	1140	1889
1044	5172	1141	3110
1045	5184	1142 (W.80)	2885
1046	5331	1143	5233
1047 (C.29)	4878	1144	5232
1048	4350	1145 (W.81)	4897
1049	4351	1146	1890
1050 (S.4)	6611	1147 (W.82)	3399
1051 (S.5)	6612	1149	4808
1052	4348	1150	5728
1053	4342	1151	4995
1054	4344	1152	4999
1055	4345	1153 (W.84)	1866
1059	2960	1154 (W.85)	1871
1064	3023	1155 (W.86)	1873
1065 (C.30)	2904	1156 (W.87)	1875
1066 (C.31)	2692	1157 (W.88)	1880
1070	2788	1158 (W.89)	1882
1071 (L.10)	20	1159 (W.90)	1887
1072	5049	1160	979
1073	3079	1161	3372
1074	3080	1162	3104
1075 (W.69)	2642	1163 (W.91)	4586
1076 (W.70)	2860	1164	4369
1077	2297	1167	2914
1078 (W.71)	2652	1168	2958
1079 (W.72)	3138	1169 (W.94)	4412
1080 (W.73)	3154	1172 (W.95)	3084
1081	2632	1173 (C.37)	4523
1082	4786	1174	4088
1085	5016	1175	4153
1086	5018	1177	1982
1087	5017	1178	5229
1088	5015	1209	2666
1089	1907	1210	4071
1090	1904	1211	4055
1091	4837	1212	4061
1092	2786	1213	4062
1093 (C.32)	4978	1230	3025
1094 (C.33)	4095	1231	3526
1095 (C.34)	4096	1232	147
1096 (W.74)	2646	1233	152
1097 (W.75)	4605	1234	2637
1098 (W.76)	1884	1235	2635
1099 (W.77)	1886	1236	2049
1100 (W.78)	1878	1237	3109
1101 (W.79)	1888	1238	3108
1102	5964	1239	3855
1103	5161	1240	2740
1104	5131	1241	2739

2000	C.L.Y.	2000	C.L.Y.
1242	1865	1369	5798
1256	3026	1370	4849
1257	3027	1371	3045
1258	3028	1372	3052
1259	3029	1373	3053
1260	3030	1374	3054
1261	3031	1375	3055
1262	3032	1376	3056
1263	3035	1377	3057
1271 (W.97)	4082	1378	3058
1276	5242	1379	3033
1279	4761	1380	5137
1280	2261	1381	3393
1281	2773	1382 (C.41)	4902
1282 (C.38)	3376	1383	1849
1283 (W.98)	3082	1384	2930
1285	3100	1396	3858
1286	3036	1397	3861
1287	3037	1398	2560
1288	3038	1399	3862
1289	3039	1401	4748
1290	3040	1402	4842
1291	3041	1403	4399
1292	3042	1404	159
1293	3043	1405	3105
1297	5376	1406	2608
1298	200	1407	1845
1300	2218	1408	3856
1305	4762	1409	5446
1306	2219	1410	4352
1307	3044	1411	2179
1308	3046	1413	2857
1309	3047	1414	2880
1310	3049	1415	2868
1311	3051	1416	2845
1312	3048	1417	2021
1313	3050	1418	2061
1314	2676	1419	2055
1315	2721	1420	2073
1317 (L.11)	380	1421	287
1320	3081	1422 (W.102)	2813
1323 (W.101)	1935	1425	1965
1324	4872	1429	59
1325	5768	1430	647
1333	2100	1431	5201
1334	4736	1432	5196
1335	4733	1433	5192
1336	2142	1434	5188
1337	2143	1435	4093
1338 (C.39)	2139	1441	5214
1339	795	1442	5206
1340	800	1443	2105
1341	798	1444	4840
1342	3821	1445	5454
1343	793	1446	5455
1344 (C.40)	2783	1447	1977
1345	5134	1458	5968
1346	5132	1459 (C.42)	2555
1348	298	1460	2255
1349	5226	1462	5154
1350	3071	1463	2286
1351	3072	1464	5163
1352	3073	1465	5209
1353	3070	1471	4821
1354	3068	1472	990
1355	3069	1473	92
1356	5152	1474	4539
1362	2867	1481 (L.12)	3933
1365	4814	1482	22
1366	4755	1483	4781
1367	991	1484	5187
1368	2797	1487	2075

2000	C.L.Y.	2000	C.L.Y.
1488.	5238	1641	201
1489.	5237	1642	3099
1490.	1839	1643	3088
1491.	4437	1644	3098
1492.	3122	1645	2819
1493.	4481	1646	5591
1502.	2636	1647	3087
1503.	2634	1648 (C.44)	4097
1504.	5211	1666	5245
1505.	2700	1667	142
1506.	5204	1668	841
1507.	5165	1669	2864
1508.	2996	1671	3113
1509.	2663	1672	5333
1510.	2662	1673	3842
1511.	3019	1674.	5231
1515.	5332	1675	2056
1516.	2598	1676	2065
1517.	5372	1677	2083
1541.	3990	1678	4157
1542.	177	1679	847
1544 (L.13)	82	1680	2604
1545 (L.14)	42	1681	2599
1546 (L.15)	24	1682	2611
1547.	5185	1683	4727
1548.	5249	1684	1818
1549.	4537	1686	153
1551.	5521	1700	2620
1552.	5186	1707 (W.114)	2808
1553.	4090	1708 (W.115)	2765
1554.	823	1709	130
1555.	4159	1710 (W.116)	3116
1556.	3827	1711	5086
1557.	3833	1712.	5085
1558.	3831	1713	5091
1559.	3829	1714	5083
1560.	3595	1715	5084
1561.	3587	1717 (W.117)	1860
1562.	5136	1718	2959
1563.	5973	1719	3012
1565.	3001	1724 (C.45)	4115
1566.	3111	1725.	2071
1587 (C.43)	1019	1726.	4056
1588.	4767	1728	4402
1593.	3003	1734	2629
1595.	1879	1735 (W.119)	3118
1596.	4770	1737	2134
1597.	1881	1738 (W.121)	2665
1598.	1877	1739	4035
1599.	1869	1748	2929
1600	1885	1749.	2849
1601.	1876	1750	1996
1602.	1867	1751	1813
1603	1868	1752.	4137
1604	1870	1763	2828
1605	1872	1764	2022
1606	1874	1765	2024
1607.	1883	1766	2042
1608	5474	1767	2047
1618	194	1768	2054
1619	214	1769	5222
1620.	1985	1770.	5213
1621.	2752	1771	262
1622.	3159	1772.	263
1623.	6683	1773.	4127
1624.	4487	1775.	3342
1625.	4488	1776.	3357
1626.	4493	1777.	1937
1627.	4478	1785 (W.122)	2993
1628.	4477	1786 (W.123)	2991
1639.	294	1787.	5404
1640	4305	1788	180

2000	C.L.Y.	2000	C.L.Y.
1789	139	1878	989
1790	140	1879	4059
1791	129	1880	6700
1792	133	1881	2731
1793	131	1882 (W.129)	1891
1794	4333	1884	4721
1795	4338	1885 (W.131)	2668
1796	3086	1887 (W.133)	2821
1797	833	1888 (S.6)	5831
1798 (C.46)	639	1917	2794
1799 (W.124)	2670	1918	2791
1800	3000	1919	2790
1801	3994	1920 (C.48)	5
1802	3964	1921	2989
1803	2729	1922	4869
1804	1969	1923	2617
1805	5189	1924	1371
1806	1812	1925 (W.134)	2681
1807	4875	1926	4784
1808	292	1927	2093
1809	4050	1928	4308
1810	4858	1929	3993
1811	3005	1930	3985
1812	2703	1937	4303
1813	2705	1938 (W.136)	1824
1814	261	1939 (W.137)	1822
1815	3813	1940 (W.138)	2253
1816	799	1941 (W.139)	1980
1817	3809	1942	2911
1818	3823	1943	2917
1819	3826	1944	2938
1820	3828	1945	2916
1821	3834	1955	4151
1822	3840	1960	1897
1823	4802	1961	2923
1824	787	1962	2912
1825	868	1963	3153
1826	299	1964	2942
1827	3999	1965	2920
1828	2220	1968 (C.49)	5478
1829	802	1969 (C.50)	3178
1830	803	1970	5199
1831	5967	1971	5203
1836	3825	1972	5195
1837	3824	1973	2275
1838	3832	1974	1859
1839	3830	1975	163
1840	3839	1977	2033
1841	2003	1978	4850
1842	5380	1979 (W.140)	1979
1843	2649	1980 (W.141)	1893
1844	2036	1981	4868
1845	2031	1982	4768
1846	2020	1983	2755
1847	2078	1984	3872
1848	1930	1985 (C.51)	3377
1849	3266	1986 (C.52; S.7)	6227
1850	4730	1987	2152
1851 (C.47)	3196	1988	6212
1864	3402	1989	2178
1865	3413	1992 (W.144)	2817
1866 (W.125)	2688	1993	4754
1867 (W.126)	1936	1994	5144
1868 (W.127)	4892	1995	5141
1870	191	2004 (C.53)	4980
1871	5060	2008	2644
1872	64	2009	897
1873	43	2012	1827
1874	88	2013	4541
1875	2536	2014	2945
1876	3968	2015	2934
1877	3967	2024	5488

2000	C.L.Y.	2000	C.L.Y.
2025	4169	2125 (C.57)	974
2026	4561	2126	971
2027	184	2127	969
2028	4766	2128	4138
2029	2631	2129	5055
2030 (W.143)	1934	2140	3853
2031	704	2141	2734
2033	2732	2142	1840
2034	2725	2143	1820
2036	1044	2144	1846
2037	3594	2145	1819
2038	3397	2146	2005
2039	5070	2147	2268
2040	5966	2148	63
2041 (W.147)	4579	2149	65
2042	2955	2150	5150
2043	2921	2151	5151
2044	2858	2152	4714
2045	1777	2154	2957
2046	1780	2155	2915
2047	1772	2156	2948
2048	1771	2157	2939
2049	1778	2158	2918
2050	5215	2169	3010
2051	2724	2170	2000
2052	2727	2171	1983
2053	2730	2172	1814
2054	2728	2173	1809
2055	154	2174	1992
2056	155	2175	1976
2057	1861	2176	1978
2058	2060	2187 (C.58)	4117
2059	2077	2188	5037
2060	4091	2189	5770
2074	4993	2190	4482
2075	5034	2192	1966
2076	5003	2193	1993
2077	4803	2194	4847
2078	5723	2195	1902
2079	5006	2196	1863
2080	4998	2197	1843
2081	5013	2198	1933
2082 (C.54)	4983	2199 (C.59)	1999
2083	4992	2207	4798
2084	4800	2208	5718
2085	4822	2210	2422
2086	5720	2211	2272
2087	3860	2212	4646
2088	703	2213	4650
2089	5036	2214	4653
2090	4816	2215	2684
2091 (C.55)	947	2225 (C.60)	641
2092 (L.16)	382	2226	3965
2093 (L.17)	32	2227	3962
2094	1039	2228 (L.18)	254
2103	4719	2229	4864
2104	5035	2230 (W.148)	2633
2110	4048	2237	3034
2111	1823	2238	60
2112	1821	2239	4780
2113	1838	2240	1847
2114 (C.56)	1853	2241	2104
2115	1848	2242 (C.61)	2140
2116	1908	2243	3326
2117	1857	2244	3267
2118	3101	2245	3271
2119	175	2246	3270
2120	3016	2247	2103
2121	1892	2250	210
2122	1931	2251	4718
2123	1835	2253	90
2124	1815	2254	2683

2000	C.L.Y.	2000	C.L.Y.
2255	4717	2408	4972
2257 (W.150)	2685	2409	5100
2264	3854	2410	5073
2265	2758	2412 (C.67)	5275
2266	3843	2413	651
2267 (L.19)	2518	2417	3255
2301	5379	2418	6487
2303	5054	2419	1988
2307	4469	2420 (C.56)	4118
2310 (L.20)	475	2421	4598
2311	4468	2422	4870
2312	2879	2423 (C.68)	37
2313	4747	2424	2091
2314	5044	2430	3008
2315	5048	2431	4387
2316	5047	2432	2470
2317	5046	2433	2839
2318	5045	2434	2883
2319 (C.62)	4977	2435	2744
2320	4306	2444 (C.69)	3378
2321	1973	2445	3362
2322	5197	2446	3355
2324	1987	2449	4300
2326	3265	2459	2804
2327	5218	2460	166
2328	3963	2463	2135
2329	968	2481	149
2330	1826	2482	2978
2331	4811	2483	5207
2332	1830	2484	5177
2333 (L.21)	3268	2485	2029
2334	839	2486	2025
2335 (W.152)	185	2487	2041
2336	4773	2488	2050
2337 (C.63)	2556	2489	2057
2338	2913	2490	2058
2339	2926	2491	2072
2340	4838	2492 (W.159)	4103
2341	2798	2493	5183
2342	2803	2494	2789
2343	4797	2522	5173
2344	5717	2523	5174
2366 (C.64)	250	2524	3844
2367	264	2526	2787
2368	251	2530	5175
2369	246	2531	822
2370	265	2532	821
2371	252	2534	3018
2372	247	2537	2427
2373	257	2539 (W.162)	1864
2374	256	2540 (W.163; C.70)	1854
2375	255	2543 (C.71)	3208
2376	266	2544 (C.72)	4885
2377	253	2545	4835
2378	248	2546	2997
2379	267	2547	2941
2380	2965	2548	2101
2381	842	2549	5059
2382 (L.22)	83	2550	4926
2383	2818	2551	5022
2384	2498	2552	4370
2385	2799	2553	2928
2386	209	2554	2768
2387	2878	2558	4732
2388 (C.65)	2709	2559 (C.73)	1855
2389	2842	2560 (W.169)	1994
2391	4713	2562	2877
2392	2935	2563	3256
2393	2809	2566	722
2394	165	2573	128
2397	5227	2576	2949
2398	5225	2585	5236

2000	C.L.Y.	2000	C.L.Y.
2599	2027	2769	3810
2600	2035	2770	3811
2601	2038	2771	845
2602	2064	2792	998
2603	2068	2793	3258
2604	2069	2794	3257
2605	2070	2795 (C.79)	4884
2606	2044	2800 (C.80)	1010
2615	3022	2801	1997
2618	3849	2802	4064
2619	2471	2803	4063
2620	3851	2810	66
2629	4836	2811	144
2630	5381	2812	2706
2631	5382	2820	2927
2641	4332	2821 (C.81)	6251
2642	4337	2822	2757
2649	3075	2823	4470
2658	5208	2824	3969
2659 (W.172)	145	2825	1834
2660	3066	2826	4371
2661	3083	2831	2975
2662	2851	2832	1909
2663	2856	2836 (C.82)	4119
2665	3262	2846	4307
2666 (C.74)	4888	2847	3062
2670	2507	2849 (C.83)	4120
2671	57	2850	4106
2672	2658	2851	4104
2676	5176	2852	4107
2686	213	2853	4105
2687	4690	2854	4866
2688	5234	2855	5087
2690	4860	2856	5090
2691	4343	2857	5076
2692	4397	2858	5094
2693	4346	2859	5089
2694	3078	2860	5081
2695	3077	2861	5093
2696	3112	2862	5088
2698 (C.76)	3379	2863	5080
2699	5101	2864	4863
2704	1986	2865	2762
2705	3004	2866	2763
2706	3881	2867	4456
2707	2988	2868	290
2710	4938	2870	2838
2711	4311	2871	3009
2724	3365	2872	1899
2725	3259	2875	5066
2726	2657	2876	4782
2727	2089	2883	4776
2728	1811	2884	4142
2729	1804	2885	2869
2730	5191	2886	2881
2735	3373	2887	2288
2736	4394	2890	160
2737 (L.23)	3934	2891	4787
2738	21	2897	843
2739	3384	2899	2793
2740 (C.77)	642	2900	3845
2741	2863	2906 (W.186)	1989
2742	4994	2907	181
2743	5730	2908	2870
2744	4810	2909	2872
2745	2987	2910	4764
2746	2986	2911	161
2764	4891	2912	1841
2765	846	2913	4148
2766	5170	2914	4347
2767	1776	2916	2761
2768 (C.78)	5159	2917 (C.84)	5276

2000	C.L.Y.	2000	C.L.Y.
2918 (L.24)	25	3061	5158
2944 (C.85)	1011	3062	3807
2945	1967	3063	4801
2948 (W.189, C.86)	4122	3064	35
2949	636	3075 (C.96)	1020
2950 (C.87)	4794	3080	1910
2952	276	3085	4384
2953	5223	3086	2289
2954	5341	3087	1825
2955	1445	3088	4376
2956	5273	3089	4489
2957 (C.88)	4559	3096	58
2958 (C.89)	4880	3097	2976
2959 (W.190)	2263	3098	297
2960	5179	3099 (C.97)	3380
2961	2746	3106	1974
2962	2747	3108	4647
2963	168	3109	2625
2974 (C.90)	5277	3110	2609
2975	4341	3111 (C.98)	3554
2976	157	3112	5004
2977	136	3114	5155
2978	5061	3115	5180
2979	5784	3116	2841
2980	4309	3118 (W.197)	2805
2981	3801	3119 (W.198)	2901
2982	2932	3120	4832
2983	4365	3121 (W.199)	2472
2984	4363	3122 (W.200)	1972
2985	4364	3123 (W.201)	138
2986	4366	3124	2846
2987 (L.25)	33	3125	2861
2988	4003	3126	171
2989 (C.91)	3179	3127	126
2990	5167	3128	3846
2991 (W.191; C.92)	2736	3132	4108
2992 (W.192; C.93)	4886	3133	5766
2993 (W.193)	2829	3134	4876
2994 (C.94)	4795	3144 (C.99)	5210
2995	5058	3145 (C.100)	5178
2996	5002	3146	5243
2997	4865	3148	964
2998	5092	3156 (W.205)	2298
3025	4353	3157	5169
3026 (W.194)	1928	3158	4936
3027 (W.195)	1932	3159	1803
3028	4388	3160	1836
3029	2900	3161	1862
3030	4774	3162	2689
3031	2785	3163	3521
3032 (S.8)	6619	3164	2537
3033 (C.95)	2266	3165	110
3040	2767	3166 (C.101)	4796
3041	2766	3171	1773
3042	132	3173	4792
3043	183	3174	4791
3044	4525	3175	4715
3045	188	3176	4753
3046	134	3177	4789
3047	2674	3179	5475
3048	2295	3180	4405
3049	2280	3181	4813
3050	2281	3182	2776
3051	2282	3183	2085
3052	2283	3184	5378
3053	3332	3185	4788
3054	56	3186	4790
3056	4132	3187	5219
3057	2410	3188	4867
3058	1901	3189	2811
3059	3802	3194	2733
3060	80	3195	197

2000	C.L.Y.	2000	C.L.Y.
3196	5162	3299	2053
3197	5202	3300	2059
3198	4358	3301	2067
3199	4480	3302 (C.105)	1051
3206	4302	3303 (C.106)	1007
3207	5181	3304	3852
3208	4576	3305	935
3209	1807	3314	3021
3212	5139	3315	4984
3213	4970	3316 (C.108)	4314
3214	2759	3317	3017
3215	5212	3318	5200
3216	4689	3319	4053
3217	5224	3320	300
3218	5228	3323	2655
3219	1788	3324	678
3223	4861	3325	650
3224	5198	3326	1794
3225	4654	3327	1806
3226	84	3328	1802
3227	3847	3329	1831
3228	4940	3330	4967
3229 (C.102)	5246	3331	4036
3230 (W.213; C.103)	1856	3332	1805
3231	2795	3335 (C.109)	4121
3232 (S.9)	6503	3336	4851
3233	5605	3337	1796
3235	2905	3338	3366
3236	644	3339 (W.217)	158
3237	4083	3340 (W.218)	203
3238	2411	3341 (W.219)	2312
3239	1898	3342	4334
3240	3803	3343 (C.110)	5278
3241	3835	3344	5099
3242	3838	3345	5082
3243	3820	3346	5077
3244	3836	3347	5078
3245	3837	3348	5079
3246	5133	3349 (C.111)	2702
3247	4966	3350 (C.113)	4982
3248	4965	3351	94
3249	93	3352	193
3250	6388	3353	3806
3251	5971	3354 (C.112)	4889
3252	5972	3355	4074
3253	5974	3356	4073
3254	5451	3357	2707
3255	4751	3359	2271
3256	2990	3360 (L.26)	1081
3269	2418	3361 (L.27)	68
3270	4531	3362 (L.28)	34
3271	3817	3363	2066
3272	4100	3364	2074
3273 (C.116)	4557	3365	2079
3274	5068	3366	2084
3275	5194	3369	1984
3276	5130	3370	1906
3277	70	3371	4335
3278	69	3372	4054
3279	71	3373	635
3280 (C.104)	6	3374	2494
3282	215	3375	2276
3283 (C.107)	955	3376 (C.114)	5248
3284	1099	3377	143
3285	2018	3378	2656
3290	2764	3379 (C.115)	4098
3291	2760	3381	2659
3294 (W.216)	127	3382 (W.220)	4577
3295	2015	3383 (W.221)	4599
3296	2023	3386	4375
3297	2032	3387 (W.224)	2660
3298	2051	3389	4720

ALPHABETICAL TABLE OF
SCOTTISH STATUTORY INSTRUMENTS 2000

The table below contains a list, in alphabetical order, of the Scottish Statutory Instruments digested by Current Law in 2000.

C.L.Y.

ALPHABETICAL TABLE OF
SCOTTISH STATUTORY INSTRUMENTS 2000

FISHERIES

FOOD

NUMERICAL TABLE OF SCOTTISH
STATUTORY INSTRUMENTS 2000

2000	C.L.Y.	2000	C.L.Y.
1	5873	83	6373
7	6302	85	6651
8	5875	86	6652
10 (C.1)	6393	87	6650
11	6389	88	6656
13	6345	89	6654
15	5862	90	6657
16	5865	91	6653
17	6340	92	6649
18	6338	93	6241
19	6334	95	6230
20	6309	96	6239
21	6341	97	6222
22	5872	98	6456
23	6402	100	6431
24	6342	101 (C.3)	6708
26	6303	102	5827
28	6412	107	6542
30	5820	108	6545
32	6678	109	6547
33	6458	110	6202
34	6305	111 (C.36)	6688
35	6380	112	6610
36	6343	113	6419
38 (C.2)	6398	118	6339
39	6648	120	6464
40	6573	121	6550
44	6408	125	6358
45	6420	127	6359
46	6390	129	6237
47	6399	130	6396
48	5844	131	6320
49	5889	132	6362
50	6409	137	6360
51	5843	143	5814
52	5857	144	5908
53	6289	145	5825
54	6403	146	6356
55	6662	148	5941
56	6666	149	6207
57	6659	150	6626
58	6663	156	6337
59	6706	157	6361
60	6451	158	5866
61	6374	159	5863
62	6372	166	6642
65	6094	167	5880
66	5911	168	6589
67	6694	169	6223
68	5826	170	6705
69	6384	171	6377
73	6630	172	5828
74	6614	173	6300
75	6344	177	6459
76	6667	178	6224
77	6615	179	6627
78	5890	180 (C.5)	6226
79	6414	181	6546
80	6695	182	6539
81	6296	183	6691
82	6298	184	5861

2000	C.L.Y.	2000	C.L.Y.
185	6238	318	6367
186	6607	319	5909
187	6608	320	6206
188	6405	322 (C.11)	6236
189	6287	323	6231
190	6411	330	6311
191	6400	337	6418
192	6366	338 (C.12)	6442
193	6629	340	6489
194	5829	341 (C.13)	6473
195	6186	342	6183
196	6185	343	6486
197	6293	344	6317
198	6297	345	6316
199	6613	346	6347
200	6200	347	5878
201	5876	352	6406
202	6413	353	6415
206	6569	354	6416
207	6575	355	6417
208	6570	359	6328
214	6318	360	6325
215	5869	361 (C.14)	6198
216	6525	364	5867
217	6319	365	5868
222	6363	366	6621
223 (C.6)	6250	369	6351
224	6404	370	6324
226	6295	371	6557
227	6310	372	6352
228	6290	378	6348
229	6379	381	6335
233	6679	382	6368
236	6712	383	6369
237	6713	387	5942
238 (C.7)	6689	388	6281
239	5949	389	6353
240	6201	390 (C.15)	6252
246	5853	391	5856
247	5855	392	6609
248	5854	393	5874
249	5859	394	6407
250	5860	395	6421
258 (C.8)	6196	396	6410
261	6643	399	6548
266	6364	400	5881
267	6331	402	6336
284	6660	403	6574
285	6645	404	6349
287	6684	405	6294
288	6376	406	6187
289	6680	407	6188
290	5870	408	5823
291	6326	409	6329
292	6182	412	5813
293	6181	413	6371
294	6711	414	6370
295	6365	418	5877
298 (C.9)	6197	419	5824
300	5884	420	5822
301	6471	421	5819
303	6327	424	6655
307	6392	425	6571
308	6397	428	6330
309	6375	429	5852
310	6714	430	5958
312 (C.10)	6233	431	6378
313	6346	432	6235
314	5894	433 (C.16)	6228
315	6076	434	6355
316	5912	435	6350
317	5910	436	6332

ALPHABETICAL TABLE OF NORTHERN IRELAND STATUTORY RULES AND ORDERS

C.L.Y.

ALPHABETICAL TABLE OF NORTHERN IRELAND STATUTORY RULES AND ORDERS

NUMERICAL TABLE OF
NORTHERN IRELAND
STATUTORY RULES AND ORDERS 2000

2000	C.L.Y.	2000	C.L.Y.
1	5736	80	5616
2	5694	81	5617
3	5732	82	5563
4	5743	83	5408
5 (C.1)	5512	84	5575
6	5508	85	5590
7	5524	86	5786
8	5523	87	5664
9	5751	91	5758
10	5434	93	5586
23	5654	94	5564
24	5422	98	5587
27	5499	99	5589
35	5657	100	5588
36	5642	101	5661
37	5753	102	5581
38	5708	103	5745
39	5551	104	5754
40	5560	105	5742
41	5677	106	5705
42	5393	107	5647
43	5623	108	5423
46	5601	109	5690
47	5709	110	5427
48	5710	113	5660
49	5702	114	5777
50	5509	115	5791
51	5583	116 (C.3)	5681
52	5415	119	5787
53	5416	120	5592
54	5417	121	5504
55	5418	122 (C.4)	5513
56	5419	125	5698
57	5577	126	5421
58	5579	128	5420
59	5790	129	5792
60	5646	131	5797
61	5597	133 (C.5)	5773
62	5598	134	5748
63	5460	135	5712
64	5650	136	5803
65	5735	138	5425
68 (C.2)	5772	139 (C.6)	5535
69	5639	140 (C.7)	5603
70	5622	142	5637
71	5692	143	5638
72	5409	144	5635
73	5413	145	5631
74	5704	146	5632
75	5747	147	5633
76	5431	148	5795
77	5562	149	5801
78	5565	150	5796
79	5615	151	5800

2000	C.L.Y.	2000	C.L.Y.
152	5794	259	5761
157	5547	260	5711
158	5543	261	5525
160	5625	262	5651
161	5810	263	5687
165	5685	264	5502
167	5684	265	5738
168	5398	266	5706
169	5799	267	5627
171	5788	268	5739
175	5497	270	5430
177	5643	278	5440
178	5644	279	5391
179	5492	282	5385
181	5696	283	5595
182 (C.8)	5774	287	5568
183	5734	292	5403
184	5621	293	5433
185	5410	295	5555
186	5572	296	5498
187	5578	297	5793
188	5558	298	5424
189	5566	299	5426
190	5561	300	5537
191	5569	301	5428
192 (C.9)	5515	302 (C.13)	5493
193	5511	303	5567
194	5585	305	5804
195	5688	306	5808
196	5746	307	5809
197	5752	308	5805
198	5399	309	5806
199	5518	310	5807
200	5539	311	5501
203	5811	312	5683
209 (C.10)	5775	314	5482
210	5636	315	5668
211 (C.11)	5462	316	5671
212	5614	317	5670
213	5495	318	5667
214	5700	319	5666
215	5703	320	5669
216	5429	321	5759
217	5580	322	5789
218 (C.12)	5463	324	5707
219	5522	325	5599
221	5600	327	5785
222	5744	328	5802
224	5411	329	5538
225	5412	331	5607
226	5470	332 (C.14)	5776
227	5389	333	5682
228	5510	334 (C.15)	5449
232	5530	335	5629
233	5414	336	5630
234	5556	339	5582
235	5557	340	5760
240	5506	341	5584
241	5764	342	5680
242	5765	344	5435
243	5394	346	5407
244	5503	347	5448
245	5695	349	5649
246	5722	350	5749
247	5606	358 (C.16)	5715
248	5548	360	5757
249	5737	361	5713
250	5500	362	5634
251	5699	363	5549
253	5609	364	5544
254	5496	365	5701
255	5750	366	5762

2000	C.L.Y.	2000	C.L.Y.
367	5697	388	5594
368	5648	389	5457
369	5771	390	5486
371	5519	391	5652
373 (C.17)	5514	392	5653
374 (C.18)	5628	393	5395
375	5593	399	5673
376 (C.19)	5624	402	5571
377	5721	403	5596
379	5505	404	5740
380	5763	405	5432
382	5641	406 (C.21)	5716
385	5494	407	5693
386	5665	408	5679
387	5477	412 (C.32)	5675

TABLE OF ABBREVIATIONS

Publishers name follows reports and journals.
(S&M = Sweet & Maxwell; ICLR = Incorporated Council of Law Reporting for England and Wales; LBC = Law Book Company of Australia; OUP = Oxford University Press; Kluwer = Kluwer Law International; Cass = Frank Cass & Co Ltd; CUP = Cambridge University Press; CLP = Central Law Publishing; TSO = The Stationery Office. LLP = Lloyd's of London Press Ltd. All other names are in full.)

A. & S.L. = Air and Space Law (*Kluwer*)
A.C. = Appeal Cases (*ICLR*)
A.D.R.L.J. = Arbitration and Dispute Resolution Law Journal (*LLP*)
A.I. & L. = Artificial Intelligence and Law (*Kluwer*)
A.L.Q. = Arab Law Quarterly (*Kluwer*)
Accountancy = Accountancy (*Institute of Chartered Accountants in England and Wales*)
Ad. & Fos. = Adoption & Fostering (*British Adoption Agency Institute*)
Admin. L.R. = Administrative Law Reports (*Barry Rose*)
Adviser = Adviser (*NACAB*)
Agri. Law = Agricultural Law (*CLP*)
All E.R. = All England Law Reports (*Butterworth Tolley Publishing*)
All E.R. (Comm) = All England Law Reports (Commercial Cases) (*Butterworth Tolley Publishing*)
All E.R. (EC) = All England Law Reports European Cases (*Butterworth Tolley Publishing*)
All E.R. Rev. = All England Law Reports Annual Review (*Butterworth Tolley Publishing*)
Amicus Curiae = Amicus Curiae (*CCH Editions*)
Anglo-Am. L.R. = Anglo-American Law Review (*Barry Rose*)
A.P.L.R. = Asia Pacific Law Review (*Kluwer Law International*)
Arbitration = Arbitration (*Institute of Arbitrators*)
Arbitration Int. = Arbitration International (*Kluwer*)
Arch. News = Archbold News (*S&M*)
Axiom = Axiom (*GT: Specialist Publishers*)

B.C.C. = British Company Law & Practice (*CCH Editions*)
B.C.L.C. = Butterworths Company Law Cases (*Butterworth Tolley Publishing*)
B.H.R.C. = Butterworths Human Rights Cases (*Butterworth Tolley Publishing*)
B.I.F.D. = Bulletin for International Fiscal Documentation (*IBFD Publications BV*)
B.J.I.B. & F.L. = Butterworths Journal of International Banking & Financial Law (*Butterworth Tolley Publishing*)
B.L.E. = Business Law Europe (*S&M*)
B.L.G.R. = Butterworths Local Government Reports (*Butterworth Tolley Publishing*)
B.L.R. = Building Law Reports (*LLB*)
B.M.C.R. = Butterworths Merger Control Review (*Butterworth Tolley Publishing*)
B.M.L.R. = Butterworths Medico-Legal Reports (*Butterworth Tolley Publishing*)
B.P.I.L.S. = Butterworths Personal Injury Litigation Services (*Butterworth Tolley Publishing*)
B.P.I.R. = Bankruptcy and Personal Insolvency Reports (*Jordan*)

B.T.C. = British Tax Cases (*CCH Editions*)
B.T.R. = British Tax Review (*S&M*)
B.V.C = British Value Added Tax Reporter (*CCH Editions*)
B.Y.B.I.L. = British Year Book of International Law (*OUP*)
Bracton L.J. = Bracton Law Journal (*University of Exeter*)
Brit. J. Criminol. = British Journal of Criminology (*OUP*)
Build. L.M. = Building Law Monthly (*Monitor Press*)
Bull. J.S.B. = Bulletin of the Judicial Studies Board
Bus. L.B. = Business Law Bulletin (*W. Green*)
Bus. L.R. = Business Law Review (*Kluwer*)

c. = chapter (*of an Act of Parliament*)
C. & E.L. = Construction & Engineering Law (*CLP*)
C. & F.L. = Credit and Finance Law (*Monitor Press*)
C. & F.L.U. = Child & Family Law Update (*SLS Legal Publications*)
C.C.L.R. = Consumer Credit Law Reports (*incorporated within Consumer Credit Control - S&M*)
C.C.L. Rep = Community Care Law Reports (*Legal Action Group*)
C.D.F.N. = Clinical Disputes Forum Newsletter (*Clinical Disputes Forum*)
C.E.C. = European Community Cases (*CCH Editions*)
C.F.I.L.R. = Company Financial and Insolvency Law Review (*Informa Publishing Group*)
C.F.L.Q. = Child and Family Law Quarterly (*Jordan*)
C.G. = Corporate Governance (*Blackwell Publishers*)
C.I.C.C. = Current Issues in Consumer Credit (*incorporated within Consumer Credit Control - S&M*)
C.I.L. = Contemporary Issues in Law (*Lawtext Publishing Ltd*)
C.I.L.L. = Construction Industry Law Letter (*Monitor Press*)
C.I.P.A.J. = Chartered Institute of Patent Agents Journal (*Chartered Institute of Patent Agents*)
C.J.Q. = Civil Justice Quarterly (*S&M*)
C.L. = Current Law Monthly Digest (*S&M*)
C.L. = Commercial Lawyer (*Commercial Lawyer*)
C.L.C. = Commercial Law Cases (*CCH Editions*)
C.L.L. Rev. = Commercial Liability Law Review (*Informa Publishing Group*)
C.L. & P. = Computer Law & Practice (*Butterworth Tolley Publishing*)

C.L. & P.R. = Charity Law and Practice Review (*Key Haven*)

C.L. Pract. = Commercial Law Practitioner (*Round Hall/S&M*)

C.L.B. = Commonwealth Law Bulletin (*Commonwealth Secretariat*)

C.L.C. = Commercial Law Cases (*CCH Editions*)

C.L.C. = Current Law Consolidation (*1947-1951*) (*S&M*)

C.L.J. = Cambridge Law Journal (*CUP*)

C.L.M. = Company Law Monitor (*Monitor Press*)

C.L.P. = Current Legal Problems (*OUP*)

C.L.S.R. = Computer Law & Security Report (*Elsevier Science*)

C.L.W. = Current Law Week (*S&M*)

C.L.Y. = Current Law Yearbook (*S&M*)

C.M. = Compliance Monitor (*CTA Financial Publishing*)

C.M.L. Rev. = Common Market Law Review (*Kluwer*)

C.M.L.R. (AR) = Common Market Law Reports (*S&M*)

C. McK. Env. L.B. = Cameron McKenna Environmental Law Bulletin

C.O.D. = Crown Office Digest (*S&M*)

C.P.L.R. = Civil Practice Law Reports (*CLT Publishing*)

C.P.N. = Civil Procedure News (*S&M*)

C.P. Rep. = Civil Procedure Reports (Online) (*S&M*)

C.P. Rev. = Consumer Policy Review (*Consumer's Association*)

C.Risk. = Clinical Risk (*Royal Society of Medicine Press*)

C.S. = case summaries (*in The Independent*)

C.S.R. = Company Secretary's Review (*Butterworth Tolley Publishing*)

C.T.L.R. = Computer and Telecommunications Law Review (*S&M ESC Publishing*)

C.T.R. = Corporate Tax Review (*Key Haven Publications Ltd*)

C.T.P. = Capital Tax Planning (*S&M*)

C.Y.E.L.S. = Cambridge Yearbook of European Legal Studies (*Hart Publishing*)

C.W. = Copyright World (*Intellectual Property*)

CA = Court of Appeal

Cambrian L.R. = Cambrian Law Review (*University of Wales*)

Can. C.L. = Canadian Current Law (*Carswell*)

CCH. T.C. = CCH Tax Cases (*CCH Editions*)

CEC = Customs and Excise Commissioners

CFI = Court of First Instance

Ch. = Chancery (*Law Reports*) (*ICLR*)

Charities M. = Charities Management (*Mitre House*)

Childright = Childright (*Children's Legal Centre*)

Civ. Lit. = Civil Litigation (*CLT Professional Publishing*)

Civ. P.B. = Civil Practice Bulletin (*W. Green*)

Clarity = Clarity (*Mark Adler*)

CMAC = Courts Martial Appeal Court

Co. Acc. = Company Accountant (*Institute of Company Accountants*)

Co. Law. = Company Lawyer (*S&M*)

Com. Cas. = Commercial Cases

Com. Jud. J. = Commonwealth Judicial Journal (*Commonwealth Magistrates & Judges Association*)

Comm. Law. = Commercial Lawyer (*Commercial Lawyer*)

Comm. Leases = Commercial Leases (*Monitor Press*)

Comm. Prop. = Commercial Property (*CLP*)

Comm. L.J. = Commercial Law Journal (*Legalease Ltd*)

Comms. L. = Communications Law (*Butterworth Tolley Publishing*)

Comp. & Law = Computers & Law (*Society for Computers*)

Comp. Law E.C. = Competition Law in the European Communities (*Bryan Harris*)

Con. L.R. = Construction Law Reports (*Butterworth Tolley Publishing*)

Cons. L. Today = Consumer Law Today (*Monitor Press*)

Cons. Law = Construction Law (*Eclipse*)

Const. L.J. = Construction Law Journal (*S&M*)

Consum. L.J. = Consumer Law Journal (*CDC Publications*)

Conv. = Conveyancer and Property Lawyer (*S&M*)

Corp. Brief. = Corporate Briefing (*Monitor Press*)

Corp. C. = Corporate Counsel (*Commercial Lawyer*)

Costs L.R. = Costs Law Reports (*CLT Professional Publishing*)

Counsel = Counsel (*Butterworth Tolley Publishing*)

Cox C.C. = Cox's Criminal Cases

Cr. App. R. = Criminal Appeal Reports (*S&M*)

Cr. App. R. (S.) = Criminal Appeal Reports (Sentencing) (*S&M*)

Crim. L.J. = Criminal Law Journal (*LBC*)

Crim. L.B. = Criminal Law Bulletin (*W. Green*)

Crim. L.R. = Criminal Law Review (*S&M*)

Crim. Law. = Criminal Lawyer (*Butterworth Tolley Publishing*)

Criminologist = Criminologist (*Barry Rose*)

D.D. & R.M. = Due Diligence & Risk Management (*CLT Professional Publishing*)

D.L.R. = Dominion Law Reports

Denning L.J. = Denning Law Journal (*University of Buckingham*)

Dir. = Directive

Disc.L.R. = Discrimination Law Reports (*Central Law Training Ltd*)

D.P. & P.P. = Data Protection and Privacy Practice (*Masons Solicitors*)

E. & L. = Education and the Law (*Carfax*)

E. & P. = International Journal of Evidence & Proof (*Blackstone Press*)

E.B.L. = Electronic Business Law (*Eclipse Group*)

E.B.L.R. = European Business Law Review (*Kluwer*)

E.C.A. = Elderly Client Adviser (*Ark Publishing*)

E.C.C. = European Commercial Cases (*S&M*)

E.C.D.R. = European Copyright and Design Reports (*S&M*)

E.C.R. = European Court Reports (*TSO*)

E.C.L. & P. = E-Commerce Law & Policy (*Cecile Park Publishing*)

E.C.L.R. = European Competition Law Review (*S&M*)

E.D.D. & R.M. = Environmental Due Diligence & Risk Management (*CLT Professional Publishing*)

E.E.F.N. = Eastern European Forum Newsletter (*International Bar Association*)

E.E.L.R. = European Environmental Law Review (*Kluwer*)

E.F.A. Rev. = European Foreign Affairs Review (*Kluwer Law International*)

E.F.S.L. = European Financial Services Law (*Kluwer*)

E.G. = Estates Gazette (*Estates Gazette Ltd*)

E.G.C.S. = Estates Gazette Case Summaries (*Estates Gazette Ltd*)

E.G.L.R. = Estates Gazette Law Reports (*Estates Gazette Ltd*)

E.H.L.R. = Environmental Health Law Reports (*S&M*)

E.H.R.L.R. = European Human Rights Law Review (*S&M*)

E.H.R.R. = European Human Rights Reports (*S&M*)

E.I.B. = Environment Information Bulletin (*Eclipse*)

E.I.P.R. = European Intellectual Property Review (*S&M*)

E.I.R.R. = European Industrial Relations Review (*Eclipse*)

E.J.E.L. & P. = European Journal for Educational Law and Policy (*Kluwer*)

E.J.H.L. = European Journal of Health Law (*Kluwer*)

E.J.I.L. = European Journal of International Law (*S&M*)

E.J.L.R. = European Journal of Law Reform (*Kluwer*)

E.J.S.S. = European Journal of Social Security (*Kluwer*)

E.L. = Equitable Lawyer (*Gostick Hall Publications*)

E.L.A. Briefing = Employment Lawyers Association Briefing (*S&M*)

E.L.B. = Environmental Law Brief (*Monitor Press*)

E.L.J. = European Law Journal (*Blackwell*)

E.L.L.R. = Environmental Liability Law Review (*Kluwer*)

E.L.M. = Environmental Law and Management (*Chancery Law Publishing Ltd*)

E.L.R. = Education Law Reports (*Jordan*)

E.L.Rev. = European Law Review (*S&M*)

E.M.L.R. = Entertainment and Media Law Reports (*S&M*)

E.O.R. = Equal Opportunities Review (*Eclipse*)

E.O.R. Dig. = Equal Opportunities Review and Discrimination Case Law Digest (*Eclipse*)

E.P.L. = European Public Law (*Kluwer*)

E.P.L.I. = Education, Public Law and the Individual (*John Wiley & Sons Ltd*)

E.P.O.R. = European Patent Office Reports (*S&M*)

E.R.P.L. = European Review of Private Law (*Kluwer*)

E.T.M.R. = European Trade Marks Reports (*S&M*)

E.W.C.B. = European Works Councils Bulletin (*Eclipse*)

EAT = Employment Appeal Tribunal

EC C.P.N. = European Commission Competition Policy Newsletter (*Commission of the European Communities*)

EC T.J. = EC Tax Journal (*Key Haven*)

EC T.R. = EC Tax Review (*Kluwer*)

Ecc. L.J. = Ecclesiastical Law Journal (*Ecclesiastical Law Society*)

Ed. C.R. = Education Case Reports (*S&M*)

EDI L.R. = Electronic Data Interchange Law Review (*Kluwer*)

ECJ = European Court of Justice

Eco M. & A. = Eco-Management & Auditing (*John Wiley & Sons Ltd*)

Ed. Law. = Education Law Journal (*Jordan*)

Ed. L.M. = Education Law Monitor (*Monitor Press*)

Edin. L.R. = Edinburgh Law Review (*T & T Clark*)

Emp. L. Brief. = Employment Law Briefing (*S&M*)

Emp. L.B. = Employment Law Bulletin (*W. Green*)

Emp L.J. = Employment Law Journal (*Legalease Ltd*)

Emp. Law. = Employment Lawyer (*CCH Editions Ltd*)

Emp. Lit. = Employment Litigation (*CLP*)

ENDS = ENDS Report (*Environmental Data Services*)

Ent. L.R. = Entertainment Law Review (*S&M*)

Env. L.B. = Environmental Law Bulletin (*W. Green*)

Env. L.M. = Environmental Law Monthly (*Monitor Press*)

Env. L.R. = Environmental Law Reports (*S&M*)

Env. Law = Environmental Law (*S&M*)

Env. Liability = Environmental Liability (*Lawtext*)

EU Focus = European Union Focus (*CCH Editions Ltd*)

Eu. L.R. = European Law Reports (*John Wiley & Sons Ltd*)

Eur. Access = European Access (*Chadwyck Healey*)

Eur. Counsel = European Counsel (*Legal & Commercial Publishing*)

Eur. J. Crime Cr. L. Cr. J. = European Journal of Crime, Criminal Law and Criminal Justice (*Kluwer*)

Euro. Env. = European Environment (*John Wiley & Sons Ltd*)

Euro. Law. = European Lawyer (*H.S. Legal Publishing*)

Euro. L.B. = European Legal Business (*Legalease*)

Euro. L.M. = European Law Monitor (*Monitor Press*)

Euro. Tax. = European Taxation (*IBFD*)

Expert = Expert (*Academy of Experts S&M*)

F & C.L. = Finance & Credit Law (*Monitor Press*)

F. & D.L.R. = Futures & Derivatives Law Review (*Cavendish*)

F.C.R. = Family Court Reporter (*Tolleys Ltd*)

F.D. & D.I.B. = Food, Drinks & Drugs Industry Bulletin (*Monitor*)

F.I. = Fraud Intelligence (*Informa Publishing Group*)

F.I.T.A.R. = Financial Instruments Tax & Accounting Review (*CTA Financial Publishing*)

F.L.R. = Family Law Reports (*Jordan*)

F.L.T. = Family Law Today (*Monitor Press*)

F.R. = Financial Regulator (*Central Banking Publications Ltd*)

F.S.B. = Financial Services Brief (*S&M*)

F.S. Bulletin = Financial Services Bulletin (*Informa Publishing Group*)

F.S.R. = Fleet Street Reports (*S&M*)

Fairplay = Fairplay (*Fairplay Publication*)

Fam. = Family Division (*Law Reports*) (*ICLR*)

Fam. L.B. = Family Law Bulletin (*W. Green*)

Fam. L.R. = Greens Family Law Reports (*W. Green*)

Fam. Law = Family Law (*Jordan*)

Fam. M. = Family Matters (*S&M*)

Fam. Med. = Family Mediation (*National Association of Family Mediation & Conciliation Services*)

Farm Law = Farm Law (*Informa Publishing Group*)

FarmT.B. = FarmTax Brief (*Monitor Press*)

Fem. L.S. = Feminist Legal Studies (*Deborah Charles*)

Food L.M. = Food Law Monthly (*Monitor*)

G.C.R. = Global Competition Review (*Law Business Research Ltd*)

G.I.L.S.I. = Gazette Incorporated Law Society of Ireland (*The Law Society*)

G.L. & B. = Global Law & Business (*Global Law & Business*)

G.L.J. = Guernsey Law Journal (*Greffier*)

G.W.D. = Green's Weekly Digest (*W. Green*)

H. & S.B. = Health and Safety Bulletin (*Eclipse*)

H. & S.M. = Health & Safety Monitor (*Monitor Press*)

H.L.J. = Hibernian Law Journal (*Law Society of Ireland*)

H.L.M. = Housing Law Monitor (*Monitor Press*)

H.L.R. = Housing Law Reports (*S&M*)

H.R.C.D. = Human Rights Case Digest (*S&M*)

H.R. & UK P. = Human Rights & UK Practice (*CLT Professional Publishing*)

H.S. = Hazardous Substances (*Monitor Press*)

HC = House of Commons

Health Law = Health Law (*Monitor Press*)

HL = House of Lords

Hold. L.R. = Holdsworth Law Review (*University of Birmingham*)

Hous. L.R. = Greens Housing Law Reports (*W. Green*)

Howard Journal = Howard Journal of Criminal Justice (*Blackwell*)

I. & C.T.L. = Information & Communications Technology Law (*Carfax*)

I. & N.L. & P. = Immigration & Nationality Law & Practice (*ButterworthTolley Publishing*)

I.B.I.S. Rep. = Information Benefits Service Report (*Charles D. Spencer & Associates Inc.*)

I.B.L. = International Business Lawyer (*Blackwell*)

I.B.R. = Irish Banking Review (*The Irish Banking Review*)

I. Bull. = Interights Bulletin (*Interights*)

I.C.C.L.J. = International and Comparative Corporate Law Journal (*Kluwer*)

I.C.C.L.R. = International Company and Commercial Law Review (*S&M*)

I.C.L.J. = Irish Criminal Law Journal (*Round Hall/S&M*)

I.C.L.Q. = International & Comparative Law Quarterly (*British Institute of International and Comparative Law*)

I.C.L.R. = International Construction Law Review (*LLP*)

I.C.L. Rev. = International Construction Law Review (*Informa Publishing Group*)

I.C.R. = Industrial Cases Reports (*ICLR*)

I.E.L.T.R. = International Energy Law and Taxation Review (*S&M*)

I.F.L. = International Family Law (*Jordan*)

I.F.L. Rev. = International Financial Law Review (*Euromoney*)

I.H.L. = In-House Lawyer (*Legalease*)

I.I.E.L. = Immigration and International Employment Law (*Eclipse Group Ltd*)

I.I.L. Rev. = International Internet Law Review (*Euromoney Institutional Investor Plc*)

I.I.R. = International Insolvency Review (*Chancery Law*)

I.J.B.L. = International Journal of Biosciences and the Law (*A B Academic*)

I.J.C.L.P. = International Journal of Communications Law and Policy (http://www.digital-Law.Net/WCLP/)

I.J.D.L. = International Journal of Discrimination and the Law (*A B Academic*)

I.J.E.C.L. & P. = International Journal of Electronic Commerce & Practice (*CLT Professional Publishers*)

I.J.E.L. = Irish Journal of European Law (*Round Hall/S&M*)

I.J.F.D.L. = International Journal of Franchising and Distribution Law (*Kluwer*)

I.J.I.L. = International Journal of Insurance Law (*LLP*)

I.J.L & I.T. = International Journal of Law & InformationTechnology (*OUP*)

I.J.L.P. = International Journal of the Legal Profession (*Carfax*)

I.J.M.C.L. = International Journal of Marine & Coastal Law (*Kluwer*)

I.J.O.S.L. = International Journal Of Shipping Law (*LLP*)

I.J.R.L. = International Journal of Refugee Law (*OUP*)

I.J.S.L. = International Journal for the Semiotics of Law (*Deborah Charles*)

I.L. & P. = Insolvency Law & Practice (*ButterworthTolley Publishing*)

I.L.J. = Industrial Law Journal (*Industrial Law Society*)

I.L.P. = International Legal Practitioner (*International BarAssociation*)

I.L.T. = Irish LawTimes (*Round Hall/S&M*)

I.L.T.R. = Irish Law Times Reports (*Round Hall/ S&M*)

I.M.L. = International Media Law (*S&M*)

I.N.L.R. = Immigration and Nationality Law Reports (*Jordan*)

I.P. = International Peacekeeping (*Kluwer*)

I.P. & I.T. Law = Intellectual Property and InformationTechnology Law (*CLP*)

I.P. Law = Intellectual Property Lawyer (*CCH Editions*)

I.P. News. = Intellectual Property Newsletter (*Monitor Press*)

I.P.D. = Intellectual Property Decisions (*Monitor Press*)

I.P.E.L.J. = Irish Planning and Environmental Law Journal (*Round Hall/S&M*)

I.P.Q. = Intellectual Property Quarterly (*S&M*)

I.P.S.P.I. = Insolvency Practitioner of the Society of Practitioners of Insolvency (*Society of Practitioners of Insolvency*)

I.R.L.A. = Insurance & Reinsurance Law Alert (*LLP Ltd*)

I.R.L.B. = Industrial Relations Law Bulletin (*Eclipse*)

I.R.L.C.T. = International Review of Law Computers & Technology (*Carfax*)

I.R.L.R. = Industrial Relations Law Reports (*Eclipse*)

I.R.T.B. = Inland Revenue Tax Bulletin (*Inland Revenue*)

I.R.V. = International Review of Victimology (*A B Academic*)

I.T. & C.L.J. = Information Technology & Communications Law Journal (*Legalease*)

IT & C.L.R. = IT & Communications Law Reports (*Legalease*)

I.T.L.J. = International Travel Law Journal (*Travel Law Centre*)

I.T.L.Q. = Internationnal Trade Law Quarterly (*LLP Ltd*)

I.T.P.J. = International Transfer Pricing Journal (*IBFD Publications BV*)

I.T.R. = Industrial Tribunal Reports

I.T.R. = International Tax Review (*Euromoney*)

I.T. Rep. = International Tax Report (*Monitor*)

I.T. rev. = International Tax Review (*Euromoney*)

I.V.M. = International VAT Monitor (*IBFD*)

IDS Brief = IDS Brief, Employment Law and Practice (*Income Data Services Ltd*)

IDS Emp. E. = IDS Employment Europe (*Income Data Services Ltd*)

IDS P.L.R. = IDS Pensions Law Reports (*Income Data Services Ltd*)

IH = Inner House of the Court of Session

IIC = International Review of Industrial Property and Copyright Law (*John Wiley & Sons Ltd*)

Imm. A.R. = Immigration Appeals Reports (*TSO*)

In Comp. = In Competition (*S&M*)

Independent = Independent Law Reports

Info. T.L.R. = Information Technology Law Reports (*Lawtext Publishing*)

Ins. L.M. = Insurance Law Monthly (*Monitor Press*)

Insolv. B. = Insolvency Bulletin (*Armstrong Information Ltd*)

Insolv. Int. = Insolvency Intelligence (*S&M*)

Insolv. L. = Insolvency Lawyer (*S&M*)

Insolvency = Insolvency (*Griffin Multimedia*)

Int. A.L.R. = International Arbitration Law Review (*S&M*)

Int. J. Comp. L.L.I.R. = International Journal of Comparative Labour Law and Industrial Relations (*Kluwer*)

Int. J. Law & Fam. = International Journal of Law, Policy and the Family (*OUP*)

Int. J. Soc. L. = International Journal of the Sociology of Law (*Academic Press Ltd*)

Int. M.L. = International Maritime Law (*S&M*)

Int. Rel. = International Relations (*David Davies Memorial Institute*)

Int. T.L.R. = International Trade Law & Regulation (*S&M ESC Publishing*)

Intertax = Intertax (*Kluwer*)

Ir. B.L. = Irish Business Law (*Inns Quay Publishing*)

Ir. T.R. = Irish Tax Review (*Institute of Taxation in Ireland*)

IT L.T. = IT Law Today (*Monitor Press*)

J.A.C.L. = Journal of Armed Conflict Law (*Nottingham University Press*)

J.A.L. = Journal of African Law (*OUP*)

J.B.L. = Journal of Business Law (*S&M*)

J.C. = Justiciary Cases

J.C. & S.L. = Journal of Conflict & Security Law (*Oxford University Press*)

J.C.L.P. = Journal of Competition Law & Policy (*OECD Publications Service*)

J. Civ. Lib. = Journal of Civil Liberties (*Northumbria Law Press*)

J. Com. Mar. St. = Journal of Common Market Studies (*Blackwell*)

J. Crim. L. = Journal of Criminal Law (*Pageant*)

J.E.C.L. & P. = Journal of Electronic Commerce Law and Practice (*Butterworth Tolley Publishing*)

J.E.L.P. = Journal of Employment Law & Practice (*Butterworth Tolley Publishing*)

J. Env. L. = Journal of Environmental Law (*OUP*)

J.E.R.L. = Journal of Energy & Natural Resources Law (*Kluwer*)

J.F.C. = Journal of Financial Crime (*Henry Stewart*)

J.F.R. & C. = Journal of Financial Regulation and Compliance (*Henry Stewart*)

J.H.L. = Journal of Housing Law (*S&M*)

J.I.B.L. = Journal of International Banking Law (*S&M*)

J.I.B.R. = Journal of International Banking Regulation (*Euromoney Publications*)

J.I.E.L. = Journal of International Economic Law (*OUP*)

J.I.F.D.L. = Journal of International Franchising & Distribution Law (*Butterworth Tolley Publishing*)

J.I.L.T. = Journal of Information, Law & Technology (*http://elj.warwick.ac.uk/jilt*)

J. Int. Arb. = Journal of International Arbitration (*Kluwer*)

J. Int. P. = Journal of International Trust and Corporate Planning (*John Wiley*)

J.L.G.L. = Journal of Local Government Law (*S&M*)

J.L.S. = Journal of Legislative Studies (*Cass*)

J.L.S.S. = Journal of the Law Society of Scotland (*Law Society of Scotland*)

J. Law & Soc. = Journal of Law and Society (*Blackwell*)

J. Leg. Hist. = Journal of Legal History (*Cass*)

J.M.L. & P. = Journal of Media Law & Practice (*Butterworth Tolley Publishing*)

J.M.L.C. = Journal of Money Laundering Control (*Henry Stewart Publications*)

J.P. = Justice of the Peace (*Justice of the Peace Ltd*)

J.P.I.L. = Journal of Personal Injury Litigation (*S&M*)

J.P.L. = Journal of Planning & Environment Law (*S&M*)

J.P.M. = Journal of Pensions Management (*Henry Stewart*)

J.P.M. & M. = Journal of Pensions Management and Marketing (*Henry Stewart*)

J.P.N. = Justice of the Peace Reports & Local Government Notes of Cases (*Justice of the Peace Ltd*)

J.P. Rep. = Justice of the Peace and Local Government Law Reports (*Justice of the Peace Ltd*)

J.R. = Judicial Review (*Hart Publishing Ltd*)

J.S.B.J. = Judicial Studies Board Journal (*Blackstone Press*)

J.S.S.L. = Journal of Social Security Law (*S&M*)

J. Soc. Wel. & Fam. L. = Journal of Social Welfare and Family Law (*Routledge*)

J.W.T. = Journal of World Trade (*Kluwer*)

Jersey L.R. = Jersey Law Review (*The Jersey Law Review*)
Jur. Rev. = Juridical Review (*W. Green*)

K.B. = Kings Bench (*Law Reports*) (*ICLR*)
K.C.L.J. = Kings College Law Journal (*King's College London*)
K.I.R. = Knights Industrial Reports

L. & T. Review = Landlord & Tenant Review (*S&M*)
L. Ex. = Legal Executive (*ILEX*)
L.E. = Lawyers' Europe (*Butterworth Tolley Publishing*)
L.F. = Litigation Funding (*Law Society Publishing*)
L.G. and L. = Local Government and Law (*Monitor Press*)
L.G. Rev. = Local Government Review (*Barry Rose*)
L.G.C. Law & Admin. = Local Government Chronicle Law & Administration (*Local Government Chronicle Ltd*)
L.G.C. = Local Government Chronicle (*Local Government Chronicle Ltd*)
L.G.L.R. = Local Government Law Reports (*S&M*)
L.I.E.I. = Legal Issues of European Integration (*Kluwer*)
L.M.C.L.Q. = Lloyd's Maritime & Commercial Law Quarterly (*LLP*)
L.P. or L.V.C. = references to denote Lands Tribunal decision (*transcripts available from the Lands Tribunal*)
L.Q.R. = Law Quarterly Review (*S&M*)
L.R. = Licensing Review (*Benedict Books*)
L.R. App. Cas. = Law Reports Appeal Cases
L.R.L.R. = Lloyd's Reinsurance Law Reports (*LLP*)
L.S. = Legal Studies (*Butterworth Tolley Publishing*)
L.S.G. = Law Society Gazette (*The Law Society*)
L. & T.R. = Landlord and Tenant Reports (*S&M*)
Law & Crit. = Law and Critique (*Deborah Charles*)
Law & Just. = Law & Justice (*Plowden*)
Law & Pol. = Law & Policy (*Blackwell*)
Law Lib. = Law Librarian (*S&M*)
Law Teach. = Law Teacher (*S&M*)
Lawyer = Lawyer (*Centaur Communications Group*)
Legal Action = Legal Action (*Legal Action Group*)
Legal Bus. = Legal Business (*Legalease*)
Legal Ethics = Legal Ethics (*Hart Publishing Ltd*)
Legal IT = Legal IT (*Global Professional Publishing*)
Legal Week = *WDIS Ltd*)
Lit. = Litigation (*Barry Rose*)
Liverpool L.R. = Liverpool Law Review (*Deborah Charles*)
Lloyd's Rep. = Lloyd's Law Reports (*LLP*)
Lloyd's Rep. Bank. = Lloyd's Law Reports Banking (*LLP*)
Lloyd's Rep. I.R. = Lloyd's Law Reports Insurance & Reinsurance (*LLP*)
Lloyd's Rep. Med. = Lloyd's Law Report Medical (*LLP*)

Lloyd's Rep. P.N. = Lloyd's Law Reports Professional Negligence (*LLP*)
Ll. Rep. = Lloyd's List Reports (*LLP*)
LVAC = Land Valuation Appeal Court

M.A.L.Q.R. = Model Arbitration Law Quarterly Review (*Simmons & Hill Publishing Ltd*)
M. Advocate = Maritime Advocate (*Merlin Legal Publishing*)
M.C.P. = Magistrates' Courts Practice (*CLP*)
M.D.U. Jour. = Medical Defence Union Journal (*Medical Defence Union*)
M.E.C.L.R. = Middle East Commercial Law Review (*S&M*)
M.I.P. = Managing Intellectual Property (*Euromoney*)
M.J. = Maastricht Journal of European and Comparative Law (*Roger Bayliss*)
M.J.L.S. = Mountbatten Journal of Legal Studies (*Southampton Institute*)
M.L.B. = Manx Law Bulletin (*Central Reference*)
M.L.J.I. = Medico-Legal Journal of Ireland (*Round Hall/S&M*)
M.L.N. = Media Lawyer Newsletter (*Tom Welsh*)
M.L.R. = Modern Law Review (*Blackwell*)
Magistrate = Magistrate (*Magistrate's Association*)
Masons C.L.R. = Masons Computer Law Reports
Med. L. Int. = Medical Law International (*A B Academic Publishing*)
Med. L. Mon. = Medical Law Monitor (*Monitor Press*)
Med. L. Rev. = Medical Law Review (*OUP*)
Med. L.R. = Medical Law Reports (*OUP*)
Med. Leg. J. = Medico-Legal Journal (*Dramrite Printers*)
Med. Lit. = Medical Litigation (*Medical Litigation Strategies*)
Med. Sci. Law = Medicine, Science & the Law (*Chiltern*)

N.I. = Northern Ireland Law Reports (*Butterworth Tolley Publishing*)
N.I.L.Q. = Northern Ireland Legal Quarterly (*SLS Legal Publications*)
N.L.J. = New Law Journal (*Butterworth Tolley Publishing*)
N.P.C. = New Property Cases (*New Property Cases Ltd*)
N.Q.H.R. = Netherlands Quarterly of Human Rights (*Kluwer*)
N.Z.L.R. = New Zealand Law Reports
Nott. L.J. = Nottingham Law Journal (*Nottingham Trent University*)

O.D. and I.L. = Ocean Development and International Law (*Taylor & Francis Ltd*)
O.J.L.S. = Oxford Journal of Legal Studies (*OUP*)
O.P.L.R. = Occupational Pensions Law Reports (*Eclipse Group*)
O.S.S. Bull. = Office for the Supervision of Solicitors Bulletin (*The Law Society's Gazette*)
O.T.R. = Offshore Taxation Review (*Key Haven*)
Offshore Red = Offshore Red (*Campden Publishing*)
Occ. Pen. = Occupational Pensions (*Eclipse*)
OJ = Official Journal of the European Communities

OJEPO = European Patent Office Official Journal

P&I Int. = P & I International (*LLP*)
P. = Probate, Divorce and Admiralty (*Law Reports*)
P. & C.R. = Property, Planning & Compensation Reports (*S&M*)
P. & M.I.L.L. = Personal and Medical Injuries Law Letter (*Monitor Press*)
P. & P. = Practice and Procedure (*S&M*)
P. & S. = Punishment & Society (*Sage*)
P. Injury = Personal Injury (*CLP*)
P.A.D. = Planning Appeal Decisions (*S&M*)
P.C.B. = Private Client Business (*S&M*)
P.C.L.B. = Practitioners' Child Law Bulletin (*S&M*)
P.E.B.L. = Perspectives on European Business Law (*European Perspectives Publications*)
P.E.L.B. = Planning and Environmental Law Bulletin (*S&M*)
P.I. = Personal Injury (*John Wiley & Sons Ltd*)
P.I.C. = Palmer's In Company (*S&M*)
P.I.Q.R. = Personal Injuries and Quantum Reports (*S&M*)
P.L. & B.I.N. = Privacy Laws & Business International Newsletter (*Privacy Law & Business*)
P.L. = Public Law (*S&M*)
P.L.B. = Property Law Bulletin (*S&M*)
P.L.C. = Practical Law for Companies (*Legal & Commercial Publishing*)
P.L.C.R. = Planning Law Case Reports (*S&M*)
P.L.J. = Property Law Journal = Property Law Journal (*Legalease*)
P.L.R. = Planning Law Reports (*Estates Gazette Ltd*)
P.N. = Professional Negligence (*Butterworth Tolley Publishing*)
P.N.L.R. = Professional Negligence and Liability Reports (*S&M*)
P.P.L. = Practical Planning Law (*CLP*)
P.P.L.R. = Public Procurement Law Review (*S&M*)
P.S.P. = Police Station Practice (*CLP*)
P.S.T. = Pension Scheme Trustee (*S&M*)
P.T. = Pensions Today (*Monitor Press*)
P.T.P.R. = Personal Tax Planning Review (*Key Haven*)
PW. = Patent World (*Intellectual Property*)
Parl. Aff. = Parliamentary Affairs (*OUP*)
Pen. Law = Pension Lawyer (*Keith Wallace*) (formerly B.P.L. = British Pension Lawyer
Pen. World = Pensions World (*Butterworth Tolley Publishing*)
Pol. J. = Police Journal (*Barry Rose*)
Policing T. = Policing Today (*Police Review*)
Prison Serv. J. = Prison Service Journal (*HM Prison, Leyhill*)
Probat. J. = Probation Journal (*National Association of Probation Officers*)
Prop. L.B. = Property Law Bulletin (*W. Green*)

Q.A. = Quarterly Account (*Money Advice Association*)
Q.B. = Queen's Bench (*Law Reports*) (*ICLR*)
Q.B.D. = Law Reports Queen's Bench Division
Q.R. = Quantum Reports (*S&M*)

R.A. = Rating Appeals (*Rating Publishers*)

R.A.D.I.C. = African Journal of International and Comparative Law (*African Society*)
R.A.L.Q. = Receivers, Administrators and Liquidators Quarterly (*Key Haven*)
R.C.I.S.G. = Review of the Convention on Contracts for the International Sale of Goods (*Kluwer*)
R.E.C.I.E.L. = Review of European Community and International Environmental Law (*Blackwell*)
R.L.R. = Restitution Law Review (*Mansfield Press*)
R.P.C. = Reports of Patent, Design and Trade Mark Cases (*The Patent Office*)
R.R.L.R. = Rent Review & Lease Renewal (*MCB University Press*)
R.T.I. = Road Traffic Indicator (*S&M*) (Ceased publication September 2000)
R.T.R. = Road Traffic Reports (*S&M*)
R.V.R. = Rating and Valuation Reporter (*Rating Publishers*)
R.W.L.R. = Rights of Way Law Review (*Rights of Way Law Review*)
Ratio Juris = Ratio Juris (*Blackwell*)
Recovery = Recovery (*Society of Practitioners of Insolvency*)
Rep. B. = Reparation Bulletin (*W. Green*)
Rep. L.R. = Greens Reparation Law Reports (*W. Green*)
Res Publica = Res Publica (*Deborah Charles*)
Rev. C.E.E. Law = Review of Central and East European Law (*Kluwer*)
ROW Bulletin = Rights of Women Bulletin (*Rights of Women*)
RPC = Restrictive Practices Court

S. & L.J. = Sport and the Law Journal (*British Association for Sport & Law*)
S. & L.S. = Social & Legal Studies (*Sage*)
S. & T.L.I. = Shipping & Transport Lawyer International (*Guthrum House Ltd*)
S. News = Sentencing News (*S&M*)
S.C. = Session Cases (*S&M/W. Green*)
S.C. (*HL*) = Session Cases (*House of Lords*)
S.C.A.L. & P. = Scottish constitutional and Administrative Law & Practice (*CLT Professional Publishing*)
S.C.C.R. = Scottish Criminal Case Reports (*The Law Society of Scotland*)
S.C.L.R. = Scottish Civil Law Reports (*The Law Society of Scotland*)
S.C.P. News = Supreme Court Practice News (*S&M*)
S.J. = Solicitors Journal (*S&M*)
S.J.L.B. = Solicitors Journal Law Brief (*S&M*)
S.L.A. & P. = Sports Law Administration & Practice (*Monitor Press*)
S.L.B. = Sports Law Bulletin (*Anglia Sports Law Research Centre*)
S.L.C.R. = Scottish Land Court Reports
S.L.C.R. Apps. = Scottish Land Court Reports (*appendix*)
S.L.G. = Scottish Law Gazette (*Scottish Law Agents Society*)
S.L.L.P. = Scottish Licensing Law & Practice (*Scottish Licensing Services Ltd*)
S.L.P.Q. = Scottish Law & Practice Quarterly (*T & T Clark*)
S.L.Rev. = Student Law Review (*Cavendish*)
S.L.T. = Scots Law Times (*S&M/W. Green*)
S.L.T. (Land Ct) = Scots Law Times Land Court Reports (*S&M/W. Green*)

S.L.T. (Lands Tr) = Scots Law Times Lands Tribunal Reports (*S&M/W. Green*)

S.L.T. (Lyon Ct) = Scots Law Times Lyon Court Reports (*S&M/W. Green*)

S.L.T. News = Scots Law Times News Section (*S&M/W. Green*)

S.L.T. (Notes) = Scots Law Times Notes of Recent Decisions (*1946-1981*) (*S&M/W. Green*)

S.L.T. (Sh Ct) = Scots Law Times Sheriff Court Reports (*S&M/W. Green*)

S.N. = Session Notes

S.P.E.L. = Scottish Planning and Environmental Law (*Planning Exchange*)

S.P.L.R. = Scottish Parliament Law Review (*W. Green*)

S.P.T.L. Reporter = Society of Public Teachers of Law Reporter (*Queen Mary*)

S.T.C. = Simons Tax Cases (*Butterworth Tolley Publishing*)

S.T.C. (SCD) = Simons Tax Cases: Special Commissioners Decisions (*Butterworth Tolley Publishing*)

S.T.I. (SCD) = Simons Tax Intelligence (*Butterworth Tolley Publishing*)

S.W.T.I. = Simon's Weekly Tax Intelligence (*Butterworth Tolley Publishing*)

SCOLAG = SCOLAG (*Scottish Legal Action Group*)

SI = Statutory Instrument

S. & C.L. = Sports and Character Licensing (*Informa Publishing Group Ltd*)

Soc. L. = Socialist Lawyer (*Haldane Society*)

Stat. L.R. = Statute Law Review (*OUP*)

Sudebnik = Sudebnik (*Simmonds & Hill*)

T. & E.T.J. = Trusts and Estates Tax Journal (*Legalease*)

T. & T. = Trusts & Trustees (*Gostick Hall*)

T.A.Q. = The Aviation Quarterly (*LLP*)

T.B. = Technical Bulletin (*Association of Business Recovery Professionals*)

T.C. or Tax.Cas. = Tax Cases (*TSO*)

T.C.L.R. = Technology and Construction Law Reports (*S&M*)

T & E.L.J. = Trusts and Estates Law Journal (*Legalease*)

T.E.L.L. = Tolley's Employment Law-Line (*Butterworth Tolley Publishing*)

T.L.P. = Transport Law & Policy (*Waterfront Partnership*)

T.N.I.B. = Tolley's National Insurance Brief (*Butterworth Tolley Publishing*)

T.O.C. = Transnational Organized Crime (*Cass*)

T.P.I.E.U.F. = Tax Planning International European Union Focus (*BNA International Inc*)

T.P.I.R. = Tax Planning International Review (*BNA International Inc*)

T.P.I. e-commerce = Tax Planning International e-commerce (*BNA International Inc*)

T.P.I.A.P.F. = Tax Planning International Asia.Pacific Focus (*BNA International Inc*)

T.P.T.S. = Tolley's Practical Tax Service (*Butterworth Tolley Publishing*)

T.P.V.S. = Tolley's Practical VAT Service (*Butterworth Tolley Publishing*)

T.S.B.P.I. = Technical Bulletin of the Society of Practitioners of Insolvency

T.W. = Trademark World (*Intellectual Property*)

TACT Review = Tolley's Practical Audit & Accounting (*The Association of Corporate Trustees*)

Tax A. = Taxation Adviser (*The Manson Group Ltd*)

Tax B. = Tax Briefing (*Office of the Revenue Commissioners*)

Tax J. = Tax Journal (*Butterworth Tolley Publishing*)

Tax. = Taxation (*Butterworth Tolley Publishing*)

Taxline = Taxline (*Tax Faculty*)

Theo. Crim. = Theoretical Criminology (*Sage Publications*)

Tr. & Est. = Trusts & Estates (*Monitor Press*)

Tr. L.R. = Trading Law Reports (*Barry Rose*)

Trans. ref. = Transcript reference number

Tribunals = = Tribunals (*OUP*)

Tru. L.I. = Trust Law International (*Butterworth Tolley Publishing*)

TSO = The Stationery Office

The Times = Times Law Reports

U.L.R. = Utilities Law Review (*Chancery Law Publishing Ltd*)

UCELNET = Universities and Colleges Education Law Network (*University of Stirling*)

UK C.L.R. = UK Competition Law Reports (*S&M*)

Uniform L.R. = Uniform Law Review (*Kluwer*)

V. & D.R. = Value Added Tax and Duties Reports (*TSO*)

V.A.T.T.R. = Value Added Tax Tribunal Reports (*TSO*)

VAT Int. = VAT Intelligence (*Gee Publishing*)

VAT Plan. = VAT Planning (*Butterworth Tolley Publishing*)

W. Comp. = World Competition (*Kluwer*)

W.B. = Welfare Benefits (*CLP*)

W.L. = Water Law (*Chancery Law Publishing Ltd*)

W.L.L.R. = World Licensing Law Report (*BNA International Inc*)

W.L.R. = Weekly Law Reports (*ICLR*)

Web J.C.L.I. = Web Journal of Current Legal Issues (*Blackstone*) http://webjcli.ncl.ac.uk

Welf. R. Bull. = Welfare Rights Bulletin (*Child Poverty*)

World I.L.R. = World Internet Law Report (*BNA International Inc*)

Worldlaw Bus. = Worldlaw Business (*Euromoney Publications*)

Writ = Writ (*Northern Ireland Law Society*)

Y.C. & M.L. = Yearbook of Copyright and Media Law (*OUP*) (formerly Y.M.E.L. = Yearbook of Media & Entertainment Law (*OUP*)

Y.E.L. = Yearbook of European Law (*OUP*)

Yb. Int'l Env. L. = Yearbook of International Environmental Law (*OUP*)

CURRENT LAW
YEAR BOOK 2000

UK, ENGLAND & WALES & EU

ACCOUNTANCY

1. **Accounting standards – annual accounts – global valuation of warranty liabilities – European Union**

    [Fourth Council Directive 78/660 based on Art.54(3)(g) of the Treaty on the annual accounts of certain types of companies Art.42.]

    B, a German building company, included a global provision based on two per cent of its total work value for warranty liabilities when calculating its annual tax liability where these arose in law prior to the date of its balance sheet but only took effect after that date. The German tax authorities agreed with the principle behind B's tax provision, but limited the provision to 0.5 per cent of B's relevant turnover for the previous two years. The national court considered that Council Directive 78/660 precluded the use of global provisions for liabilities on balance sheets, and that asset and liability items were to be valued separately. The court referred the matter to the ECJ for a preliminary ruling as to whether (1) the Directive allowed provision to be made for contingent warranty liabilities which had arisen at law, but which only became operative after the date of the balance sheet; (2) if the Directive permitted such provisions, they could be provided for globally, and (3) such global provision was to be limited to a set percentage of turnover including warranties.

    Held, that (1) the Directive required provisions to be made for contingent warranty liabilities which were effective in law prior to the date of the balance sheet but only took effect after that date; (2) a global valuation was often the most appropriate way of achieving a true and fair view of the amount involved. However, this should be in accordance with national rules and observe the requirement that accounts were to give a true and fair financial view of the company. Further, Art.42 required that provisions for charges and other liabilities had to stay within the bounds of what was necessary, and (3) national authorities had to permit global provisions for warranty claims to be determined by reference to the experiences of other companies in that sector as well as those of the company in the instant case.

    DE&ES BAUUNTERNEHMUNG GmbH v. FINANZAMT BERGHEIM (C275/97) [1999] E.C.R. I-5331, J-P Puissochet (President), ECJ.

2. **Auditors – share sales – impact of price indication in audit sheet**

    H sought a declaration that a dispute concerning the purchase price of shares was limited to the audit of the balance sheet. M contended that the audit undertaken was manifestly defective and justified an investigation of the manner in which the auditors carried out the calculation of the material amounts.

Held, giving judgment for the defendant, that an inquiry into the independent expert auditor's working papers was essential to decide whether their audit procedures were competent. Whilst the papers had played a material part in the price ascertainment process, it was not correct to use them to impose a limitation. If the parties had intended such a narrow view to be taken, indication would have been given in the agreement.

HILLSBRIDGE INVESTMENTS LTD v. MORESFIELD LTD [2000] 2 B.C.L.C. 241, Rimer, J., Ch D.

ADMINISTRATION OF JUSTICE

3. **Access to justice – membership organisations – approved bodies**

ACCESS TO JUSTICE (MEMBERSHIP ORGANISATIONS) REGULATIONS 2000, SI 2000 693; made under the Access to Justice Act 1999 s.30. In force: April 1, 2000; £1.00.

These Regulations specify bodies which are for the time being approved by the Lord Chancellor for the purpose of the Access to Justice Act 1999 s.30, which applies where a body undertakes to meet liabilities which members of the body or other persons who are parties to proceedings may incur to pay the costs of other parties. They specify an additional amount, which may be included in costs payable to a member of such a body to cover insurance or other provision made by the body against the risk of having to meet those liabilities of the member, as the likely cost to the member of the premium of an insurance policy against the risk in question.

4. **Access to Justice Act 1999 (c.22) – Commencement No.3 Order**

ACCESS TO JUSTICE ACT 1999 (COMMENCEMENT NO.3, TRANSITIONAL PROVISIONS AND SAVINGS) ORDER 2000, SI 2000 774 (C.16); made under the Access to Justice Act 1999 s.108, Sch.14 para.1, Sch.14 para.8. Commencement details: bringing into force various provisions of the Act on April 1, 2000; £2.50.

This Order brings into force, on April 1, 2000, various provisions of the Access to Justice Act 1999 relating to the Legal Services Commission and Community Legal Service; disclosure of information; services relating to foreign law; misrepresentation; conditional fee agreements; and costs.

5. **Access to Justice Act 1999 (c.22) – Commencement No.4 Order**

ACCESS TO JUSTICE ACT 1999 (COMMENCEMENT ORDER NO.4 AND TRANSITIONAL PROVISIONS) ORDER 2000, SI 2000 1920 (C.48); made under the Access to Justice Act 1999 s.108, Sch.14 para.1. Commencement details: bringing into force various provisions of the Act on July 31, 2000 and August 31, 2000; £1.50.

This Order brings into force various provisions of the Access to Justice Act 1999 relating to rights of audience and rights to conduct litigation, barristers and solicitors, the unification and renaming of the stipendiary bench, and the Greater London Magistrates' Courts Authority.

6. **Access to Justice Act 1999 (c.22) – Commencement Order No.5 and Transitional Provisions Order**

ACCESS TO JUSTICE ACT 1999 (COMMENCEMENT ORDER NO.5 AND TRANSITIONAL PROVISIONS) ORDER 2000, SI 2000 3280 (C.104); made under the Access to Justice Act 1999 s.108, Sch.14 para.1. Commencement details: bringing into force various provisions of the Act on January 8, 2001; £1.75.

This Order, which brings into force the Access to Justice Act 1999 ss. 92 to 95, relates to the execution of warrants issued by justices of the peace, together with associated repeals, on January 8, 2001.

7. **Child protection – disclosure – former allegations of sex abuse – no existence of a "pressing need" for disclosure**

[European Convention on Human Rights 1950 Art.8.]

LM applied for judicial review of the decision of a local authority and local police authority to disclose to a county council with whom he contracted to supply school transport, allegations that he had sexually abused his daughter and, while employed as an officer in a hostel for vulnerable children, a child in his care. Police investigations relating to the allegation of abuse of LM's daughter and internal investigations of the accusation of abuse whilst employed in the hostel resulted in no further action being taken against LM. LM's family name was however placed on the Central Register of Child Protection on the basis that the multi-agency conference believed that LM's daughter had been sexually abused. A previous application by a company operated by LM for the provision of school bus services had been terminated subsequent to a police check in which disclosure of the prior allegations was made. LM contended that, in relation to a pending application for the provision of school bus services and an application for a youth service teaching post, there was no cogent evidence of a pressing need for disclosure of the past allegations against him. LM argued that consideration should be given to, amongst other things, the fact that (1) he had no criminal record and no allegations against him had been proved; (2) the allegations had been made 10 years previously and there had been no further allegations, and (3) during the past 10 years he had been employed on bus runs and in teaching youths during which time no other allegation had been made.

Held, allowing the application, that (1) there was no evidence of a pressing need such as to warrant disclosure to the county council of the previous allegations against LM. The disclosure of such allegations was only required where a pressing need existed and was not a general rule, *R. v. Chief Constable of North Wales, ex p. AB* [1999] Q.B. 396, [1998] C.L.Y. 4290 applied, *L (Minors) (Sexual Abuse: Disclosure), Re* [1999] 1 W.L.R. 299, [1998] C.L.Y. 2386 and *C (A Minor) (Care Proceedings: Disclosure), Re* [1997] Fam. 76, [1996] C.L.Y. 1347 considered; (2) the provisions of the European Convention on Human Rights 1950 Art.8 established a right to a person's private life except in instances where disclosure of certain information was in the wider public interest, and (3) in the instant case the police authority when considering the merits of disclosing information about LM to the council had applied a blanket approach and thereby fallen into an error. Similarly, the local authority had failed to give consideration as to whether a pressing need for disclosure existed. Given LM's record since the allegations had been made, disclosure of those allegations to the local council would be irrational, *R. v. Ministry of Defence, ex p. Smith* [1996] Q.B. 517, [1996] C.L.Y. 383 applied.

R. v. LOCAL AUTHORITY IN THE MIDLANDS, *ex p.* LM [2000] 1 F.L.R. 612, Dyson, J., QBD.

8. **Committal orders – committal proceedings wrongly dated – error did not nullify committal order**

[Rules of the Supreme Court 1981 Ord.59 r.4 (1).]

M constructed an extension and garage without planning permission, MCC sought to have the structure lowered to comply with planning regulations and M failed to do so, resulting in his committal for breach of an injunction. M appealed, contending that (1) the application to commit had been nullified by an amendment altering it from the date when the injunction had been sealed to that of the previous day when it had been pronounced, and (2) M had not been allowed to cross examine a witness.

Held, dismissing the appeal, that (1) the wrong dates had not caused any confusion and did not invalidate the order, especially as the date of sealing was the correct date under the Rules of the Supreme Court 1981 Ord.59 r.4(1), and (2) anything raised by the cross examination of the witness would not have altered the order made.

MANCHESTER CITY COUNCIL v. McLOUGHLIN *The Times*, April 5, 2000, Roch, L.J., CA.

9. **Committal orders – community charge arrears – culpable neglect – committal in absence**

[Community Charge (Administration and Enforcement) Regulations 1989 (SI 1989 438) Reg.41 (2).]

B was liable to pay community charge for the year 1990/91 in the sum of £252.98, plus £15 costs. In February 1997, she appeared before local justices when the liability had risen to £323.78. The justices found that B's failure to pay was due to culpable neglect in terms of the Community Charge Administration and Enforcement Regulations 1989 Reg.41(2) and ordered her to serve 14 days' imprisonment postponed on payment of £2.50 per week. B failed to maintain the payments and when she failed to attend before the magistrates she was committed to prison for eight days. She was bailed after two days by an order of the High Court and applied for judicial review of the decision to commit her to prison in her absence for non payment of community charge.

Held, granting the application and quashing both the committal order and the decision that B was in culpable neglect, that (1) the magistrates had based the finding of culpable neglect on the misunderstanding that she had purchased a car for £5,000 at a time when she had community charge arrears. That in turn led them to make the committal order; (2) magistrates should not commit a person to prison in their absence where there was no positive evidence of either a refusal to attend before them or to comply with an order of the court, *R. v. Doncaster Justices, ex p. Jack (No.1)* (2000) 164 J.P. 52, [1999] C.L.Y. 11 applied, and (3) there was no such evidence in this case with the result that B should not have been committed to prison in her absence.

R. v. MEDWAY JUSTICES, *ex p.* BELLINGER [2000] R.V.R. 75, Tucker, J., QBD.

10. **Committal orders – community charge arrears – request for adjournment – failure to consider other methods of payment vitiated committal order**

B appealed a decision of the justices to refuse a further adjournment and committing her to prison for culpable neglect for failing to pay community charge. B contended that an adjournment should have been granted and that since no adequate means inquiry had been undertaken there had been no grounds for the justices' finding on the evidence that she had been guilty of culpable neglect.

Held, allowing the appeal and remitting the case to the justices that, (1) the justices' concern that the case had already taken a significant time provided no reason to refuse the application for an adjournment. The justices had failed to ensure, as they were obliged to do, that all other payment options had been exhausted before they took the decision to commit; (2) the near six year history of delay was the responsibility of the charging authority and when approached during that time B had made certain payments. These facts should have convinced the justices, on their own motion, to remit some or all the liability; (3) the justices were unclear as to whether they had addressed if B was guilty of wilful and culpable neglect for each payment period, and (4) there were no reasons given to justify the concurrent six week terms of imprisonment. The guideline available to the justices for debts between £200 and £500 was 14 days and B owed £365.

R. v. WARRINGTON BC, *ex p.* BARRETT [2000] R.V.R. 208, Turner, J., QBD.

11. **Committal orders – omission of penal notice – extent of power to commit in absence of penal notice**

[County Court Rules 1981 (SI 1981 1687) Ord.27 r.1, Ord.29 r.1 (3).]

J appealed, inter alia, against a decision to commit him to prison for 14 days for matters arising in the course of matrimonial proceedings. J argued that the order was unenforceable as it had not been endorsed with a penal notice, contrary to the County Court Rules 1981 Ord.29 r.1 (3).

Held, dismissing the appeal, that although an order which could be enforced by committal should be endorsed with a penal notice, it was within the discretion of the county court to commit a person to prison even though the breached order had not been so endorsed. Under Ord.27 r.1, the court was empowered to dispense with the requirement to serve a copy of the notice or judgment and it followed from this that the court was also empowered to dispense with the requirement for a penal notice when considering an application. However, the power was to be exercised sparingly as it was important that the express provisions of Ord.29 r.1 (3) were not undermined.

JOLLY v. HULL; JOLLY v. JOLLY; *sub nom.* JOLLY v. CIRCUIT JUDGE OF STAINES COUNTY COURT [2000 2 F.L.R. 69, Judge, L.J., CA.

12. **Committal orders – restraint orders – technical defects**

On April 27, 2000 A was found to have breached the terms of a court order restraining her from dealing with monies in a bank account but the judge indicated that he would not sign the warrant until May 5, provided that a "substantial sum" was paid into R's solicitors' bank account. The order did not cite the terms of the suspension. On May 5, A sought to argue that an offer of monies which she had made to R was substantial given her financial circumstances. A was taken into custody and refused bail by the judge. A was the same day refused bail by the Court of Appeal but an expedited hearing was arranged for May 9 in order that A could pursue an appeal on a limited basis, namely as to the deficiency in the committal order of April 27 in failing to recite the term as to suspension and as to the vagueness of the language employed.

Held, refusing the appeal, that the points taken were of a technical nature and the deficiency in the committal order did not render the judge's decision to commit A to prison flawed; she had been represented by both counsel and solicitor throughout. In relation to the use of the word "substantial" the judge was right to view the offer as inadequate in the circumstances of the case, as the complaint in the notice to show cause referred to A's having dealt with the sum of £11,000 contrary to the order restraining her from doing so.

HASTINGS v. HASTINGS, May 9, 2000, Thorpe, L.J., CA. [*Ex rel.* Nigel S Brockley, Barrister, Bracton Chambers, Bell House, 8 Bell Yard, London].

13. **Contempt of court – breach of nuisance covenant – local authority secure tenancy – sentence length**

T obtained an injunction against their tenant, L, prohibiting him from causing a disturbance to or being threatening towards his neighbours, in particular the tenant in the flat below. L kept to the terms of the injunction for over 10 months, but shortly after a new tenant moved into the flat below L was brought back before the court on contempt proceedings. The Recorder found that L had been abusive and threatening to the other tenant on five occasions and held that a custodial sentence of three months was appropriate. L appealed against the sentence.

Held, allowing the appeal, that L appeared to have learnt his lesson despite denying the allegations at the previous proceedings. He had kept to the injunction for 10 months and had not been committed before. Whilst a custodial sentence was appropriate given the severity of the breaches, the deterrent effect would be adequately served by a sentence of three weeks.

TOWER HAMLETS LBC v. LONG (2000) 32 H.L.R. 219, Butler-Sloss, L.J., CA.

14. Contempt of court – disclosure of journalist's source – discretion of court – journalistic privilege to protect identity of sources – necessity to protect interests of justice required before disclosure ordered

[Contempt of Court Act 1981 s.10.]

B, a journalist working for EN, came into possession of a leaked document from a barristers chambers which contained draft advice given by counsel concerning litigation involving J. J subsequently obtained an order pursuant to the Contempt of Court Act 1981 s.10 requiring B to reveal the source from which the document originated, on the suspicion that an employee from a contract cleaning firm was responsible for the leak. A judge ordered disclosure on the basis that the need to protect the legal professional privilege attached to the document outweighed, in the interests of justice, the desire to protect a journalists privilege. EN appealed contending that the court had a discretion to refuse an order for disclosure which should accordingly have been exercised, since the failure to conduct an internal investigation into the breach of security in chambers weighed against the necessity to protect the interests of justice.

Held, allowing the appeal, that the court must adopt a two stage reasoned approach when exercising its discretion and weigh up whether disclosure was necessary in the interests of justice, against the need to protect a journalist's privilege. In the instant case, the failure to conduct any investigation into the breach of security within chambers effectively meant that no attempt had been made by J to trace the source without recourse to the court. It was a minimum requirement that other avenues be explored before the court would order a journalist to break a professional obligation in revealing a source, *Saunders v. Punch Ltd (t/a Liberty Publishing)* [1998] 1 W.L.R. 986, [1997] C.L.Y. 21 applied. Furthermore, the nature of the document which constituted draft advice that had been discarded, was not a significant threat to legal confidentiality and as an isolated incident it did not justify placing legal privilege on a higher status than the privilege enjoyed by journalists. It followed that the court should have exercised its discretion to refuse disclosure.

JOHN v. EXPRESS NEWSPAPERS [2000] 1 W.L.R. 1931, Lord Woolf, M.R., CA.

15. Contempt of court – dishonest evidence given by bankrupt

C was adjudicated bankrupt. He failed on numerous occasions to co-operate with OR or M, his trustee in bankruptcy. He consistently refused to answer properly questions put to him by OR both in and out of court, and to comply with court orders or undertakings that he had given in court. Evidence showed that he had lied on oath in court in the course of applications arising in the administration of his estate, and had falsely exempted himself from required court attendances citing spurious ill health grounds. OR applied for C to be committed to prison for contempt of court.

Held, allowing the application and imprisoning C for 20 months, that although dishonesty in giving evidence was normally punished by a prosecution for perjury, the court had power to punish for contempt where dishonest or prevaricating answers indicative of dishonesty had been given. In the instant case, it was appropriate to consider the allegations of dishonesty in giving evidence at the same time as allegations that C had repeatedly breached court orders and undertakings, which in themselves constituted contempt of court.

OFFICIAL RECEIVER v. CUMMINGS-JOHN [2000] B.P.I.R. 320, Laddie, J., Ch D.

16. Contempt of court – freezing orders – injunction freezing assets did not apply to assets or funds not beneficially owned by defendant even though assets were held by him as bare legal owner

H was subject to a worldwide freezing order made against him by a bank, FBME, which prohibited him or his companies from disposing or dealing with assets or funds in his own name or if solely or jointly owned. Further, the court ordered H to disclose all information relating to the disposal or transfer of assets and or funds. H was held in contempt of court for failing to disclose a transfer of funds from an account held in his name into an account held in the name of his wife, for the benefit of his children. H contended that the judge had been wrong to find that he had breached the freezing order by transferring assets from bank accounts which, although held in his name, were assets beneficially owned by third parties. FMBE had not found it necessary to apply for H's committal for contempt. H appealed against the decision (*The Times*, May 28,1999) that he was in contempt of court for breaching the freezing order.

Held, allowing the appeal in part, that those assets and funds which did not beneficially belong to H but were beneficially owned by third parties were not covered in the freezing order, even though the bank account was held in his name and under his control as the bare legal owner. The main purpose of the freezing order was to safeguard FMBE against a risk of disposal of the assets pending a complete investigation and a determination by the court as to who was the beneficial owner of the assets. There was plainly no meaning within the language of the standard form freezing order to cover assets and funds which were not beneficially owned by the person being restrained.

FEDERAL BANK OF THE MIDDLE EAST v. HADKINSON (STAY OF ACTION); HADKINSON v. SAAB (NO.1) [2000] 1 W.L.R. 1695, Mummery, L.J., CA.

17. **Contempt of court – rescue of levied goods – requirement for interpleader summons – duty to offer contemnor legal aid and representation – human rights implications of penal procedure**

[County Courts Act 1984 s.92, s.101; European Convention on Human Rights 1950.]

N was subject to a judgment debt against him in favour of M, who instructed the court bailiff to levy execution on N's goods. N had the option of immediate seizure of goods or signing a walking possession order. N informed the bailiff that two of the three computers used by his business had been bought on credit and partly paid for by a third party, B, and did not belong to him but signed the walking possession order nevertheless. The computers were removed before the bailiff's return and B provided the bailiff with a statement of his ownership and documentation relating to the credit agreements. N was subsequently arrested under the provisions of the County Courts Act 1984 s.92 for contempt of court for removing levied goods and committed to prison for one month for rescue or attempted rescue of the goods. N appealed against his committal, contending that he was dyslexic and had been misled into signing the possession order.

Held, allowing the appeal, that, as a penal process with human rights implications under the European Convention on Human Rights 1950, the charge of rescue of goods should have been in writing and read out to N to ensure that he knew the extent of the case against him. Furthermore, where there was an appreciable risk of imprisonment, the court was also under a duty to give an unrepresented defendant the opportunity to seek legal advice and to apply for legal aid. On the facts, there was enough information at the disposal of the court to imply an obligation to issue an interpleader summons under s.101.

NEWMAN (T/A MANTELLA PUBLISHING) v. MODERN BOOKBINDERS LTD [2000] 1 W.L.R. 2559, Sedley, L.J., CA.

18. **Costs – setting aside – review of costs order made personally against justices**

The justices committed a sick and elderly man and a single mother of three young children to prison for non payment of council tax/community charge, in each case in the absence of the payer. In each case the prison authorities were so concerned that they immediately contacted solicitors on behalf of the ratepayer. Both were released immediately upon application. The justices filed evidence but did not attend the applications for review of their decisions. The judge hearing the applications took the view that the conduct of the justices in the circumstances was so bad that orders for costs should be made against them. He gave them 21 days within which to apply to set aside that part of his order and they did so apply.

Held, that the fresh evidence which had been filed made it apparent that the case was not as bad as it had first appeared. There was evidence that the justices could have been satisfied as to service and evidence that some form of means inquiry had been made, although it was inadequate. Further, the case of *R. v. Northampton Magistrates Court, ex p. Newell* (1993) 157 J.P. 869, [1993] C.L.Y. 2627, which had not been cited at the initial hearing but which should have been, was followed and the costs order was set aside.

R. v. DONCASTER JUSTICES, *ex p.* JACK (NO.2); R. v. DONCASTER JUSTICES, *ex p.* CHRISTISON (NO.2) [1999] R.V.R. 308, Collins, J., QBD.

19. **Councillors – bias – procedural impropriety – councillors acting as school governors – declaration of private interests**

See LOCAL GOVERNMENT: R. v. Kirklees MBC, *ex p.* Beaumont. §4087

20. **County courts – appeals**

ACCESS TO JUSTICE ACT 1999 (DESTINATION OF APPEALS) ORDER 2000, SI 2000 1071 (L.10); made under the Access to Justice Act 1999 s.56. In force: May 2, 2000; £1.50.

This Order provides that, from May 2, 2000, appeals from the county courts other than in family proceedings will lie to the High Court rather than to the Court of Appeal. Appeals from decisions of masters, registrars and district judges of the High Court will continue to lie to a judge of the High Court. Similarly, appeals from district judges in county courts will continue to lie to a judge of a county court.

21. **County courts – closure – Caerphilly**

CIVIL COURTS (AMENDMENT NO.2) ORDER 2000, SI 2000 2738; made under the Supreme Court Act 1981 s.99; and the County Courts Act 1984 s.2. In force: December 1, 2000; £1.50.

This Order amends the Civil Courts Order 1983 (SI 1983 713) by closing the county court at Caerphilly.

22. **County courts – closure – transfer of jurisdiction**

CIVIL COURTS (AMENDMENT) ORDER 2000 2000, SI 2000 1482; made under the Supreme Court Act 1981 s.99; the County Courts Act 1984 s.2, s.26; and the Insolvency Act 1986 s.374. In force: Art.3: January 2, 2001; Art.4: January 2, 2001; remainder: July 3, 2000; £1.00.

This Order amends the Civil Courts Order 1983 (SI 1983 713 as amended) to close the county court at Lichfield, with effect from July 3, 2000, and the district registry and county court at Workington, with effect from January 2, 2001. It opens a district registry at Whitehaven and confers bankruptcy jurisdiction on Whitehaven County Court.

23. **County courts – fees**

COUNTY COURT FEES (AMENDMENT) ORDER 2000, SI 2000 639 (L.2); made under the County Courts Act 1984 s.128; the Insolvency Act 1986 s.414, s.415; and the Finance Act 1990 s.128. In force: In accordance with Art.2; £1.50.

This Order amends the County Court Fees Order 1999 (SI 1999 689) so that refunds are permitted in certain cases; to take account of the establishment of the Legal Services Commission under the Access to Justice Act 1999 s.1; and to clarify the description of certain fees.

24. **County courts – fees**

COUNTY COURT FEES (AMENDMENT NO.3) ORDER 2000, SI 2000 1546 (L.15); made under the County Courts Act 1984 s.128. In force: July 3, 2000; £1.00.

This Order amends the County Court Fees Order 1999 (SI 1999 689) by specifying a fee for commencement of costs-only proceedings and extending fee 2.6 (witness summons) to cover applications for deposition orders.

25. **Court funds**

COURT FUNDS (AMENDMENT) RULES 2000, SI 2000 2918 (L.24); made under the Administration of Justice Act 1982 s.38. In force: December 1, 2000; £1.50.

These Rules amend the Court Funds Rules 1987 (SI 1987 821) by changing the period after which the Accountant General may carry over an unclaimed fund in court to an account of unclaimed balances from five to ten years.

26. **Court officers – redundancy – role of magistrates' court supervisor**

See EMPLOYMENT: Berkshire and Oxfordshire Magistrates Courts Committee v. Gannon. §2193

27. **Criminal injuries compensation – application to reopen award after final determination – relevant criteria**

The CICB appealed against a decision overturning their refusal to reopen a final award. W, a police officer, had sought judicial review of the CICB's refusal to reopen a final determination of the compensation payable to him following an incident in which he had been attacked whilst effecting an arrest. As a result of the incident, W had suffered a back injury. Following the making of the award and its acceptance by W, he had suffered an exacerbation of the original injury such that he had been unable to return to work. The CICB had refused W's request to reopen the award under the Criminal Injuries Compensation Scheme 1990 para.13 on the basis that they were not satisfied that the deterioration in his condition could be attributed to the original assault. W's application for judicial review of that decision succeeded on the basis that it had been unreasonable in the light of the available medical evidence. The CICB contended that the judge at first instance had erred in his application of the relevant causation test.

Held, dismissing the appeal, that in assessing W's eligibility under para.13 of the Scheme, the relevant test was whether there had been a "serious change attributable to the original injury". On the facts of the instant case, the CICB had erred in concluding that the chain of causation had been broken as a result of intervening events. It was clear that the exacerbation had resulted from W's increased susceptibility to injury which had been caused by the original assault. Accordingly, the exacerbation of the injury could properly be regarded as directly attributable to the assault.

R. v. CRIMINAL INJURIES COMPENSATION BOARD, *ex p.* WILLIAMS [2000] P.I.Q.R. Q339, Ward, L.J., CA.

28. **Criminal injuries compensation – buggery with child under age of consent – crime of violence despite consent**

B brought a claim for criminal injuries compensation, alleging that he had suffered injuries resulting from repeated acts of buggery which had occurred at an approved school when he was between the ages of 12 and 13. The Criminal Injuries Compensation Appeals Panel refused the claim on the ground that since he had consented to the acts complained of, he had not been the victim of a crime of violence. B applied for judicial review of that decision.

Held, allowing the application, that in the case of sexual offences, Parliament had indicated on the ground of public policy that the consent of a child under the age of consent should not constitute a defence to the offence of buggery, *R. v. Brown (Anthony Joseph)* [1994] 1 A.C. 212, [1993] C.L.Y. 920, *R. v. Coney*

(1882) L.R. 8 Q.B.D. 534 applied. Viewed from the standpoint of the "reasonable and literate man" in accordance with the approach in *R. v. Criminal Injuries Compensation Board, ex p. Webb* [1987] Q.B. 74, [1986] C.L.Y. 535, B had, even though he might have consented to the acts complained of, been the victim of a crime of violence. Accordingly, his case would have to be reconsidered by the Criminal Injuries Compensation Appeals Authority which would no doubt have to determine, pursuant to the Criminal Injuries Compensation Scheme para.13(d), whether B's consent should operate to reduce or extinguish the award to which he might otherwise have been entitled.

R. v. CRIMINAL INJURIES COMPENSATION APPEALS PANEL, *ex p.* B *The Times*, August 1, 2000, Collins, J., QBD.

29. **Criminal injuries compensation – fingers – criteria for "continuing disability"**

[Criminal Injuries Compensation Act 1995 s.2.]

E sought judicial review of the decision of the Criminal Injuries Compensation Appeals Panel, CICAP, to uphold an award of £1,500 as compensation for an injury to her finger sustained during an assault at work. E contended that the appropriate award was £3,500 since the medical evidence had indicated that she would suffer ongoing residual effects and thus her injury amounted to a "continuing disability" thereby entitling her to compensation at a higher tariff. CICAP argued that (1) many injuries resulted in permanent but minor and intermittent problems but that this did not mean that there had not been a "full recovery", and (2) as E had been able to resume her nursing career, she did not suffer from a disability that impaired her work and that there was therefore no "continuing disability".

Held, granting the application, that a continuing injury that resulted in an observable and measurable loss of function or faculty constituted a "continuing disability" and the terms "full recovery" and "continuing disability" as used in the Tariff within the Scheme drawn up by the Secretary of State, pursuant to the Criminal Injuries Compensation Act 1995 s.2, related to the state of the limb or organ rather than the general condition of the applicant. In consequence E's injury amounted to a "continuing disability".

R. v. CRIMINAL INJURIES COMPENSATION APPEALS PANEL, *ex p.* EMBLING; *sub nom.* R. v. CRIMINAL INJURIES COMPENSATION AUTHORITY, *ex p.* EMBLING [2000] P.I.Q.R. Q361, Munby, J., QBD.

30. **Criminal injuries compensation – operation of scheme in culture of public law transparency**

L had suffered a major head injury as a result of an assault outside a pub. He claimed compensation from CICA, who refused it on the ground that his conduct had "caused or contributed to the incident". L applied for a review and requested details of the reasons behind the decision and copies of any documentary evidence submitted. CICA refused to supply the information and L applied for judicial review of that refusal, arguing that it denied his right to know of the case that was being put against him and prevented him from making a proper appeal. CICA argued that disclosure was not appropriate as it had an ongoing agreement with the police that witness statements would not be disclosed except at a review hearing, it could put witnesses at risk of intimidation and would place an "intolerable and unjustified burden" on CICA.

Held, allowing the appeal, that CICA could not continue to ignore its public law role and carry out its purpose in the "closed and defensive manner" that it had adopted. To avoid unfairness, the requirement on L to give detailed grounds for seeking a review had to give rise to a corresponding requirement that the reasons for refusal be given in detail. Review was not merely an internal procedure, *R. v. Secretary of State for the Home Department, ex p. Allen The Times*, March 21, 2000, [2000] C.L.Y. 4326 distinguished, but a process upon which the right to claim an award was dependent. The processing of awards was in the arena of statute and public law and therefore decision making had to be transparent, with reasons that were "sufficient and intelligible". There was no evidence of the pleaded agreement with the police, and the other factors raised by CICA were without foundation.

R. v. CRIMINAL INJURIES COMPENSATION AUTHORITY, *ex p.* LEATHERLAND; R. v. CRIMINAL INJURIES COMPENSATION BOARD, *ex p.* BRAMALL; R. v. CRIMINAL INJURIES COMPENSATION PANEL, *ex p.* KAY *The Times*, October 12, 2000, Turner, J., QBD.

31. **Criminal injuries compensation – road traffic offences exemption – injury due to dangerous driving on private track**

M was knocked down and injured on a track by a motorcycle driven by B, an uninsured rider, who was convicted of dangerous driving. The MIB refused M's claim for compensation as the accident did not occur on the public highway. The claim was also rejected by CICB on the grounds that injuries sustained due to traffic offences were excluded under the Criminal Injuries Compensation Board Scheme 1990 para.11 unless they involved a deliberate running down. M's application for judicial review of the CICB decision was unsuccessful and he appealed.

Held, dismissing the appeal, that the wording of para.11 was unequivocal. The only exemption from the exclusion was clearly stated and therefore it would be wrong to import other exemptions contended for by M. Such a construction would also conflict with the definition of "traffic offence" in other statutes. The stance taken by the CICB in the past, whilst arguably relevant to the exercise of its discretion, could only have been relevant to construction had the wording of para.11 not been clear.

R. v. CRIMINAL INJURIES COMPENSATION BOARD, *ex p.* M (A MINOR) [2000] R.T.R 21, Auld, L.J., CA.

32. **Crown Courts – rules – cross examination – appointment of legal representative**

CROWN COURT (AMENDMENT) RULES 2000, SI 2000 2093 (L.17); made under the Supreme Court Act 1981 s.84, s.86; and the Youth Justice and Criminal Evidence Act 1999 s.38, s.65. In force: September 4, 2000; £1.50.

These Rules, which amend the Crown Court Rules 1982 (SI 1982 1109), make provision as to the time when, and the manner in which, a legal representative is to be appointed to act for the accused for the purposes of cross-examining witnesses. They also contain provisions relating to the appointment by the Crown Court of a qualified legal representative where the accused fails to appoint a legal representative to act for him.

33. **Crown courts – rules – cross examination – sexual offences**

CROWN COURT (AMENDMENT) (NO.2) RULES 2000, SI 2000 2987 (L.25); made under the Supreme Court Act 1981 s.84, s.86; the Police and Criminal Evidence Act 1984 s.81; and the Youth Justice and Criminal Evidence Act 1999 s.43, s.65. In force: December 4, 2000; £1.75.

These Rules, which amend the Crown Court Rules 1982 (SI 1982 1109), detail the procedure to be followed on an application for leave to introduce evidence or to ask questions in cross examination about the sexual behaviour of the complainant at a trial of a person charged with a sexual offence. They provide for a Crown Court judge to hold a hearing of an application for leave in chambers and disapply the rules relating to the advance notice of expert evidence where an application for leave is made in accordance with these Rules.

34. **Crown Courts – rules – evidence – video recording or television link**

CROWN COURT (AMENDMENT) (NO.3) RULES 2000, SI 2000 3362 (L.28); made under the Supreme Court Act 1981 s.84, s.86. In force: January 15, 2001; £1.50.

These Rules which amend the Crown Court Rules 1982 (SI 1982 1109) in relation to the new procedure created by the Crime and Disorder Act 1998 s.51, s.52 and

Sch.3, provide for the appropriate time by which a party that wishes to do so, shall apply for the evidence of a child or person outside the United Kingdom to be given by video recording or television link under the Criminal Justice Act 1988 s.32. In addition, they provide for a new r.24ZA so as to specify the latest date for which the first Crown Court appearance of a person sent for trial under the new procedure shall be listed and allows for the possibility of that appearance being in chambers.

35. Crown Office – forms

CROWN OFFICE (FORMS AND PROCLAMATIONS RULES) (AMENDMENT) ORDER 2000, SI 2000 3064; made under the Crown Office Act 1877 s.3. In force: November 29, 2000; £1.50.

This Order in Council amends the Crown Office (Forms and Proclamations Rules) Order 1992 (SI 1992 1730) by amending the forms for Commissions of the Peace for the City of London and the Commissions of the Peace for Greater London in consequence of the Access to Justice Act 1999. In addition, it amends the forms of letters patent creating hereditary peerages and the forms for signifying royal assent in consequence of the entry into force of the House of Lords Act 1999.

36. Crown Prosecution Service Inspectorate Act 2000 (c.10)

This Act makes provision for the inspection of the Crown Prosecution Service. This Act received Royal Assent on July 20, 2000.

37. Crown Prosecution Service Inspectorate Act 2000 (c.10) – Commencement Order

CROWN PROSECUTION SERVICE INSPECTORATE ACT 2000 (COMMENCEMENT) ORDER 2000, SI 2000 2423 (C.68); made under the Crown Prosecution Service Inspectorate Act 2000 s.3. Commencement details: bringing into force various provisions of the Act on October 1, 2000; £1.00.

This Order brings into force on October 1, 2000 the Crown Prosecution Service Inspectorate Act 2000 s.1 and s.2, which relate to the appointment, remuneration and functions of the Chief Inspector of the Crown Prosecution Service.

38. Dentists – suspension – one year suspension for driving offences – penalty out of proportion to offence and therefore unlawful

[General Dental Council Professional Conduct Committee (Procedure) Rules Order of Council 1984 (SI 1984 1517) r.11 (4).]

D, a dentist, appealed against a determination by the General Dental Council, GDC, to suspend him for 12 months following convictions for motoring offences. D had four previous convictions for driving offences, including reckless driving, failure to produce insurance documents and driving whilst disqualified. The last offence, however, was committed almost 12 months before the hearing by the GDC, and D argued that the committee should have shown leniency under the General Dental Council Professional Conduct Committee (Procedure) Rules Order of Council 1984 r.11 (4) by postponing judgment to allow D to prove that he had improved his errant driving. Moreover, it was argued that D, owner of three dental practices in Glasgow, was a hard working person who committed all the offences whilst driving to Birmingham at weekends to assist his family. The GDC argued that D was guilty of behaviour which would bring the dental profession into disrepute and undermine public confidence in the integrity of the profession.

Held, allowing the appeal, that suspension from dental practice for twelve months for driving offences was a disproportionate penalty in light of the gravity of the offences and therefore was unlawful. Although D had an appalling driving record, the important question was whether that impinged on his professionalism as a dentist. Generally, the courts would be slow to overturn the decisions by the professional standards committee of the GDC on standards which should be observed by practitioners and what should amount to derogation therefrom. Nevertheless, where the conduct relied on, as here, did not amount to professional misconduct then it would be more readily reviewable by the courts. Twelve months had passed between D's last motoring offence and the hearing by the GDC, from which one might infer that D had changed his ways and was unlikely to re-offend. Given that D owned three practices, the consequences of any suspension would be severe and out of all proportion to the offences. The judgment was postponed for two years to enable D to prove that he had improved his ways.

DAD v. GENERAL DENTAL COUNCIL [2000] 1 W.L.R. 1538, Lord Hope of Craighead, PC.

39. Drug trafficking – proceeds from drug trafficking in foreign bank – failure to comply with repatriation order

[Criminal Justice Act 1988 s.77; Drug Trafficking Act 1994 s.26.]

S was convicted of possessing heroin with intent to supply, for which he received a sentence of imprisonment of four years and a confiscation order in the sum of £47,851.45 with a sentence of 18 months in default. A restraint order was made under the Drug Trafficking Act 1994 s.26, preventing S from disposing of any assets and a repatriation order was also made requiring S to return to the UK assets held in a Jamaican bank account. Upon his failure to repatriate the money, S received a further sentence of six months for contempt of court. S appealed, challenging the power of the court to make such a repatriation order and arguing that he should not have received a further sentence for the same offence.

Held, dismissing the appeal, that the High Court had an inherent power to make a repatriation order as a means of enforcing a restraint order under the Criminal Justice Act 1988 s.77, *O (Disclosure Order), Re* [1991] 2 Q.B. 520, [1991] C.L.Y. 871 followed, and it was to be assumed that Parliament had intended a similar jurisdiction to enable the enforcement of restraint orders under the 1994 Act, otherwise they would be rendered nugatory. The sentence of six months was made under the civil jurisdiction of the High Court and was totally separate and distinct from the sentence imposed under the criminal jurisdiction.

DPP v. SCARLETT; *sub nom*. CROWN PROSECUTION SERVICE v. SCARLETT [2000] 1 W.L.R. 515, Beldam, L.J., CA.

40. Employment tribunals – registers – recording of particulars of applications

[Employment Tribunals (Constitution and Rules of Procedure) Regulations 1993 (SI 1993 2687) r.9, Sch.1 r.10 (5).]

P had exercised its right under the Employment Tribunals (Constitution and Rules of Procedure) Regulations 1993 r.9 as substituted to inspect the register of applications, appeals and decisions of tribunals kept by C. P applied for judicial review of the policy of C in relation to the particulars that were recorded in the register and the decisions of the secretary of C that the duty under r.9 was complied with by recording the existence of an application alone and that disclosure of information to P would not include, nor identify, the grounds of the claim. P submitted that the policy of C and the secretary's decisions were unlawful as the register contained less information than was required by r.9 thus a party inspecting the register did not obtain the information to which they were lawfully entitled. P contended that the secretary was under an obligation to record a summary of each of the grounds of the claim so that a party inspecting the register could identify the basis of those grounds.

Held, granting the application, that subject to limited exceptions, the register was intended to be a fairly full record of cases litigated before tribunals pursuant to Sch.1 r.10(5) to the 1993 Regulations, that the principle of open justice applied to employment tribunals and that the particulars on the register should include the details set out by P, *Storer v. British Gas Plc* [2000] 1 W.L.R. 1237, [2000] C.L.Y. 2145 considered.

R. v. SECRETARY OF THE CENTRAL OFFICE OF THE EMPLOYMENT TRIBUNALS (ENGLAND AND WALES), *ex p*. PUBLIC CONCERN AT WORK [2000] I.R.L.R. 658, Jackson, J., QBD.

41. Family proceedings – fees

FAMILY PROCEEDINGS FEES (AMENDMENT) ORDER 2000, SI 2000 640 (L.3); made under the Matrimonial and Family Proceedings Act 1984 s.41; the Insolvency Act 1986 s.415; and the Finance Act 1990 s.128. In force: in accordance with Art.2; £1.50.

This Order amends the Family Proceedings Fees Order 1999 (SI 1999 690) so that refunds are permitted in certain cases; to take account of the establishment of the Legal Services Commission under the Access to Justice Act 1999 s.1; and to remove an unnecessary fee.

42. Family proceedings – fees

FAMILY PROCEEDINGS FEES (AMENDMENT NO.3) ORDER 2000, SI 2000 1545 (L.14); made under the Matrimonial and Family Proceedings Act 1984 s.41. In force: July 3, 2000; £1.00.

This Order amends the Family Proceedings Fees Order 1999 (SI 1999 690) by specifying a fee for commencement of costs-only proceedings.

43. Family proceedings – youth courts – unification and renaming of stipendiary bench

YOUTH COURTS AND FAMILY PROCEEDINGS COURTS (CONSTITUTION) (AMENDMENT) RULES 2000, SI 2000 1873; made under the Magistrates' Courts Act 1980 s.144. In force: in accordance with r.1; £1.00.

These Rules amend the Youth Courts (Constitution) Rules 1954 (SI 1954 1711), the Family Proceedings Courts (Constitution) Rules 1991 (SI 1991 1405) and the Family Proceedings Courts (Constitution) (Metropolitan Areas) Rules 1991 (SI 1991 1426) to take account of the coming into force of the Access to Justice Act 1999 s.78 and Sch.11 which unify and rename the stipendiary bench.

44. Firearms – compensation scheme – delay – county court claim – applicability of judicial review

[Firearms (Amendment) Act 1997.]

S made an application to the Secretary of State for compensation under the Firearms (Amendment) Act 1997 on July 29, 1997 after surrendering various weapons. On October 27, 1997 S issued a County Court summons for the sum allegedly due, citing inordinate delay in the settlement of his claim. The claims submitted under options A and B of the scheme were paid on November 26, 1997 and the Secretary of State then sought to strike out the summons as disclosing no reasonable cause of action. The application was dismissed as were two subsequent appeals. The Secretary of State appealed to the House of Lords, contending that there was (1) no obligation to payment under the scheme; (2) no duty to process claims within a reasonable period of time, and (3) that a challenge other than by judicial review was an abuse of process at any time prior to final determination of the individual claim.

Held, dismissing the appeal, that (1) once all conditions of the scheme had been satisfied an applicant was clearly entitled to payment under the terms of the scheme; (2) it was clearly arguable that individual claims would be either accepted or rejected within a reasonable time and payment made shortly thereafter in cases of claims under options A and B of the scheme and in the case of option C as soon as the individual claimant agreed to accept the sum offered, and (3) since the proceedings had not sought to challenge the lawfulness of the scheme itself nor sought to take the place of a discretionary decision specifically reserved to the administration, they could not be said to constitute an abuse of process, *O'Reilly v. Mackman* [1983] 2 A.C. 237, [1982] C.L.Y. 2603, *Mercury Communications Ltd v. Director General of Telecommunications* [1996] 1 W.L.R. 48, [1995] C.L.Y. 3907 and *Trustees of the*

Dennis Rye Pension Fund v. Sheffield City Council [1998] 1 W.L.R. 840, [1997] C.L.Y. 490 considered.

STEED v. SECRETARY OF STATE FOR THE HOME DEPARTMENT; *sub nom.* STEED v. HOME OFFICE [2000] 1 W.L.R. 1169, Lord Slynn of Hadley, HL.

45. **Habeas corpus – applications for service of paper by interested parties – interveners refused joinder – proceedings criminal in origin – practice before Divisional Court and Court of Appeal (Criminal Division)**

[Rules of the Supreme Court 1965 (SI 1965 1776) Ord.54 r.2.]

HRW and AI and certain other human rights groups sought a direction that they be served with papers under the Rules of the Supreme Court Ord.54 r.2, and HRW applied to joined as intervener in P's application for habeas corpus.

Held, dismissing the applications, that although the court had power to permit interventions of this nature, the evidence that AI and HRW sought to admit could also be adduced by other parties, including P. The proceedings in the instant case were criminal in origin, and, notwithstanding the practice allowed by the House of Lords, appearances before the Divisional Court and the Court of Appeal (Criminal Division) was generally restricted to the Crown and the defendant.

PINOCHET UGARTE (HABEAS CORPUS), *Re The Times*, February 16, 2000, Rose, L.J., QBD.

46. **Injunctions – harassment – behaviour – conduct constituting harassment**

[Harassment Act 1997 s.1, s.3.]

T and S sought damages and injunctive relief against MC for harassment contrary to the Harassment Act 1997 s.1 and s.3. T and S had produced counterfeit goods and passed them off as goods having been manufactured by MC. T and S contended that they had subsequently been the victims of harassment, claiming that MC had bribed the police into raiding one of their homes, conducted oppressive litigation by bribing witnesses into giving false evidence and had telephoned one of them late at night.

Held, giving judgment for MC, that the Act had a narrow ambit and was intended to prohibit stalking, behaviour of an antisocial nature by neighbours and racial harassment. There was no definition of harassment in the Act, but having regard to the intention of Parliament it was clear what sort of behaviour the Act was aiming to control. Except for the isolated incident of the telephone call, the claim could not succeed as there was no evidence to suggest that MC had conducted itself in a manner actionable under the Act.

TUPPEN v. MICROSOFT CORP LTD *The Times*, November 15, 2000, Douglas Brown, J., QBD.

47. **Inquests – anonymity – legitimate fear for safety of police officers – judicial review of coroner's decision to grant anonymity order**

A man was shot dead by B, a member of the armed response group of the Bedfordshire police force. At the inquest the coroner considered a request from the assistant chief constable, that all four officers concerned in the incident should be granted anonymity from the assistant chief constable. The request was made on the basis that members of the deceased's family held B responsible for his death. Although no threats to B had been made, the coroner decided to grant the order. LSN, who published the local weekly newspaper applied for judicial review of the coroner's decision and sought a declaration that he was not entitled in law to make an order for anonymity in these circumstances. It was acknowledged by all parties that departures from the fundamental principle of open justice were to be strictly exceptional. LSN contended that once the coroner had accepted there were not likely to be any reprisals from the deceased's family, there were no objective grounds upon which to find cause for anonymity, and even if there were, they should have been outweighed, *R. v. Lord Saville of Newdigate, ex p. B (No.2)* [1999] 4 All E.R. 860, [1999] C.L.Y. 80 and *Jordan, Re* (Unreported), cited. It was argued on behalf of B, the Bedfordshire police force and the Coroner that there were two grounds for upholding the order, namely (1) that identification of B in this incident would increase the problems he was already suffering with local criminals in relation to another incident and which had caused him to fear for his safety, and (2) it was not in the public interest to identify to known violent criminals in the area that B was a member of the armed response team.

Held, dismissing the application, that in order to justify anonymity the facts of the case would need to establish fear for personal or family safety. The coroner was not irrational to take into account B's previous experiences in this case. He was also entitled to conclude that there was a need for special care and a risk of injury and danger to B in disclosing to the criminal fraternity that he was a member of the armed response group, nor was that in the public interest, *Jordan* followed. The existence of those grounds enabled the coroner to conclude that there was sufficient reason for anonymity provided he went on to carry out the balancing exercise laid down in *Saville*, that did not have to be done overtly. The fact that the instant case was a coroner's inquest did not weigh so heavily in favour of open justice, considering the possible detriment to B, and it was at least arguable that anonymity was necessary in order not to frustrate justice and to avoid risk of injury.

R. v. BEDFORDSHIRE CORONER, *ex p.* LOCAL SUNDAY NEWSPAPERS LTD (2000) 164 J.P. 283, Burton, J., QBD.

48. Inquests – coroners – death from eclampsia following Caesarean section – categorisation of death

[Coroners Act 1988 s.8(1).]

T, the husband of L who had died following the development of a cerebral haemorrhage, sought judicial review of a decision by the coroner not to order an inquest into her death. T maintained that the failure by hospital staff to monitor L's blood pressure for the first two and a half hours following a Caesarean section had resulted in a failure to diagnose and prevent the development of eclampsia, and that the coroner's decision that L had died as a result of natural causes had been irrational.

Held, allowing the application, that in seeking to classify the death for the purposes of the Coroners Act 1988 s.8(1), the coroner had failed to appreciate that the hospital's omission could be as significant as its commissions. There had been shortcomings in the post operative monitoring and treatment of L and there had been no evidence before the coroner which entitled him to conclude that L would have died even if effective monitoring of her condition had been undertaken, and therefore his decision had been irrational, *R. v. HM Coroner for Inner London North District, ex p. Thomas* [1993] Q.B. 610, [1993] C.L.Y. 593 applied.

R. (ON THE APPLICATION OF TOUCHE) v. HM CORONER FOR INNER NORTH LONDON DISTRICT; *sub nom.* R. v. HM CORONER FOR INNER NORTH LONDON DISTRICT, *ex p.* TOUCHE; R. v. HM CORONERS COURT OF ST PANCRAS, *ex p.* TOUCHE (2000) 164 J.P. 509, Kennedy, L.J., QBD.

49. Inquests – coroners – death in police custody – drugs and alcohol abuse by deceased – new inquest ordered following coroner's misdirection to jury on meaning of neglect

[Police and Criminal Evidence Act 1984 s.54.]

T died in police custody having been detained and held overnight as drunk and incapable. A brief search of his belongings was carried out and he was examined by a police surgeon, but it was not discovered that he had taken large amounts of prescribed drugs as well as alcohol, even though the pill bottles were in his coat pocket, labelled with that day's date and with a quantity of pills missing. No action was taken when a printout from the Police National Computer showed that T was known to have a drug problem and suicidal tendencies. At the inquest, the jury returned a verdict of "drug abuse contributed to by neglect". The Chief Constable of South Wales Police, C, applied for the verdict to be quashed on the basis that (1) there was no evidence on which the jury were entitled to find neglect and this issue should therefore not have been left to the jury and (2) the coroner's direction to the jury with regard to the issue of neglect was defective. C relied on *R. v. HM Coroner for North Humberside and Scunthorpe, ex p. Jamieson* [1995] Q.B. 1, [1994] C.L.Y. 631 in defining what constituted "neglect". C further argued that there would be nothing to gain from holding a fresh inquest, as no jury could find that the components of neglect were present.

Held, allowing the application and ordering a fresh inquest, that there was sufficient evidence to justify leaving the question of neglect to the jury, based on the following findings: (1) the failure to conduct a proper search of T was in breach of the Police and Criminal Evidence Act 1984 s.54; (2) a proper search would have revealed the pill bottles, enabling T to receive prompt medical attention; (3) the police surgeon had failed to detect that T was suffering from the effects of a drug overdose (4) no action had been taken on the Police National Computer printout and, (5) no further medical treatment was obtained during the night. The coroner had misdirected the jury by giving the impression that neglect was synonymous with simple negligence and by failing to point out that a "clear and direct causal connection" had to be found between the police's gross failure and the cause of death, *Jamieson* followed. It was important that cases such as these should be seen to be fully investigated by the coroner, and therefore a fresh inquest was appropriate.

R. v. HM CORONER FOR SWANSEA AND GOWER, *ex p.* TRISTRAM; *sub nom.* R. v. HM CORONER FOR SWANSEA AND GOWER, *ex p.* CHIEF CONSTABLE OF WALES (2000) 164 J.P. 191, Jackson, J., QBD.

50. **Inquests – interested parties – adversarial examination of witnesses – verdicts left to jury**

D died in his car which was parked in his garage with a hose pipe leading from the exhaust pipe to the car window. The alarm had been raised by H, who was the main beneficiary of D's will executed shortly before his death. The police investigated whether H had had any involvement in D's death, but no charges were brought. The coroner, C, having discussed matters with the CPS and dealt with written enquiries from H, ordered two pre-inquest reviews. At the inquest, both H and the chief constable were represented as interested parties, and cross examined witnesses. C left to the jury the verdicts of unlawful killing, suicide or an open verdict. A verdict of unlawful killing was returned. H brought an application for judicial review alleging that the verdict should not have been left to the jury as there was insufficient evidence, that a further verdict of aiding and abetting suicide should have been left to them and that there was procedural unfairness as the chief constable had turned the inquest into an adversarial process aimed at further investigation of possible criminal charges.

Held, dismissing the application, that the chief constable was a proper party to the inquest and entitled, along with the other interested parties, to ask questions of witnesses going to the purpose of the inquest which was to determine how D came by his death. It could be the case that in the process of such enquiry criminal evidence would come to light, but that did not mean that the process had been abused. There was nothing to suggest that the representative for the chief constable had stepped beyond the limits of legitimate enquiry relating to relevant facts. It was the duty of C to investigate "fully and fearlessly" and he had done so, *R. v. HM Coroner for North Humberside and Scunthorpe, ex p. Jamieson* [1995] Q.B. 1, [1994] C.L.Y. 631 applied. He had been meticulous in his procedural handling of a difficult case and there was no evidence of unfairness. The fact that assisted suicide was not mentioned to the jury was of no consequence to the outcome of the case.

R. v. HM CORONER FOR DERBY AND SOUTH DERBYSHIRE, *ex p.* HART (2000) 164 J.P. 429, Newman, J., QBD.

51. **Judicial decision making – evidence – exposure to asbestos – adequate reasons**

[Occupiers Liability Act 1957.]

T died of mesothelioma caused by exposure to asbestos. He had worked as a plumber and heating engineer and was employed by a company, JL, from 1954 to 1968. During this period T had spent approximately 50 per cent of his time working in premises belonging to LCC, pursuant to a contract with his employers, where he was regularly exposed to large quantities of asbestos dust. His executor, D, brought an action against LCC for damages claiming LCC had owed T a duty of care under the Occupiers Liability Act 1957 and had negligently failed to warn T's employers of the dangers of asbestos and failed to protect T against the risk. The trial judge dismissed the claim, preferring the evidence of LCC's expert that sufficient knowledge of the risk of asbestos would not have been known to occupiers such as LCC until the 1970's. D appealed on the ground that the judge had not given reasons for his decision.

Held, allowing the appeal and remitting the case for retrial, that the judge heard full evidence from both experts and should have provided detailed reasons explaining which elements of the evidence he favoured and why. The case would be remitted but, given that it had already been 10 years since T died and that agreement had been largely reached as to quantum, the parties were strongly encouraged to take up the option of alternative dispute resolution.

DYSON v. LEEDS CITY COUNCIL [2000] C.P. Rep. 42, Ward, L.J., CA.

52. **Judiciary – bias – danger of judicial bias – parties' representations – recusal**

At the commencement of a hearing in a possession action brought by A against C, the judge announced that he had previously acted for A until about a year before the hearing when he had ceased to be a partner in his firm. He had in fact retired from practice, although that was not then made clear. The judge had concluded that his historical involvement with A did not preclude him from hearing the claim, but he had not expressly invited representations on the point from C, who was then unrepresented. She had not made any objection and the judge had proceeded to hear the case and awarded possession to A on a discretionary ground. No criticism had been made of the manner in which he conducted the hearing. C appealed, contending that the judge had been judicially biased towards A.

Held, dismissing the appeal, that there was no question of actual bias arising in the instant circumstances, hence the judge was not required to disqualify himself automatically, *Locabail (UK) Ltd v. Bayfield Properties Ltd (Leave to Appeal)* [2000] Q.B. 451, [1999] C.L.Y. 38 applied. The issue was whether there was a "real danger of bias". In *Locabail* it had been expressly stated that previous instructions to act for a party did not, on their own, constitute such danger. Although there were "minor criticisms" that might be made of the judge's failure to give C an opportunity to address the question properly, those alone did not create a sufficient ground for disqualification. Had C been given the opportunity to make representations, it was inconceivable that the judge would have recused himself from the hearing as a result.

ALDWYCK HOUSING ASSOCIATION v. CUNNINGHAM, May 15, 2000, Judge Farnworth, CC (Luton). [*Ex rel.* Richard Colbey, Barrister, Francis Taylor Building, Temple, London].

53. **Judiciary – bias – danger of judicial bias – perceived partiality – recusal**

In a contested occupation order application, the judge became aware that he had, while at the bar some 15 years earlier, acted for one of the party's proposed witnesses.

Held, recusing himself from the case without hearing representations, that such contact prevented him from making any substantive decision in the case, *Locabail (UK) Ltd v. Bayfield Properties Ltd (Leave to Appeal)* [2000] Q.B. 451, [1999] C.L.Y. 38 applied. The judge indicated that although he did not believe that the association would lead to actual bias, he considered there had been sufficient proximity between himself and the witness to lead the parties, particularly the opposing party, to feel legitimately that there was a danger of bias.

KARAKUS v. KARAKUS, June 6, 2000, Judge Hornby, CC (Bow). [*Ex rel.* Richard Colbey, Barrister, Francis Taylor Building, Temple, London].

54. Judiciary – bias – genuine risk – unjustified allegations based on judge's ethnic and religious background found unjustified

A applied for an order that an inquiry as to damages hearing in ongoing litigation be listed before a judge other than Jacob, J. A maintained that the judge was inherently biased towards A because he was Jewish and that the judge had demonstrated his bias towards A at previous interlocutory stages of the proceedings.

Held, dismissing the application, that, although it was not possible to give a finite definition as to the circumstances in which a genuine risk of bias might arise, there was no basis for a suggestion of bias based on the individual judge's religion, ethnic background, nationality, gender, age, class, means or sexuality.

SEER TECHNOLOGIES LTD v. ABBAS (NO.1) *The Times*, March 16, 2000, Sir John Vinelott, Ch D.

55. Magistrates courts – commission areas

JUSTICES OF THE PEACE (COMMISSION AREAS) (AMENDMENT) ORDER 2000, SI 2000 677; made under the Justices of the Peace Act 1997 s.1. In force: April 1, 2000; £2.00.

This Order substitutes a new list for the list of commission areas in the Justices of the Peace (Commission Areas) Order 1999 (SI 1999 3010) to take account of changes to magistrates' courts committee areas that come into force on April 1, 2000.

56. Magistrates courts – commission areas – Avon and Somerset

COMMISSION AREAS (AVON AND SOMERSET) ORDER 2000, SI 2000 3054; made under the Justices of the Peace Act 1997 s.1. In force: January 1, 2001; £1.50.

This Order provides for the replacement of the two commission areas of Avon and Somerset by a single commission area to be known as the Avon and Somerset commission area.

57. Magistrates courts – commission areas – Devon and Cornwall

COMMISSION AREAS (DEVON AND CORNWALL) ORDER 2000, SI 2000 2671; made under the Justices of the Peace Act 1997 s.1. In force: January 1, 2001; £1.50.

This Order, which amends the Justices of the Peace (Commission Areas) Order 1999 (SI 1999 3010), provides for the replacement of the two commission areas of Devon and Cornwall by a single commission area to be known as the Devon and Cornwall commission area.

58. Magistrates courts – commission areas – Dyfed Powys

COMMISSION AREAS (DYFED POWYS) ORDER 2000, SI 2000 3096; made under the Justices of the Peace Act 1997 s.1. In force: January 1, 2001; £1.50.

This Order provides for the replacement of the two commission areas of Dyfed and Powys by a single commission area to be known as the Dyfed Powys commission area.

59. Magistrates courts – commission areas – Thames Valley

COMMISSION AREAS (THAMES VALLEY) ORDER 2000, SI 2000 1429; made under the Justices of the Peace Act 1997 s.1. In force: July 1, 2000; £1.50.

This Order, which amends the Justices of the Peace (Commission Areas) Order 1999 (SI 1999 3010), provides for the replacement of the Berkshire, Buckinghamshire and Oxfordshire commission areas by a single commission area to be known as the Thames Valley commission area.

60. Magistrates courts – commission areas – Wales

COMMISSION AREAS (NORTH WALES) ORDER 2000, SI 2000 2238; made under the Justices of the Peace Act 1997 s.1. In force: January 1, 2001; £1.50.

This Order provides for the replacement of the Clwyd and Gwynedd commission areas by a single commission area to be known as the North Wales commission area.

61. Magistrates courts – committee areas

MAGISTRATES' COURTS COMMITTEE AREAS (AMENDMENT) ORDER 2000, SI 2000 676; made under the Justices of the Peace Act 1997 s.27A. In force: April 1, 2000; £2.00.

This Order substitutes a new list for the list of magistrates' courts committee areas in the Magistrates' Courts Committee Areas Order 1999 (SI 1999 3008) to take account of changes that come into force on April 1, 2000.

62. Magistrates courts – committees – establishment – Greater London Magistrates' Court Authority

GREATER LONDON MAGISTRATES' COURTS AUTHORITY (TRANSITIONAL PROVISIONS) ORDER 2000, SI 2000 240; made under the Access to Justice Act 1999 Sch.14 para.32. In force: March 1, 2000; £1.50.

This Order contains transitional provisions in connection with the establishment of the Greater London Magistrates' Courts Authority, which will become the magistrates' courts committee for the Greater London area when the Justices of the Peace Act 1997 s.30A(2) comes into force.

63. Magistrates courts – committees and selection panels – code of conduct

CODE OF CONDUCT (MAGISTRATES' COURTS COMMITTEE AND SELECTION PANELS) ORDER 2000, SI 2000 2148; made under the Justices of the Peace Act 1997 s.39A. In force: September 1, 2000; £1.50.

This Order provides for a code of conduct to be observed by members of magistrates' courts committees and members of selection panels for choosing members of such committees.

64. Magistrates courts – extradition proceedings – unification and renaming of stipendiary bench

MAGISTRATES' COURTS (EXTRADITION) (AMENDMENT) RULES 2000, SI 2000 1872; made under the Magistrates' Court Act 1980 s.144. In force: in accordance with r.1; £1.00.

These Rules amend the Magistrates' Courts (Extradition) Rules 1989 (SI 1989 1597) to take account of the coming into force of the Access to Justice Act 1999 s.78 and Sch.11 which unify and rename the stipendiary bench.

65. **Magistrates courts – Greater London Magistrates' Courts Authority – constitution**

GREATER LONDON MAGISTRATES' COURTS AUTHORITY (CONSTITUTION) (AMENDMENT) REGULATIONS 2000, SI 2000 2149; made under the Justices of the Peace Act 1997 s.30B. In force: September 1, 2000; £1.00.

These Regulations amend the Greater London Magistrates' Courts Authority (Constitution) Regulations 1999 (SI 1999 3099) with the effect of increasing the rates for travelling and subsistence allowance payable to members of the Greater London Magistrates' Courts Authority.

66. **Magistrates courts – Greater London Magistrates' Courts Authority – financial administration**

GREATER LONDON MAGISTRATES' COURTS AUTHORITY (FINANCIAL ADMINISTRATION) REGULATIONS 2000, SI 2000 2810; made under the Justices of the Peace Act 1997 s.59D. In force: November 6, 2000; £1.50.

These Regulations apply the Local Government Finance Act 1988 Part VIII (financial administration) to the Greater London Magistrates' Courts Authority with modifications.

67. **Magistrates courts – petty sessions areas**

PETTY SESSIONS AREAS (AMENDMENT) ORDER 2000, SI 2000 675; made under the Justices of the Peace Act 1997 s.4. In force: April 1, 2000; £2.50.

This Order substitutes a new list for the list of petty sessions areas in the Petty Sessions Areas Order 1999 (SI 1999 3009) to take account of changes to magistrates' courts committee areas that come into force on April 1, 2000.

68. **Magistrates courts – procedural changes**

MAGISTRATES' COURT (AMENDMENT) RULES 2000, SI 2000 3361 (L.27); made under the Magistrates' Courts Act 1980 s.144. In force: January 15, 2001; £1.75.

These Rules, which amend the Magistrates' Courts Rules 1981 (SI 1981 552) in relation to the new procedure created by the Crime and Disorder Act 1998 s.51, s.52 and Sch.3 provide for appropriate references to being "sent" as opposed to "committed" for trial in the Crown Court and for a new r.11A to specify the documents which the magistrates' court must send to the Crown Court within four days of sending a person for trial there.

69. **Magistrates courts – warrants – enforcement**

MAGISTRATES COURTS WARRANTS (SPECIFICATION OF PROVISIONS) ORDER 2000, SI 2000 3278; made under the Magistrates Courts Act 1980 s.125A. In force: January 8, 2001; £1.50.

This Order makes provision for the manner of enforcement of warrants under statutory provisions made under the Magistrates' Courts Act 1980 ss.125A to 125D.

70. **Magistrates courts – warrants – enforcement – disclosure of information**

ENFORCEMENT OF WARRANTS (DISCLOSURE OF INFORMATION) ORDER 2000, SI 2000 3277; made under the Magistrates Courts Act 1980 s.125C. In force: January 8, 2001; £1.50.

This Order specifies that the Secretary of State for Social Security is a relevant public authority for the purpose of providing for a justices' chief executive to apply for basic personal information from a relevant public authority for the purpose of enforcing certain warrants under the Magistrates' Courts Act 1980 s.125C.

71. Magistrates courts – warrants – enforcement agencies

APPROVAL OF ENFORCEMENT AGENCIES REGULATIONS 2000, SI 2000 3279; made under the Magistrates Courts Act 1980 s.31A. In force: January 8, 2001; £2.00.

These Regulations set out the conditions that must be satisfied for an enforcement agency to be approved under the Justices of the Peace Act 1997 s.31A and the Magistrates' Courts Act 1980 s.125B which provides for the enforcement of certain warrants by enforcement agencies to be approved by a magistrates' courts committee.

72. Parliamentary privilege – Members of Parliament – waiver

See DEFAMATION: Hamilton v. Al Fayed (No.1). §1767

73. Powers of attorney – capacity to execute more than one power – earlier power not revoked by later one unless intention to do so – suitability of attorneys

[Enduring Powers of Attorney Act 1985.]

X appealed the dismissal of her objections to the registration of a power of attorney. E, a woman in her eighties and suffering from Alzheimer's disease, had executed a power of attorney in 1992 appointing two of her three daughters, Y and Z, to act on her behalf in all matters except those relating to land. In 1997 E executed a further power appointing all three daughters, X, Y and Z, which was without restriction but included a provision that "any two of my attorneys may sign". In 1998 X applied for the 1997 power to be registered as an enduring power of attorney under the Enduring Powers of Attorney Act 1985, but it was refused because the provision as to signatures meant that the attorneys would not be acting jointly or jointly and severally as required by s.11(1) of the 1985 Act. In 1999 Y and Z applied for the 1992 power to be registered. X objected on the grounds that the 1992 power had been revoked by the 1997 power and that Y and Z were not suitable to act as attorneys. Her objections were dismissed by the master and she appealed.

Held, dismissing the appeal, that the 1992 power had not been revoked. X had not shown that E had intended to revoke the earlier power, and E had not acted in a way that was inconsistent with the continuation of the 1992 power. *Law Com. No. 122 "The Incapacitated Principal"*, which had formed the basis of the 1985 Act, made it clear that donors should be allowed to execute more than one power should they so wish. Although Y and Z had been wrong to exclude X from discussions as to tax planning and to obtain E's signature to a draft document, they had generally acted in E's best interests and were trustworthy and sensible people. The difficulties between the sisters was not a reason without more to appoint a receiver, particularly as this was likely to incur expense. Weight had to be given to the fact that E wanted her family members to act for her, that they were familiar with her affairs and that she had reasons for choosing to appoint two of her three daughters.

E (ENDURING POWER OF ATTORNEY), *Re*; *sub nom.* E (A DONOR), RE; X v. Y (ENDURING POWERS OF ATTORNEY) [2001] Ch. 364, Arden, J., Ch D.

74. Powers of attorney – registration – consideration of grounds for objection – disclosure in favour of objector

C was advised by his doctor to execute a power of attorney as he was suffering from memory loss and C executed a power in favour of J, C's long term cohabitee, and M, an old business associate. C's son, S, opposed the grant on the grounds that C did not have the capacity to execute the grant and that M was an unsuitable attorney. S was concerned about the transfer of substantial assets to J and M. The judge held that the objections were without substance and ordered registration of the power of attorney. Further, the judge ordered preparation of an accountant's report into all transactions over £25,000 and notification of the Court of Protection by J and M of any transaction they had sanctioned in excess of

£5,000 and of their intention to make any transactions of £25,000 or over. The report was intended for use by the Court of Protection and the attorneys, but the court had power to disclose it to others. S's application for disclosure was refused on the grounds that it would only lead to further litigation. S appealed against the decision to register the power and sought leave to appeal against the refusal to disclose the report.

Held, dismissing the appeal and refusing leave but remitting the matter to the Court of Protection, that the first question on an application for registration of a power of attorney was whether it was necessary to make inquiries into the grounds of objection. While there had been good reasons for registering the power there had been little consideration of the need for inquiries. The reasons for the dismissal had not been expressed in a way that allowed S to see that his grounds had been considered. The judge had been entitled to decide that there was nothing to gain from disclosure and that there was a risk of distress to C and of harm to his financial affairs from further litigation. However, further inquiries into M's suitability were justified because of a transaction under which M appeared to have benefited to C's detriment was a matter which would be remitted to the Court of Protection.

C (POWER OF ATTORNEY), Re [2000] 2 F.L.R. 1, Chadwick, L.J., CA.

75. Powers of Criminal Courts (Sentencing) Act 2000 (c.6)

This Act consolidates, with amendments, certain enactments relating to the powers of courts to deal with offenders and defaulters to give effect to recommendations of the Law Commission and the Scottish Law Commission.

This Act received Royal Assent on May 25, 2000.

76. Practice directions – Crown Office – procedure changes – time limits for bundles – short notice for cases in warned list – limited transcription services

[Human Rights Act 1998.]

The Lord Chief Justice issued a Practice Direction superseding in part *Practice Direction (QBD: Crown Office List: Time Estimates, Skeleton Arguments and Paginated Bundles)* [1994] 1 W.L.R. 1551, [1994] C.L.Y. 3654 and stating that from May 2000 the number of courts sitting on Crown Office List business would be substantially increased. From May, applicants' and appellants' court bundles must be lodged at least three weeks and respondents' skeleton arguments at least 14 days prior to a substantive hearing. Cases in the warned list were considered ready for trial and might be listed at short notice, while adjournments would rarely be granted. Without notice applications would be taped and not transcribed without prior arrangement with Smith Bernal. The measures were necessary to clear the backlog of cases prior to the implementation of the Human Rights Act 1998.

PRACTICE DIRECTION (QBD: CROWN OFFICE LIST: PREPARATION FOR HEARINGS) [2000] 2 All E.R. 896, Lord Bingham of Cornhill, L.C.J., QBD.

77. Practice directions – Crown Office – renaming of Crown Office List and orders – new rules relating to judicial review

[Human Rights Act 1998.]

The Lord Chief Justice issued a Practice Direction in the Queens Bench Divisional Court which stated that the Crown Office List would be renamed the Administrative Court to reflect its primary role as a specialist court dealing with public and administrative law cases. A lead nominated judge would be appointed who would have overall responsibility for the speed, efficiency and economy with which cases would be conducted and the nominated judge who would take on this role initially would be Mr Justice Scott Baker. These changes were expected to come into effect with the coming into force of new rules relating to judicial review, at the same time as the Human Rights Act 1998 on October 2, 2000. The jurisdiction of the court to make orders would be unaffected by the new recommendations. The new rules also renamed the order for mandamus, certiorari and prohibition to a mandatory order, quashing order and a prohibiting order respectively and stated that the parties to judicial review proceedings would be described as "The Queen on the application of (name of applicant), claimant versus the public body against whom the proceedings were brought, defendant".

PRACTICE DIRECTION (QBD: ADMIN CT: ESTABLISHMENT) [2000] 1 W.L.R. 1654, Lord Woolf of Barnes, L.C.J., QBD.

78. Probate proceedings – fees – refunds

NON-CONTENTIOUS PROBATE FEES (AMENDMENT) ORDER 2000, SI 2000 642 (L.5); made under the Supreme Court Act 1981 s.130; and the Finance Act 1990 s.128. In force: April 25, 2000; £1.00.

This Order amends the Non-Contentious Probate Fees Order 1999 (SI 1999 688) by providing for refunds of fees in certain cases.

79. Reporting restrictions – undertakings not to disclose defence evidence – reporting of judgment restricted in part

[Administration of Justice Act 1960 s.12.]

T, a Swedish company, claimed £38 million, which it alleged had been misappropriated by S and LM, T's managing director and chairman respectively. T agreed that interlocutory proceedings would be held in private on the basis that S was under investigation by the Swedish authorities and any evidence he gave might encourage a criminal prosecution there. T also gave undertakings not to disclose defence affidavits, witness statements and documents except to third parties who had given a similar undertaking. S applied for an order under the Administration of Justice Act 1960 s.12 to prevent the reporting of the substantive judgment. T opposed the order, contending that it wished to inform its shareholders, from which it could not obtain undertakings, and also that it might want to disclose the findings to other courts.

Held, allowing the application in part, that there was already in principle no reason why T should not proceed to disclose the essential findings of the judgment having removed any references to protected defence material as to do so would not contravene the terms of the undertaking. It was therefore S's responsibility to satisfy the court that the proper administration of justice demanded restriction of those aspects of the judgment not covered by the existing undertaking and as it was not a function of the court to protect a litigant from embarrassment and the potential for prosecution. S had failed to discharge this burden. Although the matter did not fall within any of the categories identified in s.12, it would nevertheless be unjust to allow publication of the judgment by a law reporter to release T from its undertakings with regard to the protected material, having regard to the fact that S had conducted his defence so far on the basis that the protection afforded by the undertakings would extend beyond the handing down of any interlocutory judgment. Publication of the judgment would therefore be permitted but excluding all reference to the protected material.

TRUSTOR AB v. SMALLBONE (NO.1) [2000] 1 All E.R. 811, Rimer, J., Ch D.

80. Supreme Court – Eastern Caribbean

ANGUILLA, MONTSERRAT AND VIRGIN ISLANDS (SUPREME COURT) ORDER 2000, SI 2000 3060; made under the West Indies Act 1967 s.6, s.17; and the Anguilla Act 1980 s.1. In force: November 20, 2000; £1.50.

This Order provides for the office of Master of the Eastern Caribbean Supreme Court in the law of Anguilla, Montserrat and the Virgin Islands, following the restructuring of that Court.

81. Supreme Court – fees

SUPREME COURT FEES (AMENDMENT) ORDER 2000, SI 2000 641 (L.4); made under the Supreme Court Act 1981 s.130; the Insolvency Act 1986 s.414, s.415; and the Finance Act 1990 s.128. In force: in accordance with Art.2; £1.50.

This Order amends the Supreme Court Fees Order 1999 (SI 1999 687) so that refunds are permitted in certain cases; to take account of the establishment of the Legal Services Commission under the Access to Justice Act 1999 s.1; and to clarify the description of certain fees.

82. Supreme Court – fees

SUPREME COURT FEES (AMENDMENT NO.3) ORDER 2000, SI 2000 1544 (L.13); made under the Supreme Court Act 1981 s.130. In force: July 3, 2000; £1.00.

This Order amends the Supreme Court Fees Order 1999 (SI 1999 687) by specifying a fee for commencement of costs-only proceedings and extending fee 2.6 (witness summons) to cover applications for deposition orders.

83. Supreme Court – fees

SUPREME COURT FEES (AMENDMENT NO.4) ORDER 2000, SI 2000 2382 (L.22); made under the Supreme Court Act 1981 s.130. In force: October 2, 2000; £1.00.

This Order amends the Supreme Court Fees Order 1999 (SI 1999 687) by restructuring the fees payable in relation to claims for judicial review to take account of the new rules on judicial review contained in the Civil Procedure (Amendment No. 4) Rules 2000 (SI 2000 2092).

84. Tribunals – Transport tribunal

TRANSPORT TRIBUNAL RULES 2000, SI 2000 3226; made under the Transport Act 1985 Sch.4 para.11. In force: January 1, 2001; £2.50.

These Rules, which revoke the Transport Tribunal Rules 1986 (SI 1986 1547) apply to applications made to the Transport Tribunal under the Public Passenger Vehicles Act 1981 s.50(8) and the Goods Vehicles (Licensing of Operators) Act 1995 s.29(3). They also apply to appeals made to the Tribunal under the Public Passenger Vehicles Act 1981 s.50, the Transport Act 1985 s.111, the Goods Vehicles (Licensing of Operators) Act 1995 and the Postal Services Act 2000 s.94.

85. Tribunals – valuation tribunals – appointments

VALUATION TRIBUNALS (AMENDMENT) (ENGLAND) REGULATIONS 2000, SI 2000 409; made under the Local Government Finance Act 1988 s.143, Sch.11 para.1, Sch.11 para.5. In force: March 17, 2000; £1.50.

These Regulations amend the Valuation and Community Charge Tribunals Regulations 1989 (SI 1989 439) by providing for appointments to a tribunal to be made by a local authority and the president of the tribunal. They shorten the period after which, if no appointment is made, the Secretary of State may make an appointment in default and provide for the Secretary of State to appoint a different tribunal to deal with an appeal where, in the case of the tribunal which would normally have jurisdiction, there appears to be a conflict of interest.

86. Universities – examinations – appropriate remedy

See EDUCATION: Clark v. University of Lincolnshire and Humberside. §2001

87. Vexatious litigants – Treasury Solicitor's application for civil proceedings order – presumed acting under authority of Attorney General

[Law Officers Act 1944 s.1; Supreme Court Act 1981 s.42.]

F was the subject of a civil proceedings order made by the Treasury Solicitor under the provisions of the Supreme Court Act 1981 s.42. The application was authorised by the Attorney General under the Law Officers Act 1944 s.1 providing for the delegation of his authority to the Solicitor General. F appealed against the order, contending that the Treasury Solicitor did not have the requisite authority to act and that the Attorney General had not produced evidence proving that he had authorised the making of the application.

Held, dismissing the appeal, that where the authority of the solicitor bringing the application was challenged, it was for the challenger to substantiate that allegation with evidence in the form of a witness statement or affidavit in an early interlocutory application to stay the proceedings. The Attorney General was under no obligation to lead evidence that he had given the authority to make the application, since that authority was presumed by the court. Like any other litigant, the Attorney General could instruct solicitors to act on his behalf and solicitors were assumed to be acting with their client's authority. If a challenge to that position was not made prior to the issue of the application, by means of a letter to the Treasury Solicitor, to which he could respond with reasons for his authorisation, then the court could consider that the challenger had acted unreasonably. If a notice to stay was filed, supported by appropriate evidence, the Attorney General could respond by service of a witness statement outlining the authorisation given to the solicitor bringing the application. There was no breach of the litigant's constitutional rights in the making of a s.42 order per se and it was the court's duty to protect that right by ensuring the requirements of s.42 were made out.

ATTORNEY GENERAL v. FOLEY [2000] 2 All E.R. 609, Schiemann, L.J., CA.

88. Youth courts – London – unification of stipendiary bench

INNER LONDON YOUTH COURTS (SELECTION OF CHAIRMEN) (AMENDMENT) ORDER 2000, SI 2000 1874; made under the Children and Young Persons Act 1933 Sch.2 para.15. In force: in accordance with Art.1; £1.00.

This Order amends the Inner London Youth Courts (Selection of Chairmen) Order 1990 (SI 1990 1265) to take account of the coming into force of the Access to Justice Act 1999 s.78 and Sch.11 which unify and rename the stipendiary bench.

89. Publications

Burns, Stacy Lee; Sarat, Austin – Making Settlement Work. Law, Justice and Power. Hardback: £50.00. ISBN 0-7546-2124-3. Dartmouth.

Gerlis, Stephen M. – Practice Notes on County Court Procedure. 3rd Ed. Practice Notes. Hardback: £15.95. ISBN 1-85941-309-9. Cavendish Publishing Ltd.

Jarman, Nicholas; Cowen, Jonathan; Morgan, Adrienne; Stafford, Andrew Granville; Davis, Brendan – Butterworths Disciplinary and Regulatory Tribunals. Hardback: £130.00. ISBN 0-406-90260-7. Butterworths Law.

Morris, Gordon – Shaw's Directory of Courts in the United Kingdom: 2000-2001. Paperback: £38.50. ISBN 0-7219-1407-1. Shaw & Sons.

Murdie, Alan; Wise, Ian – Fines and Other Financial Penalties in the Magistrates' Court. Paperback: £25.00. ISBN 1-903307-01-5. The Legal Action Group.

Vidmar, Neil – World Jury Systems. Oxford Socio-Legal Studies. Hardback: £45.00. ISBN 0-19-829856-0. Oxford University Press.

ADMINISTRATIVE LAW

90. Audit Commission – publication of information by relevant authorities

AUDIT COMMISSION ACT 1988 (PUBLICATION OF INFORMATION AS TO STANDARDS OF PERFORMANCE) (VARIATION) (ENGLAND) ORDER 2000, SI 2000 2253; made under the Audit Commission Act 1998 s.44. In force: September 15, 2000; £1.00.

This Order varies the period specified in the Audit Commission Act 1998 s.44(2)(b), within which all relevant authorities in England must publish information relating to their activities in a financial year, in accordance with a direction given by the Audit Commission pursuant to s.44(1) of that Act. It reduces the period from 9 months to 7 months, beginning with the end of the financial year to which the information relates.

91. Census

CENSUS ORDER 2000, SI 2000 744; made under the Census Act 1920 s.1. In force: March 15, 2000; £2.00.

This Order provides for the taking of a census for England and Wales on April 29, 2001. It specifies the persons by whom and with respect to whom the census returns are to be made and sets out the particulars to be stated in the returns.

92. Census

CENSUS REGULATIONS 2000, SI 2000 1473; made under the Census Act 1920 s.3(1). In force: June 27, 2000; £7.30.

These Regulations provide for the detailed arrangements necessary for the conduct of the census directed to be taken by the Census Order 2000 (SI 2000 744).

93. Census

CENSUS (AMENDMENT) ORDER 2000, SI 2000 3249; made under the Census Act 1920 s.1. In force: December 13, 2000; £1.50.

This Order, which amends the Census Order 2000 (SI 2000 744), adds a new item 9A which specifies religion as a particular to be stated in the census returns.

94. Census

CENSUS (AMENDMENT) REGULATIONS 2000, SI 2000 3351; made under the Census Act 1920 s.3. In force: January 11, 2001; £7.50.

These Regulations amend the Census Regulations 2000 (SI 2000 1473) which provide for the detailed arrangements necessary for the conduct of the 2001 Census by substituting new forms H1, H2, I1 and I2. The new forms differ from the old in consequence of the Census (Amendment) Act 2000 and now include a question on religion.

95. Census (Amendment) Act 2000 (c.24)

This Act amends the Census Act 1920 to enable particulars to be required in respect of religion.

This Act received Royal Assent on July 28, 2000 and comes into force on July 28, 2000.

96. Citizenship – colonies – banishment of citizens – lawfulness of Ordinance

[British Indian Ocean Territory Order 1965 (SI 1965 1920) s.11; British Indian Ocean Territory Ordinance No.1 1971 s.4.]

B, a citizen of the Chagos Islands, applied for judicial review of the decision of the Commissioner for the British Indian Ocean Territory that his banishment pursuant to the British Indian Ocean Territory Ordinance No.1 of 1971, made under the British Indian Ocean Territory Order 1965 s.11, was lawful. The Islands had been part of the British colony of Mauritius, but became a separate colony under the 1965 Order after agreement between the United Kingdom and the United States that an American military base could be established on the main island. B contended that (1) the Ordinance and the actions taken under it ran contrary to what had been contemplated by the enabling legislation of the 1965 Order, and (2) s.4 of the Ordinance, which established that no person could enter the Islands without a permit complying with the Ordinance, could not be authorised by the general terms of s.11 of the 1965 Order, given that a British citizen had a fundamental right to live in, or return to, that part of the Queen's territory of which he was a citizen.

Held, granting the application, that (1) the tenet that constitutional or fundamental rights could only be removed by the executive through a specific provision within an Act of Parliament, or by means of Regulations given specific power under the main legislation, but could not be removed via a lesser statutory instrument the power for which derived from a general provision in the main legislation, did not apply to colonial laws, *Liyanage (Don John Francis Douglas) v. Queen, The* [1967] 1 A.C. 259, [1966] C.L.Y. 10026 applied and *R. v. Lord Chancellor, ex p. Witham* [1998] Q.B. 575, [1997] C.L.Y. 11 considered, and (2) the provisions of s.4 of the Ordinance resulted in the effective banishment of the indigenous people of the Islands. Given that s.11 (1) of the Order established that laws be made "for the peace, order and good government of the territory", the removal of citizens from that territory could not comply with s.11 (1) save in exceptionally rare circumstances. It followed that the reasons behind B's banishment were *Wednesbury* unreasonable in that they had not been conducive to the peace, order and good government of the territory. Section 4 of the Ordinance would accordingly be quashed.

R. v. SECRETARY OF STATE FOR THE FOREIGN AND COMMONWEALTH OFFICE, *ex p.* BANCOULT [2001] 2 W.L.R. 1219, Laws, L.J., QBD.

97. **Citizenship – naturalisation – British citizenship acquired by descent – entitlement to certificate of naturalisation**

[British Nationality Act 1981 s.2(1) (a), s.6(1), s.6(2).]

U sought judicial review of the Secretary of State's decision that he could not consider U's application under the British Nationality Act 1981 s.6(1) and s.6(2) for a certificate of naturalisation as a British citizen, on the basis that U had already acquired British citizenship by descent. Under s.2(1)(a) of the Act a child born outside the United Kingdom would only be a British citizen if at the time of birth either their mother or father was a British citizen other than by descent. Accordingly, in the absence of a certificate, any child born to U outside the UK would not become a citizen automatically.

Held, granting the application, that the way in which s.6 of the Act had been construed by the Secretary of State was inappropriate. The provision was to be interpreted in the light of the ordinary and natural meaning of its words, with the result that it did not exclude those who were British citizens by descent from becoming British citizens by naturalisation. The issue of a certificate of naturalisation to U would be of considerable benefit to him since it would enable him to become a British citizen "otherwise than by descent" and allow citizenship to be transmitted to any of his children who were born outside the UK.

R. v. SECRETARY OF STATE FOR THE HOME DEPARTMENT, *ex p.* ULLAH (AZAD) [2001] I.N.L.R. 74, Gibbs, J., QBD.

98. **Educational institutions – statutory interpretation – right to use title "university college" – sufficiency of time for compliance with Teaching and Higher Education Act 1998 s.39**

[Further and Higher Education Act 1992 s.77; Teaching and Higher Education Act 1998 s.39, s.40; Teaching and Higher Education Act 1998 (Commencement No. 4 and Transitional Provisions) Order 1998 (SI 1998 3237).]

A higher education institution, LHUC, applied for judicial review of the date of commencement for the coming into force of the Teaching and Higher Education Act 1998 s.39 and s.40. LHUC operated under the title "University College" without the required authorisation under the Further and Higher Education Act 1992 s.77. Such usage was prohibited upon commencement of s.39 and s.40 of the 1998 Act. Correspondence between LHUC and members of the government and Department of Education had indicated that an interval would be allowed in order for institutions to adjust to the provisions of the 1998 act. LHUC submitted that the commencement date set out under the Teaching and Higher Education Act

1998 (Commencement No. 4 and Transitional Provisions) Order 1998 did not provide adequate time for compliance thereby thwarting its legislative aim.

Held, refusing the application, that any reference to an interval between the approval process and the prohibition process was designed to give time to stop the unauthorised use of the title "University College" by institutions. There was no ambiguity in the wording of the Act and accordingly there would be sufficient time to obtain approval. LHUC had not shown any reliance on the correspondence from the Department which had resulted in any prejudice. It followed that they had been fairly treated.

R. (ON THE APPLICATION OF LIVERPOOL HOPE UNIVERSITY COLLEGE) v. SECRETARY OF STATE FOR EDUCATION AND EMPLOYMENT; *sub nom.* R. v. SECRETARY OF STATE FOR EDUCATION AND EMPLOYMENT, *ex p.* LIVERPOOL HOPE UNIVERSITY COLLEGE [2000] Ed. C.R. 330, Newman, J., QBD.

99. Fees – consular fees – payment into Consolidated Fund

CONSULAR FEES (AMENDMENT) REGULATIONS 2000, SI 2000 1017; made under the Consular Fees Act 1980 s.1. In force: May 8, 2000; £1.00.

These Regulations amend the Consular Fees Regulations 1981 (SI 1981 476) to provide for all monies received in respect of consular fees to be paid into the Consolidated Fund.

100. Health and Safety Executive – delegation – institution of proceedings by local authority

[Health and Safety at Work etc. Act 1974 s.38.]

WHS sought judicial review of the justices' decision that informations issued by the local authority for their prosecution for breaches of health and safety legislation were valid. WHS submitted that the charges could not be tried because although the local authority in instituting the proceedings had acted upon instructions from the health and safety inspector, the commencement of legal action was reserved to the inspector alone by virtue of the Health and Safety at Work etc. Act 1974 s.38.

Held, granting the application and quashing the decision, that the inspector had neither the express nor the implied authority to delegate the power conferred upon him by s.38, hence the justices had no power to hear the charges.

R. v. CROYDON JUSTICES, *ex p.* WH SMITH LTD; *sub nom.* R. (ON THE APPLICATION OF WH SMITH LTD) v. CROYDON JUSTICES [2001] E.H.L.R. 12, Elias, J., QBD.

101. Independent schools – exclusion policy not susceptible to judicial review

See EDUCATION: R. v. Muntham House School, *ex p.* R. §1964

102. Judicial review – coroners – consent to post mortems – retention of tissue samples

[Coroners Rules 1984 (SI 1984 522) r.7.]

J's wife died a year after being diagnosed as suffering from mesothelioma. The coroner decided to hold an inquest and, after consulting with J, arranged for a limited post mortem examination of her lungs. The inquest was held a year after death when the body was released to J. Two months later, J sought judicial review of the decision to order a post mortem, and an order of mandamus to return retained body parts and samples. J alleged that the coroner had asked his permission only for a piece of tissue from the lungs, and had stated that a post mortem was not necessary. His application was refused on the basis that the attack on the decision to hold a post mortem was out of time and that his wife's organs had been released to him. A renewed application was similarly refused. J sought leave to appeal against this refusal, contending that the decision to hold the post mortem formed part of the inquest, and that time should run from the inquest date.

Further, that there were still some samples mounted in paraffin blocks that had not been returned.

Held, refusing the application, that the coroner did not need J's consent to the post mortem; J's only entitlement, by virtue of the Coroners Rules 1984 r.7, was to be informed that the post mortem was going to be carried out. There was thus no good reason for granting leave for judicial review, nor for extending time for doing so. It was inappropriate to base a judicial review application on matters relating to a small number of tissue samples.

R. v. HM CORONER FOR NORTHUMBERLAND, *ex p.* JACOBS (2000) 53 B.M.L.R. 21, May, L.J., CA.

103. **Judicial review – delay – school allocation decision – challenge to precede start of term**

See EDUCATION: R. v. Rochdale MBC, *ex p.* B. §1914

104. **Local authorities powers and duties – sale of land – susceptibility to judicial review**

See LOCAL GOVERNMENT: R. v. Bolsover DC, *ex p.* Pepper. §4114

105. **Maladministration – Pensions Ombudsman – finding of maladministration against council – Personal and Occupational Pension Schemes (Miscellaneous Amendments) Regulations 1997 having retrospective effect**

[Personal and Occupational Pension Schemes (Miscellaneous Amendments) Regulations 1997 (SI 1997 786) Reg.9.]

H received superannuation payments and additional payments from WCC upon dismissal. WCC subsequently received advice that those additional payments were unlawful and reduced H's pension by that amount. H successfully appealed to the pensions ombudsman, PO, but WCC succeeded in part on appeal to the Chancery Division ([1996] 3 W.L.R. 563, [1996] C.L.Y. 4659) and on appeal to the Court of Appeal ([1998] Ch. 377, [1997] C.L.Y. 4010), on the ground that PO had no jurisdiction to investigate. H brought a second complaint to PO following the coming into force of the Personal and Occupational Pension Schemes (Miscellaneous Amendments) Regulations 1997 Reg.9, which had cured the lack of jurisdiction by adding new members to the list of those entitled to bring complaints. WCC appealed, contending that PO should not have entertained the second application because the Regulations could not have retrospective effect.

Held, dismissing the appeal, that it was clear from the language of Reg.9 that it was intended to have retrospective effect. There was little force in the argument that there was a presumption against retrospectivity in social legislation designed to protect against maladministration, *Sunshine Porcelain Potteries Pty v. Nash* [1961] A.C. 927, [1961] C.L.Y. 9283 and *l'Office Cherifien des Phosphates Unitramp SA v. Yashamita-Shinnihon Steamship Co Ltd (The Boucraa)* [1994] 1 A.C. 486, [1994] C.L.Y. 221 followed.

WESTMINSTER CITY COUNCIL v. HAYWOOD (NO.2) [2000] 2 All E.R. 634, Lightman, J., Ch D.

106. **Parliamentary ombudsman – Disability Rights Commission**

PARLIAMENTARY COMMISSIONER ORDER 2000, SI 2000 739; made under the Parliamentary Commissioner Act 1967 s.4, s.5. In force: April 13, 2000; £1.00.

This Order amends the Parliamentary Commissioner Act 1967 Sch.2 by adding the Disability Rights Commission to the list of bodies which are subject to investigation by the Parliamentary Commissioner for Administration.

107. Police – disclosure – disclosure of sensitive non conviction information – breach of government circular – public interest

[Data Protection Act 1984; Data Protection Act 1998.]

A challenged the decision of a Chief Constable to disclose sensitive non conviction information to another Chief Constable who subsequently divulged it to a local education authority following a police vetting enquiry in respect of A's application for the post of headteacher. The offer of employment was withdrawn as a result of the disclosure. A contended that the decisions to disclose the information were unlawful since they were in breach of the guidelines in Home Office Circular 9/93 and had been both irrational and procedurally unfair in that there was no pressing need in the public interest to disclose, in the absence of cogent evidence and a genuine reasonable belief in the necessity of disclosure for the protection of children. A further submitted that the disclosure was in breach of the Data Protection Act 1984 and Data Protection Act 1998.

Held, refusing the application, that a failure to comply with a government circular was not actionable on the basis of illegality although it could be relied on as evidence of unlawfulness in some other respect of the performance of administrative functions by a public body. The LEA had a lawful interest in the information and a pressing need to receive it. The police had an obligation to pass information between themselves in the exercise of their law enforcement functions, including the disclosure of sensitive information for child access vetting enquiries which was not fettered by the circular, *R. v. Chief Constable of North Wales, ex p. AB* [1999] Q.B. 396, [1998] C.L.Y. 4290 followed. It was arguable that the doctrine of procedural fairness was inapplicable in the absence of direct or indirect consequences for A as a result of the disclosure. The 1984 Act was inapplicable to manually processed material, although the information fell within sensitive personal data, it was also exempt from the 1998 Act as being data processed for the prevention and detection of crime.

R. (ON THE APPLICATION OF A) v. CHIEF CONSTABLE OF C; *sub nom.* R. v. CHIEF CONSTABLES OF C AND D, *ex p.* A [2001] 1 W.L.R. 461, Turner, J., QBD (Admin Ct).

108. Public inquiries – doctors – GP convicted of murdering patients – lawfulness of decision that inquiry should hear evidence in private

[National Health Service Act 1977 s.2; European Convention on Human Rights 1950 Art.10.]

Following the conviction of S, a GP, for the murder of 15 of his patients, the Secretary of State for Health set up an inquiry established under the National Health Service Act 1977 s.2. Its terms of reference were (a) to enquire into issues raised by the deaths of S's patients; (b) to enquire into the role and conduct of the relevant statutory bodies and authorities and consider the reasonableness of their response to available information concerning S's clinical practices, and (c) to make recommendations to the Secretary of State for Health and the Home Secretary for safeguarding patients and any related matter which public interest might require to be considered. W, a support group for the families of the victims, and representatives of the media sought judicial review of the Secretary of State's decision that the inquiry should hear evidence in private rather than in public and of the decision of the chairman of the inquiry that it would not be appropriate for the victims' families to be legally represented. The applicants argued that (1) given the width of the inquiry's terms of reference, the Secretary of State had not had the power to set up the inquiry under s.2; (2) having regard to past practice in major tragedies and to the European Convention on Human Rights 1950 Art.10, which provided for freedom of expression, a legitimate expectation had been created that a public inquiry would be held, and (3) the chairman's decision not to allow the victims' families legal representation had been irrational.

Held, granting the application for judicial review, that (1) with the possible exception of the reference to the Home Secretary, the terms of reference of the inquiry fell within the scope of the Secretary of State's powers under s.2; (2) the Secretary of State's decision that the inquiry should be held in private had been irrational. Where in the past a major disaster had occurred involving the loss of many lives, it had been considered proper to hold a public inquiry. The desirability of holding such an inquiry was enhanced where doubt existed as to how many deaths had resulted from a particular cause, where deaths occurring over a long period pointed to a breakdown in the checks and controls intended to prevent such deaths and where an event had caused a loss of confidence in a body such as the National Health Service. A public inquiry had several advantages: (a) witnesses would be less inclined to exaggerate or attempt to pass on responsibility; (b) information would become available as a result of others discovering what witnesses had said; (c) there would be a perception of open dealing which would help to restore public confidence, and (d) the risk of leaks leading to distorted reporting would be limited, and (3) the chairman's decision concerning legal representation would have to be reconsidered. It was observed that granting the victims' families legal representation would result in certain benefits, namely that lawyers would be able to obtain detailed evidence from witnesses and follow up useful leads. It would also enable the evidence of witnesses to be properly tested against evidence from other sources and allow the victims' families to play a full part in what was an important inquiry.

R. v. SECRETARY OF STATE FOR HEALTH, *ex p.* WAGSTAFF; R. v. SECRETARY OF STATE FOR HEALTH, *ex p.* ASSOCIATED NEWSPAPERS LTD; *sub nom.* R. (ON THE APPLICATION OF WAGSTAFF) v. SECRETARY OF STATE FOR HEALTH; R. (ON THE APPLICATION OF ASSOCIATED NEWSPAPERS LTD) v. SECRETARY OF STATE FOR HEALTH [2001] 1 W.L.R. 292, Kennedy, L.J., QBD.

109. Public Record Office – fees

PUBLIC RECORD OFFICE (FEES) (AMENDMENT) REGULATIONS 2000, SI 2000 964; made under the Public Records Act 1958 s.2. In force: May 1, 2000; £1.00.

These Regulations correct the omission, in the Public Record Office (Fees) (No.2) Regulations 1999 (SI 1999 3298), of the words "per negative" in Fee 8.2, which relates to colour prints where no negative exists.

110. Registration – fees – births, deaths and marriages

REGISTRATION OF BIRTHS, DEATHS AND MARRIAGES (FEES) (AMENDMENT) ORDER 2000, SI 2000 3165; made under the Marriage Act 1949 s.31; the Public Expenditure and Receipts Act 1968 s.5; and the Marriage Act 1949 Sch.3 para.1, para.2. In force: January 1, 2001; £1.50.

This Order amends the Registration of Births, Deaths and Marriages (Fees) Order 1999 (SI 1999 3311) which specifies the fees payable under the Acts relating to the registration of births, deaths and marriages and associated matters from April 1, 2000. In particular, it increases the sum payable under the Marriage Act 1949 s.27 to the sum of £30.00 and specifies the fee payable under the Marriage Act 1949 s.31 where an application is made by a party to the marriage to reduce the 15 day period mentioned in s.31 (1) and (2) of that Act.

111. Riparian rights – moorings – River Orwell – no right for local authority to grant licence or impose fee – overriding power of port authority

[Ipswich Dock Act 1805.]

M refused to obtain licences and pay an annual fee to the local authority for deepwater moorings in the River Orwell on the basis that the relevant consent had previously been obtained from the local port authority. The local authority subsequently sought to assert its riparian rights to grant or withhold licences and impose the annual fee.

Held, giving judgment for M, that by virtue of the Ipswich Dock Act 1805 the regulation of the River Orwell was entirely at the behest of the local port authority. The terms imbued in the legislation from 1805 onwards were indicative of an intention to confer an exclusive power upon the port authority to charge for facilities such as mooring. Furthermore, owing to the fact that the custom of paying dues to the council had ceased by 1877, it was incontrovertible that the local authority was debarred from exercising the right to grant permission for something which, the port authority had already licensed.

IPSWICH BC v. MOORE; IPSWICH BC v. DUKE *The Times*, July 4, 2000, Lloyd, J., Ch D.

112. Publications

Doyle, Brian – Disability Discrimination: Law and Practice. 3rd Ed. Paperback: £39.00. ISBN 0-85308-568-4. Family Law.

Thomas, Robert – Legitimate Expectations and Proportionality in Administrative Law. Hardback: £30.00. ISBN 1-84113-086-9. Hart Publishing.

Wade, H.W.R.; Forsyth, C.F. – Administrative Law. 8th Ed. Hardback: £68.00. ISBN 0-19-876526-6. Paperback: £29.99. ISBN 0-19-876525-8. Oxford University Press Inc, USA.

AGENCY

113. Agency of necessity – motor vehicle recovery charges – possibility of recovery operators proceeding both under PACE and as agents of necessity

[Police and Criminal Evidence Act 1984; Road Traffic Regulation (Special Events) Act 1994 s.101.]

L sought payment of his charges for recovering KGM's policyholder's vehicle, which had been stolen and left abandoned with its engine still running. The police were unable to disengage the engine as the ignition had been "barrelled" and, because they required the vehicle for evidential purposes in connection with possible criminal proceedings, they instructed L to attend, make the vehicle safe and to recover and store it. L was regularly appointed to recover in such situations, having had assigned to him by contract police powers to recover and store vehicles under the Road Traffic Regulation (Special Events) Act 1994. In accordance with normal practice, the police faxed confirmation of their instructions to recover the vehicle on their behalf for evidential purposes pursuant to the Police and Criminal Evidence Act 1984. After inspection of the vehicle, KGM confirmed to L that it did not wish to claim title and that L should dispose of it. It was common ground that under s.101 of the 1994 Act, and citing *Service Motor Policies at Lloyds v. City Recovery Ltd* (Unreported, July 9, 1997), [1997] C.L.Y. 3167, charges were not in those circumstances recoverable under the statutory scheme, and that there was no provision for recovery of charges from innocent owners of stolen vehicles recovered under PACE. L accepted that the vehicle had been recovered pursuant to lawful instructions issued by the police, although he contended that the vehicle was also recovered by him as an "agent of necessity". L contended that, according to the common law, he was entitled to recover his reasonable charges. KGM contended that the situation had been an emergency, necessitating immediate intervention on KGM's innocent driver's behalf, and that the instant case was therefore distinguishable from *Surrey Breakdown Ltd v. Knight* [1999] R.T.R. 84, [1998] C.L.Y. 4834.

Held, dismissing the claim, that although *Surrey Breakdown* (considered) established that an agency of necessity could arise in the course of a vehicle recovery of that type, in the instant case, no agency was established. The judge commented, obiter, that he did not rule out the possibility of a "double intention" on the recovery operators' part, namely that recovery operators could proceed under PACE and as agents of necessity. On the evidence, however, L's actions had nothing to do with preserving the property for the benefit of KGM and their policyholder, his intention was solely to comply with a request of the police. Motive and intention were relevant, and L would have needed to have acted at least partly with the intention of preserving the property for his argument to succeed. On the evidence, even if KGM's policyholder had been contacted at the time of the theft, she would not have been given the opportunity to make her own arrangements for recovery of the vehicle. The vehicle would therefore have been recovered, under the police instructions pursuant to PACE, irrespective of KGM's instructions. That fact, alone, made it impossible to say that there was an agency of necessity in the instant case.

LAMBERT (T/A LAMBERT COMMERCIALS) v. FRY, November 5, 1999, Judge Poulton, CC (Canterbury). [*Ex rel.* E Edwards Son & Noice Solicitors, 9/15 York Road, Ilford, Essex].

114. **Business cessation – ownership of monies collected by company on appointment of receivers – agency agreement**

TN appealed against a decision to refuse a declaration that payments received by SE acting as a mercantile agent for TN following the appointment of administrative receivers did not form part of SE's assets but were held on trust for TN, the principal. Placing reliance on *Farrow's Bank, Re* [1921] 2 Ch. 164 cited; TN contended that a crucial change occurred when SE went into receivership, ceasing to trade, which ended SE's right to act as agent for TN in the sale of TN's products, and to retain commission out of the proceeds of the sale of the produce. TN argued that the debtor creditor relationship between themselves and SE was based on a defeasible rather than an absolute right to recover debts, which was defeated by the cessation of SE's business as agent.

Held, dismissing the appeal, that TN could not establish that SE had lost the right to collect outstanding monies from customers following the appointment of receivers and the inevitable cessation of trading. Although the agency agreement between SE and TN had come to an end because of the appointment of receivers that was not enough to affect the right of SE to collect outstanding sums from customers which formed part of the assets of the company and were not held on trust for the principal, *Farrow's Bank* distinguished. The outstanding debts were SE's assets which became charged to the bank following the appointment of receivers.

TRIFFIT NURSERIES v. SALADS ETCETERA LTD [2000] 1 All E.R. (Comm) 737, Robert Walker, L.J., CA.

115. **Commercial agents – choice of law – US principal – express choice of law – applicability of Council Directive 86/653 – European Union**

[Commercial Agents (Council Directive) Regulations 1993 (SI 1993 3053); Council Directive 86/653 relating to self-employed commercial agents Art.17, Art.18, Art.19.]

I, a company incorporated in the United Kingdom, brought a claim ([1999] Eu L.R. 88), under the Commercial Agents (Council Directive) Regulations 1993 against E, an American company, for payment of commission, following the termination of an agency agreement under which I had acted as E's agent in the UK. The agency agreement contained a jurisdiction clause which stated that the contract would be governed by the law of the State of California. The Court of Appeal held that such a clause would only be ineffective for public policy reasons and referred the question of whether, in the circumstances, the Regulations giving effect to Council Directive 86/653 were applicable.

Held, that Arts. 17 and 18 of the Directive had to be applied in situations where the commercial agent carried on his activity in a Member State despite the fact that the principal may be established outside the Community. The aims and objectives behind the Directive, particularly Arts. 17 to 19, were to protect commercial agents in the event of termination of the contract and although Member States had a discretion to choose indemnification or compensation as the means of protection, the regime established by the Directive was mandatory in nature. Furthermore, since the Directive also aimed to protect freedom of establishment and undistorted competition in the internal market, it was essential that Arts. 17 to 19 were observed throughout the Community to ensure Community legal order.

INGMAR GB LTD v. EATON LEONARD TECHNOLOGIES INC (C381/98) [2001] All E.R. (EC) 57, M Wathelet (President), ECJ (5th Chamber).

116. **Commercial agents – EC law – payment on termination – validity of compulsory registration – European Union**

[Council Directive 86/653 on self employed commercial agents.]

C, an Italian company, acted as commercial agent for A, an Austrian company, under the terms of a contract. The contract was terminated and C claimed sums that it contended were due to it on termination. A denied liability to pay, on the grounds that C was not entered on the register of commercial agents as required by Italian law, with the result that the contract was void and unenforceable. C brought an action in Italy for recovery of the termination payment. The court stayed the proceedings and referred for a preliminary ruling the question whether compulsory registration was compatible with Council Directive 86/653.

Held, that the Directive prohibited national legislation requiring compulsory registration of commercial agents as a condition precedent to the validity of an agency contract. Where the Directive had not been transposed into domestic law, national courts had to interpret national legislation that either predated or postdated the Directive in a way consistent with the aims of the Directive, *Bellone v. Yokohama SpA (C215/97)* [1998] E.C.R. I-2191 applied.

CENTROSTEEL SRL v. ADIPOL GmbH (C456/98) [2000] 3 C.M.L.R. 711, L Sevon (President), ECJ.

117. **Commercial agents – fixed term contracts – agent's entitlement to compensation dependent upon whether contract "terminated" or "expired with the effluxion of time"**

[Rules of the Supreme Court 1965 Ord.14; Commercial Agents (Council Directive) Regulations 1993 (SI 1993 3053) Reg.17; Council Directive 86/653 relating to self employed commercial agents.]

W worked as J's agent under a contract which provided for W's appointment for a five-year period to run from January 1, 1993, with a notice period of six months. On June 30, 1997, in anticipation of the contract reaching its end, J advised W in writing that when the contract expired at the end of 1997 it would not be renewed in the same terms. The letter indicated the possibility of a new contract containing different conditions. J argued that the 1993 contract had expired with the effluxion of time, while W contended it had been terminated and that he was entitled to compensation under the Commercial Agents (Council Directive) Regulations 1993 Reg.17. W obtained judgment under the Rules of the Supreme Court Ord.14 and J appealed claiming that it had an arguable case that W was not entitled to compensation under the 1993 Regulations. J further argued that, in interpreting the Regulations, the court should have regard to Council Directive 86/653, the Directive implemented by the Regulations. It was suggested that that question of interpretation should be referred to the ECJ.

Held, allowing the appeal, that (1) in the circumstances arising on the apparent facts, there was an arguable question as to whether or not the Regulations apply when an agency contract expires with the effluxion of time. J should accordingly be given unconditional leave to defend, and (2) whether the interpretation of the Regulations required a reference to the European Court was debatable. It would be inappropriate at this stage in an appeal from an RSC Ord.14 judgment, having given leave to defend the action, to refer the matter to the ECJ. The question as to whether the matter should be referred was one for the judge hearing the action and determining the facts.

WHITEHEAD (T/A THE PATRICK WHITEHEAD PARTNERSHIP) v. JENKS & CATTELL ENGINEERING LTD [1999] Eu. L.R. 827, Smedley, J., QBD.

118. Commercial agents – marketing activities – applicability of Commercial Agents Directive

[Commercial Agents (Council Directive) Regulations 1993 (SI 1993 3053) Reg.2(4); Council Directive 86/653 relating to self employed commercial agents.]

T, a company appointed by E to market "Eastern Natural Gas" following the deregulation of the gas industry, brought an action against E alleging wrongful termination of its agency contract. T applied for determination of a preliminary issue, as to whether the Commercial Agents (Council Directive) Regulations 1993, implementing the Commercial Agents Directive 86/653, applied to its activities as commercial agents for E. E submitted that T's activities were "secondary" thus falling outside the provisions of the Regulations by virtue of Reg.2(4). T argued that since it worked exclusively for E it's activities must be described as primary and not secondary.

Held, granting the declaration, that the marketing activities of T amounted to the activities of a commercial agent since those activities had been contemplated by both parties as involving referral techniques from which E would derive long term benefits. The correct test was for the court to enquire into the primary purpose of the agency agreement to determine whether the agent had been appointed to develop goodwill in the principals' business giving the principal a commercial advantage. Such activities were not "secondary" under Reg.2(4). Accordingly, in the event of wrongful termination of a contract, T would be entitled to an indemnity or compensation.

TAMARIND INTERNATIONAL LTD v. EASTERN NATURAL GAS (RETAIL) LTD [2000] C.L.C. 1397, Morison, J., QBD.

119. Commercial agents – termination of agency – principal liable to pay retainer after date of termination

[Commercial Agents (Council Directive) Regulations 1993 (SI 1993 3053) Reg.17(6).]

D was involved in the supply of products to the plumbing trade. F was a family run, Italian company manufacturing pipe fittings for the plumbing trade. In 1992, D and F set up a company to sell F's products in the UK and Ireland. The venture failed, and the company was wound up. F and D then entered an agreement in July 1994 under which D was to be F's exclusive agent for the sale of F's products in the UK and Ireland. D was to be paid a monthly retainer for three years following the coming into force of the agreement, as well as commission on sales above an agreed threshold. The agreement was to run for an initial period of three years, and thereafter until terminated by either side subject to 12 months' written notice. D was given rights to terminate in the event of non payment of commission. Following disputes arising under the agreement, D purported to terminate it by notice in December 1996, alleging repudiatory breach by F by reason of a failure to pay commission. D brought an action seeking payment of the commission, damages for repudiatory breach of contract, and compensation for the termination of the agency pursuant to the Commercial Agents (Council Directive) Regulations 1993 Reg.17(6). F denied that monies were due, and alleged that D was the party in repudiatory breach. Further, that any rights to payment under the agreement ceased upon its termination.

Held, that (1) although D's performance of his obligations under the agreement was not as unsatisfactory as F contended, D had not devoted the diligent attention that F was entitled to expect; (2) the agreement provided for its own termination. Each of D's apparent breaches was capable of being remedied and did not, therefore, amount to repudiation on D's part. The effective cause of the termination was the lawful notice given by D; (3) on its true construction, the provision for the payment of a retainer to D ran only for the first three years of the agreement. Moreover, the provision survived the termination of the agreement, and since F had committed itself to paying the retainer for three years, and had not shown that it represented a penalty or was otherwise unconscionable, F was be obliged to make the payments until expiry of that period; (4) at common law, D had suffered no loss by reason of the termination, since the prospective commission would have been exceeded by the expense of earning it; (5) D was, entitled to compensation under Reg.17(6) up to the earliest date that the agreement could have expired, however, the agency was not profitable without the retainer, nor would it have become so. As D could not show that he had suffered a loss as a result of the termination, he was limited in the sum he could recover to £37,803, in respect of commission due on pre termination transactions and post termination retainer payments.

DUFFEN v. FRA BO SpA (NO.2); *sub nom.* DUFFEN v. FRABO SpA (NO.2) [2000] 1 Lloyd's Rep. 180, Judge Hallgarten Q.C., CC (Central London).

120. **Commercial agents – termination of agency agreement – damages for breach**

[EC Treaty Art.85 (now, Art.81); Commercial Agents (Council Directive) Regulations 1993 (SI 1993 3053).]

The applicant operated a service station owned by Esso under an Esso motor fuels agency agreement. Under that agreement he was obliged to buy all his motor fuel and lubricants from Esso at the prices charged by them. He was also precluded from selling any competing products or carrying on any other business. He had a bare licence to occupy the site, the land and equipment remaining the property of Esso, for which he paid prescribed fees. He was obliged to operate the service station in the manner required by Esso. The associated shop, the sale of lubricants and the car wash were operated by the applicant for his own benefit, but fuel was sold by him as an agent only, the title never leaving Esso until sold to the motorist. In return, the applicant was entitled to a commission. He was entitled only to use credit cards and other approved banking facilities but, subject to that, he bore the risk on non payment. The agreement was terminated on the alleged ground that he failed to keep the service station open for 24 hours a day and to supervise the operation of the site properly. He claimed, inter alia, damages for breach of the Commercial Agents (Council Directive) Regulations 1993 and the EC Treaty Art.85 (now Art.81).

Held, dismissing the appeal, that (1) under the terms of the agreement the applicant did not have authority to "negotiate the sale or purchase" or to "negotiate and conclude the sale or purchase" on behalf of Esso as referred to in the 1993 Regulations. In so far as he had a limited discretion in the method of payment, that did not indicate any process of negotiation of the sale itself, and (2) there was no breach of Art.81, which claim depended on the effects of the particular agreement together with others of similar effect. It was clear that there had been no foreclosure of the market to outside competitors and the problems in the oil retail market arose from too much commission and not too little. Further, the losses for which damages were claimed arose from predatory pricing rather than to a tie which might infringe Art.81.

PARKS v. ESSO PETROLEUM CO LTD [2000] Eu. L.R. 25, Morritt, L.J., CA.

121. **Mistake – mistake of fact as to commercial effect of agreement did not entitle mistaken party to set aside in equity**

C, a company providing investment services, had a long standing agency agreement to introduce business to N, a mutual life office. N had a standard system of allowing investors to switch investments between units in its funds, applying a system of forward pricing. C claimed that by an oral agreement N granted it special switching arrangements based on a system of historic pricing which meant funds could be switched with the benefit of having prior knowledge of unit prices. C contended that after some weeks N wrongfully terminated the agreement. Three preliminary issues were to be decided based on assertions in N's defence, for the purposes of which it was assumed the agreement existed, a fact denied by N in the main action. N argued that (1) it was an implied term of the agency agreement that C would comply with the Securities and Investments Board (SIB) principles, in particular maintaining integrity, fair dealing and minimising conflict of interest; (2) having been mistaken in relation to the subject matter of the oral agreement as to how C would exploit it and its commercial effect, they were entitled to avoid the contract in equity, and (3) the special advantage enjoyed by C put N in breach of their fiduciary duty to treat all their investors equally and so was void for public policy reasons.

Held, determining the preliminary issues in favour of C, that (1) it was not a matter of obvious inference that the SIB principles were implied into the agency agreement, *Southern Foundries (1926) Ltd v. Shirlaw* [1940] A.C. 701 applied; (2) in essence N had made a bad bargain. Its mistake had been not as to subject matter but simply as to the commercial advantage the oral agreement would give C. In such circumstances the principles of equity would not extend to relieve N from the contract, *Solle v. Butcher* [1950] 1 K.B. 671, [1947-51] C.L.Y. 8914 and *William Sindall Plc v. Cambridgeshire CC* [1994] 1 W.L.R. 1016, [1994] C.L.Y. 572 distinguished, and (3) notwithstanding that the special switching arrangement with C might have resulted in N being in breach of contract with its other policyholders, it did not constitute a fraud upon them and could not therefore be voided, *Cockshott v. Bennett* (1788) 2 Term Rep. 763 and *Milner, Re* (1884-85) L.R. 15 Q.B.D. 605 distinguished.

CLARION LTD v. NATIONAL PROVIDENT INSTITUTION [2000] 1 W.L.R. 1888, Rimer, J., Ch D.

122. Vicarious liability – port agent – secret commission as bribes

See TORTS: Petrotrade Inc v. Smith (Vicarious Liability). §5105

123. Publications

Aldridge, Trevor M. – Powers of Attorney. 9th Ed. Paperback: £49.00. ISBN 0-421-69180-8. Sweet & Maxwell.

AGRICULTURE

124. Agricultural land – compensation – set aside payments – scope of activity covered – European Union

[Council Regulation 1765/92 establishing a support system for producers of certain arable crops; Commission Regulation 762/94 laying down detailed rules for the application of Council Regulation 1765/92 with regard to the set-aside scheme, Art.2.]

J challenged MAFF's decision to refuse payment of set aside payments in respect of land that had temporary grass, used for silage, grown on it the previous year. Under Commission Regulation 762/94 Art.2, set aside meant leaving fallow a piece of land that was cultivated the previous year "with a view to harvest". J's application for set aside payments was refused on the ground that the land had not been used for agricultural production. The UK government further argued that, should the decision be in favour of J, the impact of the decision should be limited so as to avoid re-examination of up to 10,000 files. The question of the scope of Art.2 was referred to the European Court of Justice.

Held, granting the application for judicial review, that the land was eligible for set aside payments. There was no restriction as to the type of crops that must be grown for the set aside provisions to be activated. All land that was sown before the set aside year fell within Art.2. To this there were specific exceptions, namely land used permanently for pasture, permanently sown lands and forest. There was no exclusion based on types of crop sown. There was no reason to limit the impact of this decision, particularly as the UK government had not in any way been led to believe that the scope of Art.2 was limited. It was up to cultivators to show that fallow land had been sown with temporary grass, used for silage, the previous year.

R. v. MINISTRY OF AGRICULTURE, FISHERIES AND FOOD, *ex p.* JH COOKE & SONS (C372/98) *The Times*, October 18, 2000, C Gulmann (President), ECJ (6th Chamber).

125. Agricultural land – set aside – non disclosure of data by ministry – imposition of penalties – European Union

[Council Regulation 3508/92 establishing an integrated administration and control system for certain Community aid schemes Art.3(1), Art.9; Council Regulation 3887/92 laying down detailed rules for applying the integrated administration and control system for certain Community aid schemes Art.9.]

Having entered into occupation of a farm, F, who had been unable to ascertain the farm's history, asked MAFF to specify which of the fields within the farm were eligible for set aside payments under the arable area payment scheme. MAFF refused to supply the information which it held and which F needed concerning the crops that had previously been grown in the various fields. F filed a set aside form but had penalties imposed on him on the ground that two plots of land were, by reason of their cropping history, ineligible for set aside payments. F applied to the Divisional Court for an order quashing the decision to impose penalties on him. The Divisional Court asked the European Court of Justice to give preliminary rulings as to whether MAFF had the power to provide F with the information that he had asked for and, if so, whether it had been entitled to impose a penalty on him following the non disclosure of that information. For the purpose of such rulings, the court was required to interpret Council Regulation 3508/92 which established an integrated administration and control system for certain Community aid schemes.

Held, giving preliminary rulings in favour of F, that Art.3(1) of the Regulation did not exclude the possibility that the database maintained by MAFF might be consulted by parties other than MAFF itself. Furthermore, while Art.9 of the Regulation required member states to take steps to ensure the protection of data collected, it did not specify how such protection was to be given. In applying the Regulation, MAFF had to balance the interests of the individual who had provided the information against those of the individual who needed it. There was no evidence to suggest that the individual who had provided the information would be adversely affected by its disclosure. F, on the other hand, required the information to make a proper application for a compensatory payment and to avoid the imposition of a penalty. In the circumstances, MAFF was entitled to supply F with the information that he had asked for. Furthermore, MAFF could not impose a penalty under Council Regulation 3887/92 Art.9 on a party to whom the relevant information could have been supplied but to whom it had not been supplied, since the provision of incorrect information leading to a penalty would be attributable to MAFF itself.

R. v. MINISTRY OF AGRICULTURE, FISHERIES AND FOOD, *ex p.* FISHER (T/A TR & P FISHER) (C369/98) *The Times,* October 10, 2000, DAO Edward (President), ECJ (4th Chamber).

126. Agricultural policy – direct support schemes – payments

COMMON AGRICULTURAL POLICY SUPPORT SCHEMES (MODULATION) REGULATIONS 2000, SI 2000 3127; made under the European Communities Act 1972 s.2. In force: January 1, 2001; £1.75.

These Regulations implement Art.4 and Art.5 of Council Regulation 1259/1999 ([1999] OJ L160/113) establishing common rules for direct support schemes under the common agricultural policy of the European Community. They require the Minister of Agriculture, Fisheries and Food or, as the case may be, the Intervention Board to deduct a specified proportion from any payment he, or it, makes pursuant to any of the said support schemes. The amounts deducted shall be applied in accordance with Art.5(2) of the Council Regulation.

127. Agricultural policy – direct support schemes – payments

COMMON AGRICULTURAL POLICY SUPPORT SCHEMES (MODULATION) (WALES) REGULATIONS 2000, SI 2000 3294 (W.216); made under the European Communities Act 1972 s.2. In force: January 1, 2001; £2.00.

These Regulations, which implement Arts.4 and 5 of Council Regulation 1259/1999 ([1999] OJ L160/113) which establishes common rules for direct support schemes under the common agricultural policy of the European Community in relation to Wales. They require the National Assembly for Wales or, as the case may be, the Intervention Board to deduct a specified proportion from any payment they make pursuant to any of the said support schemes. The amounts deducted shall be applied in accordance with Art.5(2) of the Council Regulation.

128. Agricultural policy – integrated administration and control – payments

INTEGRATED ADMINISTRATION AND CONTROL SYSTEM (AMENDMENT) REGULATIONS 2000, SI 2000 2573; made under the European Communities Act 1972 s.2. In force: October 16, 2000; £2.00.

These Regulations, which amend the Integrated Administration and Control System Regulations 1993 (SI 1993 1317), which implement in part Council Regulation 3508/92 ([1992] OJ L355/1) and Commission Regulation 3887/92 ([1992] OJ L391/36), as amended, update references to community legislation, amend the definition of "specified payment" and insert new Regs.2A-2D to define the competent authority in relation to a holding; set out provisions to determine which authority is the competent authority in relation to a holding for the IACS year 2000; and set out provisions to determine which authority is the competent authority in relation to a holding for the IACS year 2001 and subsequent years. They make new provision in respect of the minimum size of agricultural parcel in respect of which applications may be made, provide powers for competent authorities to enter into agency arrangements with each other and provide for the sums recoverable by one competent authority to be set off against the sums payable as a specified payment by another competent authority.

129. Agricultural produce – beet seeds

BEET SEEDS (AMENDMENT) (ENGLAND) REGULATIONS 2000, SI 2000 1791; made under the Plant Varieties and Seeds Act 1964 s.16, s.36. In force: August 1, 2000; £2.00.

These Regulations amend the Beet Seeds Regulations 1993 (SI 1993 2006, as amended), insofar as they extend to England, to give effect to Council Directive 98/95 ([1999] OJ L25/1) in respect of the consolidation of the internal market, genetically modified plant resources and plant genetic resources and Council Directive 98/96 ([1999] OJ L25/27) amending, as regards unofficial field inspections, directives in respect of the marketing of seeds and the common catalogue of varieties of agricultural plant species. In particular, they amend certain definitions, including "marketing" and "official examination"; make provision in relation to marketing and marketing authorisations, tests and trials, seed as grown, selection work and other scientific purposes; provide for the marketing of genetically modified beet seeds, clear indications for genetically modified varieties and the supply of information about imported seeds; and remove provisions in respect of small packages.

130. Agricultural produce – British Wool Marketing Board

BRITISH WOOL MARKETING SCHEME (AMENDMENT) ORDER 2000, SI 2000 1709; made under the Agricultural Marketing Act 1958 s.2, Sch.1. In force: July 1, 2000; £2.00.

This Order approves amendments to the British Wool Marketing Scheme 1950 (contained in SI 1950 1326 as amended). It reduces the number of regional members of the British Wool Marketing Board from eleven to nine, and lays down details as to the timing etc. of their election; describes the nine new regions (English South Western, English Southern, English Central, English Northern, Welsh Northern, Welsh Southern, Scottish Southern, Scottish Northern, Northern Ireland), and the number of county representatives to sit on the regional committee of each; introduces an age limit beyond which no person may stand for election to either the Board or a regional committee; and describes how the number of votes each registered producer is to have in elections of regional members to the Board and of county representatives to the regional committees is to be ascertained.

131. Agricultural produce – cereal seeds

CEREAL SEEDS (AMENDMENT) (ENGLAND) REGULATIONS 2000, SI 2000 1793; made under the Plant Varieties and Seeds Act 1964 s.16, s.36. In force: August 1, 2000; £2.00.

These Regulations amend the Cereal Seeds Regulations 1993 (SI 1993 2005, as amended), insofar as they extend to England, to give effect to Council Directive 98/95 ([1999] OJ L25/1) in respect of the consolidation of the internal market, genetically modified plant resources and plant genetic resources and Council Directive 98/96 ([1999] OJ L25/27) amending, as regards unofficial field inspections, directives in respect of the marketing of seeds and the common catalogue of varieties of agricultural plant species. In particular, they amend certain definitions, including "marketing" and "official examination"; make provision in relation to marketing and marketing authorisations, tests and trials, seed as grown, selection work and other scientific purposes; provide for the marketing of genetically modified seeds, clear indications for genetically modified varieties and the supply of information about imported seeds; and amend provisions in respect of small packages.

132. Agricultural produce – energy crops – financial assistance

ENERGY CROPS REGULATIONS 2000, SI 2000 3042; made under the European Communities Act 1972 s.2. In force: December 5, 2000; £2.00.

These Regulations, which extend to England only, supplement specified Community legislation, which provides for assistance to be paid from the Guarantee Section of the European Agricultural Guidance and Guarantee Fund. They enable assistance to be paid for projects involving the establishment of miscanthus and short rotation coppice for subsequent use in equipment or a plant which produces energy through the use of such crops as a fuel supply and enable assistance to be paid for projects involving the formation of producer organisations for the purposes of managing the production and supply of short rotation coppice. They implement part of the England Rural Development Programme (ERDP) approved by the European Commission under Art.44 of Council Regulation 1257/1999 ([1999] OJ L160/80) and provide for financial assistance by the Minister of Agriculture, Fisheries and Food in respect of those projects which he has approved.

133. Agricultural produce – fodder plant seeds

FODDER PLANT SEEDS (AMENDMENT) (ENGLAND) REGULATIONS 2000, SI 2000 1792; made under the Plant Varieties and Seeds Act 1964 s.16, s.36. In force: August 1, 2000; £2.00.

These Regulations amend the Fodder Plant Seeds Regulations 1993 (SI 1993 2009, as amended), insofar as they extend to England, to give effect to Council Directive 98/95 ([1999] OJ L25/1) in respect of the consolidation of the internal market, genetically modified plant resources and plant genetic resources and Council Directive 98/96 ([1999] OJ L25/27) amending, as regards unofficial field inspections, directives in respect of the marketing of seeds and the common catalogue of varieties of agricultural plant species. In particular, they amend certain definitions, including "marketing" and "official examination"; make provision in relation to marketing and marketing authorisations, tests and trials, seed as grown, selection work and other scientific purposes; provide for the marketing of genetically modified fodder plant seeds, clear indications for genetically modified varieties, and the supply of information about imported seeds; and remove provisions in respect of small packages.

134. Agricultural produce – marketing grants

AGRICULTURAL PROCESSING AND MARKETING GRANTS REGULATIONS 2000, SI 2000 3046; made under the European Communities Act 1972 s.2. In force: December 5, 2000; £2.00.

These Regulations, which extend to England only, supplement specified Community legislation, which provides for support from the Guarantee Section of the European Agricultural Guidance and Guarantee Fund towards investment for the improvement of the processing and marketing of agricultural products. They enable grant to be paid towards expenditure incurred in connection with operations involving such improvements; implement part of the England Rural Development Programme approved by the European Commission under Art.44 of Council Regulation 1257/1999 ([1999] OJ L160/80) and provide for the payment of grants by the Minister of Agriculture, Fisheries and Food in respect of any expenditure he has approved.

135. Agricultural produce – milk – quota arrangements

DAIRY PRODUCE QUOTAS (AMENDMENT) (ENGLAND) REGULATIONS 2000, SI 2000 698; made under the European Communities Act 1972 s.2. In force: April 1, 2000; £1.50.

These Regulations amend the Dairy Produce Quotas Regulations 1997 (SI 1997 733) and implement a change to Council Regulation 3950/92 ([1992] OJ L405/1) Art.6(1) which permits Member States to specify any date in the quota year in question in respect of temporary transfers of quota. They change the date by which notice of the temporary transfer must be submitted to the Intervention Board from December 31 to March 31.

136. Agricultural produce – milk – quota arrangements

DAIRY PRODUCE QUOTAS (AMENDMENT) (ENGLAND) (NO.2) REGULATIONS 2000, SI 2000 2977; made under the European Communities Act 1972 s.2. In force: November 29, 2000; £2.00.

These Regulations amend the Dairy Produce Quotas Regulations 1997 (SI 1997 733), insofar as they apply to England, by extending the definition of "Community compensation scheme"; removing Islay from the particular milk quota arrangements applying in relation to the Scottish Islands; extending the period from 28 to 56 days within which purchasers shall notify the Intervention Board of any producers newly registering with them; clarifying who, as between an original purchaser and a new purchaser of a producer's milk, is permitted to apply for adjustments to his quota consequent upon subsequent changes to the representative fat content of that producer's milk; and making provision with respect to the transfer of quotas, temporary reallocations of surplus quotas and the Intervention Board's powers and responsibilities.

137. Agricultural produce – milk – quota arrangements – Wales

DAIRY PRODUCE QUOTAS (AMENDMENT) (WALES) REGULATIONS 2000, SI 2000 972 (W.42); made under the European Communities Act 1972 s.2. In force: April 1, 2000; £2.00.

These Regulations amend the Dairy Produce Quotas Regulations 1997 (SI 1997 733) and implement for Wales a change to Art.6(1) of Council Regulation 3950/92 ([1992] OJ L405/1) establishing an additional levy in the milk and milk products sector and which permits Member States, in respect of temporary transfers of quota, to specify any date in the quota year in question. They change the date by which notice of the temporary transfer must be submitted to the Intervention Board from December 31 to March 31.

138. **Agricultural produce – milk – quota arrangements – Wales**

DAIRY PRODUCE QUOTAS (AMENDMENT) (WALES) (NO.2) REGULATIONS 2000, SI 2000 3123 (W.201); made under the European Communities Act 1972 s.2. In force: November 29, 2000; £2.50.

These Regulations amend the Dairy Produce Quotas Regulations 1997 (SI 1997 733), insofar as they apply to Wales, by extending the definition of "Community compensation scheme"; removing Islay from the particular milk quota arrangements applying in relation to the Scottish Islands; extending the period from 28 to 56 days within which purchasers shall notify the Intervention Board of any producers newly registering with them; clarifying who, as between an original purchaser and a new purchaser of a producer's milk, is permitted to apply for adjustments to his quota consequent upon subsequent changes to the representative fat content of that producer's milk; and making provision with respect to the transfer of quotas, temporary reallocations of surplus quotas and the Intervention Board's powers and responsibilities.

139. **Agricultural produce – oil and fibre plant seeds**

OIL AND FIBRE PLANT SEEDS (AMENDMENT) (ENGLAND) REGULATIONS 2000, SI 2000 1789; made under the Plant Varieties and Seeds Act 1964 s.16, s.36. In force: August 1, 2000; £2.00.

These Regulations amend the Oil and Fibre Plant Seeds Regulations 1993 (SI 1993 2007 as amended), insofar as they extend to England, to give effect to Council Directive 98/95 ([1999] OJ L25/1) in respect of the consolidation of the internal market, genetically modified plant resources and plant genetic resources and Council Directive 98/96 ([1999] OJ L25/27) amending, as regards unofficial field inspections, directives in respect of the marketing of seeds and the common catalogue of varieties of agricultural plant species. In particular, they amend certain definitions including "marketing" and "official examination"; make provision in relation to marketing and marketing authorisations, tests and trials, seed as grown, selection work and other scientific purposes; provide for the marketing of genetically modified oil and fibre plant seeds, clear indications for genetically modified varieties and the supply of information about imported seeds; and amend provisions in respect of small packages.

140. **Agricultural produce – vegetable seeds**

VEGETABLE SEEDS (AMENDMENT) (ENGLAND) REGULATIONS 2000, SI 2000 1790; made under the Plant Varieties and Seeds Act 1964 s.16, s.36. In force: August 1, 2000; £2.00.

These Regulations amend the Vegetable Seeds Regulations 1993 (SI 1993 2008 as amended), insofar as they extend to England, to give effect to Council Directive 98/95 ([1999] OJ L25/1) in respect of the consolidation of the internal market, genetically modified plant resources and plant genetic resources. In particular, they amend certain definitions including "marketing" and "official examination"; make provision in relation to marketing and marketing authorisations, tests and trials, seed as grown, selection work and other scientific purposes; provide for the marketing of genetically modified vegetable seeds, clear indications for genetically modified varieties and the supply of information about imported seeds.

141. **Animal health – bovine animals and swine – Council Directive**

European Parliament and Council Directive 2000/20 of May 16, 2000 amending Council Directive 64/432 on animal health problems affecting intra-Community trade in bovine animals and swine. [2000] OJ L163/35.

142. Animal products – bone in beef – despatch to domestic market

BOVINES AND BOVINE PRODUCTS (TRADE) (AMENDMENT) (ENGLAND) REGULATIONS 2000, SI 2000 1667; made under the European Communities Act 1972 s.2. In force: July 17, 2000; £1.50.

These Regulations amend the Bovines and Bovine Products (Trade) Regulations 1999 (SI 1999 1103 as amended) which give effect to Commission Decision 98/692 ([1998] OJ L328/28) and Commission Decision 98/564 ([1998] OJ L273/37) which amended Council Decision 98/256 ([1998] OJ L113/32). The effect of the amendments is to permit the despatch of bone-in beef from premises approved under the Date Based Export Scheme to the domestic market.

143. Animal products – diseases and disorders – specified risk material

SPECIFIED RISK MATERIAL (AMENDMENT) (ENGLAND) (NO.3) ORDER 2000, SI 2000 3377; made under the Animal Health Act 1981 s.1, s.10, s.11, s.29, s.35, s.76, s.83, Sch.2. In force: January 19, 2001; £1.50.

This Order, which amends the Specified Risk Material Order 1997 (SI 1997 2964) and revokes the Specified Risk Material (Amendment Order) (England) (No.2) Order 2000 (SI 2000 3234), gives effect to Art.1 of Commission Decision 2001/2 ([2001] OJ L1/21), adopted on December 27, 2000, which amends Commission Decision 2000/418 ([2000] OJ L158/76) regulating the use of material presenting risk as regards transmissible spongiform encephalopathies. It brings the definition of specified risk material into line with that contained within the Commission Decision.

144. Animal products – diseases and disorders – specified risk material – Wales

SPECIFIED RISK MATERIAL (AMENDMENT) (WALES) ORDER 2000, SI 2000 2811; made under the Animal Health Act 1981 s.1, s.10, s.11, s.29, s.35, s.76, s.83, Sch.2. In force: November 7, 2000; £1.75.

This Order, which amends the Specified Risk Material Order 1997 (SI 1997 2964) in so far as it applies to Wales, gives effect to Commission Decision 2000/418 ([2000] OJ L158/76) Art.3.1 regulating the use of material presenting risks as regards transmissible spongiform encephalopathies.

145. Animal products – diseases and disorders – specified risk material – Wales

SPECIFIED RISK MATERIAL (AMENDMENT) (WALES) REGULATIONS 2000, SI 2000 2659 (W.172); made under the Food Safety Act 1990 s.16, s.17, s.19, s.26, s.48, Sch.1 para.2, Sch.1 para.3, Sch.1 para.5, Sch.1 para.6. In force: October 1, 2000; £2.00.

These Regulations, which amend the Specified Risk Material Regulations 1997 (SI 1997 2965, as amended) in so far as they apply to Wales, give effect to Art.3.1 of Commission Decision 2000/418 ([2000] OJ L158/76) regulating the use of material presenting risks as regards transmissible spongiform encephalopathies. They bring the definition of "specified risk material" into line with the definition of that phrase in the Commission Decision and provide that whole carcasses of sheep, goats and bovines are deemed to be specified risk material if they are removed from the place where they were slaughtered or died to be rendered or incinerated whole.

146. Animal products – emergency controls – contaminated products from Belgium

FOOD (ANIMAL PRODUCTS FROM BELGIUM) (EMERGENCY CONTROL) (ENGLAND AND WALES) ORDER 2000, SI 2000 587; made under the Food Safety Act 1990 s.6, s.13, s.48. In force: March 8, 2000; £2.00.

This Order revokes, and re enacts with certain changes, the Food (Animal Products from Belgium) (Emergency Control) (England and Wales) Order 1999 (SI 1999 3421) and implements, in relation to food, Commission Decision 2000/150 ([2000] OJ L50/25) on protective measures with regard to contamination by dioxins of certain products of porcine and poultry origin intended for human or animal consumption. It defines "relevant animal product", prohibits the carrying out of commercial operations relating to them, specifies the enforcement authorities and applies provisions of the Food Safety Act 1990.

147. Animal products – emergency controls – contaminated products from Belgium

FOOD (ANIMAL PRODUCTS FROM BELGIUM) (EMERGENCY CONTROL) (REVOCATION) (ENGLAND AND WALES) ORDER 2000, SI 2000 1232; made under the Food Safety Act 1990 s.6, s.13, s.48. In force: May 12, 2000; £1.00.

This Order revokes the Food (Animal Products from Belgium) (Emergency Control) (England and Wales) Order 2000 (SI 2000 587), and implements in England and Wales, in relation to food, Commission Decision 2000/301 ([2000] OJ L97/16) repealing the protective measures with regard to contamination by dioxins of certain products of porcine and poultry origin intended for human or animal consumption.

148. Animal products – import and export controls

See INTERNATIONAL TRADE. §3843, 3844, 3845, 3846

149. Animals – feedingstuffs

FEEDING STUFFS REGULATIONS 2000, SI 2000 2481; made under the Agriculture Act 1970 s.66, s.68, s.69, s.70, s.74, s.74A, s.77, s.78, s.84; and the European Communities Act 1972 c.68 s.2. In force: October 29, 2000; £10.30.

These Regulations, which principally apply to England, revoke and replace, with amendments, the Feeding Stuffs Regulations 1995 (SI 1995 1412 as amended), implement specified European Community Directives and Decisions, and provide for the enforcement of certain European Community Regulations. They prescribe permitted limits of variation in misstatements in statutory statements; prescribe the manner in which compound feedingstuffs, additives and premixtures are to be packaged and sealed; regulate the putting into circulation of feed materials; require confidentiality to be maintained in relation to commercial information relating to additives obtained by the Food Standards Agency in the course of processing applications for Community approval of an additive; restrict the marketing and use of feedingstuffs containing certain undesirable products and the putting into circulation and mixing of ingredients containing such substances; and prohibit the sale and use of compound feedingstuffs containing certain materials.

150. Animals – feedingstuffs – additives – protection of public health – European Union

[Council Directive 70/524 concerning additives in feeding stuffs Art.11; Council Regulation 2821/98 amending as regards withdrawal of the authorisation of certain antibiotics, Directive 70/524.]

P, a Belgian undertaking, was the sole manufacturer and producer of Virginiamycin, a human therapeutic antibiotic. It was administered on a regular basis to livestock, especially pigs and poultry, to promote growth by enhancing the function of the animals' intestines and reducing digestive problems. In 1998 Denmark prohibited the use of Virginiamycin in its territory and submitted a report to the Commission and to the other Member States in accordance with the procedure laid down in Directive 70/524 Art.11, to establish that its use as an additive to animal feed, although authorised under that Directive, constituted a danger to animal or human health. As a result the Council adopted Regulation 2821/98 which removed Virginiamycin from the list of authorised additives. P brought an action to annul Regulation 2821/98 and applied to suspend its operation pending judgment in the main action.

Held, dismissing the application, that (1) the applicant's argument that authorisation should not have been withdrawn because no risk to human health had been established could not be regarded as wholly unfounded and justified consideration by the Court of the other conditions for the grant of interim relief; (2) the suspension sought could be justified only if the absence of such relief would place the applicant in a situation which could endanger its existence or irremediably affect its market share; (3) on the evidence the financial harm which the applicant would suffer as a result of the operation of the Regulation would not prevent it from pursuing its activities pending judgment in the main action; (4) the applicant had failed to show that it would suffer serious and irreparable damage if the contested regulation were not suspended, and (5) the court had to balance the interests of the applicant in suspending the regulation against the interests of the other parties in its continuing. Damage to commercial and social interests could not outweigh the risk of damage to public health if the regulation were suspended. The conditions for suspending operation of the contested regulation were not satisfied.

PFIZER ANIMAL HEALTH SA/NV v. COUNCIL OF THE EUROPEAN UNION (T13/99 R) [1999] 3 C.M.L.R. 79, B Vesterdorf (President), CFI.

151. **Animals – feedingstuffs – control of contaminated feedingstuffs from Belgium**

ANIMAL FEEDINGSTUFFS FROM BELGIUM (CONTROL) (ENGLAND AND WALES) REGULATIONS 2000, SI 2000 588; made under the European Communities Act 1972 s.2. In force: March 8, 2000; £1.50.

These Regulations revoke and re enact, with changes, the Animal Feedingstuffs from Belgium (Control) (England and Wales) (No.4) Regulations 1999 (SI 1999 3422) and implement, in relation to products for animal feeding, Commission Decision 2000/150 ([2000] OJ L50/25) on protective measures with regard to contamination by dioxins of certain products of porcine and poultry origin intended for human or animal consumption. They define "controlled entity", prohibit the carrying out of specified operations in relation to them, specify the enforcement authorities and apply provisions of the Food Safety Act 1990.

152. **Animals – feedingstuffs – control of contaminated feedingstuffs from Belgium**

ANIMALS FEEDINGSTUFFS FROM BELGIUM (CONTROL) (REVOCATION) (ENGLAND AND WALES) REGULATIONS 2000, SI 2000 1233; made under the European Communities Act 1972 s.2. In force: May 12, 2000; £1.00.

These Regulations revoke the Animal Feedingstuffs from Belgium (Control) (England and Wales) Regulations 2000 (SI 2000 588) and implement in England and Wales, in relation to products for animal feeding, Commission Decision 2000/301 ([2000] OJ L97/16) repealing the protective measures with regard to contamination by dioxins of certain products of porcine and poultry origin intended for human or animal consumption.

153. **Animals – feedingstuffs – zootechnical products**

FEEDINGSTUFFS (ZOOTECHNICAL PRODUCTS) AND MEDICATED FEEDINGSTUFFS (AMENDMENT) REGULATIONS 2000, SI 2000 1686; made under the European Communities Act 1972 s.2. In force: August 1, 2000; £1.00.

These Regulations amend the Feedingstuffs (Zootechnical Products) Regulations 1999 (SI 1999 1871) by introducing a Community method of analysis for the determination of lasalocid sodium in feedingstuffs, in implementation of Commission Directive 1999/76 ([1999] OJ L207/13) in relation to zootechnical additives and products containing zootechnical additives. In addition, it brings up to date cross references in the Medicated Feedingstuffs Regulations 1998 (SI 1998 1046).

154. Cattle – diseases and disorders – brucellosis

BRUCELLOSIS (ENGLAND) ORDER 2000, SI 2000 2055; made under the Animal Health Act 1981 s.1, s.6, s.7, s.15, s.28, s.32, s.34, s.35, s.87. In force: September 1, 2000; £2.00.

This Order, which revokes and replaces the Brucellosis Order 1997 (SI 1997 758) in relation to England, implements the provisions relating to milk of Council Directive 64/432 ([1963-64] OJ Spec Ed (I) 164) on animal health problems affecting intra Community trade in bovine animals and swine and Council Directive 77/391 ([1977] OJ L145/44) introducing Community measures for the eradication of brucellosis, tuberculosis and leucosis in cattle. The principal changes relate to the arrangements for testing milk for evidence of brucellosis and the removal of the List of Approved Laboratories that were contained in Sch.1 to the 1997 Order.

155. Cattle – diseases and disorders – enzootic bovine leukosis

ENZOOTIC BOVINE LEUKOSIS (ENGLAND) ORDER 2000, SI 2000 2056; made under the Animal Health Act 1981 s.1, s.6, s.7, s.15, s.28, s.32, s.34, s.35, s.87. In force: September 1, 2000; £2.00.

This Order, which revokes and replaces the Enzootic Bovine Leukosis Order 1997 (SI 1997 757) in England, implements the provisions relating to milk of Council Directive 64/432 ([1964] OJ L121/1977) on health problems affecting intra Community trade in bovine animals and swine and Council Directive 77/391 ([1977] OJ L145/44) introducing Community measures for the eradication of brucellosis, tuberculosis and leukosis. In particular, it provides for arrangements for testing milk for evidence of enzootic bovine leukosis and the removal of the list of approved laboratories that were contained in the 1997 Order.

156. Cattle – identification and registration – labelling of beef and beef products – Council Regulation

European Parliament and Council Regulation 1760/2000 of July 17, 2000 establishing a system for the identification and registration of bovine animals and regarding the labelling of beef and beef products and repealing Council Regulation 820/97. [2000] OJ L204/1.

157. Cattle – identification and registration – movement control

CATTLE (IDENTIFICATION OF OLDER ANIMALS) REGULATIONS 2000, SI 2000 2976; made under the European Communities Act 1972 s.2. In force: December 1, 2000; £2.00.

These Regulations, which extend to England, implement the provisions of Council Regulation 1760/2000 ([2000] OJ L204/1) in relation to older cattle. They require cattle born before July 1, 1996 which are not already registered with the Ministry of Agriculture, Fisheries and Food on a voluntary basis to be registered before January 29, 2001; require the location of all cattle with passports without movement cards not already registered with the Minister to be notified; provide for the issue of movement cards to cattle born before September 28, 1998 and require notification to the Minister when these animals are moved; and provide for the notification of the death of cattle born before July 1, 1996.

158. Cattle – identification and registration – movement control – Wales

CATTLE (IDENTIFICATION OF OLDER ANIMALS) (WALES) REGULATIONS 2000, SI 2000 3339 (W.217); made under the European Communities Act 1972 s.2. In force: December 25, 2000; £2.50.

These Regulations, which implement the provisions of Council Regulation 1760/2000 ([2000] OJ L204/1) in relation to older cattle, require cattle born before July 1, 1996 which are not already registered with the National Assembly for Wales on a voluntary basis to be registered before January 29, 2001. They require the keepers of cattle to notify the National Assembly of the location of cattle not previously registered, provide for the issue of movement cards to cattle born before September 28, 1998, provide for the use of electronic notification of movement as an alternative to notification using movement cards, provide for the notification of death of cattle born before July 1, 1996, provide powers for inspectors and make it offence to obstruct these inspectors.

159. Crops – home grown cereals – levies

HOME-GROWN CEREALS AUTHORITY (RATE OF LEVY) ORDER 2000, SI 2000 1404; made under the Cereals Marketing Act 1965 s.13, s.23, s.24. In force: July 1, 2000; £1.50.

This Order specifies the rates of dealer levy, grower levy and processor levies for the purposes of financing the Home-Grown Cereals Authority's non-trading functions under the Cereals Marketing Act 1965 Part I for the year beginning July 1, 2000.

160. Environmental protection – nitrate vulnerable zones – farms – grants

FARM WASTE GRANT (NITRATE VULNERABLE ZONES) (ENGLAND) SCHEME 2000, SI 2000 2890; made under the Agriculture Act 1970 s.29. In force: November 30, 2000; £1.75.

This Scheme, which complies with Council Regulation 1257/1999 ([1999] OJ L160/80) on support for rural development from the European Agricultural Guidance and Guarantee Fund, provides for the making of grants in respect of agricultural businesses which are at least partly situated in nitrate vulnerable zones. The grant aid is available towards expenditure incurred by the agricultural business between July 31, 2000 and April 17, 2003 in relation to facilities for the handling, storage and disposal of certain farm wastes and the separation of clean and dirty water, subject to a number of restrictions. The Farm Waste Grant (Nitrate Vulnerable Zones) (England and Wales) Scheme 1996 (SI 1996 908) is revoked insofar as it applies to England.

161. Environmental protection – nitrate vulnerable zones – farms – grants

FARM WASTE GRANT (NITRATE VULNERBALE ZONES) (ENGLAND) (NO.2) SCHEME 2000, SI 2000 2911; made under the Agriculture Act 1970 s.29. In force: para.1: November 31, 2000; para.7: November 31, 2000; remainder: November 30, 2000; £1.75.

This Scheme provides for the making of grants in respect of agricultural businesses which are at least partly situated in nitrate vulnerable zones. The grant aid is available at the rate of 40 per cent towards expenditure, up to a maximum of £85,000, incurred by the agricultural business between November 30, 2000 and April 17, 2003 in relation to facilities for the handling, storage and disposal of certain farm wastes and the separation of clean and dirty water. The Farm Waste Grant (Nitrate Vulnerable Zones) (England) Scheme 2000 (SI 2000 2890) is revoked.

162. Grants – closure of applications to schemes

AGRICULTURE (CLOSURE OF GRANT SCHEMES) (ENGLAND) REGULATIONS 2000, SI 2000 205; made under the European Communities Act 1972 s.2. In force: March 1, 2000; £1.00.

These Regulations close to further applications two schemes under which grants may be made for agricultural purposes. The first scheme was established by the Agricultural Processing and Marketing Grant Regulations 1995 (SI 1995 362) and enables grants to be made towards investments or projects which fulfil objectives relating to improving the processing and marketing conditions of agricultural products. The second scheme was established under the Rural Development Grants (Agriculture) (No.2) Regulations 1995 (SI 1995 2202) and enables grants to be made towards operations which promote rural development by facilitating the development and structural adjustment of certain rural areas.

163. Horticultural Development Council – mushroom growers – levies

HORTICULTURAL DEVELOPMENT COUNCIL (AMENDMENT) ORDER 2000, SI 2000 1975; made under the Industrial Organisation and Development Act 1947 s.1, s.4, s.8. In force: October 1, 2000; £1.00.

This Order amends the Horticultural Development Council Order 1986 (SI 1986 1110) by raising to 15 pence per litre of spawn purchased for use in compost during his relevant accounting year the maximum rate of levy capable of being charged on any mushroom grower under Art.9(1)(b) of the 1986 Order. In addition, it raises to £50,000 the monetary threshold below which any other grower is exempt from the charge levied by the Horticultural Development Council under Art.9(1)(a).

164. Imports – EC law – issue of phytosanitary certificates for citrus fruits – European Union

[Council Directive 77/93 on protective measures against the introduction into the Community of organisms harmful to plants or plant products and against their spread within the community; Council Directive 91/683 amending Directive 77/93; Commission Directive 92/103 amending Directive 77/93.]

A and others, Southern Cypriot fruit producers and exporters, sought an order restraining MAAF from allowing citrus fruits from Northern Cyprus to be imported into the United Kingdom via Turkey. Following the decision of the European Court of Justice in 1994 ([1994] E.C.R. I-3087, [1994] C.L.Y. 4721) that phytosanitary certificates issued by a non Member State for citrus fruits imported into the Community should not be recognised by Member States unless they had been issued by the country of origin, C, and other Northern Cypriot producers, had agreed with a Turkish company that ships carrying C's citrus fruits would berth in Turkey for less than 24 hours where a phytosanitary certificate would be issued before the ship continued its voyage to the United Kingdom. A submitted that the issue of phytosanitary certificates in those circumstances did not comply with the requirements of the Commission Directive 92/103 amending Council Directive 77/93 on protective measures against the introduction into the Community of organisms harmful to plants. The question was referred to the ECJ for a preliminary ruling.

Held, giving a preliminary ruling, that the certificates could be issued in non member states, other than the country of origin, provided that the produce (1) had been imported into the territory of the country where checks had taken place before being exported into the Community; (2) had been in that country for sufficient time to allow proper checks to be carried out, and (3) was not subject to any specific requirements that could only be satisfied in the country of production.

R. v. MINISTER OF AGRICULTURE, FISHERIES AND FOOD, *ex p.* SP ANASTASIOU (PISSOURI) LTD (C219/98) [2000] 3 C.M.L.R. 339, GC Rodriguez Iglesias (President), ECJ.

165. Infectious disease control – movement restriction areas – pigs

SWINE FEVER (MOVEMENT RESTRICTION AREAS) ORDER 2000, SI 2000 2394; made under the Animal Health Act 1981 s.1, s.8. In force: September 8, 2000 at 4 pm; £1.75.

This Order enables the Minister of Agriculture, Fisheries and Food to make an order declaring an area within 10 km of a suspected case of swine fever to be a movement restriction area. When such an order is made, no person may move any pig off a holding in the area, move any cattle, sheep, goat or other ruminating animal off any holding in the area which has pigs on it or move any pig out of the area.

166. Infectious disease control – movement restriction areas – pigs

SWINE FEVER (MOVEMENT RESTRICTION AREAS) (AMENDMENT) ORDER 2000, SI 2000 2460; made under the Animal Health Act 1981 s.1, s.8. In force: September 12, 2000 at 5.45 pm; £1.50.

This Order amends the Swine Fever (Movement Restriction Areas) Order 2000 (SI 2000 2394) to permit the Minister Agriculture, Fisheries and Food, or an officer of the local authority acting under the written direction of the Minister, to grant a licence for the movement of animals in a movement restriction area which would otherwise be prohibited.

167. Infectious disease control – potatoes – imports – Egypt

POTATOES ORIGINATING IN EGYPT (AMENDMENT) (ENGLAND) REGULATIONS 2000, SI 2000 22; made under the European Communities Act 1972 s.2. In force: February 7, 2000; £1.00.

These Regulations implement Commission Decision 1999/842 ([1999] OJ L236/68) amending Commission Decision 96/301 ([1996] OJ L115/47) and authorising Member States temporarily to take emergency measures against the dissemination of Pseudomonas solanacearum (Smith) Smith as regards Egypt by amending the definition of "the Decision" in the Potatoes Originating in Egypt Regulations 1998 (SI 1998 201). They also substitute the references to "Pseudomonas solanacearum (Smith) Smith" in the 1998 Regulations with the term "Ralstonia solanacearum (Smith) Yabuuchi et al".

168. Infectious disease control – potatoes – imports – Egypt

POTATOES ORIGINATING IN EGYPT (AMENDMENT) (NO.2) (ENGLAND) REGULATIONS 2000, SI 2000 2963; made under the European Communities Act 1972 s.2. In force: November 30, 2000; £1.50.

These Regulations implement Commission Decision 2000/568 ([2000] OJ L238/59) amending Decision 96/301 ([1996] OJ L115/47) authorising Member States temporarily to take emergency measures against the dissemination of Pseudomonas solanacearum (Smith) Smith as regards Egypt by amending the definition of "the Decision" in the Potatoes Originating in Egypt Regulations 1998 (SI 1998 201).

169. Infectious disease control – potatoes – imports – Egypt – Wales

POTATOES ORIGINATING IN EGYPT (AMENDMENT) (WALES) REGULATIONS 2000, SI 2000 350 (W.8); made under the European Communities Act 1972 s.2. In force: February 9, 2000; £1.50.

These Regulations implement, in relation to Wales, Commission Decision 99/842 ([1999] OJ L326/68) which authorises Member States temporarily to take emergency measures against the dissemination of Pseudomonas solanacearum (Smith) Smith as regards Egypt by amending the definition of "the Decision" in the Potatoes Originating in Egypt Regulations 1998 (SI 1998 201).

170. Intervention – lenders – market in beef and veal – groups of companies – failure to act independently – European Union

[Council Regulation 805/68 on the common organisation of the market in beef and veal; Commission Regulation 859/89; Council Regulation 2456/93; Commission Decision 94/442 setting up a conciliation procedure in the context of the clearance of the accounts of the European Agricultural Guidance and Guarantee Fund (EAGGF) Guarantee Section.]

Under Council Regulation 805/68 Member States' statutory intervention agencies could buy beef and veal where the price fell below a certain level. Buying in was on the basis of tenders by the meat sellers. Commission Regulation 859/89 provided that sellers could tender only once, that they must lodge security and that they could not transfer their rights or obligations with the price for the meat being paid to direct to the seller. The Commission found in its 1992 summary report of the European Agricultural Guidance and Guarantee Fund that many UK tenderers had not complied with these requirements, and that the UK authorities should have intervened to stop these practices. The consultative body established by Commission Decision 94/442 was asked to consider the matter, and concluded that the UK had not contravened Commission Regulation 859/89, noting that it had been necessary to issue Council Regulation 2456/93 to clarify and replace Regulation 859/89. Notwithstanding this, the Commission refused to reimburse the UK in respect of certain expenses arising in intervention purchases of beef in 1992. The UK applied for annulment of this decision.

Held, dismissing the application, that (1) the UK had complied with the obligation to check that a tenderer submitted only one tender per category. Council Regulation 2456/93 provided that a group of related companies was to be regarded as one entity for the purpose of defining "tenderer", but this provision had only come into force in 1993 with the issuing of Regulation 2456/93. The UK could not be criticised for omitting to check whether tenderers were members of a group prior to 1993, *Denmark v. Commission of the European Communities (348/85)* [1987] E.C.R. 5225 followed; (2) the Commission had identified matters in its 1992 report which suggested that the restriction of one tender per tenderer had not been observed, and that tenderers who were members of groups had not acted independently in agreeing to the terms of tenders amongst themselves. Other breaches by tenderers regarding, inter alia, lodging security and receipt of payment were also identified. These matters rendered the UK's procedures under Regulation 859/89 wrongful, *Netherlands v. Commission of the European Communities (C48/91)* [1993] E.C.R. I-5611, [1994] C.L.Y. 4730, *Exportslachterijen van Oordegem BVBA v. Belgische Dienst voor Bedrifsleven en Landbouw (C2/93)* [1994] E.C.R. I-2283, [1994] C.L.Y. 4748, *BayWa v. Bundesanstalt fur Landwirtschaftliche Marktordnung (146/81)* [1982] E.C.R. 1503, [1983] C.L.Y. 1375 and *Germany v. Commission of the European Communities (8/88)* [1990] E.C.R. I-2321 followed; (3) the tenderers' unlawful conduct could have led to a false assessment of the market by the Community, and thus to excessive meat purchasing at inflated prices. The Commission had established harm to the Community budget, and the refusal of reimbursement was not excessive or disproportionate, *Commission of the European Communities v. Netherlands (11/76)* [1979] E.C.R. 245, [1980] C.L.Y. 1082, *Germany v. Commission of the European Communities (18/76)* [1979] E.C.R. 343, [1980] C.L.Y. 1081 and *Netherlands v. Commission of the European Communities (C48/91)* [1993] E.C.R. I-5611, [1994] C.L.Y. 4730 followed, and (4) there was no breach by the Commission of its duty to give reasons for its decision, given the contents of its 1992 report and its communications with the UK Government.

UNITED KINGDOM v. COMMISSION OF THE EUROPEAN COMMUNITIES (C209/96) [1998] E.C.R. I-5655, C Gulmann (President), ECJ.

171. Livestock – slaughter premiums

SLAUGHTER PREMIUM REGULATIONS 2000, SI 2000 3126; made under the European Communities Act 1972 s.2. In force: December 29, 2000; £3.00.

These Regulations lay down national implementing measures for the slaughter premium scheme for bovine animals introduced by Art.11 of Council Regulation 1254/1999 ([1999] OJ L160/21) on the common organisation of the market in beef and veal. They provide for the administration of the scheme in relation to holdings situated wholly in England, and also holdings situated partly in England and partly elsewhere in the UK, where the Minister of Agriculture, Fisheries and Food is responsible for processing the farmer's claim for premium, and for the enforcement of the scheme in relation to such holdings.

172. Machinery – tractors – emissions – Council Directive

European Parliament and Council Directive 2000/25 of May 22, 2000 on action to be taken against the emission of gaseous and particulate pollutants by engines intended to power agricultural forestry tractors and amending Council Directive 74/150. [2000] OJ L173/1.

173. Machinery – tractors – type approval

AGRICULTURAL OR FORESTRY TRACTORS AND TRACTOR COMPONENTS (TYPE APPROVAL) (AMENDMENT) REGULATIONS 2000, SI 2000 828; made under the European Communities Act 1972 s.2. In force: April 17, 2000; £4.50.

These Regulations consolidate and further amend the Agricultural or Forestry Tractors and Tractor Components (Type Approval) Regulations 1988 (SI 1988 1567) Sch.2 which specifies Community Directives establishing type approval requirements with respect to the design, construction, equipment and marking of tractors and tractor components. They implement various Commission and Council Directives.

174. Milk – Milk Development Council – functions

MILK DEVELOPMENT COUNCIL (AMENDMENT) ORDER 2000, SI 2000 878; made under the Industrial Organisation and Development Act 1947 s.1, s.4, s.8. In force: April 1, 2000; £1.50.

This Order, which amends the Milk Development Council Order 1995 (SI 1995 356), increases the specified maximum rate at which the Milk Development Council may charge producers for the expenses it incurs in the exercise of its functions, from 0.05 pence per litre to 0.08 pence and adds to the Milk Development Council's functions that of promoting or undertaking arrangements for better acquainting the public in the UK with the goods and services supplied by the industry and methods of using them.

175. Pesticides – evaluation of active substances – fees

EVALUATION OF ACTIVE SUBSTANCES FOR PESTICIDES (FEES) REGULATIONS 2000, SI 2000 2119; made under the European Communities Act 1972 s.2. In force: August 25, 2000; £1.50.

These Regulations set a fee of £4,500 for the administrative treatment and evaluation of notifications of active substances notified to the Pesticide Safety Directorate under Art.4 of Commission Regulation 451/2000 ([2000] OJ L55/25) and a fee of £120,000 for the evaluation of a dossier submitted under Art.6. The notification and evaluation are for active substances for which the UK is the rapporteur Member State in accordance with Annex I to that Regulation, where a producer wishes to secure the inclusion of that active substance in Annex 1 to Council Directive 91/414 ([1991] OJ L230/1) concerning the placing of plant protection products on the market as last amended by Commission Directive 1999/80 ([1999] OJ L210/13).

176. Pesticides – residue levels in cereals and foodstuffs – Commission Directive

Commission Directive 2000/42 of June 22, 2000 amending the Annexes to Council Directive 86/362, 86,363 and 90/642 on the fixing of maximum levels for pesticide residues in and on cereals, foodstuffs of animal origin and certain products of plant origin, including fruit and vegetables respectively. [2000] OJ L158/51.

177. Plant varieties – seeds – fees

SEEDS (FEES) (AMENDMENT) (ENGLAND) REGULATIONS 2000, SI 2000 1542; made under the Plant Varieties and Seeds Act 1964 s.16, s.36. In force: July 7, 2000; £2.50.

These Regulations amend the Seeds (Fees) Regulations 1985 (SI 1985 981 as amended) by prescribing revised fees in respect of matters arising under the Cereal Seeds Regulations 1993 (SI 1993 2005), the Fodder Plant Seeds Regulations 1993 (SI 1993 2009), the Oil and Fibre Plant Seeds Regulations 1993 (SI 1993 2007), the

Beet Seeds Regulations 1993 (SI 1993 2006), the Vegetable Seeds Regulations 1993 (SI 1993 2008) and the Seeds (Registration, Licensing and Enforcement) Regulations 1985 (SI 1985 980). They introduce new fees for examinations of crops produced from seed of a variety entered for but not added to the National List and intended to produce certified seed, certified seed of the first generation, certified seed of the second generation or certified seed for the third generation.

178. Plant varieties – seeds – fees – Wales

SEEDS (FEES) (AMENDMENT) (WALES) REGULATIONS 2000, SI 2000 719 (W.26); made under the Plant Varieties and Seeds Act 1964 s.16. In force: March 7, 2000; £1.50.

These Regulations amend the Seeds (Fees) Regulations 1985 (SI 1985 981) by providing for fees to be charged for examinations taken by crop inspectors and seed samplers.

179. Plants – plant health – harmful organisms – Council Directive

Council Directive 2000/29 of May 8, 2000 on protective measures against the introduction into the Community of organisms harmful to plants or plant products and against their spread within the Community. [2000] OJ L169/1.

180. Potatoes – seed potatoes – marketing, labelling and classification

SEED POTATOES (AMENDMENT) (ENGLAND) REGULATIONS 2000, SI 2000 1788; made under the Plant Varieties and Seeds Act 1964 s.16, s.36. In force: August 1, 2000; £2.00.

These Regulations amend the Seed Potatoes Regulations 1991 (SI 1991 2206 as amended), insofar as they extend to England, to give effect to Council Directive 98/95 ([1999] OJ L25/1) amending, in respect of the consolidation of the internal market, genetically modified plant resources and plant generic resources, directives in respect of the marketing of seeds and the common catalogue of varieties of agricultural plant species. In particular, they amend certain definitions, including "marketing" and "seed potatoes"; provide for the marketing of pre basic seed potatoes; make provision in relation to marketing for scientific purposes or selection work, genetically modified seed potatoes and the import of seed potatoes from third parties; and amend provisions with respect to the certification of seed potatoes.

181. Rural areas – agriculture and forestry – development grants

RURAL DEVELOPMENT GRANTS (AGRICULTURE AND FORESTRY) REGULATIONS 2000, SI 2000 2907; made under the European Communities Act 1972 s.2. In force: November 29, 2000; £2.00.

These Regulations, which extend to England only and amend the Agriculture (Closure of Grant Schemes) (England) Regulations 2000 (SI 2000 205) and revoke the Rural Development Grants (Agriculture) (No.2) Regulations 1995 (SI 1995 2202), supplement specified Community legislation, which provides for assistance to be paid from the Guidance Section of the European Agricultural Guidance and Guarantee Fund towards operations which promote rural development by facilitating the development and structural adjustment of certain rural areas. In the case of England, these regions are Cornwall and the Isles of Scilly, Merseyside and South Yorkshire. The Regulations operate within the scope of these provisions by enabling financial assistance to be paid by the Minister of Agriculture, Fisheries and Food in respect of operations which he has approved. Such operations may be approved if they are eligible for assistance under the Community legislation and fall within a priority set out in a Single Programming Document which has been approved by the Commission of the European Communities They provide for the making of claims for, and the payment of, financial assistance following approval, impose obligations concerning the provision of information and record keeping on those in receipt of financial assistance.

182. Rural areas – countryside stewardship

See ENVIRONMENT. §2295

183. Rural areas – rural enterprise – financial assistance

RURAL ENTERPRISE REGULATIONS 2000, SI 2000 3043; made under the European Communities Act 1972 s.2. In force: December 5, 2000; £1.75.

These Regulations, which extend to England only, supplement specified Community legislation, which provides for assistance to be paid from the Guarantee Section of the European Agricultural Guidance and Guarantee Fund. They encourage diversification by those in the agricultural sector, or rural development more generally, by enabling assistance to be paid for new agricultural or rural projects. They implement part of the England Rural Development Programme (ERDP) approved by the European Commission under Art.44 of Council Regulation 1257/1999 ([1999] OJ L160/80) and provide for financial assistance by the Minister of Agriculture, Fisheries and Food in respect of those projects which he has approved.

184. Sheep – goats – identification and registration – records and documents

SHEEP AND GOATS IDENTIFICATION (ENGLAND) ORDER 2000, SI 2000 2027; made under the Animal Health Act 1981 s.1, s.8. In force: Art.8: January 1, 2001; Art.9: January 1, 2001; Art.12: January 1, 2001; Art.15: January 1, 2001; Remainder: September 1, 2000; £2.50.

This Order, which implements the provisions relating to sheep and goats of Council Directive 92/102 ([1992] OJ L355/32) on the identification and registration of animals, makes provision for records and other documentation concerning sheep and goats and for the marking of sheep and goats. In particular, it requires any person keeping sheep and goats to notify the Minister of Agriculture, Fisheries and Food and to keep movement records. The Sheep and Goats (Records, Identification and Movement) Order 1996 (SI 1996 28) is revoked insofar as it extends to England.

185. Sheep – goats – identification and registration – Wales

SHEEP AND GOATS IDENTIFICATION (WALES) REGULATIONS 2000, SI 2000 2335 (W.152); made under the European Communities Act 1972 s.2. In force: Reg.7: January 1, 2001; Reg.8: January 1, 2001; Reg.11: January 1, 2001; Reg.14: January 1, 2001; Remainder: September 9, 2000; £3.00.

These Regulations, which implement the provisions relating to sheep and goats of Council Directive 92/102 ([1992] OJ L355/32) on the identification and registration of animals, make provision for records and other documentation concerning sheep and goats and the marking of sheep and goats. The Sheep and Goats (Records, Identification and Movement) Order 1996 (SI 1996 28) is revoked insofar as it applies to Wales.

186. Trespass to land – defences – genetically modified organisms – uprooting of crops in licensed research and development sites

M was licensed to execute research and development in trials of genetically modified, GM, plants and crops. In 1998, T and others founded an "association", whose aim was to campaign against GM research. Whilst T's opinions concerning the perceived public safety of GM crops were genuine, the association used unlawful methods to advance their campaign. The principal method employed was to uproot GM crops in order to gain publicity. M took action against T, seeking injunctions to prohibit trespass on land and interference with its plants, crops and land. Based on the defence that T's actions were justified by necessity to protect third parties and the public, unconditional leave was granted in order to defend against the action for trespass. M appealed.

Held, allowing the appeal, that T could not rely either on the defence of necessity or of public interest. Whilst in exceptional circumstances T could protect those in immediate and serious danger by uprooting the whole crop, in the instant case, only some plants had been damaged and it was clear that the real aim of the campaign had been to attract publicity, which had been further advanced by a public court hearing. Even in circumstances of emergency, trespass was not justified where a public authority was responsible for the protection of public interests, *Cresswell v. Sirl* [1948] 1 K.B. 241, [1947-51] C.L.Y. 342 and *Workman v. Cowper* [1961] 2 Q.B. 143, [1961] C.L.Y. 248 referred to.

MONSANTO PLC v. TILLY [2000] Env. L.R. 313, Stuart-Smith, L.J., CA.

187. Veterinary medicines – health – EC ban on beta-agonists – public health concerns – European Union

[Council Directive 96/22 concerning the prohibition on the use in stockfarming of certain substances having a hormonal or thyrostatic action and of beta-agonists.]

B applied for the annulment of Council Directive 96/22, which had the effect of banning the use of beta-agonists to treat animals intended for human consumption. B contended that the Directive had severe economic results for many traders.

Held, refusing the application, that Council Directive 96/22 would not be annulled because, where public health was in issue, it overrode all other considerations, even if that meant severe consequences for many traders. Although the products manufactured by the applicants contained only small doses of beta-agonists, many products containing concentrated powders and liquids contained high doses which could cause poisoning if administered to animals that were eventually consumed by humans. Although such high doses were illegal, farmers were able to claim use of one of the legal products when their animals were tested. For that reason, a near blanket ban was justified.

BOEHRINGER INGLEHEIM VETMEDICA GmbH v. COUNCIL OF THE EUROPEAN UNION (T125/96) [2000] 1 C.M.L.R. 97, A Potocki (President), CFI.

188. Vocational training – agriculture and forestry – financial assistance

VOCATIONAL TRAINING GRANTS (AGRICULTURE AND FORESTRY) REGULATIONS 2000, SI 2000 3045; made under the European Communities Act 1972 s.2. In force: December 5, 2000; £2.00.

These Regulations, which extend to England only, supplement specified Community legislation, which provides for support from the Guarantee Section of the European Agricultural Guidance and Guarantee Fund for vocational training in the agricultural and forestry sectors. They enable assistance to be paid for vocational training for those involved in agricultural and forestry activities or those involved in those sectors who wish to diversify into other activities either within or outside the agricultural and forestry sector. They implement part of the England Rural Development Programme approved by the European Commission under Art. 44 of Council Regulation 1257/1999 ([1999] OJ L160/80) and provide for the payment of financial assistance by the Minister of Agriculture, Fisheries and Food in respect of those projects which he has approved.

189. Publications

Davis, Nigel; Smith, Graham; Sydenham, Angela – Agricultural Clients Precedent Handbook. Hardback: Floppy disk. ISBN 0-85308-386-X. Jordans.

ANIMALS

190. Animal welfare – dogs – meaning of "cruel ill treatment"

[Protection of Animals Act 1911 s.1 (1) (a).]

B appealed against a conviction for cruelly ill-treating a dog, contrary to the Protection of Animals Act 1911 s.1 (1) (a). B had deliberately exposed the dog to confrontation with a wild animal in circumstances where the animal was cornered, hence risk of injury to the dog had been high. B contended that dogs were inherently inquisitive and constantly exposed themselves to risk of injury by investigating holes in the ground, and that the law was insufficiently precise as to what constituted ill treatment.

Held, dismissing the appeal, that what constituted cruelty and ill treatment was a question of fact for the magistrates and a high risk of injury was more likely to result in a finding of causation, than a low risk. The decision disclosed no error of law and the court would not interfere with it.

BANDEIRA v. RSPCA; *sub nom.* BANDEIRA v. ROYAL SOCIETY FOR THE PREVENTION OF CRUELTY TO ANIMALS (2000) 164 J.P. 307, Schiemann, L.J., QBD.

191. Animal welfare – farmed animals

WELFARE OF FARMED ANIMALS (ENGLAND) REGULATIONS 2000, SI 2000 1870; made under the Agriculture (Miscellaneous Provisions) Act 1968 s.2. In force: August 14, 2000; £3.

These Regulations, which revoke and replace, with amendments, the Welfare of Livestock Regulations 1994 (SI 1994 2126 as amended), implement Council Directive 88/166 ([1988] OJ L74/83) laying down minimum standards for the protection of laying hens kept in battery cages, Council Directive 91/629 ([1991] OJ L340/28) laying down minimum standards for the protection of calves, Council Directive 91/630 ([1991] OJ L340/33) laying down minimum standards for the protection of pigs and Council Directive 98/58 ([1998] OJ L221/23) concerning the protection of animals kept for farming purposes. They apply to all animals kept for farming purposes and lay down the general principle that owners and keepers of such animals must take reasonable steps to ensure the welfare of animals in their care and to prevent them any unnecessary pain, suffering or injury.

192. Animal welfare – habitats – interference with badger setts – meaning of "badger sett"

[Protection of Badgers Act 1992 s.3(a), s.14.]

Four men were charged with interfering with a badger sett contrary to the Protection of Badgers Act 1992 s.3(a). Digging had occurred to a maximum of two feet within an area shown to be a functional sett, but it had not disturbed the tunnel system. The prosecution contended that the dug area fell within the definition of a badger sett as specified in s.14 of the Act, but the stipendiary magistrate dismissed that argument and subsequently the charges against the men. The Crown appealed.

Held, dismissing the appeal, that the magistrate had been entitled to conclude that a badger sett did not include the area up to and including the surface area above the tunnels and chambers. The term "badger sett" in the Act referred to tunnels, chambers and immediate areas outside entrance holes, and additional interpretation was not required to achieve the intended statutory protection.

DPP v. GREEN v. GREEN; *sub nom.* GREEN v. DPP; GREEN v. LINCOLNSHIRE STIPENDIARY MAGISTRATE; CROWN PROSECUTION SERVICE v. GREEN [2001] 1 W.L.R. 505, Roch, L.J., QBD.

193. **Animal welfare – slaughter**

WELFARE OF ANIMALS (SLAUGHTER OR KILLING) (AMENDMENT) (ENGLAND) REGULATIONS 2000, SI 2000 3352; made under the European Communities Act 1972 s.2. In force: January 30, 2001; £1.50.

These Regulations amend the Welfare of Animals (Slaughter or Killing) Regulations 1995 (SI 1995 731) so as to permit a new gas mixture for killing surplus chicks.

194. **Animal welfare – transport – cleansing and disinfection**

TRANSPORT OF ANIMALS (CLEANSING AND DISINFECTION) (ENGLAND) (NO.2) ORDER 2000, SI 2000 1618; made under the Animal Health Act 1981 s.1, s.7, s.37, s.87, s.88. In force: July 6, 2000; £2.00.

This Order revokes and replaces the Transport of Animals (Cleansing and Disinfection) (England) Order 2000 (SI 2000 1412) to correct a small error. It revokes and replaces, with amendments, the Transit of Animals Order 1927 (SR & O 1927 289), the Order of the Minister dated May 9, 1927 amending the 1927 Order (SR & O 1927 399), the Horses (Sea Transport) Order 1952 (SI 1952 1291), the Transit of Animals (Road and Rail) Order 1975 (SI 1975 1024) in part, the Importation of Animals Order 1977 (SI 1977 944) in part, the Diseases of Poultry Order 1994 (SI 1994 3141) in part, and the Welfare of Animals (Transport) Order 1997 (SI 1997 1480) in part, with respect to the cleansing and disinfection of means of transport relating to animals. In addition, it implements Ch.1 para.8 of the Annex to Council Directive 91/628 ([1991] OJ L340/17) on the protection of animals during transport.

195. **Animal welfare – transport – electronic route plans**

WELFARE OF ANIMALS (TRANSPORT) (ELECTRONIC ROUTE PLANS PILOT SCHEMES) (ENGLAND) ORDER 2000, SI 2000 646; made under the Animal Health Act 1981 s.1, s.8, s.37, s.39, s.83, s.87. In force: April 3, 2000; £1.50.

This Order provides for the creation of pilot schemes to test modes of electronic submission for route plans required under the Welfare of Animals (Transport) Order 1997 (SI 1997 1480) Art.13. It provides that transporters who have been granted permission to participate in a pilot scheme may submit route plans electronically rather than on paper and that the Minister of Agriculture, Fisheries and Food may create, amend or terminate pilot schemes.

196. **Animals – personal injuries – joint keepers could sue each other**

[Animals Act 1971 s.2, s.6(3).]

H, the owner of a horse, appealed against a ruling that she was liable under the Animals Act 1971 for the death of the keeper of the horse. The keeper had been thrown from the horse after the horse had become frightened by farm machinery. F, the widower of the deceased, had issued proceedings on the basis that H was subject to strict liability as owner and keeper of the horse. H argued that one keeper could not sue another keeper as both could be regarded as having the same knowledge of the characteristics of the animal.

Held, dismissing the appeal, that an animal keeper within the meaning of s.6(3) of the Act was not prevented from relying on s.2 to sue another keeper of the animal. H, the owner of the horse, had also been a keeper of the horse. There was no restriction under the 1971 Act on those who could bring an action against the keeper of an animal.

FLACK v. HUDSON [2001] 2 W.L.R. 982, Otton, L.J., CA.

197. Diseases and disorders – approved disinfectants

DISEASES OF ANIMALS (APPROVED DISINFECTANTS) (AMENDMENT) (ENGLAND) ORDER 2000, SI 2000 3195; made under the Animal Health Act 1981 s.1, s.7, s.23. In force: December 6, 2000; £1.75.

This Order, which applies in England only, amends the Diseases of Animals (Approved Disinfectants) Order 1978 (SI 1978 32) by amending Sch.1, which lists approved disinfectants, and replacing Sch.2 which previously listed disinfectants that were approved for a transitional period until 30 June 1999. That period has now expired and there are currently no disinfectants approved on a transitional basis.

198. Dogs – houses – dangerous dogs – meaning of "public place"

[Dangerous Dogs Act 1991 s.3(1); Dangerous Dogs Act 1991 s.10(2).]

K owned two houses which were not joined but shared a common driveway with a large iron gate running across it. E lived in one house and let the other to CB. E owned two Rhodesian Ridgeback dogs, which he used to guard the premises. The dogs were normally confined in the garden to the rear of the property but were sometimes allowed to roam free in the driveway. CB's mother, SB, came to visit her son on an occasion when the dogs were free in the driveway. She was bitten by one of the dogs as she approached CB's front door. E was convicted of an offence under the Dangerous Dogs Act 1991 s.3(1) on the basis that the driveway was a public place as defined in s.10(2) of the Act, namely that it was a common part of the two houses. E appealed.

Held, allowing the appeal, that Section 10(2) of the Act stated that a public place included "the common parts of a building containing two or more separate dwellings." The case in question concerned two separate but unconnected dwellings, whereas the Act seemed to be making reference to blocks of flats. The word "building" was used in the singular and could not be reinterpreted. It was true to say that, as a tenant, CB had an absolute right to invite whom he wished to his house, but the driveway did not thereby become a public place. It remained the fact that people came to the house by invitation, thus he retained the right to require people to leave the property, *McGeachy v. Normand* 1994 S.L.T. 429, [1994] C.L.Y. 5392 considered and *DPP v. Fellowes* (1993) 157 J.P. 936, [1994] C.L.Y. 1095.

EVES v. DPP, March 2, 2000, Judge Roger Dutton, Crown Ct (Chester). [*Ex rel.* Ben Collins, Barrister, Sedan Houses, Stanley Place, Chester].

199. Fur Farming (Prohibition) Act 2000 (c.33)

This Act prohibits the keeping of animals solely or primarily for slaughter for the value of their fur and provides for the making of payments in respect of the related closure of certain businesses.

This Act received Royal Assent on November 23, 2000.

200. Infectious disease control – domestic pets – pet travel pilot scheme

PET TRAVEL SCHEME (PILOT ARRANGEMENTS) (ENGLAND) (AMENDMENT) ORDER 2000, SI 2000 1298; made under the Animal Health Act 1981 s.10. In force: June 5, 2000; £2.00.

This Order, which amends the Rabies (Importation of Dogs, Cats and Other Mammals) Order 1974 (SI 1974 2211) and the Pet Travel Scheme (Pilot Arrangements) (England) Order 1999 (SI 1999 3443), permits the entry into England of cats or dogs which have been admitted into Northern Ireland, the Republic of Ireland, the Channel Islands or the Isle of Man if they were admitted under a scheme similar to the scheme in the 1999 Order. It also adds Norway to the countries from which cats and dogs may be imported in accordance with Council Directive 92/65 ([1992] OJ L268/54). The Order removes the requirement that an animal must have been resident for six months in a qualifying country before it can be exempted from the requirement for vaccination for rabies when it is in quarantine, excludes an acaricidal collar from the permitted treatments against ticks and provides that, in countries or territories which operate an official identification system for cats and dogs, the vaccination against rabies and subsequent blood test may be carried out before the animal is identified with a microchip instead of after identification with the microchip, and permits the certificate in Sch.3 to the 1999 Order to be varied accordingly.

201. **Infectious disease control – domestic pets – pet travel pilot scheme**

PET TRAVEL SCHEME (PILOT ARRANGEMENTS) (ENGLAND) (AMENDMENT) (NO.3) ORDER 2000, SI 2000 1641; made under the Animal Health Act 1981 s.10. In force: June 22, 2000; £1.00.

This Order, which revokes the Pet Travel Scheme (Pilot Arrangements) (England) (Amendment) (No.2) Order 2000 (SI 2000 1564), makes a minor amendment to the Pet Travel Scheme (Pilot Arrangements) (England) (Amendment) Order 2000 (SI 2000 1298) Art.2(3).

202. **Mink keeping – prohibition**

MINK KEEPING (ENGLAND) ORDER 2000, SI 2000 3402; made under the Destructive Imported Animals Act 1932 s.10. In force: January 1, 2001; £1.50.

This Order, which renews in England the controls imposed in Great Britain by the Mink Keeping Order 1997 (SI 1997 3002), prohibits absolutely the keeping of mink on off-shore islands of England other than the Isle of Wight and prohibits the keeping of mink in the remainder of England except under licence. The Order ceases to have effect on January 1, 2004.

203. **Mink keeping – prohibition – Wales**

MINK KEEPING (WALES) ORDER 2000, SI 2000 3340 (W.218); made under the Destructive Imported Animals Act 1932 s.10. In force: January 1, 2001; £1.75.

This Order continues in Wales the controls imposed in Great Britain by the Mink Keeping Order 1997 (SI 1997 3002) until January 1, 2001.

204. **Personal injuries – dogs – liability for attack by police dog**

[Animals Act 1971 s.2(2).]

In the course of a pursuit of a suspect, a police officer, G, was bitten by a police dog which had been instructed to detain the suspect. G instituted proceedings for damages against C, under the Animals Act 1971 s.2(2). At first instance the claim under the 1971 Act was dismissed on the basis that there had not been any evidence of negligence on the part of the dog's handler and for the purposes of s.2(2), training was distinct from "natural inclination or characteristic". G appealed, contending that (1) the injury occurred as a result of the dog's training, and (2) such training was not generally present amongst German Shepherd dogs. C maintained that the fact that the dog had been trained did not result in it possessing characteristics not normally present in other German Shepherd dogs.

Held, dismissing the appeal, that the relevant characteristic was the ability of the dog to respond to training and instruction. That could not be termed a characteristic not normally found in German Shepherd dogs as a breed but was, conversely, precisely what made them particularly suited to police work. On the facts of the instant case the dog had acted in accordance with its training and in the characteristic way of other dogs with the same training. There was accordingly no basis for liability under s.2(2) which required damage attributable to a characteristic not normally found in the breed, *Livesey v. Chief Constable of Lancashire* (Unreported, November 10, 1994) and *Breeden v. Lampard* (Unreported, March 21, 1985) considered.

GLOSTER v. CHIEF CONSTABLE OF GREATER MANCHESTER [2000] P.I.Q.R. P114, Pill, L.J., CA.

205. Personal injuries – horses – bites – not characteristic known to owner

[Animals Act 1971 s.2.]

W, an experienced horsewoman, regularly helped A to exercise his thoroughbred gelding. On the day of the accident, W went into the horse's stable to get the horse ready for exercise. As she was removing the horse's rugs the horse bit her arm, holding on to it for a second or two. Her evidence was that the horse attacked her "in a most vicious way" and that the attack was "completely different from nipping". The skin was not broken, but W contended that as she wrenched her arm free she suffered permanent damage to the nerves of the brachial plexus. Shortly before the injury to W, A was clipping the horse when it reared up, causing A to fall to the ground. A's face was then injured badly by one of the horse's hoofs. W knew about that incident at the time of her own injury. W contended that the horse had a tendency to nip and was highly strung, unpredictable and easily frightened and that A was liable for her injury under the Animals Act 1971 s.2 in that the damage which she suffered was damage of a kind which the horse was likely to cause or which, if caused by the horse, was likely to be severe; that the likelihood of the damage or of its being severe was due to the characteristics of the horse which were not normally found in other horses at all, or were not normally to be found in other horses except at particular times or in particular circumstances, and that those characteristics were known to A. W relied on the restive and unpredictable nature of the horse and on the characteristic which she said amounted to a tendency to attack, demonstrated during the incident which injured A. A contended that there was no evidence of the horse having bitten anyone before in the way that W claimed to have been bitten.

Held, dismissing the claim, that the damage caused by the horse was not of a kind which it was likely to cause, since there was no evidence of any relevant previous tendency. However, damage caused by biting was likely to be severe. Pursuant to s.2(2)(b) of the Act, the likelihood that the damage would be severe was not due to characteristics of the horse which were not normally found in horses, or which were not normally found except at particular times or in particular circumstances. A bite by a horse was likely to have severe consequences, whatever the horse's characteristics. The severity of a horse bite was a consequence of the nature of horses' teeth and jaws. The fact that the horse was highly strung and nervous did not mean that it had characteristics not normally found in horses, or that biting or some other form of attack was more likely than normal. Accordingly, no question arose under s.2(2)(c). It was found as a fact that A's injury was not caused by an attack by the horse and that every horse keeper knew or should know that a horse bite was likely to be severe, but that did not lead to liability under s.2 unless the keeper knew that the horse was likely to attack people or attack them in particularly relevant circumstances, *Curtis v. Betts* [1990] 1 W.L.R. 459, [1990] C.L.Y. 174 and *Wallace v. Newton* [1982] 1 W.L.R. 375, [1982] C.L.Y. 842 considered.

WHITEHEAD v. ALEXANDER, August 4, 1999, Judge Hull, CC (Epsom). [*Ex rel.* Charles Foster, Barrister, 6 Pump Court, Temple, London].

206. Protection of Animals (Amendment) Act 2000 (c.40)

This Act enables provision to be made for the care, disposal or slaughter of animals to which proceedings under the Protection of Animals Act 1911 s.1 relate.

This Act received Royal Assent on November 30, 2000 and comes into force on January 30, 2001.

207. Scientific procedures – fees

ANIMALS (SCIENTIFIC PROCEDURES) ACT 1986 (FEES) ORDER 2000, SI 2000 480; made under the Animals (Scientific Procedures) Act 1986 s.8. In force: April 1, 2000; £1.00.

This Order prescribes the fees payable by the holder of a certificate issued under the Animals (Scientific Procedures) Act 1986 s.6 or s.7.

208. Veterinary medicines – Commission Directive

Commission Directive 2000/37 of June 5, 2000 amending Chapter VIa 'Pharmacovigilance' of Council Directive 81/851 on the approximation of the laws of the Member States relating to veterinary medicinal products. [2000] OJ L139/25.

209. Veterinary medicines – data sheets

MEDICINES (DATA SHEETS FOR VETERINARY DRUGS) REGULATIONS 2000, SI 2000 2386; made under the Medicines Act 1968 s.96, s.129; and the European Communities Act 1972 s.2. In force: October 1, 2000; £2.00.

These Regulations replace the Medicines (Data Sheet) Regulations 1972 (SI 1972 2076 as amended) insofar as they relate to data sheets for veterinary drugs. In particular, they prescribe the form of data sheets and the particulars to be contained in them which the holder of a product licence or marketing authorisation is required under the Medicines Act 1968 to send or deliver to practitioners in connection with any advertisement or representation.

210. Veterinary medicines – fees

MEDICINES (PRODUCTS FOR ANIMAL USE-FEES) (AMENDMENT) REGULATIONS 2000, SI 2000 2250; made under the Medicines Act 1971 s.1; and the European Communities Act 1972 s.2. In force: October 1, 2000; £2.50.

These Regulations amend the Medicines (Products for Animal Use -Fees) Regulations 1998 (SI 1998 2428 as amended), which prescribe fees in connection with applications and inspections relating to marketing authorisations under the Marketing Authorisations for Veterinary Medicinal Products Regulations 1994 (SI 1994 3142); licences and certificates granted under the Medicines Act 1968 in so far as they apply to medicinal products for animal use; and the registration of homeopathic veterinary medicinal products. In particular, they prescribe new fees and percentage amounts where the fee is charged on a percentage of turnover. The average level of such fees is increased by 2.5 per cent.

211. Veterinary medicines – marketing authorisations

MARKETING AUTHORISATIONS FOR VETERINARY MEDICINAL PRODUCTS AMENDMENT REGULATIONS 2000, SI 2000 776; made under the European Communities Act 1972 s.2. In force: April 14, 2000; £1.50.

These Regulations amend the Marketing Authorisations for Veterinary Medicinal Products Regulations 1994 (SI 1994 3142) to implement Commission Directive 1999/104 ([2000] OJ L3/18) amending the Annex to Council Directive 81/852 ([1981] OJ L317/16) relating to analytical, pharmacotoxicological and clinical standards and protocols in respect of the testing of veterinary medicinal products; Commission Regulation 649/98 ([1998] OJ L88/7) amending the Annex to Council Regulation 2309/93 ([1993] OJ L214/1), to make an amendment to the types of veterinary medicinal products which may be authorised by the Community in accordance with Part B; and the judgment of the European Court of Justice in Bruyere v. Belgium (C297/94) (1997) 38 B.M.L.R. 41, [1996] C.L.Y 4219 to prohibit importation of an unauthorised veterinary medicinal product for the purposes of placing it on the market.

212. Veterinary medicines – retailers' records

RETAILERS' RECORDS FOR VETERINARY MEDICINAL PRODUCTS REGULATIONS 2000, SI 2000 7; made under the European Communities Act 1972 s.2. In force: February 1, 2000; £1.50.

These Regulations impose certain requirements relating to record keeping on retailers of veterinary medicinal products and complete the implementation in the UK of Council Directive 81/851 ([1981] OJ L317/1) Art.50b.2 and Art.50b.3 relating to veterinary medicinal products as amended by Council Directive 90/

676 ([1990] OJ L373/15). The Medicines (Sale or Supply) (Miscellaneous Provisions) Regulations 1980 (SI 1980 1923) Reg.6 and Sch.2, which relate to pharmacy records, are revoked in so far as they apply to retail sales of veterinary medicinal products.

213. Veterinary medicines – sale and supply – exemptions

MEDICINES (EXEMPTIONS FOR MERCHANTS IN VETERINARY DRUGS) (AMENDMENT) ORDER 2000, SI 2000 2686; made under the Medicines Act 1968 s.57, s.129. In force: October 9, 2000; £2.30.

This Order amends the Medicines (Exemption for Merchants in Veterinary Drugs) Order 1998 (SI 1998 1044) Art.6 and Art.7 by providing for gloves and laminated sheets with safety warnings to be supplied by agricultural merchants on any sale or supply of organophosphorus sheep dips and removing the right of marketing authorisation holders to sell veterinary medicines directly to users. In addition, it amends Art.8 of the 1998 Order to provide that records of sales are to be kept only for products to which the 1998 Order applies which are intended for food-producing animals.

214. Veterinary surgeons – registration

VETERINARY SURGEONS AND VETERINARY PRACTITIONERS (REGISTRATION) REGULATIONS ORDER OF COUNCIL 2000, SI 2000 1619; made under the Veterinary Surgeons Act 1996 s.25. In force: June 13, 2000; £2.00.

The Regulations scheduled to this Order of Council have been approved in substitution for the Veterinary Surgeons and Veterinary Practitioners (Registration) Regulations 1999 (SI 1999 2846), which are hereby revoked.

215. Veterinary surgeons – registration

VETERINARY SURGEONS AND VETERINARY PRACTITIONERS (REGISTRATION) (AMENDMENT) REGULATIONS ORDER OF COUNCIL 2000, SI 2000 3282; made under the Veterinary Surgeons Act 1966 s.25. In force: April 1, 2001; £1.75.

The Regulations approved by this Order of Council increase the fees payable for the registration and annual retention of names on the Registers of the Royal College of Veterinary Surgeons from April 1, 2001.

216. Publications

Palmer, Julian – Animal Law. 3rd Ed. Paperback. ISBN 0-7219-0802-0. Shaw & Sons.

ARBITRATION

217. Appeals – awards – ICC Rules – right of appeal

[Arbitration Act 1996 s.68, s.69, s.82.]

SP and I entered into agreements whereby I would, in return for a lump sum payment, provide SP with finance to enable it to produce and export polyester yarn. The agreements provided that disputes would be referred to arbitration, and that they would be governed by the ICC Rules of Arbitration 1988 and by English law, save to the extent that it conflicted with Islamic Sharia law, in which case the latter would prevail. Following SP's default, I began an arbitration. The arbitrator having found in favour of I, SP sought leave to appeal against the award pursuant to the Arbitration Act 1996 s.69. SP also challenged the award under s.68 of the Act, arguing that the arbitrator had been guilty of serious irregularities which had caused it substantial injustice.

Held, refusing the applications, that (1) s.69 of the Act allowed a party to appeal on a question of law arising from an award only if the parties had not "otherwise agreed". Since the parties had, by virtue of Art.24 of the 1988 Rules, agreed to waive their right of appeal, SP was precluded from relying on s.69 of the Act, *Arab African Energy Corp v. Olie Producten Nederland BV* [1983] 2 Lloyd's Rep. 419, [1983] C.L.Y. 139 and *Marine Contractors Inc v. Shell Petroleum Development Co of Nigeria Ltd* [1984] 2 Lloyd's Rep. 77, [1984] C.L.Y. 105 applied. In any event, the issue in the arbitration had been whether the agreements had been invalidated by Sharia law. The court had no jurisdiction to determine that issue since s.82 of the Act limited its jurisdiction to issues arising out of the law of England and Wales. Moreover the arbitrator's award appeared to be clear, comprehensive and correct. SP had therefore failed to establish that the award had been "obviously wrong" for the purpose of s.69(3)(c), and (2) SP had not been able to establish either that the arbitrator had been responsible for serious irregularities, or that his findings had caused it any injustice, *Egmatra v. Marco Trading Corp* [1999] 1 Lloyd's Rep. 862, [1999] C.L.Y. 225 considered.

SANGHI POLYESTERS LTD (INDIA) v. INTERNATIONAL INVESTOR (KCFC) (KUWAIT) [2000] 1 Lloyd's Rep. 480, D Mackie Q.C., QBD (Comm Ct).

218. Appeals – awards – permission to appeal beyond High Court and county court – inter relation between Arbitration Act 1996 s.69(1) and Access to Justice Act 1999 s.55

[Arbitration Act 1996 s.69(1), s.69(8); Access to Justice Act 1999 s.55.]

HB appealed to the Court of Appeal against the refusal of the High Court to grant permission to appeal against the upholding of an arbitration award made against it in favour of MH. HB had appealed the award to the High Court under the Arbitration Act 1996 s.69(1), and when permission to appeal further was withheld, it sought to obtain permission direct from the Court of Appeal, contending that under s.69(8) of the Act the Court of Appeal had the power to grant permission to appeal, or alternatively to review the High Court refusal, if it considered that there had been an improper exercise of discretion.

Held, refusing permission to appeal (Arden, J. dissenting), that (1) the wording of s.69(8) of the Act was clear, namely that an appeal could not be brought in the Court of Appeal without permission from the court below, meaning the High Court or the county court. The availability of a review process in the Court of Appeal would be contradictory to the principle of keeping interference with arbitrators' determinations to a minimum, and (2) the Access to Justice Act 1999 s.55 was not to be interpreted as repealing s.69(8) of the 1996 Act by implication. Section 55 of the 1999 Act was not applicable to cases which were already covered by s.69(8) of the 1996 Act, with the result that, if permission to appeal to the Court of Appeal was granted in the latter instance, there was no additional requirement to obtain permission from the Court of Appeal.

HENRY BOOT CONSTRUCTION (UK) LTD v. MALMAISON HOTEL (MANCHESTER) LTD (LEAVE TO APPEAL) [2001] Q.B. 388, Waller, L.J., CA.

219. Appeals – service of process – disclosure

[Civil Procedure Rules 1998 (SI 1998 3132) Part 5 r.5.4, Part 7 r.7.7.]

C had been successful in arbitration proceedings brought by A and applied to the court to be supplied with documents relating to a possible appeal by A against the award. C contended that it had a right under the Civil Procedure Rules 1998 Part 5 r.5.4 to view such documents, as it would be party to any proceedings which ensued.

Held, granting the application, that under Part 7 r.7.7, once a claim form had been issued, proceedings existed notwithstanding that the claim had not yet been served. There was no reason why that principle should not extend to arbitration proceedings.

ADVANCED SPECIALIST TREATMENT ENGINEERING LTD v. CLEVELAND STRUCTURAL ENGINEERING (HONG KONG) LTD; *sub nom.* CLEVELAND STRUCTURAL ENGINEERING (HONG KONG) LTD v. ADVANCED SPECIALIST TREATMENT ENGINEERING LTD [2000] 1 W.L.R. 558, Colman, J., QBD (Comm Ct).

220. **Appeals – statutory interpretation – resolution of statutory drafting error**

[Arbitration Act 1979; Supreme Court Act 1981 s.18(1)(g); Arbitration Act 1996 s.9, s.107, Part I, Sch.3 para.37.]

IE appealed against a Court of Appeal decision ([1999] 1 W.L.R. 270) allowing an appeal by S and ordering, under the Arbitration Act 1996 s.9, a stay of proceedings brought by IE on the ground that the parties were contractually obliged to arbitrate in the Netherlands. IE submitted that the Court of Appeal did not have jurisdiction to hear and determine S's appeal, since the effect of the Supreme Court Act 1981 s.18(1)(g), as amended by s.107 and Sch. 3 para.37 of the 1996 Act, was that no appeal lay to the Court of Appeal from a decision of the High Court, as there was no express provision for such an appeal within s.9 or Part I of the 1996 Act.

Held, dismissing the appeal, that given the intended purpose of the legislature, as evidenced by the combined effect of s.18(1)(g) in its unamended form and the corresponding provision in the Arbitration Act 1979, it was obvious that there had been a drafting error in Sch.3 para.37 to the 1996 Act. As a result, s.18(1)(g) of the 1981 Act, as amended, had to be interpreted restrictively as being limited to High Court decisions. In the instant case the court was not precluded from adding words to resolve the obvious drafting error in Sch.3 para.37, and, as a result, S had a right of appeal from a decision under s.9. The court had to be sure of the intended purpose of the statutory provision before interpreting legislation in this manner. There had to be no doubt that there had been a drafting error such that the legislation failed to give effect to Parliament's intended purpose. The insertion, omission or substitution of words ought not to result in a substantial variation from the language of the statute.

INCO EUROPE LTD v. FIRST CHOICE DISTRIBUTION [2000] 1 W.L.R. 586, Lord Nicholls of Birkenhead, HL.

221. **Arbitrators – appointment – delay – discretion of court**

[Arbitration Act 1996 s.1, s.18.]

D, engineering contractors, entered into a contract with the Secretary of State for the refurbishment of a building. A contractual clause made provision that any disputes, differences or questions between the parties be referred, after notice, to an arbitrator. The refurbishment work was not completed until three months after the date specified in the contract and D gave notice to the Secretary of State of a claim for losses arising from the delay. Following the rejection of its claim, D, fearing the loss of future government contracts, sought to reach a compromise agreement without resorting to arbitration and therefore did not give notice of referral to arbitration until more than five years had elapsed from completion of the work. The Secretary of State rejected the claim for arbitration and D applied pursuant to the Arbitration Act 1996 s.18 for a direction that the Secretary of State request the nomination of an arbitrator pursuant to the contractual clause. Opposing the application, the Secretary of State argued that although there was a presumption in favour of arbitration, the court should not exercise its discretion under s.18, as D had been guilty of unreasonable delay in invoking the arbitration clause.

Held, granting the application, that (1) the court's discretion under s.18 had to be exercised judicially and in accordance with s.1 of the Act; (2) an application had to be refused if it would not be possible to achieve a fair resolution of the dispute by an impartial tribunal without unnecessary delay or expense, and (3) in the instant case, D's delay had, in part, resulted from the Secretary of State's lack of response to negotiations.

R DURTNELL & SONS LTD v. SECRETARY OF STATE FOR TRADE AND INDUSTRY [2001] 1 All E.R. (Comm) 41, Judge Toulmin Q.C., QBD (T&CC).

222. Arbitrators – appointment – delay – incorporation of arbitration clause by reference

[Arbitration Act 1950 s.10(1).]

The Foreign and Commonwealth Office, F, contracted for the construction of a new British Embassy building in Jordan. PT was the architect and K, the main contractor. After the building had been completed it was discovered, in 1987, that the roof leaked. In 1992 and 1993 F sought the respective agreement of PT and K for the appointment of an arbitrator. In 1996 F applied for the appointment of an arbitrator under the Arbitration Act 1950 s.10(1) and for declarations that there was a dispute between the parties, which had validly been referred to arbitration. Affidavit evidence was not forthcoming for a further 18 months. The applications were therefore heard 10 years after the discovery of the defect.

Held, refusing the applications, that (1) under the 1950 Act an arbitration clause could be incorporated by reference and the contracts with both PT and K incorporated such clauses, *Modern Building (Wales) Ltd v. Limmer & Trinidad Co Ltd* [1975] 1 W.L.R. 1281, [1975] C.L.Y. 101 and *Owners of the Annefield v. Owners of the Cargo Lately Laden on Board The Annefield (The Annefield)* [1971] P. 168 followed; (2) there was a dispute between the parties even though no formal claim had been made, *Ellerine Bros Pty Ltd v. Klinger* [1982] 1 W.L.R. 1375, [1982] C.L.Y. 92 considered; (3) the contractual provisions as to appointment had not been operated as against PT because F had not referred the matter of appointment to the President of the Chartered Institute of Arbitrators, as required under the agreement; (4) the fact that a final certificate had been issued to K would not have been a bar to the appointment sought, since the contract made no provision for a final certificate, but, on the facts, one had not been issued in any event, and (5) discretion to grant the declarations or to appoint an arbitrator was refused because of F's delay, *Frota Oceanica Brasiliera SA v. Steamship Mutual Underwriting Association (Bermuda) Ltd (The Frotanorte)* [1996] 2 Lloyd's Rep. 461, [1996] C.L.Y. 5291 followed.

SECRETARY OF STATE FOR THE FOREIGN AND COMMONWEALTH OFFICE v. PERCY THOMAS PARTNERSHIP; SECRETARY OF STATE FOR THE FOREIGN AND COMMONWEALTH OFFICE v. KIER INTERNATIONAL LTD 65 Con. L.R. 11, Judge Peter Bowsher Q.C., QBD (OR).

223. Arbitrators – bias – power of courts to investigate breach of obligations

A sought to appeal against the dismissal of its application for the removal of the chairman of an arbitration tribunal and the setting aside of three partial awards in favour of S. A had become aware of the arbitrator's position as a non executive director of a rival telecommunications company and sought his removal because of the appearance of bias. A contended that (1) the application of the bias test in *R. v. Gough (Robert)* [1993] A.C. 646, [1993] C.L.Y. 849 was not binding on an arbitrator and that a lesser test of reasonable suspicion of bias should be applied owing to the consensual nature of arbitration, and (2) the judge had wrongly accepted the submission that the ICC Rules 1998 precluded the court from an investigation into the alleged breach of an obligation to disclose, which might threaten the impartiality of the arbitrator.

Held, dismissing the appeal, that (1) the relevant test applicable in all cases was the existence of a real danger of bias and it was correctly decided in the instant case that such a danger did not exist, and (2) the finality provisions of Art.2.13 of the ICC Rules did not exclude the jurisdiction of the court. However, given that the arbitrator was not disqualified under the common law test of bias, it was unreasonable to consider that he lacked the requisite independence to which the ICC Rules referred.

AT&T CORP v. SAUDI CABLE CO [2000] 2 All E.R. (Comm) 625, Lord Woolf, M.R., CA.

224. **Arbitrators – bias – timing of objections**

[Arbitration Act 1996 s.68, s.73(1).]

R, who had purchased a cargo of sugar from GD, was ordered to pay demurrage to GD by a tribunal appointed to arbitrate on the dispute. Having questioned the arbitrator's appointment at an early stage in the proceedings, R applied pursuant to the Arbitration Act 1996 s.68 to have the award set aside on grounds of serious irregularity, contending that the arbitrator's impartiality was in doubt due to his involvement in a recent and unusually acrimonious dispute involving much the same personalities as those in the instant case. GD contended that R had continued to take part in the proceedings and was precluded by s.73(1) of the Act from challenging the decision.

Held, refusing the application, that the existence and circumstances of the earlier dispute, which had occurred two years previously, were not alone sufficient to raise doubts about the arbitrator's impartiality. R had not satisfied the requirements of s.73 because, following the arbitrator's appointment, it had participated in the proceedings; its letter asking the tribunal in general terms to consider the arbitrator's propriety, was a positive step in the proceedings and it precluded R from raising objections as to irregularities. R's submission that it was unaware of the arbitrator's continued involvement in the case until after publication of the award was rejected on the ground that it could, with due diligence, have made the discovery earlier.

RUSTAL TRADING LTD v. GILL & DUFFUS SA [2000] 1 Lloyd's Rep. 14, Moore-Bick, J., QBD (Comm Ct).

225. **Arbitrators – judicial decision making – consideration of uncontentious issues**

[Arbitration Act 1996 s.33, s.68.]

P, the seller, and R, the buyer, were parties to a contract for sale of sugar. R could not pay due to economic conditions in Russia and it communicated that fact to P, who consequently commenced arbitration under the terms of the sale contract. P contended that R had purportedly accepted liability for the goods and that it considered the arbitration to relate solely to the issue of quantum. The arbitrator conducted the arbitration as a documents only arbitration, but questioned the parties in writing as to their understanding of payment being made "as conditions allow", as specified in their contract. The arbitrator found that R had not been liable to pay at the given time under the terms of the contract. P applied to remit that decision on the basis that the arbitrator's consideration of liability constituted a serious irregularity under the Arbitration Act 1996 s.68, and that he had failed to act fairly pursuant to s.33 of the Act since P had not had an opportunity to make submissions or to adduce evidence on the issues which had formed the basis of the award.

Held, granting the application and remitting the case, that there had been a serious irregularity within s.68 of the Act. In document only arbitrations, arbitrators had to be particularly astute not to introduce into their deliberations issues which were not disputed between the parties. The arbitrator had not given sufficient information for a reasonable commercial lawyer to understand that he was planning to re-open the issue of liability, *Interbulk Ltd v. Aiden Shipping Co (The Vimeira) (No.1)* [1984] 2 Lloyd's Rep. 66, [1984] C.L.Y. 114 applied.

PACOL LTD v. JOINT STOCK CO ROSSAKHAR [1999] 2 All E.R. (Comm) 778, Colman, J., QBD (Comm Ct).

226. Arbitrators – judicial decision making – restriction of litigant's submissions – breach of rules of natural justice

[Arbitration Act 1996 s.103(2)(c).]

A appealed against an order upholding an arbitration award in favour of B, his brother and former business associate. A appeared in person and refused to restrict his assertions to the issue of whether there was a binding arbitration agreement. As a result, the judge prevented A from making any further submissions. A challenged the declaration that the award was valid and binding, contending that the award should not be recognised under the Arbitration Act 1996 s.103(2)(c) because he had been "unable to present his case".

Held, allowing the appeal in part, that A had not been given a proper opportunity to comment on the award and to present his case as to the conduct of the arbitration, with the result that the judge did not have a suitable chance to hear and determine all the issues brought by A. The findings of the award were flawed, unsatisfactory and unreasoned and the arbitrator had relied upon information which had not been made available to A. There was evidence from A's complaints that the arbitrator's conduct had arguably given rise to a breach of the rules of natural justice, which could establish that A had been "unable to present his case" for the purposes of s.103(2)(c).

IRVANI v. IRVANI [2000] 1 Lloyd's Rep. 412, Buxton, L.J., CA.

227. Arbitrators – jurisdiction – subcontracts – meaning of "dispute"

[Housing Grants, Construction & Regeneration Act 1996.]

F sought summary judgment to enforce an adjudicator's decision in its favour, in respect of a construction dispute with M. The dispute had been referred to arbitration by F following a number of interim applications for payment and the sum claimed in the notice of adjudication was substantially higher than that claimed in the last interim application. M immediately contested the jurisdiction of the adjudicator, on the basis that the dispute which had been referred had not been previously notified and rejected by M therefore at the date the notice was issued there was no "dispute" in existence. M contended that if a dispute concerned a precise basis of claim and amount, the notice of adjudication and the adjudication itself had to be concerned solely with those matters. Accordingly only the dispute in existence at the time that the notice of adjudication was served could be within the jurisdiction of the adjudicator and if that was superseded by a new claim which had not had time to develop into a dispute, then the adjudicator appointed to resolve the dispute was appointed without jurisdiction.

Held, granting the application, that (1) an adjudicator derived his jurisdiction from his appointment, which was governed by the Housing, Grants, Construction and Regeneration Act 1996. That required there to be a dispute that had already arisen between parties to a construction contract; (2) what was in "dispute" within the meaning of the Act was a question of fact. The "dispute" was all or part of whatever claims, issues or causes of action the referring party chose to refer to adjudication. A "dispute" could only arise once the subject matter had been brought to the attention of the opposing party and that party had had the opportunity to admit or reject the claim; (3) the adjudicator had jurisdiction because all the issues in the notice of adjudication had been referred to M, who had rejected them, and they were therefore disputes by the time that the notice was served *Halki Shipping Corp v. Sopex Oils Ltd (The Halki)* [1998] 1 W.L.R. 726, [1998] C.L.Y. 246 and *Monmouthshire CC v. Costelloe & Kemple Ltd* 5 B.L.R. 83, [1966] C.L.Y. 1121 followed.

FASTRACK CONTRACTORS LTD v. MORRISON CONSTRUCTION LTD [2000] B.L.R. 168, Judge Anthony Thornton Q.C., QBD (T&CC).

228. **Arbitrators – jurisdiction – tribunal's meeting with expert – procedural irregularities**

[Arbitration Act 1996 s.37(1), s.68(2).]

H, an American company, entered into a distributorship agreement in Saudi Arabia with A, the trading name used by an individual, P. A dispute arose in relation to unpaid invoices submitted to P by H. P incorporated his business and became A, allegedly without H's knowledge. Thereafter H terminated the distributorship agreement and commenced arbitration proceedings as provided for under the terms of the agreement. A counterclaimed for unpaid commission. At the conclusion of the arbitration, the panel gave judgment for H in the sum of $57,438 and for A in the sum of $602,859. H sought to set aside the award, contending that (1) the arbitrators had lacked jurisdiction to make any award in favour of A since A was not a party to the distributorship agreement, and (2) there had been serious irregularities in the way in which the tribunal had dealt with the expert evidence on Saudi Arabian law.

Held, allowing the appeal in part, that (1) if A were to succeed P under the agreement, then under Saudi Arabian law H was obliged to consent to the change. On the facts, H had been unaware of the change in status, and consent could not be implied on the basis of their knowledge at the time. The tribunal therefore had no power to make any award in favour of A, and (2) while the tribunal had been entitled to instruct an expert to assist them with Saudi Arabian law pursuant to the Arbitration Act 1996 s.37(1), they should not have met with the expert and discussed the case with him without obtaining the consent of the parties. Such conduct did amount to an irregularity but was not a serious irregularity as defined in s.68(2) of the Act, *Conder Structures v. Kvaerner Construction Ltd* 1999 A.D.R.L.J. 305 applied.

HUSSMAN (EUROPE) LTD v. AL AMEEN DEVELOPMENT & TRADE CO; *sub nom.* HUSSMANN (EUROPE) LTD v. AL AMEEN DEVELOPMENT & TRADE CO [2000] 2 Lloyd's Rep. 83, Thomas, J., QBD (Comm Ct).

229. **Awards – arbitrators – application for remission and for reasons for decision**

SW contracted with J for substantial improvements to a waterworks. The contract was completed late and the plant was defective. The parties made claims and cross claims. An arbitrator was appointed and made an award. Both parties were dissatisfied with the award and sought remission of certain parts and further reasons for other aspects of the award.

Held, allowing the applications in part, that the court would decline to make an order for further reasons where what was really sought was an appeal, or material for an appeal, from an arbitration award, *King v. Thomas McKenna Ltd* [1991] 2 Q.B. 480, [1991] C.L.Y. 199 and *Moran v. Lloyds* [1983] Q.B. 542, [1983] C.L.Y. 147 considered. In the instant case, the arbitrator had found that J was in breach of contract but that the breaches were not fundamental. Accordingly, SW's termination could not be an acceptance of a repudiatory breach and such termination would itself be a breach of contract. The arbitrator had made no findings in such a connection and accordingly the matter would be remitted on that aspect. Likewise, since the arbitrator had awarded interest up to a date different from the date of the award but without indicating why, that question would also be remitted. An order would be made for further reasons to be given for the decision that damages due to SW were not to be set off against sums owing to J at the date they became due, and for the decision that the specification of a piece of equipment demanded by SW was a variation of the design part of the contract.

JFS (UK) LTD (FORMERLY JOHNSON FILTRATION SYSTEMS LTD) v. SOUTH WEST WATER SERVICES LTD; SOUTH WEST WATER SERVICES LTD v. JFS (UK) LTD (FORMERLY JOHNSON FILTRATION SYSTEMS LTD) 65 Con. L.R. 51, Judge Humphrey Lloyd Q.C., QBD (OR).

230. **Awards – arbitrators – court's jurisdiction to remit – failure to determine jointly referred matter**

[Arbitration Act 1950 s.22(1).]

A dispute between L and K arising from construction works was referred to arbitration. The arbitrator directed that the case be pleaded in the form of a Scott Schedule. L applied under the Arbitration Act 1950 s.22(1) for one of the awards to be remitted on the ground that the arbitrator had not dealt with certain of the items in the Schedule.

Held, granting the application and remitting certain matters to the arbitrator, that the court's power to remit extended beyond the instances recognised by legal authorities, namely, awards which were wrong on their face, or those concerning misconduct or admitted mistake by the arbitrator, but the categories of case appropriate for remission were still not totally clear, *King v. Thomas McKenna Ltd* [1991] 1 All E.R. 653, [1991] C.L.Y. 199 followed. Remission was precluded where an appeal was the appropriate remedy. Insofar as L could substantiate its submission that the arbitrator had failed to decide issues the parties had jointly asked him to decide, there was jurisdiction to order remission. It did not matter that the arbitrator had not specifically referred to a Scott Schedule item as long as he had given a decision on it and in the instant case there were some matters on which no decision had been given.

LEDWOOD CONSTRUCTION LTD v. KIER CONSTRUCTION LTD 68 Con. L.R. 96, Judge John Hicks Q.C., QBD (OR).

231. **Awards – interest – unpaid awards**

[Arbitration Act 1950; Supreme Court Act 1981 s.35A; Arbitration Act 1996 s.49(4), s.66.]

W sought clarification of whether the court could award interest under the Supreme Court Act 1981 s.35A on an award that had not been paid interest had been automatically awarded under the Arbitration Act 1950, but under the Arbitration Act 1996 s.66 there was no reference to post award interest.

Held, granting the application, that the arbitrator had a discretion under s.49(4) of the 1996 Act to award interest and the court had no power to intervene in the arbitrator's determination in order to grant interest on an outstanding award.

WALKER v. ROME; *sub nom.* WALKER v. ROWE [1999] 2 All E.R. (Comm) 961, Aikens, J., QBD (Comm Ct).

232. **Building and engineering contracts – arbitrator's jurisdiction – defence founded on causes of delay**

HB and M entered into an agreement under an amended version of the JCT Standard Form Building Contract (1980 edition, Private edition with Quantities), which provided for HB to carry out certain design and construction work on the completion of a hotel. The completion date was stated as November 21, 1997 but actual completion was not achieved until March 13, 1998. On April 30, 1998 HB gave notice of intention to refer certain disputed claims for extension of time to arbitration, pursuant to the contract. An arbitrator was appointed but HB alleged that a major part of M's statement of defence raised questions outside the arbitrator's jurisdiction, in particular allegations that the delays to the contract were HB's own fault. The arbitrator held that the issues were within his jurisdiction and HB appealed.

Held, dismissing the appeal, that (1) the potential for an event to cause delays beyond the contractual completion date was a question of fact in each case, *Balfour Beatty Building Ltd v. Chestermount Properties Ltd* 62 B.L.R. 1, [1994] C.L.Y. 335 considered; (2) in the instant case, M had both negative and positive defences to HB's claim. The negative defence being that the factors relied on by HB had not caused delay as they were not capable of disrupting HB's schedule of work. The positive defence was that the delay was due to irrelevant matters that were HB's responsibility in any event. M could advance those matters by way of defence to the claim; (3) when considering contractual issues, an architect could decide matters either on a limited basis or consider if a view only taking immediate factors into account was also supported by findings made on other issues. Absolute rules could not be determined in this area, and (4) an architect could not be prevented under cl.25 of the contract from considering if a relevant event, capable of causing delay, had impacted on the progress or completion of other areas of work.

HENRY BOOT CONSTRUCTION (UK) LTD v. MALMAISON HOTEL (MANCHESTER) LTD 70 Con. L.R. 32, Dyson, J., QBD (T&CC).

233. Building and engineering contracts – ICE conditions of contract – arbitrator's jurisdiction to decide sub contract dispute – contractor serving notice requiring joinder of sub contract and main contract disputes

D&C was the main contractor under an ICE 6th edition contract and engaged D as a sub contractor on a FCEC form of subcontract, 1991 Edition. D alleged breaches of the subcontract by D&C and gave notice of dispute under cl.18(2) of the subcontract and sought the appointment of an arbitrator under cl.18(5). D&C then gave notice of a dispute to the employer's engineer under the terms of the main contract and sought an engineer's decision. D&C also gave D notice under cl.18(8) of the sub contract, requiring D to assist if there was a dispute under the main contract concerning the sub contract works. Clause 18(8) permitted the main contractor to require a sub contract dispute to be heard together with any main contract dispute. An arbitrator was appointed for the sub contract dispute but D&C disputed his jurisdiction. The arbitrator found that he had jurisdiction because D&C's cl.18(8) notice was invalid as, at the time it was made, the main contract dispute had not been referred to arbitration. Following this decision, D&C referred the main contract dispute to arbitration and issued a fresh cl.18(8) notice. The arbitrator then gave a further decision, holding that he did not have jurisdiction. Both D&C and D appealed on the issue of jurisdiction; D contending that the arbitrator had jurisdiction and D&C arguing that he did not.

Held, that the arbitrator did not have jurisdiction at the time the first notice was served. The first cl.18(8) notice was valid and did not require a pre-existing reference to arbitration. The right to require the assistance of a sub contractor in an arbitration was separate to a further right to require a joint reference and the arbitrator erred by finding that a conciliation or arbitration reference was a condition precedent to the service of a valid joinder notice. Having made his decision, the arbitrator was not entitled to make a further determination on the same issue. He was functus officio. The second decision was therefore made without jurisdiction.

DREDGING & CONSTRUCTION CO LTD v. DELTA CIVIL ENGINEERING CO LTD (NO.1); *sub nom.* DELTA CIVIL ENGINEERING CO LTD v. DREDGING & CONSTRUCTION CO LTD (NO.1) [2000] C.L.C. 213, Judge David Wilcox, QBD (T&CC).

234. Building and engineering contracts – JCT forms of contract – arbitration clause – application to additional work

[Arbitration Act 1996 s.9.]

AN, a building contractor, entered into a JCT minor works contract containing an arbitration clause with IPA to carry out specified works under the supervision of a contract administrator. Following completion of further works not specified under the contract but alleged by AN to have been carried out pursuant to a separate oral contract containing the JCT terms and no arbitration clause, AN brought proceedings seeking payment for the additional work done. IPA applied to stay the proceedings pursuant to the Arbitration Act 1996 s.9 on the basis that the further work done had been incorporated into the original contract and therefore should be determined via arbitration. Both parties requested that the judge decide the issues by reference to the affidavit evidence. The judge, while granting the stay ([1999] C.L.C. 212), refused to decide whether the issues relied on by IPA fell within the arbitration clause on the grounds that it was a matter to be dealt with in arbitration proceedings. AN appealed.

Held, dismissing the appeal, that the judge had been correct in his reasoning except in his determination not to decide whether the arbitration clause applied to the issues. The correct approach in the interests of good litigation management and the saving of costs was for the court, where applicable, to resolve the matter on the affidavit evidence, *Birse Construction Ltd v. St David Ltd* [2000] B.L.R. 57, [2000] C.L.Y. 593 considered. From the affidavit evidence in the instant case it was clear that the additional work carried out by AN had been done pursuant to a second phase of the original contract and was therefore covered by the arbitration clause.

AL-NAIMI (T/A BUILDMASTER CONSTRUCTION SERVICES) v. ISLAMIC PRESS AGENCY INC; *sub nom.* AL-NAIMI (T/A BUILDMASTER CONSTRUCTION SERVICES) v. ISLAMIC PRESS SERVICES INC [2000] 1 Lloyd's Rep. 522, Waller, L.J., CA.

235. Building and engineering contracts – RIBA form of contract – referral of disputes to arbitration

[Arbitration Act 1996 s.67.]

A employed L, a firm of architects, on a project to construct a new stand at Aintree racecourse. A contended that L had allowed the costs of the project to increase in breach of their professional duties. A made an application to refer the matter to arbitration and for the appointment of an arbitrator, on the premise that either party could make a reference and seek the appointment of an arbitrator pursuant to clause 13.1 of the contract which provided that "disputes may be dealt with as provided in paragraph 1.8 of the RIBA Condition but otherwise shall be referred to the English courts." Paragraph 1.8 of the RIBA contract provided that either party could make a reference to arbitration although the appointment of the individual arbitrator had to be mutually agreed or, in the absence of agreement, nominated by the President of the Chartered Institute of Arbitrators. L applied for relief under the Arbitration Act 1996 s.67 challenging both the jurisdiction of the arbitrator and the effectiveness of his award and contending that (1) the arbitration clause was ambiguous and therefore void for uncertainty, and (2) in the alternative the reference had no effect without the consent of both parties.

Held, refusing the declarations, that the clause was not ambiguous and once a dispute had arisen either party was entitled to make a reference to arbitration. Such an approach was in line with the way in which the English courts had repeatedly approached the same issue, namely that where it was apparent from the contract that arbitration was contemplated as a means of dispute resolution then the parties would be bound to refer to arbitration even though the clause might not have been expressed in mandatory terms, *Mangistaumunaigaz Oil Production Association v. United World Trading Inc* [1995] 1 Lloyd's Rep. 617, [1996] C.L.Y. 359 applied.

LOBB PARTNERSHIP LTD v. AINTREE RACECOURSE CO LTD [2000] C.L.C. 431, Colman, J., QBD (Comm Ct).

236. Building and engineering contracts – subcontracts – breach of contract – tripartite arbitration

L was the subcontractor to a building contract between S and a local authority, E. The main contract incorporated the ICE Standard Form of Contract for Civil Engineering Works, 5th Edition, which included, in cl.66, provision for the settlement of disputes between S and E by the engineer and, in the event of dissatisfaction with the outcome, then by arbitration. The subcontract also incorporated the F Standard Form of Subcontract (September 1984 Edition) which, by cl.18(1), allowed for arbitration between L and S. Clause 18(2) gave S the power, where cl.18(1) had not already been invoked, to require that any dispute which related to both contracts, be "dealt with jointly with the dispute under the main contract in accordance with the provisions of clause 66 thereof". The building works were not carried out according to schedule and disputes arose between the parties. In February 1995 L gave notice to S that it wished to invoke the arbitration procedure under cl.18(1). S replied that arbitration was not at that stage appropriate, and in March 1995 gave notice to L under cl.18(2) for all the disputes to be dealt with jointly. The disputes between S and E were subsequently deferred and L brought an action claiming that S was not entitled to rely on its cl.18(2) notice. The court of first instance found in favour of S, but that decision was overturned on appeal ([1999] B.L.R. 252, [1999] C.L.Y. 232), the Court of Appeal finding that L did not have to take part in tripartite arbitration. S appealed.

Held, dismissing the appeal, that given the powerlessness of L in relation to the arbitration of the disputes between S and E, it had to be an implied condition of the subcontract that S could only have the benefit of invoking cl.18(2), if it fully intended to thereafter invoke the procedure in cl.66. There was a further implied obligation that that procedure had to be invoked within a reasonable period of time. The involvement in settlement negotiations with E was not an acceptable reason for delay in implementing cl.18(2), as it was irrelevant to the subcontract. S had therefore been in breach of its obligations under cl.18(2) and it was open to L to demand instigation of the procedure under cl.18(1) instead. It was observed that clause 18(2) did not enable tripartite arbitration in the sense that all parties would have equal rights and powers. In order to make the procedure workable, (Lord Hope and Lord Clyde dissenting) contractors should endeavour to properly represent the subcontractor's case jointly with their own under the procedure specified in cl.66, with any arbitration taking place by way of concurrent hearings.

LAFARGE REDLAND AGGREGATES LTD (FORMERLY REDLAND AGGREGATES LTD) v. SHEPHARD HILL CIVIL ENGINEERING LTD; *sub nom.* LAFARGE REDLANDS AGGREGATES LTD v. SHEPHERD HILL CIVIL ENGINEERING LTD [2000] 1 W.L.R. 1621, Lord Hope of Craighead, HL.

237. **Building and engineering contracts – variation – arbitrator's revaluation powers**

W entered into a contract with L for open pit mining. Payment for the works was based on a schedule of rates. Under cl.14 of the contract, W was entitled to direct L to add to or vary the works, and L was obliged to carry out the directions as if the variations were part of the works. The contract provided that if the parties failed to agree on a value for the varied works then W could value the work at its own discretion. The contract also contained an arbitration clause. Two issues arose, (1) whether the basis upon which the value of a variation could be determined was affected by the provision allowing for sole valuation by W, and (2) whether the arbitrator had power to substitute his own valuation for that of W. At first instance it was held that (1) W did not have power under cl.14 to make binding and conclusive valuations of work which L was consequently obliged to carry out, and (2) there was no explicit restriction on the arbitrator's powers, therefore the arbitrator could determine the proper adjustment of valuations having regard to the variations made in the contract. W appealed.

Held, allowing the appeal, that (1) cl.14 conferred on W the power to make binding and conclusive valuations of the work without reference to any particular criteria, save that it was implicit that W was obliged to act honestly, reasonably and in good faith. A valuation made at W's sole discretion was made in accordance with the contract between W and L, *Campbell v. Edwards* [1976] 1 W.L.R. 403, [1976] C.L.Y. 1533 and *Jones v. Sherwood Computer Services Plc* [1992] 1 W.L.R. 277, [1992] C.L.Y. 419 considered; and (2) on a true construction of cl.14, W was the only person empowered to determine the value of the variations. There was no express power in the arbitration clause permitting the arbitrator to re value what W previously determined, *Beaufort Developments (NI) Ltd v. Gilbert-Ash (NI) Ltd* [1999] 1 A.C. 266, [1998] C.L.Y. 5055 followed. If, in the event of W acting dishonestly or unreasonably, a valuation could properly be set aside, the arbitrator could substitute his own valuation for that of W.

WMC RESOURCES LTD v. LEIGHTON CONTRACTORS PROPRIETORY LTD (2000) 2 T.C.L.R. 1, Ipp, J., Sup Ct (WA) (Full Ct).

238. **Dispute resolution – time limits – GAFTA determination of commencement date of dispute**

M appealed against a determination by the Grain and Free Trade Association, GAFTA, that a dispute relating to payments for the sale of wheat had not arisen until the final ultimatum relating to payments had been given. The decision was based on the ground that the notice for arbitration had been served within the 90 day period allowed by cl.2.2 of the GAFTA terms. It was submitted that that cl.2.2 was silent as to the point of which a dispute had arisen, stating only that once a dispute had arisen, a notice of arbitration had to be served within 90 days.

Held, allowing the appeal and remitting the award, that when an arbitration clause said nothing about the time and cause of a dispute, that dispute could be taken to have arisen at any time, depending on the individual circumstances. A dispute could arise before an invoice was sent or anytime thereafter. Moreover, cl.2.2 did not indicate that a dispute arose 90 days after receipt of an invoice, but that a notice of arbitration had to be served within 90 days of the dispute arising, which could be before or after an invoice had been received.

MARC RICH AGRICULTURE TRADING SA v. AGRIMEX LTD [2000] 1 All E.R. (Comm) 951, Langley, J., QBD (Comm Ct).

239. **International arbitration – choice of forum – determination of juridical seat of arbitration**

[Arbitration Act 1996 s.3; Civil Procedure Rules 1998 (SI 1998 3132) Part 49.]

P, a Texan company and the respondent to a dispute with D, a merchant bank, which had resulted in an arbitration award in P's favour, applied to set aside an order granting D permission to serve on it an arbitration claim form out of the jurisdiction. The arbitration scheme under which the award had been made, was based in California. P submitted that since the seat of the arbitration, within the meaning of the Arbitration Act 1996 s.3, was in the United States, and in view of the Civil Procedure Rules 1998 Part 49 PD para.8.1, which specified that such permission could only be granted where the award had been made in the United Kingdom, the judge had had no power to make that order.

Held, allowing the application, that English law demanded that an arbitration had to have a juridical seat before it began and the requirement imposed upon the court by s.3 of the Act, namely to consider the "relevant circumstances" in the determination of the appropriate jurisdiction of the seat, was one which involved consideration of the pre arbitration circumstances, not those subsequently arising. On the facts of the instant case the juridical seat was in California, since that was where D had invoked the appeal procedure, and that seat could not be unilaterally changed, *Union of India v. McDonnell Douglas Corp* [1993] 2 Lloyd's Rep. 48, [1993] C.L.Y. 175 considered.

DUBAI ISLAMIC BANK PJSC v. PAYMENTECH MERCHANT SERVICES INC [2001] 1 All E.R. (Comm) 514, Aikens, J., QBD (Comm Ct).

240. **International arbitration – jurisdiction – parties – foreign companies**

[Arbitration Act 1996; Civil Procedure Rules 1998 (SI 1998 3132) Part 49; Lugano Convention on Jurisdiction and Enforcement of Judgments in Civil and Commercial Matters 1988.]

V served an arbitration claim form seeking a declaration that S was a party to a contract of affreightment and applied for permission to serve the claim on SP, brokers based in Norway, through whom the alleged shipping contract with S had been made. SP disputed the existence of any contract and applied to have the arbitration claim set aside on the basis that the claim did not fall within the arbitration exception in the Lugano Convention, and that service of the claim form in Norway was not permitted under the Civil Procedure Rules 1998 Part 49 PD 49 para.8. Furthermore, it was argued that the court had no jurisdiction to grant declaratory relief against SP and should exercise its discretion against exercising jurisdiction over SP.

Held, refusing the application and setting aside the arbitration claim form, that the High Court had no jurisdiction either (1) as an arbitration exception to the Lugano Convention 1988; (2) under the Practice Direction contained in the third paragraph of the table in Civil Procedure Rules 1998 Part 49 PD 49 para.8.1, or (3) under the Arbitration Act 1996, to permit service of an arbitration claim form on SP, since the appropriate forum for bringing an action against SP was Norway. An arbitration agreement, being a consensual agreement, applied only to the parties to the arbitration and not to an agent. Moreover, the court had no jurisdiction to determine the issues under s.30 of the 1996 Act, as before it could do so, written agreement of all parties to the proceedings was required.

VALE DO RIO DOCE NAVEGACAO SA v. SHANGHAI BAO STEEL OCEAN SHIPPING CO LTD (T/A BAO STEEL OCEAN SHIPPING CO); *sub nom.* VALE DO RIO DOCE NAVEGACAO SA v. SHANGHAI BAO STEEL OCEAN SHIPPING CO LTD (T/A BAOSTEEL OCEAN SHIPPING CO) [2000] 2 All E.R. (Comm) 70, Thomas, J., QBD (Comm Ct).

241. **International arbitration – stay of proceedings – dissolution of arbitral body – jurisdiction to determine tortious claims – Canada**

D was a Canadian importer. J was a Polish supplier. D brought an action in Ontario against J for breach of contract, conspiracy and interference in economic relations. The contract contained an arbitration clause and J sought a stay to permit an arbitration reference.

Held, refusing the application, that the arbitration as defined in the contract could not be performed. The named arbitral body had been dissolved and the procedure to establish its replacement had yet to take place. Further, the tortious claims did not rely on the contract and were not covered by the clause in any event.

DALIMPEX LTD v. JANICKI [2000] I.L.Pr.180, Mandel, J., CJ (Gen Div) (Ont).

242. **Maritime arbitration – jurisdiction – choice of forum – enforcement of arbitration clause**

[International Arbitration Act 1974 (Australia) s.7; Trade Practices Act 1974 (Australia).]

A freight charter contract between HF and WBC provided that any dispute "arising from this charter" should be settled in London and be governed in accordance with English law. A cargo of fertiliser consigned to HF and carried by WBC on a ship owned and operated by KMC was contaminated by an earlier cargo and was not permitted to enter Australia. HF brought an action in the Australian Federal Court alleging negligence and breach of contract against both WBC and KMC and breaches under the Trade Practices Act 1974 (Australia) by WBC. WBC and KMC successfully applied for a stay of proceedings and the claims were referred for arbitration in London. HF appealed, contending that (1) the International Arbitration Act 1974 (Australia) s.7, IAA, was invalid to oust the jurisdiction of the Federal Court; (2) non contractual claims and warranties were not subject to the arbitration clause in the charterparty, and (3) claims based on the Trade Practices Act were "capable of settlement" within the meaning of s.7(2) of the IAA.

Held, allowing the appeal in part and staying the reference to arbitration on the contractual claims until after the final determination of the Federal Court proceedings that (1) the effect of s.7 of the IAA was that contractual terms in a contract which contained an arbitration clause were not to be enforced in Court proceedings. An award by an arbitrator did not, however, affect the contractual rights of a party who had not agreed to abide by that award and s.7 did not oust the power of the Federal Court; (2) contractual claims against WBC had arisen under the charter contract and should be stayed pending arbitration, but non contractual claims were not the basis of a dispute "arising from" the charter contract and there was no right to a stay in relation to those matters, nor was there any right to a stay in respect of claims made against KMC, and (3) the reference to English law in the contract's arbitration clause gave rise to no implication that claims under the Trade Practices Act 1974 (Australia) would be settled by arbitration. The clause would be ineffective if it excluded a party from a remedy under that Act.

HI FERT PTY LTD v. KIUKIANG MARITIME CARRIERS INC [1999] 2 Lloyd's Rep. 782, Beaumont, J., Fed Ct (Aus) (Full Ct).

243. Maritime arbitration – marine insurance – third party actions

[International Arbitration Act 1974 s.7(2)(b).]

D, who was master of H's fishing vessel, claimed against H in respect of injuries he suffered during the course of his employment. H brought third party proceedings against SMP, his former insurers, seeking an indemnity in relation to D's action and against B, his brokers, for failure to renew the policy. The issue of whether SMP was liable to indemnify H was in dispute in both third party actions. The insurance contract included an arbitration clause, to which the International Arbitration Act 1974 s.7(2)(b) applied. SMP's application for a stay of the third party proceedings against it, pending determination of the indemnity issue by arbitration, was unsuccessful because the judge found that determination of the dispute between SMP and H in arbitration proceedings would not determine it as between SMP and B, or between H and B, hence s.7(2)(b) was prevented from operating. SMP appealed and the question arose whether the existence of the same issue in two sets of proceedings could defeat the operation of an arbitration clause, when that same issue, litigated alone, would otherwise meet the terms of s.7(2)(b).

Held, allowing the appeal, that the word "matter" in s.7(2)(b) denoted any claim for relief which was of a type which was proper for determination in a court, and did not include every issue which might arise for decision in the course of such a claim. Section 7(2)(b) would only be defeated if the issue in the proceedings between H and SMP was incapable of settlement by arbitration, which it was not.

SHIPOWNERS MUTUAL PROTECTION & INDEMNITY ASSOCIATION (LUXEMBOURG) v. HODGETTS [2000] 1 Lloyd's Rep. 58, Fitzgerald, P., Sup Ct (QUE).

244. Maritime arbitration – time limits – stay of action – meaning of "suit" under Hague Rules

[Arbitration Act 1996 s.9, s.12; Hague Rules Art.III r.6.]

T, the claimant in a shipping dispute, sought a declaration that the commencement of proceedings in the United States within the one year time limit prescribed by the Hague Rules Art.III r.6 amounted to the issue of a "suit". Thus r.6 had been complied with notwithstanding the fact that those proceedings had been stayed on the ground that the relevant bills of lading were governed by English law and a London arbitration clause. T contended that the US court had jurisdiction to determine the merits of the case and that, in any event, C had submitted to the jurisdiction of the US court. Following the stay, T had appointed an arbitrator in order to commence arbitration proceedings in England but C contended that the claim was time barred since the one year time limit for commencing proceedings had expired. T argued that because the US proceedings had been commenced within the time limit, the arbitration proceedings were not time barred. In the alternative, T contended that the court should exercise its discretion to grant an extension of time under the Arbitration Act 1996 s.12.

Held, refusing the declaration, that for the purpose of the one year time limit, the first action had to remain valid when reliance was placed on the one year rule in the second action, with the result that where the first action had been dismissed for want of prosecution or stayed owing to the invocation of an arbitration clause, that action did not constitute a "suit", *Fort Sterling Ltd v. South Atlantic Cargo Shipping NV (The Finnrose)* [1994] 1 Lloyd's Rep. 559, [1995] C.L.Y. 4504 applied. The proposition that the institution of proceedings in any jurisdiction in the world, irrespective of any contractual obligations relating to forum, could effectively prevent the discharge of liability by reason of passage of time would lead to absurd results. C had not submitted to the jurisdiction of the US court and its plea of forum non conveniens did not amount to a step in the action under s.9. It was not appropriate for the court to exercise its discretion to grant an extension of time since T had not established that it was not reasonably practical for it to have obtained a copy of the charterparty which contained the English arbitration clause.

THYSSEN INC v. CALYPSO SHIPPING CORP SA [2000] 2 All E.R. (Comm) 97, David Steel, J., QBD (Comm Ct).

245. Publications

Arbitration Act 1996. 2nd Ed. Paperback: £49.50. ISBN 0-632-05063-2. Blackwell Science (UK).

Binder, Peter – UNCITRAL Model on International Commercial Arbitration. Hardback: £130.00. ISBN 0-421-73940-1. Sweet & Maxwell.

Harrison, Reziya; Odams de Zylva, Martin – International Commercial Arbitration. Hardback: £125.00. ISBN 0-85308-621-4. Jordans.

International Arbitration Law Review: Vol 2. 1999. Hardback: £75.00. ISBN 0-421-69730-X. Sweet & Maxwell.

Salzedo, Simon; Lord, Richard – Arbitration and Mediation. Practice Notes. Paperback: £15.95. ISBN 1-85941-302-1. Cavendish Publishing Ltd.

ARMED FORCES

246. Air Force – disciplinary procedures – custody

AIR FORCE CUSTODY RULES 2000, SI 2000 2369; made under the Air Force Act 1955 s.75M. In force: October 2, 2000; £4.00.

These Rules set out the procedures which are to apply with respect to proceedings under the Air Force Act 1955 s.75C, s.75F(1) or s.75G(1), under which the authority of a judicial officer is required to keep a person in Air Force custody for more than 48 hours without charge, or for any period after charge. In particular, it makes provisions concerning the service of documents, notification requirements, reviews under s.47H(1), the determination of the time and place of any hearing, the conduct of hearings before a judicial officer and the forms to be used by the judicial officer in recording any decision taken, or order made, in respect of keeping a person in custody.

247. Air Force – Summary Appeal Court – disciplinary proceedings

SUMMARY APPEAL COURT (AIR FORCE) RULES 2000, SI 2000 2372; made under the Air Force Act 1955 s.83ZA, s.83ZC, s.83ZF, s.83ZJ. In force: October 2, 2000; £6.30.

These Rules regulate the practice and procedure to be followed in proceedings before the summary appeal court, established under the Air Force Act 1955 s.83ZA to hear appeals against findings recorded and punishments awarded on summary dealing. In particular, they make provision in relation to the service of documents, the bringing and abandonment of appeals, appeals procedure, the constitution of the summary appeal court, the admissibility of evidence, the exercise of the court's powers to vary any punishment awarded on summary dealing and the procedure concerning applications to the court to have a case stated for the opinion of the High Court.

248. Air Force – Summary Appeal Court – oaths

ADMINISTRATION OF OATHS (SUMMARY APPEAL COURT) (AIR FORCE) ORDER 2000, SI 2000 2378; made under the Air Force Act 1955 s.83ZK, s.223. In force: October 2, 2000; £1.00.

This Order makes provision for the administration of oaths to members of the summary appeal court established under the Air Force Act 1955 s.83ZA. It specifies the person by whom the oath is to be administered and the form and manner in which the oath is to be administered.

249. Armed Forces Discipline Act 2000 (c.4)

This Act amends the Army Act 1955, the Air Force Act 1955 and the Naval Discipline Act 1957 in relation to custody, the right to elect court martial trial and appeals against findings made or punishments awarded on summary dealing or summary trial.

This Act received Royal Assent on May 25, 2000.

250. Armed Forces Discipline Act 2000 (c.4) – Commencement Order

ARMED FORCES DISCIPLINE ACT 2000 (COMMENCEMENT AND TRANSITIONAL PROVISIONS) ORDER 2000, SI 2000 2366 (C.64); made under the Armed Forces Discipline Act 2000 s.28. Commencement details: bringing into force various provisions of the Act on October 2, 2000; £2.00.

This Order brings into force on October 2, 2000 all of the provisions of the Armed Forces Discipline Act 2000 other than s.26 and s.28 which were brought into force on Royal Assent.

251. Army – disciplinary procedures – custody

ARMY CUSTODY RULES 2000, SI 2000 2368; made under the Army Act 1955 s.75M. In force: October 2, 2000; £4.00.

These Rules set out the procedures which are to apply with respect to proceedings under the Army Act 1955 s.75C, s.75F(1) or s.75G(1), under which the authority of a judicial officer is required to keep a person in military custody for more than 48 hours without charge, or for any period after charge. In particular, it makes provisions concerning the service of documents, notification requirements, reviews under s.47H(1), the determination of the time and place of any hearing, the conduct of hearings before a judicial officer and the forms to be used by the judicial officer in recording any decision taken, or order made, in respect of keeping a person in custody.

252. Army – Summary Appeal Court – disciplinary proceedings

SUMMARY APPEAL COURT (ARMY) RULES 2000, SI 2000 2371; made under the Army Act 1955 s.83ZA, s.83ZC, s.83ZF, s.83ZJ. In force: October 2, 2000; £6.30.

These Rules regulate the practice and procedure to be followed in proceeding before the summary appeal court, established under the Army Act 1955 s.83ZA to hear appeals against findings recorded and punishments awarded on summary dealing. In particular, they make provision in relation to the service of documents, the bringing and abandonment of appeals, appeals procedure, the constitution of the summary appeal court, the admissibility of evidence, the exercise of the court's powers to vary any punishment awarded on summary dealing and the procedure concerning applications to the court to have a case stated for the opinion of the High Court.

253. Army – Summary Appeal Court – oaths

ADMINISTRATION OF OATHS (SUMMARY APPEAL COURT) (ARMY) ORDER 2000, SI 2000 2377; made under the Army Act 1955 s.83ZK, s.225. In force: October 2, 2000; £1.00.

This Order, which provides for the administration of oaths to members of the summary appeal court established under the Army Act 1955 s.83ZA, specifies the person by whom, and the form and manner in which, the oath is to be administered.

254. Courts martial – appeals

COURTS-MARTIAL APPEAL (AMENDMENT) RULES 2000, SI 2000 2228 (L.18); made under the Courts-Martial (Appeals) Act 1968 s.49. In force: October 2, 2000; £1.50.

The Human Rights Act 1998 gives the Courts Martial Appeal Court the power to make a declaration that a provision of primary legislation is incompatible with the European Convention on Human Rights 1950. These Rules amend the Courts-Martial (Appeal) Rules 1968 (SI 1968 1071) to provide the procedure for the making of a declaration of incompatibility, and in particular for the service of notice on the Crown as required by s.5 of the 1998 Act. In addition, they provide for the application of the Crime (Sentences) Act 1997 to certain sentences passed by courts martial.

255. Courts martial – functions of prosecuting authority – Air Force

COURTS-MARTIAL (ROYAL AIR FORCE) (AMENDMENT) RULES 2000, SI 2000 2375; made under the Air Force Act 1955 s.75, s.103. In force: October 2, 2000; £1.50.

These Rules amend the Courts-Martial (Royal Air Force) Rules 1997 (SI 1997 171) in consequence of the changes made by the Armed Forces Discipline Act 2000 to the functions of the prosecuting authority where an accused elects to be tried by court martial. In particular, they require the higher authority to notify the prosecuting authority where the accused has elected court martial trial; make provision as to the exercise by the prosecuting authority of its functions in relation to referring back a case on withdrawal of an election for court martial trial, where the election relates to two or more charges; and require the sentencing information to be provided to a court martial to include particulars of any police caution received by the accused and notice of whether or not the accused elected court martial trial.

256. Courts martial – functions of prosecuting authority – army

COURTS-MARTIAL (ARMY) (AMENDMENT) RULES 2000, SI 2000 2374; made under the Army Act 1955 s.75, s.103. In force: October 2, 2000; £1.50.

These Rules amend the Courts-Martial (Army) Rules 1997 (SI 1997 169) in consequence of the changes made by the Armed Forces Discipline Act 2000 to the functions of the prosecuting authority where an accused elects to be tried by court martial. In particular, they require the higher authority to notify the prosecuting authority where the accused has elected court martial trial; make provision as to the exercise by the prosecuting authority of its functions in relation to referring back a case on withdrawal of an election for court martial trial, where the election relates to two or more charges; and require the sentencing information to be provided to a court martial to include particulars of any police caution received by the accused and notice of whether or not the accused elected court martial trial.

257. Courts martial – functions of prosecuting authority – navy

COURTS-MARTIAL (ROYAL NAVY) (AMENDMENT) RULES 2000, SI 2000 2373; made under the Naval Discipline Act 1957 s.58. In force: October 2, 2000; £1.50.

These Rules amend the Courts-Martial (Royal Navy) Rules 1997 (SI 1997 170) in consequence of the changes made by the Armed Forces Discipline Act 2000 to the functions of the prosecuting authority where an accused elects to be tried by court martial. In particular, they require the higher authority to notify the prosecuting authority where the accused has elected court martial trial; make provision as to the exercise by the prosecuting authority of its functions in relation to referring back a case on withdrawal of an election for court martial trial, where the election relates to two or more charges; and require the sentencing information to be provided to a court martial to include particulars of any police caution received by the accused and notice of whether or not the accused elected court martial trial.

258. Courts martial – right to fair trial – compensation – terms of settlement

[Human Rights Act 1998 Sch.1 Part I Art.6.1.]

M and five other individuals serving in the armed forces had obtained a ruling in the European Court of Human Rights that their treatment during the course of court martial proceedings infringed their right to a fair hearing by an independent and impartial tribunal under the Human Rights Act 1998 Sch.1 Part I Art.6.1. Following the hearing negotiations took place between the parties and compensation terms were agreed. The matter was thereafter referred to the court by the British government together with details of the settlement terms in order to obtain the guidance of the court as to the appropriate level of compensation for a breach of Art.6.1.

Held, striking out the applications by agreement, that the court had taken note of the terms of settlement agreed between the parties and was satisfied that it reflected appropriate respect for human rights.

MCDAID v. UNITED KINGDOM; WARD v. UNITED KINGDOM; GILES v. UNITED KINGDOM; LEECE v. UNITED KINGDOM; SHORTERS v. UNITED KINGDOM; THWAITES v. UNITED KINGDOM *The Times*, October 18, 2000, J-P Costa (President), ECHR.

259. Courts martial – right to fair trial – impartiality of convening officer

See HUMAN RIGHTS: Moore v. United Kingdom. §3215

260. Criminal injuries compensation – personal injuries – UN peacekeeper – entitlement to compensation for injuries arising from war operations or military activity

W appealed against the dismissal ([1999] 1 W.L.R. 1209, [1999] C.L.Y. 257) of his appeal against the dismissal ([1998] C.O.D. 334, [1998] C.L.Y. 255) of his application for judicial review of the MoD's refusal to pay him compensation for injuries sustained while serving as a soldier in the UN peacekeeping force in Bosnia when a Serbian tank fired a single round into the building where W was stationed. In 1979, the MoD had introduced the Criminal Injuries Compensation (Overseas) Scheme to provide discretionary ex gratia compensation to members of the armed forces injured abroad by crimes of violence at levels similar to awards under the Criminal Injuries Compensation Board scheme for victims of such crimes in Great Britain. In 1994 the Minister of State had said in a Parliamentary statement that compensation would not be awarded for injuries sustained as a result of "war operations or military activity by warring factions", and that that definition applied to the situation in Bosnia. W contended that the MoD had acted unlawfully, that his injuries were not excluded by the Scheme as a Serbian attack on a UN peacekeeping base amounted to an international crime, and that there had been unfairness as soldiers going to Bosnia had not been informed of the exclusion. W argued that compensation was paid to soldiers injured in peacekeeping duty in Northern Ireland and should be available to him.

Held, dismissing the appeal (Lord Hobhouse dissenting), that the scheme was rational in refusing to make "military activity" and criminal activity mutually exclusive so that there was no reason why the exclusion should not apply to W. Although the court had sympathy with W's position no legitimate expectation of his had been frustrated and the decision was not unfair.

R. v. MINISTRY OF DEFENCE, *ex p.* WALKER [2000] 1 W.L.R. 806, Lord Slynn of Hadley, HL.

261. Disciplinary procedures – continuation in force

ARMY, AIR FORCE AND NAVAL DISCIPLINE ACTS (CONTINUATION) ORDER 2000, SI 2000 1814; made under the Armed Forces Act 1996 s.1. In force: July 12, 2000; £1.00.

This Order enables the Army Act 1955, the Air Force Act 1955 and the Naval Discipline Act 1957 to continue in force for 12 months beyond August 31, 2001.

262. Navy – conditions of employment

ROYAL NAVY TERMS OF SERVICE (RATINGS) (AMENDMENT) REGULATIONS 2000, SI 2000 1771; made under the Armed Forces Act 1966 s.2. In force: August 1, 2000; £1.50.

These Regulations amend the Royal Navy Terms of Service (Ratings) Regulations 1982 (SI 1982 834) by reducing from 18 to 12 months the notice period required to be given by a person exercising his right under those provisions to be discharged or transferred to the reserve. In addition, they provide that all recruits are entitled to determine their service on the giving of 14 days' notice.

263. Navy – conditions of employment – royal marines

ROYAL MARINES TERMS OF SERVICE (AMENDMENT) REGULATIONS 2000, SI 2000 1772; made under the Armed Forces Act 1966 s.2. In force: August 1, 2000; £1.50.

These Regulations amend the Royal Marines Terms of Service Regulations 1988 (SI 1988 1395) by reducing from 18 to 12 months the notice period required to be given by a person exercising his right under those provisions to be discharged or transferred to the reserve. In addition, they provide that all recruits are entitled to determine their service on the giving of 14 days' notice.

264. Navy – disciplinary procedures – custody

NAVAL CUSTODY RULES 2000, SI 2000 2367; made under the Naval Discipline Act 1957 s.47N. In force: October 2, 2000; £4.00.

These Rules set out the procedures which are to apply with respect to proceedings under the Naval Discipline Act 1957 s.47D, s.47G(1) or s.47H(1), under which the authority of a judicial officer is required to keep a person in naval custody for more than 48 hours without charge or for any period after charge. In particular, it makes provisions concerning the service of documents, notification requirements, reviews under s.47H(1), the determination of the time and place of any hearing, the conduct of hearings before a judicial officer and the forms to be used by the judicial officer in recording any decision taken, or order made, in respect of keeping a person in custody.

265. Navy – Summary Appeal Court – disciplinary proceedings

SUMMARY APPEAL COURT (NAVY) RULES 2000, SI 2000 2370; made under the Naval Discipline Act 1957 s.52FF, s.52FH, s.52FL, s.52FP. In force: October 2, 2000; £6.30.

These Rules regulate the practice and procedure to be followed in proceedings before the summary appeal court, established under the Naval Discipline Act 1957 s.52FF to hear appeals against findings recorded and punishments awarded on summary trial. In particular, they make provision in relation to the service of documents, the bringing and abandonment of appeals, appeals procedure, the constitution of the summary appeal court, the admissibility of evidence, the exercise of the court's powers to vary any punishment awarded on summary dealing and the procedure concerning applications to the court to have a case stated for the opinion of the High Court.

266. Navy – Summary Appeal Court – oaths

ADMINISTRATION OF OATHS (SUMMARY APPEAL COURT) (NAVY) ORDER 2000, SI 2000 2376; made under the Naval Discipline Act 1957 s.52FQ, s.135. In force: October 2, 2000; £1.00.

This Order, which provides for the administration of oaths to members of the summary appeal court established under the Naval Discipline Act 1957 s.52FF, specifies the person by whom, and the form and manner in which, the oath is to be administered.

267. **Reserve forces – reorganisation**

RESERVE FORCES ACT 1996 (RESERVE ASSOCIATIONS) ORDER 2000, SI 2000 2379; made under the Reserve Forces Act 1996 s.110, s.119. In force: October 1, 2000; £1.50.

This Order, which winds up the Eastern Wessex Association, being one of 14 existing territorial, auxiliary and reserve forces associations in the UK, alters the areas for which the existing Wessex Association and the existing South East Association are established so that they include the counties, unitary authorities and Channel Islands that formerly belonged to the Eastern Wessex Association. In addition, it makes provision in relation to the transfer of property, rights and liabilities.

268. **Sex discrimination – equal treatment – proportionality principle – European Union**

[Council Directive 76/207 on equal treatment for men and women as regards access to employment Art.2(2).]

K applied for voluntary service in the German Army, to carry out weapon maintenance duties. K was rejected on the basis, that under German law, women volunteers were excluded from the main body of the armed services and could only enlist in medical or military music services. K brought proceedings alleging sex discrimination and a reference was made to the ECJ for a preliminary ruling as to whether Council Directive 76/207 prohibited the national provision which imposed an exclusion of women from the armed services. The German Government contended that defence matters fell outside the ambit of Community law, and the limitation on the access of women to the armed service was justified by the exemption under Art.2(2), on the basis that the sex of the worker was a determining factor given the nature of the work carried out, an example of which was the use of arms.

Held, granting the application, that (1) the Directive was applicable in such situations, *Sirdar v. Secretary of State for Defence (C273/97)* [1999] All E.R. (EC) 928, [1999] C.L.Y. 264 followed and the principle of proportionality was applicable in determining the extent of the derogation permitted under Art.2(2), and (2) adopting an exclusively male composition for the armed forces contravened the principle of proportionality.

KREIL v. GERMANY (C285/98) *The Times*, February 22, 2000, Judge not specified, ECJ.

BANKING

269. **Alliance & Leicester plc (Group Reorganisation) Act 2000 (c.iii)**

This Act provides for the transfer to Alliance & Leicester plc of the undertakings of Girobank plc and Alliance & Leicester Personal Finance Ltd.

This Act received Royal Assent on February 10, 2000 and comes into force on February 10, 2000.

270. **Banking supervision – Bank of England – test for liability for tort of misfeasance in public office**

[Council Directive 77/780 on the coordination of the laws, regulations and administrative provisions relating to the taking up and pursuit of the business of credit institutions Art.3(1).]

TRDC and other creditors of BCCI, a bank in liquidation, brought proceedings against the Bank of England for misfeasance in public office. It was alleged that senior bank officials within the Bank of England had acted in bad faith when originally granting BCCI a banking licence as they had deliberately overlooked the ongoing operation of BCCI subsequent to granting the licence and, furthermore, had failed to close down BCCI when it was known that such action was necessary. It was also alleged that the Bank of England had acted in breach of the requirements contained within Council Directive 77/780. Two issues arose for preliminary ruling; (1) whether the Bank of England could be liable to TRDC for the tort of misfeasance in a public office, and (2) whether TRDC's losses were capable in law of being caused by the Bank of England's omissions. At first instance ([1996] 3 All E.R. 558, [1996] C.L.Y. 5701) it was held that the action was bound to fail and it was accordingly struck out. TRDC appealed. The Court of Appeal upheld the decision ([2000] 2 W.L.R. 15, [1999] C.L.Y. 4854), observing that the test as to liability for misfeasance in public office could be summed up as the decision maker "knowing at the time" of his decision that "it would cause damage to the plaintiff." TRDC appealed.

Held, dismissing the appeal, that (1) liability in the tort of misfeasance in public office arose where the actions of a public officer were carried out in the knowledge of, or with reckless indifference to the probability of, injury being caused to a plaintiff, or a class of persons of which the plaintiff was a member. Two forms of liability for misfeasance in public office existed at common law. It was clear that the first, involving the exercise of public power for improper or ulterior motives, was not relevant to the instant case. Accordingly, the court was concerned with the second form of liability which arose where a public officer acted beyond his powers and in the knowledge that such actions would probably result in injury to the plaintiff. Reckless indifference was sufficient to establish liability. It followed that TRDC, in order to claim any financial losses suffered, was required to prove that officials within the Bank of England had acted with a mind set of reckless indifference in relation to the illegality of their actions and the foreseeable losses arising from them. The test set out by the Court of Appeal of knowledge or foresight that an action would cause damage did not fall sufficiently within the established standard of proof in the law of tort, and (2) no obligations were imposed on Member States under Council Directive 77/780 which provided enforceable rights under EC Law for individuals seeking damages. At the time the Directive had come into force BCCI was already legitimately carrying out business in the UK. It followed that the Bank of England had not been under an obligation, pursuant to Art.3(1), to obtain authorisation for BCCI to continue its business in the UK. Furthermore, the Directive did not establish a general duty to supervise nor, when circumstances required it, an obligation to withdraw authorisation.

THREE RIVERS DC v. BANK OF ENGLAND (NO.3) [2000] 2 W.L.R. 1220, Lord Steyn, HL.

271. **Conversion – bankers duties – choses in action – material alteration to cheque payee details – impact upon validity**

[Bills of Exchange Act 1882 s.64.]

S instituted proceedings in conversion against a bank, L, following the theft of a cheque from S's premises. The payee details had subsequently been altered and the cheque presented for payment to L which duly collected the funds from S's account. S maintained that although the material alterations to the cheque rendered the cheque itself invalid, the cheque nevertheless retained its face value for the purposes of a claim in conversion under the Bills of Exchange Act 1882 s.64 and that for sound public policy reasons the risk that a cheque might be fraudulently altered should be carried by the collecting bank. S's claim was dismissed at first instance ([2000] 1 W.L.R. 1225), the judge awarding nominal damages only and S appealed.

Held, dismissing the appeal, that the use of the word "avoided" in s.64(1) of the Act was intended to render a cheque upon which a material alteration had been made null and void. In consequence no cause of action lay in conversion upon the face value of the cheque since it no longer constituted a chose in action for that sum. The fact of invalidity could not be altered by raising arguments of estoppel since when L presented the cheque for payment in accordance with standard banking practice, such action did not amount to a representation by L that the cheque was valid.

SMITH v. LLOYDS TSB BANK PLC; HARVEY JONES LTD v. WOOLWICH PLC; *sub nom.* SMITH v. LLOYDS TSB GROUP PLC [2001] Q.B. 541, Pill, L.J., CA.

272. **Creditors – payments unauthorised payment by bank discharging customer's debt**

C, a company in liquidation, brought an action seeking repayment of a sum paid, without authority, from its account by LB, its bank, in accordance with a garnishee order nisi which had not been made absolute. The district judge rejected LB's submission that the payment had discharged an existing debt, and that C had accordingly suffered no loss, and gave summary judgment for C. The judge, in allowing LB's appeal, held that LB had reasonable grounds for relying on the equitable doctrine established in *B Liggett (Liverpool) Ltd v. Barclays Bank Ltd* [1928] 1 K.B. 48 whereby a person who, without authority, paid the debts of another was allowed the benefit of such a payment. C appealed.

Held, allowing the appeal, that there having been no authorisation or ratification by C of LB's payment to the third party, LB had not been entitled to make it, and accordingly the sum should be repaid. While LB's payment was to the benefit of C, that was not sufficient to establish an equity in LB's favour, *Cleadon Trust Ltd, Re* [1939] Ch. 286 applied and *Liggett* distinguished.

CRANTRAVE LTD (IN LIQUIDATION) v. LLOYDS BANK PLC [2000] Q.B. 917, Pill, L.J., CA.

273. **Deposits – prohibition on acceptance of deposits**

BANKING ACT 1987 (EXEMPT TRANSACTIONS) (AMENDMENT) REGULATIONS 2000, SI 2000 635; made under the Banking Act 1987 s.4. In force: April 1, 2000; £1.00.

These Regulations revoke the Banking Act 1987 (Exempt Transactions) Regulations 1997 (SI 1997 817) Reg.7 and Sch.1 so that the acceptance of deposits by certain retail and other co-operative societies is no longer exempt from the prohibition on the acceptance of deposits in the Banking Act 1987 s.3 by virtue of the society's participation in the Co-operative Deposit Protection Scheme.

274. **Disclosure – information received for dual purposes – restriction in Banking Act 1987 s.82(1)**

[Banking Act 1987 s.41, s.82.]

B brought a claim against CL and others for damages for the alleged professional negligence of accountants and auditors in the period before the collapse of B. Following the collapse, the Head of the Bank of England's Special Investigations Unit was instructed to investigate the collapse upon the request of the Chancellor of the Exchequer and he was also appointed to conduct an internal inquiry for the Bank of England under the provisions of the Banking Act 1987 s.41 (1). That resulted in the production of a large number of transcripts of interviews which the judge declared were subject to the restriction on disclosure contained in s.82 of the Act. DT, a codefendant, appealed on the grounds that (1) the information was not subject to the restriction in s.82(1) of the Act as it was obtained for a dual purpose and the primary purpose was not a purpose under, or for the Act, and (2) the information was already in the public domain and the protection of s.82(1) had been lost.

Held, allowing the appeal, that (1) both purposes of the investigation were purposes under the Act and therefore the first submission was groundless. Duality of purpose was only relevant if the non Banking Act purpose was dominant so that the Banking Act purpose could be ignored, *Bank of Credit and Commerce International (Overseas) Ltd (In Liquidation) v. Price Waterhouse (No.3)* [1998] Ch.84, [1997] C.L.Y. 316 doubted and, (2) the transcripts were in the public domain having been put forward as evidence in earlier proceedings and therefore were not protected by the restriction in s.82(1).

BARINGS PLC (IN LIQUIDATION) v. COOPERS & LYBRAND (NO.1); *sub nom.* BARINGS FUTURES (SINGAPORE) PTE LTD (IN LIQUIDATION) v. MATTER; BARINGS FUTURES (SINGAPORE) PTE LTD (IN LIQUIDATION) v. MATTAR [2000] 1 W.L.R. 2353, Lord Woolf, M.R., CA.

275. **Evidence – bankers books – disclosure in director disqualification proceedings**

See EVIDENCE: Howglen Ltd, *Re* (Application for Disclosure). §308

276. **Financial institutions – credit institutions – Council Directive**

BANKING CONSOLIDATION DIRECTIVE (CONSEQUENTIAL AMENDMENTS) REGULATIONS 2000, SI 2000 2952; made under the European Communities Act 1972 s.2. In force: November 22, 2000; £2.00.

These Regulations make consequential amendments to give effect to European Parliament and Council Directive 2000/12 ([2000] OJ L126/1) relating to the taking up and pursuit of the business of credit institutions, which codifies and repeals Council Directives 73/183, 77/780, 89/299, 89/646, 89/647, 92/30 and 92/121. They make the necessary changes to UK enactments which refer to the repealed Directives.

277. **Forgery – cheques – constructive knowledge of forgery**

BB paid out substantial sums on cheques with forged signatures and P appealed against the refusal to strike out part of BB's defence which alleged that P had constructive knowledge of the forgery. P contended that it had no actual knowledge of forgery.

Held, allowing the appeal, that the duty of care owed by a customer to its bank in respect of forged payments only arose where the customer had actual knowledge of the forgery. Those parts of the defence relating to constructive knowledge were struck out.

PRICE MEATS LTD v. BARCLAYS BANK PLC [2000] 2 All E.R. (Comm) 346, Arden, J., Ch D.

278. **Guarantees – amendments – material alteration nullity**

S, a guarantor, appealed against a decision that the guarantee he had signed had not been avoided by the insertion by the creditor bank, R, of the name and address of a purported service agent, C, without the knowledge or consent of S, after the guarantee had been signed and duly executed. R had admitted making changes to the guarantee after signature without S's approval, and S, placing reliance on the rule in *Pigot's Case* (1614) 11 Co. Rep. 266, contended that the judge had erred in failing to treat the insertion of C's details as a material alteration to the guarantee without S's approval, rendering it a nullity.

Held, dismissing the appeal, that as the insertion of C's details had not operated to alter or accelerate S's liability to make payment under the guarantee, it had not been potentially prejudicial to his legal rights and obligations and had, therefore, not been material, *Pigot's Case* distinguished. Furthermore, the alteration to the guarantee was merely procedural and had not altered the operation and the commercial use of the instrument and did not affect the enforceability of the guarantee.

RAIFFEISEN ZENTRALBANK OSTERREICH AG v. CROSSSEAS SHIPPING LTD [2000] 1 W.L.R. 1135, Potter, L.J., CA.

279. Guarantees – letters of guarantee – place of payment in absence of contractual term

B, a bank, entered into a letter of guarantee with the State Ownership Fund of Romania, SOFR, which then made a demand for payment under the terms of the letter. The payment requested was to be made to an account with a Romanian bank, although the place where the account was held was not specified. It was submitted that the place of payment was the place where the demand was to be made, which was to B in England at the address given on the guarantee letter itself. The payment was to be in dollars and the contract governed by English law.

Held, allowing the application to discharge an asset freezing order made against B and requiring that B open an interest bearing account in the name of SOFR and pay into the account the sum demanded under the guarantee, that in the absence of specific contractual provision, the place of payment was to be the place of demand since that was where B's liability crystallised. The request that payment be made into a specified Romanian account was not a term of the contract but an administrative request.

BRITTEN NORMAN LTD (IN LIQUIDATION) v. STATE OWNERSHIP FUND OF ROMANIA [2000] Lloyd's Rep. Bank. 315, Peter Leaver Q.C., Ch D.

280. Letters of credit – bankers duties – ambiguous term as to documents to be tendered – reasonable construction of ambiguous term

[Uniform Customs and Commercial Code 1993 Art.5.]

MCB issued a letter of credit which was confirmed by CAI. CAI forwarded to MCB documents, said to be required under the letter of credit, which MCB refused to accept on the basis that they were defective. CAI obtained summary judgment for damages against MCB who appealed. The question arose as to whether the disputed documents were essential for acceptance, payment or negotiation under the letter of credit.

Held, dismissing the appeal, that pursuant to the Uniform Customs and Commercial Code 1993 Art.5 it was a term of the contract that a letter of credit had to state precisely which documents were required. The wording of the letter of credit created genuine doubt as to whether the disputed documents were essential for acceptance, payment or negotiation of the letter of credit. Given the time constraints in the instant case, it was not reasonable for CAI to request elucidation from MCB. In relation to commercial credits, it was established law that an issuing banker was entitled to act upon a reasonable meaning of any ambiguous expression concerning the documents to be tendered. Although there was in law no agency relationship between an issuing bank and a confirming bank, the confirming bank was in terms of commerce the correspondent or the issuing bank and acted for it. This relationship was sufficient for the rule that an agent was to be excused for acting on a reasonable, even if wrong, interpretation of his principal instructions, to apply. The letter of credit failed to comply with the requirement of Art.5 for precise statement and therefore had to be construed against MCB, *Midland Bank Ltd v. Seymour* [1955] 2 Lloyd's Rep. 147, [1955] C.L.Y. 161 and *Commercial Banking Co of Sydney v. Jalsard Pty* [1973] A.C. 279, [1972] C.L.Y. 181 applied.

CREDIT AGRICOLE INDOSUEZ v. MUSLIM COMMERCIAL BANK LTD [2000] 1 All E.R. (Comm) 172, Sir Christopher Staughton, CA.

281. Letters of credit – bankers duties – discrepancies in documents – whether issuing bank entitled to indemnity

GB and a third party, C, agreed that GB would issue letters of credit and that C would reimburse GB for payments that GB was required to make. Both the agreement and letters of credit under it were governed by the Uniform Customs and Practice for Documentary Credits No.500 (UCP). In proceedings arising out of a letter of credit issued by GB, summary judgment was given against GB. In the summary proceedings GB was not allowed to rely on alleged discrepancies in the documents provided under the terms of the letter of credit. It fell to be determined whether the documents did in fact fail to conform with the letter of credit and, if so, whether GB was entitled to reimbursement or indemnity from C.

Held, giving judgment for C, that the documents in question failed to conform to the letter of credit. In view of the express incorporation of the UCP into the agreement between GB and C the agreement had to be construed, if possible, in a manner consistent with the UCP and the banker's duty of strict compliance. Furthermore, GB was unable to rely on Art.18(a) of the UCP having the effect that the defective documents were accepted at C's risk. Accordingly GB was not entitled to reimbursement or indemnity.

CREDIT AGRICOLE INDOSUEZ v. GENERALE BANK (NO.2) [1999] 2 All E.R. (Comm) 1016, David Steel, J., QBD (Comm Ct).

282. **Letters of credit – fraud – assignment by beneficiary to confirming bank of rights under letter of credit**

BP issued a "deferred payment" letter of credit in favour of B, requiring the filing of certain documents with BS, the confirming bank. The letter was subject to the Uniform Customs and Practice for Documentary Credits (UCP) (1993 Revision). BS informed B of the letter of credit and offered B the possibility of discounting. Having presented documents to BS which appeared to accord with the letter of credit, B wrote to BS requesting the discount which had been offered and assigning to BS its rights under the letter of credit. Approximately five months before the deferred payment date, BS transmitted the relevant funds to B. Shortly thereafter, BS discovered that the documents which had been presented by B included forgeries. When the deferred payment became due, BP refused to pay BS, on the ground that BS had no greater rights than B who had been guilty of fraud. Preliminary issues having been determined in favour of BP ([1999] 2 All E.R. (Comm) 18), BS appealed, arguing that (1) the judge had erred in ruling that B's rights had been assigned to it. BS contended that, since its transaction with B had involved the purchase of B's rights against it, the purpose of the transaction had been to extinguish B's rights under the letter of credit against BS and BP. Accordingly, there had been nothing to assign; (2) in the event that they were assignees, the normal rule that assignments take effect subject to equities should not apply in the case where a promise under a letter of credit was the subject of an assignment, and (3) since its offer of a discount had not amounted to a breach of mandate, it was entitled to reimbursement as agents of BP under the UCP.

Held, dismissing the appeal, that (1) B's rights had been assigned to BS. Given the discount which had been offered to B, it could not be said that all of B's rights had been extinguished. BS and B had intended to keep alive a joint and several obligation affecting both BS and BP, and that obligation had been assigned to BS; (2) it would not be appropriate to depart from the usual rule that a defence which was available against an assignor should also be available against the assignee. Accordingly, BS had to bear the consequences of B's fraudulent actions, and (3) the mere fact that BS's offer of a discount had not constituted a breach of mandate did not give it a right of reimbursement against BP. Whilst BS had been entitled to offer the discount, that step had not been taken with BP's authority.

BANCO SANTANDER SA v. BAYFERN LTD; *sub nom.* BANCO SANTANDER SA v. BANQUE PARIBAS [2000] 1 All E.R. (Comm) 776, Waller, L.J., CA.

283. **Letters of credit – fraud – reinbursement after authorised payment made to beneficiary**

GB issued a letter of credit nominating CA as the negotiating bank. After crediting the beneficiary under the letter of credit, CA requested reimbursement by GB. GB refused to pay alleging irregularities in the documents. CA applied for summary judgment. After the hearing had commenced GB, in the absence of any formal pleading, produced a document from the beneficiary which it claimed amounted to irrefutable evidence of the beneficiary's fraud.

Held, granting CA's application, that GB could not rely upon the fraud exception to a letter of credit unless it had done so formally. It was not possible at this stage to say that there was a clear case of fraud. In any event, the beneficiary in the present case had been paid and, since the purpose of the fraud exception was to prevent a beneficiary benefiting from his fraud, the doctrine of the fraud exception had no application once the beneficiary had been paid. Where an authorised payment had been made under a letter of credit, the paying bank was entitled to the reimbursement promised by the issuing bank.

CREDIT AGRICOLE INDOSUEZ v. GENERALE BANK (NO.1) [1999] 2 All E.R. (Comm) 1009, Rix, J., QBD (Comm Ct).

284. Letters of credit – jurisdiction – principal contractual obligation – place of payment

[Brussels Convention on Jurisdiction and Enforcement of Judgments in Civil and Commercial Matters 1968 Art.5(1).]

CAI, a French bank with a Genevan branch, gave a letter of credit to CFC in respect of a vessel to be delivered by CFC to buyers in Taipei. The letter of credit stated that on receipt of documents confirming the sale, CAI would make payment to CFC "as per your instructions". The vessel was delivered on August 21, 1998. CFC produced documents to CAI and requested payment to its bank in Taipei. CAI refused to pay on the ground that the documents were incomplete. CAI produced documents on two further occasions, on the second changing their payment instructions to London, but CAI continued to refuse, citing the fact that the letter of credit had stated that delivery had to take place between August 17 and August 20. CFC brought an application for payment of the sums outstanding, and the judge at first instance held that in accordance with the Brussels Convention 1968 Art.5(1) the contractual obligation was for the right to receive payment in London and therefore England was the appropriate forum. He therefore granted summary judgment to CFC. CAI appealed, arguing that (1) the principal contractual obligation between the parties was for CAI to examine the documents produced by CFC in Geneva and that the obligation as to payment per CFC's instructions was merely secondary, and (2) the letter of credit had clearly specified that delivery had to take place between August 17 and August 20.

Held, dismissing the appeal, that (1) the English courts did have jurisdiction. In a contractual dispute except those involving employment contracts it was not necessary to seek to pinpoint the obligation that characterised the contract but rather to identify the obligation of which performance was sought, *Shenavai v. Kreischer (C266/85)* [1987] E.C.R. 239, [1988] C.L.Y. 1468 applied. The crux of the claim was CAI's failure to pay and therefore that was the critical contractual obligation. The obligation to examine the documents was secondary. It was clear from the face of the letter of credit, and in accordance with banking practice, that CFC were entitled to choose the place of payment and that having chosen London, CAI were obliged to pay them there. This right to choose did not take the contract outside the jurisdictional rule in Art.5(1) and an allegation of forum shopping was unfounded, and (2) in relation to the discrepancy alleged by CAI, the judge had been right to find that reference to delivery between August 17 and August 20 did not form part of the description of the goods and therefore there had been no discrepancy justifying CAI's refusal to pay.

CREDIT AGRICOLE INDOSUEZ v. CHAILEASE FINANCE CORP; *sub nom.* CHAILEASE FINANCE CORP v. CREDIT AGRICOLE INDOSUEZ [2000] 1 All E.R. (Comm) 399, Potter, L.J., CA.

285. Letters of credit – summary judgments – arguable defence

B agreed to issue letters of credit to A, secured on financial guarantees. A approached P, insurance brokers, to suggest insurers who would be able to offer the guarantees. A chose M as insurers, although they were not on the Lloyds list, and P alleged that they had not recommended them. B discovered that M were not credit worthy and refused to accept the policies. Shortly afterwards P, on the understanding that it would be given the monies due under the letters of credit, entered into an unsuccessful joint venture with S for the purchase of a ship. S brought an application for summary judgment as assignees of the letters of credit. The application was refused and S appealed, arguing that B had no defence as valid letters of credit were equivalent to cash and S was entitled to the full sums outstanding.

Held, dismissing the appeal, that although the principles that a letter of credit was equivalent to cash and that a set off was not a defence were still good law, the instant case was unusual because of the extent to which B were concerned in the transaction as a whole. It would therefore be unfair to enter summary judgment against them if they were able to show a real possibility of a counterclaim that amounted to a defence. There was sufficient evidence to raise arguable defences of misrepresentation and breach of duty by P, and therefore the case should go to trial.

SAFA LTD v. BANQUE DU CAIRE [2000] 2 All E.R. (Comm) 567,Waller, L.J., CA.

286. **Misfeasance in public office – Bank of England – liability in tort to shareholders**

[Banking Act 1987.]

H was the chairman, and also a shareholder, in a family owned company, BI, which was engaged in the purchase and rental of housing stock. The business involved the taking of deposits from the public and in consequence required the regulatory approval of BE under the Banking Act 1987. BE became dissatisfied with the manner in which the company was being managed and required substantial changes to be made including the sale of all unoccupied properties. H resigned and was replaced by HA. H alleged that the housing stock had been sold off fraudulently by HA at an under value and that BE had deliberately chosen to refrain from intervening. H commenced proceedings against BE for misfeasance in public office as a result of its alleged failure to supervise adequately BI. The action was struck out at first instance ([1999] Lloyd's Rep. Bank. 478), the judge finding that H had failed to establish dishonesty on the part of BE and that the proper claimant should have been BI. H appealed, contending that (1) BE had threatened to put BI into liquidation at a meeting when H had indicated an intention to pursue an application for an injunction to prevent the sale of the properties in the absence of independent valuations; (2) BE had issued secret instructions to an independent investigator not to criticise management decisions but to restrict his commentary to the allegations of fraud, and (3) if the incidents relied upon by H were viewed as a whole, then there was a reasonably arguable case of dishonesty for BE to answer.

Held, dismissing the appeal, that (1) the response of BE to the threat of an injunction was in no way surprising given the risk to the funds of investors if injunction proceedings were ongoing; (2) there was no likelihood that H would be able to establish any improper instruction on the part of BE to W since both BE and W denied the claim and H had no cogent evidence to support the allegation; (3) if the alleged improprieties were viewed in the round then they became even less significant, and (4) it was not open to the shareholders to bring an action in tort to recover damage caused to BI.

HALL v. BANK OF ENGLAND [2000] Lloyd's Rep. Bank. 186, Sir Richard Scott V.C., CA.

287. **National Savings Bank – individual savings accounts – limitations**

NATIONAL SAVINGS BANK (INVESTMENT DEPOSITS) (LIMITS) (AMENDMENT) ORDER 2000, SI 2000 1421; made under the National Savings Bank Act 1971 s.4. In force: May 27, 2000; £1.00.

This Order amends the National Savings Bank (Investment Deposits) (Limits) Order 1977 (SI 1977 1210) by increasing the limit on the amount which may be paid into an individual savings account managed by the Director of Savings in the tax year 2000-1 and enabling the Director of Savings to accept deposits in respect of individual savings accounts transferred by account holders from other account managers pursuant to the Individual Savings Account Regulations 1998 (SI 1998 1870).

288. **Promissory notes – cheques – time of the essence**

See REAL PROPERTY: Homes v. Smith. §4621

289. **Publications**

Commercial Banking Regulatory Handbook. Paperback: £48.95. ISBN 0-7656-0653-4. M.E. Sharpe.

Consumer Banking Regulatory Handbook. Paperback: £48.95. ISBN 0-7656-0652-6. M.E. Sharpe.

Jacob, Isaac; McMaster, Peter – Law Relating to Cheques. Hardback. ISBN 0-406-10649-5. Butterworths.

McBain, Graham S. – Butterworths Banking Law Handbook. 5th Ed. Butterworth Handbooks. Paperback: £80.00. ISBN 0-406-93229-8. Butterworths Law.

Penn, Graham; Wadsley, Joan – Law and Practice of Domestic Banking. 2nd Ed. Paperback: £30.00. ISBN 0-421-41380-8. Sweet & Maxwell.

Reed, Chris; Walden, Ian – Cross Border Electronic Banking. 2nd Ed. Centre for Commercial Law Studies/Information Technology Law Unit. Hardback: £130.00. ISBN 1-85978-555-7. LLP Professional Publishing.

Securities Regulatory Handbook. Paperback: £48.95. ISBN 0-7656-0654-2. M.E. Sharpe.

Wynne, Geoffrey – Butterworths Banking Law Guide. Butterworths Guide. Paperback: £75.00. ISBN 0-406-04935-1. Butterworths.

CHARITIES

290. **Accounts – annual reports by trustees**

CHARITIES (ACCOUNTS AND REPORTS) REGULATIONS 2000, SI 2000 2868; made under the Charities Act 1993 s.42, s.44, s.45, s.86. In force: November 15, 2000; £2.00.

These Regulations, which extend only to England and Wales, amend the Charities (Accounts and Reports) Regulations 1995 (SI 1995 2724) by making new provision with respect to the form and content of the accounts of charities and the annual reports of charity trustees for financial years which begin on or after January 1, 2001.

291. **Charitable trusts – Box Moor Trust**

CHARITIES (BOXMOOR ESTATE, HEMEL HEMPSTEAD) ORDER 2000, SI 2000 844; made under the Charities Act 1993 s.17. In force: April 5, 2000; £2.50.

This Order gives effect to a Scheme of the Charity Commissioners for the charity presently known as the Boxmoor Estate. It changes the name of the charity to the Box Moor Trust and creates a new body of trustees which will in future be democratically elected. The area of benefit of the charity is now identified by means of a deposited map; the constitution and powers of the trustees are modernised; provision is made for the charity's land to be held for the purposes of public recreation; and there is a power to apply surplus income for various purposes within the area of benefit for purposes including the relief of the aged, sick, disabled and poor people, the promotion of recreational facilities and the advancement of education.

292. Charitable trusts – Bristol, Clifton and West of England Zoological Society

CHARITIES (BRISTOL, CLIFTON AND WEST OF ENGLAND ZOOLOGICAL SOCIETY) ORDER 2000, SI 2000 1808; made under the Charities Act 1993 s.17. In force: July 23, 2000; £1.50.

This Order gives effect to a Scheme sealed by the Charity Commissioners for England and Wales for the Bristol, Clifton and West of England Zoological Society which is regulated in part by the Bristol Clifton and West of England Zoological Society's Act 1901 and the Bristol Clifton and West of England Zoological Society Act 1969. The Scheme alters some of the statutory provisions contained in the Acts with the effect that the Society's power to borrow money will no longer be limited to a maximum amount of £500,000.

293. Charitable trusts – Corporation of the Hall of Arts and Science

CHARITIES (CORPORATION OF THE HALL OF ARTS AND SCIENCES) ORDER 2000, SI 2000 891; made under the Charities Act 1993 s.17. In force: April 9, 2000; £1.50.

This Order gives effect to a Scheme of the Charity Commissioners for the charity known as the Corporation of the Hall of Arts and Sciences. The Scheme alters some of the statutory provisions governing the Corporation with the effect that it shall have greater power to borrow money and to mortgage or charge its property.

294. Charitable trusts – Epsom College – administration scheme

CHARITIES (ROYAL MEDICAL FOUNDATION OF EPSOM COLLEGE) ORDER 2000, SI 2000 1639; made under the Charities Act 1993 s.17. In force: July 2, 2000; £2.50.

This Order gives effect to a Scheme of the Charity Commissioners for the charity known as Epsom College, formerly the Royal Medical Benevolent College, to be known in future as the Royal Medical Foundation of Epsom College. Changes have been made to enable the charity to carry out its two primary functions, for benevolent medical purposes and for educational purposes, more efficiently by providing for focused management, a modern administrative structure, clarity in fund-raising, simpler accounting, the removal of some outdated provisions and limited liability for those managing the School.

295. Charitable trusts – gift unlimited in time – donor's intentions

BW, a charity, was by virtue of deeds of gift dating from 1849 and 1852, the trustee of land intended to be used as a school. It sought a declaration with a view to determining whether the land was held on the trusts of the deeds or on resulting trust for the successors of the grantors of the land.

Held, granting a declaration in favour of BW, that where a gift was unlimited in time but subject to a clause of defeasance or a power of revocation, it was a question of construction whether the donor intended to supply the gift to charity in perpetuity or for a limited purpose and period. The 1849 and 1852 deeds revealed an intention by the donors to transfer the land in perpetuity for use as a school, subject only to a clause of defeasance. Since the relevant provisions for reverter were void for remoteness, BW held its possessory title for charity upon the trust of the deeds rather than upon trust for the successors of the grantors, *Cooper's Conveyance Trusts, Re* [1956] 1 W.L.R. 1096, [1956] C.L.Y. 1008 applied.

BATH AND WELLS DIOCESAN BOARD OF FINANCE v. JENKINSON (2001) 2 W.T.L.R. 353, Evans-Lombe, J., Ch D.

296. Charitable trusts – proceedings – property vested in Official Custodian – requirement for consent of Charity Commission for "charity proceedings" under Charities Act 1993 s.33(8)

[Charities Act 1993 s.22, s.33(8).]

AIM was a registered Buddhist charity which operated premises as a temple. AIM's structure was set out in a scheme of administration made in the Chancery Division in March 1996. Clause 5 of the scheme provided that AIM's management would be vested in a governing council, consisting of a patron and not more than seven other members. The patron was provided for by cl.7, which stated that N would be the first patron and would remain as such until another person was elected at a general meeting. The holding and conduct of general meetings was dealt with in cl.9 and cl.9(2), which allowed for an extraordinary general meeting to be called at any time by either the patron or the council. Clause 9(3) also provided that issues other than the removal of the patron were to be decided by a simple majority of the full members present and voting. At the material time, part of the temple was occupied by N, who claimed that he was still the patron. M and others, claiming to be the members of the governing council and trustees of AIM, were in dispute with N concerning his rights of occupation and sought an order for possession. M claimed that N had been removed as patron at an extraordinary general meeting in October 1996 when 81 members of AIM were present, 80 of whom elected S as patron. N ignored the notice to vacate the temple and changed the locks on the building, arguing that he could only be removed as patron by two thirds of all the members of AIM as provided for in cl.7(3)(e). N also claimed that M and the others had been removed from their posts within AIM by a subsequent extraordinary general meeting in November 1997. At first instance, the application for possession was dismissed, on the basis that the property was vested in the Official Custodian for Charities, who was not a party, and who should have been joined as such. Further, that N's deselection as patron in October 1996 had been ineffective. M appealed.

Held, allowing the appeal, that (1) the judge had erred in holding that M and the others were not entitled to possession on the ground that the property was vested in the Official Custodian of Charities. It was clear from the Charities Act 1993 s.22 that the Official Custodian had no basis for exercising any powers of management over the property and affairs of the charity whose property had been vested in him. The trustees of AIM were, subject to any valid claims that N might have, entitled to possession of the property of AIM. The appeal would be allowed on that ground alone, and (2) the claim for possession and N's counterclaim that he was entitled to remain in the temple would be remitted for trial to the county court. The proceedings would be stayed, however, as they concerned issues relating to the administration of AIM that fell within the definition of "charity proceedings" in s.33(8) and could not continue without the consent of either the Charity Commissioners or a judge of the Chancery Division and until an attempt at alternative dispute resolution had been made.

MUMAN v. NAGASENA [2000] 1 W.L.R. 299, Nourse, L.J., CA.

297. Charitable trusts – Rochester Bridge Trust

CHARITIES (THE ROCHESTER BRIDGE TRUST) ORDER 2000, SI 2000 3098; made under the Charities Act 1993 s.17. In force: November 30, 2000; £1.75.

The Order relates to the Charity known as The Rochester Bridge Trust which is established for the maintenance and improvement of the two adjacent bridges known as the Rochester Bridge and of the Medway Tunnel, and for purposes connected with the River Medway and for the promotion of such other charitable purposes as may from time to time be determined in the UK, primarily in the County of Kent. By a Scheme of the Charity Commissioners made on June 1, 1999 under the Charities Act 1993 s.16, the Court was reconstituted and provided with up to date objects and powers for the regulation of the Charity. This Scheme removes the restrictions imposed on the Court's powers of leasing by the Rochester Bridge Act 1846, by repealing the provisions of that Act and amending clause 5(1) of the said Scheme of 1999. It also repeals the remaining provisions of the Rochester Bridge Amendment Act 1853 as these are now redundant.

298. Charters – Licensed Victuallers' National Homes – application of funds

LICENSED VICTUALLERS' NATIONAL HOMES (CHARTER AMENDMENT) ORDER 2000, SI 2000 1348; made under the Charities Act 1993 s.15. In force: June 1, 2000; £1.00.

This Order amends the Charter of the Licensed Victuallers' National Homes to give effect to a Scheme made by the Charity Commissioners for England and Wales extending the permitted application of the funds of the Licensed Victuallers' National Homes. The funds will now benefit distressed or aged persons who have worked in breweries and distilleries and other distressed or aged persons in need, as well as continuing to benefit distressed or aged former licensed victuallers, to whom priority will be given.

299. Colleges – exempt charities – Royal College of Art

EXEMPT CHARITIES ORDER 2000, SI 2000 1826; made under the Charities Act 1993 Sch.2 para.(c). In force: August 1, 2000; £1.00.

This Order declares the Royal College of Art to be an exempt charity within the meaning of the Charities Act 1993 with effect from August 1, 2000. An exempt charity is not required to be registered with the Charity Commissioners and the Commissioners cannot exercise any powers under the Act in relation to an exempt charity except at the charity's request.

300. National Lottery – sports and arts – grants

SPORT AND ARTS JOINT SCHEME (AUTHORISATION) ORDER 2000, SI 2000 3320; made under the National Lottery etc Act 1993 Sch.3A para.2. In force: January 18, 2001; £1.50.

This Order authorises the Sport and Arts joint scheme for the distribution of National Lottery funds by Sport England and the Arts Council of England.

301. Publications

Church Schools and Charity Law. £5.00. ISBN 0-7151-4926-1. Church House Publishing.

King, Michael – Charities Act, Explained. The Point of Law Series. Paperback: £25.00. ISBN 0-11-702384-1. The Stationery Office Books.

CIVIL EVIDENCE

302. Admissibility – appeals test for admission of fresh evidence following trial – requirement of reasonable diligence

[Civil Procedure Rules 1998 (SI 1998 3132).]

A appealed the dismissal of his application to admit fresh evidence and a refusal to order a retrial following judgment against him on liability in an action brought by T, his former tenant. T had sought to recover compensation arising from the loss of her uninsured possessions in a fire at the property. At trial, an expert witness on T's behalf had given evidence that it had been impossible to pinpoint the exact source of the outbreak of the fire but that it was most likely that it had started near electrical distribution equipment. A's expert witness had suggested that it was very likely that the seat of the fire was close to T's son's bed and that it could have been caused by a naked flame. T's son, L, denied that he had been a smoker at the material time. The trial judge accepted T's evidence and, on the balance of probabilities, blamed the electrical distribution system. A appealed, submitting that (1) it had not been reasonable, on the evidence, for the judge to conclude that the seat of the fire was the electrical distribution system; (2) the judge had erred in refusing to allow him to introduce evidence, obtained by chance, from a former school friend of L's that stated that L had been a regular smoker during his schooldays, and (3) the judge had erred in concluding that the test for the reception of fresh evidence was more restrictive than the criteria set out in *Ladd v. Marshall* [1954] 1 W.L.R. 1489, [1954] C.L.Y. 2507.

Held, allowing the appeal and ordering a retrial, that whilst *Ladd* did not constitute authority when interpreting the Civil Procedure Rules 1998, it was important to consider the test therein in order to give effect to the overriding objective to deal with cases justly. There was no justification for adopting a stricter approach to that found in *Ladd* for applications to admit fresh evidence post trial, and *Ladd* applied. In the instant case the approach of the judge had been wrong as the fresh evidence had been obtained in such an unusual manner that it could not have been obtained before trial by the exercise of reasonable diligence.

TOWNSEND v. ACHILLEAS; KING v. ACHILLEAS [2001] C.P. Rep. 45, Mummery, L.J., CA.

303. Admissibility – disciplinary procedures – General Medical Council – illegally obtained evidence

The Professional Conduct Committee of the General Medical Council found I to be guilty of serious professional misconduct and suspended her registration for 12 months following her failure to return to her duties as a Senior House Officer, her failure to give any or any adequate notice of her intention to leave her post or any subsequent explanation. I's defence to the complaints made against her was based upon medical grounds. I appealed the decision contending that, whilst she had given her consent to the partial disclosure of her medical records, the committee had overstepped that consent and as such the information relied upon by the committee in reaching the decision had been obtained illegally and was therefore inadmissible.

Held, dismissing the appeal, that the admissibility of evidence in disciplinary proceedings was not dependent upon it having been obtained legally, *R. v. Khan (Sultan)* [1997] A.C. 558, [1996] C.L.Y. 1321 followed. The principle in *Khan* was not restricted to criminal proceedings and in any event the Rules of the GMC permitted wider admissibility than was generally allowed in English criminal proceedings.

IDENBURG v. GENERAL MEDICAL COUNCIL (2000) 55 B.M.L.R. 101, Lord Clyde, PC.

304. Admissibility – expert witness in same professional capacity as claimant – unsuitable nature of purported expert's report

S, a nurse manager of patients with learning disabilities, brought an action for stress at work against his employer, alleging that he was overworked and not provided with sufficient support. S disclosed an expert report from another nurse manager, now the general manager of a learning disabilities service with a different NHS Trust, who purported to give evidence in relation to liability and causation. D applied for an order debarring the witness from giving either expert evidence or evidence as a witness of fact, on the basis that he failed to recognise his duty to the court and purported to give expert evidence on matters for which he had no expertise.

Held, allowing the application, that the experience of the witness would be such as to make him capable of giving evidence as to management practice, but that he was not qualified to give expert evidence on the issues of causation of psychiatric injury or foreseeability in relation to psychiatric injury, *Stevens v. Gullis* [1999] B.L.R. 394, [1999] C.L.Y. 343 followed. He wrongly (1) made references to published material which postdated the period of alleged negligence; (2) raised issues that predated the period of alleged negligence and which were not pleaded in the particulars of claim, and (3) made findings of fact and expressed an opinion on the issue of liability, thereby trespassing on the function of the judge. As a result, and due to the intemperate language employed in the report, the report could not be said to be the objective and unbiased evidence of an expert of the court. The evidence was wholly discredited. S also intended to call at trial the manager of another home for patients with learning disabilities as a witness of fact, which was a further relevant consideration when debarring the witness from giving evidence, either as an expert or of fact at the trial.

STOREY v. DORSET COMMUNITY NHS TRUST, October 18, 1999, Judge Overend, CC (Plymouth). [*Ex rel.* Robert Weir, Barrister, Devereux Chambers, Devereux Court, London].

305. Appeals – expert evidence – solicitor's pre-trial negligence resulted in poor level of expert evidence – not in interest of justice to allow fresh evidence

[Civil Procedure Rules 1998 (SI 1998 3132).]

In reliance on a valuation provided by C, PF advanced monies to a purchaser who later defaulted. The property was subsequently sold at a value considerably under C's estimate. After some delay, PF brought proceedings against C, alleging professional negligence. C, who had initially acted in person, engaged a solicitor following the issue of a summons for directions but little further preparation was made for the case to go to trial. C was advised by counsel that an expert on lending practices be instructed but no action was taken. Following instruction from another counsel C applied, shortly before the trial, for an adjournment for the purposes of calling an expert on lending practices. It was submitted that C's solicitor had failed satisfactorily to perform his duties. The application was dismissed and C's counsel advised him on the desirability of instructing a fresh solicitor and of obtaining the services of an expert on comparables. At trial the judge found C negligent because his valuation, in the light of the evidence of PF's expert, was outside the permissible margin of deviation from the correct valuation which a reasonable surveyor would have reached. Some ten days after the judgment C obtained information relating to the comparables of PF's expert and subsequently applied for permission to appeal to adduce further evidence. C contended that due to the incompetence of the solicitor he had initially employed, he had not instructed an expert until a relatively short period before the trial. C argued that but for the misconduct of the solicitor he would have been able to adduce the additional information prior to the trial and that considering the overriding objective of the Civil Procedure Rules 1998 to deal with cases justly it was only fair that the further evidence be admitted.

Held, dismissing the application, that having regard to the overriding aim of the Rules that the court adjudicate justly, expeditiously and cost effectively it was in the interests of justice toward both parties that the case as tried should be an end to the matter, *Ladd v. Marshall* [1954] 1 W.L.R. 1489, [1954] C.L.Y. 2507 and *Mulholland v. Mitchell (No.1)* [1971] A.C. 666, [1971] C.L.Y. 3232 considered. While C's solicitor had clearly been negligent in preparing his case for trial, C could have obtained the relevant information prior to the trial. Reopening the matter would incur unnecessary costs, wasting time for both parties and was not in the interests of justice.

PARAGON FINANCE PLC (FORMERLY NATIONAL HOME LOANS CORP PLC) v. GALE [2000] C.P.Rep. 10, Mance, L.J., CA.

306. Appeals – fresh evidence – Ladd v Marshall principle not of equal application between RSC and CPR

[Rules of the Supreme Court 1965 (SI 1965 1776) Ord.59 r.10(2); Civil Procedure Rules 1998 (SI 1998 3132) r.1.2, Sch.1 Ord.59 r.59.10.]

NLF applied to adduce fresh evidence on an appeal against a decision refusing to grant a bankruptcy order against A. A contended that the application did not fulfil the requirements of the principle in *Ladd v. Marshall* [1954] 1 W.L.R. 1489, [1954] C.L.Y. 2507.

Held, refusing the application, that *Ladd v. Marshall* interpreted the Rules of the Supreme Court Ord.59 r.10(2) and, although the same words were repeated in the Civil Procedure Rules 1998 Sch.1 Ord.59 r.59.10, the effect of the overriding objective in CPR r.1.2 was such that the principle was not of equal application between the two sets of Rules. However, the principles applied to the instant case, notwithstanding that the matter in issue was procedural rather than substantive, *Ladd v. Marshall* considered and *Forward v. West Sussex CC* [1995] 1 W.L.R. 1469, [1996] C.L.Y. 886 distinguished.

LOMBARD NATWEST FACTORS LTD v. ARBIS; *sub nom.* NATWEST LOMBARD FACTORS LTD v. ARBIS [2000] B.P.I.R. 79, Hart, J., Ch D.

307. Appeals – fresh evidence – procedure for correction of errors of fact

S applied for permission to appeal against a judgment on liability for A ([2000] E.M.L.R. 478, [2000] C.L.Y. 891), contending that new evidence materially affected a finding of fact in the decision.

Held, refusing permission, that S had known about the error pre-trial, but had failed to raise it at the draft judgment stage. Where an error could be rectified by a timely application for review under the court's inherent jurisdiction, an appeal, which was costly, time consuming and uncertain, was not the appropriate procedure.

SPICE GIRLS LTD v. APRILIA WORLD SERVICE BV (PERMISSION TO APPEAL) *The Times*, September 12, 2000, Arden, J., Ch D.

308. Banks – disclosure of records by non party bank

[Bankers Books (Evidence) Act 1879 s.9(2); Civil Procedure Rules 1998 (SI 1998 3132) Part 31 r.31.17.]

R was the subject of ongoing company director disqualification proceedings and made an application against a bank, HSBC, as a non party pursuant to the Bankers Books (Evidence) Act1879 for a disclosure of records. The application was granted at first instance by the registrar and HSBC appealed.

Held, allowing the appeal, that (1) the order could not properly have been made under the 1879 Act as the records in question were not "other records used in the ordinary business of the bank" for the purposes of s.9(2), *R. v. Dadson (Peter Ernest)* (1983) 77 Cr. App. R. 91, [1983] C.L.Y. 630 and *Williams v. Barclays Bank Plc* [1988] Q.B. 161, [1987] C.L.Y. 1674 considered, and (2) on the basis that HSBC was nevertheless agreeable to the production of clearly identifiable documents, the court was obliged to consider the requirements of the Civil Procedure Rules 1998 Part 31 r.31.17. The application was deficient in that, aside from three instances, the scope of disclosure sought from the first and second class of documents was too wide and in relation to the third and fifth classes, the documents did not provide support for the case advanced by either party.

HOWGLEN LTD, *Re* (APPLICATION FOR DISCLOSURE) [2001] 1 All E.R. 376, Pumfrey, J., Ch D.

309. Contempt of court – documentary evidence – express undertakings – permission required to use documentary evidence – exercise of court's discretion

R instituted proceedings in America against a competitor company, B, alleging misuse of trade secrets. B also instituted proceedings in the US alleging that R had made fraudulent applications to secure US patents. The actions were consolidated and on the trial of the patent issue, R was found guilty of fraud. R applied to set aside the verdict of the jury and whilst the application was unsuccessful, a retrial of the damages aspect was ordered. Whilst the US proceedings were still ongoing, B instituted proceedings in England seeking the revocation of five of R's patents. The proceedings were successful and on taxation copies of certain documents were supplied to R to justify items within the bill. R's American representatives concluded that the documents disclosed would assist them in their attempts to set aside the verdict in the American proceedings. B objected on grounds of privilege and applied for an injunction to prevent collateral use in the American proceedings. The application was successful and a subsequent appeal dismissed. Meanwhile R lodged a letter with the American court seeking to force B to provide further discovery and in response B filed an antisuit application seeking to prevent R from proceeding with the application. As a preliminary matter, B gave an express undertaking not to use a certain exhibit, BEM-1, other than in connection with the antisuit application unless with the consent of R or permission of the court. B subsequently decided to pursue an application for contempt of court arising from B's alleged breach of the injunction prohibiting collateral use and made an application for permission to rely upon BEM-1, R having refused consent to its use. The application was refused and B appealed, contending that (1) permission was not required in any event or, in the alternative, if it was required it should have been granted as a matter of course since the proposed contempt proceedings did not constitute a collateral purpose, and (2) that the judge had erred in the exercise of his discretion.

Held, dismissing the appeal, that (1) it was not possible for B to maintain that permission was not required to use BEM-1 for purposes other than the antisuit motion, given the fact that B had volunteered an undertaking to that effect. B had had the option to decline to give the undertaking but had not chosen to do so, *Crest Homes Plc v. Marks* [1987] A.C. 829, [1987] C.L.Y. 2885 distinguished. Neither was it arguable that the grant of permission should have been an automatic right. The grant of permission was a matter for the exercise of discretion having regard to all the circumstances of the case, and (2) the judge had given proper consideration to all the circumstances of the case and accordingly there was no substance to the suggestion that the exercise of his discretion had been flawed.

BOURNS INC v. RAYCHEM CORP (NO.4) [2000] C.P.L.R. 155, Peter Gibson, L.J., CA.

310. **Disclosure – experts' reports provided to expert for comment – scope of "instructions" under CPR r.35.10(4) restricted to solicitors' instructions**

[Civil Procedure Rules 1998 (SI 1998 3132) Part 31 r.31.14(e), Part 35 r.35.10(4).]
BHA sought disclosure of three experts' reports to which reference had been made in some of T's disclosed experts' reports, pursuant to the Civil Procedure Rules 1998 Part 31 r.31.14(e). T argued that, since those undisclosed reports were part of the material provided to the expert for the purpose of preparing his report, they were "instructions" to which the protection of Part 35 r.35.10(4) applied.

Held, allowing the application, that for the purposes of Part 35 r.35.10(4), "instructions" did not include the material provided to an expert, such as the medical records and the reports of other experts, on which he was required to comment. Instructions, within this context, were limited to the letters from the solicitor specifying what the expert was required to do.

TAYLOR v. BOLTON HA, January 14, 2000, Judge Morland, QBD. [*Ex rel.* John Whitting, Barrister, 1 Crown Office Row, Temple, London].

311. **Disclosure – insurance agreements – order against non parties where necessary for fair disposal of credit hire claim**

[Consumer Credit Act 1974; Consumer Credit (Exempt Agreements) Order 1989 (SI 1989 869); Civil Procedure Rules 1998 (SI 1998 3132) Part 31 r.31.]
B brought an action against T for damages arising from a road traffic accident, including charges resulting from a credit hire agreement with H. B had also, upon payment of a premium, entered into an indemnity insurance contract with AA, a company within H's group. AA's underwriters, AI, paid the hire charges pursuant to the policy after the action had continued for over 51 weeks. T applied for disclosure of, inter alia, the Master agreements between AA and AI and between AA and H, pursuant to the Civil Procedure Rules 1998 Part 31 r.31.12, contending that disclosure was relevant to establish whether the insurance agreement involving H, AA and AI, which provided for subrogation rights, was a sham and therefore unenforceable, *Hart v. Jayne* (Unreported, 2000) cited. B cross applied for the case to be re-allocated to the fast track, and contended that the court had no jurisdiction to make orders against non parties in a small claims matter. Further,

that T was not entitled to go behind AA's policy because of the doctrine of res inter alios acta, *King v. Victoria Insurance Co Ltd* [1896] A.C. 250 cited. H argued that an investigation into the construction of an insurance policy was misconceived and irrelevant to the claim of an insured. AA submitted that (1) it was necessary to decide whether it was appropriate to apply the doctrine of sham before making a decision on disclosure, *Street v. Mountford* [1985] A.C. 809, [1985] C.L.Y. 1893 and *AG Securities v. Vaughan* [1990] 1 A.C. 417, [1989] C.L.Y. 2145 cited; (2) *Hart* was irrelevant because that claim was dismissed as no premium had been paid, and (3) disclosure was not relevant as B had misunderstood the Consumer Credit (Exempt Agreements) Order 1989 in that the agreement was only exempt if the obligation to pay matured during that period, actual payment was not required.

Held, granting the application for disclosure and re-allocating the case to the fast track, that a discretion to make an order against non parties pursuant to Part 31 r.31.17 of the 1998 Rules must be exercised in relation to specific documentation and only where disclosure was necessary to deal fairly with the claim, having regard to whether the request was proportionate. Disclosure in the instant case was necessary to give effect to Part 1 r.1.1 (2) because to refuse the application would put the parties on an unequal footing, since T would not have the necessary documentation on which to found his arguments. It was a matter for the trial judge to determine whether the agreement was a sham. The principle of res inter alios acta did not prevent a decision being made on disclosure, *Dimond v. Lovell* [2000] 2 W.L.R. 1121, [2000] C.L.Y. 2566 and *Hunt v. Severs* [1994] 2 A.C. 350, [1994] C.L.Y. 1530 considered. The corporate veil could be lifted sufficiently to allow T access to the documents he needed to fully argue his position fully. The complexity of the issues and the importance of the case to all parties supported the conclusion that the request was proportionate.

BURKE v. THORNTON, June 26, 2000, Deputy District Judge Thompson, CC (Hastings). [*Ex rel.* Morgan Cole Solicitors, Apex Plaza, Forbury Road, Reading].

312. Disclosure and inspection – apportionment of joint tortious liability – excess recovery – insurance agreement with third party contributor not privileged

G, a shipyard operator which, through its insurer, had settled asbestosis claims made against it by former employees, appealed against an order that its contribution proceedings against C, an independent contractor, be stayed until such time as G had disclosed to C the terms of an agreement between its insurer and another shipyard operator detailing that operators contribution in asbestosis claims. G contended that the agreement was part of without prejudice negotiations, and accordingly privileged. C maintained that it was impossible to make a sensible Part 36 payment without sight of the agreement, if it was simultaneously to ensure that G did not recover more than it had paid to its employees.

Held, allowing the appeal, that the agreement was not privileged and C was entitled to see those terms relating to the apportionment of liability in order to conduct Part 36 negotiations, and satisfy the overriding objective of enabling the court to deal with the case justly. The trial judge was only to be informed of the terms of the agreement after he had determined the parties' respective liabilities on the evidence, by way of satisfying himself that there had been no excess recovery. That principle of disclosure was to be narrowly applied to indemnity proceedings and was not to be construed in a multi defendant case as a method of ascertaining the settlement details of co defendants.

GNITROW LTD v. CAPE PLC [2000] 1 W.L.R. 2327, Pill, L.J., CA.

313. Disclosure and inspection – criteria for grant of special disclosure order

[Civil Procedure Rules 1998 (SI 1998 3132).]

An oil exploration company, A, purchased a drilling unit from BAO for the purposes of drilling in the area of the United Kingdom continental shelf.

Proceedings were subsequently commenced by A for a declaration that it had been entitled to terminate the contract on the basis that the unit had not been fit for the purpose for which it had been supplied. A applied for a special disclosure order seeking documentary evidence of any material defect in the rig between specified dates. A contended that disclosure was justified on the basis that a party was entitled to rely at trial upon the existence of defects of which he had been ignorant at the time that the contract had been terminated, *Boston Deep Sea Fishing & Ice Co v. Ansell* (1888) L.R. 39 Ch. D. 339 cited.

Held, dismissing the application, that *Boston* was not authority for unrestricted disclosure. Pleadings were required in order that the matters in issue between the parties might be defined. To make a special disclosure order in relation to unpleaded matters would result in confusion and undermine the court's case management function. The conduct of civil litigation under the Civil Procedure Rules 1998 meant special disclosure orders would require even stronger justification than they had in the past, *Cyril Leonard & Co v. Simo Securities Trust Ltd* [1972] 1 W.L.R. 80, [1972] C.L.Y. 2781 and *Boston* considered. The fact that BAO's representatives had made a prior error in relation to their disclosure obligations was also no reason to grant the order sought.

AMOCO (UK) EXPLORATION CO v. BRITISH AMERICAN OFFSHORE LTD [2000] C.P. Rep. 51, Longmore, J., QBD (Comm Ct).

314. Disclosure and inspection – documentary evidence – application for production of allegedly forged original documents

[Civil Procedure Rules 1998 (SI 1998 3132) Part 32.]

B applied for specific disclosure of the original copies of a number of documents exhibited by S to an affidavit. The application was made at a point in the proceedings at which the obligation as to disclosure had not yet arisen. B maintained that he was entitled to see the originals as a matter of course by virtue of Civil Procedure Rules 1998 Part 32 PD 32 para.13.1 and maintained that the principal reason for his request was that a number of the exhibited documents were forgeries.

Held, dismissing the application, that the allegation of forgery in respect of those original documents that were available would be finally determined by the expert instructed to report as to their authenticity. The remainder of the allegedly forged documents could not be found and that was not surprising given the fact that the documents in question were of a considerable age. B had also sought disclosure of further original documents but there was a forthcoming Part 24 hearing at which that issue could be considered. Further, classes of documents requested by B were entirely speculative and amounted to a "fishing" exercise.

SMYTH v. BEHBEHANI (DISCLOSURE) CH.1997 No.4260, Jacob, J., Ch D.

315. Disclosure and inspection – documents held in France – disclosure criminal offence in France – jurisdiction and discretion to order disclosure

[Insolvency Act 1986 s.213; Rules of the Supreme Court 1965 (SI 1965 1776); Civil Procedure Rules 1998 (SI 1998 3132) r.1.2, r.13.19(3).]

M brought an action against BAII under the Insolvency Act 1986 s.213, alleging that BAII had been involved in assisting a banking fraud connected with BCCI. Amongst other directions, an order for disclosure and inspection was made on both parties, but BAII contended that the court had no jurisdiction to order the disclosure of some 1,800 listed documents that were held in France where such disclosure would breach French law prohibiting the provision of documentary evidence of a business of a financial nature for use in foreign proceedings.

Held, that the court had a jurisdiction to order disclosure in such circumstances and could exercise its discretion in deciding whether or not to so order. The court would not have jurisdiction to order inspection where to do so would involve an offence under English law. It was, however, different where the obligation to disclose was under English law but the offence was under a foreign jurisdiction, *Brannigan v. Davison* [1997] A.C. 238, [1997] C.L.Y. 1168 applied. The existing authorities indicated that the court had a discretion whether or not to order disclosure under the Rules of the Supreme Court which was in accordance with the Civil Procedure Rules 1998 r.13.19(3) and the overriding objective under r.1.2 to consider a right or duty under a foreign jurisdiction.

MORRIS v. BANQUE ARABE ET INTERNATIONALE D'INVESTISSEMENT SA (NO.1) [2000] C.P. Rep. 65, Neuberger, J., Ch D.

316. Disclosure and inspection – payment into court – procedural default

[Insolvency Act 1986 s.423; Civil Procedure Rules 1998 (SI 1998 3132) Part 3 r.3.4.]

S appealed against the dismissal of an application seeking the striking out of T's defence or a payment into court as a condition of allowing T to continue to defend S's claim for damages following his exposure to mercury at T's South African plant. S also appealed against the refusal of an order under the Insolvency Act 1986 s.423 for disclosure of documentation concerning a prior demerger which S maintained had been arranged for the unlawful purpose of putting assets of about £20 million beyond the reach of potential creditors including S. S contended that T had failed to comply with its procedural obligations in relation to disclosure and had been guilty of other instances of procedural default.

Held, allowing the appeal, that a strike out was inappropriate but the judge had erred in rejecting the request for a payment into court, largely on the basis that T was impecunious, since the onus was on an impecunious party to demonstrate that he was unable to raise funds from friends, family and associates, *MV Yorke Motors v. Edwards* [1982] 1 W.L.R. 444, [1982] C.L.Y. 2398 applied. A payment into court in the sum of £400,000 was ordered under the Civil Procedure Rules 1998 Part 3 r.3.4. T had failed to comply with its procedural obligations including the late service of expert evidence, giving rise to a strong suspicion that the proceedings were not being conducted in good faith. The failure to produce evidence concerning the demerger appeared to indicate a prima facie breach of s.423 of the Act and T was ordered to comply with its disclosure obligations.

SITHOLE v. THOR CHEMICALS HOLDINGS LTD A2/2000/2894, Robert Walker, L.J., CA.

317. Discovery – discovery against non party – United States

[Hague Convention of the Taking of Evidence Abroad in Civil or Commercial Matters 1970; Federal Rules of Civil Procedure (United States).]

In litigation arising out of the collapse of BCCI, F sought discovery of documents held by BCCI's auditors, PW, who were based in the UK. PW resisted the discovery application. A discovery subpoena was served on a partner in PW who was at the time working in New York. PW still failed to give discovery and was found to be in contempt and subject to a rolling fine. The sanction was stayed pending an appeal.

Held, dismissing the appeal, that (1) the New York court had jurisdiction to proceed with an order for discovery under the Federal Rules of Civil Procedure since service on a partner within the jurisdiction had occurred and therefore the requirements of due process as to proper service had been satisfied; (2) there was no ruling requiring recourse to the Hague Convention for the Taking of Evidence Abroad 1970 before federal law as the means of obtaining discovery from a foreign non party witness; (3) English case law indicated that a request for production would not be contrary to any laws of confidentiality and so would not infringe the prerogative of the UK courts to interpret their own laws, and moreover that the interest in the enforcement of those laws was outweighed by the overwhelming public interest in uncovering the full extent of the BCCI frauds, and (4) the scope of the subpoena was not too wide; on the contrary, the fact that the order related to such a huge number of documents only went to show the importance of those documents to the US litigation.

FIRST AMERICAN CORP v. PRICE WATERHOUSE LLP [1999] I.L.Pr. 745, Circuit Judge Newman, US Court of Appeals, Second Circuit.

318. Doctors – professional conduct – disclosure of evidence relating to medical examinations

See HEALTH: Rajan v. General Medical Council. §2756

319. Expert evidence – admissibility of draft expert reports – "without prejudice" documents cannot be referred to at subsequent trial

U were awarded damages and interest against the defendants, B, in the Mercantile Court. The judge had disallowed interest from the period from the issue of the writ to the date of service of the final report by U's expert, so as to clarify the quantum of the claim, and refused to admit the draft report prepared by U's expert which had been served approximately two years previously. At trial B argued that the draft report was so different that it had not known the quantum until service of the final report. U appealed contending that the judge had misdirected himself by refusing to admit and take into account the draft report which was disclosed "without prejudice".

Held, dismissing the appeal, that negotiations concerning the settling of disputes were made without prejudice to any forthcoming litigation, and thus at a future trial "without prejudice" documents could not be referred to. Counsel had not cited any authorities and therefore the issue was a difficult one, although *Rush & Tompkins Ltd v. Greater London Council* [1989] A.C. 1280, [1989] C.L.Y. 1701 approved the principles of the without prejudice rule set out in *Cutts v. Head* [1984] Ch. 290, [1984] C.L.Y. 2608 which acknowledged that unless a without prejudice letter was marked "without prejudice save as to costs", it was not admissible on the costs hearing following trial. The draft report was a draft and the figures enclosed were wholly different to those in the final report. It followed that the judge had correctly disregarded the without prejudice report.

UYB LTD v. BRITISH RAILWAYS BOARD (2000) 97(42) L.S.G. 45, Waller, L.J., CA.

320. Expert evidence – claim for intimidation – cost of relying on psychiatric evidence would be disproportionate to advantage gained by its use

G entered into a contract of employment with CS, a religious organisation, to work as a volunteer in Bulawayo. CS later offered G a scholarship entitling him to come to the United Kingdom and work in the premises of an organisation connected with CS. G alleged that he was required to work at those premises under coercion and that CS had failed to provide conditions appropriate to an educational scholarship. G commenced proceedings alleging breach of contract and intimidation on the part of CS. He sought to rely on psychiatric evidence in order to substantiate his allegations. CS appealed against the decision of the master allowing the use of expert evidence contending that such evidence was not necessary to resolve the matters in issue between the parties.

Held, allowing the appeal, that the cost of calling on psychiatric evidence would be wholly disproportionate to the potential benefit gained from adducing it. The trial judge, having seen the witnesses for the parties, would be in a position to assess the merit of G's allegations and decide whether the conditions described by G amounted to intimidation or not.

GUMPO v. CHURCH OF SCIENTOLOGY RELIGIOUS EDUCATION COLLEGE INC [2000] C.P. Rep. 38, Brian Smedley, J., QBD.

321. Expert evidence – instruction of second expert – proportionality – human rights inapplicable

[Human Rights Act 1998; Civil Procedure Rules 1998 (SI 1998 3132); European Convention on Human Rights 1950 Art.6.]

W, the defendant in a personal injury claim brought by D, had agreed for an expert's report to be prepared for both parties by an occupational therapist, although the letter of instruction was prepared solely by D. W's solicitors were dissatisfied with the letter of instruction and when the report was received were concerned with its conclusions, which detailed the extent of lifelong care which D would require as a result of his injuries, and therefore applied for permission to instruct their own care expert. Permission was refused and W appealed, contending that the overriding objective of the Civil Procedure Rules 1998 was to ensure the just disposal of cases and to deny W permission to instruct another expert was unjust. Furthermore, it was argued that on the basis of the Human Rights Act 1998 and the European Convention on Human Rights 1950 Art.6, the essential or fundamental part of W's claim had been effectively barred by the refusal.

Held, allowing the appeal, that the judge had erred in refusing W permission to obtain a further report, although it had not been appropriate for W to raise human rights issues. Under the provisions of the 1998 Rules, the obtaining of a joint expert report was the correct approach, however, provided that there were sound reasons for a party wishing to obtain further evidence before deciding whether to challenge part or the whole of the joint report, then the consequential request to instruct another expert should be allowed at the discretion of the court. If however the damages claimed were modest, to ensure proportionality, the court might refuse the instruction of a second expert and merely permit the dissatisfied party to put questions to the expert who had already prepared the report. Whatever approach was taken, every effort should thereafter be made to resolve the issues between the parties and the giving of oral evidence by experts in court should be a last resort. The raising of human rights arguments was not appropriate as Art.6 of the Convention had no application to the issues raised on appeal, and the 1998 Act was not yet in force. Parties should take a responsible attitude when deciding whether to raise a human rights argument.

D (A CHILD) v. WALKER; *sub nom.* WALKER v. D (A CHILD) [2000] 1 W.L.R. 1382, Lord Woolf, M.R., CA.

322. **Expert evidence – joint expert statement resiling from previous position – application to vacate trial date and rely on additional expert evidence**

[Civil Procedure Rules 1998 (SI 1998 3132).]

R was injured in a road accident in March 1995. He sustained a whiplash injury, psychological injury and a shoulder injury. The matter was listed for fast track trial on October 13, 1999 for one day. R's orthopaedic expert had originally supported R's case that all his injuries were attributed to the road accident. He had a 30 minute telephone call with MFS's expert, following which they prepared and signed a joint statement three months before trial. They attributed whiplash injuries of only two years to the accident and some psychological factors but discounted the continuing shoulder injuries as not being attributed to the road accident. Both experts in the joint statement resiled from earlier views that the shoulder injuries were in whole or in part due to the accident. Upon receipt of the joint expert report it became clear to R that the value of his case was very much reduced as a result and R was of the view that there was no adequate explanation for why either expert had shifted position so dramatically, save that the experts referred to reconsidering the aetiology of such injuries. R had, since the joint statement was prepared, obtained advice from a leading professor in the field to suggest that rotator cuff injuries, such as R suffered from, could be caused in rear end shunts, which called into question the other experts' research on the aetiology of such injuries. R sought leave to vacate the trial date and rely on a new additional expert, which robustly supported R's continuing symptoms as being attributed to the accident.

Held, dismissing the application, that the courts could not entertain applications to resile from joint expert statements unless something was obviously and clearly wrong with the conclusions of the experts' joint meeting. Whilst a leading expert had come to a different view, there was evidence that the experts had considered the matter in detail and scrutinised all the relevant documents, and just because they had shifted opinion and there were some inconsistencies with their previous conclusions, that was not enough to give R a further bite of the cherry and try to repair the damage done by the joint expert statement. Experts were meant, where possible, to change their views and shift ground or try to win each other over when making such statements. An application to introduce further expert evidence which jeopardised the trial date would be contrary to the Civil Procedure Rules 1998 where considerations of fairness and having a full and complete picture should be tempered by considerations of cost, proportionality and avoiding delay.

RAWSON v. MIDLAND FREIGHT SERVICES (UK) LTD, October 5 1999, Deputy District Judge Hales, CC (Mansfield). [*Ex rel.* Darren Finlay, Barrister, Sovereign Chambers, 25 Park Square, Leeds].

323. **Expert evidence – personal injuries – automatic directions – restriction on number of expert witnesses**

[Civil Procedure Rules 1998 (SI 1998 3132) Part 32, Part 35.]

T appealed against the refusal to allow him to call six expert witnesses from the fields of orthopaedics, psychiatry, psychology, occupational therapy, maxillo-facial care and employment in proceedings for damages for facial injuries which T had suffered in road traffic accident. The judge had ordered that the automatic directions should apply and that accordingly expert evidence was limited to a maximum of two medical witnesses and one non medical witness. T contended that at least three medical expert reports and two non medical reports were required and that the orthopaedic report did not adequately deal with the maxillo-facial injuries.

Held, dismissing the appeal, that as a result of the coming into force of the Civil Procedure Rules 1998 Part 32 and Part 35 the court would decline to intervene with the order. The orthopaedic expert could deal with the facial injuries and either the psychiatrist or psychologist could deal with the other reports if required.

TOWNSHEND v. SUPERDRIVE MOTORING SERVICES LTD CCRTI 98/1188/2, Henry, L.J., CA.

324. **Expert evidence – personal injuries – permission to adduce additional evidence – overriding objective**

[Civil Procedure Rules 1998 (SI 1998 3132) Part 29.]

F sought to vary a decision refusing his application for permission to rely upon the evidence of a gastroenterologist and colo proctologist in proceedings for personal injuries against B. F had been injured in an accident in 1991 and maintained that the accident had resulted in stress which had exacerbated a pre-existing gastro-intestinal condition but had only obtained evidence to substantiate his claim in 1999. At a directions hearing in 1999 the judge refused an application for permission to rely upon the additional expert evidence on the basis that F had been searching in vain for some time for an expert who would support his claim and now that he had done so he should not be permitted to rely upon that evidence at trial in view of the prior procedural history. B maintained that the order, which had not been the subject of any appeal, was not now subject to challenge in view of the contents of the Civil Procedure Rules 1998 Part 29 PD 29 para.6.

Held, granting the application, that if the practice direction was the only matter to be considered, B's submissions would undoubtedly have been accepted. Having regard to the overriding objective, however, it was clear that to deny F the opportunity of adducing such evidence as he now had in his possession at trial would prevent the trial judge from doing justice as between the parties.

FOULCER v. BHATTI [2001] C.P. Rep. 37, John Mitting Q.C., QBD.

325. **Expert evidence – psychological report – not admissible where evidence by lay witness adequate**

[Civil Procedure Rules 1998 Part 35.]

S brought proceedings against T arising from a road traffic accident which occurred when S was aged 11. S sustained a back injury and obtained a psychological report which indicated that she was suffering from post traumatic stress disorder. She did not receive any psychological or psychiatric treatment. S applied to adduce the report in evidence but permission was refused. S appealed. T resisted the application, contending that (1) to obtain the report was a contempt; (2) permission to adduce the report in evidence would cause substantial prejudice to the defence as the disposal hearing was to take place very shortly, and (3) S's grandmother was to give evidence and her statement adequately covered all the matters mentioned in the report.

Held, dismissing the appeal, that (1) the Civil Procedure Rules 1998 did not prevent a party obtaining a report, but merely governed whether such a report could be adduced at a hearing, therefore obtaining the report did not in itself amount to contempt; (2) there were procedural difficulties arising from the appeal, which was brought out of time, which could result in prejudice to T; (3) the merit of the report was seriously questioned, since S did not receive any treatment and the symptoms had substantially resolved. The report did not add anything to the evidence of S's grandmother. There was a duty of the court under the Civil Procedure Rules 1998 Part 35 to restrict the evidence to that which was reasonably necessary, and it was found that expert evidence was not necessary in the instant case.

S (A CHILD) v. THORNTON, April 6, 2000, Judge RC Taylor, CC (Bradford). [*Ex rel.* Simon Dawes, Barrister, instructed by Scott Rees & Co Solicitors, Centaur House, Gardiners Place, Skelmersdale, Lancashire].

326. Expert witnesses – biased report – jointly instructed expert debarred from giving evidence at trial

A, a consulting engineer, was instructed jointly by D and K to provide a report concerning an accident on a construction site. Two weeks before the trial, KG obtained disclosure of three side letters produced by N for the attention of D's solicitors. K applied to debar N from giving evidence at trial.

Held, granting the application, that it was obvious that one of the letters was written with the purpose of assisting D's case. On its face, the letter did not indicate that N had an unbiased approach, one in which his primary duty was to the court. It was quite clearly appropriate to debar the evidence.

DUNNE v. KIER GROUP PLC, April 7, 2000, Judge Overend, CC (Plymouth). [*Ex rel.* Robert Weir, Barrister, Devereux Chambers, Devereux Court, London].

327. Expert witnesses – independence – intended witness employed by defendant housing authority

[Civil Procedure Rules 1998 (SI 1998 3132) Part 35.]

F, a local authority tenant, brought a claim against LCC, the landlord, for damages for personal injury and for specific performance arising from disrepair in the property. The district judge held that LCC's choice of surveyor was inappropriate as he was employed in its housing department and therefore not independent as required by the Civil Procedure Rules 1998 Part 35. The judge upheld the decision and LCC appealed, contending that the decision was a judicial error. F argued that the decision was correct since it related solely to the individual expert concerned.

Held, dismissing the appeal, that the fact that the expert was employed by LCC did not disqualify him as an expert, provided that he was suitably qualified. The anxiety of the judge to ensure the independence of the expert was in accord with the overall requirements of Part 35, but he had been wrong to exclude the evidence purely on the basis of the expert's employment with LCC. The fact that the hearing was due to come on shortly, however, meant that there was insufficient time to decide on the appropriateness of the witness concerned, so that LCC would have to use another witness whose credentials were not in dispute. There was a need for a procedure whereby claimants could inform authorities of the expert they intended to use, thus allowing the use of more single experts in such cases.

FIELD v. LEEDS CITY COUNCIL [2001] C.P.L.R. 129, Lord Woolf, M.R., CA.

328. **Expert witnesses – permission to instruct additional expert – circumstances where fair to refuse permission**

[Civil Procedure Rules 1998 (SI 1998 3132) Part 36.]

H brought proceedings for damages for clinical negligence against W. In addition to general damages, H claimed loss of earnings, which was the most significant element of the claim in monetary terms. Following exchange of evidence and meetings between the expert witnesses, W applied for permission to instruct an additional expert. At the time of the hearing on April 7, 2000 it was anticipated that the trial would be in October 2000. The relevant issue in the case was whether, even if clinical negligence was established, H would have had to give up work in any event at a date prior to ordinary retirement date because of various other medical conditions. Orthopaedic experts on both sides expressed a view not only as to strictly orthopaedic matters but also as to the impact of other medical conditions. After the experts' meeting, W sought to instruct a consultant physician.

Held, refusing W's application, that the issue in question was not a new issue, and the parties had previously made their decision as to the nature of the experts they wished to instruct. The stage the case had reached was one where both parties would approach and consider the case upon the basis of the evidence received and no doubt consider settlement including offers under the Civil Procedure Rules 1998 Part 36. The judge rejected W's argument that it would be unfair and contrary to the overriding objective of the 1998 Rules not to allow a further expert when it was anticipated that such an expert may well be able to report without delaying the trial date.

HUGHES v. WREXHAM MAELOR HOSPITAL NHS TRUST, April 7, 2000, Judge Edwards Q.C., CC (Chester). [*Ex rel.* Christopher Limb, Barrister, Young Street Chambers, 38 Young Street, Manchester].

329. **Hearsay evidence – claimant's reliance statements prepared for defendant by witness not called to give evidence – power to disallow such evidence under Civil Procedure Rules**

[Civil Procedure Rules 1998 (SI 1998 3132) Part 32 r.32.5(5).]

H, a film researcher, was taken by A into a part of Northern Ireland where he met and held a conversation with a person purporting to be a member of the Ulster Resistance. A television programme referring to the meeting was made by M, who later brought libel proceedings against TN. At the trial, A was not called to give evidence in spite of the fact that he had signed two statements on behalf of TN. M appealed against a ruling that he could not produce those statements in evidence for the purpose of discounting them as substantially untrue. M contended that the Civil Procedure Rules 1998 Part 32 r.32.5(5) abrogated the old rules of evidence which provided that, where a party serving a statement did not call the witness to give oral evidence, no other party could use the statement in evidence. In arguing the appeal, M stated that he would not consent to A being called and cross examined by TN on the basis that as TN had decided not to call A to give evidence in chief, it should not be permitted to place itself in a better position by having the benefit of the wider scope which cross examination would provide.

Held, dismissing the appeal, that Part 32 r.32.5(5) did not operate to change the basic principles of the law of evidence. A party could not put in evidence a statement of a witness whose evidence substantially conflicted with the case which he was putting forward with the aim of discrediting a significant part of that witness's evidence. It was clear that the court's duty was to make a decision in accordance with the admissible evidence even if it was known that further evidence existed which had not been adduced, *Air Canada v. Secretary of State for Trade (No.2)* [1983] 2 A.C. 394, [1983] C.L.Y. 2936 applied and *Anonima Petroli Italiana SpA and Neste Oy v. Marlucidez Armadora SA (The Filiatra Legacy)* [1991] 2 Lloyd's Rep. 337, [1992] C.L.Y. 3920 considered.

MCPHILEMY v. TIMES NEWSPAPERS LTD [2000] 1 W.L.R. 1732, Brooke, L.J., CA.

330. Letters of request – witnesses – pre trial discovery of non party – Canada

[Rules of Civil Procedure (Ontario) r.31.10.]

A US court issued letters rogatory to the Ontario court seeking pre trial depositions from D, the Canadian resident auditor of NT, a company subject to a class action in the US by a number of its shareholders.

Held, refusing the application to enforce the letters rogatory, that (1) in determining whether letters rogatory were being used for the purposes of pre trial discovery the recipient court was not bound to accept the language of the letters as determinative, *Westinghouse Electric Corp and Duquesne Light Co, Re* (1977) 16 O.R.(2d) 273 applied, *Friction Division Products Inc and El Du Pont de Nemours & Co Inc (No 2), Re* (1986) 56 O.R.(2d) 722 considered; (2) in determining whether to enforce letters rogatory, the evidence sought must be relevant and not otherwise obtainable, and the order must not unduly burden the witness concerned, *Re Friction Division Products Inc* considered. The circumstances in which an Ontario court would enforce letters rogatory for the purposes of pre trial discovery from non parties should not be more restrictive than those in which an Ontario court would request the assistance of a foreign court. While the court was not limited to situations in which it might make an order for discovery of non parties under the Ontario Rules of Civil Procedure r.31.10, nonetheless r.31.10 could give relevant guidance, and (3) in the instant case, the scope of the order sought was unjustifiably broad. The court had no power to narrow the request in the letters rogatory and they would be denied in their entirety.

FECHT v. DELOITTE & TOUCHE [2000] I.L.Pr. 398, RA Blair, J., CJ (Gen Div) (Ont).

331. Oral evidence – failure to secure attendance of witnesses or representatives without notice to court – claim struck out for non compliance with procedure

[Civil Procedure Rules 1998 (SI 1998 3132) Part 3 r.3.4(2)(c), Part 27 r.27.9.]

CT brought a claim for damages arising from a road traffic accident. Liability was admitted and judgment was entered for damages to be assessed. Included in the order was a direction that evidence to be relied upon must be filed and served within 28 days. CT failed to serve any witness statements dealing with quantum until the day before the hearing, when it indicated that its single witness to the facts would not be available to attend court, though no reasons were given. CT also indicated that it intended to ask the court to deal with the hearing on paper with no attendance, and enclosed a short witness statement. A replied, stating that witness evidence was required not only from the witness identified by CT but also from a further witness, and the matter could not appropriately be dealt with in the absence of oral evidence. No further communication took place and neither CT's witnesses nor representatives attended at the trial. A asked the court to exercise its powers under the Civil Procedure Rules 1998 Part 27 r.27.9 to strike out the claim on the basis of non attendance without the requisite notice or reasons being given.

Held, striking out the claim, that in addition to failing to attend without the requisite notice, CT had failed to comply with a rule, practice direction or court order in accordance with Part 3 r.3.4(2)(c).

CARROLLS TRANSPORT LTD v. ALDERMAN, March 7, 2000, District Judge Allen, CC (Brentford). [*Ex rel.* Tianne Bell, Barrister, Hardwicke Building, New Square, Lincoln's Inn, London].

332. Perjury – company bound by perjured evidence of director

In previous proceedings ([1992] 1 Lloyd's Rep 239) evidence given by S, a director and general manager of SD, on the company's behalf, was held to be credible and as a result judgment was given in favour of SD. It emerged in subsequent proceedings ([1998] Lloyd's Rep. I.R. 35), under a different judge, that the evidence given by S, since deceased, had been perjured and OIC sought to have the judgment set aside. It was common ground that, where the fraud was that of a party to the action, or, where a corporation was a party and the fraudulent evidence could be treated as that of the corporation, then the judgment could be set aside, but it was necessary to determine whether S had possessed sufficient status to make his fraudulent evidence that of OIC.

Held, allowing the appeal (Buxton L.J. dissenting), that, although the perjured evidence was that of a director and managing director of a party and not that of a party to the action, nevertheless it would be unjust not to treat it as being that of OIC, *Hunter v. Chief Constable of the West Midlands* [1980] Q.B. 283, [1980] C.L.Y. 2609 and *R. v. Andrews-Weatherfoil Ltd* [1972] 1 W.L.R. 118, [1972] C.L.Y. 594 followed.

ODYSSEY *Re* (LONDON) LTD (FORMERLY SPHERE DRAKE INSURANCE PLC) v. OIC RUN OFF LTD (FORMERLY ORION INSURANCE CO PLC) *The Times*, March 17, 2000, Nourse, L.J., CA.

333. Privilege – absolute privilege – witness statements prepared in one set of proceedings and used in another

S brought proceedings against B in Watford county court and against D in Brentford county court, alleging unlawful eviction in both cases. B, in support of his application to strike out the proceedings, swore an affidavit raising serious allegations against S concerning the proceedings. The affidavit was made available to D to assist her in her own application to strike out S's claim against her, and S subsequently sued B for damages for libel and slander, contending that defamatory statements contained in the affidavit, when used by D, were not protected by privilege. S's libel claim was struck out for being embarrassing, frivolous and vexatious, the order was subsequently affirmed by the High Court and S appealed.

Held, dismissing the appeal, that the test for deciding if absolute privilege attracted to defamatory remarks made in witness statements used in court proceedings was whether the statements were made with reference to the subject matter of those proceedings. There was no dispute that test was satisfied in respect of the use of the defamatory statements in the Watford proceedings, for which B's affidavit was originally prepared. Equally, as the affidavit included allegations referring to other cases involving S, including his claim against D, the statements had direct reference to the Brentford proceedings and thus absolute privilege applied, particularly as it was clear that the material was published to D to assist in the ongoing proceedings against her, *Seaman v. Netherclift* (1876) L.R. 2 C.P.D. 53 and *Samuels v. Coole & Haddock* (Unreported, May 22, 1997), [1997] C.L.Y. 4860 applied. The judge was therefore right to strike out S's libel claim.

SMEATON v. BUTCHER (NO.1) [2000] E.M.L.R. 985, Clarke, L.J., CA.

334. Privilege – disclosure – use at trial of without prejudice material disclosed on interlocutory application

SL issued proceedings claiming damages for negligence and breach of contract against its solicitors, SR, who counterclaimed in respect of unpaid fees. SL sought an order requiring SR to disclose documents relating to certain without prejudice discussions that had taken place between the two of them, arguing that SR had made use of those discussions for the purpose of a freezing injunction to which it had been subject. The judge dismissed the application ([2000] 1 Lloyd's Rep. 311), holding that the relevant discussions remained inadmissible owing to their without prejudice nature. SL appealed.

Held, allowing the appeal in part, that it would be unfair to allow one party to rely on without prejudice material on an interlocutory application which concerned the merits of a case without also allowing the other party to use that material at the trial. Since the merits of the case had been relevant for the purpose of SR's application for a freezing injunction, SL would be permitted to rely on the without prejudice discussions at the trial.

SOMATRA LTD v. SINCLAIR ROCHE & TEMPERLEY; SINCLAIR ROCHE & TEMPERLEY v. SOMATRA LTD [2000] 1 W.L.R. 2453, Clarke, L.J., CA.

335. Privilege – request for further information to substantiate damages claim – provision of information justified by nature of breach

[Civil Procedure Rules 1998 (SI 1998 3132) Part 18 r.18.1.]

F appealed against an order granting a request for further information pursuant to the Civil Procedure Rules 1998 Part 18 r.18.1 in favour of R, acting in the capacity of executrix, in proceedings claiming damages for inducement of breach of contract. R had succeeded in an action brought against F and others following interference with a safety deposit box kept at Harrods Ltd in which documents and tapes had been removed for copying. Some or all of the documentation had subsequently been given to B, a journalist, and had later formed the basis of a newspaper report. R sought damages for the diminution in value of the documents caused by their publication by B, and general damages for the loss of quiet enjoyment or privacy in relation to the contents of the safety deposit box. F, while conceding that R could claim general damages, sought to rely on litigation privilege or legal professional privilege as grounds for not submitting to any requests for more information. F also contended that he had no personal knowledge of the matters to which the requests related.

Held, dismissing the appeal, that it was reasonable and proportionate for R to request further information in order for her to state her case. R was entitled, in order to put the parties on an equal footing, to such information from F as was reasonably required to present her claim. It would be manifestly unjust if at the trial for damages R was unable to do any more than recover nominal damages for wrongs admitted to have taken place. Searching inquiries were justified by the clandestine nature of the underlying breach.

ROWLAND v. FAYED [2000] C.P. Rep. 35, Arden, J., Ch D.

336. Privilege – self incrimination – party facing possible contempt proceedings in same action

An asset disclosing order had been made against S who was subsequently ordered to attend for cross examination on affidavit, in contemplation of possible contempt proceedings (*The Times*, May 31, 1999, [1999] C.L.Y. 323). S claimed the privilege against self incrimination, contending that its availability should be decided at this stage. MC argued that the issue of privilege against self incrimination should not be dealt with prematurely, and that in any case the privilege should not be available where the contempt arose out of points made in the instant case.

Held, giving judgment for S, that the privilege against self incrimination could rightly be claimed by a defendant who had been ordered to be cross examined in contemplation of possible contempt proceedings in the same action. The argument that privilege was unavailable where the contempt arose out of statements made in the instant case was not borne out by the authorities, *Comet Products (UK) Ltd v. Hawkex Plastics Ltd* [1971] 2 Q.B. 67, [1970] C.L.Y. 2252 followed, *Rice v. Gordon* (1843) 13 Sim. 580 distinguished on the grounds that the defendant had already been subject to committal proceedings.

MEMORY CORP PLC v. SIDHU (NO.2) [2000] Ch. 645, Arden, J., Ch D.

337. Privilege – without prejudice – documents – restraint of use in subsequent connected proceedings

I commenced a patent action against D but eventually reached a confidential compromise agreement and subsequently a mediation agreement, containing confidentiality provisions, was drawn up between the parties. The situation deteriorated and patent actions were recommenced. M, a US subsidiary of I, brought an action in Illinois against F, a US company connected with D, in which declarations as to the validity of the assignment of licences were sought. I discovered that, during the course of those proceedings, D had supplied F with confidential without prejudice documents drawn up during the previous mediation process. I sought injunctive relief, arguing that the protection given to without prejudice documents should include the use of those documents in any litigation with the same subject matter.

Held, allowing the application, that the use of without prejudice documents in subsequent connected proceedings with the same subject matter was restrained. It was likely that the without prejudice documents were subject to an implied condition that they would not be used in litigation and, unless protection extended to subsequent litigation, the public policy aim of allowing without prejudice documents to be drawn up freely would be defeated, *Unilever Plc v. Procter & Gamble Co* [2000] F.S.R. 344, [1999] C.L.Y. 349 followed and *Stretton v. Stubbs The Times*, February 28, 1905 and *Rush & Tompkins Ltd v. Greater London Council* [1989] A.C. 1280, [1989] C.L.Y. 1701 distinguished.

INSTANCE v. DENNY BROS PRINTING LTD (INTERIM INJUNCTION) [2000] F.S.R. 869, Lloyd, J., Pat Ct.

338. **Time limits – exchange of witness statements – requirement to consider CPR Part 3 r.3.9(1) systematically**

[Civil Procedure Rules 1998 (SI 1998 3132) Part 3 r.3.9(1).]

B applied for an extension of time in which to exchange witness statements following his failure to comply with two orders providing for their exchange. The application having been dismissed, B appealed contending that the judge had failed to have regard to all of the factors set out in the Civil Procedure Rules 1998 Part 3 r.3.9(1).

Held, allowing the appeal, that the judge had failed to consider systematically the factors referred to in Part 3 r.3.9(1)(g),(h) and (i).

BANSAL v. CHEEMA [2001] C.P. Rep. 6, Brooke, L.J., CA.

339. **Witnesses – anonymity – inquests – legitimate fear for safety of police officers**

See ADMINISTRATION OF JUSTICE: R. v. Bedfordshire Coroner, *ex p.* Local Sunday Newspapers Ltd. §47

340. **Witnesses – disposal hearings – obligation on party seeking to cross examine to request attendance**

[Civil Procedure Rules 1998 (SI 1998 3132) Part 26, Part 32 r.32.6.]

D claimed damages arising out of a road traffic accident. Liability was not in dispute. D provided a statement outlining his recent symptoms. D did not attend the hearing, on the advice of his solicitor. G wished to cross-examine D at the hearing in relation to a number of heads of special damages and submitted that, because of D's absence, little weight should be attached to the statements provided and any issues on which cross-examination was desirable should be resolved in favour of G. D maintained that under the Civil Procedure Rules 1998 at any hearing other than a trial it was for the party seeking to cross-examine witnesses to request their attendance. G countered that the instant hearing, to quantify damages, was a trial and that the witnesses should have attended.

Held, finding in favour of D, that the Civil Procedure Rules 1998 Part 26 PD 26 para.12.8(4) specifically provided that unless the court otherwise directed, Part 32 r.32.6 of the 1998 Rules applied to disposal hearings. Accordingly, as G had not requested D's attendance, the evidence in the witness statements would remain unchallenged.

DORSETT v. GRANT, July 7, 2000, District Judge Rhodes, CC (Bradford). [*Ex rel.* Sean D Yates, Barrister, 10 Park Square, Leeds].

341. **Witnesses – expert witnesses – witness summons – non-payment of expert's fee**

C, an expert witness, applied to set aside the witness summons issued against her following a without notice application. C objected to giving evidence, contending that she had been informed by the claimants instructing her that they were no longer able to pay her fee, and they should not be allowed to circumvent paying her fee by the issue of a witness summons.

Held, setting aside the witness summons, that it would only be in exceptional cases that an expert who could not expect to be paid would be compelled to give evidence, and the instant case could not be called exceptional.

BROWN v. BENNETT (WITNESS SUMMONS) *The Times*, November 2, 2000, Neuberger, J., Ch D.

342. Witnesses – power of trial judge to order witness to be called – witness statements as hearsay evidence

[Civil Procedure Rules 1998 Part 32 r.32.5(5).]

The Society of Lloyd's had served a witness statement on the Lloyd's Names in accordance with pre trial directions and had decided not to call the witnesses to trial. The Names sought an order against the Society to call several witnesses for the purpose of cross examination in the trial for misrepresentation.

Held, refusing the application, that the Civil Procedure Rules 1998 Part 32 r.32.5(5) had reversed the former position under Rules of the Supreme Court, where no other party could admit the evidence at trial following the decision not to call a witness to give oral evidence where a witness statement had been served. The current stance was that the trial judge in civil proceedings had no power to order the party to call a witness to give evidence at trial or determine what evidence a litigating party tendered, *Tay Bok Choon v. Tahansan Sdn Bhd* [1987] 1 W.L.R. 413, [1987] C.L.Y. 377 considered, but that any litigating party could admit witness statements as hearsay evidence.

SOCIETY OF LLOYD'S v. JAFFRAY (WITNESS STATEMENTS) *The Times*, August 3, 2000, Cresswell, J., QBD.

343. Publications

Allen, Christopher – Practical Guide to Evidence. 2nd Ed. Paperback: £22.95. ISBN 1-85941-604-7. Cavendish Publishing Ltd.

Keane, Adrian – Modern Law of Evidence. 5th Ed. Paperback: £21.95. ISBN 0-406-92182-2. Butterworths.

Munday, R.J.C. – Butterworths Core Text: Evidence. Paperback: £12.95. ISBN 0-406-98570-7. Butterworths.

Phillips, E. – Evidence. 2nd Ed. Briefcase Series. Paperback: £10.95. ISBN 1-85941-488-5. Cavendish Publishing Ltd.

Reay, Rosamund – Evidence. Old Bailey Press 150 Leading Cases Series. Paperback: £9.95. ISBN 1-85836-383-7. Old Bailey Press.

Taylor, Alan – Evidence. 2nd Ed. Principles of Law. Paperback: £19.95. ISBN 1-85941-380-3. Cavendish Publishing Ltd.

CIVIL PROCEDURE

344. Abuse of process – delay – inordinate and inexcusable delay in progressing litigation amounted to abuse of process – striking out of actions only fair result

HB, which was owned by the State of Pakistan and which had its main office in Karachi with an office in London, made loans to a company of which GJ was a director. GJ and his codefendant, HJ, gave written personal guarantees to HB in respect of the loans. When HB's demands under the guarantees were not satisfied, it commenced parallel actions against GJ and HJ claiming £25 million. When the loans were made, Benazir Bhutto had been prime minister in Pakistan. When the government fell from power, Nawaz Sharif became prime minister, and the new government had brought criminal proceedings against Bhutto's husband, the president of HB and GJ, alleging fraud in respect of the loans. After HB had commenced the actions, Bhutto then became prime minister for a second time, and dismissed the criminal proceedings against GJ and the president of HB, before Sharif came into power. GJ and HJ contended that the actions were started by the first Sharif government, dismissed by the second Bhutto government only to be restarted by the second Sharif government. GJ and HJ then applied for HB's claims to be struck out for want of prosecution and HB conceded that it had caused inordinate and inexcusable delay for two and a half years. Despite HB's solicitors advising it repeatedly to give full discovery and to make progress with witness statements, HB was unable to make any decision and did not even communicate that fact to its own solicitors. Both actions were struck out as an abuse of process, *Arbuthnot Latham Bank Ltd v. Trafalgar Holdings Ltd* [1998] 1 W.L.R. 1426, [1998] C.L.Y. 619 and *Choraria v. Sethia* [1998] C.L.C. 625, [1998] C.L.Y. 611 considered, but HB's appeal against that order was allowed. GJ and HJ appealed.

Held, allowing the appeals and striking out the claims, that HB's inordinate and inexcusable delay in proceeding with the actions was an abuse of process. The only fair result was for the actions to be struck out. On first sight, the judge allowing HB's appeal seemed correct in stating that there had been no wholesale disregard of the rules by HB. However, the situation in Pakistan had to be considered. In ignoring the solicitors' repeated advice, HB had acted contumeliously. HB's failure to give coherent instructions to its solicitors was an affront to the court and a disregard of the norms of conducting litigation. Not only did HB wholly disregard the rules of the court in its delay, but the inference was that it did so whilst being fully aware of the consequences, therefore, HB's actions amounted to an abuse of process.

HABIB BANK LTD v. JAFFER (GULZAR HAIDER); HABIB BANK LTD v. JAFFER (HAIDER LADHU) [2000] C.P.L.R. 438, Nourse, L.J., CA.

345. **Abuse of process – disclosure and inspection – defamatory statement in privileged document – use of document in separate action**

[County Court Rules 1981 Ord.14 r.8A.]

C appealed against a finding which stayed staying his proceedings for slander and libel as they were brought in respect of and in reliance on information contained in a document which C had obtained by disclosure in other proceedings. The alleged slander was H's spoken publication to his solicitors of accusations which were then reported in a letter from H's solicitors to E, solicitors acting for receivers appointed over C's property, stating that C intended to "wreak vengeance" on those persons who acquired his land at below the market price without his authorisation. The letter was then referred to by E in an affidavit in proceedings between the receivers and C, and was subsequently sent to C pursuant to a court order. H contended that the alleged slander was on an occasion of absolute privilege, and the proceedings for slander and libel were an abuse of process, as the letter from H's solicitors was obtained on discovery by C in other proceedings. He was thus subject to an implied undertaking not to use it, or information contained in it, for the purpose of proceedings other than those in which they were compulsorily disclosed. C contended that (1) the court order was not an order for discovery, but rather an order for the production or inspection of the documents referred to in the affidavit. The relevant disclosure in the affidavit had been voluntary, and so C had been entitled to see the relevant document. Therefore there was no implied undertaking nor was there a fetter on C's use of the document, and (2) as the letter had been mentioned in open court, under the former County Court Rules 1981 Ord.14 r.8A any implied undertaking by C ceased to take effect in any event.

Held, allowing the appeal, that E's disclosure of the letter by referring to it in its affidavit had been voluntary, the subsequent court order simply requiring inspection of the document, and in open court. Therefore C had been entitled to production for inspection, so he was not subject to any implied undertaking not to use the document in an unrelated action, and it was not an abuse of process for C to use the document for other purposes, *Tejendrasingh v. Metsons*

[1997] E.M.L.R. 597, [1998] C.L.Y. 328 considered, and *Prudential Assurance Co Ltd v. Fountain Page Ltd* [1991] 1 W.L.R. 756, [1991] C.L.Y. 2870 applied.
CASSIDY v. HAWCROFT [2001] C.P. Rep. 49, May, L.J., CA.

346. **Abuse of process – former company director alleged bank had induced receiver to dismiss him – intention to relitigate issues decided in previous proceedings**

[Company Directors Disqualification Act 1986.]

In December 1988, M, the managing director of a company, was dismissed by the receiver appointed by BB, a bank which held a fixed charge over the company's premises. In July 1993, proceedings commenced against M under the Company Directors Disqualification Act 1986 were determined. The deputy judge found five allegations involving misconduct and dishonesty on M's part established. In October 1993, an action commenced by M against the bank's receiver for pay and expenses allegedly due to him was dismissed. In 1997, M issued proceedings against BB alleging, amongst other things, that BB had induced the receiver to dismiss him. The master's decision to strike out the claim was upheld on appeal by the deputy judge who concluded not only that M's case was hopeless but that it would be an abuse of process for M to relitigate issues which had been dealt with in the disqualification proceedings. M appealed arguing that, (1) he was entitled to rely on the rule that decisions in previous proceedings were binding only on the parties to those proceedings and that the decision in *Thomas Christy (In Liquidation), Re* [1994] 2 B.C.L.C. 527, [1995] C.L.Y. 2857 was wrongly decided, *Gleeson v. J Wippell & Co Ltd* [1977] 1 W.L.R. 510, [1977] C.L.Y. 1212 cited; (2) given that the findings in the disqualification proceedings flowed largely from the view which the deputy judge had taken of the reliability of M's oral evidence, it could not be said that the judge in these proceedings would make similar findings; (3) given that he had applied out of time for permission to appeal against the decision in the disqualification proceedings, this action should, at the very least, be stayed pending the determination of that application, and, (4) public policy dictated that it would be unfair for directors, disqualified under the 1986 Act, to lose the right to defend proceedings which a liquidator might later bring for compensation especially where the liquidator would not also be bound by the decision reached in the liquidation proceedings. It followed that his disqualification should not deprive him of the opportunity of pursuing his allegations against BB.

Held, dismissing the appeal, that it would be an abuse of process for M to pursue his case against BB. As BB had not been a party to the disqualification proceedings, the doctrine of res judicata did not apply. Nevertheless, M had been legally represented in those proceedings. What was more, he had taken the opportunity to call and cross examine witnesses and to produce and challenge documents. It would not be proper for M to seek to show, over 10 years after the date of his dismissal, that he had been wrongfully dismissed especially as BB would not have to prove the misconduct established against him in the disqualification proceedings. M was not to be permitted to mount a collateral attack on the final decision of a court of competent jurisdiction, *Smith v. Linskills* [1996] 1 W.L.R. 763, [1996] C.L.Y. 4496 applied. As for M's argument that he was applying out of time for permission to appeal against the decision made in the disqualification proceedings, there was no indication that that application was being pursued. Furthermore, M had made no allegations of wrongful dismissal in the action which he had commenced against the bank's receiver. That action was the appropriate forum for him to have pursued such allegations. It was observed that a disqualification order made under the 1986 Act would not automatically lead to a finding that proceedings commenced by the disqualified director and connected with his disqualification amounted to an abuse of process. Each case should be considered on their own particular facts, *Christy* and *Ashmore v. British Coal Corp* [1990] 2 Q.B. 338, [1990] C.L.Y. 3542 referred to.

MANSON v. VOOGHT (NO. 2) [2000] B.C.C. 838, Roch, L.J., CA.

347. Abuse of process – issue estoppel – claimant seeking to challenge on disclosure of evidence after compromise reached

[Civil Procedure Rules 1998 (SI 1998 3132) Part 3.]

S was involved in a road traffic accident with A in March 1998. In May 1998 a letter before action was sent by A's solicitors seeking damages for negligence. A statement from one of three eyewitnesses was included, indicating that S was responsible for the accident. S's insurers were unable to obtain instructions from S, therefore an open admission of liability was made and S's insurers paid all sums claimed by February 1999. In March 1999, S instituted proceedings for damages for negligence against A. A's insurers pleaded issue estoppel and sought to have the claim struck out as an abuse of the process of the court under the Civil Procedure Rules 1998 Part 3. S argued that he should not be estopped from bringing the claim, contending that there had been a lack of evenhandedness in the failure of A's original solicitors to disclose the existence of further independent witness evidence.

Held, dismissing the claim, that S's insurers had ostensible authority and may have had actual authority to settle the claim, having acted in their own interests and under a right of subrogation. S's delay and failure to respond to his insurers and/or loss adjusters denied him a "second bite at the cherry". If S had wished to raise the issue of A having been selective in his disclosure of evidence, the time to have done so would have been one year previously. To commence proceedings when a compromise had been reached was an abuse of process, however it was not an abuse to claim against the insurers as they had denied him the opportunity of recovering damages for the accident. A valid compromise existed that S could not challenge by issuing new proceedings

SHAFIQ v. AHMED, December 17, 1999, District Judge Duerden, CC (Bury). [*Ex rel.* Nicholas M Siddall, Barrister, 40 King Street, Manchester].

348. Abuse of process – prior action struck out for want of prosecution – second action commenced within limitation period – overriding objective

[Civil Procedure Rules 1998 (SI 1998 3132).]

A married couple, A, appealed against the dismissal of their application to strike out proceedings commenced by SF as an abuse of process. A had borrowed funds secured by a guarantee and a legal charge on their home for use by a company, TH. A failed to make payment when a request was made and SF commenced proceedings seeking payment under the guarantee. The proceedings were subsequently struck out for want of prosecution on the ground of delay but SF commenced a second action within the limitation period. A applied to strike out the second action as amounting to an abuse of process but the application was dismissed and A appealed. A maintained that SF was seeking to pursue precisely the same claim that had previously been struck out.

Held, dismissing the appeal, that following the advent of the Civil Procedure Rules 1998, the claim for payment would have been struck out as an abuse were it not for the fact that a claim for enforcement of the security by means of possession, which had not formed part of the earlier proceedings, had additionally been made. Striking out the claim for payment would still leave the substantive debt intact. In the new climate following the introduction of the Rules, a party could not seek to invoke the rule that following strike out for want of prosecution, another action commenced within the limitation period would not be struck out in the absence of exceptional circumstances. The court was obliged to have regard to the overriding objective of the Rules and in future the court should start with a presumption that if one action had been struck out on the basis of abuse then a special reason must be identified before a second action was allowed to proceed, *Arbuthnot Latham Bank Ltd v. Trafalgar Holdings Ltd* [1998] 1 W.L.R. 1426, [1998] C.L.Y. 619 followed and *Birkett v. James* [1978] A.C. 297, [1977] C.L.Y. 2410 and *Grovit v. Doctor* [1997] 1 W.L.R. 640, [1997] C.L.Y. 489 considered.

SECURUM FINANCE LTD v. ASHTON; *sub nom.* ASHTON v. SECURUM FINANCE LTD [2001] Ch. 291, Chadwick, L.J., CA.

349. Abuse of process – relitigation of claim – failure to make Part 20 claim did not debar action

[Civil Procedure Rules 1998 (SI 1998 3132) Part 1 r.1.1, Part 3 r.3.1 (3), Part 24 r.24.6.]

C, a bank, obtained summary judgment against SW, SH and the former partners of SH's firm of solicitors for £3.1 million owed on a fraudulently obtained loan. SW, who had been made bankrupt, subsequently obtained summary judgment against SH but his action against SH's former partners was rejected on the ground that SW was attempting to relitigate matters that should have been the subject of a Part 20 claim for contribution or indemnity in C's action. SW appealed.

Held, allowing the appeal, that it was an unwarranted extension of the principles against relitigation and that parties to litigation must bring their entire case forward, *Henderson v. Henderson* [1843-60] All E.R. Rep. 378 distinguished, that SW's claim should be considered an abuse of process. SW had been unrepresented and it had never been intimated to him that he should make a Part 20 claim prior to trial or risk being debarred. The court had power under the overriding objective of the pursuit of justice in the Civil Procedure Rules 1998 r.1.1 to consider the matter and under r.3.1 (3) and r.24.6 to insist on terms under which the action could proceed according to the Civil Procedure Rules 1998 Part 24 PD 24 para 5.1 and 5.2 applied. Consequently, SW was required to make full disclosure of his financial situation and make a payment in of between 70 to 80 per cent of the amount SH could expect to recover at the end of a fully contested action as security for costs.

SWEETMAN v. SHEPHERD [2000] C.P. Rep. 56, Kennedy, L.J., CA.

350. Abuse of process – statement of truth obviously incorrect – defence not afforded chance to value claim

[Civil Procedure Rules 1998 (SI 1998 3132) Part 17 r.17.2(2), Part 24, Part 34.]

BTC, a garage, brought an action against P for hire charges and storage arising from a road traffic accident. BTC's agent suffered personal injuries, and the car was unroadworthy and an economic write off. Prior to issue, P paid agreed damages for the write off and the personal injuries. Before the write off element was settled, BTC replaced the original car with another from its fleet, and stored the original car on its own premises. Three months after the accident, BTC invoiced P for hire charges and storage, giving the specific period and daily rates but no other details or reasons. P did not agree the claim. The particulars of claim referred to BTC's invoice and was accompanied by a statement of truth signed by BTC's solicitors. Subsequently, BTC's solicitors wrote to P indicating that the claim was actually for lost profit and that the particulars would need to be amended. The original hearing was adjourned until February 2000, when BTC made an application to amend to plead general damages for loss of use. P submitted that the amendment should be refused and/or that the claim should be struck out as an abuse of process, on the basis that (1) it was made so late that it would obstruct the just disposal of the proceedings; (2) the Civil Procedure Rules 1998 encouraged an open approach and the opportunity for defendants to value a claim at an early stage; (3) no witness statements had been served, in breach of the CPR; (4) the statement of truth was false; (5) in reliance upon *Birmingham Corp v. Sowsbery* (1969) 113 S.J. 877, [1969] C.L.Y. 890, the claim could not be made as a general damage claim where the company was profit making; (6) in reliance upon *Axa Insurance Co Ltd v. Swire Fraser Ltd (formerly Robert Fraser Insurance Brokers Ltd) The Times*, January 19, 2000, [2000] C.L.Y. 626 for strike out, there was now no need to show prejudice in the old sense, and (7) though the strict rules of evidence did not apply to the small claims track, Part 17, Part 22 and Part 34 were not specifically excluded, indicating that the strict rules of procedure applied. BTC submitted that no prejudice had been suffered and that P was aware of the application to amend even if it was on a different basis. Further, that as liability was admitted it would be more appropriate to sanction with costs.

Held, dismissing the application for permission to amend, that BTC's conduct amounted to an abuse of process on the grounds that (1) the application was made woefully late, the notes to Part 17 r.17.2(2) were not exclusive, BTC should have sought to amend as soon as was possible; (2) the signing of a false statement of truth was an abuse of process in itself. The important factor was not what BRC's agent meant to convey to his solicitors but what was actually stated in the particulars of claim. BTC's solicitor was duly authorised to sign the statement as true. Further, it was an abuse to proceed with a claim when the statement of truth was obviously wrong; (3) the invoice and the particulars of claim were put forward on a false basis; (4) there was a complete failure to serve any witness evidence, and (5) the claim for special damages was not in a schedule and the claim for general damages disclosed no method of calculation for the claim. In the circumstances, P could not value the claim. The action was dismissed and BTC was ordered to pay costs for the entire action which had been unreasonably incurred.

BLUE TRIANGLE CARS LTD v. PHILLIPS, February 3, 2000, Deputy District Judge Sheldrake, CC (Bristol). [*Ex rel.* Paul McGrath, Barrister, 1 Temple Gardens, Temple, London].

351. Abuse of process – vexatious litigants – court justified in making Grepe v Loam order

[European Convention on Human Rights 1950 Art.6.]

Following protracted litigation between P and WCC, a *Grepe v. Loam* order was made requiring P to obtain the leave of a circuit judge before making an application to the court relating to the litigation. P applied, without gaining the permission of a circuit judge, to set off two costs orders made in his favour against seven orders for costs made in favour of WCC. The judge having become aware of the application, an ex parte order was made preventing it from being heard and making express reference to the terms of the *Grepe v. Loam* order. P subsequently issued a similar application together with an application for permission to appeal against the *Grepe v. Loam* order. Leave to make the applications having been refused, P appealed contending, inter alia, that the restriction of his access to the court had been in breach of his rights both at common law and under the European Convention on Human Rights 1950 Art.6.

Held, dismissing the appeal, that notwithstanding that there was no record of the judge's reasons for his decision to refuse P's applications, he had been entitled to refuse those application; P had made repeated applications to the court and his application to set off the costs orders made in his favour was highly likely to have proved academic. While the right of access to the courts was recognised, both at common law and under the Convention, such recognition was tempered by the right of the court to protect itself against proceedings brought in abuse of process; in the instant case, the making of a *Grepe v. Loam* had been justified, *Wayte v. Slocombe* (Unreported, June 15, 1994) considered.

PARKINS v. WESTMINSTER CITY COUNCIL (GREPE v. LOAM ORDER) PTA 1998/6655/B1, PTA 1998/7808/B3, FC3 1999/5334/C, FC3 1999/5335/C, CCRTI 1998/1433/B1, Brooke, L.J., CA.

352. Adjournment – fast track – judge's discretion not to be interfered with

[Civil Procedure Rules 1998 (SI 1998 3132) Part 28(2).]

T was involved in two motor accidents which gave rise to two claims for damages for personal injuries. The particulars of the second claim, set out in a medical report from a consultant, did not specify any claims in respect of psychiatric injury, despite the existence of a psychiatrist's report suggesting that T was suffering from post traumatic stress disorder. There was no claim for continuing or future loss but merely modest special damages. The defendant admitted liability and subsequently both claims were allocated to the fast track procedure pursuant to the Civil Procedure Rules 1998. The court gave directions for trial in both cases under the provisions of the 1998 Rules Part 28(2). T's solicitors subsequently requested that the defendants agree to the case being allocated to the multi track and an adjournment of the hearing for assessment of damages in order that psychiatric evidence might be obtained. It was contended that the claim was potentially a substantial case on special damages in view of the potential long term damage to T's employment prospects. The request for adjournment was refused and T appealed.

Held, dismissing the appeal, that it was entirely within the judge's discretion to refuse to grant an adjournment. Any psychiatric evidence should have been served much earlier together with particulars of the loss of earnings claim. Notwithstanding the fact that T had failed in her award of damages to beat a Part 36 payment and as a result would be unlikely to receive any of the damages which were awarded to her, the fast track procedure depended on strict adherence to a fixed timetable and the judge's refusal to deviate from this had not been disproportionate.

TAYLOR v. BROCK; TAYLOR v. GRAHAM [2001] C.P. Rep. 11, Tuckey, L.J., CA.

353. **Admissions – liability – entitlement to resile from earlier admission – application of pre-action protocols**

[Civil Procedure Rules 1998 (SI 1998 3132) Part 14 r.14.1 (5), Part 24.]

T and D were involved in a road traffic accident in November 1996. D's insurers denied liability for 30 months, before indicating by letter that they were "now prepared to concede liability". However, without any further correspondence, D entered a defence to T's action for damages in December 1999, denying liability and pleading contributory negligence. T applied for summary judgment pursuant to the Civil Procedure Rules 1998 Part 24 and relied on para.3.9 of the personal injury pre-action protocol to the effect that admissions in cases worth less than £15,000 would be presumed to be binding. T also argued that (1) he had suffered prejudice through the failure to end the case; (2) the insurers ought not to be permitted to resile as a matter of policy, and (3) that it was an abuse because of the delay. D contended that he had a strong case on liability and T had suffered no more than disappointment, *Gale v. Superdrug Stores Plc* [1996] 1 W.L.R. 1089, [1996] C.L.Y. 759 and *Swain v. Hillman* [1999] C.P.L.R. 779, [1999] C.L.Y. 561 cited, and that could be appropriately dealt with by a costs sanction. D further relied on Part 14 r.14.1 (5) of the 1998 Rules and contended that the pre-action protocol para.3.9 did not apply since the instant case was multi-track, having a value exceeding £15,000.

Held, dismissing the application for summary judgment, that (1) as a matter of law, D could resile from an admission made by his insurer. Even if, which the court doubted, the admission in correspondence was that which was envisaged by Part 14 r.14.1 (5), the court had the discretion to allow it to be withdrawn. It could not be more difficult to withdraw pre-issue admissions than those made in pleadings. It was clear that D could resile, *Gale* considered, and (2) whether D ought to be allowed to resile had to be considered in all the circumstances of the case. There was a relatively short delay of six months. Even though D had lacked courtesy in failing to tell T in correspondence before the defence was entered that he intended to resile, there was no evidence of operative reliance on the admission. The admission was not within the scope of para.3.9 of the pre-action protocol because the case was worth well in excess of £15,000. Even if it did apply, the presumption was rebuttable and would have to be examined in the light of the overriding objective. That entailed consideration as to whether D had a real as opposed to a fanciful prospect of success, *Swain* considered. In the instant case, there were significant issues to be tried which went to the heart of liability. D had a real prospect of success in defending the claim. There would be overwhelmingly more prejudice to D in denying him the right to defend than to T in causing him disappointment by allowing resilement.

THOMAS v. DAVIES, June 13, 2000, District Judge Llewellyn, CC (Carmarthen). [*Ex rel.* Palser Grossman Solicitors, Discovery House, Scott Harbour, Cardiff Bay].

354. Admissions – limitations – attempt to resile from admission of liability – certainty of litigation under Civil Procedure Rules 1998

[Civil Procedure Rules 1998 (SI 1998 3132) Part 14. r.14.1 (5).]

H was involved in a road traffic accident in February 1996 when after braking successfully to avoid a car which had pulled into his path, HLBC's lorry drove into the rear of his vehicle. The offending car was not traced. HLBC's insurer subsequently admitted liability in an open letter and H indicated that he would therefore take no further steps on liability. Negotiations ensued and protective proceedings were issued in February 1999. The admission of liability was relied upon in the particulars of claim. The defence, served April 1999, denied liability on the basis of undetectable brake failure. Directions were given for a preliminary hearing as to whether HLBC should be allowed to resile from its earlier admission. H sought to rely on the admission on the basis that if the brake failure had been raised before the expiry of the three year limitation period for a claim against the Motor Insurer's Bureau, H would have had an alternative avenue, which had been lost. HLBC sought to rely upon *Gale v. Superdrug Stores Plc* [1996] 1 W.L.R. 1089, [1996] C.L.Y. 759 supporting the right of a litigant to change his or her mind. The basis of HLBC's submission was that, according to the law prior to the coming into effect of the Civil Procedure Rules 1998, a claimant had a right to withdraw from an admission unless the person relying upon it was able to establish very significant prejudice.

Held, determining the preliminary issue in favour of H, that *Gale* distinguished, did not survive the coming into force of the Rules as their purpose was to make litigation more certain. Part 14 r.14.1 (5) gave the court the power to permit a party to withdraw from an admission, the burden resting upon the party applying. Reference was also made to the PI protocol which indicated that protocol admissions were expected to hold good.

HACKMAN v. HOUNSLOW LBC, December 1, 1999, Judge A Thompson Q.C., CC (Portsmouth). [*Ex rel.* Steven Weddle, Barrister, Hardwicke Building, New Square, Lincoln's Inn, London].

355. Admissions – right to resile from mistaken admission of liability – prejudice

S suffered an injury in the course of his employment when he was hit by an excavator bucket operated by an employee of DJ. S commenced proceedings for personal injuries against DJ who denied any responsibility for the accident. Upon receipt of the summons, DJ forwarded the proceedings to its insurers, BA. BA instructed solicitors, BM, to act on the company's behalf and BM subsequently wrote to S admitting liability. After the accident, but before the admission had been made, DJ sold its assets, but did not transfer any liabilities, to another company, D, and also changed its name to TD. D later changed its name to DJ, on behalf of which the admissions were later made, although in law any liability to S lay, in reality, with TD which subsequently became insolvent. TD was later added in to S's claim as second defendant and an order made that both DJ and TD were jointly and severally liable to compensate S. DJ appealed, contending that (1) BM had never had actual authority to make an admission of liability, and (2) that the company should have been permitted to resile from the admissions made on the basis that S had not suffered any prejudice.

Held, dismissing the appeal, that (1) BM had had actual authority to make admissions, having been instructed by the insurers and having liaised with the general manager of DJ. Even if BM had not had actual authority they would in any event have had ostensible authority to make admissions on behalf of DJ, and (2) there had been serious prejudice to S because in reliance upon the admissions made, S did not avail himself of the opportunity to ascertain the true situation and protect his interests accordingly, *Gale v. Superdrug Stores Plc* [1996] 1 W.L.R. 1089, [1996] C.L.Y. 759 considered.

SOLLITT v. DJ BROADY LTD [2000] C.P.L.R. 259, Lord Bingham of Cornhill, L.C.J., CA.

356. Appeals – application for permission to appeal following refusal on paper – criteria for grant of oral hearing

[European Convention on Human Rights 1950 Art.6.]

K was the respondent to proceedings brought by his ex wife, who had been given permission to apply for financial provision in England in May 1999, in spite of the fact that the marriage had been dissolved in Jordan. K's application to the judge for permission to appeal against that order was refused. K renewed his application for permission to appeal. That application was considered by a single Lord Justice on paper and was refused. Whilst stating that he had formed a firm view as to the merit of the application, the Lord Justice commented that the issues raised in the application had been complex and that the submissions made in K's skeleton argument had been persuasive. He therefore directed that any oral renewal of the application would be considered by two Lord Justices. K renewed his application, whereupon it was listed for hearing before the Lord Justice who had refused his application and a Lord Justice new to the case. K made an application to adjourn the case, arguing that it would be unfair under common law principles of procedural fairness and under the European Convention on Human Rights 1950 Art.6 were a judge who had already made a ruling against him to be involved in determining his application again.

Held, refusing the application, that the relevant practice direction made it clear that an oral renewal of an application for permission to appeal would be determined, wherever possible, by the Lord Justice who had refused permission to appeal, either sitting alone or with another Lord Justice. The intention of the practice direction was to enable an application for permission to appeal to be dealt with by a single judge on paper in the same way as an application for permission to appeal was dealt with by the trial judge. Under the new rules, the Lord Justice had the advantage of being able to consider a full skeleton argument containing all of the relevant material and the applicant's detailed submissions. A refusal on paper was therefore likely to be considered and reasoned. The circumstances in which an oral hearing would achieve any real purpose were exceptional. They were likely to include cases where a party wished to advance fresh submissions, where a manifest error had occurred, where unexpected developments concerning the appeal had taken place or where there had been recent developments in the law. It was important to appreciate that an oral hearing was not an appeal of the previous paper refusal. There had been no breach of the common law principles of procedural fairness or of Art.6 of the Convention since the Lord Justice's decision had been reached following a consideration of a skeleton argument setting out all of the points which had been relevant to the application. There was no requirement that every application should be determined at an oral hearing.

KHREINO v. KHREINO (NO.1) [2000] C.P. Rep. 29, Thorpe, L.J., CA.

357. Appeals – applications – jurisdiction to hear appeal

[Civil Procedure Rules 1998 (SI 1998 3132) Sch.1 r.59.14(3); Civil Procedure (Amendment) Rules 2000 (SI 2000 221).]

Following the refusal of his application for permission to apply for judicial review, C sought to make a renewed application in the Court of Appeal.

Held, determining the preliminary issue in favour of C, that whilst the Court of Appeal had not had the jurisdiction to hear a renewed application made pursuant to the Civil Procedure Rules 1998 Sch.1 r.59.14(3) prior to its revocation by the Civil Procedure (Amendment) Rules 2000, it was appropriate, given the overriding objective of dealing with cases justly, for the court to employ its powers of case management under Part 3 of the 1998 Rules and accordingly hear the renewed application in the form of an appeal against the refusal to grant permission to apply for judicial review.

R. v. VALE OF GLAMORGAN COUNCIL, *ex p.* CLEMENTS *The Times*, August 22, 2000, Otton, L.J., CA.

358. Appeals – case management – multi track – directions on altered appeal procedure in private law civil proceedings – effective after May 2, 2000

[Civil Procedure Rules 1998 (SI 1998 3132) Part 8, Part 12 r.12.7, Part 14 r.14.8, Part 26 r.26.5, Part 52; Civil Procedure (Amendment No. 2) Rules 2000 (SI 2000 940) r.2; Access to Justice Act (Destination of Appeals) Order 2000 (SI 2000 1071).]

T brought an action against CM to recover business premises for rent arrears. The action was initially commenced in the High Court, but was later transferred to the county court and allocated to the multi track where a district judge gave judgment for CM and granted permission to appeal. T sought to appeal to a circuit judge in the county court, but the judge directed that, because it was a multi track claim heard by the district judge by consent, an appeal lay to the Court of Appeal. The Civil Appeal Office disagreed and advised that there was no direct route of appeal to the Court of Appeal but the county court refused jurisdiction. T applied for directions.

Held, giving directions, that the case was ordered to continue as an appeal to a circuit judge in the county court. However, as from May 2, 2000, crucial changes in the appellate regime in civil proceedings in private law matters had been made by the implementation of the Access to Justice Act (Destination of Appeals) Order 2000, which was to be read together with the Civil Procedure Rules 1998 Part 52 and the relevant practice direction, Civil Procedure Rules 1998 Part 52 PD 52. The standard route of appeal lay to the next level of judge in the court hierarchy but, as an exception, where a final decision had been made in a case allocated under r.12.7, r.14.8 or r.26.5 to the multi track by a district judge or circuit judge in the county court, or a master or district judge of the High Court, then, with certain stipulated exceptions, the Court of Appeal was the appellate court. A final decision was defined as one that would conclusively determine either the entire proceedings or a part of a claim which had been directed to be heard separately. It did not apply to striking out orders or summary judgments, nor to claims under Part 8. Except in specified cases, permission to appeal was required and would only be granted where there was a real prospect of success or for some other compelling reason. Appeals would be limited to consideration of the lower court's decision and a second appeal would be to the Court of Appeal alone and would only be allowed if a relevant issue of principle or practice was raised or there was some other compelling reason, not merely because it was "properly arguable". Generally, an appeal would only be permitted if the lower court decision was wrong, or there was a serious procedural irregularity in that court causing injustice. Apart from the exceptional cases, all appellate courts were given the same powers in respect of appeals. The importance of first instance decisions was highlighted and it was noted that there was a need to ensure accuracy in the recording of all decisions following the change of procedure. Under the Civil Procedure (Amendment No. 2) Rules 2000 r.2 the new rules would be applicable to those cases where the notice of appeal or the application for permission to appeal had been made on, or after, May 2, 2000.

TANFERN LTD v. CAMERON-MACDONALD [2000] 1 W.L.R. 1311, Brooke, L.J., CA.

359. Appeals – interlocutory judgments – power of single Lord Justice to vary perfected order

[Supreme Court Act 1981 s.58(1); Rules of the Supreme Court 1965 (SI 1965 1776) Ord.59 r.2(b)(ii).]

P appealed against the dismissal of his action in respect of the administration of his deceased uncle's estate and brought various applications to the Court of Appeal. In December 17, 1998 a directions hearing in respect of the substantive appeal was heard, the judge ordered that any future applications should be listed prior to the commencement of the substantive hearing. That procedural order was later amended. P sought permission to appeal out of time against an interlocutory order concerning the conduct and management of the substantive appeal. A single Lord Justice varied the direction so that the appeal would be heard prior to the substantive appeal. P appealed, contending that the single Lord Justice had no power to vary a perfected order of the full Court of Appeal and the varied direction was prejudicial to P by denying him a fair hearing at the substantive appeal.

Held, dismissing the appeal, that a single supervising Lord Justice had the power to make such an order under the Rules of the Supreme Court Ord.59 r.2(b)(ii) subject to the Supreme Court Act 1981 s.58(1), given that a full court had the power to vary orders. P's design was to influence the constitution of the court hearing the substantive appeal and the appeal against an interlocutory decision given prior to the trial was of a different nature from the other 13 applications listed to be heard before the substantive appeal.

PEROTTI v. WATSON (VARIATION OF PERFECTED ORDER) [2001] C.P. Rep. 5, Mummery, L.J., CA.

360. Appeals – judicial review – refusal of permission by Court of Appeal – jurisdiction of House of Lords

[Company Directors Disqualification Act 1986.]

E appealed against the refusal of the Court of Appeal to grant him permission to apply for judicial review of the Secretary of State's decision to continue proceedings against him under the Company Directors Disqualification Act 1986. A previous application for permission to seek judicial review had been refused by a single judge, and E had not requested permission to appeal against that decision either from the judge himself or from the Court of Appeal.

Held, dismissing the appeal, that the Court of Appeal only had jurisdiction to determine an appeal against a judge's refusal to grant permission to apply for judicial review if permission to appeal against that decision had been granted, and since the judge had not given permission to appeal, the Court of Appeal had by implication also refused permission to appeal. The House of Lords had no jurisdiction to entertain an appeal against a refusal of the Court of Appeal to grant permission to appeal, *Lane v. Esdaile* [1891] A.C. 210 followed and *Kemper Reinsurance Co v. Minister of Finance (Bermuda)* [2000] 1 A.C. 1, [1998] C.L.Y. 381 distinguished.

R. v. SECRETARY OF STATE FOR TRADE AND INDUSTRY, *ex p.* EASTAWAY [2000] 1 W.L.R. 2222, Lord Bingham of Cornhill, HL.

361. Appeals – new points of appeal not argued at first instance – prejudice

[Civil Procedure Rules 1998 (SI 1998 3132).]

SG was a party to three non deliverable forward foreign exchange contracts with ANZ. The contracts were subject to the terms of an agreement between the two parties stipulating the method by which losses would be calculated in the event of early termination. Following the announcement of a Russian banking moratorium, the contracts were terminated early. A dispute arose as to the calculation of losses between the parties and summary judgment granted in favour of ANZ ([1999] 2 All E.R. (Comm) 625). SG appealed, and sought permission to appeal on two new points not argued in the previous hearing, contending that, although departing from the "common ground" before the judge, the points related to matters of construction and so to points of law. It was reasonable, SG argued, that the court should approach the issues as if the two points had been submitted before the previous judge on the assumption that, however the judge might have ruled, the case would have come before the Court of Appeal. The failure to raise the points earlier would not therefore cause any prejudice to ANZ.

Held, dismissing the appeal and refusing the applications for permission to appeal, that both new points could and should have been raised before the judge at first instance. SG's request that the matters be considered was outweighed by the potential prejudice to ANZ resulting from its interest in the judgment of the lower court. The court had a duty under the Civil Procedure Rules 1998 actively to manage cases with the objective of dealing with them in a fair and expeditious manner.

AUSTRALIA AND NEW ZEALAND BANKING GROUP LTD v. SOCIETE GENERALE [2000] 1 All E.R. (Comm) 682, Mance, L.J., CA.

362. Appeals – no second chance of appeal on different aspect of judgment

T appealed against the refusal to list its application for permission to appeal against a judgment in favour of CA.

Held, dismissing the appeal, that although it was permissible to appeal against a "specified part of the judgment or order", that did not mean that one part of an appeal might be made by one notice and then another part of the judgment appealed against by a further notice. It was important in the interests of justice that appellants should present their whole case to the court at one time.

COMMERCIAL ACCEPTANCES LTD v. TOWNSEND INVESTMENTS INC [2000] C.P.L.R. 421, Lord Woolf, M.R., CA.

363. Appeals – permission to appeal – compelling reason to set aside permission

[Civil Procedure Rules 1998 (SI 1998 3132) Part 52 r.52.9.]

P applied to set aside the grant to H of permission to appeal against the setting aside of his statutory demand and the quashing of a bankruptcy order against P.

Held, refusing the application, that permission to appeal would only be set aside under the Civil Procedure Rules 1998 Part 52 r.52.9 if there was a compelling reason to do so. The guidance of earlier authorities remained relevant, *Iran Nabuvat, The (1990)* [1990] 1 W.L.R. 1115, [1990] C.L.Y. 3735, and *Smith v. Cosworth Casting Processes Ltd (Practice Note)* [1997] 1 W.L.R. 1538, [1997] C.L.Y. 501 followed.

HUNT v. PEASEGOOD *The Times*, October 20, 2000, Aldous, L.J., CA.

364. Appeals – striking out – previous litigation concerning same subject matter but different parties

[Company Directors Disqualification Act 1986 s.6.]

M was managing director of a company which ran into financial difficulties. At the instigation of B, the company went into creditors' liquidation. Three major cases involving M but not B followed. First, claims brought by M against the receivers, were dismissed. Then successful proceedings were brought against him by the Secretary of State under the Company Directors Disqualification Act 1986 s.6. It was held that his misconduct and systematic dishonesty showed that he was unfit to be concerned in the management of a company. In the third case M claimed £3 million for wrongful dismissal against the company. The claim was dismissed on the basis that, where the issue in proceedings between a director and a company had been the subject matter of a finding against the director under the Act, subsequent proceedings could be dismissed as an abuse of process of the court. Shortly before the end of the limitation period, M brought an action against the receivers, their employees and B. An application was made to strike out and M responded by requesting leave to amend his original statement of claim outside the limitation period. The proceedings were struck out and M sought leave to appeal against the finding that the action against the bank alleging the inducement of his wrongful dismissal should be struck out.

Held, granting leave to appeal, that it was arguable that leave should be given on the claim that the bank had induced the wrongful dismissal as that claim was made in the original statement of claim. The judge should have appreciated that, in general, decisions in previous proceedings are binding only between the parties and persons who are privy thereto. On an application for leave, it would not be right to refuse if in so doing the law would be extended, as it might be in this case.

MANSON v. BARCLAYS BANK PLC [1999] C.P.L.R. 825, Henry, L.J., CA.

365. Appeals – time limits – extension of time granted despite history of interlocutory delay and non compliance

[Civil Procedure Rules 1998 (SI 1998 3132) Part 3 r.3.9(1).]

C obtained interlocutory judgment for damages to be assessed in his claim against W, following W's failure to comply with the terms of an "unless" order. W appealed, and the court at first instance granted an extension of time to appeal out of time, set aside the judgment, and imposed a condition that W pay £4,000 into court within 28 days. C appealed, contending that the judge had failed to pay due regard to the Civil Procedure Rules 1998 Part 3 r.3.9(1) and in particular, that he had failed to give proper consideration to the history of interlocutory delay by W, that there was insufficient evidence to justify the order made, and that the judge should not have brought into account the extent to which W's defence was arguable.

Held, allowing the appeal, that the points against the grant of an extension of time for appeal strongly outweighed those arguments in favour, and although this had been a matter for judicial discretion, it was plain on the facts of the instant case that the judge had been wrong to exercise that discretion as he had done. Furthermore, the judge had erred in making the order subject to the requirement that W pay monies into court within a specified period, when he was plainly not in a financial position to do so. If a judge considered the imposition of a condition in any given case, the individual affected should at least possess the prospect of compliance.

CHAPPLE v. WILLIAMS [1999] C.P.L.R. 731, May, L.J., CA.

366. Appeals – time limits – statutory interpretation – extension of time limit due to closure of court office

[Housing Act 1996 s.204.]

A filed a request for the entry of an appeal under the Housing Act 1996 s.204 23 days after being notified of the decision on her review. It was held below that her appeal had been brought out of time. A contended that she had not been able to file her request within the 21 day period prescribed by s.204 because that day fell on a Saturday when the court office was closed.

Held, allowing the appeal, that the filing of a document could only be done during court opening hours, and since the last day of the prescribed period fell on a day when the court office was closed, the prescribed period was extended to the first day thereafter on which the court office was open.

AADAN v. BRENT LBC [2000] C.P. Rep. 17, Chadwick, L.J., CA.

367. Application notices – Civil Procedure Rules – striking out a disproportionate response to procedural irregularity

[Civil Procedure Rules 1998 (SI 1998 3132) Part 3 r.3.9(1).]

PH had issued proceedings on June 10, 1999 claiming greater provision from her late husband's estate using the old form N208, which form had been superseded by the new form N208 under the Civil Procedure Rules 1998. The nature of the claim, the order sought by PH and all other material facts were set out in the application. There were other defects with the papers served on the defendants. PH appealed against the striking out of her statement of case by the district judge but it was held that there were too many flaws in the proceedings. PH appealed against that decision.

Held, allowing the appeal, that the judge had correctly considered the factors set out in Part 3 r.3.9(1) but the exercise of his discretion was seriously flawed as all information necessary to understand the claim was present. The decision to strike out the claim was a disproportionate response to technical irregularities and not in the interests of justice. The Rules were intended to make civil litigation more efficient but the overriding objective was to enable the court to deal with cases justly.

HANNIGAN v. HANNIGAN [2000] 2 F.C.R. 650, Brooke, L.J., CA.

368. Automatic directions – transitional arrangements – variation by consent not inconsistent with automatic directions

[Fatal Accidents Act 1976; County Court Rules 1981 (SI 1981 1687) Ord.17 r.11; Civil Procedure Rules 1998 (SI 1998 3132) Part 51.]

D brought a claim under the Fatal Accidents Act 1976 arising out of an air crash in which her husband, the co-pilot, died. Automatic directions applied, but a consent order made in November 1998 varied the time for compliance with discovery and exchange of witness and expert statements. It also provided for the time for requesting the proper officer to fix a date for the hearing to be delayed to a later date, and that the provisions of the County Court Rules 1981 Ord.17 r.11 remained in full force and effect and the date on which the action would automatically be struck out for failure to request a date for the hearing would be August 1999. D failed to request a hearing date by August 1999. On LA's application, it was found that the order of November 1998 was a manual order, as the strike out date had been reduced to eight months from 1 December 1998. Therefore, by reason of the Civil Procedure Rules 1998 Part 51 PD 51 para.9, the order had still to be complied with. The action was accordingly struck out as at August 1, 1999. D appealed.

Held, allowing the appeal, that the order of November 1998 did not involve a variation that was repugnant to the automatic directions nor so inconsistent with them as to be displaced, *Bannister v. SGB Plc* [1998] 1 W.L.R. 1123, [1997] C.L.Y. 736 considered. Accordingly, the order did not oust the automatic directions. By virtue of Part 51 PD 51 para.6(3) of the 1998 rules the automatic directions under the 1981 Rules did not apply and D's action was not struck out. Even if the action had been struck out, it would have been appropriate to allow D's application for relief against the sanction of striking out.

DENTON v. LAMBSON AVIATION LTD, July 17, 2000, Judge Butter Q.C., CC (Central London). [*Ex rel.* Robert Weir, Barrister, Devereux Chambers, Devereux Court, London].

369. Case management – application to vary case decision to be made at early stage and by way of appeal

[Civil Procedure Rules 1998 (SI 1998 3132) Part 3 r.2.3.1 (7), Part 29.]

L and B were involved in a road accident in July 1993 and L made a high value claim against B which came before the court for a case management conference in October 1999. Both parties attended and the district judge on that occasion directed that evidence from seven expert witnesses could be given at trial. He further directed that three were to give oral evidence and four to give evidence by way of written report. In March 2000, L issued an application to vary the order. L, by that time, wished to have two of the experts whose written reports were to be relied upon attend trial for cross examination. There had been no material change of circumstances between the date of the case management conference and the application to vary. B objected to the application on the basis that L was effectively trying to appeal against the first district judge's decision out of time. B contended that L should have appealed to a circuit judge. B relied upon the Civil Procedure Rules 1998 Part 29 and Civil Procedure Rules 1998 Part 29 PD 29 para.6.3(2) which provided that a party "should" appeal in such circumstances, rather than apply back to a district judge for a variation. L countered that the expression "should" did not mean "must" and that, relying upon the general case management powers provided by Part 3 r.3.1 (7) of the 1998 Rules, the second district judge still had jurisdiction to hear the application.

Held, dismissing the application, that Part 3 r.3.1 (7) must be read in the light of the clear statement in para.6.2(1) of the Practice Direction which stressed that if variation were to be sought, the application must be made at an early stage. Paragraph.6.2(2) permitted the court to assume that a party was content with a direction if no early application had been made. In any event, para.6.2(3) made it clear that an application to vary in these circumstances "should" be made by way of an appeal to a circuit judge. The word "should" was a strong word and the distinction sought to be drawn between the expressions "should" and "must" was not an attractive one. Applications of this nature should be brought by way of an appeal unless there were exceptional circumstances, of which none were present in the instant case.

LITTLER v. BARRACLOUGH, April 12, 2000, District Judge Bellamy, QBD. [*Ex rel.* Steven Turner, Barrister, Park Lane Chambers, 19 Westgate, Leeds].

370. Case management – automatic strike out – consent orders – effect on abolition of strike out rules

[Civil Procedure Rules 1998 (SI 1998 3132) Part 51.]

B issued a personal injury claim in September 1997 and an order was made by consent on February 23, 1999 for the extension of B's time for requesting a hearing date until October 31, 1999 and that in default his claim would be automatically struck out. B did not request a hearing date within that time, but, before an automatic stay took effect under the Civil Procedure Rules 1998 Part 51 PD 51 para.19, B sought a declaration that the claim was not struck out. The judge granted the declaration, holding that the automatic strike out had been abolished so the sanction ordered could not take effect. A appealed, contending that the consent order took the action outside the old automatic directions, and that was the intention of A's solicitor in redrafting the order, and the sanction was therefore effective.

Held, dismissing the appeal, that the parties' intentions were irrelevant to the construction of an order. The order simply varied the strike out deadline. It did not oust the automatic directions, as it was not repugnant to them. Since the automatic strike out had been abolished by Part 51 PD 51 para.6, the sanction fell away.

BYRNE v. ANIXTER (UK) LTD, June 30, 2000, Judge Hull Q.C., CC (Epsom). [*Ex rel.* Ivor Collett, Barrister, No.1 Serjeant's Inn, Fleet Street, London].

371. Case management – desirability of preliminary determination of issues post Civil Procedure Rules to be decided upon the facts and circumstances of each case

[Civil Procedure Rules 1998 (SI 1998 3132).]

D applied to the court for preliminary determination of certain issues raised by R in a trade mark dispute, on the basis that if R established its case on the basis of estoppel that would be determinative of the issue and result in consequent savings of costs, delay and court time in accordance with the objectives of the Civil Procedure Rules 1998. R submitted that it was possible that not all the issues raised would be decided in favour of the same party and that some might have to be the subject of a reference to the ECJ. R maintained that costs and delay would thereby be increased because, if the preliminary issues were decided in D's favour, it was likely that there would need to be a second referral to the ECJ arising out of issues raised at trial. D suggested that extraction of potential referral points from the statements of case at the time when the preliminary issues were presented to the ECJ would avoid successive referrals.

Held, dismissing the application, that observations made in cases prior to the introduction of the 1998 Rules, regarding the desirability or otherwise of preliminary issues, remained valid, *Prudential Assurance Co Ltd v. Newman Industries Ltd (No.2)* [1982] Ch. 204, [1982] C.L.Y. 331 and *Tilling v. Whiteman* [1980] A.C. 1, [1979] C.L.Y. 1624 considered. The court had to consider the advantages and disadvantages of preliminary determination as well as the interests of all parties, savings in costs, the avoidance of litigation and reduction in the length of future hearings. In this case (1) if a reference to the ECJ were to be made it would be desirable for it to be accompanied by relevant findings of fact; (2) the case might well be determined on issues of fact rather than law rendering some or all of the points of law raised at this stage academic and possibly restricting or obviating the scope of any reference, and (3) it was always possible that a further point of European law could become apparent at trial thus resulting in a double reference despite earlier strenuous efforts to avoid this.

DUALIT LTD v. ROWLETT CATERING APPLIANCES LTD, Trans. Ref. 9901306, Neuberger, J., Ch D.

372. Case management – directions – parties' agreement as to directions overridden by judge's decision to transfer case to High Court – consent directions not binding

[Protection from Harassment Act 1997; Civil Procedure Rules 1998 (SI 1998 3132).]

After M had presented bankruptcy petitions against T and S in the county court, the parties reached an agreement concerning directions for the future conduct of the proceedings. T and S opposed the petitions by arguing that they had a claim against M under the Protection from Harassment Act 1997. After they had sought interlocutory relief against M in the High Court, M made an application to have the bankruptcy proceedings transferred to the High Court so that the petitions could be heard together with the applications which had been issued by T and S, in their harassment action. It was argued by one of the debtors that the court was precluded from acceding to M's application by virtue of the earlier agreement which had been reached between the parties regarding directions.

Held, granting the application, that, whilst the court would attach great importance to an agreement between the parties, it was not precluded from overriding such an agreement if the circumstances of the case rendered it appropriate to do so. Such an approach accorded with the spirit of the Civil Procedure Rules 1998 and did not conflict with the old rules, whereby an agreement concerning directions was not regarded as contractually binding.

DEBTORS (NO.13-MISC-2000 & NO.14-MISC-2000), *Re The Times*, April 10, 2000, Neuberger, J., Ch D.

373. Case management – failure to comply with order – striking out – reinstatement of defence

[Law of Property Act 1925 s.146; Civil Procedure Rules 1998 (SI 1998 3132) Part 3 r.3.4(2)(c), r.3.9(1).]

BA, a landlord, appealed against a refusal to reinstate its defence and counterclaim which had been struck out in proceedings commenced by C, a tenant who sought relief from forfeiture. BA had served notice upon C pursuant to the Law of Property Act 1925 s.146 alleging breaches of covenant and had subsequently re-entered the premises and forfeited the lease. C contended that the forfeiture was invalid and sought damages. Directions for the exchange of witness statements were given at an interim hearing but BA served its statement upon C two or three days after the due date and did not file it at court until some six weeks later. C made a successful application without notice under the Civil Procedure Rules 1998 Part 3 r.3.4(2)(c) to strike out BA's defence and counterclaim for failure to comply with the order. BA sought to reinstate its statements of case by way of application under Part 3 r.3.9(1) but the judge refused to grant relief and ordered that the trial on damages for C should proceed on the basis that there had been no valid forfeiture of the lease. BA appealed.

Held, allowing the appeal and restoring the defence in counterclaim, that there had been a minor, technical breach of the order. There had been no prejudice to C as a result of late service as he had already been in possession of BA's witness statement prior to the interim hearing. The witness statement had been filed at court before the defence and counterclaim were struck out and there had been no suggestion that the trial could not go ahead on the fixed date despite BA's breach of a case management direction. The judge had erred in failing to consider the checklist of matters in r.3.9(1) and had misunderstood the nature of BA's defence as he had allowed C's claim to proceed on the basis that there had been no lawful forfeiture when, in fact, BA had a substantive defence to C's claim for damages, *Biguzzi v. Rank Leisure Plc* [1999] 1 W.L.R. 1926, [1999] C.L.Y. 367 followed, *Bansal v. Cheema* (Unreported, March 2, 2000), [2000] C.L.Y. 338 followed.

CANK v. BROADYARD ASSOCIATES LTD [2001] C.P. Rep. 47, Morritt, L.J., CA.

374. Case management – proceedings commenced under CPR Part 8 – order to transfer to Part 7 at Part 8 hearing – claimant's liability for defendant's costs in preparing for Part 8 hearing;

[Civil Procedure Rules 1998 (SI 1998 3132) Part 7, Part 8.]

T lent H the deposit for a freehold commercial property. A written agreement required T's interest to be secured by a second charge on the property following completion. Up to completion, H was to pay £100 weekly, with no payments afterwards as T was to take 50 per cent of any profit from the sale following redemption and repayment of the advance. The agreement made no provision for a date for sale by T. T gave 28 days' written notice requiring sale, which H claimed not to have received. T brought an action for an order for sale and division of the proceeds, claiming that no fixed sale date had been included in the agreement so that repayment could be demanded on reasonable notice. Furthermore, that H had breached the agreement by failing to register the charge and in entering into a formal mortgage requiring the commercial lender's consent before the granting of a second charge. T commenced proceedings under the Civil Procedure Rules 1998 Part 8. H advised T that Part 8 was inappropriate to this type of case and that the matter should be the subject of a defence and then proceed to allocation. T declined to consent to the transfer to the Part 7 procedure. H therefore prepared an acknowledgement of claim and a statement in support. At the Part 8 hearing it was ordered that the matter be transferred to the Part 7 procedure for a defence and allocation. H supplied a summary assessment of costs, but it was held that costs should be dealt with at the conclusion of the case. H appealed, contending that (1) the matter should not have been brought under Part 8 as there were significant arguments of both law and fact involved of which T was aware and that his refusal had forced H to expend unnecessary costs; (2) the court had a duty summarily to assess costs which applied in the instant case; (3) use of Part 8 as a shortcut to summary judgment was to be discouraged by costs penalties, and (4) although T was only represented by a McKenzie friend at the hearing, that person was a former solicitor and T had a duty under the overriding objective to behave in a reasonable and co-operative manner in the conduct of proceedings. T asserted that there were no substantial disputed issues of fact and that the main dispute was to law only so that there was no reason why the matter could not have been dealt with at the Part 8 hearing.

Held, allowing the appeal, that (1) T was to pay H's costs of the hearing before the district judge and of the appeal, summarily assessed in the respective sums of £647.45 and £856.70 making a total sum of £1,504.15, and (2) if the whole sum of £1,504.15 was not paid by 4 pm on December 1, 1999, the action was to be stayed until payment.

TREW v. HAWES, November 3, 1999, Judge Langan Q.C., CC (Norwich). [*Ex rel.* Rogers & Norton Solicitors, The Old Chapel, 5-7 Willow Lane, Norwich, Norfolk].

375. Case management – skeleton arguments – appropriateness of sequential exchange

Held, that in complex cases the sequential exchange of skeleton arguments was more appropriate, giving the claimant an opportunity to state his case first, and for the defendant to respond. Although the usual practice in the Chancery Division was the use of simultaneous exchange of skeleton arguments, there was no indication in the rules whether simultaneous or sequential exchange was preferred, and the appropriate course depended on the individual case. The use of sequential exchange should not operate unfairly against the claimants, if used to allow the defendants to draft their skeleton arguments to reflect the claimant's case.

BROWN v. BENNETT (EXCHANGE OF SKELETON ARGUMENTS) *The Times*, June 13, 2000, Neuberger, J., Ch D.

376. Case management – striking out of primary claim – unreliable evidence

[Civil Procedure Rules 1998 (SI 1998 3132) Part 3 r.3.1 (2) (m).]
S severed a nerve in his finger in an accident at work whilst operating a lathe. S claimed he slipped on a greasy board and fell against the lathe. U alleged that S had deliberately used his finger to slow the turning lathe before it had stopped turning and was the author of his own misfortune. U alleged that S had done this before and had been warned not to on at least three occasions. In evidence, S denied that he had ever done this and denied ever having been warned. By amendment at trial, S pleaded an alternative case that if U's version was correct, then U was negligent in not removing S from working on the lathe. At the close of S's case, U applied to make a submission of no case to answer without being put to an election not to call evidence if the submission failed.

Held, dismissing the claim, that U was permitted to make the submission, *Mullan v. Birmingham City Council The Times*, July 29, 1999, [1999] C.L.Y. 361 considered, and applying the court's case management powers under the Civil Procedure Rules 1998 Part 3 r.3.1(2)(m) that the evidence of S and his consulting engineer was so unreliable that S's primary case of slipping was unsustainable and that part of his case should be struck out. The recorder considered that he could limit evidence called by U to the issues raised by the alternative case of warnings given and the question why S was not taken off the machine. As U had indicated that no evidence would be called on those issues following the striking out of S's primary case, the only evidence before the court was S's denial of touching the turning lathe and his denial that he had ever been warned. The necessary evidential base for the alternative case was therefore lacking.

SPRATLEY v. UNIVERSAL EQUIPMENT LTD, September 9, 1999, Recorder West-Knights, CC (Kingston upon Thames). [*Ex rel.* Morgan Cole Solicitors, Apex Plaza, Forbury Road, Reading].

377. Causes of action – settlements – claim for breach of contract and other losses following termination of agency agreement – impact of prior settlement agreement upon subsequent claim

An insurance company, A, acquired an agency network to sell the investment products of a company, T, a role formerly undertaken for approximately 20 years by a company, IC. Following the acquisition, T closed to new investment business and A entered into an agency agreement with IC, under which IC was appointed as A's representative. T also entered into a new agency arrangement with IC limited to existing investment plans. T subsequently terminated its agreement with IC alleging that IC had breached LAUTRO regulations. Ten days later, A gave notice of termination to IC under the agreement between IC and A. IC issued proceedings against T seeking a declaration that T was liable to meet IC's claim for commission despite the purported termination of the agreement. T defended the claim on the basis that representatives of IC had been guilty of mis-selling policies in breach of LAUTRO rules. IC went into liquidation before a trial on the preliminary issues could take place. At first instance (*The Times*, July 19, 1999, [1999] C.L.Y. 1640) the court concluded that the allegations of misselling were wholly unfounded. Following liquidation, the liquidator assigned IC's cause of action against T to the individual directors and shareholders who included H. H and others pursued the action against T and added a claim for the loss of IC as a viable business on the basis that the cessation of commission and the nature of the allegations made had led to IC's liquidation. The action against T was ultimately settled upon payment of £10 million. The agreement reached was incorporated into a Tomlin order and included an agreement between the parties that no further legal proceedings would be pursued. H subsequently commenced proceedings against A alleging breach of contract and seeking damages for the negligent publication of the misselling allegations. The impact of the prior settlement between T and IC was tried as a preliminary issue. The court at first instance held that the claim against A consisted of the same subject matter as that which had formed the basis of the claim against T. On that basis the judge concluded that the form of release contained within the Tomlin order operated to preclude the pursuit of any further proceedings in respect of those losses and accordingly struck out H's claim against A. H appealed.

Held, allowing the appeal, that (1) it was not possible to state that H's claim against A had been extinguished in view of the settlement with T since T and A were not joint tortfeasors. Instead, they had been separately responsible for consecutive breaches of two distinct contracts with IC, *Jameson v. Central Electricity Generating Board (No.1)* [1999] 2 W.L.R. 141, [1999] C.L.Y. 1386 considered. Furthermore, the claim against A did not include precisely the same matters which had been the subject of the claim against T. Additional allegations had been made concerning the publication of untrue reports and references to various parties and certain claims extended over more extensive periods of time; (2) there was no evidence of any common intention by the parties to the settlement agreement to preclude H from pursuing any further claim against A. The most realistic interpretation was that T had settled all aspects of the claim against it to include the claim for commission, which T could not realistically defend, and had made a reasonable settlement of those aspects of the claim over which it would have been possible to raise a triable issue, namely the assertion that T's actions had led to the termination of the agreement with A. On that basis, T would be unlikely to face a claim for contribution in any further proceedings between A and H, but would preserve to themselves the possibility of pursuing their own contribution claim against A. If there had been any contrary intent, then it would have been a simple matter to amend the release clause accordingly, and (3) the judge had erred in concluding that the possibility that the proceedings might eventually result in a declaration that the contract had been breached but only nominal damages be recovered was an additional reason for striking out the claim. The allegations of misselling, which had been withdrawn by T, had not been withdrawn by A and it was clearly vital to H that he should be able to seek to establish that the allegations, which had an undoubtedly serious impact upon his standing in the financial services industry, were unfounded.

HEATON v. AXA EQUITY & LAW LIFE ASSURANCE SOCIETY PLC [2001] Ch. 173, Chadwick, L.J., CA.

378. Charging orders – legal representation – sale of assets – discretionary variation of charging order

[Charging Orders Act 1979.]

P applied for permission to appeal the dismissal of his application for leave to sell his property, his assets having previously been made the subject of a freezing injunction. The property was also subject to a charging order obtained by W, the effect of which was that any equity in the property was to be used for the discharge of costs orders obtained by W earlier in the proceedings. P sought an order that the property be sold or, alternatively, that he should be able to raise money upon it to fund his legal representation.

Held, granting permission to appeal and allowing the appeal in part, that the freezing order did not restrict the sale or charge of the property for the purpose of funding legal representation, but the charging order did have that effect. The charging order would be varied under the discretion afforded the court under the Charging Orders Act 1979. Any sums obtained by the sale or charge of the property were to be paid into the client account of a solicitor, out of which up to £80,000 could be released to P for the sole purpose of funding legal advice.

PEROTTI v. WATSON (FUNDS FOR LEGAL REPRESENTATION) A3/2000/ 5456, Aldous, L.J., CA.

379. Civil Procedure Rules

CIVIL PROCEDURE (AMENDMENT) RULES 2000, SI 2000 221 (L.1); made under the Civil Procedure Act 1997 s.2. In force: r.2, r.8, r.20, r.40: 000228; Remainder: 000502; £5.80.

These Rules replace some of the most frequently used provisions of the Rules of the Supreme Court 1965 (SI 1965 1776) with rules to form an integral part of the Civil Procedure Rules 1998 (SI 1998 3132). They include new provisions on service out of the jurisdiction; representative parties; security for costs; sale of land and conveyancing counsel; and appeals. Additionally, new rules have been provided on group litigation, and on the procedure which will be used when the remaining provisions of the Defamation Act 1996 are brought into force in England and Wales.

380. Civil Procedure Rules – assessment of costs

CIVIL PROCEDURE (AMENDMENT NO.3) RULES 2000, SI 2000 1317 (L.11); made under the Civil Procedure Act 1997 s.2. In force: July 3, 2000; £2.50.

These Rules amend the Civil Procedure Rules 1998 (SI 1998 3132) to regulate proceedings where the new funding arrangements for legal proceedings, introduced by the Access to Justice Act 1999 s.27, s.29 and s.30, apply and to provide for the assessment of costs in such proceedings. Rule 17 sets out a new procedure which may be followed when only the amount of costs is in dispute. Rule 34 sets out the procedure for the assessment of costs where the court has made a Group Litigation Order under the Civil Procedure Rules Part 19 Section III.

381. Civil Procedure Rules – assessment of costs – appeals

CIVIL PROCEDURE (AMENDMENT NO.2) RULES 2000, SI 2000 940 (L.9); made under the Civil Procedure Act 1997 s.2. In force: May 2, 2000; £1.50.

These Rules amend provisions governing the procedure for appeals from detailed assessments of costs made by authorised court officers contained in the Civil Procedure Rules 1998 (SI 1998 3132 as amended by SI 2000 221). They add a new provision on service that the court must be satisfied that England and Wales is the proper place to bring the claim before giving permission to serve a claim form out of the jurisdiction.

382. Civil Procedure Rules – human rights – declaration of compatibility

CIVIL PROCEDURE (AMENDMENT NO.4) RULES 2000, SI 2000 2092 (L.16); made under the Civil Procedure Act 1997 s.1, s.2. In force: October 2, 2000; £2.50.

These Rules, which amend the Civil Procedure Rules 1998 (SI 1998 3132 as amended), add rules governing the procedure for an application under the Human Rights Act 1998 s.4 for a declaration of incompatibility and for a claim under s.7(1)(a) that a public authority has acted in a way incompatible with a Convention right; amend Part 52 to include small claims appeals; revoke Order 53 of the Supreme Court Rules in Sch.1 of the Rules, which governed applications for judicial review, and replace it with a new Part 54; and revoke Order 49, r.6 of the County Court Rules in Sch.2 of the Rules to allow the judge to direct a hearing of whether possession should be postponed.

383. Contempt of court – contempt law unchanged by Civil Procedure Rules – overriding objective to deal with cases fairly

[Civil Procedure Rules 1998 (SI 1998 3132) Part 32 r.32.14.]

M applied for permission to proceed against L for contempt of court under the Civil Procedure Rules 1998 Part 32 r.32.14, on the basis that L had made false statements in an action for breach of copyright in which judgment had been entered in favour of M. L had verified its pleadings as well as witness statements by means of statements of truth and M contended that a strong line should be taken in order to protect the benefit intended to be derived from statements of truth.

Held, refusing the application, that Part 32 r.32.14 had not created a new category of contempt and the application of that rule was still subject to the overriding objective to ensure that every case was dealt with fairly and justly. The courts would be astute, nevertheless, to ensure that the verification of documents by statements of truth should be well policed.

MALGAR LTD v. RE LEACH (ENGINEERING) LTD [2000] C.P. Rep. 39, Sir Richard Scott V.C., Ch D.

384. Contribution – third parties – nature of damage alleged against parties

[Civil Liabilities (Contribution) Act 1978 s.1 (1).]

R commissioned major building works at its hospital. After a number of disputes it entered into arbitration with the contractor, which was settled with a payment of £6.2 million to T. R had incurred over £2 million in fees and costs. It began the instant action for recovery of sums lost in the arbitration against its professional advisors, including the architect, W. W sought a contribution from T under the Civil Liabilities (Contribution) Act 1978 s.1 (1). T contended that the contribution claimed by W was not in respect of the same damage claimed against T. The claim was dismissed at first instance on that basis ([1999] B.L.R. 385) and W appealed.

Held, dismissing the appeal, that the damage alleged against T was different to that R claimed against W. The claim against T arose because of delay in completing the building work, whereas R alleged that W had reduced its ability to obtain compensation or succeed in the arbitration.

ROYAL BROMPTON HOSPITAL NHS TRUST v. HAMMOND (NO.3) 69 Con. L.R. 145, Stuart-Smith, L.J., CA.

385. Costs – adjourned case management conference – adjournment to permit amendment to particulars of claim – appeal out of time against costs order

[Civil Procedure Rules 1998 (SI 1998 3132) Sch.2 Ord.13 r.1.]

H was involved in a road traffic accident in 1996. A medical report was prepared on his behalf in September 1997. Proceedings were issued in December 1998. The pleadings made no mention of a *Smith v. Manchester* type claim. The medical report stated that the whiplash symptoms would be permanent if lasting over two years. Two years on, H asserted that he still had residual symptoms. H's witness statement referred to depression and headaches causing him to give up work in December 1998 when aged 59. A letter dated April 7, 1999 was written to S referring to the loss of employment and detriment on the labour market. H did not make it clear what his earnings were and did not clarify whether the claim was for loss of earnings or a *Smith v. Manchester* type claim. H argued that he was ready for trial. A case management conference was set for September 23, 1999. The district judge asked if the claim was for continuing loss of earnings or a *Smith v. Manchester* type claim. H's representative said that it was a loss of earnings claim arising from psychological symptoms. This had not been pleaded and was not shown in the medical report, which only dealt with whiplash symptoms. The district judge ordered that it should be pleaded and gave leave to amend the particulars of claim. He then adjourned the case management conference so that the issues could be made clear before final directions were given. The district judge ordered H to pay the costs of the same. H appealed the order under the Civil Procedure Rules 1998 Sch.2 Ord.13 r.1. The notice was sent to the court so that it arrived on September 30, 1999. The notice was not served upon S until the court sent it out in mid October. H stated that he had told S orally on September 29 that he had appealed. The fee earner in question had been on annual leave for seven days over the material five days. H argued that the order was unfair as (1) it should not have been adjourned as it was disproportionate with a claim limited to £10,000 to have two case conferences when all was ready for trial; (2) that it was a *Smith v. Manchester* type claim which did not require pleading, and (3) the notice of application under Ord.13 r.1 was only one day late as he had informed S orally and it was for the court to serve the notice of application under r.6.

Held, giving judgment for H but disallowing the costs of the appeal, that (1) H had failed to make clear whether the claim was for a *Smith v. Manchester* award or a continuing loss of earnings. S was entitled to have a written document of a binding nature that specified what the claim was for and the relevant information that would allow S to assess its value. S was entitled to that so that she could value the claim for a Part 36 payment; (2) H should reduce the claim into writing within 14 days, failing which that aspect of it be debarred from being pursued; (3) it was not necessary to plead the claim in the instant case, though loss of earnings claims were required to be pleaded; (4) to adjourn the hearing was disproportionate. The order could have been made as in (2) above. The case should then have been set down for a hearing, and (5) the notice of application was out of time. The party appealing should file and serve on the other party the notice of application within the five day time limit. It was not for the court to do so. There was no prejudice in the present case. Though the solicitor had a good excuse in this case for the five day limit being missed, she did not have a good case for failing to serve S with a copy of the notice upon her return. The oral communication on September 29 was not good enough. The 1998 Rules required a written copy of the notice to be served on S. There were two sanctions open to the court: (a) disallowing the appeal, or (b) disallowing any costs that may be recoverable on the preparation of the appeal, and the latter was the appropriate order in the present case.

HASELDINE v. SMITH, November 16, 1999, Judge Sessions, CC (Croydon). [*Ex rel.* Paul McGrath, Barrister, 1 Temple Gardens, Temple, London].

386. Costs – adverse costs orders

[Civil Procedure Rules 1998 (SI 1998 3132).]

Five test case employees had their claims for stigma damages against BCCI, their former employer, dismissed. Despite BCCI having committed a breach of the trust and confidence term of the employment contract, none of the employees proved that the damage they had suffered entailed a stigma being attached to them, which impeded them from obtaining new employment. The court then had to consider the relevant costs order.

Held, that no order for costs would be made. It was clear that under the Civil Procedure Rules 1998 the overriding objective meant that the court should make a just costs order. A costs order favouring the successful party would generally achieve justice, but the court could make a different order if, on the facts of a particular case, justice so required. The court should consider the success of the parties on parts only of their cases, and it no longer always followed that a claimant who could not prove loss but could show a breach of contract would be subject to an adverse costs order, *Elgindata (No.2), Re* [1992] 1 W.L.R. 1207, [1993] C.L.Y. 3144 considered.

BANK OF CREDIT AND COMMERCE INTERNATIONAL SA (IN LIQUIDATION) v. ALI (NO.4) *The Times*, March 2, 2000, Lightman, J., Ch D.

387. Costs – amendment of defence – no order to pay proportion until conclusion of proceedings

[Civil Procedure Rules 1998 (SI 1998 3132) Part 17 r.17.1, Part 44 r.44.3.]

F applied in July 1999 for an order pursuant to the Civil Procedure Rules 1998 Part 17 r.17.1 (2) (b) that he be permitted to amend his defence to remove an allegation of duress and make a number of substantial additions. The defence as amended would involve a change of course in the action for UN. UN opposed the amendment unless the costs of, thrown away and occasioned by the proposed amendment, were assessed immediately and paid, thus the issue arose as to what costs order should be made to safeguard UN's interests. UN referred to Part 44 r.44.3(1) of the 1998 Rules which provided that the court had discretion as to whether costs were payable by one party to another, the amount of those costs, and when they were to be paid. UN also sought to rely on Part 44 r.44.3(4), Part 44 r.44.3(6) and Part 44 r.44.3(7). On the facts of the case it was not practicable to make an order that F, as a price of his being allowed to amend his defence, pay a proportion of UN's costs. Since the final outcome of the litigation was not yet known, any proportion would be a wholly arbitrary figure. It was not suggested that the judge should order that F pay costs from or until a certain date only.

Held, ordering a detailed assessment of the costs to be made at the end of the proceedings, that although Part 44 r.44.3(7) usually applied, any order made as a proportion in the instant case would be speculative and therefore unfair. It was not right to reserve the costs to the judge at trial. In relation to the matters involved in the amendment, the court could take into account recent conduct. On general principles, there was a strong case for making some order that reflected and protected UN's interests. The overriding objective of the 1998 Rules was to enable the court to deal with the matter justly. The costs arising out of, thrown away and occasioned by the amendment, were ordered to be paid by F in any event. The judge rejected F's argument that he should make a prospective order leaving it to the trial judge to make a proportionate reduction under Part 44 r.44.3(7) in the costs to be paid to F in the event that he succeeded at trial. An order for a detailed assessment forthwith would be contrary to the general presumption in Part 47 r.47.1 that a detailed assessment should not take place until the conclusion of the proceedings, although the court may order the costs to be assessed immediately. A detailed assessment at this time would have involved a form of adversarial advocacy, a dedication of court time and would distract from the general progress of the action. These were powerful considerations against ordering a collateral trial. It would also be contrary to principle to make an order which might have the practical consequence of depriving F of further defending his claim, having regard to F's limited financial resources.

UNIVERSITY OF NOTTINGHAM v. FISHEL (AMENDMENT OF DEFENCE), July 22, 1999, Judge Paul Dean Q.C., QBD. [*Ex rel.* Daniel Lightman, Barrister, Serle Court Chambers, 13 Old Square, Lincoln's Inn, London].

388. Costs – appeals – non party funding outside jurisdiction – security for costs no bar to justice

[Civil Procedure Rules 1998 (SI 1998 3132).]

In allowing permission to appeal against summary judgment in the sum of $11.5 million, H and others were ordered to provide security for costs. They appealed, contending that under the Civil Procedure Rules 1998, permission to appeal was only granted where there was a realistic prospect of success and their appeals were being stifled by the order for costs.

Held, dismissing the appeals, that the grant of permission to appeal did not preclude the granting of security for costs, and the correct approach was to consider whether an appeal should proceed without the appellant being liable for the respondent's costs if unsuccessful. In the instant case, it was clear that none of the defendants could afford to pay FBME's costs should they lose the appeals and it was also apparent that the appeals were being funded by non parties outside the jurisdiction who wished to avoid having to pay costs if the appeals were unsuccessful. Therefore, H and the other defendants had not been denied access to justice.

FEDERAL BANK OF THE MIDDLE EAST v. HADKINSON (SECURITY FOR COSTS) (NO.2); HADKINSON v. SAAB (NO.2) [2000] 1 Costs L.R. 94, Mummery, L.J., CA.

389. Costs – appropriate level of fee earner – proportionality

[Civil Procedure Rules 1998 (SI 1998 3132) Part 1 r.1.1 (2) (c).]

B brought an action against H damages arising from a road traffic accident. Liability was not admitted in negotiation but a defence admitting liability was filed and judgment was entered for B with damages to be assessed. By consent it was subsequently agreed that B should accept £3,200 out of a payment into court, of which £3,000 represented damages in respect of B's whiplash injury. That sum was in settlement of all issues except a claim for credit hire charges which had been stayed. It was also agreed that costs to the date of acceptance should be assessed. At the subsequent assessment, H argued that it was inappropriate for B to have used a grade 1 fee earner on the grounds that the claim was a road traffic accident involving a simple whiplash injury. H's claim by comparison had been dealt with by a grade 3 fee earner.

Held, granting judgment for B, that B was not required to use unqualified or less experienced staff to progress his claim to satisfy the test of proportionality under the Civil Procedure Rules 1998 Part 1 r.1.1 (2) (c). The fact that H had chosen to use a grade 3 fee earner was his choice and would not restrict B from recovering costs for the grade 1 fee earner instructed. The court was satisfied that the claim had been dealt with expeditiously and the costs incurred were proportionate to the issues involved. B's costs were assessed at £2,886.

BROWN v. HICKS, January 28, 2000, Deputy District Judge Ball, CC (Basingstoke). [*Ex rel.* Amery-Parkes Solicitors, 12a London Street, Basingstoke, Hampshire].

390. Costs – assessment – in house solicitor's costs assessed on same principle as independent solicitor – no infringement of indemnity principle

C sought to challenge an assessment of costs on a contested taxation arising from lengthy proceedings brought by C against BT who had used an in house solicitor during the proceedings. The judge applied the principle established in *Eastwood (Deceased), Re* [1975] Ch. 112, [1974] C.L.Y. 2927 of taxing the in house solicitor's bill as if it were the bill of an independent solicitor and then applying the conventional method of taxation by identifying an hourly expense rate plus a percentage uplift figure. C contended that such an approach infringed the indemnity principle. He submitted that the instant case was special and fell into the category outlined in *Eastwood* as it appeared reasonably plain that the indemnity principle would be infringed if the principle applicable to independent solicitors was applied.

Held, dismissing the appeal, that there was insufficient evidence to conclude that, as a matter of fact, the indemnity principle had been infringed and there was a presumption in *Eastwood* that the indemnity principle was not infringed by the application of the conventional approach. The case was not special and the application of the principles in *Eastwood* ensured that the burden of a detailed enquiry into the actual costs of BT was avoided *Eastwood* applied.

COLE v. BRITISH TELECOMMUNICATIONS PLC [2000] 2 Costs L.R. 310, Buxton, L.J., CA.

391. Costs – assessment – insurer agreed to pay insured's costs – assessment sought by insurer – assessment time barred

[Solicitors Act 1974 s.70(3), s.71 (1).]

B was the subject of a claim for which it had insurance cover. As a result of that claim, B entered into a settlement agreement with its insurers, whereby the insurers agreed to pay one half of B's total outlay, including costs. The agreement provided for payment upon receipt of a sworn claim from B, such claim being "conclusive proof" that the relevant sum was due to a "third party". The agreement also provided that all disputes would be referred to arbitration. The insurers' obligations under the agreement were transferred to E, a reinsurer, who withheld a proportion of the costs claimed by L, B's solicitors, and sought a detailed assessment of L's costs pursuant to the Solicitors Act 1974 s.71 (1). Shortly thereafter, B commenced arbitration proceedings, which were initially stayed, but later reinstated. B submitted an application for a stay of the detailed assessment on the basis that the settlement agreement obliged E to pay the fixed sum referred to in the sworn claim. L agreed and also contended that E was out of time in seeking an assessment of all but seven of its bills, and that, in any event, the court should decline to exercise its discretion to allow an assessment to be carried out. E contended that it was not bound to pay the amount referred to in the sworn claim as L was not a "third party", and that an assessment was not time barred as L's bills had merely been "on account" and had contained insufficient narrative.

Held, allowing the appeal, that (1) properly construed, the settlement agreement provided that B was entitled to an indemnity in respect of its legal costs, and that L was a "third party" to whom such costs were due; (2) E had a prima facie entitlement to have L's costs assessed, but the assessment would not affect E's liability to B; (3) there had been no agreement to pay a fixed sum in costs. Whilst the agreement required the insurers to pay the amount set out in B's sworn claim, that amount was referable to the costs chargeable to B. Section 71(1) was not limited to agreements to pay a solicitor's bill; (4) E was bound by the time limits under s.70 since there had been agreement between L and B that B would receive periodic final bills, and B's choice to forego a narrative did not render the bills "on account" only; (5) concerning the bills which were not time barred, E had been unable to establish, for the purpose of s.70(3), that special circumstances existed such as to justify an assessment being carried out, and (6) the court had the power to order reimbursement of overpaid costs if an assessment resulted in a reduction of the costs, *Ingrams v. Sykes* (1987) 137 N.L.J. 1135, [1987] C.L.Y. 2956 considered.

BARCLAYS PLC v. VILLERS; VILLERS v. LOVELLS (FORMERLY LOVELL WHITE DURRANT); *sub nom.* VILLERS v. EQUITAS LTD [2000] 1 All E.R. (Comm) 357, Langley, J., QBD (Comm Ct).

392. Costs – assessment – settlement offers rejected by legally aided claimant – exercise of court's powers to take rejection into account

[Civil Procedure Rules 1998 (SI 1998 3132) Part 47 r.47.19.]

J issued proceedings for damages for medical negligence. J was legally aided and the action was settled for the sum of £25,000 on September 10, 1999. J's solicitors served a bill of costs and notice of commencement on seeking costs in the sum of £15,074. Points in dispute and replies were prepared and exchanged, and on January 18, 2000, NHA put forward an offer of £13,000 inclusive in full and final settlement. The offer was rejected, subsequently increased to GPB 13,500, and rejected again. Both offers were made "without prejudice save as to costs". The matter proceeded to a detailed assessment hearing which took place on April 17, 2000.

Held, reducing J's bill of costs to approximately £11,500, that the amount offered was substantially higher than the amount allowed, therefore it was possible to make an order in accordance with the exception referred to in the Civil Procedure Rules 1998 Part 47 r.47.19 PD 47 para.46.4 concerning settlement offers relating to assisted persons. NHA were awarded their costs of the assessment process to be set off against the costs payable to J.

JONES v. NOTTINGHAM HA, June 14, 2000, District Judge Cowling, CC (Nottingham). [*Ex rel.* Eversheds Solicitors, Fitzalan House, Fitzalan Road, Cardiff].

393. Costs – assessment – summary assessment

[Civil Procedure Rules 1998 (SI 1998 3132) Part 8, Part 44.]

C brought a claim for damages against F arising from a road traffic accident, which included personal injuries. Liability was admitted and the claim was settled without proceedings for £1,525 general and £887 special damages. C's solicitors then forwarded a schedule of costs. Following unsuccessful negotiations, C issued proceedings under the Civil Procedure Rules 1998 Part 8 to secure an assessment by the court of costs. Prior to the hearing, C served two schedules of costs; one for the costs of and incidental to Part 8 proceedings and one for those costs plus the costs of the main claim. At the hearing, C sought an order giving authority to initiate detailed assessment proceedings.

Held, that C's costs were to be summarily assessed, given (1) that C's particulars of claim referred merely to "assessment"; (2) the general presumption in favour of summary assessment as per Civil Procedure Rules 1998 Part 44 PD 44 para.4.4(1)(b); (3) F's consent to summary assessment, and (4) the disproportionality that would be involved in the case proceeding to detailed assessment. Thus, C's costs of the main claim had to be divorced from the costs of and incidental to the Part 8 hearing, as negotiations had taken place and offers had been made solely on the costs of the main action. Due to the deductions made and the offers previously put forward by F, the costs of and incidental to the Part 8 hearing were to be F's and to be offset against C's costs of the action.

CLARKE v. FOGG, February 23, 2000, District Judge Travers, CC (Birkenhead). [*Ex rel.* David Higginson, Solicitor, 8 Greenlea Close, Bebington, Merseyside].

394. **Costs – cost sharing order – group actions – conditional fee agreements**

H was involved in a group action against IT and sought an order in relation to the arrangements for cost sharing, given that each of the plaintiffs were being represented under conditional fee agreements. A proposal was put to the court whereby, if the claim was ultimately successful, only those plaintiffs still involved in the litigation would be entitled to their costs. If the claim failed, however, all the plaintiffs who had been involved at any stage would be liable to pay any costs order on a pro rata basis.

Held, refusing to make the proposed order, that the proposal was not suitable as it encouraged those plaintiffs with weaker cases to continue at all costs. The most appropriate order, in line with developed practice, would be that both the liability for, and the benefit of, costs in relation to the issues common to all the plaintiffs would be several rather than joint. A register of plaintiffs would need to be set up and a running account of costs maintained. The account would be totalled each quarter and divided by the number of plaintiffs remaining at that time. This was the first major group action involving conditional fee agreements, but the situation was analogous to plaintiffs who had the benefit of legal aid. It was not yet clear what would happen to an unsuccessful plaintiff at the end of litigation conducted under a conditional fee agreement.

HODGSON v. IMPERIAL TOBACCO LTD (NO.2) [1998] 2 Costs L.R. 27, Wright, J., QBD.

395. **Costs – costs not following event – administrative decision making – costs need not always follow event where complainant successfully challenged administrative decision of local authority**

[Magistrates Courts Act 1980 s.64(1).]

BMDC appealed by way of case stated against a costs order imposed on it following a refusal to renew B's licence to operate private hire vehicles. The magistrates' had concluded that costs should follow the event, subject to the sum being just and reasonable. BMDC contended that, (1) the correct principle which the magistrates should have followed was that a local authority should never pay costs in these circumstances unless it had acted unreasonably, improperly or dishonestly; (2) where a local authority had not acted in bad faith or unreasonably, it could never be just to order it to pay costs; (3) vehicle licensing functions were statutorily imposed on a local authority; (4) local authorities worked through sub-committees who intended to act in a quasi-judicial manner and it would not be in the public interest for authorities to be deterred from making apparently sound decisions by the fear of being subject to a costs order; (5) a local authority in the instant case had no choice practically and realistically but to appear in the magistrates court, and (6) the costs of the hearing to the successful complainant were virtually irrelevant as they should be regarded as a business expense and if this was not affordable, the complainant should go without legal representation, *R. v. Merthyr Tydfil Crown Court, ex p. Chief Constable of Dyfed Powys The Times*, December 17, 1998, [1999] C.L.Y. 399 and *R. v. Totnes Licensing Justices, ex p. Chief Constable of Devon and Cornwall* (1992) 156 J.P. 587, [1991] C.L.Y. 2329 cited.

Held, dismissing the appeal, that when exercising its power under the Magistrates' Courts Act 1980 s.64(1) in relation to costs orders, a magistrates' court did not have to conclude that costs followed the event, and should take into consideration all the relevant circumstances of the case. The court considered *Chief Constable of Derbyshire v. Goodman* (Unreported, April 2, 1998), [1998] C.L.Y. 945 which stated that it was important for the tribunal to take into account that a costs order against an authority would not generally be made, unless there was some good reason other than the other party's success, for doing so. In the instant case, the magistrates had erred in their view of s.64(1). Section 64(1) conferred a discretion on a magistrates' court to make costs orders which it thought just and reasonable, and that provision applied not only to the quantum of costs, but also to which party should pay them. Where a complainant had successfully challenged an administrative decision made by a police or regulatory authority in the proper exercise of its public duty, the court should consider in addition to any other relevant circumstances, (1) the financial prejudice to the complainant if not awarded costs, and (2) the need to encourage public authorities to make and stand by honest and reasonable administrative decisions without fear of being subject to undue financial prejudice if these decisions were successfully challenged. Ordinarily, the case would be remitted to the magistrates for further consideration. However, no further order was made as the BMDC had made it clear that its objective was to obtain guidance from the court on this matter, not to seek the recovery of costs from B. BMDC as John Blair-Gould.

BRADFORD MDC v. BOOTH; *sub nom.* BOOTH v. BRADFORD MDC (2001) 3 L.G.L.R. 8, Lord Bingham of Cornhill, L.C.J., QBD.

396. **Costs – costs not following event – extent to which courts able to make orders which do not follow the event**

[Civil Procedure Rules 1998 (SI 1998 3132).]

DEG successfully defended K's application to dismiss its application for an injunction (*The Times*, February 8, 2000, [2000] C.L.Y. 3481) and the issue of costs arose.

Held, ordering K to pay 70 per cent of DEG's costs, that under the Civil Procedure Rules 1998, the court's discretion to make an order for costs which did not follow the event was substantially the same as had been decided in previous cases, *Elgindata (No.2), Re* [1992] 1 W.L.R. 1207, [1993] C.L.Y. 3144 followed. The exercise of the court's discretion regarding costs orders in *Elgindata* had been cited approvingly by Lord Woolf in a subsequent decision, *AEI Rediffusion Music Ltd v. Phonographic Performance Ltd (Costs)* [1999] 1 W.L.R. 1507, [1999] C.L.Y. 3456 considered, in which Lord Woolf had chosen not to qualify the principles in *Elgindata*. The CPR were merely more specific in relation to the factors which had to be considered when deciding whether to make such a costs order. However, successful parties should only pay costs to losing parties, if the point taken by that party or the manner in which it was taken was unreasonable.

GWEMBE VALLEY DEVELOPMENT CO LTD (IN RECEIVERSHIP) v. KOSHY (COSTS); DEG-DEUTSCHE INVESTITIONS-UND ENTWICKLUNGSGESELLSCHAFT MBH v. KOSHY *The Times*, March 30, 2000, Rimer, J., Ch D.

397. **Costs – costs orders must be fair reflection of situation – interests behind actual parties relevant**

[Civil Procedure Rules 1998 Part 1 r.1.]

Held, ordering the defendants to bear the costs of the appeals in those cases where the claimants had financed their own proceedings, or were legally aided and therefore subject to the rights of recovery of the legal aid fund, that in general, the guidance provided by the test case was mainly of importance to those behind the defendants, being insurers and the NHS. Under the Civil Procedure Rules 1998 Part 1 r.1, the costs order had to reflect the justice of the situation. However, in those cases where the claimants had been supported by a trade union or the Police Federation, there was no order made as to the costs of the appeals, because the parties behind the claimants had similar interests to the insurers and the NHS. A claimant with "after the event" insurance was in the same position as the general pool of claimants rather than those supported by a union, because an insurance premium had been paid.

HEIL v. RANKIN (COSTS); REES v. MABCO (102) LTD (COSTS); SCHOFIELD v. SAUNDERS & TAYLOR LTD (COSTS); RAMSAY v. RIVERS (COSTS); KENT v. GRIFFITHS (COSTS); W (A CHILD) v. NORTHERN GENERAL HOSPITAL NHS TRUST (COSTS); ANNABLE v. SOUTHERN DERBYSHIRE HA (COSTS); CONNOLLY v. TASKER (COSTS) [2000] C.P. Rep. 55, Lord Woolf, M.R., CA.

398. Costs – counterclaims – defendant recovering less on counterclaim than claim – counterclaim main focus of trial

[Rules of the Supreme Court 1965 (SI 1965 1776) Ord.62 r.3(3); Civil Procedure Rules 1998 (SI 1998 3132) Part 44 r.44.3(2) (a).]

UC imported and distributed bicycles. G was a bicycle wholesaler and retailer. G ordered and received a consignment of bicycles from UC, but claimed that the goods were not of merchantable quality. G paid just over half the purchase price, and UC sued for the balance. G set up a defence and counterclaim, contending that it had already paid UC more than the value of the goods, and claiming in respect of resultant damage to its goodwill, and loss of business. UC denied this allegation throughout. At trial, the judge gave judgment for UC on its claim, but also gave judgment for G on its counterclaim. The effect of this was to reduce UC's net claim by approximately 20 per cent. The judge ordered UC to pay half of G's costs, subject to an order that G pay UC's costs up to service of the defence and counterclaim, and the costs of setting down. He justified this order on the basis that (1) neither party wanted an order that UC have the costs of the claim, and G the costs of the counterclaim, as this would prove difficult to work out on assessment; (2) the sum due to UC was never at issue; (3) the main issue was the quality of the goods supplied, on which G had won; and (4) G's counterclaim had not succeeded to the extent claimed by G, nor had G made any offer or given any explanation of the problem at the time, for which reason G was awarded only half the costs of its counterclaim. UC appealed.

Held, allowing the appeal, that (1) the question of costs was one for the discretion of the trial judge, and the appellate court would interfere only if he erred in law or principle; (2) the general rule both under the Rules of the Supreme Court Ord.62 r.3(3) and the Civil Procedure Rules Part 44 r.44.3(2)(a) was that costs followed the cause; (3) in the alternative, costs could be awarded according to the actual issues giving rise to their occurrence, the object of this principle being to encourage good behaviour by litigants, in terms of Part 44 r.44.3(4); (4) the trial judge had sought to apply Part 44 r.44.3(4) by trying to reflect the time spent on the main issues in the litigation in the costs order. He fell into error, however, in failing to take account of the fact that UC was in the right overall, but would see its recovery more than wiped out by the order to pay half of G's costs. He also erred in failing to take due account of the availability to G of a payment into court to protect its costs position, and the possibility open to UC of making a Calderbank offer of discount to reflect G's counterclaim, *Elgindata (No.2), Re* [1992] 1 W.L.R. 1207, [1993] C.L.Y. 3144, *NV Amsterdamsche Lucifersfabrieken v. H&H Trading Agencies Ltd* [1940] 1 All E.R. 587 and *Nicholson v. Little* [1956] 1 W.L.R. 829, [1956] C.L.Y. 1650 considered, and (5) the order as to costs necessary to do justice in the instant case was to award UC the costs other than those of the trial itself, in respect of which no order would be made, on the basis that it would have taken less time if UC had made realistic admissions.

UNIVERSAL CYCLES PLC v. GRANGEBRIAR LTD [2000] C.P.L.R. 42, Hale, L.J., CA.

399. Costs – default costs certificate – service of points of dispute out of time but prior to entitlement to issue of certificate

[Civil Procedure Rules 1998 (SI 1998 3132) Part 47 r.47.9(5), r.47.12(1); .]

After the successful conclusion of an action against BP, P's solicitors sent a bill and Form N252 dated January 4, 2000 to BP's solicitors allowing until January 28 for service of points of dispute. BP's solicitors served points of dispute at 4:35 pm on Friday January 28, by which time P's solicitors had applied to the court for a default costs certificate. The certificate was issued by the court on February 1, 2000. BP applied to set aside the default costs certificate.

Held, allowing the application, that P was not entitled to the default costs certificate under the Civil Procedure Rules 1998 Part 47 r.47.12(1). P's application should not have been made to the court before 10am on February 1 at the earliest, by which time the points of dispute had been served. Therefore, effectively, the court had wrongly issued the default costs certificate after the points of dispute had been served by BP, contrary to Part 47 r.47.9(5).

PARTRIDGE v. BRIAN PERKINS LTD, March 7, 2000, District Judge Bird, CC (Bristol). [*Ex rel.* Jeremy Ford, Barrister, 199 Strand, London].

400. Costs – discontinuation of proceedings before allocation

[Civil Procedure Rules 1998 (SI 1998 3132) Part 27 r.27.14(d).]

G commenced an action against R claiming damages arising out of a road traffic accident which occurred on November 1, 1998. R defended the action and allocation questionnaires were filed. By order of the court, the claim was stayed until October 19, 1999 to enable the parties to attempt settlement, without allocation to track. On October 6, 1999, G gave notice of his intention to discontinue the proceedings. R applied under the Civil Procedure Rules 1998 Part 27 r.27.14(d) for an order for their costs thrown away in defending the action on the basis of G's "unreasonable behaviour" in commencing an action which he had no intention of progressing to a final hearing. R's application was dismissed on the basis that an offer had been made earlier in the proceedings to settle without an order for costs, which offer was rejected. R appealed, contending that the judge had wrongly exercised her discretion since the case had not been allocated, therefore in accordance with Civil Procedure Rules 1998 Part 44 r.44 PD 44 para.5.1 special costs rules did not apply. R further contended that their conduct in making the earlier offer to settle did not constitute conduct justifying a departure from the "normal costs rule", therefore the judge had no proper grounds for the exercise of discretion as to costs.

Held, allowing the appeal, that G ought to pay R's costs of the action and appeal.

GREENAWAY v. ROVER GROUP LTD, February 16, 2000, Recorder Alexander Q.C., CC (Dudley). [*Ex rel.* Taylor Joynson Garrett Solicitors, Carmelite, 50 Victoria Embankment, Blackfriars, London].

401. Costs – dispute resolution – application for security for costs opposed as case suitable for alternative dispute resolution

L, a solicitor, made an application for security for the costs of an appeal brought by J, a Dutch company, in the sum of £92,117 in proceedings commenced by J for professional negligence. J maintained that the application should be dismissed in view of L's unreasonableness in refusing to refer the matter to ADR since the action was a pure money claim with no issue of principle at stake.

Held, granting the application in the sum of £60,000, that ADR was a voluntary option and there were no special features of the case that were capable of persuading the court that this was a suitable case for ADR. The claim could not be categorised as a simple money claim with no issue at stake since L as a professional was doubtless concerned to protect his reputation.

JEWO FERROUS BV v. LEWIS MOORE (A FIRM) (SECURITY FOR COSTS) [2000] C.P. Rep. 57, Gibson, L.J., CA.

402. Costs – enforcement – counterclaim – expiry of time limit for taxation – appropriate order

TW had successfully represented S in complex and lengthy slander proceedings. An order for costs was made against S's opponent, H, but she petitioned for and was granted a voluntary bankruptcy order. TW served a writ on S for payment of its fees, and was granted summary judgment in the sum of £67,000, with S given liberty to put in a defence for the balance of £117,000. As S did not file a defence, judgment was later entered for the full amount. S appealed and counterclaimed, alleging TW was negligent by failing to annul H's bankruptcy and to give an estimate of the costs at the outset, and disputing aspects of the bill such as the hourly rate and enhancement. The matter ultimately came before the Court of Appeal.

Held, allowing the appeal but dismissing the counterclaim, that given the complexity of the case TW could not be criticised for not having given an estimate of costs, and there was insufficient evidence to found a claim for negligence in relation to the bankruptcy. The case had become unnecessarily convoluted. As the bill was contested, the appropriate order, which should have been made at the start, was for the costs to be assessed notwithstanding that the time limit for taxation had passed. S would be ordered to pay TW the £67,000 as an interim payment pending that assessment.

THOMAS WATTS & CO v. SMITH [1998] 2 Costs L.R. 59, Sir Richard Scott V.C., CA.

403. Costs – entitlement to solicitor's costs at City of London rates

M claimed damages against L and the action was allocated to the fast track. Liability was not in dispute. An assessment hearing took place concerning the appropriate measure of general damages. During an adjournment, the parties compromised the action with general damages agreed at £2,500. Costs were not agreed and the judge was invited summarily to assess the costs of the action. M had instructed a firm of solicitors based in the West End of London. The relevant fee earner then moved to a firm in the City of London and continued to conduct the action. M's schedule of costs sought a rate of £165 per hour for a grade II fee earner. The claim had been issued in Wandsworth County Court, local to M's solicitor's home, before being transferred to Brentford County Court for the assessment hearing. L contended that M should not recover the costs of instructing Central London solicitors. The accident occurred in Southampton and M lived in Camberley, Surrey. L argued that M could and should have instructed provincial solicitors and the claim should have been issued and conducted in M's local county court. It was also argued that in a relatively straightforward case, where liability was not in issue and the only issue was general damages, M should recover no more than the appropriate rate for an out of London solicitor. L cited *Mann v. Powergen Plc* (Unreported, February 9, 1999), [1999] C.L.Y. 415.

Held, that the appropriate rate was the out of London Grade II rate, which was £125 per hour. Costs were assessed at a total of £3,931.

MCCAULEY v. LAMB, March 2, 2000, Judge Oppenheimer, CC (Brentford). [*Ex rel.* Charles Bagot, Barrister, Hardwicke Building, New Square, Lincoln's Inn, London].

404. Costs – expert report – engineer's report on damage to vehicle – cost of expert's report not recoverable

[Civil Procedure Rules 1998 (SI 1998 3132) Part 27.]

C and H were involved in a road traffic accident for which H was found to be liable. C claimed the pre-accident value of his vehicle, together with the cost of a vehicle engineer's report, as damages. C claimed entitlement to the cost of the report under the Civil Procedure Rules 1998 Part 27 r.27.14(3)(d).

Held, dismissing the application for the cost of the report, that an engineer's report was not recoverable as damages. *Ogejebe v. East London Bus & Coach Co* (Unreported, June 6, 2000) considered. The definition of "expert" in Part 35 r.35.2 of the 1998 Rules was not applicable to small claims by virtue of Part 27 r.27.2, which required permission to rely on expert evidence in the small claims track. Permission was not given by virtue of the standard directions for Form B. The directions in Form B stated that a party may file and serve expert's reports, but did not implicitly give permission to do so. In the instant case, permission had not been given and C could not recover the cost of the "report". The judge found that if he was wrong in holding that permission had not been given, he had a discretion whether to award the costs or not under Part 27 r.27.14(3). The vehicle engineer's report had been commissioned one month after the accident and seven months before proceedings were issued. C had never intended calling oral evidence at trial and had only sought to rely on the report. In the circumstances, the expert had not been instructed to give evidence in the case and would have given his opinion whether or not litigation ensued. Accordingly, C could not recover the cost of the report.

CROWE v. HUTT, June 12, 2000, District Judge Gilchrist, CC (Central London). [*Ex rel.* Simon Brindle, Barrister, 199 Strand, London].

405. **Costs – expert report – engineer's report on damage to vehicle – engineer's fees not part of special damages but costs – recoverable in small claims as costs only if expert**

[Civil Procedure Rules 1998 (SI 1998 3132) Part 27.]

S's insurer brought an action against I claiming the cost of an engineer's report as an item of special damage. S's insurer had commissioned an engineer to assess the nature of the damage to S's car after an accident involving I. Repairs were subsequently carried out and the cost was met by I's insurer, who also paid a £2.50 DVLA search fee and a £25 loss of use and inconvenience claim. S claimed that the engineer's fee was capable of being an item of special damage and that the obtaining of a report was both reasonable and an attempt to mitigate S's loss. I argued that the engineer's fee was not capable of being an item of special damage, it was only recoverable as costs and S had therefore erred in law by issuing proceedings for costs alone, as there was no damage to which the costs could properly attach. Since the action was brought under the small claims procedure, if the cost of the report were to be claimed as a cost of the action, it would have to be classed as an expert report under the Civil Procedure Rules 1998 Part 27 I argued that the report could not be an expert's report because (1) it was an administrative document commissioned by the insurer and not a document prepared in contemplation of litigation, and (2) the report did not assist the court.

Held, dismissing the claim, that S had not necessarily acted unreasonably in obtaining the report, but could not reasonably recover the cost because the engineer's report was not a head of damage, but a cost. As drawn, the action was misconceived as the fee was stated to be an item of special damage. However, even if the sum had been pleaded as a cost of the action, it could only be recoverable in the small claims procedure as payment for an expert report. The report did not have the status of an expert report because it was an administrative document and it had not assisted the court.

SMART CARS v. ISOTANK, May 16, 2000, District Judge Clark, CC (Birkenhead). [*Ex rel.* Helen M Mulholland, Barrister, 40 King Street, Manchester].

406. **Costs – expert report – vehicle inspection report not recoverable cost under CPR r.27 – claimant not having permission for use of expert evidence**

[Civil Procedure Rules 1998 (SI 1998 3132) Part 27 r.27.14, r.27.5, Part 35.]

R brought an action claiming damages for the cost of repairs to her car following a road traffic accident. The claim was allocated to the small claims track. Liability was in dispute and the judge found for R with a one third deduction for contributory negligence. In addition to R's own evidence about the point of impact and damage done, R relied on an inspection report setting out damage to the car, and on repair estimates and invoices. R had initially claimed the cost of the report, £42.50, as an item of special damage, but conceded at the hearing that it was a cost and sought payment of the report fee as a recoverable cost under the Civil Procedure Rules 1998 Part 27 r.27.14(3)(d) or under the court's general discretion as the report had been useful. G objected as the report was not an expert's report within the meaning of Part 35 and no permission had been granted by the court or sought by R under Part 27 r.27.5 for the use of expert evidence.

Held, giving judgment for G, that the report fee was not recoverable. It did not add much to R's own evidence or the repair documents on the damage to R's vehicle or the point of impact. It was not an expert's report, it was an inspection report for R's insurer's own purposes, not for the purposes of litigation. No application for permission for expert evidence had been made, and it would be unusual in these types of cases to have expert evidence.

ROMASCAN v. GURNEY, January 10, 2000, Deputy District Judge Greenburgh, MCLC. [*Ex rel.* Tim Petts, Barrister, 12 King's Bench Walk, London].

407. **Costs – failure to exchange witness statements within agreed time – application of CPR overriding objective**

[Civil Procedure Rules 1998 (SI 1998 3132) r.3.4, r.3.8, r.3.9.]

K sustained a serious injury to his leg and back in December 1994. Proceedings were issued in December 1997. A defence was served admitting liability but putting quantum at issue. On February 9, 1999 the parties agreed to exchange witness statements within 42 days, failing which the defaulting party would be debarred from calling such evidence. The date for exchange was subsequently extended by consent on April 16, 1999. K failed to exchange witness statements within the specified time. No trial date had been set. D applied for an order striking out K's case pursuant to the Civil Procedure Rules 1998 r.3.4. K made a cross application for relief pursuant to r.3.8 for permission to serve witness statements. The judge granted K the relief sought but penalised K's solicitors in costs. D appealed.

Held, that regard had to be had to the factors set out at r.3.9 and the overriding objective. Despite K's failure to comply with the order it was still possible to deal with the case justly. Justice could be done in terms of the overriding objective by application of the very sanction imposed by the judge. To allow the appeal would have the consequence of K being unable to pursue his claim. Whereas D had been compensated in costs and could still properly pursue his defence, *Reed v. Swanlux Cleaning Services Ltd* (Unreported, June 7, 1999), [1999] C.L.Y. 566, *Mealey Horgan Plc v. Horgan The Times*, July 6, 1999, [1999] C.L.Y. 344 and *Biguzzi v. Rank Leisure Plc* [1999] 1 W.L.R. 1926, [1999] C.L.Y. 367 considered. K was awarded the costs of the appeal. However, it was emphasised, obiter, that time orders should specify a specific date and time for compliance and the old custom of "within x days" should be dispensed with.

KOTIA v. DEWHIRST, October 6, 1999, Judge Grenfell, QBD. [*Ex rel.* Jonathan Godfrey, Barrister, St Paul's Chambers, 23 Park Square South, Leeds].

408. **Costs – failure to strike out defence at early stage – aggressive stance of defendant – known weakness of defence raised**

B, who had succeeded in a libel claim, sought an order for costs. TN in opposing the order contended that it had incurred unnecessary costs in bringing the matter to trial. It was submitted, inter alia, that the defence of fair comment, which had been struck out on the first day on the ground that the words complained of constituted a statement of fact, should have been struck out prior to the trial, a position which had been indicated by B but not eventually pursued. TN argued that had the defence been struck out it was probable that the entire action would have been settled out of court.

Held, that TN should pay B's costs, given that in the instant case the court had wide discretionary powers in respect of costs. In both its pleadings and correspondence leading up to the trial TN had taken an aggressive stance toward B. While an application to strike out at an earlier stage would have been desirable, B was a plaintiff with no obvious wealth and accordingly had shown reluctance in risking the costs that would have potentially been incurred in a strike out action. Furthermore, TN as experienced litigators should have been aware of the weakness of a defence of fair comment.

BURSTEIN v. TIMES NEWSPAPERS LTD (COSTS) HQ 9902700, Judge Richard Walker, QBD.

409. Costs – group actions – no distinction between lead claimants and common claimants when assessing costs

[Civil Procedure Rules 1998 (SI 1998 3132) Part 44 r.44.3(2).]

O and more than 100 others claimed to be suffering from hearing loss and other maladies caused by excessive levels of noise occurring in the course of their employment. Following legal advice from solicitors nominated by their respective unions, O and the other claimants settled their personal injury claims via an insurance compensation scheme. Subsequent to this settlement, O and the other claimants brought an action against their respective solicitors alleging that the settlement figures gained had been considerably lower than those likely to have been recovered in a common law action and that the solicitors had therefore been negligent in their advice on settlement. At an interlocutory stage it was ordered that there be five lead actions and that the issue of common costs be reserved to the trial judge. By the trial date, three of the claimants in the lead actions had discontinued. The judge, while finding that the solicitors did owe a duty of care, dismissed the claims on the basis that no loss had been established. Exercising her discretion and on the basis that the action had been a group action the judge ordered that 75 per cent of the costs of the defendant solicitors, WB, be recovered from O, and that the common claimants contribute 25 per cent toward the defendant's costs. O appealed, contending that the group action had been successful on a number of generic issues and therefore the costs order to reflect this should have been based as required by the Civil Procedure Rules 1998 Part 44 r.44.3(2). WB submitted by way of cross appeal that as O's action had been chosen as a test case which, if successful, the common claimants would follow, those common claimants should be taken to have known that they were potentially liable for the costs of O's action. It followed, WB argued, that the judge had erred by making a distinction between O and the common claimants when making the order.

Held, dismissing the appeal and allowing the cross appeal, that the judge had given consideration when exercising her discretion to the successful aspects of the claimants' case and had reflected this in the 25 per cent reduction. Given evidence as to the common claimants' knowledge of their potential liability which was not available to the trial judge, it was clear that they intended, or should have been so advised, to bear proportionately between them the costs of O's action. No distinction should therefore have been made between the lead claimants and the other common claimants, and as a result all the claimants should be ordered to pay 75 per cent of WB's costs. The claimants were joined in a common cause and as such shared responsibility not only for their own costs but those, if the case was defeated, of the defendants, *Davies (Joseph Owen) v. Eli Lilly & Co (No.1)* [1987] 1 W.L.R. 1136, [1987] C.L.Y. 2942 considered.

OCHWAT v. WATSON BURTON (COSTS) [2000] C.P. Rep. 45, Swinton Thomas, L.J., CA.

410. Costs – inaction of defendant and his insurers – non-allocation to small claims track

[Civil Procedure Rules 1998 (SI 1998 3132) Part 27 r.27.14.]

Following a road traffic accident in January 2000, B pursued a claim for repairs, hire and loss of use. One month later, P's insurers admitted liability for the accident and paid B the cost of repairs in March. B's solicitors sent written details of his claim for hire and wrote again two months later. P failed to reply and B issued proceedings for hire charges and loss of use, the particulars of claim being limited to damages not exceeding £1,000. P failed to file a defence and/or an acknowledgement of service and judgment was duly entered for an amount which the court would decide and costs. The matter was listed for a disposal hearing in August 2000. A day before the hearing, P's insurers appointed solicitors and a figure of £600 was agreed in settlement of B's claim. B's solicitors did not accept fixed costs, contending that P's conduct in the matter was unreasonable and the matter should either not be allocated to a track or should attract an order for costs based on P's unreasonable conduct.

Held, giving judgment for B, that unreasonable conduct became a factor to consider only when the matter was referred to the small claims track under the Civil Procedure Rules 1998 Part 27 r.27.14. P, his insurer and his solicitor must be treated as one. Their inaction had meant that B had incurred costs and it was therefore inappropriate to allocate the matter to the small claims track. Unreasonable conduct was not a specific finding but was the reasoning behind the order. B's costs of the action were assessed.

BUTLER v. PEARCE, August 24, 2000, District Judge Smedley, CC (Birkenhead). [*Ex rel.* Michael W Halsall, Solicitors, 2 The Parks, Newton-le-Willows].

411. **Costs – indemnity costs sought for unreasonable conduct of litigation – unreasonable conduct determined on facts – need to discourage unreasonableness in litigation**

[Rules of the Supreme Court 1965 (SI 1965 1776) Ord.62 r.3(4); Civil Procedure Rules 1998 (SI 1998 3132).]

Held, that in determining whether indemnity costs should be awarded under the Rules of the Supreme Court 1965 Ord.62 r.3(4), for conduct occurring prior to the coming into force of the Civil Procedure Rules 1998, the conduct complained of must be so unreasonable as to be beyond the normal run of litigation. However, the courts should be ready to make such orders where it was just to do so both in the instant case and as a means of discouraging future unreasonable conduct.

BAIRSTOW v. QUEENS MOAT HOUSES PLC (COSTS); MARCUS v. QUEENS MOAT HOUSES PLC (COSTS); HERSEY v. QUEENS MOAT HOUSES PLC (COSTS); PORTER v. QUEENS MOAT HOUSES PLC (COSTS) [2000] C.P. Rep. 44, Nelson, J., QBD.

412. **Costs – injunction granted to preserve balance of convenience pending trial**

[Civil Procedure Rules 1998 (SI 1998 3132) Part 44 r.44.3.1 (a).]

R had been employed by DEG on a contract of employment which included a restraint clause prohibiting him from working for rival businesses within six months of his contract ending. Subsequent to being informed by R that he had been offered a job with a rival company, DEG was granted an interim injunction for a short period. On the return date, the judge, finding that both sides had an arguable case, listed the matter for early trial on a preliminary issue and continued the injunction for the "balance of convenience". The judge made an order for costs against R, assessing the costs at £16,000. R appealed against the costs order, arguing that the judge had been wrong to make the order since his only reason for continuing the injunction was in order to maintain the parties' positions in the short period before trial, and that the assessed figure was too high.

Held, allowing the appeal, that the order was unjust. The judge's reasons for continuing the injunction meant that there was no winner or loser on the issue and therefore he had been wrong to label R as the unsuccessful party. The judge did not appear to have had in his mind that the question of whether a costs order should be made pursuant to the Civil Procedure Rules 1998 Part 44 r.44.3.1 (a) was a separate issue from the decision over summary assessment of those costs. It followed that the costs for both parties should be reserved to the trial judge.

RICHARDSON v. DESQUENNE ET GIRAL UK LTD; *sub nom.* DESQUENNE ET GIRAL UK LTD v. RICHARDSON [1999] C.P.L.R. 744, Morritt, L.J., CA.

413. Costs – insurance – costs exceeded indemnity limit – no exceptional circumstances to justify order for payment of costs by non party

[Supreme Court Act 1981 s.51.]

C appealed against the refusal of their application for an order under the Supreme Court Act 1981 s.51 preventing them from recovering from a non party, EIC, the professional indemnity insurer of W, the defendant surveyor, the whole of their costs of successful litigation, which exceeded the financial limit of the indemnity provided to W. C contended that (1) the judge had wrongly applied his discretion by refusing to grant an order unless there were exceptional circumstances in which a non party insurer could be ordered to pay costs; (2) that the delayed disclosure of the contractual limit of the indemnity to C constituted an exceptional circumstance warranting the order for costs, and (3) when conducting their defence, EIC's interests had been favoured over that of W.

Held, dismissing the appeal, that (1) the judge had applied the correct test as there was a need to demonstrate exceptional circumstances before a non party could be ordered to pay costs, and when considering exceptionality the court had regard to the reasonableness and good faith of the insurer, *Murphy v. Young & Co's Brewery Plc* [1997] 1 W.L.R. 1591, [1997] C.L.Y. 3113 applied; (2) the court should not impose a penalty on the insurer for non disclosure of the policy limit, which was not an exceptional course of action, and (3) the court found that it was usually the case that the insurer controlled litigation and, while its interests would usually overlap with those of the insured, when there was a risk that the cover might be exceeded the interest of the policyholder should be considered. When considering whether a non party insurer should be ordered to pay costs, it would not necessarily always have to be shown that the insurer had acted solely out of self interest, unless there was a sufficient conflict of interest, *TGA Chapman Ltd v. Christopher* [1998] 1 W.L.R. 12, [1997] C.L.Y. 3111 considered.

CORMACK v. WASHBOURNE (FORMERLY T/A WASHBOURNE & CO); *sub nom.* CORMACK v. EXCESS INSURANCE CO LTD [2000] C.P.L.R. 358, Auld, L.J., CA.

414. Costs – interim orders – interim amount payable by instalments

[Civil Procedure Rules 1998 (SI 1998 3132) Part 44 r.44.3(4).]

Held, in proceedings for an award of costs, that in determining what order to make, whether to order interim assessment and allow payment by instalments, the following circumstances ought to be taken into account having regard to the Civil Procedure Rules 1998 Part 44 r.44.3(4): (1) the general rule of giving real weight to the fact that M won overall; (2) the fact that, nevertheless, M failed on two of the three main issues; (3) the likelihood of having succeeded on the two issues on which M in fact failed; (4) the degree of evidential and conceptual overlap between the issues, and (5) the degree of departure by the parties from their case as originally presented. An overall assessment taking into account those factors led to a determination that 75 per cent of M's costs should be met by S. An interim order should not be more than that which will be made on assessment. Accordingly, an amount of £45,000 was ordered by way of interim assessment. There being credible evidence that S would be in financial difficulty by having to pay the full amount, the interim amount assessed could be paid in three monthly instalments, with the proviso that the full amount would become due if there was a default in any instalment.

SCHOLES WINDOWS LTD v. MAGNET LTD (NO.2) [2000] E.C.D.R. 266, N Underhill Q.C., Ch D.

415. Costs – interpretation of unapproved costs order – liability in so far as costs increased due to counterclaim

CDT brought proceedings against CTP for infringement of a patent. CTP counterclaimed, alleging that CDT's patent was invalid. The judge held that, whilst a valid patent existed, it had not been infringed. A dispute arose as to the unapproved costs order. CDT submitted that the order stated it should be liable for the costs of CTP in so far as they were incurred by reason of the counterclaim, and conversely CTP should be liable for the costs of the action and counterclaim in so far as they were incurred by reason of its unsuccessful challenge to the validity of the patent. CDT, while agreeing with the substance of this interpretation of the order, contended that liability should be for the costs in so far as they had been "increased" rather than "incurred". Both parties also applied for leave to appeal.

Held, granting the costs order sought by CTP and granting both parties leave to appeal, that (1) the order which best reflected the justice of the case was an order that CDT pay the costs of the action, save in so far as such costs were increased by reason of CTP's plea that the patent was invalid, and that CTP would pay the costs of the action and the invalidity counterclaim in so far as such costs were increased by reason of its plea that the patent was invalid. The central issue of the case was CDT's claim that CTP had infringed its patent, and having failed on that issue, CDT should pay the costs of it, and (2) leave to appeal should only be granted if the judge was satisfied that there was a reasonable prospect of success. If the court considered that reasonable people could differ on the conclusion they had reached, then leave should normally be given, *Pifco Ltd v. Phillips Domestic Appliances and Personal Care BV* (1999) 23(3) I.P.D. 22026, [1999] C.L.Y. 3501 applied.

CARTONNERIES DE THULIN SA v. CTP WHITE KNIGHT LTD (COSTS) [1999] F.S.R. 922, Neuberger, J., Pat Ct.

416. Costs – joint liability – one defendant controlled another

[Supreme Court Act 1981 s.51.]

QHC brought proceedings against QRF and four other defendants in relation to a funding agreement and, inter alia, patent infringement. Judgment was given for QHC and costs awarded. R, the second defendant, submitted that he should only be held liable for costs in respect of those claims made against him or in respect of unsuccessful claims made by him. QHC, disputing R's submission, contended that he should be held jointly liable with QRF for the costs of the action. QHC argued that the action had been fought for R's benefit and that he would have gained most from its success. R, QHC alleged, was effectively the controlling mind behind QRF and had funded the action for them.

Held, finding R jointly liable with QRF for the costs, that (1) the principles to be exercised in a case under the Supreme Court Act 1981 s.51 where costs were sought against a non party threw light upon the proper approach which was to be taken when payment of costs of an issue which was raised against or by only some of the parties to the action had to be considered, *Symphony Group Plc v. Hodgson* [1994] Q.B. 179, [1993] C.L.Y. 3153 applied, and (2) the defendants were to all intents and purposes "the children" of R and he operated them to maximise the benefit to him. R was at the centre of the proceedings and his actions were at the core of the dispute.

QUADRANT HOLDINGS CAMBRIDGE LTD v. QUADRANT RESEARCH FOUNDATION (COSTS) [1999] F.S.R. 918, Pumfrey, J., Pat Ct.

417. Costs – liability – personal injury claimant – unreasonable conduct and untruthful account

[Civil Procedure Rules 1998 (SI 1998 3132) Part 44.]

H brought a claim for damages for personal injury and consequential losses against his employers, BSC, and their scaffolding contractors, MAC, the latter claim being subsequently dismissed. H alleged that he fell from a defective scaffold erected by or on behalf of BSC. BSC denied liability, contending that H was never positioned on a scaffold as such, rather that he was standing on a single scaffold plank balanced between two pipes, suspended over a six to eight foot drop. H claimed £376,000 in special damages, representing losses up to his normal date of retirement plus a loss of pension. At trial, H's evidence was completely discredited as to the circumstances of the accident. The judge accepted BSC's version and criticised H for "manufacturing" some of the documents to support his special damages claim. H submitted that BSC should be liable for all the costs. BSC argued that H should not recover all his costs due to his conduct, pursuant to the Civil Procedure Rules 1998 Part 44, referring to H's inflated schedule of special damages and untruthful evidence.

Held, giving judgment for H in part, that (1) H would pay MAC's costs in their entirety, as it had been unnecessarily joined into the proceedings by H and no blame had been directed against MAC by BSC, save to say it was the relevant contractor who would have erected any scaffolding present, and (2) H would recover only 50 per cent of his costs of the action against BSC, due to his unreasonable conduct in relation to special damages and his untruthful account of the accident circumstances.

HAWKER v. BRITISH STEEL CORP, November 2, 1999, Judge Masterman, CC (Cardiff). [*Ex rel.* Dolmans Solicitors, 17-20 Windsor Place, Cardiff].

418. Costs – litigants in person – right to be heard

[Civil Procedure Rules 1998 (SI 1998 3132) Part 48 r.48.6.]

Customs presented a bankruptcy petition against C, a litigant in person who was unable to attend the hearing, based on a statutory demand for unpaid VAT. Although C had not challenged the statutory demand, he had appealed against the underlying VAT assessment. As a result, Customs successfully applied for the petition to be dismissed. However, no order was made for costs and C appealed, contending that he would have sought costs in the sum of £8,000, based on his loss of earnings for eight hours' work, increased to £17,000 on appeal, with a further £1114 for travel and other sundry expenses.

Held, allowing the appeal, that it was in the interests of justice that C should have been heard on the issue of costs, and it was assumed they would have been awarded if he had requested them at the petition hearing. Under the Civil Procedure Rules 1998 Part 48 r.48.6, however, a litigant in person was entitled to the lowest amount of (1) actual lost earnings; (2) two thirds of the appropriate lawyers' fees, or (3) £9.50 per hour. On the facts, C was entitled to £160, representing 17 hours at £9.50 per hour.

CUSTOMS AND EXCISE COMMISSIONERS v. CHITOLIE [2000] B.P.I.R. 275, Robert Walker, L.J., CA.

419. Costs – multi track – infant settlement approval hearings – additional costs incurred over and above fixed costs

[Civil Procedure Rules 1998 (SI 1998 3132) Part 8 r.8, Part 21, Part 26 r.26, Part 44 r.44.]

J issued proceedings for approval of an infant settlement in accordance with Civil Procedure Rules 1998 Part 21 PD 21 para.6.1. The settlement was in the sum of £800, and W argued that, given the settlement sum, fixed costs should apply. W conceded that allocation to the multi track was inherent in Part 8 r.8 proceedings, but requested that the court use its discretion when awarding costs under Part 44 r.44, having regard to the overriding objective. J argued that under Part 8 r.8.9(c) the case was treated as being allocated to the multi track and the provisions on allocation laid down in Part 26 r.26 were thereby excluded. J further contended that the reason such claims were allocated to the multi track was because they required additional measures to be taken in order to protect the interests of the child, specifically the appointment of a litigation friend, obtaining advice on quantum and seeking the court's approval. Costs over and above fixed costs were therefore incurred necessarily in Part 8 r.8 claims.

Held, finding in favour of J, that this was clearly a matter which was effectively allocated to the multi track although no formal allocation had occurred. Under the Civil Procedure Rules 1998 costs were necessarily incurred due to the need for an approval hearing and defendants' solicitors were aware of that. Liability for such costs must therefore follow. Fixed costs did not apply, as such cases were not allocated to the small claims track. W was ordered to pay J's costs in the sum summarily assessed.

J (A CHILD) v. WIND, March 7, 2000, District Judge Smedley, CC (Liverpool). [*Ex rel.* Scott Rees & Co Solicitors, Centaur House, Gardiners Place, Skelmersdale].

420. Costs – notice of discontinuance served in injunction proceedings – late withdrawal of application warranted indemnity costs order

[Civil Procedure Rules 1998 (SI 1998 3132) Part 38 r.38.4.]

ABG, brought an action seeking an injunction and damages against PHH and other defendants for alleged breach of covenants contained in various leases in order to restrain the establishment of companies carrying out similar business in other parts of premises which ABG occupied. A Tomlin order was entered into with a number of defendants and the action stayed in relation to them. At the beginning of the trial ABG served a notice of discontinuance under the Civil Procedure Rules 1998 Part 38 r.38.4 on the third defendant in the action, a restaurant, T, which had been operating in another part of the premises. A dispute arose as to whether such notice warranted an award of costs to T on an indemnity basis. T contended that ABG had pursued a misconceived claim for an injunction and had by its conduct acted unfairly. It was alleged that ABG had had knowledge, before T occupied the premises, that the area might be used for the purposes of a restaurant business but had made no attempt to seek an injunction to prevent this. Furthermore, upon initiating proceedings against T, ABG had made no attempt to obtain an interim injunction during the period in which T was in operation up until the time of trial.

Held, granting the application for an indemnity costs order, that it would be unjust given the conduct of ABG in bringing the action and serving notice of discontinuance at so late a stage in the proceedings for T to suffer the burden of any costs incurred in defending the claim. It had been unreasonable for ABG to have pursued the claim for an injunction up until the point of discontinuance as a continuing threat to T's business. No attempt had been made to obtain an interim injunction and as a result T's business had been seriously undermined by the ongoing portent of the injunction proceedings.

ATLANTIC BAR & GRILL LTD v. POSTHOUSE HOTELS LTD [2000] C.P. Rep. 32, Rattee, J., Ch D.

421. Costs – Part 36 offers – pre-action offer expressed to be pursuant to Part 36 – assessment of reasonable costs and disbursements – entitlement to costs to date offer accepted

[Civil Procedure Rules 1998 (SI 1998 3132) Part 36.]

P was injured in a road traffic accident, for which C admitted liability. Special damages were agreed and paid. P brought a claim for damages for personal injuries and claimed that he was entitled to his costs to be assessed on the standard basis. C made a pre-action offer expressed to be pursuant to the Civil Procedure Rules 1998 Part 36 but silent as to costs, for £800. P responded with a claimant's pre-action offer, under Part 36, for £800, but indicated that it was expressly subject to C paying his reasonable costs and disbursements, to be assessed if not agreed. C then advised P that a cheque was being requested from C's insurers, and offered £58.75 for P's profit costs, on the basis that the claim had settled below the small claims track financial limit of £1,000 for personal injuries. C argued that Part 36 offers applied to cases which would be small claims track cases. P rejected C's offer as to costs and issued proceedings. C intended that (1) there was a concluded agreement as to costs and damages; (2) the acceptance by C of P's offer, which was "subject to meeting P's reasonable costs and disbursements, to be assessed if not agreed" was also subject to an implied term that those costs would be limited to the costs awardable if the case had been allocated to the small claims track; (3) by issuing proceedings in the face of this concluded agreement, P's solicitors were abusing the process of the court; (4) there was never any reasonable expectation of the award of general damages exceeding £1,000, therefore the proceedings should be struck out, and (5) a wasted costs order should be made against P's solicitors.

Held, that (1) there was a concluded agreement as to damages and costs. The request by C for a settlement cheque from the insurers was an acceptance. The offer of £58.75 for profit costs was not inconsistent with acceptance, and was an offer towards what C perceived as P's entitlement to costs; (2) there was no implied term limiting P's costs to those allowable if the case had been allocated to the small claims track. The correspondence was clear. C's solicitors knew perfectly well that P did not intend that the offer was to be accepted, limiting them to fixed costs. An "officious bystander" would not have implied that term; (3) C had accepted P's offer and was required to pay P damages of £800 plus his reasonable costs and disbursements, to be assessed on the standard basis if not agreed, up to the date when the offer was accepted, and (4) C was ordered to pay all of P's costs after the acceptance, namely from the time when C disputed P's entitlement to anything other than fixed costs and including the costs of the proceedings on an indemnity basis to be assessed if not agreed.

PARKER v. CONNOR, April 7, 2000, Deputy District Judge Josephs, CC (Peterborough). [*Ex rel.* Hunt & Coombs Solicitors, 35 Thorpe Road, Peterborough].

422. Costs – Part 36 payments – allegation that claim was dishonest and bogus – general rule applied that claimant pay defendant's costs following failure to beat Part 36 payment

B claimed damages against BS in respect of personal injuries sustained in a motor accident for which BS admitted liability, the only issue at trial being that of quantum. Following a Part 36 payment by BS, which B failed to beat, the judge departed from the general rule by awarding costs to B up to the date of the Part 36 payment but making no order for costs thereafter on the basis that BS had made an allegation, supported by a psychiatrist's report, that B was malingering and B had been obliged to pursue the litigation to refute the allegation and to establish his honesty in bringing the claim. BS appealed.

Held, allowing the appeal, that the judge had not been entitled to depart from the general rule on costs and B was ordered to pay the costs of BS from 21 days after the Part 36 payment, excepting those relating to the malingering issue. There was no evidence to suggest that B had pursued the litigation for any reason other than that of recovering damages and the malingering allegation had been a side issue relating only to the award of costs.

BURGESS v. BRITISH STEEL [2000] C.P. Rep. 48, Swinton Thomas, L.J., CA.

423. Costs – parties not joined in proceedings – liability of non parties for costs

SBJ applied for an order that E and A, partners in AIB pay part or all of the costs of SBJ's successful action against M, an ex-employee, for breach of restrictive covenants in his contract of employment as to the soliciting of clients and breaches of confidentiality. E approached M whilst he was employed by SBJ and offered him a position at AIB which M accepted. AIB took legal advice and as a result M advised SBJ that it had breached its contract of employment by putting him on garden leave and as a result he was not bound by the soliciting restriction. When M began work for AIB he solicited SBJ's clients for AIB. SBJ began proceedings seeking injunctive relief against M only. AIB helped to pay M's costs by way of a loan, and although a cap was placed on the loan after it became clear to AIB that the action was unlikely to settle, it did agree to pay for a junior counsel at trial for M. At the trial SBJ obtained the relief it sought.

Held, allowing the application, that on the facts AIB had not agreed to indemnify M against costs arising out of the action. However AIB did take the first step of taking legal advice which began the dispute with SBJ, and continued taking legal advice until the commencement of the proceedings. Further, M was encouraged by the loan promised by AIB to fight the action which was beyond his means to pay for. Even after capping the loan AIB still paid for counsel at trial. SBJ had failed to join AIB as second defendants even though there was a strong case against it to do so, however it was understandable that SBJ wanted swiftly to prevent M from continuing to solicit its clients and therefore the quickest route was to bring proceedings directly and only against M. AIB had deliberately laid low when the question of funding arose and had resisted an order for discovery, it also remained in touch with the proceedings and ensured that M could contest. The trial would never have taken place if AIB had not funded M, and those circumstances were exceptional enough to order E and A to pay half SBJ's costs. *Symphony Group Plc v. Hodgson* [1994] Q.B. 179, [1993] C.L.Y. 3153 and *Globe Equities Ltd v. Globe Legal Services Ltd* [1999] B.L.R. 232, [1999] C.L.Y. 390 applied.

SBJ STEPHENSON LTD v. MANDY (ORDER FOR COSTS) [2000] C.P. Rep. 64, Bell, J., QBD.

424.   Costs – party succeeding on liability failing to serve costs schedule – effect of failure to comply with CPR Part 44

[Civil Procedure Rules 1998 (SI 1998 3132) Part 44 r.44.]

The court found in favour of MCC on liability in a case which was being dealt with on the fast track under the Civil Procedure Rules 1998. MCC had not served a costs schedule on W at the commencement of the trial in accordance with *Practice Direction (Sup Ct: Civil Litigation: Procedure)* [1999] 1 W.L.R. 1124, [1999] C.L.Y. 513, W had served a costs schedule. W refused to consider MCC's handwritten costs schedule at the end of the trial. W argued that, as the Rules had not been complied with, there should be no order for costs. MCC argued that the costs could be assessed by the trial judge or listed for a detailed assessment. The judge decided that summary assessment under Part 44 r.44.4.4(1)(a) was appropriate and that there would be no order for costs as MCC was in breach of the Rules and the Practice Direction. MCC appealed, contending that (1) although no costs schedule had been served before the hearing, one was available and the judge had erred in law by holding that there was no opportunity for W to investigate MCC's costs; (2) the judge should either have adjourned the summary assessment until later in the day or alternatively ordered a detailed assessment of costs, and (3) it was disproportionate in any event to disallow the whole of MCC's costs.

Held, dismissing the appeal, that (1) the trial judge's decision could only be interfered with if he had erred in law or had unreasonably exercised his discretion; (2) a costs schedule had not been served within 24 hours of the hearing and there had consequently been a breach of the Practice Direction, and (3) the trial judge had a discretion on costs and had acted within the Rules, therefore his order could not be interfered with and it was not relevant to consider the argument on the ground of proportionality.

WRIGHT v. MANCHESTER CITY COUNCIL, December 14, 1999, Judge Tetlow, CC (Altrincham). [*Ex rel.* Colemans Solicitors, Elisabeth House, 16 St Peter's Square, Manchester].

425.   Costs – payment into court – subsequent attempt to reduce payment – effect on costs order following judgment

In July 1998, A brought proceedings against W for damages following a road traffic accident. A proportion of the claim concerned A's claim for credit hire charges. On March 16, 1999 W paid into court £5,500. On April 29, 1999 the Court of Appeal gave judgment in *Dimond v. Lovell* [2000] 2 W.L.R. 1121, [2000] C.L.Y. 2566. W's solicitors regarded their case as having been strengthened by the judgment. On May 21, 1999 W retracted the payment in and sought to recover some of it. They indicated that their offer was reduced to £2,500. W's solicitors did not apply for leave to reduce the payment in. At trial in September 1999, A was awarded £5,498. The district judge ordered A to pay W's costs from the date of the payment in and A appealed.

Held, allowing the appeal, that the district judge's exercise of discretion as to costs was wrong in principle. W's solicitors had represented that the money in court should be regarded as having been reduced to £2,500. Although A did not apply to take the full payment out, the court was satisfied that had he done so, W would have objected and successfully reduced the payment in. Accordingly, where a defendant paid in one sum but later represented that only a lower sum was available for acceptance, it was wrong for the defendant to retain a protection as to costs in the higher figure, *Garner v. Cleggs* [1983] 1 W.L.R. 862, [1983] C.L.Y. 3023 applied. The correct order was for A to have his costs of the trial saved for that period of time during which the full payment into court was available for acceptance. In respect of that short period, A would pay W's costs.

ALLEN v.WHITTLE, February 29, 2000, Judge Ellis, CC (Croydon). [*Exrel.* Philip Goddard, Barrister, 4 King's Bench Walk, 2nd Floor, Temple, London].

426. **Costs – personal injuries – attempt by successful claimant to mislead court**

[Civil Procedure Rules 1998 (SI 1998 3132) Part 18, Part 36, Part 44 r.44.3.]

D, who had been involved in a road traffic accident in which his car was damaged and he suffered personal injury, claimed the cost of hiring an alternative vehicle on credit as well as loss of earnings and general damages in respect of his whiplash injury. At the time of the accident D had been working as a chauffeur or mini cab driver. D contended, supported by a medical report, that for some weeks after the accident he could hardly drive and was unable to work for about six months. It was found that these assertions were contradicted by the fact that D had hired a car within three days of the accident and the mileage recorded on the hire agreement showed that the first car hired by D had travelled over 1,000 miles in two weeks. D's evidence was further contradicted by replies to a Part 18 request which stated that he had been working within two months of the accident, albeit part time. For these reasons the judge concluded that D had misled the medical expert and had attempted to mislead the court as to the severity of his injury. However, the court accepted that D had visited his GP on the day of the accident, and that he had been unable to work for two days. P contended that as a matter of principle the court should award no general damages in circumstances where, as here, a claimant was found to have attempted to defraud a defendant's insurers, and to have lied on oath in order to do so.

Held, giving judgment for the claimant in part, that P's contention was not well founded and D was entitled to GPB 250 by way of general damages and two days' loss of earnings and expenses. When considering costs the court took into account the conduct of D as required by the Civil Procedure Rules Part 44 r.44.3, including the fact that D had exaggerated his claim. A claim of about £15,000 had been brought, whereas D had recovered total damages of £670. A month before trial P had made a Part 36 payment into court of £3,000. For these reasons the court ordered that D pay P's entire costs of the proceedings.

DESAI v. PATEL, August 31, 2000, District Judge Thomas, CC (Ilford). [*Ex rel.* Badhams Thompson Solicitors, 95 Aldwych, London].

427. **Costs – personal liability of directors of insolvent company – unreasonable litigation**

An insolvent company, FM, lost its appeal against T. An application that FM's two directors, D, be required to pay the costs personally and that the costs be summarily assessed was adjourned. D, having been joined as parties, relied on the proposition in *Taylor v. Pace Developments Ltd* [1991] B.C.C. 406, [1992] C.L.Y. 3427 that such costs orders should be made only rarely. They argued that the appeal was not unreasonably brought, that T had only itself to blame if the security for costs it had obtained turned out to be too low, and that the costs would have little significance to a company as big as T. In any event, D submitted that they should only be liable for costs after April 1999, when they had taken over the funding of the litigation from the receiver.

Held, making the costs order but refusing a summary assessment and ordering an interim payment, that the appeal was not reasonably brought and appeared to involve some element of vindictiveness. Where an individual funded litigation by an insolvent litigant, such an individual could be held liable for costs, especially where such an individual had a personal interest in the outcome of the litigation and was also aware of the risks involved. As guarantors of FM's debts, D had a personal interest in the outcome of the litigation and could therefore properly be held to have been at risk of costs. *Taylor* was distinguishable as it related to an insolvent company defending rather than pursuing proceedings. D's liability for costs would only run from April 1999, but would be unlimited. Summary assessment was not appropriate given that D disputed the amount claimed and a large sum was involved. However, an interim payment was appropriate and D was therefore required to make a payment of £20,000.

FULTON MOTORS LTD v. TOYOTA (GB) LTD (COSTS) [2000] C.P. Rep. 24, Peter Gibson, L.J., CA.

428. **Costs – proportional order for costs – issues resolved in favour of defendant and claimant's conduct before issue of proceedings**

[Civil Procedure Rules 1998 (SI 1998 3132) Part 44 r.44.3.]

WG entered into an agreement with LCC whereby LCC agreed to sell certain land to WG subject to the lapse or abandonment of an option exercisable by a third party. LCC commenced proceedings against WG seeking a determination of its rights under the agreement. At the trial, five issues had to be determined. Two issues were decided in favour of WG whereas LCC succeeded on two or three depending on whether two particular issues could be described as connected. The judge's rulings on the relevant issues meant that LCC had achieved its aim and had been the overall winner. The question of costs was then determined. WG argued that LCC's conduct before the commencement of proceedings should be reflected in the order for costs. WG contended, amongst other things, that LCC had raised only one of the five issues referred to in the particulars of claim before proceedings were issued and that it had delayed unduly in seeking a determination of the issues between the parties. As regards LCC's conduct after the issue of proceedings, WG argued that LCC had been responsible for the inclusion of a great deal of unnecessary documents in the trial bundle. LCC, on the other hand, asked the judge to take into account an offer which it had put forward and which, it argued, should have been accepted by WG.

Held, having regard to the Civil Procedure Rules 1998 Part 44 r.44.3, that it would be appropriate to award LCC a proportion of its costs. Given that LCC had been the overall winner, the fact that WG had succeeded on two of the five issues and that there had been an overlap between the various issues in terms of the evidence and arguments, such an approach would be fair. Where evidence was reasonably necessary both for a point on which LCC succeeded and for a point decided in favour of WG, the costs relating thereto were to be awarded in favour of LCC since the evidence had been reasonably required for the purpose of LCC's case and LCC had been the overall winner. Regard would be had to the Civil Procedure Rules dealing with the parties' conduct before the commencement of proceedings. The evidence revealed that LCC had left matters to the last minute. LCC had either wrongly assumed that it would succeed on the one issue which it thought needed to be determined or had buried its head in the sand without properly considering the legal position until the eleventh hour. That had led to the proceedings being conducted more hurriedly and less efficiently than was desirable. The offer relied on by LCC would not be reflected in terms of costs since (1) it having been put forward on the last working day before the trial, WG had not been given time to properly consider it; (2) it was not capable of acceptance since it had been expressed as being subject to contract and committee approval and (3) it was arguably inadmissible since it made reference to without prejudice negotiations. In all the circumstances, LCC would be awarded one half of its costs. Had LCC conducted itself reasonably before proceedings were issued, it would have recovered three quarters of its costs. Given that the trial bundle contained a great many unnecessary documents, LCC would be awarded five eighths of its costs in preparing the trial bundles.

LIVERPOOL CITY COUNCIL v. ROSEMARY CHAVASSE LTD (COSTS) [2000] C.P. Rep. 8, Neuberger, J., Ch D.

429. Costs – proportionality – appeal against master's decision on costs was rehearing

PR, who unsuccessfully defended a copyright action commenced by SME, sought to reverse the master's order requiring it to pay SME's costs. PR argued that, whereas it had at all times acted constructively and had acceded to judgment on its admissions, SME and its solicitors had, both before and after the issue of proceedings, behaved in a peremptory and aggressive fashion.

Held, dismissing the appeal, that considering the circumstances of the case, including the fact that PR had taken issue throughout with the remedy sought by SME, the master had been correct to order PR to pay SME's costs, and that SME's allegedly disproportionate conduct could be taken into account when costs were assessed. The judge on appeal was entitled to exercise his discretion in a hearing de novo concerning a costs order that had been made after the final judgment, *Singh v. Bhasin The Times*, August 21, 1998, [1998] C.L.Y. 484 applied, whereas the court would be unwilling to reopen a costs issue in interlocutory proceedings, *Hoddle v. CCF Construction* [1992] 2 All E.R. 550, [1992] C.L.Y. 3415 followed.

SONY MUSIC ENTERTAINMENT INC v. PRESTIGE RECORDS LTD [2000] 2 Costs L.R. 186, Lloyd, J., Ch D.

430. Costs – public interest – appropriateness of pre-emptive costs order – duty under Community law

[Civil Procedure Rules 1998 (SI 1998 3132).]

C sought an order that none of the parties to ongoing litigation should be obliged to pay a sum by way of costs exceeding ten per cent of their annual turnover. C submitted that to make such an order would give effect to the overriding objective laid down by the Civil Procedure Rules 1998, by ensuring that the parties were on an equal footing and that costs remained proportionate to the financial status of each party. C further contended that in the absence of such an order, it would be obliged to abandon the proceedings, and the court was therefore under a Community law duty to enable it to continue, by making the appropriate costs order.

Held, dismissing the application, that a pre-emptive costs order was only appropriate in exceptional circumstances, *R. v. Lord Chancellor, ex p. Child Poverty Action Group* [1999] 1 W.L.R. 347, [1998] C.L.Y. 412 applied. Although the instant proceedings involved a point of general public importance, the application faced substantial hurdles in terms of merit. Furthermore it could not be said that the order sought was entirely proportionate, as it would provide the applicant with greater protection than that which would be afforded to the respondent or interested parties. The court was not satisfied that, if the application were refused, C would probably abandon the proceedings, but there was no Community law duty upon it to make the order, to preclude C from doing so.

R. v. HAMMERSMITH AND FULHAM LBC, *ex p.* CPRE LONDON BRANCH (COSTS ORDER); *sub nom.* R. v. HAMMERSMITH AND FULHAM LBC, *ex p.* COUNCIL FOR THE PROTECTION OF RURAL ENGLAND (NO.2) [2000] Env. L.R. 544, Richards, J., QBD.

431. Costs – related causes of action – inherent jurisdiction to order stay pending satisfaction of earlier costs order

S contracted with BT, to provide "chatline" services. In 1992, BT suspended all payments due under various customer orders made pursuant to the contract following suspicions that the company through which S operated was not providing a bona fide service. A company identified as VTL commenced an action against BT in 1992 seeking injunctive relief to prevent BT from suspending payment. The action was unsuccessful and in 1995 S commenced an action against BT for breach of contract, contending that he personally was the contracting party. Subsequently, this cause of action and all other causes of action arising from the different customers' orders were assigned to S. In 1997, S commenced another action against BT in reliance upon those assignments. The 1995 action was struck out, on the basis that S could not establish that he was the contracting party and the 1992 action dismissed for want of prosecution. VTL were ordered to pay the costs relating to the 1992 action and when it failed to do so BT was granted a stay of the 1997 action with an order for payment within three months and strike out in default of compliance. S appealed, contending that (1) the 1992 and the 1997 actions did not arise from the same cause of action; (2) neither VTL nor S had any assets which meant that the 1997 action would be stifled, and (3) any liability for costs in the 1992 action should be postponed pending the determination of the 1997 action in order that S might have the opportunity to recover damages due to him.

Held, dismissing the appeal, that (1) S had failed to identify himself as the party to the contract in question. The actions in 1992 and 1997 undoubtedly arose from the same contract with S acting in his capacity as assignee of VTL. The court had an inherent jurisdiction to prevent a claimant from pursuing an action against a defendant which was substantially similar to the first, without satisfying obligations arising from the original action, *Eurocross Sales Ltd v. Cornhill Insurance Plc* [1995] 1 W.L.R. 1517, [1995] C.L.Y. 4011 considered; (2) the affidavit submitted by S asserting his lack of assets was wholly inadequate since it did not address the possibility of obtaining support from third parties, or deal with interests he had in the various companies carrying on the "chatline" services, which had received considerable sums of money from BT, and (3) the order was essentially a disciplinary measure and would be ineffective if it was only to require S to satisfy VTL's costs after judgment in the 1997 action.

SINCLAIR v. BRITISH TELECOMMUNICATIONS PLC [2001] 1 W.L.R. 38, Ferris, J., CA.

432. Costs – remuneration of court appointed receiver did not constitute costs

[Rules of the Supreme Court 1965 (SI 1965 1776) Ord.62 r.1 (4); Supreme Court Fees Order 1980 (SI 1980 821) Sch.1 Item 29 (d).]

The chief taxing master decided that the receivers of the estate of the late Robert Maxwell should pay a fee of £7.50 for every £100, or part thereof, of the remuneration of the receiver who had been appointed by the court upon the assessment of that remuneration by the master. The receivers appealed.

Held, allowing the appeal, that notwithstanding that "remuneration" was included in "costs" by virtue of the Rules of the Supreme Court 1965 Ord.62 r.1 (4), and that the Supreme Court Fees Order 1980 Sch.1 Item 29 (d) provided that a fee was payable upon the assessment of costs in the Chancery Division, the remuneration of a court appointed receiver was not of the character of costs in litigation. The receiver was an officer of the court and did not act on the instructions of the parties to a case.

MIRROR GROUP NEWSPAPERS PLC v. MAXWELL *The Times*, May 30, 2000, Ferris, J., Ch D.

433. Costs – security – Comptroller of Patents Designs and Trade Marks lacked jurisdiction to order – not a court for purposes of Companies Act 1985

[Patents Act 1977 s.8(1) (a), s.107 (4); Companies Act 1985 s.726 (1); Rules of the Supreme Court 1965 (SI 1965 1776) Ord.23 r.3.]

CI, a UK company, referred the question of entitlement to the grant of patents made by A to the Comptroller under the Patents Act 1977 s.8(1) (a). A filed a counterstatement but sought security for costs from CI before the matter proceeded further. A claimed that CI would not be able to pay A's costs if CI's referral was unsuccessful, and argued that the Companies Act 1985 s.726 (1) applied to inter partes proceedings before the Comptroller. A argued that the Comptroller was a "court" and that proceedings before him were "legal proceedings".

Held, refusing the application, that the Comptroller had no jurisdiction to order security for costs, that (1) an equivalent provision to the Rules of the Supreme Court 1965 Ord.23 r.3, which stated that the Order was without prejudice to any enactment which empowered the Court to require security for costs to be given in any proceedings, did not appear in s.107(4) of the 1977 Act. Accordingly, the Comptroller would not exercise any powers under any other enactment unless it was quite clear that they must apply to the Comptroller; (2) the proceedings before the Comptroller were legal proceedings, since many of the Comptroller's powers were the same as those of the High Court and the proceedings before the Comptroller determined legal rights such as ownership; (3) however, proceedings before the Comptroller were supposed to be relatively cheap, unlike the costs of proceeding before the High Court or county court. It was, therefore, not possible to conclude that Parliament could not have intended to exclude tribunals such as the Comptroller from s.726 of the 1985 Act. Indeed, the absence of the "without prejudice" condition from the 1977 Act could imply that Parliament deliberately had such an intention. The Comptroller was therefore not a Court for the purposes of s.726 and it followed that he did not have jurisdiction to order security for costs.

ABDULHAYOGLU'S PATENT APPLICATION [2000] R.P.C. 18, P Hayward, PO.

434. Costs – security – evidence of residence abroad – intention to deceive by claimant

[Rules of the Supreme Court (SI 1965 1776) Ord.23 r.1; EC Treaty Art.6 (now, after amendment, Art.12 EC).]

G brought a libel action against B in relation to matters published in Portugal. B applied for an order for security for costs under the Rules of the Supreme Court Ord.23 r.1 on the grounds that (1) G was a Portuguese resident, and (2) his address was incorrectly stated in the writ. The application was allowed by a master and upheld on appeal. G appealed, contending that he was ordinarily resident in England and, alternatively, if his address was incorrectly stated that was due to an innocent error without an intention to deceive. Further, that if he was resident in Portugal, an order for security would discriminate against him on nationality grounds, contrary to the EC Treaty Art.6 (now, after amendment, Art.12 EC).

Held, dismissing the appeal, that (1) G's evidence regarding his residence was unconvincing. Neither the master nor the judge had determined specifically that G had deliberately misled the court as to his residence, but it was clear that there was sufficient evidence to find that G had intended to deceive, and (2) although it was likely that an order for security for costs would offend against Art.6, no argument had been raised on that point and it was unnecessary to reach a conclusion on it given the finding as to G's intent to deceive.

GOODACRE v. BATES [2000] I.L.Pr. 527, Swinton Thomas, L.J., CA.

435. Costs – security – extent to which security for costs ordered against claimant ordinarily resident outside jurisdiction

[Rules of the Supreme Court 1965 (SI 1965 1776) Ord.23 r.1 (1).]

B appealed against the dismissal of his application for security for costs against L as a claimant resident outside the jurisdiction.

Held, dismissing the appeal, that under the Rules of the Supreme Court Ord.23 r.1 (1) security for costs would no longer be ordered as a matter of course against a claimant ordinarily resident outside the jurisdiction. The existing case law on such orders no longer applied and the single criterion for the court was to consider what was just in the circumstances. The existence of assets in the jurisdiction and their fixity and permanence was relevant, although the fact that a claimant was ordinarily resident within the jurisdiction did not preclude the court from ordering security. In the instant case, there was no reason to doubt L's probity considering his long residence in England and his substantial assets within the jurisdiction, and therefore it would not be just to order security for costs against him.

LEYVAND v. BARASCH *The Times*, March 23, 2000, Lightman, J., Ch D.

436. Costs – security – impecunious defendant funded by third parties

[Civil Procedure Rules 1998 (SI 1998 3132) Part 50; European Convention on Human Rights 1950 Art.6(1).]

FBME, a bank, made an application for security for costs following the grant of leave to appeal to H, an undischarged bankrupt in respect of two judgments. Previous litigation undertaken by H had been funded by third parties who were no longer willing to provide further capital. FBME submitted that, on the basis of H's impecuniosity, they were entitled to security under the Civil Procedure Rules 1998 Part 50. H opposed the application, contending that (1) an order for security would stifle an appeal for which leave had been granted since it was clear that the third parties would not provide further funds; (2) the granting of leave to appeal implied that H had a real prospect of success, therefore an order for security would result in the restraint of a reasonably arguable case. Furthermore, the court had jurisdiction to make an order for costs from the third parties after the hearing of the appeal and that should be the preferred option; (3) an order for security would restrict H's access to an independent and impartial tribunal in breach of the European Convention on Human Rights 1950 Art.6(1), and (4) there had been an inexplicable delay between the date of notice of appeal and the application for security, such delay justified either refusal of the application or a reduction in the amount of security ordered.

Held, allowing the application, that (1) H had not discharged the burden of showing that funds to pursue the appeal were unavailable from third parties. Although the third parties in question had expressed an intention not to fund any further litigation, nevertheless, as reasonable commercial men, they were likely to wish to protect the investment they had already made in the proceedings to date; (2) the granting of leave to appeal was on a without notice application and the court was not bound by a decision at that stage that the case had a real prospect of success. There were no grounds for limiting the court's powers to grant security before an appeal on the basis that, after the appeal, it was possible to make a third party order dependent on the result, especially where those third parties were resident abroad and had no assets in the UK, *Abraham v. Thompson* [1997] 4 All E.R. 362, [1997] C.L.Y. 562 distinguished; (3) an order for security for costs to be provided by an appellant did not infringe Art.6(1) and in any event the Convention was not currently incorporated into domestic legislation, *Tolstoy Miloslavsky v. United Kingdom (A/323)* [1996] E.M.L.R. 152, [1995] C.L.Y. 2647 followed, and (4) the delay was not likely to have given rise to prejudice to H. Considerable activity had taken place between the date of notice of appeal and the application for security which might have affected the judgment under appeal and that went some way to explaining the delay.

FEDERAL BANK OF THE MIDDLE EAST v. HADKINSON (SECURITY FOR COSTS) (NO.1) [2000] C.P. Rep. 31, Morritt, L.J., CA.

437. Costs – security – money borrowed on loan from bank to fund security for costs of appeal – resulting trust to bank – borrower entitled to repay money to bank on withdrawal of appeal as purpose of loan satisfied

M applied for judicial review of a decision by CPEB that she was not eligible for the Bar Vocational Course and CPEB subsequently conceded that M was eligible for a place on the course. M had borrowed the sum of £6,000 from a bank and paid it into court as security for costs. The Court of Appeal ordered that M's appeal be withdrawn and that the matter of the £6,000 be determined by the High Court. M contended that the sum was borrowed specifically to fund the security for costs of the appeal, in accordance with the terms of the loan agreement, *Barclays Bank Ltd v. Quistclose Investments Ltd* [1970] A.C. 567, [1968] C.L.Y. 459 cited. Since the matter had been conceded and the appeal withdrawn, the purpose of the loan had been satisfied and M was obliged to repay the sum to the bank. It was held at first instance that (1) on payment of the sum into court, the trust created by the agreement terminated; (2) even if the trust continued, the court had no notice of it, and (3) it was for the bank not M to make the claim. It was ordered that the sum plus interest should be paid to CPEB in satisfaction of their costs on the basis that the court had power to order payment of monies held as security for costs in satisfaction of costs orders already made in a party's favour, *London CC v. Monks* [1959] Ch. 239, [1959] C.L.Y. 2596 applied. M appealed.

Held, allowing the appeal, that (1) the loan monies were subject to the prior interest of the bank. The court only had power to make orders in respect of monies held as security for costs where the money formed part of the borrower's general assets and was owned free any prior interest of a third party, *Monks* distinguished; (2) the trust did not conclude when the money was paid into court; (3) the loan agreement provided that if M's appeal was successful and no order for costs was made against her, then the money would be returned to the bank and the loan would only continue to have effect if M's appeal failed; (4) the fact that the court had no notice of any trust was irrelevant; (5) the court had not given consideration for the money; (6) the relevant consideration was the intentions of M and the bank concerning the money and not those of the recipient of the deposit, and (7) if the trust continued after the payment into court, then M was obliged as a trustee to repay it to the bank. M was therefore entitled to recoup the money and repay her loan to the bank, *Quistclose* considered. It was confirmed that money lent as a loan could be held by the borrower as trustee on terms that the money would not become part of the borrower's general assets, would be used for a specific purpose and would otherwise be held on a resulting trust for the lender.

R. v. COMMON PROFESSIONAL EXAMINATION BOARD, *ex p.* MEALING-MCCLEOD *The Times*, May 2, 2000, Roch, L.J., CA.

438. Costs – security – order for security for costs where claim had merit and claimant's poor financial situation arguably attributable to defendant's breach

F instigated proceedings against a company, KC, alleging breach of an agreement for the extraction of coal from colliery waste deposits present in large quantities on F's land. KC made an application for security for costs which was granted in the sum of £100,000. F appealed, contending that the judge had failed to (1) pay sufficient regard to the fact that F's financial difficulties stemmed directly from KC's breach of contract; (2) give sufficient weight to the high prospect of the claim succeeding, and (3) appreciate the fact that the impact of the order would be effectively to stifle the claim.

Held, allowing the appeal, that a conclusion that a claimant would be unlikely to be in a position to meet the costs of a successful defendant's defence should not result as a matter of course in the grant of an order for security for costs. On the facts, F had a genuine claim with substantial merit and it was certainly arguable that its present poor financial situation was directly due to KC's breach of contract. In the circumstances the order made had resulted in injustice to F.

FERNHILL MINING LTD v. KIER CONSTRUCTION LTD [2000] C.P. Rep. 69, Evans, L.J., CA.

439. Costs – security – Swiss national – discrimination on grounds of nationality

[Rules of the Supreme Court 1965 (SI 1965 1776) Ord.23 r.1; Brussels Convention on Jurisdiction and Enforcement of Judgments in Civil and Commercial Matters 1968; Lugano Convention on Jurisdiction and Enforcement of Judgments in Civil and Commercial Matters 1988.]

B, a Swiss national, appealed against an order requiring him to provide security for costs.

Held, allowing the appeal, that when considering whether a Swiss national should be ordered to give security for costs under the Rules of the Supreme Court 1965 Ord.23 r.1, the court should adopt a similar approach to that taken in relation to nationals of Member States of the European Union or the European Economic Area, whereby orders for security for costs were regarded as involving covert discrimination on the ground of nationality and whereby such orders would rarely, if ever, be granted. Swiss residents were subject either to the Brussels Convention 1968 or to the Lugano Convention 1988, both of which provided for the automatic enforcement of judgments. Since no evidence had been adduced to show that enforcement of the relevant judgment against B in Switzerland would prove difficult, the order requiring security for costs to be provided would be set aside, *Fitzgerald v. Williams* [1996] Q.B. 657, [1996] C.L.Y. 726 applied.

BUNZL v. MARTIN BUNZL INTERNATIONAL LTD *The Times*, September 19, 2000, Ian Hunter Q.C., Ch D.

440. Costs – security for costs – application for security against experienced commercial litigator with skill to inflate costs and frustrate attempts at enforcement

A, the defendant to proceedings commenced by M, lodged an appeal against an order for summary judgment in favour of M which prohibited A and others from using the trade name "Morris Merryweather" in the field of security and fire protection. M applied for security for costs of the appeal in the sum of £10,000 but failed to give proper notice to A. A sought an adjournment of the application.

Held, granting the application for security for costs and dismissing the application to adjourn, that despite the lack of an adequate notice of appeal, A had had sufficient time to address the issues in the case and it would be unjust to require M to defend an appeal with the risk of further expense and delay in seeking to enforce any order for costs obtained as a result. A was an experienced commercial litigator with the ability to inflate legal costs and prolong attempts at enforcement if that was thought to be to his advantage.

MINDBENDER LTD v. ABBOTT [2000] C.P. Rep. 27, Chadwick, L.J., CA.

441. Costs – small claims – assessment – motor insurer aware of insured's deceit

H claimed damages arising out of a road traffic accident in July 1998, in which M drove into H's parked car whilst she was unloading goods from the car. M refused to give his details at the scene. H's solicitors wrote to him for insurance details but he ignored the correspondence. H eventually found the details from a DVLA search. Insurance details were subsequently discovered. H's solicitors wrote to M's insurers but were told by them that M denied contact had taken place between the vehicles. M was convicted of driving without due care and failing to report the accident in January 1999. Proceedings were issued by H in February 1999, pleading the conviction. M's insurers filed a defence denying the accident took place and denied quantum in general terms. The matter was referred to the small claims track. In July 1999, the claim was settled as per the pleadings. No agreement was reached on costs. A hearing on the question of costs took place in October 1999 and it was submitted that she was entitled to have her costs summarily assessed on an indemnity basis because M and/or M's insurers had acted unreasonably in allowing proceedings to be issued and had filed defence without merit before settling the claim.

Held, finding for H, that M's insurers were vicariously liable for M's deceit. Once they had been served with the particulars of claim they should have promptly investigated the matter, which would have led to settlement. Costs were awarded on an indemnity basis.

HELBERG-HENSEN v. MANSFIELD, October 8, 1999, District Judge Hoffman, CC (Wrexham). [*Ex rel.* Clement Jones Solicitors, Hoywell House, Parkway Business Centre, Deeside Park, Flintshire].

442. Costs – small claims – claim for reasonable costs under Consumer Credit Act 1974 s.75 – operation of Civil Procedure Rules on small claims track costs

[Consumer Credit Act 1974 s.75; Civil Procedure Act 1997; Civil Procedure Rules 1998 (SI 1998 3132).]

L brought an action against MR claiming that the contract by which MR agreed to provide a personalised vehicle registration plate was void for legal object, namely the supply of a misleading number plate, the use of which would have been an offence. MR had suggested that the licence plate could be supplied in a mixed typeface subject to L signing a disclaimer. L claimed a refund, damages for distress and inconvenience plus interest. The second defendant, BB, a credit card issuer, was joined by virtue of the Consumer Credit Act 1974 s.75, namely a debtor-creditor-supplier agreement. BB contended that it should be indemnified by MR pursuant to s.75, and that, despite the fact that the Civil Procedure Rules 1998 limited the costs allowable in the small claims track, s.75 operated such that BB should be allowed their reasonable costs. Neither the 1998 Rules nor the Civil Procedure Act 1997 repealed s.75, either expressly or impliedly. MR did not serve a defence.

Held, granting judgment for L, that BB was entitled to be indemnified by MR to the full extent of the amount awarded to L. Further, that BB was entitled to recover from MR its reasonable costs of defending L's action pursuant to s.75.

LAMPON v. MIDLAND REGISTRATION LTD, May 31, 2000, District Judge Lamdin, CC (Bromley). [*Ex rel.* Andrew J Tobin, Barrister, Chambers of Patrick Eccles Q.C., 2 Harcourt Buildings, Temple, London].

443. Costs – small claims – costs consequences of making Part 36 offer prior to allocation

[Civil Procedure Rules 1998 (SI 1998 3132) Part 27, Part 36.]

D and G were involved in a road traffic accident in November 1998. Proceedings were issued in January 2000. Prior to allocation in March 2000, G made an offer pursuant to the Civil Procedure Rules 1998 Part 36 to settle D's claim in the sum of £500 for personal injuries and £1,600 credit hire charges. The offer was accepted out of time by D in May 2000. G refused to pay D's costs on the standard basis as quantum of the claim fell within the boundaries of the small claims track and Part 27 r.27.2 confirmed that Part 36 offers did not apply to the small claims track.

Held, finding in favour of D, that Part 27 did not apply to the claim as it had not been allocated to the small claims track. As a Part 36 offer had been accepted, D was entitled to costs. Furthermore, in accordance with Part 36 r.36.15(1), a Part 36 offer had been accepted, the action was stayed and the case could not be allocated. G was ordered to pay D's costs up to 21 days after receipt of D's Part 36 offer.

DEAN v. GRIFFIN, June 7, 2000, District Judge Tynas, CC (Macclesfield). [*Ex rel.* Thorneycroft & Co Solicitors, Bridge Street Mills, Bridge Street, Macclesfield].

444. Costs – small claims – failure to notify parties of allocations – validity of restriction on costs

[Civil Procedure Rules 1998 (SI 1998 3132) Part 26 r.26.9, Part 27 r.27.14.]

P issued proceedings for damages arising from a road traffic accident. R filed a defence disputing quantum only. Unknown to either party, the court allocated the case to the small claims track, dispensing with allocation questionnaires and not sending out notices of the allocation as required under the Civil Procedure Rules 1998 Part 26 r.26.9. Damages were subsequently agreed and the only remaining issue was P's costs, which it sought in full at £1,176.39. When the case was heard the district judge made an order that C should recover fixed costs only. The fact of the allocation had still not emerged by the time of that hearing. C appealed. At the appeal, the circuit judge, inspecting the court file, informed the parties that allocation had taken place. P said that the failure to send out notices of allocation rendered the de facto allocation invalid. The restriction on costs under Part 27 r.27.14 was therefore inconsistent. R argued that the lack of a notice made no difference to the validity of the allocation, and that the costs had been correctly restricted to fixed costs.

Held, dismissing the appeal, that the judge's decision to dispense with the allocation questionnaires and the lack of notices did not invalidate the allocation; the case was allocated to the small claims track and it stayed there. Therefore the restriction to fixed costs was correct. If the case had not been formally allocated it would have made no difference to the costs order because P had rejected a reasonable offer by R to pay part of the costs. Therefore P would be rightly capped on costs in a judge's discretion. In any event, the agreed sum for damages was less than half the £1,176.39 sought by P in costs. This was out of all proportion to the claim and could not be awarded.

PORTER v. READER, January 21, 2000, Judge Curl, CC (Lowestoft). [*Ex rel.* Nigel Waddington, Barrister, 8 Stone Buildings, Lincoln's Inn, London].

445. Costs – small claims – refusal to pay credit hire charges

[Consumer Credit Act 1974.]

N brought an action against J for damages arising from a road traffic accident. N's claim was based on the cost of repairs to his vehicle, together with the cost of hire of an alternative vehicle during the repair period. The part of the claim relating to the repair costs was settled by way of an interim payment. J's insurance company, however, refused to pay the credit hire account. It stated in a letter to N's representatives that it had an offer to put forward in relation to the hire claim but gave no specific reason for the denial. N's representatives wrote to J's solicitors requesting an explanation and specific reasons as to why their client was refusing to pay the credit hire account. J's solicitors responded that it was not their client's policy nor practice to pay credit hire charges and N issued proceedings. J issued a defence based on various breaches of the Consumer Credit Act 1974, whereupon N discontinued the action and J made an application for unreasonable costs against N for the discontinuance, arguing that there had been no significant change in circumstances.

Held, awarding costs to N on a standard basis after finding that J's conduct in the matter was unreasonable, that J's refusal to explain prior to proceedings why they were not prepared to deal with the hire claim and subsequent invitation to N to issue proceedings flew in the face of the current climate of open litigation. The aim of the small claims procedure was to get away from the rituals which characterised ordinary litigation, *Afzal v. Ford Motor Co Ltd* [1994] 4 All E.R. 720, [1995] C.L.Y. 3897 considered. The court also considered the issue of proportionality given the total amount of the claim and the complex nature of the defence raised.

NORMINTON v. JOWETT, February 24, 1999, District Judge Needham, CC (Manchester). [*Ex rel.* Ison Harrison & Co Solicitors, Duke House, 54 Wellington Street, Leeds].

446. Costs – small claims – unreasonable conduct – attempt to settle

S alleged that K had driven his vehicle into the rear of S's vehicle. K denied that the accident took place. S issued proceedings, claiming a liquidated sum of £470. K stated that initially he intended to defend the action as a matter of principle, but as the hearing date approached he took a commercial view of the matter and decided to settle the claim. K was insured and had no claims bonus protection and therefore had no financial interest in the proceedings. He advised his insurance company of his intention to settle and, following his instructions, a representative from his insurance company contacted S's solicitors 17 days before the hearing and confirmed that they wanted to settle the matter in full. S's solicitor later called K's insurance company and left a message requesting a call back. No call back was received by S's solicitors. K's insurance company contacted S's solicitors once again confirming that they were prepared to pay the claim in full together with fixed costs. S's solicitors stated that they were not prepared to accept this offer and would be attending the final hearing to argue for costs to be assessed on the standard basis. They advised that this argument would be predicated on the basis that K had engaged in unreasonable conduct in settling this matter at a later stage. K's solicitors then put forward the offer in writing to S's solicitor and confirmed that they were prepared to pay S's liquidated claim in full together with interest and fixed costs. A letter was also sent to the court explaining the situation and enclosing a copy of the letter sent to S's solicitors. K's solicitors stated that S was only entitled to fixed costs and if they were to attend the hearing and force K's solicitors to attend the hearing then K's solicitors would be requesting K's costs on the basis of S's unreasonable conduct.

Held, refusing costs for both claimant and defendant, that neither K's behaviour nor that of his representatives had been unreasonable and a defendant's conduct must go somewhat further to take it outside the norm of the usual tactics of negotiation. What had happened in this case was typical of cases of this type and usual in the course of negotiation, therefore S's claim for costs on the basis of K's unreasonable conduct was not allowed. Had K wished to protect his position in a fast track manner he would have made a payment into court which would have been valid had it been made 21 days or more before the hearing. This offer was not made 21 days before the hearing and therefore K was not entitled to his costs based on S's unreasonable conduct.

STRINGER v. KORDAN, August 31, 2000, Deputy District Judge Thomas, CC (Birmingham). [*Ex rel.* Andrew Leach, Lee Crowder, Solicitors, 39 Newhall Street, Birmingham].

447. Costs – small claims – unreasonable conduct – entitlement to assessed costs in place of fixed costs

[Civil Procedure Rules 1998 Part 27 r.27.14 (2) (d).]

T, who had been involved in a minor road traffic accident with KD, appealed against an award of fixed costs in his favour, following his successful small claims action against KD, whose conduct had been found to be unreasonable. T had served a letter of claim and a witness statement, to which KD had failed to reply. T had issued proceedings in the small claims court and had obtained interlocutory judgment in the absence of a defence. The case was listed for hearing. Prior to the hearing, KD indicated a desire to settle and made an interim payment of damages. T requested the balance of the damages and provided details of his costs. T returned KD's subsequent cheque as unacceptable because it provided only for fixed costs. At the hearing, it was found that KD's general conduct had been unreasonable and judgement was awarded for T in the sum of £194.75 together with fixed costs. T appealed, contending that (1) the judge had erred in the exercise of his discretion in ordering the payment of fixed costs after making a finding of unreasonable conduct against KD; (2) pursuant to the Civil Procedure Rules 1998 Part 27 r.27.14 (2) (d), T was entitled to have his costs schedule assessed by the summary procedure, and (3) the judge had failed to have proper regard to the unreasonable conduct of KD and their insurers and their failure to settle the claim prior to issue of proceedings.

Held, allowing the appeal, that it was unreasonable for KD to have waited until after the issue of proceedings before negotiating, especially as they had been in possession of witness statements. The pre action protocol for personal injury claims stated that such matters should be negotiated when reasonably clear. It followed that costs should be assessed, but it was disproportionate for T to claim costs of more than £2,000 in respect of a claim limited to under £500. As there was no guidance available on proportionality, the judge assessed T's costs on the basis of the amount of work carried out by him at the fault of KD. As a significant amount of the initial work would have been required in any event, costs payable by KT were assessed at £950.

TAYLOR v. KD COACH HIRE LTD, June 23, 2000, Judge Marshall Evans, CC (Liverpool). [*Ex rel.* Michael W Halsall Solicitors, 2 The Parks, Newton le Willows].

448. Costs – small claims – unreasonable conduct – successive offers of settlement

F's vehicle was stationary at an entrance to a car park behind M's vehicle, when M's vehicle rolled back and hit F's vehicle. F commenced proceedings against M, who entered a defence disputing liability and the matter was referred to the small claims track. M's solicitors initially offered to pay 50 per cent of F's claim. Directions were issued from the court, one of these being to serve statements of evidence. M's solicitors then made a Part 36 offer to settle 50 per cent of F's claim. This offer was rejected by F and M's solicitors then offered to pay 75 per cent of the claim. F rejected this offer, whereupon M offered to settle the whole of the claim. F's solicitors claimed entitlement to unreasonable conduct costs on the basis that the succession of offers of settlement culminating in an offer to pay the whole claim amounted to drip feeding and M had also failed to comply with the court's direction leading F's solicitors to believe that M had no intention of pursuing the matter.

Held, making an order for costs in favour of the claimant, that M had acted unreasonably.

FOX v. MURRAY, District Judge Dodds, CC (Newcastle). [*Ex rel.* Irwin Mitchell Solicitors, 146 West Street, Sheffield].

449. **Costs – small claims – unsuccessful claim for full costs where no allocation to small claims track made**

[Civil Procedure Rules1998 (SI 1998 3132) Part 26.]

K brought proceedings against M for damages in the sum of £2,174 arising from a road traffic accident. M admitted liability and requested that the matter be referred to the small claims track. M offered £2,144 in settlement plus fixed costs. Neither K nor M filed an allocation questionnaire. K obtained summary judgment and an order that "the defendant must pay the claimant an amount which the court will decide, and costs". No further directions were given and the matter was never referred to the small claims track. K accepted the £2,144 that had been offered but indicated that they would be seeking full costs. M disputed that K was entitled to full costs, drawing K's attention to the Civil Procedure Rules 1998 Part 26 PD 26 para.12.8 and contending that the matter was a small claim from the outset and should have been referred to the small claims track. M argued that it was unreasonable to allow K to recover full costs merely because M had entered a defence admitting liability. If K was allowed to recover full costs that would appear to go against the spirit of Woolf and the principle of keeping costs to a minimum. K contended that (1) they should never have had to issue proceedings in the first place, M had admitted liability by letter; (2) they were entitled to Scale 1 costs as they had expressed the prayer to the particulars of claims to allow for this, and (3) there had been no allocation to the small claims track, and in view of (1) and (2), the judge should exercise his discretion to allow full costs.

Held, dismissing the application for Scale 1 costs, that in the particular circumstances fixed costs only were appropriate.

KAMANIA v. METROLINE, August 20,1999, District Judge Sachs, CC (York). [*Ex rel.* Berrymans Lace Mawer Solicitors, Castle Chambers, 43 Castle Street, Liverpool].

450. **Costs – statement of costs – failure to lodge in time**

[Civil Procedure Rules 1998 (SI 1998 3132) Part 44 r.44.7.]

W brought an action against D for damages for personal injuries sustained in a road traffic accident. The case was allocated to the fast track and W was awarded £4,991.83 in damages. He had failed to serve a costs schedule in accordance with the Civil Procedure Rules 1998 Part 44 r.44.7 PD 44. D asked for an explanation as to why a statement of costs had not been lodged at least 24 hours before the hearing. No explanation, save for possible administrative oversight, was offered. D contended that the explanation did not satisfy the test of exceptional circumstances and invited the judge to make no order as to costs, relying on the decision of *Crossley v. North Western Road Car Co Ltd* (Unreported, June 18, 1999), [1999] C.L.Y. 408.

Held, finding in D's favour, that W should be limited to the recovery of his counsel's brief fee plus VAT, the issue fee and the fee for preparing the medical report. All other costs would be disallowed. The rule in the practice direction was clear and W's solicitor had had ample opportunity to become acquainted with it.

WILLIAMS v. DOLIN, May 18, 2000, District Judge Wright, CC (Shoreditch). [*Ex rel.* Marcus Grant, Barrister, 1 Temple Gardens, Temple, London].

451. Costs – taxation – bill of costs omitting disputed amount of counsel's fee – no rule preventing taxation of second bill including agreed fee

A, a solicitor, had acted for O in litigation. Since O had objected to the amount of counsel's fees, A had not included that figure in the bill which he submitted, but in a covering letter he drew attention to why it was excluded. That bill proceeded to taxation. A negotiated a partial reduction in counsel's fees, which O accepted. A drew up a second bill, which included costs incurred since the first bill and counsel's reduced fee. O refused to pay the second bill, stating that she had already paid sufficient sums to A to cover counsel's fees. A brought proceedings for payment of the bill. The district judge held that O was liable to pay A's profit costs, however, since counsel's fees had not been included in the first bill O had lost her chance to ask for them to be taxed and therefore it would be unfair to allow A to pursue them. A's appeal was allowed, it being held that O had not lost her right to taxation. O appealed.

Held, dismissing the appeal, that A was right not to include counsel's fees in the first bill. He was not thereby precluded from claiming the fees in the second bill, *Cobbett v. Wood* [1908] 2 K.B. 420 applied. The second bill was adequate as it made clear why counsel's fees were now being included and that they had not been dealt with under the earlier taxation. O had therefore not been misled or deceived in any way. There was nothing in the course of action followed by A which deprived O of her right to taxation of the second bill, *Chamberlain v. Boodle & King* [1982] 1 W.L.R. 1443, [1982] C.L.Y. 3080, cited. O had chosen not to exercise that right.

AARON v. OKOYE [1998] 2 Costs L.R. 6, Hobhouse, L.J., CA.

452. Costs – taxation – contentious business agreement – costs to be calculated item by item and not globally

Following litigation, NRG had been ordered to pay BW's costs, which were in the region of £6.5 million. An issue arose as to whether the bill of costs was higher than the amount BW actually paid to its solicitors. NRG claimed that the taxing master applied a global approach and refused to look further behind the face of the bill. NRG applied for a review of the taxing master's decision.

Held, allowing the application and ordering that the bill be redrawn on an indemnity basis, that although there was no formal contentious business agreement between BW and its solicitors, there appeared to be some arrangement whereby it was charged at a lower rate than that set out on the taxed bill. It was important that taxation procedures should be consistent, and therefore even such informal arrangements had to be treated as analogous to contentious business agreements, *General of Berne Insurance Co Ltd v. Jardine Reinsurance Management Ltd* [1998] 1 W.L.R. 1231, [1998] C.L.Y. 469 followed. Therefore, an item by item approach to the taxation had to be adopted even though this might prove to be difficult and time consuming.

NEDERLANDSE REASSURANTIE GROEP HOLDING NV v. BACON & WOODROW (NO.4) [1998] 2 Costs L.R. 32, Tucker, J., QBD.

453. Costs – taxation – summary assessment in fast track cases – proportionality of costs

[Civil Procedure Rules 1998 (SI 1998 3132) Part 44.]

S brought an action for damages against W arising out of a road traffic accident in which both parties were injured. Liability was not admitted. The case was dealt with on the fast track. S was awarded £4,300 damages and W's counterclaim was dismissed. S's schedule of costs for summary assessment amounted to more than £8,500. On summary assessment, the sum of £4,500 was awarded, and S appealed, contending that (1) the judge had erred in applying the test of proportionality, having failed to have regard to material factors including those set out in the Civil Procedure Rules 1998 Part 44 r.44.5(1) (a) and r.44.5(3) and the circumstances of the action; (2) in reducing the amount of the costs award, the judge should have reviewed each item and excluded VAT from his consideration of proportionality since, in the instant case, S was unregistered and the fact that S's solicitors would have to account for VAT effectively reduced their profit costs by 17.5 per cent; (3) the judge had failed to give S's legal representative opportunity to justify items of costs which were to be disallowed, and (4) the costs incurred prior to the introduction of the 1998 Rules should have been assessed in accordance with the rules applicable at that time.

Held, dismissing the appeal, that (1) the case was a "run of the mill road traffic act claim" and S's claim for costs was wholly disproportionate in the light of the amount at issue and the lack of complexity of the case. The judge had not erred in his approach to the assessment and it was clear from his observations that he had had due regard to Part 44 of the Rules. It was important for parties to litigation to assess at the outset the likely value of the claim and its importance and complexity, and then seek to plan in advance the necessary work and time likely to be included; (2) with regard to VAT, a comparison of the amount of cost claimed with the value of the award should be made on a VAT exclusive basis; (3) it was correct in principle that costs incurred before the 1998 rules came into effect should have been dealt with in accordance with the transitional provisions, but S's costs schedule did not seek to distinguish between the two. The action itself was commenced after April 26, 1999, and although some work had been carried out prior to that it was difficult to determine how much. It was unreasonable on a summary assessment to expect a judge to make distinctions in respect of costs when the parties had not themselves sought to do so in their schedule, and (4) in relation to S's claim that his representatives had not been given an opportunity to make submissions, a summary assessment of costs was intended to be a brief procedure and if any party felt they were likely to be disadvantaged by it, they should request that the costs be dealt with by way of a detailed assessment, bearing in mind that they would have to show good reason to depart from the normal rule of summary assessment in fast track cases.

STEVENS v. WATTS, June 22, 2000, Judge Alton, CC (Birmingham). [*Ex rel.* Taylor Joynson Garrett Solicitors, Carmelite, 50 Victoria Embankment, Blackfriars London].

454. **Costs – test cases – claimant's failure to beat payment into court – appropriate order for costs**

A, a claimant, and B, the first defendant in a vibration white finger action, sought an order for costs. A and three other claimants had brought a consolidated claim against B and all had succeeded on the issue of liability. However, whilst three claimants were awarded damages in excess of the payments into court made by B, A was awarded £4,000 thus failing to beat B's payment in of £5,000. B contended that a conventional costs order should be made and that A should, therefore, pay B's costs for the period after the payment into court had been made. A argued that the court should exercise its discretion differently given that he had indicated his willingness to accept the payment in prior to trial and that B had expressed its opposition to his withdrawal from the action on the basis that he was central to the case as B wished to obtain a judgment that resolved as many issues as possible, thereby enabling it to settle many other pending proceedings out of court.

Held, granting an order for costs, that although there had been no formal agreement between the parties, they had effectively treated the four cases as test cases and that that had primarily been for the benefit of B which had wished to obtain an authoritative judgment. Whilst A's decision not to accept the payment into court had to be taken into account to some extent, it was appropriate that B should pay 90 per cent of the claimant's costs arising from the common issues from the date of the payment in and that A should pay 10 per cent of B's costs from the same date.

ALLEN v. BREL LTD C97/1097, Smith, J., QBD.

455. Costs – third parties – party joining claimant in possession – just and reasonable to order third party to pay costs

T, a US resident, had been joined as a third defendant in possession proceedings, but only in relation to costs. When the case failed, L, the successful claimant, sought to recover costs from T in relation to its action against the other defendants, B and E. Although T had given evidence on behalf of E, he knew little about the substantive issues involved in the case.

Held, allowing the application, that an order for costs against a non party would be made where it was just and reasonable to do so, *Symphony Group Plc v. Hodgson* [1994] Q.B. 179, [1993] C.L.Y. 3153 applied and this extended to making a costs order against a non party resident abroad where enforceability could be an issue, *National Justice Compania Naviera SA v. Prudential Assurance Co Ltd (The Ikarian Reefer) (No.2)* [2000] 1 W.L.R. 603, [1999] C.L.Y. 749 considered. Costs were awarded against T on the basis that he had provided help to E knowing that she would not be able to meet L's costs if unsuccessful, he had closely identified himself with E's case, even though he had no interest in the issues and had in fact been indifferent to them and E's defence had been rejected by the court.

LOCABAIL (UK) LTD v. BAYFIELD PROPERTIES LTD (NO.3); LOCABAIL (UK) LTD v. WALDORF INVESTMENT CORP (NO.3); EMMANUEL v. LOCABAIL (UK) LTD [2000] 2 Costs L.R. 169, Lawrence Collins Q.C., Ch D.

456. Costs – third party proceedings – discontinuance of main action – acceptable for merits of third party claim to be considered to determine costs award

Y brought an action for the recovery of fees alleged to be owed following his introduction to S, the seller of a property, of a purchaser, H. By consent, H was joined as a third party to the action on the basis that an alleged agreement existed whereby H would indemnify S for any liability to Y for an introduction fee. H denied any such agreement. Following the decision of Y to discontinue the action S claimed that Y was liable for the costs of the third party action. Having considered the pleadings and the evidence, a judge determined that the third party action had been more likely to fail than succeed and accordingly that Y should not be responsible for the third party costs. S appealed.

Held, dismissing the appeal, that in general the test was that a claimant on discontinuing an action would have to bear any third party costs unless the third party action had been misconceived or improperly brought. However, in the instant case, it had not been possible to determine from the pleadings the conduct of the third party action. It followed that the judge had exercised his discretion correctly, in the light of the minimal costs involved and the benefit of a summary determination, in taking the unusual step, with the parties' agreement, of examining the merits, in relation to the evidence, of the third party action. Accordingly, the judge had not erred in concluding that the evidence did not support S's claim of an agreement to indemnify.

YOUNG (T/A MICHAEL GRAHAM CHARTERED SURVEYORS) v. JR SMART (BUILDERS) LTD (COUNTERCLAIM) QBENI 99/0742/1, Mantell, L.J., CA.

457. Costs – third party proceedings – discretion in relation to proportionment of costs

[Law Reform (Married Women and Tortfeasors) Act 1935; Fatal Accidents Act 1976; Civil Liability (Contribution) Act 1978.]

J, who was suffering from an asbestos related disease, brought an action for negligence and breach of statutory duty against his former employer, BE. Shortly before his death J accepted £80,000 in full and final settlement for his claim. Subsequently J's executors brought an action under the Fatal Accidents Act 1976 for loss of dependency against CEG, the owner of power stations in which J had worked while in the employment of BE. CEG issued third party proceedings against BE seeking an indemnity and/or contribution under the Law Reform

(Married Women and Tortfeasors) Act 1935 or the Civil Liability (Contribution) Act 1978. At the hearing of preliminary issues a judge held CEG to be potentially liable to J, and that BE was potentially liable to pay a contribution under the 1935 Act. The judge went on to direct that the costs of the trial of the preliminary issues, in relation to the third party proceedings, should be costs in the cause. Both parties appealed unsuccessfully, the Court of Appeal dismissed the proceedings with costs. CEG's appeal to the House of Lords succeeded and the main action was dismissed ([2000] 1 A.C. 455, [1999] C.L.Y. 1386) on the ground that J's claim had been extinguished by his agreement with BE. Consequently, BE applied for an order dismissing the third party proceedings and, in addition, that CEG pay their costs. It was conceded in argument that the House of Lords having set aside the orders of both courts below, the question of costs in relation to the third party proceedings was a matter for the discretion of the court.

Held, allowing the application, that (1) the third party proceedings be dismissed and judgment entered for BE; (2) in relation to the costs of the third party proceedings at first instance and the Court of Appeal, BE, while succeeding in a number of its arguments against making a contribution order, had failed in substance and therefore it was proper that they be ordered to pay the costs, *Elgindata (No.2), Re* [1992] 1 W.L.R. 1207, [1993] C.L.Y. 3144 and *AEI Rediffusion Music Ltd v. Phonographic Performance Ltd (Costs)* [1999] 1 W.L.R. 1507, [1999] C.L.Y. 3456 considered; (3) the remaining costs incurred by CEG and BE in the third party proceedings should be paid by J; (4) the costs suffered by BE in the trial of preliminary issues relating to the main action, in which it had a substantial interest and had been entitled to take part, should be borne by J and paid directly to BE as opposed to the making of back to back orders. Having regard to the arguments put forward by BE in those proceedings, the germane portion for which J should be liable was two thirds, and (5) J should pay half the costs by BE in the proceedings before the House of Lords relating to the appeal of the main action.

JAMESON v. CENTRAL ELECTRICITY GENERATING BOARD (NO.2) [2000] C.P. Rep. 41, Brooke, L.J., CA.

458. Costs – trial of preliminary issues – claimant substantially successful – reservation until disposal of remaining issues

[Civil Procedure Rules 1998 (SI 1998 3132) Part 44 r.44.3(4)(b).]

In an action between A and S preliminary issues were tried in March 1999, with judgment being handed down on May 6, 1999 and A, having been substantially successful in that trial, applied for its costs. Relying on *W Lamb Ltd (t/a Premier Pump & Tank Co) v. J Jarvis & Sons Plc* 60 Con. L.R. 1, [1999] C.L.Y. 786 and *Surrey Heath BC v. Lovell Construction Ltd* 48 B.L.R. 108, [1990] C.L.Y. 411 cited, A contended that a trial of preliminary issues was an "event" for the purposes of the general principle that costs follow the event. Alternatively, that A had succeeded on a "part of its case" under the Civil Procedure Rules 1998 Part 44 r.44.3(4)(b) and the court was obliged to take that success into account. Further, that *Copthorne Hotel (Newcastle) Ltd v. Arup Associates (Costs)* 58 Con. L.R. 130 cited, in which costs of a trial of preliminary issues were reserved on the grounds that at the stage of a trial of preliminary issues the court could not be fully informed of offers or payments into court which have direct bearing on the issue of costs, was distinguishable on its facts and that different principles applied in the instant case due to the introduction of the CPR. A also argued that the costs of a trial of preliminary issues should be dealt with in the same way as the costs of an interlocutory hearing under the CPR.

Held, refusing the application, that the discretion to apply the CPR in the instant case from May 6, 1999 would be exercised. The court had regard to the parties' expectations under the pre CPR rules, and that applying the overriding objective of the CPR, and taking into account all of the relevant circumstances, the costs of the preliminary issues would be reserved until the conclusion of the trial or other disposal of the remaining issues in the action. Further, consideration of the award of costs of interlocutory hearings had little or no relevance to considerations of such awards in respect of a trial of preliminary issues, *Copthorne* considered and *Lamb* and *Surrey* distinguished.

AMEC PROCESS & ENERGY LTD v. STORK ENGINEERS & CONTRACTORS BV (COSTS ORDER) [2000] B.L.R. 70, Judge Hicks Q.C., QBD (T&CC).

459. Costs – unreasonable conduct

[Civil Procedure Rules 1998 (SI 1998 3132) r.27.14, r.44.14.]

In July 1998, Z's vehicle was damaged in a road traffic accident and repaired by her own insurers under her comprehensive policy. Z instructed solicitors to reclaim her policy excess. Judgment was obtained by default and BC's insurers immediately settled Z's excess in full but refused to pay Z's solicitors their disbursements and costs. Z's schedule of costs in respect of costs and disbursements up to and including the disposal hearing in the sum of £650 was served on BC's insurers in July 1999. BC's insurers then ceased to reply to Z's solicitors' correspondence. Z's solicitors attended the disposal hearing and asked for the full amount of costs as scheduled.

Held, allowing the claim, that Z's solicitors were only entitled to fixed costs on the small claims track under the Civil Procedure Rules 1998 r.27.14(2)(a). However, because BC's insurers had been slow in replying to correspondence and eventually had stopped corresponding with Z's solicitors, that amounted to unreasonable behaviour and misconduct under r.27.14(1) and therefore the costs claim in the sum of £650, as scheduled, was allowed in full. It was noted that had the instant case been on the fast track or multi track, then r.44.14 would have applied instead, but the result would have been the same.

ZEALANDER v. BLITZ CORP LTD, October 13, 1999, District Judge Russell, CC (Stockport). [*Ex rel.* Thorneycroft & Co Solicitors, Bridge Street Mills, Bridge Street, Macclesfield, Cheshire].

460. Costs – unreasonable conduct – claimant awarded costs of action and of appeal where defendant's conduct at fault in failing to act expeditiously

[Civil Procedure Rules 1998 (SI 1998 3132) Part 44 r.44.3, r.44.5.]

C's vehicle was damaged in a road traffic accident on July 18, 1999. The cost of repairs was estimated at £534. C instructed solicitors the following day and a letter of claim was sent on July 20, 1999, which was acknowledged by D's insurers on July 29, 1999. On August 3, 1999, C's solicitors notified D's insurers of the cost of repairs and requested an interim payment within seven days. D's insurers replied that their enquiries were continuing, and requested that C's solicitors "bear with us a little longer". On August 24, 1999, C's solicitors wrote to D's insurers advising them that, in addition to repair costs, a claim would be made for inconvenience and loss of use. The letter warned that, if no offer was made within 14 days, proceedings would be issued, including a claim for "full scale costs". D's insurers failed to acknowledge or respond to that letter. C issued proceedings on November 8, 1999, more than three months after acknowledgement of the letter of claim, at the same time again inviting D's insurers to make an offer of settlement. D filed an acknowledgement of service indicating an intention to defend, but subsequently failed to file a defence in time, whereby judgment was entered in default on December 13, 1999. By that stage, C had prepared witness statements for a contested trial. D subsequently admitted liability and offered £620 in settlement of the claim, which C accepted. At the disposal hearing the district judge, who did not allocate the claim to a track, awarded fixed costs of £140, criticising the fact that lawyers had become involved in a straightforward claim of low value. C appealed, arguing that the district judge had failed to have sufficient regard to the conduct of the parties in exercising his unfettered discretion as to costs under the Civil Procedure Rules 1998 Part 44 r.44.3 and Part 44 r.44.5.

Held, allowing the appeal, that having asked that C's solicitors bear with them a little longer, D's insurers had ample time, in accordance with the spirit of the protocols, to respond to the letter of August 24, 1999. They should have done so within a month at most. D's insurers failed to deal with the matter in a sensible way and with expedition. People who had road traffic accidents were entitled to expect that insurance companies would deal with matters much more quickly. Accordingly, the approach of the district judge was wrong. The matter should have been dealt with on the basis that, due to the conduct of D's insurers, costs were necessarily incurred by C to bring a sensible end to the litigation. There was no breach of the proportionality principal if costs were not limited as they would have been under the small claims procedure. C was awarded his costs of the action assessed at £1,486.50, and his costs of the appeal assessed at £1,712.10.

BAKEWELL v. BEVAN, March 17, 2000, Judge George, CC (Liverpool). [*Ex rel.* David Knifton, Barrister, 7 Harrington Street, Liverpool].

461. Costs – unreasonable conduct – failure to state case on liability prior to issue of proceedings

[Civil Procedure Rules 1998 (SI 1998 3132) Part 27 r.27.14 (ii) (d).]

N commenced an action against D which was compromised by agreement after issue of proceedings. N gave details of his case on liability at an early stage. D did not make its position on liability clear until it had filed a defence to N's claim and at the same time made a Part 36 offer to settle liability on a 50/50 basis. N applied for an order that D pay his costs pursuant to the Civil Procedure Rules 1998 Part 27 r.27.14 (ii) (d) on the grounds that D had behaved unreasonably. N contended that (1) it was unreasonable for D to have waited until proceedings had commenced before making an offer on liability and clarifying its case, and (2) if the Part 36 offer had been made earlier, N was likely to have accepted it but had not himself been in a position to make a Part 36 offer because D had not made clear its case. D contended that it had made a commercial decision to settle after proceedings were issued, and was perfectly entitled to do so.

Held, allowing the application, and awarding N's costs in full, that D's failure to state its case on liability prior to filing a defence amounted to unreasonable conduct for the purposes of the 1998 Rules. Once proceedings had been issued, D's commercial decision not to settle earlier had backfired and it was not entitled to argue that it had acted reasonably.

NORTHFIELD v. DSM (SOUTHERN) LTD, May 12, 2000, District Judge Fuller, CC (Basingstoke). [*Ex rel.* Stephen M Nichols & Co Solicitors, 27 Wote Street, Basingstoke, Hants.].

462. Costs – unreasonable conduct – late offers of settlement – assessment on proportionality grounds

V claimed damages arising out of a road traffic accident which occurred in June 1997. I denied liability for more than two years until an offer of settlement was made to V in December 1999, three days before the case was listed for hearing. The offer, in the sum of £1,037.73, was made on the basis of a "50/50" apportionment of liability and was rejected by V on the following day. I's solicitors explained that I would be unable to attend the hearing on December 17 due to work commitments, despite the court's notice of hearing having been received by both parties in August 1999. I's solicitors further explained that they had only recently managed to contact I after losing touch with him for several months due to I moving house without informing his solicitors of the new address. On December 16, the day before the listed hearing, I made an increased offer of settlement in the sum of £1,341.26 making no reference to the basis of apportionment of liability, together with an undertaking to pay V's fixed costs. V accepted the second offer, but made an application for unreasonable conduct costs against I in the sum of £1280.83 at the hearing, on the basis that (1) I had denied liability for a period in excess of two years but had no intention of attending court to defend V's claim, and (2) the two very late offers of settlement constituted "dripfeeding", *Woodgate v. Stafantos* (Unreported, February 18, 1997), [1997] C.L.Y. 591 and *Jancey v. Higgins* (Unreported, July 31, 1996), [1997] C.L.Y. 589 cited

Held, ordering costs against I, that I had a duty to maintain contact with his solicitors and insurers up until the conclusion of V's action, which he had failed to do. There had been no offer of settlement until it was realised that I would not be able to attend. I's conduct had indeed caused difficulties for his solicitors and insurers and there had been a degree of unreasonable conduct on his part. Considering the spirit of the civil justice reforms it was a matter of concern that such applications for unreasonable conduct costs may lead to cases not being settled where they should be, irrespective of the stage reached in the proceedings. The costs claimed by V were almost equal to the amount at which the claim had been settled. Thus, having regard to the requirement of proportionality, it was ordered that it was costs against I be assessed at £500, representing the costs which were incurred as a direct result of the late offers of settlement.

VARIA v. IHEZUE, December 17, 1999, District Judge Arnold, CC (Watford). [*Ex rel.* Ben Maltz, Barrister, 1 Essex Court, Temple, London].

463. Costs – unreasonable conduct – late settlement due to failure of solicitors to contact client

[Civil Procedure Rules 1998 (SI 1998 3132) Part 27 r.27.14(2)(d).]

C brought an action against J for damages arising from a road traffic accident. Eleven days before the small claims hearing, J's insurers agreed to settle C's claim in full. C applied for further costs under the Civil Procedure Rules 1998 Part 27 r.27.14(2)(d) on the grounds of J's unreasonable conduct. J had allowed judgment in default to be entered, which was set aside by an order date September 21, 1999. J's solicitors did not attempt to contact J until November 29, 1999, after which they tried several more times without success. Neither the defence filed nor the witness statement served contained a statement of truth. On behalf of C it was argued that (1) J had no interest in defending the proceedings, and (2) that the situation had been compounded by the unreasonable delay of J's solicitors in attempting to contact her.

Held, allowing the application and ordering J's solicitors to pay the further costs personally, that (1) although the judge was unable to say that J had acted unreasonably, it was incumbent on her solicitors immediately following the order of September 21, to ensure that a defence was filed and that the statement of truth was signed, therefore their delay had resulted in costs being incurred by C; (2) no casual link had to be shown between the unreasonable conduct and the further costs for the judge to assess costs on the basis of unreasonable conduct, but they should be proportionate, and (3) with that in mind, and the fact that the costs awarded must exclude those incurred in relation to the application to set aside, it was appropriate to assess the costs arising after September 21.

CRAVEN v. JERVIS, February 28, 2000, District Judge Silverman, CC (Edmonton). [*Ex rel.* Corries Solicitors, Rowntree Wharf, Navigation Road, York].

464. Costs – unreasonable conduct – late withdrawal from final hearing

[Civil Procedure Rules 1998 (SI 1998 3132) Part 27 r.27.14(2)(d).]

NP claimed damages from EE for credit hire, repairs and miscellaneous expenses in a small claims matter. Liability was not in dispute. The repairs and miscellaneous expenses were agreed in January 1999, one month after issue of proceedings. The sole issue was, therefore, credit hire. There were two hearings relating to credit hire and permission was given for a fully amended defence and an amended set of particular of claim. A final hearing was listed for November 3, 1999. On November 2, 1999 at 4 pm NP's solicitors called EE's solicitors and left a message concerning the possibility of settlement. At 4.30 pm NP withdrew the hire charges and attempted to settle the balance without attendance at court. NP sought the agreed damages, interest, and the issue fee, fixed costs and an engineer's fee. EE claimed that such a late withdrawal amounted to unreasonable conduct pursuant to the Civil Procedure Rules 1998 Part 27 r.27.14(2)(d) and that NP should pay for the abated brief fee and a moderate amount for solicitor's costs. NP refused and did not put forward any revised offer. Both parties attended with counsel. At the hearing, NP argued for interest on the repair charges, but had no evidence to show that they had been paid apart from an unmarked invoice. EE argued that NP must prove its case and that included the entitlement to interest, *Giles v. Thompson* [1994] 1 A.C. 142, [1993] C.L.Y. 1405 referred to. NP sought its fixed costs, as issue of the proceedings had been appropriate, and he further sought the costs of an engineer's report. The engineer had been instructed prior to any figure being put to EE, at which stage there was no issue in dispute between the parties. The engineer's report led to the original estimate being reduced by a nominal amount. No other garage had been approached. EE resisted the claim on the basis, inter alia, that there was no need for an expert as there was no issue in dispute. EE claimed the solicitor's costs of preparation and the full brief fee. NP resisted, relying on the desirability of encouraging settlement, and contending that the costs incurred could have been prevented by the solicitor preparing for the hearing himself without the assistance of counsel. The claim for hire was less than the brief fee of NP's counsel would have been had a full hearing been required. NP thought it uneconomic to proceed to a contested hearing on the issue of hire.

Held, that (1) there should be no award for interest as NP had not proved that it was entitled to interest save for £1.40 on the miscellaneous expenses; (2) the engineer's fee be disallowed as there was no issue in dispute between the parties at the time of instruction; (3) NP was entitled to the issue fee and fixed costs; (4) EE should be awarded costs pursuant to Part 27 r.27.14(2)(d) of the 1998 Rules assessed at three hours' solicitor's preparation and the full brief fee. The issues involved warranted the attendance of counsel. The issue of unreasonable conduct costs should be looked at on a case by case basis. Settlement was to be encouraged, but in the instant case it was clear from the outset, and at the very latest one month before the instant hearing, what the issues were. NP should have considered these issues before the day prior to the hearing, and should have worked out the economics of pursuing the claim at an earlier stage; certainly before briefing counsel. It was incumbent on the parties to consider all aspects of the litigation throughout the case in plenty of time. Failure to do so in the instant case amounted to unreasonable behaviour within the meaning of Part 27 r.27.14(2)(d).

NEWPOINT PLUMBING SERVICES v. EDMUNDSON ELECTRICAL LTD, November 3, 1999, District Judge Haselgrove, CC (Central London). [*Ex rel.* Paul McGrath, Barrister, 1 Temple Gardens, Temple, London].

465. Costs – unreasonable conduct – maintenance of defence an abuse

P claimed damages arising from a road traffic accident which occurred in January 1999, P's vehicle was parked and unattended when it was hit by KR's vehicle. Liability was disputed and proceedings were issued in March 1999. KR filed a defence disputing liability and quantum and the matter was referred to the small claims track. Seventeen days prior to the hearing, KR offered settlement of P's claim and fixed costs. P maintained that the defence which had been filed was an abuse and therefore represented unreasonable conduct. The hearing proceeded on the issue of costs.

Held, that the defence was an abuse as it purported to put liability in issue, when there was no issue as to liability. It followed that their conduct was unreasonable and the referral to arbitration had been improperly obtained. P's costs were assessed at the hearing.

PRATT v. KIER REGIONAL LTD, July 26, 1999, District Judge Trowmans, CC (Plymouth). [*Ex rel.* Irwin Mitchell Solicitors, Huttons Buildings, 146 West Street, Sheffield].

466. Costs – unreasonable conduct – misguided claims – unreasonable bringing of proceedings

[Civil Procedure Rules 1998 (SI 1998 3132) Part 3 r.3.4, Part 24 r.24.2.]

O, acting in person, brought vague and unparticularised claims against CC citing non existent legislation. CC applied to strike out the claims under the Civil Procedure Rules 1998 Part 3 r.3.4 and/or Part 24 r.24.2, and it emerged during the course of the hearing that the focus of O's grievance against CC was the disclosure of past criminal convictions at a child protection meeting, which were recorded and subsequently revealed to O's partner who had a right of access to those records. O's partner had not known about his previous convictions and he was upset that she had discovered them. CC contended that (1) O had no cause of action provided by any of the statutes referred to which did actually exist; (2) even if he had, he was unable to prove that he had suffered the requisite damage, and (3) none of the statutes revealed a remedy which would have been available to O in any event. CC applied for costs for unreasonable behaviour by O, arguing that O had caused a considerable amount of time wasting on the part of CC in the way that he had pleaded his claim, since he had referred to non existent statutes and in the existing statutes to which he referred, he had failed to identify the sections upon which he relied. It was clear that O had made no attempt to verify the statutory authorities on which he purported to base his claims. CC cited *Bloomfield v. Roberts* (Unreported, March 6, 1989), [1989] C.L.Y. 2948 and *Smith v. Sunseeker Leisure* (Unreported, April 13, 1993), [1993] C.L.Y. 3167 in support.

Held, giving judgment for CC, that O had brought the proceedings unreasonably. The test to be applied was an objective one. O had advanced a claim which was misguided and unparticularised. It was apparent that O had failed to pursue the proper channels in relation to his grievance against CC and had been wrong to issue proceedings without first seeking an alternative solution. There was no letter before action from O which might have given CC the opportunity to investigate O's claim objectively, and O had failed to substantiate his claim. The purpose of litigation was not to air grievances at the expense of other parties and the court's time had been wasted.

O v. CHIEF CONSTABLE OF WILTSHIRE, August 6, 1999, Judge Meston Q.C., CC (Swindon). [*Ex rel.* Lorna Skinner, Barrister, 1 Brick Court, Temple, London].

467. Costs – unreasonable conduct – scope of conduct relevant to application under CPR Part 44 r.44.14(2)

[Civil Procedure Rules 1998 (SI 1998 3132) Part 44 r.44.14(2).]

K, the claimant in proceedings against SC, sought to appeal against an order that she pay costs incurred by SC. K contended that SC's representatives had been guilty of improper and unreasonable conduct, namely misleading the court and suppressing material evidence. K maintained that in consequence the court was entitled to act under the Civil Procedure Rules 1998 Part 44 r.44.14(2) to set the order aside. K submitted that in assessing the type of misconduct which would permit the court to make an order under Part 44 r.44.14(2), it was imperative to take into consideration the totality of a party's conduct in the litigation and not simply in connection with the application under consideration.

Held, dismissing the application, that whilst the court was permitted to take into account conduct for the purposes of Part 44 r.44, such conduct was confined to that which had given rise to, or was relevant to, the application under consideration. The rule did not entitle K to raise a whole range of issues some of which concerned the very subject matter of K's claim. It was also disproportionate in relation to the sums involved in the claim to allow a lengthy examination of all the issues.

KAMINSKI v. SOMERVILLE COLLEGE 1997-K-466, Scott Baker, J., QBD.

468. Costs – wasted cost orders – unreasonable behaviour – pursuing claim with no prospect of success

[Civil Procedure Rules 1998 (SI 1998 3132) Part 27 r.27.14(2)(d).]

S brought an action against J for damages arising out of a road traffic accident. Before trial, J invited S to withdraw his claim on the basis that police evidence disclosed that S had admitted to police at the scene of the accident that he had been at fault, as he was unable to stop in time to avoid a collision. S did not attend at trial and his claim was dismissed. J sought his costs of the wasted hearing under the

Civil Procedure Rules 1998 Part 27 r.27.14(2)(d) on the basis that S had acted unreasonably in view of the police evidence and also in not attending the hearing.

Held, granting the application and awarding costs to J, that an order for costs under Part 27 r.27.14(2)(d) was appropriate as S had behaved unreasonably in (1) not attending court, and (2) persisting with a claim which he must, in all the circumstances, have known did not have a great prospect of success. The costs awarded were those of the hearing, including counsel's brief fee and an amount summarily assessed for work undertaken by J's solicitors.

SPEARING v. JACKSON, November 3, 1999, District Judge Murphy, CC (Winchester). [*Ex rel.* Amanda Gillett, Pupil Barrister, College Chambers, 19 Carlton Crescent, Southampton].

469. **Costs – wasted costs orders – breach of contract – expulsion from RICS – no statutory requirement to assess merits or limitation.**

[Courts and Legal Services Act 1990 s.4.]

F, a chartered surveyor, brought proceedings for breach of contract after he was expelled by RICS for unbefitting conduct. The claim was dismissed and on RICS's application for a wasted costs order the judge refused to order F's counsel and solicitors to show cause. RICS appealed against that decision submitting that F's counsel and solicitors had acted both negligently and with unprofessional judgment by (1) overstating the expected percentage of success to at least 60 per cent to induce the Legal Aid Board to grant a certificate; (2) not informing F that certain aspects of the case were weak and bound to fail, and (3) failing to place an appropriate limitation upon the Legal Aid certificate in light of the evidence presented.

Held, dismissing the appeal, that RICS had not produced a strong prima facie case of negligence sufficient to warrant a wasted costs order against F's counsel or instructing solicitors, *Barrister (Wasted Costs Order) (No.1 of 1991), Re* [1993] Q.B. 293, [1992] C.L.Y. 748 and *Ridehalgh v. Horsefield* [1994] Ch. 205, [1994] C.L.Y. 3623 followed. There was no statutory requirement under the Courts and Legal Services Act 1990 s.4 to limit the points that could be taken and the Code of Conduct of the Bar of England and Wales para. 3 should be used with care. The court was reluctant to interfere with the judge's decision at first instance on the grounds that (1) he was in the best position to decide whether RICS's case had been made out, *Wall v. Lefever* [1998] 1 F.C.R. 605, [1997] C.L.Y. 603 applied; (2) neither counsel or solicitors should be deterred from acting in their clients' interests by fearing subsequent personal liability to their clients' opponents, and (3) clients should not be financially prejudiced by unjustifiable conduct by their or their opponents' counsel or solicitors, *Ridehalgh v. Horsefield* approved.

FRYER v. ROYAL INSTITUTION OF CHARTERED SURVEYORS; *sub nom.* ROYAL INSTITUTION OF CHARTERED SURVEYORS v. WISEMAN MARSHALL [2000] Lloyd's Rep. P.N. 534, Clarke, L.J., CA.

470. **Costs – wasted costs orders – disproportionality**

[Civil Procedure Rules 1998 (SI 1998 3132) Part 48.]

A, a solicitor, was charged with conspiracy to defraud, following an investigation into the financial arrangements made after the dissolution of his partnership, but acquitted when the prosecution presented no evidence at trial. A commenced proceedings against the Chief Constable for false imprisonment and malicious prosecution but ultimately unilaterally vacated the trial date. The Chief Constable sought a wasted costs order against IM, A's solicitors, and T, his barrister, together with costs amounting to almost £169,000 on the basis that it had been obvious to a competent legal professional that A's claim had no prospect of success and IM and T had been negligent or had acted unreasonably in advising A to bring and continue his action.

Held, refusing the application, that a stage two hearing in the application was likely to occupy three days and the total costs involved in those proceedings would be in the region of £130,000. Therefore, the costs of the application were disproportionate to the sums claimed, *Manzanilla Ltd v. Corton Property and Investments Ltd (No.2)* [1997] 3 F.C.R. 389, [1997] C.L.Y. 608 followed. The Chief Constable had failed to establish that the wasted costs proceedings were justified notwithstanding the likely costs involved as required by the Civil Procedure Rules 1998 Part 48 PD 48 para.2.6(a)(ii). Without waiver of legal professional privilege the advice given to A by IM and T could not be known but there was no evidence to suggest that there had been any improper purpose in pursuing the proceedings against the Chief Constable. The failure of the prosecution to disclose two witness statements until a very late stage in the criminal proceedings had resulted in an arguable case for A that the police did not have an honest belief in the charges brought against A, *Glinski v. McIver* [1962] A.C. 726, [1962] C.L.Y. 1887 and *Ridehalgh v. Horsefield* [1994] Ch. 205, [1994] C.L.Y. 3623 applied. Although the Chief Constable had not been obliged to seek summary judgment of A's claim or to apply to strike out the action, the fact that he had not done so also weighed in A's favour.

CHIEF CONSTABLE OF NORTH YORKSHIRE v. AUDSLEY [2000] Lloyd's Rep. P.N. 675, Keene, J., QBD.

471. Costs – wasted costs orders – failure of solicitors to investigate evidence

T was involved in three road traffic accidents, the third involving K. Over a period of eight months K's solicitors sought disclosure from T's solicitors of the medical reports in respect of the first and second accidents and the basis upon which those actions had been settled. Disclosure of such medical reports was given two weeks before the hearing of the third accident claim, leaving insufficient time for K's insurers to make an effective payment in. T served no further evidence. As judgment had been entered in default there was no order requiring T to serve witness evidence. At the hearing of the third accident claim T led evidence that the first accident had been a rear end collision at between 50 mph and 60 mph. The second accident had been a head on collision at around 45 mph and in the third accident K's car had rolled out of a parking bay into T's car at a speed where T's car had not even moved. The personal injury claim in the third accident claim was dismissed on the basis that if T's car had not move T could not have sustained a whiplash injury. A further car repair claim of £350 was also dismissed as T's evidence at the hearing was that he had sold the car with minor damage which had not affected its sale price.

Held, making a wasted costs order, that T's solicitors had acted negligently insofar as they had (1) conducted three actions on behalf of T, a man with very limited command of English, without attending him in person once. It was clear from seeing T give evidence that it was unlikely T understood much of what was going on. Had T's solicitors seen T it was likely that the evidential problems with the third claim would have been very much apparent at the outset, and (2) failed to investigate the evidence and obtain a statement from T, which again ought to have put T's solicitors on notice of the evidential problems, *Ridehalgh v. Horsefield* [1994] Ch. 205, [1994] C.L.Y. 3623 applied. T's solicitors had acted unreasonably insofar as they had delayed without any justifiable reason handing over relevant documents to K's solicitors which were material to causation and quantum. Had these documents been disclosed this would probably have led to the third claim being resolved well short of trial. T's solicitors' conduct in this regard had also unreasonably prejudiced K's conduct of his defence and resulted in unnecessary costs being incurred. T's solicitors were ordered to pay personally K's full costs of the action and the application to show cause.

TADJEROUNI v. KADERIA, May 31, 2000, District Judge Madge, CC (West London). [*Ex rel.* Moore & Blatch Solicitors, 64 London Road, Southampton].

472. Costs – wasted costs orders – negligent behaviour of solicitor's clerk

During the course of a jury trial, a defendant decided to dispense with the services of his counsel. The solicitor's clerk, in seeking his written instructions, did so in a corridor through which he knew that the jury would progress on their way back to the court following the lunch break. The jury passed by within hearing distance and, as a result, had to be discharged. An order for wasted costs was made against the solicitors who appealed against that order. There was evidence that there had been no conference rooms available on the floor on which the trial was being held, and that the clerk had not gone to a different floor because the judge was soon to sit and might be displeased to find that the solicitor and defendant were absent.

Held, dismissing the appeal, that the clerk had behaved in a negligent fashion, given that he was experienced and had knowledge of both the court's geography and the likelihood that the jury would come along the corridor at the time he was taking instructions.

R. v. QADI [2000] P.N.L.R. 137, Rose, L.J., CA (Crim Div).

473. Counterclaims – limitations – compliance with CPR overriding objective

[Limitation Act 1980; Civil Procedure Rules 1998 (SI 1998 3132) Part 1 r.1.]

LCC sought possession on the basis of rent arrears by a summons dated May 30, 1996. J defended the action and counterclaimed for damages for disrepair from 1985. A reply and defence to the counterclaim was served on March 26, 1998, but a defence under the Limitation Act 1980 was not pleaded. The trial commenced on March 26, 1998. On the morning of the trial, LCC applied to amend the reply and defence to plead a limitation defence. The application was refused. On the second day of the trial, a further application was made which was again refused. The trial concluded and damages of £1,500 per annum was awarded for disrepair which "did not fall in the most serious category". Damages were also awarded for breaches starting from 1985 totalling £21,000. LCC appealed against the decision not to allow the amendment to plead limitation.

Held, dismissing the appeal, that the issues which fell to be considered were the strain of litigation on J; (2) the anxieties of facing new issues; (3) the raising of false hopes, and (4) the legitimate expectation that the trial would determine one way or the other, *Ketteman v. Hansel Properties Ltd* [1987] A.C. 189, [1987] C.L.Y. 2330 applied. The court also considered the Civil Procedure Rules 1998 and the overriding objective within Part 1 r.1.1 (1); the duty of the court to ensure cases were dealt with expeditiously and fairly within Part 1 r.1.1 (2) (d) and the need to identify issues at an early stage in proceedings within Part 1 r.1.4 (2) (b).

LEEDS CITY COUNCIL v. JAMES, February 20, 2000, Judge Taylor, CC (Leeds). [*Ex rel.* Adam Fullwood, Barrister, 5 Cooper Street, Manchester].

474. County courts – fees

COUNTY COURT FEES (AMENDMENT NO.2) ORDER 2000, SI 2000 939 (L.8); made under the County Courts Act 1984 s.128; and the Finance Act 1990 s.128. In force: Art.3, Art.4, Art.7 (a), Art.8, Art.9: May 2, 2000; Remainder: April 25, 2000; £1.50.

This Order amends the County Court Fees Order 1999 (SI 1999 689) so that fee 2.1 for money claims not exceeding £1,000 is no longer payable; fees 2.1 and 2.2 are no longer payable when a Group Litigation Order is made; fee 2.3 is restructured to take account of the new rules on appeals contained in the Civil Procedure (Amendment) Rules 2000 (SI 2000 221); fee 3.2 is increased from £120 to £150; fee 6 is reduced so that the fee is £1 for the first page of the first document and 20p per page for other pages; and a new fee for a request for cancellation for entry in the Register of County Court Judgments is introduced. The fees for commencing proceedings to recover a sum of money are increased.

475. County courts – fees – small claims appeals

COUNTY COURT FEES (AMENDMENT NO.4) ORDER 2000, SI 2000 2310 (L.20); made under the County Courts Act 1984 s.128; and the Finance Act 1990 s.128. In force: October 2, 2000; £1.00.

This Order amends the County Court Fees Order 1999 (SI 1999 689) by restructuring the fees payable in small claims appeals to take account of changes to the procedure for small claims appeals made by the Civil Procedure (Amendment No.4) Rules 2000 (SI 2000 2092 (L.16)).

476. **County courts – time limits – application for extension – practice at individual court – failure to serve medical report or special damages schedule within 90 day period**

B, a bus driver employed by SEKRC, claimed damages from his employer for personal injury in an accident on August 11, 1993, issuing proceedings on August 8, 1996. The particulars of claim were in the form of a general endorsement, and neither a medical report nor a schedule of special damages were served. Following a practice at the county court, B's solicitors completed a form N24 order for a 90 day extension for the service of full particulars, report and schedule. Although ostensibly an order dated August 7, 1996, the pro forma document was provided across the counter and completed without the involvement of the district judge. The documents were served outside the 90 day period but within the four month period of validity of the summons issued. SEKRC applied successfully to have the order extending time set aside, but the judge retrospectively extended time on the basis that B's solicitors had been lulled into a false sense of security by the court practice. SEKRC appealed.

Held, allowing the appeal, that there was no explanation or good reason for the delay in service. The bizarre system operated by the court did not provide such an explanation and should never have been permitted. No extension was warranted in the instant case, apart from that necessary to obtain funding from B's trade union. Further, the existence of the practice should not have been exploited by solicitors as a means of evading their professional responsibilities. Even though there was no prejudice to SEKRC, B's legal position was so lacking in validity that the claim ought to be dismissed.

BOURLET v. STAGECOACH EAST KENT ROAD CAR CO LTD [1999] P.I.Q.R. P43, Wilson, J., CA.

477. **Court of Appeal – judicial decision making – single Lord Justice not precluded from hearing substantive appeal after refusing paper application for permission to appeal**

M requested by way of a preliminary issue that a single Lord Justice who had refused M's paper application for permission to appeal should recuse himself from the substantive appeal. M contended that he would be denied a fair and impartial hearing if the same Lord Justice were to sit at the substantive appeal.

Held, refusing the request, that where the single Lord Justice was minded to refuse a paper application, a letter was to be sent, as provided for by the *Practice Direction (CA: Consolidation: Notice of Consolidation)* [1999] 1 W.L.R. 1027, [1999] C.L.Y. 507, stating that the same Lord Justice would conduct the oral hearing, either sitting alone or with another Lord Justice. Giving a preliminary view did not mean that the single Lord Justice would not conduct himself impartially and was not ground for refusal. All judges, in keeping with their oath, would listen to oral argument mindful that their first impression could have been wrong.

MAHOMED v. MORRIS (NO.1) *The Times*, March 1, 2000, Peter Gibson, L.J., CA.

478. **Court of session – temporary judge – right to fair hearing**

[European Convention on Human Rights 1950 Art.6(1).]

P's action of damages against R went to proof before a temporary judge, T. During avizandum the decision in *Starrs v. Ruxton* 2000 J.C. 208, [1999] C.L.Y. 5884 was issued. The case was put out for a hearing by order and C sought to raise as a devolution issue that a temporary judge was not an independent and impartial tribunal. T reported the case to the Inner House (2000 G.W.D. 1-4) for adjudication on that issue. P argued that (1) as a temporary judge T lacked security of tenure and therefore could not be regarded as independent and impartial under the European Convention on Human Rights 1950 Art.6(1), and (2) T's continuation in practice at the bar might present conflicts of interest. R argued, inter alia, that P had waived his right to object by failing to do so before the start of the proof.

Held, remitting the case to T to issue his decision, that (1) the appointment and use of temporary judges to hear cases, where the Crown itself was not involved in the claim, did not breach a party's Convention rights; (2) the approach to be taken was set out in a number of European cases, which had determined that impartiality and independence should be assessed by applying a subjective and an objective test, and this approach was favoured to that taken by the Canadian courts; (3) a time limited appointment in itself did not breach the Convention and security during the appointment was a vital factor. Temporary judges did have security of tenure and enjoyed the same status and immunities as a permanent judge and the absence of a guarantee of reappointment did not affect a temporary judge's independence; (4) the Lord President decided whether or not to use a temporary judge and had laid down restrictions on the use of temporary judges in potentially sensitive cases, such as judicial review; (5) though the temporary judge remained in practice, given the institutional safeguards of the judicial oath and declinature, in particular where a conflict of interest arose, this factor did not breach Art.6, especially in a system where all judges had at one time practised, and (6) the appropriate time to object to the temporary judge was before the proof started. The possible difficulty with temporary appointments had been well known in the profession by the time the proof diet was allocated and P's failure to protest about the allocation of the temporary judge at that stage meant that he had waived his right to object. Further, the case represented a private dispute which did not involve the Government or Scottish Executive, or raise matters of public interest.

CLANCY v. CAIRD (NO.1) 2000 S.C. 441, Lord Sutherland, Lord Coulsfield, Lord Penrose, Ex Div.

479. Default judgments – misunderstanding in correspondence resulted in entry of default judgment

CIL, a company, brought a claim for damages against B, the former chairman and chief executive of DTL, a company it had purchased, alleging that fraudulent or alternatively negligent oral representations had been made concerning the company's assets. Subsequent to service of the statement of case an extension of time was agreed for the service of a defence. B's solicitors then sought a further extension by agreement. The solicitors representing CIL suggested an Unless order expiring on a given date. In reply, B's solicitors stated that they would agree to a "final order" in the terms suggested. On the basis that B's solicitor had not accepted their proposal for an Unless order, CIL's representatives entered judgment in default upon expiry of the initial extension. B applied to set aside the judgment contending that (1) the time for service of the defence had not expired, and (2) they had a real prospect of success in defending the claim.

Held, allowing the application, that in the context of the correspondence between the solicitors representing both parties, a default judgment had been inappropriate. Given their exchanges, CIL's solicitors had been wrong in making a distinction between an Unless order and a final order and ought at the very least to have sought clarification from B before seeking to enter judgment. Furthermore, the decision to maintain the validity of the judgment after the receipt of a fully pleaded defence, as had been indicated in correspondence, had been misguided and amounted to good reason to set the judgment aside.

CONCORDE INVESTMENTS LTD v. BORCH [2000] C.P. Rep. 34, Langley, J., QBD (Comm Ct).

480. Disclosure – ancillary relief proceedings – evidence of tax evasion – court's discretion

In the course of proceedings for ancillary relief in two cases heard concurrently it became apparent that B and C had attempted to hide the true extent of assets and furthermore had evaded tax, or had not disclosed income, to the Revenue. After full financial disclosure had eventually been made, the judge made a consent order but indicated that he was minded to disclose papers in the case to the DPP, Law Society and the Revenue. In the event, B and C made full disclosure to the Revenue, but the judge considered that it was nevertheless appropriate to proceed to deliver judgment on the grounds that the issues raised as to the circumstances in which the court itself should initiate disclosure were of public and general importance.

Held, that (1) in the absence of any statutory rule prohibiting or restricting disclosure, there was no absolute duty of confidence and a court had a discretion to authorise or order disclosure of confidential material where to do so was in the public interest; (2) in civil proceedings, where there is an implied undertaking that material disclosed by the parties will be used only for the purposes of the proceedings, the court can release or modify that undertaking if to do so would be in the public interest; (3) there is a strong public interest that all tax, and revenue penalties due, should be paid and that evaders of tax should be convicted and sentenced. Taxpayers, in the interest of the public, have a duty to inform the Revenue as to their affairs; (4) it was doubtful that the reporting of illegal or unlawful conduct disclosed in ancillary relief material to the proper authorities where there was strong public interest in doing so would discourage full and frank disclosure in a significant number of cases. In the absence of a compelling public interest to the contrary, a court should not close its eyes to illegality or nonpayment of tax; (5) ancillary relief proceedings are not held in private in order to enable the parties to keep illegal or unlawful conduct confidential. Before a court could decide not to report illegal or unlawful conduct, it must identify a compelling public interest against such disclosure, and (6) although an innocent party in ancillary relief proceedings might suffer as a result of disclosure to the authorities in terms of delays and difficulties in obtaining and enforcing an award, that party's private interest (a) to avoid delays, and (b) to benefit from the other party's illegal or unlawful conduct did not found a public interest against disclosure.

A v. A (ANCILLARY RELIEF); B v. B (ANCILLARY RELIEF) [2000] 1 F.L.R. 701, Charles, J., Fam Div.

481. Disclosure and inspection – striking out – unless orders

[Civil Procedure Rules 1998 (SI 1998 3132) Part 1 r.1.1, Part 3 r.3.9.]

C appealed against the dismissal of its application for an extension of time to comply with an unless order and the consequent striking out of its defence in proceedings commenced by K, a former employee, for personal injuries. Following service of C's list of documents, a request had been made by K's representatives for a full set of the equipment and accompanying documentation that K had been issued with in order to fulfil her duties as a sales adviser. Following partial compliance, an unless order was made and C subsequently purported to comply. However, K's representatives maintained that certain items were still missing. C sought an extension of time for compliance on the basis that many of the items requested had to be obtained from one of its client companies. Following the striking out of the defence, C contended that (1) the judge at first instance had failed to pay due regard to the overriding objective in the Civil Procedure Rules 1998 Part 1 r.1.1, and (2) the judge had omitted to consider the various factors detailed in Part 3 r.3.9.

Held, allowing the appeal, that the judge had failed to deal specifically with the various hurdles set out in Part 3 r.3.9 and had also failed to have regard to the overriding objective of the Rules, *Bansal v. Cheema* (Unreported, March 2, 2000), [2000] C.L.Y. 338 applied. Whilst much of the blame could be attributed to C's solicitors, who had failed to adequately explain precisely why they were unable to comply with the various requests made or make any attempt to secure revision of the order to substitute items that they were able to provide, the penalty of striking out the defence was wholly disproportionate, particularly in proceedings where no trial date had been fixed.

KEITH v. CPM FIELD MARKETING LTD [2001] C.P. Rep. 35, Brooke, L.J., CA.

482. Documents – service of judicial and extrajudicial documents – Council Regulation

Council Regulation 1348/2000 of May 29, 2000 on the service in the Member States of judicial and extrajudicial documents in civil or commercial matters. [2000] OJ L160/37.

483. Estoppel – company name – wrong defendant named – no estoppel on facts

Following the loss of a cargo of lead at sea, BO, the cargo owners, instituted proceedings against DM, the shipowners. The bill of lading issued by DM's Chinese agents stated that the shippers were the "China National Non Ferrous Import and Export Corporation, Guangdong Branch", CNIECGB. BO named the "China National Non Ferrous Import and Export Corporation", CNIEC, as third defendants. DM then issued third party proceedings against CNIEC. It subsequently became apparent that CNIEC was a separate legal entity to the Guangdong company. The Chinese agents were aware of this at the time that the bill of lading was issued. Following service of the third party notice on CNIEC, the action remained dormant until 1995 when DM entered judgment in default. By then, the limitation period in respect of CNIECGB had expired. Judgment in default was set aside by consent and DM conceded that CNIECGB and CNIEC were separate companies. The matter was listed for a preliminary hearing at which DM contended that CNIEC were estopped from maintaining that they were the shippers under the bill of lading. DM maintained that the reference to "Guangdong branch" in the bill of lading was misleading and implied that CNIEC was the other party to the contract, shipping via the Guangdong branch office. DM further contended that CNIEC had given CNIEGB authority to represent itself as a branch of CNIEC.

Held, dismissing the application, that in order to establish the existence of an estoppel DM was required to prove that CNIEC had represented itself as being the shipper and had failed to do so because (1) DM had initially maintained that the representation was made by the bill of lading but this was a document of its own creation. DM had amended its claim to allege that the representation was made to its Chinese agents, but it had adduced no evidence from the agents regarding creation of the bill of lading nor any evidence concerning its understanding of the situation at the time. In any event, the agents' knowledge of the identities of CNIEC and CNIEGB would have been attributed to DM, and (2) the expert evidence adduced in relation to the use of the name clearly established that CNIEC had no control over the English version of the name used by CNIECGB.

BOLIDEN ORE & METALS CO v. DAWN MARITIME CORP [2000] 1 Lloyd's Rep. 237, Timothy Walker, J., QBD (Comm Ct).

484. Family proceedings – requirement to prepare court bundle for all hearings

See FAMILY LAW: CH (A Child) (Family Proceedings: Court Bundles), *Re*. §2554

485. Foreign jurisdictions – service of process – claim valid despite procedural omission

[Civil Procedure Rules 1998 (SI 1998 3132) Part 20, Part 6 r.6.19(3).]

VL, the Part 20 defendant, applied for summary dismissal of a claim by B for a contribution under the Civil Procedure Rules 1998 Part 20 should they be liable to a third party. VL asserted that the Part 20 contribution form was invalid as it had failed to state the grounds on which B was entitled to serve it out of the jurisdiction under Part 6 r.6.19(3) of the 1998 Rules. Moreover, the court had failed to detect the error.

Held, refusing the application, that failure to state in a Part 20 contribution form the grounds on which service was sought outside the jurisdiction did not invalidate the claim. Although r.6.19(3) was mandatory and non compliance was a serious matter, that did not justify the conclusion that there had been no valid service at all. The failure was an irregularity, but VL had not been prejudiced by it in any way.

TRUSTOR AB v. BARCLAYS BANK PLC *The Times*, November 22, 2000, Rimer, J., Ch D.

486. Foreign jurisdictions – service of process – companies – alternative methods of service

[Companies Act 1985 s.694A; Civil Procedure Rules 1998 (SI 1998 3132) Part 6 r.6.5(6).]

A company incorporated in Indonesia, PT, applied to set aside service of a claim form issued by SA and served upon PT at its registered office in London. PT contended that (1) pursuant to the Companies Act 1985 s.694A service upon its London branch was ineffective since the substance of the claim did not relate in any way to the business carried on at the branch and this was the only permissible method of service. PT further maintained that the Civil Procedure Rules 1998 Part 6 r.6.5(6) which permitted service at any place of the company's business within the jurisdiction were in consequence ultra vires, and (2) in any event PT was not "any other company" for the purposes of r.6.5(6) but rather a company incorporated in England since it had submitted relevant documentation for registration with Companies House and would therefore be required to be served at either its principal office or alternatively at a location within the jurisdiction which had some real connection with the claim pursuant to r.6.5(6).

Held, dismissing the application, that (1) s.694A was not mandatory and accordingly the alternative methods of service detailed in the Civil Procedure Rules Part 6 were available to the claimant, and (2) an overseas company which complied with the requirements of the Registrar of Companies to submit particulars for the purposes of registration was not a company registered in England since its essence was overseas, *Saab v. Saudi American Bank* [1999] 1 W.L.R. 1861, [1999] C.L.Y. 523 applied

SEA ASSETS LTD v. PT GARUDA INDONESIA [2000] 4 All E.R. 371, Longmore, J., QBD (Comm Ct).

487. Foreign jurisdictions – setting aside – registration of judgment of High Court of Pakistan

[Foreign Judgments (Reciprocal Enforcement) Act 1933.]

A sought to set aside the registration of a judgment of the High Court of Pakistan pursuant to the Foreign Judgments (Reciprocal Enforcement) Act 1993. The judgment was for a sum equivalent to approximately £5.7 million, made against A in respect of personal guarantees allegedly given by him in connection with the refinancing of his business. A contended that (1) the judgment had been obtained by fraud, and that documents relied upon by the claimant bank were forgeries; (2) the judgment had been given in his absence and without his knowledge, and (3) the Pakistani court should no longer be recognised, as a result of political upheavals, particularly as since the take over of the Pakistani government in October 1999 there had been no effective means of appeal open to him.

Held, dismissing the application, that (1) the substance of the arrangement between A and the bank had, having regard to Islamic banking practice, been fulfilled and A had not been misled; (2) the public policy grounds under which an English court could refuse to register the judgment of a foreign court did not provide a second chance to a person who had chosen not to take an opportunity to defend himself before the national court. In the instant case, A had been aware of the proceedings in Pakistan but had chosen not to participate, and (3) where a party sought to set aside a foreign judgment on the basis that it should no longer be recognised as a result of political upheavals which had taken place subsequent to the statutory instrument permitting judgments of that state to be registered under the 1933 Act, the English court should not hear arguments without first allowing the Foreign Office to make representations. In the instant case however, A's expert evidence relating to the point would be refused on grounds of lateness and irrelevance.

HABIB BANK LTD v. AHMED *The Times*, November 2, 2000, Carnwath, J., QBD.

488. Freezing injunctions – failure to disclose alterations to prescribed form of order – counsel's duty to court and to clients is balanced

M's counsel applied without notice for a freezing order and a search and seize order, unintentionally using an unorthodox draft order, which had been disapproved of in *Den Norske Bank ASA v. Antonatos* [1999] Q.B. 271, [1998] C.L.Y. 325. Counsel had informed the judge that the order was in the prescribed form, pursuant to *Practice Direction (HC: Mareva Injunctions and Anton Piller Orders: Forms)* [1996] 1 W.L.R. 1552, [1996] C.L.Y. 869. S appealed against the dismissal of his application for the immediate discharge of the orders on the ground that M had failed to disclose the amendments to the prescribed form. S further contended that the judge had erred in distinguishing between the breach of a professional duty by M's lawyers and a non-disclosure of fact by a client.

Held, dismissing the appeal, that the advocate owed to the court both a personal duty and a collective duty as part of a party's legal team and those duties could overlap. The court would consider all the relevant circumstances, including the gravity of the breach, the explanations offered, the severity and duration of the prejudice caused to the defendant, and whether the breach could be remedied in deciding on the consequential relief. The overriding objective and the principle of proportionality were prerequisite considerations to avoid injustice, *Brink's-MAT Ltd v. Elcombe* [1988] 1 W.L.R. 1350, [1989] C.L.Y. 3030 considered. It was open to a judge to dismiss a freezing order where a professional breach of duty had occurred and not just where there had been material non-disclosure by the client, *Hytec Information Systems Ltd v. Coventry City Council* [1997] 1 W.L.R. 1666, [1997] C.L.Y. 768 considered, however, in the instant case, the judge would have reached the same conclusion and the exercise of his discretion was not flawed.

MEMORY CORP PLC v. SIDHU (NO.1); *sub nom.* SIDHU v. MEMORY CORP PLC (NO.1) [2000] 1 W.L.R. 1443, Robert Walker, L.J., CA.

489. Freezing injunctions – foreign jurisdictions – consistency of orders made in domestic courts

[Civil Jurisdiction and Judgments Act 1982 s.25.]

B applied for a variation to an asset freezing order made against him in the English High Court. B was also subject to a world wide freezing order made against him in the Brunei court, which permitted him limited spending in respect of living and legal expenses.

Held, granting the application, that, notwithstanding that the domestic courts would not ordinarily grant such a variation, courts should make orders which were consistent with those of the courts in which the primary litigation was taking place. In the instant case the English High Court was exercising jurisdiction over the foreign proceedings in Brunei under the provisions of the Civil Jurisdiction and Judgments Act 1982 s.25. The court in Brunei had approved the variation and, as an ancillary court, the English court should make an order which was consistent with that of the Brunei court.

BRUNEI DARUSSALAM v. BOLKIAH *The Times*, September 5, 2000, Jacob, J., Ch D.

490. Freezing injunctions – foreign jurisdictions – order ancillary to foreign proceedings – variation

[Civil Jurisdiction and Judgments Act 1982 s.25.]

R had been granted an asset-freezing order against FD under the Civil Jurisdiction and Judgments Act 1982 s.25, ancillary to foreign proceedings. A variation of the order was subsequently sought.

Held, varying the injunction, that the following general principles should be adhered to before granting such an order, namely (1) the court was required to exercise caution prior to granting any freezing order, and particularly when an order was sought under s.25 of the Act, *Credit Suisse Fides Trust SA v. Cuoghi* [1998] Q.B. 818, [1997] C.L.Y. 893 considered. The court should bear in mind that where the primary forum for the litigation was abroad it was less likely to be fully appraised of all the facts, *Refco Inc v. Eastern Trading Co* [1999] 1 Lloyd's Rep. 159, [1998] C.L.Y. 563 considered; (2) however, if the primary grounds for making an order under s.25 were satisfied then an order should be made unless it was inexpedient to do so, particularly bearing in mind the important factors of promoting international comity and the need to prevent international fraud; (3) where a foreign court refused to grant a freezing order, it might still be appropriate for the High Court to do so, and equally, where a global freezing order had been granted by a foreign court the High Court was not prevented from granting an overlapping freezing order in relation to domestic assets and/or against defendants resident within the jurisdiction. The court would, however, need to justify the granting of an overlapping order, bearing in mind the resulting increase in court time and costs, and the danger that it might lead to the risk of double jeopardy for defendants and increased forum opportunities for claimants. As a preventative measure, where an order overlapped a global or similar order from a foreign court with primary jurisdiction, some indication of which court had the primary role for enforcement would be desirable. Whilst there might be sufficient grounds for an overlapping order made under s.25 of the Act to be in different terms to the order made by the primary court, it would be preferable for that order to follow exactly the terms of that made in the foreign court, so as to avoid inconsistency and unnecessary complications.

RYAN v. FRICTION DYNAMICS LTD *The Times*, June 14, 2000, Neuberger, J., Ch D.

491. Freezing injunctions – fraud – customer suspected by bank of money laundering

[Criminal Justice Act 1988 s.93A, s.93D.]

B, a bank, was informed by the police that A, one of its customers, was suspected of being involved in financial fraud. B made a without notice application to the court seeking directions as to the steps which it should take concerning the substantial monies that were held in A's accounts. The judge made an order of his own motion freezing the monies held in A's accounts. The order directed that the information leading to its making should remain confidential and made no provision for its service on A. A applied to discharge the order arguing, inter alia, that it had been denied the opportunity to make representations. B contended that it had had no alternative but to seek assistance from the court. B maintained that if it had drawn the criminal investigation to A's attention, it would have risked being prosecuted under the Criminal Justice Act 1988 s.93D which made it an offence to "tip off" anyone involved in money laundering, and that if it had paid out monies from A's accounts, it might have been found liable not only as constructive trustee to the beneficiaries of the monies held in the accounts but also under s.93A of the Act which made it an offence to assist another to retain the benefit of criminal conduct.

Held, discharging the order, that (1) the order had been made on the basis of evidence which made it impossible to assess the strength of the respective parties' cases. B had merely informed the judge that it harboured suspicions towards A and no evidence had been adduced to show that A had been guilty of any wrongdoing. The evidence before the court did not, therefore, justify the grant of an injunction. B could not become a constructive trustee of the monies held in A's accounts merely because it held suspicions as to the source of those monies; (2) in depriving A of its property, failing to direct that the order should be served on A and denying A the opportunity to consider the material leading to its making, the court had exceeded its powers; (3) since B could have decided to freeze A's accounts of its own volition, the making of the order had served no real purpose, and (4) in this type of case, the relevant investigating authority should provide the court with such information as was necessary to enable the court to decide whether that information should be disclosed to the defendant, *C v. S (Money Laundering: Discovery of Documents) (Practice Note)* [1999] 1 W.L.R. 1551, [1998] C.L.Y. 69 applied. The Serious Fraud Office, which had been represented before the judge, had failed to disclose any such information to the court. It was recommended that (a) if a bank feared being prosecuted under s.93A for operating an account, it should first ask the police for permission to do so and then, in the event of permission being refused, seek assistance from the court, and (b) if a bank feared being prosecuted under s.93D for refusing to operate an account, it should ask the police to identify the information which they would be prepared to allow it to disclose to the court and the customer in proceedings brought by the customer. Should the police refuse to provide the bank with adequate information, the bank should again seek assistance from the court. Were it necessary in either case for the court to be approached, the police should be invited to appear before the court to justify their position.

BANK OF SCOTLAND v. A LTD [2000] Lloyd's Rep. Bank. 271, Laddie, J., Ch D.

492. Further information – Part 18 requests – delayed response in defective format – grounds for striking out

[Civil Procedure Rules 1998 (SI 1998 3132) Part 18.]

W claimed against F in respect of damages for personal injuries sustained in a road traffic accident and for damage to goods in the vehicle at the material time. Following the issue of proceedings, F made a request pursuant to the Civil Procedure Rules 1998 Part 18 concerning the true ownership of the damaged goods, it appearing that they belonged to W's company rather than to W personally. W failed to respond to the request, and F made reference to that failure in his listing questionnaire. The court subsequently ordered of its own motion that the request be answered and set a deadline for the response to be filed, in default of which the claim would be struck out. F sought to enforce the strike-out when it failed to receive the response ordered. W submitted that the response had been served, and provided F with a copy. F contended that the response was in any event defective, since it did not comply with the format stipulated by Part 18 r.1.6(2)(a) and PD 18.

Held, striking out W's claim, that although the request had not and was not obliged to follow the suggested format in Part 18 and PD 18 of the 1998 Rules, W should have created a new document to answer the request. Part 18 r.2.3(1)(a) PD 18 had to be looked at in the light of Part 18 r.1.6(2)(a) PD 18. The questions had been properly put in order to further the overriding objective and went to the heart of the issue. As W's failure to answer remained unexplained, and he had not sought relief from the request, the court must assume that it was a contumacious breach of the Rules. In the absence of a signature or a date, which were both mandatory requirements, the answers were defective, and those defects could not be remedied simply by W swearing to the truth of them on the day of the trial. The onus was on W's solicitors to ensure that nothing was wrong with the response. There was no reason to allow them relief from the strike out.

WHITTAKER v. FARLEY, March 2, 2000, District Judge Duerden, CC (Bury). [*Ex rel.* DLA Solicitors, 101 Barbirolli Square, Manchester].

493. Injunctions – anti suit injunction application – pending forum application in Californian court

EMI, an English registered company, entered into two sales agreements which provided that the parties to it submit to the non exclusive jurisdiction of the English courts. C, an English company, but with its principal place of business in California was a party to the agreements. Following allegations by C as to breach of warranty and misrepresentation, EMI applied for an anti suit injunction, restraining C from suing on their allegations anywhere other than in England. However, C issued proceedings in California for damages. The instant application for directions was adjourned pending the outcome of EMI's application for the Californian action to be struck out on the grounds that EMI had not been properly served, or alternatively on the basis of forum non conveniens (the forum application). The forum application was, however, also adjourned. EMI contended that (1) anti suit injunction applications should be determined as quickly as possible and should not necessarily be delayed because of an existing forum application; (2) there was no longer a timescale which was oppressive to C; (3) the forthcoming forum hearing would necessarily determine the application; (4) EMI had been right to make the forum application when it did rather than waiting for the injunction to be heard in England; (5) most of the costs in the injunction proceedings had already been incurred, and (6) the injunction application might have to be heard in any event, if the forum application failed. C argued that (1) a delay of five weeks in the forum application did not justify a complete change of course; (2) EMI were guilty of delay in making the present application, albeit that this could have been due to a misunderstanding of what was said by the Californian judge; (3) there was a risk of the two hearings overlapping, which would potentially stretch the resources of both parties; (4) delaying the injunction would be likely to save substantial effort, expense and court time; (5) if the injunction were heard after the failure of the forum application, the English court would be saved the necessity of considering many of the arguments, and (6) EMI were not obliged to bring the forum application when they did, although doing so might well have been regarded as good practice in California.

Held, giving judgment for C, that on balance it was just that C's submissions should prevail over those advanced by EMI. It was ordered that the matter be relisted at a later date to consider the finding of the Californian court. EMI were required to give an undertaking that, if the injunction were rendered unnecessary by the outcome of the forum application, EMI would pay C's costs in respect of the preparation of evidence for the anti-suit injunction application.

EMI GROUP PLC v. CUBIC (UK) LTD TNS, Neuberger, J., Ch D.

494. Injunctions – breach – unrecorded legal advice not mitigation

P, a provider of open learning courses, brought proceedings against R for infringement of copyright and obtained a number of orders preventing R, inter alia, from selling courses of the same type. Following a subsequent finding that R had been in continuous breach of a consent order, P applied for an inquiry into damages and the committal of R. R by way of mitigation, claimed that its actions had been taken on legal advice.

Held, giving judgment for P in part, that (1) mitigation for breach of a consent order could not be established from the fact that actions in breach of that order had been taken on legal advice where that advice had not been recorded and there was no genuine belief as to its accuracy, and (2) although R's committal or the imposition of a fine for the breach of the injunction was inappropriate, an inquiry into damages for the breach was applicable. Damages were available in circumstances where the alleged breach constituted both a breach of an undertaking to the court and a breach of contract with another party, *Midland Marts Ltd v. Hobday* [1989] 1 W.L.R. 1143, [1989] C.L.Y. 2927 considered.

PARKER (T/A NBC SERVICES) v. RASALINGHAM (T/A MICRO TEC) *The Times*, July 25, 2000, Lawrence Collins Q.C., Ch D.

495. Injunctions – interim injunctions – confidential information – request for relief where sole supporting evidence withdrawn

M, a company engaged in the manufacture and sale of mobile telephone technology, applied on notice for an interim injunction to restrain GS, an investment banking and securities firm, from acting on behalf of V in its planned take over of M, it was contended that GS had acquired confidential information about M following involvement with M on other take over bids, creating a risk that such information could be used by GS to the detriment of M. At an earlier application for an injunction without notice M gave evidence that GS had given assurances that it would not act in a hostile bid against M. That evidence was now withdrawn, the maker suggesting that he had been mistaken in his recollection.

Held, refusing the application and discharging the interim order, that M had failed to identify any confidential information acquired by GS requiring protection and, in any event, M had now brought this information into the public domain by failing to use confidential exhibits and request that the court sit in private. The placing of false information before the court concerning the alleged assurances was to be deplored.

MANNESMANN AG v. GOLDMAN SACHS INTERNATIONAL 1999 HC 04861, Lightman, J., Ch D.

496. Injunctions – qualification – refusal as court would find it difficult to determine whether injunction breached

A telephone service provider, BT, alleged that the employees of another provider, NT, had been misrepresenting the relationship between NT and BT in order to persuade BT's existing customers to switch their custom. Following correspondence between the parties, NT provided an unconditional undertaking whereby they would not, whether by their employees or their other representatives, hold themselves out as BT or part of BT. Further incidents came to the notice of BT who commenced proceedings against NT alleging passing off, trade mark infringement and breach of the undertaking. BT obtained an interim injunction and applied for a permanent order. Whilst not disputing that BT were entitled to a permanent injunction, NT submitted that should be subject to a proviso with respect to their regulatory procedures so as to protect them against the possibility of the activities of a "rogue salesman" placing them in breach of the injunction.

Held, granting the injunction, that it was inappropriate to add a qualification to the injunction as to do so would involve the court in making many value judgments as to whether or not a breach had occurred. The degree to which it would be possible to control the salesmen as relatively low level employees within the organisation would very much depend on the company's management and systems, *Showerings Ltd v. Entam Ltd* [1975] F.S.R. 45, [1975] C.L.Y. 3421 applied. The situation could be sharply contrasted with the situation prevailing in *Microsoft Corp v. Plato Technology Ltd* [1999] F.S.R. 834, where an injunction designed to prevent the defendant from selling counterfeit copies of Microsoft software had been qualified. In *Microsoft* the defendant had acted innocently and had had no reasonable means of discovering that he had been acting otherwise due to the high quality of the counterfeit goods.

BRITISH TELECOMMUNICATIONS PLC v. NEXTCALL TELECOM PLC [2000] C.P. Rep. 49, Jacob, J., Ch D.

497. Joinder – action for recovery of land – necessity of joining person in whom legal title to land vests as claimant to action

D brought an action for possession of land and subsequently had an order for costs granted in his favour. S appealed against the order, and, arguing in reliance upon on the Supreme Court Practice 1999 Vol 2, para. 17B-83, contended that the proceedings were improperly constituted when the possession order was made, as not all holders of the legal estate had been joined as claimants in the action.

Held, dismissing the appeal, that it was not a compulsory requirement in an action for recovery of land for all claimants who owned the legal title be joined in the action. The note in para.17B-83 had first appeared in the Supreme Court Practice 1926 without authority, and it followed from the introductory note to para.17B that it was only intended to give guidance on the question of joinder of parties. The note was procedural, not substantive in nature, and although indicative of good practice, was not compulsory in application.

DEARMAN v. SIMPLETEST LTD *The Times*, February 14, 2000, Henry, L.J., CA.

498. **Joinder – limitations – hearing of joinder application – proportionality**

[Limitation Act 1980 s.33; Civil Procedure Rules 1998 (SI 3132 1998) Part 19 r.19.4.]

HB appealed against the granting of B's application to strike out her claim against him for damages arising out of a road traffic accident and against the refusal to grant her application to join B's wife, W, as a second defendant. Proceedings had been issued against B days before the limitation period expired and the two applications arose after B had filed a defence stating that HB had sued the wrong person since W had been driving at the time. The judge, having made a finding without hearing oral evidence that W had been driving, held that in order to join W as a party he would have to disapply the primary limitation period under the Limitation Act 1980 s.33, which he was not prepared to do and HB's claim was struck out.

Held, allowing the appeal, that the judge was wrong to have determined the driver's identity summarily as this involved a serious live issue between the parties which ought properly to have been determined by hearing oral evidence from all involved. Only once that had been properly determined could the question of joining W as a party be considered, in particular whether it was appropriate to substitute her under the Civil Procedure Rules 1998 Part 19 r.19.4(2), or under Part 19 r.19.4(4), the latter involving the power to disapply the 1980 Act. Arrangements had to be made for the trial of the issues of identity, limitation and joinder to be heard together, *Howe v. David Brown Tractors (Retail) Ltd* [1991] 4 All E.R. 30, [1992] C.L.Y. 2829 considered.

BRIDGEMAN v. BROWN CCRTI 99/0977.B3, Hale, L.J., CA.

499. **Judgment and orders – summary judgments – stay of execution – claim and counterclaim not sufficiently connected for defence of equitable set-off or stay**

S and Y, inventors and holders of a patent for a product called "Fingersafe", entered into a distribution agreement with H. By clause 1, they granted a licence to H to market the product in return for a royalty fee. As a condition of the agreement, by clause 2, S would form a subsidiary company, licensed to market the product outside the UK, of which H would receive 50 per cent of the shares. H defaulted on the royalty fee and was sued by S. Further, owing to a dispute concerning the voting rights no licence was granted to the subsidiary company and H counterclaimed for specific performance. S obtained summary judgment and H appealed claiming a defence of equitable set-off and further appealed the refusal of a stay pending the trial of the counterclaim. S contended that in order to resist an application for summary judgment, the defence must have substance, *National Westminster Bank Plc v. Daniel* [1994] 1 All E.R. 156, [1994] C.L.Y. 3799 referred to. S relied on late evidence that H was no longer interested in the product to demonstrate there was no basis for H seeking specific performance of clause 2.

Held, dismissing the appeal, that although the obligations arising under the clauses arose under the same commercial agreement, there were obvious differences not least that they provided for the exploitation of the invention by very different mechanisms, and therefore there was not a sufficient close connection between the claim and counter-claim to apply the doctrine of equitable set-off, *Esso Petroleum Co Ltd v. Milton* [1997] 1 W.L.R. 938, [1997] C.L.Y. 799 applied. Although the court paid no regard to the late evidence submitted by S, justice did not require a stay of the summary judgment to allow H to pursue a defence with a number of doubtful features which had not been pursued with expedition.

SANKEY v. HELPING HANDS GROUP PLC [2000] C.P. Rep. 11, Robert Walker, L.J., CA.

500. **Judgments and orders – consent orders – agreement between parties' solicitors that Civil Procedure Rules 1998 did not apply – court's management function under overriding objective**

[Civil Procedure Rules 1998 (SI 1998 3132) Part 26 r.26.6(5), Part 51.]

On reviewing the instant case, the district judge listed the matter to consider whether the Civil Procedure Rules 1998 should apply and for further directions. The parties had reached a form of agreement for the Rules not to apply. A consent order was filed and only B's solicitors attended court.

Held, ordering that S's solicitors show cause why an order for costs should not be made against them, that practitioners had to understand that the Rules conferred a managerial role on the court and removed from parties the degree of control which hitherto existed. The court wished to cooperate with the parties and would give effect to what they had agreed, if it was consistent with the overriding objective. It followed that there were key stages in the course of litigation where the court must have the direct assistance of the parties, one such instance being the pretrial review, *Baron v. Lovell* [1999] C.P.L.R. 630, [1999] C.L.Y. 520 considered. Part 26 r.26.6(5) recognised allocation as another key point. Parties were obliged to send legal representation by a person with responsibility for the case to provide the information needed and with sufficient authority to deal with the issues arising. The authors of the Rules stated that the court needed the advocates' assistance at allocation. It ought to have been clear in the instant case that the hearing listed by the judge might become an allocation hearing. If the court did not follow the parties' wishes and applied the Rules, it was bound to consider the allocation issue. The court must not be blind to the realities of practice. It would be disproportionate and in flagrant breach of the overriding objective if a consent order could not be lodged for approval and the fee earner with overall control had to be at court. There were obvious issues of proportionality where the costs were likely to be close to the value of the claim. The court encouraged consent orders but they must be lodged in time for consideration before the hearing. The court would not necessarily approve them. If not, an appropriate representative needed to be there. It was ill founded in terms of the Civil Procedure Rules 1998 Part 51 PD 51 for parties to attempt to agree to oust the Rules. The general principle was that the Rules would apply. In a case where liability was not in dispute and the court record showed a significant dispute as to quantum, the Rules should still apply. The judge found that (1) S's solicitors were given a mistaken assurance by B's solicitors as to local practice for consent orders, and (2) the parties were caught out by this being a Part 51 transitional case, as a result costs were not awarded against S's solicitors.

BAGHDADI v. SUNDERLAND, August 27, 1999, District Judge Lethem, CC (Tunbridge Wells). [*Ex rel.* Charles Bagot, Barrister, Harwicke Building, Lincoln's Inn, London].

501. **Judgments and orders – default judgments – application to set aside – unacceptable delay by applicant**

[Road Traffic Act 1998 s.151.]

K brought an action against S for damages arising from a road traffic accident. S's insurer, NS, settled all elements of the claim apart from credit hire costs incurred by K in the sum of £2,446.59. K accordingly issued costs against S in respect of the credit hire proceedings and did not issue a defence, therefore judgment was entered in default. In November 1999 a second set of proceedings was issued against NS as insurer for its breach of the Road Traffic Act 1998 s.151, namely that it had failed and/or refused to satisfy the judgment against S. S made an offer of £1,400 toward hire charges, which was rejected, and thereafter NS filed a defence, requesting a stay pending an application to set aside judgment in the first set of proceedings. An application to set aside the first set of proceedings was also filed, S arguing that, although he admitted liability, he strenuously disputed K's claim for credit hire charges, and that the reason for not filing a defence or responding to the claim was due to a number of administrative factors, including a heavy backlog following a merger with another insurance company at the time.

Held, dismissing S's application to set judgment aside, that S had failed to establish any reasonable defence and that his arguments in respect of credit hire were purely speculative. There had been an unacceptable delay by S and there was no merit in his application. Costs were assessed by the court to be paid by S.

KHAN v. SIMPSON, January 18, 2000, District Judge Wilby, CC (Bury). [*Ex rel.* David A Tubby & Co, Solicitors, Alexander House, 2a Aughton Street, Ormskirk, Lancs].

502. Judgments and orders – default judgments – Brazilian defendant's successor sought to have judgment set aside – defence on merits – seven year delay not sufficient reason in absence of other special feature

C, one of 18 coffee companies that had entered into contracts with IBC, the Brazilian Coffee Institute, in 1986, initiated proceedings in England against IBC and entered default judgment on April 20, 1990. C attempted to enforce the judgment in Europe and then brought a number of actions in Brazil. During this period IBC was being dismantled and was finally dissolved in 1992. Its liabilities were assumed by the Brazilian Government. In April 1997 C sought to substitute the Brazilian Government for IBC as the defendant. In December 1997 the Government sought to set aside the default judgment entered in 1990. The judge allowed the application on the basis that the Government had a defence on the merits ([1999] 1 All E.R. (Comm) 120). C appealed on the basis that in 1990, IBC had taken the deliberate and tactical decision not to challenge the default judgment, and a delay of seven and a half years in doing so was excessive.

Held, dismissing the appeal, that the passage of time alone was not enough to prevent set aside but where, as in this case, the court had taken the view that there was a defence on the merits which carried some degree of conviction, it was strongly inclined to allow the default judgment to be set aside even if a defendant's conduct was deserving of criticism, *Alpine Bulk Transport Co Inc v. Saudi Eagle Shipping Co Inc (The Saudi Eagle)* [1986] 2 Lloyd's Rep 221, [1987] C.L.Y. 3044 considered. Having identified such a defence, only a very special feature over and above the period of delay could lead the court to decline to set aside the default judgment. In the instant case, there was insufficient evidence for the court to conclude that IBC had taken the decision not to challenge the judgment in 1990, and even if it had, such a decision would not be sufficient to prevent set aside, given the complexity and size of the international litigation.

JH RAYNER (MINCING LANE) LTD v. CAFENORTE SA IMPORTADORA; *sub nom.* JH RAYNER (MINCING LANE) LTD v. BRAZIL; CITOMA TRADING LTD v. BRAZIL [1999] 2 All E.R. (Comm) 577, Waller, L.J., CA.

503. Judgments and orders – default judgments – setting aside – whether defence could show real prospect of successful defence

[Civil Procedure Rules 1998 (SI 1998 3132) Part 13 r.13.3(1)(a).]

M issued a claim against LLBC in October 1998 for damages for nuisance suffered from 1991 to November 1992 arising from being housed in cockroach infested accommodation. M entered judgment in default in January 1999, having served LLBC in December 1998 and failed to receive any response. LLBC applied to have the judgment set aside. In March 1999 a draft defence was served on M stating, inter alia, that the defence was one of limitation as most but not all of M's claim was time barred. LLBC did not put forward a defence on the merits. The application was refused and LLBC appealed.

Held, dismissing the appeal, that the issues to be decided were whether (1) LLBC had a real prospect of successfully defending the claim, and (2) the judgment should be set aside. The limitation defence was a defence in law and not a defence on the merits of the case. M would still recover some damages in respect of the non time barred period and the relevance of limitation was therefore one of quantum rather than LLBC's prospect of successfully defending the claim. It was found, therefore, that LLBC had no real prospect of successfully defending the claim. In considering whether to exercise its discretion under the Civil Procedure Rules Part 13 r.13.3(1)(a) the court could take into consideration LLBC's explanation for failure to enter a defence in time and the late service of the draft defence. It was not appropriate, however, in the instant case, to take the draconian step of depriving M of a judgment which had been obtained in the proper manner.

MULLIGAN v. LAMBETH LBC, January 20, 2000, Judge Cox, CC (Lambeth). [*Ex rel.* David Giles, Barrister, Verulam Chambers, Peer House, 8-14 Verulam Street, London].

504. **Judgments and orders – practice directions – settlement after sight of draft reserved judgment – delivery in open court within discretion of judge**

Both parties appealed against a ruling that a reserved judgment would be delivered in open court after a draft of the decision had been seen by the parties, and settlement had subsequently been reached. The draft decision had been made available to the legal advisors to the parties in accordance with the *Practice Statement (Sup Ct: Judgments) (No.1)* [1998] 1 W.L.R. 825, [1998] C.L.Y. 71. M and P argued that they were at liberty to reach a compromise agreement even after having seen the draft decision. Moreover, it was contended that a clause in the compromise agreement purporting to exclude formal publication of the decision was valid.

Held, dismissing the appeal, that where a judge had submitted a draft judgment to the legal advisors to the parties, following which a compromise agreement was reached, it remained within the discretion of the judge to decide whether to deliver judgment in open court or not. The discretion to make that decision resided in the judge alone and any clause in the compromise agreement purporting to exclude formal publication was unenforceable. The purpose of the Practice Statement was to ensure an orderly procedure for the handing down of reserved judgments, and not to facilitate compromise agreements, particularly as the parties themselves would normally only see the judgment an hour before its formal delivery. It remained within the discretion of the judge to alter his decision. In the instant case it was in the public interest that judgment was delivered, and the wishes of the parties were just one factor that a judge should take into account when exercising his discretion.

PRUDENTIAL ASSURANCE CO LTD v. MCBAINS COOPER [2000] 1 W.L.R. 2000, Brooke, L.J., CA.

505. **Judgments and orders – summary judgments – action for breach of contract – improbability of success resulted in making of conditional order**

B, a company involved in the brokerage of shares, entered into an agreement with N, an investment bank, to facilitate the acquisition of shares in an Italian bank by IEC, a Russian industrial company. N agreed to pay B a commission of 75% of the net fees received for the brokerage should the proposed acquisition of shares take place. N withdrew from its involvement in the transaction following changes in its senior management and the transaction subsequently failed. B brought an action for losses consisting of commission and expenses which had allegedly resulted from the lost opportunity to facilitate the transaction. N resisted the claim on the grounds that (1) the proposed acquisition would not have received the necessary regulatory approval; (2) there was no evidence to show that IEC had, or would have been able to satisfy N that it had, sufficient funds to enable the transaction to proceed, and (3) its withdrawal was not the cause of the transaction's failure. N applied for summary judgment contending that B had no real prospect of succeeding with its claim.

Held, granting B conditional permission to proceed, that, although it was improbable that the claim would succeed, it was not possible to say, whether the three grounds relied on by N were considered individually or cumulatively, that the claim had no real prospect of success. Due to the improbability of the claim succeeding, a conditional order was made whereby B was required to provide a bank guarantee to cover N's reasonable costs in defending the action.

BELGRAVE INTERNATIONAL SA v. NOMURA INTERNATIONAL PLC [2000] C.P.Rep. 5, Cresswell, J., QBD (Comm Ct).

506. Judgments and orders – summary judgments – case management – clinical negligence claim – criteria for grant of summary judgment

[Civil Procedure Rules 1998 (SI 1998 3132).]

N commenced proceedings for clinical negligence against NP. Having considered the statements of case and the allocation questionnaires filed by the parties, the master made an order requiring N to show cause why summary judgment should not be awarded in favour of NP. On the date when directions implementing that order were due to be given, N made known her opposition to the order. She argued that (1) she had the benefit of legal aid and was represented by specialist advisers who had informed the Legal Aid Board that her claim had reasonable prospects of success; (2) NP was publicly funded and was also represented by specialists in the field of clinical negligence; (3) NP had not made an application for summary judgment of its own; (4) given that the order had been made on the court's own motion, uncertainty existed as to which party should bear the costs of the application; (5) an application for summary judgment was likely to prove costly; (6) this was a substantial and complex case, the outcome of which hinged on oral evidence, and (7) the appropriate time to consider whether summary judgment should be granted was the stage when all of the evidence had been obtained and exchanged.

Held, upholding the order, that it was appropriate for the court to take an active case management role and follow the proportional approach advocated by the Civil Procedure Rules 1998. As regards the arguments put forward by N, (1) the fact that a party had specialist advisers whose views led to his case being publicly funded did not abrogate the court's responsibility to consider the pleadings and, if necessary, make an order of the type made in this case; (2) the source of NP's funding and the fact that it had specialist advisers were irrelevant; (3) NP's decision not to make an application of its own for summary judgment was similarly irrelevant. Whilst stressing that this was not suggested here, solicitors representing defendants might decide to proceed to trial with a view to achieving financial gain or pleasing their clients; (4) the court was likely to order that costs should be in the case; (5) the costs involved in an application for summary judgment were likely to be relatively inexpensive. Whereas such an application was likely to be dealt with in one day, a trial would probably last for 10 days; (6) whilst acknowledging that N's case was substantial, the costs likely to be saved if the case could be disposed of at an interlocutory hearing were enormous. Contrary to N's assertion, the merits of a case could sometimes be determined by considering the witness statements and experts' reports, and (7) it was practical for the court to consider granting summary judgment when pleadings had closed. At the time when the action was set down for trial, no provision existed for the master to read witness statements and experts' reports. It was observed that N's interests would be protected in the application for summary judgment since NP was to be required to adduce its evidence first.

NAMUSOKE v. NORTHWICK PARK AND ST MARK'S NHS TRUST (NO.1) [2000] C.P. Rep. 33, Master Murray, QBD.

507. Judgments and orders – summary judgments – imprecise pleadings – pleadings to be viewed in light of available evidence

[Civil Procedure Rules 1998 (SI 1998 3132) Part 24 r.24.2.]

M purchased a property in October 1990 with the aim of running it as a fish and chip shop. The cellar flooded on four or more occasions between December 1990 and March 1991. Having detected that some of the flood water contained raw sewage, M issued proceedings against N alleging that the flooding had been a result of the main sewage system backing up by reason of excessive burden or blockage. M sought damages for the failure of her fish and chip shop business which she argued had been caused by the reputation the property had gained as a consequence of the flooding. In her particulars of claim M did not identify the concise nature of the allegations of nuisance she wished to rely upon. N applied, pursuant to the Civil Procedure Rules 1998 Part 24 r.24.2, for summary judgment, submitting that the claim had no real prospect of success. The recorder granted summary judgment, finding that N was maintaining the sewage system to a level required of it given its considerable age. M appealed.

Held, allowing the appeal, that whilst Part 24 r.24.2 of the Rules was severe in magnitude, it was not designed to deprive a claimant where the issues of fact if found in their favour would potentially produce a successful outcome. In the instant case, the inadequacy of M's pleadings had to be viewed in the light of the available evidence which was suggestive of a reasonable prospect of success.

MUNN v. NORTH WEST WATER LTD [2001] C.P. Rep. 48, Mantell, L.J., CA.

508. Judgments and orders – summary judgments – judge's refusal to entertain renewed application

[Rules of the Supreme Court 1965 (SI 1965 1776) Ord.14, Ord.15 r.16; County Court Rules 1981 (SI 1981 1687) Ord.9 r.14.]

S was the bailee of equipment owned by D and insured by ESI which was stolen. S became bankrupt. D brought county court proceedings against S under the hire agreement and joined ESI as defendants. In successive amended statements of claim, D argued that: (1) S's insurance policy with ESI was in trust for them; (2) S held the policy under a fiduciary obligation for D; and (3) because S had failed to enforce the policy, D as the beneficiaries of the trust or fiduciary obligation were entitled to enforce the policy against ESI. They sought a declaration that ESI were obliged to indemnify S in respect of the loss of the equipment or, alternatively, that ESI were liable to indemnify D. D had sought summary judgment on the basis of the second pleading but the judge gave ESI unconditional leave to defend and D appealed. An application for summary judgment on the third pleading was dismissed as improper and D appealed. There were questions whether the judge was wrong to refuse to consider D's second application for summary judgment and, if so, whether he should have given them a declaration that ESI were liable to indemnify them.

Held, dismissing the appeals, that although the judge had been in error in refusing to entertain D's renewed application, the outcome would have been the same if he had. D were not entitled to summary judgment against ESI and there was no ground for altering the decision that ESI had leave to defend. The evidence of the insurance policy provided no basis for concluding that the insured was anyone other than S or that D had any contractual rights against ESI. S's policy did not comply with the hire agreement with D so there was no evidence that S insured the equipment as an agent for D. Neither the Rules of the Supreme Court Ord.14 nor the County Court Rules Ord.9 r.14 expressly excluded more than one application for summary judgment. The bailee S had insured his full insurable interest so had a fiduciary obligation to account to D the owner for any insurance money he recovered in excess of his own loss. The fiduciary obligation did not amount to a trust and gave D no direct rights against the insurers. *Tomlinson v. Hepburn* [1966] A.C. 45 considered. *Vanderpitte v. Preferred Insurance* [1933] A.C. 70 suggested there were circumstances where a third party could enforce an insurance policy for the insured but D's pleadings did not support the argument. The first application fell because it had not been adequately covered by the particulars of claim. The second would have fallen because, under RSC Ord.15 r.16, D could not seek a declaration because they were not parties to the insurance policy. Something more was required than an indirect interest. This was unfortunate because it meant that ESI had nothing to say other than a non-admission which was unlikely to limit costs or assist the economical conclusion of what was already drawn out litigation. *Dombey & Son v. Playfair Bros* [1897] 1 Q.B. 368, *Guaranty Trust v. Hannay* [1915] 2 K.B. 536 and *Gouriet v. Union of Post Office Workers* [1978] A.C. 435, [1977] C.L.Y. 690 considered.

DG FINANCE LTD v. SCOTT AND EAGLE STAR INSURANCE CO LTD [1999] Lloyd's Rep. I.R. 387, Hobhouse, L.J., CA.

509. **Judgments and orders – summary judgments – payment into court – permission to defend conditional upon payment into court – condition not unreasonable notwithstanding that defendant company had ceased trading**

FB, a firm of solicitors, brought an action against AEC, a company that had ceased trading, for the recovery of fees. An appeal against summary judgment having been allowed, an order was made that the defence to the claim and aspects of a counterclaim be struck out, and that permission be granted to amend the pleading so as to allege a set off. AEG were also ordered to pay into court a sum equivalent to FB's claim, in default of which the defence and counterclaim would be struck out and permission would be given to FB to enter judgment on the claim. AEG, appealed, contending that the judge had erred in requiring it to pay into court a sum of money which it could not afford to raise. AEG submitted that such a condition was equivalent to giving judgment in favour of FB.

Held, allowing the appeal in part, that (1) AEG should be granted permission to amend its pleading to allege a set off but not to challenge the quantum of FB's claim, and (2) while AEG had no assets and had ceased trading, it was evident that it had remained on the register of companies in anticipation of success in ongoing litigation; it had, when required, managed to raise money to sustain that litigation. However, given the difficulties of obtaining the money in a short period of time, AEG would be allowed 28 days in which to raise the payment into court, *MV Yorke Motors v. Edwards* [1982] 1 W.L.R. 444, [1982] C.L.Y. 2398 considered.

FOOT & BOWDEN v. ANGLO EUROPE CORP LTD PTA-A1999/6718/B1, Henry, L.J., CA.

510. **Jury trial – assessment of damages for false imprisonment – case including personal injuries claim requiring scientific investigation**

[County Courts Act 1984 s.66(3)(b).]

W brought an action against the police claiming damages arising out of false imprisonment, wrongful arrest, assault and battery and personal injuries alleged to have been sustained during arrest. CC denied liability but subsequently admitted that the arrest was unlawful and accepted liability for false imprisonment, wrongful arrest and assault and battery. However, the parties differed significantly over the facts of the arrest and whether W was restrained or assaulted in the manner that he claimed, and whether he had suffered permanent back injuries as a result. Both parties had served disputed lay evidence and were intending to serve expert medical evidence. W applied for a jury trial under the County Courts Act 1984 s.66(3)(b), contending that there was in issue a claim in respect of false imprisonment, and that s.66(3) applied irrespective of the fact that liability was admitted and despite the fact that the hearing would be for assessment of damages only. The district judge adjourned the question to the circuit judge.

Held, refusing W's application for a jury trial, that it was not open to the court to ignore *Beta Construction Ltd v. Channel Four Television Co Ltd* [1990] 1 W.L.R. 1042, [1990] C.L.Y. 2918 applied, and W was prima facie entitled to a jury. However, s.66(3) also provided that the presumption could be displaced if the court was of the opinion that the trial would require any scientific investigation which could not conveniently be made with a jury. In the instant case, the court was of the opinion that the determination of the claim for personal injuries would require such a scientific investigation.

WAKELAND-JONES v. CHIEF CONSTABLE OF DEVON AND CORNWALL, November 5, 1999, Judge Cotterill, CC (Taunton). [*Ex rel.* James Hassall, Barrister, Southernhay Chambers, 33 Southernhay East, Exeter].

511. Lands tribunal – appeals

CIVIL PROCEDURE (MODIFICATION OF ENACTMENTS) ORDER 2000, SI 2000 941; made under the Civil Procedure Act 1997 s.4. In force: May 2, 2000; £1.00.

This Order, which amends the Lands Tribunal Act 1949 following the making of a new rule for appeals in the Civil Procedure (Amendment) Rules 2000 (SI 2000 221) r.19 and Sch.5, provides that appeals from the Lands Tribunal in England and Wales to the Court of Appeal will no longer be by way of case stated.

512. Limitations – asbestosis – exposure to asbestos whilst at work – delay in bringing action caused by difficulties in funding – disapplication of limitation period to allow action to continue

[Limitation Act 1980.]

C discovered in 1992 that he had a problem with asbestos in his lungs which he claimed was caused by his exposure whilst at work in 1961 to asbestos being sprayed onto pipes by laggers employed by LT. He attempted to bring an action in 1992, but was advised that he was not eligible for legal aid. As a result, C did not proceed further until 1994 when he investigated the possibility of union funding. However the union were unwilling to fund his claim because he was no longer a member. In 1996 C was again advised by his GP to seek legal advice, which he did, resulting in proceedings being issued in 1998 under a conditional fee arrangement. The question of the application of the Limitation Act 1980 was considered as a preliminary matter.

Held, disapplying the limitation period and allowing the action to continue, that the period of delay to be considered was that from the expiry of the limitation period, being September 1995, *Donovan v. Gwentoys Ltd* [1990] 1 W.L.R. 472, [1990] C.L.Y. 2960 considered. The delay was caused by C's difficulties in funding the action, and in the circumstances this did not have any detrimental effect on T's ability to defend the action nor on the evidence likely to be adduced by the parties, *Donovan* and *Hartley v. Birmingham City Council* [1992] 1 W.L.R. 968, [1992] C.L.Y. 2811 considered. On balance it would not be inequitable to allow the action to continue. C's evidence was clear and it was common in these cases, due to the passage of time, for the evidence not to be as strong as required normally. In the circumstances, C's case was not so weak or stale as to require the court to prevent it from continuing.

CONNOLLY v. TURNER & NEWALL LTD, December 17, 1999, Judge Lyon, CC (Oldham). [*Ex rel.* John Pickering & Partners Solicitors, 9 Church Lane, Oldham].

513. Limitations – causes of action – Limitation Act 1980 s.32 applied by analogy to action for breach of fiduciary duty

[Limitation Act 1980 s.32, s.36(1).]

In September 1995 CSI issued proceedings against H alleging breaches of four written binding authority agreements made on a number of dates between May 1977 and April 1979 seeking damages for, amongst other things, dishonest breach of fiduciary duty. H filed a defence pleading limitation and the limitation point was ordered to be tried as a preliminary issue. The judge having found ([1999] 1 All E.R. (Comm) 750, [1999] C.L.Y. 466) that CSI could, with reasonable diligence, have ascertained the alleged details suppressed by H outside the limitation period within the meaning of the Limitation Act 1980 s.32, struck out those causes of action based upon breach of contract and tort as statute barred. The judge went on to find that the same limitation period should be applied by analogy in the same way pursuant to s.36(1). CSI appealed, contending that the provisions of the 1980 Act did not apply to a claim for dishonest breach of fiduciary duty.

Held, dismissing the appeal, that (1) a claim for equitable damages or equitable compensation constituted a claim for equitable relief and accordingly s.36 applied to it. Under s.36(1) the court was not required to analyse whether a limitation period had been applied to a dishonest breach of fiduciary duty by analogy prior to July 1, 1940, but rather whether one would have been applied; (2) it was apparent from the authorities prior to 1940 that equity would have applied the statute by analogy, *Knox v. Gye* (1872) L.R 5 H.L. 656, *Hovenden v. Lord Annesley* (1806) 2 Sch & L. 607, *Burdick v. Garrick* (1870) L.R. 5 Ch. App. 233, *Friend v. Young* [1897] 2 Ch. 421 and *North American Land & Timber Co Ltd v. Watkins* [1904] 1 Ch. 242 considered. Such a conclusion was reinforced by the fact that the CSI's allegations of dishonest breach of fiduciary duty arose from substantially the same facts as relied on for the alleged breaches of contract and tort, and (3) the provisions of the statute applied even where equity was acting in its exclusive jurisdiction, *Paragon Finance Plc v. Thakerar & Co* [1999] 1 All E.R. 400, [1998] C.L.Y. 536 applied.

CIA DE SEGUROS IMPERIO v. HEATH (REBX) LTD (FORMERLY CE HEATH & CO (AMERICA) LTD); *sub nom.* COMPANHIA DE SEGUROS IMPERIO v. HEATH (REBX) LTD [2001] 1 W.L.R. 112, Waller, L.J., CA.

514. Limitations – causes of action – loans – cause of action accrued on date of loan agreement

[Consumer Credit Act 1974 s.138; Limitation Act 1980 s.8, s.36.]

By a credit agreement dated October 26, 1990, J advanced £10,000 to T on the security of their home. The loan was repayable at an APR of 39 per cent over 15 years. T defaulted and O, as successor to J, issued proceedings on March 19, 1998. A defence and counterclaim was filed on June 18, 1998, alleging that the loan was an extortionate credit bargain under the Consumer Credit Act 1974 s.138. On March 31, 1999, the district judge struck out the defence and counterclaim as being statute barred under the Limitation Act 1980, since it was raised more than six years after the date of the loan. On appeal, T argued that the date of "accrual" of the cause of action was not the date of the agreement, but October 25, 1992, when, pursuant to its contractual power to vary the interest rate applicable under the agreement, the lender failed to reduce the interest rate by more than a minimal amount, such that the counterclaim was in time.

Held, dismissing the appeal, that (1) a circuit judge should follow a decision of another circuit judge unless such decision was wrong; (2) the limitation period was six years under the Limitation Act 1980 s.5 and s.9, *London North Securities Ltd v. Salt* (Unreported, November 11, 1998), [1999] C.L.Y. 2502 followed; (3) s.8 of the 1980 Act, providing for a 12 year period of limitation in actions upon a speciality, had no application, *Anker & Jerome v. J&J Securities* (Unreported, January 8, 1999) considered. Even if s.8 did apply, it was by virtue of s.8(2) of the 1980 Act, subject to any applicable shorter period of limitation, namely the six year period in s.5 or s.9 of the 1980 Act; (4) the argument that some of the relief available under s.139(2) of the 1974 Act was equitable in nature, so that by s.36 of the 1980 Act, no limitation period applied to a claim for such relief, was wrong because the relief in s.139(2) of the 1974 Act was the product of statute and not of equity, *McQuilliams v. Secured Funding Ltd* (Unreported, April 30, 1999) doubted and (5) the cause of action under s.138 of the 1974 Act accrued on the date of the agreement, *London North* followed. It was not relevant to look to any subsequent date, such a change in the interest rate.

OCWEN LTD v. TRAVIS, April 11, 2000, Judge Heppel Q.C., CC (Kingston upon Hull). [*Ex rel.* Marc Beaumont, Barrister, Harrow-on-the-Hill Chambers, 60 High Street, Harrow-on-the-Hill, Middlesex].

515. Limitations – clinical negligence – claim allowed out of time – appeal against order allowing claim after judgment on issues

[Limitations Act 1980 s.33.]

In 1973 B sustained personal injuries during childbirth while in the care of SHK, the baby died. In 1992 B raised an action seeking damages on the basis of the negligent management of her labour and applied for her action to be allowed to proceed in terms of the Limitations Act 1980 s.33. That application was dismissed and B appealed. The appeal was heard by Kennedy, J who concluded that, as the nursing staff responsible for the birth had since died, it was not possible to examine the validity of the conduct of the labour fairly and that that issue should be struck out. However, he also found that the evidence as to whether the doctor should have performed a Caesarean section was not time dependent and allowed B's appeal. The trial was heard by Garland, J. who ruled that the risks of labour so outweighed any perceived advantage as to go beyond an error of judgment, thereby constituting a breach of duty. SHK appealed the action to the Court of Appeal and also applied, in the alternative, for leave to appeal the order of Kennedy, J. out of time.

Held, dismissing the appeal and the application for leave to appeal, that (1) in considering whether to grant leave to appeal against the exercise of discretion under s.33 the court had to examine the issue in light of what occurred at trial. The facts upon which the substantive decision was based were different from those envisaged when the order allowing the claim to proceed was made. The court was required to consider the demands of justice, SHK's consent to the limitation issue being tried as a preliminary issue and the fact that the application for leave to appeal was three years out of time. The conduct of the trial could not be criticised as unfair. To allow the application could be seen as an injustice to the administration of justice itself, and (2) the case involved the trial judge weighing the evidence of witnesses and deciding what evidence he preferred. In such circumstances the trial judge's decision could only be overturned if it was plainly wrong on the whole evidence. In the instant case the judge had not been plainly wrong to accept the evidence of BN's experts.

BRIODY v. ST HELENS & KNOWSLEY AHA [1999] Lloyd's Rep. Med. 185, Ward L.J., CA.

516. Limitations – clinical negligence – date of actual knowledge – broken needle left in situ after episiotomy during birth of claimant's first child

[Limitation Act 1980 s.14.]

F had her first child in 1960 but was unaware that part of a broken needle had been left in situ following an episiotomy performed during the birth. Although she went on to have five more children, F suffered chronic pain and her sexual relationship with her husband was strained. F felt too embarrassed to discuss her problems with her male GP, but even when a female GP took over in 1983, far-reaching gynaecological investigations failed to establish the cause of the problem. In 1991 the needle was seen on an X-ray in relation to F's osteoarthritis but as it was not relevant to those investigations she was not informed of its presence until February 1994. At that point she remembered that the surgeon had remarked that the needle was broken during the episiotomy procedure. F issued proceedings for negligence in January 1997, but the court at first instance held that they were time barred as, although she did not have actual knowledge of the presence of the needle until February 1994, she had constructive knowledge some considerable time before. F appealed.

Held, dismissing the appeal, that the test of constructive knowledge within the Limitation Act 1980 s.14, as to whether a claimant could reasonably have sought medical advice, was at least in part an objective one not dependent upon personal characteristics. F knew that the problems began with the birth and they had a huge effect on her life which should have led her to seek medical help despite her reservations. Had she done so at an early stage, investigations would have centred on the birth and would have been likely either to jog her memory as to the surgeon's comment about the needle or to have resulted in an

X-ray, *Smith v. Leicestershire HA* [1998] Lloyd's Rep. Med. 77, [1998] C.L.Y. 551 applied.

FENECH v. EAST LONDON AND CITY HA [2000] Lloyd's Rep. Med. 35, Simon Brown L.J., CA.

517. Limitations – clinical negligence – unsuccessful operations – date of knowledge of injury

[Limitation Act 1980 s.14.]

J's health deteriorated after what he believed to be two routine haemorrhoidectomy operations carried out in 1987 and 1990. After discovering that he had been injured during the earlier operation, he issued a writ against EDHA in January 1997, which was held below to be outside the limitation period on the basis that J had obtained sufficient knowledge by 1992 to have issued a claim. J appealed.

Held, allowing the claim in part (Sir Christopher Staughton dissenting), that there had been nothing to indicate to that J that he had been injured rather than that the first operation in 1987 had been unsuccessful. Logically, no claim could be made for an injury until the claimant was aware both that he had been injured and that the injury was significant. Therefore, the essential precondition for the application of the Limitation Act 1980 s.14 was absent and part of the claim for the 1987 operation was within the limitation period, *Smith (Michael John) v. West Lancashire HA* [1995] P.I.Q.R. P514, [1995] C.L.Y. 3169 considered and *Forbes v. Wandsworth HA* [1997] Q.B. 402, [1996] C.L.Y. 4466 applied.

JAMES v. EAST DORSET HA (2001) 59 B.M.L.R. 196, Sedley, L.J., CA.

518. Limitations – convention estoppel – shared assumption insufficient to establish estoppel in absence of communication

[Limitation Act 1980 s.9.]

Following the compulsory acquisition of land by HLBC, a claim for compensation was submitted by the occupiers of the land A, who then entered into protracted negotiations with HLBC. In 1995, some 13 years after the original claim, A submitted a notice of reference to the Lands Tribunal which determined that the claim was statute barred pursuant to the Limitation Act 1980 s.9. The question of limitation was referred to the High Court which made the same determination that the claim was statute barred unless HLBC was precluded by its conduct from so asserting and an appeal by A to the Court of Appeal was subsequently dismissed ([1999] Ch.139, [1998] C.L.Y. 4179). A then brought a further action which claimed that HLBC was precluded from relying on the limitation period provided for in s.9 as negotiations between the parties had continued after the expiry of the limitation period. The application was allowed ([1999] 3 E.G.L.R. 125) on the basis that the parties had a shared assumption that the claim was valid, and, as a result of which, HLBC was precluded by convention estoppel. HLBC appealed, contending that the requirements for convention estoppel had not been established as there was no shared assumption of fact that the claim was not subject to a statutory period of limitation.

Held, allowing the appeal, that the evidence did not support the judge's findings. A shared assumption was insufficient to establish an estoppel unless it was communicated and the correspondence between the parties after the expiry of the limitation period failed to establish such a communication. Parties may enter into an agreement to waive the limitation defence and any such agreement would be enforced by the courts. However, there was no basis for finding that a party should be disentitled from relying on such a defence owing to continued negotiations with the other party and without an agreement having been made as to the manner of resolution of the claim in the event of the failure of negotiations.

HILLINGDON LBC v. ARC LTD (NO.2) [2001] C.P. Rep. 33, Arden, J., CA.

519. Limitations – defendant company restored to register under Companies Act 1985 s.651 – period between dissolution and restoration order disregarded for limitation purposes

[Companies Act 1985 s.651.]

WKL had been restored to the Companies Register by an order pursuant to the Companies Act 1985 s.651 on January 23, 1998 having been dissolved in 1963. S commenced proceedings against WKL in May 1999, having obtained an order under s.651 (6) declaring that the period between the dissolution and the restoration order should be disregarded for the purposes of any limitation of time within which proceedings against WKL had to be brought. There were issues in dispute between the parties as to what S's date of knowledge had been and it was clear that proceedings had been commenced some 18 months after the limitation period from the date of death had expired.

Held, that the order pursuant to s.651 (6) should be set aside because it had been made on an ex parte basis without consideration of all the relevant evidence contrary to the decision in *Workvale Ltd (No.2), Re* [1992] 1 W.L.R. 416, [1992] C.L.Y. 413, *Thomson v. Lord Clanmorris* [1900] 1 Ch. 718 and *Russo-Asiatic Bank, Re* [1934] Ch. 720 considered.

SMITH (DECEASED) v. WHITE KNIGHT LAUNDRY LTD, October 22, 1999, Judge Pryor, QBD. [*Ex rel.* Davies Arnold Cooper Solicitors, 6-8 Bouverie St, London].

520. Limitations – fraud – bank employee – position of employment established fiduciary duty

[Limitation Act 1980 s.21, s.32.]

BCCI, a bank in liquidation, brought proceedings in relation to two properties alleged to have been purchased with monies belonging to it which had been fraudulently misappropriated by a former employee, K. Both properties at issue had been purchased in 1987. The first had been registered in the name of K's mother, J, the second after a series of transfers, with two cousins of K. BCCI sought declarations that each property was held for them by the registered proprietor on a bare trust and financial compensation from K, J and K's cousins in respect of the alleged fraudulent misappropriation. The claim in relation to the property registered in the names of K's two cousins was compromised on the basis that the property be transferred to BCCI. J, by her defence submitted that she had made no contribution to the purchase of the property registered in her name and that it had been registered without her knowledge or agreement, and also that BCCI's claim against her for compensation was statute barred under the Limitation Act 1980. K claimed that his position of employment at BCCI had not given him authority to operate the relevant accounts from which the misappropriation was alleged and therefore he could not be liable as trustee. BCCI contended that no limitation period applied because their action fell within s.21 of the Act and that K owed them through his employment a fiduciary duty or alternatively had assumed the duties of a trustee in respect of BCCI's property by reason of his employment.

Held, granting the declarations and the compensation claim against K, that (1) on the evidence, K did, through his employment, have control over the relevant bank accounts; (2) the two house purchases had been financed from funds belonging to BCCI and derived from accounts under the control of K; (3) J had no knowledge of the purchase or registration under her name of the relevant property, and (4) the control over bank accounts as vested in K through his employment was such as to constitute a fiduciary duty in relation to the payment of monies from those accounts. K was therefore a constructive trustee of those funds under his control and his consequent misapplication of them constituted a breach of his duty as trustee, *Paragon Finance Plc v. Thakerar & Co* [1999] 1 All E.R. 400, [1998] C.L.Y. 536 and *Agip (Africa) Ltd v. Jackson*

[1991] Ch. 547, [1992] C.L.Y. 2039 considered. It followed that BCCI were entitled to rely on s.21 of the Act.

Observed, that given the difficulties the liquidators of BCCI had had in gaining access to the relevant documentation, and the initial absence of any records sufficient to warrant suspicion, time for the purposes of the limitation period would not in any event have begun to run until 1997 when the liquidators had first discovered the frauds. BCCI would therefore have been entitled to rely on s.32 of the Act if unable to rely on s.21.

BANK OF CREDIT & COMMERCE INTERNATIONAL (OVERSEAS) LTD (IN LIQUIDATION) v. JAN CH.1998-B-1572, Jonathan Parker, J., Ch D (Companies Ct).

521. Limitations – fraud – mortgages – reasonable diligence – fraudulent breach of retainer

[Limitation Act 1980 s.21(1).]

In September 1988 UCB, mortgage lenders, had lent money in two residential property transactions in which a solicitor, S, had acted for both UCB and the borrowers. S was employed in the firm of C at the time. The borrowers defaulted on the mortgages and UCB incurred large losses on the sale of the properties following repossession. In 1992, following the collapse of the property market and a huge increase in mortgage default, UCB instigated procedures for identifying potential claims against valuers and recovering shortfalls. In 1996 UCB discovered that the two borrowers and S had had links through various companies and other transactions of which UCB had been unaware, that false information had been given as to the borrowers' financial status and that it appeared that S had acted fraudulently. UCB brought an action in 1998 for damages for deceit, breach of trust and negligence against the partners of C who had been such in 1988. A preliminary issue arose as to limitation. UCB argued that it had not been and could not reasonably have been aware of the alleged fraud until a member of staff in the Debt Recovery Department had happened to notice the link between the borrowers, which was later traced to S.

Held, making the following findings, that UCB could with reasonable diligence have discovered the alleged breaches before 1996. The cause of action arose in 1988. There was enough information available to UCB in 1992, within the six year limitation period, to have put them on notice. Both transactions had been for large amounts, had been handled by the same broker, of whom UCB were by that time suspicious, and there had been immediate default on the mortgage payments. One of the borrowers was stated to have been separated but her husband became involved in negotiations about arrears at an early stage, a cheque issued by S, after he had left the firm of C, was dishonoured, the other borrower was found not to have been living at the property, and UCB were told of a police investigation into S's firm. Given the huge volume of arrears cases that UCB were having to deal with in the early 1990's they should have put in place more stringent measures for identifying links between and problems with professionals and individuals, with a view to possible negligence claims. However it was arguable that the limitation period would not apply in relation to the breach of trust cause of action. If UCB were able to show that S had fraudulently breached his retainer when the completion monies were held by him pending completion, in that he had given false assurances as to matters such as purchase price and sole ownership, then the Limitation Act 1980 s.21(1) would disapply the limitation period.

UCB HOME LOANS CORP LTD v. CARR [2000] Lloyd's Rep. P.N. 754, Crane, J., QBD.

522. Limitations – identity of defendant – permission to join additional defendant after expiry of limitation period

[Limitation Act 1980 s.11), s.14, s.33, s.35(1).]

R suffered serious injuries following a fall when brickwork collapsed at a construction site where he was employed on a casual "labour only" basis by W, who traded under the name "Decking and StudWelding". Following the accident, R consulted solicitors who endeavoured to ascertain the identity of the main contractor and occupier of the site. R maintained that he did not wish to commence proceedings against W as it remained his belief that W had correctly reported information that he had been given by others concerning the stability of the brickwork structure. R's solicitors wrote to two companies S&M and SMD in February 1996 in identical terms suggesting that they were the main contractor at the site. No reply was received from SMD. S&M did respond but ultimately issued a denial of liability on the basis that the main contractor at the site was in fact SMD. Eventually SMD's insurers wrote to confirm that they were considering their position but failed to clarify this prior to the expiry of the limitation period. On counsel's advice, proceedings were issued against JNR the parent company of SMD five weeks prior to the expiry of the limitation period. A defence was served to the effect that R was employed by W who had been contracted to undertake certain works by SMD but that the main contractors at the site were S&M. R sought permission to amend his particulars of claim to add S&M and SMD as additional defendants. R maintained that the service of JNR's defence was the first notification he had had that the main contractor at the site was in fact S&M. An order was granted permitting R to substitute SMD for JNR pursuant to the Limitation Act 1980 s.35(1), but his request for the addition of S&M was refused. The judge at first instance held that R had the requisite knowledge of the defendant's identity as at the date of the letter sent in February 1996 and that the application for amendment was therefore made outside the three year time limit prescribed by s.11 of the 1980 Act. R appealed contending that he had did not have the knowledge required by s.14 and therefore the three year limitation period had not expired when the application for amendment was first made. Alternatively, R maintained that the court should have made an order pursuant to s.33.

Held, allowing the appeal, that the judge at first instance had fallen into error in assuming that, because R's solicitors had sent a letter to S&M in February 1996, R had the requisite knowledge of identity. Doubt over that identity was indicated by the fact that letters had been sent to two companies in the same terms alleging that they were the main contractor. Subsequent correspondence demonstrated that R and his solicitors continued to have doubts over the identity of the main contractor on site at the relevant time. The further fact that counsel's advice was sought as to the appropriate defendant to proceedings was yet more evidence to suggest that R did not know the identity of the main contractor. R knew that S&M could be the correct defendant but he also thought two other companies might have been the main contractor. The judge's conclusion was therefore flawed because it was based upon inference rather than findings of fact.

Observed, that the court also expressed the opinion that the judge had also erred in failing to consider the possibility of a direction under s.33 of the 1980 Act.

RUSH v. JNR (SMD) LTD [2000] C.P. Rep. 12, Roch, L.J., CA.

523. **Limitations – industrial deafness – claim brought 14 years after expiry of limitation period – inequitable to exercise discretion – claimant having professional negligence claim against his solicitor**

[Limitation Act 1980 s.11, s.14, s.33.]

G worked for BS as a pole pit driver from January 4, 1971 to April 27, 1973. For the majority of the time he was protected from the factory noise by virtue of being sheltered in his cab. On March 9, 1999, more than 14 years after the expiry of the primary limitation period, G issued proceedings for noise induced hearing loss. The preliminary issues to be determined by the court were (1) the date of knowledge under the Limitation Act s.11 and s.14, and (2) whether the court should exercise its discretion under s. 33. BS contended that G had a possibility of a claim against his solicitors, which would diminish any prejudice suffered by G in the event of the court exercising its discretion in favour of BS.

Held, determining the preliminary issues in favour of BS, that it was found as a fact that it was not until the examination of G by a medical expert in October 26, 1995, that G realised that the damage was permanent and that his hearing problems, or at least some of them, were noise induced. Section 33 required the court to have regard to all the circumstances of the case, therefore the onus was on G to satisfy the court that it would be equitable to exercise the discretion in his favour, *Price v. United Engineering Steels Ltd* [1998] P.I.Q.R. P407, [1999] C.L.Y. 464 followed. The general prejudice likely to be caused to BS by the passage of time was that they would have to find witnesses and obtain evidence from them. Quantum was not likely to be substantial. In a case of this age there was clearly an onus on G and his legal advisors to progress quickly after appropriate expert evidence has been obtained. The present solicitors had been dealing with the matter since 1996 and no acceptable reason had been put forward for the delay. Whilst it was undesirable to embark on a detailed enquiry of the conduct of the matter by G's present solicitors, it was likely that they had been negligent. The possibility of a claim against G's legal advisers was clearly regarded as a significant feature. This was a case which it would not be equitable to require BS to meet. G would only suffer a slight prejudice if he was left with pursuing a remedy against his solicitors and on that basis it would not be equitable for the court to exercise the discretion in favour of G.

GELDER v. BRITISH STEEL PLC, January 20, 2000, Recorder Sycamore, CC (Bury). [*Ex rel.* Whitfield Hallam Goodall Solicitors, 23/25 Henrietta Street, Batley].

524. **Limitations – industrial injuries – claim statute barred – discretion to extend limitation period exercisable where delay attributable to solicitor's negligence**

[Limitation Act 1980 s.33.]

C, formerly employed as a metal sprayer, was informed by a chest specialist in March 1993 that he was suffering from a condition caused by iron deposits in his lungs due to the nature of his work and five months after that diagnosis, C instructed solicitors to pursue a personal injury claim. The writ was not issued until August 1996 and was consequently struck out by the High Court as falling outside the limitation period laid down by the Limitation Act 1980. C appealed, contending that the delay was entirely attributable to the negligence of his solicitors, which was outside his control, and the court should have exercised its discretion under s.33 of the Act to extend the limitation period.

Held, allowing the appeal, that there was no rule of law that the faults of solicitors should be attributed to their clients, unless as a matter of law, the client was bound by and responsible for the actions of his solicitors. The delay following C's instructions was due to the negligence of the solicitors and the judge had been wrong to attribute this failing to C when assessing whether C had acted with due diligence in pursuing his claim. C had done everything he could have been expected to do and had placed faith in his solicitors to carry out the necessary work to a professional standard. The initial five month delay had not prejudiced the fairness of the proceedings and the claim had a strong prospect of success, thus the court should have exercised its discretion by extending the limitation period and allowing C to proceed with his claim.

CORBIN v. PENFOLD METALLISING CO LTD [2000] Lloyd's Rep. Med. 247, Buxton, L.J., CA.

525. **Limitations – industrial injuries – date of knowledge**

[Limitation Act 1980 s.14, s.33.]

S was employed by B as a cleaner. Between 1983 and 1988 he was responsible for cleaning an area devoted to a chemical process. He complained that in the early part of 1984 he became aware of a burning sensation on his lips and in his throat. By 1988 his symptoms had become severe. He first consulted his GP concerning his injuries in August 1984, was referred by his GP to an ENTclinic but failed to keep his appointment. He consulted his GP again in April 1989. An ENTconsultant, to whom he had been referred, found no evidence of physical abnormalities. His solicitors, whom he consulted in 1990, arranged for him to be examined by a consultant physician who, in January 1991, reported that he had no discernible physical disability and that there was no evidence linking his symptoms to his employment. In January 1994 a medical report was obtained which was favourable to S. Additional expert reports were then sought culminating in the issue of proceedings in September 1998. The judge dealt with the question of limitation as a preliminary issue. After hearing evidence from S which showed that he had been convinced from the outset that his symptoms had been caused by his employment, the judge held that for the purpose of the Limitation Act 1980 s.14 S had acquired the requisite knowledge of his right to bring an action when he had received the favourable medical report in January 1994. The judge, however, disapplied the limitation period by exercising his discretion under s.33 of the Act in S's favour. B appealed, arguing that for limitation purposes S had acquired knowledge in August 1984 when he had concluded that his throat condition was sufficiently serious that he should see his GP.

Held, dismissing the appeal, that (1) S had acquired knowledge for the purpose of s.14 when he consulted his GP in April 1989. It was only at that time that his symptoms had become sufficiently severe for it to be said that his condition was significant. The judge had accepted his evidence that the symptoms that he had begun to experience in 1984 had been bearable. S had had a firm belief that his symptoms were linked to his working conditions, and the absence of expert medical evidence showing that he had suffered a physical disability did not prevent him from acquiring the requisite knowledge. The question of knowledge was one of fact in each case. The court should focus on the facts of a particular case rather than allow itself to be sidetracked by the many authorities which were not always easy to reconcile, *Dobbie v. Medway HA* [1994] 1 W.L.R. 1234, [1995] C.L.Y. 3171 applied, and (2) the judge had been right to disapply the limitation period under s.33 since S had made reasonable efforts to seek medical and other advice after concluding that he might have a claim against B.

SNIEZEK v. BUNDY (LETCHWORTH) LTD [2000] P.I.Q.R. P213, Bell, J., CA.

526. **Limitations – industrial injuries – limitation period wrongly disapplied – claimant failing to make full disclosure of medical condition**

[Limitation Act 1980 s.33.]

L commenced a personal injury action in 1990 in connection with a back injury sustained in 1983 whilst he was working for T. He asserted that he had not had back problems prior to 1983. Having concluded that L's injuries had only come to light in March 1987, the judge was of the opinion that the claim was within time and for that reason did not give detailed consideration to the question of exercising his discretion to disapply the limitation period under the Limitation Act 1980 s.33. Liability was established and a separate trial ordered to consider quantum. For the purpose of that trial, fresh evidence came to light which showed that L had not made full and frank disclosure of his medical condition and that he had experienced back problems before 1983. T appealed.

Held, allowing the appeal, that the discretion to disapply the limitation period could only be exercised if it was equitable to do so, having regard to all the circumstances, including the length of the delay and any prejudice which had been caused to the defendant. The judge had, when exercising his discretion under s.33, erred by failing to take into account all the relevant circumstances. There had been a delay of over four years between the date when L became aware that he had suffered a significant injury and the commencement of the action, during which time T had received no indication that a claim was pending. In light of the new and previously undisclosed evidence concerning L's back injury, it would be wrong and inequitable to disapply the limitation period.

LONG v. TOLCHARD & SONS LTD [2001] P.I.Q.R. P2, Roch, L.J., CA.

527. Limitations – industrial injuries – no prejudice to defendant in one month delay

[Limitation Act 1980 s.11, s.33; Civil Procedure Rules 1998 (SI 1998 3132) Part 2 r.2.1.]

A was involved in an accident during the course of her employment and claimed damages for personal injuries on April 27, 1998. S contended that the cause of action arose on March 29, 1995 and the claim was therefore statute barred. It was confirmed by A, following disclosure of accident documentation, that the accident occurred on that date. The court accepted that A's solicitors had received late instructions and were required to issue court proceedings at short notice. A did not have a good command of English and would have required the services of an interpreter. Unfortunately, one of the crucial forms for legal assistance had been incorrectly completed on A's behalf with the accident date set out as April 29, 1995. A argued that the court, on this occasion, should exercise their discretion under the Limitation Act 1980 s.33 in allowing the claim to proceed. S argued that the mistake lay either with A herself or with those from whom she sought legal assistance and that a great deal of delay had occurred prior to the eventual issue of proceedings.

Held, finding in favour of A, that there was no evidence of prejudice to S in allowing the claim to proceed, *Hartley v. Birmingham City Council* [1992] 1 W.L.R. 968, [1992] C.L.Y. 2811 applied, and that S had not put forward any contention of prejudice in the evidence contained in its affidavit. The judge also applied the Civil Procedure Rules 1998 Part 2 r.2.1. In all the circumstances, the period from the end of limitation to the issue of claim, 29 days, was not a very long time and there was no disadvantage or prejudice to S. The judge accordingly disapplied the time limit under s.11.

ABALA v. SURREY OAKLANDS NHS TRUST, July 23, 1999, Judge Simpson, MCLC. [*Ex rel.* Thompsons Solicitors, Congress House, Great Russell Street, London].

528. Limitations – industrial injuries – vibration white finger – absence of exceptional circumstances capable of outweighing prejudice to defendant

[Limitation Act 1980 s.14, s.33.]

T brought a claim for damages for personal injuries against G, alleging that he was suffering from a disabling form of vibration white finger. T was employed by G during the 1980s, and early 1990s during which time he operated grinding machines. The extent of his exposure to vibration was a matter of dispute between T and G. T conceded that the cause of action accrued more than three years prior to June 1997, being the date of issue of the proceedings. G defended the proceedings, claiming that they were statue barred. T conceded that he had the requisite knowledge of the injury pursuant to the Limitation Act 1980 s.14 by March 1990, but asked the judge to exercise his discretion under s.33. T contended that, although he knew the injury was significant and had been caused by his work, it was not until 1994 that he considered the condition to be sufficiently serious to justify the commencement of proceedings, being at that time more of a nuisance than a disability, *McCafferty v. Receiver for the Metropolitan Police District* [1977] 1 W.L.R. 1073, [1977] C.L.Y. 999 referred to. As time passed, T's condition deteriorated until he was experiencing constant and serious symptoms. That was supported by the fact that T was assessed for benefits purposes as having two per cent disability in 1991, rising to 20 per cent in 1995.

Held, dismissing the claim, that T had not satisfactorily explained the delay in bringing proceedings. The evidence showed that T regarded his conditions as serious by summer 1994, but did not seek further legal advice until September 1995. It was found that G would suffer very real prejudice should T be permitted to pursue his claim after such delay, and that T had failed to establish exceptional circumstances to outweigh the prejudice to G within the meaning of

Dale v. British Coal Corp (No.2) The Times, July 2, 1992, [1992] C.L.Y. 2832 considered.

THOMPSON v. GARRANDALE LTD, July 28, 1999, Judge MacDuff, CC (Nottingham). [*Ex rel.* Hopkins Solicitors, 27 Regent Street, Nottingham].

529. **Limitations – insurance contracts – replacement insurance policy providing indemnity against employee's fraud – date of accrual for claims – predating policy was date policy incepted**

[Limitation Act 1980 s.5.]

A company, U, responsible for administering the pension funds of the employees of higher education institutions instituted proceedings against RI, an insurance company providing insurance to U in respect of any fraud or dishonesty by employees of U under the terms of a fidelity insurance policy, FIP. U had had the benefit of a similar policy which had been renewed on a yearly basis until 1990 when it was replaced by the FIP. The terms of the policy provided that U would still be indemnified in respect of any losses accruing as the result of any fraud or dishonesty by employees prior to 1990 provided that certain conditions were met. The definition of "fraudulent act" within the policy specified that it consisted of acts of fraud or dishonesty committed during the currency of the policy and discovered not later than 24 months after the termination of the policy or the dismissal of the individual perpetrator whichever was the sooner. The definition was applicable to claims post 1991 and also to those predating the FIP. U discovered that an employee had perpetrated substantial frauds on the superannuation scheme in 1987, 1989 and 1991, and made a claim against RI under the FIP. A writ was not however issued until 1997, over six years after the inception of the policy. RI applied for summary judgment contending that the claim was statute barred pursuant to the Limitation Act 1980 s.5 on the basis that the date of discovery of the loss was of no consequence to the accrual of the cause of action. RI further submitted that the cause of action in respect of the 1987 and 1989 claims arose as soon as the fidelity insurance policy was concluded as RI then immediately became liable to indemnify U against the losses in question. U contended that the policy wording operated either to create a contingent liability whereby liability only arose upon discovery of the fraud within 24 months, or alternatively that discovery within the specified period was a condition precedent to liability. In either case, U submitted, until the condition was met, a cause of action did not arise.

Held, granting the application, that the reference to discovery of the fraud in the definition of "fraudulent act" was intended to be way of proviso or qualification to the acts which gave rise to the indemnity. The cause of action accrued at the time the loss was incurred rather than at the time of discovery. In consequence the cause of action in respect of the 1991 loss accrued at the date that it occurred and the cause of action in respect of the 1987 and 1989 losses accrued when the indemnity provided by the FIP in connection with those losses prior to its inception was finally agreed.

UNIVERSITIES SUPERANNUATION SCHEME LTD v. ROYAL INSURANCE (UK) LTD [2000] 1 All E.R. (Comm) 266, Langley, J., QBD (Comm Ct).

530. **Limitations – insurance policies – critical illness cover – 30 day survival rule as condition precedent**

[Civil Procedure Rules 1998 (SI 1998 3132) Part 19.4.]

V sued GL under a policy of critical illness insurance against, inter alia, V suffering a stroke. V should have sued GL's associate GLHP, and sought to amend. Leave was refused under the Civil Procedure Rules 1998 Part 19.4 which only permitted substitution of a party sued within the relevant limitation period. V had suffered a stroke on August 11, 1992, but issued proceedings on August 21, 1998, 10 days outside the limitation period if that started to run from the date of the stroke. V contended that the period started 30 days later, as condition 16 of the policy stated that the insurer would pay out 30 days after the confirmed diagnosis, if the insured survived for that period. GL contended that there was a lack of clear wording to displace the presumption that liability arose upon the occurrence of the event insured. V appealed.

Held, allowing the appeal, that condition 16 established a condition precedent to liability that V should survive for 30 days after the stroke; liability did not therefore arise until 30 days later, and GL had been sued within the original limitation period, *Callaghan v. Dominion Insurance Co Ltd* [1997] 2 Lloyd's Rep. 541, [1997] C.L.Y. 3139 distinguished. The naming of the incorrect party was careless but GHLP had suffered no prejudice.

VIRK v. GAN LIFE HOLDINGS PLC [2000] Lloyd's Rep. I.R.159, Potter, L.J., CA.

531. Limitations – personal injuries – psychiatric harm – father's reaction to child's death in utero – consequential stillbirth not part of same event – requirement of shock reaction

[Limitation Act 1980 s.33.]

T's pregnant wife was negligently treated on the day of her elective Caesarean section with the result that the baby died in utero before the operation and was stillborn by Caesarean on May 11, 1987, approximately four hours after her death. T, who was present during the operation, had been informed of the death by the hospital over the telephone 20 minutes after it occurred and had travelled to the hospital immediately. He held the dead baby at delivery and from time to time overnight and saw her placed in a metal box the next day. In 1993, during the preparation of his wife's claim, he was informed by her solicitors of the possibility of making a claim in relation to his subsequent psychiatric reaction, which had contributed to his losing his job and suffering prolonged bouts of depression. Negotiations commenced and proceedings were issued in 1995, against ELHA, the health authority.

Held, dismissing the claim, that (1) T's claim was statute barred, as he knew by May 12, 1987 that the death was caused by medical negligence; (2) the primary limitation period would however be disapplied pursuant to the Limitation Act 1980 s.33, because the evidence was intact, there was no prejudice to ELHA save in relation to interest, which prejudice could be remedied and T had relied on solicitors to pursue his claim; (3) the claim would nonetheless be dismissed as the cause of action was the death, which was a separate event to the stillbirth and at which T was not present, nor did he witness the immediate aftermath of it, *Alcock v. Chief Constable of South Yorkshire* [1992] 1 A.C. 310, [1992] C.L.Y. 3250 applied, *Tredget v. Bexley HA* [1994] 5 Med. L.R. 178 distinguished. T's injury was not caused by shock as required by *Alcock* since the Caesarean section was planned and T chose to attend, knowing that a stillbirth would occur.

TAN v. EAST LONDON AND CITY HA [1999] Lloyd's Rep. Med. 389, Judge Ludlow, CC (Chelmsford).

532. Limitations – professional negligence – date of loss – collective investment schemes

See NEGLIGENCE: Gordon v. JB Wheatley & Co. §4256

533. Limitations – professional negligence – no imputed knowledge of undervaluation by lender – negligence claim not time barred

[Limitation Act 1980 s.14A.]

L, a valuer, appealed against a decision ([1999] Lloyd's Rep. P.N. 947, [1999] C.L.Y. 478) on a preliminary issue that MC's negligence claim was not time barred, by virtue of the Limitation Act 1980 s.14A. MC lent £176,631 on the strength of L's valuation in April 1990 of a property at £250,000. The mortgagor defaulted and in 1996 the property was eventually repossessed and sold for only £100,000. During the course of attempting to obtain possession two debt collecting agents reports had suggested to MC in 1992 and June 1993 lower valuations of the property. Proceedings were issued on October 15, 1996. A contractual claim was clearly time barred, however MC argued that, as facts relevant to the cause of action were not known when the cause of action accrued, s.14A applied and limitation could run from three years from when MC first had knowledge that the property had been undervalued. L contended that MC had that knowledge prior to October 15 1993, and therefore the claim was statute barred.

Held, dismissing the appeal, that there was no evidence to support the proposition that it was reasonable for MC to have obtained the requisite knowledge by commissioning a retrospective valuation prior to October 1993. MC could not be said to have acted unreasonably by waiting to take possession before carrying out valuations of the property, including a retrospective valuation. It could not be said that MC had the requisite knowledge, actual or imputed prior to October 1993 and therefore the claim had been brought within the limitation period.

MORTGAGE CORP PLC v. LAMBERT & CO [2000] Lloyd's Rep. Bank. 207, Chadwick, L.J., CA.

534. Limitations – professional negligence – requirements for deemed concealment under the Limitation Act 1980 s.32(2)

[Limitation Act 1939; Limitation Act 1980 s.32, s.32(1)(b), s.32(2); Taxes Act 1988 s.505.]

In 1989 G, a tax specialist, provided advice to L, a charity, in relation to the applicability of the exemption under the Taxes Act 1988 s.505 to the profits made by L from the sale of alcoholic drinks. G confirmed his advice in 1992. Following the Revenue raising its assessments in 1993, L, without the knowledge of G, received guidance from others that G's advice was probably incorrect and possibly negligent. L continued to receive advice from G as to how to negotiate with the Revenue. Using G's advice L, after negotiations, reached an agreement with the Revenue in 1996 whereby only 20 per cent of the total due would be paid in satisfaction of the full claim. Subsequently, L issued proceedings against G in 1997 alleging negligence and breach of duty in relation to the advice provided in 1989, 1992 and thereafter. In a proposed amendment to their reply L sought permission to contend that the advice of G in 1989 amounted to the deliberate commission of a breach of duty within the meaning of the Limitation Act 1980 s.32(2). G applied for summary judgment in relation to L's claims in respect of his advice in 1989 on the ground that they had no prospect of success. G argued that the requirements of s.32, that the impropriety of the defendant had suspended the running of the limitation period and that facts must have been concealed, had not been met.

Held, dismissing the application, that for the purposes of s.32 of the 1980 Act, notwithstanding whether a defendant had concealed a fact from a claimant, there was a deliberate concealment in circumstances where a knowing breach of duty had been perpetrated which was not likely to be discovered for some time. The need to show dishonesty was inconsistent with the intention behind the amendment of the Limitation Act 1939. It was not necessary for the purposes of extending the limitation period under s.32(1)(b) to show deliberate concealment of the relevant fact to any extent greater than that the undertaking of the act was deliberate by way of being intentional, and that such an act was in breach of duty, regardless of whether the actor realised that consequence, *Sheldon v. RHM Outhwaite (Underwriting Agencies) Ltd* [1996] A.C. 102, [1995] C.L.Y. 3159 and *Brocklesby v. Armitage & Guest* [1999] Lloyd's Rep. P.N. 888, [2000] C.L.Y. 4274 considered.

LIVERPOOL ROMAN CATHOLIC ARCHDIOCESAN TRUSTEES INC v. GOLDBERG (NO.1) [2001] 1 All E.R. 182, Laddie, J., Ch D.

535. Limitations – service out of time – extension of time limits – general provision could not override specific provision within rules

[Civil Procedure Rules 1998 (SI 1998 3132) Part 3 r.3.9, Part 7 r.7.6(3)(b).]

C appealed a decision granting K an extension of time within which to serve a claim form, pursuant to the Civil Procedure Rules 1998 Part 7 r.7.6(3)(b), K's solicitor having served the claim out of time. C contended that the court at first instance had erred in concluding that K could be brought within the scope of Part 7 r.7.6(3)(b) on the basis that difficulties and the time taken to prepare a schedule of damages and medical report, which K was bound to serve with the particulars of claim, could be included in the consideration of whether reasonable steps had been taken to serve the particulars within the prescribed time.

Held, allowing the appeal, that (1) Part 7 r.7.6(3)(b) referred to physical service of the claim form and supporting documentation and as to whether physical service had been reasonably attempted. In the instant case there had been no adequate explanation for the failure to serve the schedule of special damage within the prescribed time, the delay having resulted simply from the solicitor's mistake in relation to the date by which he must serve the claim form, and (2) Part 7 r.7.6(3) granted the court power to extend time limits "only if" the stipulated conditions were fulfilled, which meant that the court did not possess the power to do so otherwise. Moreover, the general provision for relief from any sanction imposed, provided by Part 3 r.3.9, could not override the specific provisions detailed within Part 7 r.7.6, *Vinos v. Marks & Spencer Plc The Independent*, July 17, 2000 (C.S.), [2000] C.P.L.R. 570 applied.

KAUR v. CTP COIL LTD [2001] C.P. Rep. 34, Waller, L.J., CA.

536. Limitations – striking out – amendment to pleadings to be considered before striking out whole claim

In April 1985 S instructed GMC, solicitors, in relation to a dispute with his council over the transfer of land. Dissatisfied with them, S instructed others in October 1989 and complained to the Solicitors Complaints Bureau in February 1991. On May 17, 1991, S instructed CP in a claim against GMC on the basis that GMC disregarded S's instructions in permitting certain provisions to be included in the transfer of land. On April 28, 1997, S issued a writ against CP alleging that they had failed to bring proceedings against GMC within the limitation period, including a claim for psychological distress amounting to grievous bodily harm. On February 24, 1998 the master struck out the latter part of the claim, and five or six days prior to S's appeal out of time against that, CP notified S that if he pursued his appeal they would seek to strike out the whole claim, which they did. On appeal, the judge upheld the decision to strike out the claim in relation to personal injury, and the balance of the claim, holding that he was entitled to do so on the appeal as the matter was a rehearing. C appealed the striking out of the balance of his claim.

Held, allowing the appeal, that (1) it was not necessary for CP to serve a notice of cross appeal, as the judge's jurisdiction was not fettered by the exercise of the master's discretion; S was not taken by surprise given CP's notification of the point, although consideration should be given to embodying the practice of such informal notification in a practice direction, *Evans v. Bartlam* [1937] A.C. 473 applied; (2) the balance of the claim was struck out on the technical basis of the quality of the pleading, which could be cured by amendment; the question of a possible amendment should have been considered on the strike out application and was not; (3) S's claim independent of his personal injury claim had a six year limitation period which had not expired by the time of the hearing before the master, and (4) as S could have pursued the balance of the claim within the limitation period in fresh proceedings, leave to amend the claim should have been given.

SHADE v. COMPTON PARTNERSHIP [2000] Lloyd's Rep. P.N. 81, Robert Walker, L.J., CA.

537. Litigants in person – rights of audience – representation by lay person – husband permitted to represent wife

[Courts and Legal Services Act 1990 s.27, s.27(2)(c), s.27(2A).]

C, a litigant in person, brought proceedings against G for conspiracy, inducement to breach of contract and libel. C's husband, who had completed his Bar finals but had not been called to the Bar, applied without notice to be granted a right of audience on the grounds that C was of ill health and without means. The judge having granted permission under the Courts and Legal Services Act 1990 s.27(2)(c), G applied for the order to be set aside on the basis that the evidence before the judge in relation to C's health and means had been insufficient to justify it. The judge, finding the exercise of the discretion under s.27(2)(c) to be appropriate only in exceptional circumstances, allowed the application and set the order aside. C appealed.

Held, allowing the appeal, that (1) the fact that it would be difficult for a husband to comply with a requirement under s.27(2A) to act independently in the course of advocacy should not, in the interests of justice, preclude him from appearing for his wife. The court should, however, be satisfied that it was right in the circumstances to extend rights of audience. Accordingly, a litigant in person wishing to have someone without rights of audience act for them was required, where circumstances allowed, to explain to the court why such help was needed; (2) objections which existed to granting rights of audience to an unauthorised person who had set up an advocacy service did not apply to someone wishing to represent a member of the same family, or alternately, it was appropriate to grant rights of audience as such circumstances were exceptional, *D v. S (Rights of Audience)* [1997] 1 F.L.R. 724, [1997] C.L.Y. 49 considered, and (3) an order having been made, a litigant in person should still attend court when matters affecting their interest were discussed.

CLARKSON v. GILBERT [2000] C.P. Rep. 58, Lord Woolf of Barnes, L.C.J., CA.

538. **Magistrates courts – appeals – repairs notices – water companies – power of non party to intervene in appeal process**

[Building Act 1984 s.59, s.102; Magistrates Courts Rules 1981 (SI 1981 552) r.34.]

NWW sought judicial review of a decision by the justices refusing leave to intervene in proceedings commenced by S by way of appeal against a notice served by the local authority pursuant to the Building Act 1984 s.59. The notice stipulated that the sewer to S's property was private, that it was defective, and that accordingly he was responsible for both effecting and financing repairs. S submitted an appeal pursuant to s.102 of the Act. NWW applied to be joined in the action to protect its interests, but its application was dismissed on the basis that the justices lacked the necessary power to make such an order.

Held, granting the application, that the pending appeal process was governed by the Magistrates Courts Rules 1981 r.34. It was accordingly a civil process under which the justices were entitled to admit evidence not normally admissible in civil proceedings. It was appropriate to grant the order sought, since NWW would be directly affected by the outcome of the proceedings, potentially being liable to effect the repairs itself if the sewer was found to be in public ownership, *Lloyd v. McMahon* [1987] A.C. 625, [1987] C.L.Y. 3162 applied. Furthermore, if relief was denied there would be an undesirable duplication of proceedings, with NWW being obliged to invoke an alternative civil jurisdiction to resolve the matter.

R. v. PRESTON MAGISTRATES COURT, *ex p.* NORTH WEST WATER LTD [2000] E.H.L.R. 390, Morison, J., QBD.

539. **Part 36 offers – enhanced costs rule not applicable to summary judgments**

[Civil Procedure Rules 1998 (SI 1998 3132) Part 24 r.24.1, Part 36 r.36.21.]

P was granted summary judgment against T for $140,660 relating to gasoil supplied to T, and partly unpaid for. T appealed, contending that the judge had erred in concluding that the contract between the parties incorporated terms requiring payment in full, without any allowance for deduction, set off or counterclaim. P cross appealed the judge's refusal to award enhanced interest and indemnity costs, submitting that as the judgment made in their favour was for a sum in excess of their Part 36 offer, they were entitled to such costs pursuant to the Civil Procedure Rules 1998 Part 36 r.36.21.

Held, dismissing the appeal and cross appeal, that (1) the terms regarding payment had been incorporated, and T had no prospect of defeating the claim or advancing a successful counterclaim, and (2) with respect to P's cross appeal, the consequences of Part 36 r.36.21 applied where a trial had taken place, and therefore did not apply to summary judgment under the Civil Procedure Rules 1998 Part 24 r.24 where determination was made without trial. Nevertheless the court always had the general power to award costs on an indemnity basis and to award interest at such a rate as it considered just, and in circumstances such as these, where an offer to settle had been made by the claimant, the court ought to bear in mind that general power, otherwise claimants might be deterred from seeking summary judgment in the hope of obtaining higher interest rates after a trial. That would be contrary to the ethos and policy of the Civil Procedure Rules 1998. In the instant case, if the matter had been for his Lordships discretion at first instance, then an interest award of four per cent above base rate for 12 months, and indemnity costs from the date of the Part 36 offer may have been appropriate. However, the judge's decision would not be interfered with, as Part 36 r.36.21 had not been raised before him, and it would be wrong to interfere with his discretion where he had not had placed before him the arguments which might have compelled him to take a different view.

PETROTRADE INC v. TEXACO LTD [2001] C.P. Rep. 29, Clarke, L.J., CA.

540. Part 36 offers – offer and acceptance – withdrawal of Part 36 offers

[Civil Procedure Rules 1998 (SI 1998 3132) Part 36 r.36(5)(8), r.36(6).]

B's solicitors sent a "without prejudice" letter to P's solicitors. The offer contained therein was rejected by P. During the trial, B made an open offer which was subsequently withdrawn. Having read the draft judgment, P applied to accept the original offer, contending that it was a Part 36 offer open for 21 days and could be accepted with the court's permission.

Held, dismissing the application, that Part 36 offers could be freely withdrawn under Part 36 r.36(5)(8) without the court's permission. In the instant case, applying the rules of offer and acceptance in ascertaining whether there had been a compromise in a pending litigation, B had withdrawn the offer prior to P's acceptance.

DEW PITCHMASTIC PLC v. BIRSE CONSTRUCTION LTD (COMPROMISE); *sub nom.* PITCHMASTIC PLC v. BIRST CONSTRUCTION LTD *The Times*, June 21, 2000, Dyson, J., QBD.

541. Part 36 offers – terms of offer – determination by court where terms unclear

[Civil Procedure Rules 1998 (SI 1998 3132) Part 36.]

F successfully applied to the court for a declaration that the instant case had been settled prior to commencement of proceedings (*Malik v. FM De Rooy (No.1)* (Unreported, April 4, 2000), [2000] C.L.Y. 1456) following the acceptance of an offer made pursuant to the Civil Procedure Rules 1998 Part 36 in the sum of £5,500, stated to be in full settlement of the claim, but later qualified as being in respect of the difference in value of the vehicle, incidental expenses and other special damages. F had accepted the offer "in full and final settlement" in writing, and had sent a cheque for £500, representing the balance outstanding after an earlier interim payment. M had replied stating that the Part 36 offer had not taken into account any interim payments made. M appealed.

Held, allowing the appeal, that M's Part 36 offer and F's purported acceptance had not amounted to a concluded settlement. The words of the offer referring to the "difference in valuation" could only refer to the difference in the parties' expert's valuations of the vehicle. It followed that the offer must have excluded the £5,000 already paid on account. Indeed, since the offer did not refer to general damages, it would have been open to M to argue that they were entitled to those in addition. The judge found that even if his decision in that respect was wrong, he would have concluded in the light of the previous correspondence that M's solicitors had made a mistake and ordered rescission, OT Africa Line Ltd v. Vickers Plc [1996] 1 Lloyd's Rep. 700, [1996] C.L.Y. 1227 considered.

MALIK v. FM DE ROOY (NO.2), July 13, 2000, Judge Tetlow, CC (Manchester). [*Ex rel.* Laura Elfield, Barrister, 5 Pump Court, Temple, London].

542. Part 36 offers – validity – failure to comply with CPR r.36.5(6)(b) requirements – requirements directory not mandatory

[Civil Procedure Rules 1998 (SI 1998 3132) Part 36.]

Eight months before trial, DH wrote a letter expressed on its face to be a "formal offer made under Part 36 CPR". It complied in all respects with the requirements of the Civil Procedure Rules 1998 Part 36, save that it did not state that after 21 days the offeree could only accept the offer if the parties agreed the liability for costs, or the court gave permission, as provided by r.36.5(6)(b), nor were any words to like effect included in the letter. On the morning of the trial, L gave notice of acceptance under Part 36 r.36.12(2)(b)(i), purporting to accept DH's Part 36 offer on terms that L paid the costs of the action. DH asserted that in the absence of the words required by r.36.5(6)(b) the letter was not a valid Part 36 offer and so was not capable of acceptance under Part 36 r.36.12.

Held, that the use of the word "formal" on the face of the letter was not of itself enough to include by inference the words required by Part 36 r.36.5(6); (2) the judge was not convinced that DH was estopped from denying the assertion on the face of the letter that it was a Part 36 offer; (3) it was not open to L to waive the apparent procedural irregularity, and (4) the requirement to specify the information in Part 36 r.36.5(6)(b) was directory not mandatory and the absence of that information was not fatal. Accordingly, the letter was a valid Part 36 offer which had, in the circumstances, been accepted by L.

DAVID HALLAM LTD v. LANGFORD, February 10, 2000, Judge Bullimore, CC (Sheffield). [*Ex rel.* Graham Robinson, Barrister, Paradise Chambers, 26 Paradise Square, Sheffield].

543. Part 36 payments – case management – use as a disciplinary measure

[Civil Procedure Rules 1998 (SI 1998 3132).]

D appealed against an order upholding the master's decision, made at a case management conference at which TC had applied for summary judgment, that he should make a Part 36 payment. TC had made the application for summary judgment during a protracted dispute concerning its claim in respect of the non payment of £266,000 commission by D. D, who had not filed a sufficient defence, asserted that he had a counterclaim against an agent of TC which had not been pleaded. The master refused the application for summary judgment and ordered a Part 36 payment of £200,000 later reduced to £100,000. When D appealed following the master's decision to uphold the order, he contended that (1) the order was disproportionate and had been made to mark disapproval of the handling of the case, and (2) the summary judgment application had been flawed, having been made against the wrong party and out of time, with the result that the order providing for the Part 36 payment should not have been made.

Held, dismissing the appeal, that (1) the order was not disproportionate and had been made as a means of protecting D's opportunity to plead his counterclaim. Although the master had drawn attention to the delay in pleading the counterclaim, and to the need to encourage the progression of the case, those criteria had not been the sole reasons for the decision, and (2) the application for summary judgment had been permissible in the circumstances, and by virtue of the Civil Procedure Rules 1998. The judge had been correct not to set aside the master's order for payment in, notwithstanding the fully pleaded counterclaim which was produced to him, since to have done so would have removed the incentive to drive the case forward, which the court was required to do under the Rules. Furthermore, the judge had satisfied himself on the evidence of D's means before him that D was able to provide the sum required, notwithstanding his difficulties in achieving it, *MV Yorke Motors v. Edwards* [1982] 1 W.L.R. 444, [1982] C.L.Y. 2398 applied.

TRAINING IN COMPLIANCE LTD (T/A MATTHEW READ) v. DEWSE (T/A DATA RESEARCH CO) [2001] C.P. Rep. 46, Buxton, L.J., CA.

544. Part 36 payments – claimant seeking breakdown of payment in

[Civil Procedure Rules 1998 (SI 1998 3132) Part 36 r.36.9.]

In July 1999, EFC made a Part 36 payment and within seven days, S requested clarification pursuant to the Civil Procedure Rules 1998 Part 36 r.36.9 as to the amount included in the Part 36 payment for general damages and the amount for special damages. The request was rejected by EFC and S applied for an order that EFC provide the information requested. The application was dismissed and S appealed, contending that the overriding objective included the identification of disputes or areas of agreement, open litigation and the saving of costs. EFC submitted that the purpose of Part 36 r.36.9 could plainly be seen by considering the absence of such a Rule and the guidance contained in the Practice Direction -Offers to Settle and Payments into Court. Further, that the Practice Direction clearly referred to clarification of the terms of the offer, whereas S was requesting particularisation of the offer that went beyond the wording of both Part 36 r.36.9 and the Practice Direction.

Held, dismissing the appeal, that the offer was made in clear and acceptable terms. The Rules only required clarification of the terms of the offer itself rather than any form of breakdown.

SHARP v. EUROPA FREIGHT CORP LTD, September 27, 1999, Judge Bartfield, CC (Sheffield). [*Ex rel.* Fancy & Jackson Solicitors, Apex House, 54-56 Park St, Camberley, Surrey].

545. Part 36 payments – global settlement offer acceptable – no requirement for breakdown

[Civil Procedure Rules 1998 (SI 1998 3132) Part 36.]

M brought a claim for damages for personal injuries arising out of an accident on RBP's boat. RBP made a global offer under the Civil Procedure Rules 1998 Part 36 to settle the whole claim which was later supported by a payment into court of the same amount. M requested a breakdown of general and special damages. RBP refused and M made an application under Part 36 r.36.9 of the 1998 Rules for clarification of the Part 36 Offer, arguing that he could not be properly advised without knowing the breakdown of the offer. RBP resisted the application on the grounds that (1) Civil Procedure Rules 1998 Part 36 PD 36 para.6.1 to 6.3, there was no power to seek a breakdown of the actual offer, only a power to seek clarification of the terms of the offer; (2) if there was such a power, the court's discretion should not be exercised because of the potential practical difficulties involved, particularly regarding future assessment of costs and forcing a defendant to give a breakdown that was never intended, and (3) in any event, the application was not made in good time and failed to comply with Civil Procedure Rules 1998 Part 36 PD 36 para.3.1 by stating the terms in which RBP's Part 36 Offer was said to need clarification.

Held, dismissing the application, that (1) under Part 36 r.36.5, RBP was entitled to make a global offer in the terms that it did; (2) the interests of justice require a defendant to be able to take a commercial view of a case and to make a global offer, not necessarily arrived at by any scientific means, in order to promote settlement, and (3) it was never RBP's intention to distinguish between general and special damages and to order it to make such a distinction would be entirely artificial, *Campion v. Bradley* (Unreported, May 6, 1999), [1999] C.L.Y. 1410 and *Sharp v. Europa Freight Corp Ltd* (Unreported, September 27, 1999), [2000] C.L.Y. 544 considered.

MACDONALD v. RICHMOND BOAT PROJECT, March 16, 2000, District Judge Harvey, CC (Staines). [*Ex rel.* William Latimer-Sayer, Barrister, Cloisters, 7 Pump Court, Temple, London].

546. Part 36 payments – tender before action – notice of payment must be served

[Rules of the Supreme Court 1965 (SI 1965 1776) Ord.18 r.16, Ord.22 r.1 (2).]

W appealed against an unless order requiring service of notice of a Part 36 payment. He contended that, although the failure was a technical breach of the Rules of the Supreme Court Ord.22 r.1 (2), notice of the Part 36 payment was not required where it was made in support of a fully pleaded defence of tender before action under Ord.18 r.16.

Held, dismissing the appeal, that payment under Ord.18 r.16 had to be in accordance with Ord.22 and the Part 36 payment did not comply with Ord.22 r.1 (2) unless proper notice on the prescribed form was served.

GREENING (T/A AUTOMANIA) v.WILLIAMS [2000] C.P. Rep. 40, Ferris, J., CA.

547. Parties – joinder – financial backer – court's refusal to join as a party

[Civil Procedure Rules 1998 (SI 1998 3132) Part 48 r.48.2.]

P, a financial backer of H's unsuccessful libel action against A, applied to be joined as a party to H's application for permission to appeal. He also sought to be joined as a party to the substantive appeal should the application for permission be successful. P, relying on the Civil Procedure Rules Part 48 r.48.2 and the case of *Gurtner v. Circuit* [1968] 2 Q.B. 587, [1968] C.L.Y. 3160 argued that he should, in the interests of justice, be allowed to join the dispute. Moreover, P asserted that if he were not allowed to join the proceedings, despite his financial interest in the case, he would suffer prejudice because no opportunity would be afforded to raise any objections to the conduct of A which would be relevant in the court's decision regarding awarding costs against P.

Held, dismissing the application, that a person agreeing to provide financial assistance to a party to litigation was not entitled to be joined in the proceedings merely on the basis of his assumption of financial risk. Anyone agreeing to provide financial backing in such a manner was thereby exposed to the risk of financial loss and of not being given any opportunity to raise objections. The case of *Gurtner* was distinguishable as, in that case, the defendant was taking no part in the proceedings, and so unless the financially interested applicant was allowed to join, judgment by default would have been entered in the plaintiff's favour, and the applicant was, in any event, bound to satisfy the judgment.

HAMILTON v. AL FAYED (JOINED PARTY) *The Times*, October 13, 2000, Lord Phillips of Worth Matravers, M.R., CA.

548. Personal injuries – preliminary issues – adequacy of warning on product – issue could not be isolated as preliminary issue where evidence linked with causation

W claimed damages after contracting toxic shock syndrome caused by tampons manufactured by T. Although it was accepted that W had suffered the condition and damages were agreed, liability remained in issue. T appealed against a determination that the question of whether the warning on the product was adequate should be tried as a preliminary issue. T argued that whether the warning was adequate or not was inextricably linked with other issues, such as causation and liability, and to separate it out in this way would cause difficulties.

Held, allowing the appeal, that as the evidence on the issue of causation and the adequacy of warnings was inextricably linked, the judge was plainly wrong to isolate the issues in this way. The object of saving time and expense could not be achieved by isolating issues that were linked.

WORSLEY v. TAMBRANDS LTD (PRELIMINARY HEARING) [2000] C.P. Rep. 43, Auld, L.J., CA.

549. Pleadings – amendments – contributory negligence – failure to mitigate

[Consumer Credit Act 1974; Civil Procedure Rules 1998 (SI 1998 3132).]

P's car was written off following a road traffic accident and he subsequently claimed damages against H, inter alia, for hire car charges for an initial one month period and subsequent loss of use for 15 months. On the day of the trial H applied to amend his defence to plead (1) contributory negligence; (2) P's failure to mitigate his losses on the basis that P could have made a claim on his fully comprehensive insurance policy for the write off value of his car and/or could have borrowed monies to buy a replacement, and (3) the Consumer Credit Act 1974 in respect of P's claim for hire charges.

Held, giving judgment for P in part, that H would be permitted to amend his defence to plead contributory negligence but permission for the other amendments was refused. The purpose of pleadings under the Civil Procedure Rules 1998 was to put one's case on a clear basis such that both parties knew the case they would have to meet at trial. To allow H to amend to plead failure to mitigate would put P at an unfair disadvantage because the question of whether the "fruits of an insurance policy" could be relied upon by H in alleging such a failure was a complex legal issue that P's counsel should have time to consider. Any amendment to plead the 1974 Act should have been made some months ago in order that P have the opportunity to call a representative from the hire company to give evidence. P's damages were reduced by 25 per cent to take into account his contributory negligence.

PEETH v. HOLSTEIN, October 2, 2000, Judge Holman, CC (Manchester). [*Ex rel.* NDH Edwards, Barrister, 8 King Street Chambers, Manchester].

550. Pleadings – amendments – requirement for genuine mistake survives in Civil Procedure Rules

[Rules of the Supreme Court Ord.20 r.5; Civil Procedure Rules 1998 (SI 1998 3132) r.17.4(3), r.19.4.]

ID appealed against the refusal of its application to substitute S for four of its subsidiaries which had been included as defendants by mistake in proceedings for conversion of a shipment of champagne. ID contended that, unlike the Rules of the Supreme Court Ord.20 r.5, the Civil Procedure Rules 1998 r.17.4(3) and r.19.4 did not include a reference to the need to show either a genuine mistake or reasonable doubt as to the identity of a party.

Held, allowing the appeal, that permission to amend the writs was granted. While not formally required under simplified statement in the Rules, it would be unlikely for an application for substitution to succeed unless the mistake was genuine and there had been no real change in the law.

INTERNATIONAL DISTILLERS AND VINTERS LTD v. JF HILLEBRAND (UK) LTD *The Times*, January 25, 2000, David Foskett Q.C., QBD.

551. Pleadings – evidence – inclusion of evidence – exceptionally allowed in strike out application

[Rules of the Supreme Court 1965 (SI 1965 1776) Ord.18 r.7.]

B challenged the refusal of its application to strike out claims brought by the liquidators of an insolvent bank alleging that B was a knowing party to fraudulent trading with an intention to defraud creditors. B contended that the pleadings referred to precise words in documents, in breach of the Rules of the Supreme Court Ord.18 r.7, which required that pleadings be a summary of the facts relied upon without evidence, and that the judge had failed to apply the appropriate test in deciding whether the claims should be struck out for failing to comply with procedural rules.

Held, dismissing the appeal, that in exceptional cases the inclusion of evidence in the form of precise words from documents in a statement of claim was permissible, not only in proceedings for defamation or misrepresentation, but where the words within the documents were material. Evidence was not normally acceptable on an interlocutory application to strike out unless the application appeared likely to be successful and a full trial could be avoided and, in the instant case, B had been unable to show that no inference of knowledge in relation to the insolvent bank's activities could be made.

MORRIS v. BANK OF AMERICA NATIONAL TRUST (APPEAL AGAINST STRIKING OUT) [2000] 1 All E.R. 954, Morritt, L.J., CA.

552. Practice directions – appeals from Lands Tribunal to Court of Appeal

[Civil Procedure Rules 1998 (SI 1998 3132) Part 52; Civil Procedure (Modification of Enactments) Order 2000 (SI 2000 941).]

The Lands Tribunal issued a Practice Direction superseding *Practice Direction (Lands Tr: Appeals: Applications) (No.1 of 1999)* [1999] R.V.R. 2 concerning appeals from the tribunal to the Court of Appeal.

Held, that the requirement for appeals on points of law to be by way of case stated was removed by the Civil Procedure (Modification of Enactments) Order 2000. Such appeals are now governed by the Civil Procedure Rules 1998 Part 52 with permission being required in every case. Applications for permission must be made to the tribunal in the first instance within 28 days of the decision. Applications following a refusal by the tribunal, or seeking an extension to the time limit, are to be made to the Court of Appeal. The proposed grounds of appeal must be set out. Permission will not ordinarily be granted unless there is a real prospect that the Court of Appeal could reach a different conclusion on a point of law. Notes made by tribunal members will not ordinarily be made available to the parties and disclosure will only rarely be allowed, *Blue Circle Industries Plc v. West Midlands CC* [1994] 20 E.G. 149, [1995] C.L.Y. 671 referred to.

PRACTICE DIRECTION (LANDS TR: APPEALS: APPLICATIONS) [2000] R.V.R. 223, Judge not specified, Lands Tr.

553. Practice directions – child abuse – management of claims arising from maltreatment and assault at Kilrie Children's Home

The Lord Chief Justice issued a Practice Direction regarding personal injury claims for damages for alleged child abuse, maltreatment and assault that had taken place at Kilrie Children's Home, to be read in conjunction with the directions order of November 25, 1999. All such claims must be received by 4 pm on April 28, 2000 and should be commenced in the appropriate county court but would be transferred to the Manchester District Registry without further order. Further directions were included.

PRACTICE DIRECTION (QBD: KILRIE CHILDREN'S HOME LITIGATION) *The Times*, February 1, 2000, Lord Bingham of Cornhill, L.C.J., QBD.

554. Practice directions – Commercial Court – time estimates for summonses

A Practice Direction was published by the Queen's Bench Division (Commercial Court) concerning time estimates for commercial summonses. It provides that (1) if an individual summons is likely to exceed the time limits prescribed by the Commercial Court Guide, Appendix 1, Practice Direction (9), Supreme Court Practice para.72/A25, an application for additional time should be made to the judge responsible for the Commercial Court list supported by a written explanation for the request; (2) if no such application is made and the time allotted is subsequently discovered to be insufficient, the judge hearing the summons would possess a discretion to adjourn the matter to a date to be fixed and make such other orders including wasted costs orders as might be appropriate, and (3) a separate time estimate would be required for all summonses issued after an initial summons had been allocated a hearing date and intended to be heard in conjunction with the initial summons unless counsel or solicitors had certified that (i) the resolution of the application made in the earlier summons would prove determinative of the later application, or (ii) the subject matter of the subsequent summons was not contested.

PRACTICE DIRECTION (COMM CT: TIME ESTIMATES FOR COMMERCIAL SUMMONSES) [2000] 1 Lloyd's Rep. 626, Judge not specified, QBD (Comm Ct).

555. Practice directions – Creutzfeldt-Jakob disease litigation – transfer to Queens Bench Division

The Lord Chief Justice issued a Practice Direction in respect of Creutzfeldt-Jakob disease litigation, that all cases brought by claimants claiming damages for the contraction of Creutzfeldt-Jakob disease or psychiatric illness caused by the discovery that they were at risk should be commenced in or transferred to the Queen's Bench Division of the High Court. The assigned master would be the senior master, and the assigned judge. All documents should be marked on the top left hand side with the words "CJD Litigation".

PRACTICE DIRECTION (CREUTZFELDT-JAKOB DISEASE LITIGATION: DAMAGES) (2000) 54 B.M.L.R. 174, Lord Bingham of Cornhill, L.C.J., Court not specified.

556. Practice directions – group actions for post traumatic stress disorder and combat stress reaction – transfer of actions against Ministry of Defence

The Lord Chief Justice issued a Practice Direction concerning the conduct of group actions against the Ministry of Defence for damages for psychiatric harm.

Held, that all current actions against the Ministry of Defence for damages for psychiatric harm, whether for post traumatic stress disorder or for combat stress reaction, required immediate transfer to the Royal Courts of Justice and all new actions should be commenced there in the Central Office of the QBD. All such actions would be allocated to the multi track regardless of claim value where specific Masters were assigned to deal with them.

PRACTICE DIRECTION (QBD: POST TRAUMATIC STRESS DISORDER LITIGATION AGAINST MINISTRY OF DEFENCE: GROUP ACTIONS) *The Times*, November 26, 1999, Lord Bingham of Cornhill, L.C.J., Sup Ct.

557. Practice directions – House of Lords – amended civil appeal procedure

Held, that (1) appellants are to prepare statements of fact to be agreed between the parties on issues involved in the appeal, disputed material being included in each party's case; (2) transcripts of unreported judgments should only be cited when they contain an authoritative statement of a relevant legal principle not found in a reported case or are necessary for the understanding of another authority; (3) provide directions on the documents to be produced by the parties, the number of copies required, and the presentation of authorities, and (4) to delete the reference to *Ainsbury v. Millington* [1987] 1 W.L.R. 379, [1987] C.L.Y. 2886 in Practice Direction 42.

PRACTICE DIRECTION (HL: CIVIL PROCEDURE AMENDMENTS) [1999] 1 W.L.R. 1833, Judge not applicable, HL.

558. Practice directions – Mercantile Courts – institution of new lists

The Lord Chief Justice issued a Practice Direction in English and Welsh instituting a new Queen's Bench list in the Cardiff Registry to be named the "Cardiff Mercantile Court List" and in the Chester District Registry to be named the "Chester Mercantile Court List".

PRACTICE DIRECTION (MERC CT: WALES AND CHESTER) [2000] 1 W.L.R. 208, Lord Bingham of Cornhill, L.C.J., QBD (Merc Ct).

559. Practice directions – reading lists and hearing length estimates – Chancery and Queen's Bench Divisions

The Vice Chancellor issued a Practice Direction detailing the need for a reading list and two hearing length estimates, agreed by all advocates involved, to be produced in cases where agreed bundles have to be lodged with either the Chancery or Queen's Bench Divisions. The requirement took effect from January 11, 2000 and compliance was the claimant's or the applicant's responsibility.

PRACTICE DIRECTION (ROYAL COURTS OF JUSTICE: READING LIST: TIME ESTIMATES) [2000] 1 W.L.R. 208, Lord Bingham of Cornhill, L.C.J., Ch D.

560. Practice statements – Companies Court – end to practice of reserving company matters to companies judge for listing on Mondays

The Vice Chancellor issued a Practice Statement superseding all previous Practice Directions pertaining to the Monday list procedure in the Companies Court.

Held, that with effect from January 11, 2000 the practice of listing matters for hearing by the companies judge on Mondays was to cease. All such matters could now be issued for hearing on any day during term time and the applications judge dealing with general Chancery applications would also be available to deal with company matters previously listed for Monday hearings.

PRACTICE STATEMENT (COMPANIES CT: APPLICATIONS); *sub nom.* PRACTICE STATEMENT (COMPANIES CT: HEARINGS) [2000] 1 W.L.R. 209, Sir Richard Scott V.C., Ch D.

561. Pre-action protocols – time limits – liability for costs and interest where full payment made within three months of pre-action letter

N had claimed repair costs in respect of a cable negligently damaged by S. Liability was not in issue. S had notified N of the damage, following which N issued an invoice to S for the cost of the repairs. S ignored the invoice. N issued a 21 day letter which was also ignored by S. N instructed solicitors, who issued a seven day letter to S. Further correspondence passed between N's solicitors and S's claim handlers. N's solicitors delivered a pre-action protocol letter to S's claim handlers with a request for payment within seven days. S's claim handlers did not respond and N issued proceedings on June 24, 1999. On July 13, 1999, S's claim handlers paid the full cost of the repairs. N rejected the payment, demanding that S should pay fixed costs and interest. S disputed the claim on the basis that it had not been allowed three months after delivery of the pre-action protocol letter in which to investigate the claim. N submitted that S had had since first notification in February 1999 to investigate the claim, and that N had therefore not issued proceedings prematurely.

Held, giving judgment for S, that S had tendered cheques of £202.90 and £352.68 respectively in full and final satisfaction of the claim. It was ordered that there be no costs and interest in respect of the proceedings, including the instant application.

NORTHERN ELECTRIC PLC v. STOCKTON ON TEES BC, September 17, 1999, District Judge Robertson, CC (Middlesbrough). [*Ex rel.* Hammond Suddards Solicitors, 2 Park Lane, Leeds].

562. Rehearings – county courts – adducing fresh evidence

[Consumer Credit Act 1974; County Court Rules 1981 (SI 1981 1687) Ord.37 r.1.]

Under an agreement regulated by the Consumer Credit Act 1974, HI, a loan company, lent money to B which was secured by a charge on the matrimonial home. HI subsequently commenced possession proceedings against B following the accrual of arrears in repayments. B, in their defence to the claim, put HI to strict proof in relation to whether HI and the company that had acted as credit broker were licensed under the 1974 Act. At the trial HI produced a licence relating to the wrong broker and the claim was dismissed. HI later applied out of time for a rehearing under the County Court Rules 1981 Ord.37 r.1, arguing that it was able to produce the correct licence. The application having initially been dismissed, HI appealed successfully. The judge, whilst observing that the correct licence could with reasonable diligence have been produced at the trial, found that there would be a substantial risk of prejudice to HI if the claim was not reheard. B appealed, contending, inter alia, that the appropriate considerations for an application under Ord.37 r.1 of the Rules for a rehearing on the ground of fresh evidence were analogous to those relating to an application in the Court of Appeal on an appeal from the High Court.

Held, allowing the appeal, that in determining whether to allow the rehearing of a county court case on the ground of fresh evidence, the matters to be taken into account by a county court judge were analogous to those to which the

Court of Appeal was required to have regard when deciding whether to order a rehearing of a High Court case in equivalent circumstances. Moreover, it was imperative that litigation was not unduly prolonged and that any arguments be put forward at the earliest possible opportunity. The elements laid out in *Ladd v. Marshall* [1954] 1 W.L.R. 1489, [1954] C.L.Y. 2507, though no longer constituting immovable rules, were important guiding principles in deciding whether fresh evidence should be admitted. In the instant case, the judge had erred by carrying out a balancing exercise rather than have regard to the principles enunciated in *Ladd v. Marshall*. It was clear that the evidence could have been available at the time of the trial. *Ladd v. Marshall* considered.

HERTFORDSHIRE INVESTMENTS LTD v. BUBB [2000] 1 W.L.R. 2318, Hale, L.J., CA.

563. Restraint orders – good arguable case of fraud – restraint order should not have been set aside

UB, who alleged that the defendants had been parties to fraud, appealed against a decision setting aside a restraint order against the defendants. UB contended that the judge had misdirected himself in requiring a very high standard of proof as opposed to a good arguable case.

Held, allowing the appeal, that it was well established that a good arguable case had to be shown, therefore the judge ought not to have interfered with the restraint order.

UNITED BANK LTD v. HUSSAIN (T/A BURSLEM FILLING STATION) [2000] C.P.L.R. 270, Sir Christopher Staughton, CA.

564. Search orders – setting aside – failure to comply with formalities

[Civil Procedure Rules 1998 (SI 1998 3132) Part 25.]

B applied to set aside a search order granted to G in copyright infringement proceedings. B contended that in contravention of the appropriate practice direction, Civil Procedure Rules 1998 Part 25 PD 25, G had omitted (1) to inform the judge as required by PD 25 para 7.4(5) that the search might extend to the female defendants' homes and to stipulate that it was deviating from the standard order by employing assistant solicitors rather than a partner in the firm to supervise the search; (2) to establish, as required by PD 25 para.7.2, that the supervising solicitor had recent experience of the search procedure; (3) to provide the judge with confidential documents used in the search, and (4) to give an undertaking not to disclose the nature of the proceedings except for the purposes of the search action itself.

Held, setting aside the order, that G had materially failed to comply with the appropriate practice direction and the search order should accordingly be set aside. G's application for an interim injunction pending trial was granted.

GADGET SHOP LTD v. BUG.COM LTD [2001] C.P. Rep. 13, Rimer, J., Ch D.

565. Service of process – court's discretion to grant extensions of time – amendments to claim confined to ancillary facts

[Companies Act 1985 s.725(1); Rules of the Supreme Court 1965 Ord.20 r.5(5); Civil Procedure Rules 1998 (SI 1998 3132) Part 3 r.3.10, Part 11 r.11.1 (b).]

R applied for a declaration under the Civil Procedure Rules 1998 Part 11 r.11.1 (b) that the service of a writ by H was ineffective and should be set aside as it was not served within the time limit allowed. H submitted a counter application under Part 3 r.3.10 to remedy the error in service together with an application to amend the points of claim under the provisions of the Rules of the Supreme Court Ord.20 r.5(5) notwithstanding that the time limits for amendments had passed.

Held, granting R's declaration, that, although the Companies Act 1985 s.725(1) provided for service of a writ by sending it by post or leaving it at the registered office, service was ineffective when a writ was left with a receptionist or a security guard rather than with a managing agent of the company with a discretion to accept service. H's application under Part 3 r.3.10 was refused but the court exercised its discretion to extend the time for service, having regard to the criteria laid out in Part 7 r.7.6(3). Amendments to claims out of time under Ord.20 r.5(5), arising out of the same facts but which raised a new cause of action, would be restricted to those facts which were directly or closely connected with and ancillary to the facts originally relied upon.

AMERADA HESS v. ROME *The Times*, March 15, 2000, Colman, J., QBD.

566. Service of process – defendants domiciled in Northern Ireland – validity of service depended on existence of arguable claim against English codefendants

[Civil Jurisdiction and Judgments Act 1982 s.16.]

Z brought proceedings in England against a number of defendants, some of whom were domiciled in England and some domiciled in Northern Ireland. Subsequently it transpired that Z's only claim lay against one defendant domiciled in Northern Ireland. Z unsuccessfully sought to continue the English proceedings against the Northern Ireland defendant on the basis that, when the action was commenced, the English courts had jurisdiction because some of the defendants were domiciled in England and so the Civil Jurisdiction and Judgments Act 1982 s.16 applied. Z appealed.

Held, dismissing the appeal, that the fact that Z thought she had a valid claim against the English defendants at the time of issue of the writ did not matter if, judged objectively, there was no valid claim against a defendant domiciled within the jurisdiction. If that was so, then there was no basis for asserting jurisdiction against a defendant domiciled outside the jurisdiction.

ZAIR v. EASTERN HEALTH AND SOCIAL SERVICES BOARD [1999] I.L.Pr. 823, Waller, L.J., CA.

567. Service of process – fax number on notepaper did not amount to written indication of willingness to accept service by fax – ineffective service under CPR and Hague Convention

[Civil Procedure Rules 1998 (SI 1998 3132) Part 6; Hague Convention on the Service Abroad of Judicial and Extrajudicial Documents in Civil and Commercial Matters 1965; Brussels Convention on Jurisdiction and the Enforcement of Judgments in Civil and Commercial Matters 1968 Art.21.]

M, an English company and GD, an Italian company, were involved in a dispute concerning the payment of royalties pursuant to a licensing agreement. M commenced proceedings in England by service of a claim form on GD prior to which GD had attempted to serve a writ on M by fax. The English proceedings were set aside (*The Times*, March 1, 2000), on the basis that the Italian court was the court first seised of the action by virtue of GD's prior service by fax and under the Brussels Convention 1968 the court was obliged to stay the proceedings. GD had contended that service by fax was effective and fulfilled the requirements of the Civil Procedure Rules Part 6.2(1)(e) since the headed notepaper used by M in correspondence included a fax number which was an indication that M was prepared to accept service by fax as required by Civil Procedure Rules 1998 Part 6 PD 6 para.3.1(1)(a). M appealed.

Held, allowing the appeal, that service by fax was ineffective and did not satisfy the requirements of the 1998 Rules since the inclusion of a fax number on headed notepaper was not a sufficient written indication of M's willingness to accept service by fax. Consequently, there had been no effective service and the Italian court had not been first seised of the action, since Italian law required that service was effected before proceedings could become definitely pending before the court. The Hague Convention 1965 Art.15 required that a fax number must be expressly provided for the purpose of accepting service to amount to a written indication.

MOLINS PLC v. GD SPA [2000] 1 W.L.R. 1741, Aldous, L.J., CA.

568. Service of process – service out of jurisdiction – delay did not render service impracticable – court's discretion to extend validity

[Civil Procedure Rules 1998 (SI 1998 3132) Part 1; Rules of the Supreme Court Ord.6 r.8(1)(b), Ord.7 r.6.]

C wished to sublet the building of which it was a tenant, but could not do so without the written consent of its landlord, ME, whose offices were in Guernsey. C wrote to ME but did not receive a reply so C issued an originating summons, but did not obtain leave to serve it outside the jurisdiction. At a directions hearing the judge, on his own motion, ordered substituted service. ME appealed against the order, contending that C had not complied with the formalities required by the Rules of the Supreme Court Ord.6 r.8(1)(b) and Ord.7 r.6, which stated that leave to serve out of the jurisdiction was required and if not so marked the summons was valid for only four months. It was argued that substituted service could only be ordered where it was impracticable to serve and mere delay did not render service impracticable.

Held, allowing the appeal, that the judge was wrong to order substituted service as it had not been established that service was impracticable and C's failure to obtain leave to serve outside the jurisdiction was a fundamental flaw in the summons. As the decision had been found to be wrong, the court was required to look at the new Civil Procedure Rules 1998 in deciding how to proceed, *McPhilemy v. Times Newspapers Ltd (Re-amendment: Justification)* [1999] 3 All E.R. 775, [1999] C.L.Y. 1635 applied. As, (1) speedy resolution of the issues in the case, without additional costs, required a practical approach; (2) the court was partly to blame for the situation, and (3) no prejudice would be caused to ME as it had been aware of the proceedings throughout, it was appropriate and in the interests of justice for the court to exercise its discretion to extend the validity of the summons for a further 28 days and give C leave to issue a concurrent summons to be served outside the jurisdiction.

CADOGAN PROPERTIES LTD v. MOUNT EDEN LAND LTD [2000] I.L.Pr. 722, Peter Gibson, L.J., CA.

569. Service of process – time limits – application without notice for extension of writ – effect of non disclosure of relevant factors

[Rules of the Supreme Court 1965 (SI 1965 1776); Civil Procedure Rules 1998 (SI 1998 3132) Part 11; Civil Procedure Rules 1998 (SI 1998 33132) Part 23 r.23.10; Hague Rules Art. III r.6.]

Damage occurred to B's cargo of rice whilst being transported by HH to Nigeria. The bills of lading were in common form, but in error the reverse sides, which would normally have included by incorporation the conditions of carriage and a one year time bar under the Hague Rules Art. III r.6 in lieu of the statutory limitation of six years, were blank. Within weeks, B commenced proceedings in Nigeria, in which country a package limitation applied, and later issued a writ in England, on a date that was less that one year on from the discharge of the vessel as a whole, but more than one year on from the discharge of the particular storage area in the ship where the rice had been stored. Two applications were made by B without notice to extend the validity of the writ, the existence of which HH was still unaware. In the second application B failed to disclose that the Nigerian proceedings had by now been struck out for want of prosecution. Service of the writ was preceded by the introduction of the Civil Procedure Rules 1998. HH applied to have the orders extending the writ and service of the writ set aside arguing that (1) B's contention that the application was out of time under the Civil Procedure Rules 1998 Part 23 r.23.10, as it was not made within seven days of service of the without notice order, was incorrect; (2) B's claim was time barred and was not saved by the principle expounded in *Nordglimt, The* [1988] Q.B. 183, [1988] C.L.Y. 3219, cited as a result of the exception laid down in *Fort Sterling Ltd v. South Atlantic Cargo Shipping NV (The Finnrose)* [1994] 1 Lloyd's Rep. 559, [1995] C.L.Y. 4504, and (3) B had not shown good reason for the two extensions.

Held, granting the application, that (1) after considering the interface of the Rules of the Supreme Court 1965 and the 1998 Rules, the application would be treated as a new application under the 1998 Rules and, an application to challenge the court's jurisdiction, a period longer than seven days was applied under Part 11 of the 1998 Rules; (2) the issue of whether the claim was time barred under the Hague Rules was not a suitable one for summary determination, but, assuming that the Hague Rules did apply, *Finnrose* followed, exception to the *Nordglimt* principle would deprive B of success, and (3) the discretion to affirm the two orders made without notice would not be made in B's favour, as B had not made full disclosure of the potential time bar and the striking out of the Nigerian action, nor given a proper explanation for its delay in serving the writ at the two hearings, and had delayed serving the writ only so as to gain time to forum shop, thus maximising a tactical advantage.

BUA INTERNATIONAL LTD v. HAI HING SHIPPING CO LTD (THE HAI HING) [2000] 1 Lloyd's Rep. 300, Rix, J., QBD (Comm Ct).

570. Service of process – time limits – jurisdiction to override service provisions

[Interpretation Act 1978 s.7; Rules of the Supreme Court 1965 (SI 1965 1776) Ord.10 r.1 (3) (a), Ord.65 r.5; Civil Procedure Rules 1998 (SI 1998 3132) Part 6, Part 7.]

In mid 1993, D purchased a property with the assistance of B, a licensed conveyancer, who was in practice on his own account. In June 1999, D issued a claim form in which it was alleged that B had acted negligently by failing to advise D to conduct a survey of the property. On October 21, 1999, D unsuccessfully sought an extension of time for its service. The following day, the claim form was taken by D's solicitor to B's place of business, where it was left with a receptionist. B telephoned D's solicitor later that day to acknowledge receipt. Subsequently, B contended that by virtue of the Civil Procedure Rules 1998 Part 7 r.7.5(2), the claim form's validity expired on October 21, 1999, or that, even if it expired on October 22, by virtue of the deemed service provisions in Part 6 r.6.7, the claim form was in fact to be deemed served on October 23, at which time it was unquestionably invalid, and that this was so irrespective of the admitted fact that it had come into B's hands on October 22.

Held, that (1) since Part 7 r.7.5 of the 1998 Rules was so worded as to exclude the date of issue, the claim form expired on October 22, 1999, *Smith v. Probyn The Times*, March 29, 2000, [2000] C.L.Y. 571 applied; (2) the deemed service provisions were indeed effective to displace the reality of the receipt of the documents by B. In contrast to the position under other "deemed service" provisions, such as the Rules of the Supreme Court Ord.10 r.1 (3) (a) and Ord.65 r.5, and the Interpretation Act 1978 s.7, there were no saving words in the 1998 Rules permitting the deemed date to be displaced by proof of receipt at a different time. That was so whether receipt could be shown to have been earlier than the deemed time as in the instant case, or to have been later, where B's remedy would have been to extend time for the taking of any consequent step or to have set aside any order which had been made, and (3) there was jurisdiction to override the provisions as to service in Part 6 r.6.1 (b) and even to dispense with service altogether in Part 6 r.6.9. An application made by D at the hearing for the exercise of either form of relief as a fallback position was granted, since it would have been contrary to the overriding objective to refuse it. However, a costs award was made in B's favour.

DUTTON v. BOYDLE, May 17, 2000, Judge Overend, CC (Truro). [*Ex rel.* A Butler, Barrister, 2nd Floor, Francis Taylor Building, Temple, London].

571. Service of process – written confirmation of authorisation required for valid service on solicitors

S served a claim form accompanied by particulars of claim alleging defamation on solicitors acting for P. S failed to obtain written confirmation from the solicitors firm in question that they were authorised to accept service pursuant to the Civil Procedure Rules 1998 r.6.4(2) and proceeded instead on the mistaken assumption that they were so authorised. An application by S for confirmation that valid service had been effected or an extension of time for service was dismissed and S appealed.

Held, dismissing the appeal, that there was no basis for any suggestion that S had made every reasonable attempt to effect service and had been prevented from doing so. S had failed to obtain written confirmation of service as required by the 1998 rules and had made no attempt to effect personal service upon P.

SMITH v. PROBYN *The Times*, March 29, 2000, Morland, J., QBD.

572. **Setting aside – absence of party – wide discretion under Civil Procedure Rules**

[Civil Procedure Rules 1998 (SI 1998 3132) Part 23 r.23.11.]

B applied under the Civil Procedure Rules 1998 Part 23 r.23.11 to set aside an order for specific performance on the basis that she had not been present at the hearing.

Held, adjourning the application, that the court had a wide discretion under the Rules in general, and in particular under r.23.11, to set aside an order where one party had not attended. However, the court would be unlikely to accede to such an application either where injustice would be caused, or where it was unlikely that the original decision would be altered.

RIVERPATH PROPERTIES LTD v. BRAMMALL *The Times*, February 16, 2000, Neuberger, J., Ch D.

573. **Setting aside – failure to attend trial – no reasonable prospect of success**

[Human Rights Act 1998; Civil Procedure Rules 1998 (SI 1998 3132) Part 39 r.39(3).]

E, a man and wife, appealed against the dismissal of their application under the Civil Procedure Rules 1998 Part 39 r.39(3) to set aside a judgment entered in their absence. E had failed to attend court for the trial owing to a misunderstanding regarding the time of the hearing and judgment had been entered for BB, the creditor, ordering E to pay a substantial sum.

Held, dismissing the appeal, that the judgment should not be set aside since E's defence had no reasonable prospect of success at trial and although E were at a disadvantage in that the amount of the debt had been decided on in their absence, their interests were sufficiently protected by the undertakings entered into by BB. It was observed that legal representatives seeking to rely on the Human Rights Act 1998 should supply the court with any decisions of the European Court of Human Rights on which they intended to rely or which might assist the court.

BARCLAYS BANK PLC v. ELLIS [2001] C.P. Rep. 50, Mummery, L.J., CA.

574. **Settlement – parties under duty to forewarn court of possible compromise**

[Civil Procedure Rules 1998 (SI 1998 3132) Part 1 r.1.]

HFC appealed against the dismissal of its application in a passing off action to restrain HSBC from using that name. The court reserved judgment and between the close of argument and the delivery of the judgment, the parties met and settled. They informed the court the following day and applied for the dismissal of the appeal by consent.

Held, dismissing the appeal by consent, that it was the duty of the parties as well as their legal representatives to inform the court at the earliest opportunity of the possibility of settlement. That duty was expressly stated in the Civil Procedure Rules 1998 Part 1 r.1 where the necessity for the court's resources to be properly and efficiently deployed was confirmed.

HFC BANK PLC v. HSBC BANK PLC (FORMERLY MIDLAND BANK PLC) [2000] C.P.L.R. 197, Nourse, L.J., CA.

575. Settlement – sex discrimination – county court proceedings for personal injuries commenced after settlement of claim at employment tribunal

Twas a woman who was a victim of a series of malicious incidents while working on the assembly track at RG's car factory. She brought a claim in 1996 for sex discrimination which was settled just before the hearing for £5,000. The settlement agreement was worded, "By consent and without admitting liability, the Respondent agrees to pay and the Applicant agrees to accept the offer of £5,000 in full and final settlement of the Applicant's Industrial Tribunal Case Number B52186/96. This settlement does not affect any right the Applicant may have in relation to any industrial injuries claim." In 1997, T commenced county court proceedings against RG claiming damages for personal injury, namely psychiatric illness, anxiety and depression, and loss of earnings. In April 2000 RG applied to have the claim struck out on the ground that it had already been settled in the tribunal agreement. RG cited *Sherriff v. Klyne Tugs (Lowestoft) Ltd* [1999] I.C.R. 1170, [1999] C.L.Y. 2056, where, in similar circumstances, the victim of race discrimination had a subsequent county court claim struck out on the grounds that it had already been settled. The *Sherriff* agreement had provided that, "The applicant accepts the terms of this agreement in full and final settlement of all claims which he has or may have against the Respondent arising out of his employment or the termination thereof being claims in respect of which an employment tribunal has jurisdiction".

Held, dismissing the application, that *Sherriff* was distinguishable on the basis that in the instant case the parties had expressly provided for the personal injury claim to be held over.

TAYLOR v. ROVER GROUP LTD, May 24, 2000, Judge MacDuff Q.C., CC (Birmingham). [*Ex rel.* Thompsons Solicitors, The McLaren Building, 35 Dale End, Birmingham].

576. Small claims – adjournment of fixed date – late notification by court

[Civil Procedure Rules 1998 (SI 1998 3132) Part 27 r.27.4(2).]

The final hearing of a small claim was adjourned with a date to be fixed. The date was fixed and the parties notified less that 21 days before the hearing. At the final hearing A applied for an adjournment because the court had not given the parties 21 days' notice of the date fixed for the final hearing pursuant to the Civil Procedure Rules 1998 Part 27 r.27.4(2).

Held, dismissing the application, that Part 27 r.27.4(2) did not apply to adjournments, but only to the first giving of notice, otherwise part heard cases adjourned overnight could not be heard the next day.

ANDREW v. BELLMAN, March 16, 2000, Deputy District Judge Stephenson, CC (Watford). [*Ex rel.* Nicholas Preston, Barrister, Bracton Chambers, 8 Bell Yard, London].

577. Solicitors – ceasing to act – written application sufficient in simple cases

[Civil Procedure Rules 1998 (SI 1998 3132) Part 42 r.42.3.]

EP, a firm of solicitors, made a written application under the Civil Procedure Rules 1998 Part 42 r.42.3 for a declaration that it had ceased to act for AS. EP did not appear in court.

Held, allowing the application, that it was permissible, in appropriate cases, for a solicitor to make a written application seeking a declaration that he no longer acted for a party. In simple cases it would take up court time and add to expenses to require attendance in person. However, where a solicitor wished to withdraw from a complex case, it was advisable that he attend in person.

MILLER v. ALLIED SAINIF (UK) LTD *The Times,* October 31, 2000, Neuberger, J., Ch D.

578. Solicitors – partner involved in assault in court precincts – not acting on behalf of co partners

[Partnership Act 1890 s.10.]

F, who was taking proceedings against T, a firm of solicitors, appealed against the striking out of his claim for damages for personal injury against T for assaults allegedly carried out firstly in court and then in the court precincts by W, one of T's partners. F contended that W could be said to have been acting in the ordinary course of business under the Partnership Act 1890 s.10.

Held, dismissing the appeal, that the first assault, which had involved an altercation over documents, might have come within s.10 but F had suffered no loss and the principle of proportionality prevented trial of the claim, whereas the second assault was so far from the ordinary work of lawyers that W could not be regarded as having been acting with the authority of his co partners.

FLYNN v. ROBIN THOMPSON & PARTNERS; *sub nom*. FLYNN v. ROBINS THOMPSON & PARTNERS *The Times*, March 14, 2000, Thorpe, L.J., CA.

579. Statement of case – amendments – delay – pleading alternative case in statement of claim

[Construction (Working Places) Regulations 1966 (SI 1966 94); Rules of the Supreme Court 1965 (SI 1965 1776) Ord.18 r.14; Limitation Act 1980 s.33(3).]

P, a carpenter employed by M, suffered personal injury when he fell from the roof of a garage upon which he was working. He contended that M ought to have provided a platform for him to work upon, which would have avoided the need for him to balance upon the central roof support. He commenced proceedings against M, pleading absence of a platform in breach of the Construction (Working Places) Regulations 1966 and breach of the common law duty of care. M argued that a platform had been provided and that it was sufficient to comply with both the common law duty and the Regulations. P did not indicate the possibility of pursuing an alternative case until discussions between opposing counsel in the week before trial. P contended that if the court were to find there had been a platform, then he was entitled to rely on the alternative case that the platform was inadequate to meet the requirements of the regulations, by virtue of the Supreme Court Rules 1965 Ord.18, r.14, as a result of which assertions made in the defence are automatically put in issue. M argued that the alternative case was a new claim, which had not been pleaded, *Waghorn v. George Wimpey & Co Ltd* [1969] 1 W.L.R. 1764, [1969] C.L.Y. 2448.

Held, refusing permission to advance the proposed alternative case and dismissing the application to amend the original statement of case, that (1) the alternative case should have been pleaded as well as the original case because M's preparation of his defence was likely to have been different if specific breaches of the regulations relating to the inadequacy of the platform had been pleaded. In particular, both parties would have been likely to commission expert evidence with respect to the pleaded breaches which neither had done to date, due to the nature of the claimant's case as presently formulated, *Waghorn* followed; (2) it would not be equitable to allow the amendment to plead the new cause of action because the requirements of the Limitation Act 1980 s.33(3) were not met. P could suffer no prejudice from not being able to run a case which had never been his case and which would be run only on his lawyer's advice. The fresh allegation was inconsistent with the existing plea and the amendment substantial and made at a very late stage, *Herbert v. Vaughan* [1972] 1 W.L.R. 1128, [1972] C.L.Y. 2785 considered.

PLEDGER v. MARTIN [2000] P.I.Q.R. P31, Judge Coningsby Q.C., QBD.

580. Statements – service of witness summaries

[Civil Procedure Rules 1998 (1998 3132) Part 32 r.32.9.]

H brought an action against BC, a firm of solicitors, alleging negligence in relation to the service of a writ on a firm of accountants. BC applied without notice to H for permission to serve a witness summary on H pursuant to the Civil Procedure Rules 1998 Part 32 r.32.9 in respect of evidence given by EH, the owner of a number of garden centres at which H had lost their jobs, in an interview attended by solicitors for both BC and H. BC maintained that EH would have sold or had to sell the garden centres notwithstanding the complaint against the firm of accountants, with the result that H would have lost their jobs in any event.

Held, granting the application, that the statement had to be served in accordance with Part 32 r.32.9(2) containing either a transcript or a typed up version of the note of the conference together with the questions and answers raised. In addition, pages from a book which contained statements about or written by EH, which BC believed were not fictional, should be included with those passages it was hoped EH would support highlighted. A copy of the statement should be served on H's solicitors together with a copy of the court's judgment.

HARRISON v. BLOOM CAMILLIN (PRELIMINARY ISSUES) [2000] C.P. Rep. 83, Neuberger, J., Ch D.

581. Statements of claim – admissibility of new point raised on appeal – need for new point to be fully supported by facts

DNB brought a claim for damages for negligent valuation against BL and a limitation question arose on a trial of preliminary issues with DNB applying to raise a new point on appeal as to the date that the relevant loss began to accrue.

Held, refusing the application, that the court would not allow the new point to be raised where it was not satisfied beyond doubt that it was fully supported by the facts, *Connecticut Fire Insurance Co v. Kavanagh* [1892] A.C. 473 followed.

DNB MORTGAGES LTD v. BULLOCK & LEES [2000] Lloyd's Rep. P.N. 290, Robert Walker, L.J., CA.

582. Statements of claim – amendments – amendment to include omission by claimant's advisers – increase in value of claim – defendant not prejudiced by omission

[Civil Procedure Rules 1998 (SI 1998 3132).]

C sued SCC for damages for personal injuries. At pre trial review, C's advisers mistakenly failed to lodge an amended schedule of loss to include a claim for loss of earnings, increasing the value of the claim from £5,000 to £400,000. The mistake was not realised until two and a half weeks before trial and the judge refused an application to amend on the basis of prejudice to SCC. C appealed.

Held, allowing the appeal, that the loss of earnings claim could have been anticipated from the medical evidence and correspondence between the parties. SCC had not raised the question of the omission, which could be put down to a mistake by C's advisers. There was no prejudice over the issue of quantum as SCC could be allowed to do the work it would have wished to had the claim been made earlier. The judge had not asked for details of prejudice on liability and those suggested were not impressive. The mistake would probably have been discovered earlier if the parties had cooperated with each other in the conduct of proceedings, as required by the Civil Procedure Rules 1998.

CHILTON v. SURREY CC [1999] C.P.L.R. 525, Henry, L.J., CA.

583. Statements of claim – amendments – back injury – sustained period of heavy lifting

W appealed the dismissal of his application to amend the statement of claim in proceedings against Q for personal injuries. W had been employed as a service engineer by Q for a period of just over one year. During the entire course of his employment W had been obliged to carry cast iron heat exchanger units weighing in excess of 30 kilograms to and from domestic properties. W instituted proceedings alleging that towards the end of his period of employment with Q he had sustained a serious back injury. Two specific incidents were relied upon. W later sought to amend the statement of claim to plead the entire period of heavy lifting. Q objected to the application on the basis that the proposed amendments sought to introduce an entirely new claim which was now statute barred following the expiry of the limitation period. The judge at first instance agreed with the submissions advanced on behalf of Q and dismissed the application. W appealed.

Held, allowing the appeal, that it was clear that W was not seeking to advance a new claim. The pleadings and other documentation available clearly indicated that W alleged that the repeated lifting had resulted in a weakening of his back but that he had only experienced pain on the two occasions specifically pleaded. It was a familiar concept in cases of this nature that a back injury was sustained following a sustained period of heavy lifting. Furthermore the medical evidence previously disclosed to Q indicated that W had sustained his injury "secondary to repeated heavy lifting" and in the circumstances there could have been no possible confusion concerning the nature of W's claim.

WILLIS v. QUALITY HEATING SERVICES Trans. Ref. PTA-A 2000/5687/A2, Swinton Thomas, L.J., CA.

584. **Statements of claim – amendments – expert's report not comprehensively pleaded in statement of claim amounted to adequate notification of case**

[Civil Procedure Rules 1998 (SI 1998 3132).]

D entered into a contract with I for the supply and installation of a gas powered oven and the subsequent training and instruction of I and its employees in its operation. Following installation and a period of use, an explosion occurred after a number of I's employees had carried out some repair work. Approximately four years later, I brought proceedings against D alleging negligence and/or breach of contract. After a further four years the parties exchanged their experts' reports. D wrote to I informing it that I's report included unpleaded allegations which, unless amended via an application to the court, would not be dealt with. Subsequently I successfully applied to amend its statement of claim to include the new allegations. D appealed, contending that the application had been made too late. D submitted that they were prejudiced in their ability to investigate the new issues raised and, furthermore, prejudiced through the loss of opportunity, by reason of the expiry of the limitation period, to pass on the allegations via amendment to the applicable Part 20 defendant.

Held, dismissing the appeal, that under the Civil Procedure Rules 1998 a case could be adequately notified through an expert's report even where it had not been comprehensively pleaded in the statement of claim. The overriding objectives of the Rules were the efficient and expeditious resolution of cases, and in view of this goal it was acceptable that a case should not be set out fully a second time in the experts' reports or witness statements. In the instant case the amendment constituted new particulars which did not amount to a new case and the amendment was therefore allowed.

IBC VEHICLES LTD v. DURR LTD Trans. Ref. 1995-I-1167, Michael Tugendhat Q.C., QBD.

585. **Statements of claim – amendments – judicial discretion to allow amendment of statement of claim following delivery of final judgment and making of order before order sealed**

[Civil Procedure Rules 1998 (SI 1998 3132).]

S brought an action for damages for negligence and breach of contract against E a liquidator. E and the second defendant applied for summary judgment of the claim on the grounds that, by virtue of an agreement between the parties, E had not incurred personal liability and that he owed no duty to S for the type of loss suffered. At the summary judgment hearing the judge invited S's representatives to amend the statement of claim so as to include a claim in conversion and he repeated the invitation when he circulated his draft judgment and upon handing down the judgment. Counsel declined to make the amendment and the final judgment contained a statement that indicated counsel's refusal. S then obtained advice from leading counsel and subsequently sought permission to make the amendment. Permission was granted and E appealed.

Held, allowing the appeal (Lord Clarke dissenting), that (1) a judge retained a discretion to allow an amendment to the statement of claim and to reopen the issue after delivering judgment provided that the order had not been perfected; (2) the discretion should be used sparingly and the factors that the judge should consider under the Civil Procedure Rules 1998 were still those as stated in *Barrell Enterprises, Re* [1973] 1 W.L.R. 19, and (3) on the facts there were no exceptional circumstances to justify the exercise of the jurisdiction.

STEWART v. ENGEL (PERMISSION TO AMEND) [2000] 1 W.L.R. 2268, Sir Christopher Slade, CA.

586. **Statements of claim – amendments – jurisdiction – expiry of limitation period – amendments to writ allowed to include matters initially pleaded**

[Rules of the Supreme Court 1965 (SI 1965 1776) Ord.2 r.1, Ord.18 r.15.]

P was made bankrupt and with the consent of the Official Receiver brought an action for damages for professional negligence against SS, his former solicitors. There were protracted negotiations over the conduct of the action, which led to staying of the action, and which were finally resolved by the assignment to P of half of any resulting damages. P had served a statement of claim which included claims in relation to litigation and possession that had not been stated on the writ, contrary to the Rules of the Supreme Court Ord.18 r.15, and which were held to be time barred and his action had been dismissed. P appealed, contending that the claims had been made prior to the expiry of the limitation period. S argued that the additional claims in the statement of claim were therefore a nullity.

Held, allowing the appeal, that to treat the claims in the statement of claim as a nullity was contrary to Ord.2 r.1 and the court had jurisdiction to allow the amendment of the writ outside the limitation period where the original claim had been made within it. It was wrong to restrict the claim because of a technicality where the defendant was not prejudiced.

PHELPS v. SPON SMITH & CO *The Times*, November 26, 1999, Nicholas Strauss Q.C., Ch D.

587. **Statements of claim – amendments – mistake – party name – extension of time unnecessary**

[Civil Procedure Rules 1998 (SI 1998 3132) Part 17 r.17.4 (3), Part 19 r.19.5.]

C appealed against a decision allowing G to amend his claim form during a libel action, changing the name of the defendant. The defendant had been mistakenly named as "Channel Four Television Company Ltd", a dormant subsidiary of the correct defendant, Channel Four Television Corporation. C argued that where the mistaken name was that of some other person or entity and where, as in this case, the limitation period had expired, the court was limited to proceeding under the Civil Procedure Rules 1998 Part 19 r.19.5. It was further submitted that under this rule the court had a discretion to permit the substitution of a party, but an extension of time for service was also required, which in the instant case should be refused since it amounted to an abuse and deprived C of an accrued limitation defence. The judge had allowed the amendment under Part 17 r.17.4 (3) of the Rules.

Held, dismissing the appeal, that since the error in the naming of the defendant had been a genuine one, the judge had been right to permit the error to be corrected under Part 17. Having regard to the overriding objective of the Rules, Part 17 should not be interpreted in a restrictive way resulting in an unjust outcome. In the instant case the mistake was a genuine one and trivial in that there was no reasonable doubt caused as to the identity of the party in question.

GREGSON v. CHANNEL FOUR TELEVISION CORP (AMENDMENT OF PARTY NAME); *sub nom.* GREGSON v. CHANNEL FOUR TELEVISION CO LTD [2000] C.P. Rep. 60, May, L.J., CA.

588. Stay of proceedings – automatic stay – claim for damages for personal injuries – payment in of full claim – subsequent amendment of pleadings where injuries disclosed as more serious

P was involved in a road traffic accident and brought proceedings against D, limiting the claim to £5,000 on the basis of the medical evidence then obtained. D made a payment into court of £2,200 in 1995. P later obtained a report from a neurologist which indicated that the accident injuries were more serious than had originally been contemplated. The report was disclosed to D in September 1995. D paid a further £2,800 into court in 1997, bringing the total to £5,000. P then applied for leave to amend to claim an amount in excess of £5,000. The judge ordered the stay imposed automatically on the payment in of the whole amount of the claim to be lifted and gave leave to amend. D appealed relying on delays by P but not on any particular prejudice to D.

Held, dismissing the appeal, that once D had received the medical report it was plain that the claim had a potential well in excess of £5,000. That provided good grounds for removing the stay and granting leave to amend. Delay in making the application did not prevent that finding. The question of prejudice was important when considering whether to lift the stay and whether to give leave to amend. The potential prejudice to P far outweighed the potential prejudice that might be suffered by D.

BUXTON v. WESTMACOTT [1999] P.I.Q.R. Q115, Swinton Thomas, L.J., CA.

589. Stay of proceedings – automatic stay imposed under Part 51 – entitlement to lift automatic stay on pre-April 1999 cases

[County Court Rules 1981 (SI 1981 1687) Ord.17 r.11; Civil Procedure Rules 1998 (SI 1998 3132) Part 51.]

AP brought an action against L claiming the sum of £15,366.32, being the balance of the price of building work carried out at premises owned by L. L brought a counterclaim for defective work and loss of rent exceeding £70,000. Proceedings were commenced in March 1997. AP applied for a pre-trial review prior to April 26, 1999, but the claim was still automatically stayed pursuant to the Civil Procedure Rules 1998 Part 51. AP's application was not listed until June 13, 2000 when AP applied to lift the automatic stay.

Held, granting the application, that in the absence of guidance in the Civil Procedure Rules 1998 Part 51 PD 51 as to what circumstances were applicable to the lifting of a stay, the judge found that the purpose of the imposition of a stay was that pre April 26, 1999 cases did not remain in abeyance for too long whilst also avoiding automatic strike under the County Court Rules 1981 Ord.17 r.11. The purpose of Part 51 of the 1998 Rules was not to kill off those cases that fell within its ambit but to require any party wishing to continue with the case to ask the court for permission to do so. The two factors which were of significance in deciding whether or not to lift the stay were (1) whether the request to lift the stay was made timeously, and (2) whether it was still possible for a fair trial to be conducted. In the instant case, the request had been made before the stay came into force although it had not come before a judge prior to the trigger date of April 25 and, in the circumstances, it was appropriate to lift the stay because a fair trial was still possible.

AXTELL-POWELL v. LABOR, June 13, 2000, Judge Adams, CC (Barnet). [*Ex rel.* Giffen Couch & Archer Solicitors, Bridge House, Bridge Street, Leighton Buzzard].

590. Stay of proceedings – choice of forum – two sets of proceedings in same cause of action – determination of summary judgment prior to forum application

M brought a claim for compensation in Egypt against R, who was resident there. M had also instigated similar proceedings against R in the English courts and had applied for summary judgment in that action. R applied for a stay of the English proceedings, contending that, because the two actions concerned the same subject matter, they were vexatious.

Held, refusing the application, that in the instant case the correct approach was to allow the application for summary judgment to be heard first, and if that proved unsuccessful, the forum application could then be decided. It would normally be vexatious to issue two sets of proceedings in respect of the same cause of action, unless the claimant had sufficient justification for doing so. Accordingly the correct approach would be affected by the circumstances of each individual case, *Standard Chartered Bank v. Pakistan National Shipping Corp (No.1)* [1995] 2 Lloyd's Rep. 365 considered.

MERRILL LYNCH, PIERCE FENNER & SMITH INC v. RAFFA [2001] C.P. Rep. 44, Judge Raymond Jack Q.C., QBD.

591. **Stay of proceedings – defendant sought stay of assessment of claimant's costs pending appeal – court retained discretion to permit stay pending appeal – stay to be granted only in exceptional circumstances**

[Civil Procedure Rules 1998 (SI 1998 3132) Part 1 r.1.1 (2), Part 59 r.59.13.]

SH, a building contractor, was subject to a claim made by its subcontractor, RA, for payment for substantially completed asphalting works. SH attempted to compel RA to submit its claim to an arbitration under the main contract. In proceedings issued by RA, the Court of Appeal held ([1999] B.L.R. 252, [1999] C.L.Y. 232) that RA was entitled to proceed with the arbitration of its claim under the subcontract. RA was awarded the costs of the appeal together with 50 per cent of the costs which had been incurred in the proceedings leading up to the appeal. SH made an application to stay the assessment of RA's bill of costs on the ground that it was pursuing an appeal against the decision of the Court of Appeal. Relying on the aims set out in the Civil Procedure Rules 1998 Part 1 r.1.1 (2) (b) and r.1.1 (2) (e) namely the saving of expense and the appropriate allocation of the court's resources, SH argued that, were its appeal to succeed, the assessment of RA's costs would be rendered futile. In opposing the application, RA contended that (1) SH had delayed for three months in making its application; (2) the House of Lords was not likely to be able to hear SH's appeal for some time; (3) it would experience no difficulty in paying SH's costs should it be ordered to do so, and (4) if the aims referred to in r.1.1 (2) (b) and r.1.1 (2) (e) were to be decisive in each case, the court would effectively be deprived of its discretion to grant a stay.

Held, refusing the application, that (1) it was important to bear in mind that the overriding objective of the 1998 Rules was to deal with cases justly. Accordingly, the court should guard against selective reliance on the individual aims set out in r.1.1 (2), and (2) by virtue of Part 59 r.59.13 of the Rules, the court retained its discretion to grant a stay pending an appeal. The court should proceed by recognising that the successful party should not be deprived of the benefit of a judgment, and that a stay should be refused unless the court exercised its discretion to grant one. Where an appeal was pending, a stay would be granted only in very exceptional circumstances, *Smith, Hogg & Co Ltd v. Black Sea and Baltic Insurance Co Ltd* [1940] A.C. 997 and *Griffiths v. Bean* (1911) 27 T.L.R. 346 applied. There were no exceptional circumstances in the instant case. On the contrary, there were good reasons for refusing to grant a stay. SH had been guilty of inactivity and delay throughout the proceedings and had refused RA's offer to provide an undertaking concerning its costs.

REDLAND AGGREGATES LTD v. SHEPHERD HILL CIVIL ENGINEERING LTD (STAY OF PROCEEDINGS) [2000] C.P. Rep. 7, Auld, L.J., CA.

592. **Stay of proceedings – freezing injunctions – application to lift stay following asset transfer in contempt of court**

FBME commenced proceedings against H and others seeking the recovery of monies previously advanced and damages for breach of fiduciary duty. A world wide freezing order had previously been granted to FBME. H had been found guilty of contempt of court in failing to disclose the existence of a bank account and in transferring monies to Jersey in breach of this order. A stay was imposed precluding H from taking any further step in the action until such time as he complied fully with the order and purged his contempt. It subsequently became apparent that additional money transfers had been made. H applied to lift the stay, contending that (1) the order required the disclosure of assets of which H was the legal but not the beneficial owner and that H had complied with the terms of the order in this respect, and (2) whilst H had been guilty of an asset transfer in breach of the order, he had taken advice from his solicitors prior to the transfers and had believed that they would not breach the terms of the order since the monies were the property of third parties.

Held, granting the application and lifting the stay on terms, that whilst H had not acted with the deliberate intent of flouting the court's order when making the transfers, he had failed to take sufficient care to ensure that he was not in breach of its terms. H had acted in a cavalier fashion and his behaviour attracted a high degree of culpability. H should have sought specialist legal advice. Despite these findings it was not appropriate to permit H's Part 20 claim to be stifled by means of a stay, given that H had now been made bankrupt and a successful defence would result in the distribution of funds to his creditors. Furthermore, there was no prejudice to FBME since it had to be assumed that the monies transferred in fact belonged to third parties and would not therefore have constituted monies available to satisfy FBME's claim. In addition the breaches were not of a continuing nature, *Beeforth v. Beeforth The Times*, September 17, 1998, [1998] C.L.Y. 339 applied. H would be required to undertake all reasonable steps to secure the return to the UK of all assets transferred in breach of the order.

FEDERAL BANK OF THE MIDDLE EAST LTD v. HADKINSON (LIFTING OF STAY) Trans. Ref. HC 1999 03177, Arden, J., Ch D.

593. Stay of proceedings – judicial decision making – party sought determination only of existence of triable issue – court determined underlying issue on affidavit evidence alone

[Arbitration Act 1996 s.9; Rules of the Supreme Court 1965 (SI 1965 1776) Ord.73 r.6.]

BC, a company of development contractors, instituted proceedings against property developers, SD, claiming monies due in respect of development work done over a two year period on a project to construct luxury apartment buildings. Upon receipt of proceedings, SD made an application for a stay in accordance with the Arbitration Act 1996 s.9, on the basis that the parties were required to refer any dispute to arbitration pursuant to the terms of the underlying contract. BC disputed that any contract had ever been concluded, whilst conceding that if a contract did exist then it would contain an arbitration clause. When the application for a stay came before the court, one of the issues raised was whether the dispute concerning the existence of an arbitration agreement should be referred to the arbitrator for determination. Only brief oral submissions were made to the judge and he dealt with the application upon the affidavit evidence filed. The judge concluded that if the issues were clear then it was preferable for the court to determine whether an arbitration agreement did exist under the Rules of the Supreme Court Ord.73 r.6. The judge went on to conclude that, on the clear facts of the instant case, a contract had indeed been concluded and accordingly granted a stay ([1999] B.L.R. 194, [1999] C.L.Y. 233). BC appealed, contending that there had been no agreement between the parties to allow the issue to be determined upon the basis of the affidavits filed, and that the parties had merely been seeking a determination of whether a triable issue existed. BC maintained that if the judge had reached the conclusion that there was a triable issue, then a trial of that issue should subsequently have taken place under Ord.73 r.6.

Held, allowing the appeal and remitting the case to the Technology and Construction Court (Ward, L.J. dissenting), that it was regrettable that the parties had failed to communicate to the judge the differences in approach which had only now become apparent. BC had anticipated that a trial would take place if the existence of a triable issue was established, whereas SD had been under the impression that they were conferring upon the judge a wide discretion over the issue. If it was proposed that a judge should determine matters solely upon the basis of affidavit evidence, thereby depriving litigants of their ability to call oral evidence and cross examine opposing witnesses, then that must be made clear, and in the absence of such clarity, the judge retained only the limited jurisdiction of determining whether a triable issue existed.

BIRSE CONSTRUCTION LTD v. ST DAVID LTD [2000] B.L.R. 57, Pill, L.J., CA.

594. Stay of proceedings – ombudsman without jurisdiction on issue of writ – complaint to ombudsman should follow issue of writ and stay of action – extension of writ refused

F, an investor, made a complaint to the Personal Investment Authority Ombudsman but also issued a protective writ in April 1998, claiming damages for negligence, breach of contract and fiduciary duties in the provision of financial services by T. F, fearing the claim might become time barred, made a without notice application to extend the writ until November 1999, which was granted and T applied to set aside the order, contending that F's right to make a claim to the PIA Ombudsman was not a valid reason to extend the validity of the writ.

Held, allowing the application, that there was no valid reason for an extension of time, *Kleinwort Benson Ltd v. Barbrak Ltd (The Myrto)* [1987] A.C. 597, [1987] C.L.Y. 3125 and *Waddon v. Whitecroft-Scovill Ltd* [1988] 1 W.L.R. 309, [1988] C.L.Y. 2961 considered. By virtue of para.6.1 of the Ombudsman's terms of reference, the ombudsman had no jurisdiction where the investor had "instituted proceedings", unless the proceedings were suspended or adjourned pending the ombudsman's determination. The correct procedure was to issue a protective writ and then obtain a stay pending the ombudsman's investigation. In the instant case, a second writ had been issued in January 1999, which had been stayed pending hearing of the instant matter, and since there was no limitation issue and the proceedings were relevant only to costs, there was no good reason to extend time.

FORREST v. TOWRY LAW FINANCIAL SERVICES LTD *The Times*, December 3, 1999, Nicholas Strauss Q.C., Ch D.

595. Stay of proceedings – patents – application of stay pending determination of appeal to European Patent Office

See INTELLECTUAL PROPERTY: Unilever Plc v. Frisa NV. §3667

596. Stay of proceedings – time limits – extension of period of validity of summons

[County Court Rules 1981 (SI 1981 1687) Ord.7 r.20.]

Held, that a stay did not act as a complete stop to all aspects of proceedings. Time would not stop running under the County Court Rules 1981 Ord.7 r.20 as that provision contained a code regulating the extension of the period of validity of a summons.

ALDRIDGE v. EDWARDS [2000] C.P.L.R. 349, Brooke, L.J., CA.

597. Striking out – abuse of process – application against solicitor for negligence was not collateral attack on final decision of court

LJ, a firm of solicitors, appealed against the refusal of its application to strike out C's claim for professional negligence arising from matrimonial proceedings. C claimed that LJ had failed to adduce the necessary evidence to deal sufficiently with the issues that arose in C's wife's application for ancillary relief, and, furthermore, they had failed to furnish the district judge with proper information as to C's income, upon which the decision for ancillary relief would be based. LJ contended that the statement of claim should be struck out as an abuse of process because it represented a collateral attack on earlier decisions of the court, and because C had failed to produce fresh evidence to show that the nature of the case had changed.

Held, dismissing the appeal, that the case should not be struck out as (1) C's case was that he did not have a proper opportunity to contest the decision of the court due to incompetent counsel and inadequate preparation of evidence, and (2) C was not seeking to rely on new evidence that was not available in the first place, *Hunter v. Chief Constable of the West Midlands* [1982] A.C. 529, [1982] C.L.Y. 2382 considered, and *Arthur JS Hall & Co v. Simons* [1999] 3 W.L.R. 873, [1999] C.L.Y. 4021 applied.

CHANNON v. LINDLEY JOHNSTONE (A FIRM) [2000] 2 F.L.R. 734, Judge David Smith Q.C., QBD.

598. Striking out – abuse of process – clinical negligence claim raised as concurrent tort against separate tortfeasor

In 1969 R's back pain was investigated at NEHA's hospital with a myelogram involving 7cc of myodil being injected into his spine. After an apparent initial recovery he developed symptoms which deteriorated from 1975 onwards. In 1994 arachnoiditis was diagnosed. In 1991 those claimants in a group action against G, the manufacturers of myodil, who had also sued health authorities in relation to the administration of the drug were allowed to discontinue against them. In 1994, R joined the group action against G, and in October 1995 accepted £20,794 as part of the group settlement. In 1997, R sued NEHA, who sought to strike the claim out on the basis that R should be taken as having been fully compensated by the settlement with G, and the claim was doomed to failure and therefore an abuse of process.

Held, striking out the claim, that (1) the tort alleged against NEHA was a concurrent tort with G, showing the loss and damage; in the absence of express language to the contrary in the settlement with G in 1995, R was to be taken as being fully compensated, *Jameson v. Central Electricity Generating Board (No.1)* [1999] 2 W.L.R. 141, [1999] C.L.Y. 1386 applied, and (2) the allegations of negligence, which had to relate to 1969, appeared doomed to failure given that (i) R's expert report related to 1975 not 1969, (ii) a joint statement from the British Society of Radiologists in December 1991 was exculpatory of NEHA, and (iii) it was unlikely that the claims against the health authorities in the group action were strong when discontinued.

RAWLINSON v. NORTH ESSEX HA [2000] Lloyd's Rep. Med. 54, Mitchell, J., QBD.

599. Striking out – abuse of process – delay – failure to comply with pre-action protocol – defendant prejudiced

[Limitation Act 1980; Human Rights Act 1998; Civil Procedure Rules 1998 (SI 1998 3132) Part 3 r.3.4 (2); European Convention on Human Rights 1950 Art.6.]

J brought an action against L for damages for personal injuries in excess of £5,000. J issued proceedings on August 31, 1999 and served particulars of claim on December 13, 1999. He had first instructed solicitors on October 23, 1996, but prior to that a letter had been sent to LT on September 11, 1996 requesting confirmation that they operated the relevant bus route. LT had replied stating that since privatisation they no longer acted for L. J was referred to the correct claims handlers who sought information regarding the accident by a letter dated November 16, 1996. The first communication sent to L was a letter dated August 26, 1999, setting out the claim and asking for confirmation that L was the correct party to the proceedings. A second letter was sent to L dated December 15, 1999, informing L that proceedings had been issued. L applied for an order striking out J's statement of case pursuant to the Civil Procedure Rules 1998 Part 3 r.3.4 (2), on the basis that it was an abuse of process or likely to obstruct the just disposal of proceedings. J conceded the breach of the pre-action protocol, but argued that commencement of proceedings was governed by the relevant limitation period and that it was sufficient that a statement of case was issued and served within the prescribed time limit. L argued that the delay in it being informed about the claim was such that it was now impossible for it to enter a defence as it could no longer ascertain important details such as the bus involved and the name of the driver. The delay therefore prejudiced L to such an extent that the statement of claim ought to be struck out as an abuse of process. Further, that in the circumstances, to allow the statement of case to stand would constitute a breach of the European Convention on Human Rights 1950 Art.6 and the Human Rights Act 1998 namely the right to a fair trial.

Held, granting the application, that the Court of Appeal had approved the approach taken by the trial judge in *Biguzzi v. Rank Leisure Plc* [1999] 1 W.L.R. 1926, [1999] C.L.Y. 367 in asking the question, "Is there anything unfair in letting the case go to trial?" There had been no clear guidance from the Court of Appeal, however, on the factors to be taken into account in an application to strike out in any given case. The rule in the Limitation Act 1980 was a negative one: it was not sufficient justification that proceedings were begun before the limitation period had expired. Under the 1980 Act, two conditions had to be met: (1) the limitation period should not have expired, and (2) whether or not it had expired a claimant was obliged to proceed expeditiously, which included the obligation to comply with the pre-action protocol. Therefore, it was not enough to issue proceedings within the time limits if, in delaying, a defendant was deprived of the chance to contest the case fairly. Compliance with the 1980 Act did not preclude the need to conduct the case expeditiously and in accordance with the protocol. In the instant case, overwhelming prejudice had been caused to L due to nearly three years' delay in notification, such that L could not defend the case and it was appropriate to strike out the claim as an abuse.

JIMA ALE v. LONDON BUSES LTD, February 28, 2000, District Judge Banks, CC (Uxbridge). [*Ex rel.* Tim Sheppard, Barrister (instructed by Pitmans (Reading))].

600. Striking out – abuse of process – delay – obligation upon parties to progress claim

[Civil Procedure Rules 1998 (SI 1998 3132) Part 1 r.1.3.]

K appealed the strike out of his claim for libel. In January 1995, K had issued libel proceedings against B following the publication of newspaper articles suggesting that he had gained possession of an antique helmet knowing that it had been stolen. After B had served further and better particulars of his defence in March 1996, no steps were taken in the action until August 1999 when K applied for directions to be granted. In the intervening period, a prosecution against K on a charge of handling stolen goods had been pursued in France culminating in his acquittal. In September 1999, B applied to have the libel action struck out. Acceding to the application, the judge held that K, by delaying progress of the action, had disregarded the court rules to such an extent that he had been guilty of an abuse of process. K appealed, contending that it had been appropriate to await the outcome of the criminal action before progressing the civil action on the basis that there would have been no point in saving his reputation in the civil courts, only to have it destroyed in the criminal courts.

Held, allowing the appeal, that the judge had erred in concluding that K had been guilty of an abuse of process. When separate but related criminal proceedings were being pursued in a defamation case, it would be a question of fact and circumstance whether the trial of the defamation action should be postponed to await the outcome of those proceedings, *Gee v. BBC The Times,* November 26, 1984, [1984] C.L.Y. 2016 applied. Had K sought a stay of the action by reason of the prosecution in France, that application might well have been granted. The overriding objective of the Civil Procedure Rules 1998 was to deal with cases justly. What was more, Part 1 r.1.3 of the Rules imposed an obligation on both parties to help the court to promote the overriding objective. Accordingly, it might no longer be proper for the defendant to permit an action to lie dormant when he himself could take steps to move it forward. B had failed to take any such steps. In all the circumstances, it would be just to allow the action to proceed.

KHALILI v. BENNETT; KHALILI v.WEBB; *sub nom.* KHILILI v. BENNETT [2000] E.M.L.R. 996, Hale, L.J., CA.

601. Striking out – abuse of process – fraud on part of litigant in presenting evidence – fair trial no longer possible

[Companies Act 1985 s.459; Civil Procedure Rules 1998 (SI 1998 3132).]

A, a company under the control of T, held 24 per cent of the shares in a company, BL, the majority shareholding in which was held by B. A and LB, the cohabitee of T and a minority shareholder in BL, presented a petition for relief under the Companies Act 1985 s.459 alleging that B had acted unfairly in connection with the affairs of BL. Following the admission by T that he had, in the process of standard discovery, produced fraudulent documents, B applied to strike out the petition on the ground that a fair trial was no longer possible. Basing his finding on the evidence before him, including an affidavit of T expressing remorse, the judge dismissed the application having concluded that a fair trial was still possible. He indicated, however, that if further evidence of the attempted fraud was revealed, a renewed application would be likely to succeed. At the trial before the same judge, further evidence was submitted and a renewed application was made to strike out the petition. Despite making a finding that T had not ceased in his fraudulent behaviour, the judge dismissed the application (*The Times*, December 8, 1999) having found that a fair trial could still be held in respect of the claims in the petition which had not been affected by T's fraudulent conduct. He went on to conclude that, notwithstanding the effect on the petition of T's attempted fraud, a case for relief had still been made out. B appealed.

Held, allowing the appeal, that (1) the evidence revealed that there was no case for relief under s.459 once those allegations which had been tainted by T's fraud had been put to one side; (2) T's conduct had led to a substantial risk of injustice and had been such that he should have been deprived of the right to pursue his case, *Logicrose Ltd v. Southend United Football Club Ltd (No.1) The Times*, March 5, 1988, [1988] C.L.Y. 2828 applied; (3) it was not clear whether the judge had had regard to the overriding objective of the Civil Procedure Rules 1998. If he had done so, he should have taken into account the fact that T's conduct had made it impossible for the parties to be placed on an equal footing, that it had added significantly to the costs of the proceedings, and that it had occupied a great deal of the court's time to the detriment of other litigants, and (4) while LB had not participated in the fraud, her claim was not severable from that of A. It would therefore be unsafe to allow the petition to proceed by treating it as having been presented by her alone.

ARROW NOMINEES INC v. BLACKLEDGE [2000] C.P. Rep. 59, Chadwick, L.J., CA.

602. Striking out – abuse of process – non compliance with timetable where action still within limitation period

TD commenced an action seeking to recover payment for architectural and design services performed in respect of D's property. D counterclaimed, denying liability. The timetable set for the case was disregarded and TD successfully applied for a stay. Following further directions, the stay was lifted. D applied to strike out the claim as an abuse of process on the basis of the procedural default and asserted that TD had no intention of progressing the action to trial. The application was successful, the judge striking out the action as an abuse of process having concluded that there had been inordinate and inexcusable delay and a blatant disregard of court rules and orders. TD appealed, contending that (1) the judge failed to take account of material considerations, such as the principle of proportionality, given that the court had the opportunity to use a lesser penalty, such as peremptory or unless orders; (2) there had been no serious procedural default; (3) the limitation period had not expired, and therefore TD could issue a new writ, and (4) there was no evidence of any prejudice to D.

Held, allowing the appeal, that striking out of the action was a disproportionate sanction having regard to all the circumstances of the case, and in particular the fact that the cause of action was still within the limitation period, there was no evidence of serious prejudice caused to D, and D was proceeding with his counterclaim arising from precisely the same issues as the substantive claim.

TEKNA DESIGN LTD v. DAVENPORT PROPERTIES LTD [2000] C.P. Rep. 63, Hale, L.J., CA.

603. Striking out – abuse of process – re-entered defence admitting liability after claimant's strike out application

[Civil Procedure Rules 1998 (SI 1998 3132).]

Following the commencement of small claims unliquidated proceedings prior to the Civil Procedure Rules 1998, M's insurers conceded liability and quantum but were not prepared to meet E's solicitors' assessed costs. Due to an oversight or breakdown in communication between M and E's solicitors, M's solicitors served a defence under the 1998 Rules disputing both liability and quantum and denying each of the particulars of claim without giving any details of M's defence. E's solicitors applied under the Rules to strike out the defence as an abuse of process or otherwise likely to obstruct the just disposal of the proceedings, and did not in any event meet the criteria for a defence under the new Rules. Following the service of the application, M's solicitors filed a further defence conceding liability but not quantum.

Held, allowing the application, that the administrative problems experienced by M's solicitors were of no concern to the claimant. The defence was therefore struck out with assessed costs awarded to E.

EMMERSON v. McCLELLAND, September 14, 1999, Deputy District Judge Fink, CC (Croydon). [*Ex rel.* Aryan Stedman, Barrister, and Corries Solicitors, Rowntrees Wharf, Navigation Road, York].

604. Striking out – abuse of process – res judicata – prejudice to defendant if personal injury claim litigated

[Civil Procedure Rules 1998 (SI 1998 3132) Part 1 r.1.1.]

H brought an action against U for damage to his motor car following a road traffic accident. U had third party insurance and his insurers instructed solicitors to defend only the insured losses. A defence was filed but not a counterclaim. U informed H that he intended to bring a claim for damages for personal injuries but no agreement was made that U's claim would not be included in the proceedings. The case was dealt with under the small claims arbitration procedure and liability was apportioned 75 per cent to 25 per cent in favour of H. U subsequently issued a second action for damages for personal injury. H applied for the claim to be struck out for abuse of process on the grounds that U was seeking to relitigate matters which could or should have raised in the first action, *Henderson v. Henderson* [1843-60] All E.R. Rep. 378 and *Talbot v. Berkshire CC* [1994] Q.B. 290, [1993] C.L.Y. 1851 cited. U's claim was struck out and appealed, contending that the court should apply the overriding objective in *Biguzzi v. Rank Leisure Plc* [1999] 1 W.L.R. 1926, [1999] C.L.Y. 367 and having done so it would not have been just to strike out the claim for the reasons that (1) if the present claim had been included in the original proceedings it could not have been properly formulated or adjudicated upon. It would have been, as the district judge noted, a purely formal notice of the claim; (2) U was not seeking to go behind the finding of as to liability in the earlier action; (3) it was sensible to resolve the issue of liability while matters were reasonably fresh in the parties' minds and deal with damages for personal injuries at a later date, and (4) H had not been caused any prejudice save perhaps for the issuing of two court fees. U undertook to pay one of the claim fees and any costs which the court thought appropriate. H argued that (1) res judicata was substantive not procedural law and that the relevance of the Civil Procedure Rules 1998 was merely to broaden the category of "special circumstances" in *Henderson*; (2) he had been caused prejudice in that had U's claims been included in the original proceedings by way of counterclaim, it would not have been dealt with by arbitration.

Held, allowing the appeal, that *Henderson* was still good law. Nevertheless Part 1 r.1.1 of the 1998 Rules did modify the impact of *Henderson*, which although it had acquired by its age the character of substantive law, dealt with procedural issues. H would not be prejudiced by the claim for personal injury whereas U was at risk of severe prejudice. The 1998 Rules required and allowed greater flexibility on procedural matters. On the particular facts of the case it was just to allow the appeal.

UNDERWOOD v. HARRIS, January 31, 2000, Judge Rice, CC (Southend). [*Ex rel.* Richard Roberts, Barrister, Lamb Building, Temple, London].

605. Striking out – application of Civil Procedure Rules to cases decided prior to effective date

[Insolvency Act 1986 s.339; Civil Procedure Rules 1998 (SI 1998 3132); Civil Procedure Rules 1998 (SI 1998 3132) Part 1.]

H, a trustee in bankruptcy of the late RF, commenced proceedings in September 1994 under the Insolvency Act 1986 s.339 to set aside a transfer of RF's interest in the property to F, his ex-wife, claiming that it had been at an undervalue. In March 1996, F gave discovery, after a considerable delay, but failed to comply with court's direction for the exchange of experts' reports. H took no further steps in the proceedings until February 1998, and in July 1998 F applied for the dismissal of the s.339 application for want of prosecution. The application was granted in January 1999 and H's subsequent appeal in July 1999 was dismissed on the basis that the delay was found to be inordinate and inexcusable causing prejudice to F. H appealed again contending that (1) the length of delay should be reduced because F had contributed to the delay by failing to give discovery promptly, and it was wrong to strike out the application as the six year limitation period had not expired when the previous appeal had been heard, *Birkett v. James* [1978] A.C. 297, [1977] C.L.Y. 2410 referred to; (2) there was no evidence of prejudice to F, particularly no express averments that the passage of time would make it difficult for F's witnesses to comment on or remember salient facts, and (3) the deputy judge, in exercising his discretion, was wrong to disapply the Civil Procedure Rules 1998, especially the overriding objective in Part 1 to deal with the case justly, which on the facts would have led him to conclude that striking out was a disproportionate and inappropriate sanction.

Held, dismissing the appeal, that (1) there was no justification for reducing the period of delay; (2) it was not necessary to particularise how a witness' memory had faded if the facts supported such an inference of prejudice, which in this case, they did, *Shtun v. Zalejska* [1996] 1 W.L.R. 1270, [1996] C.L.Y. 898 applied, and (3) when exercising his discretion, bearing in mind that the striking out had been granted prior to the 1998 Rules coming into force, the deputy judge was entitled to disapply the 1998 Rules and deal with the matter applying the previous rules, save that the overriding objective of Part 1 had to be applied, *McPhilemy v. Times Newspapers Ltd (Re-amendment: Justification)* [1999] 3 All E.R. 775, [1999] C.L.Y. 1635 applied. There was no evidence that the judge had not taken Part 1 into account when exercising his discretion.

HAMBLIN v. FIELD [2000] B.P.I.R. 621, Peter Gibson, L.J., CA.

606. Striking out – automatic striking out – failure to issue directions following application for summary judgment

[County Court Rules 1981 (SI 1981 1687) Ord.17 r.11; Civil Procedure Rules 1998 (SI 1998 3132).]

S appealed against a refusal of the county court to overturn a ruling that S's action, relating to an arrears in rent, had been automatically struck out for failure to obtain a hearing date within the specified time. S obtained summary judgment on February 21, 1997, which was subsequently set aside on May 20, 1997 on terms that monies were paid into court and defences filed by June 3, 1997, at which stage automatic directions were issued. Under the directions the deadline for requesting a hearing date was September 16, 1998. S made a second application for summary judgment on June 23, 1997 on grounds which could have formed part of the first application. The application was dismissed and S contended that as a result of making the second application time had stopped running, and, as no directions had been given following dismissal of the second application, the action had been left with no time limits.

Held, dismissing the appeal, that dismissal of a second application for summary judgment which had been based upon grounds which could have been utilised at the making of the first application did not have any effect upon the time limits under the County Court Rules 1981 Ord.17 r.11 despite the new Civil Procedure Rules 1998. If the opposite was true then any litigant could frustrate the court's timetable by making applications for summary judgment. Furthermore, S's actions after the guillotine date of September 16 1997, specifically applying for specific discovery and making an application to fix a trial date out of time, indicated that S had believed that the automatic directions were still effective, *Bannister v. SGB Plc* [1998] 1 W.L.R. 1123, [1997] C.L.Y. 736 distinguished.

SEAL v. WILKINSON [2000] C.P.L.R. 1, Sedley, L.J., CA.

607. Striking out – claim for cost of building work – Tomlin order silent as to who should carry out remedial work – deficiencies in order insufficient to justify striking out of claim

C, a builder, issued proceedings against HE claiming the cost of work which had been carried out at HE's property. The proceedings were compromised by way of a Tomlin order which provided for the payment of three lump sums to C. Two of those payments were expressed as being payable following the issue of certificates confirming that certain remedial works had been satisfactorily performed. In a separate action, HE issued a third party proceedings against C relying on the Tomlin order. C applied to strike out the third party notice. Granting the application, the district judge held that the Tomlin order could not be relied on by HE as it had failed to specify which party was to carry out the remedial works. HE appealed. Reversing the district judge's decision, the judge found that notwithstanding that the Tomlin order had been badly drafted, it was to be construed as an agreement which not only provided for the payment of money to C but also for the carrying out of work by him. C appealed.

Held, dismissing the appeal, that it was arguable that the Tomlin order required C to carry out the relevant remedial works. Accordingly, C's attempt to strike out the third party notice had been inappropriate. Evidence of the circumstances in which the Tomlin order had been entered into would be admissible before the trial judge who would have to rule on the limits and effect of such evidence.

PANAYI v. HUFRAN ESTATES LTD CCRTI 99/0840/B1, Alliott, J., CA.

608. Striking out – continued failure to comply with Rules of the Supreme Court and court orders – just to order strike out in such circumstances

[Rules of the Supreme Court 1965 (SI 1965 1776).]

Acting on UCB's request, H valued a property in reliance upon which UCB granted a mortgage to a client who subsequently defaulted. UCB argued that the property had been seriously overvalued and issued proceedings alleging professional negligence on the part of H. However, UCB repeatedly failed to comply with the Rules of the Supreme Court and court orders. H succeeded in having the case struck out on the grounds that to continue would be an abuse of process. UCB appealed, arguing that there were other punitive measures available, such as an order for costs or the deduction of a part of the interest on any damages awarded.

Held, dismissing the appeal, that although other measures were within the discretion of the court, where there was a continued and blatant failure to comply with the Rules and orders of the court, striking out was the only viable option, provided it was just in the circumstances, *Arbuthnot Latham Bank Ltd v. Trafalgar Holdings Ltd* [1998] 1 W.L.R. 1426, [1998] C.L.Y. 619 applied. There was little weight in the argument that the judge fettered his discretion by not considering the other options. The breaches of Rules and orders were sufficiently serious to warrant a striking out of the action, *Biguzzi v. Rank Leisure Plc* [1999] 1 W.L.R. 1926, [1999] C.L.Y. 367 considered.

UCB CORPORATE SERVICES LTD (FORMERLY UCB BANK PLC) v. HALIFAX (SW) LTD (STRIKING OUT: BREACH OF RULES AND ORDERS) [1999] C.P.L.R. 691, Lord Lloyd of Berwick, CA.

609. Striking out – delay – discretion – 10 year delay in bringing claim – death of defendant's primary witness

[Civil Procedure Rules 1998 (SI 1998 3132) Part 1 r.1.1 (2).]

P, who had been involved in a road traffic accident in December 1989 for which C admitted liability, appealed against the striking out of his claim for personal injuries. An interlocutory judgment had been entered in P's favour in September 1994 and an order made for the assessment of damages. Subsequently considerable delays ensued during which P's advisors obtained a number of medical reports in which differences of opinion were expressed as to the likelihood of him returning to work. C's primary witness, who, having examined P, concluded that he could return to work since his injuries were relatively minor, had died in August 1998 before the matter had proceeded to trial. A judge striking out the claim had held it an abuse of the process on the grounds of delay, emanating in part from P's attempts at obtaining a more favourable medical report, which had resulted in serious prejudice to C. P contended, inter alia, that the judges' decision had not been proportional as required by the Civil Procedure Rules 1998 and that the delays that had occurred had not caused C any serious prejudice.

Held, dismissing the appeal, that the judge had taken into consideration the overriding objective of the Part 1 r.1.1 (2) of the 1998 Rules that the court deal with cases fairly and promptly had exercised his discretion justly in striking out P's claim. A period of 10 years had passed since the accident which had given rise to P's injuries, and it was no longer possible as a consequence of that delay to have a fair trial of the issues. Where such a delay had arisen the judge had a wide discretion, in the course of his case management capacity, to strike out any claim if appropriate, *Biguzzi v. Rank Leisure Plc* [1999] 1 W.L.R. 1926, [1999] C.L.Y. 367 and *UCB Corporate Services Ltd (formerly UCB Bank Plc) v. Halifax (SW) Ltd (Striking Out: Breach of Rules and Orders)* [1999] C.P.L.R. 691, [2000] C.L.Y. 608 considered. In the instant case where C's primary witness had died before the proceedings had gone to trial, it would be unfair to substitute another witness at such a late state. Any new expert would not have the benefit of prior consultation and examination of P when the effects of the accident were still evident and accordingly, such injustice, resulting from P's delay, warranted the striking out of the claim.

PURDY v. CAMBRAN [2000] C.P. Rep. 67, Swinton Thomas, L.J., CA.

610. Striking out – delay – failure to comply with mandatory time limit for service of claim form justified wasted costs order

[Civil Procedure Rules 1998 (SI 1998 3132) Part 7 r.7.4 (2), r.7.5 (2), Part 10 r.10 (3) (1) (a).]

A claim form issued on August 16, 1999 was served on L by R with a covering letter dated December 14, 1999. The letter enclosed R's expert evidence and contained a statement to the effect that, although R's solicitors acknowledged that L was entitled to a particulars of claim, they would be prepared to draft one only if L insisted that it was necessary, but they had disclosed their expert evidence in effect to take the place of the formal leading. The documents were not received by L until December 17, 1999 and the letter bore a date of receipt stamp to that effect. L's solicitors wrote to R's solicitors on January 7, 2000 acknowledging receipt. L then applied to strike out R's claim on the basis of non compliance with the Civil

Procedure Rules 1998 Part 7 r.7.4(2) and r.7.5(2), concerning time for service of particulars of claim and claim forms.

Held, striking out the claim and making a wasted costs order in favour of the defendant, that r.7.5 regarding service of a claim form was mandatory and there was no residual discretion which may be exercised by the court. It was clear from the rules that the claim form should be served within four months after the date of issue, in this case by December 16, 1999. R had not put forward any direct evidence of posting by way of a certificate of service not had there been an application for an extension of time for service of the claim form under Part 7 r.7.5 of the Rules. Under Part 7 r.7.4(2) the latest time for service of the particulars of claim would have been December 16, 1999 and the letter of L's solicitor dated January 7, 2000 did not constitute an express waiver of this requirement. R was incorrect to submit that L was not entitled to bring the application for strike out because it failed to file an acknowledgement of service. Part 10 r.10.3(1)(a) stated that the time for filing an acknowledgement of service was 14 days after service of the particulars of claim, therefore time had not yet began to run as no particulars of claim had been served.

ROBERTS v. LUTON & DUNSTABLE HOSPITAL NHS TRUST, February 11, 2000, District Judge Field, QBD. [*Ex rel.* Capsticks Solicitors, 77-83 Upper Richmond Road, London].

611. Striking out – delay – medical examinations – brain injured claimant – failure to submit to medical examination by defence

J sought permission to appeal against the dismissal of his application for an extension of time for compliance with an unless order. J had sustained serious injuries at the age of 12 in a road traffic accident but the defendants maintained that his serious mental impairment was potentially attributable to a progressive disorder rather than traumatic injury to the brain. J's mother and next friend failed to agree to arrangements for an examination by medical experts for the defence and the defendants were subsequently successful in their application for an unless order. J's mother subsequently failed to ensure his attendance at the examination and the court made an order for strike out, having dismissed J's application for an extension of time for compliance.

Held, dismissing the application, that the exercise of judicial discretion to strike out the claim could not be impugned in circumstances where a fair trial could not take place without the defendant having an opportunity to examine J and form conclusions as to whether his ongoing disability resulted from the accident or from some other cause. Furthermore there was no evidence to suggest that J's mother's attitude was likely to change, given that no explanation had been forthcoming for the repeated instances of non cooperation to date.

JASSIM v. GRAND METROPOLITAN INFORMATION SERVICES LTD [2000] C.P. Rep. 78, Chadwick, J., CA.

612. Striking out – delay – non compliance with court orders – court to exercise discretion to prevent weak and slow moving actions continuing indefinitely

[Civil Procedure Rules 1998 (SI 1998 3132) Part 3 r.3.4(ii)(c).]

O brought an action against C in 1990 claiming a failure to account for royalties in breach of agreements entered into in 1982 and 1985. Very little occurred until 1995 when, by consent, O appointed an auditor to review C's papers. He estimated that on the papers available, C only owed £6,000. In 1998, C unsuccessfully applied to strike out the claim. O vainly sought full disclosure from C, but eventually applied to set the action down for trial. On O's failure to comply with pretrial directions, the Civil Procedure Rules 1998 were found to apply and the action was struck out pursuant to Part 3 r.3.4(ii)(c) on the grounds that a fair trial was no longer possible because of the delay and failure to comply with court orders. The judge, in allowing O's appeal, found that it was inappropriate for a judge to be asked to reconsider matters already dealt with by an earlier judge in a strike out application. C appealed and O subsequently amended his claim to rely solely upon witness evidence.

Held, allowing the appeal, that the judge should have considered the overriding objective under the 1998 Rules and then determined whether the case had to be struck out as a result whilst taking into account the merits of O's claim. Litigation not conducted diligently over such a long period should not be allowed to continue indefinitely and the court now had sufficient powers under the 1998 Rules to take control of proceedings to prevent this occurring. O had no direct evidence of a failure on C's part to account for royalties, only witness evidence of events occurring up to 16 years earlier. On the merits, the claim was most unlikely to succeed, therefore it was inappropriate to allow the action to continue in light of the overriding objective. The judge had misdirected himself in finding that a judge was prevented from reconsidering matters covered by an earlier judge in deciding not to strike out. There was no order made as to costs because of C's failure to cooperate with O's legal representatives.

O'DONNELL v. CHARLY HOLDINGS INC; *sub nom.* McDONALD v. CHARLY HOLDINGS INC CCRTI 99/1216/B3, Lord Woolf, M.R., CA.

613. Striking out – delay – non compliance with directions order by claimant – significance to be attached to similar default by defendant

[Civil Procedure Rules 1998 (SI 1998 3132).]

C appealed a refusal to grant an extension of time for compliance with a directions order in an action commenced by C against P for breach of contract. The action had been commenced by C on January 2, 1997 and an order for directions made on August 13, 1997. C repeatedly failed to provide copies of documents detailed in its list of documents or replies to a request for further particulars of those documents which had been provided. All subsequent deadlines detailed in the directions order including those relating to the exchange of witness statements and expert evidence passed without either party attempting to comply. P applied to strike out the claim four weeks prior to the date fixed for the trial. The application was successful, the judge finding significant prejudice to P arising from the impact of the likely six month delay upon witness memory in an action concerning events in 1992. C appealed, contending that the judge had erred in failing to attach significance to the fact that P was equally to blame for the fact that the action was not ready for trial following the adoption of its deliberate policy of non compliance with the directions order. C maintained that under the Civil Procedure Rules 1998, P's conduct should have been viewed with more concern because of the consideration of fairness imposed by the new rules and that P should have been expected to make an application to the court to require C's compliance.

Held, dismissing the appeal, that the judge had clearly taken the issue of P's non compliance into account but had been entitled to conclude in the circumstances of the instant case, that he would refuse an extension of time for compliance. Under the regime imposed by the 1998 Rules, consideration of the issue of fairness was not confined to the individual parties but also whether there was a potential impact on other litigants whose cases might not be resolved as quickly as they might otherwise have been.

CHELTENHAM LAMINATING CO v. POLYFIBRE LTD [2001] C.P. Rep. 4, Beldam, L.J., CA.

614. Striking out – delay – prejudice – case management – criteria for consideration in strike out

A applied for the reinstatement of an action against G and S which had been struck out by order of the master.

Held, reinstating the action, that the following considerations on the applicability of strike out were considered relevant: the extent of any delay, the validity of any excuses made for it, and the contribution to the delay made by the opposing party. In addition, the parties' conduct during the litigation and general case management criteria were important.

ANNODEUS LTD v. GIBSON *The Times*, March 3, 2000, Neuberger, J., Ch D.

615. Striking out – delay – prejudice – unavailability of crucial witness

[Civil Procedure Rules 1998 (SI 1998 3132) Part 3 r.3.4(2)(c).]

By a writ issued in September 1995, C, the purchasers of a cargo of yellow maize, brought a claim against T, the owners of the vessel carrying the cargo, alleging that the ship's master had wrongly endorsed on the mate's receipt the words "cargo looks old and dusty". The points of claim were served in March 1996 and were later amended in August 1996. In September 1996 the points of defence were served, and lists of documents were exchanged in January 1997. There followed a considerable delay in the process of inspection. Following receipt of a letter in March 2000 requesting a case management conference, T applied pursuant to the Civil Procedure Rules 1998 Part 3 r.3.4(2)(c) for the claim to be struck out on the ground, inter alia, that the undue delay had caused them prejudice. T maintained that as a consequence of the delay the ship's master, whose evidence would be crucial to the case and who had previously been willing to provide evidence in court despite residing in Greece, was no longer willing to appear at court.

Held, allowing the application, that there had been a substantial and unjustified delay such as to cause T prejudice. While the ship's master had provided a written statement, it was apparent that the evidential impact of that statement would differ substantially from what might be said in court where the opportunity would be available for cross examination. Having regard to the length of delay, the lack of explanation for it, the nature of the claim and the overriding objectives of the Rules, it was appropriate that the action should be struck out.

CHENG I FOOD CO LTD v. THEOTOKO MARITIME INC 1995 Folio No.1648, Toulson, J., QBD (Comm Ct).

616. Striking out – delay – prescribed time limits – consideration of circumstances

R appealed against an order striking out his claim in negligence against RE, a firm of solicitors, on the ground that the action was an abuse of process. It was held that delays subsequent to June 1994, when interlocutory judgment for damages was granted in favour of R in default of service of notice to defend, were due to the fact that R had made a deliberate decision not to proceed which was sufficient to turn a delay into an abuse of process. RE, who had been instructed by R to act on his behalf in connection with a property development and who was supported by the Solicitors' Indemnity Fund, issued a cross notice seeking to affirm judgment on the basis that (1) R had deliberately delayed proceedings in order to conceal bankruptcy, or, alternatively, (2) the action should be dismissed for want of prosecution under the second limb of *Birkett v. James* [1978] A.C. 297, [1977] C.L.Y. 2410 on the ground that R had delayed proceedings inordinately, notwithstanding the lack of any breach of procedural time limits, which gave rise to substantial risk of prejudice. RE submitted that difficulties encountered by R in relation to legal aid and bankruptcy proceedings in no way excused the delay in applying for an assessment of damages under the judgment in default.

Held, allowing the appeal, that (1) despite a delay in proceedings there was no evidential basis on which to conclude that R had taken a decision not to proceed, and (2) it was not necessary to establish that a delay in proceeding involved a breach of procedural rules or an order of the court when considering the dismissal of a claim for want of prosecution, it depended on the consequences of that delay, *Birkett* applied. Further, in the instant case, the delay by R had been inordinate but was excusable given that R had attempted to advance his case throughout the period, had informed the Solicitors's Indemnity

Fund of his intention to proceed and had not been in breach of any prescribed time limits.

ROGERS v. RHYS EVANS (A FIRM) [2000] C.P.L.R. 400, Jonathan Parker, J., CA.

617. **Striking out – delay – professional negligence – 12 year delay – strike out of claim 12 years after relevant transaction – prejudice to defendant where recollection faded**

[Civil Procedure Rules 1998 (SI 1998 3132).]

P, a company, appealed the strike out of its claim for professional negligence against S, a firm of solicitors. P had instructed S in 1988 to act on its behalf in connection with the purchase of a leasehold interest in a property. P required permission from the landlords to carry out certain conversion works, pursuant to a covenant in the lease, and planned to carry out the works in order to realise a profit on the property. The sale was concluded and it thereafter became apparent that the requisite consents had not been obtained. P alleged that S had confirmed orally, prior to the conclusion of the purchase, that informal consent had been granted, and P instituted proceedings against S in 1994, which proceedings were thereafter subject to considerable delay. In 1999 S applied to strike out the action for want of prosecution. The judge at first instance determined the application on the basis of the principles in *Birkett v. James* [1978] A.C. 297, [1977] C.L.Y. 2410. He found that P had been guilty of inordinate and inexcusable delay, and that there would be prejudice to S in permitting the matter to proceed, having regard to the fact that the case centred around the content of unrecorded conversations, which had taken place over a decade earlier, the details of which S was by now unable to recall. P appealed, contending that the matter should have been determined under the Civil Procedure Rules 1998 rather than the decision in *Birkett v. James*, and if that had been the case, the court ought to have exercised its discretion to permit him to proceed.

Held, dismissing the appeal, that (1) the judge had been entitled to conclude that the oral evidence concerning the nature of the instructions given and the advice received was a crucial element of the claim and that to permit the action to proceed more than twelve years after those conversations had taken place, in circumstances where the contemporaneous documentation concerning the transaction was of little assistance and S's memory had faded, would have been unfairly prejudicial to S, and (2) the judge should have determined the application under the Civil Procedure Rules 1998. However, it would be an anomalous result if the application of those rules was more likely to result in the dismissal of the strike out application than the old procedure, *UCB Corporate Services Ltd (formerly UCB Bank Plc) v. Halifax (SW) Ltd (Striking Out: Breach of Rules and Orders)* [1999] C.P.L.R. 691, [2000] C.L.Y. 608 applied. Furthermore the factors which fell to be considered under the 1998 Rules were all part of the material available to, and considered by, the judge and it would be contrary to the overriding objective of the 1998 Rules to permit the instant claim to proceed.

PUREFUTURE LTD v. SIMMONS & SIMMONS [2001] C.P. Rep. 30, Clarke, L.J., CA.

618. **Striking out – delay – strike out inappropriate on basis that fair trial still possible despite significant delay**

[County Court Rules 1981 (SI 1981 1687) Ord.17 r.11; Civil Procedure Rules 1998 (SI 1998 3132) Part 3 r.3.4(2).]

W sustained serious personal injuries in a road traffic accident and commenced proceedings against the defendant driver, M, in 1992. The form N450 sent out by the court specified an incorrect date of receipt of the defence. In reliance upon that date, W's advisers calculated the deadline for requesting a trial date pursuant to the County Court Rules 1981 Ord.17 r.11. After the true date had in fact passed, W's solicitors applied for directions and an order was made for listing upon the provision of a certificate of readiness. The action did not progress and M's solicitors made enquiries of the county court as to whether the action had been struck out and received confirmation that it had, the court having mislaid their file. Following two changes of solicitors, W's new solicitors also wrote to the court stating that in their opinion the prior directions order had in fact ousted the automatic directions. The court agreed with this assessment in ignorance of the fact that the true deadline had passed before the directions order had been sought. After a further period of inaction the court made an order that the action had been struck out, having now appreciated the "true" deadline. W's solicitors successfully sought reinstatement of the action on the basis that W's former solicitors had been misled by the incorrect form N450. An application to strike out for want of prosecution was however successful in 1999. W appealed the strike out but at the hearing of the appeal the court granted M permission to appeal the earlier order for reinstatement and struck out the action under the Civil Procedure Rules 1998 Part 3 r.3.4(2). W appealed.

Held, allowing the appeal, that it had not been appropriate to strike out W's claim under the Civil Procedure Rules 1998 Part 3 r.3.4(2). Had the action progressed as it should have done, the case could have been tried in 1995. On the basis that it would still be possible to conduct a fair trial of the issues as they had been formulated in 1995, that trial should now take place, however it would be neither fair nor possible to try the additional issues raised by W in 1999 to include a substantially enlarged claim for loss of earnings. In relation to those parts of W's claim which were excluded from the present litigation, W would have an action against his former solicitors.

Observed, that the result in the instant case followed a consideration of all the relevant facts and circumstances and future cases would require similar consideration of their own particular merits.

WALSH v. MISSELDINE [2000] C.P. Rep. 74, Brooke, L.J., CA.

619. Striking out – dismissal of action inappropriate given exchange of evidence

[Rules of the Supreme Court 1965 (SI 1965 1776) Ord.18 r.19; Civil Procedure Rules 1998 (SI 1998 3132).]

R, an architect and former property developer brought a claim for damages for negligence. P issued a summons under the Rules of the Supreme Court Ord.18 r.19 to strike out R's statement of claim on the basis that what was pleaded was "frivolous and vexatious" and that the action should be dismissed, as it was an abuse of process, given that the statement of claim failed to fully plead or particularise the nature of the claim. The judge adjourned the hearing to allow R to amend the statement of claim. Following the amendment, P's application was dismissed on the ground that the newly amended pleadings were adequate. P subsequently appealed and R claimed that the application to strike out the amended claim was inappropriate under the Civil Procedure Rules 1998 in view of the fact that exchange of witness statements had already taken place.

Held, dismissing the appeal, that the application to strike out was inappropriate, given the fact that there had been an exchange of witness statements and experts' reports and a date for the trial had been fixed, prior to the appeal hearing. Under the Civil Procedure Rules 1998 such irrelevant interlocutory applications which are time consuming and costly would no longer be tolerated. The evidence which had been exchanged was crucial to the trial of the action, whereas the statement of claim merely provided the issues to be addressed. The Court of Appeal had not been informed of the fact that further directions had been given regarding the timetable of events and had they been, it would have been highly unlikely that they would have granted permission to appeal on the pleadings.

ROBERTS v. PRICE [2000] C.P. Rep. 52, Evans, L.J., CA.

620. Striking out – documentary evidence – inference from pleadings – references to extraneous material – abuse of court's jurisdiction

[Insolvency Act 1986 s.213; Rules of the Supreme Court 1965 (SI 1965 1776) Ord.18 r.19(1).]

B provided credit clearing and related banking facilities to the BCCI banking group in which B also had a minority shareholding prior to BCCI 's subsequent liquidation. The liquidators brought an action under the Insolvency Act 1986 s.213 alleging that BCCI's business had been carried on by B with intent to defraud its creditors and with other unspecified fraudulent intent and that B should be required to make a contribution to the assets of the two BCCI companies in liquidation. B applied to strike out the proceedings under the Rules of the Supreme Court 1965 Ord.18 r.19(1), contending that the pleadings disclosed no cause of action since the requisite knowledge and dishonest intent on the part of B could not be established and therefore the case had no prospect of success. Furthermore, that the complexity of the pleadings on that issue were such that if the case went to trial the burden on the court would be substantial so that to spend three weeks on a preliminary application to strike out was not out of proportion. The liquidators contended that it was an abuse of the court's striking out jurisdiction for it to become involved in lengthy interlocutory proceedings concerning pleadings and procedural matters which would require the examination of extraneous material and that the court's inherent jurisdiction to strike out should be exercised sparingly and not used to usurp the role of the trial judge. B contended that the court would not need to go beyond the material facts alleged in the pleadings, since it was likely that those represented the whole of the evidence that would be produced at trial.

Held, dismissing the applications, that in order to demonstrate B's claim that the pleadings disclosed no cause of action would necessitate a minute and protracted examination of the documents which might constitute the whole of the evidence put forward and thus would constitute the sort of "mini trial" specifically precluded by the Court of Appeal. The burden of proof at that stage of the proceedings fell on B to show that there was no chance of success, which meant that B must establish that (1) it would be impossible to infer from the documents that the requisite knowledge of the fraud was present, and (2) there was no reasonable possibility that other evidence would be produced at trial, following discovery. Those contentions could not be established with any certainty and it was clear that the documents would have to be examined in context, an exercise which the court should not embark upon during an interlocutory application, *Three Rivers DC v. Bank of England (No.4)* (Unreported, July 31, 1997) distinguished on its facts, *Saul D Harrison & Sons Plc, Re* [1995] 1 B.C.L.C. 14, [1995] C.L.Y. 2860 and *Company (No.005685 of 1988) (No.2), Re* [1989] B.C.L.C. 427, [1990] C.L.Y. 540 considered.

BANK OF AMERICA NATIONAL TRUST AND SAVINGS ASSOCIATION v. MORRIS TNS, Lloyd, J., Ch D.

621. Striking out – estoppel – claimant estopped from claiming damages for personal injuries after settlement between insurers – insufficient particulars of claim

[Civil Procedure Rules 1998 (SI 1998 3132) Part 16 r.16.4(1)(a).]

L and G were involved in a road traffic accident and L's insurers made an offer in correspondence for settlement "on a 50/50 basis". G's insurers accepted the offer on his behalf. The insurers subsequently exchanged cheques in accordance with their agreement. Later, L indicated that she did not consent to the terms of the settlement and disputed any liability for the accident. Further, she indicated she had a claim for personal injuries which had been covered in the settlement. L issued proceedings against G for damages including damages for her injuries. The particulars of claim did not give details of the circumstances of the accident, save to mention that a collision had occurred between L and G's cars. G invited the court to strike out the particulars of the claim on the grounds that it did not contain a concise statement of the facts which L relied, contrary to the requirements of the Civil Procedure Rules 1998 Part 16 r.16.4(1)(a). Further, G averred that L's claim had already been settled by the parties' insurers. The court ordered that unless L complied with Part 16 r.16.4(1)(a) her claim would be struck out. L's solicitor then filed a witness statement at court which described the circumstances of the accident in detail but this statement was not served on G.

Held, striking out the claim, that (1) the particulars of claim were insufficient for the purposes of Part 16 r.16.4(1)(a) and L could not remedy the situation by service of a witness statement and (2) even if the witness statement was accepted as a statement of case and had been served on G, L's application to reinstate the claim was refused. There had clearly been an agreement to settle the claim before L indicated her intention to dispute liability and to litigate for personal injuries. That agreement was binding on L and she was now estopped from pursuing a claim against G, *Kitchen Design & Advice Ltd v. Lea Valley Water Co* [1989] 2 Lloyd's Rep. 221, [1990] C.L.Y. 2687 applied. In refusing to reinstate the claim, the judge applied Part 3 of the 1998 Rules, holding that the statement of case was an abuse of the court's process and ought not to be litigated in view of the agreement reached. Alternatively, in the light of the documentation produced evidencing the agreement, there was no real prospect of L succeeding on the claim and G would have been entitled to summary judgment under Part 24 of the Rules. The judge also had regard to the issues of proportionality, to the prejudice of G, and to the availability of a remedy to L from her insurers if they had not been entitled to compromise her claim without her express authority.

LUCHTMANSINGH v. GROSTATE, May 5, 2000, District Judge Silverman, CC (Edmonton). [*Ex rel.* Joanna Droop, Barrister, 12 King's Bench Walk, Temple, London].

622. Striking out – failure to comply with order for disclosure – overriding objective of litigation not served by striking out

[Civil Procedure Rules 1998 (SI 1998 3132).]

S made a claim against P following an accident in 1995 to include a claim for loss of earnings. The Civil Procedure Rules 1998 were disapplied. Two years after the commencement of proceedings, an order was made requiring S to serve an updated schedule of loss and a further list of documents including a disclosure statement. An order was also made with regard to inspection. P subsequently applied for the claim to be struck out on the basis that S had failed to comply with these orders. S opposed the application and served a document in the form of a report which conformed neither to a schedule of loss nor an expert's report, and also proffered two further witness statements, contrary to a suggestion in correspondence that they would not seek to adduce further evidence beyond that which they had already served in support of their claim.

Held, refusing the application to strike out, that it would not further the overriding objective of the litigation to strike out S's claim, notwithstanding that S had been at fault in failing to comply with the orders. The correct approach was to limit S to the existing schedule of loss that he had already served and the evidence already filed in support of it. Permission was refused for further evidence to be adduced. If S wished to adduce further evidence permission from the trial judge would be required.

STOCKMAN v. PAYNE [2000] C.P. Rep. 50, Buckley, J., QBD.

623. Striking out – false imprisonment – consideration of witness statements alone

[Civil Procedure Rules 1998 (SI 1998 3132) Part 3 r.3.4(2)(a), Part 24 r.24.2.]

C was arrested by two police officers upon suspicion of burglary as he stood waiting at a taxi rank. C subsequently commenced proceedings against CCN alleging false imprisonment and assault. CCN applied to strike out the claim under the Civil Procedure Rules 1998 Part 3 r.3.4(2)(a) and Part 24 r.24.2. The judge at first instance granted the application, stating that the claim for false imprisonment was bound to fail. C appealed.

Held, allowing the appeal, that the statements which had been available to the judge clearly contained material sufficient to establish a claim for false imprisonment, based on two separate and distinct issues. Firstly, the actual suspicion of the officers and secondly the existence of reasonable grounds giving rise to that suspicion. C's account of the events leading up to his arrest, if proved to be true, would indicate that the two officers in question had possessed no reasonable grounds for suspecting that C had committed an arrestable offence since C had provided an explanation for his presence at the scene which had been confirmed prior to the arrest by an independent third party. The judge had erred in presuming that the police officer's version of events was true and effectively making a finding of fact from consideration of the statements alone that the officers had possessed reasonable grounds for suspicion.

CONLAN v. CHIEF CONSTABLE OF NORTHUMBRIA FC2-A 1999/7677/B1, Judge, L.J., CA.

624. **Striking out – libel – prospect of succeeding on single point insufficient to justify court time and cost – attempt to relitigate matters at issue in compromised proceedings was abuse of process**

[Civil Procedure Rules 1998 (SI 1998 3132).]

S was the owner of the Scottish island of Eigg from 1975 until 1995. In April 1997, BBC broadcast a radio programme in which a journalist stated that Eigg had been run on feudal lines and went on to describe how S had threatened C, a family on the island, with eviction the previous Christmas. S brought an action for defamation, claiming that the broadcast suggested that he had acted like a "feudal tyrant" towards C. BBC applied for the claim to be struck out as an abuse of process as S had commenced similar actions against two newspapers but had settled them to his detriment prior to their determination.

Held, allowing the application, that the notice to quit served by S on C was intended to have an unpleasant effect on them and no reasonable jury could find other than that it had had such an effect. Although a jury might find for S on the question of whether he intended to do damage to C's business, the court had an obligation under the Civil Procedure Rules 1998 to balance the benefits to S of succeeding on that one point against the costs and use of court time. S's compromise of the newspaper actions had allowed those newspapers to print further damaging articles about him and, although BBC could not rely on damage to S's reputation after the date of the broadcast, that factor was relevant to the court's balancing exercise, and meant that there was no real prospect that succeeding on the one issue would be of benefit to S, such as to justify the expenditure of a full trial. The claim was also an abuse of process as the main issues had been argued in the newspapers' cases and could not be relitigated by S, *Bradford & Bingley Building Society v. Seddon (Hancock t/a Hancocks)* [1999] 1 W.L.R. 1482, [1999] C.L.Y. 351 applied.

SCHELLENBERG v. BBC [2000] E.M.L.R. 296, Eady, J., QBD.

625. **Striking out – non compliance with court order – court to exercise discretion where unfair to allow claim to continue**

[Civil Procedure Rules 1998 (SI 1998 3132) Part 3 r.3.4(2).]

H suffered from pain possibly attributable to an infection caused by the aftermath of birth of her child in July 1982. H, who maintained that she had only learnt of the possible cause in April 1984, consulted solicitors, BB, in January 1987 in relation to a claim in medical negligence. In April 1989 BB issued a writ which expired a year later without being served. Subsequently, H instructed a firm of solicitors, JWT, in November 1993 to bring an action in negligence against BB. In April 1996 the court notified BB's solicitors, BLG, that the claim appeared to have been automatically struck out. BLG informed JWT in February 1997, who advised H to instruct another firm. H eventually found WB, who were able to act for her. Counsel having advised

WB in July 1998 that the action had not been automatically struck out, BLG finally concurred but in March 1999 proceeded to apply to strike out the action for want of prosecution. The order was granted and upheld on appeal on the grounds that there had been inordinate and inexcusable delay and that a fair trial was no longer possible owing to the passage of time. H appealed.

Held, dismissing the appeal, that the unqualified discretion of the court to strike out for non compliance with a court order under the Civil Procedure Rules 1998 Part 3 r.3.4(2) should be exercised, given that it would be unfair to allow the claim to continue as it could not succeed and would be a waste of public and insurance funds. There was no action in negligence where no damage had been suffered. In the instant case, BB's failure to serve proceedings had not caused loss due to the limitation period having expired within three years of the occurrence of harm to H and prior to her instructing BB. Further, H's own medical evidence did not support her claim. Accordingly it was bound to fail on the basis of both limitation and liability, *Biguzzi v. Rank Leisure Plc* [1999] 1 W.L.R. 1926, [1999] C.L.Y. 367 applied. It was observed that had the claim been viable the non compliance might not have been sufficient to justify striking out. BB would not have been able to take advantage of the time lost through the confusion surrounding the automatic strike out and, arguably, the passage of time would not have had a detrimental affect on witness evidence due to the probable reliance of the witnesses on their notes.

HARRIS v. BOLT BURDON [2000] C.P. Rep. 70, Sedley, L.J., CA.

626. Striking out – presumption that Civil Procedure Rules apply to proceedings commenced after coming into force date – criteria for striking out application – inexcusable delay punished in costs

[Civil Procedure Rules 1998 (SI 1998 3132) r.3.4(2).]

In a claim by A against S for damages for misrepresentation, A's claim was struck out for want of prosecution on the grounds of inexcusable delay. A appealed, contending that the decision could not stand because it had been decided under the old rules, and was based on the prejudice that would be caused to S if A was permitted to consolidate its action with two similar claims. The striking out application was commenced the day after the Civil Procedure Rules 1998 came into force and A argued that the old rules were of no application. S argued that the decision was correct because the delay amounted to abuse of process.

Held, allowing the appeal, that the order could not stand. There was a general presumption that the new Rules would apply and the effect of r.3.4(2) was to grant the court a wide discretion such that it was no longer valid to consider prejudice in terms of the previous authorities, *Birkett v. James* [1978] A.C. 297, [1977] C.L.Y. 2410 disapproved. There had been no decision that the delay was an abuse of process and it was not just or proportionate to strike out the whole claim, having regard to its history, *Biguzzi v. Rank Leisure Plc* [1999] 1 W.L.R. 1926, [1999] C.L.Y. 367 followed. However, some of the allegations were struck out to confine the scope of the trial and A was penalised in costs to reflect the court's disapproval of the delay.

AXA INSURANCE CO LTD v. SWIRE FRASER LTD (FORMERLY ROBERT FRASER INSURANCE BROKERS LTD) [2001] C.P. Rep. 17, Tuckey, L.J., CA.

627. Striking out – reinstatement following failure to comply with unless order – decision to reinstate fell within ambit of judicial discretion following reconsideration of all circumstances

W was injured in a road traffic accident and commenced proceedings against F. There was a history of delay by W in complying with interlocutory orders. Following an unsuccessful application to strike out, after a failure by W to comply with an order requiring the service of an updated schedule of loss and discovery, an unless order was made requiring the service of W's witness statement by a set date with the penalty of strike out in default. W did not comply and as a result the action stood struck out. W applied for reinstatement, maintaining that his failure had resulted from the instruction of a new firm of solicitors and delays in the transfer of legal aid. The application was successful and F appealed, contending that (1) the judge had paid insufficient regard to the administration of justice; (2) the application had not been made promptly contrary to the judge's findings; (3) insufficient attention had been paid to W's history of default, and (4) the threat of strike out should have been adhered to having regard to the leniency demonstrated to W in the past.

Held, dismissing the appeal, that the decision made had been within the scope of the proper exercise of judicial discretion. Whilst the judge had indicated clearly when making the unless order that the claim would be struck out for a failure to comply, he had nevertheless been obliged to reconsider the circumstances when the application for reinstatement came before him. Furthermore there had been merit to the application. The issue of liability was not contested, the damages in question were apparently significant and the trial date was unaffected, *Biguzzi v. Rank Leisure Plc* [1999] 1 W.L.R. 1926, [1999] C.L.Y. 367 applied.

WOODWARD v. FINCH [1999] C.P.L.R. 699, May, L.J., CA.

628. Supreme Court – fees

SUPREME COURT FEES (AMENDMENT NO.2) ORDER 2000, SI 2000 937 (L.6); made under the Supreme Court Act 1981 s.130; and the Finance Act 1990 s.128. In force: Art.3, Art.4, Art.8, Art.9, Art.10, Art.12: May 2, 2000; remainder: April 25, 2000; £2.00.

This Order amends the Supreme Court Fees Order 1999 (SI 1999 687) so that fees 2.1 and 2.2 are not payable after a Group Litigation Order is made; fees 2.3 and 9 are restructured to take account of the new rules on appeals contained in the Civil Procedure (Amendment) Rules 2000 (SI 2000 221); fee 7 is reduced so that the fee is £1 for the first page of the first document and 20p per page for other pages; fee 10.2 is increased from £160 to £180; and the reference to family proceedings is clarified.

629. Unless orders – failure to comply within time limit – court's power to interfere

[Civil Procedure Rules 1998 (SI 1998 3132) Part 3.]

R, a party to a consent order which required payment of a sum to I within a specified period, in default of which possession of a property would be surrendered, appealed against a possession order granted in favour of I and sought, inter alia, an extension of time within which to comply with the consent order. I submitted that the court did not have the power to vary the time within which payment was required as (1) nothing contained in the Civil Procedure Rules 1998 Part 3 gave it such power, and (2) the consent order had been entered into by agreement and had clearly stated that time was of the essence.

Held, dismissing the appeal, that (1) the court's case management powers under the Civil Procedure Rules 1998 Part 3, read in light of the overriding objective to deal with a case justly, introduced wider more flexible powers to interfere in a case and contained a power to interfere with the time within which to comply with such a consent order, and (2) that while an agreement between parties did not prevent the court from exercising its power it should be very slow in departing from a clear agreement. In the instant case it was not appropriate to extend the time for compliance.

ROPAC LTD v. INNTREPRENEUR PUB CO (CPC) LTD [2001] C.P. Rep. 31, Neuberger, J., Ch D.

630. Unless orders – request for further and better particulars – standard required for compliance

K T appealed against an order striking out parts of its defence and counterclaim on the basis that it had failed fully to comply with an unless order relating to the service of further and better particulars.

Held, dismissing the appeal, that although the judge had wrongly based his decision upon the outdated authority of *Reiss v. Woolf* [1952] 2 Q.B. 557,

[1952] C.L.Y. 2735, since in order to demonstrate compliance it was not necessary to show that each and every particular had been dealt with, had been served in good faith and that the document served was not illusory, nevertheless the judge's opinion of the requirements of the unless order and the appropriate penalty was sound. The modern authority governing proper exercise of the court's discretion in cases where breach of an unless order relating to an obligation to serve particulars was concerned was *Hytec Information Systems Ltd v. Coventry City Council* [1997] 1 W.L.R. 1666, [1997] C.L.Y. 768, and there was now no basis for construing the requirement to serve particulars in the restrictive manner detailed in *Reiss*. Breach of an order would not occur simply if one or two of the replies were inadequate and required expansion or clarification. If the replies in question could reasonably have been considered complete and adequate in that form then any inadequacy should be remedied by a further order for the provision of particulars. An order would be breached if a reply was only partially complete or clearly insufficient, but even so the discretion for strike out should only be used where, after assessing the replies as a whole, they fell significantly below what was required. This would depend upon a consideration of the individual facts of the case, including the number of defective replies in relation to the document as a whole, and their importance to the matters in issue between the parties.

QPS CONSULTANTS LTD v. KRUGER TISSUE (MANUFACTURING) LTD [1999] C.P.L.R. 710, Simon Brown, L.J., CA.

631. Vexatious litigants – application for civil proceedings order – no element of repetition in bringing actions

[Supreme Court Act 1981 s.42(1).]

The Attorney General applied to make a civil proceedings order under the Supreme Court Act 1981 s.42(1) against B, who had initiated 20 actions over a three month period but, since recovering from an illness, had not brought any further actions. The Attorney General contended that B had instituted vexatious civil proceedings without any justifiable ground in law, and most of those actions had been struck out.

Held, dismissing the application, that the Attorney General had failed to satisfy the conditions required under s.42(1). In the instant case, there was no evidence of an element of repetition to found a claim that B had habitually and persistently initiated vexatious civil proceedings, since B had not continued to litigate earlier unsuccessful actions repeatedly relying on the same cause of action.

ATTORNEY GENERAL v. BARKER (CIVIL PROCEEDINGS ORDER); *sub nom.* ATTORNEY GENERAL v. B [2000] 1 F.L.R. 759, Lord Bingham of Cornhill, L.C.J., QBD.

632. Vexatious litigants – restriction of proceedings order imposed following initiation of 13 failed actions

[Employment Tribunals Act 1996 s.33; Employment Tribunals (Constitution and Rules of Procedure) Regulations 1993 (SI 1993 2687) Sch.1 r.7(4).]

The Attorney General applied for a restriction of proceedings order under the Employment Tribunals Act 1996 s.33 against W, who had initiated 13 failed actions. W contended that he was not a vexatious litigant because whenever an order had been made under the Employment Tribunals (Constitution and Rules of Procedure) Regulations 1993 Sch.1 r.7(4), which provided that a party should pay a deposit if his claim had no reasonable prospect of success, he did not pursue the claim.

Held, granting the application, that the persistent failure of W's claims supported the assertion that he had initiated vexatious proceedings.

ATTORNEY GENERAL v. WHEEN [2000] I.R.L.R. 461, Lindsay, J., EAT.

633. Writs – service of process – renewal of concurrent writ issued under old rules – renewal ostensibly made under new rules – whether appropriate to deal with application under old rules

[Rules of the Supreme Court 1965 (SI 1965 1776); Civil Procedure Rules 1998 (SI 1998 3132).]

P applied for the renewal of a concurrent writ for service, issued prior to the implementation of the Civil Procedure Rules 1998 on January 27, 1999, and renewed on May 28, 1999 and marked "not for service out of jurisdiction".

Held, that it was appropriate to apply the principles of the old Rules of the Supreme Court 1965 when examining the merit of an application made pursuant to the 1998 Rules but relating to the renewal of a concurrent writ issued under the old rules. The 1998 Rules did not refer to concurrent claim forms, notwithstanding mention within the Commercial Court Guide. There were no grounds for reading "writ" and "claim form" on the same basis. In the instant case, it was clear that the application had only ostensibly been made under the 1998 Rules. The application related to the renewal of a writ made under the old rules and accordingly should be dealt with under the old rules. It followed that, the time for service of the writ being four months from the date of issue, the proceedings should be stayed on the basis that the writ had not been validly renewed for service.

PIRELLI CABLES LTD v. UNITED THAI SHIPPING CORP LTD [2000] 1 Lloyd's Rep. 663, Langley, J., QBD.

634. Publications

Ashford, Mark; Chard, Alex – Defending Young People in the Criminal Justice System. 2nd Ed. Paperback: £35.00. ISBN 0-905099-92-3. Legal Action Group.

Burn, Suzanne – Changing Lawyer/client Relationship in Civil Litigation. Paperback: £45.00. ISBN 0-406-98582-0. Butterworths.

Cook, Michael – Cook on Costs 2000-a Guide to Legal Remuneration in Civil Contentious and Non-contentious Business. Paperback: £55.00. ISBN 0-406-92992-0. Butterworths.

Edwards, J. Stanley; Edwards, Linda L.; Emery, Jack – Civil Procedures and Litigation: a Practical Approach. Paperback: £26.99. ISBN 0-314-12636-8. Delmar.

Fridd, Nicholas; Weddle, Steven – Basic Practice in Court, Tribunals and Inquiries. 3rd Ed. Paperback: £35.00. ISBN 0-421-68480-1. Sweet & Maxwell.

Gerlis, Stephen M. – County Court Procedure. 2nd Ed. Practice Notes. Hardback: £15.95. ISBN 1-85941-309-9. Cavendish Publishing Ltd.

Jolowicz, J.A. – On Civil Procedure: Connected Papers. Cambridge Studies in International and Comparative Law. Hardback: £60.00. ISBN 0-521-58419-1. Cambridge University Press.

Loughlin, Paula – Civil Procedure. Paperback: £22.95. ISBN 1-85941-497-4. Cavendish Publishing Ltd.

Mambro, David di – Manual of Civil Appeals. Paperback: £55.00. ISBN 0-406-92991-2. Butterworths Law.

Sheffield, Nichola; Wilson, Paul – Civil Litigation NVQ. Legal Support Practitioner Series-the Law Society's NVQ in Legal Practice. Paperback: £25.00. ISBN 1-85941-448-6. Cavendish Publishing Ltd.

COMMERCIAL LAW

635. Companies – electronic communications – members and external bodies

COMPANIES ACT 1985 (ELECTRONIC COMMUNICATIONS) ORDER 2000, SI 2000 3373; made under the Electronic Communications Act 2000 s.8, s.9. In force: December 22, 2000; £3.50.

This Order modifies various provisions of the Companies Act 1985 for the purpose of authorising or facilitating the use of electronic communications between companies and their members, debenture holders and auditors, and between companies and the registrar of companies.

636. Crown Estate – park trading regulations – designation

ROYAL PARKS AND OTHER OPEN SPACES (PARK TRADING) REGULATIONS 2000, SI 2000 2949; made under the Parks Regulation (Amendment) Act 1926 s.2. In force: November 2, 2000; £1.00.

The Royal Parks (Trading) Act 2000 s.1 (1) allows the Secretary of State for Culture, Media and Sport, as one of the successors to the Commissioners of Works, to designate particular provisions of any regulations made under the Parks Regulation (Amendment) Act 1926 s.2(1), as "park trading regulations". These Regulations, which amend the Royal Parks and Other Open Spaces Regulations 1997 (SI 1997 1639), achieve that designation.

637. Debts – commercial transactions – late payment – Council Directive

European Parliament and Council Directive 2000/35 of June 29, 2000 on combating late payment in commercial transactions. [2000] OJ L200/35.

638. Electronic commerce – Council Directive

European Parliament and Council Directive 2000/31 of June 8, 2000 on certain legal aspects of information society services, in particular electronic commerce, in the Internal Market. [2000] OJ L178/1.

639. Electronic Communications Act 2000 (c.7) – Commencement No.1 Order

ELECTRONIC COMMUNICATIONS ACT 2000 (COMMENCEMENT NO.1) ORDER 2000, SI 2000 1798 (C.46); made under the Electronic Communications Act 2000 s.16. Commencement details: bringing into force various provisions of the Act on July 25, 2000; £1.00.

This Order brings into force the Electronic Communications Act 2000 s.7, s.11 and s.12 on July 25, 2000.

640. European Economic Interest Groupings – fees – microfiche based information

EUROPEAN ECONOMIC INTEREST GROUPING (FEES) (AMENDMENT) REGULATIONS 2000, SI 2000 3412; made under the Finance Act 1973 s.56. In force: April 2, 2001; £1.50.

These Regulations, which govern the statutory fees for microfiche based information services for european economic interest groupings, amend the European Economic Interest Grouping (Fees) Regulations 1999 (SI 1999 268). They increase the fees for the inspection of a basic set of microfiche copies, for the delivery of a basic set of microfiche copies at an office of the registrar and the delivery of a paper copy of records kept by the registrar relating to a European Economic Interest Grouping delivered at the office of the registrar otherwise than at the time of the microfiche, from £5.00 to £6.50.

641. Late Payment of Commercial Debts (Interest) Act 1998 (c.20) – Commencement No.3 Order

LATE PAYMENT OF COMMERCIAL DEBTS (INTEREST) ACT 1998 (COMMENCEMENT NO.3) ORDER 2000, SI 2000 2225 (C.60); made under the Late Payment of Commercial Debts (Interest) Act 1998 s.17. Commencement details: bringing into force various provisions of the Act on September 1, 2000; £1.00.

This Order brings into force the Late Payment of Commercial Debts (Interest) Act 1998, in relation to commercial contracts for the supply of goods or services where the supplier is a small business and the purchaser is the Comptroller and Auditor General for Northern Ireland, the Metropolitan Police Authority or the London Fire and Emergency Planning Authority.

642. Late Payment of Commercial Debts (Interest) Act 1998 (c.20) – Commencement No.4 Order

LATE PAYMENT OF COMMERCIAL DEBTS (INTEREST) ACT 1998 (COMMENCEMENT NO.4) ORDER 2000, SI 2000 2740 (C.77); made under the Late Payment of Commercial Debts (Interest) Act 1998 s.17. Commencement details: bringing into force various provisions of the Act on November 1, 2000; £1.50.

This Order brings the Late Payment of Commercial Debts (Interest) Act 1998 into force on November 1, 2000, in relation to commercial contracts for the supply of goods or services where the supplier is a small business and the purchaser is a small business.

643. Royal Parks (Trading) Act 2000 (c.13)

This Act makes provision about certain offences under the Parks Regulation (Amendment) Act 1926 s.2.

This Act received Royal Assent on July 20, 2000 and comes into force on July 20, 2000.

644. Weights and measures – equipment

NON-AUTOMATIC WEIGHING INSTRUMENTS REGULATIONS 2000, SI 2000 3236; made under the European Communities Act 1972 s.2; and the Weights and Measures Act 1985 s.15, s.86, s.94. In force: January 1, 2001; £6.50.

These Regulations, which consolidate the Non-automatic Weighing Instruments (EEC Requirements) Regulations 1995 (SI 1995 1907 as amended), keep implemented Council Directive 90/384 ([1990] OJ L189/1) on the harmonisation of the laws of the Member States relating to non-automatic weighing instruments.

645. Publications

Bond, Robert – Drafting and Negotiating Software Licence Agreements. Commercial Practice Series. Paperback; Floppy disk (text document): £95.00. ISBN 0-406-91635-7. Butterworths Law.

Borrie, Sir Gordon J.; Brown, Ian – Commercial Law. 7th Ed. Paperback: £18.95. ISBN 0-406-02434-0. Butterworths.

Bradgate, Robert – Commercial Law. 3rd Ed. Paperback: £27.95. ISBN 0-406-91603-9. Butterworths Law.

Chissick, Michael; Kelman, Alistair – Electronic Commerce Law and Practice. Hardback: £135.00. ISBN 0-421-70800-X. Sweet & Maxwell.

Hooley, Richard – Commercial Law. Butterworths CoreText. Paperback: £12.95. ISBN 0-406-98142-6. Butterworths Law.

Journal of Business Law: Vol 43. Hardback: £75.00. ISBN 0-421-69760-1. Sweet & Maxwell.

Kelly, David; Holmes, Ann – Business Law. 3rd Ed. Paperback: £24.95. ISBN 1-85941-469-9. Cavendish Publishing Ltd.

Ohly, Ansgar; Spence, Michael – Law of Comparative Advertising: Directive 97/55/EC in the United Kingdom and Germany. Hardback: £30.00. ISBN 1-84113-117-2. Hart Publishing.

Pullen, Mike; Ris, Birgit – EU E-commerce-law and Policy. Paperback: £48.00. ISBN 1-902558-37-5. Palladian Law Publishing Ltd.

Smyth, Michael; Qureshi, Khawar – Business and the Human Rights Act 1998. Hardback: £50.00. ISBN 0-85308-565-X. Jordans.

COMPANY LAW

646. Auditors – resignation – statement of reasons – notice of discontinuance – appropriate costs order

[Companies Act 1985 s.394(1), s.394(3), s.394(7).]

P, who had resigned as auditors of J, sought an order for costs to be awarded on an indemnity basis following discontinuance of J's action against them. P had deposited a statement pursuant to the Companies Act 1985 s.394(1) recording the reasons for their resignation as being a disagreement with the management of J as to the presentation of certain figures in the annual accounts and a failure to secure payment for additional work undertaken since the preparation of fee estimates. J made an application to the court under s.394(3) for a declaration that the statement was being used by P to secure needless publicity for defamatory matters but the application was discontinued on the morning before the hearing. P sought (1) a declaration as to whether the court needed to make a decision on the application following discontinuance, and (2) an order for costs on an indemnity basis, contending that J had not commenced the proceedings against them in good faith and had given no good reason for the late discontinuance.

Held, granting the application, that (1) the proceedings had been brought to an end upon service of the notice of discontinuance and, for the purposes of s.394(7), that notice amounted to a decision of the court, with the result that J was required to serve P's statement on the interested parties, and (2) costs would be ordered to be paid on an indemnity basis, as the role of P was analogous to that of a trustee and they had discharged their duty to act in the public interest throughout, and J, possibly acting with ulterior motives, had failed to substantiate allegations of bad faith.

JARVIS PLC v. PRICEWATERHOUSECOOPERS [2000] 2 B.C.L.C. 368, Lightman, J., Ch D (Companies Court).

647. Companies – audits – exemptions for small companies and dormant companies

COMPANIES ACT 1985 (AUDIT EXEMPTION) (AMENDMENT) REGULATIONS 2000, SI 2000 1430; made under the Companies Act 1985 s.257. In force: May 26, 2000; £2.00.

These Regulations amend the Companies Act 1985 Part VII, which relates to the exemption of certain small companies from the requirement to have their annual accounts audited and the conditions a company must satisfy to qualify as dormant. They increase the turnover limit to qualify for exemption from £350,000 to £1 million for small companies and small groups and impose new requirements on companies claiming dormancy status.

648. Companies – club membership – distribution of proceeds of sale under scheme of arrangement – overseas members excluded from full membership status

RAC was a limited company, which owned a club and other assets. Under the articles of association, membership was conditional upon life or full membership of the club with overseas members not having the status of RAC members and excluded from voting rights. Following the sale of its motoring services division,

RAC obtained court approval of a scheme of arrangement, under which the sale proceeds would be distributed amongst its members. A number of overseas members who were claiming a right to be treated as RAC members had opposed the approval. F, an overseas member, brought proceedings seeking to set the scheme aside. RAC succeeded in having F's action set aside (*The Times*, March 3, 1999) and F appealed, contending that the lapse of a previous rule change, by which overseas members of the club were elevated to the status of full members and were thereby entitled to membership of RAC, had not acted to revert those members to their former overseas status and they were therefore entitled to a share of the sale proceeds. RAC argued that the change in the rules had merely altered the qualifying conditions for the categories of membership and had not operated to transfer any member from one category to another.

Held, dismissing the appeal, that the lapse, whilst not acting to alter the rules as if they had never changed, only had significance to the subsequent renewal by overseas members of their membership. The mere fact that overseas status was apparently not an option, was not alone sufficient to convert the membership of a former overseas member to the status of a full member. In order to participate in the windfall, overseas members would have had to opt at the renewal date preceding the cut off date to renew as a full member and pay the appropriate subscription. A member who decided to leave the club rather than upgrade his membership would not have a grievance that could lead to participation in the windfall.

FLETCHER v. ROYAL AUTOMOBILE CLUB LTD; *sub nom.* FLETCHER v. RAC Henry, L.J., CA.

649. Companies – club membership – distribution of proceeds on sale – former members claiming right to be notified

The RAC sold its motoring services business, M, in respect of which club members received the sum of £34,000. RAC was owned by a company, L, with RAC's members as its shareholders. A club member who resigned was entitled to re-apply within 3 years without the usual requirement of being proposed and seconded. P was a former member who had resigned before the sale and was aggrieved that he had received nothing from it. P alleged that (1) he should have been informed of the possibility of the sale, so that he could have re-joined prior to its taking place, and that the failure to inform him breached r.19 of the RAC's rules, which required the club committee to report annually on the work of the club, and (2) L's directors had breached their fiduciary duty toward the former members by failing to inform them of the possible sale before or at the time of their resignation. A applied for P's claim to be struck out on the basis that it had no prospect of success.

Held, allowing the application, that (1) RAC was owned by L, not its members. Accordingly, the rules did not constitute a contract between the members but were a contract between L and each member. Further, the rules did not provide for automatic reinstatement in any event, but only a right to apply for re-election without having to undergo the usual election formalities; (2) investigations into the possible sale of M did not amount to "work" in terms of r.19, and (3) the directors did not owe a fiduciary duty to the former members who had chosen to resign at a time when no particular sale was contemplated and without relying on anything said or done by the directors, *Bristol and West Building Society v. Mothew (t/a Stapley & Co)* [1998] Ch. 1, [1996] C.L.Y. 4503, *Brunninghausen v. Glavanics* (1999) 32 A.C.S.R 294, *Chez Nico (Restaurants), Re* [1992] B.C.L.C. 192, [1992] C.L.Y. 402, *Coleman v. Myers* [1977] 2 N.Z.L.R. 225, [1978] C.L.Y. 232, *Percival v. Wright* [1902] 2 Ch. 421 and *Platt v. Platt* [1999] 2 B.C.L.C. 745, [2000] C.L.Y. 685 considered.

PESKIN v. ANDERSON [2000] 2 B.C.L.C. 1, Neuberger, J., Ch D.

650. Companies – fees – payment to registrar

COMPANIES (FEES) (AMENDMENT) REGULATIONS 2000, SI 2000 3325; made under the Companies Act 1985 s.708. In force: April 2, 2001; £1.50.

These Regulations amend the Companies (Fees) Regulations 1991 (SI 1991 1206 as amended) by increasing the statutory fees payable for microfiche based information services for companies.

651. Companies – forms – Welsh language forms – Form 363s CYM

COMPANIES (WELSH LANGUAGE FORMS) (AMENDMENT) REGULATIONS 2000, SI 2000 2413; made under the Companies Act 1985 s.363, s.744. In force: October 2, 2000; £3.00.

These Regulations prescribe a new Form 363s cym, which corresponds to Form 363s prescribed by the Companies (Forms) (Amendment) Regulations 1999 (SI 1999 2356). The form is in Welsh as well as in English and will be provided by the registrar of companies to any company with a memorandum stating that it is to be registered in Wales, as opposed to England and Wales, which notifies the registrar that it wishes to receive it instead of form 363s.

652. Companies – removal from register – discretion to continue action pending restoration

[Companies Act 1985 s.653.]

A company, formed for the sole purpose of contracting with a local authority, together with its director, commenced actions in 1997 against the authority for breaches of contract. In 1998, the director, having been advised by officials at Company House that it would be appropriate to have the company struck off the register if it was no longer trading, applied for its removal from the register. That removal took place in August 1998, unbeknown to the company's solicitors who had not been consulted. The director had not appreciated that removal from the register might affect the company's claim against the authority and the solicitors became aware of the removal only after the case against the authority had been put on the warned list, although the authority's solicitors had known of the removal some three months earlier. A request was made for the case to be removed from the warned list or for it to be adjourned until the company's name was restored to the register. Those requests were refused by the authority and by a county court judge. The judge considered that, once the company had been removed from the register, it ceased to exist and was not entitled to maintain any cause of action. The company appealed, contending that where a company's name has merely been removed from the register by the administrative act of the registrar, it had not ceased to exist.

Held, allowing the appeal, that (1) the judge had a discretion to grant or refuse the applications before him. He had misdirected himself in finding that the action between the parties was automatically and irrevocably at an end when the company's name was removed from the register, and in finding that the company had no existence while its name was removed from the register; (2) once restored to the register, steps taken by a company's officers on behalf of a dormant company become the actions of the company by virtue of the Companies Act 1985 s.653, and (3) the company could have started a fresh action, but it was not in the public interest that the court time should be taken up or the parties put to the expense of repeating all the preliminary steps associated with the action. This was particularly so, as s.653 had the effect of restoring the parties to the position they were in at the time of the county court order.

TOP CREATIVE LTD v. ST ALBANS DC [2000] 2 B.C.L.C. 379, Roch, L.J., CA.

653. Company registration – valid registration of charge despite error in company number

[Companies Act 1985 s.395.]

AH borrowed monies from the Bank of Wales secured by a mortgage. A form sent to the Companies Registry for the purpose of registering the charge gave the wrong registered number for the company. The charge was registered to the company with that registered number, and the mistake was only noticed some years later when receivers were appointed to AH. The receivers applied to the court for a declaration that the mortgage had been properly registered despite the mistake.

Held, granting the declaration, that the mortgage had been properly registered. Under the Companies Act 1985 s.395 registration of a charge was not valid unless the "prescribed particulars" were provided. Provision of the correct registered number was not a "prescribed particular" because it could not be categorised as a "particular of the charge" as per s.395. Instead it constituted a particular of the mortgagor. The Registrar had not rejected the form submitted by AH and therefore it had been properly delivered to him.

GROVE v. ADVANTAGE HEALTHCARE (T10) LTD; *sub nom.* ADVANTAGE HEALTHCARE (T10) LTD, *Re* [2000] 1 B.C.L.C. 661, Lightman, J., Ch D (Companies Court).

654. **Debentures – company articles of association not followed – duomatic principle invoked to authorise debenture**

[Companies Act 1985 s.322A(1), s.322A(7).]

A company, T, granted debentures in favour of Barclays Bank, B, to the Trustees of its pension scheme, S, and to one of its directors, H. It also issued 135,000 preferred ordinary shares to another company, 3i, in return for a loan. In 1993 B appointed administrative receivers to T in order to call in its loan under the debenture. The receivers sought directions from the court as to whether the debentures had been properly made, as the procedure set out in T's Articles of Association whereby the sanction of the shareholders was required before any charges could be created, did not appear to have been followed.

Held, declaring that the S debenture was valid and granting directions in relation to the H debenture, that (1) the Duomatic principle, under which a formal procedure requiring consent by, for example, a resolution passed in general meeting, could be circumvented by all shareholders having rights of attendance and voting to agree informally on that course of action, could be applied in relation to the H debenture, *Duomatic Ltd, Re* [1969] 2 Ch. 365, [1969] C.L.Y. 412 applied. There was nothing to prevent this maxim having application to cases where a specific group of shareholders as opposed to all the shareholders were involved. The affidavit evidence appeared to suggest that 3i had attended the meeting at which the H debenture was sealed and had approved the increase in T's borrowing power necessary to transact the debenture, and therefore there appeared to be sufficient evidence to assume 3i's consent to the debenture. However in order to protect T's unsecured creditors, the matter needed to be investigated further by the receivers and the affidavit evidence tested in cross-examination, and so that part of the case would be stood down, and (2) as one of the Trustees of S was also a director of T, the S debenture came within the Companies Act 1985 s.322A(1) and so was voidable if it could be shown that the board of directors had acted outside its powers in relation to its grant. However as the debenture was made in good faith on reasonable terms and was not to T's disadvantage, and as 3i's consent could be assumed from the circumstances, the court would exercise its power under s.322A(7) to affirm it.

HUNT v. EDGE & ELLISON TRUSTEES LTD; *sub nom.* TORVALE GROUP LTD, *Re* [1999] 2 B.C.L.C. 605, Neuberger, J., Ch D (Companies Court).

655. **Directors – disqualification orders – abuse of process – striking out – delay in progress of proceedings due to error by court office**

[European Convention on Human Rights 1950 Art.6.1.]

In 1997 disqualification proceedings were brought by the Secretary of State against S as director of R which had gone into receivership in 1995. The hearing in May 1999 was not completed within the three days fixed, and a further two days were set for February 2000, which were dates convenient to counsel. In January 2000 the court discovered that the Registrar was not available on those dates and the hearing had to be moved to May. S brought an application for the proceedings to be struck out because of the delay. The application was refused and S appealed, arguing that (1) although neither party was at fault it would be an abuse of process for the proceedings to continue given the length of time that had elapsed; (2) the judge had applied the wrong test in holding that there had to be a "serious risk" of prejudice before the case could be struck out, and (3) continuing with the proceedings would be in breach of the European Convention on Human Rights 1950 Art.6.1.

Held, dismissing the appeal, that (1) continuation of the proceedings could not amount to an abuse of process since there was no party who could be properly categorised as an abuser; (2) the judge had applied the correct test and in any event there was little to distinguish the test of "real danger" used in cases of suspected bias and the test of "serious risk". Furthermore the delay had only been from February to May 2000, as S had not objected to the fixing of the hearing in February which was already some nine months since the original hearing, and (3) although the judge could be criticised for holding that a fair trial was still possible, his conclusion that there would be no breach of Art.6.1 could not be impugned. Any prejudice likely to be suffered by S was no greater than that of any defendant faced with disqualification proceedings and was outweighed by the public need to regulate directors. The Registrar could still choose to discontinue the proceedings if he felt the delay had affected his ability to conduct the trial fairly.

ROCKSTEADY SERVICES LTD, *Re*; *sub nom*. SECRETARY OF STATE FOR TRADE AND INDUSTRY v. STATON [2001] C.P. Rep. 1, Peter Gibson, L.J., CA.

656. **Directors – disqualification orders – claim to be a nominal director no defence – duty to inform liquidator from knowledge of inadequate stock records**

[Company Directors Disqualification Act 1986 s.6.]

The Secretary of State applied for an order under the Company Directors Disqualification Act 1986 s.6 that P, B and B's wife should be disqualified from acting as directors, liquidators, receivers or managers of any company, or be in any way concerned with the formation or management of a company for a specified period. The three were all directors of GPL, which had gone into voluntary liquidation in 1995, and B and his wife were also directors of GL which went into liquidation in 1991. B had also been a director of EL which went into liquidation in 1993. P had been the auditor of GL and EL. The Secretary of State contended, inter alia, that substantial sums of VAT, PAYE and NIC had not been paid on due dates by the companies and that there had been a policy of late payment or retention of monies owed and that, in respect of GPL, inadequate accounting records had been maintained.

Held, granting the disqualification orders, that (1) it was incumbent upon the directors, in circumstances where they must have known from past history that there was a real risk that a company's operations could prove unprofitable, to take proper steps to ensure that, if trading continued, creditors were not prejudiced; (2) the directors had allowed GPL to rely on the retention of Crown moneys in order to finance the company's continued trading; (3) it was the duty of a director, continuing to hold office and, in particular, receiving remuneration, to inform himself or herself as to the financial affairs of the company and to play an appropriate role in the management of its business. A director who was not prepared to do so should resign. Directorial responsibilities could not be avoided by a claim that a person was no more than a nominal director and not expected to perform any actual duties, *Westmid Packaging Services Ltd (No.2), Re* [1998] 2 All E.R. 124, [1998] C.L.Y. 663 and *Kaytech International Plc, Re* [1999] 2 B.C.L.C. 351, [1999] C.L.Y. 622 applied, and (4) where a director knew there were inadequate stock records, he was under a duty to obtain their production to the liquidator whether or not he had been specifically asked to provide that information.

GALEFORCE PLEATING CO LTD, *Re* [1999] 2 B.C.L.C. 704, Elizabeth Gloster Q.C., Ch D (Companies Court).

657. Directors – disqualification orders – debts – prejudicial payments to creditors – insufficient to justify finding of unfitness

[Company Directors Disqualification Act 1986 s.6; Insolvent Companies (Disqualification of Unfit Directors) Proceedings Rules 1987 (SI 1987 2023) r.3(3).]

B, the director of D, a company in financial difficulties, sought to proceed by way of an informal liquidation, reliant in large part upon the renegotiation of leases and payment of a debt owed to another company, I, owned by B. B paid £350,000 to trade creditors, not including I, thereby reducing D's indebtedness to them to £111,000, and £200,000 to I. The solvent liquidation failed and D went into creditors' voluntary liquidation with an estimated deficit of £400,000. B was disqualified from being a director for four years under the Company Directors Disqualification Act 1986 s.6, on the basis that he was unfit in terms of the Insolvent Companies (Disqualification of Unfit Directors) Proceedings Rules 1987 r.3(3) due to the payment to I, given its detrimental effect on the other creditors. B appealed, contending that (1) it had not been shown that the payment to I was detrimental, and (2) the unfitness decision had relied on matters not put to B at the hearing.

Held, allowing the appeal, that B had failed to show that the creditors were not prejudiced by the payment to I at the time it was made. However, the finding of unfitness was based on a factor not fully supported by the evidence and which should have been specified in a manner that B could deal with it at the hearing. When considering a director's conduct, the court was limited to the conduct given in the charge and the affidavit evidence. In the absence of dishonesty or culpable behaviour, the factors of public protection and the danger of placing directors in the unrealistic position of being liable to disqualification for each failure of duty had to be balanced. In the instant case, the making out of the detrimental payment charge did not justify a finding of unfitness. Had B been found unfit, a 30 month disqualification period would have sufficed, as opposed to four years.

DEADUCK LTD (IN LIQUIDATION), *Re; sub nom.* BAKER v. SECRETARY OF STATE FOR TRADE AND INDUSTRY [2000] 1 B.C.L.C. 148, Neuberger, J., Ch D.

658. Directors – disqualification orders – factors determining shadow director status – extent to which "directions" and "instructions" could include advice

[Company Directors Disqualification Act 1986 s.22(5).]

The Secretary of State appealed against the judge's refusal to make company director disqualification orders against D and H's shadow directors. The judge had refused to make the orders, having considered whether "directions" or "instructions" in the Company Directors Disqualification Act 1986 s.22(5) could include "advice" and the extent to which the board customarily followed the directions or instructions of the shadow in a subservient role.

Held, allowing the appeal, that the judge had construed the legislation too strictly when its purpose was to identify those with real influence in a company's affairs, *Australian Securities Commission v. AS Nominees Ltd* (1995) 133 A.L.R. 1 and *Kaytech International Plc, Re* [1999] 2 B.C.L.C. 351, [1999] C.L.Y. 622 followed. In common with "instruction" and "direction", "advice" could be classed as guidance to the board, so that it could not be excluded. However, it was not conclusive of shadow status merely to show that the board expected the directions and cast itself in a subservient role. It was also unnecessary to show that the board had surrendered its discretion to the directions of the shadow, but proof of communication to the board and its attendant consequences would suffice in the majority of cases.

SECRETARY OF STATE FOR TRADE AND INDUSTRY v. DEVERELL [2001] Ch. 340, Morritt, L.J., CA.

659. Directors – disqualification orders – inquiries into company dealings – extent of Official Receiver's powers

[Insolvency Act 1986 s.143(1), s.236(2); Company Directors Disqualification Act 1986 s.6.]

H, a former director of P, appealed against three orders directing the production of documents sought by the Official Receiver pursuant to the Insolvency Act 1986 s.236(2), which enabled inquiries to be made into company dealings in order to obtain evidence. The Official Receiver had issued proceedings seeking to disqualify H under the Company Directors Disqualification Act 1986 s.6, alleging that H had continued to act as a de facto director of P after his resignation. H had applied to strike out the s.6 proceedings and the Official Receiver had sought the production of the documents to defend that application.

Held, allowing the appeals, that the general duty of the Official Receiver as defined in the Insolvency Act 1986 s.143(1) was to realise and distribute the assets of a company for the benefit of its creditors. By virtue of s.236(2) of that Act, the Official Receiver could apply to the court to summon to appear before it, any person capable of providing information concerning the trading activities of a company in liquidation, *Esal (Commodities) Ltd (1988), Re* [1989] B.C.L.C. 59, [1989] C.L.Y. 346 applied. However, this power did not permit him to obtain evidence to be used in disqualification proceedings once those proceedings had been issued.

PANTMAENOG TIMBER CO LTD, *Re*; OFFICIAL RECEIVER v. WADGE RAPPS & HUNT; OFFICIAL RECEIVER v. GRANT THORNTON; *sub nom.* OFFICIAL RECEIVER v. MEADE-KING (A FIRM) [2001] 1 W.L.R. 730, Judge Weeks Q.C., Ch D.

660. Directors – disqualification orders – judge's findings of fact contrary to witness's evidence – subjective evaluation based on evidence and demeanour and without expert evidence

B was a director of BB, a merchant bank which was part of the Barings Group. B had been found to have been instrumental in the collapse of the Barings Group by reason of his gross incompetence. The court concluded that B had had ultimate responsibility since the end of 1993, albeit not on a proximate level, for the trading activities of L, a dealer whose unauthorised trading had caused the collapse. B's failure to discharge his management responsibilities in relation to L was found by the court to render him unfit to act as a company director and he was disqualified for six years. B appealed, disputing that his position as head of the Financial Products Group, FPG, made him responsible for L's conduct because L's unauthorised activities had started before B's appointment and because his later activities did not form part of FPG. B also challenged a number of the judge's factual conclusions on the evidence. He contended that the findings against him were contrary to his evidence and that on technical matters it was not open to the judge to reject his evidence without affirmative expert evidence to the contrary.

Held, dismissing the appeal, that the judge's findings of primary fact would not lightly be interfered with, particularly where they depended on his assessment of the credibility of the oral evidence and involved a subjective evaluation of B's fitness or otherwise to act as a company director, *Benmax v. Austin Motor Co Ltd* [1955] A.C. 370, [1955] C.L.Y. 2078 and *Grayan Building Services Ltd (In Liquidation), Re* [1995] Ch. 241, [1995] C.L.Y. 582 applied. The judge had been entitled to reject B's factual assertions without expert evidence in favour of a different sequence of events than that suggested by B. He was justified in finding that B knew, or ought to have known, about the nature of L's trading from the inception of FPG and in rejecting B's attempt to exclude the activities from his control. There was no reason to interfere with the judge's view that B's conduct involved a serious abdication of responsibility on the basis that there was no system in place to monitor L's performance and B had made no effort to instigate one.

SECRETARY OF STATE FOR TRADE AND INDUSTRY v. BAKER (NO.6); *sub nom.* BARINGS PLC (NO.6), RE; BAKER v. SECRETARY OF STATE FOR TRADE AND INDUSTRY [2000] 1 B.C.L.C. 523, Morritt, L.J., CA.

661. Directors – disqualification orders – jurisdiction to grant leave to act as a director following disqualification

[Company Directors Disqualification Act 1986 s.17(1); Insolvency Rules 1986 (SI 1986 1925) r.7.47(2); Insolvent Companies (Disqualification of Unfit Directors) Proceedings Rules 1987 (SI 1987 2023) r.2(4).]

M, a director of B, which was in the process of being wound up in the county court, was disqualified from acting as a director for six years on the ground of his misconduct. M subsequently applied to the district judge in the winding up proceedings for leave to act as a director of A, and was granted leave. The Official Receiver appealed to the High Court, contending that the order was inappropriate and the district judge had no power to make it.

Held, allowing the appeal, that (1) by virtue of the Insolvent Companies (Disqualification of Unfit Directors) Proceedings Rules 1987 r.2(4) and the Insolvency Rules 1986 r.7.47(2) a single High Court judge was the proper person to hear an appeal from leave applications; (2) where disqualification proceedings had occurred in tandem with winding-up proceedings, an application for leave to act as a director had to be made to the court presiding over the winding-up proceedings, in accordance with the Company Directors Disqualification Act 1986 s.17(1). As the county court had jurisdiction to wind up B, and as the disqualification order and leave application were made in the course of those proceedings, then it was the correct court to decide the leave application, albeit that it had no power to wind up A, and (3) although M's application was procedurally correct, the district judge's decision was irrational and could not stand.

BRITANNIA HOMES CENTRES LTD, *Re; sub nom.* OFFICIAL RECEIVER v. McCAHILL; COMPANY DIRECTORS DISQUALIFICATION ACT 1986, *Re The Times,* June 27, 2000, Richard Mawrey Q.C., Ch D.

662. Directors – disqualification orders – preferences – deliberate favouring of other creditors over Crown debts

F was a director of toymaking companies FT and TG, the latter being a dormant subsidiary of the former. By early 1996 FT was in financial difficulties. Having taken insolvency advice, F arranged the sale of stock at cost price to himself and other directors, which was then sold on to TG. Further stock was sold to TG directly. Receivers were appointed by B, a bank, the main financier of the companies. SSTI brought an application for F's disqualification as a director on the grounds that (1) F had favoured other creditors over the Crown, taking advantage of the fact that the Inland Revenue and HM Customs and Excise had not actively pursued payment of debts owed to them, and (2) the sale of stock to the directors was at an undervalue and constituted improper preferences as monies loaned by the directors to FT were effectively settled by the transaction.

Held, allowing the application in part, that (1) F had not favoured other creditors. F's practice of paying Crown debts late and keeping up to date with current VAT liabilities at the expense of VAT arrears did not amount to an intentional procedure designed to disadvantage the Crown as against other creditors which was capable of warranting F's disqualification, *Sevenoaks Stationers (Retail) Ltd, Re* [1991] Ch. 164, [1991] C.L.Y. 401 applied, and (2) the sale of stock was not in real terms at an undervalue, but did constitute preferential treatment. Although F's intention had been to find a solution that would benefit the most number of creditors and the company, he was nevertheless aware that the transactions were improper and therefore disqualification was appropriate.

FUNTIME LTD, *Re; sub nom.* SECRETARY OF STATE FOR TRADE AND INDUSTRY v. DOE [2000] 1 B.C.L.C. 247, Nicholas Strauss Q.C., Ch D (Companies Ct).

663. **Directors – disqualification orders – Scottish company – jurisdiction of English court**

[Company Directors Disqualification Act 1986 s.6(1)(b), s.6(3)d), s.7, s.8(3), s.16(1).]

F had been the director of two companies, one of which, H, was incorporated in Scotland. Following the liquidation of both companies the Secretary of State issued proceedings seeking a disqualification order pursuant to the Company Directors Disqualification Act 1986 s.8. F applied for the proceedings against him to be struck out or dismissed on the basis that the English court's powers to disqualify a director under s.8(3) were limited to companies registered in England and that therefore insofar as the Secretary of State sought to rely upon the affairs of H, the court lacked the necessary jurisdiction.

Held, allowing the application, that (1) the proceedings in relation to F's conduct whilst a director of H were a matter for the Court of Session because s.6(3)(d) of the Act limited the court's jurisdiction in the case of a company registered in Scotland to the Court of Session and the same reasoning must necessarily apply to s.8(3) which contained identical wording. Furthermore s.16(1) contemplated that a disqualification order would only be made by the court possessing jurisdiction to wind up the company, *Secretary of State for Trade and Industry v. Langridge* [1991] Ch. 402, [1991] C.L.Y. 403 considered, and (2) the Secretary of State could nevertheless bring matters relating to H into account in the ongoing English proceedings by virtue of s.6 and s.7 of the Act which entitled the Secretary of State, if it was expedient and in the public interest, to apply for a disqualification order taking into account the conduct of a person in relation to their involvement as a director with other companies. The power provided to the Secretary of State under s.6(1)(b) was not limited to companies that could only be wound up by the court in which the proceedings were taking place. It followed therefore that the Secretary of State under the powers provided by this section could bring before the English court matters relating to companies registered in Scotland.

SECRETARY OF STATE FOR TRADE AND INDUSTRY v. FORSYTHE; *sub nom.* HELENE PLC (IN LIQUIDATION), RE; BARRY ARTIST LTD, RE; SECRETARY OF STATE FOR TRADE AND INDUSTRY v. FORSYTH [2000] 2 B.C.L.C. 249, Blackburne, J., Ch D (Companies Court).

664. **Directors – disqualification orders – selective payment of debts – misconduct warranting disqualification**

The Official Receiver appealed against a decision that the directors of SC, a company in severe financial difficulty, were not guilty of misconduct in resolving to pay its bank overdraft and trade creditors in priority to its liabilities to the Inland Revenue. The directors had opted to use money due to the Inland Revenue to continue trading, in the expectation that the combination of new income, and payments following settlement of outstanding disputes with existing customers, would avoid liquidation of the company, and enable it to pay all creditors, including the Inland Revenue. The company had subsequently gone into liquidation. The judge at first instance had held that the directors were not unfit to act, in view of the fact that they had acted in good faith and had received no personal benefit and had consequently dismissed the Official Receiver's application for disqualification.

Held, allowing the appeal and ordering a period of disqualification in respect of each director, that as the judge's finding of fact was not disputed, the appellate court was entitled to determine what conclusions should be drawn with regard to unfitness, *Hitco 2000 Ltd, Re* [1995] 2 B.C.L.C. 63, [1996] C.L.Y. 993 applied. The judge had identified the correct test, but then failed to apply it correctly to the findings of fact that he had made. Applying *Secretary of State for Trade and Industry v. McTighe (No.2)* [1996] 2 B.C.L.C. 477, [1997] C.L.Y. 806 an intentional policy to favour one class of debt over another for a lengthy period would almost certainly amount to misconduct sufficient to justify disqualification, save in the most exceptional circumstances, an example of which was hard to imagine. To order otherwise would be to condone preferential and selective payment of debts.

STRUCTURAL CONCRETE LTD, *Re The Times*, July 5, 2000, Blackburne, J., Ch D.

665. **Directors – disqualification proceedings – evidence given under compulsion in insolvency proceedings did not breach right to fair trial**

[Company Directors Disqualification Act 1986 s.6; Insolvency Act 1986 s.235; European Convention on Human Rights 1950 Art.6(1).]

S, a director gave evidence under compulsion in interviews under the Insolvency Act 1986 s.235 and, as a preliminary issue, the court was called upon to decide whether the admission of that evidence in disqualification proceedings under the Company Directors Disqualification Act 1986 s.6 constituted a breach of the European Convention on Human Rights 1950 Art.6. The court at first instance dismissed the application (*The Times*, January 19, 2000), concluding that the disqualification proceedings brought by the Official Receiver against S came under civil regulatory proceedings and evidence obtained under compulsion was admissible and compatible with the Convention. S appealed against the decision allowing the case against him to proceed to a full hearing. S contended that (1) the Vice Chancellor erred by seeming to suggest that self incrimination was not an important issue in civil proceedings and that evidence which was obtained by compulsion was only inadmissible where it consisted of admissions, and (2) the disqualification proceedings should be regarded as akin to criminal proceedings for the purposes of the rule against self incrimination.

Held, dismissing the appeal, that (1) the Vice Chancellor was justified in rejecting the contention that there was a breach of Art.6(1) of the Convention with regard to the use of statements obtained under s.235 of the Insolvency Act. S had made wide general submissions and in attempting to find specific grounds for the assertion that S would not receive a fair trial he had not sought to imply that evidence given under compulsion was only inadmissible where it constituted an admission. It was imperative that all relevant factors were taken into consideration when determining the issue of a fair trial, and (2) although disqualification proceedings were not criminal, and were intended to be for the protection of the public, they included serious allegations so that issues of fairness were best decided by the trial judge either at the trial or by way of pre trial review. Civil and criminal cases were not mutually exclusive for the purposes of the rules against self incrimination and that the courts had a discretion enabling them to assess the human rights implications of compelled evidence in cases of corporate insolvency according to the facts of a particular case.

OFFICIAL RECEIVER v. STERN; *sub nom.* WESTMINSTER PROPERTY MANAGEMENT LTD, *Re* [2000] 1 W.L.R. 2230, Henry, L.J., CA.

666. **Directors – disqualification proceedings – right to fair trial**

[Company Directors Disqualification Act 1986 s.6; Insolvency Act 1986 s.235(2)(a); European Convention on Human Rights 1950 Art.6, Art.13, Protocol 1 Art.1.]

Two directors, W and M, were compelled to give answers to an examiner from the official receiver's office under the Insolvency Act 1986 s.235(2)(a). Subsequent disqualification proceedings were based on a deputy official receiver's report that relied on the answers given under compulsion. W and M complained that, although termed civil and regulatory in UK law, disqualification proceedings were actually penal in nature, with the result that they had been denied their rights under the European Convention on Human Rights 1950 Art.6. Further, that the availability of costs against them if they lost was in breach of Protocol 1 Art.1, given the breach of Art.6, and that press reports of the disqualification proceedings interfered with their private lives and reputations contrary to Art.13.

Held, refusing the applications on inadmissibility grounds, that the applications were premature as the disqualification proceedings had not yet been determined and that decision was subject to appeal in any event. Disqualification proceedings were civil in nature, *DC v. United Kingdom* [2000] B.C.C. 710, [2000] C.L.Y. 667 applied. Whilst that finding did not vitiate W's and M's right to a fair trial, it was not for the court to anticipate the fairness issue at this stage. Respect for private life had to be balanced against the need for public confidence in company management. Any damage to reputation could be subject to an action in defamation.

WGS v. UNITED KINGDOM [2000] B.C.C. 719, J-P Costa (President), ECHR.

667. Directors – disqualification proceedings – right to fair trial – regulatory nature of proceedings

[Companies Act 1985 s.151; Company Directors Disqualification Act 1986 s.6; European Convention on Human Rights 1950 Art.6.]

DC and two associates were disqualified from acting as directors by orders under the Company Directors Disqualification Act 1986 s.6 for allowing the company to finance an acquisition of its own shares, permitting the making of an unsecured interest free loan by the company that was detrimental to its creditors and for other breaches of the Companies Act 1985 s.151. DC and the others failed in an attempt to adduce character evidence at the hearing, which was dealt with under the summary procedure on an agreed statement of facts that accepted the appropriateness of disqualification. The three complained that the proceedings under the 1986 Act were unfair and constituted both civil and criminal matters that breached the European Convention on Human Rights 1950 Art.6.

Held, refusing the applications on inadmissibility grounds, that the proceedings concerned were classed as civil in UK law and disqualification was a regulatory rather than a criminal matter so that Art.6 did not apply. Exclusion of the character evidence was not unfair as it had been excluded on the grounds that it was not probative of the matters in issue. The use of compulsorily obtained statements was not unfair either, given the civil nature of the proceedings in the instant case and the fact that their use had not been challenged at the hearing, *Saunders v. United Kingdom* [1998] 1 B.C.L.C. 362, [1997] C.L.Y. 2816 distinguished.

DC v. UNITED KINGDOM [2000] B.C.C. 710, J-P Costa (President), ECHR.

668. Directors – disqualification proceedings – use of liquidated company's trading name – breach of Insolvency Act s.216 relevant to disqualification

[Insolvency Act 1986 s.216; Company Directors Disqualification Act 1986 s.2, s.9(1), Sch.1 para.4.]

During a hearing of disqualification proceedings, the judge declined to accept that a breach of the Insolvency Act 1986 s.216, preventing the use of a liquidated company's trading name, could be considered. The Official Receiver cross appealed on the ground that, since a director could be disqualified under the Company Directors Disqualification Act 1986 s.2 if convicted of a s.216 offence, therefore a breach of s.216 was relevant in disqualification proceedings.

Held, allowing the cross appeal, that the list of provisions in Sch.1 para.4 to the Company Directors Disqualification Act should be read in conjunction with s.9(1) of the same Act where the words "having regard in particular" indicated that the list was not exclusive. It was inconceivable that a director could face disqualification if convicted of an indictable offence under s.216 of the Insolvency Act 1986, but that a breach of s.216 should not be considered in disqualification proceedings.

MIGRATION SERVICES INTERNATIONAL LTD, *Re; sub nom.* WEBSTER v. OFFICIAL RECEIVER [2000] 1 B.C.L.C. 666, Neuberger, J., Ch D (Companies Court).

669. Directors – dividends paid out to shareholders – directors' liability to repay

[Trustees Act 1925 s.61; Companies Act 1985.]

In proceedings commenced against QMH by B, QMH's counterclaim had been adjourned following judgment on the main issues. QMH argued that B as directors of QMH had unlawfully paid out dividends based on the 1990 and 1991 accounts as (1) there had been insufficient funds in the company at the time, and (2) the 1991 accounts did not give a true and fair view. In consequence QMH submitted that B had therefore been in breach of the Companies Act 1985. B contended that there had been adequate funds in the group of companies as a whole and that any breach was no more than technical.

Held, allowing the counterclaim, that B were in breach of trust and their duty of skill and care as they knew or ought to have known that the dividends were unlawfully paid out in breach of s.263 and s.264 of the 1985 Act. In relation to the 1990 accounts, the dividend pay out had been unlawful because there were insufficient distributable reserves. However, there were funds in the group of companies capable of covering the dividends and so that breach was of a technical nature only. No loss had been caused to QMH. B's failure to realise that there had been insufficient funds had not been dishonest or unreasonable and therefore they were entitled to relief under s.727 of the 1985 Act and the Trustees Act 1925 s.61. The 1991 accounts did not give a true and fair view as B had deliberately not disclosed certain transactions, and therefore dividends paid out under those accounts were unlawful and could not be said to be merely a technical breach. QMH had incurred loss as a result. B's dishonest conduct in this regard meant that they were not entitled to relief and were liable to repay the sums paid out.

BAIRSTOW v. QUEENS MOAT HOUSES PLC; MARCUS v. QUEENS MOAT HOUSES PLC; HERSEY v. QUEENS MOAT HOUSES PLC; PORTER v. QUEENS MOAT HOUSES PLC [2000] 1 B.C.L.C. 549, Nelson, J., QBD.

670. Directors duties – directors in breach of fiduciary duty – shareholders agreement failing to make proper provision for creditors

[Companies Act 1985 s.151, s.263(1), s.263(2)(d).]

E appealed against a decision of the High Court ([1999] 2 B.C.L.C. 203, [1999] C.L.Y. 644) giving judgment to M, a former director and shareholder of E, in relation to monies due under an agreement between three shareholders, M, L and T, and E. Under the agreement future receipts from current contracts, after repayment of certain accrued liabilities at the date of the agreement and expenses incurred by the shareholders, would be divided pro rata between the shareholders, as payment for consultancy services provided by them to E. On the making of the agreement M resigned as director and transferred his shares to L, the majority shareholder and other director of E. E contended that the payments to M could not be enforced as (1) the directors were in breach of their fiduciary duties in causing E to enter into the agreement, at a time when E was insolvent and in circumstances where the effect of the agreement provided for the distribution to shareholders of E's assets without making proper provision for its current and future liabilities, and (2) payments made under the agreement would contravene the requirement in the Companies Act 1985 s.263(1) that a company should not make a distribution of its assets to its members except out of profits available for the purpose.

Held, allowing the appeal, that (1) the directors were in breach of their fiduciary duties in exercising powers of management for their own benefit rather than for the benefit of E. The agreement had not been intended to benefit or promote the prosperity of E, but rather it amounted to an attempt to effect an informal winding up of E and a distribution of the company's assets, and as such it failed to make proper provision for creditors, having provided for recoveries made under existing contracts to be made available to certain creditors, including the directors, to the exclusion of other current and future creditors, *Lee Behrens & Co Ltd, Re* [1932] 2 Ch. 46 applied, and (2) the agreement attempted, other than by a formal winding up, to achieve the distribution of assets on a winding up which was permissible under s.263(2)(d), and in doing so the directors acted outside their powers.

Observed that if the agreement had been otherwise enforceable, the provisions of the agreement would have constituted the giving of unlawful financial assistance for the purpose of the acquisition by L of M's shares

MACPHERSON v. EUROPEAN STRATEGIC BUREAU LTD [2000] 2 B.C.L.C. 683, Chadwick, L.J., CA.

671. Disclosure and inspection – privilege – shareholder's right to production of privileged company documents

[Companies Act 1985 s.459.]

Two shareholders of NF, a public limited company, issued a petition under the Companies Act 1985 s.459 arising from the acquisition of shares in the company by a third party. The shareholders sought specific disclosure of certain documents connected with that transaction which NF claimed were protected by legal professional privilege. NF argued that the rule in *Woodhouse & Co Ltd v. Woodhouse* (1914) 30 T.L.R. 559 whereby a shareholder was entitled to see company documents even if they were legally privileged, was restricted to small private companies with limited issues of shares and that it did not apply to substantial companies such as itself.

Held, granting the application for disclosure, that the rule in *Woodhouse* arose as a result of the fiduciary relationship between the directors of a company and its shareholders and was therefore unaffected by the size and importance of the company in question, *Woodhouse* applied.

CAS (NOMINEES) LTD v. NOTTINGHAM FOREST PLC; *sub nom.* NOTTINGHAM FOREST PLC, *Re* [2001] 1 All E.R. 954, Evans-Lombe, J., Ch D.

672. Disqualification orders – former director could take part in company management

[Company Directors Disqualification Act 1986.]

Following his disqualification under the Company Directors Disqualification Act 1986, C had been granted permission by the court to take part in the management of a company. The Secretary of State challenged the exercise of judicial discretion, contending that the judge had not observed the protective purpose of the Act and that he had erred in attributing too much weight to the respondent's needs.

Held, dismissing the appeal, that, as the judge had not misdirected himself or come to an erroneous conclusion, the exercise of his discretion in this case could not be overturned. The court advised that where possible applications for permission should be made without delay and before the same judge as heard the disqualification proceedings who should be informed of the current state of the company and the projected role of the applicant within it.

SECRETARY OF STATE FOR TRADE AND INDUSTRY v. COLLINS; *sub nom.* TLL REALISATIONS LTD, *Re* [2000] 2 B.C.L.C. 223, Peter Gibson, L.J., CA.

673. Floating charges – book debts – fixed charge over book debts

B, a company, created a fixed charge in favour of its bank to cover its business debts. Proceeds from book debts were excluded unless the bank ordered payments of the book debts into an account which the company could not operate freely. Those proceeds were to be treated as subject to a fixed charge. Otherwise the proceeds of book debts were subject to a floating charge. The Revenue, a preferential creditor, appealed against the decision that book debts were not subject to a floating charge. The question for the court was whether the company could create a fixed charge over book debts which the company could not charge or dispose of but once collected the proceeds would be subject to a floating charge.

Held, allowing the appeal, that the charge on book debts was a floating charge. The question was whether the assets were under the control of the chargee or not. Where the charged assets were book debts which the chargor was free to collect and thus extinguish the book debt, and was then free to deal with the proceeds in the normal course of its business, then the charge was a floating charge as the chargee did not have control over the charged asset.

BRUMARK INVESTMENTS LTD, *Re*; *sub nom.* INLAND REVENUE COMMISSIONER v. AGNEW [2000] 1 B.C.L.C. 353, Gault, J., CA (NZ).

674. Floating charges – liens over warehouse stock – power of sale did not make lien into equitable charge – not void for failure to register

[Companies Act 1985 s.395; Insolvency Act 1986 s.11 (3).]

T traded with IM and IN under the terms of a British International Freight Association, BIFA, agreement and the UK Warehousing Association, UKWA, agreement. Those agreements provided, inter alia, that T was entitled to a general lien over goods in its possession, together with a right to sell those goods to discharge any debts owed to T. In the event, IM and IN went into administration with outstanding debts to T. T claimed a right to exercise its lien under the Insolvency Act 1986 s.11 (3). The administrator resisted this claim on the basis that, since T had a right to possession and a power of sale over the stock, these rights were inconsistent with the ownership rights of IM and IN and thus were properly to be considered as a floating charge which was void for want of registration under the Companies Act 1985 s.395. Furthermore, the lien was based on contractual rights, and the legislative purpose behind the registration of charges, in that it allowed creditors to know who holds security over the companies' assets, would be undermined if such a right was not subject to registration.

Held, dismissing the appeal, that T did not have a floating charge over the stock held in its warehouses. Instead it had a legal possessory lien over the stock together with a right to sell that property and recoup moneys owed to T. That right was not registrable as a consequence. That there was a power of sale did not convert the lien into an equitable charge because there was no right for T to exercise a proprietary right distinct from its possession of the property further to the contract, *Great Eastern Railway Co v. Lord's Trustees* [1909] A.C. 109 applied.

HAMLET INTERNATIONAL PLC (IN ADMINISTRATION), *Re*; JEFFREY ROGERS (IMPORTS) LTD, *Re*; *sub nom.* TRIDENT INTERNATIONAL LTD v. BARLOW [1999] 2 B.C.L.C. 506, Mummery, L.J., CA.

675. Fraudulent trading – liquidation – liability of participants to make contribution to assets of company

[Insolvency Act 1986 s.213, s.213(2).]

M, the liquidator of BCCI, brought an action against BA under the Insolvency Act 1986 s.213 alleging that BA had participated in three frauds committed by BCCI with the intent to defraud its creditors and that BA should be required under s.213(2) to make a contribution to the assets of BCCI. BA sought determination of a preliminary issue, as to whether it was necessary for a person to have carried on or assisted in the carrying on of the liquidated company's business in order to fall within the ambit of s.213 of the Act.

Held, dismissing the application, that as a matter of ordinary language s.213(2) was not restricted to those who performed a managerial role. Moreover, the legislative history of the provision pointed towards a wider interpretation of s.213(2), extending not only to a person who carried on business or assisted in the carrying on of the liquidated company's business but also to a person who had participated in the fraudulent acts of the company, *Augustus Barnett & Son, Re* [1986] P.C.C. 167, [1986] C.L.Y. 301 considered and *R. v. Grantham (Paul Reginald George)* [1984] Q.B. 675, [1984] C.L.Y. 627 distinguished.

MORRIS v. BANQUE ARABE INTERNATIONALE D'INVESTISSEMENT SA (NO.2); *sub nom.* BANK OF CREDIT AND COMMERCE INTERNATIONAL SA, RE; BANQUE ARABE INTERNATIONALE D'INVESTISSEMENT SA v. MORRIS [2001] 1 B.C.L.C. 263, Neuberger, J., Ch D.

676. Mergers – schemes of arrangement – unincorporated association – distribution of sale proceeds to associate members

[Companies Act 1985 s.425.]

RACMS and RACL were both companies limited by guarantee with no share capital. RACMS provided the motoring services business of the RAC, including its breakdown service. The RAC itself was an unincorporated association having 12,000 members established by RACL and whose assets belonged to RACL. The court was called on to approve two schemes of arrangement pursuant to the Companies Act 1985 s.425 arising out of the proposed acquisition by C of RACMS and the distribution of the proceeds of sale to members of RACL. The first petition, by RACMS, proposed deleting the clauses of its memorandum of association which provided for the distribution of the proceeds of sale to the 2.5 million associate members of RACL, in effect members of the public who subscribed to the breakdown service. The second, by RACL, involved a proposal whereby the membership rights of its members would be cancelled, the members would cease to be members of RACL, but would be given separate interests in the RAC by way of shares in a new holding company. The first scheme was opposed on the basis that the clauses in question conferred a benefit on associate members amounting to a resulting trust and so could not be varied even where all members of the company agreed. The second scheme was objected to on the grounds that it was unfair to members who were not full members of the Club, the proposal to sell the motoring services should have been disclosed earlier, and the notice convening the extraordinary meeting was defective in failing to describe adequately the business to be conducted at that meeting.

Held, approving both schemes, that (1) in relation to the first scheme, associate members had no more than a hope or spes that, if the clauses of the memorandum stayed, they might one day receive a future distribution. The issue was not whether it was fair to deprive associate members of a possible future advantage but whether the scheme was fair as between members of RACMS. The court would not interfere with a bona fide majority decision taken at a meeting if the class of members had been properly consulted and the meeting had considered the matter with a view to the interests of the class which it was empowered to bind, and (2) in relation to the second scheme, the articles of the company and the Club made it clear that only full and life members of the Club were members of the company which ultimately controlled the motor services business. The board of the RACL could not reasonably have been expected to have informed members of sale proposals until it had reached a decision in principle to sell or it had been approached with a clear and potentially attractive proposal to sell. The information contained in the notice of the meeting together with the accompanying circular gave a full and fair disclosure. Such disclosure is sufficient if it enables a person to make further inquiries.

RAC MOTORING SERVICES LTD, *Re*; sub nom. ROYAL AUTOMOBILE CLUB LTD, *Re* [2000] 1 B.C.L.C. 307, Neuberger, J., Ch D (Companies Court).

677. Offer documents – right of offeror to buy out minority shareholders – failure to serve offer documents on overseas shareholders

[Companies Act 1985 s.428, s.429(1), s.430(2).]

WH, an Australian company, applied for a declaration that a notice served on it by JHG pursuant to the Companies Act 1985 s.429(1) and which required it to sell its shares in JH to JHG, was invalid. JHG had issued offer documentation to shareholders of JH for the acquisition of the entire issued share capital, but had not sent the offer documentation to overseas shareholders because of the perceived difficulties of compliance with local securities legislation. As a result of acceptances of the offer JHG's potential shareholding exceeded 90 per cent of JH's issued share capital; hence the despatch of notices under s.429(1) of the Act to the remaining shareholders, notifying them of its right to acquire their shares. WH contended that, since it had not received the offer documents and since s.429(1) of the Act applied only to the holders of shares to which the offer related, the notice served on it by JHG was invalid.

Held, refusing the application, that the failure to serve offer documentation on WH did not invalidate the subsequent s.429(1) notice served on it, with the effect that JHG was entitled and bound to acquire WH's shares in JH, pursuant to s.430(2) of the Act. On the facts JHG had made a general offer in accordance with the Companies Act 1985 s.428, to acquire all the shares in JH, and that offer was not vitiated by a failure to communicate it to a particular shareholder. The offer had therefore been applicable to WH's shares, the s.429(1) notice was valid and the compulsory purchase of WH's shareholding was legitimate.

WINPAR HOLDINGS LTD v. JOSEPH HOLT GROUP PLC; *sub nom.* JOSEPH HOLT PLC, *Re The Times*, November 14, 2000, Anthony Mann Q.C., Ch D.

678. Open ended investment companies – fees – payment to registrar

OPEN-ENDED INVESTMENT COMPANIES (INVESTMENT COMPANIES WITH VARIABLE CAPITAL) (FEES) (AMENDMENT) REGULATIONS 2000, SI 2000 3324; made under the Companies Act 1985 s.708; and the SI 1996 2827 Reg.4, Sch.1 para.5. In force: April 2, 2001; £1.50.

These Regulations amend the Open-Ended Investment Companies (Investment Companies with Variable Capital) (Fees) Regulations 1998 (SI 1998 3087) by increasing the statutory fees payable for microfiche based information services for open-ended investment companies.

679. Purchase of own shares – professional negligence – solicitors – duty of care owned to company – non client third parties

[Companies Act 1985 s.159(3), s.160(1)(a), s.271(4).]

D, a former director and shareholder of a company, B, sold 50 per cent of his shares in the company to the company itself in exchange for money and certain assets of the company. D then formally resigned from B and B was left in sole charge of B's affairs. B subsequently went into liquidation. The liquidator brought an action for professional negligence against DB, the company's solicitors, for permitting the share repurchases to be executed by the company. The liquidator contended that DB had been in breach of their duty of care owed to B both in contract and at common law by advising that the share buyback was valid. The liquidator claimed that the transaction did not meet the statutory requirements of the Companies Act 1985 in that (1) "payment" under s.159(3) of the 1985 Act referred only to money consideration given for the share repurchase whilst the instant case included property as well as cash; (2) DB had failed to draw attention to s.271(4), and as a result the accounts had failed to show that the amount of distributable profits was insufficient to purchase the shares under s.160(1)(a), rendering the transaction invalid, and (3) the cash element had been paid prior to the completion of the share repurchase contrary to the requirements of s.159(3).

Held, giving judgement for DB, that (1) "payment on redemption" for the purposes of s.159(3) was not restricted to a monetary consideration and in any event, the agreement did provide for a monetary consideration which could be satisfied by set off against property and (2) payment of the cash consideration had not taken place in advance of the sale. However, the arrangement was invalid because of the failure to obtain an auditor's statement under s.271(4) which meant that there had been insufficient distributable reserves under s.160(1)(a). Despite this, DB was not liable to B as DB had not been B's solicitor for the purposes of the share repurchase, but had instead been acting for D in his personal capacity as shareholder and since there was insufficient proximity between B and DB, it would not have been fair and reasonable to impose such a duty, *Caparo Industries Plc v. Dickman* [1990] 2 A.C. 605, [1990] C.L.Y. 3266 applied. Furthermore there was no evidence of reliance by B or any assumption of responsibility by DB.

BDG ROOF BOND LTD (IN LIQUIDATION) v. DOUGLAS [2000] 1 B.C.L.C. 401, Park, J., Ch D.

680. **Reduction of capital – takeovers – prejudice to preferential shareholders – approval of court – full and frank disclosure**

[Companies Act 1985 s.137.]

T agreed to take over RIC. The deal was structured so that a subsidiary of T, A, would acquire all of the ordinary shares in the company, most of its preference shares, and most of its convertible stock. An Australian company, W, was holder of preference shares. The proposal was to distribute shares to A and, inter alia, to cancel the share premium account. An extraordinary general meeting was called to approve this plan. W petitioned the court under the Companies Act 1985 s.137 to object that the proposal had not been explained in sufficiently clear terms and that the proposals had been generally put forward with undue haste. W further contended that the cancellation of the share premium account benefited the ordinary shareholders to the detriment of the preferred shareholders.

Held, dismissing the application, that an application under s.137 was not equivalent to ordinary litigation, given that many such applications were made by one party only. The court was required to give its approval under s.137 to proposed restructurings and therefore the applicant would be subject to a duty of full and frank disclosure which should not be diluted in any way. It was within the ambit of the discretion of the trial judge to decide, as he had done, that the proposal was fair and that it did not prejudice the rights of preferred shareholders to receipt of future dividends. There had not been any deliberate lack of openness in the company's dealings with the court and therefore the judge was entitled to sanction the cancellation on the material before him.

RANSOMES PLC, *Re*; *sub nom.* RANSOMES PLC v. WINPAR HOLDINGS LTD; WINPAR HOLDINGS LTD v. RANSOMES PLC [1999] 2 B.C.L.C. 591, Robert Walker, L.J., CA.

681. **Sale of business – warranties – construction of clause limiting liability of vendor for breach of net asset value and stock value warranties**

Under a contract for the sale of share capital in a company, the vendor, M, warranted under Sch.3 cl.7.2 and cl.7.6 for a gross margin on sales of not less than an agreed percentage and a value of net assets not less than nil. Clause 7.9.3 of the schedule excluded liability for breach of any of warranties under the agreement, limited to the extent of provisions made in the completion accounts. DG's claim for damages for breach of the cl.7.2 and cl.7.6 warranties, on the basis that the completion accounts showed a negative net value of assets and a gross margin on sales below the agreed percentage, was resisted by M on the grounds that adding back a provision in the completion accounts for obsolete and returned stock would increase the gross margin to the agreed percentage and give a positive net sale value. At first instance it was held that M could not rely on cl.7.9.3 to defeat its liability for breach of the cl.7.2 and cl.7.6 warranties, as the obsolete or returned goods provision did not apply in respect of either gross margin or net assets. M appealed, arguing that where a breach of warranty was attributable to something covered by a provision in the completion accounts, for the avoidance of double counting, the liability for the breach had to be reduced by subtracting the amount of the provision from the value of the breach.

Held, dismissing the appeal, that (1) although cl.7.9.3 could be interpreted as providing for obsolete and returned stock values to be described both in terms of the cost value and gross margin, it was more natural for it to refer only to stock; (2) as cl.7.9.3 did not expressly limit M's liability for breaches of the cl.7.2 and cl.7.6 warranties, it was not to be construed as limiting or excluding M's liability for such breaches, and (3) the judge below had correctly construed the agreement in light of the completion accounts as determining whether any provision had been made for breach of the cl.7.2 and cl.7.6 warranties.

DIXONS GROUP PLC v. MURRAY-OBODYNSKI (BREACH OF WARRANTIES) [2000] 1 B.C.L.C. 1, Clarke, L.J., CA.

682. **Schemes of arrangement – sale of business to third party – court approval on basis of shareholder agreement**

[Companies Act 1985 s.425.]

AD announced an agreement for the sale of its UK businesses to W. It asked its shareholders to approve the disposal of the business. The disposal involved a scheme of arrangement under the Companies Act 1985 s.425 and a reduction of its share capital. AD made a new arrangement for disposal of the business after a competing bid by P and W's subsequent withdrawal. AD sought court approval for the scheme of arrangement between it and its members; the court's confirmation of the reduction of capital required by the scheme and a direction for the court's order to be registered despite the reduction of its issued share capital to below the authorised minimum for a public limited company. W opposed the petition on the ground that the scheme as explained to the shareholders had as its only purpose a disposal to W and not to any other party.

Held, granting the application, that (1) the various statutory requirements had been satisfied and no minority shareholders had been coerced; (2) with regard to the reduction of capital, all statutory requirements had been met, all shareholders were treated equally and the interests of creditors or third parties had not been prejudiced, and (3) the explanation sent to the shareholders made it sufficiently clear that the scheme might be implemented even if the disposal to W did not materialise. Even if the shareholders had not been sufficiently advised on that point, a reasonable shareholder would not have taken a different voting course had that possibility been spelt out in due time.

ALLIED DOMECQ PLC, *Re* [2000] 1 B.C.L.C. 134, Blackburne, J., Ch D.

683. **Schemes of arrangement – shareholders – scheme designed to effect merger**

[Companies Act 1985 s.425, s.428.]

BTR sought the sanction of the court to a scheme of arrangement under the Companies Act 1985 s.425, together with the court's confirmation of a reduction of its capital by the cancellation, as part of the scheme, of its existing ordinary shares, ("the scheme shares"). Essentially, the scheme was designed to effect a merger between BTR and SP. The scheme provided for the cancellation of the scheme shares, the allotment to scheme share holders of new shares in SP, and for the capitalisation of the reserve from the cancellation of the scheme shares to be allotted and credited as fully paid to SP. At a meeting of share scheme holders, there was a 96.9 per cent vote in favour. Seven individual holders of scheme shares objected on the grounds that: (1) it was inappropriate to have a single meeting of all the holders of scheme shares as they would have diverse interests; (2) the chairman of the meeting had no authority to cast proxy votes given to him against a motion made to adjourn the meeting, and (3) SP should have adopted the procedure provided in relation to takeover offers contained in s.428 rather than proceeding under s.425.

Held, sanctioning the scheme, that (1) the court's function in sanctioning a proposed scheme under s.425 was not merely to see that the majority acted bona fide. It might review a majority decision where the circumstances warranted. The court could not sanction a scheme where it contained a defect, notwithstanding the fact that a majority may have voted for it, *National Bank, Ltd Re* [1966] 1 W.L.R. 819, [1966] C.L.Y. 1305 applied; (2) the fact that shareholders might have differing interests, as opposed to differing rights, did not warrant the convening of more than one meeting of holders of the scheme shares, there not being separate classes of holders of scheme shares for the purposes of the scheme in issue, *Hellenic & General Trust, Re* [1976] 1 W.L.R. 123, [1975] C.L.Y. 301 considered; (3) the chairman was entitled to use his proxy votes against the motion of adjournment, *Waxed Papers Ltd, Re* [1937] 2 All E.R. 481 applied, and (4) the Act gave BTR the choice of embarking on a s.425 scheme or on a takeover procedure under s.428.

BTR PLC, *Re* [1999] 2 B.C.L.C. 675, Jonathan Parker, J., Ch D (Companies Court).

684. Schemes of arrangement – shareholders – scheme designed to effect merger – sanction of court

[Companies Act 1985 s.425, s.428, s.429.]

N, an individual shareholder of B, sought permission to appeal against an order under the Companies Act 1985 s.425 ([1999] 2 B.C.L.C. 675, [2000] C.L.Y. 683) sanctioning a scheme of arrangement permitting the merger of B with S and the reduction of B's share capital. The merger was to be effected by the cancellation of B's ordinary shares and the replacement issue of S's fully paid up shares, in the ratio of 0.533 S shares for each B share. N contended that the scheme should have been effected under s.428 and s.429, as the scheme amounted to a takeover, so that consent of a higher percentage of shareholders was required. Further, that separate meetings should have been convened for shareholders with different interests.

Held, refusing permission to appeal, that it was the clear intention of the legislature that s.425 should operate to allow a binding compromise between companies and their members as an alternative to s.428 and s.429, *National Bank Ltd, Re* [1966] 1 W.L.R. 819, [1966] C.L.Y. 1305 considered. The court was not bound by the outcome of the meeting as a decision in favour at the meeting was only a threshold to be passed prior to obtaining the sanction of the court. This could be refused if the special interests of a group of shareholders, separate from those of the majority of shareholders, had influenced the vote. Refusal, therefore, represented a check that could be imposed where shareholders who shared the same rights could nonetheless vote in unrepresentative ways. The separate meetings for each identifiable class of shareholder contended for by N would be impractical. The Act recognised that it was for the court to consider the different interests and to refuse permission for a scheme if it was shown that certain members were taking advantage over others.

BTR PLC (LEAVE TO APPEAL), *Re* [2000] 1 B.C.L.C. 740, Chadwick, L.J., CA.

685. Share transfers – misrepresentation – misleading information inducing share transfer – valuation of shares measured at time of sale

Following a reorganisation in July 1990, the shares in LJK, a company which held a BMW dealership franchise, were allotted between three brothers, C, D and K. K held the ordinary shares and controlled the business, while C and D held preference shares with no voting rights but yielding preferential dividends. Subsequent to LJK doing poorly in the recession of the early 1990's C and D waived their dividend entitlement by a deed executed in January 1992. In March 1992, C and D refused to transfer their shares to K in return for his agreeing to "look after" them. However, in May 1992, they did transfer their shares to K for £1. They alleged that they had been told by K that the transfer was necessary to enable the business to be sold at the insistence of BMW. The alternative was said to be the withdrawal of the BMW franchise and liquidation. They further alleged that they had been told the shares would be returned to them if the business subsequently prospered. LJK did later improve and, in March 1993, BMW advised that it would not be asking for the business to be sold. A request by C and D for the retransfer of their shares was refused and LJK was eventually sold in 1996. C and D applied to the court for an award of damages for breach of contract, misrepresentation and breach of fiduciary duty.

Held, granting an order for damages, that (1) K had misled C and D by suggesting that BMW were about to withdraw the franchise and were urging him to sell, when he knew matters were not as grave as he represented; (2) the claims in contract failed as the agreement to retransfer the shares to C and D was not capable of having contractual force, because such a retransfer would have had to have been on terms as to purchase price and payment of dividends to be negotiated and agreed; (3) the shares would not have been transferred but for K's misrepresentations which were, at the least, negligent; (4) the fact that the relationship between director and shareholder did not of itself give rise to a fiduciary duty did not prevent such an obligation arising when the circumstances required it. Here there was such a duty which K broke by failing to give a candid and full account of his discussions with BMW, and (5) as the shares no longer existed the only remedy open was damages and the measure for damages for misrepresentation was the same as that for breach of fiduciary duty. Justice would be best done by valuing the shares at the time of the sale. A valuation based on future income was generally preferable to one based on net realisable value of assets, but uncertainties in LJK's income position in this case made an assets valuation the more satisfactory. Accordingly, damages should be calculated on that basis.

PLATT v. PLATT [1999] 2 B.C.L.C. 745, David Mackie Q.C., Ch D.

686. Share transfers – misrepresentation of details shown on stock transfer form – liability in damages for injurious falsehood

[Companies Act 1985 s.359(2); Financial Services Act 1986 s.3, s.5.]

L claimed that he was the owner of 100 AA ordinary shares in a golf club, H, and that P was not entitled to complete a stock transfer form transferring those shares into his name. P asserted that he was entitled to complete the stock transfer form under an agreement made with L. L had delivered a stock transfer form to P, but the inscription TBA ("to be agreed") had been inserted in the boxes relating to the transferee's name, the price to be paid and the date of execution.

Held, giving judgment for L, that (1) L had been deprived of the proceeds of the sale of the shares by P's conduct. L had similarly been deprived by H's registration of those shares; (2) L was entitled to bring a claim for injurious falsehood. The ingredients of the tort being a false statement made either recklessly or with the knowledge that it was false to a third party with the result that the claimant suffered damage; (3) H had breached the provisions of the shareholders' agreement and the supplemental deed in failing to offer L's shares for sale. H was not carrying on an investment business and, therefore, the agreement regarding the sale of L's shares was not an illegal act contrary to the Financial Services Act 1986 s.3. Even if there had been a contravention of s.3, the court would have exercised its discretion under the s.5(3) and s.5(6) of the 1986 Act to allow the agreement to be enforced, and (4) both P and H were liable to L in damages and no discretion would be exercised to order a rectification of the register under the Companies Act 1985 s.359(2), as originally sought by L.

LLOYD v. POPELY [2000] 1 B.C.L.C. 19, Peter Leaver Q.C., Ch D.

687. Shareholders – dispute between two equal shareholders – rival offers to buy each other out – likelihood of meeting valuation price

[Companies Act 1985 s.459.]

An irreconcilable dispute arose between W and B, two equal shareholders of an incorporated company. The only solution was for one shareholder to transfer his share to the other but each party's offer to sell had been criticised by the other. W applied for an order under the Companies Act 1985 s.459 that B sell his share to him at a price to be set by the court.

Held, striking out the application as an abuse of process, that the court had to consider which party was likely to be able to pay the price fixed by an independent valuer. Moreover, some thought had also to be given to the question of which of the shareholders was more actively involved in managing the company.

WEST v. BLANCHET [2000] 1 B.C.L.C. 795, Peter Leaver Q.C., Ch D (Companies Court).

688. Shareholders – unfairly prejudicial conduct – exclusion of director with majority shareholding – legitimate expectation – equitable intervention – purchase order

P was, and always had been, the majority shareholder of E, a corporate partnership, with the effect that he had voting control over the company. P made a basic agreement with M, the minority shareholders, to relinquish his stake in the company but appropriate compensation for him had not been agreed. P was subsequently excluded from control while the primary business carried on by a wholly owned subsidiary, B, was sold to a holding company in which M held the majority of votes. P sought an order that his shares be purchased by M at a value to be determined by the court. M challenged the necessity of such an order, submitting that the existence of the basic agreement was sufficient, and subsequent negotiations would ensue between the parties regarding the steps required to perform the agreement.

Held, granting the application, that P had been excluded from the running of the company without justification, and in the absence of a binding agreement between the parties for reallocation of P's shares, and extinguishment of his voting rights, P's interests had been prejudiced. Equity permitted the court to intervene and order M to purchase his shares at a fair price, *Bird Precision Bellows Ltd, Re* [1986] Ch. 658, [1985] C.L.Y. 309 considered. P's legitimate expectation that he would continue to contribute to the running of the company in the interim, was however a consequence of equitable intervention, not the cause of it. In the situation of an unwilling purchaser and an unwilling seller of shares in E which had lost its main business, it was appropriate to value E on a ongoing concern basis rather than by its assets.

PARKINSON v. EUROFINANCE GROUP LTD; *sub nom.* EUROFINANCE GROUP LTD, *Re* [2001] 1 B.C.L.C. 720, Pumfrey, J., Ch D (Companies Court).

689. Shareholders agreements – pre-emption rights not triggered by share transfer agreements

S, a shareholder in a limited company, sought a declaration that an agreement between other shareholders and an external purchaser for the sale of shares was an intention to transfer the legal title, which would invoke her pre-emption rights as contained in the company's articles of association. Furthermore, S contended that a condition requiring the purchaser to vote in favour of a special resolution to remove pre-emption rights from the articles amounted to an intention to transfer the shares.

Held, refusing the declaration, that S's pre emption rights were not triggered because the agreements for sale had explicitly declared that the buyer could not force the shareholders to prejudice existing pre-emption rights contained in the articles, *Company (No.005685 of 1988), Re* [1989] B.C.L.C. 424, [1989] C.L.Y. 356 applied. The articles were not breached even where the purchaser was required to vote for the removal of pre-emption rights from the articles. It was not necessary to serve a notice of transfer until the point where the shareholder was contractually bound to complete in breach of a pre-emption agreement.

SCOTTO v. PETCH; *sub nom.* SEDGEFIELD STEEPLECHASE CO (1927) LTD, *Re* [2000] 2 B.C.L.C. 211, Lord Hoffmann, Ch D.

690. Shares – clearing systems – insolvency of broker – clients' proprietary interest in shares

A central clearing and settlement system, CC, was operated by HK for trading in shares on the Hong Kong Stock Exchange. The scheme matched buy and sell orders and HK was interposed between buyer and seller so that shares were deemed to be sold to HK and then sold on by HK. In law a novation was effected so that the original contract was replaced by the two contracts with HK. Under the CC rules brokers were treated as principals. HK acted as custodian of the securities and the securities were registered in its name. CA carried on business as a broker on the Hong Kong Stock Exchange and participated in CC. When CA went into liquidation a question arose as to what proprietary interest, if any, was held by the clients of CA who had instructed CAPS to acquire shares where the clients had paid for shares, CA had purchased the shares and the shares had been acquired through CC.

Held, determining the preliminary issue, that when CA executed a transaction for its clients it was acting as agent for the client and so the client had a beneficial interest in the securities unless some evidence refuted that suggestion.

The fact that CA dealt as a principal under the CC did not preclude the agency relationship. A trust arose between CA and its clients because it was the clients' money that was used to acquire the securities. No formal declaration of trust was needed. Shares were fungibles and each certificate deposited with HK evidenced a bundle of rights. There was no difficulty in finding certainty of subject matter. Each client had a beneficial interest rather than being a tenant in common.

CA PACIFIC FINANCE LTD (IN LIQUIDATION), *Re* [2000] 1 B.C.L.C. 494, Yuen, J., CFI (HK).

691. **Shares – minority shareholders – legitimate expectation – unfairness in company management – jurisdiction to force share sale and make order for winding up**

[Companies Act 1985 s.459(1), s.461; Insolvency Act 1986 s.122(1).]

K, a minority shareholder in a family owned company, GL, petitioned for a forced share buyout of his interest in the company pursuant to the Companies Act 1985 s.459(1) and s.461, together with a winding up order under the Insolvency Act 1986 s.122(1). K maintained that the company had been run in a manner that was unfairly prejudicial to his interests in that the remaining shareholders had refused to agree to the sale of a hotel which comprised the company's principal asset, thus preventing him from realising the value of his investment. K further maintained that the hotel had originally been purchased on the basis that he would have the final say on matters related to it, and that in consequence his legitimate expectation that the hotel would be sold at his request had been frustrated.

Held, dismissing the petition, that there had been no unfairness in the way in which the affairs of the company had been run and there had been no agreement between the family members at any stage that K would have the final say on matters concerning the hotel. Given that there was no unfairness, it followed that there was no right to request winding up under s.122(1) since the criteria for the exercise of discretion under each jurisdiction were coextensive, *O'Neill v. Phillips* [1999] 1 W.L.R. 1092, [1999] C.L.Y. 634 applied and *Ebrahimi v. Westbourne Galleries Ltd* [1973] A.C. 360, [1972] C.L.Y. 393 considered.

GUIDEZONE LTD, *Re*; *sub nom*. KANERIA v. PATEL [2000] 2 B.C.L.C. 321, Jonathan Parker, J., Ch D (Companies Ct).

692. **Shares – minority shareholders petition under Companies Act 1985 s.459 – strike out inappropriate despite alternative remedy**

[Companies Act 1985 s.459; Civil Procedure Rules 1998.]

Y, a minority shareholder in a company, R had brought a petition under the Companies Act 1985 s.459 seeking an order that his shares be bought out by T, the managing director of R, at a price to be determined by an independent chartered accountant. T had applied to have the petition struck out, principally on the basis that the petition was an abuse of process, since Y had an alternative remedy and the costs and time involved were disproportionate to the sums at stake. Y proposed alternative dispute resolution. T appealed against the registrar's refusal to strike out the petition on the basis that directions ought to have been given allowing the application to be heard. Y contended that one of the purposes of the Civil Procedure Rules 1998 was to require that the parties cooperate in order that a saving of time and costs might be effected.

Held, dismissing the appeal, that the 1998 Rules required both active case management by the court and active attempts by the parties to narrow or resolve the issues, *North Holdings Ltd v. Southern Tropics Ltd* [1999] B.C.C. 746, [1999] C.L.Y. 629 applied. The petition was long winded and some of the allegations within it, taken in isolation, were weak, but nevertheless the petition as a whole presented an arguable case, and so striking out was not appropriate. It was reasonable to require that the parties meet to narrow the issues and the registrar's order would be varied to that effect. The alternative contention that the case should be struck out because a remedy existed under R's Articles of Association was without merit, as a shareholder was entitled to bring a s.459 petition if by doing so he felt that he would have greater confidence in the valuation of his shares being carried out by an independent accountant, as was required by s.459, rather than by R's own auditors as stipulated in the Articles.

ROTADATA LTD, *Re* [2000] 1 B.C.L.C. 122, Neuberger, J., Ch D (Companies Court).

693. **Shares – share valuation – discount applied in determining fair price for compulsory purchase of preference shares**

An order was made for the compulsory sale of shares in PO, a company involved in the sale of organic food from one retail outlet. The parties involved failed to agree on the terms, and the court had to determine a fair price of the preference shares held by nine shareholders. The preference shareholders argued that they ought to be treated as quasi partners, and that their shares should not be subject to a discounted valuation, *Ebrahimi v. Westbourne Galleries Ltd* [1973] A.C. 360, [1972] C.L.Y. 393 referred to.

Held, that the preference shareholders could not be regarded as quasi partners. Since they had essentially been investors, the court was not precluded from applying a discount and with the shareholders having taken action resulting in an order that they should be excluded from the company, they should be treated as if they were selling voluntarily and a discount of 30 per cent would apply. Furthermore, the company was extremely difficult to value, with no comparable, and having regard to uncertainty over matters such as expansion and potential competition, a valuation could be achieved by adopting a P/E ratio of 11.5 per cent multiplied by a figure for maintainable profits of £275,000, and adding on a figure for surplus cash of £270,000 excluding any element of interest.

ELLIOTT v. PLANET ORGANIC LTD; *sub nom.* PLANET ORGANIC LTD, *Re* [2000] 1 B.C.L.C. 366, Jacob, J., Ch D.

694. **Shares – shareholders – loans – capital contributions – no obligation on payee to repay money**

K appealed against the dismissal of a claim that monies paid by K to S, an insolvent company, represented shareholders' loans which were repayable to him. K contended that under Turkish company law, monies paid to S were repayable to the payer.

Held, dismissing the appeal, that the funds paid to S by K were to be treated as capital contributions and therefore created no obligation on S to repay the money to K. They would only become repayable on a distribution of S's capital and would be distributed amongst the shareholders after payment of debts in proportion to the nominal amount of their shares.

KELLAR v. WILLIAMS [2000] 2 B.C.L.C. 390, Lord Mackay of Clashfern, PC.

695. **Take overs – groups of companies – acting in concert to acquire control of target company – control demonstrated where aggregate of voting rights amounted to 30 per cent or more**

PM sought a declaration that it was entitled to terminate a licence to sell and distribute within the UK certain brands of cigarette which had been granted to a partnership comprising two of its affiliated companies and a company within the Rothman Group, RT. Under the agreement, PM was entitled to terminate the licence following a change of control of the partnership which, under cl.14, would be deemed to have occurred if there was a change in control of RIE, the parent company of RT. Following the acquisition of the Rothman group by BAT, P contended that there had been a change in control of RIE, construing cl.14 in accordance with the City Code on Take Overs and Merger, to the effect that a change in control extended to a situation where persons who had not previously had control of a company acted in concert to acquire de facto control. It was submitted that BAT had acted in concert with R, who owned one third of the ultimate parent company of RIE, by which BAT was left to control RIE.

Held, granting the declaration, that "control" of a company within the meaning of the City Code on Take Overs and Mergers section C1, could be acquired by a stranger to that company acquiring a shareholding of less than 30 per cent of the voting rights, where, at the time of the acquisition, that person had an understanding with another company whose aggregated voting rights amounted to 30 per cent or more of the votes available at a general meeting. In the instant case, before completion of the takeover of the Rothman Group's tobacco business by BAT, R and BAT had not acted in concert for the purposes of controlling RIE, however, at the point of completion there came into existence a group of persons having control of RIE who did not previously have control and accordingly, under the terms of the agreement, PM was entitled to terminate the licence.

PHILIP MORRIS PRODUCTS INC v. ROTHMANS INTERNATIONAL ENTERPRISES LTD (NO.2) [2000] U.K.C.L.R. 912, Evans-Lombe, J., Ch D.

696. Winding up – public interest – timeshare presentations – telephone canvassing companies misleading members of public

[Insolvency Act 1986 s.124A.]

The Secretary of State sought orders that four companies be wound up in the public interest. The companies were telephone canvassing companies and holiday certificate companies. Telephone canvassers would telephone members of the public to persuade them to attend timeshare presentations. The canvassers would tell the members of the public that they had won a holiday and to collect it they would have to attend a presentation. If the individual agreed they would be sent an invitation which stated that a £29 fee was payable and that the choice of airport, destination and departure date would be advised by the travel company. At the end of the presentations the individuals were given certificates which recorded an entitlement to one week's holiday at various resorts. The individuals filled in a form and returned it and the £29 fee to the holiday certificate companies. The Secretary of State alleged that the telephone canvassing companies had deceived the public by making false statements that they had won a free holiday and by not giving full details of the scheme. The travel certificate companies were alleged to have deliberately organised matters so that the minimum number of people actually went on holiday.

Held, dismissing the petition, that the Secretary of State had to show intentional and dishonest deceit of the public. For the telephone canvassers it was necessary to consider the telephone scripts and the invitations together. Although the script contained an untrue statement and did not mention the processing fee that, on its own, was not enough to merit winding the company up. On the evidence as a whole, members of the public had not been promised a free holiday. Couples taking a holiday were not a burden to the travel certificate companies as they would receive a payment from the timeshare companies for each couple that took a holiday. The Secretary of State's case against them rested on an inaccurate assumption. The companies did not deliberately make it difficult for offerees to accept holidays.

SECRETARY OF STATE FOR TRADE AND INDUSTRY v. TRAVEL TIME (UK) LTD; *sub nom.* COMPANY (NO.5669 OF 1998), *Re* [2000] 1 B.C.L.C. 427, Park, J., Ch D (Companies Court).

697. Publications

Armour, Douglas – Limited Liability Partnership: a Practical Guide. Paperback: £29.00. ISBN 0-7545-0221-X. Tolley Publishing.

Birds, John; Ferran, Eilis; et al – Boyle & Birds' Company Law. 4th Ed. Paperback: £29.99. ISBN 0-85308-629-X. Jordans.

Bratton, William W. – Corporate Law and Economics. International Library of Essays in Law and Legal Theory (second Series). Hardback: £100.00. ISBN 0-7546-2086-7. Dartmouth.

Bruce, Martha – Rights and Duties of Directors. 3rd Ed. Paperback: £65.00. ISBN 0-406-91904-6. Butterworths Law.

Griffin, Steve – Company Law. 3rd Ed. Paperback: £24.99. ISBN 0-273-64221-9. Financial Times Management.

Jofee, Victor – Minority Shareholders: Law, Practice and Procedure. Hardback: £75.00. ISBN 0-406-91445-1. Butterworths.

Joffe, Victor – Minority Shareholders: Law, Practice and Procedure. Hardback: £75.00. ISBN 0-406-91445-1. Butterworths Law.

Justice Arden; Prentice, Dan – Buckley on the Companies Acts. 15th Ed. Looseleaf/ring bound: £395.00. ISBN 0-406-14151-7. Looseleaf/ring bound: £395.00. ISBN 0-406-14151-7. Butterworths.

Kenyon-Slade, Stephen – Mergers and Take-overs in the UK and US: Law and Practice. Hardback: £125.00. ISBN 0-19-826051-2. Oxford University Press.

Lai, Jerry – Tolley's Company Secretary Handbook 2000-2001. Paperback: £49.00. ISBN 0-7545-0740-8. Tolley Publishing.

Mann, Marin; Morse, Geoffrey – Palmer's Company Law Manual. Hardback: £150.00. ISBN 0-421-63840-0. Sweet & Maxwell.

Maurice and Dwyer – Private Equity Transactions. Looseleaf/ring bound: £210.00. ISBN 0-421-69470-X. Sweet & Maxwell.

Sealy, L.S. – Cases and Materials in Company Law. 7th Ed. Paperback: £27.95. ISBN 0-406-92959-9. Butterworths Law.

Sharp, Colin G.; Bailey, Robert; Baker, Tilley – Sale and Purchase of Business. Legal Support Practitioner Series-the Law Society's NVQ in Legal Practice. Paperback: £25.00. ISBN 1-85941-443-5. Cavendish Publishing Ltd.

Taylor, M. – Joint Operating Agreements. 3rd Ed. Hardback. ISBN 0-7520-0656-8. Sweet & Maxwell.

Walmsley, Keith – Butterworths Company Law Handbook. 14th Ed. Butterworth Handbooks. Paperback: £36.00. ISBN 0-406-91961-5. Butterworths Law.

Wareham, Robert – Tolley's Company Law Handbook 2000-2001. Paperback: £49.95. ISBN 0-7545-0743-2. Tolley Publishing.

West, E. – Companies Limited by Guarantee. Hardback; Floppy disk. ISBN 0-85308-638-9. Jordans.

Wilkinson, Jacqueline – Company Law Textbook. 2nd Ed. Old Bailey Press Textbook Series. Paperback: £11.95. ISBN 1-85836-373-X. Old Bailey Press.

COMPETITION LAW

698. Anti competitive activity – excluded agreements – appealable decisions

COMPETITION ACT 1998 (NOTIFICATION OF EXCLUDED AGREEMENTS AND APPEALABLE DECISIONS) REGULATIONS 2000, SI 2000 263; made under the Competition Act 1998 s.12, s.46, s.47, s.59, s.71, Sch.13 para.19. In force: March 1, 2000; £1.50.

These Regulations apply the Competition Act s.13 to s.16 to cases where the Director has given a direction withdrawing an exclusion from the Ch.I prohibition, or is considering giving such a direction. They add to the decisions which are appealable, decisions imposing conditions or obligations or varying them in respect of parallel exemptions and decisions that an agreement would infringe the prohibition if it applied.

699. Anti competitive activity – infringement of Chapter I and Chapter II prohibitions – determination of undertakings turnover

COMPETITION ACT 1998 (DETERMINATION OF TURNOVER FOR PENALTIES) ORDER 2000, SI 2000 309; made under the Competition Act 1998 s.36, s.71. In force: March 1, 2000; £1.50.

This Order specifies how the turnover of an undertaking is to be determined for the purposes of the Competition Act 1998 s.36(8). Where an undertaking infringes either of the prohibitions contained in the Act the Director General of Fair Trading may impose on the undertaking a penalty of up to 10 per cent of its turnover as so defined.

700. Anti competitive activity – land agreements – vertical agreements

COMPETITION ACT 1998 (LAND AND VERTICAL AGREEMENTS EXCLUSION) ORDER 2000, SI 2000 310; made under the Competition Act 1998 s.50, s.71. In force: March 1, 2000; £1.50.

This Order excludes land and vertical agreements from the prohibition on anti-competitive agreements imposed by the Competition Act 1998 s.2. It provides for power to withdraw the exclusion from a particular agreement, and that an agreement to the like object and effect between the same parties to an agreement from which the exclusion is withdrawn is not excluded.

701. Anti competitive activity – penalties – immunity

COMPETITION ACT 1998 (SMALL AGREEMENTS AND CONDUCT OF MINOR SIGNIFICANCE) REGULATIONS 2000, SI 2000 262; made under the Competition Act 1998 s.39, s.40, s.59, s.71. In force: March 1, 2000; £1.50.

These Regulations specify for the purposes of the Competition Act 1998 s.39 and s.40 the category of agreements and conduct which enjoy limited immunity from the imposition of penalties for breach of the Ch.I or the Ch.II prohibitions respectively.

702. Anti competitive activity – price fixing – enforcement of copyright potentially unlawful – Commission erred in failing to investigate evidence supplied following assertion that dominant market position abused – European Union

[EC Treaty Art.85 (now Art.81 EC), Art.190 (now Art.253 EC); Council Directive 91/250 on the legal protection of computer programs.]

MLB, supplied wholesale office and computer equipment which included computer software products manufactured by an American company, MC. MLB imported copies of the French language version of MC's Canadian software into France. The software was identical to the product sold in France by MC's subsidiary, MF, but lower in price. MF took steps to prevent the sale of any French language versions of the Canadian product to anyone other than an approved MF distributor thus effectively preventing MLB from importing copies of the Canadian software. MLB made a complaint to the European Commission, contending that the activities of MF and MC breached the EC Treaty Art.85 (now Art.81 EC) and Art.190 (now Art.253 EC). The Commission dismissed the complaint. MLB then instituted proceedings in the European Court seeking annulment of the Commission's decision. MLB contended that (1) MC and MF were engaged in concerted practices designed to keep prices on the French market high, and (2) MC and MF had abused their dominant position in the French market by fixing prices at an artificially high level.

Held, allowing the application, that (1) the Commission had been correct in their conclusion that MC and MF could not have been guilty of concerted practices since they formed a single economic entity and that by virtue of Council Directive 91/250, rights of distribution into the common market were still intact following sale of a software package into Canada and therefore unauthorised importation of the Canadian product into France did amount to an unlawful infringement of MC's copyright; (2) the Commission's conclusion that the prohibition in question amounted to lawful enforcement of copyright pursuant to Council Directive 91/250 and that there had been insufficient evidence provided to substantiate the assertion of abuse of dominant market position in France was, however, flawed. Although normally enforcement under copyright was lawful, such enforcement could amount to abuse in exceptional circumstances, *Radio Telefis Eireann v. Commission of the European Communities (C241/91)* [1995] All E.R. (EC) 416, [1995] C.L.Y. 639 referred to. Evidence had been provided of alleged abusive conduct and such evidence should not have been dismissed out of hand without an investigation into whether the conduct complained of had been abusive in line with the findings in *Radio Telefis Eireann*.

MICRO LEADER BUSINESS v. COMMISSION OF THE EUROPEAN COMMUNITIES (T198/98) [2000] All E.R. (EC) 361, M Jaeger (President), CFI.

703. Anti competitive activity – supply of new cars – price discrimination

SUPPLY OF NEW CARS ORDER 2000, SI 2000 2088; made under the Fair Trading Act 1973 s.56, s.90, Sch.8 para.1, Sch.8 para.4, Sch.8 para.6, Sch.8 para.7, Sch.8 para.9, Sch.8 para.9A, Sch.8 para.12A. In force: September 1, 2000; £2.00.

This Order sets out remedies to the adverse effects on the public interest specified in the Competition Commission report entitled "New Cars: A report on the supply of new motor cars within the UK" published on April 10, 2000. In particular, it makes it unlawful for a supplier of new cars to discriminate unjustifiably between fleet customers and dealers with respect to discounts for the supply of similar volumes of new cars; requires a supplier to notify dealers at intervals of discounts and other terms and conditions of supply of a range of volumes of cars; makes it unlawful for a supplier to discriminate against a contract hire company depending on whether he supplies cars to a fleet customer or not; prohibits a supplier from withholding the supply of new cars from a dealer because of the price at which he advertises new cars for sale; and makes it unlawful for a supplier to make or carry out agreements relating to targets on which termination of a dealer's agreement may depend unless those targets may include new cars obtained from another Member State of the EEA.

704. Anti competitive activity – transitional provisions

COMPETITION ACT 1998 (CONSEQUENTIAL AND SUPPLEMENTAL PROVISIONS) ORDER 2000, SI 2000 2031; made under the Competition Act 1998 s.45, s.71, s.75. In force: Art.6: March 1, 2001; Art.8: March 1, 2001; Art.10: March 1, 2001; Art.11: March 1, 2001; Art.12: March 1, 2001; Art.13: March 1, 2001; Art.14: March 1, 2001; Art.17: March 1, 2001; Art.18: March 1, 2001; Remainder: September 1, 2000; £2.00.

This Order makes consequential amendments and supplemental provisions in connection with the commencement on March 1, 2000 of the majority of the provisions of the Competition Act 1998 not previously commenced by the Competition Act 1998 (Commencement No.5) Order 2000 (SI 2000 344). In particular, it provides that the Director General of Fair Trading may in certain circumstances terminate the transitional period in respect of an agreement which is excluded from the Ch.I prohibition by virtue of any provisions of the Competition Act 1998 (Land and Vertical Agreements Exclusion) Order 2000 (SI 2000 310).

705. Anti competitive activity – transitional provisions

COMPETITION ACT 1998 (TRANSITIONAL, CONSEQUENTIAL AND SUPPLEMENTAL PROVISIONS) ORDER 2000, SI 2000 311; made under the Competition Act 1998 s.45, s.71, s.75. In force: Art.18, Art.23, Art.29, Art.34, Art.42: March 1, 2005; Remainder March 1, 2000; £2.50.

This Order makes transitional, consequential and supplemental provisions in connection with the commencement on March 1, 2000 of the majority of the provisions of the Competition Act 1998.

706. Competition Act 1998 (c.41) – Commencement No.5 Order

COMPETITION ACT 1998 (COMMENCEMENT NO.5) ORDER 2000, SI 2000 344 (C.9); made under the Competition Act 1998 s.76. Commencement details: bringing into force various provisions of the Act on March 1, 2000; £2.00.

This Order brings into force on March 1, 2000 certain provisions of the Competition Act 1998 including the Chapter I prohibition on anti-competitive agreements and the Chapter II prohibition on abuse of a dominant position.

707. Competition agreements – tied leases of public houses – contrary to EC law – relief sought from contracting party – reliance on illegal action – directly effective rights

[EC Treaty Art.85(1) (now Art.81 (1) EC).]

CL, a brewing company, reached an agreement whereby all its public houses would be merged into Inntrepreneur Estates, I, and the tied leases relating to the properties would require the purchase of all beer from CL by the tenants. C was a tenant of two such tied houses and complained that I was infringing EC Treaty Art.85(1) (now Art.81 EC) in respect of the beer tie contained in the lease. The case proceeded as a test case seeking a preliminary ruling from the ECJ as to whether or not the arrangement fell within Art.85(1) (now Art.81 (1) EC). It was contended on behalf of C that the question whether or not the lease fell within Art.81 (1) was a question which could be disposed of by a national court and therefore sought an order that a question not be referred to the ECJ.

Held, that both the Commission and the national courts shared competence to apply Art.85 given that created directly effective rights as between individuals which could be relied on in national courts, *Delimitis v. Henninger Brau AG (C234/89)* [1991] E.C.R. I-935, [1991] C.L.Y. 3797 considered. Even were the agreement a prohibited agreement, a party to it could retain some rights under it and therefore it was necessary to refer a question to the ECJ as to whether or not damages would be payable to such a party.

COURAGE LTD v. CREHAN (NO.2) [1999] U.K.C.L.R. 407, Mance, L.J., CA.

708. Competition Commission – tribunals – appeals

COMPETITION COMMISSION APPEAL TRIBUNAL RULES 2000, SI 2000 261; made under the Competition Act 1998 s.48, s.49, s.71, Sch.8 Part II. In force: March 1, 2000; £3.50.

These Rules prescribe the procedure to be followed before a tribunal constituted by the President of the Competition Commission Appeal Tribunals to hear an appeal made pursuant to the Competition Act 1998 s.46 or s.47.

709. Concerted practices – dominant position – shipping conference line entered into exclusivity agreement – findings as to collective entity and abuse of dominant position – European Union

[EC Treaty Art.85(1) (now Art.81 (1) EC), Art.86 (now Art.82 EC).]

Three members of a shipping conference line, CEWAL, operating between Africa and Europe appealed against a decision of the Court of First Instance upholding a Commission finding that there had been an abuse of a dominant position. The Commission had found the members of CEWAL to have infringed EC Treaty Art.85(1) (now Art.81 (1) EC) by entering into a non competitive agreement by which they had desisted from operating as independent companies in order to divide between them the relevant liner market, and to have abused their collective dominant position under EC Treaty Art.86 (now Art.82 EC) by, inter alia, altering their freight rates from the tariff in force as a means of offering rates on a parity with or below those of their principal competitor. The appellants argued, inter alia, that the CFI had erred in finding that the Commission had sufficiently shown that the position of CEWAL's members on the relevant market should be assessed collectively.

Held, allowing the appeal in part, that the CFI had not erred in upholding the Commission's ruling that the members of CEWAL had abused their dominant position or in finding the Commission to have demonstrated to the necessary legal standard that the implementation of the CEWAL agreement enabled the behaviour of its members to be assessed collectively. While the same practice could result in the infringement of both Art.85 and Art.86, the objectives contained within those provisions should be distinguished. A collective dominant position could be constituted by two or more economic entities that, while independent of each other, behaved within a specific market as a collective entity. It was necessary, in establishing the existence of a collective entity, to consider the economic links or other factors which resulted in the connection between the relevant undertakings and notably those links which allowed action to be taken independently of competitors, customers or consumers. The fact that two or more undertakings were linked by an agreement, a decision of an association of undertakings or a concerted practice within the meaning of Art.85(1) was not of itself sufficient to justify a finding that they constituted a collective entity. The existence of a collective entity and a collective dominant position could, however, result from the terms of an agreement and the way in which that agreement was implemented. While a liner conference could be characterised as a collective entity, it did not automatically follow that the conference had by its conduct abused that dominant position. Against that background, it was apparent from the reasoning of the CFI that the implementation of the agreement had resulted in the members operating in the market as a collective entity. Furthermore, given that the members of CEWAL shared over 90 per cent of the relevant market and that their aim in fixing their prices below or on a level with those of a competitor had been to eliminate that competitor from the market, the CFI had been right to uphold the Commission's finding that there had been an abuse of their dominant position.

CIE MARITIME BELGE TRANSPORTS SA v. COMMISSION OF THE EUROPEAN COMMUNITIES (C395/96); *sub nom.* CIE MARITIME BELGE TRANSPORTS SA v. COMMISSION OF THE EUROPEAN COMMUNITIES (C395/96) [2000] All E.R. (EC) 385, Judge Edward (President), ECJ.

710. **Concerted practices – EU cement companies engaging in concerted practices – European Union**

[EC Treaty Art.85(1) (now Art.81(1) EC).]

In 1994, the Commission fined 42 cement companies operating in the EU 240 million euros for breaches of the EC Treaty Art.85(1) (now Art.81(1) EC), finding that they had engaged in activities designed to defend cement markets within the EU and to control certain exports to non Member States in ways that appreciably affected trade within the EU. The companies sought an annulment of the Commission's decision to impose the fines, relying, inter alia, on (1) errors by the Commission in its statement of objections; (2) a failure to grant proper access to relevant files; (3) a lack of evidence to support the Commission's findings as to guilt in breaching Art.85(1), and (4) miscalculation of the fines imposed, on the basis that the Commission had not determined precisely the length of time that individual participants had taken part in the acts complained of.

Held, allowing the application in part, that (1) the Commission had wrongly denied access to the investigation file, and this was exacerbated by a failure to provide a precise list of documents. Annulment could only be justified on this basis, however, if rights of defence were adversely affected. The error had been cured in respect of 39 companies. With regard to the remaining three, the error was such that the finding of their participation in the impugned conduct would be set aside; (2) there were errors in the statement of objections, but no damaging consequences had been shown to exist because of these errors. Therefore annulment on this ground was not appropriate; (3) the companies which had directly participated in the original agreement had infringed Art.85(1), but the Commission had erred in determining the scope and duration of the participation in some cases. To this extent, the Commission's finding was set aside. With regard to those companies alleged to have indirectly participated in the original infringing agreement, the Commission was held not to have proved its case against nine of them. The Commission's findings of concerted practices contrary to Art.85(1) were upheld, but its finding of a cartel in relation to the UK cement market was set aside. The Commission had not proved a link between the original infringing agreement and the later instances of concerted action, and could not therefore rely on participation in the later action as evidence of accession to the original infringing agreement, and (4) the fines imposed on nine companies would be annulled as their participation in the original agreement had not been proved. The remaining companies would pay reduced fines calculated on the basis of their actual participation in the infringing agreement. The Commission had applied the correct criteria for calculating the fines in all but two cases, and these two would be reduced accordingly. In total, the fines would be reduced to 110 million euros and the Commission was to bear a proportion of the costs in recognition of its administrative shortcomings.

CIMENTERIES CBR SA v. COMMISSION OF THE EUROPEAN COMMUNITIES (T25/95) [2000] 5 C.M.L.R. 204, Lindh (President), CFI.

711. **Director General of Fair Trading – exercise of concurrent functions**

COMPETITION ACT 1998 (CONCURRENCY) REGULATIONS 2000, SI 2000 260; made under the Competition Act 1998 s.54, s.71. In force: March 1, 2000; £2.00.

These Regulations make provision for the Director General of Fair Trading and regulators who can exercise functions of the Director under the Competition Act 1998 Part I concurrently with him to co-ordinate the performance of those functions. They provide for the Director and regulators to circulate information for the purposes of determining who may exercise functions in relation to a case, provide that all applications for guidance or a decision as to whether a Ch.I or Ch.II prohibition have been infringed shall be submitted to the Director, set out the steps which must be taken before a competent person exercises functions in relation to a case, provide the procedure for determining which competent person is to exercise functions in a case when agreement has not been reached; and make provision for the circumstances in which the exercise of functions by a competent person in relation to a case precludes the exercise of those functions by another competent person.

712. **Director General of Fair Trading – rules**

COMPETITION ACT 1998 (DIRECTOR'S RULES) ORDER 2000, SI 2000 293; made under the Competition Act 1998 s.51, s.53, s.71, s.74, Sch.9, Sch.13. In force: March 1, 2000; £4.50.

This Order approves the Rules made by the Director General of Fair Trading concerning procedural and other matters in connection with the carrying into effect of the Competition Act 1998 Part I.

713. **Dominant position – annulment – legality of prior undertaking not to act anti competitively – European Union**

[EC Treaty Art.86 (now Art.82 EC); Council Regulation 4064/89 on the control of concentrations between undertakings Art.3(3), Art.8(2).]

CC, a company involved in the bottling of carbonated soft drinks supplied by T, notified the Commission under Council Regulation 4064/89 of an agreement whereby shares in A, a UK subsidiary of T, were to be sold to CC, which at that time did not carry out commercial operations in the UK. By a Commission Decision it was declared that the share sale was compatible with the common market under Art.8(2) of the Regulation. The Commission found, inter alia, that (1) T controlled CC within the meaning of Art.3(3) of the Regulation; (2) the supply of cola flavoured soft drinks constituted a relevant market, and (3) CCSB, a subsidiary of A, held a dominant position in the relevant market. In reaching its decision, the Commission gave consideration to an undertaking by CC that while it controlled CCSB, the latter would follow undertakings given in prior competition proceedings by an Italian subsidiary of T. CC and T sought to annul the decision in relation to its three findings. Objections were raised by the Commission as to the admissibility of the applications on the basis that they related not to the operative part of its decision but merely to some of the grounds for the decision. CC and T argued that a finding of dominance by the Commission might result in the perception that the actions of CCSB, which would generally be considered lawful, amounted to the abuse of a dominant position, that the finding could potentially be used in pending or future cases and that it might, in the courts of certain Member States, be considered binding. T also sought a declaration that the undertaking which CC had given was void.

Held, dismissing the applications, that (1) notwithstanding that the Commission's finding that CCSB held a dominant position in the relevant market might influence the commercial strategy of the company, that finding could not be annulled as it did not have binding legal effect; the finding had resulted from an investigation into the structure of and competition within the market at the relevant time; (2) the Commission's decision had related to a notification under Council Regulation 4064/879 and not EC Treaty Art.86 (now Art.82 EC). It followed that it did not affect the power of national courts to apply Art.86. In seeking to apply Art.86, a national court would not be bound by the Commission's decision and would not be prevented from concluding that CCSB was no longer in a dominant position, *Benzine en Petroleum Handelsmaatschappij BV v. Commission of the European Communities (C77/77)* [1978] E.C.R. 1513, [1978] C.L.Y. 1345, *Deshormes (nee la Valle) v. Commission of the European Communities (C17/78)* [1979] E.C.R. 189, [1980] C.L.Y. 1188, *Rijn-Schelde-Verolme Machinefabrieken en Sheepswerven NV v. Commission of the European Communities (C223/85)* [1987] E.C.R. 4617, [1990] C.L.Y. 2218 and *Postbank NV v. Commission of the European Communities (T353/94)* [1996] All E.R. (EC) 817, [1997] C.L.Y. 2389 distinguished, and (3) T could not challenge the legality of CC's undertaking since the undertaking had no binding legal effects inasmuch as a breach of its terms would not affect the Commission's decision.

COCA COLA CO v. COMMISSION OF THE EUROPEAN COMMUNITIES (T125/97) [2000] All E.R. (EC) 460, Judge Vesterdorf (President), CFI.

714. Dominant position – franchising – withholding supplies to franchisee – action not abuse of dominant position

[EC Treaty Art.86 (now Art.82 EC).]

A became head franchisee of BS in Austria in 1994 on purchase of the business from the previous head franchisee. S, which was controlled by the same person as A, in turn had established a number of sub franchisees. BS became concerned at the way in which A was operating the franchise, and at A's payment record. BS therefore began dealing directly with the sub franchisees. BS terminated A's franchise in May 1999, and issued proceedings to recover sums outstanding from S. S served a defence and counterclaim. BS ceased making supplies to S. S applied for an injunction compelling BS to resume supplies in time for the crucial Christmas season, contending that BS was in a dominant position within the meaning of the EC Treaty Art.86 (now Art.82 EC), and was abusing that position by withholding supplies.

Held, refusing the application, that Art.86 was of direct effect and could be relied upon in the national courts. However, it was not abuse of a dominant position for an undertaking to refuse to renew a fixed term franchise agreement, just as it could not be abusive to refuse to enter into such an agreement in the first instance. The true effect of S's application would be to force itself upon BS as a franchisee and the decision as to whether a party should be a franchisee was for BS alone to make. Merely operating a franchise system did not automatically give rise to a dominant position and S had failed to identify the market within which it claimed BS was dominant.

SOCKEL GmbH v. BODY SHOP INTERNATIONAL PLC [2000] U.K.C.L.R. 262, Rimer, J., Ch D.

715. **Dominant position – investigations – validity of European Commission's decision – European Union**

[Council Regulation 17/62 implementing Art.85 and Art.86 of the Treaty Art.11.]
KG, an Irish company, had complained to the Commission in 1992 that an English company, P, and its German subsidiary, T, had abused its dominant position of the Irish market for 4 mm float glass by refusing to supply KG with this product beyond a certain limit. The Commission sent a request for information to KG under Council Regulation 17/62 Art.11. KG replied to the request, thus setting in train a process of correspondence that included further Art.11 requests directed to P and other companies engaged in the same market and an informal meeting between the Commission and P following which the Commission rejected KG's complaint. KG applied for the annulment of that decision.
Held, refusing the application, that (1) the Commission had acted with the required care, seriousness and diligence in investigating KG's complaint. It had acted properly in the way in which it had gathered information, and had given KG proper opportunities to comment on its findings, *Asia Motor France SA v. Commission of the European Communities (T7/92)* [1993] E.C.R. II-669, [1999] C.L.Y. 4259 followed. Therefore, KG's rights as a complainant had not been infringed; (2) KG had not shown that the Commission was clearly wrong in its findings and assessment as to the relevant market for 4 mm float glass *L'Oreal NV v. De Nieuwe AMCK PVBA (31/80)* [1980] E.C.R. 3775, [1981] C.L.Y. 1154 and *Nederlandsche Banden Industrie Michelin NV v. Commission of the European Communities (322/81)* [1983] E.C.R. 3461, [1985] C.L.Y. 1319 followed.
KISH GLASS & CO LTD v. COMMISSION OF THE EUROPEAN COMMUNITIES (T65/96) [2000] 5 C.M.L.R. 229, Moura Ramos (President), CFI.

716. **Dominant position – postal services – favoured treatment of subsidiary – European Union**

[EC Treaty Art.86 (now Art.82).]
UF complained that the French Post Office had infringed the EC Treaty Art.86 (now Art.82) by giving logistical and commercial assistance to its subsidiary SMFI which operated an international express mail service. The Post Office had allegedly consistently allowed SFMI to make use of its infrastructure on unusually favourable terms in order to extend its dominant position in the basic postal service market to the associated market in international express mail. The Commission rejected their complaint because of insufficient evidence that the alleged infringements were ongoing. The applicants appealed to the CFI which upheld the Commission decision which it said amounted to a rejection of the complaint for lack of Community interest. The applicants further appealed to the ECJ.
Held, granting annulment of the contested decision and referring the case back to the CFI, that (1) as the assessment of Community interest depended on the circumstances of each case the number of criteria of assessment to which the Commission might refer should not be limited. In the field of competition law where the factual and legal circumstances might differ considerably from case to case, the CFI could adopt criteria not so far considered; (2) the Commission was responsible for defining and implementing the orientation of Community competition policy and was entitled to give differing degrees of priority to the complaints before it. It had to give reasons for declining to continue to examine the complaint; (3) in deciding the order of priority of complaints the Commission had to assess in each case how serious the alleged interference with competition was and how persistent their consequences were. In particular it had to consider the duration and extent of the infringements complained of and their effect on the general competition situation; (4) if anti competitive effects continued after the practices which caused them had ceased, the Commission remained competent to act to eliminate them; (5) the Commission was not entitled to reject a complaint for lack of community interest on the grounds that the practices complained of had ceased without further ascertaining that the anti competitive effects had also ceased, and (6) the CFI erred in applying the

concept of misuse of powers by holding, without giving itself an opportunity to examine a document which the applicants wished to produce, that it did not constitute sufficient proof. The CFI was not entitled to reject a request to order production of a document which was apparently material to the outcome of a case on the ground that the document had not been produced and there was nothing to confirm its existence.

UNION FRANCAISE DE L'EXPRESS (UFEX) v. COMMISSION OF THE EUROPEAN COMMUNITIES (C119/97 P) [2000] 4 C.M.L.R. 268, J-P Puissochet (President), ECJ.

717. Dominant position – sugar beet producer – producer granting customers preferential export rates

[EC Treaty Art.86 (now Art.82), Art.190 (now Art 253).]

IS was the sole producer of sugar beet in Ireland and Northern Ireland. In 1997 it was fined by the Commission for abuse of its dominant position in the market contrary to the EC Treaty Art.86 and Art.190 (now Art.82 and Art.253 respectively). IS appealed.

Held, allowing the appeal in part, that (1) the Commission's statement of objections should supply all the information necessary to enable a company properly to defend itself and set out clearly all the essential facts upon which the Commission was relying; (2) a joint dominant position entailed a number of undertakings together adopting a common policy on the market and acting independently of their competitors, customers and consumers. Independence of the economic entities was insufficient to remove a joint dominant position; (3) undertakings occupying a joint dominant position might engage in joint or individual abusive conduct; (4) an "abuse" was an objective concept referring to the behaviour of an undertaking in a dominant position which influenced the structure of a market where the degree of competition was already weakened. Article 86 of the Treaty prohibited a dominant undertaking from eliminating a competitor and thereby reinforcing its position by means other than those within the scope of competition on its merits; (5) though the finding that a dominant position existed did not in itself imply any reproach to the undertaking concerned, it had a special responsibility, irrespective of the causes of that position, not to allow its conduct to impair genuine undistorted competition on the Common Market; (6) in deciding whether a pricing policy was abusive, it was necessary to consider all the circumstances and investigate whether the discount tended to remove or restrict the buyer's freedom to choose his source of supply; (7) the Commission was right to conclude that the practice of granting export rebates on sugar exported in processed form to other Member States was likely to distort trade in both industrial sugar and processed food products containing a significant proportion of sugar, and thereby affected trade between Member States; (8) where an undertaking in a dominant position actually implemented a practice aimed at ousting a competitor, the fact that the result hoped for was not achieved was not sufficient to prevent that being an abuse of a dominant position within Art.86, and (9) the Court of First Instance had unlimited jurisdiction to review a decision whereby the Commission imposed a fine and might cancel or reduce the fine.

IRISH SUGAR PLC v. COMMISSION OF THE EUROPEAN COMMUNITIES (T228/97) [2000] All E.R. (EC) 198, Jaeger (President), CFI.

718. Exclusive distribution agreements – distributor required to pass on information on extra territorial sales enquiries – parallel import restriction – European Community

[EC Treaty Art.85 (1) (now Art.81 (1) EC); Commission Decision 95/477.]

Under the terms of a 1982 exclusive distribution agreement between B, a German car refinishing paint manufacturer, and A, B's distributor for Belgium and Luxembourg, A agreed to pass on to B any sales enquiries from outside its territory. At B's instigation, in 1986 A stopped supplying I, a UK based distributor of B's products, and I complained to the European Commission, which conducted an investigation. The investigation showed that B had sought to identify the means whereby its products reached the UK, and that A had only supplied I under special authorisation from B. The Commission adopted Decision 95/477, which found that the passing on requirement was intended to allow B to restrict parallel imports into the UK in breach of the EC Treaty Art.85(1) (now Art.81 (1) EC). B and A were fined ECU 2.7 million and ECU 10,000, respectively, and A applied for the annulment of the Decision, contending that the Commission had not (1) respected A's rights of defence by failing to provide minutes of the hearing in French, and (2) wrongly found that the passing on requirement had breached Art.85(1) as its intended effect was to allow B to better plan its distribution and commercial strategies.

Held, refusing the application, that (1) the administrative procedure was not vitiated by a failure to supply a record to the hearing in French. A had a record of its own statement and there had been simultaneous interpretation of other parties' statements; (2) the Commission had correctly found that the passing on requirement was an unauthorised passive export sales prohibition as it differed from A's duty to inform B on the sales and market situation within its territory. The conduct of A and B could not be explained by reference to supply difficulties between 1988 and 1990 as the agreement dated from 1982 and the shortages had no bearing on A's contact with B in 1986 regarding orders from I. The agreement gave B close control over A's extra territorial activities in a way capable of affecting intra Community trade, give the size of B's UK market share and the fact that prices were higher there than in other Member States, and (3) the extent of the infringement meant that the Commission had not erred in setting the level of fines based on B's annual turnover.

ACCINAUTO SA v. COMMISSION OF THE EUROPEAN COMMUNITIES (T176/95) [2000] 4 C.M.L.R. 67, Vesterdorf (President), CFI.

719. **Exclusive distribution agreements – distributor required to pass on information on extra territorial sales enquiries – parallel import restriction – European Community**

[EC Treaty Art.85(1) (now Art.81 (1) EC).]

Under the terms of a 1982 exclusive distribution agreement between B, a German car refinishing paint manufacturer, and A, B's distributor for Belgium and Luxembourg, A agreed to pass on to B any sales enquiries from outside its territory. At B's instigation, A later stopped supplying I, a UK based distributor of B's products, and I complained to the European Commission, which conducted an investigation. The investigation showed that B had sought to identify the means whereby its products reached the UK, and that A had only supplied I under special authorisation from B. The Commission adopted Decision 95/477, which found that the passing on requirement was intended to allow B to restrict parallel imports into the UK in breach of the EC Treaty Art.85(1) (now Art.81 (1) EC). B and A were fined ECU 2.7 million and ECU 10,000, respectively, and B applied for the annulment of the Decision, contending that the Commission (1) had not respected B's rights of defence by failing to grant access to the relevant file, and (2) had wrongly found that the passing on requirement had breached Art.85(1) as its intended effect was to allow B to better plan its distribution and commercial strategies.

Held, refusing the application, that (1) sufficient access to the file had been allowed as the Commission had provided a list of documents from the case file. B had not requested any documents shown on the list and the Commission could rely on its duty of confidentiality when refusing access to certain files, *Solvay SA v. Commission of the European Communities (No.1) (T30/91)* [1995] All E.R. (EC) 600, [1996] C.L.Y. 652 considered; (2) the Commission had correctly found that the passing on requirement was an unauthorised passive export sales prohibition. The 1982 agreement gave B close control over A's extra territorial activities in a way capable of affecting intra Community trade, given the size of B's UK market share and the fact that prices were higher there than in other Member States, and (3) the extent of the infringement meant that the

Commission had not erred in setting the level of fines based on B's annual turnover.

BASF COATING AG v. COMMISSION OF THE EUROPEAN COMMUNITIES (T175/95) [2000] 4 C.M.L.R. 33,Vesterdorf (President), CFI.

720. **Imports – goods originating from People's Republic of China – imposition of EC anti-dumping duty – exporter's rights of defence not infringed during administrative procedure – European Union**

[Council Regulation 384/96 Art.20; Council Regulation 119/97.]

C manufactured ring binder mechanisms in the People's Republic of China and sold them to a US company, which resold the binders in the Community. Following a complaint by a German manufacturer the Commission initiated the anti dumping procedure and imposed a provisional anti dumping duty on imports originating in Malaysia and China. In the definitive disclosure document the Commission explained the imposition of a definitive duty set higher than the provisional duty for all Chinese exporters except one which was to be subject to a lower duty. C did not receive the final page of the disclosure document which was the page explaining the different levels of duty. During a subsequent telephone call, the details of which were disputed, the mistake was realised and an explanation as to the level of duty given. C sought the annulment of Council Regulation 119/97 which imposed the contested definitive anti dumping duties.

Held, dismissing the application, that (1) the action was admissible since, although anti dumping duties were imposed by Regulation and therefore applied to all affected economic operators, the legislative provisions could be of direct and individual concern to individual operators. In the instant case, C was directly concerned by the contested Regulation because the Regulation imposed a definitive anti dumping duty which the customs authorities of the Member States were obliged to collect. The Regulation was also of individual concern to C which was identified in it, *Gao Yao v. Council of the European Union (C75/92)* [1994] E.C.R. I-3141 distinguished, and (2) C's rights of defence were not infringed during the administrative procedure. The methodology applied to calculate the anti-dumping duty did not change after the adoption of the provisional Regulation. The individual treatment of one exporter did not constitute a clear change in methodology as C claimed. It was established law that the amount of the definitive duty constituted essential information. Owing to the missing page, the disclosure document C received did not state that the duty applicable to C would increase as a result of the individual treatment given to another exporter nor did it state the precise duty applicable to C's exports. However C became aware of the essential facts and considerations within the meaning of Council Regulation 384/96 Art.20(2) during the disputed telephone call and therefore had 10 days from the date of that telephone call to make representations pursuant to Art.20(5). Although Art.20(4) requires final disclosure to be in writing, Art.20(3) required requests for disclosure to be in writing and C had conceded that they had not submitted a written request to the Commission. Accordingly, since C was in possession of all the relevant facts, albeit by means of a telephone call, C's defence was not affected by the Commission's failure to comply with Art.20(4).

CHAMPION STATIONERY MFG CO LTD v. COUNCIL OF THE EUROPEAN UNION (T147/97); SUN KWONG METAL MANUFACTURER CO LTD v. COUNCIL OF THE EUROPEAN UNION (T147/97); US RING BINDER CORP v. COUNCIL OF THE EUROPEAN UNION (T147/97) [1999] 1 C.M.L.R. 588, P Lindh (President), CFI.

721. **Limitations – EC law – right of action in English court not precluded by earlier Commission proceedings**

[Law of Property Act 1925 s.36; Rules of the Supreme Court 1965 (SI 1965 1776) Ord.20 r.5; EC Treaty Art.85 (now Art.81 EC), Art.86 (now Art.82 EC).]

B operated container transport services between Europe and Israel. Between 1984 and 1986 B entered into agreements with other carriers for cargo sharing and setting rates, which differed according to whether a shipper shipped some or all of his containers with them. A established BC in 1988 in competition with B. B took action designed to eliminate or reduce this competition, which led to a complaint by BC to the European Commission, alleging breaches of the EC Treaty Art.85 (now Art.81 EC) and Art.86 (now Art.82 EC). In February 1991, B abandoned the activities that had led to BC's complaint. In November 1991, the Commission gave B notice that it intended to impose a fine for breaches of Art.85 committed up to February 1991; the Commission did not pursue that part of the complaint grounded on Art.86. BC went into liquidation in October 1996. A claimed that he had acquired the right to pursue BC in respect of the alleged breaches of Art.85 and Art.86 under an assignment from BC's liquidator. A brought proceedings in April 1997 against B, based on the alleged breaches of both Art.85 and Art.86. B contended that A's case on Art.85 was time barred, since it was grounded on conduct arising prior to the April 1991 cut off date. A's case on Art.86, however, was not time barred when the proceedings were issued, and A therefore sought leave to amend his pleadings so as to plead the same facts relied upon in respect of the Art.85 claim as also grounding a claim under Art.86. B applied for determination as to whether (1) A's claims were time barred; (2) A's claim was an abuse of process because of the Commission proceedings initiated by BC, and (3) A had title to sue as assignee from BC.

Held, that (1) there was a private right to sue for breach of Art.85 or Art.86 akin to a claim for breach of statutory duty, *Society of Lloyds v. Clementson* [1995] 1 C.M.L.R. 693, [1994] C.L.Y. 2684 followed; (2) the cause of action for such breach accrued when the breach first caused damage to the claimant. However, where a breach commenced prior to a limitation cut off date, and continued after it, the claim was time barred only in respect of damage occurring before the cut off date; (3) the amendment sought by A to his pleading did not rest on a substantially different factual matrix so as to preclude amendment under the Rules of the Supreme Court Ord.20 r.5(2) and (5); (4) it was not an abuse of process to raise matters in domestic proceedings that could have been raised in earlier Commission proceedings. Furthermore, it was relevant that A could not have obtained damages, interest or costs in the Commission proceedings, and (5) the assignment had sufficient width so that A could sue under either Art.85 or Art.86, and a provision in the assignment for automatic re-assignment for failure by A to conduct the action reasonably or timeously did not render it an assignment by way of charge under the Law of Property Act 1925 s.36.

ARKIN v. BORCHARD LINES LTD (PRELIMINARY ISSUE) [2000] U.K.C.L.R. 495, Colman, J., QBD (Comm Ct).

722. Mergers – merger references – Interbrew SA and Bass Holdings Ltd

MERGER REFERENCE (INTERBREW SA AND BASS PLC) (INTERIM PROVISION) ORDER 2000, SI 2000 2566; made under the Fair Trading Act 1973 s.74, s.90. In force: September 23, 2000; £1.50.

This Order requires Interbrew SA and Bass Holdings Ltd (formerly a subsidiary of Bass Plc) to maintain the business of Interbrew SA separately from those of Bass Holdings Ltd. The merger of Interbrew SA and enterprises formerly carried on by or under the control of Bass Plc has been referred to the Competition Commission. This Order, unless previously revoked, will cease to have effect 40 days after the Commission's report is laid before Parliament, or on the failure of the Commission to report within the period allowed.

723. Mergers – retail acquisition in Finland – effect on trade between Member States – Commission entitled to consider effect on both retailers and wholesalers

[Council of the European Communities Regulation 4064/89 of 21 December 1989 on the control of concentrations between undertakings Art.3, Art.22.]

K was a limited company incorporated in Finland engaged in the retail sale of daily consumer goods and speciality goods. It also sold those goods in the wholesale and cash-and-carry sectors. K acquired a competitor, T, by means of a concentration in 1996. In response to a request by the Finnish Office of Free Competition, OFC, the Commission adopted a decision prohibiting the acquisition by K of a majority shareholding in T. K appealed against that decision and the Commission indicated that it would give clearance to the merger on condition that K divested part of T's business. K applied to have the decision annulled.

Held, dismissing the action, that (1) the fact that the contractual basis for a concentration had disappeared could not in itself exclude judicial review of the legality of a Commission decision declaring that concentration incompatible with the Common Market; (2) where a company had merely complied with a Commission decision, as it was obliged to do, it could not thereby be deprived of its interest in seeking annulment of that decision; (3) it was not for the Commission to determine the competence of the OFC under Finnish law to submit a request under Council Regulation 4064/89 Art.22(3). It was required only to verify whether the request was made by a Member State within Art.22. Requests under Art.22 could be made by national authorities such as the OFC as well as by governments; (4) in deciding whether an agreement between undertakings was capable of affecting trade between Member States, it was sufficient to establish that the conduct in question was capable of having that effect; (5) the Commission was not bound, when assessing the effect of the concentration on competition, to apply the control test referred to in Art.3 to determine whether the market share of K and T should be aggregated. Having established the existence of the concentration between K and T, the Commission was required to take into account all the facts of the case, including the links between K and T and their respective retailers, in order to assess whether that concentration created or strengthened a dominant position as a result of which effective competition would be significantly impeded; (6) the Commission had not erred in finding that the effect of the concentration between K and T fell to be examined at both wholesale and retail level within Finland having regard to the links between K and T and their retailers, and that the concentration would strengthen the barriers to access to the Finnish retail and wholesale markets for daily consumer goods, and (7) the basic provisions of Council Regulation 4064/89 conferred on the Commission a power of appraisal with respect to assessments of an economic nature. Consequently review by the Community judicature of the exercise of that power had to take account of the discretionary margin of appraisal implicit in the provisions of an economic nature which formed part of the rules on concentrations.

KESKO OY v. COMMISSION OF THE EUROPEAN COMMUNITIES (T22/97) [2000] 4 C.M.L.R. 335, A Potocki (President), CFI.

724. State aids – annulment of Commission decision – adoption of new decision – no need for case proceeding to judgment – European Union

[Rules of Procedure of the Court of First Instance Art.44, Art.114.]

A 1994 Commission Decision authorised State aid to be granted to Air France in three tranches, subject to certain conditions. The decision was annulled on the ground that two points were insufficiently reasoned. In pursuance of that judgment the Commission adopted a 1998 Decision setting out further reasoning on those two points, authorising the aid grant, and approving payment of the second and third tranches. Before publication of the 1998 Decision TAT submitted that its own application to annul the 1994 Decision had yet to be determined. The Commission contended that, as no action had been brought against the 1998 Decision, an order should be made under the Rules of Procedure of the Court of First Instance Art.114 that there was no need for the case to proceed to judgment. TAT, relying on the finding in *Alpha Steel Ltd v. Commission of the European Communities (C14/81)* [1982] E.C.R. 749, [1983] C.L.Y. 1410 that a Decision replacing a Decision on the same subject matter while an action was pending was able to be seen as a new factor allowing an applicant to amend his pleadings. It also contended that its claims need not be adapted to the 1998 Decision, since it had expressed its desire to object to the authorisation of the second tranche payment.

Held, finding no need to proceed to judgment, that (1) the 1998 Decision did not merely re-adopt, with retroactive effect, the 1994 Decision. The 1998 Decision authorised anew the payment of the second and third tranches. Even though its reasoning in relation to the second tranche was indistinguishable from that in the earlier Decision, it was not purely confirmatory, but constituted a separate replacement Decision; (2) the adoption of the 1998 Decision deprived the applicant of any legitimate interest in maintaining the action inasmuch as it sought the annulment of a Decision which no longer formed part of the Community law; (3) the *Alpha* case was distinguishable as, in that case, the Commission had acted on its own initiative in replacing a Decision, whereas the 1998 Decision in this case was adopted following a court annulment of the 1994 Decision; (4) a mere expression of intent to challenge a specific measure could not be treated as equivalent to an amendment meeting the requirements of Rules of Procedure of the Court of First Instance Art.44 of claims made in an action which has already commenced, and (5) the obligation to bring a fresh action against the 1998 Decision or to amend the originating application was not purely formal, because the contested Decision was no longer part of the Community law and because the 1998 Decision, which was not the subject of any action brought within the prescribed period, had become definitive.

TAT EUROPEAN AIRLINES SA v. COMMISSION OF THE EUROPEAN COMMUNITIES (T236/95) [2000] 1 C.M.L.R. 892, Pirrung, P.C., CFI.

725. **State aids – annulment of Commission decision – Spanish subsidies to ferry service operator – European Union**

[EC Treaty Art.92 (now, after amendment, Art.87 EC), Art.93(3) (now Art.88(3) EC).]

BAI operated a shipping line between Plymouth in the UK and Santander in Spain. It complained to the EC Commission about large subsidies to be granted to a rival company by the Spanish local authorities to operate a regular shipping line between Portsmouth and Bilbao. The Commission initiated a procedure under the EC Treaty Art.93(3) (now, Art.88(3) EC) on the basis that the scheme constituted state aid under Art.92 (now, after amendment, Art.87 EC). Following a further agreement whereby the Spanish authorities agreed to purchase 26,000 travel vouchers for use on the Portsmouth to Bilbao route (the 1995 Agreement) the Commission adopted a decision to terminate the review procedure relating to the aid and BAI sought its annulment.

Held, granting the application, that (1) actions for annulment had to be brought within two months of the publication of the measure. The fact that the applicant had knowledge of the contested decision at an earlier date was irrelevant and so the application was admissible; (2) the aim of Art.92 was to prevent competition being distorted in trade between Member States. A state measure in favour of an undertaking, in the form of an agreement to purchase travel vouchers could not be excluded in principle from the concept of state aid in Art.92 merely because the parties undertook reciprocal commitments; (3) as the travel vouchers could be used only in the low season, the improved service supplied by the rival company did not in principle entail significant additional costs and the effects of the 1995 agreement on competition and trade between Member States were the same as before; (4) the relatively small amount of aid or the size of the undertaking which received it did not exclude the possibility that intra-Community trade might be affected; (5) where financial aid granted by the public authorities strengthened the position of an undertaking in relation to its competitors the aid fell within the scope of Art.92. Article 92(1) made no distinction according to the causes or aims of the aid in question but defined it in relation to its effects, and (6) the Commission's conclusion that the 1995 agreement did not constitute state aid was based on a misinterpretation of

Art.92(1). The contested decision was vitiated by an infringement of Art.92 and had to be annulled.

BRETAGNE ANGLETERRE IRLANDE (BAI) v. COMMISSION OF THE EUROPEAN COMMUNITIES (T14/96) [1999] 3 C.M.L.R. 245, Vesterdorf (President), CFI.

726. **State aids – coal industry – aid paid prior to authorisation – grant of aid dependent on undertaking's economic viability – European Union**

[Commission Decision 98/687; Commission Decision 3632/93 Art.3(2), Art.4, Art.9(5).]

The German Government notified the Commission of financial aid it planned to grant to its coal industry. The aid was granted before it had been authorised by the Commission by Decision 98/687. The applicants, a privately owned mining company established in the UK which took over the principal mining operations of British Coal, applied to have the decision annulled.

Held, dismissing the application, that (1) Decision 3632/93 establishing Community rules for State aid to the coal industry (the Code) Art.9(5) provided that the aid had to be repaid if the Commission refused its authorisation where there had been a breach of the procedural principle of prior authorisation. The Commission had the power to give ex post facto approval to aid paid prior to authorisation; (2) Art.3 of the Code required the aid plan to involve the improvement of economic viability which required only a reduction in the level of non-profitability and its non-competitiveness. This reflected the commercial reality that most Community coal industry undertakings remained uncompetitive in relation to imports from third countries; (3) under Art.3(2) of the Code improvement in viability had to be achieved by a significant reduction in production costs. Article 3(2) indicated that a trend towards a reduction by the year 2002 was sufficient but it would need to achieve a greater reduction in later years, and (4) if it appeared that a significant reduction in production costs made it possible to achieve a decrease in aid, the Commission was entitled to consider that the undertaking concerned was capable of improving its economic viability. Undertakings whose production costs were such that no real progress towards economic viability could be expected, could receive only aid for reduction of activity under Art.4.

RJB MINING PLC v. COMMISSION OF THE EUROPEAN COMMUNITIES (T110/98) [1999] 3 C.M.L.R. 445, B Vesterdorf (President), CFI.

727. **State aids – debt rescheduling – payments of lower than market rate of interest – validity of Commission Decision 97/21**

See EUROPEAN UNION: Spain v. Commission of the European Communities (C342/96). §2415

728. **State aids – monopoly broadcasting rights – territorial restriction not justified on public policy grounds – European Union**

[EC Treaty Art.52 (now, after amendment, Art.43 EC), Art.90(1) (now Art.86(1) EC); Commission Decision 97/606.]

Flemish legislation granted Va monopoly in broadcasting television advertising in Flanders, although it did not prohibit broadcasters operating from other Member States doing so. It also provided that at least 51 per cent of V's capital was to be held by publishers of Dutch language newspapers and magazines. Following a complaint, the European Commission issued Commission Decision 97/606 to the effect that the Flemish law was a State measure which was incompatible with the EC Treaty Art.90(1) (now Art.86(1) EC), read in conjunction with Art.52 (now, after amendment, Art.43 EC). The Commission found that the law was a disguised form of discrimination with a protectionist effect not justified on public interest grounds. V applied to the CFI for the annulment of the decision on the grounds, inter alia, of procedural unfairness and breach of legitimate expectation. Further, that the law was necessary in the public interest and to preserve pluralism.

Held, dismissing the application, that V, as the expressly named beneficiary of monopoly broadcasting rights, had not been denied its right to be heard. V had received relevant copies of the original complaint and the responses of both the Flemish and Belgian Governments and been afforded the opportunity to make representation prior to the Decision being adopted. Neither the manner of the Commission's examination nor the terms of its reasoned opinion had given rise to a legitimate expectation on V's part that its exclusive right would not be found contrary to Art.90(1). Reservation of V's share capital did not ensure pluralism, as ownership could be held by a single qualifying publisher. Further, the provision in the national law preventing the establishment in Flanders by a broadcaster from another Member State was contrary to Art.90(1) and Art.52 and could not be justified by reference to the public interest.

VLAAMSE TELEVISIE MAATSCHAPPIJ NV v. COMMISSION OF THE EUROPEAN COMMUNITIES (T266/97) [2000] 4 C.M.L.R. 1171, B Vesterdorf (President), ECJ.

729. **State aids – national insurance contributions – national law providing for regionally differentiated contribution**

[National Insurance Act 1997 (Norway); Agreement on a European Economic Area 1992 Art.61; Surveillance and Court Agreement 1994 Art.1 (1) Protocol 3.]

The National Insurance Act 1997 made all persons working in Norway subject to a compulsory national insurance scheme. The contribution rates were decided annually by the Norwegian Parliament, with adjustments made for different regions. The rates could be as low as zero per cent in the more isolated northern regions of Norway or as high as 14.1 per cent for urban areas in the south of the country. Decision 165/98 of the European Free Trade Association Surveillance Authority, EFTA SA, found that the system of regionally differentiated contributions constituted state aid to undertakings within the meaning of the European Economic Area Agreement 1992 Art.61(1) and was therefore incompatible with the EEA Agreement as a distortion on competition. EFTA SA further ruled that, in relation to certain sectors, part of the aid could be exempted as regional transport aid under Art.61 (3) (c), on the basis that the exposure of those sectors to intra EEA trade was limited. Other sectors that benefited from the aid, particularly manufacturing, could not be so exempted. Norway applied to the EFTA Court, seeking an annulment of Decision 165/98, arguing, inter alia, that the national insurance system was part of the general system of taxation. Norway accepted that the system was intended to benefit certain regions, but contended that, since the EEA Agreement made no provision for the harmonisation of national tax systems, it was a matter for each State to design and apply its own tax system in accordance with its own policy choices. Further, that the selectivity criterion inherent in the notion of State aid was not fulfilled, because the system was neutral as regards sector, company size, occupation, form of ownership and location of the undertaking. Norway also argued that since EFTA SA had failed to identify the aid affecting intra EEA trade, and had therefore failed to determine which parts of the system infringed Art.61 (1), the entire Decision would have to be annulled. EFTA SA and the European Commission argued that regional or geographical selectivity was capable in principle of constituting State aid within the meaning of Art.61 (1) and was comparable with sectoral selectivity.

Held, dismissing the application, that (1) while the tax system of an EEA/EFTA State was not covered by the EEA Agreement, in some instances the consequences of such a system would bring it within the scope of Art.61 (1). A primary criterion for the generality of a system was its application to all undertakings within a State. Since the Norwegian system was intended to benefit certain regions, it did in fact confer competitive advantages on regional undertakings. The regional differentiation in rates favoured certain undertakings within the meaning of Art.61 (1). The legitimacy of the policy considerations fortified this conclusion, and were instead matters to be taken into account by EFTA SA in its assessment under Art.61 (3). EFTA SA had a wide discretion in matters concerning economic and social assessment and, in the instant case, had not acted beyond its competence or wrongly applied the rules on State aid, and (2) Decision 165/98 had been taken by EFTA SA as part of its constant review and examination of State aid pursuant to the Surveillance and Court Agreement 1994 Art.1(1) Protocol 3. EFTA SA had correctly based its assessment on the characteristics of the aid scheme in question and in particular the regionally differentiated element. As regards competitive advantages in terms of intra EEA trade, EFTA SA had been entitled to examine only the characteristics of the system and whether the advantage was given by the nature of the aid or high amounts of aid, *Germany v. Commission of the European Communities (C248/84)* [1989] 1 C.M.L.R. 591, [1990] C.L.Y. 2216 applied. When State aid strengthened the position of an undertaking vis a vis another undertaking competing in intra Community trade, the latter undertaking would be regarded as affected by the aid, regardless of whether the beneficiary undertaking was actually exporting products, *Spain v. Commission of the European Communities (C278/92)* [1994] E.C.R. I-4103, [1995] C.L.Y. 656, applied, so that the Decision could not be impugned on that ground or annulled for a failure to provide adequate reasons, *Scottish Salmon Growers Association Ltd v. EFTA Surveillance Authority (E2/94)* [1995] 1 C.M.L.R. 851 followed.

NORWAY v. EFTA SURVEILLANCE AUTHORITY (E6/98) [1999] 2 C.M.L.R. 1033, Haug (President), EFTA.

730. **State aids – public television broadcasting – notice requiring Commission to define its position – failure to act within time limit – European Union**

[EC Treaty Art.85 (now Art.81 EC), Art.90 (now Art.86 EC).]

In 1993, TF1, a private television company, complained to the EC Commission concerning the methods used to finance and operate the French public television broadcasting channels. In 1995 the Commission advised that other similar complaints had been received and a study had been ordered covering all Member States but that it was not possible to specify when a report would be implemented. In the same year, TF1 advised the Commission in writing that French State aid was deliberately intended to distort competition between public and private channels and gave formal notice requesting the Commission to define its position and act upon the complaint. The Commission responded stating that the French authorities had been asked a number of questions relevant to TF1's complaint and that it would be advised of the progress of the matter. In 1997, TF1 was advised that the Commission was unable to uphold its complaint. TF1 claimed that the court should declare that the Commission, by not defining its position within two months of the formal notice, had failed to act and should either call upon the Commission to act or annul the position defined by the Commission.

Held, that (1) a person has locus standi to bring an action for failure to act not only against an institution which has failed to adopt an act which otherwise would be addressed to that person, but also against an institution which has failed to adopt a measure which would have concerned that person directly and individually. Accordingly, TF1's claim was not inadmissible on the grounds that it was not the potential addressee of the Commission's eventual decision; (2) an undertaking is directly concerned by a decision of the Commission relating to State aid where there is no doubt about the intention of the national authorities to proceed with their aid proposal. TF1 was directly concerned since the French authorities had made the financial grants an issue; (3) an undertaking is individually concerned where its interests would be affected by the grant of aid, especially if it is a competing undertaking. TF1 was therefore to be considered to be directly and individually concerned by decisions which the Commission might adopt after initiating the procedure for carrying out a preliminary examination of the grants made by the French authorities to the public television companies; (4) national remedies available to TF1 did not affect the admissibility of the claim for a declaration of failure to act; (5) the letter sent by TF1 constituted a formal notice with regard to all the submissions, including those alleging infringement of EC Treaty Art.85 (now Art.81 EC); (6) whether the duration of an administrative procedure is reasonable must be determined in relation to the circumstances of the case, its context, the necessary procedural stages, the complexity of the case and its importance for the parties involved. Here the claim for a declaration of failure to act was well founded, and (7) a definition of position terminated the Commission's failure to act and deprived the action brought of its subject-matter. There was therefore no need to adjudicate on the allegation that the Commission failed to act pursuant to the EC Treaty Art.85 and 90 (now Art.81 and 86).

TELEVISION FRANCAISE 1 SA v. COMMISSION OF THE EUROPEAN COMMUNITIES (T17/96) [2000] 4 C.M.L.R. 678, Jaeger (President), CFI.

731. **State aids – reduction in social security contributions – legality under EC law – European Union**

[Commission Decision 97/239.]

In 1981 Belgium introduced a scheme known as the "Maribel" scheme which laid down the general principles of social security for wage earners. The scheme granted employers of manual workers a reduction in social security contributions. In 1993 and 1994 the reduction was increased specifically for those employers carrying on undertakings operating in sectors most exposed to international competition. The Commission adopted Commission Decision 97/239 which provided that the increased reductions constituted illegal state aid and was incompatible with the Common Market. Belgium sought the annulment of the Decision.

Held, dismissing the application, that (1) it was not disputed that the reductions granted under the scheme conferred on the undertakings in question a financial advantage which improved their competitive position. Furthermore, the restriction of the scheme by reference to economic sector made it selective and as such it was capable of constituting aid; (2) the increased reductions were granted without any direct social or economic compensatory payment from the recipients and were not linked to the creation of jobs or to the hiring of certain groups of workers having difficulty in entering the labour market, and could not therefore be declared to be compatible with the Common Market, and (3) the aid was unlawful and should be recovered despite the attendant administrative and practical difficulties that would involve.

BELGIUM v. COMMISSION OF THE EUROPEAN COMMUNITIES (C75/97) [2000] 1 C.M.L.R. 791, PJG Kapteyn (President), ECJ.

732. **State aids – steel industry – privatisation – German's financial contribution – European Union**

[European Coal and Steel Community Treaty Art.4(c); Commission Decision 3855/91 establishing rules for aid to the steel industry Art.6(4).]

Following notification by the German government of a preliminary examination of intended financial measures in connection with the privatisation of a company in the steel sector, the EC Commission decided to initiate the procedure under Decision 3855/91 (the Fifth Steel Aid Code) Art.6(4) and concluded in Decisions 95/422, 96/178, 96/484 that intended financial contributions and loans constituted State aid prohibited by the European Coal and Steel Community (ECSC) Treaty Art.4(c). The applicants brought proceedings seeking annulment of those Decisions.

Held, dismissing the applications, that (1) since the Fifth Steel Aid Code constituted a derogation from the ECSC Treaty Art.4(c), it had to be interpreted strictly; (2) to determine whether a transfer of public resources to a steel undertaking constituted State aid within ECSC Treaty Art.4(c) it was necessary to consider whether in similar circumstances a private investor of comparable size might have provided capital of such an amount. The applicants had not shown that the Commission failed to observe the provisions of the ECSC Treaty or any rule of law relating to its application in view of the size of the undertaking concerned; (3) no distinction could be drawn between aid granted in the form of loans and of a subscription of capital; (4) the Commission did not manifestly fail to observe the Treaty or any related rules of law in considering that the undertaking was unlikely to be able to raise the sums essential to its survival and that the lender could not count on receiving any repayment from the company; (5) Art.4(c) prohibited all aid without restriction and was general and unconditional. Therefore in taking the contested decisions, the Commission did not infringe the principle of proportionality; (6) the contested decisions correctly took account of the information provided by the German Government and contained a statement of reasons which enabled the applicants to ascertain the reasons why the Commission regarded the disputed loans as State aid; (7) the applicants had not shown that the former private shareholders had withdrawn against payment of a sum and the Commission had not manifestly failed to observe the ECSC Treaty regarding the withdrawal of the private shareholders; (8) an aid which was incompatible with EC law had to be repaid. There was no power to suspend an order to repay, and (9) the applicants had the opportunity to submit their comments on the facts and assessments made by the Commission in the notice of information even if they did not take it; and so the Decisions were not unlawful by reason of an infringement of the right to be heard.

NEUE MAXHUTTE STAHLWERKE GmbH v. COMMISSION OF THE EUROPEAN COMMUNITIES (T129/95) [1999] 3 C.M.L.R. 366, Azizi (President), CFI.

733. **Tour operators – discounts – validity of delegated legislation restricting permitted discounts following Monopolies and Mergers Commission report**

[Fair Trading Act 1973 s.49, s.56; Foreign Package Holidays (Tour Operators and Travel Agents) Order 1998 (SI 1998 1945) Art.3, Art.4.]

T, a tour operator, sought to challenge the validity of the Foreign Package Holidays (Tour Operators and Travel Agents) Order 1998 Art.3 and Art.4 which prohibited tour operators from entering into contracts with travel agents aimed at restricting the holidays that the agent could offer from other operators. The Order was based on the more limited finding of the Monopolies and Mergers Commission, MMC, on a reference by the Director General of Fair Trading under the Fair Trading Act 1973 s.49 that T and A, another tour operator, were requiring agents to offer the same discounts on their holidays as those offered by other operators without funding the agents' increased costs. T's application for judicial review of the Order on the basis that it was ultra vires the powers of the Secretary of State under s.56(2) was refused and T appealed.

Held, allowing the appeal, that Art.3 and Art.4 were outside the powers of the Secretary of State as the MMC report was concerned only with contractual provisions imposing discount parity where no extra funding was provided by the tour operator, whereas Art.3(b) went wider than was necessary to prevent practices contrary to the public interest. Under s.56(2) the Secretary of State was entitled only to take action, or refuse to do so, on the basis of facts established by the MMC pursuant to s.49.

R. v. SECRETARY OF STATE FOR TRADE AND INDUSTRY, *ex p.* THOMSON HOLIDAYS LTD [2000] U.K.C.L.R. 189, Laws, L.J., CA.

734. **Unfair competition – confidential information – unlawful copying by former employees**

V, an employee of FI, resigned when the company was taken over by S. V and other former employees of FI set up a new company, F, in competition with S. It came to S's attention that documents confidential to FI, including product specifications and costing spreadsheets, had been copied from computer files and utilised by V to F's benefit. S made an interim application for an injunction restraining V and F from making use of the documents or information contained within them for a period of three months. V conceded that FI had a proprietary interest in the information but argued that little benefit had actually accrued to F and that the opportunity for unfair advantage had long since passed.

Held, refusing the application, that although V had made unlawful use of the materials it was necessary for S to show that F had obtained an unfair competitive advantage and that the advantage was continuing, *Roger Bullivant Ltd v. Ellis* [1987] I.C.R. 464, [1987] C.L.Y. 1294 applied. Product specifications were generally only used as a method of tendering for contracts with food suppliers, and F's use of them would have been of benefit to only a limited degree which certainly would not have extended more than a month after the take over of FI. The benefit of the spreadsheets would have been similarly limited, and in any event much of the information in the spreadsheets was available elsewhere. It was not unlawful for V and the other former employees to use their skills and expertise to obtain contracts. S had failed to show that an injunction was justified.

SUN VALLEY FOODS LTD v. VINCENT; SUN VALLEY FOODS LTD v. FUSION FOODS INTERNATIONAL LTD [2000] F.S.R. 825, Jonathan Parker, J., Ch D.

735. Publications

Ehlermann, Claus-Dieter; Gosling, Louisa – European Competition Law Annual 1998: Regulating Communications Markets. Hardback: £65.00. ISBN 1-84113-099-0. Hart Publishing.

Gardner, Nick – Guide to United Kingdom and European Union Competition Policy. 3rd Ed. Hardback: £45.00. ISBN 0-333-76391-2. Macmillan Press Ltd.

Lindrup, Garth – Butterworths Competition Law Handbook. 6th Ed. Paperback: £70.00. ISBN 0-406-91464-8. Butterworths Law.

Lohr, Steve; Brinkley, Joel – United States Vs Microsoft. Hardback: £15.99. ISBN 0-07-135588-X. McGraw-Hill Publishing Company.

Rodger, Barry; MacCulloch, Angus – UK Competition Act 1998: a New Era for UK Competition Law. Paperback: £35.00. ISBN 1-84113-097-4. Hart Publishing.

Smith, Martin – Competition Law: Enforcement and Procedure. Butterworths Competition Law Series. Hardback: £85.00. ISBN 0-406-90380-8. Butterworths Law.

Wesseling, Rein – Modernisation of EC Competition Law. Hardback: £35.00. ISBN 1-84113-121-0. Hart Publishing.

CONFLICT OF LAWS

736. Arbitration – notices – dissolution of foreign party to arbitration upon merger – effect upon extant arbitration proceedings

[Transformation Law 1994 (Germany) s.20.]

BL, a company of German ship owners, contracted with E, an English company, as charterers under a contract of affreightment. BL subsequently sought to pursue a claim for dead freight which resulted in a reference to arbitration. Following the appointment of arbitrators, BL merged with S as a result of which BL was dissolved. E applied to have the claim dismissed for want of prosecution, contending that on the dissolution of BL, the arbitration proceedings were also dissolved since one of the parties had ceased to exist. BL contended that upon the merger, all its rights and obligations were succeeded by S, including the arbitration proceedings.

Held, dismissing the application, that (1) under German law the doctrine of universal succession provided that assets and liabilities were transferred automatically upon merger. The contention that the proceedings would automatically be terminated if a notice were not served would run counter to that principle and German Transformation Law 1994 (Germany) s.20, and (2) under English law all matters governing the status of a foreign corporation should be determined by reference to the domestic law of that foreign corporation and to the extent that German law stated that all rights and liabilities vested in S, English law should recognise that fact, *National Bank of Greece and Athens SA v. Metliss* [1958] A.C. 509, [1957] C.L.Y. 505 applied and *Toprak Enerji Sanayi AS v. Sale Tilney Technology Plc* [1994] 1 W.L.R. 840, [1994] C.L.Y. 3798 considered.

EUROSTEEL LTD v. STINNES AG [2000] 1 All E.R. (Comm) 964, Longmore, J., QBD (Comm Ct).

737. Choice of forum – anti suit proceedings – protective proceedings raised in foreign jurisdiction – foreign court to determine jurisdiction

[Brussels Convention on Jurisdiction and Enforcement of Judgments in Civil and Commercial Matters 1968 Art.21, Art.22.]

FSBN brought proceedings in England seeking a declaration relating to the validity of a lease of an aircraft. CNAG disputed the validity of the lease, alleging that it had been terminated following the hijack at gunpoint of the vehicle carrying data associated with the aircraft. CNAG contended that this act was equivalent to a force majeure effectively bringing the lease to an end, and initiated proceedings in France as a protective measure. FSBN applied to restrain the French proceedings and sought a declaration that the English court was seised of the dispute on December 4, 1998, the date of the commencement of the English proceedings.

Held, refusing to grant the injunction sought but granting a declaration that the English proceedings had commenced on December 4, 1998, that it was not necessary to clarify the nature of the French proceedings and it was for the French courts to decline jurisdiction under the Brussels Convention Art.21 and Art.22 if appropriate. There was nothing frivolous or vexatious in CNAG bringing proceedings in France. The declaration as to the date of commencement of the English proceedings would be granted as the precise date was a possible issue in the French proceedings.

FIRST SECURITY BANK NATIONAL ASSOCIATION v. COMPAGNIE NATIONALE AIR GABON (NO.1) [1999] I.L.Pr. 617, S Tomlinson Q.C., QBD (Comm Ct).

738. Choice of forum – causes of action – foreign action involved same parties as interpleader proceedings – proceedings did not have same cause of action

[Brussels Convention on Jurisdiction and Enforcement of Judgments in Civil and Commercial Matters 1968 Art.21.]

M, the second defendant, was a company which stored, blended and traded oil. M collapsed, and GI (one of several claimants in the proceedings) claimed against M and S in respect of the proceeds of sale of seven oil cargoes which S had previously bought from M. S claimed no interest in the proceeds of sale of the cargoes, but was concerned to ensure that the proceeds were paid to the party properly entitled thereto. S therefore issued interpleader proceedings, wishing to be released from taking any further part in the proceedings. Another claimant to the proceeds of sale, BT, objected to taking part in the London proceedings, preferring that its claim against S be determined in Paris, where BT had already commenced proceedings. S agreed that the Paris court was the court first seised and that the same parties were involved. However, for the purpose of the Brussels Convention 1968 Art.21, it was necessary for the English court to decide whether the claim by BT against S in Paris involved "the same cause of action" as S's claim for interpleader relief against BT and other claimants in the London proceedings.

Held, dismissing the application, that (1) if the relevant English proceedings for the purpose of Art. 21 were BT's proceedings against S generated by S's application for interpleader relief, then the cause was the same. If the relevant proceedings were, however, the interpleader proceedings themselves, then the cause was not the same, BT's claim against S in England was merely incidental to the overall application and being based on facts and rules of law different from those to be relied on in Paris, *Owners of Cargo Lately Laden on Board the Tatry v. Owners of the Maciej Rataj (The Maciej Rataj) (C406/92)* [1999] Q.B. 515, [1995] C.L.Y. 704 considered, and *Haji-Ioannou v. Frangos* [1999] 2 All E.R. (Comm) 865, [1999] C.L.Y. 713 applied; (2) the French proceedings and the

English proceedings did not share the same object, and this was sufficient to displace BT's reliance on Art.21. BT's claim against S in Paris was that S was liable to it for the price of the relevant cargoes. S did not dispute that liability in England, where the issue was whether or not BT's claim to the proceeds of sale of the cargoes was superior to that of the other claimants, and (3) it was convenient that the adverse claims should be litigated in England, where the court appointed receivership of M was being supervised and where all the relevant parties were present, subject to BT's argument under Art.21, *De La Rue v. Herna Peron & Stockwell Ltd* [1936] 2 K.B. 164, *Sarrio SA v. Kuwait Investment Authority* [1996] 1 Lloyd's Rep.650 and *Blue Nile Shipping Co Ltd v. Iguana Shipping & Finance Inc (The Happy Fellow)* [1997] 1 Lloyd's Rep.130, [1997] C.L.Y. 4523 considered.

GLENCORE INTERNATIONAL AG v. SHELL INTERNATIONAL TRADING & SHIPPING CO LTD [1999] 2 All E.R. (Comm) 922, Rix, J., QBD (Comm Ct).

739. **Choice of forum – contract terms – place of performance – contract with German company for supply and delivery of goods to UK address**

[Brussels Convention on Jurisdiction and Enforcement of Judgments in Civil and Commercial Matters 1968 Art.5(1).]

MBM, the English subsidiary of a German company, asked E, a company based in Germany, to design, manufacture, supply and deliver a large quantity of rainscreen panels. In its order form, which formed the basis of the contract, MBM asked E to "supply and deliver" the panels to an address in England. The order form provided that the risk of loss and title to the panels would remain with E until the panels had been delivered to the address specified. During the pre contract negotiations, E sent a letter to MBM setting out separately the cost of supplying the panels and the cost of packing and shipping them. The panels having been found to be faulty owing to defects in the design or manufacturing processes, MBM issued proceedings against E claiming damages for breach of contract. E argued that the court did not have the jurisdiction to determine the action and the judge dealt with the question of jurisdiction as a preliminary issue. The court held that, for the purpose of the Brussels Convention on Jurisdiction and Enforcement of Judgments in Civil and Commercial Matters 1968 Art.5(1), the place of performance of the principal obligation under the contract had been Germany and the proceedings were therefore set aside. MBM appealed. In opposing the appeal, E argued that (1) the order having required it to supply and deliver the panels, it had had two obligations, one to supply the panels which entailed designing and manufacturing them in Germany, and the other to deliver the panels to England. E contended that, as the primary obligation involved the supply of the panels, that obligation had been discharged in Germany. In support of its construction of the contract, E relied on its earlier letter in which the cost of supplying and delivering the panels had been set out separately; (2) MBM's cause of action had arisen at the time when the defective panels were manufactured in Germany, and (3) its essential obligation under the contract had been to manufacture the panels and the breach of that obligation had been its failure to manufacture the panels correctly. Both the obligation and the breach had occurred in Germany.

Held, allowing the appeal, that the place of the performance of E's contractual obligations for the purpose of Art.5(1) of the Convention had been England. The use of the words "supply and deliver" could not convert a single contract for the supply of the panels in England into two separate contracts, one for the supply of the panels in Germany and the other for their delivery to England. This was supported by the contract terms relating to risk, title and delivery. In the context of this contract, "supply and delivery" meant supply by delivery. Even if MBM had a cause of action in Germany, doubt being expressed as to whether it did, this would not affect the nature of the action which it had brought. MBM's action was based on E's failure to supply goods of the required specification. The possibility that another cause of action existed did not invalidate the cause of action relied on by MBM. E's essential obligation for the purpose of the present action had been to supply goods complying with the contractual specification. The place for the performance of that obligation had been England and it was immaterial that the acts or omissions which led to the failure to supply the appropriate goods had occurred in Germany. *Etablissements A De Bloos Sprl v. Etablissements Bouyer SA (C14/76)* [1976] E.C.R. 1497, [1977] C.L.Y. 1280, *Custom Made Commercial Ltd v. Stawa Metallbau GmbH (C288/92)* [1994] E.C.R. I-2913, [1994] C.L.Y. 4800, *Kleinwort Benson Ltd v. Glasgow City Council (No.2)* [1999] 1 A.C. 153, [1997] C.L.Y. 904 and *Shenavai v. Kreischer (C266/85)* [1987] E.C.R. 239, [1988] C.L.Y. 1468 considered.

MBM FABRI-CLAD LTD v. EISEN UND HUTTENWERKE THALE AG [2000] C.L.C. 373, Pill, L.J., CA.

740. **Choice of forum – contracts – claimant alleging contract void for fraud – survival of jurisdiction clause – Canada**

M alleged that he had suffered losses as a result of being caught by an allegedly fraudulent scheme operated by SL, which induced him to enter into contractual relationships with SL. Accordingly the contracts with SL were completely void. M brought an action against SL in New Brunswick seeking to rely on New Brunswick securities law as a defence to claims against him. SL applied to stay the action commenced in New Brunswick relying on the jurisdiction clauses in the contracts on the basis that England was the proper forum. There were further claims in tort and it was said that the jurisdiction agreement was not operative in respect of those claims and that New Brunswick was the proper forum.

Held, granting the applications for stay conditionally, that (1) in all the circumstances New Brunswick was not the proper forum since the alleged fraud was continued until the contracts were entered into in England. In the face of the agreements to take disputes of any nature relating to M's membership at Lloyd's to English courts the onus rested with M to demonstrate strong cause why New Brunswick was the more appropriate forum than England. The court was not satisfied that they had done so, *Ash v. Lloyd's Corp* (1991) 6 O.R. (3d) 235 followed; (2) while the general principle was that the law of the place where a tort occurred generally should apply, that principle went to choice of law not the proper forum, and (3) the stay would be granted on condition that M would not be required to provide security for costs in the English action; SL waived any precondition that any judgment obtained against M should be satisfied before M could sue in England; and that SL waive any contractual requirement that M meet any contractual obligations before bringing any actions against SL.

MORRISON v. SOCIETY OF LLOYD'S; DRUMMIE v. SOCIETY OF LLOYD'S [2000] I.L.Pr. 92, Creaghan, J., QB (NB).

741. **Choice of forum – contracts – place of performance – Ireland**

[Brussels Convention on Jurisdiction and Enforcement of Judgments in Civil and Commercial Matters 1968 Art.5(1).]

An Irish company, B, bought the assets of a company, S. The contract excluded all distribution contracts but B maintained a distribution relationship with D in France. D cooperated as B's sole distributor in France. Following a dispute B gave notice of its intention to use another distributor and sought a declaration in its home court in Ireland that there was no exclusive distribution agreement with D. B argued that the Irish courts had jurisdiction because of the Brussels Convention 1968 Art.5(1). D disputed jurisdiction.

Held, declining jurisdiction, that the relevant obligation at the heart of the dispute was D's obligation to distribute the product in France and B's obligation to use only D to distribute the product. Those obligations were created by an umbrella contract and the terms of individual contracts entered into within the framework of the umbrella contract did not affect the obligations arising under the umbrella contract.

BIO MEDICAL RESEARCH LTD (T/A SLENDERTONE) v. DELATEX SA [2000] I.L.Pr. 23, McCracken, J., HC (Irl).

742. **Choice of forum – defamation – service out of jurisdiction – existence of real and substantial connection – Canada**

D bought and sold gas in Alberta and throughout North America. Its main place of business was in Alberta. It brought proceedings for defamation in Alberta against H, a member of the Saskatchewan legislative assembly residing in Saskatchewan. The alleged defamatory statements were made in circumstances which were privileged in Saskatchewan but not in Alberta. The court gave leave to serve outside the jurisdiction on the basis that Alberta was the place where the tort occurred. H applied to have the service set aside on the basis that Saskatchewan was the more appropriate forum. A Master set aside the service out of the jurisdiction but D appealed.

Held, allowing the appeal and reinstating the service, (1) the burden was on D to demonstrate that Alberta was the more appropriate forum by showing a real and substantial connection with the action, taking into account the place where the tort occurred, the applicable law, any juridical advantage and the existence of a lis alibi pendens, *Camco International (Canada) Ltd v. Porodo* (1997) 211 A.R. 71 (Q.B.) applied; (2) in all the circumstances Alberta was the most appropriate forum. It was D's principal place of business, D's identity and reputation and most of the evidence was there, and (3) potential difficulties might arise from the fact that a similar action was pending in Saskatchewan but they did not outweigh the other factors all of which pointed to Alberta as the proper forum.

DIRECT ENERGY MARKETING LTD v. HILLSON [2000] I.L.Pr.102, Kenny, J., QB (Alta).

743. **Choice of forum – delay – case relisted pending foreign court decision**

See CIVIL PROCEDURE: EMI Group Plc v. Cubic (UK) Ltd. §493

744. **Choice of forum – domicile – service of process – meaning of "sued" under Lugano Convention**

[Lugano Convention on Jurisdiction and Enforcement of Judgments in Civil and Commercial Matters 1988 Art.2, Art.6.]

A number of the defendants to proceedings brought by CT, all of whom were domiciled outside the United Kingdom, appealed against a decision ([1998] 1 W.L.R. 547, [1997] C.L.Y. 889) that the English court had jurisdiction to hear the case. The principal issue turned upon whether the concept "sued" in the Lugano Convention 1988 Art.2 and Art.6 was to be construed as referring to the date on which the writ was issued, or the date on which the proceedings were served.

Held, dismissing the appeal, that the concept "sued" had been used in the Convention interchangeably with the concepts "bring proceedings" and "instituted proceedings" and accordingly it was to be interpreted as referring to the initiation of proceedings, which, under English law, was the issue of the writ. To interpret the concept "sued" as referring to the date on which the proceedings were served would potentially pave the way for a defendant to evade service as soon as the existence of the proceedings came to his attention. There was no basis for implying that the anchor defendant had to be served first before the issue or service of the proceedings on co-defendants.

CANADA TRUST CO v. STOLZENBERG (NO.2) [2000] 3 W.L.R. 1376, Lord Steyn, HL.

745. **Choice of forum – evidence – cause of action arising in Guyana – property relevant to dispute situated in Canada – stay of Canadian proceedings – Canada**

JP and DP were brothers who had a business based in Guyana. JP lived in Ontario and brought an action in Ontario against DP arising out of an agreement relating to the business. DP sought a stay of proceedings on the basis that Guyana was the proper forum. The only connection with Ontario (other than JP's residence) was the fact that a property that was a security under the agreement was located in Ontario.

Held, granting a stay, that the subject matter of the dispute was most closely connected with Guyana where all of the material evidence was based. The presence of the security in Ontario was not a material factor and any separate proceedings relating to that property might be heard in Ontario but that was not a reason why the present dispute ought not to be heard in Guyana.

PAUL v. PAUL [1999] I.L.Pr. 839, Belleghem, J., CJ (Gen Div) (Ont).

746. **Choice of forum – Inland Revenue – accountants – jurisdiction of English courts where Irish accountant sued in connection with United Kingdom claim for tax relief**

[Civil Jurisdiction and Judgments Act 1982; Brussels Convention on Jurisdiction and Enforcement of Judgments in Civil and Commercial Matters 1968 Art.5(1).]

B and his wife moved to Ireland and instructed Y, an accountant domiciled there, to advise them in relation to their tax affairs. Subsequently B issued proceedings in England against Y alleging negligence and breach of contract. B's principal complaint was that Y had failed to secure capital gains tax retirement relief for the years 1989 and 1990. Y applied for an order setting aside service of the summons, contending that the English courts had no jurisdiction by virtue of the Civil Jurisdiction and Judgements Act 1982. Y maintained that the place of performance of his contractual obligation to B was Ireland, and that because B's pleaded case did not fall within the Brussels Convention 1968 Art.5(1), the Irish courts were the only courts possessing relevant jurisdiction. The court at first instance held that the action could not be tried in the United Kingdom under the Convention. B appealed contending that the judge had failed to identify the place of performance of the principal obligation. B contended that Y was obliged to "represent, conduct and settle" his claim for tax relief against the Inland Revenue, and that this obligation was necessarily carried out in the United Kingdom.

Held, allowing the appeal, that the pleaded retainer set out obligations that were necessarily to be performed in the United Kingdom as the place in which the Inland Revenue was located. Although advice was undoubtedly given in Dublin, the only way in which Y could perform the task he was entrusted with was by making representations to the Inland Revenue, and if required, attending the hearing before the General Commissioners in England. Although letter writing constituted part of the obligation, the vital aspect of that obligation was the communication of the opinions expressed therein to the Inland Revenue. Y's obligation to represent B could only have been performed in England, therefore Y had to submit to the jurisdiction of the English courts.

BARRY v. BRADSHAW [2000] I.L.Pr. 706, Aldous, L.J., CA.

747. **Choice of forum – insurance – commercial court providing most appropriate forum – injunction to restrain foreign proceedings**

CU provided excess insurance cover to SH and RE, who were claimants under the contracts of insurance and incorporated in the US. CU commenced an action in London for negative declaratory relief by writ. Leave to issue and serve a concurrent writ on SH and RE out of the jurisdiction was granted by the commercial court and the writ was served on RE in August 1998. On October 6, 1998, RE served points of defence and counterclaim, claiming indemnity under the contracts of insurance. At about the same time SH and RE commenced proceedings in Oregon against CU and others, but service had not been effected on CU by the time of the instant proceedings. CU sought an injunction restraining RE until trial or further order from continuing the Oregon proceedings.

Held, allowing the application and restraining the Oregon proceedings in the terms sought, that (1) the contracts were governed by English law with the commercial court being the most appropriate forum for the trial of the action; (2) in determining whether foreign proceedings would be oppressive, injustice to the parties in terms of whether or not to allow those proceedings had to be taken into account, and (3) in the interests of justice, the injustice and oppression that would occur from concurrent proceedings in a foreign jurisdiction had also to be considered, *Societe Nationale Industrielle Aerospatiale (SNIA) v. Lee Kui Jak* [1987] A.C. 871, [1987] C.L.Y. 3024 considered.

COMMERCIAL UNION ASSURANCE CO PLC v. SIMAT HELLIESEN & EICHNER INC [2000] I.L.Pr. 239, Cresswell, J., QBD (Comm Ct).

748. Choice of forum – insurance – insurance dispute – appropriate forum

C, the insurers under a policy concerning the construction, installation and transit of a boiler intended for an oil refinery in Ghana, sought a declaration of non liability after the boiler had been damaged in Belgium during shipment. The policy covered R, a Canadian corporation, R's affiliated companies and others for whom R had a responsibility to insure. C submitted that since they had not been aware that the boiler was to be unloaded in Belgium, the risk was not as described in the policy. Permission was given to C to serve out of the jurisdiction. R and one of its affiliated companies then issued proceedings in Alberta, arguing that that was the appropriate venue (1) because C had been licensed by the Superintendent of Insurance for Alberta to sell insurance, and (2) because there was an alternative claim against Canadian brokers. C applied to the Canadian court with a view to establishing that the Court of Alberta was a forum non conveniens, but it was held that the balance of convenience for all parties lay with the determination of all the issues in Alberta, and that it was in the interests of all parties to be bound by such determination, thereby avoiding a multiplicity of actions and the possibility of conflicting findings by different courts. R applied to set aside service of the proceedings brought by C in England.

Held, granting the application, that (1) the factual enquiries and evidence would primarily be directed to Canada; (2) there was no basis to C's contention that the Alberta court would apply conflict of law rules which differed from those of an English court, since the Alberta court would consider which system of law had the closest connection with the transaction; (3) C could not argue that they would be disadvantaged in having the issue of policy coverage tried in Alberta, since they had taken a commercial decision to obtain a licence to sell insurance in Alberta and had therefore accepted the risk that local law might not be to their advantage; (4) it was natural for an assured to bring a claim against the insurer in his own domicile; accordingly, the Alberta proceedings were not "contrived", and (5) the Alberta court's concern as to the multiplicity of proceedings was a valid one.

CHASE v. RAM TECHNICAL SERVICES LTD [2000] 2 Lloyd's Rep. 418, Timothy Walker, J., QBD (Comm Ct).

749. Choice of forum – jurisdiction – anti suit injunction – scope of exclusive jurisdiction clause – criteria for grant of injunction

A group of companies, A, who were based in the United States, decided to sell a group of its British based insurance companies by way of a management buy out. A entered into negotiations with D, the chairman of the insurance group, to this end. Negotiations on behalf of A were carried out by two of its executives, R and S. After the insurance group had been bought and had gone into liquidation, A brought proceedings in New York alleging that D, R and S had conspired to defraud it by inducing it to inject $42.5 million into the insurance group, buying the group through W, a company owned by them, and then using much of the sale proceeds for their own purposes. A also alleged that the conspirators had fraudulently induced it to agree to English exclusive jurisdiction clauses (EJCs) in the contracts for the sale to W. D denied the conspiracy and applied for an anti suit injunction to restrain A from bringing proceedings anywhere other than in England. Dismissing D's application, the judge held that A was not bound by the EJCs since, inter alia, its claim had arisen not from the sale agreements but from the alleged conspiracy. Under the EJCs the parties had submitted themselves "to the exclusive jurisdiction of the English courts to settle any dispute which [might] arise out of or in connection with" the agreements. D appealed contending that, when construing the EJCs, the judge had ignored the words "in connection with".

Held, allowing the appeal (Brooke, L.J. dissenting), that the judge had erred in concluding that the allegation of conspiracy to defraud was not within the scope of the EJCs; the alleged conspiracy had arisen "in connection with" the agreements. The judge's exercise of his discretion had therefore been flawed, and it was necessary to consider the matter afresh. The correct starting point was that D was entitled to the injunction in the absence of strong reasons to the contrary; it was not a case of merely deciding where the action should most conveniently be tried. Although there was much to connect the matter with the USA, there was little connection with New York other than the allegation that the conspiracy was said to have originated at a meeting there. Conversely, the proposed buy out had been concerned with the sale of a British business to a company controlled by British nationals. The judge had been wrong to conclude that there was no evidence that the New York proceedings would be no more costly than proceedings in England. As regards the ruling of the judge in New York who had dismissed D's challenge to his jurisdiction, that judge had not had the advantage of considering the finding of the judge on the injunction application to the effect that the EJCs were valid; it would not be appropriate for the court to refuse an injunction to which D would otherwise be entitled in deference to a foreign judgment with which it disagreed. There was accordingly no strong enough reason for the court not to exercise its discretion to grant the anti suit injunction sought by D.

DONOHUE v. ARMCO INC [2000] 1 All E.R. (Comm) 641, Stuart-Smith, L.J., CA.

750. **Choice of forum – jurisdiction – assignee of contractual right bound by exclusive jurisdiction clause in assignor's contract**

[Brussels Convention on Jurisdiction and Enforcement of Judgments in Civil and Commercial Matters 1968 Art.17, Art.21, Art.22.]

M, a company now in liquidation, traded in oil. M entered into contracts with I and S, two companies based in Singapore, for the sale of bunker fuel to be transported to Singapore on board the ship "The Vigour". The contracts were on similar terms and included an exclusive English jurisdiction clause. Shortly after the goods were delivered to Singapore, G, a company claiming title to the fuel transported by I and S, began proceedings in England against M seeking the delivery up of oil products alleged to be in their possession, together with damages for conversion and breach of contract. Receivers were appointed to preserve the property and receivables of M pending the outcome of the proceedings. B, a French bank that had been financing M's business operations, commenced two actions in Paris, one against I and M, and the other against S and M, to recover the amounts due under the contracts for the sale of the bunker fuel. Subsequently G joined I and S as defendants to its action and obtained leave to serve them out of the jurisdiction. S applied to join G and the receivers and liquidators as third parties to B's action against it in Paris. The receivers issued a writ in England in the name of M to recover payment from I of the price of the goods due under the contract, and I served third party proceedings on B as a means of ensuring that they would be bound by the court's decision in M's action for declaratory relief. Five applications were made to the English court in G's and M's actions seeking a stay of the various claims made by the parties. All the parties sought the consolidation of the various proceedings concerning the cargo of "The Vigour". Whereas B and S argued that those proceedings should take place in France, I, G and M's receivers submitted that England was the relevant jurisdiction.

Held, refusing B's application for a stay of the third party proceedings, that B were bound by the exclusive jurisdiction clause. B, as assignee of M's debt, took the debt together with any restrictions attached including the exclusive jurisdiction clause, *Partenreederei MS Tilly Russ v. Haven & Vervoerbedrijf Nova (C71/83)* [1985] Q.B. 931, [1985] C.L.Y. 1452 applied. B's knowledge of the existence of the clause was immaterial. The Brussels Convention 1968 Art.17 was applicable due to the existence of a valid exclusive jurisdiction agreement and overrode Arts.21 and 22, *Continental Bank NA v. Aeakos Compania Naviera SA* [1994] 1 W.L.R. 588, [1994] C.L.Y. 3715 applied. Arts.21 and 22 were unlike Art.17 in that they were essentially procedural. Art.22 did not render the imposition of a stay mandatory. Had B not been bound by the exclusive jurisdiction clause, it would have been appropriate, in accordance with Arts.21 and 22, to stay the third party proceedings in England; the actions commenced in the two jurisdictions involved the same cause of action and, as B had issued proceedings against I before being served with the third party proceedings issued by I, the French court had been seised of the proceedings first. Since it could be said that the aim of B's action had been to obtain a ruling on G's right to recover from S damages for wrongful interference with the cargo of "The Vigour", B's action involved the same cause of action relied on by G. Accordingly, Art.21 applied and it would be appropriate to stay G's action against S pending a decision of the French court on the question of jurisdiction. No grounds existed for staying the action commenced by the receivers or G's action against I.

GLENCORE INTERNATIONAL AG v. METRO TRADING INTERNATIONAL INC (NO.1); METRO TRADING INTERNATIONAL INC v. ITOCHU PETROLEUM CO (S) PTE LTD (NO.1) [1999] 2 All E.R. (Comm) 899, Moore-Bick, J., QBD (Comm Ct).

751. Choice of forum – jurisdiction – carriage by sea – construction of jurisdiction clause – Canada

TS entered into a contract with P for the carriage of a cargo of shoes between Italy and Canada. The container containing the shoes was stolen prior to delivery. TS claimed damages against P in the Canadian courts. P sought a stay on the basis that the bill of lading contained a jurisdiction clause in favour of Hamburg.

Held, refusing the application, that (1) the jurisdiction clause was inconsistent with the underlying contract as expressed in the bill of lading; (2) the court had a discretion whether or not to enforce the jurisdiction clause. This would be exercised against the clause as the main evidence was in Canada and there was only a limited connection between the parties and Hamburg. Further, TS would suffer prejudice in Hamburg as the claim could be time barred and P did not have a genuine desire to conduct the litigation in Hamburg and was only proceeding on that basis as a means of forcing a settlement.

TOWN SHOES LTD v. PANALPINA INC [2000] I.L.Pr. 172, Teitelbaum, J., Fed Ct (Can).

752. Choice of forum – jurisdiction – claim for reimbursement of monies paid over during negotiations for ship purchase – "proprietary maritime claim" given wide interpretation – Australia

[Admiralty Act 1988 (Australia) s.4(2)(a).]

CI entered into negotiations with M with a view to the purchase of a particular vessel. Whilst negotiations were ongoing, CI paid the sum of AD 197,916 to M's solicitors. The negotiations were not successful and CI sought the return of the monies paid contending that they were to be held on trust pending a concluded agreement. CI then commenced proceedings in the Admiralty jurisdiction whereupon M applied to dismiss the claim for want of jurisdiction. CI argued that the court had jurisdiction to determine its claim as it fell within the definition of a proprietary maritime claim as set out in the Admiralty Act 1988 (Australia) s.4(2)(a), namely a claim "relating to" the title to or ownership of a ship.

Held, dismissing the application, that the test to be applied was whether there existed a reasonably direct connection between the claim made by CI and the ownership of the vessel in question, *Gatoil International Inc v. Arkwright-Boston Manufacturers Mutual Insurance Co (The Sandrina)* [1985] A.C. 255, [1985] C.L.Y. 3204 applied. The words "relating to" in s.4(2)(a) were to be construed widely. The essence of the case involved the resolution of the question of the ownership of the vessel. Whereas CI contended that they had never obtained ownership of the vessel, whether equitable or otherwise, M maintained that a contract had been concluded. Such a dispute as to ownership did constitute a sufficiently direct connection for the purpose of s.4(2)(a).

CARAVELLE INVESTMENTS LTD v. MARTABAN LTD (THE CAPE DON) [2000] 1 Lloyd's Rep. 388, Finkelstein, J., Fed Ct (Aus) (Sgl judge).

753. **Choice of forum – jurisdiction – concurrent English and French proceedings – application to stay English proceedings**

S, an airline operator, and A, an aircraft manufacturer, entered into a contract which contained a French exclusive jurisdiction clause. One of S's aircraft was damaged when its landing gear collapsed on landing. MD was the manufacturer of the landing gear and its contract with A contained an English exclusive jurisdiction clause. S commenced preliminary investigative proceedings in Paris against A. MD subsequently sought a declaration of non liability to A in England. A sought to stay the English proceedings pending the outcome of the French proceedings.

Held, refusing to grant a stay, that where the parties had agreed on a forum, the court would only grant a stay of proceedings in rare and compelling circumstances. *Reichhold Norway ASA v. Goldman Sachs International* [2000] 1 W.L.R. 173, [1999] C.L.Y. 546 applied. Such circumstances did not exist in the instant case. On the contrary, there were compelling circumstances against granting a stay. The possibility that something of relevance to the English proceedings might emerge from the French proceedings was not a sufficient reason to allow A not to plead its case and make appropriate disclosure.

MESSIER DOWTY LTD v. SABENA SA (STAY OF PROCEEDINGS) [2000] 1 All E.R. (Comm) 101, Langley, J., QBD.

754. **Choice of forum – jurisdiction – construction of jurisdiction clause – agreement had to be legally binding**

[Lugano Convention on Jurisdiction and enforcement of Judgments in Civil and Commercial Matters 1988 Art.17.]

S, a Swiss company, applied to set aside a writ in proceedings brought in England by I, an English company, for recovery of damages for wrongful termination of two agreements entered into between the parties in 1996. The companies had agreed to collaborate on two projects governed by separate commercial agreements. They signed a quality assurance agreement in respect of one project providing for Swiss courts to have jurisdiction of "Court Suits" or any other disputes. A draft agreement in relation to the other project contained identical jurisdiction clauses as did a proposed replacement for the commercial agreement previously entered into. Both draft agreements were signed by I but not by S. S disputed the jurisdiction of the English Courts on the grounds that there was an agreement between the parties that the Swiss courts would have exclusive jurisdiction. I disputed the existence of an agreement sufficient to activate Art.17 of the Lugano Convention

Held, dismissing the application, that (1) an agreement conferring jurisdiction must be legally enforceable and intended to create legal relations, although not necessarily amounting to a contract under national law; (2) it could not be inferred that a jurisdiction clause in a draft agreement intended to replace an existing contract which contained no jurisdiction clause, was intended to be legally binding before the existing contract was entirely replaced by a new contract or contracts; (3) the phrase "in the event of Court Suits or any other disputes" was not a sufficiently clear reference to disputes under the already existing agreement, *IP Metal Ltd v. Ruote Oz SpA* [1993] 2 Lloyd's Rep.60, [1993] C.L.Y. 449 applied, and (4) S had not established that I's offer to contract on the terms of the previous commercial agreement was not subject to a condition as to signing of the draft agreement replacing it.

IMPLANTS INTERNATIONAL LTD v. STRATEC MEDICAL [1999] 2 All E.R. (Comm) 933, Judge McGonigal, QBD (Merc Ct).

755. Choice of forum – jurisdiction – court to restrain breaches of exclusive jurisdiction clauses

SL sought an order to restrain W, who alleged that they had been fraudulently induced to become Lloyd's Names, from pursuing a second action in Australia. W claimed that SL had failed to disclose the extent of the market's liability for asbestos claims in inducing them to become Lloyd's Names. The contract contained an exclusive jurisdiction clause in favour of the English courts but the court in Australia had refused to stay the action commenced by W. SL argued that the contract and moreover, proceedings were already underway in England in which a number of interim orders had been made.

Held, allowing the application, that the court would grant an injunction to restrain W from pursuing an action in breach of an exclusive jurisdiction clause. Though the Australian courts had refused to grant a stay, it seemed that important information concerning the proceedings in England and the interim orders relating to those proceedings had not been brought to the attention of the Australian judges. W had failed to provide any good reason as to why an injunction to restrain breach of the exclusive jurisdiction clause should not be granted.

SOCIETY OF LLOYD'S v. WHITE [2000] C.L.C. 961, Cresswell, J., QBD (Comm Ct).

756. Choice of forum – jurisdiction – exclusive jurisdiction clause in marine insurance policy – injunction to restrain action commenced in breach of jurisdiction clause

G were the principal underwriters of two Lloyd's slip policies for hull and machinery insurance on the vessel NR. The policies amounted to 50 per cent of the cover for the vessel, the balance being made up by unrelated policies taken out in Belgium. The slip policies were subject to an exclusive English jurisdiction clause. NR sustained damage and a claim was made under the slip policies. The insurers refused to pay, arguing that no loss had been caused by an insured peril. V brought an action in Belgium against G and the other insurers, in clear breach of the jurisdiction clause in relation to the slip policies. G sought an injunction to restrain V from continuing the action in Belgium.

Held, granting the injunction, that the provision in the slip policy overrode any other provisions relating to jurisdiction. There had been no good reason why V had brought the action in breach of the provision. It was the English court's duty to restrain the action, with no disrespect to the Belgian courts, *Continental Bank NA v. Aeakos Compania Naviera SA* [1994] 1 W.L.R. 588, [1994] C.L.Y. 3715 and *Japan Line Ltd v. Aggeliki Charis Compania Maritima SA (The Angelic Grace)* [1980] 1 Lloyd's Rep. 288, [1980] C.L.Y. 80 applied.

GILKES v. VENIZELOS ANESA [2000] I.L.Pr. 487, David Steel, J., QBD (T&CC).

757. Choice of forum – jurisdiction – exclusive jurisdiction clause only one of factors in determining choice of forum – Canada

F was an Ontario company that bought computer products from B, a Danish company. The sale occurred in Ontario. The products failed and F sought damages from B in the Ontario court. B sought a stay in favour of proceedings in Denmark, relying on a term in the contract conferring jurisdiction over any dispute on the Danish courts.

Held, dismissing the application, that a contractual clause dealing with the choice of forum was not determinative. Such a clause was merely one of the factors to be taken into account. By selling products in the Ontario market place B ought to assume the burden of defending those products there so long as it could be said that the forum was one which B ought reasonably to have had in mind when he offered his goods for sale.

FRESH MIX LTD v. BILWINCO A/S [1999] I.L.Pr. 775, Hermiston, J., CJ (Gen Div) (Ont).

758. Choice of forum – jurisdiction – exclusive jurisdiction clauses – anti suit injunction granted by English court where court had a sufficient interest to restrain foreign proceedings

C and S were both English companies, C having been once part of S prior to a management buy out. At all material times, however, C was managed in Beirut. C and S entered into various agreements, all of which contained exclusive jurisdiction or arbitration clauses. S gave six months' notice to terminate two of the agreements. C objected to the termination and threatened to bring proceedings under Lebanese legislation, where, as an agent, C had a right to compensation for the benefits given to the business on termination of the agency. S applied for an injunction to restrain such proceedings, but shortly prior to the hearing of S's application, C issued proceedings in Beirut against S and F. There was no time for this to be considered in the context of S's application, and although an injunction was granted to S, the proceedings already underway in Beirut were outside its scope. S thereupon issued a further summons to restrain those proceedings, subsequent to which C limited its claim to an issue which it was common ground was not subject to any exclusive jurisdiction or arbitration clauses. C argued that the amended claim had no connection with England, it was properly founded, and should not be restrained by an injunction having proper regard to the principles of comity. S submitted that the claim was vexatious, oppressive and bound to fail, and that the English court had sufficient interest in the proceedings to justify intervening by way of injunction, as the interests of justice required it to do so.

Held, granting the injunction, that (1) on the facts, C's claim was purely vexatious and bound to fail; (2) the circumstances of the case were most unusual, and given the history of the matter, the court had a very strong interest in ensuring that a party granted an order restraining the continuation of proceedings was not subject to further vexatious litigation. Further, given the status of S and C as English companies, and the fact that their previous relationship was governed by English law, the English court was the natural forum for determining whether or not C's Beirut proceedings were vexatious; (3) both England and Lebanon could be properly regarded as a natural forum for the determination of the substantive claim, but neither jurisdiction could be regarded as the sole natural forum, and (4) in the extremely unusual circumstances of this case, the English court had sufficient interest in the matter to justify making an order the effect of which would be to intervene indirectly with the foreign court, and accordingly an injunction would be granted to S, *Airbus Industrie GIE v. Patel* [1999] 1 A.C. 119, [1998] C.L.Y. 755 considered.

SHELL INTERNATIONAL PETROLEUM CO LTD v. CORAL OIL CO LTD (NO.2) [1999] 2 Lloyd's Rep. 606, Thomas, J., QBD (Comm Ct).

759. Choice of forum – jurisdiction – insurance policies – exclusive jurisdiction clauses – foreign judgments – court's duty to consider approach of foreign court

Y, an underwriter, entered into an insurance policy containing an exclusive jurisdiction clause providing that it would be subject to English law. Having obtained a judgment against the insured in Louisiana, WTC sought to enforce the judgment against Y. In doing so, it relied on the law of Louisiana which provided for a right of direct action against the insurer subject to the terms of the policy. Y sought an anti suit injunction against WTC arguing that once WTC had asserted a contractual right to claim under the insurance policies, it must be regarded as subject to the bundle of rights and obligations contained therein including the jurisdiction clause. Furthermore, there was no "good reason" why WTC should be able to evade being subject to the jurisdiction clauses. In opposing the application, WTC argued that the jurisdiction clause might be struck out by the Louisiana court as contrary to state law and the English court had to place itself in the position of the Louisiana court in that respect. Consequently, since Y had no claim to enforce the jurisdiction clauses, the right to obtain an injunction did not arise. In any event, an application for an injunction was not a cause of action thus permission to serve proceedings outside the jurisdiction should not be granted.

Held, granting the anti suit injunction, that since the policy was governed by English law, the court did not have to consider how the exclusive jurisdiction clause might be viewed by the court in Louisiana. WTC's claim against Y was contractual in nature and therefore the jurisdiction clause was binding. WTC were seeking to take advantage of insurance policies which were governed by English law therefore it was not contrary to accepted notions of judicial comity for the English court to give permission to serve proceedings on a party outside the jurisdiction when the contract relied upon in foreign proceedings contains a clause giving the English court jurisdiction.

YOUELL v. KARA MARA SHIPPING CO LTD [2000] 2 Lloyd's Rep. 102, Aikens, J., QBD (Comm Ct).

760. **Choice of forum – jurisdiction – jurisdiction clause stipulating place of business – no connection with England**

[Rules of the Supreme Court 1965 (SI 1965 1776) Ord.11 r.1 (1).]

L, a company with its place of business in Riga, was insured by I, a Russian insurer, under a contract of insurance against pollution risks. The risks were also subject to further reinsurance and voluntary agreements between tanker owners and cargo interests. I made a payment to L, who also received monies under one of the voluntary agreements. I sought to recover part of the monies it paid to L in a claim brought in England. L disputed the jurisdiction of the English court on the basis of a jurisdiction clause which stated that disputes were to be settled at either the respondent's place of business or of residence. L appealed against the refusal of its application for the writ to be struck out under the Rules of the Supreme Court Ord.11 r.1 (1).

Held, allowing the appeal, that the jurisdiction clause conferred jurisdiction on the court in Riga. Neither I nor L had a connection with England and it would be in breach of contract to permit proceedings in another jurisdiction, *Aratra Potato Co Ltd v. Egyptian Navigation Co (The El Amria)* [1981] 2 Lloyds Rep. 119, [1981] C.L.Y. 2198 applied.

INGOSSTRAKH LTD v. LATVIAN SHIPPING CO [2000] I.L.Pr. 164, Tuckey, L.J., CA.

761. **Choice of forum – jurisdiction – jurisdiction of court where prospective third party had contract containing exclusive Hong Kong jurisdiction clause – inherent power to stay proceedings**

[Rules of the Supreme Court 1965 (SI 1965 1776) Ord.11 r.1 (1); Civil Procedure Rules 1998 (SI 1998 3132) Sch.1; Brussels Convention on Jurisdiction and Enforcement of Judgments in Civil and Commercial Matters 1968 Art.17.]

A major US oil company, M, had a subsidiary in Hong Kong, MHK, which entered into a contract containing a Hong Kong jurisdiction clause with a Chinese trading company, SB, for the sale of fuel oil (the Hong Kong contract). After delivery of the oil, SB alleged that it was gas oil not fuel oil and withheld part of the price. SB had an English subsidiary, SL, which later sold a cargo of oil to MD, a US subsidiary of M. The agreement for sale (the English contract) contained an exclusive English jurisdiction clause and a term which provided for the parties' affiliated companies to set off any claims. Pursuant to this provision, MD withheld sufficient of the payment due to SL to recoup the debt owing under the Hong Kong contract. SL sued MD in England and obtained summary judgment for the balance of the sum owing but the decision was overturned by the Court of Appeal on the basis that set off had been permitted under the contract. The instant proceedings were concerned with whether SB was excused from payment under the Hong Kong contract. MD sought to join SB into the English proceedings as a Part 20 defendant, which required permission under the Civil Procedure Rules 1998 Sch.1 and the Rules of the Supreme Court 1965 Ord.11 r.1 (1). With regard to the Hong Kong contract, SB challenged the jurisdiction of the English court and contended that (1) they were merely nominees, their principal being an independent refining company, GB, and that accordingly SB did not owe any payment to MHK unless it had itself received payment from GB; (2) MHK had misdescribed the cargo, which had led to its confiscation by the Chinese authorities; (3) MHK may have been involved in a smuggling operation, amounting to a repudiatory breach of the contract, and (4) the English proceedings should be stayed to avoid multiplicity. MD contended that (1) SB was the named buyer in the Hong Kong contract and as such was liable for any claims under it; (2) the cargo had been accompanied by certificates of quality and there was no evidence that it was other than as described in the contract; (3) the allegation of smuggling was without foundation, and (4) the Hong Kong jurisdiction clause was not exclusive.

Held, allowing the application to serve a Part 20 claim, that (1) the test for distinguishing an exclusive from a non exclusive jurisdiction clause was whether it obliged the parties to resort to the relevant jurisdiction regardless of whether the word "exclusive" was used and here the language of the clause in the Hong Kong contract clearly obliged the parties to submit disputes to the Hong Kong court; (2) MD had not succeeded in showing that the convenient forum for the litigation was England rather than Hong Kong; (3) under the English contract, the exclusive jurisdiction clause was in accordance with the Brussels Convention 1968 Art.17 because one of the parties, SL, was domiciled in a contracting state. The English court nevertheless had an inherent power, if it saw fit, to stay the proceedings pending the resolution of the litigation in Hong Kong, *Harrods (Buenos Aires) Ltd (No.1), Re* [1991] 4 All E.R. 334, [1991] C.L.Y. 476 applied. However, in the instant case that would be an incorrect exercise of discretion since (a) the proceedings in England had been commenced by SL, an English company; (b) the English contract containing an exclusive English jurisdiction clause postdated the Hong Kong contract and the issues arising from it; (c) there was as yet no litigation in Hong Kong and might never be, and (d) to justify overriding an exclusive jurisdiction clause there must be strong reasons which went beyond mere convenience to the interests of justice itself, *British Aerospace Plc v. Dee Howard Co* [1993] 1 Lloyd's Rep. 368, [1993] C.L.Y. 451 considered, and such reasons were not present, and (4) having decided that the proceedings were not to be stayed, it was in the interests of justice that permission be granted to serve Part 20 proceedings against SB. This would not prevent SB from bringing proceedings in Hong Kong if it saw fit. As the English contract must be litigated in England, it was appropriate that it should be done in the presence of all interested parties. Moreover, SB was only nominally different from SL, who was already a party to the proceedings and for the purposes of the English contract they could be regarded as one entity.

SINOCHEM INTERNATIONAL OIL (LONDON) CO LTD v. MOBIL SALES AND SUPPLY CORP (NO.2) [2000] 1 All E.R. (Comm) 758, Rix, J., QBD (Comm Ct).

762. Choice of forum – jurisdiction – non contracting state

[Brussels Convention on Jurisdiction and Enforcement of Judgments in Civil and Commercial Matters 1968 Art.2, Art.5.]

Z, an insurance company domiciled in Switzerland, provided insurance to N, a Texan company, against loss and damage to their oil rigs and installations in a number of locations including Saudi Arabia. The contract contained a clause requiring all disputes to be referred to the exclusive jurisdiction of the court of Texas. Z reinsured its liability to N for locations outside the United States with A, which brokered the contract in London. Following a blow out at an oil rig owned by N in Saudi Arabia, Z settled N's subsequent claim. A claim having been made on A, A issued proceedings in England seeking a declaration that it was not liable to Z due to a number of alleged breaches of the reinsurance contract. Prior to the hearing of an application to set aside the proceedings, Z brought proceedings in Texas under the exclusive jurisdiction clause. A judge hearing the English application having set a timetable for service, Z applied to stay the proceedings on forum non conveniens grounds. Z submitted that Texas was the appropriate jurisdiction. Given that the reinsurance policy had incorporated the exclusive jurisdiction clause, Z argued, the appropriate law of the policy was that of Texas. Furthermore, the claim had been settled in Texas and the expert witnesses who would be required were not resident in London. A contended, inter alia, that the court had no power to stay the proceedings under the Brussels Convention 1968 and further, the court was required to consider only whether Z had been sued in the appropriate country, that being either the country it was domiciled in pursuant to Art.2, or the country determined by the provisions of Art.5 along with a courts decision that such a country was permitted or the submission of a defendant to the court of that country.

Held, granting the application, that (1) the proper law of the reinsurance contract was English law given that it had been brokered in London and the contractual clauses it contained were commonplace in the relevant sector of the London reinsurance market. Moreover, there were no grounds for the belief that evidence would be more accessible if the proceedings took place in Texas. However, the exclusive jurisdiction clause overrode such considerations. Accordingly, given that proceedings had been brought legitimately in Texas, and that a judge in that jurisdiction could make an order as he saw fit as to the venue for the proceedings, it was inappropriate for an English court to give permission to serve out of the jurisdiction, *Excess Insurance Co Ltd v. Allendale Mutual Insurance Co* (Unreported, March 8, 1995) applied, and (2) the Brussels Convention 1968 did not prevent the application of the doctrine of forum non conveniens to stay proceedings brought contrary to a contract term granting exclusive jurisdiction to the US courts. Although there was authority for the proposition that the courts had no power, under the Convention, to stay proceedings where the defendant was domiciled in a contracting state, the instant case was different in that the defendant was seeking, under the contract terms, to litigate in a non contracting state. The court could order a stay of proceedings on the ground of forum non conveniens in favour of a non contracting state notwithstanding a defendant being domiciled in a contracting state, *Harrods (Buenos Aires) Ltd (No.1), Re* [1991] 4 All E.R. 334, [1991] C.L.Y. 476 applied.

ACE INSURANCE SA-NV (FORMERLY CIGNA INSURANCE CO OF EUROPE SA-NV) v. ZURICH INSURANCE CO [2000] 2 All E.R. (Comm) 449, Longmore, J., QBD (Comm Ct).

763. Choice of forum – jurisdiction – non exclusive jurisdiction clauses

[Civil Jurisdiction and Judgments Act 1982 s.49; Brussels Convention on Jurisdiction and Enforcement of Judgments in Civil and Commercial Matters 1968 Art.17, Art.21.]

L, a Spanish company, had commenced proceedings in England against M, an English company, in respect of monies owed under a contract for the sale and supply of chemicals. M had issued a petition in the Spanish court and had been joined as a party to criminal proceedings that were pending in Spain. L was not a party to the criminal proceedings which involved a number of individuals connected to L. M applied for an order staying the action brought by L pending the outcome of the Spanish proceedings and requested an extension of time for serving and filing the defence. M submitted that the English court either had no jurisdiction to hear the case by virtue of the Brussels Convention 1968 Art.17 or that the court should, in its discretion, not exercise that jurisdiction by the application of Art.21.

Held, dismissing the application, that (1) M and L had contracted upon M's standard terms and conditions and the contract incorporated a clause whereby L submitted to the non exclusive jurisdiction of the English courts; (2) although Art.17 of the Convention applied to non exclusive jurisdiction clauses and generally would have given English courts exclusive jurisdiction over the matter, M had maintained the right under the contract to be a party to proceedings in other jurisdictions; (3) there were no grounds for staying the application under Art.21 as the Spanish action did not directly involve L, the causes of action were not the same and the English court had, therefore, been the first court seised of the matter, and (4) the Civil Jurisdiction and Judgments Act 1982 s.49 did not give the court the power to stay the proceedings, *Harrods (Buenos Aires) Ltd (No. 2), Re* [1992] Ch. 72, [1992] C.L.Y. 475 followed.

LAFI OFFICE & INTERNATIONAL BUSINESS SL v. MERIDEN ANIMAL HEALTH LTD [2001] 1 All E.R. (Comm) 54, Christopher Simmons Q.C., QBD.

764. Choice of forum – jurisdiction – place of contractual performance – interpretation of Brussels Convention Art.5(1)

[Brussels Convention on Jurisdiction and Enforcement of Judgments in Civil and Commercial Matters 1968 Art.5(1).]

P, a company registered in Germany, carried a cargo of wine by sea from Le Havre to Brazil. When the cargo arrived it was discovered that it was damaged. GIE, the insurer, compensated the consignee and sought to recover the monies from P in the Le Havre commercial court. The court declined jurisdiction under the Brussels Convention 1968. GIE appealed and the Court of Cassation stayed the matter pending a reference to the ECJ as to whether the words "place of performance of the obligation in question" in Art.5(1) should be interpreted by reference to where the performance had taken place, as opposed to being determined in accordance with the law governing the obligation under the conflict of laws rules of the national court concerned, as previously decided by the ECJ in cases not involving contracts of employment.

Held, that the current position as set out in the previous case law should be preserved, in that the place of performance had to be determined in accordance with the law governing the relevant obligation as determined by the conflicts of law principles of the court seised, *Industrie Tessili Italiana Como v. Dunlop AG (C12/76)* [1976] E.C.R. 1473, [1977] C.L.Y. 1281 and *Custom Made Commercial Ltd v. Stawa Metallbau GmbH (C288/92)* [1994] E.C.R. I-2913, [1994] C.L.Y. 4800 applied. Given the divergence of opinion surrounding the interpretation of Art.5, the principle of legal certainty required that a defendant should be able to foresee which courts he could be sued in, other than those of his state of domicile.

GIE GROUPE CONCORDE v. MASTER OF THE VESSEL SUHADIWARNO PANJAN (C440/97); *sub nom.* GIE GROUP CONCORDE v. MASTER OF THE VESSEL SUHADIWARNO PANJAN (C440/97) [2000] All E.R. (EC) 865, GC Rodriguez Iglesias (President), ECJ.

765. Choice of forum – jurisdiction – proceedings relating to winding up

[Civil Jurisdiction and Judgments Act 1982 Sch.3C Art.1.]

UBS had the benefit of an option agreement with O forming part of a series of transactions involving other companies. The option agreement provided for submission of any disputes arising under it to the jurisdiction of the English court. O ran into financial difficulties and the Swiss court appointed liquidators. UBS sought to prove in insolvency for a sum due under the option agreement. The liquidators accepted that UBS was entitled to prove in O liquidation but required it to give credit for payments received under the related agreements. UBS brought proceedings in England for a declaration that it did not have to give credit. O applied for a stay of proceedings in favour of the Swiss courts on the grounds of forum non conveniens. It claimed that the proceedings were not within the scope of the Civil Jurisdiction and Judgments Act 1982 Sch.3C Art.1. In so doing it relied on the second paragraph of Art.1, which provided that the underlying Lugano Convention on Jurisdiction did not apply to "proceedings relating to the winding up of insolvent companies... compositions and analogous proceedings."

Held, dismissing the application, that (1) for the para.2 exception to apply it was not enough that the claim could be said to relate to the winding up of an insolvent company. It must derive directly from it. *Gourdain (Liquidator) v. Nadler (C133/78)* [1979] E.C.R. 733, [1979] C.L.Y. 1168 applied; (2) the claim in this instance derived from the dispute between O and UBS as to the latter's rights under the preliquidation transactions in which they engaged, and (3) the court should not exercise any discretion to stay UBS action. Not only had the parties expressly agreed that the English court should have jurisdiction, but also the English proceedings were likely to serve a valuable function in aid of the disposal of the Swiss proceedings.

UBS AG v. OMNI HOLDING AG (IN LIQUIDATION) [2000] 1 W.L.R. 916, Rimer, J., Ch D.

766. Choice of forum – jurisdiction – property rights – dispute over title to foreign lands – Canada

An Italian father executed a deed in Ontario by which title to land in Italy was granted to two daughters, resident in Ontario. After the father's death the son sought to challenge the validity of the deed, contending that it should be made null and void due to his father's lack of mental competence. The daughters argued that the court in Canada had no jurisdiction to determine a dispute that related to land abroad.

Held, that the court had no jurisdiction. A general rule of Canadian law was that courts of any country had no jurisdiction to determine rights and title to land not situated in that country. An exception existed whereby Canadian courts could determine a dispute over foreign land if (1) the court had in personam jurisdiction over the defendant; (2) there was a personal obligation between the parties; (3) the local court could supervise the execution of the judgment, and (4) the order would be effective in the situs. In the instant case there was no personal obligation between the parties and the exception could not apply.

CATANIA v. GIANNATTASIO [1999] I.L. Pr. 630, Laskin, J.A., CA (Ont).

767. Choice of forum – jurisdiction – reinsurance contracts – Lugano Convention – reinsurance contract not insurance for Convention purposes

[Lugano Convention on Jurisdiction and Enforcement of Judgments in Civil and Commercial Matters 1988 Art.5; Lugano Convention on Jurisdiction and Enforcement of Judgments in Civil and Commercial Matters 1988 Title II s.3.]

A, Lloyd's underwriters, reinsured on the London market risks relating to a contract for underwater valves initially insured by L, a Swedish domiciled company. A sought to avoid claims on the basis that they were induced to enter into the reinsurance contract by alleged material misrepresentations and non disclosure by L in breach of good faith, relying on the Lugano Convention 1988 to establish English jurisdiction. L applied to strike out the claims and was unsuccessful both at first instance ([1996] 4 All E.R. 978) and on appeal ([1997] 4 All E.R. 937). L appealed, contending that (1) under the terms of Title II s.3 of the Convention the term "insurance" included reinsurance, and (2) A was not entitled to rely on Art.5, which provided for certain exceptions to the rule that persons should be sued in the jurisdiction of their domicile because the obligations of disclosure were not matters relating to contact as they were pre contractual and had arisen under the general law.

Held, dismissing the appeal (Lord Hope and Lord Millett dissenting), that (1) having referred to cases concerned with the Brussels Convention before the ECJ, academic opinion and the Schlosser Report, it was apparent that it was contrary to the structure policy of the Lugano Convention, which aimed to defend a weaker insured party, for reinsurance to be included under the term "insurance", and (2) the structure of Art.5(1) clearly provided that a claim to avoid a contract must be a matter relating to contract. The obligation to disclose required to be performed in London; the place of performance established jurisdiction. Thus Art.5(1) applied, *Kleinwort Benson Ltd v. Glasgow City Council (No.2)* [1999] 1 A.C. 153, [1997] C.L.Y. 904 and *Effer SpA v. Kantner (C38/81)* [1982] E.C.R. 825, [1983] C.L.Y. 1437 considered. A was entitled to avoid the reinsurance contract by virtue of L's failure to perform the contractual obligation in London, namely, to make a fair representation of the risk. The obligation did not give rise to an action in tort or deceit under Art.5(3).

AGNEW v. LANSFORSAKRINGSBOLAGENS AB [2001] 1 A.C. 223, Lord Woolf, M.R., HL.

768. Choice of forum – jurisdiction – submitted to jurisdiction as fourth parties by issuing summons for disclosure of documents in respect of receivership

[Brussels Convention on Jurisdiction and Enforcement of Judgments in Civil and Commercial Matters 1968 Art.2, Art.6(2); Rules of the Supreme Court 1965 (SI 1965 1776).]

MTI was in the business of storing, blending and trading in fuel oil. The oil was stored and often blended in offshore storage vessels. In February 1998, large quantities of this oil were found to be missing. MTI collapsed, and litigation followed in which the main issue was whether C, an oil trading company and various other oil claimants had title to the missing oil, or whether the oil, or proceeds from it, could be recovered. The English court appointed receivers to recover and sell the disputed oil and obtain discovery of all relevant documents. The receivership order required the shipowners to deliver up the cargo on board their vessels. One of the owners of the offshore storage vessels refused to deliver up the disputed oil in its custody. It did, however, enter into discussions with the receivers and with P as to terms for its possible delivery up. Subsequently, bankruptcy proceedings were commenced in Greece in respect of MTI, and P bid for the disputed oil in those proceedings. The Greek liquidator authorised the sale of the disputed oil to P. The English receivers thereupon sought to join P and his Liberian company, B, as fourth parties to the English proceedings. The receivers also obtained a *Mareva* injunction in respect of the disputed oil. The third defendant issued a third party notice against MTI for the court to rule on the title. P and B made an application contesting the jurisdiction of the English court. P submitted that he could only be sued in his home jurisdiction of Greece, by reason of the Brussels Convention 1968 Art.2. B submitted that it had been wrongly joined in the English proceedings as a "necessary and proper party". P and B then issued a summons seeking disclosure and inspection of documents in respect of the receivership order. P and B contended that (1) the claims against them were outwith the jurisdiction conferred over third party claims by the Rules of the Supreme Court Ord.16 r.1 (1) and r.9, and (2) since the purchase of the disputed oil by P had been effected pursuant to an order of the Greek court, the law applicable to the fourth party claims was that of Greece, and there was therefore no reasonable cause of action at English law disclosed by the fourth party notice.

Held, refusing the application, that (1) by the issue of the summons for disclosure and inspection, P and B had invoked and submitted to the jurisdiction of the English court, *Astro Exito Navegacion SA v. WT Hsu (The Messiniaki Tolmi)* [1984] 1 Lloyd's Rep. 266, [1984] C.L.Y. 351 and *Esal (Commodities) Ltd v. Mahendra Pujara* [1989] 2 Lloyd's Rep. 479, [1990] C.L.Y. 3780 applied; (2) the claim for delivery up of the disputed oil, injunctive relief and the determination of issues stated were within RSC Ord.16 r.1 (1) as matters "relating to or connected with" the subject matter of the third party notice; (3) but for P and B's submission to the jurisdiction, the tortious claims against them would be outside the scope of Art.6(2) of the Convention and RSC Ord.11; (4) despite the conflict of jurisdictions, it was impossible to say that the whole of the fourth party notice should be set aside, either on jurisdictional or discretionary grounds, notwithstanding the probability that questions of Greek law would arise, and Greek parties would be involved. Subject to the resolution of the jurisdiction question, the English court could make orders in aid of those already made by it in connection with the disputed oil; (5) B was a necessary and proper party for the purpose of RSC Ord.11. It was right that all parties with a claim to the disputed oil should be before the court concerned with the question of the missing oil as a whole. Discretion should therefore be exercised under RSC Ord.16 in favour of leave to issue the fourth party notice; (6) the propriety of raising interpleader relief under RSC Ord.17 was no bar to raising an analogous issue as to title via a third party notice, and (7) the English court had jurisdiction to grant injunctions against P and B despite the absence of any relevant cause of action against either of them, since they were otherwise subject to the jurisdiction of the court. The injunctions would have been properly granted, even in the absence of a submission to the jurisdiction, and would be maintained in support of a cause of action accruing to other parties before the court.

CALTEX TRADING PTE LTD v. METRO TRADING INTERNATIONAL INC [2000] 1 All E.R. (Comm) 108, Rix, J., QBD (Comm Ct).

769. Choice of forum – libel – claim by Russian businessman following comments in American magazine – strength of connection with jurisdiction

A Russian businessman commenced proceedings against the American publishers of a magazine, F, for libel. The proceedings were commenced in England and the claim for damage to reputation restricted to the English jurisdiction. At first instance the court imposed a stay on the proceedings on the basis that Russia was the more suitable forum since the connections that B had with the jurisdiction were not strong. The decision was reversed on appeal, the court finding that B had established the existence of a strong business reputation and a significant connection with the jurisdiction. F appealed, contending that (1) the court had erred in adopting the approach in *Cordoba Shipping Co v. National State Bank, Elizabeth, New Jersey (The Albaforth)* [1984] 2 Lloyd's Rep. 91, [1984] C.L.Y. 2671 cited; in preference to the approach in *Spiliada Maritime Corp v. Cansulex Ltd (The Spiliada)* [1987] A.C. 460, [1987] C.L.Y. 3135 cited; and (2) that the evidence suggested that either Russia or the United States of America were more suitable venues for the action.

Held, dismissing the appeal, that (1) *Spiliada* explained; had been concerned with forum issues only in a very general sense whereas the line of authority commencing with *Albaforth* considered; was well established, and (2) England was the most appropriate jurisdiction having regard to the fact that B had insignificant links with the United States and the fact that a judgment from a Russian court would not act to clear B's reputation in England.

BEREZOVSKY v. FORBES INC; GLOUCHKOV v. FORBES INC; *sub nom.* BEREZOVSKY v. MICHAELS; GLOUCHKOV v. MICHAELS [2000] 1 W.L.R. 1004, Lord Steyn, HL.

770. Choice of forum – limitations – foreign jurisdiction – statutory construction of English legislation and effect in Pakistan – court had discretion whether to test construction point in foreign court.

[Limitation Act 1980 s.14; Hague Rules; Hague Visby Rules.]

B's proceedings in the English court against P, a Pakistani shipping company, were stayed following P's waiver of reliance on the Hague Rules in favour of the Hague Visby Rules, which brought into effect an exclusive jurisdiction clause in favour of Pakistan. The court, finding that B had acted reasonably in the circumstances, had required an undertaking from P that it would not take issue with any limitation point upon commencement of proceedings in Pakistan. P subsequently indicated that it may be impossible to waive limitation by virtue of the Limitation Act 1980 s.14. B consequently applied for the stay to be lifted, but P contended that the limitation issue should be tried in Pakistan as it had complied with the term on which the stay was granted and the English court could not interfere.

Held, allowing the appeal, that the point arising under s.14 was a matter of statutory construction but it was in the discretion of the court whether the point ought to be tested in a foreign jurisdiction, *BMG Trading Ltd v. AS McKay Ltd* [1998] I.L.Pr. 691 considered. It was wrong to allow P to take a limitation defence and to force B to incur the expenditure and time of taking the matter to Pakistan, therefore the English action would be allowed to proceed.

BAGHLAF AL ZAFER FACTORY CO BR FOR INDUSTRY LTD v. PAKISTAN NATIONAL SHIPPING CO (NO.2) [2000] 1 Lloyd's Rep. 1, Waller, L.J., CA.

771. Choice of forum – patents – US patent infringement proceedings – English jurisdiction clause – effect of US proceedings in respect of lis alibi pendens

[Civil Jurisdiction and Judgments Act 1982 s.49; Brussels Convention on Jurisdiction and Enforcement of Judgments in Civil and Commercial Matters 1968.]

EL was a US company which manufactured and distributed human growth hormone (hGH) produced by recombinant DNA technology. NN was Danish company which manufactured and distributed pharmaceutical products. They entered into a licence agreement regarding certain patent rights held by NN whereby EL was granted a licence in respect of patent rights listed in a schedule to the agreement. NN subsequently brought an action claiming infringement of its patents in New Jersey. EL relied in its defence on the licence agreement which was governed by English law and gave jurisdiction to the English courts. EL made a claim in the English courts to rectify the licence to include the patent rights in the New Jersey proceedings. NN applied to set aside service of the writ for want of jurisdiction and to stay the English proceedings on the basis that by entering a defence and counterclaim in the New Jersey action, EL had waived its right to invoke the jurisdiction of the English courts as regards the licence agreement; and that New Jersey was the more appropriate forum. Those applications were refused and NN appealed.

Held, dismissing the appeal, that (1) the Brussels Convention 1968 was intended to deal with conflicts between contracting states. It did not apply to regulate jurisdictional issues between the courts of contracting states and courts of non contracting states, *Harrods (Buenos Aires) Ltd (No.1), Re* [1991] 4 All E.R. 334, [1991] C.L.Y. 476 applied; (2) the power to stay proceedings in England conferred by the Civil Jurisdictions and Judgments Act 1982 s.49 was unimpaired because it was not inconsistent with the Brussels Convention to conclude that the courts of New Jersey were the appropriate forum for the resolution of the dispute between the parties, and (3) the two claims were quite distinct and it could not be said that the New Jersey action gave rise to a lis alibi pendens; (4) it was important to take into account the parties' choice of court and in the circumstances of this case, England was the appropriate forum for the claim to rectify the licence.

ELI LILLY & CO v. NOVO NORDISK A/S (NO.1) [2000] I.L.Pr. 73, Morritt, L.J., CA.

772. Choice of forum – personal injury action – real and substantial connection to jurisdiction – Canada

C was working in Italy for an Italian company when he suffered an injury. C was a Canadian citizen and the parent company of the Italian company was based in Alberta. C brought his claim for damages in Alberta. The Canadian company contested jurisdiction.

Held, dismissing the claim, that, on the issue of forum non conveniens forum shopping is to be discouraged. Reliance on juridical advantage to a party is only relevant if there is a real and substantial connection to the jurisdiction in which the claim is to be brought. Here the claim had no real or substantial connection to the Alberta jurisdiction and the claim was more properly brought in Italy.

CORTESE v. NOWSCO WELL SERVICE LTD [1999] I.L.Pr. 767, Moore, C.J., QB (Alta).

773. Choice of forum – property rights – German creditor challenging German debtor's property transaction in France – appropriate forum

[Brussels Convention on Jurisdiction and the Enforcement of Judgments in Civil and Commercial Matters 1968 Art.16.]

R and his wife were domiciled in Germany and owed money to D. They owned property in France which they purported to transfer to their son by way of gift. D sought to challenge the transaction in the French court by an "action paulienne", a procedure available under French law whereby a creditor can challenge in his own name a transaction entered into in fraud of creditors' rights. The question arose whether the Brussels Convention 1968 Art.16 applied in its provision that courts of the contracting state in which the property is situated have exclusive jurisdiction.

Held, that Art.16 was to be construed as meaning that the exclusive jurisdiction of the contracting state in which the property is situated does not encompass all actions concerning rights in rem in immovable property but only those which both come within the scope of the Convention and are actions to decide the extent, content, ownership or possession of immovable property, or other rights in rem, and to provide holders of such rights with the protection of the powers attaching to their interest. The present action was based on D's personal claim against R, and did not require investigation of any rule or practice relating to the land as would justify conferring jurisdiction on the state where the property was situated. Accordingly such an action did not come within the scope of Art.16 and the French courts did not have jurisdiction to determine D's claim, *Sanders v. Van der Putte (C73/77)* [1977] E.C.R. 2383, [1978] C.L.Y. 1297 and *Rosler v. Rottwinkel (C241/83)* [1986] Q.B. 33, [1985] C.L.Y. 1357 considered.

REICHERT v. DRESDNER BANK (NO.1) (C115/88) [1990] I.L.Pr.105, Slynn P.C., ECJ.

774. Choice of forum – reinsurance contracts – domicile of plaintiff – Brussels Convention applied where defendant domiciled in contracting state – European Union

[Brussels Convention on Jurisdiction and Enforcement of Judgments in Civil and Commercial Matters 1968 Art.5(2), Art.8(2), Art.14(1); Brussels Convention on Jurisdiction and Enforcement of Judgments in Civil and Commercial Matters 1968 Title II.]

UG, a company incorporated in Canada, instructed its broker, E, a French company, to obtain a reinsurance contract in respect of UG's Canadian home occupiers' insurance policies. GJ, a Belgian reinsurance company, initially agreed to procure a share in the contract but later refused to pay on the ground that it had been induced to enter the contract on the basis of false information. UG commenced proceedings against GJ in France. GJ disputed the jurisdiction of the French court and the proceedings were stayed and the matter was referred to the ECJ for a preliminary ruling. GJ, relying on the Brussels Convention 1968 Title II, argued that, as it had its registered office in Belgium, only the Belgian courts had jurisdiction in the matter. UG contended that the provisions of the Convention applied only where the plaintiff was also domiciled within a contracting state. A further question for determination was whether the special rules, under Title II of the Convention, applicable to insurance also applied to reinsurance.

Held, that the jurisdiction rules contained in the Convention applied even where the plaintiff was domiciled in a non-signatory country. As long as the defendant was domiciled within a contracting state, the domicile of the plaintiff was generally not relevant. However, Art.5(2), Art.8(2) and Art.14(1) allowed, in certain exceptional cases, special preference to be given to the domicile of the plaintiff. However, this applied only where the plaintiff exercised an option under those Articles. Although special rules on jurisdiction applied by virtue of s.3 of Title II to certain insurance contracts, those rules had no application to reinsurance contracts. The purpose of s.3 was to protect the insured by providing a wider choice of jurisdiction. The insured would in most cases be in a weaker position and would not be in a position to negotiate the terms of the contract. However, such protection was not justified in the context of the relationship between a reinsurer and the reinsured.

UNIVERSAL GENERAL INSURANCE CO (UGIC) v. GROUP JOSI REINSURANCE CO SA (C412/98); *sub nom.* GROUP JOSI REINSURANCE CO SA v. COMPAGNIE D'ASSURANCES UNIVERSAL GENERAL INSURANCE CO (UGIC) (C412/98) [2001] Q.B. 68, JC Moitinho de Almeida (President), ECJ.

775. Choice of forum – representative actions – availability of legal aid – legal representation in South Africa unobtainable – matters of public interest and public policy irrelevant

L appealed against an order affirming the validity of a stay of a multi party personal injury claim instituted against C, the English parent company of a South African subsidiary involved in the manufacture of asbestos products. A writ had initially been issued by L and four other claimants in 1997. Following the granting of a stay on the basis of forum non conveniens, L appealed successfully ([1998] C.L.C. 1559, [1998] C.L.Y. 749). Subsequently writs were issued by further claimants so that the eventual number exceeded 3000. C applied to stay both actions on the basis of forum non conveniens and submitted that the claims were an abuse of process since the claimants in the first action had failed to disclose to the court their intention to launch a multi party action. The application having succeeded and been upheld on appeal ([2000] 1 Lloyd's Rep. 139), L contended that the proceedings should not be stayed since there (1) was no legal aid available in South Africa to fund such a claim; (2) was no prospect of arranging for legal representation on the basis of a contingency fee arrangement, and (3) were no other alternative sources of funding available in South Africa.

Held, allowing the appeal, that (1) whilst South Africa was the more appropriate forum, the strong probability that the claimants would be unable to obtain both the legal representation and the expert evidence required to substantiate their claims in South Africa would amount to a denial of justice, a conclusion that was reinforced by the lack of any established procedures to deal with multi party actions in South Africa, and (2) matters of public interest and public policy which had no relation to the private interests of any of the parties or to securing the ends of justice had no part to play in decisions concerning forum, *Spiliada Maritime Corp v. Cansulex Ltd (The Spiliada)* [1987] A.C. 460, [1987] C.L.Y. 3135 applied.

LUBBE v. CAPE PLC (NO.2); AFRIKA v. CAPE PLC [2000] 1 W.L.R. 1545, Lord Bingham of Cornhill, HL.

776. Choice of forum – shipping dispute – application for stay of proceedings – effect of Belgian court's ruling

[Brussels Convention on Jurisdiction and Enforcement of Judgments in Civil and Commercial Matters 1968 Art.21, Art.22.]

NE contracted with the charterer of a vessel owned by WM to supply bunker to the vessel. M entered into a similar contract with another charterer in relation to the vessel. NE and M caused the vessel to be arrested following the charterers' failure to pay for the bunker, but released it from arrest upon the provision of guarantees by WM. In June 1998 WM began proceedings in Belgium seeking to have the arrest set aside and the letters of guarantee returned. WM also issued proceedings in England, service of the writs on NE and M being effected in January 1999. WM alleged that it had reached an agreement with both NE and M that the vessel would not be arrested and claimed damages in respect of the costs of issuing the guarantees, its liabilities to the charterers and the amount which they might have to pay under the guarantees. NE and M applied to stay the proceedings in England. Prior to the hearing, the Judge of Arrest in Belgium held that NE had not renounced its right to arrest the vessel and that it had been entitled to arrest it. WM opposed the application for a stay, arguing that (1) the ruling of the Judge of Arrest had concerned the merits of the claim and accordingly under Belgian law it would not be binding on the judge who would later determine the merits of the claim with the result that the Brussels Convention 1968 Art.21 and Art.22, which concerned the staying of proceedings by the court of a contracting state where related proceedings had already been issued in a different contracting state, did not apply, and (2) in any event, since the proceedings in England involved a claim for damages and the proceedings in Belgium did not do so, the two actions did not involve the same cause of action for the purpose of Art.21.

Held, granting the application, that (1) it was necessary to decide whether the action before the Judge of Arrest had been determinative of the relevant issue, namely whether NE and M had renounced their right of arrest. Since that issue concerned the validity of the arrest rather than the merits of the claim, the ruling of the Judge of Arrest had been determinative under Belgian law and Art.21 and Art.22 could apply; (2) the actions in England and Belgium involved the same cause of action for the purpose of Art.21. The rule of law relied on, namely whether NE and M had contracted out of their right to arrest the vessel, together with the facts raised in the two actions were the same. Furthermore, the two actions had the same end in view despite the fact that there were differences in the relief claimed, such relief being merely consequential to the determination of the crucial issue, *Owners of Cargo Lately Laden on Board the Tatry v. Owners of the Maciej Rataj (The Maciej Rataj) (C406/92)* [1999] Q.B. 515, [1995] C.L.Y. 704 applied. In the circumstances, Art.21 applied and the action in England would be stayed, and (3) it would, in any event, have been appropriate to stay the proceedings under Art.22. It was unclear whether the court should decide whether to grant a stay under Art.22 by reference to the date when the application was made or the date when judgment was given. NE had filed its application before the Judge of Arrest had made his ruling. Were it necessary to consider granting a stay by reference to the date of the filing of the application, the grant of a stay would have been appropriate since the two actions involved the same issue and that issue was closely related to Belgian law. Were it necessary to consider granting a stay at the present stage, it would have been appropriate for the court to decline to exercise jurisdiction since the court in Belgium had jurisdiction in respect of both actions and the power to consolidate them. The action in Belgium against M being still pending, it would, if necessary, have been appropriate for the court to stay the action in England. The Belgian courts were more familiar with the right of arrest that had arisen in the case, the action in Belgium was well under way, and, in addition, the Belgian court would be familiar with the case against NE, which had been treated as the lead action.

WINTER MARITIME LTD v. NORTH END OIL LTD (THE WINTER); WINTER MARITIME LTD v. MARITIME OIL TRADING LTD [2000] 2 Lloyd's Rep. 298, Thomas, J., QBD.

777. **Choice of law – insurance contacts – notice of assignment – bailiff service required under French law – marine insurance policy validly assigned – service governed by English law**

[Marine Insurance Act 1906 s.50(2); Rome Convention on the law applicable to contractual obligations 1980 Art.12(2).]

R sought a declaration that a notice of assignment of a marine insurance policy had been validly served on French insurers notwithstanding a requirement under French law for bailiff service. The French insurers contended that the assignment was governed by French law and was invalid as it had not been served according to the French formalities.

Held, granting the declaration, that under the Rome Convention Art.12(2) the question of whether the assignment was governed by English or French law was determined by the law of the substantive obligation. As the insured and the insurers had agreed that the insurance contract should be governed by English law, the policy was freely assignable under the Marine Insurance Act 1906 s.50(2) and English law prescribed no formalities on the service of a notice of assignment, *Macmillan Inc v. Bishopsgate Investment Trust Plc (No.3)* [1996] 1 W.L.R. 387, [1995] C.L.Y. 693 applied and *Maudslay Sons & Field, Re* [1900] 1 Ch. 602 disapproved, following the incorporation of the Rome Convention.

RAIFFEISEN ZENTRALBANK OSTERREICH AG v. FIVE STAR GENERAL TRADING LLC (THE MOUNT I) [2000] 1 All E.R. (Comm) 897, Longmore, J., QBD (Comm Ct).

778. Declaratory judgments – forum shopping – negative declarations appropriate in domestic law – joinder inappropriate on facts – not applicable exception under Brussels Convention

[Brussels Convention on Jurisdiction and the Enforcement of Judgments in Civil and Commercial Matters 1968 Art.6.1, Art.22.]

MD designed and manufactured aircraft landing gear under an English law contract with BAA on behalf of A who had supplied an aircraft to S, a Belgian company. Following the collapse of the landing gear on S's aircraft, MD began proceedings for a declaration that it was not liable to S. S was successful in having service set aside on the grounds that (1) a negative declaration was inappropriate, and (2) the proceedings did not fall under any exception to the Brussels Convention 1968 and therefore the English court had no jurisdiction. MD appealed, arguing that the joinder of S was desirable in order to determine all the relevant issues in one forum under Art 6.1.

Held, dismissing the appeal, that (1) although the negative declaration procedure was acceptable where it was useful, the overall situation, in particular the subsequent issue by S of proceedings in France against the aircraft manufacturer, militated against the joinder of S in the English proceedings, and (2) Art.6 had to be read in conjunction with Art.22 and could not be relied on by MD since S had not issued proceedings against it.

MESSIER DOWTY LTD v. SABENA SA (APPEAL AGAINST SET ASIDE) [2000] 1 W.L.R. 2040, Lord Woolf, M.R., CA.

779. Divorce – foreign jurisdiction – validity of divorce

See FAMILY LAW: Kellman v. Kellman. §2501

780. Foreign judgemnts – injunction granted by foreign court did not afford a defence to claim for breach of confidence – foreign court not court of place of performance – injunction did not have extraterritorial effect

F was the owner of two funds administered for him by HI, the fund managers. The contract between F and HI was governed by English law and was subject to the jurisdiction of the English court. HI owed F a duty to dispose of the funds in accordance with F's instructions within, at the latest, a reasonable time from the receipt of those instructions, and not to disclose any information about the funds to a third party without a lawful excuse. In matrimonial proceedings commenced against F by his wife in Virginia, injunctive relief was granted restraining F's disposal of one of the funds (but not the other). Subsequent to the making of that order, F instructed HI to sell both funds and remit the proceeds to the Bahamas. HI told the US attorneys for F's wife of these instructions and F's wife applied for and was granted a freezing injunction in England in respect of both funds. F brought proceedings for damages against HI alleging breach of the duty of confidentiality, in the absence of a lawful excuse by disclosing F's instructions to liquidate the funds. HI denied any such breach and applied to strike out F's action. On the application to strike out, the court was required to determine, as a matter of law, whether an injunction granted by a foreign court of which HI had notice afforded a defence to the claim of breach of the duty of confidentiality, where the foreign court was neither the court of the place of performance of the contract, nor the court of the proper law of the contract.

Held, refusing the application, that F's claim would not be struck out because: (1) F had an arguable case regarding breach of confidentiality; (2) it was arguable that if HI had obeyed F's instructions to liquidate the funds within a reasonable time, it would not have been caught by the English freezing orders, and it was therefore also arguable that HI's failure to comply in time with F's instructions had caused the funds to be lost to F; (3) the question of whether F's claim for the costs incurred by him in applying to vary or discharge the freezing orders was reasonable could not be determined on a strike out application; (4) it was highly arguable that unless and until F's wife obtained an order in England, HI was bound if so instructed by F to ignore the order of the Virginia court.

Performance of F's instructions would not have been illegal under English law, since the performance of the instructions would have occurred in England and the funds then remitted to a neutral jurisdiction, *Libyan Arab Foreign Bank v. Bankers Trust Co* [1989] Q.B. 728, [1989] C.L.Y. 376 considered, and (5) the contention that F's claim was bad in law since the performance of F's instructions by HI involved a breach of the Virginia court order, was wrong. To hold otherwise would be to give the Virginia court order an extraterritorial effect which the English court did not claim for its own orders.

FOX v. HENDERSON INVESTMENT FUND LTD [1999] 2 Lloyd's Rep. 303, Timothy Walker, J., QBD (Comm Ct).

781. **Foreign judgments – enforcement – default judgment – irregularities in service not amounting to denial of natural justice – Canada**

YS obtained a default judgment in Helsinki after R defaulted on a loan. There was a clause in the loan agreement conferring jurisdiction on the Helsinki courts in the event of any disputes. Substituted service had been allowed but it subsequently transpired that R's address was readily available and that the correct procedure should have been to effect personal service. YS applied for an order recognising, registering and enforcing the judgment in Ontario where R lived. R said that the judgment should not be recognised for lack of natural justice. The Ontario court was also asked to adjudicate on quantum on the ground that YS had violated Finnish law by converting the loan agreement denominated in foreign currency to an agreement for payment of Finnish currency. R was eventually personally served with the judgment but took no action on his right to a hearing.

Held, granting the application, that (1) the three conditions for enforcement of a foreign judgment, namely jurisdiction of the foreign court over the subject matter of the judgment; finality of the judgment; and the definitiveness of the sum of money involved, had all been satisfied; (2) the only question was whether the process followed by the foreign court represented a denial of natural justice; (3) mere irregularities in prescribed procedure alone did not amount to a denial of natural justice, *Monaco (Principality) v. Project Planning Associates (International) Ltd* (1980) 32 O.R. (2d) 438 (Div.Ct.) applied; (4) in this case any suggestion of a denial of natural justice was effectively resolved when the Finnish court served R personally with the judgment and gave him the opportunity to reopen the matter. The right to have the case retried was more extensive in scope than a right of appeal, which was generally limited to points of law and unreasonable findings of fact, and (5) the court could not consider the merits of the case upon which the foreign judgment was based since errors of judgment, in fact or law, could not be considered in adjudicating on the recognition or enforcement of foreign judgments.

YRITYSPANKKI SKOP OYJ v. REINIKKA [2000] I.L.Pr.122, Pitt, J., CJ (Gen Div) (Ont).

782. **Foreign judgments – enforcement – enforcement of French judgment in Italy – European Union**

[Brussels Convention on Jurisdiction and Enforcement of Judgments in Civil and Commercial Matters 1968 Art.27(1).]

A manufacturer of motor vehicles, R, obtained judgment in an action for fraud against M who had manufactured and marketed body parts for Renault vehicles. R subsequently sought to enforce the judgment in Italy. M contended that the judgment was contrary to Italian public policy because Italy did not acknowledge the existence of property rights in car spares and the judgment was therefore unenforceable by virtue of the Brussels Convention 1968 Art.27(1). M contended that the principles of Community law and especially the right to free movement of goods and freedom of competition were in line with the Italian viewpoint and that the French court had erred in its approach.

Held, giving a preliminary ruling in favour of R, that Art. 27(1) was to be interpreted strictly and in order to invoke its effect there would have to exist a manifest breach of a rule of law viewed as essential or a right acknowledged as fundamental in the legal order of the state in question. On the facts of the instant case an error in the application of Community law was alleged which did not constitute the kind of manifest breach of a rule of law required for the operation of Art.27(1), *Krombach v. Bamberski (C7/98) The Times*, March 30, 2000, [2000] C.L.Y. 784 applied.

REGIE NATIONALE DES USINES RENAULT SA v. MAXICAR SpA (C38/98) [2000] E.C.D.R. 415, DAO Edward (President), ECJ (5th Chamber).

783. **Foreign judgments – enforcement – limitations – registration of judgments – reciprocal recognition between Canada and United Kingdom – Canada**

[Canada and United Kingdom Reciprocal Recognition and Enforcement of Judgments Act 1989 (Nova Scotia) Art.3(1).]

The Canada and United Kingdom Reciprocal Recognition and Enforcement of Judgments Act 1989 (Nova Scotia) Art.3(1) required that an application for registration of a UK judgment within Nova Scotia must be made within six years of the date of the judgment. D applied in 1999 for registration in Nova Scotia of a judgment obtained in England in 1992. For factual reasons, however, the order in the English action had not been concluded until 1997.

Held, allowing registration, that (1) the six-year limitation period under the Act did not commence until the judgment became enforceable in its state of origin. Therefore the starting point for the limitation period within which the application for registration must be made was not the date of the judgment but was the date it became enforceable in England, which was in 1997, and (2) as a pre-condition to registration, the Nova Scotia court registering the foreign judgment must be satisfied that the foreign court had jurisdiction over the litigation and over the matter that led to the judgment. In determining that issue the appropriate test was whether there was a real and substantial connection with the foreign jurisdiction, *Morguard Investments Ltd v. De Savoye* [1990] 3 S.C.R. 1077 applied.

DAVID & SNAPE v. SAMPSON [2000] I.L.Pr. 474, Joseph, P., Sup Ct (NS).

784. **Foreign judgments – enforcement – refusal to enforce foreign judgment on public policy grounds – foreign judgments – failure to follow jurisdictional rules – denial of right to present defence – European Union**

[Brussels Convention on Jurisdiction and Enforcement of Judgments in Civil and Commercial Matters 1968 Art.3, Art.27, Art.28.]

K was convicted of the involuntary manslaughter of B's daughter, a French national at the time of her death, and B sought to enforce a parallel civil judgment requiring K to pay damages in respect of the death. B, a German national, wished to enforce the judgment in his national court but it was contended that the French court had infringed the Brussels Convention 1968 Art.3 by basing its jurisdiction to commit K for trial in Paris on the nationality of B's daughter. It was further contended that the refusal to allow K to have his defence presented on his behalf in his absence was also an infringement of the Convention and for those reasons, the German court could refuse enforcement of the French civil claim on the grounds of public policy as provided for under Art.27 of the Convention. The German court referred to the ECJ the question of whether the infringements of the Convention justified that refusal.

Held, that enforcement could be refused on the second ground since the right to be defended was a fundamental element of the right to a fair trial but it could not be refused solely on the court's failure to comply with the rules relating to jurisdiction under the Convention. Article 27 of the Convention constituted an obstacle to the objective of enabling individuals to enforce judgments in whatever jurisdiction they chose by providing a simple and quick enforcement procedure, thus it had to be interpreted strictly and it would only be in exceptional cases that a court could have recourse to the public policy clause in Art.27. It was clear from the principles set out in Art.28 that the public policy test could not be applied to jurisdictional rules of the state in which enforcement was sought, even if the jurisdiction was incorrectly founded. However, depriving an individual of the right to have his defence presented in his absence constituted a fundamental breach of the right to a fair trial, an essential element of the legal order of the state, which had been enshrined in constitutional traditions common to all Member States and Art.27 could therefore be relied on.

KROMBACH v. BAMBERSKI (C7/98) *The Times*, March 30, 2000, GC Rodriguez Iglesias (President), ECJ.

785. **Foreign judgments – estoppel – Californian judgment precluding co-defendant from proceeding against another for contribution and indemnity subsequently in England – failure to establish estoppel or abuse of process**

[Code of Civil Procedure (California) s.877.6.]

B, a representative member of a Lloyd's syndicate, instituted proceedings in England in conjunction with eleven other syndicates against a firm of Lloyd's brokers, IMI. B claimed damages for deceit and an indemnity in relation to misrepresentations made by a broker employed by IMI who procured the issue of a formal policy of insurance by deception. The employee had sold 90% of the policy's risk only after a claim on the policy had been made although cover was expressed to predate the loss. The policy was issued to JAG, an American company. Proceedings were initiated in a Californian court after JAG sought to claim on its policy. Following mediation, JAG agreed to terms with all the defendants involved in the Californian proceedings except IMI. B and the other claimants made it clear that it was their intention to sue IMI in England. IMI settled JAG's claim against it subject to a declaration under the Code of Civil Procedure (California) s.877.6 that the settlement had been made in good faith. A declaration was made pursuant to the code which stated that all future claims by tortfeasors relating to the issues decided upon were barred. IMI contended that the effect of the Californian declaration was to bar claimants from pursuing any claims in the English courts. IMI also argued that the Californian decision gave rise to an estoppel per rem judicatam. Finally, IMI contended, the claimants should have made their claims in the Californian proceedings and therefore pursuit of the claim in England would constitute an abuse of process under the principle in *Henderson v. Henderson* [1843-60] All E.R. Rep. 378.

Held, determining the preliminary issue in favour of the claimants, that, (1) There was no judicial investigation of the merits of B's potential claim by the Californian judge invited to approve the settlement between JAG and IMI, and therefore there was no judicial determination of that issue capable of giving raise to a cause of action estoppel. Even if B had endeavoured to raise the issue, the Californian court would have refused to entertain it. Approval of a settlement involved an assessment of whether that settlement was within a reasonable range of the settlor's total proportional liability having due regard to any potential obligation to indemnify a co-defendant. That was not the same as determining that such a codefendant had a right to an indemnity. So far as procedural issue estoppel was concerned, the Californian court had never been seized of any substantive claim by B against IMI. B's appearance before the Californian court was limited to submissions that the court should not debar B from proceeding with their prospective claim against IMI in England; (2) There was no evidence to support the suggestion that the procedural bar created by s.877.6(c) was intended to have effect outside the jurisdiction, and (3) It would require a significant extension of the principle in *Henderson* to hold that where a claimant sues two or more defendants, any attempt by a defendant to bring a claim they may have for contribution or indemnity against another co-defendant at any time other than during the currency of those proceedings would amount to an abuse of process. There might well be numerous reasons why a defendant would opt to wait for the outcome of the substantive claim against him before launching contribution proceedings, and accordingly there was no abuse on the facts of the instant case, *DSV Silo und Verwaltungsgesellschaft mbH v. Owners of The Sennar (The Sennar) (No.2)* [1985] 1 W.L.R. 490, [1985] C.L.Y. 1291, *Carl Zeiss Stiftung v. Rayner & Keeler Ltd (Authority to Institute Proceedings: Issue*

Estoppel) [1967] 1 A.C. 853, [1966] C.L.Y. 1665, *Desert Sun Loan Corp v. Hill* [1996] 2 All E.R. 847, [1996] C.L.Y. 1102 and *Henderson* considered.
BAKER v. IAN MCCALL INTERNATIONAL LTD [2000] C.L.C. 189, Toulson, J., QBD (Comm Ct).

786. **Injunctions – anti suit injunctions – arbitration – London arbitration clause contained in contract governed by United States law – correct forum for claim;**

[Arbitration Act 1996 s.30.]
XL applied for an order to restrain OC, a Delaware corporation, from pursuing an insurance claim in Delaware, USA or any forum other than arbitration in London. XL contended that by pursuing the claim outside London, OC would be in contravention of an arbitration clause contained in the policy which stated that any dispute was to be finally determined in London, and would therefore be in breach of contract. OC argued that the policy itself, including the putative arbitration clause, was governed by New York State law under which the arbitration clause would not be recognised as enforceable in the absence of a signed written agreement containing such clause.
Held, granting the injunction, that the combined effect of the arbitration clause and the choice of law clause meant that whilst the substantive rights and obligations of the parties were governed by New York law, English law was the proper law of the arbitration agreement. It was clear that an arbitration agreement existed in English law. Whether the clause itself was valid and enforceable should be determined by the arbitral tribunal under the Arbitration Act 1996 s.30. By proceeding with any claim in the USA, OC was therefore in breach of contract and exposing XL to manifestly unjust litigation. An antisuit injunction was granted pending the tribunal ruling.
XL INSURANCE LTD v. OWENS CORNING [2001] 1 All E.R. (Comm) 530, Toulson, J., QBD (Comm Ct).

787. **Judgments and orders – revision of Brussels and Lugano Conventions**

CIVIL JURISDICTION AND JUDGMENTS ACT 1982 (AMENDMENT) ORDER 2000, SI 2000 1824; made under the Civil Jurisdiction and Judgments Act 1982 s.14. In force: in accordance with Art.1; £4.50.
This Order amends the Civil Jurisdiction and Judgments Act 1982 in consequence of a revision of the 1968 Convention on Jurisdiction and the Enforcement of Judgments in Civil and Commercial Matters (Brussels Convention), the 1971 Protocol on the Interpretation of the Convention by the Court of Justice of the European Communities and of the Lugano Convention.

788. **Jurisdiction – breach of trust – beneficiary resident in British Columbia – trust established and managed in Switzerland – Canada**

[Rules of the Supreme Court (British Columbia) r.13(10), r.14(6).]
G, a Swiss lawyer, had represented S and his associates in certain international monetary transactions as the result of which G held share certificates on trust for S in Switzerland, along with the proceeds of bank accounts in Ireland and Guernsey. Following embezzlement and money laundering charges brought against S in Thailand, G refused to deal with any of the assets and advised S that the trust had been frozen as part of the investigation. S accepted this situation, but contended that his agreement created a new trust on which he could sue. Subsequently, S demanded the return of all the assets, but G refused as the Swiss asset freezing measures still applied. S commenced proceedings for breach of trust in British Columbia, where he was resident pending the outcome of Thai extradition proceedings. G applied under the Rules of the Supreme Court (British Columbia) r.13(10) for an order setting aside service of the writ of summons

issued by S in Switzerland and a declaration under r.14(6)(c) that the Supreme Court of British Columbia either lacked or declined jurisdiction.

Held, granting the application, that any breach of trust by G, due to his failure to act on S's instructions, had not occurred in British Columbia. The trust was sited in Switzerland where the trust agreement had been made and implemented. S's residence in British Columbia was insufficient to create the necessary connection to establish jurisdiction there.

SAXENA v. GLOOR [2000] I.L.Pr. 534, Low, J., Sup Ct (BC).

789. **Jurisdiction – disclosure – documents held in France – breach of French law**

See CIVIL EVIDENCE: Morris v. Banque Arabe et Internationale d'Investissement SA (No.1). §315

790. **Jurisdiction – foreign judgments – forfeiture proceedings were a civil matter and within Brussels Convention**

[Trade Descriptions Act 1968 s.1(1)(6); Civil Jurisdiction and Judgments Act 1982; Trade Marks Act 1994 s.92(1), s.97; Brussels Convention on Jurisdiction and Enforcement of Judgments in Civil and Commercial Matters 1968 Art.1.]

UCS, a French wholesaler, which had successfully defended French actions for infringement of trade mark and forfeiture in relation to a consignment of jeans, contracted to sell the jeans to K, as a result of which they were exported to England. BH, local authority brought proceedings against K, at the instigation of LS, the trademark proprietor, for offences contrary to the Trade Marks Act 1994 s.92(1) and the Trade Descriptions Act 1968 s.1(1)(6) and a forfeiture order was granted by the magistrates court. UC appealed to the Crown Court, submitting that, the French judgments having been registered in England, the magistrates court had no civil jurisdiction to make the forfeiture order. The order was upheld, the Crown Court finding that the magistrates had been entitled to make it under their criminal jurisdiction. UC applied for judicial review of the decision, arguing that the proceedings were civil within the meaning of the Brussels Convention 1968 Art.1 and the Civil Jurisdiction and Judgments Act 1982, hence the French judgments had to be recognised by the English courts. BH submitted that the proceedings were either administrative or criminal in nature and were outside the scope of the Convention.

Held, allowing the application, that the forfeiture proceedings brought under s.97 of the 1994 Act, and any appeal by an aggrieved person to the Crown Court against an order made under that section, were civil proceedings to which the Convention applied. Forfeiture had no specific public authority character and a local authority, whilst under a duty to prosecute, was under no duty to bring forfeiture proceedings. The relief gained from such proceedings fell to the general interests of private individuals, *Lufttransportunternehmen GmbH & Co KG v. Organisation Europeenne pour la Securite de la Navigation Aerienne (Eurocontrol) (C29/76)* [1976] E.C.R. 1541, [1977] C.L.Y. 1282 and *Netherlands v. Ruffer (C814/79)* [1980] E.C.R. 3807, [1981] C.L.Y. 1037 distinguished.

R. v. HARROW CROWN COURT, *ex p.* UNIC CENTRE SARL; *sub nom.* UNIC CENTRE SARL v. BRENT AND HARROW TRADING STANDARDS SERVICE; UNIC CENTRE SARL v. HARROW CROWN COURT [2000] 1 W.L.R. 2112, Newman, J., QBD.

791. **Reinsurance contracts – implied choice of law – applicability of Rome Convention**

See INSURANCE: Tiernan v. Magen Insurance Co Ltd. §3516

792. **Publications**

Dine, Janet – Governance of Corporate Groups. Cambridge Studies in Corporate Law, 1. Hardback: £37.50. ISBN 0-521-66070-X. Cambridge University Press.

Hoecke, Mark van; Ost, Francois – Harmonisation of European Private Law. Hardback: £25.00. ISBN 1-84113-137-7. Hart Publishing.

Kaye, Peter – Procedures to Enforce Foreign Judgments. Association Of European Lawyers. Hardback: £50.00. ISBN 0-7546-2010-7. Ashgate Publishing Limited.

McClean, J.D. – Morris: the Conflict of Laws. 5th Ed. Paperback: £32.00. ISBN 0-421-66160-7. Sweet & Maxwell.

Panagopoulos, George – Restitution in Private International Law. Hardback: £40.00. ISBN 1-84113-142-3. Hart Publishing.

Potok, Richard – Cross Border Collateral: Legal Risk and the Conflict of Laws. Hardback: £85.00. ISBN 0-406-92941-6. Butterworths.

Takahashi, Koji – Claims for Contribution and Reimbursement in an International Context: Conflict of Laws Dimension of Third Party Procedure. Oxford Monographs in Private International Law. Hardback: £65.00. ISBN 0-19-826896-3. Oxford University Press.

Zimmermann, Reinhard; Whittaker, Simon – Good Faith in European Contract Law: the Common Core of European Private Law. Cambridge Studies in International and Comparative Law, 14. Hardback: £75.00. ISBN 0-521-77190-0. Cambridge University Press.

CONSTITUTIONAL LAW

793. British Virgin Islands – constitution

VIRGIN ISLANDS (CONSTITUTION) (AMENDMENT) ORDER 2000, SI 2000 1343; made under the West Indies Act 1962 s.5, s.7. In force: on a day or days to be appointed under Art.1 (4); £2.00.

This Order amends the Constitution of the Virgin Islands by making provision to revise the definition of persons deemed to belong to the Virgin Islands; defines the functions of the Deputy Governor; permits the number of Ministers to be increased to five; for the sittings of the Legislative Council; for a public register of interests and for a Complaints Commissioner; and for matters relating to the powers of the Governor, the quorum of the Executive Council, Legislative Council disqualifications, the election of the Speaker and the Public Service.

794. Disqualifications Act 2000 (c.42)

This Act removes the disqualification for membership of the House of Commons and the Northern Ireland Assembly of person who are members of the legislature of Ireland (the Oireachtas); disqualifies for certain offices which may be held by members of the Northern Ireland Assembly persons who are or become Ministers of the Government of Ireland or chairmen or deputy chairmen of committees of the Oireachtas; and makes provision with respect to who may be chairman or deputy chairman of a statutory committee of the Assembly or a member of the Northern Ireland Assembly Commission.

This Act received Royal Assent on November 30, 2000 and comes into force on November 30, 2000.

795. Montserrat – Legislative Council

MONTSERRAT CONSTITUTION (AMENDMENT) ORDER 2000, SI 2000 1339; made under the West Indies Act 1962 s.5, s.7. In force: on a day or days to be appointed under Art.1 (4); £1.50.

This Order amends the Constitution of Montserrat by abolishing the office of nominated member of the Legislative Council, increasing the number of elected members of the Council to nine, and increasing to three years the residence qualification for elected membership of the Council.

796. National Assembly for Wales – transfer of functions

NATIONAL ASSEMBLY FOR WALES (TRANSFER OF FUNCTIONS) ORDER 2000, SI 2000 253 (W.5); made under the Government of Wales Act 1998 s.22, s.24, s.42, s.151, Sch.3 para.1, Sch.3 para.3, Sch.3 para.9. In force: in accordance with Art.1 (2); £3.00.

This Order provides for the exercise by the National Assembly for Wales of certain statutory functions currently vested in Ministers of the Crown. All functions are vested in the Assembly for exercise in relation to Wales.

797. Official secrets – breach of contract – entitlement to profits from book

[Official Secrets Act 1911.]

B, a former member of the Secret Intelligence Services, SIS, who later became a Soviet agent, appealed against a decision ([1998] Ch. 439, [1998] C.L.Y. 779), that all profits derived from a book about the British secret service, including those to which he was entitled but had not yet received, be paid over to the Crown. B was employed by the SIS in 1944, and, in his contract of employment, signed an Official Secrets Act declaration not to disclose any information, in any form, about his work in the secret service. This contractual undertaking also applied after employment had ceased. B subsequently became a Soviet agent, for which he was imprisoned, but he later escaped to the Soviet Union. In 1989, B wrote the book concerned and entered into an agreement with an UK publisher. The book contained information that was no longer confidential. He received some advance payments and was entitled to more. The Crown claimed whatever amount was owing to B, who appealed the grant of an injunction preventing him from receiving any further payments from his publishers. The Attorney-General cross appealed, arguing that B had committed a breach of contract and that the restitutionary principle should apply to enable the Crown to recover any profits to which B was entitled.

Held, dismissing the appeal and allowing the cross appeal, that in exceptional cases, where normal remedies were inadequate to compensate for breach of contract, it was open to the court to order that the defendant account for all profits either received or to which he is entitled. This was an exceptional case in that the work of the secret service depends on the confidentiality of information. B had been responsible for harming the public interest by breaches of his undertaking not to divulge information. Publication of the book was a further breach of that undertaking, even though the information contained in it was no longer secret. However, it was noted that the disclosure of non-confidential information was also a criminal offence under the Official Secrets Act 1911. An absolute rule against disclosure was necessary in order to ensure that members of the secret services are able to deal with each other in complete confidence. B was able to capitalise on his notoriety as a Soviet agent and would not have been able to command such high royalties. The Crown therefore had a legitimate interest in ensuring that B did not benefit from revealing state information in breach of contract. However, as normal contractual remedies of damages, specific performance and injunction would not meet that objective, the publishers should be ordered to pay over to the Crown any amount still owing to B.

ATTORNEY GENERAL v. BLAKE [2001] 1 A.C. 268, Lord Nicholls of Birkenhead, HL.

798. Pitcairn Islands – Court of Appeal

PITCAIRN COURT OF APPEAL ORDER 2000, SI 2000 1341; made under the British Settlements Act 1887; and the British Settlements Act 1945. In force: June 15, 2000; £1.50.

This Order makes provision for the constitution of the Court of Appeal for the Pitcairn Islands, its jurisdiction and for the hearing and determination of appeals.

799. Pitcairn Islands – Court of Appeal – appeals to Privy Council

PITCAIRN (APPEALS TO PRIVY COUNCIL) ORDER 2000, SI 2000 1816; made under the Judicial Committee Act 1844 s.1. In force: August 14, 2000; £2.00.

This Order regulates appeals from judgments of the Pitcairn Court of Appeal to Her Majesty in Council by prescribing the conditions under which such appeals may be brought and the procedure which must be followed.

800. Pitcairn Islands – courts and judicial authorities

PITCAIRN (AMENDMENT) ORDER 2000, SI 2000 1340; made under the British Settlements Act 1887; and the British Settlements Act 1945. In force: June 15, 2000; £1.00.

This Order amends the Pitcairn Order 1970 (SI 1970 1434) so as to authorise courts and judicial authorities established for Pitcairn under that Order to function either in Pitcairn or in the United Kingdom or, in certain circumstances, in some other part of Her Majesty's dominions.

801. Welsh Assembly – Secretary of State for Wales – transfer of property

NATIONAL ASSEMBLY FOR WALES (TRANSFER OF PROPERTY ETC.) ORDER 2000, SI 2000 991; made under the Government of Wales Act 1998 s.25. In force: March 31, 2000; £1.50.

This Order provides for the transfer by the Secretary of State for Wales to the National Assembly of Wales all his property, rights and liabilities in respect of any of his functions which he can exercise concurrently with the Assembly by virtue of the National Assembly for Wales (Transfer of Functions) Order 1999 (SI 1999 672) Art.2(b)(c), Art.3 and Sch.1 and the National Assembly for Wales (Transfer of Functions) Order 2000 (SI 2000 253) Art.2(2)(3), Art.8 and Sch.1. It exempts from the transfer any records of the Secretary and any rights and liabilities he has in relation to the Assembly as his agent under the arrangement entered into by them under the Government of Wales Act 1998 s.41 in respect of the functions that he can exercise concurrently with the Assembly.

802. Welsh Assembly – statutory functions

NATIONAL ASSEMBLY FOR WALES (TRANSFER OF FUNCTIONS) (VARIATION) ORDER 2000, SI 2000 1829; made under the Government of Wales Act 1998 s.22. In force: August 1, 2000; £1.00.

The Order varies the National Assembly for Wales (Transfer of Functions) Order 1999 (SI 1999 672) by substituting a new entry for the Education Reform Act 1988. The effect of the variation is that the functions in that Act under s.218(6) and (6ZA), relating to the power to make regulations for prohibiting or restricting the employment of persons as teachers on medical or educational grounds and cases of misconduct, are, in relation to Wales, exercisable by both the National Assembly for Wales and the Secretary of State.

803. Welsh Assembly – statutory functions – subordinate legislation

NATIONAL ASSEMBLY FOR WALES (TRANSFER OF FUNCTIONS) (NO.2) ORDER 2000, SI 2000 1830; made under the Government of Wales Act 1998 s.22. In force: October 2, 2000; £1.00.

The Order provides that where a court is considering making a declaration of incompatibility under the Human Rights Act 1998 s.4 in relation to subordinate legislation made by the National Assembly for Wales, or made by a Minister of the Crown under a power that is also exercisable by the National Assembly, the National Assembly as well as the Minister of the Crown will be entitled under s.5(2) of that Act to be joined as a party to those court proceedings.

804. Publications

Banks, Ronald – Rights: You Pay the Bill. Paperback: £7.95. ISBN 1-901647-09-9. Othila Press.

Barnett, Hilaire – Constitutional and Administrative Law. 3rd Ed. Paperback: £27.95. ISBN 1-85941-552-0. Cavendish Publishing Ltd.

Ben-Dor, Oren – Constitutional Limits and the Public Sphere. Hardback: £35.00. ISBN 1-84113-111-3. Hart Publishing.

Herling, David – Constitutional and Administrative Law. 3rd Ed. Briefcase Series. Paperback: £10.95. ISBN 1-85941-537-7. Cavendish Publishing Ltd.

Jowell, Jeffrey; Oliver, Dawn – Changing Constitution. 4th Ed. Paperback: £22.99. ISBN 0-19-876573-8. Oxford University Press.

Klug, Heinz – Constituting Democracy: Law Gobalisation and South Africa's Political Reconstruction. Cambridge Studies in Law and Society. Hardback: £40.00. ISBN 0-521-78113-2. Paperback: £14.95. ISBN 0-521-78643-6. Cambridge University Press.

Loveland, Ian – Constitutional Law-a Critical Introduction. 2nd Ed. Paperback: £24.95. ISBN 0-406-91596-2. Butterworths Law.

Loveland, Ian D. – Constitutional Law. International Library of Essays in Law and Legal Theory (second Series). Hardback: £100.00. ISBN 0-7546-2066-2. Hardback: £99.50. ISBN 0-7546-2066-2. Dartmouth.

Parpworth, Neil – Constitutional and Administrative Law. Paperback: £12.95. ISBN 0-406-98588-X. Butterworths.

Sampford, Charles – Dare to Call It Treason. Applied Legal Philosophy. Hardback: £40.00. ISBN 1-85521-265-X. Ashgate Publishing Limited.

CONSTRUCTION LAW

805. Adjudication – building and engineering contracts – disputed payments – determination of final account

S engaged C as subcontractor under a contract incorporating DOM/2, with adjudication under the Technology and Construction Solicitors' Association Rules. Disputes arose out of C's final invoice and a letter of notice to seek adjudication was served highlighting four main issues. The adjudicator found in C's favour and that C was entitled to recover certain sums with payment in seven days. S issued a payment notice, indicating that it had interpreted the adjudicator's decision as an indication of the way in which some of the sums in issue were to be treated in a final account, arriving at a final figure of £22,246. C sought summary judgment, contending that the decision required immediate payment of all outstanding sums and which exceeded the final figure arrived at by S.

Held, refusing the application, that, on a proper construction, C's letter referring the disputes to adjudication sought a decision on a number of items in the final account. Setting the decision in the context of the subcontract's provisions, the requirement for immediate payment meant as payable under the subcontract. To find otherwise would have meant that the adjudicator had not taken account of sums already paid in respect of the disputed items. Further, the adjudicator would have exceeded his powers if he had ordered immediate payment of the final amount.

FW COOK LTD v. SHIMIZU (UK) LTD [2000] B.L.R. 199, Judge Humphrey Lloyd Q.C., QBD (T&CC).

806. Adjudication – building and engineering contracts – JCT forms of contract – set off against interim payment – effect of second adjudication on first interim payments

[Housing Grants, Construction & Regeneration Act 1996 s111.]

R employed V under a construction contract in the JCT standard form. Clause 30 provided for interim payments, applications for payment, notice of intention to withhold payment and dates for payment. Applications for interim payment were to be accompanied by an appropriate VAT invoice. V applied for payment of £1 million including VAT but did not supply a VAT invoice. An adjudicator determined that R was liable to pay V the amount applied for by V once V had provided a VAT invoice, and that R was not entitled to make any deductions since no notice had been given. V provided the VAT notice but R did not pay, instead seeking the appointment of a second adjudicator to review and revise the amount due. The second adjudicator determined that the properly calculated sum was £250,000 whereupon R notified V of its intention to deduct from that sum £200,000 for liquidated damages. V brought proceedings to enforce the decisions of both adjudicators.

Held, ordering summary judgment for V, that (1) adjudication did not take the place of arbitration and litigation in construction disputes; it was an intervening stage in the dispute resolution process. Decisions of adjudicators were binding and had to be complied with until the dispute was finally resolved, *Macob Civil Engineering Ltd v. Morrison Construction Ltd* [1999] C.L.C. 739, [1999] C.L.Y. 794 approved; (2) the Housing Grants, Construction and Regeneration Act 1996, s.111 excluded the right to deduct money as a set-off without an effective notice of intention to withhold payment and required the notice, in order to be effective, to precede the referral to adjudication; (3) the effect of the first adjudications was to require R to pay £1 million to V within the specified time after receiving the appropriate VAT invoice; (4) the effect of the second decision, since the adjudicator had no jurisdiction to set aside, revise or vary the earlier decision, was that the sum payable remained £1 million but V could not enforce it without immediately becoming liable to repay to R £750,000, and (5) the present enforcement proceedings were proceedings to enforce a contractual obligation to comply with the adjudicator's decisions. An adjudicator's decision did not have the status of a judgment.

VHE CONSTRUCTION PLC v. RBSTB TRUST CO LTD; *sub nom.* VHE CONSTRUCTION PLC v. RBSTB TRUST CO LTD (AS TRUSTEE OF THE MECURY PROPERTY FUND) [2000] B.L.R. 187, Judge Hicks Q.C., QBD (T&CC).

807. **Adjudication – building and engineering contracts – jurisdiction of adjudicator – date of contract**

[Housing Grants, Construction and Regeneration Act 1996 s.108, Part II.]

PCG sought fees which it said T had agreed to pay in connection with the conversion of a building into a nursing home. An adjudicator appointed under the Housing Grants, Construction and Regeneration Act 1996 decided that £64,975 was due. T contended that the adjudicator did not have jurisdiction, either because there was no contract, or if there was a valid contract, it was made prior to May 1, 1998, and so the Act did not apply by virtue of Part II. PCG sought to enforce the award by action and made an application for summary judgment.

Held, refusing the application for summary judgment, that (1) prima facie an adjudicator would have no jurisdiction if there was no construction agreement within the meaning of s.108 or if the agreement was reached before the material date. Accordingly, T could challenge the jurisdiction under which the award was made, *Macob Civil Engineering Ltd v. Morrison Construction Ltd* [1999] C.L.C. 739, [1999] C.L.Y. 794 distinguished; (2) on the facts, there was no voluntary submission by T to the jurisdiction of the adjudicator, and (3) T had a realistic chance of showing either that there was no contract or that it was made before the relevant date.

PROJECT CONSULTANCY GROUP v. TRUSTEES OF THE GRAY TRUST [1999] B.L.R. 377, Dyson, J., QBD (T&CC).

808. Adjudication – subcontracts – jurisdiction of adjudicator

[Scheme for Construction Contracts (England and Wales) Regulations 1998 (SI 1998 649).]

N employed J as subcontractor for construction work. When J claimed payment N issued a notice of intention to withhold payment, citing defective works and delays, but without setting a value on the delays. N treated J's subsequent withdrawal from the site as a repudiatory breach, which it accepted. J brought adjudication proceedings. The adjudicator held that N's notice of intention to withhold payment was invalid, that J was entitled to payment subject to a deduction for defective work, and did not deal with the repudiatory breach on the grounds that it did not arise under the contract. N sought declaratory relief and J sought summary judgment.

Held, finding in J's favour and ordering summary judgment against N, that (1) the adjudicator had no jurisdiction to deal with the repudiation claim as it was not a matter raised in the notice of intention to withhold payment. Although the adjudicator's reasons were wrong in law, he was right in refusing to consider the repudiation; (2) the adjudicator had given no reasons for his failure to make a deduction in respect of delay but his decision was within his jurisdiction and was binding unless challenged in arbitration or litigation; (3) an adjudicator was not given any power under the Scheme for Construction Contracts (England and Wales) Regulations 1998 to award costs. However, in this instance there was an implied agreement between the parties that he should do so.

NORTHERN DEVELOPMENTS (CUMBRIA) LTD v. J&J NICHOL [2000] B.L.R. 158, Judge Bowsher Q.C., QBD (T&CC).

809. Adjudication – summary judgments – enforcement of adjudicator's award – issue estoppel

[Housing Grants, Construction and Regeneration Act 1996 s.108.]

H applied for summary judgment following a decision of an adjudicator appointed under the Housing Grants, Construction and Regeneration Act 1996 s.108.

Held, giving judgment for H, that the adjudicator's decision was not final or binding on the parties, and it could not give rise to an estoppel precluding a party from referring the dispute to the court or to an arbitrator. Either party could refer a dispute to an adjudicator under s.108(2) at any time, but, unless the parties agreed otherwise, the adjudicator's decision could be superseded by that of either an arbitrator or the court.

HERSCHEL ENGINEERING LTD v. BREEN PROPERTY LTD [2000] B.L.R. 272, Dyson, J., QBD (T&CC).

810. Architects – limit of liability – nature of claims to which limitation clause applied – reasonableness of limitation clause

[Unfair Contract Terms Act 1977 s.11.]

M instructed Y, who practised through the defendant company, to act as his architect in the construction of a bungalow. The original contract between M and Y was made in March 1993 and incorporated the terms of the Royal Institute of British Architects' Standard Form Agreement for the Appointment of an Architect which included a clause that purported to limit the liability of Y for any loss or damage arising out of any action or proceedings for any breach of the agreement to £250,000. Later that year, M instructed Y to supervise and carry out further work relating to the initial project. In an action arising from alleged incompetent work, M claimed delivery up of various documents, damages and, by way of restitution, a sum of money that he claimed had been overpaid to Y. The issues raised by the limitation of liability clause were determined at a preliminary hearing at which the judge held that the entire contract between the parties had come into existence in March 1993, that the limitation clause had been included in the agreement, that the clause applied both to the claim in restitution and to the claim for breach of contract, and that the clause was not unreasonable within the meaning of the Unfair Contract Terms Act 1977 s.11. M appealed.

Held, dismissing the appeal, that in instructing Y to carry out further work, M had accepted Y's offer to provide additional services which had been contained in the original agreement, and the instruction to carry out further work was therefore conditional upon the acceptance of the original terms; thus, the limitation clause had been incorporated into the contract and, as a matter of construction, applied to the claim in restitution as well as to the claim in breach of contract. Both claims involved allegations of incompetence on Y's part which, if proved, would constitute a breach of the agreement. The reasonableness of the clause had to be assessed, pursuant to s.11, by reference to the circumstances known to, or in the contemplation of, the parties at the time the contract had been made, and the judge had been entitled to conclude that the limit of £250,000 had been reasonable at the time that the contract had been made.

MOORES v. YAKELEY ASSOCIATES LTD BENF1998/1589/A2, Beldam, L.J., CA.

811. **Breach of contract – building and engineering contracts – liquidated damages – architect advising employer as to most favourable assessment method – Australia**

Under a construction contract, the architect, B, had various powers to assess work done, to issue certificates of progress and completion and to assess the liability of J, the contractor, for liquidated damages. Throughout the contract, B privately advised M, the employer, of the alternative valuation methods for assessing damages. M chose the method which was most favourable to it, and made various deductions against J. M then went into liquidation and J sought to recover from B the sums deducted by M on the basis that (1) B owed J a duty of care, which had been breached, and (2) B had procured a breach of contract.

Held, giving judgment for B, that (1) there was no reliance by J or assumption of responsibility by B on which a duty of care could be established, *Pacific Associates v. Baxter* [1990] 1 Q.B. 993, [1989] C.L.Y. 2543 considered; (2) even if such a duty had existed, the correspondence between B and M was in keeping with the nature of their relationship and was neither unfair nor prejudicial to J, and (3) the more favourable valuation suggested by B and accepted by M had been honestly made and there had been no intention to incite a breach of contract.

JOHN HOLLAND CONSTRUCTION AND ENGINEERING LTD v. MAJORCA PRODUCTS (2000) 16 Const. L.J. 114, Byrne, J., Sup Ct (Vic).

812. **Building and engineering contracts – arbitration agreement – oral negotiation not sufficient for incorporation**

[Arbitration Act 1950 s.4, s.32.]

GH invited JI to tender for works at 36 flats being developed by GH. The invitation to tender envisaged a contract based on the JCT 1980 articles and conditions, which included an agreement to refer disputes to arbitration, and provided that the contract would be executed as a deal under seal. Following contract negotiations GH sent to JI a letter of intent which provided that it was GH's intention to enter into a contract with JI. The letter further provided that the contract would be in the form of the JCT 1980 edition, with amendments, and that GH would reimburse JI's reasonable costs on a quantum meruit basis if no formal contract was entered into. JI later commenced the works. On December 1, 1995 the parties met and shook hands on a price for the whole of the works. On July 26, 1996 JI issued a writ claiming sums due for work done on a quantum meruit basis and GH applied for a stay of the proceedings under the Arbitration Act 1950 s.4. JI argued that there was no agreement to arbitrate as no contract had been concluded which incorporated the JCT1980 terms or at all and further argued that there was no written agreement under s.32 of the Act to refer the dispute to Arbitration. The application for a stay was refused at first instance and GH appealed.

Held, dismissing the appeal, that the invitation to tender, envisaging a contract to be executed as a deed under seal, and of the letter of intent concerning the eventuality of GH and JI not entering into a contract, resulted in JI working subject to contract. The handshake agreement of December 1, 1995 on the price of the works was only an agreement subject to a formal contract, amounting to nothing more than negotiation preliminary to a contract which had not previously been made and was not made afterwards. Therefore, no arbitration agreement came into existence, *G Percy Trentham Ltd v. Archital Luxfer Ltd* [1993] 1 Lloyd's Rep. 25, [1993] C.L.Y. 294 considered. Further, there was no written agreement to submit any differences to arbitration as required by s.32. The dealings between the parties were subject to contract and even if, contrary to the above, there was an agreement on December 1, 1995, it was not an agreement capable of incorporating the JCT 1980 conditions. *Excomm Ltd v. Ahmed Abdul-Qawi Bamaodah (The St Raphael)* [1985] 1 Lloyd's Rep. 403, [1985] C.L.Y. 120 and *Zambia Steel & Building Supplies Ltd v. James Clarke & Eaton Ltd* [1986] 2 Lloyd's Rep. 225, [1987] C.L.Y. 155 considered.

JARVIS INTERIORS LTD v. GALLIARD HOMES LTD; *sub nom.* GALLIARD HOMES LTD v. J JARVIS & SONS PLC [2000] C.L.C. 411, Lindsay, J., CA.

813. **Building and engineering contracts – breach of contract – estoppel – alternative construction method to that specified in contract used by contractors – relevance of control officer's knowledge of method used**

M, in 1989, engaged S as consulting engineers and D as building contractors in the refurbishment of the roof of one of its dockyards. S delegated its supervisory powers under the contract to the site control officer, O, who was an employee of M's agent. In December 1993 strong winds lifted off a section of the roof. M commenced proceedings against S and D claiming damages for breach of contract. The judge concluded that the defect in the roof had resulted from the inadequacy of the fixings which had been used at the point of interface between the main frame rafters and the purlins. Primary contractual liability was found to rest with D but, on finding that S had been vicariously responsible for the conduct of O, who had failed in his supervisory capacity to observe and correct the inadequacy of the fixing method, the judge apportioned liability equally between D and S. D appealed, contending that (1) the judge had erred in his finding that there had been no positive and unequivocal agreement between the parties to use the method of fixing actually adopted. D argued that O had, in accordance with the contract conditions, instructed it to use the method of fixing which was finally chosen; (2) that promissory estoppel and waiver, which the judge had said could not be established in the absence of representation and reliance, had been established; (3) that they had a valid claim for betterment on the ground that the cost incurred in taking extra precautionary measures to secure the roof when it was rebuilt after its failure in December 1993 was an additional cost, which related to work that they had not been obliged to undertake under their original contract, and (4) that S ought to have been held not less than 75 per cent responsible for M's losses on the basis that the judge had found them vicariously responsible for O's conduct.

Held, allowing the appeal in part, that (1) there was never any instruction to vary or modify the contractual stipulations. Instead, O had gone along with the method chosen by D, believing it to be in compliance with D's contractual obligations. D did not request or believe that it needed any instructions or directions and O had not provided it with any such instructions or directions. The judge found that D would have implemented the same method of fixing regardless of whether or not O's attention had been drawn to that method; (2) the pleas of estoppel and waiver both failed. As neither the words nor the conduct of O amounted to an instruction, there was no clear or unequivocal representation on which D had relied, making it inequitable for M to hold it responsible for breach of contract. D was the main contractor and informal conversations between it and O concerning the method of fixing were not capable of transferring to M the responsibility for the inadequacy of the fixings; (3) the appeal against the judge's decision on the issue of betterment would be allowed and the damages recoverable by M reduced by £27,285.28, that being the cost of the additional materials used. Although M's decision to use straps and other fixing devices of a more expensive nature than the original contract contemplated had been reasonable, that decision could not be attributed to D's breach of contract, and (4) given that the principal duty to carry out the relevant works rested with D and that S was vicariously responsible for actions of O, the judge's apportioning of liability between the two of them would not be disturbed.

SCOTT WILSON KIRKPATRICK & PARTNERS v. MINISTRY OF DEFENCE; DEAN & DYBALL CONSTRUCTION LTD v. MINISTRY OF DEFENCE [2000] B.L.R. 20, Mance, L.J., CA.

814. **Building and engineering contracts – construction of contract – engineers duty to provide coordination drawings**

An action in relation to a major construction contract between RBH and H was largely settled. Judgment was reserved on one issue concerning the ninth to 16th defendants, AA, who were consulting engineers and subcontractors of H, which related to whether AA were obliged to provide coordination drawings showing the interrelation of pipe, electrical or other work at the site, so that the main contract could be complied with. H argued that AA's obligation was to provide the drawings prior to tender, and when they did not do so their only duty then was to provide them with "reasonable diligence". RBH argued that AA were obliged to "exercise reasonable care and skill" in supplying the drawings.

Held, allowing the application, that AA were obliged to provide the drawings using "reasonable skill, care and diligence" in time to allow H to prepare installation drawings in order to complete the main contract.

ROYAL BROMPTON HOSPITAL NHS TRUST v. HAMMOND (NO.4) [2000] B.L.R. 75, Judge Hicks Q.C., QBD (T&CC).

815. **Building and engineering contracts – guarantee entered into as condition for completion of work – guarantor seeking to rely on manifest error in certified valuation of work by contractor**

In June 1997, TB entered into a building contract with a football club, P, to construct stadium improvements. P was unable to pay the amounts due under the contract, and, after withdrawing from the site, TB obtained a guarantee from BSG in January 1998, pursuant to an agreement under a deed between P and BSG. The guarantee was entered into as one of a number of conditions on which TB returned to complete the works. The guarantee provided at cl.9.3 that a certificate delivered by TB to BSG would be conclusive evidence of the sum due, subject to an exclusion for "manifest error". TB claimed the certified sum from BSG under the guarantee. BSG disputed the amount due, contending that there was a "manifest error" in the valuation of the work and claimed rescission of the agreement underlying the guarantee on the grounds of negligent misrepresentations made by TB prior to the agreement.

Held, giving judgment for TB, that the "manifest error" must be an error in the calculation of the sums due. The agreement was not concerned with a "manifest error" in the original certified valuation. The "manifest error" must be an error which is plain and obvious on the face of the decision or which might be shown to be plain and obvious by looking at what the decision was supposed to represent, *Dixons Group Plc v. Murray-Oboynski* 86 B.L.R. 16, [1998] C.L.Y. 701 and *Beaufort Developments (NI) Ltd v. Gilbert-Ash (NI) Ltd* [1999] 1 A.C. 266, [1998] C.L.Y. 5055 applied. A defence that negligent misrepresentations had been made by TB prior to the agreement was not a defence available to BSG. The guarantee clearly and unequivocally provided for an absolute obligation to pay,

Toomey v. Eagle Star Insurance Co Ltd (No.2) [1995] 2 Lloyd's Rep. 88 distinguished.

TRY BUILD LTD v. BLUE STAR GARAGES LTD 66 Con. L.R. 90, Judge Humphrey Lloyd Q.C., QBD (T&CC).

816. **Building and engineering contracts – ICE conditions of contract – variation – valuation of work – mistake in bill of quantities**

HBC carried out engineering works for GEC, the extent of which had to be varied. The contract between the parties incorporated the ICE conditions of contract (6th edition), cl.52 of which provided, inter alia, that "where work is not of a similar character or is not executed under similar conditions...the rates and prices in the bill of quantities shall be used as the basis for valuation so far as may be reasonable". A dispute between the parties concerning the valuation of additional work carried out by HBC was referred to the arbitrator who found that whereas HBC had calculated that its charges for the supply of sheet piling in two separate locations would amount to £250,880, it had informed GEC that those charges related to the supply of the piling in one location alone. The arbitrator concluded that as the price had been arrived at by mistake, he should conduct a fair valuation of his own. HBC's appeal to a judge succeeded whereupon GEC appealed. GEC argued that for the purpose of cl.52, rates or prices in a bill of quantities should not be regarded as unalterable.

Held, dismissing the appeal, that the basis for valuation under cl.52 could not be displaced on the ground that the rates or prices in a bill of quantities had been inserted by mistake. If, however, work carried out pursuant to a variation to a contract differed significantly from the work covered by the bill of quantities, it would be open to the engineer to carry out a valuation of his own. The words "so far as may be reasonable" had been inserted in cl.52 to cater for that eventuality. The exceptions set out in cl.52(2) and cl.56(2) of the conditions supported the conclusion that the rates or prices contained in a bill of quantities were not subject to rectification. To hold otherwise would lead to uncertainty and disturb the basis of competitive tendering. In the instant case, the arbitrator should have disregarded HBC's mistake and carried out a valuation on the basis of the price which HBC had quoted.

HENRY BOOT CONSTRUCTION LTD v. ALSTOM COMBINED CYCLES LTD; *sub nom.* HENRY BOOT CONSTRUCTION LTD v. ALSTOM COMBINED CYCLES LTD (FORMERLY GEC ALSTHOM COMBINED CYCLES LTD); HENRY BOOT CONSTRUCTION LTD v. GEC ALSTOM COMBINED CYCLES LTD; HENRY BOOT CONSTRUCTION v. ALSTON COMBINED CYCLES [2000] C.L.C. 1147, Lord Lloyd, CA.

817. **Building and engineering contracts – interpretation – contractual nature of work programme**

S was engaged to design and build an oil rig and carry out certain installation work. It undertook the design work and supply of materials, but subcontracted the remainder of the works to A under a written contract. A series of major claims and counterclaims arose between the parties and a trial of preliminary issues was ordered, inter alia, as to (1) whether A's plan for the programme of the works subsequently approved by S constituted the contractual programme. Article 15 of the subcontract provided that the plan submitted by A would become the work programme when acknowledged as such by S. S argued that the plan was not contractual in nature as it did not comply with the requirements of the contract, notwithstanding its approval, and (2) the extent of S's obligations in relation to the provision of design information for the rig's pipework.

Held, on the preliminary issues, that (1) the natural construction of the contract meant the suggested plan complied with the requirements of the subcontract. S's contrary submission was unfeasible, as it did not provide for the creation of an alternative programme. S's suggestion that the contractual programme could be created by substituting in the plan submitted certain dates derived from the other documents indicating what was agreed in the contract

(a) fell foul of the requirement for acknowledgement, and (b) was practically flawed in that it presupposed that all those persons at all levels in both organisations who were putting the plan into effect knew the terms and effects of the contractual documentation relied on by S, and how they altered the written plan to which they were all working, and (2) neither the documentary evidence nor the facts revealed who was responsible for supplying the pipework design information. However, examination of the process showed that it was easier for A to follow the design information given by S. Although A was entitled to payment for variations made by S, the determination of its entitlement to extra payments under the subcontract's accelerated work provisions were to be decided by reference to the facts. A was, however, entitled to damages due to S's failure to carry out its obligations regarding A's rights or variation requests.

AMEC PROCESS & ENERGY LTD v. STORK ENGINEERS & CONTRACTORS BV (PRELIMINARY ISSUES) 68 Con. L.R. 17, Judge Hicks Q.C., QBD (T&CC).

818. **Building and engineering contracts – misrepresentation – identity of main contractor – subcontractor's right to claim rescission**

[Misrepresentation Act 1967 s.2(2).]

In April 1991, F entered into a conditional subcontract with SC to undertake ground works in connection with the construction of a bypass. SC was the main contractor, having been retained by the Welsh Office in March 1991. SC was part of a group of companies, M, which at the time was undergoing restructuring. The subcontract between F and SC was executed in October 1992. Prior to the execution of the contract, F obtained two credit references based on SC's accounts for the periods ending March 31, 1990 and March 31, 1991, both of which showed net deficiencies and reports accompanying the accounts advised that although SC was continuing to trade, it was not favourable for a credit account. On September 8, 1995, M's restructuring was formalised, with effect from March 31, 1991, on which date M purchased SC's civil engineering business. In effect, SC had ceased to trade, although its name was still used for marketing and tendering purposes for some time afterwards. In 1994 the Welsh Office treated the main contract as having been assigned to M. In October 1994, F issued proceedings against SC, including, inter alia, a claim for damages under the Misrepresentation Act 1967 s.2(2) on the grounds that SC's accounts had misrepresented the fact that it was the main contractor and continued to trade, whereas the reality was that M was the main contractor and that SC had ceased trading.

Held, dismissing the claim, that (1) the accounts did not contain any misrepresentation as to SC's financial position, although those for the year ending March 1991 represented that SC was still trading when it was not; (2) F had not relied upon an inducement to enter into the conditional contract with SC in April 1991; (3) the subcontract was entered into in October 1992, if F had knowledge of M's restructuring at that time it was inconceivable that it would not have entered into the subcontract as the work was practically complete; (4) with regard to SC's identity, at the time of entering into the contract SC was the main contractor, there could therefore be no misrepresentation of its capacity, and (5) although s.2(2) provided for damages in lieu of rescission, if the right to rescind had not already been exercised, then to claim under s.2(2) the contract must be capable of rescission at the time of the trial. It was not sufficient that the right to rescind had existed at one time, *Atlantic Lines & Navigation Co Inc v. Hallam Ltd (The Lucy)* [1983] 1 Lloyds Rep. 188, [1983] C.L.Y. 1726 and *William Sindall Plc v. Cambridgeshire CC* [1994] 1 W.L.R. 1016, [1994] C.L.Y. 572 followed, *Thomas Witter Ltd v. TBP Industries Ltd* [1996] 2 All E.R. 573, [1996] C.L.Y. 1238 not followed. It the instant case, rescission was not available as the works carried out had materially affected the rights of a third party. Even if rescission were possible, the court would have exercised its discretion to refuse it under s.2(2) as F would have contracted on the same terms with another company, such as M. Thus even if it had known the true position at the time of entering into the contract, it would have been in the same position as it was now. Further, F had had a guarantee of SC's obligations.

FLOODS OF QUEENSFERRY LTD v. SHAND CONSTRUCTION LTD (NO.3) [2000] B.L.R. 81, Judge Humphrey Lloyd Q.C., QBD (T&CC).

819. **Building and engineering contracts – performance bonds – non performance due to sub contractor's liquidation – legitimacy of claim**

BB entered into a subcontract with LL for the placing of rock for a harbour breakwater in Cardiff Bay. A performance bond was entered into by TGG as surety in favour of BB relating to the work undertaken by LL. Work was to be carried out in two phases. BB retained the right to cancel the contract in relation to the second phase and also to determine the subcontract if LL went into liquidation. BB sought to make a claim under the performance bond from TGG after LL, by reason of liquidation, failed to fulfil its obligations under the sub-contract. Summary judgment was obtained in favour of BB. TGG appealed, contending that (1) liquidation was not covered by the performance bond when given its proper construction since liquidation could not be equated with "default", and (2) BB's claim was fraudulent, being made in the knowledge that termination of the subcontract would result in savings to themselves.

Held, dismissing the appeal, that (1) while liquidation was not a breach of contract in most instances, it was not clear whether it was excluded under the construction of this subcontract. It could not be shown that liquidation was not a default under the contract or that BB did not honestly believe that the breach claimed for was in fact a breach, and, (2) there was no clear evidence of fraud either as at the date of the demand or as at the application for summary judgment, *Edward Owen Engineering Ltd v. Barclays Bank International Ltd* [1978] Q.B. 159, [1977] C.L.Y. 162 considered. None of the evidence before the court indicated that BB had acted dishonestly in making its claim. It was a legitimate expectation that a loss would be suffered by reason of LL going into liquidation .

BALFOUR BEATTY CIVIL ENGINEERING (T/A BALFOUR BEATTY/COSTAIN (CARDIFF BAY BARRAGE) JOINT VENTURE) v. TECHNICAL & GENERAL GUARANTEE CO LTD [2000] C.L.C. 252, Waller, L.J, CA.

820. **Building and engineering contracts – repairs – gas heating systems – definition of construction operations**

[Housing Grants, Construction and Regeneration Act 1996 s.105(1)(a), s.105(1)(c).]

N, a community housing association, sought a declaration that a contract it had entered into with P, a company which serviced and maintained gas heating systems and appliances, was not a construction contract within the meaning of the Housing Grants, Construction and Regeneration Act 1996 s.105(1)(a). P had invoiced N for work carried out under the contract and N had refused to pay, arguing that it had a sizeable counterclaim. P subsequently gave notice to N of adjudication under the Act. N argued that the annual service and maintenance of gas heating systems was not a construction operation within the meaning of s.105(1)(a) as gas heating systems did not form part of a building, and that s.105(1)(c) referred only to installation, and not to maintenance and repair, so excluding the latter from classification as construction operations.

Held, granting a declaration in favour of the defendant, that once installed, gas heating systems formed part of the building; therefore, maintenance and repair of heating systems was an operation that fell within s.105(1)(a) of the Act. Construing s.105 as a whole, maintenance and repair were not excluded from construction operations by the apparent redundancy of s.105(1)(c), *Walker (Inspector of Taxes) v. Centaur Clothes Group Ltd* [2000] 1 W.L.R. 799, [2000]

C.L.Y. 4912 and *Beaufort Developments (NI) Ltd v. Gilbert-Ash (NI) Ltd* [1999] 1 A.C. 266, [1998] C.L.Y. 5055 applied.
NOTTINGHAM COMMUNITY HOUSING ASSOCIATION LTD v. POWERMINSTER LTD [2000] B.L.R. 309, Dyson, J., QBD (T&CC).

821. Building inspectors – approval

BUILDING (APPROVED INSPECTORS ETC.) REGULATIONS 2000, SI 2000 2532; made under the Building Act 1984 s.1, s.16, s.17, s.35, s.47, s.49, s.50, s.51, s.52, s.53, s.54, s.56, Sch.1, Sch.4. In force: January 1, 2001; £6.30.

These Regulations, which revoke and replace the Building (Approved Inspectors etc.) Regulations 1985 (SI 1985 1066 as amended), are principally concerned with the inspection of plans and of building work. They deal with the procedures for approving inspectors, prescribe the forms of various notices and certificates to be given where an approved inspector supervises building work, prescribe the grounds on which approved inspectors' notices and certificates are to be rejected, require that approved inspectors have no professional or financial interest in the work that they supervise unless it is minor work, specify the functions of approved inspectors when supervising building work, require the calculation of an energy rating for a new dwelling where the work is being supervised by an approved inspector, specify the consultations to take place between an approved inspector and the fire authority, provide for the approval of persons to certify plans deposited with the local authority under the Building Act 1984 s.16(9), and provide that local authorities shall keep registers of all notices provided for in these Regulations that are in force and of all certificates that they have accepted in accordance with these Regulations.

822. Building regulations – consolidation of legislation

BUILDING REGULATIONS 2000, SI 2000 2531; made under the Building Act 1984 s.1, s.3, s.5, s.8, s.35, s.126, Sch.1 para.1, Sch.1 para.2, Sch.1 para.4, Sch.1 para.7, Sch.1 para.8. In force: January 1, 2001; £4.50.

These Regulations, which revoke and replace, with amendments, the Building Regulations 1991 (SI 1991 2768 as amended), consolidate all subsequent amendments to those Regulations and impose requirements on people carrying out certain building operations.

823. Building regulations – exempt bodies – Metropolitan Police Authority

BUILDING REGULATIONS (AMENDMENT) REGULATIONS 2000, SI 2000 1554; made under the Building Act 1994 s.5. In force: July 3, 2000; £1.00.

These Regulations amend the Building Regulations 1991 (SI 1991 2768) by providing that the Metropolitan Police Authority is an exempt body under the Building Act 1984 s.5(2) and is exempt from compliance with the requirements of the 1991 Regulations insofar as they are not substantive requirements.

824. Competitive tendering – building and engineering contracts – failure to follow statutory criteria – misfeasance in public office

[Public Works Contracts Regulations 1991 (SI 1991 2680) Reg.12, Reg.20.]
H, a US owned company, tendered for the fenestration work on a building constructed to house MPs and their staff, in reliance upon an invitation published in the Official Journal. However, owing to lack of response from UK firms, the tender was re-advertised, but the stated basis of the contract as being value for money remained incorrect in terms of the Public Works Contract Regulations 1991, which stipulated that the criteria should be either "lowest price" or "the most economically advantageous". All tenders submitted exceeded CO's estimates and discussions were held with the tendering parties following which SA's offer was accepted, even though it was based on a different option to that used by H and the others. Subsequently, SA's proposal was modified to bring it into line with that used by H. H brought an action for damages, alleging

breach of the law on public work contract procurement and discrimination in favour of SA in breach of both EC and domestic law.

Held, giving judgment for H on a trial of preliminary issues, that the contract had been awarded unlawfully, as (1) the provisions in Reg.12 and Reg.20 regarding the award criteria were mandatory and alternative forms could not be used; (2) although the criterion used was similar to "the most economically advantageous", the failure amounted to a defect. It followed that CO was bound to award the contract purely on price; (3) CO allowed a policy to develop that the contract should be awarded to a UK firm in breach of its duty under the Regulations, and (4) the contract had been awarded at a time when CO knew it could not do so in breach of the tort of misfeasance in public office. Therefore H was entitled to damages that would include the cost of the tender, and its intra group margin. The fact that H went into liquidation in 1998 should be also be considered. Aggravated and exemplary damages would not be awarded, however, as CO's conduct had not been directed to ensuring H's failure but to securing SA's success, *Broome v. Cassell & Co Ltd (No.1)* [1972] A.C. 1027, [1972] C.L.Y. 2745 and *AB v. South West Water Services Ltd* [1993] Q.B. 507, [1993] C.L.Y. 1598 followed.

HARMON CFEM FACADES (UK) LTD v. CORPORATE OFFICER OF THE HOUSE OF COMMONS 67 Con. L.R. 1, Judge Humphrey Lloyd Q.C., QBD (T&CC).

825. Construction Industry Training Board – levy on employers

See EMPLOYMENT. §2106

826. Delay – building and engineering contracts – delay by subcontractor – claim for liquidated damages under main contract

AM was the main contractor in the construction of a five storey building in Douglas, Isle of Man. AC was subcontracted to carry out reinforced concrete works. AC claimed an extension of time and damages with damages counter claimed by AM in respect of delays to the works. Three issues arose (1) AM relied on cl.11.1 of the subcontract which required AC to complete the subcontract work in reasonable accordance with the progress of the main contract, as meaning that AC had to comply with the programme of main contract works, AC submitted that in the absence of any provision in the subcontract for sectional completion or a phased hand over to other trades, that was not so; (2) AM had factored a "float" of five weeks into its programme of works and claimed, as well as damages for delay, an entitlement to the benefit or value of the float, and (3) AM claimed an entitlement to liquidated damages incurred under the main contract owing to delays caused by AC, the main contract final account had been first settled on the grounds that there be no payment of liquidated and ascertained damages for delay and later amended to include payment of such damages for a delay of 12 weeks to completion of the works, the final account total remained the same.

Held, dismissing the claim by AC and limiting the counter claim to a delay by AC of one and a half weeks, that (1) cl.11.1 did not require AC to comply with the detail of the main contractor's programme. However, the clause went beyond a negative duty not to unreasonably interfere with the carrying out of other work. The progress referred to was that expected and observed in the light of the facts, although the obligation was only to proceed reasonably in accordance with that progress, *Pigott Foundations Ltd v. Shepherd Construction Ltd* 67 B.L.R. 48 and *Greater London Council v. Cleveland Bridge & Engineering Co Ltd* 34 B.L.R. 50, [1987] C.L.Y. 245 considered; (2) AM's claim for the benefit of the float was misconceived. A contractor, while accepting the benefit of a float in the works programme against an employer, could not claim against the subcontractors as if that float did not exist or claim where completion within the float and no actual loss had been incurred, and (3) the substance of the settlement terms as between AMC and the employer remained materially unaltered. The claim for liquidated and ascertained damages paid to the employer could only be established where a quantifiable payment had been made to the employer for such damages in a reasonable settlement of the claim.

In the instant case none of those necessary facts to support a "reasonable settlement" had been pleaded or proved, the claim therefore failed, *Biggin & Co Ltd v. Permanite Ltd* [1951] 2 K.B. 314, [1947-51] C.L.Y. 2491 and *DSL Group Ltd v. Unisys International Services Ltd (No.1)* 41 Con.L.R. 33 applied.

ASCON CONTRACTING LTD v. ALFRED MCALPINE CONSTRUCTION ISLE OF MAN LTD 66 Con. L.R. 119, Judge John Hicks Q.C., QBD (T&CC).

827. **Engineering Construction Board – levy on employers**

See EMPLOYMENT. §2107

828. **Negligence – subcontractors – collapsed roof – combined effect of causes**

See NEGLIGENCE: Plant Construction Plc v. Clive Adams Associates (No.3). §4185

829. **Subcontractors – building and engineering contracts – subcontractor aware of design defect – implied contractual duty to warn**

J, one of several contractors to perform an installation contract, appealed against an implied finding of fact that it had a duty to warn P of a design defect, of which it was aware but for which another party was responsible, and that its failure to do so had caused P to suffer economic loss. J contended there was no such duty, but that even if there were, it had been discharged and P had not proved that any such breach had caused the loss it was claiming.

Held, allowing the appeal in part, that J had an implied contractual duty to warn and that the judge was entitled to find that it was in breach of that duty, but that he had omitted to deal with the causation issue, and therefore the case was remitted for a finding on that issue.

PLANT CONSTRUCTION PLC v. CLIVE ADAMS ASSOCIATES (NO.2); *sub nom.* PLANT CONSTRUCTION LTD v. JMH CONSTRUCTION SERVICES LTD [2000] B.L.R. 137, May, L.J., CA.

830. **Tenders – building and engineering contracts – invitation to tender – implied contractual obligations – obligation to accept only compliant tender – Canada**

D invited tenders for the construction of a pump house. The invitation to tender contained a privilege clause which provided that: "The lowest or any tender shall not necessarily be accepted". The works included the construction of a water system providing for one of three types of backfill, varying in expense, to be used at the discretion of the site engineer in various places. M submitted a tender on the basis of a standard price per linear metre of backfill. The contract was awarded to a tenderer that, although tendering at the lowest price, had added a manuscript note providing for an increase in price where more expensive backfill was required. M unsuccessfully brought an action for breach of contract, claiming that the winning tender should have been disqualified as not conforming to the tender specifications. On appeal the main issue before the court was whether the inclusion of the privilege clause allowed D to disregard the lowest conforming bid in favour of any other tender including a non conformant one.

Held, allowing the appeal, that D in awarding the contract to the non conforming tender was in breach of obligations to M arising at tender stage. Whether or not contractual obligations arose between D and M at tender stage, distinct from any obligations under the proposed building contract, depended on whether the parties intended to initiate contractual relations by the submission of a bid in response to an invitation to tender, *R in Right of Ontario v. Ron Engineering and Construction (Eastern) Ltd* [1981] S.C.R. 111 not followed, and *Blackpool and Fylde Aero Club v. Blackpool BC* [1990] 1 W.L.R. 1195, [1991] C.L.Y. 523 referred to. Here the tender documents stipulated that the contractor must submit a compliant bid and that the contractor could not negotiate the tender documents. It was reasonable to infer that D would only consider valid tenders and that D was under an implied contractual obligation only to accept a compliant bid. The privilege clause was compatible with an obligation to consider only conforming tenders as it only had a bearing on price.

MJB ENTERPRISES LTD v. DEFENCE CONSTRUCTION (1951) LTD (2000) 2 T.C.L.R. 235, Iacobucci, J., Sup Ct (Can).

831. Publications

Achieving Benefits Through Mediation: Construction Disputes. TSO Mediation Series. Paperback: £30.00. ISBN 0-11-702441-4. The Stationery Office Books.

Carnell, Nicholas J. – Causation and Delay in Construction Disputes. Hardback: £45.00. ISBN 0-632-03971-X. Blackwell Science (UK).

Chappell, David – Understanding JCT Standard Building Contracts. 6th Ed. Builders' Bookshelf Series. Paperback: £16.99. ISBN 0-415-23107-8. E & FN Spon.

Committee for Waterfront structures of the society for Harbor engineers – Recommendations of the Committee for Waterfront Structures. 7th Ed. Hardback: £75.00. ISBN 3-433-01790-5. Wiley-VCH.

Hackett, Jeremy – Construction Claims: Current Practice and Case Management. Hardback: £65.00. ISBN 1-85978-553-0. LLP Professional Publishing.

Kellerher, Thomas J.; Ansley, Robert J.; Lehman, Anthony D. – Smith, Currie & Hancock's Common Sense Construction Law. 2nd Ed. Hardback: £50.50. ISBN 0-471-39090-9. John Wiley and Sons.

New Engineering Contract. Reissue. Paperback: £35.00. ISBN 0-632-05742-4. Blackwell Science (UK).

O'Reilly – Construction Law Handbook. Paperback: £195.00. ISBN 0-7277-2883-0. Thomas Telford Ltd.

Speaight, Anthony; Stone, Gregory – Architect's Legal Handbook. 7th Ed. Paperback: £27.50. ISBN 0-7506-4375-7. Paperback: £27.50. ISBN 0-7506-4375-7. Architectural Press.

Trickey, Geoffrey; Hackett, Mark – Presentation and Settlement of Contractors' Claims. 2nd Ed. Hardback: £60.00. ISBN 0-419-20500-4. Spon Press.

CONSUMER LAW

832. Comparative advertising – misleading advertisements

CONTROL OF MISLEADING ADVERTISEMENTS (AMENDMENT) REGULATIONS 2000, SI 2000 914; made under the European Communities Act 1972 s.2. In force: April 23, 2000; £1.50.

These Regulations, which implement Council Directive 97/55 ([1997] OJ L290/18) concerning misleading advertising, amend the Control of Misleading Advertisements Regulations 1988 (SI 1988 915) by adding provisions dealing with "comparative advertisements" to the regime governing "misleading advertisements".

833. Consumer credit – advertisements and quotations – warning statements

CONSUMER CREDIT (ADVERTISEMENTS AND CONTENT OF QUOTATIONS) (AMENDMENT) REGULATIONS 2000, SI 2000 1797; made under the Consumer Credit Act 1974 s.44, s.52, s.182. In force: September 24, 2000; £2.00.

These Regulations amend the Consumer Credit (Advertisements) Regulations 1989 (SI 1989 1125), which required certain credit advertisements to carry a specified warning statement where security was or might be required in the form of a mortgage on the debtor's home, by replacing that warning statement with a new statement for two types of mortgage loan. The Consumer Credit (Content of Quotations) and Consumer Credit (Advertisements) (Amendment) Regulations

1999 (SI 1999 2725), which required the same warning statement in quotations for mortgage loans secured on the prospective debtor's home, is similarly amended.

834. Consumer credit – credit reference agencies – disclosure of information

CONSUMER CREDIT (CREDIT REFERENCE AGENCY) REGULATIONS 2000, SI 2000 290; made under the Consumer Credit Act 1974 s.157, s.158, s.159; and the Data Protection Act 1998 s.9. In force: March 1, 2000; £2.00.

These Regulations, which revoke the Consumer Credit (Credit Reference Agency) Regulations 1977 (SI 1977 329), supplement the Consumer Credit Act 1974 s.157 to s.160 and the Data Protection Act 1998 s.9(3) which relate to the disclosure to consumers of information about their financial standing held by credit reference agencies and the correction of such information where it is found to be wrong or incomplete.

835. Consumer credit agreements – interest rates – annual percentage rates as indications of price – quoting lower interest rate misleading

[Consumer Protection Act 1987 s.20(1).]

MRB, insurance brokers, were convicted of providing a misleading price indication, contrary to the Consumer Protection Act 1987 s.20(1) by giving a lower annual percentage rate for a credit facility agreement for insurance payments. MRB applied by way of judicial review against the refusal of the justices to state a case following the conviction.

Held, dismissing the application, that a statement concerning the annual percentage rate was an indication as to price and therefore within s.20(1). As the amount payable would be calculated with reference to the annual percentage rate, any figure arrived at on the basis of a lower rate would be incorrect and misleading.

R. v. KETTERING MAGISTRATES COURT, *ex p.* MRB INSURANCE BROKERS LTD; *sub nom.* R. v. KETTERING JUSTICES, *ex p.* MRB INSURANCE BROKERS LTD [2000] 2 All E.R. (Comm) 353, Douglas Brown, J., QBD.

836. Consumer credit agreements – limitations – application to re open extortionate credit bargain – limitation period applicable

[Consumer Credit Act 1974 s.139(1)(b); Limitation Act 1980 s.8.]

R entered into a credit agreement with GC which was secured against his home. A year later, a possession order was made after R had fallen into arrears with the monthly payments. R responded to subsequent attempts to enforce the possession order by making payments to GC and, following an assignment of the relevant charge, to SC. Eight years after the order had been made, R applied for it to be set aside and for permission to file a defence and counterclaim alleging that the loan amounted to an extortionate credit bargain. The district judge having dismissed those applications, R appealed to the county court judge who found that the possession order had had the effect of bringing the action to a conclusion thereby making it impossible for R to pursue his counterclaim. R appealed further, arguing that the court had the power to re open the original agreement since (1) the proceedings had not come to an end, and (2) they amounted to "proceedings to enforce" the credit agreement and a "security relating to it" for the purpose of the Consumer Credit Act 1974 s.139(1)(b).

Held, allowing the appeal, that (1) neither the district judge nor the county court judge had adjudicated on the crucial issue, namely limitation. Since R's cause of action arose from a statute and since it amounted to a claim upon a specialty, the Limitation Act 1980 s.8 applied and the appropriate limitation period was 12 years, *Collin v. Duke of Westminster* [1985] Q.B. 581, [1985] C.L.Y. 1891 applied, R's action was therefore not statute barred; (2) the court had no jurisdiction to re open a transaction which had been the subject of a judgment with the result that R could not apply for an order under s.139 of the 1974 Act setting aside the possession order. He was, however, not prevented from seeking relief of a nature that had not been the subject of the possession order, for example relief from liability to make payments in the future. Furthermore, he could do so in the present action since it had not come to an end. As R was still living in the property, SC had continued to accept monthly payments from him and the possession order had not been satisfied, it would be appropriate to allow R to pursue what was now his Part 20 claim in the present action rather than compel him to issue separate proceedings, and (3) his delay in pursuing his claim did not constitute a sufficient reason for denying him the right to pursue it. The trial judge could, however, take such delay into account when determining the application.

RAHMAN v. STERLING CREDIT LTD [2001] 1W.L.R. 496, Mummery, L.J., CA.

837. Consumer hire agreements – credit hire – quantum meruit where agreement did not stipulate rate of hire

C and L were involved in a road traffic accident. C hired a car from a credit hire company, ACR. The hire charges were disputed by L. At the first hearing C's counsel withdrew on the basis of a conflict of interest. ACR was then added as a second defendant by C who sought a declaration as to the enforceability of the hire agreement. ACR counterclaimed for the hire charges against C. At the trial, C produced her copy of the hire agreement which did not have the rate of hire included in the box on the front. C gave evidence that she assumed, or that her understanding was, that the insurer would pay the charges, although it was unclear whether this was her own or L's insurers. No assurances were given that the hire was free. On the basis of the evidence, L contended that the contract was void due to the uncertainty of its terms and relied upon *G Scammell and Nephew Ltd v. HC&JG Ouston* [1941] A.C. 251. ACR argued that the contract was not void, and even if it was, that ACR should be entitled to a quantum meruit on the basis of a reasonable price, just as a builder would be so entitled if he did work for which no price had been agreed beforehand. L's counsel requested determination of that issue before consideration of the Consumer Credit Act arguments.

Held, that the contract was void due to uncertainty. The quantum meruit claim was also dismissed although the judge stated that had it not been for C's understanding that she would not have to pay at all then it might have been different, in that it would then be like the example given of the builder where there was an understanding that payment would be required. The judge considered that it behoved hire companies to bring home to the hirer that there was a clear liability on them, even if in all probability that liability would be met by the other insurer. Therefore, the judge made a declaration that the hire contract was unenforceable and no hire charges were awarded.

CONWAY v. LAGOU, October 7, 1999, Judge Cowell, CC (West Kensington). [*Ex rel.* Tim Kevan, Barrister, 1 Temple Gardens, Temple, London].

838. Consumer hire agreements – finance company unable to exclude requirement for satisfactory quality and fitness for purpose

[Unfair Contract Terms Act 1977 s.7; Supply of Goods and Services Act 1982 s.7, s.8, s.9.]

P supplied and installed a CCTV security camera and monitor at F's farm, with specific instructions that it was to record at night. F entered into a consumer hire agreement with FNL, a finance company, who purchased the equipment from P. Following installation during the day and having seen the system operate, F signed a delivery note which stated that he accepted delivery of the goods and they were to his entire satisfaction. FNL's standard conditions stated that "FNL has had no opportunity to inspect the equipment and relies upon the customer to do so and to ensure that the equipment is of satisfactory quality and fit for the purpose for which the customer requires it. In these circumstances FNL gives no condition, warranty or undertaking, express or implied, as to the quality or fitness of the equipment". It was later discovered by F that the system did not work at night time. FNL sought to rely on the exclusion clause.

Held, finding in favour of F, that F was a consumer and the hire of the goods was covered by the Supply of Goods and Services Act 1982 s.7 to s.9, and the equipment was found not to be of satisfactory quality nor was it fit for its purpose. The hire agreement could be brought to an end. FNL was not able to escape ss. 7 to 9 of the Act by exclusion, as the agreement was caught by the Unfair Contract Terms Act 1977 s.7.

FRY v. FIRST NATIONAL LEASING LTD, June 7, 2000, District Judge Field, CC (Salisbury). [*Ex rel.* Michael Morris, Barrister, 169 Temple Chambers, Temple Avenue, London].

839. Consumer protection – distance selling

CONSUMER PROTECTION (DISTANCE SELLING) REGULATIONS 2000, SI 2000 2334; made under the European Communities Act 1972 s.2. In force: October 31, 2000; £3.50.

These Regulations, which implement European Parliament and Council Directive 97/7 ([1997] OJ L144/19) on the protection of consumers in relation to distance contracts, with the exception of Art.10, apply to certain contracts for goods or services to be supplied to a consumer where the contract is made exclusively by means of distance communication. They require the supplier to confirm in writing information already given and to provide additional information, including the conditions and procedures relating to the exercise of the right to cancel the contract; provide for a cooling off period to enable the consumer to cancel the contract by giving notice of cancellation to the supplier; and provide that on cancellation of the contract the consumer is under a duty to restore goods to the supplier if he collects them and in the meantime to take reasonable care of them. In addition, they provide that the contract must be performed within 30 days subject to agreement between the parties; provide that where the consumer's payment card is used fraudulently in connection with a distance contract the consumer will be entitled to cancel the payment; and prohibit the supply of unsolicited goods and services to consumers. The Mail Order Transactions (Information) Order 1976 (SI 1976 1812) is revoked.

840. Consumer protection – gas fires – sale of unsafe gas appliances

[Consumer Protection Act 1987 s.40(2); Gas Appliances (Safety) Regulations 1995 (SI 1995 1629) Sch.3, Reg.7(1), Reg.8.]

D was a director and majority shareholder of two limited companies, H and R, which carried on business as manufacturers and suppliers of gas fires. Between October 1998 and April 1999 both companies made supplies of "hotbox" College Coal Fires to trade purchasers. Examination and testing of one such fire following a test purchase by a trading standards officer revealed five instances of noncompliance with the essential requirements of the Gas Appliances (Safety) Regulations 1995 Sch.3. The testing body also concluded that the fire may not be safe when used in normal circumstances. Further investigations revealed that whilst an EC Type Examination Certificate had been issued in April 1998 for an "inset" version of the fire, no such certificate had been issued for the "hotbox" version. No EC Declaration of Conformity or Certificate of Conformity had been issued for either fire. Both companies were dissolved before the laying of informations and the case proceeded against D alone under the Consumer Protection Act 1987 s.40(2) D pleaded not guilty.

Held, that D was guilty of five offences of consenting in offences committed by the two companies under Reg.7(1) and Reg.8 of the 1995 Regulations. D was fined £3,500 on each information and ordered to pay prosecution costs of £9,760.

OXFORDSHIRE CC v. AMOR, February 23, 2000, Judge not applicable, MC. [*Ex rel.* A John Williams, Barrister, 13 King's Bench Walk, Temple, London].

841. Consumer protection – hazardous substances – nickel – contact with skin

DANGEROUS SUBSTANCES AND PREPARATIONS (NICKEL) (SAFETY) REGULATIONS 2000, SI 2000 1668; made under the Consumer Protection Act 1987 s.11. In force: In accordance with Reg.1; £1.50.

These Regulations, which implement European Parliament and Council Directive 94/27 ([1994] OJ L188/1), prohibit the supply of post assemblies intended to be inserted into a pierced part of the human body during epithelization of the wound caused by such piercing and containing nickel or a nickel compound unless the concentration of nickel is less than 0.05 per cent; the supply of products containing nickel or a nickel compound which are intended to come into direct and prolonged contact with the skin unless the rate of nickel release will not exceed the rate of 0.5g/cm2/per week; and the supply of products containing nickel or a nickel compound and which have a non nickel coating and which are intended to come into direct and prolonged contact with the skin.

842. Consumer protection – hazardous substances – packaging and labelling

CHEMICALS (HAZARD INFORMATION AND PACKAGING FOR SUPPLY) (AMENDMENT) REGULATIONS 2000, SI 2000 2381; made under the European Communities Act 1972 s.2; the Health and Safety at Work etc. Act 1974 s.15; and the European Communities Act 1972 s.82, Sch.3 para.1. In force: October 2, 2000; £1.50.

These Regulations, which amend the Chemicals (Hazard Information and Packaging for Supply) Regulations 1994 (SI 1994 3247), introduce a new edition of the approved supply list and make minor amendments to the provisions relating to child resistant fastenings and tactile warning devices, thereby implementing Commission Directive 2000/32 ([2000] OJ L136/1) Art.1 (1) (7) adapting to technical progress for the 26th time Council Directive 67/548 ([1967] OJ L196/1) on the approximation of the laws, regulations and administrative provisions relating to the classification, packaging and labelling of dangerous substances.

843. Consumer protection – hazardous substances – packaging and labelling

DANGEROUS SUBSTANCES AND PREPARATIONS (SAFETY) (CONSOLIDATION) AND CHEMICALS (HAZARD INFORMATION AND PACKAGING FOR SUPPLY) (AMENDMENT) REGULATIONS 2000, SI 2000 2897; made under the European Communities Act 1972 s.2; and the Consumer Protection Act 1987 s.11. In force: November 27, 2000; £10.50.

These Regulations, which revoke the Dangerous Substances and Preparations (Safety) (Consolidation) (Amendment) (No.2) Regulations 1999 (SI 1999 3193) and the Chemicals (Hazard Information and Packaging for Supply) (Amendment) (No.3) Regulations 1999 (SI 1999 3194), implement European Parliament and Council Directive 99/43 ([1999] OJ L166/87), which amended for the 17th time Council Directive 76/769 ([1976] OJ L262/201) on the approximation of the laws, regulations and administrative provisions of the Member States relating to restrictions on the marketing and use of certain dangerous substances and preparations. They amend the Dangerous Substances and Preparations (Safety) (Consolidation) Regulations 1994 (SI 1994 2844) and the Chemicals (Hazard Information and Packaging for Supply) Regulations 1994 (SI 1994 3247) by updating the lists contained in Sch.2 and Sch.6 Part IIIA respectively to include the amendments made by Directive 99/43.

844. Consumer protection – labelling – meat products – German law stipulating meat and water content – European Union

[EC Treaty Art.30 (now, after amendment, Art.28 EC); Council Directive 79/112 on the labelling, presentation and advertising of foodstuffs Art.2, Art.3(1), Art.5(1); Law on Foodstuffs and Products for Human Consumption (Germany).]

Criminal proceedings were brought in Germany against V, a Dutch meat producer. V had exported meat products to Germany, and was prosecuted under the Law on Foodstuffs and Products for Human Consumption (Germany), LMBG, and the German Food Code for marketing Dutch formed shoulder ham composed of ham pieces under the description "shoulder ham". This was alleged to be misleading in that it should have contained the word "formed". Other allegations related to the lack of labelling of an unusually high water content (up to 18 per cent) which was required under German law and of a relatively low muscle meat protein content (88 per cent as opposed to the 90 per cent stipulated in the LMBG). The case was referred to the ECJ to determine whether the LMBG was contrary to the EC Treaty Art.30 (now, after amendment, Art.28 EC).

Held, that it was contrary to Art.28 for national rules to prohibit the marketing of foodstuffs for consumer protection reasons where such goods were lawfully marketed in another Member State. Consumer protection as regards labelling matters was afforded by Council Directive 79/112. It was contrary to Art.2 and Art.5(1) of the Directive for a trade description to be used that prevented purchasers in the Member State where the goods were sold from determining their true nature. Article 3(1) required water to be listed as an ingredient where added water exceeded five per cent of the finished product's true weight.

ARNOLDOUS VAN DER LAAN (C383/97), *Re*; *sub nom*. CRIMINAL PROCEEDINGS AGAINST VAN DER LAAN (C383/97) [2000] 1 C.M.L.R. 563, P Jann (President), ECJ.

845. Consumer protection – product liability – primary agricultural products

CONSUMER PROTECTION ACT 1987 (PRODUCT LIABILITY) (MODIFICATION) ORDER 2000, SI 2000 2771; made under the Consumer Protection Act 1987 s.8. In force: December 4, 2000; £1.50.

This Order implements European Parliament and Council Directive 1999/34 ([1999] OJ L141/20), which amends Council Directive 85/374 ([1985] OJ L210/29) on the approximation of the laws, regulations and administrative provisions of the Member States concerning liability for defective products by removing the exception for primary agricultural products and game. It modifies the Consumer Protection Act 1987 by extending the scope of the provisions of Part I to primary agricultural products and game.

846. Consumer safety – cosmetics – prohibited substances

COSMETIC PRODUCTS (SAFETY) (AMENDMENT) (NO.2) REGULATIONS 2000, SI 2000 2765; made under the European Communities Act 1972 s.2. In force: October 11, 2000, October 31, 2000 and January 1, 2001; £2.00.

These Regulations amend the Cosmetic Products (Safety) Regulations 1996 (SI 1996 2925) to implement Commission Directive 2000/11 ([2000] OJ L65/22), which amends for the twenty-fifth time Council Directive 76/768 on the approximation of the laws of the Member States relating to cosmetic products and Commission Directive 2000/6 ([2000] OJ L56/42) adapting to technical progress Annexes II, III, VI and VII to Council Directive 76/768 on the approximation of the laws of the Member States relating to cosmetic products. They permit the use of specified substances, subject to restrictions, including the use of boric acid, borates and tetraborates in talcum powder, oral hygiene products and certain other products, and impose labelling requirements in respect of products intended to be used for children under three years old.

847. Consumer safety – cosmetics – prohibition of ingredients tested on animals

COSMETIC PRODUCTS (SAFETY) (AMENDMENT) REGULATIONS 2000, SI 2000 1679; made under the European Communities Act 1972 s.2. In force: June 29, 2000; £1.00.

These Regulations amend the Cosmetic Products (Safety) Regulations 1996 (SI 1996 2925), which contained a prohibition, on the supply of cosmetics which contain ingredients or combinations of ingredients tested on animals, when such testing takes place after June 30, 2000 and is undertaken in order that the products may satisfy the requirements of those Regulations. They change the date on which the prohibition will come into force from June 30, 2000 to June 30, 2002 and implement Commission Directive 2000/41 ([2000] OJ L145/25).

848. Direct sales – delivery of sales leaflet did not trigger cooling off period under SI 1987 2117 Reg.4

[Civil Procedure Rules 1998 (SI 1998 3132) Part 27 r.27.12; Consumer Protection (Cancellation of Contracts Concluded away from Business Premises) Regulations 1987 (SI 1987 2117) Reg.4; Consumer Protection (Cancellation of Contracts Concluded away from Business Premises) (Amendment) Regulations 1998 (SI 1998 3050) Reg.2(b), Reg.3(3)(b).]

H was a supplier of replacement windows. As part of its marketing strategy it delivered leaflets that included a coupon inviting the recipient to either telephone H or return the coupon requesting a visit from a salesperson. H asserted that V had done just that and had arranged an appointment for a visit on January 9, 1999. That appointment was rearranged for January 13, when H's representative provided a quote for the works and on January 14 V signed an agreement for the supply of replacement windows at a cost of £2,800. V claimed that he had neither received any leaflet nor contacted H. V claimed that the visit by H's representative had been unsolicited and that the document he had signed was a quote for replacement windows, rather than a binding agreement. The district judge at the hearing of the small claim restricted the giving of evidence to matters arising on and before January 14, 1999 and found as a preliminary point that the visit by H's representative was unsolicited and that in the absence of any cancellation clause, pursuant to the Consumer Protection (Cancellation of Contracts Concluded away from Business Premises) Regulations 1987 Reg.4, the purported contract was unenforceable. H appealed against the district judge's order under the Civil Procedure Rules 1998 Part 27 r.27.12, arguing that there had been a serious irregularity in that the district judge had prevented H from calling any evidence of matters arising after January 14 which indicated inconsistencies in V's evidence and therefore challenged his credibility on the question of whether the initial visit was solicited or not.

Held, allowing the appeal and rehearing the claim, whereupon V raised a new preliminary point that, irrespective of H's claim, the delivery of a leaflet was a visit as envisaged by Reg.3(3)(b), as substituted by the Consumer Protection (Cancellation of Contracts Concluded away from Business Premises) (Amendment) Regulations 1998 Reg.2(b), that the delivery of a leaflet through a door did not fall within Reg.3(3)(b). Regulation 3(3)(b) envisaged a visit by an individual and accordingly the delivery of a leaflet, in whatever form, did not trigger the "cooling off" requirements of Reg.4 of the Regulations.

HAVAIR LTD v. VILE, January 31, 2000, Judge Thompson, CC (Basildon). [*Ex rel.* James Fieldsend, Barrister, Second Floor, Francis Taylor Building, Temple, London].

849. Hire purchase – options – clause in agreement to purchase for nominal fee – inclusion of clause indicated hire purchase agreement

[Sale of Goods Act 1979 s.25(1).]

CAF entered into an agreement for the hire of machinery under which C paid instalments totalling £2.5 million over a seven year period. The agreement was written on a standard form used in hire purchase contracts and C was referred to throughout as the "hirer". At the expiry of the seven years a clause in the agreement gave C an option to purchase the machinery for a nominal £50. Subsequent to a further agreement under which C purported to sell the machinery to CGM, CAF brought proceedings seeking damages for wrongful interference with goods on the basis that C did not have legal title to the machinery under the Sale of Goods Act 1979 s.25(1). CAF succeeded at first instance, where it was held that the agreement was an agreement to hire rather than an agreement to buy. CGM appealed, contending that the option clause could be disregarded because, when viewed sensibly and commercially, no reasonable person looking at its terms would fail to exercise the clause, and that given the significant size of the transaction the consideration of £50 was purely nominal. It followed, CGM submitted, that the agreement was an agreement to buy the machinery.

Held, dismissing the appeal, that the inclusion of an option to buy at a nominal fee after payment of the final instalment indicated that the agreement was a hire purchase agreement. Given that an agreement to buy carried a legal obligation to buy, the agreement in the instant case provided merely an option for C to purchase the machinery, *Helby v. Matthews* [1895] A.C. 471 applied, *Forthright Finance Ltd v. Carlyle Finance Ltd* [1997] 4 All E.R. 90, [1997] C.L.Y. 972 distinguished. C had therefore made no commitment as to exercising the option and it followed that it had not taken title to the machinery.

CLOSE ASSET FINANCE v. CARE GRAPHICS MACHINERY LTD [2000] C.C.L.R. 43, Buckley, J., QBD.

850. Package holidays – tour operators and travel agents

See LEISURE INDUSTRY. §4048

851. Personal injuries – defective condom led to unwanted pregnancy – ozone damage to rubber not cause of fracture

[Consumer Protection Act 1987 s.3.]

R became pregnant after a condom worn by her husband burst during intercourse. R brought a claim against the condom's manufacturers, L, under the Consumer Protection Act 1987 s.3 for damages for personal injury, arguing that the condom must have been damaged by ozone, which would have caused the latex to weaken, or have developed some other defect, whilst it was still in the factory. L agreed that there was ozone damage but contended that it must have taken place during the time that the used condom had been left in a cupboard pending R's complaint.

Held, dismissing the application, that on the basis of both the evidence of the manufacturing process and of the experts, the evidence of the expert called for L was to be preferred and therefore the ozone damage had occurred after the latex had fractured. It was not possible to pinpoint why it had fractured, current scientific research showing that condoms did burst on occasion for no readily discernible reason. Thus the claim had not been made out.

RICHARDSON v. LRC PRODUCTS LTD [2000] P.I.Q.R. P164, Ian Kennedy, J., QBD.

852. Trade descriptions – false sun cream claims

[Trade Descriptions Act 1968 s.1, s.20, s.24.]

S, a chemist, was the managing director of a company, L, which manufactured children's protective sun cream. S was prosecuted under the Trade Descriptions Act 1968 s.1 and s.20 in respect of the cream, which was described on the outside of the tube as having a sun protection factor of 35 which provided "total sun block" and "complete protection for babies and children against harmful UVA and UVB rays". On analysis, the cream was found to have an SPF of 10 and the evidence was that even if it had had an SPF of 35 as claimed, the description would still have been false as it did not provide total sun block or complete UVA/UVB protection. S pleaded guilty to six specimen charges. L defended the charges, claiming due diligence under s.24 of the Act.

Held, that L was to be acquitted in respect of the specimen SPF 35 allegations but guilty in respect of four specimen charges concerning the descriptions "total sun block" and "complete protection". S was fined £4,000 with £5,000 costs and L fined £4,000 with £10,250 costs.

OXFORDSHIRE CC TRADING STANDARDS v. SINGH, February 29, 2000, Stipendiary Magistrate Roscoe, MC. [*Ex rel.* Guy Opperman, Barrister, 3 Paper Buildings, Temple, London].

853. Trading standards – investigation by trading standards concerning non compliance of required safety standards for baby walkers – press release published by local authority ultra vires statutory consumer protection scheme

[Local Government Act 1972 s.111 (1), s.142 (2); Consumer Protection Act 1987 s.14; General Product Safety Regulations 1994 (SI 1994 2328).]

LCC's trading standards department carried out an investigation of baby walkers manufactured by members of BPA. LCC alleged that certain walkers did not meet the required safety standards and issued a press release declaring its findings, leading to a subsequent product recall. BPA applied for a judicial review of the issue of the press release and the Secretary of State for Trade and Industry was added as a respondent.

Held, allowing the application, that the press release was ultra vires the provisions of the statutory code contained in the Consumer Protection Act 1987 and the General Product Safety Regulations 1994. Whilst the code was designed to protect the public against unsafe products, it had a dual responsibility to ensure that business interests were also adequately protected. LCC was empowered by the Local Government Act 1972 s.142 (2) and s.111 (1) to declare the issue of a suspension notice prohibiting the supply of suspected unsafe goods, but could only have publicly announced the findings if s.14 of the 1987 Act had been complied with. To issue a press release without such action was outside the statutory scheme. Neither the Secretary of State nor LCC had acted within the remit of the scheme and the press release had dispossessed manufacturers and suppliers of statutory rights and protection.

R. v. LIVERPOOL CITY COUNCIL, *ex p.* BABY PRODUCTS ASSOCIATION; *sub nom.* R. v. LIVERPOOL CC, *ex p.* BABY PRODUCTS ASSOCIATION (2000) 2 L.G.L.R. 689, Lord Bingham of Cornhill, L.C.J., QBD.

854. Weights and measures – equipment – fees

MEASURING INSTRUMENTS (EEC REQUIREMENTS) (FEES) (AMENDMENT) REGULATIONS 2000, SI 2000 689; made under the Finance Act 1973 s.56. In force: April 1, 2000; £1.00.

These Regulations amend the Measuring Instruments (EEC Requirements) (Fees) Regulations 1998 (SI 1998 1177) to provide for an increase in the fees in respect of services provided by the Department of Trade and Industry in relation to type approval and testing of measuring instruments. The hourly rate for these services is increased from £65 to £70.

855. Weights and measures – equipment – filling instruments

WEIGHING EQUIPMENT (AUTOMATIC GRAVIMETRIC FILLING INSTRUMENTS) REGULATIONS 2000, SI 2000 388; made under the Weights and Measures Act 1985 s.15, s.86. In force: July 17, 2000; £3.00.

These Regulations implement International Recommendation OIML R 61 of the Organisation Internationale de Metrologie Legale relating to automatic gravimetric filling instruments (Edition 1996 (E)), to the extent that the Recommendation applies to such instruments following the grant or renewal of a certificate of approval of a pattern by the Secretary of State under the Weights and Measures Act 1985 s.12. They define "filling instruments" to which they apply, set out general duties in terms of erection, installation, use and manner of use and provide for certain requirements which must be satisfied before a "filling instrument" is passed as fit for use for trade.

856. Weights and measures – equipment – filling machines – testing

WEIGHING EQUIPMENT (FILLING AND DISCONTINUOUS TOTALISING AUTOMATIC WEIGHING MACHINES) (AMENDMENT) REGULATIONS 2000, SI 2000 387; made under the Weights and Measures Act 1985 s.15, s.86. In force: March 17, 2000; £1.50.

These Regulations amend the Weighing Equipment (Filling and Discontinuous Totalising Automatic Weighing Machines) Regulations 1986 (SI 1986 1320) by providing an additional exception under which an inspector may test a filling machine notwithstanding the fact that the conditions for testing otherwise laid down are not met. A new Reg.23A is inserted in respect of filling machines imported from another Member State or EEA State which provides that a filling machine shall not be tested by the inspector when he is presented with the "requisite documentation".

857. Weights and measures – equipment – non automatic machines

WEIGHING EQUIPMENT (NON-AUTOMATIC WEIGHING MACHINES) REGULATIONS 2000, SI 2000 932; made under the Weights and Measures Act 1985 s.11, s.12, s.15, s.86, s.94. In force: May 2, 2000; £4.50.

These Regulations, which revoke and consolidate the Weighing Equipment (Non-automatic Weighing Machines) Regulations 1988 (SI 1988 876), prescribe non automatic weighing machines for the purposes of the Weights and Measures Act 1985 s.11 (1) so as to make it unlawful to use such machines for trade purposes unless they have been tested, passed as fit for such use and stamped by an inspector of weights and measures, or by an approved verifier under the terms of the 1985 Act as amended by the Deregulation (Weights and Measures) Order 1999 (SI 1999 503).

858. Publications

Brown, David – Producer Responsibility: Packaging Law. Paperback: £45.00. ISBN 1-902558-12-X. Palladian Law Publishing Ltd.

Cranston, Ross; Black, Julia; Scott, Colin – Consumers and the Law. 3rd Ed. Law in Context. Paperback: £24.95. ISBN 0-406-98802-1. Butterworths. Paperback: £24.95. ISBN 0-406-98802-1. Butterworths Law.

Silberstein, Sandra – Consumer Law. 3rd Ed. Nutshells. Paperback: £5.50. ISBN 0-421-68330-9. Sweet & Maxwell.

Walker, Peter M. – Practice Notes on Consumer Law. Practice Notes. Paperback: £15.95. ISBN 1-85941-573-3. Cavendish Publishing Ltd.

CONTRACTS

859. Assignment – champerty – nature of assignment of franchisees' rights

[Insolvency Act 1986 s.436.]

ANC, the franchisor of a parcel collection and delivery service appealed against a decision validating the assignments of causes of action against ANC by two former franchisees. ANC contended that (1) the terms of the franchise agreements imposed a wide prohibition on the assignment of rights, and (2) placing reliance on *Glegg v. Bromley* [1912] 3 KB 474 that an equitable assignment of the fruits of an action did not convey any rights in the action itself and thus it followed that the assignment of rights in an action constituted an independent agreement subject to the rules on champertous agreements.

Held, dismissing the appeal, that (1) the franchise agreements had been terminated prior to the assignments and upon proper construction the prohibitive terms were not intended to survive termination, and (2) there was a distinction between the assignment of the rights in the action and the assignment of the beneficial rights of the franchisee in the fruits of the action, and even if the assignment of the latter was a sale of property within the meaning of the Insolvency Act 1986 s.436, it was unconnected with the liquidator's exemption from champerty, *Linden Gardens Trust Ltd v. Lenesta Sludge Disposals Ltd* [1994] 1 AC 85, [1993] C.L.Y. 303 followed.

ANC LTD v. CLARK GOLDRING & PAGE LTD *The Times*, May 31, 2000, Robert Walker, L.J., CA.

860. **Auctions – sale without reserve – measure of damages**

[Sale of Goods Act 1979 s.51 (3).]

H, a firm of auctioneers, appealed against a judgment requiring it to pay B, a bidder, a sum of £27,600, following H's withdrawal of items from an auction without reserve. B had bid £200 for each of two engine analysers, being auctioned without reserve, which were worth £14,000. H's agent refused to sell the machines on the ground that the bid was too low and the machines were sold a few days later. B claimed damages on the basis that he was the highest bidder. H contended that (1) an auction without reserve did not create an obligation to sell to the highest bidder; (2) there was no consideration for the auctioneer's promise, and (3) as an agent for a disclosed principal, the auctioneer could not be held liable in contract.

Held, dismissing the appeal, that (1) the highest bidder at an auction without reserve could not be rejected simply because the bid was too low, *Warlow v. Harrison* (1858) 1 El. & El. 295 followed. The auctioneer was obliged, by virtue of a collateral warranty, to sell to the highest bidder and a failure to do so amounted to a breach; (2) the detriment to the bidder arising from the fact that his bid could be accepted unless withdrawn and the benefit to the auctioneer arising from the fact that the sale price was driven up by the bid, was adequate consideration, and (3) although the contract of sale existed between vendor and purchaser, a collateral agreement existed between H and B. Where the seller refused to continue with the sale, the measure of damages was to be determined with reference to the difference between the contract price and the current market value of the goods by virtue of the Sale of Goods Act 1979 s.51 (3).

BARRY v. DAVIES (T/A HEATHCOTE BALL & CO); *sub nom.* HEATHCOTE BALL & CO (COMMERCIAL AUCTIONS) LTD v. BARRY; BARRY v. HEATHCOTE BALL & CO (COMMERCIAL AUCTIONS) LTD [2000] 1 W.L.R. 1962, Sir Murray Stuart-Smith, CA.

861. **Breach of contract – arbitration – termination of contract by racing driver – nature and scope of dispute referred to sporting body**

[Arbitration Act 1996 s.9.]

D, a Formula One racing driver, sought a stay of proceedings commenced by his former team, W, for breach of contract. D had terminated his contract with W on the basis of alleged breaches of contract pursuant to clause 9.2 (b) of the agreement. W denied that it was guilty of any conduct entitling D to terminate under clause 9.2 (b) and maintained that the agreement had instead been terminated by D pursuant to clause 9.5, as a result of which D was liable to pay W the sum of $7 million. D subsequently signed a contract with another Formula One team, S, and S submitted its contract with D to the Contract Recognition Board for registration. The Board noted that the contractual periods in the two separate contracts overlapped and were subsequently invited by S to resolve the conflict. In the interim period, W issued proceedings against D in England. The Board of Recognition subsequently determined that the contract between W and D had been validly terminated, but adjourned a decision as to the basis upon which termination had been made. D sought a stay of the English action pursuant to the Arbitration Act 1996 s.9, contending that, pursuant to clause 11 of the agreement, the dispute was one which the parties had agreed should be determined by the Contract Recognition Board, such agreement effectively amounting to a reference to arbitration.

Held, dismissing the application, that whilst the proceedings before the Contract Recognition Board were arbitral in character, by virtue of clause 7.9 of the contract, the Board was limited to a decision upon which contract took preference and whether the contract between W and D had been terminated. The Board had no power to resolve the dispute over whether the contract had been terminated under clause 9.2(b) or clause 9.5 because there was no live dispute over whether the contract had in fact been terminated and, therefore, that issue did not fall within the scope of the matters referred to the Board. Thus the substance of the dispute had not been referred to the Board, a conclusion reinforced by the fact that the Board had no power to make any award of damages as a result of its findings.

WALKINSHAW v. DINIZ [2000] 2 All E.R. (Comm) 237, Thomas, J., QBD (Comm Ct).

862. Breach of contract – deductions for late completion of sections of work

[Civil Procedure Rules 1998 (SI 1998 3132) Part 24, Part 25.]

BLL, a contractor, applied for summary relief against BG, the employer, in respect of two interim applications for payment under the Civil Procedure Rules 1998 Part 24 and Part 25. BG argued that (1) it was entitled to make deductions for late completion of certain sections of the work because there had been no agreement to an extension of time, and (2) it had a valid counterclaim for damages relating to several breaches of contract by BLL which it was entitled to set off against BLL's claim.

Held, refusing the applications, that, on the evidence, (1) BG had a strong argument for entitlement to make deductions for late completion, and (2) BG had a real prospect of succeeding on its counterclaim, and in the circumstances the applications were inappropriate.

BOVIS LEND LEASE LTD (FORMERLY BOVIS CONSTRUCTION LTD) v. BRAEHEAD GLASGOW LTD (FORMERLY BRAEHEAD PARK RETAIL LTD) 71 Con. L.R. 208, Dyson, J., QBD (T&CC).

863. Breach of contract – pre contractual misconduct ground for termination – conduct prior to agreement – objective test required

B, a former international swimmer, was engaged as a facilities consultant by the Amateur Swimming Association, ASA, and received secret commissions for making commercial recommendations to ASA clients. Subsequently, B entered into an agreement formalising his appointment as a promoter of the ASA awards scheme, which included a clause stipulating that termination by ASA was permitted if the claimant was convicted of any serious criminal offence or would "otherwise be guilty" of conduct tending to bring the ASA or himself into disrepute. ASA investigated the payments and decided that such arrangements brought ASA into disrepute and purported to terminate the agreement. B's claim for damages for breach of contract was dismissed and he appealed, contending that misconduct occurring prior to the agreement could not be taken into account and, in any event, he had not considered his actions to be of an improper nature so as to qualify for termination under the clause.

Held, dismissing the appeal, that pre contractual misconduct could be relied on as a ground for termination as it was triggered by guilt which was established after the date of the agreement, notwithstanding that the conduct which was in dispute had taken place prior to the agreement. B's claim that he did not believe he had been dishonest was immaterial as B's conduct was to be judged by an objective test. Objectively, there was a real probability that B's conduct was sufficient to bring the ASA or himself into disrepute.

BLAND v. SPARKES *The Times*, December 17, 1999, Otton, L.J., CA.

864. Building and engineering contracts – breach of contract – defects in building – entitlement to nominal damages only where existence of direct remedy for third party

A, a building contractor, was employed by P to construct an office building and a car park on land belonging to UIP, an associated company of P. Defects appeared in the building and P launched arbitration proceedings against AM claiming substantial damages. AM appealed against a decision to allow a claim by P ([1998] C.L.C. 636, [1998] C.L.Y. 809), arguing that P had suffered no financial loss. No contractual relationship existed between P and UIP to complete the building work. Nevertheless, AM had entered into a separate duty of care deed with UIP, giving UIP and successive owners restricted remedies in respect of defective work. Although the case of, *Linden Gardens Trust Ltd v. Lenesta Sludge Disposals Ltd* [1994] 1 A.C. 85, [1993] C.L.Y. 303 had established the principle that a party not suffering any loss might be able to claim on behalf of a third party for the benefit of whom the contract was entered into, it was argued in the instant case that this exception did not apply as UIP had a direct remedy against AM.

Held, allowing the appeal (Lord Goff and Lord Millett dissenting), that in circumstances where a contract between a builder and an employer was for the construction of a building on the land of a third party who would own that building, the employer could seek substantial damages from the builder for any defects in the building only where the third party actually suffering the loss had no direct remedy against that builder. Where a direct remedy existed, such as in the form of a duty of care deed, the employer would be entitled to nominal damages only. The purpose of the exception to the rule that the party suffering no loss could not claim, as expounded in *Owners of the Cargo Laden on Board the Albacruz v. Owners of the Albazero (The Albacruz and The Albazero)* [1977] A.C. 774, [1976] C.L.Y. 2529, and applied in *Linden Gardens*, was to provide a remedy to third parties where no other remedy would be available. The force of that reasoning was lost, however, where the third party had a direct right to claim substantial damages. Accordingly, in the instant case, as UIP had a direct remedy, it could not be argued that P's interest in the due performance of the contract had suffered. P had not suffered substantial loss and was entitled to nominal damages only.

ALFRED MCALPINE CONSTRUCTION LTD v. PANATOWN LTD (NO.1); *sub nom.* PANATOWN LTD v. ALFRED MCALPINE CONSTRUCTION LTD [2001] 1 A.C. 518, Lord Clyde, HL.

865. **Carriage by air – standard form sales agency agreements – airlines instructing travel agents to use misleading term**

IATA, an international trade association representing the interests of airlines, contracted with a number of travel agents who were members of ABTA. The contracts were on IATA's standard terms and conditions contained within IATA Resolution 824, incorporating Resolution 814. The British Airports Authority, BAA, had for some years charged airlines for the use of its airports and these charges included a passenger service charge, PSC. Prior to 1999, the airlines did not include PSC in the total price of the tickets but absorbed the charges levied by BAA along with their other overheads. The majority of airline tickets were sold to passengers by the travel agents who received commission from IATA on each sale. The commission paid by the airlines to the travel agents was based on a percentage of the price of the ticket exclusive of taxes. In February 1999 IATA informed ABTA that PSC must be charged as a tax on all tickets issued for travel after April 1, 1999 and that the commission paid to the travel agents would be calculated on the price of the ticket exclusive of taxes and PSC. ABTA and the travel agents, who would stand to lose significant sums of commission as a result of the change, brought an action against IATA and the airlines for breach of contract claiming declarations and other relief. The judge found IATA to be in breach of contract for reducing the commission payable, and in breach of an implied term by requiring the travel agents to show PSC as a tax on tickets. IATA appealed against the orders of the judge ([2000] 1 Lloyd's Rep. 169), contending that by virtue of IATA Resolution 814 the "fares applicable" did not include PSC and that Resolution 824, section 9 gave them authority to make unilateral changes to the commission payable. ABTA argued that, (a) as PSC was not a tax, it should be treated as a part of the "fares applicable" and that therefore the travel agents were entitled to commission on that element of the ticket price, and (b) IATA were in breach of contract by requiring travel agents to refer to PSC as a tax on tickets.

Held, dismissing the appeal, that (1) "fares applicable" should not be interpreted too narrowly and did include PSC; (2) section 9 of Resolution 824 was not drafted in terms which were intended to give the airlines a unilateral right to reduce the commission in the manner that they had done. Any attempt to amend the commission payable would have to comply with the procedure for effecting amendments as set out in Resolution 824, and (3) PSC was not a tax and it was correct to make a declaration that IATA should not require travel agents to designate it as such.

ASSOCIATION OF BRITISH TRAVEL AGENTS LTD v. BRITISH AIRWAYS PLC [2000] 2 All E.R. (Comm) 204, Clarke, L.J., CA.

866. Carriage of goods – exclusion clauses – carrier's subcontractor responsible for loss of goods – statute precluded purported limitation on carrier's liability in bill of lading

[Carriage of Goods by Sea Act of the United States; Convention on the Contract for the International Carriage of Goods by Road (CMR) 1956.]

T, a bicycle manufacturer, dispatched a shipment of bicycles and bicycle frames from Wisconsin to the Netherlands via a carrier, OOCL. After arriving at port in Antwerp, the cargo was entrusted to the carrier's subcontractor, DB, who left the cargo in a locked truck on a public street from where it was stolen. T's subrogated insurers commenced proceedings against OOCL seeking the recovery of the value of the lost cargo and made an application for summary judgment. OOCL maintained that (1) the Carriage of Goods by Sea Act of the United States should be read in conjunction with clause four of the relevant bill of lading whereby responsibility for the safekeeping of the goods rested with participating carriers whilst they, their subcontractors or their agents were in possession of the goods, and not with the principal carrier, and (2) the Convention on the Contract for the International Carriage of Goods by Road was applicable and effective to limit liability.

Held, granting the application for summary judgment, that (1) the Carriage of Goods by Sea Act of the United States was applicable to the entire intermodal carriage of the goods including the period when they had been in the possession of DB. The Act prohibited the insertion of clauses in a bill of lading which sought to reduce a carrier's liability, and subsequent authority had confirmed that parties were only permitted to contract outside the ambit of its provisions where a carrier's liability was increased rather than reduced, *General Electric Co v. MV Nedlloyd* 817 F.2d 1022 and *Encyclopaedia Britannica Inc v. SS Hong Kong Producer* [1969] 2 Lloyd's Rep. 536, [1970] C.L.Y. 2652 applied, and (2) the limitation contained within the Convention on the International Carriage of Goods by Road was ineffective to limit the liability of OOCL because OOCL had not given T a fair opportunity to declare a value higher than that prescribed by the Convention, *Nippon Fire & Marine Insurance Co v. MV Tourcoing* 167 F.3d 99 considered. Furthermore, the only contract that had incorporated the Convention was that subsisting between OOCL and DB, and since T had not been a party to it, it was not binding on T or its insurers.

OOCL BRAVERY, THE [2000] 1 Lloyd's Rep. 394, Douglas F Eaton, US Court.

867. Carriers liabilities – contract terms – compensation scheme in respect of third parties

See POSTAL SERVICES: Post Office v. British World Airlines Ltd. §4555

868. **Choice of law – contractual obligations**

CONTRACTS (APPLICABLE LAW) ACT 1990 (AMENDMENT) ORDER 2000, SI 2000 1825; made under the Contract (Applicable Law) Act 1990 s.4. In force: in accordance with Art.1; £2.00.

This Order amends the Contracts (Applicable Law) Act 1990, which gives effect, in the UK, to the 1980 Convention on the law applicable to contractual obligations (Rome Convention) and the Luxembourg Convention of 1984. It makes minor amendments to the 1990 Act to reflect the revisions made to the Rome Convention on the accession of Austria, Finland and Sweden and enables the UK to ratify that Convention.

869. **Collateral contracts – warranties – beer tie in lease – effect of "entire agreement" clause**

[Misrepresentation Act 1967 s.3.]

I applied for an injunction to restrain E from breaking a beer tie contained in its lease and for an account of damages for breach of the clause. E counterclaimed that, notwithstanding an "entire agreement" clause in the lease, I had given a collateral warranty that the tie would be released. E had relied upon the undertaking given by I to the Secretary of State for Trade and Industry that the number of pubs owned by I, which were subject to a tie in agreement, would be restricted by 1992 and, that all pubs still under I's ownership would be released from the tie by 1998.

Held, giving judgment for I and dismissing the counterclaim, that the "entire agreement" clause contained in the lease not only had the effect of rendering evidence of the alleged collateral warranty inadmissible, but also deprived the warranty of all legal effect, *Deepak Fertilisers & Petrochemical Corp v. Davy McKee (London) Ltd* [1998] 2 Lloyd's Rep. 139, [1998] C.L.Y. 858 applied. Further, the agreement clause was not in breach of the Misrepresentation Act 1967 s.3 which was inapplicable to a contractual provision which defined where the terms of the contract were to be found, *McGrath v. Shah* (1989) 57 P. & C.R. 452, [1990] C.L.Y. 650 applied. In any event, the reference to a release from the tie in 1991 was insufficient to support the giving of the alleged collateral warranty to E which, owing to the passage of time, would have been invalid at the time of the execution of the agreement.

INNTREPRENEUR PUB CO LTD v. EAST CROWN LTD [2000] 2 Lloyd's Rep. 611, Lightman, J., Ch D.

870. **Computer contracts – effects of misrepresentation and delay – total failure to supply under terms of contract permitting rescission**

[Misrepresentation Act 1967 s.3; Unfair Contract Terms Act 1977 s.3(1).]

IC contracted to deliver a computer system with a required level of functionality to SW. SW claimed that it was entitled to terminate the contract when IC was unable to give an assurance that it would deliver the computer system on time and on the basis of misrepresentation arising from IC's failure to enter into a back to back agreement necessary to deliver the requisite functionality. IC argued that the contract contained an entire agreement clause, such that any prior misrepresentations were superseded. SW submitted that the entire agreement clause and the limitation clauses were subject to the test of reasonableness under the Misrepresentation Act 1967 s.3 and the Unfair Contract Terms Act 1977 s.3, respectively. IC further asserted that SW was not entitled to restitution as it had received hardware, software and management services at IC's expense.

Held, giving judgment for SW, that the delay to the contract made it clear that IC could not complete the contract by the completion date. This delay was so grave as to go to the root of the contract entitling SW to rescind it, *Universal Cargo Carriers Corp v. Citati* [1957] 2 Q.B. 401 considered, *Chilean Nitrates Sales Corp v. Marine Transportation Co Ltd (The Hermosa)* [1982] 1 Lloyds Rep 570, [1982] C.L.Y. 2455 and *Afovos Shipping Co SA v. R Pagnan & Fratelli (The Afovos)* [1983] 1 W.L.R. 155, [1983] C.L.Y. 3414 applied. An entire agreement clause was subject to the test of reasonableness under s.3 of the 1967 Act. In the instant case, the entire agreement clause purported to exclude liability for fraudulent misrepresentation made prior to the contract and therefore failed to satisfy the requirement of reasonableness, *Thomas Witter Ltd v. TBP Industries* [1996] 2 All E.R. 573, [1996] C.L.Y. 1238 applied. On the facts, IC was dealing on its standard terms and conditions, subject to modification by negotiation, which effectively left the standard terms and conditions untouched so that they were subject to the test of reasonableness under s.3(1) of the 1977 Act. The contract did not provide for the abandonment of the works or non completion of the contract. The limitation clauses were therefore unreasonable. Finally, the fact that IC had delivered hardware, which could not be used without the software, even if there was nothing wrong with the hardware, was of no significant value to SW. SW did not get any part of that for which it had paid the purchase money and was therefore entitled to restitution, *Rowland v. Divall* [1923] 2 K.B. 500 applied, *Salvage Association v. CAP Financial Services Ltd* [1995] F.S.R. 654, [1995] C.L.Y. 772 considered.

SOUTH WEST WATER SERVICES LTD v. INTERNATIONAL COMPUTERS LTD [1999] B.L.R. 420, Judge Toulmin Q.C., QBD (T&CC).

871. Contract of sale – claim that agreement for sale of health food chain intended to incorporate deferred tax – working capital to be interpreted in normal commercial sense

N agreed to buy a health food retail chain, H. The sale agreement included provision of a "working capital amount" to ensure that H could be sold as essentially cash and debt free. The question for the court was whether the working capital amount was intended by the parties to take into account deferred tax as at the date of completion. The vendor G contended that it was not so included, and therefore there were still substantial sums owed by N under the contract.

Held, giving judgment for the claimants, that deferred tax was not included in the working capital amount. Both parties were experienced commercial negotiators advised by knowledgeable accountants and solicitors. It could therefore be assumed that they construed "working capital" in its normal commercial sense as including only liabilities payable within one year. The broader interpretation necessary to bring deferred tax within the definition of the working capital amount could not be inferred. There was no mutual consensus at any stage with regard to its inclusion, and N were not therefore entitled to rectification of the sale agreement.

GEHE AG v. NBTY INC [1999] C.L.C. 1949, Moore-Bick, J., QBD (Comm Ct).

872. Contract terms – contractual obligation on software manufacturer to provide after sales service "in perpetuity" – meaning of "in perpetuity"

H's written notice terminating an agreement to supply software to G was found by the court to be effective. The court further found that a clause within the agreement requiring H to "provide support and maintenance in perpetuity" survived the termination, since it was a separate and severable obligation under the agreement. G's appeal and H's cross appeal concerned the duration of H's continuing obligation. G contended that the meaning of the words meant that it should last for ever, or, at any rate until its customers ceased to pay for it, whilst H submitted that such literal interpretation was uncertain and uncommercial and that either the clause should be rejected for uncertainty, or alternatively the court should substitute the words used for a specified shorter period, which was considered to be reasonable in the context.

Held, allowing G's appeal and dismissing H's cross appeal, that the words "in perpetuity" were inconsistent with the imposition of any time limit and, in this case, the obligation was to continue without limit of time, for as long as the contract continued to survive, which, in view of technological advances, would not be indefinitely. H's obligation would continue until G and its customers no longer required and were no longer willing to pay for the support and maintenance services and H was not released from the contract merely because it might become uneconomic for H to perform it.

HARBINGER UK LTD v. GE INFORMATION SERVICES LTD [2000] 1 All E.R. (Comm) 166, Evans, L.J., CA.

873. **Contract terms – football – season ticket holders – discretion of football club to reallocate seats**

[Unfair Contract Terms Act 1977.]

In 1994 Newcastle United Football Club, NU, offered season ticket holders at the club a package of benefits, which was named a "bond", in return for a payment of £500. One of the benefits was the opportunity to purchase a season ticket for a designated seat in the stadium for the following 10 seasons. In 1998 NU embarked upon an improvement scheme which involved the construction of a new stand to increase the seating capacity of the stadium. Letters were sent to the bondholders who had seats in the affected area informing them that their designated seats would have to be relocated. D and other bondholders brought an action against NU contending that publicity material produced by NU had purported to guarantee them a designated seat for a period of 10 years. The court held that the representations in the publicity literature did not override clause 9(b) of the contract between D and NU which gave NU the power to require the bondholders to occupy alternative seats and, further, that clause 9(b) was not unenforceable by virtue of the Unfair Contract Terms Act 1977. D appealed arguing that NU's promise of a specific seat for 10 years was enforceable and that clause 9(b) did not apply. Alternatively, D contended that if the clause did apply, NU could only exercise its power to change her seat if there was a good and sufficient reason. She maintained that the proposed improvement plans did not constitute such a reason.

Held, dismissing the appeal, that the documentation supplied to the bondholders showed that they had been made aware that whilst NU would endeavour to provide them with a particular seat, circumstances might arise where they would have to be moved to another seat. There was no inconsistency between those statements. Whilst NU's scheme had upset certain bondholders, it had been implemented for the good of the club; the judge had considered the improvement scheme carefully and had found it to be sensible, commercially viable and in the interests of the club as a whole; accordingly, NU had properly exercised its discretion under clause 9(b).

DUFFY v. NEWCASTLE UNITED FOOTBALL CO LTD *The Times*, July 7, 2000, Waller, L.J., CA.

874. **Contract terms – repudiation – local authority contract for leisure management and grounds maintenance – interpretation of contractual termination clause**

R contracted with G, a local authority, to provide leisure management and grounds maintenance services for a period of four years. The contract, which was in the standard form drafted by the Association of Metropolitan Authorities, provided that G would have the right to terminate the contract should R commit "a breach of any of its obligations under the Contract" and that G would be entitled to serve "default notices" on R specifying such breaches. Approximately three months after the contract had been entered into G began serving a number of default notices on R. Several months later G terminated the contract. R issued proceedings against G alleging that it had wrongfully terminated the contract. Despite finding certain breaches proven, the judge held that G had not been entitled to terminate the contract and ordered it to pay the sums due to R pursuant to the contract. G appealed, arguing that the judge should have construed the termination clause in the contract literally and that, had he done so, he would have found that the decision to terminate the contract had been justified. Alternatively, G contended that the cumulative effect of the breaches for which R had been responsible had been such that it had constituted a repudiation of the contract.

Held, dismissing the appeal, that (1) the judge had correctly concluded that in the context of a contract intended to last for four years, involving substantial financial input and a multitude of obligations on the part of R, the termination clause in the contract should be interpreted in a common sense way so as to limit G's right to terminate the contract to circumstances where the contract had been repudiated by R, *Hongkong Fir Shipping Co Ltd v. Kawasaki Kisen Kaisha Ltd (The Hongkong Fir)* [1962] 2 Q.B. 26, [1962] C.L.Y. 2838 and *Antaios Compania Naviera SA v. Salen Rederierna AB (The Antaios)* [1985] A.C. 191, [1984] C.L.Y. 96 applied, and (2) a contract of this kind was comparable to a building contract in that the accumulation of past breaches was relevant both on its own and for the purpose of determining what was likely to happen in the future. What was more, the court was entitled to take into account the circumstances in which breaches had occurred and whether the party seeking to bring the contract to an end had acted in a blameworthy fashion himself. Having assessed the significance of the breaches found to have been established against the background of the contract as a whole and the circumstances of the case, including the role played by G in events, the judge had been entitled to conclude that G had not had the right to terminate the contract.

RICE (T/A GARDEN GUARDIAN) v. GREAT YARMOUTH BC (2001) 3 L.G.L.R. 4, Hale, L.J., CA.

875. Contract terms – restraint of trade – equitable defences available

R appealed against a decision awarding damages to N for breach of contract. It was contended that the trial judge had made (1) an erroneous factual inference in finding that R had adopted and affirmed the management contract, and (2) an error in law by ruling that agreements found to be in restraint of trade or obtained by undue influence could be rendered enforceable by a plea of estoppel or affirmation.

Held, dismissing the appeal, that a general equitable defence such as acquiescence was available as a defence to a claim of restraint of trade.

NICHOLL v. RYDER [2000] E.M.L.R. 632, Thorpe, L.J., CA.

876. Contract terms – standard terms not incorporated into agreement between parties – collateral contract could not exist given lack of intention to contract with more than one party

S was the chief executive of W and of E, both wholly owned subsidiaries of JW. E contracted with M for the provision of computer software. S acted for E in the negotiations. M claimed that its standard conditions of sale applied. Preliminary issues were ordered to be tried concerning, inter alia, the terms of the contract and whether there was any collateral warranty by JW.

Held, that (1) M's standard terms and conditions did not apply since they included a provision that they had to be signed by both M and the customer before they became effective. On the facts of the instant case, however, as the standard terms had not been signed by either M or E they were never incorporated into the contract, *Interfoto Picture Library Ltd v. Stiletto Visual Programmes Ltd* [1989] Q.B. 433, [1988] C.L.Y. 430, [1987] C.L.Y. 445 considered. The contract contained implied terms to the effect that the software would be supplied within a reasonable time and that it would be reasonably fit for E's purposes, as known to M, and that it would be installed by M with reasonable skill and care, and (2) there was no collateral warranty by W given the complete lack of intention that M would contract with any party other than E, *Heilbut Symons & Co v. Buckleton* [1913] A.C. 30 followed.

JONATHAN WREN & CO LTD v. MICRODEC PLC 65 Con. L.R. 157, Judge Peter Bowsher Q.C., QBD (T&CC).

877. **Contract terms – variation – whether contract term concerning letter of credit varied by oral agreement**

An English company, FOM, which had exploitation rights in relation to Formula One motor racing, entered into an agreement with a Korean company, SEC, under which FOM agreed not to grant the right to stage a Grand Prix in South Korea to any party other than SEC for the year 1998. In return SEC provided FOM with an irrevocable letter of credit in the sum of $11.75 million. The contract between the parties provided that if the proposed event did not take place in 1998, FOM would be entitled to retain the entire sum. The planned event did not take place, and FOM obtained payment from the confirming bank. SEC issued proceedings seeking the recovery of the amount paid to FOM. They contended that during the course of two meetings with FOM's managing director, E, it had been orally agreed that the letter of credit would be terminated. On that basis SEC maintained either that the contractual term relating to the letter of credit had been varied or waived by agreement or that FOM was estopped from relying on the term.

Held, giving judgment for FOM, that whilst E had reassured SEC that they would not suffer any financial penalty as a result of the postponement of the Grand Prix during the first meeting, that did not amount to an agreement that the obligations under the letter of credit were no longer to be enforced; instead the statement had been intended to refer to financial penalties that might have been payable in the event of a breach by SEC. As at the conclusion of the second meeting, E and SEC had agreed that the agreement for a 1998 Grand Prix had effectively been terminated, but E had not agreed to the termination of rights that had already accrued in relation to the letter of credit. Such a conclusion was supported by the fact that the meeting had been somewhat ad hoc with no lawyers present, the contents of a draft termination agreement prepared by SEC which contemplated revocation of the letter of credit as at some future date, the fact that E had agreed to discuss the letter of credit in the future against the background of a potential new agreement for the year 2000, and the fact that there had been no mention of any revocation of the letter of credit in the minutes of a board meeting held at the relevant time by SEC.

SEPOONG ENGINEERING CONSTRUCTION CO LTD v. FORMULA ONE MANAGEMENT LTD (FORMERLY FORMULA ONE ADMINISTRATION LTD) [2000] 1 Lloyd's Rep. 602, Longmore, J., QBD (Comm Ct).

878. **Contractual liability – causes of action – effect of waiver – liability for breach of contract**

[Civil Procedure Rules 1998 (SI 1998 3132) Part 24.]

C entered into an agreement with CL for the supply of cooling water. The cooling water was subsequently used by CL to cool water required, amongst other things, for the operation of refrigerators at a meat market. The agreement contained a clause under which C indemnified CL against any losses arising from a breach in its obligations. Under a 1994 tenancy agreement with R, CL undertook to provide the cool water needed for the satisfactory operation of its refrigerators. A dispute arose between C and CL, and in 1996 C brought proceedings against CL alleging breach of contract. CL counterclaimed. On June 20, 1997 the action was settled and an agreement reached incorporating a waiver clause whereby each party agreed not to pursue any prior claims or actions arising from the supply agreement. In 1998 CL initiated proceedings for possession and arrears of rent against R, which had after previous complaints relating to the breakdown of refrigerators withheld deductions from its rent. R counterclaimed for damages, alleging that CL, in breach of the tenancy agreement, had failed to supply suitable cool water. Subsequently, CL issued Part 20 proceedings against C seeking an indemnity or contribution in relation to the counterclaims on the basis that any failure in the supply of cool water was attributable to breaches by C in the supply agreement. C applied for summary judgment under the Civil Procedure

Rules 1998 Part 24 submitting that CL's claims fell within the waiver clause of the settlement agreement and accordingly had no prospect of succeeding.

Held, refusing the application, that (1) the claim based on a breach of the supply agreement by C and the claim based on the indemnity clause contained in that supply agreement fell to be decided separately; (2) the cause of action against C for breach of contract had arisen at the date of the breach, which had occurred prior to June 20, 1997. It followed that the alleged breaches fell within the waiver clause and accordingly had no prospect of success, and (3) the cause of action against C based on the clause within the supply agreement to indemnify CL against liability to a third party had arisen, within the meaning of the waiver clause, not when liability had been incurred but when it had been quantified or realised, *Telfair Shipping Corp v. Inersea Carriers SA (The Caroline P)* [1985] 1 W.L.R. 553, [1985] C.L.Y. 2012 and *Investors Compensation Scheme Ltd v. West Bromwich Building Society (No.1)* [1998] 1 W.L.R. 896, [1997] C.L.Y. 2537 considered. Accordingly, CL's cause of action had accrued after the settlement agreement and could therefore be pursued.

CITY OF LONDON v. REEVE & CO LTD; G LAWRENCE WHOLESALE MEAT CO LTD v. CITIGEN (LONDON) LTD [2000] C.P. Rep. 73, Judge John Hicks Q.C., QBD (T&CC).

879. **Contractual liability – package holidays – asthma attack suffered at excursion on package holiday – contractual liability to use reasonable care and skill to ensure safety**

W brought an action for damages for personal injuries against a tour operator, T, after her return from a package holiday in Spain. The holiday consisted of 14 days for W and her family in an apartment complex in Benidorm. In the first few days of the holiday W purchased from T's in-resort representatives an excursion for herself and her family to a mock medieval joust event "Knights and Frights". The excursion was booked from a brochure which pictured horses and jousting, but which did not state expressly that the event was to take place indoors. W was an asthmatic and had suffered mild to moderate asthmatic attacks, although she never communicated this fact to T or its representatives. Her condition had never previously been triggered by horses or by dust and she had learned to ride and spent a good deal of time around horses as a teenager. Shortly after taking her seat in an indoor arena, and after horses had entered the arena, W felt short of breath and suffered a severe asthma attack. She used an inhaler which did not alleviate the attack and she passed out. W was taken to hospital where she spent five days in hospital, three in intensive care. W subsequently sued T for failing to warn of the risks posed by the event to persons with asthma and argued that T was in breach of a contractual duty to exercise reasonable care and skill to ensure her safety. The medical evidence was that while it was impossible to be very clear as to the cause of W's attack, it was more probable that the exposure to horses had caused her attack than any other factor. In its booking conditions T had accepted contractual liability for personal injury caused by the fault of its representatives. T relied on evidence that verbal warnings of the risks posed by Knights and Frights to asthmatics were habitually given by its representatives as a matter of company policy both at the time that the ticket was purchased and on the coach to the event and, further, that there was always a board at the indoor arena warning people of the risks posed by exposure to horses and dust to asthmatics together with a tannoy announcement in the arena to the same effect and that T argued, satisfied its contractual duty of care to W. W and her family denied having heard or seen any warnings.

Held, dismissing the claim, that (1) on the balance of probability a verbal warning was given on the coach to the event and over the tannoy at the arena; (2) there was, on the balance of probability, a warning sign at the arena; (3) in the circumstances, T had in place a system designed to minimise the risks posed by the excursion to asthma sufferers; (4) T's system was sufficient to satisfy its contractual duty to exercise reasonable care and skill in the provision of excursions to have enabled W to be safe, and (5) T could not be expected to guarantee W's safety by ensuring with certainty that she had heard and/or seen a warning.

WATERS v. THOMSON HOLIDAYS LTD, April 11, 2000, District Judge Mullis, CC (Bow). [*Ex rel.* Matthew Chapman, Barrister, Barnards Inn Chambers, Halton House, 20/23 Holborn, London].

880. **Damage to property – burden of proof – goods damaged during transit – damage resulting from defective packing assumed**

B, Ghanaian printing company, entered into a contract with an English company, X, for the supply of certain machinery to the company premises in Ghana. The machinery was packed and shipped to Ghana where it was discovered that the machinery within the container had been damaged beyond repair. B instituted proceedings against X, alleging that X had packed the machinery badly and that this had led to the damage during transit. X maintained that the machinery had been packed appropriately and securely and that the damage must have resulted from some unknown external impact during the voyage. X further maintained that B had failed to establish on the balance of probabilities that the damage had resulted from bad packing.

Held, giving judgment for B, that there was no reliable evidence in existence to indicate how the goods had been packed into the container. Nevertheless B had discharged the burden of proof since there was no evidence of any out of the ordinary occurrence which could have led to the kind of impact suggested by X and therefore on the balance of probabilities the damage had been the consequence of defective packing.

BUCKS PRINTING PRESS LTD v. PRUDENTIAL ASSURANCE CO 1988/FO/2354, Saville, J., QBD (Comm Ct).

881. **Disclosure and inspection – case management – contract for recovery of stolen painting – extent to which disclosure of identity of intermediary necessary for fair resolution of claim**

T, an art retrieval specialist, made an agreement with M to endeavour to recover a painting by Magritte which had been stolen in 1979. Under the terms of the agreement, T was entitled to receive 50 per cent of the sale proceeds when the painting was sold at auction. T recovered the painting but before it could be sold, the police intervened at M's request and removed it. M refused to make any payment to T, and T commenced proceedings for breach of contract. An interim order made at a case management hearing required T to reveal the identity of the intermediary with whose assistance he had been able to recover the painting. T appealed, contending that (1) it was an express or implied term of the agreement between the parties that the identity of the intermediary would not be revealed, and (2) disclosure would destroy his business and involve a real threat to the safety of the intermediary. M maintained that (1) the individual from whom the painting had been acquired had not been a bona fide purchaser without notice of the theft of the painting and T was therefore in effect attempting to make a profit from the handling of stolen goods, and (2) disclosure was necessary in the interests of justice.

Held, allowing the appeal, that T would not be required to disclose the identity of the intermediary at this stage of the proceedings. The judge had failed to adequately address the issue of whether the agreement contained an express or implied term that the identity of the intermediary would remain undisclosed. If the contract was found not to be unlawful by reason of illegality, then M simply had no right to demand the information. If T was ordered to disclose the intermediary's identity but declined to do so because of his fears for the intermediary's safety, he might be obliged to abandon a potentially sound and significant claim. It was not necessarily the case that disclosure was needed in order to resolve the question of the lawfulness of the contract. The parties would be required to identify the relevant issues prior to a further case management hearing to be listed preferably before the trial judge. The outcome of such a process might well prove to be that disclosure was unnecessary for the fair resolution of the principal matters in issue between the parties, or that certain issues could be tried in advance of others.

TOUSSAINT v. MATTIS [2001] C.P. Rep. 61, Schiemann, L.J., CA.

882. Distribution agreements – film industry – audits – liability for record keeping under contract where party not film producer but intermediary

P, a film company, entered into an agreement with a company, C, whereby P licensed the video distribution rights of its film output to C in certain specified countries. Both parties were aware that P was not the producer of any of the films licensed under the terms of the agreement but rather the sales agent for other third party production companies. Under the terms of the agreement C agreed to pay a non-refundable advance. The advance was calculated by reference to the production costs and costs of promotion. After some years, C exercised its audit rights pursuant to cl.17(d) of the agreement which required P, "to maintain complete books and records" and discovered that much of the information required to confirm the figures provided by P in respect of the production and promotion costs was retained by the third party producers and therefore unavailable for inspection. C suspended payment of further advances due. P instituted proceedings seeking a declaration as to the construction of the agreement and C counterclaimed for reimbursement of advances already paid. The court at first instance held that the records that P was obliged to retain pursuant to cl.17(d) of the agreement consisted solely of those documents actually provided to it by the third party producers and distributors and dismissed C's counterclaim. C appealed, contending that P was obliged to retain in its possession, or alternatively arrange for access to, all documents required to complete an audit and that the conclusions of the judge at first instance undermined the clear commercial purpose of verification contemplated by cl.17(d).

Held, allowing the appeal, that P's obligations under cl.17(d) required it to maintain, or provide access to, records of the cost of individual items of expenditure forming the costs of production and promotion. If the agreement was construed on its face it was clear that the obligation to maintain records fell to P alone. The judge had erred in his conclusion that the term "maintain" was to be interpreted solely as a reference to documents received. The inclusion of the term "complete" clearly indicated that contemporaneous records of cost such as individual invoices and receipts were included within its scope and such a conclusion was reinforced by the context of providing verification of the costs incurred by way of audit. This interpretation was not undermined by the possibility of an external audit post production as such audits were not necessarily conducted in every single case, nor by the knowledge of the parties concerning P's role as a non producer in view of the fact that the principal production companies concerned were largely owned by P.

COLUMBIA TRISTAR HOME VIDEO (INTERNATIONAL) INC v. POLYGRAM FILM INTERNATIONAL BV (FORMERLY MANIFESTO FILM SALES BV) [2000] 1 All E.R. (Comm) 385, Potter, L.J., CA.

883. Exclusion clause – defects discovered after guarantee expired – breach of express terms

See SHIPPING: China Shipbuilding Corp v. Nippon Yusen Kabukishi Kaisha (The Seta Maru, The Saikyo and The Suma). §4738

884. Exclusion clauses – effectiveness in excluding consequential losses

H, a large hotel group installed in its hotels automatic minibars known as "robobars", supplied under contract by a company HSL. The robobars were faulty in that their chiller cabinets leaked ammonia which had a corrosive effect upon the device and which also presented a potential threat to health. Eventually all of the robobars were removed by H from its hotels and H instituted proceedings for breach of contract. At first instance the court found for H on the issue of liability and awarded substantial damages. HSL appealed against the award of damages representing the cost of removal and storage of the robobars and a further award for loss of profit. HSL contended that an exemption clause within the contract excluding all liability for any indirect or consequential loss was effective to defeat these two heads of claim.

Held, dismissing the appeal, that both of the heads of loss in question were natural and direct consequences of the defects in the equipment provided by HSL and when the exemption clause was considered in its documentary and commercial context it was apparent that neither heads of loss fell within its ambit.

HOTEL SERVICES LTD v. HILTON INTERNATIONAL HOTELS (UK) LTD [2000] 1 All E.R. (Comm) 750, Sedley, L.J., CA.

885. Formation – identity of contracting parties

An oil trading company, S, entered into a written contract with another oil trading company, F, for the sale of crude oil to F over a seven month period in 1997. F had previously formed another company, C, as a joint project with a Hong Kong businessman, Z, who was also a non executive director of F. AF was employed as deputy manager of C. In the contract between S and F, C was nominated as F's operational contact. Subsequently, S entered into four additional contracts to supply crude oil, three of which were made with C and one with F. S maintained that a similar contract to that agreed with F in 1997 had been entered into with F in 1998 following an oral agreement between S and Z, acting on behalf of F. S maintained that the oral agreement had subsequently been confirmed by telex and instituted proceedings for sums outstanding under the 1998 contract. F denied that it had entered into any contract with S in 1998, contending that the agreement had in fact been made with C, which was now in liquidation, via AF.

Held, granting the declaration that F was not a party to the 1998 contract, that after hearing the evidence of the witnesses it was clear that the oral agreement had been reached during a conversation between representatives of S and Z with the minor details to be resolved later by other personnel in S together with AF. The evidence revealed that Z did not possess either actual or ostensible authority to commit F to any contractual arrangements, and accordingly F were entitled to the relief sought.

SINOCHEM INTERNATIONAL OIL (LONDON) LTD v. FORTUNE OIL CO LTD [2000] 1 Lloyd's Rep. 682, Toulson, J., QBD (Comm Ct).

886. Holidays – implied terms – guarantees

See LEISURE INDUSTRY: Marsh v. Thomson Tour Operators. §4044

887. Implied terms – contract leaving decision as to satisfaction of conditions to party's discretion – need for communication on business efficacy grounds

S entered into negotiations with SC for the sale of rights in a ladder stabilising device. In January 1989 SC sent S what purported to be draft heads of agreement. This document provided for further agreements relating to, inter alia, SC's acquisition of exclusive rights to S's patents, copyright and trademark in return for yearly royalties. Further, it provided that SC would make a payment on account of royalties in the sum of £250,000, which was made up of £150,000 to be paid after a feasibility study and a production and marketing plan and the balance to be paid after evaluation of a proposed regional advertising test market. The first stage was to be completed by June 30, 1989, with the whole process completed by September 30, 1989. In August 1989 SC discovered that a competitor had developed a similar and cheaper product. There then followed correspondence in which SC stated that it had proceeded on the basis that the subject matter was unique; that S had not completed the feasibility study by the agreed completion date and that the heads of agreement document was not legally binding. S disagreed and claimed for monies due under the agreement on the basis that SC had repudiated it. At first instance the court found that the draft heads provided for payment conditional upon satisfactory completion of the feasibility study and the judge being satisfied by S's internal documents that S had fulfilled that condition at least one month earlier and before SC had discovered the rival product, held that S was entitled to payment regardless of the fact that it failed to communicate its fulfilment of the condition to SC. SC appealed.

Held, allowing the appeal, that the terms of a commercial contract were not generally determined by the uncommunicated thoughts of one of the parties for the good practical reason that the other party may never know about them. Further, a promise which left performance at the discretion of the promisor would not be enforceable. This was because the consideration would be illusory until performance. In the instant case the terms of the agreement could not be satisfied until SC had communicated its intention to proceed to S. As a matter of business efficacy it was necessary to imply into the contract a term requiring communication that the evaluation provided for under the heads of agreement was complete by either paying the lump agreed or entering into further contracts. In situations where no licence had been granted, the court would require a clear express term to show that a party had agreed to make payments on account of royalties.

STABILAD LTD v. STEPHENS & CARTER LTD (NO.2) [1999] 2 All E.R. (Comm) 651, Peter Gibson, L.J., CA.

888. **Informers – causes of action – public policy precluded informer from maintaining an action to recover payment for information supplied**

R, who had worked for CEC as a confidential informant, brought a claim for payment and expenses. It was submitted by CEC that R had been informed at an initial stage in their dealings that any payment would be dependent on arrests or seizures resulting from his information, and that ultimately the decision as to whether to make a payment, and in what amount, resided not with R's contact but with his contact's superiors. Furthermore, there had been no intention to create legal relations between the parties since any litigation would necessarily involve inquiry by the court into areas involving public interest immunity which would have jeopardised R's safety, something which he would not have agreed to. R contended that CEC had promised to make a payment of £10,000 in return for the information and this amounted to a contractual obligation which had not been fulfilled.

Held, giving judgment for CEC, that in order for R to establish the existence of a binding contract it was necessary for him to prove that there was an intention to create legal relations, since this was not a commercial agreement where such an intention would be presumed by the court and he had failed to do this, *Balfour v. Balfour* [1919] 2 K.B. 571 considered. It was obvious to both parties that any litigation involving such agreements would involve disclosure of sensitive material, normally subject to public interest immunity and it was unthinkable that either party would have intended to create legal relations on this basis. Furthermore, even if it had been established that a contract was in existence, the terms of remuneration had been left to the absolute discretion of the Commissioners with the result that CEC was not obliged to make any payment to R. It had been made clear to R before any assistance had been given by him that there could be no certainty about future payment. It would be contrary to public policy to allow an informant to pursue a claim for reward for his services.

ROBINSON v. CUSTOMS AND EXCISE COMMISSIONERS *The Times*, April 28, 2000, Douglas Brown, J., QBD.

889. **Licences – software – tripartite agreement – fees received by distributor not held on constructive trust for copyright owner on termination**

A owned the copyright to certain software which was distributed by another company, SCL, under a distribution agreement entered into in 1994. The customers paid licence fees to SCL, which was under an obligation to make licence payments to A, not contingent upon SCL receiving the licence fees from the customers. SCL had the power to set the fees in order to provide an element of remuneration for the services it provided, this amount being the difference between the fees received and the payments made to A. The 1994 agreement was lawfully terminated in 1996, but SCL continued to receive licence fees from the customers after the date of termination. A sought to recover these monies from SCL on the basis that they were entitled to fees collected post termination under the agreement and therefore A had a proprietary claim on the fees as against L, the officers of SCL, who held the monies on a constructive trust for the benefit of A. It was held at first instance ([1999] Masons C.L.R.135, [1999] C.L.Y. 854) that licence fees remained payable to SCL on termination of the agreement and A appealed, contending that since the termination provisions of the 1994 agreement allowed A to name a different distributor to whom customers were to pay their licence fees, the obligation on the licensee to pay the fee to SCL was removed on termination.

Held, dismissing the appeal, that A did not have a proprietary claim against the post termination fees received by SCL and those monies were not held on constructive trust for A's benefit. The relationship between the parties and the consequential obligations arising from that relationship remained that of debtor and creditor, as was the position prior to termination. The alteration of the support obligation did not remove the obligation on the licensee to pay fees to SCL and, in any event, the licence agreements had not been modified by negotiation as provided for in the 1994 agreement. SCL did not have a contractual obligation to account to A for fees received. The monies received by SCL from the licensees post termination represented the discharge of a debt between SCL and the customer and the 1994 agreement did not make provision for the specific assignment of those fees to A. A constructive trust could not be inferred on the facts, but a term could be implied that SCL would be obliged to pay to A, a proportion of the monies received, or such reasonable sum as the circumstances prevailing at the time of receipt required, or in the alternative that a restitutionary remedy could be imposed to prevent SCL benefiting from unjust enrichment by keeping post termination fees in their entirety.

ANSYS INC v. LIM; *sub nom.* ANSYS INC v. LIM THUAN KHEE [2000] Masons C.L.R. 25, Waller, L.J., CA.

890. **Misrepresentation – damages – rescission no longer existing – jurisdiction of court to award damages**

[Misrepresentation Act 1967 s.2(2).]

Z, a government department, which had contracted with BA to purchase an executive jet, brought four actions, which included action 679, against BA, seeking to rescind the contract and to claim damages for misrepresentation under the Misrepresentation Act 1967 s.2(2). Upon Z's application for consolidation of the actions, it was suggested that there was only a right to damages under s.2(2) of the Act if the right to rescission still existed at the time of the hearing.

Held, dismissing action 679 on the ground of delay and another action for want of service but allowing the consolidation of the remaining actions, that even if Z had established a right to rescission, that right no longer existed, and the court by virtue of s.2(2) had no power to award damages in such circumstances.

ZANZIBAR v. BRITISH AEROSPACE (LANCASTER HOUSE) LTD [2000] 1 W.L.R. 2333, Judge Jack Q.C., QBD (Comm Ct).

891. **Misrepresentation – pop music performers in sponsorship contract – duty to reveal one member's intention to leave band**

[Misrepresentation Act 1967 s.2(1).]

S, a company formed to promote the Spice Girls, a band, sought payment of various fees pursuant to a sponsorship agreement with A. A counterclaimed for damages on the grounds that it had been induced by a film and the provision of photographic images including all five members of the band, to enter into the contract, which conduct was a misrepresentation that the group would remain intact, despite one member's express intention to leave before the end of the contract. A contended that it had considered that continuity of band membership as essential to the success of its subsequent advertising campaign.

Held, giving judgment for A, that S had been under a duty to correct a representation by conduct, arising from participation in the film, that the band membership was not about to change, and that misrepresentation had induced A to enter into the agreement. S could not discharge the burden imposed by the Misrepresentation Act 1967 s.2(1) of showing that it reasonably believed the representation to be true.

SPICE GIRLS LTD v. APRILIA WORLD SERVICE BV; *sub nom.* SPICE GIRLS LTD v. APRILLA WORLD SERVICE BV [2000] E.M.L.R. 478, Arden, J., Ch D.

892. **Mistake – contract of sale – contract providing for sampling of goods – effect of clerical error in sampling process**

S purchased a shipment of soya bean meal pellets from L. The contract of sale enabled S to claim an allowance against the agreed sale prices if the combined protein and fat content of the pellets was less than 48 per cent. The contract incorporated GAFTA 100 and provided that the "standing in" clauses relating to the sampling of goods would apply. Those clauses stipulated that S should send samples and analytical instructions to two experts, SS and I, that the mean of the tests carried out by SS and I would be regarded as final if the variation between them did not exceed 0.5 per cent, but that if the variation exceeded 0.5 per cent, either party would have the right within 14 days to request a third analysis, in which case the mean of the two tests with the closest results would be accepted as final. The sampling provisions applied by cl.18 of GAFTA 100 stipulated, inter alia, that any party failing to exercise its right to request a further analysis within the relevant time limit would be bound by the mean of the two analyses already carried out. Samples of the pellets were sent to SS and I, whose test results showed a disparity exceeding 0.5 per cent. Neither party asked for a third analysis, and S invoiced L for an allowance that was calculated on the basis of the tests performed by SS and I. L then discovered from SS that, owing to a clerical error, their test results had shown a protein content that was approximately two per cent lower than it should have been. S refused to accept a reduced allowance and referred the dispute to arbitration. S's claim was accepted by the arbitrators but dismissed by the GAFTA Board of Appeal which found that the GAFTA sampling rules did not preclude the correction of a clerical error. S appealed, arguing that the sampling provisions incorporated by the sale contract were intended to be comprehensive. L contended that the relevant provisions did not prevent an admittedly erroneous test certificate from being corrected to reflect the true result of an analysis.

Held, allowing the appeal, that in the case of international commodity sale contracts involving a chain of sales, it was desirable that contractual provisions for the resolution of mistakes should not be open to challenge by the courts. The sampling provisions forming part of the contract between the parties set out a comprehensive code for determining disputes as to quality. Accordingly, had it wished to challenge the test results, L should have requested a third analysis within the 14 day period provided for in the contract. A contrary conclusion would not make commercial sense, since uncertainty would be created as to the extent of the enquiries that could be made into the nature of a possible mistake and the time within which such enquiries could be made, *Agroexport Entreprise D'Etat pour le Commerce Exterieur v. Goorden Import Cy SA NV* [1956] 1 Lloyd's Rep. 319, [1956] C.L.Y. 351, *Alfred C Toepfer v. Continental Grain Co* [1974] 1 Lloyd's Rep. 11, [1973] C.L.Y. 3027, *Coastal (Bermuda) Ltd v. Esso Petroleum Co Ltd* [1984] 1 Lloyd's Rep. 11, [1984] C.L.Y. 3092 and *Charles E Ford Ltd v. AFEC Inc* [1986] 2 Lloyd's Rep. 307, [1987] C.L.Y. 3331 applied.

SOULES CAF v. LOUIS DREYFUS NEGOCE SA [2000] 2 All E.R. (Comm) 154, David Steel, J., QBD (Comm Ct).

893. Mobile homes – pitch fee review – relevant factors – site owner's income from bottled gas sales

Under the terms of the standard pitch agreement, the annual pitch fee for K's mobile home site was subject to a review based on the RPI, expenditure by K for the occupiers' benefit and other "relevant factors". K had sold bottled gas to site residents for a number of years. However, H, along with certain other occupiers, decided to purchase their gas from alternative suppliers, and K informed the residents that the pitch fees for those purchasing gas from other suppliers would be increased to reflect K's loss of income. At first instance it was held that K's income loss from gas sales was not a relevant factor to be considered on the annual pitch fee review. K appealed.

Held, allowing the appeal, that the loss of income from gas supplies was a relevant factor even though H was not obliged to purchase his gas from K. The agreement stipulated that K was obliged to provide that service and K had traditionally regarded the sales as a source of income. Loss of sales, therefore, had an impact on K's ability to operate the site, *Stroud v. Weir Associates* (1987) 19 H.L.R. 151, [1987] C.L.Y. 1893 followed.

HOWARD v. KINVENA HOMES LTD (2000) 32 H.L.R. 541, Simon Brown, L.J., CA.

894. Offer and acceptance – validity of acceptance of offer to Lloyd's Name – distinction between counter offers and collateral contract

SL appealed against an order setting aside a bankruptcy order against T, a former Lloyd's name. The issue turned on whether T had validly accepted the reconstruction and renewal settlement offer made by Lloyd's in 1996. T had expressed doubt as to his ability to perform his part of the contract and asked the offeror for some indulgence, contending that his qualified form of acceptance would only be effective if the offeror were prepared to perform the contract even if the indulgence were not granted.

Held, allowing the appeal, that (1) for an acceptance to be valid, it must be unconditional, and it would not be unconditional if it purported to add a new term to the contract, and (2) it was possible for an offeree to accept an offer unconditionally whilst also making a separate offer which was collateral to the original offer. In the latter case, the unconditional acceptance would be valid with regard to the original offer, regardless of whether the collateral offer were accepted. It was a question of fact as to whether an acceptance was genuinely unconditional with a collateral counter offer, or whether the making of a counter offer could be interpreted as conditional acceptance, and each case fell to be considered in its own factual context having regard to the background and language of the agreement.

SOCIETY OF LLOYD'S v. TWINN (GEOFFREY GEORGE); SOCIETY OF LLOYD'S v. TWINN (GAIL SALLY) *The Times*, April 4, 2000, Sir Richard Scott V.C., CA.

895. Oil and gas production – breach of contract – defects in gas pipeline – construction of clause imposing time limit upon liability post delivery

A company, BS, entered into a contract with BHP to supply coated steel pipes for use in an offshore oil and gas production complex. After more than two years had elapsed following the supply of pipes for a particular gas re-injection pipeline, defects became apparent. BHP instituted proceedings claiming breach of specification, quality control failures and the negligent provision of certificates and inspection reports. BS maintained that (1) any liability was excluded by clause 17.5 of the contract which purported to preclude liability for any defects discovered over 18 months post delivery, and (2) alternatively, any liability was restricted by clause 17.5 to 15 per cent of the total contract price. These issues were tried as preliminary matters and the judge at first instance held that clause 17.5 was an effective exclusion for all contractual liabilities. BHP appealed, contending that there should be no difference between the way in which limitation clauses were construed and the approach adopted in relation to exemption clauses.

Held, dismissing the appeal, that the wording of the clause had been intended as a comprehensive exclusion of all liability howsoever arising rather than limited to breaches of specific obligations. The court was permitted to adopt a less exacting approach when construing limitation, as opposed to exclusion, clauses especially where such limitation clauses were concerned with liability for contract breaches arising from negligence, *Canada Steamship Lines v. King, The* [1952] A.C. 192, [1952] C.L.Y. 610 considered and *Ailsa Craig Fishing Co v. Malvern Fishing Co and Securicor (Scotland)* [1983] 1 W.L.R. 964, [1983] C.L.Y. 440 and *George Mitchell (Chesterhall) Ltd v. Finney Lock Seeds Ltd* [1983] 2 A.C. 803, [1983] C.L.Y. 3314 applied.

BHP PETROLEUM LTD v. BRITISH STEEL PLC [2000] 2 All E.R. (Comm) 133, Evans, L.J., CA.

896. **Package holidays – weather conditions – no guarantee to supply skiing – reliance on force majeure**

See LEISURE INDUSTRY: Charlson v. Warner. §4043

897. **Public procurement – supply of services – award of contracts**

PUBLIC CONTRACTS (WORKS, SERVICES AND SUPPLY) (AMENDMENT) REGULATIONS 2000, SI 2000 2009; made under the European Communities Act 1972 s.2. In force: August 16, 2000; £6.30.

These Regulations implement European Parliament and Council Directive 97/52 ([1997] OJ L328/1) concerning the co-ordination of procedures for the award of public services contracts, public supply contracts and public works contracts respectively in its entirety for England, Wales, Scotland and Northern Ireland. The principal purpose of the Directive is to ensure that contractors, service-providers and suppliers in the European Union are treated no less favourably under the Council Directives on public procurement than third country contractors, service-providers and suppliers are treated under the WTO Government Procurement Agreement (GPA) where it applies. The Public Services Regulations 1993 (SI 1993 3228), the Public Supply Contracts Regulations 1995 (SI 1995 201) and the Public Works Contracts Regulations 1991 (SI 1991 2680) are amended accordingly.

898. **Repudiation – measure of damages – determining point in time when breach accepted – Australia**

T engaged M to build six houses. Progress payments were to be made at eight defined stages of the building works. Following disputes, T excluded M from the site and confiscated the keys. The matter was then referred to an investigatory authority which issued a rectification order, requiring certain works to be completed by August 12, 1994. M was given limited access to carry out the work, but he also issued a statement of claim for money due to him. The statement of claim did not purport to bring the contract to an end. On August 15, 1994, M gave written notice that the rectification order had been complied with, except for one outstanding matter due to illness. However, T had written to M three days earlier, purporting to terminate the contract. The letter stated that M had repudiated the contract as evidenced by the statement of claim. At first instance it was held that T's withholding of the key amounted to a repudiation, so that M's claims under the contract succeeded. T appealed against the finding on repudiation. Further, that the court had been wrong to order progress payments at contractual rates on the unperformed work as this would overcompensate M. T also sought a determination as to whether M's claim for variations would be allowed in restitution as they had not been in writing, as required under the contract.

Held, allowing the appeal in part, that M had not treated the taking of the keys as a repudiation. However, the events following T's letter showed a clear intention to end the contract. Any misapprehension on T's part as to legal rights

CONTRACTS

could not deny the words and conduct used. The judge below had correctly decided the issue of contractual damages as this placed M in the position he would have been in had T not repudiated the contract. There was no evidence to show that the contract provided for M to have all the profit at a particular stage and there was no reason why payment should not be at contractual rates. This did not segregate the contract and did not depart from the requirement to approach the matter in a way that put M in the position he would have been in if the contract had been performed. However, M's claim for variations in restitution could not succeed in the face of an inconsistent contractual provision. The variations did not have written authorisation and there was no evidence that T had agreed to pay extra for them.

TRIMIS v. MINA (2000) 2 T.C.L.R. 346, Mason, P., CA (NSW).

899. **Repudiation – wrongful interference with goods – installation of "time lock" device on computer**

[Sale of Goods Act 1979 s.12(2)(b).]

R appealed against the grant of judgment to U in proceedings for breach of contract. R had entered into a contract to supply U with a computer system. Following installation and partial payment, a dispute had arisen as to whether R was under a contractual duty to transfer information from the old system onto the new one. A representative of R had then installed a "time lock" device in the computer without the knowledge of U. The device was later activated which rendered the computer unusable and UPS was only informed about the device sometime later. R commenced proceedings for the recovery of the balance of the purchase price and U counterclaimed for the return of monies already paid, in addition to or in place of, damages on the ground that R's action had amounted to a repudiatory breach. The judge at first instance held there to have been an implied contractual term that the computer once installed would be in full working order. Accordingly, he found R's actions to have constituted a repudiatory breach. RCS appealed, contending that the installation of the device may have amounted to wrongful interference with goods but had been insufficient to repudiate the contract.

Held, dismissing the appeal, that (1) upon delivery and installation an implied term under the Sale of Goods Act 1979 s.12(2)(b) had arisen. It followed that R's installation of the "time lock" device had constituted wrongful interference with goods, *Gatoil International Inc v. Tradax Petroleum Ltd (The Rio Sun)* [1985] 1 Lloyd's Rep. 350, [1985] C.L.Y. 3152 considered; (2) the contract had been frustrated when activation of the device rendered the computer useless, *Hongkong Fir Shipping Co Ltd v. Kawasaki Kisen Kaisha Ltd (The Hongkong Fir)* [1962] 2 Q.B. 26, [1962] C.L.Y. 2838 applied. Furthermore, the action had been deliberate and had not initially been disclosed by RCS, *Suisse Atlantique Societe d'Armement SA v. NV Rotterdamsche Kolen Centrale* [1967] 1 A.C. 361, [1966] C.L.Y. 1797 considered, and (3) a repudiatory breach having been established, U was entitled to restitution. U had not been in a position to reverse the device and, consequently, the computer had been useless. It followed that the damages suffered could not be less than the purchase price.

RUBICON COMPUTER SYSTEMS LTD v. UNITED PAINTS LTD (2000) 2 T.C.L.R. 453, Mantell, L.J., CA.

900. **Set off – clause ambiguous and poorly drafted in international oil contract – interpretation governed by parties intentions – commercial purposive approach**

S and M were international oil companies trading with each other and their respective affiliates. A dispute arose when M, who was indebted to S under contract A, exercised an alleged entitlement to set off against its liability to S amounts due and unpaid to M's affiliate by S's affiliate under other contracts. The parties could not agree on the construction of a clause in contract A which purported to govern rights of set off. S applied for summary judgment, on the basis that the wording of the clause did not permit set off of an affiliate's liability unless there had been a double default by both the contracting party and the affiliate. M argued that if that was what the clause appeared to say, it was not a natural meaning of the words and it did not give effect to the parties' intentions. The judge found in favour of S ([1999] 2 All E. R. (Comm) 522) and M appealed, contending that the clause should be given a wider purposive construction, reflecting what the parties had agreed and make better commercial sense. S submitted that the meaning of the clause as drafted, although narrow, was clear and unambiguous.

Held, allowing the appeal (Kennedy, L.J. dissenting), that the drafting could not, on any view, be regarded as consistent. The court's task was to construe the provisions of the clause in a way which corresponded with its business purpose, not to impose what it thought would have been a reasonable contract, and to do so it was necessary to consider what meaning the clause conveyed to a reasonable businessman rather than the meaning of the actual words used, *Investors Compensation Scheme Ltd v. West Bromwich Building Society (No.1)* [1998] 1 W.L.R. 896, [1997] C.L.Y. 2537 applied and *Mitsui Construction Co Ltd v. Attorney General of Hong Kong* 33 B.L.R. 1 considered. Applying that test, a reasonable businessman would not have adopted the literal interpretation for which S contended.

SINOCHEM INTERNATIONAL OIL (LONDON) CO LTD v. MOBIL SALES AND SUPPLY CORP (NO.1) [2000] 1 All E.R. (Comm) 474, Mance, L.J., CA.

901. **Share valuation – contract terms – whether clause requiring determination of share value by independent accountant was condition precedent to payment**

A contract was concluded in 1990 between ST, a satellite television company, and M, a company owned by G. Under clause 6.1, ST agreed to pay to M, 55 per cent of the open market value of shares purchased in TAS, a company engaged in the business of installing satellite receiving and decoding systems and also owned by G. Clause 6.1 further specified that the share value was to be determined by an independent chartered accountant. In 1991 G, as assignee of all rights on behalf of M, instituted proceedings claiming payment pursuant to the agreement. By that stage no steps had been taken by any party to determine the value to be ascribed to the shares by appointing an independent accountant in accordance with clause 6.1 and no steps were taken to do so in the run up to the trial. In 1999 the court at first instance dismissed the claim, finding that the determination by an independent accountant was an essential constituent to any entitlement and that it was now too late to make the appointment. G appealed, contending that (1) the provision for appointment of an accountant was not a condition precedent to entitlement but merely a description of the approach to be adopted in the event of any dispute between the parties as to the appropriate share value; (2) the fact that the accountant was not named or an office holder pointed to a finding that the appointment was not a pre-condition to payment but rather mere "machinery"; (3) objective criteria existed, namely the reference to "open market value" enabling the court to fix a price, and (4) the mode of ascertainment of the price could be regarded as subsidiary and non essential in this context, *Sudbrook Trading Estate Ltd v. Eggleton* [1983] 1 A.C. 444, [1982] C.L.Y. 1776 cited.

Held, dismissing the appeal, that affording the clause its natural and ordinary meaning resulted in a finding that determination of the share value by an accountant was indeed an integral part of the definition of the payments claimed. The reference to the open market value basis for valuation did not provide an adequate basis to enable the court to fix a value since such a valuation could be on an earnings basis, an assets basis, a discounted cash flow basis or a combination of these three. A decision as to the most appropriate basis was solely a matter for the discretion of the appointed accountant. Determination by the accountant was therefore not simply a means to fall back on if the need for dispute resolution arose and this was not a case where the means for determining the value had broken down as a result of actions by the parties themselves or as a result of the expert in question refusing to assist or being unable to do so, *Sudbrook* distinguished.

GILLATT v. SKY TELEVISION LTD (FORMERLY SKY TELEVISION PLC) [2000] 1 All E.R. (Comm) 461, Mummery, L.J., CA.

902. Publications

Adams, John; Brownsword, Roger – Understanding Contract Law. 3rd Ed. Understanding Law. Paperback: £10.95. ISBN 0-421-71770-X. Sweet & Maxwell.

Allery, Philip – Overseas Supply and Installation Contracts. Hardback: £120.00. ISBN 0-421-59830-1. Hardback: £79.00. ISBN 0-421-59830-1. Sweet & Maxwell.

Beale, H.G.; Bishop, W.D.; Furmston – Contract-cases and Materials. 4th Ed. Paperback: £27.95. ISBN 0-406-92404-X. Butterworths Law.

Bix, Brian – Contract Law: Vol I & II. International Library of Essays in Law and Legal Theory (Second Series), No 8. Hardback: £210.00. ISBN 1-84014-767-9. Dartmouth.

Burnett, Rachael; Klinger, Paul – Drafting and Negotiating Computer Contracts. 2nd Ed. Hardback: £125.00. ISBN 0-406-90809-5. Butterworths Law.

Chen-Wishart, Mindy – Law of Contract. Butterworths Core Text Series. Paperback: £12.95. ISBN 0-406-03311-0. Butterworths.

Cooke, Elizabeth – Modern Law of Estoppel. Hardback: £45.00. ISBN 0-19-826222-1. Oxford University Press Inc, USA.

Cracknell, D. G. – Contract Law. 11th Ed. Cracknell's Companion. Paperback: £11.95. ISBN 1-85836-275-X. Old Bailey Press.

Davis, Martin; Oughton, David – Sourcebook on Contract Law. 2nd Ed. Sourcebook Series. Paperback: £22.95. ISBN 1-85941-584-9. Cavendish Publishing Ltd.

Jaffey, Peter – Nature and Scope of Restitution. Hardback: £30.00. ISBN 1-901362-48-5. Hart Publishing.

Kellaway, Rosalind – Negotiating International Agency and Distributorship Agreements. International Business Negotiating Guides. Looseleaf/ring bound: Floppy disk: £195.00. ISBN 0-421-63150-3. Sweet & Maxwell.

Krishnan, Vickneswaren – Obligations: Contract Law Textbook. 2nd Ed. Old Bailey Press Textbook Series. Paperback: £11.95. ISBN 1-85836-367-5. Old Bailey Press.

Mckendrick, Ewan – Contract Law. 4th Ed. Macmillan Law Masters. Paperback: £12.99. ISBN 0-333-79427-3. Macmillan Press Ltd.

Merkin, R; Faber, D – Privity-the Impact of the Contracts (Rights of Third Parties) Act 1999. Hardback: £170.00. ISBN 1-85978-598-0. LLP Professional Publishing.

Ndekugri, I.E.; Rycroft, M. – JCT98 Contracts: Law and Administration. Paperback: £24.99. ISBN 0-340-72008-5. Arnold.

One Hundred Contractual Problems and Their Solutions. Paperback: £39.50. ISBN 0-632-05517-0. Blackwell Science (UK).

Smith, J.C. – Smith and Thomas: a Casebook on Contract. 11th Ed. Paperback: £28.95. ISBN 0-421-71690-8. Sweet & Maxwell.

Stone, Richard – Principles of Contract Law. 4th Ed. Principles of Law. Paperback: £17.95. ISBN 1-85941-579-2. Cavendish Publishing Ltd.

Winternitz, I. – Electronic Publishing Agreements. Hardback: £95.00. ISBN 0-19-826872-6. Oxford University Press.

Zimmermann, Reinhard; Whittaker, Simon – Good Faith in European Contract Law. Cambridge Studies in International and Comparative Law, 14. Hardback: £60.00. ISBN 0-521-77190-0. Cambridge University Press.

CRIMINAL EVIDENCE

903. Admissibility – appeals – fresh evidence – expert witness

[Criminal Appeal Act 1968 s.23(2)(d).]

C appealed against his conviction for murder, contending that expert evidence capable of being admitted at trial cast doubt on the safety of his conviction and should be admitted on appeal.

Held, allowing the appeal and ordering a retrial, that when considering whether fresh evidence should be admitted on appeal, regard had to be paid as to whether there was a reasonable explanation for the failure to adduce the evidence at trial under the Criminal Appeal Act 1968 s.23(2)(d). However, that was not decisive and the court should also consider other factors, including the effect of the evidence if it was received and whether in light of those findings it was necessary or expedient in the interests of justice to do so, *R. v. Jones (Steven Martin)* [1997] 1 Cr. App. R. 86, [1996] C.L.Y. 1371 considered. In the instant case, the evidence was from two reliable experts and was capable of belief. Although there was no satisfactory explanation for the failure to adduce the evidence at trial, it clearly had the potential to afford grounds for allowing an appeal against conviction.

R. v. CAIRNS (ROBERT EMMETT) *The Times*, March 8, 2000, Kennedy, L.J., CA (Crim Div).

904. Admissibility – appeals – fresh evidence not available at trial

[Criminal Appeal Act 1968 s.23; Criminal Appeal Act 1995.]

J was convicted in the Crown Court of inflicting grievous bodily harm and appealed, contending that fresh evidence from a witness unavailable at trial cast doubt on the safety of the verdict.

Held, dismissing the appeal, that under the Criminal Appeal Act 1968 s.23, as amended by the Criminal Appeal Act 1995, it was necessary that an affidavit be sworn by defence solicitors outlining the background and the circumstances in which the witness came forward and in which the statement had been prepared in order to assess the validity and truthfulness of the new information. The court concentrated on the validity of the evidence before determining whether or not it was admissible, but ruled that crucially, even on the assumption that the new information was correct, it was unlikely to affect the safety of the conviction.

R. v. JAMES (WALTER JOSEPH) *The Times*, May 9, 2000, Rose, L.J., CA (Crim Div).

905. Admissibility – appeals – fresh evidence relating to different defence

[Criminal Appeal Act 1968 s.23(2); Criminal Appeal Act 1995 s.4.]

Following an unsuccessful plea of guilty to manslaughter by reason of provocation, S was convicted of murder in 1985. Following the death of his codefendant, B, S appealed, contending that B had been responsible for the death of the victim after an unsuccessful attempt to blackmail him, and that he had only admitted to the murder under duress from B.

Held, dismissing the appeal, that, provided that the elements of the Criminal Appeal Act 1968 s.23(2), as amended by the Criminal Appeal Act 1995 s.4, had been considered, the court could accept fresh evidence of a different defence even if the s.23(2) requirements were unsatisfied, *R. v. McLoughlin (John Joseph)* (Unreported, November 30, 1999) doubted, as that decision was novel, see Archbold News Issue 3, and contrary to accepted practice, *R. v. Cairns (Robert Emmett)* [2000] Crim. L.R. 473 followed. However, in the instant case, S's account was not capable of belief given that he had frequently changed substantial details to fit established evidence and was seeking to redeem himself following the death of B.

R. v. S (MARK) (A JUVENILE) [2000] 2 Cr. App. R. 431, Rose, L.J., CA (Crim Div).

906. Admissibility – confessions – personality disorders – expert evidence affecting credibility

Held, that although it was previously thought that expert evidence could only be admitted regarding a defendant's personality and propensity to give false confessions where a recognised mental illness was concerned, *R. v. Turner (Terence Stuart)* [1975] Q.B. 834, [1975] C.L.Y. 562 considered, it was now accepted that it could be admitted if it showed the defendant was suffering from a personality disorder tending to affect the reliability of their confession or evidence, *R. v. Ward (Judith Theresa)* [1993] 1 W.L.R. 619, [1993] C.L.Y. 723 considered. The criteria for admission was not whether the condition came within a recognised category of disorder, but whether the disorder could render a confession or evidence unreliable and did not require the defendant to be either a compulsive liar or known fantasist, *R. v. Roberts* (Unreported, March 19, 1998) followed. Expert evidence was to be limited, however, to instances where the disorder showed a substantial deviation from the given norm, and there was a history which pre dated the confession or evidence that was indicative of an abnormality. Where such evidence was admitted, the jury was to be directed that acceptance was not obligatory, but should be considered as illustrative of the defendant's personality, particularly with reference to facets of which they might have been unaware.

R. v. O'BRIEN (MICHAEL ALAN); R. v. HALL (DARREN DENNIS); R. v. SHERWOOD (ELLIS) [2000] Crim. L.R. 676, Roch, L.J., CA (Crim Div).

907. Admissibility – confessions – police brutality and oppression – Trinidad and Tobago

T, R and L appealed against convictions for murder. At trial their written statements were ruled inadmissible because of police brutality and oppression. The appellants contended that their oral statements and T's and R's alleged conduct in leading a policeman to where the murder weapon was hidden should similarly have been inadmissible because of their involuntary nature.

Held, allowing the appeals, that the prevalent view in Trinidad and Tobago had been that if a defendant denied making an oral statement then no objection could be taken to it. The judge had considered that the police violence had seriously undermined the reliability of the written admissions and, had it not been for that wrongly held prevalent view, he would almost certainly have ruled the evidence of conduct to be involuntary and similarly inadmissible. As that evidence had been the cornerstone of the prosecution case, the convictions were unsafe and were quashed, *Lam Chi-Ming v. Queen, The* [1991] 2 A.C. 212, [1991] C.L.Y. 628, *Ajodha v. Trinidad and Tobago* [1982] A.C. 204, [1981] C.L.Y. 415 and *Thongjai v. Queen, The* [1998] A.C. 54, [1997] C.L.Y. 1094 applied.

TIMOTHY v. TRINIDAD AND TOBAGO [2000] 1 W.L.R. 485, Lord Slynn of Hadley, PC.

908. Admissibility – confessions – police interviews – driving whilst disqualified

[Police and Criminal Evidence Act 1984 s.73.]

M appealed against conviction for driving while disqualified contending that an admission he made during a police interview failed to satisfy the evidential criteria required by the Police and Criminal Evidence Act 1984 s.73 to show that a driver was disqualified.

Held, dismissing the appeal, that a repeated admission was sufficient evidence and the magistrates were right to convict.

MORAN v. CROWN PROSECUTION SERVICE (2000) 164 J.P. 562, Silber, J., QBD.

909. Admissibility – confessions – psychiatric report – linked statements – Canada

See CIVIL PROCEDURE: Cadogan Properties Ltd v. Mount Eden Land Ltd. §568

910. Admissibility – convictions – defendants – convictions originating from same indictment

[Police and Criminal Evidence Act 1984 s.74(3).]

H was convicted of violent disorder, but the jury failed to reach a verdict on a second count of grievous bodily harm. At a retrial, evidence of H's previous conviction for violent disorder was admitted under the Police and Criminal Evidence Act 1984 s.74(3). H denied stabbing the victim and claimed that he was a mere bystander, or at the most, a reluctant participant who only became involved when attacked. H appealed against his conviction for grievous bodily harm, contending that (1) section 74(3) was not applicable to a conviction on a count which originated from the same indictment and was now subject of a retrial, and (2) the judge had erred in the summing up by failing to put H's defence properly.

Held, allowing the appeal, that (1) subsection 74(3) did not restrict the admissibility of evidence of previous convictions but should be construed as an aid in the mode of proof of that fact, however (2) the appeal was allowed on the second ground. The judge found that the evidence did not go to the essential ingredients of the offence charged. However, the evidential issue of whether H was an active participant in the violence was within the terms of s.74(3)

R. v. H (HARRY) (A JUVENILE) *The Times*, May 5, 2000, Potter, L.J., CA (Crim Div).

911. Admissibility – convictions – purpose of admission

[Police and Criminal Evidence Act 1984 s.74.]

D appealed against her conviction for attempted burglary. She had been indicted with two others, one of whom had pleaded guilty to the offence before trial. D's evidence had been that she had been with her codefendant at the material time, but that no burglary had been attempted. D submitted that the court had erred in the exercise of its discretion under the Police and Criminal Evidence Act 1984 s.74 to admit evidence of the conviction by way of guilty plea of her codefendant.

Held, allowing the appeal, that the discretion to admit evidence of the conviction of a codefendant was to be used sparingly. The judge had been quite entitled to admit evidence of the conviction, it being relevant to an issue in the trial, but he had been wrong to direct the jury that they could accept the attempted burglary as a fact, since it was for the jury to decide which account to favour.

R. v. D (SARAH LOUISE) (A JUVENILE) (2000) 164 J.P. 721, Mantell, L.J., CA (Crim Div).

912. Admissibility – DNA profiling – evidence obtained from sample which should have been destroyed – murder

[Police and Criminal Evidence Act 1984 s.64(1), s.64(3B)(b); Criminal Justice and Public Order Act 1994.]

W had been charged with drug related offences and a sample of saliva had been taken from him and submitted for DNA profiling. The charges were discontinued and W was subsequently discharged in October 1997. The sample should have been destroyed as soon as was practicable after that date in accordance with the provisions of the Police and Criminal Evidence Act 1984 s.64(1). As a result of a burglary in which one of the victims died, police accessed the DNA database and identified a match between a small blood stain on a piece of evidence and W's DNA profile. W was arrested in June 1998 on the basis of the DNA match which linked him to the attack. He provided two samples of blood which confirmed the match and was consequently convicted of murder, burglary and assault and sentenced to life imprisonment. W appealed against his conviction and contended that not only had he been entitled to the destruction of his first sample under s.64(1) but that s.64(3B)(b), as inserted by the Criminal Justice and Public Order Act 1994, excluded the admission of any evidence which had resulted from a link between the first sample, which should have been destroyed, and the second sample and any information derived therefrom.

Held, allowing the appeal and quashing the conviction, that the words used in s.64(3B)(b) were plain and had the effect of excluding both the sample and profile taken from 1997 and any information derived from that sample for the purposes of any further investigation. The purpose of the amendments to the 1984 Act was to ensure that a balance was struck between the rights of the State and the rights of the citizen and the 1994 Act clearly ruled out any discretionary power of the court, *Attorney General's Reference (No.3 of 1999), Re* [2001] 2 W.L.R. 56, [2001] 1 C.L. 110 followed.

R. v. WEIR (MICHAEL CLIVE) *The Times*, June 16, 2000, Butterfield, J., CA (Crim Div).

913. **Admissibility – DNA profiling – evidence obtained from sample which should have been destroyed – rape**

[Police and Criminal Evidence Act 1984 s.64(1), s.64(3B)(a), s.64(3B)(b).]

In 1997 a semen swab was taken from a 66 year old rape victim, who had also suffered actual bodily harm in a burglary. A DNA profile was recorded on the DNA database. Following his arrest in 1998 for an unconnected burglary, a saliva sample was taken from B without his permission and after his acquittal, his DNA profile wrongly remained on the DNA database, contrary to the Police and Criminal Evidence Act 1984 s.64(1). The sample was later DNA matched with the semen sample obtained from the rape victim and B was charged with rape. B refused to give an intimate sample but a second non intimate sample of hair was legitimately obtained and was the sole evidence against him in the rape case. The trial judge refused to admit the evidence under s.64(3B)(b) and B was acquitted of the 1997 offences. The Attorney General referred the decision to acquit B, contending that s.64(3B)(b) should not be strictly construed and claimed that the judge had a discretion to admit evidence derived from a sample which should have been destroyed but which had been used in subsequent police investigations.

Held, refusing the reference, that s.64(3B)(b) should be strictly construed together with s.64(3B)(a) and each provided that a judge had no discretion to allow any evidence that had been acquired during an investigation derived from a retained sample which should have been destroyed.

ATTORNEY GENERAL'S REFERENCE (NO.3 OF 1999), *Re*; *sub nom*. R. v. B [2000] 3 W.L.R. 1164, Swinton, L.J., CA (Crim Div).

914. **Admissibility – documentary evidence – proper operation of computer – mobile telephone bill**

[Police and Criminal Evidence Act 1984 s.69.]

M was charged with the theft of a mobile telephone from the premises where she worked as a cleaner. The telephone was never recovered but evidence was adduced, under the Police and Criminal Evidence Act 1984 s.69, in the form of an itemised bill of the calls made from the telephone in the relevant period. The bill showed calls made to telephone numbers in M's telephone book. An employee of the telephone operator working in the operator's investigation department gave evidence of the absence of any indication that the computer, which produced the itemised bill, was malfunctioning at any relevant time. The employee was unable to give evidence as to the precise details of the operation of the computer. The computerised record was allowed to stand as evidence and M was convicted of theft. M appealed on the grounds that the evidence of the operator's employee should not have been admitted.

Held, dismissing the appeal, that the evidence of the operator's employee satisfied the test laid down by Lord Griffiths in *R. v. Shephard (Hilda)* [1993] A.C. 380, [1993] C.L.Y. 636. The employee's familiarity with the workings of the computer and his assertion that there was no malfunction of the computer at the relevant time, based on the fact that there was no record or report of malfunction, were sufficient to satisfy the provisions of the Act. Further, the jury was entitled to take into account that the records were produced by a large company providing a substantial public service which was the subject of licensing and audit by the Department of Trade and Industry, *DPP v. McKeown (Sharon)* [1997] 1 W.L.R. 295, [1997] C.L.Y. 1093 considered.

R. v. MARCOLINO (ANA) [1999] Masons C.L.R. 392, Henry, L.J., CA (Crim Div).

915. Admissibility – documentary evidence – transferral of images via the Internet – certification

See CRIMINAL LAW: R. v. Waddon (Graham). §996

916. Admissibility – entrapment – drug offences – audio tape recordings and journalist's notes

[Police and Criminal Evidence Act 1984 s.78.]

W and his codefendants were accused of supplying a journalist, A, and a local heroin addict, K, with heroin, as part of a newspaper "sting" operation carried out in May 1998. The case was listed for a two day voir dire to determine whether the entrapment constituted an abuse of process and whether the evidence should be excluded under the Police and Criminal Evidence Act 1984 s.78. All parties submitted skeleton arguments and *Teixeira de Castro v. Portugal* (1999) 28 E.H.R.R. 101, [1998] C.L.Y. 3122, *R. v. Smurthwaite (Keith)* [1994] 1 All E.R. 898, [1994] C.L.Y. 669 and *R. v. Singfield* (Unreported, November 23, 1999) were cited. The Crown's case against W was that, although not a regular dealer, W had supplied K with heroin in the previous two days and when asked for some by K had supplied A with two foil wraps a couple of hours later. He did not comment when interviewed but A had a tape of most of the meetings. W denied the allegations. The voir dire focused at the outset on whether K expected to be paid or was paid by A and the quality of A's recording or noting of conversations.

Held, staying the case as an abuse of process, that (1) the conversations had not been fully taped and the quality of A's notes, which were not contemporaneous, was poor; (2) there was a clear difference between K's and A's evidence regarding payment; (3) there was a delay of three months between the operation and the date of statements made to the police; (4) the taped conversations did not answer the key issue of who prompted the sale of drugs, *Teixeira* referred to; (5) the fact that K was a heroin addict placed in question the quality of his recall and evidence; (6) there was insufficient corroboration from interviews, voice recognition evidence, photographs or parades, and (7) there was no police or legal involvement for three months after the operation.

R. v. WOODS (ALAN), March 2, 2000, Judge Taylor Q.C., Crown Ct. [*Ex rel.* Guy Opperman, Barrister, 3 Paper Buildings, Temple, London].

917. Admissibility – entrapment – drug offences – malpractice outside the criminal justice system

[Police and Criminal Evidence Act 1984 s.78.]

H and T, partners in a motor scooter business, appealed against their convictions for supplying a Class A drug, namely heroin. The two had supplied the drugs to News of the World journalists who had posed as wealthy Arabs seeking to purchase scooters for export to the Middle East. The purpose of the newspaper had been to obtain evidence of drug offences against the two. At trial, the judge had refused applications to stay proceedings as an abuse of process or to exclude the evidence of what took place, pursuant to the Police and Criminal Evidence Act 1984 s.78, on the ground that any alleged criminal behaviour on the part of the journalists was venial in comparison to the criminal behaviour of H and T. H and T submitted that the judge had erred in not holding that the journalist's actions had amounted to commercial lawlessness which outweighed any criminal behaviour on their part.

Held, dismissing the appeals, that the court was obliged to balance the interests of avoiding an affront to the criminal justice system against the public interest that those charged with serious crime should be prosecuted. In exercising that discretion, it was necessary to differentiate between malpractice by law enforcement agencies, and commercial lawlessness, which carried less force because the investigator allegedly guilty of malpractice was outside the criminal justice system. In the instant case, the trial judge had considered the relevant circumstances and had exercised his discretion appropriately, *R. v. Latif (Khalid)* [1996] 1 W.L.R. 104, [1996] C.L.Y. 1432 distinguished.

R. v. HARDWICKE (JOSEPH PHILIP); R. v. THWAITES (STEFAN PETER) *The Times*, November 16, 2000, Kennedy, L.J., CA (Crim Div).

918. Admissibility – entrapment – drug offences – supply to journalists

[Police and Criminal Evidence Act 1984 s.78; Human Rights Act 1998 Sch.1 Part I Art.6.]

C appealed against convictions for supplying cocaine, a Class A drug, and a small quantity of cannabis resin, a Class B drug. C had supplied these drugs to a newspaper journalist who had posed as an Arab sheikh. The purpose of the newspaper had been to obtain evidence of drug offences against C. Prior to trial, C argued that (1) all the prosecution evidence, being agent provocateur evidence, should be excluded under the Police and Criminal Evidence Act 1984 s.78 for being unfairly obtained and likely to have an adverse effect on the fairness of the trial, and (2) reliance on the unfairly obtained evidence was contrary to the Human Rights Act 1998 Sch.1 Part I Art.6 in that it deprived C of a right to a fair trial. The judge ruled the evidence admissible and C was convicted. On appeal, relying on passages from *Teixeira de Castro v. Portugal* (1999) 28 E.H.R.R. 101, [1998] C.L.Y. 3122, C propounded a general objection to evidence obtained by agents provocateurs, irrespective of whether the trial as a whole was fair or not.

Held, dismissing the appeal, that there was no general objection to agent provocateur evidence requiring it to be excluded irrespective of any consideration of its impact on the fairness of the proceedings. It was within the discretion of the judge whether to exclude such evidence, on the basis of the impact of the evidence on the procedural fairness of the trial and the reliability of prosecution evidence. The question that had to be asked was whether admitting agent provocateur evidence would compromise the fairness of the trial. This would be the case, for example, if the prosecution evidence was unreliable or tainted in some other way. However, there was no general objection, based on policy considerations, to the admission of such evidence. It was clear from the case of *Teixeira*, that national courts were given considerable discretion on the admissibility of evidence, subject to a duty to ensure the fairness of the proceedings. Moreover, the *Teixeira* case contained no discussion of the meaning of "fair trial" and had been concerned with the actions of police officers. More importantly, there was no evidence in the present case to suggest that there had been actual incitement or instigation to commit the drugs offences.

R. v. SHANNON (JOHN JAMES); *sub nom*. R. v. ALFORD (JOHN JAMES) [2001] 1 W.L.R. 51, Potter, L.J., CA (Crim Div).

919. Admissibility – entrapment – taxis – plain clothed policemen

[Police and Criminal Evidence Act 1984 s.78; Human Rights Act 1998; European Convention on Human Rights 1950 Art.6.]

A, a taxi driver, was driving outside his licensed area without his sign lit up when he was stopped and hired by plain clothed policemen. A stipendiary magistrate refused to admit the policemen's evidence, in the exercise of his discretion under the Police and Criminal Evidence Act 1984 s.78, on the ground that the officers had acted as agents provocateurs. The local authority appealed by way of case stated.

Held, allowing the appeal and remitting the case with a direction to convict, that the admission of the officers' evidence would not prejudice a fair trial. Contrary to A's own evidence, he had not referred to a pre-arranged fare nor been under a mistake of identity when he had picked up the two policemen. Furthermore, there was no evidence of any pressure being exerted upon A to take the fare and commit the offence. The magistrate had been wrong to rule that, although not yet implemented, admission of the evidence was contrary to the intention of the Human Rights Act 1998 and unfair under the European Convention on Human Rights 1950 Art.6.

NOTTINGHAM CITY COUNCIL v. AMIN [2000] 1 W.L.R. 1071, Lord Bingham of Cornhill, L.C.J., QBD.

920. Admissibility – interception – evidence obtained by police from call logging system without warrant

[Telecommunications Act 1984 s.42; Interception of Communications Act 1985 s.1, s.9.]

M appealed against part of a decision (*The Times*, December 29, 1998) dismissing his appeal against a decision upholding his conviction of fraudulently using a telecommunication system under the Telecommunications Act 1984 s.42. The evidence on which the prosecution case was based had been obtained by placing a call logging system on M's telephone line, without obtaining a warrant. Printouts from the system established that it had been used to secure access to the computer systems of certain companies, thereby gaining unauthorised access to outside telephone lines at the companies' expense. M argued that under the Interception of Communications Act 1985 s.9(1), evidence obtained in breach of s.1 of that Act would be inadmissible. Section 1 stated that the intercepting of a communication was an offence. It had been held by the Divisional Court that s.9 merely prohibited questions regarding the way in which the evidence was obtained, but not its actual admissibility.

Held, allowing the appeal, that s.1 and s.9 of the 1985 Act disallowed the admission of evidence obtained by intercepting communications by a person listed in s.9(2), except where that evidence was obtained in accordance with s.1(3) of the 1985 Act. The Act preserved the practice of separating acts of surveillance from the prosecution of offenders, *R. v. Preston (Stephen)* [1994] 2 A.C. 130, [1994] C.L.Y. 864 applied. As the intercept had been made without a warrant, questioning was prohibited both as to the circumstances surrounding the intercept and the evidence obtained as a result, *R. v. Effik (Godwin Eno)* (1992) 95 Cr. App. R. 427, [1993] C.L.Y. 665 overruled.

MORGANS v. DPP [2001] 1 A.C. 315, Lord Hope of Craighead, HL.

921. Admissibility – interception – evidence obtained by telephone tapping by police authority of another Member State

[Criminal Evidence Act 1984 s.78; Interception of Communications Act 1985; Criminal Procedure and Investigations Act 1996 s.35(1); European Convention on Human Rights 1950 Art.6, Art.8.]

X and two others appealed pursuant to the Criminal Procedure and Investigations Act 1996 s.35(1) against the decision of a judge to admit prosecution evidence derived from telephone intercepts carried out by the police authority of another Member State. The judge, having found that the evidence had been obtained lawfully in the foreign jurisdiction, held it to be admissible. X had applied under the Criminal Evidence Act 1984 s.78 to have the evidence excluded. X contended that (1) the interception of telephone calls constituted a breach of the European Convention on Human Rights1950 Art.8, and accordingly the admission of such evidence was contrary to Art.6, and (2) the provisions within the Interception of Communications Act 1985 extended to foreign intercepts whether or not lawfully obtained and therefore the evidence was not admissible.

Held, dismissing the appeal, that (1) the judge had correctly heard the application seeking to exclude the evidence as if the Human Rights Act 1998 were currently in force since it was certain that any appeal would not be heard until after October 2000, *R. v. DPP, ex p. Kebilene* [1999] 3 W.L.R. 972, [1999] C.L.Y. 1045 applied; (2) the judge had not erred in his finding that both the telephone intercepts and subsequent conveying of that evidence to the UK authorities had been lawful and justifiable under Art.8(2). The 1985 Act was limited to telephone intercepts that were carried out in the UK and did not amount to the introduction of a public policy with wider jurisdiction, *R. v. Preston (Stephen)* [1994] 2 A.C. 130, [1994] C.L.Y. 864 considered. Accordingly it had been a matter for the judge's discretion whether or not the evidence should be excluded either under common law or s.78 of the 1984 Act. It was necessary that the legal grounds for carrying out telephone intercepts be accessible and foreseeable so as to enable a person to regulate their conduct accordingly, perhaps with appropriate advice, *Malone v. United Kingdom (A/82)* (1985) 7 E.H.R.R. 14 considered. While it was desirable that all areas of potential interference with privacy be subject to some form of regulation, the absence of such regulation did not automatically result in such information and its uses being unlawful; (3) a balance had to be struck between the provisions of Art.8 and the need to interfere with privacy in the interests of crime prevention. The judge, having found the evidence to have been lawfully obtained, had correctly exercised his discretion in allowing the evidence, *R. v. Aujla (Ajit Singh)* [1998] 2 Cr. App. R. 16, [1997] C.L.Y. 1130 followed, and (4) it was observed that the ruling of the ECHR in *Khan v. United Kingdom* 8 B.H.R.C. 310, [2000] C.L.Y. 3249 did not alter the decision in the instant case. The court was required to follow established principles in circumstances where an alleged breach of Art.8 occurred which did not obviously result in a breach of Art.6, *R. v. Khan (Sultan)* [1997] A.C. 558, [1996] C.L.Y. 1321 considered.

R. v. P; R. v. Y; R. v. Z; *sub nom.* R. v. X *The Times*, May 23, 2000, Potter, L.J., CA (Crim Div).

922. Admissibility – police interviews – suspect not told of more serious offence during questioning

[Police and Criminal Evidence Act 1984 s.78.]

The police arrested K in respect of an assault on N and theft of N's handbag. N was treated in hospital following the assault, and, although she received appropriate treatment, died from post operative complications the day after the offence. K declined the offer of legal representation during interviews. Although the police had all the material information to arrest K on a charge of robbery or manslaughter, they decided to proceed without doing so with a view to seeing what assistance K's answers would first give them on those charges. K was convicted of robbery and manslaughter in part on the basis of evidence then obtained, and appealed, contending that it ought to have been excluded under the Police and Criminal Evidence Act 1984 s.78.

Held, allowing the appeals against conviction for robbery and manslaughter, that where the police had arrested someone for one offence and proposed to question him in relation to another more serious offence, they should charge him with it or make him aware of the true nature of the investigation so as to inform the suspect's decision whether to exercise his right to obtain free legal advice. The Act and its codes presume that suspects knew why they are being interviewed and the level of offence concerned. If, as a result of not knowing, answers were given contrary to their interests, the evidence should normally be excluded because of the seriously adverse effect on the fairness of the proceedings.

R. v. KIRK (ALFRED ALEXANDER) [2000] 1 W.L.R. 567, Kennedy, L.J., CA (Crim Div).

923. Admissibility – searches – breach of PACE codes of practice

[Police and Criminal Evidence Act 1984.]

S, a postmaster, appealed against his conviction for theft on the ground that evidence obtained as a result of a police search was inadmissible since he had not consented to the search as required by the Police and Criminal Evidence Act 1984 Codes of Practice Code B. S, who had reported an alleged armed robbery in his post office, had complied with a request for police access to the premises but had not been asked for his consent. S contended that the search was therefore unlawful. The Crown argued that the search was a routine scene of crime search to which Code B did not apply under para.1.3, which was not intended to cover circumstances where a prolonged occupation of the premises was required. Moreover, since S was regarded as a victim at the time the search took place, no contravention of the Code B had occurred since the Code was designed to protect suspects not victims.

Held, dismissing the appeal, that Code B applied generally to the search of premises, regardless of whether the occupier was a victim or a suspect and written consent was required from the occupiers of the premises. The police search had turned into something more than just a routine scene of crime search. However, notwithstanding the breach of Code B, it was not unfair under s.78 of the Act for the search findings to be adduced as admissible evidence since there was no question as to the reliability of that evidence, *R. v. Keenan (Graham)* [1990] 2 Q.B. 54, [1990] C.L.Y. 813 distinguished. The judge had been correct to exercise his discretion in admitting the evidence since the police had acted in a bona fide manner, and if it had not been admitted for the jury to consider, the error would have resulted in an interference with justice. Furthermore, there was nothing to suggest that consent would not have been granted had it been requested.

R. v. SANGHERA (RASHPAL) [2001] 1 Cr. App. R. 20, Lord Woolf of Barnes, L.C.J., CA (Crim Div).

924. Admissibility – similar fact evidence – evidence of complainant in previous rape trial despite defendant's acquittal

Z was charged with rape. He had previously faced four allegations of rape, one of which resulted in a conviction, the other three in acquittal. The Crown wished to call the four previous complainants to give evidence regarding Z's conduct towards them, with a view to negate Z's defence that the complainant in the present case had consented to sexual intercourse, under the similar facts rule. The Court of Appeal refused to admit the evidence ((2000) 164 J.P. 240), on the ground that it pointed to the guilt of Z in respect of offences of which he had previously been acquitted and accordingly would in effect place him in a double jeopardy position. The Crown appealed.

Held, allowing the appeal, that the evidence could be admitted since the defendant was not being placed in a position of double jeopardy as he was not being prosecuted on the same facts which had given rise to the earlier acquittals. The evidence of the earlier complainants was clearly relevant and fell within the similar fact rule, despite the fact that it showed that the defendant was guilty of the offences of which he had earlier been acquitted, *Sambasivam v. Public Prosecutor, Federation of Malaya* [1950] A.C. 458, [1947-51] C.L.Y. 1979 distinguished.

R. v. Z (PRIOR ACQUITTAL); *sub nom.* R. v. X (PRIOR ACQUITTAL) [2000] 2 A.C. 483, Lord Hutton, HL.

925. Admissibility – similar fact evidence – war crimes – disclosure of offences other than those charged

S was charged with the murder in 1942 of two Jews in Belorussia, in violation of the laws and customs of war. The trial judge refused S's application to stay the proceedings as an abuse of process. The allegation was that S was one of several killers employed on a search and kill operation after a massacre of nearly 3000 Jews. There was eye witness evidence that S was the killer in relation to the two counts of murder and also evidence that S was a policeman involved in the search and kill operation, and a member of the group which included the killer of those identified in the murder counts. S argued that the evidence of two witnesses should be excluded as it was of no relevance to the issues the jury had to resolve, but the trial judge admitted their evidence. S was convicted, and appealed on the basis that the trial judge should have stayed proceedings and was wrong to admit the evidence of the two witnesses.

Held, dismissing the appeal, that (1) on the stay the judge had correctly directed himself, *Attorney General's Reference (No.1 of 1990), Re* [1992] Q.B. 630, [1992] C.L.Y. 615 applied and rightly concluded that, despite the unprecedented lapse of time since 1942, S had not discharged the burden of showing that there was such prejudice to him that a fair trial could not be held, and (2) on the admission of the evidence, in order to make a rational assessment of evidence more directly relating to a charge it might sometimes be necessary for a jury to hear evidence of context and circumstances; therefore evidence of S's involvement in the operation to hunt down and execute survivors of the massacre was probative and admissible even if it disclosed the commission of criminal offences other than those charged.

R. v. SAWONIUK (ANTHONY) [2000] 2 Cr. App. R. 220, Lord Bingham of Cornhill, L.C.J., CA (Crim Div).

926. Admissibility – statements – witnesses in fear – failure to give reasons for admission of statement

[Criminal Justice Act 1988 s.23, s.26.]

D appealed against his conviction for affray. The trial judge had admitted two witness statements under the Criminal Justice Act 1988 s.23 on the ground that the two witnesses were in fear. D contended that there had been insufficient evidence that the witnesses were in fear such as to warrant their statements being read under s.23. It was submitted that the judge had not exercised his discretion under s.26 of the Act correctly or at all when deciding whether the statements should be read and, furthermore, that the judge had not provided reasons for the admission of those statements.

Held, dismissing the appeal, that a conviction would not inevitably be unsafe where a judge had neglected to provide reasons for the exercise of his discretion under s.26 of the Act to allow the admission of evidence in the form of witness statements under s.23. However, it was necessary to show that the judge had properly exercised his discretion and that a finding of guilt had been the only reasonable and proper outcome. In the instant case, the judge had been entitled to conclude that fear precluded the witnesses' attendance. His discretion to admit the witness statements had been properly exercised and the directions he had provided had not only been adequate but had been favourable to the defence. Although reasons should have been given, the failure to do so was not fatal to the conviction, *Stirland v. DPP* [1944] A.C. 315 applied.

R. v. DENTON (CLIVE) [2001] 1 Cr. App. R. 16, Rose, L.J., CA (Crim Div).

927. Admissibility – witness statements – translation by interpreter – inclusion of statements in committtall papers

[Magistrates Courts Act 1980 s.5A(3) (a), s.5B, s.6(2).]

R appealed against his conviction for assault occasioning actual bodily harm and common assault, arising from an attack on two Chinese men. R admitted striking one of the men but claimed to have been acting in self defence. Statements, which formed part of the committal papers, had been taken from the two victims with the aid of an interpreter. The translated statements were verified with each victim and agreement reached as to the contents. Given that, for the purposes of a committal under the Magistrates Courts Act 1980 s.6(2), a witness statement had to comply with the requirements of s.5A(3)(a) and 5B of the Act, R submitted that his committal had been invalid as the statements constituted the account of the interpreters rather than the two victims.

Held, dismissing the appeal, that in order to comply with the requirements of s.5A(3)(a) a witness statement should be the actual statement of a witness rather than a translation, via an interpreter, of what that witness said, *R. v. Derodra (Kishor)* [2000] 1 Cr. App. R. 41, [1999] C.L.Y. 873 distinguished. Accordingly, there had been an irregularity in the committal proceedings, although one for which the magistrates had not been answerable. Given such an irregularity, the court was required to consider whether it had resulted in a demonstrable injustice, *R. v. Gee (Arthur)* [1936] 2 K.B. 442 and *Neill v. North Antrim Magistrates Court* [1992] 1 W.L.R. 1220, [1993] C.L.Y. 680 applied. In the instant case R, notwithstanding the witness statements, was subject to a strong prima facie case against him. He had admitted striking one of the victims, albeit in alleged self defence. Moreover, other witnesses had identified him. It followed that R had not been prejudiced sufficiently to warrant his committal being quashed.

R. v. RAYNOR (STEPHEN) (2001) 165 J.P. 149, Latham, L.J., CA (Crim Div).

928. Burden of proof – summary offences – failure to display vehicle excise licence

[Vehicle Excise and Registration Act 1994 s.29, s.46.]

The Secretary of State laid an information against H in respect of an alleged offence of failing to display a vehicle excise licence contrary to the Vehicle Excise and Registration Act 1994 s.29. According to the Secretary of State's records, H was the registered keeper of the vehicle and had failed to reply to a notice under s.46 requesting details of the person responsible for it on the date of the offence. The Secretary of State contended that the evidence adduced had been sufficient to convict H of the offence. The court held that the fact that H was the registered keeper of the vehicle was insufficient evidence in itself that he was guilty of the offence as there had been no corroborative evidence that H was the driver on the day in question and the burden of proof was on the Secretary of State to show that H was the driver on that day. The Secretary of State appealed.

Held, allowing the appeal and remitting the case to the magistrates court with a direction to convict, that (1) the burden of proof remained on the Crown to show that H was the keeper of the vehicle on the date of the offence; (2) the burden was not discharged by showing merely that H was the registered keeper of the vehicle, and (3) in the instant case, the burden had, however, been discharged because H had failed to respond to the s.46 notice. The justices had been entitled to draw an adverse inference from that failure, *Elliott v. Loake* [1983] Crim. L.R. 36, [1983] C.L.Y. 634 applied.

SECRETARY OF STATE FOR THE ENVIRONMENT, TRANSPORT AND THE REGIONS v. HOLT [2000] R.T.R. 309, Alliott, J., QBD.

929. Burden of proof – summary offences – proof of possession of insurance and MOT certificates

[Road Traffic Act 1988 s.47, s.143.]

K collided with a motorcycle. Informations were issued that he drove carelessly and had used a motor vehicle on a road without insurance, contrary to the Road Traffic Act 1988 s.143, and without an MOT certificate, contrary to s.47. K had not produced either. The justices convicted K of careless driving, but dismissed the other charges on the basis that there had been no requests for production. The DPP appealed by way of case stated on the question of whether the justices had been correct to acquit K when he had not been asked to produce evidence of his insurance or MOT.

Held, allowing the appeal, that once it was proved that K had used the vehicle on the road, the burden shifted to K to prove possession of the insurance policy and the MOT certificate. On the facts, there was no oppression by the police who might have been able to call evidence that there had been a request, even though they had not attended the scene of the accident, *John v. Humphreys* [1955] 1 W.L.R. 325, [1955] C.L.Y. 1632 followed.

DPP v. KAVAZ [1999] R.T.R. 40, Garland, J., QBD.

930. Cross examination – defendants – discrepancies in defence statement – necessity for leave

[Customs and Excise Management Act 1979 s.170(2).]

W was convicted for an offence contrary to the Customs and Excise Management Act 1979 s.170(2) following his arrest at Gatwick airport when he was found to be concealing drugs internally. At trial, an inconsistency had become apparent between the evidence in W's defence statement which had been served by his solicitors, where W said he knew he was carrying the drugs when he arrived in the UK and his evidence during cross examination, in which he maintained that he believed he had vomited up all of the packets before travelling to the UK. The defence statement had not been signed and W alleged that his solicitor had made a mistake in serving an incorrect statement of his case. Whilst referring to the alleged mistake in his summing up, the trial judge had provided the jury with no special guidance. Neither the defence or the prosecution counsel had commented on the discrepancy and W appealed.

Held, allowing the appeal, that the judge had erred in failing to give specific directions as to the inconsistency given that the jury would be affected by it. Defence counsel had correctly believed that she had no right to object to the evidence since the obligation to serve the statement lay with the accused and the solicitor was acting on behalf of the accused and could be assumed to have verified the statement with them. Prosecution counsel also required leave before commenting on the evidence. The conviction was therefore unsafe. It was advisable that defence statements be signed by a defendant in preference to them being permitted to be served by solicitors on a defendant's behalf without procedures being followed to verify accuracy.

R. v. WHEELER (LESLIE); *sub nom.* LESLIE WHEELER [2001] 1 Cr. App. R. 10, Potter, L.J., CA (Crim Div).

931. Cross examination – defendants – discrepancies in defence statement and examination in chief – inferences to be drawn

[Criminal Procedure and Investigations Act 1996 s.11.]

T was convicted of supplying a controlled class B drug, cannabis. T stated in his defence statement that he had been asked to deliver three bin liners containing cannabis, which he believed contained rolling tobacco, for which he was to be paid £100. However, during examination in chief, he stated he would be paid £150. The prosecution applied to the recorder to be permitted to cross examine T as to the discrepancies between his evidence at trial and his defence statement. T appealed against his conviction on the ground that it was wrong for the recorder to allow the jury to consider whether to draw an inference from the differences between his defence statement and the evidence he had given at trial. T contended that there was a distinction between the defence at trial and a defence statement, and that was brought to light by the Criminal Procedure and Investigations Act 1996 s.11(1)(d), where T could comply with s.5(6) by merely describing his defence in the broadest terms, such as "self defence". Furthermore, T claimed s.11 did not apply as the differences were not so substantial as to warrant a direction to the jury from the recorder.

Held, dismissing the appeal, that giving the word "defence" a limited legal meaning would frustrate the purpose of the Act and as a result, its provisions would be unworkable. The aim of the Act was to ensure both parties had the opportunity to investigate matters relied on by the opposite side and to prevent miscarriages of justice. It would be difficult to compare a restrictive defence statement with T's defence given at trial. The defence statement was defined generally as the nature of the defence, the matters on which issue was taken, and the reasons why issue was being taken. It was unnecessary under s.11 (3) to apply for leave to cross examine the accused on differences in the defence and the defence statement. However, under s.11 (3) the interests of the accused were protected by the discretion conferred on the judge in deciding whether such differences justified comment and the drawing of an inference. In the instant case, the discrepancies in the amount of payment for delivery were significant and of fundamental importance to justify the recorder's discretion in allowing the drawing of an inference by the jury.

R. v. TIBBS (JOHN) [2000] 2 Cr. App. R. 309, Beldam, L.J., CA (Crim Div).

932. Cross examination – police officers – previous fabrication of interview record

M was charged, with four others, with conspiracy to supply heroin. The prosecution alleged that money and articles found in his possession were derived from drug dealing. There was also evidence of extensive expenditure. One of the codefendants had pleaded guilty and gave evidence against M, who challenged the bona fides of a witness and accused a police officer, inter alia, of suborning the witness to give false evidence. The defence sought to cross examine the police officer about his involvement in a previous case in which it had been alleged that an interview record had been fabricated. The trial judge ruled that cross examination of the police officer as to credit on the basis of the earlier case was not permissible, because an allegation of subornation was different in kind from an allegation of fabrication. In relation to the evidence of M's possessions and expenditure, the judge did not direct the jury in terms that if the explanation for them might be other than drug dealing, that evidence would not be probative. M was convicted and appealed on the grounds that the judge had erred in drawing a distinction between subornation and fabrication as entirely unrelated types of malpractice, and that the direction concerning M's possessions and expenditure was inadequate.

Held, dismissing the appeal, that (1) if there was clear evidence that a police officer, whose credit and credibility were significant in the case before the jury, had been guilty of serious malpractice on an earlier occasion, that necessarily damaged his credibility when it fell to be judged on the second occasion, even though the malpractice was of a different kind. Accordingly, it was not a ground for denying cross-examination as to credit that the type of malpractice in the case before the jury was different from that alleged in the earlier case and therefore the trial judge had erred in drawing the distinction between subornation and fabrication. However, on the facts of the case the denial of such cross-examination did not render the conviction unsafe, *R. v. Edwards (John)* [1991] 1 W.L.R. 207, [1991] C.L.Y. 732 applied, and (2) that it was not necessary as a matter of law for the judge to tell the jury that they could only hold evidence of M's wealth and expenditure against him if satisfied that it was not the product of innocent commercial activity, even if they rejected the explanation given by M and his witnesses in relation to his wealth and expenditure, they must also rule out the possibility of any explanation other than the prosecution's before treating this as evidence of a conspiracy.

R. v. MALIK (WASEEM) (APPEAL AGAINST CONVICTION) [2000] 2 Cr. App. R. 8, Lord Bingham of Cornhill, L.C.J., CA (Crim Div).

933. Disabled persons – children – facilitated communication – evidence relating to alleged sexual abuse

See FAMILY LAW: D (A Child) (Evidence: Facilitated Communication), *Re*. §2558

934. Disclosure – criminal investigations – initiation of proceedings by third party following disclosure of police evidence

The prosecuting authorities had sought to prosecute M, a councillor and officer of PBC, for corruption and deception. Some of the charges were dismissed and the remaining charges were ordered to lie on the file. The police disclosed material obtained during the course of their investigations, with the consent of the witnesses, to PBC. PBC initiated proceedings against M for breach of his fiduciary duty in relation to an alleged financial inducement received whilst a councillor. M applied to strike out PBC's action as an abuse of process, on the basis that the information had not been obtained with the proper authority of a court of competent jurisdiction. M contended that the prosecuting authorities were bound by an implied undertaking to the court not to use the material obtained in the course of a criminal investigation, other than for the purpose of criminal proceedings, and they were therefore in contempt of court. The court dismissed M's application and M appealed.

Held, dismissing the appeal, that the prosecuting authorities were not subject to an implied undertaking to the court not to use the material obtained in the course of a criminal investigation, other than for the purpose of criminal proceedings, *Taylor v. Director of the Serious Fraud Office* [1999] 2 A.C. 177, [1998] C.L.Y. 1768 considered. In the instant case, the information tended to indicate a prima facie case of corruption perpetrated against PBC, and therefore it was in the interests of justice that the police were entitled to reveal such information. It was also consistent with their duty of returning property to its true owner. The duty of confidence owed by the police to the owner of the documents could be waived if it was in the public interest for the information to be disclosed. However, in the absence of the owner's consent, it was desirable for the police to obtain a subpoena and inform the owner, prior to disclosure, thereby allowing the court to determine whether the duty of confidence should be overridden. The only avenue of redress for a party without ownership rights in the documents was by way of judicial review, as the police owed a general public duty, *Marcel v. Commissioner of Police of the Metropolis* [1992] Ch. 225, [1992] C.L.Y. 3581 applied.

PRESTON BC v. McGRATH *The Times*, May 19, 2000, Waller, L.J., CA.

935. Documents – service by prosecution

CRIME AND DISORDER ACT 1998 (SERVICE OF PROSECUTION EVIDENCE) REGULATIONS 2000, SI 2000 3305; made under the Crime and Disorder Act 1998 Sch.3 para.1. In force: January 15, 2001; £1.50.

These Regulations, which revoke the Crime and Disorder Act 1998 (Service of Prosecution Evidence) Regulations 1998 (SI 1998 3115), relate to circumstances where a person is sent by a magistrates' court to the Crown Court for trial pursuant to the Crime and Disorder Act 1998 s.51 by providing that copies of the documents containing the evidence on which the charge or charges are based shall be served on the person sent for trial and given to the Crown Court within 42 days from the date of the first hearing in the Crown Court, that the prosecutor may apply for an extension or further extension of the period prescribed by making an oral or written application to the Crown Court at the place specified in the notice under s.51 (7) of the 1998 Act, and provide for the procedures to be followed on an oral application for the extension or further extension of the prescribed period, where the application is made after the first Crown Court appearance of the person who was sent for trial and on a written application for the extension or further extension of the prescribed period.

936. Drink driving offences – blood tests – admissibility of breath test result following Camicintoximeter's failure to calibrate

[Road Traffic Act 1988 s.7 (3).]

S was stopped while driving and a roadside breath test showed positive. At a police station, the lowest of two breath test readings showed 102 micrograms of alcohol per 100 millilitres, but the Camic intoximeter failed to calibrate so S was required to provide a blood specimen, pursuant to the Road Traffic Act 1988 s.7 (3). The blood sample was placed in two bottles but one of them was cracked and the blood from there was transferred with a new syringe to a different bottle. It was unclear whether the police or S had retained the original sample, but subsequent analysis revealed that the prosecution specimen contained 246 milligrams of alcohol per 100 millilitres of blood. When charged, S contended that contamination had occurred. The prosecution was given leave to adduce evidence of the breath test result to show its compatibility with the blood sample on the basis that it was more probative than prejudicial. S appealed by way of case stated, relying on *Badkin v. Chief Constable of South Yorkshire* [1988] R.T.R. 401, [1988] C.L.Y. 3123 to contend that the breath test evidence should not have been admitted.

Held, dismissing the appeal, that evidence of breath test results was admissible in prosecutions based on blood analysis for particular purposes, subject to the discretion of the court. If the breath test result had been compatible with the blood test, in a broadly equivalent sense, it would have tended to support the reliability of the blood test, aside from the reason why S was required to give blood, as it would have been a singular coincidence for both tests to have been broadly equivalent yet unreliable for different reasons. However, such evidence should be adduced as expert evidence and not as the evidence of a police officer. In the instant case, although it was unclear whether the evidence had been adduced as expert evidence or not, it had been admitted solely in relation to the question of contamination. In any event, the conviction was safe because the justices had clearly stated that they considered the blood sample to be completely reliable even without the breath test evidence, *Yhnell v. DPP* [1989] R.T.R. 250 and *Smith v. Geraghty* [1986] R.T.R. 222, [1986] C.L.Y. 2870 considered and *Badkin* distinguished because in that case the prosecution had been based on an unreliable breath test, despite a subsequent blood test.

SLASOR v. DPP [1999] R.T.R. 432, Rose, L.J., QBD.

937. Drink driving offences – blood tests – negative breath sample later provided – adjournment sought to instruct expert

P appealed by way of case stated against his conviction for driving with excess alcohol. P's blood sample tested positive but he gave a negative breath test shortly afterwards. His application for an adjournment to enable him to adduce expert evidence to contradict the test results was refused by the justices on the basis that such evidence would be of no value to P.

Held, allowing the appeal, that P was entitled to have the proceedings adjourned so that expert evidence on the alcohol metabolism rate could be adduced to contradict the findings of the blood test, *Snelson v. Thompson* [1985] R.T.R. 220, [1985] C.L.Y. 3058 considered. Such evidence would clearly have been of value to P and the justices had wrongly refused the adjournment.

PARISH v. DPP [2000] R.T.R. 143, Tuckey, L.J., QBD.

938. Drink driving offences – breath tests – defective Lion intoximeter – validity of using blood specimen in evidence

[Road Traffic Act 1988 s.5 (1) (a), s.8 (2).]

B provided two specimens of breath using a Lion Intoximeter 3000 and one specimen of blood, all of which showed that B was above the prescribed drink drive limits contrary to the Road Traffic Act 1988 s.5 (1) (a). The police officer who arrested B believed the intoximeter to be accurate but this was disproved later in court. B appealed against conviction on the basis that, as the intoximeter had not been working properly at the time of his arrest, the necessary prerequisites to the provision of a blood specimen under the 1988 Act were not met, thereby prohibiting the use of that specimen in evidence.

Held, dismissing the appeal, that the prosecution did not have to prove that an intoximeter was actually working accurately when a driver was put to his election under s.8 (2) of the 1988 Act to supply a specimen of blood in order to rely on that specimen in court. As B had provided a blood specimen, the accuracy or otherwise of the intoximeter was irrelevant, *Prince v. DPP* [1996] Crim. L.R. 343 applied.

BRANAGAN v. DPP; *sub nom.* R. v. DPP, *ex p.* BRANAGAN [2000] R.T.R. 235, Simon Brown L.J., QBD.

939. Drink driving offences – urine tests – application of one hour time limit

[Road Traffic Act 1972; Road Traffic Act 1988 s.7(5).]

B was arrested after providing a positive breath test and subsequently taken to a police station where he was required to provide two specimens of urine. The first sample was discarded in accordance with standard procedures and the second sent for analysis. The analysis revealed a level of blood alcohol in excess of the prescribed limit. B was acquitted by the justices of a charge of driving with excess alcohol on the basis that the urine sample had not been taken within the time limits prescribed by the Road Traffic Act 1988 s.7(5). The DPP appealed, contending that failure to comply with the one hour time limit specified in s.7(5) did not render the specimen inadmissible.

Held, allowing the appeal, that s.7(5) contained nothing to indicate that cases decided under its precursor, the Road Traffic Act 1972, were no longer valid. On that basis, the only reason for the imposition of a one hour time limit was to make clear to a driver to whom a request had been made, the time available for compliance before he became liable to a charge of failing to supply a specimen. Therefore the fact that a specimen was provided after the one hour period, at the discretion of the police officer, did not render the sample inadmissible, *Poole v. Lockwood* [1981] R.T.R. 285, [1981] C.L.Y. 2332 and *Roney v. Matthews* (1975) 61 Cr. App. R. 195, [1975] C.L.Y. 2950 applied.

DPP v. BALDWIN (2000) 164 J.P. 606, Butterfield, J., QBD.

940. Drug offences – driving – proof of unfitness to drive owing to cannabis consumption

[Road Traffic Act 1988 s.4(1).]

L was stopped by police officers who had observed him driving too fast and erratically. L admitted taking cannabis, his eyes were red, his speech slurred and he gave answers slowly. A blood sample taken by a police surgeon was analysed by M, a forensic scientist, and found to contain a cannabis derivative. L was charged with driving while unfit through drugs, contrary to the Road Traffic Act 1988 s.4(1). M, not the surgeon, gave evidence with the police officers at the trial. L was convicted and appealed by way of case stated, arguing that for unfitness to be proved a medically qualified witness had to give evidence to that effect and that adverse inferences could be drawn from the failure to do so.

Held, dismissing the appeal, that (1) there was no reason to draw adverse inferences from the failure to call a doctor, and (2) there was ample evidence from the police witnesses to justify the finding that drugs had impaired L's ability to drive.

LEETHAM v. DPP [1999] R.T.R. 29, Rose, L.J., QBD.

941. Expert evidence – foreign jurisdictions – proof of conduct constituting criminal offence abroad

O was convicted of handling stolen cars in Germany from a hire company and was sentenced to 30 months' imprisonment. O appealed against conviction, contending that the Crown had failed to prove that his actions amounted to an offence under German law and that the trial judge, rather than calling and relying upon expert legal advice, erroneously drew inferences from the facts that an offence had been committed, namely that the cars had been reported stolen to the police and that two employees of the hire company had prepared documents in German which were produced at court without a translation and relied on as crime reports.

Held, allowing the appeal and quashing the conviction, that where the Crown alleged that offences had been committed abroad, it had to be proved by proper expert evidence that the conduct constituted an offence in the relevant foreign jurisdiction. It was not permissible for a judge to rely on the rebuttable presumption that foreign laws were the same as English law. The two employees of the hire company could not be considered competent witnesses and foreign law could not be the subject of judicial notice *R. v. Ofori (Noble Julius) (No.2)* (1994) 99 Cr. App. R. 223, [1995] C.L.Y. 1216 followed.

R. v. OKOLIE (FRANK) *The Times*, June 16, 2000, Henry, L.J., CA (Crim Div).

942. Harassment – conduct – sufficient nexus between incidents

[Protection from Harassment Act 1997 s.2, s.7(3).]

L was convicted of harassment under the Protection from Harassment Act 1997 s.2 following two incidents separated by a period of four months in which he first slapped his former girlfriend and latterly threatened her companion. L appealed by way of case stated on the basis that there had to exist a sufficient nexus between the incidents complained of so as to give rise to a "course of conduct" for the purposes of s.7(3).

Held, allowing the appeal, that whilst no more than two incidents were needed to constitute harassment, the fewer the number of incidents and the wider the time lapse, the less likely such a finding would be justified. On the facts of the instant case there was insufficient evidence upon which to find harassment proved.

LAU v. DPP [2000] 1 F.L.R. 799, Schiemann, L.J., QBD.

943. Identification – video evidence – covert video made in breach of PACE codes of practice

[Police and Criminal Evidence Act 1984 s.66; European Convention on Human Rights Art.5, Art.6, Art.8.]

P appealed against his conviction on three counts of robbery. He had unsuccessfully opposed the admission of prosecution evidence in the form of a covert video taken by the police and used for identification purposes. While criticising the video evidence as being in clear breach of the Codes of Practice established under the Police and Criminal Evidence Act 1984 s.66, the judge allowed the evidence on the ground that the video was nevertheless fair. P contended that, having found the police to have knowingly committed the relevant breaches, the judge had erred in admitting the evidence. P argued that the video evidence had been obtained pursuant to the 1984 Home Office surveillance guidelines which had no status in law, and that the obtaining of the evidence breached the European Convention on Human Rights Art.5, Art.6 and Art.8.

Held, dismissing the appeal, that the video evidence had been admissible notwithstanding clear breaches of the Code. The Home Office guidelines were neither illegal nor ultra vires, *Govell v. United Kingdom* (Unreported, January 14, 1998) considered. Reference to the Convention had not been appropriate given that domestic law could adequately deal with P's appeal. It was observed that unnecessary references to the Convention resulted in wasted court time and had the effect of lowering the veneration held for human rights law.

R. v. PERRY (STEPHEN ARTHUR) *The Times*, April 28, 2000, Swinton Thomas, L.J., CA (Crim Div).

944. Witnesses – anonymity – public interest – informers – identity not to be revealed

Held, that where it was accepted by the judge in an action for wrongful imprisonment and malicious prosecution that to admit evidence as to the identity of an informer would hinder future police investigations and endanger the informer, then it was not open to the court to devise a means for circumventing that, such as requiring the evidence to be given in camera. The court was required to balance the interests of someone seeking damages, with those of the public interest in maintaining the anonymity of informers. Once it was accepted that the public interest in concealing the identity of the informer was greater, and any benefit to the claimant minimal, then there was no residual discretion to order evidence to be given in camera, *Marks v. Beyfus* (1890) L.R. 25 Q.B.D. 494 followed.

POWELL v. CHIEF CONSTABLE OF NORTH WALES *The Times*, February 11, 2000, Schiemann, L.J., CA.

945. Witnesses – attendance – role of CPS in making enquiries and securing attendance

C was arrested in July 1997 as a consequence of his involvement in a violent incident and subsequently charged with assault occasioning actual bodily harm. One of the witnesses, S, failed to attend at the trial in January 1998 and the matter was adjourned until April 1998, the CPS having obtained a witness summons. In April 1998, S again failed to attend and it transpired that the witness summons had not been served and S had at some stage been in America. The Crown were prepared to proceed in the absence of S, but C required her attendance and maintained that her evidence was crucial to the defence. The proceedings were stayed and the matter was eventually listed again for trial in December 1999. C applied for the case to be stayed as an abuse of process, as S still did not attend. It was discovered that S was concerned about her immigration status in the US and that her application for a Green Card may be jeopardised if she returned to England. No evidence was produced to that effect. C contended that the Crown had taken the view that S's immigration concerns were more important than C's liberty, and had approached the issue of this witness on entirely the wrong basis, *R. v. Radak (Jason Dragon)* [1999] 1 Cr. App. R. 187, [1998] C.L.Y. 885 and *R. v. Cavanagh (James Michael)* [1972] 1 W.L.R. 676, [1972] C.L.Y. 645 referred to.

Held, ordering a stay of proceedings, that (1) the CPS had failed to take all reasonable steps to secure S's attendance in that it had failed to establish whether S's fears regarding her Green Card were genuine and had failed to make any enquiries with US Immigration, and (2) had overlooked the fact that a witness had a duty to give evidence. Given that conclusion, it was unnecessary to consider the second stage of the test established by *Cavanagh*, namely, whether S's non attendance would cause prejudice to C.

R. v. CHALMERS (ANDREW ROBERT), December 15, 1999, Judge Balston, Crown Court (Maidstone). [*Ex rel.* Trobridges Solicitors, 1 Ford Park Road, Mutley Plain, Plymouth].

946. Youth Justice and Criminal Evidence Act 1999 (c.23) – Commencement No.2 Order

YOUTH JUSTICE AND CRIMINAL EVIDENCE ACT 1999 (COMMENCEMENT NO.2) ORDER 2000, SI 2000 1034 (C.27); made under the Youth Justice and Criminal Evidence Act 1999 s.68. Commencement details: bringing into force various provisions of the Act on April 14, 2000; £1.50.

This Order brings into force the Youth Justice and Criminal Evidence Act 1999 s.59, s.60 and Sch.4 para.15 to para.17 and para.22 on April 14, 2000. It also commences a number of repeals consequential upon the coming into force of s.60 together with repeals of provisions in the Children and Young Persons Act 1969 and the Crime and Disorder Act 1998 which serve no purpose following the coming into force of the provisions in Sch.5 to the 1999 Act on January 1, 2000.

947. Youth Justice and Criminal Evidence Act 1999 (c.23) – Commencement No.4 Order

YOUTH JUSTICE AND CRIMINAL EVIDENCE ACT 1999 (COMMENCEMENT NO.4) ORDER 2000, SI 2000 2091 (C.55); made under the Youth Justice and

Criminal Evidence Act 1999 s.64, s.68. Commencement details: bringing into force various provisions of the Act on September 4, 2000; £1.00.

This Order brings into force the Youth Justice and Criminal Evidence Act 1999 s.34, s.35, s.38, s.39 and s.40, which make provision, in relation to certain offences, for protecting witnesses from cross examination in person by an accused. In addition, it brings into force Sch.7 para.4 which applies the provisions only to proceedings instituted on or after September 4, 2000.

948. **Publications**

Sharpe, Sybil – Search and Surveillance: the Movement from Evidence to Information. Hardback: £50.00. ISBN 0-7546-2062-X. Ashgate Publishing Limited.

CRIMINAL LAW

949. **Aircraft – safety – use of mobile telephone – statutory construction of "likely to endanger safety of an aircraft"**

[Air Navigation (No.2) Order 1995 (SI 1995 1970) Art.55.]

W was convicted of an offence of behaving in a manner likely to endanger the safety of an aircraft, contrary to the Air Navigation (No.2) Order 1995 Art.55, by the persistent use of a mobile telephone in mid flight. W contended that the use of a mobile telephone was not likely to endanger an aircraft. The prosecution relied on evidence from three expert witnesses on the risk and W argued that the judge had erred in his summing up by putting forward "a real risk not to be ignored" as a meaning of the word "likely" in the statute.

Held, dismissing the appeal, that the word "likely" had been correctly construed in its statutory context as meaning "a real risk which should not be ignored", *H (Minors) (Sexual Abuse: Standard of Proof), Re* [1996] A.C. 563, [1996] C.L.Y. 632 applied and the judge had been correct to include such a direction in his summing up.

R. v. WHITEHOUSE (NEIL) *The Times*, December 10, 1999, Pill, L.J., CA.

950. **Arrest – breach of the peace – arrest of bailiff levying distress – criteria for exercise of common law powers**

B, a county court bailiff, attended at the premises of a debtor, D, for the purposes of levying distress against D's property. D told B to leave in forceful terms and indicated that if he did not, then D would invite friends to assist in preventing the removal of any goods. Both D and B then called the police. The police officer concluded that a breach of the peace was likely and arrested B, after he refused to leave voluntarily. B was taken to the police station in handcuffs and later released without charge. B commenced proceedings against CCE for assault and false imprisonment. At first instance his claim was dismissed, the judge concluding that the police officer had acted reasonably in the light of provocation from B. B appealed, contending that in order for a common law arrest to be lawful, there had to be (1) a real threat to the peace, and (2) unreasonable conduct on the part of the individual to be arrested, the natural consequence of which was violence, which was not entirely unreasonable, from a third party.

Held, allowing the appeal, that B's submissions correctly summarised the law in relation to common law arrest, *Foulkes v. Chief Constable of Merseyside* [1998] 3 All E.R. 705, [1998] C.L.Y. 4258 applied and *Redmond-Bate v. DPP* (1999) 163 J.P. 789, [1999] C.L.Y. 949 and *Nicol and Selvanayagam v. DPP* (1996) 160 J.P. 155, [1995] C.L.Y. 1240 approved. In the instant case, although the officer had correctly determined that a breach of the peace was likely, B had nevertheless been acting lawfully and reasonably in seeking to remove D's goods unless payment was forthcoming. Furthermore the "threat" had emanated from D rather than B. A violent reaction by D to B's conduct would have been unreasonable and B's arrest was not justified.

BIBBY v. CHIEF CONSTABLE OF ESSEX (2000) 164 J.P. 297, Schiemann, L.J., CA.

951. Arrest – police officers – information given by arresting oficer

[Animals Act 1971 s.2(2); Police and Criminal Evidence Act 1984 s.28.]

D, who had been involved in a violent incident, hid in some wasteland to avoid being caught by the police, who were pursuing him with a police dog. Despite being warned, D did not give himself up, whereupon the dog was released. D was bitten by the dog several times in the ensuing struggle. He was informed by the arresting officer to walk to another officer, who handcuffed D and informed him of his arrest for affray. D's claim for aggravated and exemplary damages for wrongful arrest, false imprisonment, trespass to the person and breach of statutory duty had failed. D appealed, arguing that under the Police and Criminal Evidence Act 1984 s.28 he should have been informed of the reason for arrest by the arresting officer, not told to go to another officer. Moreover, D sought damages under the Animals Act 1971 s.2(2), in respect of the dog bites.

Held, dismissing the appeal, that it was not a requirement of s.28 that the arresting officer supply a reason for the arrest, as long as a reason is provided as soon as practicable after the arrest. D was provided with a reason for his arrest soon after being apprehended and it was not relevant that the arresting officer did not give the reason. Moreover, D's claim for damages under the 1971 Act would fail as by resisting apprehension he had voluntarily accepted the risk of suffering damage.

DHESI v. CHIEF CONSTABLE OF THE WEST MIDLANDS *The Times*, May 9, 2000, Stuart-Smith, L.J., CA.

952. Conspiracy – jurisdiction – acts taking place abroad – distinguishing substantive offences and conspiracy

N was indicted with others, inter alia, on three counts of conspiracy to defraud. The counts, subject to differences of name and date, were in identical form, although on the facts there were differences. N controlled companies operating in England and abroad and the conspiracy alleged was that he and others conspired to defraud those who might be dishonestly induced to enter into business with one or other of his various companies relating to performance bonds, or their equivalent, involving companies abroad. At the commencement of the trial, the question of territorial jurisdiction arose. The Crown submitted that it was insufficient to ground jurisdiction in inchoate crimes, such as conspiracy, on the fact that the agreement was made in England but it was necessary to look at the actual conduct contemplated by the conspirators. In counts 3, 4 and 5 the victims were deprived of their funds within the jurisdiction, or it was clearly the contemplation of the conspirators that that might be so. N submitted that the loss occurred where the victim was resident and that was where the defrauding occurred and it was not enough that the unlawful act might be carried out here in any of the three counts. The judge ruled that, whatever might have been the nature of the agreement as to who were to be the victims, it was clearly part of it that payment and the whole of the defrauding might well take place within the jurisdiction of the court and N thereupon changed his plea to one of guilty. N appealed against the judge's ruling.

Held, dismissing the appeal, that (1) in determining issues of jurisdiction a distinction was to be drawn between charges of substantive offences and charges of conspiracy, *Liangsiriprasert v. United States* [1991] 1 A.C. 225, [1991] C.L.Y. 1743 and *R. v. Manning (John Laurence)* [1999] Q.B. 980, [1998] C.L.Y. 957 applied; (2) the courts of England and Wales had no jurisdiction to try a defendant on a count of conspiracy, if the conspiracy although made here, was to do something in a foreign country, or which could only be done in a foreign country, *Board of Trade v. Owen* [1957] A.C. 602, [1957] C.L.Y. 696, *R. v. Cox (Peter Stanley)* [1968] 1 W.L.R. 88, [1968] C.L.Y. 652 and *Attorney General's Reference (No.1 of 1982), Re* [1983] Q.B. 751, [1983] C.L.Y. 574 considered; (3)

the courts did have such jurisdiction if the conspiracy, wherever made, was to do something here or to do something which might be done here, whether wholly or in part, even if no overt act pursuant to the conspiracy was done in England or Wales. The residence of the party who suffered the loss did not determine where the crime of defrauding took place, *R. v. Kohn* (1864) 4 F. & F. 68, *Board of Trade v. Owen, R. v. Cox (Peter Stanley), Liangsiriprasert, R. v. Sansom (Alec James)* [1991] 2 Q.B. 130, [1990] C.L.Y. 948 and *R. v. Manning (John Lawrence)* considered, and (4) applying the above principles, the court had jurisdiction to try N, because it was within the contemplation of the conspirators that the unlawful acts which they agreed to do in that count might well be done here. The court substantially agreed with the trial judge, save that his reliance on where the last act took place was misplaced in a case of conspiracy as opposed to a case in which the substantive offence was charged.

R. v. NAINI (JAMSHID HASHEMI) [1999] 2 Cr. App. R. 398, Lord Bingham of Cornhill, L.C.J., CA (Crim Div).

953. Counterfeiting – euro – Council Decision

Council Framework Decision 2000/383 (JHA) of May 29, 2000 on increasing protection by criminal penalties and other sanctions against counterfeiting in connection with the introduction of the euro. [2000] OJ L140/1.

954. Crime and Disorder Act 1998 (c.37) – Commencement No.7 Order

CRIME AND DISORDER ACT 1998 (COMMENCEMENT NO.7) ORDER 2000, SI 2000 924 (C.24); made under the Crime and Disorder Act 1998 s.121. Commencement details: bringing into force various provisions of the Act on April 1, 2000 and June 1, 2000; £1.50.

This Order brings into force the remaining youth justice provisions of the Crime and Disorder Act 1998. Provisions on reprimands and warnings, which have already been commenced for certain areas, are further commenced on April 1, 2000 for specified areas and are commenced nationally on June 1, 2000. Provisions on appeals against parenting orders, appeals against child safety orders, and supervision orders are commenced on June 1, 2000. The remaining provisions included in this Order come into force on April 1, 2000.

955. Crime and Disorder Act 1998 (c.37) – Commencement No.8 Order

CRIME AND DISORDER ACT 1998 (COMMENCEMENT NO.8) ORDER 2000, SI 2000 3283 (C.107); made under the Crime and Disorder Act 1998 s.121. Commencement details: bringing into force various provisions of the Act on January 15, 2001; £1.75.

This Order brings the Crime and Disorder Act 1998 s.51, 52 and Sch.3, which provide that there shall be no committal proceedings for indictable-only offences, into force on January 15, 2001.

956. Crime prevention – implementation of strategies – cooperation with local authorities and chief officers of police – prescribed bodies

CRIME AND DISORDER STRATEGIES (PRESCRIBED DESCRIPTIONS) (AMENDMENT) ORDER 2000, SI 2000 300; made under the Crime and Disorder Act 1998 s.5. In force: March 10, 2000; £1.00.

This Order amends the Crime and Disorder Strategies (Prescribed Descriptions) Order 1998 (SI 1998 2452) by adding the National Assembly for Wales to the description of persons or bodies who are required to co-operate with local authorities and chief officers of police in the formulation and implementation of strategies for the reduction of crime and disorder within local government areas.

957. Drink driving offences – breath tests – failure to provide – ignorance of medical inability

[Road Traffic Act 1988 s.7(6).]

F was charged with the offence of failing to provide a breath specimen under the Road Traffic Act 1988 s.7(6) and acquitted. The DPP appealed, contending that F's unawareness of his inability to provide a breath specimen for medical reasons, at the time when the test was requested, was not a defence to the charge.

Held, allowing the appeal, that a defendant who deliberately refused to provide a breath sample, unaware of his inability to do so for medical reasons, did not have an excuse for failing to provide a sample. In the instant case, there was no link between F's failure to provide a sample and his medical condition. The position would be different, however, where the defendant had made a genuine attempt to provide a sample but was unable to do so for medical reasons. In such cases it would be open to the police to require a blood or urine specimen.

DPP v. FURBY [2000] R.T.R. 181, Kennedy, L.J., QBD.

958. Drink driving offences – breath tests – failure to provide – offer of blood or urine test – failure to specify

[Road Traffic Act 1988 s.7(6).]

B had an accident whilst driving. At hospital, she refused a breath specimen to a police officer, P. P then told B that she was required to provide either a blood or urine sample at his election but that she could make representations as to the decision. B replied, "No, no, no," and questioned the legality of the request, referring to the European Court of Justice. P did not go on to choose the type of sample and put the request again. B was convicted of failing to provide a blood/urine specimen, contrary to the Road Traffic Act 1988 s.7(6) and appealed on the basis that a proper request had not been made for the purposes of s.7(6).

Held, dismissing the appeal, that to prove an offence under s.7(6), it was necessary to establish only that the defendant had been required to provide a specimen in pursuance of s.7 and that the defendant had without reasonable excuse failed to do so, it was therefore not essential to specify or ask B about her willingness to provide a particular type of specimen.

BURKE v. DPP [1999] R.T.R. 387, Mitchell, J., QBD.

959. Drink driving offences – breath tests – failure to provide – panic attacks

[Road Traffic Act 1988 s.7(6).]

The DPP appealed against F's acquittal on a charge of failure to provide a breath specimen. Evidence from F's doctor confirmed that she was liable to suffer panic attacks requiring medical intervention when faced with stressful situations. Moreover, F had not taken medication to control her panic attacks for several days prior to the arrest. The court below decided that although the medical evidence asserted that the panic attacks did not impair her ability to understand what was being said to her and that there were no physical or mental reasons why a specimen could not have been provided, F had provided a reasonable excuse, under the Road Traffic Act 1988 s.7(6), for her failure.

Held, dismissing the appeal, that the justices had been entitled to hold that a lawful excuse for failure to provide a breath test had been given where medical evidence showed that the defendant was liable to suffer panic attacks when faced with stressful situations. The justices had rightly stressed the need for evidence of a physical or mental impediment to providing a breath specimen and had surveyed the evidence before them in a comprehensive manner. It was clear from the evidence that F would become very short of breath when feeling stressed. There was, therefore, a direct causative link between her condition and the failure to provide a breath specimen, *R. v. Lennard (Michael)* [1973] 1 W.L.R. 483, [1973] C.L.Y. 2896 and *DPP v. Pearman* (1993) 157 J.P. 883, [1993] C.L.Y. 3500 considered.

DPP v. FALZARANO; *sub nom.* R. (ON THE APPLICATION OF FALZARANO) v. CROWN PROSECUTION SERVICE (2001) 165 J.P. 201, Potts, J., QBD.

960. Drink driving offences – breath tests – failure to provide – request to see law book

[Road Traffic Act 1988 s.7.]

N was stopped by the police whilst driving and provided a positive breath test. Having been arrested and taken to a police station, N was requested to provide two specimens of breath but refused until given the opportunity to see a law book. An officer, having denied N's request, later charged him under the Road Traffic Act 1988 s.7. The justices held that N had genuinely believed that he was entitled to have access to a law book and had had a lawful excuse not to provide a sample of breath. The DPP appealed.

Held, allowing the appeal, that the imposition of a condition requiring sight of a law book before providing a specimen of breath had amounted to a refusal to provide a specimen. It followed that N did not have a lawful excuse for failing to provide the two samples of breath. There was no right enabling a defendant to consult a solicitor, or to consult the PACE Codes of Practice before supplying a sample of breath and, similarly, as in the instant case no right to set a precondition of seeing a law book, *Smith v. Hand* [1986] R.T.R. 265, [1986] C.L.Y. 2879, *DPP v. Skinner* [1990] R.T.R. 254, [1991] C.L.Y. 3118 and *DPP v. Billington* [1988] 1 W.L.R 535, [1988] C.L.Y. 3094 considered.

DPP v. NOE [2000] R.T.R. 351, Roch, L.J., QBD.

961. Drink driving offences – breath tests – failure to provide – second test refused on medical grounds but blood test provided

[Road Traffic Act 1988 s.7(6), s.7(3).]

M failed a roadside breath test. At the police station he was required to give two breath specimens. M gave one, and told the officer that its reading above the legal limit related not to alcohol but medication. M refused to give a second breath specimen, but offered a blood specimen, which was taken. M was convicted of failing to provide a breath specimen, contrary to the Road Traffic Act 1988 s.7(6). The justices found that M had had no difficulty in providing the first specimen and was capable of providing a second, but made no findings on whether the officer had had reasonable cause to believe that for medical reasons a breath specimen could not be provided or should not be required, or had concluded that M's conduct amounted to a refusal to give a specimen. M was convicted and appealed.

Held, allowing the appeal and remitting the case for rehearing, that (1) matters had plainly not ended with M's refusal over the second breath specimen; (2) the power to take blood was strictly governed by the Road Traffic Act 1988 s.7(3) and that if the police officer had been relying on paragraph (a) he might have formed the opinion that there were medical reasons why a breath specimen should not be required, and (3) in the absence of any finding on that there was no factual basis against which to consider the appeal and the case would be remitted.

MAY v. DPP [2000] R.T.R. 7, Lord Bingham of Cornhill, L.C.J., QBD.

962. Drugs offences – drug trafficking – inference from possession and offer to buy – Mauritius

[Constitution of Mauritius s.10(7); Dangerous Drugs Act 1986 (Mauritius) s.38.]

A search revealed 35 sealed plastic sachets of heroin and 50 empty plastic bags at S's flat. He was charged with knowingly having in his possession 395 grams of heroin and wilfully offering to buy the drug under the Dangerous Drugs Act 1986 and it was alleged that it could reasonably be inferred that he was trafficking in drugs under s.38. S did not give evidence at trial where it was held that S had been trafficking at the time, so that he was liable to a more severe sentence, and he was convicted of the two offences under the Act without a further opportunity to give evidence. S's appeal to the Court of Appeal of Mauritius was dismissed and he appealed to the Privy Council, contending that by adopting the inference, for the purposes of deciding on penalty, he was found to have been trafficking prior to his conviction in breach of his right to silence under the Constitution of Mauritius s.10(7).

Held, dismissing the appeal, that there was nothing in the Act to exclude the common law rule that facts could be established by inference from proven facts, and the judge had applied the appropriate standard of proof. The concept of "trafficking" was sufficiently clear so that s.38 did not offend against the principle that a criminal offence should be defined so that a person could judge whether his acts rendered him liable to prosecution. Section 38 laid down a statutory aggravation of the offences specified, not a separate and distinct offence. Aggravation, therefore, was a question of fact which had to be established at trial at the same time as the offence, so that the judge was entitled to make a finding of trafficking without giving S a further opportunity to give evidence. By failing to give evidence, S had not been deprived of his right to silence but had taken the risk that the court would make an adverse finding on the trafficking issue prior to reaching a verdict on the offence with which he was charged.

SABAPATHEE v. MAURITIUS [1999] 1 W.L.R. 1836, Lord Hope of Craighead, PC.

963. Drugs offences – supply of drugs – applicability of rules on offer and acceptance

D was convicted of offering to supply a class A drug to an undercover policeman. D asserted that the offer to supply heroin had been made earlier by his brother and had been accepted by the policeman so that there could be no evidence of an ensuing or continuing offer. The judge directed the jury that there was a continuing and incomplete offer. D appealed against conviction contending that, under the principles of contract law, once an offer had been accepted, it was no longer an offer.

Held, dismissing the appeal, that the principles of contract law had no place in a criminal trial. There was sufficient evidence for the jury to determine the existence of an offer to supply and D was either offering the drug or participating in an offer.

R. v. DHILLON (KARAMJIT SINGH); *sub nom.* [2000] CRIM. L.R. 760 *The Times*, April 5, 2000, Hooper, J., CA (Crim Div).

964. Firearms – certificates – fees

FIREARMS (VARIATION OF FEES) ORDER 2000, SI 2000 3148; made under the Firearms Act 1968 s.43; and the Firearms (Amendment) Act 1988 s.11. In force: January 1, 2001; £1.50.

This Order, which extends to Great Britain, varies certain fees payable under the Firearms Act 1968 and the Firearms (Amendment) Act 1988.

965. Firearms – Firearms Consultative Committee

FIREARMS (AMENDMENT) ACT 1988 (FIREARMS CONSULTATIVE COMMITTEE) ORDER 2000, SI 2000 177; made under the Firearms (Amendment) Act 1988 s.22. In force: February 1, 2000; £1.00.

This Order continues in existence the Firearms Consultative Committee established under the Firearms (Amendment) Act 1988 s.22(8) for a further period of two years from the date of the expiry of the current period of its existence.

966. Firearms offences – possession – proving commission of scheduled offence

[Firearms Act 1937 s.23(2); Firearms Act 1968 s.17(2).]

N was arrested on suspicion of theft of a chicken sandwich, searched and a small imitation firearm was found in his possession. N was convicted of possessing an imitation firearm, contrary to the Firearms Act 1968 s.17(2) based on a ruling that there was no requirement to prove the alleged theft in order to convict on the firearms offence. N was sentenced to six months' imprisonment and he appealed.

Held, dismissing the appeal, that under s.17(2) there was no requirement for the prosecution to prove that N had committed the alleged theft in order to convict on a charge of possessing a firearm, or an imitation firearm. The statute was clear and unambiguous and stated that the possession of a firearm or imitation firearm was an offence if it were carried whilst a scheduled offence was either being committed or when someone was arrested for a scheduled offence, *R. v. Baker (Henry)* [1962] 2 Q.B. 530, [1961] C.L.Y. 3568 disapproved as referring to the Firearms Act 1937 s.23(2) and decided in earlier times when penalties for firearms offences were lower.

R. v. NELSON (MARK JONES); *sub nom.* R. v. NELSON (DAMIEN); R. v. SUTHERLAND (JASON) [2001] Q.B. 55, Rose, L.J., CA (Crim Div).

967. Food safety – restaurants – meaning of "proprietor"

[Food Safety Act 1990 s.11, s.53; Food Safety (General Food Hygiene) Regulations 1995 (SI 1995 1763).]

A was convicted in May 1999 of offences contrary to the Food Safety (General Food Hygiene) Regulations 1995. He appealed by way of case stated against conviction, contending that he had ceased to be a "proprietor" of the restaurant after May 1998, the date that LCC decided to prosecute, by reason of his exclusion from the premises following a disagreement with his business partner. The magistrate had convicted A on the basis that he had made no attempt to terminate his responsibility as a business partner, whether sleeping or acting and he was liable to prosecution regardless of any exclusion.

Held, dismissing the appeal, that a "proprietor" had a wider meaning than "owner" and under the Food Safety Act 1990 s.11 it was not necessary for a "proprietor" to be in daily charge of the business or even to visit the premises in order to be legally responsible, *Curri v. Westminster City Council* [2000] E.H.L.R. 16 approved. Normally, "proprietor" equated to "owner", but the definition of "proprietor" was clearly stated in s.53. It was for the magistrate to determine if A was the person, or one of the people, by whom the business was carried on. Despite A's exclusion from the premises the magistrate had correctly applied judgement to the established facts.

AHMED v. NICHOLLS; *sub nom.* AHMED v. LEICESTER CITY COUNCIL [2000] E.H.L.R. 182, Kennedy, L.J., QBD.

968. Football – offences – designation of association football matches

FOOTBALL (OFFENCES) (DESIGNATION OF FOOTBALL MATCHES) ORDER 2000, SI 2000 2329; made under the Football (Offences) Act 2000 s.1. In force: October 1, 2000; £1.00.

This Order designates association football matches for the purposes of the Football (Offences) Act 1991 which introduced penalties for certain types of misconduct at designated football matches.

969. Football – spectators – legal aid – advice and assistance

FOOTBALL (DISORDER) (LEGAL ADVICE AND ASSISTANCE) ORDER 2000, SI 2000 2127; made under the Football (Disorder) Act 2000 s.3. In force: August 28, 2000; £1.50.

This Order, which is consequential upon the Football (Disorder) Act 2000, modifies the effect of the Legal Aid Act 1988, the Legal Advice and Assistance (Scope) Regulations 1989 (SI 1989 550) and the Legal Advice and Assistance Regulations 1989 (SI 1989 340) in respect of proceedings, under the Football Spectators Act 1989 s.14B (banning orders made on a complaint), s.14D (appeals), s.14G(2) (additional requirements of orders), s.14H (termination of orders), s.21B (summary measures), and s.21D(2) (compensation).

970. Football – spectators – offences – corresponding Belgian offences

FOOTBALL SPECTATORS (CORRESPONDING OFFENCES IN BELGIUM) ORDER 2000, SI 2000 1108; made under the Football Spectators Act 1989 s.22. In force: May 24, 2000; £2.00.

This Order specifies offences under the law of Belgium which appear to correspond to certain of the offences specified in the Football Spectators Act 1989 Sch.1. Under s.22 of that Act proceedings may be commenced before magistrates against a person who resides in an area in England or Wales if that person has been convicted of such an offence and an international football banning order may be made. Under s.19 the person to whom such an order applies may be required to report to a police station in England or Wales and to comply with any other conditions imposed on the occasion of a football match played in any country outside England and Wales.

971. Football – spectators – regulated football matches

FOOTBALL SPECTATORS (PRESCRIPTION) ORDER 2000, SI 2000 2126; made under the Football Spectators Act 1989 s.14, s.18, s.22A; and the Football (Disorder) Act 2000 s.3. In force: August 28, 2000; £1.50.

This Order, which is made in consequence of the Football (Disorder) Act 2000, revokes and replaces the Football Spectators (Designation of Football Matches outside England and Wales) Order 1990 (SI 1990 732), the Football Spectators (Designation of Enforcing Authority) Order 1999 (SI 1999 2459), the Public Order (Domestic Football Banning) Order 1999 (SI 1999 2460), and the Football Spectators (Designation of Football Matches in England and Wales) Order 1999 (SI 1999 2461) which relate to international football banning orders under the Football Spectators Act 1989 and domestic football banning orders under the Public Order Act 1986. It describes the football matches in, and outside, England and Wales which are regulated football matches for the purposes of Part II of the 1989 Act. The effect of a banning order is to prohibit attendance at football matches both inside and outside England and Wales and to report to a police station when required to do so on the occasion of those matches.

972. Football spectators – offences – corresponding Dutch offences

FOOTBALL SPECTATORS (CORRESPONDING OFFENCES IN THE NETHERLANDS) ORDER 2000, SI 2000 1109; made under the Football Spectators Act 1989 s.22. In force: May 24, 2000; £1.50.

This Order specifies offences under the law of the Netherlands which appear to correspond to certain of the offences specified in the Football Spectators Act 1989 Sch.1. Under s.22 of that Act proceedings may be commenced before magistrates against a person who resides or is believed to reside in an area in England or Wales if that person has been convicted of such an offence and an international football banning order may be made. Under s.19 the person to whom such an order applies may be required to report to a police station in England or Wales on the occasion of a football match played in any country outside England and Wales.

973. Football (Disorder) Act 2000 (c.25)

This Act provides for the prevention of violence or disorder at or in connection with association football matches.

This Act received Royal Assent on July 28, 2000.

974. Football (Disorder) Act 2000 (c.25) – Commencement Order

FOOTBALL (DISORDER) ACT 2000 (COMMENCEMENT) ORDER 2000, SI 2000 2125 (C.57); made under the Football (Disorder) Act 2000 s.5.

Commencement details: bringing into force various provisions of the Act on August 28, 2000; £1.00.

This Order brings the Football (Disorder) Act 2000 s.1 into force on August 28, 2000. The remainder of the Act came into force on Royal Assent.

975. Harassment – conduct – existence of sufficient nexus between incidents

See CRIMINAL EVIDENCE: Lau v. DPP. §942

976. Harassment – conduct – two victims – duplicity of charges

[Protection from Harassment Act 1997 s.1, s.2.]

The DPP appealed against a decision to allow an appeal by D against his conviction for harassment contrary to the Protection from Harassment Act 1997 s.2. D had been accused by a couple living next door to him of pursuing a course of harassment against them, both in the presence of one or other of them and in their absence. D had successfully argued that the charge was duplicitous because it was not aimed at both of the victims together on at least two separate occasions.

Held, allowing the appeal, that a harassment charge involving two victims did not become duplicitous merely because the charge was not aimed at both victims together on at least two occasions. It was quite possible that the conduct was aimed at both victims when only one was present. A course of conduct could amount to the harassment of more than one victim as the use of the singular in s.1 of the Act was not to be construed as excluding the plural.

DPP v. DUNN [2001] 1 Cr. App. R. 22, Bell, J., QBD.

977. Harassment – restraint orders – identification of protected party

[Protection from Harassment Act 1997 s.5.]

M appealed against a restraining order made under the Protection from Harassment Act 1997 s.5 as a result of his guilty plea to harassment offences. He contended that the order was deficient because it failed to identify the protected party.

Held, that an order made under s.5 of the Act required the protected party to be identified and the order was amended accordingly.

R. v. MANN (ANDREW) *The Times*, April 11, 2000, Sachs, J., CA (Crim Div).

978. Illegal entrants – asylum seekers – facilitating entry – requirement of actual entry

[Immigration Act 1971 s.25(1)(a), s.25(1)(b).]

E and H had driven two vans onto a British registered ferry destined for the UK. Fifteen Afghans were found in the back of E's van. E denied that he knew of their presence but was convicted of being knowingly concerned in facilitating illegal entry into the UK contrary to the Immigration Act 1971 s.25(1)(a). Twelve asylum seekers were found in H's van and he was convicted of facilitating the entry into the UK of asylum claimants contrary to s.25(1)(b). E and H appealed against conviction, contending in E's case that the judge had failed to direct the jury that a distinction could be made between facilitating the arrival and facilitating the entry of such persons and both E and H contended that the offences were not committed until entry had been completed.

Held, dismissing the appeal, that provided the accused knew or had reasonable cause to believe that a person was an illegal immigrant or asylum seeker, actual entry into the UK was not necessary in order to secure a conviction, *R. v. Adams* [1996] Crim. L.R. 593, [1997] C.L.Y. 2928 approved and *R. v. Naillie (Yabo Hurerali)* [1993] A.C. 674, [1993] C.L.Y. 2196 distinguished. As the judge had correctly directed the jury to decide whether (1) the passengers intentionally sought to enter the UK illegally or to claim asylum, and (2) E and H were knowingly concerned in executing this intention, the convictions were safe.

R. v. EYCK (DENNIS JERREL); R. v. HADAKOGLU (YAKUP) [2000] 1 W.L.R. 1389, Mantell, L.J., CA (Crim Div).

979. Juvenile offenders – Youth Justice Board – functions

YOUTH JUSTICE BOARD FOR ENGLAND AND WALES ORDER 2000, SI 2000 1160; made under the Crime and Disorder Act 1998 s.41. In force: April 20, 2000; £2.00.

This Order confers new functions on the Youth Justice Board for England and Wales, established by the Crime and Disorder Act 1998 s.41, by adding new paragraphs to s.41 (5) of the 1998 Act. It lists functions exercisable by the Secretary of State in relation to the youth justice system and provides that they shall be exercisable by the Youth Justice Board for England and Wales concurrently with the Secretary of State.

980. Manslaughter – corporate liability – proof of guilty mind and identified individual – directing mind and will rule

GWT, a train operating company, had faced seven charges of manslaughter following a collision. The judge had ruled that it was a condition precedent to a conviction for corporate manslaughter by gross negligence, that a guilty mind and the guilt of an identified individual be proved. As a result, GWT was fined for not providing transport so as to ensure the public were not exposed to risks to their health and safety, and only the train driver was prosecuted. The Attorney General referred to the court two questions of law concerning evidence of GWT's state of mind, and secondly, evidence establishing the guilt of an identified individual for the same crime. The Attorney General contended that it was not necessary to inquire into GWT's state of mind and submitted that large companies should be as susceptible to conviction for manslaughter as one man companies. GWT contended that liability was based on the identification principle, which attributed to the company the mind and will of senior directors, and that the appropriate rule of attribution was determined with regard to whether Parliament had intended companies to be liable. The Attorney General argued that the law would be brought into disrepute if every act and state of mind of an employee was attributed to a blameless company, and that personal liability should be considered, *Meridian Global Funds Management Asia Ltd v. Securities Commission* [1995] 2 A.C. 500, [1996] C.L.Y. 969, *R. v. British Steel Plc* [1995] 1 W.L.R. 1356, [1996] C.L.Y. 3020, *Director General of Fair Trading v. Pioneer Concrete (UK) Ltd* [1995] 1 A.C. 456, [1995] C.L.Y. 576, *R. v. Associated Octel Co Ltd* [1996] 1 W.L.R. 1543, [1996] C.L.Y. 3019 and *R. v. Gateway Foodmarkets Ltd* [1997] 3 All E.R. 78, [1997] C.L.Y. 2611 cited.

Held, allowing the reference in part, that there was no evidence that the courts in their recent decisions had started to move from identification to personal liability as a basis for corporate liability for manslaughter. In relation to the rule of attribution, the courts had considered that the "directing mind and will" rule applied, thereby affirming the existence of the identification theory, *Meridian Global Funds Management Asia Ltd v. Securities Commission* [1995] 2 A.C. 500, [1996] C.L.Y. 969 considered. That approach was also consistent with the Law Commission's Report No.237 of March 4, 1996 entitled "Legislating the Criminal Code: Involuntary Manslaughter".

ATTORNEY GENERAL'S REFERENCE (NO.2 OF 1999), *Re* [2000] Q.B. 796, Rose, L.J., CA (Crim Div).

981. Money laundering – using or possessing proceeds of crime – burden of proving adequate consideration

[Criminal Justice Act 1988 s.93B.]

G, a property developer, managed a property which he contended was rented out to B, who had lent him £28,000. G repaid the money a month later, with £500 added as interest, but no record in writing had been made of the transaction. The prosecution contended that B had died before the money was lent and that the money in fact came from G's co-accused, A, who had used the property for the purpose of laundering money concealed from B's executors. G was convicted of acquiring, using or having possession of the proceeds of crime, contrary to the Criminal Justice Act 1988 s.93B. G appealed against his conviction, contending that, by paying interest on the money received, he had given adequate consideration for it and that the burden was on the prosecution to establish otherwise.

Held, dismissing the appeal, that the burden of proof was not on the prosecution to disprove the defence claim that money had been acquired, used or possessed for adequate consideration, as only the defence would know the facts about how much, if any, consideration had been given. It was clear that when G acquired the money, no consideration had been given and there had been no obligation to account for it. Whether adequate consideration had been given was within the knowledge of the defence on whom the burden of proof lay and G had failed to discharge that onus.

R. v. GIBSON (LEONARD) *The Times*, March 3, 2000, Beldam, L.J., CA (Crim Div).

982. **Murder – diminished responsibility – availability of defence following finding of unfitness to plead**

[Homicide Act 1957 s.2; Criminal Procedure (Insanity) Act 1964 s.4A(2).]

A, aged 16 and his codefendant M, aged 17 were charged with the murder or manslaughter of a 15 year old boy. M pleaded guilty to manslaughter on the grounds of diminished responsibility and was committed under a restriction order without limit of time to hospital. A, however, was found unfit to plead by reason of his mental disability following the evidence of psychiatrists that he was a paranoid schizophrenic. A hearing was commenced before a different jury pursuant to the Criminal Procedure (Insanity) Act 1964 s.4A(2) in which A applied for a ruling on whether he could raise a defence of diminished responsibility under the Homicide Act 1957 s.2, on the basis that if the defence was made out, then the judge would not be obliged to make a hospital order without limit of time. The judge at first instance held that the defence was not applicable and that the prosecution must prove both the actus reus and the mens rea. The jury found that A had committed the act of murder charged and the judge made a hospital order with a restriction order without a time limit. The Court of Appeal upheld the decision ([1999] 3 W.L.R. 1204, [1999] C.L.Y. 933) and A appealed, contending that the "act" of murder included a mental element to which the defence of diminished responsibility was relevant.

Held, dismissing the appeal, that the Court of Appeal had correctly held that the s.2 defence could not apply to the hearing. It was only applicable where a defendant would be liable to be convicted of murder. Under s.4A(2) of the 1964 Act, the jury had determined that A was under a mental disability and the trial was terminated so that A was no longer liable to be convicted of murder and, therefore, could not raise the statutory defence of diminished responsibility, although the defences of mistake, self defence and provocation were available at such a hearing. However, the prosecution was not required to prove the mental elements of the offence, *R. v. Egan (Michael) (Theft)* [1998] 1 Cr. App. R. 121, [1996] C.L.Y. 3885 disapproved and *Attorney General's Reference (No.3 of 1998), Re* [1999] 3 W.L.R. 1194, [1999] C.L.Y. 942 approved especially as s.4A(2) referred to the word "act" and not "offence". The main objective of s.4A(2) was to balance the protection afforded to persons found to be unfit to plead at trial with the need to safeguard the public from defendants who had committed injurious acts which would constitute crimes if done with the required mental element.

R. v. ANTOINE (PIERRE HARRISON) (A JUVENILE) [2001] 1 A.C. 340, Lord Hutton, HL.

983. Murder – intention – felony/murder rule – failure to direct on manslaughter alternative owing to intoxication – Trinidad and Tobago

[Supreme Court of Judicature Act (Trinidad and Tobago) 1980 s.44(1).]

S and M were convicted of murdering V. The prosecution submitted that they, together with S's son, had planned to frighten V and taken her to a quiet place where M slapped her then killed her with a cutlass passed to him, at his request, by S's son. M's defence was that he was drunk. S's defence was that he was party only to a joint enterprise to slap the woman. With regard to S, the judge directed the jury according to the constructive malice principle of the felony/murder rule, that S was guilty of murder if he was a party to a plan to commit acts of violence on V, who died from injuries sustained whilst that plan was being implemented. S did not give evidence. With regard to M, the judge directed the jury that they should acquit M if they found he lacked, through intoxication, the intent required for murder, but did not direct them in relation to manslaughter. S and M appealed to the Privy Council after their appeals to the Court of Appeal of Trinidad and Tobago were dismissed.

Held, dismissing the appeals, that (1) the judge had misdirected the jury on the basis of the felony/murder rule, since the rule no longer applied, *Moses v. Trinidad and Tobago* [1997] A.C. 53, [1996] C.L.Y. 1484 followed, but the proviso to the Supreme Court of Judicature Act (Trinidad and Tobago) 1980 s.44(1) should be applied, as it was clear from S's statement to the police that he had contemplated that M might use the cutlass to kill or cause really serious injury to V. His knowledge at the outset that the cutlass was in the car, his awareness of M's request for it to be passed to him, his failure to stop the enterprise, as well as his assistance in the departure from the scene, gave him the necessary degree of foresight to render him liable for murder, and (2) in the case of M, there was no evidence to establish that the effect of intoxication was such as to cause M to lack the specific intent for murder, particularly in view of the fact that, on his own admission, he was following instructions given by S and he was able to give the police a lucid account of his actions. The degree of intoxication fell far below that which would preclude the formation of specific intent required for murder. Consequently, there had been no miscarriage of justice in the judge's failure to direct the jury on an alternative charge.

SOOKLAL v. TRINIDAD AND TOBAGO [1999] 1 W.L.R. 2011, Lord Hope of Craighead, PC.

984. Murder – intention – felony/murder rule – Trinidad and Tobago

[Supreme Court of Judicature Act (Trinidad and Tobago) 1980 s.44(1).]

J was arrested near the scene of V's murder. In a confession admitted in evidence, he stated that he and M, who had a gun, were looking for a car to steal, saw V by a car and approached him wearing masks with M drawing his gun. V also had a gun and both V and M were shot dead. In evidence J denied knowing M or participating in any offence with him. No evidence was given in relation to any contemplation by J as to whether the gun was loaded or for what M might use it. The judge directed the jury in accordance with the principle of constructive malice under the felony/murder rule, whereby intention was not an element to be proved when a felony involving violence took place and a death occurred. J contended that since the decision in *Moses v. Trinidad and Tobago* [1997] A.C. 53, [1996] C.L.Y. 1484, which retrospectively disapplied that rule from 1979, the summing up was a fundamental misdirection and the failure to examine J's intention meant that the jury's conviction was unsafe. J was convicted and appealed. The Court of Appeal of Trinidad and Tobago dismissed his appeal, on the basis that had the issue of intention been addressed, then conviction was still a likely outcome and the proviso to the Supreme Court of Judicature Act (Trinidad and Tobago) 1980 s.44(1) would be applied. Although the proviso had not been applied in *Moses*, the instant case was clearly distinguishable on the basis that J knew of the existence of the gun and had witnessed M take the gun out ready for use, despite which he continued in the act. J appealed to the Privy Council.

Held, allowing the appeal and remitting the case to the Court of Appeal to consider whether a retrial be ordered, that the judge had misdirected the jury, which as a result had not considered the crucial issue of intention. It was not safe to assume that the jury would have inevitably convicted J of murder, if properly directed, in the absence of evidence about J's contemplation as to the use to which M might have put the gun, so that the Court of Appeal had erred in applying the proviso, *Moses* applied.

JOHNSON v. TRINIDAD AND TOBAGO [1999] 1 W.L.R. 2000, Lord Hutton, PC.

985. Murder – intention – felony/murder rule – Trinidad and Tobago

[Supreme Court of Judicature Act (Trinidad and Tobago) 1980 s.44(1).]

G and C were convicted of the murder of V. They appealed to the Court of Appeal of Trinidad and Tobago on the basis that the trial judge gave the traditional felony/murder direction that, as this was a case of a killing alleged to have been committed in the course of a robbery, it was sufficient for a conviction of murder for the State to prove that both G and C were participating in the robbery. Following *Moses v. Trinidad and Tobago* [1997] A.C. 53, [1996] C.L.Y. 1484, which retrospectively abolished the constructive malice principle, the Court of Appeal applied the proviso to the Supreme Court of Judicature Act (Trinidad and Tobago) 1980 s.44(1) and dismissed the appeals of G and C, on the grounds that the jury's verdict would have been the same, even if the proper directions had been given, G and C appealed to the Privy Council, contending that the proviso ought not to have been applied.

Held, allowing the appeals, substituting the verdicts of murder for manslaughter and setting aside the death sentences, that the Court of Appeal correctly approached the issue of the abolition of the felony/murder issue, but were wrong to apply the proviso, since (1) in G's case, evidence had been taken into account which the jury had been told to reject by the trial judge, without giving a reason for taking a different view to that of the judge, and (2) in both cases the court should have considered the law on intent and joint enterprise. The trial having been conducted on the issue of intent as to robbery, there was insufficient evidence for a jury to have concluded that either G or C had contemplated murder, such as to make conviction inevitable.

STAFFORD v. TRINIDAD AND TOBAGO [1999] 1 W.L.R. 2026 (Note), Lord Hope of Craighead, PC.

986. Murder – provocation – relevance of personal characteristics in application of objective test

[Homicide Act 1957 s.3.]

S was convicted of murder after he stabbed M during a violent row one evening when both men had been drinking heavily. S successfully appealed, reducing the conviction to manslaughter ([1999] Q.B. 1079, [1998] C.L.Y. 960), on the basis of provocation since he had many unresolved grievances against M, and M's repeated denials in the face of allegations that M had stolen the tools of his trade had inflamed his anger. The trial judge had directed the jury not to take account of factors personal to S, such as his clinical depression, when deciding whether a reasonable man would have acted as S had done under the same circumstances. On appeal it was contended that the judge had erred in his direction to the jury and characteristics personal to S were relevant when deciding whether the objective element of the provocation test had been satisfied. The Crown appealed against the decision of the Court of Appeal, contending that the Homicide Act 1957 s.3 had not changed the previous common law position established by *R. v. Camplin (Paul)* [1978] A.C. 705, [1978] C.L.Y. 558 and *Luc Thiet Thuan v. Queen, The* [1997] A.C. 131, [1996] C.L.Y. 1456 cited, whereby the only personal characteristics relevant to the objective test were the age and sex of the accused. According to authorities these were only relevant to the gravity of the provocation and not to matters effecting the powers of self control of the accused.

Held, dismissing the appeal (Lord Hobhouse dissenting), that the trial judge had erred in his direction to the jury in telling them to disregard personal characteristics of the defendant when considering whether the provocation was such that it would have made the reasonable man lose his self control and act in the way S had done. The defence of provocation involved two tests: the subjective test which questioned whether the person provoked had temporarily been deprived of the power of self control resulting in the unlawful act causing death, and the objective test where the jury had to consider whether the provocation was such that a reasonable man would have lost his self control and acted in such a way. The common law position had been modified by the Homicide Act 1957 s.3 which provided for the objective element to be a matter for the jury and, in making their decision, they could take into account everything both done or said, thus widening the circumstances which could amount to provocation. In *Camplin*, it was decided that the age and sex of the defendant could be taken into account, but the majority decision in *Luc Thiet Thuan* which had been followed by the trial judge, had held that the S's brain damage, which diminished his ability to control his actions, was not relevant. The judge had erred in telling the jury that the depressive illness, making S less inhibited and adversely effecting his power of self control, was not something to which they should have regard. Such a direction was contrary to s.3 of the Act although it was still necessary for the jury to apply an objective standard of behaviour which society was entitled to expect. *Camplin* and *Luc Thiet Thuan* considered.

R. v. SMITH (MORGAN JAMES) [2001] 1 A.C. 146, Lord Slynn of Hadley, HL.

987. **Obstruction of highway – demonstrations – relevance of motive when not attempting to prevent imminent offence**

B was convicted of obstructing the highway during a peaceful demonstration in which he sat in the road outside commercial premises and refused to move. He contended that there was a lawful reason for his act because he was attempting to prevent illegal activities on the premises. The magistrate refused to admit evidence of alleged illegal acts on the ground that it went to "motive" rather than "purpose" and convicted B, who appealed by way of case stated.

Held, dismissing the appeal, that, in the instant case there was no material difference between "purpose" and "motive", since B was not attempting to prevent an activity which might result in an imminent breach of the peace or some other serious offence. Therefore, B's motive was not relevant and the magistrate had been entitled to refuse to admit the evidence.

BIRCH v. DPP *The Independent*, January 13, 2000, Rose, L.J., QBD.

988. **Obstruction of police – police powers – vehicle examination – determination of status as road**

[Police Act 1996 s.89 (2).]

Held, that it was a question of fact for determination by the justices as to whether a given location was a "road", *Griffin v. Squires* [1958] 1 W.L.R. 1106, [1958] C.L.Y. 3016 followed, so that where a police officer asked for the keys to a motor vehicle in Trafalgar Square for the purposes of undertaking an examination and to prevent it being driven away, a finding that the Square constituted a road meant that the officer was acting within the execution of his duties under the Police Act 1996 s.89 (2).

SADIKU v. DPP [2000] R.T.R. 155, Tuckey, L.J., QBD.

989. **Offences – forgery and counterfeiting**

CRIMINAL JUSTICE ACT 1993 (EXTENSION OF GROUP A OFFENCES) ORDER 2000, SI 2000 1878; made under the Criminal Justice Act 1993 s.1. In force: August 1, 2000; £1.00.

The Criminal Justice Act 1993 Part I makes provision about the jurisdiction of courts in England and Wales in relation to certain offences of dishonesty and blackmail set out in s.1 of that Act. This Order amends s.1 (2) of the Act by extending the Group A offences to which Part I of the Act applies so as to include various offences contained in the Forgery and Counterfeiting Act 1981 Part II.

990. Offences – freezing of funds – Burma

BURMA (FREEZING OF FUNDS) REGULATIONS 2000, SI 2000 1472; made under the European Communities Act 1972 s.2. In force: June 7, 2000; £1.50.

These Regulations provide that breaches of certain provisions of Council Regulation 1081/2000 ([2000] OJ L122/29) prohibiting the sale, supply and export to Burma/Myanmar of equipment which might be used for internal repression or terrorism, and freezing the funds of certain persons related to important governmental functions in that country, are to be criminal offences. They provide for information to be requested by or on behalf of the Treasury or the Bank of England for the purposes of ensuring compliance with the Council Regulation and that failure to do so, the provision of false information or the suppression of information is a criminal offence.

991. Offences – freezing of funds and prohibition on investment – Federal Republic of Yugoslavia

FEDERAL REPUBLIC OF YUGOSLAVIA (FREEZING OF FUNDS AND PROHIBITION ON INVESTMENT) (AMENDMENT) REGULATIONS 2000, SI 2000 1367; made under the European Communities Act 1972 s.2. In force: May 20, 2000; £1.00.

These Regulations amend the Federal Republic of Yugoslavia (Freezing of Funds and Prohibition on Investment) Regulations 1999 (SI 1999 1786) in consequence of Council Regulation 723/2000 ([2000] OJ L86/1) which amended Council Regulation 1294/1999 ([1999] OJ L153/63) concerning a freeze of funds and a ban on investment in relation to the Federal Republic of Yugoslavia. They amend the numbering of cross references and provide that breach of the requirement to provide information to facilitate compliance with the 1999 Council Regulation shall be a criminal offence.

992. Perverting public justice – bail – assisting bailed person to flee – bail lapsing on arraignment

[Criminal Law Act 1967 s.6(3); Bail Act 1976; Criminal Attempts Act 1981 s.1.]

D was convicted of an offence of perverting the course of justice, in that he made arrangements for and gave assistance in the flight from the UK of Asil Nadir, knowing that Nadir was due to stand trial and was prohibited by reason of his bail conditions from leaving the country. On appeal it was contended, inter alia, that it was incumbent on the prosecution to prove that Nadir was granted bail subject to a condition that he should not leave the jurisdiction and that such condition remained in force in May 1993 when the act charged against D took place. Bail was first granted to Nadir in the magistrates' court. The conditions included requirements that he live and sleep at a named London address and that he surrender his passport and make no application for other travel documents. The grant of bail continued until Nadir first surrendered to the Crown Court where counsel agreed it was unnecessary for Nadir to surrender to the custody of the court, bail was not mentioned by counsel or the judge, and Nadir was arraigned. At a subsequent hearing, Nadir applied to vary those bail conditions which were believed by all present to be in force but that application was rejected and no further ruling on bail was made and Nadir was then re-arraigned. Nadir left the country. It was submitted that there was, as a matter of fact, no grant of bail to Nadir at the first hearing, because of a misapprehension under which all parties laboured and that there had been no subsequent grant of bail.

Held, allowing the appeal, that arraignment caused the grant of bail to lapse. Further, the Bail Act 1976 clearly envisaged that the grant of bail comprised of a judicial decision and a judicial act. Following the hearing Nadir was therefore neither on bail nor was he unlawfully at large. He was either technically in the custody of the court or was subject to an indictment and liable if he did not attend his trial to be compelled to do so. Since the indictment against D made express reference to the bail conditions and there were no bail conditions in force at the material time, they were an ingredient of the offence as charged but not proved. In the circumstances of the case, it would be wrong to substitute an alternative conviction for attempting to do what was alleged by virtue of the Criminal Law Act 1967 s.6(3) and the Criminal Attempts Act 1981 s.1 (1) and s.1 (2).

R. v. DIMOND (PETER CHARLES) [2000] 1 Cr. App. R. 21, Lord Bingham of Cornhill, L.C.J., CA (Crim Div).

993. Pornography – children – Internet – ignorance of possession in computer cache – meaning of "making"

[Criminal Justice Act 1988 s.160(1).]

A appealed against conviction of possessing indecent photographs of children he had downloaded unknowingly to the cache of his computer and the Crown cross appealed against a verdict of no case to answer on 21 charges of making such photographs. G appealed against his conviction, under the Criminal Justice Act 1988 s.160(1) of possession of an indecent pseudo photograph comprising two photographs taped together so that the naked body of a woman could be superimposed over that of a child.

Held, allowing the appeals, that (1) A could not be convicted of possessing an indecent photograph unless he knew that he had the photograph in his possession. In the case of a defendant claiming to be carrying out research into child pornography, it was a question of fact whether such research constituted a legitimate reason for being in possession of an indecent photograph and the court was entitled to be sceptical; (2) the "making" of an indecent photograph included copying, downloading or storing it on a computer, provided that it was done knowingly, *R. v. Bowden (Jonathan) The Times*, November 19, 1999, [1999] C.L.Y. 947 applied, and (3) parts of two different photographs taped together could not be said to constitute a photograph, although a reproduction of it might be.

ATKINS v. DPP; GOODLAND v. DPP; *sub nom.* DPP v. ATKINS [2000] 1 W.L.R. 1427, Simon Brown, L.J., QBD.

994. Pornography – children – specific knowledge of content of video recordings

[Customs and Excise Management Act 1979 s.170(2).]

F was apprehended by Customs attempting to import two videos which showed naked boys under 16 engaging in indecent acts. F's defence was that although he believed that the videos were banned titles in the UK he had not known they contained indecent material. F was convicted under the Customs and Excise Management Act 1979 s.170(2) and sentenced to two concurrent terms of imprisonment of six months. F appealed, contending that the Crown was required to prove the extent of his knowledge and specifically that he knew the videos contained indecency with children.

Held, dismissing the appeal, that there was no such burden on the prosecution, *R. v. Shivapuri* [1987] A.C. 1, [1986] C.L.Y. 482 applied and *R. v. Hussain (Mohammed Blayat)* [1969] 2 Q.B. 567, [1969] C.L.Y. 854 followed. The jury had clearly rejected F's defence and decided that F knew the material was pornographic and it was not necessary for the fact that the videos showed children under 16 to be known to F.

R. v. FORBES (GILES) *The Times*, April 4, 2000, Rose, L.J., CA (Crim Div).

995. Pornography – incitement – impossibility defence where police officer had no intention to supply

A was accused of attempting to incite a police officer to supply him with pornographic pictures of under age girls above the age of 12. The officer stated under cross examination that, although he had access to such photographs, he had no intention of supplying A with them. A contended that the incitement was, therefore, impossible and the magistrate agreed, finding that there was no case to answer on the basis of the decisions in *R. v. Shaw* [1994] Crim. L.R.

365, [1994] C.L.Y. 836 and *R. v. Curr (Patrick Vincent McGinley)* [1968] 2 Q.B. 944, [1967] C.L.Y. 1656. The DPP appealed by way of case stated.

Held, allowing the appeal, that there was no necessity for the person being incited to commit an offence to have a mens rea corresponding to that of the inciter. In the instant case, the officer had access to illegal child pornography and the fact that he had no intention of providing A with the material requested did not render incitement impossible, *Shaw, Curr, R. v. Sang (Leonard Anthony)* [1980] A.C. 402, [1979] C.L.Y. 448 and *DPP v. Nock (David Michael)* [1978] A.C. 979, [1978] C.L.Y. 430 considered.

DPP v. ARMSTRONG (ANDREW) [2000] Crim. L.R. 379, Tuckey, L.J., QBD.

996. Pornography – obscenity – Internet – transmission by computer

[Obscene Publications Act 1959 s.2(1), s.1(3)(b); Police and Criminal Evidence Act 1984 s.69, Sch.3 Part II para.11.]

W was charged with publishing obscene articles contrary to the Obscene Publications Act 1959 s.2(1). Images were transferred to a number of websites, via an Internet service provider, ISP. W contended that (1) due to the nature of the Internet, publication occurred abroad so that the court did not have jurisdiction, and (2) that the Police and Criminal Evidence Act 1984 s.69 had not been complied with as a certificate had not been produced for each computer involved in the transmission of the data to show that the information had been correctly received and processed, and therefore there was no admissible evidence of publication.

Held, giving judgment for the prosecution, that (1) under s.1(3)(b) of the 1959 Act, publishing an article included, where the data was stored electronically, transmitting that data. In the instant case, an act of publication took place when the data was transmitted by W or his agent to the ISP. As the data was sent and received within the jurisdiction, it was immaterial that the transmission left the jurisdiction in the interim period, and (2) many computers could be involved in the process of transmitting from sender to receiver via the Internet, both within and outside the jurisdiction involved in the process. However, the intermediate computers were mere post boxes. It was sufficient to certificate the original sending computer and the ultimate receiving computer for the purposes of complying with s.69 and Sch.3 Part II para.11 of the 1984 Act, *R. v. Cochrane* [1993] Crim. L.R. 48, [1993] C.L.Y. 633 distinguished.

R. v. WADDON (GRAHAM) [1999] I.T.C.L.R. 422, Judge Hardy, Crown Ct (Southwark).

997. Road traffic offences – arrest – driving whilst disqualified – defendant not driving at time of arrest

[Road Traffic Act 1988 s.103(3).]

S was charged with resisting a police constable in the execution of his duty. The prosecution case was that S had been driving a vehicle while disqualified, and the constable had attempted to arrest S pursuant to the Road Traffic Act 1988 s.103(3). The justices held that S had not been the driver and dismissed the information. The Crown appealed by way of case stated, contending that for the purposes of s.103(3) "a person driving a motor vehicle on a road" was to be construed as including someone who was reasonably suspected of having been the driver of the vehicle in question.

Held, dismissing the appeal, that, however desirable it might be for the police to have such a power, there was no need to read any extra words into s.103(3); as the justices had found as a fact that S was not the driver, there was no power of arrest pursuant to s.103(3).

DPP v. SWANN (2000) 164 J.P. 365, Forbes, J., QBD.

998. Road traffic offences – fixed penalties

FIXED PENALTY ORDER 2000, SI 2000 2792; made under the Road Traffic Offenders Act 1988 s.53. In force: November 11, 2000; £1.75.

This Order, which revokes and replaces the Fixed Penalty Order 1992 (SI 1992 346) and the Fixed Penalty (Increase) (Scotland) Order 1992 (SI 1992 435 (S.50)), prescribes fixed penalties for fixed penalty offences. It increases fixed penalties from £40 to £60 for offences involving obligatory endorsement and for parking offences committed in Greater London on a red route, from £30 to £40 for other parking offences committed in Greater London and from £20 to f 30 for other fixed penalty offences.

999. Road traffic offences – speeding – incorrect siting of restriction signs

[Road Traffic Regulation Act 1984 s.14, s.84(1), s.89(1).]

W was convicted of exceeding the speed limit contrary to a speed restriction order made under the Road Traffic Regulation Act 1984 s.14 and contrary to s.84(1) and 89(1) of the Act. W appealed by way of case stated, contending that the restriction signs invalidated the speed limit.

Held, dismissing the appeal, that, although the signs had been incorrectly sited, they sufficiently advised drivers of the lawful maximum speed on the part of the road subject to the order. Whilst they indicated that the length of the restriction was longer than the section of road normally affected, the signs did not invalidate the speed limit.

WAWRZYNCZYK v. CHIEF CONSTABLE OF STAFFORDSHIRE *The Times*, March 16, 2000, Schiemann, L.J., QBD.

1000. Road traffic offences – summary offences – motorised scooters as mechanically propelled vehicles

[Road Traffic Act 1988 s.185(1).]

The DPP appealed against the dismissal of two informations which had been laid against S for offences of driving whilst disqualified and driving without third-party insurance. S had been stopped whilst riding an unregistered motorised scooter which the DPP contended was a "motor vehicle" for the purposes of the Road Traffic Act 1988 s.185(1). S disputed this, arguing that the scooter would not be recognised for registration and was not technically roadworthy.

Held, allowing the appeal, that a reasonable person would regard the user of such a scooter as a road user, *Burns v. Currell* [1963] 2 Q.B. 433, [1963] C.L.Y. 3038 applied. General use of scooters on the road was within contemplation. The roadworthiness of the scooter was not the crucial issue as to whether its use on the road was to be contemplated. The motorised scooter was a mechanically propelled vehicle which was designed and intended for road use, and therefore the statutory requirements of a licence and third-party insurance applied.

DPP v. SADDINGTON; *sub nom.* CHIEF CONSTABLE OF NORTH YORKSHIRE v. SADDINGTON (2001) 165 J.P. 122, Pill, L.J., QBD.

1001. Road traffic offences – tractors – use involving danger of injury

[Road Traffic Act 1988 s.40A.]

P was driving a tractor with lowered front link arms, along a C class road in a rural locality. An oncoming car crossed into P's path and collided with P, without P being at fault. The other driver was killed. The justices dismissed a charge that P had used the tractor on the road when its equipment was such that the use involved a danger of injury, contrary to the Road Traffic Act 1988 s.40A. The Crown appealed.

Held, dismissing the appeal, that the question of whether there was a danger for the purposes of s.40A, was a matter which required the justices to consider the condition of the vehicle independent of the fact that an accident had occurred. Further, the justices were entitled to take into account the rural nature of the locality, the classification of the road, and conclude that the lowered arms did not amount to a danger on that occasion.

DPP v. POTTS [2000] R.T.R. 1, Otton, L.J., QBD.

1002. Sexual offences – gross indecency – inciting girl under 14 – honest subjective belief that victim was 14 or over

[Sexual Offences Act 1956; Indecency with Children Act 1960 s.1 (1), s.6(3).]

B, a boy aged 15, repeatedly requested a 13 year old girl to perform oral sex during a bus journey. He was charged with inciting a girl under 14 to commit an act of gross indecency, contrary to the Indecency with Children Act 1960 s.1 (1). B maintained a not guilty plea on the basis that he had honestly believed that the girl was over 14. He altered his plea to guilty after a decision by the justices that his state of mind concerning the victim's age could not provide a defence. An appeal by way of case stated was dismissed ([1999] 3 W.L.R. 116). B appealed to the House of Lords, contending that as the 1960 Act was silent as to the mental element of the offence, the common law presumption that mens rea was necessary should apply. The Crown argued that the offence was one of strict liability, that the law in this area had been regarded as settled since the decision in *R. v. Prince* (1875) L.R. 2 C.C.R. 154, and that subsequent legislation, namely the Sexual Offences Act 1956 and the 1960 Act itself, had not been intended to change this approach, especially since an express exception had been created in s.6(3) of the 1960 Act whereby belief as to age could provide a defence in prescribed circumstances.

Held, allowing the appeal, that (1) the common law presumption of mens rea applied in the case of s.1(1) of the 1960 Act. The presumption was well established in the absence of a specific contrary intent expressed by Parliament, *Sweet v. Parsley* [1970] A.C. 132, [1969] C.L.Y. 2210 applied. The submission that the 1956 Act had reinforced the decision in *Prince* was ill founded in view of the fact that the disparate offences within the 1956 Act displayed no clear pattern. The interpretation of s.1 of the 1960 Act could not be based on the contents of another piece of legislation unless that legislation gave cogent guidance. Further, the decision in *Prince* ran counter to the presumption established by *Sweet v. Parsley*; (2) a defendant was entitled to be acquitted of the offence if he honestly believed that the child in question was aged 14 or over and it was not necessary that his belief had to be based on reasonable grounds. There had been a general move from an objective to a subjective assessment, *DPP v. Morgan* [1976] A.C. 182, [1975] C.L.Y. 682 and *Beckford v. Queen, The* [1988] A.C. 130, [1987] C.L.Y. 825 applied and *R. v. Williams (Gladstone)* [1987] 3 All E.R. 411, [1984] C.L.Y. 504 approved and (3) the burden of proving that the defendant lacked honest belief that the child was aged 14 or over lay with the prosecution.

B (A CHILD) v. DPP [2000] 2 A.C. 428, Lord Nicholls of Birkenhead, HL.

1003. Sexual offences – indecent assault – consent given under belief as to defendant's medical qualifications

T appealed against his conviction on three counts of indecent assault after he had deceived three women into consenting to allowing him to demonstrate breast self examination on the basis that he was medically qualified. There was no evidence of a sexual motive and T contended that the judge had wrongly concluded that T's lack of medical qualification or training had fundamentally altered the nature and quality of the act thus vitiating consent.

Held, dismissing the appeal, that the acts were indecent if performed without consent and there was no genuine consent because the complainants had consented only to an act of a medical nature and not for any other reason. The fundamental quality of the act was so significantly different that it rendered any consent irrelevant, *R. v. Clarence* (1888) L.R. 22 Q.B.D. 23 and *R. v. Linekar (Gareth)* [1995] Q.B. 250, [1995] C.L.Y. 1290 distinguished as the nature of the act had not affected the victim's consent.

R. v. TABASSUM (NAVEED); *sub nom.* R. v. TABASSUM (NAVID) [2000] 2 Cr. App. R. 328, Rose, L.J., CA (Crim Div).

1004. Sexual offences – indecent assault – genuine belief that victim was 16 years or over

[Sexual Offences Act 1956 s.14(1), s.14(3), s.14(4); Human Rights Act 1998 Sch.1 Part I Art.6(2).]

The CPS appealed against an interlocutory decision that when seeking to prove an offence of indecent assault on a girl under 16, it was necessary for the prosecution to establish the absence of a genuine belief on the part of the accused that the girl was 16 years of age or older. The CPS argued that the Sexual Offences Act 1956 s.14 excluded the presumption that mens rea was required before a criminal offence was committed by way of necessary implication. Authorities had established that the offence was one of strict liability except in those situations whereby a defence was afforded under s.14(3) and s.14(4). K disputed these arguments and further contended that to read the offence as absolute was a violation of the Human Rights Act 1998 Sch.1 Part I Art.6(2).

Held, allowing the appeal, that had the legislature intended genuine belief to be a defence to a charge under s.14(1), then it would have been unnecessary to enact s.14(3) and s.14(4), under which genuine belief was a defence in specified circumstances. The presumption that mens rea was an ingredient of the offence was thus impliedly excluded and the only elements of the offence which the prosecution were required to prove were that the victim was under 16 and that an assault had taken place in indecent circumstances, *R. v. Maughan* (1934) 24 Cr. App. R. 130 and *R. v. Forde* [1923] 2 K.B. 400 considered. That interpretation was not incompatible with the Act as it was reasonable for Parliament to strike the balance between the protection of society and the rights of the offender, *Salabiaku v. France (A/141-A)* (1991) 13 E.H.R.R. 379 considered. The prosecution did not have to prove that K at the time of the incident did not honestly believe that the complainant was 16 years old.

R. v. K; *sub nom.* CPS v. K [2001] 1 Cr. App. R. 35, Roch, L.J., CA (Crim Div).

1005. Sexual offences – indecent assault – joinder of offences committed over 20 year period

O was convicted of five counts of indecent assault committed between 1972 and 1975 and between 1994 and 1998. All the offences concerned young boys at a school where O had been head teacher. O appealed against conviction, arguing that the offences should not have been joined and tried together as there was too long a gap between them.

Held, allowing the appeal, that where there was such a long gap between offences, a clear nexus between them would have to be shown before they could be joined. Although events separated by long periods of time were capable of being part of a series of events, in the instant case there was no historical continuum linking them. Moreover, the evidence in relation to each offence should have strong probative force in order to be readily cross admissible in relation to other offences, which clearly was not the case.

R. v. O'BRIEN (ROBERT FRANCIS) *The Times*, March 23, 2000, Rose, L.J., CA (Crim Div).

1006. Sexual Offences (Amendment) Act 2000 (c.44)

This Act reduces the age at which, and makes provision with respect to the circumstance in which, certain sexual acts are lawful; and makes it an offence for a person aged 18 or over to engage in sexual activity with or directed towards a person under that age if he is in a position of trust in relation to that person.

This Act received Royal Assent on November 30, 2000.

1007. Sexual Offences (Amendment) Act 2000 (c.44) – Commencement No.1 Order

SEXUAL OFFENCES (AMENDMENT) ACT 2000 (COMMENCEMENT NO.1) ORDER 2000, SI 2000 3303 (C.106); made under the Sexual Offences (Amendment) Act 2000 s.7. Commencement details: bringing into force various provisions of the Act on January 8, 2001; £1.50.

This Order brings the Sexual Offences (Amendment) Act 2000 into force on January 8, 2001 for England, Wales and Northern Ireland.

1008. Terrorism – emergency provisions – extension

PREVENTION OF TERRORISM (TEMPORARY PROVISIONS) ACT 1989 (CONTINUANCE) ORDER 2000, SI 2000 835; made under the Prevention of Terrorism (Temporary Provisions) Act 1989 s.27. In force: March 22, 2000; £1.00.

This Order continues in force for a period of 12 months from March 22, 2000, the Prevention of Terrorism (Temporary Provisions) Act 1989 Part I, Part III, Part IV, Part IVB, Part V and s.27 (6) (c) and the Criminal Justice (Terrorism and Conspiracy) Act 1998 s.4.

1009. Terrorism Act 2000 (c.11)

This Act makes provision with respect to terrorism. In particular, it makes temporary provision for Northern Ireland relating to the prosecution and punishment of certain offences, the preservation of peace and the maintenance of order.

This Act received Royal Assent on July 20, 2000.

1010. Terrorism Act 2000 (c.11) – Commencement No.1 Order

TERRORISM ACT 2000 (COMMENCEMENT NO.1) ORDER 2000, SI 2000 2800 (C.80); made under the Terrorism Act 2000 s.128. Commencement details: bringing into force various provisions of the Act on October 12, 2000; £1.50.

This Order brings into force various provisions of the Terrorism Act 2000 for the making of certain codes of practice and orders relating to such codes on October 12, 2000. The codes in question are those relating to the exercise of functions by members of the Royal Ulster Constabulary or the armed forces in Northern Ireland, the exercise of functions by authorised and examining officers and the audio or video recording of certain interviews by the police of suspected terrorists or as part of port or border controls.

1011. Terrorism Act 2000 (c.11) – Commencement No.2 Order

TERRORISM ACT 2000 (COMMENCEMENT NO.2) ORDER 2000, SI 2000 2944 (C.85); made under the Terrorism Act 2000 s.128. Commencement details: bringing into force various provisions of the Act on October 31, 2000; £1.50.

This Order brings into force on October 31, 2000 various provisions of the Terrorism Act 2000 in relation to regulations with respect to applications for deproscription, the establishment of the Proscribed Organisations Appeal Commission (POAC), orders specifying certain monetary instruments as 'terrorist cash', rules of court relating to detention and forfeiture of terrorist cash, regulations to apply or disapply to certain Crown servants provisions relating to terrorist property offences and terrorist information, the procedure of POAC and rules for appeals to POAC, rules of court for enforcement of certain forfeiture and restraint orders, Crown Court Rules or Act of Adjournal for applications for customer information orders, orders specifying classes of persons as 'financial institutions' and classes of information as 'customer information', and orders relating to the supplying of information by ship or aircraft passengers, ship or aircraft owners or agents to examining officers.

1012. Theft – appropriation – gifts

[Theft Act 1968 s.1 (1), s.3(1).]

H appealed against her conviction for theft. H persuaded F, a man of limited intelligence for whom she cared, to make a series of transfers from his bank account to her own. She maintained that the transfers had constituted a gift. Her conviction having been upheld by the Court of Appeal ([2000] 1 Cr. App. R. 1), the question before the House of Lords was: "whether the acquisition of an indefeasible title to property [was] capable of amounting to an appropriation of property belonging to another for the purposes of the Theft Act 1968 s.1 (1)." It was contended that following the decisions in *Lawrence v. Commissioner of Police of the Metropolis* [1972] A.C. 626, [1971] C.L.Y. 2814 and *DPP v. Gomez (Edwin)* [1993] A.C. 442, [1993] C.L.Y. 994, appropriation could only take place where the owner preserved some proprietary interest or the right to take up again or restore a proprietary interest in the relevant property.

Held, dismissing the appeal (Lord Hutton and Lord Hobhouse dissenting), that an indefeasible title to property acquired by means of taking a gift from a person who was easily influenced could constitute "appropriation" under the Act. "Appropriation" for the purposes of s.3(1) should not be interpreted too strictly and was an objective term relating to any adoption of an owner's rights. It was not dependent on the consent of the owner, *Lawrence* applied. Furthermore, the gift of property whereby the owner relinquished his entire proprietary interest in the property transferred could constitute theft where the recipient had acted dishonestly, *Gomez* applied. There was no requirement for appropriation to be unlawful for it to constitute theft as the requirement for the prosecution to show dishonesty and the intention to permanently deprive provided adequate protection against injustice, and any narrowing of the definition of appropriation could lead to the acquittal of dishonest persons whose conduct merited conviction.

R. v. HINKS (KAREN MARIA) [2000] 3 W.L.R. 1590, Lord Steyn, HL.

1013. Theft – appropriation – presentation of cheques

[Theft Act 1968 s.1, s.15.]

W, a builder, was convicted of fraudulent trading and theft and was sentenced to five years and six months' imprisonment. The offences of theft related to the dishonest overcharging of clients for work carried out. The judge had found that W had acquired property belonging to another when he had attempted to cash cheques paid to him for the work. W appealed against his conviction and sentence contending that the judge had erred in his approach given that the decision of *R. v. Preddy (John Crawford)* [1996] A.C. 815, [1996] C.L.Y. 1530 made it clear that where it was not possible to identify property belonging to another, a defendant could not be found guilty of obtaining property by deception.

Held, dismissing the appeal, that a distinction should be made between "appropriation" by taking on the rights of an owner, and "obtaining" in relation to the specific offences under the Theft Act 1968 s.1 and s.15. A conviction for theft prescribed that appropriation of property belonging to another be displayed. *Preddy*, however, related to offences under s.15 of obtaining by deception and involved funds being transferred by CHAPS order so that the defendant did not initiate the process which debited the victim's account. Moreover, it had been difficult to identify the "property of another" as there had been a new chose in action upon presentation of the relevant cheques, *Preddy* distinguished. The appropriation in the instant case occurred when W presented the cheques or caused them to be presented, *R. v. Kohn (David James)* (1979) 69 Cr. App. R. 395, [1980] C.L.Y. 591 and *R. v. Hallam* [1995] Crim. L.R. 323 considered, and although persons would intervene unless the processing of the cheque was automatic, they would be innocent agents.

R. v. WILLIAMS (ROY) [2001] 1 Cr. App. R. 23, Turner, J., CA (Crim Div).

1014. Vagrancy – buildings – meaning of "inclosed area"

[Vagrancy Act 1824 s.4.]

T was apprehended in an office within a university building and convicted of an offence contrary to the Vagrancy Act 1824 s.4, which specified several areas where the offence could be committed. T appealed by way of case stated against the conviction contending that an office did not fall within the ambit of an "inclosed area" as defined by s.4, and that the words had to be taken in context with the rest of the section which referred to the outdoors and buildings other than office buildings.

Held, allowing the appeal and quashing the conviction, that a room within a building did not constitute an enclosed area for the purposes of s.4, *Knott v. Blackburn* [1944] K.B. 77 applied, wherein Viscount Caldecote, L.C.J. had held that "inclosed area" had to be taken in context with the rest of the section including the words "yard" and "garden".

TALBOT v. DPP; *sub nom.* TALBOT v. OXFORD CITY MAGISTRATES COURT; TALBOT v. OXFORD CITY JUSTICES [2000] 1 W.L.R. 1102, Gage, J., QBD.

1015. Violent offences – assault – defences – mistaken belief as to lawfulness of arrest

[Offences Against the Person Act 1861 s.38.]

L appealed against his conviction for two offences of assault with intent to resist arrest contrary to the Offences Against the Person Act 1861 s.38. L had been stopped by the police and failed a roadside breath test. Upon being told that he was to be arrested, he punched both of the officers. L, having conceded that the breathalyser test had provided evidence upon which the jury could have reasonably concluded that the officers had been acting lawfully, contended that the judge had failed to direct the jury that his genuinely mistaken belief that he had passed the test, and that his arrest had therefore been unlawful, provided a defence.

Held, dismissing the appeal, that a genuine mistake may afford a defence to a criminal offence but the mistake had to be one of fact. In the instant case, after the lawfulness of the purported arrest had been established, L must have intended to resist arrest in order for an offence to have been committed under s.38. On that basis, L's belief as to the lawfulness of the arrest was irrelevant since the arrest had been properly attempted on reasonable grounds.

R. v. LEE (DENNIS PERCIVAL) (CONVICTION) [2001] 1 Cr. App. R.19, Rose, L.J., CA (Crim Div).

1016. Violent offences – common assault – actus reus – causing injury through third party

[Criminal Justice Act 1988 s.39.]

H appealed against his conviction on a charge of common assault contrary to the Criminal Justice Act 1988 s.39. He had been accused of beating a child by punching the child's mother causing the child to fall and hit his head. He argued that battery required the direct application of force which involved direct physical contact with the victim either with the body or with a medium such as a weapon.

Held, dismissing the appeal, that the correct approach to the actus reus of battery was set out in Smith and Hogan, Criminal Law (9th edition (1999) p.406) which revealed that battery did not require the direct infliction of violence. Furthermore, even if the definition of battery argued for by H was correct, H had committed battery. The child's fall to the floor had resulted directly from H's assault on his mother. No distinction could be drawn between using the mother or a weapon as the relevant medium save that the latter involved intention and the former recklessness. In the circumstances, H had committed the offence of assault by beating.

HAYSTEAD v. CHIEF CONSTABLE OF DERBYSHIRE; *sub nom.* HAYSTEAD v. DPP [2000] 3 All E.R. 890, Laws, L.J., QBD.

1017. Violent offences – grievous bodily harm – mens rea – objective test for causation

M, aged 16 at the time, was among a group of people who broke into the victim's hostel room, whereupon she fell or jumped into the street and was seriously injured. M appealed against conviction for grievous bodily harm, contending that in directing the jury on foreseeability, the judge had failed properly to direct the jury that they should consider it in terms of a person of the same age and sex as M involved in similar circumstances.

Held, dismissing the appeal, that the test of causation was objective, *R. v. Roberts (Kenneth Joseph)* (1972) 56 Cr. App. R. 95, [1972] C.L.Y. 576 and *R. v. Mackie (Robert)* ((1973) 57 Cr. App. R. 453, [1973] C.L.Y. 564 applied. The "reasonable man", as defined in *R. v. Camplin (Paul)* [1978] A.C. 705, [1978] C.L.Y. 558, would have foreseen the victim's conduct as a natural result of M's actions. It was only when considering intention that the subjective approach was relevant. The directions on causation, therefore, could not be faulted, *R. v. Williams (Barry Anthony)* [1992] 1 W.L.R. 380, [1992] C.L.Y. 796 considered.

R. v. M (RICHARD) (A JUVENILE) [2000] Crim. L.R. 372, Roch, L.J., CA (Crim Div).

1018. Witnesses – intimidation – evidence of investigation in progress

[Criminal Justice and Public Order Act 1994 s.51 (1).]

The appellants, who were members of the same family, were charged with causing grievous bodily harm with intent and with intimidating a witness. The prosecution alleged that the victim, MG, who was married to a member of the appellants' family, had visited the local council, the police and the official receiver, and implicated the appellants in a substantial housing benefit fraud. MG gave evidence that in late 1995 and early 1996 BS and JS had sought to involve him in making false claims for housing benefit. When he refused to do this they threatened him with violence. The appellants and another coaccused arrived at MG's home where he was punched, kicked and beaten with a hockey stick, sustaining serious injuries. The principal issue for the jury was whether all the coaccused had taken some part in the beating, or whether MG had attacked CS first who had hit him in self defence whilst the others attempted to separate them. A housing benefit fraud officer confirmed that he had visited and interviewed BS and CS in connection with housing benefit applications and had taken a witness statement from MG. The judge directed the jury in relation to the offence of intimidating a witness, that the Crown had to prove that the appellants knew or believed that there was an investigation into an offence but not that such an investigation was in fact under way. The appellants were all convicted of both offences. They appealed against conviction, on the grounds that the judge's direction was wrong.

Held, dismissing the appeal, that although the Criminal Justice and Public Order Act 1994 s.51 (1) (b) spoke of the state of mind of a defendant when it stated that he had to know or believe that the person whom he was intimidating was assisting in the investigation of an offence, the words in s.51 (1) (c), "intending thereby to cause the investigation or the course of justice to be obstructed, perverted or interfered with", necessarily required that an investigation was in fact being carried out. Accordingly, there needed to be evidence before the jury that an investigation was in fact in progress. In this case there was such evidence before the jury, if it chose to accept it, and therefore the convictions were safe.

R. v. SINGH (B); R. v. SINGH (C); R. v. SINGH (J) [2000] 1 Cr. App. R. 31, Brooke, L.J., CA (Crim Div).

1019. Youth Justice and Criminal Evidence Act 1999 (c.23) – Commencement No.3 Order

YOUTH JUSTICE AND CRIMINAL EVIDENCE ACT 1999 (COMMENCEMENT NO.3) ORDER 2000, SI 2000 1587 (C.43); made under the Youth Justice and

Criminal Evidence Act 1999 s.68. Commencement details: bringing into force various provisions of the Act on June 26, 2000; £1.00.

This Order brings into force the Youth Justice and Criminal Evidence Act 1999 Part I and Sch.1 on June 26, 2000. These provisions enable, and in some circumstances require, courts to refer young offenders who have been convicted of certain offences to youth offender panels. It also commences a number of minor and consequential amendments and transitional provisions relating to such panels.

1020. Youth Justice and Criminal Evidence Act 1999 (c.23) – Commencement No.5 Order

YOUTH JUSTICE AND CRIMINAL EVIDENCE ACT 1999 (COMMENCEMENT NO.5) ORDER 2000, SI 2000 3075 (C.96); made under the Youth Justice and Criminal Evidence Act 1999 s.64, s.68. Commencement details: bringing into force various provisions of the Act on December 4, 2000; £1.75.

This Order brings into force the Youth Justice and Criminal Evidence Act 1999 s.41 and s.43, which provide, in connection with sexual offences, for the restriction of evidence or questions about a complainant's sexual history. In addition, it brings into force the repeal of the Sexual Offences (Amendment) Act 1976 s.2 and s.3.

1021. Publications

Alldridge, Peter – Relocating Criminal Law. Applied Legal Philosophy. Hardback: £50.00. ISBN 1-85521-268-4. Ashgate Publishing Limited.

Bennett, Wayne W.; Hess, Karen – Criminal Investigation. 6th Ed. Hardback: £29.99. ISBN 0-534-57659-1. Wadsworth.

Bennett, Wayne W.; Hess, Karen – Management and Supervision in Law Enforcement. 3rd Ed. Hardback: £29.99. ISBN 0-534-55434-2. Wadsworth.

Bibbings, Lois; Nicolson, Donald – Feminist Perspectives on Criminal Law. Feminist Perspectives Series. Paperback: £19.95. ISBN 1-85941-526-1. Cavendish Publishing Ltd.

Bloy, Duncan J.; Parry, Philip; Molan, Michael; Lanser, Denis – Principles of Criminal Law. 4th Ed. Principles of Law. Paperback: £17.95. ISBN 1-85941-580-6. Cavendish Publishing Ltd.

Buchanan, Alec – Psychiatric Aspects of Justification, Excuse and Mitigation in Anglo-American Criminal Law. Forensic Focus, 17. Paperback: £18.95. ISBN 1-85302-797-9. Jessica Kingsley Publishers.

Card, Richard – Public Order Law. Hardback: £50.00. ISBN 0-85308-595-1. Jordans.

Cavadino, Paul; Gibson, Bryan – A to Z of Criminal Justice. Paperback: £20.00. ISBN 1-872870-10-4. Waterside Press.

Cobley, Cathy – Sex Offenders. Paperback: £35.00. ISBN 0-85308-622-2. Jordans.

Crawford, Adam; Goodey, Jo – Integrating a Victim Perspective Within Criminal Justice. Advances in Criminology. Hardback: £40.00. ISBN 1-84014-486-6. Dartmouth.

Doherty, Michael – Criminal Justice and Penology: Textbook. Paperback: £11.95. ISBN 1-85836-372-1. Old Bailey Press.

Doherty, Michael – Criminology Textbook. 2nd Ed. Old Bailey Press Textbook Series. Paperback: £11.95. ISBN 1-85836-362-4. Old Bailey Press.

Dupont-Morales, M.A.; Hooper, Michael K.; Schmidt, Judy H. – Handbook of Criminal Justice Administration. Public Administration and Public Policy, Vol 84. Hardback. ISBN 0-8247-0418-5. Marcel Dekker.

Fairchild, Erika S.; Dammer, Harry – Comparative Criminal Justice Systems. 2nd Ed. Paperback: £33.00. ISBN 0-534-51480-4. Wadsworth.

Fionda, Julia; Bryant, Michael – Briefcase on Criminal Law. 2nd Ed. Briefcase Series. Paperback: £10.95. ISBN 1-85941-487-7. Cavendish Publishing Ltd.

Houghton, Peter – Face of Mammon. Hardback: £18.99. ISBN 0-7494-2264-5. Kogan Page.

Hoyle, Carolyn – Negotiating Domestic Violence: Police, Criminal Justice and Victims. Clarendon Studies in Criminology. Paperback: £17.00. ISBN 0-19-829930-3. Oxford University Press.

King, Roy; Wincup, Emma – Doing Research on Crime and Justice. Paperback: £17.99. ISBN 0-19-876540-1. Oxford University Press.

Levi, Michael; Pithouse, Andrew – White Collar Crime and Its Victims. Clarendon Studies in Criminology. Hardback: £45.00. ISBN 0-19-826254-X. Clarendon Press.

MacDonald, Ziggy; Pyle, David – Illicit Activity: the Economics of Crime, Drugs and Tax Fraud. Hardback: £55.00. ISBN 0-7546-2047-6. Ashgate Publishing Limited.

Miller, C.J. – Contempt of Court. 3rd Ed. Hardback: £125.00. ISBN 0-19-825697-3. Oxford University Press.

Morton, James – Sex, Crimes and Misdemeanours: from Oscar Wilde to Lorena Bobbitt. Paperback: £7.99. ISBN 0-7515-2526-X. Warner.

Otlowski, Margaret – Voluntary Euthanasia and the Common Law. Paperback: £25.00. ISBN 0-19-829868-4. Paperback: £25.00. ISBN 0-19-829868-4. Oxford University Press.

Padfield, Nicola – Criminal Law. 2nd Ed. Butterworths Core Text Series. Paperback: £12.95. ISBN 0-406-91602-0. Butterworths Law.

Padfield, Nicola – Texts and Materials on the Criminal Justice Process. 2nd Ed. Paperback: £24.95. ISBN 0-406-98147-7. Butterworths.

Sanders, Andrew; Young, Richard – Criminal Justice. 2nd Ed. Paperback: £19.95. ISBN 0-406-99989-9. Butterworths. Paperback: £19.95. ISBN 0-406-99989-9. Butterworths Law.

Simester, A.P.; Sullivan, G.R. – Criminal Law. The Juridical Studies Series. Hardback: £50.00. ISBN 1-901362-60-4. Paperback: £22.50. ISBN 1-901362-61-2. Hart Publishing.

Turlington, Shannon – Cyberscams. Behind the Headlines. Paperback: £3.50. ISBN 1-902932-10-2. South Street Press.

Tyrer, Jane; Lawton, David – Criminal Litigation. Legal Support Practitioner Series-the Law Society's NVQ in Legal Practice. Paperback: £25.00. ISBN 1-85941-440-0. Cavendish Publishing Ltd.

CRIMINAL PROCEDURE

1022. Appeals – acquittals – no case to answer – Bermuda

[Court of Appeal Act 1964 (Bermuda) s.17(2).]

S had been acquitted of murder following a direction given to the jury by the trial judge based upon his finding that there had been no case to answer. The Attorney General lodged an appeal pursuant to the provisions of the Court of Appeal Act 1964 (Bermuda) s.17(2). The Court of Appeal ordered a retrial, having concluded that the judge should have left the case to the jury. S appealed, contending that a submission of no case to answer inevitably involved issues of both law and fact and, as such, did not satisfy the requirements of s.17(2) which allowed an appeal on grounds involving a question of law alone, *R. v. Galbraith (George Charles)* [1981] 1 W.L.R. 1039, [1981] C.L.Y. 513 cited. The Attorney General countered that any decision by a judge in relation to a submission of no case to answer under either limb in *Galbraith* was always a question of law.

Held, allowing the appeal, that the provisions of s.17(2) gave effect to the clear intention of the legislature that appeal by the Attorney General should be restricted to pure questions of law. Furthermore, it was an established principle of English law that an acquittal by a court of competent jurisdiction was final and could not generally be questioned by any other court, *Attorney General of Northern Ireland's Reference (No.1 of 1975), Re* [1977] A.C. 105, [1976] C.L.Y. 1917 distinguished, *Benson v. Northern Ireland Transport Board* [1942] A.C. 520 cited.

SMITH (JUSTIS RAHAM) v. QUEEN, THE [2000] 1 W.L.R. 1644, Lord Steyn, PC.

1023. Appeals – Criminal Review Commission – dock identifications – current standards of fairness

[Criminal Appeal Act 1995 s.9.]

J was convicted of aggravated robbery in 1968 and sentenced to eight years' imprisonment. His conviction had been based substantially on the identification evidence of one witness. That witness having picked out J in an identity parade later identified him in clearer terms during the trial. The Criminal Cases Review Commission referred his conviction to the Court of Appeal under the Criminal Appeal Act 1995 s.9. It was submitted that the identification evidence was unsound and could not be regarded as safe.

Held, allowing the appeal, that in considering criminal appeals, it was appropriate to take into account current standards of fairness rather than those prevailing at the time of conviction, *R. v. Bentley (Derek)* [1999] Crim. L.R. 330, [1998] C.L.Y. 1051 applied and *R. v. Gerald (Clovis Lloyd)* [1999] Crim. L.R. 315 considered. The rules regarding the admission of identification evidence had become much stricter, in particular, identification of an accused whilst in the dock was not now generally permitted. Applying current standards of fairness to the instant case, it was apparent that the conviction was unsafe and should accordingly be quashed.

R. v. JOHNSON (HAROLD ROBERT) [2001] 1 Cr. App. R. 26, Lord Woolf of Barnes, L.C.J., CA (Crim Div).

1024. Appeals – delay – judicial review of magistrates' decision to refuse adjournment leading to dismissal of charge

N was charged with indecently assaulting his next door neighbour. In defence he claimed to have been so inebriated that he had entered the wrong house and mistaken his neighbour for his girlfriend. When the complainant failed to appear in court on the day of the trial, N's solicitor argued that it was because she did not wish to pursue the case further. On that basis, the magistrates refused to grant a prosecution application for adjournment of the hearing and dismissed the case. The complainant was in fact unaware of the trial date. The prosecution applied for judicial review of the decision to refuse an adjournment. The important issue before the court was whether relief should be refused, on the ground that a long delay had elapsed since the trial date.

Held, allowing the application, that the court's discretion whether to grant relief had to be exercised having regard to all the circumstances and, on the facts, the case should be returned to the justices. Although a long delay had elapsed since the trial date, that had no adverse impact either on the complainant or N. The charge of indecent assault was a serious charge and the delay had not affected the evidence in any way. Moreover, N had contributed to the delay by suggesting that the complainant no longer wished to proceed with the case.

R. v. NEATH AND PORT TALBOT MAGISTRATES COURT, *ex p.* DPP; *sub nom.* R. v. NEATH AND PORT TALBOT JUSTICES, *ex p.* DPP [2000] 1 W.L.R. 1376, Blofeld, J., QBD.

1025. Appeals – pleas – criteria for overturning conviction following guilty plea

[Criminal Justice Act 1988 s.23, s.26.]

M was charged with offences of false imprisonment, making a threat to kill and causing a noxious substance to be administered. At the outset of the trial the Crown applied for the statements of the two victims to be read under the Criminal Justice Act 1988 s.23. The judge found on the evidence that the victims were absent through fear, and that the requirements of s.23 were satisfied. He then ruled under s.26 that it was in the interests of justice for the statements to be read to the jury. Following that ruling, M pleaded guilty, having been strongly advised by his legal representatives that he could still appeal against the judge's rulings. M challenged the rulings on appeal.

Held, dismissing the appeal, that (1) a conviction following a plea of guilty could only be overturned on appeal if it appeared (a) that the appellant did not appreciate the nature of the charge, or did not intend to admit that he was guilty of it, or (b) that on the admitted facts he could not in law have been convicted of the offence charged; (2) where a guilty plea followed an erroneous ruling of law the court had jurisdiction to entertain the appeal only where the guilty plea was founded upon the ruling, and it was only where the erroneous ruling of law, coupled with the admitted facts, made acquittal legally impossible that a plea of guilty could properly be said to have been founded on the ruling so as to enable a successful appeal against the conviction. The fact that an erroneous ruling of law as to the admissibility of certain prosecution evidence drove a defendant to plead guilty because it made the case against him factually overwhelming was insufficient, and (3) the guilty plea prevented M appealing against the judge's ruling. There was no evidence that he had not intended to plead guilty and the convictions were not unsafe, based as they were on the guilty pleas of a man who had legal advice available to him, *R. v. Forde* [1923] 2 K.B. 400 and *R. v. Chalkley (Tony Michael)* [1998] Q.B. 848, [1998] C.L.Y. 1073 applied and *R. v. Mullen (Nicholas Robert) (No.2)* [1999] 3 W.L.R. 777, [1999] C.L.Y. 972 considered.

R. v. THOMAS (MATTHEW) [2000] 1 Cr. App. R. 447, Roch, L.J., CA (Crim Div).

1026. Appeals – pleas – jurisdiction of court to intervene – material irregularities

[Misuse of Drugs Act 1971 s.20; Human Rights Act 1998.]

T and his codefendants appealed against their convictions following guilty pleas to an offence under the Misuse of Drugs Act 1971 s.20 involving 33 kilogrammes of a Class A drug, namely cocaine, seized in Madrid. T contended that the same ground of unlawful prosecution misconduct applied to the instant appeal as had applied to his contemporaneous conviction on a second indictment for the importation of a Class A drug which had been stayed at retrial.

Held, dismissing the appeal, that whilst in the present case the convictions were safe, of the two competing lines of authority regarding the court's jurisdiction to intervene in convictions following guilty pleas, the broad approach following *R. v. Mullen (Nicholas Robert) (No.2)* [2000] Q.B. 520, [1999] C.L.Y. 972 which allowed intervention following a material irregularity was preferred. The introduction of the Human Rights Act 1998 had strengthened the common law requirement for a fair trial and had made clear that where an abuse of process had occurred prior to trial a conviction could be unsafe notwithstanding a guilty plea, *Mullen* applied. Although the common law and statutory tests were different, there could rarely be a situation where a conviction would be considered safe if the defendant had not received a fair trial. The contrary authority of *R. v. Chalkley (Tony Michael)* [1998] Q.B. 848, [1998] C.L.Y. 1073 which advocated a narrow approach was not followed.

R. v. TOGHER (KENNETH) (APPEAL AGAINST CONVICTION); R. v. DORAN (BRIAN PETER) (APPEAL AGAINST CONVICTION); R. v. PARSONS (ROBERT) (APPEAL AGAINST CONVICTION) [2001] 1 Cr. App. R. 33, Lord Woolf of Barnes, L.C.J., CA (Crim Div).

1027. Bail – appeals – non compliance with time limits

[Bail (Amendment) Act 1993 s.1.]

O sought judicial review of a decision that the Crown Court had jurisdiction to hear the prosecutor's appeal against a grant of bail. O had been charged with an offence of robbery and on June 7, 2000 had been granted bail by the justices subject to conditions. The prosecution had exercised the right of appeal against a grant of bail pursuant to the Bail (Amendment) Act 1993 s.1 and had appealed to the Crown Court. The appeal had been listed to be heard at 3pm on June 9 and O contended that the prosecution had lost the right of appeal as, on the proper construction of s.1 (8) of the Act, the hearing of an appeal had to be commenced within the prescribed time limit of 48 hours from the giving of the oral notice of appeal. On that basis, the appeal had been scheduled for three hours later, as a result of which the Crown Court had no jurisdiction to hear the appeal.

Held, dismissing the application, that s.1 (8) was not to be construed literally. In contrast with the other sub-sections of s.1 of the Act, the wording of s.1 (8) was intended to be interpreted as meaning that the appeal had to be commenced within two working days of the decision to grant bail in accordance with the legislature's intention. The provision had to be construed as striking a balance with the practical realities within which it was intended to work. The consequence that the right of appeal could be lost in the event of a delay in the hearing, was inconsistent with the construction of the provision.

R. v. MIDDLESEX GUILDHALL CROWN COURT, *ex p.* OKOLI [2001] 1 Cr. App. R. 1, Laws, L.J., QBD.

1028. Bail – custodial sentences – discount for detention during trial

[Criminal Justice Act 1967 s.67; Bail Act 1976 s.4, s.5.]

The Secretary of State appealed against the dismissal of his application for summary judgment in proceedings brought by B, a prisoner, for damages for false imprisonment. B had claimed aggravated damages in respect of the last five days of his eight year prison sentence for rape on the basis that his trial lasted five days and although he had been granted bail during that time, it was subject to the condition that he submit to custody an hour before the hearing and would not be released until half an hour after the hearing ended. B submitted that those times counted as a "relevant period" under the Criminal Justice Act 1967 s.67 for which he should have received a discount. The Secretary of State contended that the requirement that B submit to custody was by reason of the Bail Act 1976 and B's further detention was within the discretion and power of the judge, therefore his detention was not "by reason of having been committed to custody by an order of the court" under the 1967 Act.

Held, allowing the appeal, that the s.4 and s.5 of the 1976 Act did not impose any duty upon the court to consider the grant of bail for periods immediately before or after the trial was proceeding when an order for the defendant's detention had been made solely for the purposes of ensuring the orderly or efficient conduct of the trial. The time that B spent in the dock also did not fall to be credited against sentence, *R. v. Governor of Kirkham Prison, ex p. Burke* (Unreported, March 18, 1994) applied.

BURGESS v. SECRETARY OF STATE FOR THE HOME DEPARTMENT; *sub nom.* SECRETARY OF STATE FOR THE HOME DEPARTMENT v. BURGESS; BURGESS v. HOME OFFICE [2001] 1 W.L.R. 93, Lord Phillips of Worth Matravers, M.R., CA.

1029. Committals – sentencing – legitimate expectation – adjournment for pre sentence reports

[Magistrates Courts Act 1980 s.38; Criminal Procedure and Investigations Act 1996 s.49.]

E had pleaded guilty to burglary charges in the magistrates court and consented to summary trial under the "plea before venue" provisions of the Magistrates Courts Act 1980, as amended by the Criminal Procedure and Investigations Act 1996 s.49. The magistrates adjourned the case, stating that their powers of sentence might be adequate, but after receipt of a pre sentence report E was committed for sentence at the Crown Court pursuant to s.38 of the 1980 Act. E applied for judicial review of the decision, contending that by adjourning for pre sentence reports, the court had created a legitimate expectation in him that he would be sentenced within the summary jurisdiction.

Held, dismissing the application, that the creation of a legitimate expectation depended on the facts of each case but the mere fact of an adjournment for a pre sentence report could not amount to a promise sufficient to create a legitimate expectation, so long as nothing had been said or done to indicate that committal to the Crown Court had been ruled out, *R. v. Gillam (Leslie George)* (1980) 2

Cr. App. R. (S.) 267, [1981] C.L.Y. 525.41 considered and *R. v. Warley Magistrates Court, ex p. DPP* [1999] 1 W.L.R. 216, [1998] C.L.Y. 1009 applied.

R. v. NORWICH MAGISTRATES COURT, *ex p.* ELLIOTT; R. v. SOUTH EAST NORTHUMBERLAND MAGISTRATES COURT, *ex p.* KNOX; R. v. MILTON KEYNES MAGISTRATES COURT, *ex p.* LONG; R. v. BRENT YOUTH COURT, *ex p.* A (A JUVENILE) [2000] 1 Cr. App. R. (S.) 152, Otton, L.J., QBD.

1030. Committals – sentencing – legitimate expectation – announcement that defendant would not be committed

R was charged with drug offences and pleaded guilty at a plea before venue hearing in the magistrates court. The justices accepted jurisdiction, ordered a pre sentence report and announced in open court that all sentencing options would be kept open, apart from committal to the Crown Court. The matter came back before a stipendiary magistrate who committed R to the Crown Court for sentence. R applied for judicial review of that decision, arguing that he had a legitimate expectation that he would be sentenced in the magistrates court.

Held, allowing the application, that no new circumstances had arisen after the first hearing to justify a departure from the assurance given by the justices, and therefore the stipendiary magistrate was bound by it, *R. v. Warley Magistrates Court, ex p. DPP* [1999] 1 W.L.R. 216, [1998] C.L.Y. 1009 applied.

R. v. HORSEFERRY ROAD MAGISTRATES COURT, *ex p.* RUGLESS [2000] 1 Cr. App. R. (S.) 484, Potts, J., QBD.

1031. Committals – sentencing – legitimate expectation – prior indication of summons disposal

O sought judicial review of a decision by a stipendiary magistrate to commit him for sentence to the Crown Court following his guilty plea to two charges of using and one charge of possessing a false passport. O contended that he had had a legitimate expectation that the magistrate would deal with the charges, which had been supported by the magistrate's adjournment for a pre-sentence report and the evidence of his solicitor who was experienced in criminal cases.

Held, allowing the application, that this was a clear case in which to apply the doctrine of legitimate expectation which was applicable to the magistrates in a case where an indication had been given as to the sentence to be passed *R. v. Norwich Magistrates Court, ex p. Elliott* [2000] 1 Cr. App. R. (S.) 152, [2000] C.L.Y. 1029 applied. O had discharged the burden of proof upon him to show that there had been conduct amounting to a clear and unequivocal representation that sentence would be determined by the magistrates.

R. v. SHEFFIELD MAGISTRATES COURT, *ex p.* OJO (2000) 164 J.P. 659, Gibbs, J., QBD.

1032. Committals – sentencing – power to remit to magistrates – decision to commit made on erroneous facts

[Customs and Excise Management Act 1970 s.170; Powers of Criminal Courts Act 1973 s.42 (1); Magistrates Court Act 1980 s.38.]

B appeared before a magistrates' court charged with being knowingly concerned in the fraudulent evasion of the prohibition on the importation of a Class A drug, cocaine. B had been detained at Heathrow Airport and was found to have swallowed 55 packages, which were thought to contain 300 grams of cocaine. B indicated that he would plead guilty and he was committed to the Crown Court for sentence under the Magistrates' Courts Act 1980 s.38. Following the committal, but before his appearance in the Crown Court, it was discovered that the packages did not contain cocaine but sodium bicarbonate. When B appeared before the Crown Court, the Court remitted B to the magistrates' court. B appealed contending that the Crown Court had no power to remit him to the magistrates' court.

Held, dismissing the appeal, that the power of the Crown Court to deal with an offender who had been committed to the court under the Magistrates Courts

Act 1980 s.38 was found in the Powers of Criminal Courts Act 1973 s.42(1). This section did not empower the Crown Court to remit a defendant to the magistrates' court. In the normal case where there had been a decision to commit for sentence on the wrong view of the facts it seemed that the proper approach would be to allow a defendant to make an application to change his plea. If a defendant had advanced an early indication of plea on a wrong view of the facts, it was difficult generally to see why an application to change the plea should not be allowed. This would allow the Crown Court to remit the case to the magistrates' court where the matter could be considered on a proper view of the facts for the purposes of s.38. However in the instant case there was no application for a change of plea. The offence to which the applicant indicated his willingness to plead guilty was charged under the Customs and Excise Management Act 1970 s.170. This section included offences of attempting to evade the prohibition on importation as well as doing so. In the circumstances the applicant was guilty of the offence to which he had indicated his willingness to plead guilty. The Court would accordingly quash the decision of the Crown Court remitting the matter to the magistrates' court. This would have the effect that the matter remained at the Crown Court and the Crown Court could proceed to sentence the applicant.

R. v. ISLEWORTH CROWN COURT, *ex p.* BUDA [2000] 1 Cr. App. R. (S.) 538, Moses, J., QBD.

1033. Committals – trials – definition of "criminal investigation" to determine procedure – series of offences

[Criminal Procedure and Investigations Act 1996.]

The Criminal Procedure and Investigations Act 1996 Part I, Sch.1 and Sch.2, applied a new committal procedure to alleged offences where no criminal investigation had commenced before the appointed date of April 1, 1997. P applied for judicial review of a stipendiary magistrate's decision to order a new style "paper" committal for two offences committed after the introductory date and to order an old style oral committal in respect of one alleged offence committed prior to that date. P was committed for trial in a hybrid style committal where live evidence would be adduced for the first charge and written evidence for the latter charges. In a joined case, C applied for judicial review of a justices' decision to commit him for trial under the old style committal procedure for 14 offences allegedly committed prior to the appointed date and to employ the new style "paper" committal for 20 alleged offences committed after that date. In both decisions it had been determined that no criminal investigation could have begun before the appointed date and the alleged offences which had occurred after April 1, 1997 were therefore subject to the new style of committal in which live evidence was not permitted. P and C argued that their alleged offences constituted a series of offences which formed part of a single investigation of offences of the same nature and contended that the criminal investigations had been begun before the appointed date so that the new style committal procedure should not apply.

Held, allowing the applications, that the definition of "criminal investigation" in the Code of Practice issued under s.23 included investigations begun in the belief that a crime might have been committed. The words "criminal investigation" had the same meaning in Part I and Part II of the Act for suspected or alleged offences. It was possible for a criminal investigation to be begun before the alleged commission of the offence, particularly where either surveillance or a series of offences was involved, some of which occurred before and some after the appointed date. In both cases, the justices were misdirected in law, *R. v. Norwich Stipendiary Magistrate, ex p. Keable* [1998] Crim. L.R. 501, [1998] C.L.Y. 964 not followed. It was a question of fact in each case for the court to determine whether a series of offences formed part of one investigation and when the said investigation of the offences began. In P's case the matter was remitted for the stipendiary to decide whether to adopt the above approach, or reject such a view, and hold a committal in a hybrid form. In C's case both committal orders were quashed, and the examining justices would need to consider, on the facts, whether the second series of offences was subject to an investigation before the appointed date.

R. v. UXBRIDGE MAGISTRATES COURT, *ex p.* PATEL; R. v. LONDON MAGISTRATES COURT, *ex p.* CROPPER; *sub nom.* R. v. UXBRIDGE JUSTICES, *ex p.* PATEL; R. v. LONDON CITY JUSTICES, *ex p.* CROPPER (2000) 164 J.P. 209, Simon Brown L.J., QBD.

1034. **Convictions – road traffic offences – ignorance of disqualification following imposition in absence**

[Magistrates Courts Act 1980 s.14; Road Traffic Act 1988 s.103(1)(b).]

In March 1997, S was convicted in his absence of an offence contrary to the Road Traffic Act 1988 s.103(1)(b). Sentence was adjourned to April 1997, when in his absence he was disqualified for six months, and S was informed by a letter dated April 25, 1997. Later that day S was stopped when driving, and was charged with driving while disqualified. S was later convicted, notwithstanding that on July 4, 1997 he had sworn a statutory declaration that he had not been aware of the earlier process or hearing dates, pursuant to the Magistrates Courts Act 1980 s.14. S appealed, contending that the statutory declaration had the effect of rendering the April 1997 disqualification void.

Held, dismissing the appeal, that s.14 of the 1980 Act did render the earlier proceedings and disqualification void, but not ab initio; the disqualification was voidable until S took advantage of s.14, which meant that on April 25, 1997, he had indeed been driving while disqualified.

SINGH (JASPAL) v. DPP (2000) 164 J.P. 82, Kennedy, L.J., QBD.

1035. **Costs – defendant's costs order – pre charge costs of obtaining legal advice prior to questioning**

[Prosecution of Offences Act 1985; Criminal Justice Act 1987 s.2.]

Held, that in the exceptionally serious circumstances of an investigation under the Criminal Justice Act 1987 s.2 a defendant was entitled to consult a solicitor and could claim for pre charge costs for advice prior to his attendance to answer questions. The term "proceedings" was not exhaustively defined in the Prosecution of Offences Act 1985 and so could cover matters arising before charge.

R. v. MAHON (PATRICK) [1999] 2 Costs. L.R.151, Chief Taxing Master, Court not applicable.

1036. **Costs – defendant's costs orders – defendants claim for own disbursements**

[Prosecution of Offences Act 1985 s.16(1); Costs in Criminal Cases (General) Regulations 1986 (SI 1986 1335) Reg.7(1).]

W successfully defended a criminal prosecution and was awarded a defendant's costs order, pursuant to the Prosecution of Offences Act 1985 s.16(1). W's solicitors applied for their costs and subsequently W applied for repayment of his own expenses for preparation of his case. The justices' clerk refused to consider W's claim and he applied for judicial review of the decision.

Held, allowing the application, that the clerk had been obliged to consider the claim objectively and to determine whether the costs were justifiable under the Costs in Criminal Cases (General) Regulations 1986 Reg.7(1).

R. v. BEDLINGTON MAGISTRATES COURT, *ex p.* WILKINSON (2000) 164 J.P. 156, Moses, J., QBD.

1037. **Costs – defendant's costs orders – non legally aided applicant – basis of determination**

[Rules of the Supreme Court 1965 (SI 1965 1776) Ord.62.]

M was acquitted of fraudulent trading, having privately funded his defence by way of a loan to his company and he successfully applied for a defendant's costs order. M appealed against the determining officer's decision regarding (1) the amount of weight to be accorded to a fee agreement M had reached with counsel; (2) the fact that M had not applied for legal aid; (3) interest and other payments made in the course of financing his defence, and (4) whether the standard basis taxation principles in the Rules of the Supreme Court Ord.62 applied to the instant case.

Held, dismissing the appeal, that (1) in a privately funded case the determining officer was not bound by the terms of any arrangement between client and counsel relating to the brief fee. In determining what work should be paid for out of public funds, the determining officer would have to consider the appropriateness of counsel being engaged on particular tasks; (2) non application for legal aid was not a relevant consideration in determining costs; (3) the amount of expenses payable under a defendant's costs order was governed by the same principles as applied in the common law rule so that the costs of proceedings did not include the methods used to finance payment of those costs, *Westminster City Council v. Wingrove* [1991] 1 Q.B. 652, [1991] C.L.Y. 725 applied, and (4) while the actual basis for a taxation on the standard basis under Ord.62 was not to be imported into the assessment of expenses properly recoverable under a defendant's costs order, the determination of the issue was essentially the same as that in Ord.62.

MORRIS v. LORD CHANCELLOR [2000] 1 Costs L.R. 88, Ian Kennedy, J., QBD.

1038. **Costs – defendant's costs orders – validity of formula used by trial judge**

[Prosecution of Offences Act 1985 s.16(7).]

T pleaded guilty to an offence of possessing a controlled drug on an indictment containing counts of supplying and possessing and was sentenced to a fine of £100 with seven days' imprisonment in default. T was granted a defendant's costs order pursuant to the Prosecution of Offences Act 1985 s.16(7) of one third of the taxed costs figure. T argued before the determining officer that the trial judge was precluded from fixing costs by reference to a formula and that he was therefore entitled to full costs. The determining officer applied the trial judge's order and T appealed.

Held, dismissing the appeal, that (1) when directing payment of T's costs out of central funds under the 1985 Act the trial judge was entitled to direct that he should receive only a fixed percentage of the costs as taxed, and (2) the determining officer had no discretion to disobey an order made by the trial judge whatever its vires. However it was open to T to make a further application to the trial judge regarding the defendant's costs order.

R. v. TAYLOR (COSTS) [2000] 1 Costs L.R. 32, Master GN Pollard, Supreme Court Taxing Office.

1039. **Costs – defendants – remuneration of court appointed legal representative**

COSTS IN CRIMINAL CASES (GENERAL) (AMENDMENT) REGULATIONS 2000, SI 2000 2094; made under the Prosecution of Offences Act 1985 s.19, s.20. In force: in accordance with Reg.1; £1.00.

These Regulations amend the Costs in Criminal Cases (General) Regulations 1986 (SI 1986 1335) to provide that the system set out in Part III for the payment of defendants' costs out of central funds should apply with any necessary modifications to the remuneration of a legal representative appointed by the court to cross examine a witness under the Youth Justice and Criminal Evidence Act 1999 s.38(4).

1040. **Costs – legal aid – fee for cracked trial**

[Legal Aid in Criminal and Care Proceedings (Costs) Regulations 1989 (SI 1989 343) Reg.2(1), Reg.9.]

On August 27, 1997 B indicated his intention to plead guilty to a number of charges and on September 1, 1997 he was committed for trial. A plea and directions hearing was held on September 26, 1997 at which B pleaded not guilty to each count. B's counsel, T, indicated that the plea was not a real plea of guilty and that B would plead guilty at the next hearing. The subsequent hearing on October 17, 1997 was also listed as a plea and directions hearing, at which B pleaded guilty and was sentenced. T claimed the fee for a cracked trial for the hearing on October 17, 1997, rather than the fee for a guilty plea. The Legal Aid in Criminal and Care Proceedings (Costs) Regulations 1989 Reg.2(1) and Reg.9 provided that a hearing which was fixed for arraigning a person was a plea and directions hearing unless it had been decided a trial would follow immediately if the defendant pleaded not guilty. T argued therefore that the hearing on October 17, 1997 was not a plea and directions hearing. The taxing master allowed T the fee for a cracked trial and LC appealed. T did not resist the appeal.

Held, allowing the appeal, that the facts clearly showed that the case had proceeded on the basis of a guilty plea from the beginning. Although the plea of not guilty on September 26, 1997 was unreal, it required B to be arraigned again at the subsequent hearing. The hearing of October 17, 1997 was not a cracked trial because there was no question of B being tried immediately had he not changed his plea, *R. v. Dawson (Stuart Ian)* [1999] 1 Costs L.R. 4, [2000] C.L.Y. 3978 distinguished. T therefore was entitled to the fee only for a guilty plea.

Observed, that nothing in the Regulations prevented more than one plea and directions hearing in a case or that a plea and directions hearing could not be adjourned part heard.

LORD CHANCELLOR v. TAYLOR [2000] 1 Costs L.R. 1, Ebsworth, J., QBD.

1041. Costs – prosecutions – jurisdiction of Crown Court to increase costs order

[Supreme Court Act 1981 s.48(2); Prosecution of Offences Act 1985 s.18(1).]

H was convicted of 19 offences of causing unnecessary suffering to animals and was ordered to pay £260 towards the RSPCA's costs of prosecution. H's appeal was dismissed by the Crown Court, which ordered her to pay £28,500 in costs to the RSPCA. H appealed.

Held, dismissing the appeal, that the Crown Court did have jurisdiction upon the dismissal of a defendants appeal from a magistrates court to make an order for costs that the magistrates court had refused. While there was no statutory right of appeal to the Crown Court open to either party on a costs order from a magistrates court, the Crown Court did have the power under the Prosecution of Offences Act 1985 s.18(1) in dismissing an appeal to "make such order as to costs ... as it considers just and reasonable" or, alternatively, under the Supreme Court Act 1981 s.48(2) to alter any part of an appealed decision including those elements which had not been appealed. In the instant case there was no evidence that H was unable to pay the costs, which were not excessive. It was observed that in the case of an unsuccessful appeal, the Crown Court should hesitate before interfering with an order for costs made by magistrates. Furthermore, a prosecutor should give an appellant ample notice of any intention to ask the Crown Court to vary an order for costs.

HAMILTON-JOHNSON v. RSPCA; *sub nom.* HAMILTON-JOHNSON v. ROYAL SOCIETY FOR THE PREVENTION OF CRUELTY TO ANIMALS [2000] 2 Cr. App. R. (S.) 390, Schiemann, L.J., QBD.

1042. Costs – wasted costs order – poor drafting – negligent and unreasonable conduct

H, a firm of solicitors representing M on charges of gross indecency against his daughter, discovered on the day of the trial that M's daughter had made a complaint to the Social Services Department, SSD, as well as her statement to the police. The trial was adjourned and H sent a letter to SSD asking for the record of the complaint. SSD refused to disclose it and H issued a witness summons expressed in very general terms. The judge set aside the witness summons as being too general and, having examined the SSD document and compared it to the statement given to the police, held that it should not be disclosed and made a wasted costs order against H, which H appealed.

Held, allowing the appeal, that despite the poor drafting of the summons, SSD were nevertheless aware, from the letter, of what they were being asked to provide. No costs had actually been wasted as a hearing would have been necessary in any event since SSD sought to oppose the summons, and the judge had been able to make a finding on the admissibility of the statement, *Barrister (Wasted Costs Order) (No.1 of 1991), Re* [1993] Q.B. 293, [1992] C.L.Y. 748 applied. Wasted costs orders should not be used as a way of penalising solicitors unless costs had actually been wasted through negligence or unreasonableness.

R. v. M (WASTED COSTS ORDER); *sub nom.* HOWELLS (SOLICITORS), *Re* [2000] P.N.L.R. 214, Roch, L.J, Rougier, J, Wright, J., CA (Crim Div).

1043. Costs – wasted costs orders – solicitor relying on counsel – counsel failing to refer to unreported case

[Prosecution of Offences Act 1985 s.19.]

HR, solicitors, acted for a defendant in a murder trial. At the commencement of the trial the court extended the custody time limit but the trial was subsequently aborted because of the unavailability of a witness. Counsel advised HR that as no application to extend the custody time limit had been made an application for bail was appropriate and HR subsequently notified the court and the prosecution that such an application was to be made. At the hearing the prosecution referred defence counsel to the unreported Divisional Court decision *Bozkurt, Re* (Unreported, October 3, 1997), which determined that custody time limits did not apply after the swearing in of a jury. Although defence counsel offered to withdraw the application, the prosecution obtained a wasted costs order against HR alleging negligent conduct. HR appealed.

Held, allowing the appeal, that for a wasted costs order to be made under the Prosecution of Offences Act 1985 s.19, costs had to be sustained via improper, unreasonable or negligent conduct. HR had relied on the advice of senior junior counsel and it could not be shown that HR had acted in a way that no competent and reasonably well informed solicitor would act, *Ridehalgh v. Horsefield* [1994] Ch. 205, [1994] C.L.Y. 3623, followed.

R. v. A (WASTED COSTS ORDER); *sub nom.* R. v. HICKMAN & ROSE; HICKMAN & ROSE (WASTED COSTS ORDER) (NO.10 OF 1999), *Re* [2000] P.N.L.R. 628, Clarke, L.J., CA (Crim Div).

1044. Criminal appeals – human rights compatibility – notice of issues

CRIMINAL APPEAL (AMENDMENT) RULES 2000, SI 2000 2036; made under the Supreme Court Act 1981 s.84, s.86; and the Human Rights Act 1998 s.5. In force: October 2, 2000; £1.50.

These Rules amend the Criminal Appeal Rules 1968 (SI 1968 1262) so as to provide the Crown with notice of issues relating to the human rights compatibility of primary legislation. The Human Rights Act 1998 s.4 provides the Court of Appeal with the power to make a declaration of incompatibility in respect of a provision of primary legislation; s.5 provides the Crown with an entitlement to notice, where a court is considering whether to make such a declaration. It further provides various parties with an entitlement to be joined in the proceedings.

1045. Criminal charges – amendments – dates in informations

[Magistrates Courts Act 1980 s.127; Magistrates Courts Rules 1981 (SI 1981 552).]

Held, that, although no specific power existed under the Magistrates Courts Act 1980 nor under the Magistrates Courts Rules 1981, a magistrate was able to amend the date in an information so that it fell within the six month time limit in s.127 of the 1980 Act if it did not interfere with any evidence before the court, delay the trial or prejudice the defendant.

R. v. BLACKBURN JUSTICES, *ex p.* HOLMES (2000) 164 J.P. 163, Jowitt, J., QBD.

1046. Criminal charges – amendments – fresh count added to indictment before retrial

[Protection from Harassment Act 1997 s.5.]

S applied for permission to appeal against his convictions, following a retrial, on four counts of breaching a restraining order contrary to the Protection from Harassment Act 1997 s.5. Prior to the retrial, the court had dismissed S's contention that it was either not permissible or an abuse of process for the Crown to add an additional count, and that the additional count amounted to the first on the new indictment on which he was convicted.

Held, refusing the application, that there was manifestly a power to amend the indictment by the introduction of a new count before a retrial. This power was available where, as in the instant case, no injustice would be caused by its exercise, *R. v. Bloomfield (Mark Andrew)* [1997] 1 Cr. App. R. 135, [1997] C.L.Y. 1255 distinguished.

R. v. SWAINE (ROBERT EDWARD) *The Times,* November 1, 2000, Swinton Thomas, L.J., CA (Crim Div).

1047. Criminal charges – summonses – failure to disclose offence – amendments

[Food Safety Act 1990 s.15(1)(b), s.34.]

W, the former owner of a football club, appealed his conviction for 12 breaches of the Food Safety Act 1990 s.15(1)(b). W maintained that (1) the summonses in their original form were so poorly drafted that they did not disclose any offence, and (2) a subsequent application to amend should not have been allowed, following an initial refusal, since it had been made long after the expiration of the 12-month period prescribed for laying an information under s.34.

Held, allowing the appeal and quashing the conviction, that (1) the summonses in their original form were badly drafted. It was necessary to ask whether in that form they enabled the defendant to identify the precise nature of the alleged wrongdoing. On the facts of the instant case the answer must be that they did not since there were two distinct offences contained within s.15(1) but it was not clear from the wording of the summons what was the precise nature of the wrongdoing charged, and (2) in consequence the information was void at the expiration of the 12 month period and the justices should accordingly have refused the application to amend, *Simpson v. Roberts The Times,* December 21, 1984, [1985] C.L.Y. 2095 and *R. v. Scunthorpe Justices, ex p. M* (1998) 162 J.P. 635, [1998] C.L.Y. 1038 applied.

WARD v. BARKING AND DAGENHAM LBC [2000] E.H.L.R. 263, Kennedy, L.J., QBD.

1048. Criminal charges – time limits – actual bodily harm charge amended to common assault

[Offences against the Person Act 1861 s.47; Magistrates Courts Act 1980 s.127; Criminal Justice Act 1988 s.39.]

S was charged with assault occasioning actual bodily harm contrary to the Offences against the Person Act 1861 s.47. More than six months after the commission of the alleged offence the prosecution applied to the stipendiary magistrate to amend the charge to one of common assault contrary to the Criminal Justice Act 1988 s.39. S applied for judicial review of the magistrate's decision to accept jurisdiction to hear the summary matter on the grounds that it was irrational and wrong in law. S contended that the prosecution had not amended the original charge but had withdrawn it and replaced it with a summary charge. S argued that the information relating to the summary charge was therefore laid out of time by virtue of the provisions of the Magistrates Courts Act 1980 s.127 and that it was unjust for the matter to proceed.

Held, dismissing the application, that the application before the magistrate was in reality an application to amend the original charge and thus s.127 of the 1980 Act did not apply. If the amended charge arose out of the same or substantially the same facts as the original charge, then the court could consider if it was just to allow the amendment, *R. v. Scunthorpe Justices, ex p. M* (1998) 162 J.P. 635, [1998] C.L.Y. 1038 followed. In the instant case there had been no injustice to S and the magistrate had applied the principles correctly.

R. v. THAMES MAGISTRATES COURT, *ex p.* STEVENS (2000) 164 J.P. 233, Klevan, J., QBD.

1049. Criminal damage – classification – jurisdiction of the Crown Court

[Criminal Law Act 1967 s.6; Interpretation Act 1978 Sch.1; Magistrates Courts Act 1980 s.17, s.22, Sch.1 para.29; Criminal Justice Act 1988 s.40.]

F was indicted on counts of racially aggravated criminal damage and racially aggravated assault occasioning actual bodily harm. The trial judge also left to the jury the alternative counts of criminal damage and assault occasioning actual bodily harm and the jury returned verdicts of guilty to both of those lesser offences. F appealed against his conviction for criminal damage on the grounds that, although criminal damage was an offence triable either way, the effect of the Magistrates Courts Act 1980 s.22 was to render it an offence triable summarily only when the amount of the damage did not exceed £5000. He therefore contended that the Crown Court had no jurisdiction to try the summary matter pursuant to the Criminal Law Act 1967 s.6 unless the alternative counts had been added to the indictment under the provisions of the Criminal Justice Act 1988 s.40. The Crown countered that the effect of the Interpretation Act 1978 Sch.1 was that the way in which an offence was triable was to be construed without regard to the effect of s.22 of the 1980 Act on the mode of trial in any particular case.

Held, dismissing the appeal, that the effect of s.22 of the 1980 Act was to determine the mode of trial but that it did not change the classification of the offence and that s.17 and Sch.1 para.29 of the same Act clearly stated that criminal damage was an offence triable either way. The court accepted the Crown's submission in respect of the 1978 Act, *R. v. Burt (Sean David)* (1997) 161 J.P. 77, disapproved.

R. v. FENNELL (PETER) [2000] 1 W.L.R. 2011, Rose, L.J., CA (Crim Div).

1050. Criminal Justice and Court Services Act 2000 (c.43)

This Act establishes a National Probation Service for England and Wales and a Children and Family Court Advisory and Support Service; it makes further provision for the protection of children and about dealing with persons suspected of, charged with or convicted of offences and it amends the law relating to access to information held under the Road Traffic Act 1988 Part III.

This Act received Royal Assent on November 30, 2000.

1051. Criminal Justice and Court Services Act 2000 (c.43) – Commencement No.1 Order

CRIMINAL JUSTICE AND COURT SERVICES ACT 2000 (COMMENCEMENT NO.1) ORDER 2000, SI 2000 3302 (C.105); made under the Criminal Justice and Court Services Act 2000 s.80. Commencement details: bringing into force various provisions of the Act on January 11, 2001 and February 1, 2001; £1.50.

This Order brings the Criminal Justice and Court Services Act 2000 Part II and Sch.4, which give powers to courts in certain circumstances to disqualify individuals from working with children, into force on January 11, 2001. In addition s.56, relating to reprimands and warnings, s.62, relating to conditions as to monitoring on release on licence etc., and s.63, in so far as it relates to requirements for electronic monitoring of young offenders after release, are brought into force on February 1, 2001.

1052. Custody – time limits – effect of prior custodial sentence

L applied for judicial review of a decision of the Crown Court to refuse to determine an application by the Crown for an extension of the custody time limit in respect of an offence of indecent assault on a female under 14 for which L had been charged. L was remanded into custody but on committal was sentenced to four months' detention for other offences. The Crown contended that the custody time limit for the second offence was suspended until the time served for the first offences had passed, as L could not have been a serving prisoner and in the custody of the Crown Court at one and the same time. The judge refused to grant an extension of time or hear a bail application on the ground that it was premature, since L had been both in custody and on remand awaiting trial and the custody time limit could not have been running during that time.

Held, granting the application, that the judge should have adjudicated on the matter. The Crown Court had no common law powers to suspend the running of custody time limits and, given the lack of statutory provision, a prisoner was entitled to have the period spent in custody taken into account when calculating the custody time limits, *R. v. Manchester Crown Court, ex p. McDonald* [1999] 1 W.L.R. 841, [1998] C.L.Y. 1025 applied.

R. v. PETERBOROUGH CROWN COURT, *ex p.* L [2000] Crim. L.R. 470, Rose, L.J., QBD.

1053. Custody – time limits – effort made in fixing trial date within custody limits

[Prosecution of Offences Act 1985 s.22(3); Crime and Disorder Act 1998 s.43(2); Prosecution of Offences (Custody Time Limits) Regulations 1987 (SI 1987 299) Reg.5(3).]

N applied for judicial review of a decision to extend his time in custody by 85 days under the Prosecution of Offences Act 1985 s.22(3) as amended by the Crime and Disorder Act 1998 s.43(2). N argued that the prosecution had not acted with due diligence and expedition in providing information and gathering its evidence and his case should have been transferred to another circuit so as to ensure an earlier trial date.

Held, refusing the application, that a trial date within the custody time limits should be fixed at an early stage, preferably at the plea and directions hearing, especially in a complex case or when a specially authorised judge was required. The onus was on the court and the prosecution to fix a trial date within the time limits laid down in the Prosecution of Offences (Custody Time Limits) Regulations 1987 Reg.5(3). In the instant case the prosecution had acted correctly and the court had made appropriate efforts to find a judge and court able to deal with the trial within the time limit.

R. v. WORCESTER CROWN COURT, *ex p.* NORMAN [2000] 3 All E.R. 267, Smith, J., QBD.

1054. Customs and excise – drug trafficking – seizure of proceeds – application for release

[Drug Trafficking Act 1994 s.42, s.43.]

Magistrates allowed S's application under the Drug Trafficking Act 1994 for the release of money seized by Customs officers who believed that they had reasonable grounds to suspect the money represented the proceeds of trafficking in accordance with s.42(1) of the Act. The magistrates, by reason of applying a balance of probabilities test, had concluded that the money was not necessarily used for drug trafficking and directed its release. Customs requested the magistrates to state a case, suggesting that they had applied the wrong test and considered the origin and destination of the money, not the s.42 test of whether there were reasonable grounds for suspicion that it represented the proceeds of drug trafficking. The magistrates insisted that, despite the reasons given, they had applied the s.42 test in their deliberations. The chairman swore an affidavit confirming that the magistrates had been aware and proceeded on the basis that the burden of showing there were no longer reasonable grounds for Customs to suspect that the money was drug trafficking proceeds lay with S, pursuant to s.42(6), and that they accepted S's evidence of the origin of the money as discharging this burden. Customs applied for judicial review, contending that the magistrates had applied the wrong test and thereby reversed the burden of proof.

Held, allowing the application, that the magistrates' reasons at the time of making the decision were material and indicated that they had concerned themselves with the fact of whether the money was the proceeds of drug trafficking, which was not the issue they had to resolve. In doing so, they had reversed the burden of proof under s.42(6). Under that section, it was for S to exclude the presence of reasonable grounds for Customs' suspicion and in applying the s.43 balance of probabilities test, the magistrates had considered it the duty of Customs to satisfy them that the money represented the proceeds of drug trafficking and they had pre-empted the decision to be made at the forfeiture stage.

CUSTOMS AND EXCISE COMMISSIONERS v. SHAH (1999) 163 J.P. 759, Auld, L.J., QBD.

1055. Customs and excise – drug trafficking – seizure of proceeds – defective procedure

[Drug Trafficking Act 1994 s.42(1), s.63.]

Customs officers at Luton Airport seized cash from A under the provisions of the Drug Trafficking Act 1994 s.42(1) consisting of £23,960 sterling and £900 in pesetas on the basis that there were reasonable grounds for suspecting that the money was the proceeds of or intended for drug trafficking. The following day an order for detention of the cash was granted by the magistrates and following an unsuccessful application on behalf of A for the return of the cash, a order for further detention was granted. A date was fixed for the hearing of an application for forfeiture of the cash. A appealed against the decision to refuse judicial review of the magistrates orders relating to the forfeiture proceedings. It was contended that due to procedural error the initial order for detention was a nullity, the customs officer making the application was not duly authorised to do so and the application was made in bad faith since Customs and Excise had stated that they were undecided about whether they would pursue an application for forfeiture.

Held, dismissing the appeal, that the procedural issue was irrelevant as A had received notice of, and had attended, the detention hearing and in substance the rules had been complied with without A suffering any prejudice as a consequence. Secondly, the customs officer was authorised to apply for forfeiture under the provisions of the Act since he was by statutory definition a constable under s.63. The customs officer's decision to apply for forfeiture was a legitimate step in the public interest taken on the spur of the moment, to preserve the proper possibility of a forfeiture notwithstanding procedural difficulties and therefore was not taken in bad faith.

R. v. LUTON JUSTICES, *ex p.* ABECASIS (2000) 164 J.P. 265, May, L.J., CA.

1056. Disclosure – informers – failure by police to disclose information – juror's unsolicited visit to murder scene

[Criminal Appeal Act 1968 s.2; Criminal Appeal Act 1995; Human Rights Act 1998 s.2, s.3(1); European Convention on Human Rights 1950 Art.6(1).]

D and R were arrested on suspicion of murder and robbery during a police raid at the house where they were staying. Also occupying the house was a registered police informant who had provided the police with information which suggested the involvement of another man, C, in the offence. J was later arrested and all three defendants convicted for the offences of murder and robbery. During the trial, the police failed to disclose any material relating to the informant. An appeal against their conviction having failed, D and R applied to the ECHR contending that material irregularities in the trial had breached the European Convention on Human Rights

1950 Art.6(1). The Criminal Cases Review Commission, CCRC, subsequently ordered an inquiry into the case. The CCRC inquiry found, amongst other things, that the police had failed to disclose that the informant had been in contact with his handler prior to the arrest of D and R, and that there had been discussions about the possibility of giving the informant a reward. Concern was also expressed in relation to the possibility that the jury foreman had visited the murder scene during the trial, in addition to other relevant locations. The CCRC referred the case to the Court of Appeal. The ECHR having found ([1999] Crim L.R. 410) that Art.6(1) had been violated, it was argued that in addition to the CCRC's findings, the ECHR ruling raised a strong presumption that the convictions were unsafe.

Held, allowing the appeals, that the jurisdiction of the ECHR was to examine the fairness of the trial not to express an opinion on the safety of the conviction under domestic law. Despite the finding by the ECHR that Art.6(1) had been violated, that would not necessarily lead to the quashing of a conviction, since it was for the domestic court to examine the safety of the conviction in accordance with the Criminal Appeal Act 1968 s.2 as amended by the Criminal Appeal Act 1995. The duty under s.2 of the 1968 Act extended to a consideration of abuse of the pre trial process, with regard to the particular circumstances of the case, notwithstanding future obligations under s.3(1) of the 1998 Act to give effect to legislation in a way which was compatible with the Convention. If a trial was found to be unfair, that could have an impact on the safety of the conviction even in the face of overwhelming evidence, *R. v. Mullen (Nicholas Robert) (No.2)* [1999] 3 W.L.R. 777, [1999] C.L.Y. 972 and *R. v. Weir (Michael Clive) The Times*, June 16, 2000, [2000] C.L.Y. 912 applied. In the instant case, the failure by the police to disclose information about their informant, and the fact that a juror had visited the murder scene, were serious material irregularities. Furthermore, owing to the informant concealing his status he had been forced to lie to the jury about his whereabouts at the time of the arrest of D and R which had amounted to a conspiracy to give perjured evidence. It could not be said with any certainty what impact the undisclosed material might have had on the jury, and accordingly the convictions were rendered unsafe. Although the Human Rights Act 1998 s.2 would place an obligation on the court to take into account judgments of the ECHR, which appeared to be a lesser obligation than adopting the judgment, it was not necessary to determine the extent to which such judgments would become binding upon the Court of Appeal since the court had reached the same conclusion on unfairness. It was observed that in future jurors should be given directions warning against visiting a crime scene if the judge considered there was a risk of a juror doing so acting on his own initiative. Notwithstanding the finding that the convictions were unsafe, it did not amount to a finding of innocence in view of the overwhelming evidence against all three defendants.

R. v. DAVIS (MICHAEL GEORGE) (NO.3); R. v. JOHNSON (RANDOLPH EGBERT); R. v. ROWE (RAPHAEL GEORGE) [2001] 1 Cr. App. R. 8, Mantell, L.J., CA (Crim Div).

1057. **Disclosure – journalists – safeguards against self incrimination – fulfilment of access conditions**

[Police and Criminal Evidence Act 1984 s.9, Sch.1 para. 2; Official Secrets Act 1989; European Convention on Human Rights 1950 Art.6.]

R, the editor of the Guardian newspaper and B, a correspondent of the Observer newspaper, were both subject to production orders made by a judge pursuant to the Police and Criminal Evidence Act 1984 s.9 and Sch.1 para.2, following an application by a police officer with the Metropolitan Police Special Branch. The orders concerned a letter written to the Guardian from S, a former employee of the Security Services under investigation for alleged breaches of the Official Secrets Act 1989, and material relating to a front page article published in the Observer, written by B, alleging that the names of agents involved in an assassination plot against G had been made known to the Observer but could not be publicly disclosed for legal reasons, and referring to S making known full details of the plot in a letter to the Home Secretary. R and B applied for judicial review of the decision to grant the orders contending that their privilege against self incrimination was in danger of being infringed and that the access conditions set out in Sch.1 para.2 of the Act had not been fulfilled.

Held, allowing the application by R and allowing the application by B in part, that the judge had to be satisfied, from an examination of the evidence, that the requirements under Sch.1 para 2 of the Act were fulfilled and it was not enough for the judge to have made the orders solely on the basis of the police officer's assertions. A persons right against self incrimination was safeguarded by the access conditions but domestic legislation also had to be considered in view of the European Convention on Human Rights 1950 Art.6.1 and Art.6.2 and the relevant decisions of the European Court of Justice considering those provisions in the context of domestic legislation. In this regard the court was bound by the reasoning of superior courts on the interpretation of these decisions, *R. v. Hertfordshire CC, ex p. Green Environmental Industries Ltd* [2000] 2 W.L.R. 373, [2000] C.L.Y. 2300 and *R. v. Director of Serious Fraud Office, ex p. Smith* [1993] A.C. 1, [1992] C.L.Y. 980 followed. *Smith* directed that the question of whether a statute excluded the right against self incrimination was a matter of construction. Section 9 and Sch.1 of the Act did not provide enough authority for the submission that B should give access to material which might incriminate him. Even if such a conclusion was incorrect, when exercising discretion whether to grant the order the possible consequence of self incrimination was highly relevant. When deciding whether the access conditions had been met, it was necessary to consider the purpose of the production order, which, in the instant case, had been to enable the police to have access to material in the possession of journalists which was relevant to the criminal activities of the individual who had provided the material. The access provisions could only be said to have been fulfilled in relation to the letter referred to by B, written to the Home Secretary, and therefore the production order would be limited to that item alone. The evidence against the Guardian was unspecific, and the access conditions had not been fulfilled.

R. (ON THE APPLICATION OF BRIGHT) v. CENTRAL CRIMINAL COURT; R. v. CENTRAL CRIMINAL COURT, *ex p.* ALTON; R. v. CENTRAL CRIMINAL COURT, *ex p.* RUSBRIDGER; *sub nom.* R. v. CENTRAL CRIMINAL COURT, *ex p.* BRIGHT; R. v. CENTRAL CRIMINAL COURT, *ex p.* OBSERVER; R. v. CENTRAL CRIMINAL COURT, *ex p.* GUARDIAN [2001] 1 W.L.R. 662, Judge, L.J., QBD.

1058. Disclosure – public interest immunity – Crown's duty to present accurate information – ex parte applications

J was convicted of possession of heroin with intent to supply. During the course of the trial, a police officer informed the prosecution that a point raised by the defence in open court was incorrect. The judge subsequently adjourned to consider matters of public interest immunity and was informed by prosecuting counsel of the police officer's assertion. It later transpired that the point made by the defence was in fact true. J appealed.

Held, allowing the appeal and ordering a retrial, that this was a serious case which showed the need to ensure absolute accuracy when deciding public interest immunity issues in chambers as the defence would not usually know what was being discussed.

R. v. JACKSON (STEVEN ALLAN) [2000] Crim. L.R. 377, Alliott, J., CA (Crim Div).

1059. Disclosure – public interest immunity – evidence in chambers

[Human Rights Act 1998.]

D and two other applicants sought to adjourn a public interest immunity hearing pending their fresh substantive appeal. The applicants cited the European Court of Human Rights case of *Rowe v. United Kingdom The Times*, March 1, 2000, [2000] C.L.Y. 3219 and contended that as that judgment had not been determined and the Human Rights Act 1998 was not in force, they would be deprived of their sole remedy if the public immunity evidence was analysed in chambers.

Held, refusing the application, that having considered *Rowe,* there was nothing to suggest that the public interest immunity procedure developed in the instant case and in *R. v. Keane (Stephen John)* [1994] 1 W.L.R. 746, [1994] C.L.Y. 876 had been disapproved. The court would accordingly hear the prosecution's public interest immunity application in chambers.

R. v. DAVIS (MICHAEL GEORGE) (NO.2); R. v. ROWE (RAPHAEL GEORGE); R. v. JOHNSON (RANDOLPH EGBERT) *The Times,* April 24, 2000, Mantell, L.J., CA (Crim Div).

1060. Juries – discharge – discovery of new material within exhibit

A appealed against conviction for facilitating the entry of an illegal immigrant, arguing that the jury should have been discharged as it had discovered, after retiring, that an exhibit contained further material. The jury had returned after retiring to say that an envelope, which had been available for inspection, in fact contained two landing cards and not one. An application to have the jury discharged was refused by the judge.

Held, dismissing the appeal, that there was no reason why a jury should be discharged following a discovery that an exhibit which it had been free to inspect in fact contained further evidence. As the exhibit had been available for inspection, this was not a case of new evidence coming to light. Moreover, the new material did not in any way conflict with A's case, *R. v. Devichand* [1991] Crim. L.R. 446, [1992] C.L.Y. 908 distinguished.

R. v. ABRAR (MUNAWAR HABIB) *The Times,* May 26, 2000, Alliott, J., CA (Crim Div).

1061. Juries – intimidation – presence of associates of accused in public gallery – improper influence

T appealed against his conviction for burglary. During the trial the jury had declined to nominate a foreman, having been intimidated by the presence of a group of people, wrongly believed by the jury to be friends of T, who had entered the public gallery. The judge had taken steps to identify those persons who actually were connected with T to the jurors and had declined an application to discharge them.

Held, allowing the appeal, that whilst it was inappropriate to enquire of the individual jurors whether they had been influenced by incidents in the courtroom, it was necessary to pose the question whether a fair minded person would be of the opinion that an injustice had occurred. On the facts the appeal would be allowed since it was not possible to ascertain whether the jury might have been subject to improper influence as a result of prior events.

R. v. THORPE (CRAIG STUART) *The Times,* November 2, 2000, Kay, L.J., CA (Crim Div).

1062. Jury directions – codefendants – more than one possible cause of death – murder

[Human Rights Act 1998 Sch.1 Part I Art.6.]

Held, that where it was possible that a murder may have been committed in one of two ways, a jury should be directed that, before any defendant could be convicted, they must all agree on which basis he was guilty. That might include a direction that, provided the jury were agreed on one basis for each defendant, it would not matter if some also thought that another basis also applied. Where two possible means of a killing are completely different acts, happening at different times, the jury ought to be unanimous on which act has lead them to a decision to convict. Where an appeal against conviction has succeeded, the order of a retrial does not constitute a breach of the Human Rights Act

1998Sch.1 Part I Art.6. Further, a conviction was not unsafe where an offer to accept a lesser plea had been made and rejected.

R. v. BOREMAN (VICTOR); R. v. BYRNE (MALCOLM MATTHEW); R. v. BYRNE (MICHAEL JOHN) [2000] 1 All E.R. 307, Otton, L.J., CA (Crim Div).

1063. Jury directions – consent – honest belief – rape

[Sexual Offences (Amendment) Act 1976 s.1 (2).]

A appealed against his conviction for rape. Having identified the primary issue in the case as one of consent, the judge directed the jury that it had to be established either that A had known that the complainant had not consented to sexual intercourse or that he had been reckless as to whether she had consented. A argued that the judge had erred by failing to direct the jury that an honest but mistaken belief in the complainant's consent would result in his acquittal. A submitted that where consent was in issue, a jury should be directed as a matter of course as to the defence of honest belief, and that the requirement to provide such a direction had been recognised by the Sexual Offences (Amendment) Act 1976 s.1 (2). In the alternative, A contended that such a direction was necessary where the question of reckless rape was before the court.

Held, dismissing the appeal, that (1) there was no requirement that the judge should give a direction as to honest belief in every case where consent was in issue. In the instant case where the facts did not give rise to the possibility of the jury reaching a decision that A had had a mistaken but genuine belief that the complainant had consented, the judge had correctly surmised that such a direction was unnecessary, *R. v. Taylor (Robert Peter)* (1985) 80 Cr. App. R. 327, [1985] C.L.Y. 681 applied. Such an approach was consistent with the fundamental principle that a jury should not be subjected to elaborate and unnecessary directions. The provisions of s.1 (2) of the 1976 Act only applied where the question of honesty had arisen in a case, and (2) the question of honest belief did not always arise where reckless rape was under consideration. It was possible for a defendant to fail to address his mind to the question of consent, or be indifferent thereto, in circumstances where, if he had addressed his mind to the question, there could be no question of a genuine belief that the complainant had consented.

R. v. A (PATRICK) [2000] 2 All E.R. 185, Roch, L.J., CA (Crim Div).

1064. Jury directions – convictions – explanation of significance – burglary

S contended that his burglary conviction was unsafe following the failure of the judge to explain to the jury the implications of prosecution evidence relating to his substantial criminal record for offences of a similar nature.

Held, allowing the appeal and quashing the conviction, that the jury had been given inadequate directions by the judge. The jury should have been directed that the previous convictions were not necessarily relevant and that the evidence went only to show a history of S relying on a legitimate purpose for his presence at the scene in common with the instant case. The important issue was not the admissibility of such evidence but the failure of the judge to properly explain to the jury how to deal with it.

R. v. SOFFE (NICHOLAS) *The Times*, April 5, 2000, Swinton, L.J., CA (Crim Div).

1065. Jury directions – duress – prejudicial remarks on failure to call witnesses – drugs offences

S appealed against a conviction for the fraudulent evasion of the prohibition against cocaine. S argued that the judge had erred (1) by making a reference to the defence's failure to call S's boyfriend and mother as witnesses, and (2) by giving a confusing and unnecessary direction on the proximity of W's boyfriend in relation to her defence of duress.

Held, allowing the appeal and ordering a retrial, that (1) it had been inappropriate for the judge to comment on the failure of the defence to call particular witnesses, *R. v. Wheeler (Paul Howard Francis)* [1967] 1 W.L.R. 1531, [1967] C.L.Y. 848 applied. Both counsel had adverted to the error and the judge should not have ignored their advice, and (2) the judge had erred by raising the issue of the proximity of W's boyfriend in relation to threats to kill or seriously injure. It was important that when complex legal issues requiring directions arose, they should be discussed with counsel in the absence of the jury prior to closing speeches, so that counsel could address the jury appropriately.

R. v. WRIGHT (SHANI ANN) *The Times*, March 3, 2000, Kennedy, L.J., CA (Crim Div).

1066. Jury directions – evidence – inconsistencies in defence statement and corss examination – drugs offences.

See CRIMINAL EVIDENCE: R. v. Wheeler (Leslie). §930

1067. Jury directions – good character – appropriateness of rhetorical questions – indecent assault

In April 1975 L was deputy warden at a boys' camp in Wales. The complainant, who was aged 14 at that time, was on a weekend break from a children's home. In 1997 he complained to the police that while at the camp L had made indecent suggestions and subsequently buggered him. When interviewed in 1998 L denied the allegations made against him. At L's trial on charges of indecent assault and buggery, the complainant admitted that before the alleged incident he had been involved in 16 burglaries and had also absconded from the children's home. L was of good character. The judge, in summing up to the jury, gave a good character direction in the form of rhetorical questions. L was convicted. He appealed against conviction on the grounds that the character direction was insufficient and inappropriate to the circumstances of the case.

Held, allowing the appeal, that (1) character directions should not be given in the form of a question, they should be given in the form of an affirmative statement, and that applied even if the question was a leading question, and (2) in a case such as this one which turned almost entirely on the question of credibility as between the complainant and L, the question of credibility was of the greatest importance and relevance so that, in the absence of an appropriate direction as to good character, the convictions were unsafe.

R. v. LLOYD (DAVID) [2000] 2 Cr. App. R. 355, Pill, L.J., CA (Crim Div).

1068. Jury directions – good character – discretion to exclude propensity – robbery

M appealed against his conviction on two counts of robbery. At his trial, the judge, in giving a good character direction to the jury, only gave that part of the direction that related to credibility. The judge did not mention the question of propensity as M had previously been cautioned for possessing offensive weapons on two occasions.

Held, dismissing the appeal, that it was well within the discretion of the judge to omit the reference to propensity as M must have admitted committing an offence prior to being cautioned. To have given the full direction would therefore have been inappropriate.

R. v. MARTIN (DAVID PAUL) [2000] 2 Cr. App. R. 42, Mantell, L.J., CA (Crim Div).

1069. Jury directions – intention – jury's request for further directions – murder

W appealed against his conviction on counts of aiding and abetting attempted suicide and of murder. W had helped to tie nooses made from bed sheets around the necks of the victims, while on remand. During the course of the trial, the jury had sought further directions from the judge in the form of questions, after the initial directions on the proof of murder had been given. W cited *R. v. Nedrick (Ransford Delroy)* [1986] 1 W.L.R. 1025, [1986] C.L.Y. 651 and *R. v. Woollin (Stephen*

Leslie) [1999] 1 A.C. 82, [1998] C.L.Y. 1052 in asserting that those further directions should have taken into account the uncertainties that the jury had experienced over the approach to be taken to recklessness or intention. On behalf of the Crown it was submitted that dicta in *Woollin* suggested that the jury directions should be kept as simple as possible.

Held, dismissing the appeal, that the jury had been given straightforward and simple directions on the real question which was intention. There had been no need to digress into an analysis of such complex concepts as purpose and foresight of consequences. The trial judge had been in the best position to determine whether anything more than a simple direction was required and in the light of all the directions received had been in no doubt as to the requirements for a finding of murder, *Nedrick* considered and *Woollin* followed.

R. v. WRIGHT (GLENN PAUL) *The Times*, May 17, 2000, Beldam, L.J., CA (Crim Div).

1070. Jury directions – intoxication – effect on intent – murder

M was convicted of murder following the fatal stabbing of her partner in a violent struggle. At the time of the offence, M had had a blood alcohol level of approximately 300 mg of alcohol per 100ml of blood. At her trial, the judge had not given a direction to the jury as to the effect of intoxication on her intent. M appealed.

Held, dismissing the appeal, that it was necessary to establish the factual background in order to determine whether a drunken intention direction was required. Where the facts of a case so indicated, it was not essential that the jury be given the standard direction relating to the effect of alcohol on intent, *R. v. Sheehan (Michael)* [1975] 1 W.L.R. 739, [1975] C.L.Y. 604 and *Sooklal v. Trinidad and Tobago* [1999] 1 W.L.R. 2011, [2000] C.L.Y. 983 considered. In the instant case the facts indicated that M had had the requisite intention for murder despite her level of intoxication. It followed that the judge had not erred in not giving a direction to the jury relating to the effect of alcohol on her intent.

R. v. McKNIGHT (SONIA) *The Times*, May 5, 2000, Henry, L.J., CA (Crim Div).

1071. Jury directions – Lucas directions – adoption of forbidden line of reasoning – burglary

M appealed against convictions for aggravated vehicle taking and burglary, arguing that the judge had failed to give a Lucas direction to the jury.

Held, dismissing the appeal, that a Lucas direction was to assist the jury and was clearly inappropriate in the instant case as there was no risk of the jury determining the issues using a prohibited line of reasoning. A Lucas direction would merely have confused the issues.

R. v. MIDDLETON (RONALD) *The Times*, April 12, 2000, Judge, L.J., CA (Crim Div).

1072. Jury directions – possession – knowledge, control or proximity to knife

[Criminal Justice Act 1988 s.139.]

D appealed against conviction for possession of a bladed article in a public place for which D had received six months' imprisonment. D submitted that the knife found in his vehicle was used solely as a garden tool and that he had been unaware that the weapon was in his van. D contended that the judge had misdirected the jury in directing that they were able to convict on the fact that D had known that the knife was in the van, as that alone could not be sufficient for a conviction under the Criminal Justice Act 1988 s.139.

Held, allowing the appeal, that the judge's summing up could have misled the jury and there had been insufficient knowledge, control or proximity to establish that D was aware of the weapon being in his van, and accordingly the conviction was unsafe.

R. v. DAUBNEY (GARRICK JAMES) (2000) 164 J.P. 519, Laws, L.J., CA (Crim Div).

1073. Jury directions – right to silence – adverse inferences – murder

[Criminal Justice and Public Order Act 1994 s.34; Human Rights Act 1998 Sch.1 Part I Art.6.]

F and four others appealed against their conviction for the murder of a young schizophrenic woman. Despite it having been agreed at the trial that the jury would be directed not to draw inferences from the failure of three of the defendants to mention relevant facts to the police, the judge had subsequently failed expressly to give a direction in accordance with the guidance set out in *R. v. McGarry (Patrick John)* [1999] 1 W.L.R. 1500, [1998] C.L.Y. 1062 and the Judicial Studies Board Specimen Direction No.44. It was contended that the judge's failure to give directions regarding the drawing of adverse inferences under the Criminal Justice and Public Order Act 1994 s.34 had rendered the convictions unsafe.

Held, dismissing the appeals, after examining the adverse inference direction in the light of the Human Rights Act 1998 Sch.1 Part I Art.6 and the right to a fair trial, that despite the reference to unfairness there had been a non direction rather than a misdirection. The circumstances of fairness related to the entire prosecution process and were not restricted to the safety of the conviction. It was found that the case in its entirety had been conducted in accordance with the right to silence, and in a manner consistent with no adverse inference being drawn with the result that there had been no unfairness, *Condron v. United Kingdom (No.2)* 8 B.H.R.C. 290, [2000] C.L.Y. 1075 considered. The court was satisfied that no reasonable jury, directed correctly, could have come to a different conclusion from that reached by the trial jury and that the appellants had been given a fair and safe trial.

R. v. F (MARK FRANK); R. v. L (CLAIRE LOUISE); R. v. L (M) (A JUVENILE); R. v. B (CHRISTOPHER JOHN) (A JUVENILE); R. v. H (ANN NOLENE) (A JUVENILE) [2001] 1 Cr. App. R. 17, Lord Woolf of Barnes, L.C.J., CA (Crim Div).

1074. Jury directions – right to silence – adverse inferences in isolation – grievous bodily harm with intent

[Offences Against the Person Act 1861 s.18; Criminal Justice and Public Order Act 1994 s.34.]

D appealed against conviction of causing grievous bodily harm with intent, contrary to the Offences Against the Person Act 1861 s.18. D failed to give an explanation of the incident in interview but subsequently relied upon as evidence at trial the assertion that the actual culprit was A, his associate. D contended that the judge had failed to direct the jury that an adverse inference could not be drawn from his earlier silence under the Criminal Justice and Public Order 1994 s.34 unless they were satisfied that the prosecution evidence had proved there was a case to answer.

Held, allowing the appeal, that where s.34 was concerned the decision to convict could not be based on the inference alone but had to be considered together with both the defence and prosecution evidence, *R. v. Cowan (Donald)* [1996] Q.B. 373, [1996] C.L.Y. 1511 followed.

R. v. D (ILHAN) (A JUVENILE) *The Times*, December 7, 1999, Auld, L.J., CA (Crim Div).

1075. Jury directions – right to silence – police interviews – drugs offences

[European Convention on Human Rights 1950 Art.6.1.]

WC and KC were convicted of drug related offences following a jury direction by the trial judge stating that they had the option of drawing an adverse inference from silence during police interview. Their solicitor, believing them to be suffering from heroin withdrawal symptoms, had advised them to say nothing. WC and KC were found guilty and whilst the Court of Appeal considered the direction to be flawed, it did not find the conviction to be unsafe. C complained to the European Court of Human Rights contending that he did not receive a fair trial within the meaning of the European Convention on Human Rights 1950 Art. 6.1.

Held, allowing the application, that C had not received a fair trial under Art. 6.1 as the jury should have been directed that if the silence could not be attributed to C having no answer, or none that would stand up in cross examination, no adverse inference should be drawn. The reason for the silence, if proffered, and its plausibility should have been taken into account.

CONDRON v. UNITED KINGDOM (35718/97) (NO.2) (2001) 31 E.H.R.R. 1, J-P Costa (President), ECHR.

1076. **Jury directions – right to silence – undisclosed information during interview – drugs offences**

[Criminal Justice and Public Order Act 1994 s.34.]

G appealed against a conviction for possession of a Class A drug with intent to supply. During his police interview G had answered questions concerning his drug usage, but at trial G had given evidence, which had not been previously disclosed, claiming that he was a customer and not a dealer. The judge directed that an adverse inference could be drawn from G's silence under the Criminal Justice and Public Order Act 1994 s.34. G contended that the direction had not been correctly given.

Held, allowing the appeal, that the direction had rendered the conviction unsafe. The judge should not have left the matter to the jury and had not given clear directions regarding two of the requirements defined in *R. v. Argent (Brian)* [1997] 2 Cr. App. R. 27, [1997] C.L.Y. 1163 to assist the jury to identify the relevant precise fact and to consider whether that fact was something that G could reasonably have been expected to mention. In addition, the judge had failed to direct that any inference by itself did not establish guilt and that the jury had to be satisfied of a prima facie case against G and conclude that his justification for silence could not be explained or could offer no explanation that would survive cross examination. That was an essential requirement following *R. v. Cowan (Donald)* [1996] Q.B. 373, [1996] C.L.Y. 1511. The direction might have led the jury to draw an adverse inference without being satisfied of those elements, *R. v. Argent (Brian)* [1997] 2 Cr. App. R. 27, [1997] C.L.Y. 1163, *R. v. Cowan (Donald)* [1996] Q.B. 373, [1996] C.L.Y. 1511 and *Condron v. United Kingdom (No.2)* 8 B.H.R.C. 290, [2000] C.L.Y. 1075 applied.

R. v. GILL (STEPHEN IAN) [2001] 1 Cr. App. R. 11, Bracewell, L.J., CA (Crim Div).

1077. **Juvenile offenders – custody – time limits – Crown Court's failure to give reasons – due diligence**

[Prosecution of Offences Act 1985 s.22(3)(b); Prosecution of Offences (Youth Courts Time Limits) Regulations 1999 (SI 1999 2743) Reg.4.]

B sought judicial review of a decision of the Crown Court to allow the Crown's appeal against the refusal of the youth court to extend the custody time limit for B's prosecution for attempted robbery. B contended that the decision should be quashed on the basis that (1) the judge had given no reasons for the decision, and (2) the delay in bringing the matter to trial was mainly attributable to the prosecution's late primary disclosure. DPP argued that (a) although reasons should have been given for the decision, the absence of them did not invalidate the judge's conclusion, and (b) it had only been necessary to seek an extension of the time limit beyond that permitted under the Prosecution of Offences (Youth Courts Time Limits) Regulations 1999 Reg.4 because B had previously made a successful application for an adjournment.

Held, granting the application and quashing the decision, that (1) the Crown Court, sitting in its capacity as an appellate court, was under a duty to give reasons unless those reasons were obvious or the subject of the appeal was simple or unimportant, *R. v. Harrow Crown Court, ex p. Dave* [1994] 1 W.L.R. 98, [1994] C.L.Y. 1064 applied, and (2) there was a causal link between the delay in disclosure by the prosecution and the need to seek an extension of the

99-day time limit laid down in Reg.4. On the facts, it was clear that the prosecution had not proceeded with due diligence and expedition as required by the Prosecution of Offences Act 1985 s.22(3)(b).

R. v. KINGSTON CROWN COURT, *ex p.* B (A JUVENILE) (2000) 164 J.P. 633, Jackson, J., QBD.

1078. Juvenile offenders – trial in Crown Court – right to fair trial

[European Convention on Human Rights 1950 Art.3, Art.6.]

C, an 11 year old boy, was convicted in the Crown Court of attempted robbery and sentenced to 30 months' detention. The trial judge had ruled that C could be tried in an adult court notwithstanding submissions relating to the European Convention on Human Rights 1950 Art.3 and Art.6 and psychiatric evidence of a troubled past and learning difficulties. C applied for leave to appeal by reference to Art.3 and Art.6.

Held, refusing the application, that the trial judge had not erred in the exercise of his discretion. The judge had given due consideration to the provisions of Art.3 and Art.6. Furthermore, regard had been given to the stipulations relating to the trials of children contained in *T v. United Kingdom* [2000] 2 All E.R. 1024 (Note), [2000] C.L.Y. 3198 and to the appropriate adjustments made for C.

R. v. C (A JUVENILE) *The Times*, July 5, 2000, Tuckey, L.J., CA (Crim Div).

1079. Magistrates – judicial decision making – extent of magistrates' entitlement to rely on personal knowledge of facts

C appealed against three convictions for having uprooted trees in 1998, which were subject to tree preservation orders made in November 1994 by EBC, the local authority. The order protected trees existing at the date upon which it was made, but not trees subsequently planted. At the trial EBC produced photographs of the site, showing various uprooted trees, and relied upon the oral testimony of EBC's planning officer and an independent arboriculturalist, both of whom answered questions on the photographs. C maintained, inter alia, that EBC had failed to show that the trees in question had existed at the time of the order. The Justices concluded on the evidence that the trees photographed were from the area covered by the Tree Preservation Order, and relied upon their own knowledge and experience of trees and woodland to determine from the girth of the trees photographed that they were more than four years' old, and therefore in existence when the order was made.

Held, allowing the appeal, that the justices were not entitled to rely on their own personal knowledge of facts. The questions regarding the age of the trees, and whether they existed at the time of the order should have been determined by reference to evidence, and not to the personal beliefs of the justices.

CARTER v. EASTBOURNE BC (2000) 164 J.P. 273, Lord Bingham of Cornhill, L.C.J., QBD.

1080. Magistrates – preliminary rulings – availability of duress – robbery

A wanted to raise the defence of duress to a charge of robbery, claiming that two strangers had threatened to kill him if he did not rob an identified victim. On a preliminary point of law, the justices heard evidence from A on oath, and read the police interview and statements from police officers who were present when the offence was committed. The justices ruled that duress was not a sustainable defence and A changed his plea to guilty. A appealed by way of case stated, and asked the court to consider whether the justices should have heard evidence on the voir dire when determining if the defence was available to A, and whether they had been entitled to rule that the defence was not raised in the case, considering the evidence in the voir dire.

Held, allowing the appeal, that the justices had not followed the correct approach when determining as a preliminary issue whether a prima facie case of duress had been raised. The justices should not have described the procedure as voir dire as such a hearing was not appropriate for justices, although there was no general rule regarding when justices should state their decision on preliminary points and whether such points should be taken, *F (An Infant) v. Chief Constable of Kent* [1982] Crim. L.R. 682, [1982] C.L.Y. 1949 followed. It had been appropriate in the instant case to seek a ruling but it was necessary to take care in exercising the relevant discretion. Justices must be aware of the limited nature of their role in determining whether the defence could be tried, and they had not considered that separately from the merits of the defence of duress. The justices had also relied on their decision that the threat to kill did not overcome A's will, as there was a physical distance between A and his assailants when the offence took place. It was not appropriate to assess the merits of the defence in such a way and their analysis of effective threats was flawed. A had been deprived of a full hearing of his case as the justices had rejected the merits of his defence, which was made out prima facie, without the benefit of cross-examination, character evidence and further legal submissions.

A (A CHILD) v. DPP (2000) 164 J.P. 317, Douglas Brown, J., QBD.

1081. **Magistrates courts – bills of indictment**

INDICTMENTS (PROCEDURE) (AMENDMENT) RULES 2000, SI 2000 3360 (L.26); made under the Administration of Justice (Miscellaneous Provisions) Act 1933 s.2. In force: January 15, 2001; £1.50.

These Rules, which amend the Indictments (Procedure) Rules 1971 (SI 1971 2084) in relation to the new procedure created by Crime and Disorder Act 1998 s.51, s.52 and Sch.3, provide for a bill of indictment to be preferred within 28 days of the service of the prosecution case and to make appropriate reference to the new procedure in relation to applications to the High Court for voluntary bills of indictment.

1082. **Mode of trial – codefendants – individual right of election**

[Magistrates Courts Act 1980 s.25.]

G was charged with handling cheques stolen by R, who had already been committed for trial. The stipendiary magistrate rejected the prosecution's application that G be committed for trial, and the case was adjourned for summary trial. At a subsequent hearing the Crown asked the court to embark on the trial of G and then revert, using their powers under the Magistrates Courts Act 1980 s.25, to examining justices and commit G to the Crown Court to link with R's trial. Whilst not objecting to the procedure, G's solicitor would not consent to committal because of the seriousness of the offences. The justices decided to commit G in the interests of justice, and G sought judicial review of that decision.

Held, quashing the decision and remitting the case to the justices for summary trial, that each co-accused had a right to elect their own mode of trial unaffected by the elections of others and s.25 was not to be used as a means of defeating that right, *R. v. Brentwood Justices, ex p. Nicholls* [1992] 1 A.C. 1, [1992] C.L.Y. 942 followed. In any event, there was no requirement that G and R should be before the Crown Court together, *R. v. West Norfolk Justices, ex p. McMullen* (1993) 157 J.P. 461, [1994] C.L.Y. 750 followed.

R. v. BRADFORD MAGISTRATES COURT, *ex p.* GRANT [1999] 163 J.P. 717, Rose, L.J., QBD.

1083. **Money laundering – drug trafficking – proceeds from drug trafficking and criminal conduct**

[Criminal Justice Act 1988 s.93A(7); Drug Trafficking Act 1994.]

E appealed against a conviction on two counts of conspiracy to remove from the jurisdiction property which represented the proceeds of criminal conduct and two counts of conspiracy to convert property which represented the proceeds of criminal conduct. He was sentenced to 14 years' imprisonment but had been acquitted of the alternative counts of acts involving the proceeds of drug trafficking. By implication, the finding of guilt showed that the jury did not believe the money to have come from drug trafficking, which was excluded from the definition of criminal conduct for the purposes of the Criminal Justice Act 1988 s.93A(7). At trial, there had been clear evidence that money had been laundered, but no conclusive evidence of the origins of the money. E contended that this cast doubt on the safety of the conviction as the Crown had failed to establish that the money was either the proceeds of drug trafficking or of criminal conduct. The judge had refused a submission of no case to answer and had left the counts before the jury, directing that they should be considered in the alternative. E argued that this opened the possibility of speculation by the jury although the Crown had submitted that at the close of the prosecution case, the jury had before them material which could lead to a secure inference that the money had been received as proceeds of either drug trafficking, criminal conduct, or both.

Held, dismissing the appeal, that the case highlighted the unfortunate dichotomy between the 1988 Act and the Drug Trafficking Act 1994. It was unsatisfactory that the indictment had gone before the jury without the addition of a compendious count of conspiracy which would avoid the necessity for the jury to decide on the exact origins of the money. Whilst the judge had erred in leaving the counts in the alternative, as there was ample evidence to convict on both, the conviction was safe in the light of the overwhelming evidence and the clear directions. Although the offences were serious, E's sentence was reduced to 12 years' imprisonment as the maximum penalty was not justified and it was important not to equate them with those under the 1994 Act.

R. v. EL-KURD (USSAMA SAMMY) *The Independent*, October 26, 2000, Latham, L.J., CA (Crim Div).

1084. Non molestation order – breach – failure to hear full account at committal

W was the subject of injunctions, backed with the power of arrest, restraining him from using or threatening violence against a former girlfriend and her family. An interim injunction was granted on an ex parte application in November 1998 and continued until May 1999 when, three days later it was widened to exclude W from the vicinity of either the former girlfriend's or her parents' homes. However, W breached the injunction on four occasions soon afterwards, including an attempt to force his way into the parents' home. The police brought W immediately before the court. Whilst there was no notice to show cause, there were manuscript witness statements relating to the three final breaches, and the judge dealt with the matter on the basis of those and W's admissions, without allowing M's solicitor to give a full account. The judge sentenced W to 6 weeks' imprisonment suspended for 12 months. M appealed on the basis that it had been denied natural justice. W argued that, by analogy with cases where the Divisional Court considered a magistrate's decision on the admissibility of evidence, intervention was only justified if injustice had arisen because of a substantial error.

Held, allowing the appeal, that the judge had failed to ensure that sufficient time and care was taken to establish the facts and a reasoned decision given. It was not necessary to decide whether the Court of Appeal's power of intervention was as limited as argued by W, because in the instant case the judge's errors had led to injustice, *Neill v. North Antrim Magistrates Court* [1992] 1 W.L.R. 1220, [1993] C.L.Y. 680 considered.

MANCHESTER CITY COUNCIL v. WORTHINGTON [2000] 1 F.L.R. 411, Auld, L.J., CA.

1085. Plea bargaining – indecent assault – representations giving rise to legitimate expectation – subsequent referral

The Attorney General applied for leave to refer a suspended sentence of 18 months' imprisonment imposed on P following his guilty plea to nine offences of indecent assault on the ground that it was unduly lenient. The offences were committed between 1969 and 1977 when P was the deputy headteacher and subsequently headteacher of a preparatory school. At trial, the defence and the prosecution counsel approached the judge on the basis that the Crown would accept a guilty plea, P having stated that he would not plead guilty if the consequence was imprisonment. The judge imposed a suspended sentence, having concluded that the length of time since the offences had been committed and the fact that P had voluntarily ceased the offending conduct constituted exceptional circumstances. It was contended that prosecuting counsel had acted beyond his duty by discussing the question of sentence with the judge and that accordingly such conduct fell outside the responsibility of the Attorney General.

Held, refusing the application, that where the Crown, acting as prosecuting authority, provided representations to a defendant upon which that defendant was permitted to rely and in fact did rely to his detriment, such representations could be interpreted as giving rise to a legitimate expectation that the Crown would not later attempt to retreat from those representations by way of an Attorney General's reference or other means. There was no sensible distinction, with regard to the prosecution of criminal offences under the auspices of the Crown, to be drawn between the Crown Prosecution Service, the Inland Revenue or Customs and Excise. The court, in reaching its decision, had regard to the following considerations: (1) prosecuting counsel had unconditionally accepted the approach of the judge; (2) prosecuting counsel had been instructed by the Crown Prosecution Service for which the Attorney General was responsible, and (3) given the previous history of the case, to re-open the sentence imposed could potentially be considered an abuse, *Attorney General's Reference (Nos.80 and 81 of 1999), Re* [2000] 2 Cr. App. R. (S.) 138 applied. The instant case graphically illustrated how inappropriate plea bargaining could be. Counsel should only have recourse to seeing the judge in private in wholly exceptional circumstances.

ATTORNEY GENERAL'S REFERENCE (NO.44 OF 2000), *Re*; *sub nom*. R. v. PEVERETT (ROBIN) [2001] 1 Cr. App. R. 27, Rose, L.J., CA (Crim Div).

1086.   Plea bargaining – road traffic offences – refusal to reinstate charge – abuse of process

The DPP appealed by way of case stated against the refusal of the magistrates to reinstate a charge of drink driving against E, who had been charged with offences of driving while over the limit prescribed in relation to alcohol, failing to stop after an accident and failing to report an accident. The prosecutor had asked for the first charge to be withdrawn, believing that the correct procedure had not been followed in relation to the intoximeter tests. E had entered a guilty plea in respect of the two remaining charges and the magistrates had retired to consider sentence. The prosecutor, having made consultations in relation to the intoximeter testing, then sought to reinstate the excess alcohol charge as she realised that she had made an error in interpretation of the law relating to that offence. The magistrates reinstated the charge and adjourned the case. When the case had resumed, E informed the magistrates that DPP had agreed to withdraw the alcohol charge prior to the court proceedings in return for E's guilty plea to the two other charges. The magistrates did not reinstate the excess alcohol charge, holding that it would be an abuse of process. DPP appealed, contending that the case stated by the magistrates did not disclose that there had been an agreement between DPP and E and that the magistrates had erred in holding that the attempt to reintroduce the charge was an abuse of process.

Held, dismissing the appeal, that the case stated by the magistrates did reveal that they had considered that an agreement had been reached between DPP and E. Given that a compromise had been made, the magistrates had been entitled to regard the attempt to reinstate the drink driving charge as an abuse of process, *R. v. Latif (Khalid)* [1996] 1 W.L.R. 104, [1996] C.L.Y. 1432 followed.

DPP v. EDGAR (2000) 164 J.P. 471, Schiemann, L.J., QBD.

1087. Police records – recordable offences

NATIONAL POLICE RECORDS (RECORDABLE OFFENCES) REGULATIONS 2000, SI 2000 1139; made under the Police and Criminal Evidence Act 1984 s.27. In force: June 1, 2000; £2.00.

These Regulations, which revoke and replace the National Police Records (Recordable Offences) Regulations 1985 (SI 1985 1941), provide for the recording in national police records of convictions, cautions, reprimands and warnings for the offences specified in the Schedule and for any offence punishable with imprisonment in the case of an adult.

1088. Practice direction – Court of Appeal – criminal appeals – provision of case summaries

The Lord Chief Justice issued a Practice Direction amending with immediate effect *Practice Direction (CA (Crim Div): Criminal Appeal Office Summaries) (No.1)* [1992] 1 W.L.R. 938, [1992] C.L.Y. 681 to extend the provision of case summaries, which had been prepared for the assistance of the Court of Appeal, to solicitor advocates and to appellants representing themselves. The Registrar of Criminal Appeals or a High Court judge retained a discretion to direct otherwise if the summary contained explicitly sadistic or prurient material.

PRACTICE DIRECTION (CA (CRIM DIV): CRIMINAL APPEAL OFFICE SUMMARIES) (NO.2) [2000] 1 W.L.R. 1177, Lord Bingham of Cornhill, L.C.J., CA (Crim Div).

1089. Practice directions – criminal appeals – taxation of costs – legally aided appellants

See LEGAL AID: Practice Direction (HL: Taxation Procedure Amendment). §3995

1090. Practice directions – Crown Court – directions for trial of young defendants in Crown Courts

[Children and Young Persons Act 1933 s.39; Youth Justice and Criminal Evidence Act 1999 s.45.]

The Lord Chief Justice issued a Practice Direction applying the decision of the European Court of Human Rights in *T v. United Kingdom The Times*, December 17, 1999, [2000] C.L.Y. 3198, to the way that cases in Crown Courts involving children and young people, to be known as "young defendants" should be conducted so that they were not subjected to distressful or humiliating situations. Where a young defendant was indicted jointly with an adult the normal procedure should be separate trials unless that would be contrary to the interests of justice and the young defendant would not be unreasonably prejudiced. Where a joint trial took place, then the ordinary procedures might have to be modified. Visits to the court room before the trial could be arranged to prevent intimidation of the young defendant. During the trial all participants should be seated on the same level, where possible and the young defendant should be allowed to sit with family and within comfortable communicating distance with his lawyers. Rigorous formality should be avoided, wigs, robes and uniforms should not be worn and consideration should be given to frequent breaks because of a young defendant's shorter concentration span. Where media interest was high, the police should assist in preventing intimidation or abuse of the young defendant and both attendance and reporting restrictions could be imposed, although alternative facilities for the media must be provided, subject to directions under the Children and Young Persons Act 1933 s.39 and the Youth Justice and Criminal Evidence Act 1999 s.45.

PRACTICE DIRECTION (CROWN CT: TRIAL OF CHILDREN AND YOUNG PERSONS); *sub nom.* PRACTICE NOTE (QBD: CROWN CT: TRIAL OF CHILDREN AND YOUNG PERSONS) [2000] 1 W.L.R. 659, Lord Bingham of Cornhill, L.C.J., Sup Ct.

1091. Practice directions – Crown Courts – allocation of court business

[Magistrates Courts Act 1980 s.6, s.7; Criminal Justice Act 1987 s.4; Criminal Justice Act 1991 s.53; Crime and Disorder Act 1998 s.51.]

The Lord Chancellor issued a Practice Direction amending *Practice Direction (CA (Crim Div): Crown Court: Allocation of Court Business) (No.2)* [1998] 1 W.L.R. 1244, [1998] C.L.Y. 1076 so that, save for certain offences in class 2 and offences in class 3, a magistrates' court, on committing a person for trial under the Magistrates Courts Act 1980 s.6 or transferring a defendant under the Criminal Justice Act 1987 s.4 or the Criminal Justice Act 1991 s.53 or sending a defendant under the Crime and Disorder Act 1998 s.51 should, if the offence or one of the offences was included in classes 1 or 2, specify the most convenient location of the Crown Court where a High Court judge regularly sat. Where the presiding judge had directed otherwise, the magistrates' court was required to specify the location. In order to establish "the most convenient location", the guidance contained in the Magistrates' Courts Act 1980 s.7 should be considered. Committals for sentence should be directed to the Crown Court where the substantive order had been made, unless impractical, or otherwise to the most convenient location. Civil appeals were to be heard at the Crown Court designated by the presiding judge. To expedite hearings, directions for the transfer of proceedings to another Crown Court could be given by the presiding judge and any party could apply to a Crown Court judge to challenge the direction. The allocation of proceedings to various levels of the judiciary was specified and directions on the transfer of proceedings between circuits given.

PRACTICE DIRECTION (CROWN CT: ALLOCATION OF BUSINESS) (NO.3) [2000] 1 W.L.R. 203, Lord Bingham of Cornhill, L.C.J., Sup Ct.

1092. Practice directions – House of Lords – amended criminal appeal procedure

The House of Lords issued a Practice Direction amending previous directions establishing the procedure to be followed in criminal appeals.

Held, that (1) time limits start to run from the day of decision or refusal of an application and not the following day; (2) appellants are required to prepare for discussion and the parties to agree a statement of facts and issues involved in the appeal. Disputed material is to be included in each party's case; (3) transcripts of unreported judgments will only be cited if they contain an authoritative statement of a relevant principle of law not to be found in a reported case or are necessary for the understanding of some other authority, and (4) previous directions on the number of copies to be lodged and their presentation are repealed and replaced.

PRACTICE DIRECTION (HL: CRIMINAL PROCEDURE AMENDMENTS) [1999] 1 W.L.R. 1830, Judge not applicable, HL.

1093. Practice directions – magistrates clerks – duties of legal advisers to lay bench – role in ensuring fair trial

[Human Rights Act 1998.]

The Lord Chief Justice issued a practice direction with immediate effect on October 2, 2000 giving detailed guidance concerning the responsibilities of justices' clerks and legal advisers who were members of the clerks' staff. It was directed that the clerks were responsible for the provision of advice by other staff members and for effective case management. The principal duties of advisers were (1) to assist on legal matters, taking care not to not make findings of fact, but only to remind the justices of the evidence when necessary; (2) to assist unrepresented parties without arguing the case on their behalf; (3) to question witnesses when necessary in order to clarify the evidence, and (4) to ensure a fair trial. In order to ensure a fair trial it was directed that any advice other than that given in open court was provisional until submissions from the parties had been heard. Further, proceedings for the enforcement of financial penalties in the absence of the prosecuting authorities were held to be compatible with the Human Rights Act 1998.

PRACTICE DIRECTION (QBD: JUSTICES: CLERK TO COURT) [2000] 1 W.L.R. 1886, Lord Woolf of Barnes, L.C.J., QBD.

1094. Practice directions – stay of proceedings – written notice of stay on ground of abuse of process

The Lord Chief Justice issued a Practice Direction dealing with the procedure where a defendant on trial on indictment in the Crown Court sought to stay an indictment on the ground of abuse of process.

Held, with immediate effect, that in such cases, written notice of the application had to be given to the prosecuting authority and to any codefendant no later than 14 days before the fixed date or warned date for trial, "the relevant date". The notice was required to include the case name, indictment number, fixed or warned date for trial, and set out the grounds of the application. The applicant's counsel had to lodge with the court and serve on every other party a skeleton argument at least five clear working days before the relevant date. The prosecuting counsel had two clear days to lodge their skeleton argument and serve it. The skeleton arguments were required to specify any points of law to be argued, and include a chronology and dramatis personae. It would be advisable for the defence counsel to raise with the judge the possibility of bringing an application for abuse of process at the plea and directions hearing, thereby giving the judge an opportunity to order additional directions and a different timetable.

PRACTICE DIRECTION (CROWN CT: ABUSE OF PROCESS); *sub nom.* PRACTICE DIRECTION (CROWN CT: ABUSE OF PROCESS APPLICATIONS) [2000] 1 W.L.R. 1322, Lord Bingham of Cornhill, L.C.J., CA (Crim Div).

1095. Practice directions – tariffs – juveniles convicted of murder

The Lord Chief Justice issued a practice statement on July 27, 2000, following a decision of the European Court of Human Rights in *T v. United Kingdom* [2000] 2 All E.R. 1024 (Note), [2000] C.L.Y. 3198 referred to, that ministers should not set tariffs for juveniles sentenced to detention at Her Majesty's pleasure. The practice statement dealt with the review of tariffs for all those sentenced for murder as juveniles, pending the introduction of legislation under which tariffs for defendants under the age of 18 would be set by the trial judge in open court. The Home Secretary had proposed that he would set new tariffs in accordance with recommendations made by the Lord Chief Justice as to both existing and new cases. Before making those recommendations, which would be made in open court, the Lord Chief Justice would invite written representations from the detainee's legal advisers and from the Director of Public Prosecutions, who could include representations on behalf of the victim's families. The approach that his Lordship would adopt was based on that applied when establishing a tariff period to recommend to the Home Secretary in relation to adult offenders sentenced to a mandatory life sentence for murder, in that the usual length of tariff would be a period of 14 years which might be increased or reduced to allow for aggravating or mitigating factors. The Lord Chief Justice detailed those factors which might aggravate or mitigate such offences.

PRACTICE STATEMENT (CA (CRIM DIV): JUVENILES: MURDER TARIFF); *sub nom.* PRACTICE STATEMENT (LIFE SENTENCES FOR MURDER) [2000] 1 W.L.R. 1655, Lord Woolf of Barnes, L.C.J., CA (Crim Div).

1096. Prosecutions – Crown Prosecution Service – reasons for non prosecution – test for bringing prosecution – death in custody

The sisters of AM, who had died of asphyxia whilst being restrained by prison officers, applied for judicial review of the decision of the DPP not to prosecute any of the officers involved. A coroner's inquest, having found that the asphyxia had been attributable to the way in which AM had been held by one of the prison officers, returned a verdict of unlawful killing. Following police investigations into the incident the papers were passed on to a special casework lawyer of the CPS who concluded that there was insufficient evidence to create a realistic prospect of conviction. A senior CPS caseworker assigned to review the decision not to prosecute determined that the responses of the prison officers during cross examination at the coroner's inquest tended to support the allegation that excessive force had been used. However, whilst able to establish the officer responsible for causing the asphyxiation, the caseworker concluded that insufficient evidence existed to support a criminal prosecution and accordingly that the case did not have a realistic prospect of success. His decision was subsequently communicated to the solicitors acting for AM's sisters by a letter and a press release issued by the DPP the following day. It was contended that (1) while no general duty existed for the CPS to give reasons for a decision not to prosecute, the circumstances of the instant case imposed an obligation to supply coherent and sensible reasons for their decision, and (2) the caseworker had erred in his application of the Code for Crown Prosecutors.

Held, allowing the application, that (1) while the DPP was not under a general duty to give reasons for a decision not to prosecute, it was reasonable where no compelling grounds existed otherwise, that in circumstances where an individual had died whilst in the custody of the State and a properly directed inquest had reached a verdict that the killing had been unlawful, reasons be given for a decision not to prosecute. The right to life was a fundamental human right which could only be denied in extremely limited circumstances. The coroner's verdict had created an ordinary expectation that a prosecution would result. Accordingly, it was desirable that the DPP in deciding to go against such an expectation should provide grounds for that decision, and (2) the caseworker had failed to take into account certain critical evidential matters and had applied, in considering the prospect of success, a higher test than was required under the provisions of the Code. The Code required that a prosecution if brought would "more likely than not" result in a conviction. The CPS was not required to establish an equivalent standard of proof as that of jury or magistrates court when considering whether or not to bring a conviction.

R. v. DPP, *ex p.* MANNING [2001] Q.B. 330, Lord Bingham of Cornhill, L.C.J., QBD.

1097. Prosecutions – drug trafficking – authorisation by Customs and Excise

[Misuse of Drugs Act 1971 s.3(1); Criminal Law Act 1977 s.4(3); Customs and Excise Management Act 1979 s.145.]

K appealed against a conviction for conspiring to evade the prohibition on the importation of controlled drugs under the Misuse of Drugs Act 1971 s.3(1), contending that only the Customs and Excise Commissioners could authorise the proceedings. K relied on *R. v. Pearce (Stephen John)* (1981) 72 Cr. App. R. 295, [1981] C.L.Y. 462 in arguing that the Criminal Law Act 1977 s.4(3) prevented any evasion of the requirement for obtaining consent prior to prosecution.

Held, dismissing the appeal, that s.4(3) had to be read together with the Customs and Excise Management Act 1979 s.145(1) and (6) and it was clear that the authorisation of the Commissioners was not necessary to commence a prosecution for an offence under the 1979 Act, except where the offence was summary or conspiracy to commit such an offence, *Pearce* distinguished.

R. v. KEYES (ANTHONY MATTHEW); R. v. EDJEDEWE (THOMAS); R. v. CHAPMAN (LORRAINE) [2000] 2 Cr. App. R. 181, Pill, L.J., CA (Crim Div).

1098. Prosecutions – Inland Revenue – conspiracy – Attorney General's consent to prosecute

[Prosecution of Offences Act 1985 s.3(2).]

H sought judicial review of the refusal of the Criminal Cases Review Commission to refer to the Court of Appeal his conviction for conspiring to cheat the Inland Revenue. H argued that (1) his conviction had been a nullity since the Inland

Revenue had not had the power to conduct a prosecution in the Crown Court without the consent of the Attorney General; (2) given that he had been charged by a police officer, the prosecution should have been brought by the Crown Prosecution Service, and (3) his conviction had been unsafe since the judge had omitted to direct the jury on the significance of dishonesty as an element of the offence. He was given permission to proceed with his application for judicial review on the first of those grounds but not in respect of the remaining two.

Held, refusing the application, that (1) despite the absence of express statutory authority, the Revenue could pursue prosecutions in the Crown Court and did not need the consent of the Attorney General to do so. To hold otherwise would be inconsistent with the right that was enjoyed by members of the public to bring prosecutions, *R. v. Bradbury* [1921] 1 K.B. 562, *R. v. Hudson (Alan Harry)* [1956] 2 Q.B. 252, [1956] C.L.Y. 1885, *R. v. Inland Revenue Commissioners, ex p. Rossminster Ltd* [1980] A.C. 952, [1980] C.L.Y. 2278 and *R. v. W* [1998] S.T.C. 550, [1998] C.L.Y. 990 considered; (2) permission to pursue the contention that the prosecution should have been brought by the Crown Prosecution Service had been rightly refused. H had relied on the Prosecution of Offences Act 1985 s.3(2) which provided that it was the duty of the DPP to take over the conduct of all criminal proceedings "instituted on behalf of a police force". Proceedings were only instituted on behalf of a police force, however, where the police force had investigated the case, arrested the suspect and brought him before the custody officer, *R. v. Stafford Justices, ex p. Customs and Excise Commissioners* [1991] 2 Q.B. 339, [1991] C.L.Y. 1864 followed and *R. v. Ealing Justices, ex p. Dixon* [1990] 2 Q.B. 91, [1990] C.L.Y. 1023 not followed, and (3) given that the Commission was only approached in cases where the applicant had already exercised his rights in the court below, the court should be wary of allowing an application for judicial review to be pursued against it save where valid grounds were put forward.

R. (ON THE APPLICATION OF HUNT) v. CRIMINAL CASES REVIEW COMMISSION; *sub nom.* R. v. CRIMINAL CASES REVIEW COMMISSION, *ex p.* HUNT [2001] 2 W.L.R. 319, Lord Woolf of Barnes, L.C.J., QBD.

1099. Remand – time limits

PROSECUTION OF OFFENCES (CUSTODY TIME LIMITS) (AMENDMENT) REGULATIONS 2000, SI 2000 3284; made under the Prosecution of Offences Act 1985 s.22, s.29. In force: January 15, 2001; £1.75.

These Regulations amend the Prosecution of Offences (Custody Time Limits) Regulations 1987 (SI 1987 299) so as to provide for cases where a person is sent from a Magistrates' Court to the Crown Court for trial under the Crime and Disorder Act 1998 s.51. The Prosecution of Offences (Custody Time Limits) (Modification) Regulations 1998 (SI 1998 3037) are revoked.

1100. Summing up – fraud – observations of implausibility – repeated interruptions during cross examination and closing speech

T was convicted of participation in an elaborate multi million pound fraud, involving the operation of bogus companies. T appealed against his conviction and a five year sentence of imprisonment. T contended that (1) the judge had erred in rejecting without consideration T's invitation to add an alternative count to the indictment to reflect T's contention that he had not been involved with the fraud from the outset but had only come to appreciate that the various investment schemes offered were dishonest at a much later stage. T further argued that the judge had further erred in dismissing this aspect of the defence in his summing up as an "unnecessary complication"; (2) the judge's repeated interruptions of counsel's closing speech and during T's cross examination had been unfairly prejudicial; (3) the use of "unused" material by the prosecution during the course of cross examination had resulted in unfairness; (4) the suggestion by the prosecution that they possessed evidence capable of clearly refuting T's evidence concerning travel to America had been improper since the prosecution had never possessed such evidence at any stage, and (5) there had been a lack of balance in the judge's summing up.

Held, dismissing the appeal, that (1) the determination of whether or not to add an additional count to the indictment had been entirely a matter of judicial discretion and it could not be argued that the refusal in the instant case amounted to a decision outside the scope of that discretion. Further, counsel and the trial judge had expressly confirmed to the jury that they should only proceed to return a guilty verdict in respect of T if satisfied that he had been involved in the fraud from the outset; (2) the number of questions posed by the judge during the trial and counsel's closing speech had not been excessive nor had their content been objectionable; (3) there was no basis for objection to the use of the unused material by the Crown since the documents in question belonged to T, had been disclosed in accordance with standard procedures, and a substantial proportion comprised part of the Crown case; (4) the suggestion made by the prosecution that they possessed irrefutable evidence concerning T's travel to America had been inappropriate, but had played no significant part in the proceedings and any adverse impact upon T's overall credibility would have been minimal, and (5) whilst a judge was under an obligation to present both sides of a case impartially he was not precluded from pointing out implausibilities or inconsistencies, *R. v. Nelson (Garfield Alexander)* [1997] Crim. L.R. 234 considered.

R. v. TUEGEL (PETER JOHANNES); R. v. SAIA (SEBASTIANO CLAUDIO); R. v. MARTENS (GERHARD WERNER) [2000] 2 All E.R. 872, Rose, L.J., CA (Crim Div).

1101. Summing up – jury trial – duty of trial judge to inform jury of all relevant evidence

Held, that a trial judge in his summing up of the evidence had a duty to draw the attention of the jury to all possible conclusions open to them, even if neither of the parties to the action made explicit mention of them in their submissions. The only instance where evidence could be put aside by a trial judge was when it was vague and unreliable to the extent that a reasonable jury would refuse to accept it.

VON STARCK v. QUEEN, THE [2000] 1 W.L.R. 1270, Lord Clyde, PC.

1102. Summing up – sexual offences – judge's failure to review evidence

AT was charged with two counts of rape and one of indecent assault against three women. There were five days of evidence in a trial lasting seven days. The judge gave appropriate directions on the law but did not review the evidence, telling the jury that they had received sufficient assistance from counsel's closing speeches and that they would have copies of AT's police interviews available on retirement. AT was convicted only on one count of rape, and appealed against conviction on the ground that the judge had not summed up the evidence.

Held, allowing the appeal and ordering a retrial, that counsel's closing speeches were no substitute for an impartial review of the evidence by the trial judge; it was the judge's task to arrange the evidence issue by issue, and identify succinctly those pieces of conflicting evidence so that the jury's attention was focused on the issues to be resolved.

R. v. AMADO-TAYLOR (IAN WALMSLEY) [2000] 2 Cr. App. R. 189, Henry, L.J., CA (Crim Div).

1103. Trials – Crown Courts – alteration of venue to comply with custody time limits

[Supreme Court Act 1981 s.76 (1); Crime and Disorder Act 1998 s.51.]

B, who was remanded in custody facing trial on indictment for the supply of drugs to his codefendants, S and W, sought judicial review of a decision of the Croydon Crown Court to transfer the trial to another Crown Court in order that the case could be heard within custody time limits. B argued that, since the case had been sent to Croydon by the magistrates under the Crime and Disorder Act 1998 s.51, brought into force in parts of the country as a pilot scheme, it was not possible to transfer it to a different venue because that was prohibited by the Supreme Court Act 1981 s.76(1), as amended.

Held, refusing the application, that s.76(1) of the 1981 Act should not be read as providing an exhaustive list of circumstances in which a trial venue could be varied. The Crown Court had the power to alter the trial venue of an indictable only case which had been transferred directly to the Crown Court without committal proceedings having taken place.

R. v. CROYDON CROWN COURT, *ex p.* BRITTON (2000) 164 J.P. 729, Hooper, J., QBD.

1104. Trials – delay – right to fair trial – police and DPP's inaction: Mauritius

[European Convention on Human Rights 1950 Art.6(1); Constitution of Mauritius 1968 s.10(1).]

D was arrested in December 1985 on provisional charges of forgery and held in custody for 17 days. He made a number of statements to the police in which he allegedly admitted to the charges subsequently brought against him. Thereafter the DPP and the police took no further action toward bringing a prosecution until in September 1988 the Solicitor General made the decision to prosecute. Following a trial by an intermediate court in May 1993, D was convicted of embezzlement and forgery. He appealed to the Supreme Court of Mauritius contending that the delay prior to his trial had been contrary to the Constitution of Mauritius 1968 s.10(1) which guaranteed, inter alia, the disposal of proceedings within a reasonable time. The court, finding the period of delay to have started only from the time of the Solicitor General's decision to prosecute, dismissed the appeal in July 1998. D appealed to the Privy Council.

Held, allowing the appeal, that (1) the relevant period of delay prior to D's trial commenced upon his arrest, *Deweer v. Belgium (A/35)* [1980] E.C.C. 169 applied. It followed that there had been a delay of six years and nine months prior to the ruling of the intermediate court. Such a delay had been the result of the inaction of the police and the DPP. Given the nature of the charges and the available evidence including purported confessions by D, the pre trial delay had been inordinately long and accordingly contrary to s.10(1); (2) the provisions of s.10(1) applied equally to the post conviction delay of over five years in disposing of D's appeal. Section 10(1) required a purposive and generous reading. It would be perverse were a defendant granted protection under the provisions of s.10(1) with regard to a pre trial delay alone. Furthermore, the Constitution which had been substantially modelled on the European Convention on Human Rights 1950 should be interpreted in the light of Art.6(1) which extended to the appellate process, and (3) given the proceedings had been ongoing for almost 15 years and that the delay had been inordinate and inexcusable, D's conviction should be quashed. The Constitution set out guaranteed rights. Accordingly and notwithstanding the strength of the prosecution's case against D, it was inappropriate to affirm the conviction and substitute a lesser sentence.

DARMALINGUM v. MAURITIUS [2000] 1 W.L.R. 2303, Lord Steyn, PC.

1105. Trials – evidence – private consultation with solicitor following admissions – refusal to permit re-examination

D, who had been charged with burglary, made certain admissions when giving evidence as a result of which the stipendiary magistrate allowed his solicitor to take private instructions from him. When the stipendiary returned to court, D's solicitor asked for permission to re-examine him. That request having been refused, the stipendiary was asked to state a case as to whether it was lawful for a defence advocate to take instructions whilst his client was giving evidence, and if so, where re-examination could lawfully be refused. The stipendiary refused to state a case and D sought judicial review of his decision. For the purpose of the application, affidavits were sworn by the stipendiary and by D's solicitor. The stipendiary stated that, at the time when D's solicitor had asked for permission to speak with him believing D had completed his evidence, he had wrongly assumed that his solicitor wanted to speak about a possible change of plea, and that upon his return to court he refused D's solicitor's request to re-examine D, on the ground that his evidence might be tainted by the conversation with his solicitor. D's solicitor asserted that, when he had asked for permission to speak with D, D having not left the witness box, he had given the stipendiary no indication that he did not intend to re-examine D, and that the need to re-examine him only became apparent as a result of the consultation.

Held, refusing the application, that whereas a defendant should not be denied his right to give evidence in re-examination, the stipendiary had been entitled to assume that D's evidence had been concluded and that his solicitor had only wanted to speak with him about the possibility of altering his plea. It followed that the stipendiary had been entitled to refuse to permit D's re-examination and to decline to state a case.

Observed that where a solicitor was minded to take the unusual step of consulting with his client during the giving of evidence, the onus was on him to explain to the court his reasons for taking that step and, if appropriate, to provide assurances as to the matters to be discussed with his client.

R. v. READING AND WEST BERKSHIRE STIPENDIARY MAGISTRATES, *ex p.* DYAS (2000) 164 J.P. 117, Rose, L.J., QBD.

1106. Verdicts – acquittals – grounds on which trial judge may halt prosecution

[Criminal Justice Act 1972 s.36.]

The Attorney General referred, pursuant to the Criminal Justice Act 1972 s.36, a point of law to the Court of Appeal after W, who had been charged with an offence of being in possession of an offensive weapon, was acquitted by a jury following directions from the trial judge. The judge had instructed the jury to return a verdict of not guilty on the apparent basis that the accused had a reasonable excuse, and consequently a conviction was unlikely.

Held, allowing the reference, that a trial judge was empowered to halt a prosecution in limited circumstances only, those being where the prosecution amounted to an abuse of process, the indictment was held to be defective, the court had no jurisdiction to hear the matter, the accused had successfully pleaded autrefois acquit or convict or where a nolle prosequi had been entered by the Attorney General. It was the responsibility of the Crown Prosecution Service to conduct a prosecution, and a trial judge should intervene in a case, which had been properly laid before the court, only where the prosecution amounted to an abuse of process and was oppressive. In the instant case, it was apparent that the trial judge had directed the jury acquit on the basis that a conviction was unlikely and, in doing so, had acted contrary to the relevant authorities, *R. v. Middlesex Quarter Sessions, ex p. DPP* [1952] 2 Q.B. 758, [1952] C.L.Y. 1868 applied and *DPP v. Humphrys (Bruce Edward)* [1977] A.C. 1, [1976] C.L.Y. 488 followed.

ATTORNEY GENERAL'S REFERENCE (NO.2 OF 2000), *Re*; *sub nom.* R. v. W [2001] 1 Cr. App. R. 36, Kennedy, L.J., CA (Crim Div).

1107. Verdicts – actual bodily harm – inconsistency

W appealed against his conviction for assault occasioning actual bodily harm, contending that (1) the verdict was inconsistent with a not guilty verdict on a count of racially aggravated assault, and (2) he should not have been cross examined about his dismissal from previous employment for making racist statements.

Held, dismissing the appeal, that (1) the verdicts were consistent as the jury had obviously been unsure of the racial element, and (2) although the cross examination had been inadvisable given the shortcomings of W's dismissal hearing, and should have therefore been assessed by the judge before its presentation to the jury, there was no resulting prejudice to W.

R. v. WRIGHT (DEREK) *The Times*, May 31, 2000, Henriques, J., CA (Crim Div).

1108. Verdicts – careless driving – time barred conviction set aside – subsequent alternative verdict to dangerous driving

[Magistrates Courts Act 1980 s.142; Road Traffic Offenders Act 1988 s.24 (1).]

W sought judicial review of a conviction for careless driving. W had been convicted of offences of careless driving and threatening behaviour but acquitted of an offence of dangerous driving. The careless driving summons had subsequently been found to be out of time and was accordingly set aside by the justices under the Magistrates Courts Act 1980 s.142. The justices had been invited by the prosecution to convict for the same offence of careless driving on the valid summons of dangerous driving which they accepted and as a result of which W was duly convicted. W maintained that his conviction was unlawful on the ground that the justices were functus officio since a verdict had been handed down on the dangerous driving summons which had thereby terminated their jurisdiction.

Held, dismissing the application, that no sensible distinction could be drawn between the instant case and the cases where a jury had been accidentally discharged before returning a verdict. In such a case where a verdict had been reached and there was no question of any further deliberation, there could be no question of injustice and the alternative verdict was clearly available to the justices under the Road Traffic Offenders Act 1988 s.24(1), *R. v. Alowi (Zia)* (Unreported, March 8, 1999) applied.

R. v. HAYWARDS HEATH JUSTICES, *ex p.* WHITE (2000) 164 J.P. 629, Judge, L.J., QBD.

1109. Verdicts – drug offences – sentence on lesser charge on loss of offer to plead guilty

Y was charged with a single count of possessing heroin with intent to supply and entered a plea of not guilty. The Crown refused to accept his offer to plead guilty to the offence of possessing the drug. The jury subsequently returned a not guilty verdict in relation to the single count contained in the indictment. The judge then proceeded to sentence Y to three years' imprisonment for the offence of possession on the basis that Y had offered to plead guilty to that offence. The Crown had not sought a conviction on that basis and the jury had received no direction concerning the possibility of Y's conviction for the lesser offence. Y appealed, contending that the judge had no power to sentence him for an offence with which he had not been charged and in relation to which the Crown had refused to accept a guilty plea.

Held, allowing the appeal, that there had been no effective conviction. Once the Crown had taken the decision to reject the plea of guilty to simple possession, that plea became a nullity, and the only valid plea put to the jury had been that of not guilty to the charge of possession with intent to supply. Consequently, there had been no lawful basis for Y's sentence, *R. v. Hazeltine (Clifford)* [1967] 2 Q.B. 857, [1967] C.L.Y. 855 applied. It was observed that in cases where offenders were charged with the possession of drugs with an intent to supply and the quantities of drugs involved were such as to render a charge of simple possession not unfeasible, it would be advisable for simple possession to be charged by way of an additional count.

R. v. YEARDLEY (PETER) (APPEAL AGAINST CONVICTION) [2000] Q.B. 374, Roch, L.J., CA (Crim Div).

1110. Verdicts – murder – exhumation of deceased defendant for DNA profiling

In appeal proceedings commenced by the family of H, who had been executed following his conviction for murder in 1962, the Crown sought a direction for exhumation. The Crown maintained that exhumation for the purposes of DNA sampling would provide definitive evidence linking H with one of the victims of the original attack. The family opposed the application, contending that there was a significant possibility that trial exhibits had been contaminated.

Held, granting a direction for exhumation, that it was in the interests of justice to grant an exhumation order as part of the ongoing process to ensure that the verdict of the jury at the original trial had in fact been correct.

R. v. HANRATTY (JAMES) (DECEASED) *The Times*, October 26, 2000, Lord Woolf of Barnes, L.C.J., CA (Crim Div).

1111. Verdicts – murder – imposition of time limit – clerk of court's statement – Trinidad and Tobago

Following the judge's summing up at D's trial for murder, the clerk of the court asked the jury whether they had reached a verdict or whether they wished to retire. They retired for three hours, returning with certain queries which the judge said he could not deal with. He then told them that they had a further 30 minutes in which to reach a decision, and they returned a verdict of guilty 20 minutes later. D appealed.

Held, allowing the appeal and remitting to the Court of Appeal the question of a retrial, that the clerk's question to the jury could have planted the idea in their minds that the verdict was a foregone conclusion and there was nothing to discuss. It was therefore an irregularity even though it had not been put by the judge, *Crosdale v. Queen, The* [1995] 1 W.L.R. 864, [1996] C.L.Y. 1604 applied. The judge's 30 minute time limit had put pressure on the jury perhaps to reach a verdict that they might not otherwise have reached had they been given unlimited time, and they should have been reminded that it was open to them to inform the court if they were unable to agree.

DE FOUR v. TRINIDAD AND TOBAGO [1999] 1 W.L.R. 1731, Sir Patrick Russell, PC.

1112. Youth courts – committals – 11 year old defendant – criteria for committal

[Children and Young Persons Act 1933 s.44, s.53(2); Criminal Damage Act 1971 s.1; Magistrates Courts Act 1980 s.24(1)(a); Human Rights Act 1998 Sch.1 Part I Art.6.]

A was charged with arson offences under the Criminal Damage Act 1971 s.1. The magistrates decided to commit him for trial in the Crown Court notwithstanding the fact that he had been 11 years old at the time of the alleged offence and 12 at the time of his appearance in the youth court. A applied for judicial review of the justices' decision contending that (1) no reasonable youth court could have reached that decision under the Magistrates Courts Act 1980 s.24(1)(a); (2) the justices had not had sufficient regard for his welfare; (3) the case had not been sufficiently serious to justify his committal for trial, and (4) there had been a breach of the Human Rights Act 1998 Sch.1 Part I Art.6 in that he had been denied the right to a fair trial.

Held, dismissing the appeal, that (1) if the justices formed the opinion, as they had in this case, that it was possible to sentence a juvenile defendant to detention under the provisions of the Children and Young Persons Act 1933 s.53(2), then they were bound to commit him for Crown Court trial under s.24(1) of the 1980 Act, *R. v. M (Aaron Shaun)* [1998] 1 W.L.R. 363, [1998] C.L.Y. 1281 considered; (2) the considerations of s.44 of the 1933 Act relating to the welfare of a juvenile offender should not deflect the magistrates from doing what was prescribed by s.24(1) of the 1980 Act; (3) given that the conditions set out in s.24(1) had been met, the magistrates had been bound to apply that subsection and had had no discretion to hear the case themselves, and (4) there had been no cases that had determined that a trial before a judge and jury was not a fair mode of trial. The Crown Court judge would, in the exercise of his discretion, have to determine how the trial was to be conducted, who should participate in it and what, if any, publicity should be allowed.

R. v. DEVIZES YOUTH COURT, *ex p.* A (2000) 164 J.P. 330, Brooke, L.J., QBD.

1113. Youth courts – committals – offences found to be grave crimes – committal of remitted case

[Children and Young Persons Act 1933 s.56(1); Magistrates Courts Act 1980 s.6(2), s.24, s.37.]

A, aged 16, was committed to the Crown Court for trial on charges of arson, burglary and attempted burglary under the Magistrates Court Act 1980 s.24, following the finding of the youth court that the charges were "grave crimes". At the Crown Court, no evidence was offered in relation to the arson charge. A pleaded guilty to the remaining charges and the case was remitted to the youth court for sentence. Having taken guilty pleas from A on other charges, the youth court committed A to the Crown Court for trial by reference to s.6(2) on all the matters before it. A appealed against the sentence of 22 months' detention handed down by the Crown Court. At the appeal the question was raised as to whether the youth court had the power to commit the remitted cases back to the Crown Court for sentence. A contended that the committal under s.6(2) was unlawful, as the magistrates had no power to commit A for trial on the remitted cases, and the purported committal under s.37 could only have occurred if A had been convicted by the magistrates.

Held, dismissing the appeal, that the intention of the magistrates was that A was being committed for sentence under s.37, even though the court endorsement stated otherwise. Section 37 empowered the youth court to commit the matters for sentence, since the Children and Young Persons Act 1933 s.56(1) effectively gave it the powers it would have had if it had tried A on those charges and found him guilty. Thus, the youth court had the power to commit for sentence but not for trial. The Crown Court should not have remitted the cases for sentence to the youth court, given that they had found that the matters were "grave crimes".

R. v. A (DAVID ROY) (A JUVENILE); R. v. L (ROBERT) (A JUVENILE) (1999) 163 J.P. 841, Holland, J., CA (Crim Div).

1114. Youth courts – magistrates – requirement for female magistrate

[Youth Courts (Constitution) Rules 1954 (SI 1954 1711) r.12(1), r.12(2).]

F, who was aged 13, was charged with an offence of robbery. Having pleaded not guilty, his trial in the youth court was carried out before two male magistrates. The Youth Courts (Constitution) Rules 1954 r.12(1) stipulated that the court should be constituted of a minimum of three justices and that it should include representatives of both sexes. Neither the prosecution nor the defence raised the point as to the absence of a female magistrate. Following an adjournment, the trial resumed before the two male magistrates who found F guilty. F appealed to the Crown Court. At his appeal hearing the Crown Court, which was also subject to the requirement of being constituted of both sexes, consisted of a male recorder and two male magistrates. Counsel for F having made the submission that the court was wrongly constituted, the hearing was adjourned. F subsequently applied for judicial review of the decision of the youth court on the ground that there had been a breach of r.12(1). It was submitted by the prosecution that the youth court had properly exercised its discretion pursuant to r.12(2) to continue without a female member, and, further, that the point had not been raised before the youth court.

Held, granting the application, that the requirements of r.12(1) were mandatory unless there had been a proper exercise by the justices of their discretion under r.12(2) to continue in the absence of a female magistrate. In exercising their discretion under r.12(2), it was in the interests of fairness that the issue be expressed and the submissions of both parties sought. In the instant case the decision to proceed had been reached in private and accordingly amounted to procedural unfairness. It followed that F's conviction would be quashed and a retrial ordered.

R. v. BIRMINGHAM JUSTICES, *ex p.* F (A JUVENILE); *sub nom.* R. v. BIRMINGHAM YOUTH COURT, *ex p.* F (A CHILD) (2000) 164 J.P. 523, Laws, L.J., QBD.

1115. **Youth courts – mode of trial – wounding with intent – serious unprovoked attack**

[Offences Against the Person Act 1861 s.18; Children and Young Persons Act 1933 s.53.]

DPP applied to quash a decision of the youth court that K and C, both aged 15 years, should be tried summarily, having been jointly charged with unlawful wounding with intent to do grievous bodily harm contrary to the Offences Against the Person Act 1861 s.18 following an assault upon C, also 15. DPP contended that the case should have been committed to the Crown Court for trial in order to keep open the option of a lengthy custodial sentence under the Children and Young Persons Act 1933 s.53(2).

Held, allowing the application and quashing the decision of the justices, that the instant case was clearly one where the option of sentencing under s.53 should have been kept open owing to the deliberate and unprovoked nature of the attack and that would only be possible if the defendants were tried on indictment.

R. v. NORTH HAMPSHIRE YOUTH COURT, *ex p.* DPP (2000) 164 J.P. 377, Pill, L.J., QBD.

1116. **Publications**

Archbold – Archbold: Criminal Appeal Office Index: No.1, 2000. Paperback: £35.00. ISBN 0-421-69050-X. Sweet & Maxwell.

Archbold: Criminal Pleading, Evidence and Practice 2000: CD-ROM. CD ROM: £225.00. ISBN 0-421-69270-7. Sweet & Maxwell.

Bobb-Semple, Colin – Sourcebook on Criminal Litigation and Sentencing. Sourcebook Series. Paperback: £23.95. ISBN 1-85941-101-0. Cavendish Publishing Ltd.

Brewer, D.; et al – Magistrates' Courts Criminal Practice. Hardback: £100.00. ISBN 0-85308-392-4. Jordans.

Enright, Sean; Grant, Gary – Bail. Paperback: £27.50. ISBN 0-406-00250-9. Butterworths.

Nobles, Richard; Schiff, David – Understanding Miscarriages of Justice. Hardback: £45.00. ISBN 0-19-829893-5. Oxford University Press Inc, USA.

Padfield, Nicola – Texts and Materials on the Criminal Justice Process. 2nd Ed. Paperback: £24.95. ISBN 0-406-98147-7. Butterworths.

Richardson, James – Archbold: Criminal Pleading, Evidence and Practice: 2001. Hardback: £215.00. ISBN 0-421-73160-5. Sweet & Maxwell.

CRIMINAL SENTENCING

1117. **Actual bodily harm – common assault on police officer**

C appealed against a sentence of three years' imprisonment for assault occasioning actual bodily harm and common assault to a police officer. C was driving in his car when he was seen by police officers driving on the wrong side of a bollard at a junction. The police officers stopped him and required him to take a breath test. When C attempted to move away the officer took hold of him and C punched the officer in the face and then punched him five or six times to the head. The officer fell to the ground, and C sat astride him and continued to punch him in the face. A member of the public intervened and C leaned back on this person's leg, causing damage to his knee.

Held, allowing the appeal, that the judge correctly described C as carrying out a frenzied attack on the police officer. It must be clear that such behaviour would not be tolerated. The court paid attention to the fact that the maximum sentence for assault occasioning actual bodily harm was five years' imprisonment. The sentence imposed was too long and a sentence of two years and three months would be substituted.

R. v. CASEY (BRIAN MICHAEL) [2000] 1 Cr. App. R. (S.) 221, Gage, J., CA (Crim Div).

1118. **Actual bodily harm – consecutive sentences – failure to indicate pleas taken into account**

[Criminal Justice and Public Order Act 1994 s.48.]

B appealed against a total sentence of 18 months' imprisonment, having pleaded guilty to two offences of assault occasioning actual bodily harm. Both offences related to the same victim, a woman with whom B had lived for several years. Following an argument, B punched the victim on the back of the head, causing a cut to her head. Three days later, following a further argument, B struck the woman on the head and shoulders with a saucepan, causing wounds to the head. Sentenced to six months' imprisonment for the first offence, and 12 months' consecutive for the second, B argued that the judge when sentencing him did not indicate that the court had taken into account his early pleas of guilty referring to the Criminal Justice and Public Order Act 1994 s.48 and *R. v. Fearon (Paul)* [1996] 2 Cr. App. R. (S.) 25, [1996] C.L.Y. 1745 . B argued that as a matter of principle, the Court of Appeal was bound to reduce the sentence in any case where the sentencing judge had failed to mention that account had been taken his plea or pleas of guilty.

Held, dismissing the appeal, that in the Court's judgment, that was not what *Fearon* decided. The Court in *Fearon* stressed that it was highly desirable in every case where a defendant pleaded guilty in the Crown Court for the sentencing judge to say so in his sentencing remarks. The Court did not say that it was inevitable that a reduction in sentence would follow a failure to do so. It was possible to imagine a number of circumstances which might affect the decision of the Court of Appeal whether in the circumstances of the particular case it was bound to proceed on the basis that there might reasonably be a possibility that the sentencing court did not take a plea or pleas of guilty into consideration. The nature of the sentence, when measured against the facts of the crime and the mitigation other than the plea, might provide a strong indication that the sentencing court must have given B credit for his plea. Conversely, the nature of the sentence might be more consistent with the sentence which would be appropriate after a contested trial. In this particular case, it seemed to the Court that the sentences which were imposed were more consistent with the judge and justices having given B due credit for his pleas than having neglected to do so. These were serious assaults with aggravating features, committed within a few days of each other, in one case with a weapon. The two assaults were separate, although involving the same victim, and called for consecutive sentences, provided that the total sentences were not excessive.

R. v. BISHOP (ALAN) [2000] 1 Cr. App. R. (S.) 432, Bell, J., CA (Crim Div).

1119. **Actual bodily harm – doctors – assault on member of hospital medical staff**

M appealed against a sentence of 12 months' imprisonment on conviction of assault occasioning actual bodily harm. M assaulted a hospital doctor involved in the treatment of his baby son when he became concerned as to the treatment his son was receiving. M struck the doctor a single blow to the face which resulted in him falling backwards and hitting his head against a table.

Held, allowing the appeal, that, although assaulting a member of hospital staff required an immediate custodial sentence, mitigating factors were to be taken into account when determining the length of the sentence, *R. v. Ollerenshaw (Paul Michael)* [1999] 1 Cr. App. R. (S.) 65, [1998] C.L.Y. 1169 considered. Sentencing in such cases was dependant on the facts of the individual case, which might include aggravating features, such as a repeated or sustained attack, or striking more than one person, or mitigating factors, such as remorse, previous good behaviour or a guilty plea. On the facts of the instant case, a sentence of six months' imprisonment was substituted as that adequately reflected the mitigating factors.

R. v. McNALLY (JOHN STEPHEN) [2000] 1 Cr. App. R. (S.) 535, Rose, L.J., CA (Crim Div).

1120. Actual bodily harm – police officer – assault during arrest

E appealed against a sentence of 12 months' imprisonment imposed following his guilty plea to assault occasioning actual bodily harm. E had been involved in a disturbance outside a nightclub, and when a police officer had attempted to arrest him, he had struck the officer twice on the back of the head, causing him to fall to the ground. E had then dragged the officer along the ground in an attempt to escape. The officer suffered bruising.

Held, allowing the appeal and reducing the sentence to eight months' imprisonment, that E had pleaded guilty on the basis that when he struck the first blows, he was unaware that the victim was a police officer. Any attack on a police officer, particularly one dealing with a difficult situation, was a serious matter and would lead to a custodial sentence, however E's sentence was longer than was necessary, *R. v. Fletcher (Stephen Augustus)* [1998] 1 Cr. App. R. (S.) 7, [1998] C.L.Y. 1107 considered.

R. v. ELLIOTT (STEPHEN JAMES) [2000] 1 Cr. App. R. (S.) 264, Kay, J., CA (Crim Div).

1121. Actual bodily harm – teachers – disturbance on school premises – assault on school teacher by parent

B appealed against a sentence of 15 months' imprisonment for assault occasioning actual bodily harm and causing a disturbance on school premises. B went to the school where his son was a pupil, forced his way into the staff room and assaulted a teacher he believed had assaulted his son. There was no basis for this belief.

Held, allowing the appeal and reducing the term to nine months' imprisonment, that a custodial sentence was justified. School teachers were in a vulnerable position. However, the sentencer had started from too high a starting point in determining the length of the sentence.

R. v. BYRNE (JOSEPH) [2000] 1 Cr. App. R. (S.) 282, Judge Beaumont Q.C., CA (Crim Div).

1122. Actual bodily harm – violence – attack on motorist

S appealed against a sentence of 12 months' imprisonment on conviction of assault occasioning actual bodily harm. S was in his car at a shopping centre. The victim, who was also in a car, was waiting for a parking space to be vacated when S drove past him, and began to reverse into the space. When the victim went to remonstrate with S, he butted him in the face, breaking his nose.

Held, allowing the appeal and reducing the sentence to eight months' imprisonment, that incidents involving a violent attack on a motorist, arising in the course of parking or other motoring altercations, were on the increase and courts must indicate that they are not to be tolerated. Custody was almost inevitable and where any significant injury was caused the period in question would be months rather than weeks, even if the offender was a person of previous good character. If there was a view that courts treated this sort of incident more leniently than other types of violence, the sooner that people were disabused of that view the better, *R. v. Arnold (Michael John)* [1996] 1 Cr. App. R (S.) 115 and *R. v. Maben (Matthew)* [1997] 2 Cr. App. R. (S.) 341, [1998] C.L.Y. 1110 considered.

R. v. SHARPE (SABYN JOHN) [2000] 1 Cr. App. R. (S.) 1, Scott Baker, J., CA (Crim Div).

1123. Actual bodily harm – violence to child

R appealed against a sentence of 15 months' imprisonment having pleaded guilty to assault occasioning actual bodily harm. R was left in charge of the 18 month old son of his then girlfriend. He telephoned the girlfriend and said that he had accidentally dropped the boy. Examination of the boy at hospital revealed marked and extensive bruising to the left side of the face and bruising over other parts of the face and an arm. The pattern of bruising indicated that the child had been struck two or three times with considerable force by an open hand.

Held, allowing the appeal, that in the light of the authorities the sentence was too severe. A sentence of six months' imprisonment was substituted, *R. v. S (Jason Lee)* [1999] 2 Cr. App. R. (S.) 126, [1999] C.L.Y. 1067, *R. v. Todd (Thomas)* (1990) 12 Cr. App. R. (S.) 14, [1991] C.L.Y. 1006 and *R. v. Barnes (Stephen)* (1993) 14 Cr. App. R. (S.) 547, [1994] C.L.Y. 1173 considered.

R. v. RAYSON (DAVID RALPH) [2000] 2 Cr. App. R. (S.) 317, Goldring, J., CA (Crim Div).

1124. Administering poison – children – solvents – absence of any sexual connotation

L pleaded guilty to two counts of causing a noxious thing to be administered or taken with intent. L was visited by two brothers aged five and six years, who were the children of a family who lived in the same street. L allowed them to inhale a solution of isobutyle nitrate, as a result of which they felt dizzy and unwell. L was sentenced to three years' imprisonment on the basis that the offences had no sexual connotation. L appealed.

Held, allowing the appeal, that it was significant that the offence had no sexual connotation. The offence fully merited a custodial sentence, but three years was too long, bearing in mind the L's plea; a sentence of two years would be substituted.

R. v. LILES (ANTHONY) [2000] 1 Cr. App. R. (S.) 31, Moses, J., CA (Crim Div).

1125. Administering poison – pleas – administering sleep inducing tablets to victims

N appealed against a total sentence of 12 months' imprisonment having pleaded guilty to three counts of causing a noxious thing to be administered or taken with intent. On three separate occasions the appellant administered some form of sleep inducing tablet to neighbours and friends. On one occasion, N placed a woman who had been rendered unconscious into a suitcase and removed her from her house into a car with a view to removing her to another house. All three victims lost consciousness, and two were taken to hospital.

Held, dismissing the appeal, that the sentencer had to approach the case on the basis that N knew what she was doing and acted deliberately, although not with the intention of causing any permanent harm. The sentence was fully merited.

R. v. NASAR (AZRAM) [2000] 1 Cr. App. R. (S.) 333, Otton, L.J., CA (Crim Div).

1126. Aggravated vehicle taking – passengers – inappropriate to order passenger to take extended driving test

W appealed against a sentence of 12 months' imprisonment and a two year disqualification period with an order for an extended retest having been plead guilty to an incident in which he was a passenger in a stolen vehicle, which his co accused drove dangerously at high speed. W contended that there should be a differentiation between the sentence imposed on the driver with that of the passenger.

Held, allowing the appeal, that having regard to the fact that W had attempted to stop his co accused from driving dangerously, and the fact that he himself had no driving convictions, the court reduced the two year disqualification period to 18 months, and quashed the order requiring W to take an extended re test. It was inappropriate to impose an order on a passenger to undertake an extended driving test, *R. v. Bradshaw (Wayne Martin) The Times*, December 31, 1994, [1995] C.L.Y. 1304 followed. Furthermore, the 12 month sentence was reduced to eight months' imprisonment.

R. v. WIGGINS (JAMIE MARK) (2001) 165 J.P. 210, Langley, J., CA (Crim Div).

1127. **Aircraft – intoxication – drunken aircraft passenger – refusal to refrain from smoking in prohibited area**

A appealed against a sentence of nine months' imprisonment, having pleaded guilty before a magistrates' court to being drunk on an aircraft and to smoking in a prohibited part of an aircraft. He was committed to the Crown Court for sentence. A boarded an international flight having drunk about eight cans of beer. He was seated in a non smoking section of the plane but smoked repeatedly, despite requests from the cabin crew to extinguish his cigarette. When the cabin staff refused to serve him a drink during the flight, he approached the galley and demanded more drink. Police officers boarded the plane on its arrival and arrested A, who was still considered to be drunk three and a half hours later.

Held, allowing the appeal, that A was very drunk throughout much of the flight and persisted in smoking knowing that he should desist, causing annoyance to his fellow passengers and defying repeated requests from cabin staff to stop doing so. Offences by drunken airline passengers were becoming too prevalent, and strong deterrent sentences were needed. The court would, however, reduce the sentence from nine months to six months' imprisonment, *R. v. Beer (Carmel Anne)* [1998] 2 Cr. App. R. (S.) 248, [1998] C.L.Y. 1113, *R. v. Vincent* (Unreported, May 13, 1998) and *R. v. Hunter (Glen Ronald) The Times*, February 26, 1998, [1998] C.L.Y. 1114 considered.

R. v. ABDULKARIM (KHALID IBRAHIM) [2000] 2 Cr. App. R. (S.) 16, Auld, L.J., CA (Crim Div).

1128. **Aircraft – intoxication – psychiatric illness did not excuse drunken behaviour on aeroplane**

A, a schizophrenic, appealed against a sentence of eight months' imprisonment having pleaded guilty to an offence of being drunk on an aeroplane. A had persistently smoked on board the plane, and in one incident had stubbed out his cigarette against a bulkhead which had resulted in ash falling between floor panels so that a fire extinguisher had to be used. A had also been abusive to a female flight attendant. A contended that the remark made by the sentencing judge that the "passengers must have been utterly terrified" illustrated that the judge had acted as if he were sentencing for the more serious offence of endangering the aircraft, which had led to an excessive sentence.

Held, dismissing the appeal, that the sentence was appropriate as A's behaviour had been particularly unpleasant and had lasted a long period of time, terrifying fellow passengers. Such behaviour could not be excused by reason of A's mental illness as he had embarked on the aircraft without his medication and had deliberately become intoxicated to relieve himself from the symptoms of schizophrenia.

R. v. AYODEJI (JULIAN) [2001] 1 Cr. App. R. (S.) 106, Maurice Kay, J., CA (Crim Div).

1129. **Arson – alcohol abuse – setting fire to matrimonial home**

H appealed against a sentence of four years' imprisonment. He lived with his wife and children in a semi detached council house. Following a period of matrimonial difficulty, H became drunk and a violent argument developed between H and his wife; one of the children left the house, and a short while afterwards H's wife's brother returned and took H's wife and the other children away. Shortly afterwards neighbours saw that a number of fires were alight in different rooms in the house. H eventually admitted setting fires in various rooms, which caused extensive fire damage or smoke damage. The adjoining house, occupied by a lady aged 85, was damaged by smoke.

Held, dismissing the appeal, that the offence was aggravated by the closeness of the elderly neighbour and the fact that some damage was caused to her property. The court took a serious view of arson where life was endangered, even though this was not intentional, because of the propensity of fire to spread rapidly and unpredictably. The sentence of four years was not wrong in principle or manifestly excessive, *R. v. Gannon (Christopher)* (1990) 12 Cr. App. R. (S.) 545, [1992] C.L.Y. 1139, *Attorney General's Reference (No.5 of 1993), Re* (1994) 15 Cr. App. R. (S.) 201, *Attorney General's Reference (No.61 of 1996), Re* [1997] 2 Cr. App. R. (S.) 316, [1997] C.L.Y. 1399 considered.

R. v. HARDING (IVOR WILLIAM) [2000] 1 Cr. App. R. (S.) 327, Maurice Kay, J., CA (Crim Div).

1130. Arson – damage to property – setting fire to estranged wife's home – unduly lenient sentence

The Attorney General referred as unduly lenient a sentence of five years' imprisonment, K having been convicted of arson, threatening to destroy property and arson with intent to endanger life. K set fire to the duvet on his estranged wife's bed after she rejected his sexual advances and later poured petrol through the letter box of her flat and threatened to burn her out. A few days later, K poured petrol through the letter box and set fire to it while two children and a babysitter were in the flat. The fire was extinguished after some damage had been caused to the flat, but the babysitter and children were rescued with minor injuries.

Held, allowing the reference, that following a trial, a sentence within the bracket of eight to 10 years' imprisonment would have been appropriate. The Court would substitute a sentence of seven years *R. v. Cheeseborough (Colin Ian)* (1982) 4 Cr. App. R. (S.) 394, [1983] C.L.Y. 768; *Attorney General's Reference (No.66 of 1997), Re* [2000] 1 Cr. App. R. (S) 149, [2000] C.L.Y. 1133, and *Attorney General's Reference (Nos. 78, 79 & 85 of 1998), Re* [2000] 1 Cr. App. R. (S) 371, [2000] C.L.Y. 1132 considered.

ATTORNEY GENERAL'S REFERENCE (NO.57 OF 1998), *Re; sub nom.* R. v. KERSWELL (JOHN WILLIAM) [2000] 1 Cr. App. R. (S.) 422, Rose, L.J., CA (Crim Div).

1131. Arson – intent to endanger life

M appealed against a sentence of six years' imprisonment. M lived with a woman and her children in a semi-detached house. Following an argument with the woman, the appellant became angry, seized her arm and used some violence on her. The appellant then brought a petrol can containing an inflammable liquid into the house, poured the contents over the hall and other rooms and attempted to set light to it. The woman tried to prevent him from setting fire to the liquid, but the appellant succeeded in causing a fire which spread to worktops in the kitchen. The appellant attempted to prevent the woman's son from escaping from the house and subsequently prevented the woman herself from doing so. Eventually the woman jumped from an open window.

Held, dismissing the appeal, that the sentencer described the offence as a very serious case of arson with intent to endanger life. It was sustained course of action intended to terrify and destroy the woman and her son and the appellant himself. The sentence was not manifestly excessive or outside the accepted tariff for this type of crime *Attorney General's Reference (No.1 of 1997), Re* [1998] 1 Cr. App. R. (S.) 54, [1997] C.L.Y. 1402.

R. v. McGRATH (JAMES ANDREW) [2000] 1 Cr. App. R. (S.) 479, Ognall, J., CA (Crim Div) Court of Appeal (Criminal Division).

1132. Arson – intent to endanger life – causing grave injuries to children – unduly lenient sentence

The Attorney General referred as unduly lenient sentences of eight years' imprisonment in the case of the R, five years' detention in a young offender institution in the case of M and a combination order in the case of O. R and M were convicted on two counts of arson with intent to endanger life and O was convicted on two counts of arson, being reckless whether life would be in danger. R felt a long standing resentment towards his father. He decided to buy petrol and make petrol bombs in order to carry out an attack on his father's house. Together with M and O, R bought a small quantity of petrol which was poured into two milk bottles. R and M each threw a lighted petrol bomb at a row of houses which contained the father's house. The bottles each hit a different house, neither of which was the house occupied by R's father. One of the houses caught fire and two small children living in the house suffered grave injuries which were likely to lead to extensive and permanent scarring.

Held, refusing the reference, that the appropriate bracket of sentences in the case of M was one of eight to 10 years. It followed that the court did not accept the submission that the sentence imposed by the judge was unduly lenient. It fell at the bottom of the bracket, it was not outside it and the court could not conclude that the sentence which the judge imposed was outside the range of options open to a reasonable and properly directed sentencing judge. This was a proper sentence to impose, it was a very severe sentence for young man with no record of committing offences of this type. There was no ground for criticising the distinction which was drawn between R, M and O and the court would accordingly refuse leave to the Attorney General in all three cases *R. v. Cheeseborough (Colin Ian)* (1982) 4 Cr. App. R. (S.) 394, [1983] C.L.Y. 768, *R. v. Mahood (Stephen Charles)* (1986) 8 Cr. App. R. (S.) 188, [1987] C.L.Y. 868, *R. v. Thomas (Derek)* (1988) 10 Cr. App. R. (S.) 386, [1990] C.L.Y. 1193, *R. v. Mitchell (Nicholas Charles) The Times*, September 4, 1998, [1998] C.L.Y. 1119, and *Attorney General's Reference (No.67 of 1998), Re* [2000] 1 Cr. App. R. (S.) 149 considered.

ATTORNEY GENERAL'S REFERENCE (NOS.78, 79 & 85 OF 1998), *Re; sub nom.* R. v. RUSSELL (ROBERT JOHN); R. v. O (JASON PATRICK) (A JUVENILE); R. v. M (SARAH RUTH) (A JUVENILE) [2000] 1 Cr. App. R. (S.) 371, Lord Bingham of Cornhill, L.C.J., CA (Crim Div).

1133. Arson – intent to endanger life – setting fire in bungalow where four people were asleep – unduly lenient sentence

The Attorney General referred as unduly lenient a sentence of three years' imprisonment, R having been convicted of arson with intent to endanger life. R entered the bungalow where his mother in law lived, in the early hours of the morning, using a key which he had removed from his wife's key ring. R squirted petrol from a plastic container onto a carpet, and set fire to the carpet outside bedrooms where his wife, mother in law, son and brother in law were sleeping. R left the scene. The fire was discovered and extinguished before very much damage had been done.

Held, allowing the reference, that the offence involved premeditation and planning and R had deliberately set fire to carpet outside three bedrooms where members of the family were sleeping and then left the fire to take hold and endanger the lives of four people. The offence of arson was always serious, and the degree of seriousness was much affected by the intention of the offender. R's intention to endanger life put the offence into a very serious category. The court would have expected that following a trial, the sentencer would have imposed a sentence within the range of eight to 10 years. Taking into account the element of double jeopardy, the court substituted a sentence of seven years, *R.*

v. Cheeseborough (Colin Ian) (1982) 4 Cr. App. R. (S.) 394, [1983] C.L.Y. 768 considered.

ATTORNEY GENERAL'S REFERENCE (NO.66 OF 1997), *Re; sub nom.* R. v. ROBERTS (ANTHONY CHARLES) [2000] 1 Cr. App. R. (S.) 149, Rose, L.J., CA (Crim Div).

1134. Arson – intent to endanger life – setting fire to house with intent to endanger life – unduly lenient sentence

The Attorney General referred as unduly lenient a sentence of six years' imprisonment, B having been convicted of arson with intent to endanger life. B placed a can of petrol under the bed in which her husband was sleeping and lit a fire. Her husband awoke and shouted for help, but sustained extensive injuries.

Held, that the sentence was unduly lenient but that it was not appropriate for the court to intervene. In the present case the court would have expected, following a trial, a sentence of at least eight years. It followed that the sentence passed by the judge could properly be described as unduly lenient. On reference by the Attorney General, the court had to take into account the element of double jeopardy. For that reason any sentence which the court would now impose would be significantly less than the term of eight years. The court, in the exercise of its discretion, would therefore not interfere with the sentence, *R. v. Cheeseborough (Colin Ian)* (1982) 4 Cr. App. R. (S.) 394, [1983] C.L.Y. 768 and *Attorney General's Reference (No.66 of 1997), Re* [2000] 1 Cr. App. R. (S.) 149, [2000] C.L.Y. 1133 considered.

ATTORNEY GENERAL'S REFERENCE (NO.4 OF 1999), *Re; sub nom.* R. v. BLUNDELL (JACQUELINE LOUISE) (UNDULY LENIENT SENTENCE) [2000] 2 Cr. App. R. (S.) 5, Rose, L.J., CA (Crim Div).

1135. Arson – recklessness – unduly lenient sentence

The Attorney General referred as unduly lenient a sentence of three years' imprisonment, H having pleaded guilty to arson, being reckless as to whether life was endangered. H had a relationship with a woman which came to an end. He pursued the woman with a combination of letters, presents and telephone calls. The woman made no positive response except to involve the police. Early one morning, H poured petrol into her kitchen and set it alight. The woman woke up, smelled the smoke and escaped through the front door without serious injury. Damage to the extent of £10,000 was done to the house.

Held, refusing the reference, that the fire was started deliberately at a time when H must have known that the woman would be in the house, probably asleep. H did nothing to alert the complainant or the emergency services. The court would not, however, increase the sentence for two reasons. The first was that the judge had given an indication of his view of the right level of sentence before the offender pleaded guilty. That would not bind the Court of Appeal, as was made clear in *Attorney General's Reference (No.40 of 1996), Re* [1997] 1 Cr. App. R. (S.) 357, [1997] C.L.Y. 1540 but it was a factor to which consideration ought to be given. The second was the element of double jeopardy which was particularly relevant where the offender had actually served the sentence and been released before the application had been heard. In those circumstances, the court was not disposed to order an increase in the sentence, *Attorney General's Reference (No.5 of 1993), Re* (1994) 15 Cr. App. R. (S.) 201, *R. v. Sparks (Seth Joseph)* (1995) 16 Cr. App. R. (S.) 480, *Attorney General's Reference (No.35 of 1996), Re* [1997] 1 Cr. App. R. (S.) 350, [1997] C.L.Y. 1401 and *Attorney General's Reference (No.1 of 1997), Re* [1998] 1 Cr. App. R. (S.) 54, [1997] C.L.Y. 1402 considered.

ATTORNEY GENERAL'S REFERENCE (NO.84 OF 1998), *Re; sub nom.* R. v. HINES (MALCOLM) [1999] 2 Cr. App. R. (S.) 380, Judge, L.J., CA (Crim Div)

1136. Assault – common assault – causing noxious substance to be taken with intent to injure

S appealed against a total sentence of 24 months' imprisonment having pleaded guilty to causing a noxious thing to be taken with intent to injure, aggrieve or annoy, theft and common assault. S was seen to steal a bottle of vodka from a shop. When a security guard attempted to arrest him, S sprayed a substance into his face. The substance temporarily blinded the security guard, caused him difficulty in breathing and led to a burning sensation. S admitted that he had been given a substance by another man and that he did not know what it was.

Held, dismissing the appeal, that the Court had considered the necessity for deterrence and the fact that the injury was not long lasting. The sentence of 21 months for causing a noxious substance to be taken was not excessive, *R. v. Jones (Ronald Gordon)* (1990) 12 Cr. App. R. (S.) 233, [1992] C.L.Y. 1135, *R. v. Robertson (Malcolm)* [1998] 1 Cr. App. R. (S.) 21, [1998] C.L.Y. 1399, *R. v. Doak (John)* (1993) 14 Cr. App. R. (S.) 128, [1993] C.L.Y. 1306, *R. v. Nawrot (Michael James)* (1988) 10 Cr. App. R. (S.) 239, *R. v. Hunt (Nigel John)* [1997] 1 Cr. App. R. (S.) 414, [1997] C.L.Y. 1403 and *R. v. Flanagan (Sean Patrick)* (1994) 15 Cr. App. R. (S.) 300 considered.

R. v. SKY (TRE) [2000] 2 Cr. App. R. (S.) 260, Owen, J., CA (Crim Div).

1137. Assault – robbery – use of ammonia spray – unduly lenient sentence

The Attorney General applied to refer as unduly lenient a sentence of 30 months' imprisonment imposed concurrently for two offences of assault with intent to rob. D had entered a restaurant with the aim of stealing monies from the cash till and had subsequently sprayed ammonia into the faces of the restaurant owners and fled. The application centred on the number of aggravating features including the use of an ammonia spray on the victims, its effect on them, the premeditated nature of the offences, the fact that a small business had been targeted and that D had previous convictions for robbery and carrying an imitation firearm with intent.

Held, allowing the reference, that the sentence had been unduly lenient. There were no mitigating factors and the sentence had failed to reflect the severity of the offences charged. Having regard to the element of double jeopardy inherent in the resentencing process sentences of four years and six months' imprisonment on each count concurrent was substituted, *Attorney General's Reference (No.2 of 1989), Re* (1989) 11 Cr. App. R. (S.) 481, [1991] C.L.Y. 1208 and *Attorney General's Reference (No.9 of 1989), Re* (1990) 12 Cr. App. R. (S.) 7, [1991] C.L.Y. 1214 considered.

ATTORNEY GENERAL'S REFERENCE (NO.16 OF 2000), Re; *sub nom*. R. v. DOWNEY (THOMAS) [2001] 1 Cr. App. R. (S.) 27, Rose, L.J., CA (Crim Div).

1138. Bail – contempt of court – failure to surrender to bail

C appealed against a sentence of nine months' imprisonment imposed having been arrested in connection with an allegation of being involved in the fraudulent evasion of excise duty in 1997. He was released on bail but failed to attend. C was eventually arrested and acquitted of the offence. C claimed to have been subjected to threats by others involved in the offence with which he had been charged.

Held, allowing the appeal, that the sentencer was entitled to take account of the effect of C's absence on the administration of justice in the cases which had been tried, but he allowed the involvement in those cases to influence his view of the possible consequences to an undesirable degree. As a result of C's absence, the whole process of the trial had to be repeated for him. The court did not accept the argument that C should receive some credit in relation to the bail offence because he was acquitted of the principal offence. Where a person was bailed to appear to attend the trial, the criminality if they failed to attend was not affected by whether or not they were subsequently acquitted or convicted of the principal offence. Allegations of intimidation could easily be made. It was in the interests of the proper determination of such issues that they would be looked at by the judge following a rigorous and demanding approach. The sentencer probably did take too high a starting point in view of the fact that the maximum sentence was 12 months. In the circumstances the sentence was reduced to seven years and six months' imprisonment.

R. v. CLARKE (CHRISTOPHER) [2000] 1 Cr. App. R. (S.) 224, Newman, J., CA (Crim Div).

1139. Blackmail – threatening to publish ex girlfriend's photographs

K appealed against a sentence of 18 months' imprisonment imposed having pleaded guilty to blackmail. K had a relationship with a young woman, over a period of three years until they decided to end their relationship. The young woman moved out of their accommodation, leaving a forwarding address. She made no arrangements for the payment of a certain joint debt. K attempted to contact her to obtain funds to cover earlier joint financial commitments but received no response from the young woman. K subsequently wrote to the young woman, threatening to distribute embarrassing photographs of her if she did not pay a total of £900. The young woman contacted the police and K was arrested.

Held, allowing the appeal, that the sentencing judge took the view that K had adopted a grossly improper way of enforcing what he perceived to be a justifiable demand. The necessary element of deterrence could be met by a sentence of 12 months' imprisonment, having regard to K's youth, plea and previous good character, *R. v. Hadjou (George)* (1989) 11 Cr. App. R. (S.) 29, [1990] C.L.Y. 1209 and *R. v. Mason (John Leslie)* (1995) 16 Cr. App. R. (S.) 968 considered.

R. v. KEWELL (DAVID EDWARD) [2000] 2 Cr. App. R. (S.) 38, Ebsworth, J., CA (Crim Div).

1140. Breach of non molestation order – family case

See FAMILY LAW: Hale v. Tanner (Practice Note). §2541

1141. Buggery – children

D was convicted of indecently assaulting his daughter between 1982 and 1984 and of attempted buggery of his adopted son between 1982 and 1983. He attempted to commit buggery on his adopted son, who was the son of his wife, when the boy was about 10 years old. He indecently assaulted his daughter when she was aged four or five years. The offences were not reported to the police until 1998. D was sentenced to four years' imprisonment for attempted buggery, with 12 months consecutive for indecent assault, and appealed.

Held, dismissing the appeal, that a sentence of five years after a contested trial for attempted buggery of an adopted son could not reasonably be called manifestly excessive, the sentence of four years made appropriate allowance for D's age and health, *R. v. Willis (Peter Charles)* [1975] 1 W.L.R. 292, [1975] C.L.Y. 714, *R. v. Hayes (George Markie)* (1992) 13 Cr. App. R. (S.) 626, [1993] C.L.Y. 1027, *R. v. Fisher (Robert Butler)* (1987) 9 Cr. App. R. (S.) 462, [1990] C.L.Y. 1216, *R. v. D* [2000] 1 Cr. App. R. (S.) 120, [2000] C.L.Y. 1279 and *R. v. D (George Ernest)* (1993) 14 Cr. App. R. (S.) 776, [1994] C.L.Y. 1180 considered.

R. v. DR (APPEAL AGAINST SENTENCE: APPELLANTS AGE) [2000] 2 Cr. App. R. (S.) 314, Sir Charles McCullough, CA (Crim Div).

1142. Buggery – children – 12 year old victim

M, aged 36, became friendly with a 12 year old girl. Over a period of about 18 months there was a sexual relationship between them, in the course of which various sexual activities took place. These included one of act of anal intercourse, several acts of vaginal intercourse, and various other indecent acts. M was sentenced to five years' imprisonment on the count of buggery, five years' imprisonment on each count of indecent assault and 21 months' imprisonment on each count of unlawful sexual intercourse, all concurrent and appealed.

Held, dismissing the appeal, that the case had proceeded on the basis that the complainant had consented. The offences represented a course of conduct over a period of time and had resulted in physical abnormalities on the part of the complainant. This was not the case of an isolated act of sexual interference; it was a sustained course of conduct involving an underage and vulnerable child. The sentence of five years' imprisonment was not manifestly excessive or wrong in principle, *R. v. Palmer (Dale Stephen)* (1995) 16 Cr. App. R. (S.) 642, [1996] C.L.Y. 1950, *R. v. Davies (Tarian John)* [1998] 1 Cr. App. R. (S.) 380, [1997] C.L.Y. 1413 and *Attorney General's Reference (No.17 of 1990), Re* (1991) 92 Cr. App. R. 288, [1991] C.L.Y. 1219 considered.

R. v. I (MICHAEL) [2000] 2 Cr. App. R. (S.) 167, Judge Richard Gibbs Q.C., CA (Crim Div).

1143.   Buggery – children – 16 year old victim under influence of alcohol

D pleaded guilty to buggery of a woman. D, aged 19, met a girl aged 16 in a public house. The girl had been drinking. She approached D and they embraced. She then performed an act of oral sex, and they went down an alleyway, where sexual intercourse occurred. One of the girl's friends tried to persuade her to come away but the girl declined to do so. The girl stood up and stumbled so as to lean over a bench. D had intercourse from behind, entering her anus. They then had vaginal intercourse. Shortly afterwards the girl became distressed and went to join her friends. When D was arrested, he admitted that he had had intercourse with the girl both vaginally and anally, but claimed that she had consented. D was sentenced to six months' detention in a young offender institution and appealed.

Held, allowing the appeal, that the sentencer was entitled to come to the factual conclusions that he had reached, that D must have been satisfied that the girl was drunk and that he had taken advantage of the situation. This was an offence of buggery committed by an experienced 19 year old on a 16 year old girl who was plainly drunk. It could not be said that the sentence was wrong in principle or manifestly excessive. However, since D has been in custody twice, when arrested and when sentenced, the sentence would be reduced to three months' detention.

R. v. DALTON (RICHARD CHARLES) [2000] 2 Cr. App. R. (S.) 87, Toulson, J., CA (Crim Div).

1144.   Buggery – children – indecent assault

B was convicted of five offences of unlawful sexual intercourse with a girl under 16, four offences of indecent assault on a female, and one of buggery. B, aged about 36, started a relationship with the mother of the girl aged about 13. After the girl's fourteenth birthday B was involved in various sexual acts with the girl over a period of five months. On one occasion B inserted his penis into her anus. B appealed against a sentence of four years' imprisonment for buggery, with two years imprisonment concurrent for each of the other offences.

Held, allowing the appeal, that the present case was more serious than *Davies* in that it involved a grave abuse of B's position of trust in relation to the girl, the offences were committed over a long period and there was a substantial difference in age. The offence was, however, a single act of buggery which was to be treated as consensual, and the sentence was too high; a sentence of three years would be substituted, *R. v. Davies (Tarian John)* [1998] 1 Cr. App. R. (S.) 380, [1997] C.L.Y. 1413 considered.

R. v. BRIERLEY (ANTHONY MICHAEL) [2000] 2 Cr. App. R. (S.) 278, Richards, J., CA (Crim Div).

1145. Buggery – children – willing participation of 14 year old victim

[Criminal Justice Act 1991 s.44.]

A appealed against a sentence of three and a half years' imprisonment with an order extending his licence under the Criminal Justice Act 1991 s.44 having pleaded guilty to one count of buggery and one count of gross indecency with a child. The victim of the offences, a boy aged 14, left home following an argument with his family and went to stay with A's brother. A visited his brother and went for a walk accompanied by the victim. They went to some waste ground, where A penetrated the victim's anus with his penis, and encouraged the victim to do the same to him, which he did. At some stage A performed oral sex on the victim. Some days later, A went into the victim's bedroom, got into bed, and kissed him on the lips for a period of several minutes. A admitted the offences in interview. It was accepted that the victim consented and participated willingly with no threats or pressure.

Held, allowing the appeal, that the court had concluded that by reason of A's good character, his plea at the earliest opportunity, his remorse, and the fact that the victim was a willing participant, the sentences were manifestly excessive. The appropriate sentence would be 21 months' imprisonment, *R. v. Bradley (Paul Richard)* [1998] 1 Cr. App. R. (S.) 432, [1998] C.L.Y. 1125 considered.

R. v. A (S) [2000] 1 Cr. App. R. (S.) 36, Bracewell, J., CA (Crim Div).

1146. Burglary – aggravated burglary – intent to inflict grievous bodily harm

D was convicted of aggravated burglary with intent to inflict grievous bodily harm, and attempted burglary with intent to inflict grievous bodily harm. D was attacked in the street while walking home in the early hours of the morning. Some time later D kicked open the door of a flat in the house where his own flat was situated and entered the flat, carrying a knife and demanding to know where unspecified people were. D searched the flat and then left. D subsequently knocked on the door of another flat, shouted at the occupants and threatened to kill them. D later attacked the door with a hammer, causing extensive damage. Police officers arrived and arrested the appellant. D was sentenced to four and a half years' imprisonment on each count concurrent, and appealed.

Held, allowing the appeal, that D would not have offended had it not been for the attack on himself, in which he sustained a significant injury. His intention in breaking into the flat was to seek out his assailant. He intended no harm to the occupants of the flat and did not in fact cause any harm. Having regard to the authorities to which the court's attention had been drawn, the court would substitute sentences of two and a half years concurrent on each count, *Attorney General's Reference (No.47 of 1997), Re* [1998] 2 Cr. App. R. (S.) 68, [1998] C.L.Y. 1127; *Attorney General's Reference (No.16 of 1994), Re* (1995) 16 Cr. App. R. (S.) 629, [1996] C.L.Y. 1737 considered.

R. v. DANIEL (CRAIG) [2000] 2 Cr. App. R. (S.) 184, Dyson, J., CA (Crim Div).

1147. Burglary – aggravated burglary – stabbing nurse after entering nurses' home – unduly lenient sentence

The Attorney General referred as unduly lenient a sentence of 18 months' imprisonment for an offence of aggravated burglary. S had entered a nurses' home and gained access to a room where a nurse was asleep. He kissed the nurse and then began stabbing her with a pair of small scissors which he had picked up in her room. S then ran off and escaped through the window. The victim sustained minor stab wounds to the arm, neck and chest.

Held, allowing the reference, that this was plainly a very serious offence, causing terror to the victim in the middle of the night and involving repeated stabbing with scissors. The court would have expected, on a plea of guilty, a sentence of the order of five years' imprisonment. Taking into account the element of double jeopardy, the court would substitute a sentence of four years' imprisonment, *Attorney General's Reference (No.16 of 1994), Re* (1995) 16 Cr. App. R. (S.) 629, [1996] C.L.Y. 1737, *Attorney General's Reference (No.1 of 1995), Re* [1996] 1 Cr. App. R. (S.) 11, [1996] C.L.Y. 1692, *Attorney General's*

Reference (No.36 of 1997), Re [1998] 1 Cr. App. R. (S.) 365, [1998] C.L.Y. 1129 considered.
ATTORNEY GENERAL'S REFERENCE (NO.1 OF 2000), *Re; sub nom.* R. v. SHIOUI (RASHID) [2000] 2 Cr. App. R. (S.) 340, Rose, L.J., CA (Crim Div).

1148. **Burglary – consecutive sentences – categorisation of prisoners**

P appealed against a sentence of 12 months' imprisonment, having pleaded guilty to affray. The affray arose from an incident with the woman with whom he was living and her family, in which he abused her, threatened her with violence and brandished a knife. The sentence was consecutive to a sentence of three and a half years' imprisonment for burglary, which had been imposed between the commission of the affray and his appearance in the Crown Court for that offence. The effect of the imposition of the sentence of 12 months consecutive to the existing sentence of three and a half years was to make M a long term prisoner in respect of the whole of the aggregate term, rather than a short term prisoner.

Held, dismissing the appeal, that the effect of the imposition of the later sentence was to delay the date on which P was entitled to be released from July 1, 2000 until October 1, 2000, two thirds of the way through the combined sentence. The court noted that the Parole Board could at its discretion release P six months after July 1, 2000. The effect of the combined sentence could be that P would be released 15 months later than he would have been released but for the 12 month sentence. The court had been referred to *R. v. Waite (Glen Anthony)* (1992) 13 Cr. App. R. (S.) 26, [1992] C.L.Y. 1157, *R. v. Cozens (Alan William)* [1996] 2 Cr. App. R. (S.) 321, [1997] C.L.Y. 1475, *R. v. Secretary of State for the Home Department, ex p. Francois* [1999] 1 A.C. 43, [1998] C.L.Y. 1155 and *R. v. Brown (Anthony Azuris)* [1999] 1 Cr. App. R. (S.) 47, [1999] C.L.Y. 1108. The authorities established that the effect of a sentence in converting a short term prisoner to a long term prisoner was a relevant consideration for the sentencing judge. If the effect was or might be to impose on the defendant an additional sentence disproportionate to what was required, then the judge might find it necessary to make an appropriate discount. That of course involved the consideration of what was the least sentence that was appropriate for the instant offence. In the present case, the judge had considered the matter and decided that the longest sentence which would avoid converting P to the status of a long term prisoner would not meet the seriousness of the case. The offence was far too serious to be dealt with by means of a sentence of five months or less. It was plain that the judge had considered the matter and had exercised his discretion. He had reached the view that a sentence of five months or less. It was plain that the judge had considered the matter and had exercised his discretion. He had reached the view that a sentence of five months or less was not an appropriate or possible sentence. It followed that this was one of those cases in which despite the conversion of the defendant to the status of long term prisoner it was appropriate for the sentencer to pass the sentence which did. If it were not so, it would mean that even if the first court had passed a sentence which deliberately kept the defendant below the four year barrier. That consequence could not be right.

R. v. PARKER (DAVID ANDREW) [2000] 2 Cr. App. R. (S.) 294, Crane, J., CA (Crim Div).

1149. **Burglary – elderly persons**

B appealed against a sentence of seven years' imprisonment having been convicted of aggravated burglary. He entered a bungalow occupied by a woman aged 70, threatened her with a chisel and demanded money from her. B left the bungalow, taking £50 and a radio, having pulled the telephone from the socket. He had numerous previous convictions, including three for robbery.

Held, dismissing the appeal, that the Court agreed with the sentencer's observation that B was a man from whom the public required protection for a long time *R. v. Stewart (Trevor Mathew)* [1996] 2 Cr. App. R. (S) 302, [1997] C.L.Y. 1420 [1997] C.L.Y. 1420 considered.

R. v. BRADY (DEREK) [2000] 1 Cr. App. R. (S.) 410, Rougier, J, CA (Crim Div).

1150. Burglary – elderly persons – burglaries in elderly people's homes

[Criminal Justice Act 1991 s.40.]

W appealed against a sentence of seven years' imprisonment on two counts of burglary. W went to the home of an elderly lady, knocked at the front door and told her that he needed to check the windows. He was admitted to her home and began to measure the windows. W persuaded the lady to go into a bedroom while he went into the kitchen; he then left the house, taking £14, a key and a bus pass. A few hours later W knocked at the front door of a flat occupied by a man aged 77. W claimed that he had been sent by the council and the police and was admitted to the flat. He told the occupier that he had come to measure the property for alarms on the windows. W eventually left the flat having stolen about £30. W had various previous convictions, including convictions for burglary in 1994 in respect of which he had been sentenced five years' imprisonment. The sentences of seven years' imprisonment on each count concurrent, were consecutive to an order under the Criminal Justice Act 1991 s.40 returning him to prison in respect of the earlier sentence.

Held, dismissing the appeal, that W was a professional operator who chose vulnerable people, entered their houses by using a subterfuge and then stole. The sentences of seven years were severe but not manifestly excessive, *R. v. McCamon (Andrew)* [1998] 2 Cr. App. R. (S.) 81, [1998] C.L.Y. 1134, *R. v. Henry (Christopher Stephen)* [1998] 1 Cr. App. R. (S.) 289, [1998] C.L.Y. 1131, *R. v. Brewster (Alex Edward)* [1998] 1 Cr. App. R. 220, [1997] C.L.Y. 1423 considered.

R. v. WOODLIFFE (MARK ALEXANDER) [2000] 1 Cr. App. R. (S.) 330, Hooper, J., CA (Crim Div).

1151. Burglary – handling stolen goods – burglary of isolated country homes

G appealed against a sentence of 10 years' imprisonment having pleaded guilty to seven counts of burglary, with eight years on six counts of handling, all concurrent, with a confiscation order in the amount of about £70,000, a compensation order in the amount of about £47,000 and an order to pay £7,000 prosecution costs. G burgled a series of relatively isolated country homes over a period of about seven months. The homes were spread over a significant geographical area. Property stolen in other burglaries was recovered from a house in Portugal belonging to G, who had eighteen previous convictions for offences of dishonesty, including burglary.

Held, dismissing the appeal, that the sentencer was justified in imposing a sentence of 10 years' imprisonment on a man who was properly described as a very serious professional burglar. Such a sentence for simple (as opposed to aggravated) burglary was at the top of the permissible bracket, but the sentence was not manifestly excessive, *R. v. Brewster (Alex Edward)* [1998] 1 Cr. App. R. 220, [1997] C.L.Y. 1423, *R. v. Brewster (David Edward)* (1980) 71 Cr. App. R. 375, [1981] C.L.Y. 525.18, *R. v. Winn (Stephen)* (1995) 16 Cr. App. R. (S.) 53, [1996] C.L.Y. 1744, *R. v. Lee (David)* (1995) 16 Cr. App. R. (S.) 60, [1996] C.L.Y. 1743, *R. v. Henry (Christopher Stephen)* [1998] 1 Cr. App. R. (S.) 289, [1998] C.L.Y. 1131, *R. v. Carawana* (Unreported, May 23, 1997), *R. v. Whittaker (Barrington)* [1998] 1 Cr. App. R. (S.) 172, [1998] C.L.Y. 1133, *R. v. Hawkins* (Unreported, January 15, 1999) considered.

R. v. GIBBS (BARRY EDWARD) [2000] 1 Cr. App. R. (S.) 261, Rose, L.J., CA (Crim Div).

1152. Burglary – houses – criminal record of similar offences

B, aged 19, appealed against a sentence of five years' detention in a young offender institution and an order to be deprived of a motor car having pleaded guilty before a magistrates' court to three charges of burglary and was committed to the Crown Court for sentence. B entered three houses during the day while the occupiers were present. In two cases the occupiers encountered B. In the third case B stole jewellery worth over £17,000 from a couple aged 84 and 94 respectively. B asked for five further offences of burglary to be taken into consideration.

Held, dismissing the appeal, that B had an appalling record, having committed 37 burglaries. His offences had been committed to subsidise his addiction to drugs. The sentence was therefore not excessive.

R. v. BURNS (PAUL RUDI) [2000] 2 Cr. App. R. (S.) 198, Tucker, J., CA (Crim Div).

1153. **Burglary – return orders – order to serve whole of relevant period**

[Criminal Justice Act 1991 s.40.]

G appealed against an order to return to custody under the Criminal Justice Act 1991 s.40 for a period of 20 months and 21 days, with 15 months' imprisonment consecutive for burglary pleaded guilty before a magistrates' court to burglary. He was committed to the Crown Court for sentence. In March 1998 G broke into a flat and stole various items of property to the value of £2,000. In 1994, G had been convicted of manslaughter and was sentenced to six years' imprisonment. He was released in December 1997, and his sentence would expire on November 21, 1999.

Held, allowing the appeal, that the sentence of 15 months' imprisonment for burglary of a dwelling could not be said to be excessive, particularly as the offence was committed shortly after the appellant's release from custody. In respect of the appellant's return to prison for the entirety of the balance of the original sentence outstanding at the date of the new offence, the fact that the appellant had made progress during the relevant period was very much to his credit. It was plainly right in principle to order him to serve part of the outstanding sentence, but the circumstances did not warrant an order that the appellant should serve the entire outstanding balance of his sentence. It would have been sufficient to order the appellant to return to custody for six months of the balance of the original sentence. The court would accordingly substitute a term of six months for the original order under s.40 of the 1991 Act, with the sentence of 15 months consecutive, *R. v. Secretary of State for the Home Department, ex p. Probyn* [1998] 1 W.L.R. 809, [1997] C.L.Y. 1654 considered.

R. v. GRIFFITHS (COLIN BARRY) [2000] 2 Cr. App. R. (S.) 224, Richards, J., CA (Crim Div).

1154. **Burials and cremation – drug addiction – preventing burial of corpse**

P appealed against a sentence of 18 months' imprisonment having pleaded guilty to preventing the burial of a corpse. Police officers who attended at P's flat found the badly decomposed body of a man who had died about six weeks previously. P claimed that the deceased had visited his flat to share some heroin with him. Both P and the deceased injected heroin. When P woke up the next morning, he found the man dead.

Held, allowing the appeal, that the offence was callous, thoughtless and cruel to the family of the deceased, who had experienced real distress during the period when the deceased was missing. The offence impeded the ability of the authorities properly to investigate the circumstances of death and made it impossible to discover the true facts surrounding his death. The court considered that a sentence of 18 months' imprisonment could be appropriate in such cases. However, in view of the fact that since the offence P had attended a drug rehabilitation centre, the court would reduce the sentence to 12 months' imprisonment, *R. v. Parry (Jonathan Anthony)* (1986) 8 Cr. App. R. (S.) 470, [1988] C.L.Y. 890, *R. v. Doyle (David Martin)* [1996] 1 Cr. App. R. (S.) 341, [1996] C.L.Y. 1708 and *R. v. King (Dianne Susan)* (1990) 12 Cr. App. R. (S.) 76 considered.

R. v. PEDDER (TIMOTHY) [2000] 2 Cr. App. R. (S.) 36, Latham, J., CA (Crim Div).

1155. Careless driving – death – excess alcohol

T appealed against a sentence of three years' imprisonment and disqualification from driving for five years on conviction of causing death by careless driving, having consumed alcohol so as to be above the prescribed limit. T was driving his car at about 5 am on a day in November when two pedestrians who were wearing dark clothing started to cross the road ahead of him. T's car collided with them and one of the pedestrians suffered head injuries from which he died. T was found to have a breath alcohol level of 52 mg of alcohol per 100 ml of breath. Witnesses described the pedestrians as running across the road and one expressed the view that T would have had little chance of avoiding them.

Held, allowing the appeal, that T was one and a half times over the legal limit, and that clearly affected his reactions, but all the other familiar aggravating factors were absent from the case. There were many personal mitigating factors. This was a case where the driving itself did not have the aggravating features which were present in many of the cases where sentences in the region of three years or more had been imposed. An appropriate sentence on the facts of the case would have been two years' imprisonment, *Attorney General's Reference (No.11 of 1998), Re* [1999] 1 Cr. App. R. (S.) 145, [1999] C.L.Y. 1321, *R. v. Corcoran (Terence)* [1996] 1 Cr. App. R. (S.) 416, [1996] C.L.Y. 1768, *R. v. Nunn (Adam John)* [1996] 2 Cr. App. R. (S.) 136, [1996] C.L.Y. 1836 and *Attorney General's Reference (No.66 of 1996), Re* [1998] 1 Cr. App. R. (S.) 16, [1997] C.L.Y. 1689 considered.

R. v. THOMPSON (EMRAH JOSEPH) [2000] 1 Cr. App. R. (S.) 85, Ebsworth, J., CA (Crim Div).

1156. Child abduction – threatening to kill – abduction of child by stranger

[Child Abduction Act 1984; Criminal Justice Act 1991 s.2(2)(b).]

D appealed against a sentence of five years' imprisonment having been convicted of abducting a child, contrary to the Child Abduction Act 1984. D encountered a four year old boy who had been sent by his mother to collect a loaf of bread from a friend. As he was returning to his home, D approached him and told him to come to him. He told him to close his eyes and threatened to kill him. The boy's mother found D holding the boy by the hand; the boy managed to break free and escaped. D drove away in his car but was subsequently arrested.

Held, dismissing the appeal, that the sentencer felt constrained to sentence on the basis that he did not know what D's intention was in relation to the boy, and that the offence of abduction was not a sexual offence within the meaning of the Criminal Justice Act 1991 s.2(2)(b). The sentencer took the view that the offence was planned and that D had set out deliberately to find a child. In the Court's view the circumstances of the offence gave rise to grave concern. D had offered no innocent explanation of his conduct, or at any time stated what his intention was towards the boy. It was plain that he had been deliberately looking for a young child and had threatened violence. It was a matter of great good fortune that the child's mother brought the incident to an early end. D had fought the case and lacked the mitigation of a plea. The sentence was severe but not excessive, *R. v. Dootson (Robert)* (1995) 16 Cr. App. R. (S.) 223, [1995] C.L.Y. 1416 considered.

R. v. DEAN (PAUL ASHLEY) [2000] 2 Cr. App. R. (S.) 253, Richards, J., CA (Crim Div).

1157. Child abuse – sexual offences – schoolboy victims – unduly lenient sentence

The Attorney General referred as unduly lenient a sentence of 10 years' imprisonment, S having been convicted, on 19 counts in total, of attempted buggery, child abduction, indecent assault and indecency with a child, following attacks on schoolboys aged between 11 and 14 years over a four year period. All the attacks had taken place on a common over which the boys walked on their way to and from school. The abuse was lengthy, perverted and involved threats of violence and death.

Held, allowing the reference, that in the absence of a guilty plea, and taking into account the fact that the attacks were planned, carried out over a long period of time on vulnerable boys, and involved particularly gross sexual abuse, the sentence of 10 years' imprisonment was unduly lenient. A sentence of 18 years would have been justified following a trial for abuse of this type, but taking into account the element of double jeopardy inherent in the resentencing process, the sentence was reduced to one of 15 years' imprisonment.

ATTORNEY GENERAL'S REFERENCE (NO.89 OF 1998), *Re; sub nom.* R. v. S (PAUL WILLIAM) [2000] 1 Cr. App. R. (S.) 49, Rose, L.J., CA (Crim Div).

1158. Community service orders – revocation – breach – inability to comply with order on grounds of ill health

J appealed against a sentence of six months' imprisonment imposed for the breach of the community service element of a combination order imposed following conviction for assisting illegal entry. J was unable to comply with the community service as a result of a chronic spinal problem.

Held, allowing the appeal, that J had suffered from a chronic back spinal problem for a number of years. This was mentioned in the pre-sentence report. The probation officer who recommended the combination order was satisfied that there would be work of a light character available for J. Both the probation service and the court were aware when the combination order was made that J was unfit for heavy work. J was unable to carry out the work to which he was assigned and a medical certificate was obtained. It was established in the case of *R. v. Fielding (Craig)* (1993) 14 Cr. App. R. (S.) 494, [1994] C.L.Y. 1201 applied, that it was inappropriate to impose a custodial sentence where through no fault of the offender he was unable to complete his obligations under a community service order. In the subsequent decision of *R. v. Hammon (Terry Mark)* [1998] 2 Cr. App. R. (S.) 202, [1998] C.L.Y. 1146 applied, it was established that where the offender had failed to disclose his condition to the court when the order was made, the fact that he was unable to carry out the community service order could not be used to persuade the court not to impose a custodial sentence in its place. It was impossible to contend that J had misled the original court as to his medical condition. The court was bound to conclude that the custodial sentence was wrong. The sentence would be quashed and a probation order for 12 months would be substituted.

R. v. JACKSON (CHRISTOPHER) [2000] 1 Cr. App. R. (S.) 405, Dyson, J., CA (Crim Div).

1159. Confiscation orders – adjournment – postponement of determination – inherent jurisdiction of the court

[Drug Trafficking Act 1994 s.3.]

L was convicted in June 1998 of two offences of being knowingly concerned in the fraudulent evasion of the prohibition or restriction on the importation of Class A drugs and a date was fixed within six months of the conviction, for a hearing concerning a confiscation order. Several days before the hearing, L changed his solicitors resulting in the postponement of the hearing, the hearing eventually taking place in May 1999 after a further postponement due to the unavailability of the judge. A confiscation order was subsequently made and L appealed contending that it was made without jurisdiction since the order was made more than six months from the date of conviction, and the decision to postpone was not made for a purpose permitted by the Drug Trafficking Act 1994 s.3 that is, for time to gather further information in order for a decision to be made.

Held, dismissing the appeal, that the judge's decision to postpone the confiscation order was not one to which s.3 applied, and under its inherent jurisdiction the court was entitled to decide when a case should be heard and whether to order an adjournment provided it acted reasonably, which the judge had done in this case. Section 3 did not remove this jurisdiction and did not mean that the only circumstance in which delay could be sanctioned was to obtain more information, since this would lead to absurd results where for example, delay was necessary due to illness. It was clearly not Parliament's intention to remove the court's inherent jurisdiction.

R. v. LINGHAM (GARY) [2001] 1 Cr. App. R. (S.) 46, Jowitt, J., CA (Crim Div).

1160. Confiscation orders – adjournments – postponement of determination – special circumstances

[Criminal Justice Act 1988 s.71, s.72(2), s.72A.]

M had been convicted of conspiracy to defraud. Proceedings under the Criminal Justice Act 1988 s.71 to determine the extent to which M had benefited from his crimes began on July 6, 1998, the same date as his guilty plea. However, as M disputed any benefit, the proceedings were adjourned so that further information could be obtained. A custodial sentence and confiscation order were imposed on April 1, 1999. M appealed against the confiscation order, arguing that as the process of deciding whether he had benefited from his crime, under s.71, began on July 6, so the six month time limit under s.72A applied. The Crown contended that under s.72(2), a primary determination was to be made, which, in the instant case, had not been made until April 1, 1999. It was further argued that time had not begun to run under s.72A as at no time were the proceedings postponed.

Held, allowing the appeal, that confiscation order proceedings under s.71 began as soon as the court began the process of deciding whether to make such an order, which occurred on July 6, 1998. As M disputed any statement on the extent to which he benefited from his crime, any adjournments for the purpose of obtaining more information must have been under s.72A. There were no exceptional circumstances and the six month time limit therefore applied so that the court had no jurisdiction to make the order.

R. v. MIRANDA (JUAN CARLOS); R. v. SHAYLER (JAMES ARTHUR) [2000] 2 Cr. App. R. 164, Nelson, J., CA (Crim Div).

1161. Confiscation orders – appeals – limitations

[Criminal Appeal Act 1968 s.9(1); Drug Trafficking Act 1994.]

N sought leave to appeal against the imposition of a confiscation order, having pleaded guilty in March 1996 to three counts of conspiring to supply class B drugs. In June 1996 he was sentenced to a total of six years' imprisonment. He applied for leave to appeal against sentence. That application was refused by the Full Court of the Court of Appeal in January 1997. In July 1997 proceedings under the Drug Trafficking Act 1994 took place and a confiscation order was made in the amount of £248,208, with two and a half years' imprisonment in default. N applied for leave to appeal against the confiscation order.

Held, refusing the application, that the question was whether the Court of Appeal had jurisdiction to hear an application with regard to the confiscation order, when N's application for leave to appeal against the sentence of imprisonment had previously been refused. The 1994 Act expressly provided for postponed determinations, but required them to take place within six months beginning with the date of conviction unless there were exceptional circumstances. There was no doubt that N had acted correctly in applying for leave to appeal against his prison sentence without waiting for the conclusion of the 1994 Act proceedings. He was required to make his application within 28 days of the day on which the sentence was passed. The Criminal Appeal Act 1968 s.9(1) provided that a person who had been convicted on indictment might appeal against any sentence passed on him for the offence either on conviction or in subsequent proceedings. "Sentence" included any order made by a court when dealing with an offender, and the question was how many appeals against sentence could a convicted person pursue in relation to the same conviction. Section 11 of the 1968 Act did not prevent N from making an application for leave to appeal against the confiscation order, notwithstanding that he had previously applied for leave to appeal against the sentence of imprisonment. The confiscation order had not been made on the same day as the sentence was passed, and the court did not say that it was treating the sentences as substantially one sentence. Such a statement would not have been appropriate. Accordingly, there were not two sentences "passed in the same proceedings". N's appeal against this prison sentence could not be seen as an appeal against a confiscation order that had yet to be made. However, on the merits of the application there were no grounds to grant leave.

R. v. NEAL (JOHN FREDERICK) (SENTENCING) [1999] 2 Cr. App. R. (S.) 352, Maurice Kay, J., CA (Crim Div).

1162. Confiscation orders – evasion of excise duty – forfeiture of goods at time of arrest – no accrual of benefit

[Criminal Justice Act 1988 s.71 (4), s.71 (5).]

S was arrested following the discovery by customs and excise officers of 1.2 million cigarettes on board a boat arriving in the UK. Upon his arrest the cigarettes and the boat were forfeited. Having pleaded guilty, S was convicted of fraudulent evasion of excise duty and sentenced to 21 months' imprisonment. In addition the trial judge, having calculated the value of the cigarettes and boat and reduced the figure in view of S's realisable assets, made a confiscation order in the sum of £46,450. S appealed against the confiscation order, contending that since both the boat and cigarettes had been forfeited at the time of his arrest no benefit had accrued to him within the meaning of the Criminal Justice Act 1988 s.71 (4) or s.71 (5). S submitted that the forfeiture had removed all arguable benefit and accordingly there could not be double jeopardy or double recovery.

Held, allowing the appeal, that where an individual upon arrival in the UK was apprehended with goods on which they intended to evade paying excise duty and those goods were confiscated prior to their sale, the value of such goods could not be said to be a benefit or the proceeds of crime for the purposes of confiscation order proceedings. Liability for duty on such goods having been incurred upon entry into the UK, notwithstanding the confiscation of those goods, an individual would remain liable for the duty they had attempted to evade, *R. v. Dimsey (Dermot Jeremy) (No.2)* [2000] 2 All E.R. 142, [1999] C.L.Y. 910 distinguished. In the instant case, given that the cigarettes were immediately forfeited upon S's arrest, no benefit had accrued from his criminal conduct for the purposes of s.71 of the Act. It followed that the confiscation order would be quashed.

R. v. SMITH (DAVID CADMAN) [2001] 1 Cr. App. R. (S.) 61, Burton, J., CA (Crim Div).

1163. Confiscation orders – fraudulent trading – postponement of determination – power of court to specify period exceeding six months

[Criminal Justice Act 1988 s.72A.]

K appealed against the imposition of a confiscation order in the amount of £110,000. K had appeared in the Crown Court on three occasions and pleaded guilty to various counts of fraudulent trading, managing a company while bankrupt, and procuring the execution of a valuable security by deception. He was sentenced to a total of four and a half years' imprisonment. He appealed against the sentence to the Court of Appeal (Criminal division) and his appeal was allowed in March 1998, when the sentences were reduced in total to three years and nine months' imprisonment. Confiscation hearings were mentioned in the Crown Court on various occasions and in June 1998 an application was made for an extension of time under the Criminal Justice Act 1988 s.72A. A postponement was granted due to exceptional circumstances.

Held, allowing the appeal, that in the absence of exceptional circumstances the court had no power to specify a period of postponement which exceeded six months beginning with the date of verdict for plea. If the court was to determine that there were exceptional circumstances, it must do so before the expiry of the six-month period. The court was bound by the decisions in *R. v. Cole (Andrew Stanley) The Independent*, April 30, 1998, [1998] C.L.Y. 1011 and

R. v. Shergill (Sukdev Singh) [1999] 1 W.L.R. 1944, [1999] C.L.Y. 1106 considered, so the confiscation order was quashed.

R. v. KHAN (KHALID MAHMOOD) [2000] 2 Cr. App. R. (S.) 76, Hidden, J., CA (Crim Div).

1164. Confiscation orders – matrimonial home – wife's entitlement to property

[Drug Trafficking Offences Act 1986.]

N was convicted of drug trafficking offences and a restraint order was made against the matrimonial home under the Drug Trafficking Offences Act 1986. Customs sought to enforce the restraint order after N failed to discharge the confiscation order that had been made against his assets. N's wife's application to have the order varied, on the ground that she alone was legally and beneficially entitled to the property, was dismissed and she appealed.

Held, dismissing the appeal, that it would be an abuse of process for a third party to relitigate a case where it had been decided on substantially the same evidence as was now being offered. Moreover, N's wife, though not directly represented, had a common cause with her husband and their joint interests were represented. N's wife had ample opportunity to argue her case and had in fact given detailed evidence about the ownership of the property. That evidence was disbelieved and it would be wrong now to re-open the case on the basis of that evidence alone. In appropriate cases, relitigation would be allowed, where, for example, fresh evidence had emerged or where the interests of a third party had not been represented.

NORRIS (CLIFFORD), *Re* [2000] 1 W.L.R. 1094, Tuckey, L.J., CA.

1165. Confiscation orders – obtaining by deception – assessment of proceeds – sharing proceeds with accomplice

[Criminal Justice Act 1988 s.71; Proceeds of Crime Act 1995.]

P pleaded guilty to conspiring to obtain property by deception. P was the postmaster at a sub post office. Stolen benefit books were used to obtain a total of £51,950 in 89 encashments. All of the encashments took place at the sub post office where P was postmaster. P admitted that the stolen benefit books came into his possession when he was approached by a man who had the books and who offered to share the proceeds of the fraud equally. P was provided with the blank stolen books, wrote a fraudulent signature on the orders by way of receipt, and then took amounts matching the value of the orders in cash from the post office till or safe. He then paid half of the proceeds to his accomplice. P was sentenced to 21 months' imprisonment, with a confiscation order under the Criminal Justice Act 1988, as amended by Proceeds of Crime Act 1995, in the amount of £51,920, with two years' imprisonment in default. P appealed.

Held, dismissing the appeal, that P admitted receiving a total of £51,920. That figure represented his benefit from his relevant criminal conduct for the purpose of the Act. The fact that he had subsequently given some of the money to his fellow conspirator was irrelevant for the purposes of s.71. Under the provisions of the Criminal Justice Act 1988 s.71 as amended by the Proceeds of Crime Act 1995, which applied to the present case, it was the duty of the court, if the prosecution had given notice, to determine the amount of the defendant's benefit from his criminal conduct and to order the defendant to pay that amount. Contrary to the position in earlier cases, subject to the provisions of the Criminal Justice Act 1988 in their original form, the judge had no discretion once statutory conditions were met. The judge had found that P had assets at the relevant time in the form of funds on deposit with the bank amounting to £55,000. It was accepted that that money was available to P and that the amount that might be realised at the time the order was made. The sentencing judge had correctly ordered P to pay the lesser of those two amounts in accordance with s.71 (6) of the 1988 Act.

R. v. PATEL (ASSESH) [2000] 2 Cr. App. R. (S.) 10, Douglas Brown, J., CA (Crim Div).

1166. Confiscation orders – pleas entered in the magistrates court – power to make order following committal to Crown Court

[Powers of Criminal Courts Act 1973 s.35, s.42; Magistrates Courts Act 1980 s.38; Criminal Justice Act 1988 s.71; Crime and Disorder Act 1998 s.83, Sch.9, para.8.]

W pleaded guilty before a magistrates' court to three counts of being knowingly concerned in dealing with goods with intent to defraud the Revenue of duty payable. W was committed to the Crown Court for sentence under the Magistrates Courts Act 1980 s.38. W acquired possession of hand rolling tobacco, cigarettes, spirits and wine which were chargeable with a total of £18,795 excise duty that had not been paid. He admitted purchasing 15,000 cigarettes and 20 kilograms of hand rolling tobacco from foreign lorry drivers, for sale through his business. He was sentenced to 12 months' imprisonment with a confiscation order under the Criminal Justice Act 1988 s.71 in the amount of £35,243. It was argued that the Crown Court had no power to make a confiscation order following a committal for sentence as W was not a person convicted by the Crown Court. W further contended that the correctness of this interpretation was shown by the Crime and Disorder Act 1998 s.83 which amended the s.71 of the 1988 Act by inserting a further subsection (subsection (9A)).

Held, allowing the appeal, that subsection 9A did not come into force until September 30, 1998. The Crime and Disorder Act 1998 Sch.9, para.8 provided that s.83 of the 1998 Act, which inserted the subsection, did not apply where the offence was committed before the commencement of the section. Further, where a defendant pleaded guilty in a magistrates' court it could not be said that he had been convicted before the Crown Court. Section 42 of the 1973 Act gave the court power to deal with such a defendant in any manner as if he had been convicted on indictment but the power in s.71(1) did not arise save in a court where he was convicted. In this case that was the magistrates court. W's submission that s.71 (9A) was inserted to remove the lacuna was a good point. The fact that it was specifically provided that it should not apply where the offence was committed before the commencement of s.83 of the 1998 Act added considerable force to the construction. Accordingly, the confiscation order would be quashed. The court would substitute for the confiscation order a compensation order under the s.35 of the 1973 Act in the amount of £18,795.

R. v. WHELLEM (STUART CHARLES) [2000] 1 Cr. App. R. (S.) 200, Gage, J., CA (Crim Div).

1167. Confiscation orders – pleas entered in the magistrates court – power to make order following committal to Crown Court

See SENTENCING: R. v. Whellem (Stuart Charles). §1166

1168. Confiscation orders – supply of drugs – assessment of proceeds of drug trafficking

[Drug Trafficking Act 1994 s.4.]

C appealed against the imposition of a confiscation order of £26,920 under the Drug Trafficking Act 1994 having pleaded guilty to possessing and supplying a Class A drug. The order was made following a drug trafficking offences assessment. £25,000 of the sum related to an assessment of C's proceeds from drug trafficking, the Recorder having found it to be the amount by which his expenditure during the course of a three year period exceeded his legitimate income. The remaining £1,920 constituted the money found in C's possession at the time of his arrest. C contended, inter alia, that the Recorder had erred in holding him not to have satisfied the burden of proof necessary to displace the assumptions required under s.4(3) of the Act.

Held, dismissing the appeal, that the Recorder had not erred in his findings. C had failed to keep any records of his alleged business dealings and the Recorder having assessed the evidence before him had correctly concluded that C had not displaced the assumptions that the court was required to apply under s.4(3) of the Act. Any suggestion that the assessment was unduly harsh was misguided. It was not open to the court to show mercy or discretion once the proceeds from drug trafficking had been established.

R. v. CROFT (TERENCE GEORGE) *The Times*, July 6, 2000, Wright, J., CA (Crim Div).

1169. **Confiscation orders – supply of drugs – failure to pay confiscation order – default term of imprisonment – no breach of European Convention on Human Rights**

[Drug Trafficking Act 1994; European Convention on Human Rights 1950 Art.6, Art.7.]

M appealed against a sentence of 11 years' imprisonment together with a confiscation order, the latter requiring repayment within 12 months and embracing a default term of 21 months' imprisonment, having been convicted of conspiring to supply a Class A drug under the Drug Trafficking Act 1994. M contended that the length of the default term was excessive and that the confiscation procedure breached the European Convention on Human Rights 1950 Art.6 and Art.7.

Held, dismissing the appeal, that where a confiscation order was not paid, the imposition of a default term of imprisonment did not breach the 1950 Convention. Whilst an agreed order could be the subject of an appeal, *R. v. Emmett (Brian)* [1998] A.C. 773, [1997] C.L.Y. 1470 followed, there was no evidence of a relevant mistake of law or fact in the instant case. In relation to Art.6, there was no conflict with the confiscation procedure and the relevant powers of the 1994 Act were not in question, *Welch v. United Kingdom (A/307-A)* (1995) 20 E.H.R.R. 247, [1995] C.L.Y. 2650 applied. It was established that a defendant could bear an onus, but not the whole burden of proof, *Lingens v. Austria (No.1) (8803/79)* (1982) 4 E.H.R.R. 373 applied, and that certain reasonable presumptions were permissible, *Salabiaku v. France (A/141-A)* (1991) 13 E.H.R.R. 379 applied. In addition, there was no breach of Art.7 as the default term was simply a means of enforcing the order and did not constitute the imposition of a more severe penalty.

R. v. MALIK (ALEEM MUSHTAQ) *The Times*, May 30, 2000, Henry, L.J., CA (Crim Div).

1170. **Confiscation orders – supply of drugs – postponement of determination – exceptional circumstances**

[Drug Trafficking Act 1994 s.3.]

E pleaded guilty in October 1997 to being concerned in the supply of a Class A drug and other drug trafficking offences. The case was adjourned for a *Newton* hearing, which took place in January 1998, when E was sentenced to various terms of imprisonment. An appeal against those sentences was determined by the Court of Appeal on July 16, 1998. One day before the hearing of the appeal, the Crown Court purported to extend time under the Drug Trafficking Act 1994, and on July 22, 1998 the Crown Court made a confiscation order against E. It was argued that the Crown Court had no jurisdiction to make a confiscation order, as more than six months had elapsed since the date of E's conviction.

Held, allowing the appeal, that it was clear that E had the right to appeal against the confiscation order, even though he had already appealed against the principal sentence for the offence. The sentencer in the Crown Court had purported, retrospectively, to extend the time within which the confiscation order had to be made. Section 3 of the Act allowed the Crown Court to postpone making a confiscation order for up to six months, or longer if there were exceptional circumstances. The Act would not permit a finding of exceptional circumstances to be made retrospectively. The provisions of the Act were clear. A confiscation order was normally to be made within six months of conviction. In exceptional circumstances, the period might be exceeded. The judgment whether the circumstances were exceptional was to be made by the court considering whether to make the confiscation order, and the decision must be made before the six month period had elapsed. It followed that the confiscation order would be quashed, *R. v. Neal (John Frederick) (Sentencing)* [1999] 2 Cr. App. R. (S.) 352, [2000] C.L.Y. 1161, *R. v. Cole (Andrew Stanley) The Independent*, April 30, 1998, [1998] C.L.Y. 1011 and *R. v. Shergill (Sukdev Singh)* [1999] 1 W.L.R. 1944, [1999] C.L.Y. 1106 considered.

R. v. EDWARDS (DUNCAN) [2000] 1 Cr. App. R. (S.) 98, Blofeld, J., CA (Crim Div).

1171. Confiscation orders – supply of drugs – postponement of determination – validity of order

[Drug Trafficking Act 1994 s.3.]

K appealed against a sentence totalling five years' imprisonment and a confiscation order of £96,450 having pleaded guilty to conspiring to supply cannabis resin, possession of cannabis resin, possession of cocaine, possession of a prohibited weapon, and possession of a document with intent to deceive. K was concerned in a conspiracy to distribute cannabis resin. K argued that the sentence was inconsistent with an indication given by the judge before the plea was entered, and that the confiscation order was made without jurisdiction. Further, it was argued for K that there was no effective postponement under the Drug Trafficking Act 1994 s.3 before the expiry of six months from the date of conviction, *R. v. Cole (Andrew Stanley) The Independent*, April 30, 1998, [1998] C.L.Y. 1011 and *R. v. Shergill (Sukdev Singh)* [1999] 1 W.L.R. 1944, [1999] C.L.Y. 1106 referred to.

Held, allowing the appeal, that there had been no effective postponement under s.3 of the Act as that could only be constituted by a judicial decision taken in open court with the reasons given. It therefore followed that the confiscation order was made without jurisdiction and was quashed.

R. v. KELLY (MARTIN PATRICK) [2000] 2 Cr. App. R. (S.) 129, Laws, L.J., CA (Crim Div).

1172. Confiscation orders – theft – assessment of proceeds – burden of proof

[Criminal Justice Act 1988 s.71, s.73(6).]

B appealed against a confiscation order for £450,000 imposed following a guilty plea to 21 counts of theft and one count of evading liability by deception after B had elicited in excess of £500,000 from three women whom he had befriended and persuaded to lend him money. B contended that the judge had erroneously placed the burden of proof on him to establish that he had no realisable assets and how the proceeds had been spent. B claimed that the onus of proving the benefit and also the amount of tangible assets was upon the prosecution, and unless this could be established a confiscation order could not be imposed. Furthermore, it was submitted that the judge had incorrectly increased the value of actual proceeds which might be realised by adjusting the figure in accordance with the inflation rate.

Held, dismissing the appeal, that the judge had adhered to the correct approach, namely, that once the prosecution had established the receipt of a benefit, the Criminal Justice Act 1988 s.71 as amended gave the court power to impose the order, and thereafter it was for B to prove, on a balance of probabilities, that he no longer had the proceeds or that their realisability had diminished, *R. v. Rees* (Unreported, July 19, 1990) considered. Under s.73(6) of the Act, it was the responsibility of the defendant to establish that the realisable amount was less than the court's assessment of benefit. The judge had been entitled to infer on the facts of the case that B had invested the money and thus could take into account the changes in the value of the money in determining the starting figure for the actual proceeds of his offences.

R. v. BARWICK (ROBERT ERNEST); *sub nom.* R. v. BARWICK (ROBERT EARNEST) [2001] 1 Cr. App. R. (S.) 129, Holman, J., CA (Crim Div).

1173. Consecutive sentences – custodial sentences – incorporation of licence periods – power to extend

[Criminal Justice Act 1991 s.44, s.51 (2D); Crime and Disorder Act 1998 s.58.]

B appealed against a total sentence of 10 years' imprisonment with a 10 years' extended licence period for various sexual offences involving young boys, to which he had pleaded guilty. B submitted that the court had no power under the Crime and Disorder Act 1998 s.58 to impose consecutive extended custodial sentences incorporating extended licence periods, since the effect was to render his sentence manifestly excessive. He drew attention to his guilty pleas, his cooperation with the court and the proposed enforcement of legislation to lower the age of homosexual consent to 16, which would have decriminalised some of his behaviour.

Held, allowing the appeal, reducing the term of imprisonment to eight years and the extended licence period to five years, that (1) although there was no prohibition in s.58 of the 1998 Act itself on the passing of consecutive extended sentences and although the Criminal Justice Act 1991 s.44 and s.51 (2D) supported the view that such sentences were permitted, the total sentence imposed was, on the facts of the case, excessive. The purpose of s.58 of the 1998 Act was to protect the public and to aid rehabilitation by ensuring that where a normal licence period was inadequate, an extended sentence could be passed, which would have the effect of substituting the normal licence period with one which would expire at the end of the extended sentence, and (2) it was acceptable, in appropriate cases, for a sentencing judge to consider the impact of proposed legislation before it came into force, but in the instant case the individual sentences imposed were justified and the mere fact that a literal interpretation of s.58 could lead to disproportionate licence periods did not warrant the adoption of a non literal construction of the section.

R. v. BARKER (PETER ANDREW) [2001] 1 Cr. App. R. (S.) 142, Roch, L.J., CA (Crim Div).

1174. Consecutive sentences – dangerous driving – offences arising from same facts

K appealed against his sentence having pleaded guilty before a magistrates' court to dangerous driving and driving while unfit through drink or drugs. He was committed to the Crown Court for sentence. K was seen early one morning driving a lorry in an erratic manner. The lorry eventually collided with a car which had been stopped in a lay by, flinging the driver into the air, and then stopped. The driver of the car suffered serious injuries including a fracture to the base of the spine and head injuries. K was found to have traces of diazepam and barbiturates in his blood. K admitted having taken diazepam that morning, having taken five or six doses the previous day, and that he had had no sleep since the previous morning. K was sentenced to six months' imprisonment for driving while unfit and two years' imprisonment consecutive for dangerous driving, and disqualified from driving for five years.

Held, allowing the appeal, that it was wrong to pass the maximum sentence for each offence as K had pleaded guilty, and that it was wrong to pass consecutive sentences for offences arising out of the same facts. This was a serious case which was aggravated by the drugs that had been taken. The imposition of the maximum sentence for each offence was however excessive, and it was wrong to order the sentences to run consecutively, as both offences arose out of the use of drugs by K. The sentence for dangerous driving would be reduced to 18 months and the sentence for driving while unfit would be reduced to four months, the sentences to run concurrently. The period of disqualification would stand.

R. v. KING (JAMES GEORGE) [2000] 1 Cr. App. R. (S.) 105, Aikens, J., CA (Crim Div).

1175. Consecutive sentences – sentence length – appropriateness of imposing longer than commensurate sentences

[Criminal Justice Act 1991 s.2(2)(b); Crime and Disorder Act 1998 s.58.]

S appealed against a total sentence of six years' imprisonment having pleaded guilty to one count of theft and one count of robbery. He went to the home of a lady aged 84, where he had cleaned the windows on a previous occasion. He entered the home through an open door and asked the lady for a cup of tea. The lady went to get her next door neighbour who told S to leave the flat. After S had left, the lady found that her pension book and some cash were missing. A few days later S returned to the lady's home and again entered. When the lady screamed, S grabbed her by the neck, put his hand over her mouth and dragged her into the bedroom. He left the lady on the floor and stole her purse, pension book and a sum in cash. The lady was taken to hospital where she was found to have suffered bruising to her face and elsewhere. She suffered the loss of two teeth, and several other teeth were loosened. S had numerous convictions for offences including inflicting grievous bodily harm, assault occasioning actual bodily harm and manslaughter. S also had previous convictions for burglaries at the homes of elderly people. He was sentenced to 12 months' imprisonment for theft, with five years' imprisonment consecutive for robbery, passed as a longer than commensurate sentence under the Criminal Justice Act 1991 s.2(2)(b), with an extension period of four years under the Crime and Disorder Act 1998 s.58. S argued that it was wrong in principle to order a longer than commensurate sentence to run consecutively to the sentence of 12 months' imprisonment for theft, relying on *R. v. Walters (Desmond Arthur)* [1997] 2 Cr. App. R. (S.) 87, [1997] C.L.Y. 1585.

Held, dismissing the appeal, that the essential submission on behalf of S was that the consecutive sentence fell foul of the principle identified in *Walters*. The court was bound to follow that principle. However, the court asked itself first whether the total sentence of six years' imprisonment was appropriate given S's offending behaviour, when viewed in the context of the order under s.58. In the court's judgment, a total sentence of six years' imprisonment was entirely correct. The circumstances of the robbery were such that it was unnecessary for the sentencer to invoke the provisions of s.2(2)(b) of the 1991 Act. A sentence of five years' imprisonment for the offences of robbery could properly have been imposed without reliance on those provisions. The sentence of five years' imprisonment was correct in principle without regard to s.2(2)(b) of the 1991 Act and the consecutive sentence of 12 months' imprisonment for the separate offence of theft was also correct. Accordingly, the principle identified in *Walters* did not operate.

R. v. SOWDEN (CLIVE BRIAN) [2000] 2 Cr. App. R. (S.) 360, Potts, J., CA (Crim Div).

1176. Consecutive sentences – sentence on serving prisoner – failure to reconvene court during variation of sentence – variation

[Supreme Court Act 1981 s.47.]

H appealed against the variation of his sentence, having pleaded guilty to possession of heroin and with intent to supply. At the time of sentence, the appellant was serving a sentence of detention in a young offender institution for other offences. He was sentenced to three and a half years' detention in a young offender institution. The sentencer did not make any order as to whether the sentence of three and a half years was concurrent or consecutive to the existing sentences. Two days later, the Crown Court was asked to clarify whether the sentence was concurrent or consecutive, and the sentencer ordered that the sentence should be served consecutively to the existing sentence. The sentencer did not reconvene the court or give the appellant or his counsel any opportunity to be heard on the question. It was argued that the sentencer should not have made the order that the new sentence be served consecutively to the existing sentence. H challenged the manner in which the power was exercised contending that he was afforded no hearing or opportunity to make representations.

Held, allowing the appeal, that the Supreme Court Act 1981 s.47 empowered a sentencer to vary the sentence. In the court's judgment, the sentencer should not have varied the sentence except in open court, *R. v. Dowling (Stephen)* (1989) 88 Cr. App. R. 88, [1989] C.L.Y. 1132 considered. Having regard to be potentially prejudicial consequences which could flow from the variation, the sentencer should not have done so without giving the appellant an opportunity to be heard. Prior to the variation, the effect of the sentence imposed on the appellant would have been that it would take effect on the day it was imposed and the terminal date of all the sentences to which the appellant was subject would be the terminal date of the new sentence. H would have remained a short term prisoner. The court was satisfied that the judge should not have varied the sentence to three and a half years consecutive. By doing so he acted contrary to the requirements of procedural fairness, and also inconsistently with his own expressed intention so far as it could be gathered from the original sentencing remarks. The sentencer might have been influenced by *R. v. Davies (Gwyn George)* [1998] 1 Cr. App. R. (S). 252, [1997] C.L.Y. 1478 considered, and the suggestion in Current Sentencing Practice that the normal approach in circumstances such as these was to make the second sentence consecutive to the sentence which was being served. However as was pointed out in Current Sentencing Practice a sentencer should always have regard to the totality of the sentence. This meant that the sentencer should have accurate information as to sentences which were being served, and that the defendant's representative should be given the opportunity to make representations with regard to the totality of the single term which sentences would comprise. The case illustrated the need for all counsel to be vigilant in assisting the judge in drawing his attention to facts which were material to the details of sentencing. The sentence of three and a half years would be ordered to run concurrently with the existing sentence.

R. v. H (CHOUDHRY FIAZ) (A JUVENILE) [2000] 1 Cr. App. R. (S.) 181, Newman, J., CA (Crim Div).

1177. Consecutive sentences – totality of sentence – term consecutive to sentence already in operation

W appealed against a sentence of five years and six months' imprisonment having pleaded guilty to robbery, burglary, theft, false accounting and perverting the course of justice. He asked for 68 offences of dishonestly obtaining benefit to be taken into consideration. The term was consecutive to a sentence of three years' imprisonment imposed on a previous occasion which W was already serving.

Held, allowing the appeal, that in *Stevens* the Court had reiterated the principle that although it may be proper to make a sentence consecutive to one passed on an earlier occasion, particularly where the second offence was committed while M was on bail for the first offence, the sentencing court must have regard to the totality of the sentence to be served. If all the offences had been dealt with at the same time, would the same total sentence have resulted? If not, the total produced by making the sentences consecutive might be disproportionate and excessive. It was right in principle in the present case to make the sentences for the later offences consecutive to the sentence which M was already serving. Despite the seriousness of some of the individual offences, M would not have received a total sentence of eight and a half years' imprisonment if all the matters had been dealt with together. The component sentences could not be subject to criticism considered on their own. The combination of the sentences passed by the judge with the sentence that M was already serving did produce a total term that was disproportionate to the overall criminality of M. The court would reduce the overall total term to a total of seven years, by making appropriate adjustments to the latest sentences. *R. v. Stevens (Alan)* [1997] 2 Cr. App. R. (S.) 180, [1997] C.L.Y. 1480 considered.

R. v. WATTS (DARREN LEE) [2000] 1 Cr. App. R. (S.) 460, Richards, J, CA (Crim Div).

1178. Consecutive sentences – variation of sentences – distinction between recall for breach of early release licence and return order

[Criminal Justice Act 1991 s.39, s.40, s.51 (2); Crime and Disorder Act 1998 s.101, s.102(1).]

C appealed against the variation of a sentence of imprisonment of three years and six months imposed in 1999 to make it run consecutive to an earlier four year prison sentence imposed in 1996, for which he had been released on licence but subsequently recalled to prison following breach. The judge had been unaware of the four year sentence when the 1999 sentence was imposed or that C had been recalled to prison. Consequently, he imposed the variation on the basis that without it C would shortly be released as the recent sentence would be subsumed by the earlier one. C contended that such a variation was unlawful, citing the Criminal Justice Act 1991 s.51 (2), as amended by the Crime and Disorder Act 1998 ss.101 and 102(1).

Held, allowing the appeal, that there was a difference between sentences imposed where a prisoner was recalled for breach of licence and that where he was ordered by the court to be returned to custody. The varied sentence which was the subject of the appeal had been imposed under s.39 of the 1991 Act dealing with recalls and not as a return order under s.40 of the 1991 Act. The amendments to s.51 (2) meant that the two sentences would not be treated as a single sentence and the situation envisaged by the judge would not have arisen. C had previously been released from the four year sentence, with the effect that he was covered by the prohibitions under s.102(1) of the 1998 Act and the court could not make the later sentence consecutive to the earlier sentence.

R. v. CAWTHORN (ROBERT) [2001] 1 Cr. App. R. (S.) 136, Henriques, J., CA (Crim Div).

1179. Conspiracy – handling stolen goods – obtaining by deception

D and E appealed against respective sentences of seven and four years' imprisonment. D was convicted of conspiracy to steal, and E pleaded guilty to six counts of handling stolen goods and one of obtaining property by deception. D and E were involved in "ringing" stolen cars. 33 vehicles were involved and their identities were applied to other vehicles. Vehicles with false identities were then sold or disposed of.

Held, allowing the appeal, that this was not the kind of case which demanded the maximum sentence; it was not so extensive, involved, ruthless or profitable as some cases which came before the court. The sentence of seven years on D was reduced to five years and the sentence of four years on E was reduced to three years.

R. v. DENNARD (WILLIAM); R. v. DRAPER (JOHN) [2000] 1 Cr. App. R. (S.) 232, Judge Myerson, CA (Crim Div).

1180. Conspiracy – handling stolen goods – stolen computer equipment – unduly lenient sentence

The Attorney General referred as unduly lenient a sentence of 12 months' imprisonment, R having been convicted of conspiracy to handle stolen goods and conspiracy to steal. He pleaded guilty to taking part in the management of a company while an undischarged bankrupt, and to a further count of conspiracy to handle stolen goods. R ran a computer supply and repair business. Over a period of some months he received a substantial quantity of stolen computer equipment from a variety of sources, and sold the stolen equipment through his business. R agreed to buy a lorry load of computers worth about £250,000, which were to be stolen by one of his suppliers.

Held, allowing the reference, that it appeared to the court that the sentencer was over impressed by the personal qualities of R and paid too much regard to them in comparison with the gravity of those offences, which could properly have been expected to attract a total sentence of at least four years' imprisonment. Taking into account the element of double jeopardy, and the fact that the offender had already been released from the sentence imposed by the trial judge, the court would impose sentence totalling 30 months' imprisonment, *R. v. Sutcliffe (Brian)* (1995) 16 Cr. App. R. (S.) 69, [1996] C.L.Y. 2091, *R. v. Patel (Moussa Mohammed)* (1984) 6 Cr. App. R. (S.) 191, [1986] C.L.Y. 831, *R. v. Amlani (Chanudula)* (1995) 16 Cr. App. R. (S.) 339, *R. v. Connor (Vincent)* (1981) 3 Cr. App. R. (S.) 225, [1982] C.L.Y. 684.39 and *R. v. Byrne (James)* (1994) 15 Cr. App. R. (S.) 34 considered.

ATTORNEY GENERAL'S REFERENCE (NO.70 OF 1999), *Re*; *sub nom*. R. v. RANCE (RICHARD) [2000] 2 Cr. App. R. (S.) 28, Rose, L.J., CA (Crim Div).

1181. **Conspiracy – theft – vehicles broken into and items stolen – unduly lenient sentence**

The Attorney General referred as unduly lenient a two year probation order, M having admitted that he had broken into about 25 vans, stealing drills and power tools which had been left in the vehicles overnight. The total value of the property stolen was estimated to be £25,000. M was placed on probation for two years with the condition that he should attend a probation centre for 30 days.

Held, refusing the reference, that had M had contested the allegations and had been convicted following a trial, the sentence would have been in the range of 18 months to two years' imprisonment. On a plea of guilty, a sentence of 12 months would not have been excessive. The question was whether the sentence imposed on M was outside the range of sentences reasonably open to the sentencer, having regard to the mitigating factors. M had a long record of offences and had begun to commit the present offences shortly after his release from an earlier sentence. He had admitted the offences and cooperated with the police; he had made determined efforts to overcome his addiction to drugs. The court reminded itself that the sentencing court must retain an element of discretion. In this case the sentence imposed was merciful but not unduly lenient. The court would not accordingly disturb the sentence.

ATTORNEY GENERAL'S REFERENCE (NO.48 OF 1999), *Re*; *sub nom*. R. v. MORTON (STEPHEN RICHARD) [2000] 1 Cr. App. R. (S.) 472, Lord Bingham of Cornhill, L.C.J., CA (Crim Div).

1182. **Counterfeiting – Trade Marks Act offences – dealing with falsely labelled goods – professional enterprise leading to substantial profit**

[Trade Marks Act 1994 s.92(1)(c).]

A and three others appealed against sentences imposed having pleaded guilty to offences against the Trade Marks Act 1994 s.92(1)(c). They played various roles in producing, distributing and storing clothing which was to be sold as having been made by well known fashion houses. Goods worth between £800,000 and £900,000 were involved. They were sentenced to terms of three years' or two years' imprisonment according to their involvement.

Held, dismissing the appeals, that their conduct tended to undermine reputable companies; it was a professional enterprise likely to lead to substantial profit. The sentences fully took into account all relevant matters, *R. v. Yanko (Wayne John)* [1996] 1 Cr. App. R. (S.) 217, [1996] C.L.Y. 1848 considered.

R. v. ANSARI (MOHAMMED); R. v. HORNER (DAVID); R. v. LING (PETER); R. v. ANSARI (SAYED) [2000] 1 Cr. App. R. (S.) 94, Curtis, J., CA (Crim Div).

1183. **Custodial sentences – discounts – previous period spent on remand**

E pleaded guilty to robbery, and D pleaded guilty to robbery and unlawful wounding. E and D were concerned with another man in an attack on a security van which they thought was delivering cash to a bank. A police officer who was pretending to be a security guard was sprayed with liquid from a bottle. A dummy cash box was stolen, but E and D were immediately arrested by other officers. D was involved some months later in a fight in which a man was kicked in the face. Sentenced to seven years' imprisonment for robbery in each case, with 12 months' imprisonment consecutive imposed on D for unlawful wounding, E and D appealed.

Held, dismissing the appeal, that D had been convicted in 1993 for participating in a robbery committed in 1992. He was sentenced to 12 years' imprisonment for this offence. In 1995 the Court of Appeal (Criminal Division) allowed an appeal against his conviction and ordered a retrial. The jury failed to agree on the retrial and prosecution did not proceed further. The applicant had accordingly spent three and three quarter years in custody for an offence for which he was never convicted. It was argued that the sentencer should have given the applicant some discount against the current sentence in respect of that period in custody. A similar issue had been considered in *Wiwczaryk (Stephen Michael)* (1980) 2 Cr. App. R. (S.) 309, in which the Court indicated that the fact that the applicant had spent time in prison prior to the offences for which he was sentenced for offences in respect of which his conviction was subsequently quashed did not give him credit on which he could draw for subsequent crimes. It was made clear in that decision, as a matter of principle, that it was not open to a person who was about to be sentenced to argue that he should be given credit for the previous sentence in such circumstances.

R. v. EXLEY (WARREN); R. v. DAY (MARK ALAN) [2000] 2 Cr. App. R. (S.) 189, Otton, L.J., CA (Crim Div).

1184. Custodial sentences – discounts – refusal to give discount following Newton hearing

H pleaded guilty before a magistrates' court to assault occasioning actual bodily harm, criminal damage and affray. He was committed to the Crown Court for sentence. H and three other men spent an afternoon in a public house. A dispute arose between H and the landlord over the price of some packets of crisps. One of H's friends grabbed the landlord by the neck, and H vaulted over the bar, punched the landlord on the head and continued to punch and kick him. In the course of the attack a dishwasher and an ice maker were damaged, together with the landlord's spectacles. The landlord was treated for bleeding and bruising and was off work for two weeks. Although H pleaded guilty to the charges, he denied certain aspects of the evidence, and there was a *Newton* hearing in the Crown Court, during the course of which the landlord, his wife and a customer gave evidence. H was sentenced to 15 months' imprisonment. In passing sentence, the sentencer indicated that H had forfeited any credit for his plea of guilty by requiring a factual issue to be tried. H appealed.

Held, allowing the appeal, that the court had said on more than one occasion that a judge was entitled to reduce the discount that would otherwise be given for a plea of guilty when there had been a *Newton* hearing and the defence version was disbelieved. In the court's judgment, the sentencer was wrong to give H no credit for his plea of guilty, although he would have been fully entitled to reduce the discount. Apart from this there was nothing wrong with the sentence, even on a plea of guilty, for such a serious attack. The sentence would be reduced from 15 months to 12 months, *R. v. Stevens (David)* (1986) 8 Cr. App. R. (S.) 297, [1988] C.L.Y. 914, *R. v. Jauncey (Jeffrey James)* (1986) 8 Cr. App. R. (S.) 401, [1988] C.L.Y. 901 and *R. v. Williams (Timothy James)* (1990) 12 Cr. App. R. (S.) 415, [1992] C.L.Y. 1291 considered.

R. v. HASSALL (RICHARD DAVID) [2000] 1 Cr. App. R. (S.) 67, Penry-Davey, J., CA (Crim Div).

1185. Custodial sentences – extradition – discount for period spent in custody

L had been convicted of drug offences. Before sentence could be imposed, however, he absconded to the Netherlands, where he was apprehended and spent nearly eight months in custody. On return to the UK, L was sentenced to five years' imprisonment for drug offences and appealed, contending that credit should have been given for the period spent in Dutch custody.

Held, allowing the appeal, that defendants who absconded after conviction were entitled to credit in respect of time spent in foreign custody. On the facts of the instant case, L would not be given credit for the whole period as he should have been aware that failure to meet a bail condition would lead to an extra three months' imprisonment. Moreover, the period in Dutch custody had been prolonged by L's attempt to resist extradition on grounds of entrapment, an argument already rejected at his original trial in England. Therefore credit would only be given for three of the eight months spent in Dutch custody.

R. v. LODDE (DAVID); R. v. LODDE (ANN) *The Times*, March 8, 2000, Henry, L.J., CA.

1186. Custodial sentences – legitimate expectation – indications of sentencing judge – unduly lenient sentence

[Criminal Justice Act 1988 s.36; European Convention on Human Rights 1950 Art.6.]

The Attorney General sought leave to refer a sentence to the court on the grounds that it was unduly lenient under the Criminal Justice Act 1988 s.36. W and S had been convicted of conspiracy to cheat, cheating at common law, and false accounting in matters relating to monies improperly gained from the Inland Revenue. The sentences imposed had consisted of financial penalties to repay the tax and make compensation. The Attorney General highlighted the aggravating features which included a breach of trust over a long period of time. W and S contended that the reference should not result in custodial sentences as the sentencing judge had indicated both prior to sentence and in his remarks in open court that he had not considered custody to be appropriate. It was argued that this had raised a legitimate expectation on the part of W and S and that an increase in the sentence would be unfair in any event due to the delay of 17 months since trial.

Held, allowing the reference, that the appropriate sentence was one which included the repayment of the tax, financial penalties, and custody. A term of 18 months' imprisonment was therefore imposed on W, and six months' on S. The indications given by the judge were relevant but in the absence of any guilty plea having been proffered as a result, any detrimental reliance by W and S, or the acquiescence of the prosecution at trial, the court's discretion was not fettered, *Attorney General's Reference (No.44 of 2000), Re The Times*, October 25, 2000, [2000] C.L.Y. 1085 distinguished. Further, the delay was not so great as to constitute a breach of the European Convention on Human Rights 1950 Art.6 and did not prevent the imposition of a more appropriate sentence, *Howarth v. United Kingdom The Times*, October 10, 2000, [2000] C.L.Y. 3216 distinguished. Questions arising from the application were referred to the House of Lords.

ATTORNEY GENERAL'S REFERENCE (NOS.86 AND 87 OF 1999), *Re*; R. v. SIMPSON (MOIRA); *sub nom*. R. v. WEBB (ROBERT EDWARD) [2001] 1 Cr. App. R. (S.) 141, Kennedy, L.J., CA (Crim Div).

1187. Custodial sentences – pre sentence reports – first term of imprisonment

A applied for an extension of time in which to apply for leave to appeal against his sentence of five years' imprisonment following his conviction for conspiracy to kidnap, robbery, and having an imitation firearm with intent to kidnap. The Court of Appeal had held in *R. v. Gillette (Arthur Stanley) The Times*, December 3, 1999, [2000] C.L.Y. 1188, that the court when considering sending an offender to prison for the first time, with the possible exception of sentencing to very short periods of time, should as a matter of course obtain a pre sentence report prior to passing such sentence. A contended that given the decision in *Gillette* the judge had erred in failing to order a pre sentence report prior to passing the custodial sentence, which was his first term of imprisonment.

Held, refusing the application, that the sentencing judge had not been obliged to obtain a pre sentence report as there had been no request by counsel for a report and as every possible assumption had been made by the judge in A's favour, *Gillette* distinguished. In circumstances where the court was willing to make every possible assumption in favour of an offender, it was required to decide whether a pre sentence report was necessary. In the instant case a pre sentence report would have provided the sentencing judge with no assistance with regard to the sentence which should be imposed for the three offences.

R. v. ARMSARAMAH (ROBERT) [2001] 1 Cr. App. R. (S.) 133, Steel, J., CA (Crim Div).

1188. Custodial sentences – pre sentence reports – first term of imprisonment – 72 year old in poor health

G, a 72 year old man in poor health, appealed against seven concurrent sentences of 12 months imprisonment for indecent assault. G contended that pre sentence and medical reports should have been obtained.

Held, dismissing the appeal, that obtaining pre sentence and social enquiry reports prior to handing down a first custodial sentence was essential unless the term was very short. In the instant case, although neither pre sentence reports nor medical reports had been produced, G had been given the minimum sentence applicable to the offence. The reports, which had subsequently been provided to the Court of Appeal, were unfavourable and revealed that G had refused to accept any responsibility for his offences or to take part in any work with the probation service.

R. v. GILLETTE (ARTHUR STANLEY) *The Times*, December 3, 1999, Wright, J., CA (Crim Div).

1189. Custodial sentences – remand awaiting extradition – discount in sentence

[Criminal Justice Act 1967 s.67; Criminal Justice Act 1991 s.34, s.47; Crime (Sentences) Act 1997 s.28.]

D was convicted in 1987 of offences of attempting to obtain property by deception, forgery, using false instruments and using a copy of a false instrument. He was sentenced to a total of six years' imprisonment. D absconded during his trial and was convicted and sentenced in his absence. He was arrested in Switzerland in 1996 and eventually extradited to the UK in August 1997, having spent a period of 10 months in custody in Switzerland pending extradition. D argued on appeal that the sentence should be reduced to take account of the period spent in custody in Switzerland waiting extradition.

Held, allowing the appeal, that before the Criminal Justice Act 1991, there was no legislative basis whereby time in custody awaiting extradition could be taken into account, but the Court of Appeal had held that it should in fairness and in justice be taken into account when fixing the sentence. The Criminal Justice Act 1991 s.47 made provision for the case of an extradited prisoner. It empowered the court by which he was being sentenced to order that the period spent awaiting extradition should be treated as a relevant period for the purposes of the Criminal Justice Act 1967 s.67. The difficulty about that section was that it defined an "extradited prisoner" as a person who had been extradited to the UK before being tried for the offence in respect of which his sentence was eventually imposed. It presumed that the extradition had taken place before the sentence was passed. The court had been referred to *R. v. Howard (Curtis)* [1996] 2 Cr. App. R. (S.) 419, [1996] C.L.Y. 1988, which was concerned with the deduction of time spent in custody awaiting extradition in the case of a person sentenced to life imprisonment, and required to serve a specified period under the Criminal Justice Act 1991 s.34 (now the Crime (Sentences) Act 1997 s.28). Some allowance should be made in calculating the s.34 period for the fact that D had spent time in custody pending extradition but the whole period spent in custody should not be taken into account because D had made an attempt to avoid extradition and had played the system. In the present case, part of the delay before D had been extradited was caused by the need for the UK government to supply further information to supplement the initial extradition request. On the circumstances it was appropriate to make some deduction from the sentence passed in 1987 to achieve fairness to D. The court was not persuaded that the original sentence was too long. Doing the utmost to give D appropriate credit, the sentence would be reduced to a total of four and a half years' imprisonment.

R. v. DE SIMONE (GIANNI) [2000] 2 Cr. App. R. (S.) 332, Brian Smedley, J., CA (Crim Div).

1190. Custodial sentences – return orders – sentencing powers of Crown Court

[Criminal Justice Act 1967 s.56; Criminal Justice Act 1991 s.40; Crime (Sentences) Act 1997 s.57(3); Crime and Disorder Act 1998 Sch.7 para.43, Sch.8 para.9(1)(b); Crime (Sentences) Act 1997 (Commencement No.2 and Transitional Provisions Order) 1997 (SI 1997 2200).]

D was sentenced to a total of 26 months' imprisonment in March 1997. He was released from that sentence in April 1998. A few days later, D was arrested for an offence of possessing cocaine. He was released on bail but failed to surrender. In May 1998, D committed offences of driving while disqualified and taking a vehicle without consent. He pleaded guilty to these offences before a magistrates' court and was sentenced to five months' imprisonment. No order was made under the Criminal Justice Act 1991 s.40. In June 1998, D appeared in the Crown Court and was sentenced to three months' imprisonment for burglary. He was released from custody in August 1998 and was arrested again in September 1998 for taking a motor vehicle without consent and driving while disqualified. He appeared at a magistrates' court, where he pleaded guilty to possessing a controlled drug in April 1998 and taking a motor vehicle without consent and driving while disqualified in September 1998. He was committed to the Crown Court to be dealt with under s.40 of the 1991 Act in respect of the sentence passed in March 1997, and in respect of the other offences under the Criminal Justice Act 1967 s.56. In the Crown Court he was ordered to return to custody for 12 months in respect of the sentence of March 1997, and for a consecutive period of five weeks in respect of the sentences imposed in May and June 1998. He was sentenced to consecutive terms of four months' imprisonment for taking a motor vehicle, two months' imprisonment for driving while disqualified and six months' imprisonment for being in possession of a controlled drug. D argued that (1) the Crown Court had no power to sentence him for the offences of possessing a class A controlled drug, taking a motor vehicle and driving while disqualified, as he was not lawfully committed for sentence for those offences; (2) the Crown Court had exceeded its powers in ordering the sentence of six months' imprisonment for possessing a class A drug to run consecutively to the sentences for taking a vehicle and driving while disqualified, and (3) the orders under s.40 of the 1991 Act failed to identify correctly the relevant offences and were made in excess of the court's discretion.

Held, allowing the appeal, that (1) the magistrates' court purported to commit D to the Crown Court for the later offences under s.56 of the 1967 Act. However, the Crime (Sentences) Act 1997 (Commencement No.2 and Transitional Provisions Order) 1997 which purported to amend s.56 of the 1967 Act to refer to s.40(3) of the 1991 Act was invalid. The Order purported to be made under the Crime (Sentences) Act 1997 s.57(3), allowing the Secretary of State to make transitional provisions and savings in connection with any provision brought into force by the Order but it did not empower the Secretary of State to amend the text of an Act. The Secretary of State was therefore acting beyond his authority and the amendment was ultra vires and ineffective. These were no transitional provisions or savings and the amendment should have been made by Parliament. The necessary amendments had now been made by the Crime and Disorder Act 1998 Sch.8 para.9(1)(b), but those did not become effective until after committal by a magistrates' court. It could not retrospectively validate the committal. The Crown Court had no power to sentence D for the later offences on the basis of the committal under s.40(3) of the 1991 Act. The decision of the Court of Appeal in *R. v. Russell (John Paul)* [1998] 2 Cr. App. R. (S.) 375, [1999] C.L.Y. 1231 had been reversed by amendments to s.40 of the 1991 Act made by Sch.7 para.43 to the 1998 Act. The effect of the amendment reversed the decision in *Russell* and came into effect before D was sentenced in the Crown Court but contained no provision saving cases where the offender had already been committed for sentence. It followed that the Crown Court had no power to sentence D for the offences of taking a vehicle without consent, driving while disqualified or possessing cocaine; (2) the Crown Court had to deal with an offender committed under s.56 of the 1967 Act in the same way as the magistrates' court, so that the order making the sentence for possession consecutive to the motoring offences was unlawful, and (3) there was no indication in respect of which of the offences that the s.40 orders had been made and it was unlawful to order such periods to be served consecutively. The orders were reduced to six months with a five month consecutive sentence for the later offences.

R. v. DIVERS (SAUL ANDREW) [1999] 2 Cr. App. R. (S.) 421, Klevan, J, CA (Crim Div).

1191. **Custodial sentences – suspended sentences – substantial conspiracy to defraud – activating suspended sentence**

C was convicted of conspiring fraudulently to evade the duty chargeable on certain goods. C owned a warehouse in which goods on which no customs duty had been paid were stored prior to distribution. The offence was committed during the operational period of a suspended sentence imposed for conspiracy to handle stolen goods. C was sentenced to three years' imprisonment, with the suspended sentence activated consecutively. He appealed.

Held, dismissing the appeal, that a court confronted with an offender who had been given the exceptional benefit of a suspended sentence was now likely to consider that the fact that he had kept free of conviction of a substantial portion of the period of suspension should result in the reduction in the length of sentence which was activated, unless there were good reasons for doing so. C had been convicted of handling stolen goods, and given the exceptional benefit of a suspended sentence, but during the period of the suspension, had involved himself in a very substantial conspiracy to defraud the Revenue. There was no justification for concluding that he should not serve the whole period of the sentence which had been so exceptionally suspended.

R. v. CHUNI (NARINDER) [2000] 2 Cr. App. R. (S.) 64, Latham, J., CA (Crim Div).

1192. **Dangerous driving – criminal records – return orders**

[Magistrates' Courts Act 1980 s.38; Criminal Justice Act 1991 s.40.]

C appealed against the length of a return order having pleaded guilty before a magistrates' court to two offences of dangerous driving. C was committed to the Crown Court for sentence under the Magistrates' Courts Act 1980 s.38. C cut in front of another car, forcing it to stop, and then reversed into it, causing damage. A short while later, C drove alongside another vehicle and pushed it into a parked car. When the driver of the other vehicle stopped, C rammed it with his own car whilst the driver and his wife and children were inside it. C was sentenced to two consecutive terms of four months' imprisonment, consecutive to an order under the Criminal Justice Act 1991 s.40 returning him to prison for two years and 73 days, being the balance of a sentence of eight years' imprisonment for robbery and related offences imposed in 1993, from which C had been released in March 1997. C appealed arguing that the order for return under s.40 gave him no credit for the efforts he had made since his release to change his previous pattern of hardened criminality.

Held, allowing the appeal, that the sentencer did not appear to have applied his mind to the question of whether the return period should be reduced in accordance with *R. v. Taylor (Adrian Edward)* [1998] 1 W.L.R. 809, [1997] C.L.Y. 1632. The period of two years and 73 days was too long, a period of 12 months and 73 days would be substituted, to which the sentences for dangerous driving would be consecutive.

R. v. COX (ALLAN) [2000] 2 Cr. App. R. (S.) 57, Ebsworth, J., CA (Crim Div).

1193. Dangerous driving – death – 18 year old driver in sports car

N, aged 18 at the time of the offence, appealed against a sentence of four years' detention in a young offender institution having been convicted of two offences of causing death by dangerous driving. N was given a Porsche sports car by his father for an 18th birthday present. He took two friends for a ride in the car one lunchtime. He drove along a road which was subject to a speed limit of 30 miles an hour, overtaking another car at a speed in excess of 60 miles an hour. N eventually lost control of the car, which mounted the pavement and collided with two elderly women, who were killed instantly.

Held, allowing the appeal, that sentencing in cases of this kind was one of the most difficult tasks facing judges in the Crown Court. They had to take into account the loss and grieving of the relatives of those killed and the public concern at lives needlessly wasted; on the other hand they had to take into account the facts of each particular case, including the circumstances, the character and attitude of the defendant. Nothing done by way of sentencing could compensate a bereaved family and friends. No sentence could in any way be a comment on the value of a human life. The sentence had to be set within the parameters which emerged from the decisions of the Court of Appeal. In the instant case, there were aggravating features: the speed was grossly excessive and there was overtaking in dangerous circumstances. Two women were killed. The case did not involve many of the aggravating features: seen on other cases, such as drink or drugs or racing. The driving took place over a short time and was not prolonged. There were significant mitigating factors: N was young and had no previous convictions; He was full of remorse and suffered from depression. In the court's judgment the proper sentence would have been three years' detention.

R. v. NIJJER (SATVINDER SINGH) [1999] 2 Cr. App. R. (S.) 385, Judge Brian Walsh Q.C., CA (Crim Div).

1194. Dangerous driving – death – falling asleep during driving – unduly lenient sentence

The Attorney General referred as unduly lenient a combination order for an offence of causing death by dangerous driving. G was driving a van along a motorway when other drivers noticed that his vehicle was weaving from one lane to another. The van entered the hard shoulder and continued along it until the van collided with a car which had broken down. The car was protected by cones which had been placed on the hard shoulder by police. The driver of the car, who was lying under the car attempting to repair it, was killed instantly and three passengers in the car suffered serious injuries. G left the scene and telephoned his brother to ask him to collect him. G admitted that he had had four hours sleep on the night before the accident and thought that he was travelling at between 60 and 70 miles an hour. It was accepted that G had fallen asleep at the wheel, that the dangerous driving had continued for a distance of not more than one mile and that when the G had left the scene of the accident he was unaware that the collision had caused death or serious injuries. G was sentenced to a combination order consisting of 100 hours community service and 12 months' probation, and was disqualified from driving.

Held, allowing the reference, that in the court's view leaving the scene by an offender was an important aggravating factor not least because it deprived the authorities of the opportunity to establish whether or not he had had an excessive amount to drink. The court did not accept that this was a momentary falling asleep since this was always the culmination of a period during which the driver was conscious of drowsiness and difficulty in keeping his eyes open. The court could not accept the sentencer's judgment that a custodial sentence was not necessary. If the case had been contested at trial a sentence of 30 months' imprisonment would have been appropriate, taking into account the perseverance of G in driving after the signs of drowsiness must have been apparent, and G's conduct in leaving the scene. On a plea of guilty the appropriate sentence would have been 21 months' imprisonment. Taking into account the element of double jeopardy and the fact that G had completed the community service order the court would substitute a sentence of nine months' imprisonment.

ATTORNEY GENERAL'S REFERENCE (NO.26 OF 1999), *Re; sub nom.* R. v. GASTINGER (NEALE ARTHUR) [2000] 1 Cr. App. R. (S.) 394, Lord Bingham of Cornhill, L.C.J., CA (Crim Div).

1195. Dangerous driving – death – head on collision with approaching car

C appealed against a sentence of two years' imprisonment and disqualification from driving for five years, having been convicted of causing death by dangerous driving. C drove his motor car closely behind another car at a speed between 55 and 60 mph. Eventually as the cars approached a wide left-hand bend, C started to overtake the other car, accelerating to a speed of between 65 and 70 mph. C's car collided head on with an approaching car. The driver of the other car was killed.

Held, dismissing the appeal, that there was no clear explanation of why C was substantially over the centre line of the road when the accident occurred. It appeared that he must have failed to concentrate on his driving in the moments after an overtaking manoeuvre when he was proceeding at a speed in excess of the relevant speed limit. The sentence was severe but not excessive *R. v. Le Mouel (Andre Marcel)* [1996] 1 Cr. App. R. (S.) 42, [1996] C.L.Y. 1831, *R. v. Bevan (Paul Martin)* [1996] 1 Cr. App. R. (S.) 14 and *R. v. Boswell (James Thomas)* [1984] 1 W.L.R. 1047, [1985] C.L.Y. 770 considered.

R. v. CUSICK (COLIN) [2000] 1 Cr. App. R. (S.) 444, Turner, J., CA (Crim Div).

1196. Dangerous driving – death – overtaking in left hand drive vehicle

K appealed against a sentence of 12 months' imprisonment and disqualification from driving for four years. K, an officer in the Finnish army, pleaded guilty to causing death by dangerous driving. K was posted to the United Kingdom for postgraduate studies. While driving in a left hand drive car on a single carriageway road he came up behind a line of traffic led by a slow moving heavy vehicle. He began an overtaking manoeuvre, moving into the opposing lane. Road markings indicated that drivers should pull back to the left, but K maintained his position in the outside lane, travelling at about 55 miles an hour. K continued over a blind incline and collided head-on with an oncoming car. A passenger in the car died from her injuries, and the driver and another passenger were seriously injured. K also suffered injuries. He contended that he believed that he was on a dual carriageway and had been confused by the road mark up.

Held, allowing the appeal, that K had deliberately undertaken a dangerous overtaking manoeuvre in an attempt to pass the slow moving vehicle. In the court's judgment *R. v. Le Mouel (Andre Marcel)* [1996] 1 Cr. App. R. (S.) 42, [1996] C.L.Y. 1831 and *R. v. Obermeier (Manfred)* [1997] 2 Cr. App. R. (S.) 346, [1998] C.L.Y. 1363 considered, were distinguishable on the basis that in those cases the dangerous driving was the result of inattention by foreign motorists, rather than the result of a deliberate dangerous manoeuvre. K had no previous convictions and could be said to be of impeccable character. His military career had probably been wrecked and he had been seriously injured. On the facts the court felt able to reduce the sentence from 12 months to eight months.

R. v. KOSOLA (JYRI JAAKKO) [2000] 1 Cr. App. R. (S.) 205, Sullivan, J., CA (Crim Div).

1197. Dangerous driving – death – racing in built up area

P appealed against a sentence of five and a half years' detention in a young offender institution and disqualification from driving for six years on conviction of causing death by dangerous driving. P was driving his motor car when he met another young man who was filling his car with petrol. He challenged him to a race, but the young man ignored him and drove away. Some time later P met a different young man, and they agreed to race their cars down an undivided single carriageway road in a built-up area. The two cars were driven down the road at speeds estimated to be between 70 and 80 mph. The driver of the first car lost control of his car, which veered across the road, flew through the air and collided with a brick wall. A girl sitting on the back seat of the car was killed, and the front seat passenger suffered severe head injuries. P was interviewed but denied that he had been racing with the other driver. The driver of the car which crashed, who pleaded guilty, was sentenced to four years' imprisonment.

Held, dismissing the appeal, that in cases of causing death by dangerous driving arising out of racing on the highway, offenders would lose their liberty for five years or more. P was not the driver of the car that crashed, but had instigated the whole procedure. The sentence imposed on P was appropriate in the circumstances, *Attorney General's Reference (Nos.14 and 24 of 1993), Re* [1994] 1 W.L.R. 530, [1994] C.L.Y. 1193 and *R. v. Hodder* (Unreported, November 18, 1997) considered.

R. v. PADLEY (IAN) [2000] 2 Cr. App. R. (S.) 201, Wright, J., CA (Crim Div).

1198. Dangerous driving – death – removal of tachograph

W pleaded guilty to three counts of causing death by dangerous driving. W was driving a horse box in the early afternoon. He approached a point on the road at which an accident had caused a build-up of traffic. A warning sign had been placed in advance of the build-up, and a police car displaying its warning lights had been positioned to give warning of the hazard. W did not significantly reduce the speed of his vehicle, and collided with the line of stationary traffic. A motor car was crushed by the impact, and the three occupants of the car were killed. The tachograph recording showed that W's vehicle had been travelling at 51 mph at the moment of impact. After the accident W removed the tachograph and replaced it with an earlier tachograph. W was sentenced to three years' imprisonment and disqualified from driving for six years. He appealed.

Held, dismissing the appeal, that there was medical evidence that W was subject to a condition which might have affected his attention to his driving. The sentencer had taken that evidence into account, but in addition had taken account of the fact that W ignored warnings from his passenger and had removed the tachograph from his vehicle following the accident. The sentencer had properly taken account of all relevant factors. This was a case in which three people lost their lives. The sentence was not manifestly excessive.

R. v. WAGSTAFF (TREVOR CLIFFORD) [2000] 2 Cr. App. R. (S.) 205, Judge Rhys Davies Q.C., CA (Crim Div).

1199. Dangerous driving – death – risk of custodial sentence

N appealed against a sentence of 12 months' imprisonment and disqualification from driving for four years having been convicted of causing death by dangerous driving. N was driving a low loader lorry carrying a dumper truck. N had attempted to deliver the dumper truck to an address but was unable to do so and decided to return with the dumper to his employer's premises. On the way back he needed to cross the north bound carriageway of a dual carriageway with a view to entering the south bound carriageway. N drove his vehicle through a gap in the central reservation with a view to turning right into the southbound carriageway. As he waited for a gap in the southbound traffic, the rear of his vehicle was protruding into the outside lane of the north bound carriageway, in which cars were travelling at high speed, and were unable to see the rear lights of his vehicle. A car being driven in the outside lane of the north bound carriageway collided with the rear of his lorry and the driver was killed. Another car collided with the rear of that car.

Held, that this was a very dangerous piece of driving, although wholly unintended. N could have approached the southbound carriageway by a nearby roundabout. The court considered that the custody threshold had been passed. Motorists must realise that if they drove dangerously and thereby killed somebody they would be in danger of imprisonment. The court was unable to say that the sentence of 12 months was manifestly excessive. However, the disqualification would be reduced from four years to two.

R. v. NEAVEN (DAVID JOHN) [2000] 1 Cr. App. R. (S.) 391, Swinton Thomas, L.J., CA (Crim Div).

1200. Delay – period between original sentence and Attorney General's Reference – right to hearing within reasonable time

See HUMAN RIGHTS: Howarth v. United Kingdom. §3216

1201. Drink driving offences – disqualification – additional penalty points

[Road Traffic Act 1972 s.101; Transport Act 1981 s.19; Road Traffic Offenders Act 1988 s.44 (1).]

M was convicted of a drink driving offence, for which he was subject to an obligatory disqualification from driving for two years. He was also convicted of the offence of driving without insurance, which had been committed on the same occasion and for which his licence was endorsed with eight penalty points. M appealed by way of case stated against the addition of the penalty points.

Held, allowing the appeal, that the drink driving offence was punishable by obligatory disqualification under the Road Traffic Offenders Act 1988 s.44(1), which consolidated the previous law relating to penalty points under the Transport Act 1981 s.19 and the Road Traffic Act 1972 s.101. Both these measures provided that a period of disqualification was to be determined by taking account of all the circumstances of the case where more than one offence had been committed. The presumption pertaining to consolidating legislation applied so that s.44(1) of the 1988 Act did not change the meaning of s.101(1) of the 1972 Act, in the absence of a clear indication that Parliament intended it to do so, *Ahmed (Baria) v. McLeod* 1998 J.C. 242, [1998] C.L.Y. 5695 followed. The penalty points would therefore be removed from M's licence.

MARTIN v. DPP; *sub nom.* MARTIN v. CROWN PROSECUTION SERVICE [2000] 2 Cr. App. R. (S.) 18, Simon Brown L.J., QBD.

1202. Drink driving offences – disqualification – special reasons – incorrect information given at police station regarding automatic ban

[Road Traffic Act 1988 s.7(3), s.7(6); Road Traffic Offenders Act 1988 s.34(1).]

B failed a roadside breath test. At a police station, B offered to provide another breath specimen. Officer D informed him, in Officer G's hearing, that the breathalyser was not working properly, and G then requested a specimen of blood or urine pursuant to the Road Traffic Act 1988 s.7(3). B asked the officer if a refusal meant a definite disqualification and was told it did not. On the basis of that, he refused. The justices convicted B of failing to provide a specimen of blood, contrary to the Road Traffic Act 1988 s.7(6), fined and disqualified him for 18 months. The Crown Court upheld the conviction holding that there were no matters capable of amounting to special reasons within the meaning of the Road Traffic Offenders Act 1988 s.34(1), but reduced the sentence to the statutory minimum of 12 months. B appealed against conviction and sentence.

Held, dismissing the appeal against conviction but allowing that against sentence and remitting the matter of sentence for further consideration by the Crown Court, that (1) s.7(3) of the 1988 Act required only that the requesting officer had cause to believe that there was no reliable device available and that the driver be informed, it was therefore not required that the requesting officer be the person who informed the driver, and (2) given that the Crown Court had found that B's decision had been affected by the inaccurate information, that was capable of amounting to a special reason within s.34(1) as a matter of law.

BOBIN v. DPP [1999] R.T.R. 375, Brian Smedley, J., QBD.

1203. Drink driving offences – disqualification – special reasons for not imposing ban – intention of offender

The Crown appealed by way of case stated against the justices' decision that there were special reasons not to ban H from driving following his arrest while attempting to drive a car under the influence of alcohol. H admitted that he had intended to steal and drive the car that he was found in, but that the fact that he had not succeeded in starting the engine, and had only travelled two car lengths as the result of the car being pushed by a friend, amounted to a special reason not to disqualify him. The Crown contended that the justices should have focused on H's intention to drive, as opposed to what H had actually achieved.

Held, allowing the appeal, that the justices should have considered what B intended to do, which by his own admission was to drive home while intoxicated, rather than what he had achieved. The guidelines given in *Chatters v. Burke* [1986] 1 W.L.R. 1321, [1998] C.L.Y. 2914 were considered, but it was noted that, although they recognised that special reasons could exist for not imposing a ban, they did not stipulate when that conclusion was to be reached in any given case.

CROWN PROSECUTION SERVICE v. HUMPHRIES; *sub nom*. DPP v. HUMPHRIES [2000] 2 Cr. App. R. (S.) 1, Tuckey, L.J., QBD.

1204. Drink driving offences – disqualification – special reasons not to disqualify

[Road Traffic Offenders Act 1988 s.34.]

O challenged the dismissal of his appeal against sentence. O was convicted by a magistrates' court of driving with excess alcohol. O was seen by a police officer manoeuvring a car in the car park of a public house. O was asked to take a breath test, and was found to have 103 milligrams of alcohol per 100 millilitres of breath. The applicant lived a few minutes' walk from the public house, and said that he was not going to drive out of the car park, but was simply attempting to move his car a few yards to clear the access to the car park. Sentenced to a fine of £750, with £120 costs, and disqualified from driving for 20 months, subject to a reduction of five months on the successful completion of a drink driving course. The magistrates' court found that special reasons existed within the meaning of the Road Traffic Offenders Act 1988 s.34 but exercised their discretion to disqualify in any event.

Held, allowing the application, it was unusual for a court to find that special reasons existed for not disqualifying, and then to impose a period of disqualification longer than the mandatory minimum of 12 months. It could not be said that such an approach would never be appropriate. Where special reasons were found to exist, and where it was not suggested that the actual driving undertaken or contemplated could have posed any appreciable risk of danger to anyone it would be hard to justify a period of disqualification in excess of the mandatory 12 months. The magistrates' court and the Crown Court paid more attention to the guidelines suggested by the Magistrates' Association than these particular facts warranted. The guidelines were of little assistance in cases where special reasons had been found to exist. The court would substitute a period of 12 months disqualification for the 20 months imposed by the magistrates' court.

R. v. ST ALBANS CROWN COURT, *ex p*. O'DONOVAN (WILLIAM JOSEPH) [2000] 1 Cr. App. R. (S.) 344, Simon Brown, L.J., QBD.

1205. Drug offences – pleas – cultivation of cannabis for personal use

E appealed against a sentence of 12 months' imprisonment having pleaded guilty to cultivating cannabis. Police officers searching his house found a room which had been converted for the growth of cannabis plants by the hydroponic system. Twenty one plants in various stages of growth were found, together with harvested leaves and equipment designed to promote plant growth. E pleaded guilty on the basis that the cannabis was intended for his personal consumption only.

Held, allowing the appeal, that the sentence was manifestly excessive and a sentence of nine months was substituted, *R. v. Bennett (John)* [1998] 1 Cr. App. R. (S.) 429, [1998] C.L.Y. 1193 and *R. v. Marsland (Anthony John)* (1994) 15 Cr. App. R. (S.) 665, [1995] C.L.Y. 1359 considered.

R. v. EVANS (ROGER PAUL) [2000] 1 Cr. App. R. (S.) 107, Scott Baker, J., CA (Crim Div).

1206. Drug offences – supply of drugs – cannabis – conspiring to supply on a large scale

C and others pleaded guilty to conspiring to supply class B drugs. Over a period of about 15 months they were concerned in importing large quantities of cannabis or amphetamine. Sentenced to 11 years' imprisonment in the case of C, with lesser sentences on the other appellants.

Held, allowing the appeals, that it was submitted that a sentence of 11 years on a plea of guilty was too long, given that the maximum sentence for the offence was 14 years' imprisonment. It was conceded that the quantities of drugs involved were rightly described as "massive" and that the case was properly placed in the top bracket, *R. v. Aramah (John Uzu)* (1983) 76 Cr. App. R. 190, [1983] C.L.Y. 764.19 and *R. v. Ronchetti (Jonathan)* [1998] 2 Cr. App. R. (S.) 100, [1998] C.L.Y. 1183 considered. It was argued that room should be left for even larger quantities which were found from time to time in other conspiracies. The court was prepared to recognise some limited force in these submissions. To justify the sentence of 11 years on a plea of guilty, the judge's starting point had to be almost at the maximum sentence. That was to pitch the gravity of the case somewhat too high. It was, however, a most serious and persistent offence and C's sentence would be reduced by one year. The sentences on the other appellants would be varied accordingly.

R. v. CHISHOLM (JOHN); R. v. FLYNN (MICHAEL PATRICK); R. v. WATERS (CARL); R. v. KILTY (STEPHEN); R. v. WRIGHT (FREDERICK MARTIN); R. v. TOBIN (ALAN) [1999] 2 Cr. App. R. (S.) 443, Simon Brown, L.J., CA (Crim Div).

1207. Drug offences – supply of drugs – Class A and B drug – social supply

B appealed against a sentence of a total of nine months' imprisonment having pleaded guilty to possessing a Class A substance, ecstasy, and a Class B substance, amphetamines, in each case with intent to supply. B was found at a nightclub in possession of 14 ecstasy tablets and four amphetamine tablets. B admitted that he intended to share the tablets with two friends.

Held, allowing the appeal, that even if the case were analogous to a case of simple possession, it did not follow that a custodial sentence was inappropriate. Possession on behalf of others was more serious than possession on behalf of oneself, and possession with a view to getting a much used drug into a night club might be more serious than possession in other circumstances. The sentencer was right to conclude that a custodial sentence was appropriate, but the sentence could be reduced to six months *R. v. Denslow (Paul)* [1998] Crim. L.R. 566, *R. v. Aramah (John Uzu)* (1983) 76 Cr. App. R. 190, [1983] C.L.Y. 764.19 and *R. v. Ollerenshaw (Paul Michael)* [1999] 1 Cr. App. R. (S.) 65, [1998] C.L.Y. 1169 considered.

R. v. BUSBY (NICKY MARK) [2000] 1 Cr. App. R. (S.) 279, Hughes, J., CA (Crim Div).

1208. Drug offences – supply of drugs – Class A drugs – social supply

R appealed against a sentence of 18 months' imprisonment, having pleaded guilty to possessing a Class A drug, ecstasy, with intent to supply. R was driving a car which was stopped by police officers as a result of the manner in which R was driving. Drugs were found in R's car and two passengers were arrested. R's address was searched and a box containing 28 ecstasy tablets was found. The tablets were divided into wraps of six, five and three tablets. R admitted that he intended to supply the tablets to five persons, but claimed that he was not involved in commercial supply beyond recouping the money that he had spent in obtaining the tablets. He appealed contending that the sentence was excessive in view of his intention to supply the drug on a small scale to friends and not for commercial profit.

Held, allowing the appeal, that was argued that a sentence of 18 months' imprisonment was excessive in view of the appellant's intention to supply ecstasy on a small scale to friends and not for commercial profit. The court would not wish to give the impression that offences involving the supply or intended supply of ecstasy were not of the utmost gravity, but the Court felt constrained by the authorities to reduce the sentence to 12 months' imprisonment *R. v. Byrne (Thomas Ross)* [1996] 2 Cr. App. R. (S.) 34, [1996] C.L.Y. 1849 and *R. v. Wakeman (Paul)* [1999] 1 Cr. App. R. (S.) 222, [1999] C.L.Y. 1144 considered.

R. v. ROBERTSON (TIMOTHY) [2000] 1 Cr. App. R. (S.) 514, Scott Baker, J., CA (Crim Div).

1209. **Drug offences – supply of drugs – Class A drugs – social supply**

S appealed against a sentence of four years and six months' imprisonment having pleaded guilty to possessing heroin with intent to supply. Police officers saw S approach a woman and exchange something with her. When the officers approached, S cycled off and then ran away after discarding his bicycle. He was seen to discard a package which was found to contain 1.82 grams of heroin of unknown purity. S pleaded guilty on the basis that he had agreed to buy a small quantity of heroin on behalf of a group of friends for their own use. The plea was not set out in writing.

Held, allowing the appeal, that if a plea was offered on a particular basis, and the material available to the Crown indicated that that basis might well be true, the Crown ought to accept that basis. If the Crown took the view that the evidence of circumstances were such that the Crown could not support any suggestion that the version put forward by the defence was wrong, the Crown should make that clear. If the Crown felt unable to go that far, it should leave the defence to put forward its version and leave the sentencer to decide whether to accept it or to enquire further, by way of a Newton hearing or other wise. The Crown should not indicate that it could not dispute the defendant's version, and then introduce material which tended to contradict it. The Court was bound to consider the sentence on the basis of the version of the facts put forward by the defendant. The question arose, on that basis, as to whether the sentence was manifestly excessive. The Court had been referred to *R. v. Spinks (Gary)* (1987) 9 Cr. App. R. (S.) 297, [1989] C.L.Y. 1032 and *R. v. Denslow (Paul)* [1998] Crim. L.R. 566. In this case, the consumers were not present when the purchase was made. A custodial sentence was inevitable but the sentence imposed was longer than was necessary. A sentence of two years was substituted *R. v. Tolera (Nathan)* [1999] 1 Cr. App. R. 29, [1998] C.L.Y. 1331 considered.

R. v. SMYTHE (SCOTT LEE) [2000] 1 Cr. App. R. (S.) 547, Judge Mellor, CA (Crim Div).

1210. **Drug offences – supply of drugs – Class B drugs – judicial error**

[Misuse of Drugs Act 1971 s.4(3)(d); Customs and Excise Management Act 1979 s.170(2).]

B appealed against a sentence of a total of 42 months' imprisonment with a confiscation order in the amount of £699 having been convicted of possessing a Class B drug with intent to supply, and of being concerned in the supply of a Class B drug. B was tried jointly with his sister who was convicted on six counts of assisting another to retain the proceeds of drug trafficking. On an afternoon in December 1996 police officers stopped B while he was driving his car, and found five small bags containing cannabis in his possession. A search of his home resulted in the discovery of scales, self sealing bags and building society account books showing that £43,000 had been deposited in the accounts between 1994 and 1996. B admitted buying cannabis, but denied supplying or intending to supply cannabis. He denied knowledge of the scales and plastic bags and cash found in a house. The sentencer passed sentence on the basis that a compendious or global count was justified and lawful; the offence of which the accused was convicted was an activity offence; although the jury convicted on the basis that the appellant was involved on one occasion only, a sentencer was entitled, when assessing the appropriate penalty, to look at the wider picture as was manifestly the case; the offence of which the accused was convicted covered a continuous course over a period of 33 months and involved profits of £25,000, *R. v. Martin (Ellis Anthony)* [1998] 2 Cr. App. R. 385, [1998] C.L.Y. 1021 cited.

Held, allowing the appeal, that the important question whether the offence under the Misuse of Drugs Act 1971 s.4(3)(d) was an "activity" offence by analogy with Customs and Excise Management Act 1979 s.170(2). That point would have to be decided at some stage, but need not be decided in the present case. The sentencer accepted that the jury had convicted on the basis of one occasion only, but had considered that he had the right to look at the wider picture. Whether he had such a right had to be considered in the light of recent decisions of the court, dealing with circumstances where sentences had been passed in relation to activity that had neither been indicated or admitted *R. v. Doyle (Julie Marie)* [1998] 1 Cr. App. R. (S.) 79, [1998] C.L.Y. 1186 and *R. v. Evans (Cheryl Eleanor)* [2000] 1 Cr. App. R. (S.) 144 considered. It was clear on the basis of those decisions that the sentencer was bound to sentence for that which had been established in front of and by the jury and that was a single offence. The facts of the case were simple. What was established by the convictions on the two counts on which B was convicted was the possession of five sealed bags of cannabis on a particular date, and an involvement in the supply of cannabis on one occasions during the period covered by the indictment. The sentencer fell into error in proceeding to sentence the appellant on a much wider basis. It was not open to the sentencer to sentence B other than as a person who had supplied or been concerned in the supply of drugs on one occasions and had possession of a further modest quantity of the same drug on the day of his arrest. In those circumstances, sentences totalling 42 months were manifestly excessive. The court would reduce the sentences to a total of 18 months. The court pointed out that the difficulties which arose in the case would have been avoided if the prosecution had drafted six substantive counts which reflected the six counts laid against his sister.

R. v. BROWN (ALVA LORENZO) [2000] 1 Cr. App. R. (S.) 300, Maurice Kay, J., CA (Crim Div).

1211. Drug offences – supply of drugs – criteria for purity analysis

M, convicted of possession with intent to supply quantities of heroin, cocaine and ecstasy, appealed against a sentence of five years' imprisonment. At trial M had contended that the drugs were for his own personal use, representing about one month's supply. He appealed against the sentence on the basis that the judge had not been entitled to impose a sentence of such duration without ordering a purity analysis of the drugs.

Held, dismissing the appeal, that a purity analysis would only be essential for sentencing purposes in cases where the weight of the drugs exceeded 500g, such as importation cases or where the prosecution had reason to believe that the defendant was acting as a wholesaler rather than a retailer. In such circumstances, the purity of the drugs would be a good indicator as to the defendant's proximity to the source of supply and the court might wish to proceed on a more serious basis. The amount of drugs involved in the offence, as determined by weight at 100 per cent purity, was an important but not a determinative factor in sentencing and the judge should have regard to all the other circumstances of the case. Amount was not to be assessed on the street value of the drugs although this might be a useful cross reference, *R. v. Aramah (John Uzu)* (1983) 76 Cr. App. R. 190, [1983] C.L.Y. 764.19 and *R. v. Aranguren (Jose de Jesus)* (1994) 99 Cr. App. R. 347, [1995] C.L.Y. 1364 considered. Although weight depended on purity, which could only be accurately ascertained by analysis, generally such analysis would not be necessary, particularly in view of the delay it would cause and the cost involved in cases where there was a small quantity of drugs indicating personal use or limited supply to others, *Attorney General's Reference (No.13 of 1995), Re* [1996] 1 Cr. App. R. (S.) 120, [1996] C.L.Y. 1766 and *R. v. McPhail (Daniel)* [1997] 1 Cr. App. R. (S.) 321, [1996] C.L.Y. 1858 considered. Assumptions on purity could be made in the case of ecstasy and LSD in certain circumstances.

Guidance issued by the Crown Prosecution to prosecutors did not accurately reflect the law in this regard.

R. v. MORRIS (HAROLD LINDEN) [2001] 1 Cr. App. R. 4, Rose, L.J., CA (Crim Div).

1212. Drug offences – supply of drugs – cultivation of cannabis – social supply

D appealed against a sentence of 12 months' imprisonment having indicated his intention before a magistrates' court to plead guilty to possession of a Class B drug, cannabis, with intent to supply, and to producing cannabis. He was committed to the Crown Court for sentence. Police officers executing a search warrant at D's premises found a number of cannabis plants growing in the bedroom and in a garage. It was estimated that the plants would have yielded about 400 g of cannabis. D admitted that he had grown the cannabis with a view to sale to his friends who were already users.

Held, dismissing the appeal, that the sentencer observed that the growing of cannabis had been planned, premeditated and professional, with considerable effort being devoted to ensure that the plants had optimum growing conditions. Previous decisions suggested that people who grew cannabis could be divided into four different categories: those who grew cannabis for their own use; those who grew cannabis for their own use and for the use of their friends at no charge; those who grew cannabis to supply to friends for money, and those who grew cannabis in massive quantities for supply to all and sundry. This case came into the third category of commercial supply to friends in which a sentence of two years was reduced to 12 months, on the basis that D had grown cannabis for non commercial supply. The sentence of 21 months in the present case could not be considered manifestly excessive, *R. v. Blackham (Brian Francis)* [1997] 2 Cr. App. R. (S.) 275, [1997] C.L.Y. 1505 considered.

R. v. DIBDEN (LAWRENCE) [2000] 1 Cr. App. R. (S.) 64, Judge Allen, CA (Crim Div).

1213. Drug offences – supply of drugs – fatal effect on victim

A appealed against a sentence of three years' imprisonment having pleaded guilty before a magistrates' court to supplying heroin and was committed to the Crown Court for sentence. A was living in a bail hostel under the terms of a probation order. He had started to prepare an injection of heroin for his own use, when another resident of the hostel came in and asked for some of the heroin. Eventually A offered some of the heroin to the other man. The other man injected himself with heroin and collapsed. He died during the night. It was discovered that the deceased had a substantial quantity of alcohol in his blood and the cause of death was asphyxia owing to the swallowing of vomit caused by alcohol and heroin poisoning. It was accepted that the heroin was not causative of death.

Held, allowing the appeal, that the sentence was manifestly excessive and a sentence of two years' imprisonment would be substituted, *R. v. Clarke (Anthony John)* (1992) 13 Cr. App. R. (S.) 552, [1993] C.L.Y. 1223, *R. v. Lucas (Andrew)* [1999] 1 Cr. App. R. (S.) 78, [1999] C.L.Y. 1146 considered.

R. v. ASHFORD (DAVID LEONARD) [2000] 1 Cr. App. R. (S.) 389, Owen, J., CA (Crim Div).

1214. Drug offences – supply of drugs – fatal effect on victim

B appealed against a sentence of 18 months' imprisonment have pleaded guilty before a magistrates court to supplying a Class A drug, ecstasy. B gave two ecstasy tablets to a friend. The friend died after apparently consuming one of the tablets. His medical history indicated that he suffered from a heart abnormality which might have predisposed him to a sudden death due to a heart rhythm disturbance, and that the ingestion of ecstasy contributed to the heart failure from which he died.

Held, allowing the appeal, that the case illustrated the dangers to young people of taking ecstasy. Those who contributed to its availability, even at the lowest end of the chain, must be appropriately punished. Supply of the drug to another, even where the supply was between friends without financial return, was necessarily a more serious offence than possession of the same quantity of the drug for personal consumption. In determining the appropriate sentence for B however, it was important to concentrate on his actions. He should not receive a disproportionate sentence because of the tragic and appalling consequences. B gave two ecstasy tablets to a friend at no profit to himself. There was no evidence that he was a dealer even at the lowest level. The Court had been referred to a number of reported decisions in relation to the supply of relatively small quantities or ecstasy in similar circumstances. Having regard to those decisions, the sentence of 18 months' imprisonment was out of line and manifestly excessive. The court would substitute a sentence of nine months' imprisonment.

R. v. BULL (JAMIE) [2000] 2 Cr. App. R. (S.) 195, Holman, J., CA (Crim Div).

1215. Drug offences – supply of drugs – Newton hearings – reliance on adverse witness statement

G appealed against a sentence of three years' imprisonment having pleaded guilty to being in possession of a Class A controlled drug, ecstasy, with intent to supply. G was seen in a club to put a handful of tablets into his mouth. Security staff retrieved 19 tablets from his mouth and called police. A search of the appellant revealed a further quantity of tablets concealed in his clothing, amounting to 25 in all. G stated that he had gone to the club with his girlfriend and another friend, and that they had bought the ecstasy tablets between them, each contributing towards the purchase of 20 tablets. G claimed that it was his intention to share the tablets with friends who were with him at the nightclub. The sentencer declined to pass sentence on that basis and a Newton hearing was conducted. The prosecution did not call any further evidence, but the defendant gave evidence. The judge stated that after hearing the evidence he was satisfied that the defendant had taken the ecstasy tablets to the club to sell the tablets for commercial gain. In the course of passing sentence, the sentencer referred to a witness statement in which the witness stated that he had seen the defendant selling drugs in the club. The witness who made the statement was not called in the Newton hearing and no reference to his statement was made by the judge in the course of the hearing. It was submitted for G that the fact that the judge made explicit reference to the contents of the witness statement only five minutes after the conclusion of the Newton hearing justified the conclusion that the judge must have had the contents and effect of the statement in mind in reaching conclusions adverse to G at the Newton hearing. The Court accepted that submission.

Held, allowing the appeal, that the sentencer fell into significant error in placing reliance on the contents of the witness statement in the absence of the maker of the statement and proper of opportunity to test his evidence. The consequence was that the Court was constrained to sentence on the basis originally advanced by G and not on the basis of the sentencer's conclusion at the end of the Newton hearing. On that basis the sentence was too long and a sentence of two years' imprisonment would be substituted. *R. v. Ahmed (Nabil)* (1985) 80 Cr. App. R. 295, [1985] C.L.Y. 828, *R. v. Spalding (Phillip Peter)* (1995) 16 Cr. App. R. (S.) 803, [1996] C.L.Y. 1856, and *R. v. Byrne (Thomas Ross)* [1996] 2 Cr. App. R. (S.) 34, [1996] C.L.Y. 1849 considered.

R. v. GASS (ANTHONY) [2000] 1 Cr. App. R. (S.) 475, Ognall, J., CA (Crim Div).

1216. Drug offences – supply of drugs – opium – sentencing policy

M appealed against a sentence of 14 years' imprisonment imposed after pleading guilty to the offence of possessing opium, a Class A drug, with intent to supply. M argued that as the street value of opium was considerably lower than that of other Class A drugs, such as heroin and cocaine, a lesser sentence should be imposed. Further, opium was not commonly sold on the streets, it was generally imported for personal use and there was no evidence to suggest that its use was likely to increase. As offences concerning opium were rare, the matter was referred to the Sentencing Advisory Panel.

Held, allowing the appeal and substituting a sentence of nine years' imprisonment, that the fact that the street value of opium was considerably less than that of other Class A drugs should be taken into account at the sentencing stage. As suggested by the Panel, the determining factor should be the weight of the drug, with a sentence of 14 years and upwards being appropriate for opium weighing 40 kg or more at 100 per cent purity and sentence of 10 years or more for opium weighing four kilos or more. In some cases the equivalent in street value of other Class A drugs could be used a cross check. Nevertheless, using the equivalent value of other drugs should be treated with caution and should be disregarded where it would be likely to produce an unacceptably high or low sentence. The normal yardstick for determining sentence should, therefore, be the weight of the drug. However, a different method of calculating sentence would be appropriate where there is evidence to suggest that the opium is being imported for conversion into heroin or morphine. In such a case, the sentence should be based on the amount of heroin or morphine that can be produced from the opium. In the case of heroin or cocaine, it was normal to assess the relative purity of the substances, so that any sentence can be based on the amount of the illicit product seized and not on any lawful additives. However, in the case of opium, even when it was treated for use for non-medical purposes, it remained essentially a natural derivative of the opium plant. Opium should therefore be assumed to be 100 per cent pure, though it should be open to defendants to introduce evidence to show that it was less than pure.

R. v. MASHAOLLAHI (BEHROOZ); *sub nom*. R. v. MASHAOLLI [2001] 1 Cr. App. R. 6, Rougier, J., CA (Crim Div).

1217. Drug offences – supply of drugs – paracetamol sold as cocaine

[Criminal Justice Act 1991 s.40.]

P appealed against a sentence of 18 months' imprisonment, together with an order under the Criminal Justice Act 1991 s.40 to serve 224 days of an earlier sentence for robbery, having pleaded guilty to offering to supply a class A controlled drug, cocaine. P was seen at a place where police officers were maintaining a surveillance operation with a view to observing drug deals. P approached an undercover policewoman and asked her what she wanted; the policewoman indicated that she wanted crack cocaine. P gave her a cling film wrap containing a white substance and accepted £20 from her. Analysis of the substance showed that it contained crushed paracetamol which was not a controlled drug. P said that he deliberately sold paracetamol, knowing what it was, to "rip the buyer off".

Held, allowing the appeal, that it was arguable that P's criminality was more akin to obtaining by deception than to drug dealing, and that the sentencer did not sufficiently take into account that P supplied paracetamol and knew that that was what he was supplying. In the court's view, it was important that the sentence should reflect the fact that what P sold and supplied was a non controlled and relatively harmless substance. The sentencer did not make clear whether the order under s.40 should be served before or concurrently with the later sentence. The court would make it clear that that term must be served in advance of the sentence for the later offence, but the period would be reduced to six months.

R. v. PRINCE (CARLTON) [1999] 2 Cr. App. R. (S.) 419, Holman, J., CA (Crim Div).

1218. Drug offences – supply of drugs – possession of cannabis in role as courier

F, convicted of possessing a Class B drug, cannabis resin, with intent to supply, appealed against a sentence of seven years' imprisonment. F was stopped while driving his car, and a search disclosed 48 kg of cannabis resin concealed under the rear seat. He was sentenced on the basis that he had acted as a courier for substantial payment in a professional operation. F had two previous convictions for offences involving the supply or exportation of cannabis, one of them abroad.

Held, allowing the appeal, that despite the seriousness of the case, the sentence of seven years' imprisonment was too long and a sentence of five years was substituted, *R. v. Aramah (John Uzu)* (1983) 76 Cr. App. R. 190, [1983] C.L.Y. 764.19, *R. v. Ronchetti (Jonathan)* [1998] 2 Cr. App. R. (S.) 100, [1998] C.L.Y. 1183 and *R. v. Netts (Alan Frank)* [1997] 2 Cr. App. R. (S.) 117, [1997] C.L.Y. 1510 considered.

R. v. FREEDER (DAVID) [2000] 1 Cr. App. R. (S.) 25, Penry-Davey, J., CA (Crim Div).

1219. Drug offences – supply of drugs – possession of drugs for personal consumption

G appealed against sentences totalling five years' imprisonment having pleaded guilty to possession of heroin with intent to supply and to other counts charging possession of cannabis, producing cannabis and possession of methadone, temazepam and ecstasy. Police officers searching the G's home found 120.9 grams of heroin, and small quantities of cannabis, methadone, temazepam and ecstasy. G said that all the drugs were for his personal use. He had bought the heroin cheaply as he had a long standing habit; he did not supply drugs to the public, but would have supplied the heroin to his girlfriend and other drug taking friends in order to obtain monies to feed his habit.

Held, dismissing the appeal, that a substantial custodial sentence was necessary, and the sentence was not manifestly excessive.

R. v. GIUNTA (SANTO) [2000] 1 Cr. App. R. (S.) 365, Owen, J, CA (Crim Div).

1220. Drug offences – supply of drugs – prison visitors – appropriateness of imposing disproportionate sentence

B was sentenced in 1995 to life imprisonment for murder. In 1998 a woman visiting him in prison was found to be in possession of a package containing 13.6 g of heroin at 48 per cent purity. A search of the woman's home resulted in the discovery of a quantity of amphetamine and a large amount of correspondence with B, in which he asked her to supply him with heroin because he was in debt and needed heroin to pay off his debts. B told the woman how the drugs were to be packaged. B was sentenced to 12 years' imprisonment, and appealed.

Held, allowing the appeal, that the sentence had been imposed on a wrong basis, and that a proportionate sentence should have been imposed. The sentence would be reduced to six years, to run concurrently with the sentence of life imprisonment.

R. v. BLACK (CRAIG ADAM) [2000] 2 Cr. App. R. (S.) 41, Ebsworth, J., CA (Crim Div).

1221. Drug offences – supply of drugs – prison visitors – attempt to smuggle heroin into prison for use by prisoner – mitigating factors not exceptional

H appealed against a sentence of two years' imprisonment having pleaded guilty to possession of heroin with intent to supply. H visited a prison to see a prisoner who was an associate of her former husband. H was observed by a prison officer to remove something from her blouse and put it in her mouth; when challenged she surrendered a knotted condom containing 6.02 g of heroin.

Held, dismissing the appeal, that H was 32 years old and of good character; she was the sole carer for three children aged between nine and 15, one of whom had disabilities leading to behavioural problems. H had committed the offence at the suggestion of her ex husband. The court acknowledged that there were mitigating features about the case, but such mitigating features were frequently found in such cases. There were no exceptional circumstances which would justify suspension of the sentence. The sentence was not excessive or wrong in principle, *R. v. Prince (James Peter)* [1996] 1 Cr. App. R. (S.) 335, [1996] C.L.Y.1853 considered.

R. v. HAMILTON (LINDA KELLY) [2000] 1 Cr. App. R. (S.) 91, Hidden, J., CA (Crim Div).

1222. Drug offences – supply of drugs – prison visitors – Class A drugs

C appealed against a sentence of four years' imprisonment having pleaded guilty to possessing a Class A drug, cocaine, with intent to supply. C went to visit her boyfriend who was serving a sentence of imprisonment. She was found in possession of a wrap containing half a gram of cocaine of 96 per cent purity, concealed in her mouth.

Held, dismissing the appeal, that the taking of drugs into prison was a common occurrence which caused havoc within the prison system. There could be no criticism of the sentence.

R. v. COWAP (TRACEY) [2000] 1 Cr. App. R. (S.) 284, Brian Smedley, J., CA (Crim Div).

1223. Drug offences – supply of drugs – prison visitors – smuggling drugs into prison

Y appealed against a sentence of a total of two and a half years' imprisonment having pleaded guilty to possessing a Class A drug, heroin, with intent to supply, and possessing a Class B drug, cannabis, with intent to supply. Y went to a prison to visit a prisoner. When she was told that she would be searched for drugs, she handed over two balloons. One contained 10.7 grams of heroin, and the other 25.9 grams of cannabis.

Held, dismissing the appeal, that her boyfriend, who was serving a life sentence at the prison, had asked her to bring a quantity of cannabis into the prison in return for a payment of £75. She had been given the two balloons by a man she met outside the prison, and did not know that one contained heroin. The court had observed frequently in recent cases that the offence of smuggling drugs into prison was one of extreme gravity which had become more and more prevalent. If Y had known that she was taking heroin into prison, she could have expected a sentence of five years. The sentence of two and half years was entirely correct, *R. v. Bilinski (Edward)* (1988) 86 Cr. App. R. 146, [1988] C.L.Y. 930, *R. v. Savage (Jefferson Scott)* (1993) 14 Cr. App. R. (S.) 409, [1994] C.L.Y. 1250 and *R. v. Batt (Jeanne)* [1999] 2 Cr. App. R. (S.) 223, [1999] C.L.Y. 1141 considered.

R. v. YOUNG (SUSAN) [2000] 2 Cr. App. R. (S.) 248, Judge Martin Stephens Q.C., CA (Crim Div).

1224. Drug offences – supply of drugs – supplying cannabis resin to pupils at school

K was convicted of three charges of supplying cannabis resin and two charges of supplying herbal cannabis. K was employed as a cleaner at a school. On five separate occasions he supplied pupils at school, who were aged between 15 and 17, with small quantities of the herbal cannabis or cannabis resin. K was sentenced to a total of two years' imprisonment and appealed.

Held, allowing the appeal, that these were very serious offences which merited immediate custodial sentences. However, the case did not involve a breach of trust. K was a school cleaner who was not in any relationship of trust with the boys. The correct sentence would have been 18 months' imprisonment, *R. v. Nolan (Leroy)* (1992) 13 Cr. App. R. (S.) 144, [1993] C.L.Y. 1138 considered.

R. v. KITCHING (STEVEN) [2000] 2 Cr. App. R. (S.) 194, Dyson, J., CA (Crim Div).

1225. **Drug offences – supply of drugs – supplying Class A drugs to regular customers**

W appealed against a sentence of six and a half years' imprisonment, and X, Y and Z appealed against sentences of six years, five years and three years respectively. W, Y and Z having pleaded guilty to conspiring to supply Class A drugs, cocaine and heroin. Police officers carried out observations of the first appellant's address and noted visits by large numbers of people, most of them lasting a very short period of time. A police undercover officer made a number of test purchases inside the house, buying heroin from W and observing him making a sale of cocaine to another person. The officer bought heroin from each of other codefendants. A search of the address revealed packages of heroin and cocaine. W pleaded guilty on the basis that he had started to sell drugs to pay off debt and had supplied drugs to a limited number of regular customers.

Held, allowing the appeal, that W had pleaded guilty on a particular basis. The sentencer decided not to hear evidence about the factual matters which were in issue between the Crown and the defence in relation to the basis of the plea. In the court's judgment, the sentencer was obliged to sentence on the basis of the plea submitted by the codefendants. In those circumstances the sentences were too long. The sentence on W was reduced to six and a half years' imprisonment on each count concurrent. The sentences on X, Y and Z were reduced proportionately, *R. v. Tolera (Nathan)* [1999] 1 Cr. App. R. 29, [1998] C.L.Y. 1331 and *R. v. Djahit (Turkesh)* [1999] 2 Cr. App. R. (S.) 142, [1999] C.L.Y. 1137 considered.

R. v. WILLIAMS (DEREK ANTHONY); R. v. DRYDEN (SANDRA LEE); R. v. JAMES (MARTIN SYLVESTER) [2000] 2 Cr. App. R. (S.) 308, Penry-Davey, J., CA (Crim Div).

1226. **Drug offences – supply of drugs – supplying cocaine to undercover police officer**

Z appealed against a sentence of four years and six months' imprisonment having pleaded guilty to possession of crack cocaine, possession of crack cocaine with intent to supply and failing to surrender to bail. Z was approached by a police officer and asked the police officer what he wanted. The officer said "rocks" and Z spat two rocks of crack cocaine into his hand. Three rocks of cocaine were removed from his mouth, and a further amount of crack cocaine was produced from his sock. The total amount of cocaine amounted to 3.594 g at approximately 80 per cent purity.

Held, dismissing the appeal, that the court took the view that the sentence of four and a half years was at the upper limit of what would be described as the existing tariff but it was not satisfied that the sentence was manifestly excessive, *R. v. Edwards (Sean Karl)* (1992) 13 Cr. App. R. (S.) 356, [1993] C.L.Y. 1139, *R. v. Virgo (Devon)* [1996] 2 Cr. App. R. (S.) 443, [1997] C.L.Y. 1521 and *R. v. Howard (Barrington)* [1996] 2 Cr. App. R. (S.) 273, [1997] C.L.Y. 1520 considered.

R. v. IQBAL (ZAHIR) [2000] 2 Cr. App. R. (S.) 119, Newman, J., CA (Crim Div).

1227. **Drug offences – supply of drugs – supplying cocaine to undercover police officers**

D pleaded guilty to two counts of supplying a Class A controlled drug, cocaine, to possession of a quantity of cannabis resin and possession a quantity of ecstasy. Undercover police officers telephoned D and two meetings took place, at each of which D sold the officer £50 worth of cocaine. When D's address was searched, 37.7 grams of cannabis resin and eight ecstasy tablets were found. D appealed against a sentence of five and a half years' imprisonment concurrent on each count of supplying cocaine, with concurrent sentence for the other offences.

Held, allowing the appeal, that a sentence of four years' imprisonment was appropriate in this case and in line with sentencing decisions in cases of this class. A sentence of four years' imprisonment would be substituted, *R. v.*

Howard (Barrington) [1996] 2 Cr. App. R. (S.) 273, [1997] C.L.Y. 1520 considered.

R. v. DAY (MARIO) [2000] 2 Cr. App. R. (S.) 312, Judge Peter Crawford Q.C., CA (Crim Div).

1228. Drug offences – supply of drugs – supplying drugs to undercover police officers – persistent offender

[Crime (Sentences) Act 1997 s.3.]

H, convicted of two counts of supplying a Class A controlled drug, heroin, appealed against a sentence of seven years' imprisonment. H on two occasions supplied small quantities of heroin to undercover police officers who were engaged in an operation targeting drug dealers. H had various convictions for dishonesty and offences in relation to cannabis, and two previous convictions for possession of heroin with intent to supply in 1990 and 1994 respectively. H was sentenced to seven years' imprisonment. The sentence imposed was in accordance with the Crime (Sentences) Act 1997 s.3 which provided that where a person was convicted of a Class A drug trafficking offence committed at a time when he was over 18 and had been convicted of two other Class A drug trafficking offences on different occasions, the court was required to impose a custodial sentence of at least seven years, unless the court was of the opinion that there were circumstances which would make the prescribed custodial sentence unjust in all the circumstances. H appealed contending that the sentence was unjust and manifestly excessive.

Held, dismissing the appeal, that the sentencer observed that the conditions for the application of s.3 were fulfilled. The offences were very serious and H had shown himself to be a persistent offender. The offences were aggravated by H's record and the fact that he was on bail in connection with other drug offences at the time when the offences were committed. The sentencer rejected the submission that a sentence of seven years would be unjust in all the circumstances. The court had formed the view that it was impossible to conclude that the present sentence was manifestly excessive *R. v. Munson* (Unreported, November 23, 1998) considered. In any event, the court regarded that approach to the construction of the section as inappropriate. The purpose of the section was, in the absence of specific or particular circumstances which would render it unjust to do so, to oblige the court to impose the prescribed custodial sentence. Parliament had chosen a term of seven years as a standard penalty on a third drug trafficking conviction meeting the conditions in s.3(1). The object of the section plainly was to require courts to impose a sentence of at least seven years in circumstances, where but for the section, they would not or might not do so. If that were not the intention of the section, it was very difficult to see what the intention of the section was. In this case the sentencer had concluded that it was not unjust in all circumstances to impose the prescribed custodial sentence. It would be necessary to show that that was a wrong judgment before the court could interfere. In the court's view, it was a judgment which the sentencer was fully entitled to reach. It would be wrong to say what might on the facts of any given case amount to a circumstance which would make it unjust to impose the prescribed custodial sentence. That task must await a case in which the issue arose. H had a long record of criminal activity involving drug offences. The sentencer had reached a correct conclusion and there were no grounds for interfering with it.

R. v. HARVEY (WINSTON GEORGE) [2000] 1 Cr. App. R. (S.) 368, Lord Bingham of Cornhill, L.C.J., CA (Crim Div).

1229. Drug trafficking – conspiracy to import 88,000 ecstasy tablets

E and others appealed against sentences of 18 and 22 years' imprisonment respectively, having been convicted of conspiring to import a Class A drug, ecstasy. They were concerned in a scheme to import a total of 115,000 tablets of ecstasy at 75 per cent purity, equivalent to 88,000 tablets at 100 per cent purity. The importation did not take place as an accomplice was arrested in Belgium in possession of the tablets.

Held, allowing the appeal, that the Crown did not seek to distinguish between the roles played by E and the others, and they fell to be sentenced at the same level. The question was, what was the appropriate sentence for conspiring to import the equivalent of 88,000 tablets of pure ecstasy? The cases indicated that the bracket was between 14 and 20 years. This was a conspiracy which was not brought to fruition, and the court would substitute sentences of 16 years' imprisonment on both appellants. *R. v. Warren (John Barry)* [1996] 1 Cr. App. R. 120, [1996] C.L.Y. 1879, *R. v. Van Tattenhove (Frans Willem)* [1996] 1 Cr. App. R. 408 and *R. v. Main (Ronald Alan)* [1997] 2 Cr. App. R. (S.) 63, [1997] C.L.Y. 1502 considered.

R. v. ELLIS (PAUL EDWARD); R. v. AVIS (EDWARD) [2000] 1 Cr. App. R. (S.) 38, Garland, J., CA (Crim Div).

1230. Drug trafficking – conspiracy to import and supply drugs – unduly lenient sentence

The Attorney General asked the court to review the sentences of D and E on the ground that they were unduly lenient. D and E were convicted of conspiring to import a Class B drug, cannabis resin. D and E were concerned in a conspiracy to import and supply 400 kg of cannabis resin. Sentenced to seven years' imprisonment in the case of D, who was treated as principal in the conspiracy, and to less terms in the case of E who played lesser roles.

Held, allowing the reference in part, that the sentence on D was unduly lenient, and a sentence of nine years' imprisonment would be substituted. The sentences imposed on E were also lenient, but the court would not interfere with them.

ATTORNEY GENERAL'S REFERENCE (NOS.36, 37, 38, 39 OF 1999), *Re*; R. v. BRIGNULL (SEAN); R. v. HUNT (JAMES); R. v. NORRIS-COPSON (BRIAN); *sub nom.* R. v. DOUGHTY (BARRY MICHAEL) [2000] 2 Cr. App. R. (S.) 303, Kennedy, L.J., CA (Crim Div).

1231. Drug trafficking – exporting ecstasy tablets

P appealed against his sentence of 10 years' imprisonment having pleaded guilty to being knowingly concerned in the exportation of a Class A drug, ecstasy. P had sent a total of 9,245 ecstasy tablets in the post to a contact in the United States under an arrangement whereby he had received payment in dollar bills via a foreign exchange bureau.

Held, dismissing the appeal, that the exportation of controlled drugs was just as serious as the importation of such drugs. The arrangement that P had made in relation to receiving payment conveyed a level of professionalism. Furthermore, the offence had been committed within three months of his release from prison following a conviction for the exportation of amphetamines. Having regard to the guidelines set out in *R. v. Warren (John Barry)* [1996] 1 Cr. App. R. 120, [1996] C.L.Y. 1879, the appropriate sentence, taking into account the quantity of tablets involved, was in the order of 10 years. It followed that P's sentence was not manifestly excessive, *Warren* considered.

R. v. POWELL (MATTHEW TRISTAN) *The Times*, October 5, 2000, Rougier, J., CA (Crim Div).

1232. Drug trafficking – importation of cannabis

G appealed against a sentence of seven years' imprisonment having pleaded guilty to being knowingly concerned in the importation of a Class B drug, cannabis. G entered the UK in June 1998, driving a refrigerated lorry. He transferred a number of boxes from the lorry to his own car, and subsequently began to transfer the boxes to a car belonging to another man. At this time G was arrested, and the boxes were found to contain 141 kg of cannabis resin. G subsequently admitted that he had been asked to smuggle tobacco into the UK and had agreed to do so. He was to be paid £1,400 for each box, and had smuggled six boxes on an earlier occasion. G pleaded guilty on the basis that he knew that the later consignment had been drugs, but that he did not know that the earlier consignment had consisted of drugs.

Held, allowing the appeal, that the basis of G's plea was accepted by the prosecution and by the judge; G fell to be sentenced on the basis of the importation of 141 kg of cannabis resin. It seemed that a sentence of seven years' imprisonment on a plea of guilty for importation of 141 kg of cannabis resin was clearly excessive. The court would substitute a sentence of five and a half years' imprisonment, *R. v. Ronchetti (Jonathan)* [1998] 2 Cr. App. R. (S.) 100, [1998] C.L.Y. 1183 followed.

R. v. GOLDER (RICHARD ANTHONY) [2000] 1 Cr. App. R. (S.) 59, Keene, J., CA (Crim Div).

1233. Drug trafficking – importation of cocaine

D appealed against a sentence of two years' imprisonment having pleaded guilty to two counts of being knowingly concerned in the fraudulent evasion of the prohibition on the importation of cocaine. Customs officers intercepted two envelopes addressed to D, each of which was found to contain cocaine. One contained 21.5 grams at 26 per cent purity, equivalent to 5.59 grams at 100 per cent purity; the second contained 21.5 grams at 23 per cent purity, equivalent to 4.94 grams at 100 per cent purity. The cocaine was replaced with an innocuous substance and the envelopes were sealed and delivered. D claimed that the cocaine was intended exclusively for his personal use.

Held, dismissing the appeal, that D was entitled to discount in sentence if the sentencing court accepted that the importation was solely for the personal consumption of D. However, the larger the amount of the drugs the smaller would be the discount. This was because the larger the amount of the drugs the greater was the danger that the drugs might pass into the hands of others. In assessing that danger, the court should also take into account the purity and therefore the value of the drugs. In the present case the sentencer was right to conclude that the amount and purity of the drugs were so small that he could disregard the possibility that they would fall into other hands. This was a case towards the very bottom of the scale. It would be a rare case in which a sentence of less than two years' imprisonment would be imposed for the importation of Class A drugs, even where the amounts involved were small and the importation was solely for personal use. The sentence of two years could not be criticised, *R. v. Aramah (John Uzu)* (1983) 76 Cr. App. R. 190, [1983] C.L.Y. 764.19, *R. v. Singh (Satvir)* (1988) 10 Cr. App. R. (S.) 402, [1990] C.L.Y. 1290, *R. v. Aranguren (Jose de Jesus)* (1994) 99 Cr. App. R. 347, [1995] C.L.Y. 1364, *R. v. Keach (Walter Stacy)* (1984) 6 Cr. App. R. (S.) 402, [1985] C.L.Y. 803, *R. v. Dolgin* (1988) 10 Cr. App. R. (S.) 447, [1991] C.L.Y. 1094, *R. v. Meah (Brian)* (1991) 92 Cr. App. R. 254, [1991] C.L.Y. 1117, *R. v. McLean (Lancelot)* (1994) 15 Cr. App. R. (S.) 706, [1995] C.L.Y. 1361 considered.

R. v. DE BRITO (MAX DOMINGOS) [2000] 2 Cr. App. R. (S.) 255, Dyson, J., CA (Crim Div).

1234. Drug trafficking – jurisdiction – reduction in sentence length in accordance with statutory provisions

[Crime (Sentences) Act 1997 s.3.]

S, convicted of four offences of drug trafficking, appealed against concurrent terms of seven years' imprisonment which was the minimum sentence allowed for repeated Class A drug trafficking offences under the Crime (Sentences) Act 1997 s.3. S contended that s.3(2) enabled the court to pass a lower sentence where "particular circumstances" permitted.

Held, allowing the appeal, that the fact that S's last previous conviction had resulted in a probation order, together with other mitigating features, amounted to "particular circumstances" within the meaning of the Act. The sentence was therefore unjust and was accordingly reduced to concurrent terms of three years' imprisonment.

R. v. STENHOUSE (JAMES CAMERON) [2000] 2 Cr. App. R. (S.) 386, Henry, L.J., CA (Crim Div).

1235. **Drug trafficking – remand – time spent in custody**

[Criminal Justice Act 1967 s.67.]

R, who had pleaded guilty to being concerned in the importation of 19.3 kilograms of cannabis, appealed against a sentence of 42 months' imprisonment. R had been in custody on remand, but for two and half months of the time when he was in custody he was serving a sentence for other offences imposed by a magistrates' court. The sentence imposed by the magistrates' court was subsequently quashed on appeal, but the quashing of the sentence did not allow for the period during which R was in custody on remand, and at the same time serving the sentence imposed by the magistrates' court, to be treated as a relevant period for the purposes of the Criminal Justice Act 1967 s.67, and to be deducted from the sentence imposed by the Crown Court.

Held, allowing the appeal, that the Court would reduce the sentence of 42 months by five months, to 37 months.

R. v. ROBERTS (KARL ERIC) [2000] 1 Cr. App. R. (S.) 569, Jowitt, J., CA (Crim Div).

1236. **Employees – diseases and disorders – Legionnaires' Disease – responsibility of director**

[Health and Safety at Work etc. Act 1974 s.37.]

D pleaded guilty to neglecting his duty as a director, whereby a body corporate committed an offence under the Health and Safety at Work etc. Act 1974 s.37. D was a director of the company which made plastic cases. The manufacture of these cases involved the use of machinery which created a substantial amount of heat. The heat was cooled by water which was held in cooling towers. The operation of the water cooling towers gave rise to the danger of a bacteria of the virus which led to Legionnaires' Disease. The company employed a person who was responsible for health and safety. Over a period of time, the company or its predecessor was advised that the towers were infected with bacteria and that appropriate remedial measures should be taken. A contractor was engaged to carry out the appropriate treatment and issued certificates from time to time to the effect that the appropriate treatment had been carried out. An employee of the company contracted Legionnaires' Disease and died as a result. D appealed against a fine of £25,000 and an order to pay £10,000 prosecution costs. The company, which did not appeal, was fined a total of £30,000 and two contracting companies were each fined £15,000 and ordered to pay £15,000 prosecution costs.

Held, allowing the appeal in part, that D claimed that the fines imposed on himself and the company were excessive as the company and D relied on the contractors to deal with the potential problems in the cooling system. Neither the company nor its employees were experts in the relevant field; they had chosen a competent independent third party contractor and were let down by the contractors. In the court's view, the answer was that the purpose of health and safety legislation was to ensure, so far as possible, that employees worked in a healthy and safe place and atmosphere. The primary responsibility for ensuring their safety and their health remained with their employers, and it was not adequate for an employer to seek to transfer responsibility for all matters to an expert third party. It must be for the employers to supervise the independent contractor. The court could see no reason in principle why the employer should not face up to the fact that it must carry greater responsibility for the safety of the employees than those who were engaged on a part time basis to assist them in that regard. D had pleaded guilty on the basis that the only neglect on his part was his failure to ensure that the company employee responsible for health and safety issues had undergone a training course. On that basis, the company could be treated as responsible for the activities of D and other employees. The fine imposed on the appellant was excessive and would be reduced to £15,000. The order for payment of costs would not be disturbed.

R. v. DAVIES (CERI) [1999] 2 Cr. App. R. (S.) 356, David Steel, J., CA (Crim Div).

1237. False accounting – dishonesty – attempt to conceal thefts by falsifying documents

G appealed against a sentence of a total of 21 months' imprisonment, having pleaded guilty before a magistrates' court to one offence of theft, one of false accounting, one of making a false instrument, and one of using a false instrument. He was committed to the Crown Court for sentence. G was treasurer and secretary of a voluntary football club and was responsible for dealing with the club's bank account and financial affairs. G admitted that he had stolen a sum of between £7,300 and £7,500 from the club's accounts over a period of seven years. He used various means in an attempt to conceal the offences.

Held, allowing the appeal, that the amount of money stolen should be taken as a starting point but it was not the sole consideration. The offences were committed over a period of nearly eight years, and when clarification was sought, G told a series of lies reinforced by the falsification of accounts and other documents. However applying the guidance in *R. v. Clark (Trevor)* [1998] 2 Cr. App. R. 137, [1998] C.L.Y. 1392 applied, and giving an appropriate discount for G's admissions and early plea, the total sentence should have been 12 months' imprisonment.

R. v. GRIFFITHS (PETER WYN) [2000] 1 Cr. App. R. (S.) 240, Sullivan, J., CA (Crim Div).

1238. False accounting – fraudulent trading – unduly lenient sentences

The Attorney General asked the court to review sentences on the ground that they were unduly lenient. T, aged 46, pleaded guilty to fraudulent trading. R, aged 70, pleaded guilty to three offences of false accounting. T and R were respectively managing director and chairman of a company which sent invoices to a factoring company, on terms that the factoring company would advance three quarters of the face value of the invoices to T and R's company, and would then recover the full invoice sum from the debtors. When the full sum was recovered from the debtors, the factors would pay the balance to the offenders' company, less a percentage. The prosecution case was that T and R sent a number of bogus invoices relating to bogus claims and bogus companies to the factors, and thereby dishonestly obtained a substantial sum from the factors. Over a period of about 17 months, 159 false invoices with a face value of over £1 million were raised. Other valid invoices were also raised during the same period. T and R were sentenced to a conditional discharge and an absolute discharge respectively, with orders to pay prosecution costs in the amounts of £750 and £150 respectively.

Held, refusing the reference, that it would be unfair to reopen the sentences to the detriment of T and R. While the court wished to make it plain that these were serious offences, the court did not consider it appropriate to grant leave to the Attorney General.

ATTORNEY GENERAL'S REFERENCE (NOS.80 AND 81 OF 1999), *Re; sub nom.* R. v. THOMPSON (WILFRID FRANK); R. v. RODGERS (ANDREW CAMPBELL) [2000] 2 Cr. App. R. (S.) 138, Lord Bingham of Cornhill, L.C.J., CA (Crim Div).

1239. False imprisonment – confessions – victim detained in own house with intention of securing confession to alleged crime

A appealed against a sentence of four years' imprisonment having pleaded guilty to false imprisonment. A's daughter complained that she had been indecently assaulted by another man, M, who denied the offence and the Crown Prosecution Service decided that there was insufficient evidence for prosecution. M was assaulted and A was arrested and charged with that offence. He was remanded in custody for six months and subsequently acquitted. A became obsessed with the alleged indecent assault. Some time later he went to M's house early in the morning, and smashed the windows. A got into the house carrying a five litre oil can. He forced the M to lie in the corner of the bedroom and threatened to set light to him. Police officers arrived, but A detained M for a period of seven hours, threatening to set light to him if the officers stormed the house. He forced M to write a confession to the indecent assault. He eventually released M and surrendered himself. It was discovered that the oil can contained only water. A claimed that he had no intention of harming M, but simply wanted a confession so that M could be prosecuted.

Held, allowing the appeal, that the Court accepted that A took the law into his own hands only when he realised that his campaign for prosecution had not succeeded. He had brought great suffering to himself and his family. The Court did not consider that the sentence of four years was improper, but in the unusual circumstances of the case would extend mercy and reduce the sentence to three years.

R. v. AS [2000] 1 Cr. App. R. (S.) 491, Owen, J., CA (Crim Div).

1240. False imprisonment – kidnapping of former partner – offence committed in presence of small child

L appealed against a sentence of two years' imprisonment on conviction of false imprisonment. L had a relationship with a woman over a period of 18 years. They had three children. Some months before the offence they separated, but L continued to have access to one of the children. L went to the woman's home, struck her on the head so as to render her unconscious, and then took her and the child in his car. He then made the woman drive to a park, where he said he had dug a grave for her. The woman managed to jump out and call for help. L forced the woman back into the car and drove off again, but eventually took her back to her home.

Held, dismissing the appeal, that this was not a transitory false imprisonment; it was a terrifying experience for the victim, committed in the presence of the small child. Significant violence was used and L had never shown contrition or remorse. The sentence was not wrong in principle or excessive in any way.

R. v. LUCAS (LAWRENCE OWEN) [2000] 1 Cr. App. R. (S.) 5, Scott Baker, J., CA (Crim Div).

1241. Fines – corporate crime – level of penalty – Trade Descriptions Act offences

[Trade Descriptions Act 1968 s.13.]

DE, an estate agency business, was convicted in the Crown Court of three offences contrary to the Trade Descriptions Act 1968 s.13. In each case it had erected signs outside properties to suggest that it had acted as the estate agent in their sale. DE was a modest business with no previous convictions and profits of £16,000 and £33,000, respectively, for its previous two years of trading. It was fined £7,500 on each count, giving a total penalty of £22,000 with costs. DE appealed, contending that the fines were excessive as justices frequently imposed fines of around £100 for similar offences under the 1968 Act and the Town and Country Planning legislation.

Held, allowing the appeal, that the fines would be reduced to £2,000 for each conviction taking into account the seriousness of the offences and DE's means. However, the low level of fines that appeared generally to be applied in the magistrates courts for these offences was inappropriate for commercial crime and should be increased to the level of the instant appeal.

R. v. DOCKLANDS ESTATES LTD [2001] 1 Cr. App. R. (S.) 78, Lord Woolf of Barnes, L.C.J., CA (Crim Div).

1242. Firearms offences – conspiracy – possession of prohibited ammunition with intention to enforce payment of debt

K, T and W pleaded guilty to having a firearm with intent to commit an indictable offence, and, in the case of T, possessing prohibited ammunition. K, T and W were observed by police officers making a number of journeys in different motor vehicles.

They were eventually stopped, and a search of the vehicle disclosed a small handgun and various other items including a number of live rounds of ammunition. A large amount of ammunition was later found at the home of one of K,T and W. They pleaded guilty on the basis that they were seeking to enforce the payment of a debt and their intention was to show the gun to the debtor to induce him to pay off the debt. K,T and W appealed against sentences of seven and a half years' imprisonment for possessing a firearm with intent in the case of K and T and six years in the case of a W, with 18 months' imprisonment consecutive in the case of one of the appellants for possessing prohibited ammunition. The total sentences were seven and a half years, nine years and six years' imprisonment respectively.

Held, allowing the appeal, that the sentencer had deliberately imposed severe sentences in view of the problem of the use of firearms in the locality. These were very serious offences, and there could be no criticism of the sentencer's determination to impose severe sentences to respond to the local position and to include a significant deterrent element in the sentences. There was force in the argument that the starting point was too high on the basis of the agreed basis of plea. The sentences would be reduced from seven and half years to six years, from nine years to seven years and from six years to five years respectively, *R. v. Lewis (Martin) (1986)* (1986) 8 Cr. App. R. (S.) 314, [1988] C.L.Y. 966, *R. v. Francis (Andrew Donald)* (1995) 16 Cr. App. R. (S.) 95, [1996] C.L.Y. 1893 and *R. v. Avis (Tony)* [1998] 1 Cr. App. R. 420, [1998] C.L.Y. 1214 considered.

R. v. LAVIN (THOMAS); R. v. LAVIN (KEVIN); R. v. WHEELER (STEPHEN) [2000] 1 Cr. App. R. (S.) 227, Kennedy, L.J., CA (Crim Div).

1243. Firearms offences – explosives – extended campaign against banks and supermarkets

P appealed against a total sentence of 21 years' imprisonment, imposed following his guilty plea to nine counts of blackmail, three counts of assault occasioning actual bodily harm, one count of causing an explosion likely to endanger life, one count of doing an act with intent to cause an explosion likely to endanger life, one count of unlawful wounding, two counts of possessing firearms with intent to commit an indictable offence, one count of possessing explosives, and one count of possessing a prohibited weapon. Over a period of three and a half years P had waged campaigns against a bank and a supermarket chain. Over that period, P placed 25 explosive devices of six different types, each intended to produce an explosion involving risk of harm to anyone in the vicinity. One device was designed to fire a shotgun cartridge when the box was opened. Other devices sent to members of the public contained a mechanism designed to fire a rifle bullet when the package was opened. Various other explosive devices were used. On one occasion a device exploded causing a car to be engulfed in flames.

Held, dismissing the appeal, that the sentence was correct in principle and entirely appropriate.

R. v. PEARCE (EDGAR) [2000] 2 Cr. App. R. (S.) 32, Johnson, J., CA (Crim Div).

1244. Firearms offences – intent to cause fear of violence – unduly lenient sentence

[Firearms Act 1978 s.16A.]

The Attorney General asked the court to review a sentence on the ground that it was unduly lenient. H pleaded guilty to possessing an imitation firearm with intent to cause fear of violence, contrary to the Firearms Act 1978 s.16A. H spent an evening drinking, and then hired a taxi to take him to his home address. When the taxi arrived at the offender's home and the driver asked for the fare, the offender went into the house and returned with what appeared to be a gun. H made movements which indicated that he was cocking the gun. Following a conversation, the taxi driver drove away and called the police. H's house was surrounded by armed police officers and he was arrested after half an hour.

Officers searching H's house found a replica hand gun and replica ammunition. He was sentenced to a community service order.

Held, allowing the reference, that the sentence of less than two years' imprisonment would have been inappropriate on the facts of this case. The sentence of 100 hours' community service was quashed and a sentence of 12 months' imprisonment was substituted, having regard to the element of double jeopardy *R. v. Avis (Tony)* [1998] 1 Cr. App. R. 420, [1998] C.L.Y. 1214, *R. v. Roker (Stuart Caleb)* [1998] 2 Cr. App. R (S.) 254, [1998] C.L.Y. 1218, *R. v. Thompson (Steven)* [1997] 2 Cr. App. R. (S.) 188, [1997] C.L.Y. 1542, *R. v. Thompson (Tony)* [1999] 2 Cr. App. R. (S.) 292, [1999] C.L.Y. 1167, *R. v. Mercredi (Barbara)* [1997] 2 Cr. App. R. (S.) 204, [1997] C.L.Y. 1541 considered.

ATTORNEY GENERAL'S REFERENCE (NO.49 OF 1999), *Re*; *sub nom.* R. v. HINCHLIFFE (ALLEN PATRICK) [2000] 1 Cr. App. R. (S.) 436, Kennedy, L.J., CA (Crim Div).

1245. Firearms offences – intention to cause fear of violence – threatening police officers with air rifle

C appealed against a sentence of two years' imprisonment, having been convicted of possessing a firearm with intent to cause fear of violence. Police officers attended at the home of C following reports that a man had fired an airgun in a street. C pointed a firearm out of the window and threatened the police officers. Subsequently a shot was fired from an upstairs rear window. Eventually C was arrested and a search of his house revealed two air rifles and a quantity of pellets.

Held, dismissing the appeal, that it was not submitted that the sentence of two years was in any way excessive for the offence, although it was argued that the sentence was mistaken in relation to the amount of time spent in custody on remand which would be taken into account. In the court's view, the fact that the sentencer might have been mistaken about the time in custody which would be credited towards C's sentence did not mean that the sentencer would have given a shorter sentence if he had known the actual position or that the sentence was manifestly excessive. This was a serious offence involving the use of a firearm. Guidelines had been set out in *R. v. Avis (Tony)* [1998] 1 Cr. App. R. 420, [1998] C.L.Y. 1214 considered, which pointed to the need for sentences to reflect public concern over the use of firearms. The sentence could not possibly be said to be manifestly excessive.

R. v. CAREY (STEPHEN) [2000] 1 Cr. App. R. (S.) 179, Gage, J., CA (Crim Div).

1246. Firearms offences – pleas – storing guns on behalf of unidentified criminal

C appealed against a sentence of three and a half years' imprisonment, having pleaded guilty to possessing a shortened shotgun and a prohibited weapon. Police officers searched the C's house in connection with unrelated offences and found a plastic bin liner containing a dismantled sawn off shotgun and a suitcase containing an automatic machine pistol, together with a quantity of ammunition. C pleaded guilty on the basis that he had agreed to store unspecified property for a friend; that the property had been in his possession for about 10 days; that he believed the property to be stolen goods and had not examined the property. He had received no financial reward for allowing the items to be stored in his home and was not fearful of disclosing the identity of the person who brought them to his home. The prosecution did not accept this account, but did not call any evidence to challenge it.

Held, allowing the appeal, that the judge would have been entitled, if he took the view that what was being put forward was likely to be a false factual basis of plea, to refuse to accept it and give C the opportunity to call evidence so that the issue could be determined. That was a matter for the judge. The stance taken by the Crown was relevant but not determinative. Once the factual basis on which C was to be sentenced had been accepted, the sentence must proceed on that basis. The court was persuaded that it had not done so. A sentence of three and a half years imprisonment on a plea of guilty would have been entirely appropriate for a man storing guns for a criminal and indeed might not be enough. But if C was quite unaware of what he had, that must make a substantial difference. C had afforded a secure place to an unidentified criminal to store what turned out to be very dangerous weapons; he had made no inquiry and had deliberately closed his eyes. There must be a significant difference between a man who did that believing what he had was stolen goods and a man had knowingly stored weapons which were apt to be lethal. The proper sentence was one of two years' imprisonment.

R. v. CAMPBELL (DALE) [2000] 1 Cr. App. R. (S.) 291, Hughes, J., CA (Crim Div).

1247. Firearms offences – possession – threatening man with loaded sawn off shotgun

[Firearms Act 1968 s.16A.]

C appealed against a sentence of seven years' imprisonment having pleaded guilty to possessing a firearm with intent to cause fear of violence, contrary to the Firearms Act 1968 s.16A. C went to the house of a man whom he had known for some time and pointed a shortened shotgun at him. The man closed the front door of the house and the shotgun was discharged into the door. C pleaded guilty on the basis that he had intended only to threaten the man, and that the shotgun had been discharged by his companion.

Held, allowing the appeal, that the sentencer passed sentence on the basis that C had gone with another man to threaten the victim with a loaded sawn off shotgun, but had not discharged the shotgun himself. An appropriate starting point in the light of *R. v. Avis (Tony)* [1998] 1 Cr. App. R. 420, [1998] C.L.Y. 1214 was six years, with a limited discount for the plea; the appropriate sentence was five years' imprisonment.

R. v. CORRY (RAYMOND RONALD) [2000] 1 Cr. App. R. (S.) 47, McKinnon, J., CA (Crim Div).

1248. Firearms offences – possession – used to commit theft

[Firearms Act 1968 Sch.1.]

T pleaded guilty to possessing a firearm at the time of committing an offence specified in the Firearms Act 1968 Sch.1, and to theft. T stole a bag containing £122 in cash from a reception desk. He was chased by the cashier through the streets and eventually stopped by a police officer. He was searched and an imitation handgun was found in the waistband of his jeans. T stated that he had not shown the imitation shotgun to the cashier and the cashier would not have known that he had it on him. T was sentenced to 15 months' detention in a young offender institution for possessing a firearm at the time of committing an offence, with three months' detention consecutive for theft. T appealed.

Held, dismissing the appeal, that the law on imitation firearms existed to prevent or deter anyone minded to commit a criminal offence from carrying a firearm or imitation firearm. In normal circumstances a person in possession of a firearm or imitation firearm when an offence was committed could expect a substantial custodial sentence. The sentence of 15 months could not be described as excessive.

R. v. T (MARCUS) (A JUVENILE) [2000] 2 Cr. App. R. (S.) 155, Judge Richard Gibbs Q.C., CA (Crim Div).

1249. Firearms offences – possession of firearm without certificate

[Firearms Act 1968.]

W appealed against a sentence of six months' imprisonment, having pleaded guilty to possession of a firearm without a certificate. Police officers searching his home found a revolver hanging on the wall of the living room. The revolver was found to be a modern reproduction of an antique revolver. It was fitted with a replacement cylinder, the chambers of which were blocked so as to prevent the gun from being fired. A separate cylinder which could be fitted to the revolver so as to convert it into a working firearm was found in a cupboard. The revolver and the separate cylinder together constituted a firearm subject to the Firearms Act 1968. W stated that the gun was an ornamental copy of a revolver made in 1814 which he had bought a number of years previously.

Held, allowing the appeal, that the appropriate sentence would have been two months' imprisonment.

R. v. WHARTON (THOMAS LESLIE) [2000] 2 Cr. App. R. (S.) 339, Forbes, J., CA (Crim Div).

1250. Firearms offences – possession of prohibited weapons and ammunition

[Firearms (Amendment) Act 1997.]

A pleaded guilty before a magistrates' court to 10 charges of possession of prohibited weapons and five charges of possession of prohibited ammunition. He was committed to the Crown Court for sentence. A had been a registered firearms dealer. Following the passing of the Firearms (Amendment) Act 1997, A arranged for a number of firearms which had become prohibited as a result of the Act to be taken to Germany and stored at the premises of a shooting club. After some time, this arrangement came to an end, and A had to remove the firearms. He attempted unsuccessfully to sell the firearms in Germany, and then brought them back into the UK without appropriate authorisation. For some months the firearms were stored in a garage at the home of a friend, but following a fire at the home they were discovered by officers of the fire brigade. A was sentenced to three years' imprisonment on each charge, all concurrent, and appealed.

Held, allowing the appeal, that the essential purpose of the 1997 Act was the safety of the public. The gravamen of the offences committed by A was that he flatly ignored the purpose of the legislation. He treated himself as being above the law. He had kept a number of lethal weapons and some ammunition in insecure conditions for no proper reason other then that he hoped to surrender them for the purpose of obtaining compensation. The court had no doubt that these offences were so serious that only a custodial sentence was appropriate. The length of the sentence should reflect not just the gravity of A's flagrant disregard of the legislation but also that as a former firearms dealer he knew that he was exposing his friends and others to a significant level of risk. The case fell outside the guidelines discussed in *R. v. Avis (Tony)* [1998] 1 Cr. App. R. 420, [1998] C.L.Y. 1214. The sentence of three years' imprisonment was significantly longer than it needed to have been. A sentence of 18 months was substituted.

R. v. APLIN (MALCOLM) [2000] 2 Cr. App. R. (S.) 89, Turner, J., CA (Crim Div).

1251. Firearms offences – possession of sawn off shotgun – weapon acquired with the intention of committing suicide – weapon left in unsecured car

H pleaded guilty before a magistrates' court to possession of a firearm whilst a prohibited person, possession of a shortened shotgun without a certificate, and possession of a loaded shotgun in a public place. He was committed to the Crown Court for sentence. Police officers who were summoned to an empty car found a sawn off shotgun loaded with two cartridges. H was traced as the hirer of the car. H admitted that the gun belonged to him, and said that he had bought it with the intention of committing suicide. H appealed against sentences of two and a half years' imprisonment on each count concurrent, with an order for forfeiture and disposal of the shotgun and cartridges.

Held, dismissing the appeal, that although H came into the possession of the shortened shotgun with the intention of committing suicide, he had acted with extreme irresponsibility and recklessness. The gun was left readily visible to a passing member of the public in an unsecured car. The court did not accept the submission that H's intention to commit suicide rendered it less culpable to leave a weapon visible and available to the public. The sentence was not manifestly excessive.

R. v. HOLMES (ANTHONY) [1999] 2 Cr. App. R. (S.) 383, Alliott, J., CA (Crim Div).

1252. Firearms offences – possession of short barrelled revolver

H appealed against a sentence of two years' imprisonment having pleaded guilty to possessing a prohibited weapon, a short barrelled revolver, and possessing ammunition. Police officers searching H's house in connection with other matters found a revolver with a shortened barrel and 104 rounds of live ammunition. H claimed that the revolver had been left with her by her stepson.

Held, dismissing the appeal, that there was no lawful purpose to which the weapon could be put; its barrel had been shortened and it could be used only for crime. The offence was extremely serious and the sentence was not manifestly excessive, *R. v. Avis (Tony)* [1998] 1 Cr. App. R. 420, [1998] C.L.Y. 1214 considered.

R. v. HAIR (LORRAINE) [2000] 1 Cr. App. R. (S.) 118, Curtis, J., CA (Crim Div).

1253. Firearms offences – possession of short barrelled revolver for self protection – no intention to use

W appealed against sentence of four years' imprisonment for the possession of a prohibited weapon, with concurrent sentences for the other offences, having pleaded guilty to possessing a prohibited weapon, possessing ammunition without a certificate, possessing a firearm when prohibited, and possessing a Class B drug, cannabis. Police officers searching W's house found a short barrelled revolver loaded with six rounds of ammunition. W admitted buying the gun for his own protection, having given assistance to the police following the murder of his friend.

Held, allowing the appeal, that although the weapon was loaded, it had not been used and W had had it for only a short time; there was no allegation of an intention to use the weapon. The sentence was manifestly excessive; sentences totalling two years' imprisonment would be substituted, *R. v. Avis (Tony)* [1998] 1 Cr. App. R. 420, [1998] C.L.Y. 1214 considered.

R. v. WRIGHT (RICHARD) [2000] 1 Cr. App. R. (S.) 109, Elias, J., CA (Crim Div).

1254. Firearms offences – prohibited persons – possession of firearm by former prisoner

[Firearms Act 1968 s.21.]

B appealed against a sentence of four years' imprisonment on conviction of possessing a firearm while a prohibited person. B was seen by police officers apparently concealing an object in a hedge; the object was discovered to be a semi-automatic pistol. B had been sentenced to a term of five and a half years' imprisonment in 1992 and was a prohibited person for the purpose of the Firearms Act 1968 s.21.

Held, allowing the appeal, that the maximum sentence for the offence was five years' imprisonment, the gun was not in a condition in which it could have been fired and there was no evidence that B had used the gun himself or had any ammunition for it. The sentence of four years was manifestly excessive; a sentence of two and a half years would be substituted, *R. v. Rout (Christopher)* (1993) 14 Cr. App. R. (S.) 584, [1994] C.L.Y. 1263, *R. v. Smith (Patrick O'Neill)* (1989) 11 Cr. App. R. (S.) 55, [1990] C.L.Y. 1383 and *R. v. Hill (Norman David William)* [1999] 2 Cr. App. R. (S.) 388, [1999] C.L.Y. 1160 considered.

R. v. BRIZZI (RAPHELLO) [2000] 1 Cr. App. R. (S.) 126, Harrison, J., CA (Crim Div).

1255. Forgery – passport – possession of false passport for use by others – notice recommending deportation not served

[Immigration Act 1971 s.6.]

S pleaded guilty to possessing forged passports. S had arrived at Heathrow airport on an international flight and was searched by Customs officers, who found four forged Greek passports concealed in his trousers. H claimed that he had been asked to bring them into the country and that he was to be paid £150 for doing so. He was visiting the country for a legitimate purpose. S appealed against the sentence of 12 months' imprisonment and recommendation for deportation.

Held, allowing the appeal, that H was not using a false passport, but transporting false passports for others to use. In the view of the court an appropriate sentence for what he had done would be six months rather than 12 months' imprisonment. No notice had been served on the appellant in relation to the recommendation, as was required by the Immigration Act 1971 s.6, and the recommendation would accordingly be quashed, *R. v. Singh (Daljit)* [1999] 1 Cr. App. R. (S.) 490, [1998] C.L.Y. 1227 considered.

R. v. SILIAVSKI (BOYAN YOSSIFOV) [2000] 1 Cr. App. R. (S.) 23, Garland, J., CA (Crim Div).

1256. **Fraud – company directors – giving false impression of value of company**

[Companies Act 1985 s.450; Financial Services Act 1986 s.47(2); Company Directors Disqualification Act 1986.]

C and H pleaded guilty to two counts charging them with engaging in a course of conduct which created a false or misleading impression as to the market in or the price or value of investments, contrary to the Financial Services Act 1986 s.47(2). C also pleaded guilty to making or being privy to making false entries in a document affecting or relating to the property or the finances of a company, contrary to Companies Act 1985 s.450. C was the principal shareholder and managing director of a company, and H was the finance director of the company. Over a period of about two years C and H used various devices to create a false or misleading impression in the company's accounts, thereby permitting the company to proceed to flotation when it would otherwise have been unable to do so. The company eventually failed with a deficiency of £4.32 million, of which £1.344 million represented investments. C and H were sentenced to 18 months' imprisonment with five years' disqualification under Company Directors Disqualification Act 1986, and five years' imprisonment with 10 years' disqualification respectively, and appealed.

Held, allowing the appeal, that this was a very serious fraud persisted in over a period of time which resulted in a large deficiency. In view of all the mitigation relevant to H, the sentencer had failed to give sufficient discount for the plea in the case of the second appellant. The Court would substitute a sentence of four years' imprisonment. The appeal of C would be dismissed, *R. v. Buffrey (Paul Edward)* (1993) 14 Cr. App. R. (S.) 511, [1994] C.L.Y. 1267 considered.

R. v. CHAUHAN (RASHMIKANT BHIKHUBHAI); R. v. HOLROYD (JOHN MALCOLM) [2000] 2 Cr. App. R. (S.) 230, Dyson, J., CA (Crim Div).

1257. **Fraud – conspiracy – advertising of devices on internet – loss of broadcaster's profits**

[Powers of the Criminal Courts Act 1973 s.43.]

W, who pleaded guilty to conspiracy to defraud, had made and sold devices which enabled members of the public to watch television programmes broadcast by a commercial broadcasting company to paying subscribers. W advertised his devices on an internet newsgroup and interacted with purchasers via email, offering discounts on bulk purchases. His activities caused estimated potential losses to the broadcasting company of £50,000 per annum. His profits were in the region of £5,000. W had no previous convictions.

Held, sentencing the defendant, that a five-month term of imprisonment was appropriate and W would be deprived of his rights to certain equipment pursuant to the Powers of the Criminal Courts Act 1973 s.43, *R. v. Carey (Harold Christopher)* [1999] 1 Cr. App. R. (S.) 322, [1999] C.L.Y. 1173 considered.

R. v. WHITTAKER (FRAUD), August 10, 2000, Judge Bennett, CC (Burnley). [*Ex rel.* Richard Mullan, Barrister, Sedan House, Stanley Place, Chester].

1258. Fraud – insurance claims – conspiracy to defraud insurance companies

M was convicted of four offences of conspiracy to defraud and pleaded guilty to three further similar offences. M was concerned with others in a series of conspiracies to defraud insurance companies by making false claims arising out of traffic accidents. He made seven claims for a total of £34,162 in respect of traffic accidents which had either not happened, or had not happened in the manner stated in the claim. M appealed against a sentence of five years' imprisonment concurrent on each count in respect of which he was convicted, and three and a half years concurrent on each count to which he pleaded guilty, all concurrent total sentence, five years' imprisonment.

Held, allowing the appeal, that the sentence treated M as the central figure in a series of conspiracies, saying that he had instigated the offences which required a degree of ingenuity and planning. However, the totality of the sentences was too long. The sentences on the counts in respect of which M had been convicted would be reduced to four years' imprisonment, and on those counts which he pleaded guilty to three years' imprisonment, all concurrent bringing total sentence to four years' imprisonment.

R. v. MEHBOOB (CHAND) [2000] 2 Cr. App. R. (S.) 343, Penry-Davey, J., CA (Crim Div).

1259. Grievous bodily harm – attack on victim with baseball bat – unduly lenient sentence

[Offences Against the Person Act 1861 s.18; Criminal Justice Act 1988 s.36.]

The Attorney General sought leave to refer D's sentence of 200 hours' community service for wounding with intent to cause grievous bodily harm to the Court of Appeal under the Criminal Justice Act 1988 s.36 on the basis of undue leniency. The Attorney General submitted that the sentence was unduly lenient bearing in mind the aggravating features of the offence that D had used a baseball bat to strike his victim, and that the blows continued whilst the victim was on the ground, where D had kicked him twice.

Held, granting leave and allowing the reference, that, as in nearly all convictions for offences committed contrary to the Offences Against the Person Act 1861 s.18, public interest required a custodial sentence to be imposed. A sentence of between two and three years' imprisonment would have been appropriate, but taking into account the element of double jeopardy, the fact that D was now losing his liberty and that he had performed a substantial amount of his community service, a sentence of nine months imprisonment was imposed.

ATTORNEY GENERAL'S REFERENCE (NO.56 OF 2000), *Re*; *sub nom*. R. v. DICKERSON (NIGEL ROY) [2001] 1 Cr. App. R. (S.) 127, Rose, L.J., CA (Crim Div).

1260. Grievous bodily harm – children – pleas – injuries inflicted on baby

H appealed against a sentence of four years' imprisonment, having pleaded guilty before a magistrates' court to inflicting grievous bodily harm to his son aged three months. He was committed to the Crown Court for sentence. H and his wife took their child to hospital on two occasions within a few days. On the second visit the child was found to have a fracture of the parietal with subdural bleeding. H admitted that having been left alone with the baby, he had become agitated and distressed when the baby cried. He had picked the baby up and shaken him and then accidentally dropped him so that he fell on his head.

Held, allowing the appeal, that H was of low intellectual ability and prone to anxiety and depression. It was uncertain whether the child had sustained any lasting injuries. The court had been referred to *R. v. Scott (Paul James)* (1995) 16 Cr. App. R. (S.) 451. The Court considered that an immediate custodial sentence was required, but that the sentence of four years did not adequately reflect H's plea. The sentence was reduced to two years.

R. v. JH [2000] 1 Cr. App. R. (S.) 551, Potts, J., CA (Crim Div).

1261. Grievous bodily harm – conspiracy – throwing nitric acid over victim – imposition of extended sentence

[Criminal Justice Act 1991 s.2(2)(b).]

R and E were convicted of conspiring to cause grievous bodily harm with intent. E was also convicted of causing grievous bodily harm with intent. R and E had been in prison together. R had formerly had a girlfriend who had ended their relationship when he was sentenced to imprisonment. While serving his sentence, he continually telephoned her and would not accept that the relationship was over. He was warned to stay away from the complainant. Some time later E ran up to her in the street and threw nitric acid over her head. The acid struck the side of her head and face, causing serious injury. The victim required several operations to remove damaged tissue and suffered the loss of her ear along with significant scarring of her face, neck, scalp and chest. She was likely to require further surgery. R and E were sentenced to 15 years' imprisonment in each case under the Criminal Justice Act 1991 s.2(2)(b). R and E appealed.

Held, dismissing the appeal, that the recent decision of the court indicated that attacks of this nature would be met by condign punishment and that a sentence of 15 years was not appropriate on that basis. It was not necessary for the sentencer to invoke the Criminal Justice Act 1991 s.2(2)(b) to justify the sentence. The fact that the sentencer had erroneously invoked s.2(2)(b) did not required the court to reduce the sentence. It should be known that if the Court of Appeal had to consider a case when the sentencer had purported to invoke s.2(2)(b) and passed a longer than commensurate sentence, but the sentence passed was correct within normal tariff principles, then the Court of Appeal would not reduce the sentence, even if it considered the purported use of s.2(2)(b) to be in error, *R. v. Ismail (Ibrahim)* (1992) 13 Cr. App. R. (S.) 395, [1993] C.L.Y. 1184, *R. v. Newton (Paul Joseph)* [1999] 1 Cr. App. R.(S.) 438, [1999] C.L.Y. 1181 and *R. v. Jones (Russell Thomas)* [1999] 1 Cr. App. R. (S.) 473, [1999] C.L.Y. 1180 considered.

R. v. RAI (KRISHAN RAJA); R. v. ROBINSON (EARL) [2000] 2 Cr. App. R. (S.) 120, Judge Norman Jones Q.C., CA (Crim Div).

1262. Grievous bodily harm – drug abuse – repetitive assaults on pregnant partner – unduly lenient sentence

[Criminal Justice Act 1988 s.36.]

The Attorney General referred a sentence of 30 months' imprisonment to the Court of Appeal under the Criminal Justice Act 1988 s.36 on the ground of undue leniency. P had pleaded guilty to the offences of false imprisonment, threatening to kill and assault occasioning actual and grievous bodily harm, but only after he had heard the evidence in chief of his girlfriend as to the attacks on her, for he had no recollection of the events due to the intake of drugs. Three of the offences had been committed during the currency of a 30 months' custodial sentence, which had been imposed for offences of violence. P was ordered to serve the remaining 11 months of the first sentence, followed by a further 30 month term. The Attorney General maintained that a harsher sentence had been merited in view of the fact that the victim had been pregnant at the time of the offences of false imprisonment and grievous bodily harm, the sustained nature of the attacks and the fact that they had been committed during the currency of another sentence imposed for offences of violence, *Attorney General's Reference (No.52 of 1996), Re* [1997] 2 Cr. App. R. (S.) 230, [1997] C.L.Y. 1718 and *R. v. Spence (Clinton Everton)* (1983) 5 Cr. App. R. (S.) 413, [1984] C.L.Y. 876 referred to.

Held, allowing the reference and increasing the sentence of 30 months to five years, that (1) a sentence of six to seven years would have been justified. The actual sentence imposed did not reflect the repetitive nature of the criminal behaviour against P's pregnant girlfriend, some of it in the presence of children, and (2) three of the offences had been committed during the currency of a custodial sentence, although some discount would be allowed by reason of the witness statement.

ATTORNEY GENERAL'S REFERENCE (NO.42 OF 2000), *Re; sub nom.* R. v. PINKNEY (DALE) [2001] 1 Cr. App. R. (S.) 114, Rose, L.J., CA (Crim Div).

1263. Grievous bodily harm – extended sentences – length of extension

[Criminal Justice Act 1991 s.2(2); Crime and Disorder Act 1998 s.58.]

G pleaded guilty to wounding with intent to cause grievous bodily harm. G went into a public house where he spent the evening with a friend. A number of arguments broke out between them, and eventually G punched his friend to the head and body. When the friend attempted to defend himself, G picked up a half pint glass, grasped the base of the glass with his right hand and drove the glass into his friend's head around his ear. The friend was found to have a large laceration extending from the neck over the chin as far as the ear. G had several previous convictions for offences including affray and unlawful wounding. G was sentenced to an extended sentence of 10 years under the Crime and Disorder Act 1998 s.58, consisting of a custodial term of five years' detention in a young offender institution, with an extension period of five years. G appealed.

Held, allowing the appeal, that reports before the sentencing judge referred to G's over indulgence in alcohol and drugs and the risk that he would become involved in further violent offences. The first question for the court was whether the five-year sentence which the judge imposed as the custodial term was excessive. The court's judgment was that the sentence was entirely appropriate for the offence on the plea of guilty. The second question was whether it was appropriate for the judge to invoke the Crime and Disorder Act 1998 s.58. Certain conditions were necessary before the section could be invoked. The court must be proposing to impose a custodial sentence for the sexual or violent offence, and the court must consider that the ordinary licence period would not be adequate for the purpose of preventing the commission by the offender of further offences and securing his rehabilitation. An extended sentence had two parts: a custodial term and an extension period. The Criminal Justice Act 1991 s.2(2) applied only to the custodial term. In the court's judgment, it was proper to invoke s.58 on the facts of this case. While there were signs that G recognised the need to reform his pattern of behaviour, there was a risk of further violent offending if he did not. The judge was fully justified in imposing an extension period both the prevent the commission of future offences and to secure the rehabilitation of G. The next question was whether the five-year extension period was too long. The imposition of the extended term did lead to the possibility that G might end up serving a 10-year sentence for this offence. That would be true only if he reoffended. The court was obliged to address the question whether it could accept the possibility, even if G were to offend again, that he would face a sentence as long as that. The court answered that question in the negative. While the judge was entitled to invoke s.58, the period of the extension was longer that the purpose of imposing it justified. The extension period would be reduced to two years.

R. v. GOULD (STEVEN LEWIS) [2000] 2 Cr. App. R. (S.) 173, Lord Bingham of Cornhill, L.C.J., CA (Crim Div).

1264. Grievous bodily harm – extended sentences – ordered to run consecutively to return order

[Offences against the Person Act 1861 s.20; Criminal Justice Act 1991 s.2(2)(b), s.40.]

S pleaded guilty to two counts of inflicting grievous bodily harm contrary to the Offences against the Person Act 1861 s.20. He was sentenced to four years' imprisonment, passed as a longer than commensurate sentence under the Criminal Justice Act 1991 s.2(2)(b), consecutive to an order under the Criminal Justice Act 1991 s.40, returning him to custody for a period of 167 days in respect of an earlier sentence of 18 months' imprisonment. It was submitted on appeal that it was wrong in principle to order a sentence passed under s.2(2) to be served consecutively to the unexpired portion of the earlier sentence, relying on *R. v. Johnson (Adrian)* [1998] 1 Cr. App. R. (S.) 126, [1998] C.L.Y. 1159 and *R. v. King (Samuel Nathaniel)* (1995) 16 Cr. App. R. (S.) 987, [1996] C.L.Y. 2065.

Held, allowing the appeal, that authority covered the situation. The appeal would be allowed to the extent that the period of 167 days would be ordered to run concurrently to the sentence of four years.

R. v. SULLIVAN (ALAN) [2000] 2 Cr. App. R. (S.) 318, Judge Grigson, CA (Crim Div).

1265. Grievous bodily harm – intention – inflicting life threatening injuries on victim

J and O appealed against sentences of six years' imprisonment having pleaded guilty to causing grievous bodily harm with intent. Following an incident in a public house, one of the appellants was evicted, but waited outside. Some time later J and O confronted the victim, who had been involved in the incident at the public house, and a fight began. J took an estate agent's sign from a neighbouring garden and struck the victim with its wooden post. O kicked the victim in the head. The victim was found to have suffered fractured ribs and a ruptured spleen. The injuries were considered to be life threatening. His spleen was removed with the result that his immune system was permanently affected. His hearing and vision were permanently damaged.

Held, dismissing the appeal, that the victim in the present case had suffered permanent injuries. J and O had pleaded guilty on the basis that they were jointly responsible for the violence. The pleas had been entered six months after the date on which the case had originally been listed, and J and O could not expect the full normal discount. A sentence of seven or eight years would not have been excessive following a trial, and a reduction to six years to give some credit for the late pleas did not involve any error of principle. This was a sustained and brutal attack which had permanent consequences for the victim. The sentences were neither wrong in principle nor manifestly excessive, *R. v. Coles (Barrie)* [1997] 2 Cr. App. R. (S.) 95, [1997] C.L.Y. 1559 distinguished.

R. v. JAMA (HUSSEIN); R. v. OLIVER (AUSTEN MICHAEL) [2000] 2 Cr. App. R. (S.) 98, Toulson, J., CA (Crim Div).

1266. Grievous bodily harm – intention – inflicting serious injuries on victim – unduly lenient sentence

[Offences Against the Person Act 1861 s.18.]

The Attorney General asked the court to review a sentence on the ground that it was unduly lenient. B pleaded guilty on re-arrangement to one count of wounding with intent contrary to the Offences Against the Person Act 1861 s.18 having previously pleaded guilty to an offence contrary to s.20. He was standing outside an Indian restaurant with a beer glass which he had taken from the restaurant when two young men walked past him. For no particular reason, the offender approached one of the young men from behind and an altercation took place, in the course of which he smashed the young man in the face with the beer glass. The victim was found to have lacerations to the face which remained painful and unsightly for several months and left some permanent scarring. B was sentenced to eight months' detention in a young offender institution and order pay £500 compensation which was offered by the offender and paid.

Held, allowing the reference, that the sentencer had adopted a level of sentence for a glassing offence which was significantly below that indicated by the decided cases. There was a difference between offences under s.18 and those under s.20. The sentence imposed was unduly lenient. The least sentence that the sentencer could properly have imposed, bearing in mind the plea of guilty and other mitigation, would have been 18 months' detention in a young offender institution. Bearing in mind the element of double jeopardy, the court would substitute a sentence of 12 months' detention in a young offender institution, *Attorney General's Reference (No.20 of 1993), Re* (1994) 15 Cr. App.

R. (S.) 797, [1995] C.L.Y. 1495, *Attorney General's Reference (No.41 of 1994), Re* (1995) 16 Cr. App. R. (S.) 792, [1996] C.L.Y. 1919 considered.

ATTORNEY GENERAL'S REFERENCE (NO.79 OF 1999), *Re*; *sub nom*. R. v. BRANCH (DAVID) [2000] 2 Cr. App. R. (S.) 124, Lord Bingham of Cornhill, L.C.J., CA (Crim Div).

1267. **Grievous bodily harm – intention – inflicting serious injuries on victim resulting in loss of one eye**

[Offences against the Person Act 1861 s.18; Crime (Sentences) Act 1997 s.2, s.28.]

M and C were convicted of wounding or causing grievous bodily harm with intent. They were involved, with others, in a fight in a public house in the course of which the victim was knocked to the floor. M punched and kicked him in the head, and then stamped on his head. M struck the victim's head on four occasions with a chair. The victim suffered grave injuries including the loss of sight in one eye and the reduced vision in the other. M was sentenced to life imprisonment under the Crime (Sentences) Act 1997 s.2 with a specified period for the purposes of s.28 of six years less 261 days. C was sentenced to 12 years' imprisonment, consecutive to a term which he was serving for other offences.

Held, allowing the appeal in part, that M had a previous conviction for manslaughter and was liable to an automatic life sentence by virtue of s.2 of the Act unless there were exceptional circumstances, *Attorney General's Reference (No.53 of 1998), Re* [2000] Q.B. 198, [1999] C.L.Y. 1249 considered. The Court was in agreement with the sentencer that there were no exceptional circumstances which would have justified the court in not imposing a life sentence. Had the manslaughter conviction stood alone as a solitary act of violence in his record, and had that offence been of the most venial nature, it might have been possible to contend that he was not a man who posed a threat to the public from whom the public needed to be protected. Such a finding, if properly made, might justify the non-imposition of a life sentence which could in such circumstances be criticised as disproportionate and unjust. That was not the case. M had a record of violence. The Court had next to consider whether the sentencer was wrong to sentence M to 12 years' imprisonment, and to treat 12 years as the notional determinate sentence for the purposes of the s.28 in the case of M. It was submitted on behalf of both the appellants that the sentence of 12 years was shown by the authorities to be appropriate to attempted murder as opposed to an offence under the Offences against the Person Act 1861 s.18. In the Court's judgement it was plain that the 12 years sentence was at or towards the top of that or any relevant bracket. The Court was not constrained by authority to conclude that it fell out of the relevant bracket. The Court was not constrained by authority to conclude that it fell out of the relevant bracket so as to compel the Court to reduce the sentence. The offence was an appalling display of sadistic and sustained cruelty. The sentence was not excessive in view of lifelong harm which it had inflicted on the victim. The sentencer was entitled to impose a sentence of 12 years' imprisonment on M, and to treat 12 years as the notional sentence for the purpose of the s.28 in the case of M. The sentence in the case of C would be ordered to run concurrently with the earlier sentence. *R. v. Friemel (Peter Godfrey)* (1987) 9 Cr. App. R. (S.) 99, [1989] C.L.Y. 930, *R. v. Burton (Lawrence John)* (1990) 12 Cr. App. R. (S.) 559, [1992] C.L.Y. 1150, *R. v. White (Edward)* (1992) 13 Cr. App. R. (S.) 108, [1992] C.L.Y. 1152, *R. v. D (John)* [1998] 1 Cr. App. R. (S.) 110, [1998] C.L.Y. 1311, *R. v. Bedford (Roy John)* (1993) 14 Cr. App. R. (S.) 336, [1994] C.L.Y. 1314, *R. v. Dearn (Franklyn)* (1990) 12 Cr. App. R. (S.) 526, [1992] C.L.Y. 1149, *Attorney General's Reference (No.33 of 1996), Re* [1997] 2 Cr. App. R. (S.) 10, [1997] C.L.Y. 1622, *Attorney General's Reference (No.2 of 1997), Re* [1998] 1 Cr. App. R. (S.) 27, [1997] C.L.Y. 1621, *R. v. Lloyd (Paul Gabriel)* [1990] 12 Cr. App. R. (S.) 354, [1992] C.L.Y. 1287, *R. v. Pollin (Steven Lee)* [1997] 2 Cr. App. R. (S.) 356, [1998] C.L.Y. 1403, and *Attorney General's*

Reference (Nos.8 and 9 of 1997) [1998] 1 Cr. App. R. (S.) 98, [1997] C.L.Y. 1566 considered.

R. v. MEREDITH (CHRISTOPHER); R. v. CRAVEN (ADRIAN) [2000] 1 Cr. App. R. (S.) 508, Lord Bingham of Cornhill, L.C.J., CA (Crim Div).

1268. Grievous bodily harm – petrol – setting fire to victim

P appealed against a sentence of 10 years' imprisonment, having been convicted of causing grievous bodily harm with intent. P and the victim were known to each other and each had a flat in the same block, although the victim also had another address. In the early hours of the morning P returned to his flat and decided that someone had made an unauthorised entry. With two other men he went to the victim's address, where he accused him of entering the flat. The victim was then taken by car to his own flat by P and two other men. P had a petrol container in his possession. P continued to make accusations against the victim and threatened to burn him if he did not admit by 11 am that he had made an unauthorised entry into P's flat. At 11 am P counted off passing minutes and then splashed petrol over the victim's head and body and ignited the fumes with a cigarette lighter. The victim ran from the flat ablaze. P pulled of his coat and threw water on him. The victim sustained burns to his head, chest, arms and both hands.

Held, dismissing the appeal, that in the climate of today's sentencing a sentence of 10 years' imprisonment could not be described as either wrong in principle or manifestly excessive, *R. v. Medland (Eric William)* (1990) 12 Cr. App. R. (S.) 557, [1992] C.L.Y. 1288 considered.

R. v. PARKER (TIMOTHY) [2000] 2 Cr. App. R. (S.) 60, Alliott, J., CA (Crim Div).

1269. Grievous bodily harm – rugby players – fracture of opposing player's eye socket

M appealed against a sentence of eight months' imprisonment having been convicted of maliciously inflicting grievous bodily harm. M was taking part in a rugby union match. Half way through the second half M punched another player in the face knocking him to the ground. The other player was taken to hospital, where he was found to have a fractured eye socket. M denied punching the other player but was convicted by the jury.

Held, dismissing the appeal, that nothing in the cases cited on behalf of M suggested that the sentence passed was wrong in principle. The sentencer had observed that rugby was not a licence for thuggery. The offence involved an assault off the ball and after play had moved on. It caused serious injury. The sentencer's approach could not be faulted. The sentence was neither inappropriate nor excessive, *R. v. Shervill (David Anthony)* (1989) 11 Cr. App. R. (S.) 284, *R. v. Lincoln (Peter Alan)* (1990) 12 Cr. App. R. (S.) 250, [1992] C.L.Y. 1144, *R. v. Davies (Robert Paul)* (1990) 12 Cr. App. R. (S.) 308, [1992] C.L.Y. 1145, *R. v. Rogers (Martin John)* (1994) 15 Cr. App. R. (S.) 393, *R. v. Goodwin (Reginald Barry)* (1995) 16 Cr. App. R. (S.) 885, *R. v. Ollerenshaw (Paul Michael)* [1999] 1 Cr. App. R. (S.) 65, [1998] C.L.Y. 1169 considered.

R. v. MOSS (MARK DAVID) [2000] 1 Cr. App. R. (S.) 307, Potts, J., CA (Crim Div).

1270. Grievous bodily harm – unprovoked attack on stranger

C appealed against a sentence of 18 months' detention in a young offender institution, having pleaded guilty to maliciously inflicting grievous bodily harm. C, aged 19, attended a function at a night club. C was involved in an incident with the doorman and was asked to leave the club. C left the club and approached a man who was a complete stranger to him. C lashed out at the stranger, punching him in the face with the back of his fist. The stranger fell to the ground and hit his neck against a wall of an adjoining building. He was later found to have sustained a fracture at the base of the skull for which specialist treatment was necessary. He was unable to return to work and was thought likely to have to wear a halo jacket holding his neck in a stable position for six months. A medical report on the victim indicated that the prognosis was good, but that the fracture had been potentially fatal with the risk of irreparable neurological damage.

Held, allowing the appeal, that it was argued that the sentence was excessive as the offence involved the use of a single blow, and the injuries sustained by the victim were caused by his fall against the wall. C had surrendered to the police and pleaded guilty. He was 19 years old and of impeccable character. The court considered that for any unprovoked blow of this nature, which caused the serious injuries which this blow caused, the assailant must expect to go straight to custody. In view of the mitigation, however, the court considered the right sentence would be one of six months' detention.

R. v. CLARKE (JONATHAN) [1999] 2 Cr. App. R. (S.) 400, Simon Brown, L.J., CA (Crim Div).

1271. Harassment – 13 year old victim – fear of violence due to persistent and threatening phone calls

[Protection from Harassment Act 1997 s.4.]

H pleaded guilty to harassment causing fear of violence contrary to the Protection from Harassment Act 1997 s.4. H came into possession of a bus pass belonging to a girl aged 13. Using information from the pass, he made many telephone calls to her at her home. When the girl answered the telephone, H would sometimes hang up and sometimes start heavy breathing and asking her questions. On one occasion, H threatened to rape the girl. As a consequence, she was very frightened and became afraid to leave the house. H was sentenced to 18 months' imprisonment, with a restraining order under s.4. H appealed.

Held, allowing the appeal, that the victim was a young girl at a vulnerable stage in her life who was clearly frightened by H's actions. Plainly a sentence of imprisonment was necessary. Having regard to the H's early pleas, the court had concluded that the sentence was too severe. A sentence of 12 months' imprisonment would be substituted.

R. v. HILL (JASON LEE) [2000] 1 Cr. App. R. (S.) 8, Bracewell, J., CA (Crim Div).

1272. Harassment – actual bodily harm – stalking over nine month period – female victim suffering from generalised anxiety state

N appealed against a sentence of two years' imprisonment having been convicted of assault occasioning actual bodily harm in the form of stalking a female building society branch manager. N frequently looked into her office, and on several occasions mouthed obscenities through her window. N watched the woman leaving work and left a note on the windscreen of her car. N on various occasions stared at her in the street, made obscene gestures towards her, banged on her car roof and made lewd comments to her. The victim suffered from a generalised anxiety state brought about by these incidents.

Held, allowing the appeal, that N had engaged in a course of conduct lasting at least nine months which led to psychiatric injury to the victim. The case could be distinguished on its facts from *R. v. Smith (Peter Leonard)* [1998] 1 Cr. App. R. (S.) 138, [1997] C.L.Y. 1578, where the conduct extended over a period of four years, and where the victim required medical treatment. The court had come to the conclusion that the sentence was manifestly excessive. Notwithstanding that this was a serious case causing upset and distress to the victim over many months, the right sentence would have been 15 months' imprisonment, *R. v. Burstow (Anthony Christopher)* [1997] 1 Cr. App. R. 144, [1996] C.L.Y. 1438 considered and *Smith* distinguished.

R. v. NOTICE (JEFFREY) [2000] 1 Cr. App. R. (S.) 75, Scott Baker, J., CA (Crim Div).

1273. Ill treatment – children – mother failing to protect child from violence

C appealed against a sentence of a total of five years' imprisonment having pleaded guilty to two offences of cruelty to a child. C was the mother of a child. She lived with a man who was not the child's father. Over a period of several months, the man assaulted the child on a number of occasions. On one occasion, C received a telephone call at work and returned immediately to her home. Half an hour after returning home she called an ambulance. The child was taken to hospital where she was found to be dead. A post mortem examination revealed a large number of bruises, most of them recent, together with a haemorrhage to the intestines, a fractured rib and split liver. This injury would have caused death within 15 to 20 minutes of its infliction and it would have been obvious that the child was in need of urgent medical attention. The prosecution case against C was that over a period of seven months she had failed to protect the child from violence inflicted by the man with whom she was living and that on the occasion of the child's death she had caused unnecessary suffering by the delay in calling for an ambulance. The man was convicted of murder and sentenced to life imprisonment.

Held, dismissing the appeal, that C had acted with utter selfishness, relegating the interests of the child below her own interest in pursuing a relationship with the man. This was a horrific case involving an extreme form of child cruelty or neglect on the part of C. In the court's judgment the sentences were entirely appropriate.

R. v. SLC [2000] 1 Cr. App. R. (S.) 304, Maurice Kay, J., CA (Crim Div).

1274. Ill treatment – children – parents leaving children unsupervised for long periods

C and S appealed against respective sentences of 12 and 15 months' imprisonment, having pleaded guilty to three counts of cruelty to a child. S was the mother of the three children, aged 13, nine and seven. She lived with C. One afternoon C and S went out at about 3.30 pm, leaving the children unsupervised. They returned at about 9.30 pm. The 13 year old boy was taken to hospital the following morning where he died from pneumonia caused by methadone poisoning. C was a drug addict to whom methadone and other drugs had been prescribed. The methadone was normally kept in their bedroom into which the children were not normally allowed. The prosecution case was based on the allegation that C and S had left the children unsupervised for a period of about seven hours, during which the oldest boy had consumed methadone which killed him.

Held, dismissing the appeal, that the question was whether 12 months' imprisonment was manifestly excessive in relation to the conduct of C and S, bearing in mind their pleas and personal circumstances. The court was unable to conclude that the sentences were manifestly excessive.

R. v. C (PAUL JOHN); R. v. S (JACQUELINE ROSEMARY) [2000] 2 Cr. App. R. (S.) 329, Rose, L.J., CA (Crim Div).

1275. Illegal entrants – facilitating illegal entry into United Kingdom

[Immigration Act 1971 s.25(1)(a).]

F and D were convicted and E pleaded guilty to facilitating the entry of immigrants, contrary to the Immigration Act 1971 s.25(1)(a). They were concerned in arranging to transport 20 illegal immigrants into the UK in a lorry. They appealed against their sentence of four years' imprisonment in each case.

Held, allowing the appeal, that F, D and E played a vital part in the enterprise. The sentencer had indicated that he had taken six years as a starting point and made appropriate allowances for the good character of F, D and E. In the court's view, this starting point was incorrect and the court would reduce sentences to three years in each case, *R. v. Le (Van Binh)* [1999] 1 Cr. App. R. (S.) 422, [1998] C.L.Y. 1245, *R. v. Ungruh (Helmut)* [1996] 2 Cr. App. R. (S.) 205, [1996] C.L.Y. 1936, *R. v. Brown (Nicholas Alexander)* [1997] 1 Cr. App. R. (S.) 112, [1997] C.L.Y. 1579 and *R. v. Winn (James Derrick)* [1999] 1 Cr. App. R. (S.) 154, [1999] C.L.Y. 1191 considered.

R. v. LIDDLE (FREDERICK); R. v. VAN ACKEREN (MICHAEL STANELEY); R. v. SINGH (BHUPINDER) [2000] 2 Cr. App. R. (S.) 282, Curtis, J., CA (Crim Div).

1276. Illegal entrants – facilitating illegal entry of two men into UK – no evidence of involvement in immigration syndicate

A appealed against a sentence of two years' imprisonment having pleaded guilty before a magistrates' court to facilitating illegal entry, and was committed to the Crown Court for sentence. A arrived at the UK Customs area at Coquelles in a car accompanied by his girlfriend and their baby. A search of the car disclosed two Yugoslav nationals hiding in the boot. A claimed that he had been asked by an acquaintance to give the two men a lift from Holland into France, and that the two men had subsequently persuaded him to take them to England. They were not members of his family.

Held, allowing the appeal, that this was an isolated offence involving two illegal entrants, with no evidence of financial gain, commercial organisation or sophisticated planning. It was accepted that a custodial sentence was inevitable. A had strong emotional reasons for becoming involved in the offence, as a former Yugoslav national himself. The sentence would be reduced to 18 months' imprisonment.

R. v. AHMETAJ (ESAD) [2000] 1 Cr. App. R. (S.) 66, Butterfield, J., CA (Crim Div).

1277. Indecent assault – attempting to kiss woman without consent

T, aged 42, appealed against a sentence of nine months' imprisonment, having been was convicted of one count of indecent assault. He worked as a cleaner at a shopping centre. He made himself known to an 18 year old woman who worked at a shop as a sales assistant. On one occasion he followed her into a stock room and asked her to meet him, which she refused to do. Some time later she returned to the stock room to have lunch. When the young woman left, T grabbed her in a hug, pushed her backwards on to some cases and tried to kiss her twice and then kissed her hand.

Held, allowing the appeal, that the sentencer commented that the serious aspect of the case was the difference in age between T and the victim, and the fact that his actions had made her unhappy and frightened. In the court's view, this was not the most serious offence of indecent assault. The court took into account T's previous good character. The sentence of nine months was longer than necessary. A sentence of four months' imprisonment would be substituted, *R. v. Drysdale (Andrew McDonald)* (1993) 14 Cr. App. R. (S.) 15, [1993] C.L.Y. 1190 considered.

R. v. TABIT (ELABBES) [2000] 2 Cr. App. R. (S.) 298, Brian Smedley, J., CA (Crim Div).

1278. Indecent assault – children – appellant involved in sexual acts with consenting teenage boys

F, a woman with three children, pleaded guilty to five counts of indecent assault on a male and to two counts of permitting premises to be used for smoking cannabis resin. She admitted that on a number of occasions she had been involved in sexual activities, including sexual intercourse, with two boys aged 15. On other occasions F had allowed young people to smoke cannabis at her house. F was sentenced to 12 months' imprisonment concurrent on each count of indecent assault, with nine months' imprisonment on each count of permitting premises to be used for smoking cannabis, and appealed.

Held, allowing the appeal, that these were serious offences which crossed the custody threshold and justified a sentence of imprisonment. The question was whether the sentence of 12 months' imprisonment was too long. The court came to the conclusion that it was, in view of the mitigating circumstances, and a sentence of six months' imprisonment could be substituted on each count, all concurrent, *R. v. Sant (Vicky)* (1989) 11 Cr. App. R. (S.) 441, [1991] C.L.Y. 1141, *R. v. Tozer (Kerry Anne)* (1994) 15 Cr. App. R. (S.) 807, [1995] C.L.Y. 1409 and *R. v. B (Sharon Kristine)* (1994) 15 Cr. App. R. (S.) 815, [1995] C.L.Y. 1405 considered.

R. v. TF (INDECENT ASSAULT: MENTAL HEALTH) [2000] 2 Cr. App. R. (S.) 292, Penry-Davey, J., CA (Crim Div).

1279. Indecent assault – children – assault and attempted buggery of 14 year old step daughter – sentenced on basis of attempted rape

D was convicted of two offences of indecent assault and one of attempted buggery. D was convicted of indecently assaulting his stepdaughter, aged between 12 and 14, by having sexual intercourse with her and attempting to bugger her when she was 14. D was sentenced to 18 months' imprisonment on each count of indecent assault with seven years for attempted buggery, all concurrent. D appealed.

Held, allowing the appeal, that D was not charged with attempted rape in respect of the attempted buggery, but with attempted buggery. An offender was to be sentenced only for the offence of which he had been found guilty. The sentence was manifestly excessive; a sentence of three years would be substituted, *R. v. Davies (Tarian John)* [1998] 1 Cr. App. R. (S.) 380, [1997] C.L.Y. 1413 considered.

R. v. D [2000] 1 Cr. App. R. (S.) 120, Aikens, J., CA (Crim Div).

1280. Indecent assault – children – assault on niece – unduly lenient sentence

The Attorney General asked the court to review sentences on the ground that they were unduly lenient. T was convicted on three counts of indecent assault. T indecently assaulted his niece on three occasions between her tenth and eleventh birthdays. The offences were committed at T's home, when the niece and her family were staying overnight. T would put his hand inside the girl's underwear and touch her vagina, occasionally exposing his penis to her. Following his conviction, T admitted his responsibility for the offences and expressed remorse. T was sentenced to a probation order for three years in respect of the offences.

Held, refusing the reference, that the sentencer was well aware that such offences usually merited immediate imprisonment, especially where there was a breach of trust. The sentencer added that he had decided that that was not appropriate in the present case. He took into account the fact that the defendant had no previous convictions of the same nature, that he had shown remorse and had accepted what he had done. The judge was told there was a real prospect of rehabilitation. He concluded that it was an unusual case in which an unusual course should be taken. In the light of these considerations, the court was not persuaded that the sentence passed, albeit lenient, was unduly lenient. Sentencing was an art, not a science. There were cases within the residual discretion of the sentencing judge where it was appropriate to take an exceptional course. This was such a case and the sentence, though lenient, was not unduly lenient, *Attorney General's Reference (No.35 of 1994), Re* (1995) 16 Cr. App. R. (S.) 635, [1996] C.L.Y. 1782, *Attorney General's Reference (No.34 of 1997), Re* [1998] 1 F.L.R. 515, [1997] C.L.Y. 1450 considered.

ATTORNEY GENERAL'S REFERENCE (NO.77 OF 1999), *Re; sub nom.* R. v. T (JOHN) [2000] 2 Cr. App. R. (S.) 250, Rose, L.J., CA (Crim Div).

1281. Indecent assault – children – attempted sexual intercourse with girl of 15 years

M met a 15 year old girl who was walking home after drinking a considerable amount of cider. M realised the girl was drunk and that she was a danger to herself and to traffic. They made their way down a footpath and began kissing each other. The complainant removed her lower clothing and M attempted unsuccessfully to have intercourse with her. He then placed one of his fingers into her vagina. She then became nauseous and sexual activity stopped. The girl then told appellant to leave her as she could look after herself. She was later found lying on the ground in a drunken condition. M went to the police station the next day and admitted that he had been involved. He subsequently made a full admission. M was sentenced to two years' imprisonment and appealed.

Held, allowing the appeal, that the activity was consensual and the offence could have been charged as attempted unlawful sexual intercourse. Had it been so charged the maximum sentence would have been two years' imprisonment. The Court had observed in *R. v. I (Matthew Joseph)* [1998] 2 Cr. App. R. (S) 63, [1998] C.L.Y. 1262 applied, that where a defendant was convicted of indecent assault on the basis of a single act of intercourse with a consenting girl under 16, it was proper to approach the matter on the basis that the maximum sentence should be regarded as two years, because the court was in reality dealing with an act of unlawful sexual intercourse. The Court had been referred also to *R. v. Wilson (Tyrell)* (Unreported, July 22, 1997) and *R. v. Goodwin* (Unreported, August 4, 1995). M was a man of previous good character who was entitled to credit for volunteering himself to the police and for pleading guilty. There was no substantial disparity in the ages of M and the girl. The sentence of two years was too high. The sentence would be reduced to nine months' imprisonment.

R. v. M (MICHAEL NEIL) [2000] 1 Cr. App. R. (S.) 416, Ebsworth, J., CA (Crim Div).

1282. Indecent assault – children – father sexually abusing 11 year old daughter – sexual activity over four year period – unduly lenient sentence

The Attorney General referred as unduly lenient a sentence of three years and three months' imprisonment for CB, a 37 year old sex offender. Following the breakdown of his marriage, CB had maintained contact with his 11 year old daughter, X, who visited him at his home every alternate weekend and during the school holidays. When X was between the ages of 11 and 14, CB had indecently assaulted her with increasing severity, beginning with fondling of the chest and pubic areas, progressing to masturbation, digital vaginal penetration and oral sex and culminating in regular sexual intercourse and attempted anal penetration. He had also taught her to perform indecent acts upon him, and had claimed he had a relationship tantamount to a boyfriend and girlfriend partnership with X. Sexual activity had ceased when X, who had had no prior sexual experience, had mistakenly believed herself to be pregnant. The Attorney General contended that the sentence failed to reflect the gravity of the offences given that they had occurred over a considerable period of time and the fact that a young girl had been corrupted by a person in a position of trust. CB argued that the sentence could not be categorised as unduly lenient in the light of his early guilty plea, frank admissions, genuine remorse and previous good character.

Held, allowing the reference, that a sentence of five and a half years' imprisonment was appropriate in view of the range of sexual activity involved, its duration and the end result, which was total corruption of an 11 year old girl. A sentence of seven to eight years would have been appropriate, and the reduction from that bracket to the substituted sentence reflected the element of double jeopardy.

ATTORNEY GENERAL'S REFERENCE (NO.32 OF 2000), *Re*; *sub nom*. R. v. CB 2000/3359/R2, Rose, L.J., CA (Crim Div).

1283. Indecent assault – children – indecent assault on daughter 40 years previously – age of offender

W, aged 80, appealed against a sentence of three and a half years' imprisonment, having pleaded guilty to 14 counts of indecent assault and one of gross indecency with a child. The offences were committed against the daughter of W beginning about 40 years before the proceedings and extending over about four years while his daughter was between the ages of 11 and 15. W indecently assaulted his daughter in various ways. The daughter, who was now 51 years old, stated that she frequently suffered from nightmares and had never forgotten the offences.

Held, dismissing the appeal, that if the crimes had been disclosed and dealt with at an earlier date, a much longer sentence, of the order of eight years imprisonment, would have been appropriate. The sentencer had reduced the sentence on account of the plea of guilty, the time which had passed since the offences were committed and the advanced age of W. The only question was whether he had reduced the sentence sufficiently on account of these matters. In cases such as this, the time which had passed since the offence had been committed was normally a consequence of the offence itself, and an indicator of the depth of the injury which had been done. Delay was a factor to be taken into account, but the weight to be attached to it was likely to be limited. Great caution was required lest discount was granted for what was in truth an aspect of the crime itself. An offender's age was obviously a relevant factor, but in this case there was no particular ailment or hardship which would affect W by reason of his age. To reduce the sentence further could send out a message of support to W's misconceived notions and serve to prolong his lack of insight. It could weaken the message as to the consequences which other who perpetrated such offences should realise would be meted out to them. The sentencer conducted the difficult balancing exercise in a way which could not be impugned.

R. v. W (J) [2000] 1 Cr. App. R. (S.) 234, Newman, J., CA (Crim Div).

1284. Indecent assault – children – recidivists – extended sentences

[Criminal Justice Act 1991 s.2(2)(b), s.40.]

C indicated before a magistrates' court that he would plead guilty to indecent assault on a female. He was committed to the Crown Court for sentence. C entered a house through an open window, and indecently assaulted a 12 year old girl who was asleep in bed. The offence was committed five months after C's release from a sentence of seven years' imprisonment imposed for a similar offence. A psychiatric report indicated that there was a high risk of C repeating the offence. C appealed against a sentence of eight years' imprisonment, passed as a longer than commensurate sentence under the Criminal Justice Act 1991 s.2(2)(b) consecutive to an order under the Criminal Justice Act 1991 s.40 returning C to prison for 682 days in respect of the earlier sentence. The sentencer should have asked himself what would have been the appropriate sentence commensurate with the offence, and then gone on to consider what if anything should be added to protect the public under s.2(2)(b). Unfortunately, the sentencer did not go through that exercise so it was impossible to know how the sentence of eight years was divided.

Held, allowing the appeal, that the sentencer should have added the appropriate number of years to cover the danger to the public under s.2(2)(b). In the court's view, having regard to the aggravating features of the offence, the appropriate commensurate sentence would have been in the region of four years, *R. v. Crow (William John)* (1995) 16 Cr. App. R. (S.) 409 considered. The sentencer had also to bear in mind that this was a case where C had pleaded guilty. This was particularly important in cases involving sex offences as it avoided requiring young girls or boys to give evidence in court. It was necessary that the court did bear in mind the importance of giving and appearing to give a discount in relation to a plea of guilty. The sentence of eight years was excessive. The appropriate sentence, taking account of s.2(2)(b), would have been six years. The order returning C to prison for 682 days under the Criminal Justice Act 1991 s.40 and ordering the sentence for the later offence to run consecutively to that order, was contrary to the approach which the court adopted in *R. v. Johnson (Adrian)* [1998] 1 Cr. App. R. (S.) 126, [1998] C.L.Y. 1159. The headnote stated "a longer than the normal sentence passed under Criminal Justice Act 1991 s.2(2)(b) should not be ordered to run consecutively to a period for which the offender is returned to prison under the Criminal Justice Act 1991 s.40." *Johnson* followed the earlier case of *R. v. King (Samuel Nathaniel)* (1995) 16 Cr. App. R. (S.) 987, [1996] C.L.Y. 2065 considered. While the court indicated in *Johnson* that such a course was generally undesirable, implying that there might be cases where such a course was not improper, there was nothing in the present case to take it outside the principle set out in *Johnson*. Accordingly the court would substitute a sentence of six years' imprisonment for the eight years imposed by the Crown Court, and order it to run concurrently with the order return the defendant to prison for 682 days under s.40. The court similarly ordered a return to prison order of 150 days for C to run concurrently with a six year sentence for two indecent assaults, instead of consecutively to it.

R. v. C (NEIL DAVID); R. v. J [2000] 1 Cr. App. R. (S.) 359, Collins, J., CA (Crim Div).

1285. Indecent assault – children – sentencing not gender specific

B, a care assistant in a residential school for boys, appealed against her sentence of five years imprisonment following a conviction for 10 offences of indecent assault against five boys aged between 12 and 14.

Held, dismissing the appeal, that the sentence was appropriate, having regard to the fact that it was a serious abuse case involving a breach of trust, and having taken into account the mitigating circumstances. Gender specific factors were not taken into account when sentencing, notwithstanding that if a man of the same age as B had committed an indecent assault on a young girl in similar circumstances, he would have received a very long sentence.

R. v. B (CAROLINE) [2001] 1 Cr. App. R. (S.) 74, Rose, L.J., CA (Crim Div).

1286. Indecent assault – children – sexual abuse – 71 year old offender in extreme ill health – unduly lenient sentence

The Attorney General referred to the court the sentences imposed on G, a 71 year old male, who was convicted of nine counts of indecent assault on a female, four counts of indecent assault on a male, and two counts of indecency with a child. The victims were G's three children and the abuse was over a prolonged period when G was in his late thirties to late forties. The abuse of his eldest daughter took place when she was between nine and 15 years' old and included digital vaginal interference, self masturbation in her presence and mutual genital contact. Thereafter G's adopted son was abused between the ages of five and 12, during which time he was required to masturbate G, including taking G's penis into his mouth and was subjected to anal intercourse and masturbation by G. The abuse of G's adopted daughter occurred when she was aged 12 to 13 years' and consisted of digital vaginal penetration, oral sex and attempted intercourse. The Attorney General referred as unduly lenient a concurrent sentence of two years' imprisonment on each count of indecent assault and 12 months' imprisonment on both counts of indecency, suspended for a term of two years, citing aggravating features including there being three separate victims, the lengthy period of abuse and the particularly adverse effect on the boy, who tried on several occasions to run away from home. In mitigation G relied upon his extreme ill health, the fact that he had no previous convictions and that the last offence had occurred 22 years before conviction.

Held, allowing the reference, that the sentence could not fail to be characterised as being unduly lenient. The judge had not given due regard to the public's requirements for punishment and deterrence in such cases. Taking into account G's personal circumstances, a sentence of six years would normally have been expected. Having regard to the element of double jeopardy and to the harassment G had suffered since conviction, a sentence of four years' would be substituted.

ATTORNEY GENERAL'S REFERENCE (NO.15 OF 2000), *Re*; *sub nom*. R. v G (RICHARD) [2001] 1 Cr. App. R. (S.) 23, Rose, L.J., CA (Crim Div).

1287. Indecent assault – children – unduly lenient sentence

The Attorney General asked the court to review sentences on the ground that they were unduly lenient. F lived with his wife and children, including a daughter aged between 10 and 11. The daughter alleged that on the various occasions when her mother was either asleep or out of the house, F indecently assaulted her by placing his penis on her vaginal area and by placing her hand on his penis. F denied all of the allegations and was convicted on three specific counts. F was sentenced to a total of six months' imprisonment.

Held, allowing the reference, that the sentence of six months' imprisonment was outside the range of appropriate sentences and unduly lenient. The appropriate sentence for these offences following conviction on a plea of not guilty was 15 and 18 months. F had however completed his sentence and had attempted to re-establish his life and employment. If the court were to substitute a longer sentence, it would make an appropriate deduction on account of the impact of double jeopardy. In the circumstances the sentence which the court would substitute would be of the order of nine months. As F had already served a sentence of six months, no relevant public interest would be served by substituting a sentence which would result in the offender being returned to prison for a relatively short time. In those circumstances although the sentences were unduly lenient, the Court would not substitute another sentence, *Attorney General's Reference (No.50 of 1997), Re* [1998] 2 Cr. App. R. (S.) 155), [1998] C.L.Y. 1249 considered.

ATTORNEY GENERAL'S REFERENCE (NO.43 OF 1999), *Re*; *sub nom.* R. v. M (GG) [2000] 1 Cr. App. R. (S.) 398, Lord Bingham of Cornhill, L.C.J., CA (Crim Div).

1288. **Indecent assault – children – unduly lenient sentence**

The Attorney General asked the court to review a sentence on the ground that it was unduly lenient. W was convicted of seven counts of indecent assault. W's wife died in 1990, leaving him to care for four children, including two daughters then aged 10 and eight and a baby daughter. W began to abuse the eldest girl when she was about 12, placing his fingers in her vagina and touching her breasts. There was at least one incident of simulated intercourse. The offences against the first daughter were committed over a period of two years and ended when she left home at the age of 13. W indecently assaulted the second daughter on a number of occasions when she was eight or nine years old, and indecently assaulted the youngest daughter aged eight by making her masturbate him and by lying on top of her and ejaculating on top of her. W was sentenced to a total of 30 months' imprisonment.

Held, allowing the reference, that the sentences were unduly lenient for abuse of three daughters in succession. The appropriate total sentence would have been of the order of four to five years. A sentence of three and a half years was substituted, *Attorney General's Reference (No.54 of 1997), Re* [1998] 2 Cr. App. R. (S.) 324, [1998] C.L.Y. 1266, *Attorney General's Reference (No.20 of 1998), Re* [1999] 1 Cr. App. R. (S.) 280, [1999] C.L.Y. 1201, *Attorney General's Reference (No.32 of 1998), Re* [1999] 1 Cr. App. R. (S.) 316, [1999] C.L.Y. 1210, *Attorney General's Reference (No.2 of 1995), Re* [1996] 1 Cr. App. R. (S.) 274, [1996] C.L.Y. 1788, *R. v. L (Indecent Assault: Sentencing)* [1999] 1 Cr. App. R. 117, [1998] C.L.Y. 1257, *R. v. L (Kenneth Peter)* [1999] 1 Cr. App. R. (S.) 347, [1999] C.L.Y. 1203, and *Attorney General's Reference (No.34 of 1997), Re* [1998] 1 F.L.R. 515, [1997] C.L.Y. 1450, *R. v. Demel (Gem Delantha)* [1997] 2 Cr. App. R. (S.) 5, [1997] C.L.Y. 1445 considered.

ATTORNEY GENERAL'S REFERENCE (NO.66 OF 1999), *Re*; *sub nom.* R. v. BW [2000] 1 Cr. App. R. (S.) 558, Roch, L.J., CA (Crim Div).

1289. **Indecent assault – female passenger on underground train**

D appealed against his conviction and sentence of three months' imprisonment for indecent assault on a female passenger on an underground train. D was observed by police officers riding on underground trains. He was observed to stand close behind a woman passenger, who felt an intermittent rubbing motion across her buttocks. D was arrested by officers who had observed the incident.

Held, dismissing the appeal, that the sentencer formed the view that D had entered on a planned and premeditated expedition with a view to committing indecent assaults. The offence could not be treated as a result of a momentary aberration. D was not entitled to the credit which he would have received for a plea of guilty, *R. v. Neem (Zohair)* (1993) 14 Cr. App. R. (S) 18, [1993] C.L.Y. 1195 and *R. v. Townsend (Scott)* (1995) 16 Cr. App. R. (S) 553, [1994] C.L.Y. 1284 considered.

R. v. MD [2000] 1 Cr. App. R. (S.) 426, Alliott, J., CA (Crim Div).

1290. **Indecent assault – medical treatment – osteopath assaulting patients – unduly lenient sentence**

The Attorney General asked the court to review a sentence on the ground that it was unduly lenient. M was convicted of four counts of indecent assault on a female. He was a qualified osteopath, and the victims of the assaults were patients who came to him for treatment. On four occasions between 1991 and 1993, M indecently assaulted patients during periods of treatment. The assaults involved asking the women to remove their clothing, massaging them on or between the breasts and, in respect of two patients, exposing his erect penis. M was sentenced to 12 months' imprisonment on each count, suspended for two years.

Held, allowing the reference, that the sentencer was confronted with a particularly difficult problem. The court was satisfied that the sentencer paid too much regard to the requirements of M and his family and too little regard to the public concern generated by offences of this kind committed under the guise of medical treatment against female patients who might well be vulnerable. The sentence of 12 months' imprisonment suspended was unduly lenient. In all the circumstances of the case, including the period of time over which the offences were committed, the fact that there were four separate victims and that M's professional body had intervened before two of the offences were committed, the court would have expected a total sentence of at least 30 months' imprisonment. Taking into account the element of double jeopardy, the court would substitute a sentence of 18 months' immediate imprisonment on each count to run concurrently, *R. v. Pike (Colin)* [1996] 1 Cr. App. R. (S.) 4, *R. v. Prokop (Xavier Alexander)* (1995) 16 Cr. App. R. (S.) 598 and *R. v. Ghosh (Deb Baron)* [1999] 1 Cr. App. R. (S.) 225, [1999] C.L.Y. 1202 considered.

ATTORNEY GENERAL'S REFERENCE (NO.6 OF 1999), *Re*; *sub nom.* R. v. MIDDA (JULIAN ELLERY) (UNDULY LENIENT SENTENCE) [2000] 2 Cr. App. R. (S.) 67, Rose, L.J., CA (Crim Div).

1291. **Indecent assault – offences committed against prostitute – unduly lenient sentence**

The Attorney General asked the court to review a sentence on the ground that it was unduly lenient. W engaged the victim through an escort agency for the purposes of sexual services. In the course of sexual activities, W without the knowledge of the victim placed live maggots in her vagina. W admitted subsequently threatening the victim with a knife. The victim ran out of his house naked and drove off in her car. W pleaded guilty to indecent assault and was sentenced to twelve months' imprisonment.

Held, allowing the reference, the sentence was unduly lenient for an exceptionally unpleasant and serious sexual assault which had caused the victim significant psychological harm. A sentence of three years' imprisonment was substituted.

ATTORNEY GENERAL'S REFERENCE (NO.65 OF 1999), *Re*; *sub nom.* R. v. W (ROBERT) [2000] 1 Cr. App. R. (S.) 554, Swinton Thomas, L.J., CA (Crim Div).

1292. **Indecent assault – offensive weapons – deliberately planned attack on victim – threat with knife**

S pleaded guilty to two counts of indecent assault on a female. S had had a sexual relationship with the victim for about six years. During the course of this relationship S had used objects on the victim, such as a carrot and a vibrator. On the occasion of the offence, S and the victim went for a drive in S's taxi to a remote area and he eventually proposed sexual intercourse to the victim, which she refused. S then produced a knife from under the driver's seat, together with a cucumber, applied vaseline to the victim and inserted the cucumber into her. He also forced his fingers into her anus. He then attempted to make her take his penis in her mouth and ejaculated over her face. S was sentenced to seven years' imprisonment on one count and three years' imprisonment concurrent on the second count. S appealed.

Held, dismissing the appeal, that the sentencer was correct to say that S had treated the victim as a sex object and made a planned and deliberate attack upon her. This was a dreadful case, demanding a very long sentence. The sentence of seven years, while severe, could not be described as manifestly excessive.

R. v. S (WAYNE) [2000] 1 Cr. App. R. (S.) 62, Butterfield, J., CA (Crim Div).

1293. Indecent assault – partner

C appealed against a sentence of three and half years' imprisonment, having pleaded guilty to indecent assault. He lived with a woman who had been his partner for 10 years. After they had retired to bed, C suddenly removed the quilt from the bed, and attempted to perform oral sex on her. He then demanded that she perform oral sex on him, but she refused. C inserted his fingers into her anus and then threatened to insert his penis into her anus unless she performed oral sex on him, which she did. C continued to threaten her while she did so. The victim attempted to escape, but C forced her to return to the bedroom and made her perform oral sex again. The victim eventually ran across the road to her mother's house covered only in blanket.

Held, allowing the appeal, that C had lived with the victim for 10 years and had three children. There had been no violence in the relationship apart from this offence. Although a severe sentence was justified for an unpleasant, serious and sustained attack, the appropriate sentence would have been two and a half years' imprisonment, *R. v. Kowalski (Roy)* (1988) 86 Cr. App. R. 339, [1988] C.L.Y. 1654, and *R. v. Basnett (Wayne)* [1996] 2 Cr. App. R. (S.) 305, [1996] C.L.Y. 1945 considered.

R. v. C (CLIFFORD PAUL) [2000] 1 Cr. App. R. (S.) 533, Penry-Davey, J., CA (Crim Div).

1294. Indecent assault – perverting public justice – unqualified person posing as doctor

The Attorney General asked the court to review a sentence on the ground that it was unduly lenient. G was convicted of four offences of indecent assault, 16 of obtaining property by deception, three of unlawful wounding, two of supplying prescription only medicines and on a second indictment of nine offences of doing an act tending and intended to pervert the course of justice. G, who had no medical qualifications, training or experience, practised as a doctor and in the course of doing so committed indecent assaults on female patients in the form of vaginal examinations. He also prescribed medicines and administered injections. On a number of occasions he acted as an expert witness in drink driving cases in the magistrates' court or Crown Court and gave false evidence. G was sentenced to a total of five years' imprisonment.

Held, refusing the reference, that at the time when the sentence was imposed, the overall sentence was unduly lenient. An appropriate sentence for the first indictment would have been of the order of five to six years, with a consecutive sentence of the order of two years for the offences of perverting justice. The total sentence would have been no less than seven years. In view of the element of double jeopardy, the age of the offender and his state of health, it was not necessary in public interest at this stage to substitute an increased sentence, *R. v. Prokop (Xavier Alexander)* (1995) 16 Cr. App. R. (S.) 598, *R. v. Pike (Colin)* [1996] 1 Cr. App. R. (S.) 4, *R. v. Ghosh (Deb Baron)* [1999] 1 Cr. App. R. (S.) 225, [1999] C.L.Y. 1202, *Attorney General's Reference (No.44 of 1994), Re* [1996] 1 Cr. App. R. (S.) 256, [1995] C.L.Y. 1449 and *Attorney*

General's Reference (No.4 of 1989), Re [1990] 1 W.L.R. 41, [1990] C.L.Y. 1207 considered.

ATTORNEY GENERAL'S REFERENCE (NO.62 OF 1998), *Re*; *sub nom*. R. v. ONUBOGU (GODWIN) [2000] 2 Cr. App. R. (S.) 286, Kennedy, L.J., CA (Crim Div).

1295. Indecent assault – pleas – appropriateness of imposing extended sentence

[Crime and Disorder Act 1998 s.58.]

B pleaded guilty to indecent assault on a female. He met a girl at a public house and fell into conversation with her. They began to kiss and eventually B touched her over her clothes and put his finger into her vagina. B took her hand and put it on his penis over his trousers. B was sentenced to an extended sentence under the Crime and Disorder Act 1998 s.58 consisting of a custodial term of four years with an extension period of three years. B appealed.

Held, allowing the appeal, that B was 36 and had no previous convictions. A sentence of four years' imprisonment could not be justified, following an early plea of guilty. There was nothing to suggest that any particular matters had been taken into account by the sentencer in deciding to impose an extended sentence under the Crime and Disorder Act 1998 s.58. the sentence would be quashed and a sentence of 18 months' imprisonment substituted.

R. v. BARROS (JOSO MANUEL) [2000] 2 Cr. App. R. (S.) 327, Scott Baker, J., CA (Crim Div).

1296. Indecent assault – private hire vehicles – driver assaulting sleeping passenger

S, convicted of indecent assault, appealed against a sentence of three years' imprisonment. The complainant left a bar in company with her friend and they shared a minicab driven by S. The complainant fell asleep in the minicab. S stopped to drop off the complainant's friend, and got into the back of the cab, where he put his hand inside her underwear and inserted his fingers into her vagina. S returned to the driver's seat when the complainant woke up and screamed, and then drove her home. S claimed that he had done nothing indecent and had simply tried to wake the complainant.

Held, allowing the appeal, that this was a serious indecent assault committed by a person who was in a position of trust. The sentence was not excessive, but in view of the exceptional personal mitigating circumstances affecting the appellant's family the sentence would be reduced to two years' imprisonment.

R. v. S (ABDUL) [2000] 1 Cr. App. R. (S.) 40, Butterfield, J., CA (Crim Div).

1297. Indecent assault – probation orders – sexual assault on woman working alone

[Criminal Justice Act 1988 s.36.]

The Attorney General referred a sentence of three years' probation with a condition of sex offender treatment for indecent assault to the Court of Appeal pursuant to the Criminal Justice Act 1988 s.36. D had tricked his way into the vehicle of his victim and had begun to assault her, indicating that he had a knife, but had fled when his victim had begun to resist. The Attorney General contended that an appropriate sentence would have been not less than three years' imprisonment as the assault had been premeditated, undertaken with the threat of a knife, and on a woman working alone. D had shown little remorse and had a record of serious sexual offences, including rape, which indicated a risk of reoffending.

Held, refusing the reference, that D's guilty plea, the fact that he had desisted from the assault when his victim resisted, and the hardship imprisonment would have caused his family were exceptional circumstances and that, whilst a sentence of three years' imprisonment, extended by three years, would have been acceptable, the judge had been entitled to impose the non-custodial term. A successful programme of treatment would be more beneficial to the public than the service of a lengthy term of imprisonment and this too was a consideration which the judge had been entitled to consider, *R. v. Knibbs (Gordon Ralph)* (1991) 12 Cr. App. R. (S.) 655, [1992] C.L.Y. 1317 considered.

ATTORNEY GENERAL'S REFERENCE (NO.46 OF 2000), *Re; sub nom*. R. v. DYSON (GERALD FRANK) [2001] 1 Cr. App. R. (S.) 118, Lord Woolf of Barnes, L.C.J., CA (Crim Div).

1298. Indecent assault – recidivists – extended sentences

[Criminal Justice Act 1991 s.2(2)(b); Crime and Disorder Act 1998 s.58.]

T pleaded guilty to indecent assault. He approached a woman as she was walking home in the early hours of the morning, grabbed her by the arm, attempted to pull her into a nearby street, put his hand up her skirt and pulled down her tights. T had convictions for five previous offences of indecent assault on women committed of the period between 1982 and 1996. T was sentenced to five years' imprisonment passed as a longer sentence than commensurate sentence under the Criminal Justice Act 1991 s.2(2)(b), on the basis that an appropriate commensurate sentence would have been two years, with an additional three years for the protection of the public. T had voluntarily admitted the offence to a member of the staff of the hostel where he lived, who had contacted the police. T gave an incomplete account of what had happened, and a *Newton* hearing was necessary to determine the precise facts of the offence. The identity of T would never have been known without his voluntary confession. T appealed.

Held, allowing the appeal, that the sentencer had properly given a smaller amount of credit for T's plea of guilty because he had given an account of the offence which required a *Newton* hearing and put the victim through the trauma of reliving a frightening experience. T's voluntary surrender was a countervailing factor which might have increased the extent of his credit for the plea of guilty. The judge had concluded on the basis of T's previous conviction that there was a considerable risk of serious harm being caused to women on the streets. It was difficult to look at T's record with any confidence that T did not pose a risk of serious harm. The pre-sentence report indicated that T suffered from Asperger's Syndrome, but there was a high risk of reoffending, particularly when T was under the influence of alcohol. It had been suggested that the appropriate sentence might be an extended sentence under the Crime and Disorder Act 1998 s.58. After anxious consideration the court had concluded that it should substitute an extended sentence under s.58 of the longer than commensurate sentence passed by the sentencer under the s.2(2)(b) of the 1991 Act. The court would substitute an extended sentence with a custodial term of two years and an extension period of three years. The total term of the extended sentence would be five years.

R. v. THORNTON (PETER) [2000] 2 Cr. App. R. (S.) 47, Mance, L.J., CA (Crim Div).

1299. Indecent assault – recidivists – indecent assault committed on underground train

[Criminal Justice Act 1991 s.2(2).]

O appealed against a sentence of 30 months' imprisonment, having pleaded guilty before a magistrates' court to indecent assault and was committed to the Crown Court for sentence. O was seen travelling on an Underground train. He sat down next to a woman and touched her on the bottom through his jacket. The woman pushed O on the chest and complained. O had several convictions for indecent assault on a female.

Held, allowing the appeal, that O had become a persistent offender and the sentencer was justified in concluding that he was more prone to take risks than previously. The sentencer had taken into account the distinct risk that O would continue to cause distress and embarrassment to women in the future. This had led him to impose a longer sentence than O had hitherto received. That approach was not consistent with the Criminal Justice Act 1991 s.2(2)(a), which required any custodial sentence to be "for such term (not exceeding the permitted maximum) as in the opinion of the court is commensurate with the seriousness of the offence". Notwithstanding the aggravating features it was impossible to say that the gravity of the offence justified a 30-month imprisonment. The offence happened in a public place, the victim was with a friend, the indecent assault, although deliberate consisted brief physical contact by O through the victim's clothing. He did not touch her private parts and quickly desisted when she protested. This was not a case in which s.2(2)(b) was or could possibly have been invoked. While it was a sexual offence, it was not one from which the public required protection from serious harm. The sentence was substantially longer than was commensurate with the offence. An appropriate sentence would have been 12 months' imprisonment.

R. v. OSMAN (YACOUB) [2000] 2 Cr. App. R. (S.) 112, Judge Richard Gibbs Q.C., CA (Crim Div).

1300. Indecent assault – sentence length – violent indecent assault on woman – unduly lenient sentence

The Attorney General asked the Court of Appeal to review a sentence on the ground that it was unduly lenient. J was sentenced to four months' imprisonment having been convicted of an indecent assault on a female. J saw the victim in a public house, and left the public house at the same time as the victim. The victim attempted to avoid him, but J waited for her and approached her. He made advances to her which she rejected. He then placed his hand inside her clothing and pushed her into the driveway of a bungalow where he removed her clothing and masturbated himself. He ejaculated over her body and rubbed semen on her. J then left her. J was arrested the next morning. He admitted the act, but claimed that the victim consented.

Held, allowing the reference, that having regard to the seriousness of the offence, the proper sentence at the end of the trial would have been three and a half to four years' imprisonment. Bearing in mind the element of double jeopardy, the court would substitute a sentence of two years and nine months' imprisonment *R. v. Hiscock (John Andrew)* (1992) 13 Cr. App. R. (S.) 24, [1992] C.L.Y. 1305, *R. v. Rance (Ian James)* [1996] 1 Cr. App. R. (S.) 301, [1996] C.L.Y. 1939, *R. v. Currie (James)* (1988) 10 Cr. App. R. (S.) 85, [1990] C.L.Y. 1334, and *Attorney General's Reference (No.39 of 1997), Re* [1998] 2 Cr. App. R. (S.) 336, [1998] C.L.Y. 1264 considered.

ATTORNEY GENERAL'S REFERENCE (NO.29 OF 1999), *Re; sub nom.* R. v. J [2000] 1 Cr. App. R. (S.) 209, Kennedy, L.J., CA (Crim Div).

1301. Indecent assault – Sex Offenders Register – period of registration – extended licence supervision order not included as term of imprisonment

[Sex Offenders Act 1997 s.1; Crime and Disorder Act 1998 s.58(2).]

S pleaded guilty to indecent assault and was sentenced to two years' imprisonment. The judge, exercising his powers under the Crime and Disorder Act 1998 s.58, added to the sentence a two-year extended licence supervision order and ordered S's indefinite registration as a sex offender under the Sex Offenders Act 1997 s.1. S appealed, contending that the judge had erred in that (1) insufficient consideration had been given to his early plea of guilty; (2) the assault had been minor and limited, and (3) his conviction had had devastating repercussions upon his life.

Held, allowing the appeal in part, that the judge had considered all relevant mitigating factors when sentencing but had erred when determining the length of the registration period as required by the 1997 Act. Section 1 of the 1997 Act established that an indefinite period of registration would be imposed where the term of imprisonment relating to the offence was more than 30 months. The judge had incorrectly included the extended licence period imposed under s.58(2) of the 1998 Act within his calculation of the term of imprisonment. A period of extended licence imposed a liability that an offender might be imprisoned and accordingly was not to be interpreted as a term of imprisonment. It followed that as s.1 of the 1997 Act stated that the period of registration for terms of imprisonment not exceeding 30 months would be 10 years, this would be substituted.

R. v. S (GRAHAM) [2001] 1 Cr. App. R. 7, Rougier, J., CA (Crim Div).

1302. **Indecent assault – sexual behaviour – intercourse with mentally disabled person**

J appealed against sentences of four months' imprisonment for indecent assault and 18 months' imprisonment concurrent for unlawful sexual intercourse with a mentally disabled victim, having pleaded guilty to both counts. J was a night porter at a hotel. A woman aged 49 with learning difficulties who was naive in sexual matters obtained work as a cleaner at the hotel. J indecently assaulted her by sucking her breast and touching her between her legs. A week later the appellant locked the woman in a lavatory cubicle and had sexual intercourse with her. J claimed that the woman had consented on each occasions.

Held, allowing the appeal, that the maximum sentence for the offence was two years, J was entitled to a discount for his plea. An appropriate sentence after a trial would have been between 13 and 14 months; allowing a discount for J's plea, the appropriate sentence would be nine months' imprisonment.

R. v. A (DJ) [2000] 1 Cr. App. R. (S.) 563, Jackson, J., CA (Crim Div).

1303. **Indecent assault – sustained attack on lone female – probation order inappropriate – unduly lenient sentence**

[Criminal Justice Act 1988 s.36.]

The Attorney General applied for a sentence to be referred under the Criminal Justice Act 1988 s.36 on the ground that it was unduly lenient. T, aged 18, was charged with offences of indecent assault and common assault, to which he pleaded guilty. He was made the subject of a three-year probation order with conditions of residence at a hostel for 12 months and participation in a sexual offender group work programme. The Attorney General contended that the offence contained the aggravating features that it had taken place following a degree of premeditation against a lone female at night, which had continued despite the presence of passers by and had only ended by their active intervention. The victim had been severely affected by the assault, and was now scared to go out and subdued. In mitigation, it was pleaded that T was of previous good character and was working well within the offender's group.

Held, allowing the reference and imposing 18 months' detention, that despite T's age, his plea, and the element of double jeopardy, the probation order was inappropriate for a sustained sexual attack of that nature. Whilst the mitigation led to a lesser sentence than would otherwise have been imposed, the sentence had to reflect the mental and physical suffering of the victim.

ATTORNEY GENERAL'S REFERENCE (NO.31 OF 2000), Re; *sub nom.* R. v. T (LEIGH) (A JUVENILE) [2001] 1 Cr. App. R. (S.) 112, Swinton Thomas, L.J., CA (Crim Div).

1304. **Indecent exposure – children – recidivists – extended sentences**

[Criminal Justice Act 1991 s.2 (2) (b), s.40, s.44.]

P was convicted of gross indecency with a child. P approached a group of girls aged 13 and 14, who were with a younger boy, masturbating and with his penis exposed. He said nothing. The girls were frightened and embarrassed and reported the matter to the police. P denied the offence. He had a long record of indecent assaults or indecent exposure to women, having been convicted of 28 offences since the age of 13. He had been sentenced in 1994 to four years' imprisonment for attempted abduction of a girl under 16. P was sentenced to six years' imprisonment, imposed as a longer than commensurate sentence under the Criminal Justice Act 1991 s.2(2)(b), consecutively to a period of 11 months under the Criminal Justice Act 1991 s.40 in respect of the earlier sentence, and an order for extended supervision under the Criminal Justice Act 1991 s.44. P appealed contending that the six years imprisonment was excessive.

Held, allowing the appeal, that the maximum sentence for the offence of gross indecency with a child had been increased from two years to 10 years with effect from October 1, 1997. The increase reflected Parliament's view that offending of this type, involving indecency towards children, was potentially very serious and damaging, and should be dealt with more severely than had hitherto been possible. Reports before the sentencer indicated that the appellant was a recidivist sex offender and that there was no evidence to indicate that any treatment he had received to date had had any significant beneficial effect. P exhibited a number of distorted beliefs regarding his offending, for example that the victim enjoyed the assault. He had not attended sex offender treatment programmes in prison. The decision of the sentencer that this was an appropriate case for the use of s.2(2)(b) could not be criticised. P's most recent conviction gave rise to serious concern that his offending behaviour was likely to escalate. The question was whether six years imprisonment for this offence was manifestly excessive. The offence itself, and looked at in isolation, was not the most serious of offences of indecency towards a child. As the Court had made clear in *R. v. Bowler (Kevin)* (1994) 15 Cr. App. R. (S) 78, that was not the whole point. If there was clear evidence that an offender was a danger, then the fact that the particular offence did not in itself involve particularly serious conduct did not prevent the court from carrying out its obligation to protect the public from people such as this by imposing a sentence which was longer than appeared commensurate with the offence. That was the whole purpose of s.2(2)(b). In *Bowler* itself a sentence of six years' imprisonment for an indecent assault committed by an appellant with a dreadful history was not considered excessive. However, the sentencer should not have imposed a consecutive order under s.40 in respect of the earlier sentence. The Court had held in *R. v. Johnson (Adrian)* [1998] 1 Cr. App. R. (S) 126, [1998] C.L.Y. 1159 that where a longer than normal sentence was passed under s.2(2)(b), it should not be ordered to run consecutively to a period of return to prison under s.40.

R. v. P (PAUL ANDREW) [2000] 1 Cr. App. R. (S.) 428, Collins, J., CA (Crim Div).

1305. Judgments and orders – forfeiture – basis for order

[Powers of Criminal Courts Act 1973 s.43.]

R indicated his intention to plead guilty before a magistrates' court to three offences of facilitating the entry of an illegal immigrant. He was committed to the Crown Court for sentence. He was concerned in securing the entry of four people into the UK. R obtained visas for the persons concerned by making false statements at a British embassy. Sentenced to three years' imprisonment concurrent on each count, with an order for the forfeiture of various documents and £1,043 in cash, and recommended for deportation. R appealed against the forfeiture order.

Held, dismissing the appeal, that, although the judge did not make an express finding of the basis on which the forfeiture order was made, his failure to do so did not invalidate his order in the circumstances of this case. It was always desirable for a judge to make an express finding before making an order under the Powers of Criminal Courts Act 1973 s.43. The sentence of three years' imprisonment was not challenged.

R. v. RANASINGHE (ROHANA) [1999] 2 Cr. App. R. (S.) 366, Smith, J., CA (Crim Div).

1306. Juvenile offenders – anonymity – reporting restriction lifted in the public interest

[Children and Young Persons Act 1933 s.49(4A); Theft Act 1968 s.12(1); European Convention on Human Rights 1950 Art.8, Art.10.]

M, aged 15 at the time of his trial in the magistrates court, pleaded guilty to a charge under the Theft Act 1968 s.12(1). The justices then considered an application by a newspaper editor that reporting restrictions be dispensed with under the Children and Young Persons Act 1933 s.49(4A). A journalist was allowed to address the court, though the prosecution remained neutral. Reporting restrictions were lifted with reference to the name of the offender but remained to the extent of identifying his address or school details. It was stated that anonymity was being dispensed with because M constituted a serious danger to the public. M appealed by way of case stated, contending that the purpose of the newspaper was to shame him. Further, that the justices should not have allowed the journalist to address the court.

Held, dismissing the appeal, that the power to dispense with reporting restrictions in cases involving juvenile offenders should be exercised with great caution, particularly as the UK was party to a number of international treaties guaranteeing the welfare of juvenile offenders. There was a tension between the need to protect juvenile offenders against unnecessary and adverse publicity, in line with the European Convention on Human Rights 1950 Art.8, and the need to ensure freedom of expression, as guaranteed by Art.10. This tension could be resolved by dispensing with anonymity only where it was in the public interest to do so. In the instant case, the justices had directly addressed the issue by holding that M constituted a serious danger to the public. It was entirely proper for the court to afford the journalist an opportunity to address the court, particularly as the prosecution remained neutral on the issue.

MCKERRY v. TEESDALE AND WEAR VALLEY JUSTICES; *sub nom*. McKERRY v. DPP (2000) 164 J.P. 355, Lord Bingham of Cornhill, L.C.J., QBD.

1307. Juvenile offenders – arson – fire in school building

L, aged 16 at the time of the offence, appealed against a sentence of two years' detention having pleaded guilty to damaging property and arson. Shortly after leaving school L and another youth returned and broke windows by throwing stones at them, causing damage to the amount of £800. Some weeks later L started a fire in the art block at the school which caused damage to the extent of £400,000. L admitted that he had gone to the school, entered the art block and started the fire by lighting and dropping pieces of paper. When the fire started it got out of hand and L panicked and ran away.

Held, dismissing the appeal, that L pleaded guilty to arson on the basis that he had been reckless as to whether property would be destroyed. It was accepted that there had been no pre-planning and that no accelerant had been used. The sentencer referred to *R. v. Dewberry (Rodney Brian)* (1985) 7 Cr. App. R. (S.) 202, [1986] C.L.Y. 772 where a sentence was reduced from three years to 12 months, but said that the normal sentencing powers for young offenders had since been increased. There was evidence that at the time of the offence the appellant was suffering from a depressive illness for which he could be treated. The court had also been referred to *R. v. Innes (Philip Gordon)* (1985) 7 Cr. App. R. (S.) 52, [1986] C.L.Y. 902.1. In the court's view, there could be no criticism of the judge's decision to impose a custodial penalty, and there were no grounds for concluding that the sentence was manifestly excessive. If L had not been young and of good character, a significantly longer sentence would have been justified. The cases relied on by L dated from 1985. It might be that since then greater emphasis had been placed on the effects of the crime, including arson. Apart from the damage done to the school, the work of many students had been destroyed. A sentence of less than two years could not be justified.

R. v. L (DAVID) (A JUVENILE) [2000] 1 Cr. App. R. (S.) 185, Sullivan, J., CA (Crim Div).

1308. Juvenile offenders – arson – intent to endanger life

[Children and Young Persons Act 1933 s.53(3).]

J, aged 16, appealed against a sentence of nine years' detention under the Children and Young Persons Act 1933, s.53(3) having pleaded guilty to arson with intent to endanger life, unlawful wounding, escape and various other offences. J entered the unlocked garage of a house. Clothes were taken from a dryer and petrol was taken from the garage and poured on to the ground near the house and lit. Three weeks later J and a co-defendant entered the flat of an older man who was drunk. When he became intoxicated they attacked him, knocking him unconscious. They then set fires in various places within the flat, leaving the victim unconscious inside the flat. The victim was rescued by members of the public. J was arrested and detained in a secure unit. While so detained he and other youths attacked a member of staff and escaped.

Held, dismissing the appeal, that although only 15, J had been before courts on five separate occasions. Presentence reports were gloomy in the extreme. The court accepted that a sentence of nine years' detention was a very long one for a young man of 15 or 16, but this was a very serious case involving an appalling catalogue of offending. J was extremely lucky that the fire did not result in the death of the victim and a charge of murder. It was clear that the appellant remained a substantial risk to the public. Making due allowance for J's age and pleas, the court was satisfied that the sentence of nine years' detention was not excessive.

R. v. J (CHRISTOPHER KENNETH) (A JUVENILE) [2000] 2 Cr. App. R. (S.) 235, Richards, J., CA (Crim Div).

1309. Juvenile offenders – arson – life imprisonment excessive and unreasonable

[Children and Young Persons Act 1933 s.53(3); Crime (Sentences) Act 1997 s.28.]

E, aged 14, appealed against two concurrent life sentences imposed under the Children and Young Persons Act 1933 s.53(3), with a recommendation, under the Crime (Sentences) Act 1997 s.28, that he serve at least 2 years, on conviction of arson with the intent to cause damage to property or being reckless as to whether property would be damaged.

Held, allowing the appeal, that in considering the appropriate sentence a balance had to be struck between the welfare of the offender and the interest of the public. It was wrong in principle and inappropriate to have imposed concurrent terms, and a sentence of three years' imprisonment would be substituted, *R. v. Pither (Stephen George)* (1979) 1 Cr. App. R. (S.) 209 considered.

R. v. E (PAUL MARTIN) (A JUVENILE) *The Times*, December 3, 1999, Johnson, J., CA (Crim Div).

1310. Juvenile offenders – arson – reduction in term of detention

[Children and Young Persons Act 1933 s.53.]

T, aged 14, pleaded guilty to arson. T was one of a group of youths who were seen to enter a waste paper yard where bales of waste paper were stacked. Shortly afterwards, flames were seen coming from the yard and the fire brigade attended. The fire spread and eventually caused damage to the extent of £250,000. T was sentenced to three years' detention under the Children and Young Persons Act 1933 s.53(2) and 53(3) and appealed.

Held, allowing the appeal, that the sentencer was right to order T to be detained under s.53(3), but a term of two years' detention would meet the needs of justice in the instant case, *R. v. Storey (Stephen David)* (1984) 6 Cr. App. R. (S.) 104, [1985] C.L.Y. 810, *R. v. Innes (Philip Gordon)* (1985) 7 Cr. App. R. (S.) 52, [1986] C.L.Y. 902.1 and *R. v. Swallow (Mark Paul)* (1985) 7 Cr. App. R. (S.) 22, [1986] C.L.Y. 895 considered.

R. v. T (SIMON WILLIAM) (A JUVENILE) [2000] 1 Cr. App. R. (S.) 45, McKinnon, J., CA (Crim Div).

1311. Juvenile offenders – attempted rape – detention term

[Children and Young Persons Act 1933 s.53(3).]

M, aged 14 at the time of the offences, appealed against concurrent terms of five years' detention under the Children and Young Persons Act 1933 s.53(3), having pleaded guilty to two offences of attempted rape. M followed a young woman who was returning home late at night. He offered to help her find a telephone box and led her to a secluded place. M made advances to the young woman, grabbed her breasts and squeezed her vagina. He pulled down her trousers and attempted to penetrate her anus and vagina. Police officers arrived and M desisted.

Held, allowing the appeal, that the sentencer referred to the mitigation available to M, his age, his pleas of guilty and his background. The offence was committed while M was subject to a conditional discharge for offences of indecency. These were grave offences, aggravated by the nature of the conduct in question, the use of violence and the fact that the offences were committed shortly after the imposition of a conditional discharge. There was plainly no alternative to a sentence of detention. It was submitted that the sentence of five years' detention was too long, *R. v. Billam (Keith)* [1986] 1 W.L.R. 349, [1986] C.L.Y. 868 and *R. v. N (John Robert)* (1989) 11 Cr. App. R. (S.) 437, [1991] C.L.Y. 1191 considered. The court was satisfied that the sentencer might have taken too high a starting point or not have given sufficient discount for the plea of guilty. The court was persuaded that there were grounds for reducing the sentence. The court would substitute a term of three and a half years' detention.

R. v. M (A JUVENILE) [2000] 1 Cr. App. R. (S.) 188, Newman, J., CA (Crim Div).

1312. **Juvenile offenders – breach of supervision order – power of youth court to commit juvenile to Crown Court**

[Children and Young Persons Act 1969 s.15; Crime and Disorder Act 1998 s.72.]

M, aged 16, appeared before the Crown Court in June 1998 and was made the subject of a supervision order. In October 1998, he appeared before the youth court for breach of the order and for offences of handling stolen goods and theft. He was committed to the Crown Court, where the supervision order was revoked and sentences totalling two years' detention in a young offender institution were imposed for the offences in respect of which the order was made and the other offences. The youth court had purported to act under the Children and Young Persons Act 1969 s.15, as amended by the Crime and Disorder Act 1998 s.72, which allowed a magistrates' court dealing with an offender for breach of a supervision order made by the Crown Court to commit the offender to the Crown Court to be dealt with. Section 72 of the 1998 Act came into effect on September 30, 1998, a date after any of the breaches of the supervision order had taken place.

Held, allowing the appeal, that it in the absence of any clear and express transitional provisions, the terms of s.72 amending s.15 of the 1969 Act did not allow the justices to give retrospective effect to the amendment, and accordingly they had exceeded their jurisdiction. Before September 30, 1998, a juvenile who appeared before the youth court for breach of a supervision order was not liable to be committed to the Crown Court to be dealt with, even where the supervision order had been made by the Crown Court. The question therefore arose as to whether s.72, amending s.15 of the 1969 Act, gave the youth court jurisdiction to commit the appellant to the Crown Court to be dealt with for breaches of a supervision order committed prior to the commencement of the amending legislation. The presumption in any criminal legislation was against retrospectivity. In the absence of any transitional provisions governing the situation, the court did not accept that the youth court could commit the appellant to the Crown Court for breaches of the supervision order committed before September 30, 1998. Accordingly, the youth court had no jurisdiction to commit M to the Crown Court in respect of those breaches, and consequently the Crown Court had no jurisdiction to make any order or pass any sentence in respect of the breaches. The sentence imposed in respect of the offences for which the supervision order was made would be quashed.

R. v. M (ABDUL) (A JUVENILE) [2000] 1 Cr. App. R. (S.) 27, Ognall, J., CA (Crim Div).

1313. Juvenile offenders – burglary – elderly persons

[Children and Young Persons Act 1933 s.53(3).]

B, who was aged 16 at the time, appealed against a total sentence of 10 years' detention imposed under the Children and Young Persons Act 1933, s.53(3), having pleaded guilty to two counts of burglary and one of aggravated burglary. B entered the home of an elderly lady in a sheltered housing complex and stole £90 in cash and some property. As a result of the burglary the victim became afraid to stay in the flat alone and was admitted to hospital where she died. On the same day B committed a similar burglary in another sheltered flat. Some months later B entered another flat in the same complex occupied by a lady aged 72. When the lady woke up attempted to put on the light, B pulled her out of her bed and stabbed her repeatedly with a knife. The lady was found to have two wounds to the abdomen and two in the back. B told his brother about the incident and his brother telephoned the police for advice. B was subsequently arrested.

Held, dismissing the appeal, that the offences of this type, targeting old people, required lengthy sentences of detention or imprisonment. Even allowing for B's age and pleas, the requirement to protect the public, and particularly elderly women who lived on their own, demanded a sentence which would deter others from such behaviour.

R. v. B (DALE JOHN) (A JUVENILE) [2000] 2 Cr. App. R. (S.) 376, Kay, J., CA (Crim Div).

1314. Juvenile offenders – burglary – unoccupied flat

[Children and Young Persons Act 1933 s.53(3).]

C, aged 17, pleaded guilty to burglary. C broke into a flat occupied by a woman after she had left for work. C was arrested whilst still in the flat. C had previously broken into business premises used by the occupier of the flat. C was sentenced to four years' detention under the Children and Young Persons Act 1933 s.53(3) and appealed.

Held, allowing the appeal, that this was a case where a substantial custodial sentence was inevitable. Burglary of a dwelling was an offence for which detention under s.53(3) was available, and the offence justified a sentence of detention, but four years was too long; a sentence of two and a half years' detention would be substituted.

R. v. C (ANTHONY) (A JUVENILE) [2000] 1 Cr. App. R. (S.) 115, Mitchell, J., CA (Crim Div).

1315. Juvenile offenders – criminal damage – obstructing railway by placing objects on track

[Children and Young Persons Act 1933 s.53(3).]

H, aged 14 at the time of he offences, appealed against a sentence of five years' detention under the Children and Young Persons Act 1933 s.53(3) having pleaded guilty to three counts of obstructing the railway. H, in company with an older person, placed obstructions on railway lines on three occasions. On each occasion, the obstruction was struck by a train. No injuries or accident resulted.

Held, allowing the appeal, that the sentencer rightly took a very serious view of the offences, which called for substantial custodial sentences. The element of public danger was extremely grave. However, in view of the extreme youth of H and the fact that the offences were committed in the company of somebody much older, the Court would reduce the sentence to three years' detention.

R. v. AH (A JUVENILE) [2000] 2 Cr. App. R. (S.) 280, Judge Peter Crawford Q.C., CA (Crim Div).

1316. Juvenile offenders – detention and training orders – account taken of time spent in custody on remand when determining sentence length

[Crime and Disorder Act 1998 s.73, s.74(5).]

A sought judicial review of the decision of a youth court sentencing him under the Crime and Disorder Act 1998 s.73 to a four month detention and training order. It was submitted that guidance was necessary since magistrates' courts were deploying detention and training orders without making inquiry as to the amount of time spent on remand.

Held, allowing the application, that (1) a magistrates' court was under a duty to determine the length of time spent in custody on remand prior to considering what term to be imposed, and (2) where a court was minded to impose a detention and training order its intention should be indicated in open court in order for the period of time spent by an offender on remand in custody to be established and accordingly taken into account in determining the length of the order as required under s.74(5) of the Act.

R. v. HARINGEY YOUTH COURT, *ex p.* A (A JUVENILE) *The Times*, May 30, 2000, Laws, L.J., QBD.

1317. **Juvenile offenders – detention and training orders – credit for time spent in custody on remand – relevant statutory provisions**

[Crime and Disorder Act 1998 s.79(1), s.79(5).]

C, aged 17 at the date of the offence and 18 when sentenced, appealed against a detention and training order of 18 months, following his pleas of guilty, for offences of robbery and burglary. C submitted that the judge had intended that the time on remand should count towards his sentence, however he had misdirected himself as to the applicability of the Crime and Disorder Act 1998 s.79(5). C had been sentenced on the flawed basis that because he was 18 at the time of sentence, the detention and training order would be treated as a period of detention in a young offender institution, thus attracting a reduction for the time that C had spent in custody on remand.

Held, allowing the appeal, that the recorder had been correct in his view that a substantial custodial sentence was justified in C's case and that there should be a deduction given C's early guilty plea, his age and genuine remorse. The recorder had clearly intended that credit should be given for the time that C had spent on remand. However, by virtue of s.79(1), s.79(5) applied only in cases where an offender was being re-sentenced and did not permit a detention and training order to be treated as a sentence of detention in a young offender institution. Thus, it had not been possible to discount C's sentence in this manner. The correct approach was to sentence C as a 17 year old and impose a four month detention and training order but, in view of the fact that C had been released on bail and a four month order would necessitate his return to custody for 12 days, it was more convenient to quash the sentence imposed by the recorder and substitute a 12 month conditional discharge, *R. v. Danga* [1992] Q.B. 476, [1992] C.L.Y. 1450 applied.

R. v. C (DAVID ANTHONY) (A JUVENILE) *The Times*, October 13, 2000, Rose, L.J., CA (Crim Div).

1318. **Juvenile offenders – detention and training orders – recidivists – meaning of "persistent offender"**

[Crime and Disorder Act 1998 s.73(2)(a); Powers of Criminal Courts (Sentencing) Act 2000 Sch.12.]

C, aged 15, appealed against a sentence of a 12 month detention and training order made following convictions for burglary, allowing himself to be carried in a vehicle taken without consent, and further acts of burglary and aggravated vehicle taking committed while on bail for the first offences. C asserted that in imposing the sentence the judge had been wrong to refer to him as a "persistent offender" for the purposes of the Crime and Disorder Act 1998 s.73(2)(a) because a Home Office circular, entitled "Tackling Delays in the Youth Justice System", defined "persistent young offenders" as those who had been sentenced "on three or more separate occasions for one or more recordable offence".

Held, dismissing the appeal, that the definition of "persistent offender" in s.73, depended on the facts of each case and was not defined by the Home Office circular. The fact that C had burgled a second time while on bail demonstrated a sufficient degree of persistence to satisfy s.73. Section 73 was repealed by the Powers of Criminal Courts (Sentencing) Act 2000 Sch.12 on August 25, 2000.

R. v. C (A JUVENILE) (PERSISTENT OFFENDER); *sub nom.* R. v. C (YOUNG PERSON: PERSISTENT OFFENDER) *The Times*, October 11, 2000, Astill, J., CA (Crim Div).

1319. Juvenile offenders – detention and training orders – sentencing guidelines

[Children and Young Persons Act 1933 s.53 (3); Criminal Justice Act 1991 Part 1; Criminal Appeal Act 1995; s.11 (3) 9b); Crime and Disorder Act 1998; Crime and Disorder Act 1998 (Commencement No 6) Order 1999 (SI 1999 3426) para.4.]

G, a juvenile offender, appealed against a sentence of 18 months' detention imposed on him following his conviction on a charge of inflicting grievous bodily harm.

Held, allowing the appeal and substituting the period of detention with a detention and training order, that (1) the provisions of the Crime and Disorder Act 1998 s.73 to s.79, which related to detention and training orders for offenders under the age of 18, applied. The Court of Appeal was, by virtue of the Criminal Appeal Act 1995 s.11 (3) (b), empowered, when passing a different sentence from that imposed in the court below, to pass a sentence which "the court below had power to pass". The court was under a duty, pursuant to the Crime and Disorder Act 1998 (Commencement No 6) Order 1999 para.4, when considering the sentence that might or could have been imposed in the court below, to presume that s.73 to s.79 of the 1998 Act, which came into force on April 1, 2000, had been in force; (2) detention in young offender institutions and secure training orders had been abolished under s.73 (7) of the 1998 Act and were replaced by detention and training orders under s.73 (1). Such orders constituted custodial sentences within the Criminal Justice Act 1991 Part 1, and accordingly it was necessary that the requirements of s.1 (2) (a) or (b) of the 1991 Act were met; (3) where a defendant was under the age of 15 at the time of conviction, a detention and training order should not be made unless that person was a persistent offender. Similarly, such an order should not be made where an offender was below the age of 12 unless a custodial sentence was the only means of preventing further offences, and the offence had been committed on or after a day to be appointed; (4) the court could not impose terms of less than four months consecutively so as to result in a total sentence of four months, *R. v. Dover Youth Court, ex p. K* [1999] 1 W.L.R. 27, [1998] C.L.Y. 1290 considered. The term imposed should not exceed the maximum available to the Crown Court in relation to an offender over the age of 21; (5) the power to impose detention under the Children and Young Persons Act 1933 s.53 (3) remained unaffected. Equally the principles relating to such a sentence and the undesirability of long periods of detention under the age of 18 continued to apply, *R. v. M (Aaron Shaun)* [1998] 1 W.L.R. 363, [1998] C.L.Y. 1281 considered, and (6) any time spent in custody on remand was not to be deducted from the period to be served under a detention and training order, although it was to be considered by the sentencer. However, the court should have regard when dealing, on the same occasion, with offenders both above and below the age of 18, to the fact that time in custody on remand would automatically be deducted from the sentence imposed on the older offender.

R. v. G (STEPHEN) (A JUVENILE) [2001] 1 Cr. App. R. (S.) 17, Rose, L.J., CA (Crim Div).

1320. Juvenile offenders – detention and training orders – youth custody – consideration of remand period – pro rata reduction

[Crime and Disorder Act 1998 s.74 (5).]

I challenged the dismissal of her appeal against a four month detention and training order for assault. I contended that the court had failed to take into account the period during which she had been remanded in custody.

Held, refusing the application, that under the Crime and Disorder Act 1998 s.74 (5) time spent remanded in custody should always be considered but the court was not obliged to discount the sentence pro rata. In the instant case I had spent less than 24 hours in custody and the decision not to discount was not irrational.

R. v. INNER LONDON CROWN COURT, *ex p.* I (A JUVENILE) *The Times*, May 12, 2000, Laws, L.J., QBD.

1321. Juvenile offenders – electronic monitoring – disparate sentences – older codefendant eligible for early release subject to tagging and curfew

[Criminal Justice Act 1991 s.34A; Crime and Disorder Act 1998.]

C, aged 17, and his codefendant, aged 19, were each sentenced to nine months' detention for unlawful wounding. C appealed against the sentence on the ground that the judge had expressly ordered identical sentences and his codefendant, being over the age of 18, would be eligible for early release subject to electronic tagging and a curfew order under the Criminal Justice Act 1991 s.34A, whereas C would not.

Held, dismissing the appeal, that, although an apparent injustice had been created by the decision to release an older, equally culpable codefendant earlier, the Secretary of State was empowered under the Crime and Disorder Act 1998 s.73 to s.79, which came into effect on April 1, 2000, to operate the release provisions in a way which did justice between offenders of different ages. The decision was all the more anomalous considering that younger offenders were generally dealt with less severely than older ones. It was therefore the duty of the Secretary of State to analyse the impact on the fairness to a younger offender before considering early release of a equally culpable older codefendant.

R. v. C (TOBY) (A JUVENILE) *The Times*, April 5, 2000, Judge, L.J., CA (Crim Div).

1322. Juvenile offenders – grievous bodily harm – stabbing bus driver – unduly lenient sentence

[Children and Young Persons Act 1933 s.53.]

The Attorney General asked the court to review a sentence on the grounds that it was unduly lenient. H, a 16 year old youth, pleaded guilty to wounding with intent to cause grievous bodily harm. He was travelling on a bus when he became involved in an argument with the driver about the validity of his ticket. He stabbed the driver, apparently aiming at his ribs, but the victim pulled up his arms to protect himself and sustained a deep cut in his arm. H was arrested two days later and admitted responsibility for the attack. H was sentenced to a probation order for two years.

Held, allowing the reference, that the sentencer had allowed herself to be over persuaded by the personal circumstances of the offender, to the extent that the requirements of the victim and the public in relation to offences of this type were obscured. The sentence was unduly lenient. The court would have expected a sentence of the order of three and a half years' detention under the Children and Young Persons Act 1933 s.53. Taking account of the element of double jeopardy, and progress made by H on probation, the court would substitute a sentence of two and a half years' detention under s.53, *Attorney General's Reference (Nos.59, 60 and 63 of 1998), Re* [1999] 2 Cr. App. R. (S.) 128, [1999] C.L.Y. 1371 considered.

ATTORNEY GENERAL'S REFERENCE (NO.69 OF 1999), *Re*; *sub nom*. R. v. H (BILAL) (A JUVENILE) [2000] 2 Cr. App. R. (S.) 53, Rose, L.J., CA (Crim Div).

1323. Juvenile offenders – grievous bodily harm – stabbing victim during fight – unduly lenient sentence

[Offences Against the Person Act 1861 s.18; Children and Young Persons Act 1933 s.53(3).]

The Attorney General asked the court to review a sentence on the ground that it was unduly lenient. G, aged 17, was convicted of wounding with intent to inflict grievous bodily harm. He was standing outside a shop with his friends when a man left the shop accompanied by his younger son. The man heard G's friend swearing and asked him to be quiet. G then attacked the man, caught him in a headlock and punched him several times in the head. He was taken to the hospital and found to have a 2 cm transverse laceration on his left calf. A swelling developed and he needed an operation. G told some friends that he had stabbed the man with a knife. G was sentenced to 15 months' detention in a young offender institution.

Held, allowing the reference, that the court felt bound to conclude that the sentence was unduly lenient. This was a serious offence committed deliberately which gave rise to a conviction under the Offences Against the Person Act 1861 s.18. An appropriate sentence at trial would have been four years' detention under the Children and Young Persons Act 1933 s.53(3). Allowing for the double jeopardy element, the court would substitute a sentence of three years' detention, *Attorney General's Reference (No.28 of 1995), Re* [1996] 1 Cr. App. R. (S.) 410, [1996] C.L.Y. 1967 and *Attorney General's Reference (Nos.59, 60 and 63 of 1998), Re* [1999] 2 Cr. App. R. (S.) 128, [1999] C.L.Y. 1371 considered.

ATTORNEY GENERAL'S REFERENCE (NO.75 OF 1999), *Re*; *sub nom*. R. v. G (WESLEY STUART) (A JUVENILE) [2000] 2 Cr. App. R. (S.) 146, Lord Bingham of Cornhill, L.C.J., CA (Crim Div).

1324. Juvenile offenders – grievous bodily harm – sustained assault on vulnerable individual – unduly lenient sentence

The Attorney General referred to the court a sentence of three years' detention that had been imposed on E for an offence of causing grievous bodily harm with intent. E, who was 16 at the time of the offence, had entered the flat of a middle aged man, shouted abuse at him and assaulted him with his fists, feet and various implements, namely a walking stick, a saucepan and a crutch. The assault took place in the victim's bedroom, kitchen and garden and was renewed following the intervention of a neighbour. The victim, who was known to be vulnerable owing to physical and mental handicaps, was rendered unconscious by the assault, sustained extensive bruising together with four fractured ribs and had to be moved to hospital as a place of safety following a psychiatrist's report which concluded that the incident had had a significant effect on his social functioning. The Attorney General argued that the sentence imposed on E had been unduly lenient.

Held, allowing the reference, that the offence had been a very serious one; the victim was a vulnerable individual; he had been attacked in his home; various weapons had been used; the assault had been prolonged and had taken place in different locations; the victim had suffered significant physical injuries and psychological damage. Furthermore, E had committed the offence while on bail for other offences. Having regard to those matters, E's age at the time of the offence and his plea of guilty, albeit at a late stage, a sentence of five years' detention would have been appropriate. Taking into account the element of double jeopardy a sentence of four years' detention would be imposed.

ATTORNEY GENERAL'S REFERENCE (NO.33 OF 2000), *Re*; *sub nom*. R. v. E (NICHOLAS) (A JUVENILE) [2001] 1 Cr. App. R. (S.) 102, Rose, L.J., CA (Crim Div).

1325. Juvenile offenders – handling stolen goods – return orders

[Children and Young Persons Act 1933 s.53(2); Powers of Criminal Courts Act 1973 s.42(2); Magistrates Courts Act 1980 s.37, s.38, s.56; Criminal Justice Act 1991 s.40(3), s.41.]

N pleaded guilty before a youth court to handling stolen goods and attempting to obtain property by deception. He was remitted to another youth court where he pleaded guilty to further offences. N was committed to the Crown Court under the Magistrates Courts Act 1980 s.56 in relation to the other offences. N was sentenced in the Crown Court to a total of 16 months' detention in a young offender institution in respect of the offences for which he had been committed for sentence, consecutive to a period of custody which he was ordered to serve under the Criminal Justice Act 1991 s.41 in respect of an earlier sentence of detention under the Children and Young Persons Act 1933 s.53(2).

Held, allowing the appeal, that N had not been committed by the youth court under the s.40(3) of the 1991 Act. The powers of the Crown Court following a committal under the s.37 of the 1980 Act were set out in the Powers of Criminal Courts Act 1973 s.42(2). That section provided that where an offender was committed by the magistrates' court to the Crown Court, the Crown Court might sentence him to a term of detention in a young offender institution or "deal with him in any manner in which magistrates' court might have dealt with him". The Crown Court had wider powers where an offender over the age of 18 was committed for sentence under the s.38 of the 1980 Act. The Crown Court had no power to make an order under the s.40 of the 1991 Act. Moreover the powers of the Crown Court were limited to those set out in s.42(2)(a) and s.42(2)(b) of the 1973 Act which were alternative. The Crown Court could not deal with an offender under both s.42(2)(a) and s.42(2)(b). The Crown Court was accordingly entitled to sentence N to a term of detention in a young offender institution, but did not have the power to impose an additional sentence under the s.40 of the 1991 Act. The order for return imposed under s.40 was unlawful and would be quashed.

R. v. N (DUANE) (A JUVENILE) [2000] 2 Cr. App. R. (S.) 105, Pill, L.J., CA (Crim Div).

1326. Juvenile offenders – indecent assault – children

B aged between 14 and 15 at the time of the offences, appealed against a sentence of two years' detention in a young offender institution, having pleaded guilty to three counts of indecent assault on a female, one count of indecent assault on a male, and one count of committing an act of gross indecency with a child. B lived with his stepmother and two half-sisters aged four and six years. Over a period of several months the appellant regularly looked after the children in the evenings and also looked after two sons of a friend of his stepmother. B admitted indecently assaulting one of the boys, aged three, by touching and sucking his penis. B admitted indecently assaulting both of his half sisters by touching them in the vaginal area and on one occasion encouraging one of the girls to perform oral sex on him.

Held, allowing the appeal, that sentencing a man as young as this for this type of offence always posed problems. It was necessary to balance the interest of B in seeking a way to prevent further offences against the damage to his victims and public abhorrence of this type of crime. It was not wrong in principle for B to be given a custodial sentence, but bearing in mind the recommendations for treatment put forward in the presentence report, the court would substitute a supervision order.

R. v. B (A JUVENILE) [2000] 1 Cr. App. R. (S.) 177, Gage, J., CA (Crim Div).

1327. Juvenile offenders – indecent assault – children – assault on victims over period of four years

R appealed against a sentence of a total of four years' imprisonment, having pleaded guilty to four counts of indecent assault. The offences were committed between 1971 and 1975 against a boy and girl who were R's nephew and niece. At the time the offences began, R was 14 and the victims were eight and 10 respectively. The victims complained of various forms of indecency, committed while R was baby-sitting for them.

Held, allowing the appeal, that these were extremely serious offences involving penetration. Even allowing for R's young age at the time of the offences, there was a significant degree of breach of trust. The correct approach in a case of this kind was to sentence R on the basis of what would have been the appropriate sentence had he been brought before the court within a reasonably short time after the commission of the offences. It appeared to the court that the sentencer might have lost sight of the fact that R at the time of the offences was little more than a child himself. In these circumstances the sentences would be reduced to a total of two years' imprisonment.

R. v. R (COLIN OLIVER) (A JUVENILE) [2000] 1 Cr. App. R. (S.) 244, Wright, J., CA (Crim Div).

1328. Juvenile offenders – indecent assault – children – supervision orders – unduly lenient sentence

[Children and Young Persons Act 1933 s.53(3).]

The Attorney General asked the court to review a sentence on the ground that it was unduly lenient. B aged 14, pleaded guilty to indecent assault. He met a girl aged 12 who attended the same school, as she was walking home from school. He persuaded her to go into some bushes and asked her if she would have sex with him. When she refused, the offender pushed her to the ground, removed some of her clothing and forced his penis into her mouth. He then withdrew and ejaculated over her leg. When arrested B eventually said that the girl had approached him and that she had consented to his actions. B was sentenced to a supervision order for three years.

Held, allowing the reference, that the sentencer had been under the misapprehension that the effective choices were an order of three years' detention under the Children and Young Persons Act 1933 s.53(3) or a supervision order. That understanding was incorrect. The Court had no hesitation in concluding that the sentence imposed on B was unduly lenient. Such behaviour was wholly unacceptable and did not become less unacceptable by virtue of the B's age. It caused concern and outrage to parents and called for a punitive sentence which would be recognised by the public and B as such. B did plead guilty, and his youth told in his favour. The appropriate sentence for the Crown Court to have passed would have been 12 months' detention under the Children and Young Persons Act 1933 s.53(3). In view of the element of double jeopardy, and B's behaviour since the sentence was imposed, the public interest would not be served by imposing that would be a very short period of detention. While the sentence was unduly lenient, the Court would not substitute any other sentence. *R. v. Hiscock (John Andrew)* (1992) 13 Cr. App. R. (S.) 24, [1992] C.L.Y. 1305, *R. v. Pilgrim (Dennis Decosta)* (1993) 14 Cr. App. R. (S.) 432, [1994] C.L.Y. 1287, *R. v. Wilson (Iain Malcolm)* (1993) 14 Cr. App. R. (S.) 627, [1994] C.L.Y. 1283, *R. v. M (Aaron Shaun)* [1998] 1 W.L.R. 363, [1998] C.L.Y. 1281. *R. v. Fairhurst (Jonathan)* [1986] 1 W.L.R. 1374, [1987] C.L.Y. 1079, *R. v. Storey (Stephen David)* (1984) 6 Cr. App. R. (S.) 104, [1985] C.L.Y. 810, *R. v. McFarlane (Cyril)* (1988) 10 Cr.App.R.(S.) 10, [1990] C.L.Y. 1478 considered.

ATTORNEY GENERAL'S REFERENCE (NO.61 OF 1999), *Re*; *sub nom.* R. v. B (WAYNE) (A JUVENILE) [2000] 1 Cr. App. R. (S.) 516, Lord Bingham of Cornhill, L.C.J., CA (Crim Div).

1329. Juvenile offenders – indecent assault – young woman assaulted at night

[Children and Young Persons Act 1933 s.53(3).]

O, aged 16, pleaded guilty to indecent assault on a female. O encountered a young woman who was walking home in the early hours of the morning. He grabbed her from behind, pushed her to the floor and placed his hand inside her trousers and touched her vagina. A man heard the woman's screams and came to her assistance and O ran off, taking the victim's purse containing £19. O, initially denying the offence but later pleading guilty, was sentenced to four years' detention under the Children and Young Persons Act 1933 s.53(3), with six months' detention concurrent for theft. O appealed.

Held, allowing the appeal, that it seemed to the court that the sentencer had arrived at the sentence more with the offence of attempted rape in mind than the offence of indecent assault to which O had pleaded guilty. The proper sentence was three years' detention in relation to the indecent assault, *R. v. Guiver (Stuart Harold)* (1987) 9 Cr. App. R. (S.) 407, [1990] C.L.Y. 1491 considered.

R. v. O (STEPHEN MARK) (A JUVENILE) [2000] 1 Cr. App. R. (S.) 73, Hidden, J., CA (Crim Div).

1330. Juvenile offenders – manslaughter – offensive weapons – victim stumbling on to knife

H was sentenced to four years' detention in a young offender institution and appealed, having been convicted of manslaughter. The victim had assaulted H on two occasions, and suggested through an intermediary that H should meet him at the address where he was staying. H went to the address, taking a knife. When the victim arrived he challenged H to a fight, but H did not respond. Eventually H produced the knife from his pocket and held it out in front of him, fearing that the victim was about to attack him. The victim fell forward onto the knife, which penetrated his chest. H ran off, discarding the knife. The sentencer accepted that the death of the victim was the result of the victim falling or stumbling on to the knife held by H.

Held, dismissing the appeal, that although it was accepted that H did not stab or lash out at the deceased and was seeking to avoid a confrontation, he had taken the serious step of arming himself with a knife. The sentence fell within the bracket open to the sentencing judge even if it was towards the top end.

R. v. A-H (A JUVENILE) [2000] 2 Cr. App. R. (S.) 158, Lord Bingham of Cornhill, L.C.J., CA (Crim Div).

1331. Juvenile offenders – murder – appropriate tariff – children's welfare and progress relevant factors

V and T, both aged 18, had been convicted of murdering a child at the age of 10 and were sentenced to be detained at her Majesty's pleasure. In *T v. United Kingdom* [2000] 2 All E.R. 1024 (Note), [2000] C.L.Y. 3198, it had been held that it was unlawful for the Secretary of State to set the tariff. Accordingly, the matter was referred to the Court of Appeal to make a tariff recommendation pursuant to the *Practice Statement (CA (Crim Div): Juveniles: Murder Tariff)* [2000] 1 W.L.R. 1655, [2000] C.L.Y. 1095.

Held, reducing the tariff, that in reviewing the tariffs of children sentenced to be detained at Her Majesty's Pleasure, it was appropriate to take into account the welfare of the children and any progress they had made in redeeming themselves. Any representations received from the victim's family should be limited to the effect of the crime on the victim's family and should not contain recommendations on what tariff should be set. Although the crime was a particularly horrendous one, it had to be remembered that the offenders were only 10 when it was committed and had spent the last seven years in custody. Now, aged 18, they would be due to be transferred to a young offender institution. However, it was clear that such a change would undo all the good work that had been done in their upbringing during detention. It was in the public interest that the tremendous amount of skill invested in the upbringing of the children should not be wasted. Moreover, release would not mean the end of punishment for these children, who would, in any case, be on licence and be liable to be recalled to custody. Given that the children had done all that they could to improve themselves, a tariff of 8 years was appropriate. Such a tariff would expire on February 21, 2001. If the tariff were to be set to expire immediately, it would be after February 2001 that the parole board would decide whether to release the children. Accordingly, the tariff would be set to expire immediately.

THOMPSON (TARIFF RECOMMENDATIONS), *Re*; VENABLES (TARIFF RECOMMENDATION), *Re* [2001] 1 All E.R. 737, Lord Woolf of Barnes, L.C.J., CA (Crim Div).

1332. Juvenile offenders – probation orders – order made on the same occasion as the imposition of a custodial sentence

[Criminal Justice Act 1948; Criminal Courts Act 1973 s.2(1); Supreme Court Act 1981 s.48.]

C appeared before a youth court and admitted three breaches of a community service order imposed by the Crown Court in January 1999. She was committed to the crown court for sentence. A few weeks later, she appeared again at the youth court, and pleaded guilty to using threatening words or behaviour. She was sentenced to two months' detention in a young offender institution for that offence. One week later, on her appearance in the Crown Court, the Crown court revoked the community service orders and made probation orders in respect of the offences for which the community service orders had been made. At the same time the Crown Court dismissed C's appeal against the sentence that probation orders should not have been made in view of the sentence of two months' detention in a young offender institution imposed in the youth court and maintained in the Crown Court. C appealed.

Held, allowing the appeal, that two questions arose for consideration, firstly whether the Crown Court in dismissing C's appeal against the sentence of detention was imposing a sentence, and secondly whether in the circumstances the Crown Court could properly make probation order: (1) the court was satisfied that in dismissing C's appeal against the sentence of detention in a young offender institution and maintaining that sentence, the Crown court was imposing sentence on C, *R. v. Knutsford Crown Court, ex p. Jones* (1985) 7 Cr. App. R. (S.) 448 considered. The Supreme Court Act 1981 s.48 provided that on the determination of an appeal to the Crown Court, the Crown court might award any punishment whether more or less severe than that awarded by the magistrates' court. It followed that in dismissing C's appeal against sentence, the Crown Court "decided how C should be sentenced" and imposed sentence on her; (2) it had been held in *R. v. Evans (Raymond Frederick)* [1959] 1 W.L.R. 26, [1959] C.L.Y. 2013 that making a probation order which could not immediately take effect was contrary to the spirit and intention of the Criminal Justice Act 1948. That principle had not changed. Powers of the Criminal Courts Act 1973 s.2(1) provided that the purposes of a probation order were to be either securing the rehabilitation of offender, protecting the public from harm from him or preventing the commission by him of further offences. It was impermissible to combine a probation order with an immediate custodial sentence whether in respect of the same offence or of different offences sentenced on the same occasion. It was inconsistent with the purpose and spirit of s.2(1). The Crown Court was wrong to make probation orders in respect of C's breaches of the earlier community service orders. The probation orders would accordingly be quashed, and in view of the passage of time since the matter was before the Crown Court, no separate penalty would be imposed in respect of the breaches of the community service order.

R. v. C-T (SARAH) (A JUVENILE) [2000] 2 Cr. App. R. (S.) 335, Potts, J., CA (Crim Div).

1333. Juvenile offenders – rape – jurisdiction of youth court – referral to Crown Court required

[Children and Young Persons Act 1933 s.53.]

M, aged 17, was charged with the attempted rape and indecent assault of a 15 year old girl. In February 1998 the justices decided, without referring to legal advice, that as there were no aggravating features a sentence of more than two years was not justified and therefore the Children and Young Persons Act 1933 s.53, requiring transfer to the Crown Court, did not apply. However, in March, when the case came back before the court, the justices held that the case should be transferred, and the CPS served a notice of transfer. The CPS applied for judicial review of the February decision and M for judicial review of the March decision.

Held, quashing the February decision, that the justices had applied the wrong test. They should not have considered whether a sentence of more than two years was actually appropriate, but whether it was appropriate that the sentencing court should have such a sentence available to it. It was always appropriate that a juvenile charged with rape should be tried on indictment, and there was no reason in this case for not treating the charge of attempted rape as equally serious, *R. v. Billam (Keith)* [1986] 1 W.L.R. 349, [1986] C.L.Y. 868 applied. The justices had no power to overturn their earlier decision on mode of trial, *R. v. Liverpool Justices, ex p. Crown Prosecution Service* (1990) 90 Cr. App. R. 261, [1990] C.L.Y. 999 applied. Equally, a notice of transfer served by the CPS could not reverse a decision on mode of trial.

R. v. FAREHAM YOUTH COURT, *ex p.* CROWN PROSECUTION SERVICE; R. v. FAREHAM YOUTH COURT, *ex p.* M; *sub nom.* R. v. FAREHAM YOUTH COURT, *ex p.* DPP (1999) 163 J.P. 812, Kennedy, L.J., QBD.

1334. Juvenile offenders – rape – statutory limitations on periods of detention

[Childrens and Young Persons Act 1933 s.53(2) and s.53(3); Criminal Appeals Act 1968 s.11(3); Criminal Justice Act 1982 s.1B(4) and s.1B(5).]

G, aged 17, pleaded guilty to rape, indecent assault on a female and three counts of robbery. On two occasions G approached male persons in a wooded area, threatened them each with a meat cleaver and demanded money. On a third occasion G approached a woman, threatened her with a meat cleaver, ordered her to masturbate him and raped her. G then took £9 from her purse. G was sentenced "to be detained" for a total of eight years and appealed arguing that as the sentencer did not refer to the Childrens and Young Persons Act 1933 s.53(2) and s.53(3), the sentence took effect as a sentence of detention in a young offender institution and that by virtue of the Criminal Justice Act 1982 s.1B(4) and s.1B(5) the sentence was automatically reduced to two years' detention in a young offender institution.

Held, allowing the appeal, that to understand a sentence expressed as being of "detention" and to reach a conclusion whether it was ambiguous it was necessary to look at its context. In the present case no properly advised defendant could have considered that there was any prospect of any sentence other than a long sentence which could be passed only under s.53. Any informed observer would have realised that the sentencer was acting under s.53 since that was the only conclusion which gave due credit to those involved in the sentencing exercise and made sense of what occurred.

Observed, that sentencing judges should avoid any risk by stating expressly the statutory basis on which they were acting at the time they passed sentences on offenders under 18 and that counsel for the Crown should be alert to this and should draw the judge's attention to any failure on his part to express his intentions. It did not in any event appear self evident from the language of the Criminal Appeals Act 1968 s.11(3) that the Court of appeal was precluded absolutely from exercising the power which it would otherwise have itself to invoke s.53(3) in circumstances where the judge could and should obviously have done so, but had instead dealt with the appellant by passing a sentence of "detention on a young offender institution" which by its length infringed s.1B(4). On the merits of the case, the sentence of six years imposed for rape was too high, and would substitute a sentence of four years' detention under s.53(3) was substituted. The sentences for robbery of two years' detention in each case, concurrent but consecutive to the sentence for rape, would remain leaving a total of six years detention under s.53(3).

R. v. GF (A JUVENILE) [2000] 2 Cr. App. R. (S.) 364, Mance, L.J., CA (Crim Div).

1335. Juvenile offenders – robbery – accomplices – robbery of young man in lift

M aged 18 on date of conviction, pleaded guilty in the Crown Court to robbery. Together with a younger accomplice, M attacked a young man in a lift. The victim was knocked to the floor and a ring and some cash were stolen. M appealed against a sentence of two years' detention in a young offender institution. M's accomplice, who was 17, was convicted by a youth court and sentenced to four months' detention in a young offender institution.

Held, dismissing the appeal, that the sentencer in the Crown Court commented on the apparent leniency of the sentence passed by the youth court, but stated that he would pass a sentence on M which he considered appropriate to the offence. It was conceded that the sentence of two years' detention could not be criticised but it was argued that the disparity between M's sentence and the sentence passed on his accomplice was unacceptably wide. The court would apply the test stated in *R. v. Fawcett (Kenneth John)* (1983) 5 Cr. App. R. (S.) 158, [1984] C.L.Y. 836 applied, which was "would right thinking members of the public, with full knowledge of all the relevant facts and circumstances, learning of the sentence, consider that something had gone wrong with the administration of justice?" In the court's judgment right thinking members of the public would not consider that something had gone wrong. There were three grounds for differentiating between M and his accomplice: M had struck a blow to the victim which inflicted injuries; M was older than his accomplice; and M had a more serious criminal record. It was likely that the two offenders would receive different sentences. Undue credit had been given to the accomplice for his youth and the fact that he played a lesser role in the robbery. That was not a reason to reduce the two year sentence which was properly imposed on M. The court wished to say that a great deal of difficulty and cost would have been avoided if both offenders had been sentenced on the same occasion by the same court. The youth court ought to have committed the accomplice to the Crown Court for sentence. The court had in the past deplored the practice of magistrates' courts in dealing with one offender, when the coaccused was to be dealt with in the Crown Court. There might be special cases where it was appropriate to deal with the young offender in a youth court, but the present case did not fall into that category. Wherever possible, those who committed offences jointly should all be sentenced by the same court.

R. v. MS (A JUVENILE) (OFFENCE: ROBBERY) [2000] 1 Cr. App. R. (S.) 386, Jackson, J., CA (Crim Div).

1336. Juvenile offenders – robbery – elderly persons – probation orders – unduly lenient sentence

The Attorney General referred to the court the case of B, aged 17 at the time of the offence, who met a man aged 69 who was walking in the street. B ran up behind the victim, pushed him to the ground and then stood over him and demanded his wallet. When the victim shouted for help, B placed his hand over the victim's mouth and repeated his demand. B was arrested shortly afterwards following a chase by police officers. A probation order was imposed. The Attorney General asked the Court of Appeal to review the sentence on the ground that it was unduly lenient contending that the offence was aggravated by the fact that a vulnerable victim was targeted by a young man, considerable force was used, and a significant injury was inflicted which left a degree of permanent disfigurement. B argued that he was young and of previous good character, and that he pleaded guilty at the first available opportunity. *Attorney General's Reference (No.6 of 1994), Re* (1995) 16 Cr. App. R. (S.) 343, *Attorney General's Reference (No.39 of 1996), Re* [1997] 1 Cr. App. R. (S.) 355, [1997] C.L.Y. 1692, *Attorney General's Reference (No.44 of 1997), Re* [1998] 2 Cr. App. R. (S.) 105, [1998] C.L.Y. 1381 and *Attorney General's Reference (No.13 of 1998), Re* [1999] 1 Cr. App. R. (S.) 140, [1999] C.L.Y. 1238 referred to.

Held, allowing the reference, that sentence in the case of an adult would be three years' imprisonment. The appropriate sentence on a young man who was in effect being sentenced for a second time was 18 months' detention in a young offender institution.

ATTORNEY GENERAL'S REFERENCE (NO.21 OF 1999), *Re; sub nom.* R. v. N (STEPHEN JAMES) (A JUVENILE) [2000] 1 Cr. App. R. (S.) 197, Kennedy, L.J., CA (Crim Div).

1337. **Juvenile offenders – robbery – offensive weapons – attacking victim with knife**

W pleaded guilty to robbery and possessing a bladed instrument. W aged 18, became acquainted with the victim who was 45. The victim found W's visits a nuisance and attempted to cut off contact with him. Some time later, W met the victim at a public house and invited the victim back to his home. When they were there, the victim alleged that W attacked him from behind, held him by the throat and demanded money. Eventually he took the victim's wallet containing two cash cards and required the victim to accompany him to a cash dispensing machine. W took a kitchen knife and held it to the victim's back until the victim was able to escape. In the presentence report, W alleged that the older man had raped him, and that W had retaliated by attacking him with such ferocity that the victim offered him his cash cards as a means of stopping the attack. The Crown indicated that they would not accept that basis of plea, and the case was adjourned to allow W's claim to be investigated. When the case was relisted, the prosecution indicated that they would not pursue a Newton hearing and outlined the Crown's case. Defence counsel mitigated in accordance with W's account of the offence given in the pre-sentence report. The sentencer rejected the W's version of events as simply not credible and sentenced W to a total of 12 months' detention in a young offender institution. W appealed.

Held, dismissing the appeal, that the sentencer should not have proceeded to sentence without a Newton hearing. Where there was a substantial conflict in the versions of the facts of the offence, and the court was not willing to sentence on the basis of the defendant's version, the court must proceed to hear evidence on the question, whether or not counsel for the defence wished such a hearing to take place. The judge did not give any indication to counsel that he was rejecting the basis of plea that appeared in the pre-sentence report and arrived at his conclusion on the facts without any inquiry or taking evidence. The court had accordingly invited counsel for W to address the court on the basis of the version of facts set out in the pre-sentence report. The court had reached the view that even assuming a sexual approach had been made by the victim, a sentence of 12 months' detention in a young offender institution was the irreducible minimum sentence that could be passed.

R. v. W (JONATHAN) (A JUVENILE) [2000] 1 Cr. App. R. (S.) 488, Douglas Brown, J., CA (Crim Div).

1338. **Juvenile offenders – robbery – supervision orders – unduly lenient sentence**

The Attorney General asked the court to review sentences on the grounds that they were unduly lenient. L, aged 17, pleaded guilty before two youth courts to two offences of robbery and was convicted of burglary and theft. G, aged 16, pleaded guilty to robbery and burglary, and was convicted of a further robbery. L and G were committed to the Crown Court for sentence. The victim of two of the robberies was a 12 year old girl who was known to both of the offenders. She was approached by L and G when walking home from school; one offender grabbed her arm while the other pulled off her jacket. Subsequently, both offenders went to the girl's home, entered the house uninvited and stole vouchers to the value of £30. A few days later G met the girl in a park and stole from her a total of £30. On a different occasion L assisted in an attempt to rob a woman of her handbag. Sentenced in each case to a supervision order for 12 months.

Held, refusing the application, L and G had previous convictions but reports before the Court of Appeal in each case suggested that L and G were taking advantage of the opportunities afforded by the supervision order. The court had concluded that the sentences were unduly lenient. It was easy to view offences of this type through the eyes of the offender alone and form a judgment as to what might be in the best interest of the offender. That was not the only matter to take into account. There was a public dimension to offending of this kind which could not properly be overlooked. Parents were justifiably incensed when children on the way to school or on the way home from school were victimised by older children. The court appreciated the considerations which led the sentencer to adopt the course he did, but the sentences were unduly lenient and custodial sentences of some months should have been imposed. However, in view of the personal situations of L and G as they now were, it would be destructive to impose custodial sentences on L and G at this stage. For that reason the Court would not disturb the orders made by the sentencer. *R. v. Robinson (Darren Lee)* (1992) 13 Cr. App. R. (S.) 104, [1992] C.L.Y. 1455, *R. v. Hiscock (Nicholas Stephen)* (1994) 15 Cr. App. R. (S.) 287 and *Attorney General's Reference (Nos.44 and 46 of 1995), Re* [1996] 2 Cr. App. R. (S.) 128, [1996] C.L.Y. 2058 considered.

ATTORNEY GENERAL'S REFERENCE (NOS.57 AND 58 OF 1999), *Re*; R. v. G (JOANNE RAINEY) (A JUVENILE); *sub nom.* R. v. L (CATHERINE FIONA) (A JUVENILE) [2000] 1 Cr. App. R. (S.) 502, Lord Bingham of Cornhill, L.C.J., CA (Crim Div).

1339. Juvenile offenders – robbery – unduly lenient sentence

The Attorney General the sentences imposed on four juveniles, K, W, P and S for robbery and attempted robbery perpetrated against three passengers aged between 16 and 18 whilst on a train and using an imitation firearm in the attack. K had been sentenced to four months' detention and the three other offenders had received community sentences.

Held, allowing the reference, that although the court had had regard to all relevant mitigation and the risk of double jeopardy, the sentences were unduly lenient. K and W's sentences would be increased to 12 months' detention, and P and S would receive six months' detention, subject to detention and training orders. It was stated that offenders who committed robberies on public transport should receive custodial sentences, unless there were exceptional circumstances to the contrary.

ATTORNEY GENERAL'S REFERENCE (NOS.7, 8, 9 AND 10 OF 2000), *Re*; *sub nom.* R. v. K (IMRAN) (A JUVENILE); R. v. S (JOE) (A JUVENILE); R. v. P (GARETH) (A JUVENILE); R. v. W (LEE) (A JUVENILE) [2001] 1 Cr. App. R. (S.) 48, Swinton Thomas, L.J., CA (Crim Div).

1340. Juvenile offenders – robbery – use of imitation firearms – pre planned offence – unduly lenient sentence

[Children and Young Persons Act 1933 s.53.]

The Attorney General asked the court to review sentences on the basis that they were unduly lenient. T, L, B and J pleaded guilty to an offence of robbery. The four juvenile offenders carried out a pre planned robbery of a sub post office armed with imitation firearms. In the course of the robbery one of the guns was discharged causing members of staff to believe they were facing imminent death. Following his arrest and the granting of bail, L, having been refused the use of a mobile phone by R, produced a Stanley knife and held it to the side of R's stomach. R, fearing that he might be stabbed, freed himself and ran away. L was consequently arrested but denied the offence. T, L, B and J were sentenced to two years' detention in a young offender institution in respect of the robbery of the sub post office and L was sentenced in respect of the subsequent offence of attempted robbery to a concurrent sentence of 12 months detention.

Held, allowing the reference, that considering *R. v. Turner (Bryan James)* (1975) 61 Cr. App. R. 67, [1975] C.L.Y. 559 and *R. v. Dacres (Robert Clive)* (1995) 16 Cr. App. R (S.) 176, [1996] C.L.Y. 2060 there were aggravating circumstances to the robbery and the sentences had been unduly lenient. The robbery had been pre planned and imitation firearms, one of which was subsequently discharged, were used. Giving consideration to their youth, their relative cooperation whilst in custody and the requirements of the Children and Young Persons Act 1933 s.53, sentences of five years detention were more appropriate. In respect of the offence of attempted robbery L would serve an additional 12 month concurrent sentence.

ATTORNEY GENERAL'S REFERENCE (NOS.52, 53, 54 AND 55 OF 1999), *Re*; R. v. L (A JUVENILE); R. v. B (A JUVENILE); R. v. J (A JUVENILE); *sub nom.* R. v. T (A JUVENILE) [2000] 1 Cr. App. R. (S.) 450, Kennedy, L.J., CA (Crim Div).

1341. Juvenile offenders – robbery – use of mask and imitation gun – detention and training orders – unduly lenient sentence

The Attorney General referred a sentence of an eight month detention and training order imposed on S for the attempted robbery of a garage shop on the ground of undue leniency. S, a juvenile, had used a disguise and a toy gun, which the Attorney General contended were aggravating features which would have justified a sentence of five to seven years' imprisonment had S been an adult, rather than the two to three years stated by the judge to be an appropriate tariff.

Held, that the sentence was unduly lenient but that it was not appropriate for the court to intervene. An appropriate sentence for an adult would have been three and a half to seven years' imprisonment, *Attorney General's Reference (Nos.41 and 42 of 1995), Re* [1996] 2 Cr. App. R. (S.) 115, [1996] C.L.Y. 2057 followed. An appropriate sentence for S would have been a detention order of three years. In view of the long period of uncertainty which had surrounded his sentence, and of which S had been aware, and the inherent element of double jeopardy, the court would have reduced this to two years. However, in view of the progress made by S while in custody and his impending release, the court declined to interfere with the sentence imposed.

ATTORNEY GENERAL'S REFERENCE (NO.62 OF 2000), *Re; sub nom.* R. v. S (DANIEL EDWARD) (A JUVENILE) 200004847/R2, Rose, L.J., CA (Crim Div).

1342. Juvenile offenders – robbery – use of weapons – premeditated offence – unduly lenient sentence

The Attorney General sought leave to refer sentences imposed on T and F, both aged 17, for series of robberies perpetrated against young boys, amounting to eight and six months' detention respectively, to the Court of Appeal. The Attorney General contended that the offences were aggravated by the fact that they had been planned, knives had been carried and brandished and the fact that the offences had been committed by a group in public with the aid of a disguise.

Held, allowing the reference, that sentences substantially in excess of those imposed would have been justified, but having regard to the element of double jeopardy and the mitigation advanced on behalf of both offenders, detention and training orders would be imposed of 12 and six months respectively effective from the hearing of the application before the court.

ATTORNEY GENERAL'S REFERENCE (NOS.11 AND 12 OF 2000), *Re*; R. v. F (NICHOLAS) (A JUVENILE); *sub nom.* R. v. T (JAMES) (A JUVENILE) [2001] 1 Cr. App. R. (S.) 10, Swinton Thomas, L.J., CA (Crim Div).

1343. Juvenile offenders – robbery of elderly persons when boarding buses

[Children and Young Persons Act 1933 s.53(3).]

P and B, aged 16 and 14 respectively, pleaded guilty to five offences of theft and one of robbery. They accosted elderly women as they were boarding buses, jostled them and stole their purses. They were sentenced to five years' detention under the Children and Young Persons Act 1933 s.53(3) in each case and appealed.

Held, allowing the appeal, that the campaign mounted by P and M caused great fear and distress, but bearing in mind their youth and their pleas of guilty, the sentences were manifestly excessive. The court would substitute a sentence of four years' detention on P and three and a half years on B.

R. v. M (PATRICK) (A JUVENILE); R. v. M (BERNARD) (A JUVENILE) [2000] 1 Cr. App. R. (S.) 6, Butterfield, J., CA (Crim Div).

1344. Juvenile offenders – robbery of youth by group of young offenders – appropriateness of detention

[Children and Young Persons Act 1933 s.53(3).]

J and C, aged 14, L, aged 16 and W, aged 17, pleaded guilty to robbery and assault occasioning actual bodily harm. W was convicted of false imprisonment and assault occasioning actual bodily harm. They subjected a 15 year old boy to a brutal assault at a railway station and extorted money from him. He sustained extensive injuries and was hospitalised for five days. J and C were sentenced to two years' detention under the Children and Young Persons Act 1933 s.53(3) for robbery, with no separate penalty for assault occasioning actual bodily harm; L was sentenced to two years' detention in a young offender institution for robbery with no separate penalty for assault occasioning actual bodily harm; W was sentenced to 21 months' detention in a young offender institution on each count of false imprisonment and assault occasioning actual bodily harm. The issue in the appeal concerned the powers of the Crown Court to impose the sentences imposed on the appellants. It was contended that the serious feature of the incident was not the robbery but the assault, and the serious violence which caused the victim actual bodily harm was a distinct and separate offence from the robbery. It was further argued that it was wrong in principle for the court to impose detention under s.53 for robbery when in reality it was passing sentence for the assault.

Held, dismissing the appeal, that this was a dreadful sustained attack by a gang on a defenceless and harmless youth of their own age which went on for a very long time. The question was whether the court could pass appropriate sentences on offenders of this age range. For those aged 14, a sentence of detention under s.53(3) was available on conviction for robbery or false imprisonment, but not for assault occasioning actual bodily harm. The correct approach to the facts of the case was that the attack on the victim began for the purposes of robbery, which was achieved with only minor violence. The attack proceeded to protracted and gratuitous violence with continuing echoes of the original robbery. It was a prolonged but single incident or episode against the same victim at the same place. The court had not the slightest doubt that if the victim had not succumbed to the early pressure, he would have been subjected to the more serious violence until he did. Although in the technical sense the robbery was complete before the violence continued, the offences were inextricably linked. The actual bodily harm could, therefore, be taken into account when considering the seriousness of the robbery, and in those circumstances the sentences of detention under s.53 were correct. As W had played a lesser role, and he had acted to reduce the violence, his sentence was reduced to 15 months' detention.

R. v. M (JODIE) (A JUVENILE); R. v. L (WAYNE) (A JUVENILE); R. v. C (LEANNE) (A JUVENILE); R. v. M (STUART) (A JUVENILE) [2000] 1 Cr. App. R. (S.) 17, Judge, L.J., CA (Crim Div).

1345. **Juvenile offenders – secure accommodation – non secure council accommodation with curfew – time not automatically deducted from sentence**

[Criminal Justice Act 1967 s.67(1A).]

A, who had been convicted of handling stolen goods, had spent 43 days in non secure council accommodation on remand before being sentenced. A successfully applied for judicial review of the decision not take into account the period spent in non secure accommodation for the purpose of reducing his sentence. The Secretary of State appealed, arguing that, under the Criminal Justice Act 1967 s.67(1A), only a period spent in accommodation designed for "restricting liberty" could be taken into account, whereas the doors had not been locked and A had in fact absconded. A argued that, although the accommodation was not secure, he was subject to restrictive conditions, including a curfew, which had the effect of restricting his liberty.

Held, allowing the appeal, that an offender who spent time in non secure accommodation was not entitled to have his custodial sentence automatically reduced by the amount spent in that accommodation, *R. v. Collins (Daniel)* (1995) 16 Cr. App. R. (S.) 156, [1996] C.L.Y. 1963 overruled. The fact that restrictive conditions, including a curfew, had been attached did not alter the fact that the accommodation was not secure. The court could have imposed similar conditions as conditions of bail.

R. v. SECRETARY OF STATE FOR THE HOME DEPARTMENT, *ex p.* A (A JUVENILE); *sub nom.* R. v. HOME OFFICE, *ex p.* A (A JUVENILE) [2000] 2 A.C. 276, Lord Hope of Craighead, HL.

1346. Life imprisonment – arson – prisoners – recklessly starting fire in prison cell endangering life

[Criminal Justice Act 1991 s.2(2)(b); Crime (Sentences) Act 1997 s.28.]

W appealed against a sentence of life imprisonment with a specified period under the Crime (Sentences) Act 1997, s.28 of five years, having pleaded guilty to arson being reckless as to whether life was endangered. He was serving a sentence of eight years' imprisonment imposed for serious sexual offences when he set fire to his cell at the prison where he was detained. Prison officers saw smoke coming from the door of his cell and when they looked through the hatch they saw that a large part of the cell was on fire. The fire brigade was called, and a fire extinguisher was used in an attempt to extinguish the flames. W was removed from the cell. He said that he had been in a turmoil when he started the fire and had seen the fire as a way of escaping from the situation.

Held, quashing the indeterminate sentence and substituting a sentence of 10 years' imprisonment under the Criminal Justice Act 1991 s.2(2)(6), that psychiatric witnesses considered that W suffered from a personality disorder, but that he was not suffering from a mental illness. He was not suitable for a hospital order. The criteria for the imposition of an indeterminate sentence had been set out in *R. v. Hodgson (Rowland Jack Forster)* (1968) 52 Cr. App. R. 113, [1968] C.L.Y. 848 and more recently in *R. v. Chapman (Jamie Lee)* [2000] 1 Cr. App. R. 77, [1999] C.L.Y. 1250. In *Chapman* it had been made clear that the criteria laid down in *Hodgson* were still good law, and that the first pre-condition for imposing an indeterminate life sentence was that the offender had committed an offence grave enough to merit an extremely long sentence. The court agreed with the submission that in this case the first pre-condition was not satisfied. It seemed to the court that the offence of reckless arson in this case was not an offence which called for an extremely long sentence. An appropriate sentence for the offence to which W had pleaded guilty would have been three years, *R. v. Hales (Robert)* [1999] 2 Cr. App R. (S.) 113, [1999] C.L.Y. 1078 considered. However, the court was also bound to consider s.2(2)(b). This was a case where there was the clearest possible evidence that the requirements of s.2(2)(b) were satisfied. It was therefore decided that, in addition to the three years which would be appropriate as a commensurate sentence for the offence to which W pleaded guilty, there would be added for the purposes of public protection under s.2(2)(b) a further period of seven years. The total sentence would be 10 years' imprisonment, consecutive to the sentence W was already serving, passed as a longer than commensurate sentence under s.2(2)(b).

R. v. WILSON (GODFREY) [2000] 2 Cr. App. R. (S.) 323, Kennedy, L.J., CA (Crim Div).

1347. Life imprisonment – automatic sentences – scope of "exceptional circumstances"

[Crime (Sentences) Act 1997 s.2; European Convention on Human Rights 1950 Art.3, Art.5.]

O appealed against the imposition of an automatic life sentence pursuant to the Crime (Sentences) Act 1997 s.2 subsequent to his guilty plea to an offence of robbery. Section 2 provided for the automatic imposition of a life sentence on certain offenders where a second offence had been committed, except where there were "exceptional circumstances". It was contended that the Act should be read in the light of the European Convention on Human Rights 1950, or alternatively, that s.2 was incompatible with the Convention.

Held, allowing the appeal, that (1) the purpose behind the enactment of s.2 was the protection of the public. It followed that where an offender did not pose a considerable risk to the public, that constituted an exceptional circumstance and accordingly the court would not impose an automatic life sentence. Moreover, the time that had elapsed between the offences was a relevant consideration in deciding the degree of risk a defendant posed to the public. Similarly, the age of a defendant and the potentially different nature of the offences could, in some circumstances, give rise to the conclusion that the case was exceptional, *R. v. Buckland (Andrew)* [2000] 1 W.L.R. 1262, [2000] C.L.Y. 1359 and *Attorney General's Reference (No.53 of 1998), Re* [2000] Q.B. 198, [1999] C.L.Y. 1249 considered, and (2) where an offender posed a considerable risk to the public, the imposition of an automatic life sentence under s.2 would not contravene the provisions of the Convention. While it was possible to envisage situations in which the imposition of an automatic life sentence could be regarded as arbitrary under Art.5 and a form of punishment contrary to Art.3, such a problem only arose where an unduly restrictive approach was taken to interpreting s.2. This problem could be avoided if it was interpreted in accordance with the policy and purpose of Parliament, which was to protect the public.

R. v. OFFEN (MATTHEW BARRY) (NO.2); R. v. McGILLIARD (PETER WILSON); R. v. McKEOWN (DARREN); R. v. OKWUEGBUNAM (KRISTOVA); R. v. S (STEPHEN) [2001] 1 W.L.R. 253, Lord Woolf of Barnes, L.C.J., CA (Crim Div).

1348. **Life imprisonment – buggery – second serious offence – comparison with rape – consent was differentialising factor**

[Offences Against the Person Act 1861 s.18; Criminal Justice and Public Order Act 1994 s.142; Crime (Sentences) Act 1997 s.2(5).]

W was convicted of an offence of buggery in July 1990 and, following a *Newton* hearing, in which the offence was adjudged non consensual, was sentenced to four years' imprisonment. Nine years later W was convicted of an offence of wounding with intent to cause grievous bodily harm under the Offences against the Person Act 1861 s.18 and was sentenced to life imprisonment in accordance with the Crime (Sentences) Act 1997 s.2, although the trial judge felt that a term of three years was more appropriate. W appealed against the sentence contending that buggery did not fall within the list of serious offences contained in s.2(5) of the 1997 Act.

Held, allowing the appeal, that buggery did not amount to a serious offence within s.2 of the 1997 Act. The trial judge had made an error in deciding that, after the change in the law effected by the Criminal Justice and Public Order Act 1994 s.142, the offence of rape, which did fall within s.2(5), embraced buggery and would therefore lead to a mandatory life sentence. Rape and buggery could not be equated with one another as a lack of consent was an essential ingredient in the former offence, but not in the latter. The court substituted a sentence of three years' imprisonment.

R. v. W (STEPHEN ROBERT) [2000] 1 W.L.R. 1687, Roch, L.J., CA (Crim Div).

1349. **Life imprisonment – child murders – full lifelong sentence appropriate for heinous crimes**

[Murder (Abolition of Death Penalty) Act 1965.]

H was convicted of the murder of two children in 1966. In 1985 the Secretary of State reached the provisional conclusion that a tariff of 30 years should be imposed on H as a mandatory life prisoner and in 1987 H confessed to her participation in the murders of a further three children. In 1990 the Home Secretary concluded that a "whole life" tariff was merited, a decision affirmed by the subsequent Home Secretary in 1997. An application for judicial review of the decision both to make and affirm this decision was dismissed together with a subsequent appeal. H appealed, contending that (1) under the Murder (Abolition of Death Penalty) Act 1965 it was anticipated that a prisoner would be released after a finite period of imprisonment; (2) that the policy in relation to "whole life" tariffs as operated by successive Home Secretaries was *Wednesbury* unreasonable; (3) that the imposition of a "whole life" tariff amounted to an unlawful increase in the 30 year tariff imposed in 1985, and (4) that the sentence was excessive having regard to the applicant's age at the time the time the offences were committed and the influence exercised over H by her codefendant.

Held, dismissing the appeal, that (1) there was no reason why a particularly heinous crime should not attract the imposition of a life long term of imprisonment; (2) given the fact that the Home Secretary was prepared to constantly reassess the decision he had made in the light of such further information as became available, it could not be said that he had unlawfully fettered his discretion; (3) the 30 year tariff had been a provisional sentence never communicated to H until 1994, at which juncture she was also informed of the 1990 decision to impose a whole life sentence. Furthermore the 1985 decision had been taken at a time when the H's involvement in three further murders was not known to the then Home Secretary, and (4) the crimes which H had committed were uniquely wicked and without H's active involvement it was likely that the five children in question would still have been alive.

R. v. SECRETARY OF STATE FOR THE HOME DEPARTMENT, *ex p.* HINDLEY [2001] 1 A.C. 410, Lord Steyn, HL.

1350. Life imprisonment – criminal record – failure of counsel to give correct advice

[Crime (Sentences) Act 1997 s.2(3).]

S had been convicted of an offence of causing grievous bodily harm with intent. Counsel at trial had failed to advise S that he risked mandatory life imprisonment for a second serious offence, S having a previous conviction of a serious nature. Had S been aware of the length of sentence he faced he may have changed his plea to guilty to a lesser offence, which would have been acceptable to the Crown.

Held, allowing the appeal, that where a defence barrister did not explain to his client that because of his previous conviction for unlawful sexual intercourse with a girl under the age of 13, there was a possibility of him receiving a mandatory life sentence for an offence of causing grievous bodily harm with intent, that would amount to an exceptional circumstance under the terms of the Crime (Sentences) Act 1997 s.2(3) and a life sentence could not fairly be imposed.

R. v. STEPHENS (MICHAEL) [2000] 2 Cr. App. R. (S.) 320, Rose, L.J., CA (Crim Div).

1351. Life imprisonment – firearms offences – length of specified period

[Firearms Act 1968 s.16, s.17(2), s.18; Crime (Sentences) Act 1997 s.2, s.28.]

S pleaded guilty to possessing a firearm when committing a specified offence, contrary to the Firearms Act 1968 s.17(2), and to possessing a firearm and ammunition when a prohibited person. S visited the home of his stepfather, taking with him a handgun. He removed the magazine, dropped a number of rounds of ammunition on the floor and threw the gun down. He then became agitated and the family spent two hours trying to calm him down. Later S was in the company of a woman at a nightclub. When she told him she was going home S assaulted her by grabbing her throat and pushed the barrel of the gun into her stomach. S was arrested shortly afterwards. He was seen to discard a gun, which was found to be a semi-automatic pistol in working order with six live rounds in the magazine. S had various previous convictions, including a conviction in 1994 for wounding with intent to cause grievous bodily harm and for carrying an imitation firearm with intent to commit an indictable offence contrary to the Firearms Act 1968 s.18. He had been convicted in 1996 of an offence contrary to the Firearms Act 1968 s.16. It followed that, in the absence of exceptional circumstances, S was liable to the imposition of an automatic life sentence under the Crime (Sentences) Act 1997 s.2. S was sentenced to life imprisonment with a period specified for the purposes of the Crime (Sentences) Act 1997 s.28, four years for possessing a firearm when committing a specified offence, and 30 months' imprisonment concurrent for each of the other offences. S appealed.

Held, allowing the appeal, that S did not challenge the imposition of an automatic life sentence. It was argued that the period specified for the purposes of the Crime (Sentences) Act 1997 s.28 was wrongly calculated, *R. v. M (Young Offender: Time in Custody on Remand)* [1999] 1 W.L.R. 485, [1998] C.L.Y. 1269 considered. The court would assume that the judge had started with a notional determinate term of eight years. This was high but not outside the bracket of terms reasonably to be considered for offences of kind. The sentencer should, however, have given credit for the time spent by S in custody before sentence. The court would reduce the specified period by eight and a half months on that ground.

R. v. SQUIRES (LLOYD CHARLES) [2000] 2 Cr. App. R. (S.) 160, Lord Bingham of Cornhill, L.C.J., CA (Crim Div).

1352. **Life imprisonment – firearms offences – robbery and possession of firearm – specified period**

[Crime (Sentences) Act 1997 s.2.]

A was convicted of robbery, having a firearm (a revolver) with intent to commit robbery, and having a firearm (a stun gun) with intent to commit robbery. B, the codefendant, was convicted of two counts of robbery and one of the attempted robbery, of having a firearm with intent to commit robbery on each of those occasions, and causing grievous bodily harm with intent. B was concerned in three robberies or attempted robberies in which security guards were attacked while delivering cash, threatened with firearms and robbed. In one case one of the security guards was shot in the leg. They were sentenced in each case to life imprisonment under Crime (Sentences) Act 1997 s.2 with specified periods in the case of A of nine years and B, 15 years. A and B appealed.

Held, allowing the appeal in part, that the sentencer based the specified period in the case of A on a notional determinate sentence of 16 years, and the specified period of 25 years in the case of B on a notional determinate sentence of 25 years. The Court had considered the matter of specified periods in *R. v. M (Young Offender: Time in Custody on Remand)* [1999] 1 W.L.R. 485, [1998] C.L.Y. 1269, *R. v. Secretary of State for the Home Department, ex p. Furber* [1998] 1 All E.R. 23, [1997] C.L.Y. 1593, *R. v. E* [2000] 1 Cr. App. R. (S.) 78, [2000] C.L.Y. 1355 and *R. v. Darke (Anthony)* [2000] 1 Cr. App. R. (S.) 123, [2000] C.L.Y. 1360. From those cases, a number of propositions could be derived. These were that in arriving at the specified period it was necessary first to decide what the proper determinate sentence would have been had it not been necessary to impose a life sentence. This applied whether the life sentence was discretionary or imposed under the Crime (Sentences) Act 1997. The determinate part of the sentence was that which was necessary to reflect punishment, retribution and the need for deterrence. The determinate part of the sentence should not be enlarged with a view to protecting the public. In arriving at the determinate part of sentence, it was relevant to have regard to the feelings of uncertainty and hopelessness experienced by a prisoner who had been made subject to a life sentence. The specified period should normally be half of the determinate period, less the whole of any time spent in custody on remand. Applying those principles, the Court had to ask whether 25 years was appropriate as the notional determinate period in the case of B, who was convicted of three separate armed robberies and one offence of using a firearm to inflict grievous bodily harm. Taking the starting point indicated by *R. v. Turner (Bryan James)* (1975) 61 Cr. App. R. 67, [1975] C.L.Y. 559, it had to be remembered that *Turner* was decided at a time when the sentencing climate was different. A more recent example of sentencing levels was provided by *R. v. Schultz (Karl)* [1996] 1 Cr. App. R. (S.) 451, [1996] C.L.Y. 2059, in which sentences of 25 years were upheld in the case of an armed robber found guilty of more than one offence. The Court considered that the appropriate determinate sentence for B would have been 22 years. It followed that the specified period was 11 years, less one year and six days on remand that is, nine years and 359 days. In the case of A, the specified period based on the unaltered determinate period of 16 years would be six years and 359 days.

R. v. ADAMS (DAVID ANTHONY); R. v. HARDING (WILLIAM HENRY) [2000] 2 Cr. App. R. (S.) 274, Mantell, L.J., CA (Crim Div).

1353. Life imprisonment – manslaughter on grounds of diminished responsibility – mental health – second serious offence

[Mental Health Act 1983 s.37, s.41; Crime (Sentences) Act 1997 s.2.]

N appealed against a sentence of life imprisonment imposed under the Crime (Sentences) Act 1997 s.2 on conviction of manslaughter on a plea of diminished responsibility, a second qualifying offence for the purposes of the 1997 Act.

Held, dismissing the appeal, that psychiatric evidence showed that N was suffering from a paranoid psychotic illness at the time of the offence, requiring a hospital order under the Mental Health Act 1983 s.37 and s.41. However, s.2 of the 1997 Act applied and N's mental state did not amount to an "exceptional circumstance" justifying the imposition of a hospital order, as opposed to a sentence of life imprisonment. Although it was regrettable that N had to be sentenced to prison, the main difference in the mode of disposal existed in the release and recall procedures, rather than in the treatment he would receive.

R. v. NEWMAN (DEAN DAVID) [2000] 2 Cr. App. R. (S.) 227, Lord Bingham of Cornhill, L.C.J., CA (Crim Div).

1354. Life imprisonment – rape – 15 year old victim – specified period

[Crime (Sentences) Act 1997 s.28.]

P was convicted of rape. He followed a 15 year old girl who got off a bus to walk home. He came up behind her, seized her by the neck and mouth and forced her into an alleyway, where he raped her several times over a period of several hours. Between the commission of that offence and his conviction, he was convicted of offences of vaginal and anal rape and indecent assault committed against a different victim in a similar manner. P was sentenced to life imprisonment on each count of rape, with a specified period for the purposes of the Crime (Sentences) Act 1997 s.28 of 12 years, and a sentence of five years' imprisonment concurrent for indecent assault. P appealed arguing that the period of 12 years specified for the purposes of s.28 was too long.

Held, allowing the appeal, that the court in *R. v. M (Young Offender: Time in Custody on Remand)* [1999] 1 W.L.R. 485, [1998] C.L.Y. 1269 had considered the factors which would influence a court in deciding on an appropriate period for the purposes of s.28 of the Act. In that case the court indicated that the specified period should normally be fixed at one half of the determinate sentence which would have been appropriate in the circumstances of the case, although there might be exceptional cases where a longer period was appropriate. The court did not give any indication of what might be the type of circumstances which would justify the decision to make the specified period something in excess of one half of the notional determinate sentence. In the present case, given the grave aggravating features, a determinate sentence of 16 years' imprisonment would have been justified. It was clear that P would represent a risk to the public for a number of years in future. The task of determining whether it was safe to release P into the community was a function committed by statute to the Parole Board. It was not the function of the court to make any future assessment of risk. The court was not persuaded that there were such exceptional circumstances as would justify concluding that the specified period should be more from one half of the notional determinate sentence. In those circumstances the specified period would be reduced to eight years.

R. v. PULLEN (STUART) [2000] 2 Cr. App. R. (S.) 114, Turner, J., CA (Crim Div).

1355. Life imprisonment – rape – committed while on licence for earlier rape

[Crime (Sentences) Act 1997 s.2, s.28.]

E pleaded guilty to two counts of rape and one of false imprisonment. E was released on licence from a sentence of 10 years' imprisonment for rape of his stepdaughter, imposed in 1992. He forced his way into a flat occupied by a woman aged 58, raped her twice and then held her against her will in his own flat for most of a day. E was sentenced to an automatic life sentence under the Crime (Sentences) Act 1997 s.2 on each count of rape, with eight years' imprisonment concurrent for false imprisonment, together with a specified period under s.28 of 12 years. E appealed.

Held, allowing the appeal, that the sentencer indicated that the determinate sentence she would have passed but for the automatic life sentence would have been 18 years, and the period of 12 years was calculated as two thirds of that term. It was argued that that term was too high, and that the judge should have fixed a date of eligibility for parole at half and not at two thirds of the notional determinate sentence. The court agreed that the notional determinate sentence was too high, having regard to E's plea. The appropriate determinate sentence would have been 15 years. It was appropriate to take half of the notional determinate sentence as the basis of the specified period, unless there was a good reason to fix a higher proportion. The court would fix the appropriate period at eight years, taking a period which was marginally higher than one half of the notional determinate sentence and taking into account the period E had spent remanded in custody, *R. v. Secretary of State for the Home Department, ex p. Furber* [1998] 1 All E.R. 23, [1997] C.L.Y. 1593 and *R. v. M (Young Offender: Time in Custody on Remand)* [1999] 1 W.L.R. 485, [1998] C.L.Y. 1269 considered.

R. v. E; *sub nom.* R. v. ABE [2000] 1 Cr. App. R. (S.) 78, Curtis, J., CA (Crim Div).

1356. Life imprisonment – rape – specified period

[Crime (Sentences) Act 1997 s.2, s.28.]

S pleaded guilty to seven counts of indecent assault, seven counts of rape and one count of attempted rape. S committed a series of offences in respect of the same victim. He had been convicted of attempted rape in 1994. S appealed against a sentence of life imprisonment under Crime (Sentences) Act 1997 s.2 with a period of five and a half years specified for the purpose of Crime (Sentences) Act 1997 s.28.

Held, allowing the appeal, that the correct approach to determining specified periods for the purposes of Crime (Sentences) Act 1997 s.28 was set out in *R. v. M (Young Offender: Time in Custody on Remand)* [1999] 1 W.L.R. 485, [1998] C.L.Y. 1269, where the Court indicated that in the normal case the sentencing court should take half of the determinate sentence that would have been passed and deduct from that a period equivalent to the period spent in custody on remand. In the present case, the sentencer indicated that he considered a term of nine years would have been appropriate as a determinate sentence. He deducted three years from that figure and a further six months, reflecting the period spent on remand, to reach the final specified period of five and a half years. If the judge's attention had been drawn to *R. v. M,* he would have calculated the period by taking half of nine years and then deducting the period spent in custody on remand, which was approximately equal to four months. Recalculating the period in this way, the Court would specify a period for the purposes of s.28 of four years and two months.

R. v. S (KENNETH MERVYN) [2000] 2 Cr. App. R. (S.) 187, Holman, J., CA (Crim Div).

1357. Life imprisonment – rape – specified period – unduly lenient sentence

The Attorney General applied for a sentence to be referred on the ground that it was unduly lenient. G, was convicted of rape and false imprisonment. On sentencing G to a mandatory life sentence, the judge indicated that the notional determinate sentence would have been nine years' imprisonment and that the specified period before which parole could be considered would be four years. The Attorney General contended that the judge had wrongly speculated on the future decision of the parole board and that attention should be drawn to the aggravating factors that G had planned the offence, carried a weapon, used excessive violence, raped the victim twice, and had a previous conviction of rape.

Held, allowing the reference, that the sentence was unduly lenient as the severity of the offence warranted an appropriate level of punishment and it was not for the judge to speculate any future approach of the parole board. Furthermore in view of the aggravated features of the offence, the notional determinate sentence should have been 14 years' imprisonment. However, with regard to double jeopardy and the time spent in custody before sentencing, the appropriate sentence was 13 years' imprisonment and the specified period before which parole could be considered was six years.

ATTORNEY GENERAL'S REFERENCE (NO.6 OF 2000), *Re; sub nom*. R. v. GOLDSMITH (SIMON) [2001] 1 Cr. App. R. (S.) 20, Rose, L.J., CA (Crim Div).

1358. Life imprisonment – robbery – exceptional circumstances

[Crime (Sentences) Act 1997 s.2, s.28.]

O pleaded guilty to robbery. O entered a building society branch, approached the counter and took a toy gun from a sports bag. He pointed the toy gun at one of the cashiers and demanded money. The cashier handed over a bundle of notes amounting to £960. O prevented the staff from activating an alarm, and then apologised and left. He was followed by a customer who recovered the sports bag into which O had placed the money. O admitted to some friends that he had committed the robbery and they contacted the police. O had a previous conviction for robbery. O was sentenced to an automatic life sentence under the Crime (Sentences) Act 1997 s.2, with a specified period for the purposes of s.28 of 14 months.

Held, dismissing the appeal, that when s.2 applied, the sentencer was obliged to impose a sentence of life imprisonment, unless there were exceptional circumstances relating either to the offences or the offender which justified the sentencer in not doing so. The Court had to consider whether there were exceptional circumstances in the present case. It was said that the robbery was amateurish, with no violence, shouting or raised voices. O apologised after committing the offence; the stolen money was recovered soon after the offence and O put up no struggle to retain it. O had committed the offence wearing bedroom slippers and had admitted the offence to friends soon after it had been committed. In the Court's view, this was a planned robbery; O successfully accomplished the robbery even though his sports bag was quickly taken from him, the amount taken was not insubstantial and the victims were put in fear. The Court found it impossible to say that there were exceptional circumstances relating to the offence which would justify the court in not imposing a life sentence. O had suffered from psychiatric difficulties since childhood; he was diagnosed as suffering from an unstable personality disorder but was not regarded as a danger to the public. Serious crime was not infrequently committed by persons who might be suffering from depression, or were otherwise unwell. Again, the Court could not say that there were circumstances relating to the offender which were exceptional so as to justify the court in not imposing a life sentence. *Attorney General's Reference (No.53 of 1998), Re* [2000] Q.B. 198, [1999] C.L.Y. 1249 considered.

R. v. OFFEN (MATTHEW BARRY) (NO.1) [2000] 1 Cr. App. R. (S.) 565, Jowitt, J., CA (Crim Div).

1359. Life imprisonment – robbery – second serious offence – attempts did not constitute a serious offence

[Crime (Sentences) Act 1997 s.2.]

B was convicted of attempted robbery and possession of a firearm, following an incident in which he entered a bank with a handwritten note stating that he intended to carry out a robbery and was carrying a firearm. B was in fact carrying an imitation firearm which he never produced, but the bank clerk raised the alarm believing that the threat would be carried out and B was subsequently arrested without protest. At trial B, who had a previous conviction for having an imitation firearm with intent to resist arrest, was convicted and sentenced to two concurrent life sentences under the provisions of the Crime (Sentences) Act 1997 s.2, which obliged the court to impose a life sentence after the commission of a second serious offence. B appealed against the sentence, contending that, despite having a previous conviction for a similar serious offence, it was open to the judge not to impose a life sentence in exceptional circumstances and, furthermore, that attempted robbery and possession of an imitation firearm were not serious offences for the purposes of s.2.

Held, allowing the appeal, that, in construing the words of the statute, attempted robbery was not a serious offence since attempts had been specifically referred to in other sections and omitted from s.2. Possession of an imitation firearm, however, was a serious offence since the offences mentioned in parenthesis in s.2 were not an exhaustive list. However, the judge had erred by declining to impose a life sentence in such an exceptional circumstances as revealed in the instant case, where no physical injury was or could have been caused, the firearm had never been produced and B had made no gain.

R. v. BUCKLAND (ANDREW) [2000] 1 W.L.R. 1262, Lord Bingham of Cornhill, L.C.J., CA (Crim Div).

1360. Life imprisonment – robbery – specified period

[Crime (Sentences) Act 1997 s.2, s.28(3)(b).]

D, aged 52, was convicted of robbery which took place at a railway station while armed with an imitation revolver. He had previously been convicted of armed robbery at a post office in 1983, and was on that occasion sentenced to nine years' imprisonment. D was sentenced to an automatic life sentence imposed under the Crime (Sentences) Act 1997 s.2 with a specified period of seven years, together with a sentence of nine years' imprisonment for possessing an imitation firearm with intent to commit robbery, and concurrent sentences for other unrelated offences. D appealed against the specified period of seven years and further contended that the trial judge had failed to take into consideration the six month period spent in custody on remand.

Held, allowing the appeal, that the sentencer simply specified a period of seven years without indicating how he had arrived at that figure. The sentencer did not make clear what notional determinate sentence he had in mind, and whether he had taken one half or two thirds of that figure as a basis for the specified period. The Court of Appeal was entitled to exercise for the judge the discretion that he did not exercise for himself, *R. v. Secretary of State for the Home Department, ex p. Furber* [1998] 1 All E.R. 23, [1997] C.L.Y. 1593 considered. The court's view was reinforced by *R. v. M (Young Offender: Time in Custody on Remand)* [1999] 1 W.L.R. 485, [1998] C.L.Y. 1269, where the court said that, in many cases, half the notional determinate sentence would be the appropriate period, although there would be certain cases where it would be appropriate to fix the specified period as a larger portion of the determinate sentence that would have been passed. The proper notional determinate sentence would have been nine years and the appropriate portion to specify was one half of that period; this led to a period of four and a half years. D had spent precisely six months in custody on remand prior to sentence, and under s.28(3)(b) time spent on remand had to be taken into account by the judge in fixing the specified period. The judge made no reference whatever to time spent in custody, and the court had to exercise its discretion in place of that of the sentencing judge. The court was not obliged to grant credit but in the circumstances of the case the appropriate credit should be given by deducting the six months from the specified period of four and a half years' reducing it to four years.

R. v. DARKE (ANTHONY) [2000] 1 Cr. App. R. (S.) 123, Curtis, J., CA (Crim Div).

1361. Life imprisonment – violent offences – conviction of second serious offence – 33 year interval did not amount to exceptional circumstances

[Offences Against the Person Act 1861 s.18; Crime (Sentences) Act 1997 s.2.]

T appealed against the imposition of an automatic life sentence. T was convicted of manslaughter in 1967 at the age of 22 and sentenced to three years' imprisonment. Some 33 years later, T was convicted of an offence contrary to the Offences Against the Person Act 1861 s.18 for which T was sentenced to life imprisonment as required by the Crime (Sentences) Act 1997 s.2. T contended that the passage of time since his first offence and his defence of provocation for the instant offence amounted to exceptional circumstances within the meaning of the 1997 Act and that his life sentence should be reduced accordingly.

Held, dismissing the application, that provocation and passage of time did not amount to exceptional circumstances under the provisions of the 1997 Act and although it was surprising that there had been no submissions to the court with regard to European human rights law and despite the fact that both courts had acknowledged the injustice of the penalty, the sentence could not be altered.

R. v. TURNER (IAN) [2000] 2 Cr. App. R. (S.) 472, Rougier, J., CA (Crim Div).

1362. Manslaughter – death caused by single fist blow

H appealed against a sentence of four years' imprisonment having pleaded guilty to manslaughter. H's wife went out one evening leaving H in charge of their two young children. H's wife went to a public house where she met a man who had been at school with her. They left the public house together shortly before midnight. H spent the evening with his wife's parents, and left, leaving one of the children with them. He stopped the car outside the public house where his wife had been, and then saw her walking down the street with the man whom she had met, with their arms linked and kissing each other. H punched the man in the face with his right fist. The blow caused the man to fall backwards, striking his head on a manhole cover. The man was taken to hospital and died a few days later. The cause of death was injury to his skull and brain consistent with falling heavily on to the right side of his head. A fracture of the condyle of his lower jaw was consistent with a heavy fist blow. H was arrested and subsequently charged with murder. He eventually admitted that he had punched the victim after seeing him kiss his wife.

Held, allowing the appeal, that the judge indicated that he accepted the mitigating effect of H's plea, his remorse and good character, but considered that H had lost his temper and struck a blow of considerable force. This was not a case where a lesser act of violence had horrific consequences arising out of some unexpected circumstance. The judge had misclassified the offence. To fall within the type of case considered in *R. v. Coleman (Anthony Neville)* (1992) 95 Cr. App. R. 159, [1992] C.L.Y. 1338, it was not necessary that the victim should have a thin skull or that the blow struck should not be extremely forceful. The extreme forcefulness of the blow was not irrelevant; the fact that this blow was of such force as to break the victim's jaw must be regarded as a serious aggravating feature of the case. The fact remained that it was not the blow which inflicted the fatal injury. In the court's view, given the wealth of mitigation available to H, the proper sentence would have been 18 months' imprisonment.

R. v. HENRY (CHRISTOPHER GEORGE) [1999] 2 Cr. App. R. (S.) 412, Simon Brown, L.J., CA (Crim Div).

1363. Manslaughter – diminished responsibility – depressive husband killing wife to conceal financial problems

S, sentenced to five years' imprisonment, appealed, having pleaded guilty to manslaughter by reason of diminished responsibility on an indictment charging him with murder. S and his wife ran a small business which fell into difficulties. S mortgaged his house and put the proceeds into the business, but the business continued to fail. S was eventually made bankrupt, but concealed this fact from his wife. In October 1998, bailiffs repossessed the matrimonial home under a court order, but S re-entered the house and changed the locks, taking steps to prevent his wife knowing anything of what had happened. A few days later as S and his wife were leaving the house together S suddenly seized a spade and hit his wife hard across the head. She fell to the ground and as she lay there he strangled her. S placed her body in the boot of his car, and changed his clothing. He spent the next 28 days driving around with his wife's body in the boot of the car, and eventually surrendered to the police. Psychiatric reports concluded that S was sane but suffering from such a degree of depression as substantially to impair his responsibility for his actions.

Held, allowing the appeal, that the court bore in mind that S was not a violent man. It was his desire to protect his wife from a full appreciation of their financial position and the impending loss of the home. The crime was the result of love rather than hatred. That did not excuse S; his responsibility was impaired but not absent. The taking of human life, even in such circumstances, was a terrible thing which called for punishment. The extent of the punishment must reflect all the circumstances and, even taking account of the events after the killing, the crime did not in the court's judgment merit a term of five years' imprisonment. The court would substitute a sentence of three years' imprisonment, *R. v. Davis (Jennifer Anne)* (1983) 5 Cr. App. R. (S.) 425, [1984] C.L.Y. 888 and *R. v. Jewsbury (Barry)* (1983) 3 Cr. App. R. (S.) 1 considered.

R. v. SEXTON (CLIFFORD JOHN) [2000] 2 Cr. App. R. (S.) 94, Lord Bingham of Cornhill, L.C.J., CA (Crim Div).

1364. Manslaughter – driving over victim unintentionally – unduly lenient sentence

The Attorney General asked the court to review a sentence on the ground that it was unduly lenient. H was convicted of conspiracy to cause actual bodily harm, theft and manslaughter. H's accomplice had a long standing dispute with another man, The accomplice asked H to frighten the other man by telephone calls or visits and relatively minor assaults. H drove a stolen car which hit the other man after he had been knocked to the ground while making his way home from a public house where he had been drinking. H made no attempt to stop and drove away at speed. The other man was found to have suffered a severe head injury from which he later died. The evidence suggested that the deceased had been lying in the road when the vehicle passed over him. H subsequently set fire to the car and was sentenced to five years' imprisonment for manslaughter, with concurrent sentences for the other offences.

Held, refusing the reference, that the sentencer passed sentence on the basis that H had attacked the victim, knocked him to the ground and driven off over him, but had not intended to kill him. The sentencer treated the matter as a deliberate attack leading to an accidental death. Accepting the basis on which the sentencer had passed sentence, the court did not consider that the sentence was unduly lenient *R. v. Gault (Michael Paul)* (1995) 16 Cr. App. R. (S.) 1013; *R. v. Ripley (Samuel)* [1997] 1 Cr. App. R. (S.) 19; *Attorney General's Reference (Nos.14 and 24 of 1993), Re* [1994] 1 W.L.R. 530, [1994] C.L.Y. 1193: and *R. v. Elton (Andrew)* [1999] 2 Cr. App. R. (S.) 58, [1999] C.L.Y. 1260 considered.

ATTORNEY GENERAL'S REFERENCE (NO.16 OF 1999), *Re*; *sub nom.* R. v. HARRIS (TIMOTHY JOHN); R. v. MARSH (PETER MICHAEL) [2000] 1 Cr. App. R. (S.) 524, Lord Bingham of Cornhill, L.C.J., CA (Crim Div).

1365. Manslaughter – gross negligence – pedestrian stepping in front of motorcyclist causing death

D was convicted of manslaughter. He had spent an evening drinking in various public houses, and had taken several prescribed drugs which he knew should not be taken in combination with alcohol. The victim was riding a motorcycle down a one way street when D either jumped, ran or walked into his path. The motorcyclist was unable to avoid colliding with him; he fell from the motorcycle and received multiple injuries when his body struck a lamp post. He died shortly afterwards. D claimed that he was on his way home after purchasing a meal in a restaurant when he went to cross the road; seeing bright headlights coming towards him he tried to jump out of the way, but by error of judgment jumped into the motorcyclist's path. D denied deliberately jumping in front of the motorcycle. Sentenced to three and a half years' imprisonment for manslaughter, with three months' imprisonment consecutive for other unrelated offences.

Held, allowing the appeal, that cases of manslaughter by gross negligence were notoriously difficult as the jury was left to find the point at which the defendant's conduct was so grossly negligent or reckless as to be properly branded as criminal. The judge stated that D had either jumped or stepped in front of the motorcyclist, waving his arms to make him stop. D submitted that the sentence was in line with sentences passed on reckless motorists who caused death, and was therefore inappropriately high for the facts of the instant case. The judge was faced with a unique sentencing problem. The offence was serious and called for a substantial term of imprisonment. The offence was serious and called for a substantial term of imprisonment. The court would substitute a sentence of two years and three months for the sentence of three and a half years for manslaughter, with the three month term for other offences still consecutive.

R. v. DEVINE (ANDREW MALEY) [1999] 2 Cr. App. R. (S.) 409, Simon Brown, L.J., CA (Crim Div).

1366. Manslaughter – intoxication – series of violent incidents

B was sentenced to six years' detention in a young offender institution, having pleaded guilty to manslaughter. He had spent the day drinking with some friends, one of whom was the victim. During the evening B and the victim became increasingly argumentative. Eventually there was a scuffle between them and B challenged the victim to a fight which then took place. Neither of the participants was badly hurt in the fight and they shook hands. Subsequently a further fight broke out in which the victim attempted to punch B, who retaliated and knocked him over. The victim made a provocative remark, and B struck him a single blow which knocked him to the ground. The victim cracked his head against the ground and suffered extensive fractures to the skull from which he died.

Held, allowing the appeal, that the case did not fall within the most venial category of manslaughter, which comes close to being an accident. There was a background of violence, both in B's previous record and in the course of the evening. This was not a case of an isolated blow struck with fatal results, but a blow struck on a man who was unsteady and confused at the end of an evening of violence. Plainly, the offence called for a substantial penalty but the court felt to some extent constrained by the authorities to conclude that the sentence of six years' detention in a young offender institution was excessive. A sentence of four and a half years' detention would be substituted, *R. v. Eaton (Spencer William)* (1989) 11 Cr. App. R. (S.) 475, [1991] C.L.Y. 1166, *R. v. Silver (Michael)* (1994) 15 Cr. App. R. (S.) 837 and *R. v. Bamborough (David)* (1995) 16 Cr. App. R. (S.) 602 considered.

R. v. BOSANKO (STEPHEN) [2000] 2 Cr. App. R. (S.) 108, Lord Bingham of Cornhill, L.C.J., CA (Crim Div).

1367. Mitigation – victim impact statements – sentencing guidelines

[Criminal Justice Act 1967 s.9.]

P appealed his sentence of four years' imprisonment for robbery of a middle aged woman whilst she was on her way home from shopping, to which he had pleaded guilty. P contended that his previous good character and work record, genuine remorse and his attempts to overcome his heroin addiction should have been taken into account in mitigation. The victim had provided a witness statement some five months after the attack, however P was concerned that a strongly worded letter from the victim's husband detailing the devastating physical and mental impact of the attack on his wife, which had not been disclosed to the defence, had been included in the judge's case papers and might have influenced him when sentencing.

Held, allowing the appeal and reducing four years' imprisonment to three, that there were matters other than P's plea which should have been taken into account in mitigation. Further, the letter from the victim's husband was to be disregarded, *R. v. Nunn (Adam John)* [1996] 2 Cr. App. R. (S.) 136, [1996] C.L.Y. 1836 applied, and the victim's witness statement, whilst taken into account, was treated with caution, *R. v. Hobstaff (Anthony)* (1993) 14 Cr. App. R. (S.) 605, [1994] C.L.Y. 1275 applied. The court made certain propositions, established from case law, concerning the use of victim impact statements, (1) if an offence had had a particularly damaging effect upon a victim then that fact should be made known to the court and taken into account, but such information must be in proper evidential form, for example conforming with the Criminal Justice Act 1967 s.9 or an expert's report, and be served in advance upon the defence, *Hobstaff* referred to. Evidence from the victim alone on the impact of the offence on his life should be approached with caution, especially if it related to matters the defence could not realistically be expected to investigate, and (2) so that the courts could act with some degree of consistency when sentencing, a court must pass sentence in accordance with governing sentencing considerations, and the opinions of the victims or their close relatives on the appropriate level of sentence should not be taken into account, always bearing in mind that the facts of each case should be considered individually, *Nunn* referred to. However there were two exceptions to that general rule, firstly, where the victim's distress was aggravated by the offender's sentence, the sentence might be moderated, and secondly, where the victim's forgiveness or unwillingness to press charges suggested that their mental suffering might be much less than was normally the case, *R. v. Roche (Gerard Martin)* [1999] 2 Cr. App. R. (S.) 105, [1999] C.L.Y. 1320 referred to.

R. v. PERKS (JAMES BENJAMIN) [2001] 1 Cr. App. R. (S.) 19, Garland, J., CA (Crim Div).

1368. Murder – conspiracy to murder – disparate roles of appellant and codefendant

C had been convicted of conspiracy to murder and was serving a term of imprisonment when he met his codefendant who persuaded him to take part in a scheme to kill a woman with whom the codefendant had been living. C and the codefendant exchanged letters in which the plan to kill the woman was discussed. C was arrested for the offence while still in prison. He admitted that he had discussed plans to kill the woman with his codefendant, but claimed that he had played along with the other man to keep him quiet and had no intention of carrying out his part of the scheme. Both were sentenced to eight years' imprisonment for the offence.

Held, allowing the appeal, that the sentencer had stated that there was no difference between C and his codefendant. The court agreed with the submission that a difference should have been made between C and his codefendant on account of their previous convictions, and because the codefendant was the prime mover. In view of those matters a significant distinction should have been drawn between C and the codefendant. C's sentence would be reduced to six years' imprisonment.

R. v. CHAPMAN (KRAIGE ANDREW) [1999] 2 Cr. App. R. (S.) 374, Smith, J., CA (Crim Div).

1369. Murder – firearms offences – shooting victim at public house

S was convicted of murder and of attempted murder. He went with another man to a club, carrying a loaded gun. They encountered two other men and S gave the gun to his companion and encouraged him to fire at each of the other men. One of the men was killed. S was sentenced to custody for life for murder, and to 25 years' imprisonment for attempted murder. S appealed against the sentence of 25 years for attempted murder.

Held, allowing the appeal, that the authorities showed that for attempted murder committed as a vengeance crime, either in the course of organised crime or some more petty rivalry, the range of sentences was from 14 years to 20 years. In the absence of any clear motive, the court had to conclude that there was a grievance between the two groups of men. The sentence for attempted murder would be reduced to 18 years, *R. v. Donnelly (Francis Gray)* (1983) 5 Cr. App. R. (S.) 70, [1984] C.L.Y. 821, *R. v. Al-Banna (Marwan)* (1984) 6 Cr. App. R. (S.) 426, [1985] C.L.Y. 760, *R. v. Burton (Lawrence John)* (1990) 12 Cr. App. R. (S.) 559, [1992] C.L.Y. 1150, *R. v. Grant (Martin Charles)* (1992) 13 Cr. App. R. (S.) 54, [1992] C.L.Y. 1151, *R. v. White (Edward)* (1992) 13 Cr. App. R. (S.) 108, [1992] C.L.Y. 1152, *R. v. Clift (Sean Kenneth)* (1995) 16 Cr. App. R. (S.)

1022, [1996] C.L.Y. 1725, *R.v Doyle (Stephen)* [1996] 1 Cr. App. R. (S.) 239, [1996] C.L.Y. 1727, *R. v. Mortiboys (Derrick Godfrey)* [1997] 1 Cr. App. R. (S.) 141, [1997] C.L.Y. 1625, *R. v. Powell (Shaka)* [1998] 1 Cr. App. R. (S.) 84, [1998] C.L.Y. 1306 considered.

R. v. SMITH (SHEVON) [2000] 1 Cr. App. R. (S.) 212, Newman, J., CA (Crim Div).

1370. **Obtaining by deception – social security offences – conspiring to fraudulently claim benefits**

B, sentenced to 15 months' imprisonment, appealed, having pleaded guilty to conspiracy to obtain property by deception. B admitted conspiring to fraudulently claim income support and jobseekers' allowance between April 1994 and September 1998. He was party to making a claim on the basis of a fictitious, unemployed male person. A false passport bearing the appellant's photograph was used to support the claim. B was sentenced on the basis that he was involved in the conspiracy for a period of about four years, and that about £10,000 had been received by virtue of his activities.

Held, allowing the appeal, that it might be that in the future the Court would need to reconsider the level of sentence indicated in *Stewart* for cases of social security fraud. For the purpose of the present appeal, the Court would substitute a sentence of 10 months' imprisonment, *R. v. Ellison (John James)* [1998] 2 Cr. App. R. (S.) 382, [1999] C.L.Y. 1274 and *R. v. Stewart (Livingstone)* [1987] 1 W.L.R. 559, [1987] C.L.Y. 1015 considered.

R. v. BENDRIS (FAOUZI) [2000] 2 Cr. App. R. (S.) 183, Rose, L.J., CA (Crim Div).

1371. **Offences – unduly lenient sentences – review by Court of Appeal**

CRIMINAL JUSTICE ACT 1988 (REVIEWS OF SENTENCING) ORDER 2000, SI 2000 1924; made under the Criminal Justice Act 1988 s.35. In force: August 21, 2000; £1.00.

This Order extends the range of offences triable either way which, under the Criminal Justice Act 1988 Part IV, the Attorney General may refer to the Court of Appeal, with the leave of that Court, where he considers that a sentence imposed in the Crown Court was unduly lenient.

1372. **Offences against public morals – extended sentences – committing act against public decency**

[Criminal Justice Act 1991 s.2(2)(b), s.31, s.40.]

G, convicted of outraging public decency, appealed against a sentence of five years' imprisonment. G was seen in an alleyway near a primary school. He went towards a wall overlooking the playground of the school in which children were playing, withdrew his penis from his trousers and masturbated himself. He was arrested by police officers who had seen his activities. G had numerous previous convictions for indecent assaults on females and males, leading to custodial sentence for terms of up to five years' imprisonment. He had been released from custody one month before the present offences. G was sentenced to five years' imprisonment consecutive to an order under the Criminal Justice Act 1991 s.40 returning him to custody for the balance of the earlier sentence. G argued that the sentence was not commensurate with the seriousness of the offence.

Held, allowing the appeal, that the sentencer had said that G was a danger to young people. While this was correct, it could justify a sentence only under s.2(2)(b) of the Act. The court could not pass a sentence under that section because the offence of which G had been convicted was not a sexual offence within the meaning of the Act. The sentencer was therefore limited to passing a sentence commensurate with the seriousness of the offence. While it might be said that s.2(2)(b) was enacted specifically for defendants such as F, the fact that the definition of "sexual offence" in s.31 did not include the offence of which G was convicted on this occasion meant that s.2(2)(b) was not available and the sentencer was limited to passing a sentence which was commensurate with the seriousness of the offence. Although G was near to the school playground, he was not in the physical presence or earshot of any child and he was not gesticulating or calling to any child. The sentence was manifestly excessive, a proper sentence for the offence of committing an act outraging public decency was three years' imprisonment, consecutive to the order returning G to custody in respect of the earlier sentence.

R. v. GAYNOR (LEE) [2000] 2 Cr. App. R. (S.) 163, Hidden, J., CA (Crim Div).

1373. Offences against the person – administering noxious substances

C appealed against a sentence of six years' imprisonment on conviction of causing a noxious thing to be taken so as to endanger life. C, a woman aged 62, placed a number of containers of petrol and other liquids in the loft of her mother's house and arranged pipes so that petrol was carried through the cavity wall into the house next door, where the occupants became ill and suffered nausea as a result.

Held, allowing the appeal, that there was no clear explanation of the reasons for the offence; C had not shown any symptoms of major mental illness though she had undergone psychiatric treatment. As the neighbours had not suffered more than a general feeling of being ill and nauseous, the sentence would be reduced to four years' imprisonment.

R. v. CRONIN-SIMPSON (JUNE) [2000] 1 Cr. App. R. (S.) 54, Moses, J., CA (Crim Div).

1374. Offensive behaviour – threatening to damage property by setting fire to premises

M appealed against a sentence of six years' imprisonment, having pleaded guilty to threatening to destroy property. M became involved in a dispute with the proprietor of a kebab shop. He returned to the shop in the early hours of the morning, whilst the shop was still open, splashed diesel fuel on to the shop floor and threatened to burn the place down. Customers ran from the shop and the proprietor managed to seize the M's cigarette lighter and a petrol can which he was carrying. M claimed that he had no intention of setting fire to the premises, but that he intended merely to scare people into thinking that he was going to kill them.

Held, allowing the appeal, that this was a serious offence which demanded a substantial custodial sentence, but the sentence of six years' imprisonment was manifestly excessive. The Court would substitute a sentence of three years' imprisonment *R. v. Kavanagh (John William)* [1998] 1 Cr. App. R. (S.) 241, [1998] C.L.Y. 1166

R. v. McCANN (SEAN) [2000] 1 Cr. App. R. (S.) 495, Ognall, J., CA (Crim Div).

1375. Offensive weapons – possession of kitchen knife concealed under sock in public place

[Criminal Justice Act 1988 s.139.]

B appealed against a sentence of 18 months' imprisonment having pleaded guilty to having a bladed article in a public place, contrary to the Criminal Justice Act 1988 s.139. B entered a supermarket and filled a trolley with goods to a substantial value. He left the trolley near the exit and went in the direction of the lavatories. He was stopped and arrested by a store detective. Police officers were called and B produced a kitchen knife with a five inch blade from his sock. B claimed that he had the knife with him for his own protection.

Held, allowing the appeal, that the maximum sentence for the offence was two years' imprisonment. Serious though it was to carry a knife, there was no indication of its presence until he produced it to police officers following his arrest. It appeared to the court that insufficient credit had been given for his plea and the circumstances in which the offence was committed. A sentence of six months' imprisonment would be substituted.

R. v. BALDWIN (KEITH ALAN) [2000] 1 Cr. App. R. (S.) 81, Mitchell, J., CA (Crim Div).

1376. Offensive weapons – possession of plastic bottle containing ammonia solution

P was convicted of possessing an offensive weapon. P attended a police station in connection with unrelated matters and on being searched was found to be in possession of a plastic bottle containing a solution of ammonia. P admitted that he was carrying the bottle for protection and had done so for several days. Analysis of the liquid indicated that it could cause extreme discomfort if sprayed into the eyes but would not cause permanent injury. P appealed against the sentence of nine months' imprisonment.

Held, dismissing the appeal, that the sentencer was fully justified in passing an immediate custodial sentence. The sentence of nine months' imprisonment was severe but not excessive, *R. v. Hopkins (Stephen)* [1996] 1 Cr. App. R. (S.) 18 considered.

R. v. PROCTOR (JONATHON MARK) [2000] 1 Cr. App. R. (S.) 295, Judge Rivlin Q.C., CA (Crim Div).

1377. Perverting public justice – careless driving – motorist attempting to conceal evidence of involvement in fatal accident

W pleaded guilty to doing acts tending and intended to pervert the course of public justice. W left a public house and drove his car to meet a friend. While driving his car, he collided with two elderly men who were crossing the road having alighted from a bus. Both men died shortly afterwards. W's car was seriously damaged. W did not stop but drove his car to a wood a few miles away where he removed a cowling from the ignition socket so as to make it look as if the car had been stolen. He returned to the public house and asked a friend to drive him home; when he returned home he told his wife to tell the police that his car had been stolen. When police officers arrived at his home, W denied any knowledge of the accident and maintained the story that his car had been stolen. W persisted in this story throughout several interviews but eventually admitted the truth 24 hours after the accident. W said that his attention had wandered while he was driving; he had not consumed alcohol so as to be above the limit. He was prosecuted for driving without due care and attention and was dealt with by a magistrates' court for that offence. W appealed against a sentence of four and a half years' imprisonment.

Held, allowing the appeal, that the judge described the offence as a serious attempt to cover up W's involvement in a hit and run accident, and indicated that the sentence must be longer than would have been imposed if W had pleaded guilty to charges of causing death by dangerous driving. In the court's view, the judge erred in his approach. There were two completely distinct offences. First, the driving offence itself which resulted in the deaths, and secondly, the offence of perverting the course of justice by deliberately trying to cover up W's involvement. Each offence had to be considered and sentenced separately. W had not, by his actions, avoided a charge of causing death by dangerous driving; the prosecution elected not to charge him with that offence. The impression was left that the judge was sentencing W for the motoring offences with an "uplift" for the cover up. Any attempt to cover up and deny responsibility for a fatal accident was a serious matter, particularly when some other person was drawn into the deception. A sentence of four and a half years' imprisonment was disproportionate to the scale of the cover up and its duration. A custodial sentence was inevitable but a sentence of two years' imprisonment would have been appropriate.

R. v. WAKE (LESLIE) [1999] 2 Cr. App. R. (S.) 403, Holman, J., CA (Crim Div).

1378. Perverting public justice – dangerous driving – destroying car involved in fatal accident

D and E appealed against their sentences, having pleaded guilty to perverting the course of justice. E pleaded guilty also to driving without due care and attention. E was driving his father's car with D as his passenger when the car collided with a couple who were walking along the right hand side of an unlighted road. One of the pedestrians died immediately and the other suffered severe injuries. E immediately drove to the home of a girlfriend, and later D and E returned to the scene of the accident intending to retrieve missing pieces of the car. D and E then left the scene of the accident and agreed to dispose of the car. The car was driven to a field and set on fire; D and E were then driven away by friends in a second car. E then reported to the police that the car had been stolen, and the group agreed upon a false version of the events which would be used if they were asked to give an account of them. E was then told that the pedestrian had died and that a witness had given his name to the police. E then went to the police station and said that he had been in an accident and that the car had been stolen afterwards. Both had previous convictions; E had served a six month sentence for perverting the course of justice. They were sentenced to 18 months' and three years' imprisonment respectively for perverting the course of justice; E was conditionally discharged for driving without due care and attention and disqualified from driving for three years.

Held, allowing the appeal, that the proper sentences were nine months and 18 months' imprisonment respectively, *Attorney General's Reference (Nos.62, 63, 64 and 65 of 1996), Re* [1998] 1 Cr. App. R. (S.) 9, [1997] C.L.Y. 1658, *R. v. Ocego (Stephen Mark)* [1998] 1 Cr. App. R. (S.) 408, [1998] C.L.Y. 1175, *Attorney General's Reference (No.19 of 1993), Re* (1994) 15 Cr. App. R. (S.) 760, [1995] C.L.Y. 1448, *R. v. Walsh (John)* (1993) 14 Cr. App. R. (S.) 671, [1994] C.L.Y. 1215 considered.

R. v. DOWD (JEFFREY); R. v. HUSKINS (MALCOM) [2000] 1 Cr. App. R. (S.) 349, Hooper, J., CA (Crim Div).

1379. Perverting public justice – falsification – conspiring to give false account of ownership of vehicle

C and M were sentenced to a total of three years' imprisonment and appealed having pleaded guilty to conspiracy to pervert the course of justice and C alone pleaded guilty to perverting the course of justice. C and M were concerned in a car repair business. A customer took his wife's car to the business for repairs and was lent a car belonging to the business for her use while the repairs were undertaken. The customer's wife was driving the loan car when it was involved in a head on collision as a result of which she died. Police officers found that the tyres on the car were in a poor condition. It was discovered that the car was not insured and C and M agreed to tell the police that the car had been received by the business as payment for work carried out on another car and had been sold by M to C. Their story was that the car had been lent to the customer by C. C maintained the story in interview under caution and produced receipts as proof of the transfer of ownership. Eventually C and M admitted that the receipts were false and that the vehicle had been lent to the customer by the company.

Held, allowing the appeal, that the sentences were too long. The court would substitute a sentence of 18 months' imprisonment in the case of the M and 15 months in the case of C, with a sentence of three months' imprisonment in the case of C consecutive for other matters, *R. v. Reid (Stephen Anthony)* (1992) 13 Cr. App. R. (S.) 513, [1993] C.L.Y. 1241 considered.

R. v. CHARLTON (MARK ROBERT); R. v. MEALING (DAVID) [2000] 2 Cr. App. R. (S.) 102, Hidden, J., CA (Crim Div).

1380. Pleas – discounts – failure of judge to expressly mention plea

[Criminal Justice Act 1967 s.56; Criminal Justice and Public Order Act 1994 s.48.]

A appealed against sentences of eight months' imprisonment for attempting to obtain by deception, with four months consecutive for a bail offence, having pleaded guilty before a magistrates' court. A acquired a copy of a credit card statement relating to another person's credit card account. A ordered goods by telephone worth about £3,000, giving the name and address of the other person. The dealer taking the order was suspicious, and the goods were eventually delivered by undercover police officers. A was waiting in the road outside the house of the other person, introduced himself as the other person and signed a receipt for the goods. A was released on bail but failed to surrender and was eventually arrested. He was committed to the Crown Court for sentence.

Held, allowing the appeal, that fraudulent use of credit cards or information about credit cards was a serious offence, generally calling for immediate and substantial terms of imprisonment. The court could see nothing wrong in principle with the sentence of eight months' imprisonment. However, the sentencing remarks made no reference to any credit begin given for the plea of guilty. Clearly it was appropriate to give some credit for the plea of guilty, albeit that A had been caught red handed. The Criminal Justice and Public Order Act 1994 s.48 required the court to take into account the stage of the proceedings at which the defendant indicated his intention to plead guilty. In the instant case the Crown Court either did not give any credit for the guilty plea, or failed in its duty under the statute to state in open court that it had done so. The court would emphasise the decision in *R. v. Fearon (Paul)* [1996] 2 Cr. App. R. (S.) 25, [1996] C.L.Y. 1745, in which the same principles applied, in that it was desirable for a sentencing judge to indicate in his sentencing remarks that the defendant's plea of guilty had been taken into account. For that reason the sentence for attempting to obtain by deception would be reduced to seven months' imprisonment. In respect of the bail offence, A had been committed to the Crown Court under the Criminal Justice Act 1967 s.56. The powers of the Crown Court to deal with him for that offence were limited to those which the magistrates' court could have exercised. It followed that the maximum sentence for that offence was three months' imprisonment. The sentence imposed by the Crown Court for the bail offence was therefore unlawful and a sentence of two months would be substituted, consecutive to the sentence for attempting to obtain by deception. It was correct to make the two sentences consecutive. Failure to surrender to bail was a serious and discrete matter and in principle should attract a separate and consecutive sentence.

R. v. ARORIDE (TOBARE) [1999] 2 Cr. App. R. (S.) 406, Holman, J., CA (Crim Div).

1381. Pornography – children – Internet – downloading and distribution of images

[Protection of Children Act 1978 s.1 (1) (a), s.1 (1) (b); Criminal Justice Act 1988 s.160(1).]

T, who had been convicted of 30 offences of taking indecent photographs of children contrary to the Protection of Children Act 1978 s.1 (1) (a) and two offences under s.1 (1) (b) of distributing the same, appealed against a total sentence of 24 months' imprisonment. He contended that insufficient credit had been given for his guilty plea and the extent of his co-operation with the investigation. P and M, who had been sentenced to three years' and three months' imprisonment respectively for offences of the same nature, also appealed against sentence.

Held, allowing the appeals, that the nature and quantity of the material and the extent of commercial gain and distribution were relevant sentencing factors for offences of this kind. The maximum statutory penalty of three years' imprisonment was appropriate in cases involving large scale or commercial exploitation or distribution, particularly where the defendant had similar previous convictions. A non custodial sentence was appropriate for isolated possession cases without commercial gain or where material had been passed between two individuals. An early guilty plea, the level of co-operation with investigations and the character of the defendant were also relevant, *R. v. Travell (Richard John)* [1997] 1 Cr. App. R. (S.) 52, [1997] C.L.Y. 1638 and *R. v. Bolingbroke (Leslie John) The Times*, August 16, 2000, [2000] C.L.Y. 1382 considered. Accordingly, T's sentence would be reduced to 18 months' imprisonment for the s.1 (1) (b) offences, to be served concurrently with the 12 month term imposed under s.1 (1) (a). M's sentence would be quashed and substituted by a 12 month conditional discharge in the light of the offence being isolated and P's sentence for similar offences, including an offence under the Criminal Justice Act 1988 should be reduced to 18 months.

R. v. TOOMER (MARTIN CHARLES); R. v. POWELL (MICHAEL EDMUND); R. v. MOULD (DAVID FREDERICK) [2001] 2 Cr. App. R. (S.) 8, Kennedy, L.J., CA (Crim Div).

1382. Pornography – children – Internet – possession and distribution of indecent photographs

B appealed against a sentence of four years' imprisonment for possession and distribution of indecent photographs. B had been convicted of 10 counts of possession, for which he received two years' imprisonment for each, to run concurrently, and six counts of distribution, for which he also received two years' imprisonment for each to run concurrently. The judge ordered that the sentences imposed for possession and distribution should run consecutively, making a total sentence of four years. It was contended that B had effectively been sentenced twice for the same offence, since the distribution of the images could not take place without their possession and the sentence was excessive in view of B's previous good character and the fact that the offences had not been committed for gain.

Held, allowing the appeal in part, that the sentences for possession and distribution be served concurrently but the sentence for distribution would be increased to the maximum possible for the offence, namely three years, thus reducing the overall sentence to three years. In offences of this kind a very firm line would be taken even if the defendant was of good character and no profit had been made, since the material could be made available to an extremely wide audience and might have a corrupting effect.

R. v. BOLINGBROKE (LESLIE JOHN) [2001] 1 Cr. App. R. (S.) 80, Lord Woolf of Barnes, L.C.J., CA (Crim Div).

1383. Pornography – children – taking indecent photographs

[Sexual Offences Act 1956; Protection of Children Act 1978.]

B pleaded guilty to three counts of taking indecent photographs of a child, and one count of unlawful sexual intercourse with a girl under 16. B encountered a girl aged 15 who was working as a prostitute. He took her to his home where sexual intercourse occurred. On that occasion he made videos of the act of sexual intercourse and on subsequent occasions took a series of indecent photographs of the girl. On a different occasion B made contact with a girl aged 13 through an escort agency and took a series of indecent photographs of her. B was sentenced to a total of nine months' imprisonment and appealed against the sentence.

Held, dismissing the appeal, that the court had to consider whether an act of consensual sexual intercourse with a girl of 15, together with three offences of taking indecent photographs, represented a course of conduct of such gravity that it could only be dealt with by a custodial sentence. The relevant provisions of the Protection of Children Act 1978 and of the Sexual Offences Act 1956 were intended for the protection of children from sexual abuse. B had pleaded guilty on the basis that he believed the girls to be over the age of 16; the sentencer had concluded that B was at least reckless as to whether the girls were 16, basing his judgment on his own assessment of the age of the girls. It did not appear to the court that the sentencer was in any way unfaithful to the basis upon which the appellant had pleaded. He was entitled to make a judgment on the facts of the case. It was reasonable to conclude that whatever B said he believed, he had been reckless in reaching that belief. The public policy of the protection of girls from themselves had to be looked at against previous decisions of the Court of Appeal and the individual circumstances of the appellant. B was a man of 52 of previous good character. In the court's view the attitude of society to teenage prostitution and the taking of sexually suggestive and explicit photographs of under-age girls had changed since the case of *R. v. Taylor (Derek Roy)* [1977] 1 W.L.R. 612, [1977] C.L.Y. 658. It was apparent from cases dealing with the taking of indecent photographs of children, particularly where there was a commercial aspect, that the court would take a strong line to discourage this kind of activity. This was not a case where there was any commercial benefit from the taking of the photographs; however, the sentence of imprisonment was right in principle and could not be considered excessive in length.

R. v. B (ANTHONY RICHARD) [2000] 1 Cr. App. R. (S.) 412, Ebsworth, J, CA (Crim Div).

1384. Pornography – internet – children – downloading obscene publication from internet

J pleaded guilty to six offences of making indecent photographs. Police officers executing a search warrant at the house belonging to another man where the appellant lived seized the J's computer and computer disks, which were found to contain 18,500 images of a sexual nature, depicting young children. J admitted that he had downloaded the images from the Internet for his own personal use. He had no intention of selling them or distributing them to anyone else. J had on a previous occasion been sentenced to a term of imprisonment for possessing indecent photographs of children. J was sentenced to two years' imprisonment, and appealed.

Held, allowing the appeal, that this was a disgusting trade and a custodial sentence was inevitable. However, a sentence of 18 months' imprisonment would meet the justice of the matter.

R. v. JAMES (KENELM) [2000] 2 Cr. App. R. (S.) 258, Klevan, J., CA (Crim Div).

1385. Prostitution – coercion – living on earnings

[Sexual Offences Act 1956 s.30.]

P appealed against a sentence of five years' imprisonment following his conviction for living on the earnings of prostitution contrary to the Sexual Offences Act 1956 s.30. The complainant, aged 19, had moved into P's flat a few weeks after meeting him and P had ordered that she work as a prostitute in a sauna. Although the complainant had not led a promiscuous lifestyle, she agreed to P's demands because she was scared of him, and over the duration of six weeks she earned approximately £7000, all of which was given to P. Eventually she persuaded P to let her see her family, and after suffering a nervous breakdown and attempting self harm, she never returned to him.

Held, dismissing the appeal, that five years' imprisonment was not inappropriate where coercion and corruption was evidenced. In the case of *R. v. Farrugia (Francis)* (1979) 69 Cr. App. R. 108, [1979] C.L.Y. 540 the judge had stated that a sentence in excess of two years' imprisonment applied where there was strong evidence of corruption or coercion. In the instant case the complainants age, sexual inexperience, unwillingness to be a prostitute and P's control of her earnings satisfied the required criteria. Whilst five years was a long sentence, the maximum sentence was seven years, and the trial judge had been in the best position to assess how the aggravating factors should be reflected in the sentence. *Farrugia* considered.

R. v. POWELL (ASHNA GEORGE) [2001] 1 Cr. App. R. (S.) 76, Tuckey, L.J., CA (Crim Div).

1386. Racially aggravated offences – harassment – abuse directed at police officer on duty

[Crime and Disorder Act 1998 s.31.]

J appealed against a sentence of nine months' imprisonment having pleaded guilty before a magistrates' court to racially aggravated harassment contrary to the Crime and Disorder Act 1998 s.31. He was committed to the Crown Court for sentence. Police officers, including one officer of Asian origin, went to a disturbance on a housing estate. When they tried to arrest the appellant's cousin,

J interfered, and abused the officer. On a number of occasions J placed his face close to the officer's face and shouted racial abuse at him.

Held, allowing the appeal, that the court entirely agreed that the offence was so serious that only a custodial sentence could be justified. However, in view of J's early plea, his remorse, apology to the officer and the fact that the offence was not racially motivated but consisted of racial abuse, the court found it unnecessary to pass a sentence of nine months' imprisonment. A sentence of six months would have been sufficient.

R. v. JESSON (GARY MARTIN) [2000] 2 Cr. App. R. (S.) 200, Judge Martin Stephens Q.C., CA (Crim Div).

1387. Racially aggravated offences – offensive behaviour – threatening words directed at train conductor and police officer

[Criminal Justice Act 1967 s.56; Magistrates Court Act 1980 s.38; Public Order Act 1986 s.4; Crime and Disorder Act 1998 s.31.]

M appealed against a sentence of 18 months' imprisonment for racially aggravated threatening words and one month's imprisonment concurrent for travelling on a train without a ticket, on conviction on a guilty plea before a magistrates' court. He was committed to the Crown Court for sentence under the Magistrates Courts Act 1980 s.38 and the Criminal Justice Act 1967 s.56. M was travelling on a train when a conductor asked to see his ticket. M, who had not got a ticket, pretended that he had one and said that he had lost it. M became abusive and the conductor ordered him to leave the train. M then addressed words of racial abuse to the conductor. The conductor feared that he was going to be hit and was upset by the incident. M was arrested when the train arrived at its destination, and was abusive to the police officers who arrested him.

Held, dismissing the appeal, that the basic offence of using threatening words was set out in the Public Order Act 1986 s.4. This created a summary offence with a maximum term of six months' imprisonment. The Crime and Disorder Act 1998 s.31 created an offence of racially aggravated threatening, abusive or insulting words which was punishable as an either way offence with a term of imprisonment of up to two years. While M pleaded guilty before the magistrates' court, he was committed for sentence under s.38 of the 1980 Act and the Crown Court had power to deal with him as if he had been convicted in the Crown Court. It was plain from the legislation that Parliament regarded racial aggravation as a very significant factor, which increased the maximum penalty from six months for the basic offence to two years for the aggravated offence. Against that background, the court had to decide whether the sentence of 18 months' imprisonment was manifestly excessive. Although M pleaded guilty, he had no option but to do so: the evidence against him was overwhelming and the discount for his pleas was marginal. He had a record of many previous convictions, some of them serious. In the judgement of the court, this was a bad example of this type of offence. The sentence was severe, as it needed to be, to reflect public concern about conduct which damaged good racial relations within the community. The discount for M's plea was entirely proper. The sentence was fully justified.

R. v. MILLER (STEPHEN) [1999] 2 Cr. App. R. (S.) 392, Judge Colston Q.C., CA (Crim Div).

1388. Racially aggravated offences – sentencing guidelines

[Crime and Disorder Act 1998 s.29(1)(b)(ii).]

S appealed against a sentence of 42 months' imprisonment for an offence of racially motivated assault occasioning actual bodily harm. S relied on *R. v. Clarke (Simon) (1992)* 13 Cr. App. R. (S.) 640, [1993] C.L.Y. 1011 to contend that, despite the racism, the length of the sentence was manifestly excessive.

Held, dismissing the appeal, that the sentence was not manifestly excessive, racism would not be tolerated by society in general, and racially motivated offences would be punished more severely by the courts than an ordinary offence. The Crime and Disorder Act 1998 s.29(1)(b)(ii) had increased the maximum sentence for racially motivated actual bodily harm to seven years, implying that up to a further two years should be added to the sentence which would have been handed down had the offence not been racially motivated, *Clarke* distinguished. The appropriate procedure was to sentence for the substantive offence before adding a further term for the racial aspect prior to deciding on the total sentence proportionate to the criminality exhibited. The nature of the racial aggravation, whether issued by word or deed, and the location and number of people involved were all significant factors in assessing sentence and normal mitigation would affect any discount from sentence. The court would not shrink from extending the sentence to cross the custody threshold where the basic offence had not done so.

R. v. SAUNDERS (JOSEPH BRIAN) [2000] 1 Cr. App. R. 458, Rose, L.J., CA (Crim Div).

1389. Rape – adult victim threatened with knife – infliction of sexual indignities – victim's children present for part of time

B, aged 19, pleaded guilty to rape. B went to the home of a relative, where he was a frequent visitor. After some conversation, he threatened his relative's wife with a knife. B made her children go to a bedroom, and then forced the victim to go to her bedroom, where he raped her and committed other sexual indignities on her. The children managed to escape and the police were called. B admitted the offence in interview and pleaded guilty. B was sentenced to nine years' detention in a young offender institution and appealed.

Held, dismissing the appeal, that this was a very serious case with several aggravating features. These included the use of a weapon to frighten both the victim and her children, the infliction of sexual indignities over and above the rape, the fact that children were present in their own home when the offence was committed, and an abuse of trust in that B was a regular visitor to the home as a member of the extended family. The sentence was not manifestly excessive.

R. v. B (DAVID WAYNE) [2000] 1 Cr. App. R. (S.) 3, Bracewell, J., CA (Crim Div).

1390. Rape – children – attempted rape – 13 year old victim

[Criminal Justice Act 1991 s.2(2)(b).]

T was convicted of attempted rape and rape. He encountered a 13 year old girl who was reading on some grassland. T threatened the girl by holding a knife to her throat, undressed her and attempted to place his penis in her vagina. He then placed his penis in her anus. The complainant saw T a few days later and he was arrested. T subsequently admitting committing sexual acts with the girl, but claimed that she had consented. T was sentenced to 14 years' imprisonment on each count concurrent, and appealed.

Held, allowing the appeal, that the court assumed that the judge had not passed a longer than commensurate sentence under the Criminal Justice Act 1991 s.2(2)(b) and considered that the sentence of 14 years' imprisonment was justified by the seriousness of the offences themselves. While these were offences of the utmost seriousness with a number of aggravating features the appropriate sentence was 12 years' imprisonment, *R. v. Drabble (Stephen Jeffrey)* [1996] 2 Cr. App. R. (S.) 322, [1996] C.L.Y. 2040 considered.

R. v. TRIGGS (DAVID LAWRENCE) [2000] 2 Cr. App. R. (S.) 179, Dyson, J., CA (Crim Div).

1391. Rape – children – child aged seven

M appealed against a sentence of 14 years' imprisonment, having pleaded guilty to two counts of rape and one of assault occasioning actual bodily harm. The victim of the offences was a child aged seven who lived at a public house where her stepfather was the landlord. The child spent Christmas Day with her family and returned to the public house and went to bed in due course. M who rented a room at the public house, entered the room where the child was sleeping and carried her to his own room. When the child called for her mother M punched her in the eye, undressed her, and had intercourse with her both vaginally and anally. The next day it was noticed that the child had facial injuries and she was taken to hospital. The child later complained to her uncle and eventually gave a full account to her mother.

Held, dismissing the appeal, that there was evidence before the sentencer that the offence had changed the personality of the victim. The offence was aggravated by the youth of the victim, the discrepancy in age between the child and M, the fact that there were two rapes, the fact that there was violence both before and after the sexual activity, the fact that there was an attempt to perform oral sex, the devastating effect of the offence on the victim, and the breach of trust which resulted from fact that M was living within the home of the child and was trusted by her family. Although a discount was to be allowed for the plea of guilty, the likelihood of a conviction if there had been a trial was overwhelming and the discount for pleading guilty would not make a substantial reduction from the proper starting point for the offence. Had there been a trial, the appropriate sentence would have been in the region of 14 to 16 years. Although the sentence of 14 years on a plea of guilty was at the top of the permissible bracket the Court was unable to say that it was manifestly excessive.

R. v. M (PETER KENNETH) [2000] 1 Cr. App. R. (S.) 419, Ebsworth, J., CA (Crim Div).

1392. Rape – children – eight year old victim – unduly lenient sentence

[Criminal Justice Act 1991 s.44.]

The Attorney General asked the court to review a sentence on the ground that it was unduly lenient. N was convicted of three counts of rape, one count of indecent assault and one count of gross indecency. He married a woman who had a young daughter. Over a period of about nine months, when the daughter was seven or eight years old, N had intercourse with her on a number of occasions and indecently assaulted her in various ways. N was sentenced to six years' imprisonment on each count of rape, with sentences of two years' imprisonment on each count of indecent assault and gross indecency, all concurrent, with an order under the Criminal Justice Act 1991 s.44.

Held, allowing the reference, that the sentences imposed were unduly lenient. Where a stepfather raped his stepdaughter several times and subjected her to other sexual indignities, and the victim was as young as seven or eight years, the sentence should have been in the order of 10 or 11 years following a contested trial. Making allowance for the element of double jeopardy, the court would substitute sentence of nine years' imprisonment on each count of rape and three years on each count of indecent assault and gross indecency, the sentence to run concurrently, *R. v. Billam (Keith)* [1986] 1 W.L.R. 349, [1986] C.L.Y. 868 considered.

ATTORNEY GENERAL'S REFERENCE (NO.71 OF 1999), *Re*; *sub nom.* R. v. AN [2000] 2 Cr. App. R. (S.) 83, Roch, L.J., CA (Crim Div).

1393. Rape – children – failure to impose automatic life sentence – unduly lenient sentence

[Criminal Justice Act 1991 s.44; Crime (Sentences) Act 1997 s.2, s.44.]

The Attorney General submitted to the court to review sentences on ground that they were unduly lenient. J pleaded guilty to five counts of indecent assault, two counts of indecency with a child, five counts of rape and one count of unlawful sexual intercourse with a girl under the age of 13. J had indecently assaulted and raped his stepdaughter over a period of five years beginning when she was 11, and had committed other acts of indecency towards her. He had also indecently assaulted and raped his natural daughter when she was between the ages of 12 and 14. J was sentenced to a total of six years' imprisonment, with an order under the Criminal Justice Act 1991 s.44.

Held, allowing the reference, that J had various previous convictions, including a conviction for unlawful sexual intercourse with a girl under the age of 13, when the offender was 16. It followed that by reason of the Crime (Sentences) Act 1997 s.2, it was obligatory for the court to impose an automatic life sentence for one of the offences of rape committed after the commencement date of the 1997 Act. It was conceded that there were no exceptional circumstances which would have entitled the sentencer not to impose a life sentence *Attorney General's Reference (No.53 of 1998), Re* [2000] Q.B. 198, [1999] C.L.Y. 1249 considered. The Court would impose a sentence of life imprisonment on the count of rape which was committed after the commencement of the Crime (Sentences) Act 1997, with a specified period of five and a half years. The sentences imposed on the other counts of rape, which were committed before the commencement of the Crime (Sentences) Act 1997, were manifestly too lenient. Sentences of eight years would be substituted on some of the counts, and 12 years on another. It was inappropriate in this case to have regard to the element of double jeopardy.

ATTORNEY GENERAL'S REFERENCE (NO.35 OF 1999), *Re*; *sub nom.* R. v. S (DAVID JOHN) [2000] 1 Cr. App. R. (S.) 440, Kennedy, L.J., CA (Crim Div).

1394. Rape – children – father raping daughter over period of nine years

D appealed against a sentence of 16 years' imprisonment, having pleaded guilty to three counts of indecent assault, three counts of rape and three counts of incest. All of the offences related to the appellant's daughter. D admitted that over a period of nine years beginning when the daughter was 13, he committed various sexual offences against her. The offences took place in an attic room in D's house which had been furnished for the purpose.

Held, allowing the appeal, that D had pleaded guilty just before summing up and his daughter had given her evidence and been cross examined. There were a number of reasons why courts gave credit to somebody who pleaded guilty. They included saving court time and public money, and the recognition that by a plea of guilty the offender was facing up to what he had done. In this class of case, over and above those factors, there was the factor that an early plea of guilty spared the victim the ordeal of anticipating the trial, of giving evidence at the trial and being cross examined on the basis that she was lying. In the present case, the plea came at a late stage. The victim was spared none of those stresses or indignities. It followed that this was a case in which only a relatively small reduction in sentence could be given to reflect the eventual plea of guilty. The fact that there had been an interval of over five years between the last offence and their coming to light was a fact to which very little weight could be attached. The main reason for such delay was frequently the inability of the abused person to divulge what had happened. People who committed this type of offence needed to understand that later if not sooner the truth might come out and their past would catch up with them. It afforded little if any mitigation to say that in the meantime there had been a number of years during which the offender had had to live with the possibility of the truth coming out. Having regard to the cases which had been drawn to the Court's attention, the sentence of 16 years was too high, despite the gravity and depravity of the offences. The court would substitute a sentence of 14 years' imprisonment, *R. v. W (John Thomas)* [1998] 1 Cr. App. R. (S.) 24, [1998] C.L.Y. 1341, *R. v. M (Adrian Alexander)* [1996] 2 Cr. App. R. (S.) 286, [1997] C.L.Y. 1452, *R. v. D (David John)* (1993) 14 Cr. App. R. (S.) 639, [1994] C.L.Y. 1330 and *R. v. R (Peter John)* (1993) 14 Cr. App. R. (S.) 328, [1994] C.L.Y. 1334 considered.

R. v. DR (APPEAL AGAINST SENTENCE: GUILTY PLEA) [2000] 2 Cr. App. R. (S.) 239, Holman, J., CA (Crim Div).

1395. Rape – children – indecent assault – attempted rape of child – unduly lenient sentence

The Attorney General asked the Court of Appeal to review sentences on the ground that they were unduly lenient. G pleaded guilty to two counts of attempted rape, four counts of indecent assault, and one count of indecency with a child. G met a woman who was the mother of a child aged six and moved into her home. Eventually they made plans to marry. Following a complaint by the child, G admitted a series of incidents in which he had placed his penis between the child's legs, put his finger into her vagina and put his penis between the cheeks of the child's bottom. There was evidence that since the incidents, the child had become quiet, withdrawn and tearful. G was sentenced to 30 months' imprisonment on each count, all the sentences to run concurrently.

Held, allowing the reference, that the court's opinion was that if G had been convicted of the two offences of attempted rape after a trial, the appropriate sentence would have been of the order of six years' imprisonment on each count concurrent. On a plea of guilty and in particular an early plea the appropriate sentence at trial would have been four years. It followed that the sentence of 30 months' imprisonment was unduly lenient. Allowing for the discount which was normally granted on a reference by the Attorney General to reflect the element of double jeopardy, the Court of Appeal considered that a sentence of three years' imprisonment should be substituted. An increase of that order would not be justified, and the court would not disturb the existing sentence, having made plain that the sentence was considered unduly lenient *R. v. Billam (Keith)* [1986] 1 W.L.R. 349, [1986] C.L.Y. 868, *R. v. McCarthey* (1988) 10 Cr. App. R. (S.) 443, [1991] C.L.Y. 1017, *Attorney General's Reference (No.3 of 1995), Re* [1996] 1 Cr. App. R. (S.) 26, [1996] C.L.Y. 1775, *Attorney General's Reference (No.5 of 1996), Re* [1996] 2 Cr. App. R. (S.) 434, [1997] C.L.Y. 1454 considered.

ATTORNEY GENERAL'S REFERENCE (NO.28 OF 1999), *Re*; *sub nom.* R. v. G [2000] 1 Cr. App. R. (S.) 314, Lord Bingham of Cornhill, L.C.J., CA (Crim Div).

1396. Rape – children – indecent assault – offences committed over 19 year period

K appealed against a sentence of 18 years' imprisonment on conviction of one count of rape, two counts of buggery and 16 counts of indecent assault. Over a period of 19 years, K committed sexual offences against a total of seven children. The offences began with K targeting children from vulnerable and deprived backgrounds by buying them presents and taking an interest in them, then progressing to sexual abuse, which involved genital touching, masturbation, oral sex and in the case of one girl, sexual intercourse and in the case of one boy, buggery.

Held, dismissing the appeal, that a long sentence was required for prolonged insatiable depravity involving children of both sexes over a protracted period of time. The court had come to the conclusion that the sentence was severe but not manifestly excessive. It was needed for the punishment of the appellant, the protection of young children and for general deterrence, *R. v. C (John Francis)* (1993) 14 Cr. App. R. (S.) 562, [1994] C.L.Y. 1255, *R. v. R (Peter John)* (1993) 14 Cr. App. R. (S.) 328, [1994] C.L.Y. 1334 and *R. v. M (Adrian Alexander)* [1996] 2 Cr. App. R. (S.) 286, [1997] C.L.Y. 1452 considered.

R. v. KING (MICHAEL JOHN) [1999] 2 Cr. App. R. (S.) 376, Douglas Brown, J., CA (Crim Div).

1397. Rape – children – step father

[Criminal Justice Act 1991 s.2 (2) (b).]

L pleaded guilty to two charges of rape on a male person, and one of indecent assault on a male. L on the two occasions committed buggery on his stepson, who was 12 at the time. L had previous convictions for various offences including two indecent assaults on a female and one attempted rape, committed in 1970, 1982 and 1984. L was sentenced to nine years' imprisonment on each count of buggery with five years' imprisonment for indecent assault, all concurrent, and passed as a longer than commensurate sentence under the Criminal Justice Act 1991 s.2(2)(b) and appealed.

Held, allowing the appeal, that these were plainly very serious offences, particularly in view of the breach of trust on the part of L and the youth of the victim. L's last sexual offence had been committed 15 years before the latest offences and it was submitted that the conditions for imposing a longer than commensurate sentence were not present. The judge should not have relied on the previous convictions to justify a longer than commensurate sentence. The correct sentence would have been seven years' imprisonment for each of the offences of rape on a male and four years for indecent assault, all concurrent.

R. v. L (MICHAEL JOHN) [2000] 2 Cr. App. R. (S.) 177, Dyson, J., CA (Crim Div).

1398. Rape – DNA profiling – violent offenders

M pleaded guilty to rape. He encountered a 17 year old girl who was walking home alone in the early hours of the morning. M attempted to engage her in conversation and then followed her as she continued her journey. M caught up with her and moved in front of her so as to block her path. He then seized her by the shoulders and pinned her against a wall. He slapped or punched her on the head several times and eventually he raped her. The girl got up and made her way home; M followed her into her house. The victim immediately complained to her brother who found that M had left. M was arrested 12 hours later. He initially denied the offence but made an admission when confronted by DNA evidence. M was sentenced to eight years' imprisonment. M appealed contending that in the light of *R. v. Bamforth (Jason)* [1999] 1 Cr. App. R. (S.) 123, [1999] C.L.Y. 1314, *R. v. Doe (Clayton Christopher)* (1995) 16 Cr. App. R. (S.) 718, [1996] C.L.Y. 2051, *R. v. McCue* (1987) 9 Cr. App. R. (S.) 17, [1988] C.L.Y. 975 and *R. v. Ford (Kevin Dexter)* [1998] 2 Cr. App. R. (S.) 74, [1998] C.L.Y. 1351 cited, the starting point was eight years and that the appropriate sentence on a plea was accordingly six years.

Held, allowing the appeal, that the sentencer expressed the view that the gratuitous violence and the youth of the victim, the offence would have warranted a sentence of 10 years' imprisonment following a contested trial. The Court had considered all the cases and was satisfied that this submission was well founded. The Court reached this conclusion with a degree of reluctance, but it was the duty of the Court to ensure that there was harmony of sentencing in like cases. The Court would substitute a sentence of six years' imprisonment.

R. v. M (MARK) [2000] 1 Cr. App. R. (S.) 457, Ognall, J, CA (Crim Div).

1399. Rape – indecent assault – elderly offender – relevance of age

W appealed against a sentence of 12 years' imprisonment imposed for seven offences of indecent assault and seven offences of rape. W, who was 75 years of age when the sentence was passed, argued that his age should have been taken into account. The trial judge had refused to take age into account on the ground that W had committed his last offence only two years ago.

Held, allowing the appeal, that although these were appalling offences, it was appropriate to take age into account so that any prison term imposed did not result in W being released when he was well over 80 years of age. Age could not be entirely excluded from consideration in this case. The sentence would therefore be reduced to eight years.

R. v. W (RONALD DOUGLAS); *sub nom.* R. v. W (SENTENCING: AGE OF DEFENDANT) *The Times*, October 26, 2000, Richards, J., CA (Crim Div).

1400. Rape – indecent assault – rape of child by stepfather – unduly lenient sentences

The Attorney General asked the Court of Appeal to review sentences on the ground that they were unduly lenient. P was convicted of two counts of indecent assault and one of rape. In 1975, the mother of the victim, who was then aged 11, married P who went to live with the mother and her four children.

Shortly before the marriage P had been released from a term of imprisonment for unlawful sexual intercourse with a girl under the age of 13. A few months later, P indecently assaulted the girl by touching her vagina. The following year P took the girl to hospital; she fell asleep in P's car on the way home and P removed her underwear and tried to force open her legs, but was unable to do so when she struggled. Some time later P came into her bedroom where she was asleep, climbed on top of her and raped her. The victim reported the offences to the police in 1998. P was sentenced to a total of four years' imprisonment.

Held, allowing the reference, that the total sentence passed by the sentencer was unduly lenient. The court would have expected a total sentence of the order of nine years' imprisonment. Taking account of the element of double jeopardy, the court would substitute a sentence of seven years' imprisonment *Attorney General's Reference (No.32 of 1992), Re* (1994) 15 Cr. App. R. (S.) 149 and *Attorney General's Reference (No.8 of 1991), Re* (1992) 13 Cr. App. R. (S.) 360 considered.

ATTORNEY GENERAL'S REFERENCE (NO.23 OF 1999), *Re*; *sub nom.* R. v. PR [2000] 1 Cr. App. R. (S.) 258, Rose, L.J., CA (Crim Div).

1401. Rape – indecent assault – robbery – rape on female – unduly lenient sentence

The Attorney General asked the Court to review a sentence on the ground that it was unduly lenient. B was convicted of having a firearm with intent to commit a robbery, robbery, indecent assault on a female, and rape. B and another man knocked at the door of a house and forced their way in. A boy was threatened with a loaded firearm. The men then demanded jewellery, money and drugs from the people present. A 19 year old girl who was present at the house was forced to give up various items of jewellery. She was then threatened with the gun by B's accomplice and taken to another room where she was asked to suck the man's penis. The woman was then raped by the accomplice. Subsequently B threatened the same woman with a gun, forced his penis into her mouth and raped her. The two men then left the house. B was identified some months later and was sentenced to a total of nine years' imprisonment.

Held, allowing the reference, that the victim had made a statement which showed that she was seriously traumatised by the offence. The offences committed by B were aggravated by various features in the case: the offender raped the victim after she had already been raped by his accomplice; the offender and the accomplice gained entry forcefully into the house where the victim was a visitor; they used violence and a gun over and above the force necessary to commit the rape; and the victim was made to suck B's penis. Guidelines for sentencing in cases of rape were laid down in *R. v. Billam (Keith)* [1986] 1 W.L.R. 349, [1986] C.L.Y. 868. Five of the aggravating features mentioned in *Billam* were present. The sentence which should have been passed at the end of the trial would have been 14 years' imprisonment. Allowing for the element of double jeopardy, the Court would substitute a sentence of eleven and a half years.

ATTORNEY GENERAL'S REFERENCE (NO.47 OF 1999), *Re*; *sub nom.* R. v. B (K) [2000] 1 Cr. App. R. (S.) 446, Kennedy, L.J, CA (Crim Div).

1402. Rape – kidnapping – rape by former husband – unduly lenient sentence

The Attorney General asked the Court to review sentences on the ground that they were unduly lenient. L was convicted of rape and kidnapping and sentenced to 18 months' imprisonment. L had known the victim for about 10 years and they were married in 1993. The marriage broke down and divorce proceedings began in 1997. Following an attempted reconciliation the divorce proceedings were delayed. In April 1998 the victim decided to end the relationship and the divorce proceedings were reinstated. A few days later L visited the matrimonial home, smashed a window and ripped out telephone wires. He later returned to the home and threatened the victim with a knife. Several weeks later the victim was approached by L while she was in a public house. She left the public house and

L held her as she was crossing the car park, pushed her into his car and drove her to a plot of land in a dark neighbourhood. The victim attempted to escape on two occasions but was unable to do so. L then lay on top of the victim and raped her.

Held, allowing the appeal, that the Court was obliged to proceed on the basis that L had not deliberately sought out his wife on the occasion of the offence. The cases showed that a plea of guilty had been treated as a factor of very considerable importance; an association between L and the victim had been regarded as important because it might lessen the extent of personal violation. The presence of physical violence or threats was a relevant matter, as was the breach of an injunction or court order or a bail condition. In the present case there was no plea of guilty and L had been convicted of kidnapping. The sentence of 18 months' imprisonment was outside the limits of the sentences open to the sentencer. On conviction of these offences following a trial, a sentence of at least four years' imprisonment should have been imposed, even on the view of the facts most favourable to L. Making allowance for double jeopardy, sentences of three years' imprisonment on each count concurrent would be substituted *R. v. Billam (Keith)* [1986] 1 W.L.R. 349, [1986] C.L.Y. 868, *R. v. Berry (Arthur John)* (1988) 10 Cr. App. R. (S.) 13, [1990] C.L.Y. 1394; *Attorney General's Reference (No.7 of 1989), Re* (1990) 12 Cr. App. R. (S.) 1, [1991] C.L.Y. 1194; *R. v. Maskell (David John)* (1991) 12 Cr. App. R. (S.) 638, [1992] C.L.Y. 1377; *R. v. Haywood (Alan John)* (1992) 13 Cr. App. R. (S.) 175, [1993] C.L.Y. 1266; *R. v. C (Robert)* (1994) 15 Cr. App. R. (S.) 757, [1995] C.L.Y. 1457; *Attorney General's Reference (No.27 of 1998), Re* [1999] 1 Cr. App. R. (S.) 259, [1999] C.L.Y. 1309; *R. v. H (Paul Raymond)* (1994) 15 Cr. App. R. (S.) 373; *R. v. T (Robert Leonard)* (1994) 15 Cr. App. R. (S.) 318; *R. v. Pearson (Kirk Paul)* [1996] 1 Cr. App. R. (S.) 309, [1996] C.L.Y. 2053; and *R. v. M (Paul Richard)* (1995) 16 Cr. App. R. (S.) 770 considered.

ATTORNEY GENERAL'S REFERENCE (NO.64 OF 1999), *Re*; *sub nom.* R. v. L (DAVID ALBERT) [2000] 1 Cr. App. R. (S.) 529, Lord Bingham of Cornhill, L.C.J., CA (Crim Div).

1403. Rape – spouses – violent repeated rapes

G was convicted of three counts of rape, one of assault occasioning actual bodily harm and one of common assault. G had been married for about 13 years when he became depressed and began to behave violently towards his wife. He forced his wife to have sexual intercourse without her consent, using violence towards her as they did so. On one occasion G placed a tie around his wife's neck and tied it in such a way as to restrict her breathing. G was sentenced to 10 years' imprisonment concurrent on each count of rape, with concurrent sentences for the other offences. G appealed.

Held, dismissing the appeal, that G's behaviour was not attributable to mental illness, but probably to jealousy and possessiveness. This was a particularly distasteful and persistent serious of sexual misconduct in a domestic setting over a considerable period of time. The court had concluded that although the sentence was undoubtedly severe, it could not be said to be manifestly excessive.

R. v. G (W) [2000] 1 Cr. App. R. (S.) 70, Judge Fabyan Evans, CA (Crim Div).

1404. Rape – unduly lenient sentence

The Attorney General referred to the court as unduly lenient a sentence of four year's imprisonment H having been convicted of rape. H gained access to the home of a woman with whom he was acquainted and began to have sexual intercourse with her while she was asleep. When the woman woke up and told him to desist, he did so. H was sentenced to four years' imprisonment.

Held, allowing the reference, that this was undoubtedly a serious case of rape. Although no violence was used, H took advantage of the victim while she was asleep in her own home. The sentence of four years' imprisonment was unduly lenient. Making allowance for the element of the double jeopardy, the court would substitute a sentence of six years' imprisonment.

ATTORNEY GENERAL'S REFERENCE (NO.51 OF 1999), *Re*; *sub nom*. R. v. DH [2000] 1 Cr. App. R. (S.) 407, SwintonThomas, L.J., CA (Crim Div).

1405. Repatriation – prisoners – sentence of foreign court need not be converted into English sentence

[Repatriation of Prisoners Act 1984; Convention on the Transfer of Sentenced Persons 1983 (Council of Europe).]

Held, that where a repatriated prisoner had been sentenced in a foreign court, there was no requirement for it to be converted into an English court sentence under the Repatriation of Prisoners Act 1984, or the Convention on the Transfer of Sentenced Persons 1983.

R. v. SECRETARY OF STATE FOR THE HOME DEPARTMENT, *ex p*. OSHIN [2000] 1 W.L.R. 2311, Tuckey, L.J., QBD.

1406. Restriction orders – mental health – requirement of medical evidence before imposition of restriction order

[Mental Health Act 1983 s.41 (1).]

R, an acute paranoid schizophrenic and a regular cannabis user, appealed against the imposition of a restriction order under the Mental Health Act 1983 s.41 (1) following his guilty pleas to offences of wounding and assault occasioning actual bodily harm. R had randomly attacked two members of the public and, while in police custody, a police officer. Notwithstanding that the medical evidence did not prescribe the need for a restriction order, the trial judge had found that by his experience in court R's mental state was at the very least aggravated by his smoking cannabis daily. It was contended that the judge should not have imposed the order in the absence of supporting medical evidence.

Held, allowing the appeal, that when imposing a restriction order under the Act, it was necessary that there be grounds for doing so within the medical evidence. In the instant case there had been no basis for the imposition of a restriction order. It was observed that the subsections of s.41 established the requirements before a restriction order could be imposed. It was however possible that in appropriate circumstances a judge upon hearing oral evidence might not be willing to accept it.

R. v. R (DANIEL F) *The Times*, November 1, 2000, Judge Fawcus, CA (Crim Div).

1407. Road traffic offences – disqualification – dangerous driving causing serious injuries

B appealed against a sentence of 18 months' imprisonment and disqualification from driving for four years having pleaded guilty to dangerous driving. He was the driver of one of two cars which were seen driving at high speed along a suburban road subject to a 30 mph speed limit. Witnesses thought that they were racing. B's car clipped the kerb and he lost control. His car spun across the road and collided with another vehicle. The driver and passenger in the other vehicle suffered serious injuries. B pleaded guilty on the basis that he was driving at about 60 mph and that he was not racing with the other vehicle. Rather, he said, he was driving in a fast convoy.

Held, allowing the appeal, that a sentence of imprisonment was inevitable for this offences of dangerous driving. The court bore in mind that the maximum sentence for the offences was two years' imprisonment, and that B was entitled to credit for his plea of guilty. In the court's view, the appropriate starting point would have been 18 months' imprisonment and when B was afforded the appropriate credit for his plea, the proper sentence would be 12 months' imprisonment. The disqualification would be reduced to three years.

R. v. BURMAN (RAKESH) [2000] 2 Cr. App. R. (S.) 3, Connell, J., CA (Crim Div).

1408. Road traffic offences – disqualification – pleas – sentence length

[Criminal Attempts Act 1981 s.9; Road Traffic Act 1988 s.103.]

M pleaded guilty before a magistrates' court to interfering with a motor vehicle contrary to the Criminal Attempts Act 1981 s.9, and driving while disqualified contrary to the Road Traffic Act 1988 s.103. M was sentenced to one month's detention in a young offender institution for interfering with a motor vehicle and five months' detention in a young offender institution for driving while disqualified, to run consecutively. M appealed to the Crown Court, where his appeal was dismissed, and then to the Divisional Court by case stated. M argued that by imposing the maximum sentence available under its sentencing powers the court had given no credit for the pleas of guilty and had not reflected the totality principle.

Held, dismissing the appeal, that the offences to which M pleaded guilty were both triable only summarily. The maximum sentence for interfering with a motor vehicle was three months' imprisonment, and the maximum for driving while disqualified was six months' imprisonment. Considered individually, it could be said that in respect of each of the offences M had received some discount from the maximum sentence available to the court.

M (NEIL) (A JUVENILE) v. DPP [2000] 2 Cr. App. R. (S.) 43, Turner, J., QBD.

1409. Road traffic offences – disqualification – totting up procedure – magistrates' discretion

[Road Traffic Offenders Act 1988 s.34, s.34(2), s.35.]

J appealed against sentence claiming that the six-month period of disqualification he had received under the totting up procedure was longer than the ban he would have received for the single offence of driving at speeds of up to 100 miles per hour on a single carriageway. J contended that the justices were required to consider whether to disqualify him under the Road Traffic Offenders Act 1988 s.34 prior to considering whether to disqualify him under s.35, the totting up procedure.

Held, dismissing the appeal, that consideration should be given firstly to the imposition of discretionary disqualification under s.34(2), such consideration taking into account the whole record of the accused. If a longer sentence was required than that allowed for the single offence, then disqualification should not be under s.34 but penalty points should be imposed thereby leading to a longer disqualification due to the totting up procedure. Where the single offence did not justify disqualification, a ban under s.35 was not an anomaly as the penalty was in accordance with the offender's history. To decide otherwise would be to remove the justices' statutory discretion under s.34.

JONES v. CHIEF CONSTABLE OF WEST MERCIA; *sub nom.* JONES v. DPP (2001) 165 J.P. 6, Buxton, L.J., QBD.

1410. Road traffic offences – driving without due care – endorsement of driving licence

[Road Traffic (New Drivers) Act 1995.]

E was convicted of driving without due care and attention on an indictment charging him with dangerous driving. E approached a school crossing at which two vehicles had stopped to allow a child to cross the road. E overtook the two vehicles on the inside and crossed the crossing, missing the child who was crossing the road. E was sentenced to a fine of £100 and six penalty points. E appealed.

Held, allowing the appeal, that the sentencer had indicated that in the exercise of his discretion he would not disqualify E. By virtue of the Road Traffic (New Drivers) Act 1995, the effect of awarding six or more penalty points to E was to require the revocation of his driving licence. As E lived in a remote area there were difficulties in supervising him as a provisional licence holder, and the practical effect of the award of six penalty points was to disqualify him from driving. The number of penalty points which could be awarded on conviction for driving without due care and attention could range between three and nine.

The interests of justice would be met if the number of points were reduced from six to five.

R. v. EDMUNDS (DAMIEN JOSEPH) [2000] 2 Cr. App. R. (S.) 62, Ebsworth, J., CA (Crim Div).

1411. Road traffic offences – tachographs – owner driver switching off tachograph so as to prevent recording of journeys

[Transport Act 1968 s.99(5).]

P appealed against a sentence of nine months' imprisonment having pleaded guilty to five offences of knowingly making a false statement, contrary to the Transport Act 1968 s.99(5), and to other related offences. P was the owner driver of a 38 tonne bulk carrier. His vehicle was involved in an accident as a result of a mistake by another driver, and was examined by a police accident investigator. The tachograph showed that the vehicle had been stationary for some period before the accident. Further investigation showed that a switch had been installed and wired to the tachograph unit so that the driver could switch off the record of speed and distance. P admitted that he had switched off the tachograph on a number of occasions. Analysis of his records showed that on a number of occasions P had not taken the required periods of rest.

Held, allowing the appeal, that the court accepted that P was an owner driver; he was not in a managerial position and had not persuaded employees to break the law. As there was no element of corruption of others, a shorter sentence than nine months would have sufficed. A sentence of three months would be substituted, *R. v. Raven (Cyril William)* (1988) 10 Cr. App. R. (S.) 354, [1990] C.L.Y. 1356 and *R. v. McCabe (James)* (1989) 11 Cr. App. R. (S.) 154, [1991] C.L.Y. 1224 considered.

R. v. POTTER (DAVID) [1999] 2 Cr. App. R. (S.) 448, Garland, J., CA (Crim Div).

1412. Robbery – disparate sentences – attempted robbery at shop claiming to be armed with CS gas

B appealed against a sentence of five years' imprisonment having pleaded guilty to two counts of attempted robbery. B went into an estate agent's office wearing a false beard and a hat which covered most of his face. He pointed a small aerosol can in the direction of the cashier, indicated that it contained CS gas and demanded money. The cashier replied that she did not have any money and activated an alarm. B then walked out of the premises. A short while later he entered a small shop wearing the same disguise and behaved in the same way. B fled from the shop when one of the proprietors operated a panic button. B was driven off in a car by another person and the registration number of the vehicle was noted.

Held, allowing the appeal, that it was submitted that B was previously of good character; the offences had been committed when he was under particularly severe personal stress and were so inept that detection was almost inevitable. The court recognised that it was important that any sentence should properly reflect the need for the law to protect staff who worked in small premises of this kind, but considered that the sentence was manifestly excessive. This was not one of the more serious robberies of this nature, and insufficient credit was given for the guilty plea and B's character. There was some disparity between the sentence and a sentence of two years imposed on the driver of the car. A sentence of three years was appropriate.

R. v. BISHOP (HARRY) [2000] 1 Cr. App. R. (S.) 89, Elias, J., CA (Crim Div).

1413. Robbery – elderly victim – attack on victim at home – unduly lenient sentence

[Criminal Justice Act 1988 s.36.]

The Attorney General sought leave to refer a sentence of four years' imprisonment to the Court of Appeal under the Criminal Justice Act 1988 s.36 on the basis of undue leniency. J had forced entry to the flat of a 79 year old man, assaulted him and stolen monies from him. The Attorney General contended that the offence was aggravated by the age and infirmity of the victim, the fact that the offence was committed in the victim's own home, the use of violence and the fact that only 13 months earlier J had been released from imprisonment for committing a series of offences possessing the same character.

Held, granting leave but refusing the reference, that whilst the sentence was lenient it could not be categorised as unduly lenient, *Attorney General's Reference (No.1 of 1999), Re* [1999] 2 Cr. App. R. (S) 398, [1999] C.L.Y. 1334 and *Attorney General's Reference (Nos.19 and 20 of 1990), Re* (1990) 12 Cr. App. R. (S.) 490, [1991] C.L.Y. 1027 considered.

ATTORNEY GENERAL'S REFERENCE (NO.48 OF 2000), *Re*; *sub nom*. R. v. JOHNSON (MARTIN CLIVE) [2001] 1 Cr. App. R. (S.) 123, Roch, L.J., CA (Crim Div).

1414. **Robbery – elderly victim robbed in own home for second time – weapon and violence used – defendant on licence at time of offence – unduly lenient sentence**

[Criminal Justice Act 1991 s.40.]

The Attorney General referred to the court a sentence of six years' imprisonment for robbery on the ground of undue leniency. The victim was an elderly man, whom F knew lived on his own and had previously robbed the same victim in his home. F threatened the victim with a six inch blade and a telephone cable, which he wrapped around the victim's neck. As a result, F obtained £120 in cash and a souvenir coin worth £20. F had previously been sentenced for 29 offences, many of which were dishonesty offences. The Attorney General submitted that the sentence imposed was unduly lenient, considering the aggravating features of the targeting of a known vulnerable victim, the use of a weapon and violence and the fact that F was still on licence for offences of robbery and burglary.

Held, allowing the reference, that the sentence was increased to eight years' imprisonment with the remaining period of the licence period to be served. Where an elderly victim was violently attacked and injured within the home, the sentence would be in double figures, *Attorney General's Reference (Nos.32 and 33 of 1995), Re* [1996] 2 Cr. App. R. (S.) 346, [1997] C.L.Y. 1421 and *Attorney General's Reference (No.1 of 1999), Re* [1999] 2 Cr. App. R. (S.) 398, [1999] C.L.Y. 1334 considered. The appropriate starting point was a sentence of 10 years reduced to eight years to reflect the element of double jeopardy. The judge had erred by failing to invoke the powers under the Criminal Justice Act 1991 s.40 and to order that F serve the 443 days of unexpired licence. It was in the public interest to make it clear to defendants that if they committed further offences during the licence period there was a real penalty to pay, *R. v. Blades (Selhurst)* [2000] Crim. L.R. 62, [1999] C.L.Y. 1280 followed.

ATTORNEY GENERAL'S REFERENCE (NO.89 OF 1999), *Re*; *sub nom*. R. v. FARROW (NEIL JACK) [2000] 2 Cr. App. R. (S.) 382, Kennedy, L.J., CA (Crim Div).

1415. **Robbery – elderly victims collecting pensions from post office**

B pleaded guilty to two counts of robbery. B robbed two women, aged 77 and 79 respectively, who had just collected their pensions from a post office. Each woman was attacked from behind and one was subjected to some degree of force. B had numerous previous convictions for various offences. B was sentenced to six years' imprisonment on each count concurrent and appealed.

Held, allowing the appeal, that deliberately targeting elderly women in the street after they had drawn their pensions was a different category of case from roughing someone up in the lavatory of a public house and stealing a wallet. The appropriate sentences, if B had been sentenced on each count separately, would have been five years in one case, where force was used against the victim, and four years in the other. The question was, what was right total sentence? The court agreed that the appropriate total sentence for the two offences was six years, but would vary the sentences to three years and three years on each count, consecutive, *R. v. Thomas (Robert Sean)* (1994) 15 Cr.

App. R. (S.) 848, [1995] C.L.Y. 1466 and *R. v. Perez-Pinto (Stephen)* [1996] 1 Cr. App. R. (S.) 22 considered.

R. v. BUCK (CAMERON) [2000] 1 Cr. App. R. (S.) 42, Garland, J., CA (Crim Div).

1416. Robbery – false imprisonment – attack on doctor making house call – unduly lenient sentence

[Criminal Justice Act 1988 s.36.]

The Attorney General sought leave to refer W's sentence for the offences of false imprisonment and robbery to the Court of Appeal under the Criminal Justice Act 1988 s.36 on the basis of undue leniency. W had been sentenced to two years and six months' imprisonment and, as the conviction was within a licence period, a return order of 166 days was also imposed. The Attorney General contended that the total sentence of just under three years was unduly lenient, bearing in mind the aggravating features of the offences that (1) W attacked a doctor making a house call late at night in unfamiliar surroundings who was thus highly vulnerable; (2) the robbery was committed to obtain drugs which the doctor had to carry as part of his duties; (3) there was reliance on the use of a knife, and (4) W had an appalling record which included offences of violence and dishonesty and was on licence at the time.

Held, granting leave but refusing the reference, that although in the court's view a sentence of between four and five years would have been appropriate, the sentence imposed, whilst on the low side, was still within the appropriate sentencing bracket, and could not therefore be said to be unduly lenient.

ATTORNEY GENERAL'S REFERENCE (NO.45 OF 2000), *Re*; *sub nom.* R. v. WEST (STEWART JONATHAN) [2001] 1 Cr. App. R. (S.) 119, Lord Woolf of Barnes, L.C.J., CA (Crim Div).

1417. Robbery – firearm offences – robberies of taxi drivers – use of imitation firearms

H was convicted of two counts of robbery and sentenced to eight years' detention, having been involved in the robberies of two taxi drivers within 28 hours whilst armed with an imitation firearm. The judge indicated that his starting point for the sentence was 10 years. H appealed, contending that the starting point of 10 years was too high and that the tariff for an offence of this nature was four years, *R. v. Murphy (Vincent Thomas)* (1988) 10 Cr. App. R. (S.) 468, [1991] C.L.Y. 1209 and *R. v. Jackson (Christopher Anthony)* [1998] 1 Cr. App. R. (S.) 259, [1998] C.L.Y. 1376 cited.

Held, dismissing the appeal, that the cases of *Murphy* and *Jackson* considered, did not lay down any tariff for this type of offence. The use of a replica firearm was an aggravating feature. This was an attack on a vulnerable group in a similar category to small shop owners who served the public and who were entitled to look to the court for protection, otherwise the levels of service would fall away because of such attacks when they decided that their business was not worth the risk. The public, especially women unable to make their way home safely at night, would suffer should night time taxi services be lost in a particular locality. The two offences could properly have attracted consecutive sentences and it could not be said that the 10 year starting point was manifestly excessive. The sentences were harsh but not excessive.

R. v. HERBERT (STEVIE JEFFREY), March 24, 2000, Judge Wright, CA (Crim Div). [*Ex rel.* Ian Strongman, Barrister, No. 8 Chambers, Fountain Court, Steelhouse Lane, Birmingham].

1418. Robbery – firearms offences – defendant suffering from psychopathic disorder – unduly lenient sentence

The Attorney General asked the court to review a sentence on the ground that it was unduly lenient. W pleaded guilty to robbery and to being in possession of a firearm, an air pistol, with intent. W went into a public house where he drank two pints of lager and spoke to the barmaid. He left the public house briefly and returned with a gun, which he pointed towards the barmaid and demanded that she open up the till. W then required barmaid to go upstairs where he tied her up. He then fired the air gun into the wall. W was sentenced to six years' imprisonment for robbery, with one year consecutive for possession of a firearm with intent, with sentences of 12 months' imprisonment for other offences, concurrent.

Held, allowing the reference, that the offender had numerous convictions starting in 1977 which included assault occasioning actual bodily harm, inflicting grievous bodily harm, robbery, burglary and aggravated burglary. A psychiatric report indicated that the offender was not subject to mental illness, but had longstanding and severe personality difficulties and was considered to be suffering from a longstanding untreatable psychopathic disorder. W presented a significant risk to the public and must be detained until such time as it was safe for him to be released. The court would quash the sentence of six years and impose a life sentence.

ATTORNEY GENERAL'S REFERENCE (NO.56 OF 1999), *Re*; *sub nom.* WARD (ALAN JOHN) [2000] 1 Cr. App. R. (S.) 401, Swinton Thomas, L.J., CA (Crim Div).

1419. Robbery – juvenile codefendants – unduly lenient sentence

The Attorney General asked the court to review a sentence on the ground that it was unduly lenient. C, aged 23, pleaded guilty to robbery. C was one of a group of several young men who encountered two boys, one aged 16, shortly after midnight. C and two others approached the boys and demanded money from them. C searched the pockets of one of the boys and found a mobile telephone. C's accomplice attacked the boy and subsequently demanded a ring which was on his finger. The accomplice punched him several further times and he fell over a wall. C joined in punching the victim and eventually the victim surrendered the ring and a pair of sunglasses. C and the accomplice were arrested shortly afterwards. The sentencer accepted that the accomplice, who was 16, was the main aggressor, although C had taken a full part in the robbery. The sentencer made a supervision order in respect of the accomplice, on grounds which were personal to him. In order to avoid a sense of injustice on the part of C, the sentencer imposed a community service order on him.

Held, allowing the reference, that the court had emphasised that robberies committed in streets made members of the public afraid to walk out alone, and that sentences for such offences required an element of deterrence. Even a first offender must expect a custodial sentence for such an offence. The authorities showed that mitigation available to one offender did not entitle another offender, who could not rely on the mitigation, to take advantage of it considering *Attorney General's Reference (Nos.62, 63 and 64 of 1995), Re* [1996] 2 Cr. App. R. (S.) 223, [1996] C.L.Y. 2062. The submissions made on behalf of the Attorney General were sound in principle. There were strong and special factors which indicated an unusual sentence in the case of the co-defendant. The offender was not in the first flush of youth, he had played a full part in a frightening robbery and he had no excuse to advance to explain or justify his behaviour. Allowing for his good character, his plea and personal mitigation relating to his family circumstances, the judge's sentence did fall outside the range of sentences which was reasonably open to him. On conviction after a trial, the offence would have earned a sentence of three years' imprisonment. On a plea of guilty the appropriate sentence would be two years' imprisonment. Allowing for the element of double jeopardy, the court would substitute a sentence of 18 months' imprisonment, *Attorney General's Reference (No.44 of 1997), Re* [1998] 2 Cr. App. R. (S.) 105, [1998] C.L.Y. 1381, *Attorney General's Reference (No.39 of 1996), Re* [1997] 1 Cr. App. R. (S.) 355, [1997] C.L.Y. 1692 and *Attorney General's Reference (No.6 of 1994), Re* (1995) 16 Cr. App. R. (S.) 343 considered.

ATTORNEY GENERAL'S REFERENCE (NO.73 OF 1999), *Re*; *sub nom.* R. v. C (MARK) [2000] 2 Cr. App. R. (S.) 209, Lord Bingham of Cornhill, L.C.J., CA (Crim Div).

1420. Robbery – mental health – unduly lenient sentence

[Criminal Justice Act 1988 s.36.]

The Attorney General referred a sentence on the ground undue leniency. S, a 33 year old male, pleaded guilty to robbery and possession of a Class A drug and was sentenced to 10 months' imprisonment. The Attorney General submitted that four aggravating features were present: (1) the premeditated nature of the robbery which gave rise to the wearing of a balaclava; (2) the vulnerability of the small business targeted; (3) the threatening use of a weapon during the robbery, and (4) the shop assistants had been placed in fear. S, whilst conceding that a longer sentence could not have been criticised in relation to the offence of robbery, submitted that, in the light of his unsettled mind and psychiatric evidence which pointed to possible signs of depression, a much lower sentence had been justified.

Held, allowing the reference, that the sentence was unduly lenient. Given the grave features of the offence, but taking into account a guilty plea, a sentence of five or six years' imprisonment would have been expected. Having regard to the element of double jeopardy, the court increased the sentence to four years.

ATTORNEY GENERAL'S REFERENCE (NO.16 OF 2000), *Re*; *sub nom*. R. v. SKITTLETHORPE (STUART) [2001] 1 Cr. App. R. (S.) 42, Rose, L.J., CA (Crim Div).

1421. Robbery – offensive weapons – attempted robbery at post office – unduly lenient sentence

The Attorney General asked the court to review a sentence on the ground that it was unduly lenient. L was convicted of theft, attempted robbery and having an imitation firearm with intent to commit an indictable offence. He was one of the two men who entered a sub post office in a village. One of the men produced what appeared to be a handgun and the other produced a knife. They demanded money and pushed an assistant towards the post office counter. Two customers were forced to lie down on the floor. The two men failed to open the safe and ran off. They were arrested shortly afterwards driving in a car which had been stolen earlier. A small handgun was found near the post office. It was a low-powered air pistol which was not in working order. L was sentenced to three years' imprisonment on each count.

Held, allowing the reference, that the court had no hesitation in concluding that the sentence of three years' imprisonment was unduly lenient. On a conviction following a contested trial a sentence of six years would have been the minimum sentence which could properly have been imposed. Allowing for the element of double jeopardy, the court would substitute a sentence of five years' imprisonment, *Attorney General's Reference (No.9 of 1989), Re* (1990) 12 Cr. App. R. (S.) 7, [1991] C.L.Y. 1214, *R. v. Tidiman (Ian Lee)* (1991) 12 Cr. App. R. (S.) 702, [1992] C.L.Y. 1155, *Attorney General's Reference (No.7 of 1992), Re* (1993) 14 Cr. App. R. (S.) 122, [1993] C.L.Y. 1278 and *R. v. Gould (Anthony Lawrence)* (1983) 5 Cr. App. R. (S.) 72, [1984] C.L.Y. 790 considered.

ATTORNEY GENERAL'S REFERENCE (NO.74 OF 1999), *Re*; *sub nom*. R. v. LEVITT (DARREN PAUL) [2000] 2 Cr. App. R. (S.) 150, Lord Bingham of Cornhill, L.C.J., CA (Crim Div).

1422. Robbery – pleas – giving evidence in defence of codefendant – discount for plea

H pleaded guilty to robbery. H and an accomplice accosted a man who was walking home in the early hours of the morning. The victim was threatened with a knife and money was demanded. The victim was knocked to the ground and kicked about the head and body. H and his accomplice then ran off, chased by the victim. H and his accomplice were arrested shortly afterwards. H pleaded guilty, but gave evidence in the trial of his accomplice to the effect that his accomplice was not involved in a robbery. His accomplice was convicted. The sentencer indicated that he would not give H the normal discount of a plea of guilty in view of the fact that he had given evidence in support of his accomplice's untrue story. H was sentenced to four years' imprisonment and appealed.

Held, allowing the appeal, that it was wrong in principle to deny the defendant credit for his plea because he had given evidence on behalf of a codefendant which was not believed by the jury. It was important that a codefendant should not be inhibited from giving evidence on the basis that if that evidence was disbelieved, he would lose the credit which he would otherwise get for his plea. The court would reduce his sentence to three and a half years' imprisonment, *R. v. Lawless (Frank)* [1998] 2 Cr. App. R. (S.) 176, [1998] C.L.Y. 1327 applied.

R. v. HICKMAN (PHILIP) [2000] 2 Cr. App. R. (S.) 171, Kennedy, L.J., CA (Crim Div).

1423. Robbery – threatening to kill – attempted robbery at office of estate agent – unduly lenient sentence

The Attorney General asked the court to review a sentence on the ground that it was unduly lenient. T was convicted of attempted robbery. He was unexpectedly made redundant from his work early in the morning. After spending the day drinking he set off home. He entered an estate agent's office and after some time demanded money from a member of staff of the agency, using his fingers concealed in his jacket pocket to pretend he had a weapon. One of the employees attempted to get the cash from the petty cash tin, but was unable to do so. T threatened to kill one of the members of staff. Eventually, one of the staff members was able to escape and the police were called. T fled from the shop, leaving behind his rucksack. He was arrested an hour later. T was sentenced to six months' imprisonment.

Held, allowing the reference, that this case was outside the normal category of attacks upon vulnerable premises with an imitation firearm. An appropriate sentence in the Court Court would have been of the order of three years' imprisonment, a sentence significantly below the appropriate bracket normally merited by attempted robbery on this sort of premises. Taking account of the element of double jeopardy, the court would substitute a sentence of two years' imprisonment, *R. v. Wilson (Edward John)* (1992) 13 Cr. App. R. (S.) 397, [1993] C.L.Y. 1275, *Attorney General's Reference (No.2 of 1994), Re* (1995) 16 Cr. App. R. (S.) 117, [1996] C.L.Y. 2070 and *Attorney General's Reference (No.12 of 1993), Re* (1994) 15 Cr. App. R. (S.) 424, [1993] C.L.Y. 1276 considered.

ATTORNEY GENERAL'S REFERENCE (NO.68 OF 1999), *Re*; *sub nom.* R. v. THOMAS (NIGEL WYNN) [2000] 2 Cr. App. R. (S.) 50, Rose, L.J., CA (Crim Div).

1424. Robbery – violence – injuries of extreme severity on victim during armed robbery

E appealed against a sentence of 10 years' imprisonment having pleaded guilty to robbery. He entered an antique shop run by a lady aged 59. He distracted the attention of the shopkeeper, and then produced an implement from a carrier bag with which he struck the shopkeeper on the side of the head, knocking her unconscious. He then stole various items to the value of £1,200 and left. The shopkeeper was taken to hospital where she was found to have serious injuries including bruising and swelling of parts of the brain. These would lead to hearing difficulties, and a problem with balance. She was unable to continue with her work and was unlikely to regain hearing in her right ear or the sense of taste or smell.

Held, allowing the appeal, that it was plain from the authorities that injuries inflicted in the course of carrying out a robbery were features which the court was entitled to take into account. The injuries and the effect on the victim of the robbery were horrific, but no firearm was used; the use of a firearm was always an aggravating feature. Looking at the authorities, the Court took the view that the sentence was excessive for the offence with which the sentencer was dealing. The appropriate sentence would have been eight years' imprisonment, *R. v. Hewitt (Raymond Frederick)* (1990) 12 Cr. App. R. (S.) 466, [1992] C.L.Y.

1201, *Attorney General's Reference (No.29 of 1995), Re* [1996] 2 Cr. App. R. (S.) 60, [1996] C.L.Y. 2074, *Attorney General's Reference (No.36 of 1992), Re* (1994) 15 Cr. App. R. (S.) 117 and *R. v. Woodruff (John William)* [1998] 1 Cr. App. R. (S.) 424, [1998] C.L.Y. 1374considered.

R. v. EVANS (GLENN CLIFFORD) [2000] 1 Cr. App. R. (S.) 454, Brian Smedley, J., CA (Crim Div).

1425. Robbery – vulnerable victim known to assailant – unduly lenient sentence

[Criminal Justice Act 1988 s.36.]

The Attorney General referred sentences of 15 months' and 13 months' imprisonment for robbery on the ground of undue leniency. The Attorney General contended that the sentences imposed were unduly lenient and that, on a guilty plea, a three year sentence of imprisonment would have been justified. The Attorney General further submitted that the offence had been aggravated by the fact that it had been committed by F and T together against a single victim known to them and rendered vulnerable by alcoholism, that the monies stolen had been disability benefit, that force had been used against the victim resulting in injury and that F had a conviction for robbery and T had been on probation at the time.

Held that the sentences were unduly lenient but that they were not varied in the exercise of the court's discretion owing to the element of double jeopardy. It would not be in the interests of justice to increase the tariff given that F had now been released from prison and obtained full time employment, *Attorney General's Reference (No.44 of 1997), Re* [1998] 2 Cr. App. R. (S) 105, [1998] C.L.Y. 1381 applied.

ATTORNEY GENERAL'S REFERENCE (NOS.37 AND 38 OF 2000), *Re*; R. v. THOMSON (CAMERON KIRKWOOD); *sub nom.* R. v. FISHER (MALCOLM) 2000/03478/R2, 2000/03479/R2, Lord Woolf of Barnes, L.C.J., CA (Crim Div).

1426. Sexual abuse – children – sexual abuse by parents over period of 13 years

M and W, husband and wife aged 68 and 67 respectively, were convicted of numerous counts of rape, buggery, and indecent assault. They had sexually abused their own children over a period of 13 years between 1961 and 1974, and their grandchildren between 1982 and 1995. The children were subjected to vaginal and anal intercourse and oral sex, and a variety of objects, including razor blades and knitting needles, were inserted into their bodies. M appealed against a sentence of a total of 25 years' imprisonment and W appealed against a sentence of a total of 14 years.

Held, dismissing the appeal, that the case was one of unusual, possible unique, gravity. The sentences were not manifestly excessive or wrong in principle.

R. v. M (G); R. v. M (E) [2000] 1 Cr. App. R. (S.) 296, Kennedy, L.J., CA (Crim Div).

1427. Sexual offences – child victims – sentencing considerations

Held, that sentencing those convicted of sexual offences against children depended to a greater extent than normal on the special facts of the individual case. Judges were not bound by previous authority to make a probation order and had to consider both the interests of the victim and the wider public interest, as opposed to focusing solely on the offender's circumstances, although they were to be borne in mind.

ATTORNEY GENERAL'S REFERENCE (NO.82 OF 1999), *Re The Independent*, February 28, 2000 (C.S.), Lord Bingham of Cornhill, L.C.J., CA (Crim Div).

1428. Sexual offences – children – Sex Offenders Register – unduly lenient sentence

[Sex Offenders Act 1997.]

G was convicted of eight counts of indecent conduct inflicted upon two children and was sentenced to 12 months' imprisonment. The Attorney General contended that the sentence was too lenient.

Held, allowing the reference, that the court had a duty to protect children by passing appropriate deterrent sentences. In addition, and when convicting sexual offenders, judges should explicitly deal with the issue of registration under the Sex Offenders Act 1997. Although the matter had been referred to, as an order had been made for a registration period of 10 years, the issue had not been expressly dealt with. The sentence was unjustifiably lenient and was increased to two and a half years imprisonment with a registration period for life.

ATTORNEY GENERAL'S REFERENCE (NO.72 OF 1999), *Re; sub nom.* R. v. MG; R. v. G (SEX OFFENCE: REGISTRATION) [2000] 2 Cr. App. R. (S.) 79, Roch, L.J., CA (Crim Div).

1429. Sexual offences – children – unlawful sexual intercourse with 13 year old – single consensual episode

[Criminal Justice Act 1991 s.44.]

H, a man aged 52, pleaded guilty to unlawful sexual intercourse with a girl under 16, indecent assault on a female and indecency with a child. H met a 13 year old girl who had left her foster mother's home with the intention of visiting a friend. The girl approached H and asked him for some money for her bus fare. H ordered a taxi and took the girl to his flat, after visiting a supermarket to buy lager and cigarettes. H gave the girl some lager and then indecently assaulted her. Sexual intercourse took place, and the girl masturbated H at his request, before sexual intercourse took place again. The girl claimed that she had told H her age. H was sentenced to 18 months' imprisonment, with an order under the Criminal Justice Act 1991 s.44. H appealed.

Held, allowing the appeal, that a custodial sentence was plainly appropriate, and the only question related to the length of the sentence. The maximum sentence for the offence was two years' imprisonment. This was not a case where H was in a position of trust, and he was entitled to credit for his guilty plea. Bearing in mind the cases to which the court had been referred, the court considered that a sentence of 18 months' imprisonment for an offence involving one consensual episode not involving a breach of trust was too long. A sentence of nine months' imprisonment would be substituted, *R. v. Hill (Graham)* [1997] 2 Cr. App. R. (S.) 243, [1997] C.L.Y. 1458, *R. v. Carter (Jahroy)* [1997] 1 Cr App. R. (S.) 434, [1997] C.L.Y. 1459 and *R. v. O (Gordon Edward)* [1999] 1 Cr. App. R. (S.) 327, [1999] C.L.Y. 1350 considered.

R. v. H [2000] 1 Cr. App. R. (S.) 82, Harrison, J., CA (Crim Div).

1430. Sexual offences – children – unlawful sexual intercourse with girls under 16

C, aged 26, pleaded guilty to three counts of unlawful sexual intercourse with girls under the age of 16. C had intercourse with a 14 year old girl in her parents' home while they were away. The girl became pregnant. C had intercourse with the same girl on a number of subsequent occasions. C subsequently had intercourse with two other girls, aged 13. C was sentenced to a total of four years' imprisonment and appealed.

Held, allowing the appeal, that this case was towards the more serious end of the category of offences of its kind. C was involved in a campaign of sexual intercourse with under age girls, one of whom became pregnant. The court had however concluded that a total sentence of four years was manifestly excessive and would reduce the sentences to a total of three years, *R. v. Carter (Jahroy)* [1997] 1 Cr. App. R. (S.) 434, [1997] C.L.Y. 1459 considered.

R. v. CLEMENT (CERI CARTER) [2000] 2 Cr. App. R. (S.) 153, Turner, J., CA (Crim Div).

1431. Sexual offences – public nuisance – making indecent suggestions to women in public places

W pleaded guilty to two counts of causing a public nuisance. On two occasions W approached women in public places and made indecent suggestions to them. He had an extensive record of previous convictions for sexual offences extending over a period of 20 years. W appealed against a sentence of two years' imprisonment on each count concurrent.

Held, allowing the appeal, that the sentence of two years' imprisonment was not wrong in principle, but W had spent 11 months on bail in a bail hostel, subject to restrictive conditions which required him to remain in the building itself at all times and permitted him to leave only once each fortnight under supervision. It was argued that the circumstances of confinement in a bail hostel were analogous to a prison and that credit for that period should have been given by the sentencer. A period in a bail hostel, however restrictive, was not to be equated with a period of imprisonment; however the degree of loss of liberty experienced by W in this case ought to have been taken into account to a greater extent than it had been. Having regard to the period of restricted liberty which W experienced before being sentence in the Crown Court, the court would substitute a sentence of 18 months' imprisonment on each count concurrent.

R. v. WATSON (STEPHEN DAVID) [2000] 2 Cr. App. R. (S.) 301, Judge Peter Crawford Q.C., CA (Crim Div).

1432. Tax evasion – criminal record – removal of spirits from bonded warehouses under pretext of exporting

F and G were convicted of being knowingly concerned in the evasion of excise duty. They were involved in removing spirits from bonded warehouses under the pretext that they were intended to be exported, when in fact the spirits were sold within the United Kingdom. The total amount of duty evaded was estimated to be more than £1,200,000. F and G appealed against sentences of four years' and five years' imprisonment respectively.

Held, dismissing the appeal, that the sentencer had correctly taken seven years as a starting point and reduced the sentence to reflect the roles of F and G and their previous good characters. The sentences were appropriate, *R. v. Dosanjh (Barjinder)* [1998] 3 All E.R. 618, [1998] C.L.Y. 1390 considered.

R. v. FLAHERTY (MARK GORDON); R. v. McMANUS (MICHAEL FRANCIS) [2000] 1 Cr. App. R. (S.) 250, Gray, J., CA (Crim Div).

1433. Tax evasion – VAT – evading £440,000 in VAT

[Value Added Tax Act 1994.]

B pleaded guilty to conduct involving the commission of one or more offences under the Value Added Tax Act 1994, and to cheating the Inland Revenue. B was concerned in a fraud on the Customs and Excise over a period of about four years. B conducted the affairs of a number of businesses in such a way as to conceal the true takings of the businesses, and concealed from the Inland Revenue the amount he was paying to his staff. It was agreed that a total of £440,000 in VAT had been avoided. Sentenced to four years' imprisonment for the VAT offences, with two years concurrent for cheating the Inland Revenue and a confiscation order in the amount of £401,498.

Held, allowing the appeal, that the sentencer indicated that he took six years as a starting point, and gave B credit for his plea of guilty and his previous good character. The court had been persuaded that the sentences were manifestly excessive. The sentencer started at too high a level. The correct sentence would have been three years' imprisonment for the VAT offences, with 18 months' imprisonment concurrent for the Inland Revenue offences, *R. v. Aziz (Abdul)* [1996] 1 Cr. App. R. (S.) 265, [1996] C.L.Y. 2080 considered.

R. v. BLUNDELL (RAYMOND JOHN) [1999] 2 Cr. App. R. (S.) 415, Owen, J., CA (Crim Div).

1434. Theft – false imprisonment – robbery of elderly lady

R pleaded guilty to false imprisonment and theft. He went to the home of a lady aged 89 with whom he was acquainted. He asked to be allowed to use the lavatory and was permitted to do so. When the lady asked him to leave the house, he refused to do so and became aggressive. He pushed the lady into a chair and demanded money, and pushed her back into the chair when she attempted to get out of it. R eventually left the house, taking £20 from her purse and pulling the telephone lead from the wall. Sentenced to five years' imprisonment on each count concurrently, R appealed.

Held, allowing the appeal, that the court had to take account of the fact that R pleaded guilty to theft and not to robbery. R had surrendered himself to the police before coming a suspect and made admissions so as to avoid the victim from having any anxiety about having to appear in court. The sentence would be reduced from five years' imprisonment to four years, *R. v. Lee (David)* (1995) 16 Cr. App. R. (S.) 60, [1996] C.L.Y. 1743 and *R. v. Hearne (Simon John)* [1999] 1 Cr. App. R. (S.) 333, [1999] C.L.Y. 1337 considered.

R. v. RICHARDSON (MARK IAN) [2000] 2 Cr. App. R. (S.) 373, Roch, L.J., CA (Crim Div).

1435. Theft – police officers – theft of handbag

M pleaded guilty before a magistrates' court to theft and was committed to the Crown Court for sentence. M went into a shoe shop and took a handbag from a female undercover police officer who was posing as a member of the public trying on shoes in the shop. M was seen to give the bag to a second man who disappeared. M had 36 previous convictions, most for dishonesty. Sentenced to three years' imprisonment, M appealed.

Held, dismissing the appeal, that the sentence was severe but it was not manifestly excessive.

R. v. MULLINS (CHRISTOPHER) [2000] 2 Cr. App. R. (S.) 372, Rose, L.J., CA (Crim Div).

1436. Theft – post office clerks – altering records to conceal theft

J appealed against a sentence of 14 months' imprisonment, having pleaded guilty to two offences of stealing from the post office. J was employed as a counter clerk by the post office. She stole a total of £5,318 from her till on two occasions, altering records of her stock to conceal the thefts. J, a single parent, had got into debt and was threatened by bailiffs.

Held, allowing the appeal, that the sentencer had started at too high a point in the sentencing bracket. The sentence would be reduced to nine months, *R. v. Barrick (John)* (1985) 81 Cr. App. R. 78, [1985] C.L.Y. 765 and *R. v. Clark (Trevor)* [1998] 2 Cr. App. R. 137, [1998] C.L.Y. 1392 considered.

R. v. JAMES (MARIA) [2000] 1 Cr. App. R. (S.) 285, Hughes, J., CA (Crim Div).

1437. Theft – recidivists – stealing handbag from victim

J pleaded guilty to theft. He approached a woman who was waiting at the reception desk of a hotel and was seen to take a purse from her bag. J had numerous previous convictions, including nine previous convictions for stealing handbags or their contents. J was sentenced to 18 months' imprisonment and appealed.

Held, dismissing the appeal, that the offence was bold, it was committed inside a hotel with an accomplice. J had a bad record for dishonesty. Such offences were prevalent and people needed to be protected from persistent offenders such as J, who could be properly be described as a professional pickpocket. The sentence was within the appropriate range.

R. v. JARRETT (JOHN GORDON) [2000] 2 Cr. App. R. (S.) 166, Nelson, J., CA (Crim Div).

1438. Threatening to kill – manslaughter – verbal threats made to relatives of victim – unduly lenient sentence

The Attorney General asked the court to review sentences on the ground that they were unduly lenient. J was convicted of two counts of threatening to kill. Between 1975 and 1990 the offender lived with a woman. J killed the woman in 1992 and eventually pleaded guilty to manslaughter by reason of diminished responsibility and was sentenced to two years' imprisonment. Following his release from prison he made threats towards members of the woman's family. On one occasion he met the deceased woman's brother, who was shopping. J stood close to the brother and threatened to kill him. On the same occasion he made threats to kill the deceased woman's sister. The brother and sister were both terrified by the threats, which they treated as genuine. J was arrested and repeated the threats to police officers. J was sentenced to 15 months' imprisonment on each count concurrent.

Held, allowing the reference, that the offence was aggravated by the fact that the threats were issued to close relatives of a woman whom J had killed, that they were the culmination of a campaign of threats extending over several years and that they had real effects on the victims. J had expressed no remorse. In the court's view the sentence was unduly lenient. Following conviction at trial, an appropriate sentence would have been between three and a half and four years' imprisonment. Making allowance for the element of double jeopardy, particularly as J had been released from custody, the court would substitute sentences of three years' imprisonment, *R. v. Kandola (Sundar Singh)* (1987) 9 Cr. App. R. (S.) 162, [1989] C.L.Y. 1125, *R. v. Martin (Caroline Ann)* (1993) 14 Cr. App. R. (S.) 645, [1994] C.L.Y. 1372, *R. v. Serzin (Bisunas Viadas)* (1995) 16 Cr. App. R. (S.) 4, [1996] C.L.Y. 2025, *R. v. Parker (Robbie)* (1995) 16 Cr. App. R. (S.) 525, *R. v. Shepherd (Paul)* [1998] 1 Cr. App. R. (S.) 397, [1998] C.L.Y. 1395, and *R. v. Gidney (Rebecca Jane)* [1999] 1 Cr. App. R. (S.) 138, [1999] C.L.Y. 1365 considered.

ATTORNEY GENERAL'S REFERENCE (NO.84 OF 1999), *Re*; *sub nom*. R. v. JENNISON (COLIN ALBERT) [2000] 2 Cr. App. R. (S.) 213, Lord Bingham of Cornhill, L.C.J., CA (Crim Div).

1439. Unlawful wounding – knives – stabbing victim during fight

[Offences Against the Person Act 1861 s.20.]

M pleaded guilty to unlawful wounding contrary to the Offences Against the Person Act 1861 s.20, on an indictment which alleged wounding with intent to do grievous bodily harm. M became involved in an argument with a friend. The argument developed into a fight, and the friend struck the appellant with a meat cleaver causing a wound to his shoulder. M then stabbed his friend four times, in the shoulder and the arm, and twice in the chest, with a knife which he had been using to open bottles. The victim was found to have life-threatening injuries to the heart. He was in intensive care for four days and remained in hospital for a further 24 days. M was sentenced to four and a half years' imprisonment and appealed contending that that in passing a sentence of four and half years' imprisonment, the sentencer failed to give an appropriate measure of discount to reflect M's plea of guilty.

Held, dismissing the appeal, that the case was not alone in raising a situation where in the view of the Court a plea of guilty to unlawful wounding ought never to have been accepted by the prosecution. While there were features of the Crown's evidence which might been susceptible to challenge, the Court's view was that where a very serious crime of violence took place from which a jury could have drawn the conclusion that it was accompanied by the requisite element of intent, the matter should in normal circumstances be tried out. If it was not, the sentencer would face particular problems if he felt in his own mind that the facts gave rise to a prima facie inference of intent but was called on to sentence for the offence without that distinguishing element. The court had to consider what was the appropriate sentence for the offence, treated as an offence contrary to s.20, giving proper account to the plea of guilty. The sentence did not cross the threshold of manifest excessiveness. It was undoubtedly a severe sentence for an offence contrary to s.20, but it could not be characterised as manifestly excessive.

R. v. McNELLIS (ANTHONY) [2000] 1 Cr. App. R. (S.) 481, Ognall, J., CA (Crim Div).

1440. Waste disposal – pollution control – dumping lorry tyres – custodial sentence inappropriate

[Environmental Protection Act 1990 s.33.]

O and E appealed against sentence of eight months' imprisonment for guilty pleas to offences contrary to the Environmental Protection Act 1990 s.33. They contended that a custodial sentence was inappropriate given that the offence was a minor pollution offence of dumping of lorry tyres which did not expose the public to hazardous substances.

Held, allowing the appeal, that a term of imprisonment was unreasonable in the light of the fact that the offences were at the lower end of the scale, did not expose the public to a significant risk, had not been repeated and that there had been no lasting adverse effect on the environment, *R. v. Garrett (Terence William)* [1997] 1 Cr. App. R. (S.) 109, [1997] C.L.Y. 2354 distinguished.

R. v. O'BRIEN (PAUL); R. v. ENKEL (ANDREW) [2000] 2 Cr. App. R. (S.) 358, Goldring, J., CA (Crim Div).

1441. Wounding with intent – delay – stabbing during fight in night club – unduly lenient sentence

The Attorney General asked the court to review a sentence of 15 months' imprisonment on the ground that it was unduly lenient. H was convicted of wounding with intent to cause grievous bodily harm. A confrontation between two groups took place at a night club, and fighting broke out outside the night club. In the course of the fighting the offender stabbed a man in the buttocks. The victim was found to have 11 lacerations to his buttocks. H claimed that he had not been involved in the original confrontation or fighting; he admitted picking up a Swiss army knife and throwing it away.

Held, allowing the reference, that there was considerable delay between the offence and the trial for which H was not responsible. It seemed to the court that a sentence substantially more severe than that imposed by the sentencer was required. Taking into account the mitigating circumstances, a proper sentence would have been two and a half years' imprisonment. The court would accordingly substitute a sentence of 22 months' imprisonment, to reflect the element of double jeopardy.

ATTORNEY GENERAL'S REFERENCE (NO.27 OF 1999), *Re*; *sub nom*. R. v. HIGGS (CHRISTOPHER DAVID) [2000] 1 Cr. App. R. (S.) 237, Kennedy, L.J., CA (Crim Div).

1442. Wounding with intent – licensed premises – glassing in public house

D appealed against a sentence of six years' imprisonment, having pleaded guilty to wounding with intent to do grievous bodily harm. D attacked a man in a public house, striking him on the back of the head with a pint glass and punching him on the back of the head. The victim suffered four lacerations which required 17 stitches. D claimed that the victim had insulted D's sister.

Held, allowing the appeal, that the court was satisfied that the sentence was significantly above the tariff even on a plea of not guilty. In all the circumstances, the right sentence was four years' imprisonment, *Attorney General's Reference (No.14 of 1994), Re* (1995) 16 Cr. App. R. (S.) 376 considered.

R. v. DOOLEY (LEE PETER) [1999] 2 Cr. App. R. (S.) 364, Dyson, J., CA (Crim Div).

1443. Wounding with intent – licensed premises – unprovoked glassing – unduly lenient sentence

[Offences Against the Person Act 1861 s.18.]

The Attorney General referred a sentence of two years' imprisonment on conviction of wounding with intent contrary to the Offences Against the Person Act1861s.18. B, aged 35, attacked his 17 year old victim in a wine bar, breaking a pint glass in his face and causing deep lacerations to the face requiring 44 stitches. Scarring was still visible at trial and was expected to be permanent and the victim had recurring difficulties with his right eye. B pleaded self defence and claimed that he suffered from psychiatric problems from a previous similar attack on himself. The Attorney General contended that the unprovoked attack with a weapon in licensed premises demonstrated aggravating features which clearly rendered the sentence excessively lenient.

Held, allowing the reference, that the sentence was unduly lenient and a term of imprisonment of 42 months was substituted. The victim's serious injuries, the use of the glass, the lack of mitigation and the contested trial, made the sentence inappropriate, *Attorney General's Reference (No.24 of 1998), Re* [1999] 1 Cr. App. R. (S.) 278, [1999] C.L.Y. 1373 considered.

ATTORNEY GENERAL'S REFERENCE (NO.14 OF 2000), *Re; sub nom*. R. v. BOFFEY (KEVIN PAUL) [2001] 1 Cr. App. R. (S.) 16, Roch, L.J., CA (Crim Div).

1444. Publications

Ashworth, Andrew – Sentencing and Criminal Justice. 3rd Ed. Paperback: £21.95. ISBN 0-406-91490-7. Butterworths Law.

CULTURE

1445. Museums – art galleries – transfer of objects and documents

MUSEUMS AND GALLERIES ACT 1992 (AMENDMENT) ORDER 2000, SI 2000 2955; made under the Museums and Galleries Act 1992 s.6. In force: November 23, 2000; £1.50.

This Order amends the Museums and Galleries Act 1992 Sch.5 to include the Historic Buildings and Monuments Commission for England, Historic Royal Palaces and the National Trust for Places of Historic Interest or Natural Beauty, with the effect of enabling the Historic Buildings and Monuments Commission for England to transfer objects and documents to any specified body and enabling all three bodies to receive such objects and documents from any specified body.

DAMAGES

1446. Clinical negligence – surrogacy – claimant victim of clinical negligence – cost of surrogacy irrecoverable as general damages – claim contrary to public policy

[Human Fertilisation and Embryology Act 1990 s.30.]

HKHA negligently performed a Caesarean section and hysterectomy on B, whose child was stillborn, with the result that B could have no more children. B subsequently came to a commercial agreement with a woman in California to have a surrogate child, by using her own eggs fertilised by the sperm of her unmarried partner. B argued that the cost of that arrangement should be recoverable from HKHA as general damages.

Held, that damages were awarded in the sum of £69,618 for pain and suffering but were not awarded for the proposed commercial surrogacy. Such an award would be contrary to public policy as surrogacy agreements were unenforceable under English law and commercial surrogacy agreements were punishable by criminal sanction. Although the arrangements would be made pursuant to Californian law, if a child were born, a guardian for the child and court proceedings would be necessary in England. B and her partner would not qualify in adoption proceedings or proceedings for a parental order under the Human Fertilisation and Embryology Act 1990 s.30 as such applicants had to be married. A court could retrospectively sanction breaches of statute in the paramount interests of an existing child, but it was asking too much for a court to enable a claimant to enter into an unlawful contract. B's age of 46 years also had to be considered as the arrangement would most likely fail and therefore it would be unreasonable to require HKHA to fund it. The facts of the case were exceptional, and the court did not exclude a claim for the costs of surrogacy brought within the law, for example by a young married woman who had been rendered incapable of having children.

BRIODY v. ST HELENS AND KNOWSLEY HA (CLAIM FOR DAMAGES AND COSTS) [2000] 2 F.C.R. 13, Ebsworth, J., QBD.

1447. Consumer credit – measure of damages – mitigation of loss – failure to accept offer of courtesy car

L's car was damaged in a road traffic accident, but remained drivable. L arranged a replacement hire car through DAS, his legal expenses insurer, commencing 13 days after the accident, for a total charge of £624. Meanwhile O's insurance company, A, offered L a free courtesy car while his own was being repaired. In addition, L's insurance company, HHH, advised that if he had his car repaired by one of their approved garages then he would have the benefit of a free courtesy car. Both offers were received by L before he commenced his hire with DAS. O admitted liability but disputed L's right to recover the hire charges contending that where no-cost alternatives were available, then L was under a duty to mitigate his loss by availing himself of them and he had had 13 days to organise his replacement car before the repairs were carried out. The DAS cover was for recovery of L's uninsured losses. With the option of free alternatives, in particular from his own insurance company, there should have been no uninsured loss. L argued that as he had the benefit of a DAS policy it was reasonable for him to utilise it and that the acceptance of the offer by A would have invalidated his own insurance policy.

Held, dismissing L's claim, that there was a clear duty on L to mitigate his loss. Therefore, even if A's offer was not accepted, the offer from L's insurance company should have been, *Fitton v. Goss* (Unreported, April 23, 1996) considered

LOUCA v. O'NEILL, June 1, 2000, District Judge Brett, CC (Bromley). [*Ex rel.* Nigel Ffitch, Barrister, Phoenix Chambers, Gray's Inn, London].

1448. Contributions – surveyor liable to lender for negligent valuation – purchaser liable to lender for non payment of loan – applicability of Civil Liability (Contribution) Act 1978

[Civil Liability (Contribution) Act 1978 s.1 (1).]

H, valuers who had accepted their liability to compensate A, a building society which had suffered loss after having advanced a loan in reliance upon H's negligent valuation, appealed against a decision that they were not entitled to partial reimbursement from T, the party which had defaulted on the loan repayments. A had loaned the funds to a property development company, of which T was a director, and the money was used to purchase property. T defaulted on the repayments, and A sold the property at a loss. H compensated A, but sought a contribution from T pursuant to the Civil Liability (Contribution) Act 1978, submitting that T had been partially responsible for A's loss.

Held, dismissing the appeal, that although H and T were both liable to A, they were not liable in respect of the "same damage" for the purpose of s.1 (1) of the Act. Whereas H were liable in negligence for the losses arising from the loan, which would not have been advanced if the valuation had been accurate, T was responsible for losses accruing as a result of the non payment of a debt. Since neither H nor T could extinguish or reduce the liability of the other, the 1978 Act did not apply and H were not entitled to claim a contribution from T.

HOWKINS & HARRISON v. TYLER [2001] Lloyd's Rep. P.N. 1, Sir Richard Scott V.C., CA.

1449. Dilapidations – valuation – expert evidence – unsatisfactory evidence of diminution in value – appropriate to calculate with reference to potential buyer

[Landlord and Tenant Act 1927 s.18(1).]

C, the landlord of a large multi storey mill complex, sought damages for dilapidations against S, a former tenant, who admitted to allowing the building to fall into disrepair. In assessing the level of damages pursuant to the Landlord and Tenant Act 1927 s.18(1), both parties submitted expert evidence from surveyors as to the diminution in value of the reversion of the property. Whilst agreement was reached concerning the open market value of the building in a state of disrepair at £245,000, it was argued by the surveyor representing C, that the freehold value in repair amounted to £585,000, on the basis that demand existed for similar buildings despite a widespread over supply. C's surveyor also considered that possible future demand might originate from potential users of the building in sectors other than its existing ones. The surveyor for S submitted, that due to a prevailing economic recession, and more particularly a general economic decline in the sectors from which potential users were likely to be drawn, no demand existed for similar buildings. He argued that the design of such buildings did not meet with modern requirements, and maintained that the value of the building in a state of repair was no more than that of it in disrepair.

Held, giving judgment for C, that the correct assessment of damages was £40,000. The expert evidence as to diminution in value was unsatisfactory but, in so far as it was of relevance, the evidence of the expert called on behalf of S was to be preferred. The schedule of works submitted by C could not be regarded as cogent evidence of the diminution in value of the reversion or of the actual diminution, *Crewe Services & Investment Corp v. Silk* [1998] 2 E.G.L.R. 1, [1998] C.L.Y. 122 considered. Accordingly, in the instant case, it was reasonable to assume a likely purchaser would have been a speculator who viewed the property from the perspective of its future potential in a more buoyant property market. The level of disrepair would be a cause of some concern and would, when reflecting on future expenditure required to rectify the disrepair, have an effect on the price realisable, *Portman v. Latter* [1942] W.N. 97 applied.

CRAVEN (BUILDERS) LTD v. SECRETARY OF STATE FOR HEALTH [2000] 1 E.G.L.R. 128, Neuberger, J., Ch D.

1450. Economic loss – disabled child born following negligent advice – compensation for economic loss beyond age of majority

N were the parents of a disabled child, born following allegedly negligent advice provided by WHA. N claimed damages for negligence, including economic loss arising from the future care of the child. On a preliminary issue, WHA argued that N should only receive compensation for the period up until the child's eighteenth birthday, as after that age there was no longer a legal duty on the parents to care for the child and they would be doing so voluntarily.

Held, that N were entitled under the normal compensatory principles in default of being restored to the position they would have been in had the advice not been given. Therefore, N were entitled to compensation beyond the child's eighteenth birthday, *Allen v. Bloomsbury HA* [1993] 1 All E.R. 651, [1993] C.L.Y. 1416 considered.

NUNNERLEY v. WARRINGTON HA [2000] P.I.Q.R. Q69, Morison, J., QBD.

1451. Fatal accidents – measure of damages – calculation of past and future dependency – regard to paid and unpaid care actually provided

[Fatal Accidents Act 1976.]

PB brought an action for damages under the Fatal Accidents Act 1976 following the death of his wife from injuries sustained in the process of her treatment during labour, at a hospital, SM. The treatment concluded in a Caesarean section as a result of which AB was born. Liability having been admitted, judgment was entered for PB by consent. The subsequent hearing for the assessment of damages was adjourned following the failure of PB to attend, and an unless order was made requiring his attendance at the future hearing. An order was made joining AB as second claimant so that his rights could be preserved. At the reconvened assessment hearing, PB again failed to attend, despite sufficient warning. The judge indicated that, while he intended to dismiss PB's claim in compliance with the unless order, such action should be postponed until after the assessment so that, if the matter arose, the issue of what was claimable by PB and AB, respectively, could be dealt with effectively. AB contended that the appropriate measure for past and future care should be based upon AB's actual care since the death of his mother, both paid and unpaid. SM maintained that the proper basis for calculating past and future dependency was the care which the mother would, in fact, have provided AB.

Held, giving judgment for the second claimant, that the correct basis for the calculation of past and future dependency was to have regard to the care, both paid and unpaid, actually provided to AB. Giving consideration to the provisions of the 1976 Act, it was appropriate to examine the expense incurred in replacing AB's mother's services. Given that there was clear authority for compensating the expense incurred through the employment of a nanny even where one had not in fact been employed, it followed that there was strong reason for compensating for the expense when one actually had been employed, *Hay v. Hughes* [1975] Q.B. 790, [1975] C.L.Y. 722 considered. The court was required in adopting such an approach to ensure that the claimant was not over compensated, *Spittle v. Bunney* [1988] 1 W.L.R. 847, [1988] C.L.Y. 1056 and *Stanley v. Saddique* [1992] Q.B. 1, [1991] C.L.Y. 1307 considered. If travelling costs had been incurred as a integral element of replacing the services of AB's mother, either in the payment of a nanny's travelling expenditure or expenditure on travelling to a nanny, it was appropriate to include those costs in the assessment, provided they were reasonable.

BORDIN v. ST MARY'S NHS TRUST [2000] Lloyd's Rep. Med. 287, Crane, J., QBD.

1452. Fraudulent misrepresentation – transaction less profitable as a result of misrepresentation – requirement to prove loss before damages recoverable

[Limitation Act 1980.]

C agreed to purchase and distribute S's products in France, on the understanding that the prices at which S were offering the products to C were the lowest available. It later transpired that S had been selling the products to bulk customers in the UK at much lower prices. The judge in the court below awarded damages with simple interest against S for breach of contract and fraudulent misrepresentation. S appealed, arguing that (1) no actual loss had been caused to C by the deception, as its only effect had been that C were deprived of the opportunity to make a larger profit than they had done, and (2) the Limitation Act 1980 rendered aspects of the claim statute barred. C counter appealed against the awarding of simple as opposed to compound interest on the ground that S should not be allowed to benefit from the fraud.

Held, dismissing the appeal and the cross appeal, that (1) it was not necessary for C to show that it had made a loss. It was enough to show that without the fraud it would have entered into a more profitable arrangement, *East v. Maurer* [1991] 1 W.L.R. 461, [1991] C.L.Y. 1306 and *Smith New Court Securities Ltd v. Scrimgeour Vickers (Asset Management) Ltd* [1997] A.C. 254, [1996] C.L.Y. 996 applied. The judge had been entitled to find that if the misrepresentation had not been made C would have secured a more advantageous arrangement on price with S, and (2) the claim was not time barred as the fraud had only been discovered in 1996 and the writ was issued that year. Although it could have been discovered had C made more extensive enquiries, C could not be criticised for failing to do so since it had reasonably assumed that the business relationship was based on trust and openness. To require more from C would have been to impose "exceptional measure" as the test rather than "reasonable diligence", *Paragon Finance Plc v. Thakerar & Co* [1999] 1 All E.R. 400, [1998] C.L.Y. 536 applied.

CLEF AQUITAINE SARL v. LAPORTE MATERIALS (BARROW) LTD; *sub nom.* CLEF AQUITAINE SARL v. SOVEREIGN CHEMICAL INDUSTRIES LTD [2001] Q.B. 488, Simon Brown, L.J., CA.

1453. Interest – award following non acceptance of Part 36 offer – vires of CPR r.36.21

[Supreme Court Act 1981 s.35A; Civil Procedure Act 1997; Civil Procedure Rules 1998 (SI 1998 3132) Part 1 r.1.1, Part 36 r.36.21.]

A made a Part 36 offer under the Civil Procedure Rules 1998 which M did not accept. At trial, M was held liable for more than the proposals in the offer and A claimed interest on the sum awarded under the Supreme Court Act 1981 s.35A and under Part 36 r.36.21 of the 1998 rules. Interest under s.35A was conceded, but M claimed that the imposition of interest under r.36.21 exceeded the requirement to compensate A and was punitive and unjust and because it was penal in nature and was ultra vires the enabling legislation. M argued that (1) relying upon *President of India v. La Pintada Compania Navegacion SA (The La Pintada) (No.1)* [1985] A.C. 104, [1984] C.L.Y. 123 per Lord Brandon, the award of interest was a matter of substantive law; (2) the 1998 Rules were concerned with practice and procedure not substantive law; (3) the award of interest was a matter of substantive law, therefore s.35A and not the Civil Procedure Act 1997 founded the power to award interest under r.36.21 but the function of an award of interest under s.35A was to compensate a party for being kept out of its money, not to penalise; (4) Part 36 r.36.21 had penal effect and therefore could not be within s.35A; (5) s.35A did not contemplate two awards of interest and the statutory power was not hindered by the words "subject to Rules of Court", and (6) Part 36 r.36.21 was therefore ultra vires.

Held, refusing to stand the issue down to be dealt with by way of judicial review on the grounds that the validity of r.36.21 was an essential component of the interest claim but granting permission to appeal on the award of costs and interest, *R. v. Reading Crown Court, ex p. Hutchinson* [1988] Q.B. 384, [1988] C.L.Y. 593 applied, that interest under s.35A was not the same as that under Part 36 r.36.21. Section 35A conferred a power for the award of simple interest that could be circumscribed by the Rules of Court. On its true construction, a single award was contemplated to compensate a party for being kept out of its money. The rate and duration of interest were subject to the court's discretion, but it must have been contemplated that the discretion would be exercised in accordance with the law at the date s.35A was passed. The enabling power for Part 36 r.36.21 lay in s.1 of the 1997 Act and under s.1(3) the power was to be exercised "with a view to securing that the civil justice system is accessible, fair and efficient". This was translated in Part 1 r.1.1 of the 1998 Rules into the overriding objective. Part 36 r.36.21 was designed to encourage parties to focus on the need for fair and early settlement of actions and it was a policy of the 1998 Rules to ensure compliance with its provisions and any directions made under its powers, by the imposition of sanctions. In the instant situation, sanctions and penalties were synonymous. The power to award enhanced interest under Part 36 r.36.21 was a sanction against a party failing to accept a reasonable offer, thereby unnecessarily prolonging the litigation, and it had never been suggested that the 1998 Rules could not impose sanctions, *Little v.*

George Little Sebire & Co (Enhanced Interest) The Times, November 17, 1999, [1999] C.L.Y. 443 considered.

ALL-IN-ONE DESIGN & BUILD LTD v. MOTCOMB ESTATES LTD *The Times*, April 4, 2000, Recorder Michael Black Q.C., QBD (T&CC).

1454. Interim payments – corporate insolvency – impact of insolvency upon discretion to award interim payment

[Civil Procedure Rules 1998 (SI 1998 3132) Part 25 r.25.7.]

H, a company in insolvent liquidation, applied for an interim payment following a ruling that it was entitled to recover damages from HOC for breach of contract and misfeasance in public office. H maintained that it was entitled to interim damages on account of tender costs and loss of profit. HOC contended that (1) if an interim payment were to be made it could not be recovered from the liquidator should H's claim fail at trial but would be expended in the liquidation, and (2) H had failed to prove that they would recover damages on account of lost profits or tender costs at trial and would in any event have sustained no loss as a result of HOC's actions since, if the contract had been awarded, the company would have gone into liquidation before the contract had been completed.

Held, granting the application and awarding the sum of £1,848,456 by way of interim payment, that (1) the fact that an interim payment might prove to be irrecoverable was irrelevant to the making of an order under the Civil Procedure Rules 1998 Part 25 r.25.7 since the aim of an interim payment was to provide a party with part of the monies that he was entitled to receive and courts were not in the habit of refusing such applications because of the prospect of a successful appeal. Furthermore, there was no provision under r.25.7 for an order to be made subject to conditions, nor was there any other provision with that effect, reflecting the attitude that the court was not concerned with the eventual manner in which any monies awarded were used, and (2) if the contract had been awarded to H, the company would not have gone into liquidation but would have made a significant profit.

HARMON CFEM FACADES (UK) LTD v. CORPORATE OFFICER OF THE HOUSE OF COMMONS (INTERIM PAYMENT) [2001] C.P. Rep. 20, Judge Humphrey Lloyd Q.C., QBD (T&CC).

1455. Interim payments – misapplication of building society advances – solicitors' liability for whole of advance since entire transaction fraudulent

[Rules of the Supreme Court (SI 1965 1776) Ord.29 r.11 (1), r.12 (c).]

A applied for interim payments in three related actions against E, their solicitors, who acted in relation to advances made by A for the purchases of six hotels. In each case A had been misled as to the actual cost of the buildings with much of the advances being applied to goodwill, fixtures and fittings. Additionally, an intermediate vendor had, in each case, been inserted between the vendor and A's borrower, with no money passing on the sale by that party to the borrower. In each case, E's instructions required them to report to A before completion where various matters had arisen including "any other matters which ought to be brought to the attention of the society as mortgagee". E argued that they could only be liable for that part of the advances which had been improperly applied. It was further submitted that in the case of the four hotels covered by a single action, there was a single claim limiting liability thereon to £1,000,000 under the Solicitors' Indemnity Rules 1989.

Held, allowing the application and ordering interim payments, that (1) the entire transactions were frauds on A which could not have happened without the connivance or the gross negligence of E and no disbursement of the society's funds was within E's authorisation. Under the provisions of Rules of the Supreme Court Ord.29 r.11 (1) and r.12 (c) interim payments would be ordered where the court was satisfied that "substantial damages" or a "substantial sum of money apart from any damages or costs" would be obtained by the claimant. This did not require the claimant to present a water tight case with no prospect of failure, but did require that the defendant had not been granted unconditional leave to defend the action. Thus the extent of E's liability met the required standard to enable A to claim interim payments, and (2) E were engaged to act in respect of the four hotels under separate retainers and gave separate undertakings to act in accordance with instructions. There were four separate transactions and it was not to the point that they had been brought in one action rather than in four separate ones.

ALLIANCE & LEICESTER BUILDING SOCIETY v. EDGESTOP LTD; ALLIANCE & LEICESTER BUILDING SOCIETY v. DHANOA; ALLIANCE & LEICESTER BUILDING SOCIETY v. SAMRA [1999] Lloyd's Rep. P.N. 868, Hoffmann, J., Ch D.

1456. Interim payments – offer of sum in full and final settlement – interim payments later stated not to be taken into account by Part 36 r.36 offer – original offer binding due to acceptance

[Civil Procedure Rules 1998 (SI 1998 3132) Part 36 r.36.]

M brought an action for damages for personal injuries arising out of a road traffic accident in March 1999. In May 1999, D made an interim payment to M in the sum of £5,000 stated to be on account of special damages, specifically in settlement of the claim for the pre-accident value of the vehicle. Various correspondence followed in respect of the value of the vehicle, hire charges and general damages only. By a letter dated November 1999, M's solicitors offered to settle the claim in accordance with the Civil Procedure Rules 1998 Part 36 r.36, stating that they were instructed to offer the sum of £5,500 in full settlement of M's claim. The letter also stated that the offer to settle was in respect of the difference in valuation, hire/recovery storage invoice, incidental expenses, loss of holidays, replacement damaged spectacles and telephone calls to Europe. D replied accepting the offer "in full and final settlement of your client's claim", and attaching a cheque for £500 to represent the balance outstanding after the interim payment. M returned the cheque and stated that the Part 36 r.36 offer did not take into account any interim payments made. M issued proceedings against D. D applied for a declaration that the case was settled prior to commencement of proceedings.

Held, granting D's application, that the letter from M's solicitors in November 1999 represented a clear and unambiguous offer to settle M's claim fully and finally in the sum of £5,500. It was not adequate for M's solicitors to seek to rely on the "small print". Neither was it open to them to state, after the event, that their intention had only been to settle the claim in part. Upon acceptance by D, M was bound by the clear and unambiguous terminology of the letter, *Mutton v. Osarinwian* (Unreported, May 25, 1999), [1999] C.L.Y. 492 referred to.

MALIK v. FM DE ROOY (NO.1), April 4, 2000, Deputy District Judge Smith, CC (Manchester). [*Ex rel.* Laura Elfield, Barrister, 5 Pump Court, Temple, London].

1457. Interim payments – payment by insurer in respect of pre-accident value of car – failure to apply for repayment conclusion of proceedings – County Court Rules inapplicable

[County Court Rules 1981 (SI 1981 1687) Ord.29 r.17; Civil Procedure Rules 1998 (SI 1998 3132) Part 25 r.25.8.]

M brought an action in July 1998 for damages in respect of personal injuries and other losses sustained as a result of a road traffic accident in August 1997. In December 1997 LUB's insurers made a voluntary interim payment of £1,700 to M in respect of the pre-accident value of his car which had been a write off. LUB continued to deny liability and when the action was tried in November 1999 the claim was dismissed in its entirety. LUB however neglected to apply for repayment of the £1,700 when judgment was given, only issuing an application in January 2000. M resisted the application, claiming that (1) the appropriate time to apply for repayment of the interim payment was at the conclusion of the proceedings and that, having neglected to apply at that time, LUB could not do so afterwards, and (2) the sum had long since been spent by M and he would be prejudiced by an order to repay it. Because the Civil Procedure Rules 1998 were silent on the question of when it was permissible to apply for adjustment of interim payments, M's counsel sought to rely on the County Court Rules 1981 Ord. 29 r.17 in support of the proposition that such applications could only be made during the currency of proceedings or at their conclusion and ought not to be granted after the proceedings were over.

Held, that Part 25 r.25.8 was drafted in less restrictive terms that Ord. 29 r.17 intentionally to permit applications for adjustments of interim payments to be made in a wider range of circumstances than previously, and that since the CPR was intended to create a new regime for civil justice it was not appropriate to look to the old rules for guidance. The words "may make an order to adjust the interim payment" in Part 25 r.25.8 gave the court a general discretion to order repayment or not as it judged appropriate in the circumstances. While the judge agreed that it was desirable that such applications be made at the conclusion of proceedings, in the absence of evidence of specific prejudice caused to M by LMB's delay, he thought it just to order M to repay the interim payment plus interest thereon from the date of payment to the date of trial of the action. Since the necessity for the application came about through LUB's failure to apply for repayment at the appropriate time, LUB was not entitled to its costs of the application.

MANOTTA v. LONDON UNITED BUSWAYS LTD, February 22, 2000, District Judge Carlton, CC (Uxbridge). [*Ex rel.* Joanne Wardale, Barrister, 3 Paper Buildings, Temple, London].

1458. Interim payments – payments pending final damages assessment – interest accruing to claimant not to be taken into account in final damages assessment

Held, that where interim payments had been made after judgment as to liability but prior to the final assessment of damages, interest accruing on such payments was to be regarded as the claimant's property and was not to be taken into account when determining the final amount of damages.

PARRY v. NORTH WEST SURREY HA *The Times*, January 5, 2000, Penry-Davey, J., QBD.

1459. Interim payments – personal injuries – care of claimant with severe head injuries – use of payment to change care regime – effect of status quo on trial

C claimed damages for a catastrophic head injury suffered in a road traffic accident for which M was liable. C obtained an interim payment of £100,000, which did not exceed a reasonable proportion of the damages likely to be recovered by him. M appealed, as C had indicated that the money was to be used to set up a home care regime on a permanent basis when, until then, for much of the week he was cared for at an NHS unit. M had disclosed a report that C was effectively in a persistent vegetative state, and challenged C's expert's assertion that home care improved the quality of his life. M argued that the trial on this issue would not be on a level playing field if the status quo was that C was being permanently cared for at home.

Held, dismissing the appeal, that (1) the "level playing field" factor had only been dealt with by the judge as an afterthought, so that the Court of Appeal could review the exercise of the judge's discretion, as the factor was one to be taken into account; (2) C was already spending some of his time at home, and even that required considerable expenditure; (3) part of the interim payment was to repay sums already spent by C's parents; (4) questions of bed availability at the unit would be the same at trial as they were now because C continued to spend some time there; (5) it was C's money, and (6) judges were trained to act dispassionately and if the evidence showed that the home regime was not to C's benefit, the judge would not allow it, and that decision might be informed by knowing how C fared at home; the playing field had not been angled all one way, *Stringman v. McArdle* [1994] 1 W.L.R. 1653, [1994] C.L.Y. 1482 applied.

CAMPBELL v. MYLCHREEST [1999] P.I.Q.R. Q17, Sir John Balcombe, CA.

1460. **Losses – hire charges – motor insurance – subrogation – recovery of hire charges by motor insurer**

C brought an action against D for damages arising out of a road traffic accident. Liability was not in dispute and the only claim outstanding at the date of issue of proceedings was a claim for hire charges in the sum of £1,085.64. C had the benefit of an insurance policy, provided by AA, under which AA provided that it would indemnify C against the cost of hiring a replacement vehicle provided that (1) the period of hire did not exceed 21 days, and (2) it was reasonably satisfied that C would be able to recover the whole of the hire costs, whether initially paid by the insured or the insurer. The policy further provided that AA was entitled to pursue recovery of the costs on C's behalf. C maintained that he was unaware of the provisions of the insurance policy. The day following the accident, C was provided with a replacement car by EUK, the hire company. AA paid the charges of the hire vehicle and no invoice was ever sent to C. AA brought a claim in the name of C for the recovery of the hire charges on the basis that it was subrogated to C's rights of recovery against D. It was held that C had no liability to pay the hire charges as there was no enforceable agreement between C and EUK, therefore C had incurred no loss and could not recover the hire charges from D. Further, on a true construction of the insurance policy, the right of subrogation only arose where C had been indemnified for a liability that he had incurred. As there was no liability on the part of C to pay the hire charges, no right of subrogation arose. C appealed, contending that (1) C had suffered a loss in that he had been deprived of the use of his car and the hire charges were a measure of such loss, *Giles v. Thompson* [1994] 1 A.C. 142, [1993] C.L.Y. 1405 cited; (2) the circumstances of the hiring were irrelevant and there was no difference in principle between car repairs and car hire, and (3) even if C had incurred no financial liability, AA had incurred a loss such as to entitle it to subrogation as a restitutionary remedy for unjust enrichment, *Banque Financiere de la Cite SA v. Parc (Battersea) Ltd* [1999] 1 A.C. 221, [1998] C.L.Y. 2521, *Austin v. Zurich General Accident and Liability Insurance Co Ltd* [1944] 2 All E.R. 243 and *King v. Victoria Insurance Co Ltd* [1896] A.C. 250 cited.

Held, dismissing the appeal, that it had been found as a fact that there was no agreement between C and EUK as C had been provided with a replacement vehicle at no cost to himself and with no enforceable liability to pay. C had therefore incurred no loss and could not recover the hire charges from D, *Giles* distinguished. There was a fundamental difference between the cost of repair and the hire charges, *Taylor v. Cook* (Unreported, August 6, 1999), [1999] C.L.Y. 2504 applied. The method of calculating loss was unrelated to the question of liability to pay. The doctrine of subrogation as a restitutionary remedy for unjust enrichment was a developing area of the law on which there were few authorities, but the remarks of Lord Steyn in *Banque Financiere* were referred to as indicative of a granting trend towards its recognition. The instant case turned on the fact that there was no obligation on the part of C to the hire company, distinguishing *King* where the right to recover on the part of the insurance company was limited to the rights of the insured against the defendant. Further, the right to an indemnity by the claimant was determined by the claimant primary liability, *Austin* considered, and no primary liability arose on C's part in the instant case.

CUNNINGHAM v. DAMON, December 1, 1999, District Judge Diamond, CC (Medway). [*Ex rel.* Patrick McMorrow, Barrister, 169 Temple Chambers, Temple Avenue, London].

1461. **Measure of damages – benefits – pure economic loss – deduction of benefits paid to parents of disabled child**

[Social Security (Recovery of Benefits) Act 1997 s.1 (1), Sch.2.]

R, parents of a child born with Down's Syndrome, had been awarded damages ([2000] Lloyd's Rep. Med.181, [2000] C.L.Y. 4200) for the negligent omission of EDHA to inform them that the mother's pregnancy could result in the birth of a disabled child and the resultant loss of opportunity to terminate the pregnancy.

R were in receipt of a number of benefits, including income support, jobseeker's allowance, unemployment benefit, attendance allowance, and the care and mobility components of disability living allowance. R submitted that the Social Security (Recovery of Benefits) Act 1997 s.1(1) applied with the result that those benefits that fell within Sch.2 of the Act should not be deducted from the award. In the alternative, it was submitted that if common law principles applied, as established in *Hodgson v. Trapp* [1989] A.C. 807, [1989] C.L.Y. 1285, only income support, unemployment benefit and jobseeker's allowance should be deducted.

Held, giving judgment for R, that (1) the Act did not apply to an action brought for the recovery of damages in tort for economic loss, and (2) common law principles applied to all the benefits R were in receipt of. Given that EDHA had been liable to compensate R rather than their child, there was no reason at common law that any benefits paid to them as a result of that child's disability should be deducted from the award. With regard to invalid care allowance, which was received by R for the care of the child, EDHA was liable for any reasonable expenditure arising from the child's disability. The allowance did not cover such expenditure on providing equipment, holidays and therapies which R had incurred. Accordingly EDHA would be liable for such expenditure. It was not appropriate in the interests of justice or in view of the principle of double recovery for invalid care allowance to be deducted from the award, *Hodgson v. Trapp* applied.

RAND v. EAST DORSET HA (DEDUCTION OF BENEFITS) [2001] P.I.Q.R. Q1, Newman, J., QBD.

1462.   Measure of damages – breach of warranty – award for diminution in value as at date of sale

[Civil Procedure Rules 1998 (SI 1998 3132) Part 35 r.35.15.]

In October 1998, C purchased a horse from A for £5,000. The sale was subject to an examination by a vet and, more importantly, the assurance put in writing by A that the horse was free of "stable vices" in response to a specific enquiry by C. Upon delivery it was quickly noted that the horse did have a stable vice known as "windsucking". C had the vice verified by his vet and attempted to rescind the contract for breach of warranty. A refused to take the horse back and so C kept the horse and sought damages for diminution of value. It was at no time suggested that the vice affected the performance of the horse as a show jumper for C's teenage son. The claim was based on the premise that purchasers would be reluctant to buy a horse with a stable vice and that a sale would only be achieved by discounting the price. It was noted that A had sought the same assurance as to stable vices when she had purchased the horse in about April 1998. The judge sat with an assessor, a barrister knowledgeable in matters equine, appointed by the Court under the Civil Procedure Rules 1998 Part 35 r.35.15.

Held, granting judgment in C's favour, that the warranty as to stable vices was a term of the contract and that the evidence showed that the horse was a "windsucker" as at the date of the sale. That left only the quantum of damages. A argued that each horse was individual and that there were many which commanded huge sums on sale by virtue of counterbalancing favourable factors. It was found that there was no evidence to show that the horse was exceptional and indeed many potential purchasers, like C, would decline to view the horse if they knew it was a "windsucker". C's expert evidence showed that "windsucking" potentially lowered a horse's value by 50 per cent. The court held that the correct measure of damages was the diminution in value, by reason of the breach, as at the date of sale. The sum of £2,500 plus interest was awarded, being 50 per cent of the purchase price.

CONLON v. ALLEN, April 3, 2000, District Judge Davies, CC (Chichester). [*Ex rel.* David McHugh, Barrister, Bracton Chambers, 2nd Floor, 95A Chancery Lane, London].

1463. Measure of damages – choice of forum – assessment of quantum

[Private International Law (Miscellaneous Provisions) Act 1995 s.11, s.12, s.14(3).]

E, an English citizen who had suffered a severe head injury in Spain while travelling as a passenger in a hire car driven by S, sought damages for personal injury from S. The principles governing the determination of liability were the same in both Spanish and English law, but the quantification of damages differed, with the result that Spanish law was likely to produce a substantially lower award. E sought resolution of the case under English law and submitted that since the assessment of damages was a procedural process as opposed to a substantive one, quantification fell to be determined in accordance with the law of the forum, namely the same law as that which was applied to determine liability issues. S maintained that Spanish law was applicable because all issues, including quantification, were subject to the Private International Law (Miscellaneous Provisions) Act 1995 s.11 and s.12.

Held, giving judgment for E, that although heads of damages were matters of substantive law, the quantification of damages was a procedural task and where a tort had been committed in a foreign country, damages were to be assessed in accordance with the law of the forum. Section 14(3) of the Act specifically provided for procedural issues to be determined in that way and s.12 permitted displacement of the general rule contained in s.11 in circumstances where the tort was connected more to another country than the one in which the tort had taken place. In the instant case, the fact that both parties were English coupled with the fact that the principal heads of damage had arisen in England, firmly indicated that it was more appropriate to assess damages according to English law, *Boys v. Chaplin* [1971] A.C. 356, [1969] C.L.Y. 469 followed.

E v. SIMMONDS [2001] 1 W.L.R. 1003, Garland, J., QBD.

1464. Measure of damages – clinical negligence – failed sterilisation resulting in birth of severely disabled child – value of mother's care – discount rate on multipliers – rate of interest for general damages

T was awarded judgment in her action against SHA for negligent performance of a sterilisation operation. Damages fell to be assessed and T claimed damages for pain, suffering and loss of amenity, including the loss of amenity in caring for J, her unwanted fifth child, who was conceived and born severely disabled after the operation. T also sought the cost of past and future care of J, based on the discounted commercial value of her own services, and her loss of earnings during pregnancy. T contended for a two per cent discount rate for the multiplier for future losses and interest of three per cent on general damages. SHA, whilst not disputing that the general damages claim should reflect the additional burden of rearing a handicapped child, argued that the value of T's services properly fell within the assessment of her past and future loss of amenity, and could not constitute a separate head of claim because no commercial care costs had been incurred. SHA also submitted that her claim for future costs was limited to those she was likely to and could afford to incur, and that her claim for future loss of earnings ought to be heavily discounted because her emotional instability and poor employment record indicated that she was unlikely to have worked full time in any event. SHA opposed any change in the discount and interest rates.

Held, giving judgment for T, that T was entitled to recover the reasonable cost of bringing up and caring for J for the rest of their joint lives, *Housecroft v. Burnett* [1986] 1 All E.R. 332, [1986] C.L.Y. 989 and *Emeh v. Kensington and Chelsea and Westminster AHA* [1985] Q.B. 1012, [1985] C.L.Y. 2322 applied. General damages included a lump sum for the additional stress and worry arising from the burden of rearing a disabled child. Past and future care costs were valued in accordance with commercial rates with a 25 per cent discount and although other past expenses were restricted to what had actually been spent, future costs were those which T would reasonably wish to incur to meet J's needs and were not limited to what she could have afforded, *Robinson v. Salford*

HA [1992] 3 Med L.R. 270, [1992] C.L.Y. 1544 considered and *Anderson v. Forth Valley Health Board* 1998 S.L.T. 588, [1998] C.L.Y. 6115 applied. The guideline discount rate of three per cent would remain as there had not been a sufficient change in economic circumstances to justify a reduction, *Wells v. Wells* [1999] 1 A.C. 345, [1998] C.L.Y. 1446 followed, and the rate of interest was three per cent, *Burns (Craig) v. Davies (Joseph Cyril)* [1999] Lloyd's Rep. Med. 215, [1999] C.L.Y. 1424 followed.

TAYLOR v. SHROPSHIRE HA (NO.2) [2000] Lloyd's Rep. Med. 96, Judge Nicholl, DR (Birmingham).

1465. Measure of damages – computer contracts – inflated claim and failure to mitigate loss contended

[Unfair Contract Terms Act 1977.]

A company, P entered into a contract with W, a supplier of computer hardware and software, for the supply of an integrated computer system. W committed numerous breaches of contract and eventually abandoned the contract altogether. P accepted the repudiation and commenced proceedings in the Commercial Court seeking damages under 12 separate heads of claim. W admitted liability but maintained that the damages claim was inflated, that P had failed to mitigate its loss and that the effect of certain clauses in the contract was to limit or exclude its own liability. W also sought rectification of clause 43(a)(i) which was relied upon by P as imposing liability for consequential losses. W maintained that during the course of contractual negotiations, P's representatives had accepted that W would not be liable for such losses.

Held, giving judgment for P in the sum of £9,047,113, on a claim for £22,898,472, that there was no cogent evidence to suggest that an agreement had been entered into between the parties' representatives to exclude liability for consequential losses and therefore no basis for the suggested rectification. The Unfair Contract Terms Act 1977 applied, as P was dealing on W's written standard terms of business, rendering the exclusion of liability clauses unenforceable as being unreasonable. Furthermore there was no evidence that P had failed to mitigate its loss under any of the heads of damage.

PEGLER LTD v. WANG (UK) LTD (NO.1) [2000] B.L.R. 218, Judge Bowsher Q.C., QBD (T&CC).

1466. Measure of damages – contract of sale – oil – damages sought for late delivery – normal measure of damages applied – cost of hedging instruments recoverable

A sold 950,000 barrels of crude oil f.o.b. to AP. Owing to AP's default, the oil was not delivered until eight days after the contractual delivery date. A had purchased the oil from a third party. As they thought that oil prices were due to drop, they purchased the oil by choosing a deferred price option rather than a back to back arrangement. After selecting that option, they entered into four contracts for differences. Following the late delivery of the oil, A entered into futures contacts to cover their outright risks. They issued proceedings against AP claiming the profit that they would have received had the oil been delivered on time together with the costs of entering into the contracts for differences and the futures contracts. Liability having been admitted by AP, the court was asked to assess damages. AP argued that A's losses had resulted not from the late delivery of the oil but from the contracts for differences which had proved unfavourable to A. AP contended that such losses were either too remote or not recoverable under the contract which excluded liability for indirect or consequential losses. A argued that damages should be assessed in the usual way namely by calculating the difference between the value of the oil at the contractual delivery date and its value at the date of its actual delivery.

Held, giving judgment on the basis argued for by A, that A's loss was to be calculated with reference to the difference between the price that they had received for the oil and the price that they would have received had delivery been made on time. The parties were experienced oil traders, and AP ought to have foreseen that A would enter into a separate contract to obtain the oil. It was observed that if damages were not to be calculated in such a way, there would be no good reason for depriving A of the costs of the hedging instruments. Given that the slightest movement in the price of oil could have a marked impact on the profitability of a transaction, such costs were foreseeable and could not be described as too remote or as consequential losses.

ADDAX LTD v. ARCADIA PETROLEUM LTD [2000] 1 Lloyd's Rep. 493, Morison, J., QBD (Comm Ct).

1467. Measure of damages – damages awarded for repair costs assessed at date of judgment – unjust to award damages as at date of breach owing to inflation and claimant's lack of resources to repair – claimant entitled to wait for liability to be established

B claimed that AM's smelting plant emitted pollutants and noxious gases into the atmosphere, causing corrosion to B's roof. B repaired the damage, but further damage appeared for which B was unable to pay. B commenced proceedings against AM and submitted a figure for special damages for the repair costs. Subsequently, B was given permission to amend the initial figure, and at trial B was awarded the amended sum for special damages. AM appealed, contending that the original figure which represented the cost of repair when the physical damage occurred was the correct figure and that B was in breach of his duty to mitigate his damage by waiting for a decision on AM's liability before making repairs. Furthermore, AM claimed that B was prevented from claiming the amended sum as it was B's impecuniosity that had caused the delay in repairing the building, which was not a result of AM's breach of duty, *Dredger Liesbosch v. SS Edison (The Edison)* [1933] A.C. 449 cited.

Held, dismissing the appeal, that the general tortious rule stipulated that damages should be assessed at the date of breach, *Miliangos v. George Frank (Textiles) Ltd (No.1)* [1976] A.C. 443, [1975] C.L.Y. 2657 considered, but the instant case was an exception because a strict application of the rule would have resulted in an injustice to B, who had lacked the resources to pay for the repairs at that time. The increase in repair costs was due to rapid inflation and B was not in breach of a duty to mitigate his damage as he was entitled to wait until liability had been established, *Dredger Liesbosch* distinguished.

ALCOA MINERALS OF JAMAICA INC v. BRODERICK [2000] 3 W.L.R. 23, Lord Slynn of Hadley, PC.

1468. Measure of damages – date for determining damages for loss of opportunity – medical evidence available after notional trial date admissible

HJJJ, a firm of solicitors, appealed against an assessment of damages made against them in a professional negligence action following the automatic striking out of C's personal injury claim. HJJJ contended that the date for assessment of damages was the notional trial date and that medical evidence made available thereafter should be inadmissible in the assessment of damages hearing.

Held, dismissing the appeal, that the date for assessment of damages for loss of opportunity was the date of a notional trial of the personal injury action. Although evidence relating to a completely new head of damage arising after the notional trial date might have to be refused, medical evidence coming to light after the notional trial date which related to an existing head of damage could be of assistance to the judge and could be considered in an appropriate case.

CHARLES v. HUGH JAMES JONES & JENKINS [2000] 1 W.L.R. 1278, Swinton Thomas, L.J., CA.

1469. Measure of damages – fatal accidents – calculation of financial dependency – deceased disabled prior to accident

[Law Reform (Miscellaneous Provisions) Act 1934; Fatal Accidents Act 1976.]
K appealed against the level of damages awarded to T, following the death of T's wife, who was in poor health, from a pulmonary embolism three weeks after

breaking her femur in K's shop. At the time of the accident, T's wife had been suffering from osteoarthritis, osteoporosis, diabetes and high blood pressure. She had not been able to walk very far, but helped in the garden and did the cooking and cleaning. T had been awarded £50,000 under the Fatal Accidents Act 1976 and £5,000 for pain and suffering under the Law Reform (Miscellaneous Provisions) Act 1934. K submitted that the award was too high.

Held, allowing the appeal, that the claim had been seriously overvalued with regard to both heads of claim. The purpose of the 1976 Act was to assess the financial dependency of the claimant on the deceased. It was not within the power of the court to award damages for emotional dependency. T's wife had been in poor health and the extent of her future domestic assistance was impossible to determine. The multiplier and multiplicand approach was accordingly inappropriate. At the time of death she had been carrying out a large part of the household duties which could be given a monetary value, even though they had not actually been replaced by an outside agency. The award of £50,000 was replaced by £20,000. The award of £5,000 was reduced to £2,500, on the basis that the deceased had only suffered on K's account for a period of three weeks.

THOMAS v. KWIK SAVE STORES LTD *The Times*, June 27, 2000, Latham, L.J., CA.

1470. Measure of damages – inappropriate to employ higher multiplier to compensate for higher tax rate abroad

GI appealed against a decision awarding VO, a 31 year old Dutch national, £1,203,508 in damages for personal injury, including £969,335 for future loss of earnings. GI argued that the judge had erred by accepting evidence submitted by VO relating to the comparatively higher rates of tax in Holland, thereby applying a higher multiplier in reaching a final figure for future loss of earnings. GI put before the court as further evidence a report which, with reference to the calculation established in *Duxbury v. Duxbury* [1992] Fam. 62, indicated that applying Dutch income tax, rather than a wealth tax which potentially would be abolished in the near future, the fund would be exhausted three years earlier than applying the UK tax rates. On the basis of those calculations GI argued that £50,000 would be required to account for the difference in the two tax rates, involving an increase of the multiplier to 22.5 per cent. VO contended that liability to the higher rate of tax was an exceptional circumstance such as to justify the application of a higher multiplier, or a reduction in the discount rate.

Held, allowing the appeal, that (1) the *Duxbury* calculation while a beneficial method of comparing and calculating the effect of tax did not make reference to mortality, an element which the *Ogden* tables accounted for and from which the multiplier was derived. It was unnecessary to apply *Wells v. Wells* [1999] 1 A.C. 345, [1998] C.L.Y. 1446 in making the calculation, which was merely a means of ensuring that a reduction from 3.5 per cent gross to 3 per cent net was a correct approximation; (2) there was insufficient evidence to support consideration being given to the wealth tax when concluding whether the circumstances in the instant case were exceptional, and (3) the court was not concerned with how a claimant would actually apply the money awarded when calculating the multiplier. However in exceptional cases it was just to refer to all the circumstances of the claimants case in order to ascertain whether those circumstances warranted exceptional treatment. In the instant case, evidence that Dutch income tax was higher than UK income tax was not sufficient to establish exceptional circumstances, and therefore did not justify a lower discount rate or higher multiplier.

VAN OUDENHOVEN v. GRIFFIN INNS LTD [2000] 1 W.L.R. 1413, Stuart-Smith, L.J., CA.

1471. Measure of damages – industrial diseases – benefits to be deducted in full from personal injury damages awards

[Pneumoconiosis etc (Workers' Compensation) Act 1979.]

B, who had contracted malignant mesothelioma following environmental exposure in his teens to asbestos around N's factory premises, and later during his employment with N, claimed a statutory compensation award of £39,228 under the Pneumoconiosis etc (Workers' Compensation) Act 1979. He subsequently brought an action for damages for personal injuries against N, but died before the claim was concluded. Liability was ultimately admitted and quantum agreed in the sum of £144,473. The only issue to be determined at trial was whether, and to what extent, the 1979 Act payment was to be deducted from the damages award. The judge ordered ([2000] P.I.Q.R. Q57) that it should be set off against the heads of loss of nursing care and loss of earnings, but not against general damages. N appealed, contending that in order to avoid double recovery by B, all collateral benefits directly attributable to the injury should be deducted, in accordance with the general principle in *Hodgson v. Trapp* [1989] A.C. 807, [1989] C.L.Y. 1285 cited. B argued that the purpose of the 1979 Act payment was solely in respect of the loss of the chance to sue, hence B should not have to give any credit for the payment.

Held, allowing the appeal, that the 1979 Act provided compensation for contracting a disease, and all of the consequences arising from that disease. The amount payable was calculated according to an applicant's age and the extent of his disability. It was not determined by the prospects of success of any future litigation and the likely quantum of damages, hence B's argument was entirely artificial. As a matter of principle, and to avoid overcompensation in respect of the same illness, the entire statutory award was deductible from B's damages, as general damages were in no different category from special damages, *Hodgson* applied.

BALLANTINE v. NEWALLS INSULATION CO LTD [2001] I.C.R. 25, Aldous, L.J., CA.

1472. Measure of damages – injury following road accident – pecuniary loss

[Civil Procedure Rules 1998 (SI 1998 3132) Part 1 r.1 (2).]

C was involved in three road accidents within a period of 33 months in which she sustained repeated whiplash injuries. She also suffered from soft tissue injury to her cervical spine causing continuing pain in the area of her neck, shoulder and thoracic spine which limited her movement. Liability was admitted by the three defendants involved in the accidents. C maintained during the trial that she continued to suffer residual pain with medical evidence also summarising her condition as falling between that of minor nuisance symptoms and the category of intrusive, intermittent symptoms with loss of work. Prognosis at the trial showed improvement in her condition and that C was likely to be stable with no likelihood of her condition further deteriorating. In awarding damages, the judge took into consideration the total loss suffered by C and apportioned the award between the defendants.

Held, giving judgment for C, that as the prognosis was that C's condition was unlikely to deteriorate further but was likely to continue to suffer chronic pain and experience the attendant difficulties, a general damages award of £12,000 would be appropriate. However, given the emphasis in the Civil Procedure Rules 1998 Part 1 r.1 (2) of dealing "justly" with cases, the court could take account of the guidance given in Law Com. No.257 Recommendations on *General Damages* in Personal Injury Cases, which recommended that general damages in personal injuries cases be increased by a factor of 1.5. It would not be in accordance with the CPR to await a Court of Appeal ruling before implementing the Law Commission guidance, and the award would therefore be increased to £18,000, apportioned equally between E and D. It would also be appropriate to make a *Smith v. Manchester* award of £3,000 to reflect potential disadvantage C could suffer in the open labour market.

CUTLER v. EGERTON [2000] P.I.Q.R. Q84, Judge Anthony Thompson, CC (Portsmouth).

1473. Measure of damages – loss of earnings – late amendment increasing value of claim – resulting vacation of trial inappropriate

G was injured in accident caused by B on 30 June 1996. Proceedings were issued in March 1998, limiting the claim to £50,000. In G's statement of October 1999, he confirmed the accuracy of the Schedule setting out a claim for lost earnings of about £40,000. On January 14, 2000 the district judge gave G permission to update the schedule, allowing him until March 2000 to do so. The parties agreed to extend that time to early April. A schedule was produced by G in March reducing the claim for lost earnings to £29,000 and a hearing for assessment of damages was set for May 9, 2000. On April 13, the district judge allowed G's application at a telephone hearing to amend the schedule so as to increase the claim to £135,000, on the basis that recent evidence obtained by G showed the earnings of a roofer, G's pre-accident employment, to be considerably greater than that pleaded. The trial was vacated and listed for December 2000. B appealed.

Held, allowing the appeal, that it was wholly inappropriate to allow the amendment and consequent vacation of the trial. It was far too late to allow all previous calculations of the claim for lost earnings to be abandoned in favour of evidence as to the present level of earnings of roofers from an individual who had only employed G post-accident. The explanation of G's employment expert that he had tried several times to get hold of the witness but failed, was deemed to be unsatisfactory.

GREGORY v. BARTLETT (DECEASED), May 3, 2000, Judge Thompson, CC (Winchester). [*Ex rel.* Robert Weir, Barrister, Devereux Chambers, Devereux Court, London].

1474. Measure of damages – mitigation – specialist machine stolen whilst on hire – claimant not bound to purchase replacement at auction or to take steps beyond its means

FPH hired a highway trenching machine to W. The machine having been stolen whilst in W's possession, FPH issued proceedings against W claiming damages in respect of its loss. Liability was admitted by W, and the court was asked to assess damages. FPH's expert, C, who had offered to sell a similar machine to FPH for £138,000, gave evidence stating that he had been asked by FPH to search for a suitable replacement machine and that he had found such a machine in Germany which would cost £87,000, representing the machine's market value, the cost of putting it into an acceptable condition, his commission and the cost of a warranty. W's expert relied on the auction prices of comparable machines which, he submitted, were in the region of £20,000 to 30,000. The judge awarded FPH damages of £87,000 as compensation for the loss of the machine together with the sum of £15,000, representing the profit which FPH could have expected to have received in hiring the machine had it not been stolen. W appealed, arguing that (1) by not rejecting its expert's valuation in his judgment, the judge should have accepted that valuation thereby preventing FPH from being overcompensated for its loss; (2) the judge had not dealt adequately with FPH's duty to mitigate its loss, and (3) in the absence of evidence that FPH had been impecunious, the judge had erred in concluding that FPH had not acted unreasonably in declining to purchase a replacement machine, and in awarding FPH damages for its lost profits.

Held, dismissing the appeal, that (1) the judge had been correct to proceed by considering the value of the machine to FPH, and accordingly by assessing the cost of replacing the machine. Given the specialist nature of the machine and the limited availability of comparable machines, it would have been reasonable for FPH to have purchased a machine which had the benefit of a warranty and service history as against a machine at an auction with an unknown history. The judge had been entitled to conclude that it would not have been reasonable for FPH to buy the machine for £138,000, and that it had acted reasonably in instructing C to shop around for a replacement. No distinction could effectively be drawn between assessing the reasonable value of the machine and the question of mitigation of loss, and (2) concerning the award for FPH's lost profits, FPH had not acted unreasonably in declining to purchase a replacement machine in the prevailing market. A party in the position of FPH could not be expected to mitigate its loss by taking action beyond its means, *Dodd Properties (Kent) Ltd v. Canterbury City Council* [1980] 1 W.L.R. 433, [1980] C.L.Y. 642 applied.

FERNGOLD PLANT HIRE LTD v. WENHAM (T/A BW CONTRACTORS); *sub nom.* FERNGOLD PLANT HIRE LTD v. BW CONTRACTORS CCRTF 1999/0293/B2, Ward, L.J., CA.

1475. Measure of damages – moderate back injury – amount increased in line with Law Com. No. 257

[Social Security (Recovery of Benefits) Act 1997.]

In a reserved judgment, after argument on the issue, the judge accepted A's submission to act on Law Com. No.257 Recommendations on *General Damages* in Personal Injury Cases by increasing the award in a JSB "moderate back injury" case by a factor of 1.5 from £6,000 up to £9,000. The judge decided that it would be wrong simply to hold that H was a matter for other judges in other courts when the recommendation was addressed to the judiciary at large. There were other issues of controversy between the parties, including what order for costs should be made where the total gross award was less than an effective payment into court, but the net receipt of A after judgment was significantly greater than would have been the effect of accepting the payment into court, because the effect of the judgment limited D's entitlement to withhold sums from damages pursuant to the Social Security (Recovery of Benefits) Act 1997. The parties mutually agreed not to pursue any points on appeal, as a result of which all other consequential orders were agreed.

ADAMS v. DORSET AMBULANCE NHS TRUST, November 11, 1999, Judge Thompson Q.C., CC (Southampton). [*Ex rel.* Allan Gore, Barrister, 12 King's Bench Walk, Temple, London].

1476. Measure of damages – personal injuries – assessment of future loss of earnings – inadequacy of judicial reasoning

S, who had suffered a whiplash injury to his neck in a road traffic accident for which J had admitted liability, appealed against an order for damages for personal injuries. At the trial as to damages, before a district judge by consent of the parties, considerable conflicting medical and accountancy evidence was adduced. The judge made an order in S's favour for damages and interest in excess of £43,000 which included an award of £15,000 for pain, suffering and loss of amenity, but he rejected S's claim for future loss of earnings arising from his inability to continue his mobile catering and delivery trade. S appealed, contending that the judge had failed to make coherent findings in relation to both the extent of his injuries and the reasons for the rejection of the claim for future loss of profits from his business and that a refusal to make such an award was inconsistent with an award of £15,000 by way of general damages.

Held, allowing the appeal, that in a High Court action where there were disputed and complex issues to be resolved, trial by a district judge of the assessment of damages was inappropriate and the matter would be remitted for retrial before a circuit judge on the issue of loss of earnings only. The trial judge in the instant case had failed to give adequate reasons for his decision, *Flannery v. Halifax Estate Agencies Ltd (t/a Colleys Professional Services)* [2000] 1 W.L.R. 377, [1999] C.L.Y. 37 applied.

SANDRY v. JONES *The Times,* August 3, 2000, Swinton Thomas, L.J., CA.

1477. Measure of damages – personal injuries – judge entitled to conclude that injuries would cause successful accountant to retire early

A, who had admitted liability for a road traffic accident in which S, a highly successful accountant, had suffered multiple injuries, appealed against the judge's assessment of S's lost future earnings resulting from his probable early retirement. S, who had become a partner at 31 and commanded an annual salary of £425,250, had argued that, due to the consequences of the accident, there was an increased likelihood of his retiring earlier than he otherwise would have done. He complained of increased fatigue and pain resulting from his day to day work activities. Having concluded that S's salary would continue to increase at the rate of six per cent annually until he reached 50 and that it would remain stable thereafter, the judge found that it was probable that S would be forced to retire earlier than anticipated, but discounted the award by 30 per cent to reflect the element of uncertainty. She accordingly awarded S £925,512.70. A contended that (1) the judge had overestimated the probability that S's injuries would result in retirement earlier than envisaged. A submitted that there had been a likelihood of S seeking to retire early before the accident, given that he would be in a position of financial comfort prior to retirement age and that it was common practice for partners in his firm to retire early, and (2) the judge had not been justified in concluding that S's salary would increase at the rate of six per cent each year.

Held, dismissing the appeal, that (1) the judge had been entitled to conclude that there was a significant probability that S would have to retire early. The nature of the injuries sustained and their consequences on S in the form of day to day pain, fatigue and anxiety resulting from short term memory loss all indicated an increased probability of early retirement from what was a highly responsible and stressful job. While the award had been generous, the judge had applied a 30 per cent discount which adequately reflected the inherent level of uncertainty, and (2) there were no grounds for assuming that a salary increase of six per cent each year would not be sustained. That increase had been based on the assumption that S's firm's profits would remain constant. It was observed that S had had a recent increase of 12 per cent in his salary.

SMEE v. ADYE QBENF 1999/0781/A2, Stuart-Smith, L.J., CA.

1478. **Measure of damages – personal injuries – revised levels of award for pain, suffering and loss of amenity – retention of conventional principles of general damages assessment**

Law Commission recommendations contained in Law Com. No.257 Recommendations on General Damages in Personal Injury Cases for an increase in the level of damages to be awarded for non pecuniary loss were submitted to the court for final consideration. It was argued that the conventional approach for the assessment of damages was producing awards that were far too low in modern society, and that the courts should produce guidelines to facilitate awards of compensation that were consistently fair, just and reasonable, having regard to the current value of money. The contrary submissions were that current guidelines and the use of the RPI already ensured fair awards and any change should be legislative in nature. A group of cases was identified in relation to which the court could express its views on the Commission's proposals.

Held, granting a general declaration and giving individual judgments on the respective cases, that (1) it was the established role of the judiciary to review levels of award for pain, suffering and loss of amenity, and whilst Parliament could intervene, it had shown no inclination to do so; (2) the court would retain conventional principles for the assessment of general damages, but a modest increase was required to some awards to ensure a fair, just and reasonable sum. Balancing the importance of consistency against the dangers of rigidity, the updated level must not be unjust to the defendant and must be consistent with public perceptions of reasonableness; (3) after considering all relevant factors, including levels of award in other Member States, increased life expectancy, the evolution of medical science, NHS resources, increased earnings, inflation and the manner of pleading special damages, it was the awards for catastrophic injuries which were in most need of increase and, at the highest level, that increase should be approximately one third. Awards presently below £10,000 were to remain untouched and awards between the higher and lower brackets would be subject to a downward taper. It was expected that the Judicial Studies Board Guidelines would be revised in light of this decision, but the present edition would remain valid in the interim. Although GDP had been taken into account in determining the level of awards in the instant cases, the RPI would continue to provide a less complex means of measuring monetary value and this should be used to update appropriate future cases.

HEIL v. RANKIN; REES v. MABCO (102) LTD; SCHOFIELD v. SAUNDERS & TAYLOR LTD; RAMSAY v. RIVERS; KENT v. GRIFFITHS; W (A CHILD) v. NORTHERN GENERAL HOSPITAL NHS TRUST; ANNABLE v. SOUTHERN DERBYSHIRE HA; CONNOLLY v. TASKER [2001] Q.B. 272, Lord Woolf, M.R., CA.

1479. Measure of damages – personal injuries – severe brain damage – cost of long term care in specialist unit

[Civil Procedure Rules 1998 (SI 1998 3132) Part 35 r.35.7.]

J, who had suffered severe head injuries in a road traffic accident, sought damages for past and future care. J submitted that he would continue to need the level of care which he had been receiving at a specialist transitional rehabilitation unit for the rest of his life, costing £890.40 per week. G disputed the costs, seeking to admit further evidence of a care expert on the basis that (1) the amount included in the fees for accommodation and ordinary living expenses should be deducted from future costs; (2) the notional wage earned by J in the workshop constituted earnings and should thus be deducted from the overall cost of care, and (3) the rate of return, with regard to the mulitiplier, should be different from that established in *Wells v. Wells* [1999] 1 A.C. 345, [1998] C.L.Y. 1446.

Held, giving judgment for J, that (1) "ordinary living expenses" should be deducted from the cost of care *Lim Poh Choo v. Camden and Islington AHA* [1980] A.C. 174, [1976] C.L.Y. 663 applied; (2) as J should not be in a worse position than he would have been if the accident had not occurred, the logical result was to deduct the total future loss of notional wage from the total future cost of care, thus calculating the cost of future care at £800 per week, and (3) in the absence of any evidence supporting G's submission, the appropriate rate of return was 3 per cent, *Wells* applied. It was held on a preliminary issue that, although a single jointly instructed expert was preferable as specified in the Civil Procedure Rules 1998 Part 35 r.35.7, the evidence of G's care expert was not sufficiently prejudicial to J to be excluded.

J v. GROCOTT [2001] C.P. Rep. 15, Hale, J., QBD.

1480. Measure of damages – professional negligence – solicitors – quantification of loss of chance action – discounted damages – interest rates – calculation of costs

H sued B, their former solicitors, for damages of £1,000,000 for loss of the chance to sue T, on the basis that B had negligently failed to serve H's claim against T within the limitation period. Negligence was admitted, and at trial, damages of £95,000 plus interest were awarded ([2000] Lloyd's Rep. P.N. 89, [1999] C.L.Y. 1421), H's estimated loss had been assessed by the court at £190,000, but discounted by 35 per cent to reflect the uncertainty of H proving negligence against T, the reduced amount then suffering a further 20 per cent reduction for the uncertainty of establishing causation. Issues arose after the handing down of the judgment, namely (1) B contended that the judge had erred in his method of applying the discounts, and that the damages should have been discounted by a total of 55 per cent, with T's potential cross claim of £15,000 deducted in its entirety from the damages before discount, as there was no uncertainty about its recovery, (2) at what rate interest should be awarded, and (3) the appropriate order to be made as to costs in the light of the discrepancy between the amount of H's claim, and the ultimate award.

Held, granting declaratory relief, that (1) the discounts had been applied correctly, as they were independent of each other, and the 20 per cent reduction had to be applied to the 65 per cent chance of establishing negligence. T's potential cross claim should however have been deducted before discount; (2) interest would be awarded at the short term investment rate which reflected changes in monetary value and interest rates more realistically than the judgment debt interest rate, which tended to be too high, and was inappropriate to the instant case, as there was no reason to penalise B, dictum of Bingham LJ in

Watts v. Morrow [1991] 1 W.L.R. 1421, [1992] C.L.Y. 1548 applied; (3) H were allowed their costs, save for those incurred in pursuing the unsuccessful heads of claim. On the facts of the case, H's claim was not exaggerated and the unrecovered items had not made a material difference to the time or disbursements incurred. Although the costs claimed by H of £366,000 appeared high in relation to the amount recovered, the issues involved had been difficult, and the financial value of the claim was not therefore a reliable guide on the question of proportionality.

HARRISON v. BLOOM CAMILLIN (COSTS) [2000] Lloyd's Rep. P.N. 404, Neuberger, J., Ch D.

1481. Measure of damages – professional negligence – surveyors – negligent overvaluation of system built property

FP, a firm of surveyors, was retained by A, a mortgagee, to carry out a valuation report on a maisonette in 1988. The report stated that the property consisted of a concrete panel and timber clad structure constructed using the Jesperson 12M system, and was valued by FP at £42,000. Subsequently, structural defects were discovered and the property was initially let by I before being repossessed and sold by A for £6,000. At first instance, FP was held to have been negligent on the basis of expert evidence as to the state of knowledge of this type of structure in 1988. The actual valuation was accepted as £14,000. FP appealed against liability and quantum of £67,859.77, inclusive of interest and costs, allowed under four heads: (a) the difference between the mortgage valuation of £42,000 and the expert's figure of £14,000; (b) a sum allowed for heating appliances; (c) actual mortgage payments, less rent receipts from the date I moved out until repossession, and (d) a second bank loan taken out by I.

Held, dismissing the appeal against liability but allowing that against quantum (Brooke L.J. dissenting on quantum), that no award should have been made under (c) as this represented a loss that had already been compensated under (a) and also because the damages should not have been increased on the basis that the property had been let rather than sold when I first vacated. The figure allowed under (d) would also be deleted, as no damages should have been awarded under that head. Quantum, therefore, was reduced to £28,250 with interest to be recalculated accordingly.

IZZARD v. FIELD PALMER [2000] 1 E.G.L.R. 177, Kennedy, L.J., CA.

1482. Measure of damages – psychiatric harm – future loss of earnings – hypothetical subsequent tort

H, who had been a police officer since 1975, suffered from post traumatic stress disorder as a result of a serious shooting incident that occurred while he was on duty in 1987. In 1993, he was the victim of a road traffic accident caused by R, a drunken driver. Although the physical injuries sustained by H were minor, the accident exacerbated H's psychiatric condition and subsequently led to his permanent discharge from the police force in 1994 on the grounds of ill health. H claimed damages for personal injury against R, liability was admitted, and an award of £32,837 was made by the judge to include H's future loss of earnings. H appealed that award. H submitted that, while his psychiatric condition originated from the shooting incident, the more serious recurrence that led to his early retirement from the police force had been triggered by the commission of R's tort. H thus contended that the judge had erred in taking into account a hypothetical future tort which may have shortened H's career when assessing the damages to be awarded against tortfeasor R, *Baker v. Willoughby* [1970] A.C. 467, [1970] C.L.Y. 1862 cited, *Jobling v. Associated Dairies* [1982] A.C. 794, [1981] C.L.Y. 835 cited.

Held, allowing the appeal, that there was no general rule that subsequent tortious acts should be ignored when assessing damages for personal injury even if they were a foreseeable or likely cause of early termination of employment. However, in H's case the judge had discounted the chances of him working to retirement too heavily and had used a multiplier that was too low.

HEIL v. RANKIN (APPEAL AGAINST DAMAGES) [2001] P.I.Q.R. Q3, Otton, L.J., CA.

1483. Measure of damages – real propoerty – date of loss – solicitors' failure to obtain coal mining report

H, a company which acquired and ran private nursing homes, made a claim in negligence against its solicitors, G, who had been retained in connection with the purchase of a derelict property in 1987 and who had omitted to obtain a coal mining report. H had renovated the property, following which subsidence had occurred as a result of coal mining, causing H to suffer various losses. H had been aware of minor cracking in some of the walls in February 1990, but had not discovered the cause of the cracking until August 1990 when the structure of the building had further deteriorated. A writ had been issued on February 8, 1996, and it fell for preliminary determination whether the claim was statute barred. H contended that but for G's negligence it would not have purchased the property and incurred the refurbishment costs, but that nevertheless loss had only been suffered when the cracks became significant enough to warrant investigation and repair. G submitted that the date of loss had to be backdated to a time earlier than February 1990, because although the first signs of damage had appeared in that month and were not then considered to be a significant problem, the subsequent discovery of the mining activities indicated that considerable physical damage must have occurred before February 1990. G further maintained that, as the property had not depreciated in value below the price for which H had purchased it and as diminution in value was the primary measure of loss, H was not entitled to recover damages for renovation costs and loss of profit.

Held, determining the preliminary issue in favour of H, that (1) the question of when loss was suffered was to be carefully considered, since loss was not necessarily contemporaneous with expenditure, especially where future contingencies were involved. It was the cracking and consequential loss to business which gave rise to the wasted expenditure and loss of profit for which H claimed; accordingly, no loss had been suffered outside the six year period from the date on which the proceedings had been issued, and (2) a nil diminution in value did not automatically mean that other measures of damages were not recoverable, and there was to be some flexibility at least in claims against solicitors, *County Personnel (Employment Agency) Ltd v. Alan R Pulver & Co* [1987] 1 W.L.R. 916, [1987] C.L.Y. 3551 applied. It was for the trial judge to select an approach which would result in realistic compensation for H. A fair formula might be to adopt a measure of damages based on expenditure incurred minus the net profit earned and the value of the property as refurbished, *Oates v. Anthony Pittman & Co* [1998] P.N.L.R. 683, [1998] C.L.Y. 4008 and *Reeves v. Thrings & Long* [1996] P.N.L.R. 265, [1996] C.L.Y. 4501 considered.

HAVENLEDGE LTD v. GRAEME JOHN & PARTNERS [2000] Lloyd's Rep. P.N. 614, Richards, J., QBD.

1484. Motor vehicles – claim for diminution in value of vehicle following repairs – no evidence as to standard of repair

S and L were involved in a road traffic accident and judgment was entered in default of filing a defence, although liability was admitted. S brought a claim for, among other things, diminution in the value of his vehicle. S contended that his vehicle was valued at the time of the accident at £6,500 and, in reliance on an engineer's report, that its value had diminished by five per cent, by virtue of it being a repaired vehicle, *Payton v. Brooks* [1974] 1 Lloyd's Rep. 241, [1974] C.L.Y. 841 and *Warwick Motor Auctions v. Bennett* (Unreported, October 14, 1996), [1997] C.L.Y. 1815 cited. L contended that (1) there was no evidence that S's engineer had inspected the vehicle either before or after repairs, nor that the repairs were not carried out to a satisfactory standard of a competent and/or approved repairer; (2) there was no evidence to suggest that S was not satisfied with the standard of repairs, and (3) any repairs carried out by an approved repairer would carry a 12 month guarantee and any defects would be covered by this warranty.

Held, dismissing the claim, that there was no evidence that S's engineer had inspected the vehicle, nor that repairs had not been carried out to a satisfactory standard. S was ordered to pay L's costs of the hearing.

SMITH v. LOUGHLIN, January 6, 2000, District Judge R Weston, CC (Kingston upon Hull). [*Ex rel.* Ford & Warren Solicitors, Westgate Point, Westgate, Leeds].

1485. Noise – air routes – damages sought from surveyor failing to investigate possibility of aircraft noise – noise did not amount to physical discomfort – requirement to consider contract as a whole to determine whether its purpose had been to provide pleasure

F, who intended to purchase a property located in the vicinity of a major airport, instructed S, a surveyor, to inspect and prepare a report on the property. S was asked, inter alia, to investigate whether the property might be affected by aircraft noise. Having bought the property, F complained that his enjoyment of it had been significantly affected by aircraft noise. He issued proceedings alleging negligence on the part of S. The judge found that S had been negligent and awarded F damages of £10,000 for distress and inconvenience. Whilst he did not challenge the judge's finding of negligence, S appealed against the award of damages.

Held, allowing the appeal (Clarke, L.J. dissenting), that F had not been entitled to damages for distress and inconvenience since (1) the evidence revealed that he had not suffered physical discomfort and inconvenience. Whilst persistent high levels of noise could cause physical discomfort, F had by no means been subject to noise of such a degree, and (2) S had not been retained under a contract to provide pleasure, relaxation or peace of mind and therefore did not fall within the exceptional category of cases referred to in *Watts v. Morrow* [1991] 1 W.L.R. 1421, [1992] C.L.Y. 1548 where damages for non physical distress and annoyance could be recovered. It being necessary to consider the contract as a whole, the contract in the instant case had been an ordinary surveyor's contract.

FARLEY v. SKINNER (NO.2) 73 Con. L.R. 70, Stuart-Smith, L.J., CA.

1486. Pecuniary loss – injury following accident at work – demotion – reduction in earnings recoverable from employer

C, an employee, was injured following an accident at work. A disciplinary hearing was held in consequence of the accident as a result of which C was demoted, suffering a £5,000 loss in income. Proceedings were brought by C against M, the parties apportioning liability 85 per cent to M and 15 per cent to C by consent. At the subsequent assessment of damages hearing C was awarded a sum representing his lost income having regard to his agreed 15 per cent liability. M appealed, contending that C's loss of income was a result of the demotion rather than the accident itself.

Held, dismissing the appeal, that where a number of factors led to a situation where a person had suffered a loss, it might be necessary to decide what was the predominant cause of that loss. In usual circumstances, where a claimant's conduct which had led to an accident was objectively reviewed and as a result he was demoted and suffered a loss of income, it was likely that the relevant cause of that loss would be his conduct alone even where the employer's breach of duty had been a factor contributory to the accident. That was still the case even though a possibility existed that as a result employers might discipline employees more frequently following accidents. It was to be hoped that when they did discipline, they would do so objectively, disregarding any potential claim that been made against them by the employee. In the instant case, the disciplinary hearing against C was inconsistent with the subsequent finding of M's high level of responsibility. Had that been accepted at the time, the disciplinary hearing and subsequent loss of pay would not have taken place. The relevant cause of C's loss of income was not, therefore, his conduct but rather the accident itself, which had been predominantly M's fault. The additional disadvantage in terms of loss of pay flowed from the accident and should therefore form part of the sums recoverable for M's breach of duty, *Stapley v. Gypsum Mines Ltd* [1953] A.C. 663, [1953] C.L.Y. 2287 and *South Australia Asset Management Corp v. York Montague Ltd* [1997] A.C. 191, [1996] C.L.Y. 4519 applied.

CASEY v. MORANE LTD [2001] I.C.R. 316, Henry, L.J., CA.

1487. Personal injuries – attempt to mislead court – entitlement to general damages

See CIVIL PROCEDURE: Desai v. Patel. §426

1488. Personal injuries – ex gratia payments – retirement of employee on medical grounds – ex gratia payment followed by award of damages – disregard of benevolent payments – double recovery

W, who was employed by BOC and who had been off sick following aggravation of a pre-existing back condition, was dismissed on grounds of ill health and given an ex gratia payment calculated by reference to his length of service and earnings. The payment was described as "an advance against damages that may be awarded", even though there was no claim pending. W subsequently brought a personal injury action against BOC, which was successful and BOC was ordered to pay the agreed damages despite the fact that the payment already made far exceeded its liability to W. BOC appealed and it was debated whether the payment was a "benevolent gift" within the dicta of *Parry v. Cleaver* [1970] A.C. 1, [1969] C.L.Y. 906 and subsequent case law, or whether it was a genuine intention to benefit W.

Held, allowing the appeal, that as a matter of public policy, employers ought to be encouraged to make ex gratia payments without the gesture being interpreted as encouragement to the employee to sue them for an additional sum. The judge of first instance had placed too much weight on the disregard of acts of benevolence by the tortfeasor despite recent case law which had reaffirmed principles militating against double recovery, *McCamley v. Cammell Laird Shipbuilders Ltd* [1990] 1 W.L.R. 963, [1990] C.L.Y. 1718 distinguished and *Hunt v. Severs* [1994] 2 A.C. 350, [1994] C.L.Y. 1530 applied. Allowance was prima facie to be made for benevolent gifts made by a tortfeasor against any compensation that it was subsequently ordered to pay.

WILLIAMS v. BOC GASES LTD [2000] I.C.R. 1181, Brooke, L.J., CA.

1489. Personal injuries – interest rates – proposed alteration of rate of interest payable on general damages

[Damages Act 1996 s.1.]

L appealed in a personal injury case against a decision whereby interest on general damages was assessed at the usual rate of two per cent per annum. It was argued that the guideline rate should be increased to three per cent in accordance with the decision in *Wells v. Wells* [1999] 1 A.C. 345, [1998] C.L.Y. 1446 which set the discount rate to be used in calculating damages for future losses and expenses at such a rate. Alternatively, it was contended that, once the Lord Chancellor had prescribed a rate under the Damages Act 1996 s.1, that rate should serve as the guideline rate for interest on general damages.

Held, dismissing the appeal, that it would not be appropriate to increase the guideline rate. Interest on general damages and the rate of return used to calculate future losses served different purposes; whereas the former was intended to provide compensation for the delay in payment of a sum that was notionally payable at an earlier date, the latter was a component of an actuarial calculation of future loss. As general damages were awarded on amounts that were conventional, and as an award of interest was discretionary, a rigid mathematical approach to the calculation of interest was inappropriate. The guideline rate of interest should be certain so as to facilitate settlements and minimise costs. It should be altered only if a strong economic case for change was established, *Birkett v. Hayes* [1982] 1 W.L.R. 816, [1982] C.L.Y. 791 and *Wright v. British Railways Board* [1983] 2 A.C. 773, [1983] C.L.Y. 1063 applied. Furthermore, there was no basis for establishing a guideline whereby the rate of interest on general damages should be the rate prescribed from time to time by the Lord Chancellor under s.1 of the 1996 Act.

L (A PATIENT) v. CHIEF CONSTABLE OF STAFFORDSHIRE [2000] P.I.Q.R. Q349, May, L.J., CA.

1490. Personal injuries – multipliers – amendment to rate of discount for future loss of earnings

[Damages Act 1996 s.1 (1).]

B brought a claim against AC, in respect of serious injuries suffered during the course of his employment with AC. Following a significant award of damages to B, the issue arose as to the appropriate discount rate upon which to base the multiplier for future loss of earnings. The current guideline rate of three per cent was laid down in *Wells v. Wells* [1999] 1 A.C. 345, [1998] C.L.Y. 1446 pending the making of an order by the Lord Chancellor under the Damages Act 1996 s.1 (1) and it was established in that case, that multipliers should be based upon the yield from index linked government securities. The case also indicated the possibility of the courts effecting future variations of the rate, in the event of a "marked change in economic circumstances"

Held, giving judgment for B, that having regard to the principles relied upon by the House of Lords in their determination of the rate in *Wells* and in the light of the lower rate of interest from index linked government securities and the absence of a new statutory discount rate from the Lord Chancellor, a reduction in the discount rate to two per cent was appropriate, *Wells* followed.

BARRY v. ABLEREX CONSTRUCTION (MIDLANDS) LTD [2000] P.I.Q.R. Q263, Latham, J., QBD.

1491. Real property – diminution in value – solicitor failing to request copy of established use certificate revealed in local search – quasi industrial use affecting value of residential property

DLA, a firm of solicitors acting for M and D in the purchase of a property, admitted liability for failing to request a copy of an established use certificate, as revealed in the local search, and for failing to notify M and D of its existence. The property was a converted barn that had previously belonged to the adjacent farm, and both properties were covered by the certificate. The certificate permitted the owner of the farm to store road planings immediately to the rear of M and D's property. The planings only began to appear once M and D had exchanged contracts for the property, and finally reached a height of 40 to 50 feet after they had moved in. Bulldozers were used to grade the mounds, floodlights were used to enable work to continue after dark, and a portacabin was placed overlooking M and D's garden. The property had been bought for £168,000 in 1996 and subsequently sold in 1999 for £190,000. M and D claimed the diminution of the value at the date of completion in 1996, the costs involved in moving and damages for inconvenience and distress.

Held, on assessment of damages, that (1) M and D would not have bought the property had they been aware of the existence of the certificate; (2) although some stigma attached to the property by reason of its position next to the farm, the certificate permitted activities that exceeded purely agricultural use and were quasi industrial in nature. The diminution in value was therefore greater, and was awarded at 10 per cent of the property's value at the date of purchase in 1996; (3) all the costs involved in moving were recoverable, and (4) an award of £800 in total was made for inconvenience and distress.

MYATT v. DIBB LUPTON ALSOP, October 4, 1999, District Judge Greenwood, QBD. [*Ex rel.* Kate Bentley, Pupil Barrister, 2 Crown Office Row, Second Floor, Temple, London].

1492. Structured settlements – discount rate in damages calculations not open to judicial alteration

[Damages Act 1996 s.1 (1).]

W, a child disabled with cerebral palsy as a result of medical negligence, appealed against a decision rejecting his request for a reduction in the discount rate of three per cent employed in calculating his pecuniary loss. W was awarded £3.1 million including £135,000 for pain and suffering, subsequently increased to £175,000 (*The Times*, March 24, 2000) and argued that a drop in the gross return for index linked government securities was precisely the type of change in economic circumstances contemplated by the House of Lords in its judgment in *Wells v. Wells* [1999] 1 A.C. 345, [1998] C.L.Y. 1446 that would justify a rate change. Furthermore, W contended that the impact of taxation fell unfairly on larger awards, which should be compensated for either by an increase in the multiplier or by a decrease in the discount rate.

Held, dismissing the appeal, that the judgment in *Wells* clearly allowed no change prior to the announcement of a new rate by the Lord Chancellor under the Damages Act 1996 s.1 (1), *Barry v. Ablerex Construction (Midlands) Ltd The Times*, March 30, 2000, [2000] C.L.Y. 1490 disapproved, and that, in any event, the drop in the return rate of about 0.5 per cent was not a sufficient change of overall economic circumstances to trigger a rate change, especially where it was known that the Court of Protection as a prudent investor would obtain a higher return than that obtainable from index linked government securities. Although claimants who received larger awards were relatively worse off because of taxation, except in exceptional cases, prudent investment in equities and gilts over a long period would rectify the disparity.

W (A CHILD) v. NORTHERN GENERAL HOSPITAL NHS TRUST (STRUCTURED SETTLEMENTS) [2000] 1 W.L.R. 1404, Stuart-Smith, L.J., CA.

1493. Trespass to goods – shoplifting – repeat offences – supermarket awarded damages for apprehending and arranging for prosecution

[Civil Procedure Rules 1998 (SI 1998 3132) Part 27.]

C was convicted of two separate incidents of shoplifting from AS's supermarket. On the first occasion C stole goods valued at £116.89 and on the second, goods worth £22.42. On each occasion, the goods were recovered undamaged. AS sought damages at large, for trespass to goods, based upon the financial loss incurred in detecting and apprehending C, and arranging for her prosecution. Exemplary damages were also sought.

Held, that although AS could not produce evidence of financial loss directly linked to C's actions, it must have caused a great deal of aggravation in dealing with C, which was beyond measure. It was therefore appropriate to take an intuitive approach to assessing AS's loss. A damages award of £70 was made, taking into account the value of the goods involved. It might not have been appropriate to make an award of damages for a single incident of shoplifting. However, where special circumstances existed, such as repeat offending, it was important to make it clear that people could not get away with such behaviour. In the circumstances, it would be wrong to make any award of punitive damages, given that C had been dealt with on each occasion by the criminal courts. Interest and costs were awarded to AS in accordance with the Civil Procedure Rules 1998 Part 27.

ASDA STORES LTD v. CROKE, December 20, 1999, District Judge Merrick, CC (Brighton). [*Ex rel.* Sally Ann Smith, Barrister, Crown Office Row Chambers, Blenheim House, 120 Church Street, Brighton].

Personal Injuries or Death – Quantum

Details have been received of the following cases in which damages for personal injuries or death were awarded. The classification and sequence of the classified awards follows that adopted in Kemp and Kemp. *The Quantum of Damages*, Vol.2.

Unless there is some statement to the contrary, the age of the applicant is his age at the time of the court hearing. Unless specified the damages are stated on the basis of full liability, *ie.* ignoring any deduction made for contributory negligence. The sum is the total amount of the damages awarded unless otherwise stated. For a cumulative guide to *quantum* of damages cases reported in Current Law during 1998, see the *Quantum* of Damages table. We must stress that we are entirely dependent on the contributor of an unreported case for the accuracy of his or her report; it is impracticable for us independently to check the facts stated to us. We welcome contributions and are most grateful for all the reports received. We would appreciate reports of any alterations to awards noted here, either in, or in anticipation of, appeal.

Paraplegia

1494.   T, male, aged 23 at the date of the accident and 32 at trial, was injured whilst engaged in a trampolining event in August 1991. T had a learning disability and a mental age of 12. His spinal column was severed at C4/5 which resulted in him being confined to a wheelchair. T required extensive care which was expected to be provided by his parents. T had received post nursing care and care from the local social services department. T was successful in a trial on liability and thereafter a bungalow was purchased and adapted so as to be suitable for T's needs. In respect of future loss, the judge, having heard conflicting evidence as to longevity, found a life expectancy of 28 years from the date of the accident. Awards for future loss were also made in respect of aids and equipment, accommodation, transport, medical therapy and Court of Protection expenses. *General Damages*: £135,000. Award for part care by family: £132,372. Award for part care provided by local authority: £85,727. Award for past nursing care: £169,531. Award for future care £817,843 (based on multiplicand of £: 52,101 and multiplier of 15.1, but with an additional £10,396 for the last three years to take account of extra assistance his mother would need by reason of her age). Award for conversion of property: £59,607. Total award: £1,882,890.

THORNTON v. KINGSTON UPON HULL CITY COUNCIL [2000] 5 Q.R. 7, Judge Bennett, QBD.

Multiple injuries

1495.   J, male, aged 32 at the date of the injury and 37 at the hearing, a serving police officer, suffered an attempt on his life by two assailants who cut his throat, slashed his face and arms, smashed his skull with a hammer and attempted to sever his left wrist. J gripped the knives with his hands in self defence and as a result suffered severe injuries to the tendons and nerves in the palms of both hands. Before the assault he was fit and healthy with good promotion prospects and was "ideally suited to the police force". After the assault, J was in hospital for 11 days undergoing multiple operations on his fractured skull, plastic surgery on his neck and face and severed tendons in his hands. He was then cared for by his parents and girlfriend. He underwent three further operations on his hands. He was a determined and good patient and he returned to light work within 11 months. He was then transferred to non-operational training duties, a job which he could hold for a maximum period of 10 years at which time he would be forced to leave the force due to a career management policy of the Metropolitan police which would require him to return to operational duties at that time. J had various permanent injuries and disabilities, namely (1) the fracture of the skull had left a dent and hypersensitivity to cold; (2) a large visible scar across the neck with a dent and flap and multiple less visible scars on the face; (3) loss of parts of both ears; (4) reduced concentration and short term memory, loss of confidence and regular headaches three times per week; (5) post traumatic stress disorder which was severe in nature for one year and continuing emotional lability; (6) a damaged median nerve in the left shoulder; (7) a large ugly scar on the left forearm; (8) visible hypertrophic scarring of the left hand with clawing of the tips of all fingers necessitating the use of an arm brace three times each week with cold intolerance, and (9) clawed index finger and visible scarring to the right hand. The award was made in the light of decision in *Heil v. Rankin* [2000] 2 W.L.R. 1173, [2000] 4 C.L.144. *General Damages*: £50,000. Past care award: £5,000. Future loss of earnings award: £137,088. *Smith v. Manchester* award: £10,000. Future pension loss award: £62,031. Total Award: £286,419.

JONES (CICA: QUANTUM: 2000: MULTIPLE INJURIES), *Re* [2000] 6 Q.R. 5, Judge Eric Stockdale (Chairman), CICA (London).

Multiple injuries

1496. L, male, aged 61 at the date of the assault and 67 at the date of the appeal hearing, sustained injuries when, whilst employed as a gate keeper in a dock area, he attempted to stop the escape of thieves from his employer's premises by shutting the dock gates. The thieves drove their transit van at him and went through the dock gates. L suffered a fracture dislocation of the right elbow together with a dislocation of the radius at the elbow and a fracture of the ulna. An operation was needed to relocate the dislocation, reduce the fracture and insert a plate. L was left with diminished range of movement in the arm, elbow and wrist. L also sustained a displaced fracture of the mandible in two places with injuries to the left mental nerve. The fractures of the jaw were held with plates and a bone graft was needed. L underwent further operations to remove the plates. He could not wear dentures for 15 months and was left with persistent discomfort to the left side of his jaw. He had difficulty eating and the pain caused sleep disturbance. The symptoms were permanent. L was also left with a laceration of the left ear and facial lacerations and still had continuing tenderness to touch in cold weather. He was left with a minor head injury causing poor short term memory and concentration but there was a good prognosis in that respect. *General Damages*: £22,500. Past loss of earnings award: £10,855. Past care award: £18,028. Award for past gardening expenses and car and boat maintenance: £3,712. Future care award: £34,150. Award for future gardening expenses and car and boat maintenance: £3,650. Total award (after deduction on account of benefits): £88,952.

L (CICB: QUANTUM: 2000), *Re*, January 27, 2000, Gee (Chairman), CICB. [*Ex rel.* Hough Halton & Soal, Solicitors, 32 Abbey Street, Carlisle].

Multiple injuries

1497. A, male, aged 21 at the date of the accident and 24 at trial, was knocked off his motorcycle when a car pulled out in front of him. He suffered initial impairment of vision with developing stiffness and pain in his neck and shoulder. He wore a collar intermittently for six months. He suffered swelling of the right knee, requiring fluid to be aspirated on four occasions. His knee ached and was initially painful on movement. His left arm was painful and in a sling for four weeks. There were no bones broken in either arm or leg. Analgesics were prescribed and a course of physiotherapy undertaken. A was off work for three weeks and returned to work on crutches, which were used for a short period. He was initially restricted in walking distance and his return to gym training was delayed. A's minor shoulder and leg injuries resolved over a short period. The residual neck symptoms were an intermittent nuisance, but by the date of trial had largely resolved and it was anticipated that they would completely resolve within a further six months. A's knee symptoms were less frequent by the date of trial and recovery was anticipated within a further six months. *General Damages*: £8,500.

ATA v. HELLENN; *sub nom.* ATA v. HELLEN [2000] 4 Q.R. 3, Judge Collins, CC (Wandsworth).

Multiple injuries – psychiatric damage

1498. S, male, aged 18 at the date of the road traffic accident and 24 at trial, was involved in a collision in which his girlfriend was killed and S was seriously injured. S suffered multiple frontal lobe contusions and acute brain swelling from a severe head injury, a fractured jaw, a closed fracture of the distal shaft of the left humerus, a closed fracture of the base of the first metacarpal of the left hand, a laceration below his left kneecap and fractures to his left foot. He also suffered a collapsed lung and pneumonia while in hospital. The fracture to his humerus was eventually treated by open reduction and internal fixation. The fracture to the jaw was treated conservatively because of his grave ill health. The fracture united in a slightly abnormal position as a result. At the time of the accident, S was an apprentice maintenance fitter, he was due to take final exams in maintenance fitting before applying to join the Royal Navy, which had always been his ambition. He had been a healthy, fit, young man. The accident changed S completely. He was severely depressed, took to heavy drinking and suffered severe mood swings. In the first nine months after the accident he tried to commit suicide three times. He suffered from loss of memory. As a result of the combination of frontal lobe damage and post traumatic stress disorder, his symptoms were unlikely to improve significantly with the further passage of time. S clearly could not enlist in the Royal Navy and damages for future loss of earnings and fringe benefits were calculated on loss of chance, assessed at 75 per cent. S made a good recovery from his orthopaedic injuries, but continued to suffer from some aching in cold weather. S returned to his pre-accident work five months after the accident but he had undergone a considerable personality change and his attendance and attitude were poor and his conduct questionable. He was dismissed soon after for gross misconduct. S then obtained and lost a total of 13 jobs between the date of the accident and trial, all due to violent mood swings. S was incapable of holding any job for any reasonable length of time and would face longer periods of unemployment. *General Damages*: £40,000. Award for loss of congenial employment: £9,375. Future loss of earnings award: £155,000. Future loss of pension award: £17,500.

SMALL v. SOMERVILLE ROBERTS [2000] 5 Q.R. 5, Judge Nicholl, QBD.

Multiple injuries – leg

1499. H, male, aged 12 at the date of the accident and 16 at trial, suffered multiple injuries when struck by a car whilst crossing the road. He sustained an avulsion fracture of the tibia, four chipped front teeth, a suspected undisplaced fracture of the nasal bones and multiple abrasions to the face and both knees. His left leg was in plaster for 6 weeks after the accident. H was off school for three months after the accident. He was unable to resume his sporting activities, which included football, cycling and cricket, for six months after the accident. The most serious injury was that sustained to the tibia from which H made a good recovery over a period of 18 months or so. The only ongoing symptom at the date of trial was some minor residual aching discomfort in the left knee which, according to the medical evidence, might persist indefinitely. After the accident, H developed headaches and dizziness which persisted for nearly three years after the accident. At the date of trial, all four teeth chipped in the accident were firm and alive to vitality tests and it was considered unlikely that they would die as a result of the accident. There was a future possibility that H would need to have the teeth crowned. As a result of the abrasions to the face and knees, H was left with minor scarring to the face, which was not obvious to the casual observer, and scarring to the left knee which made H feel self-conscious when wearing shorts. *General Damages*: £6,500.

H (A CHILD) v. REED, February 16, 2000, Judge HDH Jones, CC (Swansea). [*Ex rel.* David Harris, Barrister, Iscoed Chambers, 86 St. Helens Road, Swansea].

Multiple injuries – foot

1500.   C, female, a hairdresser, aged 17 at the date of the road traffic accident and 22 at trial, sustained multiple injuries, the most serious of which was a closed uncomplicated fracture to the left os calcis. C also sustained a complex fracture to the sacrum and left hemi-pelvis, a closed head injury, with a short period of post traumatic amnesia, multiple cuts and grazes and slight but permanent scarring to her hands and arm. C remained in hospital for two months, for the first six weeks of which she was bedridden. She was able to return to part time work six months post accident, and full time one year thereafter. She was left suffering from ongoing residual symptoms; a painful left foot and heel, the height of which had been reduced; distortion to the subtalar joint, and some back and groin pain. She walked with a slight limp. C had to give up her previous sporting activities. Whilst she had initially suffered from substantial morbid depression with symptoms of post traumatic stress disorder, for which she had received treatment, she had largely recovered from that condition some four years after the accident. There was a 15 per cent risk that she would develop lumbar spinal disease within 15 years, and a 50 per cent chance that within 10 years post accident she would require a subtalar fusion, at which stage she would no longer be able to continue in her chosen profession as a stylist at a hairdressing salon. The general damages award included on uplift of £1,250 pursuant to *Heil v. Rankin* [2000] 2 W.L.R. 1173, [2000] C.L.Y. 1478. *General Damages*: £26,250. *Smith v. Manchester* award: £14,000 (representing one year's net income).
    CHAMBERS v. FLYNN, June 21, 2000, District Judge Wilson, CC (Portsmouth). [*Ex rel.* Paul Hepher, Barrister, 2 Gray's Inn Square Chambers, 2 Gray's Inn, London].

Multiple injuries – foot

1501.   C, female aged 63 years at the date of the accident and 67 at the hearing, suffered multiple injuries in a road traffic accident. Prior to the accident she was a gregarious, fit and active lady, who worked as a barmaid in a hotel, carried out her own gardening and decorating, and enjoyed dancing and badminton. The accident resulted in several injuries, namely (1) a whiplash injury to the neck and lower back, together with fractured ribs on the left side, which produced pain and stiffness and from which C was fully recovered in five to six months; (2) a comminuted fracture of the right heel bone, requiring C to be detained in hospital for four weeks with her leg in plaster, followed by extensive physiotherapy. C was effectively non-weight bearing on a zimmer frame for approximately three months, after which she required crutches for approximately seven months and a walking stick until approximately 18 months after the accident. C had been left with permanent pain on weight-bearing, which restricted her ability to walk to approximately 30 minutes, prevented her from driving, and severely interfered with her household and leisure activities, in consequence of which she was no longer as independent as previously. It was found that this injury had severely debilitated a previously active lady, affecting every aspect of her life; (3) a psychological reaction, diagnosed as post traumatic stress disorder for the first two months, during which time C suffered from anxiety with depressive features, including loss of confidence and anxiety in cars, requiring referral to a psychiatrist approximately two years and six months after the accident and a prescription of anti-depressants. The loss of her ability to pursue her job and her active hobbies had been an important factor in her psychiatric illness, although C had taken up painting and continued to play the piano. The prognosis was for resolution of her psychiatric symptoms within approximately three years 10 months from the date of the accident. In consequence of the neck injury, C developed vomiting and dizziness for approximately six weeks, since which time she had been affected by moderate to severe tinnitus in both ears which kept her awake at night, such that she preferred to fall asleep with the television on in an attempt to mask it. The tinnitus was found to be permanent, and might become worse with ageing, requiring the provision of a tinnitus masker. It was found that this was a disabling factor, quite separate from the disability associated with the heel. In assessing the damages, the judge had regard to the JSB Guidelines and to *King v. Co-Steel Sheerness Plc* (Unreported, July 9, 1998), [1998] C.L.Y. 1686 and *Fuller v. Haymills (Contractors) Ltd* (Unreported, September 26, 1997), [1998] C.L.Y. 1687 considered; with regard to the heel injury, *Dyer v. Commissioner of Police of the Metropolis* (Unreported, October 26, 1998) and *Aylesbury v. Hale* (Unreported, November 9, 1994), [1995] C.L.Y. 1691 considered; with regard to the tinnitus and *Hurst v. Pigott* (Unreported, November 9, 1989), [1989] C.L.Y. 1258 and *Lymer v. Henson* (Unreported, December 16, 1996), [1997] C.L.Y. 1863 considered; with regard to the psychiatric damage. *General Damages*: £25,000 broken down as follows: neck, back and rib £2,000, heel injury £12,000, tinnitus £10,000, psychiatric reaction £3,500; totalling £27,500, and then discounted to reflect some overlap.

PATTERSON v. BUNCLARK, November 26, 1999, District Judge McCullagh, CC (Birkenhead). [*Ex rel.* David Knifton, Barrister, 7 Harrington Street, Liverpool].

Very severe brain damage

1502. L, a boy, born on June 27, 1991 and aged eight at the date of the infant settlement approval hearing, suffered birth asphyxia resulting in cerebral palsy. Liability was conceded by BHA. L was benefiting from a conductive education regime which was put in place some time before the trial, the costs of which were not met by the LEA. At trial, BHA conceded that the conductive education was beneficial but argued that the costs of it should be met by the LEA and that L should be protected by an education indemnity. L refused BHA's standard indemnity. It was agreed that BHA would fund L's day education costs until the age of 19, up to a maximum of £50,000 index linked. Life expectancy was argued by BHA to be 28 and by L to be 60. The settlement which was reached represented a life expectancy in the mid 30s. *General Damages* (approved settlement): £145,000. Award for past costs of education: £37,850. Future care award to age 19: £380,000.

L (A CHILD) v. BERKSHIRE HA [2000] 4 Q.R. 4, Buckley, J., QBD.

Very severe brain damage

1503. S, a boy born on December 10, 1990, and aged eight and a half at the date of trial, sustained irreversible brain damage shortly after birth due to failure by the hospital and midwife to recognise signs of hypoglycaemia, resulting in severe developmental retardation and mild spastic quadriplegic cerebral palsy. S had the mental age of a child aged between 12 and 18 months. He had a limited degree of insight into the nature and extent of his disability. S was doubly incontinent, unable to walk, feed or care for himself and experienced severe difficulties in communication. S suffered from epileptic seizures with daytime fits and tantrums and night time fits. It was found that S's whole life expectancy was 37 years, based upon the preferred evidence of S's consultant paediatrician. By agreement, the multipliers were increased on appeal, taking a three per cent discount rate for accelerated payment, *Wells v. Wells* [1999] 1 A.C. 345, [1998] C.L.Y. 1446 applied. The multiplier fixed for future whole life pecuniary losses was 22 (increased from 16 at first instance based upon actuarial multiplier of 17.86 taking a four and a half per cent discount rate for accelerated payment and a further 10 per cent for "life's manifold contingencies"). The multiplier for future loss of earnings was fixed at 8.64 (increased from 7 at first instance taking an overall working life of 27 years from leaving school at 16). *General Damages*: £125,500. Future loss of earnings (multiplier 8.64): £81,370. Future care (multiplier 22): £1,158,783. Court of Protection fees: £48,000. Total award: £1,873,345.

S (A MINOR) v. PORTSMOUTH AND SOUTH EAST HAMPSHIRE HA, July 30, 1999, May, L.J., CA. [*Ex rel.* Frank R. Moat, Barrister, 3 Pump Court, Temple, London].

Very severe brain damage

1504. P, male, aged 14 years and nine months at the date of trial, suffered severe brain damage as a result of surgery carried out the day after his birth to repair a congenital cardiac condition. The surgery, known as a mustard operation, involved the insertion of an artificial atrial septum to allow oxygenated blood to pass into the right ventricle instead of the left ventricle. The operation was carried out successfully, but the blood in the supporting cardiopulmonary bypass unit had clotted, resulting in multiple cerebral emboli which caused P's brain damage. P suffered catastrophic injuries. He had a right sided hemiparesis with severe spasticity of the right arm, but with less effect on the left leg. P had a right homonymous hemianopia which effectively meant that his sight was restricted to objects ahead of him and in an arc of only 45 degrees to the left. He had severe learning difficulties, compounded by behavioural problems, and lacked the ability to concentrate. P functioned at the level of a three year old, although physically an appropriate size for his age. P was extremely disruptive, easily distracted and required intensive supervision or one to one care whilst awake. P had no concept of danger and was not readily biddable. He had limited speech. Until 1995, P was cared for at home by his mother but after that attended a residential school, as a result of which there was improvement in his ability to function, and in particular he ceased to be doubly incontinent. P was able to use the lavatory to pass urine but still required a pad for when he passed faeces. At night, he usually awoke twice to go to the lavatory. Shortly after the operation, P suffered fits but these had largely resolved by the date of trial. P was, however, still taking anti-convulsion medication. An EEG in 1996 showed epileptiform discharges. The evidence showed that there was no prospect of any real improvement, except possibly in relation to P's behaviour as he grew older. P's life expectancy was found to be 25 years. It was envisaged that P would remain at the residential school until the age of 19. He returned home on alternate weekends and for school holidays, and was cared for by his mother and her partner at those times. It was found, that from the age of 19, P would benefit from being cared for in a residential setting rather than at home. *General Damages* (agreed): £120,000. Past care (including respite care): £68,500. Past expenses: £46,115. Future care up to 19 (multiplier 3.93, multiplicand £6,103.20): £23,985. Future care after 19 (multiplier 13.74, multiplicand £1,680 per week): £1,131,626. Lost earning capacity (multiplier 12.17): £212,731. Other future losses (including case management): £36,085. Total award (including interest): £1,699,231.

P (A CHILD) v. HAMMERSMITH AND QUEEN CHARLOTTE'S SPECIAL HA [2000] 3 Q.R. 3, Latham, J., QBD.

Very severe brain damage

1505. D, female, aged 14 at the date of the accident and 20 at trial, a US citizen, suffered a serious head injury in a coach crash on October 4, 1993. D's injuries included head injury, contusions and severe oedema, she was fitting and comatose on arrival at hospital. D suffered a fractured right femur, fractured right clavicle and a fractured phalanx meta-carpal of the right hand. She remained unresponsive for about 10 days. Thereafter, a neuropsychologist assessed D's age equivalent scores to range from about age two to age six. D's communication skills were extremely limited and her full scale IQ only 50. She would never reach a level of independent thinking, judgment or behaviour sufficient to be able to live independently, manage her affairs or work. D's continued disability and cognitive, motor neuro behavioural deficits rendered her totally dependent upon others for her care and safety. D required supervision 24 hours per day. D was profoundly deficient in initiation, planning, self care, executive functions and thinking/problem solving. She had severe short term memory deficits. D did have a degree of insight into her condition and an awareness of her difference from others which caused periods of sadness. D's parents, particularly her mother, a trained nurse, had devoted their lives from 1993 to 1998 to caring for C to a remarkably high standard. D had since November 1998 been cared for in a specialist brain injury facility in the US, where her needs were fully met and her abilities were maximised. D was intended to stay there for the rest her natural life. D, though only 14 years old at the time of the accident, was an "honour roll" student from a high achieving family who would in all probability have been an above average earner during her lifetime. Her life expectancy was reduced by about six years. It was recognised that the level of supervision might decrease slightly in future. Continuing therapies were justified on the basis that they should gradually increase the level of D's independence and reduce her behavioural problems. The cost of future institutional care was discounted to give credit for what C would otherwise have had to spend on her accommodation, heat, light and food if the accident had not occurred. Awards for past care: £151,250 (for gratuitous care provided by the parents) and £137,500 (for the first year of residential care). Cost of past medical expenses: £153,675. Future cost of residential care: £3,412,104 (made up of £3,618,210 (based upon a whole life multiplier of 27.22, split 1.91 for a further two years in the educational programme at the facility and 25.31 in the vocational programme at the facility)). Total deduction (for accommodation and other expenses avoided based on £7,527 pa): £206,106. Future medical expenses: £364,049 (for speech therapy and occupational therapy sessions once per week). Future legal expenses: £271,729 (for the US equivalent of the English Court of Protection fees). Future loss of earnings: £631,200 based upon $60,000 per annum (including fringe benefits) which was equivalent to $48,000 net of tax plus a small sum for holiday earnings while she would have been at college.

DASHIELL v. LUTTIT; *sub nom.* DASHIELL v. LUTTITT [2000] 3 Q.R. 4, Judge Buckley, QBD.

Very severe brain damage

1506. O, a boy, was born in June 1994 at King's College Hospital. It was alleged on his behalf that the cerebral palsy from which he suffered was caused by the negligence of the obstetric staff at the hospital. The hospital admitted breach of duty of care in failing to deliver O on time but disputed causation, alleging that he would have been brain damaged in any event. A previous application for an interim payment of £25,000 (less CRU benefits) had been made by consent. An argument was put forward on behalf of O for a further interim payment of £400,000. The interim award was made on the basis that, aside from the issue of causation, the negligence admitted would merit substantial damages. The court was satisfied that there was a reasonable and proper purpose for the money to help O's family to care for him. A second interim payment of £400,000 was ordered to be paid into court (subject to sums due to CRU).

O (A MINOR) v. KING'S HEALTHCARE NHS TRUST, June 21,1999, Master Rose, QBD. [*Ex rel.* Alexander Johnson Solicitors, 10-11 Lanark Square, Glengall Bridge, London].

Very severe brain damage – epilepsy

1507. H, a girl, born on September 6, 1990 and aged eight at the date of the infant settlement approval hearing, suffered birth asphyxia resulting in cerebral palsy and a severe form of epilepsy which had a greater impact on her life than the cerebral palsy. HHA conceded liability for the cerebral palsy but denied liability for the epilepsy. H had to take steroids which resulted in obesity, and suffered from tiredness and lethargy. Her learning capacity was reduced. She suffered from drop attacks which necessitated her wearing a helmet outside and her life expectancy was significantly reduced. As a result of her disabilities, H would never be able to work. She had difficulties with regard to communication and movement and required regular physiotherapy. She would need stimulation and motivation when no longer attending school. She would progressively need computer and environmental aids to assist her and future travel costs would be significant. *General Damages*: £132,000. Past gratuitous care award: £120,000. Future loss of earnings award (multiplier 10): £117,000. Future care award (based on the assumption of care by her parents to age 19 and professional care thereafter): £836,500. Total award: £1.75 million.

H (A CHILD) v. HILLINGDON HA [2000] 4 Q.R. 4, Latham, J., QBD.

Severe brain damage

1508.   T, female, aged eight at the date of the accident and 16 at trial, was struck by a motor car as she walked out into the road behind an ice cream van. T suffered a right temporo-parietal skull vault fracture. A CT scan revealed gross brain swelling through a contre-coup injury, partial obliteration of the basal cisterns and compressions of the third ventricle. A tracheotomy was required. T was in a coma for four months and discharged from hospital after 18 months, whereupon she underwent intensive therapy. T was left with a marked spastic gait affecting the left arm, trunk and left leg but was able to walk. No significant future deterioration was anticipated. T suffered arrested development, lack of judgement and insight, emotional lability, impulsiveness and a volatile temperament. She had a tracheotomy scar. Management in the home was difficult and behavioural rehabilitation was required. T was in need of supervision and care in the home. She was unlikely to obtain any remunerative employment. T was accepted on a two year course for disabled and brain injured adolescents and adults. T's life expectancy was reduced by 17.5 years. *General Damages*: £100,000. Past care award: £75,000 (including 25 per cent reduction from commercial rates). Future care award: £698,200. Future loss of earnings award: £130,757. Total award: £1,157,352.

T (A CHILD) v. PAGE [2000] 5 Q.R. 6, Judge Diehl Q.C., QBD.

Severe brain damage

1509.   J, male aged 24 at the date of the incident and 28 at the date of the hearing, was on leave from the RAF when he was attacked by three men. He was struck on the back of his head and knocked to the ground. Although he later went to his parents' house, his mother found him unconscious in the middle of the night and he was rushed to hospital with a Glasgow Coma Scale of four over 15 and a dilated right pupil. A CT brain scan revealed a large right extra dural haematoma and a right temporal parietal depressed skull fracture. He underwent a front temporal craniotomy to evacuate the haematoma. He remained in intensive care for two days after which he was transferred for rehabilitation. He was then transferred to an RAF rehabilitation centre where he remained for six months, following which he was discharged to his parents' home. An interim payment enabled J to benefit from a further period of physical rehabilitation. In July 1996, J moved to a centre for the young and physically disabled. As a result of the brain injury, J suffered physical disability. He had a residual spastic tetra paresis, which was worse on the left than on the right side. He normally used a wheelchair, but was able to walk slowly with the aid of two elbow crutches. J also began to suffer from a neural behavioural disorder comprising a lack of insight, lack of judgement, rigid thinking, unrealistic attitudes and aspirations, coarse and slightly disinhibited social behaviour, lack of tolerance, impulsiveness, poor money management and a neglect of personal hygiene. He also had language problems. Loss of earnings was claimed on the basis that J would have left the RAF in October 1998, some three and a half years after the accident. Thereafter earnings were claimed at the rate for all manually employed males in the new earnings survey of 1998. Although J was significantly disabled, he wanted to be as independent as possible. The care package assumed that J would have a home of his own and would need residential carers working opposite each other in overlapping shifts during daytime with the facility for him to access the emergency support overnight. A case manager was recommended. *General Damages*: £100,000. Past loss of earnings award: £34,412. Award for past personal care support (after discount): £12,500. Part rehabilitation costs: £149,406. Award for future loss of earnings and pension: £251,775. Future care award: £1,053,630. Accommodation award: £151,600. Aid and equipment award: £139,050. Transport award: £63,000. Care manager award: £49,000. Total award: £2,014,383.

JONES (CICA: QUANTUM: 2000: HEAD INJURIES), *Re*, November 24, 1999, Tony Summers (Chairman), CICA (Liverpool). [*Ex rel.* Irwin Mitchell Solicitors, St Peter's House, Hartshead, Sheffield].

Severe brain damage – epilepsy

1510.   C, female, aged 39 at the date of the road traffic accident and 45 at trial, was seriously injured and her husband was killed. C suffered severe head injuries and brain damage. She was taken to hospital and then to a specialist head unit. She was paralysed and required ventilation. A right parietal elevation of a depressed skull fracture and a tracheostomy were carried out. C developed an acinetobacter infection. She was disorientated in time and place with complete closure of the right eyelid. She also had a severe left hemiparesis and was agitated and aggressive, she suffered from convulsions and became paranoid. C had been of average intelligence and in full time work as a civil servant before the accident. Her IQ was substantially reduced by her brain injury. The eyelid opened slowly but she was left with an abnormal eye. She walked with a markedly hemiplegic gait. Although able to carry out many household tasks, C needed supervision. She lacked motivation and had to be reminded to eat regular meals. She was at times frustrated and angry over the changes to her life and the loss of her driving licence due to epilepsy. The epilepsy required daily medication. C could use local shops but could not use public transport and was reliant on others for transport. Although C achieved a substantial degree of autonomy, she would always require domestic help and supervision and the services of a case manager. Her personality was altered from that of a competent mother, wife and employee to that of a person with a high degree of dependency. She would not work again. C's husband had been a self employed farm worker. His estate suffered loss of earnings and pension. His wife and son were dependent upon him. *General Damages*: £85,000 (agreed and approved). Past loss of earnings award: £56,908. Past care award: £41,500. Future loss of earnings award: £122,056. Future care award: £310,000. Total Award: 908,562.

C (A PATIENT: HEAD INJURIES) v. EWIN, July 25, 2000, District Judge Holloway, QBD. [*Ex rel.* David Mason, Barrister, Milburn House Chambers, Floor A, Milburn House, Dean Street, Newcastle-upon-Tyne].

Severe brain damage – sight

1511.   S, male, a university student, aged 25 at the date of the assault and 33 at the hearing, was hit over the head causing diffuse brain injury and complete loss of vision in the left eye, and loss of the peripheral vision in the right. His sight was reduced to 10 degrees tunnel vision, with reduced visual acuity. S was able to read half inch lettering at 35 cm for 10 minutes. In addition, he suffered permanent significant deterioration in his cognitive function. His verbal intellectual level was reduced to below the lower limit of average. Prior to the assault, S had obtained three A levels. The deterioration represented an estimated 20 points reduction in IQ. The assault caused temporary hemiparesis, and some remaining left sided weakness was permanent. S had no prospect of employment. He had intended to become a fashion designer. S was treated for depression and needed assistance in cooking and going out of the house. Past loss of earnings was awarded on the basis of an average of £23,000 gross p.a. earnings to the date of the hearing. A commercial hourly rate of £4 was applied for the past care award. Future loss of earnings were calculated on the basis of an average annual income of £30,000 to £35,000 gross, applying a multiplier of 18. A multiplier of 24.66 was applied to the commercial rate of £5 for the future care award. *General Damages*: (including an element to compensate for loss of job satisfaction) £145,000. Past loss of earnings award: £100,000. Past care award:

£36,956. Future loss of earnings award: £405,000. Future care award: £134,643. Total award: £824,000 (before deduction on account of benefits).

SMITH (CICB: QUANTUM: 2000), *Re*, May 3, 2000, John Leighton Williams Q.C. (Chairman), CICB (Durham). [*Ex rel.* Richard Power, Barrister, 6 Pump Court, Temple, London].

Moderate brain damage

1512.   R, male, hairdresser, aged 22 at the date of the accident and 32 at trial, was the front seat passenger in a motor car which was involved in a road traffic accident. R suffered a severe diffuse cerebral injury. He was rendered unconscious and suffered retrograde amnesia of about two days and post traumatic amnesia of about six weeks. R was unconscious for 48 hours and spent one month in hospital. Although there was no fracture of the skull, a CT scan showed areas of haemorrhage in the right frontal lobe and the left temporal and occipital lobes. R was incontinent of urine following discharge from hospital. He developed post traumatic epilepsy requiring treatment with anticonvulsant drugs which continued to the date of hearing. R's residual symptoms included change of character, becoming somewhat quiet and docile, impaired memory and concentration, unsteady gait, right sided headaches, post traumatic epilepsy and double vision when looking to the right or downwards. R would never be able to work or lead an independent life without supervision and would not make any further recovery. He was unable to choose appropriate clothing without being prompted. He had a tendency to drop things, misjudge distances and was generally clumsy. R tired easily and was slow to respond. He found it difficult to follow television programmes or read more than two or three paragraphs of a book or magazine without forgetting what went before. His IQ was reduced from a pre-accident average range to a borderline 71-78. His memory had been very severely impaired and was in the defective range. R became easily confused and his word selection was impaired. R needed support and assistance with showering and personal hygiene; taking his medication; dealing with paperwork; planning and organising his activities and structuring his day; going shopping; cooking and with domestic jobs such as cleaning, washing and ironing. R also required an enabler or companion to get him out of the house, accompany him to social or leisure pursuits and bring him home safely. *General Damages*: £80,000. Past loss of earnings: £98,833 (based upon earnings rising to about £17,000 net per annum by 1999). Past care: £57,390. Future loss of earnings: £314,500 (based upon multiplicand of £17,000 net per annum. Future care: £333,099 (including cost of an enabler/companion for 12 hours per week).

RUSHTON v. JERVIS [2000] 3 Q.R. 3, Master Foster, QBD.

Moderate brain damage

1513.   G, male, aged 56 at the date of the accident and 61 at trial, fell 25 feet from a ladder, sustaining multiple injuries, including severe and diffusive cerebral brain injury, his coma score being 10 on the Glasgow Coma Scale, together with a fracture of the left maxilla, tear of left rotator cuff muscles, injuries to his knees and lacerations to his face. G was unconscious and in intensive care for nine days. He remained in hospital for approximately one month. G suffered permanent brain damage, which included significant post-traumatic amnesia and difficulties with memory, concentration, motivation and personality change. He suffered minimal effects from the left hemiparesis, including clumsiness in his left arm and clumsiness and weakness in his left leg. G was unable to work in any capacity. He was incapable of managing his own affairs. The general damages award took into account an uplift by a factor of up to two on the basis of a successful appeal, relying upon Law Com. No.257 Recommendations on *General Damages* in Personal Injury Cases. The multiplier applied for the award for future loss of earnings was 3.25. the future care award was based upon unpaid care by G's wife and a paid carer for 14 hours per week and applying a multiplier of 12.31. A multiplier of 12.31 was applied to the future care management award. *General Damages*: £80,000. Future loss of earnings award: £29,737. Future care award: £100,973. Future care management award: £23,008. Award for future home maintenance and DIY: £4,500.

GASSON v. OCS GROUP LTD, February 16, 2000, Sir Oliver Popplewell, QBD. [*Ex rel.* Frank R Moat, Barrister, 3 Pump Court, Temple, London].

Moderate brain damage

1514.   K, a boy, aged 15 at the hearing, suffered cerebral palsy due to the mismanagement of his birth. Liability was admitted, and a payment into court of £1.5 million was made by PSEH. K suffered from athetoid cerebral palsy, was only moderately physically disabled, but had very poor speech and learning difficulties which give him a functional IQ of about 65 (borderline subnormal). He tired easily, could only walk about 100 metres on his own and had difficulty with uneven ground and slopes. He could scarcely use his right hand and had a tremor in his left hand. He had difficulty with drinking and speech. Associated epilepsy was under control. His mother intended to provide care for K for as long as she was able. An award was approved by the Court, including the following awards for specific heads of loss. The award was to be structured in part. *General Damages*: £80,000. Past care award: £50,000. Future care award: £750,000 based on £7,500 per annum, from date of trial to age 19: £12,500, per annum from age 19 to 23: £35,000 per annum from age 23 for rest of life. Future loss of earnings award (multiplier 18): £300,000.

K (A CHILD) v. PORTSMOUTH AND SOUTH EAST HAMPSHIRE HA, November 22, 1999, Judge Astill, QBD. [*Ex rel.* George Ide, Phillips Solicitors, 52 North Street, Chichester, West Sussex].

Moderate brain damage

1515.   S, male aged 44 at the date of the accident and 49 at trial, suffered a fractured skull, bruising to the left temporal lobe of his brain, a ruptured left tympanic membrane and damage to his olfactory nerve following a fall from a ladder during his work as a gardener/handyman. S was left with daily headaches, bilateral anosmia, a significant loss of cognitive function, a change of personality, depression and irritability. Thirteen weeks after the accident S returned to work. He had difficulty coping and was only able to work for one to two weeks. He then had a breakdown and was unable to continue. He had not worked since. After the accident, S experienced psychotic episodes which led to his occasional admission to a psychiatric hospital. It was not disputed that these episodes were caused by the accident and that the prognosis was poor. The main issues on the assessment of damages were a claim for past and future care, a claim for cost of future medical treatment and a claim for accommodation made on the basis of *Roberts v. Johnstone* [1989] Q.B. 878, [1989] C.L.Y. 1202 applied. Liability was in dispute, but a settlement was agreed and approved by the court. *General Damages*: £60,000. Past loss of earnings award: £33,725. Past care award: £110,291. Award for loss of congenial employment: £5,000.

S v. METHODIST HOMES FOR THE AGED, January 10, 2000, Judge Butter Q.C., CC (Central London). [*Ex rel.* Hodge Jones & Allen Solicitors, Twyman House, 31-39 Camden Road, London].

Moderate brain damage

1516.   K, male, aged 65 at the date of the accident and 70 at the date of the hearing, was knocked down by a car whilst using a pedestrian crossing. K suffered a skull fracture on the right side of the head and was rendered unconscious. He remained unconscious for two weeks and was unable to communicate for four weeks. There was a right subdural haematoma, swelling of the right cerebral hemisphere and contusion of the left temporal lobe. There was post traumatic amnesia of at least two weeks duration. The head injury caused cognitive impairment, memory loss and personality change. There were typical features of organic frontal lobe syndrome. K suffered from mood swings, lability, frustration, loss of interest in previous hobbies, disinhibition and obsessional behaviour. Although not physically aggressive, he could be argumentative and had displayed inappropriate behaviour, including accosting strangers with excessive and argumentative conversation. He had reverted to an almost childlike dependence on his wife and was not capable of managing his own affairs. He was independent in terms of personal care and did not require nursing but required constant support, company and encouragement which had been and was likely to continue to be provided mainly by his wife, with regular respite care. There was a risk of post traumatic epilepsy, but no fits had occurred and at the date of the hearing the agreed medical evidence was that the risk had fallen below 5 per cent and would continue to fall to a fixed level of 2 per cent 10 years post accident, assuming no fits. On that basis the judge approved abandonment of the pleaded claim for provisional damages and approved the compromise on a full and final basis of assessment. Other injuries included damage to the left optic nerve aggravating the effects of chronic glaucoma of the right eye and accelerating the loss of useful vision in that eye by two to three years. There were also fractures of the right sixth and seventh ribs, right pubis, right sacrum, right radial head and right ankle and soft tissue injury to the cervical spine. There was persistent aching of the right arm, restriction of movement of the right ankle and discomfort and restriction of movement in the neck and shoulders.

General Damages (agreed and approved): £60,000. Total award (including special damages, past and future care, interest and Court of Protection fees): £190,000.

K v. HICKMAN, October 18, 1999, Morison, J., QBD. [*Ex rel.* Philip A Butler, Barrister, Deans Court Chambers, 24 St John Street, Manchester].

Moderate brain damage

1517. S, male, aged five at the date of the road traffic accident and 11 at the date of the infant settlement approval hearing, sustained a severe closed head injury causing brain damage, left hemiparesis and damage to the right fourth and sixth cranial nerves causing cranial nerve palsy and loss of binocular vision. Because of the head injury and hemiparesis, S developed left foot drop requiring orthosis and there was reduced co-ordination of left arm and leg. S would never be able to carry out work requiring fine manipulation of the upper limbs or heavy manual work. He suffered a fit on the way to hospital, but no subsequent frank epileptic seizures so that the agreed medical evidence was to the effect that although the post traumatic epilepsy risk remained above the general population level, it had fallen, six years after the accident, to less than three per cent and would reduce still further in the absence of fits. On that basis the court approved the abandonment of the pleaded claim for provisional damages in favour of compromise on a full and final assessment basis. S would continue to require regular physiotherapy to assist with the effects of left sided weakness. In addition to the adverse effect on future employability caused by physical weakness, the head injury had caused a degree of cognitive/intellectual impairment most obviously manifested in poor reading ability, (S's reading age at age 11 being equivalent only to that of a child of six). *General Damages* (agreed): £40,000. *Smith v. Manchester* award (agreed): £72,000. Total award (including special damages, interest, future physiotherapy, future equipment needs: £150,000.

S (A CHILD) v. FORRESTER, September 14, 1999, District Judge Wells, QBD. [*Ex rel.* Philip A Butler, Barrister, Deans Court Chambers, 24 St John St, Manchester].

Less severe brain damage – multiple injuries

1518. S, male, aged 86 at the date of the accident and 88 at trial, was knocked down by a car whilst crossing the road. He sustained a closed head injury, a closed comminuted fracture to the right tibia and fibula, cuts to the left hand, right knee and head, bruising to the left knee and a sprained neck. S was detained in hospital. The tibia was pinned and screwed. The cut to the left wrist and right knee required stitching. S commenced partial weight-bearing after seven weeks and was discharged to his home after eight weeks. S continued to mobilise partial weight-bearing, being dependant on two crutches. Prior to the accident he could mobilise with or without a stick. The tibial fracture did not unite. S was medically advised to undergo revision surgery, which entailed a 15 per cent chance of death. If he did not undergo such surgery the failure of the metalwork was said to be inevitable, and any revision surgery at that time would have a 20 per cent risk of death. These matters caused concern to S and his wife. The neck sprain exacerbated pre-existing symptoms by a period of four to 12 months. The cuts to the left wrist and right knee resulted in permanent scarring. S suffered a degree of traumatic brain injury with post-traumatic concussion of one hour. He suffered intermittent headaches every day, which would be permanent. His gait apraxia and age-related deterioration in memory and other cognitive functioning were accelerated by a period of more than three years. In addition a pre-existing essential tremor was exacerbated, rendering his writing illegible. At the date of trial S complained of confusion, pain and swelling in the right leg and headaches. The judge accepted that before the accident he had been active and independent, and he had now lost his mobility, confidence and independence. The judge took into account S's age, in that his life expectancy was less than five years, but also that the accident had cast "a severe blight over his remaining years". The judge made no adjustment to the award in the light of the Law Com. No.257 Recommendations on *General Damages* in Personal Injury Cases, but instead extended S's time for leave to appeal. *General Damages*: £27,500; Future Losses: £16,375; Total Award: £53,668.05. [Editorial Note: The defendant is applying to the Court of Appeal for leave to appeal.]

STENNETT v. HOOK, February 18, 2000, Judge Marr-Johnson, MCLC. [*Ex rel.* Richard Menzies, Barrister, 8 Stone Buildings, Lincoln's Inn, London].

Psychiatric damage

1519. B, male aged 27 at the date of the incident and 33 at the date of the hearing, was injured when four men broke into the house where he was staying, armed with baseball bats and a Rottweiler dog. The other occupants of the house escaped, but B was attacked. B was taken to hospital, where a wound to the forehead was sutured. B moved out of the area, but continued to believe that he was likely to be assaulted again. B moved home every two to three months in an effort to hide from his attackers. He gave evidence against his attackers and believed that he would be subjected to assaults from them or their friends. B suffered post-traumatic stress, with nightmares, flash-backs and panic attacks at any reminder of the incident. He had a psychotic disorder which was compounded by the PTSD together with ongoing anxiety and depression related to his real fear of suffering further violence from his assailants. B had frequent outbursts of anger, was weepy and his mood fluctuated. He would avoid people and public houses and was unable to use public transport. B suffered from panic attacks during which he hyperventilated, his heart raced and he shook and stuttered. B was careless in appearance. His former partner had refused him contact to his children because of his condition. His condition was not likely to improve, even with professional help, which he had sought, but which had failed. The psychiatrist had stated that this was one of the most severe and disabling anxiety depressive states that he had seen. It was likely that he would be disabled for several years and there was a risk that the psychiatric disorder would become lifelong. B had been unemployed at the time of the incident, though he had prospects of employment. It was unlikely he would work again, but a return to employment could not be ruled out. *General*

Damages: £45,000. Past loss of earnings (after deductions for benefits and the likelihood of unemployment) £13,090. Future loss of earnings (multiplier 17, multiplicand £5,618): £95,472. Total award: £153,562.

B (CICB: QUANTUM: 2000), *Re*, February 23, 2000, Donald Robertson Q.C., CICB (Durham). [*Ex rel.* Joseph PAP O'Brien, Barrister, Broad Chare Chambers, 33 Broad Chare, Newcastle-upon-Tyne].

Psychiatric damage

1520.   D, male, aged 10 at the date of the road traffic accident in which his father was killed and his mother seriously injured, and 15 at trial, suffered only minor physical injuries and was not detained in hospital. D's mother's injuries resulted in epilepsy and a change of personality. She came to rely heavily on D for emotional and practical support. D and his mother moved home so as to be near to his maternal grandparents, who were heavily involved in looking after his mother. This meant moving to a different town and school. D became depressed and distressed over the death of his father and, as he saw it, effectively the death of his mother as he had known her, due to the severity of her change of personality. He became upset when trying to talk about his father. He suffered from repetitive thoughts and nightmares about the accident and was nervous at first in travelling by car. There were indications of a post traumatic stress disorder. Over a period of about two years D's mental state improved. He did well at school and coped with caring for his mother and his other interests, including football and his pets. He largely overcame his emotional state over the accident and was found to cope well with the responsibility he had assumed in helping to care for his mother. *General Damages*: £11,000 (agreed and approved).

C (A PATIENT: DEPENDENCY) v. EWIN, July 25, 2000, District Judge Holloway, QBD. [*Ex rel.* David Mason, Barrister, Milburn House Chambers, Floor A, Milburn House, Dean Street, Newcastle-upon-Tyne].

Psychiatric damage

1521.   C, male, aged 47 at the date of the incident and 50 at trial, was the landlord of the Royal Oak public house in Didsbury, Manchester at the date of the attack. He was mugged, tied up and had spirits poured all over him by a number of intruders, who threatened to set him alight and then emptied the pub safe and threatened to kill him. C escaped but suffered a significant psychological reaction to the extent that he had to give up working as a pub landlord some 15 months later. C's physical injuries included bruising to the back and neck, but C made a quick and complete recovery from these injuries. C suffered psychological symptoms, including flashbacks and nightmares relating to the incident approximately two to three times a week during the year following the incident. C also suffered loss of confidence which affected his everyday life and manifested itself in nervousness, anxiety, mood swings and depression. C also suffered loss of energy which resulted in disorganisation, disinterest in day to day life and lack of concentration, which had a severe effect on his personal relationships. C also suffered from poor libido, loss of appetite and consequent weight loss. C's symptoms were attributed to post traumatic stress disorder and a depressive disorder of moderate severity. Expert evidence suggested that treatment with antidepressants and cognitive behaviour therapy should result in C becoming asymptomatic within 12 to 18 months of the hearing. C had not undergone psychological treatment as recommended, at an earlier stage, by a consultant psychiatrist, who had predicted that C's symptoms would be relieved within 12 months of the commencement of treatment. *General Damages*: £7,500. Loss of earnings: £10,000. *Smith v. Manchester*: £20,000. Total award: £37,500.

CROLLA (CICB: QUANTUM: 1999), *Re*, August 4, 1999, Chairman: Edward Gee, CICB (Manchester). [*Ex rel.* Rowlands Solicitors, 3 York Street, Manchester].

Psychiatric damage – whiplash type injury

1522. W, female, aged 18 at the date of the accident and 20 at trial, was injured in a road traffic accident and sustained a soft tissue injury to her cervical spine. This caused her severe discomfort for one month. She wore a soft collar for two months and was unwilling to attend college for that period. On examination after 10 months, she had a full range of movement, with some discomfort at the extremes. W suffered occasional discomfort on turning her head sharply, and her neck was occasionally stiff in the mornings. She made a complete recovery within 18 months. There was also a psychological reaction, which fell short of post traumatic stress disorder. There was a mild situational driving anxiety state. W had become depressed after the accident and taken an overdose within three months of the same, and her depression was still evident after two years; however, there were a number of causes of that depression which were unrelated to the accident and this state appeared to have been evident prior to the accident. Nonetheless, the accident continued to contribute to her psychological difficulties some two years afterwards. *General Damages*: £3,115.

WALKER v. MIRICKI [2000] 4 Q.R. 4, Judge Machin, CC (Chesterfield).

Psychiatric damage after sexual abuse

1523. W, female, aged 25 at the date of the hearing, was subjected to incidents of rape between 1985 and 1991 when aged between 12 and 18. The intercourse was perpetrated by a family friend and took place at least twice a week over that period. It went unreported until another victim made a similar complaint. Subsequent prosecution was stopped, although the offender served 12 months' imprisonment for offences relating to the other victim. The offender continued to live in the same locality as W. The Board heard expert evidence that although there had been no finding of depression, the trauma had led to feelings of low self esteem and self blame, which continued until the date of the hearing. W was vulnerable to abusive and exploitative relationships with men, and did not derive sexual intimacy or pleasure from her private relationships. It was hoped that the situation would improve with therapy, and W acknowledged the need for the same. *General Damages*: £20,000.

W (CICB: QUANTUM: 1999), *Re*, June 7, 1999, Chairman: David Barker Q.C., CICB (London). [*Ex rel.* Graham Watson, Barrister, Pump Court Chambers, 31 Southgate Street, Winchester].

Psychiatric damage after sexual abuse

1524. F, a girl, born in 1979, was sexually abused by her stepfather for four to five years between the ages of nine and 13. At first her stepfather would kiss her good night and one night he got into bed and started to touch her. The abuse occurred on a daily basis. It also occurred occasionally out of the house. The abuse progressed to include touching of breasts and the genital area, fingering and digital penetration of the vagina, touching and masturbation of the stepfather's penis, attempts to make her perform oral sex, oral sex performed by the stepfather upon F's breasts and vagina, masturbation and ejaculation upon F's body and attempted sexual intercourse on numerous occasions throughout the four year period including many attempts of incomplete penetration. The abuse resulted in F suffering thrush and an unnecessary appendectomy following abdominal pain which initially was considered to be psychological in origin but was ultimately the result of abuse. F left school in 1995 but her GCSE grades were affected, as the GCSE exams took place at the time of her stepfather's trial. F's grades were worse than predicted. F was described as having an inability to concentrate at school and it was contended that the abuse led to a deterioration in F's previously high academic achievement. F felt "dirty and disgusting" and felt great distress and inferiority amongst her peers. She also experienced flashbacks to the abuse. F experienced powerful outbursts of aggression and anger and an inability to relate comfortably with male friends. She developed an eating disorder and withdrew from normal social activities. It was not anticipated that she would make a full recovery from her psychological and physical scarring. *General Damages*: £17,500.

F (CICB: QUANTUM: 2000), *Re* [2000] 4 Q.R. 4, D Robertson Q.C. (Chairman), CICB (London).

Psychiatric damage after sexual abuse

1525.   A, male, aged 31 at the date of the hearing, suffered extensive and repeated sexual abuse from his football coach between the ages of about 11 and 14. A received football coaching on a frequent basis and was sexually assaulted by the coach when he stayed the night at his home, before and after coaching sessions. The sexual assaults took place on almost every occasion, and during trips involving football away from home and abroad. A was forced to masturbate and to perform oral sex upon his assailant, and was forced to receive the same. A was also buggered on many occasions. He found that the most physically and emotionally distressing aspect of the abuse. A felt coerced to co-operate with his assailant's treatment due to the favourable promotion he believed he would receive in terms of a career as a juvenile professional footballer, his assailant having a considerable reputation locally as a football coach. The assailant was eventually convicted of a large number of sexual offences involving A and other young boys in both the US and the UK and was sentenced to imprisonment. The assailant was not convicted of any offence of buggery upon A, but it was accepted for the purpose of compensation that events had occurred as described. At the time of the abuse, A felt unable to report it, and suffered in silence for many years. He experienced considerable feelings of guilt, and felt that he had lost a normal experience of growing up, particularly in terms of his sexual development. At times of normal day to day stress he felt unable to cope and would experience intrusive memories and thoughts about the abuse. By the time of the hearing, A continued to suffer some of those symptoms from time to time, but had been able to establish a settled pattern of employment and family life. A was initially refused an award by the single member on the basis of his delay in reporting the crime and that no crime of violence had occurred. That was overturned on appeal and A received a full award. The award was inclusive of a sum to contribute towards the cost of some private psychotherapeutic treatment. *General Damages*: £15,000.

A (CICA: QUANTUM: 2000), *Re* [2000] 6 Q.R. 6, Judge not specified, CICA (London).

Psychiatric damage after sexual abuse

1526.   N, male, aged 19 at the date of the hearing, was sexually abused between the ages of seven and 12 by a family friend. The abuse involved mutual masturbation, oral sex, digital interference and penile penetration. N subsequently sexually abused his sister, on occasions receiving instruction from the family friend. N was placed into residential care and committed minor offences, receiving cautions. N underwent psychotherapy for two years and other counselling, but continued to suffer anger and guilt and was sexually disinhibited with poor impulse control. The CICB initially refused to make an award (1) on evidential grounds, and (2) because N's behaviour justified refusing an award in any event. At the rehearing, further evidence was presented including psychiatric evidence that his antisocial behaviour was a typical reaction of those who had suffered abuse and that, but for the abuse N had suffered, he would not have gone on to abuse his sister. On the basis of *Meah v. McCreamer* [1985] 1 All E.R. 367, [1985] C.L.Y. 967, it was argued that the Board was not precluded from making an award. The Board found that the abuse described had occurred and awarded damages, but this was reduced by 20 per cent due to N's unlawful conduct. *General Damages*: (£8,000 less 20 per cent reduction): £6,400.

N (CICB: QUANTUM: 2000), *Re*, January 26, 2000, Charles Whitby Q.C. (Chairman), CICB (Plymouth). [*Ex rel.* Carol Mashembo, Pupil Barrister, King's Bench Chambers, 115 North Hill, Plymouth].

Psychiatric damage after sexual abuse

1527. L, female, aged 23 at the date of the incident and 31 at the hearing, was raped by a known assailant, T. T had systematically manipulated and controlled L by threats of violence. When L refused T's advances she was raped on two separate occasions. L was put in such fear that she relocated and decided not to report the incidents at all. Nearly two years later, L was approached by police investigating similar offences against other women. L co-operated fully with the investigation and gave evidence at T's trial. T was convicted for some offences but acquitted of the rape of L. L's symptoms included depression, haunting memories and nightmares, anxiety, irritability and a fear of her children playing outside. L had become mistrustful of men and had been unable to have a sexual relationship with her partner. L's application for compensation was rejected by a single member on the basis that (a) the rape was not proven and therefore her injuries were not directly attributable to "a crime of violence" under the Criminal Injuries Compensation Scheme 1990 para.4 and (b) that she had failed to report the incident to the police contrary to para.6 of the 1990 Scheme. It was found on appeal that L's was an exceptional case, in that T was an extremely violent criminal with considerable underworld influence. Although L had been raped, some of her fears regarding T had existed prior to those actual incidents. Therefore, not all her psychological damage could be attributed to the criminal injury. T had threatened L in such a manner that it was completely understandable why she had not reported him to the police. The Board did not consider it appropriate to make any reduction on the grounds of non reporting and made a full award. *General Damages*: £7,500.

L (CICB: QUANTUM: 1999), *Re*, June 8, 1999, CICB (Bath). [*Ex rel.* Vershal Relan, Barrister, 3 Paper Buildings, Lorne Park Road, Bournemouth].

Psychiatric damage after sexual abuse

1528. S, male, aged 27 at the date of the hearing, was sexually abused at the age of 12 by one of his carers in a local authority residential home. The abuse took the form of touching of the applicant's penis on two occasions. The long term psychological symptoms fell within the description of post traumatic stress disorder. S experienced symptoms of reliving the trauma in the form of nightmares and avoidance of activities reminiscent of the trauma, such as watching television programmes relating to sexual abuse, and when attempting sexual intercourse. S had had an on off relationship with his partner who was now his fiancee. There was little intimacy in their relationship. S had great difficulty receiving or giving affection and found sexual intercourse distressing. S's condition had failed to respond to therapy and the prognosis was poor. In making the award, the Board took into account that S already had problems relating to his natural family when he entered the care system. *General Damages*: £7,300.

S (CICB: QUANTUM: 1999) (SEXUAL ABUSE), *Re*, October 20, 1999, Chairman: Lord Carlisle Q.C., CICB (Manchester). [*Ex rel.* Ian Huffer, Barrister, Young Street Chambers, 38 Young Street, Manchester].

Post traumatic stress disorder

1529. H, female, aged 43 at the date of the incident and 51 at the hearing, witnessed the murder of her daughter, whose ex boyfriend burst into H's home, attacked H with a knife and murdered H's daughter, aged 18, who was eight months pregnant. The unborn child was lost. H was taunted by the attacker while her daughter was dying. H fled onto the street after her daughter was stabbed, but was caught and dragged back inside by the attacker. H suffered survivor guilt, particularly as she had originally introduced the attacker to the family, and because she had fled during the attack. H was fearful and moved accommodation several times, slept briefly and poorly, had recurrent nightmares, avoided the area of the attack, suffered anxiety and panic attacks, had low self esteem and confidence, experienced thoughts of suicide, vivid flashbacks and reliving of the attack and reduced concentration and short term memory, irritability, loss of temper and a lack of direction and was uninterested in relationships. Anti-depressants helped her quality of sleep but not the other symptoms. Community psychiatric treatment had proved unsuccessful. H could not work due to her symptoms and had not worked since the attack, although probably would not have done so anyway due to an unrelated pre-existing physical condition. There was some history of heavy alcohol abuse. H, a widow, lived alone but relied on her surviving daughters for emotional support and day-to-day care. H found it stressful to leave her house even to socialise with friends, her only real recreation being seeing her grandchildren. Her usual day consisted of watching television, drinking and smoking, from waking until the small hours, followed by a brief period of sleep. In evidence at the hearing, H could not remember simple facts such as a basic history of her accommodation moves or what she had watched on television the night before, and confirmed that this was now usual for her. Two psychiatrists' reports concluded that H was suffering from post traumatic stress disorder and had a markedly impaired ability to pursue a normal lifestyle. The medical evidence differed on whether the diagnosis was of PTSD alone or of a depressive disorder or other psychiatric illness in addition.

The court proceeded on the basis of the more recent evidence which suggested PTSD only. There had been some improvements in some aspects of H's condition, but others had worsened. The prognosis was poor. Even if some symptomatic improvement occurred H would have persisting PTSD which would continue to impede her from returning to a normal lifestyle. Physically, H had suffered division of the right ulnar nerve but this had been repaired with excellent function. H had some tendon damage and ongoing weakness of grip in the left dominant hand and generally used her right hand instead. H was left with a box-shaped scar on the cheek measuring 3 cm x 2 cm, a prominent raised 2.5 cm scar on the left hand and three longer but less prominent scars on the right forearm. The scarring and ongoing weakness were significant injuries but their effects were somewhat overshadowed by the PTSD. The panel considered *Heil v. Rankin* [2000] 2 W.L.R. 1173, [2000] C.L.Y. 1478 in making the award. *General Damages*: £50,000. *Smith v. Manchester* award: £5,000.

H (CICB: QUANTUM: 2000), *Re* [2000] 6 Q.R. 6, David Williamson (Chairman), CICB (Bath).

Post traumatic stress disorder

1530.   L, female, aged 25 at the date of injury and 30 at the hearing, was injured when she attempted to arrest a shoplifter in her capacity as deputy manageress of a clothing store. The shoplifter was joined by seven other youths who assaulted L and ran riot in the store. L suffered bruising to her back, elbow, eye and leg, all of which resolved within weeks. L was able to continue working, but several months after the assault received notice of the court hearing date at which she was expected to give evidence. She fainted and began to suffer from panic attacks and other psychological sequelae, including diminished self confidence, depression and anxiety. She recovered sufficiently to return to work within a month on a part time basis, but used a taxi for all travel and refused to leave the store whilst at work. A marginally distressing incident at work some months after her return led to her being unable to work. L was diagnosed as suffering from post traumatic stress disorder, and some two years after the assault, ceased working. L had not worked for three years by the date of the assessment, and did not anticipate being able to do so. She could not venture out alone, needing to be accompanied by her husband or family at all times. Attempts to overcome her fear of the city centre resulted in panic attacks. She was undergoing weekly psychotherapy. Her marriage had suffered, and all aspects of her life had been touched. *General Damages*: £25,000. Total award: £112,000.

LONG (CICB: QUANTUM: 1999), *Re*, September 29, 1999, Chairman: J. Leighton Williams Q.C., CICB (Nottingham). [*Ex rel.* Richard Gregory, Barrister, 24 The Ropewalk, Nottingham].

Post traumatic stress disorder

1531.   M, a male infant aged 21 months at the date of the incident and seven years and eight months old at the date of the hearing, witnessed his mother being killed by his father. M saw his father throw his mother out of the front door and bang her head repeatedly against a brick wall. Notwithstanding his mother's struggles and bloodied state, she was then kicked severely to the head and body by M's father. M screamed throughout and was very distraught and was found by his mother's side on police arrival. His mother died two days later from severe head injuries, having never regained consciousness. The father was convicted of manslaughter. M's father informed him of the death of his mother two years after the assault. The principal psychiatric evidence was a report prepared three years after the mother's death, which found that (1) M had loss of speech for seven months after the killing; (2) when M next saw his father in prison one month after his mother's death, he vomited over him; (3) M did not sleep for the first three months following the death of his mother; (4) when initially placed in foster care he appeared disconnected, traumatised and unable to respond to anyone. He was only jolted from his unconnected state when a familiar piece of music was heard on the radio which he connected to his natural mother; (5) M was severely traumatised by the loss of his mother at his father's hands and was diagnosed as being in a depressed state and having a post traumatic stress disorder state. The PTSD symptoms were marked by his mourning the loss of his mother having witnessed the killing of his "major love object" but also the loss of the other most significant person in his life, his father. That caused him to regress substantially, losing skills attained, particularly of speech and language; (6) he exhibited disturbed behaviour at school from the age of four, and (7) he would require lengthy psychotherapy to make sense of the information he had been given and to integrate his traumatic memories. Medical experts agreed that young children who had suffered similarly might retain confused images of the violence they had witnessed. In many cases, the trauma was not spoken because it occurred before the child acquired language but could be observed in the child's play. M was made the subject of a care order and placed for adoption. He had been assessed as having special care needs. The Board were only prepared to make an award once satisfied that M and his natural father had stopped living together for good. The Board took into account the circumstances of the killing that M witnessed in noting that M screamed throughout the incident and was very distraught. *General Damages*: £15,000.

M (A CHILD) (CICB: QUANTUM: 1999), *Re*, June 15, 1999, Chairman: John Archer Q.C., CICB (London). [*Ex rel.* Anthony Rimmer, Barrister, Francis Taylor Building, Temple, London].

Post traumatic stress disorder – psychiatric damage

1532.   DB, a girl aged 16 at the date of the incident and 20 at the date of the hearing, and YB, a girl aged 14 and a half at the date of the incident and 19 at the date of the hearing were present with their father during the course of an armed robbery. Both were manhandled, but the actual level of violence was fairly minor. There were continual threats of violence throughout the raid. Both girls subsequently suffered a significant dip in performance at school. They were considered to be intelligent children but failed to achieve their anticipated academic results. Both lost confidence and became quiet, withdrawn and reserved. Socialising and being in the presence of strangers continued to present difficulties. They turned to each other for support. Both were found to be suffering from post traumatic stress disorder. A full resolution of the condition was anticipated for both within five and a half to six years from the date of the incident. Both were also found to be suffering from a phobic anxiety disorder, which involved marked episodes of anxiety and was difficult to treat. To resolve the problem it would be necessary for them to reintroduce themselves into company so as to learn to cope once more in a social situation. It was thought likely that this process would be slow, taking several years, although there was a risk that the condition was permanent.

DB also suffered a severe depressive episode lasting for approximately one year. She was preoccupied with the knowledge that she and her family could have been killed and that she and her sister could have been raped. She felt vulnerable and frightened and was constantly vigilant. She would not go out on her own and did not like leaving home. When out with friends, she thought she was being followed and looked round corners. Her mood was snappy and changeable. A few months after the attack, DB suffered severe stomach pains and stomach cramps diagnosed as Crohn's disease. She found it difficult to come to terms with the illness. Both girls experienced flashbacks and frightening dreams, which diminished with time. Four years after the incident, DB experienced such events on a twice weekly basis and YB on a weekly basis. DB had intended to go to university and believed that the effect of the attack robbed her of that opportunity. The type of work she could undertake was restricted by the possibility of a continuing persistent anxiety state. In particular, she could not work with the public. Four years after the incident, B began studying to be a teacher, therefore her future prospects appeared to have been delayed but not destroyed. *General Damages*: DB (including *Smith v. Manchester* award) £20,000. YB had educational aspirations which were initially thwarted, but had commenced a YTS course, again indicting future prospects delayed rather than ruined. YB (including *Smith v. Manchester* award) £17,500.

DB AND YB (CHILDREN) (CICA: QUANTUM: 2000), *Re*, November 3, 1999, Campbell Q.C., CICA (Manchester). [*Ex rel.* Rowlands Solicitors, 3 York Street, Manchester].

Post traumatic stress disorder – psychiatric damage

1533.   FB, male aged 43 at the date of the incident and 48 at the date of the hearing, was present with his daughters during the course of an armed robbery at a club owned and operated by him. During the robbery, FB was threatened with a shotgun, the barrel of which was at one point thrust into his throat, and a hammer, continual threats of violence were made to FB and his daughters, though the level of violence actually suffered was minor. He was extremely frightened for the safety of his daughters and feared that he would be badly assaulted or shot. FB had a history of work related anxiety symptoms in the years prior to the attack, but there was no suggestion of ongoing symptoms at the date of the attack. FB's post-attack symptoms included difficulty sleeping and vivid intrusive imagery of the attack when asleep. Four years after the incident he was experiencing flashbacks on a weekly basis. He remained confined to his own home for two years during which time he even struggled if left alone in the property. He was irritable, snappy and lost his appetite. He became socially withdrawn. By the date of the hearing he still would not visit crowded public places alone. FB described four main consequences arising from the incident, being loss of earnings and of his home; continuing social restrictions; distress and depression and a sense of loss of all that he had worked for. FB was diagnosed as suffering from post traumatic stress disorder which persisted at the date of the hearing, but was likely to improve slowly with treatment. He was also suffering from a severe depressive episode which was likely to resolve within 12 months of the date of the hearing with proper treatment. H also suffered from a phobic anxiety disorder. The final prognosis was guarded and it was likely that his earning capacity would be greatly restricted for the rest of his life. Total award: £145,000.

B (FRANCIS) (CICA: QUANTUM: 2000), *Re*, November 3, 1999, Campbell Q.C., CICA (Manchester). [*Ex rel.* Rowlands Solicitors, 3 York Street, Manchester].

Post traumatic stress disorder – nose

1534.   S, male, aged 32 at the time of the incident and 37 at the hearing, was the victim of a robbery when his three assailants held him captive for 13 hours. During his ordeal he was handcuffed, beaten, stabbed and shot at with a shotgun. He escaped by throwing himself out of a moving car. S suffered post traumatic stress disorder. S was still receiving counselling at the date of the hearing. He suffered nightmares two to three nights every week and sometimes had flashbacks in the daytime. He suffered from anxiety and depression and had taken Prozac intermittently. He had suffered outbursts of anger but they had ceased by the hearing. He had been employed in several short-term jobs since the incident. He was no longer able to care for his two children, although that was partly because he did not want them to be involved in a witness protection programme. S's physical injuries included a broken nose which by the hearing date had required two operations. S had a displaced septum so that he was still unable to breathe through his left nostril and suffered from sneezing and bleeding. Cosmetically, his nose was not significantly disfigured. The prognosis was uncertain. S also sustained neurological damage to his right hand from the handcuffs which resulted in numbness in his fourth and fifth fingers. S was no longer able to play the guitar. The Panel agreed that the injuries to the nose appeared to fall between the categories of injuries given in the Judicial Studies Board Guidelines. *General Damages*: £16,500 (including £3,500 for the injury to the nose and £12,000 for the post-traumatic stress disorder).
    S (CICB: QUANTUM: 2000), *Re*, May 22, 2000, Lord Carlisle Q.C. (Chairman), CICB (London). [*Ex rel.* Jake Harris, Pupil Barrister, Goldsmith Chambers, Temple, London].

Head

1535.   W, a boy, aged five at the date of the accident in July 1997 and seven at trial, was struck on the head by another child guest who had jumped onto him from a roof during a garden party hosted by K. W collapsed two hours later and a CT scan revealed an extradural haematoma. W underwent an emergency right parietal craniotomy to remove the blood clot that evening. W made an excellent post operative recovery and was discharged from hospital four days after the accident. There was no primary brain injury nor residual neurological deficit. There was a small risk that W might develop post traumatic epilepsy. The initial risk of this was between five per cent and 10 per cent, diminishing progressively the longer he remained seizure free. The long term (after about seven years) risk of W developing later fits was around two per cent, that of the general population. *General Damages* (provisional award, with entitlement to return for further damages if epilepsy developed within eight years of the accident): £4,500.
    W (A CHILD) v. KERRY, November 24, 1999, District Judge Sparrow, CC (Norwich). [*Ex rel.* Anthony Bate, Barrister, East Anglian Chambers, 57 London Street, Norwich].

Head – multiple injuries

1536.   P, male, aged 39 at the date of the assault and 43 at the hearing, was attacked outside his home with an iron bar sustaining blows to his head, face and left arm. P sustained cuts to his head and face from a Stanley knife. P was detained in hospital for seven days. At the date of the assault P was not in employment, having taken leave of absence to care for his terminally ill wife, and following her death to provide care for his son, aged seven. It was accepted that he would have returned to his former employment when circumstances allowed, but for the injuries sustained in the assault. P sustained a comminuted fracture of the right zygomatic arch which was fixed with a titanium bone plate. His cheek ached in cold weather and he had a loss of sensation on the right side of the forehead over the distribution of the infra orbital nerve. There was a fracture to the left mandibular condyle and an undisplaced fracture of the left mandibular parasymphysis. Both were treated surgically by the placement of bridle wire. P's mouth opening was decreased and there was a decrease in his ability to perform right and left lateral excursive movements. His right and left jaw joints clicked when performing excursive movement. P experienced difficulty in eating certain foods. The prognosis was that the limitation of movement was permanent. P sustained tinnitus and deafness to the left ear, which was described as slight in nature. There was damage to the left ulnar nerve causing mild disability in the left forearm and hand characterised by weakness and pins and needles thereto. Lacerations were present to the pinna of both ears with the left ear almost severed, together with multiple deep lacerations to the scalp. He was left with a scar from the coronal flap running from the apex of the right ear across the top of the head to the apex of the left ear and two one cm scars on the right cheek and a single one cm scar on the left. The head injuries gave rise to post traumatic stress syndrome consisting of (1) severe memory impairment in that he could not remember facts or events (he left food cooking, causing fires, and returned home from shopping by foot unaware that he had travelled outward by car); (2) severe headaches several times per week; (3) mood changes, including being short tempered and frustrated; (4) momentary feelings of disequilibrium, and (5) speech disturbance. The prognosis was that such symptoms would be permanent and any recovery considerably limited. The medical evidence was that his symptoms had and would in the future render him totally unsuitable to undertake any form of employment. P was unable to resume his previous hobby of motorcycling, which he had performed on a semi professional basis, or to carry out gardening tasks. *General Damages*: £50,000. Total award: £237,476.

PERKINS (CICB: QUANTUM: 1999), *Re*, August 11, 1999, Chairman: Charles Whitby Q.C., CICB (York). [*Ex rel.* Jonathan Godfrey, Barrister, St. Paul's Chambers, 23 Park Square South, Leeds].

Head – psychiatric damage

1537. H, female, aged 27 at the date of the incident and 32 at the hearing, was in a restaurant with her husband at the time of the incident. They were both seated near to the window. H recalled seeing a young man outside. A brick was thrown through the window, striking H on the head. She felt her eyes popping and the left side of her face going numb, following which she believed she blacked out. H was taken to hospital by ambulance. As a result of this incident, H suffered a severe head injury, namely a compound fracture of the right parietal region and an underlying extradural haematoma. She needed neurosurgical intervention whereby the fracture was elevated. H was discharged from hospital in December 1995 to the care of her husband who had been looking after their children, a two year old daughter and a 12 week old baby. H was prescribed anticonvulsants and advised to rest. H's husband and his mother helped care for her while she convalesced. Following the accident, H suffered from severe headaches which were post traumatic in nature. As a result, she had to take strong painkillers. The headaches were sometimes accompanied by violent sickness. She also felt that her left side was weak. In addition, she experienced flashbacks of the incident which caused her psychological distress. She was therefore diagnosed as suffering from post traumatic stress disorder. H saw a consultant psychiatrist and counselling therapy was arranged for her for a duration of approximately three months. Following this, H was prescribed antidepressants by her GP as she was still suffering from depressive episodes. As a result of these symptoms, H could not leave the house alone for nearly one year following the incident. This was due to her fear of being stalked after a report was published in the paper detailing the attack. In addition, she was unable to dine in a restaurant after the incident and had a phobia of glass windows. H became nervous and apprehensive of crowded places, having developed a fear of men who resembled the assailant. Other symptoms included bouts of insomnia and crying. H returned to work approximately 18 months after the incident, working one day per week as a betting shop cashier. She remained unable to return to working at her previous level of seniority as a manageress of a betting shop and had to work reduced hours. That was due to poor manual dexterity and slowness in her work following the incident. It was found to be unlikely that H would ever return to her pre-accident level of employment. It was also expected that her post traumatic migraines would continue indefinitely to some degree. H remained at an increased risk of epilepsy of two per cent for the rest of her life as a direct result of the incident. As a consequence of the above symptoms, H lost confidence in everyday social intercourse and at the date of the hearing was only just recovering from the post traumatic stress disorder. *General Damages*: £40,000. Future loss of earnings: £43,290. Total award: £87,199.

HULME (CICB: QUANTUM: 2000), *Re* [2000] 3 Q.R. 4, Lord Carlisle (Chairman), CICB (Manchester).

Head – neck

1538.   P worked for G as a panel beater and paint sprayer. On October 3, 1995 he was struck by a car which fell from a hydraulic ramp and hit him on the right side of the head. D was knocked unconscious and suffered post traumatic amnesia. D suffered a sore neck and lump on the side of the head. There was a whiplash type injury to his neck from the impact. D was detained overnight in hospital and discharged the next day. D spent four weeks mainly in bed. D attended his GP's surgery on October 31, 1995 and was deemed fit for work from November 6, 1995. D was unable to cope and gave up work due to pain in his neck. D contended that he was suffering from short term memory loss. D's doctor administered a simple memory test and D was unable to remember two out of three items. D could not remember the month of the year and could not remember TV programmes which he had watched the previous night. D was subsequently made redundant for reasons unconnected with the accident. D's clinical psychologist concluded that D was suffering from an information and memory processing disorder. Further tests indicated impairment of memory and cognitive deficiency. D's neck continued to be problematic. D was then seen by G's neurologist who could not detect any significant brain injury and could not understand D's memory difficulties. D's condition appeared to be deteriorating as opposed to improving. D was referred to G's clinical psychologist who undertook a full range of memory test functions. It was subsequently determined that D had grossly under performed and if the results had truly reflected the state of his brain, D would have been admitted to a brain injury unit. Further joint tests were undertaken by D's and G's clinical psychologists, when it was again confirmed that D had under performed. The trial judge rejected the case entirely with regard to a brain injury. It was concluded that there was no memory deficit. D had received a blow the head and a whiplash type injury to the neck and there was post concussional amnesia. D then started to exaggerate the severity of his symptoms and other non organic factors intervened. D's claim for loss of earnings after redundancy was rejected. D's claim for a *Smith v. Manchester* award was rejected. *General Damages*: £8,500.

DOWLE v. GRAHAM, March 26, 1999, Judge O'Malley, CC (Taunton). [*Ex rel.* Bond Pearce Solicitors, Darwin House, Southernhay Gardens, Exeter].

Cheekbone – psychiatric damage

1539.   C, male aged 41 at the time of the assault, and 46 at the hearing, was punched and kicked repeatedly in the face and body when he intervened in a domestic dispute in the course of his work as a police officer. C sustained severe trauma to the face with multiple, significantly displaced fractures to the right zygomatic arch. He underwent an operation one week after the attack to reduce the fractures and insert titanium plates to stabilise the bones. Pre-operatively, C was noted to have profound numbness in the distribution of the right infra-orbital nerve affecting the cheek, lateral aspect of the nose, upper lip and teeth in the right upper quadrant. He experienced some diplopia and "floaters" in the right eye. He suffered paraesthesia on the right side of his face which was likely to be permanent, which was worse in cold weather and he avoided very hot or very cold food and drink. The right side of his face felt as if he had been anaesthetised and that was a constant reminder of the event. The psychiatric consequences of the attack led to the development of a major chronic depressive illness with symptoms of post-traumatic stress syndrome. C developed alcohol dependency and experienced significant anxiety and stress. He had been medically retired after an unsuccessful attempt to return to his police work. C experienced night sweats, early morning vomiting, shakiness, dizziness, headaches, anorexia and a fear of encountering his assailant. He had an intense fear of the unknown. Anti-depressant medication had been unsuccessful as had treatment by psychologists and the prognosis was poor. *General Damages* (including award for loss of congenial employment): £37,500. Past loss of earnings award: £7,089. Future loss of earnings award: £56,750. Total award: £101,339.

CALVERT (CICB: QUANTUM: 2000), *Re*, December 14, 1999, John Crowley Q.C., CICB (London). [*Ex rel.* James Laughland, Barrister, 1 Temple Gardens, Temple, London].

Cheekbone – teeth

1540.   J, male, aged 23 at the date of the incident and 27 at the hearing, was assaulted by two nightclub doormen, and sustained a fracture to his left zygotic arch. J was prescribed painkillers. He experienced severe pain for a period of approximately three weeks and thereafter intermittent discomfort for a few months. His cheekbone healed within four months of the incident without the need for operative treatment. A front incisor was abridged under general anaesthetic. *General Damages*: £3,500.

JACKSON (CICB: QUANTUM:1999), *Re*, February 22, 1999, Chairman: Charles Whitby Q.C., CICB (York). [*Ex rel.* Edward Legard, Barrister, York Chambers, 14 Toft Green, York].

Teeth

1541.   F, a boy aged 12 at the date of the accident and 17 at the date of the infant settlement approval hearing, was injured when using a water slide at D's pool. The upper left front tooth was knocked out and subsequently had to be replaced with a denture. The upper right front tooth was fractured with the loss of one third of its crown, and displaced upwards into the bone of the jaw. It was re-implanted under local anaesthetic on the day of the accident and the missing part of the crown later rebuilt. Despite subsequent root canal filling the tooth had to be extracted four years later as it was painful and discoloured. That involved five visits to the dentist for extraction and fitting a new denture. Prior to the accident, F had had perfect dentition with healthy teeth. F was unable to play sports for about six months after the accident. The denture was uncomfortable at first and F was unable to bite and enjoy firm or hard food. The agreed medical evidence was that a denture should not be considered a permanent solution, and that replacement of F's missing teeth by implants would be the most effective method of restoring his teeth as closely as possible to their pre-accident condition. That would involve lengthy treatment for up to two years with bone regeneration and grafting at the sites of the implants prior to fixing of the implants and crowns. Thereafter the crowns would require replacement every 10 to 15 years and the ceramic abutments to the crowns would need to be replaced every 20 to 30 years. *General Damages*: £4,000. Award for future cost of restorative dentistry (agreed): £7,650. Award for future cost of replacement of crowns and ceramic abutments: £5,000.

F (A CHILD) v. BEDFORD BC, March 17, 2000, Judge Charles Harris Q.C., CC (Northampton). [*Ex rel.* Jonathan Hand, Barrister, 35 Essex Street, Temple, London].

Teeth

1542.   G, a girl, aged eight at the date of the accident and 10 at trial, sustained facial and oral injuries when she fell from her bicycle. She was taken to hospital where it was noted that her front lower and upper teeth were loose and hypersensitive; there was traumatic ulceration of the labial mucosa with "tatooing"; extra-orally the lower lip was extremely swollen and there were signs of trauma to the chin and lower border of the mandible. On review one week later, the symptoms were the same and G was unable to open her mouth or eat solids. A liquid diet was recommended. G was reviewed again approximately six weeks after the accident when she was able to open her mouth normally but complained of discomfort and clicking on opening wide. She was able to eat solids but her anterior teeth were still sensitive and unable to tolerate temperature extremes. By the time of review eight months after the accident G's symptoms had resolved, save there was still some less pronounced discomfort and clicking associated with the right tempro-mandibular joint. The accident had caused damage to the nerves of the upper four front teeth, which were slightly discoloured. The likely prognosis was that the teeth would have to be root treated and crowned in a few years' time. An award was made to cover the anticipated cost of further dental treatment. *General Damages* (agreed): £3,000.

     G (A CHILD) v. GRINDAL [2000] 4 Q.R. 6, District Judge Cotterill, CC (Nuneaton).

Teeth

1543.   F, female, a housewife, aged 30 at the date of the incident and 33 at trial, attended upon W, a dentist, for treatment between September 1995 and October 1996. Some of the treatment was negligent, and some constituted an assault, W having been suspended from practising by the General Dental Council and not having informed F. The negligent treatment constituted the failure to recognise decay in a tooth, in September 1995, which demanded prompt treatment. The failure to treat led to pain and the extraction of the tooth, which needed replacing with an implant retained crown. Its absence had caused soreness on the open gum for three years and six months. When it was extracted, the mesial root broke off. W was unaware that the root remained, F suffered pain for three weeks before it was removed and her holiday during that period was ruined. W also unnecessarily extracted a wisdom tooth and removed and replaced a filling. The general damages award included an element for future inconvenience, as the crown would have to be replaced every seven years. In addition, there was an award representing damages for the treatment which took place on four occasions while W was suspended, to which treatment F would not have consented if aware of the suspension, and therefore it constituted assault. *General Damages*: £3,000. Award for dental treatment amounting to assault: £500.

     FINNEGAN v. WILTSHIRE, April 5, 2000, District Judge Cowling, CC (Mansfield). [*Ex rel.* Richard Gregory, Barrister, 24 The Ropewalk, Nottingham].

Facial scars

1544.   M, male, aged 29 at the time of the incident and 37 at the date of the hearing was attacked with broken glass and sustained lacerations to the left forearm, left little finger and under the surface of his chin. He was taken to hospital where his lacerations were explored and sutured under general anaesthetic. During the healing process the scar became hypertrophic and contracted. Scar revision was therefore undertaken. As that did not produce a satisfactory result, further revision surgery was carried out. However, after that some of the stitches came out in the early operative period so re-stitching was required. M suffered some embarrassment from scarring measuring 5 cm below the submental region, which scarring stretched to 1.5 cm in width at the maximum point. Puckering of the skin at each end produced a bulge or fold. There was no expectation of spontaneous improvement. The scarring to the forearm and finger were minor. *General Damages*: £11,000.

MARTIN (CICB: QUANTUM: 2000), *Re* [2000] 4 Q.R. 5, Sir Derek Bradbeer (Chairman), CICB (Durham).

Facial scars

1545.   C, a girl aged four at the time of the incident and 10 at trial, received facial injuries when attacked by a dog owned by T. C sustained cuts to the area around her left eyebrow, the left side of the bridge of her nose, the right cheek below the right eye and the side of the right nostril and right side of the mouth. The wounds were cleaned and steri-stripped. The wounds healed leaving scars representing obvious cosmetic defects. The most severe scars were under the right eye and to the right side of the mouth where there was a clear contour deformity and pigmentation making the scarring readily apparent. C also suffered a psychological injury manifesting itself in a phobic anxiety in relation to animals in general, dogs in particular, bedwetting and heightened awareness of the appearance of her face. After approximately two years, the most noticeable scars remained the two on the right cheek. C underwent surgical revision of those scars four years after the incident which produced a significant improvement in the cosmetic appearance of the scars. By the date of hearing, C had fully recovered from the psychological effects of the incident and the scars represented a barely noticeable cosmetic defect which no longer troubled her. *General Damages*: £7,000.

C (A CHILD) v. TAYLOR, January 12, 2000, Deputy District Judge Wilson, CC (Nottingham). [*Ex rel.* Nelsons, Solicitors, Pennine House, 8 Stanford Street, Nottingham].

Facial scars

1546.   H, male, aged 29 at the date of the accident and 32 at trial, a restaurateur, tripped and fell through glass doors badly lacerating his lip and chin, necessitating 35 sutures. H was unable to work for five weeks. H's wounds healed reasonably well, to leave a 2 cm horizontal scar along the underside of the lower lip, a 3 cm vertical scar from his lip to his chin, and a circular scar to the chin, some 3 cm in diameter. The first two scars had begun to fade by the time of the assessment, but were still visible at conversational distances. The third scar was the most cosmetically apparent, and distorted the left side of the chin. It would not improve, and would always be visible. There was a loss of sensation at the skin within the circular scar, and a raised area on the left lip which sometimes caused embarrassing dribbling when H ate or drank. The court had particular regard to those functional deficiencies in making the award. *General Damages*: £5,850.

HUSSAIN v. NAWAZ, November 25, 1999, Recorder Aspley, CC (Derby). [*Ex rel.* Richard Gregory, Barrister, 24 The Ropewalk, Nottingham].

Facial scars

1547.   B, female, aged four at the time of the accident and five at trial, was riding her new bicycle when the frame snapped and she collided with metal railings. She suffered a 7mm laceration at the lateral margin of her left eyebrow and associated bruising. The wound was cleaned and closed with skin tape and healed soundly. However it was expected to leave a visible and permanent scar. B was off nursery school for one day, and was reluctant to ride her bicycle for some months. *General Damages* (agreed): £4,750.

B (A CHILD) v. LITTLEWOODS PLC, October 19, 1999, District Judge Ing, CC (Cheltenham). [*Ex rel.* Davis Gregory Solicitors, 25 Rodney Road, Cheltenham, Gloucs].

Facial scars

1548. K, male, electrical engineer, aged 27 at the date of the injury and 29 at trial, was injured when he was headbutted over the left eye in a hotel by a member of the hotel staff. He suffered a laceration above the eyebrow which bled profusely. He attended hospital, where three steristrips were required to close the wound. The laceration healed, leaving a scar 2.5 cm long in the shape of a "v", which was easily visible at normal conversational distance. The scar was lumpy and a source of embarrassment to K as it attracted comment. It remained slightly tender to the touch although this was likely to resolve in the near future. *General Damages*: £4,500

KING v. BRITANNIA HOTELS LTD, June 29, 2000, Judge Carter Q.C., CC (Bury). [*Ex rel.* Russell & Russell Solicitors, Colmar House, Middleton Gardens, Middleton].

Facial scars – psychiatric damage

1549. C, male, a self employed painter and decorator, aged 30 at the date of the incident and 34 at the hearing, was attacked by a group of football hooligans. He was severely beaten and kicked in the head. He suffered an undisplaced skull fracture and lacerations to his face and abdomen. His concussive head injury gave rise to headaches which resolved within a year, and a very small increase in the risk of epilepsy. He suffered a modest hearing loss in his left ear, which although described as a five per cent disability, caused significant difficulties in ordinary social conversation. He lost a tooth, which was crowned, and others were loosened. The crowned tooth became infected and an apicectomy was necessary. The tooth continued to ache after four years. The lacerations left a curved scar through C's lip measuring approximately 4.5 cm, and a longer scar to the cheek and neck. After cosmetic surgery, this scar improved slightly, but was still prominent on the neck, and bled occasionally when shaved. C suffered from post traumatic stress disorder, characterised by nightmares and intrusive thoughts. At the time of the assessment, that was described as an enduring personality change, with his confidence permanently lowered. Both the attack and the scars, which were a daily reminder thereof, created significant psychological sequelae. The applicant had changed his social habits. *General Damages*: £23,500.

CARRINGTON (CICB: QUANTUM: 2000), *Re* [2000] 4 Q.R. 5, Michael Lever Q.C. (Chairman), CICB (York).

Facial scars – psychiatric damage

1550. P, female, aged 20 at the date of the accident and 24 at trial, was injured when she fell against a glass panelled door. P's head went through the glass panel, which shattered causing severe lacerations to the left side of her face. P was left with only partial sensation of the left infra-orbital nerve, mild weakness of the upper lip and a scar commencing approximately 4 mm from the mid-point of the left lower eyelid lash margin and extending down medially for a distance of approximately 2.6 cm to the left nasolabial area. The scar then extended downwards obliquely and laterally to the left corner of the mouth for a distance of just under 2 cm, and then along the vermilion of the left lower lip for a distance of 1 cm. The upper part of the scar from the lower eyelid to the nose was white in colour, flat and with a maximum width of 3 mm. The lower component, extending in the nasolabial crease, from the side of the nose down to the corner of the mouth, was slightly hypertrophic, pale and raised. The scar on the left lower lip was barely visible unless P were to bare her teeth, in which case a white line across the lower lip was visible. The whole area adjacent to the scar for a circumference of 4 cm had slightly diminished sensation compared with the right side of the face. There was some weakness leading to dribbling immediately after the accident for about six to eight months. There was numbness to the left upper lip and some discomfort from the teeth behind the upper lip. The left cheek felt heavy and P complained of a dragging sensation. Initially, due to pain in the area, P found it difficult and frustrating to eat and the upper left eyelid would not close properly. After 18 months it was confirmed that the pattern of scarring and sensation was unlikely to change significantly. Revisional surgery was an option but there was no guarantee of success. At the time of the trial P decided that she did not wish to have such surgery, but would like the option in the future. P was referred for cosmetic camouflage advice, the cost of which was included in her special damages claim. Two psychiatric consultants confirmed that P had a previous history of mood disturbance and depression and that this had been aggravated by the accident. P was more vulnerable to the fears, anxieties and discomforts of a facial injury at a crucial time in her life than the average girl and more vulnerable than she would otherwise have been because of her previous history. Both experts were in agreement that the symptoms experienced by P were essentially a post traumatic depression. They agreed that she experienced a considerable level of self consciousness about her appearance and that there was substantial loss of confidence which was recovering. There was a substantial impairment of concentration and sleep and nightmares with flashbacks of the accident continued for some 18 months. P argued that her future employment prospects were affected by the accident. P was unemployed at the time of the accident and there was no loss of earnings claim. With regard to future loss of earnings a *Smith v. Manchester* claim was made. The judge accepted P's submissions that her injuries fell into the upper bracket of the Judicial Studies Board Guidelines on facial injuries for females. *General Damages*: £22,500. *Smith v. Manchester* award (agreed): £2,500. Award for future losses (including cosmetic camouflage and possible cosmetic surgery): £12,255.

PENFOLD v. DA SILVA, November 1, 1999, Judge Bond, CC (Bournemouth). [*Ex rel.* The Andrew Isaacs Practice, Solicitors, Wessex Chambers, 21 Lansdowne Road, Bournemouth].

Facial scars – psychiatric damage

1551.   S, male, aged eight at the date of the road traffic accident and 11 at the infant settlement approval hearing, suffered two deep lacerations from glass to his right cheek, each about 7mm long. S was admitted to hospital for one day to have the wounds cleaned and stitched under general anaesthetic. The glass damaged a facial nerve on the right hand side, which left S with a deformed smile. The nerve damage was 90 per cent healed within two months of the accident and had fully healed by the next appointment, five months after the accident, with no adverse future consequences. The injuries took some months to heal, though the scars healed well leaving only a minor cosmetic blemish. In addition, S suffered a psychological reaction which was particularly acute during the months after the accident during which time S suffered from bad dreams and flashbacks. S was also worried about his mother, who was more seriously injured in the accident. S was an anxious passenger for some time, being more anxious generally than before the accident, and that was still the case three years after the accident. S developed an occasional twitch in his right cheek, first noticed by his family about one year after the accident, which was said to be anxiety related rather than due to the nerve damage. The twitch was most often present when S was relaxing. That and his post accident appearance had led to S being teased at school. The prognosis was that S's general anxiety would improve with time, possibly years rather than months, and no treatment was recommended in view of S's dislike of further medical intervention. *General Damages* (agreed): £6,750.

S (A CHILD) v. BLOOMFIELD, October 7, 1999, District Judge Levinson, CC (Chichester). [*Ex rel.* Tim Petts, Barrister, 12 Kings Bench Walk, Temple, London].

Ear

1552.   W, female, 11 at the time of the incident and 12 at trial, underwent piercing of the upper outer part of her right ear. Within days the ear had become swollen and W developed vomiting and high temperature. A diagnosis of perichondritis and abscess formation was made. The ear remained swollen after treatment by intravenous antibiotics and so the ear was incised under general anaesthetic. There was noted to be a perforation in the cartilage; a drain was inserted in the ear and the wound dressed. Culture of the pus from the ear showed pseudomonas species and she was put on a course of Ciprofloxacin. The loss of cartilage resulted in swelling of the upper pole and kinking of the helical rim. Behind the ear was a 13 mm vertical scar medial to the helix. The ear remained tender to firm pressure and painful in the cold although those symptoms were expected gradually to subside. W remained, and was found to be likely to remain, self conscious and would not wear her hair otherwise than so as to conceal the ear. The deformation of the ear was anticipated to be permanent. *General Damages*: £4,850.

W (A CHILD) v. CLASSIC CUTS, October 7, 1999, District Judge Evans, CC (Kingston upon Hull). [*Ex rel.* Paul W Miller, Barrister, Wilberforce Chambers, 7 Bishop Lane, Hull].

Ear – facial scars

1553.   H, female, a police officer, aged 27 at the date of the incident in 1995 and 32 at the date of the hearing, was attacked by a prisoner in the rear of a police van. The prisoner bit 40 per cent of her right ear off and then spat it onto the floor of the van. Over a period of three years, H underwent three reconstructive operations. At the first operation, the missing part of the ear was sewn back on, but that gave rise to a purulent discharge and the tissue died. During subsequent operations, cartilage and skin was removed from her left ear and her neck to rebuild her right ear. H was left with disfiguring and distressing scarring consisting of a scar measuring 6.5 cm on her neck, and a scar measuring 4.5 cm behind her right ear, both of which were visible, and a small scar behind her left ear at the donor site which was hidden by the ear. H suffered increased sensation and pain to the lower part of her right ear and numbness at the top of the ear. Her sleep was disturbed due to pain from the ear, cold weather made it painful and she could no longer carry out her main form of exercise which was swimming. Washing her hair was also difficult. A significant consequence of the injury was the psychological effect. Although she was able to continue work as a police officer after brief periods of recuperation following each operation, H suffered humiliating and upsetting comments from both prisoners and some fellow officers, as she was expected to wear her hair up at work. H felt diminished by the disfigurement and her ability to deal with confrontational situations was affected. H could no longer wear earrings as she used to, or support sunglasses. *General Damages*: £22,500.

HOLLOWAY (CICB: QUANTUM: 2000), *Re* [2000] 4 Q.R. 5, Michael Lewis Q.C. (Chairman), CICB (London).

Sight

1554.   A, male, aged 16 at the date of the incident and 20 at the hearing, was injured as a result of an air rifle being fired in his direction. A pellet went into A's right eye causing devastating injury and loss of that eye. A sustained anuclination of the right eye causing immediate and continual blindness in that eye and extensive haemorrhaging. The eye was removed immediately after the accident and hydroxy apatite implants were inserted into the eye socket. A was initially treated with oral and intravenous antibiotics and he continued to take antibiotics and anti-inflammatory tablets following his discharge from hospital the day after the incident. He took antibiotic eye drops for approximately three months. Two and a half months after the incident the injury had healed apart from a small area in the centre of the conjunctiva. After six and a half months, A was fitted with an artificial eye. Recovery from the injury was generally good, but A's monocular vision continued to cause him problems in terms of driving and performing other functions. Additionally, the right eye was noticeably sunken and lacked range of movement, which caused A embarrassment and loss of confidence. There was a risk that over time the weight of the artificial eye and lack of movement would cause the lower eyelid to sink and preventative surgery would be required to reduce that. There was a possibility that plastic surgery might eventually become necessary. The artificial eye would require replacing approximately every two years as the ageing process caused changes within the eye socket. A's employers at Manchester Airport confirmed that as a result of the loss of his eye, A was unable to obtain promotion within that firm due to his inability to hold an HGV driving licence. Employment consultants identified the difficulty A would have in obtaining alternative employment, due to his loss of vision. A multiplier of 23 was applied in calculating future loss of earnings. *General Damages*: £27,500. Past loss of earnings: £2,670. Future loss of earnings: £115,000. Award for future medical treatment: £8,500.

AVGERINOS (CICB: QUANTUM: 1999), *Re*, May 18, 1999, Chairman: Edward Gee, CICB (Manchester). [*Ex rel.* Rowlands Solicitors, 3 York Street, Manchester].

Hearing and speech

1555.   N, male, aged 67 at the date of trial, suffered from hearing loss and tinnitus during the mid to late 1980's. N was exposed to industrial noise for a period of 19 years during his employment with UEC between 1971 and 1990. He was also exposed to industrial noise at 86 dB (A) with other employers between 1961 and 1971 and at 93 dB (A) for one year prior to 1963. Between 1949 and 1957, N also worked for the Royal Navy and was exposed to occasional engine room noise, small arms fire and noise from a "Bofors gun". A tone audiogram performed by N's medical expert in 1994 revealed a moderate high tone sensori-neural hearing loss, with a dip at 6 Khz on the right and 4 Khz on the left, consistent with noise damage and ageing. Averaging thresholds for 1, 2 and 3 Khz was 26.6 dB and at 6 Khz 52.5 dB. It was common ground between the experts that the hearing loss due to noise was 7 dB after correction was made for age related loss. However, a further audiogram performed in 1999 showed significant deterioration, particularly in the lower frequencies. The thresholds across all frequencies on both sides showed a fall below 40 dB and although on the left side this was in part due to wax, N's hearing on the right side had also significantly deteriorated, in particular at the frequencies of 500 Hz and 1 Khz. The audiometric pattern therefore no longer showed the characteristic 4 or 6 Khz dip that was considered to be a diagnostic factor for noise damage. N's symptoms caused him to turn up the television, and he had difficulty understanding a conversation on the telephone. He had no difficulty understanding a conversation in a quiet room, but he did have difficulty in a noisy room or in a crowd. N suffered from tinnitus every day, and disturbed sleep approximately once a week. N did not consult his GP about the tinnitus, nor did he wear a tinnitus masker. Discounts were made from the general damages award totalling 25 per cent, comprising of 15 per cent and 10 per cent to reflect hearing damage during N's employment with the Royal Navy and other employers respectively. The judge referred to *Fry v. Ford Motor Co Ltd* (Unreported, March 1999). N's injury was considered to be of greater severity because of the mixed hearing loss. *General Damages*: £7,000.

NEIL v. UEC INDUSTRIES, January 20, 2000, Judge Urquart, CC (Liverpool). [*Ex rel.* J. Keith Park & Co Solicitors, Claughton House, 39 Barrow Street, St. Helens Merseyside].

Hearing and speech

1556.   M, female, born on August 22, 1990 and aged nine at the date of the infant settlement approved hearing, brought a claim for negligent failure to diagnose congenital profound sensorineural hearing loss in both ears which was present from birth but not diagnosed until July 1, 1993 when she was almost three years old, notwithstanding regular hearing tests from March 11, 1991. M experienced profound hearing loss in both ears in excess of 96 dB which was unlikely to improve. Hearing aids had been supplied since the delayed diagnosis and would be required for the rest of M's life. The failure to diagnose M's hearing loss caused speech and language delay and behavioural difficulties. She underwent intensive speech therapy from September 1998 and that improved her speech to such an extent that she became able to speak and be understood. The award took into account risk in establishing liability, causation and quantum. Total award (approved) (including general damages and future loss of earning capacity): £50,000.

M (A CHILD) v. NORTH & MID HAMPTONSHIRE HA, October 11, 1999, Judge Hidden, QBD. [*Ex rel.* Frank R Moat, Barrister, 3 Pump Court, Temple, London].

Neck

1557.   M, female, aged 47 at the date of the accident and 49 at trial, was overtaking a parked bus which turned into her car without warning, sending it spinning across the road. As a result, M suffered an acute neck sprain affecting, in particular, the right side of the neck. She visited her GP who advised painkillers. M suffered significant constant pain for about four weeks and thereafter suffered intermittent neck pain radiating into her right shoulder. That affected such activities as reversing when driving, carrying anything heavy in her right hand and writing reports at work. M was also nervous in traffic, particularly when passing buses. The medical evidence was that M would in all probability be symptom free by 21 months after the accident. However, M's evidence was that at the date of trial, two years after, she was still suffering intermittent symptoms. It was found that she would make a full recovery within a short period. *General Damages*: £3,000. Total award: £4,687.

MAMCZYNSKI v. GM BUSES (NORTH) LTD, January 11, 2000, District Judge Stockton, CC (Oldham). [*Ex rel.* Andrew Granville Stafford, Barrister, 4 King's Bench Walk, Temple, London].

Neck – pre-existing disability or condition: aggravated by whiplash

1558.   W, female, aged 41 at the date of the accident and 46 at the date of the assessment hearing suffered a neck strain and a major depressive episode and travel phobia when involved in a low speed road traffic accident. W had exhibited some discomfort and variable restriction in her neck prior to the accident. Following the accident the levels of pain and restriction were much more persistent and the court found that the effect of the accident was to have accelerated W's degenerative changes by four years. It was agreed that W had suffered a major depressive episode and travel phobia for a period of 20 months. W's intermittent neck, shoulder and back pain, suffered prior to the accident had not prevented her from working as a piece worker in a textile factory nor had it affected her home and social life. Following the accident W was unable to return to work and required assistance in the home and around the garden. W retrained and was able to return to work for another employer on a reduced salary and on lighter duties three years after the accident. *General Damages*: £8,500. Total award: £37,443.

WESLEY v. COBB (DECEASED), January 19, 2000, District Judge Clegg, CC (Altrincham). [*Ex rel.* Myers Lister Price, Solicitors, 376 Palatine Road, Northenden, Manchester].

Neck – pre-existing disability or condition: aggravated by whiplash

1559.   C, male, aged 30 at the date of the accident and 34 at trial, was involved in a collision where there was a front impact to the passenger side of the car. He was taken to hospital and two hours later suffered stiffening in his neck and pain radiating down his right shoulder into the right arm, with a heavy sensation. C was advised to keep his arm in a sling for seven days and was referred for physiotherapy. C suffered continuing pain despite using analgesia and anti-inflammatory drugs. He suffered immediate numbness in the fifth finger of his right hand. C stopped playing squash and could not swim, but continued to work. Eighteen months after the accident, C was continuing to suffer some neck pain, pain radiating down the right arm, weakness of the right arm and sensory disturbance in the medial fingers of the right hand. An MRI scan showed that he had cervical spondylotic disease. There were two disc protrusions, of which at least one had occurred as a consequence of the accident. The onset of pain in the neck radiating down and weakening the right arm was a direct consequence of the accident and medical evidence suggested that a five year acceleration in the spondylotic process had taken place. *General Damages*: £8,000.

CALFORD v. CAMPBELL [2000] 3 Q.R. 5, District Judge Hayworth, CC (Rawtenstall).

Neck – pre-existing disability or condition: aggravated by whiplash

1560.   D, female, aged 57 at the date of the road traffic accident and 59 at trial, suffered a whiplash injury. Initially D was symptom free. After three days, D began to suffer pain in her neck, shoulders and right arm. She also suffered headaches. There were no psychological sequelae. D's GP prescribed painkillers. She continued to work. She undertook physiotherapy and osteopathy, but that only gave her transient benefit and her symptoms remained. In August 1998 she retired on the grounds of ill health unrelated to the accident. Over the years the pain in her neck and shoulders improved, although on the day of the trial D was still complaining of suffering such pain intermittently but on a daily basis. The medical evidence confirmed that the neck and shoulder pain was unlikely to improve further because the accident had probably brought forward, by a period of between five and 10 years, symptoms from pre-existing degenerative change in her cervical spine. It was found that the injury fell just within Section 6(A)(b)(i) (more serious moderate neck injuries) of the Judicial Studies Board Guidelines. *General Damages*: £7,000.

DIAMOND v. WYLIE [2000] 6 Q.R. 7, District Judge Kesterton, CC (Nuneaton).

Neck – back

1561.   G, male, aged 24 at the date of the road traffic accident and 28 at the date of assessment, sustained a jarring soft tissue injury to his neck and lower back. G attended hospital where X-rays were taken but no bony injury was found. G was off work for four weeks initially and then for a further six weeks over the next 12 months. Eighteen months after the accident G was off work for a further 23 weeks when, with the help of physiotherapy, the pain gradually diminished. G was left with stiffness and intermittent severe pain to his neck and lower back which would probably continue for a period of four to five years from the accident with a risk of residual discomfort and intermittent pain continuing in the future. Prior to the accident, G was fit and an enthusiastic marathon runner, but afterwards he was unable to run long distances or carry out heavy manual tasks. *General Damages*: £6,750.

GIMBLETT v. SWANSEA CITY COUNCIL [2000] 3 Q.R. 5, District Judge Batcup, CC (Neath and Port Talbot).

Neck – whiplash type injury

1562.   C, a girl, aged 15 at the time of the road traffic accident and 18 at trial, sustained a whiplash type injury. She immediately complained of a dull ache in the front of her neck, but did not attend a hospital, preferring to attend her GP and a physiotherapist. C began physiotherapy one week after the accident continuing for 10 months. C also relied on a combination of simple analgesics, requiring painkillers at least two or three times a week on average. From the date of the accident, C was never symptom free. She suffered from pain in the upper cervical region radiating into the occipital region of her head. Often the pain would result in her having to go to bed and sleep it off. She suffered from an acute phase of symptoms for two months and thereafter the symptoms remained static. The symptoms were increased by physical activity and by sitting holding her neck in a flexed position. Participating in school sports such as netball, hockey and volley ball resulted in neck pain and headaches but that was a price she was prepared to pay. She did however have to give up playing badminton. The predominant effect on her life was the loss of the sport of trampolining in which she excelled. C started trampolining at the age of five and started competing at seven. She won the regional championships for the next eight years until she was 14. In 1992 she won the national championship and the under 15's world championship in 1994. The year before the accident C came third in the world championships in a different age group. She was competing at the highest level in her sport. Before the accident she trained four to five times per week. She was unable to trampoline following the accident for one month. She resumed trampolining after that time but found that she could not do all of the required exercises, jumping caused dizziness. She was unable to do more than three one hour training sessions per week and those resulted in headaches and dizziness. The reduced amount of training was insufficient to keep her at the level of fitness or competition that she had enjoyed. C entered a national competition in the year after her accident, but instead of coming in the top four she ranked twenty seventh. S eventually decided to retire from her sport. It was found that C would have had a good chance of qualifying to take part in the 2004 Olympic games, but for the accident. The award for loss of amenity took account of the fact that C had excelled in her chosen sport and but for the accident had the prospect of achieving real excellence. *General Damages*: £16,500 (including an award of £10,500 for loss of amenity).

C (A CHILD) v. KITCHEN, August 2, 2000, District Judge Dancey, CC (Poole). [*Ex rel.* Lyons Davidson Solicitors, Victoria House, 51 Victoria Street, Bristol].

Neck – whiplash type injury

1563.   C, female aged 45 at the date of the road traffic accident and 50 at the date of the assessment, sustained soft tissue injuries to her neck and thoracic spine. She was conveyed to hospital where X-rays revealed no bony injury and was discharged with a cervical collar and advised to take analgesics. C wore the collar for one month after which she was able to return to work as a domestic assistant at a hospital, but remained on light duties for a further three months. When examined eight months after the accident, C complained of a constant burning pain in the neck and mid back area. The judge found that C had made a substantial recovery by three to four years after the accident and had only minimal ongoing symptoms which could be controlled by analgesics and avoiding heavy physical activity. C also suffered from symptoms of a stress disorder including tension, anxiety, ruminations about the accident and insomnia. She was fearful of motor travel and avoided any driving. The psychological symptoms were associated with the development of a moderate form of depression which required medication. C was a vulnerable person who had previously been prescribed antidepressant medication but had not been symptomatic for three years pre-accident. Four years after the accident, C required near continuous antidepressant medication and had not regained her confidence in respect of motor travel. She remained partially handicapped by residual symptoms of the stress disorder and it was highly unlikely that she would improve significantly in the foreseeable future. In the year following the accident C had taken eight tablets of Co-Dydramol during each 24 hour period which was the maximum stated dose. That had a constipating effect and C had developed an anal fissure, which had required two separate surgical procedures to remedy the tear and provide a complete resolution of the condition. *General Damages*: £13,500 (£7,500 in respect of the whiplash injury, £3,500 in respect of the psychiatric injuries and £2,500 in respect of the constipation and remedial surgery).

GILES v. GOSS, March 24, 2000, Judge D Glyn Morgan, CC (Newport, Gwent). [*Ex rel.* Andrew Arentsen, Barrister, 33 Park Place, Cardiff].

Neck – whiplash type injury

1564.   S, female, aged 22 at the date of the road traffic accident in October 1995, and 27 at trial, sustained a whiplash injury to the neck. Five years after the accident, S continued to experience muscle spasms in her neck on an almost daily basis, with symptoms commonly lasting for a couple of hours and spreading down between her shoulder blades. S had difficulty managing her household chores and looking after her young daughter. She still found that her neck would hurt after 20 minutes of driving. The orthopaedic experts, agreed that S had a permanent whiplash injury but that the symptoms would not worsen with time. S was fit to return to work in a job where her neck was not placed at any extremes of its range of movement for anything other than a short time and also in employment where the work was not regularly strenuous or heavy. At the time of the accident S had worked as a care assistant, having been in that job since the age of 18. S was off work as a result of the accident and her employment was terminated on grounds of ill heath nine months later. S underwent two courses of physiotherapy treatment. Three years after the accident she gave birth to her daughter and four months later, was pronounced by the DSS to be fit for work. Five years after the accident, S had not returned to work because she was looking after her daughter full time. At the time of the accident, S had just started a part time evening Access to Higher Education course because she only had one GCSE. S had hoped then to go onto university so that she could retrain as a social worker on the management side. The judge found that it was too speculative to suggest S would have achieved that aim and in all likelihood she would have continued as a care assistant but for the accident. The judge found that S should have mitigated her losses and found equally well paid work by June 1999. S also suffered from an adjustment disorder associated with her anxiety about driving and being a passenger in a car. Those symptoms had settled by the date of the trial. *General Damages*: £12,750 (whiplash injury: £12,000; psychological injury, £750). *Smith v. Manchester* award: £10,000. Award for loss of congenial employment: £2,500.

STEVENS v. LONDON & COUNTY LTD, March 16, 2000, Judge Cook, CC (Epsom). [*Ex rel.* Robert Weir, Barrister, Devereux Chambers, Devereux Court, London].

Neck – whiplash type injury

1565.   C, male, aged 48 at the date of the road traffic accident and 51 at trial, sustained bruising to his left lower leg, subungual haematoma subsequently leading to temporary loss of big toe nail, other bruises and contusions and shock. C was a retired schoolteacher, a polyarthritic condition had led to his retirement before the accident. A few days after the accident, C developed neck pain which was diagnosed as cervical spinal whiplash (C5/6 and C6/7) with an exacerbation of a previously subsided crico-thyroid injury. C experienced headaches and also developed post traumatic stress disorder and anxious depression. The neck pain significantly affected his daily activities including watching TV. He had to take care bending forward, in picking things up, when travelling in friends' cars or on public transport, when he wore a cervical collar, and had difficulty sleeping on his back. C developed nightmares and flashbacks of the accident, he continued to suffer headaches for a while, and there were some uncharacteristic episodes of uncontrollable aggression. C was prescribed a large number of drugs, including sleeping pills, relaxants and pain killers, and he saw numerous specialists. A psychiatrist said of him that his "neat, methodical, punctual, approach to life has made it more difficult for him to adjust to the effect of the accident" and that he had an "egg shell personality with extensive psychosomatic problems prior to the index episode". C's symptoms had improved but there was a possibility of them continuing indefinitely. The judge took account of a possibility of further expenditure on investigation and treatment which C was still undergoing at trial, and applied Guidelines 3(A)(c) and 3(B)(c) of the JSB Guidelines for the psychiatric injuries, and Guideline 6(A)(b)(ii) for the neck injuries, the lower of the two moderate brackets. *General Damages*: £11,250 (apportioned £7,250 for the neck, crico-thyroid and other physical injuries, and £4,000 for the psychiatric injuries). Award for possible future treatment: £1,500.

CORNER v. OSMENT, December 15, 1999, Judge Edwards, CC (Brentford). [*Ex rel.* Lawrence Caun, Barrister, Lamb Chambers, Lamb Buildings, Temple, London].

Neck – whiplash type injury

1566.   P, male, aged 57 at the date of the road traffic accident and 60 at the disposal hearing, suffered a whiplash injury when his stationary vehicle was hit from behind. He did not initially seek medical help. Following his arrival home he began to experience "flu like symptoms" which he treated by bed rest. The following day he awoke feeling shaken and nauseous, and developed stiffness of the neck, restricting his movements. P attempted to carry on his work as an electronic engineer, attending work as normal on the day following the accident, but was unable to continue past lunch time. Five days after the accident P was seen by his GP and noted to have a tenderness on the right side of the neck restricting rotation and abduction of the right shoulder. Pain was noted over the right trapezius muscle. P was advised to take analgesic tablets and to gradually mobilise his neck. He was able to return to work six days after the accident, but was unable to do any heavy lifting or perform several of his normal tasks. Five and a half months post accident, P was suffering continuing pain on the right side of the neck and restricted movements. He underwent a number of sessions of physiotherapy and other treatments which produced short term improvements, but no long term change in symptomology. Nine and a half months post accident P still experienced problems with restriction of movement and painful episodes. Further courses of physiotherapy were recommended for the next two years consisting of up to 20 treatments. P had suffered from degenerative changes prior to the accident making him vulnerable to further episodes of discomfort. Medical opinion was that had the accident not occurred, P would have remained symptom free for at least 10 years. Two and a half years post-accident, P was still experiencing pain and discomfort in his neck. On X-ray and clinical examination, evidence was noted of post-traumatic spondylosis. P's symptoms were thought to have reached a peak and residual symptoms were likely to remain for an extended period. At trial three years post accident, P described how he was continuing to use painkillers on an occasional basis and sought physiotherapy treatment whenever appropriate. He had had to give up his main pastime of cycling as he was unable to look over his right shoulder due to continued restricted movements and pain. Cycling was particularly important as he had been advised to undertake such exercise by his heart specialist following two heart attacks in the previous four years. His other main hobby of motor cycling had been severely curtailed due to neck pain suffered when wearing a crash helmet. P's employment continued to be affected due to his restricted movements and he had had to adapt new working practices to overcome those problems. *General Damages*: £7,500.

PARSLOW v. BRITISH WATERWAYS BOARD, July 7, 2000, Deputy District Judge Powell, CC (Scunthorpe). [*Ex rel.* Martin & Haigh Solicitors, 12-18 Frances Street, Scunthorpe, North Lincolnshire].

Neck – whiplash type injury

1567.   G, female, aged 24 at the date of the accident and 29 at trial, suffered severe whiplash injury to her neck with immediate pain radiating from her neck to her shoulders with some restriction of movement. The pain was severe and disabling for two to three months. G suffered pins and needles in her right hand for three months. She suffered dizziness and headaches over four months with sleep disturbance. G wore a collar for six weeks. Analgesics were prescribed and 20 sessions of physiotherapy. G was unable to continue her work as a library assistant driving a mobile library lorry, for two months due to the lorry not having power assisted steering. G was a keen horse rider who competed in national events. The accident prevented her from competing in the 1996 season. It was found that G had experienced significant pain and discomfort over the first two to three months and thereafter less significant pain up to four months after the accident. G was left with intermittent residual symptoms in the nature of a nuisance which would appear after exertion, particularly after competing on her horse. It was accepted that those symptoms were likely to be permanent. The other driver, who was found to be drunk at the scene of the accident, had verbally threatened G with physical violence prior to the arrival of the police. It was found that that had given rise to G's minor psychological symptoms of nervousness and anxiety when driving. Her symptoms were not perceived to be of great significance but impacted on G's psychological state for a few months after the accident, although she did tend to persist in being a "back seat" driver. *General Damages*: £7,250.

GUDGE v. MILROY [2000] 4 Q.R. 6, Judge Serota Q.C., CC (Hitchin).

Neck – whiplash type injury

1568.   F, female, aged 20 at the date of the road traffic accident and 23 at trial, sustained a whiplash injury. Within a few days her neck had stiffened and she developed severe headaches. The headaches continued, with about six or seven severe episodes over the next 13 months. F suffered a constant ache in her neck, lower skull, and across her shoulders. Sitting, looking downwards, for 30 minutes or more, or driving for about an hour could lead to an aggravation of the problem. A five month course of physiotherapy treatment resolved the headaches, but the ache persisted. The evidence at trial was that the ache was permanent. It affected her every day, and certain activities would aggravate the injury. F had taken up yoga to try to ease her muscular pain, and had developed ways of minimising her exposure to pain. She used an analgesic gel daily to ease the aching. The agreed medical evidence was that the injury represented a "considerable nuisance and inconvenience to her, but would not represent a disability apart from strenuous physical activity." The judge found that the injury fell within the moderate band of the JSB neck injury guidelines. He considered it a (b)(i) type of injury, namely permanent/recurring pain/discomfort. *General Damages*: £7,000.

FRYERS v. HIRST, August 4, 2000, District Judge Jordan, CC (Bradford). [*Ex rel.* David S Dixon, Barrister, Sovereign Chambers, 25 Park Square, Leeds].

Neck – whiplash type injury

1569.   P, male, aged 54 at the date of the accident and 58 at trial, sustained a soft tissue injury to his neck when he took avoiding action to prevent a head on collision and drove into a concrete post. P was off work for two weeks. Neck rotation was restricted to the right, by 30 per cent to 40 per cent of the normal range and to the left, by 40 per cent of the normal range. Extension was limited by 25 per cent. There was pain in the shoulder blade and internal rotation was limited. His symptoms were aggravated by sitting at a desk with a PC. P took paracetamol for headaches, which occurred two to three times per week. His ability to carry out gardening was restricted and he had given up sporting activities. At trial, his symptoms had not improved and medical opinion was that there would be neither improvement not deterioration for the remainder of P's working life. *General Damages*: £6,750.

PALFREY v. STAGECOACH LTD, May 18, 2000, District Judge Tromans, CC (Exeter). [*Ex rel.* Crosse & Crosse Solicitors, 14 Southernhay West, Exeter EX1 1PL].

Neck – whiplash type injury

1570. D, male, aged 41 at the date of the accident and 45 at trial, was injured in a road traffic accident, sustaining a whiplash injury to his neck and a mild sprain of the ligaments to his lumbar spine, together with psychological trauma. D attended hospital on the day of the accident and was fitted with a soft collar and advised, to take analgesics. He was away from work for five weeks and wore the collar for one month. He experienced difficulty in sleeping. D's neck symptoms had almost completely resolved two months after the accident, with only occasional twinges thereafter and he was able to resume his hobby of golf. It was thought that the residual symptoms, although minimal, continued for about two years post accident. The court held that there was no significant injury to the lumbar spine, with no tearing of ligaments and all effects of the sprain spent within a year. D's psychological symptoms following the accident consisted of mood and sleep disturbance, reactive to discomfort, and reduced socialisation. The symptoms caused by the accident were found to have continued for approximately one year from the date of the accident, but had substantially reduced after about six months. An MRI scan three and a half years after the accident was normal, showing no evidence of degenerative disease. There was no loss of disc height, nor disc protrusion. The spinal canal and exit foramina were of normal dimensions and all the facet joints were normal. *General Damages*: £6,500.

DAVIES v. HAYTER, February 28, 2000, Michael Harvey Q.C., QBD. [*Ex rel.* Not applicable].

Neck – whiplash type injury

1571. L, male aged 25 at the date of the road traffic accident and 26 at trial suffered whiplash injuries to the cervical spine, together with mid back and lower back pain. He also suffered from headaches. He was off work for eight weeks, two of which were over Christmas. Six months after the accident, L was still suffering from persistent back and neck pain. He had undergone 17 sessions of physiotherapy and had seen his GP on several occasions. His work involved lifting weights of up to 25 kg which aggravated the back and neck injury. L had tried on one occasion to return to his pre-accident hobby of playing football, but a year after the accident, he still complained of neck and back pain. The amount of pain was dependent upon the extent of physical activity during the day. He also continued to suffer headaches and lower back pain which he described as a dull ache but which on occasions could become painful. He had the occasional shooting pain on turning to the left. He had not returned to playing football and had encountered difficulties at home when playing with his two young children. Thereafter there had been an improvement and it was such that it was L's intention to go snow boarding and skiing approximately 17 months after the accident. The prognosis given three months prior to the trial, was for a complete recovery within 18 to 24 months of the accident. *General Damages*: £6,000.

LEACH v. PRO DELTA SYSTEMS LTD, January 31, 2000, District Judge Wilby, CC (Bury). [*Ex rel.* Tarran & Co, Solicitors, 5th Floor, Old Bank Chambers, 2 Old Bank Street, Manchester].

Neck – whiplash type injury

1572. G, male aged 34 at the date of the accident and 36 at trial, was injured when an HGV lorry was driven into the side of his moving car. The accident resulted in multiple small lacerations, which resolved within a few weeks, a soft tissue injury to the right wrist and forearm and a whiplash injury. The right forearm injury caused pain for three months and then some minor wrist discomfort which had fully resolved at the date of the trial. The whiplash injury caused immediate pain in both sides of the neck, in both shoulders and between the shoulder blades. For the first three months there was constant pain in those areas and restrictions on movement. By 18 months, there was a constant ache in the right side of the neck and shoulder blade area which became more painful after a period of activity. There were no restrictions on movement, although G suffered pain at extremes of movement in the neck and right shoulder. The prognosis was that G would continue indefinitely to suffer those residual symptoms, which he described as more of an irritation and inconvenience rather than a restriction. X-rays showed no degenerative change. His ability to work as a project manager for an insurance company was unimpaired. *General Damages*: £6,000.

GOUDIE v. NIGHT FREIGHT (EAST) LTD, October 20, 1999, District Judge Bazley White, CC (Ipswich). [*Ex rel.* Jackaman, Smith & Mulley Solicitors, 7 Northgate Street, Ipswich].

Neck – whiplash type injury

1573.   U, male, aged 42 at the date of the road traffic accident and 46 at trial, sustained whiplash injuries to his cervical spine. He was intending to start his own business at the time of the accident, as a self employed joiner. Over the three years following the accident, U required periods of time away from work, which were found to be slightly more than six months in total. His hobbies of golf and swimming were initially affected, but those were not passions and he could have undertaken them, but did not thereafter do so due to pressures of time. U's symptoms improved between the time of accident and trial, but some remained. U experienced pain in his neck which occurred once or twice a month and which could last for several days at a time. That occurred after heavy work. U's condition had stabilised and no further deterioration was expected but his intermittent symptoms were expected to continue for the foreseeable future. *General Damages*: £5,500.

UTLEY v. PARKER [2000] 3 Q.R. 5, Recorder Harrison, CC (Sheffield).

Neck – whiplash type injury

1574.   K, male, aged 41 at the date of the road traffic accident and 45 at trial, sustained a whiplash injury to his neck. Analgesics were prescribed and K wore a collar for about one week. His neck was noticeably painful for a similar period. K was certified unfit for work for a period of one week. No other treatment was prescribed and the symptoms gradually settled down over a further period of six weeks. Thereafter, K suffered only minor residual symptoms if he turned his head quickly, or when he was playing darts. At the trial, which took place four years after the accident, it was accepted that K had no previous history of neck pain. Although the symptoms had all but resolved, K was left with ongoing residual symptoms which were a nuisance in terms of a stiff neck in the morning for a short period of time. It was likely that this would persist for the foreseeable future. *General Damages*: £5,500.

KEMPSTER v. ASHFIELD, November 11, 1999, District Judge Cooper, CC (Southampton). [*Ex rel.* Kevin Haven, Barrister, 2 Gray's Inn Square Chambers, Gray's Inn, London].

Neck – whiplash type injury

1575.   H, a female aged 33 at the date of the road traffic accident and 36 at trial, was injured when her vehicle was struck from the side by B's vehicle and pushed across the road. H started to experience stiffness in her neck a couple of days later. H did not seek medical assistance at the time and did not take any time off work. However, five months later she still had persistent neck pain and went to her GP. He advised painkillers, which she continued to take on and off thereafter. H also attended physiotherapy for about six months after consulting her GP. H's neck symptoms eased to the point where they were intermittent and only brought on by activities in which her head stayed in the same position for a long time, such as long car journeys. However, she was still experiencing those symptoms at trial, nearly three and a half years after the accident. A joint medical report indicated that a complete resolution was to be expected, though no timescale was given in which that would happen. H had also suffered "clunking" in her left shoulder since the accident. The judge indicated that he was prepared to accept that there was some link with the accident, however it was not as significant to H's claim as her neck problems. It was also said that damages awards made in many whiplash quantum reports were on the low side, failing to take into account the recent trend to give higher awards for general damages. *General Damages*: £5,000.

HARVEY v. BLOUNT [2000] 5 Q.R. 6, Deputy District Judge Coward, CC (Luton).

Neck – whiplash type injury

1576.   F, female, a student, aged 19 at the date of the road traffic accident and 22 at trial, sustained a whiplash injury to the neck and a soft tissue injury to the groin. She attended her GP the day after the accident and was prescribed anti-inflammatories and pain killers. She was referred for physiotherapy for three months and subsequently underwent chiropractic treatments for five months. Two years after the accident, F had sought to relieve her symptoms by way of osteopathy. In total she had undergone in excess of 20 sessions of therapy. She was unable to attend 60 per cent of her lectures during the autumn term and was registered disabled by her university for examination purposes. An MRI scan taken 29 months after the accident revealed minimal forward slipping of the discs at C2/3 with no evidence of disc herniation. Eighteen months post accident F was experiencing twinges of pain and muscle spasm in the neck radiating down the back. She also felt discomfort in the upper arms and tingling in the hands. She began to experience pain daily. At trial her symptoms were persisting and such residual symptoms were expected to be permanent. She was unable to pursue her pre-accident hobbies of swimming, cycling and aerobics. She was however able to participate in light step classes. *General Damages*: £5,000.

FALLON v. BATEMAN, August 14, 2000, District Judge Edwards, CC (Bournemouth). [*Ex rel.* Nigel S Brockley, Barrister, Bracton Chambers, Bell House, 8 Bell Yard, London].

Neck – whiplash type injury

1577.   C1, male, aged 65 at the date of the accident and 68 at trial, and C2, female, aged 61 at the date of the accident and 63 at trial, sustained injuries in a road traffic accident. Both were taken to hospital on the day of the accident and attended their GP the following day. C1 complained of a whiplash type injury to his neck and underwent physiotherapy one month after the accident, twice a week for six to eight weeks. Backache was noticed some months after the accident but was considered to be unrelated. The neck symptoms subsequently returned. Ten months after the accident, C1 was experiencing constant neck pain. He was unable to play golf, which had been a favourite pastime, and found getting to sleep difficult. He underwent further physiotherapy 13 months post accident. Two years post accident, painkillers were taken almost every night and his sleep was broken two to three times each night. His range of movement was between half and three quarters of normal with a complaint of discomfort at the extreme of all movements. A diagnosis of a pre-existing asymptomatic degenerative neck condition was made. Symptoms at the date of trial were assessed as being 20 per cent due to the pre-existing condition. Symptoms were expected to continue indefinitely, but were expected to be eased by further physiotherapy. C2 suffered superficial seatbelt bruising and pain to the neck. Three months after the accident, back pain developed, which the medical evidence attributed to the accident. C2 underwent a course of physiotherapy. A year post accident, she could still not carry shopping, ironing was difficult, and walking for half an hour resulted in pain. Two years post accident, pain was still provoked by movement, and painkillers were taken daily. Although no difficulty was experienced getting to sleep, C2 woke early most mornings with pain to the neck. The symptoms were expected to continue indefinitely but would be eased by further physiotherapy. *General Damages*: C1 £4,800. C2 £6,000.

DORSETT v. GRANT (QUANTUM), July 7, 2000, District Judge Rhodes, CC (Bradford). [*Ex rel.* Sean D. Yates, Barrister, 10 Park Square, Leeds].

Neck – whiplash type injury

1578. H, female, aged 27 at the date of the accident and 32 at trial, suffered a soft tissue whiplash injury to her neck in a rear end shunt road traffic accident. H attended her GP, and was initially able to return to her clerical work with the Metropolitan Police. H's symptoms did not improve, and she had to cancel a pre-booked skiing holiday. H attended hospital, where she was fitted with a cervical collar, which she wore for several weeks. She was also prescribed strong painkillers. H was signed off work, and her employer arranged intensive physiotherapy. She received a month's treatment as an inpatient. After that treatment her symptoms were greatly improved, but she continued to suffer significant problems with strenuous activity. Outpatient physiotherapy continued several times per week, and she was signed off work for a total of seven months. A year after the accident, H's symptoms were much improved, although she was continuing to have physiotherapy. Exertion and housework continued to be difficult, and sporting activities were disrupted. H fully recovered from the effects of the injury 18 months to two years after the accident. In the first couple of months after the accident H also occasionally suffered from some generalised and nebulous symptoms, which were attributable to the collision. Those included the aggravation of a previous back injury with some radiation of pain into the legs, paraesthesia and dizziness. The judge found that the injury had had a serious effect on H, whom he characterised as an honest yet anxious person. In making the award he took account of the long and intensive physiotherapy she had to endure, and her loss of enjoyment of the holiday. He granted H permission to appeal against his award on the basis of the Law Commission's recommendation that general damages be increased. *General Damages*: £4,500.

HARBIGE v. EARL, January 27, 2000, Judge Kenny, CC (Reading). [*Ex rel.* Benjamin Williams, Barrister, 1 Temple Gardens, Temple, London].

Neck – whiplash type injury

1579. N, male, aged 51 at the date of the accident and 53 at trial, was proceeding slowly in traffic when W's car collided with his nearside. Agreed medical evidence was that N had sustained a jerking action on his neck. Onset of symptoms was delayed for a day or so, but thereafter N had significant neck pain radiating into his shoulder and arm for a period of about four weeks. Following that, the symptoms subsided, but N was left with residual discomfort. N suffered little episodes of discomfort for up to two years after the accident. These affected his hobby of cycling, although they did not stop him altogether from engaging in it. N suffered discomfort when driving long distances. N did not take time off work and did not visit his GP, but did have one session of physiotherapy and about five visits to a chiropractor one year after the accident. *General Damages*: £2,750.

NEWTON v. WHITTAKER, January 7, 2000, District Judge Hawkesworth, CC (Sheffield). [*Ex rel.* Andrew Granville Stafford, Barrister, 4 King's Bench Walk, Temple, London].

Neck – whiplash type injury

1580. M, female, aged 54 at the date of the accident and 56 at trial, suffered a whiplash injury affecting the neck. M did not lose consciousness but began to experience pain some 30 minutes after the accident. M's symptoms were severe for between seven and 10 days but had resolved completely within a further 10 to 14 days. M was prescribed Diazepam for five days but did not take any time off work. She attended an office party the day after the accident and her enjoyment of that was affected as indeed was the entirety of the Christmas period. In assessing general damages, the judge took account of the fact that the claim had proceeded on the small claims track, *Frost v. Furness* (Unreported, July 14, 1997), [1997] C.L.Y. 1886, *Tilbury v. Soundlab (UK) Ltd* (1996) 96(1) Q.R. 5, [1996] C.L.Y. 2360 and *A (A Minor) v. Sullivan* (1999) 99(5) Q.R. 8, [1999] C.L.Y. 1595, applied. *General Damages*: £600.

MORLEY v. SUSSEX COASTLINE BUSES LTD, December 9, 1999, Deputy District Judge Hebbert, CC (Southampton). [*Ex rel.* Nigel S Brockley, Barrister, Bracton Chambers, Bell House, 8 Bell Yard, London].

Spine

1581.　A, male, aged 38 at the date of the incident and 48 at the hearing, was injured as a result of falling 15 to 20 feet following an assault. He suffered a fracture of the lower part of his cervical spine at C5/6, a tear drop fracture of the inferior body of C6, and a fracture of the C5 lamina causing spinal cord damage resulting in incomplete tetraplegia. By the date of the hearing A was left with left sided low lumbar and left leg pain which disturbed his sleep and was not relieved by medication. As a result of this A suffered impairment of concentration, fatigue and severe depression which was continuing. At the hearing, there remained a mild wasting of the right forearm, slight weakness and slight reduction in power of the right arm, impaired sensation to pin below the C7 dermatome, which was relatively mild, slightly impaired muscle power on the right more than the left and risk of spinal cord cyst formation in the future. There remained diminution of neck movement and a risk of arthritis. As a result of neurological damage, bladder function was not normal. A could not run, he suffered spasms in the right arm and abdomen and occasionally in the right leg. A suffered from sexual dysfunction resulting from impairment to his sense of masculinity and which contributed to his depression. His ability to walk without sticks was limited to two or three miles. At the hearing, he continued to need general psychological and emotional support but could live physically independently. He was only fit for less demanding, sedentary work, such as clerical work, and was unlikely to remain fit for work beyond the age of 60. He was in need of psychological counselling, occupational therapy and physiotherapy. His life expectancy was reduced to 72. *General Damages*: £50,000. Future loss of earnings award: £67,000. Future care award: £15,000. Award for future medical and other treatment: £15,000. Total award: £154,850.

AOUDIA (CICB: QUANTUM: 2000), *Re* [2000] 5 Q.R. 6, Raymond Walker Q.C. (Chairman), CICB (London).

Spine – neck

1582.　O, a female nurse aged 33 at the date of trial, was forced to retire from nursing duties due to spinal injuries caused by lifting and handling heavy patients. Liability was admitted. O first consulted her GP with pain in her cervical spine in February 1994 aged about 27 years. In April 1994, she was also complaining of low back pain. She was referred for investigations and for a specialist opinion. The symptoms resolved with physiotherapy. O then worked normally until April 1996 when her neck pain recurred severely. An MRI scan in August 1996 disclosed a posterior prolapse at C5/6 and changes at C6/7. O was treated with further physiotherapy and transferred to lighter duties. In March 1997, the symptoms recurred. O had traction, which was unhelpful. She was then referred for a neurosurgical opinion and on May 27, 1997 had a surgical decompression and fusion at C5/6. In the aftermath of that surgery, she again developed low back pain. She returned to work in June 1998, but the pain in her neck and low back recurred immediately and she had to give up. O was medically retired a little over a year later. At the date of trial, O had very restricted movement in her cervical spine. Her neck was intermittently painful and further deterioration was likely. She had a scar to the font of her neck from the operation. O suffered constant low back pain. Her injuries interfered with a lot of mundane activities, such as sitting for a long time or driving a car. O was retraining to become a counsellor. *General Damages*: £17,500; Award for loss of congenial employment: £5,000; Award for loss of earnings up to July 2000 (when training would be completed) £44,953; Award for future loss of earnings: (multiplier 14) £61,446; *Smith v. Manchester* Award: £11,000; Loss of pension award: 20,000; Total Award: £167,521.

O'REGAN v. BEDFORD HOSPITAL NHS TRUST, December 6, 1999, Judge Reid Q.C., CC (Clerkenwell). [*Ex rel.* Richard Davison, Barrister, Thomas More Chambers, 51/52 Carey Street, Lincoln's Inn, London].

Spine below neck

1583.   G, male, aged 33 at the date of the incident and 54 at the date of assessment, sustained a lower back injury while in the course of his work as a police dog handler in October 1977. A laminectomy was performed and G was found to have a major disc protrusion at L5/S1. G was hospitalised for five weeks and absent from work for seven months. Thereafter G returned to work but continued to experience residual pain and discomfort. G received an award from the CICB of £950. In January 1985 he noticed acute pain in his lower back and as a result was forced to transfer to CID. He received numerous facet joint blocks which provided him with temporary pain relief. He also underwent facet joint denervation. By the end of 1985 G had deteriorated further and was unable to work at all. In March 1986 he was readmitted to hospital with severe back pain and sciatica. In October 1986 a large central disc protrusion at L4/5 was removed and in order to relieve his leg pain the right L5/S1 discs were divided. G was left with right foot drop, significant back pain, sciatica and sensory disturbance around L5. In 1987 G was medically retired from the police force. Between 1987 and 1995 G continued to suffer continuous and acute pain. His injuries prevented him from doing any of the activities he had enjoyed prior to the incident. He would spend most of his time in bed due to the pain and used a wheelchair. He was unable to perform any transfers from either his bed or his wheelchair without assistance. He was prescribed high dosages of morphine and other strong analgesics. In 1993 he was admitted as an emergency suffering from a medication induced "zombie" like state. He received an epidural catheterisation of morphine which provided pain relief for one month. Repeat epidurals however proved unsuccessful. G then suffered a cardiac infarction. In April 1995 a spinal cord stimulator was inserted at his lower thoracic level. The mechanism did not alter the permanency of G's condition but allowed him to be completely pain free. At the date of the assessment he was able to drive an adapted car, and walk a maximum of 15 yards if necessary. The CICB considered that G had been through a traumatic and painful existence up until the spinal cord stimulator had been implanted. He had been a highly decorated dog handler who it was accepted would have completed his 30 years' service and then would have had a successful career outside the police force. He had received various treatments including acupuncture, physiotherapy, hydrotherapy, formal rhizolysis, cortisone blocks, catheterisation and three operations on his spine. *General Damages*: £40,000. Award for loss of congenial employment: £5,000. Past loss of earnings award: £5,529. Award for past care: £30,000. Award for past medical care: £3,000. Award for past expenses: £31,196. Future care award: £9,000. Award for future expenses: £39,000. Total award: £158,725 (less £90,000 deductions).

GOODALL (CICB: QUANTUM: 1999), *Re*, May 13, 1999, Chairman: C Whitby Q.C., CICB (London). [*Ex rel.* Paul Cairnes, Barrister, 3 Paper Buildings at Bournemouth, Lorne Park Road, Bournemouth].

Spine below neck

1584.   B, male, aged 40 at the date of injury and 46 at the hearing, was stabbed in the back in the course of a robbery in September 1993. He suffered a very serious spinal cord injury causing nerve damage and resulting in loss of sensation on the right side from leg to nipple level. There was total loss of sexual function and consequential loss of enjoyment of marriage. Viagra was prescribed, but was not only ineffective but also produced side effects and so was discontinued. B's mobility was impaired. He could walk only with the aid of elbow crutches and was subject to sudden leg spasm with risk of falling. Although not incontinent, B suffered urgency of micturition and also constipation. On anything other than short trips out of doors, he needed a wheelchair. B's home was on two levels with stairs, the bathroom being upstairs, and by reason of his mobility problems and bowel/bladder problems, adaptations were required. There was no reduction of B's life expectancy and no prospect of improvement of his symptoms. Prior to the attack, B managed and supervised his own business, with occasional unpaid help from his wife, but after the attack he was able to carry on the business only with the regular unpaid help of his wife, the paid help of his two daughters and the employment of a series of part time employees. B's claim was advanced on the basis of a continuing need for care, to be valued either on the basis of commercial care or alternatively on the basis of continuing gratuitous care by his wife, the latter alternative being feasible only if the award were to include an element for the payment of a full time employee. On the issue of pain, suffering and loss of amenity reference was made to the JSB Guidelines (1999) classification 6(B)(a)(ii) and *Michalski v. Martin Stabin* (Unreported, January 18, 1993), [1993] C.L.Y. 1429. *General Damages*: £37,500. Past loss of earnings: £19,356.74. Future loss of earnings (multiplier 12): £73,057.92. Further costs of equipment/adaptations/accommodation conversion: £31,468.41. Past care: £24,000. Future care (assuming wife as primary carer, multiplier 20): £80,000. Total award (including past and future treatment costs and miscellaneous expenses, but before deduction of benefits): £287,418.

BHAVSAR (CICB: QUANTUM: 2000), *Re* [2000] 3 Q.R. 6, E Lowther, CICB (Manchester).

Spine below neck

1585.   G, male, a steel fixer, aged 33 at the date of the accident and 36 at trial, suffered a back injury whilst at work when a stone wall on which he was standing collapsed and he fell some seven feet, landing face down on some sharp underlying rubble. G suffered an injury to his back and two broken ribs. G had a previous history of lower back pain, but had been clear of associated trouble for 18 months prior to the accident. G spent four days in hospital, where it was confirmed that he had sustained a compressed fracture to the vertebrae. G suffered a fracture to the third and fourth thoracic vertebrae in his back and a low back strain. He had to attend as an outpatient following discharge from hospital and he underwent extensive physiotherapy. He continued to suffer from pain as a result of the wedge fracture of the fourth thoracic vertebra. Pain extended from the back of his chest to the mid line. Activity brought on severe pain. He was unable to play with his young children. Sneezing and deep breathing caused pain. G was unable to pursue his hobbies of swimming, jogging, amateur boxing/coaching, and golf. He continued to be in constant pain and discomfort and that was expected to continue for the rest of his life. He was unable to return to his former occupation as a steel fixer or to resume any heavy manual work in the future. G was consequently disadvantaged on the labour market, although he had been able to take on a part time job working for a friend. G would be able to continue to undertake physically undemanding work for the rest of his working life, but was unemployed at the time of the trial having recently lost his part time job. The judge found that it would take him six months to find another job and three years to build up to his full earning capacity, leaving him with a continuing future partial loss of earnings. H was awarded damages for disadvantage on the labour market representing three times his anticipated residual annual earning capacity. *General Damages*: £15,000. *Smith v. Manchester* award: £37,110. Total award: £133,555.

GRIFFITHS v. RICHARD MEDLINS CONTRACTS, November 30, 1999, Judge Bursell, QBD. [*Ex rel.* Veale Wasbroughs Solicitors, Orchard Court, Orchard Lane, Bristol].

Spine below neck

1586.   C, male, aged 34 at the date of the road traffic accident and 37 at assessment of damages hearing, was a front seat passenger in a car struck from behind at 40 to 50 mph. C immediately felt pain in his neck and back in the area between his shoulder blades. Five hours later he attended hospital and the pain in his neck and shoulders was noted. There was no neurological deficit. C was X-rayed and discharged with a soft collar. The following morning, C was very stiff in his cervical and lumbar spine. Shortly afterwards, C's GP gave him a 14 day medical certificate for neck strain. Over the course of the following two weeks, the pain in the neck and shoulders subsided but the low back pain became worse. Anti-inflammatories alleviated that. The pain remained significant on C's return to work as a bricklayer. A month after first seeing his GP, C attended again complaining of left sided sciatica. He was referred for physiotherapy. He struggled on at work for a further few weeks then took time off. When he tried to go back to work a month later, he only managed two days work on account of low back pain and left leg pain. A month later, C bent forward to pick up his 16 week old son when he felt a popping in his back. He saw his GP who initially signed him off work for three weeks and then extended that period to a further month. Three months later, given that there had been a six to seven month period of intractable left sided sciatica since the accident, C was seen by a consultant orthopaedic surgeon. A clinical diagnosis of L4/L5 disc prolapse was made, which was confirmed by a MRI scan. Two months later L4/L5 discectomy and lateral nerve root decompression was carried out. Two years later C still experienced some back pain which fluctuated daily. C was reluctant to take painkillers for fear of damaging the lumbar spine further. C had not played golf since the accident and was unable to play with his young children to a normal extent. He could no longer do any jobs around the house or his own motor maintenance, but had managed to find employment as a supervisor in a packaging company which was better than the forecast predicted by the employment consultant. He had no history of back pain prior to the accident.
      The judge found that the case fell near the boundary of para.6B (b) (i) and (ii) of the JSB Guildelines, 4th Edition, for moderate back injuries. A multiplier of 16 was used for the award for future loss of earnings and of 12 for future loss of DIY/maintenance award. *General Damages*: £14,000. Special damages (including past loss of earnings): £18,716. *Smith v. Manchester* award: £8,000. Future loss of earnings: £19,136. Future loss of DIY/maintenance: £3,600. Total award (inclusive of interest): £64,747.
      CHAPPELL v. TDC MOTOR FACTORS, November 1, 1999, Smedley, J., QBD. [*Ex rel.* Giles Colin, Barrister, Crown Office Row Chambers, Bleinhein House, 120 Church St, Brighton].

Spine below neck – whiplash type injury

1587.   O, male, aged 32 at the date of the accident and 35 at trial, suffered soft tissue injuries to his neck and lower back as a result of a road traffic accident. O noticed neck symptoms within a few hours, and lower back symptoms within a couple of days of the accident. O was off work for a week. He attended his GP once and was treated with a soft collar, which he wore for around five days, analgesics, and a six week course of physiotherapy. The neck injury caused pain and stiffness for around one month, and thereafter caused about 15 isolated incidents of muscle spasm and pain, each lasting for a few minutes, with a complete recovery within approximately one year of the accident. The lower back injury caused a minimal protrusion of the L5/S1 disc. Symptoms of intermittent pain and stiffness in the lower back brought on by driving for more than an hour, walking for more than half an hour, standing for more than half an hour, or prolonged sitting, continued at the date of trial and were likely to be permanent. O was employed at the date of trial as a factory quality controller and laboratory technician, earning in excess of £20,000 per annum gross. There was a risk that he could lose his job in the future because of the possible closure of his factory, two out of three of the departments having recently been closed down. O would be disadvantaged in the open labour market as he would have difficulty in carrying out a job involving manual work and would suffer discomfort in any job involving prolonged standing or sitting. His skills, however, would make it possible for him to transfer to quality control work in a different type of factory. O stated that he was free to move to any part of the country in order to seek work similar to his current employment, and that he would seek manual work only as a last resort. It was therefore found that O's handicap on the open labour market was not a significant one. *General Damages*: £8,000. *Smith v. Manchester* award: £4,000.

OLIVER v. BURTON, December 13, 1999, District Judge Marley, CC (Newcastle). [*Ex rel.* Mark Henley, Barrister, 9 Woodhouse Square, Leeds].

Spine below neck – whiplash type injury

1588.   C, male, aged 53 at the date of the accident and 57 at trial, suffered a whiplash injury affecting the neck. C had suffered from neck pain with associated paraesthesia affecting the hands for some eight years prior to the occurrence of the accident. Additionally, there was evidence of some minor disc degeneration at C5/6. Historically, the neck pain had been treated with analgesics and the episodes lasted for periods of two to three days. The day after the accident, C's neck was stiff and painful and within about a day he started to suffer from bouts of dizziness. A week later, he consulted his GP who advised that the dizziness would wear off and prescribed a course of three physiotherapy treatments. Some nine months after the accident the neck pain had become so severe that C was required to undergo further physiotherapy and took seven weeks off work. The medical evidence attributed the need for further physiotherapy directly to the accident. In order to reduce the number of hours he spent driving, C changed his job and reduced his hours to part time. C underwent a third period of physiotherapy which he found to be beneficial but which he had been unable to continue due to lack of funds. C was also diagnosed as suffering from bilateral carpal tunnel syndrome but complained of pain affecting all of the fingers and thumbs of both hands. Consequently, it was concluded that at least some of the paraesthesia affecting the hands was caused by the injury to the cervical spine. At trial, more than four years after the accident, C had been symptom free for a period of approximately one year and had been able to resume full time employment. *General Damages*: £5,500.

MCPHERSON v. SHIASSON, December 9, 1999, Deputy District Judge Hebbert, CC (Wakefield). [*Ex rel.* Nigel S. Brockley, Barrister, Bracton Chambers, Bell House, 8 Bell Yard, London].

Back

1589.   S, female, aged 23 at the date of the incident and 28 at trial, suffered a soft tissue injury to her lower back giving rise to persistent and severe backache as a result of repetitive and awkward handling of heavy loads at work. X-rays, CT scans and MRI scans revealed no significant abnormalities. Both consultant orthopaedic surgeons who examined her agreed that, while it was unusual, it was not unknown for soft tissue injuries not to be revealed by presently available diagnostic tools. S's level of disability was assessed by relying on her own account of the pain and discomfort she endured on a daily basis and she gave evidence that it was severe. S was unable to lift heavy weights, could not travel any distance without discomfort and walking was limited to half a mile. S's husband had to undertake many of the routine household chores in the family home. S was unable to endure the travelling necessary to enjoy foreign holidays or resume any of the sporting and leisure activities she enjoyed prior to her injury. S sought pain relief from a variety of sources, both conventional and alternative. She had undergone facet joint injections, physiotherapy, hydrotherapy, acupuncture, epidural and steroid injections; none of which made any significant improvement to her condition. S was considered to have "substantial residual disability". S was unable to return to work and it was held that she had no residual earning capacity. Her ability to enjoy motherhood and family life had been severely restricted by her injury. *General*

Damages: £25,000. Future loss of earnings: £301,006 (multiplier 17.68 allowing for five years off work to raise family). Total award: £374,443.

STONE v. COMMISSIONER OF POLICE OF THE METROPOLIS, September 16, 1999, Judge Serota Q.C., CC (Milton Keynes). [*Ex rel.* Giles Harrap, Barrister, 3 Pump Court, Temple, London].

Back

1590. M, male, aged 29 at the date of the first incident, 32 at the date of the second incident and 34 at trial, sustained injuries to his back. The first injury occurred when M lifted a heavy kerbstone and the second when he slipped whilst dismounting from a flat bed wagon. In respect of both injuries, liability was established against CCC. Both medical experts agreed that M had sustained a permanent back disability and was permanently unfit for heavy labouring. The medical picture was clouded by the fact that M's back had already been degenerating before the first accident and that there was specific reference within his GP and medical records to a back injury which had occurred whilst M had been helping to push start a car in February 1995. However, the judge was satisfied that, cumulatively, the two accidents constituted the major significant causes of M's back condition and that but for the happening of those accidents, he would not be in the condition that he was in and would remain in for the foreseeable future. The first accident, which occurred in June 1995, caused low back pain and sciatica. M was able to return to work after three weeks to light duties at first and then to normal heavy labouring, but was left with a vulnerable back. The second accident, which occurred in May 1997, caused further trauma to the lower back, resulting in low back pain and sciatica. M's condition then became irreversible and he was permanently unfit for heavy work. There was some evidence that M might need an operation on the degenerative disc in the future. During the course of the hearing, CCC sought an adjournment in order to interview M for alternative employment as a car park warden. M indicated that he would accept such employment. The judge considered that the claim fell within the category of a back injury of moderate severity with substantial acceleration of back degeneration for the purposes of the Judicial Studies Board Guidelines and the appropriate bracket was £13,250 to £18,500. *General Damages*: £14,500. Past loss of earnings (including interest): £11,362. Future loss of earnings: £56,597. *Smith v. Manchester* award: £7,793. Past care: £500. Loss of pension: £14,481. Total award: £109,405.

MCHUGH v. CARLISLE CITY COUNCIL [2000] 3 Q.R. 6, Judge Brown, CC (Carlisle).

Back

1591. M, male, aged 53 at trial, began to suffer stiffness and pain in his back three days after the accident. That steadily became worse over the next few days. The pain remained very bad for about a week and then began to ease to some extent. Over the following year, M was never pain free but the severity of the pain varied from day to day. He reacted a lot more slowly in the work place as a consequence. Eighteen months after the accident M was pain free about 20 per cent of the time and the remaining 80 per cent he had a variable amount of backache. The pain was localised over the lower back on the left side and over the left side. When the pain was at its worst it radiated down into the upper part of his left buttock, but never into the left leg. The backache was related to cold and particularly damp conditions. The pain was at its worst on waking. On some days M was aware of a constant aching in his back. The medical opinion was that due to degenerative changes he would have experienced the same symptoms in five to eight years from the date of the accident in any event. *General Damages*: £9,000.

MCKERCHAR v. CAMPBELL, April 6, 2000, District Judge Pickup, CC (Rawtenstall). [*Ex rel.* Paul Clark, Barrister, Exchange Chambers, Pearl Assurance House, Derby Square, Liverpool].

Back

1592.   D, male, aged 38 at the date of the road traffic accident and 41 at trial, sustained a whiplash injury to his neck, seatbelt bruising to his chest, lumbar back strain and bruising to both knees. The bruising to the chest and knees resolved with six to eight weeks of the accident. A blow to C's left knee exacerbated a pre-existing patellofemoral arthritic condition for a period of six months. Neck pain with associated restriction of movement radiating to upper back resolved within six months of the accident. Severe lower back pain remained as the main symptom six months post accident. This interfered with C's ability to work as a self employed landscape gardener and resulted in the employment of subcontractors for the more arduous tasks in the first year after the accident. The back problems persisted and X-rays revealed that there was a previously asymptomatic back condition of the lumbar spine which would have become symptomatic by 45 years of age in any event as a result of the type of work C carried out as a landscape gardener. The judge accepted that C's back injuries had also restricted his social activities. He was unable to launch the family fishing boat, go camping or play with his young children to the extent that he would have otherwise have expected. The medical prognosis was that the accident accelerated the pre-existing lumbar spine symptoms by between five to seven years. General damages were awarded after considering *Sheil v. Chamberlain* (Unreported, April 3, 1991), [1991] C.L.Y. 1405 and *Desborough v. Carlisle City Council* (Unreported, January 22, 1990), [1990] C.L.Y. 1634. *General Damages*: £8,500.

LLOYD-DAVIES v. LYTH, February 9, 2000, District Judge Newman, CC (Chester). [*Ex rel.* Kevin Haven, Barrister, 2 Gray's Inn Square Chambers, Gray's Inn, London].

Back

1593.   C, male, aged 40 at the date of the accident and 44 at trial, sustained injuries when he tripped and fell over a pipe in a factory causing a strain to the lumbar spine at L5/S1. The accident aggravated pre-existing asymptomatic degenerative changes in the back. C consulted his GP who prescribed painkillers and rest, and C undertook a private course of physiotherapy. C's medical evidence was preferred, namely, that the accident had brought forward the onset of the symptoms by five to 10 years, but that the degenerative changes themselves had not been specifically worsened by the accident. It was found that C's symptoms would continue indefinitely but would not prevent C from continuing in his occupation as a sample printer up to normal retirement age. *General Damages*: £7,500.

COOTS v. STEAD MCALPINE & CO LTD [2000] 3 Q.R. 7, Judge Philips, CC (Carlisle).

Back

1594.   W, female, aged 50 at the date of injury and 56 at trial, a midwife of 28 years' experience, worked in the community delivering two or three babies per annum until 1994 when her supervisors required her to work in the delivery suite in the local hospital to ensure that her training was kept up to date. Her work in the delivery suite involved heavy manual handling of patients, for instance moving mothers after epidural injection who did not have control over their legs. W had a long history of back complaints and a small disc prolapse in her lower spine and it was found as a fact that WHHA were aware of the back problem. The manual handling work in the delivery suite aggravated W's lower back problem and increased the disc prolapse such that she had to have surgery within one year and was retired on ill health grounds in November 1996. *General Damages*: £5,000. Loss of earnings award: £31,612. Total Award: £41,638.

WELLS v. WEST HERTFORDSHIRE HA (QUANTUM) [2000] 6 Q.R. 7, N Baker Q.C., QBD.

Back – pre-existing disability or condition: aggravated by whiplash

1595.   B, female, aged 70 at the date of the accident and 75 at trial, was injured in a road traffic accident. She sustained a whiplash type injury which accelerated her pre-existing condition of osteoporosis. Her injuries were followed by depression, loss of appetite, disorientation and forgetfulness. Before the accident B was a voluntary worker, carrying out church work and meals on wheels amongst other things. She was quite stoical and attended her GP only eight times following the accident. Two years after the accident she saw a consultant psychiatrist who diagnosed a degree of underlying depression. There was a history of back pain prior to the accident. *General Damages*: £6,750.
        BROWN v. OWEN [2000] 6 Q.R. 8, Deputy District Judge Harvey, CC (Chichester).

Back – whiplash type injury

1596.   R, aged 27 at the date of the road traffic accident and 31 at trial, sustained soft tissue injuries to his neck and lower back. Three years and six months after the accident he was suffering from daily background neck pain, with exacerbations causing pain lasting up to two weeks. He also suffered from constant lower back pain, which he described as being "like a bad bruise", which again would be aggravated by activity. He had not been able to return to sporting activities, including football, boxing, tennis and ice hockey. He found that pilates treatment relieved pain for a few days, but to gain effective relief he had to attend for treatment three times a week. R also suffered from frequent headaches. At the time of the trial, those occurred about three times a day and would last between one and two hours each but would be relieved by taking paracetamol. The prognosis was for gradually reducing symptoms over the following three to five years, with the expectation that R would be symptom free in a further 10 years. *General Damages*: £10,000.
        RUSHTON v. GEE, November 5, 1999, Recorder Byrne, CC (Salford). [*Ex rel.* Daniel Barnett, Barrister, 2 Gray's Inn Square Chambers, Gray's Inn, London].

Back – whiplash type injury

1597.   B, female aged 19, at the date of the road traffic accident and 23 at trial, suffered injuries to her neck and lower back. Her neck injury settled within five weeks but the back pain persisted. B was off work as a recreational assistant for six weeks and on return she avoided heavy work and ultimately changed employment two and a half years later due to her symptoms. B's treating physiotherapist stated eight months after the accident that B was pain free, a view never accepted by B. At hearing, four years post accident, B complained of back aches in the morning and daily discomfort precipitated by household chores, or if she stood or walked for more than 30 minutes. B owned a horse and rode it on a regular basis, but since the accident only undertook occasional light riding. The judge was satisfied that (i) there was no back trouble prior to the accident; (ii) all doctors at some time detected symptoms; (iii) the neck injury cleared up quickly which was strange if B was unconsciously motivated by the claim; and (iv) she only took 31 days off work, which was not consistent with a lady who was consciously or subconsciously influenced by a claim. The judge proceeded to find that B's enduring symptoms were caused by the accident, commenting that the courts had on a number of occasions made awards for continuing symptoms not medically explained. It was not necessary in each case to have a report from a psychologist or pain management expert. *General Damages*: £7,000.
        BROOK v. FAULKNER, February 10, 2000, District Judge Hallet, CC (Chelmsford). [*Ex rel.* Michael Morris, Barrister, 169 Temple Chambers, Temple Avenue, London].

Back – excretory organs

1598. W, female, aged 41 at the date of the accident and 46 at trial, sustained a low back injury and consequent low back pain following a fall down the stairs at work. Prior to the accident, W had suffered from pre-existing degenerative disc disease in the lower lumbar spine which would have progressed naturally. However, the agreed medical evidence was that the fall had accelerated by approximately 10 years the symptoms suffered since the accident. Those symptoms comprised mild but constant pain, which restricted W's employment to either a sedentary occupation or an occupation involving light duties. The back injury also caused an abnormality of her detrusor (ie. bladder) muscle which resulted in W having to empty her bladder hourly by day and getting up two to four times at night with incontinence on occasions. The prognosis was that W would never have normal bladder function again. Although her voiding pattern might be controlled with drugs, it was not suggested that the bladder problems would have occurred had it not been for the accident. Damages were assessed, as W did not succeed on liability. *General Damages*: £15,500 (split for the back injury: £6,500, and for the bladder malfunction: £9,000.

WALE v. LONDON UNDERGROUND LTD, October 30, 1998, Judge Dean Q.C., CC (Central London). [*Ex rel.* Jackaman Smith & Mulley, Solicitors, Oak House, 7 Northgate Street, Ipswich, Suffolk].

Whiplash type injury – other conditions

1599. M, female aged 19 at the date of the accident and 21 at trial, suffered whiplash injuries to her neck and right shoulder, a mild driving related anxiety and hair loss caused by the stress of the accident. M immediately attended hospital where she was examined and X-rays were taken of her neck. She was provided with a soft collar and asked to return the following day as her neck was swollen. The next day she was told she had sustained no broken bones and was advised to exercise and to wear the collar intermittently. M was off work for two days as a result of her injuries. She used the collar daily for three weeks following the accident, particularly whilst working at a VDU. M also sustained minor injuries to her back and right shoulder and experienced headaches and nightmares and particular anxiety when travelling in a vehicle for two weeks following the accident. The symptoms in M's right shoulder settled within two weeks of the accident as did her flash backs and nightmares. M continued to be a more nervous driver and passenger, although she returned to driving within six weeks of the accident. After several weeks, M still continued to experience pain and stiffness in her upper back and although the acute symptoms in M's neck and upper back resolved within two months of the accident, she continued to experience aching and stiffness in her neck and upper back on occasions over the following ten months. A few weeks after the accident, M noticed that her hair was falling out in clumps. She was prescribed stress relieving herbal tablets by her GP and referred to a consultant dermatologist. Over a two week period, approximately 40 per cent of M's hair fell out and was extremely thin at the front and on top. Over the following two months her hair began to grow again and she was left with thinner hair but no obvious baldness. Twelve months after the date of the accident, M was symptom free. Her hair loss abated within approximately two months of the accident and by the date of trial, hair growth had returned to normal. *General Damages*: £2,750 (£750 of which was in respect of hair loss).

BICKLEY v. BRADLEY, March 2, 2000, District Judge Jones, CC (Manchester). [*Ex rel.* Pannone & Partners Solicitors, 123 Deansgate, Manchester].

Shoulder

1600. F, female aged 60 at the date of the accident and 68 at trial, was injured when her right arm was pulled behind her by an escaping youth. F was able to finish her work and that night went on a previously planned holiday. Pain around the right shoulder increased, forcing her to cut short her holiday after one week. She had intended to work until aged 65 but was unable to continue working and her employment was terminated nine months after the accident. The pain in her shoulder increased over time, but subsided completely two to three years after the incident when all sensation in her right arm was lost. Thereafter there were periods of pain in the shoulder and neck and periods of complete numbness. F attended pain management and neurological appointments but no organic explanation for her symptoms was found. In 1997 she was diagnosed as suffering from reflex sympathetic dystrophy. No firm prognosis was possible. At the date of the hearing, F was still heavily reliant on the care of her family as she was unable to carry out many basic tasks for herself and would be for the foreseeable future. She described the right arm as being practically useless. *General Damages*: £12,500. Past care award: £15,000. Future care award: £20,000.

FLETCHER (CICB: QUANTUM: 2000), *Re*, February 9, 2000, Judge not specified, CICB (Nottingham). [*Ex rel.* Nick Blake, Barrister, 24 The Ropewalk, Nottingham].

Shoulder

1601.   M, female, aged 31 at the date of the incident and 36 at the hearing, was assaulted whilst working as a nurse in a residential care home. The assailant held on to her lower right arm while she struggled to get free. Her right arm, wrist and shoulder immediately began aching. She visited her GP who diagnosed a soft tissue injury and prescribed ibuprofen. Just over a month after the assault, M was unable to continue working due to extreme pain if she tried to do any lifting. At first she was absent from work on sick leave, but she proceeded to resign her employment four months later, not having returned to work in the interim. M underwent physiotherapy and ultrasound treatment for two months, beginning a month after the incident, and she also had injections into her shoulder. Eight months after the assault, M had an MRI scan which showed that she was suffering from tendonitis. Six months later, she had a manipulation under anaesthetic to try to improve the range of movement. By the date of hearing, some four years and six months after the assault, M continued to have difficulties when doing activities such as ironing or vacuuming and she avoided carrying heavy shopping. She was not able to return to any nursing job which would involve lifting. M had begun her own video rental business in the interim. *General Damages*: £8,500 (including an element of future loss of earnings).

M (CICB: QUANTUM: 2000), *Re*, June 6, 2000, C Whitby Q.C. (Chairman), CICB (Bath). [*Ex rel.* Rebecca Tuck, Barrister, Old Square Chambers, 1 Verulam Buildings, Gray's Inn, London].

Shoulder

1602.   M, male, aged 52 at the date of the accident and 56 at trial, was a prison inmate who slipped in a prison kitchen and struck his left non-dominant shoulder sustaining a contusion. He was prescribed painkillers and was able to continue working in the kitchen, albeit on light duties for the first seven to eight months. M then developed chronic rotator cuff tendonitis and impingement syndrome. M underwent two courses of physiotherapy. Three years after the accident the shoulder had a full range of movement, but a painful arc, and M suffered episodes of pain. An operation was expected to relieve the symptoms. The accident had accelerated the onset of the problems by three and a half years. *General Damages*: £6,000.

MORRISSEY v. HOME OFFICE [2000] 6 Q.R. 8, District Judge Horan, CC (Liverpool).

Shoulder – psychiatric damage

1603. H, male, a process worker, aged 51 at the date of the road traffic accident and 53 at trial, suffered a serious injury to his right dominant shoulder. His right arm was in a sling for three weeks. He suffered some deformation around the outer side of the clavicle. Mobility in his shoulder was permanently limited. Abduction without pain was only possible to 120 degrees. Pain would move up his shoulder and into his neck. Flexion was limited permanently to 130 degrees and external rotation to 20 degrees. He could not easily use his right arm for heavy tasks. His shoulder would ache from time to time and would keep him awake at night. An associated soft tissue injury to the cervical spine resolved within one year of the accident. H also suffered bruising and abrasions to his groin, left shoulder, left hand, left knee and otherwise down the left hand side of his body. These healed within weeks. Prior to the accident, H had been exceptionally fit and was able to run and cycle long distances, training up to five times per week. He engaged in fell running and hill walking. The accident left H unable to pursue his fitness activities and unable to ride his bicycle. That led him to develop a post traumatic anxiety condition, which left him depressed, anxious, tearful and angry. He lost some close friends and it affected his relationship with his wife of 30 years. At times he felt suicidal. Although his mental condition was serious for some time, it had improved sharply by the trial and the judge found that, after the litigation was over, H would be likely to improve further. The judge categorised the psychiatric injury as "moderate" in nature due to the limited duration of severe effects. H suffered headaches after the accident which a neurologist associated with the stress, anger and depression of his psychiatric condition. Although the headaches were at times painful, they were improving by the trial. H had changed jobs by the time of the trial and was no longer required to perform heavy work. *General Damages*: £14,500.

HUTCHINSON v. CUNNINGHAM, May 11, 2000, District Judge Gaunt, CC (Tameside). [*Ex rel.* BT McCluggage, Barrister, 9 St John Street, Manchester].

Arm

1604. K, male, aged 27 at the date of the road traffic accident and 30 at trial, suffered a displaced fracture of the right hand dominant middle and lower two thirds of the radius of his right arm. An operation was required to reduce the fracture and a six hole semitubular bone plate was inserted. The bone failed to unite and a second operation was required two months later when bone was grafted from the left iliac crest. K's arm was placed in a full plaster cast. The bone still failed to unite and a second graft took place. K's arm was finally removed from plaster a year after the accident. K was a self employed artexer but at the time of the accident was working in a managerial position in a car bodyshop. The medical evidence showed that he would continue to suffer from constant discomfort in his right forearm and would suffer considerable weakness and loss of grip in his hand thus disadvantaging him significantly on the open labour market. *General Damages*: £21,000. *Smith v. Manchester* award: £15,000.

KIRKPATRICK v. TODD, April 13, 2000, District Judge Tennant, CC (Basingstoke). [*Ex rel.* Shoosmiths Solicitors, Quantum House, Basing View, Basingstoke, Hants].

Work related upper limb disorders

1605. M, female aged 41 at the date of the injury and 45 at trial, was employed to service and repair diving suits for the offshore industry. Her job involved hanging up suits to dry from a high rail using bulldog clips, and tightening face-plates with wing nuts. After five weeks, M suffered an overuse syndrome in both upper limbs which caused bilateral pain, exacerbated by manual tasks. She found gripping difficult which rendered her unemployable, experienced pain in ordinary household chores and her hobbies of knitting and gardening were affected. M was despondent and angry. The symptoms, which had continued unabated for four years, had been misdiagnosed as carpal tunnel syndrome, for which she had undergone ineffective decompression surgery to her left wrist. She was expected to recover after six months of active management and to find work within nine months. *General Damages*: £7,000.

MOLVAER v. WHIRLY BIRD SERVICES LTD, March 6, 2000, Judge Holt, CC (Norwich). [*Ex rel.* Philip Kolvin, Barrister, 2-3 Gray's Inn Square, London].

Work related upper limb disorders

1606. W, male, aged 35 at the date of the injury and 39 at trial, suffered inflamed tendons in his right bicep. The injury was caused by the repeated forceful flexion of his right dominant arm, whilst operating a machine at work. He struggled on working for a few weeks after initial mild symptoms presented. The injury was aggravated one night when, after operating the machine, W found himself in considerable pain. He took anti-inflammatory medication and analgesia. He was unable to drive for two weeks and was off work for nearly three weeks. When he returned to work he still suffered discomfort. The pain radiated into his right hand and fingers. For 12 to 18 months he suffered regular and repeated episodes of pain. He found difficulty in pursuing his hobbies, which included motor racing and golf. W switched to a much lighter job, which calmed his symptoms. If he chose to return to heavy work he would be at further risk. Symptoms occurred for between two and two and a half years, being acute at first, then diminishing, but having an impact on his enjoyment of life. By the end of that period, the symptoms had all but disappeared. *General Damages*: £3,500.

WILLIAMS v. KAYE PRESTEIGNE LTD [2000] 6 Q.R. 8, Judge Brunning, CC (Derby).

Elbow

1607. P, male, a driver and meat porter aged 45 at the date of the accident and 48 at trial, slipped and fell off a loading platform. He suffered a Type II fracture of the radial head of the right elbow. He wore a sling and underwent physiotherapy. He had difficulty sleeping for three months. Two and a half years after the accident, he had recovered 25-135 degrees extension compared with 0-140 degrees on the left elbow. His supination was, however, limited to 40 degrees, preventing him from holding his palm upwards. P could not straighten the arm, which caused modest cosmetic and functional anxiety. He also had difficulty with screwing and twisting motions. His ability to carry was reduced from weights of 200 lb to 175 lb. He suffered pain and aching on heavy exertion. In addition, there was secondary capsular tightness in the right shoulder, with movement reduced by 20 degrees. There was an onset of mild osteoarthritis, notwithstanding his successful adaption to his mild disability. *General Damages*: £10,000.

PLUME v. MASON BROS (BUTCHERS) LTD [2000] 4 Q.R. 6, District Judge Butler, CC (Burton on Trent).

Wrist

1608. W, a childminder and mother, aged 27 at the date of the accident and 29 at trial, sustained injuries to her wrists and neck when a van collided with the back of her car. W suffered pain in her neck for four months but the symptoms subsided completely within six months. At the date of trial she continued to experience pain and discomfort in her wrists, particularly in her right dominant wrist. W wore splints on both wrists at night and was sometimes forced to wear one on her right wrist during the day when, for instance, she was pushing children in their pushchairs. Pressure on her right wrist caused pain down her arm, weakness in her hand and inability to grip. W had problems picking up her youngest child and was unable to cope fully with her duties as mother and childminder. W was also unable to undertake activities such as gardening and decorating. W had suffered carpal tunnel syndrome in the past and there were references to previous trauma to the right wrist. The trial judge accepted however that the symptoms complained of were very different to those she had experienced in the past and were indeed caused by the accident. W had noticed some small improvement but it was generally accepted that the problems were permanent. *General Damages*: £6,750.

HAVILL v. WILSON, December 15, 1999, District Judge Weintroub, CC (Bournemouth). [*Ex rel.* Paul Cairnes, Barrister, 3 Paper Buildings, 20 Lorne Park Rd, Bournemouth].

Wrist

1609.　H, female, aged 36 at the date of the accident and 38 at trial, right hand dominant, sustained a completely displaced angulated fracture of the distal 1 cm of the right radius. The fracture was manipulated under regional anaesthetic and the forearm was immobilised in a plaster cast for four weeks. Thereafter H wore a splint on her wrist all of the time for two weeks. She was unable to work for nine weeks, unable to drive for four weeks and unable to swim for six weeks. After eight weeks she was fit to resume housework, light gardening, and the care of her children. For the purpose of the assessment of damages, the court found it to be a significant factor that she had four children, who at the date of the accident, were 10 years, three years and twins of 14 months. At the date of trial, flexation in the right wrist was restricted, which expert evidence predicted would be permanent. The ulnar bone was prominent as a result of the accident and prone to being knocked with resulting pain. Although able to continue with her work as a housewife, mother and part time support worker, some necessary tasks could only be performed more slowly than before the accident. H had difficulty cleaning windows and gardening, and suffered aches in cold weather. She continued to wear a support on her wrist occasionally. Discomfort and aching resulted from ordinary daily domestic tasks. H was not prevented from undertaking her job. Expert medical evidence had explored the opinion that residual discomfort would resolve 20 months post accident and that any continuing discomfort would be slight. However, the court found that the symptoms which H had continued to suffer at 20 months were not slight. Damages were awarded on the basis that discomfort would lessen soon after the trial. *General Damages*: £5,250.

HAMMANT v. STOCKPORT MBC, June 20, 2000, District Judge Jack, CC (Stoke-on-Trent). [*Ex rel.* Glaisyers Solicitors, 6th Floor, Manchester House, 18-20 Bridge Street, Manchester].

Wrist

1610.　R, male, aged 35 at the date of the accident and 39 at trial, tripped in a pothole in the middle of a pathway, falling and landing on his outstretched left wrist, as a result of which he sustained a fracture to the base of the radial styloid. R's wrist remained in plaster for six weeks, during which period he took painkillers on a daily basis. R was unable to return to work as a farm labourer for some four months. The injury and consequent period of immobilisation left R with a stiff and painful wrist, resulting in a significant disability. R wore a supporting wrist splint for nine months, and thereafter an elastic support bandage. He also underwent some basic physiotherapy. Whilst R had managed to return to lighter duties by the end of the four month period, it took him some 20 months to regain normal function. In awarding general damages at the top of the JSB Guidelines' bracket 6(H)(d), the judge found that R had been a fit and active man who had been unable to pursue his normal sporting hobbies of weight training, tennis and squash. R was, at trial, at a slightly increased risk of developing osteoarthritis in his left radiocarpal joint in five to 10 years time. *General Damages*: £5,000.

RICHARDS v. HAMPSHIRE CC, January 28, 2000, Judge Lauriston, CC (Portsmouth). [*Ex rel.* Paul Hepher, Barrister, 2 Gray's Inn Square Chambers, 2 Gray's Inn Square, London].

Wrist

1611.   H, female, aged 63 at the date of the accident, right hand dominant and 67 at trial, tripped over a clod of earth falling heavily onto her left wrist. X-ray examination revealed that the wrist was fractured. She also had lacerations to the forearms and face and several abrasions to her face and legs. On the following day the wrist was set in plaster from the fingers to above the elbow. After about four weeks the arm became very painful and H returned to hospital where it was found that the laceration had become infected. It was dressed, H was given antibiotics, and the wrist was replastered. It remained in plaster for a further three weeks. She then kept the arm in a sling for six weeks. H was left with a painful and slightly deformed wrist. She found most household chores painful, in particular opening bottles and jars, vacuuming, ironing and carrying shopping. H's husband was disabled and H found his care difficult. Further deterioration or improvement was unlikely. H relied on her daughter to take her out of the house as she was left with a fear of further falls. She was taking antidepressants because of depression and anxiety resulting from the accident. In addition to the symptoms in her wrist, H was left with 1.5 mm scars on her left wrist and her upper lip. *General Damages*: GPB 7,500.

HOBSON v. NTL TEESSIDE LTD, August 16, 2000, District Judge Bullock, CC (Newcastle-upon-Tyne). [*Ex rel.* David Mason, Barrister, Milburn House Chambers, Floor A, Milburn House, Dean Street, Newcastle-upon-Tyne].

Fingers

1612.   C, girl aged nearly three at the date of the accident and nine at trial, caught the fingers of her right dominant hand in an escalator. She underwent surgery on the day of the accident and again two days later. The ends of her index, middle and ring fingers were severed. The index finger was severed through the tip, with just half the nail bed remaining, and there was a hang nail deformity. The middle finger was amputated just distal to the distal interphalangeal joint, with an ulnar based flap covering the amputation tip. The ring finger was amputated through the distal interphalangeal joint, and there was a scar over the dorso-ulnar aspect of the middle phalanx. Flexion of the proximal interphalangeal joints of the three damaged fingers was impaired. Pinch grip was reduced between the thumb and index finger. The girl's deformed hand severely reduced her chances of obtaining a husband through an arranged marriage, in that she came from a traditional Muslim family of Pakistani origin. In that community, any physical blemish made a woman undesirable as a wife. Although the girl was of at least average intelligence, she was severely handicapped in the labour market at a time when keyboard skills were assuming increasing importance in the marketplace. *General Damages*: £28,000. General damages for loss of marriage prospects: £12,000. *Smith v. Manchester* award: £15,000. Total award: £55,000. [Damages were assessed without implementing the Law Commission's recommendation that general damages awards be increased].

C (A CHILD) v. LONDON UNDERGROUND LTD, March 9, 2000, Judge Ryland, CC (Central London). [*Ex rel.* Stephen Shay, Barrister, 1 King's Bench Walk, Temple, London].

Fingers

1613.   H, male, aged 59 at the date of the accident and 64 at trial, suffered a traumatic amputation of the tip of the ring finger of the left non dominant hand. The remains of the finger were amputated through the distal inter-phalangeal joint three months after the accident. H was off work for four months. H's finger continued to feel stiff and was still painful at times, particularly in cold weather. H had reduced grip. The judge did not feel bound by the bracket in the Judicial Studies Board Guidelines s.6(I)(l) which he stressed were only guidelines. *General Damages*: £4,500.

HARDING v. BASINGSTOKE AND DEANE BC [2000] 3 Q.R. 7, District Judge Field, CC (Salisbury).

Fingers

1614.   W, a girl aged six at the date of the accident and eight at trial, had the tip of her little finger on her left, non dominant hand crushed in the frame of a classroom door which was closed suddenly. The bone extruded, and the wound was treated initially by dressings and antibiotics. Ten weeks later the protuberant end of the distal phalanx was removed using a bone nibbler, under general anaesthetic. W lost nearly 1cm of her little finger and the remaining part was thinner in diameter than on her right hand. New nail growth curled around the end of her finger. W found the injury and subsequent treatment very distressing for about nine months. She was left with permanent disfigurement which was not particularly noticeable, but affected the distance she could stretch when playing musical instruments. *General Damages* (agreed): £3,500.

W (A MINOR) v. GLOUCESTERSHIRE CC, September 10, 1999, District Judge Exton, CC (Cheltenham). [*Ex rel.* Davis Gregory Solicitors, 25 Rodney Road, Cheltenham, Gloucestershire].

Sacrum, pelvis and hips

1615.   C, female, aged 34 at the date of the road traffic accident and 41 at trial, an American citizen temporarily in the UK, sustained life-threatening injuries including a severely comminuted displaced fracture of the floor of the acetabulum with the proximal femur displaced towards the pelvis, fractures of the superior and inferior pubic rami on the right side and the inferior pubic ramus on the left, a laceration in the left external iliac vein necessitating a laparotomy and 34 units of blood transfusion, a multi-fragmented displaced fracture of the left clavicle and nerve damage to the shin and the dorsum of the left foot. She spent five days in intensive care followed by a period of traction, then a six and a half hour operation to repair the acetabulum with screws and plates. After four weeks in hospital and four months on crutches, C was left with permanent restriction of movement requiring use of a cane to aid stability, and stiffness when sitting or standing for more than 20 minutes. Many social and domestic activities were painful or impossible. Previously a keen sportswoman, she was forced to give up all sports including tennis, racquetball and kite-flying. She had intended to return to full time work when her youngest child reached 13 in July 2000 but was unlikely to be able to obtain or cope with even part time work; a multiplier of 12.5 was used to reflect the possibility of her finding a sympathetic employer and the need for her to care for her husband, who now suffered from multiple sclerosis. On her return to the USA in 1995, C's injuries prevented her from obtaining any private medical insurance. There was extensive scarring to the hip, the total length of which was 55 cm, an unsightly mass of jellied tissue on her thigh and a laparotomy scar. She would require at least four hip replacement operations to repair damage resulting from the accident. She also required surgery to her knee in respect of an unrelated injury. *General Damages*: £45,000. Future loss of earnings award: £149,006 (multiplier of 12.5. Award for the discounted cost of future hip operations: £79,470. Award for the inability to obtain medical insurance: £31,788.

RATTRAY v. HINDS, June 9, 2000, John Mitting Q.C., QBD. [*Ex rel.* Richard Bendall, Barrister, 33 Bedford Row, London].

Sacrum, pelvis and hips – respiratory organs and chest

1616.   U, female, aged 58 at the time of the road traffic accident and 62 at trial, suffered a fractured sternum and multiple bruising. U was not detained in hospital but was prescribed painkillers and physiotherapy. She suffered severe pain in her chest for about six weeks but it gradually resolved thereafter. Although the bruising gradually subsided U was left with continuing pain in her right hip and buttock which was subsequently agreed as being trochanteric bursitis. Five months after the accident U was markedly restricted in her mobility, only able to walk a few hundred yards and was taking daily painkillers. Her hobbies of gardening and walking were significantly curtailed. Despite an attempt to return to work as a post office counter clerk five months after the accident, she was unable to do so because of the pain in her right hip region. U finally returned to work a year after the accident and, with assistance from colleagues, continued until her retirement six months later. U had considerably, improved 21 months after the accident. She was no longer limping but still had some pain in the hip region if she walked for more than 800 yards. Shopping was possible but with discomfort and the heavier aspects of her gardening were disrupted. U was a keen gardener. Ibuprofen was taken on a regular basis. Three years after the accident the symptoms in the right upper leg were not grossly restricting, her discomfort was more of a nuisance than a handicap, but she could not undertake the pre-accident level of gardening and now had to be careful in her daily activities. She still had aching in the buttock and right upper leg but not a sharp pain. She was not as active as before or would hope to have been in retirement. She still occasionally took painkillers. The prognosis was that while there might be slight improvement, little change was likely in the near future. *General Damages*: £7,000 (apportioned, £2,500 for the fractured sternum and the bruising and £4,500 for the trochanteric bursitis).

UTER v. WILLIAMS, October 21, 1999, District Judge Exton, CC (Bristol). [*Ex rel.* Christopher Taylor, Barrister, Queen Square Chambers, 56 Queen Square, Bristol].

Leg

1617.　B, a boy aged 14 at the time of the accident and 16 at trial, was on holiday with his parents in Great Yarmouth. B attended P's Go Kart Centre. When B was about to get into a go kart, it was struck from behind by another go kart already racing on the track. The impact caused the empty kart to strike both B's legs. B suffered a transverse fracture of the lower third of his right tibia and fibula. B underwent a manipulation under anaesthetic. He was released from hospital two days after the accident. B's right leg was in plaster for a period of eight weeks, during which time B was non weight bearing. When the plaster was removed, B attempted to weight bear but developed pain and swelling of the right tibia. The leg was therefore replastered for a further four weeks. B was off school for a full term from September to December 1998 and as a result of this he had to resit the whole of that academic year. B had hoped to join the armed forces but that ambition was lost due to the injury. It was also discovered that B was asthmatic, therefore it was unlikely that he would have been able to enrol in the armed forces in any event. Arguments were put to the court that this claim fell outside the bottom bracket of the JSB Guidelines (Section 6) (A) (c) (iii)) which dealt with simple fractures to the tibia or fibula. The medical evidence suggested that B would have complete resolution of all symptoms 22 months after the accident. *General Damages*: £5,250.

B (A MINOR) v. PLEASURE & LEISURE CORP, November 16, 1999, Deputy District Judge Jeffries, CC (Skegness). [*Ex rel.* Hodgkinsons Solicitors, The Old Manse, 14 Lumley Avenue, Skegness, Lincolnshire].

Leg – arm – non facial scars

1618.　H, female aged 10 at the date of the road traffic accident and 14 at trial suffered a compound fracture of the left tibia and fibula, fracture of the neck of the left humerus and a fracture of the right clavicle. The clavicular fracture was treated with a sling, worn for six weeks. Thereafter H only suffered minor discomfort upon vigorous physical activity. The injury to the left leg required four surgical procedures under general anaesthetic, including fixing of an external fixator, replacing it with plates and screws and an external cast. A further operation was needed to remove the plate. H was in a wheelchair for two months post accident and in considerable pain with her leg for four months. Four years post accident, there had been good orthopaedic recovery with no loss of movement or any arthritis risk, but there was extensive scarring to the lower leg. The largest surgical scar,was 32 cm by 5 cm, there were five other scars representing the points of insertion of the fixator pins, and a mass of scars caused traumatically including a vertical scar 9 cm by 2 cm, a scar of 2 cm and one of 3 cm which were de-pigmented, contoured and had altered sensation along their edges and surfaces associated with some cutaneous nerve damage. The scarring was described by a plastic surgeon as very significant and clearly visible. There was no prospect of any significant improvement, although they would fade to some extent, they would always represent a very serious cosmetic deficit. H had some psychiatric reaction to the scars, she refused to wear skirts and only wore trousers with boots underneath to protect the scar surface. She had expressed to a psychiatrist a wish that she was a boy and had been hurt by malicious comments of school children and by unthinking reactions of siblings and friends. She had suffered from post traumatic stress disorder of mild to moderate intensity which was continuing at the date of trial but was thought likely to resolve slowly. At the time of the trial, the psychiatric reaction to the scarring was more serious than the post traumatic stress disorder and was expected to persist through her teenage years into early adulthood. *General Damages*: £33,500.

H (A CHILD) v. COOPER, February 16, 2000, District Judge Batcup, CC (Neath & Port Talbot). [*Ex rel.* Gareth John Jones, Barrister, 33 Park Place, Cardiff].

Leg – non facial scars

1619.　E, a boy, aged 10 years and seven months at the date of the accident and 13 years and two months at trial, suffered an injury to his right leg while playing football on land belonging to C. E fell while playing and caught his right leg on a piece of stone or concrete hidden by the grass. E attended the casualty department at the local hospital and was found to have a 3 cm laceration on the right tibia. The laceration was cleaned and closed with steristrips and a double tubigrip was applied. Nine days later the steristrips were removed and a further dressing applied. On the following day, E again attended the casualty department as the wound was inflamed and discharging, and a further dressing was applied and a course of antibiotics prescribed. The wound then healed and on examination three months later there was an obvious scar, 2.5 cm by 0.5 cm on the right leg. At the date of the examination this was described as very unsightly but improvement was expected over the following nine months. E continued to complain of aching around the scar and pain on the scar whenever it was knocked. It was expected that this would settle over the following six months. At the date of trial, the scar was pale and not readily visible. E stated that it was more visible during the summer months. E did not have any functional problems with the leg. *General Damages* were assessed at £2,000.

E (A CHILD) v. CALDERDALE MBC [2000] 4 Q.R. 7, District Judge Slim, CC (Halifax).

Loss of leg below knee

1620.　M, male, aged 17 at the date of the road traffic accident in April 1988 and 28 at trial, suffered a complete dislocation of the talus bone in the left foot and a splintered displaced fracture of the upper part of the left femur with a moderately severe concussional head injury. He underwent operative treatment at the time of the accident for the cleaning and excision of the wound as well as reduction of the talus bone in relation to the left ankle. He suffered from clawing of the toes throughout 1990 and 1991. In 1992 he underwent operative treatment for elongation of the Achilles tendon and a posterior capsulotomy of the left ankle. Symptoms of pain in the ankle and foot continued due to arthritis in the ankle joint and avascular necrosis of the talus and Volkmans contracture to the foot with clawing of the toes. Ultimately M underwent a below knee amputation of the left leg in November 1995. He was affected by sudden cramps and pains in the stump. He needed time off work due to stump breakdown and abscess formation. He had an increased chance of developing osteoarthritis in the remaining joints of both lower limbs all the more so given the fact that he was employed as an HGV driver. The agreed neuropsychology evidence was that he was left with altered personality and impairment of memory and concentration as a result of the head injury. He had difficulty renewing verbal learning and had a relatively poor speed of information processing. Following amputation of his leg, he consulted another firm of solicitors who proceeded with an action in professional negligence against his former solicitors for failure to prosecute an action against the original tortfeasor. It was accepted that if a personal injury action had progressed with competent legal advice it would not, in the circumstances, have been possible for the assessment for damages to take place much before the date of trial in the professional negligence action in any event, and accordingly the action progressed to a normal assessment hearing as if the action had been a personal injury action. The district judge expressed the opinion that an increase in general damages by a factor of 1.5 was long overdue. *General Damages*: £55,000. Past loss of earnings award: £97,500. Past care and attendance award: £6,500. Future loss of earnings award: £159,500. Future care award: £50,000. Award for cost of artificial limbs: £122,803. Award for cost of accommodation: £166,690. Award for cost of aids and equipment: £10,000. Award for transport costs: £35,000. Total award: £724,477.

MCFARLANE v. CLIFFORD SMITH & BUCHANAN, September 26, 1999, District Judge Holloway, QBD. [*Ex rel.* Hough Halton & Soal, Solicitors, 32 Abbey Street, Carlisle].

Severe leg injuries

1621. S, male, aged 44 at the date of the attack and 50 at the date of the assessment, suffered multiple stab wounds during an unprovoked attack. An artery was severed in the left leg that led to an above knee amputation leaving a 10 inch stump. His right leg was also severely injured due to damage caused to the lower quadriceps and to the cruciate ligament resulting in a loss of power and instability. The last 15 degrees of extension of the right leg were missing. He was an inpatient for a period of 13 weeks. S's mobility was severely restricted in that he could only walk for 100 yards at a time at a reduced pace. The prognosis was that the restriction in mobility would not improve, and due to degenerative changes to his right leg it would deteriorate when he was much older with the result that he might need to use a wheelchair. S experienced significant problems with the prosthesis to his left leg, which caused him to have pain and fall on regular intervals. He also suffered phantom pains on a continuing basis. S sustained superficial stab wound injuries to his face, neck, abdomen and upper arm. A pre-existing psychological condition, which included cognitive impairment hearing loss and difficulty with articulation of speech, was exacerbated. S was considered to be an anxious man, whose relationship with his partner and six children had deteriorated as a result of his inability to cope with his physical injuries. *General Damages*: £75,000.

SCHREMBRI (CICB: QUANTUM: 1999), *Re* [2000] 3 Q.R. 7, Michael Brent Q.C. (Chairman), CICB (London).

Severe leg injuries – psychiatric damage

1622. C, male, ex-paratrooper, aged 32 at the date of the incident and 36 at the hearing, was attacked with a knife. C's most serious physical injury was the complete severance of the left sciatic nerve at the thigh which was treated, unsuccessfully, with peripheral nerve surgery. His other wounds were sutured. The only significant scarring was to his thigh. He remained an inpatient for five weeks, immobilised in a hip spica, during which time he suffered a marked psychiatric reaction with anxiety, depression and nightmares relating to the incident. C was left with near paralysis of the left foot which was markedly unstable, altered sensation and constant lower leg pain. He limped and used a stick intermittently. The sole of his foot remained exquisitely tender. He was unable to walk on uneven ground. He could only walk a quarter to half a mile on a good day and on some days scarcely at all. The instability caused frequent falls and sprains. His sleep was regularly disturbed by pain, and constant pain-relieving medication made him feel groggy. He could not drive a manual car. Having been a fit, confident, outgoing individual who enjoyed training and all racket sports he had become largely housebound with mood, memory, concentration and libido all affected. He lived in constant fear of reprisal, moving away from his former home for that reason. He was disturbed by images of violence. Although he had only had limited psychological therapy his ongoing physical sequelae, which were permanent, would continue to have a marked affect on his psychiatric health quite apart from his continuing fear of reprisal. The incident occurred just before he was due to commence new employment in sales. He was unlikely to resume any form of employment but the multiplier of 18 was reduced to 10 to reflect the fact of non-continuous pre-incident employment and the remote possibility of obtaining part time non-secure work. *General Damages*: £37,500. Past loss of earnings award: £56,085. Future loss of earnings award: £200,690. Total award: £302,797.

CURRIE (CICB: QUANTUM: 1999), *Re*, September 21, 1999, George Lowther (Chairman), CICB (Durham). [*Ex rel.* Simon E Wood, Barrister, Plowden Buildings, Temple, London].

Less severe leg injuries

1623.   D, male, aged 18 at the date of the accident and 23 at trial, sustained injuries when his lower left leg became trapped between two metal structures, one of which was being lifted by a mechanical digger. He had a pre-existing lateral ligament instability of the left ankle which was asymptomatic at the time of the accident. As a result of the accident, he sustained two undisplaced segmental fractures to the lower left fibia just above the ankle. A below the knee plaster cast was applied and D's leg was in plaster for eight weeks. Within 10 weeks of the plaster being removed, D began to experience discomfort and instability in the left ankle, caused by lateral ligament laxity. The trauma to the left tibia had aggravated the pre-existing injury, causing symptoms of pain, discomfort and instability. Corrective surgery would be necessary. *General Damages*: £8,000. Award for cost of future surgery: £2,500.

DAVIES v. GRAVELLE PLANT LTD, July 1, 1999, Judge Diehl, Q.C., CC (Swansea). [*Ex rel.* Bryan Thomas, Barrister, 33 Park Place, Cardiff].

Knee

1624.   G, female, aged 38 at the date of the accident and 44 at trial, was injured whilst travelling as a standing passenger on a bus, when it pulled away sharply with a sudden jolt, causing her left leg to be jerked forwards and back. She sustained an osteochondral fracture of her left knee, and there was localised damage to the medial femoral condyle. F remained troubled by a constant gnawing pain in the left knee, which was worse in cold or wet weather. The knee swelled up most days, clicked intermittently and gave way once or twice a week. Her walking distance was limited and she could not run. She suffered a sharp pain in the joint when weight bearing, turning or twisting. Housework aggravated the pain. There was a possibility of knee replacement and knee revision. An award for loss of earnings was made on the basis that G had intended to return to work as a care escort. *General Damages*: £33,000.

GRACE v. STAGECOACH LTD, June 23, 2000, District Judge Wainwright, CC (Exeter). [*Ex rel.* Crosse & Crosse Solicitors, 14 Southernhay West, Exeter].

Knee

1625. L, a boy, aged 14 at the date of the road traffic accident and 17 at the child settlement approval hearing, suffered a serious open fracture dislocation of the right patella which required urgent surgical treatment and subsequent split skin grafting. L suffered severe degloving to tissue around the knee that had left him with an anterior knee scar of 20 cm in length, with patchy discolouration which required a skin graft. On the lateral aspect of the knee there was a skin graft area measuring 10 cm by 14 cm. L also suffered an undisplaced fracture of the proximal right tibia which also required surgery with repair to a partial, 40 per cent, division of the posterior tibial nerve. L also suffered abrasions to the right arm, scalp and lumbar spine which injuries settled and did not cause any ongoing problems. The appearance and contour of the popliteal fossa on the right side would never return to normal and resulted in an abnormal appearance of the right knee. Revisional surgery would be unlikely to produce any significant improvement in the cosmetic appearance of the scars. L was left with an area of numbness on the lateral part of his right foot due to the disruption of the posterior tibial nerve, and this numbness was a permanent consequence. *General Damages*: £26,000.

L (A CHILD) v. BACON, May 3, 2000, District Judge Bower, CC (Doncaster). [*Ex rel.* Frank Allen Pennington Solicitors, Hill House Chambers, 6/7 Regent Terrace, South Parade, Doncaster].

Knee

1626. M, male, a police officer, aged 39 at the date of the accident and 46 at the assessment hearing, sustained an injury to the right knee when he tripped in a hole, whilst pursuing a burglar. The right knee swelled up and became painful. M initially took five days off work, thereafter taking time off intermittently when the knee became swollen. M had had a meniscectomy in the right knee some 11 years previously, but the knee was symptomless prior to the accident. At the date of the hearing the knee still became swollen and locked every few months. Painkillers were taken four times a week to control pain, which was described as being present 50 per cent of the waking time. M, who, before the accident had taken part in football at a high level, had to give it up after the accident. Medical evidence confirmed that pre-existing asymptomatic arthritis had been accelerated by a period of 10 years and would probably prevent him from working as a police officer at some point in the future. *General Damages* Award: £8,500. Award for possibility of loss of congenial employment within 10 years post accident: £2,500.

MORTON (CICA: QUANTUM: 2000), *Re*, July 13, 2000, Lord Carlisle Q.C. (Chairman), CICA (York). [*Ex rel.* Jonathan Saul Godfrey, Barrister, St. Paul's Chambers, 23 Park Square South, Leeds].

Knee

1627. C, female, aged 22 at the date of the accident and 25 at trial, was injured whilst a pillion passenger on a motorcycle which collided with A's vehicle. C was taken to hospital. X-rays confirmed that she had not sustained a fracture to her left knee but there was air in the pre-patellae. A pressure dressing was applied and she was treated with antibiotics. C also sustained cuts and grazes to her hand and a wound to her left knee which required stitches. C was then discharged. Two days later she attended the fracture clinic for the stitches to be removed and a further attendance at casualty was required five days later for the dressing to be replaced because of bleeding. C was off work for two weeks after the accident and had to sit with her leg up for most of that time. Her mother provided a small degree of care to her. During the year after the accident, C's knee would give way on a regular basis, particularly when she was walking. Her knee ached when she walked or exercised. Those symptoms prohibited her from continuing her hobbies, which included aerobics, swimming and horse riding, for six months after the accident.

Following the first anniversary of the accident the symptoms improved. At that time, C still found that her knee ached if she walked for more than half a mile and it would give way, less often than it did after the first year, but approximately two to three times per week. The symptoms continued to affect her whilst driving as the knee became uncomfortable if it was left in a constant position. C was examined by an orthopaedic surgeon and a diagnosis of chondromalacia patellae or anterior knee pain was made six months before trial. The consultant confirmed that the impact of the left knee had rendered it persistently tender and that episodes of the knee giving way were considered most likely to be related to sudden pain in the knee. The consultant indicated that recovery would usually take place over a period of five years and he expected improvement during the next two years but he could not be certain of this. Occasionally, the symptoms could persist indefinitely. Degenerative changes were not normally associated with this condition and surgical treatment was usually fairly ineffective. *General Damages*: £8,000.

CARNELL v. A-B AEGON, January 4, 2000, District Judge Crosse, CC (Exeter). [*Ex rel.* Crosse & Crosse Solicitors, 14 Southernhay West, Exeter].

Knee

1628. P, male, aged 52 at the date of accident and 55 at trial, suffered a mild whiplash injury that subsided within 24 hours and an impact injury to his left knee, that immediately began to swell in a road traffic accident. Pain to the knee was experienced for five months after the accident but was controlled by painkillers and a support stocking. Around five months after the accident, P experienced a painful locking of the knee and re-attended hospital. Internal investigation revealed the existence of a pre-existing degenerative condition, albeit one that had been asymptomatic prior to the accident. After this date, the knee caused discomfort especially in cold weather and in the cold conditions where P worked. P was unable to continue with his hobbies of fishing and gardening. It was agreed that the accident had accelerated the symptoms by six to eight months. As at the date of assessment of damages, the knee was continuing to deteriorate. *General Damages*: £2,250.

PATTERSON v. MIDLAND BANK PLC, January 31, 2000, District Judge Wood, CC (Pontefract). [*Ex rel.* Sean D Yates, Barrister, 10 Park Square, Leeds].

Knee – neck

1629. R, male, aged 59 at the date of the accident and 62 at trial, was injured when a pile of scaffolding poles was dropped on him by a forklift truck. R suffered two fractured vertebrae in his neck and a right knee injury including fractures. His neck injuries consisted of fractures to the spinous process of the sixth and seventh cervical vertebrae, with lamina fractures of the seventh. Those were undisplaced, therefore there was no risk of neurological damage.

Pre-existing degenerative changes were present in the cervical spine. A disc prolapse at C6/7 was also thought to have occurred before the accident. It was felt likely that the accident had initiated symptoms from the pre-existing conditions. The neck was initially very painful but the pain gradually diminished. Fifteen months after the accident, R was experiencing lower back pain and problems turning his neck and was unable to drive. He also experienced slight weakness of the left arm arising from a distortion of the biceps muscle. At 25 months post accident, R still experienced an aching neck. At trial, turning the neck was still uncomfortable. The knee injuries consisted of a comminuted right tibial plateau fracture with avulsions of the insertions of both posterior and anterior cruciate ligaments and lateral meniscal tear, requiring open reduction and internal fixation of the tibial eminence fractures. A large avulsion fracture of the tibial eminence was re-attached and a posterior cruciate ligament inserted. A separate anterior approach was used to re-attach the anterior tibial eminence fracture. Tears of the a.c. ligament and meniscus were repaired. R suffered severe knee pain with sharp pains down the side of his right leg and numbness over the anterior aspect of the right knee, which gradually resolved. Physiotherapy was required initially to treat a fixed flexion deformity. At 25 months his right knee was painful especially when walking down steps or slopes. Numbness was still present at the front of the knee, which lacked two to three degrees of full extension. Those post accident symptoms were likely to be permanent. At trial, it was found that R had no residual earnings capacity. *General Damages*: £22,000.

REES v. PALMER, January 4, 2000, District Judge Daniel, CC (Bristol). [*Ex rel.* Veale Wasbrough Solicitors, Orchard Court, Orchard Lane, Bristol].

Knee – spine below neck

1630.   H, male, aged 28 at the date of the accident 33 at trial, was injured when driving a forklift truck which went into a large pothole. H was thrown around violently and suffered a fracture to his coccyx and an injury to his knee. The knee injury did not yield symptoms for three or four weeks after the accident as H alleged he was unable to walk and remained in bed with his back injury. H became depressed after the accident. The medical evidence indicated he had developed pain amplification syndrome. B's psychiatric evidence indicated that H was a malingerer who was deliberately exaggerating and elaborating his symptoms for the purpose of financial gain. H's case was that it was unlikely he would work again and he claimed full future loss of earnings. H attempted to return to work two months after the accident, but had to give up. At trial, the judge found that H's symptoms were genuine. H gave evidence that he was making an improvement and on that basis the judge made an award for two years' future loss of earnings. *General Damages*: £11,750. Total award £107,611.19.

HARVEY v. BECK & POLLITZER, February 17, 2000, Roderick Denyer Q.C., CC (Bristol). [*Ex rel.* Veale Wasbrough Solicitors, Orchard Court, Orchard Lane, Bristol].

Knee – shoulder

1631.   D, female aged 63 at the date of the accident and 65 at trial, suffered a fracture of her left malleolus and a soft tissue injury to her shoulder when she tripped in a pothole. D was in below-knee plaster for seven weeks and received eight or nine sessions of physiotherapy. By the date of trial she was left with some permanent restriction of movement and intermittent pain, and had difficulty when walking over uneven surfaces. *General Damages* (agreed): £7,250 (apportioned £5,000 to the knee injury and £2,250 to the shoulder injury).

DINGLEY v. BROMLEY LBC (QUANTUM) [2000] 5 Q.R. 7, Recorder Baillie, CC (Bromley).

Ankle

1632.   D, male aged 67 at the time of the accident and 68 at trial was leading a flock of sheep down a rural two road when he tripped and fell. D felt immediate pain to his right ankle and foot. He attended hospital whereupon he was diagnosed with a fracture to his right foot and right ankle. In particular there was a fracture to the base of the fifth metatarsal bone and an undisplaced fracture to the lateral malleolus bone of the right ankle. D was treated in a plaster back slab for seven weeks. He was unable to carry out any farming duties for five to six weeks and was unable to drive for eight weeks. Following his discharge from hospital D still tended to walk with a slight limp and his ankle became painful when walking across rough ground. He was left with a slightly reduced range of movement in the right ankle. The recovery process was anticipated to take 12 months and thereafter D was expected to suffer a low grade discomfort on a permanent basis. *General Damages* £6000.

DAVIES v. SHROPSHIRE CC, February 29, 2000, District Judge Hearne, CC (Telford). [*Ex rel.* Hodgkinsons Solicitors, The Old Manse, 14 Lumley Avenue, Skegness, Lincolnshire].

Ankle

1633. H, male, aged 38 at the date of the accident and 43 at trial, stepped into a hole on a playing field at premises owned by HO. H twisted his left ankle, which was immediately painful and swollen. H attended hospital where examination confirmed a minor avulsion flake fracture at the tip of his left lateral malleolus as well as injury to his left lateral ligament and his left capsule. H was in plaster for a fortnight and then wore an aircast splint for a month. When it was removed he had physiotherapy treatment. In spite of that, H continued to experience some discomfort and instability in his ankle. Further examination revealed that the lateral ligament had been stretched and rendered partially deficient. It was not susceptible to treatment and meant that H was left with permanent moderate instability in his ankle joint. H worked in an office and his job was secure. The residual symptoms did not affect his work. *General Damages*: £4,000.

HANRAHAN v. HOME OFFICE [2000] 3 Q.R. 8, Assistant Recorder Gateshill, CC (Leeds).

Ankle

1634. M, male, aged 67 at the date of the accident and 70 at trial, was a pedestrian whose foot was hit by the rear wheel of a car. He had pre-existing glaucoma and diabetes mellitus and documented diabetes peripheral neuropathy. He suffered bimalleollar fracture of the right ankle. There was severe displacement of the ankle joint with some fragmentation of the tibia and fibula. M underwent an operation which involved internal fixation of the ankle. Two screws were inserted through the medial malleolus and a plate and seven screws put on the fibula and lateral malleolus. The leg was then elevated on a Brauns frame and M was treated with antibiotics. A below knee cast was applied and he remained in hospital for 12 days. Upon discharge M was able to mobilise using crutches, but was non-weightbearing. The plaster was removed after four weeks but M suffered severe pain for several weeks and was unable to go out for four months. He was unable to bathe himself and his pre-accident twice weekly social services home help was increased to an additional daily attendance. The scars healed. Movements were restricted with some plantar flexion but no eversion or inversion and very little mid-tarsal movement. M continued to take painkillers. Before the accident M could walk for an hour but his injuries reduced that to half an hour. After two years the symptoms stabilised. By the date of the trial he had developed osteoarthritis in the right ankle which was likely to deteriorate. *General Damages*: 7,500.

MCCLEAN v. BOULT [2000] 4 Q.R. 8, Judge Cox, CC (Lambeth).

Foot

1635. P, male, aged 34 at the date of the road traffic accident and 39 at trial, sustained a severe degloving injury to the left foot, involving loss of skin and subcutaneous tissues, a grossly displaced fracture, dislocation of the neck of the third left metatarsal, a displaced fracture of the cuboid with separation of the fractured fragment and a fracture of the base of the cuboid bone. A split skin graft was taken from the left thigh to the 8 cm wound and the head of the third metatarsal was removed. P was discharged from hospital in a left backslab and crutches after nine days but developed an infection in the sole of the foot which required incision and drainage two months post accident. The wound healed within eight months of the accident and physiotherapy followed for a further seven months. Custom made insoles were then fitted. Full weight bearing without crutches was not possible until nearly 12 months post accident. At trial, the agreed medical evidence was that ongoing symptoms of aching and pain in the left foot would continue, the third toe would require amputation and fusion of the calcaneo cuboid joint would be necessary in 10 to 12 years. P would not be able to return to any of his pre-accident sporting activities save for swimming, he would need insoles for life and would require an automatic transmission car. Two weeks before the date of the accident, P had been dismissed from his job as a graphics operator. At trial, the judge accepted P's evidence that, but for the accident, he would have worked as a freelancer in that field whereas the pain and lack of mobility occasioned by his injury prevented him from working for a period of 14 months and thereafter justified him in setting up his own graphics and design business at home, notwithstanding that the business had yielded no profit by the date of trial. A multiplier of 15 was applied to a multiplicand of £6,000 for the future loss of earnings award. *General Damages*: £22,500. Past loss of earnings award: £79,500. Additional cost of working from home (*Roberts v. Johnston* award): £30,000. Future loss of earnings award £90,000. Total award (including interest) £243,555.

PATON v. FEKADE [2000] 5 Q.R. 7, Judge Hardy, CC (Central London).

Foot

1636. G, aged 29 at the date of the accident and 34 at trial, suffered a puncture wound to the sole of his right foot when the top of a stake he was stamping into the ground pierced his boot. G sustained a penetrating wound which was contaminated by pieces of the boot itself. Following initial treatment for cleaning and debridement, the foot was extremely swollen and painful, and it became infected. After a number of procedures to alleviate pain, it was discovered that the cuboid bone had become diseased and, at a sixth operation, G required a bone graft from his pelvis to the foot. The foot arch proceeded to collapse. Residual symptoms included painful scarring, throbbing pain, disturbed sleep and inability to take normal weight on the right foot. Walking and standing were limited to some extent and G limped. All those symptoms were permanent. G was a resolute man and had managed to complete his combat fitness tests, but only having taken painkillers. There was some doubt whether G would complete his full army career and there was a risk his injury would prevent his being promoted to sergeant which, but for the accident, would inevitably have been the case. The judge found that G, who held an LGV licence, was likely to seek work in the transport industry on leaving the army in 2004 and would then be at a disadvantage on the open labour market. *General Damages*: £16,000. *Smith v. Manchester* award: £10,000.

GEORGE v. MINISTRY OF DEFENCE, October 8, 1999, Judge Tetlow, CC (Manchester). [*Ex rel.* William Waldron, Barrister, Exchange Chambers, Pearl Assurance House, Derby Square, Liverpool].

Foot

1637. G, male, aged 31 at the date of the accident and 34 at trial, was injured when a heavy freezer chill cabinet fell on his right foot. Despite his protective shoes, G experienced immediate pain, bruising and swelling of the foot. X-rays revealed undisplaced transverse fractures at the base of both the second and third metatarsals. G was initially given a bandage and crutches but returned to hospital when the swelling subsided to have a plaster back slab applied. The plaster was removed after three weeks at which time the foot remained swollen and stiff. G then underwent a course of physiotherapy. Two months post injury, G was still having problems weight bearing and had found the physiotherapy painful. No further active treatment was recommended and he was discharged from hospital care. G made a brief attempt to return to work but was signed off due to increased swelling of the foot. G was away from work for seven months. An arch support was later fitted and when further X-rays were taken they showed that the fractures had united well. Eighteen months post injury, G complained of an aching in the foot depending on his level of activity. The foot tended to be stiff in the morning but there was no pain at rest. G avoided using ladders, pushing wheelbarrows and other activities which placed undue pressure on the foot. He used a strap for support. Three years and six months post injury, G described a "niggling" pain in the foot on activity. The pain was worse in cold weather, if he attempted to lift heavy objects, or if he ran or walked over rough ground. The foot had occasionally given way. G had not played football or golf since the accident and had not ridden his bicycle. He favoured his left foot. There was some tenderness across the base of the foot, together with a slight reduction in mid foot movement and toe flexion. His persisting minor symptoms were expected to be permanent. Premature degenerative changes were not expected as a result of the injury. Shortly before the disposal hearing G had worked for approximately one month as a coal delivery man, lifting heavy bags of coal. The medical evidence concluded that he was at a "slight" disadvantage on the labour market but the claim for a *Smith & Manchester* award was rejected. *General Damages*: £4,300.

GOODWIN v. GKN SHEEPBRIDGE STOKES LTD, January 10, 2000, District Judge Cochrane, CC (Chesterfield). [*Ex rel.* Craig Moore, Barrister, Park Lane Chambers, 19 Westgate, Leeds].

Foot

1638. J, female, aged 69 at the date of the accident and 73 at trial, sustained a fracture to the left os calcis when she fell from the stage in a village hall. Immediately after the accident she was in excruciating pain. She was admitted to hospital. Two days later a screw was inserted under general anaesthetic. J spent nine days in hospital followed by eight weeks immobilisation in a plaster cast. The pain became much worse when J attempted to mobilise after the removal of the plaster. It was very severe for three months, gradually improving over a further three months. Eighteen months after the accident J complained of discomfort in the left heel bone after standing or walking for more than 15 minutes. She required regular analgesics. Three and a half years after the accident the pain was only occasional. Prior to the accident J had suffered from a dull backache after standing for more than 30 minutes or when she had been lifting heavy weights. Following the accident her back symptoms increased in severity and she required additional analgesics. On examination approximately 18 months after the accident she was able to stand for only 15 minutes before the ache commenced. The frequency of symptoms had increased from two to three times a week. The prognosis was that with a course of physiotherapy the symptoms caused by the accident should improve within a further six to 12 months. J was virtually housebound for three months after the accident, during which time she was unable to do any housework. She was unable to work as a caretaker for six months after the accident, or to return to her main hobby of ballroom dancing for five months. When she started dancing again, she found that she was unable to perform the faster dances, and participation was reduced by a half. She was depressed, anxious and tearful for three months after the accident. Eighteen months after the accident she was still wary of walking out alone. Her confidence improved within a further 12 months. *General Damages*: £4,000.

JONES v. MANAGEMENT TRUSTEES OF PONTESBURY PUBLIC HALL, January 25, 2000, Judge Hughes, CC (Telford). [*Ex rel.* Erica Power, Barrister, 1 Paper Buildings, Temple, London].

Foot

1639. S, female, aged 26 at the date of the accident and 28 at trial, was a part time insurance agent. She visited a car boot sale in YAS's field, where she tripped and fell in a rabbit hole suffering immediate pain and swelling to the ankle. At the hospital, S was found to have an avulsion fracture to the navicular (tarsal) bone caused when a chip of bone was pulled away by excessive tension in the attached soft tissues. The fracture was treated conservatively with an initial back cast which was then replaced after two days with a below the knee back slab for four weeks. Following removal of the back slab, S was mobilised with physiotherapy. She improved quite rapidly and the pain and swelling had largely settled three months after the accident. On examination at eight months post accident, S reported occasional twinges and discomfort. The injury had completely resolved within 12 months. During the first six weeks after the accident, S had been restricted in playing with her toddler, driving and doing general household chores. Relatives provided help during this period. She was, however, fit enough to return to work two months after the accident. There was no long term risk of degeneration. *General Damages*: £4,000.

SHORT v. TRUSTEES OF YEOVIL AGRICULTURAL SOCIETY, September 24, 1999, Deputy District Judge King, CC (Yeovil). [*Ex rel.* Jonathan Dingle, Barrister, South Western Chambers, 12 Middle Street, Taunton].

Facial and non facial scars

1640. F, a girl aged two at the date of the injury and four at trial, was bitten by a dog sustaining multiple lacerations of the right side of the forehead. F was left with four scars measuring 16 x 2 mm, 10 x 2 mm, 3 x 2 mm and 5 x 3 mm. The scars were permanent and, although they could be concealed by cosmetics in due course, they could not be treated by plastic surgery. They were not expected to alter in appearance. The scarring became more noticeable when exposed to the sun. The scarring was significant and noticeable from six to eight feet. There was genuine and real cosmetic disability, but not serious disfigurement. *General Damages*: £9,000.

F (A MINOR) v. SLATER, September 14, 1999, District Judge Buckley, CC (Blackpool). [*Ex rel.* Blackburn & Co Solicitors, 7 Crescent East, Thornton Cleveleys, Lancashire].

Burns

1641. M, male, aged 55 at the date of injury and 62 at trial, right hand dominant, was an engineer working on a merchant vessel when the engine exploded whilst at sea, trapping M in the flaming engine room. M suffered full thickness burns to the face, hands and forearms. Skin grafts were carried out from donor sites on the thighs and calves. There were three further operations to the hands to relieve contractures over the following years. At the date of trial, M's hands remained severely scarred and clawed, especially the left, with considerable loss of abduction and adduction of the fingers. M had difficulty in carrying out most everyday tasks. M's family carried out cooking, cleaning and personal services for him on a daily basis. The scarring to M's face was not obvious, but he was very self conscious of his hands and arms and would not wear shorts because of visible donor sites. M underwent physiotherapy for two years and three months, and wore pressure garments for three years. Within six months, M was diagnosed as suffering from post traumatic stress disorder with mixed anxiety and depression. The latter developed into a fixed phobic anxiety of fire and being trapped indoors. M was taking sleeping tablets and occasionally anxiolytic drugs and analgesics. M was formerly a sociable individual and a moderate to heavy drinker but had become alcohol dependent and short tempered with no interests and few friends. M got no benefit from counselling and the prognosis was poor. M was unfit for work. The judge agreed that M was in the "severe" category of the JSB Guidelines for post traumatic stress disorder with his life severely affected by anger and phobia of fire. *General Damages*: £55,000 (the judge gave an indication that, bearing in mind cumulative effects, the award for general damages comprised £28,000 for psychological injury, £15,000 for loss of hand function and £12,000 for scarring). Total award: £245,403.

MIZON v. COMCON INTERNATIONAL LTD, August 19, 1999, Judge Bowers, CC (Kingston-upon-Hull). [*Ex rel.* Stephen J. Glover, Barrister, 37 Park Square, Leeds].

Burns

1642. L, female, aged 27 at the time of the accident and 34 at the hearing, was using a hired steam wallpaper stripper when steam shot out causing burns to her right cheek, right side of the chest and right upper limb. L was taken to hospital where dressings were applied and analgesics were administered. It was necessary for L to attend hospital daily for the following three weeks for dressings. After eight weeks L was able to return to normal household duties. The burns to the face and chest were superficial; the burns to the upper arm were superficial and dermal. The evidence was that the post-burn mark on the face should disappear within 12 to 18 months of the accident. On the upper arm L suffered permanent scarring to the extent that a patch of freckles damaged by the burns would not return and that area would look different from normal skin which was heavily freckled. A keloid scar had formed on the inside of the upper arm which, by the time of the hearing, had flattened but remained white and would be permanent. Its position meant that it had no cosmetic effect. The right breast and nipple had some discolouration of the skin which would be permanent. No sensation was affected in any area. L would remain cosmetically aware of the patch of skin without freckles, and was no longer willing to wear sleeveless or short sleeve tops. *General Damages*: £5,000.

LINDSAY v. TAYLOR, August 21, 2000, District Judge Brougham, CC (Middlesborough). [*Ex rel.* Marc Davies, Barrister, Durham Barristers Chambers, 27 Old Elvet, Durham].

Burns – psychiatric damage

1643.   T, female, aged 32 at the date of the accident in August 1997 and 33 at trial, was on holiday at a hotel when a waitress spilt scalding water over her lap and left forearm. T suffered superficial burns to both legs and her arm, which subsequently formed large blisters, wept and burst. T's wounds were dressed and she was confined to bed for one week, and suffered limited mobility for a further two weeks thereafter. During that time the burns were dressed daily for one week, and once every two days for a further two weeks, during which time she was dependent upon her family for assistance in getting about and reliant upon them for running the house. T's wounds healed after about five weeks. T was pregnant at the time of the accident and suffered anxiety about the health of her unborn child, heightened by a vaginal bleed one week after the accident. Her pregnancy also meant that she was only able to take limited analgaesia for the treatment of what were extremely painful injuries. At six months post accident, T presented with discoloured skin measuring 29 cm by 17 cm on the front of her left leg and 14 cm by 11 cm on her right leg, and over her left arm. Two years post accident the scars were practically invisible, only becoming apparent in either cold or very warm conditions. That appearance was expected to improve with time. There were no other ongoing physical symptoms. T was acutely aware of the presence of the residual scars and, although no psychiatric evidence was adduced, it was apparent that she had also suffered psychological trauma as a result of the accident which was still present at trial, manifesting itself as anxiety, intrusive thought and hypervigilence, improvement of which was again anticipated in due course. *General Damages*: £7,500 (£5,500 for the physical injury and £2,000 for the psychological sequelae).

TERRY v. SANDS FARM COUNTRY HOUSE HOTEL, June 1, 2000, District Judge Weston, CC (Telford). [*Ex rel.* Nicholas E Starks, Barrister, St Ive's Chambers, Whittall Street, Birmingham].

Burns – post traumatic stress disorder

1644.   S, female, aged 44 at the date of the assault and 50 at the hearing, was injured in an acid attack. At hospital she was estimated to have eight per cent full thickness burns to her face, right arm, dorsum of both hands and the left upper chest plus damage to both eyes. The following day S became severely ill from septicaemia. An endotracheal tube was inserted for three weeks.

S underwent the first skin graft three weeks after the assault. She underwent further skin grafts 10 months, two years eight months and two years 11 months after the assault. S was left with extensive scarring to her whole face, save for a 5 cm x 8 cm patch in front of the right ear, loss of hair above the left forehead, severe scarring to the right arm and left forearm and scarring to both hands. All scarring was permanent. Pressure garments were worn for some two years post assault. S's left earlobe was destroyed in the attack and only limited improvement was obtained after two operations, 10 months and two years eight months post assault. S suffered a perforated left eardrum, likely to have been caused by chemical burns. Unsuccessful myringoplasty surgery was conducted four years post assault. S suffered permanent hearing loss, tinnitus and a persistent and foul smelling variable discharge from the left ear. S also experienced pain in the throat and on the left side of the face and ear, particularly when in the cold. Swabs revealed methicillin resistant staphylococcus aureus. S experienced soreness in her eyes with extensive watering on a permanent basis. There was some visual impairment. S also suffered from headaches, dizziness and a loss of balance. Prior to the attack S had worked full time in a supermarket which she ran with her husband and was outgoing and sociable. Following the attack she developed agoraphobic tendencies and suffered from sleep disturbance, anxiety, frequent flashbacks, excessive sensitivity to heat and became socially withdrawn and more distant in her relationships. There was a diagnosis of severe post traumatic stress disorder and a moderately severe depressive reaction. The prognosis for the psychiatric injuries was poor although there had been some small improvement by the hearing. Due to the severity of her injuries, S was unable to work again. *General Damages*: Assessed at £86,250 including a 15 per cent uplift in the light of *Heil v. Rankin* [2000] 2 W.L.R. 1173, [2000] C.L.Y. 1478.

S (CICB: QUANTUM: 2000) (BURNS), *Re*, March 23, 2000, Not specified; CICB (London). [*Ex rel.* David W Brounger, Barrister, Lamb Building, Temple, London].

Skin conditions

1645.   P, female, aged 21 at the date of the injury and 27 at trial, worked as a manager of one of K's mini labs, processing films. In October 1994, she was given a powerful industrial cleaning agent "ChemKwik" to shift heavy stains left by photo processing chemicals. P used that three times daily for three weeks. She wore rubber gloves, but due to lack of training did not used them properly or replace them sufficiently frequently, as a result of which contamination got onto the inside of the gloves. P developed dermatitis to both hands, characterised by a red papulovesicular scaly eczema on the front of the right wrist, in the centre of the left palm, on both thenar eminences and on all fingers of both hands and the right thumb. The dermatitis waxed and waned and was aggravated by irritants such as household cleaners and by manual work such as heavy shopping. P was forced to leave her job and started a family. The dermatitis interfered with her care of her baby and was likely to be lifelong. P was only able to seek work that was "clean and dry", avoiding occupations such as nursing or catering. As a result the judge found that P was handicapped on the labour market. *General Damages*: £8,500. *Smith v. Manchester*: £15,000.

PUTTOCK v. KODAK LTD, March 31, 2000, Judge Parry, CC (Guildford). [*Ex rel.* Richard Davison, Barrister, Thomas More Chambers, Lincoln's Inn, London].

Respiratory organs and chest

1646.   D, male, aged 34 at the date of accident and 38 at trial, suffered a severe and potentially fatal penetrating wound following an accident at work. He had been undertaking demolition work in the basement of a five storey building when concrete rubble dropped from above. In turning to escape, he tripped and fell, impaling himself on a steel bar which measured approximately three inches in diameter. The bar penetrated under the left armpit and through the chest wall. He was in extreme pain, breathless, barely able to talk and in fear of losing his life. On arrival at hospital he was found to have sustained a collapsed left lung, multiple rib fractures and early signs of pneumothorax. There was no direct damage to any other internal organs. An inter costal chest drain was inserted and his pneumothorax settled rapidly. He was discharged from hospital approximately one week later. There were permanent scars below his left armpit, but they were of limited cosmetic significance. Over a year later D was still experiencing pain in the anterior and lateral chest wall but this gradually diminished and he had made a full functional recovery within two years of the accident. The judge found that D's injuries fell squarely within bracket (d) of the "Chest Injuries" section of the JSB Guidelines. *General Damages*: £7,250.

DRABBLE v. DEMOLITION SERVICES LTD, May 8, 2000, District Judge Jordan, CC (Bradford). [*Ex rel.* Edward T Legard, Barrister, York Chambers, 14 Toft Green, York].

Respiratory organs and chest

1647. M, female, aged 33 at the date of the road traffic accident and 36 at trial, suffered a rupture of a right breast implant. M had undergone a right subcutaneous mastectomy 11 years prior to the accident, with immediate silicone implant. Seven years after the mastectomy, the first implant ruptured and was replaced with an expander type implant. It was the second implant which was damaged in the accident. After the accident M experienced discomfort in the right breast. Within weeks of the accident the right breast had reduced in size and become distorted. Ultrasound examination showed leakage of the implant and M's name was put on the waiting list for a replacement implant. The surgery was carried out some 11 months after the accident. M was in hospital for one week after the operation due to complications. The agreed award for general damages reflected the 11 month period when M suffered the discomfort and embarrassment of the misshapen breast and the additional surgery which M had to undergo and which she found very traumatic. *General Damages* (agreed): £6,500.

MCCARTHY v. DAVIS, January 19, 2000, Judge Kenny, CC (Reading). [*Ex rel.* Alison McCormick, Barrister, 35 Essex Street, Temple, London].

Respiratory organs and chest – asthma

1648. B, female, aged 54 at the onset of symptoms and 58 at trial, developed asthma as a result of exposure to Glutaraldehyde in the course of her employment as a theatre nurse. B was employed in this position from 1971 until her retirement on health grounds in September 1996. Her asthma developed in 1995. While dealing with the Glutaraldehyde, B experienced watering of the eyes and dryness of the throat. Eventually she developed a cough and took a lengthy period off work during 1995. It was found that her condition improved when away from work and there was a prompt recurrence on re-exposure. She described a cough keeping her awake, feeling of chest tightness, wheezing from time to time, worsening later in the day. *General Damages*: £15,000 (agreed).

BROBBEY v. NORTH MANCHESTER HEALTHCARE NHS TRUST (QUANTUM), March 22, 2000, Judge Holman, CC (Manchester). [*Ex rel.* Thompsons Solicitors, Acresfield, 8 Exchange Street, Manchester].

Respiratory organs and chest – asthma

1649. C, male, aged seven at the date of trial, suffered repeated chest infections throughout his childhood and was eventually diagnosed as suffering from asthma. C's mother was employed by GUS between 1991 and June 1992. In November 1991, C's mother became pregnant with C. Her job required her to work in a large room containing approximately 100 employees of which approximately 90 per cent smoked freely at their desks through the course of the working day. C claimed that there was insufficient ventilation within the room and accordingly his mother was exposed to an excessive amount of cigarette smoke throughout the period of her pregnancy. C was born with a reduced birth weight and between the ages of four months and three and a half years C was treated on 13 separate occasions by his GP for chest infections. Thereafter, C continued to attend his GP but on a less frequent basis. In 1999 C was diagnosed as suffering from mild asthma. The prognosis was that there was a 50 per cent chance of improvement although the possibility of a deterioration in the severity of symptoms could not be excluded. The long term effect was thought to be unclear but the general view was that there was unlikely to be any adverse effect on lung function in adult life. C's expert consultant was satisfied of a causal link between the repeated chest infections and diagnosis of mild asthma and C's mother's exposure to tobacco smoke. GUS denied liability throughout but did not produce any evidence to counter the medical evidence. An offer of settlement was accepted and approved. *General Damages*: GBP 5,000 (approved).

C (A CHILD) v. GREAT UNIVERSAL STORES PLC, March 31, 2000, Deputy District Judge Rigby, CC (Burnley). [*Ex rel.* Waddington & Son Solicitors, 28 Manchester Road, Burnley, Lancashire].

Respiratory organs and chest – asbestos related injury and disease

1650.   S, male, aged 56 at the onset of illness and 60 at death, worked for BRB for 40 years prior to taking voluntary redundancy in March 1993. During the course of his employment he was exposed to very extensive asbestos dust. As a result, he developed a mesothelioma, being a tumour of the lung caused by asbestos exposure. S's symptoms began in August 1993 and he died on September 5, 1997. S therefore suffered an extensive period of illness for a mesothelioma victim. S suffered a severe amount of distress and pain, breathlessness, weakness, swelling of the chest, gastrointestinal symptoms, depression and paralysis of the legs. There was a large tumour which extended massively through the chest wall, and caused much embarrassment. In addition he suffered considerable depression at the thought of his pending death and as a result became resistant to going out and being seen by friends. *General Damages*: £58,000. Total award: £301,737.

SANDFORD v. BRITISH RAILWAYS BOARD, September 9, 1999, Judge Rutherford, QBD. [*Ex rel.* Townsends Solicitors, 42 Cricklade Street, Swindon, Wiltshire].

Respiratory organs and chest – asbestos related injury and disease

1651.   L, male, died at age 50 in 1995 as a result of mesothelioma which he contracted as a result of exposure to asbestos dust whilst working at C's factory from March 1966 to July 1966. Onset of symptoms occurred in early 1994 with an intermittent pain in the upper part of the chest. In late 1994 and early 1995 he experienced pain in the back of his left shoulder and pleural effusion was found at the base of his left lung. Malignant pleural mesothelioma was diagnosed in February 1995. L deteriorated rapidly and suffered severe abdominal pain and vomiting until his death in May 1995. L was particularly young to die of mesothelioma, and although his period of suffering was relatively short, he suffered significant pain and underwent major surgery and other intrusive medical treatment. The instant case justified an award at the upper end of the JSB guidelines. *General Damages*: (including interest) £46,719. Future loss of pension award: £38,524. Total award: £284,652.

O'LOUGHLIN v. CAPE DISTRIBUTION LTD 99 NJ 580/1997-0-1132, Forbes, J., QBD.

Respiratory organs and chest – asbestos related injury and disease

1652.   E, aged 49 at the date of trial, worked as a lagger for D for approximately 10 years from between the ages of 16 and 26. E was exposed to asbestos in the course of his work which involved feeding asbestos into a limpet spraying machine, mixing up asbestos and applying it to pipes and boilers, cutting sections, making mattresses and occasionally delagging. E was diagnosed as having a pleural plaque, a 10 per cent risk of developing mesothelioma, a five per cent risk of developing lung cancer, a five percent risk of developing asbestosis and a one per cent risk of developing pleural thickening. E had suffered a significant psychiatric reaction to the knowledge that he had an asbestos related disease due in part to the fact that his father, uncle and grandfather had worked as laggers and had all died from asbestos related conditions. E had formed the view that he was likely to succumb to an early death due to an asbestos related illness and was diagnosed as suffering from a depressive illness. The psychiatric symptoms included becoming bad tempered and irritable, sleep disturbance, impaired concentration and losing interest in hobbies and in his social life. E was undertaking cognitive therapy with a clinical psychologist and it was anticipated that he would need an immediate course of some 20 sessions and thereafter approximately one session every two months until aged 55. E was a self employed taxi driver with a small net annual profit of £4,722. E opted for damages on a final basis. General damages were awarded for E's psychiatric condition and for the risks of contracting further asbestos related diseases. The judge made an award for the prospect of losing income in the so called lost years should E develop a malignancy. *General Damages*: £20,000. Award for prospect of losing income: £2,000. An award for future psychiatric counselling costs: £2,800.

ELDERBRANT v. CAPE DARLINGTON LTD, March 13, 2000, Judge Pailing, CC (Newcastle). [*Ex rel.* Frank Burton Q.C., 12 King's Bench Walk, London].

Respiratory organs and chest – asbestos related injury and disease

1653.   M, male, aged 66 at trial, was exposed to asbestos dust between 1973 and 1983 in the course of M's work as a dock worker. He developed pleural plaques and left sided diffuse pleural thickening attributable to asbestos exposure, which was diagnosed in 1995. M suffered severe breathlessness on exertion. He had a total respiratory disability of 60 per cent but only 10 per cent of this was due to asbestos related disease, the remaining 50 per cent being due to emphysema. It was found that M had a one per cent risk of asbestosis, a three per cent risk of mesothelioma, a 15 per cent risk of lung cancer (multiplicative effect of asbestos exposure and smoking) and a 20 per cent risk of the pleural thickening worsening sufficiently to lead to increased disablement. The judge expressly found no evidence of anxiety. An award of provisional damages was made on the basis of the existing condition only and with no reference to future risks. General damages (provisional): £10,000.

MEACHEN v. HARWICH DOCK CO LTD [2000] 5 Q.R. 7, Judge Simpson, MCLC.

Excretory organs – psychiatric damage after sexual abuse

1654.   W, female aged 45 years at the date of the incident and 52 at the date of the hearing, was falsely imprisoned and raped both vaginally and anally by a man with whom she had formed a relationship and who had spiked her drink with amphetamines at his flat. During the course of the imprisonment, W was also subjected to sexual assault with a broom handle. The assaults happened on three occasions during a 20 hour period. The events had a severe impact on W both physically and emotionally. W suffered pelvic injuries and had to undergo two major operations in order to repair a grossly unstable bladder caused by nerve damage. The first procedure undertaken was an ileocystoplasty, but the initial success of this operation soon waned and W suffered intermittent periods of incontinence and then difficulty passing urine. That necessitated the second operation, which was an ileal loop diversion allowing the bladder to drain into a bag. Soon after that operation W suffered two episodes involving sub acute intestinal obstructions and in 1999 was readmitted to hospital because of a urinary tract infection. W was distressed by the cosmetic consequences of the surgery. She continued to suffer from pelvic discomfort which remained impossible to control. Future risks included stone formation in the kidneys, recurrent urinary tract infections and slow deterioration in kidney function. Before the attack, W had suffered depressive episodes in 1974 and between

1988 and 1990. She suffered reactive depression subsequent to the attack. Her fear and distress was increased when her assailant persisted to contact her and serious threats were made during these calls. Two years after the incident, W was described as weepy, frightened and apprehensive. She was still having nightmares on a weekly basis although their frequency had lessened. She was afraid to go out and remained indoors except to visit her local shops when accompanied. In addition, W's eating habits were affected and she put on weight. W was diagnosed as suffering from post traumatic stress syndrome and depression. Four years after the incident, there was some improvement, albeit fairly modest. The nightmares were continuing and their frequency depended on the level of stress she was experiencing at the time. It was estimated that they occurred approximately once or twice each week. W remained agoraphobic and preoccupied with the incident and her concentration was poor. She also suffered a daily visual reliving experience upon waking which caused her distress, and continued to suffer depressive mood swings. It was found that W's non specific fear symptoms would persist indefinitely. Her post traumatic stress disorder would decrease in its severity but would never entirely disappear and her reactive depression would gradually settle with the improvement in her health. However, it was unlikely that she would ever be able to conduct a normal sexual relationship and neither would she be able to return to work. It was anticipated that she would need to be escorted on leaving her home for the remainder of her life. Part of her claim included future care by her partner. Multipliers of 10 and of 20 were applied for the future loss of earnings award and for the future care award respectively. *General Damages*: £50,000. Past loss of earnings award: £16,868. Future loss of earnings award: £53,728. Past care award: £8,000. Future care award: £50,000.

W (CICB: QUANTUM: 2000), *Re*, November 4, 1999, Campbell Q.C., CICB (Manchester). [*Ex rel.* Rowlands Solicitors, 3 York Street, Manchester].

Reproductive organs: male

1655. [Civil Procedure Rules 1998 (SI 1998 3132) Part 36.]
H, a boy aged 12 years and 11 months at the date of the incident and 15 at the date of the infant settlement approval hearing, awoke in August 1997 with severe abdominal pain and feeling sick. His mother took him to his GP's surgery, where gastro-enteritis was diagnosed by a locum GP, whom, it was contended, had been negligent in his examination. Two days later, H again awoke with severe abdominal pain. He was limping and his mother noticed that the right testicle was swollen. She summoned the duty doctor who immediately referred him to hospital. There H underwent surgical removal of the right testicle. H's claim was that if H had been properly examined he would have been referred to hospital for surgery which would have avoided loss of the testicle. H made an offer to settle under the Civil Procedure Rules 1998 Part 36, which included a sum for a low risk of infertility. That was accepted by P without admission of liability and approved by the court. *General Damages* (approved): £14,500.

H (A CHILD) v. PARSONS, September 29, 1999, Deputy District Judge Matthews, CC (Leicester). [*Ex rel.* Holyoak & Co Solicitors, 6 Peacock Lane, Leicester].

Other conditions

1656. R, male, a patient under the Mental Health Act 1983, was aged 36 in February 1993 when GPs treating his erratic and agitated behaviour began to prescribe doses of chlorpromazine, a neuroleptic drug used to treat schizophrenia and as a tranquilliser, at or in excess of 1,500 mg per day, considerably in excess of the recommended maximum. Other neuroleptic drugs, droperidol and zuclophenthixol, were also prescribed. R became drowsy, over sedated and withdrawn, Parkinsonian, incontinent, and refused food and drink. Three months later, R was admitted to hospital where he was noted as being physically unwell, hot and sweaty, with a tremor, mute and confused, incontinent of urine, pyrexial and tachycardiac. R was diagnosed as suffering from neuroleptic malignant syndrome, a potentially fatal condition. The neuroleptic medication was stopped and he was treated for the condition. R's condition gradually improved, and six months later, he was discharged, and his condition remained reasonably stable thereafter. *General Damages* (agreed and approved): £6,800.

R v. GARDNER, September 9, 1999, Judge Simpson, MCLC. [*Ex rel.* Anthony Gold Lerman & Muirhead Solicitors, New London Bridge House, 25 London Bridge Street, London].

Toxicosis – food poisoning

1657.   M, male, aged 48 at the time of the incident and 50 at trial, claimed damages for personal injury after suffering illness in the form of diarrhoea and vomiting, later diagnosed as a shingella infection caused by contaminated food. The illness continued for the whole of his holiday and for three weeks after M's return. He was unable to work for three weeks. M was awarded 60 per cent of the cost of the holiday together with one week's loss of wages. *General Damages*: £2,000. Award for loss of enjoyment of the holiday: £500.

MIDDLEGE v. THOMSON HOLIDAYS [2000] 5 Q.R. 8, District Judge Bird, CC (Bristol).

Toxicosis – food poisoning

1658.   D, female, aged 23 at the date of infection and 25 at trial, booked a fortnight's honeymoon with F, a tour operator, in the Dominican Republic. Two days after arrival D developed central abdominal pain associated with watery stools every 30 minutes. Medication prescribed by a local doctor led to vomiting, and there was also difficulty giving intravenous and intermuscular injections. The diarrhoea and cramps continued severely for 48 hours, then gradually subsided, taking about four weeks until she was fully recovered. During the height of the illness, D felt feverish and then anorexic. She lost half a stone in weight and was restricted to a bread and water diet. Medical evidence concluded that D suffered acute gastroenteritis, most likely due to infection with entero-toxigenic eschericia coli, the commonest cause of traveller diarrhoea. The most likely source was from contaminated drinks, either ice or the glasses in which the drinks were served. The award took into account disappointment and distress for the spoilt honeymoon and damages for the diminution in value of the holiday. *General Damages* (agreed): £1,500.

DUFFY v. FIRST CHOICE HOLIDAYS & FLIGHTS LTD [2000] 4 Q.R. 8, Judge Cook, CC (Guildford).

Toxicosis – food poisoning

1659.   A, a boy, aged seven months at the date of the incident and three years and nine months at the infant settlement approval hearing, was fed milk which gave rise to salmonella food poisoning. He suffered from diarrhoea and vomiting which was acute for 14 days. A lost two pounds in weight. At its worst, A needed to be changed every hour, but there were periods within this fortnight when his condition could be controlled, although that was through avoiding milk or food. A was supplied with rehydrating fluid. Thereafter, the condition improved, and although stool samples showed that salmonella was present for a further six months, he suffered only intermittent symptoms, namely diarrhoea and vomiting, on perhaps 10-12 occasions. At least some of those could be explained as the result of inevitable childhood infections, and were unconnected to his food poisoning. A's sleep was disrupted, and he was irritable when suffering from the effects of the illness.

A's grandmother was a district nurse, and gave advice which avoided the need to attend upon A's GP more than once. *General Damages*: £1,300.

A (A CHILD) v. MILUPA LTD [2000] 4 Q.R. 8, District Judge Cleary, CC (Stourbridge).

Minor injuries

1660. L, female aged 60 at the date of the road traffic accident and 62 at the date of assessment hearing sustained a soft tissue neck injury and a laceration to the occipital region of the scalp. Five sutures were inserted into the laceration and L was not detained in hospital. L developed pain and stiffness at the back of the neck on the morning after the accident although the symptoms were never severe. She also developed more acute pain and stiffness in the lumbar spine. When examined two months after the accident she had virtually no neck pain and the pain in her lumbar spine had gradually improved and gave only occasional discomfort. The prognosis was for a full recovery within 12 to 18 months. L suffered a psychological reaction to the accident with some symptoms of a post traumatic stress disorder. She was diagnosed as having suffered from the lesser syndrome of acute stress disorder with an associated moderate depression. L suffered from panic attacks, insomnia and intrusive thoughts about the accident. She closed her haberdashery shop because she felt unable to cope. The psychiatric evidence suggested that she was unfit for work for a six month period. After that time period she made a good recovery and at trial had substantially recovered from any psychiatric injury attributed to the accident. She had obtained work as a barmaid but had not returned to running her own shop. *General Damages*: £4,000.

LORD v. TAYMIX TRANSPORT LTD, March 17, 2000, Recorder Valerie Davies, CC (Cardiff). [*Ex rel.* Andrew Arentsen, Barrister, 33 Park Place, Cardiff].

Minor injuries

1661. M, male, aged 37 at the date of the accident and 40 at trial, a coal process operator, fell from machinery onto a coal pile some 10 feet below. M suffered a neck strain involving slight scarring of the ligaments. M was unable to work for two weeks, and was in considerable pain during that period. His sleep was disrupted, and his Christmas ruined. M was prescribed analgesia, but was not required to wear a collar. On his return to work, he had difficulty reversing a forklift truck, having to turn his entire body to do so. After three months, his symptoms began to improve. After five months, M resumed his hobby of fishing. After six months, he complained only of occasional residual symptoms, which resolved entirely within 18 months of the accident. M also sustained a laceration to his right wrist, which was embedded with coal pigment. The resulting blackened scar was four cm long, although it was very thin. Some of the pigment faded in time. M also suffered a strain to his back, which recovered within a few months, and a graze to his forehead. The judge had particular regard to the whiplash injury and the scar in his award. *General Damages*: £3,300.

MORRIS v. COAL PRODUCT HOLDINGS LTD, November 24, 1999, District Judge Babington, CC (Barnsley). [*Ex rel.* Richard Gregory, Barrister, 24 the Ropewalk, Nottingham].

Minor injuries

1662. M, male, aged 34 at the date of the accident and 37 at the hearing, was a passenger in a vehicle which was struck head on by another vehicle in May 1997. M sustained a whiplash type injury to his neck together with bruising and stiffness to his left knee. He was also shaken and distressed by the accident. The neck symptoms resolved completely within four months and the psychological injury resolved within two months. It was anticipated that his knee injury would resolve within three and a half months, but at the date of the hearing he still had some stiffness in his knee after exercising at his gym, otherwise he had fully recovered within four months of the accident. *General Damages*: £2,500.

MIRTHA v. SERIWALA, April 19, 2000, District Judge Turner, CC (Preston). [*Ex rel.* Robert McGinty, Barrister, New Bailey Chambers, 10 Lawson Street, Preston, Lancs.].

Minor injuries

1663. S, male aged 22 at the date of the road traffic accident and 23 at trial, sustained personal injuries to his neck and shoulder together with an injury to his thigh when it was trapped against a door after the collision. S was unable to work for three days and thereafter returned to light duties only for a considerable time. S consulted his GP and received hospital treatment. The injuries to his neck and shoulder were resolved within approximately 12 months of the date of the accident, although he suffered ongoing headaches. The Judge found that these were not proven to arise from the original accident. It was found that S had suffered symptoms involving the neck, shoulders, some headaches and anxiety for a period of 12 months. *General Damages*: £2,250.

SUMMERFIELD v. MR GOOSTRY (A FIRM), February 16, 2000, Judge Tetlow, CC (Manchester). [*Ex rel.* Betesh Fox & Co Solicitors, 16-17 Ralli Courts, West Riverside, Manchester].

Minor injuries

1664. G, male, aged 49 at the date of the accident and 51 at trial, was knocked off his motorcycle sustaining multiple abrasions to both palms, left hand, left iliac crest and left hip. He bruised his left shoulder, left forearm and left leg and exacerbated his pre-existing condition of lower backache. He was off work as a guest house proprietor for eight days during which time the pain was acute. The abrasions, bruising and lacerations healed in about three weeks. The pain and stiffness in his left wrist and shoulder resolved in about six months by which time the backache had subsided to its pre-accident level. G was left with some reddened scarring on his shin and a faint scar 1 cm in length on his ankle. There was no cosmetic embarrassment. At trial, 20 months after the accident, G's ankle still tended to give way once a week with a feeling of instability, but physiotherapy was likely to remedy the situation. Clinically, the ankle was stable. *General Damages*: £2,000.

GRAHAM v. MORINI [2000] 5 Q.R. 8, District Judge Buckley, CC (Blackpool).

Minor injuries

1665. E, male aged 14 at the time of the accident and 16 at the infant settlement approval hearing, was injured in a road traffic accident. He was shaken and upset as a result of the collision. He was immediately aware of pain in his right shin, which was bleeding. After a restless night E awoke with pain over the front of his left shoulder and some bruising, and pain in the right shin. The pain and bruising gradually settled over a period of around six months. Following the accident E also suffered distress and anxiety, to such an extent that he was off school for two to three weeks after the accident. He suffered flashbacks for three to four weeks after the accident, but no nightmares. He spent some time away from the area in an attempt to forget the accident. At the time of the hearing, E was still a nervous passenger, but this was expected to resolve within a few months. There was a small 1 cm by 1 cm depressed scar on the shin, which was permanent. That caused no embarrassment or concern and was not particularly noticeable. *General Damages*: £2,000.

E (A CHILD) v. ANDERSON, March 30, 2000, Deputy District Judge Eyley, CC (Ashford). [*Ex rel.* Richard Menzies, Barrister, 8 Stone Buildings, Lincoln's Inn, London].

Minor injuries

1666. G, male, a fireman aged 41 at the date of the accident and 43 at trial, was struck in the face by a fire hose before falling to the floor and being struck forcibly across various parts of his body, principally the lower chest and abdomen. G was conveyed to hospital where he remained overnight before being discharged after X-rays and ultrasound scans revealed no internal injury. The bruising to the face caused bilateral black eyes and his vision was blurred for nine days. A full recovery was made from the facial bruising within 10 days. The significant pain in the chest and abdomen persisted for 10 days during which period G remained in bed unable to undertake any physical activity. Thereafter he recovered slowly and gradually became more mobile. The pain in his chest resolved after four and a half weeks, and G returned to work after five weeks. When examined four months after the accident there were no abnormal clinical findings and a full recovery had been made. G's wife had taken time off work to look after him and he was not able to play with his children for 10 days. *General Damages*: £1,500.

GREIG v. SOUTH WALES FIRE SERVICE, January 19, 2000, District Judge North, CC (Cardiff). [*Ex rel.* Andrew Arentsen, Barrister, 33 Park Place, Cardiff].

Minor injuries

1667. A, male, aged 16 at the time of the accident and 17 at the time of the hearing, had profound and multiple disabilities. He spent some time in residential respite care arranged through the local authority social services department. On entering the respite care home, A's mother provided a detailed list of A's needs, which specified that a bed guard was not to be used on A's bed. However, a bed guard was used on A's bed and A's head became trapped between the bars of the bed guard for a period of approximately one hour. A suffered blistering and swelling to his right ear which was slightly flattened. He also sustained a line across his right cheekbone thought compatible with a reaction over the bone which was still visible 18 months later. Due to A's disabilities, it was exceptionally difficult to ascertain the psychological impact of the accident on him, but some disruption to his behaviour was noticeable which included sleep disruption up to one year after the accident and increased attachment to his parents. It was not possible to ascertain the psychological effect that the injuries had on A's self image. At the infant approval hearing, some 18 months after the accident, the district judge accepted the difficulties in assessing the psychological impact on A due to his disabilities and accepted that the parties were correct to use an analogy with a new born baby as the basis for assessment of general damages. Further, the district judge accepted that due to A's disabilities he would not be in a position to assume control of the settlement monies when he reached the age of 18 and accepted that due to the level of damages agreed a trust would be too cumbersome. Damages were ordered to be paid to A's mother on his attaining the age of 18. *General Damages*: £1,500.

A (A CHILD) v. WESTMINSTER SOCIETY FOR PEOPLE WITH LEARNING DISABILITIES, October 13, 1999, District Judge Hasan, CC (Central London). [*Ex rel.* David Levene & Co Solicitors, Bedford House, 125-133 Camden High Street, London].

Minor injuries

1668. Z, a boy aged nine at the date of the accident and 10 at trial, was injured in a road traffic accident and sustained minor injuries. Liability was not in issue. Z suffered a blow to the head causing headaches which lasted for a period of seven weeks and a laceration of the frenulum which healed over a period of seven days. Z also suffered nightmares of the accident which lasted for a period of seven days. *General Damages*: £1,250.

Z (A CHILD) v. GREATER MANCHESTER POLICE AUTHORITY, November 16, 1999, Deputy District Judge Jeffries, CC (Skegness). [*Ex rel.* Hodgkinsons Solicitors,The Old Manse, 14 Lumley Avenue, Skegness, Lincolnshire].

Minor injuries

1669.   J, male, aged 14 at the date of the accident and 15 at the date of the infant settlement approval hearing, was injured in a road traffic accident when he was knocked off his bicycle and dragged along by a car. H sustained grazing to his forehead, right arm and hand, right shoulder, right hip and a superficial laceration to his left knee followed by severe headaches and aching in his shoulder and knee for a period of two weeks. Six months after the accident J suffered from occasional headaches, but the prognosis was that he would make a full recovery. *General Damages*: (agreed and approved) £1,000.

J (A CHILD) v. JONES, November 23, 1999, District Judge Gambrill, CC (Uxbridge). [*Ex rel.* Paul Tropp, Barrister, Hardwicke Building, New Square, Lincoln's Inn, London].

Minor injuries

1670.   K, a boy, aged seven at the date of the accident and nine at trial, was injured when an automatic door failed to open. He sustained minor injuries including a graze over the left eyebrow, nausea, dizziness and headache, which lasted one day, and a bruise which lasted approximately one week. The settlement was approved. *General Damages*: £500.

K (A CHILD) v. TESCO STORES LTD, October 7, 1999, District Judge Banks, CC (Uxbridge). [*Ex rel.* The Woodbridge Partnership Solicitors, Windsor House, 42 Windsor Street, Uxbridge, Middlesex].

Minor injuries – psychiatric damage

1671.   G, male, aged 19 at the date of the road traffic accident and 23 at trial, sustained soft tissue injuries to his lower back, soft tissue injuries to his neck which resolved after 10 days, bruising to his shoulder, knees and right thigh, which settled over four weeks, and a scar to his right thigh. He was off work for seven days and was unable to pursue his hobby of weight training for six weeks. G attended a chiropractor for six sessions of treatment to his lower back. G suffered psychological symptoms for 18 months as a result of the accident, including headaches, intrusive thoughts, flashbacks, mood and sleep disturbance and travel anxiety. The judge found that, while G's psychological symptoms stopped short of post traumatic stress disorder, he was entitled to be compensated in respect of them. *General Damages*: £5,250 (comprising £2,250 for the orthopaedic injuries and £3,000 for the psychological injury).

GIBBENS v. WOOD, July 4, 2000, District Judge Corrigan, CC (Plymouth). [*Ex rel.* Clare Vines, Barrister, 35 Essex Street, London].

Minor injuries – psychiatric damage

1672.   W, female, aged 22 at the date of the accident and 26 at trial, was walking to a football match when she was knocked to the ground and then stood upon by a police horse. W sustained extensive abrasions to her left knee and grazes to her shin as a result of the fall. There was bruising to her calf where the horse had stood on her. W's leg was stiff and painful for six weeks; there was temporary scarring to her knee that had faded by the time of trial. W developed mild post traumatic stress disorder, suffering occasional nightmares for several months after the accident. She was scared when she saw horses, including horse racing on television. She became anxious when encountering a police presence at football matches. On one occasion she had a panic attack and was forced to return home without watching the match. W was breastfeeding at the time of the accident. Her supply of breast milk dried up. There was a gradual recovery over three years but minor symptoms of anxiety persisted at the time of trial. *General Damages*: £3,000.

WATKINSON v. CHIEF CONSTABLE OF THE WEST MIDLANDS, December 8, 1999, Judge Mayor Q.C., CC (Leicester). [*Ex rel.* Nicholas George, Barrister, 27 New Walk, Leicester].

Minor injuries – psychiatric damage

1673.   L, a girl aged six years and three months at the time of the accident and eight at the date of the infant settlement approval hearing, was shaken, upset and tearful as a result of a road traffic collision. She had a graze on her left temple and was aware of pain in her lower abdomen. L had a restless night after the accident, and awoke with a sore head. Noticeable bruising had developed on her lower abdomen. She suffered daily pain for about a week. After this L suffered intermittent pain brought on by active play. L was off school for two to three days and upon her return was a less active participant in games lessons for two to three weeks. The physical symptoms resolved within three to four months. After the accident L was a nervous passenger. She did not suffer any nightmares. The nervousness was still present at a reduced level at the time of the hearing. This was expected to resolve within a few months. *General Damages*: £1,275.

L (A CHILD) v. ANDERSON [2000] 5 Q.R. 8, Deputy District Judge Eyley, CC (Ashford).

Minor injuries – head

1674.   K, male, aged 22 at the date of the incident and 26 at trial, was subjected to a serious attack by two assailants. He was punched about the head and face then kicked in the head whilst on the ground causing him to lose consciousness. His physical injuries included a cut to the left eyebrow which required stitches and later scarred, bruising to the right eye and a severe abrasion affecting the left temporal and parietal parts of his head. He was hospitalised for four days and for the first couple of days he remained confused and amnesic about the events of the assault. For some weeks following his discharge K experienced pain in his head, clumsiness of his limbs, slurring of his speech and poor co-ordination, all of which were worse when tired. Anxiety was a significant problem. He stayed in a lot, lost confidence and was uneasy when walking alone in the street. The initial medical evidence identified those symptoms of anxiety as being consistent with post traumatic stress disorder. K's father allowed him to return to work in the family building business after just two weeks but due to his clumsiness he could not use ladders, power tools or electric cutting devices. A year after the accident, there had largely been a clinical recovery with respect to motor function and K had become far steadier on his feet. The headaches lasted between six to nine months and were often of three to four hours' duration. The second medical report was able to identify all of the symptoms collectively as post concussional syndrome. The judge found that K had fully recovered 18 months after the accident, but for those 18 months K had been a shadow of his former self. The judge concluded that the injuries were within the minor head injuries category of the JSB Guidelines and within the minor post traumatic stress disorder category as there had been a recovery within two years. *General Damages*: £5,000.

KELLY v. HEMMING, April 22, 1999, Recorder Critchlow, CC (Slough). [*Ex rel.* Adrian Posta, Barrister, South Western Chambers, 12 Middle Street, Taunton, Somerset].

Minor injuries – head

1675.   M, a girl, aged seven at the date of injury and 11 at trial, was kneeling down to look at some clothing on the bottom shelf of a rack in a department store. Some racking fell off a shelf above M, and hit her in the middle of the forehead near the hairline, causing a haematoma but no laceration. M sustained bruising which lasted a few days and headaches for about six weeks, but M suffered no neurological deficit. M was left with subcutaneous scarring, causing a slight depressed area on her forehead that became more pronounced when she frowned or looked upward, approximately 1.5cm x 1cm in a crescent shape. The scarring was likely to be permanent. Surgery was not appropriate. *General Damages*: £4,000.

    M (A MINOR) v. DEBENHAMS PLC, August 19, 1999, Deputy District Judge Iacopi, CC (Cheltenham). [*Ex rel.* Davis Gregory Solicitors, 25 Rodney Road, Cheltenham, Gloucestershire].

Minor injuries – head

1676.   W, male aged 31 at the date of the accident and 33 at trial, struck his head on an oil pipe protruding from a wall. There was no loss of consciousness but he felt stunned by the injury and fell to the ground. He had a laceration to the right eyebrow and another to the right side of the nose, and a major cut to the right lower eyelid. Plastic skin was applied to the major wound. W was off work for a week. His eye was painful and swollen for several weeks and he was referred to hospital for X-rays. Initially, it was felt that he had sustained a fractured cheekbone, although that was not confirmed. W occasionally felt that the vision in his right eye was less clear than in the left and he experienced an occasional sensation of double vision. The right eye watered. There was pain and discomfort around the right orbit accompanied by headaches which occurred intermittently. There was also altered sensation in the right cheek. W took painkillers for the headaches but otherwise received no treatment. His symptoms were initially expected to resolve within 12 to 18 months of the injury. At the date of trial, approximately two years and nine months post injury, he was still complaining of right sided headaches around the right eye most evenings and a tightness around the right eye. He also complained of occasional blurring of vision. He took painkillers for the headaches as required. The persisting symptoms were described as a "nuisance" rather than a disability and W had not sought any further help from his doctor. The revised prognosis was that the remaining symptoms would persist until approximately three years from the date of injury but there was no likelihood of any long term disability. There was a small scar in the crease below the right eye measuring approximately 1.5 cm. That was not visible at conversational distance but went purple in cold weather. *General Damages*: £3,750.

    WILLIAMS v. CATERPILLAR (PETERLEE) LTD, January 11, 2000, District Judge Hall, CC (Sunderland). [*Ex rel.* Craig Moore, Barrister, Park Lane Chambers, 19 Westgate, Leeds].

Minor injuries – head

1677.   P, male, aged 53 at the date of the assault and 56 at the hearing, was punched twice in the face by a neighbour. Falling to the ground, he suffered a blow from another assailant to the base of his back with a metal bar and further punches and kicks to his face and body. He was not rendered unconscious and a dislocation to his jaw spontaneously relocated the following day. Severe bruising developed across the base of his back and both hands. He also suffered from severe headaches and disturbed vision which prevented him from working as a self employed tool maker for one week. Less severe headaches persisted for 12 months. *General Damages*: £2,000.

    PERKINS v. WAKELIN [2000] 6 Q.R. 8, District Judge Field, CC (Milton Keynes).

Minor injuries – head

1678.   F, male, aged 36 at the date of the accident and 39 at trial, suffered a blow to his forehead from a protruding shaft on a cutter bar whilst working at C's premises. F sustained a graze to his forehead which did not bleed and was not sutured. There was no visible scar when F was examined by a neurosurgeon. F complained of headaches immediately after the incident and was prescribed paracetamol. He subsequently complained of headaches which occurred about two to three times a week, for which he took at least one paracetamol tablet on most days. Sometimes, F had a week free of headaches. F did not need to consult his GP nor take any time off work, and did not feel his day to day life had been changed by his injury. Concussion and post traumatic syndrome of headaches were diagnosed. The prognosis was for complete resolution within three to six months. F stated in his evidence that the headaches had disappeared after 15 months and during the later months they had become both less frequent and less severe. It was noted that F had not mentioned headaches when he underwent an annual works medical some months after the accident. *General Damages*: £1,250.

   FARRELLY v. COURTAULDS CHEMICALS, August 11, 1999, Judge McDuff Q.C., CC (Nottingham). [*Ex rel.* Timothy Mayer, Barrister, 5 Fountain Court, Steelhouse Lane, Birmingham].

Minor injuries – cheekbone

1679.   R, male, aged 43 at the date of assault and 47 at trial, was head butted, knocked to the ground, and then punched. R suffered a displaced zygomatic fracture, anterior to the tempero-mandibular joint, from the impact of the head butt, which hit him on the left side of his face at the top of the cheekbone just behind the end of the left eyebrow. He also suffered a graze to his forehead on the right hand side from falling to the ground. Ten days after the accident, the fracture had to be united by surgery requiring a general anaesthetic, two nights in hospital and seven stitches. The stitches were above the hairline and were not visible. For a two and a half week period following the assault, R was unable to work. He suffered pain in his cheekbone and jaw and headaches, and had to take painkillers every day. He could not speak properly and could not eat solid food because of restriction of movement in his jaw. From two weeks after the assault until three to four months later, R suffered occasional pain at the fracture site, and had to take painkillers occasionally. The injury resulted in no cosmetic impairment, and a complete recovery was made within four months. *General Damages*: £2,850.

   RALL v. WALLAGE, May 8, 2000, Judge Armstrong, CC (Pontefract). [*Ex rel.* Mark Henley, Barrister, 9 Woodhouse Square, Leeds].

Minor injuries – sight

1680.   M, male, aged 52 at the date of the accident and 55 at trial, was struck in the right eye by factory floor debris. Metallic particles were removed from the eye on three separate hospital outpatient visits. M was off work for 13 days. At the date of the medical examination two years after the accident, M's vision levels were normal and acceptable for distance and near viewing. By the date of the trial, M continued to experience slight blurring of vision in strong light. The blurring occurred occasionally and was of a few minutes' duration. The medical evidence indicated that the blurring of vision had no deleterious effect from a functional point of view and would not persist. The district judge commented that the injury fell at the very bottom of the "minor" eye injury bracket of the JSB Guidelines. *General Damages*: £1,850.

   MORGAN v. FORD MOTOR CO LTD, June 6, 2000, District Judge Jenkins, CC (Bridgend). [*Ex rel.* Michael Brace, Barrister, 33 Park Place, Cardiff].

Minor injuries – neck

1681.   S, male, aged 51 at the date of the road traffic accident and 56 at trial, suffered a whiplash injury to the neck. He went to hospital but was discharged after X-rays had been taken. Symptoms developed over the next few days with severe pain radiating from the neck down the right arm. At the time of the accident S was recovering from an operation to fuse discs in his cervical spine. After the accident he was in severe pain for about three months with consistent loss of sleep. His right arm was weak and he was unable to pursue his only pre-accident leisure activity of swimming. The evidence showed that the delay in recovery from the operation which would have been made but for the accident was about 12 months. The symptoms persisted for about 12 months in total. As an additional head of claim, S suffered considerable anxiety over as to whether he would lose the benefit of the fusion operation, and the possibility that a further neck operation would be required. That anxiety resolved approximately 18 months after the accident. *General Damages*: £4,000.

SHANAHAN v. WILLMOTT, May 9, 2000, District Judge Edwards, CC (Brentford). [*Ex rel.* Mark Lyne, Barrister, 1 Essex Court, Temple, London].

Minor injuries – neck

1682.   D, male aged 24 at the time of the road traffic accident and 27 at trial, was thrown forward in his car, striking his head on the roof. He was shaken and distressed but was not aware of any injury and so drove home. A few hours later he began to experience pain and stiffness in the neck and right shoulder and his wife took him to hospital. X-ray examination revealed no bony injury and he was discharged. He suffered considerable pain and stiffness in the neck and top of the right shoulder for two or three weeks before it started to ease. D undertook eight sessions of physiotherapy in the weeks following the accident. He returned to work after four weeks at which stage he estimated he was some 60 to 70 per cent better but suffering constant "mild to moderate" aching in the neck and the top of the right shoulder. His work, driving a waste compactor, involved a great deal of neck movement which hindered recovery. Two years after the accident D was signed off work as a result of the continuing complaints and was referred to a consultant. An MRI scan revealed no frank disc damage. He remained off work for four weeks, undertook further physiotherapy and a pain relief specialist administered injections. When he returned to work his employers changed his duties to ones which were less physically demanding. Within a further three months his symptoms resolved entirely and were not expected to recur. He suffered symptoms for a total of 27 months. *General Damages*: £3,750.

DOWNIE v. WILLIAMS, August 16, 2000, Judge Bernstein, CC (Birkenhead). [*Ex rel.* Richard Menzies, Barrister, 8 Stone Buildings, Lincoln's Inn, London].

Minor injuries – spine below neck

1683.   B, female, aged 60 at the date of the accident and 63 at trial, suffered a jarring soft tissue injury to her lumbosacral spine when she slipped and fell onto her back whilst ballroom dancing. B experienced immediate pain and discomfort within her pelvis, lower spine and legs and sustained bruising. A few days after the accident, B went on a long planned overseas holiday. She experienced aggravation of her symptoms during the trip, which ruined her holiday. On her return to the UK, B consulted her GP and underwent a course of physiotherapy and her symptoms gradually improved. B had a history of spondylitic change within her spine which had been symptomatic. The increased pain and discomfort caused disruption and inconvenience to her day to day activities. She was unable to enjoy her hobbies of badminton, cycling and ballroom dancing. Damages for the loss of enjoyment of the holiday were agreed at a sum equivalent to the cost of the holiday. *General Damages*: £3,000. Award for loss of enjoyment of holiday (agreed): £440.

BURGESS v. ELECTRICITY SPORTS & SOCIAL CLUB, October 13, 1999, Recorder Britton, CC (Cardiff). [*Ex rel.* Bryan Thomas, Barrister, 33 Park Place, Cardiff].

Minor injuries – back

1684. B, male, aged 43 at the date of the accident and 46 at trial, slipped on some water on the floor in a prison and fell over. B had a pre-existing prolapsed disc in his lower back and a history of neck injury. His low back and neck symptoms were aggravated by the fall, and he also injured his right hip, thigh and arm, although not seriously. The neck exacerbation lasted for six to seven months and the back exacerbation for 12 months, requiring periodic analgesics. *General Damages*: £4,000.

BLEAKLEY v. HOME OFFICE, April 17, 2000, Deputy District Judge Hebbert, CC (Bolton). [*Ex rel.* Titus Gibson, Barrister, Oriel Chambers, 14 Water Street, Liverpool].

Minor injuries – back

1685. P, female, aged 20, hit her head on the windscreen and was dazed when H drove a removal van around a blind bend on the wrong side of the road, causing a head on collision with P's car. P was aware of pain in her right knee and ankle. That evening she became aware of pain in her low back and the back of her neck. P attended hospital the next day, where her neck was noted to be tender with a restricted range of movement. P was given a collar which she wore for one week and her neck ached for a further week before resolving. Her ankle was swollen for two days and her knee was bruised for two weeks. P had a constant headache for 24 hours. She was off work for one week. P's main complaint was an ache in her back which was constant for around a month before it became intermittent. P's back then ached every morning, following prolonged driving or sitting and upon lifting. P treated her back with ibuprofen tablets and gel. She underwent six sessions of physiotherapy around one year after the accident. After that, the ache occurred only occasionally and was less intense. The judge found that P did not exaggerate her injury and that it was still a cause of some inconvenience to her at trial, two years after the accident. A completely full recovery was expected within three years of the accident. *General Damages*: £3,500.

PEARCE v. HUMPIT REMOVALS LTD, October 13, 1999, District Judge Burgess, CC (Reading). [*Ex rel.* Richard Menzies, Barrister, 8 Stone Buildings, Lincoln's Inn, London].

Minor injuries – back

1686. C, female, aged 28 at the date of the accident and 31 at trial, was injured whilst descending the stairs in her rented accommodation when one of the steps collapsed, resulting in her falling a distance of five steps to the floor. C became aware of discomfort in her neck and back, radiating into her shoulders and causing nausea. She attended hospital the following day. Her symptoms were made worse due to her being in the early stages of pregnancy and due to pre-existing intermittent low back pain. C experienced pins and needles and pain and discomfort in her right hand leading to sleep disturbance. C sustained soft tissue injuries to her neck and back. The neck injuries resolved within approximately four weeks of the accident, whereas the back pain was exacerbated for six to 12 months post accident. *General Damages*: £3,000.

CHAMBERS v. CARDIFF COMMUNITY HOUSING ASSOCIATION LTD, March 28, 2000, District Judge Carson, CC (Cardiff). [*Ex rel.* Julian Reed, Barrister, 9 Park Place, Cardiff].

Minor injuries – whiplash type injury

1687.   D, female, aged 24 at the date of the road traffic accident and 28 at trial, was not immediately aware of any injuries, but within hours of the accident she began to experience pain and stiffness in her neck and back. She attended hospital where she was provided with a soft cervical collar. D was absent from work for 18 weeks and used the cervical collar on an intermittent basis during that time. D suffered a psychological reaction to the accident and developed a specific phobia in relation to travelling by motor car. The accident also exacerbated D's pre-accident depressive condition, extending it by a period of about 12 months. D's neck symptoms had almost resolved by the second anniversary of the accident, and had completely resolved by the third anniversary. D's phobia in relation to motor car travel still troubled her, but mainly as a passenger, rather than as a driver. The judge indicated that the physical injuries alone would have warranted an award of £3,850, and that the psychological injuries in isolation would have warranted an award of £2,000. Owing to the overlap between the loss of amenity caused by the physical injuries and that caused by the psychological injuries, a discount of £150 was made. *General Damages*: £5,700.

DIMELOW v. GRADWELL, June 21, 2000, District Judge Lingard, CC (Bradford). [*Ex rel.* Dermot Hughes, Barrister, 26 Paradise Square, Sheffield].

Minor injuries – whiplash type injury

1688.   S, and J, both male police officers aged 31 and 49 respectively at the date of the accident and 34 and 52 respectively at the date of the assessment hearing, suffered injuries when their police car was involved in a rear shunt collision. S sustained a soft tissue cervical injury. He suffered significant pain and discomfort in the neck and undertook light duties at work for three months. He underwent two separate courses of physiotherapy which gradually reduced his symptomatology. He was examined 11 months post accident and had restricted neck movement as well as intermittent pain associated with any physical activity. He was unable to play golf and gave up jogging. The prognosis was for a full recovery within a two year period with no long term complications. At trial S described a regular intermittent ache which was described as a nuisance and he still felt unable to return to playing golf. J sustained soft tissue injuries to the neck and back. J wore a soft collar for two weeks but his symptoms continued such that he underwent physiotherapy at the Police Rehabilitation Centre. He was off work for a five month period. Ten months after the accident he had a constant aching pain in the neck and intermittent pain in the lower back and still took regular oral analgesia. The prognosis was that the injury would resolve gradually such that after a two year post accident period there would be a complete resolution. Three years after the accident, J described mild ongoing symptoms particularly early in the morning and at the end of a working day. Damages were assessed upon the basis that a full recovery would occur shortly after the hearing. *General Damages*: for S: £4,750, for J: £5,000.

STANDING v. WERRETT, March 15, 2000, District Judge Dawson, CC (Pontypridd). [*Ex rel.* Andrew Arentsen, Barrister, 33 Park Place, Cardiff].

Minor injuries – whiplash type injury

1689.   T, female, aged 43 at the date of the accident and 46 at trial, suffered a whiplash neck injury in a heavy rear end collision. T suffered immediate pain, headache and shock. The following morning T woke in great pain and went to hospital. T was given a collar which she wore for two weeks and on and off for two weeks thereafter. T saw her GP on two occasions in the following weeks and was prescribed painkillers. T underwent nine sessions of chiropractic treatment. Her symptoms improved over the first two months. By six months after the accident, T still had an ache in the root of her neck, which was worse after exercise. By the date of trial, two and a half years after the accident, T still had some stiffness and aching, described as nuisance symptoms. Those were provoked if she kept her neck in one position for a length of time, but did not occur every day. T had given up her hobby of swimming because it provoked her symptoms. The medical evidence was that the nuisance symptoms were likely to be permanent. *General Damages*: £4,750.

TWYCROSS v. HILTON, November 17, 1999, District Judge Robinson, CC (Lincoln). [*Ex rel.* Andrew Stafford, Barrister, 4 King's Bench Walk, Temple, London].

Minor injuries – whiplash type injury

1690.   H, female, aged 46 at the date of the road traffic accident and 49 at the date of trial, sustained soft tissue injuries to her lower back and dominant shoulder. Immediately aware of pain, H attended a local hospital. Following examination she was discharged with painkillers. After three weeks she returned to the hospital complaining of severe, persisting pain in the lumbar spine, with radiation into the right leg. There was also limited movement with discomfort in the shoulder and arm. H received physiotherapy treatment, which proved of limited benefit. Six months after the accident she was referred by her GP to an orthopaedic consultant who provided her with a lumbar support. Her practical and recreational activities remained restricted. Family members and eventually, a cleaner assisted her with housework. She was unable to enjoy her hobby of walking and, due to her immobility, gained four stones in weight. Prior to the collision H had experienced problems with her lower back and her shoulder. The medical experts concluded that the accident had caused symptoms suffered in the lumbar spine during the initial 18 to 24 months post accident, and secondly, had aggravated a pre-existing condition in the shoulder. Any physical sequelae persisting beyond two years was entirely constitutional and could not be attributed to the collision. *General Damages*: £4,250.

HILL v. HOLMES, September 9, 1999, District Judge Mildred, CC (Reading). [*Ex rel.* Elaine Strachan, Barrister, 1 Alfred St, Oxford].

Minor injuries – whiplash type injury

1691.   S, female, a housekeeper, aged 35 at the date of the road traffic accident and 38 at trial, suffered a whiplash injury to her neck and lower back, and a blow to her chest and right shoulder. She also bit her tongue, causing a laceration which required three stitches. Her mouth was swollen, and eating was difficult for a week. At trial, over three years later, she was still occasionally aware of the injury to her tongue. Her other injuries slowly improved, and had been thought likely to resolve within 18 months of the accident. In fact at trial she was still suffering occasional clicking in the neck, infrequent lower back pain, and pain in the shoulder. S had been unable to drive for two months as a result of the injuries, and did not return to work for five months. *General Damages*: £4,000.

SCREETON v. EAST RIDING DC, April 13, 2000, Judge Barber, CC (Kingston upon Hull). [*Ex rel.* Richard Gregory, Barrister, 24 The Ropewalk, Nottingham].

Minor injuries – whiplash type injury

1692.   F, female, aged 25 at the date of the road traffic accident and 28 at trial, sustained a whiplash type injury to her neck and a blackened left eye when, as a rear seat passenger, she banged her head on the head rest in front during the collision. F attended hospital where she was treated with a soft collar which she wore for one week. F's symptoms were severe for six weeks during which time she could not drive her children to school. It had been anticipated that a full recovery would be made within one year of the accident. However 18 months after the accident F suffered a muscle spasm diagnosed as a torticollis. It was accepted that the soft tissue injuries to the neck increased F's vulnerability to a torticollis and that as a consequence full recovery was delayed to two years after the accident. *General Damages*: £3,750.

FITZPATRICK v. ROYAL TAXIS, June 1, 2000, Deputy District Judge Ayres, CC (Oldham). [*Ex rel.* Bruce Henry, Barrister, 15 Winckley Square, Preston].

Minor injuries – whiplash type injury

1693.   T, male, aged 41 at the date of the accident and 44 at trial, suffered a soft tissue neck injury when A's car ran into the side of his car. The pain worsened and T attended hospital four days later. T made one visit to his GP a month later. The pain and stiffness in his neck meant that for a period of about six months T had to reduce the length of shifts that he did as a minicab driver. The injury interfered with his sex life and his hobby of darts for a few months. The symptoms had improved two years and six months after the accident. However, T continued to experience occasional neck discomfort in cold weather or after a long spell of driving. *General Damages*: £3,750.

TOWLER v. ALI, October 14, 1999, District Judge Jones, CC (Clerkenwell). [*Ex rel.* Andrew Granville Stafford, Barrister, 4 King's Bench Walk, Temple, London].

Minor injuries – whiplash type injury

1694.   W, female aged 27 at the date of the road traffic accident and 29 at the hearing, suffered a soft tissue injury to her lower spine and her neck. At the time of the accident W was six months into her first pregnancy. Her first thought was for her unborn child, but she was reassured at hospital that no harm had been done. Over the next few days she developed pain and stiffness in her neck and back. This interfered with her ability to perform household chores and exercise. She had two days off work as a secretary. For a week or so after the collision she felt awful, but was unable to take painkillers because of her pregnancy. She was referred for physiotherapy, but again, her pregnancy hindered treatment, and little could be done for her. She gave up after three sessions. W's neck injury resolved after four weeks, but her back remained symptomatic, being painful and stiff, especially with lifting or with static posture, as when at her VDU at work. After approximately 11 or 12 months W's back was much improved. She only experienced occasional symptoms, when lifting, although there was also a tendency for her back to "go" occasionally with exertion. At trial, 20 months after the accident, there had been two such episodes, one when sharply lifting her child. After each episode, W suffered pain for a week. As a result, W avoided lifting heavy weights, such as washing. Otherwise, W's symptoms no longer troubled her, and no long term problems were anticipated in the medical report. W had also suffered slight nervousness when driving, but it was never extreme enough to cause her to avoid car travel. *General Damages*: £3,300.

WALTON v. MAGNA CARTA POLO, March 8, 2000, Judge Parry, CC (Staines). [*Ex rel.* Benjamin Williams, Barrister, 1 Temple Gardens, Temple, London].

Minor injuries – whiplash type injury

1695.   E, male, aged 29 at the date of the accident and 31 at trial, suffered a soft tissue injury to his cervical spine in a rear end shunt road traffic accident. He was immediately aware of pain in his neck and attended casualty where a severe whiplash injury was diagnosed. He was discharged with a cervical collar and co-proxamol. The pain, which radiated into his shoulders and upper back, prevented him from sleeping initially, and he was prescribed Diazepam. He was off work for four weeks. Six months after the accident he was taking eight paracetamol per day to keep his symptoms at a manageable level. He was unable to swim or cycle with his family for nine months. At around 15 months after the accident, E had made good progress after physiotherapy treatment and a full recovery was expected 17 to 18 months after the accident. At trial, around two years after the accident, E was only suffering from occasional pain which was no more than a nuisance. *General Damages*: £3,300.

EVANS v. LEWIS, May 12, 2000, District Judge Batcup, CC (Merthyr Tydfill). [*Ex rel.* Matthew White, Barrister, St. John's Chambers, Small Street, Bristol].

Minor injuries – whiplash type injury

1696. A, male, plant fitter, aged 19 at the date of the road traffic accident and 21 at trial, suffered whiplash injury to his neck and strain to his left shoulder for which he attended hospital the following day. No treatment other than simple analgesia was recommended. A was off work for a week by which time the symptoms in his shoulder had resolved. He was in significant pain for a week and thereafter experienced recurrent discomfort in his neck which was noticeable upon exertion, which was required by the heavy nature of his work. A's neck tended to "lock" on occasions. Seven months after the accident A had minimal symptoms and a slight restriction of movement in the neck although by the anniversary of the accident he was entirely symptom free with no suggestion of any recurrence of symptoms in the future. *General Damages*: £3,200.

APPLETON v. JB TAXIS, September 22, 1999, District Judge Wilby, CC (Bolton). [*Ex rel.* Timothy White, Barrister, 15 Winckley Square, Preston].

Minor injuries – whiplash type injury

1697. S, female, aged 22 at the date of the road traffic accident and 23 at trial, sustained a whiplash injury to her neck and bruising to her chest. She continued to her place of work but her symptoms worsened and within an hour she attended the accident and emergency department of the local hospital. She was given a soft collar, prescribed painkillers and then discharged. The following day, discomfort was also felt in the lower back. She took only one night away from her work, but attended only because she thought she might otherwise lose her job. She was unable to continue with aerobics which she had performed two to three times each week pre-accident. Two months after the accident S was still experiencing stiffness to her neck in the mornings and upon sudden movement. S also experienced chest pain after work, which involved sitting for long periods using the telephone. After nine months, the neck pain had resolved as had the chest pain. However, there was still some severe discomfort to the lower back, mainly when sitting at work. The prognosis was for a full recovery in 15 to 18 months. At the date of the hearing, 15 months after the accident, some discomfort was still being experienced. *General Damages*: £3,000.

SHAW v. DIVERS, July 20, 2000, District Judge Lawton, CC (Bradford). [*Ex rel.* Sean D Yates, Barrister, 10 Park Square, Leeds].

Minor injuries – whiplash type injury

1698. H1, male and H2, female, aged 54 and 50 respectively at the date of the road traffic accident, both suffered whiplash injuries. H1 was aware of immediate symptoms in his neck and two days later attended hospital where he was prescribed analgesia. He suffered severe symptoms in the neck for approximately 10 days, during which time he also suffered headaches and sleep disturbance. Although he remained nervous about driving he had no time away from his work as a television engineer. Two months post-accident he had a full range of movement in his neck, but with pain at the extremes, and was stiff suffering intermittent headaches. All symptoms were expected to resolve within nine to 12 months of the accident. However, H1's witness statement confirmed that he had suffered minor residual symptoms in his neck for up to 17 months. H2 suffered multiple minor injuries in the accident including neck pain radiating into the right shoulder, headaches, pain and tenderness across the chest wall from a seat belt injury, jarring injury to the right leg and significant psychological disturbance. At the time of her examination two months post-accident she became extremely distressed when asked to recount the accident details. A full recovery was made from the injury to her right leg and the seat belt injury within a few days but it was expected that she would continue to suffer pain and stiffness in the neck with intermittent headaches for up to 16 months after the accident. In respect of her psychological symptoms she was diagnosed as suffering from post traumatic stress and was treated with anti-depressants. However, as expected she made an almost full recovery within 18 months, although she continued to report minor residual symptoms amounting to nervousness in traffic. *General Damages*: H1: £3,000, H2: £4,500.

HINDE v. COCKSEDGE, March 10, 2000, District Judge Duerdon, CC (Bury). [*Ex rel.* John Parr, Barrister, 8 King Street, Manchester].

Minor injuries – whiplash type injury

1699.   S, male, aged 20 at the date of the accident and 21 at trial, was a front seat passenger in a motor car which was struck by M's vehicle on S's side of the car. S suffered whiplash and soft tissue injuries to his neck and lower back and received a not insignificant blow to his left elbow, thereby sustaining further soft tissue damage. S was in considerable pain which gradually eased over a two month period. The elbow injury healed within two months. At the time of trial, S was still suffering from minor, but nevertheless irritating, stabbing pains in his lumbar region whenever he carried out any sporting activities or attempted to lift any significant weight. S was unable to play sport or snooker for several months. In addition to his physical injuries, S suffered flashbacks of the accident and anxiety whilst driving and travelling in motor cars, which was still persisting at the time of trial. S also suffered from insomnia for several months after the accident. *General Damages*: £2,900.

SINGH v. M&N CONTRACTORS LTD [2000] 4 Q.R. 7, District Judge Jordan, CC (Bradford).

Minor injuries – whiplash type injury

1700.   V, male, aged 19 at the date of the road traffic accident and 21 at trial, suffered soft tissue injuries to his neck and back, but only felt discomfort later the same day when he was working as a panel beater. He became aware of pain in his lower back and stiffness in his neck along with an ache at the back of his head. V consulted his GP and was prescribed painkillers. Five months post accident V was seen by a consultant who diagnosed a hyperflexion sprain of the soft tissues in the neck and a mild low back strain. The neck discomfort initially involved stiffness and mild pain upon certain movements or when sitting for about half an hour and it had been accompanied by what V described as severe headaches. The discomfort began to improve about two months after the accident and had fully resolved after 12 months. The lower back injury was the most intrusive. It ached continually for about six weeks during which time V took painkillers. Thereafter there was improvement but five months after the accident, V still had a constant mild ache which was exacerbated by the twisting and bending he was required to undertake at work. The pain did not prevent him from working or interfere with his social life. By the date of the hearing some 27 months post accident, the back had substantially improved so that he could undertake heavy lifting and twisting at work with only spasmodic discomfort. The judge accepted V's evidence that he still felt short duration spasms of back pain approximately once every two weeks which he dealt with by standing up straight so as to stretch out his back. No long term disability or degeneration was expected and it was anticipated that even if a full recovery were not achieved any remaining symptoms would only be minor and intermittent. *General Damages*: £2,800.

VANNECK v. SLUGGETT, August 18, 1999, District Judge Smith, CC (Yeovil). [*Ex rel.* Adrian Posta, Barrister, South Western Chambers, 12 Middle Street, Taunton].

Minor injuries – whiplash type injury

1701.   N, female aged 28 at the date of the accident and 29 at the assessment of damages hearing, sustained a soft tissue injury to the region of her cervical spine and an aggravation of an on-going back problem. The symptoms of the former were at their worst for two to three weeks and involved pain over the right side of her neck radiating down to her right shoulder. They were aggravated by strenuous work and sitting in one position for any great length of time but gradually diminished in severity. In relation to her back, the period of exacerbation was no more than three weeks, prompting her to visit her chiropractor. G was unable to return to her previous activity of swimming for approximately one month after the accident and it was several months before she could attend the gym although she did not take any time off work. Sixteen months after the accident, an examination revealed full movement in her neck and it was the opinion of the orthopaedic surgeon that she was left with minor residual symptoms which were occasionally intrusive but in no way restrictive of her activities, although permanent in nature. *General Damages:* £2,750.

GADDIE v. MITIE GROUP PLC, January 13, 2000, District Judge Wade, CC (Cheltenham). [*Ex rel.* Archna Dawar, Barrister, Assize Court Chambers, 14 Small Street, Bristol].

Minor injuries – whiplash type injury

1702.   P, female, aged 36 at the date of the accident and 37 at trial, was involved in a five car shunt. As a result she received a flexion extension injury to her cervical spine. As neck pain increased she took painkillers and, two days after the accident, consulted her GP. She had two sessions of physiotherapy, and there was a diminution of her symptoms in the two weeks following the accident. Thereafter her symptoms reached a plateau. A year after the accident she continued to be troubled by stiffness and discomfort in the neck and shoulders which was made worse by activities such as lifting her son and reversing her car. Medical evidence indicated that she would become symptom free by 18 to 20 months after the accident. *General Damages* (agreed): £2,500.

PAWSON v. NEIL, December 16, 1999, District Judge Meredith, CC (Torquay). [*Ex rel.* Andrew Granville Stafford, Barrister, 4 King's Bench Walk, Temple, London].

Minor injuries – whiplash type injury

1703.   F, male, aged 27 at the date of the accident and 29 at trial, was injured in a road traffic accident in which he sustained a sudden hyper-flexion injury to his cervical spine. He suffered from severe pain for a week to 10 days. F had a gradual, but impressive improvement up to three months after the accident. Thereafter, F suffered an exacerbation of discomfort but physiotherapy led to a rapid improvement in his symptoms. It was thought, on examination shortly after the exacerbation that it would be short lived and his symptoms were unlikely to be recurrent. Some 11 months later, F did still suffer from problems with his neck and shoulders, particularly during cold weather. The aching and discomfort was infrequent but affected F's ability to play golf as frequently as desired. *General Damages:* £2,500.

FAULKNER v. SHAMJI, February 11, 2000, District Judge Field, CC (Milton Keynes). [*Ex rel.* Pannone & Partners Solicitors, 123 Deansgate, Manchester].

Minor injuries – whiplash type injury

1704.   M, a boy aged 12 at the date of the accident and 13 at the infant settlement approval hearing, was injured in a road traffic accident. As a result of impact, M struck his left eyebrow on the nearside passenger window. He was dazed but did not lose consciousness and there was no laceration. M developed low back ache and neck ache as a result of the accident. He attended hospital and was treated with analgesics. M visited his GP four days after the accident, and he was prescribed further analgesics and advised to rest. The low back pain resolved a week after the accident and M returned to school. The neck pain persisted and necessitated another visit to his GP several weeks after the accident, when further analgesics were prescribed. Over the following months, the symptoms became intermittent, mainly manifesting themselves at night. Six months after the accident, M was seen by a consultant who noted that M still suffered intermittent right-sided neck pain, mostly prevalent at night, and occasionally required analgesics. Right cervical rotation and extension were each limited to 80 per cent of normal range. The diagnosis was of a sprain injury of the right-sided facetal joints of the cervical spine. M had commenced physiotherapy and the prognosis was that full resolution of the symptoms was to be expected over the next three to six months. At the date of the hearing, 10 months after the accident, the symptoms had fully resolved as a result of the physiotherapy. *General Damages*: £2,500.

M (A CHILD) v. BUKHARI, February 16, 2000, District Judge Trent, CC (Barnet). [*Ex rel.* Anna Kotzeva, Barrister, 1 Temple Gardens, London].

Minor injuries – whiplash type injury

1705.   V, male, aged 34 at the date of the road traffic accident and 36 at trial, experienced a stiffening up of his neck and back on the day of the accident, which worsened overnight. He took five days off work during which he visited his GP and took paracetamol. During the first month after the accident, V avoided flying and was unable to play with his young children. He was able to go to the gym and resume jogging one month after the accident, although he had to be cautious for a further month. For five months he experienced some stiffness in his neck most days, particularly on waking. Thereafter those symptoms became less frequent, and had completely resolved one year after the accident. *General Damages*: £2,500.

BUNYAN v. VASSOR, June 1, 2000, District Judge Burgess, CC (Reading). [*Ex rel.* Matthew Brunning, Barrister, Wessex Chambers, 48 Queens Road, Reading, Berkshire].

Minor injuries – whiplash type injury

1706.   NB and JB, both female aged 17 and 26 respectively at the date of the accident and 19 and 28 respectively at trial, sustained whiplash type injuries to the neck. NB was shocked and dazed after the accident, but did not experience any significant pain. She went to school the next day, but her neck became stiff and painful as the day continued. She attended hospital and was diagnosed with a soft tissue injury to her neck, and was given a cervical collar, advised to rest and take analgesia. NB wore the collar for seven to 10 days, during which time the situation improved. She did not take any time off school, although she experienced intermittent pain and discomfort after a full day's work at school, and she was unable to clean her bedroom for two weeks. NB was also unable to go to ballet classes for a couple of weeks. She experienced a dull ache for one month, but over the summer holidays her neck improved. The aching resumed upon her return to school, but occurred only intermittently, about once every couple of weeks, lasting for a day at a time. She became pregnant just over a year after the accident, and that accentuated her neck stiffness. When her son was born, she had to give up breast feeding him after three weeks, because of the neck pain it caused. NB tried to avoid taking painkillers, instead relying on alternative methods of pain relief, namely aromatherapy, reflexology and massage. After 22 months she experienced only intermittent stiffness in her neck, and the prognosis was for complete resolution of her symptoms and no permanent disability. JB experienced shock and pain between her shoulder blades after the accident. Pain and discomfort in her upper back and neck developed that night, and continued throughout the next day without improvement. JB attended hospital the following day and was diagnosed with a soft tissue injury to her neck and upper back, and advised to rest and take analgesia. The pain significantly improved over the first two weeks, with only occasional continuing discomfort and stiffness. She did not require any time off work as a computer operator. She was initially apprehensive when driving after the accident, but no significant difficulty was experienced. She saw an osteopath three times and underwent three sessions of physiotherapy, and also saw a reflexologist. Her hobby of aerobics was curtailed as she found it painful in the initial period after the accident. After 22 months, she was continuing to experience intermittent pain in the side of her neck, which was aggravated by her job, which required her to sit in one position with her head bent. A "clunk" noise could be heard from cervical spine movement, which was due to the muscles. The injury only amounted to a fairly minor whiplash, with some continuing symptoms, with which she had "learned to live" with. *General Damages*: for NB: £2,250, for JB: £1,750.

BEVINGTON v. DOYLE, February 15, 2000, District Judge Tetlow, CC (Milton Keynes). [*Ex rel.* Amanda Drane, Barrister, 4 King's Bench Walk, 2nd Floor, Temple, London].

Minor injuries – whiplash type injury

1707.   H, female, aged 25 at the date of the accident and 27 at trial, suffered a whiplash injury when her vehicle was hit from the side by another vehicle. H attended hospital and was given a soft collar to wear. She experienced constant pain and stiffness in the right side of her neck for three weeks and did not return to work for five weeks. During this period, H visited her GP five times, had 10 sessions of physiotherapy and took pain killers. H's sleep was affected and her discomfort was increased by seat belt injuries to the chest. H required assistance with household chores for three months and during this period did not drive. She was unable to go to the gymnasium for eight months, by which time the physical symptoms had entirely resolved. After the accident, H was anxious as both a passenger and a driver and remained so for 16 months after the accident. *General Damages*: £2,200 (apportioned £1,900 for the physical injuries and £300 for the psychological symptoms).

HUGHES v. BLOOR, December 14, 1999, Deputy District Judge Gatter, CC (Birmingham). [*Ex rel.* James Morgan, Barrister, St. Philip's Chambers, Fountain Court, Steelhouse Lane, Birmingham].

Minor injuries – whiplash type injury

1708.   B, male, aged 22 at the date of the accident and 23 at trial, was injured in a road traffic accident, sustaining a whiplash injury. Maximal pain lasted for one week, after which the headaches and the neck symptoms abated. However, after one month B was still suffering sleep problems due to his neck injury, and after five months he was still suffering from frequent bouts of pain and stiffness which were worse if he was obliged to sit for long periods, and which affected him at work. The medical evidence suggested that B would be asymptomatic at one year post trauma, but evidence given at trial one year and four months after the injury showed he still suffered from minor residual symptoms. *General Damages*: £2,000.

BUTLAND v. O'CONNOR, April 12, 2000, District Judge Wilson, CC (Portsmouth). [*Ex rel.* Daniel Jones, Barrister, Phoenix Chambers, Chancery Lane, Gray's Inn, London].

Minor injuries – whiplash type injury

1709.   W, male, aged 64 at the date of the road traffic accident and 65 at trial, sustained a whiplash injury to his neck and lower back. He attended his GP 48 hours after the accident and was prescribed analgesics. W experienced neck pain which was at its worst two days after the accident, and had become intermittent one week later. Five months after the accident W was still experiencing occasional pain when at work at a VDU, and when fell walking. One year post accident W still suffered sporadic pain in the neck and back but only after long periods of exertion. He experienced some nervousness when driving. *General Damages*: £2,000.

WILLIAMS v. THOMPSON, July 4, 2000, District Judge Clegg, CC (Altrincham). [*Ex rel.* David Calvert, Barrister, 68 Quay Street, Manchester].

Minor injuries – whiplash type injury

1710.   N, female, aged 12 at the date of the road traffic accident and 14 at the assessment hearing suffered a whiplash injury. N was able to get out of the car and walk around after the accident, but was immediately aware of pain in her neck. She was taken to hospital where she was examined, diagnosed with a whiplash injury to her neck, given a cervical collar and advised to take analgesia. She wore the collar continuously for about a week, and then gradually weaned herself off it. She was in significant pain for about a month and during that period she was unable to participate in school sports. N became a nervous passenger after the accident, preferring to sit in the front rather than the rear of vehicles. After the first month, N found that her neck ached at the end of the school day, although not in significant pain. She continued to experience intermittent aching in her neck, particularly after prolonged bending over a desk or computer and about once a week she woke up with a stiff neck, which would last for a couple of hours. She occasionally required analgesia, but generally coped without. N's symptoms settled within about 12 months, with no long term sequelae. *General Damages*: £2,000.

N (A CHILD) v. SMITH & WHITEINCH GROUP, March 20, 2000, Deputy District Judge Durman, CC (Croydon). [*Ex rel.* Amanda Drane, Barrister, 4 King's Bench Walk, 2nd Floor, Temple, London].

Minor injuries – whiplash type injury

1711.   C, male, aged 29 at the date of the road traffic accident and 32 at the assessment hearing, sustained a whiplash type injury to his neck. C was badly shaken following the accident and was taken to hospital. He was provided with a neck brace and advised to rest his neck for a few days and then mobilise it. C, who was employed as a mortgage salesman, was unable to drive for two weeks following the accident and was off work for the same period, due to stiffness in his neck and referred shoulder pain. He slowly improved over a four month period. He was unable to return to his previous activities of squash and football for three months, and his social activities were curtailed during this period. Four months after the accident he was virtually asymptomatic, save for occasional twinges, especially on cold mornings, ceasing as he loosened up. C then began to develop migraine type headaches which initially affected him twice a week, but gradually began to resolve, then ceased completely. *General Damages*: £1,700.

ROWE v. ROGERS, June 23, 2000, District Judge Asplin, CC (Newport). [*Ex rel.* Jane H S Foulser McFarlane, Barrister, Temple Chambers, 32 Park Place, Cardiff].

Minor injuries – whiplash type injury

1712.   M1 and M2, sisters, aged seven and 11 respectively at the date of the accident and 10 and 14 respectively at the date of the infant settlement approval hearing, sustained injuries in a road traffic accident. M1 suffered a whiplash injury to her neck and was shocked and shaken. She was immediately aware of pain and subsequent stiffness of movement. Her GP prescribed analgesics. The initial symptoms were acute but quickly improved. Five months after the accident only niggling residual symptoms remained which fully resolved after a further month. M1 had no time off school and suffered minimal impairment of her social and domestic activities over the first two to three weeks. M2 suffered symptoms almost identical to M1 except that five months after the accident her residual symptoms were slightly more pronounced. However, those symptoms fully resolved within a further two months. *General Damages*: M1 = £1,625. M2 = £2,000.

M (A CHILD) v. ORAHA, February 10, 2000, District Judge Southcomb, CC (Central London). [*Ex rel.* Kevin Haven, Barrister, 2 Gray's Inn Square Chambers, Gray's Inn, London].

Minor injuries – whiplash type injury

1713.   E, male, aged 18 at the time of the accident and 20 at trial, was involved in a rear end shunt. E sustained a whiplash injury. For 10 days, he suffered pain to the posterior aspect of his neck and shoulders most of the time. The pain was described as "intermittent" thereafter, being associated with waking and activities such as driving for 20 minutes or more and lifting objects at work. E saw his GP on the Monday after the accident and was prescribed a course of non steroidal anti inflammatory analgesics. E had no time off work as he was seeking a promotion, which he subsequently obtained. Following the accident, E was unable to enjoy his hobby of ten pin bowling, an activity at which he had represented his county and had been considered for the national youth team. The medical evidence was that he was able to resume bowling six to eight weeks after the accident, but E made no attempt to return. He was able to play football after four weeks. It was observed that E's symptoms had been improving constantly over a period of eight months, after which time any residual problems had completely cleared up. *General Damages*: £1,600.

EDWARDS v. PRYCE, August 23, 1999, District Judge Gee, CC (Liverpool). [*Ex rel.* Stephen Cottrell, Pupil Barrister, 3 Paper Buildings, Temple, London].

Minor injuries – whiplash type injury

1714.   S, male, aged 41 at the date of the accident and 42 at the date of disposal, sustained a whiplash injury to his neck. After initial distress and shock, S attended his local accident and emergency department where he was advised to take pain killing relief. S was off work for five days. Pain and discomfort lasted for approximately four to five months and adversely affected S's ability to enjoy working out in the gym. S sought no other medical treatment. *General Damages*: £1,500.

SIMPSON v. GRANT, November 15, 1999, District Judge Harrison, CC (Manchester). [*Ex rel.* Betesh Partnership Solicitors, P.O. Box No. 180, 2nd Floor Cardinal House, 20 St. Mary's Parsonage, Manchester].

Minor injuries – whiplash type injury

1715.   C, female, aged 14 at the date of the road traffic accident and 15 at the hearing, was thrown forward and backward in her seat, sustaining a mild to moderate whiplash injury, and moderate spinal sprain to her thoracic spine. The accident occurred on a Sunday, and C rested for the remainder of that day. She experienced pain in her back that evening, and took paracetamol. Her sleep was disturbed, and her neck was stiff in the morning. C went to school, but experienced pain in her neck and middle back. C's concentration was disturbed for about two weeks. Physical education was painful for two weeks. Two days after the accident, C saw her GP complaining of neck and back pains and was prescribed analgesia. C was tender over the left trapezius muscle in the neck. C took paracetamol for one week and the discomfort lasted for three weeks. Five months after the accident, C still suffered some intermittent lower back pain. C experienced discomfort on extension, and discomfort in the muscle on the right side on lateral flexion. C was expected to have fully recovered within about eight months of the accident. *General Damages*: (agreed) £1,500.

C (A CHILD) v. PEERS, November 26, 1999, District Judge Eaton, CC (Leicester). [*Ex rel.* Andrew Skelly, Barrister, 1 Gray's Inn Square, London].

Minor injuries – whiplash type injury

1716.   C, female, aged 34 at the date of the accident and 36 at trial, sustained a whiplash injury when her stationary car was shunted from behind. She later attended hospital where a mild whiplash injury was diagnosed and was discharged with a soft collar and Ibuprofen painkillers. C experienced pain and stiffness in her neck within 24 hours which was acute for two to three weeks causing lost sleep and during this time she wore a collar constantly. It was found that the pain had continued intermittently for several months thereafter. C was off work for five weeks, was obliged to postpone her camping holiday and then had the enjoyment of that holiday reduced (although not ruined) by the discomfort which she was still suffering and the lack of a car large enough to carry all the camping equipment. C, who later found she was pregnant at the time of the accident, was distressed about having taken Ibuprofen during the early states of pregnancy. However, it was found that this anxiety was more attributable to her having recently suffered a miscarriage than to the accident. There was no recurrence of symptoms, although C was nervous about driving for some 11 months. *General Damages*: £1,400.
    CAVE v. CROME, February 3, 2000, District Judge Shanks, CC (Chelmsford). [*Ex rel.* Neil Ashley, Barrister, 63 Wickham Road, Witham, Essex].

Minor injuries – whiplash type injury

1717.   S, male, aged 27 at the date of the road traffic accident and 29 at the date of assessment, suffered a whiplash injury to the neck. He attended hospital that day and was given a collar to wear, which he wore for two days. He took two weeks off work, one week sick and one week as holiday. S had consistent pain in his neck for eight to nine weeks after the accident and experienced sleepless nights for about eight weeks caused by neck pain. He experienced a full recovery within 12 weeks. His hobbies of DIY and playing pool were affected for about four weeks. *General Damages*: £1,400.
    SIMMS v. WALLS, October 12, 1999, District Judge Cooper, CC (Southampton). [*Ex rel.* Andrew Lorie, Barrister, College Chambers, 19 Carlton Crescent, Southampton].

Minor injuries – whiplash type injury

1718.   J, male aged 25 years at the date of the road traffic accident, was immediately aware of pain at the base of his cervical spine. He was off work for two days after which the pain had resolved. One week later attended his GP complaining of low back pain, irritable bowel syndrome, resolving shoulder pain and pain and bruising to the left leg. For a period of two months, J avoided lifting and carrying heavy objects at work and attending the gym, and had to ensure that he was always in quite close proximity to a toilet because the symptoms of his irritable bowel syndrome were then at their worst. An examination three months after the accident revealed a full range of movements to his cervical and lumbar spine, although the movements were painful at extremes in the respect of the latter. J suffered some stiffness in the lower back together with occasional pain in his left leg and abdominal discomfort attributable to irritable bowel syndrome. The prognosis was for a full recovery in all respects within six to nine months of the accident. *General Damages*: (agreed) £1,350.
    JAMES v. JOHNSON, December 3, 1999, Deputy District Judge Woodburn, CC (Gloucester). [*Ex rel.* Archna Dawar, Barrister, Assize Court Chambers, 14 Small Street, Bristol].

Minor injuries – whiplash type injury

1719.   H, female aged 12 at the date of the road traffic accident and 13 at the hearing, was injured when the vehicle in which she was travelling was involved in a head on collision. H was examined seven months after the accident whereupon the diagnosis was that H had suffered a minor neck sprain. This caused particular pain and stiffness for 10 days after the accident and there were ongoing symptoms which completely resolved six weeks after the accident. H missed three days of school. *General Damages*: £1,300.

H (A CHILD) v. GRAY, April 6, 2000, District Judge Brown, CC (Telford). [*Ex rel.* Hodgkinsons Solicitors, The Old Manse, 14 Lumley Avenue, Skegness, Lincolnshire].

Minor injuries – whiplash type injury

1720.   C, male aged 33 at the date of the accident and 34 at the hearing, sustained injuries in a road traffic accident. C was examined by a doctor three months later and it was found that he had sustained a sudden hyperflexion, hyperextension force to the cervical spine leading to soft tissue injury. C experienced pain and stiffness of movement in the neck for two weeks and three days. These symptoms then fully resolved. C was also emotionally shaken and distraught in a general sense for two weeks, displaying physical features of stress, trembling and nausea, and on three occasions vomiting. For two weeks he had difficulty sleeping and after the incident was somewhat anxious driving. There was no evidence to suggest that C had sustained any bony damage likely to cause future long term arthritic changes in the cervical spine, nor any neurological trauma that could lead to future loss of function. *General Damages*: £1,000

DONEGAN v. DUNNIGAN, February 22, 2000, District Judge Richardson, CC (Birkenhead). [*Ex rel.* Michael W Halsall Solicitors, 2 The Parks, Newton-le-Willows].

Minor injuries – whiplash type injury

1721.   KA, male, aged 23 at the date of the road traffic accident and 24 at the date of the hearing, suffered a soft tissue whiplash injury to his neck and strained both wrists. KA was in no immediate pain, but stiffness developed in his neck and left shoulder overnight. He slept badly. KA attended his GP the next day, and took two days off work as a waiter. He took painkillers, and attended his GP on a second occasion a few weeks later, when he was still having difficulty lifting heavy objects. He was prescribed anti-inflammatories. KA's symptoms of discomfort and stiffness in his neck, between his shoulders and in his wrists gradually improved, and he had made a full recovery two months after the accident. *General Damages*: £900.

KALAM v. KHAN (QUANTUM), February 4, 2000, District Judge Sanghera, CC (Nuneaton). [*Ex rel.* Benjamin Williams, Barrister, 1 Temple Gardens, Temple, London].

Minor injuries – whiplash type injury

1722.   A, female, aged 36 at the date of the accident and 38 at trial, was injured in a road traffic accident when the car in which she was travelling was struck from behind. A suffered a minor whiplash injury. There were no immediate symptoms, but the next day A telephoned the casualty department of her local hospital, reporting pain in her lower back and left sided sciatica. A contacted her GP who advised analgesics, which she took for five days. The back pain and sciatica persisted for three weeks before resolving completely. In addition, A suffered from a general travel anxiety, whereby she became nervous and anxious when cars followed closely behind her. Although A continued to drive, it was accepted that it was not until 16 months after the accident that her psychological problems resolved fully. *General Damages*: £850 (including an award of £100 for travel anxiety).

ASHOURI v. PENFOLD, October 22, 1999, District Judge James, CC (Southampton). [*Ex rel.* Vershal Rehan, Barrister, 20 Lorne Park Road, Bournemouth].

Minor injuries – whiplash type injury

1723.   C, female, aged 30 at the date of the accident and 31 at the hearing, was injured in a road traffic accident and sustained a minor whiplash injury. The first onset of neck pain and headache was at work the following day. On telephoning her GP's surgery, C was advised to go to the local accident and emergency department, where C was advised to use painkillers and a gel. C sought no further treatment. C had no time off work but was in pain at work and went to bed early. The worst of the pain lasted three to four days, and the symptoms had resolved fully within about seven to 10 days. There were no long term problems or complications. The judge rejected C's comparisons with more severe cases such as *Evans v. Jibb* (Unreported, October 16, 1995), [1995] C.L.Y. 1804 and *Mitchell v. Rivett* (1998) 98 (2) Q.R. 6, [1998] C.L.Y. 1733 and accepted D's valuation, saying the case was closest to *Knight v. Hooper* (Unreported, October 14, 1993), [1993] C.L.Y. 1584. *General Damages*: £600.
    HUGHES v. HUNT, December 13, 1999, District Judge Enzer, CC (Epsom). [*Ex rel.* Tim Petts, Barrister, 12 King's Bench Walk, Temple, London].

Minor injuries – whiplash type injury

1724.   N, female, aged 69 at the date of the accident and 70 at trial, was injured in a road traffic accident. She started to experience aching of the neck and shoulders some 24 hours later. N consulted her GP three days after the accident, whereupon an examination determined that she had slight restriction of forward flexion in the neck. Paracetamol tablets were recommended to ease the neck and shoulder discomfort. There was some disturbance of sleep for the first few nights. After two weeks the symptoms resolved. *General Damages*: £580.
    NICKLESS v. OSBORNE, October 1, 1999, District Judge Meredith, CC (Torquay). [*Ex rel.* Adrian Posta, Barrister, South Western Chambers, 12 Middle Street, Taunton].

Minor injuries – whiplash type injury

1725.   B, male aged 23 at the date of the accident and 25 at the hearing, was injured in a road traffic accident. He was examined by a doctor and was found to have sustained injuries to his neck. There was no major damage. The symptoms resulted from a soft tissue injury. B had two sessions of physiotherapy. His symptoms had resolved within approximately two weeks from the date of the accident. B also suffered a minor nervous reaction to the accident in relation to driving, which gradually settled over several months without the need for psychological assessment. General damages; £1,000.
    BOLD v. NOON, February 21, 2000, District Judge Mornington, CC (Birkenhead). [*Ex rel.* Michael W Halsall Solicitors, 2 The Parks, Newton-le-Willows].

Minor injuries – whiplash type injury

1726.   K, female, aged 14 at the date of the accident and 15 at the infant settlement approval hearing, was injured in a road traffic accident. The same day she developed a gradually progressive ache and stiffness in the neck with referred headaches. The day after the accident she attended hospital where a diagnosis of a whiplash injury to the neck was made. She was advised to take pain relief as required and to rest. She took two days off school after which she resumed her normal studies but was unable to participate in physical education for about one month. K was a keen ballet dancer and normally attended lessons three times a week. She missed lessons for about a month and thereafter failed her ballet exams, attributing the failure to the accident and injuries. K suffered from sleep disturbance due to an inability to find a comfortable sleeping position. She did not suffer any psychological effects from the accident and was not nervous travelling in cars. The neck symptoms and headaches gradually settled down over three months but she continued to suffer from a clicking, grinding sensation in the neck for approximately a year after the accident. By the date of the approved settlement she had made a full recovery. General damages (approved): £1,800.

K (A CHILD) v. GOBBI, March 6, 2000, District Judge Tennant, CC (Southampton). [*Ex rel.* Amanda Gillett, Pupil Barrister, College Chambers, 19 Carlton Crescent, Southampton].

Minor injuries – shoulder

1727. B, aged 36 at the date of the accident and 40 at the assessment hearing, was electrocuted while using a pneumatic drill at work. He sustained an injury to his right shoulder and was taken to hospital, where an ECG was performed. B was prescribed painkillers and underwent physiotherapy. He visited his GP every two weeks for four months post accident. He was given a steroid injection by his GP and 11 months post accident was given a cortisone injection. B's symptoms resolved 12 months post accident. *General Damages*: £3,500.

BROWN v. EOM CONSTRUCTION LTD, July 19, 2000, District Judge Duerdan, CC (Bury). [*Ex rel.* David Calvert, Barrister, 68 Quay Street, Manchester].

Minor injuries – shoulder

1728. R, female, aged 17 at the date of the road traffic accident and 18 at trial, suffered an injury to her upper back and left shoulder. She also sustained a minor neck injury which resolved after two weeks, and swelling and bruising to the head with associated headaches, which resolved after a few days. R suffered disturbed sleep, including nightmares, for several weeks. She underwent physiotherapy which provided some benefit. Three and a half months after the accident, the pain and stiffness in the shoulder continued and tenderness in the shoulder area was noted, as was a slight limitation of abduction of the left arm. R, who worked on a farm, was off work for six weeks and upon her return was moved to lighter duties, where she remained for seven months. About seven months post accident she suffered aching in the shoulder after a hard day at work. Her sleep was not disturbed but she would wake the next morning with an ache. Analgesics were used when required. That remained the position at the time of the hearing. The prognosis was for recovery some 15 months after the accident. In addition, R was anxious when driving, particularly at junctions, and was a nervous passenger. The prognosis for those symptoms, although not from a psychologist or psychiatrist, was that they would also resolve themselves within the same time period. *General Damages*: £3,000.

R (A CHILD) v. TAYLOR, June 22, 2000, Judge Downes, CC (Norwich). [*Ex rel.* Michael Morris, Barrister, 169 Temple Chambers, Temple Avenue, London].

Minor injuries – shoulder

1729. S, male, aged 25 at the date of the accident and 26 at trial, was injured in a road traffic accident. The following day he had pain in his left shoulder region and lower back and attended hospital where soft tissue injuries were diagnosed. For two to three weeks following the accident, S suffered moderate pain continually in both his left shoulder and lumbar back. He was off work for three days following the accident. Upon examination two months after the accident there was some tenderness over the left shoulder and slight pain on extension, but otherwise movements were full and normal. S experienced a constant dull ache in the lumbar spine region but upon examination the lumbar spine was normal. S worked as an electronic engineer and his job involved sitting at a computer screen and driving long distances. Both of these activities caused him occasional problems. Prior to the accident he had enjoyed playing badminton once a week but he was unable to play for four weeks. The prognosis was for a full recovery within six to 12 months of the accident. *General Damages*: (agreed) £1,750.

SCHNOOR v. CAGE, March 7, 2000, District Judge Dancey, CC (Weymouth). [*Ex rel.* Amanda Gillett, Pupil Barrister, College Chambers, 19 Carlton Crescent, Southampton].

Minor injuries – arm

1730.   C, female, aged 21 months at the date of the accident and four at the hearing, fell down some steps at her home injuring her right arm. C was taken to L, an NHS hospital, where a doctor examined the arm, which caused C to start screaming and crying. He had rolled C's pyjama sleeve about halfway up the right arm and, seeing that she could move her fingers, concluded that C had just bruised the arm. He did not, however, examine the upper forearm or consider an X-ray. Thirteen days later, C's mother noticed swelling was present on the forearm as well as a bony prominence and returned her to the hospital. A different consultant organised X-rays which revealed a fracture mid-shaft of the right radius with some slight angulation. There was also evidence of early callus formation on the ulna and some plastic deformation as opposed to a complete fracture. The injury was treated by means of an above elbow slab which was kept on for some 19 days. L admitted liability in failing to make an accurate diagnosis at the time of C's original admission. The effect of the delay in the diagnosis had caused C some 10 days of pain and discomfort which should have resolved had she been placed in plaster at the time of her initial injury. The delay did not affect the outcome of the fracture and C went on to make a full and complete recovery, giving no rise to long term disability. *General Damages*: £600.

C (A CHILD) v. LEEDS NHS TEACHING NATIONAL TRUST [2000] 3 Q.R. 7, District Judge Heath, CC (Leeds).

Minor injuries – hand

1731.   B, male, aged 52 at the date of the accident and 56 at trial, was injured in a road traffic accident, suffering a fracture to the head of the second metacarpal in his left non-dominant hand. A plaster slab was applied to the hand and wrist. After two weeks the fracture was found to have displaced and it was reduced under local anaesthetic. B wore the plaster for another two weeks. He was off work for six weeks and unable to drive for five weeks. He attended 17 physiotherapy sessions over three months. Five months after the accident, B's hand was functioning reasonably well but there were still problems. He was unable to play golf for a year. Three years after the accident his grip was still weaker than before the accident but still above average. He had a little extra difficulty with fine manipulation in cold weather. His residual problems represented a nuisance rather than a significant disability. B had also suffered a whiplash injury and wore a collar continuously for three weeks but there was a complete resolution of symptoms after five months. B suffered a laceration to the chin which required sutures. *General Damages*: £3,750 (£1,500 for the whiplash injury, £250 for the injury to the chin and £3,000 for the hand injury, discounted overall by £1,000).

BENNETT v. HEWITT, April 13, 2000, District Judge Short, CC (Luton). [*Ex rel.* David Allen, Barrister, 9 Bedford Row, London].

Minor injuries – hand

1732.   G, male, a sewerage worker, aged 42 at the date of the incident and 45 at the hearing, was bitten by a rat through his protective gloves on the right hand at the webbing between thumb and index finger. The gloves were worn to protect against Weil's disease (leptospirosis) being contracted from the infected water, and although the wound did not touch the water, G initially suffered anxiety in relation to the danger of contracting the disease. G did not contract the disease. G was unable to work for 12 weeks in all. His hand was useless for the first six weeks.

It was extremely painful, and red and swollen. His sleep was disrupted for two weeks. There were occasional periods of numbness and tingling down the entire arm. G required physiotherapy and electro-magnetic therapy. He visited his general practitioner on eight occasions, and he was unable to play snooker for six months. On examination after 30 months, his grip and pinch strength was reduced by about 10 per cent, although it was expected to return to normal. G continued to suffer occasional aching and swelling in the cold weather or after heavy work, which generally subsided over a two hour period. Those symptoms were continuing at trial, but were expected to resolve. *General Damages*: £3,000.

GREEN v. LEICESTER CC [2000] 4 Q.R. 7, Recorder Critchlow, CC (Mansfield).

Minor injuries – hand

1733.   Y, female, aged 42 at the date of trial, developed five callouses affecting her right dominant hand whilst employed by S as a hand cutter for a period of several weeks. The medical evidence confirmed that the callouses were caused by repeated pressure when using hand scissors to cut different types of garment. The development of such callouses identified a clear case of occupational overuse. Y's callouses were visible for some three years but had completely disappeared within three months of undertaking alternative work. *General Damages*: £1,688.

YATES v. JOHN SMEDLEY LTD, June 13, 2000, Judge Hunt, CC (York). [*Ex rel.* Morrish & Co Solicitors, First Floor, Oxford House, Oxford Row, Leeds].

Minor injuries – hand

1734.   M, a boy aged 11 years and four months at the date of the accident and 13 years and two months at trial, was injured whilst on a fairground ride belonging to D. M's left hand was trapped between metal bars which were at the side of a moving conveyor belt. M suffered bruising and tenderness to his left hand and a fracture of the left fifth metacarpal. A plaster cast was applied and the left arm was placed in a sling. The cast was removed three weeks later and M was discharged from hospital, receiving no further treatment. For approximately a week, M had no use of his left arm. The accident occurred during the school holidays and M did not miss any schooling but his enjoyment of the Christmas holiday was severely disrupted. *General Damages* (approved by court): £1,400.

M (A MINOR) v. DE KONING, November 16, 1999, District Judge Slim, CC (Halifax). [*Ex rel.* Rhodes Thain & Collinson Solicitors, 27 Harrison Road, Halifax].

Minor injuries – hand

1735.   P, female, bakery operative aged 24 at the date of the accident and 26 at trial, suffered a crush injury when her left hand was jammed between a bakery trolley and a metal bar. P sustained bad bruising and an abrasion over her left middle finger. X-rays revealed no bony injury and she was prescribed strapping which remained in place for a total of seven days. For four to six weeks immediately following the accident P endured considerable discomfort and inconvenience. Although P continued to work she found her job difficult. Thereafter her symptoms improved significantly and when examined three months after the accident she had only occasional episodes of shooting pain. P had a full range of finger and hand movement and junction and it was anticipated that symptoms would settle entirely within six months of the accident. *General Damages*: £750.

PEPPERALL v. MEMORY LANE CAKES LTD, November 19, 1999, District Judge John, CC (Cardiff). [*Ex rel.* Andrew Arentsen, Barrister, 33 Park Place, Cardiff].

Minor injuries – hand

1736.   R, male, aged 46 at the date of the accident and 50 at trial, sustained a burn injury to the back of his right dominant hand when a paint stick melted on contact with hot steel running onto the back of his hand. The paint came into contact between the second and third metacarpal heads across a two cm square area. The burnt area blistered and required dressings. It took five weeks to heal during which time the skin kept breaking, causing pain and discomfort. R made a complete recovery with full movement of the hand and no residual scarring. Four years after the accident, there were no continuing difficulties. The judge observed that the injury was initially painful but that a speedy and full recovery had taken place. *General Damages*: £750

   RITTER v. BRITISH STEEL PLC, November 26, 1999, Deputy District Judge Morgan, CC (Cardiff). [*Ex rel.* Andrew Arentsen, Barrister, 33 Park Place, Cardiff].

Minor injuries – fingers

1737.   D, male, aged 45 at the date of accident and 47 at trial sustained a laceration of the right, dominant index finger close to the distal interphalangeal joint when his hand was caught by a conveyor belt. The laceration was 1cm in length and did not involve any tendons or nerves. The wound was closed, but could not be stitched due to its position. D was absent from work for one week and the wound healed after two weeks, leaving scarring and some tenderness at the date of trial. *General Damages*: £1,500.

   DUFFY v. CARNABY, March 24, 2000, District Judge Weston, CC (Kingston upon Hull). [*Ex rel.* Graham & Rosen Solicitors, 8 Parliament Street, Hull].

Minor injuries – fingers

1738.   B, male, aged 22 at the date of the accident and 25 at trial, was employed upon the manufacture of UPVC windows when he was provided with faulty bits for use with an air driver used for driving screws. The bits tended to slip off the screws and in February and March 1996, on two occasions, a bit slipped penetrating the left index finger of B's non dominant hand. The puncture wounds bled and had to be treated with plasters. B noticed a small lump underneath the skin and experienced discomfort in using the finger when it banged against items. Two years and six months later, B experienced another accident to his finger, which resulted in the lump growing. It proved to be a cyst and required excision under local anaesthetic. After excision, B's symptoms resolved and he was left with a small white scar. The judge discounted a causal link between the formation of the cyst and the two accidents in 1996, in making an award in respect of those accidents. *General Damages*: £1,100.

   BURROWS v. KINGSTON UPON HULL CITY COUNCIL [2000] 3 Q.R. 7, Judge Brunning, CC (Nottingham).

Minor injuries – leg

1739.   D, male, aged 22 at the date of the accident and 24 at the date of trial, had an accident at work which caused a fracture to the lower fibula and a puncture wound above the lateral malleolus. A below knee plaster case was applied and due to weeping from the wound he was admitted to hospital for a period of two days. D was unable to bear any weight for three and a half weeks and the plaster case remained in place for six weeks. D was absent from work for approximately seven weeks. Six months after the accident, D had made a virtually full recovery, but there were some slight twinges of pain in cold weather which were expected to resolve within 18 months of the accident. D was also left with a scar of a quarter of an inch by an eighth of an inch behind the right lateral malleolus. *General Damages*: £3,600.

DEAN v. WUNDPETS LTD, September 16, 1999, District Judge Slim, CC (Halifax). [*Ex rel.* Rhodes Thain & Collinson Solicitors, 27 Harrison Road, Halifax].

Minor injuries – leg

1740.   G, a boy aged two years and six months at the date of the accident and five at the hearing, was initially very quiet after a road traffic accident, and upon examination it became apparent that he had sustained minimally displaced fractures to his left tibia and fibula. His leg was placed in a plaster cast, which he wore for six weeks. His mother was advised to give him Calpol for analgesia. G was "not himself" for the first two weeks after the accident and preferred to be driven by his father than his mother, often repeating, "Don't crash the car, Mummy" when his mother was driving. His conversations about the accident gradually reduced in frequency, and he did not otherwise appear to be unduly distressed by the accident. After six weeks the plaster cast was removed, he was discharged and his parents were advised to allow him to get back to normal at his own pace. He limped a little initially, but that soon settled. The leg injuries resolved fully and there were no long term sequelae. General damages: £4,000.

G (A CHILD) v. PITT (T/A KP GROUP), April 4, 2000, District Judge Raskin, CC (Trowbridge). [*Ex rel.* Amanda Drane, Barrister, 4 King's Bench Walk, Temple, London].

Minor injuries – knee

1741.   J, a girl, aged 11 years at the date of the accident and 16 at the assessment hearing, sustained a medial collateral ligament strain to her knee whilst she was taking part in a tobogganing activity on a dry ski slope. She suffered immediate pain and was taken to hospital, where the knee was aspirated and strapped. She was referred to a fracture clinic and wore a plaster of paris cast for three weeks. An acute strain of the medial collateral ligament was diagnosed. J was initially unable to attend school, but began a gradual return to school just prior to the summer holiday. She was weightbearing on crutches throughout the holiday and on her return to school in the autumn term. J gradually mobilised, initially wearing a knee support daily, and afterwards during sporting activities. J continued to undergo physiotherapy treatment for over two years after the accident as the symptoms endured. Two and a half years post accident J had regained full function in her knee, but suffered occasional throbbing pains in her knee on walking or performing physical activity, but functionally she had made a full recovery. The knee did not swell, lock or give way, and did not interfere with her day to day activities. The judge concluded that the injury had caused considerable disruption to J's social life, her education and sporting activities. She had suffered a loss of amenity in that she was no longer able to participate in ballroom dancing, which she had previously enjoyed and earned medals, even teaching young children. She had incurred the costs of a private maths tutor for one hour per week for 11 weeks as she had fallen behind in the subject during her absence from school. It was held that J's mother had not failed to mitigate by omitting to seek to persuade the school to make special arrangements for J's education as such arrangements would have placed too high a burden on the school. *General Damages*: £3,500. Award for cost of private tutor: £110.

J (A CHILD) v. URDD GOBAITH CYMRU, July 7, 2000, District Judge T John, CC (Cardiff). [*Ex rel.* Jane HS Foulser McFarlane, Barrister, Temple Chambers, 32 Park Place, Cardiff].

Minor injuries – knee

1742.   M, male, aged 16 at the date of the accident and 18 at the assessment of damages hearing, was struck by a car which had mounted the pavement outside his school. He received a glancing blow below his left knee, was knocked over and suffered minor grazing to other parts of his body. No bony injury was noted on X-ray. M suffered pain on weight bearing for five weeks, during which time he took painkillers. He was off work for five weeks from his summer job, working in a fast food restaurant. Three months after the accident he was walking normally and able to play football, cricket and games at school. One year after the accident, on examination, there were no clinical signs. On full flexion of the left knee M reported discomfort over the patella ligament which was expected to disappear over the following two to three months. There was no scarring and a full recovery was expected. *General Damages*: £2,000.

M (A CHILD) v. KHAN, March 8, 2000, District Judge Jones, CC (Slough). [*Ex rel.* Owen White Solicitors, Senate House, 62-70 Bath Road, Berkshire].

Minor injuries – ankle

1743. C, male, aged 40 at the date of the accident and 41 at trial, suffered a fractured lateral malleolus of his right ankle when he twisted this in a hole in some cobblestones. There was an inversion type injury to the right ankle. After the fracture was confirmed, the ankle was treated by plaster immobilisation. The plaster cast was retained for six weeks. C worked on light duties answering telephones during this period. C continued to suffer discomfort over the lateral aspect of the ankle in colder weather. The medical evidence indicated that a full recovery was likely within a period of 12 to 18 months from the date of the accident. *General Damages*: £3,500.

COLES v. LEWIS [2000] 4 Q.R. 7, District Judge TJ Lewis, CC (Swansea).

Minor injuries – ankle

1744. A, male aged 32 at the date of the accident and 34 at trial, tripped on a sunken paving stone and suffered an acute sprain to the ligaments of his left ankle. For several years previously, A had suffered low back pain, but he had been reasonably free of symptoms for approximately two to three months prior to the accident. A few days after the accident, A became aware of worsening back pain and he consulted a physiotherapist privately. Three months after the accident, he continued to suffer aching in the left foot and ankle, weakness in the left foot and a tendency of the foot to "give way". The agreed medical evidence was that the accident had caused an aggravation of underlying constitutional symptoms in the lumbo-sacral spine for a period of up to three months following the accident. It was also agreed that by two years after the accident the residual ankle symptoms had resolved. The Judge "had in mind" the recommendations of Law Com. 257 encouraging courts to increase the level of general damages within the bracket £2,000 to £3,000 by up to 1.5. *General Damages* £3,250.

AHMED v. CARDIFF CC, December 17, 1999, Judge Masterman, CC (Cardiff). [*Ex rel.* Helen Gower, Barrister, Old Square Chambers, Hanover House, 47 Corn Street, Bristol].

Minor injuries – foot

1745. B, male, a fireman aged 27 at the date of the accident and 29 at trial, sustained a soft tissue injury to his left foot when it was struck by a heavy fire hose. B attended hospital where the foot was found to be very swollen and bruised. It was strapped and B was discharged and provided with crutches. B remained unable to weight bear for two weeks before gradually improving thereafter. B returned to work after four weeks and commenced playing football after six weeks. When examined seven months after the accident, the only residual symptom was pain in the foot whilst playing football. Examination revealed a small amount of swelling but there was a full range of movement. Remaining symptoms were described as "very low grade"and a full resolution was anticipated within a short period thereafter. *General Damages*: £800.

BEVAN v. SOUTH WALES FIRE SERVICE, January 19, 2000, District Judge North, CC (Cardiff). [*Ex rel.* Andrew Arentsen, Barrister, 33 Park Place, Cardiff].

Minor injuries – toe

1746.   M, male, aged 35 at the date of the operation and 38 at the assessment hearing, alleged that he had unnecessarily suffered the wrong surgical procedure to the second and fourth toes of his right foot. The judge rejected the allegation of negligence but assessed what would have been the appropriate quantum for an unnecessary operation of this sort. The operation was the FETTS procedure which took an hour and was carried out under general anaesthetic. It required 2.5 cm long incisions to be made along the tops of the second and fourth toe, the cutting of the flexor tendons within each and then attaching each cut tendon to each toe's extendor tendon. M was in hospital for two days. He was on crutches until the stitches were removed after 10 days. His foot was swollen and heavily bruised. By eight weeks the swelling had reduced, the bruising had gone and the scars had healed well. M suffered the usual period of between three to six month's pain for such an operation. The judge took into consideration that credit should be given for the fact that part of the pain, suffering and loss of amenity had also been sustained as a result of the contemporaneous necessary operations also performed on the third and fifth toes of the right foot. The judge assessed the appropriate *General Damages* as being £3,000.

MCBRIDE v. BASILDON AND THURROCK HOSPITAL NHS TRUST [2000] 3 Q.R. 8, Judge Rice, CC (Southend).

Minor injuries – disease

1747.   D1 and D2, children, suffered a cockroach infestation at their home for a period of three years. Both children had suffered insect bites which became infected and required lancing. Both had then developed a disease, Henoch Schonlein Pupura (HSP), the effects of which were that they suffered with a rash, swollen joints and abdominal pains that lasted intermittently for a year. Expert evidence was given by a consultant haematologist to the effect that the cockroach infestation was likely to have caused HSP either through the infected bites or by heavy exposure to the bacteria carried by the cockroaches over a number of years. The bites were likely to have been caused by the cockroaches but even if the original bites were due to other insects, the cockroaches were the likely cause of the infection. SMBC settled the claim which was approved by the court. *General Damages*: £2,000 (awarded to each child).

D (A CHILD) v. SEFTON MBC, January 20, 2000, Judge Urquhart, CC (Liverpool). [*Ex rel.* Tracey Bloom, Barrister, Doughty Street Chambers, 11 Doughty Street, London].

Minor injuries – toxicosis

1748.   D, female, aged five at the date of the incident and seven at the hearing, suffered from an outbreak of dysentery caused by consumption of fruit salad. D became listless, lethargic, anorexic and feverish within a couple of days of consuming the product. Diarrhoea developed together with faecal incontinence and abdominal pain later in the same day. The diarrhoea lasted for five days. The medical evidence concluded that D was suffering from an episode of gastroenteritis, most likely, Shingella Flexineri, from which her parents were also suffering. D was a diabetic who needed two injections of insulin per day and glucose tests. The effects of the dysentery impacted upon her blood sugar and insulin requirements which fluctuated for several weeks that was indicative of poorly controlled diabetes. D's diabetic condition was not stabilised for four weeks. During that time she lost a lot of weight due to the dysentery and the poorly controlled diabetes. D recovered fully after that with no ongoing symptoms. *General Damages*: £1,250 (agreed and approved).

D (A CHILD) v. J SAINSBURY PLC, March 24, 2000, Deputy District Judge Hammond, CC (Brighton). [*Ex rel.* Donne Mileham & Haddock Solicitors, 100 Queens Road, Brighton, East Sussex].

Claims for death of husband

1749.   [Law Reform (Miscellaneous Provisions) Act 1970 s.4(1).]
J, male, aged 27 at the date of death, was a musician in the Royal Marines and was killed by a bomb on September 22, 1989. The award was calculated on the basis that J would have remained as a musician in the Marines until 1994, when he would have been 32 years old, and it was assumed that he would have continued to work as a musician in civilian life. J's widow also worked, and was two years younger than he was. J's salary in the Marines would have increased with promotion. His widow had remarried, but that was ignored under the provisions of the Law Reform (Miscellaneous Provisions) Act 1970 s.4(1). The tribunal accepted the Ministry of Defence's career projection for J, but concluded that it was somewhat optimistic, and therefore delayed all promotions and wage increases by three years. The multipliers were (1) 22.24 for loss of earnings related dependency to the age of 65; (2) 9.93 for loss of pension related dependency from age 50, and (3) 18.88 for loss of DIY domestic services. The tribunal discounted the lump sum that J would have received on leaving the Marines by multiplying it by 0.5067 (23 years' acceleration). The Board deducted J's widow's pension to the date of her remarriage, when it ceased. Award for bereavement: £3,500. Past earnings based dependency: £57,000. Future earnings based dependency: £161,577. Pension dependency: £74,912. Total award: £311,592.

JONES (CICB: QUANTUM: 1999), *Re*, August 12, 1999, Eric Stockdale, J., CICB (London). [*Ex rel.* Simon Levene, Barrister, 199, Strand, London].

Claims for death of husband

1750.   M, male, aged 26 at the date of death, was a musician in the Royal Marines and was killed by a bomb on September 22, 1989. The award was calculated on the basis that M would have remained as a musician in the Marines until 1995, when he would have been 32 years old, and it was assumed that he would have continued to work as a musician in civilian life. M's widow also worked and had not remarried. His salary in the Marines would have increased with promotion. The tribunal accepted the Ministry of Defence's career projection for M, but concluded that it was somewhat optimistic and therefore delayed all promotions and wage increases by three years. The multipliers were (1) 22.56 for loss of earnings related dependency; (2) 9.64 for lost of pension related dependency, and (3) 18.88 for loss of DIY domestic services. It discounted the lump sum that M would have received on leaving the Marines by multiplying it by 0.5067 (23 years' acceleration). M's widow's pension to the date of the hearing was deducted. Award for bereavement: £3,500. Past earnings based dependency: £63,533. Future earnings based dependency: £184,259. Pension dependency: £78,848. Total award: £277,715.

MCMILLAN (CICB: QUANTUM: 1999), *Re*, August 12, 1999, Eric Stockdale, J., CICB (London). [*Ex rel.* Simon Levene, Barrister, 199, Strand, London].

Claims for death of parent

1751.   E, a boy born on May 21, 1993, brought a claim under the Fatal Accidents Act 1976 in respect of the death of his mother, T, on February 14, 1994 as a result of an anaesthetic accident at the defendant's hospital. On February 10, 1994 T had undergone a thorascopic sympathectomy operation under general anaesthetic as a result of which she died four days later from brain damage caused by cerebral hypoxia. Liability was admitted. T was aged 30 when she died and was unmarried. E was her only child. T had worked as a computer operator prior to E's birth and was intending to return to work at the earliest possible opportunity. She did not wish to become dependent on benefits in the long term. E suffered from Klinefelter's Syndrome, being a chromosomal abnormality resulting in excessive growth in height, incomplete sexual development in puberty with ascent or mal-descent of testes (35 per cent requiring surgical correction) and development of breasts (60 per cent requiring surgical intervention), the need for hormonal supplementation, mildly reduced intellectual development and behavioural difficulties. Although Klinefelter's Syndrome was described as mild, the evidence showed that he was beginning to show signs of retarded intellectual development and difficult behaviour at school. E had problems with reading and writing, social interaction with his peers, poor co-ordination, poor concentration and a short attention span for reading and writing skills. He needed one to one adult supervision at home and at school. E's claim consisted of (1) financial dependency on his mother; (2) practical dependency based upon the cost of replacing the care and services she provided; (3) an element to reflect the attention given especially by a mother and irreplaceable elsewhere, and (4) special damages including reasonable funeral costs. Approved settlement: £275,000.

E (A CHILD) v. NORTH MIDDLESEX HOSPITAL NHS TRUST, December 13, 1999, Judge John Rogers Q.C., QBD. [*Ex rel.* Bolt Burdon Solicitors, 1 Providence Place, Islington, London].

Claims for death of parent

1752.   W, an infant was aged four when his mother was murdered and nine at the date of the hearing. W's mother was separated from his father and was in fact killed by W's father. W was cared for by his maternal grandmother. W's mother was employed as a part time dental nurse earning £3,265 a year. In addition she received annually child benefit of £530, single parent benefit of £320 and family credit of £2,769. At the date of death W's grandmother was employed as a dinner lady by the local authority and earned £4,500 net per annum. At the date of her daughter's death the grandmother was aged 54 and intended to work until the age of 60. She gave up work to care for W. At the hearing the Board dealt with the matter in two parts. For financial dependency, the Board set the multiplicand at £2,300 and the multiplier at 11.5, giving a total of £26,450. From that the CICB deducted £4,461 which had been recovered from the killer of W's mother in a separate civil action, giving a sum of £21,989 which was rounded up to £22,000. For the services up to the date on which W's grandmother would have retired the multiplicand was set at £4,500 and a multiplier of 5.5 applied. For loss of services following her retirement the multiplicand was £2,000 and the multiplier 6. The total claim for loss of services therefore amounted to £36,750. £10,223 was deducted from that sum to account for benefits received. The sum left of £25,437 was rounded up to £26,000. An award of £973 for funeral expenses was also made.

W (A CHILD) (CICB: QUANTUM: 1999), *Re*, July 28, 1999, E Gee, Chairman, CICB (Manchester). [*Ex rel.* Rhodes, Thain & Collinson Solicitors, 27 Harrison Road, Halifax].

1753. **Publications**

Kemp and Kemp: Personal Injury Practice: CD-ROM. £350.00. ISBN 0-421-64820-1. Sweet & Maxwell.

DEFAMATION

1754. Affidavits – privilege

See EVIDENCE: Smeaton v. Butcher (No.1). §333

1755. Defamation Act 1996 (c.31) – Commencement No.2 Order

DEFAMATION ACT 1996 (COMMENCEMENT NO. 2) ORDER 2000, SI 2000 222 (C.7); made under the Defamation Act 1996 s.19. Commencement details: bringing into force various provisions of the Act on February 28, 2000; £1.00.

This Order brings into force on February 28, 2000 all the provisions of the Defamation Act 1996 which apply in England and Wales and which have not so far been brought into force, with the exception of the repeal of the Broadcasting Act 1990 Sch.20 para.3.

1756. Defences – foreign jurisdictions – public policy defence – adjudication on integrity of friendly state's judiciary

[Civil Liability (Contribution) Act 1978 s.1 (4); European Convention on Human Rights 1950 Art.6, Art.10.]

S, a Malaysian legal firm, sought to strike out parts of the defence to an application for a contribution under the Civil Liability (Contribution) Act 1978 s.1 (4), in respect of some £2.9 million paid out in settlement of defamation proceedings. The proceedings had been brought by a number of persons in Malaysia in respect of statements attributed to two partners of S, in an article published by E. S submitted that the public policy defence raised by the defendants under the European Convention on Human Rights 1950 Art.6 and Art.10, alleging that the Malaysian judiciary lacked independence from the government and that its defamation laws were used to stifle freedom of expression, were not issues on which the court should adjudicate.

Held, allowing the application in part, that the court would not decide on issues involving the integrity and independence of a friendly state's judiciary in the determination of substantive contribution proceedings, *Buttes Gas and Oil Co v. Hammer (No.3)* [1982] A.C. 888, [1981] C.L.Y. 1473 and *Lubbe v. Cape Plc (No.2)* [2000] 1 W.L.R. 1545, [2000] C.L.Y. 775 considered. Moreover, there had been no infringement of Art.6 as a result of the partial strike out of the defence because under the 1978 Act the court would only order the defendants to pay a contribution that was just and equitable. Nor was there any discrepancy between Art.10 and the common law, *Tolstoy Miloslavsky v. United Kingdom (A/323)* [1996] E.M.L.R. 152, [1995] C.L.Y. 2647 and *John v. MGN Ltd* [1997] Q.B. 586, [1996] C.L.Y. 5673 considered. The public policy defence had not been pleaded in relation to the defence of fair comment and had no relevance to it, therefore it remained open for a defence of fair comment to be tried as a preliminary issue.

SKRINE & CO v. EUROMONEY PUBLICATIONS PLC [2001] E.M.L.R. 16, Morland, J., QBD.

1757. Libel – justification – amendment of defence – restriction of peripheral issues

TN published newspaper articles alleging that T had donated some £100,000 to the Conservative Party from his companies at a time when the assets of the company were subject to UN sanctions because T was associated with the Bosnian Serb leadership then involved in the Bosnian war. T brought an action for libel in which TN applied for permission to amend its defence for the fifth time to plead further particulars of justification. The application was refused and TN appealed, contending that its additional plea was relevant to the substance of the original newspaper article.

Held, dismissing the appeal, that a decision as to whether a plea of justification raised issues essential to the resolution of matters in dispute or alternatively raised matters of merely a peripheral nature was pre-eminently one for determination by the judge at first instance, who had correctly exercised his discretion. In general, TN should be allowed to develop its defence to the full, but peripheral issues were to be restricted in the interests of case management and on proportionality grounds, *McPhilemy v. Times Newspapers Ltd (Re-amendment: Justification)* [1999] 3 All E.R. 775, [1999] C.L.Y. 1635 followed.

TANCIC v. TIMES NEWSPAPERS LTD; *sub nom.* TIMES NEWSPAPERS LTD v. TANCIC *The Times*, January 12, 2000, Brooke, L.J., CA.

1758. Libel – measure of damages – mitigation – suitability of summary disposal

[Defamation Act 1996 s.8, s.9.]

B commenced libel proceedings against TN following the publication of an article alleging that B, together with other like minded individuals, had formed a group with the aim of disrupting the performance of modern atonal concerts. TN applied (1) to rely upon certain aspects of its defence in relation to mitigation of damages, despite the fact that the defence of justification and fair comment had already been adjudged unsustainable. TN maintained that matters relating to the claimant's conduct should be available to the judge when assessing damages, *Godfrey v. Demon Internet Ltd* [1999] 4 All E.R. 342, [1999] C.L.Y. 1636 cited, and (2) that the issue of damages was suitable for summary disposal by judge alone pursuant to the Defamation Act 1996 s.8 and s.9 under which the recoverable damages would be limited to £10,000.

Held, dismissing the application, that (1) it would only be appropriate to permit the introduction of evidence which fell outside the criteria in *Pamplin v. Express Newspapers Ltd (No.2)* [1988] 1 W.L.R. 116, [1988] C.L.Y. 2123 in an exceptional case. While exceptional circumstances may have existed in *Godfrey*, where the claimant had sought to invite defamatory comment in order that he might commence vexatious libel proceedings, the circumstances could not be said to be similarly exceptional in the instant case, *Kelly v. Sherlock* (1866) L.R. 1 Q.B. 686 distinguished, and (2) it was not appropriate to determine the issue of damages summarily under the s.9 procedure and limit the damages recoverable to £10,000. Following publication, TN had refused to apologise and had aggressively defended the litigation. There was also the possibility that when the damages fell to be assessed, issues put to B in cross examination, if not found to be correct, could potentially result in an increase in the total damages award.

BURSTEIN v. TIMES NEWSPAPERS LTD 1999 TLQ (J) 1205, Judge Richard Walker, QBD.

1759. Libel – publications – foreign jurisdictions – liability for harmful event – Ireland

[Brussels Convention on Jurisdiction and Enforcement of Judgments in Civil and Commercial Matters 1968 Art.5(3).]

Claims for damages for libel were brought against GD and BC, respectively, the publisher and author of a booklet about the trial of the "Birmingham Six". H, a member of that group, contended that the libel arose in Ireland from the republication of the booklet there. BC sought a declaration that the Irish courts had no jurisdiction in the matter on the ground that under the Brussels Convention 1968 Art.5(3) the place where the harmful event occurred was restricted to a place where it was natural and probable for republication to occur and that was not Ireland, since he had requested GD to refrain from distributing the booklet there.

Held, refusing the application, that the contract between GD and BC did not prohibit publication or dissemination of the information in Ireland. A mere request that the work should not be distributed in Ireland did not mean that publication would not occur. Considering the issues covered in the booklet, the proximity of England to Ireland and the likely interest by the Irish in the subject matter, it was almost inevitable that the booklet would be published in Ireland. That was a natural and probable consequence of the English publication and BC was responsible for the alleged harmful event occurring in Ireland.

HUNTER v. GERALD DUCKWORTH & CO LTD [2000] I.L.Pr. 229, Kelly, J., HC (Irl).

1760. **Libel – qualified – privilege – solicitors – expression of personal opinions – scope of solicitor's general retainer**

R, a magazine editor, brought a libel action against T, a solicitor who had represented A in separate libel proceedings resulting from allegations that A had been guilty of sexual abuse. T's verbal criticism of R's journalistic and ethical standards, which was made during the course of media representations on A's behalf, was published and R alleged the words used to have been defamatory. T, who had been given general authority by A to deal with the media, pleaded, inter alia, qualified privilege. At the beginning of the trial, summary judgment had been granted in T's favour (Unreported, April 29, 1999, [1999] C.L.Y. 1629) on the ground that R had no real prospect of rebutting the defence of qualified privilege. In seeking to have the judgment set aside, R conceded that an agent had the same right to qualified privilege as his principal, but submitted that the defence did not extend to the circumstances of the instant case where T had expressed his personal views and those views had not been adopted by A or made with his authority. He further submitted that to allow T to rely on the defence of qualified privilege would be contrary to the public interest because it would represent a licence to libel. R also argued that T's comments had amounted to a breach of the solicitors' professional rules of conduct. T contended that his statement had been within the scope of his general instructions and duty to A.

Held, dismissing the appeal (Chadwick L.J. dissenting), that the scope of T's retainer was a question of fact and inference. Modern practice might frequently require a solicitor to rely on his own experience in the representation of a client rather than on direct instructions. Privilege did not depend on the solicitor having specific express authority and a broad authority to protect a client's interests was implicit in the retainer, *Baker v. Carrick* [1894] 1 Q.B. 838 and *Watts v. Times Newspapers Ltd* [1997] Q.B. 650, [1995] C.L.Y. 3133 considered. In the instant case, T's comments had been relevant to the authority conveyed on him by A, had not been said in malice and would have been endorsed by A. The allegations pertaining to the public interest and the professional rules of conduct were ill founded and there was no reason to restrict the ambit of the privilege defence to non lawyer agents.

REGAN v. TAYLOR [2000] E.M.L.R. 549, May, L.J., CA.

1761. **Libel – qualified privilege – factors for consideration**

[Defamation Act 1996 s.8.]

A series of newspaper articles published by M alleged that JG, a ball manufacturer, used an Indian subcontractor that employed child labour. The third article asserted that JG had broken an earlier promise to send employees to India to investigate the allegations. JG brought an action for libel in respect of that article, in which it sought summary disposal under the Defamation Act 1996 s.8. JG argued that the words complained of were obviously defamatory and that the only substantive defence, namely qualified privilege, had no realistic prospect of success with the result that there was no other reason to try the claim.

Held, granting the application for summary disposal, that (1) the test to be applied under s.8 was whether the defence had a real prospect of success, *Swain v. Hillman* [1999] C.P.L.R. 779, [1999] C.L.Y. 561 applied; (2) qualified privilege in media publications to the world at large had to be determined in line with established common law principles; (3) the matters to be taken into account included the seriousness of the allegation; the nature of the information and the extent to which it was a matter of public concern; the source of the information and the steps taken to verify it; the status of the information; the urgency of the matter; whether comment was sought from the claimant; whether the article contained the gist of the claimant's version of the story; the tone of the article and the circumstances of the publication, including timing, *Reynolds v. Times Newspapers Ltd* [1999] 3 W.L.R. 1010, [1999] C.L.Y. 1630 applied, and (4) applying those factors to the instant case, the publication of the allegations in the third article was not in the public interest and M did not have a duty to publish them.

JAMES GILBERT LTD v. MGN LTD [2000] E.M.L.R. 680, Eady, J., QBD.

1762. Libel – qualified privilege – malice – preliminary issues – case management

[Civil Procedure Rules 1998 (SI 1998 3132) Part 3 r.3.1 (1), Part 32 r.32.]

G brought a libel action against Y, claiming that an article published by Y was defamatory. The court ordered that the issues of qualified privilege and malice be determined on a trial of preliminary issues prior to determination of the issue of justification. G appealed, contending that the judge's approach was novel and unfair, because it was impossible to consider whether the article was published on an occasion of qualified privilege without determining initially whether the article was in the public interest, having regard to all the issues.

Held, dismissing the appeal, that the judge's unique approach was in accordance with the overriding objective under the Civil Procedure Rules 1988, as it enabled libel cases to be dealt with justly, economically and expeditiously. The judge was entitled to determine the preliminary issues of qualified privilege and malice before determining the justification plea. The court in furtherance of the overriding objective was given wide case management powers under Part 3 r.3.1 (1), allowing it to direct a separate trial of any issues, and exclude admissible and relevant evidence which it considered to be time consuming and costly under Part 32 r.32. The truth of the publication was not a material factor to the preliminary issues, nor was any determination of the journalist's reliability.

GKR KARATE (UK) LTD v. YORKSHIRE POST NEWSPAPERS LTD (NO.1) [2000] 1 W.L.R. 2571, May, L.J., CA.

1763. Libel – qualified privilege – newspapers – journalist's duties to make enquiries

G ran karate classes in Leeds. Y published a free local newspaper, for which H was a journalist. H wrote an article alleging malpractice by G, based on information supplied by G and quoting two people involved in karate; B, a local instructor, and P, the general administrator of the English Karate Governing Body. H left a message asking G to contact her about the article but G failed to do so. H made enquiries with the local trading standards office, which confirmed that it had had no complaints about G. Y published H's article. G brought an action for libel. Y raised defences of justification, fair comment and qualified privilege and an order was made that the latter should be determined first at a preliminary hearing.

Held, dismissing the action, that Y had shown qualified privilege. The test was whether it was H's social or moral duty to pass on information which the public had a right to know. That had to be assessed in the context as a whole, with the court giving weight to freedom of expression and favouring publication where appropriate, *Reynolds v. Times Newspapers Ltd* [1999] 3 W.L.R. 1010, [1999] C.L.Y. 1630 applied. L's readership was local to Leeds and had a proper interest in knowing about the practices of G in the area. H had acted reasonably in relying on the information supplied by all three sources, particularly that of P given his position of responsibility in the karate world. Factors in G's favour were that (1) H had been wrong to frame P's comments as though they were fact, and (2) H should have made more effort to allow G to respond to the article and should have mentioned the trading standards enquiry. However, those factors were insufficient to outweigh the interests of publication and the defence was made out.

GKR KARATE (UK) LTD v. YORKSHIRE POST NEWSPAPERS LTD (NO.2) [2000] E.M.L.R. 410, Sir Oliver Popplewell, QBD.

1764. Libel – qualified privilege – political statements – New Zealand

[Defamation Act 1992 (New Zealand) s.19.]

L, a former prime minister of New Zealand, appealed to the Privy Council against a decision of the New Zealand Court of Appeal (4 B.H.R.C. 573, [1998] C.L.Y.1781) upholding a first instance decision ([1997] 2 N.Z.L.R. 22) refusing L's application to strike out a plea of political expression as a defence of qualified privilege available to A in a defamation action brought by L. The Privy Council allowed the appeal and remitted the matter back to the New Zealand Court of Appeal for reconsideration following the House of Lord's decision in *Reynolds v. Times Newspapers Ltd* [1999] 3 W.L.R. 1010, [1999] C.L.Y. 1630.

Held, dismissing the appeal, that the *Reynolds* decision added to the uncertainties surrounding qualified privilege and could further restrict public comment. Societal differences between England and New Zealand required the court to adopt a different approach to that taken in *Reynolds*. Also, the Defamation Act 1992 (New Zealand) s.19 allowed the New Zealand courts to take a wider view when defining what constituted misuse of an occasion of qualified privilege. Thus in the law of New Zealand, (1) qualified privilege could apply to generally published political statements; (2) the nature of New Zealand democracy meant that the public had an interest in statements about the present and future performance of their elected representatives, and there was particular interest in comments about their actions and qualities, as well as their abilities in discharging public responsibilities; (3) such concerns were dependent on whether the matters in issue were public or private in nature; (4) the width of public concern was in relation to the extent of the publication, and (5) to attract privilege the statement had to be published on a qualifying occasion, *Reynolds* not followed.

LANGE v. ATKINSON (NO.2) 8 B.H.R.C. 500, Richardson (President), CA (NZ).

1765. Libel – striking out – prospect of succeeding on single point insufficient to justify court time and cost – attempt to relitigate matters at issue in compromised proceedings was abuse of process

See CIVIL PROCEDURE: Schellenberg v. BBC. §624

1766. Malicious falsehood – aggravated damages

See TORTS: Khodaparast v. Shad. §5116

1767. Privilege – parliamentary privilege – individual member of Parliament

[Defamation Act 1996 s.13.]

H, a former member of Parliament, instituted proceedings against AF for defamation following allegations that H had been engaged in the corrupt practice of accepting cash in return for asking parliamentary questions. AF applied to stay the claim on the basis that to permit it to proceed would constitute a breach of parliamentary privilege. The application was refused at first instance and AF launched an unsuccessful appeal. Thereafter AF lodged a further appeal, contending that of all the distinct types of parliamentary privilege, only a very few belonged to individual members of Parliament, as opposed to the House as a whole. AF further maintained that those privileges belonging exclusively to the House included its autonomous jurisdiction over specific matters, a privilege which H, as a former member of Parliament, was not entitled to waive.

Held, dismissing the appeal, that the arguments raised on behalf of AF were flawed. All of the privileges in existence belonged to the House exclusively not to individual members of Parliament. If the Defamation Act 1996 s.13 had not been enacted the case would necessarily have been the subject of a stay because parliamentary privilege would have precluded any attempt by either party to put in issue the evidence previously adduced before the parliamentary committee, which had conducted an inquiry into H's conduct. Nevertheless s.13 permitted an individual member of Parliament to waive the privilege afforded to him by virtue of his role. Such a waiver was also effective to override the privilege of the House as a whole in relation to those matters under s.13(2)(b). In consequence, any challenge to parliamentary procedures and even a challenge to the actual findings made by a prior parliamentary inquiry into conduct would not infringe parliamentary privilege.

HAMILTON v. AL FAYED (NO.1) [2001] 1 A.C. 395, Lord Browne-Wilkinson, HL.

1768. Publications

Hooper, David – Winners and Losers in the Libel Business. Hardback: £25.00. ISBN 0-316-64833-7. Little, Brown & Company.

Loveland, Ian – Political Libels: a Comparative Study. Hardback: £22.50. ISBN 1-84113-115-6. Hart Publishing.

DISPUTE RESOLUTION

1769. Publications

Achieving Benefits Through Mediation: an Effective Business Tool. TSO Mediation Series. Paperback: £30.00. ISBN 0-11-702443-0. The Stationery Office Books.

Achieving Benefits Through Mediation: Personal Injury Disputes. TSO Mediation Series. Paperback: £30.00. ISBN 0-11-702440-6. The Stationery Office Books.

ECCLESIASTICAL LAW

1770. Burials and cremation – exhumation – reburial in Jewish cemetery

[Human Rights Act 1998.]

The relatives of the deceased, a Jewish man who had married outside the faith and who had died in 1981, petitioned for a faculty to have his remains exhumed for the purpose of his reburial in a Jewish cemetery. The deceased had been buried, at the request of his wife, on consecrated ground, and it was out of respect for her that the petitioners had delayed in applying for the faculty.

Held, granting the faculty, that the beliefs of the Christian and Jewish faiths relating to burial, in particular those teachings that concerned the permanence of burial and the rejection of the concept of portable remains, were sufficiently similar to warrant the granting of the faculty. While the passage of time and an intention to bury remains in unconsecrated ground constituted factors which under normal circumstances militated against the granting of a faculty, the petitioners in the instant case had exhibited good cause for their delay in applying, *Christ Church (Alsager), Re* [1999] Fam. 142, [1998] C.L.Y. 1786 and *Church Norton Churchyard, Re* [1989] Fam. 37, [1989] C.L.Y. 1301 considered. It was observed that the refusal of the faculty might have constituted a breach of the freedom of religion under the Human Rights Act 1998 were that Act in force.

DURRINGTON CEMETERY, *Re* [2001] Fam. 33, Chancellor Hill, Cons Ct (Chichester).

1771. Church of England – faculty jurisdiction – care of places of worship

FACULTY JURISDICTION (CARE OF PLACES OF WORSHIP) RULES 2000, SI 2000 2048; made under the Care of Churches and Ecclesiastical Jurisdiction Measure 1991 s.14, s.26. In force: in accordance with r.1; £6.30.

These Rules lay down the procedure for faculty proceedings involving buildings, objects, structures or land which are brought within the faculty jurisdiction under the Care of Places of Worship Measure 1999. Although the provisions of the Rules in general mirror those of the Faculty Jurisdiction Rules 2000 (SI 2000 2047), some of them make special provision for the 1999 Measure.

1772. Church of England – faculty jurisdiction – procedure

FACULTY JURISDICTION RULES 2000, SI 2000 2047; made under the Care of Churches and Ecclesiastical Jurisdiction Measure 1991 s.14, s.26. In force: January 1, 2001; £7.30.

These Rules revoke and replace the Faculty Jurisdiction Rules 1992 (SI 1992 2882) which introduced various changes in procedure in conjunction with the implementation of the Care of Churches and Ecclesiastical Jurisdiction Measure 1991. These Rules continue the general framework of the procedure and introduce various changes.

1773. Church of England – registered patron – incapacitated or under disability

PARSONAGES MEASURE RULES 2000, SI 2000 3171; made under the Parsonages Measure 1938 s.15. In force: January 1, 2001; £2.00.

These Rules, which are required to take account of the changes made by the Church of England (Miscellaneous Provisions) Measure 2000, make provision where the registered patron is incapacitated or under disability and, where objections to proposals are received, requires the relevant Board to pass the objections to the Church Commissioners for consideration.

1774. Church of England (Miscellaneous Provisions) Measure 2000 (c.m.1)

This Measure, which was passed by the General Synod of the Church of England, transfers certain functions of the Church Commissioners to diocesan bodies. It provides for the performance of a rural dean's functions during a vacancy, absence or illness and enables dioceses to rename rural deans as area deans. In addition, it amends the Consecration of Churchyards Act 1867 s.1, the City of London (Guild Churches) Act 1952 s.12(10), the Church Funds Investment Measure 1958 Sch, the Ecclesiastical Jurisdiction Measure 1963 s.8, the Repair of Benefice Buildings Measure 1972 s.21, the Ecclesiastical Fees Measure 1986 s.4, the Patronage (Benefices) Measure 1986 s.3 and the Church of England (Legal Aid and Miscellaneous Provisions) Measure 1988 s.6.

This Act received Royal Assent on July 28, 2000.

1775. Churches – alterations – criteria for grant of faculty for millennium window

P, the treasurer of a parochial church council, applied for a faculty to replace the existing stained glass in a Victorian window at an ancient Norman church with abstract glazing by a local stained glass artist as part of a millennium project. The application was opposed on the grounds that the proposed design was not in keeping with other windows within the church, that the existing window was attractive and did not need repairing, that the church was a listed building, and that the design was neither educational nor inspirational.

Held, granting the faculty, that in considering a faculty for a millennium window, the court was obliged to have regard to the strong presumption against any change to a listed building which would have a detrimental effect on its character as a building of architectural or historic interest. In the instant case that presumption had been rebutted since the existing windows within the church were not all of the same type or age and the window to be replaced bore no specific Christian motive, *St Luke the Evangelist (Maidstone), Re* [1995] Fam. 1, [1995] C.L.Y. 1867 applied. Whilst there was undoubted opposition to the proposal, it was nevertheless clear from the available evidence that the majority of villagers were in favour.

ST GREGORY OFFCHURCH, *Re* [2000] 1 W.L.R. 2471, Sir William Gage (Chancellor), Cons Ct (Coventry).

1776. Clergy – age limits – Channel Islands

ECCLESIASTICAL OFFICES (AGE LIMIT) (CHANNEL ISLANDS) ORDER 2000, SI 2000 2767; made under the Channel Islands (Church Legislation) Measure 1931 s.2; and the Ecclesiastical Offices (Age Limit) Measure 1975 s.7. In force: November 1, 2000; £1.75.

This Order applies the Ecclesiastical Offices (Age Limit) Measure 1975 to the Channel Islands in accordance with a Scheme prepared by the Bishop of Winchester.

1777. Faculty proceedings – ecclesiastical offences – fees

ECCLESIASTICAL JUDGES, LEGAL OFFICERS AND OTHERS (FEES) ORDER 2000, SI 2000 2045; made under the Ecclesiastical Fees Measure 1986 s.6. In force: January 1, 2001; £2.50.

This Order revokes and replaces the fees fixed by Table I of the Ecclesiastical Judges and Legal Officers (Fees) Order 1999 (SI 1999 2110) in relation to faculty proceedings, proceedings for an injunction or a restoration order under the Care of Churches and Ecclesiastical Jurisdiction Measure 1991 s.13(4)(5) and proceedings under the Care of Cathedrals (Supplementary Provisions) Measure 1994 s.4, and the fees fixed by Table III for proceedings in respect of ecclesiastical offences under the Ecclesiastical Jurisdiction Measure 1963. Other increases are made to miscellaneous fees.

1778. Fees – baptism, marriages and burials

PAROCHIAL FEES ORDER 2000, SI 2000 2049; made under the Ecclesiastical Fees Measure 1986 s.1. In force: January 1, 2001; £2.00.

This Order, which revokes the Parochial Fees Order 1999 (SI 1999 2113), establishes a new table of fees payable for certain matters in connection with baptisms, marriages and burials, for the erection of monuments in churchyards and for other miscellaneous matters.

1779. Grants – Churches Conservation Trust

GRANTS TO THE CHURCHES CONSERVATION TRUST ORDER 2000, SI 2000 402; made under the Redundant Churches and other Religious Buildings Act 1969 s.1. In force: April 1, 2000; £1.00.

This Order specifies the period April 1, 2000 to March 31, 2003 for the purposes of the Redundant Churches and other Religious Buildings Act 1969, thus enabling the Secretary of State to make grants to the Churches Conservation Trust during that period of such amounts, payable at such times and subject to such conditions as he may from time to time determine. It specifies the sum of £8,829,000 as the maximum aggregate amount of the grants that may be paid over that period.

1780. Legal officers – fees

LEGAL OFFICERS (ANNUAL FEES) ORDER 2000, SI 2000 2046; made under the Ecclesiastical Fees Measure 1986 s.5. In force: January 1, 2001; £2.00.

This Order, which revokes and replaces the Legal Officers (Annual Fees) Order 1999 (SI 1999 2108), increases the annual fees for diocesan registrars and fixes new annual fees for the provincial registrars.

1781. United Reformed Church Act 2000 (c.ii)

This Act, which amends the United Reformed Church Act 1972 and the United Reformed Church Act 1981, makes provision as to property held on behalf of the Congregational Union of Scotland, its member churches and the Scottish Congregational College, and for purposes incidental to or consequential upon the unification of the Congregational Union of Scotland with the United Reformed Church in the UK.

This Act received Royal Assent on February 10, 2000 and comes into force on February 10, 2000.

1782. Publications

Macmorran, Kenneth M.; Briden, Timothy – Handbook for Churchwardens and Parochial Church Councillors. Paperback: £9.99. ISBN 0-264-67486-3. Mowbray.

ECONOMICS

1783. Structural funds – National Assembly for Wales – exercise of functions

STRUCTURAL FUNDS (NATIONAL ASSEMBLY FOR WALES) REGULATIONS 2000, SI 2000 906; made under the European Communities Act 1972 s.2. In force: March 31, 2000; £2.00.

These Regulations enable the National Assembly for Wales to exercise, in relation to Wales, certain functions under Council Regulation 4253/88 ([1988] OJ L374/1) laying down provisions for implementing Regulation 2052/88 relating to coordination of the activities of the different Structural Funds between themselves and with the operations of the European Investment Bank and the other existing financial instruments and under Council Regulation 1260/1999 ([1999] OJ L161/1) laying down general provisions on the Structural Funds. The Structural Funds concerned are the European Regional Development Fund, the Financial Instrument for Fisheries Guidance and the Guidance Section of the European Agricultural Guidance and Guarantee Fund.

1784. Publications

Bouckaert, Boudewijn; de Geest, Gerrit – Encyclopedia of Law and Economics: Vols I-V. Hardback: £865.00. ISBN 1-85898-565-X. Edward Elgar.

Glassner, Martin Ira – Bibliography on Land-locked States, Economic Development and International Law. 5th Ed. Hardback: £95.00. ISBN 0-7656-0675-5. M.E. Sharpe.

Hahn, Robert W. – Reviving Regulatory Reform. Hardback: £22.50. ISBN 0-8447-4121-3. Paperback: £12.50. ISBN 0-8447-4122-1. The AEI Press.

Posner, Eric A. – Law and Economics. International Library of Essays in Law and Legal Theory (second Series). Hardback: £90.00. ISBN 0-7546-2098-0. Dartmouth.

Watt, Richard – Copyright and Economic Theory: Friends or Foes? Elgar Monographs. Hardback: £49.95. ISBN 1-84064-312-9. Edward Elgar.

EDUCATION

1785. Barristers – bar vocational course – failed assessments – extent to which mitigating circumstances considered by review board – visitor's power to intervene

J, a man of Asian origin, enrolled at the Inns of Court School of Law, ICSL, for the Bar Vocational Course in 1995/6. He failed both the civil and criminal multiple choice tests, MCTs, both initially and on a retake, and the negotiation and EC competition law assessments. J submitted mitigating circumstances in relation to his first attempts at the MCTs. Although the board of examiners accepted his mitigating circumstances, they were not persuaded that but for those circumstances J would have passed the MCTs. J applied unsuccessfully to the review board in relation to the MCTs, but citing different mitigation. In June 1996, J retook the MCTs and failed. In the January 1997 resits, J passed the negotiation assessment but failed the MCTs. J submitted the death of his father in law as a mitigating circumstance to the board of examiners, but the board was again not satisfied that but for those circumstances he would have passed the MCTs, although he was allowed to resit the tests on a further occasion. J's application to the review board was dismissed. On his final attempt at the resits, J passed the criminal MCT but failed the civil MCT. J did not plead any mitigation before the board of examiners, but he did apply to the review board, referring to the family pressure on him to succeed as the eldest son. He did not refer expressly to the Assessment of Regulations 1995/6 Reg.12(2)(b) in his application, and the review board did not deal expressly with the mitigation points in the reasons for confirming the decision of the board of examiners. J appealed to the Visitor, arguing that, having regard to his particular personal difficulties as a man from a working class Asian family, he should be given the opportunity to resit the civil MCTa further time.

Held, dismissing the appeal, that (1) despite the failure of the review board to refer to the mitigating circumstances in its reasons, it was accepted on the basis of its standard practice that the board would consider and deal with all the material that was placed before it, irrespective of the particular ground of appeal expressly relied on; (2) while the Visitor had a very wide jurisdiction to redress grievances, that power was to be exercised with care in relation to educational decisions properly taken. In particular, the Visitor should only intervene in exceptional circumstances in cases concerning matters of academic judgment in relation to examinations, *Sealey v. Inns of Court School of Law* (Unreported, December 17, 1997) applied. The threshold for intervention was analogous to the *Wednesbury* unreasonableness test. Applying that test to the facts of the instant case, the review board's decision to confirm the decision of the board of examiners was one that it was entitled to take. J had failed the civil MCT by a considerable margin on every occasion on which he had taken it. The mitigating circumstances put forward by J did not take the case into a different realm, since the review board was already well aware of the parental pressure faced by J and the other matters. Consequently, the review board would have appreciated the serious implications that its decision would have for J and his family, but that did not make the case exceptional.

JHAMAT v. INNS OF COURT SCHOOL OF LAW [1999] E.L.R. 450, Dyson, J., VIC.

1786. Barristers – examinations – review board's duty to provide reasons – formula based decision inappropriate

O appealed to the review board of the Inns of Court School of Law against the decision of the examination board concerning the bar final vocational examinations which he had taken. He argued that there were mitigating reasons for his failure to pass the examinations, in that his father and brother had been subject to a police investigation for alleged dishonesty at the time of his exams, a fact which he had been reluctant to bring to the board's attention because of possible adverse implications for his career. The review board did not accept that he had provided a satisfactory reason for his failure to make the board aware of his mitigating circumstances. The review board's reasons were recorded in a formulaic manner. O appealed to the Visitors to the ICSL.

Held, dismissing the appeal, that there was a duty to provide reasons individually, concisely and clearly. Although the use of a formula to express the reasons was unsatisfactory, the manner in which the reasons had been expressed was not so inadequate as to render the decision unlawful. The paucity of reasons could not have made any difference to the case since no complex point of law had to be determined. The issue put before the review board by O was simple and straightforward and had been adequately dealt with by the board. The decision of the board to reject O's reasons for his failure to reveal his mitigating circumstances could not be considered perverse.

O'DOHERTY v. INNS OF COURT SCHOOL OF LAW [1999] E.L.R. 364, Smith, J., VIC.

1787. Colleges – complaints – appeal procedures – academic committee's duties

N, a student at CC, sought judicial review of the academic committee's refusal to consider the details of her sexual harassment complaint as an extenuating circumstance in respect of an appeal against her exam results. N had been informed that the appeal would be heard by the academic committee in accordance with Reg.8(3) of the Academic Affairs Handbook and that the only consideration would be the existence of a material irregularity on the part of the Board of Examiners. N had requested a list of the documents to be presented to the committee and had been informed of the limited grounds of appeal by the chairman of the committee. N had not received the list and papers which she had provided to the committee members at the appeal were not considered as they did not fulfil the requirements of Reg.8(3). N's appeal was dismissed and she challenged the decision, contending that the committee had acted unfairly by its refusal to consider her documentation and by not disclosing to her the list of documents upon which it had relied.

Held, granting the application, that (1) the refusal to consider N's submissions had amounted to a breach of the proper appeal procedure and could not be justified on the basis of confidentiality. N's arguments could not properly have been made without reference to the harassment allegations and any decision as to the limiting of submitted material should have been made by the committee as a whole and not just the chairman, *R. v. Schools Appeals Tribunal of the Wakefield Diocesan Board of Education, ex p. J* (1999) 1 L.G.L.R. 216, [1999] C.L.Y. 1871 followed, and (2) relevant material should not have been considered by the committee without first giving N the opportunity to comment upon it, *Wiseman v. Borneman* [1971] A.C. 297, [1969] C.L.Y. 1748 applied. The committee's failure to disclose the material had amounted to a breach of the principles of fairness and had resulted in a risk of prejudice towards N, *Lake District Special Planning Board v. Secretary of State for the Environment* 236 E.G. 417, [1975] C.L.Y. 20 applied.

R. v. CHELSEA COLLEGE OF ART AND DESIGN, *ex p.* NASH [2000] Ed. C.R. 571, Elias, J., QBD.

1788. Colleges – dissolution – Walford College Shropshire

WALFORD COLLEGE, SHROPSHIRE (DISSOLUTION) ORDER 2000, SI 2000 3219; made under the Further and Higher Education Act 1992 s.27. In force: January 1, 2001; £1.50.

This Order dissolves the further education corporation established to conduct Walford College, Shropshire. It provides for the transfer of its property, rights and liabilities to the North Shropshire College, Oswestry and secures the rights of its employees by applying the Further and Higher Education Act 1992 s.26(2)(3)(4).

1789. Colleges – exempt charities – Royal College of Art

See CHARITIES. §299

1790. Councillors – bias – procedural impropriety – councillors acting as school governors – declaration of private interests

See LOCAL GOVERNMENT: R. v. Kirklees MBC, *ex p.* Beaumont. §4087

1791. Courses – subsidies – deregistration from entitlement – legitimate expectation – absence of value for money

AT, a provider of IT training services, applied for judicial review of a decision of the Secretary of State to deregister a course which it ran from an entitlement to an 80 per cent subsidy on the ground that the course did not provide value for money. AT had applied to register on the individual learning account scheme offered by the Secretary of State. The application pack provided no guidance on the maximum cost of providing courses that could be subsidised. The Secretary of State expressed concern at the figure set by AT for running the course and AT responded to those concerns, but AT took bookings from students before receiving a final decision from the Secretary of State. The Secretary of State decided to de-register the course, although he agreed to honour course bookings already taken. AT argued that there was a legitimate expectation that it would remain on the register as no costs ceiling had been imposed.

Held, refusing the application, that (1) the Secretary of State had not created a legitimate expectation on the part of AT that the course would remain on the register and had not given an unambiguous representation that AT could begin accepting bookings from students, and (2) whilst there was a duty to consult, a duty with which the Secretary of State had failed properly to comply, consultation in the instant case would have made no difference to the Secretary of State's decision as there had been an opportunity for AT to make representations and the course did not provide value for money, a factor which the Secretary of State was entitled to take into account in reaching his decision.

R. (ON THE APPLICATION OF AMRAF TRAINING PLC) v. SECRETARY OF STATE FOR EDUCATION AND EMPLOYMENT, *ex p.* AMRAF TRAINING PLC; *sub nom.* R. v. SECRETARY OF STATE FOR EDUCATION AND EMPLOYMENT, *ex p.* AMRAF TRAINING PLC [2001] E.L.R. 125, Elias, J., QBD.

1792. Education action zones – establishment – Bristol

BRISTOL EDUCATION ACTION ZONE ORDER 2000, SI 2000 865; made under the School Standards and Framework Act 1998 s.10, s.11, s.138, Sch.1 para.2. In force: April 17, 2000; £2.00.

This Order establishes the Bristol Education Action Zone and provides for the membership of the Education Action Forum for the zone.

1793. Education action zones – establishment – Derby North East

DERBY NORTH EAST EDUCATION ACTION ZONE ORDER 2000, SI 2000 864; made under the School Standards and Framework Act 1998 s.10, s.11, s.138, Sch.1 para.2. In force: April 17, 2000; £2.00.

This Order establishes the Derby North East Education Action Zone and provides for the membership of the Education Action Forum for the zone.

1794. Education action zones – establishment – East Manchester

EAST MANCHESTER EDUCATION ACTION ZONE (VARIATION) ORDER 2000, SI 2000 3326; made under the School Standards and Framework Act 1998 s.10, s.11. In force: January 15, 2001; £1.50.

This Order varies the East Manchester Education Action Zone Order 1999 (SI 1999 3015) by adding Cedar Mount School to the schools which comprise the Zone and provides for circumstances in which members of the Forum may be removed from office.

1795. Education action zones – establishment – Great Yarmouth Achievement

GREAT YARMOUTH ACHIEVEMENT EDUCATION ACTION ZONE ORDER 2000, SI 2000 867; made under the School Standards and Framework Act 1998 s.10, s.11, s.138, Sch.1 para.2. In force: April 17, 2000; £2.00.

This Order establishes the Great Yarmouth Achievement Education Action Zone and provides for the membership of the Education Action Forum for the zone.

1796. Education action zones – establishment – Newham

NEWHAM EDUCATION ACTION ZONE (VARIATION) ORDER 2000, SI 2000 3337; made under the School Standards and Framework Act 1998 s.10, s.11. In force: January 15, 2001; £1.50.

This Order varies the Newham Education Action Zone Order 1998 (SI 1998 1960) by adding Britannia Village Primary School to the schools which comprise the Zone and provides for circumstances in which members of the Forum may be removed from office.

1797. Education action zones – establishment – North Stockton Community

NORTH STOCKTON COMMUNITY EDUCATION ACTION ZONE ORDER 2000, SI 2000 866; made under the School Standards and Framework Act 1998 s.10, s.11, s.138, Sch.1 para.2. In force: April 17, 2000; £2.00.

This Order establishes the North Stockton Community Education Action Zone and provides for the membership of the Education Action Forum for the zone.

1798. Education action zones – establishment – North West Shropshire

NORTH WEST SHROPSHIRE EDUCATION ACTION ZONE (NO.2) ORDER 2000, SI 2000 422; made under the School Standards and Framework Act 1998 s.10, s.11, s.138, Sch.1 para.2. In force: Art.1, Art.3: 000229; remainder: 000403; £2.00.

This Order, which revokes and replaces the North West Shropshire Education Action Zone Order 2000 (SI 2000 295), establishes the North West Shropshire Education Action Zone and provides for the membership of the Education Action Forum for the zone.

1799. Education action zones – establishment – South East Sheffield

ACTION FOR EDUCATION AND EMPLOYMENT SOUTH EAST SHEFFIELD EDUCATION ACTION ZONE ORDER 2000, SI 2000 863; made under the School Standards and Framework Act 1998 s.10, s.11, s.138, Sch.1 para.2. In force: April 17, 2000; £1.50.

This Order establishes the Action for Education and Employment South East Sheffield Education Action Zone and provides for the membership of the Education Action Forum for the zone.

1800. Education action zones – establishment – South of England

SOUTH OF ENGLAND VIRTUAL EDUCATION ACTION ZONE (NO.2) ORDER 2000, SI 2000 423; made under the School Standards and Framework Act 1998 s.10, s.11, s.138, Sch.1 para.2. In force: Art.1, Art.3: 000229; remainder: 000403; £2.00.

This Order, which revokes and replaces the South of England Virtual Education Action Zone Order 2000 (SI 2000 296), establishes the South of England Virtual Education Action Zone and provides for the membership of the Education Action Forum for the zone.

1801. Education action zones – establishment – Westminster

WESTMINSTER EDUCATION ACTION ZONE ORDER 2000, SI 2000 1022; made under the School Standards and Framework Act 1998 s.10, s.11, s.138, Sch.1 para.2. In force: May 1, 2000; £2.00.

This Order establishes the Westminster Education Action Zone and provides for the membership of the Education Action Forum for the zone.

1802. Education action zones – establishment   Withernsea and Southern Holderness

WITHERNSEA AND SOUTHERN HOLDERNESS RURAL ACHIEVEMENT EDUCATION ACTION ZONE (AMENDMENT) ORDER 2000, SI 2000 3328; made under the School Standards and Framework Act 1998 s.10, s.11. In force: January 15, 2001; £1.50.

This Order, which amends the Withernsea and Southern Holderness Rural Achievement Education Action Zone Order 1999 (SI 1999 3400), provides for additional members to be appointed to the Education Action Forum for the zone. The Forum may now appoint an extra person representing the local community interests, and may also appoint a representative of the Local Education Authority's Joint Consultative Committee, a representative of the zone's schools' support staff and up to four representatives of teachers or of organisations representing teachers. In addition, it provides for circumstances in which members of the Forum may be removed from office.

1803. Education associations – dissolution – North East London

NORTH EAST LONDON EDUCATION ASSOCIATION (DISSOLUTION) ORDER 2000, SI 2000 3159; made under the School Inspection Act 1996 s.39, s.45. In force: December 15, 2000; £1.50.

This Order, which provides for the dissolution of the North East London Education Association on December 20, 2000, transfers property rights and liabilities of the Association to the Secretary of State.

1804. Education Transfer Council – dissolution

EDUCATION TRANSFER COUNCIL (WINDING UP) REGULATIONS 2000, SI 2000 2729; made under the School Standards and Framework Act 1998 s.137, s.138. In force: October 31, 2000; £1.50.

These Regulations make provision for the dissolution of the Education Transfer Council by order of the Secretary of State and for dealing with the property, rights and liabilities of the Council in connection with their dissolution. In particular, they deal with the preparation of a plan for the disposal of the property of the Council, the exercise of the functions of the Council prior to the dissolution date and property, rights and liabilities of the Council on dissolution, legal proceedings and construction of documents.

1805. Educational institutions – educational awards – listed bodies

EDUCATION (LISTED BODIES) (ENGLAND) ORDER 2000, SI 2000 3332; made under the Education Reform Act 1988 s.216. In force: December 22, 2000; £2.50.

This Order, which amends the Education (Listed Bodies) Order 1999 (SI 1999 834), lists the name of each body which is not a recognised body within the Education Reform Act 1988 s.214(2)(a) or (b) but which either provides any course which is in preparation for a degree to be granted by such a recognised body and is approved by or on behalf of that body; or is a constituent college, school, hall or other institution of a university which is such a recognised body. Recognised bodies are universities, colleges or other bodies which are authorised by Royal Charter or by or under Act of Parliament to grant degrees and other bodies for the time being permitted by these bodies to act on their behalf in the granting of degrees.

1806. Educational institutions – recognised bodies – degrees

EDUCATION (RECOGNISED BODIES) (ENGLAND) ORDER 2000, SI 2000 3327; made under the Education Reform Act 1988 s.216. In force: December 22, 2000; £2.00.

This Order lists all those bodies which appear to the Secretary of State to be recognised bodies within the Education Reform Act 1988 s.214(2)(a) or (b). These are universities, colleges or other bodies which are authorised by Royal Charter or by or under Act of Parliament to grant degrees and other bodies for the time being permitted by these bodies to act on their behalf in the granting of degrees. An award granted by such a body is not an award of a kind referred to in s.214(1), which makes it an offence to grant, offer to grant, or issue any invitation relating to certain unrecognised degrees and awards.

1807. Educational institutions – transfer of property

EDUCATION (NEW PROCEDURES FOR PROPERTY TRANSFERS) REGULATIONS 2000, SI 2000 3209; made under the School Standards and Framework Act 1998 s.137, s.138, s.144. In force: January 1, 2001; £3.00.

These Regulations make provision for dealing with transfers of property, rights and liabilities under various provisions in the Education Reform Act 1988, the Further and Higher Education Act 1992 and the School Standards and Framework Act 1998 when the Education Transfer Council has been dissolved.

1808. Foreign nationals – discrimination – refusal by local education authority to give full educational grant – action for damages under Race Relations Act inappropriate

[Race Relations Act 1976.]

N, a Swedish national, claimed damages under the Race Relations Act 1976 against W, the LEA, for discrimination contrary to EC law, following W's refusal to give her a full educational grant. N contended that her claim was similar to that available to a British national in domestic law and invited the court to grant the relief provided for such claims under the Act.

Held, refusing to grant the relief sought, that there were no legitimate grounds for bringing the action for damages under the Act, firstly because, in the absence of any Community mechanism for the domestic law of each Member State to make rules for the assertion of Community rights, such an action was ill founded, and secondly because the Act did not cover the circumstances in which N's claim had arisen.

NABADDA v. WESTMINSTER CITY COUNCIL; GOMILSEK v. HARINGEY LBC [2000] I.C.R. 951, Buxton, L.J., CA.

1809. Further education – colleges – governance – Wiltshire College

WILTSHIRE COLLEGE (GOVERNMENT) REGULATIONS 2000, SI 2000 2173; made under the Further and Higher Education Act 1992 s.20, s.21, s.89, Sch.4. In force: September 1, 2000; £3.00.

These Regulations prescribe the form of the instrument of government and articles of government for Wiltshire College.

1810. Further education – governors powers and duties – grounds for removal of academic staff member

[Education (Government of Further Education Corporations) Regulations 1992 (SI 1992 1957) Sch.1.]

B, a lecturer at CB, was appointed to the board of governors as an academic staff member for a term of four years from November 1995. In that year, CB introduced a code of conduct for governors which dealt with matters such as the expectation that members would stand by decisions even if they disagreed with them and a statement of the general principle of openness and accountability, subject to confidentiality over sensitive matters. New board members did not have to sign the code, but it was expected that they would do so as it was seen as a statement of good practice. In addition, cl.13(4) of the instrument of government, contained in the Education (Government of Further Education Corporations) Regulations 1992 Sch.1, provided that an academic staff board member had to withdraw from any board meetings at which his own remuneration or terms and conditions of service were to be discussed. B found himself in disagreement with his fellow board members from the commencement of his term, and after attending three meetings, the board resolved to terminate his membership in accordance with cl.9(2)(b) of the instrument, on the grounds that he had refused to accept the conditions of membership, and that the governors had lost confidence in him. Following a complaint by B to the Secretary of State, his removal was reconsidered and again confirmed in February 1998, this time on the basis that the board's effectiveness had been adversely affected by his inability to accept the membership conditions. The main complaints against B concerned his refusal to accept the chairman's rulings on confidentiality; his refusal to sign the code of conduct; his refusal to withdraw from meetings dealing with staff pay at a time when he was on the union negotiating team; his personal attacks on the principal and his failure to support the collective view of the board. J sought judicial review of the decision to remove him from the board, contending that it was tainted with procedural unfairness and based on a mistake of law.

Held, refusing the application, that (1) the decision was not vitiated by the express failure to mention the statutory grounds of B's unfitness or inability to discharge his board functions. Considered against the whole factual background, it was clear that the board had decided that B was unfit to be a member by reason of his unwillingness to accept the conditions of board membership; (2) the instrument of government was not an exhaustive code. In particular, cl.13 did not prohibit a board from requiring a staff member to withdraw from meetings other than in the circumstances expressly stated. It followed that the board had acted properly in seeking to exclude B from board discussions about general staff terms and conditions. In any event, the main complaint against B was not the fact of his disagreement, but his manner of pursuing it, which evidenced a continuing and damaging refusal to accept the board's working practices. The board was therefore entitled to conclude that B was unfit to discharge his functions as a member; (3) similarly, B's refusal to sign the code showed that he was unable to discharge his functions, notwithstanding that he was not legally obliged to do so; (4) B's membership of the union negotiating team exposed him to a clear conflict of interest and the board's decision on this matter could not be criticised; (5) the board had been entitled to regard B's criticisms of the principal as a relevant factor in determining his fitness. Since college well being depended on mutual trust between the principal and the board, the board had clearly been right to take B's personal attacks into account, and (6) examined either individually or collectively, the various complaints made by the board against B showed no error in reasoning which was susceptible to judicial review.

R. v. CITY OF BATH COLLEGE CORP, *ex p.* BASHFORTH [1999] E.L.R. 459, Dyson, J., QBD.

1811. Further education corporations – dissolution – Chippenham, Lackham and Trowbridge Colleges

CHIPPENHAM, LACKHAM AND TROWBRIDGE COLLEGES (DISSOLUTION) ORDER 2000, SI 2000 2728; made under the Further and Higher Education Act 1992 s.27. In force: November 1, 2000; £1.50.

This Order dissolves the further education corporations established to conduct Chippenham College, Lackham College, Wiltshire and Trowbridge College. It provides for the transfer of the property, rights and liabilities of each corporation to Wiltshire College, and secures the rights of its employees by applying the Further and Higher Education Act 1992 s.26(2) to (4).

1812. **Further education corporations – dissolution – College of Care and Early Education**

COLLEGE OF CARE AND EARLY EDUCATION (DISSOLUTION) ORDER 2000, SI 2000 1806; made under the Further and Higher Education Act 1992 s.27. In force: August 1, 2000; £1.00.

This Order, which dissolves the further education corporation established to conduct the College of Care and Early Education, provides for the transfer of its property, rights and liabilities to City of Bristol College and secures the rights of its employees by applying the Further and Higher Education Act 1992 s.26(2)(3)(4).

1813. **Further education corporations – dissolution – Hendon College**

HENDON COLLEGE (DISSOLUTION) ORDER 2000, SI 2000 1751; made under the Further and Higher Education Act 1992 s.27. In force: August 1, 2000; £1.00.

This Order, which dissolves the further education corporation established to conduct Hendon College, provides for the transfer of its property, rights and liabilities to Barnet College and secures the rights of its employees by applying the Further and Higher Education Act 1992 s.26(2)(3)(4).

1814. **Further education corporations – dissolution – Kingsway: Camden's College**

KINGSWAY: CAMDEN'S COLLEGE (DISSOLUTION) ORDER 2000, SI 2000 2172; made under the Further and Higher Education Act 1992 s.27. In force: September 1, 2000; £1.00.

This Order, which dissolves the further education corporation established to conduct Kingsway: Camden's College, provides for the transfer of its property, rights and liabilities to Westminster College, London and secures the rights of its employees by applying the Further and Higher Education Act 1992 s.26(2)(3)(4).

1815. **Further education corporations – dissolution – Melton Mowbray College**

MELTON MOWBRAY COLLEGE (DISSOLUTION) ORDER 2000, SI 2000 2124; made under the Further and Higher Education Act 1992 s.27. In force: September 1, 2000; £1.00.

This Order, which dissolves the further education corporation established to conduct Melton Mowbray College, provides for the transfer of its property, rights and liabilities to Brooksby College, Melton Mowbray and secures the rights of its employees by applying the Further and Higher Education Act 1992 s.26(2)(3)(4).

1816. **Further education corporations – dissolution – Pencoed College – Wales**

PENCOED COLLEGE (DISSOLUTION) ORDER 2000, SI 2000 974 (W.44); made under the Further and Higher Education Act 1992 s.27. In force: April 1, 2000; £1.50.

This Order dissolves the further education corporation established to conduct Pencoed College. It provides for its property, rights and liabilities to transfer to Bridgend College of Technology Further Education Corporation and secures the rights of its employees by applying the Further and Higher Education Act 1992 s.26(2) to s.26(4).

1817. **Further education corporations – dissolution – Phoenix College**

PHOENIX COLLEGE (DISSOLUTION) ORDER 2000, SI 2000 354; made under the Further and Higher Education Act 1992 s.27. In force: April 1, 2000; £1.00.

This Order dissolves the further education corporation established to conduct Phoenix College. It provides for the transfer of its property, rights and liabilities to Merton College, Morden and secures the rights of its employees.

1818. Further education corporations – dissolution – Rutland Sixth Form College

RUTLAND SIXTH FORM COLLEGE, OAKHAM (DISSOLUTION) ORDER 2000, SI 2000 1684; made under the Further and Higher Education Act 1992 s.27. In force: August 1, 2000; £1.00.

This Order dissolves with effect from August 1, 2000 the further education corporation established to conduct Rutland Sixth Form College, Oakham. It provides for the transfer of its property, rights and liabilities to Tresham Institute, Kettering, and secures the rights of its employees by applying the Further and Higher Education Act 1992 s.26 (2) (3) (4).

1819. Further education corporations – establishment – Wiltshire College

WILTSHIRE COLLEGE (INCORPORATION) ORDER 2000, SI 2000 2145; made under the Further and Higher Education Act 1992 s.16, s.17. In force: September 1, 2000; £1.00.

This Order establishes a further education corporation called Wiltshire College under the Further and Higher Education Act 1992 s.16(1) for the purpose of conducting the educational institution called by the same name and appoints November 1, 2000 as the operative date for the purposes of Part 1 of that Act.

1820. Further Education Funding Councils – additional functions

FURTHER EDUCATION FUNDING COUNCIL FOR ENGLAND (SUPPLEMENTARY FUNCTIONS) (AMENDMENT) ORDER 2000, SI 2000 2143; made under the Further and Higher Education Act 1992 s.8. In force: September 1, 2000; £1.00.

This Order amends the Further Education Funding Council for England (Supplementary Functions) Order 1999 (SI 1999 2269) by conferring on the Further Education Funding Council for England functions exerciseable in connection with the Education (Grants) (Dance and Drama) (England) Regulations 2000 (SI 2000 2144) as well as the Education (Grants) (Dance and Drama) (England) Regulations 1999 (SI 1999 2264), and the functions of specifying requirements which must be complied with under the Dance and Drama Regulations.

1821. Grants – assisted places – incidental expenses

EDUCATION (ASSISTED PLACES) (INCIDENTAL EXPENSES) (AMENDMENT) (ENGLAND) REGULATIONS 2000, SI 2000 2112; made under the Education (Schools) Act 1997 s.3. In force: September 1, 2000; £1.00.

These Regulations amend the Education (Assisted Places) (Incidental Expenses) Regulations 1997 (SI 1997 1969) in relation to England and in respect of a school year beginning on or after September 1, 2000, by relaxing the means test and increasing the amount of grant payable for uniform grant in respect of clothing expenditure incurred in relation to the 2000/2001 and subsequent school years. They provide that £71 is payable where the relevant income does not exceed £10,901 and £37 is payable where the relevant income exceeds that figure but does not exceed £11,718. In addition, they relax the means test for travel grant and increase the amount of grant payable.

1822. Grants – assisted places – incidental expenses – Wales

EDUCATION (ASSISTED PLACES) (INCIDENTAL EXPENSES) AMENDMENT (WALES) REGULATIONS 2000, SI 2000 1939 (W.137); made under the Education (Schools) Act 1997 s.3. In force: September 1, 2000; £1.50.

These Regulations amend the Education (Assisted Places) (Incidental Expenses) Regulations 1997 (SI 1997 1969) in respect of a school year beginning on or after September 1, 2000 by relaxing the means test and increasing the uniform grant payable in respect of clothing expenditure incurred in relation to the 2000/2001 and subsequent school years. In addition, they relax the means test for travel grant and increase the amount of grant payable.

1823. **Grants – assisted places – qualifying income limits**

EDUCATION (ASSISTED PLACES) (AMENDMENT) (ENGLAND) REGULATIONS 2000, SI 2000 2111; made under the Education (Schools) Act 1997 s.3. In force: September 1, 2000; £1.50.

These Regulations amend the Education (Assisted Places) Regulations 1997 (SI 1997 1968) in respect of a school year beginning on or after September 1, 2000. They increase the reductions to be made in relevant income in relation to dependent relatives under Reg.10(4)(6) from £1,300 to £1,400 and relax the means test for the remission of fees. The level of income at or below which fees are to be wholly remitted is set at £10,901 instead of £10,670.

1824. **Grants – assisted places – qualifying income limits – Wales**

EDUCATION (ASSISTED PLACES) AMENDMENT (WALES) REGULATIONS 2000, SI 2000 1938 (W.136); made under the Education (Schools) Act 1997 s.3. In force: September 1, 2000; £1.50.

These Regulations amend the Education (Assisted Places) Regulations 1997 (SI 1997 1968) in respect of a school year beginning on or after September 1, 2000 by increasing from £1,300 to £1,400 the deduction to be made in "relevant" income in relation to dependent relatives under Reg.10(4)(6) of the 1997 Regulations. In addition, the level of income at or below which fees are to be wholly remitted is set at £10,901 instead of £10,670 with corresponding increases in the extent of remission where "relevant" income exceeds that sum.

1825. **Grants – disabled students – additional expenditure**

EDUCATION (GRANTS FOR DISABLED POSTGRADUATE STUDENTS) REGULATIONS 2000 (AMENDMENT) REGULATIONS 2000, SI 2000 3087; made under the Teaching and Higher Education Act 1998 s.22, s.42, s.43. In force: December 11, 2000; £1.75.

These Regulations, which amend the Education (Grants for Disabled Postgraduate Students) Regulations 2000 (SI 2000 2330), provide for grants to eligible students undertaking designated courses whether they attend their courses or whether they pursue their courses through open learning. They provide that a person is ineligible for a grant where the payment received from his institution to meet additional costs incurred due to his disability is part of an allowance, bursary or other such award made by his institution and that eligible students must be ordinarily resident in England and Wales on the first day of each academic year, not just at the start of the course.

1826. **Grants – disabled students – additional expenditure**

EDUCATION (GRANTS FOR DISABLED POSTGRADUATE STUDENTS) REGULATIONS 2000, SI 2000 2330; made under the Teaching and Higher Education Act 1998 s.22, s.42, s.43. In force: September 22, 2000; £2.00.

These Regulations make provision for grants to disabled postgraduate students to meet additional expenditure incurred in attending their courses by reason of their disability. They provide for the method of application for grant, transfers between courses, termination of eligibility and the provision of information by students to the Secretary of State for the purpose of exercising his functions under the Regulations, on a similar basis to those applying to undergraduate student support, and enable the Secretary of State to pay grant at such time and in such manner as he considers appropriate.

1827. **Grants – education maintenance allowances**

EDUCATION MAINTENANCE ALLOWANCE (PILOT AREAS) REGULATIONS 2000, SI 2000 2012; made under the Education Act 1996 s.518, s.569. In force: August 21, 2000; £3.00.

These Regulations, which revoke and replace the Education Maintenance Allowance (Pilot Areas) Regulations 1999 (SI 1999 2168) and the Education

Maintenance Allowance (Pilot Areas) (Amendment) Regulations 2000 (SI 2000 838), provide for the payment of allowances by specified local education authorities in respect of students over compulsory school age. In particular, they set down conditions relating to residence and income and prescribe further circumstances in which the allowances can be paid.

1828. **Grants – education maintenance allowances**

EDUCATION MAINTENANCE ALLOWANCE (PILOT AREAS) (AMENDMENT) REGULATIONS 2000, SI 2000 838; made under the Education Act 1996 s.518, s.569. In force: April 17, 2000; £1.00.

These Regulations amend the Education Maintenance Allowance (Pilot Areas) Regulations 1999 (SI 1999 2168) to correct a drafting error and to change the provisions which apply for payment of a weekly allowance where a week falls partly outside the term of an institution.

1829. **Grants – education standards**

EDUCATION STANDARDS FUND (ENGLAND) REGULATIONS 2000, SI 2000 703; made under the Education Act 1996 s.484, s.489, s.569. In force: April 1, 2000; £3.00.

These Regulations, which revoke and replace the Education (Education Standards Etc. Grants) (England) Regulations 1999 (SI 1999 606), revise, delete or amend some of the purposes for which grants are payable by the Secretary of State to local education authorities in England.

1830. **Grants – education standards**

EDUCATION STANDARDS FUND (ENGLAND) (AMENDMENT) REGULATIONS 2000, SI 2000 2332; made under the Education Act 1995 s.484, s.489, s.569. In force: September 22, 2000; £1.50.

These Regulations amend the Education Standards Fund (England) Regulations 2000 (SI 2000 703) by adding seven new purposes for or in connection with which grants are payable. The new purposes relate to the transforming Key Stage 3 pilot programme, extra support for teaching of literacy and numeracy to some Key Stage 2 pupils, the development of Excellence in Cities plans, planning and establishing a fresh start school, improving the standards of education of pupils whose parents are asylum seekers, support for pupils with behavioural difficulties admitted in-year to schools in the Excellence in Cities project and improving standards at Key Stage 4 through partnership arrangements between schools. In addition, they provide for a new list of additional education authorities.

1831. **Grants – education standards**

EDUCATION STANDARDS FUND (ENGLAND) (AMENDMENT NO.2) REGULATIONS 2000, SI 2000 3329; made under the Education Act 1996 s.484, s.569. In force: January 12, 2001; £1.50.

These Regulation, which amend the Education Standards Fund (England) Regulations 2000 (SI 2000 703), add two new purposes for or in connection with which grant is payable. The new purposes relate to developing and extending the services offered by maintained nursery schools and schemes by LEAs to pilot new methods of providing education services.

1832. **Grants – education standards – Wales**

EDUCATION (EDUCATION STANDARDS GRANTS) (WALES) REGULATIONS 2000, SI 2000 834 (W.32); made under the Education Act 1996 s.484, s.489, s.569. In force: April 1, 2000; £3.00.

These Regulations, which revoke and replace, with amendments, the Education (Education Standards Grants) (Wales) Regulations 1999 (SI 1999 521), provide for the payment of grants, under the Education Act 1996 s.484, in respect of expenditure incurred by local education authorities for or in connection with educational purposes which are deemed to be in the interests of education in Wales by the National Assembly for Wales.

1833. Grants – higher education – discretionary grant refused – evidence of financial hardship

[Education Act 1962 s.1, s.2.]

R applied for a discretionary grant to enable her to undertake a higher education diploma course in the performing arts. Her application and subsequent appeal were turned down twice. She was told that a discretionary award could only be made if she could demonstrate exceptional circumstances as set out in the guidance notes. Her third application was refused on the ground that she had failed to provide any evidence of her family's financial hardship. R sought judicial review of the decision on the ground, that the financial information, which showed that she was experiencing severe financial hardship, had been before the sub committee in her previous applications.

Held, granting the application, quashing the decision and remitting the matter to the sub committee for reconsideration of the financial information submitted by R in support of her first two applications. The sub committee's decision had been based on the erroneous fact that R had provided no details of her financial position.

R. v. BIRMINGHAM CITY COUNCIL, *ex p.* REECE [1999] E.L.R. 373, Dyson, J., QBD.

1834. Grants – mandatory awards

EDUCATION (MANDATORY AWARDS) REGULATIONS 2000 (AMENDMENT) REGULATIONS 2000, SI 2000 2825; made under the Education Act 1962 s.1, s.4. In force: November 7, 2000; £1.50.

These Regulations amend the Mandatory Awards Regulations 2000 (SI 2000 2123) so that grant may be paid in respect of a dependent child who attends a city academy and to extend the disregard of grants to students to facilitate teacher training, in calculating their income, to payments in respect of such training by institutions which receive funding under the Further and Higher Education Act 1992 s.65(3). •

1835. Grants – mandatory awards

EDUCATION (MANDATORY AWARDS) REGULATIONS 2000, SI 2000 2123; made under the Education Act 1962 s.1, s.4, Sch.1 para.3, Sch.1 para.4; and the Education Act 1973 s.3. In force: September 1, 2000; £6.30.

These Regulations, which revoke and replace the Education (Mandatory Awards) Regulations 1999 (SI 1999 1494 as amended), provide expressly that members of the armed forces are treated as falling within the temporary employment abroad exemption from the residence conditions of Reg.13; provide that a new grant is available for a student who is entitled to receive a dependant's grant in respect of a dependent child; and extend the requirement to disregard grants to students to facilitate their training as teachers, in ascertaining the student's income, to payments in respect of such training by institutions receiving funding under the Education Act 1994 s.5 for students starting postgraduate courses of initial teacher training in the academic year 2000/2001. In addition, they make provision relating to the calculation of an eligible student's income for the purposes of determining his contribution.

1836. Grants – Purcell School

EDUCATION (GRANTS) (PURCELL SCHOOL) REGULATIONS 2000, SI 2000 3160; made under the Education Act 1996 s.485, s.489. In force: January 1, 2001; £1.50.

These Regulations authorise the Secretary of State to pay a grant to the Governors of the Purcell School, to help meet the expenditure incurred in refurbishing the school's premises at Aldenham Road, Bushey, Hertfordshire.

1837. Grants – Royal Ballet School

EDUCATION (GRANTS) (ROYAL BALLET SCHOOL) REGULATIONS 2000, SI 2000 443; made under the Education Act 1996 s.485, s.489. In force: March 17, 2000; £1.00.

These Regulations authorise the Secretary of State to pay on or before March 31, 2000, a grant to the governors of the Royal Ballet School of 155 Talgarth Road, Barons Court, London W14 9DE, in respect of expenditure to be incurred by them in acquiring and transferring to new premises for the Upper Division of the School.

1838. Grants – schools for performing arts

EDUCATION (GRANTS) (MUSIC, BALLET AND CHOIR SCHOOLS) (AMENDMENT) (ENGLAND) REGULATIONS 2000, SI 2000 2113; made under the Education Act 1996 s.485, s.489, s.569. In force: September 1, 2000; £1.00.

These Regulations amend the Education (Grants) (Music, Ballet and Choir Schools) Regulations 1995 (SI 1995 2018) by increasing to £1,400 the reduction to be made in relevant income in respect of dependent relatives; relaxing the means test for the remission of fees, uniform grant and travel grant; and increasing the amount of uniform and travel grant payable.

1839. Grants – students – calculation of parental contribution

EDUCATION (STUDENT SUPPORT) REGULATIONS 2000 (AMENDMENT) REGULATIONS 2000, SI 2000 1490; made under the Teaching and Higher Education Act 1998 s.22, s.42, s.43. In force: June 28, 2000; £1.00.

These Regulations amend the Education (Student Support) Regulations 2000 (SI 2000 1121) Sch.3, Part II. They provide, in the case of a student whose course begins before September 1, 2000, for the gross amount of loan interest on which relief is given under the Income Tax Acts to be deducted in determining the parent's residual income for the purposes of ascertaining the parental contribution under the Regulations.

1840. Grants – students – eligibility

EDUCATION (STUDENT SUPPORT) REGULATIONS 2000 (AMENDMENT) (NO.2) REGULATIONS 2000, SI 2000 2142; made under the Teaching and Higher Education Act 1998 s.22, s.42, s.43. In force: September 1, 2000; £1.50.

These Regulations amend the Education (Student Support) Regulations 2000 (SI 2000 1121) by introducing a definition of end-on courses and providing that certain provisions of the 2000 Regulations do not affect students attending an end-on course. In addition, provision is made in relation to dependent children, hardship loans and teacher training grants.

1841. Grants – students – eligibility

EDUCATION (STUDENT SUPPORT) REGULATIONS 2000 (AMENDMENT) (NO.3) REGULATIONS 2000, SI 2000 2912; made under the Teaching and Higher Education Act 1998 s.22, s.42, s.43. In force: November 21, 2000; £1.75.

These Regulations amend the Education (Student Support) Regulations 2000 (SI 2000 1121) by providing for support for students undertaking part time designated courses whether they attend the course or whether they pursue the course through open learning. However, students must still attend designated courses in order to be eligible for full time support. In addition, they insert an additional eligibility criterion for part time students; exclude prisoners serving custodial sentences from eligibility for loans and grants for disabled part time students' living costs; provide that where the student has already made an application for a loan after his eligibility has been converted from that of an eligible student under Part II of the 2000 Regulations, he may apply further for the maximum amount of loan or increased maximum to which he was entitled under Reg.20; and extend the disregard of grants to students to facilitate teacher training, in calculating their income, to payments in respect of such training by institutions which receive funding under the Further and Higher Education Act 1992 s.65(3).

1842. Grants – students – eligibility

EDUCATION (STUDENT SUPPORT) REGULATIONS 2000, SI 2000 1121; made under the Teaching and Higher Education Act 1998 s.22, s.42, s.43. In force: May 11, 2000; £7.30.

These Regulations provide for support for students attending higher education courses beginning on or after September 1, 2000. In particular, they prohibit a student, in respect of whom the first academic year of the course begins on or after September 1, 2000, from receiving support at any one time for more than one designated course or for a designated course and a designated part-time course and enable a student who has not applied for support in respect of his attendance at a designated course in the first academic year of his course to do so in a subsequent academic year. A new grant is available for a student who is entitled to receive a dependant's grant in respect of a dependent child.

1843. Grants – students – eligibility – European institutions

EDUCATION (STUDENT SUPPORT) (EUROPEAN INSTITUTIONS) REGULATIONS 2000, SI 2000 2197; made under the Teaching and Higher Education Act 1998 s.22, s.42, s.43. In force: September 1, 2000; £2.00.

These Regulations, which amend the Education (Student Support) (European Institutions) Regulations 1999 (SI 1999 2270), make provision for grants by the Secretary of State for postgraduate study at three European institutions: the College of Europe, the European University Institute and the Bologna Centre. In particular, they amend the eligibility criteria to take account of the fact that eligible students will not be resident in England and Wales on the first day of their course; provide that living costs for the College of Europe allow for variations in the number of extra weeks for the academic year 2000-2001; make provision in relation to eligibility for grants for dependants and disabled students' living costs; and provide that where a student is absent from his course for more than 60 days because of illness or is absent for any other reason, he will not be eligible to receive support except at the Secretary of State's discretion.

1844. Grants – students – eligibility – European institutions

EDUCATION (STUDENT SUPPORT) (EUROPEAN INSTITUTIONS) (AMENDMENT) REGULATIONS 2000, SI 2000 923; made under the Teaching and Higher Education Act 1998 s.22, s.42, s.43. In force: April 21, 2000; £1.50.

These Regulations amend the Education (Student Support) (European Institutions) Regulations 1999 (SI 1999 2270) to include an additional eligibility requirement that, where a student has previously undertaken postgraduate study of more than two years, an award will not normally be made in respect of any of the three institutions, and to include further provisions for travel costs at the College of Europe.

1845. Grants – students – eligibility – European institutions

EDUCATION (STUDENT SUPPORT) (EUROPEAN INSTITUTIONS) (AMENDMENT) (NO.2) REGULATIONS 2000, SI 2000 1407; made under the Teaching and Higher Education Act 1998 s.22, s.43. In force: July 1, 2000; £1.00.

These Regulations amend the Education (Student Support) (European Institutions) Regulations 1999 (SI 1999 2270 as amended) by correcting an error in the drafting of Reg.3(1)(e).

1846. Grants – students – performing arts

EDUCATION (GRANTS) (DANCE AND DRAMA) (ENGLAND) REGULATIONS 2000, SI 2000 2144; made under the Education Act 1996 s.485, s.489, s.569. In force: September 1, 2000; £2.00.

These Regulations, which revoke and replace the Education (Dance and Drama) (England) Regulations 1999 (SI 1999 2264), provide for grants to be paid by the Secretary of State to specified institutions, in respect of dance and drama students selected by the institutions.

1847. Grants – students – performing arts

EDUCATION (GRANTS) (DANCE AND DRAMA) (ENGLAND) (AMENDMENT) REGULATIONS 2000, SI 2000 2240; made under the Education Act 1996 s.485, s.569. In force: September 1, 2000; £1.00.

These Regulations amend the Education (Grants) (Dance and Drama) (England) Regulations 2000 (SI 2000 2144) by making an alteration to one of the figures in the Table in Sch.2.

1848. Grants – Wells Cathedral School

EDUCATION (GRANTS) (WELLS CATHEDRAL SCHOOL) REGULATIONS 2000, SI 2000 2115; made under the Education Act 1996 s.485, s.489. In force: September 1, 2000; £1.00.

These Regulations authorise the Secretary of State to pay a grant to the Governors of the Wells Cathedral School, to help meet the expenditure to be incurred by them in acquiring additional new premises for the School. Payment is subject to such conditions and requirements as the Secretary of State may specify.

1849. Higher education corporations – dissolution – Kent College for the Careers Service

COLLEGE OF GUIDANCE STUDIES HIGHER EDUCATION CORPORATION (DISSOLUTION) ORDER 2000, SI 2000 1383; made under the Education Reform Act 1988 s.128. In force: August 1, 2000; £1.00.

This Order dissolves the College of Guidance Studies higher education corporation originally established as Kent College for the Careers Service. It provides for its property, rights and liabilities to transfer to Canterbury Christ Church University College and secures the rights of employees by applying the Education Reform Act 1988 s.127.

1850. Higher education corporations – dissolution – North Riding College

NORTH RIDING COLLEGE HIGHER EDUCATION CORPORATION (DISSOLUTION) ORDER 2000, SI 2000 355; made under the Education Reform Act 1988 s.128. In force: August 1, 2000; £1.00.

This Order dissolves North Riding College higher education corporation, provides that the property, rights and liabilities of the dissolved corporation transfer to the University of Hull and secures the rights of employees.

1851. Independent schools – school exclusions – exclusion decision not susceptible to judicial review – specific performance not available for contract between school and fee paying parents

L, a pupil at IFE, an independent co-educational day school, unsuccessfully appealed to a committee of school governors against a decision to exclude her following allegations of theft. L's parents made an application for interim relief in the form of a mandatory order requiring IFE to accept L back pending the outcome of an application for judicial review of the decision to exclude her. A mandatory order was made ex parte and when the matter returned before the court, IFE applied for its discharge on the ground that, as a private body, it was not susceptible to judicial review. L's parents had also issued a notice of motion seeking a mandatory injunction requiring specific performance of the contract between IFE and themselves as fee payers. The affidavit evidence showed that L had been accepted back into the school by her fellow pupils and her immediate teachers.

Held, discharging the mandatory order and refusing the judicial review application, that (1) although IFE operated within a statutory framework, the relationship between IFE and its students was founded on the contract between the school and the fee paying parents. Such a contract was completely private and had no statutory basis, and it followed that such schools were not public bodies. The only remedy available to parents in such cases was to seek a declaration that some of their contractual rights had been infringed because of the manner in which the school had treated their child, *R. v. Fernhill Manor School, ex p. A* [1993] 1 F.L.R. 620, [1993] C.L.Y. 1683 applied. There was accordingly no basis for any judicial review application in the instant case and the interim injunction would be discharged, and (2) in the context of private contractual relationships, it was generally undesirable that specific performance should be used to maintain relationships notwithstanding the parties' earlier willingness to do so. Specific performance was an equitable remedy and the courts had a discretion as to whether it should be granted in any particular case. The courts would be particularly reluctant to exercise the discretion in favour of making an order where the contract involved daily personal contact, *CH Giles & Co Ltd v. Morris* [1972] 1 W.L.R. 307, [1972] C.L.Y. 520 applied. Leaving aside the supervisory difficulties, the instant case presented difficulties due to the breakdown of trust in the educational relationship.

R. v. INCORPORATED FROEBEL EDUCATIONAL INSTITUTE, *ex p.* L [1999] E.L.R. 488, Tucker, J., QBD.

1852. Learning and Skills Act 2000 (c.21)

This Act establishes the Learning and Skills Council for England and the National Council for Education and Training for Wales and makes other provision about education and training.

This Act received Royal Assent on July 28, 2000.

1853. Learning and Skills Act 2000 (c.21) – Commencement No.1 Order

LEARNING AND SKILLS ACT 2000 (COMMENCEMENT NO.1) ORDER 2000, SI 2000 2114 (C.56); made under the Learning and Skills Act 2000 s.154. Commencement details: bringing into force various provisions of the Act on August 3, 2000, August 10, 2000 and September 1, 2000; £1.50.

This Order brings into force various provisions of the Learning and Skills Act 2000 on August 3, 2000, August 10, 2000 and September 1, 2000.

1854. Learning and Skills Act 2000 (c.21) – Commencement No.1 Order – Wales

LEARNING AND SKILLS ACT 2000 (COMMENCEMENT NO.1) (WALES) ORDER 2000, SI 2000 2540 (W.163; C.70); made under the Learning and Skills

Act 2000 s.154. Commencement details: bringing into force various provisions of the Act on September 19, 2000; £2.00.

This Order brings into force certain provisions of the Learning and Skills Act 2000, which relate to the establishment of the National Council for Education and Training for Wales and consequential provisions. In addition, it brings into force Sch.4 of the Act which includes provisions relating to the membership, staffing, proceedings and accounting requirements of the Council.

1855. Learning and Skills Act 2000 (c.21) – Commencement No.2 Order

LEARNING AND SKILLS ACT 2000 (COMMENCEMENT NO.2 AND SAVINGS) ORDER 2000, SI 2000 2559 (C.73); made under the Learning and Skills Act 2000 s.152, s.154. Commencement details: bringing into force various provisions of the Act on October 1, 2000, November 1, 2000 and January 1, 2001; £1.50.

This Order brings certain provisions of the Learning and Skills Act 2000 into force on October 1, 2000, November 1, 2000, and January 1, 2001.

1856. Learning and Skills Act 2000 (c.21) – Commencement No.2 Order – Wales

LEARNING AND SKILLS ACT 2000 (COMMENCEMENT NO.2) (WALES) ORDER 2000, SI 2000 3230 (W.213; C.103); made under the Learning and Skills Act 2000 s.154. Commencement details: bringing into force various provisions of the Act on January 1, 2001; £2.00.

This Order brings into force certain provisions of the Learning and Skills Act 2000 in relation to Wales on January 1, 2001 which impose duties on the National Council for Education and Training for Wales; require the Council to have due regard to the promotion of equality of opportunity in the exercise of its functions; give the Council supplementary powers necessary to enable it to carry out its functions and to establish committees; empower the National Assembly to make schemes for the transfer to the Council of property, rights and liabilities associated with the acquisition by the Council of its functions; allow induction periods for teachers to be served in further education institutions in some circumstances; and empower the National Assembly to direct companies with whom it has contracted in respect of the provision of training not to take certain actions.

1857. Learning and Skills Council for England – interim functions

LEARNING AND SKILLS COUNCIL FOR ENGLAND (INTERIM FUNCTIONS) ORDER 2000, SI 2000 2117; made under the Learning and Skills Act 2000 Sch.10 para.5. In force: September 1, 2000; £1.50.

The Learning and Skills Act 2000 Sch.10 para.5 provides for the Secretary of State to confer powers on the Learning and Skills Council for England, if it is established before it acquires its full functions, to help it carry out its full functions when it acquires them. This Order confers power on the Council to do anything necessary or expedient in preparation for the exercise of functions under s.2, s.3, s.8, s.12(6) or s.13 of the Act when those sections come into force together with an associated power to give financial assistance.

1858. Local education authorities – budget statements

EDUCATION (BUDGET STATEMENTS) (ENGLAND) REGULATIONS 2000, SI 2000 576; made under the School Standards and Framework Act 1998 s.52, s.138. In force: March 6, 2000; £6.30.

These Regulations prescribe the form and contents of the budget statement of a local education authority in England for the financial year beginning on April 1, 2000.

1859. Local education authorities – expenditure – outturn statements

EDUCATION (OUTTURN STATEMENTS) (ENGLAND) REGULATIONS 2000, SI 2000 1974; made under the School Standards and Framework Act 1998 s.52, s.138, s.144. In force: August 21, 2000; £3.50.

These Regulations prescribe the form and content of the outturn statement of a local education authority in England, in relation to the financial year beginning on April 1, 1999, under the School Standards and Framework Act 1998 s.52(2). The statement gives details of expenditure by the local education authority, and of other resources allocated by them to schools which they maintain, during the financial year to which it relates.

1860. Local education authorities – expenditure – outturn statements – Wales

EDUCATION (OUTTURN STATEMENTS) (WALES) REGULATIONS 2000, SI 2000 1717 (W.117); made under the School Standards and Framework Act 1998 s.52, s.138, s.142. In force: July 31, 2000; £3.00.

These Regulations, which partially revoke the Education (School Financial Statements) (Prescribed Particulars etc.) Regulations 1995 (SI 1995 208 as amended) in relation to Wales, specify the information about local education authorities' expenditure on education which must be contained in an outturn statement required to be prepared by each LEA after the end of the financial year under the School Standards and Framework Act 1998 s.52(2). In addition, they specify the form which outturn statements must take and the manner of, and time for, publication of such statements.

1861. Local education authorities – post compulsory education awards

LOCAL EDUCATION AUTHORITY (POST-COMPULSORY EDUCATION AWARDS) (AMENDMENT) (ENGLAND) REGULATIONS 2000, SI 2000 2057; made under the Education Act 1996 s.518, s.569. In force: September 1, 2000; £1.50.

These Regulations, which amend the Local Education Authority (Post-Compulsory Education Awards) Regulations 1999 (SI 1999 299), provide LEAs with the power to grant post-compulsory education awards but this power does not apply in a financial year in relation to which an LEA has determined that it should not do so. In addition, they provide for the requirements for annual determinations, that the effect of them does not apply where the award is a "school access fund award", and that a determination made in respect of the 2000-01 financial year does not apply in respect of the granting of any school access fund award on or after September 1, 2000.

1862. Local education authorities – transfer of assets – Inner London Education Authority

EDUCATION (INNER LONDON EDUCATION AUTHORITY) (PROPERTY TRANSFER) (MODIFICATION) ORDER 2000, SI 2000 3161; made under the Education Reform Act 1988 s.187, s.231, s.232. In force: January 1, 2001; £1.75.

This Order modifies the effect of the Education (Inner London Education Authority) (Property Transfer) Order 1990 (SI 1990 124) so that Conditions A and C now cease to apply in their entirety.

1863. Local education authorities – transfer of assets – London Residuary Body

EDUCATION (LONDON RESIDUARY BODY) (PROPERTY TRANSFER) (AMENDMENT) ORDER 2000, SI 2000 2196; made under the Education Reform Act 1988 s.187, s.231, s.232. In force: September 1, 2000; £1.00.

This Order amends the Education (London Residuary Body) (Property Transfer) Order 1992 (SI 1992 587) Art.4(7), as amended, which imposes a condition that part of the site of the former Wandsworth Boys' Secondary School should be brought into use by the Council of the London Borough of Wandsworth as a site for a school by September 1, 2000. It substitutes a new date of September 1, 2003 as the date by which the part of the site subject to the condition must be brought into use as the site for a new school or as the site for a school transferring to that site.

1864. National Council for Education and Training for Wales – functions

NATIONAL COUNCIL FOR EDUCATION AND TRAINING FOR WALES (INTERIM FUNCTIONS) ORDER 2000, SI 2000 2539 (W.162); made under the Learning and Skills Act 2000 Sch.10 para.13. In force: September 19, 2000; £1.75.

This Order confers power on the National Council for Education and Training for Wales to do anything necessary or expedient in preparation for the exercise of functions under the Learning and Skills Act 2000 s.31, s.32, s.40(1)(6) and s.41 when those sections come into force together with an associated power to give financial assistance. The relevant functions are the Council's main duties in respect of education and training both for persons aged 16 to 19 years and for persons aged over 19 years, the Council's power to secure facilities for information, advice or guidance in connection with education or training and its duties with respect to persons with learning difficulties.

1865. National Curriculum – assessment arrangements – key stage 1

EDUCATION (NATIONAL CURRICULUM) (KEY STAGE 1 ASSESSMENT ARRANGEMENTS) (ENGLAND) (AMENDMENT) ORDER 2000, SI 2000 1242; made under the Education Act 1996 s.356, s.568. In force: April 28, 2000; £1.00.

This Order amends the Education (National Curriculum) (Key Stage 1 Assessment Arrangements) (England) Order 1999 (SI 1999 1236), which specifies the assessment arrangements for the core subjects in the final year of the first key stage, by introducing a statutory duty on the part of the head teacher to provide a signed statement to the local education authority confirming that the assessment arrangement test and tasks were administered in accordance with the provisions of the document in which they were published.

1866. National Curriculum – attainment targets – art – Wales

EDUCATION (NATIONAL CURRICULUM) (ATTAINMENT TARGETS AND PROGRAMMES OF STUDY IN ART) (WALES) ORDER 2000, SI 2000 1153 (W.84); made under the Education Act 1996 s.356. In force: August 1, 2000; £2.00.

The National Curriculum for Wales for Art will be revised from August 1, 2000. This Order, which revokes and replaces the Education (National Curriculum) (Attainment Targets and Programmes of Study in Art) (Wales) Order 1998 (SI 1998 1886), gives legal effect to the new programmes of study and attainment targets for them. Details of these are set out in a document entitled Art in the National Curriculum which is available from the Qualifications, Curriculum and Assessment Authority for Wales.

1867. National Curriculum – attainment targets – art and design

EDUCATION (NATIONAL CURRICULUM) (ATTAINMENT TARGETS AND PROGRAMMES OF STUDY IN ART AND DESIGN) (ENGLAND) ORDER 2000, SI 2000 1602; made under the Education Act 1996 s.356, s.568. In force: August 1, 2000; £1.00.

This Order, which revokes the Education (National Curriculum) (Attainment Targets and Programmes of Study in Art) (England) Order 1998 (SI 1998 1990), provides for the attainment targets and programmes of study set out in the document published by the Stationery Office entitled Attainment Targets and Programmes of Study in Art and Design to have effect for the purposes of specifying those elements of the national curriculum in art and design in relation to schools in England.

1868. **National Curriculum – attainment targets – citizenship**

EDUCATION (NATIONAL CURRICULUM) (ATTAINMENT TARGETS AND PROGRAMMES OF STUDY IN CITIZENSHIP) (ENGLAND) ORDER 2000, SI 2000 1603; made under the Education Act 1996 s.356, s.568. In force: August 1, 2002; £1.00.

This Order provides for the attainment target and programmes of study set out in the document published by the Stationery Office entitled Attainment Target and Programmes of Study in Citizenship to have effect for the purposes of specifying those elements of the national curriculum in citizenship in relation to schools in England.

1869. **National Curriculum – attainment targets – design and technology**

EDUCATION (NATIONAL CURRICULUM) (ATTAINMENT TARGETS AND PROGRAMMES OF STUDY IN DESIGN AND TECHNOLOGY) (ENGLAND) ORDER 2000, SI 2000 1599; made under the Education Act 1996 s.356, s.568. In force: August 1, 2000; £1.00.

This Order, which revokes the Education (National Curriculum) (Attainment Targets and Programmes of Study in Technology) (England) Order 1998 (SI 1998 1986), provides for for the attainment targets and programmes of study set out in the document published by the Stationery Office entitled Attainment Targets and Programmes of Study in Design and Technology to have effect for the purposes of specifying those elements of the national curriculum in design and technology in relation to schools in England.

1870. **National Curriculum – attainment targets – English**

EDUCATION (NATIONAL CURRICULUM) (ATTAINMENT TARGETS AND PROGRAMMES OF STUDY IN ENGLISH) (ENGLAND) ORDER 2000, SI 2000 1604; made under the Education Act 1996 s.356, s.568. In force: August 1, 2000; £1.00.

This Order, which revokes the Education (National Curriculum) (Attainment Targets and Programmes of Study in English) Order 1995 (SI 1995 51) provides for the attainment targets and programmes of study set out in the document published by the Stationery Office entitled Attainment Targets and Programmes of Study in English to have effect for the purposes of specifying those elements of the national curriculum in English in relation to schools in England.

1871. **National Curriculum – attainment targets – English – Wales**

EDUCATION (NATIONAL CURRICULUM) (ATTAINMENT TARGETS AND PROGRAMMES OF STUDY IN ENGLISH) (WALES) ORDER 2000, SI 2000 1154 (W.85); made under the Education Act 1996 s.356. In force: August 1, 2000; £2.00.

The National Curriculum for Wales for English will be revised from August 1, 2000. This Order, which revokes and replaces the Education (National Curriculum) (Attainment Targets and Programmes of Study in English) Order 1995 (SI 1995 51), gives legal effect to the new programmes of study and attainment targets for them. Details of these are set out in a document entitled English in the National Curriculum which is available from the Qualifications, Curriculum and Assessment Authority for Wales.

1872. **National Curriculum – attainment targets – geography**

EDUCATION (NATIONAL CURRICULUM) (ATTAINMENT TARGETS AND PROGRAMMES OF STUDY IN GEOGRAPHY) (ENGLAND) ORDER 2000, SI 2000 1605; made under the Education Act 1996 s.356, s.568. In force: August 1, 2000; £1.00.

This Order, which revokes the Education (National Curriculum) (Attainment Targets and Programmes of Study in Geography) (England) Order 1998 (SI 1998 1989), provides for the attainment targets and programmes of study set out in the document published by the Stationery Office entitled Attainment Targets and Programmes of Study in Geography to have effect for the purposes of specifying those elements of the national curriculum in geography in relation to schools in England.

1873. National Curriculum – attainment targets – geography – Wales

EDUCATION (NATIONAL CURRICULUM) (ATTAINMENT TARGETS AND PROGRAMMES OF STUDY IN GEOGRAPHY) (WALES) ORDER 2000, SI 2000 1155 (W.86); made under the Education Act 1996 s.356. In force: August 1, 2000; £2.00.

This Order, which revokes the Education (National Curriculum) (Attainment Targets and Programmes of Study in Geography) (Wales) Order 1998 (SI 1998 1885), provides for the attainment targets and programmes of study set out in the document entitled Geography in the National Curriculum, to have effect for the purposes of specifying those elements of the national curriculum in geography in relation to schools in Wales.

1874. National Curriculum – attainment targets – history

EDUCATION (NATIONAL CURRICULUM) (ATTAINMENT TARGETS AND PROGRAMMES OF STUDY IN HISTORY) (ENGLAND) ORDER 2000, SI 2000 1606; made under the Education Act 1996 s.356, s.568. In force: August 1, 2000; £1.00.

This Order, which revokes the Education (National Curriculum) (Attainment Targets and Programmes of Study in History) Order 1998 (SI 1998 1988), provides for the attainment targets and programmes of study set out in the document published by the Stationery Office entitled Attainment Targets and Programmes of Study in History to have effect for the purposes of specifying those elements of the national curriculum in history in relation to schools in England.

1875. National Curriculum – attainment targets – history – Wales

EDUCATION (NATIONAL CURRICULUM) (ATTAINMENT TARGETS AND PROGRAMMES OF STUDY IN HISTORY) (WALES) ORDER 2000, SI 2000 1156 (W.87); made under the Education Act 1996 s.356. In force: August 1, 2000; £2.00.

This Order, which revokes the Education (National Curriculum) (Attainment Targets and Programmes of Study in History) (Wales) Order 1998 (SI 1998 1888), provides for the attainment targets and programmes of study set out in the document entitled History in the National Curriculum, to have effect for the purposes of specifying those elements of the national curriculum in history in relation to schools in Wales.

1876. National Curriculum – attainment targets – information and communication technology

EDUCATION (NATIONAL CURRICULUM) (ATTAINMENT TARGETS AND PROGRAMMES OF STUDY IN INFORMATION AND COMMUNICATION TECHNOLOGY) (ENGLAND) ORDER 2000, SI 2000 1601; made under the Education Act 1996 s.356, s.568. In force: August 1, 2000; £1.00.

This Order, which revokes the Education (National Curriculum) (Attainment Targets and Programmes of Study in Technology) (England) Order 1998 (SI 1998 1986), provides for the attainment targets and programmes of study set out in the document published by the Stationery Office entitled Attainment Targets and Programmes of Study in Information and Communication Technology to have effect for the purposes of specifying those elements of the national curriculum in information and communication technology in relation to schools in England.

1877. National Curriculum – attainment targets – mathematics

EDUCATION (NATIONAL CURRICULUM) (ATTAINMENT TARGETS AND PROGRAMMES OF STUDY IN MATHEMATICS) (ENGLAND) ORDER 2000, SI 2000 1598; made under the Education Act 1996 s.356, s.568. In force: August 1, 2000; £1.00.

This Order, which revokes the Education (National Curriculum) (Attainment Targets and Programmes of Study in Mathematics) Order 1995 (SI 1995 52), provides for the attainment targets and programmes of study set out in the document published by the Stationery Office entitled Attainment Targets and Programmes of Study in Mathematics to have effect for the purposes of specifying those elements of the national curriculum for mathematics in relation to schools in England.

1878. National Curriculum – attainment targets – mathematics – Wales

EDUCATION (NATIONAL CURRICULUM) (ATTAINMENT TARGETS AND PROGRAMMES OF STUDY IN MATHEMATICS) (WALES) ORDER 2000, SI 2000 1100 (W.78); made under the Education Act 1996 s.356. In force: August 1, 2000; £2.00.

The National Curriculum for Wales for mathematics will be revised from August 1, 2000. This Order, which revokes and replaces the Education (National Curriculum) (Attainment Targets and Programmes of Study in Mathematics) Order 1995 (SI 1995 52), gives legal effect to the new programmes of study and attainment targets for them. Details of these are set out in a document entitled Mathematics in the National Curriculum which is available from the Qualifications, Curriculum and Assessment Authority for Wales.

1879. National Curriculum – attainment targets – modern languages

EDUCATION (NATIONAL CURRICULUM) (ATTAINMENT TARGETS AND PROGRAMMES OF STUDY IN MODERN FOREIGN LANGUAGES) (ENGLAND) ORDER 2000, SI 2000 1595; made under the Education Act 1996 s.356, s.568. In force: August 1, 2000; £1.00.

This Order, which revokes the Education (National Curriculum) (Attainment Targets and Programmes of Study in Modern Foreign Languages) Order 1995 (SI 1995 57), provides for the attainment targets and programmes of study set out in the document published by the Stationery Office entitled Attainment Targets and Programmes of Study in Modern Foreign Languages to have effect for the purposes of specifying those elements of the national curriculum in modern foreign languages in relation to schools in England.

1880. National Curriculum – attainment targets – modern languages – Wales

EDUCATION (NATIONAL CURRICULUM) (ATTAINMENT TARGETS AND PROGRAMMES OF STUDY IN MODERN FOREIGN LANGUAGES) (WALES) ORDER 2000, SI 2000 1157 (W.88); made under the Education Act 1996 s.356. In force: August 1, 2000; £2.00.

The National Curriculum for Wales for modern foreign languages will be revised from August 1, 2000. This Order, which revokes and replaces the Education (National Curriculum) (Attainment Targets and Programmes of Study in Modern Foreign Languages) (Wales) Order 1995 (SI 1995 57), gives legal effect to the new programmes of study. Details of these are set out in a document entitled Modern Foreign Languages in the National Curriculum which is available from the Qualifications, Curriculum and Assessment Authority for Wales.

1881. National Curriculum – attainment targets – music

EDUCATION (NATIONAL CURRICULUM) (ATTAINMENT TARGETS AND PROGRAMMES OF STUDY IN MUSIC) (ENGLAND) ORDER 2000, SI 2000

1597; made under the Education Act 1996 s.356, s.568. In force: August 1, 2000; £1.00.

This Order, which revokes the Education (National Curriculum) (Attainment Targets and Programmes of Study in Music) (England) Order 1998 (SI 1998 1991), provides for the attainment targets and programmes of study set out in the document published by the Stationery Office entitled Attainment Targets and Programmes of Study in Music to have effect for the purposes of specifying those elements of the national curriculum in music in relation to schools in England.

1882. **National Curriculum – attainment targets – music – Wales**

EDUCATION (NATIONAL CURRICULUM) (ATTAINMENT TARGETS AND PROGRAMMES OF STUDY IN MUSIC) (WALES) ORDER 2000, SI 2000 1158 (W.89); made under the Education Act 1996 s.356. In force: August 1, 2000; £2.00.

The National Curriculum for Wales for music will be revised from August 1, 2000. This Order, which revokes and replaces the Education (National Curriculum) (Attainment Targets and Programmes of Study in Music) (Wales) Order 1998 (SI 1998 1889), gives legal effect to the new programmes of study and attainment targets. Details of these are set out in a document entitled Music in the National Curriculum which is available from the Qualifications, Curriculum and Assessment Authority for Wales.

1883. **National Curriculum – attainment targets – physical education**

EDUCATION (NATIONAL CURRICULUM) (ATTAINMENT TARGETS AND PROGRAMMES OF STUDY IN PHYSICAL EDUCATION) (ENGLAND) ORDER 2000, SI 2000 1607; made under the Education Act 1996 s.356, s.568. In force: August 1, 2000; £1.00.

This Order, which revokes the Education (National Curriculum) (Attainment Targets and Programmes of Study in Physical Education) Order 1998 (SI 1998 1987), provides for the attainment targets and programmes of study set out in the document published by the Stationery Office entitled Attainment Targets and Programmes of Study in Physical Education to have effect for the purposes of specifying those elements of the national curriculum in physical education in relation to schools in England.

1884. **National Curriculum – attainment targets – physical education – Wales**

EDUCATION (NATIONAL CURRICULUM) (ATTAINMENT TARGETS AND PROGRAMMES OF STUDY IN PHYSICAL EDUCATION) (WALES) ORDER 2000, SI 2000 1098 (W.76); made under the Education Act 1996 s.356. In force: August 1, 2000; August 1, 2001; August 1, 2002; £2.00.

The National Curriculum for Wales for physical education will be revised from August 1, 2000. This Order, which revokes and replaces the Education (National Curriculum) (Attainment Targets and Programmes of Study in Physical Education) (Wales) Order 1998 (SI 1998 1887), gives legal effect to the new programmes of study and attainment targets. Details of these are set out in a document entitled Physical Education in the National Curriculum which is available from the Qualifications, Curriculum and Assessment Authority for Wales.

1885. **National Curriculum – attainment targets – science**

EDUCATION (NATIONAL CURRICULUM) (ATTAINMENT TARGETS AND PROGRAMMES OF STUDY IN SCIENCE) (ENGLAND) ORDER 2000, SI 2000 1600; made under the Education Act 1996 s.356, s.568. In force: August 1, 2000; £1.00.

This Order, which revokes the Education (National Curriculum) (Attainment Targets and Programmes of Study in Science) Order 1995 (SI 1995 53), provides for the attainment targets and programmes of study set out in the document published by the Stationery Office entitled Attainment Targets and

Programmes of Study in Science to have effect for the purposes of specifying those elements of the national curriculum for science in relation to schools in England.

1886. National Curriculum – attainment targets – science – Wales

EDUCATION (NATIONAL CURRICULUM) (ATTAINMENT TARGETS AND PROGRAMMES OF STUDY IN SCIENCE) (WALES) ORDER 2000, SI 2000 1099 (W.77); made under the Education Act 1996 s.356. In force: August 1, 2000; £2.00.

The National Curriculum for Wales for science will be revised from August 1, 2000. This Order, which revokes and replaces the Education (National Curriculum) (Attainment Targets and Programmes of Study in Science) (Wales) Order 1995 (SI 1995 53), gives legal effect to the new programmes of study. Details of these are set out in a document entitled Science in the National Curriculum which is available from the Qualifications, Curriculum and Assessment Authority for Wales.

1887. National Curriculum – attainment targets – technology – Wales

EDUCATION (NATIONAL CURRICULUM) (ATTAINMENT TARGETS AND PROGRAMMES OF STUDY IN TECHNOLOGY) (WALES) ORDER 2000, SI 2000 1159 (W.90); made under the Education Act 1996 s.356. In force: August 1, 2000; £2.00.

The National Curriculum for Wales for technology will be revised from August 1, 2000. This Order, which revokes and replaces the Education (National Curriculum) (Attainment Targets and Programmes of Study in Technology) (Wales) Order 1998 (SI 1998 1890), gives legal effect to the new programmes of study and attainment targets. Details of these are set out in documents entitled Design and Technology in the National Curriculum and Information Technology in the National Curriculum which are available from the Qualifications, Curriculum and Assessment Authority for Wales.

1888. National Curriculum – attainment targets – Welsh – Wales

EDUCATION (NATIONAL CURRICULUM) (ATTAINMENT TARGETS AND PROGRAMMES OF STUDY IN WELSH) ORDER 2000, SI 2000 1101 (W.79); made under the Education Act 1996 s.356. In force: August 1, 2000; £2.00.

The National Curriculum for Wales for Welsh will be revised from August 1, 2000. This Order, which revokes and replaces the Education (National Curriculum) (Attainment Targets and Programmes of Study in Welsh) Order 1995 (SI 1995 69), gives legal effect to the new programmes of study and attainment targets for them. Details of these are set out in a document entitled Welsh in the National Curriculum which is available from the Qualifications, Curriculum and Assessment Authority for Wales.

1889. National Curriculum – exceptions – Key Stage 4

EDUCATION (NATIONAL CURRICULUM) (EXCEPTIONS AT KEY STAGE 4) (ENGLAND) REGULATIONS 2000, SI 2000 1140; made under the Education Act 1996 s.363, s.368, s.569. In force: August 1, 2000; £2.00.

These Regulations revoke the Education (National Curriculum) (Exceptions at Key Stage 4) Regulations 1998 (SI 1998 2021) and replace them with an expanded set of exceptions to the National Curriculum at Key Stage 4. They retain the provision for the National Curriculum to be disapplied for pupils at Key Stage 4 in maintained schools in England to allow participation in an extended work related learning programme. They allow schools to disapply the requirement for a pupil to study design and technology and/or a modern foreign language where he has demonstrated strengths in a particular curriculum area and is emphasising this curriculum area and also where he is making significantly less progress than others of his age.

1890. National Curriculum – foundation subjects – citizenship – art and design

FOUNDATION SUBJECT (AMENDMENT) (ENGLAND) ORDER 2000, SI 2000 1146; made under the Education Act 1996 s.354, s.568. In force: May 2, 2000 save as provided in Art.1 (1); £1.50.

This Order amends the Education Act 1996 s.354 so that citizenship is to become a foundation subject in relation to the third and fourth key stages as from the start of the school year beginning in 2002. It provides that the existing foundation subject of art is to be replaced by art and design.

1891. National Curriculum – foundation subjects – modern languages – Wales

FOUNDATION SUBJECT (AMENDMENT) (WALES) ORDER 2000, SI 2000 1882 (W.129); made under the Education Act 1996 s.354. In force: July 20, 2000; £2.00.

This Order amends the Education Act 1996 s.354, which lists the subjects which are foundation subjects for the purposes of the National Curriculum, so that modern foreign languages need no longer be specified in an order of the National Assembly under that section. Instead, an order under s.354 may provide that any modern foreign language is to constitute a modern foreign language for the purposes of the National Curriculum.

1892. National Curriculum – individual pupil exemptions

EDUCATION (NATIONAL CURRICULUM) (TEMPORARY EXCEPTIONS FOR INDIVIDUAL PUPILS) (ENGLAND) REGULATIONS 2000, SI 2000 2121; made under the Education Act 1996 s.365, s.366, s.367, s.569; and the School Standards and Framework Act 1998 s.144. In force: August 25, 2000; £2.00.

These Regulations revoke and replace, with modifications, the Education (National Curriculum) (Temporary Exceptions for Individual Pupils) Regulations 1989 (SI 1989 1181) in relation to England. They enable head teachers of county, voluntary or foundation schools or community or foundation special schools not established in hospitals to direct that the provisions of the National Curriculum should not apply to a pupil, or should apply with modifications, and apply only in relation to maintained schools in England.

1893. National Curriculum – modern languages – Wales

EDUCATION (NATIONAL CURRICULUM) (MODERN FOREIGN LANGUAGES) (WALES) ORDER 2000, SI 2000 1980 (W.141); made under the Education Act 1996 s.354. In force: August 1, 2000; £1.50.

This Order, which revokes and replaces, in relation to Wales, the Education (National Curriculum) (Modern Foreign Languages) Order 1991 (SI 1991 2567 as amended), provides that a modern foreign language which is not an official language of the European Community is not a "modern foreign language" for the purposes of the Education Act 1996 s.354 unless the school at which the language is taught offers all pupils in the third key stage, in respect of whom there is a requirement to study a modern foreign language as a foundation subject, the opportunity of studying one or more of the official languages of the European Community as a foundation subject.

1894. Nursery education – grants – elegibility

NURSERY EDUCATION (ENGLAND) REGULATIONS 2000, SI 2000 107; made under the Nursery Education and Grant-Maintained Schools Act 1996 s.1, s.8, Sch.2 para.1; and the School Standards and Framework Act 1998 Sch.26 para.6, para.13. In force: February 11, 2000; £2.00.

These Regulations revoke and replace the Nursery Education (England) Regulations 1998 (SI 1998 655). They prescribe matters relating to the making of grants in respect of nursery education and the inspection of relevant nursery education for the purposes of the Nursery Education and Grant-Maintained Schools Act 1996 and the School Standards and Framework Act 1998 Sch.26.

They prescribe the time after which education provided for a child is nursery education; the authorities and persons to whom grants in respect of nursery education may be made; the method of calculating the amount of grant to be paid in respect of the provision of nursery education; the information relating to a claim for child benefit which constitutes "social security information" for the purposes of Sch.2 of the 1996 Act; the period within which a report of an inspection of relevant nursery education is to be made and the authorities and persons to whom copies of such a report must be sent; and the intervals at which relevant nursery education is to be inspected for the purposes of Sch.26 para.6(1)(a) of the 1998 Act.

1895. Practice directions – Special Educational Needs Tribunal – translation of decisions

The President issued a Practice Direction in respect of translation of decisions, that where a foreign language interpreter interpreted for the parents of a child at a hearing of the Special Educational Needs Tribunal, or the parents were visually impaired and read braille, they must be offered the choice of a translated version of the decision upon condition that it would be issued at the same time as the English version, which was likely to take longer than the normal 10 working days and that the English version would be the official record of the decision.

PRACTICE DIRECTION (SENT:TRANSLATIONS OF DECISIONS) [2000] E.L.R. 469, Trevor Aldridge Q.C. (President), SENT.

1896. Pupils – academic records – disclosure of educational records

EDUCATION (PUPIL INFORMATION) (ENGLAND) REGULATIONS 2000, SI 2000 297; made under the Education Act 1996 s.408, s.563, s.569. In force: Reg.11: May 1, 2000; Remainder: March 1, 2000; £3.50.

These Regulations, which revoke and replace the Education (School Records) Regulations 1989 (SI 1989 1261), the Education (Individual Pupils' Achievements) (Information) Regulations 1992 (SI 1992 3168), the Education (Individual Pupils' Achievements) (Information) Regulations 1997 (SI 1997 1368) and the Education (Individual Pupils' Achievements) (Information) (Amendment) Regulations 1998 (SI 1998 877), make provision for the keeping of records about the academic achievements, skills and abilities and the progress of pupils at schools maintained by local education authorities and special schools not so maintained. They make provision for the disclosure of educational records by the head teachers of all schools maintained by local education authorities and special schools not so maintained. The major change made by the regulations is the omission of provisions relating to the right to access information by pupils which, from March 1, 2000 will be governed by the Data Protection Act 1998.

1897. Qualifications – professionals – recognition

EUROPEAN COMMUNITIES (RECOGNITION OF PROFESSIONAL QUALIFICATIONS) (AMENDMENT) REGULATIONS 2000, SI 2000 1960; made under the European Communities Act 1972 s.2. In force: August 28, 2000; £2.00.

These Regulations amend the European Communities (Recognition of Professional Qualifications) Regulations 1991 (SI 1991 824) which give effect in the UK to Council Directive 89/48 ([1989] OJ L19/16) on a general system for the recognition of higher education diplomas awarded on completion of professional education and training of at least three years' duration. In particular, they clarify the application of the term "designated authority" and substitute a reference to the profession of chartered certified accountant for the profession of certified accountant.

1898. Schools – Chief Inspector of Schools – appointment

EDUCATION (CHIEF INSPECTOR OF SCHOOLS IN ENGLAND) ORDER 2000, SI 2000 3239; made under the School Inspections Act 1996 s.1. In force: December 14, 2000; £1.50.

This Order appoints Michael John Tomlinson to be Her Majesty's Chief Inspector of Schools in England for the period from December 14, 2000 to November 30, 2001.

1899. Schools – foundation bodies

EDUCATION (FOUNDATION BODY) (ENGLAND) REGULATIONS 2000, SI 2000 2872; made under the School Standards and Framework Act 1998 s.21, s.35, s.138, s.144, Sch.4 para.5, Sch.8 para.2, Sch.8 para.3, Sch.8 para.4, Sch.8 para.5, Sch.12 para.1. In force: November 15, 2000; £4.00.

These Regulations make provision for and in connection with the establishment, membership, functions and winding up of foundation bodies and the steps to be taken in connection with schools joining or leaving a group of schools for which a foundation body acts. A foundation body is a body corporate established under the School Standards and Framework Act 1998 s.21 in relation to a group of three or more schools, each of which is either a foundation or a voluntary school, to hold property for the purposes of the schools, appoint foundation governors, and promote cooperation between schools in the group.

1900. Schools – infant class size limit

INFANT CLASS SIZES (ADMISSION AND STANDARD NUMBERS) (ENGLAND) REGULATIONS 2000, SI 2000 180; made under the School Standards and Framework Act 1998 s.93, s.138. In force: February 21, 2000; £2.00.

These Regulations make transitional provisions in connection with the imposition of a limit on the size of infant classes at maintained schools in England under the School Standards and Framework Act 1998 s.1. They apply in relation to the admission of children to such schools for education in infant classes in the 2000/2001 school year. They disapply certain provisions of the 1998 Act concerning the fixing of the number of children to be so admitted.

1901. Schools – inspectors – appointments

EDUCATION (INSPECTORS OF SCHOOLS IN ENGLAND) ORDER 2000, SI 2000 3058; made under the School Inspectors Act 1996 s.1. In force: December 18, 2000; £1.50.

This Order appoints certain named persons as Her Majesty's Inspectors of Schools in England.

1902. Schools – maintained schools – change of category

EDUCATION (CHANGE OF CATEGORY OF MAINTAINED SCHOOLS) (ENGLAND) REGULATIONS 2000, SI 2000 2195; made under the School Standards and Framework Act 1998 s.35, s.138, s.144, Sch.4 para.5, Sch.8 para.2, Sch.8 para.3, Sch.8 para.4, Sch.8 para.5, Sch.12 para.1. In force: September 1, 2000; £6.30.

These Regulations, which revoke the Education (Change of Category of Maintained Schools) (England) Regulations 1999 (SI 1999 2259), make provision for community, voluntary controlled, voluntary aided, and foundation schools to become another category of school within those categories, and for a community special school to become a foundation special school and a foundation special school to become a community special school.

1903. Schools – maintained schools – finance

FINANCING OF MAINTAINED SCHOOLS (ENGLAND) REGULATIONS 2000, SI 2000 478; made under the School Standards and Framework Act 1998 s.46, s.47, s.48, s.138, s.144, Sch.14 para.1. In force: February 29, 2000; £4.00.

These Regulations prescribe the expenditure which makes up a local education authority's "local schools budget" for the financial year beginning on April 1, 2000 and specify the nature of the planned expenditure which a local education authority may deduct from their local schools budget in order to arrive at their "individual schools budget" for that financial year.

1904. Schools – maintained schools – finance – additional budget shares

FINANCING OF MAINTAINED SCHOOLS (ENGLAND) (NO.2) REGULATIONS 2000, SI 2000 1090; made under the School Standards and Framework Act 1998 s.47, s.138. In force: April 19, 2000; £1.50.

These Regulations make additional provision for the redetermination of schools' budget shares in the financial year beginning on April 1, 2000. Additional amounts are to be added to budget shares depending on whether the school is a primary, secondary or special school and, except in the case of a special school or certain middle deemed primary schools, depending on the numbers of registered pupils at the school.

1905. Schools – maintained schools – finance – Wales

FINANCING OF MAINTAINED SCHOOLS (AMENDMENT) (WALES) REGULATIONS 2000, SI 2000 911 (W.40); made under the Standards and School Framework Act 1998 s.46, s.47. In force: March 24, 2000; £2.00.

These Regulations allow local authorities to distribute additional funding arising from teachers' pay restructuring to schools in response to the need in individual schools for a transitional period of up to three years or to incorporate a factor relating to it in Local Education Authorities' distribution formulae from 2000/01. They amend The Financing of Maintained Schools Regulations 1999 (SI 1999 101) so that any consultation with schools on changes to the distribution formula in respect of funding for teachers' pay restructuring or the employment of advanced skills teachers on or after November 30, 1999 will fulfil the certain consultation requirements; to reduce from 80 per cent to 75 per cent the percentage of the budget shares for primary and secondary schools which must be determined by pupil led factors; and to allow local education authorities, for the financial years 2000/01, 2001/02 and 2002/03, to deduct from the local schools budget and retain centrally, provision for the costs of teachers' pay restructuring and the employment of advanced skills teachers.

1906. Schools – maintained schools – pupils – information

EDUCATION (INFORMATION ABOUT INDIVIDUAL PUPILS) (ENGLAND) REGULATIONS 2000, SI 2000 3370; made under the Education Act 1996 s.537A, s.569. In force: January 18, 2001; £1.75.

These Regulations, which revoke and replace the Education (Information About Individual Pupils) (England) Regulations 1999 (SI 1999 989), require the governing body of any maintained school on receiving a written request from the local education authority by which the school is maintained to supply specified information within 14 days.

1907. Schools – performance – information

EDUCATION (SCHOOL PERFORMANCE INFORMATION) (ENGLAND) (AMENDMENT) REGULATIONS 2000, SI 2000 1089; made under the Education Act 1996 s.537, s.569. In force: May 15, 2000; £1.00.

These Regulations replace the Education (School Performance Information) (England) Regulations 1999 (SI 1999 1178) Reg.9 which relates to the collection and publication of information about the performance of schools. The new Reg.9

requires the governing body of every maintained school to provide information directly to the Secretary of State within two weeks of receiving a written request from him and replaces the duty under the old Reg.9 to provide that information to the local education authority and the authority's duty to pass this on to the Secretary of State.

1908. Schools – performance – information

EDUCATION (SCHOOL PERFORMANCE INFORMATION) (ENGLAND) (AMENDMENT NO.2) REGULATIONS 2000, SI 2000 2116; made under the Education Act 1996 s.29, s.408, s.537, s.569. In force: August 24, 2000; £1.50.

These Regulations amend the Education (School Performance Information) (England) Regulations 1999 (SI 1999 1178) which relate to the collection and publication of information about the performance of schools. They remove the requirement that local education authorities publish the information required by the 1999 Regulations before February 24 in each year; require the governing body of every maintained secondary school except a middle deemed secondary school, and the proprietor of every non-maintained special school or independent school with pupils aged 15 to provide the Secretary of State with information as to the numbers of pupils aged 15 who have special educational needs instead of the numbers of registered pupils aged 15 who have statements of special educational needs; and require that information be provided to the Secretary of State and published by local education authorities as to the number of registered pupils at or near the end of the final year of the second key stage who have special educational needs instead of the numbers of registered pupils who have statements of special educational needs.

1909. Schools – performance – information

EDUCATION (SCHOOL PERFORMANCE INFORMATION) (ENGLAND) (AMENDMENT NO.3) REGULATIONS 2000, SI 2000 2832; made under the Education Act 1996 s.537, s.569. In force: November 8, 2000; £1.75.

These Regulations, which amend the Education (School Performance Information) (England) Regulations 1999 (SI 1999 1178), add a new Reg.15 which requires a local education authority when publishing information about pupils at or near the end of the final year of the second key stage under Reg.14(2)(3)(3A) to exclude from the number a pupil whose first language is not English when directed to do so by the Secretary of State on application made by the school in question.

1910. Schools – religious character designation

DESIGNATION OF SCHOOLS HAVING A RELIGIOUS CHARACTER (ENGLAND) ORDER 2000, SI 2000 3080; made under the School Standards and Framework Act 1998 s.69, s.138. In force: November 1, 2000; £1.50.

This Order designates further voluntary schools in England which have a religious character in addition to those already listed in the Designation of Schools Having a Religious Character (England) Order 1999 (SI 1999 2432).

1911. Schools – school admissions – alterations to admission arrangements – selection by ability – adjudicator's jurisdiction

[Education Act 1996 s.573; Schools Standards and Framework Act 1998 s.103; Education (Objection to Admission Arrangements) Regulations 1999 (SI 1999 125) Reg.2.]

Objections had been raised to WLBC's proposals for admission arrangements to three of its schools and the matter was referred to D, an adjudicator appointed under the Schools Standards and Framework Act 1998. The objections concerned the schools' policies of selecting a proportion of their pupils through ability tests, it was asserted that these policies had an adverse effect on the provision of education in the locality as a whole, as the three schools "creamed off" the higher ability pupils to the detriment of other schools in the area, and that a system of banding would be fairer. D determined that the policies were not in the best interests of local children and that the proportion of children admitted through tests should be reduced. WLBC sought judicial review of the determination on the grounds, inter alia, that (1) the objectors' desire to end selection procedures amounted to a request for a "significant change in the character of the school" and by virtue of the Education (Objection to Admission Arrangements) Regulations 1999 Reg.2 the objections should not have been referred to D, and (2) D's decision to alter the admission policies also amounted to a "significant change" which, under s.103 of the 1998 Act, he was not authorised to make.

Held, granting the application, that it was clear from government circulars, school practice and the underlying purpose of the Education Act 1996, in particular from the now repealed s.573 (4) and (5), that alterations to admission procedures were likely to constitute a significant change in the function of schools, and as the substance of the objections concerned that issue, D had had no jurisdiction to adjudicate. It was apparent from his determination that he had not considered the limitation of his powers under s.103 and he had therefore not taken account of a material factor. As his proposals would constitute a significant change, his determination would be quashed.

R. v. DOWNES, *ex p.* WANDSWORTH LBC [2000] E.L.R. 425, Sullivan, J., QBD.

1912. Schools – school admissions – appeals – power of Education Appeals Committees to hear new evidence

[Education Act 1996 Sch.33 Part II para.11A; School Standards and Framework Act 1998 s.1.]

SS had refused places to two children, J and M, at a popular infants' school in order to restrict class sizes to 30 children in anticipation of the effect of the School Standards and Framework Act 1998 s.1. On hearing fresh evidence, the Education Appeals Committee found that SS's decisions in relation to J and M were ones which no reasonable authority would have reached, as per the Education Act 1996 Sch.33 Part II para.11A. There was evidence that J lived with his grandparents within the school's catchment area, rather than with his mother who lived outside the area, and there were medical reasons why M should be given a place. SS sought judicial review of the committee's decisions on the ground that the committee had erred in law in treating the appeals as rehearings and receiving fresh evidence. The committee argued that para.11A should be interpreted to mean that there should be a rehearing.

Held, refusing the application, that an education appeal committee should not hear fresh evidence, as in order to be fair to all applicants for school places it was incumbent on parents to put all relevant information before the education authority at the time that it was making the allocation. However, as there had been sufficient evidence available to SS at the time of its decision to show that J lived with his grandparents, the committee was entitled to find that SS's decision had been unreasonable. Equally, SB had been entitled to find that SS had not properly brought to the attention of M's parents the fact that medical evidence could be submitted. The committee was therefore entitled to take into account that medical evidence, and to find that M should have been offered a place.

R. v. SOUTHEND BOROUGH EDUCATION APPEALS COMMITTEE, *ex p.* SOUTHEND ON SEA BC [2000] Ed. C.R. 368, Hooper, J., QBD.

1913. Schools – school admissions – change of catchment area – effect on parental preference

[Education Act 1996 s.411.]

B applied for judicial review of RLBC's decision that, as a result of the change in admissions policy by one secondary school, CH, those children who might have gone to that school in the 1998/1999 academic year would be placed in the catchment area of another school, MHS, which did not have as good an academic record. B argued that RLBC's decision ignored parental preference, as required under the Education Act 1996 s.411, by elevating the importance of the catchment area.

Held, refusing the application, that the decision had not affected parental preference because a preference for CH could still be expressed, and provided that the children from its catchment area did not fill its places, it was possible for children outside the catchment area to gain a place there. Further, the application could not be dealt with until after the start of the next term, with the result that there was no benefit in granting leave. Challenges to decisions based on admissions policies should be brought with the utmost expedition, *R. v. Appeal Committee of Brighouse School, ex p. G and B* [1997] E.L.R. 39, [1997] C.L.Y. 2108 and *R. v. Bradford City Council, ex p. Ali (Sikander)* (1994) 6 Admin. L.R. 589, [1995] C.L.Y. 1910 considered.

R. v. REDBRIDGE LBC, *ex p.* B [1999] Ed. C.R. 959, Popplewell, J., QBD.

1914. Schools – school admissions – delay in bringing judicial review proceedings

[Supreme Court Act 1981 s.31 (6); Education Act 1996 s.411.]

B, C and K were 11 year old pupils who had been allocated places at school X by RMBC, the LEA, where they would commence their secondary education in the 1999 autumn term. During their final year at primary school, each of their parents had expressed a preference under the Education Act 1996 s.411 (1) for school Y. The parents were dissatisfied with RMBC's allocation decision and believed that the selection criteria had not been reasonably or properly applied. The decision was communicated to the parents on February 26, 1999 and on June 10 they were informed that their appeals against the decision had been unsuccessful. On June 25 they instructed solicitors, who made an application for legal aid, which was granted on July 22. A letter before action was sent to RMBC on July 28, and a reply received on August 10. Applications for permission to bring judicial review proceedings challenging the allocation decisions were lodged on September 6. The issue before the court was whether there had been undue and inexcusable delay by the applicants in commencing judicial review proceedings, so that leave should be refused on the basis that it would be detrimental to good administration pursuant to the Supreme Court Act 1981 s.31 (6).

Held, refusing the applications, that, very exceptional circumstances aside, it was essential that challenges of this nature were determined before the new school year began. This was in the interests of all parties, including the applicants, the school, its teachers and other pupils. In the instant case, the court would not consider the merits of the applications because the applications for permission had been brought too late for the purposes of s.31 (6) of the 1981 Act. Any decision in favour of B, C and K would clearly involve very substantial disruption to both schools, particularly in light of the fact that school Y was fully subscribed. The applicants would have had to commence proceedings by early August at the latest in order for the court to have been able to entertain the applications.

R. v. ROCHDALE MBC, *ex p.* B [2000] Ed. C.R. 117, Judge David Pannick Q.C., QBD.

1915. Schools – school admissions – letter mistakenly stated child accepted at preferred school – legitimate expectation

[Education Act 1996 s.423.]

The mother of L sought judicial review of BCC's refusal to grant L a place at the secondary school of his choice. L had previously been allocated a place at a secondary school that was not his preferred choice. His mother's appeal, made pursuant to the Education Act 1996 s.423 against the decision was refused and L did not attend school for a year. L's mother made a second appeal seeking a place at the preferred school and on that occasion nominated another school that L was prepared to accept as second choice. The minutes of the appeal hearing showed that the decision reached by the committee was that L should be allocated a place at the second choice school but the letter informing L's mother of the decision stated that L had been allocated a place at both schools. L's mother interpretation of the letter was that L had been allocated a place at his preferred school. When the mistake came to light, BCC offered a rehearing of L's appeal. L's mother refused and lodged her application for judicial review of BCC's decision, contending that BCC was bound by the contents of the letter and that the error in the letter gave rise to a legitimate expectation that L would be allowed to attend his preferred school.

Held, refusing the application, that there was no doubt as to the decision reached at the appeal hearing and there was no justification for changing that decision because of a clerical error. An unequivocal promise could give rise to a legitimate expectation in circumstances where there were no contrary public interest considerations, *R. v. North and East Devon HA, ex p. Coughlan* [2000] 2 W.L.R. 622, [1999] C.L.Y. 2643 followed. In the instant case, however, there had been no such clear and unambiguous promise.

R. v. BIRMINGHAM CITY COUNCIL, *ex p.* L (A CHILD) [2000] Ed. C.R. 484, Latham, J., QBD.

1916. **Schools – school admissions – limit on pupil numbers – preservation of ability spread – limit in keeping with efficient use of resources**

[Education Act 1996 s.411.]

M sought judicial review of a decision of the LEA's appeal committee refusing him admission to a particular school. The LEA had accepted the school's limit of 230 admissions per year. M was ninth on the waiting list above that limit. There were no special circumstances applicable to his application and the committee refused his admission, contending that admitting pupils in excess of 230 would be detrimental in terms of the efficient provision of education and the efficient use of resources under the Education Act 1996 s.411 (3). In reaching its decision, the committee had before it the LEA's reasons for limiting the pupil intake, which stated that with intakes of 240 there would be serious problems in accommodating children regardless of gender or ethnic origin. M submitted that there was nothing in that statement which satisfied the s.411 (1) parental preference obligation. Further, that the statement amounted to the reservation of places for persons who might later come in, to the detriment of those actually applying at a particular time, and amounted to a policy of reverse discrimination.

Held, refusing the application, that (1) there were no reserved places for persons coming from outside, but a desire for flexibility when a place occurred for a new child; (2) that flexibility was not simply to allow for gender or ethnic considerations, but also for a spread of abilities and an even distribution of children from feeder schools; (3) there was no ground upon which it could be found that the committee's decision was perverse, and (4) the committee had correctly reached a decision that to increase pupil numbers would prejudice the provision of efficient education or the efficient use of resources.

R. v. SHEFFIELD CITY COUNCIL, *ex p.* M [2000] E.L.R. 85, Burton, J., QBD.

1917. **Schools – school admissions – parental rights – refusal of LEA to admit pupil to preferred primary school**

[School Standards and Framework Act 1998 s.86(2), Sch.24 para.12.]

J, the parents of B, a child aged four, applied for judicial review of the decision of SG, the LEA, not to admit B to the primary school of their choice. SG claimed it was not obliged to comply with B's parental preference and contended that it had acted within its powers in offering a place at an alternative school within the statutory walking distance of two miles. Moreover, SG submitted that the admission of B to the preferred school would have resulted in it exceeding the statutory maximum on infant class sizes. In challenging SG's decision J contended that (1) the education appeal committee had failed to ensure that SG's admission arrangements and selection criteria had been implemented in accordance with the School Standards and Framework Act 1998 Sch.24 para.12 and had failed to ensure that parental preference was complied with under s.86(2) of the Act; (2) SG had based its decision on catchment areas, when there was no mention of catchment areas in its admission criteria policy, and (3) four places at the school currently existed for children who might move into the area and therefore there was no evidence to show that infant class size prejudice would result if B were to be placed in the preferred school.

Held, refusing the application, that (1) SG had properly adopted the geographical criteria for its admissions policy in applying the "closest to, and/or furthest from, criterion". SG had looked at the walking distances travelled by children to the nearest school, compared to the distances which would have to be walked to alternative schools, and this criterion had been misconstrued as a catchment area; (2) the procedure applied by the school known as "ghost funding" did not mean that there were an extra four available school places, and (3) class size prejudice had been proved given that additional resources would be required to enable B to attend the preferred school.

R. v. SOUTH GLOUCESTERSHIRE EDUCATION APPEALS COMMITTEE, *ex p.* B (A CHILD) [2000] E.L.R. 602, Hidden, J., QBD.

1918. **Schools – school admissions – primary schools – limitation on power of appeals committee to overturn decision on school admission – discretion to admit additional evidence**

[Education Act 1996 Sch.33 para.11A; School Standards and Framework Act 1998.]

C, a five year old child, appealed against the dismissal of his application for judicial review following a decision by the local education authority, RLBC, to refuse to admit him to his parent's preferred choice of infant school and a subsequent decision of the appeals committee to uphold the refusal. The school in question had been oversubscribed when C made his application and his parents had provided medical evidence in support of their contention that special circumstances existed justifying his application being treated as a priority. The local education authority sub committee rejected the contention that C should be afforded priority on that basis. Before the appeals committee C's parents had sought to adduce additional medical evidence but their request was dismissed and the appeal itself was dismissed on the basis that the committee's powers on appeal were strictly circumscribed by the Education Act 1996 Sch.33 para.11A.

Held, dismissing the appeal, that (1) following the introduction of limits upon infant class sizes in the School Standards and Framework Act 1998, local education authorities were entitled to take class size into account when formulating admissions policies for the academic year 1999/2000 and where an application had been refused on the basis that accepting the child would result in the school being oversubscribed, an appeals committee would only be entitled to overturn the decision in two strictly defined circumstances pursuant to Sch.33 para.11A of the 1996 Act; (2) in disputes concerning school admissions the relevant applicant was the parent rather than the child and in future the parent should proceed to make the application. Any applications launched in the name of the child in order to avoid potential adverse costs orders would be viewed as an abuse of process in the absence of special circumstances, and (3) the burden of proof was on the applicant to furnish all relevant evidence in support of an application for admission to a particular school but the appeals committee did possess a discretion to admit further evidence and had erred in declining the request in the instant case. The hearing before the appeals committee did not amount to a rehearing but was instead confined to a consideration of whether the decision was not one that could have been reached by a reasonable admissions authority in the circumstances.

R. v. RICHMOND LBC APPEAL COMMITTEE, *ex p.* JC (A CHILD); *sub nom.* R. v. RICHMOND LBC, *ex p.* C (A CHILD); R. v. RICHMOND LBC, *ex p.* JC (A CHILD) [2001] E.L.R. 21, Kennedy, L.J., CA.

1919. Schools – school admissions – procedure – extent of adjudicator's jurisdiction to consider objection

[School Standards and Framework Act 1998 s.84.]

WMBC challenged the school adjudicator's decision that its admissions procedures for secondary schools did not meet the criterion of fairness set out in the Code of Practice under s.84 of the School Standards and Framework Act 1998 s.84. WMBC contended that the adjudicator had misdirected himself in law by substituting his judgment for that of the local education authority and that he had acted unfairly as WMBC had not been given the opportunity to expand on the policy arguments for the admissions procedures adopted.

Held, refusing the application, that the adjudicator had the jurisdiction to consider the objection and that WMBC had been given every opportunity to advance full submissions.

R. v. SCHOOLS ADJUDICATOR, *ex p.* WIRRAL MBC [2000] Ed. C.R. 355, Latham, J., QBD.

1920. Schools – school admissions – publication of admission arrangements – LEA's duties

[Education Act 1996 s.414; Education (School Information) (England) Regulations 1994 (SI 1994 1421) Reg.7(3).]

Local education authorities had a statutory duty under the Education Act 1996 s.414 to publish their school admission arrangements. The Education (School Information) (England) Regulations 1994 Reg.7(3) provided that particulars of those arrangements were to be distributed free of charge or made available for inspection on request. In the instant case, the LEA's admission policy provided for parental preferences to be prioritised where a school was oversubscribed. The first priority was based on residence in a defined admissions area. The parents of six pupils refused a place at their preferred school lost their appeals to the LEA's appeal committee and an initial judicial review application was refused. They then re-applied for judicial review, contending that the LEA had acted unlawfully by (1) not supplying a map of the admission area; (2) not publishing its policy on the admission of pupils moving into the admissions area; (3) claiming that the school was full despite the fact that children new to the area might be accommodated, and (4) not consulting over changes to the admissions area.

Held, refusing the re-application, that (1) the LEA had not acted unlawfully by not supplying a map along with the admissions information. A map would have been difficult to interpret and it was not wrong to leave it to the people concerned to make an enquiry as to the admission area in which they lived; (2) the admissions policy indicated that the LEA would do its best to accommodate a child moving into its area. This did not breach any statutory obligation and did not prejudice any legitimate expectation of the parents; (3) the description of a school as a feeder school did not ensure that a child going there would necessarily be offered a place at the preferred high school, and (4) admission area amendments could have been discovered by the parents on an application to the LEA.

R. v. STOCKTON ON TEES BC, *ex p.* W [2000] E.L.R. 93, Stuart-Smith, L.J., CA.

1921. Schools – school admissions – refusal of local education authority to admit pupil to preferred secondary school – contention of procedural unfairness

The parents of R, an 11 year old girl, applied for judicial review of the dismissal of their appeal against SG's refusal to admit R to their preferred secondary school, which her older sister attended. The parents contended that it had been procedurally unfair not to give them an opportunity to present their case in relation to the issues arising through the older sisters' attendance and that the appeals committee had failed to give sufficient reasons for its decision.

Held, refusing the application, that the committee was not under a duty to comply with parental preference if admitting a child would in its opinion prejudice efficient education after conducting the two stage test required by *R. v. Commissioner for Local Education, ex p. Croydon LBC* [1989] 1 All E.R. 1033, [1989] C.L.Y. 2328. It was unnecessary to provide detailed grounds for the refusal as this did not impair the parent's ability to understand the basis of the decision. There was no procedural unfairness as the sibling link point had been taken into account.

R. v. SOUTH GLOUCESTERSHIRE EDUCATION APPEALS COMMITTEE, *ex p.* C [2000] Ed. C.R. 212, Dyson, J., QBD.

1922. Schools – school admissions – selection criteria favouring pupils with ability in music and dance – duty of LEA to provide information to adjudicator

[Schools Standards and Framework Act 1998 s.90.]

An adjudicator appointed under the Schools Standards and Framework Act 1998 s.90 assessed the admissions policy of a comprehensive school, MH, and found that in the event of over subscription a 10 per cent preference was given to children with a particular aptitude in music, that a 5 per cent preference was given to children with a particular aptitude for dance and that a 30 per cent preference was given to children with an aptitude for technology. The adjudicator determined that such a policy was discriminatory in view of the difficulties faced by children from families who were unable or unwilling to meet the cost of music or dance tuition. The existing system was therefore replaced by a policy whereby a 10 per cent preference was shown towards pupils gifted in music, dance or technology. The adjudicator had not been informed that the local education authority provided free musical tuition and musical instruments to those children whose parents were otherwise unable to meet the cost. J, a child, sought judicial review of the determination.

Held, granting the application, that where a local authority had no basis to foresee an adjudicator's criticism of a particular admissions policy, it was unreasonable for that adjudicator to rely on or anticipate any relevant information being forthcoming and accordingly the decision had been unreasonable.

R. v. CLARK, *ex p.* JD *The Times*, May 26, 2000, Kay, J., QBD.

1923. Schools – school admissions – special educational needs – power of local authority to compel school outside its own area to admit pupil

[Education Act 1996, s.324, s.495, s.496 Sch.27 para.3(4).]

T, aged 12, was assessed by his local education authority, SLBC, as having special educational needs. His mother, M, was asked to specify her preferred choice of school, and she chose ASS, which was outside SLBC's area. T went through the normal admissions procedure for ASS and was refused a place. Although SLBC formally nominated ASS in T's statement of special educational needs and insisted that ASS should accept T, ASS continued to maintain its stance, and T applied for judicial review of that decision. T argued that (1) ASS was named in the statement; (2) the Education Act 1996 s.324(5)(b) placed a mandatory duty on a school so named to accept the child concerned, and (3) the wording of Sch.27 para.3(4) clearly implied that a school could be nominated by an authority outside its own area. AAS contended, inter alia, that s.324 had to be read as giving no power to compel schools outside an LEA's area to accept a particular child with special educational needs.

Held, granting the application, that once named in a statement, a school was under a duty to accept the relevant child. Taken together, s.324 and Sch.27 showed that the scheme under the Act was intended to allow authorities to send children to schools outside their areas, particularly since school catchment areas did not always correspond with authority areas. As the language of s.324 was clear and compelling, it could not be given the meaning argued for by ASS. The requirement that an authority should consult with the school under Sch.27 and the appeal procedure available to an aggrieved school under s.495 and s.496 were sufficient protection to the schools involved.

R. v. GOVERNORS OF A SCHOOL, *ex p.* T; *sub nom.* R. v. GOVERNORS OF A&S SCHOOL, *ex p.* T; R. v. CHAIR OF GOVERNERS AND HEADTEACHER OF A SCHOOL, *ex p.* T [2000] Ed. C.R. 223, Jackson, J., QBD.

1924. Schools – school admissions – vires of admissions policy giving priority to residents of catchment area – LEA boundary coinciding in part with catchment area

[Education Act 1996 s.411.]

LT appealed against a decision refusing an application for judicial review of RMBC's school admissions policy. LT lived outside the borough but her parents had expressed a preference for a school within RMBC's area. However, LT was refused a place because the school was oversubscribed, and in such situations RMBC's policy gave priority to applicants living within the individual school's catchment area. The catchment area concerned coincided with the borough boundary for part of its length and LT contended, in reliance upon *R. v. Shadow Education Committee of Greenwich LBC, ex p. Governors of John Ball Primary School* 88 L.G.R. 589, [1990] C.L.Y. 1772, that adopting a catchment based policy, given the geographic boundaries of the instant case, was contrary to the Education Act 1996 s.411.

Held, dismissing the appeal, that proximity to a school was a valid consideration in determining a school admissions policy and the fact that the catchment area coincided with the borough boundary did not serve to make RMBC's admissions policy ultra vires, as to do so would mean that applicants living outside the borough could gain preference to borough residents, contrary to the intention of Parliament. LEAs had to have a realistic and practical admissions policy, and the use of catchment areas could be a valid primary consideration, *R. v. Shadow Education Committee of Greenwich LBC, ex p. Governors of John Ball Primary School* and *R. v. Wiltshire CC, ex p. Razazan* [1997] E.L.R. 370, [1997] C.L.Y. 2107 considered.

R. v. ROTHERHAM MBC, *ex p.* T; *sub nom.* R. v. ROTHERHAM MBC, *ex p.* LT [2000] B.L.G.R. 338, Stuart-Smith, L.J., CA.

1925. Schools – school exclusions – natural justice – refusal to reveal witness statement on ground of confidentiality unfair

A schoolboy appealed against the dismissal of his challenge to a decision to permanently exclude him from school following an incident of theft. The boy maintained that the school's failure to disclose the contents of a written statement made by another pupil breached the rules of natural justice.

Held, allowing the appeal, that the refusal to disclose the nature of the serious allegations, which the school had attempted to justify on the basis of confidentiality, amounted to procedural unfairness. B had a right to be heard but that right was of no avail unless he knew what was being said against him.

R. v. GOVERNORS OF DUNRAVEN SCHOOL, *ex p.* B (A CHILD); *sub nom.* R. v. GOVERNING BODY OF DUNRAVEN SCHOOL, *ex p.* B (A CHILD) [2000] B.L.G.R. 494, Sedley, L.J., CA.

1926. Schools – school exclusions – natural justice – relevance of parental influence

Two sisters were permanently excluded from their secondary school after a series of disruptive incidents. Their behaviour had been influenced by their father, who was a former headteacher of the school and who had been very critical of the school and its management since his departure. Their appeals against the decision to exclude them were dismissed and both sought judicial review.

Held, refusing the applications, that, in relation to the elder girl, it was a case of exclusion rather than a refusal to admit. There had been no breach of natural justice since the girl had walked out of school, thus preventing the headteacher from interviewing her or enabling her to make representations. Furthermore, she had not asked to be heard before the headteacher, the disciplinary committee or the appeal committee. It was clear that the relevant guidance suggesting that exclusion should be used in the last resort had been taken into account, although it had not been specifically referred to in the decision. The headteacher had taken into account the girl's previous good record and was entitled to consider the likely effect of her father's influence on her behaviour were she to remain at the school. He had also been entitled to consider the interests of the other pupils at the school, as well as the interests of the girl concerned. The decision to consider whether the conduct was extreme enough to merit exclusion, and then to consider whether exclusion was appropriate in all the circumstances, could not be faulted. In relation to the younger girl, there was no breach of natural justice since a sufficient inquiry into the events leading to her exclusion had been conducted. The girl's previous good record had been taken into account and the incidents reflected the girl's general attitude to the school and her likely conduct in the future were she to remain at the school. The girl had been excluded because of her behaviour and her father's conduct was relevant simply for the purpose of determining whether there was likely to be any change in her behaviour. The headteacher and the committee had been entitled to conclude that, notwithstanding that it was a measure of last resort, there was no way of dealing with the situation other than to exclude the girl.

R. v. BOARD OF GOVERNORS OF BRYN ELIAN HIGH SCHOOL, *ex p.* W [1999] E.L.R. 380, Kay, J., QBD.

1927. Schools – school exclusions – prescribed period for representations about exclusion

EDUCATION (EXCLUSION FROM SCHOOL) (PRESCRIBED PERIODS) (AMENDMENT) (ENGLAND) REGULATIONS 2000, SI 2000 294; made under the School Standards and Framework Act 1998 s.66, s.138. In force: March 1, 2000; £1.00.

These Regulations amend the Education (Exclusion from School) (Prescribed Periods) Regulations 1999 (SI 1999 1868) in relation to maintained schools in England so that where a head teacher excludes any pupil in circumstances where the pupil would be excluded from the school for between 5 and 15 school days in any one term, the governing body must take each of the steps referred to in the School Standards and Framework Act 1998 s.66(2) within 50 school days of receiving notification of the exclusion.

1928. Schools – school exclusions – prescribed period for representations about exclusion

EDUCATION (EXCLUSION FROM SCHOOL) (PRESCRIBED PERIODS) (AMENDMENT) (WALES) REGULATIONS 2000, SI 2000 3026 (W.194); made under the School Standards and Framework Act 1998 s.66, s.138. In force: January 1, 2001; £1.75.

These Regulations amend the Education (Exclusion from School) (Prescribed Periods) Regulations 1999 (SI 1999 1868) in relation to maintained schools in Wales. They provide that where a pupil at such a school would, as a result of an exclusion, be excluded for a fixed period of more than five but not more than 15 school days in total in any one term, a governing body must normally take each of the steps referred to in the School Standards and Framework Act 1998 s.66(2) not later than 50 school days after receiving notification of the exclusion.

1929. Schools – school exclusions – reinstatement – industrial action of teachers – use of pupil support centres

[School Standards and Framework Act 1998 s.39(2), s.67(4).]

W applied for judicial review of the governors' interim decision that she should not be reintegrated into the classroom but should work outside the principal's office in the mornings and attend a pupil support centre in the afternoons. W contended that the new regime was contrary to an appeal committee's decision to reinstate her and that the decision should not have been influenced by the threat of industrial action from the teaching staff.

Held, refusing the application, that the interim educational arrangements did not amount to continuing exclusion from the school and sufficiently constituted reinstatement for the purposes of the School Standards and Framework Act

1998 s.67(4). The governors had been entitled to consider the interests of all the pupils and even if the threatened industrial action was irresponsible, that was not a reason to interfere with the governors' exercise of their discretion. Furthermore, the use of a pupil support unit under s.39(2) in such cases was unassailable.

R. v. GOVERNORS OF B SCHOOL, *ex p.* W *The Times*, November 14, 2000, Richards, J., QBD.

1930. Schools – school government – governing bodies and meetings

EDUCATION (SCHOOL GOVERNMENT) (ENGLAND) (AMENDMENT) REGULATIONS 2000, SI 2000 1848; made under the School Standards and Framework Act 1998 s.44, s.138, Sch.9 para.4, Sch.11 para.1, Sch.11 para.2, Sch.11 para.3, Sch.11 para.4, Sch.11 para.8. In force: September 1, 2000; £1.50.

These Regulations amend the Education (School Government) (England) Regulations 1999 (SI 1999 2163) by making provision to ensure that when the Secretary of State nominates the chairman of the governing body of a school in special measures the governing body's duty to elect a chairman does not apply and the governing body cannot remove the Secretary of State's appointee. They rationalise the requirements for the quorum for governing body meetings; provide that a governing body's decision to discontinue a school must be confirmed at a second meeting held at least 28 days after the initial decision; prohibit the delegation by governing bodies of decisions about membership of their committees and clarify that staff dismissal committees and dismissal appeal committees set up with two governor members cannot consider cases or vote unless both members are present.

1931. Schools – school management – governing bodies – role of head teacher

EDUCATION (SCHOOL GOVERNMENT) (TERMS OF REFERENCE) (ENGLAND) REGULATIONS 2000, SI 2000 2122; made under the School Standards and Framework Act 1998 s.38, s.44, s.138. In force: September 1, 2000; £2.00.

These Regulations, which apply to the governing bodies and head teachers of maintained schools, set out two principles to operate as terms of reference for governing bodies. They provide that governing bodies are to carry out their functions with a view to fulfilling a largely strategic role in the school; the head teacher has responsibility for the internal organisation, management and control of the school, for advising the governing body in relation to the strategic framework and implementing the framework set out by the governing body; and confer particular functions on the governing body and head teacher in respect of the preparation of a policy for the school curriculum and the establishment of a performance management policy for the school.

1932. Schools – school management – role of head teacher and governing bodies – Wales

SCHOOL GOVERNMENT (TERMS OF REFERENCE) (WALES) REGULATIONS 2000, SI 2000 3027 (W.195); made under the School Standards and Framework Act 1998 s.38, s.138. In force: January 1, 2001; £2.00.

These Regulations, which apply to the governing bodies and head teachers of maintained schools in Wales, lay down a number of principles which are to serve as terms of reference for governing bodies and deal with the respective roles and responsibilities of governing bodies and head teachers. They impose a duty on the governing body and the head teacher to promote equal opportunities and good relations between persons of different racial groups and different genders, provide that the governing bodies are to establish a strategic framework for each school by setting aims and objectives and policies and targets for achieving those aims and objectives.

1933. Schools – school management – school organisation proposals

EDUCATION (SCHOOL ORGANISATION PROPOSALS) (ENGLAND) (AMENDMENT) REGULATIONS 2000, SI 2000 2198; made under the School Standards and Framework Act 1998 s.28, s.29, s.33, s.138, s.144, Sch.5 para.5, Sch.6 para.3, Sch.6 para.5, Sch.7 para.2, Sch.7 para.5, Sch.7 para.8, Sch.7 para.9, Sch.8 para.5. In force: September 1, 2000; £2.00.

These Regulations amend the Education (School Organisation Proposals) (England) Regulations 1999 (SI 1999 2213). In particular, they include the making of an agreement for the establishment of a new category of school, to be known as a city academy, as an event which can be specified in a conditional approval; require a school organisation committee to notify interested parties of any notification they receive of a local education authority's determination to implement proposals to which there were no objections by the end of the objection period; require the publication of proposals to increase the number of pupils in any relevant age group in cases where the increase will amount to 27 or more pupils; and provide that this requirement does not apply in the case of any increase in the admission of pupils to sixth form education.

1934. Schools – school management – school session times – Wales

CHANGING OF SCHOOL SESSION TIMES (WALES) REGULATIONS 2000, SI 2000 2030 (W.143); made under the School Standards and Framework Act 1998 s.41, s.138. In force: September 1, 2000; £2.00.

These Regulations set out the procedures to be taken by the governing body of a community, voluntary controlled or community special school before making any change in its session times. They do not apply to foundation, voluntary aided or foundation special schools. In particular, they specify when a change in the times of school sessions takes effect and provide for the meeting with parents, required to be held before any change in school session times is made, to be under the control of the governing body.

1935. Schools – school management – school session times – Wales

EDUCATION (SCHOOL DAY AND SCHOOL YEAR) (WALES) REGULATIONS 2000, SI 2000 1323 (W.101); made under the Education Act 1996 s.551, s.569. In force: May 1, 2000; £2.00.

These Regulations, which revoke and replace the Education (Schools and Further Education) Regulations 1981 (SI 1981 1086) Reg.10 in relation to Wales only, provide for the length of the school day and school year. In addition, they provide that not more than six school sessions devoted to the training of teachers in school teachers' appraisal, pay system or school staffing structures during the period May 1, 2000 to July 31, 2001 may be treated as sessions on which the school has met.

1936. Schools – school management – transition to new schools framework – Wales

EDUCATION (TRANSITION TO NEW FRAMEWORK) (NEW SCHOOLS, GROUPS AND MISCELLANEOUS) REGULATIONS 1999 (AMENDMENT) (WALES) REGULATIONS 2000, SI 2000 1867 (W.126); made under the School Standards and Framework Act 1998 s.138, s.144, Sch.10 para.1. In force: July 31, 2000; £2.00.

These Regulations amend the Education (Transition to New Framework) (New Schools, Groups and Miscellaneous) Regulations 1999 (SI 1999 362) Reg.54 to provide that property other than land, and associated rights and liabilities, of a grouped governing body held for the purposes of a school should vest in the new individual governing body of the school concerned. They also provide for any property other than land, and any associated rights and liabilities which have already passed to the local education authority under the 1999 Regulations to vest in the individual governing body of the appropriate school.

1937. Schools – school meals – nutritional standards

EDUCATION (NUTRITIONAL STANDARDS FOR SCHOOL LUNCHES) (ENGLAND) REGULATIONS 2000, SI 2000 1777; made under the School Standards and Framework Act 1998 s.114, s.138. In force: April 1, 2001; £1.50.

These Regulations introduce nutritional standards for school lunches for registered pupils at maintained nursery schools, community, foundation and voluntary schools and community and foundation special schools.

1938. Schools – selective grammar schools – parental ballots – vires of Education (Grammar School Ballot) Regulations 1998

[School Standards and Framework Act 1998 s.104; Human Rights Act 1998 s.6(1); Education (Grammar School Designation) Order 1998 (SI 1998 2219); Education (Grammar School Ballot) Regulations 1998 (SI 1998 2876); European Convention on Human Rights 1950.]

SMC was a designated grammar school under the Education (Grammar School Designation) Order 1998 and the School Standards and Framework Act 1998 s.104, in respect of which the Secretary of State was entitled to make the Education (Grammar School Ballot) Regulations 1998, the Ballot Regulations, which provided for a ballot of parents to be held at their request to decide whether such schools should retain their selective status. The Ballot Regulations created three categories of schools: (1) grammar schools within defined areas; (2) groups of grammar schools, and (3) individual grammar schools. For schools in both categories (1) and (2), parents of children at feeder schools could take part in the ballot, but for category (2) schools, including SMC, parents of current pupils could not take part in the ballot, whereas for schools in category (1), they could do so. R, a pupil currently attending SMC, sought to challenge the Ballot Regulations on the grounds that they were irrational, and, along with s.104 to s.108 of the Act, incompatible with the European Convention on Human Rights 1950, as embodied in English law by the Human Rights Act 1998 s.6(1).

Held, refusing the application, that it was logical for different parental participation rights to be applied in respect of the three categories, as in category (1) any change would affect an entire area, whereas children already attending category (2) schools would not be so directly affected by the end of selection as children coming from feeder schools. The Ballot Regulations effectively reflected Parliament's intention, as expressly provided for in the Act, and so could not be struck down on irrationality grounds in the absence of exceptional circumstances. The Human Rights Act 1998 s.6(1) was not yet in force and did not therefore confer any rights that were justiciable in an English court. Further, the application had been brought outside the relevant three month time limit. In the case of schools required to operate ballot procedures, it was necessary to ensure finality prior to the start of the next academic year.

R. v. SECRETARY OF STATE FOR EDUCATION AND EMPLOYMENT, *ex p.* RCO (A CHILD) [2000] Ed. C.R. 441, Scott Baker, J., QBD.

1939. Special educational needs – appeals – expedited appeal to House of Lords against SENT decision – child attending school during appeal process

B, a profoundly disabled five year old child, was the subject of a statement of special educational needs by HLBC. That statement named W as the appropriate school to meet B's needs. B's mother, who wanted B to attend G school in a neighbouring borough, appealed unsuccessfully against that decision to the SENT. The appeal against the SENT's decision was dismissed at first instance but upheld on appeal to the Court of Appeal, which remitted the matter to the SENT. The Court of Appeal refused to order that the rehearing be stayed pending the outcome of an appeal to the House of Lords. At the time, leave to appeal to the House of Lords had not been given and the Court of Appeal concluded that it would be contrary to B's interests for her to be shuttled back and forth between two schools. In February 1999, the second SENT concluded that it would be an inefficient use of general resources to send B to G. B was then attending W for half a day per week. In the meantime, HLBC obtained leave to appeal against the

Court of Appeal's judgment to the House of Lords. B then sought to appeal against the decision of the second SENT on a point of law. In April 1999, on application by HLBC, a master ordered that the appeal against the decision of the second SENT be stayed pending the outcome of the appeal to the House of Lords. B appealed against the order granting the stay, arguing that the appeal should be expedited. HLBC contended that the stay should be maintained, because if it succeeded at the House of Lords, the second SENT decision would be undermined and B's appeal against that decision would be a waste of time and money.

Held, allowing the appeal, that B's interests were the most important factor in the case and the courts should try to ensure that the litigation process did not result in her being shuttled back and forth between schools. That danger was more acute now that B was attending W and an effort was being made to integrate her there. The outcome of the appeal against the second SENT decision would not be resolved until the beginning of the new academic year. If matters were expedited that would be unlikely to result in B leaving W in the interim period. However, the refusal of a stay and allowing the appeal to be heard would not necessarily, even if that appeal were successful, result in B leaving W, at least until the outcome of the House of Lords appeal. A House of Lords decision in HLBC's favour would preserve the status quo. The costs of the appeal might well in that case be a waste of time and money. On the other hand, if the stay was maintained and there was no expedition of the appeal against the decision of the second SENT, all the time between the date of the instant hearing and the House of Lords judgment would be wasted. Although the matter was finely balanced, the damage that would result from the delay in expediting the statutory appeal outweighed the factor that the costs of the appeal could be wasted if the House of Lords ruled in HLBC's favour. The stay would therefore be lifted, B having stated that she would not contend that the House of Lord's decision was purely academic, *Smith Hogg & Co Ltd v. Black Sea and Baltic General Insurance Co Ltd* [1939] 2 All E.R. 855 considered.

R. v. HARROW LBC, *ex p.* B [1999] E.L.R. 495, Moses, J., QBD.

1940. **Special educational needs – delay in amending statement to name specific school – effect on right of appeal**

[Education Act 1996 s.313, s.314.]

A, a 12 year old autistic boy, was also diagnosed with dyspraxia and complex epilepsy. He had moderate to severe learning difficulties and KCC, the LEA, maintained a statement of his special educational needs. A was due to begin secondary education in September 1998 and in December 1997 KCC amended A's statement to name C, a non residential special school. A's parents appealed against the naming of C to the SENT, seeking a placement for A at D, an independent residential school which had specialised provision for children with epilepsy. The appeal was settled by KCC agreeing to fund a two term placement at D, beginning in September 1998. A's placement at D was successful and his parents wanted to ensure that he continued his education there. In March 1999, KCC agreed to a further extension of the placement by one term, to end in July 1999. A's parents obtained medical evidence with a view to launching an appeal in the event that KCC decided to amend the statement to name another school. In May, KCC decided that there were no medical grounds for continuing A's placement at D or any social reasons why A needed a residential placement. KCC decided not to amend the statement immediately but rather canvassed a number of different non residential schools regarding suitability and availability of places. On July 6, 1999 C indicated that it had a place available for the autumn term and, after further consultation, A's statement was amended on July 27, 1999, naming C. A's parents applied for judicial review of KCC's decision to amend, arguing that it was perverse on the grounds that there had been an undue and unjustified delay and that A's statutory right to an effective appeal had been stifled. It was argued that A's appeal would not be heard until November 24, 1999, and that because he would have to leave D in the interim, a successful appeal would have a disruptive effect on his schooling. Further, KCC could have made an amended statement naming a type of school rather than a specific school by mid May at the latest, thus allowing sufficient time for an appeal, and the failure to adopt this course of action showed a deliberate decision to proceed in a manner likely to stifle A's right of appeal.

Held, dismissing the appeal, that (1) in the context of amendments made to a statement of special educational needs, the Code of Practice issued under the Education Act 1996 s.313 and s.314 made it clear that any amendments and any arrangements arising there from should be made both in good time and in such a way as to cause as little disruption as possible to the education of the child. In the instant case, it was apparent that if KCC named C it knew or ought to have known that A's parents would be likely to appeal against that decision, and that an appeal would take some time. However, it could not be accepted that the decision to name C, and the consequent delay to the amendment of A's statement was perverse. It had been open to KCC to form the view that the issue regarding the amendment of the statement was whether a particular named school, and specifically C which A had previously attended, would be appropriate to meet A's complex needs. While it would have been open to KCC to amend the statement at an earlier stage merely to refer to placement at a non residential school and then re-amend to name a specific school later, such a process would not have been desirable in the circumstances. In order to substantiate its view that a non residential placement was more appropriate for A, KCC had been entitled to take steps to find a school and name it so as to facilitate a debate on the matter in the event that there was an appeal. In the circumstances, KCC's approach could not be described as involving an intentional delay calculated to stifle an appeal; (2) even when an appeal was likely against an amended statement, an LEA was not bound to consider whether it would be better to avoid delay by amending the statement without naming a specific school. In the instant case, KCC had reasonable grounds for concluding that a specific school should be named, and, assuming that there had been a failure to consider an earlier amendment without naming a school, that did not show perversity, and (3) in any event, A's parents were still entitled to have their appeal heard, and while a successful appeal would result in some disruption to A's education, that may have occurred in any case. The mere fact of disruption could not be equated with stifling the right to an effective appeal.

R. v. KENT CC, *ex p.* AMS (A MINOR) [2000] Ed. C.R. 68, Moses, J., QBD.

1941. Special educational needs – disabilities – child suffering from autism and severe language disorder – suitability of mainstream school

[Education Act 1996 s.316 Sch.27 para.3(3).]

A, the father of F, a 10 year old child with mild autism and severe specific language disorder, appealed against a decision of the special educational needs tribunal that F should continue to attend a mainstream school. A, who wished him to attend a special autistic school, had previously appealed against the statement of special educational needs of the local education authority, BLBC, in which it was recommended that F continue attending the mainstream school. The special educational needs tribunal, having found that F should be placed in a school able to deal with his mild degree of autism, went on to hold that the mainstream school was suitable, notwithstanding the fact that it was not protecting F from bullying and did not have a teacher sufficiently qualified to give F the language therapy he required. A appealed, contending that (1) the tribunal had failed to appreciate that under the Education Act 1996 Sch.27 para.3(3) it was for BLBC to prove that the special school was unsuitable and they had not done so. A submitted that the tribunal's finding that there was no evidence to show that it was unsuitable had therefore been inadequate; (2) the tribunal's decision that the mainstream school was suitable had been perverse given its findings that the school was failing F in relation to the problem of bullying and the provision of specialised therapies, combined with the fact that it had a policy of not admitting autistic children, and (3) the tribunal had not properly applied s.316 of the Act which gave a parent the right to veto their child's integration into mainstream education.

Held, dismissing the appeal, that (1) it was clear that there had been sufficient evidence before the tribunal in relation to both schools for it to have made a finding that the mainstream school was more suitable and for that decision to have been in accordance with Sch.27 para.3(3) of the 1996 Act; (2) the tribunal's findings in relation to the school's failures did not outweigh their general finding that the school as a whole was able to meet F's needs. It followed that the decision had not been perverse, and (3) s.316 of the Act contained no express intention to provide a parental veto. It was accordingly open to the tribunal to prefer BLBC's assessment of F's needs and how they could be met.

F (A MINOR) v. BRENT LBC; *sub nom.* R. v. F (A MINOR); R. v. BRENT LBC, *ex p.* AF [2000] Ed. C.R. 425, Owen, J., QBD.

1942. Special educational needs – failure to specify level of teaching in statement

[Education (Special Educational Needs) Regulations 1994 (SI 1994 1047).]

H, the parents of a child with severe learning difficulties, appealed against a tribunal's decision to endorse the LEA's selection of a school for their child. H contended that (1) the tribunal had erred by failing to take into consideration the willingness of the LEA to pay for a placement with the result that any difference in cost between a private and a local authority specialist school was negligible; (2) the tribunal had failed to specify clearly the level of teaching, and (3) the tribunal had failed to give sufficient consideration to an expert's report.

Held, allowing the appeal in part, that the tribunal's consideration of the use of the authority's resources had been appropriate. The tribunal had properly reviewed the available evidence and therefore its decision could not be considered irrational. There had been no breach of the requirement to provide a statement of reasons. However, the tribunal's amendment to the special educational provisional statement was insufficiently specific under the Education (Special Educational Needs) Regulations 1994 and the Code of Practice para.4.28.

H v. LEICESTERSHIRE CC; *sub nom.* R. v. LEICESTERSHIRE CC, *ex p.* H [2000] E.L.R. 471, Dyson, J., QBD.

1943. Special educational needs – funding – liability of LEA for travelling costs

[Education Act 1996 s.324(5)(a)(i).]

A, who was brain damaged and had special educational needs, sought judicial review of the decision of the LEA, ILBC, to refuse payment of the costs of travelling to an independent school, located 75 miles from his parental home and at which he was a weekly boarder. In its assessment of A's educational needs ILBC had not named a local school. The principal special education officer had informed A's parents that ILBC would fund A's attendance at the boarding school on the basis that his parents would provide transport. Upon A becoming seriously ill, necessitating a greater number of journeys, his parents asked ILBC to reconsider its decision. In response, ILBC restated its position that it was able to make local provision for A's education and that attendance at the school was funded on the basis that travel was the responsibility of his parents. A argued that ILBC was under a duty, pursuant to the Education Act 1996 s.324(5)(a)(i), to make arrangements for his attendance at the school, failing which the statement of special educational needs had to be amended to specify a suitable local school.

Held, granting the application, that ILBC had been *Wednesbury* unreasonable in failing to take account of the extra journeys necessitated by A's illness and in failing to give consideration to the ability of his parents to pay for the travel arrangements. It was not open to ILBC to rely on the belief that A's education could be provided locally where no local school had been mentioned in the statement of special needs.

R. v. ISLINGTON LBC, *ex p.* A (A CHILD) *The Times,* October 20, 2000, Jack Beatson, Q.C., QBD.

1944. Special educational needs – independent schools – Secretary of State's refusal to consent to school admission based solely on child's age

[Education Act 1996 s.347(5)(b).]

P, the mother of J, a child suffering from attention deficit hyperactivity disorder and dyslexia, sought judicial review of the Secretary of State's refusal to allow him to be educated at an independent school on the basis that the school did not have the appropriate registration to teach primary school children. P contended that the Secretary of State had erred in concentrating on the issue of registration rather than the possibility of granting an individual consent under the Education Act 1996 s.347(5)(b) for J, and that he had failed to provide proper reasons for his decision.

Held, granting the application, that the Secretary of State had applied departmental policy too rigidly in relation to J, his decision having been based solely on J's age without regard being had to the individual circumstances of the case.

R. v. SECRETARY OF STATE FOR EDUCATION AND EMPLOYMENT, *ex p.* P [2000] Ed. C.R. 669, Dyson, J., QBD.

1945. Special educational needs – local education authorities – genuine administrative error in special needs statement – power to amend statement

[Education Act 1996 s.324(5)(a)(i), s.326(3)(b).]

B, the parents of an eight year old child, J, who suffered from cerebral palsy, applied for judicial review after an administrative error had been made on J's statement of special educational needs. The statement followed an agreement reached at a Special Educational Needs Tribunal and the error concerned the amount of individual support which J needed and which was available from support assistants at her primary school. B contended that even if a mistake had been made, the local authority, WMBC, were under a duty to make provision for J in accordance with the statement, pursuant to the Education Act 1996 s.324(5)(a)(i). WMBC argued that a subsequent amended form of the statement was applicable.

Held, refusing the application, that a genuine administrative error had been made. The correct version of the statement was the one which had been amended under s.326(3)(b) of the Act and which accurately reflected the decision of the tribunal. Upon a proper construction, the amended statement did not impose a duty upon WMBC to provide classroom support exclusively to J.

R. v. WIRRAL MBC, *ex p.* B (A CHILD) [2000] B.L.G.R. 541, Maurice Kay, J., QBD.

1946. Special educational needs – local education authorities – resources of sending and receiving authorities

[Education Act 1996 s.411, Sch.27 para.3(3).]

H, a local education authority, appealed against a decision ([1998] 3 F.C.R. 231, [1998] C.L.Y. 1970) that in assessing a request to send a special needs child to a school situated outside its area, it was to take into account the resources of the receiving authority as well as its own resources. H drew attention to the Education Act 1996 Sch.27 para.3(3), which stated that once an LEA had decided that a child had special needs, it was to state the name of the school to be attended, unless that would be "incompatible with an efficient use of resources" H argued that Sch.27 para.3(3) referred to the resources of the sending authority in contradistinction to the position with regard to schools that did not cater for special needs pupils, where general resource constraints might be taken into account.

Held, allowing the appeal, that there was a distinction to be drawn between schools that catered for pupils with special needs and those that did not do so. In the case of special needs schools, the LEA was entitled to take into account only its own resources. In the case of schools that did not cater for pupils with special needs, there was a specific right to send a child outside the LEA's area and under s.411 the authority was required to take into account resource constraints generally, whereas no comparable right existed in relation to special needs schools. The cost of sending a child to a special needs school outside the LEA's area was likely to be higher than the cost of sending a child to a school that did not cater for pupils with special needs and for that reason there were two schemes in place.

B v. HARROW LBC (NO.1); *sub nom.* F v. HARROW LBC; B v. SPECIAL EDUCATIONAL NEEDS TRIBUNAL; F v. SPECIAL EDUCATION NEEDS TRIBUNAL [2000] 1 W.L.R. 223, Lord Slynn of Hadley, HL.

1947. Special educational needs – local education authorities – vicarious liability

[Supreme Court Act 1981 s.33(2).]

P and three others suffered from various learning difficulties, including in the case of three of them, dyslexia, resulting in their experiencing academic as well as social difficulties and in one case suffering from clinical depression. P. had brought an action against her local authority, alleging that its failure to provide appropriate education for pupils with special educational needs and its failure to mitigate the effects of the condition had been a direct cause of her failure to find employment and the consequential loss of wages. In a decision of the Court of Appeal ([1999] 1 W.L.R. 500, [1998] C.L.Y. 3945) allowing the appeal of the local authority from the QBD decision ([1997] 3 F.C.R. 621, [1997] C.L.Y. 2142), it was held that dyslexia could not constitute a personal injury and that there were strong policy reasons for not imposing a duty of care on the employee of a local authority. On appeal, it was contended by the appellants that they had a right to claim damages from the local authority since they had suffered personal injuries caused as a direct result of the educational psychologist's breach of duty, for which the local authority was vicariously liable.

Held, that a local education authority could be vicariously liable for the acts of its employees and there was no justification for a blanket immunity policy in respect of education officers performing the authority's functions with regard to children with special educational needs, *X (Minors) v. Bedfordshire CC* [1995] 2 A.C. 633, [1995] C.L.Y. 3452 doubted. An employee, such as an educational psychologist, exercising a particular skill or profession, might owe a duty of care to particular pupils where it could be foreseen that those pupils might be injured if due skill and care were not exercised in the performance of that duty. Such a situation would arise where an educational psychologist was specifically engaged to offer advice in relation to the assessment of and future provision for a specific child and it was clear that the parents of the child and the child's teachers would rely on the advice and act upon it. Where a duty of care existed, if that duty was breached by failing to diagnose specific learning difficulties such as dyslexia and failing to take steps to ameliorate the condition, the local authority could be held vicariously liable for the consequential loss suffered. However, the court also had to have regard to any public policy reasons for not imposing such liability and should be slow to find negligence since such a finding might interfere with the performance of the authority's duties. A failure to diagnose a congenital condition such as dyslexia and to take the necessary action, resulting in a child's level of academic achievement being reduced and a consequential loss of wages, could constitute damage for the purpose of a claim and could give rise to a claim for personal injuries under the Supreme Court Act 1981 s.33(2).

PHELPS v. HILLINGDON LBC; ANDERTON v. CLWYD CC; G (A CHILD) v. BROMLEY LBC; JARVIS v. HAMPSHIRE CC, *Re*; *sub nom.* G (A CHILD), *Re* [2000] 3 W.L.R. 776, Lord Slynn of Hadley, HL.

1948. Special educational needs – parental rights – choice of school for disabled child – weight to be accorded to parental wishes

[Education Act 1996 s.9, s.316, s.324, s.411, Sch.27.]

L, a child suffering from cerebral palsy and Turner's syndrome, appealed against a decision of the Special Educational Needs Tribunal that her needs would be adequately catered for at a mainstream state day school rather than at the independent special school which was the preferred choice of her mother, M. L's appeal to the High Court was dismissed and L appealed, contending that the tribunal had paid insufficient regard to M's wishes. L maintained that a similar balancing act to that required to be carried out under the Education Act 1996 s.411 and Sch.27 was required under s.316, and that under s.316, the LEA or tribunal was first required to determine whether the conditions for mainstream schooling in s.316(2) were satisfied so as to give rise to the duty to provide mainstream education and then ascertain whether mainstream education contradicted parental wishes. L argued that if a contradiction was found to exist then the relevant authority or tribunal was required to perform a balancing exercise between parental wishes on the one hand and the resource implications and other benefits of mainstream provision on the other.

Held, dismissing the appeal, that the duty to provide mainstream education under s.316 had been negatived by M's objections. In consequence s.316 ceased to have relevance and the only obligations requiring consideration were those ordinary obligations arising under s.324 and the general duty to take account of parental wishes in s.9, *S (A Minor) v. Special Educational Needs Tribunal* [1995] 1 W.L.R. 1627, [1995] C.L.Y. 1937 and *South Glamorgan CC v. L and M* [1996] E.L.R. 400, [1997] C.L.Y. 2136 applied. On that basis the tribunal had made no discernible error of law, *C v. Buckinghamshire CC* [1999] B.L.G.R. 321, [1999] C.L.Y. 1896 considered.

L (A MINOR) v. HEREFORD AND WORCESTER CC; *sub nom.* L v. WORCESTERSHIRE CC [2000] Ed. C.R. 492, Hale, L.J., CA.

1949. Special educational needs – schools – relocation – effect of statement naming particular school

After moving from the area of one LEA to another, the parents of S, a child who was the subject of a statement of special educational needs, were informed that S could no longer attend the school named in that statement. On the parents' application for judicial review the LEA accepted that it had acted unlawfully, but contended that as the school was full and since responsibility for the child's education now rested with another LEA, relief should not be granted.

Held, that the statement naming an appropriate school for the child was still valid and operative. Although responsibility for the child's education had passed to another LEA, until a decision by that LEA had been reached, the court should make reasonable orders to ensure that the child continued his education at the named school in accordance with the statement.

R. v. MANCHESTER CITY COUNCIL, *ex p.* S [1999] E.L.R. 414, Scott Baker, J., QBD.

1950. Special educational needs – Special Educational Needs Tribunal – need to hear evidence before striking out appeal

[Special Educational Needs Tribunal Regulations 1995 (SI 1995 3113) Reg.36(2)(b).]

SGC had issued a statement of special educational needs in relation to G's son. The parties could not agree upon the choice of school to be named in the statement, each having rejected the preferences of the other. SGC eventually issued a final statement naming a different grant maintained school to those previously proposed. G appealed against SGC's choice on the basis that the school was unable to meet the provisions set out in the statement. The Special Educational Needs Tribunal considered G's grounds of appeal and a letter from the Director of Education and struck out the appeal pursuant to the Special Educational Needs Tribunal Regulations 1995 Reg.36(2)(b) on the grounds that it was scandalous, frivolous or vexatious. G appealed against the striking out, contending that this was a first appeal in relation to the choice of this particular school and its suitability to meet the special educational needs of his son. G maintained that having established that it had jurisdiction to hear the appeal, the tribunal had, by striking it out without a hearing, preferred one set of facts over another without hearing any evidence, an approach which was not permitted by Reg.36. SGC contended that G's appeal against the school named in the final statement was an attempt to relitigate the issue of his own choice of school, as he was not adducing any fresh evidence or raising any new issues.

Held, allowing the appeal, that although the history of the litigation was long and involved, this was a first appeal to attempt to establish that this particular school was not an appropriate choice and the tribunal had erred in law because it had determined factual issues without hearing any evidence, *White v. Aldridge (President of the Special Educational Needs Tribunal)* [1999] Ed. C.R. 488, [1998] C.L.Y. 1981 considered.

G (A CHILD) v. SOUTH GLOUCESTERSHIRE COUNCIL [2000] Ed. C.R. 401, Hidden, J., QBD.

1951. Special educational needs – Special Educational Needs Tribunal – procedural impropriety – unlawful to order production of papers relating to previous decisions

F applied to quash a decision of the SENT that papers relating to a decision and appeal brought by F in the previous year should be considered when determining F's second appeal.

Held, granting the application, that the tribunal was not entitled to demand the papers relating to the appeals to the earlier tribunal and to the High Court. The decision would therefore be quashed.

R. v. SPECIAL EDUCATIONAL NEEDS TRIBUNAL, *ex p.* F [1999] E.L.R. 417, Ognall, J., QBD.

1952. Special educational needs – special schools – attention deficit disorder – appropriateness of placement at special school

M, aged 11 years, was diagnosed as suffering from attention deficit disorder. He had been excluded from school two years earlier and had since been taught at home. The local authority formed the view that he should be reintroduced to a special school for children with emotional or behavioural problems. M's parents wanted him to attend a mainstream primary school and appealed to the SENT, which concluded that the parents' choice of school would not cater for M's needs and that the special school was more appropriate for the time being. The parents appealed to the High Court on the grounds that the tribunal (1) had been wrong to rely on the evidence of the educational psychologist, who had relied mainly upon written reports, and that of the head teacher of the special school, who had no personal knowledge of the child; (2) had failed to consider schools other than the LEA's choice; (3) had been wrong to consider the fact of the child's earlier exclusion from school, and (4) had failed to consider properly the evidence of the child's father.

Held, dismissing the appeal, that the SENT had not acted irrationally by taking into account the evidence of the psychologist and deciding what weight to attach to it. The tribunal had been entitled to reach its conclusion about the appropriateness of the special school for M and to take into account the fact that M had been excluded from school two years earlier. Furthermore, the tribunal had not ignored the father's evidence, but had instead decided not to accept his arguments, so that there had been no procedural error.

AE v. SPECIAL EDUCATIONAL NEEDS TRIBUNAL [1999] E.L.R. 341, Keene, J., QBD.

1953. Special educational needs – special schools – effect of transport and occupational therapy costs

[Education Act 1996 Sch.27 para.3; Education (Special Schools) Regulations 1994 (SI 1994 652).]

B, who was born in 1993, was diagnosed in 1995 as having Rett syndrome. She was not independently mobile and had severe learning difficulties. HLBC, the LEA, maintained a statement of special educational needs for B. The statement named X, a school for children with profound and severe learning difficulties located close to

B's family home as the appropriate school to meet B's needs. B's mother had previously expressed a preference for Y, another school for children with severe and profound learning difficulties but located in another borough about three miles from the family home, as she was entitled to do under the Education Act 1996 Sch.27 para.3. B's mother appealed to the SENT against the naming of X school. The SENT upheld HLBC's decision to name X school on the grounds that (1) B's attendance at Y would not be an efficient use of resources, within the meaning of Sch.27 para.3(3)(b). The finding was based on a conclusion that B's attendance at Y school would result in the expenditure of an additional £7,000 per year: £6,000 on transport costs and £1,000 on occupational therapy, and (2) the placement of B at Y school would entail a breach of the Education (Special Schools) Regulations 1994, in that Y had already accepted numbers in excess of the total approved by the Secretary of State. B's mother appealed, arguing that the SENT had been wrong in law to include the transport costs, and that the occupational therapy costs by themselves could not be a basis for the decision on the use of resources. Further, the transport costs should not be included because B's mother had committed herself to drive B to Y school and it was unfair of the SENT to hold that HLBC would need to meet the transport costs without allowing B's mother the opportunity of showing that she could meet her commitment. The SENT had held that, on the evidence, it was likely that HLBC would have to meet the costs because B's mother had had difficulty ensuring B's regular attendance at X school, which was much closer to the family home.

Held, dismissing the appeal, that (1) the SENT's conclusion that on the evidence it was likely that B's mother would be unable to fulfil her commitment to transport B to school was difficult to challenge as a matter of law. It followed from that finding that it was open to the SENT to hold that either the transport costs would have to be met by HLBC or that X school was the only appropriate school. If B was not able to attend Y school regularly it could not be said to be the appropriate school to meet her special educational needs, and (2) the SENT was justified in finding, as a matter of educational judgment, that the additional cost of £1,000 for occupational therapy was by itself sufficient to base a conclusion that B's attendance at Y school would be incompatible with the efficient use of resources. Provided that an approved limit was in place under the 1994 Regulations, it was open to an LEA to refuse to name a particular school in a statement of special educational needs on the ground that to do so would involve a breach of the approval given under the Regulations. It followed that the SENT had been entitled to use this as an additional ground for dismissing B's appeal.

B v. HARROW LBC (NO.2) [2000] Ed. C.R. 62, Latham, J., QBD.

1954. Special educational needs – special schools – preferred school over subscribed

[Education Act 1996 s.9, Sch.27 para.3; Education (Special Schools) Regulations 1994 (SI 1994 652) Part VI para. 8.]

S's son, B, had special educational needs and attended a special school, V, which was maintained by BCC as the relevant LEA. V's headmaster believed that B could transfer to W, another special school maintained by BCC, and S therefore asked D, his LEA, to name W in B's statement. D accepted that W was an appropriate placement, and did not suggest that B's attendance there would be incompatible with the efficient use of resources or the education of other pupils, but refused S's request on the basis that W was oversubscribed and no place could be allocated. S appealed to the Special Educational Needs Tribunal, which dismissed the appeal in reliance upon *Sunderland City Council v. P and C* [1996] E.L.R. 283, [1996] C.L.Y. 2496, finding that the amendment sought could not be allowed as the Education (Special Schools) Regulations 1994 Part VI, para.8 provided that the number of pupils at W could not exceed that specified. S appealed.

Held, allowing the appeal, that the tribunal had failed to consider whether there was a conflict between the Education Act 1996 s.9 and Sch.27 para.3, on the one hand, and Part VI para.8 of the Regulations on the other. It was inevitable that Sch.27 para.3 would come into play when parents sought the naming in a statement of special educational needs of a school that was already up to its permitted capacity; *Sunderland* was to be distinguished as the decision in that case was concerned with the criteria for attending a specified school.

S v. DUDLEY MBC [2000] Ed. C.R. 200,Turner, J., QBD.

1955. Special educational needs – special schools – provision of education at day school for autistic child – mother's opposition properly considered by SENT

[Education Act 1996 s.9.]

T, a 10 year old autistic boy with severe learning difficulties, had had no formal education since October 1997 when his mother, W, withdrew him from school and sought to provide him with an education at home. The educational experts, including those instructed by W, agreed that T's educational needs would best be served at a residential school. However, W was opposed to such a placement. SMBC, the LEA, carried out an assessment of T's special educational needs and produced a statement of those needs in July 1998. The statement named M, a maintained special day school, as the school which would best meet T's needs and enable him to re-enter formal education. W wanted T to attend S, a specialist residential school for autistic children, as a day pupil. W unsuccessfully challenged the choice of M before the SENT and she appealed, contending that (1) she had agreed before the tribunal that it was an essential aspect of her challenge to the statement that, as and when T became accustomed to formal education, his placement at S should gradually become residential, and (2) the SENT had not properly considered her case and had not given sufficient regard to her parental preference, contrary to the Education Act 1996 s.9.

Held, dismissing the appeal, that (1) on the basis of the affidavit evidence and the SENT's reasons it was clear that W had been opposed throughout to a residential placement for T. It was not her case that S should be named because it would later enable a smooth transition to be made to residential education for T when he was ready. It followed that the SENT had not misunderstood her case and that it had dealt with it on the basis that she had wished, namely the question of what was the appropriate day provision for T, and (2) the issue as to whether the SENT had complied with its duty under s.9 did not depend solely on whether it had considered W's preference, it was also necessary to consider whether the reasons for that preference had been adequately addressed, *C v. Buckinghamshire CC* [1999] B.L.G.R. 321, [1999] C.L.Y. 1896 applied. In the instant case, the SENT had dealt fully and properly with each of the reasons advanced by W for her preference for S. In particular, the SENT had considered W's contention that T would be better cared for and taught in a school specialising in the education of autistic children and had given adequate reasons, including the greater level of out of school support at M and the availability of integrated services provided by SMBC, for rejecting that contention. Having dealt with the merits of S, as advanced by W, it had not been necessary to embark on a full assessment of S and the mere fact that W had preferred S did not alter the position.

W-R v. SOLIHULL MBC [1999] E.L.R. 528, Latham, J., QBD.

1956. Special educational needs – special schools – unsuitability of placement at residential school

S and M, two brothers of school age, had very poor school attendance records. According to an educational psychologist, S suffered from moderate learning difficulty, a contributory cause of which was probably his lack of regular schooling. In M's case, the educational psychologist concluded that he was suffering from low self esteem and that he would need a great deal of support and encouragement to return to education. MCC, the local education authority, recommended that both brothers should continue their education at a residential school. The matter came before the Special Educational Needs Tribunal, SENT, which rejected MCC's recommendations. The SENT found that S did not suffer from "emotional and behavioural difficulties" within the meaning of the relevant

Code of Practice, and that M did not do so sufficiently to warrant his being educated at a residential school. The SENTconcluded that whilst S displayed certain features referred to in the Code of Practice as being indicative of emotional and behavioural difficulties, it could not be said that his educational problems fell within the category of emotional and behavioural difficulties. In M's case, the SENT found that his fundamental problem was one of non attendance and that he would not be assisted by going to a residential school and mixing with children who suffered from emotional and behavioural difficulties. MCC appealed against the decision contending that the SENT's findings conflicted with those of the educational psychologist and were therefore irrational. MCC argued that the SENT had erred in treating the guidance in the Code of Practice as a list of criteria, all of which had to be present in order to justify a finding that a child suffered from emotional and behavioural difficulties.

Held, dismissing the appeal, that the SENT had been entitled to reject MCC's recommendations and had not misdirected itself in its interpretation of the Code of Practice. The SENT had not been bound to follow the findings of the educational psychologist if persuaded that the conclusions reached by the psychologist were not justified on the evidence. It was not correct to say that the SENT had concluded that all of the criteria mentioned in the Code of Practice should be present in order to justify a finding that a child suffered from emotional and behavioural difficulties. In this case, the SENT had considered the criteria and concluded that certain elements of those criteria were absent. Since the SENT had made no specific directions as to the nature and extent of the boys' individual tuition, the case would be remitted to the SENT for such directions to be given.

MANCHESTER CITY COUNCIL v. SPECIAL EDUCATIONAL NEEDS TRIBUNAL [2000] Ed. C.R. 80, Collins, J., QBD.

1957. **Special Educational Needs Tribunal – appeals – costs – liability of Special Educational Needs Tribunal**

[Rules of the Supreme Court 1965 (SI 1965 1776) Ord.55; Civil Procedure Rules 1998 (SI 1998 3132).]

S successfully appealed ([2000] Ed. C.R. 200, [2000] C.L.Y. 1954) against a decision of a Special Educational Needs Tribunal dismissing S's appeal against a statement of special educational needs made by DMBC. The tribunal was ordered to pay S's costs, with liberty being given to apply for the order to be discharged. The tribunal applied, contending that it could not appear on the appeal as of right by reason of the Rules of the Supreme Court Ord.55 and that there were no factors in the instant case capable of justifying the costs order.

Held, granting the application and discharging the costs order, that whilst the tribunal had surprisingly preferred delegated legislation over a statutory provision in its initial decision which had not been reviewed in terms of the Civil Procedure Rules 1998 overriding objective, that conduct was not perverse and did not exceed the stringent criteria to be met before the tribunal could be held liable for an appellant's costs, *R. v. Lincoln Justices, ex p. Count* (1996) 8 Admin. L.R. 233, [1995] C.L.Y. 129 applied.

S v. DUDLEY MBC (COSTS) [2000] Ed. C.R. 410, Turner, J., QBD.

1958. **Special Educational Needs Tribunal – appeals procedure**

[Rules of the Supreme Court 1965 (SI 1965 1776) Ord.55.]

On February 8, 1999, H's child was the subject of a Special Educational Needs Tribunal decision that she wished to challenge. The decision letter sent to H's former representative stated that a challenge was only possible on appeal to the High Court. H made a written application to the tribunal for a review, but solicitors acting for her subsequently wrote to the tribunal, stating that they had now been instructed and seeking guidance as to the relevant appeal procedure. H's solicitors' notes of a subsequent telephone call revealed that what was being talked about was a review, not an appeal. The tribunal replied on March 2, 1999, indicating that it was not prepared to review the decision. H's solicitors proceeded on the basis that the reference to review meant judicial review. They sought legal aid on that basis, writing to the tribunal on March 18, 1999 to inform it of the grant of legal aid, subject to counsel's opinion, to apply for judicial review. The tribunal replied on April 1, 1999, stating that an appeal was required, and that the time limit for an application was 28 days from the date of the decision. H's solicitors stated that the time limit was 3 months, to which the tribunal replied, identifying authority for the proposition, that the correct route of appeal was pursuant to the Rules of the Supreme Court Ord.55. H's solicitors finally accepted the proposition and lodged papers for an appeal on April 26, 1999. H applied for an extension of time for the filing of the notice of appeal.

Held, refusing the application, that (1) the matter of extending the time in which to file notice of appeal had to be approached by keeping the need for a tight timetable for such appeals firmly in mind. In the instant case, it was also relevant that the child's special educational needs were due to be reconsidered in November 1999, and (2) H's former representative had been told of the appropriate route, and H's newly instructed solicitors had been given a clear indication of the appropriate procedure in the letter of April 1. The unexplained or unjustified delays and the periods involved meant that it would be inappropriate to extend the time for appealing.

H v. NORTHAMPTONSHIRE CC [2000] Ed. C.R. 238, Latham, J., QBD.

1959. Special Educational Needs Tribunal – expert evidence – justification for adjournment

W was the subject of a special educational needs statement naming CGS as the school that could best meet his needs. CGS came into being in 1995 following the merger of DSS and another school. W's mother did not believe that CGS was appropriate and instructed an educational psychologist, H, to provide an assessment report. H had previously been headteacher of DSS and had unsuccessfully applied for the headship of CGS, as a result of which he had given an undertaking not to have any involvement with CGS. H indicated to W's mother that he could not complete his assessment of CGS without gaining access to the school and to the teaching staff involved in the provision of special educational needs tuition. Having regard to the history of the matter, and to the terms of H's undertaking, CGS refused to allow H access to the school. Prior to the hearing before the SENT, W's mother unsuccessfully sought an adjournment. She then applied for an order directing that the SENT adjourn the proceedings on the basis that otherwise she would be disadvantaged, due to the lack of H's full report.

Held, refusing the application, that having regard to the SENT's procedural rules a court should be slow to interfere with the conduct of a case before the tribunal. In the instant case, even if the court or the tribunal had the power to direct CGS to grant access to H, such an order could not be made as a matter of discretion. Having regard to the antipathy towards H, it would not be possible for him to obtain a proper assessment as to how CGS would fulfil the requirements of the special educational needs statement. W's mother had to make a choice between proceeding with the hearing before the SENT on the basis of H's evidence as it was, or of asking for an adjournment in order to instruct another educational psychologist to make the assessment.

R. v. HEAD TEACHER AND GOVERNING BODY OF CRUG GLAS SCHOOL, *ex p.* W (A MINOR) [1999] E.L.R. 484, Latham, J., QBD.

1960. Special Educational Needs Tribunal – jurisdiction – removal of statement of child over age of 16

[Education Act 1996 s.312(5), Sch.27 para.11.]

S appealed against the decision of the Special Educational Needs Tribunal that it did not have jurisdiction to hear S's appeal against the LEA's decision to cease to maintain a statement of special educational needs for her son. S contended that the tribunal had wrongly concluded that her son who was not a registered pupil at a school and aged over 16 at the time of the appeal, was not a child for the purposes of the appeal under the Education Act 1996 Sch.27 para.11.

Held, allowing the appeal, that the tribunal had jurisdiction to hear the appeal. S had received notice of the authority's intention to cease maintenance of the statement at a time when her son was of compulsory school age and a registered pupil. The definition of a "child" under s.312(5) included any child who had been the subject of a statement at the time that the LEA made the decision and gave notice to cease to maintain a statement.

S v. ESSEX CC [2000] Ed. C.R. 471, Turner, J., QBD.

1961. **Special Educational Needs Tribunal – special schools – tribunal's inability to resolve fundamental differences between parties concerning extent of educational need**

[Education Act 1996 s.324.]

S, aged 13, suffered from attention deficit hyperactivity disorder, ADHD, Asperger's Syndrome and dyspraxia, together with a communication disorder. SCC issued a statement of S's special educational needs under the Education Act 1996 s.324, concluding that S's local comprehensive school would be suitable. S appealed on the ground that his needs could only be properly met at a specialist residential school. At the conclusion of the hearing before the SENT the parties appeared to have reached agreement on the statement, the appeal was dismissed and the tribunal found that the local school was adequate. S appealed, arguing that the tribunal, (1) had not properly ascertained the nature of the agreement between the parties, and had ignored the fact that there was significant variance in the parties' views as to the extent of his condition; (2) had been wrong to identify a school before it had fully explored what was required to meet his needs; (3) had heard insufficient evidence to enable it to reach a decision about the facilities that would be provided by the local school, and (4) had failed to give in its determination an adequate level of specific detail about the programme and facilities to be provided to him.

Held, allowing the appeal and remitting the case, that the tribunal's decision was fatally flawed in that (1) the tribunal had failed to appreciate that differences between the parties remained in relation to S's needs arising as a result of the ADHD, Asperger's Syndrome and the communication disorder, and, consequently, had failed to address those issues in its findings; (2) although it was clear that the tribunal had to make findings in respect of S's condition and consequent needs before seeking a solution, it was, however, entitled to "lean" towards a particular school, given the need to find a workable solution, provided that it had satisfied itself that that school was capable of fulfilling the needs which it had identified in part 2 of the statement of special educational needs, *R. v. Secretary of State for Education and Science, ex p. E* [1992] 1 F.L.R. 377, [1992] C.L.Y. 1877 and *R. v. Secretary of State for Education, ex p. W* (Unreported, May 27, 1994) applied; (3) expert evidence had identified specific therapies needed by S, including occupational therapy. The latter was unavailable at the local school and there was little or no evidence before the tribunal capable of satisfying it that the experts' recommendations could be carried out at that school, and (4) the statement had to be "so clear as to leave no room for doubt as to what has been decided is necessary in the individual case", *L v. Clarke* [1998] E.L.R. 129, [1998] C.L.Y. 1978 applied. In the instant case the experts' views were very specific, but the statement did not reflect that level of specificity and was therefore inadequate.

S v. SWANSEA CITY AND COUNTY COUNCIL [2000] E.L.R. 315, Sullivan, J., QBD.

1962. Special Educational Needs Tribunal – witnesses – LEA giving evidence through representative as well as by two witnesses

[Special Educational Needs Tribunal Regulations 1995 (SI 1995 3113) Reg.29(1).]

H, the mother of a child with special educational needs, appealed against a SENT decision refusing her appeal against the school placement allocated by GCC, the LEA. H contended that GCC had wrongly been allowed to give evidence through its representative and two witnesses, contrary to the Special Educational Needs Tribunal Regulations 1995 Reg.29(1), which provided that no more than two witnesses could give evidence orally for each party.

Held, dismissing the appeal, that GCC was permitted to give evidence through its representative as well as to call the evidence of two witnesses. It was the intention of Reg.29 that both parties should be treated as equals in the proceedings. GCC was a corporate entity which could only act in the appeal through its appointed representative, who was not acting as a witness and was not precluded from giving evidence of the child's circumstances.

H v. GLOUCESTERSHIRE CC; *sub nom.* R. v. GLOUCESTERSHIRE CC, *ex p.* H [2000] E.L.R. 357, Elias, J., QBD.

1963. Special schools – judicial review – non resuscitation policy

[Education Act 1996 s.19.]

D, a physically disabled child with special educational needs, attended C, a special school. In 1998 the headteacher gave instructions that D was not to be resuscitated if she stopped breathing. The policy was changed soon afterwards following a complaint from D's grandparents to the school governors. The grandparents complained to the Secretary of State, who concluded that an independent review was unnecessary. Due to D's ill health, the LEA provided her with home tuition. The grandparents lost confidence in C and decided not to return D until they had a satisfactory response to their complaint. D subsequently obtained legal aid in December 1998 to seek judicial review of (1) the headteacher's decision to introduce the non resuscitation policy; (2) the adequacy of the governors' investigation, and (3) the LEA's failure under the Education Act 1996 s.19 to provide her with an adequate education. The application for leave was not made until March 1999.

Held, refusing the application, that (1) the decision complained of had been taken in April 1998 and the length of delay alone justified refusal; (2) the non resuscitation policy had existed for only a few days and had been promptly withdrawn. Accordingly, judicial review would serve no useful purpose; (3) the LEA's decision not to hold an independent investigation was confirmed by the Secretary of State and could not be said to be *Wednesbury* unreasonable. Further, the headteacher was now on sick leave and it was doubtful that she could give evidence to an inquiry, and (4) the exchange of correspondence between the grandparents and the LEA revealed differences as to the discharge of the LEA's duties under s.19 where a child was kept away from school when well enough to attend. However, D could not attend school and was receiving home tuition, so it would be inappropriate to give permission in respect of that issue. Although the court was mindful of D's interests and wider public concerns, the issues were such that D's best interests would not be furthered by judicial review of the decisions concerned.

R. v. HEAD TEACHER OF CRUG GLAS SCHOOL, *ex p.* D (A CHILD); R. v. GOVERNING BODY OF CRUG GLAS SCHOOL, *ex p.* D (A CHILD); R. v. SWANSEA CITY COUNCIL, *ex p.* D (A CHILD) [2000] E.L.R. 69, Sullivan, J., QBD.

1964. Special schools – judicial review – susceptibility of non maintained school to judicial review

[Education Act 1996 s.342.]

R was excluded from a non maintained special needs school on disciplinary grounds. The school received most of its funding from a local authority but was non maintained. R applied for judicial review of the decision to exclude him.

Held, refusing the application, that the decisions of the school were not amenable to judicial review because although the school was generally under controls pursuant to the Education Act 1996 s.342, there was no statutory regulation of its admission and exclusion policy.

R. v. MUNTHAM HOUSE SCHOOL, *ex p.* R; *sub nom.* R. v. MUNTHAM HOUSE SCHOOL, *ex p.* C [2000] B.L.G.R. 255, Richards, J., QBD.

1965. Students – grants – eligibility

EDUCATION (MANDATORY AWARDS) (AMENDMENT) REGULATIONS 2000, SI 2000 1425; made under the Education Act 1962 s.1, s.4. In force: June 16, 2000; £1.50.

These Regulations amend the Education (Mandatory Awards) Regulations 1999 (SI 1999 1494) by providing that students who become entitled to an award after September 1, 1999 for a course that began before September 1, 1998 shall be eligible for an award under the 1999 Regulations and for the payment, as soon as reasonably practicable after the award, of any fees due to be paid as part of the award. In addition, they remove the duty on authorities to bestow a fees award in respect of any student who is participating in the ERASMUS scheme where all periods of study during the academic year are undertaken at an institution outside the UK and make provision in relation to fees.

1966. Students – grants – eligibility – trainee teachers

EDUCATION (FEES AND AWARDS) (AMENDMENT) (ENGLAND) REGULATIONS 2000, SI 2000 2192; made under the Education (Fees and Awards) Act 1983 s.2. In force: September 1, 2000; £1.00.

These Regulations amend the Education (Fees and Awards) Regulations 1997 (SI 1997 1972) to make it lawful for the Teacher Training Agency and institutions funded by it under the Education Act 1994 s.5 to adopt rules of eligibility for awards to students training to become teachers which confine eligibility to persons having a specified connection with the UK.

1967. Students – grants – eligibility – trainee teachers

EDUCATION (FEES AND AWARDS) (AMENDMENT NO.2) (ENGLAND) REGULATIONS 2000, SI 2000 2945; made under the Education (Fees and Awards) Act 1983 s.2. In force: November 23, 2000; £1.75.

These Regulations amend the Education (Fees and Awards) Regulations 1997 (SI 1997 1972) to make it lawful for the Higher Education Funding Council for England and institutions funded by it to adopt rules of eligibility for awards to students training, otherwise than by way of a course leading to a first degree, to teach persons over compulsory school age, which confine eligibility to persons having the connection with the UK specified in paras.1, 2 and 5 to 8 of the Schedule to those Regulations.

1968. Students – loans – grants

EDUCATION (STUDENT SUPPORT) (AMENDMENT) REGULATIONS 2000, SI 2000 1120; made under the Teaching and Higher Education Act 1998 s.22, s.42, s.43. In force: May 10, 2000; £1.50.

These Regulations amend the Education (Student Support) Regulations 1999 (SI 1999 496) by amending the definition of "disability related benefit"; providing an additional income disregard of £905 for an only or eldest child when assessing grants for dependants; and providing that all disability and incapacity related benefits, whether taxable or not, are to be disregarded when determining a dependant's net income. The provisions relating to overpayments are amended and Sch.1 para.3(a) has been amended so that a person who applied for refugee status before July 1, 1993 and who has been granted indefinite leave to enter or remain in the UK under the Backlog Clearance Measures will be eligible for financial support.

1969. Students – loans – mortgage style repayment loans

EDUCATION (STUDENT LOANS) (AMENDMENT) (ENGLAND AND WALES) REGULATIONS 2000, SI 2000 1804; made under the Education (Student Loans) Act 1990 s.1, Sch.2 para.1. In force: August 1, 2000; £1.50.

These Regulations amend the Education (Student Loans) Regulations 1998 (SI 1998 211), which govern mortgage style repayment loans made, primarily to students who began their courses on August 1, 1998, under the Education (Student Loans) Act 1990. They amend the definition of "metropolitan police district", provide expressly that members of the regular armed forces are treated as falling within the temporary employment abroad exemption from the residence conditions, and increase the maximum amounts which may be lent in relation to an academic year in line with inflation.

1970. Students – loans – repayments

EDUCATION (STUDENT LOANS) (REPAYMENT) REGULATIONS 2000, SI 2000 944; made under the Education (Scotland) Act 1980 s.73; the Education (Scotland) Act s.73B; and the Teaching and Higher Education Act 1998 s.22, s.42. In force: April 1, 2000; £4.50.

These Regulations apply to students who started higher education courses in September 1998 or later and provide for repayments to be collected by the Inland Revenue through self assessment, by employers and by the Secretary of State where borrowers are living and working abroad. Borrowers may also make voluntary repayments to the Secretary of State at any time.

1971. Teachers – compensation for redundancy and retirement

TEACHERS (COMPENSATION FOR REDUNDANCY AND PREMATURE RETIREMENT) (AMENDMENT) REGULATIONS 2000, SI 2000 664; made under the Superannuation Act 1972 s.24. In force: Reg.5: April 1, 2000; remainder: March 30, 2000; £1.50.

These Regulations amend the Teachers (Compensation for Redundancy and Premature Retirement) Regulations 1997 (SI 1997 311) by adding to the definition of "relevant employment" employment as a teacher by a person who is performing functions on behalf of a local education authority and who has been accepted for the purposes of the teachers' pension scheme by the Secretary of State. They provide a rate of supplementary death grant payable to a teacher whose retirement benefits become payable on or after April 1, 2000 and insert a new paragraph to provide for the payment to the Secretary of State of a lump sum equal to the actuarial value of the total compensation payable by an accepted function provider.

1972. Teachers – compulsory registration – Wales

TEACHERS (COMPULSORY REGISTRATION) (WALES) REGULATIONS 2000, SI 2000 3122 (W.200); made under the Education Reform Act 1988 s.218. In force: February 1, 2001; £1.75.

These Regulations provide that no qualified teachers, save for certain exceptions, are to be employed in maintained schools or in non-maintained special schools unless they are registered by the General Teaching Council for Wales.

1973. Teachers – conditions of employment – remuneration

EDUCATION (SCHOOL TEACHER'S PAY AND CONDITIONS) (NO.3) ORDER 2000, SI 2000 2321; made under the School Teachers' Pay and Conditions Act 1991 s.2, s.5. In force: September 1, 2000; £1.50.

This Order, which applies to all school teachers in England and Wales, refers to a document entitled School Teachers' Pay and Conditions Document 2000 published by Her Majesty's Stationery Office and directs that the provisions set out in the Document shall have effect, with modifications, from September 1, 2000.

1974. Teachers – conditions of employment – remuneration

EDUCATION (SCHOOL TEACHERS' PAY AND CONDITIONS) (NO.4) ORDER 2000, SI 2000 3106; made under the School Teachers' Pay and Conditions Act 1991 s.2, s.5. In force: December 13, 2000; £3.00.

This Order amends the School Teachers' Pay and Conditions Document 2000, to which the Education (School Teachers' Pay and Conditions) (No.3) Order 2000 (SI 2000 2321) gave effect, with modifications, on September 1, 2000. It amends the professional duties' section of the Document to introduce professional duties for head teachers and others in relation to carrying out threshold assessments.

1975. Teachers – contract of employment – performance related pay – adequacy of consultation

See EMPLOYMENT: R. v. Secretary of State for Education and Employment, *ex p.* National Union of Teachers. §2216

1976. Teachers – General Teaching Council for England – maintenance of records

GENERAL TEACHING COUNCIL FOR ENGLAND (ADDITIONAL FUNCTIONS) ORDER 2000, SI 2000 2175; made under the Teaching and Higher Education Act 1998 s.7, s.42. In force: September 1, 2000; £2.00.

This Order confers on the General Teaching Council for England, a body corporate established by the Teaching and Higher Education Act 1998 s.1 (1), the additional function of maintaining records in a written or electronic form relating to specified categories of persons. In addition, it specifies the type of information to be included in the records.

1977. Teachers – General Teaching Council for England – membership

GENERAL TEACHING COUNCIL FOR ENGLAND (CONSTITUTION) (AMENDMENT) REGULATIONS 2000, SI 2000 1447; made under the Teaching and Higher Education Act 1998 s.1, s.42, Sch.1 para.3. In force: June 30, 2000; £1.00.

These Regulations amend the General Teaching Council for England (Constitution) Regulations 1999 (SI 1999 1726) to provide for the Disability Rights Commission to appoint one member of the Council. The membership of the Council is thereby increased to 64 members.

1978. Teachers – General Teaching Council for England – registered teachers

GENERAL TEACHING COUNCIL FOR ENGLAND (REGISTRATION OF TEACHERS) REGULATIONS 2000, SI 2000 2176; made under the Teaching and Higher Education Act 1998 s.3, s.4, s.5, s.14, s.42. In force: Reg.12: February 1, 2001; Reg.16: February 1, 2001; Reg.17: February 1, 2001; Remainder: September 1, 2000; £2.50.

These Regulations, which relate to the functions of the General Teaching Council for England, a body corporate established by the Teaching and Higher Education Act 1998 s.1 (1), provide for the form and manner in which the register of teachers is to be kept and other matters relating to registration; prescribe additional circumstances in which teachers are ineligible for registration; authorise the Council to issue, and from time to time revise, a Code of Practice laying down standards for the professional conduct and practice expected of registered teachers; and require the Council to supply copies of information held about them to registered teachers and other persons such as qualified teachers who are not registered about whom the Council hold records pursuant to the General Teaching Council for England (Additional Functions) Order 2000 (SI 2000 2175).

1979. Teachers – General Teaching Council for Wales – functions

GENERAL TEACHING COUNCIL FOR WALES (FUNCTIONS) REGULATIONS 2000, SI 2000 1979 (W.140); made under the Teaching and Higher Education Act 1998 s.3, s.4, s.5, s.14, s.42. In force: Regs.12: February 1, 2001; Reg 17: February 1, 2001; Reg.16: December 1, 2000; Remainder: September 1, 2000; £3.50.

These Regulations relate to the functions conferred on the General Teaching Council for Wales by the Education Act 1998, including the establishment and maintenance of a register of teachers. They prescribe the form and manner in which the register is to be kept, other matters relating to registration, and circumstances in which teachers are eligible and ineligible for registration.

1980. Teachers – General Teaching Council for Wales – maintenance of records

GENERAL TEACHING COUNCIL FOR WALES (ADDITIONAL FUNCTIONS) ORDER 2000, SI 2000 1941 (W.139); made under the Teaching and Higher Education Act 1998 s.7, s.42. In force: September 1, 2000; £2.50.

This Order confers on the General Teaching Council for Wales the additional function of maintaining records in a written or electronic form relating to specified categories of persons and specifies the type of information to be included in the records.

1981. Teachers – induction periods

EDUCATION (INDUCTION ARRANGEMENTS FOR SCHOOL TEACHERS) (AMENDMENT) (ENGLAND) REGULATIONS 2000, SI 2000 1001; made under the Teaching and Higher Education Act 1998 s.19, s.42. In force: May 1, 2000; £1.50.

These Regulations, which amend the Education (Induction Arrangements for School Teachers) (England) Regulations 1999 (SI 1999 1065), enable any local education authority to act as the appropriate body in relation to teacher induction at an independent school; prescribe an additional circumstance for the completion of an induction period in an independent school that either a local education authority or the persons or body determined by the Secretary of State must have agreed to act as the appropriate body; and permit appropriate bodies to give notice of their decisions in relation to induction by facsimile or electronic mail or similar means.

1982. Teachers – induction periods

EDUCATION (INDUCTION ARRANGEMENTS FOR SCHOOL TEACHERS) (AMENDMENT NO.2) (ENGLAND) REGULATIONS 2000, SI 2000 1177; made under the Teaching and Higher Education Act 1998 s.19, s.42. In force: May 25, 2000; £1.00.

These Regulations amend the Education (Induction Arrangements for School Teachers) (England) Regulations 1999 (SI 1999 1065) Reg.13 to enable the Secretary of State to determine different standards for the satisfactory completion of an induction period for different categories of persons.

1983. Teachers – induction periods

EDUCATION (INDUCTION ARRANGEMENTS FOR SCHOOL TEACHERS) (AMENDMENT NO.3) (ENGLAND) REGULATIONS 2000, SI 2000 2171; made under theTeaching and Higher Education Act1998 s.19, s.42. In force: September1, 2000; £1.50.

These Regulations amend the Education (Induction Arrangements for School Teachers) (England) Regulations 1999 (SI 1999 1065) by providing that from September 1, 2000 an induction period can be served in a sixth form college where the governing body of the college has agreed with a local education authority that they will act as the appropriate body. Where a teacher is serving induction at more than one school or sixth form college, the head teachers of those institutions must agree that one of them will act as lead head teacher with responsibility for the teacher's supervision and training.

1984. Teachers – performance appraisals

EDUCATION (SCHOOL TEACHER APPRAISAL) (AMENDMENT) (ENGLAND) REGULATIONS 2000, SI 2000 3369; made under the Education (No. 2) Act 1986 s.49, s.63. In force: Reg.1: December 31, 2000; Reg.2: December 31, 2000; Reg.4: December 31, 2000; remainder: January 15, 2001; £1.50.

These Regulations amend the Education (School Teacher Appraisal) (England) Regulations 2000 (SI 2000 1620), by extending the deadline for which the governing body of a school to which the Regulations apply to secure that the head teacher's objectives have been agreed from December 31, 2000 to April 6, 2001. If the governing body decides that the head teacher's first appraisal cycle under the Regulations should be a period of less than one year then each year starting from 2001, the governing body must ensure that the head teacher's objectives have been agreed or set before December 31 in that year.

1985. Teachers – performance appraisals

EDUCATION (SCHOOL TEACHER APPRAISAL) (ENGLAND) REGULATIONS 2000, SI 2000 1620; made under the Education (No.2) Act 1986 s.49, s.63. In force: September 1, 2000; £2.00.

These Regulations, which revoke and replace the Education (School Teacher Appraisal) Regulations 1991 (SI 1991 1511 as amended), provide for the appraisal of the performance of school teachers, including unqualified teachers and those employed on fixed term contracts of one year or more, employed at not more than two community, voluntary, foundation, community special, or foundation special schools. By virtue of the Teaching and Higher Education Act 1998 s.19(7), these Regulations do not apply to teachers serving an induction period under s.19.

1986. Teachers – qualifications – independent schools

EDUCATION (TEACHERS' QUALIFICATIONS AND HEALTH STANDARDS) (ENGLAND) (AMENDMENT) REGULATIONS 2000, SI 2000 2704; made under the Education Reform Act 1988 s.218, s.232. In force: October 25, 2000; £2.00.

These Regulations amend the Education (Teachers' Qualifications and Health Standards) (England) Regulations 1999 (SI 1999 2166) to enable certain teachers employed in independent schools to be awarded qualified teacher status. They provide that a teacher is eligible for qualified teacher status if he is currently employed as a teacher in an independent school, has been assessed as meeting the standards for qualified teacher status, holds one of the qualifications specified in these Regulations and was employed as a teacher at an independent school before September 1, 1989.

1987. Teachers – remuneration

SCHOOL TEACHERS' REMUNERATION ORDER 2000, SI 2000 2324; made under the School Teachers' Pay and Conditions Act 1991 s.5. In force: September 1, 2000; £1.00.

The School Teachers' Pay and Conditions Act 1991 authorises the Secretary of State to make pay and conditions orders containing provision about the statutory conditions of employment of school teachers. This Order provides that, for the purposes of the 1991 Act, incentive payments known as "golden hellos" for newly qualified school teachers or school teachers who have successfully completed their induction periods taking up or occupying posts in shortage subjects, are not to be regarded as remuneration.

1988. Teachers – restriction of employment – child protection

EDUCATION (RESTRICTION OF EMPLOYMENT) REGULATIONS 2000, SI 2000 2419; made under the Education Reform Act 1988 s.218, s.232; the Teaching and Higher Education Act 1998 s.15, s.42; and the Protection of Children Act 1999 s.6. In force: October 2, 2000; £2.50.

These Regulations revoke the Education (Teachers) Regulations 1993 (SI 1993 543) and make fresh provision for the restriction of the employment of persons as teachers or workers with children or young persons. In particular, they provide for a person's relevant employment to be prohibited or restricted on four grounds: medical grounds, misconduct, that he is not a fit and proper person to be employed as a teacher or in work that brings him into contact with children or young persons, or that he has been placed on the list of people considered unsuitable to work with children kept by the Secretary of State for Health under the Protection of Children Act 1999 s.1.

1989. Teachers – restriction of employment – child protection – Wales

EDUCATION (RESTRICTION OF EMPLOYMENT) (WALES) REGULATIONS 2000, SI 2000 2906 (W.186); made under the Education Reform Act 1988 s.218, s.232; and the Teaching and Higher Education Act 1998 s.15, s.42. In force: November 1, 2000; £2.00.

These Regulations, which revoke the Education (Teachers) Regulations 1993 (SI 1993 543) Reg.10A and the Education (Teachers (Amendment) Regulations 1998 (SI 1998 1584) Reg.3 (4), make provision with regard to services provided by those whose employment as a teacher or worker with children or young persons is prohibited or restricted under regulations made under the Education Reform Act 1988 s.218 (6) and require the employers of teachers to report misconduct to the National Assembly for Wales.

1990. Teachers – sex discrimination – homosexual abuse from pupils – direct liability of school

See EMPLOYMENT: Pearce v. Governing Body of Mayfield Secondary School. §2206

1991. Teachers – Teacher Training Agency – additional functions

TEACHER TRAINING AGENCY (ADDITIONAL FUNCTIONS) ORDER 2000, SI 2000 1000; made under the Education Act 1994 s.16. In force: May 1, 2000; £1.00.

This Order, which revokes the Teacher Training Agency (Additional Functions) Order 1998 (SI 1998 1194), confers on the Teaching Training Agency the additional function of arranging the assessment of candidates for national tests for teacher training candidates in literacy, numeracy and information and communications technology. Numeracy tests will be administered to teachers undertaking induction under the Education (Induction Arrangements for School Teachers) (England) Regulations 1999 (SI 1999 1065) who qualify on or after May 1, 2000 and before May 1, 2001. Teachers qualifying on or after May 1, 2001 will need to have passed all three tests.

1992. **Teachers – Teacher Training Agency – additional functions**

TEACHER TRAINING AGENCY (ADDITIONAL FUNCTIONS) (NO.2) ORDER 2000, SI 2000 2174; made under the Education Act 1994 s.16. In force: September 1, 2000; £1.00.

This Order confers on the Teacher Training Agency, established under the Education Act 1994 s.1, the additional function of paying grants as incentives to encourage the governing bodies of maintained schools and non-maintained special schools, local education authorities, city technology colleges, city colleges for the technology of the arts and city academies to recruit, employ and secure the provision of training for graduate teachers. Graduate teachers are unqualified teachers participating in employment-based training designed to lead to the award of qualified teacher status.

1993. **Teachers – training – bursaries**

EDUCATION (BURSARIES FOR SCHOOL TEACHER TRAINING PILOT SCHEME) (ENGLAND) REGULATIONS 2000, SI 2000 2193; made under the Education (No.2) Act 1986 s.50, s.63. In force: September 1, 2000; £1.50.

These Regulations authorise the Secretary of State to pay bursaries and grants to facilitate and encourage the training of qualified school teachers, other than head teachers, employed in schools, or by the local education authorities, included in a pilot scheme. The scheme runs from September 1, 2000 to March 31, 2002. Bursaries and grants are payable up to a total of £500 for each teacher for training approved by the Secretary of State, or £700 where the teacher is employed to work in one or more publicly maintained schools participating in one of the Excellence in Cities projects or in one of the specified education action zones. Teachers are eligible provided their training is not subsidised by other public funds.

1994. **Teachers – training – incentive grants – Wales**

TEACHER TRAINING INCENTIVE (WALES) REGULATIONS 2000, SI 2000 2560 (W.169); made under the Education (No.2) Act 1986 s.50, s.63. In force: September 22, 2000; £2.00.

These Regulations partially revoke the Education (Mathematics and Science Teacher Training Incentive) (Wales) Regulations 1999 (SI 1999 2816), which provided for the payment of grants by way of incentives to encourage more people to undergo college-based post-graduate teacher training courses to teach mathematics or science at secondary level. They provide that incentive grants may be paid in respect of such courses to teach all subjects and, where a person receives any instalments of grant in respect of a course at an institution in England for which incentive grants are payable under parallel arrangements, they enable the National Assembly to pay any remaining instalments to which that person would have been entitled by virtue of these Regulations had he or she completed a course in Wales in respect of which grant was paid under these Regulations. In addition, they include a new provision enabling grants to be paid to encourage schools to take on and train graduate teachers.

1995. **Teachers – training – institutions eligible for funding**

EDUCATION (FUNDING FOR TEACHER TRAINING) DESIGNATION ORDER 2000, SI 2000 57; made under the Education Act 1994 s.4. In force: February 7, 2000; £1.50.

This Order designates Barking and Dagenham LBC, Birmingham City Council, Buckinghamshire CC, Bury MBC, Camden LBC, Cheshire CC, Cornwall CC, Dorset CC, Dyslexia Institute Ltd, East Sussex CC, Haringey LBC, Kensington and Chelsea LBC, Kirklees MBC, Manchester City Council, Newham LBC, Oxfordshire CC, Rotherham MBC, Sefton MBC, Southwark LBC, Staffordshire CC, Thurrock BC, and West Sussex CC as institutions eligible for funding under the Education Act 1994 Part I with the result that the Teacher Training Agency may make grants, loans or other payments in respect of expenditure incurred or to be incurred by the designated institutions for the purposes of the provision of teacher training and the provision of facilities, and the carrying on of other activities, which the institution considers it necessary or desirable to provide or carry on for the purpose of or in connection with the provision of teacher training.

1996. Teachers – training – institutions eligible for funding

EDUCATION (FUNDING FOR TEACHER TRAINING) DESIGNATION (NO.2) ORDER 2000, SI 2000 1750; made under the Education Act 1994 s.4. In force: August 1, 2000; £2.00.

This Order designates specified institutions and bodies as institutions eligible for funding under the Education Act 1994 Part I. The effect of this Order is to enable the Teacher Training Agency to make grants, loans or other payments in respect of expenditure incurred or to be incurred by the designated institutions for the purposes of the provision of teacher training and the provision of facilities.

1997. Teachers – training – institutions eligible for funding

EDUCATION (FUNDING FOR TEACHER TRAINING) DESIGNATION (NO.3) ORDER 2000, SI 2000 2801; made under the Education Act 1994 s.4. In force: November 2, 2000; £1.50.

This Order designates the Mathematical Association, a charitable unincorporated association, and Start Education (EM) Ltd as institutions eligible for funding under the Education Act 1994 Part I, with the effect that the Teacher Training Agency may make grants, loans or other payments in respect of expenditure incurred or to be incurred by the designated institutions for the purposes of the provision of teacher training and facilities, which the institutions consider it necessary or desirable to provide for the purpose of or in connection with the provision of teacher training.

1998. Teaching and Higher Education Act 1998 (c.30) – Commencement No.6 Order

TEACHING AND HIGHER EDUCATION ACT 1998 (COMMENCEMENT NO.6) ORDER 2000, SI 2000 970 (C.24); made under the Teaching and Higher Education Act 1998 s.46. Commencement details: bringing into force various provisions of the Act on April 5, 2000 and September 1, 2000; £1.00.

This Order brings into force certain provisions of the Teaching and Higher Education Act 1998 relating to the establishment and functions of the General Teaching Council for England and the General Teaching Council for Wales on April 5, 2000 and September 1, 2000.

1999. Teaching and Higher Education Act 1998 (c.30) – Commencement No.7 Order

TEACHING AND HIGHER EDUCATION ACT 1998 (COMMENCEMENT NO.7) ORDER 2000, SI 2000 2199 (C.59); made under the Teaching and Higher Education Act 1998 s.46. Commencement details: bringing into force various provisions of the Act on August 15, 2000; £1.00.

This Order brings into force the Teaching and Higher Education Act 1998 s.15, which empowers the Secretary of State to make regulations requiring employers of teachers and workers with children and young persons to supply information relating to their dismissal or resignation to the Secretary of State, the General Teaching Council for England or the General Teaching Council for Wales.

2000. Training – funding

TRAINING PROGRAMMES (CESSATION OF FUNDING) (PRESCRIBED ACTIONS) ORDER 2000, SI 2000 2170; made under the Learning and Skills Act 2000 s.141. In force: August 10, 2000; £1.50.

This Order, which applies to Training and Enterprise Councils and Chambers of Commerce, Training and Enterprise in England, specifies actions which are prescribed for the purposes of the Learning and Skills Act 2000 s.141 (2). Such actions include changes to contractual terms and conditions of employees and company executives, other than routine increases in salary; any new expenditure in excess of £20,000 and any new contractual commitments which extend beyond March 25, 2001; the transfer of any asset of a value in excess of £10,000, other than at full market value; and any transaction or agreement which decreases the fixed or current asset base of the company by more than £10,000 of its net book value. No such action is prescribed, however, if it is carried out or procured by the company after the company has fulfilled all of its contractual obligations under arrangements with the Secretary of State and has discharged all of its financial indebtedness to the Secretary of State.

2001. Universities – causes of action – student's right of action in contract

C, a student of ULH, failed her finals owing to plagiarism on one of the papers she had submitted, but was allowed by the academic appeals board to resubmit the paper for marking since the board accepted that she had not set out to deceive the university. The board of examiners awarded a zero mark, which on appeal was held to be an inappropriate academic response by the governors' appeal committee, but which was confirmed by the academic board. C was allowed a final attempt to resit her finals leading to an award of a third class degree, which was outlined in the student regulations as being the usual award in such cases. C then commenced proceedings against ULH, contending that the academic board had misconstrued the meaning of plagiarism and awarded a mark outside academic convention without taking her explanation into account. Later C amended her pleadings to argue that the academic board had failed to comply with a decision of the governors' appeal committee in confirming the zero mark previously held to be inappropriate. Furthermore, she argued that ULH was in breach of its contractual regulations in limiting the possible class of degree that could be awarded at a second attempt. C's claim was struck out on the basis that issues relating to a student's academic performance were not susceptible to adjudication by the court and that, as a public law matter, the appropriate remedy was to seek judicial review. C appealed, contending that the court had jurisdiction to deal with the contractual claim.

Held, allowing the appeal, that in the case of a new university with no provision for the supervisory function of a visitor, the judge had been right to strike out the claim as originally pleaded because it was concerned with the award of marks reflecting C's academic competence and therefore fell outside the matters which were capable of adjudication by the court, *Hines v. Birkbeck College* [1986] Ch. 524, [1985] C.L.Y. 3552 applied. However, following the amendment of the pleadings, the issue was based on the contractual relationship between C and ULH governed by the student regulations, which C alleged had been breached. The fact that the dispute concerned issues of public law did not prevent C from pursuing the matter by means of an action in contract despite the more generous time limits applicable to private law proceedings, *O'Reilly v. Mackman* [1983] 2 A.C. 237, [1982] C.L.Y. 2603 doubted. Under the Civil Procedure Rules 1998 what was crucial was whether there had been an abuse of process in which the court could intervene even where the limitation period was still current. The ability of the court to invoke sanctions under the Rules meant that there was no longer a need to prohibit the use of the contractual route where both public and private law were involved.

CLARK v. UNIVERSITY OF LINCOLNSHIRE AND HUMBERSIDE [2000] 1 W.L.R. 1988, Sedley, L.J., CA.

2002. Universities – funding – public procurement Directives – meaning of "public law body" – categorisation of specific forms of funding – European Union

[Council Directive 92/50 relating to the coordination of procedures for the award of public service contracts; Council Directive 93/36 coordinating procedures for the award of public supply contracts; Council Directive 93/37 concerning the coordination of procedures for the award of public works contracts.]

CU sought judicial review of the decision of the Treasury to maintain universities on the list of public bodies falling within the scope of Council Directive 92/50, Council Directive 93/36 and Council Directive 93/37 on the coordination of procedures for the award of public service contracts. Questions were referred to the European Court of Justice concerning the scope of Art.1 of Directive 93/37 which defined a "public law body" as any body which (1) was established for the purpose of meeting needs in the general interest, not having a commercial character; (2) had a legal personality, and (3) was financed for the most part by the state or other bodies governed by public law. Clarification was sought regarding the issue of whether universities were financed "for the most part" by the entities mentioned in the Directive with reference to specific forms of funding.

Held, that a university was a contracting authority within the meaning of the Directive if at least half of its income came from public authorities during the budgetary year. For the purpose of the Directives the notion of a financial link had to be understood as indicating the close dependency of a given body on the State or other public entity and only payments which went to financing the activities of the body concerned, without any specific consideration, could therefore be described as "public funding". Funding in the form of awards and grants for the support of research work was to be regarded as financing by a contracting authority, as were student grants. However, sums paid for the supply of services such as the organisation of conferences, consultancy or research work could not be regarded as public financing. On the question of whether the public funding identified represented the university's funding "for the most part", that phrase had to be given its ordinary meaning which was "more than half". All sources of income were to be taken into account, including income from commercial activities over a 12 month period covering the budgetary year, notwithstanding that there might be variations in sources of income during the year. Provisional figures could be used, if necessary.

R. (ON THE APPLICATION OF UNIVERSITY OF CAMBRIDGE) v. HM TREASURY (C380/98); *sub nom.* R. v. HM TREASURY, *ex p.* UNIVERSITY OF CAMBRIDGE (C380/98) [2000] 1 W.L.R. 2514, DAO Edward (President), ECJ (5th Chamber).

2003. Universities – qualifying examinations – medical profession

MEDICAL ACT 1983 (MEDICAL EDUCATION) ORDER 2000, SI 2000 1841; made under the Medical Act 1983 s.8. In force: August 3, 2000; £1.00.

This Order amends the Medical Act 1983 s.4(2) by adding a combination of Leicester University and Warwick University to the bodies and combinations of bodies entitled to hold qualifying examinations for the purposes of Part II of the Medical Act 1993.

2004. Universities – sex discrimination – exclusion from vocational course for absence due to pregnancy – comparison with claim in employment sphere

[Sex Discrimination Act 1975 s.1, s.22; Council Directive 76/207 on equal treatment.]

SBU appealed against an order quashing its decision to terminate the studies of C, a radiography student, who had been absent for much of the final year of her course, partly as a result of pregnancy related illness. The examination board had concluded that C should withdraw from the radiography course and her appeal to the University's Appeal Panel had subsequently been dismissed. C sought judicial review of the decisions, arguing discrimination on the ground of her sex. Shortly afterwards, she commenced separate proceedings in the county court under the Sex Discrimination Act 1975. The application for judicial review was granted and it was held that s.1 of the 1975 Act was equally applicable to the dismissal of pregnant women in an educational context as it was to those dismissed from their employment. The matter was remitted to the board for reconsideration. SBU, contended that the decision to withdraw C had been lawful, that she had not been discriminated against on the ground of sex and that if she still wanted to obtain her degree, she would have to reapply for admission. C claimed that she was validly enrolled on the course and that she was entitled to complete it without having to reapply for admission.

Held, dismissing the appeal, that the judge had correctly concluded that full consideration had not been given to C's mitigating circumstances and the case had been properly remitted. The examination board was, however, relieved from acting in accordance with the judge's ruling on sex discrimination, as there was the possibility that he had misinterpreted the 1975 Act and the Equal Treatment Directive 76/207. He had had no jurisdiction to draw a parallel between the dismissal of pregnant women from employment and the exclusion of C from an educational establishment within the meaning of s.22 of the Act, as that finding had the effect of broadening the applicability of the Directive, the decisions made under it, and the interpretation of the Act, *Webb v. EMO Air Cargo (UK) Ltd (No.2)* [1995] 1 W.L.R. 1454, [1996] C.L.Y. 2622 distinguished. The sex discrimination claim was the subject of proceedings in the county court, the determination of which was restricted to the jurisdiction of that court, *R. v. Secretary of State for Employment, ex p. Equal Opportunities Commission* [1992] 1 All E.R. 545 applied.

R. v. SOUTH BANK UNIVERSITY, *ex p.* COGGERAN [2000] I.C.R. 1342, Mummery, L.J., CA.

2005. Vocational training – individual learning accounts – grants

INDIVIDUAL LEARNING ACCOUNTS (ENGLAND) REGULATIONS 2000, SI 2000 2146; made under the Learning and Skills Act 2000 s.105, s.108, s.152. In force: September 1, 2000; £2.00.

These Regulations define "qualifying arrangements", referred to in the Learning and Skills Act 2000 s.105, and provide for a payment of grant to persons who are parties to qualifying arrangements, known as individual learning account holders. In particular, they provide that qualifying arrangements must take the form of registration by an eligible person with a body approved by the Secretary of State; set down conditions of eligibility; provide that grants may be paid in respect of any education or training specified by the Secretary of State other than secondary or higher education; stipulate that the Secretary of State shall decide the amount of grant payable; and provide for the payment of grant to the person providing the education or training.

2006. Voluntary aided schools – compensation – provision of site by LEA – assessment of compensation

[Education Act 1946 Sch.1 para.6, Sch.1 para.7, Sch.1 para.8.]

Q, a charity, had until 1990 run a voluntary controlled school, that is one unable to bear all its expenses out of its charitable assets. As such, under the Education Act 1946 Sch.1 para.6, the LEA and its predecessors had a duty to provide any necessary new sites for the school, and convey them to the trustees of Q. That occurred in 1962, when the school moved from two sites to a new single site. Under the Act, the LEA was entitled to compensation for conveying the land, under para.7 if either of the old sites was sold by Q, or under para.8 if Q sold the new site. Both paragraphs stated that the level of compensation should have regard to the value of the land conveyed to the trustees. In 1968, one of the old sites was sold, and compensation was paid under para.7. When the school closed and the new site was sold in 1993, compensation was paid under para.8. In 1994, the remaining old site was sold, and the LEA sought further compensation under para.7. The Secretary of State refused, claiming that by applying a current market valuation to the land conveyed, the LEA had already been reimbursed in full. The LEA sought review, contending that the relevant valuation applied to the land conveyed should be its outlay plus a suitable uplift, bearing in mind that it had waited 30 years for the reimbursement of its monies.

Held, refusing the application, that the purpose of paras.7 and 8 was to put the LEA back into a position in which it would have been had it not conveyed the site, and the Secretary of State's approach of assessing the value to mean the value at the time that either of the events in paras.7 and 8 occurred achieved that result justly and in a relatively uncomplicated way. It was therefore the preferred approach.

R. v. SECRETARY OF STATE FOR EDUCATION AND EMPLOYMENT, *ex p.* ROCHDALE MBC [2000] Ed. C.R. 415, Hooper, J., QBD.

2007. Publications

Education Case Reports: Vol 1, 1999. Hardback: £150.00. ISBN 0-421-69540-4. Sweet & Maxwell.

Game Plan for Getting Into Law School. £12.99. ISBN 0-7689-0394-7. Vacation Work Publications.

Gold, Richard; Szemerenyi, Stephen – Running a School 2000/01: Legal Duties and Responsibilities. 3rd Ed. Paperback: £29.95. ISBN 0-85308-507-2. Jordans.

Law Schools 2001. 3rd Ed. £17.99. ISBN 0-7689-0437-4. Vacation Work Publications.

White, John; Ruebain, David – Taking Action! 2nd Ed. Paperback: £14.99. ISBN 1-84190-010-9. Questions Publishing Co.

ELECTORAL PROCESS

2008. Elections – Greater London Authority – early voting

GREATER LONDON AUTHORITY ELECTION (EARLY VOTING) ORDER 2000, SI 2000 826; made under the Greater London Authority Act 1999 s.3. In force: March 24, 2000; £2.50.

This Order, which has been made in consequence of a defect as to the dates of early voting in the Greater London Authority (Early Voting) Order 2000 (SI 2000 725), specifies the days and times for early voting in the first ordinary election of the Greater London Authority and the polling stations at which early voting may take place.

2009. Elections – Greater London Authority – expenses

GREATER LONDON AUTHORITY ELECTIONS (EXPENSES) ORDER 2000, SI 2000 789; made under the Representation of the People Act 1983 s.75, s.76. In force: March 17, 2000; £1.50.

This Order prescribes the maximum expenditure which may be incurred at Greater London Authority elections by candidates or their agents.

2010. Elections – Greater London Authority – expenses

GREATER LONDON AUTHORITY ELECTIONS (NO.2) (AMENDMENT) RULES 2000, SI 2000 1040; made under the Representation of the People Act 1983 s.36, s.81, s.82. In force: May 4, 2000; £2.00.

These Rules amend the Greater London Authority Elections (No.2) Rules 2000 (SI 2000 427). They amend r.41 (8) of the London Members Election Rules, set out in Sch.2, and r.41 (7) of the Mayoral Election Rules, set out in Sch.3, to make these provisions correspond more closely to r.40(B) of the Constituency Members Election Rules, set out in Sch.1. They insert new forms relating to the return as to election expenses which the election agent for the candidates included in a registered political party's list is required to make in connection with the election of the London members of the London Assembly, to the declaration by election agents as to election expenses of list candidates at elections of the London members and to the declaration by list candidates as to election expenses at elections of the London members.

2011. Elections – Greater London Authority – returning officer – acceptance of office

GREATER LONDON AUTHORITY (ELECTIONS AND ACCEPTANCE OF OFFICE) ORDER 2000, SI 2000 308; made under the Greater London Authority Act 1999 s.3, s.28, s.405, s.406, s.420, Sch.4 para.8. In force: March 7, 2000; £1.50.

This Order makes provision in relation to elections for the Greater London Authority by designating who is to be the returning officer at the first ordinary election of the Mayor and the members of the London Assembly, prescribing the form of declaration of acceptance of office to be made by the Mayor, and by members of the Assembly and designating for the purposes of the first ordinary election, the officer who is to receive returns and declarations as to election expenses.

2012. Elections – Mayor of London – London Assembly

GREATER LONDON AUTHORITY ELECTION RULES 2000, SI 2000 208; made under the Representation of the People Act 1983 s.36. In force: February 29, 2000; £10.30.

These Rules make detailed provision for elections to the office of Mayor and of the members of the London Assembly, prescribe the forms to be used in some or all of the elections and, in relation to some of the forms, directions for their printing. The rules are also concerned with amendments and modifications to the Local Elections (Principal Areas) Rules 1986 (SI 1986 2214) where the poll at a Greater London Authority election is combined with the poll at an election of London borough councillors.

2013. Elections – Mayor of London – London Assembly

GREATER LONDON AUTHORITY ELECTIONS (NO.2) RULES 2000, SI 2000 427; made under the Representation of the People Act 1983 s.36. In force: March 15, 2000; £8.80.

These Rules, which revoke the Greater London Authority Elections Rules 2000 (SI 2000 208), make detailed provision for elections to the office of Mayor and of the members of the London Assembly.

2014. Elections – Mayor of London – London Assembly – disqualification

GREATER LONDON AUTHORITY (DISQUALIFICATION) ORDER 2000, SI 2000 432; made under the Greater London Authority Act 1999 s.21. In force: February 24, 2000; £1.50.

This Order designates the offices and appointments which disqualify the holders from being elected or being the Mayor of London or a member of the London Assembly.

2015. Local elections – Ashfield

DISTRICT OF ASHFIELD (ELECTORAL CHANGES) ORDER 2000, SI 2000 3295; made under the Local Government Act 1992 s.17, s.26. In force: In accordance with Art.1; £1.75.

This Order, which revokes the District of Ashfield (Electoral Arrangements) Order 1976 (SI 1976 180) and amends the Nottinghamshire (District Boundaries) Order 1988 (SI 1988 61), abolishes the existing wards of the district, provides for the creation of 15 new wards and makes provision for the names and areas of, and numbers of councillors for, the new wards. The changes have effect in relation to local government elections to be held on and after May 1, 2003.

2016. Local elections – Barking and Dagenham

LONDON BOROUGH OF BARKING AND DAGENHAM (ELECTORAL CHANGES) ORDER 2000, SI 2000 780; made under the Local Government Act 1992 s.17, s.26. In force: October 10, 2001 and May 2, 2002; £1.50.

This Order, which revokes the London Borough of Barking (Electoral Arrangements) Order 1977 (SI 1977 1427), abolishes the existing wards of the London borough of Barking and Dagenham and provides for the creation of 17 new wards. The changes have effect in relation to local government elections to be held on and after May 2, 2002.

2017. Local elections – Barnet

LONDON BOROUGH OF BARNET (ELECTORAL CHANGES) ORDER 2000, SI 2000 333; made under the Local Government Act 1992 s.17, s.26. In force: October 10, 2001 and May 2, 2002; £1.50.

This Order, which revokes the London Borough of Barnet (Electoral Arrangements) Order 1977 (SI 1977 1817), abolishes the existing wards of the borough and provides for the creation of 21 new wards. The changes have effect in relation to local government elections to be held on and after May 2, 2002.

2018. Local elections – Bassetlaw

DISTRICT OF BASSETLAW (ELECTORAL CHANGES) ORDER 2000, SI 2000 3285; made under the Local Government Act 1992 s.17, s.26. In force: In accordance with Art.1; £2.00.

This Order, which revokes the District of Bassetlaw (Electoral Arrangements) Order 1976 (SI 1976 1095), abolishes the existing wards of the district, provides for the creation of 25 new wards and makes provision for a whole council election in 2002 and for reversion to elections by thirds in subsequent years. The changes have effect in relation to local government elections to be held on and after May 2, 2002.

2019. Local elections – Bexley

LONDON BOROUGH OF BEXLEY (ELECTORAL CHANGES) ORDER 2000, SI 2000 312; made under the Local Government Act 1992 s.17, s.26. In force: October 10, 2001 and May 2, 2002; £1.50.

This Order, which revokes the London Borough of Bexley (Electoral Arrangements) Order 1977 (SI 1977 1763), abolishes the existing wards of the London borough of Bexley and provides for the creation of 21 new wards. The changes have effect in relation to local government elections to be held on and after May 2, 2002.

2020. Local elections – Brent

LONDON BOROUGH OF BRENT (ELECTORAL CHANGES) ORDER 2000, SI 2000 1846; made under the Local Government Act 1992 s.17, s.26. In force: In accordance with Art.1; £1.50.

This Order, which revokes the London Borough of Brent (Electoral Arrangements) Order 1977 (SI 1977 1810), abolishes the existing wards of the borough and provides for the creation of 21 new wards. The changes have effect in relation to local government elections to be held on and after May 2, 2002.

2021. Local elections – Bridgnorth

DISTRICT OF BRIDGNORTH (ELECTORAL CHANGES) ORDER 2000, SI 2000 1417; made under the Local Government Act 1992 s.17, s.26. In force: October 10, 2002 and May 1, 2003; £1.50.

This Order, which gives effect to recommendations by the Local Government Commission for England for electoral changes in the district of Bridgnorth, abolishes the existing wards of the district and provides for the creation of 21 new wards and their names and areas. The District of Bridgnorth (Electoral Arrangements) Order 1976 (SI 1976 1691) is revoked.

2022. Local elections – Bromley

LONDON BOROUGH OF BROMLEY (ELECTORAL CHANGES) ORDER 2000, SI 2000 1764; made under the Local Government Act 1992 s.17, s.26. In force: In accordance with Art.1; £1.50.

This Order, which revokes the London Borough of Bromley (Electoral Arrangements) Order 1977 (SI 1977 2141), abolishes the existing wards of the borough and provides for the creation of 22 new wards. The changes have effect in relation to local government elections to be held on and after May 2, 2002.

2023. Local elections – Broxtowe

BOROUGH OF BROXTOWE (ELECTORAL CHANGES) ORDER 2000, SI 2000 3296; made under the Local Government Act 1992 s.17, s.26. In force: In accordance with Art.1; £1.75.

This Order, which revokes the District of Broxtowe (Electoral Arrangements) Order 1975 (SI 1975 2202), abolishes the existing wards of the borough, provides for the creation of 21 new wards and makes provision for the names and areas of, and numbers of councillors for, the new wards. The changes have effect in relation to local government elections to be held on and after May 1, 2003.

2024. Local elections – Camden

LONDON BOROUGH OF CAMDEN (ELECTORAL CHANGES) ORDER 2000, SI 2000 1765; made under the Local Government Act 1992 s.17, s.26. In force: In accordance with Art.1; £1.50.

This Order, which revokes the London Borough of Camden (Electoral Arrangements) Order 1977 (SI 1977 1864), abolishes the existing wards of the borough and provides for the creation of 18 new wards. The changes have effect in relation to local government elections to be held on and after May 2, 2002.

2025. Local elections – Cheshire

COUNTY OF CHESHIRE (ELECTORAL CHANGES) ORDER 2000, SI 2000 2486; made under the Local Government Act 1992 s.17, s.26. In force: In accordance with Art.1 (2); £2.00.

This Order, which revokes the County of Cheshire (Electoral Arrangements) Order 1980 (SI 1980 1805), abolishes the existing divisions of the county and provides for the creation of 51 new divisions. The changes have effect in relation to local government elections to be held on or after May 3, 2001.

2026. Local elections – City of Westminster

CITY OF WESTMINSTER (ELECTORAL CHANGES) ORDER 2000, SI 2000 788; made under the Local Government Act 1992 s.17, s.26. In force: October 10, 2001 and May 2, 2002; £1.50.

This Order, which revokes the City of Westminster (Electoral Arrangements) Order 1978 (SI 1978 48), abolishes the existing wards of the City and provides for the creation of 20 new wards. The changes have effect in relation to local government elections to be held on and after May 2, 2002.

2027. Local elections – Craven

DISTRICT OF CRAVEN (ELECTORAL CHANGES) ORDER 2000, SI 2000 2599; made under the Local Government Act 1992 s.17, s.26. In force: In accordance with Art.1 (2) (3); £2.00.

This Order, which revokes the District of Craven (Electoral Arrangements) Order 1977 (SI 1977 864), abolishes the existing wards of the district, provides for the creation of 19 new wards and makes provision for a whole council election in 2002 and for reversion to elections by thirds in subsequent years. The changes have effect in relation to local government elections to be held on and after May 2, 2002.

2028. Local elections – Croydon

LONDON BOROUGH OF CROYDON (ELECTORAL CHANGES) ORDER 2000, SI 2000 781; made under the Local Government Act 1992 s.17, s.26. In force: October 10, 2001 and May 2, 2002; £1.50.

This Order, which revokes the London Borough of Croydon (Electoral Arrangements) Order 1977 (SI 1977 1564), abolishes the existing wards of the borough and provides for the creation of 24 new wards. The changes have effect in relation to local government elections to be held on and after May 2, 2002.

2029. Local elections – Cumbria

COUNTY OF CUMBRIA (ELECTORAL CHANGES) ORDER 2000, SI 2000 2485; made under the Local Government Act 1992 s.17, s.26. In force: In accordance with Art.1 (2); £2.00.

This Order, which revokes the County of Cumbria (Electoral Arrangements) Order 1981 (SI 1981 79), abolishes the existing divisions of the county and provides for the creation of 84 new divisions. The changes have effect in relation to local government elections to be held on or after May 3, 2001.

2030. Local elections – Ealing

LONDON BOROUGH OF EALING (ELECTORAL CHANGES) ORDER 2000, SI 2000 334; made under the Local Government Act 1992 s.17, s.26. In force: October 10, 2001 and May 2, 2002; £1.50.

This Order, which revokes the London Borough of Ealing (Electoral Arrangements) Order 1977 (SI 1977 1414), abolishes the existing wards of the borough and provides for the creation of 23 new wards. The changes have effect in relation to local government elections to be held on and after May 2, 2002.

2031. Local elections – Enfield

LONDON BOROUGH OF ENFIELD (ELECTORAL CHANGES) ORDER 2000, SI 2000 1845; made under the Local Government Act 1992 s.17, s.26. In force: In accordance with Art.1; £1.50.

This Order, which revokes the London Borough of Enfield (Electoral Arrangements) Order 1980 (SI 1980 732), abolishes the existing wards of the borough and provides for the creation of 21 new wards. The changes have effect in relation to local government elections to be held on and after May 2, 2002.

2032. Local elections – Gedling

BOROUGH OF GEDLING (ELECTORAL CHANGES) ORDER 2000, SI 2000 3297; made under the Local Government Act 1992 s.17, s.26. In force: In accordance with Art.1; £1.75.

This Order, which revokes the Borough of Gedling (Electoral Arrangements) Order 1975 (SI 1975 2089) and amends the Nottinghamshire (District Boundaries) Order 1987 (SI 1987 221) and the Nottinghamshire (District Boundaries) Order 1988 (SI 1988 61), abolishes the existing wards of the borough, provides for the creation of 22 new wards and makes provision for the names and areas of, and numbers of councillors for, the new wards. The changes have effect in relation to local government elections to be held on and after May 1, 2003.

2033. Local elections – Greenwich

LONDON BOROUGH OF GREENWICH (ELECTORAL CHANGES) ORDER 2000, SI 2000 1977; made under the Local Government Act 1992 s.17, s.26. In force: October 10, 2001 and May 2, 2002; £1.50.

This Order, which revokes the London Borough of Greenwich (Electoral Arrangements) Order 1977 (SI 1977 1764), abolishes the existing wards of the borough and provides for the creation of 17 new wards. The changes have effect in relation to local government elections to be held on and after May 2, 2002.

2034. Local elections – Hackney

LONDON BOROUGH OF HACKNEY (ELECTORAL CHANGES) ORDER 2000, SI 2000 782; made under the Local Government Act 1992 s.17, s.26. In force: October 10, 2001 and May 2, 2002; £1.50.

This Order, which revokes the London Borough of Hackney (Electoral Arrangements) Order 1977 (SI 1977 1765), abolishes the existing wards of the borough and provides for the creation of 19 new wards. The changes have effect in relation to local government elections to be held on and after May 2, 2002.

2035. Local elections – Hambleton

DISTRICT OF HAMBLETON (ELECTORAL CHANGES) ORDER 2000, SI 2000 2600; made under the Local Government Act 1992 s.17, s.26. In force: In accordance with Art.1 (2); £2.00.

This Order, which revokes the District of Hambleton (Electoral Arrangements) Order 1978 (SI 1978 1814) and the Parish of Northallerton (Wards) Order 1977, abolishes the existing wards of the district and provides for the creation of 30 new wards. The changes have effect in relation to local government elections to be held on and after May 1, 2003.

2036. Local elections – Hammersmith and Fulham

LONDON BOROUGH OF HAMMERSMITH AND FULHAM (ELECTORAL CHANGES) ORDER 2000, SI 2000 1844; made under the Local Government Act 1992 s.17, s.26. In force: In accordance with Art.1; £1.50.

This Order, which revokes the London Borough of Hammersmith (Electoral Arrangements) Order 1977 (SI 1977 1565), abolishes the existing wards of the borough and provides for the creation of 16 new wards. In addition, it modifies the names of certain wards. The changes have effect in relation to local government elections to be held on and after May 2, 2002.

2037. Local elections – Haringey

LONDON BOROUGH OF HARINGEY (ELECTORAL CHANGES) ORDER 2000, SI 2000 783; made under the Local Government Act 1992 s.17, s.26. In force: October 10, 2001 and May 2, 2002; £1.50.

This Order, which revokes the London Borough of Haringey (Electoral Arrangements) Order 1977 (SI 1977 2067), abolishes the existing wards of the borough and provides for the creation of 19 new wards. The changes have effect in relation to local government elections to be held on and after May 2, 2002.

2038. Local elections – Harrogate

BOROUGH OF HARROGATE (ELECTORAL CHANGES) ORDER 2000, SI 2000 2601; made under the Local Government Act 1992 s.17, s.26. In force: In accordance with Art.1 (2) (3) (4); £3.00.

This Order, which revokes the Borough of Harrogate (Electoral Arrangements) Order 1979 (SI 1979 1327), abolishes the existing wards of the borough, provides for the creation of 35 new wards and makes provision for a whole council election in 2002 and for reversion to elections by thirds in subsequent years. The changes have effect in relation to local government elections to be held on and after May 2, 2002.

2039. Local elections – Harrow

LONDON BOROUGH OF HARROW (ELECTORAL CHANGES) ORDER 2000, SI 2000 316; made under the Local Government Act 1992 s.17, s.26. In force: October 10, 2001 and May 2, 2002; £1.50.

This Order, which revokes the London Borough of Harrow (Electoral Arrangements) Order 1978 (SI 1978 89), abolishes the existing wards of the borough and provides for the creation of 21 new wards. The changes have effect in relation to local government elections to be held on and after May 2, 2002.

2040. Local elections – Havering

LONDON BOROUGH OF HAVERING (ELECTORAL CHANGES) ORDER 2000, SI 2000 313; made under the Local Government Act 1992 s.17, s.26. In force: October 10, 2001 and May 2, 2002; £1.50.

This Order, which revokes the London Borough of Havering (Electoral Arrangements) Order 1977 (SI 1977 1545), abolishes the existing wards of the London borough of Havering and provides for the creation of 18 new wards. The changes have effect in relation to local government elections to be held on and after May 2, 2002.

2041. Local elections – Hertfordshire

COUNTY OF HERTFORDSHIRE (ELECTORAL CHANGES) ORDER 2000, SI 2000 2487; made under the Local Government Act 1992 s.17, s.26. In force: In accordance with Art.1 (2) and (3); £2.00.

This Order, which revokes the County of Hertfordshire (Electoral Arrangements) Order 1980 (SI 1980 1769) and the District of Three Rivers (Parishes and Electoral Changes) Order 1998 (SI 1998 2556) Art.5, abolishes the existing divisions of the county and provides for the creation of 77 new divisions. The changes have effect in relation to local government elections to be held on or after May 3, 2001.

2042. Local elections – Hillingdon

LONDON BOROUGH OF HILLINGDON (ELECTORAL CHANGES) ORDER 2000, SI 2000 1766; made under the Local Government Act 1992 s.17, s.26. In force: In accordance with Art.1; £1.50.

This Order, which revokes the London Borough of Hillingdon (Electoral Arrangements) Order 1977 (SI 1977 1673), abolishes the existing wards of the borough and provides for the creation of 22 new wards. The changes have effect in relation to local government elections to be held on and after May 2, 2002.

2043. Local elections – Hounslow

LONDON BOROUGH OF HOUNSLOW (ELECTORAL CHANGES) ORDER 2000, SI 2000 317; made under the Local Government Act 1992 s.17, s.26. In force: October 10, 2001 and May 2, 2002; £1.50.

This Order, which revokes the London Borough of Hounslow (Electoral Arrangements) Order 1977 (SI 1977 1278), abolishes the existing wards of the borough and provides for the creation of 20 new wards. The changes have effect in relation to local government elections to be held on and after May 2, 2002.

2044. Local elections – Isle of Wight

ISLE OF WIGHT (ELECTORAL CHANGES) ORDER 2000, SI 2000 2606; made under the Local Government Act 1992 s.17, s.26; and the Local Government and Rating Act 1997 s.14, s.23. In force: In accordance with Art.1 (2) (3); £2.00.

This Order, which revokes and replaces the Isle of Wight (Electoral Changes) Order 1999 (SI 1999 2393) and amends the Isle of Wight (Structural Change) Order 1994 (SI 1994 1210), abolishes the existing divisions of the county and provides for the creation of 48 new divisions. The changes have effect in relation to local government elections to be held on and after May 3, 2001

2045. Local elections – Islington

LONDON BOROUGH OF ISLINGTON (ELECTORAL CHANGES) ORDER 2000, SI 2000 784; made under the Local Government Act 1992 s.17, s.26. In force: October 10, 2001 and May 2, 2002; £1.50.

This Order, which revokes the London Borough of Islington (Electoral Arrangements) Order 1977 (SI 1977 1566), abolishes the existing wards of the borough and provides for the creation of 16 new wards. The changes have effect in relation to local government elections to be held on and after May 2, 2002.

2046. Local elections – Kensington and Chelsea

ROYAL BOROUGH OF KENSINGTON AND CHELSEA (ELECTORAL CHANGES) ORDER 2000, SI 2000 785; made under the Local Government Act 1992 s.17, s.26. In force: October 10, 2001 and May 2, 2002; £1.50.

This Order, which revokes the Royal Borough of Kensington and Chelsea (Electoral Arrangements) Order 1977 (SI 1977 1818), abolishes the existing wards of the borough and provides for the creation of 18 new wards. The changes have effect in relation to local government elections to be held on and after May 2, 2002.

2047. Local elections – Kingston upon Thames

ROYAL BOROUGH OF KINGSTON UPON THAMES (ELECTORAL CHANGES) ORDER 2000, SI 2000 1767; made under the Local Government Act 1992 s.17, s.26. In force: In accordance with Art.1; £1.50.

This Order, which revokes the Royal Borough of Kingston upon Thames (Electoral Arrangements) Order 1977 (SI 1977 1588), abolishes the existing wards of the borough and provides for the creation of 16 new wards. The changes have effect in relation to local government elections to be held on and after May 2, 2002.

2048. Local elections – Lambeth

LONDON BOROUGH OF LAMBETH (ELECTORAL CHANGES) ORDER 2000, SI 2000 319; made under the Local Government Act 1992 s.17, s.26. In force: October 10, 2001 and May 2, 2002; £1.50.

This Order, which revokes the London Borough of Lambeth (Electoral Arrangements) Order 1977 (SI 1977 2068), abolishes the existing wards of the borough and provides for the creation of 21 new wards. The changes have effect in relation to local government elections to be held on and after May 2, 2002.

2049. Local elections – Lewisham

. LONDON BOROUGH OF LEWISHAM (ELECTORAL CHANGES) ORDER 2000, SI 2000 1236; made under the Local Government Act 1992 s.17, s.26. In force: October 10, 2001 and May 2, 2002; £1.50.

This Order, which revokes the London Borough of Lewisham (Electoral Arrangements) Order 1977 (SI 1977 1391), abolishes the existing wards of the borough and provides for the creation of 18 new wards. The changes have effect in relation to local government elections to be held on and after May 2, 2002.

2050. Local elections – Lincolnshire

COUNTY OF LINCOLNSHIRE (ELECTORAL CHANGES) ORDER 2000, SI 2000 2488; made under the Local Government Act 1992 s.17, s.26. In force: In accordance with Art.1 (2) and (3); £2.00.

This Order, which revokes the County of Lincolnshire (Electoral Arrangements) Order 1980 (SI 1980 1829) and the District of West Lindsey (Electoral Changes) Order 1998 (SI 1998 2366) Art.4, abolishes the existing divisions of the county and provides for the creation of 77 new divisions. The changes have effect in relation to local government elections to be held on or after May 3, 2001.

2051. Local elections – Mansfield

DISTRICT OF MANSFIELD (ELECTORAL CHANGES) ORDER 2000, SI 2000 3298; made under the Local Government Act 1992 s.17, s.26. In force: In accordance with Art.1; £1.75.

This Order, which revokes the District of Mansfield (Electoral Arrangements) Order 1976 (SI 1976 751), abolishes the existing wards of the district, provides for the creation of 19 new wards and makes provision for the names and areas of, and numbers of councillors for, the new wards. The changes have effect in relation to local government elections to be held on and after May 1, 2003.

2052. Local elections – Merton

LONDON BOROUGH OF MERTON (ELECTORAL CHANGES) ORDER 2000, SI 2000 318; made under the Local Government Act 1992 s.17, s.26. In force: October 10, 2001 and May 2, 2002; £1.50.

This Order, which revokes the London Borough of Merton (Electoral Arrangements) Order 1977 (SI 1977 1819), abolishes the existing wards of the borough and provides for the creation of 20 new wards. The changes have effect in relation to local government elections to be held on and after May 2, 2002.

2053. Local elections – Newark and Sherwood

DISTRICT OF NEWARK AND SHERWOOD (ELECTORAL CHANGES) ORDER 2000, SI 2000 3299; made under the Local Government Act 1992 s.17, s.26. In force: In accordance with Art.1; £2.00.

This Order, which revokes the District of Newark (Electoral Arrangements) Order 1976 (SI 1976 810), abolishes the existing wards of the district, provides for the creation of 26 new wards and makes provision for the names and areas of, and numbers of councillors for, the new wards. The changes have effect in relation to local government elections to be held on and after May 1, 2003.

2054. Local elections – Newham

LONDON BOROUGH OF NEWHAM (ELECTORAL CHANGES) ORDER 2000, SI 2000 1768; made under the Local Government Act 1992 s.17, s.26. In force: October 10, 2001 and May 2, 2002; £1.50.

This Order, which revokes the London Borough of Newham (Electoral Arrangements) Order 1977 (SI 1977 1613), abolishes the existing wards of the borough and provides for the creation of 20 new wards. The changes have effect in relation to local government elections to be held on and after May 2, 2002.

2055. Local elections – North Shropshire

DISTRICT OF NORTH SHROPSHIRE (ELECTORAL CHANGES) ORDER 2000, SI 2000 1419; made under the Local Government Act 1992 s.17, s.26. In force: October 10, 2002 and May 1, 2003; £2.00.

This Order, which gives effect to recommendations by the Local Government Commission for England for electoral changes in the district of North Shropshire, abolishes the existing wards of the district and provides for the creation of 24 new wards and their names and areas. The District of North Shropshire (Electoral Arrangements) Order 1976 (SI 1976 196) is revoked.

2056. Local elections – North Warwickshire

BOROUGH OF NORTH WARWICKSHIRE (ELECTORAL CHANGES) ORDER 2000, SI 2000 1675; made under the Local Government Act 1992 s.17, s.26. In force: In accordance with Art.1; £2.00.

This Order, which revokes the Borough of North Warwickshire (Electoral Arrangements) Order 1976 (SI 1976 1132), abolishes the existing wards of the borough and provides for the creation of 17 new wards. The changes have effect in relation to local government elections to be held on and after May 1, 2003.

2057. Local elections – Northamptonshire

COUNTY OF NORTHAMPTONSHIRE (ELECTORAL CHANGES) ORDER 2000, SI 2000 2489; made under the Local Government Act 1992 s.17, s.26. In force: In accordance with Art.1 (2); £2.00.

This Order, which revokes the County of Northamptonshire (Electoral Arrangements) Order 1981 (SI 1981 49), abolishes the existing divisions of the county and provides for the creation of 73 new divisions. The changes have effect in relation to local government elections to be held on or after May 3, 2001.

2058. Local elections – Northumberland

COUNTY OF NORTHUMBERLAND (ELECTORAL CHANGES) ORDER 2000, SI 2000 2490; made under the Local Government Act 1992 s.17, s.26. In force: In accordance with Art.1 (2) and (3); £2.00.

This Order, which revokes the County of Northumberland (Electoral Arrangements) Order 1980 (SI 1980 738), the District of Tynedale (Electoral Changes) Order 1998 (SI 1998 2343) Art.3 and the Borough of Castle Morpeth (Electoral Changes) Order 1998 (SI 1998 2344) Art.2, abolishes the existing divisions of the county and provides for the creation of 67 new divisions. The changes have effect in relation to local government elections to be held on or after May 3, 2001.

2059. Local elections – Nottingham

CITY OF NOTTINGHAM (ELECTORAL CHANGES) ORDER 2000, SI 2000 3300; made under the Local Government Act 1992 s.17, s.26. In force: In accordance with Art.1; £1.75.

This Order, which revokes the City of Nottingham (Electoral Arrangements) Order 1976 (SI 1976 114), abolishes the existing wards of the city, provides for the creation of 20 new wards and makes provision for the names and areas of, and numbers of councillors for, the new wards. The changes have effect in relation to local government elections to be held on and after May 1, 2003.

2060. Local elections – Nuneaton and Bedworth

BOROUGH OF NUNEATON AND BEDWORTH (ELECTORAL CHANGES) ORDER 2000, SI 2000 2058; made under the Local Government Act 1992 s.17, s.26. In force: October 10, 2001 and May 2, 2002; £1.50.

This Order, which revokes the Borough of Nuneaton (Electoral Arrangements) Order 1977 (SI 1977 732), abolishes the existing wards of the borough and provides for the creation of 17 new wards. The changes have effect in relation to local government elections to be held on October 10, 2001 and May 2, 2002.

2061. Local elections – Oswestry

BOROUGH OF OSWESTRY (ELECTORAL CHANGES) ORDER 2000, SI 2000 1418; made under the Local Government Act 1992 s.17, s.26. In force: May 25, 2000, October 10, 2002 and May 1, 2003; £1.50.

This Order, which gives effect to recommendations by the Local Government Commission for England for electoral changes in the borough of Oswestry, abolishes the existing wards of the borough and provides for the creation of 14 new wards and their names and areas. The Borough of Oswestry (Electoral Arrangements) Order 1975 (SI 1975 2200) is revoked.

2062. Local elections – Redbridge

LONDON BOROUGH OF REDBRIDGE (ELECTORAL CHANGES) ORDER 2000, SI 2000 335; made under the Local Government Act 1992 s.17, s.26. In force: October 10, 2001 and May 2, 2002; £1.50.

This Order, which revokes the London Borough of Redbridge (Electoral Arrangements) Order 1977 (SI 1977 1546), abolishes the existing wards of the borough and provides for the creation of 21 new wards. The changes have effect in relation to local government elections to be held on and after May 2, 2002.

2063. Local elections – Richmond upon Thames

BOROUGH OF RICHMOND UPON THAMES (ELECTORAL CHANGES) ORDER 2000, SI 2000 314; made under the Local Government Act 1992 s.17, s.26. In force: October 10, 2001 and May 2, 2002; £1.50.

This Order, which revokes the London Borough of Richmond upon Thames (Electoral Arrangements) Order 1977 (SI 1977 1567), abolishes the existing wards of the London borough of Richmond upon Thames and provides for the creation of 18 new wards. The changes have effect in relation to local government elections to be held on and after May 2, 2002.

2064. Local elections – Richmondshire

DISTRICT OF RICHMONDSHIRE (ELECTORAL CHANGES) ORDER 2000, SI 2000 2602; made under the Local Government Act 1992 s.17, s.26. In force: In accordance with Art.1 (2); £2.00.

This Order, which revokes the District of Richmondshire (Electoral Arrangements) Order 1977 (SI 1977 1674), abolishes the existing wards of the district and provides for the creation of 24 new wards. The changes have effect in relation to local government elections to be held on and after May 1, 2003.

2065. Local elections – Rugby

BOROUGH OF RUGBY (ELECTORAL CHANGES) ORDER 2000, SI 2000 1676; made under the Local Government Act 1992 s.17, s.26. In force: In accordance with Art.1; £2.00.

This Order, which revokes the Borough of Rugby (Electoral Arrangements) Order 1978 (SI 1978 1862), abolishes the existing wards of the borough and provides for the creation of 20 new wards. The changes have effect in relation to local government elections to be held on and after May 2, 2002.

2066. Local elections – Rugby

BOROUGH OF RUGBY (ELECTORAL CHANGES) (NO.2) ORDER 2000, SI 2000 3363; made under the Local Government Act 1992 s.17, s.26. In force: In accordance with Art.1 (2) (3) (4); £2.00.

This Order, which revokes and replaces the Borough of Rugby (Electoral Changes) Order 2000 (SI 2000 1676), depicts the boundaries of the Dunchurch and Knightlow ward omitted from the map referred to in the 2000 Order and establishes the electoral cycle for the parishes mentioned or referred to in Art.6. This Order gives effect to recommendations by the Local Government Commission for England for electoral changes in the borough of Rugby, abolishes the existing wards of the borough and provides for the creation of twenty new wards, makes provision for a whole council election in 2002 and for reversion to elections by thirds in subsequent years. The changes have effect in relation to local government elections to be held on and after May 2, 2002. The Borough of Rugby (Electoral Arrangements) Order 1978 (SI 1978 1862) is revoked.

2067. Local elections – Rushcliffe

BOROUGH OF RUSHCLIFFE (ELECTORAL CHANGES) ORDER 2000, SI 2000 3301; made under the Local Government Act 1992 s.17, s.26. In force: In accordance with Art.1; £1.75.

This Order, which revokes the Borough of Rushcliffe (Electoral Arrangements) Order 1975 (SI 1975 1669), abolishes the existing wards of the borough, provides for the creation of 28 new wards and makes provision for the names and areas of, and numbers of councillors for, the new wards. The changes have effect in relation to local government elections to be held on and after May 1, 2003.

2068. Local elections – Ryedale

DISTRICT OF RYEDALE (ELECTORAL CHANGES) ORDER 2000, SI 2000 2603; made under the Local Government Act 1992 s.17, s.26. In force: In accordance with Art.1 (2); £2.00.

This Order, which revokes the District of Ryedale (Electoral Arrangements) Order 1979 (SI 1979 1110), abolishes the existing wards of the district and provides for the creation of 20 new wards. The changes have effect in relation to local government elections to be held on and after May 1, 2003.

2069. Local elections – Scarborough

BOROUGH OF SCARBOROUGH (ELECTORAL CHANGES) ORDER 2000, SI 2000 2604; made under the Local Government Act 1992 s.17, s.26. In force: In accordance with Art.1 (2); £2.00.

This Order, which revokes the Borough of Scarborough (Electoral Arrangements) Order 1977 (SI 1977 1065), abolishes the existing wards of the borough and provides for the creation of 25 new wards. The changes have effect in relation to local government elections to be held on and after May 1, 2003.

2070. Local elections – Selby

DISTRICT OF SELBY (ELECTORAL CHANGES) ORDER 2000, SI 2000 2605; made under the Local Government Act 1992 s.17, s.26. In force: In accordance with Art.1 (2); £1.50.

This Order, which revokes the District of Selby (Electoral Arrangements) Order 1978 (SI 1978 45), abolishes the existing wards of the district and provides for the creation of 20 new wards. The changes have effect in relation to local government elections to be held on and after May 1, 2003.

2071. Local elections – Shrewsbury and Atcham

BOROUGH OF SHREWSBURY AND ATCHAM (ELECTORAL CHANGES) ORDER 2000, SI 2000 1725; made under the Local Government Act 1992 s.17, s.26. In force: October 10, 2001 and May 2, 2002; £2.00.

This Order, which revokes the Borough of Shrewsbury and Atcham (Electoral Arrangements) Order 1975 (SI 1975 2107), abolishes the existing wards of the borough and provides for the creation of 24 new wards. It provides for a whole council election in 2002 and for reversion to elections by thirds in subsequent years.

2072. Local elections – Somerset

COUNTY OF SOMERSET (ELECTORAL CHANGES) ORDER 2000, SI 2000 2491; made under the Local Government Act 1992 s.17, s.26. In force: In accordance with Art.1 (2) and (3); £2.00.

This Order, which revokes the County of Somerset (Electoral Arrangements) Order 1980 (SI 1980 1725), the District of Mendip (Electoral Changes) Order 1998 (SI 1998 2464) Art.3 and the District of Sedgemoor (Electoral Changes) Order 1998 (SI 1998 2465) Art.3, abolishes the existing divisions of the county and provides for the creation of 58 new divisions. The changes have effect in relation to local government elections to be held on or after May 3, 2001.

2073. Local elections – South Shropshire

DISTRICT OF SOUTH SHROPSHIRE (ELECTORAL CHANGES) ORDER 2000, SI 2000 1420; made under the Local Government Act 1992 s.17, s.26. In force: October 10, 2002 and May 1, 2003; £1.50.

This Order, which gives effect to recommendations by the Local Government Commission for England for electoral changes in the district of South Shropshire, abolishes the existing wards of the district and provides for the creation of 23 new wards and their names and areas. The District of South Shropshire (Electoral Arrangements) Order 1976 (SI 1976 67) is revoked.

2074. Local elections – South Shropshire

DISTRICT OF SOUTH SHROPSHIRE (ELECTORAL CHANGES) (AMENDMENT) ORDER 2000, SI 2000 3364; made under the Local Government Act 1992 s.17, s.26. In force: December 22, 2000; £1.50.

This Order, which corrects an error in the District of South Shropshire (Electoral Changes) Order 2000 (SI 2000 1420), provides for two councillors to be elected for the Worthen ward and has effect in relation to local government elections to be held on and after May 1, 2003.

2075. Local elections – Southend-on-Sea

BOROUGH OF SOUTHEND-ON-SEA (ELECTORAL CHANGES) ORDER 2000, SI 2000 1487; made under the Local Government Act 1992 s.17, s.26. In force: In accordance with Art.1 (2) (3); £1.50.

This Order, which revokes the Borough of Southend-on-Sea (Electoral Arrangements) Order 1975 (SI 1975 1698) and the Essex (Boroughs of Colchester, Southend-on-Sea and Thurrock and District of Tendring) (Structural, Boundary and Electoral Changes) Order 1996 (SI 1996 1875) Art.7, abolishes the existing wards of the borough of Southend-on-Sea and provides for the creation of 17 new wards. The changes have effect in relation to local government elections to be held on and after May 3, 2001.

2076. Local elections – Southwark

LONDON BOROUGH OF SOUTHWARK (ELECTORAL CHANGES) ORDER 2000, SI 2000 786; made under the Local Government Act 1992 s.17, s.26. In force: October 10, 2001 and May 2, 2002; £1.50.

This Order, which revokes the London Borough of Southwark (Electoral Arrangements) Order 1977 (SI 1977 1392), abolishes the existing wards of the borough and provides for the creation of 21 new wards. The changes have effect in relation to local government elections to be held on and after May 2, 2002.

2077. Local elections – Stratford on Avon

DISTRICT OF STRATFORD ON AVON (ELECTORAL CHANGES) ORDER 2000, SI 2000 2059; made under the Local Government Act 1992 s.17, s.26. In force: October 10, 2001 and May 2, 2002; £2.00.

This Order, which revokes the District of Stratford-on-Avon (Electoral Arrangements) Order 1977 (SI 1977 1393), abolishes the existing wards of the district and provides for the creation of 31 new wards. The changes have effect in relation to local government elections to be held on October 10, 2001 and May 2, 2002.

2078. Local elections – Sutton

LONDON BOROUGH OF SUTTON (ELECTORAL CHANGES) ORDER 2000, SI 2000 1847; made under the Local Government Act 1992 s.17, s.26. In force: In accordance with Art.1; £1.50.

This Order, which revokes the London Borough of Sutton (Electoral Arrangements) Order 1977 (SI 1977 1275), abolishes the existing wards of the borough and provides for the creation of 18 new wards. The changes have effect in relation to local government elections to be held on and after May 2, 2002.

2079. Local elections – Taunton Deane

BOROUGH OF TAUNTON DEANE (ELECTORAL CHANGES) (AMENDMENT) ORDER 2000, SI 2000 3365; made under the Local Government Act 1992 s.17, s.26. In force: December 22, 2000; £1.50.

This Order, which corrects errors in the District of Taunton Deane (Electoral Changes) Order 1998 (SI 1998 2461), clarifies that the parish included in the Bradford-on-Tone ward is the parish of Langford Budville and provides that the area of the ward of Stoke St. Gregory comprises the parishes of Burrowbridge and Stoke St. Gregory.

2080.   Local elections – Tower Hamlets

LONDON BOROUGH OF TOWER HAMLETS (ELECTORAL CHANGES) ORDER 2000, SI 2000 787; made under the Local Government Act 1992 s.17, s.26. In force: October 10, 2001 and May 2, 2002; £1.50.

This Order, which revokes the London Borough of Tower Hamlets (Electoral Arrangements) Order 1978 (SI 1978 63), abolishes the existing wards of the borough and provides for the creation of 17 new wards. The changes have effect in relation to local government elections to be held on and after May 2, 2002.

2081.   Local elections – Waltham Forest

LONDON BOROUGH OF WALTHAM FOREST (ELECTORAL CHANGES) ORDER 2000, SI 2000 336; made under the Local Government Act 1992 s.17, s.26. In force: October 10, 2001 and May 2, 2002; £1.50.

This Order, which revokes the London Borough of Waltham Forest (Electoral Arrangements) Order 1977 (SI 1977 1766), abolishes the existing wards of the borough and provides for the creation of 20 new wards. The changes have effect in relation to local government elections to be held on and after May 2, 2002.

2082.   Local elections – Wandsworth

LONDON BOROUGH OF WANDSWORTH (ELECTORAL CHANGES) ORDER 2000, SI 2000 315; made under the Local Government Act 1992 s.17, s.26. In force: October 10, 2001 and May 2, 2002; £1.50.

This Order, which revokes the London Borough of Wandsworth (Electoral Arrangements) Order 1977 (SI 1977 1962), abolishes the existing wards of the London borough of Wandsworth and provides for the creation of 20 new wards. The changes have effect in relation to local government elections to be held on and after May 2, 2002.

2083.   Local elections – Warwick

DISTRICT OF WARWICK (ELECTORAL CHANGES) ORDER 2000, SI 2000 1677; made under the Local Government Act 1992 s.15. In force: In accordance with Art.1; £1.50.

This Order, which revokes the District of Warwick (Electoral Arrangements) Order 1979 (SI 1979 1328), abolishes the existing wards of the district and provides for the creation of 20 new wards. The changes have effect in relation to local government elections to be held on and after May 1, 2003.

2084.   Local elections – Waverley

BOROUGH OF WAVERLEY (ELECTORAL CHANGES) (AMENDMENT) ORDER 2000, SI 2000 3366; made under the Local Government Act 1992 s.17, s.26. In force: December 22, 2000; £1.50.

This Order, which has effect in relation to local government elections to be held on and after May 1, 2003, corrects errors in the Borough of Waverley (Electoral Changes) Order 1999 (SI 1999 2482). The amendments provide for two councillors to be elected for each of the Godalming Binscombe, and Haslemere East and Grayswood wards, and for three councillors to be elected for the Hindhead ward.

2085.   Political parties – registration requirements – financial regulation

REGISTERED PARTIES (NON-CONSTITUENT AND NON-AFFILIATED ORGANISATIONS) ORDER 2000, SI 2000 3183; made under the Political

Parties, Elections and Referendums Act 2000 s.26. In force: December 14, 2000; £1.75.

The Political Parties, Elections and Referendums Act 2000 s.26(1) prohibits the registration of a party unless it has adopted a scheme which sets out the arrangements for regulating its financial affairs for the purposes of that Act. The scheme must determine whether the party is to be taken to consist of a central organisation. This Order exercises the power in s.26(8)(c) of the Act to specify organisations falling within this provision and descriptions of organisations.

2086. Political Parties, Elections and Referendums Act 2000 (c.41)

This Act establishes an Electoral Commission to make provision about the registration and finances of political parties; to make provision about donations and expenditure for political purposes; to make provision about election and referendum campaigns and the conduct of referendums; to make provision about election petitions and other legal proceedings in connection with elections; to reduce the qualifying periods set out in the Representation of the People Act 1985 ss.1 and 3 and to make pre-consolidation amendments relating to European Parliamentary Elections.

This Act received Royal Assent on November 30, 2000.

2087. Representation of the People Act 2000 (c.2)

This Act provides for a new system of registration of voters for the purposes of parliamentary and local government elections and makes provision in relation to voting at such elections.

This Act received Royal Assent on March 9, 2000.

ELECTRICITY INDUSTRY

2088. Electricity – renewable energy sources – internal market – draft Council Directive

Amended proposal for a European Parliament and Council Directive on the promotion of electricity from renewable energy sources in the internal electricity market. [2000] OJ C311E/320.

2089. Electricity generation – non fossil fuel sources

ELECTRICITY FROM NON-FOSSIL FUEL SOURCES SAVING ARRANGEMENTS ORDER 2000, SI 2000 2727; made under the Utilities Act 2000 s.67. In force: October 27, 2000; £2.00.

This Order amends the Electricity Act 1989 by providing for the modification of arrangements which have been made by public electricity suppliers in compliance with s.32 of the 1989 Act to coincide with the commencement of trading under the new electricity trading arrangements (NETA). They oblige public electricity suppliers in England and Wales to ensure that a person nominated by them makes the new arrangements which secure the availability of a certain amount of generating capacity from non fossil fuel generating stations; oblige the nominated person to offer for sale the electricity made available to him under the arrangements to all licensed electricity suppliers in England and Wales and to use his reasonable endeavours to receive the best price reasonably attainable for it; and provide that the nominated person must be approved by the Secretary of State.

2090. Electricity supply industry – improvements to distribution system – power to recover expenditure

[Electricity Act 1989 s.19.]

A village trust which owned 88 dwellings installed electricity night storage heating in those dwellings resulting in reinforcement works to the distribution system totalling £44,693. LE, the electricity supplier, held a licence which provided that no charge would be made for the reinforcement of an existing distribution system if the new or increased load requirement did not exceed 25 per cent of the existing effective capacity. An application was made to LE by the individual tenants of the dwellings with a view to an agreement being reached concerning the relevant works. LE decided that the "25 per cent rule" did not apply to a case where the request for an increased supply did not amount to an independent request but instead related to a larger scheme giving rise to an increase exceeding 25 per cent of the relevant capacity. LE's decision was referred to the Director General of Electricity Supply who held that the "25 per cent rule" did apply. LE sought judicial review of that decision.

Held, allowing the application, that the appropriate test was one of causation, such an approach accorded with the charging regime set out in the relevant statutory and licensing provisions. Where an increased demand arose from a single project, it would be contrary to the aim of the Electricity Act 1989 s.19, which enabled the supplier to recover expenses from the individual requiring its supply, to permit the demand to be divided between the individual customers thereby avoiding payment of the relevant charges. In reality the project represented a single cause of the increased supply. In the circumstances, the tenants involved were liable for a proportionate share of the expenses reasonably incurred by LE in the provision of the relevant works.

R. v. DIRECTOR GENERAL OF ELECTRICITY SUPPLY, *ex p.* LONDON ELECTRICITY PLC *The Times*, June 13, 2000, Harrison, J., QBD.

2091. Electricity supply industry – licences – exemptions

ELECTRICITY (CLASS EXEMPTIONS FROM THE REQUIREMENT FOR A LICENCE) (AMENDMENT) (ENGLAND AND WALES) ORDER 2000, SI 2000 2424; made under the Electricity Act 1989 s.5, s.111. In force: October 1, 2000; £1.00.

This Order amends the Electricity (Class Exemptions from the Requirement for a Licence) Order 1997 (SI 1997 989) by granting, for a period of one year, exemption from the requirement to hold a licence to generate electricity to two new classes of persons whose generating stations were connected to the transmission system in England and Wales or a distribution system in England and Wales on September 30, 2000. The new Class C covers persons whose stations are not normally capable of exporting more than 100 megawatts and the new Class D covers persons with stations which were not subject to central despatch on September 30, 2000.

2092. Electricity supply industry – performance standards

ELECTRICITY (STANDARDS OF PERFORMANCE) (AMENDMENT) REGULATIONS 2000, SI 2000 840; made under the Electricity Act 1989 s.39, s.60. In force: April 1, 2000; £1.00.

These Regulations amend the Electricity (Standards of Performance) Regulations 1993 (SI 1993 1193) by reducing from 24 to 18 hours the time public electricity suppliers have to restore interrupted supplies before making penalty payments to affected customers.

2093. Environmental impact assessments – electricity works

ELECTRICITY WORKS (ENVIRONMENTAL IMPACT ASSESSMENT) (ENGLAND AND WALES) REGULATIONS 2000, SI 2000 1927; made under the European Communities Act 1972 s.2. In force: September 1, 2000; £3.00.

These Regulations implement Council Directive 85/337 ([1985] OJ L175/40) as amended by Council Directive 97/11 ([1997] OJ L73/5) on the assessment of certain public and private projects on the environment insofar as it relates to applications for consent to construct, extend or operate a power station or install or keep installed overhead electricity lines under the Electricity Act 1989 s.36 and s.37. The Electricity and Pipe-line Works (Assessment of Environmental Effects) Regulations 1990 (SI 1990 442), the Electricity and Pipe-line Works (Assessment of Environmental Effects) (Amendment) Regulations 1996 (SI 1996 422) and the Electricity and Pipe-line Works (Assessment of Environmental Effects) (Amendment) Regulations 1997 (SI 1997 629) are revoked.

EMPLOYMENT

2094. Annual leave – EC Law – entitlement – exclusions under Working Time Directive

[Working Time Regulations 1998 (SI 1998 1833) Reg.13, Reg.18; Council Directive 93/104 concerning certain aspects of the organisation of working time.]

B, a clerical worker employed by a parcel delivery operator, T, appealed against an employment tribunal's ruling that she was not entitled to four week's paid annual leave. The tribunal had held that B was excluded from the Working Time Regulations 1998 Reg.13 by virtue of Reg.18 as she was a worker in the road transport industry. B appealed, arguing that Reg.13 should be given a purposive construction.

Held, staying the appeal, that the matter should be referred to the ECJ for a ruling on interpretation. It had not been possible to derive assistance as to the correct interpretation of Reg.18 from the Regulations themselves, from other national legislation nor from the Working Time Directive 93/104. Although there was clearly an intention to exclude certain classes of workers from the right to holidays, it was not clear whether the exclusions listed in Reg.18 were intended to be applied to all workers in the named sectors of activity.

BOWDEN v. TUFFNELLS PARCELS EXPRESS LTD [2000] I.R.L.R. 560, Lindsay, J., EAT.

2095. Annual leave – EC Law – Working Time Directive 93/104 Art. 7 did not have direct effect

[Council Directive 93/104 on the organisation of working time Art.7.]

G, a part time swimming instructor, was paid an hourly rate but was not entitled under her contract to annual leave. She brought an action against her employer, E, alleging, inter alia, that E had failed to provide her with a proper statement of the terms and conditions of her employment. As regards her entitlement to annual leave, G sought to rely on the Working Time Directive 93/104 Art.7 which provided that Member States were to ensure that every worker should receive four weeks' paid annual leave. It having been agreed that E, as a local authority, was an emanation of the State and that G was a "worker" within the meaning of the Directive, the issue arose as to whether Art.7 had direct effect. The employment tribunal held Art.7 not to be directly effective. G appealed to the Employment Appeal Tribunal ([1999] 3 C.M.L.R. 190, [1999] C.L.Y. 2018) which found Art.7 to have direct effect on the ground that it was clear, precise and unambiguous. E appealed.

Held, allowing the appeal, that Art.7 was insufficiently precise and did not therefore have direct effect. While it clearly established a precise minimum period of paid annual leave of four weeks, it contained no guidelines as to how a worker's entitlement was to be determined where he was in the initial stages of his employment, where he had more than one employer or where he was employed on a part time or commission basis.

EAST RIDING OF YORKSHIRE DC v. GIBSON; *sub nom.* GIBSON v. EAST RIDING OF YORKSHIRE DC [2000] 3 C.M.L.R. 329, Mummery, L.J., CA.

2096. Appeals – employment tribunal – time limits – notice served one day out of time – delay attributable to computer failure

[Interpretation Act 1978 s.7; Employment Appeal Tribunal Rules 1993 (SI 1993 2854) r.3(2), r.35.]

M served notice of an appeal from a decision of an employment tribunal 43 days from the date on which extended written reasons for the decision were sent to M. The Employment Appeal Tribunal Rules 1993 r.3(2) provided that an appeal was to be instituted within 42 days from that date. The delay was attributed to a last minute failure of the computer in the office of the appellant's then counsel. It was argued that, by reason of the provisions of r.35 of the 1993 Rules and/or the Interpretation Act 1978 s.7, the words "were sent" meant "were received".

Held, dismissing the appeal, that (1) the provisions relied on related to service by post, whereas r.3(2) dealt with the calculation of the date from which time started to run for the purposes of serving notice of appeal, *Immigration Advisory Service v. Oommen* [1997] I.C.R. 683, [1997] C.L.Y. 2227 distinguished. That rule defined a specific date at which an act was done, namely the date on which the decision was entered onto the register. This rule meant that both parties would know the time limit of the appeal and thus was both practical and just, and (2) time limits should be strictly applied and not used as a guideline. The delay caused by the computer failure did not provide a satisfactory excuse justifying an extension of time, as it was open to M to have presented the notice of appeal, other than through use of a computer.

MOCK v. INLAND REVENUE COMMISSIONERS [1999] I.R.L.R. 785, Morison, J., EAT.

2097. Barristers – pupillage – entitlement to minimum wage

[National Minimum Wage Act 1998 s.54; National Minimum Wage Regulations 1999 (SI 1999 584) Reg.12.]

E accepted an unpaid 12 month pupillage with a barristers' chambers. In friendly litigation brought at the Bar Council's instigation, E sought and was granted declarations ([2000] I.R.L.R. 18) that her acceptance of the pupillage created an apprenticeship contract, that she was a "worker" within the meaning of the National Minimum Wage Act 1998 s.54(3)(a) and that, being over 26 years old, she was entitled by virtue of the National Minimum Wage Regulations 1999 Reg.12 to be paid the national minimum wage during her pupillage. L, a barrister belonging to the chambers, appealed, contending that the offer to provide E with education and training was not enforceable as a contract since there had been no intention to create legal relations and E had provided no consideration. Furthermore, L argued, the relationship between the parties was regulated by Bar Council guidelines relating to pupillage which rendered a further contract unnecessary.

Held, allowing the appeal, that (1) there was a binding contract for the provision of education and training which impliedly incorporated regulatory materials governing pupillage; (2) a broad view had to be taken of the relationship between E and the barristers' chambers. It was in the chambers' long term interests to attract talented pupils and, regardless of whether E was a prospective candidate for tenancy or not, her agreement to that potentially productive relationship had been consideration for the offer, and (3) the construction of "apprenticeship" in s.54(2) of the 1998 Act was intended to be unlegalistic and covered learned professions. However, a cardinal ingredient of an apprenticeship was a mutual covenant whereby the master undertook to educate and train the apprentice, who, in return, was bound to serve and work for the master. In the instant case, there had been no expectation on E to provide valuable service and she was not obliged to do anything which was not conducive to her own training, hence she did not work under a contract of apprenticeship or an equivalent contract.

EDMONDS v. LAWSON; *sub nom.* EDMUNDS v. LAWSON [2000] Q.B. 501, Lord Bingham of Cornhill, L.C.J., CA.

2098. Bonus payments – employers duties – exercise of discretion

C, who had formerly been employed as a senior equities trader by N, instituted proceedings for breach of contract against N following N's decision to pay him a nil bonus in respect of a period during which he had earned profits in excess of £22 million for the company. The decision had followed an alteration to N's bonus scheme so as to replace the traditional "formulaic" bonus payment with a discretionary bonus dependent upon individual performance. C contended that the assessment of individual performance related solely to profitability whereas N maintained that other factors, including the needs of its business and whether it desired to retain the employee in question, were also significant.

Held, giving judgment for C in the sum of £1.35 million, that "individual performance" meant the performance by C of his contract and excluded N's business needs and the need, or the absence of the need, to retain and motivate C. Further, in assessing C's bonus entitlement, N had a duty not to act irrationally or perversely. In relying upon C's summary dismissal to opt not to make any bonus payment to him and seeking to justify that decision on the basis of unfounded allegations of non participation and disruption, N had acted irrationally.

CLARK v. NOMURA INTERNATIONAL PLC [2000] I.R.L.R. 766, Burton, J., QBD.

2099. Casual workers – employment agencies – deployment across EU – social security status

[Council Regulation 1408/71 on the application of social security schemes to employed persons, to self-employed persons and to members of their families moving within the Community Art.14(1)(a); Council Regulation 574/72 Art.11(1)(a).]

F, an employment agency, deployed casual workers in both Ireland and the Netherlands. All of F's operations were carried out from Ireland and all its employment contracts for workers in Ireland and in the Netherlands were issued in Dublin and were thus subject to the Irish social security system. F deployed only Irish nationals who were resident in Ireland. Council Regulation 1408/71 Art.14(1)(a) provided that a worker sent by an "undertaking to which he is normally attached" to a temporary position in another Member State remained subject to the social security system of the sending state. In respect of workers posted to the Netherlands, E101 certificates were issued by F pursuant to Council Regulation 574/72 Art.11(1)(a). The Netherlands submitted that the posted workers did not fall within Art.14(1)(a) and requested that F pay employer's contributions. The Dutch Court referred a number of issues to the ECJ, namely (1) whether an undertaking in a Member State providing temporary staff to another undertaking in another Member State must have "ties" with the first Member State in the sense that it must normally carry on its business there; (2) the criteria for determining whether an undertaking which provided casual workers normally carried on its operations in the state of establishment, and (3) to what extent an E101 certificate was binding on the social security institutions of other states.

Held, giving a preliminary ruling, that (1) an undertaking providing temporary staff originating in one Member State for work in another Member State was normally obliged to carry on its activities in the first state, *Manpower Sarl, Strasbourg Regional Office v. Caisse Primaire d'Assurance Maladie de Strasbourg (C35/70)* [1971] C.M.L.R. 222, [1971] C.L.Y. 4508 applied; (2) the undertaking providing temporary workers normally carried on its activities in the Member State in which it was established if it habitually carried on significant activities in that state. In order to determine the extent of the activities carried on, it was necessary to consider various factors to include the place of administration of the undertaking, the place in which employment contracts were concluded, the place where workers were recruited and the turnover during a given period; (3) a Member State could not subject temporary personnel to its own social security system where a valid E101 certificate was in force, but the state issuing the certificate must reconsider or withdraw it if the information it contained did not accord with the requirements of Art.14(1)(a). Regulation 574/72 Art.11 (1)(a) was to be interpreted as meaning that such a certificate was binding on other Member States to the extent that posted workers were covered by the social security system of the Member State in which the undertaking was established.

FITZWILLIAM EXECUTIVE SEARCH LTD (T/A FITZWILLIAM TECHNICAL SERVICES) v. BESTUUR VAN HET LANDELIJK INSTITUUT SOCIALE VERZEKERINGEN (C202/97) [2000] Q.B. 906, GC Rodriguez Iglesias (President), ECJ.

2100. Children – agricultural and horticultural work – street trading – increase in minimum age

CHILDREN (PROTECTION AT WORK) REGULATIONS 2000, SI 2000 1333; made under the European Communities Act 1972 s.2. In force: June 7, 2000; £1.00.

These Regulations, which implement, in England and Wales, Council Directive 94/33 ([1994] OJ L216/12) on the protection of young people at work, amend the Children and Young Persons Act 1933 by raising to 13 the minimum age at which children may be authorised by local authority by laws to be employed in light agricultural or horticultural work; providing that local authority by laws authorising children to take part in street trading must contain provisions determining the days and hours during which, and the places at which, they may do so and that only persons aged at least 16 and who are over compulsory school age may take part in performances of a dangerous nature.

2101. Children – hours of employment – limitation during term time

CHILDREN (PROTECTION AT WORK) (NO.2) REGULATIONS 2000, SI 2000 2548; made under the European Communities Act 1972 s.2. In force: October 11, 2000; £1.00.

These Regulations give effect, in England and Wales, to Council Directive 94/33 ([1994] OJ L216/12) on the protection of young people at work. Art.17(1)(b) provided a derogation to Art.8(1)(b) which relates to the maximum number of hours which may be worked by children in term time but this derogation has now come to an end. In particular, they amend the Children and Young Persons Act 1933 s.18, to place a limit on the number of hours that a child may be employed in any week in which they are required to attend school.

2102. Childrens welfare – performing arts – performances and rehearsals

See FAMILY LAW. §2498

2103. Codes of practice – disciplinary and grievance procedures

EMPLOYMENT CODE OF PRACTICE (DISCIPLINARY AND GRIEVANCE PROCEDURES) ORDER 2000, SI 2000 2247; made under the Trade Union and Labour Relations (Consolidation) Act 1992 s.200. In force: September 4, 2000; £1.00.

This Order appoints September 4, 2000 as the day on which the Code of Practice on Disciplinary and Grievance Procedures, which takes account of the right to be accompanied under the Employment Relations Act 1999 s.10, comes into effect. The Code, which replaces the Code of Practice on Disciplinary Practice and Procedures in Employment which came into effect on February 5, 1998, is available from The Stationery Office, ISBN 0 11 782318 X.

2104. Codes of practice – industrial action ballots

EMPLOYMENT CODE OF PRACTICE (INDUSTRIAL ACTION BALLOTS AND NOTICE TO EMPLOYERS) ORDER 2000, SI 2000 2241; made under the Trade

Union and Labour Relations (Consolidation) Act 1992 s.204. In force: September 18, 2000; £1.00.

This Order appoints September 18, 2000 as the day on which the revised Code of Practice on Industrial Action Ballots and Notice to Employers comes into effect. The revised Code replaces that which came into effect on November 17, 1995.

2105. Codes of practice – trade union recognition – ballots

EMPLOYMENT CODE OF PRACTICE (ACCESS TO WORKERS DURING RECOGNITION AND DERECOGNITION BALLOTS) ORDER 2000, SI 2000 1443; made under the Trade Union and Labour Relations (Consolidation) Act 1992 s.204. In force: June 6, 2000; £1.00.

This Order brings into force the Code of Practice on Access to Workers during Recognition and Derecognition Ballots, which is issued by the Secretary of State under the Trade Union and Labour Relations (Consolidation) Act 1992 s.204(2).

2106. Construction industry – Construction Industry Training Board – levy on employers

INDUSTRIAL TRAINING LEVY (CONSTRUCTION BOARD) ORDER 2000, SI 2000 434; made under the Industrial Training Act 1982 s.11, s.12. In force: February 23, 2000; £2.00.

This Order imposes a levy on employers in the construction industry for the purpose of raising money towards meeting the expenses of the Construction Industry Training Board. The levy is to be limited to 0.5 per cent of payroll in respect of employees employed under contracts of service or apprenticeship and 2.28 per cent of payments made by the employers to persons under labour-only agreements.

2107. Construction industry – Engineering Construction Board – levy on employers

INDUSTRIAL TRAINING LEVY (ENGINEERING CONSTRUCTION BOARD) ORDER 2000, SI 2000 433; made under the Industrial Training Act 1982 s.11, s.12. In force: February 23, 2000; £2.00.

This Order imposes a levy on employers in the engineering construction industry for the purpose of raising money towards meeting the expenses of the Engineering Construction Industry Training Board.

2108. Constructive dismissal – implied terms – reasonableness of reference

H, a savings and investment advisor with TSB, was given a final written warning, following an incident in which she forged a client's initials on a corrected form entry. Various unconnected complaints were made against her by customers which, as part of standard practice, were investigated without her knowledge. When H applied for another job she informed her prospective employers about the forgery, but TSB supplied a reference in which they stated that 17 complaints had been made against her, four of which had been made out and eight of which were still to be investigated. H was not offered the job. She resigned and claimed constructive dismissal. The employment tribunal found that the reference breached the implied term in H's employment contract of trust and confidence in that it did not give the full picture and was likely to be injurious to H's career, and that H had been constructively dismissed and the dismissal was unfair. TSB appealed.

Held, dismissing the appeal, that the tribunal was entitled to reach the conclusions that it had. The fact that H had had no opportunity to refute the complaints was capable of being a fundamental breach of the implied term of trust and confidence, *Spring v. Guardian Assurance Plc* [1995] 2 A.C. 296, [1994] C.L.Y. 1918 applied. TSB were under a duty to provide a reference that was fair and reasonable. The fact that the procedure for investigating complaints was the standard one in the industry did not justify the misleading nature of the reference. Bald accuracy was not necessarily enough to make a reference reasonable. TSB could have ensured that H was not taken by surprise by the allegations being revealed for the first time in the arena of her application for another job. The tribunal were right to find that H had been constructively dismissed as the fact that she had intended to leave in any event did not alter the fact that when she actually left she had no other job to go to.

TSB BANK PLC v. HARRIS [2000] I.R.L.R. 157, Judge John Altman, EAT.

2109. **Constructive dismissal – mobility clauses – jurisdiction where dismissal abroad**

[Civil Jurisdiction and Judgments Act 1982 s.42(3).]

T was employed as a solicitor by HL, a company incorporated in Ireland but with offices in London. The terms and conditions in his contract of employment provided that he would be based in London but might be transferred elsewhere as required. T agreed with HL to move from London to Spain from where T intended to continue working in the same capacity and handle the same workload as when based in London. Subsequent to his move, HL forwarded to T in Spain all his work which was still being sent to their London office. T maintained the London office address on his Solicitors Practising Certificate and continued to indicate it as the address at which service would be accepted by him on HL's behalf. Salary payments to T continued on the same basis and were subject to English taxation. T retained a home in London. During the total period of T's employment only 35 days were spent in Spain. T brought an action against HL for unfair dismissal on grounds that he had been constructively dismissed. As a preliminary issue, the tribunal held that it did have jurisdiction to hear the case. HL appealed, contending that (1) the tribunal had made no finding as to T's base, that the decision had been perverse and unsupported by evidence and that the tribunal had been in error by drawing inferences from the evidence available that T would be returning to work in London; (2) under the Civil Jurisdiction and Judgments Act 1982 s.42(3) the tribunal did not have jurisdiction to deal with the contractual and unfair dismissal claims because HL was incorporated in Ireland; (3) on the basis of *Rutten v. Cross Medical Ltd (C383/95)* [1997] All E.R. (EC) 121, [1997] C.L.Y. 2199 T was working in Spain at the time of his dismissal and therefore the tribunal had no jurisdiction, and (4) the tribunal chairman at the hearing of the preliminary issue had exhibited clear bias by way of comments made to both counsel that were disparaging toward HL and had erred by refusing a request for postponement and transfer to another region.

Held, dismissing the appeal, that (1) the tribunal had not erred in law by drawing inferences from the evidence available that T was likely to return at a future date to work in London. T had acted consistently with that intention. He retained a property in London and had taken only a six month tenancy in Spain. During his eight years of employment with HL, only a total of 35 days had been spent in Spain; (2) although HL's "registered office" was in Ireland, its sole business was carried out in the UK. On that basis HL had its central management and control in the UK and fell within s.42(3) of the 1982 Act; (3) it would be unjust to exclude jurisdiction where a mobility clause existed in a contract of employment on the basis that an employee was dismissed while abroad, *Rutten* considered, and (4) the tribunal chairman had been unnecessarily aggressive toward HL but this did not indicate the presence of bias. There was no evidence that the chairman had had his mind irrevocably set against HL, *R. v. HM Coroner for Inner London West District, ex p. Dallaglio* [1994] 4 All E.R. 139, [1995] C.L.Y. 872 and *R. v. Gough (Robert)* [1993] A.C. 646, [1993] C.L.Y. 849 considered.

HARADA LTD (T/A CHEQUEPOINT UK LTD) v. TURNER [2000] I.L.Pr. 574, Lindsay, J., EAT.

2110. **Constructive dismissal – vicarious liability – acts of elected councillors – breach of terms of trust and confidence**

M, an employee of BS, was subject to abusive comments and allegations of dishonesty during the course of his work by P, a councillor. Although P was censured by a full meeting of the council, M resigned claiming constructive dismissal for which he contended BS was vicariously liable. The employment tribunal refused to hold that there had been a breach of M's contract of employment on the basis that P had no authority over M in the course of her duties. M appealed, arguing that BS was vicariously liable for P's acts, which amounted to a breach of the implied term of trust and confidence.

Held, allowing the appeal (Lindsay, J dissenting), that the tribunal had erred in basing its decision on the issue of P's lack of express authority. Elected members could still undermine the relationship of trust and confidence, even though they lacked express authority to engage or dismiss the employee concerned, *Hilton International Hotels (UK) Ltd v. Protopapa* [1990] I.R.L.R. 316, [1991] C.L.Y. 1614 applied. Councillors did not act on their own behalf so that BS was vicariously liable for P's acts where these were capable of undermining the employment relationship between BS and M.

MOORES v. BUDE-STRATTON TOWN COUNCIL [2001] I.C.R. 271, Lindsay, J., EAT.

2111. Continuity of employment – fixed term contracts – existence of arrangement preserving continuity

[Employment Rights Act 1996 s.213(3)(c).]

B, E and G were employed by the US Army as maintenance workers on a series of fixed term contracts until the final termination of their employment in 1996. At the employer's insistence, all of the fixed term contracts were for a period of less than two years, and between every contract there was a break of at least two weeks before employment commenced again on another contract. At the end of each contract, B, E and G were paid any outstanding holiday pay or other benefits and had to complete new documentation before they commenced employment on the new contract. During the breaks in employment, E and G registered as unemployed and claimed unemployment benefit. Following the termination of their contracts in 1996 and confirmation that no further employment would be offered, B, E and G commenced proceedings in employment tribunals claiming a redundancy payment and, in the case of E, unfair dismissal. The employer contended that the tribunal did not have jurisdiction to hear the claims, since neither B, E nor G had the necessary qualifying period of two years' continuous employment. B, E and G argued that their continuity of employment had not been affected by the breaks because the breaks were by "custom or arrangement" pursuant to the Employment Rights Act 1996 s.213(3)(c). The tribunal upheld the employer's arguments and B, E and G appealed.

Held, dismissing the appeal, that "by arrangement" under s.213(3)(c) required some action or statement by the employer that indicating that the parties viewed the employment relationship as continuing, notwithstanding the break between fixed term contracts, *Letheby & Christopher Ltd v. Bond* [1988] I.C.R. 480, [1988] C.L.Y. 1339 followed. In this sense, an "arrangement" demanded that there had been some agreement, not necessarily amounting to a contract, prior to the break in employment. A "custom" for the purposes of s.213(3)(c) meant an industrial "custom and practice" rather than the custom of an individual trade. It followed that a break in employment would not break continuity if either an arrangement was made that the employment should be regarded as continuing or by an established custom and practice employment was treated as continuing through such breaks. In the instant case, the tribunal had been justified in finding that there was no arrangement or custom to the effect that, despite the breaks between the various fixed term contracts the employment of B, E and G would be regarded as continuing. The most that could be said was that there was a "settled expectation" that the employees would return to their old jobs after the break. It was very clear that the employer neither regarded the employment relationships as continuing nor wanted them to do so, and there was insufficient evidence to satisfy the statutory test that the employment of B, E and G was to be regarded as continuing despite the breaks. While it was generally desirable that employees should benefit from the statutory employment protection rights, if an employer was lawfully able to arrange its employment practices so that its employees were denied such rights then that was a matter for the employer, and it was for Parliament to close any perceived loopholes in the legislation.

BOOTH v. UNITED STATES [1999] I.R.L.R. 16, Morison, J., EAT.

2112. **Contract of employment – employment status – rent officers**

[Rent Act 1977; Employment Rights Act 1996.]

J was promoted from the post of administrative officer to the position of rent officer with the local authority. She signed a contract of employment that was in similar terms to her previous one, and was paid by RBKC's personnel department. J subsequently made an application claiming unfair and constructive dismissal, and the preliminary issue of whether she was an employee arose. An employment tribunal found that she was an office holder under the Rent Act 1977 and was not an employee. J appealed.

Held, allowing the appeal and remitting the case to the employment tribunal, that the tribunal had erred in not considering the fact that a person could be both an office holder and an employee. There was no case law on the treatment of rent officers for the purposes of unfair dismissal. Therefore, since the Employment Rights Act 1996 was aimed at safeguarding employees' rights determination of the issue should be weighted in J's favour. A finding that her promotion had deprived her of the employment rights she had previously enjoyed would be unfair and contrary to the aim of the Act. She was therefore an employee of the authority which had the power to dismiss her and were responsible for paying her.

JOHNSON v. RYAN [2000] I.C.R. 236, Morison, J., EAT.

2113. **Contract of employment – fiduciary duty – undertaking private work – employee obligations**

F was employed full time by NU as a scientific director of its infertility clinic. NU claimed that F was in breach of his contract of employment by undertaking paid work at private clinics without NU's authorisation and also in breach of his fiduciary duty by receiving remuneration for organising the supply of other trained embryologists employed by NU to those clinics. F contended that no loss had occurred to NU from his breach of contract in failing to obtain NU's prior consent and, therefore, the court could not award damages to NU.

Held, allowing the claim in part, that an employment relationship was not normally considered fiduciary and therefore, an employee's fiduciary duty not to pursue his own interests only arose where the employee was under a specific contractual duty to act only in the interests of his employer. F was not obliged to inform NU that he was undertaking external work. F had, however, breached a specific fiduciary duty by receiving payment for directing his trainees to work outside the university for his own interests and NU was entitled to an account of F's profits therefrom.

UNIVERSITY OF NOTTINGHAM v. FISHEL [2000] I.C.R. 1462, Elias, J., QBD.

2114. **Contract of employment – garden leave clause – enforceability during notice period**

J was employed as an international sales executive by S, a company engaged in the development and exploitation of internet software. His contract of employment included terms designed to protect S's interests in the event of its termination, including a clause imposing garden leave during a six-month termination period. In March 2000 J accepted a job in a different capacity with M, another software company, commencing on April 1, 2000. S obtained an injunction at first instance, restraining J from working for, or advising, M during the term of the garden leave period. J applied for permission to appeal against that decision.

Held, dismissing the application, that (1) the garden leave clause remained in force during the life of the employment contract, including the notice period; (2) the clause could only be limited if notice to do so had been given that applied to the notice period. However, this would also have required detailed provisions to cater for such modification, including S's liability to pay C's salary during that time; (3) there was no basis for making such far reaching changes where they were unnecessary for either commercial efficacy reasons or to satisfy the officious bystander test; (4) the restraint of trade doctrine invalidated contractual terms from the date the restraint was imposed, unless the term was justified on reasonableness grounds in terms of its effect on the parties and the wider public interest. On that basis the validity of the garden leave clause had to be tested as at the date of the employment contract and could include restraints imposed during the life of the contract, *Esso Petroleum Co Ltd v. Harper's Garage (Stourport) Ltd* [1968] A.C. 269, [1967] C.L.Y. 3906 and *A Schroeder Music Publishing Co Ltd v. Instone (formerly Macaulay)* [1974] 1 W.L.R. 1308, [1978] C.L.Y. 1270 applied; (5) applying that principle to the instant case, the garden leave clause remained valid and was justified, and (6) the court below had taken C's undertakings into account, but concluded that an injunction was justified. That was a matter for the judge and it was immaterial that an appellate court could have reached a different conclusion.

SYMBIAN LTD v. CHRISTENSEN [2000] U.K.C.L.R. 879, Morritt, L.J., CA.

2115. Contract of employment – penalty clauses – failure to work notice period

S's application for unfair constructive dismissal against his former employers, G, was dismissed. The tribunal also found that a clause in S's contract which required S to pay a sum to G if he failed to give and work the four weeks' notice as required by the contract was illegal as it constituted a penalty rather than a lawful liquidated damages clause. G appealed.

Held, dismissing the appeal, that the clause was unenforceable. As G would have had little difficulty in replacing S, the clause created a no win situation for S which went far beyond compensating G for any possible loss, and therefore constituted a penalty and not a "genuine pre estimate of loss", *Dunlop Pneumatic Tyre Co Ltd v. New Garage & Motor Co Ltd* [1915] A.C. 79 applied.

GIRAUD UK LTD v. SMITH [2000] I.R.L.R. 763, Maurice Kay, J., EAT.

2116. Contract of employment – restrictive covenant – extent of information protected – confidentiality clauses

In the course of his employment with S, an insurance broker, M signed a service agreement containing clauses preventing the disclosure of confidential information and restrictive covenants relating to competitive activities and non solicitation of staff for 12 months post termination. In October 1998, M was offered a job with another broker, A, on the basis that he would bring in new business. M accepted the offer but did not submit his notice until December 11, 1998. M's letter stated that he wanted to terminate his employment with immediate effect. M's notice period was six months. Following discussion, S wrote to M, reserving the right to send M on garden leave. M subsequently agreed to terms permitting him to leave S on agreeing to be bound by the restrictive covenants and confidentiality clause. S claimed that M wanted to take legal advice and it was agreed that he would not come into the office for a few days. M however claimed that he was sent on garden leave and that by doing so S was in breach of contract and could no longer rely on the covenants contained in the contract. M commenced work with A in January 1999 and S commenced proceedings against M and obtained an interim injunction. In an affidavit M disclosed that he had approached 27 of S's clients and that 8 had appointed A as their brokers in place of S. S sought continuation of the injunction.

Held, allowing the application and awarding damages to S, that the confidentiality clause was not invalid because it potentially included information M carried in his head. The distinction between deliberately learning information and information innocently carried was not definitive of what could be legitimately protected. Information protected by the clause included that used in S's business, dissemination of which S limited and which, if disclosed to a competitor, could cause S real or significant harm; the class was wider than trade secrets but narrower than confidential information, *Lansing Linde Ltd v.*

Kerr [1991] 1 W.L.R. 251, [1991] C.L.Y. 446 and *FSS Travel & Leisure Systems Ltd v. Johnson* [1998] I.R.L.R. 382, [1998] C.L.Y. 2193 followed. On a plain reading of the clause, a person of ordinary honesty would understand it as referring to the property of an old employer. The confidentiality clause included client names, policy coverage and renewals, and fee and premium information. The non solicitation clause was also valid, as S's staff were a prime asset which S had a legitimate interest in protecting. On the facts, S had not repudiated M's contract or sent him on garden leave. Damages were assessed at £44, 424 for net loss of clients and £45, 000 for future losses after 1999, on a loss of chance basis, being an approximation to one third net lost commission for a multiplier of three years.

SBJ STEPHENSON LTD v. MANDY [2000] I.R.L.R. 233, Bell, J., QBD.

2117. Contract of employment – unfair contract terms – dismissal without recourse to disciplinary procedure

[Unfair Contract Terms Act 1977 s.3, s.12.]

B appealed against the dismissal of his claim for damages for breach of contract on the basis that a provision denying him the benefit of the disciplinary procedures was void as being unreasonable pursuant to the Unfair Contract Terms Act 1977 s.3. B commenced employment with AEB on July 6, 1998 and was summarily dismissed on September 24, 1998. The disciplinary procedure was not implemented, but B was given three months' salary in lieu of notice. A provision in the written contract of employment provided that an employee of less than two years' standing could be dismissed by notice and/or payment in lieu of notice without implementation of the disciplinary procedure.

Held, dismissing the appeal, that (1) in order to rely on s.3 of the Act it had to be shown that one of the parties to the contact dealt "as consumer" in relation to the other party within the meaning of s.12. Here the claimant dealt as a consumer in relation to the defendant because he neither made the contract in the course of a business nor held himself out as doing so, but the defendant did make the contract in the course of business, but (2) the disputed provision in the written contract of employment regarding dismissal was not void. It set out the claimant's entitlement and the limits of his rights. It was not a contract term excluding or restricting liability of the defendant in respect of breach of contract or entitling the defendant to render a contracted performance substantially different from that which was reasonably expected or to render no performance in respect of any part of its contractual obligation.

BRIGDEN v. AMERICAN EXPRESS BANK LTD [2000] I.R.L.R. 94, Morland, J., QBD.

2118. Contract of employment – wrongful dismissal – power to exclude contractual right to payment in lieu of notice

T&K employed S as a double glazing sales and marketing director. S's contract of employment gave T&K the option to terminate S's employment by paying him in lieu of notice, however S had no right to expect payment in lieu unless that option had been applied. The contract also included a clause that T&K could dismiss S without prior notice or payment in lieu in nine specific circumstances, including missing performance targets. S was dismissed "with immediate effect" and without payment, and the employment tribunal ruled that S had been wrongfully dismissed and was entitled to payment in lieu. T&K appealed to the Employment Appeal Tribunal, but the appeal was dismissed. T&K further appealed.

Held, dismissing the appeal, that a contractual provision empowering an employer to dismiss an employee immediately was, when read in the contract's entirety, insufficient cause to exclude an employees contractual right to payment in lieu of notice. Whilst meeting sales targets was an important part of S's duties, and T&K should have some redress if sales targets were not being met, it was unacceptable that the power to dismiss with immediate effect could automatically be construed as eliminating the contractual clause permitting payment in lieu of notice.

SKILTON v. T&K HOME IMPROVEMENTS LTD; *sub nom.* T&K HOME IMPROVEMENTS LTD v. SKILTON [2000] I.C.R. 1162, Pill, L.J., CA.

2119. Disability discrimination – contract workers – liability of employment agency as principal

[Disability Discrimination Act 1995 s.12.]

A company, ALA, appealed against a reversal of an employment tribunal's decision holding that ALA was to be regarded as the principal for the purposes of the Disability Discrimination Act 1995 s.12. T, a computer consultant, was employed by a company, I, of which he was the sole shareholder, and which contracted with MHC, an employment agency, for the supply of his services to ALA. MHC received fees from ALA and paid I and T himself received a salary from I. T was dismissed after being diagnosed as suffering from diabetes and brought an action for unfair dismissal and breach of contract based on disability discrimination.

Held, dismissing the appeal, that, although there was no direct contract between T or I and ALA, the latter had made the work available to T, and clearly fell within the definition of principal in s.12(6) as the party which made the work available to a contract worker. It was irrelevant that the employment contract had been made between ALA and MHC and not with I.

MHC CONSULTING SERVICES LTD v. TANSELL; *sub nom.* ABBEY LIFE ASSURANCE CO LTD v. TANSELL [2000] I.C.R. 789, Mummery, L.J., CA.

2120. Disability discrimination – deaf persons – vicarious liability for sexual harassment

[Sex Discrimination Act 1975 s.41 (3).]

C brought complaints against her former employers, EYC, of sex discrimination in relation to the acts of another employee who had sexually harassed her, and of disability discrimination in relation to its failure to provide facilities to prevent her being disadvantaged by her profound deafness. Both complaints were dismissed and C appealed, arguing that the tribunal (1) had erred in applying the principles of *King v. Great Britain China Centre* [1992] I.C.R. 516 to its decision on disability discrimination, and (2) had misdirected itself on the question of whether EYC could avail itself of the defence to vicarious liability for an employee's actions set out in the Sex Discrimination Act 1975 s.41 (3).

Held, allowing the appeal in part, that (1) *King* was relevant to race and sex discrimination cases but did not appear relevant to the instant case. However, basing its decision on *King* did not make the decision of the tribunal wrong as it had approached the issue of disability discrimination correctly overall, and (2) the tribunal had erred in its consideration of the statutory defence by asking itself whether any steps that could have been taken by EYC to prevent the harassment would have made any difference. The correct test was to look at what, if any, steps had been taken and whether there were any other reasonably practicable steps that should have been taken. Although the tribunal had identified that EYC had implemented a policy on personal harassment in the workplace, as there was a known perpetrator and victim it was necessary to investigate whether other, more direct steps could have been taken, and the tribunal was therefore wrong to hold that the defence was made out without more evidence. The matter was remitted to a fresh tribunal for a rehearing on that issue alone.

CANNIFFE v. EAST RIDING OF YORKSHIRE COUNCIL [2000] I.R.L.R. 555, Burton, J., EAT.

2121. Disability discrimination – drivers – diabetes – driving ban during review period – justification

[Health and Safety at Work etc. Act 1974; Disability Discrimination Act 1995 s.5, s.6, s.8(2).]

PO appealed against a finding of unlawful discrimination under the Disability Discrimination Act 1995 s.5 against J, a diabetic delivery driver who had developed insulin dependency. PO had reconsidered its policy of automatically deeming J unfit to drive following a complaint by J and had issued him with new terms of employment restricting his driving duties, which it argued were justified in the circumstances taking into account its responsibilities under the Health and Safety at Work etc. Act 1974. PO conceded that the total ban on driving had been discriminatory but contended that there had been no discrimination whilst a review of J's position was being undertaken or once the new terms had been issued.

Held, allowing the appeal in part, that (1) although discrimination could be justified while the employer assessed the situation, in the instant case the period of such assessment was inexplicably long and could not be justified. The tribunal's findings in relation to the review period would not therefore be disturbed; (2) in their determination upon the period after new terms had been offered to J, the tribunal had seriously misdirected itself in finding that s.6 of the 1995 Act did not apply, leading to a failure to enquire as to what steps PO had taken to minimise any discrimination and whether those steps had been reasonable. The tribunal's recommendation that J should be returned to his driving duties had been inadequate as an employer had to be allowed to reconsider what steps to take to comply with s.6 in the light of its other duties imposed by common law and the 1974 Act. A recommendation should have been made under s.8(2) of the 1995 Act that PO take appropriate action to reduce the adverse effect of its proposals.

JONES v. POST OFFICE; *sub nom.* POST OFFICE v. JONES (SC) [2000] I.C.R. 388, Holland, J., EAT.

2122. Disability discrimination – exemptions – small businesses – group of companies – parent company with seven employees

[Disability Discrimination Act 1995 s.7.]

G, the parent company of a multi national group of companies, had seven employees. When C was dismissed by CG she brought an application under the Disability Discrimination Act 1995 and the employment tribunal considered the preliminary issue of whether the claim was excluded under s.7 because CG was a company with less than 20 employees. The tribunal held that it was entitled to look behind the Act to the Parliamentary debate on the Bill as s.7 would lead to an absurd result if it allowed CG to be excluded. The tribunal held that Parliament had intended to prevent small businesses with little expertise from being hampered by the legislation, and that the s.7 exemption should therefore not apply to large groups of companies. CG appealed.

Held, allowing the appeal, that s.7 had to be given its natural meaning and the tribunal had approached the issue incorrectly. Section 7 was clear on its face. Its underlying purpose was to exclude certain employers from the ambit of the Act and the use of the total number of employees as a basis for doing so was not absurd. Parliament would have been aware of the issue of groups of companies when it chose that method. There was therefore no absurdity to justify the tribunal's approach, *Pepper (Inspector of Taxes) v. Hart* [1993] A.C. 593, [1993] C.L.Y. 459 distinguished. The coverage of the Act was a matter for Parliament and it could not be extended by the tribunal, *Hardie v. C D Northern Ltd* [2000] I.C.R. 207, [2000] C.L.Y. 2123 applied.

COLT GROUP LTD v. COUCHMAN [2000] I.C.R. 327, Charles, J., EAT.

2123. Disability discrimination – exemptions – small businesses – lifting of corporate veil

[Disability Discrimination Act 1995 s.7.]

H's claim of disability discrimination made against CDN was dismissed by an employment tribunal as, at the time of the dismissal, CDN had only 19 employees and was so exempted under the Disability Discrimination Act 1995 s.7. On appeal it was submitted that the term "employer" in that Act should be interpreted as including "associated employers" since they were included in other statutes dealing with discrimination. It was further suggested that it had been a legislative oversight not to include "associated employers" in the definition of "employer" in the 1995 Act. Alternatively, it was argued that the corporate veil should be lifted thereby revealing a single economic unit of more than 20 employees.

Held, dismissing the appeal, that (1) there is nothing in the 1995 Act which extends the meaning of "employer" to other bodies; (2) there is no available presumption requiring that Parliamentary provisions chosen in relation to sex and race discrimination should necessarily be the ones chosen for disability discrimination; (3) it is not for the courts to legislate where Parliament has not done so, and (4) there was no economic unit other than CDN which was the employer and there was no reason to look behind that corporation.

HARDIE v. CD NORTHERN LTD [2000] I.C.R. 207, Lindsay, J., EAT.

2124. Disability discrimination – expert evidence – consent to medical examination – agreement to disclose

[Disability Discrimination Act 1995 s.1.]

LLBC appealed against an employment appeal tribunal's finding ([2000] I.R.L.R. 14) that K, who was bringing an action for disability discrimination, was disabled within the meaning of the Disability Discrimination Act 1995 s.1. K had given evidence on his own behalf and called on two expert witnesses, his GP and a consultant psychologist, who both stated that K was suffering from a mental impairment, reactive depression, which substantially adversely affected his day to day activities. K had also undergone a medical examination by LLBC's medical expert but refused the disclosure of the subsequent medical report. K was receiving treatment for the condition at the time of the hearing as a result of which his symptoms were controlled. LLBC contended that K had failed to discharge the burden of proof to show that his mental impairment adversely affected his daily activities, despite the medical evidence from the expert witnesses stating that it did.

Held, dismissing the appeal, that at the relevant time K was disabled, a conclusion supported by the direct evidence of two medical experts. There was no contrary evidence put before the tribunal and no challenge to the factual basis underlying those opinions. The tribunal had clearly erred in not reaching the conclusion that K had proved his case and in failing to make a finding of fact, the EAT was correct in its decision not to remit the case for a rehearing by the tribunal. It was observed that a person having consented to a medical examination, K could not then decline its disclosure. Such conduct impeded the fair and expeditious conduct of a claim. It followed that good practice required the disclosure of the report.

KAPADIA v. LAMBETH LBC [2000] I.R.L.R. 699, Schiemann, L.J., CA.

2125. Disability discrimination – expert evidence – extent of impairment

[Disability Discrimination Act 1995 s.1 (1), Sch.I.]

V, who was employed by BT as a clerical officer, had an upper arm complaint and complained that she had been discriminated against on the grounds of disability. BT resisted her complaint, arguing that she was not disabled within the meaning of the Disability Discrimination Act 1995 s.1 (1). The tribunal heard evidence from V and M, BT's medical officer, and found that V could not undertake a range of tasks, including preparing vegetables, cutting meat, carrying pans of water, opening jars or tins or holding up a book to read. Despite these findings, the tribunal accepted BT's argument that V was not disabled because her impairment did not substantially affect her ability to carry out normal day to day activities. The tribunal held that loss of strength was not the same as loss of function and that V's inability to cut up meat did not show that her impairment was substantial. Further, that V could modify her behaviour to prevent or reduce the effects of the impairment. The tribunal noted that, while V's inability to carry a pan of water was covered by the guidance issued by the Secretary of State for Education and Employment, carrying a chair did not fall within the concept of ordinary daily activities. The tribunal relied heavily on the medical evidence provided by M to the effect that V's impairment was not substantial and that Sch.I of the Act required an overall assessment of a person's ability to use their upper limbs, regardless of an inability to lift or move particular everyday objects. V appealed, arguing that the tribunal's decision was perverse, that it had given no proper consideration to the meaning of "substantial", that it had misdirected itself concerning the use of the guidance and in the way it had dealt with M's evidence.

Held, allowing the appeal, that (1) in determining whether V's impairment had a "substantial impact on her ability to carry out normal daily activities", the tribunal should have focused on what V could not do, as opposed to what that she could, *Goodwin v. Patent Office* [1999] I.C.R. 302, [1998] C.L.Y. 2114 applied. Having regard to the range of activities that V could not do, the tribunal's decision that she was not disabled was perverse; (2) the tribunal erred in not considering the proper interpretation of the word "substantial"; (3) the tribunal misunderstood the proper function of the guidance, which was to be used in marginal cases where it was not immediately clear whether or not someone had a disability and had used it instead in a literal and legalistic fashion to conclude that V's impairment was not substantial. Stating that V's inability to prepare vegetables and cut meat could not, on its own, make her impairment substantial demonstrated a misunderstanding of the tribunal's role. Such matters were clearly daily activities and V's inability to perform them obviously meant that she was disabled within the meaning of s.1 (1). Further, the tribunal's statement that ironing was not a daily activity as given in the guidance showed a misunderstanding of its illustrative function. It was obvious that the tasks concerned were normal day to day activities, and (4) the tribunal also erred by misdirecting itself as to the relevance of M's evidence. It was not for the expert medical witness to determine what were daily activities, or whether an impairment was "substantial", since those were matters for the tribunal to determine.

VICARY v. BRITISH TELECOMMUNICATIONS PLC [1999] I.R.L.R. 680, Morison, J., EAT.

2126. Disability discrimination – local authorities – adequacy of redeployment procedures

[Disability Discrimination Act 1995 s.5.]

M had been employed as an assistant cook for some years until going on sick leave after injuring his back. He returned to work as a classroom assistant and it was recommended that he be redeployed as a Category B redeployee under KCC's clearing house procedures. Those procedures were designed to match internal job vacancies within KCC with existing redeployees. Category A staff were those at risk, or under notice, of redundancy, while category B staff were those deployed on incapability/ill health. Category A staff were best placed to obtain redeployment. Subsequently a new category was introduced to cover staff with a disability but M was not recategorised. M applied for a new post, but was turned down on the grounds that it would involve heavy lifting. He applied for a further post but was informed it was reserved for category A staff. When his supernumerary post came to an end he was dismissed following an incapability hearing. He appealed to a tribunal relying on the Disability Discrimination Act 1995 s.5(1) and s.5(2). The tribunal found that category A staff were appropriate comparators under s.5(1). They were satisfied that M had received less favourable treatment by being categorised as a category B redeployee, and by being retained in that category when the revised procedures were introduced. The tribunal found that he had been unfairly dismissed on the basis of his incapability. KCC appealed.

Held, dismissing the appeal, that (1) the tribunal was entitled to consider that the redeployment procedures of KCC did not adequately reflect the statutory duty on employers under the Act. Preferential treatment had been given to redundant or potentially redundant employees, which meant that those with disabilities were relatively handicapped in the system of redeployment; (2) on the facts found, had M been treated as a category A employee he would have been redeployed and not dismissed; (3) the structure of the Act required employers to take reasonable steps to accommodate disabled staff and the tribunal had found, on the evidence, that KCC had failed to consider whether reasonable adjustments could be made to jobs for which M had applied, and (3) the tribunal was entitled to find that the dismissal was unreasonable and unfair.

KENT CC v. MINGO [2000] I.R.L.R. 90, Morison, J., EAT.

2127. Disability discrimination – recruitment – withdrawal of job offer – discovery of past mental health record – justification

[Disability Discrimination Act 1995 s.5(1).]

F was offered a job by HF after interview. HF's occupational health physician discovered that F had a history of mental illness and voiced concerns that a recurrence would affect her work attendance. The job offer was withdrawn on the grounds that satisfactory medical clearance had not been obtained and F complained that she had been discriminated against under the Disability Discrimination Act 1995 s.5. The employment tribunal found that F had a reference from her previous employment showing that she had not lost any time through ill health but that HF had not taken this into account. Further, that HF had assumed that F's attendance would be poor because of her mental health and that she had been discriminated against because of her disability. On appeal, HF argued that it had no actual knowledge of the disability.

Held, dismissing the appeal, that knowledge on the part of HF was not relevant for the purposes of assessing whether there was, as a fact, discrimination under s.5(1)(a), nor was it necessarily relevant for the purposes of assessing justification under s.5(1)(b), *Clark v. TDG Ltd (t/a Novacold Ltd)* [1999] 2 All E.R. 977, [1999] C.L.Y. 2022, *HJ Heinz Co Ltd v. Kenrick* [2000] I.C.R. 491 followed and *O'Neill v. Symm & Co Ltd* [1998] I.C.R. 481, [1998] C.L.Y. 2116 not followed.

HAMMERSMITH AND FULHAM LBC v. FARNSWORTH [2000] I.R.L.R. 691, Charles, J., EAT.

2128. Disability discrimination – time limits – outcome of internal appeal

R appealed against a decision of the employment tribunal that it did not have jurisdiction to hear his claim for disability discrimination against PO because the claim had been submitted out of time. R had been diagnosed as suffering from chronic discoid lupus erythematosus, and, following a considerable period of absence from work, he had been dismissed from his employment with PO by reason of incapability. R contended that (1) the tribunal had failed to consider the debilitating effects of his medical condition on his state of mind, and (2) he had been concentrating on an internal appeal which, if successful, could have resulted in him getting his job back which was a reasonable ground for delay in accordance with the ruling in *Aniagwu v. Hackney LBC* [1999] I.R.L.R. 303, [1999] C.L.Y. 2099.

Held, dismissing the appeal, that (1) as the tribunal had taken R's medical condition into account and the difficult circumstances which he had been facing at the relevant time, it had been fully justified in finding that R had been able to present his case and had been capable of understanding the advice of his trade union official on the time limit within which he had to present a claim to the tribunal, and (2) in the instant case, the tribunal had been aware of R's concentration on the internal appeal which it had addressed accordingly, *Aniagwu* distinguished. Further, in the absence of a legislative provision that time should only begin to run from the conclusion of domestic procedures, the time limit for submitting a claim to the employment tribunal had to be strictly upheld.

ROBINSON v. POST OFFICE [2000] I.R.L.R. 804, Lindsay, J. (President), EAT.

2129. Disability discrimination – unfair dismissal – knowledge of disability at time of dismissal

[Disability Discrimination Act 1995 s.5(3), Sch.1; Employment Rights Act 1996 s.98(4).]

K, who was employed by H as a process worker, became ill and was off work. Despite consultation with a number of doctors, K's illness was not satisfactorily diagnosed. When the expiry of K's nine month contractual sick pay entitlement was approaching, H advised there was a risk of dismissal if K was unable to indicate a probable date for his return to work. K suspected he was suffering from chronic fatigue syndrome, CFS, and requested H to take no further action until after his pending appointment with an appropriate specialist. In the meantime, H's medical advisor noted K's continuing unfitness to work and K was dismissed. A diagnosis of CFS was subsequently made. K brought proceedings against H for unfair dismissal and disability discrimination. It was conceded by H that K had been suffering from CFS at the time of his dismissal and that the condition was a disability recognised under the Disability Discrimination Act 1995 Sch.1. The tribunal upheld the claim for disability discrimination, and concluded that K had also been unfairly dismissed. H appealed, contending that (1) the tribunal had erred in its finding that disability discrimination automatically resulted in unfair dismissal, and (2) H had no knowledge at the time of K's dismissal that he was suffering from CFS and had been justified in its consequent action.

Held, allowing the appeal in part and setting aside the decision as to unfair dismissal, that (1) the tribunal had erred in concluding that K's dismissal on the ground of his disability led automatically to a finding that he had been unfairly dismissed. It had failed to give separate consideration to the fairness of K's dismissal as required by the Employment Rights Act 1996 s. 98(4), hence the matter should be remitted for fresh consideration; (2) H had been aware of the nature of K's symptoms and the fact that they fell within Sch.1 of the 1995 Act, which was sufficient and possibly more than was necessary to justify a finding of discrimination, *O'Neill v. Symm & Co Ltd* [1998] I.C.R. 481, [1998] C.L.Y. 2116 considered, and (3) justification for the treatment of an employee under s.5(3) of the 1995 Act required analysis of the relevant circumstances of both parties, *Baynton v. Saurus General Engineers Ltd* [1999] I.R.L.R. 604, [1999] C.L.Y. 2024 applied. In the instant case, the tribunal's finding that H had not acted reasonably in failing to adequately consider whether K was suitable for part-time work, lighter duties or alternative employment could not be disturbed.

HJ HEINZ CO LTD v. KENRICK [2000] I.C.R. 491, Lindsay, J., EAT.

2130. Discrimination – causes of action – death of complainant – survival of claim

[Law Reform (Miscellaneous Provisions) Act 1934 s.1(1); Race Relations Act 1976 s.53(1), s.54(1).]

A brought a complaint of racial discrimination against her employer, LG, but died prior to the hearing before the employment tribunal. The tribunal found that A's complaint survived her death, but LG's appeal was successful, the Employment Appeal Tribunal holding ([1999] I.C.R. 774, [1999] C.L.R. 2053) that a claim under the Discrimination Acts was not a cause of action, but a non assignable personal right, and that there was no express provision in the Acts, or in other legislation, which provided for the substitution of a deceased party. H, A's personal representative, appealed arguing that A's complaint survived her death by virtue of the Law Reform (Miscellaneous Provisions) Act 1934 s.1 (1). LG argued that (1) the Race Relations Act 1976 s.54(1) indicated that a complaint could only be made by an individual complainant and not by somebody on his behalf, and (2) s.53(1) of the 1976 Act had the effect of excluding the operation of the Act of 1934.

Held, allowing the appeal, that (1) a claim under the Discrimination Acts was a cause of action and satisfied the definitions of that term in *Read v. Brown* (1888) L.R. 22 Q.B.D. 128 and *Letang v. Cooper* [1965] 1 Q.B. 232, [1964] C.L.Y. 3499. The Employment Appeal Tribunal had erred in looking to the Discrimination Acts for an express provision regarding the substitution of a deceased complainant and ought instead to have focused on whether there were any provisions which expressly excluded the rights conferred by the 1934 Act; (2) whilst s.54(1) of the 1976 Act did not confer rights on a personal representative, it did not take away the rights that were provided by the Act of 1934, and (3) the purpose of s.53(1) was to ensure that proceedings were brought in the appropriate forum. Claims for wrongful and unfair dismissal survived the death of the complainant and Parliament could not have intended the position to be any different regarding claims for discrimination.

ANDREWS (DECEASED) v. LEWISHAM AND GUYS MENTAL HEALTH NHS TRUST; *sub nom.* HARRIS (PERSONAL REPRESENTATIVES OF ANDREWS (DECEASED)) v. LEWISHAM AND GUYS MENTAL HEALTH NHS TRUST; LEWISHAM AND GUYS MENTAL HEALTH NHS TRUST v. ANDREWS (DECEASED) [2000] 3 All E.R. 769, Stuart-Smith, L.J., CA.

2131. Dismissal – summary dismissal – continuity of employment – damages to reflect lost opportunity to claim unfair dismissal

R, employed by UNSL as a post office counter assistant, was summarily dismissed for gross misconduct three weeks before she had completed two years' service. Following concerns raised about the disappearance of considerable amounts of cash from the shop in which R worked, UNSL installed closed circuit security cameras to monitor her actions. As a result of the video footage thus obtained, UNSL reported R to the police and a criminal investigation commenced. After her dismissal and the subsequent appeal against dismissal the matter was dropped by the police and no charges were ever brought. R was interviewed by two managers at a disciplinary hearing at which no details of the allegations made against her were provided. She was suspended and then dismissed with no further disciplinary hearing. An internal appeal also proved unsuccessful and R's dismissal was confirmed. She presented a complaint of wrongful dismissal to an employment tribunal. The tribunal found the dismissal wrongful and in breach of UNSL's contractual disciplinary procedure. R was awarded one week's pay as damages in lieu of notice and a sum representing her loss of wages for breach of contract in respect of the period that she would have remained in employment had the disciplinary procedure been properly followed. R also asked the tribunal to make an award of damages to reflect her loss of opportunity to bring a claim for unfair dismissal, on the basis that, if the disciplinary procedure had been properly operated, she would have obtained the necessary qualifying period of two years' service to bring such a claim. The tribunal rejected that submission and R appealed.

Held, allowing the appeal and remitting the matter to an employment tribunal, that the fundamental principle concerning the measure of damages for breach of contract was that the party who had suffered a loss as a result of the breach should, so far as possible, be placed in the same position with regard to damages as if the contract had been performed, *Robinson v. Harman* [1843-60] All E.R. Rep. 383 applied. In the instant case, that principle required a comparison between what actually happened and what would have happened had the breach of contract not occurred, namely that R would have been dismissed at a time when an unfair dismissal claim could have been brought, or alternatively that she might not have been dismissed at all. If she had been dismissed then the dismissal might have been fair or unfair, with differing financial consequences for R. While the investigation of those various possibilities and the assessment of both the chances of each one occurring, together with the resultant financial loss, was complicated, the exercise was one with which tribunals were familiar, *HW Smith (Cabinets) Ltd v. Brindle* [1972] 1

W.L.R. 1653, [1973] C.L.Y. 1032, *Robert Cort & Son Ltd v. Charman* [1981] I.C.R. 816, [1982] C.L.Y. 1099 and *Stapp v. Shaftesbury Society* [1982] I.R.L.R. 326, [1982] C.L.Y. 1101 considered. In particular, the tribunal erred in holding that *Focsa Services (UK) Ltd v. Birkett* [1996] I.R.L.R. 325, [1996] C.L.Y. 2522 was binding on them and prevented them from including as a head of damages for breach of contract R's loss of opportunity to bring a claim for unfair dismissal. The decision in *Focsa* was distinguishable because in that case there was no question of the applicant, who was dismissed four months into a six month probationary period, approaching the limits of the necessary period of qualifying service in order to bring a claim of unfair dismissal.

RASPIN v. UNITED NEWS SHOPS LTD [1999] I.R.L.R. 9, Judge Hicks Q.C., EAT.

2132. Dismissal – summary dismissal – failure to disclose secret profits – breach of fiduciary duty and confidence

N was appointed as organist and choir master of Westminster Abbey in January 1988 and his wife, A, was appointed as his part time secretary and concert secretary. Overall government of the Abbey was vested in the Dean and Canons, while responsibility for administration lay with the assistant Receivers General, F and G. The choristers included lay vicars who received a salary from the Abbey, subject to PAYE under Sch.E. In addition to his salary, N received fees for special events that took place in the Abbey. The lay vicars received fees charged to tax under Sch.D for these events and for other events such as broadcasts and outside concerts. After December 1991 the special events were arranged by N and A alone. The financial arrangements and the payment of fees to the lay vicars were carried out by the Abbey Finance Department. In April 1994, the Inland Revenue informed the Abbey that any fees paid to Abbey employees above their salaries were to be taxed at source under Sch.E. N claimed that F then advised him that the lay vicars could preserve Sch.D tax status in relation to their fees for special events if they were paid through a separate account, and that such an arrangement would be sanctioned by the Abbey's internal auditors. F insisted that while the issue was discussed he did not sanction any specific arrangement or suggest that a separate account would be approved by the internal auditor. A separate account was opened in 1994 in the name of "Neary Music" to receive fixing fees paid by external promoters and to make payments to the lay vicars and a company, NML, was incorporated in 1997 with A as sole shareholder and director. From April 1994 until March 1998, A received fixing fees of £11,900 and a dividend of £1,500 in lieu of fees. The fees were not disclosed to the Abbey until March 1998, whereupon N and A were summarily dismissed for gross misconduct. The Abbey relied on a number of grounds in support of the dismissals, including the unauthorised taking of fixing fees by A on the Abbey choir, and the failure by N and A in their duty of openness to the Abbey. N petitioned the Queen as Visitor to the Abbey to resolve the dispute.

Held, dismissing the petition, that (1) it was well established that the fiduciary relationship between employer and employee required that the employee would not make a profit out of his position of trust and would not act for his own benefit without the informed consent of his employer, *Hivac Ltd v. Park Royal Scientific Instruments Ltd* [1946] Ch. 169, *Reading v. Attorney General* [1951] A.C. 507, [1947-51] C.L.Y. 3579 and *Attorney General v. Blake* [1998] Ch. 439, [1996] C.L.Y. 1121 applied. The extent and degree of the duty would vary according to the facts of each case. In the instant case, the Abbey was a religious collegiate institution and as such its senior members were entitled to expect a degree of openness and integrity that differed from a commercial organisation, and (2) the main issue was whether N and A's conduct amounted to a sufficiently serious breach of fiduciary duty to justify summary dismissal. There was no rule of law that gross misconduct justifying summary dismissal must always have an element of dishonesty, *Keppel v. Wheeler* [1927] 1 K.B. 577 and *Kelly v. Cooper* [1993] A.C. 205, [1993] C.L.Y. 72 distinguished, *Regal (Hastings) Ltd v. Gulliver* [1967] 2 A.C. 134 (Note) and *Sinclair v. Neighbour* [1967] 2 Q.B. 279, [1967] C.L.Y. 1429 applied. Summary dismissal would be justified if the employee had behaved in a manner so inconsistent with the employment as to undermine the fundamental duty of trust and confidence, *Lewis v. Motorworld Garages* [1986] I.C.R. 157, [1986] C.L.Y. 1261 applied. By running a business, whose main source of income were the Abbey choristers, for three and a half years, and by deriving secret profits in the form of fixing fees and surpluses on special events, N and A were clearly in breach of their duty of fidelity owed to the Abbey. N and A had had every opportunity and reason to inform the Abbey of what they were doing and yet they had continued to make secret profits from the music fixing business. Such conduct fatally undermined the trust and confidence in the employment relationship and justified their summary dismissal.

NEARY v. DEAN OF WESTMINSTER [1999] I.R.L.R. 288, Lord Jauncey of Tullichettle, Visitor (Westminster).

2133.   Employees rights – insolvency – Irish company with UK branches – protection under EC law – European Union

[Employment Rights Act 1996 Pt XII; Council Directive 80/987 relating to the protection of employees in the event of insolvency of their employer Art.3.]

The Irish High Court ordered the winding up of a company, BL, incorporated in Ireland, with branches throughout the UK in one of which E was employed. E applied for arrears of pay, holiday pay and compensation to the Secretary of State as the relevant guarantee institution as required by Council Directive 80/987 Art. 3(1) and the Employment Rights Act 1996 Pt.XII. The Secretary of State refused the application on the basis that he had no responsibility, citing *Danmarks Aktive Handelsrejsende v. Lonmodtagernes Garantifond (C117/96)* [1998] 1 All. E.R. (E.C.) 112, [1997] C.L.Y. 2232. E contended that the instant case could be distinguished from *Danmarks* because BL had UK branches and E was paid through these branches, and the collection of taxes and social security contributions were made under English law. The employment tribunal referred to the ECJ the question of which guarantee institution was responsible for settling the claims, the state where the insolvency proceedings had been commenced or the state in which E had been employed.

Held, giving a preliminary ruling, that the protection given by the Directive to employees in the event of their employer being declared insolvent was available in the country in which the employees worked. That was the most appropriate interpretation of the Directive in the light of its social objectives. BL had a significant presence in the UK, employing over two hundred people, and collected tax and national insurance contributions in accordance with English law, *Danmarks* distinguished.

EVERSON v. SECRETARY OF STATE FOR TRADE AND INDUSTRY (C198/98) [2000] All E.R. (EC) 29, L Sevon (President), ECJ.

2134.   Employees rights – time off work for public duties

TIME OFF FOR PUBLIC DUTIES ORDER 2000, SI 2000 1737; made under the Employment Rights Act 1996 s.50. In force: August 14, 2000; £1.00.

The Employment Rights Act 1996 s.50(2) provides for an employee who is a member of a public body to be permitted to take time off during working hours in order to attend meetings or for other purposes connected with the functions of the body. The right to time off is available only in relation to bodies specified in s.50(2), but the Secretary of State has power to modify it by adding or removing particular bodies. This Order adds Scottish water and sewerage authorities and Water Industry Consultative Committees to the list of bodies specified.

2135.   Employees rights – time off work for public duties

TIME OFF FOR PUBLIC DUTIES (NO.2) ORDER 2000, SI 2000 2463; made under the Employment Rights Act 1996 s.50. In force: October 5, 2000; £1.50.

The Employment Rights Act 1996 s.50 requires an employer to allow time off during working hours to an employee of his who is a justice of the peace or who is a member of a body set out in s.50(2) including a "relevant education body". This

Order amends s.50(9) by adding the General Teaching Council for England and the General Teaching Council for Wales to the list of relevant education bodies whose members are covered by s.50.

2136. Employment Appeal Tribunal – appeals – elaboration of reasons requested

R had been summarily dismissed on the grounds of misconduct. His application to an employment tribunal complaining of unfair dismissal and racial discrimination was dismissed. He appealed to the EAT, arguing that the tribunal had not taken into consideration all 10 comparators that he had raised in evidence. The EAT adjourned the appeal hearing and ordered that the tribunal should give a further elaboration of its reasons, under the procedure established in *Yusuf v. Aberplace* [1984] I.C.R. 850, [1985] C.L.Y. 1271.

Held, allowing the appeal and remitting the case to a different tribunal, that the previous EAT had erred in allowing the tribunal to add to its determination, *Yusuf* not followed. Following the promulgation of its determination the tribunal's judicial function was complete and it could only be asked to comment, on procedural aspects alone, where allegations of bias had been made. Where the tribunal's reasons were, as in the instant case, clearly lacking in relation to an evidential point, the appropriate order was to remit the matter to a fresh tribunal.

REUBEN v. BRENT LBC [2000] I.C.R. 102, Morison, J., EAT.

2137. Employment Relations Act 1999 (c.26) – Commencement No.4 Order

EMPLOYMENT RELATIONS ACT 1999 (COMMENCEMENT NO.4 AND TRANSITIONAL PROVISION) ORDER 2000, SI 2000 420 (C.11); made under the Employment Relations Act 1999 s.45. Commencement details: bringing into force various provisions of the Act on February 22, 2000; £1.00.

This Order brings into force the Employment Relations Act 1999 s.24, which relates to the appointment of the members of the Central Arbitration Committee and contains a transitional provision relating to existing members of the Committee.

2138. Employment Relations Act 1999 (c.26) – Commencement No.5 Order

EMPLOYMENT RELATIONS ACT 1999 (COMMENCEMENT NO.5 AND TRANSITIONAL PROVISION) ORDER 2000, SI 2000 875 (C.20); made under the Employment Relations Act 1999 s.45. Commencement details: bringing into force various provisions of the Act on April 24, 2000; £1.00.

This Order brings into force, on April 24, 2000, the Employment Relations Act 1999 s.16 and Sch.5. These provisions amend the Trade Union and Labour Relations (Consolidation) Act 1992 Part V to provide that an employee is regarded as unfairly dismissed for the purposes of the Employment Rights Act 1996 Part X if dismissed, in certain circumstances, because he or she took part in official industrial action. They also make consequential amendments to s.105 of the 1996 Act which relates to unfair selection for redundancy.

2139. Employment Relations Act 1999 (c.26) – Commencement No.6 Order

EMPLOYMENT RELATIONS ACT 1999 (COMMENCEMENT NO.6 AND TRANSITIONAL PROVISIONS) ORDER 2000, SI 2000 1338 (C.39); made under the Employment Relations Act 1999 s.45. Commencement details: bringing into force various provisions of the Act on June 6, 2000; £1.50.

This Order brings into force the Employment Relations Act 1999 s.1, s.2, s.6, s.25 and Sch.1, which amend the Trade Union and Labour Relations (Consolidation) Act 1992 Part I and Part VI, insert a new Sch.A1 into that Act and amend the Employment Rights Act 1996, in connection with the right of trade unions to be recognised in certain circumstances as entitled to conduct collective bargaining on behalf of workers.

2140. Employment Relations Act 1999 (c.26) – Commencement No.7 Order

EMPLOYMENT RELATIONS ACT 1999 (COMMENCEMENT NO.7 AND TRANSITIONAL PROVISIONS) ORDER 2000, SI 2000 2242 (C.61); made under the Employment Relations Act 1999 s.45. Commencement details: bringing into force various provisions of the Act on September 4, 2000 and September 18, 2000; £1.50.

This Order brings into force on September 4, 2000 the Employment Relations Act 1999 ss.10-12, s.13(4)-(6), s.14 and s.15, which provide a right to be accompanied in disciplinary and grievance hearings. In addition, it brings into force on September 18, 2000 s.4 and Sch.3 to the Act, which amend the Trade Union and Labour Relations (Consolidation) Act 1992 Part V.

2141. Employment tribunals – appeals – time limits – discretion to refuse extension and to strike out notice of appearance

C presented a complaint to an employment tribunal, alleging that she was entitled to equal pay with named comparators, that she had been unfairly dismissed and had been discriminated against on grounds of her sex. C's IT1 was received on July 27, 1998. On September 7, 1998, C's former employer, I, responded with a notice of appearance, IT3, in which only cursory treatment was given to C's complaint. C sought further and better particulars of the IT3, on September 10, 1998. At the directions hearing on November 6, 1998, an order was made, inter alia, for the further and better particulars C had requested. It was indicated that failure to comply with that order might result in the whole or a part of the notice of appearance being struck out, and possibly a direction being made to debar I from defending altogether. I's then representatives served an unsatisfactory reply to the further and better particulars out of time on November 30, 1998. The chairman was invited by C's representatives to make an order striking out the notice of appearance. Accordingly an unless order was made on December 8, 1998, giving I 10 days in which to make submissions or provide particulars. None were forthcoming, and on January 6, 1999 the chairman ordered the notice of appearance to be struck out. No representations were made on behalf of I at the directions hearing on January 12, 1999. I changed its representatives, and in February 1999 the new representatives requested the tribunal to review its decision to strike out the notice, although the time limit for a review had expired on January 21. The tribunal rejected the request as any further postponement would prejudice C. On February 25, 1999 I filed a notice of appeal to the EAT, outside the time limit with respect to the unless order and the order striking the case out, but within the limit in relation to the employment tribunal's decision not to review the last order. An extension of time was requested because I and its new representatives had been ignorant of the two orders until at least February 21, 1999.

Held, dismissing the appeal and refusing leave to appeal, that (1) a discretionary extension of time with respect to the two orders was refused, the fault for the delay rested entirely with I and its representatives; (2) even if the appeal with respect to the unless order and the decision to strike out had been made within time it would not have been allowed; (3) I had been sensibly given a further period of time by the unless order on December 8, 1998 in which to comply with the previous order; (4) I's then representatives made no further communication with the tribunal before January 6, 1999, and in the circumstances the tribunal had been entitled to strike the case out; (5) the tribunal was entitled to take account of the absence of any proper or satisfactory explanation for the non compliance and that factor predominated over the question of injustice to the parties; (6) the tribunal had been entitled to hold that the application for review was without any merit, even if extended time had been granted, and (7) the EAT should support the employment tribunal's exercise of discretion in attempting to case manage in a proper way.

ILION GROUP PLC v. CONNOR [1999] Disc. L.R. 200, Morison, J., EAT.

2142. Employment tribunals – conciliation

EMPLOYMENT TRIBUNALS ACT (APPLICATION OF CONCILIATION PROVISIONS) ORDER 2000 (REVOCATION) ORDER 2000, SI 2000 1336; made under the Employment Tribunals Act 1996 s.18. In force: May 19, 2000; £1.00.

This Order revokes the Employment Tribunals Act (Application of Conciliation Provisions) Order 2000 (SI 2000 1299) due to a discrepancy between the title in the heading and the title, set out in Art.1, by which the Order may be cited.

2143. Employment tribunals – conciliation – conciliation officers

EMPLOYMENT TRIBUNALS ACT 1996 (APPLICATION OF CONCILIATION PROVISIONS) ORDER 2000, SI 2000 1337; made under the Employment Tribunals Act 1996 s.18. In force: June 6, 2000; £1.00.

This Order directs that the Employment Rights Act 1996 s.80(1) be added to the list in the Employment Tribunals Act 1996 s.18(1)(d) and specifies the Trade Union and Labour Relations (Consolidation) Act 1992 s.70B and Sch.A1 para.156 as provisions to which the Employment Tribunals Act 1996 s.18(1)(f) applies. The effect of this direction is that the provisions of s.18 providing for conciliation officers appointed by the Advisory Conciliation and Arbitration Service to conciliate between the parties, or possible parties, to proceedings before employment tribunals are applied in relation to proceedings arising out of a contravention, or alleged contravention, of the provision.

2144. Employment tribunals – employee representatives – extent of party's right to be represented by person of their choice

[Employment Tribunals Act 1996 s.6(1); Employment Tribunals (Constitution and Rules of Procedure) Regulations 1993 (SI 1993 2687) Sch.1 r.9.]

B appealed against an EAT decision that the employment tribunal had power to hold that B's lay representative should only assist her during the tribunal hearing and not act as her representative. B contended that she had an absolute right under the Employment Tribunals Act 1996 s.6(1) to be represented by the person of her choice.

Held, dismissing the appeal on the ground that B would not have succeeded in any event, that, although a tribunal had the power under the Employment Tribunals (Constitution and Rules of Procedure) Regulations 1993 Sch.1 r.9 to control a party's conduct, the tribunal could not exceed its power to control proceedings in such a way that it could require a representative to act merely as a litigation friend. Section 6(1) conferred an absolute right that could not be qualified in the absence of clear statutory authority. To obviate difficulties, however, tribunals were required to promote procedural fairness between parties, and could require parties to act fairly and reasonably in presenting their cases, or when challenging the other side's evidence. A party disagreeing with a tribunal ruling had a right of appeal where the error concerned constituted an error of law. However, even if such an error was found to exist, it did not mean that an appeal would succeed if the EAT held that the decision itself was correct, notwithstanding the procedural error.

BACHE v. ESSEX CC [2000] 2 All E.R. 847, Peter Gibson, L.J., CA.

2145. Employment tribunals – hearings – public access – hearing held in office protected by coded security locks in excess of tribunal's jurisdiction

[Employment Tribunals (Constitution and Rules of Procedure) Regulations 1993 (SI 1993 2687) Sch.1 r.8(2).]

S appealed against the dismissal by the EAT of his appeal against a finding of the employment tribunal that S's unfair dismissal claim had been brought out of time. S contended before the EAT that the tribunal hearing had not been held in public as it had taken place in the regional chairman's office, due to lack of available room, and the presence of a coded security door lock meant that public access was precluded.

However, the EAT held that the hearing was still in public as no member of the public had been prevented from attending.

Held, allowing the appeal, that the requirement to sit in public was fundamental to the administration of justice, and, although there were exceptions in the case of employment tribunals, the wording of the Employment Tribunals (Constitution and Rules of Procedure) Regulations 1993 Sch.1 r.8(2) gave rise to the inference that a failure to do so on the part of a tribunal meant that any decision reached was unlawful. An employment tribunal hearing conducted in a room protected by a coded security lock was not a hearing in public. Moreover, though no member of the public was actually prevented from entering the room, the real question was whether any member of the public would have been able to enter the room had they wished to do so.

STORER v. BRITISH GAS PLC; *sub nom.* STORER v. BG PLC (FORMERLY BRITISH GAS PLC) [2000] 1 W.L.R. 1237, Henry, L.J., CA.

2146. Employment tribunals – inspection of registers

See ADMINISTRATION OF JUSTICE: R. v. Secretary of the Central Office of the Employment Tribunals (England and Wales), *ex p.* Public Concern at Work. §40

2147. Employment tribunals – judicial decision making – majority decision with chairman dissenting – contradictory findings of fact not grounds for appeal

K, a police constable, brought an application claiming that she had been victimised and discriminated against on the ground of sex in relation to assessment of her work and refusals to promote her. An employment tribunal found in her favour by a majority, the Chairman dissenting. CC appealed.

Held, dismissing the appeal, that the tribunal did not err in reaching its decision and it was not one which no reasonable tribunal could have reached. The issues were largely ones of fact, and therefore the tribunal's omission to set out the legal principles in the determination was not fatal. The lay members' variance of opinion from that of the chairman, the fact that they did not find for K on every allegation and the length of their reasons showed that a detailed analysis of the facts had been undertaken, and the findings were supported by the evidence.

CHIEF CONSTABLE OF THAMES VALLEY v. KELLAWAY [2000] I.R.L.R. 170, Morison, J., EAT.

2148. Employment tribunals – jurisdiction – award of costs on indemnity basis – vexatious acts of trade union representatives

[Transfer of Undertakings (Protection of Employment) Regulations 1981 (SI 1981 1794) Reg.10, Reg.11; Employment Tribunals (Constitution and Rules of Procedure) Regulations 1993 (SI 1993 2687) Sch.1 r.12.]

B and 12 others, members of the trade union Unison, were employed in a care home run by UR. In May 1997, the shareholders of UR agreed to sell their shares to HH, another company, which then took over the running of the home. On behalf of its members, Unison sought a meeting with the directors of UR concerning the provision of information and consultation in relation to what it viewed as the transfer of an undertaking under the Transfer of Undertakings (Protection of Employment) Regulations 1981. It was also suggested that UR should grant Unison recognition for the purposes of representing its staff. UR replied that it did not intend to recognise Unison and that since there had only been a share transfer there was not a relevant transfer for the purposes of the Regulations and the obligation to consult and provide information did not arise. Further communications between UR and Unison failed to resolve the issue and B complained to an employment tribunal, alleging a failure to provide information and consult with staff affected by a transfer of an undertaking, contrary to Reg.10 and Reg.11. The chairman dismissed the complaints as there had been no relevant transfer and ordered costs on an indemnity basis on the ground that Unison had acted vexatiously in pursuing the claims which had been brought for the collateral purpose of obtaining recognition. B appealed, contending that the chairman had wrongly taken the means of the union into account.

Held, dismissing the appeal, that (1) the test for the tribunal was whether it had properly exercised the discretion to award costs under the Employment Tribunals (Constitution and Rules of Procedure) Regulations 1993 Sch.1 r.12, in the sense that it was just in the circumstances to do so. The exercise of that discretion would only be interfered with on the ground of perversity; (2) it could not be said that a failure to inquire into a party's means would necessarily vitiate an exercise of discretion to award costs, *Wiggin Alloys v. Jenkins* [1981] I.R.L.R. 275, [1981] C.L.Y. 958 considered, *Omar v. Worldwide News Inc (t/a United Press International)* [1998] I.R.L.R. 291, [1998] C.L.Y. 2167 not followed. In the instant case, no evidence was presented to the chairman on the subject; (3) where a union had supported and assisted a case there was nothing inherently wrong in considering whether the union had objectives beyond success in those proceedings, and such a consideration was not limited to cases where the union had provided members with an indemnity as to costs, *Dorney v. Chippenham College* (Unreported, EAT, May 12, 1997) applied; (4) there was no need for an applicant to be at fault to justify a costs award on the grounds that it had acted vexatiously in bringing the proceedings and there was nothing improper in identifying parties with their advisers and in particular the conduct of their advisers. No evidence was tendered in the instant case that the applicants were not at fault; (5) in the circumstances, the chairman had been entitled to hold that Unison had acted vexatiously, having regard to the clear state of the law and its collateral purpose in pursuing the proceedings; (6) having regard to Unison's conduct, the chairman did not err in having regard to its means in making the costs award, and (7) the award of costs on an indemnity basis was correct, *Munkenbeck & Marshall v. McAlpine* 44 Con. L.R. 30, [1996] C.L.Y. 742 considered.

BEYNON v. SCADDEN [1999] I.R.L.R. 700, Lindsay, J., EAT.

2149. **Employment tribunals – jurisdiction – breach of contract – no jurisdiction to consider complaint made before termination of employment**

[Wages Act 1986; Employment Rights Act 1996 Part II; Employment Tribunals Extension of Jurisdiction (England and Wales) Order 1994 (SI 1994 1623) Art.7.]

C, who had been employed by LCC, was dismissed following an incident in April 1994. Subsequent to an internal appeal the effective date of termination of his employment was July 7, 1995. C made three applications to the employment tribunal in November 1994 claiming, inter alia, unfair dismissal and various breaches of his contract of employment. The tribunal having found the dismissal to have been fair, held, pursuant to the Employment Tribunals Extension of Jurisdiction (England and Wales) Order 1994 Art.7, that it did not have jurisdiction to consider the breach of contract claims on the ground that they had been made prematurely. The Employment Appeal Tribunal having reversed the decision, LCC appealed. C cross appealed against the failure of the tribunal to consider whether it had jurisdiction to determine claims arising from LCC's alleged failure to pay him his full salary during his suspension under the Wages Act 1986, now re-enacted in the Employment Rights Act 1996 Part II.

Held, allowing the appeal and cross appeal, that (1) notwithstanding that LCC would not be prejudiced by an early claim, the tribunal did not have jurisdiction under the 1994 Order to hear a claim for breach of contract brought prior to the effective date of termination. Article 7 of the 1994 Order prohibited the exercise of jurisdiction over complaints which did not fall within the specified time periods. The jurisdiction of the tribunal to consider breach of contract claims only existed upon the termination of employment, and (2) the tribunal having rejected jurisdiction under Art. 7 ought, given that C was without legal representation, to have considered whether they had jurisdiction to hear the complaints under the 1986 Act. It followed that C's claims should be remitted to the tribunal.

CAPEK v. LINCOLNSHIRE CC [2000] I.C.R. 878, Mummery, L.J., CA.

2150. Employment tribunals – procedural impropriety – chairman's failure to exchange written submissions

O, an employee of BDLBC, successfully presented a complaint to an employment tribunal alleging racial discrimination and victimisation. At the close of the second day of the hearing the chairman addressed the parties as to the shortage of time and the need to conclude the proceedings expeditiously. Counsel for BDLBC who had a further witness to call informed the tribunal that he would not be calling him. A written statement of the witness had been included in the papers served on the tribunal. Further agreement was reached that the parties would put their closing submissions in writing, but no direction was provided as to their mutual exchange. Subsequent to the receipt of the tribunal decision, that BDLBC had racially discriminated against O, BDLBC expressed disquiet that the decision had been made without opportunity for prior sight of the written submissions and sought a review. The tribunal enquired of both parties how their submissions would have differed if the submissions had been exchanged and refused the review application on the grounds that it did not have a reasonable prospect of success. BDLBC appealed, contending that (1) the procedure by which the tribunal reached its decision amounted to a breach of the rules of natural justice. The responsibility for ensuring the exchange of written submissions was on the tribunal and its failure to do so was a serious procedural irregularity; (2) the decision not to call the second witness had resulted from the unspoken pressure of time and knowledge that opposing counsel was unwell. Furthermore the tribunals subsequent decision not to give consideration to that witness's statement had been unjust, and (3) the tribunal had erred in its finding of discriminatory conduct before the commencement date of the discriminatory conduct relied upon.

Held, dismissing the appeal, that (1) the tribunal chairman, having secured the consent of both parties to make written submissions, was under a duty to serve each party with the submissions of the other. In failing to do so the tribunal was in breach of the rules of natural justice. The breach had however been remedied by the subsequent request made for the comments of both parties and the tribunal's subsequent reconsideration; (2) responsibility resided with counsel as to whether or not a witness should be called in support of his client's case. There were no grounds for counsel, in view of his overriding obligation to serve his client's best interests, to excuse the exercise of that discretion on the basis alleged, and (3) the tribunal had been entitled to their finding that discriminatory conduct toward O had extended prior to the commencement date of the conduct relied upon. The determined date was of significance only in respect of O's entitlement to compensation which could not extend prior to it. It was not desirable that the tribunal comprehensively set out their findings as to the nature of the discriminatory conduct prior to the commencement date.

BARKING AND DAGENHAM LBC v. OGUOKO [2000] I.R.L.R. 179, Judge Byrt Q.C., EAT.

2151. Employment tribunals – procedure – amendment to included disability discrimination claim – time limit

[Disability Discrimination Act 1995 s.8, Sch.3 para.3 (1); Employment Rights Act 1996 s.111 (2).]

H, who had a history of back problems and had undergone corrective surgery, was made redundant from his post with PTL on December 31, 1996. On February 7, 1997 he presented a complaint to an employment tribunal, alleging that he had been unfairly dismissed on the grounds of inadequate consultation. He did not mention a possible claim under the Disability Discrimination Act 1995. In April 1997, H saw PTL's IT3, which stated that he had been selected for redundancy because he could not perform the full range of his duties owing to his back problems. In September 1997, following a period of depression, H sought to amend his IT1, to add a complaint that he had been discriminated against on the grounds of a disability, contrary to the Act. PTL objected to the amendment, on the basis that it had not been presented within three months of the alleged act of discrimination, as required by Sch.3, para.3(1). Leave for the amendment was refused on the basis that it amounted to an new cause of action which was time barred on March 30, 1997. As to whether the complaint could be allowed on "just and equitable" grounds, the chairman considered various matters concerning prejudice and hardship that would be suffered by both parties. As regards delay, the chairman referred to H's depression during the period between April and September 1997. On balance, the chairman decided that, in the circumstances, it would not be just and equitable to allow the amendment. H appealed, contending that the three month time limit under Sch.3 para.3(1) was not applicable when the disability complaint was, as in the instant case, being added by way of amendment to an existing complaint of some other kind, as opposed to the presentation of a complaint under s.8 as a wholly new case. H also argued that the chairman had erred in the exercise of his discretion on whether it would be just and equitable to allow the amendment.

Held, dismissing the appeal, that in considering whether leave to add an amendment to an existing complaint should be granted, an employment tribunal would first have to consider whether the original application was itself presented within the time limit applicable to the type of claim put forward. It was only if that question could be answered in the affirmative that the tribunal would then consider whether, as a matter of discretion, leave to make the amendment should be granted, *Cocking v. Sandhurst Ltd* [1974] I.C.R. 650, [1975] C.L.Y. 1119 applied. In order to secure certainty of litigation and not encourage abusive or speculative applications, which may or may not, depending on evidence obtained, be supplanted by the real complaint, it was necessary that the strict time limits applicable to employment tribunal proceedings applied to the presentation of new complaints by way of amendment. It followed that the word "presented" in the Employment Rights Act 1996 s.111(2) referred, in the context of the three month time limit for complaints, not only to the lodging of originating applications, but also to applications for leave to make amendments to those applications, *British Newspaper Printing Corp (North) Ltd v. Kelly* [1989] I.R.L.R. 222, [1990] C.L.Y. 1893 not followed. The same reasoning applied to Sch.3 para.3(1) of the 1995 Act, which required that complaints were presented within three months of the alleged act occurring. It followed that the three month time bar applied to H's application for leave to amend, and that since the amendment concerned a new cause of action not pleaded in the original IT1, the tribunal had no discretion to allow it. In the alternative, the chairman's decision that leave to amend should not be allowed on just and equitable grounds must stand. H had not shown that the chairman had either failed to take a relevant matter into account or taken into account an irrelevant matter.

HARVEY v. PORT OF TILBURY (LONDON) LTD [1999] I.C.R. 1030, Lindsay, J., EAT.

2152. Employment tribunals – procedure – disclosure of information

EMPLOYMENT TRIBUNALS (CONSTITUTION AND RULES OF PROCEDURE) (AMENDMENT) REGULATIONS 2000, SI 2000 1987; made under the Employment Tribunals Act 1996 s.7, s.11, s.41. In force: August 17, 2000; £1.50.

These Regulations amend the Employment Tribunals (Constitution and Rules of Procedure) Regulations 1993 (SI 1993 2687) with respect to the amount of information to be placed by the Secretary on the Register, which is open to public inspection, in relation to applications and appeals.

2153. Employment tribunals – procedure – power to strike out claim summarily

[Employment Rights Act 1996; Employment Tribunals (Constitution and Rules of Procedure) Regulations 1993 (SI 1993 2687) Sch.1 r.7(4), r.9, r.13; Civil Procedure Rules 1998 (SI 1998 3132).]

C appealed against an EAT decision that an employment tribunal had made no error of law in refusing to strike out a claim before the hearing of evidence. M, an employee, had commenced proceedings against C for victimisation contrary to the Employment Rights Act 1996 and, prior to the opening of the case, C had made an application under the Employment Tribunals (Constitution and Rules of Procedure) Regulations 1993 Sch.1 r.9 and Sch.1 r.13, to strike out the claims on the basis that they had no real prospect of success. It was held that the tribunal did not have jurisdiction to strike out a claim before hearing evidence and the application had been dismissed. C contended that the EAT had failed to have sufficient regard to r.9 of the Regulations which enabled an employment tribunal to conduct the proceedings in the manner which it thought most appropriate for the just handling of the proceedings in the same way as a court applied the Civil Procedure Rules 1998 when a claimant had no reasonable prospect of success.

Held, dismissing the appeal, that r.9 and r.13 of the Regulations were procedural in nature and did not give an employment tribunal the power to strike out a claim summarily. Rule 9 enabled a tribunal to stop proceedings after hearing a claimant's evidence but not before. In any event, to allow a tribunal to strike out a claim prior to the hearing of evidence would be inconsistent with r.7(4) of the Regulations which provided for cases in which a claimant's contentions had no real prospect of success at the pre hearing stage of the proceedings. Further, to combine the case management powers contained in the Civil Procedure Rules 1998 with those of the employment tribunals would be contrary to the object of the Regulations which had been formulated prior to the Rules.

CARE FIRST PARTNERSHIP LTD v. ROFFEY; *sub nom.* ROFFEY v. CARE FIRST PARTNERSHIP LTD [2001] I.C.R. 87, Aldous, L.J., CA.

2154.   Employment tribunals – reporting restrictions – transsexualism – validity of order

[Employment Tribunals (Constitution and Rules of Procedure) Regulations 1993 (SI 1993 687) r.13, r.14; Employment Appeal Tribunal Rules 1993 (SI 1993 2854) r.23; Council Directive 76/207 on equal treatment for men and women as regards access to employment.]

A, a transsexual, claimed sex discrimination arising from the refusal of West Yorkshire Police to employ her as a constable on the ground that she would be unable to carry out intimate searches of female suspects because she was still legally male. The employment tribunal made a restricted reporting order, RRO, relying on the Employment Tribunals (Constitution and Rules of Procedure) Regulations 1993 r.13(1) and, in the alternative, A's rights under the Equal Treatment Directive, as without the RRO, A would have been unable to bring her case against the Chief Constable, CC, an emanation of the State. The order was to continue until the promulgation of the tribunal's decision. The tribunal found that there had been discrimination and adjourned to consider a remedy. CC appealed against liability and an issue arose as to whether the RRO had been correctly made and whether it was still in force.

Held, making an RRO in perpetual terms, that the employment tribunal had no power to make the RRO under r.13. The power to do so under r.14 was not applicable as A's treatment could not be said to come within the definition of "sexual misconduct" merely because it was related to her gender. The decision on liability only was not a promulgation of the tribunal's decision, so that the RRO made in consequence of the Directive remained in force. The EAT's powers to make an RRO under the Employment Appeal Tribunal Rules r.23 was so restrictive as to make it almost impossible for A to exercise her rights under the Directive, as it was not in dispute that exposure of her identity could severely disrupt her life. In the circumstances, therefore, the EAT would make the order under the jurisdiction created by the Directive.

CHIEF CONSTABLE OF WEST YORKSHIRE v. A [2001] I.C.R. 128, Lindsay, J., EAT.

2155.   Employment tribunals – time limits – reasonableness of steps to ensure compliance

L was dismissed on November 2, 1998. An application was sent by first class post to the employment tribunal on January 18, 1999. The solicitor made a diary note to check on February 2, 1999 whether any acknowledgement had been received from the tribunal. After checking on February 3, the solicitor found that the application had not been received by the tribunal and a copy was sent by fax and post on February 4, 1999. The tribunal held that it was not reasonably practicable for the application to be presented within time. The system the solicitors had for checking was a quality system; all reasonable steps had been taken to ensure the application was received in time. The employer appealed.

Held, allowing the appeal, that the tribunal had erred in holding that it was not reasonably practicable for the complaint to be presented within time, when the system for checking whether the complaint had been received involved a check after the three month period had expired. Where an applicant was represented and the application was entrusted to the post, it must be shown that all reasonable steps had been taken to ensure compliance with the time limits. This meant that there must be a system in place, which, if followed correctly, would provide for a check that the complaint had been received within time before the expiry of the time limit.

LISTERS SOLICITORS LTD v. LAMBERT, January 27, 2000, Judge not specified, EAT. [*Ex rel.* John Worrall, Barrister, 10 Park Square, Leeds].

2156. **Equal pay – comparators – annual increments based on length of service**

[Equal Pay Act 1970 s.1.]

In 1987, E, who had been employed as a district chief speech therapist by NHHA since 1983, made a claim under the Equal Pay Act 1970. She contended that her work was of equal value to that of a male comparator, M, who had been employed for less than a year by NHHA as a clinical psychologist. The pay scale under which M was employed provided for annual increments over the succeeding four years. The employment tribunal determined that at the relevant time E's work was of equal value to M's and that, accordingly, she should be entitled to the annual salary paid to M in 1987. E appealed, contending that her salary should have included the four increments that M would have received had he been appointed at the time when she had begun work as a district chief speech therapist. The EAT having dismissed her appeal ([1999] I.R.L.R. 155), E appealed, submitting that, since her own and M's contracts of employment contained a clause providing for annual increments to be determined solely by reference to the number of years served, s.1 dictated that her salary should be assessed in the manner in which she had argued for. She maintained that otherwise she would be wrongly deprived of her entitlement to annual increases based upon length of service.

Held, dismissing the appeal, that in finding that E's work was of equal value to that of M, the tribunal had paid regard to the length of service and experience of both E and M. The work done by E and M increased in its value to the employer over time. E had to be compared with her chosen comparator. She therefore had to be paid at the level in the scale which M had reached. If E were permitted to enter a pay scale on the same level as M but incrementally higher, the situation would result whereby E would be paid at a level higher than the comparator to whom she had established equal value. Such a result would effectively allow E to "double count" her experience.

ENDERBY v. FRENCHAY HA (NO.2); EVESHAM v. NORTH HERTFORDSHIRE HA; HUGHES v. WEST BERKSHIRE HA [2000] I.C.R. 612, Roch, L.J., CA.

2157. **Equal pay – comparators – interpretation of EC law – transfer of undertakings from public to private sector**

[Transfer of Undertakings (Protection of Employment) Regulations 1981 (SI 1989 1794); EC Treaty Art.119 (Arts.117 to 120 of the EC Treaty have been replaced by Arts.136 to 143 EC).]

L, and other female workers employed by R as cleaners/caterers in school premises, appealed against the dismissal of their appeal of an order that, with regard to the equal pay principle, they were not permitted to compare themselves with male comparators employed by a different and unconnected employer. As a result of compulsory competitive tendering, there had been a transfer of undertaking from the local authority to R which paid L at a lower rate. L unsuccessfully litigated in an employment tribunal for equal pay, using as comparators male employees of the local authority who performed jobs of equal value. On appeal, their contentions for a wider interpretation of the EC Treaty Art.119 (Arts.117 to 120 of the EC Treaty have been replaced by Arts.136 to 143 EC), were dismissed in favour of a ruling that the chosen comparators were not in the same establishment or service as L because R did not control the pay of both groups of employees. On appeal L argued that (1) there were special circumstances, namely the combined effects of compulsory competitive tendering, the Transfer of Undertakings (Protection of Employment) Regulations 1981 and a job evaluation study prepared by the local authority prior to the transfer, for Art.119 to confer upon them a directly effective right to claim equal pay with the chosen comparators, and (2) the issue was not one of justifying the difference, but of explaining the discrepancy, between the two rates of pay. Such explanation could be provided by R, without them having to ascertain from the local authority why the male comparator was paid at a higher rate.

Held, referring the case to the ECJ, that since L's submissions raised two complex issues, namely (1) the direct applicability of Art.119, and (2) the identification of appropriate comparators under Art.119, being important throughout the Community particularly with regard to the transfer of undertakings from public authorities to the private sector, ought to be interpreted by the ECJ.

LAWRENCE v. REGENT OFFICE CARE LTD [2000] I.R.L.R. 608, Mummery, L.J., CA.

2158. **Equal pay – comparators – jurisdiction of tribunal to determine claim without independent expert report**

[Equal Pay Act 1970 s.2A(1); Employment Tribunals (Constitution and Rules of Procedure) Regulations 1993 (SI 1993 687) Sch.2 para.8A.]

W, one of nine women employed as cleaner/packers failed in an equal pay claim which alleged that they were engaged in work of equal value to that undertaken by men employed as picker/packers. The tribunal had concluded that the work was obviously of a different value and that no expert's report was needed to elucidate that fact. The claim was dismissed as having no reasonable prospect of success. Under the Equal Pay Act 1970 s.2A(1) (as amended in 1996) the tribunal had power to determine an equal value question without reference to an independent expert's report where it was satisfied on the facts that the claim was without merit. However, under the Employment Tribunals (Constitution and Rules of Procedure) Regulations 1993 Sch.2 para.8A that jurisdiction was qualified by placing an obligation on the tribunal to give parties an opportunity to make representations as to whether an expert should be required and, following a decision not to require an expert report, to give the parties an opportunity to adduce expert evidence before the tribunal adjudicated on the issue. It was contended that this two stage process had not been adopted by the tribunal, which had determined the matter without giving the parties an opportunity to adduce their own expert evidence. W appealed.

Held, allowing the appeal and remitting the case to a freshly constituted tribunal, that there had been a procedural mishap in that the tribunal had concluded that no expert evidence would alter their finding and they had determined the matter without giving the parties the opportunity to persuade it to arrange for the appointment of an independent expert. W should have been told that her rights were going to be fully determined by the tribunal in the event that she failed to persuade it to arrange for the appointment of an independent expert. In light of the changes brought about by the 1993 Regulations, the law now required the tribunal to allow the parties to adduce expert evidence after it had decided the claim had no reasonable prospect of success, *Sheffield City Council v. Siberry* [1989] I.C.R. 208, [1989] C.L.Y. 1427 not followed.

WOOD v. WILLIAM BALL LTD [1999] I.C.R. 277, Morison, J., EAT.

2159. Equal pay – comparators – supplementary pay for shift working and unsociable hours – European Union

[EC Treaty Art.119 (Arts.117 to 120 of the EC Treaty have been replaced by Arts.136 to 143 EC); Council Directive 75/117 on equal pay.]

J, a Swedish equal opportunities ombudsman, brought an equal pay claim on behalf of two midwives employed by O, who were paid at a lower rate than medical technicians for work of a similar nature, although the midwives received supplements for working inconvenient hours and shifts. The standard working week was 40 hours but for those on shift work the weekly hours were reduced to 34. Before the labour court, J argued that the supplementary payments and the lower hours ought not to be taken into account. O contended that there was no difference in pay levels if those matters were taken into account. The labour court sought a preliminary ruling from the ECJ as to whether the supplementary payments were to be taken into account for comparative purposes in an equal pay claim under the EC Treaty Art.119 (Arts.117 to 120 of the EC Treaty have been replaced by Arts.136 to 143 EC) and Council Directive 75/117.

Held, giving a preliminary ruling, that in calculating the salary to be used as the basis for assessing equal pay no account was to be taken of such supplementary payments as to do so would undermine the effectiveness of Art.119, *Barber v. Guardian Royal Exchange Assurance Group (C262/88)* [1991] 1 Q.B. 344, [1990] C.L.Y. 1915 followed. Where there was a difference in pay between two groups and it was shown that women constituted a substantial proportion of the lower paid group, it was for the employer to justify the difference by reference to objective factors not related to discrimination on gender grounds.

JAMSTALLDHETSOMBUDSMANNEN v. OREBRO LANS LANDSTING (C236/98) [2000] 2 C.M.L.R. 708, JC Moitinho de Almeida (President), ECJ.

2160. Equal pay – families – conditions imposed on married female workers but not to male counterparts – European Union

[EC Treaty Art.119 (Arts.117 to 120 of the EC Treaty have been replaced by Arts.136 EC to 143 EC); Council Directive 75/117 on equal pay for men and women; Council Directive 79/7 on equal treatment for men and women in matters of social security Art.4(1); Constitution of Greece 1975 Art.4.]

Greek legislation providing for the payment of family allowances imposed conditions on married female workers which were not imposed on their male counterparts. The EC Treaty Art.119 (Arts.117 to 120 of the EC Treaty have been replaced by Arts.136 EC to 143 EC) came into force in Greece in January 1981, requiring the adoption of measures to ensure compliance with the principle of equal pay. Although Greece had incorporated the principle of equal pay into the Constitution of Greece 1975 Art.4, the European Commission argued that (1) collective agreements in Greece contained conditions imposing certain benefits upon female workers which were not imposed on their male counterparts, and (2) although the Government had introduced legislation altering such provisions in these agreements, this was not retrospective in effect as from the date Art.119 came into force. As a consequence, female employees had been deprived of benefits, and the calculation of their pensions would be adversely affected, which amounted to a violation of the principle of equal pay. Greece argued that (1) the equal pay provision in Art.4 of the Constitution satisfied the requirements of Art.119 of the EC Treaty; (2) if the female workers' lost benefits equated to pay, Greece would have to demand additional social security contributions which would be contrary to the principle of proportionality, and (3) due to the status of collective agreements on pay and benefits under Greek law, it was not always possible for the Government to end the operation of rules and practices which were inconsistent with EC law and/or the Constitution.

Held, giving a preliminary ruling, that (1) under Art.119, pay meant any remuneration received by a worker, either directly or indirectly, as a result of employment, which included family allowances. Discrimination in their payment, therefore, was contrary to Art.119 and to Council Directive 75/117. Since female workers' pensions were also affected thereby, this also constituted direct discrimination contrary to Council Directive 79/7 Art.4(1), *R. v. Secretary of State for Employment, ex p. Seymour-Smith (C167/97)* [1999] 2 A.C. 554, [1999] C.L.Y. 2141 followed; (2) Art.4 of the Constitution was insufficient to give effect to the requirements of EC law, which required unequivocal provisions setting out the requisite rights and obligations, *Sex Discrimination Laws (248/ 83), Re* [1985] E.C.R. 1459, [1986] C.L.Y. 1457 distinguished and *Equal Pay Concepts (143/83), Re* [1985] E.C.R. 427, [1986] C.L.Y. 1460 followed; (3) Member States could not rely on practical, administrative or financial difficulties to justify a failure to comply with the requirements of Directives, *Commission of the European Communities v. Belgium (C42/89)* [1990] E.C.R. I-2821 followed, and (4) while it was legitimate to leave the implementation of the equal pay principle to be worked out between management and workers in the first instance, Member States retained the responsibility of ensuring that legal and administrative measures were in operation to guarantee the operation of the principle, *Commission of the European Communities v. Denmark (143/83)* followed.

COMMISSION OF THE EUROPEAN COMMUNITIES v. GREECE (C187/98); *sub nom.* COMMISSION OF THE EUROPEAN COMMUNITIES v. HELLENIC REPUBLIC (C187/98) [2000] 1 C.M.L.R. 465, PJG Kapteyn (President), ECJ.

2161. **Equal pay – maternity rights – air crew – loss of pregnant employee's flying allowance on transfer to ground job**

[Equal Pay Act 1970; Employment Rights Act 1996 s.67(2); EC Treaty Art.119 (Arts.117 to 120 of the EC Treaty have been replaced by Arts.136 to 143 EC).]

M, a cabin crew member, was given ground duties prior to her maternity leave. In accordance with her contract, such was mandatory in any event, after the 16th week of pregnancy, although M requested and was granted the same earlier. Once on ground duties, no flying allowances were paid to M. BA appealed the tribunal's decision that by not paying flying allowances they were in breach of their obligations as to (1) remuneration on suspension on maternity grounds, in particular the Employment Rights Act 1996 s.67(2), and (2) equal pay as provided by the Equal Pay Act 1970 and/or the EC Treaty Art.119 (Arts.117 to 120 of the EC Treaty have been replaced by Arts.136 EC to 143 EC). M cross appealed the dismissal of her deductions claim. BA contended that (1) there was no difference between the terms and conditions applicable to M's work in the air and on the ground, and the tribunal had made inadequate findings of fact in relation to the nature of the flying allowances, and (2) maternity conditions in general, including remuneration on suspension on maternity grounds, were governed by domestic legislation, and no separate claim could arise under the 1970 Act or Art.119, *Gillespie v. Northern Health and Social Services Board (C342/93)* [1996] All E.R. (EC) 284, [1996] C.L.Y. 2570 referred to.

Held, allowing the appeal in part and dismissing the cross appeal, that (1) employees were entitled to flying allowances when on normal flying duties, but not on the ground. The tribunal's decision that a considerable part of the flying allowances represented profit to the cabin crew recipient was adequate, and they were not obliged to make a detailed differentiation between profit and expenses. Subsequently the tribunal had been entitled to conclude, that whilst the kind of alternative work offered to M was suitable, the terms and conditions applicable to those alternative ground duties were substantially less favourable than the corresponding terms of her normal cabin crew work within the meaning of the 1996 Act, and (2) With regard to equal pay, no distinction should be drawn between a worker physically absent on maternity leave and one moved to alternative work in the interests of her health and safety, therefore applying *Gillespie*, adequate allowance of maternity rights was made under the 1996 Act, and no claim arose under either the 1970 Act or Art.119. In respect of the cross appeal, under the terms of M's contract she was offered suitable alternative employment, upon basic pay, which she agreed to, and therefore there had been no unlawful deductions under her contract.

BRITISH AIRWAYS (EUROPEAN OPERATIONS AT GATWICK) LTD v. MOORE; *sub nom.* BRITISH AIRWAYS (EUROPEAN OPERATIONS) GATWICK LTD v. MOORE [2000] 2 C.M.L.R. 343, Judge Peter Clark, EAT.

2162. **Equal pay – part time workers – retrospective membership of occupational pension schemes – compatibility of statutory time limits – European Union**

[Equal Pay Act 1970 s.2(4), s.2(5).]

The claimants, part time workers, commenced proceedings under the Equal Pay Act 1970 claiming retroactive membership of their occupational pension schemes for service prior to amendments to the schemes giving part time workers equal rights to membership in line with their full time colleagues. Following the issue of 60,000 claims before the UK courts, in three test cases the claimants sought the right to join their schemes in situations where respectively, (1) the scheme had been amended more than two years before the proceedings had begun; (2) the claimants had ceased to be employed more than six months before commencement of proceedings, and (3) the claimants had worked on a series of intermittent short term contracts with the same employer. Under s.2(4) workers were required to bring such equality actions within six months following their cessation of employment, and s.2(5) provided that retroactive membership of the schemes would only be allowed for up to two years before the date equality proceedings began. The employment tribunal having made a preliminary ruling that those time limits applied, the House of Lords made a reference to the ECJ asking whether those national rules regarding time limits were compatible with EC law.

Held, giving a preliminary ruling, that in the absence of Community provisions, it fell upon the Member States to lay down procedural rules concerning the actions based on rights arising from the direct effect of Community law, including applicable time limits for bringing such actions, which were essential for the maintenance of legal certainty. The imposition of a six month time limit on the institution of proceedings under the Act giving effect to Community law rights, was not precluded by Community law, provided that the principle of equivalence was not infringed by the limitation period being less favourable than that which applied to actions based on rights arising from domestic law, *Levez v. TH Jennings (Harlow Pools) Ltd (C326/96)* [1999] All E.R. (EC) 1, [1999] C.L.Y. 2067 applied. However, the rule providing that a claimant's pensionable service was to be calculated only by reference to service after a date falling no earlier than two years prior to the date of claim, infringed the principle of effectiveness, rendering it impossible to exercise rights conferred by the Community and thus was precluded by Community law. The claims brought under s.2(5) were not concerned with arrears of benefits but rather to secure recognition of the right to retroactive membership of the pension scheme, in order to evaluate benefits payable in the future and the section discounted the whole period of service prior to the two years for the purpose of calculating future pension benefits. As to workers on intermittent consecutive short term contracts, if there was a stable relationship in existence between the claimant and the employer, the starting point for the limitation period should be fixed on the date on which the stability of such short term contracts was interrupted, provided the contracts related to the same employment.

PRESTON v. WOLVERHAMPTON HEALTHCARE NHS TRUST (NO.1) (C78/98); PRESTON v. SECRETARY OF STATE FOR HEALTH (NO.1) (C78/98); FLETCHER v. MIDLAND BANK PLC (NO.1) (C78/98); *sub nom.* PRESTON v. WOLVERHAMPTON HEALTH CARE NHS TRUST (NO.1) (C78/98) [2001] 2 W.L.R. 408, GC Rodriguez Iglesias (President), ECJ.

2163. **Equal pay – retirement – pre retirement payments to female employee – categorisation of payment – European Union**

[EC Treaty Art.119 (Arts.117 to Art.120 of the EC Treaty have been replaced by Arts.136 to 143 EC); Treaty on European Union (Maastricht) 1992 Protocol No.2;

Council Directive 76/207 on equal treatment for men and women as regards access to employment Art.5; Council Directive 86/378 on implementation of principle of equal treatment for men and women in occupational social security schemes Art.2, Art.4.]

D was employed by S from 1960 to 1986. From 1984 she was paid a pre retirement premium by S, and from 1986 until she was 60 in November 1991, S paid her an unemployment benefit supplement. Both payments being provided for under Belgian law. In 1993, following the decision in *Commission of the European Communities v. Belgium (C173/91)* [1993] E.C.R. I-673, [1993] C.L.Y. 4276, which held that such payments constituted "pay" pursuant to the EC Treaty Art.119 (Arts.117 to 120 of the EC Treaty have been replaced by Arts.136 to 143 EC), D sought an order in the national court that the supplement should be paid until she reached 65, as it would have been for a male worker. At first instance, it was held that the payment was part of an "occupational social security scheme" and was paid prior to 1990, which meant that the Treaty on European Union (Maastricht) 1992 Protocol No.2 applied so that the payment did not come within the equal pay provisions of Art.119. D appealed and the court referred to the ECJ the question of whether Protocol No.2 applied to the payments and whether they complied with Council Directive 76/207 Art.5.

Held, giving a preliminary ruling, that the payments were part of an occupational scheme designed to support employees facing unemployment close to retirement and therefore were within the definition of an "occupational social security scheme" for the purposes of Council Directive 86/378 Art.2 and Art.4. However, Protocol No.2 applied as the payments were made before 1990 and D had not instituted proceedings prior to that date, so that the payments were not required to comply with Art.119. As the payments were "pay" in terms of Art.119 they were excluded from the scope of Directive 76/207.

DEFREYN v. SABENA SA (C166/99) [2000] Pens. L.R. 261, DAO Edward (President), ECJ.

2164. Equal pay – statutory maternity pay – entitlement during maternity leave

[Social Security Contributions and Benefits Act 1992 s.164; EC Treaty Art.119 (Arts.117 to 120 of the EC Treaty have been replaced by Arts.136 to 143 EC); Council Directive 92/85 on the safety and health at work of pregnant workers and workers who have recently given birth Art.11.]

B, who worked part time for T, took maternity leave, but was refused statutory maternity pay because her weekly earnings were below the minimum required under the Social Security Contributions and Benefits Act 1992 s.164. B failed to qualify for any other form of payment, such as maternity allowance, or alternatively incapacity benefit, as she did not satisfy the conditions required. She made an application to an employment tribunal, arguing that under the EC Treaty Art.119 (Arts.117 to 120 of the EC Treaty have been replaced by Arts.136 to 143 EC) maternity pay had to be of a sufficient level to ensure that the principle of maternity leave was not threatened. The tribunal refused the application and B appealed on the basis that the domestic law had unlawfully limited her rights to statutory maternity pay.

Held, dismissing the appeal, that Council Directive 92/85 was aimed at ensuring that taking maternity leave would not jeopardise the objective of safeguarding a woman's career before and after giving birth. However, Art.11 of the Directive allowed Member States to set criteria for eligibility, and this was not in conflict with the equal pay requirements of Art.119 (now Art.141 EC) of the Treaty. Where a woman was otherwise eligible for maternity pay, the rate payable could not be set so low that it frustrated the purpose of the Directive, *Gillespie v. Northern Health and Social Services Board (C342/93)* [1996] All E.R. (EC) 284, [1996] C.L.Y. 2570, applied. Such minimum payment requirements were not intended to apply to women such as B who did not qualify under the criteria, and therefore B did not have a claim by way of the Treaty which she would not have had under domestic law.

BANKS v. TESCO STORES LTD [2000] 1 C.M.L.R. 400, Morison, J., EAT.

2165. Equal pay – statutory maternity pay – entitlement to benefit of pay rise

[Equal Pay Act 1970; Employment Rights Act 1996; Statutory Maternity Pay (General) Regulations 1986 (SI 1986 1960) Reg.21 (3); EC Treaty Art.119 (Arts.117 to 120 of the EC Treaty have been replaced by Arts.136 to 143 EC).]

A, an employee of W, commenced her maternity leave on January 8, 1996, being paid in accordance with her contract a higher earnings rate for a period of 10 weeks which had been calculated taking into account her normal weekly earnings during the "relevant period" as defined by the Statutory Maternity Pay (General) Regulations 1986 Reg.21 (3). On December 1, 1995 she received a pay increase but that was not included in her maternity pay, and as a result A claimed that she had been discriminated against contrary to the Equal Pay Act 1970 and EC Treaty Art.119 (Arts.117 to 120 of the EC Treaty have been replaced by Arts.136 to 143 EC). An amendment to the Regulations had been designed to implement the decision in *Gillespie v. Northern Health and Social Services Board (C342/93)* [1996] All E.R. (EC) 284, [1996] C.L.Y. 2570 where the application of Art.141 had been considered, however A contended that full implementation had not taken place as the Regulations applied to backdated pay rises only.

Held, dismissing the appeal, that Reg.21 (7) had failed to give effect to the fact that (1) a woman was entitled to a pay rise whether backdated or not which occurred at any point between the start of the relevant period and the end of her maternity leave. She could not however take advantage of a pay increase which took effect after her higher pay rate had finished, *Gillespie* followed. A was therefore entitled to the benefit of the pay increase in the calculation of her earnings related higher rate pay and her rights under Art.119 had been breached. That entitlement could not however be enforced under the 1970 Act as there was no appropriate comparable. The correct procedure was to bring a claim under the Employment Rights Act 1996 for an unlawful deduction, however she was out of time for bringing such a claim. Permission to appeal was granted.

ALABASTER v. WOOLWICH PLC [2000] I.C.R. 1037, Judge Peter Clark, EAT.

2166. Equal pay – time limits – distinction between actual job and overall employment relationship

[Equal Pay Act 1970 s.1, s.2 (4).]

NP appealed against a decision of an EAT ([2000] I.C.R. 78) that a claim by a former employee, Y, under the Equal Pay Act 1970 s.1 had been made in time. Y was made redundant in October 1996 having worked for NP in various departments since 1969, including as an analyst in the internal audit department until May 1995. Y lodged an application in April 1997 alleging that she had been entitled to the same rate of pay as two male colleagues in the audit department, as her work had been of equal value. NP submitted that the application was made out of the six month time limit because the words "employed in the employment" within s.2 (4) of the Act applied to the job on which the claim was based and not the overall employment relationship.

Held, dismissing the appeal, that under s.2 (4), properly construed, an application by an employee under s.1 had to be made within six months of the termination of that employee's employment. There was a distinction between "employment" and "work" in both sections, in that "employment" referred to the employment contract and "work" to the actual job being undertaken. It followed that the words "employed in the employment" should be read as meaning "employed under a contract of service". In the instant case, Y had lodged her application within six months of the termination of her employment with NP and it was accordingly valid.

YOUNG v. NATIONAL POWER PLC; *sub nom.* NATIONAL POWER PLC v. YOUNG [2001] 2 All E.R. 339, Smith, J., CA.

2167. Equal treatment – Council Directive

Council Directive 2000/43 of June 29, 2000 implementing the principle of equal treatment between persons irrespective of racial or ethnic origin. [2000] OJ L180/22.

2168. Equal treatment – direct effect of Art.119 EC – application of time limit on national provisions prohibiting discrimination – European Union

[EC Treaty Art.119 (Arts.117 to 120 of the EC Treaty have been replaced by Arts.136 to 143 EC).]

V, a female part time employee of DT, was disaffiliated from the occupational pension scheme because her hours of work did not reach the required level and brought proceedings under national law provisions claiming a pension entitlement equivalent to that which she would have received had she been affiliated to the scheme. The Court of First Instance granted the applications on the basis that the national provisions she relied upon embodied the principle of equal treatment by placing an obligation on the state to take action to remove existing disadvantages. DT appealed contending that prior to the judgment in *Defrenne v. SABENA (C43/75)* [1981] 1 All E.R. 122, [1976] C.L.Y. 1164 on April 8 1976 which had established the direct effect of EC Treaty Art.119 (Arts.117 to 120 of the EC Treaty have been replaced by Arts.136 to 143 EC), V could not rely on Art.119 since the principle of legal certainty imposed time limits on individuals bringing claims on the basis of Art.119 and that took precedence over the national law provisions. A reference was made to the ECJ asking whether the Community law principle of legal certainty affected national legislation which prohibited discrimination.

Held, giving a preliminary ruling, that national legislation aiming to prevent discrimination by applying the principle of equal pay for male and female workers, was instrumental in implementing Art.119 and was not affected by the time limit. It was clear that a pension scheme related to an individual's employment constituted pay, thus falling within the remit of Art.119 and the exclusion of part time workers from such a pension scheme was a potential breach of the Article. The time limit imposed in respect of pay claims based on the direct effect of Art.119 before the ruling in *Defrene* was designed to secure legal certainty and not to deprive workers of the opportunity to place reliance on their own national provisions dealing with equal treatment. Furthermore, the primary purpose of Art.119 was a social one, safeguarding the fundamental human right not to be discriminated against on the grounds of sex, an objective which prevailed over the economic aim of eliminating the distortion of competition between undertakings established in different Member States.

SCHRODER v. DEUTSCHE TELEKOM AG (C50/96); DEUTSCHE TELEKOM AG v. VICK (C234/96); DEUTSCHE POST AG v. SIEVERS (C270/97) [2000] I.R.L.R. 353, R Schintgen (President), ECJ.

2169. Equal treatment – medical profession – effect of provision reducing value of practice on sale – European Union

[Council Directive 76/207 on equal treatment for men and women as regards access to employment; Council Directive 86/613 on equal treatment between men and women engaged in an activity in a self-employed capacity.]

Danish legislation provided that the payment due on the sale of a specialist medical practice was to be determined by whether it was a full or part time practice. J, a female medical practitioner with a full time medical practice, was informed that the effect of the legislation meant her practice would be valued on a part time basis due to its level of turnover. The reason that the turnover of her practice was modest was because J had devoted part of her time to family commitments. She argued that the legislation was indirectly discriminatory because more women spent time raising children than men and the national court referred questions as to the interpretation of Council Direction 76/207 and Council Directive 86/613 in relation to the effects of the scheme to the ECJ.

Held, giving a preliminary ruling, that there had to be a separate assessment of each of the main elements affecting a significant number of persons in the relevant category for reasons of transparency. While budgetary considerations alone could not justify indirect discrimination, social policy measures could be justification for such a policy where they had a legitimate aim and determination of such matters was reserved to the Member State. The goodwill value of a medical practice was not equivalent to a pension since the time of its acquisition was not fixed and the sum received was not linked to specific payments, as was the case with a pension.

JORGENSEN v. FORENINGEN AF SPECIALLAEGER (C226/98) [2000] I.R.L.R. 726, JC Moitinho de Almeida (President), ECJ.

2170. **Equal treatment – positive discrimination – compatibility with Equal Treatment Directive – European Union**

[EC Treaty Art.119 (Arts.117 to 120 of the EC Treaty have been replaced by Arts.136 to 143 EC); Council Directive 76/207 on equal treatment for men and women as regards access to employment Art.2.]

Swedish law provided that positive discrimination could be allowed in making professorial appointments due to the under representation of women at that level. Four candidates, A, D, F, and M were short listed for a professorial post of whom D, F and M were women and A was male. A was found to be better qualified, but the post was initially offered to D. However, she declined and it was then offered to F. A complained to the University Appeals Board and the matter was referred to the ECJ for a preliminary ruling as to whether Council Directive 76/207 Art.2 prohibited positive discrimination in terms of recruitment for members of an under represented gender. Further, if there could be positive discrimination where there was little difference in the candidates' merits and there were only a limited number of posts involved.

Held, giving a preliminary ruling that positive discrimination was prohibited by Art.2(1) and (4) and the EC Treaty Art.119 (Arts.117 to 120 of the EC Treaty have been replaced by Arts.136 to 143 EC) where it required that the person from the under represented gender, having relevant qualifications, was to be chosen in preference to the person that would otherwise have been appointed. The actual number of posts involved was immaterial. However, Art.2(1) and (4) did not preclude the granting of a preference to a candidate from one gender over candidates from the other gender where they displayed equal merit and the assessment was based on an objective determination of their personal situations, *Badeck's Application (C158/97), Re* [2000] All E.R. (EC) 289, [2000] C.L.Y. 2171, *Kalanke v. Freie und Hansestadt Bremen (C450/93)* [1996] All E.R. (EC) 66, [1996] C.L.Y. 2624 and *Marschall v. Land Nordrhein-Westfalen (C409/95)* [1997] All E.R. (EC) 865, [1998] C.L.Y. 2146 considered.

ABRAHAMSSON v. FOGELQVIST (C407/98) [2000] I.R.L.R. 732, DAO Edward (President), ECJ.

2171. **Equal treatment – positive discrimination – public sector posts – legality of scheme giving women priority – European Union**

[Council Directive 76/207 on the equal treatment of women as regards access to employment, vocational training and promotion, and working conditions Art.2.]

The applicants, who included the Prime Minister and State Attorney of the Landtag of Hesse, sought review of the legality of a Hesse law that aimed to provide equal access to public sector posts for men and women by adopting advancement plans. The applicants asserted that the law was contrary to the constitutional duty to ensure that only the best people were chosen for the job and gave preference on the basis of sex in breach of Council Directive 76/207 Art.2(1), which prohibited discrimination of all forms, and Art.2(4), which allowed measures to correct inequalities where, for example, women were under represented in a particular field.

Held, giving a preliminary ruling, that it was not unlawful to adopt measures to give priority to women in sectors in which they were under represented, as the purpose of such schemes was to introduce greater equality by removing an imbalance. Nevertheless, it was important that such measures did not give an automatic priority to women over equally qualified men. It was important to ensure that all candidates, irrespective of sex, were subject to an objective assessment taking account of all personal qualities and strengths. Subject to that condition, it was lawful to adopt a plan aiming to reverse under-representation by providing in particular that a certain percentage of the academic service staff should be female and by allocating half of training places to women in certain fields. It was equally lawful to provide that suitably qualified women would be guaranteed an interview in fields in which they were under represented.

BADECK'S APPLICATION (C158/97), Re; sub nom. BADEK'S REVIEW PROCEEDING (C158/97), Re [2000] All E.R. (EC) 289, GC Rodriguez Iglesias (President), ECJ.

2172. Equal treatment – pregnancy – refusal to employ for indefinite period illegal – European Union

[Council Directive 76/207 on the implementation of the principle of equal treatment for men and women as regards access to employment, vocational training and promotion, and working conditions Art.2.]

Held, that Council Directive 76/207 Art.2(1) and Art.2(3) prevented employers from refusing to appoint a pregnant woman to a position for an indefinite period on the basis that she was prevented from working during pregnancy by statute.

MAHLBURG v. LAND MECKLENBURG VORPOMMERN (C207/98) [2000] I.R.L.R. 276, PJG Kapteyn, ECJ (6th Chamber).

2173. Equitable remedies – compromise agreements – effect on "stigma" claims owing to employer's fraud

E, former employees of BCCI, a bank in insolvent liquidation, signed form COT3 of the Advisory, Conciliation and Arbitration Service to settle "all and any claims whether under statute, common law, or in equity" arising from their employment with BCCI in return for payment. Following BCCI's liquidation, it attempted to recover loans made to E, which resulted in E bringing counterclaims for damages for "stigma damages" since, as a result of the fraudulent and dishonest manner in which the bank had conducted business, they were disadvantaged in the labour market. BCCI contended that E were precluded from bringing their claims by virtue of the COT3 agreements and E argued that the agreements were voidable on the basis that they did not know they had such a claim and BCCI had breached their duty to disclose its own breaches of the contract of employment by virtue of the implied term of trust and confidence. E submitted that BCCI was in breach of its duty by failing to inform E that it was insolvent and was carrying on a dishonest business. The questions for the court were: (1) whether the agreement should be classified as a compromise or a release, and (2) whether BCCI had a duty of disclosure under the contract of employment. At first hearing ([1999] 2 All E.R. 1005), it was held that the agreements entered into by E were valid and binding, therefore precluded E from claiming damages for breach of contract and misrepresentation. E appealed.

Held, allowing the appeal, that if read literally the COT3 agreements acted as a bar to all claims but that the literal meaning of such a document could be changed so as to reflect the intentions of the parties which must be ascertained objectively, Investors Compensation Scheme Ltd v. West Bromwich Building Society (No.1) [1998] 1 W.L.R. 896, [1997] C.L.Y. 2537 followed. There was no particular rule of equitable construction specifically applicable to releases, but the general rule of construction based on the objective ascertainment of the parties intentions applied. Equity would intervene where it would be unconscionable to allow one of the parties to rely on the strict legal construction of the document. In the present case it was not the intention of the parties that the COT3 release barred a claim based on BCCI's dishonest business conduct of which E was ignorant. To hold otherwise would allow BCCI to obtain an unconscionable advantage from E's ignorance of the facts.

BANK OF CREDIT AND COMMERCE INTERNATIONAL SA (IN LIQUIDATION) v. ALI (NO.1) [2000] 3 All E.R. 51, Sir Richard Scott V.C., CA.

2174. Fixed term contracts – teachers – fairness of dismissal on expiry – relevance of financial resources of individual school

[Employment Rights Act 1996 s.98.]

E, a school teacher, was employed on a contract expressed as being temporary "because funding is available for this period only". The school did not renew the contract when it expired, but employed another teacher to replace E. The school had only a finite sum of money from the LEA to meet its outgoings and was bound by nationally negotiated pay scales for remunerating teachers and thus had no discretion in what E was paid. The replacement teacher, being at a significantly lower point on the pay spine, cost £6,810 per annum less than E. E, who had been at the school in excess of the minimum qualifying period, claimed unfair dismissal.

Held, dismissing the claim, that the dismissal was fair, *Terry v. East Sussex CC* [1977] 1 All E.R. 567, [1977] C.L.Y. 1139 followed. The non renewal of a fixed term contract was capable of amounting to "some other substantial reason" within the Employment Rights Act 1996 s.98(1)(b) where, firstly, E knew from the outset that the contract was for a fixed period and, secondly, he knew the reason why it was limited in time. Further, given the budgetary constraints within which the school had to operate, and the non negotiability of teachers' salaries, the decision to dismiss was just and equitable within s.98(4).

EDWARDS v. SOMERSET CC, January 31, 2000, CG Toomer (Chairman), ET (Employment Tribunal). [*Ex rel.* County Solicitor, Somerset County Council, County Hall, Taunton].

2175. Freedom of movement – workers – compensation on termination of employment at employee's initiative – compatibility with EC law

[Law on Employees (Austria) para.23; EC Treaty Art.48 (now, after amendment, Art.39 EC).]

G, a German national, terminated his contract of employment with F, an Austrian company with whom he had been employed for more than three years, in order to take up new employment in Germany. G claimed a compensation payment on termination of employment from F pursuant to the Law on Employees (Austria) para.23(1) and F refused the payment on the basis of para.23(7), namely that G had given notice or left for no important reason. G's claim was dismissed by the Austrian court on the basis that para.23(7) did not conflict with the EC Treaty Art.48 (now, after amendment, Art.39 EC) on the removal of obstacles to free movement of workers since it did not restrict mobility and the amount of compensation lost was insufficient to result in a restriction of such free movement. G appealed, contending that it could not be inferred that a restriction on freedom of movement had to be "perceptible" in order to fall within Art.48, *Union Royale Belge des Societes de Football Association (ASBL) v. Bosman (C415/93)* [1996] All E.R. (EC) 97, [1996] C.L.Y. 3149 referred to. The court found that (1) there was a lack of comparable case law; (2) recent Austrian legal literature took the view that loss of compensation on an employee's termination of his employment was inconsistent with the principle of freedom of movement; (3) it was doubtful if public interest objectives could justify an exclusion from a broad entitlement to compensation, within the meaning of para.23(7), in view of the court's existing case law concerning proportionality, and (4) expressed doubts over the validity of *Bosman*. The court therefore submitted to the ECJ the question of whether Art.48 took precedence over a national law which excluded a right to compensation in respect of an employee's termination of his employment for the sole reason that he intended to take up employment in another Member State.

Held, giving a preliminary ruling that Art.48 was designed to prohibit discrimination on the basis of nationality between the workers of Member States. The legislation in question applied irrespective of the nationality of the worker in question. Furthermore, compensation was denied to a worker who terminated his contract irrespective of whether he was leaving to take up the opportunity of employment in the same or another Member State. *Bosman* was authority for the proposition that Art.48 prohibited national rules which were applicable irrespective of nationality but which had the effect of impeding freedom of movement. G had contended that the national rule in question had a comparable effect to that in *Bosman*. The legislation in question, however, would not deter a worker from terminating his contract to take up the opportunity of other employment because the entitlement to compensation was not dependent upon whether he chose to stay or go but instead upon a future hypothetical occurrence, specifically termination of the contract without termination being at the worker's own instigation or otherwise attributable to him. Such an occurrence was too vague and indirect to amount to a hindrance of free movement.

GRAF v. FILZMOSER MASCHINENBAU GmbH (C190/98) [2000] All E.R. (EC) 170, GC Rodriguez Iglesisas (President), ECJ.

2176. **Freedom of movement of workers – qualifications – recognition – Spanish educational qualification requirements – validity – European Union**

[EC Treaty Art.48 (now Art.39); Council Directive 89/48 EC on a general system for the recognition of higher education diplomas Art.1 (d); Council Directive 92/51 EC on a second general system for the recognition of professional education and training to supplement Directive 89/48 EC Art.1 (f).]

B was a Spanish national resident in Madrid. With the help of a grant from the Prado, she undertook post graduate studies in the UK, after which she worked part time for the Prado under a temporary contract as an art restorer. Under a collective agreement between the Prado and staff representatives, the post of a restorer was only to be available with a Spanish qualification or with a foreign qualification which was officially recognised by the competent body. B applied to have her qualification recognised but was refused pending her passing an examination to test her knowledge in 24 subjects. B's application for a permanent post as a restorer at the Prado was rejected on the ground that she did not meet the terms of the collective agreement. The ECJ was asked to rule on whether the provision, requiring prior validation of qualifications obtained in another Member State, infringed the right to freedom of movement for workers protected under the EC Treaty Art.48 (now Art.39)

Held, giving a preliminary ruling, that Art.39 had not been breached in that 1) Community law did not preclude a public body from making a post conditional on the candidate's demonstrating the necessary qualifications, provided that requirement did not represent an unjustified barrier to the right of freedom of movement for workers; (2) where a profession is not regulated for the purpose of Directive 89/48 Art.1 (d) or Directive 92/51 Art.1 (f) (regarding the recognition of professional qualifications and educational training), the public body seeking to fill the post must investigate whether a qualification or experience obtained in another Member State is to be regarded as equivalent to the qualification required, and (3) such an obligation is even more necessary where the public body has made a grant to the applicant to pursue those studies in another Member State and has employed that person on a temporary basis in the post to be filled.

DE BOBADILLA v. MUSEO NACIONAL DEL PRADO (C234/97) [1999] 3 C.M.L.R. 151, GC Rodriguez Iglesias (President), ECJ.

2177. Holiday pay – apportionment – method of calculation

[Apportionment Act 1870; Working Time Regulations 1998 (SI 1998 1833) Reg.16.]

T appealed against the method of calculation of the holiday pay owing to him following the termination of his employment with E.T, who had received an annual salary, contended that the Apportionment Act 1870 setting out the calculation method for holiday pay as one 365th of a year's pay for each day owing, as illustrated by *Thames Water Utilities Ltd v. Reynolds* [1996] I.R.L.R. 186, [1996] C.L.Y. 2673, did not apply. He argued that his annual salary should be divided by his actual number of working days, excluding weekends in order to evaluate the correct daily rate. Alternatively, he submitted, if the *Thames Water* method applied, then two legal errors had been made in the calculation, namely (1) that the number of days in the particular month of T's termination had been used in the calculation, and (2) that since he was entitled to 10 days' holiday, this amounted to two working weeks and he was actually entitled to 14 days' pay.

Held, allowing the appeal in part, that the 1870 Act applied since there was no express stipulation in T's contract of employment to suggest otherwise, *Thames Water* followed. However, there had been errors in the calculation since, (1) taking a pragmatic approach, the calculation should not be subject to monthly variations, and (2) the working week would be "grossed up" to a seven day week giving T an entitlement to 14 days since this was more consistent with the method employed in *Thames Water* and the policy underpinning recently enacted legislation, for example the Working Time Regulations 1998 Reg.16.

TAYLOR v. EAST MIDLANDS OFFENDER EMPLOYMENT; *sub nom.* TAYLOR v. LOWE [2000] I.R.L.R. 760, Maurice Kay, J., EAT.

2178. Minimum wage – increase

NATIONAL MINIMUM WAGE REGULATIONS 1999 (AMENDMENT) REGULATIONS 2000, SI 2000 1989; made under the National Minimum Wage Act 1998 s.1, s.2, s.3, s.51. In force: October 1, 2000; £1.50.

These Regulations increase the minimum hourly rate of the national minimum wage from £3.60 to £3.70 and make miscellaneous amendments to the National Minimum Wage Regulations 1999 (SI 1999 584).

2179. Minimum wage – young persons

NATIONAL MINIMUM WAGE (INCREASE IN DEVELOPMENT RATE FOR YOUNG WORKERS) REGULATIONS 2000, SI 2000 1411; made under the National Minimum Wage Act 1998 s.3, s.51. In force: June 1, 2000; £1.00.

These Regulations, which amend the National Minimum Wage Regulations 1999 (SI 1999 584), increase the minimum hourly rate of the national minimum wage applying to young workers who have reached 18 but are not yet 22 from £3.00 to £3.20.

2180. Parental leave – Directive 96/34 – validity of implementing Regulations – interim relief

[Maternity and Parental Leave etc. Regulations 1999 (SI 1999 3312) Reg.13(3); Council Directive 96/34 on parental leave.]

The TUC appealed against the court's refusal to grant a declaration that the Maternity and Parental Leave etc. Regulations 1999 Reg.13(3) should be rendered ineffective pending a decision by the ECJ on its validity. The Regulations, which purported to give effect to Council Directive 96/34, gave an entitlement to an authorised period of parental leave for employees with children aged five and under, but Reg.13(3) limited that right to those employees whose children were born after the date of commencement of the Directive. The TUC, which had challenged the validity of that restriction by way of judicial review ([2000] I.R.L.R. 565), submitted that parents who were disadvantaged by the refusal to grant interim relief would suffer an irrevocable breach of their Community rights.

Held, dismissing the appeal, that a request for the grant of an interim declaration to render national legislation inoperative was rare, and the court had correctly found that the TUC's arguments against the validity of Reg.13(3) had not been sufficiently strong to justify the exceptional step of restraining its enforcement *R. v. Secretary of State for Transport, ex p. Factortame (No.2)* [1991] 1 A.C. 603, [1991] C.L.Y. 4032 followed. The guidance in *Factortame* had been correctly applied by the court, and full consideration had been given to the potential deprivation of parental rights pending the decision of the European Court of Justice. In the meantime, there was a presumption in favour of the national law being applicable.

R. v. SECRETARY OF STATE FOR TRADE AND INDUSTRY, *ex p.* TRADES UNION CONGRESS [2001] 1 C.M.L.R. 8, Buxton, L.J., CA.

2181. Race discrimination – compensation – joint and several liability of employer and two named employees

[Race Relations Act 1976 s.56(1)(b).]

GB, who was born in Nigeria, succeeded before the employment tribunal in his complaint of race discrimination against his employer, DHL, and two fellow employees, S and H. At a subsequent remedy hearing, the tribunal awarded GB £3,750 compensation against DHL, comprising £2,750 for injured feelings and £1,000 for detrimental effects to GB's health. GB appealed, contending that the tribunal had failed to consider whether an award of aggravated damages should have been made. Further, that awards should also have been made against S and H.

Held, dismissing the appeal, that an employment tribunal could only order compensation for racial discrimination under the Race Relations Act 1976 s.56(1)(b). In concluding that there were no aggravating factors, the tribunal had correctly considered the authorities on the appropriateness of such damages, *Alexander v. Secretary of State for the Home Department* [1988] 1 W.L.R. 968, [1988] C.L.Y. 1295 and *McConnell v. Police Authority for Northern Ireland* [1997] N.I. 244, [1998] C.L.Y. 5150 considered. The tribunal's decision not to award compensation against DHL, S and H on a joint and several basis was founded on its decision that the conduct complained of was due to a lack of training, rather than intentional acts. It was open to the tribunal to make DHL, S and H jointly liable, with contribution to be decided between them, however the sum awarded had been paid in full by DHL and it was unnecessary to set the award aside.

GBAJA-BIAMILA v. DHL INTERNATIONAL (UK) LTD [2000] I.C.R. 730, Lindsay, J., EAT.

2182. Race discrimination – compensation – mitigation of loss in choosing to retrain – calculation of awards for injury to feelings and aggravated damages

ICTS, a security firm, appealed against findings of the employment tribunal that they had committed three acts of direct racial discrimination and victimisation against T, a former security guard, and further appealed the level of the compensatory award made to T. T had brought his claim following his dismissal after an incident in which the deputy security manager of ICTS had forced entry to the building where T was working and made allegations that he had been asleep on the job. The tribunal found that there had been victimisation, and that ICTS had conducted an unfair disciplinary hearing. The tribunal awarded T £20,000 for loss of earnings, £22,000 for injury to feelings and £5,000 aggravated damages. ICTS appealed, arguing inter alia that (1) T had failed to mitigate his loss as he had undertaken further training rather than pursuing another security job; (2) the award for injury to feelings should not have been calculated globally and was excessive, and (3) the tribunal had failed to apply the correct principles in awarding aggravated damages.

Held, allowing the appeal in part, that the tribunal had been entitled to find (1) that T was likely to have had difficulty finding a job in the security industry because of the nature of his dismissal and that retraining was, thus, a reasonable step for him to take; (2) by analogy with personal injury cases, and given the connected nature of the incidents of victimisation, the tribunal were right to take a global approach to the award for injury to feelings. The award had to be compensatory not punitive and given that the victimisation had occurred over a short period of time and that T was content to retrain, the award was excessive and would be reduced to £7,500, and (3) aggravated damages had also to be compensatory not punitive. The tribunal had been entitled to find that the actions of ICTS were motivated by a desire to catch T out and that, therefore, aggravated damages were justified, however the amount awarded was too high and would be reduced to £2,500. *McConnell v. Police Authority for Northern Ireland* [1997] N.I. 244, [1998] C.L.Y. 5150 applied.

TCHOULA v. ICTS (UK) LTD; *sub nom.* ICTS (UK) LTD v. TCHOULA [2000] I.C.R. 1191, Judge Peter Clark, EAT.

2183. **Race discrimination – constructive dismissal – minor individual instances of discrimination – policy of discrimination**

[Race Relations Act 1976 s.33.]

Throughout a period of employment of six years with A, J consistently received high appraisals, a number of promotions and substantial increases in salary. However, A appointed a new finance director, who, according to J, from their very first meeting, began a four-year racially motivated campaign to get rid of him. The individual incidents consisted of disparaging remarks and treatment in front of other members of staff, downgrading J's responsibilities and giving him less favourable assessments and much smaller increments in salary. There were also allegations of petty vindictiveness, such as making J share a telephone and preventing him from using the senior staff car park which he had been given permission to use while attending work on crutches. J contended that the actions of the new finance director constituted a policy of discrimination that began on the day he took up the post and continued until J left A, *Owusu v. London Fire and Civil Defence Authority* [1995] I.R.L.R. 574, [1996] C.L.Y. 2583 and *Cast v. Croydon College* [1998] I.C.R. 500, [1998] C.L.Y. 2200 cited. On the basis of the guidance given in *Glasgow City Council v. Zafar* [1997] 1 W.L.R. 1659, [1998] C.L.Y. 5810, the tribunal were invited to infer racial discrimination. J sought a finding of unfair dismissal as a result of being constructively dismissed following the finance director's actions.

Held, giving judgment for J, that the allegation of racial discrimination had been made out. The finance director's conduct was such that it was inconceivable that he would have treated anyone in such a way whom he did not consider inherently inferior. On the balance of probabilities, the treatment of J derived from the assumption of racial inferiority. J was awarded £20,000 for injury to feelings, although it was accepted that the instances of discrimination fell short of the seriousness of those in *HM Prison Service v. Johnson* [1997] I.C.R. 275, [1997] C.L.Y. 2242. The tribunal was critical of the fact that, although A had an equal opportunities policy, no-one who gave evidence at the hearing had read it. All the acts of racial discrimination were found to have been intentional, and most were found to have been malicious even though the discriminator may not have been aware that he was motivated by racism. As such the case was one where aggravated damages were appropriate, *Johnson* and the Race Relations Act 1976 s.33 considered. An award of £5,500 was made for aggravated damages.

JHA v. AMERICAN LIFE INSURANCE CO, January 13, 2000, Professor Rideout (Chairman), ET. [*Ex rel.* Melvyn Harris, Barrister, 7 New Square, Lincoln's Inn, London].

2184. **Race discrimination – constructive dismissal – provisions under Race Relations Act as compared with Sex Discrimination Act;**

[Sex Discrimination Act 1975; Race Relations Act 1976 s.4(2)(c); Sex Discrimination Act 1986.]

H, who was black and of Jamaican origin, was employed as a nurse by WNHS. On December 12, 1995 she presented an application to an employment tribunal, alleging racial discrimination, which was settled by compromise on May 7, 1996 On May 1, 1997 H presented a second application, alleging racial discrimination and victimisation with respect to a particular incident of non selection for training on February 4, 1997. The second complaint was dismissed in October 1997 and H's appeal to the EAT was dismissed on April 6, 1998. On October 20, 1997 H gave four weeks notice of resignation on grounds of discrimination and victimisation since March 1993, and WNHS accepted her resignation on October 23, 1997. On February 6, 1998, H presented a third application, alleging unfair constructive dismissal, particulars of which included allegations contained in the two previous complaints and a further specific allegation with respect to the promotion of a white colleague in September 1997. H alleged that WNHS had not advised her that the post had been available. It was concluded following a preliminary hearing, that (1) the act complained of was the promotion of H's colleague, and (2) the complaint had been presented outside the three month time limit under the Race Relations Act 1976 s.68. H appealed to the EAT, arguing that (1) the act complained of for the purposes of starting time was H's unfair dismissal; (2) the dismissal did not take effect until November 16, 1997 when H's notice expired, and (3) the complaint on February 6, 1998 had been within the time limit.

Held, dismissing H's appeal, that (1) dismissal was not defined within the 1976 Act and the Act had not been amended to include constructive dismissal and expiry of fixed term contracts by the Sex Discrimination Act 1986 s.82(a), as was the case with the Sex Discrimination Act 1975. The tribunal concluded that it should be assumed that Parliament had deliberately not intended to define dismissal within the 1976 Act; (2) racially discriminatory behaviour leading to the resignation of an employee in circumstances amounting to constructive dismissal amounted to "some other detriment" under s.4(2)(c) of the 1976 Act, it did not amount to dismissal within the meaning of that provision, *Weathersfield (t/a Van & Truck Rental) v. Sargent* [1999] I.C.R. 425, [1999] C.L.Y. 2091 distinguished; (3) the latest date on which the act complained of took place was correctly found to be the date of H's resignation letter and not the date the notice expired; (4) H's complaint had therefore been out of time, and (5) in absence of any material factual dispute, discretion could properly be exercised to determine the limitation point at a preliminary rather than full hearing.

HARROLD v. WILTSHIRE HEALTHCARE NHS TRUST [1999] Disc. L.R. 232, Judge Peter Clark, EAT.

2185. **Race discrimination – disciplinary procedures – discriminatory application of procedure**

[Race Relations Act 1976 s.1, s.32.]

S, a Sikh, was subject to a racial attack by a fellow employee SK, whilst attending a social function organised by his employers, ACT. S claimed he had picked up a chair during the attack in self defence, although some witnesses claimed he had used it aggressively. Following internal disciplinary hearings, both S and SK were summarily dismissed for "violence against a fellow employee" in accordance with ACT's disciplinary code. S applied to the employment tribunal complaining of discrimination contrary to the Race Relations Act 1976 and unfair dismissal. The tribunal found the dismissal to be unfair but dismissed S's allegation of racial discrimination ([1999] I.R.L.R. 683). S appealed against the discrimination finding and the Employment Appeal Tribunal set aside the tribunal's decision on the grounds that (1) ACT were vicariously liable for SK's actions, the tribunal in finding otherwise had not applied the correct statutory test under s.32 of the Act, and (2) ACT's ignoring of the fact that the attack against S was racial when considering appropriate disciplinary action against him, in accordance with their policy of disregarding provocation or mitigating factors when deciding whether an employee had used violence, did amount to racial discrimination within s.1 of the Act and the tribunal had erred in concluding otherwise. ACT appealed.

Held, allowing the appeal, that (1) the Employment Appeal Tribunal had been unduly analytical of the wording of the tribunal's decision and the tribunal's occasional use of a non statutory expression did not mean that they had failed to apply the correct statutory test under s.32, *Tower Boot Co Ltd v. Jones* [1997] 2 All E.R. 406, [1997] C.L.Y. 2246 applied. Although a different tribunal might have determined that the social function was "in the course of employment" as defined by s.32, on the facts the tribunal's decision was not so unreasonable that it should be interfered with, and (2) although ACT, in pursuing its disciplinary policy, might have acted unreasonably in not taking into account matters of provocation, in the instant case, given the racial element of the attack on S, this did not assist in determining whether they had treated him less favourably on racial grounds. The fact remained that S was unable to evince satisfactory comparator evidence to prove that he had been less favourably treated because of his race in the course of ACT's disciplinary process against him.

SIDHU v. AEROSPACE COMPOSITE TECHNOLOGY LTD [2001] I.C.R.167, Peter Gibson, L.J., CA.

2186. **Race discrimination – leave of absence denied – appropriate choice of comparator**

[Race Relations Act 1976 s.2 (1) (a).]

B, was employed by a company, TNT, as a delivery van driver. B lodged a complaint with the employment tribunal citing alleged racial discrimination, harassment, and unauthorised interference with wages. He subsequently arranged an appointment with an adviser at the local Racial Equality Council, who was assisting him with the presentation of his claim. B requested a leave of absence from TNT to attend the appointment, but his request was refused. B attended the appointment despite the refusal. When B returned to work he was suspended, given a final written warning for disciplinary matters already outstanding, and then summarily dismissed for taking unauthorised leave of absence. B amended his complaint to the employment tribunal to include allegations of unfair dismissal and victimisation. The tribunal upheld his complaint of discrimination in relation to the refusal of a leave of absence, and also held the dismissal to be an act of victimisation, and unfair. TNT lodged an appeal with the Employment Appeal Tribunal, contending that the tribunal's determination that the appropriate comparator was an employee seeking leave of absence for the purposes of consultation about litigation unrelated to his employment was flawed. TNT maintained that the true comparator would be an individual seeking leave of absence in connection with the pursuit of a claim against TNT. The appeal was dismissed and TNT appealed.

Held, dismissing the appeal, that the court was obliged to follow the approach of the Court of Appeal in *Chief Constable of West Yorkshire v. Khan The Times*, March 15, 2000, [2000] C.L.Y. 2187 and the comparator was to be identified by looking at what was requested. In the instant case the correct comparator was an individual making a similar request, namely leave of absence. The reason for making the request was not something that the tribunal needed to consider. Despite this apparent flaw in the tribunal's reasoning it would not affect the overall decision, given the fact that the tribunal correctly concluded that the comparator would be another employee seeking leave of absence and their resultant finding of fact that ordinarily, an employee making a similar request to TNT, and providing at least a day's notice, would have had their request granted.

TNT EXPRESS WORLDWIDE (UK) LTD v. BROWN; *sub nom.* BROWN v. TNT EXPRESS WORLDWIDE (UK) LTD [2001] I.C.R.182, Peter Gibson, L.J., CA.

2187. **Race discrimination – victimisation – prior claim alleging direct discrimination – carrying out protected act**

[Sex Discrimination Act 1975; Race Relations Act 1976 s.2(1)(a).]

K, a sergeant in the West Yorkshire Police force, made a complaint of racial discrimination to an employment tribunal arising from CC's failure to support his application for promotion to inspector. Subsequently, K applied for an inspector's position in Norfolk. The Norfolk Police requested a reference from CC in respect of K's suitability for the post. CC declined to provide the reference, on the ground that to do so could prejudice his case in the pending employment tribunal hearing. K amended his application to include a complaint of victimisation under the Race Relations Act 1976 s.2(1)(a). The employment tribunal dismissed K's direct discrimination claim, but the victimisation complaint succeeded. CC's appeal to the EAT against the finding that K had been unlawfully victimised was dismissed. CC appealed against that decision, contending that both tribunals had erred in concluding that he had acted "by reason" that K had brought proceedings under the Act, and by choosing the wrong comparator in considering the issue of victimisation.

Held, dismissing the appeal, that s.2(1)(a) should be interpreted in its context within the 1976 Act, as its function was to safeguard those who had brought proceedings alleging racial discrimination under s.2(1) from being victimised for having done the protected act. The "but for" test from the comparable provisions of the Sex Discrimination Act 1975 was equally applicable to the 1976 Act, *R. v. Birmingham City Council, ex p. Equal Opportunities Commission (No.1)* [1989] A.C. 1155, [1989] C.L.Y. 1371 and *James v. Eastleigh BC* [1990] 2 A.C. 751, [1990] C.L.Y. 2565 considered. If it had not been for the proceedings brought under the 1976 Act a reference would have been provided. In assessing the most appropriate comparator, the correct approach was to identify what had actually been requested, and not to look at the reasons why the reference requested had not been provided.

CHIEF CONSTABLE OF WEST YORKSHIRE v. KHAN [2000] I.C.R. 1169, Lord Woolf, M.R., CA.

2188. **Redundancy – consultation – employer's duty – dismissal to effect change in terms and conditions post merger**

[Trade Union and Labour Relations (Consolidation) Act 1992 s.188; Employment Rights Act 1996 s.95(1); Council Directive 98/59 relating to collective redundancies.]

Following a merger, M served notices terminating the contracts of employment of the employees concerned, with an offer of re-engagement on new terms to be accepted by the employees reporting for work. GMB, the union representing the employees affected, complained to an employment tribunal, contending that there had been a failure to consult with employee representatives as required under the Trade Union and Labour Relations (Consolidation) Act 1992 s.188. The tribunal declined jurisdiction on the ground that no dismissals had taken place in terms of s.188. GMB appealed, arguing that the tribunal had failed to consider the construction of the words "dismiss" and "dismissal" under the Employment Rights Act 1996 s.95(1), which provided that a dismissal occurred on a termination of employment, either with or without notice. M argued that the tribunal's conclusion had been correct, as, despite the terms of the letters, it had never envisaged any redundancies or changes in the workforce so long as the new terms were accepted.

Held, allowing the appeal, that the tribunal had failed to give effect to the unambiguous provisions of the legislation by attempting to equate them with the actual loss of jobs. However, s.188 of the 1992 Act did not require such a restricted meaning to be substituted for that under s.95(1) of the 1996 Act. The aims of Council Directive 98/59 would not be fulfilled if consultation was limited only to situations where actual job losses were envisaged. M was, therefore, under a duty to consult that arose when it sent out the letters notifying the change.

GMB v. MAN TRUCK & BUS UK LTD [2000] I.C.R. 1101, Howell, Q.C. (Commissioner), EAT.

2189. Redundancy – payments in lieu of notice – effective date of termination for equal pay claim

[Equal Pay Act 1970 s.2(4).]

D was employed by H as an education officer. On September 2, 1997 she was informed by letter that her post was no longer needed and that she was to be retired on grounds of redundancy. The letter stated that she was entitled to six months' notice of termination and that her "last day of service" would be March 1, 1998, however, as there would be no work for her to do after September 30, 1997, she would receive a lump sum payment as compensation in lieu of notice, and that the period to which that payment related would not be regarded as service for the calculation of D's pension entitlement. D's last day of work was September 22, 1997, and, following correspondence between her trade union and H, it was agreed by H that her termination would be deferred until September 30, 1997 and that the lump sum payment would cover the period from that date until expiry of the notice period on March 31, 1998. On August 5, 1998, D presented an application to an employment tribunal claiming equal pay with inspectors/advisors and assistant education officers employed by H. The tribunal found that D's employment had ended on March 31, 1998 and that accordingly the application had been presented within the six month time limit. H appealed, arguing that the words "employed in the employment" in the Equal Pay Act 1970 s.2(4) did not mean "employed under a contract of employment" but working under a contract of employment in the employment in respect of which the equal pay claim was brought.

Held, dismissing the appeal, that (1) H's argument that D's employment ended on September 30, 1997 could not be accepted. A distinction had to be drawn between cases of summary dismissal with pay in lieu of notice, when the employment ended on the last day of work, and termination on notice where the employee was not required to work out the notice period and where the employment ended when the notice period expired. In the instant case, having regard to the constant reference by H to the expiry of D's notice period on March 1, 1998 and later on March 31, 1998, the tribunal had correctly found that D's employment had been terminated on notice and that D had not been required to work out that notice. The fact that she received a lump sum described as a payment in lieu of notice did not alter the conclusion that her employment had been terminated with notice, and (2) the phrase "employed in the employment" meant "employed under a contract of employment in which the equality clause relied upon for the purpose of the claim applied". When that contract of employment was terminated, time began to run for the purposes of s.2(4), *Etheridge v. Strathclyde RC* [1992] I.C.R. 579, [1992] C.L.Y. 1933 considered and the fact that she was not physically required to carry out any duties under that contract was irrelevant.

HQ SERVICE CHILDREN'S EDUCATION (MOD) v. DAVITT [1999] I.C.R. 978, Judge Peter Clark, EAT.

2190. Redundancy – selection – fairness – failure to consider reinstatement

C was employed as a forklift truck driver by M. Other employees were required to undertake work in addition to forklift truck driving, but C was reluctant to do such work and regarded forklift truck driving as his speciality. M elected to make selective redundancies and drew up redundancy criteria without consultation with union representatives contrary to its own stated procedure. The criteria included a points grading for attitude and flexibility. C was awarded a low points rating in both areas and was selected for redundancy. He made a claim for unfair dismissal. The employment tribunal concluded that M's failure to consult with both the union and C, together with its unclear and misleading selection criteria, rendered the dismissal unfair. The tribunal also concluded that even if a proper procedure had been followed, C would still have been selected for redundancy and awarded him £350 representing his notional loss of wages for a period of two weeks. C appealed against the award, contending that consideration should have been given to his reinstatement which had been specifically requested in his originating application, and challenging the finding that he would have been dismissed in any event.

Held, allowing the appeal and remitting the case to the employment tribunal, that (1) even where a finding that dismissal was inevitable had been made, the options of reinstatement or re-engagement should not be discounted, *Polkey v. AE Dayton Services Ltd* [1988] A.C. 344, [1988] C.L.Y. 1353 applied. The tribunal had also erred in considering the facts as at the time of dismissal rather than at the remedies stage, and (2) the tribunal had erred in determining whether C was likely to have been dismissed in any event by applying the "balance of probabilities" test. C should have been compensated for the loss of the chance that he would have been retained by M, either indefinitely or at least for longer than two weeks, had M adopted a fair procedure in dismissing him, *Polkey* and *Sillifant v. Powell Dufryn Timber Ltd* [1983] I.R.L.R. 91, [1983] C.L.Y. 1348 applied.

CONSTANTINE v. MCGREGOR CORY LTD [2000] I.C.R. 938, Lindsay, J., EAT.

2191. Redundancy – selection – fairness – procedural defect cured at appeal

L was employed by T as a quantity surveyor together with one other quantity surveyor. He was advised in September 1997 that he was "potentially redundant". T, having failed to find acceptable alternative employment for him, confirmed his redundancy and his employment ceased on October 6, 1997. At his request an inquiry was held at which he was told, for the first time, of the selection criteria under which he had been chosen as the surveyor to be made redundant. Two appeals were made against his dismissal. Both appeals were by way of rehearing and L had the opportunity to challenge many points and to dispute the selection criteria. An appeal to the Employment Appeal Tribunal was lodged on the basis that a failure to declare the principles of selection for redundancy until eight weeks after the date of termination did not remedy a failure to consult. It was further argued that the employment tribunal's finding had been perverse.

Held, dismissing the appeal, that (1) a procedural defect at the dismissal stage may be cured at the appeal stage, provided that the appeal represents a rehearing, and not merely a review, of the original decision. The tribunal was entitled to find that the defect in the consultation prior to dismissal was cured by rehearing at the appeal stages, and (2) the tribunal's findings were not perverse, but were within the range of reasonable responses open to an employer to make. The fairness of the selection criteria and their application was not dependent on their being written down and the appeals were heard by parties who had previously been uninvolved in the process and who could therefore have reached a different conclusion if that had been appropriate.

LLOYD v. TAYLOR WOODROW CONSTRUCTION [1999] I.R.L.R. 782, Judge Peter Clark, EAT.

2192. Redundancy payments – agricultural workers – calculation of basic weekly wage

[Agricultural Wages Act 1948 s.7; Employment Rights Act 1996 s.221 (2); Agricultural Wages Board Order 1997.]

B had worked for WAA as an agricultural worker from June 1977 until his dismissal by way of redundancy in January 1998. WAA appealed against the employment tribunal's calculation of the redundancy payment due to B on the basis of his weekly wage under the contract of employment. WAA contended that B's gross basic wage was the total amount set out in the Agricultural Wages Order 1997, namely £160.85 less £60.32 which was paid to B's mother in respect of board and lodgings. WAA maintained that the balance of £100.53 was a week's pay as defined by the Employment Rights Act 1996 s.221 (2) upon the basis of which B's redundancy entitlement should have been calculated.

Held, dismissing the appeal, that the minimum rate of wages payable to B under the terms of the contract of employment had to comply with the Agricultural Wages Act 1948 and the 1997 Order which amounted to £160.85, namely the minimum specified by the 1997 Order. The minimum rate of wages could be partially satisfied by the provision of board and lodging under s.7 of the 1948 Act, however, such a provision did not alter the obligation of the employer to pay the statutory minimum wage.

WA ARMSTRONG & SONS LTD v. BORRILL [2000] I.C.R. 367, Charles, J., EAT.

2193. Redundancy payments – court officers – delegated responsibility – nature of employment in calculating redundancy entitlement

[Justices of the Peace Act 1949 (Compensation) Regulations 1978 (SI 1978 1682) Reg.3(1).]

BOMCC appealed against an employment tribunal's decision allowing the claims of P, a court supervisor, and G, a family and maintenance assistant, for additional redundancy payments under the Justices of the Peace Act 1949 (Compensation) Regulations 1978, following termination of their employment at a magistrates' court. At least 40 per cent of P's working time had been spent on duties delegated by the justices' clerk.

Held, allowing the appeal and remitting the case for redetermination, that the tribunal had misdirected itself in finding, for the purpose of Reg.3(1), that P's employment in assisting the justices' clerk did not need to be more than an "appreciable" part of P's duties. Such employment needed to be wholly or primarily devoted to providing such assistance. However, it was unclear how delegated and non delegated functions were to be determined as it would not have been unreasonable in the circumstances to describe P's non delegated work as "assisting the clerk".

BERKSHIRE AND OXFORDSHIRE MAGISTRATES COURTS COMMITTEE v. GANNON [2000] I.C.R. 1003, Carnwath, J., QBD.

2194. Redundancy payments – insolvency – payment from Secretary of State – effect on continuity of employment;

[Redundancy Payments Act 1965; Employment Protection (Consolidation) Act 1978 s.106; Employment Rights Act 1996 s.166.]

L applied to the Secretary of State for a redundancy payment under the provisions of the Employment Protection (Consolidation) Act 1978 s.106, now the Employment Rights Act 1996 s.166 following the insolvency of his employer, R, and received a payment in respect of the period he had been employed ending with the date on which the notice of redundancy had been issued. Shortly afterwards, L was reemployed by PGI, the company who had bought the insolvent business as a going concern, and which also went into receivership some years later. L made another application to the Secretary of State for a redundancy payment and received a payment calculated from the date when L had commenced employment with PGI. L appealed to the employment tribunal contending that the payment should have been calculated from the date when he had commenced employment with R, since there had been no break in his continuity of employment owing to the transfer of undertakings from R to PGI. The appeal was allowed and the Secretary of State appealed against the decision.

Held, allowing the appeal, that the redundancy payment made in respect of L's employment with R had operated to break his continuity of employment and the Secretary of State had been correct to conclude that L had not been employed immediately prior to the transfer and had satisfied himself, as required by the 1978 Act, that L was therefore entitled to a redundancy payment. The introduction of statutory redundancy payments by the Redundancy Payments Act 1965 aimed to provide income for an employee while he was seeking new employment and the Secretary of State's decision to award a redundancy payment had been based on the law at the time the application was made and could not be criticised merely on the basis that later developments in the law cast doubt upon that decision.

LASSMAN v. SECRETARY OF STATE FOR TRADE AND INDUSTRY; *sub nom.* SECRETARY OF STATE FOR TRADE AND INDUSTRY v. LASSMAN [2000] I.C.R.1109, Beldam, L.J., CA.

2195.   References – employers duties – extent of duty of care

K, a self employed financial services agent, brought an action against A for damages for breach of duty in relation to the provision of a reference in which A had referred to complaints received from investors and the resulting reviews of K's work demanded by LAUTRO, the relevant regulatory body. In addition, A had not answered a question concerning K's honesty. K claimed that A was in breach of its duty of care to disclose fully all relevant matters by failing to state that the K disputed the complaints and had not been investigated. K had given his notice to A after accepting an offer from a competitor, AD, which was subject to a reference. On the basis of A's reference, AD had decided not to employ K.

Held, granting judgment for A, that A did not owe K a duty of care in contract or in tort to provide him with a reference that was full and comprehensive. There was only a tortious duty to take reasonable care not to give misleading information about K, such as selective provision of information, or comment which could give rise to a false or mistaken inference in the mind of a reasonable recipient, thereby having a detrimental result for K. The nature and extent of the duty contended for by K, if imposed, would be impossible to define, and would often act against the interests of employees, as it would have to include bad as well as good points. In the instant case, the information in the reference was not misleading and not negligently provided.

KIDD v. AXA EQUITY & LAW LIFE ASSURANCE SOCIETY PLC [2000] I.R.L.R. 301, Burton, J., QBD.

2196.   Remuneration – expenses – fixed rate subsistence allowance – unilateral reduction unlawful

S paid its employees a subsistence allowance at a flat rate of £62.50. Subsequently S decided to reduce that rate and began paying all its employees at a new, reduced rate. H's application to have that decision declared unlawful was allowed on grounds that the unilateral reduction in the rate payable was contrary to the terms of the contract. S appealed.

Held, dismissing the appeal, that on a proper construction of the contractual terms, it was clear that the scheme provided for a fixed rate to be paid subject to specific exceptions. There was nothing in the contract to indicate that a general power to vary the rate of payment was intended.

SECURITY AND FACILITIES DIVISION v. HAYES; *sub nom.* HAYES v. SECURITY FACILITIES DIVISION [2001] I.R.L.R. 81, Peter Gibson, L.J., CA.

2197.   Remuneration – wages – deductions during enforced sick leave – entitlement to pay

B, an employee of KLM, had significant periods of absence from work due to ill health which wholly depleted her entitlement to sick pay. B produced a certificate from her doctor indicating that she would be fit to return to work in February 1999. KLM refused to permit B to return until such time as its own doctor had certified that she was fit to do so. A six week period elapsed at the end of which KLM found that B was suitably fit. B made a claim to the employment tribunal for unlawful deduction of wages in respect of the six week period. The employment tribunal dismissed B's claim and she appealed. B submitted that (1) in the absence of an express contractual term entitling an employer to refuse payment, an employee who presented himself as fit for work had a contractual right to payment at common law, and (2) under the terms of B's contract the refusal to permit B to work amounted to a suspension on medical grounds for which she was entitled to be paid.

Held, allowing the appeal, that (1) if an employee made himself available for work then at common law he was entitled to be paid unless a particular clause of his contract of employment stated otherwise, and (2) the tribunal reserved their position on the issue of whether or not the period in question had amounted to a medical suspension since a resolution was not necessary for the disposal of the appeal.

BEVERIDGE v. KLM UK LTD [2000] I.R.L.R. 765, Lord Johnston, EAT.

2198. Remuneration – wages – deductions to fund holiday pay – lawfulness

[Working Time Regulations 1998 (SI 1998 1833) Reg.16(1).]

D appealed against an employment tribunal's finding that W, a firm of painters and decorators, had not made unauthorised deductions from his wages. Prior to the implementation of the Working Time Regulations 1998, W operated a scheme whereby the sum of £20 was deducted from each employee's wage per week and paid into a fund which was then used to pay £40 per day for each day of an employee's statutory and annual holiday entitlement. Following the introduction of the Regulations, this scheme was replaced by a deduction of the hourly rate in order to fund the cost of meeting statutory holiday entitlement. D argued that the tribunal had erred in law in determining that W's scheme discharged its liability under the Regulations.

Held, allowing the appeal, that the tribunal had fallen into error in finding that W was entitled to unilaterally vary its employees' contractual entitlement to remuneration in order to fund the paid annual leave to which workers were entitled pursuant to Reg.16(1).

DAVIES v. MJ WYATT (DECORATORS) LTD [2000] I.R.L.R. 759, Judge David Wilcox, EAT.

2199. Restrictive covenants – consultants – extent and enforceability – uncertainty of "negotiations" in relation former employer's clients

H was employed as a consultant by ICS under a contract of employment which contained a clause restricting him, for 12 months from the end of his employment, from approaching or soliciting ICS's customers or persons with whom ICS had been "negotiating" or who were "in the habit of dealing with" ICS. H entered into discussions with a prospective customer, UTA, on behalf of ICS, but then continued to negotiate with them without ICS's knowledge and ultimately obtained their custom for his own business, which he left ICS in order to pursue. ICS applied for an injunction restraining H in accordance with the contractual clause.

Held, allowing the application, that the clause was enforceable and was not uncertain. In order to constitute "negotiations", dealings with a customer would have to involve mutual consideration of a contract that had a realistic prospect of coming into being. H's contact with UTA on behalf of ICS clearly came into this category. The extension of the clause to include those "in the habit of dealing with" ICS was also reasonable, given that a relationship with a potential customer could build up over a number of years and a consultant in the position of H could form a bond with such a customer even if he were not directly involved in negotiations.

INTERNATIONAL CONSULTING SERVICES (UK) LTD v. HART [2000] I.R.L.R. 227, Nicholas Strauss Q.C., QBD.

2200. Restrictive covenants – enforceability – standard form covenants – non specific restrictions

C was employed by W, a haulage company, as their European Operations Manager but left to work for another haulage company, SDM, which also employed several other former employees of W. W discovered that SDM was carrying out haulage work for customers who had previously used W.

Furthermore, it was alleged that during C's employment with W, SDM had been given preferential treatment over other sub contractors receiving substantial premium rates, at W's expense. W's applied for injunctive relief relying on a non competition clause and a non solicitation clause in C's contract of employment. The application was refused on the basis that the covenants were too wide to be enforceable as the clauses referred to "any business carried on" and there was no real evidence of damage. W appealed.

Held, dismissing the appeal, that the non competition clause had been made intentionally wide in an attempt to cover all possible situations and such standard form covenants were fatal to the enforceability of the restrictions, *Littlewoods Organisation Ltd v. Harris* [1977] 1 W.L.R. 1472, [1978] C.L.Y. 2941 distinguished. There had been no attempt by W to formulate the covenant so as to "focus on the particular restraint necessary in respect of a particular employee", *JA Mont (UK) Ltd v. Mills* [1993] I.R.L.R. 172, [1993] C.L.Y. 1732 followed. However, the judge had erred in finding the non solicitation clause unenforceable since that clause was restricted to the services which C had himself been engaged in providing during his employment with W and persons with whom he had dealt. Although that clause would have been enforceable, it was not in the balance of convenience to grant injunctive relief since the covenant had only three months left to run and even if injunctive relief were to be granted, there was nothing to prevent C's continued dealing with those customers already solicited, *Universal Thermosensors Ltd v. Hibben* [1992] 1 W.L.R. 840, [1992] C.L.Y. 1910 applied.

WINCANTON LTD v. CRANNY [2000] I.R.L.R. 716, Simon Brown, L.J., CA.

2201. Restrictive covenants – payment to accept covenant significant factor but not decisive

Held, that payment made to an employee to gain acceptance of a restrictive covenant was a relevant but not a conclusive factor, so that restraint still required justification by the employer.

TURNER v. COMMONWEALTH & BRITISH MINERALS LTD [2000] I.R.L.R. 114, Waller, L.J, Butler-Sloss, L.J., CA.

2202. Restrictive covenants – sale of business by founder – three year non solicitation covenant

TSC purchased ACL, a call centre management company, from M in 1996. TSC stressed that it regarded the continued presence of M as crucial to the ongoing success of ACL's business. Given the highly competitive nature of ACL's business and the fact that its skills were at a premium at that time, TSC understood that the continued success of ACL depended on the skills and abilities of the existing workforce. Accordingly, TSC insisted on the inclusion of restrictive covenants in both the share purchase agreement and M's contract of employment, which provided that for three years from the date of the agreement, or for a year following the termination of his employment, whichever was the later, M would not solicit the services of any ACL or TSC employee. M's employment was terminated by ACL in August 1997 and shortly afterwards he became a director of a new company, R. Three ACL employees joined R and in January 1998 TSC issued proceedings against M, claiming damages on the grounds that he had encouraged them to leave ACL in breach of the covenants. M's application to strike out TSC's claim was allowed at first instance and TSC appealed.

Held, dismissing the appeal, that (1) in approaching the question of the reasonableness of the restraint, it was first necessary to ascertain the legitimate interests of ACL and TSC that they were entitled to protect, and then consider whether the restraints were adequate for that purpose. The question had to be considered in view of the overall commercial bargain between TSC and M, and accordingly M's contract of employment could not be viewed in isolation from the share purchase agreement, *Dawnay Day & Co Ltd v. de Braconier d'Alphen* [1997] I.R.L.R. 285 applied. In considering the substance of the transactions, M's express acknowledgement that the restrictions were reasonable was important. Further, although the reasonableness of the restraint was to be judged in the light of the circumstances at the time it was entered into, the parties' reasonable expectations, including growth of the business, had to be taken into account; (2) ACL had a legitimate interest in maintaining a stable, trained workforce and could properly protect that interest within the limits of reasonableness, *Dawnay Day* and *Hanover Insurance Brokers Ltd v. Schapiro* [1994] I.R.L.R. 82, [1994] C.L.Y. 1927 followed, and (3) while the issue of reasonableness had to be considered in the context of the overall commercial bargain, the covenant had two clear faults: (a) the prohibition against solicitation was made without any reference to the knowledge, skill or importance to ACL of the employee being solicited, and (b) the prohibition embraced those employees who joined ACL after M had left. The fact that at the time the covenant was concluded all but one of ACL's employees was considered important by TSC was no answer to these faults, since it could reasonably have been expected that the business would expand and employ more staff who would not all be of vital importance to the company. The covenant therefore went further than was reasonably necessary for the protection of ACL's and TSC's interests and was therefore unenforceable.

TSC EUROPE (UK) LTD v. MASSEY [1999] I.R.L.R. 22, Judge Peter Whiteman Q.C., Ch D.

2203. **Restrictive covenants – solicitors – parties' intentions – reasonableness of geographical restriction**

S, an assistant solicitor, appealed against the grant of an injunction in favour of his former employers. S had been employed by H, a small firm with an established client base, but left to work at another firm in the locality as he felt he was being treated unfairly. H successfully applied for an injunction preventing S from working at the firm on the basis that he had breached the restrictive covenant contained in his contract of employment which purported to restrict S from working for a period of 12 months within a 10 mile radius of H's premises. S appealed, contending that the restrictive covenant was prima facie unenforceable and that H had not discharged the burden of proving that the restrictions were reasonably required. It was argued that the clause was too wide in that it prevented S from carrying on work of any kind as the clause did not specifically refer to working as a solicitor and that the ten mile radius was not necessary to protect H's business. It was further contended that the balance of justice did not favour the grant of an injunction and damages were a more appropriate remedy.

Held, dismissing the appeal, that the restrictive covenant had to be interpreted objectively and by seeking to ascertain the intentions of the parties and it was clear that the clause sought to prevent S from working as a solicitor rather than to prevent him from carrying out any type of work. The judge had been correct to find that the 10 mile radius was reasonable since he had particular knowledge of the area and it was open to S to work in branch offices outside the 10 mile radius. On the balance of convenience issue, the judge had also reached the correct conclusion since damages were not an appropriate remedy where it was not clear that S had suffered any loss and it was not possible for H to quantify their damage.

HOLLIS & CO v. STOCKS [2000] U.K.C.L.R. 658, Aldous, L.J., CA.

2204. **Sex discrimination – collective agreements – bonus paid to full time workers – European Union**

[EC Treaty Art.119 (Arts.117 to 120 of the EC Treaty have been replaced by Arts.136 to 143 EC); Council Directive 76/207 EC on the implementation of the principle of equal treatment for men and women as regards access to employment, vocational training, promotion and working conditions.]

K was employed on a full time basis by KE until taking statutory childcare leave from June 20, 1995. From September 20, 1995 she again worked for KE in "minor employment" classified as a normal working week of less than 15 hours and normal pay not exceeding a fraction of the monthly baseline. K requested payment to her of the annual bonus allowance for 1995, an allowance payable for public sector workers under a collective agreement, ZTV. This was refused on the grounds that ZTV applied only to persons whose employment relationship was governed by the collective agreement for public sector employees, BAT, from which persons in minor employment were excluded. The national court asked the ECJ to determine whether the EC Treaty Art.119 (Arts.117 to 120 of the EC Treaty have been replaced by Arts.136 to 143 EC) should be interpreted as meaning that exclusion by a collective agreement from a bonus provided under that agreement of persons in minor employment constituted indirect discrimination against women, where that exclusion affected a considerably higher proportion of women than men, it being common ground that the exclusion did not constitute direct sex discrimination. Furthermore, it was asked whether the application of the relevant national law in question was compatible with Council Directive 76/207.

Held, giving a preliminary hearing, that (1) under Art.119 the exclusion constituted indirect discrimination based on sex, where that exclusion applied independently of the sex of the worker but actually affected a considerably higher percentage of women than men; (2) an exclusion in respect of pay differs from a measure relating to social policy which is a matter for the Member States to determine, and (3) Council Directive 76/207 was not applicable to the present case since it did not cover pay within the meaning of Art.119 and a bonus allowance paid in respect of a worker's employment constituted pay for the purposes of the directive, *Gillespie v. Northern Health and Social Services Board (C342/93)* [1996] All E.R. (EC) 284, [1996] C.L.Y. 2570 considered.

KRUGER v. KREISKRANKENHAUS EBERSBERG (C281/97) [1999] E.C.R. I-5127, G Hirsch (President), ECJ.

2205. Sex discrimination – compensation – effect of contract based on illegality

[Sex Discrimination Act 1975 s.6(2)(b); Council Directive 76/207/EC on equal treatment for men and women as regards access to employment, vocational training and promotion, and working conditions.]

H successfully brought a complaint of unfair dismissal on the ground that she had been discriminated against contrary to the Sex Discrimination Act 1975 s.6(2)b, following her dismissal from her job as a chef when she became pregnant. However, upon discovering that her employers, with her acquiescence, had failed to deduct income tax and national insurance contributions, the tribunal refused to award compensation to H on the basis that to award compensation based on an illegal contract offended against the principle that the judiciary would not enforce an illegal contract. H appealed.

Held, allowing the appeal, that H should be awarded compensation despite the illegality of the contract since Council Directive 76/207 unambiguously guaranteed the principle of fair treatment between men and women with regard to working conditions and the court had a duty to interpret the national law so as to give effect to the Directive and provide the individual with an effective remedy. Furthermore, the tribunal had failed to adopt the correct approach in regarding the sex discrimination complaint as based on the contract of employment. The illegality concerned only the means by which wages were paid and there was no causal link between H's acquiescence in that matter and her complaint of sex discrimination. As such, there were no public policy reasons for not awarding H compensation, *Leighton v. Michael* [1995] I.C.R. 1091, [1995] C.L.Y. 2045 approved. The court expressed the view that it was not impossible that in more extreme cases a different conclusion as to whether an employee would be afforded the protection of the Directive would be reached. The case was remitted for determination of the amount of compensation.

HALL v. WOOLSTON HALL LEISURE LTD [2001] 1 W.L.R. 225, Peter Gibson, L.J., CA.

2206. Sex discrimination – homosexuality – teacher subject to abuse from pupils – direct liability of school

[Sex Discrimination Act 1975.]

P, a lesbian employed by MS as a science teacher, appealed against an employment tribunal finding that her subjection by pupils to abuse relating to her sexual orientation did not constitute sexual discrimination under the Sex Discrimination Act 1975. The tribunal had found that MS, which had taken no steps to reduce the abuse, would have been directly liable had there been a finding of discrimination. P contended that the nature of the abuse had been gender specific and accordingly was discrimination on the ground of sex. It followed, P argued, that the tribunal had erred in its finding that homophobic abuse directed specifically at her gender had not been sexual discrimination.

Held, dismissing the appeal, that P had been subjected to homosexual discrimination, not sexual discrimination, and as such there had been no breach of the 1975 Act which provided protection from discrimination on the grounds of sex not sexual orientation. Abuse, albeit gender specific, directed at a person's sexual orientation did not amount to discrimination under the 1975 Act, *Smith v. Gardner Merchant Ltd* [1998] 3 All E.R. 852, [1998] C.L.Y. 2197 applied. In the instant case, P's treatment could not be said to have been less favourable on the grounds of her sex.

Observed, in relation to the tribunal's finding that had discrimination occurred MS would have been directly liable, that the question for consideration was the degree of control an employer had such as to prevent or reduce the extent of any harassment, *Burton v. De Vere Hotels Ltd* [1997] I.C.R. 1, [1996] C.L.Y. 2587 considered. Accordingly it was recommended that the Department of Education issue new guidelines to schools, as a matter of some urgency, detailing the appropriate measures to be taken in similar instances.

PEARCE v. GOVERNING BODY OF MAYFIELD SECONDARY SCHOOL; *sub nom.* GOVERNING BODY OF MAYFIELD SECONDARY SCHOOL v. PEARCE [2000] I.C.R. 920, Burton, J., EAT.

2207. Sex discrimination – new allegation advanced at hearing – tribunal correct to decline to exercise jurisdiction

S brought an application in the employment tribunal alleging that her line manager, L, had sexually harassed her and that her employer, Z, had been vicariously liable for his conduct. S's complaint against L was settled but her claim against Z was dismissed by the tribunal which held that Z had taken all steps reasonably practicable to prevent the conduct of which L had been accused. At the hearing S asked the tribunal to consider whether Z's treatment of her harassment complaint amounted to harassment on its part. The tribunal declined to entertain that allegation. S appealed, arguing that the tribunal should have determined her allegation on the ground that she had merely been placing a different label on facts which had previously been asserted.

Held, dismissing the appeal, that the tribunal had been correct to decline to determine the claim which S had sought to introduce at the hearing. It had not been referred to in her originating application, it had not been introduced by way of amendment to that application, and her witness statement would not have alerted Z to the possibility that it might be raised. The fresh allegation was a serious one which, if established, might have damaged Z's reputation and caused it financial loss. It followed that it should have been given a fair opportunity to deal with it, *Selkent Bus Co Ltd v. Moore* [1996] I.C.R. 836, [1996] C.L.Y. 2661 applied and *Quarcoopome v. Sock Shop Holdings Ltd* [1995] I.R.L.R. 353, [1995] C.L.Y. 2025 considered.

SMITH v. ZENECA (AGROCHEMICALS) LTD [2000] I.C.R. 800, Charles, J., EAT.

2208. Sex discrimination – promotion – separate incidents – objective assessment of whole

D brought an action against her employers, PBS, in an employment tribunal on grounds of sex discrimination and unfair dismissal, following a series of sexual comments by her manager, H, and remarking that D should wear revealing clothes to an interview to be conducted by H in relation to her potential promotion. When D refused to work with H any longer she was dismissed. The employment tribunal dismissed her applications, finding that none of the alleged incidents, standing alone, amounted to sexual discrimination as D had not complained about them at the time and were not meant offensively, and that her dismissal had been within the band of reasonable responses opened to PBS as her refusal to work with H had put them in the difficult position of having to dismiss one of the two. D appealed.

Held, allowing the appeal on the ground of sex discrimination only, that the tribunal had erred in its approach. It was required to make findings of fact based on the incidents as a whole, rather than separately, and then assess objectively whether they amounted to D being treated to her detriment, taking into account her subjective attitude to the incidents and the spirit in which they were made but giving those matters their proper weight in the circumstances. It was important to remember that sexual banter by a man towards a woman often had a wholly different effect on the recipient than banter between members of the same sex. The interview incident should have been looked at in the context of all the previous incidents. The remark made by H undermined D's dignity as a woman and because he would not have similarly treated a man, it was clearly discriminatory; D's failure to complain was not sufficient to dislodge that inference. The tribunal's findings in relation to unfair dismissal could not be criticised and therefore that aspect of the decision would not be overturned.

DRISKEL v. PENINSULA BUSINESS SERVICES LTD [2000] I.R.L.R.151, Holland, J., EAT.

2209. Sex discrimination – transsexualism – gender reassignment – causal link between dismissal and gender

[Sex Discrimination Act 1975 s.6 (2); Disability Discrimination Act 1995 s.1.]

A appealed against the dismissal of her allegations of sex discrimination and disability discrimination against CC, her former employer. A, who had been born a male, had been diagnosed as suffering from gender identity dysphoria following which, she had started gender reassignment. A had subsequently been moved to another department and had then been dismissed from her employment as a probationary police officer for poor work performance.

Held, dismissing the appeal, that, although A's poor work performance was linked to the side effects of the medical treatment involved in gender reassignment, she had failed to establish the requisite causal link between her dismissal and her sex for the purpose of the Sex Discrimination Act 1975 s.6 (2) nor could her condition fall within the definition of "disability" for the purpose of the Disability Discrimination Act 1995 s.1, *P v. S and Cornwall CC (C13/94)* [1996] All E.R. (EC) 397, [1996] C.L.Y. 2536 distinguished.

ASHTON v. CHIEF CONSTABLE OF WEST MERCIA [2001] I.C.R. 67, Judge Peter Clark, EAT.

2210. Sex discrimination – unfair dismissal – qualifying period indirectly discriminatory

[Unfair Dismissal (Variation of Qualifying Period) Order 1985 (SI 1985 782); EC Treaty Art.119 (Arts.117 to 120 of the EC Treaty have been replaced by Arts.136 to 143 EC); Council Directive 76/207 on equal treatment for men and women as regards access to employment; .]

S claimed that the Unfair Dismissal (Variation of Qualifying Period) Order 1985 was indirectly discriminatory against women, and therefore incompatible with the principle of the Equal Treatment Directive, since fewer women than men were able to comply with it. The Court of Appeal referring to the Directive declared that the 1985 Order was indirectly discriminatory and stated that the Secretary of State had failed to discharge the burden of proving that there was an objective justification for the indirect sex discrimination, but were unable to grant relief as it was unclear whether compensation for unfair dismissal constituted "pay" within the meaning of the EC Treaty Art.119 (Arts.117 to 120 of the EC Treaty have been replaced by Arts.136 to 143 EC). The Secretary of State appealed ([1997] 1 W.L.R. 473) against a decision allowing S's appeal and the declaration was discharged as it did not allow S to bring an unfair dismissal claim and the appeal adjourned pending a preliminary ruling from the ECJ. The ECJ ruled ([1999] A.C. 554) that compensation for a breach of the right not to be unfairly dismissed constituted "pay" for the purposes of Art.119 and stated that the national court had to determine whether there was a persistent and continuous disparity which constituted indirect discrimination under Art.119.

Held, allowing the appeal, that the extension of the qualifying period in 1985 had a considerable adverse effect on women, because a smaller percentage of women, as compared to men were able to satisfy the qualifying period, that disparity in the effect of the 1985 Order constituted indirect discrimination, contrary to Art.119. However, the government had justified by objective factors unrelated to sexual discrimination, that the main objective of the 1985 Order was to encourage recruitment by employers. Following the judgment of the ECJ, the national courts should not restrict the wide discretionary powers afforded to the government, as that would burden governments which attempted in good faith to implement and adopt social and economic policies in order to achieve a legitimate aim.

R. v. SECRETARY OF STATE FOR EMPLOYMENT, *ex p.* SEYMOUR-SMITH (NO.2) [2000] 1 W.L.R. 435, Lord Nicholls of Birkenhead, HL.

2211.   Sex discrimination – vicarious liability of Chief Constable – social events within course of employment

[Sex Discrimination Act 1975 s.17, s.41 (1); Police Act 1996.]

S, a female police officer, complained to an employment tribunal that a fellow officer, W, had sexually harassed her during social events which were connected with work. At the time of the acts complained of, S was on secondment to the North East branch of the Regional Crime Squad, RCS, which had no statutory or independent legal personality. The tribunal upheld her complaint, ruling that W had discriminated against S in the course of his employment and that LC, as his home force and his employer, was vicariously liable for those acts under the Sex Discrimination Act 1975 s.41 (1). Section 17(1) of the 1975 Act provided that the holding of the office of constable would be treated as employment by the chief officer of police in respect of any act done by him in relation to that constable. It was argued that the tribunal had failed to determine whether W could be said to be "any other person" within the meaning of s.17(7)(b), so that the Chief Constable of LC was the officer in control. The tribunal had not considered the application of s.17(7)(b) because it had held that W and S were "persons appointed" to the LC for the purposes of s.17(7)(a), that their secondment to RCS did not alter that state of affairs, and that accordingly the Chief Constable of LC was a "chief officer of police" under s.17(7)(a). The Chief Constable submitted that on their secondment to RCS, W and S had ceased to be "persons appointed" to the LC under the Police Act 1996 and that since they were not "persons appointed" to the RCS, the tribunal had therefore erred in holding that s.17(7)(a) applied.

Held, dismissing the appeal, that the tribunal had not erred in holding that s.17(7)(a) applied. W was a "person appointed" under the 1996 Act to the LC. The argument that that appointment ceased on his secondment to the RCS was not sustainable, as the Home Office circular made it clear that all seconded officers remained at all times members of their home forces for all purposes. That conclusion was reinforced by the fact that RCS did not have separate legal status or personality. Section 17(7)(b) of the 1975 Act was limited to those officers, such as Ministry of Defence police, who were not appointed to a Home Office controlled police force under the 1996 Act. The argument that W fell within both s.17(7)(a) and 17(7)(b) could not be sustained. Although the two incidents took place away from the actual work place, they occurred during work based social gatherings. In that context they could be seen as occurring in the course of employment in an extended version of the work place, *Tower Boot Co Ltd v. Jones* [1997] 2 All E.R. 406, [1997] C.L.Y. 2246 and *Waters v. Commissioner of Police of the Metropolis* [1997] I.C.R. 1073, [1997] C.L.Y. 4150 applied.

CHIEF CONSTABLE OF LINCOLNSHIRE v. STUBBS [1999] I.C.R. 547, Morison, J. (President), EAT.

2212. Social workers – Department of Health – vires of consultancy service index

[Human Rights Act 1998 Sch.1 Part I Art.6.]

C was employed as an unqualified social worker in a local authority run residential care home. A child, S, became a resident of the home and was later fostered by C and his family. S subsequently made allegations of abuse against C. During investigations into these allegations further claims were made alleging violence toward two female partners and physical abuse of two children. C was dismissed following a disciplinary hearing and his subsequent complaint of unfair dismissal and consequent appeal were later dismissed. C was informed that his name had been included on the consultancy service index, a list maintained by the Department of Health which gave details of those individuals deemed unsuitable to work with children. C sought judicial review of the decision to include his name on the index. The application was dismissed and C appealed, contending that (1) the lack of statutory authority rendered the list unlawful, and (2) the list breached the Human Rights Act Act 1998 Sch.1 Part I Art.6 on the basis that he had been denied the opportunity of a fair hearing.

Held, dismissing the appeal, that (1) the Crown possessed all the same liberties as a private individual in this instance and a private individual was entitled to act as he or she pleased, subject to the constraints imposed by the substantive law or the requirement not to infringe the rights of others, *R. v. Somerset CC, ex p. Fewings* [1995] 1 W.L.R. 1037, [1995] C.L.Y. 3253 and *Entick v. Carrington* (1795) 19 St. Tr. 1029 considered. C had not been deprived of any qualification and there was no suggestion that any rights he possessed, such as protection from discrimination on the grounds of race, sex or disability or the requirements as to references, were being interfered with, *Nagle v. Fielden* [1966] 2 Q.B. 633, [1966] C.L.Y. 12099 distinguished. As long as these rights were observed there was no bar to the maintenance of such a list, and (2) the list did not breach Art.6(1) because inclusion of a name on the list was not in any way determinative of C's rights and responsibilities, *Fayed v. United Kingdom (A/294-B)* (1994) 18 E.H.R.R. 393, [1995] C.L.Y. 2622 and *Le Compte v. Belgium (A/43)* (1982) E.C.C. 240 applied. Information was only provided once the decision to offer employment had been taken and the nature of that information was strictly limited, leaving the decision whether to offer the position entirely at the discretion of the individual employer.

R. v. SECRETARY OF STATE FOR HEALTH, *ex p.* C [2000] 1 F.L.R. 627, Hale, L.J., CA.

2213. Suspension – local authority inquiries – reasonable cause – breach of implied term of trust and confidence

See SOCIAL WELFARE: Gogay v. Hertfordshire CC. §4890

2214. Teachers – conditions of employment – remuneration

EDUCATION (SCHOOL TEACHERS' PAY AND CONDITIONS) ORDER 2000, SI 2000 868; made under the School Teachers' Pay and Conditions Act 1991 s.2, s.5. In force: April 1, 2000; £3.50.

This Order amends the School Teachers' Pay and Conditions Document 1999, given effect by the Education (School Teachers' Pay and Conditions) (No.2) Order 1999 (SI 1999 2160), by uprating the amounts of salary and certain allowances and revising the provisions concerning the award of experience points to classroom teachers.

2215. Teachers – conditions of employment – remuneration

EDUCATION (SCHOOL TEACHERS' PAY AND CONDITIONS) (NO.2) ORDER 2000, SI 2000 929; made under the School Teachers' Pay and Conditions Act 1991 s.2, s.5. In force: April 1, 2000; £1.50.

This Order amends the School Teachers' Pay and Conditions Document 1999, given effect by the Education (School Teachers' Pay and Conditions) (No.2) Order 1999 (SI 1999 2160), by introducing new professional duties for head teachers and other teachers in relation to assessments as to whether teachers have passed the performance threshold.

2216. Teachers – contract of employment – performance related pay – adequacy of consultation

[School Teachers' Pay and Conditions Act 1991 s.2; Education Act 1996 s.10, s.11; Education (School Teachers' Pay and Conditions) (No.2) Order 2000 (SI 2000 929).]

NUT sought judicial review of the Education (School Teachers' Pay and Conditions) (No.2) Order 2000 which purported to change the contracts of employment of school teachers and of the threshold standards set by the Secretary of State to determine teachers' eligibility for higher rates of pay. The Secretary of State proposed to implement a system of performance related pay for school teachers whereby experienced teachers would be eligible for additional remuneration if they were able to demonstrate certain competencies relating to classroom skills and pupil progress. The Order purported to amend teachers' contracts of employment so as to incorporate the new scheme and an information note, which was sent to all schools and which was published in the Department of Education and Employment newsletter, set out the threshold standards required of teachers. NUT contended that the Secretary of State had (1) failed to employ the appropriate statutory procedure for altering teachers' pay and conditions as detailed in the School Teachers' Pay and Conditions Act 1991 s.2; (2) failed to consult relevant bodies in the correct order, and (3) used a consultation process that was unfair. The Secretary of State countered that he had not acted ultra vires as he had a general power under the Education Act 1996 s.10 and s.11 to administer policies that promoted education and that a four day consultation period had been sufficient.

Held, allowing the application and quashing both the threshold standards and the statutory instrument, that (1) the Secretary of State had not used any of the three statutory methods available to him to amend teachers' contracts of employment and that, in publishing the threshold standards in an information note, he had bypassed the independent review that was required when a significant and controversial change was to be made to teachers' pay and conditions of service; (2) s.2 of the 1991 Act did not impose any requirement for the Secretary of State to consult the relevant bodies in a specific order, and (3) the four day consultation period was wholly inadequate, notwithstanding that there had been a much longer general period of consultation, because the Order introduced a change that was outside the scope of previous consultations.

R. v. SECRETARY OF STATE FOR EDUCATION AND EMPLOYMENT, *ex p.* NATIONAL UNION OF TEACHERS [2000] Ed. C.R. 603, Jackson, J., QBD.

2217. Termination of employment – payments in lieu of notice – right to reimbursement on insolvency

[Employment Rights Act 1996 s.183.]

W was dismissed when her employers ran into financial difficulties. She was not paid in lieu of notice and brought an application to an employment tribunal. The tribunal joined the Secretary of State as a party on the question of the applicability of an employee's right under the Employment Rights Act 1996 s.183 to be reimbursed by the National Insurance Fund where their former employers had become insolvent. The Secretary of State made written representations to the tribunal stating that no evidence had come to light that W's employers had been made insolvent. The tribunal found that although the definition of insolvency in s.183, that a winding up order had been made, a receiver appointed or a voluntary arrangement entered into, had not been met by the evidence, it could be inferred from the fact that the company had been dissolved shortly after W's dismissal. The Secretary of State appealed.

Held, allowing the appeal, that the tribunal's decision was wrong in that it was based on a misunderstanding of the effects of company dissolution and ignored the evidence submitted by the Secretary of State which had not been countered by W. The requirements of s.183 were comprehensive. An applicant in the position of W had to prove that one of the events set out in that section had occurred in order to benefit from its provisions.

SECRETARY OF STATE FOR TRADE AND INDUSTRY v. WALDEN [2000] I.R.L.R. 168, Judge Peter Clark, EAT.

2218. Trade unions – recognition – collective bargaining

TRADE UNION RECOGNITION (METHOD OF COLLECTIVE BARGAINING) ORDER 2000, SI 2000 1300; made under the Trade Union and Labour Relations (Consolidation) Act 1992 Sch.A1 para.168. In force: June 6, 2000; £2.00.

This Order specifies, for the purpose of certain provisions of the Trade Union and Labour Relations (Consolidation) Act 1992 Sch.A1, the method by which collective bargaining might be carried out. The specified method is required to be taken into account by the Central Arbitration Committee (CAC) when, following an application for trade union recognition under Sch.A1, it is required to specify a method by which the union and employer concerned are to conduct collective bargaining.

2219. Trade unions – recognition – collective bargaining – ballots

RECOGNITION AND DERECOGNITION BALLOTS (QUALIFIED PERSONS) ORDER 2000, SI 2000 1306; made under the Trade Union and Labour Relations (Consolidation) Act 1992 Sch.A1 para.25, para.117. In force: June 6, 2000; £1.00.

The Trade Union and Labour Relations (Consolidation) Act 1992 Sch.A1 provides that where the Central Arbitration Committee arranges a ballot on the recognition or derecognition of a trade union for collective bargaining, it must appoint a "qualified independent person" to conduct the ballot. This Order specifies conditions which must be satisfied in order for an individual or partnership to be a qualified person and specifies certain persons by name as qualified persons.

2220. Trade unions – recognition – industrial action – offshore employment

EMPLOYMENT RELATIONS (OFFSHORE EMPLOYMENT) ORDER 2000, SI 2000 1828; made under the Trade Union and Labour Relations (Consolidation) Act 1992 s.287; and the Employment Rights Act 1996 s.201, s.236. In force: August 14, 2000; £1.50.

This Order applies certain provisions of the Trade Union and Labour Relations (Consolidation) Act 1992 and the Employment Rights Act 1996, relating to trade union recognition and industrial action, to employment for the purposes of activities in the territorial waters of the UK and specified areas of the Continental Shelf. It has no application in respect of ships in navigation, or engaged in fishing or dredging.

2221. Trade unions – trade union rules – membership of national executive – reserved seats

[Trade Union and Labour Relations (Consolidation) Act 1992 s.108A(1).]

H, a trade union member, sought a declaration pursuant to the Trade Union and Labour Relations (Consolidation) Act 1992 s.108A(1) that UNISON had been in breach of its rule D2.2.4 in that it had allowed S to retain her seat on its national executive. S occupied a seat reserved for low paid female members and H argued that S had ceased to be eligible for the seat on the basis that her hourly rate of pay had risen above £5.25. H contended that (1) S's earnings had been just below the level stipulated at the time of her election and that she had been dishonest to sign a declaration that her earnings would not exceed the limit during the next year; (2) UNISON had failed to make adequate checks as to the eligibility of those nominated for reserved seats, and (3) even if S had been properly elected, UNISON's decision to allow her to remain on the executive when her earnings exceeded the stated threshold was illogical. UNISON countered that S could not have been aware of any future pay increases and that the union rules should not be interpreted as strictly as a statute but construed to give effect to the underlying purpose which was to ensure female representation on the executive which was dominated by men despite the fact that the members of the union were predominantly female.

Held, granting a declaration in favour of H, that UNISON had been in breach of rule D2.24. The correct interpretation of the rule, as it would be understood by ordinary members, was that a person holding a reserved seat should cease to be eligible when their level of pay rose above the stipulated level. Although S's earnings had been below the threshold at the time of her election she no longer met the requirements of the seat to which she had been elected. Whilst there had been a breach of the rules, an enforcement order was not appropriate as S's term of office had ended and any mischief had been minor.

HILL v. UNISON, August 31, 2000, Judge not applicable, Certification Officer. [*Ex rel.* Certification Office, 180 Borough High Street, London].

2222. Training – funding of training programmes

See EDUCATION. §2000

2223. Tranfer of undertakings – consultation – liability of transferee

[Transfer of Undertakings (Protection of Employment) Regulations 1981 (SI 1981 1794) Reg.5(2)(a), Reg.5(2)(b).]

C and his colleagues were employed by a sausage production company, L. L encountered financial difficulties and receivers were appointed. The receivers intended to sell the business as a going concern if a sale could be concluded within a 14 day period. During this period there was sufficient stock to enable L to carry on trading. Ten employees were dismissed immediately and, on the same date that L was acquired by K, 10 more were dismissed. C brought a complaint of unfair dismissal against K. The tribunal held that there had been a relevant transfer to which the Transfer of Undertakings (Protection of Employment) Regulations 1981 applied and that responsibility for the applicants' contracts of employment had therefore transferred to K. The tribunal also held, however, that the dismissals had been connected with the transfer and had been carried out for an economic, technical or organisational reason entailing changes in the workforce. The tribunal found that the applicants had been dismissed by reason of redundancy and that their dismissal had been unfair on the ground that K had not offered them alternative employment. The tribunal made a protective award against K on the basis that there had been a failure to consult. K appealed, contending that (1) there had been no relevant transfer; (2) assuming that a relevant transfer had taken place, the dismissals had not occurred by reason of, or in connection with, the transfer; (3) C had not been employed by the relevant undertaking immediately before the transfer, since the employees had been dismissed by the receivers; (4) C had not been entitled to a protective award, and (5) as transferee of the undertaking, it could not be held liable to pay a protective award.

Held, dismissing the appeal, that (1) there had been a relevant transfer to which the Regulations applied and responsibility for the individual contracts of employment had therefore transferred to K. K had continued to make sausages as L had done without any interruption to production. It had sold its products to the same customers and had taken steps to protect the goodwill of the business; (2) the dismissals had resulted from the transfer. This was clearly the case in relation to those employees who had been dismissed on the day of the transfer. The reason for their dismissal was the closure of L's factory and the closure of the factory had been caused by the transfer of the business. The earlier dismissals were more problematic since it may have been the case that the business was being reorganised prior to the transfer. The tribunal had held, however, that the transfer had been the principal reason for the dismissal and that had been an issue of fact for them to determine. Having reached the conclusion that there had been a transfer, and that the transfer had been the main reason for the dismissal, the tribunal had no power to consider whether the dismissals had occurred for an economic, technical or organisational reason. Having made their findings regarding the transfer, no question of fairness arose for determination. Furthermore, since the dismissals had resulted from the transfer, redundancy payments were not payable; (3) applying the principle in *Litster v. Forth Dry Dock and Engineering Co Ltd* [1990] 1 A.C. 546, [1989] C.L.Y. 4304, the applicants had been employed in the undertaking immediately before the transfer, and (4) it had been the receivers' obligation to ensure effective consultation with the employees and that responsibility had transferred to K. The duty to consult arose from an individual's contract of employment. Such an interpretation was supported by the nature of the remedy for a failure to consult, which belonged to the individual and was regarded as part of his contractual entitlement. Such a liability fell within the ambit of Reg.5(2)(a) and Reg.5(2)(b) of the Regulations.

KERRY FOODS LTD v. CREBER [2000] I.C.R. 556, Morison, J., EAT.

2224. Transfer of undertakings – administrative receivership – hiving down – effect on employees' rights

[Transfer of Undertakings (Protection of Employment) Regulations 1981 (SI 1981 1794) Reg.4; Council Directive 77/187 relating to the safeguarding of employees' rights in the event of transfers of undertakings.]

MF went into administration. The business of MF was ultimately transferred as a going concern to FDM, through D, but there remained a question of whether the rights of the employees had been transferred thereby. Although it was common for an administrator to adopt a hive down mechanism to enable viable parts of a business to continue, the purpose of the instant scheme had been to defeat the rights of the employees.

Held, that the scheme was in effect a single transfer for the purposes of the Transfer of Undertakings (Protection of Employment) Regulations 1981 Reg.4 and liability for the employees therefore also passed. The purpose of Reg.4 was to enable a hiving down to be achieved without in any way compromising the rights of workers under Council Directive 77/187.

MAXWELL FLEET AND FACILITIES MANAGEMENT LTD (IN ADMINISTRATION) (NO.2), Re [2000] 2 All E.R. 860, David Mackie Q.C., Ch D (Companies Court).

2225. Transfer of undertakings – application of Council Directive 77/187 – European Union

[Council Directive 77/187 relating to the safeguarding of employees rights in the event of transfer of undertakings Art.4(2).]

E went into voluntary liquidation. S had been working for them for 21 years and was made redundant with 22 months' notice. He was then informed that part of E's business had been transferred to a second undertaking, A, and that S would continue his employment with A. However, this would require him to engage in different work and to be based in Brussels. S objected to the proposals and rejected his new contract with A. S claimed that E had either unilaterally breached or terminated the contract of employment. S brought an action in the Brussels Labour Court on this basis and it referred two questions regarding Council Directive 77/187 to the ECJ namely, (1) whether the Directive applied to undertakings in voluntary liquidation which transferred all or part of their assets to another undertaking from which the worker then took his orders, and (2) whether the Directive prevented a worker employed by the transferor from objecting to the transfer of his contract or relationship to the transferee.

Held, that (1) the Directive applied to undertakings in voluntary liquidation transferring all or part of their assets to another undertaking, so long as there was continued trading, and (2) the Directive was only inapplicable where the employee himself resolved to terminate his employment, and that being the case, it was for the national court to look at the reasons why S refused the contract of employment offered to him and to determine whether the contract created a substantial and detrimental change in his working conditions sufficient to activate Art.4(2).

EUROPIECES SA v. SANDERS (C399/96) [1999] All E.R. (EC) 831, G Hirsch (President), ECJ.

2226. Transfer of undertakings – continuity of employment – existence of economic entity where no assets or workforce transferred

[Transfer of Undertakings (Protection of Employment) Regulations 1981 (SI 1981 1794).]

RCO, corporate cleaning contractors, appealed against a finding of the employment tribunal that there had been the transfer of an undertaking pursuant to the Transfer of Undertakings (Protection of Employment) Regulations 1981. I had provided cleaning services to W, a hospital, and RCO provided the same services at another hospital, F. Following the transfer of much of the work at W to F, RCO had successfully retained the cleaning contract at F. A number of the cleaners at W lost their jobs as a result of the reorganisation and claimed unfair dismissal by reason of a transfer and unfair selection for redundancy. The tribunal held that the cleaning services at F amounted to a recognisable economic entity which had maintained its identity pursuant to the transfer by I as the activities had stayed the same. RCO appealed, contending that the business of hospital cleaning was a "people business" in view of its labour intensive nature and that since none of I's existing employees had been transferred, there had not been any transfer capable of fulfilling the definition in the Regulations.

Held, dismissing the appeal, that the transfer of employees was not decisive even in labour intensive areas of employment. The question of the existence of a transfer of an undertaking had to be looked at as a whole, taking all the facts characterising the transaction into account, on which basis the tribunal had been justified in reaching its conclusion *ECM (Vehicle Delivery Services) Ltd v. Cox* [1999] 4 All E.R. 669, [1999] C.L.Y. 2133 followed.

RCO SUPPORT SERVICES LTD v. UNISON; AINTREE HOSPITAL TRUST v. UNISON [2000] I.C.R. 1502, Lindsay, J. (President), EAT.

2227. Transfer of undertakings – contract of employment – entitlement to profit related pay

[Transfer of Undertakings (Protection of Employment) Regulations 1981 (SI 1981 1794) Reg.5.]

W was employed by A which was engaged to carry out a works contract for a county council. W's remuneration package included a profit sharing bonus scheme, the PRP scheme. The works contract was put out to tender and UCS was successful, with the result that W was transferred from A to UCS. W applied to an employment tribunal claiming that UCS was liable to pay profit related pay under or by reference to the PRP scheme entered into before the transfer. The scheme provided that all eligible employees employed by A during the profit period should participate in the scheme and that only those employed "in the employment unit" at the first of the month preceding the month in which payment of PRP was to be made would receive payment. An employment tribunal upheld the application and UCS appealed to the Employment Appeal Tribunal.

Held, dismissing the appeal, that (1) this issue to be determined was the proper construction of the PRP scheme having regard to the transfer itself, the terms of and the purpose of the Transfer of Business Undertakings (Protection of

Employment) Regulations 1981 (TUPE). The agreement between A and W that part of W's pay was PRP under the scheme was to have effect after the transfer as if it had been made between UCS and W; and (2) The phrase "in the employment unit" was to be construed as employment in the undertaking transferred and not as continued employment by A when the contract of employment was, as a consequence of the transfer and TUPE, to have effect as if originally made between UCS and W.

UNICORN CONSULTANCY SERVICES LTD v. WESTBROOK [2000] I.R.L.R. 80, Charles, J., EAT.

2228. Transfer of undertakings – contract of employment – substantial detrimental change – effect of notice of objection

[Transfer of Undertakings (Protection of Employment Regulations) 1981 (SI 1981 1794) Reg.5(4A), Reg.5(4B).]

H was employed by OU as an A level examination moderator. In 1995, OU indicated that it intended to transfer H's contract of employment to the AEB, a different examination board. Since the proposed transfer involved a substantial detrimental change to H's terms and conditions, he served a notice of objection to the transfer under the Transfer of Undertakings (Protection of Employment) Regulations 1981 Reg.5(4A). The proposed transfer took place, and H claimed damages against OU, the transferor, for wrongful dismissal on the basis that the inevitable changes to his working conditions amounted to constructive dismissal. OU applied to strike out the claim, contending that H had waived his right to be treated as constructively dismissed by raising objections prior to the transfer and that any liability had moved to the transferee. The application was refused and OU appealed.

Held, dismissing the appeal, that an employee was entitled to treat his contract of employment as terminated by serving a notice of objection to the transfer, where the proposed transfer necessarily involved substantial detrimental changes to working conditions. An anticipatory repudiatory breach could be accepted or rejected by H, giving rise to an entitlement to recover damages for constructive dismissal against the transferor at common law or under the Regulations. In the absence of a consensual or statutory novation between the employee and the transferee, which was excluded by Reg.5(4A) in the event of the employee objecting to the transfer, the detrimental changes could be treated as a repudiation of contract by the transferor giving rise to a claim for wrongful dismissal. Prior to the transfer taking effect, the proposed changes amounted to an anticipatory repudiatory breach, which it was open to H to either accept or reject. Due to the effect of Reg.5(4A), once H had objected to the transfer, the transfer of his contract to the transferee was not affected, leaving OU liable for the termination of his contract. The Regulations should be construed purposively in that the aim was to afford the employee with protection in the event of a transfer of undertakings, *Katsikas v. Konstantinidis (C132/91)* [1992] E.C.R. I-6577, [1993] C.L.Y. 4280 and *Litster v. Forth Dry Dock and Engineering Co Ltd* [1990] 1 A.C. 546, [1989] C.L.Y. 1508 considered. It was therefore entirely within the spirit of that aim to interpret Reg.5(4B) to the extent that an employee would not lose his right to claim constructive dismissal if the contract was terminated due to a substantial detrimental change in working conditions. This interpretation was supported by Reg.5(5) which protected the common law right to terminate and sue for constructive dismissal. The fact that H had treated himself as constructively dismissed before the transfer did not preclude a remedy, since if the change to working conditions was inevitable, it took place from the moment of the transfer.

OXFORD UNIVERSITY v. HUMPHREYS; *sub nom.* HUMPHREYS v. OXFORD UNIVERSITY [2000] 1 All E.R. 996, Potter, L.J., CA.

2229. Transfer of undertakings – contracting out – termination of cleaning contracts ancillary to main business – European Union

[Council Directive 77/187 relating to the safeguarding of employees' rights in the event of transfers of undertakings Art.1 (1).]

References were made to the ECJ posing two questions: (1) whether the term "legal transfer" under Council Directive 77/187 Art.1 (1) applied when an undertaking that had previously contracted out cleaning operations, on the basis of annual contract renewals, which were not the main activity of its business, terminated the contract and brought the work back in house, and (2) whether the cleaning work could be considered "part of a business" albeit the work was an activity ancillary to the main business.

Held, answering the questions referred as follows, that, the question whether there had been a transfer under Art.1 (1) was to be answered by reference to whether the entity in question had retained its identity following the alleged transfer, *Spijkers v. Gebroeders Benedik Abattoir CV (C24/85)* [1986] E.C.R. 1119, [1986] C.L.Y. 1362 and *Suzen v. Zehnacker Gebaudereinigung GmbH Krankenhausservice (C13/95)* [1997] All E.R. (EC) 289, [1997] C.L.Y. 2278 applied. Since the Directive could apply where a contractor terminated a cleaning contract with one undertaking and concluded, in relation to the same cleaning activity, a new contract with another undertaking, it followed that the Directive could likewise apply when that contractor resumed the cleaning activity itself. The fact that the activity was ancillary to the main business activity of the contractor would not of itself exclude the application of the Directive, *Rask and Christensen v. ISS Kantineservice A/S (C209/91)* [1993] I.R.L.R. 133, [1993] C.L.Y. 4281 applied. However, it was necessary that the transfer related to a stable economic entity whose activities went beyond one single cleaning contract, *Ledernes Hovedorganisation v. Dansk Arbejdsgiverforening (C48/94)* [1996] 3 C.M.L.R. 45, [1995] C.L.Y. 2072 applied. "Entity" referred to an organised group of persons and assets enabling an economic activity to pursue a specific objective. In sectors such as cleaning, an organised group of staff permanently assigned to a specific task might amount to an "economic entity", provided it had sufficient structure and autonomy. A high degree of similarity between the activities carried out before and after the transfer was not sufficient to hold that there had been a transfer, since an entity could not be defined solely by the activity undertaken, *Suzen* applied. The importance attached to the various factors was a matter for the national courts, however it should be borne in mind that groups of workers in labour intensive sectors engaged permanently on a specific activity could constitute an economic entity capable of maintaining its identity where a new employer pursued the activity and retained the majority of those workers.

FRANCISCO HERNANDEZ VIDAL SA v. PEREZ (C127/96); SANTNER v. HOECHST AG (C229/96), MONTANA v. CLARO SOL SA (C74/97) [1999] I.R.L.R. 132, J-P Puissochet (President), ECJ.

2230. Transfer of undertakings – local authorities – Greater London Authority

TRANSFER OF UNDERTAKINGS (PROTECTION OF EMPLOYMENT) (GREATER LONDON AUTHORITY) ORDER 2000, SI 2000 686; made under the Greater London Authority Act 1999 s.405, s.406. In force: April 1, 2000; £1.00.

This Order applies the Transfer of Undertakings (Protection of Employment) Regulations 1981 (SI 1981 1794) to transfers of staff by means of transfer orders under the Greater London Authority Act 1999 s.408 or transfer schemes under s.409 of that Act.

2231. Transfer of undertakings – public bodies – termination or expiry of contracted out services – European Union

[Council Directive 77/187 relating to the safeguarding of employees' rights in the event of transfers of undertakings Art.1 (1).]

H provided home help services and was employed by a company, M. Following the expiry of the contract, another company, A, took over the provision of the services, employing H and her colleagues. H's previous service with M was not recognised by A. On an application to the Spanish court it was held that there had not been a transfer of an undertaking according to the provisions of the Spanish legislation. In the joined case, Z was a guard employed by a company which held the contract for maintaining surveillance of the medical supplies depot of the German Armed Forces. The contract was put out to tender and the company employing Z lost the contract. The company which was awarded the contract did not take on Z and he brought a complaint that he had been unlawfully dismissed for a reason relating to a transfer. References were made to the ECJ as to whether Council Directive 77/187 Art.1 (1) applied when a public body contracted out services to another contractor on the expiry or termination of an earlier contract.

Held, giving a preliminary ruling, that the question whether there had been a transfer of an undertaking for the purposes of Art.1 (1) was to be answered by reference to whether the entity in question had retained its identity following the disputed transfer, *Spijkers v. Gebroeders Benedik Abattoir CV (C24/85)* [1986] E.C.R. 1119, [1986] C.L.Y. 1362 and *Suzen v. Zehnacker Gebaudereinigung GmbH Krankenhausservice (C13/95)* [1997] All E.R. (EC) 289, [1997] C.L.Y. 2278 applied. The absence of any contractual relationship between the transferor and transferee or between two successive contractors in the context of a public service tender, did not conclusively establish that no transfer had taken place, although it was evidence pointing in that direction. In order for the Directive to apply, it was necessary to show that the transfer related to an economic entity that was not limited to performing a single contract, *Ledernes Hovedorganisation v. Dansk Arbejdsgiverforening (C48/94)* [1996] 3 C.M.L.R. 45, [1995] C.L.Y. 2072 applied. In this context, an entity was an organised group of persons and assets carrying out an economic activity in furtherance of a specific objective, *Suzen* applied. In labour intensive sectors such as surveillance, an organised group of staff permanently assigned to a specific task could be an economic entity, provided it had sufficient structure and autonomy. The fact that the undertaking in question would frequently be subject to compliance with precise contractual obligations imposed by the tendering body would not affect the existence of an economic entity as a matter of principle. In order to determine whether an economic entity existed and if it had been transferred, the national court had to consider all the relevant facts surrounding the particular transaction. Similarities between a service carried out by a new contractor and that previously performed by another contractor did not justify a finding that that service constituted an economic entity which had been transferred between the two contractors. The identity of the economic entity had to be ascertained by reference to the workforce, management and operating methods, and not merely the activity carried out.

SANCHEZ HIDALGO v. ASOCIACION DE SERVICIOS ASER (C173/96); ZIEMAN v. ZIEMAN SICHERHEIT GmbH (C247/96) [1999] I.R.L.R. 136, J-P Puissochet, (President), ECJ.

2232. Transfer of undertakings – redundancy – identifiable economic entity

[Transfer of Undertakings (Protection of Employment) Regulations 1981 (SI 1981 1794) Reg.3.]

A company, WL, appealed against a finding of the employment tribunal that there had been no transfer of undertaking under the Transfer of Undertakings (Protection of Employment) Regulations 1981 Reg.3. WL had obtained a management contract to run a leisure centre owned by a local authority, E. Following the expiration of the contract term, E's relevant in-house department succeeded to the contract following a process of compulsory competitive tendering. B, together with other former employees of WL, was made redundant and instituted proceedings in the employment tribunal. The tribunal concluded that there had been no relevant transfer of an undertaking since there had been no transfer of any tangible assets and the majority of the workforce did not transfer to E. WL contended that the tribunal had failed to address the issue of whether a stable and discrete economic entity existed and that had it done so, it might have reached a very different conclusion on the facts.

Held, dismissing the appeal, that the tribunal had not reached an independent conclusion on the existence of an economic entity, instead it had assumed that a stable entity had existed, *Spijkers v. Gebroeders Benedik Abattoir CV (C24/85)* [1986] E.C.R. 1119, [1986] C.L.Y. 1362 applied. Although the tribunal's findings had been reached without having severally addressed the two relevant questions separately, namely (1) existence of a stable and discrete economic entity, and (2) whether there had been a relevant transfer, the tribunal would inevitably have reached the same conclusion had it addressed the issue in the appropriate manner, *Betts v. Brintel Helicopters Ltd (t/a British International Helicopters)* [1997] 2 All E.R. 840, [1997] C.L.Y. 2270 applied.

WHITEWATER LEISURE MANAGEMENT LTD v. BARNES [2000] I.C.R. 1049, Burton, J., EAT.

2233. Transfer of undertakings – subsidiary companies – re engagement on less favourable terms – European Union

[Council Directive 77/187 relating to the safeguarding of employees' rights in the event of transfers of undertakings.]

An employment tribunal sought a ruling from the ECJ as to whether Council Directive 77/187 applied to a transfer between two subsidiary companies with the same management and ownership. ACC and AMS, although two distinct legal entities, were owned and managed by the same corporation, AMCO, however AMS's terms of employment were less favourable. In 1994, ACC won mine working contracts which it subcontracted to AMS prior to the eventual dismissal of a number of its employees, including A. A was shortly engaged by AMS. ACC, following concern over AMS's employment terms and conditions, withdrew the subcontract and re-engaged A on terms better than he had had at AMS, but worse than those he had previously enjoyed during his employment with ACC. A, claiming entitlement to his earlier conditions of employment, contended that his rights were protected under the Directive since the two transfers constituted a transfer of undertaking. ACC submitted that no transfer had taken place.

Held, ruling in favour of A, that Directive 77/187 could apply to a transfer between two subsidiary companies as long as it involved a transfer of some "economic entity", in the sense of an organised group of persons and assets working toward a given objective. The Directive required there to be a natural or legal change in the person of the employer, regardless of whether or not ownership of the undertaking was transferred, so that shared management and ownership did not preclude the transfer of an economic entity.

ALLEN v. AMALGAMATED CONSTRUCTION CO LTD (C234/98) [2000] All E.R. (EC) 97, DAO Edward (President), ECJ.

2234. Transfer of undertakings – tortious liability – transfer of employee's cause of action

[Transfer of Undertakings (Protection of Employment) Regulations 1981 (SI 1981 1794); Council Directive 77/187 relating to the safeguarding of employees' rights in the event of transfers of undertakings.]

M commenced proceedings for damages for negligence in respect of injuries suffered at work against his employer, LCC. LCC transferred their waste disposal business and refuse service to LWS. LCC claimed that M had a cause of action against LWS, as M's rights against LCC had been transferred to LWS by virtue of the Transfer of Undertakings (Protection of Employment) Regulations 1981. The judge ruled that the Regulations did not transfer tortious liability from LCC to LWS. LCC appealed.

Held, allowing the appeal, that LCC's tortious liability had been transferred to LWS by virtue of the Regulations. The rights and obligations fell within the ambit of liability, as it was liability "in connection with" a contract of employment within the meaning of Reg.5(2)(a). The wording of Reg.5(2)(a) could be widely interpreted to encompass tortious rights and liabilities, as it did not restrict the rights to those of a contractual nature. Alternatively, a liability could be construed as falling within the meaning of an obligation arising from an employment relationship or contract within the meaning of the Council Directive 77/187. The relevant provisions of the Directive could be construed purposively to enable M not to be deprived of benefits which he would otherwise have enjoyed, but for the transfer. In a joined case, the primary issue in respect of whether liability in tort had transferred was determined in the same manner as above, however, it was found that a transferor's rights to indemnity under an employers' liability insurance effected by the transferor were also transferred by the Regulations.

MARTIN v. LANCASHIRE CC; BERNADONE v. PALL MALL SERVICES GROUP LTD; HARINGEY HEALTHCARE NHS TRUST v. INDEPENDENT INSURANCE LTD [2000] 3 All E.R. 544, Peter Gibson, L.J., CA.

2235. Transport Salaried Staffs'Association (Amendment of Rules) Act 2000 (c.v)

This Act amends the rules of the Transport Salaried Staffs' Association so that income which would otherwise be applied to the Provident Benefit Fund may be applied by the Association from time to time to meet expenses other than the application of provident benefits.

This Act received Royal Assent on March 9, 2000 and comes into force on March 9, 2000.

2236. Unfair dismissal – employment status – introduction of reformulated claim – estoppel

[Sex Discrimination Act 1975 s.9.]

E appealed against a decision of the employment tribunal on a preliminary issue relating to the status of T's employment. The tribunal had dismissed T's claim for unfair dismissal having found that she was not an employee, but had alerted her to her right to bring a claim as a contract worker under the Sex Discrimination Act 1975 s.9. E contended that (1) the tribunal's jurisdiction was limited to the issues presented to it; (2) the introduction of a claim under s.9 effectively raised a new issue whichT should be estopped from pursuing since her unfair dismissal claim had already been dismissed; (3) the s.9 issue had been raised outside the three month time limit applicable to claims for unfair dismissal and was therefore time barred, and (4) the introduction of the s.9 issue at the end of the hearing was contrary to natural justice, since E was given no opportunity to deal with the matter and suffered prejudice in that, whereas it had succeeded on the points to be determined by the tribunal, T had been allowed to proceed to a final hearing.

Held, dismissing the appeal, that (1) the introduction of the s.9 issue was merely a different formulation of the dismissal claim originally brought and therefore did not constitute a new factual element in the case. The jurisdiction of the tribunal had therefore not been exceeded, *Chapman v. Simon* [1994] I.R.L.R. 124, [1994] C.L.Y. 1967 distinguished; (2) the claim under s.9 was introduced during the currency of the proceedings even though the hearing had in fact been completed. Accordingly, the principle of estoppel did not apply, *Divine-Bortey v. Brent LBC* [1998] I.C.R. 886, [1998] C.L.Y. 2163 distinguished; (3) the three month time limit was not relevant since no new factual elements were being introduced outside this period, and (4) on the issue of natural justice, it was necessary to balance the question of prejudice between the parties. E had been prejudiced by having had no opportunity to respond to the issue raised at the end of the preliminary hearing, but, if the claim proved to be sound, T would be substantially prejudiced by being prevented from pursuing it. Such prejudice would far outweigh the prejudice suffered by E, who would have the opportunity to prepare a defence prior to the substantive hearing.

ELTEK (UK) LTD v. THOMSON [2000] I.C.R. 689, Lord Johnston, EAT.

2237. Unfair dismissal – employment tribunals – approach to reasonableness

[Employment Rights Act 1996 s.98.]

H and PO, employers of M and F respectively, appealed against decisions of the EAT ([2000] 2 All E.R. 741) and (Unreported, April 16, 1998) respectively, upholding complaints of unfair dismissal. PO and H contended that the EAT had erred in its approach to the reasonableness or unreasonableness of an employee's dismissal.

Held, allowing the appeals, that an employment tribunal should not employ its own view of what it would have done had it been the employer when considering the reasonableness of a dismissal under the Employment Rights Act 1996 s.98, *Haddon v. Van Den Bergh Foods Ltd* [1999] I.C.R. 1150, [2000] C.L.Y. 2239 overruled, but should continue to apply the approach laid out in *Iceland Frozen Foods Ltd v. Jones* [1983] I.C.R. 17, [1983] C.L.Y. 1325, namely, to consider whether the dismissal was within the band or range of reasonable responses which a reasonable employer would adopt, *Iceland* applied. Where dismissal was based on belief of an employee's misconduct, tribunals should continue to apply the approach followed in *British Home Stores Ltd v. Burchell* [1980] I.C.R. 303, [1980] C.L.Y. 1004 as approved in *W Weddel & Co v. Tepper* [1980] I.C.R. 286, [1980] C.L.Y. 1005, namely, to determine whether an employer had reasonable grounds to sustain a belief of misconduct and whether that employer had carried out as much investigation as was reasonable in the circumstances, *Burchell* approved and *Weddell* followed. In relation to M, the tribunal had erred in substituting itself in place of H when evaluating the quality and weight of evidence which sustained the belief of M's involvement in misappropriation. In the case of F, the EAT had been wrong to reverse the decision of the tribunal which had determined that PO did have a reason to dismiss F related to his conduct within s.98(2)(b) and that PO had acted reasonably in treating that conduct as a reason for dismissal.

FOLEY v. POST OFFICE; HSBC BANK PLC (FORMERLY MIDLAND BANK PLC) v. MADDEN; *sub nom.* POST OFFICE v. FOLEY [2001] 1 All E.R. 550, Mummery, L.J., CA.

2238. Unfair dismissal – gross misconduct – summary dismissal – blameworthy conduct

[Employment Rights Act 1996 s.122(2), s.123(6).]

K, head of O's screen printing department, was allowed to carry out his own private printing work using O's premises and facilities, providing that he only did so outside working hours and paid for any materials used. K had been warned about past breaches of these conditions, but subsequently instructed another employee to assist him with a private job during working hours. Although the work only took approx five minutes and cost £2 in materials he was summarily dismissed for gross misconduct. K's complaint to an employment tribunal that he had been unfairly dismissed was upheld on the ground that no reasonable employer would have summarily dismissed for such a minor breach of the conditions regarding private work. K was awarded £10,575.66 compensation for unfair dismissal, including £7,635.66 as a compensatory award. O appealed against the tribunal's finding on the issue of the reduction of the basic and compensatory awards on account of K's conduct.

Held, allowing the appeal in part, that for the purposes of reducing the basic and compensatory awards by reason of a K's contributory conduct in accordance with the Employment Rights Act 1996 s.122(2) and s.123(6), the tribunal first had to satisfy itself that K was guilty of blameworthy conduct. Such an inquiry must be directed solely at his conduct and not that of O. If blameworthy conduct causing the dismissal was found then the tribunal was obliged under s.123(6) to reduce the compensatory award. It did not have the option of choosing not to reduce the award, *Parker Foundry Ltd v. Slack* [1992] I.C.R. 302, [1992] C.L.Y. 1989 applied. By contrast, in relation to reductions to the basic award by reason contributory conduct, the tribunal had a wide discretion under s.122(2) as to whether to make any reduction and the authorities showed that different proportionate reductions could be made to the basic and compensatory awards, *Parker Foundry Ltd* and *Rao v. Civil Aviation Authority* [1994] I.R.L.R. 240, [1992] C.L.Y. 1985 considered. Similarly, the tribunal had no power to rule that K's causative contributory conduct was overridden by the grossly disproportionate reaction of O. In relation to the wider discretion applying to reductions to the basic award, on the facts, the tribunal had been entitled to find that it was equitable that no reduction should be made to the basic award by reason of K's contributory conduct. Taking into account the tribunal's finding that K's contributory conduct was of a minor nature, a 20 per cent reduction to the compensatory award would be made under s.123(6).

OPTIKINETICS LTD v. WHOOLEY [1999] I.C.R. 984, Judge Peter Clark, EAT.

2239. Unfair dismissal – gross misconduct – summary dismissal – test for determining reasonableness of decision

[Employment Rights Act 1996 s.98(4).]

H, a technical operator with VDBF, was invited to attend a ceremony to mark his 15 years' service with the company. On the day of the ceremony, H was rostered to work a shift commencing at 2.00 pm and finishing at 10.00 pm. The ceremony was to begin at 5.15 pm and conclude at 7.30 pm. A week before the ceremony G, a manager, told H that he would be required to complete his shift after the ceremony because of staffing problems. Another manager said later that most people did not return to work because they had usually had something to drink, but that H should sort out the matter with G. H did not speak to G about it again. H drank at the ceremony and decided not to return to work. He was then summarily dismissed for gross misconduct and complained to an employment tribunal that he had been unfairly dismissed. The tribunal, although recognising the harshness of the decision and that few reasonable employers would have taken such action, nevertheless regarded itself as bound to hold that the dismissal was fair under the reasonable responses test and in light of VDBF's disciplinary rules. H appealed, contending that the tribunal erred by applying the reasonable responses test given the clear words of the Employment Rights Act 1996 s.98(4).

Held, allowing the appeal but finding H liable on the basis 25 per cent contributory fault, that (1) in deciding whether a particular dismissal was unfair, the tribunal had to consider the reasonableness of the decision to dismiss under s.98(4) having regard to the equity and substantial merits of the particular case. Whilst it had to recognise that its own views might not accord with what was "reasonable", it was not sufficient to answer the question by stating that it would not have dismissed in the circumstances. The tribunal's task was essentially that of an "industrial jury" and it was perfectly proper to begin to assess the reasonableness of the decision by asking themselves what they would have done in the circumstances. They must then determine as a matter of fact and an object basis, the reasonableness of the employer's decision to treat the particular conduct as sufficient to dismiss, *Bessenden Properties Ltd v. Corness* [1974] I.R.L.R. 338, [1975] C.L.Y. 1178 and *Grundy (Teddington) v. Willis* [1976] I.C.R. 323, [1976] C.L.Y. 1002 applied; (2) the reasonable responses test was not helpful in this context because it had resulted in tribunals applying what amounted to a test of perversity before being prepared to make a finding of unfair dismissal, *Rolls Royce Ltd v. Walpole* [1980] I.R.L.R. 343, [1980] C.L.Y. 1025, *British Leyland (UK) Ltd v. Swift* [1981] I.R.L.R. 91, [1981] C.L.Y. 945 and *Iceland Frozen Foods Ltd v. Jones* [1983] I.C.R. 17, [1983] C.L.Y. 1325 considered. Tribunals should simply ask, as a question of fact, whether the employer acted reasonably or unreasonably, *Gilham v. Kent CC (No.2)* [1985] I.C.R. 233, [1985] C.L.Y. 1259 applied, and (3) in the instant case, the tribunal erred in applying a test of perversity in judging whether H's dismissal was fair. The reference to "equity" in s.98(4) required a consideration of the matter from the employee's point of view, which the tribunal had failed to do in the instant case.

HADDON v. VAN DEN BERGH FOODS LTD [1999] I.C.R. 1150, Morison, J., EAT.

2240. **Unfair dismissal – misconduct – first breach of discipline – reasonable response test**

B was dismissed by his employer, W, following a fight with another employee. His claim of unfair dismissal was dismissed but his claim of wrongful dismissal was allowed. B appealed, arguing that the tribunal had erred in finding that W had reasonable grounds for dismissal and in ignoring the ACAS Code of Practice which stated that dismissal should not result from a first breach of discipline unless it was accompanied by gross misconduct.

Held, dismissing the appeal, that despite a recent somewhat confusing line of authority, it was still the case that a tribunal was not permitted to substitute its own opinion of what an employer should have done at the time of dismissal and was required to look at whether the employer's conduct fell within the "band of reasonable responses", *Iceland Frozen Foods Ltd v. Jones* [1983] I.C.R. 17, [1983] C.L.Y. 1325 applied. In assessing reasonableness, it was necessary to find that an employer had "reasonable grounds based on a reasonable investigation", *Gilham v. Kent CC (No.2)* [1985] I.C.R. 233, [1985] C.L.Y. 1259 applied. In the instant case, the tribunal had applied the appropriate tests correctly and was entitled to reach the conclusion that it had. Its failure to mention the ACAS Code of Practice was of no consequence, since W's disciplinary procedure specifically stated that violent behaviour could lead to dismissal, *Lock v. Cardiff Railway Co Ltd* [1998] I.R.L.R. 358, [1998] C.L.Y. 2235 distinguished.

BEEDELL v. WEST FERRY PRINTERS LTD [2000] I.C.R. 1263, Judge Peter Clark, EAT.

2241. **Unfair dismissal – termination of employment – abusive behaviour from another employee – "danger" to cover acts of employees**

[Employment Rights Act 1996 s.100(1)(d); Council Directive 89/391 on the introduction of measures to encourage improvements in the safety and health of workers at work.]

M worked as a nightshift machine minder with one other person, H. Following abusive behaviour towards him by H, M, fearing for his personal safety left the workplace in the middle of his shift and immediately thereafter telephoned his manager reporting the incident. He subsequently reported the matter to a more senior manager, saying his return to work was contingent on the receipt of an assurance about his safety, which in effect meant the removal or dismissal of H. The account of the incident given by H was accepted by his employer, HP, which claimed that M had resigned by walking out in the middle of a shift. M's claim for unfair dismissal was upheld by an employment tribunal under the Employment Rights Act 1996 s.100(1)(d). Under that provision an employee is regarded as having been unfairly dismissed if the reason for his dismissal is that he left a place of work in circumstances where he reasonably believed there was a serious or imminent danger. HP, the employer, appealed to the Employment Appeal Tribunal, claiming that M had not been dismissed but had resigned as the company had not complied with his ultimatum that H should be moved. The company further submitted that the word "danger" in the Act was limited to dangers relating to circumstances of the workplace itself and did not include dangers caused by an individual action of a fellow employee.

Held, dismissing the appeal, that (1) the tribunal was correct in concluding that M had been dismissed and there was no arguable point of law. He had sought to secure his employment by persuading HP to take appropriate action with regard to H so as to make his place of work safe, and (2) having regard to Council Directive 89/391, it was clear that Parliament, in enacting the 1996 Act intended the word "danger" to be construed without limitation and was intended to cover any danger, however it arose.

HARVEST PRESS LTD v. McCAFFREY [1999] I.R.L.R. 778, Morison, J., EAT.

2242. Unfair dismissal – time limits – failure of internal appeal – effective date of termination

[Employment Rights Act 1996 s.111 (2).]

D, a teacher with 18 years service, was dismissed for gross misconduct following allegations of improper behaviour towards six female pupils. A letter dated February 17 informed D that he was summarily dismissed. D appealed but on March 13 the appeal was dismissed. On June 11, D presented an originating application to the employment tribunal claiming unfair dismissal citing March 13 as his last working day, a date within the three month period limitation period imposed by the Employment Rights Act 1996 s.111 (2). An employment tribunal and subsequently the Employment Appeal Tribunal held in the employer's favour that the date the employment ended was February 17, when D had been informed of his summary dismissal and not March 13, when his appeal was dismissed. D appealed.

Held, allowing the appeal, that the effective date of termination was the date of the appeal. It was clear that D had been suspended with the possibility of his dismissal not being confirmed, rather than summarily dismissed with a possibility of reinstatement. The fact that his salary had paid until the date of the appeal was strong evidence in support of that finding, *J Sainsbury Ltd v. Savage* [1981] I.C.R. 1, [1981] C.L.Y. 968 distinguished as involving a different contractual scheme and *Cook v. Ministry of Defence* (Unreported, May 14, 1984) distinguished because in that case the employee had received his National Insurance card, no pay and been told he was free to take up other employment forthwith.

DRAGE v. GOVERNING BODY OF GREENFORD HIGH SCHOOL; *sub nom.* DRAGE v. GOVERNORS OF GREENFORD HIGH SCHOOL [2000] I.C.R. 899, Simon Brown, L.J., CA.

2243. Unfair dismissal – time limits – misrepresentation – unsatisfactory reference provided outside three month period

[Employment Rights Act 1996 s.111 (2) (a).]

S, an employee of PO, was investigated by the police in relation to items he had purchased from a jeweller, but no action was taken against him. At a subsequent meeting with PO, at which S's union representative was present, S alleged that he was told PO intended to dismiss him, but if he chose to resign he would be given a satisfactory reference. Six months later a job offer that had been made to him was revoked because the reference provided by PO was not acceptable. S made a claim to the employment tribunal for unfair dismissal. The tribunal, after hearing evidence only from S, held that S's claim was not time barred even though it was made outside the three month time limit prescribed by the Employment Rights Act 1996 s.111 (2) (a), because S had believed that he had an agreement with PO and it was only when the unsatisfactory reference was given that he realised he had a possible claim for unfair dismissal. PO appealed contending that (1) the tribunal should not have decided the jurisdictional issue on the basis of S's evidence alone as PO disputed S's version of events, and (2) the tribunal had not applied the test set out in *Machine Tool Industry Research Association v. Simpson* [1988] I.C.R. 558, [1988] C.L.Y. 1355, which was authority for the proposition that whilst it was reasonable for S not to have been aware that the reference was unsatisfactory within the three month time limit. Nevertheless as at the date of his dismissal he had knowledge of all necessary facts upon which to contend that he had been dismissed, and the knowledge that he subsequently acquired concerning the content of the reference was not an essential element of his decision to bring a claim, neither did it bring about a change in his opinion that he could do so.

Held, quashing the decision and remitting the case, that (1) the tribunal erred in basing its decision on S's evidence alone since the factual dispute was crucial to the resolution of the jurisdictional issue. The words "reasonably practicable" in the Act required a test of fact not of reasonableness and matters concerning which the applicant was mistaken or ignorant related to knowledge of the right to bring a claim, not knowledge as to the likely merits of any such claim, *London Underground Ltd v. Noel* [2000] I.C.R. 109, [1999] C.L.Y. 2146 considered. Whilst the test set out in *Machine Tools* and *Noel* and guidance in other authorities was helpful, it should not be rigidly applied in place of the statutory test which was clear and in ordinary language, *Sevenoaks Stationers (Retail) Ltd, Re* [1991] Ch. 164, [1991] C.L.Y. 401 applied, and (2) S's claim was based upon the allegation that PO had made a fraudulent misrepresentation to him in relation to the reference at the time that he left his employment. It was arguable that such a misrepresentation was capable of rendering S's resignation a dismissal by PO. Therefore, on S's version of the facts, the giving of the reference was the crucial event which gave rise to his knowledge of his right to make a claim, since until that point he had had no reason to believe that the representation made by PO was false. As PO denied ever having made the representation, the jurisdictional issue could only be resolved by a finding on the factual issue of whether the representation was made, which necessarily required hearing evidence from both parties. Such a disputed issue of fact should not be left until the final hearing of the substantive claim because if S was found not to be telling the truth that would be decisive of his claim as a whole.

POST OFFICE v. SANHOTRA [2000] I.C.R. 866, Charles, J., EAT.

2244. Unfair dismissal – waiver – extensions of fixed term contract

[Employment Rights Act 1996 s.95(1)(b), s.197.]

B was employed by CWH under a fixed term contract of three years' duration. The contract provided for the waiver of B's right to claim unfair dismissal in the event of its non renewal. Upon the expiry of the fixed term, B's employment was extended on several occasions for periods which varied in length. Each of CWH's letters offering B an extension to his contract incorporated a waiver clause. In proceedings issued by B, the Employment Appeal Tribunal found ([1998] I.C.R. 576, [1997] C.L.Y. 2198) that B had waived his right to claim unfair dismissal by virtue of the Employment Rights Act 1996 s.197(1) which provided that an employee could waive his right to claim unfair dismissal in the case of the non renewal of "a contract for a fixed term of one year or more". B appealed arguing that s.197(1) should be construed so as to limit its application to the initial fixed term of his contract with the result that the extensions to his contract were outside its ambit.

Held, dismissing the appeal, that the court was bound by the decision in *BBC v. Kelly-Phillips* [1998] 2 All E.R. 845, [1998] C.L.Y. 2151 followed. The Court of Appeal in *Kelly-Phillips* had been right to conclude that s.197(1) was to be construed in the light of s.95(1)(b) which recognised the possibility of an extension to the fixed term of a contract "under the same contract", that s.95(1)(b) applied to any extension of the initial term of a contract on identical, or substantially identical, terms to that contract, and that it was not necessary that the extension should be effected pursuant to a provision in the initial contract. Such a conclusion was supported by the terms of s.197(3) and (5). Furthermore, it was sometimes necessary when construing statutory provisions to take a common sense approach. In the instant case, it was clear that B's initial contract had been extended and that the extensions to that contract did not constitute new contracts, *BBC v. Ioannou* [1975] Q.B. 781, [1975] C.L.Y. 1091 applied.

BHATT v. CHELSEA AND WESTMINSTER HEALTHCARE NHS TRUST (UNFAIR DISMISSAL) A1/97/1378, Buxton, L.J., CA.

2245. Vicarious liability – employees offering secret commission as bribes

See TORTS: Petrotrade Inc v. Smith (Vicarious Liability). §5105

2246. Wrongful dismissal – public health – employee's right to take steps to protect public

[Employment Rights Act 1996 s.100(1)(e); Council Directive 89/391 on the introduction of measures to encourage improvements in the safety and health of workers at work.]

M, who had been employed as a chef by C for just over a month, left the restaurant premises having refused to cook chicken which he considered was a health hazard to the customers. His subsequent claim for wrongful dismissal was rejected by an employment tribunal. He appealed to the Employment Appeal Tribunal on the basis that he had been dismissed for taking steps "to protect other persons from danger" as referred to in the Employment Rights Act 1996 s.100(1)(e) and that the tribunal should not have limited that phrase to a reference to other employees. He also appealed against the tribunal's finding that he did not have the requisite period of employment to entitle him to any statutory notice period.

Held, allowing the appeal and remitting the case to a fresh employment tribunal, that (1) in the absence of any limitation to "other workers" or other "persons employed" the expression "other persons" in s.100(1)(e) extended to members of the public, particularly having regard to the general aim behind Council Directive 89/391 to improve health and safety provisions in the work place; (2) no period of continuous employment was required for the common law claim of damages for wrongful dismissal. At common law there was implied into every contract of employment, a term giving every employee reasonable notice of termination in the absence of any express term as to notice, and (3) whether the alleged danger perceived by M was "serious and imminent" as required by s.100(1)(e) had to be judged by reference to "all the circumstances" and as such could not be determined on the basis of pleadings alone.

MASIAK v. CITY RESTAURANTS (UK) LTD [1999] I.R.L.R. 780, Judge Peter Clark, EAT.

2247. Wrongful dismissal – summary dismissal – failure to give adequate notice under contract

R was employed by CS under the terms of a contract terminable on six months' notice by either party, with a provision allowing CS to make a payment in lieu of notice. CS summarily dismissed R without making any payment in lieu of notice. R obtained new employment at a higher rate of pay five weeks later and brought an action against CS for wrongful dismissal. The employment tribunal held that he had been wrongfully dismissed. CS argued that R was under a duty to mitigate his loss and that CS were entitled to the benefit of the fact that R had obtained new employment at a higher salary within two months of his summary dismissal. The tribunal rejected this argument, holding that, where an employment contract expressly provided for summary termination on payment of salary in lieu of notice, a summary dismissal accompanied by such payment was a lawful act and not a breach of contract. It followed that a claim in respect of a failure to make such a payment was a claim for a sum due under the contract rather than a claim for damages for wrongful dismissal, and the duty to mitigate loss did not apply in those circumstances. CS appealed, arguing that the contract did not give R a right to payment in lieu, but rather gave CS an option to make such a payment if it chose. In the instant case, it had chosen instead to wrongfully dismiss R, whereupon R was entitled to bring a claim for damages but the normal rules concerning mitigation of loss applied so that R had to give credit for sums earned in his new employment.

Held, dismissing the appeal, that the tribunal had correctly decided that R was not under a duty to mitigate his loss. A summary dismissal by an employer on payment of a sum in lieu of notice in reliance on an express contractual provision would be a lawful termination of employment, *Delaney v. RJ Staples (t/a De Montfort Recruitment)* [1992] 1 A.C. 687, [1992] C.L.Y. 2028 considered. In the instant case, CS was entitled to terminate R's contract either by giving six months' notice, or by making an equivalent payment in lieu of such notice. There was no third option to choose to dismiss wrongfully thereby entitling R to bring an action for damages for breach of contract. The contractual provisions were intended to give R the protection of six months' notice or an "up front" payment in lieu, regardless of any mitigation. The purpose of a payment in lieu in such circumstances would be to cushion R against the difficulties of searching for new employment while unemployed. The failure by CS to make the payment of monies in lieu of notice constituted a breach by CS of its promise to make such a payment in the event of summary dismissal. The payment in lieu could be claimed either as a sum due under the contract or as damages for breach of contract, but however the claim was put the payment was not subject to the duty to mitigate.

CERBERUS SOFTWARE LTD v. ROWLEY; *sub nom.* ROWLEY v. CERBERUS SOFTWARE LTD [2000] I.C.R. 35, Morison, J., EAT.

2248. Publications

Achieving Benefits Through Mediation: Employment and Discrimination Claims. TSO Mediation Series. Paperback: £30.00. ISBN 0-11-702442-2. The Stationery Office Books.

Allen, A.; et al – Employment Law and the Human Rights Act 1998. Paperback: £25.00. ISBN 0-85308-503-X. Jordans.

Barnard, Catherine – EC Employment Law. 3rd Ed. Oxford European Community Law Series. Hardback: £60.00. ISBN 0-19-876564-9. Paperback: £24.99. ISBN 0-19-876565-7. Oxford University Press.

Barrow, Charles – Sourcebook on Employment Law. Sourcebook Series. Paperback: £24.95. ISBN 1-85941-184-3. Cavendish Publishing Ltd.

Barrow, Charles; Blunt, Steve; Gibbons, Steve; Manley, Isabel – Blackstone's Guide to the Employment Relations Act 1999. Blackstone's Guides. £25.00. ISBN 1-84174-125-6. Blackstone Press.

Bercusson, Brian – European Labour Law. 2nd Ed. Butterworths Law in Context. Paperback: £36.95. ISBN 0-406-98254-6. Butterworths Law.

Berry, Adrian – Dealing with Your Dismissal in a Week. Successful Business in a Week. Paperback: £6.99. ISBN 0-340-78092-4. Hodder & Stoughton General.

Bourn, Colin – Transfer of Undertakings in the Public Sector. Employment and European Union Law. Hardback: £40.00. ISBN 1-84014-772-5. Ashgate Publishing Limited.

Brading, Jean; Curtis, John – Disability Discrimination. 2nd Ed. Paperback: £19.95. ISBN 0-7494-2778-7. Kogan Page.

Chandler, Peter – A-Z of Employment Law: a Complete Reference Source for Managers. 3rd Ed. Hardback: £45.00. ISBN 0-7494-3067-2. Kogan Page.

Chandler, Peter – Waud's Employment Law 2000-2001. 13th Ed. Paperback: £25.00. ISBN 0-7494-3137-7. Kogan Page.

Du Feu, V.; Gillero, E.; Hopkins, M. – EU and International Employment Law. £200.00. ISBN 0-85308-590-0. Jordans.

Employee Share Schemes: Law and Practice. Hardback. ISBN 0-421-48200-1. Sweet & Maxwell.

Employment Relations Act. Legal Essentials Series. Paperback: £29.99. ISBN 0-85292-850-5. Institute of Personnel and Development.

Fairclough, Murray – Working for Justice: the Employee's Guide to the Law. 2nd Ed. Paperback: £9.95. ISBN 1-899053-13-1. Otter Publications.

Hammond Suddards – Data Protection. Legal Essentials. Paperback: £29.99. ISBN 0-85292-861-0. Institute of Personnel and Development.

Hunt, Melanie – Employment Law Guide. Paperback: £9.99. ISBN 1-902646-61-4. Law Pack Publishing.

Hyams, Oliver – Employment in Schools: a Legal Guide. Paperback: £35.00. ISBN 0-85308-567-6. Jordans.

Jefferson, Michael – Employment Law. 4th Ed. Principles of Law. Paperback: £20.95. ISBN 1-85941-468-0. Cavendish Publishing Ltd.

Kibling, Thomas; Lewis, Tamara – Employment Law: an Adviser's Handbook. 4th Ed. Paperback: £23.00. ISBN 0-905099-93-1. Legal Action Group.

Labour Laws and Global Trade. Paperback: £20.00. ISBN 1-84113-187-3. Hart Publishing.

LawCards: Employment Law. 2nd Ed. LawCards Series. Paperback: £5.50. ISBN 1-85941-568-7. Cavendish Publishing Ltd.

Lewis, David; Sargeant, Malcolm – Essentials of Employment Law. 6th Ed. Paperback: £19.95. ISBN 0-85292-796-7. Institute of Personnel and Development.

McColgan, Aileen – Discrimination Law: Text, Cases and Materials. Paperback: £22.50. ISBN 1-84113-146-6. Hart Publishing.

McMullen, John – Redundancy: Law and Practice. 2nd Ed. Hardback: £100.00. ISBN 0-421-68390-2. Sweet & Maxwell.

Morris, Gillian S.; Archer, Timothy J. – Collective Labour Law. Hardback: £45.00. ISBN 1-84113-096-6. Hart Publishing.

Muntigl, Peter; Weiss, Gilbert; Wodak, Ruth – European Union Discourses and Unemployment: an Interdisciplinary Approach to Employment Policy Making and Organizational Change. Dialogues on Work and Innovation, 12. Paperback: £29.00. ISBN 90-272-1782-3. John Benjamins Publishing Company.

O'Dempsey, Declan – Employment Law and the Human Rights Act 1998. Paperback: £25.00. ISBN 0-85308-596-X. Jordans.

Peck, Lib; Cooper, Jonathan; Owers, Anne – Race Discrimination: Developing and Using a New Legal Framework. The Justice Series: Putting Rights Into Practice. Paperback: £15.00. ISBN 1-84113-167-9. Hart Publishing.

Phillips, Jeremy – Employees' Inventions. Hardback: £55.00. ISBN 1-902558-28-6. Palladian Law Publishing Ltd.

Sargeant; Lewis; Wilkinson; Marchington – Core Personnel and Development (Updated Ed)/ Essentials of Employment Law (6th Ed). Paperback: £43.98. ISBN 0-85292-882-3. Institute of Personnel and Development.

Selwyn, Norman – Selwyn's Law of Employment. 11th Ed. Paperback: £24.95. ISBN 0-406-91357-9. Butterworths Law.

Shaw, Josephine; More, Gillian – Workers' Europe: Social and Labour Law of the European Union. Hardback: £40.00. ISBN 1-85521-777-5. Dartmouth.

Smith, Ian; Thomas, Gareth – Industrial Law. 7th Ed. Paperback: £29.95. ISBN 0-406-90411-1. Paperback: £29.95. ISBN 0-406-90411-1. Butterworths.

Szyszczak, Erika – EC Labour Law. EULS. Paperback: £16.99. ISBN 0-582-30814-3. Longman Higher Education.

TUC Guide to Your Rights At Work. Paperback: £8.99. ISBN 0-7494-3364-7. Kogan Page.

Working Time Regulations. 2nd Ed. Legal Essentials. Paperback: £29.99. ISBN 0-85292-870-X. Chartered Institute of Personnel and Development (CIPD).

ENVIRONMENT

2249. Abatement notices – form of notice – remedial work not specified

[Environmental Protection Act 1990 s.80.]

M, a pig farmer, was served with an abatement notice by WMBC because it was satisfied that a statutory nuisance existed from smells emanating from the pig farm. The notice, served pursuant to the Environmental Protection Act 1990 s.80, required the abatement of the specified nuisance and prohibited its recurrence but did not state what work or other steps were required to do so. The farmer appealed on the ground that the notice was defective because it failed to specify the works to be undertaken. The magistrate quashed the notice, finding it was defective because the necessary works had not been specified. The council sought judicial review of that decision.

Held, remitting the matter for rehearing, that a local authority was entitled, within the terms of s.80 and depending on the circumstances, to serve an abatement notice either requiring the abatement of the nuisance or specifying the works necessary to abate the nuisance. In the present case, the magistrate made his ruling by reference to a purported finding of fact in circumstances where there was no agreed statement of facts upon which that ruling of law could have been based. The ruling was fatally flawed by an error of law in purporting to make a critical finding of fact, without having heard evidence upon which that finding of fact could properly be founded.

R. v. WAKEFIELD MAGISTRATES COURT, *ex p.* WAKEFIELD MBC [2000] E.H.L.R. 81, Forbes, J., QBD.

2250. Abatement notices – local authorities powers and duties – liability for breach of common law duty of care

G appealed against an order striking out two actions against H's enforcement of an abatement notice preventing G using his vehicle. G contended that H had negligently enforced the environmental regulations and made reference to him maliciously and without legal authority in a letter.

Held, dismissing the appeal, that the issues had already been litigated in a competent court, and therefore could not be litigated again, *Hunter v. Chief Constable of the West Midlands* [1982] A.C. 529, [1982] C.L.Y. 2382 applied. Furthermore, G's contentions would fail because no common law duty had arisen when H exercised its statutory duty in enforcing the abatement notice.

GRIBLER v. HARROW LBC [2000] E.H.L.R. 188, Walter Aylen Q.C., QBD.

2251. Abatement notices – validity – particularity of notice

[Local Government (Miscellaneous Provisions) Act 1976 s.16(1); Housing Act 1985; Environmental Protection Act 1990 s.80(1).]

ELBC served an abatement notice on S under the Environmental Protection Act 1990 s.80(1) in relation to refuse in the front yard of a property owned by him. The notice required S to clear the existing refuse and to provide proper facilities for the storage and collection of refuse in the future. ELBC then served a separate notice on S under the Local Government (Miscellaneous Provisions) Act 1976 s.16(1) requiring him to provide it with information relating to the occupancy of the property in order to enable it to "take appropriate action under the provisions of the Housing Act 1985". S was convicted of failing to comply with the notices and appealed by way of case stated, arguing that (1) the abatement notice was invalid in that it did not clearly set out what he was required to do in order to provide proper storage facilities for his refuse; (2) the abatement notice had not made it clear that recurrence of the nuisance complained of was prohibited, and (3) the notice served under the 1976 Act was invalid as it did not set out the sections of the 1985 Act upon which ELBC was relying.

Held, allowing the appeal in part, that (1) the particularity of an abatement notice was a question of fact. In this case, the question of how to store refuse was not a difficult or complicated one and it was reasonable for ELBC to take a common sense approach and leave the practical details to S, *Sterling Homes (Midlands) Ltd v. Birmingham City Council* [1996] Env. L.R. 121, [1996] C.L.Y. 2689 applied; (2) the issue of recurrence was implicit in both the wording of the notice and the obvious inference that the requirement to provide refuse storage facilities gave rise to a future duty, and (3) although it did not have to refer to specific sections of the 1985 Act, the 1976 Act notice was invalid since ELBC had failed to make it clear in relation to which of its functions under the 1985 Act the information sought was required.

STANLEY v. EALING LBC [2000] E.H.L.R. 172, Jowitt, J., QBD.

2252. Air pollution – air quality reviews

AIR QUALITY (ENGLAND) REGULATIONS 2000, SI 2000 928; made under the Environment Act 1995 s.87, s.91. In force: April 6, 2000; £2.00.

These Regulations prescribe the relevant period for the purpose of the Environment Act 1995 Part IV which requires local authorities to conduct a review of the quality of air within their area. That review must consider the air quality for the time being and the likely future air quality within a relevant period and must be accompanied by an assessment of whether any prescribed air quality standards or objectives are being achieved or are likely to be achieved within such a period.

2253. Air pollution – air quality reviews – Wales

AIR QUALITY (WALES) REGULATIONS 2000, SI 2000 1940 (W.138); made under the Environment Act 1995 s.87, s.91. In force: August 1, 2000; £2.50.

The Environment Act 1995 Part IV, requires county and county borough councils in Wales to review air quality within their area for the time being and the likely future air quality during a relevant period. These Regulations, which revoke the Air Quality Regulations 1997 (SI 1997 3043), prescribe the relevant period and the air quality objectives to be achieved by the end of that period.

2254. Air pollution – emissions – motor vehicles – Council Decision

European Parliament and Council Decision 1753/2000 of June 22, 2000 establishing a scheme to monitor the average specific emissions of CO2 from new passenger cars. [2000] OJ L202/1.

2255. Air pollution – liquid fuels – sulphur content

SULPHUR CONTENT OF LIQUID FUELS (ENGLAND AND WALES) REGULATIONS 2000, SI 2000 1460; made under the European Communities Act 1972 s.2. In force: June 27, 2000; £2.00.

These Regulations, which revoke the Marketing of Gas Oil (Sulphur Content) Regulations 1994 (SI 1994 2249) in relation to England and Wales, implement Council Directive 1999/32 ([1999] OJ L121/13) relating to the sulphur content of certain liquid fuels. They make it an offence to use heavy fuel oil on or after January 1, 2003 with a sulphur content exceeding one per cent and to use gas oil or marine oil on or after July 1, 2000 with a sulphur content exceeding 0.2 per cent by mass and to use such oil on or after January 1, 2008 with sulphur content exceeding 0.1 per cent. In addition, they require the Secretary of State to check compliance with these requirements by sampling sulphur content of fuels, set out technical requirements for analysis of samples, and provide for the granting of permits to enable combustion plant operators to take advantages of certain exemptions.

2256. Conservation areas – habitats – EC law – prohibited activities – geographical scope – continental shelf

[Conservation (Natural Habitats etc) Regulations 1994 (SI 1994 2716); Council Directive 92/43 on the conservation of natural habitats and of wild fauna and flora.]

A number of oil and gas companies had applied to the Secretary of State for licences to search and bore for oil in the Atlantic Frontier, an area outside UK territorial waters but located on the UK's continental shelf. In exercising his licensing function, the Secretary of State had to construe the Conservation (Natural Habitats etc) Regulations 1994 which implemented Council Directive 92/43. G challenged the 1994 Regulations, contending that the limitation to UK territorial waters was contrary to the scope and overall aim of the Directive, stated in Art.2(1) as ensuring biodiversity through conservation. In commenting on the Directive's reference to the "European territory" of a Member State, the Secretary of State relied on the accepted meaning of "territory" in international law, being that which extended only to a country's territorial waters in the strict sense. G contended that certain species afforded protection under the provisions of the Directive, such as, cetaceans (whales, porpoises and dolphins) and a type of coral, would be denied protection if the Regulations were limited to territorial waters. To give full effect to the Directive the Regulations must extend to the UK continental shelf and the waters above. The species mentioned were listed in the Directive and in relation to that list, there were certain prohibited activities. That requirement was implemented by Reg.39(1), but G contended that the list of prohibited activities should be given a broad interpretation and "deliberate disturbing" extended to activities which were potentially disruptive. Furthermore, Reg.40(3)(c), which provided a defence for activities on the basis that they were unavoidable and incidental to a lawful activity, was an impermissible derogation.

Held, allowing the application in part, that, in order to give it full effect, the Directive was to be construed purposively and in the context of other relevant Community, international and domestic legislation with the result that its geographical scope extended beyond the UK's territorial waters to its continental shelf and associated waters up to a limit of 200 nautical miles from the baseline at which the territorial sea was measured. However, the list of prohibited activities was definitive and would not be given a wider interpretation. The defence provided by Reg.40(3)(c) was not impermissible. Although the application had been delayed, G was representing the public interest and that factor outweighed the general principle applicable when granting extensions of time, *R. v. Secretary of State for Trade and Industry, ex p. Greenpeace Ltd (No.1)* [1998] Eu. L.R. 48, [1998] C.L.Y. 2252 considered.

R. v. SECRETARY OF STATE FOR TRADE AND INDUSTRY, *ex p.* GREENPEACE LTD (NO.2) [2000] 2 C.M.L.R. 94, Maurice Kay, J., QBD.

2257. **Conservation areas – selection and definition criteria – relevance of economic social or cultural matters – European Union**

[Council Directive 92/43 on the conservation of natural habitats and of wild fauna and flora Art.2(3), Art.4(1).]

A question on the correct interpretation of the Habitats Directive 92/43 Art.4(1) was referred to the ECJ for a preliminary ruling. F, the statutory port authority for Bristol, had applied for judicial review of the Secretary of State's decision to propose to the European Commission that the Severn Estuary be designated as a special area of conservation under the Directive. F argued that when selecting and defining the boundaries of the proposed areas, the Secretary of State was obliged under Art.2(3) to take account of economic, social and cultural requirements and regional and local characteristics.

Held, giving a preliminary ruling, that when selecting and defining the boundaries of proposed areas of special conservation under Art.4(1) a Member State must have regard only to conservation issues and not to economic, social or cultural or other matters. Annex III to the Directive specified the criteria for selecting sites for special conservation and those criteria were concerned solely with conserving the natural habitat and wild fauna and flora. The Commission was obliged, under Art.4(2), to produce a draft list of sites of Community importance, which was based on lists of sites of ecological importance produced at national level. Any favourable conservation status was then to be assessed in relation to the entire territory of the European Community. To allow Member States in to exclude sites on economic, social or cultural grounds or any other grounds not related to conservation which otherwise met the ecological criteria would defeat the purpose of preserving natural habitats on a European wide basis.

R. (ON THE APPLICATION OF FIRST CORPORATE SHIPPING LTD) v. SECRETARY OF STATE FOR THE ENVIRONMENT, TRANSPORT AND THE REGIONS (C371/98); *sub nom.* R. v. SECRETARY OF STATE FOR THE ENVIRONMENT, TRANSPORT AND THE REGIONS, *ex p.* FIRST CORPORATE SHIPPING LTD (C371/98) [2001] All E.R. (EC) 177, GC Rodriguez Iglesias (President), ECJ.

2258. **Conservation areas – wild bird habitats – designation of special protection areas – European Union**

[Council Directive 79/409 on the conservation of wild birds Art.4; Council Directive 92/43 on the conservation of natural habitats and of wild fauna and flora.]

Council Directive 79/409, the Wild Birds Directive, required the designation of certain areas as special protection areas, SPAs, on ornithological criteria and for appropriate steps to be taken to protect those areas. Council Directive 92/43, the habitats directive, required appropriate steps to be taken to avoid the deterioration of habitats and disturbance of species in special conservation areas, including SPAs. The effect of projects that could have a significant impact upon a site were to be assessed and only allowed to proceed if the site's integrity would not be adversely affected or the overriding public interest required that the project should be carried out. The Commission applied to the ECJ for a declaration that France had failed to fulfil its obligations under the Directives because certain areas designated as SPAs within an area of marshland were insufficient to meet the obligations imposed by the Directives.

Held, granting the declaration, that (1) the Commission's complaints would be upheld as France had failed to classify a sufficient area within the marsh as SPAs during the prescribed period; (2) on the evidence, France had failed in its obligation to take appropriate measures to avoid deterioration of the classified areas in breach of Art.4(4) of the Wild Birds Directive. Article 4(4) required Member States to take appropriate steps to avoid deterioration of habitats in areas most suitable for the conservation of wild birds, even where the areas concerned had not been classified as SPAs, provided that they should have been so classified, *Commission of the European Communities v. Spain (C355/90)* [1993] E.C.R. I-4221, [1994] C.L.Y. 4833 applied; (4) the evidence showed that France had not taken the measures necessary to avoid deterioration of some, but not all, areas which should have been classified as SPAs, and (5) a motorway construction route had been marked out to avoid all areas which the French Government intended to classify as SPAs. Part of that area had subsequently mistakenly been classified as an SPA. Thus its removal from that classification corrected that mistake and did not amount to a declassification of part of an SPA through a reduction in its surface area contrary to Art.4.

COMMISSION OF THE EUROPEAN COMMUNITIES v. FRANCE (C96/98) [2000] 2 C.M.L.R. 681, L Sevon (President), ECJ.

2259. Countryside and Rights of Way Act 2000 (c.37)

This Act to makes new provision for public access to the countryside; to amend the law relating to public rights of way; to enable traffic regulation orders to be made for the purpose of conserving an area's natural beauty; to make provision with respect to the driving of mechanically propelled vehicles elsewhere than on roads; to amend the law relating to nature conservation and the protection of wildlife and to make further provision with respect to areas of outstanding natural beauty.

This Act received Royal Assent on November 30, 2000.

2260. Energy – energy efficiency – fluorescent lighting – Council Directive

European Parliament and Council Directive 2000/55 of September 18, 2000 on energy efficiency requirements for ballasts for fluorescent lighting. [2000] OJ L279/33.

2261. Energy conservation – grants

HOME ENERGY EFFICIENCY SCHEME (ENGLAND) REGULATIONS 2000, SI 2000 1280; made under the Social Security Act 1990 s.15. In force: June 1, 2000; £2.00.

These Regulations, which revoke and replace, with amendments, in so far as they apply to England, the Home Energy Efficiency Scheme Regulations 1997 (SI 1997 790), enable the Secretary of State to make or arrange for the making of grant for the improvement of energy efficiency in dwellings occupied by persons on low incomes with children, elderly persons on low incomes or persons in receipt of benefit relating to ill health.

2262. Energy conservation – grants – Wales

HOME ENERGY EFFICIENCY SCHEME (AMENDMENT) (WALES) REGULATIONS 2000, SI 2000 1039 (W.68); made under the Social Security Act 1990 s.15. In force: April 6, 2000; £2.00.

These Regulations amend the Home Energy Efficiency Scheme Regulations 1997 (SI 1997 790) setting out the the Home Energy Efficiency Scheme which provides grants towards the cost of work or advice to improve thermal insulation or to reduce or prevent energy wastage in dwellings. They change the limitation on the purposes for which a grant may be awarded under the 1997 Regulations, from "...not more than one.." to "...one or more..." of the purposes set out and provide new maximum amounts for grants.

2263. Energy conservation – grants – Wales

HOME ENERGY EFFICIENCY SCHEMES (WALES) REGULATIONS 2000, SI 2000 2959 (W.190); made under the Social Security Act 1990 s.15. In force: November 6, 2000; £2.50.

These Regulations, which set out the schemes to provide grants towards the cost of work or advice to improve thermal insulation or otherwise to reduce or prevent energy wastage in dwellings under the Social Security Act 1990 s.15. They deal with who is eligible to receive a grant, determination by the Assembly of the categories of works and the maximum levels of grants available, the purposes for which grants may be approved and the method of applying for a grant. They also revoke the Home Energy Efficiency Scheme (Amendment) (Wales) Regulations 2000 (SI 2000 1039) and the Home Energy Efficiency Scheme Regulations 1997 (SI 1997 790) in relation to Wales.

2264. Environment – eco-label award scheme – Council Regulation

European Parliament and Council Regulation 1980/2000 of July 17, 2000 on a revised Community eco-label award scheme. [2000] OJ L237/1.

2265. Environment Act 1995 (c.25) – Commencement No.16 and Saving Provision Order – England

ENVIRONMENT ACT 1995 (COMMENCEMENT NO. 16 AND SAVING PROVISION) (ENGLAND) ORDER 2000, SI 2000 340 (C.8); made under the Environment Act 1995 s.125. Commencement details: bringing into force various provisions of the Act on April 1, 2000; £2.00.

This Order brings various provisions of the Environment Act 1995, including s.57, which inserts a new Part 11A into the Environmental Protection Act 1990 providing for a regime for identification and remediation of contaminated land, into force on April 1, 2000.

2266. Environment Act 1995 (c.25) – Commencement No.18 Order – England and Wales

ENVIRONMENT ACT 1995 (COMMENCEMENT NO.18) (ENGLAND AND WALES) ORDER 2000, SI 2000 3033 (C.95); made under the Environment Act 1995 s.125. Commencement details: bringing into force various provisions of the Act on December 1, 2000; £1.75.

This Order brings into force the Environment Act 1995 Sch.21 para.1 (1), which substitutes a new s.221 in the Water Industry Act 1991, and s.116 insofar as it relates to that provision.

2267. Environmental impact assessments – mining permission – expiry of time limit for determination of permission conditions – requirement for assessment

[Planning and Compensation Act 1991 s.22(3), Sch.2 s.6.]

H lived adjacent to a quarry owned by S and in respect of which an old mining permission was held. By virtue of the Planning and Compensation Act 1991 s.22(3) the permission could not authorise any mining development unless an application was made to determine the conditions to which the permission should be subject. If the mineral planning authority had not determined those conditions within three months of the making of the application, the permission was to be deemed, in accordance with the Planning and Compensation Act 1991 Sch.2 s.6, to be subject to the conditions contained in the application. S sought the imposition of such conditions by the mineral planning authority, which, in turn, requested an environmental statement. S applied to the Secretary of State for a direction whether an environmental statement was necessary. The Secretary of State advised that it was not, but that, given the nature of the proposed development, environmental information should be considered before consent was granted. The three month period under the 1991 Act expired and S claimed that it had deemed permission on the conditions included in its application. H and the mineral planning authority disagreed, but the authority changed its view on advice of counsel. H sought leave to apply for judicial review of the authority's decision. S opposed the application on the grounds that H had failed to disclose material matters regarding his expertise in mining and that there had been a delay in bringing the proceedings. H's complaints regarding the quarry related to both personal considerations such as time of working and noise, and wider issues relating to the protection of the environment. S claimed that it would be caused extreme hardship if an interim injunction was granted and that H was not in a position to offer recompense for any resultant financial loss.

Held, granting permission and allowing the application, that (1) H had made a sufficient disclosure to the court; (2) it was only once the authority had changed its position regarding the deemed permission that H had a decision which he could challenge. There was a reasonable explanation for H's delay and it would be wrong to refuse permission on the basis of delay; (3) where H's concerns were limited to his personal considerations an injunction would not be granted. The relevant adverse effects could be limited without the mining itself being prevented; (4) the consequences of work starting without an environmental assessment might make irreversible any harm that might be caused, and (5) in the absence of any indication that appropriate steps could be taken to prevent the envisaged environmental harm, an interim injunction should be granted. This was so despite the fact that H was not in a position to offer any undertaking as to any financial loss.

R. v. DURHAM CC, *ex p.* HUDDLESTON (LEAVE TO APPEAL); *sub nom.* R. v. DURHAM CC, *ex p.* HUDDLESTONE (LEAVE TO APPEAL) [2000] J.P.L. 409, Kay, J., QBD.

2268. Environmental protection – Antarctica – restricted areas

ANTARCTIC (AMENDMENT) REGULATIONS 2000, SI 2000 2147; made under the Antarctic Act 1994 s.9, s.10, s.15, s.25, s.32. In force: September 1, 2000; £2.50.

These Regulations amend the Antarctic Regulations 1995 (SI 1995 490) Sch.1 and Sch.2 by adding further restricted areas and an historic site.

2269. Environmental protection – contaminated land – remediation scheme

CONTAMINATED LAND (ENGLAND) REGULATIONS 2000, SI 2000 227; made under the Environmental Protection Act 1990 s.78C, s.78E, s.78G, s.78L, s.78R. In force: April 1, 2000; £3.50.

These Regulations make provision for certain aspects of a new scheme under the Environmental Protection Act 1990 Part IIA for the remediation of contaminated land. They designate responsibility for enforcement of the scheme which is to be shared between local authorities and the Environment Agency and contain provisions relating to remediation notices, compensation and appeals.

2270. Environmental protection – dangerous substances – disposal of polychlorinated biphenyls

ENVIRONMENTAL PROTECTION (DISPOSAL OF POLYCHLORINATED BIPHENYLS AND OTHER DANGEROUS SUBSTANCES) (ENGLAND AND WALES) REGULATIONS 2000, SI 2000 1043; made under the European Communities Act 1972 s.2. In force: May 4, 2000; £3.00.

These Regulations implement provisions of Council Directive 96/59 ([1996] OJ L243/31) on the disposal of polychlorinated biphenyls and polychlorinated terphenyls, "PCBs", which require decontamination or disposal of PCBs and equipment containing them and make associated provisions for inventories, labelling and monitoring. They are additional to the existing relevant requirements of the waste management licensing regime under the Environmental Protection Act 1990.

2271. Environmental protection – dangerous substances – disposal of polychlorinated biphenyls

ENVIRONMENTAL PROTECTION (DISPOSAL OF POLYCHLORINATED BIPHENYLS AND OTHER DANGEROUS SUBSTANCES) (ENGLAND AND WALES) (AMENDMENT) REGULATIONS 2000, SI 2000 3359; made under the European Communities Act 1972 s.2. In force: January 1, 2001; £1.50.

These Regulations amend the Environmental Protection (Disposal of Polychlorinated Biphenyls (PCBs) and other Dangerous Substances), (England and Wales) Regulations 2000 (SI 2000 2143) so as to enable those who applied before January 1, 2001 for a direction under the 2000 Regulations to continue to hold equipment containing PCBs until March 31, 2001.

2272. Environmental protection – financial assistance

FINANCIAL ASSISTANCE FOR ENVIRONMENTAL PURPOSES (NO.2) ORDER 2000, SI 2000 2211; made under the Environmental Protection Act 1990 s.153. In force: September 8, 2000; £1.00.

This Order varies the Environmental Protection Act 1990 s.153 (1) so as to enable the Secretary of State, with the consent of the Treasury, to give financial assistance to, or for the purposes of, the Pollution Emergency Response Services programme, the Waste and Resources Action Programme and the Protocol on Energy Efficiency and Related Environmental Aspects to the Energy Charter Treaty.

2273. Environmental protection – financial assistance – radon management and support for remedial works

FINANCIAL ASSISTANCE FOR ENVIRONMENTAL PURPOSES ORDER 2000, SI 2000 207; made under the Environmental Protection Act 1990 s.153. In force: March 1, 2000; £1.00.

This Order varies the Environmental Protection Act 1990 s.153 (1) to enable the Secretary of State to give financial assistance to, or for the purposes of, the programme known as Radon Management and Support for Remedial Works Campaigns in England.

2274. Environmental protection – nuisance – service of process – service effected upon a company's registered office or a principal office

[Environmental Protection Act 1990 s.79 (1), s.82 (6), s.160 (4).]

H, who considered that works being carried out by MH near to his property constituted a statutory nuisance under the Environmental Protection Act 1990 s.79(1), provided notice to MH's director and general manager by a letter, pursuant to s.82(6), that he was minded to issue proceedings by which MH would be required to cease the alleged nuisance. The letter was sent to MH's principal office rather than its registered office. The justices dismissed the summons on the ground that the letter, not having been sent to MH's registered office, had not amounted to proper service within the meaning of s.160 of the Act. H appealed.

Held, allowing the appeal, that (1) the 1990 Act was designed to provide a remedy to lay persons and it was, therefore, inappropriate to adopt an unduly technical method of construction, *R. v. Birmingham City Council, ex p. Ireland* [1999] 2 All E.R. 609, [1999] C.L.Y. 2214 applied; (2) the requirements relating to service set out in s.160 of the Act were permissive as opposed to compulsory. Moreover other methods of service were available and a failure to comply with the section could be corrected; (3) service could be effected at a company's registered office or its principal office. There were no grounds for interpreting the words within s.160(4) of the Act relating to a company's principal office as applicable only to companies registered outside the United Kingdom, and (4) in the instant case, there had been sufficient evidence before the justices that notice had been served on MH and received by a person in authority who had acted upon it. No prejudice had resulted from notice being sent to the principal rather than registered office.

HEWLINGS v. MCLEAN HOMES EAST ANGLIA LTD [2001] 2 All E.R. 281, Rafferty, J., QBD.

2275. Environmental protection – pollution control regime – Council Directive

POLLUTION PREVENTION AND CONTROL (ENGLAND AND WALES) REGULATIONS 2000, SI 2000 1973; made under the Pollution Prevention and Control Act 1999 s.2. In force: August 1, 2000; £8.80.

These Regulations set out a pollution control regime for the purpose of implementing Council Directive 96/61 ([1996] OJ L257/26) and for regulating other environmentally polluting activities not covered by the Directive.

2276. Environmental protection – waste – packaging

PRODUCER RESPONSIBILITY OBLIGATIONS (PACKAGING WASTE) (AMENDMENT) (ENGLAND AND WALES) REGULATIONS 2000, SI 2000 3375; made under the Environment Act 1995 s.93, s.94. In force: December 31, 2000; £1.50.

These Regulations amend the fee which is to be charged by the Environment Agency on an application for registration of a scheme under the Producer Responsibility Obligations (Packaging Waste) Regulations 1997 (SI 1997 648) Reg.14 and Reg.15. The fee is now calculated at the rate of £460 per member of the scheme, rather than on a scale according to the number of members of the scheme. They also increase the targets from 2001 onwards, provided for by Directive 94/62 ([1994] OJ L365/10), to 56 per cent for recovery and 18 per cent for recycling.

2277. Environmental protection – waste management – air pollution – incineration of pet carcasses – classification as non clinical waste

[Waste Management Licensing Regulations 1994 (SI 1994 1056); Council Directive 91/156 on waste.]

TF, who farmed land adjacent to an incinerator operated by TR used for the destruction of pet animal carcasses, sought judicial review of an authorisation granted by DDC permitting the emission of pollutants within prescribed limits so as to comply with the guidance issued by the Secretary of State in PG5/3(95). TF contended that (1) the waste should have been treated as clinical waste pursuant to Council Directive 91/156 and that, as a consequence, DDC had wrongly applied the pollution limits in PG5/3(95) rather than the tighter constraints present in PG5/1(95) applicable to the disposal of clinical waste, and (2) DDC had consequently omitted to take into account the relevant statutory objectives under the Waste Management Licensing Regulations 1994.

Held, refusing the application, that (1) pet carcasses did not constitute clinical waste for the purposes of Council Directive 91/156. DDC had accordingly been entitled to rely on the guidance in PG5/3(95) which set a higher emission level, and (2) DDC had not blindly followed the guideline requirements, but had properly sought advice as to how best to fulfil the statutory requirements and had therefore had the relevant objectives properly in mind.

R. v. DAVENTRY DC, *ex p.* THORNBY FARMS [2001] Env. L.R. 20, Collins, J., QBD.

2278. Environmental protection – waste management – objectives of Directive on waste – local authorities' obligations

[Waste Management Licensing Regulations 1994 (SI 1994 1056) Sch.4 para.4; Council Directive 75/442 on waste.]

A local authority, LCC, granted planning permission for the extraction of coal and clay and the disposal of 3.9 million tonnes of household waste on a local site. Local residents formed a company, B, to oppose the scheme and made an application for permission to move for judicial review. B contended that LCC had paid insufficient regard to the objectives contained within Council Directive 75/442 as implemented by the Waste Management Licensing Regulations 1994 Sch.4 para.4, taking account of them simply as material considerations rather than taking real steps to achieve them, as required. LCC opposed the application and challenged the locus standi of B to bring proceedings on the basis that the company had been incorporated solely to avoid adverse costs implications should the challenge prove unsuccessful.

Held, dismissing the application, that (1) the arguments propounded by B ran counter to established authority and would in any event, if accepted, result in an unsatisfactory situation whereby the objectives would have an uncertain status, *R. v. Bolton MBC, ex p. Kirkman* [1998] Env. L.R. 719, [1998] C.L.Y. 4236 considered. The objectives were to be treated as goals at which to aim and in consequence, on the facts of the instant case, LCC had considered them in an entirely appropriate manner, and (2) the incorporation of a company which was formerly a local action group need not prevent it from pursuing proceedings for judicial review. There was no evidence that the avoidance of costs was the prime motivation for forming B and the risk to LCC could be adequately dealt by means of an application for security for costs, *R. v. Hammersmith and Fulham LBC, ex p. People Before Profit Ltd* 80 L.G.R. 322, [1982] C.L.Y. 3165 and *R. v. Secretary of State for the Environment, ex p. Kirkstall Valley Campaign Ltd* [1996] 3 All E.R. 304, [1996] C.L.Y. 4679 considered.

R. v. LEICESTERSHIRE CC, *ex p.* BLACKFORDBY AND BOOTHORPE ACTION GROUP LTD; *sub nom.* R. v. LEICESTER CITY COUNCIL, *ex p.* BLACKFORDBY AND BOOTHORPE ACTION GROUP LTD; R. v. LEICESTERSHIRE CC, *ex p.* BLACKFORDBY AND BOOTHCORPE ACTION GROUP LTD [2001] Env. L.R. 2, Richards, J., QBD.

2279. Environmental protection – waste recycling payments

ENVIRONMENTAL PROTECTION (WASTE RECYCLING PAYMENTS) (AMENDMENT) (ENGLAND) REGULATIONS 2000, SI 2000 831; made under the Environmental Protection Act 1990 s.52. In force: April 17, 2000; £1.50.

These Regulations increase, by an average of 15 per cent, the figures for determining a waste disposal authority's net saving of expenditure where this could not be determined by other means for the purposes of the Environmental Protection Act 1990 s.52(1) and s.52(3) which require waste disposal authorities to pay waste collection authorities amounts representing their net savings on the disposal of waste retained by collection authorities for recycling.

2280. Environmentally sensitive areas – designation

ENVIRONMENTALLY SENSITIVE AREAS (STAGE I) DESIGNATION ORDER 2000, SI 2000 3049; made under the Agriculture Act 1986 s.18. In force: December 5, 2000; £2.50.

The Agriculture Act 1986 s.18 gives the Minister of Agriculture, Fisheries and Food power to designate areas in England as environmentally sensitive areas where it appears to him particularly desirable to conserve, protect or enhance environmental features in those areas by the maintenance or adoption of particular agricultural methods. This Order designates areas in the Broads, Pennine Dales, Somerset Levels and Moors, South Downs and West Penwith as environmentally sensitive areas and specifies what capital activities may attract aid and the maximum rates of payment which are payable in respect of various management activities in accordance with s.18(3) of the Act. It implements Arts.22-24 and Art.43(2) of Council Regulation 1257/1999 ([1999] OJ L160/80).

2281. Environmentally sensitive areas – designation

ENVIRONMENTALLY SENSITIVE AREAS (STAGE II) DESIGNATION ORDER 2000, SI 2000 3050; made under the Agriculture Act 1986 s.18. In force: December 5, 2000; £2.00.

The Agriculture Act 1986 s.18 gives the Minister of Agriculture, Fisheries and Food power to designate areas in England as environmentally sensitive areas where it appears to him particularly desirable to conserve, protect or enhance environmental features in those areas by the maintenance or adoption of particular agricultural methods. This Order designates areas in Breckland, Clun, North Peak, Suffolk River Valleys and Test Valley as environmentally sensitive areas and specifies what capital activities may attract aid and the maximum rates of payment which are payable in respect of various management activities in accordance with s.18(3) of the Act. It implements Arts.22-24 and Art.43(2) of Council Regulation 1257/1999 ([1999] OJ L160/80).

2282. Environmentally sensitive areas – designation

ENVIRONMENTALLY SENSITIVE AREAS (STAGE III) DESIGNATION ORDER 2000, SI 2000 3051; made under the Agriculture Act 1986 s.18. In force: December 5, 2000; £2.00.

The Agriculture Act 1986 s.18 gives the Minister of Agriculture, Fisheries and Food power to designate areas in England as environmentally sensitive areas where it appears to him particularly desirable to conserve, protect or enhance environmental features in those areas by the maintenance or adoption of particular agricultural methods. This Order designates areas in the Avon Valley, Exmoor, Lake District, North Kent Marshes, South Wessex Downs and South West Peak district as environmentally sensitive areas and specifies what capital activities may attract aid and the maximum rates of payment which are payable in respect of various management activities in accordance with s.18(3) of the Act. It implements Arts.22-24 and Art.43(2) of Council Regulation 1257/1999 ([1999] OJ L160/80).

2283. Environmentally sensitive areas – designation

ENVIRONMENTALLY SENSITIVE AREAS (STAGE IV) DESIGNATION ORDER 2000, SI 2000 3052; made under the Agriculture Act 1986 s.18. In force: December 5, 2000; £2.00.

The Agriculture Act 1986 s.18 gives the Minister of Agriculture, Fisheries and Food power to designate areas in England as environmentally sensitive areas where it appears to him particularly desirable to conserve, protect or enhance environmental features in those areas by the maintenance or adoption of particular agricultural methods. This Order designates areas in the Blackdown Hills, the Cotswold Hills, Dartmoor, the Essex Coast, the Shropshire Hills and the Upper Thames Tributaries as environmentally sensitive areas and specifies what capital activities may attract aid and the maximum rates of payment which are payable in respect of various management activities in accordance with s.18(3) of the Act. It implements Arts.22-24 and Art.43(2) of Council Regulation 1257/1999 ([1999] OJ L160/80).

2284. Habitats – conservation – European sites register

CONSERVATION (NATURAL HABITATS, &C.) (AMENDMENT) (ENGLAND) REGULATIONS 2000, SI 2000 192; made under the European Communities Act 1972 s.2. In force: February 28, 2000; £1.50.

These Regulations amend the Conservation (Natural Habitats, &c.) Regulations 1994 (SI 1994 2716), which make provision for implementing Council Directive 92/43 ([1992] OJ L206/7) on the conservation of natural habitats and of wild fauna and flora, by adding a further category of sites to the meaning of "European site" in Reg.10. Consequential amendments are made to Reg.11 of the 1994 Regulations to provide for registration of this new category of sites in the register of European sites compiled and maintained by the Secretary of State under that regulation.

2285. Harbours – environmental impact assessments

See SHIPPING. §4713

2286. Land drainage – Internal Drainage Boards – reorganisation – Lower Alde and Middle Alde

AMALGAMATION OF THE LOWER ALDE AND MIDDLE ALDE INTERNAL DRAINAGE DISTRICTS ORDER 2000, SI 2000 1463; made under the Land Drainage Act 1991 s.3. In force: May 24, 2000; £1.50.

This Order confirms a Scheme submitted by the Environment Agency for the abolition of the Lower Alde and Middle Alde Internal Drainage Boards. These boards are replaced by a new "Lower Alde Internal Drainage Board" and the two former internal drainage districts are amalgamated together to form the corresponding new internal drainage district.

2287. Motor vehicles – end of life vehicles – Council Directive

European Parliament and Council Directive 2000/53 of September 18, 2000 on end-of-life vehicles. [2000] OJ L269/34.

2288. Noise pollution – mobile homes – compensation

HIGHWAYS NOISE PAYMENTS AND MOVABLE HOMES (ENGLAND) REGULATIONS 2000, SI 2000 2887; made under the Land Compensation Act 1973 s.20A. In force: November 23, 2000; £2.00.

The Land Compensation Act 1973 s.20A enables regulations to be made providing for payments to persons living in caravans and other structures which are not buildings which are, or are likely to be, affected by noise caused by the construction or use of public works. Such dwellings do not qualify for noise insulation or grant under the Noise Insulation Regulations 1975 (SI 1975 1763 as amended). These Regulations provide that a noise payment of £1,650 shall be made, where specified qualifying conditions are met, to the occupier of a caravan or movable home by the appropriate highway authority.

2289. Noise pollution – mobile homes – compensation

HIGHWAYS NOISE PAYMENTS AND MOVABLE HOMES (ENGLAND) (AMENDMENT) REGULATIONS 2000, SI 2000 3086; made under the Land Compensation Act 1973 s.20A. In force: November 23, 2000; £1.50.

These Regulations correct defects in the Highways Noise Payments and Movable Homes (England) Regulations 2000 (SI 2000 2887) to make it clear that noise payments under Reg.3 are discretionary and that the figure of £1,650 in Reg.5 is the maximum noise payment that may be made.

2290. Noise pollution – outdoors equipment – Council Directive

European Parliament and Council Directive 2000/14 of May 8, 2000 on the approximation of the laws of the Member States relating to the noise emission in the environment by equipment for use outdoors. [2000] OJ L162/1.

2291. Oil pollution – strict liability – appropriate level of fine – public status and financial position determining factors

[Water Resources Act 1991 s.85(1).]

A tanker, the "Sea Empress", grounded upon rocks as she was being guided into port by a pilot employed by H, a subsidiary of the local port authority, M. As a result of the collision substantial quantities of crude oil were discharged into the sea. The Environment Agency, EA, commenced criminal proceedings against M which included a charge of causing polluting matter to enter controlled waters, contrary to the Water Resources Act 1991 s.85(1). M entered a guilty plea on the basis that the offence was one of strict liability whilst not accepting any blame for the incident. The court imposed a fine of £4 million and M appealed. M contended that (1) the judge paid insufficient regard to M's relative lack of fault for the incident; (2) the judge erred in failing to allow M full credit for its guilty plea; (3) the position of M as a public trust authority was relevant when determining the level of any fine as the burden of payment would fall either upon the port itself, the port's customers or the general public, and (4) the judge failed to appreciate the true financial status of the company.

Held, allowing the appeal and reducing the fine to £750,000, that (1) the court had erred in failing to have regard to the agreed basis upon which the guilty plea was entered, namely that M did not accept that it had been at fault; (2) the court had erred in failing to give full credit for the guilty plea. M were not to be criticised for failing to enter a plea at an earlier stage given that they were obliged to commission expert evidence to rebut accusations of fault by EA before the basis of the plea could be agreed; (3) the judge failed to give sufficient consideration as to how the fine was to be paid and there had been no evidence before him that the fine could be paid by simply raising charges, and (4) the judge had taken too positive a view of M's financial position although not all of the relevant material had been available to him for consideration. Whilst a substantial fine was needed to mark the seriousness of the offence, it should not be so heavy so as to destroy M's business with consequent impact upon the local economy.

ENVIRONMENT AGENCY v. MILFORD HAVEN PORT AUTHORITY (THE SEA EMPRESS); *sub nom.* R. v. MILFORD HAVEN PORT AUTHORITY [2000] 2 Cr. App. R. (S.) 423, Lord Bingham of Cornhill, L.C.J., CA (Crim Div).

2292. Ozone depletion – air pollution – Council Regulation

European Parliament and Council Regulation 2037/2000 of June 29, 2000 on substances that deplete the ozone layer. [2000] OJ L244/1.

2293. Pollution Prevention and Control Act 1999 (c.24) – Commencement No.1 Order – England and Wales

POLLUTION PREVENTION AND CONTROL ACT 1999 (COMMENCEMENT NO.1) (ENGLAND AND WALES) ORDER 2000, SI 2000 800 (C.18); made under the Pollution Prevention and Control Act 1999 s.7. Commencement details: bringing into force various provisions of the Act on March 21, 2000; £1.00.

This Order brings into force the Pollution Prevention and Control Act 1999 s.6(1) and Sch.2 in so far as they extend to England and Wales.

2294. Rights of way – roads – meaning of "byway open to all traffic"

[Wildlife and Countryside Act 1981 s.66(1).]

M issued proceedings challenging the Secretary of State's decision to uphold a modification order which had altered the status of a road used as a public path to a byway open to all traffic. The relevant route had been recorded as a public road since 1929 and since the publication in 1972 of the definitive map as a road used as a public path. Whereas there was little evidence that the route had been used by vehicles in living memory, the route had been shown on maps predating 1929 as a public right of way for vehicular traffic. The judge at first instance upheld the Secretary of State's decision ([2000] 2 All E.R. 788, [1999] C.L.Y. 4272), holding that the definition of "byway open to all traffic" contained in the Wildlife and Countryside Act 1981 s.66(1), namely "a highway over which the public have a right of way for vehicular and all other kinds of traffic, but which is used by the public mainly for the purpose for which footpaths and bridleways are so used", should be construed purposively rather than literally. M appealed, arguing that the definition in s.66(1) could only be satisfied if the evidence revealed not only that the route was currently being used by vehicles, pedestrians and equestrians but also that the combined use of the route by pedestrians and equestrians exceeded its use by vehicles. M contended that such evidence had plainly been absent in the instant case.

Held, dismissing the appeal, that s.66(1) was to be construed purposively rather than literally. When passing the 1981 Act and similar legislation, Parliament had intended to define the concept or character of a route and to enable local authorities to record routes in definitive maps and statements for the benefit of ramblers and equestrians. Parliament had not intended that routes classified as roads used as public paths should disappear from definitive maps and statements merely because no evidence of current use could be established or because the evidence showed that the current use of the route did not accord with the literal definition contained in s.66(1). Were s.66(1) to be construed literally, local authorities might have to review maps and statements each time evidence was put to them showing that the use of a route had altered and such an absurd situation could not have been contemplated by Parliament.

MASTERS v. SECRETARY OF STATE FOR THE ENVIRONMENT, TRANSPORT AND THE REGIONS; *sub nom*. R. v. SECRETARY OF STATE FOR THE ENVIRONMENT, TRANSPORT AND THE REGIONS, *ex p.* MASTERS [2001] Q.B. 151, Roch, L.J., CA.

2295. Rural areas – countryside stewardship

COUNTRYSIDE STEWARDSHIP REGULATIONS 2000, SI 2000 3048; made under the Environment Act 1995 s.98. In force: December 5, 2000; £3.00.

These Regulations, which apply to England including the Isles of Scilly, revoke and replace with savings the Countryside Stewardship Regulations 1998 (SI 1998 1327). They provide for payments to be made to any person who enters an agreement with the Minister of Agriculture, Fisheries and Food requiring him to carry out an activity which is conducive to a specified purpose on land in which he has an interest. In addition, they revoke the Countryside Stewardship Regulations 1999 (SI 1999 1177).

2296. Sewers and drains – statutory power to lay public sewers – whether pipe a sewer or a drain

[Public Health Act 1936 s.15.]

In 1973 M was given a notice under the Public Health Act 1936 s.15 to the effect that BLBC intended to lay public sewers through his private land. In 1996 M blocked the pipe, so that repairs had to be carried out. BLBC proceeded against him for the cost of those repairs and sought a declaration that the pipe was a sewer. M unsuccessfully claimed that the pipe laid was a drain rather than a sewer and that since BLBC had no statutory power to lay the pipe they had committed a trespass on M's land. M appealed.

Held, dismissing the appeal, that the status of a pipe, namely whether it is a drain or a sewer, depended on the function for which the pipe was constructed. If constructed as a sewer it remained a sewer even if only receiving, as a drain did, effluent from one property, *Beckenham UDC v. Wood* (1896) 60 J.P. 490 followed.

BROMLEY LBC v. MORRITT [2000] E.H.L.R. 24, Mummery, L.J., CA.

2297. Smoke control – authorisation of fuel

SMOKE CONTROL AREAS (AUTHORISED FUELS) (AMENDMENT) (ENGLAND) REGULATIONS 2000, SI 2000 1077; made under the Clean Air Act 1993 s.20, s.63. In force: May 9, 2000; £1.50.

These Regulations amend the Smoke Control (Authorised Fuels) Regulations 1991 (SI 1991 1282) so that Aimcor Supercoke and Supabrite Coke Doubles are authorised fuels for the purpose of the Clean Air Act 1993 s.20 which provides that where smoke is emitted from a chimney in a smoke control area and that chimney is either a chimney of a building or a chimney serving the furnace of a fixed boiler or industrial plant, the occupier of the building, or the person having possession of the boiler or plant, is guilty of an offence. It is a defence to show that the alleged emission was caused solely by the use of an authorised fuel.

2298. Smoke control – authorisation of fuel – Wales

SMOKE CONTROL AREAS (AUTHORISED FUELS) (AMENDMENT) (WALES) REGULATIONS 2000, SI 2000 3156 (W.205); made under the Clean Air Act 1993 s.20, s.63. In force: December 1, 2000; £1.75.

These Regulations, which extend to Wales only, amend the Smoke Control (Authorised Fuels) Regulations 1991 (SI 1991 1281) so that Aimcor Supercoke and Supabrite Coke Doubles are authorised fuels for the purposes of the Clean Air Act 1993 s.20 which provides that where smoke is emitted from a chimney in a smoke control area and that chimney is either a chimney of a building or a chimney serving the furnace of a fixed boiler or industrial plant, the occupier of the building, or the person having possession of the boiler or plant, is guilty of an offence. It is a defence to show that the alleged emission was caused solely by the use of an authorised fuel. The Regulations also amend the 1991 Regulations to take account that Beacon Beans are no longer manufactured, that the place of manufacture of Sunbrite is now different, that Coal Products Limited is now the manufacturer of Supertherm, Supertherm II and Thermac briquettes and that Taybrite briquettes are now also manufactured without any markings.

2299. Warm Homes and Energy Conservation Act 2000 (c.31)

This Act requires the Secretary of State to publish and implement a strategy for reducing fuel poverty and to require the setting of targets for the implementation of that strategy.

This Act received Royal Assent on November 23, 2000.

2300. Waste disposal – EC law – statutory request for factual information – self incrimination – protection of public health

[Police and Criminal Evidence Act 1984; Environmental Protection Act 1990 s.71(2); Council Directive 91/156 on waste; European Convention on Human Rights 1950 Art.6(1).]

H, a local waste regulation authority, had found and disposed of a large quantity of clinical waste on G's land and subsequently served a request for information pursuant to the Environmental Protection Act 1990 s.71(2) concerning the source of the waste and G's business practices. G, who was not licensed to keep waste on the site, refused to reply without confirmation from H that its replies would not be used against it in a prosecution. G argued that the request was an attempt to deprive it of a right to silence, which it would have had if interviewed under the Police and Criminal Evidence Act 1984 as part of a criminal investigation. H issued a summons for non compliance, which was adjourned pending an unsuccessful application for judicial review. G appealed to the House of Lords. Whilst conceding that s.71(2) impliedly excluded the privilege against self incrimination, G submitted that as the 1990 Act gave effect to Council Directive 91/156, it had to be interpreted in accordance with the principles of European law including the European Convention on Human Rights 1950 Art.6(1), which afforded a privilege against self incrimination.

Held, dismissing the appeal, that the jurisprudence underpinning Art.6(1) was concerned with the fairness of a trial and not with extra judicial inquiries, *Saunders v. United Kingdom* [1998] 1 B.C.L.C. 362, [1997] C.L.Y. 2816 distinguished. The authority was entitled to request factual information, particularly in view of the urgent need to protect public health from an environmental hazard, even if potentially incriminating, but was not entitled to invite an admission of wrongdoing. Since none of the questions put to G invited such an admission, G was obliged to respond to them, *Orkem SA (formerly CdF Chimie SA) v. Commission of the European Communities (C 374/87)* [1989] E.C.R. 3355, [1990] C.L.Y. 2069 considered.

R. v. HERTFORDSHIRE CC, *ex p.* GREEN ENVIRONMENTAL INDUSTRIES LTD; *sub nom.* GREEN ENVIRONMENTAL INDUSTRIES LTD, RE; GREEN ENVIRONMENTAL INDUSTRIES LTD v. HERTFORDSHIRE CC [2000] 2 A.C. 412, Lord Hoffmann, HL.

2301. Waste disposal – failure to comply with previous judgment – calculation of payment penalty – Eurpoean Union

[EC Treaty Art.171 (now Art.228 EC); Council Directive 75/442 on waste Art.4, Art.6; Council Directive 78/319 on toxic and dangerous waste Art.12.]

Following receipt of a complaint concerning the uncontrolled tipping of waste at the mouth of the River Kouroupitos in Chania, Crete, the Commission expressed its concern to the Greek Government. The Greek Government in response drew attention, inter alia, to the opposition of the population of Chania to plans to develop new landfill sites. The Commission subsequently brought proceedings against the Greek Government ([1995] 3 C.M.L.R. 589, [1992] C.L.Y. 4729) in which it was held that the failure of the Government to adopt measures which enabled waste to be disposed of without endangering human health and without harming the environment pursuant to the Framework Waste Directive 75/442 Art.4, and its failure to establish waste disposal plans pursuant to Art.6 of the Directive and toxic and dangerous waste disposal plans pursuant to Council Directive 78/319 Art.12 could not be excused by pleading internal circumstances. Following continued communications between the Commission and the Greek Government, the Commission issued a reasoned opinion stating that the Greek Government in not drawing up or implementing the required waste disposal plans had thereby failed to comply with the earlier judgment. The Commission consequently brought an action under the EC Treaty Art.171 (now Art.228 EC).

Held, granting the declaration under Art.171, that the Greek Government had persisted in its failure to comply with the earlier judgment. The Government had stated that tipping would cease after August 1998, but, the fact remained that it had not been done. Article 171 did not specify a time limit within which a judgment had to be complied with, however, the nature of the immediate and uniform application of Community law dictated that the process of compliance be initiated immediately and completed forthwith. The Commission had adopted guidelines for the determination of penalty payments as provided for in Art.171 (2), the purpose of which was the effective enforcement of Community law, namely, that the breach of obligations be remedied as soon as possible. Such payments were to be calculated on the basis of the duration and severity of the infringement, and the ability of the Member State to pay, while, at the same time, ensuring the penalty carried the desired deterrent effect. On that basis, the duration of G's infringement had been considerable, its severity was indisputable owing to the fact that Art.4 of the Framework Waste Directive provided for the protection of human health and the environment. Consequently the Government would be ordered to pay a slightly reduced penalty payment to be paid daily until compliance with the original judgment.

COMMISSION OF THE EUROPEAN COMMUNITIES v. GREECE (C387/97); *sub nom.* COMMISSION OF THE EUROPEAN COMMUNITIES v. HELLENIC REPUBLIC (C387/97) *The Times*, July 7, 2000, GC Rodriguez Iglesias (President), ECJ.

2302. Waste disposal – licences – breach of conditions – validity

[Finance Act 1996 s.40, s.66.]

In 1994 H, a farmer, had been granted a waste disposal licence with conditions attached permitting him to operate a landfill site at his farm. H exceeded a maximum input as determined by one of the conditions attached to the licence. Although the local authority issued a stop notice as to the breach in January 1997, it was only in August 1997 that the licence was actually suspended. H was convicted of being knowingly concerned in the fraudulent evasion of landfill tax. H appealed, contending that, as no taxable disposal had taken place under the Finance Act 1996 s.40, no tax was due. Under s.40(2) a taxable disposal could only be made at a landfill site, which, according to s.66 existed where a site licence was in force in relation to the land. H asserted that where waste disposal activity took place in breach of any conditions attached to the licence, it could not be regarded as being authorised and therefore the land was not at the relevant time a landfill site as defined by the Act.

Held, dismissing the appeal, that the breach of conditions attached to a waste disposal licence did not prevent the licence from being valid. Neither did the issue of a stop notice, by the local council, affect its validity. It remained in force until suspended in August 1997.

R. v. HARRIS (ANDREW WILLIAM) [2001] Env. L.R. 9, Swinton Thomas, L.J., CA (Crim Div).

2303. Waste management – recycling – obligation to prioritise – waste oils – European Union

[EC Treaty Art.169 (now Art.226 EC); Council Directive 75/439 on the disposal of waste oils Art.3(1); Council Directive 87/101.]

Council Directive 75/439 Art.3(1), as amended by Council Directive 87/101, required Member States to give priority to the recycling over the thermal processing of waste oils, to the extent permitted by economic and technical restraints. The European Commission considered that, in the legislation introduced by Germany to give effect to the Directive, parity, rather than priority, had been accorded to recycling, and that there had therefore been a failure to transpose Art.3(1). Germany argued that its relevant domestic law gave priority to recycling, and that there were economic and technical restraints on recycling. The Commission did not accept this, and addressed a reasoned opinion on the point to Germany, requiring compliance within two months. Germany did not reply to the opinion, and the Commission brought proceedings against Germany.

Held, that Germany had failed to transpose the Council Directive 75/439, (1) although transposition did not require the importation of the exact words of that Directive into relevant domestic law, it must be fully applied in clear and precise words. In the instant case, it was not clear that the relevant German legislation prioritised recycling over other forms of processing, *Commission of the European Communities v. Netherlands (C339/87)* [1990] E.C.R. I-851 followed; (2) one of the aims of Directive 87/101 gave priority to the regeneration of waste oils. If this was technically, economically and organisationally impracticable in a Member State, Directive 75/439 Art.3(2) laid down a subsidiary requirement that combustion of the waste oil be effected in an environmentally appropriate way, unless this was likewise constrained by technical, economic or organisational reasons. Only then was a Member State obliged to ensure the storage or destruction of waste oils; (3) the expression "technical, economic and organisational restraints" in Directive 75/439 Art.3(1) was not to be interpreted restrictively, and was not intended to provide exceptions, but rather to define the scope of the duty imposed. Its interpretation could not be left to individual Member States, as to do so would reduce uniformity or make the duty worthless; (4) Member States were obliged to take measures under Directive 75/439 proportionate to the goal of according priority to the processing of waste oils by regeneration. If the existence of constraints made the adoption of such measures impossible, then Directive 75/439 would be deprived of any effect. Germany had adopted its own definition of constraints, and had thereby justified fiscal measures the effect of which was to encourage the continued burning of certain oils, and (5) it was not the function of the court to prescribe the measures to be taken to give effect to a Directive, but it was obliged to consider if there were measures which could have been taken within the criteria it laid down. Germany had failed to take such measures.

COMMISSION OF THE EUROPEAN COMMUNITIES v. GERMANY (C102/97) [1999] 3 C.M.L.R. 631, J-P Puissochet (President), ECJ.

2304. **Water pollution – abatement of nuisance – consultation with perpetrator of nuisance prior to service of abatement notice**

[Public Health Act 1936 s.259(1); Environmental Protection Act 1990 s.80(3).]
A port health authority, FTPHA, served an abatement notice upon a water provider, SWW, requiring the cessation of sewage discharge into a local estuary. SWW sought judicial review of the decision to serve the abatement notice. At first instance the court held that (1) SWW had had a legitimate expectation of consultation which had been unfairly denied to it; (2) the notice was null and void due to a failure to detail the works required to abate the nuisance; (3) the waters which formed the subject of the notice did not constitute a "watercourse" as define by the Public Health Act 1936 s.259(1), and (4) SWW was not restricted to its right of statutory appeal under the Environmental Protection Act 1990 s.80(3), but was entitled to proceed by way of judicial review. FTPHA appealed.

Held, dismissing the appeal, that (1) in the absence of any duty to consult, a clear assurance would be required before legitimate expectation could arise and that was not present in the correspondence from FTPHA. Furthermore, it was inappropriate to categorise the authority's refusal to exercise its discretion to consult as Wednesbury unreasonable; (2) the local authority was free to leave the means by which the nuisance was to be abated to the discretion of the perpetrator. If, however, the authority chose to prescribe the form of abatement, then the method to be employed must be specified within the notice, *Network Housing Association Ltd v. Westminster City Council* [1995] Env. L.R. 176, [1996] C.L.Y. 2745 and *Sterling Homes (Midlands) Ltd v. Birmingham City Council* [1996] Env. L.R. 121, [1996] C.L.Y. 2689 considered and *Kirklees MBC v. Field* (1998) 162 J.P. 88, [1997] C.L.Y. 2374 overruled; (3) in its historical context the term "watercourse" had not been intended to apply to estuary waters and it was inappropriate to give the term a wider definition than had been afforded to it in 1936 given the fact that protection from sewage pollution could be effected by other means and the fact that a wider definition would still not bring the open sea within its scope, and (4) it had been inappropriate to grant such a wide ranging permission to move for judicial review.

Observed, that where a statutory right of appeal existed then permission to move for judicial review should be granted only in exceptional circumstances, particularly so where the case involved issues of public safety.

R. v. FALMOUTH AND TRURO PORT HA, *ex p.* SOUTH WEST WATER LTD; *sub nom.* FALMOUTH AND TRURO PORT HA v. SOUTH WEST WATER LTD [2001] Q.B. 445, Simon Brown, L.J., CA.

2305. **Water pollution – escape of creosote into surface water – prior authorisation exceptional or even impossible – European Union**

[Council Directive 76/464 on pollution caused by certain dangerous substances discharged into the aquatic environment of the Community; Council Directive 76/769 relating to restrictions on the marketing and use of certain dangerous substances and preparations; Council Directive 94/60 amending Directive 76/769.]

Council Directive 76/464 provided for Member States to take action to eliminate water pollution caused by substances specified in List I of the Annex, and to reduce pollution by other substances detailed in List II. Use of substances in either list required prior authorisation. N used creosote, a List I substance, in shoring up operations without prior authorisation. Article 6 of the Directive provided that creosote was actually to be treated as if it were a List II substance, for which no emissions limit had been set under Directive 76/464. N applied to the national court for regularisation of the situation, which in turn referred the interpretation of Directive 76/464 to the ECJ.

Held, giving a preliminary ruling that (1) "discharge" in Art.1 (2) (d) of Directive 76/464 meant the introduction of any of the dangerous substances in either List I or List II into waters within the scope of the Directive; (2) Community law laid down two systems for combating surface water pollution. The first was a system of authorisation where the discharge was attributable to an identified person, and the second was a system of programmes to counter pollution which came from multiple sources; (3) "discharge" in Art.1 (2) (d) included the escape of creosote used by N into surface water where the resultant pollution was attributable to a specific person; (4) any discharge of a List I substance required prior authorisation. Member States were free under Art.10 to impose requirements in this regard additional to those contained in the Directive, even if this made the grant of authorisation exceptional or even impossible; (5) it was irrelevant that the Council had laid down no emissions limit for creosote, since Member States were obliged in any event to eliminate all pollution emanating from List I substances, and (6) it was permissible for Member States to introduce additional authorisation criteria even if the effect was to make authorisation exceptional or even impossible. Further, limitations on the use of creosote contained in Council Directive 76/769, as amended by Council Directive 94/60, did not prevent Member States from establishing assessment criteria making the use of creosote impossible or exceptional.

NEDERHOFF v. DIJKGRAAF EN HOOGHEEMRADEN VAN HET HOOGHEEMRAADSCHAP RIJNLAND (C232/97) [2000] 1 C.M.L.R. 681, PJG Kapteyn (President), ECJ (6th Chamber).

2306. **Water pollution – nitrate pollution of spring water – intensive farming – test of hypothetically good farmer.**

See NUISANCE: Savage v. Fairclough. §4289

2307. **Publications**

Austen, Mark; Richards, Tamara – Basic Legal Documents on International Animal Welfare and Wildlife Conservation. Hardback: £140.00. ISBN 90-411-9780-X. Kluwer Law International.

Environmental Law and Procedures Management. Unbound/looseleaf: £95.00. ISBN 0-7545-0378-X. Tolley Publishing.

Environmental Law Reports. Hardback: £275.00. ISBN 0-421-70360-1. Sweet & Maxwell.

Fijalkowski, Agata; Fitzmaurice, Malgosia – Right of the Child to a Clean Environment. Programme on International Rights of the Child. Hardback: £50.00. ISBN 0-7546-2012-3. Ashgate Publishing Limited.

Garbutt, John – Environmental Law: Practical Handbook. 3rd Ed. Paperback: £45.00. ISBN 1-902558-24-3. Palladian Law Publishing Ltd.

Gillespie, Alexander – International Environmental Law, Policy, and Ethics. Paperback: £17.99. ISBN 0-19-829872-2. Oxford University Press.

Jackson, R.P.; Legge, D.; Parry, J.; Ruddock, F.; Longworth, E.J.; Regan, P. – Environmental Law and Techniques for the Built Environment. Paperback: £22.95. ISBN 1-85941-597-0. Cavendish Publishing Ltd.

Knill, Christoph; Lenschow, Andrea – Implementing EU Environmental Policy: New Directions and Old Problems. Issues in Environmental Politics. Hardback: £45.00. ISBN 0-7190-5928-3. Manchester University Press.

Kosobud, Richard F. – Emissions Trading: Environmental Policy's New Approach. Hardback: £48.50. ISBN 0-471-35504-6. John Wiley and Sons.

Kummer, Katharina – International Management of Hazardous Wastes: the Basel Convention and Related Legal Rules. Oxford Monographs in International Law. Paperback: £25.00. ISBN 0-19-829827-7. Oxford University Press.

Lucas, Alastair R.; Tilleman, William A. – Environmental Law and the Energy Sector. Hardback: £45.00. ISBN 0-19-825824-0. Oxford University Press.

Randolph, Bryan; Meinzen-Dick, Ruth – Negotiating Water Rights. Paperback: £14.95. ISBN 1-85339-484-X. Intermediate Technology Publications.

Revesz, Richard L.; Sands, Philippe; Stewart, Richard B. – Environmental Law, the Economy, and Sustainable Development: the United States, the European Union and the International Community. Hardback: £40.00. ISBN 0-521-64270-1. Cambridge University Press.

Schmidt, Carsten – Designing International Environmental Agreements: Incentive Compatible Strategies for Cost Effective Cooperation. New Horizons in Environmental Economics. Hardback: £55.00. ISBN 1-84064-352-8. Edward Elgar.

Somsen, Han – Yearbook of European Environmental Law. Hardback: £80.00. ISBN 0-19-876463-4. Oxford University Press Inc, USA.

Spedding, Linda S. – Materials Sourcebook on Environmental Law. Old Bailey Press: Law in Practice. Paperback: £23.95. ISBN 1-85836-077-3. Old Bailey Press.

Stroup, Richard L.; Meiners, Roger E. – Cutting Green Tape: Pollutants, Environmental Regulation, and the Law. Hardback: £29.50. ISBN 1-56000-429-0. Transaction Publishers.

Stroup, Richard L.; Meiners, Roger E. – Cutting Green Tape: Pollutants, Environmental Regulation and the Law. Paperback: £18.50. ISBN 0-7658-0618-5. Transaction Publishers.

Tromans, Stephen; Irvine, Gillian – Taking Responsibility: Personal Liability Under Environmental Law. Business and Environment Practitioner Series. Paperback: £35.00. ISBN 1-85383-597-8. Paperback: £35.00. ISBN 1-85383-597-8. Earthscan.

Tromans, Stephen; Turrall-Clarke, Robert – Contaminated Land: the New Regime. Hardback: £65.00. ISBN 0-421-66120-8. Sweet & Maxwell.

Weale, Albert; Pridham, Geoffrey; Cini, Michelle; Konstadakopulos, Dimitrios; Porter, Martin; Flynn, Brendan – Environmental Governance in Europe: an Ever Closer Ecological Union? Hardback: £55.00. ISBN 0-19-829708-4. Oxford University Press.

Woolley, David; Pugh-Smith, John; Langham, Richard; Upton, William – Environmental Law. Hardback: £125.00. ISBN 0-19-826008-3. Oxford University Press.

ENVIRONMENTAL HEALTH

2308. Abatement notices – noise pollution – dog kennels in residential area – "best practical means" of counteracting effect of nuisance

[Environmental Protection Act 1990 s.79(1)(g); Statutory Nuisance (Appeals) Regulations 1995 (SI 1995 2644) Reg 2(2)(e).]

M bred dogs as a business in a residential area. NFDC, the local planning authority, served an abatement notice on the grounds that barking, howling and whining amounted to a statutory nuisance under the Environmental Protection Act 1990 s.79(1)(g). M appealed against the notice on the basis that he had used the "best practical means" of preventing the nuisance within the meaning of the Statutory Nuisance (Appeals) Regulations 1995 Reg.2(2)(e). The Crown Court, concluding that the notice was justified, since "best practical means" included moving the kennels to another location, stated a case on the issue of whether "best practical means" extended to removal of the kennels elsewhere.

Held, allowing the appeal, that the Regulations could not be interpreted to mean that carrying on a business at another location was within the available "best practical means". To require the elimination of the business from the premises to which the notice related defeated the intention of Parliament which was to allow an applicant to defeat a notice if, notwithstanding that a nuisance had been created, he could show on the balance of probabilities that the best practical means had been used to counteract its effects.

MANLEY v. NEW FOREST DC [2000] E.H.L.R. 113, Simon Brown, L.J., QBD.

2309. Burials and cremation – body parts removed during post mortem examination

CREMATION (AMENDMENT) REGULATIONS 2000, SI 2000 58; made under the Cremation Act 1902 s.7. In force: February 14, 2000; £2.00.

These Regulations, which do not apply to Scotland, amend the Cremation Regulations 1930 (SR & O 1930 1016), making provision concerning the cremation of parts of the body of a deceased person, those parts having been removed in the course of a post-mortem examination.

2310. Environmental protection – waste management – suspension of waste disposal licences

[Environmental Protection Act 1990 s.38.]

P had been granted waste disposal and management licences. In 1997 one such licence was suspended by the Environment Protection Agency, in exercise of its powers under the Environmental Protection Act 1990 s.38(6), after local concern had been expressed about the level of fumes emanating from the plant. The notice informed P that the suspension would cease when the agency notified P that disposal activities could be carried out without serious risk of pollution. P applied for judicial review of the decision, arguing that the terms of the notice gave the agency the power to prolong the suspension for as long as it saw fit. Moreover, P contended that under s.38(12) of the Act, the suspension was to cease on either a specified date or on the occurrence of an event. Notification by the agency, P argued, could not amount to an event since it was dependent upon the agency's state of mind.

Held, dismissing the application, that it was within the power of the agency to issue a notice in the terms of that served upon P. The word "event", as used in s.38(12), was to be construed purposively and without limitation. There was no reason why receipt of a notification of a decision that suspension would cease should not amount to an event.

R. v. SECRETARY OF STATE FOR THE ENVIRONMENT, TRANSPORT AND THE REGIONS, *ex p.* PREMIERE ENVIRONMENT LTD [2000] Env. L.R. 724, Sullivan, J., QBD.

2311. Food hygiene – butchers' shops – licensing

FOOD SAFETY (GENERAL FOOD HYGIENE) (BUTCHERS' SHOPS) AMENDMENT REGULATIONS 2000, SI 2000 930; made under the Food Safety Act 1990 s.16, s.19, s.26, s.45, s.48, Sch.1 para.5. In force: Reg.1, Reg.5: May 1, 2000; Reg.2, Reg.3, Reg.4: November 1, 2000; £2.00.

These Regulations further amend the Food Safety (General Food Hygiene) Regulations 1995 (SI 1995 1763) in relation to England only by introducing a requirement for the premises of butchers' shops to be licensed by food authorities. They provide that a charge of £100 is payable for the issue of a licence which will remain in force for periods of a year.

2312. Food hygiene – butchers' shops – licensing – Wales

FOOD SAFETY (GENERAL FOOD HYGIENE) (BUTCHERS' SHOPS) (AMENDMENT) (WALES) REGULATIONS 2000, SI 2000 3341 (W.219); made under the Food Safety Act 1990 s.16, s.19, s.26, s.45, s.48, Sch.1 para.5. In force: Reg.1 and Reg.5, December 31, 2000, Reg.2 to Reg.4, June 30, 2001; £2.50.

These Regulations amend the Food Safety (General Food Hygiene) Regulations 1995 (SI 1995 1763) in relation to Wales, by introducing a requirement for butchers' shops to be licensed by food authorities. They provide that provisions relating to the licensing of butchers' shops do not apply to those businesses to which the sectoral provisions listed in Reg.3 of the 1995 Regulations apply. They provide for licence applications, licence conditions, suspension and revocation of licences and amend the 1995 Regulations so that using premises as a butcher's shop otherwise than in accordance with a licence is a criminal offence.

2313. Publications

Garbutt, John – Waste Management Law-practical Handbook. 3rd Ed. Paperback: £48.00. ISBN 1-902558-25-1. Palladian Law Publishing Ltd.

EQUITY

2314. Attempted misrepresentation – preservation of equitable interest

See SHIPPING: Standard Chartered Bank v. Pakistan National Shipping Corp (No.2). §4681

2315. Constructive trusts – breach of trust – dishonesty not essential to knowing receipt – state of knowledge test

The liquidators of B appealed against a decision ([1999] B.C.C. 669, [1999] C.L.Y. 648) refusing the recovery of $6.79 million from A, a Nigerian businessman, on the ground that proof of A's dishonesty, which was required to find him liable as a constructive trustee under both heads of knowing assistance and knowing receipt, had not been established. In 1985, A had given ICIC, a company controlled by B, a sum of $10 million. The sum was advanced under an artificial loan agreement designed to give the impression that certain dummy loans were performing as normal. In 1988, A received $16.79 million, under the agreement, as divestiture payments. The claimants argued that A's dishonesty could be inferred from his knowledge of the artificially arranged loan transaction and from his receipt of an unusually high rate of return of 15 per cent compound interest.

Held, dismissing the appeal, that A's state of knowledge of the situation in 1985 was not such as to make it unconscionable for him to enter into the transaction. Furthermore, it was not unconscionable for A to retain the benefits of the divestiture payments, notwithstanding the rumours which were circulating about the integrity of B's management. There was nothing to alert A to the fact that the particular transaction, entered into some years earlier, might be tainted. Nevertheless, the court below had erred by not distinguishing between dishonesty and knowledge in knowing receipt cases. Dishonesty was not a necessary ingredient for the establishment of liability under the knowing receipt head of constructive trust, *Belmont Finance Corp v. Williams Furniture (No.2)* [1980] 1 All E.R. 393, [1980] C.L.Y. 279 considered. The categorisation of degrees of knowledge, accepted in, *Baden v. Societe Generale pour Favoriser le Developpement du Commerce et de l'Industrie en France SA* [1993] 1 W.L.R. 509, [1992] C.L.Y. 214, was not particularly helpful in cases of knowing receipt. In such cases a single test, asking whether it would be unconscionable for the recipient to retain the benefits of the receipt, was sufficient, and in the instant case the evidence satisfied the test. *Baden* considered.

BANK OF CREDIT AND COMMERCE INTERNATIONAL (OVERSEAS) LTD v. CHIEF LABODE ONADIMAKI AKINDELE [2001] Ch. 437, Nourse, L.J., CA.

2316. Constructive trusts – dishonesty required for knowing assistance

D, the second defendant, made an interlocutory appeal against summary judgment for F in the sum of £473,237. D contended that there was a factual dispute over whether he had received £398,162 of the sum beneficially, in which case a claim could be made out only for knowing assistance.

Held, allowing the appeal, that D was granted partial leave to defend. Although a finding of dishonesty was not required for D to be a constructive trustee of sums received in breach of trust, knowing assistance required evidence of dishonesty, which had not been shown on the facts, *Royal Brunei Airlines Sdn Bhd v. Tan* [1995] 2 A.C. 378, [1995] C.L.Y. 2193 followed.

HOUGHTON v. FAYERS [2000] Lloyd's Rep. Bank. 145, Nourse, L.J., CA.

2317. Constructive trusts – joint ventures – oral contract to acquire site by joint venture unenforceable – equity to intervene – shares in joint venture company held on constructive trust

After finding in favour of BH ([2000] 2 W.L.R. 772), that equity could intervene after LD's failure to fulfil the terms of an oral contract between BH and LD, the court gave the parties an opportunity to make submissions as to the terms of the order to be granted. The oral contract had provided for the creation of a company, S, as a joint venture to be owned equally by BH and LD, for the purposes of acquiring certain premises. S had, with funding from LD, proceeded to purchase the premises and the court had found that it was inequitable for LD to be allowed to treat the property as its own. BH sought an order that one half of the issued share capital in S be held upon trust for BH.

Held, granting an order for the shares in S to be held by LD on trust for BH and LD equally, that equity, as described in *Pallant v. Morgan* [1953] Ch. 43, [1952] C.L.Y. 3571, could not be invoked in relation to the property itself, because it was not inequitable to allow S to treat the premises as its own. BH and LD had always intended that S should acquire the premises as its own asset and LD could not be treated as trustee of the premises because it was neither the legal nor beneficial owner. However, prior to the acquisition of the property and prior to LD acquiring the shares in S, BH and LD had contemplated that the shares purchased would be the subject of a joint venture. LD had acquired the shares in S, therefore it was appropriate to treat those shares as being subject to a trust held by LD for the benefit of it and BH equally, *Pallant* applied.

BANNER HOMES HOLDINGS LTD (FORMERLY BANNER HOMES GROUP PLC) v. LUFF DEVELOPMENTS LTD (NO.2) [2000] Ch. 372, Chadwick, L.J., CA.

2318. Documents – rectification of trust – letter granting interest to applicant – letter not amounting to rectification of document

C applied to have a document rectified so that lump sum death benefits payable under J's occupational pension scheme would be conferred on her. C argued that a letter written by the settlor, J, was effective to nominate her to the class of beneficiaries under the terms of the discretionary trust.

Held, dismissing the application, that although it might have been J's intention to benefit C, it was not in fact possible to do so by means of rectification which would turn the document into something different from that which was intended at the time it was created.

COLLINS v. JONES *The Times*, February 3, 2000, Judge Stanley Burnton Q.C., Ch D.

2319. **Employment – employers – dishonest conduct – claims subsequent to COT3 agreement**

See EMPLOYMENT: Bank of Credit and Commerce International SA (In Liquidation) v. Ali (No.1). §2173

2320. **Equitable principles – overpayments – entitlement to recoup overpaid royalties**

[Limitation Act 1980 s.35.]

PC, the management company for C, a singer, sought a declaration as to the construction of contracts, and recovery from D and another musician who had performed on a tour, alleged overpayment of royalties arising from recordings of the tour released as a live album. Between 1990 and 1997, D and the other band members, had been paid royalties calculated in accordance with a formula set out in their respective contracts. The payments had never been discounted to reflect the fact that D had performed in only five of the 15 album tracks. Upon realising its mistake, PC commenced the instant proceedings, contending that on a proper interpretation of D's contract, the royalties paid to him ought to have been proportional to the number of tracks in which he featured, and that the overpayment could be recouped by setting it off against future royalties. D, denying overpayment, submitted that (1) the contract rightly provided that he was entitled to royalties on the entire album, so long as he had participated in at least one track, and PC's conduct to date endorsed that view; (2) that he was entitled to retain all past royalties, and be paid on the same basis in the future, by virtue of the principle of estoppel by convention. Alternatively, estoppel by representation prohibited recovery of past payments; (3) D had relied on the payments to the extent that he had insufficient funds to repay them, and (4) the claim was statute barred.

Held, granting judgment for PC, that (1) the construction of the contract sought by D, was devoid of commercial logic and inconsistent with recognised practice in the music industry, as it would enable D to claim royalties on entire future albums, even if he had performed on only one of the tracks. PC's conduct was not to be used as an aid to construction of the contract; (2) the defence of estoppel by convention failed with regard to future payments, because to allow it would be to suggest that the doctrine could be used to change the future meaning of an agreement, and the facts did not satisfy the minimum requirements laid down in *India v. India Steamship Co Ltd (The Indian Endurance and The Indian Grace) (No.2)* [1998] A.C. 878, [1997] C.L.Y. 875. Likewise, estoppel by representation also failed because the tender of payment under a contract was not an indication that such payment was due; (3) recovery of the over-payments was not a matter of appealing to the court's discretion, but was governed by legal principle, *Lipkin Gorman v. Karpnale Ltd* [1991] 2 A.C. 548, [1991] C.L.Y. 502 applied. On the facts, notwithstanding that D had not incurred a specific expense in reliance upon the payments, the extended duration of the payment period had led to a general change in lifestyle, such that recovery was limited to 50 per cent of the amount of the overpayment, and (4) since the case concerned equitable set off, as opposed to legal set off, the Limitation Act 1980 s.35 was not applicable, hence PC's claim was not backdated *Westdeutsche Landesbank Girozentrale v. Islington LBC* [1996] A.C. 669, [1996] C.L.Y. 4149 applied.

PHILIP COLLINS LTD v. DAVIS [2000] 3 All E.R. 808, Jonathan Parker, J., Ch D.

2321. **Estoppel – equitable principles – repeated assurances of inheritance made by benefactor to employee gave rise to estoppel**

G, who was then aged 12, met H, a wealthy landowner, in 1952 and a close friendship developed between the two. At the age of 15, G left school and began to work for H on a full time basis. Although it was initially intended that G should attend agricultural college, this idea was later abandoned as H persuaded G that he could learn more if he continued to work for him. G met S whom he subsequently married. Prior to the marriage, G and S were taken out for a meal by H during which H stated that G would eventually take over the running of the farm and that on his death, the entire business would be left to G. At the christening of G's first child, H stated that the child's birth would enable the farm to continue through to the next generation. Further assurances were made over subsequent years. In 1992, H met W. A relationship developed between them, and by 1994 W had taken the place of G as the principal beneficiary of H's will. H initiated a police investigation into G's management of the accounts relating to the farm business and other associated businesses which G was by then involved with. As a result of the investigation, G and S were the subject of disciplinary proceedings and thereafter summarily dismissed. G issued proceedings against H and W seeking equitable relief on the basis of proprietary estoppel. The judge held ([1998] 3 All E.R. 917) that whilst G's evidence in relation to the assurances made by H was true, there had nevertheless been no assurance from H capable of amounting to an irrevocable promise that G would inherit his estate despite subsequent changes in circumstances, and the claim therefore failed. The court also held that there was insufficient evidence of detriment. G appealed.

Held, allowing the appeal, that (1) the fact that a testamentary disposition was always capable of revocation could not defeat a promise of the kind made by H, whereby he had effectively assured G that "all this will be yours", *Taylor v. Dickens* [1998] 1 F.L.R. 806, [1997] C.L.Y. 4736 considered. On the facts, it was intended that G should rely on the assurances given and they were clearly relied on. Reliance would in any event be presumed, *Greasley v. Cooke* [1980] 1 W.L.R. 1306, [1980] C.L.Y. 1066 referred to. The judge had misdirected himself with regard to the necessary elements of proprietary estoppel. In particular he had exaggerated the extent to which a promise had to be expressly irrevocable in order to give rise to an estoppel, and had further erred in suggesting that there had been a need to find a definite agreement as per the doctrine of mutual wills, and (2) G's case on detriment was compelling. He had left school in the face of opposition from his headmaster and concern from his parents to work for a much older man who had influenced both his social and his working life. In effect, for a period exceeding 30 years, G and his family had acted as a surrogate family to H. In many ways G had been denied the opportunity of bettering himself in reliance on H's oft repeated assurances, and in those circumstances detriment had clearly been established.

GILLETT v. HOLT [2001] Ch. 210, Robert Walker, L.J., CA.

2322. **Estoppel – second arbitration – attempt to raise same issues**

H employed J to extend and refurbish a residential home. H alleged various defects and other breaches in response to J's claim for payment and the matter was referred to arbitration. H sought unsuccessfully to persuade the arbitrator to allow amendment of his pleadings and the matter was subsequently settled by way of a consent order. H then began a second arbitration, claiming damages for various breaches committed by J, including some that had been alleged during the course of the first arbitration. J appealed against an interim award in the second arbitration, contending that there was no jurisdiction to make an award where H was estopped from raising points in the second arbitration that should have been either raised in the first arbitration or had been dealt with by the consent order. Alternatively, that the doctrine of res judicata applied.

Held, allowing the appeal, that H was estopped from raising matters that could have been decided by the first arbitrator, subject to the existence of special circumstances, *Henderson v. Henderson* [1843-60] All E.R. Rep. 378 followed. However, for these to apply, it was not sufficient that the items were known about but not pleaded because of lack of care or inadvertent omission. In the instant case, therefore, the second arbitrator should not have permitted H to put forward points that should have been raised or proceeded with before the first arbitrator.

JONES v. HALL; *sub nom.* RON JONES (BURTON ON TRENT) LTD v. HALL (2000) 2 T.C.L.R. 195, Judge Humphrey Lloyd Q.C., QBD.

2323. **Fiduciary duty – confidential information – proposal to purchase island – no fiduciary duty arose in relation to proposal where offer to represent prospective purchaser rejected**

A company, AI, became interested in purchasing an island off the coast of New Zealand with the aim of developing it for residential and leisure purposes. The island was owned by a forestry company in receivership. AI approached FAR, a group of companies which operated a merchant banking business, with the aim of securing finance for the purchase. FAR dispatched written details of the terms on which they were prepared to act, but these proved unacceptable to AI. FAR gave formal notice of the withdrawal of its offer but subsequently acted as intermediary with third parties in relation to the sale of the island, which was eventually concluded. A company from the FAR group purchased a mill and associated land on the island. AI instituted proceedings in New Zealand contending that FAR had breached a fiduciary duty of loyalty, and that furthermore, they had been in receipt of confidential information which had subsequently been misused, again in breach of a duty to AI. At first instance the court gave judgment for AI but the ruling was reversed on appeal. AI appealed.

Held, dismissing the appeal, that (1) there was no relationship between the parties sufficient to give rise to the duties of a fiduciary, *Bristol and West Building Society v. Mothew (t/a Stapley & Co)* [1998] Ch. 1, [1996] C.L.Y. 4503 considered. There was never any explicit or implicit agreement that FAR would act on behalf of AI and its offer to act as such had been rejected by AI upon receipt, and (2) whilst the information provided by AI to FAR was confidential, there was no evidence to suggest misuse of that information in order to negotiate the purchase, particularly having regard to the time lapse between provision of the information and the eventual sale.

ARKLOW INVESTMENTS LTD v. MacLEAN [2000] 1 W.L.R. 594, Henry, J., PC.

2324. **Fiduciary duty – knowing assistance – provision of fraudulent loans – appellant in receipt of proceeds – insufficient knowledge of fraudulent activities**

JB, a bank, issued proceedings against S, its former managing director, alleging that S had acted in breach of his fiduciary duty in making various loans which resulted in losses to JB in excess of £46 million. H, who was named as a codefendant in those proceedings, was found by the judge to have knowingly assisted S as some of the relevant monies were paid through accounts connected with H's companies. Judgment was entered against H in the sum of £4,572,910. H appealed.

Held, allowing the appeal, that there was insufficient evidence for the judge's finding against H. An inference could not be drawn from H's handling of the transactions that money had been transferred between accounts solely for the purpose of hiding where it had come from. Although H may have had some suspicions about S's activities, he did not have the requisite level of knowledge. There was a risk that the judge, in what was a very lengthy and complex case, had allowed his opinion of H to be tainted by his proximity to the key players in the fraud. In addition, H's lack of full legal representation at the trial had put him at a disadvantage. Furthermore, the judge was wrong to find that JB had lost its right to reclaim the monies by affirming the loan contracts after they had discovered S's fraud. The contracts were not binding on JB since S did not have the authority to enter into them. No beneficial interest in the monies had been transferred to the "borrower" companies. Instead those monies were held on constructive trust for JB, *Rolled Steel Products (Holdings) Ltd v. British Steel Corp* [1986] Ch. 246, [1985] C.L.Y. 306 applied.

JYSKE BANK (GIBRALTAR) LTD v. SPJELDNAES (NO.2) CHANF 1998/0315/3, 0317/3, 0318/3, 0319/3, 0320/3, 0322/3, 0323/3, Nourse, L.J., CA.

2325. Fiduciary duty – limitations

See CIVIL PROCEDURE: Cia de Seguros Imperio v. Heath (REBX) Ltd (formerly CE Heath & Co (America) Ltd). §513

2326. Forfeiture – relief – relief from forfeiture available in case of finance lease

MG, who had granted four finance leases of video and editing equipment to OD, appealed against an order of the High Court ([1999] 2 All E.R. 811, [1999] C.L.Y. 3290) that the court had jurisdiction to grant relief from forfeiture following OD's breach of the leases, and OD appealed against an order that it had lost the right to relief as a result of selling the equipment. All four leases, under which MG had retained title, were subject to a primary rental period of 36 months and thereafter a secondary rental period if such was desired by OD. Following the primary period, OD had the option to be appointed as the sales agent of MG for the purpose of negotiating a sale of the equipment. In the event of a sale being negotiated, OD would receive 95 per cent of the sale proceeds. In February 1998, at which point the primary rental had been paid on all but one of the agreements, OD went into receivership, which constituted a repudiatory breach under the lease terms. Wishing to achieve a speedy sale of OD as a going concern, the receivers obtained leave to sell the equipment with good title with the proceeds being held in escrow. OD then pursued its application for relief from forfeiture, requesting that MG should receive such of the sale proceeds as it would have done had the equipment been sold in accordance with the lease terms. On the appeal against the High Court decision, MG contended that the court had no jurisdiction to grant relief from forfeiture in ordinary commercial contracts that were unconnected with interests in land.

Held, dismissing the appeals, that (1) a finance lease was in principle capable of attracting relief from forfeiture providing that the provision occasioning forfeiture in the lease satisfied one of the conditions referred to by Lord Wilberforce in *Shiloh Spinners Ltd v. Harding (No.1)* [1973] A.C. 691, [1973] C.L.Y. 1867. In the instant case MG's right to forfeit satisfied the condition that it was essentially security for the payment of money. OD had sufficient possessory rights under the leases, and the fact that those leases were commercial contracts with chattels as subject matter as opposed to land went to the question of whether discretion should be exercised rather than jurisdiction, *Shiloh Spinners Ltd*, *BICC Plc v. Burndy Corp* [1985] Ch. 232, [1985] C.L.Y. 2604 and *Transag Haulage Ltd (IAR) v. Leyland DAF Finance Plc* [1994] 2 B.C.L.C. 88, [1995] C.L.Y. 2827 applied, and (2) relief from forfeiture, which essentially involved the continuation of a lease, could not be granted where the lease was in effect extinct. In the instant case the equipment had been sold, and relief could not be granted in respect of the sale proceeds.

ON DEMAND INFORMATION PLC (IN ADMINISTRATIVE RECEIVERSHIP) v. MICHAEL GERSON (FINANCE) PLC [2001] 1 W.L.R. 155, Robert Walker, L.J., CA.

2327. Joint ventures – constructive trusts – agreement to acquire site – acquisition by one party to agreement – shares held on constructive trust

BH and LD entered into an oral agreement, whereby a joint venture company, S, was to be formed to effect the purchase of a development site, under which the shares in S were to be held equally between the parties. Preliminary issues as to the differences in the shareholders' agreement were not concluded prior to exchange of contract, and shortly thereafter LD failed to honour the agreement and the site was subsequently acquired by S with finance supplied by LD. BH commenced proceedings claiming that, prior to the acquisition of the site by S, an oral agreement existed between the parties, alternatively, in the absence of a binding agreement, that circumstances had given rise to a constructive trust in favour of BH over 50 per cent of the shares in S. BH's claim was dismissed on the ground that equity could not convert a common arrangement, which was qualified by the right to withdraw into an unqualified arrangement which precluded such a right. Further, that BH had failed to prove that it had acted to its detriment in reliance on the oral agreement. BH appealed.

Held, allowing the appeal, that the oral arrangement preceded the actual acquisition of the site by LD, and it was inequitable to allow the acquisition of the site solely by LD, as that conflicted with the agreement, *Pallant v. Morgan* [1953] Ch. 43, [1952] C.L.Y. 3571 approved. It was irrelevant that the agreement was contractually unenforceable as equity could intervene. LD had not informed BH that it wished to withdraw from the understanding, and in the circumstances it was the existence either of a detriment suffered to BH, or the advantage gained by LD as of a result of the pre-acquisition arrangement, which led to LD being treated as a trustee. BH did not have to show both to succeed and the judge below had erred by holding that equity could not intervene on the basis that BH had not shown it had acted in detrimental reliance upon the agreement.

BANNER HOMES HOLDINGS LTD (FORMERLY BANNER HOMES GROUP PLC) v. LUFF DEVELOPMENTS LTD (NO.1) [2000] 2 All E.R. 117, Chadwick, L.J., CA.

2328. Life insurance – insurance premiums – tracing – monies could be traced through insurance policy

M controlled a company that obtained money from a number of prospective purchasers to acquire and develop land in the Algarve in Portugal. Although the land was purchased, the development did not take place and the funds were found to have been dissipated. In the meantime M had insured his life for £1 million and subsequently committed suicide. F and 219 other investors in the Portuguese land development discovered that M had used £20,440 of their investment monies to pay 40 per cent of the insurance premiums on his life policy and claimed a proportionate share of the policy's proceeds. F appealed against a decision that the purchasers were entitled only to the refund of the premiums together with interest. The beneficiaries, M's children, cross appealed claiming that (1) the insurance policy would have paid out the whole sum as a result of the first two premiums that M had paid from his own resources and therefore the disputed premium payments had not affected the insurance policy, and (2) the purchasers had already been recompensed by obtaining the land, shares in the company, and a settlement of £600,000 from the bank from which the moneys had been dissipated.

Held, allowing the appeal (Lord Steyn and Lord Hope of Craighead dissenting) and dismissing the cross appeal, that the purchasers had a proprietary right to receive 40 per cent of the policy fund. The equitable interests of the purchasers were directly traceable into the policy moneys and the court had no discretion in the matter. There was no question of resulting or constructive trusts, nor fairness and reasonableness, just the straightforward enforcement of property rights. With regard to the cross appeal, what the purchasers had received was a remedy from different proceedings and they had been put to no election in relation to it. This was not an action for damages where the loss could be mitigated by recovery elsewhere and no adjustment was therefore necessary.

FOSKETT v. McKEOWN [2001] 1 A.C. 102, Lord Browne-Wilkinson, HL.

2329. Limitations – mortgagees powers and duties – power of sale as equitable remedy

See REAL PROPERTY: Raja v. Lloyds TSB Bank Plc. §4657

2330. Quantum meruit – unjust enrichment – claimant entitled to payment for services rendered despite lack of contract

C, a public relations and communications company, claimed damages of £375,000 for breach of contract, or alternatively a quantum meruit in the sum of £55,481 in respect of work done for ICL, a company who had secured a contract to supply a computerised payment system to two national organisations. Before the contract was secured, ICL and G had been members of a consortium of companies bidding for the contract. In the meantime, G had asked C to carry out preliminary work on the basis that, if the consortium were successful, C would be appointed as public relations consultants to the project. Following the withdrawal of G from the consortium, ICL appointed a different company to the project in place of C. C contended that (1) a binding contract had been entered into at the time when G originally invited C to commence work; (2) ICL were estopped from denying the existence of that contract as they had induced C to expect that they would be appointed if ICL's bid were successful and had allowed that expectation to continue, and (3) if it was found that no contract had been entered into, a quantum meruit assessment should be carried out in respect of the work done in anticipation of the contract.

Held, giving judgment for C, that (1) no contract had been concluded between C and ICL. Both parties were aware that detailed negotiations were necessary and it could not be inferred that there was any intention to enter into a binding contract before negotiations were concluded; (2) C could not rely on the principle of estoppel since ICL had not led them to expect that they would be offered a contract, and (3) despite the general rule that a person who carried out work in the hope of gaining a contract did so at his own risk, there were exceptional cases such as this where the court could impose an obligation to pay depending on the individual facts. It would be inequitable for C not to be paid for the work which they carried out since they were induced to carry out the work free of charge by an assurance that ICL would be prepared to negotiate a contract with them if the bid succeeded. The assurance given suggested that the work required from C went far beyond what would normally be expected from a potential sub contractor who would only have an option to bid for the sub contract if the main contractor's bid were to prove successful. The assurance placed the case in a different category far removed from the usual "subject to contract" case where the risks to the potential sub contractor were obvious. This was not a case where the work done by C was defective, or where there had been a disagreement about terms. Instead what had occurred was outside the various risks of working without remuneration which C could fairly be said to have accepted, *Regalian Properties Plc v. London Docklands Development Corp* [1995] 1 W.L.R. 212, [1995] C.L.Y. 794 distinguished and *William Lacey (Hounslow) Ltd v. Davis* [1957] 1 W.L.R. 932, [1957] C.L.Y. 356 considered, and, (4) C's services provided ICL with a benefit for which they would otherwise have had to pay and it would be unjust for ICL to enrich themselves by not paying for C's services. C was duly awarded the sum of £38,370 on a quantum meruit basis.

COUNTRYWIDE COMMUNICATIONS LTD v. ICL PATHWAY LTD [2000] C.L.C. 324, Nicholas Strauss Q.C., QBD.

2331. Restitution – overpayments – recovery of overpayment – estoppel in absence of changed position insufficient to establish defence

D received a redundancy payment of £125,000 from which he invested £90,000 by way of single premium in an individual pension policy with SE. D enquired about the possibility of early retirement benefit and upon exercising that option received a tax-free payment of £36,588 together with a residual life pension of £4,655 per annum escalating at three per cent each year from the date of the first payment. When he reached the age of sixty five D approached SE about the consequences of his forthcoming receipt of a state pension. SE sent D a statement in which a fund of over £201,000 was shown. After queries as to this amount from D and a financial advisor under his instruction SE confirmed both verbally and in writing that the statement was correct. D, exercising an option under the policy, later received a tax-free payment of £51,333 and invested a further £150,604 in an alternative pension scheme. SE then discovered an administrative error had resulted in a failure to update D's record after his initial early retirement benefit payment. The error had resulted in an overpayment to D of £172,451. SE sought recovery of the funds overpaid on the basis of unjust enrichment and mistaken fact. D disputed SE's claim contending that SE's carelessness or refusal to investigate the matter properly prevented restitution. D argued that he had changed his position and that SE were estopped from recovering the funds paid to him.

Held, giving judgment for SE, that (1) while SE had made a number of serious administrative errors they were prima facie entitled to recover the money overpaid. Mere carelessness did not by itself preclude recovery of the money, *Kelly v. Solari* (1841) 9 M. & W. 54 and *Barclays Bank Ltd v. WJ Simms Son & Cooke (Southern) Ltd* [1980] Q.B. 677, [1979] C.L.Y. 157 considered; (2) there was no causal link between D's receipt of the payment and his change of position. D's general financial and other difficulties constituted problems that he would have faced with or without the error having been made, *Lipkin Gorman v. Karpnale Ltd* [1991] 2 A.C. 548, [1991] C.L.Y. 502 and *South Tyneside MBC v. Svenska International Plc* [1995] 1 All E.R. 545, [1995] C.L.Y. 764 considered, and (3) on the facts of the instant case it was not appropriate for a plea of estoppel to provide a complete defence following the recognition of the defence of change of position in *Lipkin Gorman* because D had acted to his detriment only in relation to £9661 and it would therefore be inequitable to permit him to retain the entirety of the overpayment, *Avon CC v. Howlett* [1983] 1 W.L.R. 605, [1983] C.L.Y. 1210 distinguished. It was observed that statements made concerning the inappropriateness of the doctrine of estoppel as a complete defence where a change of position was not established in relation to the whole of the sum mistakenly paid should not be read as a general statement of principle but were confined to the particular facts of the instant case.

SCOTTISH EQUITABLE PLC v. DERBY [2000] 3 All E.R. 793, Harrison, J., QBD.

2332. Solicitors – fraudulent breach of trust – causation – right to restitutionary remedy

In an action brought by C against his solicitor, B, for damages for breach of trust, breach of contract and negligence, C appealed against a finding that he was not permitted to recover from B the sum of £524,100, which sum B had misappropriated in breach of trust, and which C contended had resulted in his losing a much greater amount. The sum had been part of the purchase price of shares in J, a company. C had argued that, upon receipt of the money, B had dealt with it in such a way that he had been unable to implement an agreement whereby he would secure a majority shareholding in J. This, he maintained, had caused him to advance and borrow large sums of money which he would not otherwise have had to expend. The court of first instance had found that since C had received the shares that he had paid for, B's fraud had not been causative of his alleged loss of the sum of £524,100. In his appeal, C submitted that fraud was an appropriate case to order a restitutionary remedy in accordance with equitable principles, *Swindle v. Harrison* [1997] 4 All E.R. 705, [1997] C.L.Y. 3822 cited.

Held, dismissing the appeal, that C could not rely on equity to obviate the need to prove causation. There was no principle upon which C could rely to claim equitable compensation for B's breach of trust in respect of losses which had not been caused by that breach. The payment of £524,100 to B and the subsequent creation of the trust for that sum had resulted directly from the transaction concerning the sale and purchase of the shares in J. That transaction had been completed when C had received his shares, and his decision to make further advances to J had been unrelated to B's breach of trust. To oblige B to reconstitute the trust fund would be to effect a double recovery for C, which would not be an equitable result. Furthermore, an award of an identical amount to that of the trust fund would not be equitable, since it would bear no relation to C's actual loss. *Target Holdings Ltd v. Redferns (No.1)* [1996] A.C. 421, [1995] C.L.Y. 2195, which had been relied upon in *Swindle*, had been correctly applied by the lower court, since the principles emerging from that case were applicable to actions for fraudulent breach of trust.

COLLINS v. BREBNER [2000] Lloyd's Rep. P.N. 587, Tuckey, L.J., CA.

2333. Unconscionability – mortgages – mortgage taken out by elderly man to assist son – duties of mortgage

D applied for a mortgage with PBS at the age of 72, the aim of the transaction being to provide a means for D's son, S, to purchase a supermarket business. S acted as guarantor for the loan. The mortgage was granted but S defaulted and PBS commenced possession proceedings. D defended the claim on the basis of non est factum, undue influence and unconscionability relying on the decision in *Credit Lyonnais Bank Nederland NV v. Burch* [1997] 1 All E.R. 144, [1996] C.L.Y. 2784. Judgment was granted to PBS and D appealed, contending that the judge at first instance had not fully dealt with the defence of unconscionability. D maintained that he was poor, illiterate and in receipt of a very low income and on that basis PBS should have declined the advance,

Held, dismissing the appeal, that whilst the transaction had clearly been very unwise from D's point of view there had been no obligation upon PBS to ensure that D as a parent had been acting appropriately in seeking to assist his son. None of the vital ingredients normally found in a case of unconscionable bargain, which were similar to those necessary to establish undue influence, were to be found in the instant case, *Burch* distinguished on the basis that D had received independent legal advice, *Royal Bank of Scotland v. Etridge (No.2)* [1998] 4 All E.R. 705, [1998] C.L.Y. 4358 and *Barclays Bank v. O'Brien* [1994] 1 A.C. 180, [1994] C.L.Y. 3300 considered. D was not at a serious disadvantage to PBS, neither D nor S had been indebted to PBS beforehand and D was not exploited by PBS nor did they act in any morally questionable way towards him. Whilst the agreement had been unwise the bargain as a whole had not been "overreaching and oppressive".

PORTMAN BUILDING SOCIETY v. DUSANGH [2000] 2 All E.R. (Comm) 221, Simon Brown, L.J., CA.

2334. Undue influence – transactions in favour of third party – applicability of doctrine

N applied to set aside a land transaction made in favour of B alleging that, in entering into the transaction, she had relied on the advice of B's husband, a solicitor who had placed undue influence on her.

Held, giving judgment for N, that the doctrine of undue influence was not limited to transactions which were in favour of, or which had been instigated by, the individual on whom reliance had been placed. The basis on which the transaction could be impugned was the abuse of a position of trust and the doctrine of undue influence applied where the wrongdoer had personal reasons for wishing the complainant to deal with the person in whose favour the transaction was made. It made no difference that the transaction originated with the third party if it could be shown that the relationship of trust and confidence between the complainant and the wrongdoer had been abused in order to induce the complainant to enter into the transaction. The onus then rested upon the wrongdoer to rebut the presumption of undue influence by showing that the complainant had acted independently, evidenced in most cases by the receipt of independent legal advice by the complainant. It was not sufficient to show that the complainant understood the nature and effect of the transaction; the advisor had to establish that the complainant was free from improper influence.

NAIDOO v. NAIDU *The Times*, November 1, 2000, Blackburne, J., Ch D.

2335. Publications

Doherty, Michael – Equity and Trusts. 2nd Ed. Old Bailey Press Revision Workbook Series. Paperback: £7.95. ISBN 1-85836-353-5. Old Bailey Press.

Halliwell, Margaret – Equity and Trusts. 2nd Ed. Old Bailey Press Textbook Series. Paperback: £11.95. ISBN 1-85836-363-2. Old Bailey Press.

Smith, Lionel D. – Restitution. International Library of Essays in Law and Legal Theory (second Series). Hardback: £100.00. ISBN 0-7546-2057-3. Hardback: £100.00. ISBN 0-7546-2057-3. Dartmouth.

EUROPEAN UNION

2336. **Agricultural produce – fruit – importation of cherries from third country – levying of countervailing duties**

[Council Regulation 2707/72; Commission Regulation 1395/94 Art.1.]
L imported sour cherries into Germany from Romania. Under Commission Regulation 1395/94 Art.1 the consignment was subjected to a countervailing charge equivalent to the difference between the price paid by L and the minimum Community price. When delivered, the fruit was in fact decaying and L was compelled to sell the entire consignment to a distillery at a substantial discount. Accordingly customs authorities imposed increases to the countervailing charge to reflect the discounted price and L's reduced transport costs. The German Finance Court referred the question to the European Court of Justice.
Held, giving a preliminary ruling, that the preamble to Council Regulation 2707/72 which provided the framework for protective measures for fruit and vegetables emphasised that measures should be in keeping with circumstances so that they have none but the desired effect of equalising prices. The sale of spoiled cherries to a distillery did not affect the Community market in fresh fruit. Commission Regulation 1395/94 Art.1 must be interpreted as meaning that a countervailing charge may not be levied in respect of sour cherries released for free circulation within the Community at a low price, where that low price was attributable to circumstances beyond the control of the importer and was unconnected with the origin of the goods, such as significant and unexpected deterioration of the fruit, *Dinter GmbH v. Hauptzollamt Bad Reichenhall (C81/92)* [1993] E.C.R. I-4601, [1994] C.L.Y. 4758 followed.
LUKSCH v. HAUPTZOLLAMT WEIDEN (C31/98) [2000] 2 C.M.L.R. 472, P Jann (President), ECJ.

2337. **Agricultural produce – milk products – butter – intervention agencies – adequacy of checks carried out by Member State to prevent fraud**

[EC Treaty Art.190 (now Art.253 EC); Council Regulation 729/70 on the financing of the common agricultural policy Art.8(1), Art.8(2); Council Regulation 283/72 Art.3, Art.4.]
The European Agricultural Guidance and Guarantee Fund, E, was entitled under Council Regulation 729/70 to stabilise market prices for agricultural produce, but only if the intervention complied with certain rules. Art.8(1) of Regulation 729/70 required Member States to ensure that transactions financed by E were carried out correctly and to prevent irregularities. Art.8(2) of Regulation 729/70 provided that any financial irregularities were to be borne by the relevant Member State. Council Regulation 283/72 Art.3 and 4 required Member States to notify the Commission promptly of any irregularities discovered by the Member States. Under the rules, E was authorised to purchase butter only if it conformed to precise compositional requirements. Following an investigation, the Commission determined that most butter produced in N did not comply and that N was aware of that fact. The Commission also found that, although there had been fraud, N had never demanded repayments from the undertakings concerned or notified the Commission of those irregularities. The Commission therefore reduced the accounts presented by N for reimbursement of intervention expenditure on butter. N applied to the Court for partial annulment of that decision.
Held, dismissing the application, that (1) there was sufficient evidence of N's infringement of Regulation 729/70 Art.8(2). Where the Commission refused to charge expenditure to E on the grounds that it was incurred as a result of breaches of Community rules for which breach a Member State could be held responsible, the Commission need only adduce evidence of serious and reasonable doubt. The Commission was not obliged to demonstrate exhaustively that the checks carried out by N were inadequate, *Exportslachterijen van Oordegem BVBA v. Belgische Dienst voor Bedrifsleven en Landbouw (C2/93)* [1994] E.C.R. I-2283, [1994] C.L.Y. 4748, *France v.*

Commission of the European Communities (C235/97) [1998] E.C.R. I-7555 and *Germany v. Commission of the European Communities (C54/95)* [1999] E.C.R. I-35 followed, (2) the obligation within Council Regulation 283/72 Art.3 and 4 to communicate irregularities to the Commission encompassed incidents of fraud which came to the attention of N, and (3) the extent of the duty to state reasons for a decision as laid down in EC Treaty Art.190 (now Art.253 EC) depended on the nature of the act and the context in which it was adopted. N was fully aware of the reasons for the Commission's decision not to charge the contested amounts to E, *Germany v. Commission of the European Communities (C54/91)* [1993] E.C.R. I-3399, [1993] C.L.Y. 4207 and *Netherlands v. Commission of the European Communities (C27/94)* [1998] E.C.R. I-5581 followed.

NETHERLANDS v. COMMISSION OF THE EUROPEAN COMMUNITIES (C28/94) [2000] 2 C.M.L.R. 436, PJG Kapteyn (President), ECJ.

2338. Beef – exports – implementation of Directive 64/433 – incorporation of later amendments to Directive

[Products of Animal Origin (Import and Export) Regulations 1992 (SI 1992 3298); Council Directive 64/433 on health problems affecting intra-Community trade in fresh meat Art.3.1 (A) (f) (iii); Commission Decision 94/474; Commission Decision 94/794; Commission Decision 95/287.]

M appealed against a conviction of being involved in the transportation of beef without accompanying valid health certificates, contrary to the Products of Animal Origin (Import and Export) Regulations 1992. M appealed, arguing that there was no legal justification for the contention that at the material time the UK had been a "restricted region or area" within the definition in Council Directive 64/433 Art.3.1 (A) (f) (iii).

Held, allowing the appeal, that the Directive had been amended by Commission Decision 94/474, Commission Decision 94/794 and Commission Decision 95/287, which had placed progressively greater restrictions on the export of British beef culminating in its absolute ban. Although to avoid a nonsensical result those Decisions had to be treated as having established the UK as a restricted area requiring health certification, the Regulations implementing the Directive had been made prior to the amendments. As the Regulations did not state that they would incorporate future amendments of EC law, such incorporation could not be construed and therefore the Regulations had to be taken as implementing only the unamended version of the Directive, which did not require health certification.

MAYNE v. MINISTRY OF AGRICULTURE, FISHERIES AND FOOD; CHITTY WHOLESALE LTD v. MINISTRY OF AGRICULTURE, FISHERIES AND FOOD [2001] E.H.L.R. 5, Kennedy, L.J., QBD.

2339. Community Acts – loans – Commission's refusal to recognise amendments – non addressee's right to seek annulment

[EC Treaty Art.173 (now, after amendment, Art.230 EC); Commission Regulation 1897/92; Council Decision 91/658.]

The Council of the European Communities by adopting Council Decision 91/658 authorised a medium term loan to the USSR and subsequently to the Russian Federation to enable the purchase of food. S was a supplier of grain and entered into a contract of supply with Russia. Under Commission Regulation 1897/92 the European Commission was only able to make loans provided that it recognised the supply contract as conforming with the requirements of Council Decision 91/658. The Commission recognised the conformity of the contract in issue. The contract was, however, subsequently amended, on terms which required Russia to pay an increased price for the grain supplied by S. The Commission refused to recognise the amendments, and communicated this refusal to Russia's designated commercial agent, V. S learned of this refusal, ceased deliveries of grain, and applied to the ECJ for annulment of the Commission's refusal to recognise the amendments to the contract. The matter was referred to the CFI, which held that S's claim for annulment was inadmissible, since the decision did not directly concern S under the EC Treaty Art.173 (now, after amendment, Art.230 EC). S appealed to the ECJ against the dismissal of its claim for annulment.

Held, allowing the appeal, that (1) a person was directly concerned with a Community measure if the measure directly affected their legal situation and if it left no discretion on its implementation to those to whom it was addressed directly. The Commission's refusal to recognise the contractual amendments deprived S of any real prospect of performing the contract, or of obtaining payment for supplies made under it. Therefore, although the refusal had been addressed to V, it directly affected S's legal position, and S was therefore directly concerned with the refusal.

SOCIETE LOUIS DREYFUS & CIE v. COMMISSION OF THE EUROPEAN COMMUNITIES (C386/96) [1999] 1 C.M.L.R. 481, GC Rodriguez Iglesias (President), ECJ.

2340. Counterfeiting – confidential information – disclosure of consignee's identity;

[Protection of Confidential Information Act (Sweden); Council Regulation 3295/94 laying down measures to prohibit the release for free circulation, export, re-export or entry for a suspensive procedure of counterfeit and pirated goods.]

The Swedish Customs Office suspended the release of certain goods bearing a certain registered mark into free circulation having formed the view that they were counterfeit. A inspected the goods and concluded that they were indeed counterfeit. A applied for the detention of the goods under Council Regulation 3295/94. Under this Regulation the goods could only be detained for one month if A did not institute an ordinary court action. However A could not commence an action as it had no knowledge of the identity of the declarant or the consignee against whom an action could be brought. The Swedish authorities refused to divulge the relevant information on the basis that it was confidential so that its release was precluded under the Protection of Confidential Information Act (Sweden). A appealed against the refusal and the national court referred the issue to the ECJ as to whether the Regulation precluded the operation of domestic laws preventing the disclosure of the identity of the parties concerned.

Held, giving a preliminary ruling, that the Regulation did prevent the application of the Act in withholding the identity of either the declarant or consignee of imported counterfeited goods.

ADIDAS AG (C223/98), *Re*; *sub nom.* ADIDAS AG'S REFERENCE (C223/98) [1999] 3 C.M.L.R. 895, DAO Edward (President), ECJ.

2341. Counterfeiting – search an seizure – applicability to goods in transit through Community

[Council Regulation 3295/94 laying down measures to prohibit the release for free circulation, export, re-export or entry for a suspensive procedure of counterfeit and pirated goods.]

Austrian customs, at the request of P, seized T-shirts, which were suspected of been counterfeits of P's brands and which were being transported from Indonesia to Poland. In subsequent court proceedings, the Austrian Supreme Court sought a preliminary ruling from the ECJ as to whether Council Regulation 3295/94 allowing customs authorities of Member States to impound suspected counterfeit goods applied to goods in transit moving through Community territory from one non Member State to another non Member State.

Held, giving a preliminary ruling, that it was clear that the Regulation applied to goods in such cases, and it did not matter whether the company holding rights in the goods had a registered office in the Community or not. The transit of such non-Community goods could have an effect on the internal market, and there was no apparent reason from the facts to question the applicability of the Regulation to the case.

POLO/LAUREN CO LP v. PT DWIDUA LANGGENG PRATAMA INTERNATIONAL FREIGHT FORWARDERS (C383/98) [2000] E.T.M.R. 535, L Sevon (President), ECJ (1st Chamber).

2342. **Court of First Instance – jurisdiction – error of law – court substituting its own reasoning for that of Commission**

[EC Treaty Art.85(3)(now Art.81(3) EC), Art.173 (now, after amendment, Art.230 EC), Art.190 (now Art.253 EC); Council Decision 90/685 implementing an action programme to promote the development of the European audiovisual industry (MEDIA).]

U, a film distribution company owned equally by three international film companies and a number of its subsidiaries, applied for distribution funding under the MEDIA programme established by Council Decision 90/685, which provided interest free loans to assist in the distribution of films in different Member States. U's application was rejected on the grounds that its status was uncertain because of a pending application to renew an exemption under the EC Treaty Art.85(3) (now Art.81(3) EC) and that distribution by subsidiaries did not fulfil MEDIA's funding criteria. U's application to annul the decision was refused and U appealed, contending that the CFI had erred in law when it had found that the Commission had discretion to refuse U's application on the basis that it did not further the aims of MEDIA or that its status was uncertain pending its exemption application. Further, that the court had substituted its own reasoning for that of the Commission in contravention of Art.173 (now, after amendment, Art.230 EC) and Art.190 (now Art.253 EC).

Held, allowing the appeal, that the court had correctly interpreted MEDIA's funding criteria, in that applications were to be submitted by at least three distributors with no prior history of substantial co-operation. Funding applications could also be validly rejected where there were grounds for believing the loan would not be repaid, compatibility with Art.85 being a precondition. However, in finding that U's application could be rejected on the basis of its uncertain status, the court's reasoning was based on an erroneous interpretation of the Commission's decision, which had not expressly referred to the Art.85(3) procedure. This error of law meant that the court had substituted its own reasoning for that of the Commission.

DIR INTERNATIONAL FILM SRL v. COMMISSION OF THE EUROPEAN COMMUNITIES (C164/98 P) [2000] 1 C.M.L.R. 619, Schintgen (President), ECJ.

2343. **Court of First Instance – jurisdiction – state aids – classification of exemptions and concessions**

[EC Treaty Art.92 (now, after amendment, Art.87 EC).]

France appealed against a decision of the CFI ([2000] 3 C.M.L.R. 611, [1998] C.L.Y. 740) that a European Commission decision should be annulled. The CFI had found, contrary to the Commission decision, that certain exemptions and concessions granted to PMU, an economic interest group concerned with the management of off-course betting, constituted State aid, contrary to the EC Treaty Art.92 (now, after amendment, Art.87 EC).

Held, dismissing the appeal that, (1) the CFI's jurisdiction was not limited to deciding whether the Commission had made a clear error of assessment in classifying the reduction in public levy payments. State aid was a legal concept to be interpreted on the basis of objective factors and the CFI's role was to examine comprehensively whether the disputed measure qualified as aid within the meaning of Art.92(1). The CFI had made no error of law in this regard. Neither had it erred in its assessment of the criteria used by the Commission in relation to this point. Further, the CFI's findings of fact were legally correct and, in any event, findings of fact by the CFI could not be reviewed on appeal; (2) the CFI's reasoning for its ruling was sufficiently detailed and correct in law, *Compagnie Nationale Air France v. Commission of the European Communities*

(T358/94) [1996] E.C.R. II-2109 followed; (3) the CFI had found that France's contentions regarding a VAT deduction exemption were based on factual errors, which made it impossible to determine if State aid was involved. A substantial assessment of this point was beyond the ECJ's appellate jurisdiction, and (4) the CFI had correctly concluded that the Commission had not given reasons for its findings that a national court decision that the obligation to repay sums wrongly exempted from a housing levy arose at the time the investigation commenced in 1991 and gave rise to a legitimate expectation that aid received prior to that date was lawful.

FRANCE v. LADBROKE RACING LTD (C83/98) [2000] 3 C.M.L.R. 555, GC Rodriguez Iglesias (President), ECJ.

2344. **Court of First Instance – practice note – criteria for hearings before single judge**

The Practice Note sets out the criteria under which a single judge is able to hear and decide cases which come before the Court of First Instance. The Judge Rapporteur, sitting as a single judge, may decide cases which do not involve difficult questions of fact or law, which are of limited importance, or involve any other special circumstances concerning (1) Community officials; (2) decisions of Community institutions where the case is a direct action brought by the person to whom the decision is addressed, provided that the case raises only questions already clarified by established case law or forms part of a series of cases and of which one has already been finally decided, and (3) the arbitration of a dispute arising out of a contract concluded by or on behalf of the Community. There must be a unanimous decision by the chamber comprised of three judges before a case may be delegated all the parties must have been heard. Where a party which is a Member State or Community institution objects to the delegation of the case it must be heard by or referred to the chamber to which the Judge Rapporteur belongs. Certain specified classes of cases cannot be heard by a single judge, including those raising issues as to the legality of an act of general application.

PRACTICE NOTE (CFI: CONSTITUTION) [2000] All E.R. (EC) 1, Judge not specified, CFI.

2345. **Customs administration – customs charges – recovery – compatibility of national time limits – Italy**

Italian national rules for the imposition of charges for customs operations were held by the ECJ to be contrary to the EC Treaty. Those national rules were subsequently amended to comply with that judgment but only after legislation had been introduced laying down a time limit of five years (later reduced to three years) for the bringing of claims for the refund of sums paid in connection with customs operations. On a claim for reimbursement of sums unduly paid as customs charges on behalf of a Milan customs agent it was argued that the claim was statute barred by reason of the three year time limit. The national court asked the ECJ to determine (1) whether Community law precluded the application of a national provision which introduced, in relation to customs charges, a limited time limit instead of the ordinary 10 year limitation period, and (2) whether Community law precluded a Member State from relying on a national time limit to resist actions for repayment of taxes levied in breach of Community provisions at a time when that state had not amended its national rules to comply with those provisions.

Held, giving a preliminary ruling, (1) that Community law did not preclude the legislation of a Member State from laying down, alongside a limitation period applicable under the ordinary law to actions between private individuals for the recovery of sums paid but not due, special procedural rules which are less favourable. On the evidence, the legislation at issue was not to be regarded as amended specifically to limit the consequences of the ECJ's rulings. Community law did not preclude the application of a national provision which imposed a special time limit for actions for repayment of customs charges, instead of a longer period for actions for recovery of other sums, and (2) the conduct of the Italian authorities did not have the effect of depriving the plaintiff company of enforcing its rights before the national courts. Community law did not prohibit a Member State from resisting actions for repayment of charges levied in breach of Community law by relying on a time limit under national law, even if that member state had not yet amended those national rules to render them compatible with those provisions.

APRILE SRL v. AMMINISTRAZIONE DELLE FINANZE DELLO STATO (C228/96) [2000] 1 W.L.R. 126, GC Rodriguez Iglesias (President), ECJ.

2346. **Customs duty – dumping – calculation of constructed normal value – comparables**

[Council Regulation 2423/88; Council Regulation 5/96 imposing definitive anti dumping duties on imports of microwave ovens originating in China, Korea, Malaysia and Thailand and collecting definitively the duty imposed.]

Council Regulation 2423/88 set out rules to combat subsidised imports of goods from outside the European Community. Article 2(3)(6)(ii) contained methods of calculating the anti dumping duty to be imposed, based on the constructed normal value of the relevant product, where there were no sales of a like product on the exporting country's domestic market and which required a number of factors to be taken into account so as to provide an appropriate comparison. Where this was not possible, Art.2(3)(6)(ii) permitted the calculation to be made "by any other reasonable method". A manufactured microwave ovens in Thailand, but did not sell them there. There was, therefore, no domestic market. Nor, in this case, were the other factors present which would otherwise have fallen to be considered in assessing the constructed normal value of A's microwave ovens. Accordingly, the Community institutions, proceeding on the "any other reasonable method" basis, calculated A's manufacturing costs, increased by an amount representing sales, administrative and general expenses, and also employed a comparison with the Korean domestic market. This calculation was then used to determine the anti dumping duty to be imposed under Council Regulation 5/96 upon A, which was assessed at 14 per cent on all imports of microwave ovens from Thailand. A sought the annulment of Regulation 5/96, contending that (1) the choice of method for determining the sales, general and administrative expenses, and profit margin was in breach of Regulation 2423/88; (2) the use of the Korean data was unreasonable, and (3) account had been taken of import duties and indirect charges in assessing the constructed normal value contrary to Regulation 2423/88 Art.2(10)(6).

Held, that Regulation 2423/88 Art.2 was not infringed by the provisions of Regulation 5/96, (1) the Council had been justified in rejecting as unreliable data provided by A's parent company upon which A had sought to rely in relation to its expenses and profit margins, and had not acted unreasonably in so doing; (2) in relation to the Korean data, Regulation 2423/88 Art.2(3)(6)(ii) allowed the use of data from third parties where the method employed was reasonable. The Korean market was the only market covered by the present anti dumping proceedings where sales of the like product were made in comparable quantities. Moreover, adjustments had been made to allow for pertinent differences so that use of the data was reasonable. There was therefore no manifest error, nor any breach of the principles of equity, in employing it, *Nakajima All Precision Co Ltd v. Council of Ministers of the European Communities (C69/89 R)* [1991] E.C.R. I-2069 and *Crispoltoni v. Fattoria Autonoma Tabacchi (C133/93)* [1994] E.C.R. I-4863 followed, and (3) with regard to the treatment of import duties and indirect charges, there was no dispute that import duty would have been payable by A had it sold the microwaves on the Thai market. Since these would have been reimbursed on export, the Council deducted them from the constructed normal value. Article 2(10(6) further provided that the constructed normal value be further reduced by the equivalent of any import charges or indirect taxes. Deduction of amounts higher than such import charges or indirect taxes was not therefore liable to be made.

ACME INDUSTRY CO LTD v. COUNCIL OF THE EUROPEAN UNION (T48/96) [1999] 3 C.M.L.R. 823, Cooke (President), CFI.

2347. Customs duty – dumping – retrospective exemption

[Council Regulation 1567/97 Council Regulation (EC) No 1567/97 concerning a definitive anti-dumping duty on imports of leather handbags originating in the People's Republic of China.]

MG, together with another company, L, manufactured handbags in China. The Commission undertook an investigation into dumping in relation to handbags imported from China, which led to the imposition of anti dumping duties under Council Regulation 1567/97, initially set at 38 per cent. Following a review, the Commission set L's duty at 0 per cent, as it found that L had not been involved in any dumping, but it refused to back date the reviewed duty. MG applied for a refund of duty it had paid on L's products and for the Regulation to be annulled.

Held, allowing the application, that the application was admissible as MG had a legitimate interest in, and was individually affected by, the Regulation as it had the effect of not allowing retroactive implementation of the reviewed duty. The Commission had selected an investigation period during which L had not been involved in any dumping, and it had therefore to give retroactive effect to that fact. The provision for imposing duty was aimed at ensuring that duties could be enforced on all relevant undertakings and was not meant to be a way of penalising them. The giving of retroactive effect was permissible where the recipient would thereby be in a better legal position and its legitimate expectations protected, as would be the situation in the instant case. The relevant parts of the Regulation would therefore be annulled in order to give the reviewed duty retroactive effect.

MEDICI GRIMM KG v. COUNCIL OF THE EUROPEAN UNION (T7/99) [2000] 3 C.M.L.R. 374, Tiili (President), CFI.

2348. Customs duty – investigations – fraud – duty of customs authorities to inform principal

[Council Regulation 1430/79 on the repayment or remission of import or export duties Art.13(1); Commission Regulation 2454/93 laying down provisions for the interpretation of Council Regulation 2913/92 establishing the Community Customs Code; Commission Decision 98/372 on animal health conditions and veterinary certification for imports of live animals of bovine and porcine species.]

D, a Dutch customs agent, issued seven customs certificates for consignments of cigarettes between July and September 1993, whilst acting in the capacity of a principal. The cigarettes were meant for export out of the Community under the external transit system. However, the Dutch Customs authorities had strong grounds to believe that the cigarettes were not leaving the Community and that this would give rise to a Customs debt for which D would be liable. They did not inform D. On investigation it was found that there was a fraud, but that D was entirely innocent of either fault or dishonesty. However, the Customs authority required D to pay the customs debt. D challenged this decision in the national courts. Proceedings were stayed and the following questions were referred to the ECJ: (1) whether the Customs authorities were obliged under the external transit regime to inform a principal of their suspicion of fraud, to enable him to avoid liability for a customs debt, and (2) if there was such an obligation, what were the consequences if it was not complied with.

Held, giving a preliminary ruling, that although the content of the second was altered as a matter of procedural expediency: (1) Community law does not impose a duty on customs authorities, who have been informed of a possible fraud within the external transit regime, to inform principals, even where the principal would be liable for customs duty, and had acted in good faith, and (2) Council Regulation 1430/79 Art.13(1) referred to certain special situations where a principal could avoid the payment of customs duties. In such situations a principal must be innocent of any deception or negligence. Although the situations listed within the meaning of Art.13(1) were not exhaustive, one of the special situations was where, as in the present case, customs authorities were conducting an investigation and a principal had not been informed and the offences had been allowed to be committed in the interests of the investigation. It followed that, Commission Decision C(98) 372, reached under Commission Regulation 2454/93 was invalid.

DE HAAN BEHEER BV v. INSPECTEUR DER INVOERRECHTEN EN ACCUNZEN TE ROTTERDAM (C61/98) [1999] All E.R. (EC) 803, J-P Puissochet (President), ECJ.

2349. Customs duty – repayments – penalty for breaching time limits under Community Customs Code

[Council Regulation 2913/92 establishing the Community Customs Code; Community Regulation 2454/93 laying down provisions for the interpretation of Council regulation 2913/92.]

S imported non Community goods into the Community for later re-export. Upon their arrival in Germany, the goods were presented to Customs and released to S for temporary storage. Council Regulation 2913/92, the Community Customs Code laid down time limits for the completion of customs clearance. S told Customs that it would not always be able to meet the time limits, and following a number of failures by S, Customs refused to grant S's requests for extensions of time, and warned S about the incurring of customs debt as a result of its failure to comply. During 1995, Customs issued notices of assessment for customs duties, all of which S challenged. S sought annulment of the duties assessed and challenged Customs' rejection of its appeal for repayment of duties in proceedings before the national court. The court ordered the two issues to be joined, and referred a number of points to the ECJ relating to the proper interpretation of the Code, and the validity of Commission Regulation 2454/93 Art.859 an exhaustive code of non significant customs failures incurring debt under the Code, and Art.900 of Regulation 2454/93 providing for repayment of duties in relation to goods eligible either for Community treatment or preferential tariff treatment.

Held, giving a preliminary ruling, that (1) in respect of Art.204 and Art.249 of the Code, the Council had laid down essential rules regarding customs debt, and was empowered to delegate power to the Commission to adopt all necessary measures, provided these conformed with the essential rules and/or implementing legislation adopted by the Council, *Germany v. Commission of the European Communities (C240/90)* [1992] E.C.R. I-5383, [1993] C.L.Y. 4195, *Zuckerfabrik Franken GmbH v. Hauptzollamt Wurzburg (C121/83)* [1984] E.C.R. 2039, *Netherlands v. Commission of the European Communities (C478/93)* [1995] E.C.R. I-3081, [1996] C.L.Y. 2809 and *Belgium v. Commission of the European Communities (C9/95)* [1997] E.C.R. I-645 followed; (2) Art.859 of Regulation 2454/93 met the Code's aim of ensuring uniform application and avoiding fraud. It contained a full and valid code of non significant customs failures incurring customs debt; (3) repayment of duties required strict compliance with the relevant provisions. Lack of obvious negligence by the trader, *R. v. Commissioners of Customs and Excise, ex p. EMU Tabac Sarl (C296/95)* [1998] Q.B. 791, [1998] C.L.Y. 4643 followed, was a prerequisite to any repayment, *Hauptzollamt Giessen v. Deutscher Fernsprecher GmbH (C64/89)* [1990] E.C.R. I-2535 followed, and was required even where the circumstances set out in Art.900 of Regulation 2454/93 applied; (4) traders had the right to appeal against refusals to grant time extensions under Art.234 of the Code. Under Art.245 of the Code, it was for the Member States to establish the appeals procedure; (5) only exceptional circumstances justified the granting of extensions, and it was for the national courts to determine if such circumstances existed; (6) time limits could only be extended under Art.49 of the Code prior to their initial expiry, and (7) in determining an application for repayment of duties, a customs authority must look at all the circumstances set out in Art.900 to Art.904 of Regulation 2454/93. If unable to make a decision, it must verify whether a special situation existed under Art.905 and remit the matter if necessary to the Commission for determination, *Woltmann (t/a Trans-ex-Import) v. Hauptzollamt Potsdam (C86/97)* [1999] E.C.R. I-1041 followed.

FIRMA SOHL & SOHLKE v. HAUPTZOLLAMT BREMEN (C48/98) [2000] 1 C.M.L.R. 351, Schintgen (President), ECJ.

2350. Customs duty – repayments – refusal by EC Commission

[EC Treaty Art.190 (now Art.253 EC); Council Regulation 1430/79 on the repayment or remission of import or export duties Art.13; Commission Regulation 2454/93 laying down provisions for the implementation of Council Regulation 2913/92 establishing the Community Customs Code.]

M, a Dutch customs agent, made 98 customs declarations in respect of certain imports made by a third party over a 16 month period. The declarations were based on invoices subsequently found to be fraudulent. As a result, M was liable to pay a higher rate of tax, but it later sought a repayment, and the Dutch tax authorities forwarded the application to the European Commission. The Commission refused M's application, but later revoked its refusal in the light of the decision in *France Aviation v. Commission of the European Communities (T346/94)* [1996] All E.R. (EC) 177, [1996] C.L.Y. 2791. The Dutch authorities then sought further information from M in support of its repayment application, which was forwarded to the Commission. The Commission refused the re-application and M sought annulment of the second refusal.

Held, refusing the application, that (1) although the Commission had correctly annulled its first decision on the grounds that M's right to be heard had been infringed, *France Aviation* followed, the second decision refusing repayment was tainted with a number of irregularities, causing the Commission to exceed its powers under Commission Regulation 2454/93 and to fail to have regard to the principle of legal certainty; (2) M had a guaranteed right to be heard at both the national level and in subsequent proceedings before the Commission. However, the statement which M had to file only guaranteed this right in the national proceedings, *Eyckeler & Malt AG v. Commission of the European Communities (T42/96)* [1998] ECR II-401 and *Primex Produkte Import-Export GmbH & Co KG v. Commission of the European Communities (T50/96)* [1998] ECR II-3773, [1999] C.L.Y. 2261 followed; (3) however, the Commission's second refusal would not be annulled because of these irregularities as it could not be shown that the outcome would have been different had they not occurred; (4) there had been no breach of the principle of legitimate expectation, since the Commission had given no assurances that there would be a repayment. On the contrary, the Commission was obliged to decide the matter afresh following annulment of its first refusal; (5) there were no special circumstances capable of justifying the operation of the equitable principle under Council Regulation 1430/79 Art.13 whereby a trader could be relieved of a loss it would otherwise have incurred, and (6) The grounds of the second refusal had been duly brought to M's attention and the Commission had complied with its duty to give reasons for its decisions under the EC Treaty Art.190 (now Art.253 EC).

MEHIBAS DORDTSELAAN BV v. COMMISSION OF THE EUROPEAN COMMUNITIES (T290/97) [2000] 2 C.M.L.R. 375, Cooke (President), CFI.

2351. Direct effect of Working Time Directive

See EMPLOYMENT: East Riding of Yorkshire DC v. Gibson. §2095

2352. Directives – annulment – locus standi of private company

[Council Directive 98/43 on the approximation of laws, regulations and administrative provisions relating to the advertising of tobacco products.]

S, a company licensed to sell footwear under a tobacco related trade mark, sought the annulment of Council Directive 98/43, due to be implemented in Member States by 30 July 2001. S argued that it would be adversely affected by the Directive's ban on advertising connected with tobacco products. A parallel application had also been lodged with the ECJ and S asked the CFI to stay the proceedings in the instant case pending the decision of the ECJ.

Held, refusing the application, that there was no scope for a private body to challenge Directives that only imposed duties directly on Member States. In any event, the ban on advertising would be enforced by national legislation implementing the Directive, not by the Directive itself, so that S could not argue that the Directive would directly effect its activities. Further, S was not being deprived of a legal remedy as the proceedings before the ECJ were ongoing.

SALAMANDER AG v. EUROPEAN PARLIAMENT (T172/98) [2000] All E.R. (EC) 754, K Lenaerts (President), CFI.

2353. **Directives – implementation – failure to set adequate penalty payments**

[Council Directive 92/13 on the procurement procedures of entities operating in the water, energy, transport and telecommunications sectors Art.13.]

The Commission complained that France had failed adequately to transpose into its domestic law certain provisions of Council Directive 92/13, designed to harmonise the law and practice concerning the procurement procedures for entities operating in the water, energy, transport and telecommunications sectors. The Commission referred specifically to failures (1) to set penalty payments for infringements of the Directive at a level high enough to be of dissuasive effect, coupled with provisions giving discretion to the national courts that were limited by vague considerations; (2) to transpose provisions in the Directive requiring the setting up of an attestation system for contracting parties, and (3) properly to transpose the provisions of the Directive requiring the establishment of a conciliation procedure.

Held, upholding the complaint in part with the result that France had failed to comply with Art.13 of the Directive, that (1) in relation to penalty payments, the Directive did not specify whether these were to be fixed by national legislation or a competent court. A penalty payment was itself a deterrent and not reinforced as such by a provision setting out the amount of the penalty to be paid. It was not contrary to the Directive, therefore, for a court to assess the conduct and situation of the party before it when considering the amount and nature of the appropriate penalty; indeed, this approach was consonant with the requirements of a fair trial. The Commission's complaint on this ground would be dismissed; (2) French claims to have given the Directive's attestation provisions sufficient publicity were ineffective as the measure had not been properly transposed into domestic law within the requisite time limit. Transposition of this provision was obligatory, not optional, *Commission of the European Communities v. Germany (C59/98)* [1991] E.C.R. I-2607 followed, and (3) the transposition of the conciliation procedure into national law was required so that interested parties could know of its existence and of their right to exercise it. France had not made the necessary transposition within the required time period.

COMMISSION OF THE EUROPEAN COMMUNITIES v. FRANCE (C225/97) [1999] E.C.R. I-3011, PJG Kapteyn (President), ECJ.

2354. **Directives – implementation – national court's power of review**

[Council Directive 85/337 on the assessment of the effects of certain public and private projects on the environment Art.1 (5), Art.5(1), Art.6(2).]

A Luxembourg Court referred various questions to the ECJ regarding the legality of the adoption of a motorway construction project in the absence of an environmental impact assessment. It was contended that the adoption of the project by the national executive through legislative provisions passed specifically for the purpose was in breach of Council Directive 85/337 Art.5(1) and Art.6(2) which required the carrying out of an environmental impact assessment or public enquiry prior to the adoption of projects likely to have a significant effect on the environment. The ECJ was asked to clarify whether the national court had a power to review the legislative process by which the project had been adopted, having regard to the fact that Art.1 (5) of the Directive exempted projects which had been adopted "by a specific act of national legislation" on the basis that the Directive's objectives were met through the legislative process.

Held, giving a preliminary ruling, that (1) a national court was empowered to review whether the legislature had kept within the limits of discretion set out in the Directive when choosing the manner of implementation, and the provisions of the Directive could be taken into account in that process of review; (2) Art.1(5) was to be construed as referring to legislative acts which enabled the objectives of the Directive to be met, in that the supply of information relating to the project was equivalent to that which was supplied to the competent authority in an ordinary procedure for granting consent for a project, and, in addition, public access to that information was ensured, and (3) the adoption of a project likely to have a significant effects on the environment, in the absence of information which would have been supplied under an ordinary procedure, would amount to a breach of the Directive.

LUXEMBOURG v. LINSTER (C287/98) *The Times*, October 5, 2000, GC Rodriguez Iglesias (President), ECJ.

2355. Directives – implementation – stay pending revision of legislation

[Council Directive 96/9 relating to the protection of databases.]

Luxembourg failed to implement EC Directive 96/9 relating to the legal protection of databases by January 1, 1998. The Directive was due to be implemented in Luxembourg but the implementing legislation also contained a complete revision of the country's copyright law and had been delayed. Luxembourg requested that the proceedings brought against it by the Commission be stayed as they would become redundant as soon as the legislation was enacted.

Held, giving a preliminary ruling, that Luxembourg had failed to fulfil its obligations under the Directive and had presented no grounds justifying a stay of the proceedings.

COMMISSION OF THE EUROPEAN COMMUNITIES v. LUXEMBOURG (C348/99) [2000] E.C.D.R. 246, Advocate General Philippe Leger, AGO.

2356. Directives – interim injunctions – validity of Directive 98/43 – appropriateness of relief pending decision

[Council Directive 98/43 on the approximation of laws, regulations and administrative provisions relating to the advertising of tobacco products.]

The Secretary of State appealed against the grant of an interim injunction (*The Times*, November 16, 1999, [1999] C.L.Y. 2233), preventing the Government from making regulations to implement a ban on tobacco advertising and sponsorship under Council Directive 98/43. Leave to seek judicial review of the decision to proceed by way of secondary legislation had been given prior to a reference to the ECJ on the validity of the Directive and the judge granting the injunction had held, inter alia, that Community law considerations did not apply. The Secretary of State contended that the injunction was an obstacle to both Government and Community policy.

Held, allowing the appeal (Laws, L.J. dissenting), that the judge had erred in failing to consider Community law. The threshold conditions of *Zuckerfabrik Suderdithmarschen AG v. Hauptzollamt Itzehoe (C143/88)* [1991] E.C.R. I-415, [1991] C.L.Y. 4051 had been met in respect of determining the Directive's invalidity, and a failure to consider the issue of irreparable damage as germane to his enquiry meant that the conclusion of the judge could not be accepted. Further, he had placed too much reliance on the fact that the legislation was not yet in force, when the primary consideration was the effect the injunction posed to the Government's ability to legislate in an area of public interest. The injunction was inappropriate given that a major public health issue was involved even though the regulations would be subject to uncertainty, pending the outcome of the reference to the ECJ.

R. v. SECRETARY OF STATE FOR HEALTH, *ex p.* IMPERIAL TOBACCO LTD [2000] 2 W.L.R. 834, Lord Woolf, M.R., CA.

2357. Dominant position – pension funds – compulsory affiliation to sector fund – legal monopoly

[EC TreatyArt.3 (now, after amendment, Art.3 EC), Art.5 (now Art.10 EC), Art.85 (now Art.81 EC), Art.86 (now Art.82 EC), Art.90 (now Art.86 EC).]

A, a Dutch company, was obliged by Dutch law to affiliate to a supplementary pension fund for workers within its industrial sector. A had been affiliated to the Fund since 1975, and in 1981, having concluded that the Fund was not sufficiently generous, A entered into an arrangement providing enhanced benefits for its employees with an insurer. In 1989, the basis on which benefits under the compulsory scheme were paid out was improved, making it comparable with A's private arrangement. A therefore applied to be exempted from affiliation to the fund. The fund refused A's application and refused to follow the advice of the Insurance Board, requiring it, inter alia, to grant an exemption. The national court adopted the Board's decision, but stayed proceedings pending a reference to the ECJ as to whether the Fund was an undertaking within the meaning of the EC Treaty Art.85 (now Art.81 EC), Art.86 (now Art.82 EC) and Art.90 (now Art.86 EC), and if so, whether compulsory fund membership nullified the effectiveness of competition rules applicable to undertakings, and if not, whether there were circumstances which could render compulsory membership incompatible with Art.90.

Held, giving a preliminary ruling, that (1) agreements made in the context of collective negotiations between employers and employees in pursuit of recognised social policy objectives were not caught by Art.85(1). To hold otherwise would seriously undermine such objectives; (2) Art.3(g) (now, after amendment, Art.3 EC), Art.5 (now Art.10) and Art.85 do not prevent compulsory affiliation to a sectoral pension fund at the request of employers and employees in the relevant industry; (3) for competition law purposes, an undertaking includes any entity engaged in economic activity; (4) the fund was an undertaking within the meaning of Art.85 (now Art.81 EC), as although it was not profit making, it competed with insurance companies; (5) the fund's sole right to collect and administer monies paid in by reason of the compulsory affiliation amounted to an exclusive right within the meaning of Art.90 (now Art.86 EC). The fund therefore held a legal monopoly giving it a dominant position within the meaning of Art.86 (now Art.82 EC) which was justified under Art.90(2) (now Art.86(2) EC), given the social solidarity basis of the sectoral scheme, and (6) it was for the Dutch Government to consider whether the alternative of laying down minimum pension requirements would meet the requirement of ensuring minimum levels of pension payments currently achieved by compulsory fund affiliation.

ALBANY INTERNATIONAL BV v. STICHTING BEDRIJFSPENSIOENFONDS TEXTIELINDUSTRIE (C67/96) [2000] 4 C.M.L.R. 446, GC Rodriguez Iglesias (President), ECJ.

2358. Dominant position – pension funds – compulsory affiliation to sector fund – legal monopoly

[EC Treaty Art.3 (now, after amendment, Art.3 EC), Art.5 (now Art.10 EC), Art.85(1) (now Art.81(1) EC), Art.86 (now Art.82 EC), Art.90 (now Art.86 EC).]

B, a Dutch company, made pension arrangements for its employees with an insurer in 1968. The Dutch government had established an industrial sector pension fund, the Fund, to which all employers in B's industrial sector were obliged to affiliate. The Fund learned of B's existence, and required B to affiliate as from 1990. It exempted B from paying contributions prior to this date, in the light of the level of benefits provided under B's own scheme. B asked to be exempted from affiliation entirely, contending that its pension benefits exceeded those of the Fund. The Fund refused B's exemption request and this decision was upheld by the Insurance Board. B subsequently challenged demands for payment by the Fund in the national court which stayed proceedings pending an application to the ECJ for a preliminary ruling as to whether (1) the EC Treaty Art.85(1) (now Art.81(1) EC) applied to agreements between employers and employees establishing a single sectoral pension scheme requiring compulsory affiliation, the scheme having the sole right to collect and administer the relevant pension contributions; (2) compulsory affiliation infringed Art.3 (now, after amendment, Art.3 EC), Art.5 (now Art.10 EC) and Art.85 (now Art.81 EC); (3) the compulsory scheme was an undertaking within the meaning of competition provisions of the Treaty, and (4) Art.86 (now Art.82 EC) and Art.90 (now Art.86 EC) prohibited the granting of exclusive rights to sectoral pension schemes, the effect of which was to seriously restrict the freedom to make separate pension arrangements with a private insurer.

Held, giving a preliminary ruling, that (1) whilst certain restrictions on competition inevitably arose from collective agreements between employers and employees, to treat such agreements as subject to Art.85(1) would seriously undermine the scheme's social policy objectives. They would be regarded as falling outside the provisions of Art.85(1); (2) compulsory affiliation was not a legislative measure capable of undermining the provisions of Art.3(g), Art.5 and Art.85; (3) for competition law purposes, an undertaking included any entity engaged in economic activity; (4) the fund was an undertaking within the meaning of Art.85, as although it was not profit making, it competed with insurance companies; (5) the fund had exclusive rights under Art.90 as it had the sole right to collect and administer monies paid in by reason of the compulsory affiliation; (6) the fund held a legal monopoly giving it a dominant position within the meaning of Art.86; (7) the fund's exclusive right of administration was not contrary to Art.86 and Art.90 and was justified in that there was a danger that insurers might cream off the good risks, leaving the fund to deal with an increasing proportion of bad risks, rendering it less competitive than comparable private sector services; (8) removal of the exclusive right could prevent the fund from performing its allotted function under acceptable economic conditions; (9) Dutch law provided guidelines for exemption from affiliation, the principle being that funds might agree to exemption, provided that this would not affect their financial equilibrium. Exemption could be refused where this would be necessary to ensure performance of the social task entrusted to the relevant state organ, and (10) it was for the Dutch government to consider whether the alternative of laying down minimum pension requirements would meet the requirement of ensuring minimum levels of pension payments currently achieved via compulsory fund affiliation.

BRENTJENS HANDELSONDERNEMING BV v. STICHTING BEDRIJFSPENSIOENFONDS VOOR DE HANDEL IN BOUWMATERIALEN (C115/97) [2000] 4 C.M.L.R. 566, GC Rodriguez Iglesias (President), ECJ.

2359. **Dominant position – pension funds – compulsory affiliation to sector fund – legal monopoly**

[EC Treaty Art.3 (now, after amendment, Art.3 EC), Art.5 (now Art.10 EC), Art.85 (now Art.81 EC), Art.86 (now Art.82 EC), Art.90 (now Art.86 EC).]

DB, a Dutch company operated floating derricks which it hired out to the offshore and chemical industries. The Dutch government had established a fund for the provision of pensions to dock workers, affiliation to which was compulsory for employers. DB had taken the view that it was not covered by the law establishing the fund, and had made separate arrangements with an insurer for its employees' pensions. Compulsory affiliation to the fund was extended in 1991, and in 1993, DB received a demand for contributions to the fund for those years. DB's appeal against the order for contribution was upheld at first instance but overturned on appeal. DB appealed to the Supreme Court, which stayed proceedings pending reference to the ECJ for a preliminary ruling as to whether (1) the fund was an undertaking within the meaning of the EC Treaty Art.85 (now Art.81EC), Art.86 (now Art.82EC) and Art.90 (now Art.86EC); (2) agreements between organisations representing employers and employees whereby affiliation to the fund was compulsory under Dutch law amounted to agreements between undertakings affecting trade within the Common Market under Art.85(1) (now Art.81 (1) EC); (3) compulsory affiliation infringed Art.85, and if not, whether there were circumstances making compulsory affiliation to the fund contrary to

Art.90, and (4) whether compulsory affiliation gave the fund an exclusive right under Art.90(1) (now Art.86(1) EC) the mere exercise of which amounted to abuse of the fund's dominant position.

Held, giving a preliminary ruling, that (1) whilst certain restrictions on competition inevitably arose from collective agreements between employers and employees, to treat such agreements as subject to Art.85(1) would seriously undermine the social policy objectives of such schemes. They would be regarded as being beyond the scope of Art.85(1); (2) Art.3(g), Art.5 and Art.85 did not prevent public authorities from making affiliation to a particular sectoral pension fund compulsory if requested to do so by organisations representing employers and employees in a given sector; (3) for competition law purposes, an undertaking included any entity engaged in economic activity; (4) the fund was an undertaking within the meaning of Art.85, as although it was not profit making, it competed with insurance companies; (5) the fund's exclusive right to manage contributions gave it a dominant position within the meaning of Art.86; (6) the removal of the exclusive right conferred on the fund could make it impossible for it to carry out the tasks committed to it within economically acceptable conditions; (7) the fund's exclusive right to administer the relevant supplementary pension provisions did not infringe Art.86 and Art.90, and (8) it was for the Dutch government to determine whether the alternative of laying down minimum pension requirements would meet the requirement of ensuring minimum levels of pension payments currently achieved via compulsory affiliation to the Fund.

MAATSCHAPPIJ DRIJVENDE BOKKEN BV v. STICHTING PENSIOENFONDS VOOR DE VERDOER-EN HAVENBEDRIJVEN (C219/97) [2000] 4 C.M.L.R. 599, GC Rodriguez Iglesias (President), ECJ.

2360. EC law – correct implementation of Directive – individual's right to enforce

See PLANNING: R. v. Hammersmith and Fulham LBC, *ex p.* CPRE London Branch (Leave to Appeal) (No.2). §4462

2361. EC law – embargoes – prohibition of Iraqi claims – validity and permanency

See INTERNATIONAL LAW: Shanning International Ltd (In Liquidation) v. Lloyds TSB Bank Plc (formerly Lloyds Bank Plc). §3808

2362. EFTA Court of Justice – practice directions – advisory opinion procedure

To make the co-operation between the EFTA Court and national courts and tribunals through the advisory opinion procedure under the ESA/Court Agreement Art.34 more effective and enable the EFTA Court to better meet the requirements of national courts, a note for guidance has been addressed to all interested parties, in particular to all national courts and tribunals. The note contains practical information based on the experience in applying the advisory opinion procedure.

Held, that (1) any court or tribunal of an EFTA State which is a party to the EEA Agreement may ask the EFTA Court to interpret a rule of EEA law; (2) the request for an advisory opinion must be limited to the interpretation of a provision of EEA law since the EFTA Court does not have jurisdiction to interpret national law; (3) the request for an advisory opinion to the EFTA Court may be in any form allowed by national procedural law; (4) the request for an advisory opinion to the EFTA Court may be expressed in the language of the national court but will be translated into English, the language of the EFTA Court; (5) the request should contain a statement of reasons which is succinct but sufficiently complete to give the court and those who must be notified a clear understanding of the factual and legal context of the main proceedings; (6) the aim of the statement of reasons is to put the EFTA Court in a position to give the national court an answer which will be of assistance to it; (7) the national court should ensure that the order for reference itself includes all the relevant information; (8) a national court or tribunal may refer a request for an advisory opinion to the EFTA Court as soon as an opinion on the point of interpretation of EEA law is necessary to enable it to give judgment; (9) the request for an advisory opinion should be sent by the national court directly to the EFTA Court, by registered post, to: EFTA Court, Registry, 1, Rue du Fort Thungen, L-1499 Luxembourg. Tel: (352) 42 10 81. Fax: (352) 43 43 89; (10) the Court registry will remain in contact with the national court until the advisory opinion is given, and will send copies of the various documents (in particular written observations and the report for the hearing). The Court will also send its advisory opinion to the national court, and (11) proceedings for an advisory opinion before the EFTA Court are free of charge. The Court does not rule on costs.

PRACTICE DIRECTION (EFTA: GUIDANCE ON REQUESTS BY NATIONAL COURTS FOR ADVISORY OPINIONS) [1999] 3 C.M.L.R. 525, Judge not applicable, EFTA.

2363. **Energy – nuclear power – failure to submit information regarding origin of supply to ESAI – time limits**

[Euratom Treaty Art.61.]

K operated a nuclear power plant in Germany. It contracted with B for the supply of uranium. The contract could only take effect with the approval of E, the Euratom Supply Agency. B was also obliged to advise K and E of the country of origin of each delivery. E's rules required that E sign or reject the contract within 10 working days. The contract was submitted to E on November 29, 1993. In a letter of December 10, 1993 received by K and B on December 13, 1993, the last day of the specified period, E asked for information regarding the origin of the uranium. On December 14, 1993 B informed E that the source of the supply would be C, the Commonwealth of Independent States. As K had already contracted to buy a large amount of uranium from C, E expressed concern on December 20, 1993 at over reliance on C as a source of supply. On January 6, 1994 E signed the supply contract between B and K but stipulated that the uranium be sourced otherwise than from C. K considered that the supply contract could not be performed and through B purchased the uranium elsewhere at greater cost. K appealed unsuccessfully to the EC Commission. K thereafter appealed unsuccessfully to CFI, and appealed to the ECJ.

Held, dismissing the appeal, that (1) E was entitled to extend the time limits in its rules. K and B could have submitted the information as to the origin of the supplies at the time of the original submission to E. Therefore the 10 day rule did not prohibit E from requiring the relevant information within the period if the original documentation was incomplete, *Commission of the European Communities v. Brazzelli Lualdi (C136/92)* [1994] E.C.R. I-1981, *San Marco Impex Italiana Srl v. Commission of the European Communities (C19/95)* [1996] E.C.R. I-4435 and *John Deere Ltd v. Commission of the European Communities (C7/95 P)* [1998] All E.R. (EC) 481 (Note), [1998] C.L.Y. 2317 followed; (2) the lapse of time before E took its decision did not infringe the rules, because the obligation on E to decide quickly on the conclusion of a contract existed only if the documentation contained all the necessary information. Where it did not, the period of time referred to in the rules did not start to run until receipt of the complete documentation; (3) such of the arguments by K which merely reiterated pleas put forward at first instance constituted requests for re-examination of the application brought before the Court of First Instance and were inadmissible on appeal, *Kupka-Floridi v. Economic and Social Committee (C244/92)* [1993] E.C.R. I-2041, *John Deere Ltd v. EC Commission* (C7/95P) [1998] E.C.R. I-3111 and *Eppe v. Commission of the European Communities (C354/92)* [1993] E.C.R. I-7027 followed; (4) E had not misused its powers. A decision could amount to a misuse of powers only where it appeared, on the basis of objective, relevant and consistent evidence, that it had been taken for purposes other than those stated; (5) a finding of fact by the Court of First Instance did not constitute a point of law which could be reviewed unless the clear sense of the evidence had been distorted; (6) E's obligations under Euratom Treaty Art.61 inter alia to ensure a regular and equitable supply of nuclear fuel gave E a broad discretion to ensure diversification of supply. This obligation constituted a legal obstacle to the contract within the meaning of Art.61, and (7) since neither E nor the Commission was guilty of illegality the claim for damages would also be dismissed.

KERNKRAFTWERKE LIPPE-EMS GmbH v. COMMISSION OF THE EUROPEAN COMMUNITY (C161/97 P) [2000] 2 C.M.L.R. 489, Jann (President), ECJ.

2364. **Equal treatment – armed forces – proportionality**

See ARMED FORCES: Kreil v. Germany (C285/98). §268

2365. **European Commission – comfort letters – subsequent exemption decision – annulment application**

[EC Treaty Art.85 (now Art.81 EC).]

SA, a company incorporated under Dutch law, manufactured bottling machinery. It complained to the Commission that a mutual exclusive supply agreement it had entered into with SG, a French manufacturer, was contrary to the EC Treaty Art.85(1) (now Art.81(1)). The Commission decided that the agreement was not of sufficient economic importance at Community level to justify a formal investigation and the matter was closed. However, on a subsequent application by SG, the Commission re-opened the file and exempted the agreement under Art.85(3). SA sought the annulment of that decision.

Held, allowing the application, that (1) any measure capable of producing a binding effect on an applicant's interests could be the subject of an annulment application. Only the final decision was open to challenge and not intermediate measures in preparation for the final decision. The form in which the decision was adopted was immaterial for the purpose of a challenge by an action for annulment, *IBM Corp v. Commission of the European Communities (C60/81)* [1981] E.C.R. 2639, [1981] C.L.Y. 1266 and *Automec Srl v. Commission of the European Communities (T24/90)* [1992] E.C.R. II-2223, [1993] C.L.Y. 4251 followed; (2) the Commission's comfort letter dealing with SA's original complaint contained a clear appraisal of the agreement and its economic importance. That appraisal indicated that the decision to take no further action on the matter constituted the final step in the administrative procedure whereby the institution's position was finally determined. The decision could not be followed by any other measure capable of being the subject of annulment proceedings, *Syndicat Francais de l'Express International (SFEI) v. Commission of the European Communities (C39/93 P)* [1994] E.C.R. I-2681, [1994] C.L.Y. 4797 followed; (3) the decision to re-open the administrative procedure that resulted in the adoption of the contested decision was not based on any new points of fact or law requiring a re-examination of the matter; (4) the Commission was not entitled to adopt a fresh decision on a complaint, relating to a matter which had already been closed because of its limited economic importance at Community level, without properly stating the reasons, in particular the existence of fresh evidence, for re-opening the administrative procedure which had led to that decision, and (5) comfort letters, such as those sent to SA by the Commission in relation to its original application, did not prevent a national court from reaching a different decision as regards compatibility with Art.85 based in the information available to it. However, the opinion contained in the letters should be taken into account by the national court, *L'Oreal NV v. De Nieuwe AMCK PVBA (31/80)* [1980] E.C.R. 3775, [1981] C.L.Y. 1154 followed.

STORK AMSTERDAM BV v. COMMISSION OF THE EUROPEAN COMMUNITIES (T241/97) [2000] 5 C.M.L.R. 31, Moura Ramos (President), CFI.

2366. European Commission – complaints – anti dumping proceedings – locus standi of European consumers' organisation

[Council Regulation 384/96 on protection against dumped imports from countries not members of the European Community.]

The European Commission had given notice of the commencement of anti dumping proceedings in respect of imports of unbleached cotton fabrics. B, an international association representing European consumer organisations' interests at Community level, sought recognition as a party interested in the proceedings, and to be provided with a copy of the complaint and other non confidential information. The Commission refused to recognise B as an interested party, on the grounds that the imported items were not generally sold at retail level, it being the Commission's view that B could only be recognised as an interested party where good were sold at this level in light of the GATT Anti Dumping Code 1994 and Council Regulation 384/96. B sought annulment of the Commission's decision refusing it recognition as an interested party, and a declaration that consumer organisations should be regarded as interested parties in anti dumping proceedings generally.

Held, granting the application in part and annulling the contested decision, that (1) B's claim for a declaration that consumer organisations should be regarded as interested parties in anti dumping proceedings generally was inadmissible as standing could only be determined at the time particular proceedings were lodged, *Cityflyer Express Ltd v. Commission of the European Communities (T16/96)* [1998] E.C.R. II-757 followed. However, its claim that the Commission's decision to exclude B from the present anti dumping proceedings should be annulled was admissible; (2) the GATT Anti Dumping Code was binding on the Community and since Regulation 384/96 purported to transpose the Code into Community law, it was to be interpreted in the light of the Code, *International Fruit Co NV v. Produktschap voor Groenten en Fruit (No.3) (C21/72)* [1972] E.C.R. 1219, [1975] C.L.Y. 1267 and *Nakajima All Precision Co Ltd v. Council of the European Communities (C69/89 R)* [1991] E.C.R. I-2069 followed; (3) the Code obliged authorities to provide opportunities for consumer organisations in relation to goods commonly sold at retail level. However, this did not apply only to products sold at this level so that the Commission could not interpret the Regulation as confining B's right to be considered as an interested party solely to proceedings relating to products commonly sold at retail level; (4) a party seeking recognition as an interested party had to show a link between its activities and the product in question. The Commission could not automatically exclude such a party, but had to afford it an opportunity to explain its interest before a recognition decision was made, and (5) in the instant case, B represented all consumers of goods and services. The fact that the goods in issue were processed further prior to retail sale was not a valid ground for the Commission's refusal to recognise B as an interested party in the anti dumping proceedings.

BUREAU EUROPEEN DES UNIONS DE CONSOMMATEURS (BEUC) v. COMMISSION OF THE EUROPEAN COMMUNITIES (INTERPRETATION: ADMISSIBILITY CRITERIA) (T256/97) [2000] 1 C.M.L.R. 542, Cooke (President), CFI.

2367. European Commission – complaints – failure to act – applicable time limits

[EC Treaty Art.86 (now Art.82 EC), Art.92 (now, after amendment, Art.87 EC), Art.93 (now Art.88 EC), Art.175 (now Art.232 EC); Council Regulation 17/62 implementing Art.85 and Art.86 of the Treaty; Commission Regulation 99/63 on the hearings provided for in Art.19(1) and Art.19(2) of Council Regulation No.17/62.]

UPS, an international parcel distribution company, lodged a complaint with the European Commission about the conduct of DP, the German post office. UPS claimed that there had been breaches of the EC Treaty Art.86 (now Art.82 EC), Art.92 (now, after amendment, Art.87 EC), and Art.93 (now Art.88 EC). The Commission initiated the proper procedure under Council Regulation 17/62. There then followed an exchange of correspondence, during which the

Commission advised it had suspended the investigation relating to Art.86 and in December 1997 it sent a formal letter pursuant to Commission Regulation 99/63 Art.6 requiring UPS to submit its observations. These were submitted in February 1998. However, by June 1998 the Commission had failed to make a definitive decision whether to reject the complaint and UPS wrote a formal letter pursuant to Art 175 (now Art.232 EC), requesting one. After the two months permitted by Art.175 the Commission had failed to make a decision and UPS brought the present action for a declaration of failure to act in relation to its complaint.

Held, granting the declaration, that the Commission was required to either activate the procedure against DP or reject the complaint within a reasonable time, *Guerin Automobiles v. Commission of the European Communities (C282/ 95 P)* [1997] E.C.R. I-1503 followed. A reasonable time was to be determined by the circumstances of each case and guidance was given as to important factors. In the instant case UPS submitted its observations when the investigation was in its final stage. At that point the Commission should have been in a position to make a decision. Further, there were no exceptional circumstances to justify the delay.

UPS EUROPE SA v. COMMISSION OF THE EUROPEAN COMMUNITIES (T127/ 98) [1999] All E.R. (EC) 794, Moura Ramos (President), CFI.

2368. **European Commission – decisions – effect of contested Decision on undertaking**

[EC Treaty Art.85 (now Art.81 EC); Council Regulation 17/62; Council Regulation 4064/89.]

The Commission adopted a decision under Council Regulation 4064/89 (the Merger Regulation) that the creation of a joint venture to carry on insurance business in the fields of life assurance, capitalisation and retirement funds did not constitute a concentration within the meaning of Art.3 of the Regulation and so did not come within the scope of that Regulation. AG applied for annulment of that decision. The Commission raised an objection that the action was inadmissible on the ground that the contested decision produced no immediate legal effects which affected the interests of AG. AG took the view that the contested decision constituted a definitive legal act capable of forming the subject matter of an action for annulment.

Held, dismissing the application, that (1) any decision which brought about a distinctive change in the legal position of the undertakings concerned by producing definitive legal effects was actionable; (2) the contested decision which found that the setting up of the joint venture did not constitute a concentration and thus fell outside the scope of Council Regulation 4064/89 had the effect of bringing that operation within the prohibition on agreements, decisions and concerted practices under the EC Treaty Art.85 (now Art.81 EC) and the separate and distinct procedure provided for in Council Regulation 17/ 62. The contested decision constituted a definitive decision which could be challenged by an action for annulment in order to secure the protection of AG's rights under Regulation 4064/89; (3) although Council Regulation 4064/89 expressly conferred on undertakings the right to be heard before the adoption of certain specified decisions, it did not include decisions finding, as in this case under Art.6(1)(a), that the operation notified was not covered by Council Regulation 4064/89, and (4) observance of the right of the defence was a fundamental principle of Community law and had to be applied prior to the adoption of any decision likely to have an adverse effect on the undertakings concerned. When requesting information, the Commission had to state the purpose of its request and in this case the Commission had done so.

ASSICURAZIONI GENERALI SpA v. COMMISSION OF THE EUROPEAN COMMUNITIES (T87/96) [2000] 4 C.M.L.R. 312, B Vesterdorf (President), CFI.

2369. European Commission – decisions – failure to authenticate – breach of essential procedural requirement

[EC Treaty Art.173 (now, after amendment, Art.230 EC); Commission Decision 91/300.]

The Commission fined ICI for its activities on the soda ash market, as the result of Commission Decision 91/300. However, the decision was not authenticated by the signatures of either the President or Executive Secretary of the Commission, as required by the Commission's Rules of Procedure Art.12(1). As a result, ICI succeeded in its application to the CFI for the decision to be annulled and the court held that the failure to authenticate amounted to an infringement of an essential procedural requirement under the EC Treaty Art.173 (now, after amendment, Art.230 EC). The Commission appealed.

Held, dismissing the appeal, that authentication was a crucial procedure which had to be completed prior to the notification of a Decision to ensure compliance with the principle of legal certainty. Failure to carry out authentication, even if there was no other defect or omission, was sufficient to amount to a breach justifying annulment under Art.173.

COMMISSION OF THE EUROPEAN COMMUNITIES v. ICI PLC (C286/95 P) [2000] 5 C.M.L.R. 413, L Sevon (President), ECJ.

2370. European Commission – decisions – failure to authenticate before notification – requirement for legal certainty

[EC Treaty Art.173 (now, after amendment, Art.230 EC).]

The European Commission imposed fines on S for breach of Community law, but its decision to do so was annulled on the ground that the decision was void because it had not been authenticated by the president and executive secretary of the Commission before it was sent to S. The Commission appealed, submitting that its failure to authenticate had not prejudiced S, and in the absence of any other irregularity, that alone was not sufficient to vitiate the decision.

Held, dismissing the appeal, that it was absolutely vital that authentication preceded notification, as it was crucial for legal certainty that the notified text was identical to the text adopted by the Commission. Authentication was an essential procedural requirement within the meaning of EC Treaty Art.173 (now, after amendment, Art.230 EC) and infringement of that requirement would result in annulment. It was immaterial that no harm had been caused to any party.

COMMISSION OF THE EUROPEAN COMMUNITIES v. SOLVAY SA (C287/95 P); COMMISSION OF THE EUROPEAN COMMUNITIES v. ICI PLC (C286/95 P); *sub nom.* COMMISSION OF THE EUROPEAN COMMUNITIES v. IMPERIAL CHEMICAL INDUSTRIES PLC (C286/95 P) [2001] All E.R. (EC) 439, L Sevon (President), ECJ (5th Chamber).

2371. European Commission – disclosure and inspection – access to legally privileged documents

The European Commission found that documents certifying the authenticity of Argentine beef had been falsified and the German Government sought to recover import duty from I, who unsuccessfully argued that it had presented the certificates in good faith. I made a request to inspect documents held by the Commission that related to the inquiry. The Commission refused on the ground that some documents originated from Argentina or other Member States and therefore any application for sight of those documents must be made directly to the states concerned and all the other Commission documents fell under the exception in the Code of Conduct of December 6, 1993 in relation to documents forming the subject of legal proceedings. I applied to annul the refusal decision.

Held, allowing the application in part, that the public was to have the broadest possible access to Commission and Council documents. Access should only be refused where documents had been produced specifically for particular court proceedings, not only those subject to normal legal privilege but also correspondence about the case between the individual Directorate General and the relevant lawyer or legal office. Purely administrative documents, even if prejudicial to the Commission's case, should not be withheld. Access could not be granted, however, to documents produced by Member States or other countries.

INTERPORC IM-UND EXPORT GmbH v. COMMISSION OF THE EUROPEAN COMMUNITIES (T92/98) [2000] 1 C.M.L.R. 181, B Vesterdorf (President), CFI.

2372. European Commission – disclosure and inspection – prevalence of public interest

[Council Regulation 1468/81 on customs and agricultural matters; Council Regulation 515/97 on customs and agricultural matters; Commission Decision 94/90 on public access to Commission documents.]

JT, a textile importer which was involved in a dispute with the UK customs authorities concerning import duties claimed on goods from Bangladesh, challenged the European Commission's refusal to disclose documents pertaining to investigative missions in Bangladesh. The Commission had refused to grant access to the documents on the basis of Council Regulation 1468/81, as repealed and replaced by Council Regulation 515/97, maintaining that any information gathered as a result of the missions was confidential.

Held, granting the application, that although Regulation 1468/81 imposed significant limits on the distribution of information, it did not prevail over the Code of Conduct forming part of Commission Decision 94/90, the purpose of which was to ensure a general policy of openness with regard to the disclosure of information. In any event, given that JT's request for access to the documents had been made in the context of a legal action, Art.19(2) of the Regulation, which provided for the use of information in legal actions notwithstanding its confidentiality, was applicable.

JT'S CORP LTD v. COMMISSION OF THE EUROPEAN COMMUNITIES (T123/99) [2001] 1 C.M.L.R. 22, V Tiili (President), CFI.

2373. European Commission – illegality – milk quota allocation – failure to remedy

[EC Treaty Art.117 (Arts.117 to 120 of the EC Treaty have been replaced by Arts.136 EC to 143 EC), Art.155 (now Art.211), Art.215 (now Art.288); Council Regulation 1078/77 introducing a system of premiums for the non marketing of milk and milk products and for the conversion of dairy herds; Council Regulation 857/84 adopting general rules for the application of the levy in the milk and milk products sector; Council Regulation 2055/93.]

E was a agricultural company which held nine farms. In 1976 four of the farms were let to a partnership, C. E was a partner in C. C was part of the non marketing scheme under Council Regulation 1078/77 for five years from November 14, 1980. E was part of the Milk Quota scheme under Council Regulation 857/84. C was dissolved on September 30, 1984 and the four farms reverted to E. E then made applications to the Ministry of Agriculture, Fisheries, and Food in 1989 and 1991, under the Milk Quota scheme, SLOM Quota. The applications failed. As a result E applied to the High Court seeking judicial review of the decisions. The case was referred to the CFI. In *R. v. Ministry of Agriculture, Fisheries and Food, ex p. H&R Ecroyd Holdings Ltd (C127/94)* [1996] E.C.R. I-2731 the CFI ruled that Council Regulation 857/84 Art.3a(1), as amended by Council Regulation 764/89, was invalid. The European Commission refused to take corrective measures on the basis that the invalidity had been cured by Council Regulation 2055/93.

Held, that the European Commission's decision not to take action was annulled. It was settled case law that the Commission had to adopt measures to remedy illegality when it was identified by the ECJ under the EC Treaty Art.117 (Arts.117 to 120 of the EC Treaty have been replaced by Arts.136 EC to 143 EC). That was also true under EC Treaty Art.155 (now Art.211). The Commission was not entitled to rely on the measures it had taken in the form of the adoption of Council Regulation 2055/93, since the specific problem in the instant case was that of transferees of non marketing obligations, *R. v. Ministry of Agriculture,*

Fisheries and Food, ex p. H&R Ecroyd Holdings Ltd (C127/94) [1996] E.C.R. I-2731 followed and *Wehrs v. Hauptzollamt Luneburg (C264/90)* [1992] E.C.R. I-6285, [1993] C.L.Y. 4223 distinguished. The Commission had failed to satisfy either its duty to remedy the illegality or its duty to make good the damage suffered by E pursuant to Art.215 (now Art.288 EC) of the EC Treaty.

H&R ECROYD HOLDINGS LTD v. COMMISSION OF THE EUROPEAN COMMUNITIES (T220/97) [1999] 2 C.M.L.R. 1361, Moura Ramos (President), CFI.

2374. **European Commission – investigations – State aids – Decision based on inadequate analysis**

[EC Treaty Art.92(3)(a) (now, after amendment, Art.87(3) EC), Art.93 (now Art.88 EC), Art.174 (now Art.231 EC); Commission Decision 92/317; Commission Decision 97/242.]

The European Commission had investigated the taking over of a Spanish company, H, by an arm of the Spanish Government, and had requested information as to the level of capital contributions Spain had made to cover H's liabilities. Spain provided the information, and the Commission found in Commission Decision 92/317 that certain of the capital contributions paid as the result of an intended privatisation constituted state aid contrary to the EC Treaty Art.92 (now, after amendment, Art.87 EC) and should therefore be repaid. Spain's application for an annulment of this decision succeeded before the ECJ ([1994] E.C.R. I-4103), on the ground that the Commission's analysis of the compatibility of the alleged state aid with the provisions of Art.92(3)(a) was inadequate. The Commission therefore undertook a more detailed analysis, but again reached its original conclusion in Commission Decision 97/242. Spain sought annulment of this latest decision.

Held, refusing the application, that (1) the decision in the earlier case obliged the Commission to substitute lawful performance for unlawful performance at the point where the unlawful performance had occurred. The Commission's investigation had been lawful; it was its analysis of that investigation which had been unlawful. Compliance with the earlier judgment therefore required only that the Commission should undertake a fresh analysis. There was no breach of EC Treaty Art.93 (now Art.88 EC) or EC Treaty Art.174 (now Art.231 EC), *Asteris AE v. Commission of the European Communities (C97/86)* [1988] E.C.R. 2181, [1990] C.L.Y. 2200, *1986 Budget (34/86), Re* [1986] E.C.R. 2155, [1986] C.L.Y. 1396 and *R. v. Minister of Agriculture, Fisheries and Food, ex p. Federation Europeene de la Sante Animale (FEDESA) (331/88)* [1990] E.C.R. I-4023, [1991] C.L.Y. 3765 followed, and (2) Spain's right to be heard had not been infringed, and neither had the principles of legitimate expectation nor legal certainty been breached, since the Commission's new analysis was based on the original information provided to it, on which Spain had already expressed a position.

SPAIN v. COMMISSION OF THE EUROPEAN COMMUNITIES (C415/96) [1999] 1 C.M.L.R. 304, PJG Kapteyn, ECJ.

2375. **European Court of Justice – Advocates General – role – status of opinion – right to submit written responses**

[EC Treaty Art.165 (now Art.221 EC), Art.166 (now, after amendment, Art.222 EC); European Convention on Human Rights 1950 Art.6(1); Rules of Procedure of the Court of Justice Art.61.]

E applied for leave to submit written observations in response to an opinion of the Advocate General in proceedings before the ECJ. E contended that, as a party to a civil trial, it was entitled to have knowledge of and comment on all evidence adduced or observations filed, in order to influence the court's decision, a fundamental right under the European Convention on Human Rights 1950 Art.6(1). E placed reliance on *Vermeulen v. Belgium* (Unreported, February 20 1996) concerning the role of the Procureur General at the Belgium Court of Cassation, which involved delivering an opinion which was objective and reasoned in law, but which had the ultimate intention of influencing the court. The European Court of Human Rights found that a refusal to allow V to reply to the opinion before the end of the hearing amounted to a breach of Art.6(1) and E contended that the same principle applied to opinions delivered by the Advocate General, due to the incorporation of fundamental constitutional rights into EC law. It was submitted that it was part of the ECJ's role to ensure compliance with those fundamental principles, particularly those which were established in international treaties, such as the ECHR.

Held, refusing the application, that there was no provision for the parties to submit written observations in response to the Advocate General's opinion as under the EC Treaty Art.165 (now Art.221 EC) and Art.166 (now, after amendment, Art.222 EC) the role of the Advocate General was synonymous with that of ECJ judges in that they assisted the court in its interpretation of the Treaty and compliance with its provisions. The Advocate General's opinion brought the oral proceedings to an end and did not form part of the proceedings, but rather instigated the court's deliberations. The role, therefore, was integral to the court rather than originating from an external authority. This role differed fundamentally from that of the Procureur, thus the ECHR was not relevant, *Vermeulen* distinguished. There already existed a safeguard in the form of procedures to re-open the oral proceedings at the request of the Advocate General, or the parties themselves under the Rules of Procedure of the Court of Justice Art.61, which prevented the ECJ from being influenced by material which the parties had been unable to discuss.

EMESA SUGAR (FREE ZONE) NV v. ARUBA (C17/98) (NO.1) *The Times*, February 29, 2000, GC Rodriguez Iglesias (President), ECJ.

2376. European Court of Justice – appellate jurisdiction – CFI's refusal to admit evidence after close of oral procedure

[Commission Decision 86/398; Statute of the Court of Justice Art.37(4).]

Following an investigation by the European Commission, H was found to have taken part in the operation of a European wide cartel between polypropylene producers and was fined 2,750,000 ECUs. The fine was reduced on appeal to the CFI but the court refused a request to re-open the oral hearing and other measures of inquiry. In support of the request H had relied on certain factual evidence of which it became aware after the conclusion of the oral procedure and, in particular, after the rehearing and delivery of the judgment of the CFI in *BASF AG v. Commission of the European Communities (T4/89)* [1992] E.C.R. II-1591, [1992] C.L.Y. 4703. That evidence allegedly showed that Commission Decision 86/398 was vitiated by serious procedural defects for the examination of which fresh measures of inquiry into the evidence was required. H appealed to the ECJ with D joined as intervener on the grounds that the CFI was in breach of procedural requirements and had infringed Community law by refusing to hold the Decision was non existent, or to annul it for breach of essential procedural requirements by refusing to re-open the oral procedure and to order the necessary measures or organisation and inquiry. Further, that it had also erred when reviewing the facts to assess the individual responsibility of those participating in the infringement, and in settling the amount of the fine.

Held, dismissing the appeal, that (1) the fact that D had been given leave to intervene did not preclude a fresh examination of the admissibility of its intervention at the hearing; (2) D's claim that the ECJ should declare the Decision non existent or annul it as regards all its addressees, or at least as regards D, specifically concerned D and was not identical to the forms of order sought by H. Therefore it did not satisfy the conditions laid down in the Statute of the Court of Justice Art.37(4) which would make it inadmissible; (3) an appeal to the ECJ was limited to points of law and might rely only on the grounds listed therein, to the exclusion of any fresh appraisal of the facts. However, it was incumbent on the ECJ to verify whether, in making that assessment, the CFI committed an error of law by infringing the general principles of law; (4) acts of Community institutions were in principle presumed to be lawful and produce legal effect even if they were tainted with irregularities, until they were annulled or withdrawn. Only an irregularity whose gravity was so obvious that it could not be tolerated by the Community legal order must be regarded as legally non existent. That exception was reserved for extreme situations; (5) the alleged procedural irregularities were not of such obvious priority that the decision should be regarded as legally non existent, and (6) the CFI had not erred in law in refusing to re-open the oral hearing or order measures of organisation and inquiry; nor did it infringe the rules of evidence or fail to comply with the obligation to give reasons for its conclusions.

HULS AG v. COMMISSION OF THE EUROPEAN COMMUNITIES (C199/92 P) [1999] 5 C.M.L.R.1016, PJG Kapteyn (President), ECJ.

2377. European Court of Justice – appellate jurisdiction – CFI's refusal to annul Commission Decision 86/398

[EC Treaty Art.81 (now Art.77 EC); Commission Decision 86/398.]

Following an investigation by the European Commission, H was found to have been involved in the operation of a European wide cartel between polypropylene producers. The Commission adopted Commission Decision 86/938, imposing a fine on H for breach of EC Treaty Art.81(1) (now Art.77 EC), the Decision was upheld on H's appeal to the CFI ([1992] 4 C.M.L.R. 84). H appealed to the ECJ, arguing that the adoption of the Decision by the CFI had been flawed by procedural defects and that there was a breach of H's rights of defence because the Commission refused to inform it of the replies of other polypropylene producers against whom the Commission's investigation was directed. Further, that the CFI was in breach of its obligation to deliver judgments on a "single infringement" at the same time, also that there were contradictions between the reasoning and the operative part of the contested judgment and that the CFI had failed to apply the rule of law laid down in *Orkem SA (formerly CdF Chimie SA) v. Commission of the European Communities (C374/87)* [1989] E.C.R. 3355, [1990] C.L.Y. 2069. Furthermore, that the CFI had erred in refusing to reduce the fine imposed on H.

Held, dismissing the appeal, that (1) the complaints of procedural defects and failure to apply the rule in *Orkem* were inadmissible before the ECJ as they had not been raised before the CFI; (2) H had access to the replies of other producers after the appeals before the CFI were joined for the purpose of the hearing but had failed to establish that those replies were of use in its defence and conferred rights of defence whose breach might lead to annulment of the Commission's decision; (3) H had failed to show that the delivery of the judgments on different dates was prejudicial to it. Simultaneous delivery of judgments was at the direction of, and not mandatory for, the Community judicature. Consequently, the choice of the CFI not to deliver judgment on the same date in all the cases did not run counter to Community law and was legally unobjectionable; (4) it was not open to the ECJ to review the CFI's finding of fact and assessment of the evidence. The CFI was entitled to conclude that H had participated in the cartel, and (5) there was no evidence that the CFI had erroneously assessed the level of the fine imposed on H and there was no obligation to reduce the amount of the fine.

HERCULES CHEMICALS NV v. COMMISSION OF THE EUROPEAN COMMUNITIES (C51/92 P) [1999] 5 C.M.L.R. 976, PJG Kapteyn (President), ECJ.

2378. European Court of Justice – appellate jurisdiction – CFI's refusal to re open oral hearing

[Commission Decision 86/398; Statute of the Court of Justice Art.37(4); Rules of Procedure of the Court of Justice Art.113(2).]

Following an investigation by the European Commission, S was fined for its involvement in the operation of a European wide cartel of polypropylene producers, pursuant to Commission Decision 86/398. On appeal to the CFI, S's request that the court re-open the oral hearing and order measures of inquiry was refused. The request arose following statements made by the Commission at the hearing of a similar appeal against a decision whereby fines were imposed on members of a PVC cartel where the court ruled that the Decision applicable in that case was non existent because of procedural irregularities. On appeal to the ECJ, S argued that the CFI's refusal to re-open the hearing and order the necessary measures of inquiry was in breach of procedure and general infringement of Community law. D had been fined for taking part in the same cartel and intervened in support of S.

Held, dismissing the appeal, that (1) an order giving leave to D to intervene in support of S did not preclude a fresh examination of the admissibility of its intervention; (2) the claim of an intervener, with which it was specifically concerned, and which was not identical to the order sought by the party it was supporting, was admissible as it did not satisfy the conditions of inadmissibility laid down in the Statute of the Court of Justice Art.37(4); (3) a plea to the effect that the CFI wrongly concluded that there were no procedural irregularities and which did not change the subject matter of the CFI proceedings, supported by existing material which did not constitute new material was not contrary to the Rules of Procedure of the Court of Justice Art.113(2); (4) an appeal might rely only on grounds relating to the infringement of rules of law, to the exclusion of any appraisal of the facts. The appraisal by the CFI of evidence put before it did not constitute, a point of law which was subject, as such, to review by the ECJ, save where the clear sense of that evidence had been distorted; (5) the request for measures of inquiry or the re-opening of oral procedure could be admitted only if it related to acts which might have a decisive influence on the outcome of the case and could not be put forward before the close of oral procedure; (6) indications of a general nature concerning an alleged practice of the Commission and emerging from a judgment delivered in other cases, or statements made on the occasion of other proceedings, could not, as such, be regarded as decisive, and (7) the CFI was not obliged to order that the oral procedures be re-opened on the ground of public policy objections to the way the decision was adopted. That obligation only existed on the basis of the factual evidence in the case file.

SHELL INTERNATIONAL CHEMICAL CO LTD v. COMMISSION OF THE EUROPEAN COMMUNITIES (C234/92) [1999] 5 C.M.L.R. 1142, PJG Kapteyn (President), ECJ.

2379. **European Court of Justice – appellate jurisdiction – CFI's refusal to re-open oral hearing**

[Commission Decision 86/398; Statute of the Court of Justice Art.37(4).]

Following an investigation by the European Commission, ICI was fined for its part in the operation of a European wide cartel of polypropylene producers, pursuant to Commission Decision 86/398. When ICI appealed to the CFI its request that the court re-open the oral hearing and order measures of inquiry was refused. The request arose as a result of statements made by the Commission in a similar appeal against a Decision, whereby fines were imposed on members of a PVC cartel where the court ruled that the Decision applicable in that case was non existent because of procedural irregularities. ICI appealed to the ECJ, arguing that the CFI's refusal to re-open the hearing constituted a breach of procedure and infringement of Community law. D, which had also been fined for its part in the cartel intervened in support of ICI.

Held, dismissing the appeal, that (1) an intervener could use arguments different from those used by the party it was supporting, provided the intervener sought to support that party's submissions; (2) D's claim as regards the Decision specifically concerned D and was not identical to the form of order sought by ICI. Therefore it did not satisfy the conditions laid down in the Statute of the Court of Justice Art.37(4) to make the intervention inadmissible; (3) an appeal might rely only on grounds relating to the infringement of rules of law, to the exclusion of any appraisal of the facts. In so far as they challenged the CFI's appraisal of the evidence before it in connection with the request that the oral procedure be re-opened, ICI's complaints could not be examined on appeal; (4) a request for the reopening of the oral procedure or measures of inquiry made after the oral proceedings were closed might be admitted only if it related to facts which might have a decisive influence on the outcome of the case and which could not have been put forward earlier; (5) indications of a general nature concerning an alleged practice of the Commission emerging from a judgment delivered in other cases, or statements made in other proceedings, could not be decisive; (6) the CFI was not obliged to re-open oral proceedings on the basis of public policy objections to the way in which the decision was adopted, and (7) acts of the Community institutions were in principle presumed lawful and to produce legal effects, even if tainted by irregularities, until they were annulled or withdrawn. Only where the gravity of the irregularity was so obvious that it could not be tolerated by the Community legal order should it be treated as legally non existent.

ICI PLC v. COMMISSION OF THE EUROPEAN COMMUNITIES (C200/92) [1999] 5 C.M.L.R. 1110, PJG Kapteyn (President), ECJ.

2380. **European Court of Justice – jurisdiction – cause of action arising in EFTA Member State prior to EU accession**

[EC Treaty Art.234 (now, after amendment, Art.307 EC); Agreement on a European Economic Area 1992 Art.6, Art.108(2); Agreement between the EFTA States on the Establishment of a Surveillance Authority and a Court of Justice Art.34; Council Directive 80/987 on the protection of employees in the event of the insolvency of their employer.]

A's employer became insolvent in 1994, prior to Sweden's accession to the EU, but while it was a Member State of EFTA. A's claim for lost wages was precluded under national law, as the employer was owned by her son, however, she would have had such an entitlement had Council Directive 80/987 been correctly transposed into national law. A contended that Sweden was liable to pay compensation in reliance upon the principle in *Francovich v. Italy (C6/90)* [1991] E.C.R. I-5357, [1992] C.L.Y. 4815 cited, by virtue of the Agreement on a European Economic Area 1992 Art.6. The national court sought a preliminary ruling from the ECJ and the issue arose whether an EFTA Member State that subsequently became a Member State of the EU could be liable for damage arising from a failure to transpose Directive 80/987 correctly into national law, at a time prior to its EU accession.

Held, refusing to give a preliminary ruling, that (1) the ECJ did not have jurisdiction to give a ruling on the application of the EEA Agreement within EFTA Member States, such matters being reserved to the EFTA court by Art.108(2) of the EFTA Agreement and the EFTA Surveillance Agreement Art.34, *R & V Haegeman sprl v. Belgium (181/73)* [1975] 1 C.M.L.R. 515 and *Demirel v. Stadt Schwabisch Gmund (C12/86)* [1989] 1 C.M.L.R. 421 followed. Although the ECJ had jurisdiction under the EC Treaty Art.234 (now, after amendment, Art.307 EC) to give a preliminary ruling on the interpretation of the EEA Agreement, that jurisdiction only applied to EU Member States, and (2) A could not rely on rights derived directly from Directive 80/987 as the events triggering the protection guarantee took place prior to Sweden's accession to the EU, *Maso v. Istitutio Nazionale Della Previdenza Sociale (INPS) (C373/95)* [1997] E.C.R. I-4051 followed.

ANDERSSON v. SVENSKA STATEN (C321/97); *sub nom.* ANDERSSON v. SWEDEN (C321/97) [2000] 2 C.M.L.R. 191, GC Rodriguez Iglesias (President), ECJ.

2381. **European Court of Justice – preliminary rulings – Swedish Revenue Board – right of reference**

[EC Treaty Art.177 (now Article 234 EC).]

The Swedish Revenue Board was asked for a preliminary decision on the VAT treatment of an assignment of film rights. The Board's two divisions, respectively charged with dealing with direct and indirect taxes, were headed by two full time members, who were trained judges. Under Swedish law, the Board could give preliminary decisions on taxation matters, which could be appealed to the Supreme Administrative Court of Sweden. The question arose as to whether the

Board, when giving a preliminary decision, was a "court or tribunal" able to refer a question to the ECJ for a preliminary ruling under the EC Treaty Art.177 (now Article 234 EC).

Held, that the Revenue Board was carrying out an administrative, rather than a judicial function when giving its preliminary decisions, notwithstanding its composition or statutory guarantee of independence. Its role was not to review the legality of a decision that the tax authorities could reach, but rather to determine how a particular transaction was to be assessed for tax. The Board could not, therefore, refer questions to the ECJ under Art.177, *Criminal Proceedings against Unterweger (318/85)* [1986] E.C.R. 955 and *Job Centre Coop ARL (C111/94), Re* [1995] E.C.R. I-3361, [1996] C.L.Y. 2795 followed.

VICTORIA FILM A/S v. RIKSSKATTEVERKET (C134/97); *sub nom.* VICTORIA FILM A/S'S REFERENCE (C134/97), *Re* [1998] E.C.R. I-7023, G Hirsch (President), ECJ.

2382. Excise duty – alcohol – harmonisation of beer and wine duty

[EC Treaty Art.95 (now, after amendment, Art.90 EC), Art.99 (now Art.93 EC), Art.190 (now Art.253 EC); Council Directive 92/83 on the harmonisation of the structures of excise duties on alcohol and alcoholic beverages; Council Directive 92/84 on the approximation of the rates of excise duty on alcohol and alcoholic beverages.]

In proceedings before the national court, S argued that Council Directive 92/83 and Council Directive 92/84 were invalid, contending that the Directives had the effect of requiring a major rise in taxation on beer under national law and of requiring a new standard of taxation assessed by reference to alcohol content, as opposed to volume. S argued that the change was discriminatory and contrary to the EC Treaty Art.95 (now, after amendment, Art.90 EC) as (1) imported drinks would be taxed at a higher rate than nationally produced comparable products; (2) the difference in duty between wine and beer that would result was not justifiable on an objective basis, and (3) the minimum zero rate for wine created a permanent exemption for the wine producing countries of southern Europe. Further, that the Directives would not lead to a harmonisation of the taxation treatment of alcoholic drinks, contrary to Art.99 (now Art.93 EC) of the Treaty and that the Council had failed to give reasons for promulgating the Directives, contrary to Art.190 (now Art.253 EC). The national court referred the matter to the ECJ for a preliminary ruling.

Held, giving a preliminary ruling, that (1) the purpose of Art.95 was to guarantee the free movement of goods unhindered by discriminatory national taxation. Member States had a wide discretion as to how to implement the Directives so as to comply with the Treaty. In the instant case, only commonly consumed low cost wine could be considered as competing with beer, so that only these should be taken into account in the instant proceedings, *VAT Rates on Wine, Re (C356/85)* [1987] E.C.R. 3299, [1990] C.L.Y. 2237 and *Wachauf v. Germany (5/88)* [1989] E.C.R. 2609, [1991] C.L.Y. 3730 followed; (2) the purpose of Art.99 was to achieve harmonisation between the taxation provisions relating to beer and wine. It was not their function to harmonise taxation between beer and wine. Moreover, Member States could introduce harmonisation in stages, having regard to the complexity of existing national laws in this area, *Rewe-Zentrale AG v. Direktor de Landwirtschaftskammer Rheinland (37/83)* [1984] E.C.R. 1229, [1985] C.L.Y. 1427 and *Germany v. European Parliament (C233/94)* [1997] E.C.R. I-2405 followed, and (3) the purpose of Directive 92/84 was to harmonise national legislation and set minimum rates for duty and did not require a specific statement of reasons.

SOCIETE CRITOURIDIENNE DE DISTRIBUTION (SOCRIDIS) v. RECEVEUR PRINCIPAL DES DOUANES (C166/98) [2000] 3 C.M.L.R. 669, J-P Puissochet (President), ECJ.

2383. Free movement of capital – land registration – precluded for second residences in other Member States

[EC Treaty Art.73b (now Art.56 EC); Agreement on a European Economic Area 1992; Act of Accession of Norway, Austria, Finland and Sweden to the European Communities 1994 Art.70.]

K, a German national, acquired land in Austria, intending to transfer his principal residence there. However, a 1993 Austrian law required that K obtain authorisation for the transfer, conditional on his showing that the land would not be used for a secondary residence. Austrian nationals were not required to make such a declaration under the 1993 law. The law was declared unconstitutional in 1996, as it represented an excessive fetter on the right to property. Austria then introduced a fresh provision, extending the declaration procedure to all acquiring land, regardless of nationality. Certain restrictions still applied to foreigners, however, except for those who showed they were exercising freedoms under the EC Treaty or the Agreement on a European Economic Area 1992. K succeeded before the Austrian Constitutional Court, on the ground that the whole of the 1993 law had been declared unconstitutional and he then commenced proceedings for compensation for Austria's breach of Community law under both the 1993 and 1996 provisions. The court referred questions to the ECJ for a preliminary ruling, concerning the impact of the 1993 and 1996 laws on the freedom of establishment and movement of capital within the European Union, and Austria's terms of accession to the European Union under the Act of Accession of Norway, Austria, Finland and Sweden to the European Communities 1994.

Held, giving a preliminary ruling, that (1) the 1993 law discriminated against nationals of other Member States regarding the free movement of capital, contrary to the Art.73b (now Art.56 EC). However, under Art.70 of the Act of Accession, Austria could maintain its existing legislation on secondary residences for five years following accession. Since the 1993 law had been declared unconstitutional by an Austrian court, it was for that court to determine whether it was part of domestic law at the date of Austria's accession. If so, then it did not contravene Art.73b; (2) although the 1996 law had not been applied in K's case, it was incompatible with Art.73b in that it had been exercised in a discriminatory manner. Further, in the light of other measures available, the 1996 law was a restriction on the free movement of capital, *Union Royale Belge des Societes de Football Association (ASBL) v. Bosman (C415/93)* [1996] All E.R. (EC) 97, [1996] C.L.Y. 3149 and *Robert Fearon & Co Ltd v. Irish Land Commission (C182/83)* [1984] E.C.R. 3677, [1985] C.L.Y. 1402 applied, and (3) Member States had to make provision for non contractual reparation to individuals suffering damage if they breached Community law. Member States could not escape liability by relying upon the distribution of power and responsibility between their various organs, *Brasserie du Pecheur SA v. Germany (C46/93)* [1996] Q.B. 404, [1996] C.L.Y. 2803 applied.

KONLE v. AUSTRIA (C302/97) [1999] E.C.R. I-3099, GC Rodriguez Iglesias (President), ECJ.

2384. Free movement of goods – angling licences – general right to fish throughout Finland – issue confined to single Member State

[EC Treaty Art.59 (now, after amendments, Art.49 EC).]

In 1996, Finland enacted legislation whereby anyone could take part in angling, even in privately owned waters without the owner's permissions on payment of a fee in each department in which they intended to fish. The fees collected were distributed to the owners of the waters on an annual basis after deduction of administration expenses. G paid a licence fee and proceeded to fish in J's waters. J brought proceedings in the Finnish court, seeking a declaration that G was not entitled to fish in his waters on the basis that the Finnish legislation contravened the provisions of the EC Treaty concerning the free movement of goods, arguing that fishing rights constituted "goods" for this purpose. The Finnish court referred the matter to the ECJ.

Held, giving a preliminary ruling, that (1) goods were products capable of monetary valuation and of transfer pursuant to commercial transactions. However, not all things valued in money and capable of commercial transfer were goods, *Export Tax on Art Treasures, Re (C7/68)* [1968] E.C.R. 617, [1969] C.L.Y. 1396 considered. Making fishing rights available was properly to be regarded as the provision of a service under the EC Treaty Art.59 (now, after amendments, Art.49 EC) provided that the service had a cross border character. In the instant case, however, the parties were both Finns, living and established in Finland. The matter was therefore confined within a single Member State, and the provisions of the Treaty relating to the freedom to provide services were of no application, *Customs and Excise Commissioners v. Schindler (C275/92)* [1994] Q.B. 610, [1994] C.L.Y. 4907 followed.

JAGERSKIOLD v. GUSTAFSSON (C97/98) [2000] 1 C.M.L.R. 235, Hirsch (President), ECJ.

2385. **Free movement of goods – labelling – language requirement – not a "technical regulation" under Directive 83/189**

[Council Directive 83/189 laying down a procedure for the provision of information in the field of technical standards and regulations.]

A dispute arose between C and B, each claiming that the other was selling various products which did not bear any labelling or sufficient labelling in the language of the area, namely Dutch, contrary to the relevant Belgian legislation. The Court was asked to interpret Council Directive 83/189 which lays down the procedure for the provision of information requiring Member States to notify the Commission of all draft technical regulations.

Held, giving a preliminary ruling, that (1) the obligation to give mandatory labelling particulars instructions for use and guarantees for products in the language of the area in which they are sold did not constitute a "technical regulation" within the meaning of Council Directive 83/189, and (2) Member States may adopt national measures requiring information appearing on imported products to be given in he language of the area in which the products are sold or another language which is understood by consumers in that area provided that the measures are applied without distinction to all national and imported products and are proportionate to the objective of consumer protection.

COLIM NV v. BIGG'S CONTINENT NOORD NV (C33/97) [2000] 2 C.M.L.R. 135, J-P Puissochet (President), ECJ.

2386. **Free movement of goods – marketing – risk of consumer being misled – power of national court to override Community law**

[EC Treaty Art.30 (now, after amendment, Art.28 EC), Art.36 (now, after amendment, Art.30 EC); Council Directive 76/768 relating to cosmetic products Art.6(3).]

EL and L were German subsidiaries of competing multinational cosmetics companies. EL sought an injunction against L in the Landgericht Koln. The subject of the application was the marketing of a facial cosmetic cream which was manufactured in Monaco and distributed by L throughout Germany and other parts of Europe. The essence of the dispute was a contention by EL that use of the word "lifting" in the marketing of the cream was misleading as it could lead to the impression that use of the cream had equivalent effect to that of a face lift operation. EL contended that promotion and distribution of the cream was thereby inconsistent with national unfair competition legislation prohibiting misleading advertising. L countered that an injunction would force them to incur expenditure by repackaging the cream for its German customers only, thus impeding the free movement of goods throughout the Community. The German court, in reliance on the authorities, adopted the view that there was a possibility that consumers could be misled by the use of the word "lifting" but submitted a reference to the ECJ. The issue for determination was whether, having regard to the risk of a proportion of consumers being misled as to any permanent effect of the cream, Community law could override domestic legislation which prohibited the importation and distribution of a cosmetic product whose name included the word "lifting", notwithstanding that the product was being distributed without objection in other Member States. In particular, reference was made to the EC Treaty Art.30 (now, after amendment, Art.28 EC) and Art.36 (now, after amendment Art.30 EC) and Council Directive 76/768 Art.6(3).

Held, giving a preliminary ruling, that EC Treaty Art.30 and Art.36 and Council Directive 76/768 Art.6(3) did not prevent the German court from applying its national legislation. However, in order to justify the grant of an injunction, the German court must first be satisfied that an average German consumer who was reasonably observant, well informed and circumspect would be sufficiently confused as to the attributes of the product by reason of the marketing description applied to it so as to believe that the product possessed properties which it did not in fact possess, *Gut Springenheide GmbH v. Obekreisdirektor des Kreises Steinfurt -Amt fur Lebensmitteluberwachung (C210/96)* [1998] E.C.R. I-4657, [1999] C.L.Y. 814 applied. There were additional factors to be taken into account in the application of that test to the instant case, namely, that particular social, cultural or linguistic features in a Member State might need to be considered and specifically whether the use of the word "lifting" would tend to mislead German consumers, despite its apparent lack of ill-effect in other German speaking Member States. It might also be the case that the usage instructions were sufficiently clear as to the duration of the product's effects to negate any false impression which might have arisen as a result of the use of the word "lifting".

ESTEE LAUDER COSMETICS GmbH & CO OHG v. LANCASTER GROUP GmbH (C220/98) [2000] All E.R. (EC) 122, Judge Edward, ECJ.

2387. Free movement of persons – discrimination – private sector employer requiring evidence of bilingual status

[EC Treaty Art.48 (now, after amendment, Art.39 EC); Council Regulation 1612/68 on freedom of movement for workers within the Community Art.3(1), Art.7.]

C, a private banking company, had a staff recruitment requirement, under a collective agreement, that applicants must possess a certificate proving their bilingual ability which was only issued by the public authority in one Italian province. A was refused entry to C's recruitment competition because, although he had evidence that he was bilingual, he did not possess the certificate in question. The ECJ had to determine whether the condition was contrary to Community law by virtue of Council Regulation 1612/68 Art.3 or Art.7 or EC Treaty Art.48 (now, after amendment, Art.39 EC).

Held, giving a preliminary ruling, that the requirement breached Art.48 of the Treaty, that (1) Art.3(1) of the Regulation applied only to the laws of Member States; (2) the collective agreement did not permit C to adopt discriminatory criteria in relation to workers who were nationals of other Member States and, by itself, did not infringe Art.7 of the Regulation which did not apply to the requirement in issue; (3) Art.48 of the Treaty was not restricted to only Member States and the free movement of persons was not to be adversely affected by measures imposed by the private sector; (4) the fact that certain Treaty provisions were addressed to Member States did not preclude rights from being conferred on an interested individual, *Defrenne v. SABENA (C43/75)* [1981] 1 All E.R. 122, [1976] C.L.Y. 1164 applied. Article 48 applied to private persons with an interest in the observance of Treaty obligations; (5) a measure that affected nationals of the Member State concerned could be discriminatory on nationality grounds and it was not necessary for all workers in a territory to be disadvantaged by it or for it to apply only against nationals of other Member States, and (6) although requiring evidence of linguistic competence could be legitimate, an exclusive requirement to provide evidence of that skill solely by reliance upon a qualification issued in one part of a Member State was contrary to Art.48 of the Treaty.

ANGONESE v. CASSA DI RISPARMIO DI BOLZANO SpA (C281/98) [2000] All E.R. (EC) 577, GC Rodriguez Iglesias (President), ECJ.

2388. Free movement of persons – sportspersons – national rules governing transfer

[EC Treaty Art.48 (now, after amendment, Art.39 EC).]

FRB's rules provided that basketball players coming from non Member States, and certain other named European States, were subject to a transfer deadline of 31 March for participation in championship matches. However, players from other Member States were subject to a transfer deadline of 28 February. The ECJ was asked whether the EC Treaty Art.48 (now, after amendment, Art.39 EC) precluded the application of rules that prevented a club from fielding players from other Member States in matches in the national championship, where the transfer took place after the date given in the rules.

Held, giving a preliminary ruling, that Art.48 did not prevent the exclusion of foreign players for non economic reasons. However, such restrictions had to be limited to their proper objectives and not used to exclude such players from the entire sporting activity concerned. On the facts, FRB's rules constituted an obstacle to the free movement of workers, but it was for the national court to determine whether the rule was capable of objective justification. Taken as a whole, however, rules that prevented a club from fielding players from another Member State transferred by the set deadline, which was earlier that that applicable in the case on players from non Member States, breached Art.48 where there were no objective reasons for the difference in treatment.

LEHTONEN v. FEDERATION ROYALE BELGE DES SOCIETES DE BASKET-BALL ASBL (FRBSB) (C176/96) [2001] All E.R. (EC) 97, R Schintgen (President), ECJ.

2389. Free movement of persons – workers – education funding – part time frontier worker

[EC Treaty Art.48 (now, after amendment, Art.39 EC), Art.52 (now, after amendment, Art.43 EC); Council Regulation 1612/68 on freedom of movement for workers within the Community Art.7 (2).]

Dutch law provided that finance was available to Dutch nationals and those living in the Netherlands in respect of courses in the Netherlands and those undertaken at certain specified foreign institutions. M was a Belgian national living in Belgium studying at a specified institution located in Belgium. Her parents were Belgian and resided there but her father owned a company established in the Netherlands where her mother worked part time. M appealed against a decision refusing finance for her studies to the Dutch study finance tribunal, arguing that the right to finance should not be subject to the requirement that she resided in the Member State where her parents were employed by virtue of Council Regulation 1612/68 Art.7. The tribunal stayed the proceedings and made a reference to the ECJ for a preliminary ruling as to whether M's mother was an employee for the purposes of the freedom of movement of workers in EC Treaty Art.48 (now Art.39 EC) and Regulation 1612/68.

Held, giving a preliminary ruling, that (1) a person was an employee if they acted under the direction of another person for a certain period of time in return for remuneration. The activity had to be effective and genuine as opposed to marginal, *Lawrie-Blum v. Land Baden-Wurttenberg (C66/85)* [1986] E.C.R. 2121, [1987] C.L.Y. 1569 applied; (2) whether the activities were performed under the direction of another person entrusted with overall responsibility for the management of a firm was a question of fact and marriage to the company's owner did not preclude the existence of a qualifying subordinate employment relationship as a "worker" for purposes of Art.48 of the Treaty and Art.7 of the Regulation; (3) permanent frontier workers had a right of free movement under the Regulation that was to be enjoyed without discrimination. Further, the principle of equal treatment contained in Art.7 included the prevention of discrimination to the worker's dependants, *Bernini (MJE) v. Netherlands Ministry of Education and Science (C3/90)* [1992] E.C.R. I-1071, [1992] C.L.Y. 4767 followed; (4) M, as the dependant child of a national of one Member State, who worked in another Member State, but who lived in the state of which she was a national, could rely on Art.7(2) to claim study finance, subject only to the same conditions that applied to the children of Dutch nationals, and (5) under Art.52 (now, after amendment, Art.43) of the Treaty, nationals of one Member State working as self employed persons in another Member State were entitled to the same treatment as the nationals of the host state, and this precluded residential requirements of a discriminatory nature, *Commission of the European Communities v. Luxembourg (C111/91)* [1993] E.C.R. I-817, [1993] C.L.Y. 4376 applied.

MEEUSEN v. HOOFDDIRECTIE VAN DE INFORMATIE BEHEER GROEP (C337/97) [2000] 2 C.M.L.R. 659, J-P Puissochet (President), ECJ.

2390. Free movement of services – legal profession

See LEGAL PROFESSION. §4019

2391. Freedom of establishment – aircraft – registration subject to residence requirements

[EC Treaty Art.6 (now, after amendment, Art.12 EC), Art.52 (now, after amendment, Art.43 EC).]

Under a provision of Belgian law, Community operators were required to be resident or established for one year in Belgium before they could register aircraft there. The Commission claimed that this showed a failure by Belgium to fulfil its obligations under EC Treaty Art.6 and Art.52 (now, after amendment, Art.12 and Art.43). The Commission drew the attention of the Belgian authorities to the restrictions encountered by operators wishing to carry out aerial photography over Belgium and the authorities replied to the effect that a law was being prepared establishing the conditions for aerial work. The relevant amendments not having been produced, the Commission brought an action against Belgium. Belgium claimed in its defence its intention to amend the offending provision and pointed out that, pending introduction, the authorities had undertaken not to apply the offending provisions to legal and natural persons from other Member States.

Held, declaring a failure to fulfil obligations, that (1) the conditions laid down for registration of aircraft constituted discrimination on the grounds of nationality which impeded the exercise of the freedom of establishment of natural and legal persons from other Member States, and (2) the administrative practice of not applying the provisions in question could not be regarded as constituting proper fulfilment of obligations under the Treaty. These were mere administrative practices which, by their nature, were alterable at will by the authorities.

COMMISSION OF THE EUROPEAN COMMUNITIES v. BELGIUM (C203/98) [2000] 1 C.M.L.R. 866, Kapteyn (President), ECJ.

2392. Freedom of information – asylum – failure to disclose – duty to give reasons on basis of individual documents

[Council Decision 93/731 on public access to Council documents Art.4(1).]

K, a university lecturer and researcher, appealed against a refusal by the Council of the European Union, CEU, to allow access to documents containing information on the situation prevailing in countries from which the majority of asylum seekers originated. The documents consisted of reports drawn up by the Centre for Information, Discussion and Exchange on Asylum, CIREA, reports drawn up by member states and submitted to CIREA and details of persons in Member States involved in asylum cases. Access was allowed to only ten documents prepared by the Danish authorities. As to the remaining documents, access was refused under Council Decision 93/731 Art.4(1) on the ground that they contained sensitive information which, if disclosed, could harm diplomatic relations between the countries concerned and the EU. K argued that, whereas diverse situations prevailed in all the countries concerned, the CEU had used a short and identically worded refusal in the case of each country, which showed that the documents had not in fact been individually examined. The CEU countered that the countries concerned shared common features that justified the use of an identically worded refusal.

Held, allowing the appeal, that the CEU had failed to carry out an assessment of each document individually. The reports contained information on very different third countries with which the EU had variable diplomatic relations. The reasons given by the CEU failed to show that each document had been assessed individually. Moreover, Art.4(1) was subject to the principles guaranteeing the right to information and proportionality and by refusing to grant even partial access to the documents, the CEU had acted disproportionately.

KUIJER v. COUNCIL OF THE EUROPEAN UNION (T188/98) [2000] 2 C.M.L.R. 400, Moura Ramos (President), CFI.

2393. **Freedom of information – disclosure – decision precluding MEP access to report arms exports – international relations**

[Council Decision 93/731 on public access to Council documents Art.4(1).]

A Member of the European Parliament applied for the annulment of a Council Decision of November 4, 1997 whereby the Council refused her access to a report from the Working Group on Conventional Arms Exports on the ground that its disclosure might harm the public interest as regards the EU's international relations. She argued that the Decision infringed Decision 93/731 Art.4(1) by which the Council adopted a Code of Conduct which aimed to improve public access to Council documents.

Held, granting the application, that (1) Decision 93/731 applied to all Council documents irrespective of their content, *Svenska Journalistforbundet v. Council of the European Union (T174/95)* [1998] All E.R. (EC) 545, [1998] C.L.Y. 2327 followed. As a general rule the public should have the greatest possible access to documents held by the Council and exceptions to that principle were to be construed restrictively; (2) the Council had to determine the possible consequences which disclosure of a contested report might have for international relations of the EU. Review of its refusal of access to the report by the court was limited to verifying whether the procedural rules had been complied with, the contested Decision was properly reasoned, the effects had been accurately stated, and there had been a manifest error of assessment of the facts or a misuse of powers; (3) as Decision 93/731 was a measure of internal organisation, the Council was entitled to grant partial access if it so wished, and (4) the principle of proportionality required that derogations remained within the limits of what was appropriate and necessary for achieving the aim in view. Decision 93/731 Art.4(1) had to be interpreted in the light of the principle of the right of information and the principle of proportionality. The Council was obliged to examine whether partial access should be granted to the information not covered by exceptions. As the Council did not make such an examination in this case the contested Decision was vitiated by an error of law and should be annulled.

HAUTALA v. COUNCIL OF THE EUROPEAN UNION (T14/98) [1999] 3 C.M.L.R. 528, B Vesterdorf (President), CFI.

2394. **Freedom of information – environment – implementation of Directive 90/313**

[EC Treaty Art.169 (now Art.226 EC); Council Directive 90/313 on the freedom of access to information on the environment Art.2(b), Art.3(2), Art.5.]

The EC Commission brought an action under EC Treaty Art.169 (now Art.226 EC) for a declaration that German provisions transposing EC Directive 90/313 on the freedom of access to information on the environment into national law (UIG) and imposing charges for that information were incompatible with the Directive. In support of its action the Commission relied on four grounds: (1) the general exclusion of courts, criminal prosecution authorities and disciplinary authorities from the scope of the UIG; (2) the exclusion of the right to obtain information during "administrative proceedings"; (3) the lack of provision for information to be supplied in part, and (4) the provision for a charge to be made even if a request for information was refused and the absence of any provision that the charge must be limited to a reasonable sum.

Held, allowing the application in part, that (1) it was for the Commission to prove the existence of the alleged failure to fulfil obligations and it might not rely on the presumption that in Germany all courts and other bodies acting in the exercise of their judicial functions must be regarded as public authorities for the purposes of the Directive. The Commission had failed to show that in Germany authorities acting normally in the exercise of their judicial powers and therefore not covered by the Directive might also have information on the environment when acting outside their strictly judicial functions; (2) the exclusion of access to information during "administrative proceedings" as provided for in the UIG went beyond the scope of the derogation allowed for in Art.3(2) of the Directive. Art.3(2) referred to "preliminary investigation proceedings" which covered all administrative proceedings prior to judicial proceedings the outcome of which was capable of forming the subject matter of judicial review in the administrative courts; (3) Art.3(2) of the Directive permitted Member States to refuse to grant a request for information in specified cases but required them to communicate information from which it was possible to detach information covered by the requirements of confidentiality or privilege. In the absence of an express provision in the UIG regarding partial communication, persons seeking information might not be aware of the full extent of their rights and public authorities to whom a request for information was addressed might be dissuaded from granting it, and (4) Art.5 expressly permitted Member States to impose a reasonable charge for supplying information on the environment in accordance with the objective of the Directive to provide freedom of access to information. The Commission had not shown that Art.5 was incorrectly transposed into German law in this respect. However the imposition of a charge to be made even when a request for information was refused was incompatible with Art.5.

COMMISSION OF THE EUROPEAN COMMUNITIES v. GERMANY (C217/97) [1999] 3 C.M.L.R. 277, PJG Kapteyn (President), ECJ.

2395. **Freedom of information – European Commission – Commission acting as legal or economic adviser – refusal of disclosure subject to national law**

[EC Treaty Art.85 (now Art.81 EC), Art.86 (now Art.82 EC); Commission Decision 94/90 on public access to Commission documents; European Convention on Human Rights 1950 Art.6.]

V, a lawyer, sought access to certain documentation prepared by the European Commission in response to questions posed by national courts concerning Notice 93/C39/05 dealing with the application of the EC Treaty Art.85 (now Art.81 EC) and Art.86 (now Art.82 EC). The documentation comprised legal and economic analysis of information supplied by national courts regarding competition issues and the interpretation of Community law. The Commission refused access to the documents on the basis that they were concerned with current legal proceedings creating a requirement to protect the public interest, in conformity with specified grounds for refusal outlined in Commission Decision 94/90. That refusal was upheld by the CFI ([1998] All E.R. (EC) 289, [1998] C.L.Y. 2326), which found that the decision whether to grant public access to such documentation was retained by the national court on the basis of the principle of procedural autonomy derived from the European Convention on Human Rights 1950 Art.6. V appealed.

Held, allowing the appeal, setting aside the decision of the CFI and annulling the Commission's decision, that access to Commission documents could not be refused purely on the basis that they were prepared in response to questions raised by national courts during proceedings, without any enquiry into whether disclosure infringed national law. The right under Art.6 could not be construed as restricting the decision about disclosure of documents to the national court hearing the dispute. Often the information requested from the Commission by the national court on the application of Art.85 and Art.86, would be of a general nature and may not have been specifically prepared with particular proceedings in mind or bear any relation to the information provided by the national court. Each piece of documentation must be assessed individually. The procedural rules relating to disclosure were to be applied in the usual way where the documentation had been prepared on the basis of specific data and the Commission was acting as a legal or economic adviser to the national court. Access to a whole category of documents could not be refused since the Decision 94/90 had to be strictly applied giving the public the widest possible access to Council and Commission documents. It was sound administration to allow general access to documentation with the proviso that the national court could object if disclosure infringed national rules.

VAN DER WAL v. COMMISSION OF THE EUROPEAN COMMUNITIES (C174/98); VAN DER WAL v. COMMISSION OF THE EUROPEAN COMMUNITIES (C189/98) *The Times*, February 22, 2000, GC Rodriguez Iglesias (President), ECJ.

2396. Freedom to provide services – competitive tendering – award of contract to state-owned financing company – involvement of single Member State

[EC Treaty Art.55 (now Art.45 EC), Art.90(2) (now Art.86(2) EC).]

A municipal council, CI, acting under a provision of Italian law, set up a company, IA, to run its solid urban waste service. The share capital of IA was held as to 51 per cent by CI and 49 per cent by G, a state-owned financing company. Subsequently the municipality decided to award IA the solid urban waste collection service, previously provided by R. R claimed that the choice of private partner should have been brought about by public tender and that the waste collection service should also have been awarded under a public tender procedure. The national court asked the ECJ to rule on the applicability and interpretation of EC Treaty Art.55 (now Art.45 EC) and EC Treaty Art.90(2) (now Art.86(2) EC).

Held, giving a preliminary ruling, that (1) Art.55 did not apply where the facts giving rise to the proceedings concerned a single Member State only. In such a situation there were no Community law issues relating to freedom of movement of persons or freedom to provide services. R had its seat in Italy and did not operate on the Italian market in reliance on freedom of establishment or freedom to provide services, and (2) it was not possible, in the absence of sufficient information in the present case, to give any ruling as to whether Art.90(2), which derogates from competition rules of the Treaty, was applicable.

RISAN SRL v. COMUNE DI ISCHIA (C108/98) [2000] 4 C.M.L.R. 657, J-P Puissochet (President), ECJ.

2397. Freedom to provide services – gambling – prohibition on arranging bets

[EC Treaty Art.55 (now Art.45 EC), Art..56 (now, after amendment, Art.46 EC).]

Z was an intermediary working in Italy for a licensed English bookmaker. His job was to arrange bets for Italian clients on foreign sporting events. Italian law forbade the taking of bets except in certain circumstances for which licences were required. Z did not have one, and he was ordered to cease his activities. Z brought proceedings for a review of that decision before the Italian Council of State, which held that the matter called for an interpretation of the provisions of the EC Treaty relating to the freedom to provide services. It was the view of the Council that the Italian legislation was analogous to English legislation forbidding lotteries, and the effect of the decision in *Customs and Excise Commissioners v. Schindler (C275/92)* [1994] Q.B. 610, [1994] C.L.Y. 4907 was that such national legislation was not precluded. Z argued that the two situations were not truly analogous, since lotteries were activities of pure chance, whereas betting required a degree of skill and judgment on the part of the participant. The question as to whether the Italian legislation was contrary to the EC treaty was referred to the ECJ

Held, giving a preliminary ruling, that (1) although betting did not, unlike lotteries, involve the application of pure chance and nothing more, in view of the money staked by way of betting and the prizes offered there was scope for crime and fraud to the same extent as with lotteries. It was therefore appropriate for Member States to assess whether or not such activities should be restricted or even prohibited, provided that any restrictions or prohibitions were not discriminatory, *Schindler (C275/92)* followed; (2) the Italian legislation was prima facie a restriction on the freedom to provide services. Article 55 (now Art.45 EC) and Art.56 (now, after amendment, Art.46 EC) permitted such restrictions for reasons of public health, public policy or public security. Case law of the ECJ permitted restrictions for overriding reasons related to the public interest. It was for the national courts to verify whether the legislation concerned was genuinely directed to carrying out the aims which were capable of justifying it, and whether the restrictions imposed were proportionate in the light of those aims, *Vereinigte Familiapress Zeitungsverlags und Vertriebs GmbH v. Heinrich Bauer Verlag (C368/95)* [1997] E.C.R. I-3689 distinguished and *Stichting Collectieve Antennevoorziening Gouda v. Commissariaat voor de Media (C288/89)* [1991] E.C.R. I-4007 followed.

QUESTORE DI VERONA v. ZENATTI (C67/98) [2000] 1 C.M.L.R. 201, GC Rodriguez Iglesias (President), ECJ.

2398. Freedom to provide services – minimum wage – French company to pay Belgian minimum wage

[EC Treaty Art.60 (now Art.50), Art.59 (now, after amendment, Art.49).]

A French construction company, A, was contracted to work on the construction of sugar silos in Belgium. Under Belgian law, construction companies, resident and non resident, operating within Belgium were obliged to pay their workers a minimum remuneration, to contribute to a social fund used for workers' benefits and to keep specific records of individual workers and a register of all employees. Non compliance with the regulations was a criminal offence and A was prosecuted for failure to comply. A contended that the legal requirements restricted its right to provide services in a Member State and were in breach of the EC Treaty Art.59 (now, after amendment, Art.49) and Art.60 (now Art.50). The national court referred the matter to the ECJ.

Held, giving a preliminary ruling, that Community law did not prevent Member States from enacting minimum wage legislation for the protection of workers and it would be applicable to non resident contractors. However, requiring the employer to contribute to a social fund for the benefit of workers and to maintain employee records could not be imposed if the employer was subject to an objectively similar scheme in its own Member State of residence. Criminal proceedings would only be justified where the relevant legislation breached had been formulated with precision and clarity and was readily ascertainable by a non resident employer.

CRIMINAL PROCEEDINGS AGAINST ARBLADE (C369/96) [2001] I.C.R. 434, GC Rodriguez Iglesias (President), ECJ.

2399. Freedom to provide services – security companies – Belgian legislation establishing residence and authorisation requirements

[EC Treaty Art.48 (now, after amendment, Art.39 EC), Art.52 (now, after amendment, Art.43 EC), Art.59 (now, after amendment, Art.49 EC); Law of April 10, 1990 on security firms, security systems firms and internal security services (Belgium).]

Belgium enacted the Law of 10 April 1990 on security firms, security systems firms and internal security services, which required, inter alia, that such undertakings were to have a Belgian place of business; that certain employees were to have Belgian residence; that all employees were to obtain a Belgian identity card and that any such undertaking from another Member State acquired authorisation from the Belgian authorities. The European Commission sought a declaration that the law failed to comply with the obligations under the EC Treaty Art.48 (now, after amendment, Art.39 EC), Art.52 (now, after amendment, Art.43 EC) and Art.59 (now, after amendment, Art.49 EC).

Held, granting the declaration sought, that (1) the requirement that an undertaking had a Belgian place of business was in breach of the freedom to provide services, under Art.59 (now, after amendment, Art.49 EC). The defence of public policy was to be interpreted restrictively and there had to be a genuine and sufficiently serious threat affecting one of the fundamental interests of society. Belgium's argument that any security firm was a threat to public policy and public security was unfounded and could not justify such a broad restriction on the freedom to provide services; (2) the residence requirements constituted a restriction on the free movement of persons, under Art.48 (now, after amendment, Art.39 EC) and on freedom of establishment, under Art.52 (now, after amendment, Art.43 EC). The need to acquire information as to the undertaking's managers could be achieved without such a restriction and through co-operation between Member States; (3) in relation to freedom to provide services the legislation in issue exceeded what was necessary to secure the objective sought. A defence based on the public interest would be required to apply to all such undertakings in the jurisdiction, and (4) the requirement that every staff member carry a Belgian identity card was a restriction on the freedom to provide services.

COMMISSION OF THE EUROPEAN COMMUNITIES v. BELGIUM (C355/98) [2000] 2 C.M.L.R. 357, JC Moitinho de Almeida (President), ECJ.

2400. Import controls – alcohol – Finnish import controls – justification on public order grounds

[Council Regulation 918/83 setting up a Community system of reliefs from customs duty; Council Directive 69/169 relating to exemption from turnover tax and excise duty on imports in international travel.]

For many years prior to its accession to the EU in 1995, Finland prohibited the importation of alcohol on return trips overseas lasting less than 24 hours. These provisions were relaxed in 1995, but were reintroduced in 1996. They prevented the importation of alcohol by those arriving in Finland from outside the EEA, except by air, and whose journey lasted no more than 20 hours. The measure was justified on the grounds that public order and safety had declined since the original restrictions had been relaxed; the Finnish alcohol industry had suffered; and the country had lost significant alcohol related revenue. H returned to Finland by boat from Estonia, after a journey of less than 20 hours, with 19 cans of beer. Finnish customs confiscated the beer and ordered H to pay a fine. H argued that under Council Regulation 918/83 he could import beer without being liable to a criminal penalty.

Held, finding that the restriction was justified on public order and health grounds, that (1) Regulation 918/83 and Council Directive 69/169 allowed Member States to regulate imports and exports in a manner that restricted the free movement of goods on certain public policy grounds. These provisions only pertained to the tax position; they did not deal with the relevant public policy requirements, which remained matters for regulation under national law. In the instant case, the restrictions were imposed on the basis that they were necessary in the interests of public morality, public safety and the preservation of human health and life. They did not, therefore, contravene either the Regulation or the Directive; (2) economic considerations, such as the damage to the Finnish alcohol industry and loss of national revenue, did not justify restrictions on imports. Considerations of public order and the maintenance of internal security did provide justification, however, *Criminal Proceedings against Franzen (C189/95)* [1997] E.C.R. I-5909 followed, and (3) the national legislation had to be examined in the light of the basic principle of free movement of goods in the internal market. The legislation was only a minor derogation from the Community wide system of customs and tax reliefs, and was justified in the light of the specific problems which the Finnish government faced and was attempting to deal with. In such circumstances, the legislation contravened neither the Regulation nor the Directive.

CRIMINAL PROCEEDINGS AGAINST HEINONEN (C394/97) [1999] E.C.R. I-3599, J-P Puissochet (President), ECJ.

2401. Import controls – association agreements – national court's jurisdiction to make interim order

[EC Treaty Art.131 (now, after amendment, Art.182 EC).]

As the result of a dispute over a decision of the Council of the European Union restricting imports of sugar into the Community from the overseas territory of a Member State, E sought an interim order prohibiting the Aruban authorities from refusing movement certificates for sugar packed in its factories on the island and the Dutch court referred the question to the ECJ as to whether a national court could make an order for interim measures against a non EC authority to prevent the imminent infringement of Community law.

Held, giving a preliminary ruling, that a national court could make such an order where it seriously doubted the validity of the Community measure, as implemented by the authority, and had referred the matter to the ECJ. The applicant must be faced with the serious threat of damage and the national court had to have taken the Community's interests into account when making the order. Such an order could be made against an overseas territory mentioned in the EC Treaty Art.131 (now, after amendment, Art.182 EC) having a special relationship with a Member State, given the need to ensure the temporary protection of individuals in a dispute concerning Community law.

EMESA SUGAR (FREE ZONE) NV v. ARUBA (C17/98) (NO.2) *The Times*, February 29, 2000, GC Rodriguez Iglesias (President), ECJ.

2402. Import controls – import licences – retrospective application

[Council Regulation 338/97 on the protection of species of wild fauna and flora by regulating trade therein Art.4(1); Commission Regulation 939/97 laying down detailed rules concerning the implementation of Council Regulation 338/97 Art.8(3).]

R appealed against a refusal by the Commissioner to restore two antique ivory elephants which had been seized by Customs officers on the basis that they had been imported without a valid import licence, in violation of Council Regulation 338/97 Art.4(1). The regulations were made in accordance with the Convention on International Trade in Endangered Species of Wild Fauna and Flora 1976. R's legal representatives sought to obtain a retrospective import licence from the Department of the Environment, Transport and the Regions, DETR. The DETR claimed that it did not have the requisite power to grant a retrospective import permit. R successfully appealed to the VAT and duties tribunal. The Commissioners appealed.

Held, allowing the appeal, that (1) the tribunal had erred by disregarding the fact that the task of deciding whether a retrospective import licence should be granted lay not with Commissioners but with the DETR, as the "competent management authority" of the UK and for the purposes of the Convention. The tribunal had wrongly stated that the Commissioners had acted unreasonably in accepting the decision of the DETR in the absence of any consideration of the reasonableness of the DETR's refusal. There was no obligation upon the Commissioners to consider the reasonableness or otherwise of the DETR's decision, and (2) for the purpose of determining whether a retrospective import licence was to be granted under Commission Regulation 939/97 Art.8.3(a), it was arguable that "irregularities" did not encompass the innocent or inadvertent acts or omissions of an importer.

CUSTOMS AND EXCISE COMMISSIONERS v. RAY [2000] 3 C.M.L.R. 1095, Evans-Lombe, J., Ch D.

2403. Import controls – quotas – Chinese imports – replacement of national quota with Community wide quota

[Council Regulation 3420/83; Council Regulation 519/94 on common rules for imports from certain third countries and repealing Regulations 1765/82, 1766/82 and 3420/83 Art.1 (2).]

Imports of certain products from China into the EU had been subject to quantitative restrictions applicable in certain Member States under Council Regulation 3420/83, rather than subject to a Community wide import quota. By Council Regulation 519/94 Art.1 (2), these restrictions were replaced with a Community wide quota. Certain reasons for the introduction of the measure, such as harmonisation and greater uniformity in relation to import rules, were recited in the preamble to Regulation 519/94. However, the UK sought annulment of Art.1 (2) on the grounds that the Council had (1) not given adequate reason for enacting the Regulation; (2) imposed arbitrary quotas; (3) failed properly to appreciate the relevant facts, and (4) infringed the principles of proportionality and equal of treatment. Prior to the coming into force of the disputed Regulation, only Spain had imposed a national quantitative restriction, and this had involved less than two per cent of the Community's import of the products concerned. The UK argued that the Regulation had a significant impact at Community level, whereas the previous regime had had a minimal impact, and that the Council ought to have explained why it had brought this about.

Held, that (1) the measure was of general application, and it was accordingly appropriate to give general reasons for its introduction. The Council was not specifically required to go into technical detail in explaining its decision, nor, since the general objective was to abolish national restrictions, to explain why restrictions were to be imposed at Community level. Neither was there a requirement to make an express reference to the principle of proportionality; (2) the Council's action was proportionate, given the aim of the measure, the Council's own broad discretion in the matter and the pressure of Chinese imports, *Germany v. Council of the European Communities (C280/93) (No.2)* [1994] E.C.R. I-4973 followed, and (3) the Council was free to decide upon the necessary restrictions and had not breached the principle of equal treatment, *Wuidart v. Laiterie Cooperative Eupenoise Societe Cooperative (C267/88)* [1990] E.C.R. I-435 followed.

UNITED KINGDOM v. COUNCIL OF THE EUROPEAN UNION (C150/94) [1999] 1 C.M.L.R. 367, PJG Kapteyn, ECJ.

2404. Import controls – quotas – fruit – privatised undertaking seeking additional licences

[Council Regulation 404/93 creating a common market organisation for bananas Art.30.]

F was a fruit trading company, a previously State owned undertaking in the former GDR. It was privatised and administered by T, the body established under public law with responsibility for restructuring such undertakings. Following completion of new ripening facilities, F applied to the Commission for a special grant of licences for the importation of bananas under the tariff quota, pursuant to Regulation 404/93 on the common organisation of the market in bananas. The application was refused by the contested decision which the applicant sought to annul because it was incompatible with Art.30 of the Regulation.

Held, dismissing the application, that (1) Regulation 404/93 Art.30 empowered the Commission to take specific transitional measures intended to deal with disturbances in the internal market brought about by the replacement of the various national arrangements by the common organisation of the market; (2) F was able, when it took its decision to build a new ripening plant, to foresee the consequences that this would have within the context of the common organisation of the market in bananas established by Regulation 404/93. Accordingly, the Commission, which had a broad discretion in assessing the need for transitional measures, was justified in rejecting F's request for additional licences; (3) before it started to build the ripening plant, F needed to assess its profitability. The fact that the quantities of bananas ripened in the former plant were attributed to F in calculating its import rights did not imply that F was justified in inferring that there was continuity in the ripening business from the privatisation to the opening of the new plant; (4) there had been no breach of the principle of equal treatment as the difficulties of privatised undertakings from the former GDR were not due to the establishment of the common organisation of the market. No economic operator could claim a right to property in a market share held before the adoption of the common market in bananas, and (5) the contested Decision did not constitute a misuse of powers. There was no evidence that it had been taken to achieve an end other than that stated.

FRUCHTHANDELSGESELLSCHAFT MBH CHEMNITZ v. COMMISSION OF THE EUROPEAN COMMUNITIES (T254/97) [1999] 3 C.M.L.R. 508, Cooke (President), CFI.

2405. Limitations – repayments – claim for return of government charges – disparity between national and Community provisions

S sought to recover from M ITL 93 million. This represented sums paid in accordance with an annual administrative charge levied by M for entering companies on the register of companies. The charge was levied in breach of a directive. M opposed S's claim for the return of the monies paid on the basis of the domestic limitation period of three years with respect to governmental charges. The limitation period in civil law claims between private individuals was 10 years. The national court referred the following questions to the ECJ (1) whether a Member State's reliance on a national limitation period, which as applicable only to specified actions and which was less favourable than the usual civil limitation period, was contrary to Community law, and (2) whether Community law prohibited a Member State from relying on a limitation period which ran from the date of payment of the charges, even if the Directive with which the charge was incompatible, had not been properly transposed into domestic law as at that date.

Held, giving a preliminary ruling, that (1) Community law did not prohibit a Member State from relying on a time limit of three years under national law. This was true even if it represented a derogation from the normal, and more favourable, limitation period used in civil actions between private individuals. However, such a limitation period must apply to both domestic and Community actions, and not render the exercise of Community rights either virtually impossible or excessively difficult, *Haahr Petroleum Ltd v. Abenra Havn* (C90/94) [1998] 1 C.M.L.R. 771, [1998] C.L.Y. 4634, and (2) in the present circumstances, Community law did not prohibit the Member State from taking as the start date of a limitation period the date of payment of the said charges. This was so even if the Directive concerned had not been properly transposed into domestic law.

MINISTERO DELLE FINANZE v. SPAC SpA (C260/96) [1999] C.E.C. 490, GC Rodriguez Iglesias (President), ECJ.

2406. Limitations – taxation – recovery provisions under national law – compatibility

[EC Treaty Art.95 (now, after amendment, Art.90 EC).]

Under Italian law a consumption tax imposed on banana products deriving from other Member States was subsequently declared contrary to of the EC Treaty Art.95 (now, after amendment, Art.90 EC) by the European Court of Justice (*Commission of the European Communities v. Italy (184/85)* [1987] E.C.R. 2013). D, an Italian company, applied unsuccessfully for reimbursement, falling foul of the three year time limit for recovery of taxes stipulated by the domestic law provisions. D subsequently sought an order stipulating that repayment be made, but the national court, considering that the provisions of the domestic law might violate Community principles, stayed the proceedings and referred a number of questions to the ECJ for a preliminary ruling, specifically whether (1) the time limits imposed for recovery and conditions of proof, being more restrictive than those applicable to general rules of civil law, offended the principles of equivalence and effectiveness; (2) the retroactive application of the domestic provision, and (3) the national court's acceptance of the presumption that taxes had been passed onto the consumer thus precluding recovery, were contrary to Community law.

Held, giving a preliminary ruling that (1) in the interests of legal certainty a Member State was entitled to impose limitation periods and procedural requirements in the field of taxation notwithstanding that those provisions were less favourable than those applicable in similar actions between private individuals, *Rewe-Zentralfinanz eG v. Landwirtschaftskammer fur das Saarland (C33/76)* [1976] E.C.R. 1989, [1977] C.L.Y. 1247 applied. Furthermore, the time limit applied without distinction to all actions for repayment whatever their basis and a limit of three years was not unreasonable. Given the absence of specific Community rules on the reimbursement of payments not due, it was a matter for the legal system of each Member State to define which courts would have jurisdiction and what procedural requirements were necessary in accordance with the principle of equivalence; (2) it was not incompatible with Community law to implement legislative changes relating to the recovery of taxes subsequently judged to have been imposed unlawfully, providing that the changes ensured the availability of proceedings to secure repayment, *Aprile Srl v. Amministrazione delle Finanze dello Stato (C228/96)* [2000] 1 W.L.R. 126, [2000] C.L.Y. 2345 applied, and (3) to accept a presumption that taxes had been passed on to consumers was contrary to Community principles and it was for the national court in each case to consider the issue as a matter of fact having regard to all the evidence, *Amministrazione delle Finanze dello Stato v. San Giorgio SpA (C199/82)* [1983] E.C.R. 3595, [1985] C.L.Y. 1433 applied.

DILEXPORT SRL v. AMMINISTRAZIONE DELLE FINANZE DELLO STATO (C343/96) [2000] All E.R. (EC) 600, J-P Puissochet (President), ECJ.

2407. **Linguistics – Decisions – implementation of linguistic diversity programme – challenge to legal basis**

[EC Treaty Art.128 (now, after amendment, Article 151 EC), Art.130 (now Article 157 EC); Council Decision 96/664 on the adoption of a multiannual programme to promote the linguistic diversity of the Community in the information society.]

The European Parliament applied for the annulment of Council Decision 96/664 adopting the multi-annual MLIS programme to promote linguistic diversity of the Community in the information society. Parliament objected to the legal basis of the Decision, which was adopted under the EC Treaty Art.130 (now Article 157 EC), whereas Parliament contended that the Decision should also have been based on Art.128 (now, after amendment, Article 151 EC), concerning Community action in the cultural field.

Held, dismissing the action, that the choice of legal basis for a measure had to be based on objective factors susceptible to judicial review, including the measure's aim and content. In determining whether the dual legal basis contended for by Parliament was necessary, it was appropriate to consider whether the contested Decision was indissociably concerned both with industry and culture, *European Parliament v. Council of the European Union (C271/94)* [1996] E.C.R. I-1689 and *European Parliament v. Council of the European Union (C22/96)* [1998] E.C.R. I-3231, [1999] C.L.Y. 2228 applied. The contested decision was directly intended to benefit small and medium sized enterprises, although some recitals referred to citizens they were not identifiable as directly targeted beneficiaries. In any event, citizens benefited from linguistic diversity in general in the information society. In contrast, small and medium sized enterprises were seen as beneficiaries of concrete actions undertaken in accordance with the MLIS programme. Although some of the Directive's provisions referred to cultural aspects of the information society these were general aspirations in line with Art.128(4) of the Treaty and did not amount to objectives. Article 2 of the Decision related to the development of infrastructures, the use of technologies and resources and the reduction of costs through the use of centralised language tools and by promoting technical standards in linguistic fields. Such actions did not have the direct effect of improving the dissemination of culture under Art 128(2). The main aim of the Directive was to ensure that competitiveness was not undermined by the costs of linguistic diversity. The object of programme therefore was essentially economic.

EUROPEAN PARLIAMENT v. COUNCIL OF THE EUROPEAN UNION (C42/97) [2000] 2 C.M.L.R. 73, PJG Kapteyn (President), ECJ.

2408. Locus standi – local authorities – application for partial annulment of Council Regulation 1013/97

[Council Regulation 1013/97 on aid to certain shipyards under restructuring; EC Treaty Art.173 (now, after amendment, Art.230 EC).]

Council Regulation 1013/97 made provision for aid to publicly owned shipyards in Spain up to a predetermined aggregate amount. In accordance with the Regulation, the Spanish government agreed to reduce capacity in its publicly owned yards by, inter alia, discontinuing ship conversions in Astander shipyard for as long as that facility remained in public ownership. CAC brought an action under the EC Treaty Art.173(2) (now, after amendment, Art.230(2) EC, and Art.173(4) (now, after amendment, Art.230(4) EC) seeking partial annulment of the Regulation, Astander shipyard being located within CAC's region. The Council of the European Union, argued that CAC, as a regional authority within a Member State, had no legal standing to bring proceedings under Art.173(2), and that it was not able to bring itself within Art.173(4) as CAC was neither directly nor individually concerned by the provisions of the Regulation, as required by Art.173(4).

Held, finding the application inadmissible, that (1) for the purposes of Art.173(2), the term "Member State" applied only to government authorities and did not extend to regional governments or autonomous communities, whatever the extent of their powers. CAC did not, therefore, have legal standing under Art.173(2), *Regione Toscana v. Commission of the European Communities (C180/97)* [1997] E.C.R. I-5245 and *Vlaams Gewest (Flemish Region) v. Commission of the European Communities (T214/95)* [1998] E.C.R. II-717 followed, and (2) the CAC had only a general interest in the effect of the Regulation, in so far as it affected the level of employment within its area. Thus, despite being a legal person under Spanish law, and thereby having legal capacity to proceed under Art.173(4), it did not have sufficient direct and individual interest in the operation of the Regulation to bring itself within the category of persons entitled to invoke Art.173(4), *Federazione Nazionale del Commercio Oleano (FEDEROLIO) v. Commission of the European Communities (T122/96)* [1997] All E.R. (EC) 929, [1998] C.L.Y. 2334 followed.

COMUNIDAD AUTONOMA DE CANTABRIA v. COUNCIL OF THE EUROPEAN UNION (T238/97) [1999] 3 C.M.L.R. 656, B Vesterdorf (President), CFI.

2409. Ministers – designated powers

EUROPEAN COMMUNITIES (DESIGNATION) ORDER 2000, SI 2000 738; made under the European Communities Act 1972 s.2. In force: April 6, 2000; £1.50.

This Order designates ministers who, and departments which, may exercise the power to make regulations conferred by the European Communities Act 1972 s.2 and specifies the matters in relation to which that power may be exercised.

2410. Ministers – designated powers

EUROPEAN COMMUNITIES (DESIGNATION) (NO.4) ORDER 2000, SI 2000 3057; made under the European Communities Act 1972 s.2. In force: December 18, 2000; £1.50.

This Order designates certain authorities which may exercise the power to make regulations conferred by the European Communities Act 1972 s.2(2) and specifies the matters in relation to which that power may be exercised.

2411. Ministers – designated powers

EUROPEAN COMMUNITIES (DESIGNATION) (NO.5) ORDER 2000, SI 2000 3238; made under the European Communities Act 1972 s.2. In force: January 24, 2001; £1.75.

This is a further Order in the series designating authorities which may exercise the power to make regulations conferred by the European Communities Act 1972 s.2(2) and specifying the matters in relation to which that power may be exercised.

2412. Single currency – conversion rates – Council Regulation

Council Regulation 1478/2000 of June 19, 2000 amending Regulation 2866/98 on the conversion rates between the euro and the currencies of the Member States adopting the euro. [2000] OJ L167/1.

2413. Social security – E101 certificate – self employment

See SOCIAL SECURITY: Banks v. Theatre Royal de la Monnaie (C178/97). §4817

2414. Social security – equal treatment – different pensionable age – breach of EC law

See SOCIAL SECURITY: R. v. Department of Social Security, *ex p.* Scullion. §4819

2415. State aids – debt rescheduling – payments of lower than market rate of interest – validity of Commission Decision 97/21

[EC Treaty Art.92(1) (now, after amendment, Art.87(1) EC), Art.118 (Arts.117 to 120 of the EC Treaty have been replaced by Arts.136 to 143 EC); Commission Decision 97/21.]

In June 1992 a Spanish private company became insolvent and suspended debt repayments. In October 1993 that suspension was lifted as a result of an agreement with creditors. Pursuant to their legal obligation to do so, F, an agency in the Ministry of Employment and Social Security, and SS, the Social Security Fund, paid the wages of the company's workers during its insolvency. F and SS thereby gained the subrogated rights of the workers to recoup those payments of wages from the company. F and SS, as two of the company's creditors, agreed to reschedule repayments of those sums by the company to F and SS. As part of that debt rescheduling F and SS applied to the repayments a rate of interest which was below the market rate for loans. In Commission Decision 97/21 the EC Commission ruled that the measures adopted by F and SS, including the application to the repayments of a lower than market rate of interest, contained illegal aids. The Spanish government, G, applied to the European Court of Justice to annul the decision, arguing that the Commission's decision infringed EC Treaty Art.92(1) (now, after amendment, Art.87(1) EC) and EC Treaty Art.118 (Arts.117 to 120 of the EC Treaty have been replaced by Arts.136 to 143 EC).

Held, annulling in part the Commission decision, that (1) the measures taken by F and SS were not in the nature of a loan. The interest applied was default interest, intended to make good the loss suffered by F and SS because of the company's delay in paying its existing debts to F and SS. Such default interest imposed by a creditor of an existing debt fulfilled a different purpose to commercial interest on lending, *Spain v. Commission of the European Communities (C42/93)* [1994] E.C.R. I-4175, [1995] C.L.Y. 655 followed. Therefore (a) whether a State measure including reduced rate loans constituted aid for the purposes of Art.92 depended on whether the recipient undertaking received an economic advantage which it would not have received under normal market conditions. F did not make loans to undertakings but merely settled all valid claims put forward by employees and then recovered that money from the undertakings concerned. The rescheduling of those repayments did not amount to aid for these purposes. A similar view would be taken of the rescheduling of debt payments to SSF, and (b) accordingly G did not act as a public investor whose conduct was to be compared to the conduct of a private investor investing with a view to a profit. G was a public creditor which, like private creditors, could conclude repayment agreements with debtors. It was significant that the agreements did not create any new debts to the public authorities but drew solely on existing obligations.

Observed, that it would have been an infringement of Art.92 if the rate of default interest applied by F and SS had been different from the rate of default interest which would have been charged by a private creditor, and (2) Art.118 which recognised the importance of the social dimension of the EU was without prejudice to the other provisions of the Treaty. Although the role of F and SS related to employment law and social security rules, the social character of State aid was not sufficient in itself to exclude it from being categorised as aid for the purposes of Art.92, *Germany v. Commission of the European Communities (European Parliament Intervening) (281/85)* [1987] E.C.R. 3203, [1988] C.L.Y. 1498 and *France v. Commission of the European Communities (C241/94)* [1996] E.C.R. I-4551, [1997] C.L.Y. 2399 followed.

SPAIN v. COMMISSION OF THE EUROPEAN COMMUNITIES (C342/96) [2000] 2 C.M.L.R. 415, G Hirsch (President), ECJ.

2416. Tenders – public sector contracts – tenderor not required to award contract to sole tenderee

[Council Directive 93/37 concerning the coordination of procedures for the award of public works contracts Art.18(1), Art.30(1).]

M was amongst a number of companies that tendered for work on an Austrian motorway scheme organised by A. The list of tenderees was narrowed down to M, but A then decided to cancel the contract. M applied to the national court for an order annulling the decision, and the court referred the matter to the ECJ for a preliminary ruling on the application of Council Directive 93/37 to the awarding of public works contracts.

Held, giving a preliminary ruling, that Art.18(1) of the Directive did not require a tenderor to award a contract having gone through the tender procedure, and there was nothing to suggest that a contract could only be cancelled in extreme circumstances. The purpose of the Directive was to ensure fair competition, and to allow a tenderor to make an objective decision based on established criteria, such as those under Art.30(1).

METALMECCANICA FRACASSO SpA v. AMT DER SALZBURGER LANDESREGIERUNG FUR DEN BUNDENMINISTER FUR WIRTSCHAFTLICHE ANGELEGENHEITEN (C27/98) [1999] E.C.R. I-5697, PJG Kapteyn (President), ECJ.

2417. Tobacco products – advertising ban – legal basis for Directive 98/43 – challenge to validity

[EC Treaty Art.57(2) (now, after amendment, Art.47(2) EC), Art.66 (now Art.55 EC), Art.100a (now, after amendment, Art.95 EC), Art.129(4) (now, after amendment, Art.152(4) EC); Council Directive 98/43 relating to the advertising and sponsorship of tobacco products.]

Germany applied for the annulment of Council Directive 98/43 which banned any advertising or sponsorship of tobacco products in the Community on the ground that it could not legally be founded on any of the Articles stated in the preamble, namely EC Treaty Art.57(2) (now, after amendment, Art.47(2) EC), EC Treaty Art.66 (now Art.55 EC) or EC Treaty Art.100a (now, after amendment, Art.95 EC). In a joined case, an English court referred the question of the validity of the Directive.

Held, annulling Council Directive 98/43, that none of the Articles referred to in the preamble provided a legal basis for the prohibitions. EC Treaty Art.129(4) (now, after amendment, Art.152 EC) prevented EU institutions from legislating to harmonise national laws on human health. Nevertheless, such a concern formed part of all EU policies, and it was possible for Community legislation in other areas to have an impact on human health, provided that such legislation was not adopted with a view to circumventing the provisions of Art.129(4). Measures adopted on the basis of Art.100a had to be genuinely intended to improve the functioning of the internal market and measures adopted on the basis of Art.57(2) and Art.66 had to be intended to make it easier for persons to take up and pursue activities by way of services. Differences in national laws on tobacco advertising within the community could affect the free movement of media and press products containing tobacco advertising which could in turn impede the functioning of the market by restricting the freedom to provide services in that area. As regards advertising services it was true that some Member States imposed fewer restrictions than others, leading to possible distortions of competition. A limited ban on advertising within the press sector could therefore have been based on Art.100a, however, it was not possible for the court to partially annul the Directive as that was a matter for the legislature alone. There was no need to rule on the joined case as the Directive had been entirely annulled.

GERMANY v. EUROPEAN PARLIAMENT (C376/98); R. v. SECRETARY OF STATE FOR HEALTH, *ex p.* IMPERIAL TOBACCO LTD (C74/99) [2000] All E.R. (EC) 769, GC Rodriguez Iglesias (President), ECJ.

2418. Treaties – agreements – Switzerland

EUROPEAN COMMUNITIES (DEFINITION OF TREATIES) (AGREEMENT BETWEEN THE EUROPEAN COMMUNITY AND ITS MEMBER STATES AND THE SWISS CONFEDERATION ON THE FREE MOVEMENT OF PERSONS) ORDER 2000, SI 2000 3269; made under the European Communities Act 1972 s.1. In force: in accordance with Art.1 (2); £1.50.

This Order declares the Agreement between the European Community and its Member States and the Swiss Confederation on the Free Movement of Persons, signed on June 21, 1999, to be a Community Treaty as defined in the European Communities Act 1972 s.1. The object of the Agreement is to accord rights of entry, residence and rights of access to work, to facilitate the provision of services in the territory of the Contracting Parties and to accord equal treatment as regards living, employment and working conditions.

2419. Publications

Armstrong, Kenneth A. – Regulation, Deregulation, Reregulation. European Dossier. Paperback: £9.99. ISBN 0-7494-2995-X. Kogan Page.

Arnull, Anthony; Dashwood, Alan; Ross, Malcolm – Wyatt and Dashwood's European Union Law. 4th Ed. Paperback: £28.95. ISBN 0-421-68040-7. Sweet & Maxwell.

Bankowski, Zenon; Scott, Andrew – European Union and Its Order: the Legal Theory of European Integration. Paperback: £14.99. ISBN 0-631-21504-2. Blackwell Publishers.

Brown, L. Neville; Kennedy,T. – Court of Justice of the European Communities. 5th Ed. Paperback: £24.95. ISBN 0-421-68120-9. Sweet & Maxwell.

Cuthbert, Mike – Nutshells: European Union Law. 3rd Ed. Nutshells. Paperback: £5.50. ISBN 0-421-68300-7. Sweet & Maxwell.

Hanlon, James – European Community Law. 2nd Ed. Paperback: £14.95. ISBN 0-421-71020-9. Sweet & Maxwell.

Horspool, Margot – European Union Law. 2nd Ed. Butterworths Core Texts. Paperback: £12.95. ISBN 0-406-91601-2. Butterworths Law.

Joyce, Eva – European Union Law. 2nd Ed. Principles of Law. Paperback: £15.95. ISBN 1-85941-464-8. Cavendish Publishing Ltd.

Kaczorowska, Alina – EU Law for Today's Lawyers. 1st Ed. Paperback: £16.95. ISBN 1-85836-356-X. Old Bailey Press.

Kenner, Jeff – Law of the European Union Social Chapter. Hardback: £22.50. ISBN 1-901362-69-8. Hart Publishing.

Mills, Shaun – Constitutional and Administrative Law of the EC. Paperback: £24.95. ISBN 1-85941-223-8. Cavendish Publishing Ltd.

Neunreither, Karlheinz; Wiener, Antje – European Integration After Amsterdam: Institutional Dynamics and Prospects for Democracy. Hardback: £50.00. ISBN 0-19-829641-X. Paperback: £18.99. ISBN 0-19-829640-1. Oxford University Press.

Robinson, O.F.; Fergus, David; Gordon, W.M – European Legal History. 3rd Ed. Paperback: £29.95. ISBN 0-406-91360-9. Butterworths Law.

Skiadas, Dimitros – European Court of Auditors: the Financial Conscience of the European Union. European Dossier Series. Paperback (C format): £12.99. ISBN 0-7494-3338-8. Kogan Page.

Stefanou, Constantin; Xanthaki, Helen – Legal and Political Interpretation of Article 215(2) [new Article 288(2)] of the Treaty of Rome. Hardback: £39.95. ISBN 1-84014-428-9. Ashgate Publishing Ltd.

Stone Sweet, Alec – Governing with Judges: Constitutional Politics in Europe. Paperback: £16.99. ISBN 0-19-829771-8. Oxford University Press.

Sweet, Alec Stone – Governing with Judges: Constitutional Politics in Europe. Hardback: £35.00. ISBN 0-19-829730-0. Oxford University Press.

Tillotson, John – European Union Law: Text, Cases and Materials. 3rd Ed. Paperback: £19.95. ISBN 1-85941-550-4. Cavendish Publishing Ltd.

Ward, Angela – Judicial Review and the Rights of Private Parties in EC Law. Hardback: £60.00. ISBN 0-19-826822-X. Oxford University Press.

EXTRADITION

2420. Appeals – stay of proceedings – right of appeal or judicial review in absence of statutory entitlement

[Supreme Court Act 1981 s.29(3); Human Rights Act 1998 Sch.1 Part I Art.6.]

B, the subject of extradition proceedings, sought permission to appeal to the Court of Appeal, or seek judicial review in the Queen's Bench Divisional Court, following the refusal of his application for a stay for abuse of process in criminal proceedings. B submitted that (1) he was entitled to challenge a refusal of a stay by virtue of the Human Rights Act 1998 Sch.1 Part I Art.6, since to delay seeking a remedy until the end of the trial would mean that there would be an unacceptable postponement of the question whether there should have been a trial in the first place, and also of any available remedy; (2) despite the provisions of the Supreme Court Act 1981 s.29(3) and the decision in *R. v. Manchester Crown Court, ex p. DPP* [1994] 1 A.C. 9, [1993] C.L.Y. 15, a Crown Court order was open to review by the Divisional Court since extradition abuse was a different category of abuse from those already established, and (3) the prosecution having failed to make full disclosure to the lower courts, there had been an abuse of process.

Held, refusing permission to appeal and to move for judicial review, that (1) there was no interlocutory right of appeal except where one was conferred by statute. There was no statute permitting a right of appeal against a refusal to stay proceedings for abuse of process, and Art.6 did not provide such a right where the domestic legislation failed to do so; (2) there was no justification for placing extradition cases in a category of their own so as to enable the Divisional Court to circumvent s.29(3) of the 1981 Act, *ex p. DPP* applied, and (3) the duty upon the prosecution was to effect full disclosure, not prior to committal, but by the time of the trial.

R. v. B (EXTRADITION: ABUSE OF PROCESS) *The Times*, October 18, 2000, Rose, L.J., CA (Crim Div).

2421. Convictions – conviction in absence – retrial guarantee acceptable

P entered Switzerland from Kosovo and, having been refused asylum there, was granted asylum in England. P was convicted of the supply of drugs in his absence in Switzerland and sentenced there. Switzerland sought P's extradition, giving assurances that he would be given a retrial on his return if he applied within 20 days of formal notification of sentence. At committal, P's contention that he had received no guarantee of a retrial was rejected and he applied for habeas corpus, arguing that the decision of the judge on retrial would be a formality.

Held, dismissing the application, that, without evidence of bad faith, the court was entitled to take the assurances of the Swiss government at face value. It was in the interest of comity that the unconditional guarantees of signatories to the relevant extradition treaties should be accepted.

PECI v. GOVERNOR OF BRIXTON PRISON *The Times*, January 12, 2000, Moses, J., QBD.

2422. **Fugitive offenders – forms – renaming of stipendiary bench**

FUGITIVE OFFENDERS (FORMS) (AMENDMENT) REGULATIONS 2000, SI 2000 2210; made under the Extradition Act 1989 s.28. In force: In accordance with Reg.1; £1.00.

These Regulations amend the Fugitive Offenders (Forms) Regulations 1967 (SI 1967 1257) to take account of the coming into force of the Access to Justice Act 1999 s.78 and Sch.11 which unify and rename the stipendiary bench.

2423. **Habeas corpus – committals procedure – particulars of offences to be laid at committal – Bahamas**

C appealed against a decision of the Court of Appeal of the Bahamas upholding a refusal of his application for a writ of habeas corpus to prevent his extradition to the United States on charges of drug trafficking. C contended that his committal into custody to await extradition was procedurally unfair and that the accusations made against him were not made in good faith in the interest of justice.

Held, dismissing the appeal, that C had suffered no procedural injustice concluding that despite the lack of proper particulars before the magistrates at committal, the offences of which C had been accused had been plain from the documentation. Further the respondent clearly had jurisdiction and a prima facie case.

CHARRON (ALAIN) v. UNITED STATES [2000] 1 W.L.R. 1793, Lord Hutton, PC.

2424. **Habeas corpus – non custodial sentences – supervisory release period – extradition to US**

[Extradition Act 1989 s.7 (2); United States of America (Extradition) Order 1976 (SI 1976 2144) Sch.1 Art.III (4), Art.VII (4).]

B pleaded guilty to bank theft and was sentenced in the US to five years' imprisonment followed by five years' supervised release. B completed the custodial sentence, but during the supervisory period he left the US without authorisation and failed to report to his probation officer. B was arrested and detained awaiting extradition under the Extradition Act 1989 s.7 (2). B appealed against the refusal (*The Times*, April 15, 1999, [1999] C.L.Y. 2287) of his application for a writ of habeas corpus. B contended that he was not subject to extradition as it was valid only during the term of custodial imprisonment which he had completed.

Held, dismissing the appeal (Lord Hutton and Lord Hobhouse dissenting), that "sentence" for the purpose of the United States of America (Extradition) Order 1976 Sch.1 Art.VII (4) was not expressly limited to the sentence of imprisonment referred to in Art.III (4) of the 1976 Order, but could include other penalties. B, had received the requisite custodial sentence under Art III (4) and the failure to carry out the supervisory period, which formed part of the total sentence under Art.VII (4), rendered B liable to extradition.

BURKE, *Re*; *sub nom*. R. v. GOVERNOR OF BRIXTON PRISON, *ex p.* BURKE [2001] 1 A.C. 422, Lord Hope of Craighead, HL.

2425. Habeas corpus – suspended sentences – meaning of "punishment awarded"

[European Convention on Extradition 1957 Art.2.1.]

L applied for a writ of habeas corpus having been convicted by a Norwegian court of assault and sentenced to 120 days' imprisonment with a further 60 days' suspended. Under the European Convention on Extradition 1957 Art.2.1, extradition would only be granted where "the punishment awarded" exceeded four months. L contended that the suspended term of his sentence did not form part of the "punishment awarded".

Held, refusing the application, that the term "punishment awarded" within Art.2.1 encompassed the suspended part of a prison sentence. The Convention should be interpreted with a common sense approach. Article 2.1 was intended to provide general principles to highlight the seriousness of the offence committed.

LEES v. NORWAY *The Times*, November 1, 2000, Buxton, L.J., QBD.

2426. Publications

Woodhouse, Diana – Pinochet Case: a Legal and Constitutional Analysis. Hardback: £30.00. ISBN 1-84113-102-4. Hart Publishing.

FAMILY LAW

2427. Adoption – child protection – disclosure of information

PROTECTION OF CHILDREN (ACCESS TO LISTS) (PRESCRIBED INDIVIDUALS) REGULATIONS 2000, SI 2000 2537; made under the Care Standards Act 2000 s.103. In force: October 9, 2000; £1.00.

These Regulations provide that, before the commencement of the Protection of Children Act 1999 s.8 and the Care Standards Act 2000 s.102, a prospective adopter whose suitability to adopt a child is being considered under the Adoption Agencies Regulations 1983 (SI 1983 1964), is an individual of a prescribed description for the purposes of s.103(2)(b) of the 2000 Act. A person is therefore entitled, upon making an application to the Secretary of State, to information as to whether the prospective adopter is included either in the list kept under the Protection of Children Act 1999 s.1, the list kept for the purposes of regulations made under the Education Reform Act 1988 s.218(6), or any list kept of persons disqualified under the Education Act 1996 s.470 or s.471 for the purpose of considering his suitability to adopt.

2428. Adoption – consent – change of mind by birth mother – baby living with prospective adopters for eight months – mother unreasonably withholding consent

P, who had a history of eating disorders and of threatening self harm, became pregnant with L when she was aged 18. P sought advice from a voluntary adoption agency as to the possibility of adoption and was informed, incorrectly, that she could change her mind and take the baby back at any time prior to giving formal consent to the reporting officer. In reality, however, return was only permitted by court order after the adoption application was made. L was placed with prospective adopters, A, who applied for adoption in the county court five weeks later. P then sought to recover L, contending that she had changed her mind about the adoption. It was five months before the contested matter came to court and eight months before the full hearing. L had become settled with the adopters in the meantime and P had no bond with the child. The contested application was transferred to the High Court, with A seeking an adoption order and P applying for the return of L.

Held, making the adoption order and refusing P's application, that the lack of a bond between P and L, along with considerations of L's welfare, meant that L should remain with A. P's application was motivated by her emotional response to the situation. Her circumstances and her previous responses to stressful situations were a cause for concern as to the consistency of care that L would receive. Viewed objectively, therefore, P had unreasonably withheld her consent to L's adoption.

A (ADOPTION: MOTHER'S OBJECTIONS), Re [2000] 1 F.L.R. 665, Sumner, J., Fam Div.

2429. **Adoption – freeing orders – parental consent not witnessed by reporting officer – consent valid where unconditional and with knowledge of implications**

[Adoption Act 1976 s16(1).]

In an application for an adoption order in respect of two children, the issue was whether the mother had given free and unconditional consent to the order being made. Under the Adoption Act 1976 s16(1), an adoption order could only be made if the court was satisfied that any parental consent was freely given. In the instant case, the mother had given written consent, but the reporting officer had not witnessed it.

Held, granting the application, that it was clear from the written statement and from conversations that the mother had freely and unconditionally agreed to the adoption. The fact that the reporting officer had not witnessed the consent did not make it invalid. The mother was fully aware of the implications of what she was consenting to.

D (CHILDREN) (ADOPTION: FREEING ORDER), Re [2001] 1 F.L.R. 403, Connell, J., Fam Div.

2430. **Adoption – freeing orders – parental consent withheld – contact with siblings**

A freeing order in respect of an adoption application concerning A, a two year old child, was refused by a county court judge on the basis that consent had been withheld by the child's natural father. When considering the reasonableness of the withholding of consent, the judge directed himself primarily to the issue of A's contact with her three older siblings who were to remain in care, since the basis of the father's objections was that isolation from her natural family would be disadvantageous to A. The guardian ad litem appealed against the refusal, contending that the judge had erred in his approach to what the reasonable parent would do, and had failed to consider the wider issues of current social values and the advantages of adoption to A.

Held, allowing the appeal, that the judge had wrongly restricted his considerations of reasonableness to the sibling contact issue. It was clearly advantageous to A to be placed in a permanent home where she could form family attachments. Looking at the circumstances of the instant case, there was no possibility of any of the children being returned to the natural parents, due to the deficiencies in the mother's ability to care for them and the allegations of sexual abuse that had been directed at the father. The judge should have adopted a less legalistic approach when addressing the issue of reasonableness, and assessed whether the advantages of adoption to the welfare of the child outweighed the disadvantages of the loss of sibling contact, C (A Minor) (Adoption: Parental Agreement: Contact), Re [1993] 2 F.L.R. 260, [1994] C.L.Y. 3087 and W (An Infant), Re [1971] A.C. 682, [1971] C.L.Y. 5831 considered.

F (CHILDREN) (ADOPTION: FREEING ORDER), Re [2000] 2 F.L.R. 505, Thorpe, L.J., CA.

2431. **Adoption – freeing orders – replacement with care order – placement with natural father**

[Children Act 1989 s.34(4).]

A child, D, born in February 1999, was made the subject of care and freeing orders in September 1999. Shortly after the hearing D's mother, M, abducted him during a contact visit, and the police had to secure his return. M had no further contact with

D, and D's father, F, came forward as a possible carer. He was assessed as suitable by OMBC, which applied to substitute a care order for the freeing order under the inherent jurisdiction of the court so that D could be placed with F immediately. M consented to this course of action but resisted the termination of contact with D.

Held, granting the application, that the threshold criteria had clearly been met and OMBC's proposed course of action was in the best interests of D in the circumstances. Contact to M would be suspended until OMBC's pending application under the Children Act 1989 s.34(4) was determined. M would have the opportunity to file a statement and be heard on that application, which would be heard as soon as possible by the county court judge who had initially heard the matter.

OLDHAM MBC v. D [2000] 2 F.L.R. 382, Bracewell, J., Fam Div.

2432. Adoption – freeing orders – revocation under court's inherent jurisdiction

[Adoption Act 1976 s.20.]

A local authority applied to have a freeing order, which had been made in respect of J, revoked on the ground that it was no longer relevant as circumstances had changed. The original plan had been to place J for adoption, but as J had become settled in a foster placement, the local authority intended to allow the placement to continue on a long term basis without the need to resort to adoption. Under the Adoption Act 1976 s.20, only J's mother, M, could apply to have the order revoked once the twelve month period following the making of the order had passed. As M was unlikely to apply for the revocation of the order, the local authority argued that the court should exercise its inherent jurisdiction to revoke the order as it was in J's best interests to do so.

Held, granting the application, that there was nothing in the 1976 Act to prevent a court from exercising its inherent jurisdiction to revoke a freeing order where the best interests of the child so dictated. It was clearly in J's interests that the local authority should be able to make plans for him, particularly as adoption was no longer appropriate.

J (A CHILD) (FREEING FOR ADOPTION), *Re*; *sub nom.* JS, RE; J (A CHILD) (ADOPTION: REVOCATION OF FREEING ORDER), *Re* [2000] 2 F.L.R. 58, Black J., Fam Div.

2433. Adoption – intercountry adoption – adoption order made by Russian court – dispensing with mother's consent

[Adoption Act 1976 s.16(4).]

A was born in Russia and placed in a children's home when she was two days old following the decision of her mother, M, to put her up for adoption. B, an English couple with business and social connections in Russia, adopted A a year later and were granted an adoption order by the Russian court. M did not attend the hearing although she had been informed of it, and she did not appeal against the order. B were required to obtain an adoption order in the English court as the Russian court's order was not recognised in English law. The appointed guardian ad litem was concerned that M had given her consent to the adoption less than six weeks after the birth, contrary to the Adoption Act 1976 s.16(4), but when inquiries were made the Russian court stated that any attempt to contact M could lead to civil proceedings being brought against B for violating M's right to confidentiality concerning the adoption. B made an application for M's consent to be dispensed with in accordance with s.16.

Held, granting the application and the adoption order, that the court had to look at whether any reasonable steps could be taken to obtain M's consent, practicality being an important factor in assessing reasonableness. The likelihood that attempts to contact M could lead to disruptive and inconvenient proceedings being brought against B and the fact that M had been informed of the Russian court hearing and had chosen to have no involvement with it meant that it would not be reasonable for her consent to be sought. A had developed a good bond with B and they were providing her with a caring home and a knowledge of her country of birth. An adoption order was therefore appropriate.

A (A CHILD) (ADOPTION OF A RUSSIAN CHILD), *Re* [2000] 1 F.L.R. 539, Charles, J., Fam Div.

2434. Adoption – intercountry adoption – consent – foreign guardianship

[Adoption Act 1976 s.16(1)(b).]

A, an unmarried Englishwoman, sought to adopt N, a 12 year old Romanian orphan, who had been abandoned at birth by his natural mother and taken immediately to an orphanage where A had been a volunteer. Before returning to England, A obtained a Romanian adoption order for N with the full consent of both his natural mother and the orphanage. Given that under the Adoption Act 1976 s.16 the consent of a parent or guardian was required prior to the granting of an adoption order, the issue arose as to whether, and under what context, a foreign person or institution could form a guardian within the meaning of s.16(1)(b).

Held, granting the application, that a foreign guardian with rights of guardianship provided under a foreign order that was recognised by English law was capable of giving consent to an adoption under s.16 and accordingly this consent could be obtained or dispensed with prior to the granting of an adoption order, *Adoption Application 96 AO 147, Re* (Unreported, January 31, 1997) and *AMR (Adoption: Procedure), Re,* [1999] 2 F.L.R. 807, [2000] C.L.Y. 2436 considered. In the instant case the declarations of abandonment and consensual adoption by N's natural mother satisfactorily demonstrated that the consent given by the orphanage to A to proceed with the adoption fulfilled the criteria of s.16(1)(b).

N (A CHILD) (ADOPTION: FOREIGN GUARDIANSHIP), *Re; sub nom.* AGN (ADOPTION: FOREIGN ADOPTION), *Re* [2000] 2 F.L.R. 431, Cazalet, J., Fam Div.

2435. Adoption – intercountry adoption – consent – Romanian hospital as guardian

[Adoption Act 1976 s.16; Children Act 1989 s.5.]

J, a Romanian girl, was given up by her mother at birth and raised in a number of institutions. When she was 13 the hospital in which she was living was given parental rights over her, and formally approved of her removal to England by a British couple, A, who had developed a bond with her whilst they were working in Romania. When J was 17 A applied to adopt her. The adoption was supported by the local authority, despite their initial reservations, by the Official Solicitor and by J's mother. The issue arose as to whether the hospital's consent was required since the consent of the guardian was a requirement under the Adoption Act 1976 for the granting of an adoption order.

Held, granting the application and making the adoption order, that under the Adoption Act 1976 a "guardian" under s.16 could only mean a guardian appointed under the Children Act 1989 s.5 "unless the context otherwise requires". The word "requires" had to be given its due weight, and there was nothing in s.16 of the 1976 Act to suggest that a different definition was required. Therefore, the hospital's formal consent was not necessary as it was not a guardian appointed in accordance with the 1989 Act.

D (ADOPTION: FOREIGN GUARDIANSHIP), *Re* [1999] 2 F.L.R. 865, Holman, J., Fam Div.

2436. Adoption – intercountry adoption – consent of Polish guardian required – consent of natural parents not required

[Adoption Act 1976; Children Act 1989 s.5.]

A was raised in Poland by her great grandmother, GG, who was appointed her guardian by a court order which also removed parental authority from A's natural parents, NP. GG brought A to England and left her in the care of A's great aunt, GA. GA applied to adopt A and the issue for the court was whether consent was required from NP or GG. The questions which fell to be decided were whether the Polish orders granting guardianship to GG, and depriving the natural parents of parental authority, should be recognised under English law.

Held, that GG's but not NP's consent was required and that as Polish "parental authority" was broadly analogous to parental responsibility in English law, it was appropriate and in accordance with judicial comity for the Polish order to be recognised, *Valentine's Settlement, Re* [1965] Ch. 831, [1965] C.L.Y. 3556 applied. The removal of parental authority from NP had the effect of leaving them only with rights accorded to natural parents, such as the right to apply for contact. Therefore, they were no longer "parents" for the purposes of the Adoption Act 1976 and their consent was not required. In relation to GG, the Act defined a "guardian" as one appointed under the Children Act 1989 s.5 "unless the context otherwise requires". That phrase had to be given a wide meaning, with "context" referring to all the circumstances of the case, which here required a different definition, making GG a guardian within the 1976 Act, *D (Adoption: Foreign Guardianship), Re* [1999] 2 F.L.R. 865, [2000] C.L.Y. 2435 not followed.

AMR (ADOPTION: PROCEDURE), *Re* [1999] 2 F.L.R. 807, Judge David Gee, Fam Div.

2437. **Adoption – jurisdiction – Isle of Man adopters – court empowered to transfer adoption application to county court**

[Adoption Act 1976 s.62(3); Adoption Rules 1984 (SI 1984 265) r.3(4); Children (Allocation of Proceedings) Order 1991 (SI 1991 1677) Art.13(1).]

J, a minor, was placed with a married couple in the Isle of Man after a care order and freeing order had been made in England. However, as freeing orders made in England were no longer recognised in the Isle of Man, the prospective adopters applied for an adoption order in the English courts. As the child was not in Great Britain at the time of the application, the Adoption Act 1976 s.62(3) required that any application be made to the High Court. Nevertheless, where appropriate, the court was empowered to transfer the proceedings to a county court under the Children (Allocation of Proceedings) Order 1991 Art.13(1).

Held, exercising the power of transfer under Art.13(1), that the court was empowered to order a transfer where it had sufficient information to reach a decision and it was appropriate to do so. Moreover, the power of transfer was not restricted to the High Court, but could also be exercised by the proper officer under the Adoption Rules 1984 r.3(4).

J (A CHILD) (ADOPTION PROCEDURE: ISLE OF MAN), *Re; sub nom.* H (A CHILD) (ISLE OF MAN: ADOPTION), *Re* [2000] 2 F.L.R. 633, Sumner, J., Fam Div.

2438. **Adoption (Intercountry Aspects) Act 1999 (c.18) – Commencement No.1 Order**

ADOPTION (INTERCOUNTRY ASPECTS) ACT 1999 (COMMENCEMENT NO.1) ORDER 2000, SI 2000 52 (C.1); made under the Adoption (Intercountry Aspects) Act 1999 s.18. Commencement details: bringing into force various provisions of the Act on January 31, 2000; £1.00.

This Order brings the Adoption (Intercountry Aspects) Act 1999 s.13 into force on January 31, 2000, in so far as it inserts a new s.72(3A), which provides that making arrangements for adoption includes arrangements for an assessment to indicate whether a person is suitable to adopt a child, into the Adoption Act 1976.

2439. **Child abduction – acquiescence – burden of proof**

[Children Act 1989; Hague Convention on the Civil Aspects of International Child Abduction 1980 Art.13.]

M, who was Swedish, and F, who was British, the mother and father of H, met in Sweden in 1994. They separated there shortly after H's birth in 1996 but F continued living in Sweden and had frequent contact with H. In September 1998, M commenced a course which required her to spend nine months in Spain and three months in the UK, and M and F agreed that H should live with F during that time. In March 1999, F and H moved to Wales, and M had contact with H there and in the UK where she was studying. In July 1999, M did not return H to F after contact. F commenced proceedings under the Children Act 1989 and was granted an order prohibiting M from removing H from the jurisdiction. The case was listed for a full hearing on residence, but it was not until M consulted different solicitors in September that she was advised to make an application for H's return to Sweden under the Hague Convention on the Civil Aspects of International Child Abduction 1980. F contended that M had consented to or acquiesced in H living in the UK.

Held, granting the application for H's return to Sweden, that the facts showed that H had retained his habitual Swedish residence throughout so that his retention in the UK was unlawful. M was his main carer and it was never her intention not to return to Sweden on completing her course. Her conduct had not been such as to imply consent to, or acquiescence in, H living permanently in the UK. Under Art.13 of the Convention the burden was on F to prove consent and he had failed to do so, *C (Minors) (Abduction: Consent), Re* [1996] 1 F.L.R. 414, [1996] C.L.Y. 521 applied.

Observed, that it should have been noted much earlier by the parties' representatives or the court that this was a case to which the Convention applied.

H (A CHILD) (ABDUCTION: HABITUAL RESIDENCE: CONSENT), *Re*; *sub nom*. H (CHILD ABDUCTION: WRONGFUL RETENTION), *Re* [2000] 2 F.L.R. 294, Holman, J., Fam Div.

2440. Child abduction – acquiescence – court's discretion to order child's return to United States

[Hague Convention on the Civil Aspects of International Child Abduction 1980 Art.13.]

A five year old child, J, was removed from her home in the USA by M, her English mother. Her American father, F, took legal advice in the USA but was not told about the power of summary return under the Hague Convention on the Civil Aspects of International Child Abduction 1980. He wrote to M requesting a reconciliation and indicated that if it failed he would agree to M and J settling in the UK. He came to England in February 1998 and took further legal advice, but again was not informed about the Convention. He was granted a contact order on the basis that he was attempting to settle in the UK. Contact having broken down, he unsuccessfully applied for a penal order and then, following a visit to the US Embassy, applied for J's return to the USA under the Convention. M argued that returning J would put her at grave risk of harm under Art.13(b) and that F had acquiesced in her removal under Art.13(a).

Held, refusing the application, that there was insufficient evidence to support M's Art.13(b) defence. However, F had by his conduct acquiesced. He had not brought proceedings in the USA, and in the UK had applied only for contact. He had made no requests for J's return and had set out on a process towards living in England himself. Only when there were problems with contact did he bring proceedings under the Convention, which was clearly a change of mind. Since acquiescence had been established, the court was not bound to order J's return to her former home, but it did have a discretion. Although M's removal of J was wrongful in view of the fact that F had custody rights which he was exercising immediately prior to J's removal, the court had to balance all the factors affecting J's welfare. As J had been settled in the UK for 19 months, had successfully commenced her formal education and lived close to her maternal grandparents, it was not appropriate that the court should exercise its discretion to return her to the USA, *AZ (A Minor) (Abduction: Acquiescence), Re* [1993] 1 F.L.R. 682, [1994] C.L.Y. 3145 and *D (Abduction: Acquiescence: Mother's Removal from Australia to Wales), Re* [1998] 1 F.L.R. 686 considered.

B (A CHILD) (ABDUCTION: ACQUIESCENCE), *Re* [1999] 2 F.L.R. 818, Kirkwood, J., Fam Div.

2441. Child abduction – acquiescence – delay in applying for return – child attaining 16 in meantime

[Hague Convention on the Civil Aspects of International Child Abduction 1980 Art.4, Art.12.]

Two children, K and R, aged 14 and 11 respectively, were wrongfully removed from Australia by their mother, M. Their father, F, thought that the family had taken an extended holiday. He had no information as to their location for eight months and then M moved house without notifying him of the new address. F eventually applied for the return of K and R, but by the time of the hearing of the application K had reached 16, and an issue arose as to whether the Hague Convention on the Civil Aspects of International Child Abduction 1980 Art.4 precluded an order for K's return. Further, M submitted that R had settled in England and that F had acquiesced in their removal.

Held, ordering R's return and relisting K's case for a determination of her views under the inherent jurisdiction, that the Convention did not apply to K by virtue of Art.4. As regards R, Art.12 provided that he should be returned unless he had settled into the new environment, but the reasons for the delay in applying for return were relevant as an abducting parent should not to be able to benefit from his or her own deception. In the instant case, M had concealed her whereabouts and could not take advantage of the settlement argument, *N (Minors) (Abduction), Re* [1991] 1 F.L.R. 413, [1991] C.L.Y. 2530 applied. Acquiescence could be determined by reference to the wronged parent's state of mind and was a question of fact with two distinct elements: a subjective determination and actual behaviour, *H v. H (Child Abduction: Acquiescence)* [1998] A.C. 72, [1997] C.L.Y. 387 and *P v. P (Abduction: Acquiescence)* [1998] 2 F.L.R. 835, [1999] C.L.Y. 2317 considered. On the facts, F had been deceived as to the initial reason for the children's absence and had then sought to find out where K and R were. M's attempts to hide from F were inconsistent with acquiescence on his part.

H (ABDUCTION: CHILD OF 16), *Re*; *sub nom.* H (CHILD ABDUCTION: CHILD OF SIXTEEN), *Re* [2000] 2 F.L.R. 51, Bracewell, J., Fam Div.

2442. Child abduction – consent – discretion to order children's return to France

[Child Abduction and Custody Act 1985 s.9(b); European Convention on Recognition and Enforcement of Decisions Concerning Custody of Children 1980.]

M, the mother of two children, applied for their summary return to France, where the children had been born and brought up. After the parents' separation, a French court made a residence order in favour of M, with F, the father, to have the children for holidays. The father, F, kept the children in England at the end of a holiday, arguing that M had consented to the children living with him in England.

Held, granting the application, that M had consented to the children living with F, but the court had a discretion in deciding whether or not to order their return to France. There were some concerns about the children's life with M, her new partner and his children. More importantly, however, if the court refused to order the children's return to France, it would conflict with the French court's residence order, thus making it difficult for the children to visit France in the future. Accordingly, notwithstanding M's consent to the children's removal from France, it was right that the court should exercise its discretion in favour of returning the children to France for the issues to be resolved there. The court also stated that the position whereby under the Child Abduction and Custody Act 1985 s.9(b) a decision on the merits of custody should include a decision whether to recognise and enforce a foreign decision under the European Convention on Recognition and Enforcement of Decisions Concerning Custody of Children 1980 was possibly inconvenient in practice, and that a judicial discretion would be more expedient.

D (ABDUCTION: DISCRETIONARY RETURN), *Re* [2000] 1 F.L.R. 24, Wilson, J., Fam Div.

2443. Child abduction – defences – age and maturity of child – child's views – return to country of habitual residence inappropriate

[Hague Convention on the Civil Aspects of International Child Abduction 1980 Art.13.]

The parents of G, aged 11, and T, aged six, were British nationals who had been resident in Spain since 1993. In 1997 the mother commenced divorce and custody proceedings and obtained an order from the Spanish court in her favour. The father then removed the children from their mother in breach of her custody rights and set up home with them in England. At first instance, a defence under the Hague Convention on the Civil Aspects of International Child Abduction 1980 Art.13(b) was rejected on the basis that G lacked sufficient age and maturity for her wishes to be taken into account. It was further held that even if the defence had been established, it would have been wrong for the court to exercise its discretion against the spirit of the Convention, which was for the children's future to be decided in their country of habitual residence. G subsequently wrote to her mother in terms which made it clear that she objected to being returned to Spain and alluding to her mother's alcohol abuse. The father appealed against the decision to return the children to Spain.

Held, allowing the appeal, that the relevant factors were (1) whether the child objected to being returned to the country of habitual residence and, if so, why; (2) the age and degree of maturity of the child, and (3) whether it was appropriate to take account of the child's views, *S (A Minor) (Abduction: Custody Rights), Re* [1993] Fam. 242, [1993] C.L.Y. 2796 and *S (Minors) (Abduction: Acquiescence), Re* [1994] 1 F.L.R. 819, [1995] C.L.Y. 3430 applied. The issue of objection was essentially a matter of fact, but the question of maturity was a matter on which the court was required to exercise its judgment. In the instant case, it was accepted that G objected to being returned to her mother's care, and this was supported by a medical report indicating that she had suffered emotional abuse in her earlier life. Her consistent approach and the letter to her mother indicated that G was of a maturity beyond her years and the Art.13 defence was therefore made out. With regard to T, the issue was whether there was a grave risk that to order his return without his sister would place him in an intolerable situation, notwithstanding that the Spanish authorities had established that he was not at risk of harm. Again, due to the exceptional circumstances of the case, an Art.13 defence was made out. It was noted that the general rule of the UK court was to uphold the Convention in order to avoid sanctioning the unlawful abduction of a child, but this rule was not to be followed at the expense of the welfare of the child involved in the particular case.

T (CHILDREN) (ABDUCTION: CHILD'S OBJECTIONS TO RETURN), *Re; sub nom.* T (CHILDREN) (ABDUCTION: CUSTODY RIGHTS), *Re* [2000] 2 F.L.R. 192, Ward, L.J., CA.

2444. Child abduction – defences – risk of harm – protection offered by Norwegian court

[Hague Convention on the Civil Aspects of International Child Abduction 1980 Art.13(b).]

A Somali born father, F, and mother, M, were divorced from each other and lived in Norway. F had been imprisoned there having been convicted of murder. M obtained passports for herself and the children by forging F's signature and removed the children to England. F, who was due for release in 2000 or 2001 applied to have the children returned to Norway. He gave a number of undertakings in identical terms to the Norwegian court and in this jurisdiction not to harass M or the children. M sought to adduce oral evidence as to her fear of returning and contended under the Hague Convention on the Civil Aspects of International Child Abduction 1980 Art.13(b) that she and the children would be at risk of harm.

Held, granting the application by F, that in abduction proceedings oral evidence would not assist the court in deciding factual disputes. The court proceeded on the basis that M's fears were genuine and then objectively considered the reasons for her fears. On the facts, however, the Norwegian court could offer M various forms of protection and therefore she had not established a defence to the abduction under Art.13(b).

M (A CHILD) (ABDUCTION: INTOLERABLE SITUATION), Re [2000] 1 F.L.R. 930, Charles, J., Fam Div.

2445. Child abduction – ex parte applications – whether ex parte order violated right to fair trial

F, the unmarried father of J, made ex parte applications for parental responsibility and prohibited steps orders. The following day J's mother, M, left with J for South Africa. F then renewed his applications and the judge made ex parte orders directing M's return with J to the jurisdiction on the basis that the court had rights of custody once it was seised of proceedings to determine rights of custody at either the first or second ex parte hearings. M argued that her human rights had been infringed in that she had not been given notice of the hearings and had been deprived of a fair trial.

Held, refusing M's application for permission to appeal, that M had not been deprived of a fair trial since she had always had the opportunity to apply to set aside the ex parte orders and had subsequently had a full trial. F had been entitled to make the ex parte applications in the circumstances of the case.

J (A CHILD) (ABDUCTION: DECLARATION OF WRONGFUL REMOVAL), Re; *sub nom.* J (A CHILD) (ABDUCTION: RIGHTS OF CUSTODY), Re [2000] 1 F.L.R. 78, Swinton Thomas, L.J., CA.

2446. Child abduction – foreign judgments – custody proceedings commenced in Spain after English consent order obtained – choice of forum

[Hague Convention on the Civil Aspects of International Child Abduction 1980.]

M's parents, both of whom were British, went to live in Spain soon after M's birth in 1993. They separated in 1998. M lived with his father, A, in England for a short period, but in January 1999 his mother, B, was granted temporary custody of him in Spain. A brought M to England with B's consent, but failed to return him to Spain whereupon B commenced proceedings under the Hague Convention on the Civil Aspects of International Child Abduction 1980. In March 1999 an order was made by agreement in the English court that M should live with A in England. In June 1999 B commenced custody proceedings in Spain. It was not clear whether the Spanish court was aware of the English consent order. Custody was awarded to B in October 1999. When A failed to return M to Spain after a Christmas holiday in England, B made a second application under the Hague Convention.

Held, granting the application, that M should be returned to Spain so that the Spanish court could deal with the substantive case. Despite the worrying possibility that the Spanish court had not been fully informed of the situation when it made its order that order was valid and M had been habitually resident in Spain since June 1999. The English court was bound by that order. It was for the Spanish court to investigate and adjudicate upon the merits of the case.

M (ABDUCTION: CONFLICT OF JURISDICTION), Re [2000] 2 F.L.R. 372, Dame Elizabeth Butler-Sloss (President), Fam Div.

2447. Child abduction – Ireland – removal of child in breach of Irish court's custody rights

[Hague Convention on the Civil Aspects of International Child Abduction 1980 Art.3, Art.8.]

F, an Irish national and the unmarried father of H, commenced proceedings for guardianship and access in the Irish district court and later sought an order for the return of H after M had taken her to England without his consent. F contended that the wrongful removal amounted to a breach of the rights of custody that were vested in the Irish court, upon which he was entitled to rely in this jurisdiction when seeking an order for the return of H. M appealed against the decision of the Court of Appeal ([2000] Fam. Law. 80) allowing F's appeal against the refusal of an order to return H to Ireland.

Held, dismissing the appeal, that the Irish court possessed custody rights in respect of H by virtue of F's pending guardianship application; such a conclusion accorded with a purposive interpretation of the Hague Convention on the Civil Aspects of International Child Abduction 1980 Art.3 and Art.8. F had invoked the jurisdiction of the Irish court, as a result of which that court had rights of custody in respect of H and therefore F was entitled to apply to the country to which H had been wrongly removed for an order for H's return.

H (A MINOR) (ABDUCTION: RIGHTS OF CUSTODY), *Re*; *sub nom*. H (A CHILD) (REMOVAL FROM JURISDICTION), *Re* [2000] 2 A.C. 291, Lord Mackay of Clashfern, HL.

2448. **Child abduction – Jewish law – Orthodox Jewish mother removing children to England – jurisdiction of Israeli Beth Din**

[Hague Convention on the Civil Aspects of International Child Abduction 1980.]

M and F, Orthodox Jews, were married in 1992 in Israel where their first two children were born in 1994 and 1995. When M was eight months pregnant with the third child she flew to England with the other children. Mediation attempts by a series of rabbis failed and F sought the return of the two older children under the Hague Convention on the Civil Aspects of International Child Abduction 1980 and the return of the child born in England under the court's inherent jurisdiction. M resisted, inter alia, on the basis that she would not get justice from the Beth Din chosen by F in Israel and would be discriminated against as a woman as she would be unable to obtain a get without F's consent.

Held, granting the application, that the children would be returned to Israel as this was clearly in their best interests. M had chosen to raise her children in the Orthodox faith and submit to the jurisdiction of the Beth Din. She could not therefore claim that the religious jurisdiction breached either her own or her children's human rights. The court would not investigate the law and practice of the Beth Din, nor would it treat Israel any differently from other Convention signatories on the ground of the dual civil and religious system operated there. Further, F had undertaken not to remove the children from M in Israel pending the hearing and to consent to a get.

S (ABDUCTION: INTOLERABLE SITUATION: BETH DIN), *Re* [2000] 1 F.L.R. 454, Connell, J., Fam Div.

2449. **Child abduction – residence – one parent's change of habitual residence – effect on children**

[Hague Convention on the Civil Aspects of International Child Abduction 1980.]

A married couple had three children, all born and habitually resident in England. In November 1999 the family went to live in Spain. The father, F, contended that the move was the culmination of careful discussion. The mother, M, stated that she had only agreed to it at the last minute as a means of saving the marriage. In February 2000 M left Spain with the children and returned to England without F's knowledge or consent. F applied for the children to be returned to Spain under the Hague Convention on the Civil Aspects of International Child Abduction 1980 on the basis that he was resident in Spain. M, however, asserted that she had never lost her habitual residence in England.

Held, refusing the application, that where one parent had changed habitual residence but the other had not done so, the parent who had done so could not argue that a child's habitual residence had necessarily also changed. On the facts, the children had not lost their habitual residence in England nor had they become habitually resident in Spain at any time before they left with M.

N (CHILD ABDUCTION: HABITUAL RESIDENCE), *Re*; *sub nom*. N v. N (CHILD ABDUCTION: HABITUAL RESIDENCE) [2000] 2 F.L.R. 899, Black, J., Fam Div.

2450. Child abduction – solicitors – order requiring parent's solicitors to disclose whereabouts of child – lawfulness of secrecy provision in order

A court order obtained pursuant to a without notice application by the claimant required the proposed defendant's solicitors to disclose the whereabouts of the proposed second defendant who was the child of the claimant and the proposed first defendant. The solicitors did not know the child's whereabouts, although they did disclose all notes of an introductory meeting with the proposed first defendant. The solicitors objected to a provision in the order that prevented them from informing the proposed defendant that the order had been made, contending that it was wrong in principle for them to keep information from their client.

Held, discharging part of the order sought, that the relationship between the solicitors and the first defendant was covered by professional privilege and the solicitors would be in breach of their duty to their client if they disclosed any communication from that client other than in compliance with a court order. The secrecy provision was only tenable if it was necessary to assist in tracing the whereabouts of the child. It would be inappropriate in general terms to make an order requiring a solicitor to mislead a client and which prevented the solicitor from giving full advice to that client, *B (Minors) (Abduction: Disclosure), Re* [1995] 1 F.L.R. 774 followed. On the facts, the solicitors had disclosed all the information in their possession, therefore the secrecy provision of the court order would be removed. In general terms, however, there was no objection to such a provision being included in an order for a limited period, determined by reference to the facts of the case, where that might lead to the discovery of the whereabouts of a child and protect the solicitors during the recovery phase.

H (CHILD ABDUCTION: WHEREABOUTS ORDER TO SOLICITORS), *Re* [2000] 1 F.L.R. 766, Hughes, J., Fam Div.

2451. Child abduction – United States – cooperation with US court

[Hague Convention on the Civil Aspects of International Child Abduction 1980 Art.7.]

H and W met in America, where W was a citizen and H, who was English, had permission to reside. Their first child, M, was born in October 1991, and they married in 1994. Following H's imprisonment for drug offences, M went to live permanently with his maternal great grandmother, GGM, in May 1995. GGM and M's maternal grandmother, MGM, were appointed as co guardians of M. H continued to have further periods of imprisonment both before and after a second child, J, was born in September 1997. When W was remanded in custody for drug offences in June 1998, J also went to live with GGM. In September 1998, H was deported and returned to England. W was released on probation in November 1998 and lived with GGM and the children until January 1999 when she removed both children to England and set up home with H. GGM and MGM applied for the children's summary return under the Hague Convention on the Civil Aspects of International Child Abduction 1980. W contended that returning the children to the USA was likely to cause them harm as H could not return with them and W would be arrested on her arrival for breach of her probation conditions. The case came before the High Court and after hearing evidence the judge spoke directly to the American judge involved in the criminal case, who revoked the warrant for W's arrest and gave an assurance that no action would be taken against her until the case relating to the children had been dealt with in the American court. He also spoke to the American family judge, who confirmed that the matter would be dealt with expeditiously on the children's return. The Official Solicitor submitted a report suggesting that if the American court decided at the substantive hearing that the children should live in England, they could be made wards of court with the Official Solicitor as their next friend to monitor their progress and report back to the American Court. The High Court judge adjourned the case to allow the parties to consider their positions. H and W withdrew their opposition to the children being returned, and a hearing took place before the American family judge attended by GGM and lawyers acting for H and W, at which undertakings were given by all parties regarding living arrangements for the children in America pending the outcome of the substantive hearing.

Held, ordering the children's return and incorporating the American court's order in a consent order, that although the case had been more protracted than was usual in Hague Convention cases, the course taken had achieved a result where the benefits had outweighed the requirement for a speedy resolution. The collaboration between the courts had been within the remit of Art.7 of the Convention and had been in the best interests of the children, as it had allayed concerns about what would happen to the children on their arrival in America and had established a structure for the ongoing resolution of the children's future interests. It was important in cases of judicial collaboration for the parties to be involved in the process and to be kept informed of the content of the discussions between the courts.

M AND J (CHILDREN) (ABDUCTION: INTERNATIONAL JUDICIAL COLLABORATION), *Re* [2000] 1 F.L.R. 803, Singer, J., Fam Div.

2452. Child abduction – unmarried fathers – child's removal to Spain by mother – effect of father's application for parental responsibility order

[Hague Convention on the Civil Aspects of International Child Abduction 1980 Art.3.]

An unmarried father, F, applied for contact and parental responsibility orders in respect of his child, C, which were adjourned in order to allow for negotiations. The child's mother, M, took C to Spain to visit her new partner, indicating through her solicitors that it was a temporary visit. However, it became apparent that she was not planning to return, and F applied for a declaration that M had wrongfully removed C in breach of the Hague Convention on the Civil Aspects of International Child Abduction 1980 Art.3. The issue arose as to whether, in the absence of custody rights of the unmarried father, the removal was in breach of the custody rights vested in the court by virtue of the pending action.

Held, granting the declaration, that the court was seised of proceedings in relation to C, albeit that they had been suspended and that no final orders had been made. There had been several hearings and a consent order had been drawn up. It was an offence for a child to be taken out of the UK without the consent of a person with parental responsibility. Proceedings for a parental responsibility order were commensurate with proceedings for an order prohibiting removal, and therefore came within the definition of proceedings relating to rights of custody in the Convention, *Practice Note: Hague Convention: Applications by Fathers Without Parental Responsibility* [1998] 1 F.L.R. 491, [1998] C.L.Y. 2379 not followed.

C (A CHILD) (ABDUCTION: WRONGFUL REMOVAL), *Re*; *sub nom*. C (A CHILD) (ABDUCTION: UNMARRIED FATHER) [1999] 2 F.L.R. 859, Hale, J., Fam Div.

2453. Child abduction – unmarried fathers – rights and status

[European Convention on Human Rights 1950; Hague Convention on the Civil Aspects of International Child Abduction 1980.]

An unmarried father, F, applied for parental responsibility and other orders. The mother, M, took the child, B, to Italy. F unsuccessfully sought B's return under the Hague Convention on the Civil Aspects of International Child Abduction 1980, the court having concluded that F had no formal rights of custody. F complained to the European Court of Human Rights that his rights as an unmarried father were not protected in the same way as those of a married father.

Held, declaring the application inadmissible, that in relation to applications brought under the Hague Convention there was an objective and reasonable justification why F, who merely had contact with the child, should not be treated as being on an equal footing with an applicant who had the child in his care. A father having parental responsibility for a child bore different responsibilities from those of a father having only the right of contact with the child. There had been no discrimination as between married and unmarried fathers. Accordingly, the different treatment of the applicant was not in breach of the European Court of Human Rights.

B v. UNITED KINGDOM [2000] 1 F.L.R. 1, J-P Costa (President), ECHR.

2454. Child protection – failure of local authority to take effective and practical steps

See HUMAN RIGHTS: KL v. United Kingdom. §3169
See HUMAN RIGHTS: Z v. United Kingdom. §3170

2455. Child support – maintenance orders – financial resources of absent parent's new partner – child support officer's power to obtain information – mother's rights

[Child Support Act 1991 s.50, Sch.1.]

H, who had divorced in 1991 and subsequently remarried, appealed against the decision of a Child Support Commissioner to dismiss his appeal against a decision of the Child Support Appeal Tribunal. The tribunal had dismissed his appeal against the refusal of a Child Support Officer, CSO, to review a decision not to cancel an interim maintenance assessment made pursuant to the Child Support Act 1991. Following the issuing of a maintenance enquiry form, H sought reassurances from the Child Support Agency, CSA, that financial details concerning his income and expenditure and that of his second wife would not be made available to his first wife. CSA refused to provide the requested assurance and after H failed to return a second enquiry form an interim maintenance assessment under s.12 of the 1991 Act was made. H contended that (1) CSO was not entitled in accordance with Sch.1 para.1 to para.5 to the 1991 Act and associated Regulations to request information in relation to an absent parent's new family until at least one completed maintenance assessment had been made. H argued that Sch.1 para.6(1) established that the power to require such information under the relevant regulations was only available in circumstances where one or more assessments had already been made, and (2) the failure of CSO to guarantee the non disclosure of financial information supplied by him had been unlawful under s.50(1) of the 1991 Act.

Held, dismissing the appeal, that (1) the reference to a maintenance assessment within Sch.1 para.6(1) was a reference to a preliminary calculation of what would be prima facie payable if para.6(1) did not apply. To hold otherwise would result in a situation whereby a completed assessment would be made without reference to any new partner's income. That would necessitate a second phase of enquiries if it produced a result, whereby the income of the absent parent would be likely to be reduced below the protected level in the absence of any additional household income, and (2) the requirements of natural justice and the need to ensure the confidence of the recipient demanded that the information used to formulate an assessment should be communicated to both parties, and such communication by a civil servant acting in his official capacity was authorised by s.50(6) of the 1991 Act.

HUXLEY v. CHILD SUPPORT OFFICER [2000] 1 F.L.R. 898, Hale, L.J., CA.

2456. Child support – occupational pensions – injury pension to be taken into account when assessing child maintenance

[Child Support (Maintenance Assessments and Special Cases) Regulations 1992 (SI 1992 1815) Sch.1 para.9, Sch.2 para.5.]

W, a fireman, was forced to retire after an injury at work. W received a pension in two parts, an ill health pension and an injury pension. W's ex wife applied for a child support assessment of the maintenance to be paid by W. The child support officer took into account the two pensions when calculating W's assessable income on the application. W appealed to the Child Support Appeal Tribunal on the ground that the injury pension should not have been assessed as part of his income for the purposes of the Child Support (Maintenance Assessments and Special Cases) Regulations 1992 Sch.1 para.9. W contended that the payment of an injury pension under his occupational pension scheme should be disregarded as the absent parent's income as it amounted to "compensation for personal injury" under Sch.2 para.5. W's contentions were rejected at first instance and he appealed.

Held, dismissing the appeal, that W's injury pension had been calculated by reference to the extent of his disablement, not by reference to his likely losses of income or to any expenses related to the injury. Were it not for W's injury, neither pension would have been paid, and therefore payments made as a result of an injury under W's occupational pension scheme did not constitute "compensation" for the purposes of the Regulations. W's income resulting from both the ill health and injury the pensions could be taken into account in assessing child maintenance.

WAKEFIELD v. SECRETARY OF STATE FOR SOCIAL SECURITY; *sub nom.* WAKEFIELD v. CHILD SUPPORT OFFICER [2000] 1 F.L.R. 510, Wilson, J., CA.

2457. Children – care orders – ancillary injunction to secure child's attendance at college

[Supreme Court Act 1981 s.37; Children Act 1989 s.33(3), s.100.]

P was a poor school attender, despite being academically gifted. Her parents did not assist in the local authority's attempts to improve her school attendance, eventually withdrawing her from school. P was removed into foster care under a recovery order, but was returned home under a care order. P wished to attend a sixth form college and the local authority applied for an injunction compelling P's parents to allow her to attend.

Held, granting the application, that the court had the power under the Supreme Court Act 1981 s.37 to make the order sought in support of the rights conferred by the Children Act 1989 s.33(3) and it was clearly in P's best interests that it be made. Section 100 of the 1989 Act did not apply to this power and therefore leave was not required for the order to be made, but even if it was, it would have been granted under the inherent jurisdiction as P was likely to suffer significant harm without the order.

P (A CHILD) (CARE ORDERS: INJUNCTIVE RELIEF), *Re* [2000] 2 F.L.R. 385, Charles, J., Fam Div.

2458. Children – care orders – failure to take effective action against abusive parents – guidance for social services

The local authority applied for care orders in respect of three children who had been physically ill treated and showed signs of emotional disturbance. Social services had originally supported the children, but despite warnings from teachers and without proper consideration of the file, had decided to take no further action because of the parents' failure to cooperate. After the case had been re-opened after a referral from a concerned school, an emergency protection order was made in respect of two of the children and care proceedings were commenced in respect of all three of them.

Held, granting the applications, that it was clear that the children had been left to suffer in totally inadequate conditions for many years. Lessons should be learnt by social services. In particular, every case file should have, at the top or on the front, a chronology recording every significant event. Lack of parental cooperation should lead to a closer investigation of the case. Health visitors and teachers were an important source of information and any referrals by them should be treated with the utmost seriousness. Where children were part of a sibling group, they should not be considered individually but in the wider family context. Finally, in order to prevent cases from drifting into the background and losing urgency, work with families should be scheduled by setting a timetable within which effective action should be taken.

E (MINORS) (CARE PROCEEDINGS: SOCIAL WORK PRACTICE), *Re* [2000] 2 F.L.R. 254, Bracewell, J., Fam Div.

2459. Children – care orders – local authority applying to withdraw proceedings – opposition by guardian ad litem

[European Convention on Human Rights 1950 Art.8(1).]

LA, the local authority, commenced care proceedings in respect of N, a baby born in 1998. M, the mother of N, had four other children by three different fathers. Two of the children had behavioural and health problems and had been placed in foster care, where they were settled and wished to remain. Relations between social services and the parents were acrimonious. However, it was accepted that the parents' care of N was exemplary and LA applied to withdraw the application for a care order. G, the guardian ad litem, who had not been consulted by LA prior to the making of the application, opposed it on the grounds that LA had failed to investigate the wealth of evidence concerning the care of the older children and the parents' failure to accept or cooperate with the advice given to them by the professionals and experts. The parents sought to rely on the European Convention on Human Rights 1950 Art.8(1).

Held, refusing leave to withdraw the application, that the court could only interfere with the parents' right to family life if to do so was necessary to fulfil a pressing social need. The court was only concerned with the fact that N was not currently suffering any harm and was not currently at risk but was entitled to rely on the evidence of the past care of the children in order to assess the parents' ability to safeguard N's welfare in the future. LA's case assessment had failed to consider the evidence concerning the two older children in foster care and the only way in which LA's evidence could be tested was in court. Therefore there was a clear need for the application to be heard in court for the benefit of N.

N (A CHILD) (LEAVE TO WITHDRAW CARE PROCEEDINGS), *Re* [2000] 1 F.L.R. 134, Bracewell, J., Fam Div.

2460. Children – care orders – removal of young siblings after elder children taken into care – local authority response disproportionate to concerns for children's welfare

[European Convention on Human Rights 1950 Art.8.]

M and F had four children, K, aged 12, CM, aged six, J, aged 18 months and C aged eight months. K and CM were taken into foster care following two instances when K was found at home alone at the age of eight. At least one of the incidents took place at a time when M was on home leave from hospital where she was being treated following a mental breakdown. Reports prepared indicated significant concerns over the effect that M's parenting had had on K's intellectual and emotional development. Both K and CM remained in a foster placement thereafter. Whilst in foster care, K made allegations of sexual abuse against her grandfather. After J was born, a report was prepared by an independent social worker which concluded that whilst J was thriving physically and there were no concerns for him at that time, it was highly likely that he would suffer "similar significant harm as his sisters in future". An interim care order and a recovery order were made and J, when aged 10 months, was removed from M and F at the hospital, together with C, to whom M had just given birth. C was returned to M after four days but removed again two months later. A final hearing followed at which care orders were made in respect of J and C and authority was given for the local authority to refuse all contact between the parents and K and CM. M and F appealed, contending that there was insufficient evidence upon which to conclude that J and C were likely to suffer emotional harm in future since the only evidence of harm had been in relation to K. Further, the reports had assumed that CM had suffered harm when there was no real evidence to support such a conclusion.

Held, allowing the appeal, discharging the care orders in relation to J and C, and remitting the case for consideration by a High Court judge, that the possibility of future harm could never have justified the removal of such young children from their parents and the cutting of all ties. Such a response was not proportionate to the concerns expressed for the children. Such a view was in line with the jurisprudence of the European Court and the requirements of the

European Convention on Human Rights 1950 Art.8. The order for permission to refuse contact in relation to K and CM would stand, although the parents would retain the option of seeking permission in the future.

C AND B (CHILDREN) (CARE ORDER: FUTURE HARM), *Re*; *sub nom.* C AND J (CHILDREN), *Re* [2001] 1 F.L.R. 611, Hale, L.J., CA.

2461. Children – care orders – residence – determination of designated local authority

[Children Act 1989 s.31, s.105.]

Following J's birth in Plymouth, PCC immediately obtained an interim care order and J went with her mother to live with the maternal grandmother and later to a residential assessment centre in Plymouth. Following a placement away from Plymouth, and about four months prior to the court hearing, J was separated from her mother and placed with the paternal grandmother in Liverpool. At first instance it was held that J's ordinary place of residence was Plymouth, where her mother lived, and that, in any case, by virtue of the Children Act 1989 s.31 (8) (b), PCC was the assumed designated local authority as Plymouth was where the circumstances leading to the care order arose. The father appealed, relying on *Northamptonshire CC v. Islington LBC* [2000] 2 W.L.R. 193, [1999] C.L.Y. 2312 to contend that when applying the disregard provision and s.31 (8) (a), a judge had a discretion to depart from the statutory constraint.

Held, dismissing the appeal, that the general approach to adopt was to interpret s.31 and s.105 so that the ordinary place of residence was that which applied immediately before any period of disregard. It was clear that for a new born baby in its mother's care, the residence of dependency was that of the mother. The facts of the instant case should not have given rise to litigation as PCC had accepted responsibility throughout and matters of this nature were only to be litigated in exceptional cases, *Northamptonshire* followed.

C (A CHILD) v. PLYMOUTH CITY COUNCIL; *sub nom.* PLYMOUTH CITY COUNCIL v. C; C v. PLYMOUTH CC [2000] 1 F.L.R. 875, Thorpe, L.J., CA.

2462. Children – care orders – teenage mothers – care plans for mother and baby – local authority responsibilities during pregnancy

Care orders were made in respect of a 13 year old mother and her four month old daughter, who were living with foster parents. Guidance was given for the benefit of local authorities with regard to their duties in caring for young teenage mothers and their babies.

It was held that it was not to be assumed that babies of young teenagers should be adopted. Each case turned on its own facts, depending on the extent of care offered elsewhere. However if local authority care was a possibility, then (1) as soon as the pregnancy was declared, planning for both mother and baby had to begin straightaway, and the mother's welfare did not take priority over that of the unborn baby; (2) social work and expert reports were to be finished well in advance of the birth; (3) any care proceedings should be issued on the same day as the birth, and in the case of a very young mother, prompt transfer to the High Court and appointment of separate guardians ad litem was required; (4) there should be an urgent early hearing for the court to determine the baby's interim placement; (5) it was imperative that the Family Court heard the case, using the standby procedure if necessary, to make an early final determination; (6) where adoption was contemplated, twin track and/or concurrent planning was crucial, *D and K (Children) (Care Plan: Twin Track Planning), Re* [2000] 1 W.L.R. 642, [1999] C.L.Y. 2359 considered, and (7) suitable adopters could be identified before the final decision of the court, so long as no steps had been taken to implement the adoption process.

R (A CHILD) (CARE PROCEEDINGS: TEENAGE PREGNANCY), *Re*; *sub nom.* R (A CHILD) (CARE PROCEEDINGS: TEENAGE MOTHER), *Re* [2000] 2 F.L.R. 660, Bracewell, J., Fam Div.

2463. Children – care orders – uncertainty as to whether child's injuries attributable to parents or childminder

[Children Act 1989 s.31(2); European Convention on Human Rights 1950 Art.8.]

A, a child of pre school age, was cared for when her parents were at work by a childminder at the childminder's home and otherwise by her parents at their home. Having sustained serious head injuries caused by violent shaking, responsibility for which could not safely be attributed to any party, A was made the subject of a care order, which was upheld on appeal ([2000] 2 W.L.R. 346). A's parents appealed, contending that as they had not been shown to be responsible for causing the injuries, the threshold conditions under the Children Act 1989 s.31(2) were not met, and that a family upbringing was only to be disturbed by state intervention where the primary carers were inadequate, not where harm had been unforeseeably inflicted during a temporary period of care with a third party. Further, the order was in breach of the European Convention on Human Rights 1950 Art.8, which guaranteed respect for their family life.

Held, dismissing the appeal, that (1) s.31(2) of the Act was satisfied even though the court was unable to ascertain which of the carers had caused the injury. It would be dangerously irresponsible, where shared care was commonplace and where it was often impossible to distinguish between primary carers and other carers, to limit intervention only to those incidents where the assailant had been identified. The proper construction of the words "care given to the child" in s.31(2) of the Act was care given by any carer of the child, and (2) the care proceedings were a necessary and legitimate process to protect A from future harm and were within the exceptions set out in Art.8(2) of the Convention.

LANCASHIRE CC v. B (A CHILD) (CARE ORDERS: SIGNIFICANT HARM); *sub nom.* LANCASHIRE CC v. W (A CHILD) (CARE ORDERS: SIGNIFICANT HARM); LANCASHIRE CC v. A (A CHILD); BW (CARE ORDERS), RE; B AND W (CHILDREN) (THRESHOLD CRITERIA), *Re* [2000] 2 A.C. 147, Lord Nicholls of Birkenhead, HL.

2464. Children – care orders – validity of refusing legal aid for children

See LEGAL AID: R. v. Legal Aid Board, *ex p.* W (Children). §3982

2465. Children – care proceedings – disclosure sought of expert's reports obtained in criminal proceedings

[Children Act 1989.]

A father, F, was subject to criminal proceedings in relation to injuries caused to one of his children. Care proceedings were also commenced by the guardian ad litem appointed in relation to that child. In the criminal proceedings, F obtained leave to instruct different medical experts from those that had been instructed in the civil proceedings. The guardian ad litem sought disclosure of the notes and reports of experts who had been instructed in the criminal proceedings. F contended, in reliance upon *R. v. Derby Magistrates Court, ex p. B* [1996] A.C. 487, [1996] C.L.Y. 1402, that the experts had been instructed through his solicitors and therefore their reports were subject to legal professional privilege. The guardian ad litem relied on *L (A Minor) (Police Investigation: Privilege), Re* [1997] A.C. 16, [1996] C.L.Y. 502 to argue that the welfare of the child ought to be put first and the reports disclosed.

Held, that the material prepared by the experts in the criminal proceedings remained subject to an absolute right to legal professional privilege. Privilege applied to material relating to direct or indirect communications with experts instructed solely for the purposes of the criminal proceedings. Witnesses should not volunteer legally privileged material and should not be compelled by the court to make such disclosure without the consent of the person who had the right to privilege. Therefore F could refuse to disclose the names of the experts instructed in the criminal proceedings, *Derby Magistrates* followed and *L (A Minor)* distinguished on the ground that the majority judgments in that case were concerned with the issue of legal privilege in care proceedings under the Children Act 1989.

S CC v. B [2000] Fam. 76, Charles, J., Fam Div.

2466. **Children – care proceedings – duties of advocates – wasted costs orders**

In care proceedings, an early report by a medical expert, M, indicated that sight of the relevant GP records was vital to her consideration of the case. However, when the GP records were disclosed by the guardian ad litem, they were not shown to M, a fact which only came to light when M was giving evidence. M had to write a further report and return to finish her evidence a few days later. It also became apparent that another expert, F, had not been shown the father's most recent statement. F was able to read the statement and finish her evidence on the same day. The judge gave judgment in open court as to wasted costs orders and the duties of advocates at pre hearing reviews.

Held, making a wasted costs order against counsel for the local authority, that although parents were often fighting a losing battle in care proceedings, they retained the right to have their case put properly. As costs did not follow the event, it fell to the court to keep checks on the build up of costs as part of its case management function, which could quite properly include instigating wasted costs order proceedings. Counsel for a local authority led a team with responsibility to conduct the case effectively, collate evidence appropriately and ascertain that all expert witnesses were completely up to date. At pre hearing reviews all the advocates in a case had to ensure collectively that (1) the issues were clear; (2) the evidence was available, or that directions would be sought to make it available; (3) experts had been informed of any matters that had arisen since their reports, and that additional reports would be written where necessary; (4) witnesses had been identified, timetabled and their required time slot calculated, with particular attention being given to ensuring that the evidence of expert witnesses would not run over on to another day; (5) written evidence was properly presented in bundles with a chronology; (6) the guardian's report would be available in good time, and (7) the judge had sufficient reading time. The failures in the instant case in relation to the expert evidence had no reasonable explanation and were negligent. However, despite the collective nature of the advocates' responsibilities identified above, it was only appropriate to make a wasted costs order against counsel for the local authority, and only in relation to M's evidence since there had been no actual loss of time in relation to F's evidence, *Ridehalgh v. Horsefield* [1994] Ch. 205, [1994] C.L.Y. 3623 considered.

G (CHILDREN) (CARE PROCEEDINGS: WASTED COSTS), *Re*; *sub nom*. G, S AND M (CHILDREN) (WASTED COSTS), RE; G, S AND H (CARE PROCEEDINGS: WASTED COSTS), *Re* [2000] Fam. 104, Wall, J., Fam Div.

2467. **Children – care proceedings – exclusion orders – procedural requirements**

[Children Act 1989 s.38A(2), s.44A(2); Family Proceedings Courts (Children Act 1989) Rules 1991 (SI 1991 1395) r.25A.]

W appealed against an order committing him to two months' imprisonment, suspended for a period of six months, for his breach of an exclusion order with a power of arrest attached, which formed part of an interim care order in respect of his three children. W contended that the order was manifestly excessive in the light of changed circumstances. W accepted that he had breached the exclusion order, having spent a night at the family home, but asserted that a statement made for the purpose of obtaining the exclusion order was inadequate and that he had not been served personally with appropriate documents in compliance with the Family Proceedings Courts (Children Act 1989) Rules 1991 r.25A.

Held, allowing the appeal, that the order was excessive in the light of developments and would be quashed and replaced with an order of suspension of one month. The children had been taken into care and therefore the exclusion order was redundant. The purpose of r.25A was to ensure that the relevant party was made aware of the evidence on which an exclusion order had been made in order to give him an opportunity to vary or discharge the order. The statement relied upon in support of an exclusion order should be separate, clearly setting out the factual material relied upon together with evidence supporting the requirements for the obtaining of such an order under the Children Act 1989 s.38A(2) and s.44A(2). The statement should state clearly what the relevant person was required to do in order to comply with an order. Where, in the absence of the relevant person, the court had made an exclusion order of its own motion, it should direct that a statement of evidence be prepared and served upon that person, and it would not be necessary to serve a separate statement at subsequent renewals of an exclusion order unless the grounds for the application had changed.

W (EXCLUSION: STATEMENT OF EVIDENCE), Re; sub nom. W v. A LOCAL AUTHORITY (EXCLUSION REQUIREMENT); W v. MIDDLESBROUGH BC (EXCLUSION ORDER: EVIDENCE) [2000] 2 F.L.R. 666, Cazalet, J., Fam Div.

2468. Children – care proceedings – extent of parent's culpability in neglect of child recorded in consent order – court's power to go behind consent order

JH was the mother of M, who was aged five, and L. In proceedings in Scotland it was proved that JH had neglected M in a manner likely to cause suffering to his health, although the expert evidence was inconclusive as to whether JH's treatment of M had been deliberate or merely careless. Shortly after L's birth the local authority sought an order that he should be placed in interim care. A split hearing was ordered whereby the issue of the threshold criteria would be determined first. Negotiations on the day of the hearing resulted in an order being made which recorded a concession on the part of JH that she had failed to supervise M causing his admission to hospital on various dates. At the hearing the judge ordered assessments to be prepared by a consultant psychologist and a consultant psychiatrist. Both experts commented that without an adjudication by the court they were unable to say whether JH had deliberately abused M or whether she had merely been careless in supervising him. When the case came before the court again, the judge decided that that issue would have to be tried. JH appealed, arguing that the local authority was bound by the principle of issue estoppel from going behind the order that had been made by agreement whereby she had conceded that she had failed to supervise M. Alternatively, she argued that if the judge possessed a discretion enabling him to depart from the agreed order, he had erred in exercising that discretion, since she would be prejudiced by the lengthening of the case and the consequent lengthening of her separation from L.

Held, dismissing the appeal, that in discharging his principal responsibility to promote the welfare of the child as the paramount consideration the judge had to retain a discretion and a degree of flexibility. The principle of issue estoppel had no application to a case of this nature. Where a local authority had reached a considered decision as to the extent of findings to be made in respect of issues involving a parent, the local authority would only be allowed to go behind those findings if very good reasons were established. In the instant case although the local authority had been at fault in failing to realise that the central issue of the extent of JH's culpability would have to be resolved, the inability of the experts to proceed justified the judge's decision to order a trial of that issue, and it could not be said that the judge had erred in the exercise of his discretion.

D (A CHILD) (THRESHOLD CRITERIA: ISSUE ESTOPPEL), Re [2001] 1 F.L.R. 274, Thorpe, L.J., CA.

2469. Children – care proceedings – solicitor for guardian ad litem previously represented father – ability of solicitor to continue acting

[Courts and Legal Services Act 1990 s.27(4).]

Care proceedings were brought in respect of two children and during the course of the proceedings the father, A, was joined as a party. A was cross examined by the solicitor acting for the guardian ad litem. A recognised the solicitor as the same person that had acted for him in an unrelated case many years earlier. A's application under the Courts and Legal Services Act 1990 s.27 (4) for an order that the solicitor should not be heard was dismissed and A appealed.

Held, dismissing the appeal, that though sensitivity was of the utmost importance in family cases, for the solicitor to be removed from the case there had to be a real possibility of injustice being caused. The solicitor had no recollection of ever representing A and checks on records held at her firm revealed no potential conflict of interest or risk of injustice, *Bolkiah v. KPMG* [1999] 2 A.C. 222, [1999] C.L.Y. 1 followed and *R. v. Dann (Anthony Ian)* [1997] Crim. L. R. 46 distinguished.

T AND A (CHILDREN) (RISK OF DISCLOSURE), *Re; sub nom.* T (CHILDREN) (CARE PROCEEDINGS: GUARDIAN AD LITEM), *Re* [2000] 1 F.L.R. 859, Ward, L.J., CA.

2470. Children – child protection – child care organisations

PROTECTION OF CHILDREN (CHILD CARE ORGANISATIONS) REGULATIONS 2000, SI 2000 2432; made under the Protection of Children Act 1999 s.12. In force: October 2, 2000; £1.50.

These Regulations prescribe enactments for the purposes of the Protection of Children Act 1999 s.12(1), which requires the Secretary of State to keep a list of persons considered unsuitable to work with children. The Act requires that child care organisations must submit individuals to the Secretary of State for inclusion on that list and in certain circumstances, it will prohibit them from offering employment in a child care position to any individual who is included in the list.

2471. Children – child protection – tribunal procedure

PROTECTION OF CHILDREN ACT TRIBUNAL REGULATIONS 2000, SI 2000 2619; made under the Protection of Children Act 1999 s.9, Sch.para.2. In force: October 2, 2000; £3.50.

These Regulations make provision with respect to the proceedings of the Tribunal, established by the Protection of Children Act 1999 s.9, on an appeal or determination under s.4 of the Act or regulations made under s.6. In particular, they provide for the initiation of appeals and applications for leave, case management and related powers, hearings, the making, pronouncement and notification of the Tribunal's decision, and supplementary provision including the curing of irregularities, the death of the applicant and proof and certification of documents.

2472. Children – Children's Commissioner – appointment – Wales

CHILDREN'S COMMISSIONER FOR WALES (APPOINTMENT) REGULATIONS 2000, SI 2000 3121 (W.199); made under the Care Standards Act 2000 s.118, Sch.2 para.2. In force: December 8, 2000; £1.75.

These Regulations make provision for the appointment of the Children's Commissioner for Wales whose office is established under the Care Standards Act 2000 Part V. They make provision for the appointment to be made by the Assembly First Secretary following advice from any committee of the Assembly which has been established for the purpose of advertising as to the appointment and advice as to their suitability for appointment, as to the term of office, and as to the circumstances in which the Commissioner may be relieved of office. The First Secretary is also under a duty to take account of the views of children resident in Wales as to the proposed appointment.

2473. Children – contact orders – Californian court permitting contact conditional on mirror order – court's jurisdiction to make mirror order

[Family Law Act 1986 s.1, s.2, s.3(1); Hague Convention on the Civil Aspects of International Child Abduction 1980.]

A mother, M, who had joint British and US nationality, removed her child to California where she commenced divorce proceedings. The father, F, an Iranian with no right of entry into the US, obtained an order under the Hague

Convention on the Civil Aspects of International Child Abduction 1980 whereby the child could visit him for one week per year, conditional on F obtaining an order in identical terms in this jurisdiction. F therefore applied for the order and the issue arose as to whether the English court was precluded from making such an order under the Family Law Act 1986 s.1 by s.2(2) and s.2(3)(a), which limited the court's jurisdiction under s.3(1) to children who were either habitually resident here or present within the jurisdiction at the time the order was made.

Held, granting the application, that as a matter of comity and common sense it was desirable to continue the practice of making mirror orders so that the court in one jurisdiction could be confident that there would be redress in another jurisdiction should the parent refuse to comply. On the facts of the instant case, the mirror order would only have effect when the child was in the jurisdiction and therefore the inherent jurisdiction of the court could be relied upon by virtue of s.2(3)(b) where the child was in the country on the relevant date and the court considered that the immediate exercise of its powers was necessary for the purposes of protection. The power to make such orders would only rarely be exercised and was reserved for Family Division judges.

P (A CHILD) (MIRROR ORDERS), *Re*; *sub nom*. P (A CHILD) (JURISDICTION: MIRROR ORDER) [2000] 1 F.L.R. 435, Singer, J., Fam Div.

2474. Children – contact orders – decision to terminate contact – applicability of European Convention on Human Rights

[Children Act 1989 s.34; European Convention on Human Rights 1950 Art.6.1, Art.8.]

Care orders were made in relation to three children because of the harm that they had suffered by way of neglect. The local authority proposed, under a care plan, the quick placement of the children for adoption. In care proceedings the local authority sought leave to terminate the mother's contact with the children under the Children Act 1989 s.34(4) on the grounds of her opposition to the care plan and the potential for her to become a destabilising influence. Permission having been granted, the mother appealed contending, inter alia, that the decision to terminate contact infringed her rights under the European Convention on Human Rights 1950 Art.6.1 and Art.8. The mother submitted that the decision of the local authority to terminate contact subsequent to the order being made would be an administrative decision from which she would have no effective remedy.

Held, dismissing the appeal, that (1) having given consideration to the children's long term welfare, the justices had been correct in granting leave to terminate contact. Whilst the 1989 Act established in principle that a child was best brought up at home by his parents, continued habitation with the mother in the instant case could not be considered to be in the children's long term interest; (2) having applied the 1989 Act, the justices had given consideration to the provisions of Art.6 and Art.8 of the Convention. Where the needs of a case made it appropriate, the application of the provisions of s.34 as an integral part of a care plan and as a means of eschewing delay in the best interests of the children did not infringe the Convention, and (3) the use of the Convention as a means of bolstering appeal grounds should be discouraged.

F (CHILDREN) (CARE: TERMINATION OF CONTACT), *Re*; *sub nom*. F (CHILDREN) (CARE PROCEEDINGS: CONTACT), *Re* [2000] 2 F.C.R. 481, Wall, J., Fam Div.

2475. Children – contact orders – effect of domestic violence

[Children Act 1989 s.1, s.3.]

L's father, F, made applications for parental responsibility and direct contact. The judge, finding that there had been a history of violent domestic incidents since the birth of L and that L's mother, M, opposed direct contact because of a genuine fear of F, dismissed the application for parental responsibility and made an order for indirect contact. F appealed and the court heard his appeal with the appeals of the fathers of V, M and H, who had each had an application for direct contact refused against a background of domestic violence.

Held, dismissing the appeals, that the court had a duty to apply the principle in the Children Act 1989 s.1 that the welfare of the child was paramount and to take into account all relevant considerations in each individual case. In family proceedings, the courts should be aware of expert psychiatric evidence relating to the potential emotional harm that could be suffered by children who were exposed to domestic violence. There was no prima facie assumption that there should be no direct contact between a parent and a child in cases where allegations of domestic violence had been proven, but the effect of the violence on the child and the parent with care and control, the behaviour of the parties towards each other and the child, and the motivation of the parent seeking direct contact were factors that should be taken into account by the court when exercising its discretion to make an order. In L's case, there were obvious risks to the child if a direct contact order were to be made. In making an order for indirect contact, the judge had made a decision that was consistent with the advice in the psychiatric report and which enabled L to understand her cultural background. Similarly, in the cases of V, M and H, the decisions not to order direct contact had been made with the welfare of the child as the overriding consideration and after applying the welfare checklist in s.3 of the Act.

L (A CHILD) (CONTACT: DOMESTIC VIOLENCE), *Re*; V (A CHILD) (CONTACT: DOMESTIC VIOLENCE), RE; M (A CHILD) (CONTACT: DOMESTIC VIOLENCE), RE; H (CHILDREN) (CONTACT: DOMESTIC VIOLENCE), *Re* [2001] 2 W.L.R. 339, Dame Elizabeth Butler-Sloss (President), CA.

2476. **Children – contact orders – father sought contact to son not seen for nine years – mother's allegations of sexual abuse unproven – mother's hostility such that chance of rapprochement lost**

F, the father of children aged 11 and 13, made an application for direct contact to the younger child, having accepted that his application for contact to his elder daughter would not succeed due to her opposition. The parents had separated in 1991 and M had subsequently made allegations that F was responsible for sexually abusing the children when they were aged two and five. A therapist, to whom the children were referred for treatment, concluded that they had been abused, although the techniques used to reach this conclusion breached the Cleveland Guidelines in that they had involved the use of leading questions and substantial encouragement. The judge found the allegations of sexual abuse not proven but dismissed the application and ordered the continuance of arrangements for indirect contact to both children ([1999] 2 F.L.R. 92). F appealed, contending that the judge had erred by (1) neglecting to conduct a proper balancing exercise between the risk of short term harm and the risk of long term harm if the younger child were to be denied meaningful contact with F, particularly during adolescence; (2) accepting the reasoning of the experts called on M's behalf so far as future contact was concerned when their evidence concerning the allegations of abuse had been so decisively rejected, and (3) failing to provide adequate reasons for rejecting the psychiatric evidence adduced on his behalf.

Held, dismissing the appeal, that the judge had been well aware of the law to be applied in a case such as this. The weight to be afforded to the competing factors when conducting the balancing exercise in question was a matter for the judge's discretion, and on the facts of the case, the judge's decision did not fall outside the ambit of that discretion; (2) the decision as to what evidence to accept and reject was again a matter for the judge, and it was not possible to say that it had clearly been wrong to accept the views of the therapist called on M's behalf with respect to future contact despite the criticism of her conclusions on the issue of abuse, and (3) the reasons for the rejection of the psychiatric evidence adduced on F's behalf concerning the benefit of future direct contact were plain. The judge had appreciated that the child was so determined that there should be no contact with F due to the hostility engendered by M that he should not be forced to have contact with F. Essentially, the window of opportunity had now passed and the opportunity for any meaningful rapprochement between the child and F had been lost. The court directed that the Official Solicitor should explain the court's decision to the children in person and emphasise the court's conclusion that F was a devoted and loving father who could bring substantial benefit to their lives should they decide to approach him in the future.

M (SEXUAL ABUSE ALLEGATIONS: INTERVIEWING TECHNIQUES), *Re* FAFMI 1999/0777/B1, Ward, L.J., CA.

2477. Children – contact orders – history of domestic violence – indirect contact appropriate – mother's intention to return to Cyprus

[Hague Convention on the Civil Aspects of International Child Abduction 1980.]

F had behaved aggressively to M and her relatives, attacking M and threatening to rape and kill her. After their divorce, he had supervised contact with their daughter, D, but no contact with the son, S, in respect of whom he denied paternity. M, a Greek Cypriot, obtained leave to take the children to Cyprus, where they lived for a year. F did not write to his daughter, D, while she was in Cyprus, but attempted to make telephone contact with her. M said that D would not speak to him, although D did eventually send two cards. F made aggressive telephone calls to Cyprus, threatening to abduct D and to kill M. M and the children returned to England on discovering that F had commenced without notice proceedings under the Hague Convention on the Civil Aspects of International Child Abduction 1980, applying for contact with both children and a prohibited steps order to prevent their removal.

Held, granting the application for contact by making an order for indirect contact and refusing the application for a prohibited steps order, that (1) the application for contact with S was properly made given that F now wished to be named on S's birth certificate; (2) M could return to Cyprus if she wished, where she had the means to support herself, provided that indirect contact was established with F which could lead to supervised direct contact later, and (3) there was to be no attempt at direct contact between D and F for the time being as D was frightened of F. Such contact could not take place until the necessary preparations had been made and F had built a relationship with the child, *M (Minors) (Contact: Violent Parent), Re* [1999] 2 F.L.R. 321, [1998] C.L.Y. 2421 followed.

S (VIOLENT PARENT: INDIRECT CONTACT), *Re; sub nom.* S (CONTACT: INDIRECT CONTACT), *Re* [2000] 1 F.L.R. 481, Cazalet, J., Fam Div.

2478. Children – contact orders – indirect written contact

A 12 year old boy, P, had had no contact with his father, F, for four or five years following F's imprisonment for armed robbery. P had memories of F being violent to his mother, M, during their cohabitation but was not opposed to receiving cards from F when this was suggested by the court welfare officer, CWO. The CWO recommended indirect contact, but the justices made an order for no contact on the ground that any contact at such a stage might disrupt P's life. F appealed. He was released from prison the day before the hearing.

Held, allowing the appeal and making an order for indirect contact restricted to the sending of birthday and Christmas cards, that the justices had failed to take into account the circumscribed nature of indirect contact. P knew his father and receiving cards from him was likely to foster their relationship without being detrimental to P's stability.

P (CONTACT: INDIRECT CONTACT), *Re* [1999] 2 F.L.R. 893, Sir Stephen Brown, Fam Div.

2479. Children – contact orders – interim supervision orders – programme of therapy to facilitate future contact

Z, aged 11, and A, aged 7, lived with their mother, M, who had a diagnosed personality disorder. Z and A had contact with their father, F, but began to show fear and reluctance to see him. Various private law applications by both parents were heard at the same time as the local authority's application for supervision orders. The court held that the threshold criteria had been met, that M's allegations that F was a danger to the children were unfounded and that she had been influencing the children regarding contact with F. The local authority commenced proceedings in public law, seeking interim supervision orders in respect of both Z and A.

Held, granting the application, that interim supervision orders should be made and the private law applications adjourned to the final hearing. Interim orders were appropriate to allow for the implementation and monitoring of a package of therapy for the whole family, aimed at enabling contact between A and F, and supporting Z towards the resumption of future contact, with the proviso that if the package failed the matter could come back before the court. Questions as to the appropriateness of care orders and the need for a change in residence for either Z or A would need to be addressed at a later date. M's full cooperation would be required for the successful implementation of the therapy package but the court was confident that a sufficient level of cooperation would be forthcoming.

Z AND A (CHILDREN) (CONTACT: SUPERVISION ORDER), *Re* [2000] 2 F.L.R. 406, Charles, J., Fam Div.

2480. **Children – contact orders – order in favour of grandparents resident in France – enforceability of order**

[Child Abduction and Custody Act 1985; European Convention on Recognition and Enforcement of Decisions concerning Custody of Children 1980 Art.10(1)(b), Art.11(2).]

Following a breakdown in the relationship between the grandparents and the parents of N, aged seven, and C, aged three, the grandparents, who were French and residing in France, applied to the English court to enforce a French order entitling them to fortnightly contact with the children in France. An important factor in the making of the French order was the proximity of the two households, as N and C had been living in France with their parents for some time. However, the parents had relocated to England with N and C without the knowledge of the French court or the grandparents. The parents relied upon the Child Abduction and Custody Act 1985, which incorporated the European Convention on Recognition and Enforcement of Decisions concerning Custody of Children 1980 Art.10(1)(b), contending that the order was contrary to natural justice and that contact with the grandparents in France was manifestly adverse to the children's interests. The grandparents disputed that the provisions of Art.10(1)(b) were satisfied and while conceding that it was not in the children's interests to make the journey to France, argued that the order could be varied under Art.11(2) to provide for contact in England.

Held, refusing the application, that the basic premise on which the contact order had been granted initially was that contact should take place in France since that was where the children were residing at the time. In view of the grandparents' concession and the hostile relations between the adults, the defence to enforcement under Art.10(1)(b) had been made out. The court would not exercise its discretion under Art.11(2) because the grandparents had not made any firm proposals for contact in England.

L (ABDUCTION: EUROPEAN CONVENTION: ACCESS), *Re* [1999] 2 F.L.R. 1089, Bennett, J., Fam Div.

2481. **Children – contact orders – order restricting applications**

[Children Act 1989 s.91 (14).]

Three children were the subject of care orders as a result of M's inadequate care. M applied to discharge the care orders, alternatively for defined contact with the children. At the hearing, M accepted that there was no prospect of rehabilitation and withdrew her application to discharge the care orders. The judge agreed to the local authority's request for a reduction in contact. The local authority, supported by the guardian ad litem, then sought an order under the Children Act 1989 s.91(14) on the grounds that M was unlikely for some time to accept that she was never going to look after the children again and the order was required to safeguard the children's welfare. The judge made the order because of the vacillation of the local authority in planning the children's future, not because M had been making an unreasonable number of applications. M appealed.

Held, allowing the appeal, that orders under s.91 (14) were appropriate where repeated unmeritorious applications were being made, or pre-emptively where it was in the best interests of the children to prevent unmeritorious applications. A balance had to be struck between the interests of the child and the right of the litigant to have unrestricted access to the courts and the judge had correctly balanced the interests of the children against the restriction upon M. The children had been subject to deplorable vacillation and urgently needed to settle down away from M and it was likely that the reduction in contact would encourage her to make further contact applications which would be disruptive and confusing for the children. It was, therefore, in the interests of the children that M should have to overcome a modest hurdle if she wished to make further applications. However, a restriction of 12 months would be adequate to allow matters to settle.

M (CARE ORDERS: RESTRICTING APPLICATIONS), *Re; sub nom*. M (A CHILD) (SECTION 91 (14) ORDER), *Re* [1999] 3 F.C.R. 400, Butler-Sloss, L.J., CA.

2482. Children – parental contact – local authorities' powers and duties

[Children Act 1989 s.34(2); Contact with Children Regulations 1991 (SI 1991 891) Reg.3.]

W was in local authority care. An order made under the Children Act 1989 s.34 (2) prohibited any future parental contact. On the mother's application for contact, an interim order was made granting contact at the discretion of the local authority. The guardian ad litem sought an order prohibiting the local authority from permitting staying contact. It was argued that it was the duty of the court to promote the welfare of the child, which meant that the court had the power to prohibit a local authority from allowing contact. Further, it was asserted that the wording of s.34 was sufficiently wide to lead to such a conclusion. A final order allowing contact at the discretion of the local authority was made and the guardian ad litem appealed.

Held, dismissing the appeal, that the court could not order the local authority to prohibit contact which the local authority considered beneficial as the obligation under s.34 was a positive one requiring local authorities to promote contact and the restriction was on the power to refuse contact, *Kent CC v. C* [1993] Fam. 57, [1993] C.L.Y. 2782 overruled in part. Moreover, the local authority could lawfully circumvent any order by agreement with the parent under the Contact with Children Regulations 1991 Reg.3. Although the wording of s.34 seemed to give wide powers, the whole policy of the 1989 Act was to shift power from the court to the local authority once an order had been made, *L (Minors) (Sexual Abuse: Standard of Proof), Re* [1996] 1 F.L.R. 116, [1996] C.L.Y. 482 approved.

W (A CHILD) (PARENTAL CONTACT: PROHIBITION), *Re; sub nom*. W (A CHILD) (SECTION 34(2) ORDERS), *Re* [2000] Fam. 130, Thorpe, L.J., CA.

2483. Children – parental responsibility agreements – effect of care order

[Children Act 1989 s.4(1) (b), s.33.]

X and Y were subject to interim care orders in favour of the local authority, despite opposition from their unmarried parents. The father's application for a parental responsibility order was refused. Both parents subsequently entered into a parental responsibility agreement under the Children Act 1989 s.4(1) (b), whereby the mother agreed that the father should have parental responsibility. The father appealed against the decision to refuse to allow him parental responsibility and a preliminary point arose in the appeal as to whether the agreement was valid, given that the children were subject to a care order. The local authority argued that as it had shared parental responsibility by virtue of s.33, it could determine the way in which the mother exercised her parental responsibility.

Held, allowing the appeal, that the parents were at liberty to enter into a parental responsibility agreement notwithstanding that a care order in favour of the local authority was in force. In making the agreement, the parents were not exercising parental responsibility, as that only took effect when the agreement was filed with the Principal Registry. The power of the parents to enter into an agreement under s.4(1)(b) was not an exercise of parental responsibility but formed instead a separate process by which parents could make arrangements for their children. If the parents were to marry, the father would acquire parental responsibility in a way that the local authority could not prevent and there was no reason to prevent its acquisition by another route.

X (CHILDREN) (CARE PROCEEDINGS: PARENTAL RESPONSIBILITY), *Re*; *sub nom.* X (A CHILD) (PARENTAL RESPONSIBILITY AGREEMENT: CHILD IN CARE), *Re* [2000] Fam. 156, Wilson, J., Fam Div.

2484. Children – prohibited steps orders – circumcision – consent of both parents required

[Children Act 1989 s.2(7).]

M, the English mother of J, aged five, was granted a prohibited steps order preventing J's Muslim father, F, from making arrangements to have J circumcised without a court order. F appealed against the decision to grant the order, contending that the judge had been wrong to place greater emphasis on the fact that J had been brought up in a secular environment than on the fact that J had been born a Muslim. F argued that the judge had given too much weight to M's opposition, whilst not appreciating the impact that F's views would have on J.

Held, dismissing the appeal, that where there was a dispute concerning an important decision regarding a child, the matter should be referred to the court. Ritual circumcision was an irreversible operation which was not medically necessary, bearing physical and psychological risks and in such cases the Children Act 1989 s.2(7), stated that the consent of both parents was essential. The issue of what was in the best interests of the child would depend on the facts and, in the instant case, the judge had correctly found that circumcision at the age of five which was not medically necessary was not in the child's best interests.

J (A MINOR) (PROHIBITED STEPS ORDER: CIRCUMCISION), *Re*; *sub nom.* J (A MINOR) (SPECIFIC ISSUE ORDERS: MUSLIM UPBRINGING AND CIRCUMCISION), RE; J (CHILDS RELIGIOUS UPBRINGING AND CIRCUMCISION), RE; U (A CHILD), *Re* [2000] 1 F.L.R. 571, Thorpe, L.J., CA.

2485. Children – removal from jurisdiction – right to family life – balancing rights of parents

[European Convention on Human Rights 1950 Art.8.]

A's mother, M, wished to move to the US to further her career as a harpist, and was granted permission to take A, aged 10 months, with her, upon giving an undertaking to return A to the UK at least twice a year for contact with her father, F. F applied for leave to appeal against the order on the ground that it interfered with his right to family life under the European Convention on Human Rights 1950 Art.8.

Held, refusing the application, that Art.8 enshrined a right to private life as well as family life, and the court was required to balance those rights. The judge had approached the task correctly, and had not erred in finding that M was acting reasonably as her job prospects were likely to be better in America, *H (Application to Remove from Jurisdiction), Re* [1998] 1 F.L.R. 848, [1998] C.L.Y. 2441 applied.

A (A CHILD) (PERMISSION TO REMOVE CHILD FROM JURISDICTION: HUMAN RIGHTS), *Re*; *sub nom.* G-A (A CHILD), *Re* [2000] 2 F.L.R. 225, Ward, L.J., CA.

2486. **Children – residence orders – application – public hearing in accordance with right to fair trial**

See HUMAN RIGHTS: B v. United Kingdom (Hearing in Private) (36337/97). §3211

2487. **Children – residence orders – application for interim order – views of mentally disabled child**

[Civil Procedure Rules 1998 (SI 1998 3132) Part 25 r.25 r.1.]

In 1983 J sustained brain damage, leaving him mentally and physically disabled at the age of two. In 1986 and after his parents had separated, his mother, M, was granted custody with reasonable access being given to his father, F, who had regular contact with him, including staying contact. In 1999, after a period of staying contact, F did not return J to M but wrote informing her that J had expressly stated that he wanted to remain with him. M applied for an interim declaration that J should reside with her pending the hearing of the substantive case.

Held, refusing the application, that although the court had the power to grant an interim declaration under the Civil Procedure Rules 1998 Part 25 r.25.1, the application in the instant case was premature because the issue of J's capacity had not been determined. At his age there was a presumption, which could only be displaced by clear evidence, that he had the capacity to decide where he should reside.

R v. R (INTERIM DECLARATION: ADULT'S RESIDENCE) [2000] 1 F.L.R. 451, Bracewell, J., Fam Div.

2488. **Children – residence orders – costs – father's unreasonable conduct**

F agreed that his aim of shared residence was unrealistic during mediation over contact to M and F's two children. As a result, M gained residence with alternate weekend contact, overnight contact on Tuesdays, and staying contact during school holidays being given to F. Subsequently, F sought contact every weekend, and M suggested replacing the Tuesday contact with Sunday contact on those weekends when F did not have contact. F then announced that the children should live with him and refused mediation other than through lawyers, unless M first agreed to share residence, which M refused. F, who had significantly greater assets than M, commenced residence and contact proceedings. M represented herself initially and later took out a mortgage to cover her legal fees. The welfare office reported that the children, probably following F's lead, had expressed a wish for shared residence. F strongly criticised M's ability as a mother, but later acknowledged that she was as good a parent as he was and withdrew the residence proceedings. M applied for costs on the ground of F's unreasonable conduct.

Held, granting the application and awarding M 75 per cent of her costs, that the bulk of the costs had been incurred as the result of F's failed residence application, which should never have been brought. F's conduct and allegations against M, along with his improper encouragement of the children to further his desire for shared residence, justified the making of the order. Further, he had continued with this course of action knowing the effect that the costs would have on M and had threatened the residence application as a means of securing a compromise on the contact issue by oppression.

M v. H (COSTS: RESIDENCE PROCEEDINGS) [2000] 1 F.L.R. 394, Michael Harrison Q.C., Fam Div.

2489. **Children – residence orders – removal from jurisdiction – refusal of permission not to be disturbed where no error of law on part of judge**

M appealed against the refusal to grant leave for her to remove her six year old daughter, S, from the UK, so that they could both settle in Singapore with C, whom M planned to marry. S had lived with M since her parents' marriage broke down in 1996, but had regular contact with her father, F. On being informed of M's intention to marry and settle in Singapore, F had applied for residence and for a prohibited steps order. M had cross applied for leave. M had made it clear throughout that if permission to remove S was refused, she too would remain in the UK and C would depart alone. At first instance it was held that although there was a presumption that leave would be granted if a reasonable decision had been made to leave the country, that presumption was outweighed in the circumstances of the instant case by the fact that S's bond with her father would be frustrated. M's application was refused despite the judge's knowledge of the adverse consequences on M's relationship with C. M appealed on the ground that the judge had erred in failing to take into account the risk of emotional harm to S caused by the dissolution of her new family and the emotional impact of that dissolution on M.

Held, dismissing the appeal (Thorpe L.J. dissenting) that the instant case was not one in which the judge could be said to have failed to direct himself as to the correct approach to take in reaching his decision, *MH v. GP (Child: Emigration)* [1995] 2 F.L.R. 106, [1996] C.L.Y. 543 applied. He had correctly observed that there was a presumption in favour of M's application, but that the best interests of S negated that presumption. It was a difficult and finely balanced decision for the judge to make, but in the absence of judicial error, it was not for the appellate court to interfere with his discretion, *G v. G (Minors: Custody Appeal)* [1985] 1 W.L.R. 647, [1985] C.L.Y. 2594 and *Piglowska v. Piglowski* [1999] 1 W.L.R 1360, [1999] C.L.Y. 2421 considered.

C (A CHILD) (LEAVE TO REMOVE FROM JURISDICTION), *Re*; *sub nom.* C (A CHILD) (REMOVAL FROM JURISDICTION), *Re* [2000] 2 F.L.R. 457, Thorpe, L.J., CA.

2490. Children – residence orders – views of child same as those of father – no requirement for separate representation

[Children Act 1989 s.1, s.10(8).]

S, a boy aged 12, sought leave to apply for a residence order in the course of his parents' divorce proceedings. Having consulted two solicitors, who both satisfied themselves as to his understanding and maturity, it was established that S understood the nature of his expressed desire to live with his father, F.

Held, refusing the application, that although S had sufficient understanding for the purposes of the Children Act 1989 s.10(8) to instruct a solicitor in his own right, there was no difference between S's wishes and those of F so that S's concerns could form part of F's submissions in the divorce proceedings. The wishes of a child were an important but not decisive factor in the context of s.1 of the Act. In consequence, while the court could theoretically decide against S's wishes, proper account would be taken of them as it would be undesirable to impose an unwanted result upon him.

H (RESIDENCE ORDER: CHILD'S APPLICATION FOR LEAVE), *Re* [2000] 1 F.L.R. 780, Johnson, J., Fam Div.

2491. Children – secure accommodation – effect of child attaining 16 during period of order;

[Children Act 1989 s.20, s.25; Children (Secure Accommodation) Regulations 1991 (SI 1991 1505) Reg.5.]

G, a girl aged 15, had been under the wardship of the local authority for a considerable period. An order had been made in 1995 that G should remain in wardship whilst in her minority, that she should be accommodated by the local authority and that she should not be removed by her parents without prior consultation. G's behaviour led to serious concerns and the local authority sought the approval of the court for G's removal to secure accommodation. The court gave approval for a period of 28 days' secure accommodation. However, G was due to attain the age of 16 by the end of 28 day period. The Official Solicitor appealed, contending that on a proper construction of the Children Act 1989 s.20 and s.25, read in conjunction with the Children (Secure Accommodation) Regulations 1991 Reg.5, the order was invalid because from the date of G's sixteenth birthday to the end of the secure accommodation order she would be accommodated under s.20(5) of the 1989 Act and restrictive accommodation of such persons was prohibited under Reg.5 of the 1991 Regulations.

Held, dismissing the appeal, that when the secure accommodation order was sought, G was accommodated under s.25 of the 1989 Act because she was under 16. The judge had been entitled to make the secure accommodation order as Reg.5 of the 1991 Regulations did not apply to s.25 of the 1989 Act. All the judge had to decide was whether the criteria for a secure accommodation order been met on the date of the hearing. What happened after G reached 16 was irrelevant to the exercise of the judge's discretion when granting the order.

G (A CHILD) (SECURE ACCOMMODATION ORDER), *Re* [2000] 2 F.L.R. 259, Thorpe, L.J., CA.

2492. Children (Leaving Care) Act 2000 (c.35)

This Act makes provision about children and young persons who are being, or have been, looked after by a local authority; and replaces the Children Act 1989 s.24.

This Act received Royal Assent on November 30, 2000.

2493. Childrens rights – HIV testing – baby born to HIV positive mother – testing of baby

A baby, C, was born to M, who was infected with the HIV virus. M, who was breast feeding the baby, refused to allow her to be tested for the presence of HIV infection due to her scepticism about conventional medical treatment for HIV and AIDS. She sought permission to appeal against a decision that it was in the interests of the baby's welfare that the test should take place. M contended that there was no point to the test as she did not believe that the result could be conclusive and she did not wish her baby to be put into a category of special risk and subjected to aggressive medical intervention unnecessarily.

Held, dismissing the appeal, that the primary issue of concern was the child's welfare and not the rights of the parents. The advantages of the test were overwhelming and it would not be in the best interests of the child to live in ignorance of the state of her health. She had both national and international rights of her own and the case had to be determined by reference not only to her welfare but also to her physical needs, her background and to the risk of harm to which she would be subjected.

C (A CHILD) (HIV TESTING), *Re*; *sub nom.* C (A MINOR) (HIV TEST), *Re* [1999] 2 F.L.R. 1004, Butler-Sloss, L.J., CA.

2494. Childrens welfare – family proceedings

CHILDREN AND FAMILY COURT ADVISORY AND SUPPORT SERVICE (MEMBERSHIP, COMMITTEE AND PROCEDURE) REGULATIONS 2000, SI 2000 3374; made under the Criminal Justice and Court Services Act 2000 Sch.2 para.2, para.4. In force: January 18, 2001; £2.00.

These Regulations make provision for the membership, committees and procedure of the Children and Family Court Advisory and Support Service. The main functions of the Service are to promote the welfare of children, to give advice in any court about any application, to make provision for the children to be represented and to provide information, advice and other support for the children and their families.

2495. Childrens welfare – medical treatment – best interests of child paramount in medical intervention dispute

E was born 16 weeks premature in April 1999 with severe medical problems, including chronic lung disease, as a result of which E had to be kept on a ventilator. By September 1999 E's condition had greatly deteriorated, and medical opinion was that death was inevitable, that further ventilation would serve no long term purpose, and that it would only lead to prolonged suffering without hope of recovery or any future quality of life. E's parents, who had lost confidence in R, the hospital trust, wanted the ventilation to continue, believing that there was a possibility that E could recover. R made an emergency application to the High Court for an order that non medical intervention by removal from the ventilator was appropriate. The Official Solicitor, on behalf of E, contended that it was inappropriate for the court to make a declaration in a matter concerning a doctor's clinical expertise.

Held, granting the declaration, that it was the duty of the court to serve the best interests of E, but given that the court could not override the opinions of those clinically responsible for E, the Official Solicitor's approach would ordinarily be appropriate. However, in view of the absence of trust between the parties, it was in E's best interests for a permissive order to be made to the effect that R could treat E in such a manner as its clinicians thought to be in her best interests.

ROYAL WOLVERHAMPTON HOSPITALS NHS TRUST v. B (MEDICAL TREATMENT) [2000] 1 F.L.R. 953, Bodey, J., Fam Div.

2496. Childrens welfare – medical treatment – difference of opinion as to treatment for immunodeficiency

M, a seven year old Russian child, suffered from immunodeficiency for which he was receiving immunostimulant therapy, a treatment which had the approval of his parents prior to M coming to the UK. However, doctors who saw the child in this country recommended that he be treated with immunoglobin, a treatment that would have to continue for the rest of his life. The parents were not happy with this due to an early misdiagnosis by English doctors and because the Russian treatment had been working well. They were also concerned about the quality and availability of blood products on their return to Russia. The parties agreed to an order before the hearing.

Held, that in accordance with the agreed order, the immunoglobin treatment would continue but the parents were to be closely involved in decision making. The parents' wish that doses be as small as possible was also noted. It would in any event be open to any of the parties to return to the court for further directions. In the instant case, the parents' misgivings would have been overridden in the absence of agreement because of the overwhelming medical evidence in favour of the immunoglobin treatment.

MM (A CHILD) (MEDICAL TREATMENT), *Re* [2000] 1 F.L.R. 224, Black, J., Fam Div.

2497. Childrens welfare – performing arts – grant of licence by local authority

CHILDREN (PERFORMANCES) AMENDMENT REGULATIONS 2000, SI 2000 10; made under the Children and Young Persons Act 1963 s.37. In force: February 1, 2000; £1.00.

These Regulations revoke, in relation to England only, the Children (Performances) Regulations 1968 (SI 1968 1728) Reg.6, to remove restrictions preventing local authorities from granting a licence allowing a child to take part in a public performance if the child would, in the twelve months before that performance, have taken part in other performances on more than a certain number of days, and requiring them to take certain other matters into account when deciding whether to grant a licence. From the coming into force of these Regulations, local authorities in England will not be subject to those restrictions when considering the grant of a licence in respect of a performance by a child.

2498. Childrens welfare – performing arts – maximum duration of performances or rehearsals

CHILDREN (PERFORMANCES) AMENDMENT (NO.2) REGULATIONS 2000, SI 2000 2384; made under the Children and Young Persons Act 1963 s.37. In force: September 29, 2000; £1.50.

These Regulations amend the Children (Performances) Regulations 1968 (SI 1968 1728) in relation to children aged nine or over to increase the maximum length of time to four hours in which a child may take part in a continuous performance or rehearsal without a break. In addition, they extend the permitted hours in the working day and the total number of hours in which these children may be present at the place of performance or rehearsal.

2499. Contact orders – domestic violence – relevance of domestic violence

M, the child's mother, started cohabiting with F, the child's father, shortly before the child, T, was born in September 1998. M alleged that F was violent towards her throughout the cohabitation, and F pleaded guilty to one charge of assault in December 1998. In January 1999 M was granted a non molestation injunction and F applied for contact to T. F failed to attend appointments with the Court Welfare Officer, CWO, and one hearing. At a directions hearing a residence order was made in M's favour pending the final hearing and contact was ordered to take place fortnightly at a contact centre, with two sessions to be observed by the CWO. M appealed against the making of the contact order, arguing that it should be limited to the two sessions with the CWO to allow him to make his report, and that it was pre-emptive of the final hearing to be ordering a full reintroduction of T to F.

Held, allowing the appeal, that the judge had taken the wrong approach in holding that as T was only 15 months old he was unlikely to be affected by the risk that contact could be resumed only for it to be ended following the final hearing. The judge had placed too little weight on the effect that contact would have on M and on the background of domestic violence, and had been wrong to distinguish the case of *D (A Minor) (Contact: Interim Order), Re* [1995] 1 F.L.R. 495, [1995] C.L.Y. 3480, which was to be applied.

M (A CHILD) (INTERIM CONTACT: DOMESTIC VIOLENCE), *Re* [2000] 2 F.L.R. 377, Thorpe, L.J., CA.

2500. Divorce – decrees – decree absolute void owing to procedural error – human rights

[Human Rights Act 1998; Family Proceedings Rules 1991 (SI 1991 1247); European Convention on Human Rights 1950 Art.8, Art.12.]

A wife, W, successfully petitioned for divorce, with decree nisi being granted in July 1998. In October 1998, her husband, H, applied for the decree to be made absolute. The court processed the application contrary to the requirements of the Family Proceedings Rules 1991 treating it as an application by the petitioner. H, unaware of the mistake, remarried in Singapore in March 1999 and brought his new wife to the UK where she was granted leave to remain. The parties were informed of the mistake in August 1999 and the matter was transferred to the High Court to determine whether the decree absolute was void under the principles in *Manchanda v. Manchanda* [1995] 2 F.L.R. 590, [1995] C.L.Y. 2307. The judge requested the intervention of the Queen's Proctor as H had raised the issue of the applicability of the Human Rights Act 1998. H argued that, although the Act was not yet in force, the court in ordering a hearing of its own motion had acted as a "public authority" within the meaning of the Act. Any such act that breached the European Convention on Human Rights 1950 would be retrospectively unlawful once the Act came into force in October 2000. A decision that the decree absolute was void would breach H's right to family life and right to marry under Art.8 and Art.12 of the Convention so that the public authority had to be mindful of that fact when carrying out the act.

Held, that the court's act in setting up a hearing did not establish new proceedings and therefore did not trigger a potential future application of the

Act. The existing divorce proceedings were incomplete and the court was merely facilitating their continuation and resolution. In any event, no Convention right had been breached. There had simply been a procedural error which meant that H had not been legally entitled to marry his second wife when he had done so. There was no right to divorce under the Convention and the fact that the decree absolute was void, *Manchanda* applied, did not breach Art.8 or Art.12.

DENNIS v. DENNIS [2000] Fam. 163, Wall, J., Fam Div.

2501. **Divorce – foreign jurisdictions – "effectiveness" of divorce granted by Guam court**

[Family Law Act 1986 s.46, s.49, s.51.]

H and W were US citizens who married in the USA in 1980. Having moved to the UK in 1982, they had sought a divorce in 1987. A deed of separation was agreed between them under which W could remain in the matrimonial home for 10 years following the separation, and the couple agreed to obtain a divorce in Guam. This State was then a US territory where divorce was permitted on postal application, conditional upon both parties accepting the jurisdiction of the Guam court. The final order was granted by the Guam Superior Court in 1989. Both H and W considered themselves to have been divorced and behaved on that basis, with H remarrying in France in 1991. At the end of the 10 year period, however, W obtained fresh legal advice and contended that the power to grant such divorces was now recognised as having been ultra vires Guam law. The Guam Superior Court refused W's application to vacate the divorce order on the basis of equitable estoppel. W petitioned for a divorce in England and H applied to strike out that application on the basis that the Guam divorce was valid.

Held, granting the strike out application, that overseas divorces were recognised under the Family Law Act 1986 s.46 on the basis that they were "effective" in the jurisdiction where they were granted. In the instant case, it was also necessary to consider Guam's then status as a US territory, as s.49 required that the divorce was recognised throughout the USA. As the word "effective" was less rigorous than the word "valid", the divorce, even though now deemed invalid in Guam, retained its validity on the ground of estoppel. Further, it was not contrary to public policy to recognise it as such, Accordingly, the court would not exercise its discretion under s.51 to disallow the Guam divorce.

KELLMAN v. KELLMAN [2000] 1 F.L.R. 785, Paul Coleridge Q.C., Fam Div.

2502. **Divorce – Orthodox Jewish husband refusing get – court's jurisdiction to refuse husband's application for decree absolute**

[Matrimonial Causes Act 1973 s.9; County Courts Act 1984 s.38.]

H and W were Orthodox Jews. W obtained a decree nisi but H refused to grant her a get, despite encouragement to do so from the Beth Din. Without the get the marriage continued under Jewish law, to W's detriment, even after the grant of a decree absolute. H then applied under the Matrimonial Causes Act 1973 s.9(2) for a decree absolute and the issue was whether the court had jurisdiction to refuse the decree until H granted the get.

Held, refusing the application, that the court had a wide jurisdiction under s.9 which was not confined to issues governed by the Act and which was designed to ensure that neither party suffered an injustice. In the instant case, justice could not be done as long as H was able to hold W to the burden of the marriage, *N v. N (Jurisdiction: Pre Nuptial Agreement)* [1999] 2 F.L.R. 745, [1999] C.L.Y. 2407 considered. There was also an inherent jurisdiction, which extended to the county court by reason of the County Courts Act 1984 s.38, to refuse a decree absolute where there were special reasons to do so, *Smith v. Smith (Divorce)* [1990] 1 F.L.R. 438, [1990] C.L.Y. 2284 followed.

O v. O (JURISDICTION: JEWISH DIVORCE) [2000] 2 F.L.R. 147, Judge Viljoen, CC (Watford).

2503. Divorce – pensions

See PENSIONS. §4349

2504. Divorce – solicitors – one off consultation with solicitor by wife – solicitor's duties when instructed later by husband

In 1991 W had a lengthy one off consultation with a solicitor, T, about problems in her marriage. When she issued divorce proceedings in 1998 she discovered that her husband, H, had instructed T to act for him. T refused to stand down, asserting that as he had no recollection of the consultation with W there was no conflict of interest, and that there was no support for the contention that there was a likelihood of prejudice. W issued a summons for an order that T should be barred from acting, but in order to avoid delays and further costs offered to withdraw it on the basis that the parties should pay their own costs. H refused the offer. The judge gave leave for the summons to be withdrawn, and made a costs order against H on the ground that the application had been properly brought as there was a likelihood of prejudice. H appealed.

Held, dismissing the appeal, that the judge had been right to find that this had been a proper application. The interests of justice strictly demanded that solicitors who had been given confidential information should not be seen in any way to risk its disclosure to opposing parties, *Bolkiah v. KPMG* [1999] 2 A.C. 222, [1999] C.L.Y. 1 applied. W's offer to withdraw had been based on practical considerations and was not an admission of defeat. In ordering H to pay the costs the judge had made a proper finding on the merits of the application which could not be disturbed.

DAVIES v. DAVIES [2000] 1 F.L.R. 39, Sir Stephen Brown, CA.

2505. Divorce – Talaq divorce – validity – registration with Sharia court

[Family Law Act 1986 s.46(1), s.51.]

H and W entered into a valid polygamous marriage under the law of Lebanon in April 1981. They lived apart for most of their marriage, with H remaining in Lebanon. W retained domicile in Lebanon but was resident in Europe and the USA. In December 1981, H pronounced a Talaq divorce in front of witnesses and had the divorce registered with the Sharia court in Lebanon, as required by Lebanese law. W only became aware of the divorce 16 years later when H withdrew financial support. W subsequently petitioned the English courts for divorce, whereupon H contended that there was no marriage to dissolve.

Held, giving judgment for H, that it was not necessary for W to have notice of the Talaq divorce for it to be effective. The Family Law Act 1986 s.46(1) provided for recognition of a divorce in foreign proceedings where either party was domiciled in the foreign jurisdiction and where some form of proceedings had been gone through. The provision of Lebanese law catering for registration of the divorce with the Sharia court constituted sufficient proceedings for the purposes of s.46(1), *Chaudhary v. Chaudhary* [1985] Fam. 19, [1985] C.L.Y. 1080 followed. On the facts, the court would not exercise its discretion under s.51 to decline recognition of the divorce.

EL FADL v. EL FADL [2000] 1 F.L.R. 175, Hughes, J., Fam Div.

2506. Domestic violence – committal orders – suspension order could be indefinite

[Rules of the Supreme Court 1965 (SI 1965 1776) Ord.52 r.7(1).]

G appealed against a decision to activate a suspended committal order which had been expressed to last "until further order of the court". G asserted that the suspended committal order failed to comply with the Rules of the Supreme Court 1965 Ord.52 r.7(1), which provided that suspension should be "for such period or on such terms or conditions" as the court specified.

Held, dismissing the appeal, that it was within the power of the court to suspend a committal order, even indefinitely, for so long as the contemnor continued to comply with the original order. The power of the court to make a suspended committal order derived primarily from common law and r.7(1) merely prescribed the procedure for the exercise of that discretion. Moreover, there was nothing in r.7(1) to suggest that suspension had to be for a finite period. The argument that suspension should be for a finite period was more persuasive in the case of ordinary criminal cases, because it would be unjust if a suspended sentence were to be activated for minor or totally unrelated offences. In the case of contempt of court, the sentence would be activated only in the event of a precisely worded order being breached. The alleged breaches in the instant case took place within 18 days of the order. Had the judge suspended the term for a definite period, it would most certainly have been for a longer period than that. No injustice had been caused to G.

GRIFFIN v. GRIFFIN [2000] C.P.L.R. 452, Hale, L.J., CA.

2507. Family proceedings – allocation of proceedings

CHILDREN (ALLOCATION OF PROCEEDINGS) (AMENDMENT) ORDER 2000, SI 2000 2670; made under the Children Act 1989 Sch.11 Part 1. In force: October 23, 2000; £1.50.

This Order amends the Children (Allocation of Proceedings) Order 1991 (SI 1991 1677) so as to include Barnet County Court in the list of Family Hearing Centres.

2508. Family proceedings – applications without notice – procedural requirements

M applied without notice for the discharge of an order granted on F's without notice application requiring her to surrender her passport and prohibiting each parent from removing the child from the jurisdiction.

Held, granting the application, that an applicant seeking injunctive relief without notice in the Family Division was obliged to disclose all relevant material and a failure to do so would entitle the court to refuse to grant the relief sought regardless of the merits of the case. An applicant granted injunctive relief without notice and his legal representatives were obliged, whether or not an express undertaking had been given, (1) to issue proceedings within a specified time; (2) to provide sworn statements of truth for any unsworn evidence given before the court, and (3) to serve on the respondent, as soon as practicable, the proceedings, a sealed copy of the order, the sworn evidence relied upon, and notice of the return date together with details of any application to be made thereon. The applicant's legal representatives had a duty to ensure that a without notice injunction order contained full details of the evidence that had been before the judge together with any legal authorities cited during the application and a further duty to comply promptly with a respondent's reasonable request for information about the hearing. The court recognised that such a procedure might not be appropriate in all injunctive without notice applications, particularly in cases involving children where the court might be required to take quick and firm steps to protect the child.

S (A CHILD) (FAMILY DIVISION: WITHOUT NOTICE ORDERS), *Re; sub nom.* S (A CHILD) (EX PARTE ORDERS), *Re* [2001] 1 W.L.R. 211, Munby, J., Fam Div.

2509. Family proceedings – blood tests – paternity – refusal of parent with care and control to allow blood test

[Family Law Reform Act 1969 s.20(1), s.21.]

X obtained an order in the county court under the Family Law Reform Act 1969 s.20(1) requiring that a sample of blood be taken from O and J, two minors, to determine the issue of paternity. In each case the mother had care and control of the child and opposed any blood sample being taken. X sought to enforce compliance with the order.

Held, refusing the application, that the court could not enforce compliance with an order requiring that a blood sample be taken from a child to determine paternity. It was clear from s.21(1) and s.21(3) that the parent with the care and control of a child could refuse any blood sample being taken for the purposes of determining paternity. The court had neither inherent jurisdiction nor the power under s.21 to override any decision of the parent despite the fact that it might be in the best interests of the child that the issue of paternity was settled. It would be for Parliament to rectify the situation.

O AND J (CHILDREN) (BLOOD TESTS: CONSTRAINT), *Re; sub nom.* O AND J (CHILDREN) (PATERNITY: BLOOD TESTS), RE; J (A CHILD) (BLOOD TESTS), *Re* [2000] Fam. 139, Wall, J., Fam Div.

2510. Family proceedings – expert evidence – inappropriate for expert treating child to provide report

Allegations of sexual abuse of a child by F were made in family proceedings and a report was produced by a child psychiatrist who had been treating the child under instructions from M. F's applications for an independent report from a jointly instructed psychiatrist and opposing the admission of M's expert's report were rejected and F appealed.

Held, allowing the appeal, that it was clearly inappropriate for an expert who had previously been involved in the treatment of a patient to produce a report that purported to be independent for use in litigation.

B (A CHILD) (SEXUAL ABUSE: EXPERT'S REPORT), *Re; sub nom.* B (A CHILD) (SEXUAL ABUSE: INDEPENDENT EXPERT), *Re* [2000] 1 F.L.R. 871, Thorpe, L.J., CA.

2511. Family proceedings – expert evidence – lay evidence preferred to expert evidence

The local authority appealed against preliminary findings of fact in care proceedings whereby the evidence of the maternal grandmother was preferred to that of two radiologists as to the timing of non accidental injuries sustained by B. The authority contended that the judge had erred in setting aside expert medical evidence in preference for the lay evidence of the grandmother and that the findings of fact in relation to the injuries were crucial to the final outcome.

Held, allowing the appeal, that the trial judge had erred in principle by failing to give any logical reasons for a decision so crucial to the final care decision. It was within the jurisdiction of the Court of Appeal to allow an appeal based on findings of fact, where those findings were central to the final decision.

B (A CHILD) (SPLIT HEARINGS: JURISDICTION), *Re* [2000] 1 W.L.R. 790, Dame Elizabeth Butler-Sloss, CA.

2512. Family proceedings – fees

FAMILY PROCEEDINGS FEES (AMENDMENT NO.2) ORDER 2000, SI 2000 938 (L.7); made under the Matrimonial and Family Proceedings Act 1984 s.41. In force: April 25, 2000; £1.50.

This Order amends the Family Proceedings Fees Order 1999 (SI 1999 690) so that a new fee of £80 for applications for ancillary relief is introduced as fee 4.4; fee 7 is reduced so that the fee is £1 for the first page and 20p per page for other pages; the fee for a detailed assessment hearing is increased from £80 to £130 and is the new fee 8.2; a new fee of £40 for a request for the issue of a default costs certificate is introduced as the new fee 8.3; and a new fee £50 is introduced for a request or application to set aside a default costs certificate as part of the new fee 8.4.

2513. Family proceedings – guardian ad litem – separation of conjoined twins – propriety of Official Solicitor's actions

Q, the director of a pressure group, ProLife Alliance, appealed against the decision of the President of the Family Division not to remove the Official Solicitor, OS, and appoint Q as guardian. The OS had decided not to appeal against a decision which had authorised an operation to separate conjoined twins resulting in the death of the weaker twin, M, in order to give her stronger sister, J, a better chance of life. Q contended that (1) the President's finding that the OS could only be removed on grounds of negligence or incompetence was incorrect and the proper test was the lower one of improper conduct objectively assessed; (2) in referring to his "broader responsibilities" the OS had shown that he lacked a singleminded dedication to M's best interests, which was required of him in his role; (3) the conclusion that M's prospects of survival were nil and that an appeal to the House of Lords raised no question of public importance was incorrect in law and represented a manifest failing in the OS's duties, and (4) the approval of the court should have been sought before the OS made the decision not to proceed with an appeal.

Held, dismissing the appeal, that (1) the President was not required to make a comprehensive statement of the circumstances in which a guardian ad litem could be removed and had in the context been referring to a consideration of whether the OS had been guilty of a manifest failure to discharge his duty; (2) the OS did have broad and heavy responsibilities in dealing with a variety of cases raising difficult legal and ethical issues and had not failed in his duty to M by suggesting that any development in this area of law had to be cautious; (3) the OS had acted with total propriety when considering whether to proceed with an appeal and could not be said to have failed in his duties in any way, and (4) notwithstanding that the OS could have sought directions from the court on how to proceed, approval of the court was not a requirement, particularly when the President would have reached the same conclusion in any event. Furthermore, in view of Q's position within the pressure group it would have been inappropriate for him to act as a guardian ad litem.

A (CHILDREN) (CONJOINED TWINS: MEDICAL TREATMENT) (NO.2), *Re* [2001] 1 F.L.R. 267, Ward, L.J., CA.

2514. Family proceedings – joinder – intervention of child's older sister in care proceedings

The parents appealed against a decision to allow their 17 year old daughter, D, to intervene in care proceedings involving her younger sister where there had been allegations of sexual abuse by the children against the parents.

Held, allowing the appeal, that although the court had the power to give leave to intervene to a person who was not directly involved in the proceedings, whether it was appropriate to do so depended on the facts of each case. The judge had erred by failing sufficiently to consider that D's intervention in these proceedings would not benefit her because she would remain unprotected in parallel criminal proceedings for perjury and seeking to pervert the course of justice, *S (Minors) (Care: Residence: Intervener), Re* [1997] 1 F.L.R. 497, [1997] C.L.Y. 371 considered.

H (A CHILD) (CARE PROCEEDINGS: INTERVENER), *Re* [2000] 1 F.L.R. 775, Dame Elizabeth Butler-Sloss (President), CA.

2515. Family proceedings – jurisdiction – recognition and enforcement of judgments – Council Regulation

Council Regulation 1347/2000 of May 29, 2000 on jurisdiction and the recognition and enforcement of judgments in matrimonial matters and in matters of parental responsibility for children of both spouses. [2000] OJ L160/19.

2516. Family proceedings – records – child subject of care proceedings – guardian ad litem's right to see report into death of child's brother

[Children Act 1989 s.42 (1) (b).]

The guardian ad litem of R sought access to a report compiled by the Area Child Protection Committee relating to the circumstances of the death of R's brother and the inter agency approach to the problems of R's family. Following the refusal of the local authority to allow access to the report on the ground that he had no right to see it, the guardian ad litem made an interlocutory application in care proceedings relating to R to view the report. Finding that the report fell within the Children Act 1989 s.42(1) (b) and related to R, the judge ordered the local authority to allow the guardian ad litem to have access to it. The local authority appealed contending, inter alia, that the report should not be disclosed as a matter of policy on the basis that it might limit honest assessment of the agency concerned.

Held, dismissing the appeal, that the report constituted a record held by a local authority, and accordingly the guardian ad litem did have the right to read it under s.42(1)(b). In light of the proceedings, the guardian ad litem had a legitimate interest in obtaining a full copy of the report. Such a right did not, however, mean that sensitive or irrelevant information should be disclosed.

R (A CHILD) (CARE PROCEEDINGS: DISCLOSURE), *Re* [2000] 2 F.L.R. 751, Dame Elizabeth Butler-Sloss, CA.

2517. Family proceedings – reporting restrictions – factors to be taken into account

M, the mother of C, made allegations against F, C's father, during proceedings concerning residence and contact. Some of the allegations were dismissed by the court but were subsequently repeated by M to the media. The High Court granted an injunction restraining M and her partner from revealing the contents of court documents in the public domain. M then withdrew from these proceedings but F sought a further injunction to restrain the continued publication of allegations which had been made in the proceedings concerning C.

Held, granting the injunction, that the court had inherent jurisdiction to grant injunctions to promote the welfare of C and to protect C from any damage, which did not depend on the proceedings being held in private. That approach was not based on any duty of confidentiality. Repeated publication of material already in the public domain could be damaging to C. The welfare of C was of paramount importance and the court was required to balance the public interest in the freedom of the press against the likelihood of damage being done to C if the allegations made in the proceedings continued to be made public. It was in the overall public interest in the circumstances of the case that the injunctions be granted.

A v. M (FAMILY PROCEEDINGS: PUBLICITY) [2000] 1 F.L.R. 562, Charles, J., Fam Div.

2518. Family proceedings – rules

FAMILY PROCEEDINGS (AMENDMENT) RULES 2000, SI 2000 2267 (L.19); made under the Matrimonial and Family Proceedings Act 1984 s.40. In force: October 2, 2000 and December 1, 2000; £3.00.

These Rules amend the Family Proceedings Rules 1991 (SI 1991 1247) by providing a procedural code for cases concerning the Human Rights Act 1998 and for applications for pension sharing and pension attachment orders, in cases where one or both parties have pension rights.

2519. Financial provision – agreements – effect on subsequent claims

[Matrimonial Causes Act 1973 s.25.]

W had moved from South Africa upon her marriage and had invested her capital in her ex husband's home. Following her divorce, W was reduced to a standard of living much removed from that which she had been used to, whilst her former spouse was financially secure. W appealed against a decision that the existence of an agreement for financial provision, which she had entered into upon divorce, disentitled her from any further claims. W contended that the judge had placed too much significance on the agreement and had failed to take proper account of the principles laid down in the authorities.

Held, allowing the appeal, that an agreement betwen the parties was merely one of the factors to be considered when assessing their positions according to the criteria under the Matrimonial Causes Act 1973 s.25. The judge had wrongly disregarded the proper approach elucidated in *Camm v. Camm* (1983) F.L.R. 577, [1983] C.L.Y. 1100. He had also failed to take account of other relevant considerations, including the position in which W had been left upon the dissolution of the marriage and the principles to be adopted in cases concerning short marriages, *S v. S* [1977] Fam. 127, [1976] C.L.Y. 782 applied. Having considered all those factors, a lump sum of £60,000 would be awarded to W to assist her in purchasing a house.

SMITH (LETITIA) v. SMITH (RICHARD) [2000] 3 F.C.R. 374, Thorpe, L.J., CA.

2520. Financial provision – children – court's jurisdiction to make maintenance orders for benefit of children – Mesher orders

[Matrimonial Causes Act 1973 s.23(1)(a); Child Support Act 1991 s.8(5).]

H appealed against an order made during ancillary relief proceedings that he should pay his wife £999 per month for the benefit of their three children, that sum to be reduced pro tanto by any amount arrived at by the Child Support Agency, and that his share in the matrimonial home should be transferred to W absolutely. H contended, inter alia, that (1) since there was neither consent between the parties nor a substantive entitlement to spousal maintenance, the judge had not had jurisdiction to make the order, and (2) given the financial position of each of the parties, the judge had erred in failing to give H a deferred charge over the matrimonial home.

Held, allowing the appeal, that (1) the court had no jurisdiction to make a maintenance order for the benefit of children in ancillary relief proceedings, unless it was made under the Child Support Act 1991 s.8(5) and both parties consented to it. The 1991 Act deprived courts of the jurisdiction to make discretionary decisions on the extent of a husband's duty to maintain his children. It was, however, common practice for spousal maintenance orders made under the Matrimonial Causes Act 1973 s.23(1)(a) to incorporate payments in respect of the children. These could be reduced pro tanto by any amount determined by the Child Support Agency. Importantly, it was necessary for such orders to contain a substantial amount of spousal maintenance, and (2) a Mesher order retained utility in circumstances where the assets of a family were sufficient for both parties to be rehoused if the matrimonial home was sold, and where it was in the best interests of the children that they remained in the home until their majority, *Clutton v. Clutton* [1991] 1 W.L.R. 359, [1991] C.L.Y. 1804 applied. In the instant case, given that there were sufficient assets to rehouse both parties, the judge had erred in refusing to grant a Mesher order.

DORNEY-KINGDOM v. DORNEY-KINGDOM [2000] 2 F.L.R. 855, Thorpe, L.J., CA.

2521. Financial provision – disclosure – no jurisdiction to order production appointment under Children Act 1989 Sch.1

[Children Act 1989 Sch.1; Family Proceedings Rules 1991 (SI 1991 1247) r.2.62(7).]

M and F, an unmarried couple, had a child. M applied under the Children Act 1989 Sch.1 for financial provision for the child. M was unhappy about the state of F's disclosure prior to trial and sought a production appointment against an agent of F under the Family Proceedings Rules 1991 r.2.62(7). F objected, contending that (1) r.2.62(7) applied to ancillary relief after divorce, and that Sch.1 applications were not ancillary relief applications, and (2) r.4.14 referred to the directions that could be made under Sch.1 and a production appointment did not feature among those directions.

Held, refusing the application, that there was no jurisdiction to make an order for a production appointment. M would have to rely on a subpoena duces tecum. It was noted, however, that production appointments were useful additional tools in the preparation of cases for trial, and that the present position was unsatisfactory. The point would be referred to the rules committee.

B v. H, May 11, 2000, District Judge Bradley, Fam Div. [*Ex rel.* DA Pears, Barrister, Francis Taylor Building, Temple, London].

2522. Financial provision – evidence required for hearing

[Matrimonial Causes Act 1973 s.25.]

Held, that in divorce cases, where financial dispute resolution had failed and it was necessary for the case to proceed to a substantive hearing, evidence with regard to the parties' financial circumstances should be broadened to include information about the financial situation of the couple during the marriage and details of their present individual financial circumstances, particularly where there was greater wealth involved. Directions for the provision of narrative affidavits would enable the court to properly consider all aspects and the financial history of the case before them as required by the Matrimonial Causes Act 1973 s.25

W v. W (ANCILLARY RELIEF: PRACTICE) [2000] Fam. Law 473, Wilson, J., Fam Div.

2523. Financial provision – hearings – recorder reserving hearing to himself

[Matrimonial Causes Act 1973 s.25.]

After commencing divorce proceedings, H applied for an occupation order relating to the matrimonial home. The recorder granted the order and directed that H's application for ancillary relief should be reserved to himself. At the hearing W argued that H, who had been made bankrupt and who had been sentenced to a term of imprisonment for handling stolen goods, should receive nothing from the matrimonial assets. The recorder, however, accepted H's arguments and made an order providing for the sale of the matrimonial home and an equal division of the proceeds of sale. W appealed.

Held, allowing the appeal, that the recorder had erred by (1) failing to consider systematically the factors set out in the Matrimonial Causes Act 1973 s.25, most notably the conduct of the parties, which had been the principal issue in the case, and (2) reserving the application to himself, thereby circumventing the arrangements in the county court which were aimed at ensuring that such applications were determined by someone with the necessary skill and experience. It followed that the application would have to be retried.

COOPER v. KAUR [2001] 1 F.C.R. 12, Thorpe, L.J., CA.

2524. Financial provision – homosexual couple – discriminatory legislation

See HUMAN RIGHTS: Attorney General for Ontario v. M. §3254

2525. Financial provision – lump sum payments – Duxbury calculations inappropriate in case of elderly couple

H and W had married in 1955 and at the time of the divorce were aged 79 and 76 respectively. Although the judge found that both parties had made a full contribution throughout the marriage it was also found that W's business had become so successful that her assets, totalling £1.034 million, far exceeded those of H, which amounted to £61,000. The judge ordered W to pay H a lump sum of £389,000 to enable him to purchase a house and to provide him with an income of £16,000 per year while leaving the income producing fund intact. W appealed on the ground that sufficient income could be produced by a quasi Duxbury fund of £87,000 having regard to H's age and requirements so that the lump sum awarded should be reduced to £226,000.

Held, that the judge had erred in assuming that the income producing fund would remain intact and be used solely to produce income, that the attributable income was five per cent gross, that inflation and tax changes should be ignored and that H's reasonable needs would remain at £16,000 per year, *Preston v. Preston* [1982] Fam. 17, [1981] C.L.Y. 714 followed. There was a real possibility that H, having reached the age of 79, would live longer than the life expectancy tables used in a Duxbury calculation so that Duxbury principles would not assist at all. The lump sum was reduced to £350,000.

A v. A (DUXBURY CALCULATIONS); *sub nom.* A v. A (ELDERLY APPLICANT: LUMP SUM) [1999] 2 F.L.R. 969, Singer, J., Fam Div.

2526. Financial provision – lump sum payments – effect of maintenance arrears

H and W separated in August 1995 after a childless marriage of almost 10 years. H petitioned for divorce in April 1996 and decree absolute was pronounced in October 1996. Both parties were professional in background but W had been wholly dependent on H from the outset of the marriage due to a continuing back injury. Upon separation H began to dispose of his assets and capital so as to reduce or extinguish his liabilities to W. An interim periodical payments order was made in W's favour, against which H appealed and which he did not pay. The court of first instance set aside transfers of cash totalling £95,506.62 to H's uncle. The court also ordered H to make periodical payments of £14,400 per year net, to repay immediately the arrears then outstanding, and to pay W a lump sum of £82,500. H appealed, arguing that (1) as no application to set aside the transfers of his funds had been made, the judge had been wrong to set aside those dispositions; (2) the judge had erred in taking his conduct into account when calculating the lump sum payable to W, the relevant calculation being inaccurate in any event; (3) in ordering payment of all the arrears, the judge had taken no account of the fact that some of the arrears were more than 12 months' old, and (4) in quantifying the periodical payments, the judge ought not to have accepted W's budget and should have made a periodical payments order expiring after three to five years so as to encourage W to earn her own living.

Held, allowing the appeal to a limited extent, that (1) it had not been necessary to set aside the transfers of H's funds since ownership of those funds remained with H; (2) the dominant criterion for the determination of the lump sum was not H's conduct but W's need for housing. The starting point of the calculation was to see how much capital was available to each party. The lump sum was reduced to £65,000 in recognition of the extent to which W's own deposit account would be restored by the enforcement in full of the maintenance arrears; (3) the judge had been entitled to enforce maintenance arrears beyond the conventional period of 12 months because H's defiance of the maintenance order had been flagrant and W had had to rely upon her nest egg whilst H had enjoyed a substantial salary which exceeded his own needs, and (4) the judge had made a realistic overall assessment of W's ability to work and had considered the appropriate proportion of H's income that should be used to support her. She had established a total dependency on him and it had been appropriate to make a periodical payments order which was not limited in duration.

PURBA v. PURBA [2000] 1 F.L.R. 444, Thorpe, L.J., CA.

2527. Financial provision – maintenance orders – cessation on cohabitation – evidence of cohabitation

[Social Security Contributions and Benefits Act 1992.]

H and W were divorced in December 1998. By consent, it was ordered that H would pay £1000 per month until W either remarried or cohabited for more than three months. L moved into W's bed and breakfast establishment in December 1998 and they became engaged. In January 1999 W went to America with L to meet his family, following which L returned to the United Kingdom on March 5, 1999 and continued to live with W. On April 20, 1999 H told W that he would stop the payments because of her cohabitation. W arranged for L to become the tenant of a friend, but he spent some nights with her, helped with the business, and took part in the upbringing of W's dependent child. W denied cohabitation and sued for arrears of six months' maintenance.

Held, that although a complete list of factors indicative of cohabitation could not be given, the Social Security Contributions and Benefits Act 1992 and the authorities indicated that it was relevant that W and L were living in the same household save for the arrangement brought about by H's warning and had an established and continuing sexual relationship. The stability of the relationship was evidenced by their financial arrangements. Further, L had a close bond with W's child. The motive for W's arrangements and the denial of her engagement to L was her desire to continue to receive maintenance. On the facts, a reasonable person would have considered L and W to be cohabiting. However, as the evidence showed that the cohabitation had commenced only at the beginning of March 1999, H had stopped payments one month early and so was liable to pay W £1000 under the terms of the consent order.

KIMBER v. KIMBER; *sub nom*. K v. K (ENFORCEMENT) [2000] 1 F.L.R. 383, Judge Tyrer, Fam Div.

2528. Financial provision – maintenance orders – maintenance pending suit – provision for legal fees

[Matrimonial Causes Act 1973 s.22.]

A wife, W, whose legal aid certificate had been discharged following the making of a maintenance order pending suit and whose unpaid legal costs amounted to some £40,000, made an interlocutory application for the maintenance payments to include a specific sum for the payment of her legal fees. W, who had no independent means and was dependent upon her husband, H, who had considerable assets, submitted that she had no means at her disposal to pay her mounting legal fees.

Held, granting the application, that maintenance payments covered recurring living expenses of an income nature which could include legal fees incurred in the course of litigation. Such payments were not restricted to daily living expenses in a literal sense, *Dennis (Deceased), Re* [1981] 2 All E.R. 140, [1981] C.L.Y. 2887 and *Espinosa v. Bourke* [1999] 1 F.L.R. 747, [1999] C.L.Y. 4639 considered. The Matrimonial Causes Act 1973 s.22 empowered the court, when ordering maintenance pending suit, to include an element towards the payee's legal costs of the suit. In the instant case, W had no other means of meeting her legal fees, and the payment of those fees was her most pressing need, comparable to her need for food and shelter.

A v. A (MAINTENANCE PENDING SUIT: PROVISION FOR LEGAL FEES); *sub nom*. A v. A (MAINTENANCE PENDING SUIT: PROVISION FOR LEGAL COSTS) [2001] 1 W.L.R. 605, Holman, J., Fam Div.

2529. Financial provision – Mareva injunctions – court's inherent jurisdiction

[Matrimonial Causes Act 1973 s.37; Supreme Court Act 1981 s.37; Matrimonial and Family Proceedings Act 1984 Part III.]

K and KH, husband and wife respectively, had their marriage dissolved in Jordan and entered into a separation agreement. K subsequently sought to abandon the terms of the agreement by pleading poverty, although he had put a London property on the market, which was allegedly owned by an off shore bearer share company, with an asking price of £2.25 million. KH obtained a Mareva injunction and applied to vary the separation agreement and for leave to bring proceedings under the Matrimonial and Family Proceedings Act 1984 Part III, since he was unable to bring proceedings under the Matrimonial Causes Act 1973. K sought permission to appeal against the injunction, contending that the effect of the decision in *Richards v. Richards* [1984] A.C. 174, [1983] C.L.Y. 1861 coupled with the existence of the statutory jurisdiction to restrain the anticipatory disposition of assets under s.37 of the 1973 Act, meant that the court no longer had any inherent jurisdiction under the Supreme Court Act 1981 s.37 or otherwise.

Held, refusing permission to appeal, that there was clear House of Lords authority in *Harrow LBC v. Johnstone* [1997] 1 W.L.R. 459, [1997] C.L.Y. 2703 that the court retained its inherent jurisdiction to make orders to protect financial and proprietary remedies in order to protect one spouse from unscrupulous dealing on the part of the other, even if the conditions of s.37 of the 1981 Act were not satisfied.

KHREINO v. KHREINO (NO.2) [2000] 1 F.C.R. 80, Thorpe, L.J., CA.

2530. Financial provision – matrimonial property – guidance given by House of Lords on division of matrimonial assets

[Matrimonial Causes Act 1973 s.25.]

A divorced couple, who had been deemed by the court to have been equal partners in a lucrative farming enterprise throughout their 33-year marriage, appealed against the decisions made on their respective applications for ancillary relief ([1999] Fam. 304, [1998] C.L.Y. 2447), which had resulted in W receiving approximately 40 per cent of the total available property. The applications had proceeded on a "clean break" basis, since the offspring were adult and no longer dependent. H submitted that the award was excessive because it represented far more than W's "financial needs" within the meaning of the Matrimonial Causes Act 1973 s.25, even if those words were to be given the benefit of a liberal interpretation and called "reasonable requirements". He contended for adherence to the approach enunciated in *Dart v. Dart* [1996] 2 F.L.R. 286, [1996] C.L.Y. 2858 and maintained that the court had wrongly exercised its discretionary powers. W cross appealed, arguing that the pool of resources ought to have been divided equally, notwithstanding the fact that H's father had made a significant financial contribution to the farming business early in the marriage.

Held, dismissing the appeal and the cross appeal, that although there should be no presumption of equal division, equality should not be departed from unless there were good reasons for doing so. In order to reach a fair decision, the court had to consider the facts of each case, but a judge would be well advised to check his tentative views against the yardstick of equal division before reaching a conclusion. Furthermore, the parties' financial needs were not to be regarded as determinative; instead, they were merely one of the factors to be taken into account. There were no grounds for disturbing the decision of the Court of Appeal. The couple, by their joint input throughout the marriage, had built up a valuable business partnership; whereas W had taken primary responsibility for the family and the home, H had concentrated on the business. Where the assets exceeded the financial needs of both parties, there was no justification for confining W's share to her actual needs, with H, who had similar needs, being permitted to keep any surplus of assets. Appropriate weight was to be given in the instant case to the contribution made by H's father to the business and to W's wish to be able to make provision in her will for her children.

WHITE (PAMELA) v. WHITE (MARTIN) [2001] 1 A.C. 596, Lord Nicholls of Birkenhead, HL.

2531. Financial provision – receivers – receiver appointed over foreign income paid in England

A husband and wife, H and W, divorced after a short marriage. They had one child. An application for ancillary relief was decided in 1991 and there was a subsequent order for periodical payments to be made by H for the child and provision for the payment by H of private school fees. H was resident abroad and the majority of his assets were held by family trusts or foreign companies. H's true financial position was unclear. H fell into arrears with the payments. W applied to increase the payments and there was a cross application by H to remit the arrears and reduce the payments. H then ceased making payments altogether and indicated that he would not be participating in the pending proceedings. H had no assets in England and the English bank account through which he had paid the periodical payments was no longer in existence. However, H was in receipt of an annuity from an Italian company, which was paid through the company's branch office in London. W applied ex parte for the appointment of her solicitor as receiver of the annuity payments.

Held, granting the application, that W's solicitor was to be appointed receiver of the annuity payments pending further consideration of the issues by the court.

D v. A, May 11, 2000, District Judge Bradley, Fam Div. [*Ex rel.* DA Pears, Barrister, Francis Taylor Building, Temple, London].

2532. Financial provision – separation agreements – weight accorded to agreement on divorce

A couple met when the husband, H, was 54 and the wife, W, was 35. Both had children from previous marriages. When they married, H was already wealthy, with assets exceeding £4 million, and W had an interest in a property and an annual income of £10,000. Prior to the marriage, H and W signed a deed drawn up by H's solicitor which, although wrongly stating that H and W had received independent advice, made provision for W as to the cost of secondary education for her children, household expenses and capital for her to purchase a house equivalent in value to the house which she had owned before the marriage. H and W separated four years after the marriage and a separation agreement was drawn up. A property worth £250,000 had already been purchased for W and the agreement provided for her to receive a regular income, calculated on the basis of the ages of the children of the marriage residing with her and their educational status. Throughout the litigation, both H and W sought to set aside the agreement and by the time of the hearing outstanding questions remained as to the status of the agreement, whether the periodical payments ought to be varied to a lump sum and W's maintenance eligibility, based on the length of the marriage.

Held, that the separation agreement was persuasive in nature given the conduct of H and W in the periods before and after its execution. The agreement, therefore, formed the basis for the order, but finality was required. A lump sum of £240,000 would be substituted for the payments provided for under the separation agreement, calculated to take H's generosity in buying the property for W into account.

G v. G (FINANCIAL PROVISION: SEPARATION AGREEMENT) [2000] 2 F.L.R. 18, Connell, J., Fam Div.

2533. Financial provisions – periodical payments – court's jurisdiction to vary or extend expired order

[Matrimonial Causes Act 1973 s.31 (1).]

H and W's marriage was dissolved in 1992 and a consent order was entered into providing for periodical payments to be made by H to W until 1998, when it was expected that W would be earning for herself. Four days before the expiry of the order, W applied for an extension and variation of the periodical payments order, and the judge ruled in her favour. H appealed and the court held that it did not have jurisdiction to vary the order pursuant to the Matrimonial Causes Act 1973 s.31, since the period referred to in the consent order had expired. W appealed, contending that the judge had erred in law.

Held, allowing the appeal, that a court had the jurisdiction to extend or vary an expired order on condition that the application citing the court's statutory power had been issued during the period referred to in the original order. *Richardson v. Richardson (No.2)* [1996] 2 F.L.R. 617, [1997] C.L.Y. 2477 followed and *G v. G (Periodical Payments: Jurisdiction to Vary)* [1998] Fam. 1, [1997] C.L.Y. 2489 disapproved.

JONES v. JONES (PERIODICAL PAYMENTS) [2001] Fam. 96, Dame Elizabeth Butler-Sloss (President), CA.

2534. Fostering – convictions – effect of foster parent's conviction for indecent assault

[Offences Against the Person Act 1861 s.62; Children and Young Persons Act 1933 Sch.1; Sexual Offences Act 1956 s.15; Foster Placement (Children) Regulations 1991 (SI 1991 910) Reg.3(4A).]

Two children, C, aged 13, and K, aged 11, had been cared for by their maternal grandmother, G, and her partner, N, since 1991 under care orders. G and N were approved as foster parents in 1994, despite the fact that N had convictions for indecent assault on a boy in 1954 under the Offences Against the Person Act 1861 s.62, and buggery with an adult in 1973. When it became apparent that the children's mother, M, was considering applying for a residence order, G made applications (1) for a decision that the Foster Placement (Children) Regulations 1991 Reg.3(4A) did not apply to the convictions so as to prohibit N from being a foster carer on the ground that the offence under s.62 of the 1861 Act was a specified offence under the Children and Young Persons Act 1933 Sch.1, and (2) for a direction that the details of the conviction should not be disclosed to M as she might pass the information around the community. M was not present at the hearing but instructed her representatives to receive the information on a "lawyer only" basis.

Held, refusing the applications, that (1) the 1991 Regulations applied. Although the Sexual Offences Act 1956 had repealed s.62 of the 1861 Act and removed it from Sch.1 to the 1933 Act, it had been replaced by s.15 of the 1956 Act. As s.62 of the 1861 Act and s.15 of the 1956 Act were essentially the same, and in order to avoid a loophole that could not have been intended by Parliament, both Sch.1 to the 1933 Act and the 1991 Regulation, had to be construed as including offences under both Acts, and (2) G had not shown that there was a real possibility, as opposed to a mere likelihood, that M would spread the information inappropriately and risk harm to the children, *D (Minors) (Adoption Reports: Confidentiality), Re* [1996] A.C. 593, [1996] C.L.Y. 474 applied. M was prepared to give an undertaking that she would not do so, and it was in the best interests of the children that she should be able to play an active and fully informed role in decision making for the children's future.

S (CHILDREN) (FOSTER PLACEMENT: REGULATIONS 1991), *Re* [2000] 1 F.L.R. 648, Bodey, J., Fam Div.

2535. Fostering – newspapers – disclosure of local authority's fostering policy

[Human Rights Act 1998 s.12(4), Sch.1 Part I Art.10.1, Sch.1 Part I Art.10.2.]

A, a newspaper publisher, applied for an order to vary an injunction granted to the local authority which restrained foster parents from disclosing to the newspaper information concerning the local authority's policies in respect of transracial fostering. A contended that the welfare of the child was not the paramount consideration and that the court was not required to conduct a balancing exercise when considering how to exercise its discretion, but was instead obliged, pursuant to the Human Rights Act 1998 Sch.1 Part I Art.10.1, to give priority to a newspaper's right to publish information which was in the public interest. A contended that there was a legitimate public interest in the disclosure of the information and that the restrictions on publication did not fall within the derogations set out in Art.10.2.

Held, granting the application, that the injunction was too wide and was varied accordingly, although the identity of the social workers involved was not permitted to be published. In the instant case the welfare of the child was not the paramount consideration and therefore the court was able to consider whether it was appropriate to permit the disclosure of the information, *M and N (Minors), Re* [1990] Fam. 211, [1990] C.L.Y. 3190 and *Z (A Minor) (Freedom of Publication), Re* [1997] Fam. 1, [1996] C.L.Y. 547 considered. In considering whether to grant an injunction to prevent the publication of information, the court was obliged to have paramount regard to the right of a newspaper to publish information contained in Art.10 unless one of the derogations applied. An exception would not apply unless there was a pressing social need, proportionality and sufficient evidence to show that there should not be publication. There was insufficient evidence to enable the court to find that any of the derogations applied and there was a legitimate public interest in the disclosure of the information, in accordance with the s.12(4).

RICHMOND UPON THAMES LBC v. H; *sub nom.* X (A CHILD) (INJUNCTIONS RESTRAINING PUBLICATION), *Re* [2001] 1 F.C.R. 541, Bracewell, J., Fam. Div.

2536. Maintenance orders – enforcement facilities – unification and renaming of stipendiary bench

MAINTENANCE ORDERS (FACILITIES FOR ENFORCEMENT) (AMENDMENT) RULES 2000, SI 2000 1875; made under the Magistrates' Courts Act 1980 s.144. In force: in accordance with r.1; £1.00.

These Rules amend the Maintenance Orders (Facilities for Enforcement) Rules 1922 (SR & O 1922 1355) to take account of the coming into force of the Access to Justice Act 1999 s.74 and s.75, which modify the territorial organisation of magistrates and magistrates' courts, and s.78 and Sch.11, which unify and rename the stipendiary bench.

2537. Marriage – immigration purposes – reporting procedure

REPORTING OF SUSPICIOUS MARRIAGES AND REGISTRATION OF MARRIAGES (MISCELLANEOUS AMENDMENTS) REGULATIONS 2000, SI 2000 3164; made under the Marriage Act 1949 s.27, s.27B, s.31, s.74; the Registration Service Act 1953 s.20; and the Immigration and Asylum Act 1999 s.24. In force: January 1, 2001; £3.00.

These Regulations, which set out the procedure for reporting certain marriages to the Secretary of State where it is suspected that the marriage is to be or has been entered into for immigration purposes, amend the Marriage (Authorised Persons) Regulations 1952 (SI 1952 1869), the Registration of Marriages Regulations 1986 (SI 1986 1442) and the Registration of Marriages (Welsh Language) Regulations 1999 (SI 1999 1621) respectively to reflect amendments made to the Marriage Act 1949 by the Immigration and Asylum Act 1999. In particular, they remove references to marriage by certificate and licence and omit the relevant forms for this. In addition, they insert a new regulation which sets out the procedure for making an application to the Registrar General to reduce the 15-day waiting period imposed under the Marriage Act 1949 s.31, as amended, for all marriages which are to be solemnized on the authority of certificates issued by a superintendent registrar and they insert a new form 8A into Sch.1 to those Regulations and the Welsh Regulations for that purpose.

2538. Marriage – nullity – physical inter-sex – consideration of psychological and hormonal factors

H did not contest W's divorce petition but sought a decree of nullity during ancillary relief proceedings. H contended that the marriage was void because W was not a woman but a physical inter-sex.

Held, refusing the application, that where the gonadal, chromosomal and genital tests gave differing results, the biological test was inadequate so that additional developmental, psychological, and hormonal factors together with the secondary sexual characteristics could be considered, *Corbett v. Corbett (otherwise Ashley) (No.1)* [1971] P. 83, [1970] C.L.Y. 808 distinguished. W had been registered as a boy at birth on the basis of chromosomal and gonadal evidence and a diagnosis of partial androgen insensitivity together with evidence of her ambiguous genitalia showed that W was not a transsexual but a physical inter-sex. From the time when W had been able to choose her sexuality she had lived as a woman and had undergone gender reassignment surgery which had allowed the marriage to be consummated and that was sufficient to demonstrate that W was a woman for the purposes of the marriage.

W v. W (NULLITY: GENDER); *sub nom.* W v. W (PHYSICAL INTER-SEX) [2001] Fam. 111, Charles, J., Fam. Div.

2539. Marriage – transsexualism – legal gender at time of marriage

B, the female partner in a marriage, petitioned the court for a declaration that her marriage was valid. B had been born genetically male but had undergone gender re-assignment prior to her marriage to become female. B contended that the law in its present state was not in keeping with the social and medical advances that had been made in recent years.

Held, refusing the application, that the court was not the forum for the introduction of the legal reform. The law in its present state clearly determined that the marriage would only be valid if B's sex had been female at the time of birth, *Corbett v. Corbett (otherwise Ashley) (No.1)* [1971] P. 83, [1970] C.L.Y. 808. Any change in the law was a matter for the legislature.

B v. B (VALIDITY OF MARRIAGE: TRANSSEXUAL) [2001] 1 F.L.R. 389, Johnson, J., Fam Div.

2540. Matrimonial home – occupation orders – application by divorced father – mother proposing sale

[Family Law Act 1996 s.33, s.35.]

H and W were divorced in 1994. They had two children, N, a boy aged 17, and a girl, S, who was aged 15 at the time of trial. The couple had a matrimonial home in London. No ancillary relief application was made at the time of the divorce, but the parties agreed that W would remain in the London home with the children so that they could complete their education. H moved to Kuala Lumpur. H contended that he had a beneficial interest in the London home by virtue of his contributions. While N and S were visiting H in Kuala Lumpur in July 1999, W announced that she was leaving the matrimonial home and moving to Somerset. N refused to move with W. On her return to the UK, S was collected by another relative and taken to the country, while N was left with nowhere to go until he was taken in by H's sister. H obtained an order preventing the sale of the former matrimonial home or a disposal of the proceeds and applied for an order under the Family Law Act 1996 s.33 permitting him to occupy the home with N.

Held, granting the application, that the application was to proceed by way of s.35 given the lack of evidence as to H's beneficial interest. Under s.35(6) the housing needs and resources of the parties had to be considered. The effect on the parties' health and well being, their conduct and the length of separation also had to be taken into account. On the facts, H's financial position was more precarious than that of W. On balance, therefore, the order sought by H would provide greater security in comparison to W's short term inconvenience. Furthermore, in relation to conduct, W was responsible in part for the situation. Therefore, H would be permitted to return to the property for six months or until ancillary matters as to the discharge of the mortgage were resolved, with leave being given to W to apply to discharge the order if H failed to comply with his undertaking to pay the mortgage.

S v. F (OCCUPATION ORDER) [2000] 1 F.L.R. 255, Judge Cryan, Fam Div.

2541. Non molestation orders – breach – appropriate sentence length

[Criminal Justice Act 1991 s.1, s.2, s.3; Criminal Justice and Public Order Act 1994 s.48.]

T appealed against the imposition of a suspended sentence of six months' imprisonment following her admitted breach of a non molestation order made in relation to her ex-boyfriend, H. Under the order T was restricted from intimidating, harassing or pestering H. T, who had not been present when the order was made, had subsequently harassed H and his new partner, M, by making repeated threatening and abusive telephone calls. She was arrested, under the power attached to the order, at the conclusion of proceedings brought against her by M relating to complaints of harassment. T contended, amongst other things, that the sentence was manifestly excessive given her early admission of the breach. Such admission, she argued, should have been treated as equivalent to an early guilty plea in criminal cases and accordingly the court should have followed the principles contained in the Criminal Justice and Public Order Act 1994 s.48 and, by analogy, the aims of the Criminal Justice Act 1991 s.1, s.2 and s.3.

Held, allowing the appeal and imposing a sentence of 28 days' imprisonment suspended for the full duration of the non molestation order, that there were no grounds for concluding as a general rule that the statutory provisions in respect of sentencing in criminal proceedings should be followed in proceedings for contempt. The court should have regard to the fact that cases relating to contempt of court could only come before the court on an application to commit. While committal to prison would not always result from any breach, the fact that a person had breached an order for the first time did not preclude his or her committal to prison, *Thorpe v. Thorpe* [1998] 2 F.L.R. 127, [1998] C.L.Y. 1161 considered. The objective of contempt of court proceedings was to mark the court's disapproval of a breach and to secure compliance with the relevant order in the future. It was, in most circumstances, good practice for the court to set out brief reasons for its decision in any specific case. In the instant case, given that T (a) had immediately admitted the breach, which was, furthermore, her first; (b) had not had the benefit of a warning about the consequences of any breach since she had not been present in court when the order was made, and (c) was the mother of a young child, the sentence of six months' imprisonment had been manifestly excessive.

HALE v. TANNER (PRACTICE NOTE) [2000] 1 W.L.R. 2377, Hale, L.J., CA.

2542. Non molestation orders – cohabitation – jurisdiction – statutory provisions purposively construed so as to include borderline cases

[Family Law Act 1996 s.42, s.62(3).]

The Family Proceedings Court refused to hear an application for a non molestation order pursuant to the Family Law Act 1996 s.42 on the basis that the parties were not "associated persons" within the meaning of s.62(3)(b) or (c) of the Act. The applicant appealed on the grounds that the justices had misdirected themselves in that they had made findings against the weight of the evidence and had refused to hear oral evidence from the applicant in relation to cohabitation.

Held, allowing the appeal and remitting the case for rehearing, that the justices had misdirected themselves in that they had (1) considered s.62(3)(c) of the Act first and, having found that the parties did not live in the same house, had precluded themselves from determining whether or not the parties were cohabitants within the meaning of s.62(3)(b), and (2) failed to address the main thrust of the respondent's statement which provided evidence of cohabitation against interest, and had refused to hear oral evidence from the applicant for clarification on the point. In cases of domestic violence there should be a purposive construction of s.62(3) and courts should not decline jurisdiction unless, on the facts, the case was clearly incapable of being brought within the statutory framework, *Crake v. Supplementary Benefits Commission* [1982] 1 All E.R. 498, [1982] C.L.Y. 3035, followed.

G v. F (NON MOLESTATION ORDER: JURISDICTION); *sub nom.* G v. G (NON MOLESTATION ORDER: JURISDICTION) [2000] Fam. 186, Wall, J., Fam Div.

2543. Non molestation orders – contempt of court – repeated breaches by son terrorising mother

M, who was aged 21 at the time of the appeal, had been taken into care at the age of six and had not seen his mother, R, between the age of eight and the time when he came out of care. On his release from care, M repeatedly molested and terrorised R, causing her to attempt suicide. Non molestation orders were made but M disregarded them. The police attended on a number of occasions but no substantive penalty was imposed. In January 2000, however, three breaches of the injunctions were proved in court, the first relating to an incident in November 1999 and the other two to an incident in December 1999. M was sentenced to three months' imprisonment for the first incident and to two consecutive six month terms, to run concurrently, for the latter. M appealed, contending that the earlier breach had been proved in error and that the consecutive six month terms were excessive, given the absence of violence or threats of violence.

Held, allowing the appeal in part, that the sentence for the November 1999 breach would be quashed as it had been proved in error. However, despite there having been no violence on the occasion of the other two breaches, M's conduct had seriously terrorised R. Taken together with the continuing contempt of court, those breaches justified a total of six months' imprisonment.

RAFIQ v. MUSE [2000] 1 F.L.R. 820, Ward, L.J., CA.

2544. Non molestation orders – time – indefinite nature of order justified

[Family Law Act 1996 s.42(5), s.47(2).]

The father of a child, BJ, appealed against the making of a non molestation order. The parents, who had been unmarried, separated in 1995. In 1999, the father applied for a parental responsibility order. The judge, finding a background of various incidents between the parents, granted the order and in addition made a non molestation order. The non molestation order was made for an indefinite period and had a power of arrest attached to it for a period of two years as provided for under the Family Law Act 1996 s.47(2). The father placed reliance on *M v. W (Non Molestation Order: Duration)* [2000] 1 F.L.R. 107, [2000] C.L.Y. 2545, contending that the nature of a non molestation order was such that it was designed to give the parties space in which to settle down and should only be made for a specific period of time unless unusual circumstances dictated otherwise. He maintained that it was perverse for the duration of the power of arrest to be shorter than the duration of the order to which it was attached.

Held, dismissing the appeal, that non molestation orders were designed for a range of purposes and were intended to be flexible, *M v. W* overruled. It was not beneficial for the courts to be required to distinguish exceptional circumstances. The duration of a power of arrest did not have to mirror the duration of the non molestation order. In the instant case the order had been made for the benefit of the child and the mother in compliance with s.42(5) of the Act, and its indefinite nature had been justified owing to the relationship between the parents.

B-J (A CHILD) (NON MOLESTATION ORDER: POWER OF ARREST) [2001] 2 W.L.R. 1660, Hale, L.J., CA.

2545. Non molestation orders – time – length of order

[Family Law Act 1996.]

M, the father, unsuccessfully sought to discharge a non molestation order made "till further order" and appealed.

Held, allowing the appeal, that the object of non molestation orders was to give the parties a breathing space, and orders should be for a specified period of time unless there existed exceptional or unusual circumstances. The family proceedings court in this case had been wrong to state that case law decided prior to the Family Law Act 1996 had no relevance to the case. Earlier decisions could certainly help to indicate what would be the appropriate length of an order. The court should have made a finite order and, accordingly, an order would be made extending the non molestation order to a specified date.

M v. W (NON-MOLESTATION ORDER: DURATION) [2000] 1 F.L.R. 107, Cazalet, J., Fam Div.

2546. Occupation orders – enforcement – no power to enforce orders for payment of outgoings

[Debtors Act 1869 s.4; Administration of Justice Act 1970 Sch.8; Family Law Act 1996 s.40.]

H and W married in 1992 and had two children aged five and three. In 1998 W obtained an occupation order against H. In March 1999 an order was made under the Family Law Act 1996 s.40(1) requiring H to pay a monthly sum to the local housing association in respect of rent and a number of other specified outgoings. Following his failure to comply with that order, W sought his committal to prison for contempt of court. The judge, finding that an order under s.40 fell neither within the exceptions to the Debtors Act 1869 s.4 nor within the Administration of Justice Act 1970 Sch.8, dismissed W's application. W appealed, contending that Parliament must have intended that an order to pay money was to be enforced in the same way as the occupation order to which it was linked.

Held, dismissing the appeal, that while the court had the power under s.40 of the 1996 Act, when making an occupation order, to require a person to make payments in relation to rent and other outgoings on a property, there was no power to enforce such an order. Section 40 could not be interpreted as implying a partial repeal of s.4 of the 1869 Act which limited the circumstances under which a debtor could be imprisoned. It was observed that in the absence of a power of enforcement, s.40 was of no value to a spouse or cohabitee who remained in occupation of a property. Such an omission needed to be addressed by Parliament.

NWOGBE v. NWOGBE [2000] 2 F.L.R. 744, Robert Walker, L.J., CA.

2547. Occupation orders – family divided into two warring camps – eviction of wife sought

[Family Law Act 1996 s.33(6), s.33(7); Housing Act 1996.]

H and W occupied the matrimonial home with their two children, R, who was 16 and expecting a child of her own, and J, who was 13. Disputes between the parties resulted in H applying for a non molestation order and an occupation order. By the time that the latter application came to be heard, the parties had given undertakings not to molest each other. In determining H's application for an occupation order, the recorder found that the family had become divided into two camps, with H and J in one and W and R in the other, and that an extremely tense atmosphere had existed in the home for several years, particularly between H and R. Having concluded that greater harm would be caused by maintaining the status quo than by not doing so, and that the local authority would be able to house W and R more easily than it would H and J, the recorder ordered W to vacate the home. W appealed arguing that the recorder had misapplied the Family Law Act 1996 s.33(7).

Held, allowing the appeal, that the recorder had erred in finding that s.33(7) had been applicable. In order for that provision to apply, the court had to be satisfied, inter alia, that the applicant or a relevant child would be likely to suffer "significant harm attributable to the conduct of the respondent" if an occupation order was not made. Although H had been registered as disabled, there had been no finding that either he or J was likely to suffer significant harm. What was more, the recorder had made no finding that any harm suffered by H had been attributable to the conduct of W. The behaviour of W, who had been guilty of no more than failing to control R in her hostility towards H, had been no worse than H's own behaviour. Furthermore, the recorder had failed to deal with the harm likely to be caused to R, who had been faced with the choice of either remaining in the home with a parent who disliked her, or being accommodated by the local authority at a time when she was in an advanced state of pregnancy. As far as the parties' rehousing prospects were concerned, H, with his disability, was more likely than W to receive assistance from the local authority under the homelessness provisions of the Housing Act 1996. In the circumstances, it was necessary for the court to exercise its discretion under s.33(6) of the Family Law Act. In doing so, it had to be borne in mind that the eviction of one co owner from the matrimonial home was a draconian remedy and one of last resort. Taking into account the relevant considerations, in particular the fact that the parties could be accommodated in the matrimonial home until the determination of a pending application for ancillary relief, and the fact that the undertakings which the parties had given had proved effective, it was appropriate to dismiss the occupation order.

Y (CHILDREN) (OCCUPATION ORDER), *Re; sub nom.* Y (CHILDREN) (MATRIMONIAL HOME: VACATION), *Re* [2000] 2 F.C.R. 470, Ward, L.J., CA.

2548. Occupation orders – intention – conduct of former spouse sharing home

[Family Law Act 1996 s.33(6), s.33(7).]

H and W were married with two teenage children. W commenced divorce proceedings, but H and W continued to live in the same house. There was a tense atmosphere, largely attributed to H's conduct and W applied for an occupation order under the Family Act 1996 s.33. The judge at first instance, having found that the children had suffered harm because of the tension, held however that H's conduct was unintentional so that the ensuing harm was not attributable to him. The s.33 application was therefore dismissed and a direction made for a final hearing of W's application for residence orders and ancillary relief. W appealed.

Held, dismissing the appeal, that an occupation order was to be made under s.33(7) if it was found to be likely that either the applicant or a relevant child would suffer significant harm because of the alleged conduct, unless making the order would cause even greater harm. In considering the likelihood of harm, intention was immaterial as the important factor was the effect of the relevant conduct. Even if an order was not made as a mandatory step under s.33(7), the court still had a discretion under s.33(6) to make an order. The judge below had erred in focusing on H's intentions, but his conclusions would be upheld. There was no violence in the instant case and the direction for a final hearing meant that the outstanding issues between the parties would soon be determined.

G v. G (OCCUPATION ORDER: CONDUCT) [2000] 2 F.L.R. 36, Thorpe, L.J., CA.

2549. Practice directions – arrest – breach of non molestation or occupation order – need for arresting officer's attendance when arrested person brought before judge within 24 hours of arrest dispensed with

The President of the Family Division issued a Practice Direction dealing with the requirement for the attendance of the arresting officer when a person arrested under a power of arrest for breach of a non molestation or occupation order was brought before a judge or magistrate within 24 hours of arrest. Attendance of the arresting officer was not required, except where the arrest itself was in issue. Where the arresting officer was also a witness to events prior to the arrest, attendance could be arranged for subsequent hearings.

PRACTICE DIRECTION (FAM DIV: ARRESTING OFFICER: ATTENDANCE); *sub nom.* PRESIDENT'S DIRECTION (FAMILY LAW ACT 1996: ATTENDANCE OF ARRESTING OFFICER) [2000] 1 W.L.R. 83, Dame Elizabeth Butler-Sloss, Fam Div.

2550. Practice directions – case management – contents of court bundles for use in family proceedings

The President of the Family Division issued a Practice Direction replacing *Practice Direction (Family Proceedings: Case Management)* [1995] 1 W.L.R. 332, [1995] C.L.Y. 2296 para.5 and para.8 on the nature and organisation of court bundles for use in family proceedings in the High Court and the Royal Courts of Justice with effect from May 2, 2000. Bundles should be paginated and indexed and should contain all and only relevant documents in chronological order within separate sections for applications and orders; statements and affidavits; expert and other reports; and miscellaneous documents. Bundles should be agreed, if possible, and should include a summary, a statement of issues, a chronology and skeleton arguments together with copies of all authorities to be cited. The bundles should be clearly marked with the case title and number and the judge's name, if known, and should be lodged two clear days prior to the hearing.

PRACTICE DIRECTION (FAM DIV: FAMILY PROCEEDINGS: COURT BUNDLES) [2000] 1 W.L.R. 737, Dame Elizabeth Butler-Sloss (President), Fam Div.

2551. Practice directions – family proceedings – costs

[Access to Justice Act 1999 s.29, s.30; Civil Procedure Rules 1998 (SI 1998 3132).]

Held, that all current and future editions of the Civil Procedure Rules 1998 Part 43 to 48 PD 43 to 48 applied to family proceedings. The new edition, dated July 3, 2000, included changes due to the Access to Justice Act 1999. It was emphasised that family proceedings were not subject to conditional fee agreements, although legal costs insurance premiums and the funding costs of certain membership organisations were recoverable under s.29 and s.30 of the Act.

PRACTICE DIRECTION (FAM DIV: COSTS: CIVIL PROCEDURE RULES 1998); *sub nom.* PRACTICE DIRECTION (FAM DIV: PROCEEDINGS: COSTS) [2000] 1 W.L.R. 1781, Dame Elizabeth Butler-Sloss (President), Fam Div.

2552. Practice directions – family proceedings – financial dispute resolution – pre action protocol – joint experts

[Civil Procedure Rules 1998 (SI 1998 3132) Part 35; Family Proceedings (Amendment No.2) Rules 1999 (SI 1999 3491 (L. 28)).]

The President issued a Practice Direction, with the concurrence of the Lord Chancellor, on the coming into force of the Family Proceedings (Amendment No.2) Rules 1999 on June 5, 1999. The Practice Direction applied from the same date, replacing *Practice Direction (Fam Div: Family Proceedings: Financial Dispute Resolution)* [1997] 1 W.L.R. 1069, [1997] C.L.Y. 2497. Provision was made for a pre action protocol indicating the steps to be taken before proceedings were commenced and for a Financial Dispute Resolution, FDR, appointment for the purposes of negotiation. Anything said or done in the course of an FDR meeting would not be admissible in evidence except in exceptional circumstances, *D (Minors) (Conciliation: Disclosure of Information), Re* [1993] 2 W.L.R. 721, [1993] C.L.Y. 2865 applied. Those representing the parties at such a meeting would be expected to have full knowledge of the case. Provision was made for the use of single joint experts, with power of appointment reserved to the court under the Civil Procedure Rules 1998 Part 35 where the parties failed to agree.

PRACTICE DIRECTION (FAM DIV: ANCILLARY RELIEF PROCEDURE) [2000] 1 W.L.R. 1480, Dame Elizabeth Butler-Sloss (President), Fam Div.

2553. Practice directions – family proceedings – use of authorities in human rights cases – allocation of certain human rights issues to particular judges

[Human Rights Act 1998 s.4.]

The President of the Family Division issued a Practice Direction dealing with the procedure to be followed by parties seeking to rely upon human rights authorities in family proceedings. With effect from 2 October 2000 the court had to be provided with a comprehensive list of the cases to be cited, together with authoritative reports and the full texts of those cases. The cases were available on the court's judgment website, http://www.echr.coe.int/hudoc. Where the issue involved, or might involve, declarations of incompatibility under the Human Rights Act 1998 s.4, it had to be determined by a High Court judge. Proceedings issued under the Act in respect of judicial acts had to be reserved in the High Court to a High Court judge or in the county court to a circuit judge.

PRACTICE DIRECTION (FAM DIV: HUMAN RIGHTS ACT 1998: CITATION OF AUTHORITIES); *sub nom.* PRACTICE DIRECTION (FAM DIV: PROCEEDINGS: HUMAN RIGHTS) [2000] 1 W.L.R. 1782, Dame Elizabeth Butler-Sloss (President), Fam Div.

2554. Practice directions – solicitors – court bundles – solicitors' duties

[Civil Procedure Rules 1998 (SI 1998 3132) Part 44 r.44.14.]

In proceedings brought in the Family Division a judgment was given relating to the applicability of *Practice Direction (Fam Div: Family Proceedings: Court*

Bundles) [2000] 1 W.L.R. 737, [2000] C.L.Y. 2550 to an application concerning the adoption of a seven month old child.

Held, granting directions, that the requirement to prepare a court bundle relating to the application before the court as provided for in the Practice Direction applied to all hearings of whatever duration. The only exception was in circumstances where because of the urgency of the application, it was not reasonably practicable to prepare a bundle. In the instant case the hearing concerned was a straightforward application for directions in adoption proceedings, but no bundle had been prepared summarising the background or stating the issues to be determined. Consequently, a hearing which should have been disposed of in 20 minutes had lasted an hour and a half. Under the Civil Procedure Rules Part 44 r.44.14 the court was entitled to make an order disallowing half the fees which would otherwise have been awarded to the applicants because of their legal representatives' failure to prepare the necessary court bundle. Further, there would normally be no reason not to identify the lawyers concerned, *G (Children) (Care Proceedings: Wasted Costs), Re* [2000] 2 W.L.R. 1007, [2000] C.L.Y. 2466 considered.

CH (A CHILD) (FAMILY PROCEEDINGS: COURT BUNDLES), *Re*; *sub nom.* H (A CHILD) (COURT BUNDLES: DISALLOWANCE OF FEES), *Re* [2000] 2 F.C.R. 193, Wall, J., Fam Div.

2555. Protection of Children Act 1999 (c.14) – Commencement No.1 Order

PROTECTION OF CHILDREN ACT 1999 (COMMENCEMENT NO.1) ORDER 2000, SI 2000 1459 (C.42); made under the Protection of Children Act 1999 s.14. Commencement details: bringing into force various provisions of the Act on June 5, 2000; £1.00.

This Order brings into force the Protection of Children Act 1999 s.3(1) and s.3(2), which make provision relating to the inclusion of individuals in the list kept by the Secretary of State for the purposes of s.1 of the Act on transfer from the Consultancy Service Index.

2556. Protection of Children Act 1999 (c.14) – Commencement No.2 Order

PROTECTION OF CHILDREN ACT 1999 (COMMENCEMENT NO.2) ORDER 2000, SI 2000 2337 (C.63); made under the Protection of Children Act 1999 s.14. Commencement details: bringing into force various provisions of the Act on September 1, 2000 and October 2, 2000; £1.00.

This Order brings into force the Protection of Children Act 1999 s.3(3) (in part), s.5, s.6, s.9 (in part) and s.12 on September 1, 2000. In addition, it brings into force the remaining provisions of the Act, except s.8 and s.10, on October 2, 2000.

2557. Right to family life – adoption – freeing order dispensing with mother's consent

See HUMAN RIGHTS: Scott v. United Kingdom. §3238

2558. Wardship – disabled persons – unreliability of evidence obtained by "facilitated communication"

The parents of D, a boy aged 17 suffering from serious autism and with a cognitive thinking age of not more than two, sought the discharge of a wardship order following the local authority's unreserved withdrawal of allegations of sexual abuse made against the father. D, who was unable to speak had been assisted by a care worker in giving information about the alleged abuse by facilitated communication, a treatment for autism first developed in America and Australia in the early 1990s, whereby a helper supported the arm of the impaired person while using a keyboard or similar device.

Held, granting the application, that the wardship order should be discharged. It was observed that the manner in which D had come to give evidence was a matter of public interest. In a resolution adopted by the American Psychological

Association in August 1994 it had been stated that "facilitated communication is a controversial and unproven communicative procedure with no scientifically demonstrated support for its efficacy". The resolution went on to conclude that responses obtained by facilitated communication should not be used to confirm or deny any allegations of abuse. A report prepared with the agreement of both parties by a professor of clinical psychology had concluded that responses obtained by facilitated communication should be viewed with scepticism. It followed that it would be dangerous for the court in family proceedings to rely on evidence supplied by such a method where an individual had impaired cognitive abilities.

D (A CHILD) (EVIDENCE: FACILITATED COMMUNICATION), *Re; sub nom.* D (A CHILD) (WARDSHIP: EVIDENCE OF ABUSE), *Re* [2001] 1 F.L.R. 148, Dame Elizabeth Butler-Sloss (President), Fam Div.

2559. Publications

Barker, Richard W. Newcastle – Child Protection: Practice, Policy and Management. Paperback: £14.95. ISBN 1-85302-319-1. Jessica Kingsley Publishers.

Barnett, Hilaire – Family Law Textbook. Paperback: £23.95. ISBN 1-85941-496-6. Cavendish Publishing Ltd.

Bates, Phil – Family Law. Butterworths Core Text. Paperback: £12.95. ISBN 0-406-92954-8. Butterworths Law.

Bird, Roger – Ancillary Relief Handbook. 2nd Ed. Paperback: £45.00. ISBN 0-85308-633-8. Family Law.

Black, Jill; Bridge, Jane; Bond, Tina – Practical Approach to Family Law. 6th Ed. A Practical Approach. Paperback: £28.95. ISBN 1-85431-874-8. Blackstone Press.

Black; Waller; White, Ken – Family Proceedings: a Guide for Urgent Business and Emergencies. Book and floppy disk: £75.00. ISBN 0-406-99294-0. Butterworths Law.

Blomfield, R.; Brooks, H. – Practical Guide to Family Proceedings. Paperback: £29.50. ISBN 0-85308-647-8. Family Law.

Clout, Imogen; Taylor, James – Money and Divorce: a Mediation Handbook. Paperback: £19.50. ISBN 0-85308-431-9. Family Law.

Cretney, S M – Family Law. 4th Ed. Textbook Series. Paperback: £18.95. ISBN 0-421-66980-2. Sweet & Maxwell.

Davies, Richard; Mornington, Marilyn – Matrimonial Proceedings. 2nd Ed. Practice Notes. Paperback: £15.95. ISBN 1-85941-306-4. Cavendish Publishing Ltd.

Davies, Richard; Mornington, Marilyn – Family and Matrimonial Practice. 3rd Ed. Practice Notes. Paperback: £25.00. ISBN 1-85941-445-1. Cavendish Publishing Ltd.

Dodds, Malcolm – Family Law. Old Bailey Press 150 Leading Cases Series. Paperback: £9.95. ISBN 1-85836-366-7. Old Bailey Press.

Dowd, Nancy E. – Redefining Fatherhood. Hardback. ISBN 0-8147-1925-2. New York University Press.

Duckworth, P. – Matrimonial Property and Finance. 6th Ed. Unbound/looseleaf: £125.00. ISBN 0-85308-525-0. Family Law.

Eekelaar, John; Maclean, Mavis; Beinart, Sarah – Family Lawyers: the Divorce Work of Solicitors. Paperback: £14.00. ISBN 1-84113-186-5. Hart Publishing.

Heinze, Eric – Of Innocence and Autonomy: Children, Sex and Human Rights. Programme on International Rights of the Child. Hardback: £40.00. ISBN 1-84014-484-X. Ashgate Publishing Limited.

Jacobs, Edward; Douglas, Gillian – Child Support: the Legislation 1999. 4th Ed. Book (details unknown): £22.00. ISBN 0-421-74070-1. Sweet & Maxwell.

James, Rebecca; Mulholland, Shona – Children Act, Explained. The Point of Law Series. Hardback: £25.00. ISBN 0-11-702385-X. The Stationery Office Books.

Murphy, John – Ethnic Minorities, Their Families and the Law. Hardback: £25.00. ISBN 1-901362-59-0. Hart Publishing.

Pertman, Adam – Adoption Nation. Hardback: £15.50. ISBN 0-465-05650-4. Basic Books.

Seymour, John – Childbirth and the Law. Hardback: £45.00. ISBN 0-19-826468-2. Oxford University Press.

Smith, John – Cohabitation Rights. Paperback: £9.99. ISBN 1-902646-52-5. Law Pack Publishing.

FINANCE

2560. African Development Bank – capital stock subscription

AFRICAN DEVELOPMENT BANK (FURTHER SUBSCRIPTION TO CAPITAL STOCK) ORDER 2000, SI 2000 1398; made under the Overseas Development and Co-operation Act 1980 s.4. In force: May 17, 2000; £1.00.

This Order provides for the payment to the African Development Bank of a subscription equivalent of 139,900,000 Units of Account to the increased authorised capital stock of the Bank. It provides for the payment of any sum which may be required to maintain the value of that subscription, for the redemption of non-interest-bearing and non-negotiable notes issued by the Secretary of State in payment of that subscription, and that certain sums that may be received by the UK Government from the Bank shall be paid to the Consolidated Fund.

2561. Conditional sales – regulated agreements – third party payments – effect on contractual relationship

ABC was the employer of R, who had entered into a regulated conditional sale agreement with PSA, a finance company, for a van to use in ABC's business. The deposit and instalments were paid by ABC. When R left ABC's employment, the van remained in their possession and payment ceased. The van was repossessed by PSA, and ABC claimed the return of the deposit and instalments paid.

Held, dismissing the claim, that the payment by ABC on behalf of the debtor did not create any relationship of contract or tort with PSA since it was of no concern to the finance company who made payment, which was accepted for and on behalf of the signatory to the agreement.

ABC CARS v. PSA FINANCE PLC, July 4, 2000, Deputy District Judge Frazer, CC (Winchester). [*Ex rel.* Nicholas Preston, Barrister, 8 Bell Yard, London].

2562. Consumer credit – credit hire agreements – common intention that payment would only fall due on settlement of third party proceedings

[Consumer Credit Act 1974 s.8.]

D brought an action against S for damages arising from a road traffic accident. S did not dispute liability. D claimed the cost of hiring a replacement vehicle on a credit hire basis, amounting to some £3,666. S disputed D's claim in respect of the hire. D had been introduced to a car rental company, AC, through solicitors acting on his behalf. AC had thereafter delivered a vehicle to D and collected it at the end of the hire period some 48 days later. At the commencement of the hire, D signed an agreement, the only agreement ever used by AC, which provided for payment on demand and made no reference to credit. The period of hire concluded on December 29, 1997. AC posted to D an invoice in respect of the hire charge and two reminder letters in March and June 1998, although D had no recollection of receiving them. A director of AC gave evidence that the company did not pursue outstanding hire charges in circumstances where a third party claim was outstanding. D gave evidence that he could not have afforded to pay the hire charge at the time of the hire and further that he had simply assumed that his insurer would pay for the hire. As part of the agreement, D had signed an authority for the hire charge to be collected through a debit card. No attempt had been made by AC to use the authority. Despite the authority being sought and obtained, no details of a debit or credit card had been taken. In addition, no deposit was taken.

Held, finding as a preliminary issue that the hire agreement was an agreement for credit, that, although the written agreement contained no reference to credit, both parties had a common intention that payment for hire would not be made until such time as the third party proceedings were settled. Insofar as the written agreement provided for payment on demand it was a sham, since the common intention of the parties was that credit would be afforded until such time as the third party proceedings were settled. As the agreement was an agreement for credit, it fell within the provisions of the Consumer Credit Act 1974 s.8. The action was stayed pending the decision in the House of Lords in *Dimond v. Lovell* [2000] Q.B. 216, [1999] C.L.Y. 2457.

DUFFUS v. SOUTHGATE, December 2, 1999, District Judge Morley, CC (Edmonton). [*Ex rel.* Ian Bridge, Barrister, Mitre Court Chambers, Temple, London].

2563. Consumer credit – credit hire agreements – disclosure – insurance agreements ordered against non parties where necessary for fair disposal of cr

See CIVIL EVIDENCE: Burke v. Thornton. §311

2564. Consumer credit – credit hire agreements – enforceability – failure to specify number of instalments

[Consumer Credit Act 1974; Consumer Credit (Exempt Agreements) Order 1989 (SI 1989 869) Art.3.]

N and B were involved in a road traffic accident. Liability was not in dispute. N hired a replacement car from ABV. The hire agreement contained a clause requiring payment of the hire charges within 51 weeks of the date of the agreement but did not specify the number of instalments in which they should be paid. N contended that (1) from the nature of the agreement it was obvious that it was intended that the hire charges should be paid in one lump sum and that if necessary that could be implied into the agreement so that it would be exempt from the Consumer Credit Act 1974 by virtue of the Consumer Credit (Exempt Agreements) Order 1989, and (2) if the hire agreement was a regulated consumer credit agreement, it had been improperly executed and was, therefore, unenforceable against her. B argued that because the number of instalments was not specified, Art.3 of the Order did not apply, and the court could not imply the number of repayments into the agreement, *Zoan v. Rouamba* [2000] 1 W.L.R. 1509, [2000] C.L.Y. 2589 cited.

Held, dismissing the claim for hire charges, that in the light of *Zoan v. Rouamba* the court could not imply the number of instalments into the hire agreement. Accordingly, the agreement did not meet the requirements of Art.3, it was not exempt from the provisions of the 1974 Act and therefore was unenforceable against N.

NEWBY v. BIRD, May 31, 2000, Judge Trigger, CC (Birkenhead). [*Ex rel.* Tim Grover, Barrister, 7 Harrington Street, Liverpool].

2565. Consumer credit – credit hire agreements – enforceability – hire charges payable on demand

M and H were involved in a road traffic accident. Liability was not disputed. M's insurers arranged for him to hire a replacement car from HD. M claimed the hire charges from H. M gave evidence that HD had delivered a replacement vehicle to his home and had collected his damaged vehicle for repairs. He had signed a form in respect of the replacement vehicle but had not read the terms and conditions. No representations had been made to him about payment for the hire but he had assumed that as he held fully comprehensive insurance he would not be personally liable for any of the charges. M's counsel suggested that irrespective of M's assumptions about the agreement he had signed, it was not a credit hire agreement and was clearly enforceable against M. M had at all times been liable to pay the cost of hire and the fact that HD had foregone their right to enforce the debt was irrelevant. H contended that HD had misrepresented the position to M and the agreement was unenforceable as a sham. In the alternative, H contended that it was a credit hire agreement and relying upon *Dimond v. Lovell* [2000] 2 W.L.R. 1121, [2000] C.L.Y. 2566 was unenforceable.

Held, allowing the application in part, that the agreement had not specifically provided for credit but instead included a term requiring payment on demand. M had signed the agreement in four places. Despite the fact that M had had no intention of paying the hire charges, the agreement was clearly not a credit agreement. The court could not be satisfied on the balance of probabilities that the agreement was not enforceable against M. There was certainly a prospect of the agreement being enforced against him and it would be wrong to hold it unenforceable as a credit hire agreement, when it clearly was not such agreement. M had acted reasonably in using HD upon the recommendations of his insurers, and they had offered an exceptional service. M was entitled to recover the cost of hire for a reasonable hire period of five days, but he was not entitled to recover the cost of collection or delivery as they were "additional benefits", *Dimond* followed.

MILLER v. HULBERT, May 15, 2000, District Judge Jackson, CC (Romford). [*Ex rel.* Victoria Ling, Barrister, 1 Temple Gardens, Temple, London].

2566. **Consumer credit – credit hire agreements – enforceability – improper execution of agreement**

[Consumer Credit Act 1974 s.61 (1).]

D's car was damaged as a result of an accident caused by L. She hired a car from a specialist company under an agreement which provided that the company would have conduct of any litigation, and that the costs of the hire would not be payable until the conclusion of the case. In proceedings commenced against L, the recorder awarded D damages equivalent to the car hire charges which had been payable under the agreement. L appealed to the Court of Appeal which held that (1) the agreement was regulated by the Consumer Credit Act 1974; (2) the agreement having been unenforceable by the company against D on the ground that it had not been properly executed under s.61 (1) of the Act, D could not recover the hire charges from L, and (3) had the agreement been properly executed, D would have been entitled to recover the hire charges in full. D appealed.

Held, dismissing the appeal (Lord Nicholls dissenting in part), that (1) since all of the terms of the agreement stipulated that the company's right to recover the hire charges was to be deferred, credit had been granted to D with the result that the agreement was a "regulated agreement" for the purposes of the 1974 Act; (2) the agreement having been improperly executed and therefore unenforceable by the company against D, it could not be said that D had been unjustly enriched by not having to pay the hire charges since the 1974 Act contemplated that a debtor might benefit from the improper execution of an agreement; (3) D could not claim against L as trustee for the company as the company would thereby acquire rights resulting from an agreement which had been held to be unenforceable. Furthermore, she could not recover damages for the notional cost of hiring the car as this would lead to double recovery, *Hunt v. Severs* [1994] 2 A.C. 350, [1994] C.L.Y. 1530 applied. In the circumstances, D was not entitled to recover damages for the loss of the use of her car, and (4) had the agreement been enforceable, D would have been entitled to recover the hire charges that she would have had to pay had she entered into an agreement with an ordinary hire company. Although she had acted reasonably in approaching a specialist company, L should not have to pay for the extra benefits such as the cost of investigating the accident and the cost of supplying D with credit which the company had provided, *British Westinghouse Electric and Manufacturing Co Ltd v. Underground Electric Railways Co of London Ltd* [1912] A.C. 673 applied.

DIMOND v. LOVELL [2000] 2 W.L.R. 1121, Lord Hoffmann, HL.

2567. Consumer credit – credit hire agreements – enforceability – legal expenses insurer separate from vehicle lessor

[Consumer Credit Act 1974 s.15; Financial Services Act 1986 s.132.]

C claimed damages from H arising from a road traffic accident in March 1999. Liability was conceded. A claim for a replacement vehicle was made in respect of a hire car which was provided to C after the accident. The rental agreement between MLG, the lessor, and C did not limit the period of hire to three months. H contended that this meant that the agreement was a regulated consumer hire agreement, pursuant to the Consumer Credit Act 1974 s.15, and further that it was unenforceable against C due to its being improperly executed. Therefore C had suffered no loss and could not make a claim under this head of damage from H. C contended that the agreement with MLG was not in fact a hire agreement but merely an agreement which regulated the use of the car. It was argued that the claim was a subrogated one on behalf of DAS, a legal expenses insurer, since it had provided the car pursuant to an insurance policy, the policy document being produced in court. It was argued that MLG were merely subcontractors performing DAS's obligations. C further contended that DAS had paid MLG the hire charges pursuant to a Master Agreement which was also produced to the court. C relied upon *Department of Trade and Industry v. St Christopher Motorists Association Ltd* [1974] 1 W.L.R. 99, [1974] C.L.Y. 1900.

Held, dismissing the claim, that the agreement signed by C used the words "rental agreement" and referred to him as the "hirer". The Master Agreement provided for MLG to investigate the claim and also potentially to provide to C a written rental agreement in MLG's standard form. There was no absolute obligation on MLG to provide a car. It was conditional upon, for example, investigating the claim. This was inconsistent with the analysis that this was merely subcontracting the functions of MLG. Further, DAS were required to pay MLG the sums "due". It was therefore held that MLG were a separate contractor rather than a subcontractor of DAS, with DAS meeting the cost of hire under a separate agreement. Therefore, the separate contract was governed by the 1974 Act and regulated thereunder, rendering it unenforceable. C was not obliged to pay MLG for the hire and DAS were not obliged to pay MLG and therefore there could be no right of subrogation. DAS had also been put to proof that they were authorised to provide not only legal expenses but also insurance for the provision of a car. No proof of authorisation had been given, and they had not produced evidence of any reasonable belief that they were so authorised, pursuant to the Financial Services Act 1986 s.132. However, in the light of the other findings, it was not necessary to address the question of the effect of this on the hire claim and whether it was tainted by any illegality.

CASEY v. HARTLEY, January 17, 2000, District Judge Green, CC (Ashford). [*Ex rel*. Tim Kevan, Barrister, 1 Temple Gardens, Temple, London, instructed by Karen Green of McGoldricks].

2568. Consumer credit – credit hire agreements – enforceability – no requirement for payment with 12 months of agreement date

[Consumer Credit Act 1974 s.127(3), s.173; Consumer Credit (Exempt Agreements) Order 1989 (SI 1989 869).]

W brought an action against BCHP for damages arising from a road traffic accident. Liability was not in dispute. W hired a car from F on a credit hire basis. The agreement stated that W was entitled to interest free credit in respect of the hire charges until the conclusion of the claim for damages against the third party, or the conclusion of any proceedings to recover such damages, or within 364 days, whichever was the earlier. It was contended that W could consent to the hire charges being enforced against him and waive any defects in the agreement, pursuant to the Consumer Credit Act 1974 s.173.

Held, dismissing the appeal, that the agreement was not exempt by virtue of the Consumer Credit (Exempt Agreements) Order 1989 because (1) the number of payments was not stated and could not be inferred, *Majeed v. Incentive Group* (Unreported, August 27, 1999), [1999] C.L.Y. 2465 followed; (2)

payment was not required to be made within 12 months, therefore the period of interest free credit was not tied to any particular date, the contract was construed contra proferentem and the limit in the agreement was also to be construed exclusively, *Trow v. Ind Coope (West Midlands) Ltd* [1967] 2 Q.B. 899, [1967] C.L.Y. 3259 followed; (3) the effect of s.127(3) of the 1974 Act was that the court could not consent to an order enforcing the agreement, *Wotton v. Flagg* [1998] C.C.L.R. 63, [1997] C.L.Y. 959 and *Hatfield v. Hiscock* [1998] C.C.L.R. 68, [1998] C.L.Y. 2501 not followed; (4) any consent on the part of W had to be real and not presumed, and (5) any such consent would in any event constitute a failure to mitigate.

WOODBURN v. BCH PRESTIGE, November 4, 1999, District Judge Tetlow, CC (Manchester). [*Ex rel.* NDH Edwards, Barrister, 8 King Street Chambers, Manchester].

2569. Consumer credit – credit hire agreements – enforceability – payment required on conclusion of claim or within 364 days

[Consumer Credit Act 1974; Consumer Credit (Exempt Agreements) Order 1989 (SI 1989 869) Art.3(1).]

C brought an action against W for damages, including credit hire charges, arising from a road traffic accident. W admitted liability for the accident. C hired a car on a credit hire basis for 29 days from F. C claimed £1,218.18 for the credit hire costs. W denied that C was entitled to recover the charges, averring that the agreement was regulated by the Consumer Credit Act 1974. C contended that the agreement fell within the 12 month exemption under the Consumer Credit (Exempt Agreements) Order 1989 Art.3(1) on the basis that the agreement included a clause which provided that the hirer was entitled to interest free credit in respect of the hire charges until the conclusion of any claim or any proceedings for damages against the party that the hirer alleged was liable for the damages, or within 364 days, whichever was the earlier. This question was heard as a preliminary issue, as it was conceded by C that a finding in W's favour would result in the charges being irrecoverable.

Held, dismissing the credit hire claim, that the clause did not exempt the agreement because the hire agreement was inconclusive as to when payment was required and how many payments the hirer was required to make. Accordingly, the clause had to be construed contra proferentem and the agreement was not exempt.

COOKE v. WHITELEY, October 27, 1999, District Judge Goudie, CC (Doncaster). [*Ex rel.* Helen Waddington, Barrister, Park Lane Chambers, 19 Westgate, Leeds].

2570. Consumer credit – credit hire agreements – enforceability – sham terms as to credit time limit and repayment

[Consumer Credit Act 1974; Consumer Credit (Exempt Agreements) Order 1989 (SI 1989 869).]

A brought an action against P arising out of a road traffic accident, claiming hire charges of £3,626. A had hired a car on a credit basis from a credit hire company for a period from September 11 to November 3, 1998. The credit hire agreement specified that the hire must not exceed three months and that the hire company would defer A's payment of the charges. However, A had to repay the charges within 11 months of the date of the agreement and in less than three instalments. The hire company also presented A with a standard letter at the same time as he signed the hire agreement. The letter stated "we take this opportunity to advise you that credit hire is more expensive than spot hire because payment of your hire invoice is deferred until the conclusion of your claim". At the date of hearing, 13 months after the date of the agreement, A had not paid the hire charges and had not been asked to do so. A argued that the hire agreement was exempt from the provisions of the Consumer Credit Act 1974 by virtue of the inclusion of a clause requiring repayment in less than 12 months and in less than four instalments, in accordance with the Consumer Credit (Exempt Agreements) Order 1989. P argued that the fact of non payment and the terms of the letter were evidence that the terms and conditions of the agreement were a sham device and that they did not reflect the true contractual intention of the parties.

Held, dismissing the claim for hire charges, that (1) as the hire agreement stood it was exempt from the provisions of the Act. However, the letter reflected what the parties to the hire agreement expected to happen and it certainly reflected the way that the credit hire trade operated. The letter was sufficient to prevent the hire company from succeeding in a claim against A for the hire charges before conclusion of the claim, and (2) it was necessary to look at the whole bargain, and in particular the letter from the hire company to A. Since that letter reflected the reality of the position, the condition of the agreement purporting to limit credit to 11 months and requiring repayment within that time was a sham. Accordingly, the agreement was not exempt from the provisions of the Act and fell to be considered under *Dimond v. Lovell* [2000] 2 W.L.R. 1121, [2000] C.L.Y. 2566 and as such was unenforceable, *Dimond* applied.

ARMSTRONG v. PEARCY, October 26, 1999, Deputy District Judge Wilkinson, CC (Bury). [*Ex rel.* Simon McCann, Barrister, Deans Court Chambers, 24 St John Street, Manchester].

2571. **Consumer credit – credit hire agreements – enforcement where creditor under hire agreement not party to proceedings**

[Consumer Credit Act 1974 s.127.]

H claimed damages from S following a road traffic accident. H hired a replacement vehicle and claimed the hire charges from S. The issue between the parties was whether the contract for hire was a hire agreement within the meaning of the Consumer Credit Act 1974 and whether the prescribed terms had to be in a prescribed form.

Held, dismissing the claim, that no enforcement order pursuant to s.127 was available between the parties because the creditor to the hire agreement was not a party to the proceedings.

HAAGMAN v. SADEG, October 20, 1999, District Judge Back, CC (Uxbridge). [*Ex rel.* Nicholas Preston, Barrister, Bracton Chambers, 8 Bell Yard, London].

2572. **Consumer credit – credit hire agreements – exempt agreement not comparable to instalment borrowing agreement**

[Consumer Credit (Exempt Agreements) Order 1989 (SI 1989 689).]

H brought an action against N for damages, including credit hire charges, arising from a road traffic accident. Liability was not in dispute. The credit agreement provided that "The credit period extended by this agreement shall expire in any event 51 weeks from the date of this agreement. At the expiry of the credit period you shall then become liable to pay the hire charges in full. If the hire charges are subsequently recovered from the third party, the credit hire company will refund them to you". The only issue was whether this clause sufficed to render the credit hire agreement exempt under the Consumer Credit (Exempt Agreements) Order 1989. N argued on appeal that it did not, relying on the report of the Commission on Consumer Credit Cmnd 4596.

Held, dismissing the appeal, that the agreement was exempt. N's argument that the agreement was not exempt because it did not forbid voluntary early instalment repayments was completely unsustainable. The agreement was obviously not an agreement for instalment borrowing. There was no liability to pay for 51 weeks, and then there was a liability to pay the charges "in full". The Commission Report on Consumer Credit was therefore irrelevant to the instant case. It showed that the committee had intended not to exempt agreements for instalment borrowing from regulation. The agreement in the instant case was nothing like an instalment borrowing agreement. N's contention that the word "liable" was fatal to the agreement was also completely unsustainable. The only reasonable construction of the agreement was that there was a contractual liability to pay the credit hire charges after 51 weeks. There was no valid distinction between the wording of the agreement and the wording of the 1989 order, nor would it matter if the company had decided to enforce the liability to pay after 51 weeks. D's contention that the terms of the agreement were ambiguous also failed.

NORTHERN CONTRACTORS v. HOPWOOD Judge Kenny, CC (Reading).

2573. Consumer credit – credit hire agreements – exempt agreements – enforceability

[Consumer Credit Act 1974; Consumer Credit (Exempt Agreements) Order 1989, Art.3(1)(a).]

P brought an action for damages against D following a road traffic accident in June 1999. Liability was admitted and only quantum remained an issue at the hearing. P obtained a replacement vehicle from H whilst his was being repaired and P's garage arranged payment of the repair invoice once the repair had been completed. P signed a credit repair agreement and a credit hire agreement. Both agreements contained the following clause: "The credit period extended by this Agreement shall expire in any event 51 weeks from the date of this Agreement. At the expiry of the credit period you shall then become liable to pay the [repair charges/hire charges] in full....." D argued that the agreements were regulated by the Consumer Credit Act 1974 and that the clause limiting the credit period did not exempt the agreements from the provisions of the Act because it failed to comply with the requirements of the Consumer Credit (Exempt Agreements) Order 1989 Art.3(1)(a). P conceded that if the agreements were not exempt then they failed to comply with the Act and would not be enforceable against P. The court was concerned to determine the matter by way of preliminary issue.

Held, dismissing the claim for credit hire and credit repair, that the consumer credit legislation was a minefield for consumers and as such it was not correct that a liberal approach should be adopted. Instead, it was necessary to look closely at the Regulation. The agreements simply stated that the credit period would come to an end at the expiry of 51 weeks and that the hirer then became liable. It did not require payment. The 1989 order was prescriptive and therefore the agreement must require payment. The agreement should also state the number of payments to be made and the dates on which those payments were to be made, if it was to comply with the regulations.

PAYNE v. DEAN, May 26, 2000, District Judge Dancey, CC (Poole). [*Ex rel.* Lyons Davidson Solicitors, Victoria House, 51 Victoria Street, Bristol].

2574. Consumer credit – credit hire agreements – exempt agreements – no valid agreement for provision of credit – mitigation of loss

[Consumer Credit Act 1974 s.11(1)(b), s.13(a); Consumer Credit (Exempt Agreements) Order 1989 (SI 1989 869) Art.4(1)(9).]

D claimed damages from H arising out of a road traffic accident. Liability was admitted, and the only item of dispute was a claim for car hire charges. D had hired a vehicle from M, a company her business used on a regular basis. On the face of the hire document, it was not a credit agreement, since there was no mention of credit. However, an invoice later sent to D described her as a "credit customer", and referred to the method of payment as "credit". H submitted that the agreement was a consumer credit agreement regulated by the Consumer Credit Act 1974, and was therefore unenforceable, *Dimond v. Lovell* [2000] 2 W.L.R. 1121, [2000] C.L.Y. 2566 cited. H further contended that the daily hire charge of £45 plus VAT was excessive, and that D had failed sufficiently to mitigate her loss, since she had rejected her insurers' offer of a courtesy car. D argued against the existence of an agreement, maintaining that M, who had known that D was claiming damages from H, had extended the use of its vehicle to D as a "mere indulgence", and that although a courtesy car had been available from her insurers, their select repairers were some 60 miles away from her home, whereas M was local.

Held, allowing the claim for hire charges, that there was no "agreement" for the provision of credit between D and M. If there had been such an agreement, it would have been exempt in any event under the Consumer Credit (Exempt

Agreements) Order 1989 Art.4(1)(9) since it was a restricted use debtor creditor agreement under s.11 (1)(b) and s.13(a) of the 1974 Act, and there was no charge being made for the credit. It had been reasonable for D to decline to use her insurers' repairers notwithstanding the availability of a courtesy car, since they were a considerable distance from her home, and she had wanted to use an authorised Volkswagen repairer, as her car was new and she was concerned about the warranties.

DOWNES v. HAMMOND, June 19, 2000, District Judge Mitchell, CC (Bow). [*Ex rel*. Katya Melluish, Barrister, 3 Paper Buildings, Temple, London].

2575. Consumer credit – credit hire agreements – exempt agreements – payment required in full upon expiration of 51 weeks

[Consumer Credit Act 1974; Consumer Credit (Exempt Agreements) Order 1989 (SI 1989 689) Art.3(1)(a)(i).]

After an accident caused by D, C hired a car on credit. It was conceded that the hire agreement did not comply with the Consumer Credit Act 1974 and would be unenforceable if it was regulated by the Act. C argued that it was an exempt agreement, and referred to the words of the agreement, "the credit period extended by this agreement shall expire no later than 51 weeks from the date of this agreement. At the expiry of the credit period, payment must be made in full." C claimed that the clause brought the agreement precisely within the terms of the Consumer Credit (Exempt Agreements) Order 1989 Art.3(1)(a)(i), as payment was required within 12 months beginning with the date of the agreement, and then payment had to be made "in full" which meant in a single payment. D admitted that the 12 month limb of the test was satisfied, but argued that under the agreement there was nothing to stop C from paying off the credit in a series of voluntary interim payments before the expiry of 51 weeks, for example, in 50 instalments of £20. D referred to Cmnd 4596, which stated that agreements where multiple instalment payments were "required or permitted by the terms of the contract" should be regulated. In the absence of a prohibition on such voluntary payments, D argued that multiple instalment payments were permitted, and as such the agreement could not be exempt.

Held, giving judgment for C, that the reference in the Order to the number of payments to be made was a reference to payments which were provided for by the credit agreement itself. The Commission's Report referred to instalments permitted by the "terms of the agreement". Moreover, the language of the Order itself in referring to the number of payments "to be made", and later use of the word "required" suggested that it was referring to payments which there was some obligation to make. Neither the Commission's Report nor the Order was intended to encompass purely voluntary payments of the sort posited by D, which were not instalment payments as such, being neither required nor provided for by the agreement. There was, therefore, no ambiguity in the agreement at all; the words "in full" clearly meant that a single payment was required at the conclusion of 51 weeks. The agreement came firmly within the Order, and was exempt from the Act. C was awarded the hire charges in full.

KALAM v. KHAN, February 4, 2000, District Judge Sanghera, CC (Nuneaton). [*Ex rel*. Benjamin Williams, Barrister, 1 Temple Gardens, Temple, London].

2576. Consumer credit – credit hire agreements – exempt agreements – purposive drafting acceptable in absence of fraud or sham

[Consumer Credit Act 1974; Consumer Credit (Exempt Agreements) Order 1989 (SI 1989 869) Art.3(1)(a)(i).]

Following a road traffic accident, D claimed damages from J, including car hire charges. D had entered into a credit hire agreement with H for a period of approximately two weeks whilst his own vehicle was being repaired. J refused to meet the hire charges contending that (1) the credit hire agreement, although on the face of it being exempt from the Consumer Credit Act 1974 by virtue of the Consumer Credit (Exempt Agreements) Order 1989 Art.3 (1)(a)(i), was not actually intended to be an exempt agreement, but had been drafted as such solely to overcome problems in the subsequent recovery of the charges, and (2) D had failed to mitigate his loss by not making use of a courtesy car which was available under his own insurance policy.

Held, finding in favour of D, that (1) in the absence of fraud or sham, it was irrelevant whether H had constructed its agreement purposely to make it exempt. The agreement was exempt because of the lack of provision for payment by instalments, *Northern Contractors v. Hopwood* (Unreported, March 24, 2000) followed. Despite the existence of an insurance agreement with AA, there was no evidence of sham, and (2) D had acted reasonably in following the advice of his insurance brokers to contact H, hence he had not failed to mitigate his loss.

DOWALL v. JOHNSON, July 4, 2000, District Judge Field, CC (Salisbury). [*Ex rel.* Scott Rees & Co Solicitors, Centaur House, Gardiners Place, Skelmersdale, Lancashire].

2577. Consumer credit – credit hire agreements – exempt agreements – specification of number of payments required

[Consumer Credit Act 1974; Consumer Credit (Exempt Agreements) Order 1989 (SI 1989 869) Art.3 (1) (a) (i).]

F brought an action against M for damages following a road traffic accident. The claim included car hire charges for 19 days hire. F had hired the car from H, at the same time taking out uninsured loss insurance with AA, whereby AA would pay H's charges if recovery from M had not been achieved within a 51 week credit period. Clause 14 of the agreement stated that at the expiry of the credit period, the hirer would become "liable to pay" the hire charges in full. M admitted liability, but maintained that the hire charges were unenforceable against him, by virtue of the agreement being regulated under the Consumer Credit Act 1974. F argued that (1) M was estopped from pursuing his contention at trial because he had omitted to plead it in his defence, and (2) the agreement was an exempt agreement under the Consumer Credit (Exempt Agreements) Order 1989 Art.3 (1) (a) (i), and since the wording of clause 14 was ambiguous, it ought to be purposively construed to the effect that, as the charges were to be paid in a single instalment, the requirement of the Order to specify the number of payments be dispensed with, and since the term "liable to pay" was a legal one and thereby actionable, that satisfied the requirements of the 1989 Order.

Held, finding in favour of M, that (1) as no details of the hire agreement had been served with the statement of case, M could not have known that the case concerned a credit hire agreement, hence he was permitted to raise the issue at trial; (2) the 1989 Order was to be narrowly construed and its working strictly interpreted. Accordingly the number of payments had to be expressed and could not be inferred, and (3) the phrase "liable to pay after 51 weeks" was permissive and did not amount to a "requirement for payment within 12 months", therefore the agreement did not comply with the requirements of the Order and was a regulated agreement, and as it was common ground that the provisions of the 1974 Act had not been complied with, it was unenforceable, *Dimond v. Lovell* [2000] 2 W.L.R. 1121, [2000] C.L.Y. 2566, *Cooke v. Whiteley* (Unreported, October 27, 1999), [2000] C.L.Y. 2569 and *Woodburn v. BCH Prestige* (Unreported, November 4, 1999), [2000] C.L.Y. 2568 followed.

FRENCON BUILDERS v. MARASHI, June 14, 2000, District Judge Plaskow, CC (Brentford). [*Ex rel.* Nigel Ffitch, Barrister, Phoenix Chambers, Gray's Inn Chambers, Gray's Inn, London].

2578. Consumer credit – credit hire agreements – exempt agreements – time for payment of hire charges

[Consumer Credit Act 1974; Consumer Credit (Exempt Agreements) Order 1989 (SI 1989 869).]

J and G were involved in a road traffic accident in August 1999. J hired a replacement vehicle for a period of 20 days. The daily rate charged for the hire vehicle was £34 per day, plus a £15 delivery charge, plus VAT. The written agreement between J and the hire company provided that the hire charges would become payable by the hirer in a single payment on conclusion of the proceedings against the party responsible for the accident or within 12 months of the date of the hire agreement, whichever was the sooner. J brought an action against G claiming damages for loss of use and the car hire charges. G contended that the agreement was not exempt on the basis that it did not specifically require J to make payment within a period of 12 months beginning with the date of the agreement in that the words "become payable" did not create an obligation on the hirer to pay the hire charges and, relying upon *Dimond v. Lovell* [2000] 2 W.L.R. 1121, [2000] C.L.Y. 2566, damages could not therefore be recovered against G. Further, G contended that the daily rate of £34 per day included a charge for additional services over and above the hiring of the vehicle, which was not recoverable against G on the basis of the obiter comments of the majority of the House of Lords in *Dimond*. G sought to rely on evidence of alternative rates.

Held, allowing the hire charges, that the agreement was exempt from the Consumer Credit Act 1974 by virtue of the Consumer Credit (Exempt Agreements) Order 1989 and was therefore distinguishable from *Dimond*. There could not be any reasonable construction of the agreement other than a requirement to pay within 12 months. The words "become payable" were absolutely and abundantly clear and created an obligation to pay the hire charges. The daily rate of £34 per day was recoverable against G. There was no reliable evidence before the court of alternative rates for hire vehicles available to J at the time of the hiring. J had demonstrably mitigated his loss and was therefore entitled to recover the hire charges in full.

JONES v. GERRARD, May 15, 2000, District Judge Harrison, CC (Chester). [*Ex rel.* Michael Jones, Barrister, Cobden House Chambers, 19 Quay Street, Manchester].

2579. Consumer credit – credit hire agreements – fees "payable on demand" amounted to provision of credit

[Consumer Credit Act 1974.]

B brought an action against S for damages arising out of a road traffic accident, including a claim for hire charges in respect of a replacement motorcycle. The hire agreement provided that any sums due in respect of the hire were "payable on demand". No fee was paid up front in respect of the hire and an invoice was levied at the end of the hire stating "payment now due". The hire agreement was limited to a maximum period of three months' rental. B stated that he had understood from his insurers that he would only have to pay the hire charges if his claim failed on liability. The hire company contended that the motorcycle had been hired "on a credit hire basis", but that credit was only extended in so far as the hirer did not enforce the agreement. In fact the hire charges remained unpaid at trial, approximately two years and six months after hire commenced. At the time of the hearing, the hirer had a licence to conduct consumer credit business and was applying to back date the same to cover the hire agreement in question. However, neither at the time of the arbitration nor at the subsequent appeal was evidence available to show that the licence had been backdated. At a small claims track hearing it was held that no credit had been extended and that the hire company was merely indulging B. The hire charges were therefore recoverable. S appealed.

Held, allowing the appeal, that credit had been extended, since under the agreement the hirer was provided with services in the form of hiring the motorcycle before payment was required in respect of the same. This was credit within the meaning of the Consumer Credit Act 1974 since services were provided, in the form of the motorcycle, for a substantial period, up to three months, before payment was required at the end of hire. Furthermore, there was sufficient evidence to imply a term or a collateral agreement providing for credit. The judge's decision was therefore reversed: since credit had been extended, the agreement was a regulated consumer credit agreement within the meaning of s.8 of the Act. The agreement was improperly executed for a variety of reasons. Following *Dimond v. Lovell* [2000] 2 W.L.R. 1121, [2000] C.L.Y. 2566 the hire charges were irrecoverable. B conceded that, in the absence of a licence having been backdated by the Office of Fair Trading, an application under s.7 of the 1974 Act would be futile as the agreement was unenforceable in any event.

BURROWS v. STEVENS, June 16, 2000, Judge Farnworth, CC (Watford). [*Ex rel.* Richard Miles, Barrister, 2 King's Bench Walk, Temple, London].

2580. Consumer credit – credit hire agreements – hire costs disallowed where consumer hire agreement unenforceable against claimant

[Consumer Credit Act 1974 s.15.]

W's car was damaged in a road traffic accident and W signed a rental agreement with M. M had an agreement with D, W's legal expenses insurers, that M would provide cars to D's policyholders in such circumstances. W claimed the cost of hire from S. W argued that (1) D was entitled to exercise subrogation rights under the policy; (2) W was entitled to claim for the loss of use of his car, which could be best represented by the cost to D of providing him with a replacement, *Everson v. Flurry* (Unreported, February 22, 1999), [1999] C.L.Y. 3411 referred to; (3) S was not entitled to have taken into account the fruits of an insurance policy entered into by W before the accident, otherwise S would benefit from a windfall; (4) it was not a credit hire case but hire provided under an insurance policy, therefore *Dimond v. Lovell* [2000] 2 W.L.R. 1121, [2000] C.L.Y. 2566 cited was not relevant. S argued that the hire charges were not recoverable, because (1) the rental agreement was between W and M and it was capable of subsisting for more than three months in the absence of any term to the contrary, it was a regulated consumer hire agreement under the Consumer Credit Act 1974 s.15 which was improperly executed and so was unenforceable against W; (2) since W was not liable to M, D could not be in any better position than W to claim the hire charges from S; (3) the reasoning in *Everson v. Flurry* on the measure of W's loss had been overruled by the Court of Appeal in *Dimond v. Lovell*, and (4) S was not improperly making use of the pre-accident insurance policy to claim a windfall, since the relevant agreement was the one between W and M upon which W's claim was based, and the fact that W had only entered into the agreement because of his insurance with D was irrelevant, *Golding v. Mason* (Unreported, September 14, 1999), [1999] C.L.Y. 2477 and *Casey v. Hartley* (Unreported, January 17, 2000), [2000] C.L.Y. 2567 cited.

Held, dismissing the application for hire costs, that the agreement was clearly within s.15 of the 1974 Act and was a consumer hire agreement. It was improperly executed and so W could not recover the sum claimed from S, as the agreement was unenforceable against W.

WOOD v. SIBLEY, April 17, 2000, District Judge Wainwright, CC (Exeter). [*Ex rel.* Tim Petts, Barrister, 12 King's Bench Walk, London].

2581. Consumer credit – credit hire agreements – incorporation of prescribed terms

[Consumer Credit Act 1974 s.127.]

A claimed damages from J following a road traffic accident. A hired a replacement vehicle and claimed the hire costs from J. The issue between the parties was whether the contact for hire was a hire agreement within the meaning of the Consumer Credit Act 1974 and whether the prescribed terms had to be in a prescribed form.

Held, allowing the claim, that even if not in the prescribed form, all the prescribed terms were incorporated in the agreement and s.127 of the Act gave power to the court of its own motion to make an enforcement order as there was no prejudice to J.

AGARD v. JETHA, October 18, 1999, District Judge Naqvi, CC (Bow). [*Ex rel.* Nicholas Preston, Barrister, Bracton Chambers, 8 Bell Yard, London].

2582. Consumer credit – credit hire agreements – incorporation of terms without fresh consideration

F's vehicle was damaged in an accident for which S was at fault and F required a replacement vehicle. He was contacted by a hire firm who informed him that as he was not at fault for the accident the charges would be recovered from S's insurer. Following that representation a hire car was supplied and an accompanying delivery note signed. Two days after supply of the hire car an agreement was sent to F which appeared to require payment at the cessation of hire, and which F duly signed.

Held, finding that the hire charges were not recoverable, that this was an attempt to incorporate terms into the contract after the contract was concluded and without any fresh consideration, hence the terms had not been validly incorporated. The provision of a hire car was an offer and the acceptance of the car by F constituted an acceptance of that offer. The consideration provided by F was the subrogated right to sue on his behalf. The terms as to payment were that payment would be made by S's Insurer and not F.

FLINT v. SOWERBY, May 31, 2000, District Judge Ward, CC (Newcastle). [*Ex rel.* NDH Edwards, Barrister, 8 King Street Chambers, Manchester].

2583. Consumer credit – credit hire agreements – legal expenses insurance – insurers right to bring subrogated claim

[Consumer Credit Act 1974.]

B and U were involved in a road traffic accident and B hired a replacement vehicle from MLP. This vehicle was provided pursuant to B's legal expenses insurance policy with DAS and an agreement between MLP and DAS. Liability was not in dispute and DAS sought to bring a subrogated claim in B's name for the recovery of the hire charges. U argued that those charges could not be recovered on the alternate grounds that (1) DAS had not proved that B had taken out a policy with them and that a premium had been paid; (2) DAS had not proved that they had paid the charges, and (3) the hire agreement was a regulated hire agreement under the Consumer Credit Act 1974 and was unenforceable by reason of non-compliance with the provisions of that Act.

Held, dismissing the claim for hire charges, that as DAS had not proved that B had taken out the policy and paid a premium, or that DAS had paid the charges, they were not entitled to bring a subrogated claim, *Everson v. Flurry* (Unreported, February 22, 1999), [1999] C.L.Y. 3411 distinguished. Not being invited to do so, the court did not make a decision in respect of the 1974 Act issue.

BRAIN v. UDDIN, May 18, 2000, Deputy District Judge Bull, CC (Birmingham). [*Ex rel.* James Morgan, Barrister, St Philip's Chambers, Fountain Court, Steelhouse Lane, Birmingham].

2584. Consumer credit – credit hire agreements – motor vehicles – "sham" agreements

[Consumer Credit Act 1974; Consumer Credit (Exempt Agreements) Order 1989 (SI 1989 869) Art.3(1).]

N was involved in a road traffic accident in June 1999 and claimed damages from Y including credit hire charges. After the accident N had contacted his insurers who told him that they would provide him with a courtesy car while his own car was being repaired on condition that he took it to a repairer of their choice. N preferred to use a different repairer, who referred him to H. H advised N that they would pay for the repairs to N's car provided he was not responsible for the accident. N was given a replacement car the same day as the accident. He was then sent two documents purporting to be a credit hire agreement and a credit repair agreement. The agreements were blank and N's evidence was that he accepted them on the basis that he would not be paying. N was concerned with a clause purporting to end the agreement within 51 weeks of its commencement, but H told him that he had paid £10 to protect his liability by taking out insurance with AA who were owned by H. N was not asked to make any payment under either agreement.

Held, dismissing the credit hire claim, that the wording of the agreements did create a liability on N to pay the charges within a period of a year. On the face of it, they were exempt agreements within the meaning of the Consumer Credit (Exempt Agreements) Order 1989 Art. 3(1) and not subject to regulation by the Consumer Credit Act 1974. However, that did not represent the true position and the agreements should be struck down as a sham. The '51 week clauses' were an open and deliberate attempt to circumvent the mechanics of the agreement, the true mechanics being an attempt by H to interpose a third party into the equation in the person of AA. The payment of £10 as insurance against a liability of about £4,000 did not ring true as a commercial venture. The judge was not satisfied on the evidence that the relevant sums had been paid by AA but in any event, as it was owned by H, the money was simply revolving around one organisation. For an agreement to be struck down as a sham it was not necessary to find that there was any common intention to deceive or any deceit at all, *Street v. Mountford* [1985] A.C. 809, [1985] C.L.Y. 1893 and *Smithson v. Checketts* (Unreported, April 3, 2000) followed.

NEILSON v. YOUNG, June 6, 2000, District Judge Bullock, CC (Newcastle). [*Ex rel.* Joanna Droop, Barrister, 12 King;s Bench Walk, Temple, London].

2585. Consumer credit – credit hire agreements – no demand for payment nor express agreement for forbearance

R and M were involved in a road traffic accident in December 1998. R hired a replacement vehicle from HD whilst his own vehicle was being repaired for the period December 15, 1998 to January 6, 1999. The daily rate of hire, inclusive of a £10 supplement for dual control, was £42.50 per day with an additional delivery charge of £75. Further, R incurred collision damage waiver charges at the rate of £6 per day. The total hire charges including VAT were £1,398.84. The terms and conditions of the hire agreement provided inter alia that R would pay on demand the rental charges and excess waiver and that the period of the agreement would not exceed 90 days. M argued that the agreement was unenforceable because credit had been extended and based on the fact that the charges had not been paid some 18 months later, no demand had been made and R had signed a retainer with his broker to the effect that R's solicitor would pay any hire charges received from M's insurers directly to the hire company, the intention of the parties was clearly that R would be granted credit on the hire charges until the conclusion of the claim for damages, bringing the agreement between R and the hire company within the ambit of *Dimond v. Lovell* [2000] 2 W.L.R. 1121, [2000] C.L.Y. 2566. R contended that, at the time of signing the hire agreement, he assumed that M would pay the hire charges because M was liable for the accident. R stated that no oral or written representations were made to him to the effect that he would not be liable for the hire charges or that he would be extended credit on the hire charges.

Held, allowing the claim for hire charges in full and distinguishing *Dimond v. Lovell*, that on the face of the terms and conditions no credit was extended to R. There had been no variation of the terms and conditions of the hire agreement. The fact that no demand had been made for payment by the hire company was a commercial decision on the part of the hire company, but forbearance to sue did not grant R a contractual entitlement to credit and there had been no express agreement for forbearance in this case. Similarly, the fact that the hire charges remained unpaid at the time of the hearing did not of itself constitute an agreement between the hire company and R that R would be extended credit. It was open to the hire company to sue R for outstanding hire charges on the basis of the written terms and conditions.

RADCLIFFE v. McKEOWN, June 7, 2000, District Judge Smedley, CC (Liverpool). [*Ex rel.* Michael Jones, Barrister, Cobden House Chambers, 19 Quay Street, Manchester].

2586. Consumer credit – credit hire agreements – no provision for payment by instalments – reasonableness of hire period where repairs delayed

[Consumer Credit Act 1974; Consumer Credit (Exempt Agreements) Order 1989 (SI 1989 869).]

SW brought an action for damages against BW following a road traffic accident. Liability was not in dispute. As a result of the accident, SW's car was undriveable but repairable. Due to the Christmas and New Year holiday period, repairs to her vehicle could not be started until January 6. The repairs were commenced immediately thereafter and completed within a reasonable time. Two days after the accident, SW hired a replacement vehicle from FAM and the period of hire ran until immediately after the repairs to her vehicle had been completed. The hire agreement included a provision that credit would be extended until the claim against the responsible third party had been concluded or 11 months from the date of the agreement had expired, whichever was the soonest. BW contended that (1) an unreasonable delay had occurred, and (2) the agreement was unenforceable, being a regulated agreement which fell foul of the provisions of the Consumer Credit Act 1974.

Held, allowing the claim by SW in full, except for delivery and collection charges not previously notified as payable, that (1) it was entirely reasonable that repairs should not have commenced until after the Christmas and New Year holiday and accordingly it was entirely reasonable that SW should have hired a vehicle for the period that her car was being repaired, and (2) the agreement was exempt from regulation under the Act by virtue of the Consumer Credit (Exempt Agreements) Order 1989. The absence of a provision for payment by instalments did not thereby take the agreement out of the ambit of the Order. The agreement did not refer to instalment payments at all, and therefore it would have been perverse to find that the agreement was regulated. The plain meaning of the words of the agreement was that the sum due for hire was payable in full, either when the claim had been concluded or at the expiration of 11 months, whichever occurred soonest. A submission that the court should look at BW's circumstances to determine whether or not there was a likelihood that SW could pay the hire charges was not a relevant consideration to the interpretation of the agreement.

WALKER v. WORTH, August 20, 1999, District Judge McCullagh, CC (Birkenhead). [*Ex rel.* David A Tubby & Co Solicitors, Alexander House, 2a Aughton Street, Ormskirk, Lancs.].

2587. Consumer credit – credit hire agreements – repair agreement but not car hire agreement exempt under Consumer Credit Act 1974

[Consumer Credit Act 1974; Consumer Credit (Exempt Agreements) Order 1989 Art.3 (1) (a); Civil Procedure Rules 1998 (SI 1998 3132) Part 27 r.27.14.]

J brought action against B for damages for credit car hire and credit repair costs arising from a road traffic accident. J had hired the car from H who also provided credit for the repair of her car. B admitted liability but denied that J was entitled to recover damages under either agreement averring that both agreements were regulated by the Consumer Credit Act 1974 and were enforceable pursuant to *Dimond v. Lovell* [2000] 2 W.L.R. 1121, [2000] C.L.Y. 2566. J contended that both were exempt under the Consumer Credit (Exempt Agreements) Order 1989 Art.3(1) (a) (i), as payment was required within 12 months. Clause three of the agreements stated "The period extended by this Agreement shall expire, in any event, 51 weeks from the date of this Agreement. At the expiry of the credit period you shall then become liable to pay the hire charges in full". J argued that the wording of the Order should be construed widely, that the clause therefore complied with its requirements and that payment in one instalment, although not expressed, could be inferred. In the alternative J argued that the credit repair fell outside *Dimond* and therefore remained enforceable and recoverable. B argued, inter alia, that (1) as the 1974 Act had been enacted to protect consumers any exemption from its protective measures should be construed narrowly; (2) the number of payments to be made had to be expressed to comply with the terms of the 1989 Order and could not be inferred; (3) a liability for payment after 51 weeks did not amount to a requirement for payment to be made within 12 months; (4) the credit repair agreement was ad idem with the credit hire agreement and as both provided a service to J they should stand or fall together; (5) in the alternative, both agreements were enforceable as J had relied on and been induced by a promise by H not to enforce the agreement against her. H was therefore estopped from resiling on their promise and (6) the engineer's fee of £70.50 claimed was not recoverable as a repair estimate and invoice had been provided and the quantum of repair costs was not an issue.

Held, finding in favour of the defendant, that (1) the 1989 Order should be construed narrowly and its wording strictly interpreted; (2) the number of repayments must be expressed and could not be inferred; (3) liability for payment after 51 weeks did not amount to a requirement for payment within 12 months, therefore the agreement for credit car hire did not comply with the requirements of the Order and the agreement was regulated by the 1974 Act. By consent the provisions of the Act had not been complied with and the agreement was therefore unenforceable, *Dimond* and *Cooke v. Whiteley* (Unreported, October 27, 1999), [2000] C.L.Y. 2569 applied; (4) the credit repair agreement was different to the credit car hire and was enforceable, *Jones v. Stroud DC* [1986] 1 W.L.R. 1141, [1986] C.L.Y. 343 applied, (5) H was estopped from resiling on their promise not to enforce the agreement against J, *City and Westminster Properties (1934) Ltd v. Mudd* [1959] Ch. 129, [1958] C.L.Y. 1788 applied, and (6) as the repair estimate and invoice were available and the quantum of repair was not disputed, the engineer's report was unnecessary and under the principle of proportionality was not recoverable, therefore fixed costs only were allowed in accordance with the Civil Procedure Rules 1998 Part 27 r.27.14.

JORDAN v. BASHFORD, May 8, 2000, Judge Ellis, CC (Croydon). [*Ex rel.* Nigel Ffitch, Barrister, Phoenix Chambers, Gray's Inn, London].

2588. Consumer credit – credit hire agreements – repairs carried out under unenforceable consumer credit agreement

[Consumer Credit Act 1974.]

S's car was damaged in an accident in July 1998. It was repaired and an invoice was produced. S had not claimed on his insurance for the repairs and did not pay the invoice himself. S dealt with a company, A, who arranged repairs and car hire. S had not signed any documents relating to the hire and had not paid for the hire. No terms and conditions relating to payment for repairs or hire were ever disclosed. S argued that he was entitled to recover the costs of repairs, these being the best evidence of the diminution in value of his car, *Taylor v. Cook* (Unreported, August 6, 1999), [1999] C.L.Y. 2504 referred to. O argued that the hire charges were irrecoverable for failure to comply with the Consumer Credit Act 1974. O also argued that the repairs had been carried out under an unenforceable consumer credit agreement, therefore the car had been repaired at no cost to S and O had no liability to pay S. O argued that the relevant question was what the repairs had cost S, not what the cost of the repairs was, *Taylor v. Cook* cited.

Held, disallowing the claim for hire and repair charges, that there was no evidence that the repairs had been paid for and there was no evidence that S was liable to pay for the repairs. S had been put back into the pre-accident position by having his car repaired with the cost being met by a third party of which there was little information. Notwithstanding *Taylor v. Cook*, the claim failed. The hire charges were also irrecoverable for failure to comply with the 1974 Act.

STUMP v. OTUAGOMAH, March 10, 2000, District Judge Worthington, CC (Lambeth). [*Ex rel.* Tim Petts, Barrister, 12 King's Bench Walk, London].

2589. Consumer credit – credit hire agreements – time limit for payment – compliance with Consumer Credit (Exempt Agreements) Order 1989

[Consumer Credit Act 1974; Consumer Credit (Exempt Agreements) Order 1989 (SI 1989 869).]

Z claimed damages from R arising from a road traffic accident. Liability was not in dispute. Z had hired a car on credit hire from S. A credit hire agreement was made, in which it was stated that payment was due on the anniversary of the agreement and also that it was due 12 months after the date of the agreement. At the hearing, Z successfully argued that the contract was exempt from the Consumer Credit Act 1974 under the Consumer Credit (Exempt Agreements) Order 1989, and therefore enforceable, with the result that Z would recover from R pursuant to *Dimond v. Lovell* [2000] 2 W.L.R. 1121, [2000] C.L.Y. 2566. R appealed.

Held, allowing the appeal, that the 1989 Order required payment within 12 months beginning with the date of the agreement. In counting time, the date the agreement was made should be included. In counting time for 12 months "after" or "from" the date of the agreement, the date of the agreement would not be included, therefore this period did not come within the prescribed period set out in the 1989 Order, nor did the use of the words "on the anniversary". Therefore, the hire agreement in question was regulated by and unenforceable under the 1974 Act.

ZOAN v. ROUAMBA [2000] 1 W.L.R. 1509, Chadwick, L.J., CA.

2590. Consumer credit – credit hire charges – payment not requested by hirer – intention to offer credit

K and O were involved in a road traffic accident in November 1998. Liability was not in dispute. K entered into a car hire agreement with S for a period of 34 days. This was evidenced by two agreements, the first allowing for 28 days and being signed by K, and the second being for a period of six days' hire and not signed by K. K claimed to have no knowledge of the second agreement. The terms and conditions made no mention of any deferral of a debt. The preamble to the agreements stated that no relaxation or forbearance on behalf of S was to be taken as any form of waiver or in any way affecting S's legal rights. The agreement stated that the terms and conditions did not come into effect until the charges had been paid in full and before the commencement of hire. K had not paid any of the charges and had been told by an intermediary between herself and S that "she would not have to worry about it". No request was ever made for payment from S. K argued that there was no contractual right to defer the agreement and that the fact that the charges had not been paid was a mere indulgence on behalf of S, not amounting to a credit agreement. O argued, inter alia, that the terms and conditions did not apply as the agreement stipulated that they did not come into force until the charges were paid in full. As a result O contended that the agreement was oral and the agreement to defer was apparent not only from the express term that she "did not have to worry about it", but also evidenced by the fact that S's normal practice was to charge before hire, and that this was an indication that a contrary agreement had been made.

Held, giving judgment for K, that (1) being told "not to worry about it", on the evidence, meant that she did not have to worry about the cost of the hire charges as they would be recovered from some other party. At the very most, she would be liable to pay at the conclusion of litigation; (2) credit was given, as K was led to believe that she would not be paying for the car, or that the charges would not be due until the conclusion of litigation. This was supported by the evidence that no request had ever been made for the charges, and (3) the case should be looked at as a whole to assess the true intention of the parties. On the facts, credit was clearly envisaged. It was necessary to give effect to what was agreed rather than what was printed as the whole of the circumstances needed to be evaluated; a matter of particular importance in the area of consumer law.

KATON v. O'REILLY, September 13, 1999, District Judge Smith, CC (Yeovil). [*Ex rel.* Paul McGrath, Barrister, 1 Temple Gardens, Temple, London].

2591. Consumer credit – credit reference agencies – disclosure of information

CONSUMER CREDIT (CONDUCT OF BUSINESS) (CREDIT REFERENCES) (AMENDMENT) REGULATIONS 2000, SI 2000 291; made under the Consumer Credit Act 1974 s.26, s.147. In force: March 1, 2000; £1.00.

These Regulations amend the Consumer Credit (Conduct of Business) (Credit References) Regulations 1977 (SI 1977 330) which supplement the Consumer Credit Act 1974 s.157 to s.160, certain provisions of the Data Protection Act 1998 s.7 to s.9 and the Consumer Credit (Credit Reference Agency) Regulations 2000 (SI 2000 290), which deal with the disclosure to consumers of information about their financial standing held by credit reference agencies and the correction of such information where it is found to be wrong or incomplete.

2592. Consumer credit – repairs – credit repair agreements – no distinction between credit hire and credit repairs

[Consumer Credit Act 1974.]

C and E were involved in a road traffic accident. C's vehicle was repaired on a credit basis and C was successful at the disposal hearing in recovering the full amount of the repairs from E. E appealed, contending that there was no difference between the issue of credit hire and credit repairs and the judge had been wrong to draw a distinction between the two where (1) the hire agreement between the hire company and the claimant was unenforceable and the hire charges were therefore irrecoverable pursuant to *Dimond v. Lovell* [2000] Q.B. 216, [1999] C.L.Y. 2457, and (2) the credit repair agreement was likewise unenforceable but the car repair figure was found to be a method of measuring the diminution in value of the claimant's car. Therefore, if a credit repair agreement was unenforceable against a claimant, then the same argument would prevail as in *Dimond*. E further argued that it was not possible to quantify C's loss or diminution in value by the cost of repairs, nor state that C's loss had crystallised at the time of the accident. C contended that the repair costs were a direct loss and not a consequential loss *Dimond*, *Jones v. Stroud DC* [1986] 1 W.L.R. 1141, [1986] C.L.Y. 1993 and *Taylor v. Cook* (Unreported, August 6, 1999), [1999] C.L.Y. 2504 cited.

Held, allowing the appeal, that the credit repair agreement fell foul of the Consumer Credit Act 1974, and the court should not "permit by the back door that which it struck down at the front door". The agreement was a commercial agreement and should not be equated with authorities where a trust could be said to exist, *Hunt v. Severs* [1994] 2 A.C. 350, [1994] C.L.Y. 1530 considered. A trust would only arise in cases involving the provision of voluntary services by a close friend or relative. The unenforceable agreement was that of the repairer, and according to the principles of equity, as he was not "coming to equity with clean hands", it would be wrong to impute a trust. The award of damages and costs made by the District Judge in respect of vehicle repair was set aside, and the assessment of damages and costs incurred before the District Judge was stayed pending determination of *Dimond* by the House of Lords.

CARTER v. EASON, February 18, 2000, Judge Trigger, CC (Liverpool). [*Ex rel.* Beachcroft Wansbroughs Solicitors, 13 Police Street, Manchester].

2593. Consumer credit – storage of vehicle – no credit agreement with storage company – charges enforceable

[Consumer Credit Act 1974.]

M brought an action against E for damages arising out of a road traffic accident. Following the accident M's vehicle went into storage and M was provided with an invoice for storage fees. E contended that the storage agreement was a credit agreement pursuant to the Consumer Credit Act 1974 and as such was unenforceable against M and thereafter E, *Dimond v. Lovell* [2000] 2 W.L.R. 1121, [2000] C.L.Y. 2566 cited.

Held, giving judgment for the storage charges, that there was no contract between M and the storage company which could lead to an inference of credit. The storage company were prepared to allow more time for payment as they were aware litigation was being pursued to recover the debt. M was responsible for the debt and therefore it was enforceable against M and against E.

MANITO v. ELLIOTT, June 13, 2000, District Judge Chapman, CC (Salford). [*Ex rel.* J Keith Park & Co Solicitors, 23 Westway, Maghull, Liverpool].

2594. Consumer credit agreements – exemptions – loan to former employee

[Consumer Credit Act 1974, s.8; Consumer Credit (Exempt Agreements) (No.2) Order 1985 (SI 1985 757) Art.4.]

Questions arose as to whether loan agreements between BCCI and two former employees, S and H, were regulated within the meaning of the Consumer Credit Act 1974 s.8 or were exempt pursuant to the Consumer Credit (Exempt Agreements (No.2) Order 1985 Art.4. BCCI argued that the agreements were exempt and were therefore enforceable without the need for compliance with the requirements of the 1974 Act. S and H contended that the loans were excluded from exemption because the only charges arising on them were interest payments and it was theoretically possible that the interest rate could have exceeded 13 per cent following termination of their employment, so as to fall outside the provisions of Art.4(1)(c) of the Regulations.

Held, giving judgment for BCCI, that (1) Art. 4(1) provided that a consumer credit agreement covered by the descriptions in Art.4(1)(a), (b) or (c) would not be regulated, and (2) if an agreement satisfied the requirements of any of those categories it was unnecessary to consider whether it also fell into another exempt category. In the instant case the agreements were exempt by virtue of Art.4(1)(a) and Art.4(3).

BANK OF CREDIT AND COMMERCE INTERNATIONAL SA (IN LIQUIDATION) v. ALI (NO.2) [2000] C.C.L.R. 1, Lightman, J., Ch D.

2595. Consumer credit agreements – interest – term requiring borrower to pay interest on capital sum after judgment

[Consumer Credit Act 1974 s.129(2), s.136; County Courts Act 1984; County Courts (Interest on Judgment Debts) Order 1991 (SI 1991 1184); Unfair Terms in Consumer Contracts Regulations 1994 (SI 1994 3159) Reg.3, Reg.4(1).]

FNB, a provider of credit, used standard agreements which incorporated a term providing that interest on amounts outstanding would be charged both before and after judgment. Following complaints received from members of the public, the Director General applied for an injunction restraining FNB from relying on the term. Refusing the application, the judge held ([2000] 1 W.L.R. 98) that whilst the fairness of the term could be assessed under the Unfair Terms in Consumer Contracts Regulations 1994 Reg.3, the term was neither substantively nor procedurally unfair. Arguing that the term fell within the exceptions set out in Reg.3(2), FNB appealed against the judge's finding that he had jurisdiction to assess the fairness of the term. The Director General appealed against the judge's finding that the term was not unfair. It was argued that borrowers suffered unfairness in discovering that they had to pay interest after being ordered to pay a judgment by instalments without the court having been asked to use its power under the Consumer Credit Act 1974 s.136 to amend the relevant agreement.

Held, allowing the Director General's appeal and dismissing FNB's cross appeal, that (1) the judge had been right to assess the fairness of the disputed term. The term did not fall within the exceptions set out in Reg.3(2). For the purpose of Reg.3(2)(a), it did not define the subject matter of the contract. As regards Reg.3(2)(b), it could not be said that the term was concerned with the adequacy of the price or remuneration of the goods or services which had been sold or supplied, and (2) the term was unfair within Reg.4(1) of the 1994 Regulations. As the term had the effect of surprising and defeating the reasonable expectations of borrowers, it offended the requirement of good faith. It also created a significant imbalance in the parties' rights and obligations by enabling FNB to recover interest after judgment in circumstances where the County Courts Act 1984 and the County Courts (Interest on Judgment Debts)

Order 1991 prevented it from doing so. The court's powers to make a time order under s.129(2) of the 1974 Act and to amend the terms of an agreement under s.136 did not prevent the term from operating unfairly in the many cases where instalment orders were made without those powers having been relied on.

DIRECTOR GENERAL OF FAIR TRADING v. FIRST NATIONAL BANK PLC [2000] Q.B. 672, Peter Gibson, L.J., CA.

2596. Debts – assignment – defective notice of assignment

CL claimed, inter alia, that debts owed by S to B had been assigned to it and sought summary judgment, relying on a notice of assignment which had been signed on behalf of S in confirmation. The notice had been sent by B and stated that the debts owed by S to B were to be assigned to SO and payable to CL.

Held, making no order on the application, that although a notice to a debtor stating that the debt should be paid to another person could amount to a notice of assignment, the reference to the assignment to SO, with no specific mention of an assignment to CL, created the possibility that CL was only a collection agent, and in the absence of further evidence, did not justify summary judgment.

CREDIT LYONNIAS COMMERCIAL FINANCE LTD v. SINGH AND KAUR (T/A MANDER FASHIONS), November 30, 1999, Master Leslie, QBD. [*Ex rel.* Sunil Iyer, Barrister, Bracton Chambers, 8 Bell Yard, London].

2597. Gambling – provision of credit to client – unlicensed consumer credit business

[Consumer Credit Act 1974 s.40.]

CI accepted bets on the movement of various Stock Exchange indices over specific periods. Before being allowed to bet, a client was required either to pay a deposit or to place bets on the basis of a given credit allocation. A client exceeding the level of his deposit or credit allocation was required to provide extra funding, termed a "margin", before betting could continue. N was given a credit allocation and, following losses, was required to make a margin payment. As he could not do so, CI served a statutory demand on him for £48,453. N applied for the demand to be set aside but was unsuccessful at first instance and on appeal. N appealed, contending that CI's business involved providing credit, and, as it was not licensed to conduct consumer credit business, the agreement was unenforceable under the Consumer Credit Act 1974 s.40.

Held, dismissing the appeal, that when N entered into the contract with CI it was not possible to determine whether he would become indebted to CI in the future. N's credit allocation, therefore, did not grant him credit in respect of what would otherwise be an indebtedness payable at an earlier date. The credit allocation simply meant that N did not have to provide security against possible future indebtedness until his losses exceeded the amount of the credit allocation, *Dimond v. Lovell* [2000] Q.B. 216, [1999] C.L.Y. 2457 distinguished.

NEJAD v. CITY INDEX LTD [2000] C.C.L.R. 7, Stuart-Smith, L.J., CA.

2598. Government securities – transfer

EXCHANGE OF SECURITIES (GENERAL) (AMENDMENT) RULES 2000, SI 2000 1516; made under the National Loans Act 1968 s.14. In force: July 1, 2000; £1.00.

These Rules amend the Exchange of Securities (General) Rules 1979 (SI 1979 1678) to allow for securities which are transferable through the medium of the CGO Service being transferred instead in accordance with the Uncertificated Securities Regulations 1995 (SI 1995 3272), under which title to securities may be evidenced otherwise than by a certificate and transferred without a written instrument by means of a relevant system operated by an approved person, currently only CRESTCo.

2599. Government securities – transfer

GOVERNMENT STOCK (AMENDMENT) REGULATIONS 2000, SI 2000 1681; made under the Finance Act 1942 s.47. In force: July 1, 2000; £1.50.

These Regulations amend the Government Stock Regulations 1965 (SI 1965 1420) to enable stock which has been transferable through the medium of the CGO Service by means of an exempt transfer to be transferred instead in accordance with the Uncertificated Securities Regulations 1995 (SI 1995 3272) by means of a relevant system operated by a person, currently only CRESTCo Ltd, who has been approved under the 1995 Regulations.

2600. Hire purchase – agreement void due to fraudulent impersonation – mistake as to hirer's identity

[Hire Purchase Act 1964 s.27, s.29.]

R obtained a vehicle on hire purchase from SF through a dealer by impersonating P, producing P's driving licence and forging his signature, thereby satisfying SF's credit checks. P was a man of good character unaware of this transaction. R then purported to sell the vehicle to H, a dealer in vehicle spare parts, who purchased it unaware of the fraud. SF sought the return of the vehicle from H or, damages in the alternative, contending that (1) the identity of the hire purchaser was crucial to the agreement and the mistake thereto rendered the agreement void rather than voidable, thereby preventing R from passing title to H, and (2) as the signature on the agreement was a forgery, the agreement was void. H contended that, the identity of the rogue was not crucial to the agreement and that the mistake rendered the agreement merely voidable rather than void; (2) SF had failed to avoid the agreement prior to the sale to H, and (3) H was a private purchaser in good faith under the Hire Purchase Act 1964 s.27 and therefore entitled to take good title.

Held, giving judgment for SF, that (1) SF intended to contract with P, in whose name the agreement was made and whose signature had been forged by R, rather than with R, *King's Norton Metal Co v. Edridge Merrett & Co* (1897) 14 T.L.R. 98 and *Cundy v. Lindsay* (1878) L.R. 3 App. Cas. 459 applied; (2) the lack of direct contact between SF and R, and the fact that the agreement was in writing rather than oral, prevented this being an inter praesentes agreement, *Lewis v. Averay (No.1)* [1972] 1 Q.B. 198, [1971] C.L.Y. 1801 distinguished; (3) although R had conducted negotiations with the dealer, the dealer had not acted as the agent of SF, *Branwhite v. Worcester Works Finance Ltd* [1969] 1 A.C. 552, [1968] C.L.Y. 1766 applied; (4) the hirer's identity was crucial to the agreement and the mistake as to his identity rendered the agreement void. Although not relevant to the decision, it was further found that vehicle spare parts were not "mechanically propelled vehicles" for the purposes of s.29 of the Act, *Smart v. Allen* [1963] 1 Q.B. 291, [1962] C.L.Y. 2723 applied; (5) H's dealings in spare parts did not make him a dealer in vehicles, and (6) had the agreement been voidable rather than void, H would have been able to rely on the defence of private purchaser under s.27.

SHOGUN FINANCE LTD v. HUDSON, January 13, 2000, Not specified, CC (Leicester). [*Ex rel.* Sunil Iyer, Barrister, Bracton Chambers, 8 Bell Yard, London].

2601. Hire purchase – default – measure of damages

[Consumer Credit Act 1974 s.39(2), s.100.]

B sued M for damages arising out of default on a contract of hire purchase for a motor vehicle. Two issues arose in the case, whether (1) the agreement remained enforceable against M where B sued in the name of the company but the hire purchase agreement was in a trading name of B as B's licence under the Consumer Credit Act 1974 authorised it to trade only under the name of the company, and (2) the court was able to award a lesser sum than the measure of damages set out in s.100(1) on the ground that B's loss within the meaning of s.100(3) was less than the prima facie measure of damages.

Held, giving judgment for B, that (1) there had been a breach of s.39(2) but that did not make the agreement unenforceable against M, and (2) the question was whether "loss" within the meaning of s.100(3) included the owner's lost profits that he would have received but for the hirer's termination. The court held that "loss" included the owner's lost profits and that the power in s.100(3) to award a lesser sum should be exercised accordingly.

BOOTH & PHIPPS GARAGES LTD v. MILTON, October 1, 1999, District Judge Bowman, CC (Oxford). [*Ex rel.* Alexander Pelling, Barrister, New Court Chambers, 5 Verulam Buildings, Gray's Inn, London].

2602. Hire purchase – fraud – mistake as to identity of contracting party – adequacy of steps taken to verify identity

[Hire Purchase Act 1964 s.27.]

CT, a finance company, purchased a car for the purposes of letting it on hire purchase to X. X was a fraudster who had assumed the identify of HC, a real person. X produced a driving licence in HC's name, which turned out to be a forgery. The only check carried out by CT was to verify with a credit agency that there was a person by the name of HC living at the address given on the driving licence and that he did not have a bad credit history. CT entered the agreement and allowed X to take the car. CT subsequently discovered the fraud. Twelve days after entering the hire purchase agreement, CT informed the police and placed a security marker on the vehicle with Equifax HPI. Two days later, C purchased the vehicle for cash, unaware that it was subject to a hire purchase agreement. CT then exercised its right under the hire purchase agreement to send a notice of termination of the agreement and repossessed the car from C. C brought an action for conversion against CT, invoking the innocent purchaser protection in the Hire Purchase Act 1964 s.27. CT contended that this protection was not available to her on the basis that the agreement was not subsisting at the date she bought the car because (1) the agreement was void ab initio on the grounds of unilateral mistake as to the identify of the person CT was contracting with, induced by the fraud of X, *Lewis v. Averay (No.2)* [1973] 1 W.L.R. 510, [1973] C.L.Y. 2637, and *Chartered Trust Plc v. Bamford* (Unreported, April 22, 1999), [1999] C.L.Y. 2512 cited, and (2) alternatively, by informing the police and Equifax HPI of the fraud, CT had effectively avoided the contract prior to C's purchase, *Car and Universal Finance Co Ltd v. Caldwell* [1965] 1 Q.B. 525, [1964] C.L.Y. 3286 cited.

Held, finding in favour of C on a preliminary issue, that the hire purchase agreement was not void ab initio nor had it been effectively avoided at the date of C's purchase. CT had failed to take all reasonable steps to verify the identity of X and could not, therefore, later rely on identity as being of importance, Cheshire, Fifoot and Furmston's Law of Contract, 13th edn, p.262 cited. The approach taken to establishing that X was who he claimed to be was limited to taking a driving licence from him. The hire purchase agreement was therefore not void for unilateral mistake. Further, the notice that CT gave terminating the agreement was inconsistent with its claim that the agreement was void ab initio, in that CT was purporting to terminate something which did not exist. The agreement subsisted until that notice was served, which was well after the car came into C's hands. The agreement was therefore not avoided by notifying the police and Equifax HPI that a fraud had taken place.

CAWSTON v. CHARTERED TRUST PLC, February 29, 2000, Judge Brandt, CC (Colchester). [*Ex rel.* Andrew Granville Stafford, Barrister, 4 King's Bench Walk, 2nd Floor, Temple, London].

2603. Loan agreements – interest rates – bank's entitlement to use current practice for calculation – duty to notify customer of changes

A couple, K, appealed against the dismissal of their claim against a bank, HSBC for the return of overpaid interest. K had taken out a long term loan for business purposes. The loan agreement specified that interest would accrue on a daily basis and that it would be "debited and compounded in accordance with the bank's current practice from time to time". HSBC's established practice was to debit and compound interest on a quarterly basis, with the effect that the amount of the monthly repayments remained unchanged but the outstanding amount of the loan altered. K submitted that such interpretation of the relevant clause was unacceptable, since the practice was not described in the agreement, and was subject to variation at HSBC's whim, hence the true cost of borrowing was concealed. K contended for an alternative construction so as to provide that interest would be debited and capitalised on a daily basis.

Held, dismissing the appeal, that the bank's interpretation of the agreement was correct, and in accordance with established English banking practice, which entitled the bank to charge its customers compound interest, *National Bank of Greece v. Pinios Shipping Co (No.1)* [1990] 1 A.C. 637, [1990] C.L.Y. 267 applied. The interpretation of the agreement contended for by K was inconsistent with the agreement they had signed, the words used having been given their natural and ordinary meaning.

KITCHEN v. HSBC BANK PLC [2000] 1 All E.R. (Comm) 787, Brooke, L.J., CA.

2604. Local government finance – stocks and bonds – transfer

LOCAL AUTHORITY (STOCKS AND BONDS) (AMENDMENT) REGULATIONS 2000, SI 2000 1680; made under the Companies Act 1989 s.207. In force: July 1, 2000; £1.50.

These Regulations, which amend the Local Authority (Stocks and Bonds) Regulations 1974 (SI 1974 519), enable stock and bonds which have been transferable through the medium of the CGO Service by means of an exempt transfer to be transferred instead in accordance with the Uncertificated Securities Regulations 1995 (SI 1995 3272) by means of a relevant system operated by a person, currently only CRESTCo Limited, who has been approved under the 1995 Regulations.

2605. Mortgages – arrears – estoppel on basis of earlier possession proceedings

UCB brought proceedings against C for arrears under a mortgage agreement, seeking possession of the land and a money judgment for the arrears. By the time of the hearing C had given possession voluntarily and an unopposed possession order was made. Two years later, UCB brought proceedings to recover the amount of the arrears and obtained summary judgment against C. C's appeal against summary judgment was dismissed and he appealed on the basis that there had been a claim for arrears in the initial proceedings and so the doctrine of res judicata applied, barring UCB from bringing a second claim.

Held, dismissing the appeal, that the mere fact that a judgment granting possession had been given where there was also a money claim did not give rise to an estoppel on the basis of res judicata or on the basis of the doctrine in *Henderson v. Henderson* [1843-60] All E.R. Rep. 378 distinguished; C would not have agreed to judgment being entered on the money claim at the time the possession order was made and it could not be said that there was an agreement that the money claim had been abandoned at that time. It could not be right that a judgment limited to granting possession could release C from all financial liability to UCB.

UCB BANK PLC v. CHANDLER (2000) 79 P.& C.R. 270, Evans, L.J., CA.

2606. Mortgages – joint and several liability – interpretation of mortgage deed

G appealed against a judgment that because of the interpretation of a mortgage between AIB and M and G as mortgagors, he was liable for the debts of M to AIB. M had conducted property dealings in three separate capacities; on his own account, in partnership with G, and in partnership with S. G was only entitled to the profits of the dealings attributable to his partnership. M and G signed a facility letter in favour of AIM, which contained a condition that M's and M and G's borrowings should be reduced, and executed a mortgage, which contained a standard joint and several liability clause, and which defined the mortgagor as the two of them. G contended that all the circumstances surrounding the execution of the mortgage, including the parties' intentions, as illustrated by the facility letter, should be used to aid the interpretation of the mortgage deed.

Held, dismissing the appeal, that the only meaning one could draw from the mortgage deed was that there was joint and several liability. The terms of the facility letter did nothing to dispel that conclusion.

AIB GROUP (UK) PLC (FORMERLY ALLIED IRISH BANK PLC AND AIB FINANCE LTD) v. MARTIN; AIB GROUP (UK) PLC (FORMERLY ALLIED IRISH BANK PLC AND AIB FINANCE LTD) v. GOLD (2000) 97(30) L.S.G. 42, Morritt, L.J., CA.

2607. Mortgages – mistake – advance complete when funds transferred to client account – loan contract and resulting mortgage distinct transactions – rectification impossible where principal not acting on agent's behalf

B applied to H for a mortgage advance naming D as solicitors acting in the transaction but received a mortgage pack from SRF, an associated mortgage company sharing premises with H, due to an error. The error was not identified until after the contract had been entered into and funds transferred from H to D's client account, by which time completion had occurred. The mortgage deed executed by B was in favour of SRF as was the life policy and following B falling into arrears, SRF was registered as proprietor of a charge over the property resulting in possession proceedings and the ultimate sale of the property. H claimed the shortfall between the sale proceeds and the original advance but leave to substitute SRF as claimants was granted, resulting in H being named in pleadings as lending money on behalf of SRF. The issue to be decided on appeal was whether the original advance was made by H acting as principal was on behalf of SRF who later ratified the act and whether the solicitors owed a duty of care to SRF.

Held, dismissing the appeal, that when the original advance was transferred into D's client account H was acting as principal issuing the monies from its own resources and thus the act could not be later ratified under the laws of agency by SRF, since H were not purporting to act on their behalf, *Keighley Maxsted & Co v. Durant* [1901] A.C. 240 considered. At the point of transfer the advance was complete as H had performed their obligations under the contract which they had entered into with B which had been concluded by B's initial acceptance of the mortgage offer. The initial loan contract and the mortgage that followed were two distinct transactions and there had been no mistake affecting the initial contract, *National Home Loans Corp Plc v. Giffen Couch & Archer* [1998] 1 W.L.R. 207, [1997] C.L.Y. 3829 applied. The law of agency did not play a part in the correction of mistakes such as in the present case as other appropriate remedies such as rectification, rescission or estoppel existed. The issue of whether D owed a duty of care to SRF was therefore a moot point.

SECURED RESIDENTIAL FUNDING PLC v. DOUGLAS GOLDBERG HENDELES & CO *The Times*, April 26, 2000, Laws, L.J., CA.

2608. Multilateral Investment Guarantee Agency – capital stock subscription

MULTILATERAL INVESTMENT GUARANTEE AGENCY (FURTHER SUBSCRIPTION TO CAPITAL STOCK) ORDER 2000, SI 2000 1406; made under the Multilateral Investment Guarantee Agency Act 1988 s.2. In force: May 17, 2000; £1.00.

This Order provides for the payment to the Multilateral Investment Guarantee Agency of a subscription equivalent to $40,088,100 to the increased authorised capital stock of the Agency. It provides for the redemption of non-interest-bearing and non-negotiable notes issued by the Secretary of State in payment of that subscription, and that certain sums that may be received by the UK Government from the Agency shall be paid to the Consolidated Fund.

2609. National Savings – certificates – authority to make payments

SAVINGS CERTIFICATES (AMENDMENT) REGULATIONS 2000, SI 2000 3110; made under the National Debt Act 1972 s.11. In force: December 13, 2000; £1.50.

These Regulations amend the Savings Certificates Regulations 1991 (SI 1991 1031) to provide that an application for payment of an amount payable in respect of a National Savings certificate implies authority to the Director of Savings to make payment by such means, other than by warrant, as may be provided for in the terms and conditions subject to which the certificate is held. The amendment ensures that such authority is not terminated by the death of the applicant, but requires the Director not to initiate payment if he receives notice that the applicant has died or countermanded the authority.

2610. Possession orders – mortgage arrears – interpretation of mortgage contract – calculation of arrears

[Administration of Justice Act 1970 s.36.]

L appealed against a possession order obtained by BS on the basis of substantial mortgage arrears. L contended that the amount of arrears depended on the construction of the mortgage contract, and that on its true interpretation it was likely that those arrears would be discharged within the mortgage term, and the court should therefore have refused possession pursuant to the Administration of Justice Act 1970 s.36.

Held, allowing the appeal, that the quantum of arrears depended on the construction of the contract, and was more than a matter of factual calculation. There was evidence that L had validly exercised an option to pay interest at a lower charging rate. Furthermore, calculation of the amount of arrears was dependent upon whether the option had been exercised, whether an unauthorised charge of compound interest had been made, and the correct total of sums already repaid by L. As those matters had not been considered by the trial judge, it was appropriate to direct a retrial.

BANK OF SCOTLAND v. LADJADJ; *sub nom.* LADJADJ v. BANK OF SCOTLAND [2000] 2 All E.R. (Comm) 583, Laws, L.J., CA.

2611. Securities – uncertificated securities – transfer

UNCERTIFICATED SECURITIES (AMENDMENT) REGULATIONS 2000, SI 2000 1682; made under the Companies Act 1989 s.207. In force: July 1, 2000; £1.50.

These Regulations amend the Uncertificated Securities Regulations 1995 (SI 1995 3272) to allow for securities which have been transferable through the medium of the CGO Service to be transferred instead in accordance with those Regulations by means of a relevant system operated by an Operator, currently only CRESTCo Ltd.

2612. Swap agreements – termination – calculation of amount payable on early termination following insolvency

P entered into an agreement with R incorporating the Master Agreement (Multicurrency-Cross Border) (1992) of the International Swaps and Derivatives Association Inc. There was provision for the agreement to be terminated by insolvency, which under s.5 amounted to an event of default, whereupon a fixed formula would be used to calculate early termination payments. P became insolvent and R, who was also in financial difficulties, calculated the sum payable based on the market quotation formula, involving an open market valuation of the obligation which R as the non defaulting party had lost or gained as a result of the default. P, seeking to challenge the use of the formula, sought a declaration that it was entitled to require R to use an alternate method of calculation known as the loss payment method, which was a permitted method within the agreement. P contended that the method used had failed to produce a commercially reasonable result as it undervalued R's gain and that both parties had contemplated that the two methods would yield a broadly similar result. P submitted that the loss payment method was intended broadly to reflect the loss of bargain and therefore gave a more reasonable result in the circumstances.

Held, granting the declaration, that it had been the intention of both parties when making the agreement that the two methods of calculation used to formulate the early termination payment would yield a similar result and that a number of factors, including R's financial difficulties, resulted in a discrepancy between the two. Whilst the agreement provided that the parties had chosen the market quotation formula rather than the "loss" formula, R, as the non defaulting party, had been impliedly required by the agreement to take into account factors which would have led it to conclude that the market quotation formula would not produce a commercially reasonable result. While R's belief that the market quotation method was viable had been honestly held, the method was flawed in that it failed to take into account the nominal value of the obligation and the amount payable to P and was not, therefore, a belief that a reasonable person acting in its position in accordance with the agreement had been entitled to hold. Accordingly, the court found that R had been in breach of the agreement and P was entitled to require R to use the loss payment method of calculation which took no account of R's credit worthiness.

PEREGRINE FIXED INCOME LTD (IN LIQUIDATION) v. ROBINSON DEPARTMENT STORE PLC [2000] Lloyd's Rep. Bank. 304, Moore-Bick, J., QBD (Comm Ct).

2613. Publications

Compliance Link. Paperback: £11.50. ISBN 0-7656-0656-9. M.E. Sharpe.

Cousins, Edward; Kennedy, Paul – Law of Mortgages. 2nd Ed. Property and Conveyancing Library. Hardback: £125.00. ISBN 0-421-52950-4. Sweet & Maxwell.

Finance Act Handbook 2000. Butterworth Handbooks. ISBN 0-406-91448-6. Butterworths Law.

Jackson, John H. – Jurisprudence of GATT and the WTO. Hardback: £45.00. ISBN 0-521-62056-2. Cambridge University Press.

Macgregor, Laura; Prosser, Tony; Villiers, Charlotte – Regulation and Markets Beyond 2000. Hardback: £65.00. ISBN 0-7546-2017-4. Dartmouth.

Parlour, Richard – Butterworths International Guide to Money Laundering Law and Practice. 2nd Ed. Paperback: £135.00. ISBN 0-406-90435-9. Butterworths.

PricewaterhouseCoopers Regulatory Handbook Series. Paperback: £225.00. ISBN 0-7656-0649-6. M.E. Sharpe.

Reynolds, Barnabus – International Financial Markets. Special Issue. Paperback: £150.00. ISBN 0-421-70780-1. Sweet & Maxwell.

Salter, Richard – Modern Law of Guarantees. Paperback: £175.00. ISBN 0-406-12781-6. Butterworths.

Shaw, Paul; Bologna, Jack – Preventing Corporate Embezzlement. Paperback: £29.99. ISBN 0-7506-7254-4. Butterworth-Heinemann.

Tennekoon, Ravi C. – Law and Regulation of International Finance. 2nd Ed. Hardback: £150.00. ISBN 0-406-08158-1. Butterworths.

Trust Regulatory Handbook. Paperback: £48.95. ISBN 0-7656-0650-X. M.E. Sharpe.

FINANCIAL SERVICES

2614. Building societies – Commission expenses – fees

BUILDING SOCIETIES (GENERAL CHARGE AND FEES) REGULATIONS 2000, SI 2000 668; made under the Building Societies Act 1986 s.2, s.116. In force: April 1, 2000; £2.00.

These Regulations, which revoke the Building Societies (General Charge and Fees) Regulations 1999 (SI 1999 738), provide for a charge to be paid by building societies towards the expenses of the Building Societies Commission.

Societies with assets of £50 million or less are required to pay a sum of £3,750 plus a sum equal to 0.00124 per cent of their assets; societies with assets of more than £50 million are required to pay a sum of £5,000 plus a sum equal to 0.00124 per cent of their assets up to £30,000 million and 0.00062 per cent of their assets above that amount. They also provide for fees to be paid in respect of functions of the Building Societies Commission and the Central Office of the Registry of Friendly Societies.

2615. Electronic money – prudential supervision of institutions – Council Directive

European Parliament and Council Directive 2000/46 of September 18, 2000 on the taking up, pursuit of and prudential supervision of the business of electronic money institutions. [2000] OJ L275/39.

2616. Financial institutions – credit institutions – Council Directive

European Parliament and Council Directive 2000/12 of March 20, 2000 relating to the taking up and pursuit of the business of credit institutions. [2000] OJ L126/1.

2617. Financial markets – regulation – insider dealing

INSIDER DEALING (SECURITIES AND REGULATED MARKETS) (AMENDMENT) ORDER 2000, SI 2000 1923; made under the Criminal Justice Act 1993 s.60, s.62, s.64. In force: July 20, 2000; £1.

This Order amends the Insider Dealing (Securities and Regulated Markets) Order 1994 (SI 1994 187) Art.9 and Sch, by changing the list of markets which are "regulated markets" for the purposes of insider dealing. In addition, it adds to the list, in Art.10 of the 1994 Order, of regulated markets which are "regulated in the United Kingdom" for the purposes of the territorial scope of the offence of insider dealing.

2618. Financial Services and Markets Act 2000 (c.8)

This Act makes provision about the regulation of financial services and markets. In particular, it provides for the transfer of certain statutory functions relating to building societies, friendly societies, industrial and provident societies and certain other mutual societies.

This Act received Royal Assent on June 14, 2000.

2619. Friendly societies – Commission expenses – fees

FRIENDLY SOCIETIES (GENERAL CHARGE AND FEES) REGULATIONS 2000, SI 2000 674; made under the Friendly Societies Act 1992 s.2, s.114; and the Friendly Societies Act 1974 s.104. In force: April 1, 2000; £2.50.

These Regulations provide for a charge to be paid by friendly societies towards the expenses of the Friendly Societies Commission with respect to the Commission's accounting year beginning April 1, 2000. Each society is required to pay 0.55 per cent of its "specified income" for the year to December 31, 1999, subject to a minimum charge of £350 and a maximum of £47,000. They also require and prescribe fees to be paid for matters transacted under the Friendly Societies Act 1974 or the Friendly Societies Act 1992. The Friendly Societies (General Charge and Fees) Regulations 1999 (SI 1999 736) are revoked.

2620. Friendly societies – insurance business

FRIENDLY SOCIETIES (INSURANCE BUSINESS) (AMENDMENT) REGULATIONS 2000, SI 2000 1700; made under the Friendly Societies Act 1992 s.45, s.121. In force: August 1, 2000; £1.50.

These Regulations amend the Friendly Societies (Insurance Business) Regulations 1994 (SI 1994 1981) Part V which relates to the determination of a friendly society's liabilities by aligning them with the regulations applicable to insurance companies.

2621. Independent financial advisers – professional negligence – negligent "investment advice" – limitation period

[Financial Services Act 1986 s.62.]

In 1991, after approaching an insurance company, LA, and receiving advice from S, a self employed financial advisor, who was also an authorised LA representative, M entered into a package of transactions consisting of the remortgage of the matrimonial home, the surrender of a number of life policies, the taking out of a pension policy, and an endowment policy, the latter being used as collateral security for the mortgage advance. In October 1992, due to difficulties in making the requisite payments, M stopped contributing to the pension policy. In 1994, M wrote to the compliance officer at LA communicating his concerns as to the suitability for his interests of the endowment policy, and seeking reimbursement with interest of the premiums paid. During 1994 the long term insurance business of LA was transferred to B which, conceding S's bad advice, cancelled the endowment policy, and refunded the premiums with interest. By a writ issued on July 29, 1997 M brought an action for damages, alleging that S had provided negligent advice. M submitted, inter alia, that S had failed to discharge his duty of care to give, and to ensure M's understanding of advice on the overall degree of the financial commitments involved, such that M had entered into a series of transactions which were not affordable. M further alleged that B was liable under the Financial Services Act 1986 s.62. B contended, inter alia, that the claims were statute barred, and that LA/B were not, in any event, liable for the consequences of the remortgage, since that element of the advice given by S was outside the scope of S's authority from LA.

Held, giving judgment for B, that (1) the claims, whether in tort or pursuant to s.62 of the 1986 Act were statute barred, because the policies came into being on the date on which they were issued, not the later date, on which the premiums were paid *Forster v. Outred & Co* [1982] 1 W.L.R. 86, [1982] C.L.Y. 1849, *DW Moore v. Ferrier* [1988] 1 W.L.R. 267, [1988] C.L.Y. 2154, *Bell v. Peter Browne & Co* [1990] 2 Q.B. 495, [1991] C.L.Y. 2343 and *Knapp v. Ecclesiastical Insurance Group Plc* [1998] Lloyd's Rep. I.R. 390, [1997] C.L.Y. 645 considered; (2) by reason of his agreement with LA to provide "investment advice", S had actual authority to advise M on the remortgaging of his matrimonial home, because even though that aspect was not investment advice for the purposes of the 1986 Act, it was ancillary to other advice given, and LA/B were liable for it, and (3) the advice provided by S had fallen short of the standard of care reasonably to be expected of him, and had been in breach of the Code of Conduct established under the LAUTRO Rules 1988. M had suffered loss by proceeding in reliance upon it, and but for the limitation issue, would have been entitled to damages under the 1986 Act.

MARTIN v. BRITANNIA LIFE LTD [2000] Lloyd's Rep. P.N. 412, Jonathan Parker, J., Ch D.

2622. Industrial and provident societies – credit unions – registration – fees

INDUSTRIAL AND PROVIDENT SOCIETIES (CREDIT UNIONS) (FEES) REGULATIONS 2000, SI 2000 669; made under the Industrial and Provident Societies Act 1965 s.70, s.71. In force: April 1, 2000; £2.00.

These Regulations increase some of the fees payable for registration and other transactions under the Industrial and Provident Societies Act 1965, the Industrial and Provident Societies Act 1967 and the Credit Unions Act 1979. Taking all the fees together, some of which remain unchanged, the overall increase is about 4 per cent. The Industrial and Provident Societies (Credit Unions) (Fees) Regulations 1999 (SI 1999 739) are revoked.

2623. Industrial and provident societies – registration – fees

INDUSTRIAL AND PROVIDENT SOCIETIES (FEES) REGULATIONS 2000, SI 2000 673; made under the Industrial and Provident Societies Act 1965 s.70, s.71. In force: April 1, 2000; £1.50.

These Regulations, which revoke the Industrial and Provident Societies (Fees) Regulations 1999 (SI 1999 740), increase the fees payable for registration and other transactions under the Industrial and Provident Societies Act 1965 and the Industrial and Provident Societies Act 1967. Taking all the fees together, some of which remain unchanged, the overall increase is about 3 per cent.

2624. Mortgages – deeds of priority – simple or compound interest

Two mortgagees, W and U, entered into a deed of priority assigning to U priority in respect of all sums owing by the borrower under an all-moneys charge not exceeding the capital sum of £160,000, "together with interest thereon". At first instance it was held that the interest referred to in the deed of priority represented simple interest on the capital sum and not compound interest. U appealed, contending that the interest referred to in the deed represented the compound interest payable between the borrower and U under the loan agreement between them which conferred the right to capitalise the interest, *Bank of New South Wales v. Brown* (1983) 151 C.L.R. 514 cited. W contended that "interest" should be construed as simple interest since the deed of priority did not make any specific provision for compound interest, *National Bank of Greece SA v. Pinios Shipping Co (No.1)* [1990] 1 A.C. 637, [1990] C.L.Y. 267 and *Bank of Credit and Commerce International SA v. Blattner* (Unreported, November 20, 1986) cited.

Held, allowing the appeal, that it must have been within the contemplation of the parties that the borrower's loans with UCB may have provided for compound interest. The loan in question in fact provided for the amount outstanding to be compounded on a monthly basis. The purpose of the deed of priority was to set out the priorities between W and U regarding their respective rights against the borrower. There was no provision for interest to be paid between W and U. Thus, the reference in the deed of priority to "interest" related to the interest paid by the borrower to U under the loan agreement. That agreement provided for capitalisation of the interest, however for the purposes of the deed of priority it was to be treated as interest and not capital. *Brown* was pertinent to the issue as it concerned the rights of a third party in relation to whether interest was to be interpreted as simple or compound, and it supported the contention that the deed of priority did not envisage the payment of simple interest only, *Pinios* and *Blattner* distinguished.

WHITBREAD PLC v. UCB CORPORATE SERVICES LTD [2000] 3 E.G.L.R. 60, Pill, L.J., CA.

2625. Personal equity plans – depositary interests

PERSONAL EQUITY PLAN (AMENDMENT) REGULATIONS 2000, SI 2000 3109; made under the Income and Corporation Taxes Act 1988 s.333; and the Taxation of Chargeable Gains Act 1992 s.151. In force: December 13, 2000; £1.50.

These Regulations, which amend the Personal Equity Plan Regulations 1989 (SI 1989 469), add depositary interests which represent existing qualifying or permitted investments, other than cash, to the qualifying investments for general plans or the investments which may be made or held under single company plans.

2626. PIA ombudsman – jurisdiction – investor issuing proceedings

See CIVIL PROCEDURE: Forrest v. Towry Law Financial Services Ltd. §594

2627. Privilege – informers – communications between financial regulator and informant

[Financial Services Act 1986.]

T entered into a transaction with R concerning the purchase of shares. A dispute arose between the parties regarding the value of the deal which resulted in the involvement of the Serious Fraud Office (SFO). Having received an assurance that it would not be prosecuted, R supplied SFO with information about the share deal. SFO subsequently contacted TSA, the regulatory body involved in the process of granting authorisations to conduct investment business under the Financial Services Act 1986. Having been assured by TSA of complete confidentiality, R wrote a letter to them incriminating T. Consequently M, T's managing director, was arrested on a charge of conspiracy to defraud TSA. Following a ruling that there was no case to answer, M commenced libel proceedings against R, later amending the claim to include an allegation of malicious prosecution. R contended that its letter attracted absolute privilege, and appealed against a preliminary finding that it did not do so. R submitted that since the absolute protection afforded to statements made in the course of judicial proceedings had been extended to tribunals exercising functions equivalent to those of a court, the authorisation tribunal proceedings were absolutely protected, as was written material obtained by TSA and used as evidence in those proceedings.

Held, allowing the appeal, that (1) proceedings before a TSA authorisation tribunal did attract absolute privilege, *Trapp v. Mackie* [1979] 1 W.L.R. 377, [1979] C.L.Y. 1282 followed; (2) absolute privilege also attached to communications between a financial services regulatory body and its informants where the information was disclosed to assist the association in its investigation into a person's fitness to carry on investment business. The court considered the competing considerations of public policy, namely administering justice for a defendant on the one hand and serving the public interest in the detection and punishment of crime on the other, and found that if informants feared libel proceedings, they might not be forthcoming with information, thereby jeopardising the purpose of the Act to protect the public from unfit investment advisers. The long established rule that an informant was only entitled to qualified privilege was no longer appropriate and the letter to TSA therefore warranted absolute immunity from suit, *Mahon v. Rahn (No.1)* [1998] Q.B. 424, [1997] C.L.Y. 475 and *Taylor v. Director of the Serious Fraud Office* [1999] 2 A.C. 177, [1998] C.L.Y. 1768 considered, and (3) a claim for malicious prosecution against an informant would not succeed where the evidence against the claimant had come from a number of sources and the prosecuting authority had exercised its discretion as to which evidence to adduce.

MAHON v. RAHN (NO.2) [2000] 1 W.L.R. 2150, Brooke, L.J., CA.

2628. Securities – listing – change of competent authority

OFFICIAL LISTING OF SECURITIES (CHANGE OF COMPETENT AUTHORITY) REGULATIONS 2000, SI 2000 968; made under the European Communities Act 1972 s.2. In force: Reg.8: April 5, 2000; remainder: May 1, 2000; £2.00.

These Regulations amend the Financial Services Act 1986 by changing the competent authority for the purposes of Part IV relating to official listing of securities from the International Stock Exchange of the UK and the Republic of Ireland Ltd to the Financial Services Authority with effect from May 1, 2000.

2629. Self regulating organisations – designated dates

FINANCIAL SERVICES AND MARKETS (TRANSITIONAL PROVISIONS) (DESIGNATED DATE FOR CERTAIN SELF-REGULATING ORGANISATIONS) ORDER 2000, SI 2000 1734; made under the Financial Services and Markets Act 2000 s.428, Sch.21 para.1, Sch.21 para.2. In force: July 25, 2000; £1.00.

The Personal Investment Authority Limited and the Investment Management Regulatory Organisation Limited are recognised self-regulating organisations and recognised self-regulating organisations for friendly societies under the

Financial Services Act 1986. The Financial Services and Markets Act 2000 Sch. 21 makes transitional provisions concerning the position of such organisations pending the repeal of those provisions of the 1986 Act relating to their recognition and subsequent supervision, including provisions which are applicable, from a date to be designated by the Treasury, in relation to such organisations. This Order designates July 25, 2000 as the designated date for the Personal Investment Authority Limited and for the Investment Management Regulatory Organisation Limited.

2630. **Publications**

Blair, Michael; Minghella, Loretta; Taylor, Michael; Threipland, Mark – Blackstone's Guide to the Financial Services and Markets Act 2000. Paperback: £30.00. ISBN 1-84174-116-7. Blackstone Press.

Lee, Ruben – What Is an Exchange?: Automation, Management and Regulation of Financial Markets. Paperback: £14.99. ISBN 0-19-829704-1. Oxford University Press.

Regulatory Reporting Handbook. Paperback: £48.95. ISBN 0-7656-0655-0. M.E. Sharpe.

Regulatory Risk Management Handbook. Paperback: £48.95. ISBN 0-7656-0651-8. M.E. Sharpe.

Sabalot, Deborah – Guide to the Financial Services and Markets Act 2000. Paperback: £35.00. ISBN 0-406-93141-0. Butterworths.

Whitehouse, Chris – Finance and Law for the Elderly Client (in Associate with the Society of Trust and Estate Pratitioners). Unbound/looseleaf: £155.00. ISBN 0-7545-0233-3. Tolley Publishing.

FISHERIES

2631. **Conservation – edible crabs**

UNDERSIZED EDIBLE CRABS ORDER 2000, SI 2000 2029; made under the Sea Fish (Conservation) Act 1967 s.1, s.6, s.15, s.20. In force: August 28, 2000; £2.00.

This Order prescribes minimum sizes for the landing of edible crabs (Cancer pagurus) in certain areas in England and provides an exemption from the minimum landing size for the landing of edible crabs from foreign fishing boats. In addition, it prohibits the landing in England or Northern Ireland by relevant British fishing boats or Scottish fishing boats of edible crabs which have not attained a size of 130 mm and have been caught in any waters within British fishery limits which are outside the Eastern Sea Fisheries District and gives British sea-fishery officers further enforcement powers in relation to British fishing boats. The Undersized Crabs Order 1986 (SI 1986 497) and the Undersized Crabs (Variation) Order 1989 (SI 1989 2443) are partially revoked.

2632. **Conservation – enforcement of Community measures**

SEA FISHING (ENFORCEMENT OF COMMUNITY CONSERVATION MEASURES) ORDER 2000, SI 2000 1081; made under the Fisheries Act 1981 s.30. In force: May 15, 2000; £3.00.

This Order, which revokes the Sea Fishing (Enforcement of Community Conservation Measures) Order 1997 (SI 1997 1949) and the Sea Fishing (Enforcement of Community Conservation Measures) (Amendment) Order 1997 (SI 1997 2841), re enacts provisions for the enforcement of Council Regulation 894/97 ([1997] OJ L132/1) Art.11 laying down technical measures for the conservation of fishery resources and provides for the enforcement of restrictions and obligations contained in Council Regulation 850/98 ([1998] OJ L125/1), for the conservation of fishery resources through technical measures for the protection of juveniles of marine organisms.

2633. Conservation – enforcement of Community measures – Wales

SEA FISHING (ENFORCEMENT OF COMMUNITY CONSERVATION MEASURES) (WALES) ORDER 2000, SI 2000 2230 (W.148); made under the Fisheries Act 1981 s.30. In force: September 11, 2000; £4.50.

This Order, which revokes the Sea Fishing (Enforcement of Community Conservation Measures) Order 1997 (SI 1997 1949) and the Sea Fishing (Enforcement of Community Conservation Measures) (Amendment) Order 1997 (SI 1997 2841) in so far as they apply to Wales, re-enacts provisions for the enforcement of Art.11 of Council Regulation 894/97 ([1997] OJ L132/1) laying down certain technical measures for the conservation of fishery resources. In addition, it provides for the enforcement of restrictions and obligations contained in Council Regulation 850/98 ([1998] OJ L125/1) for the conservation of fishery resources through technical measures for the protection of juveniles of marine organisms, as amended.

2634. Conservation – lobsters

UNDERSIZED LOBSTERS ORDER 2000, SI 2000 1503; made under the Sea Fish (Conservation) Act 1967 s.1, s.15, s.20. In force: June 30, 2000; £2.00.

This Order, which revokes the Undersized Lobsters Order 1993 (SI 1993 1178) in relation to England and Northern Ireland, prescribes a minimum size for the landing of lobsters (Homarus gammarus) in England and provides for an exemption from the minimum landing size in relation to foreign fishing boats. In addition, it prescribes a minimum size for the sale of lobsters in England and for the carriage of lobsters on a relevant British fishing boat, or on a Scottish fishing boat which is in waters within relevant British fishery limits. It gives British sea-fishery officers further enforcement powers in relation to British fishing boats.

2635. Conservation – prohibition of landing of crab claws

CRAB CLAWS (PROHIBITION OF LANDING) (REVOCATION) ORDER 2000, SI 2000 1235; made under the Sea Fish (Conservation) Act 1967 s.6, s.20. In force: June 15, 2000; £1.50.

This Order revokes, except in so far as it forms part of Scots law or applies to landings in Wales, the Crab Claws (Prohibition of Landing) Order 1986 (SI 1986 496), which prohibited the landing of crab claws in the United Kingdom if they have been detached from edible crabs (Cancer pagurus) caught within British fishery limits.

2636. Conservation – spider crabs

UNDERSIZED SPIDER CRABS ORDER 2000, SI 2000 1502; made under the Sea Fish (Conservation) Act 1967 s.1, s.15. In force: June 30, 2000; £2.00.

This Order prescribes a minimum size for the landing of male spider crabs (Maia squinado) in England and provides for an exemption from the minimum landing size in relation to foreign fishing boats. It gives British sea-fishery officers further enforcement powers in relation to British fishing boats.

2637. Conservation – whiting

UNDERSIZED WHITING (REVOCATION) ORDER 2000, SI 2000 1234; made under the Sea Fish (Conservation) Act 1967 s.1, s.15, s.20. In force: June 15, 2000; £1.00.

This Order revokes, except in so far as it forms part of the law of Scotland or has effect in relation to Wales, the Undersized Whiting Order 1992 (SI 1992 1212), which prescribed minimum sizes for the landing and sale in Great Britain, and for carriage on a British fishing boat, of whiting (Merlangius merlangus).

2638. **Fish – imports – validity of Commission Decision banning imports from Japan from publication date – European Community**

[Council Directive 90/675 laying down the principles governing the organisation of veterinary checks on products entering the Community from third countries Art.19(1); Commission Decision 95/119 concerning certain protective measures with regard to fishery products originating in Japan.]

The European Commission was empowered under Council Directive 90/675 Art.19(1) to suspend the entry of products into the Community from third countries where veterinary experts had uncovered a serious risk to public health. Following adverse findings by Community veterinary experts in relation to Japanese fishery products, the Commission adopted Decision 95/119 under the Regulation banning the importation into the Community of all fishery products from Japan. I had already concluded contracts for the importation of white tuna from Japan, and had landed and cleared the first consignment through Spanish customs prior to the adoption of the Decision. The rest of the tuna was dispatched from Japan in three consignments, the first of which was refused customs clearance into the Community in reliance upon the Decision. I sought an order annulling the decision to the extent that it related to products already en route to the Community.

Held, refusing I's application, that (1) imports into the Commission were prohibited by the Decision not exports from third countries, and the prohibition applied from the date of publication. It was not, therefore, retroactive, nor in breach of the principle of legal certainty; (2) I had no legitimate expectation that its particular economic circumstances would be taken into account when protective measures were being adopted, either generally, or in relation to products already dispatched; (3) in relation to the principle of proportionality, a complete ban was justified in the light of the prohibitive costs of an extensive individual inspection scheme. The Decision was not a disproportionate interference with the freedom to trade, having regard to the general interest objectives pursued by the Community. The ban was justified on public health grounds, given the nature of the risk involved and the disproportionate cost of examining all imported products; (4) the fact that the products were already en route to the Community had no bearing on the equality of the decision, which applied equally to all imports from Japan after the date of publication; (5) in the light of the nature of the Decision and the time within which it had to be implemented, the Commission was justified in confining itself to the recitals to the Decision stating the basis of its assessment, without going into greater detail, and (6) there was no evidence that the Commission was pursuing an objective other than that for which power was conferred upon it by Directive 90/675, *Affish BV v. Rijksdienst (C183/95)* [1997] E.C.R. I-4315 followed.

INDUSTRIA DEL FRIO AUXILIAR CONSERVERA SA v. COMMISSION OF THE EUROPEAN COMMUNITIES (T136/95) [1999] 3 C.M.L.R. 667, A Kalogeropoulos (President), CFI.

2639. **Fisheries policy – collection and management of data – Council Regulation**

Council Regulation 1543/2000 of June 29, 2000 establishing a Community framework for the collection and management of the data needed to conduct the common fisheries policy. [2000] OJ L176/1.

2640. **Fisheries policy – quotas – allocation of quota – discriminatory practices**

[EC Treaty Art.34(3) (now, after amendment, Art.29(3) EC); Council Regulation 3759/92 on the common organisation of the market in fishery and aquaculture products Art.4.]

Member States were responsible under the Common Fisheries Policy for administering a quota of the total allowable catch for each fish stock in a particular sea area. MAFF discharged this function in the UK. In relation to certain white fish stocks, MAFF established quota allocations for three groups of fishermen, termed "sector", "non sector" and vessels under 10 metres. A was a "non sector" group member. The "sector" group, which had the largest quota allocation, comprised vessels owned by members of producers' organisations, POs. The POs, under a scheme established by Council Regulation 3759/92 Art.4, managed the allocations within the "sector" group. Most imposed monthly or annual restrictions on members' catches, but these restrictions did not operate as conditions of individual members' licences. A, as a "non sector" operator under MAFF's direct regulation, was free to fish against all "non sector" stock quota, but its licence was subject to a monthly catch limit. This was set by reference to factors which had the effect of conferring greater catch limits on "non sector" vessels which commonly fished a particular stock than on those which did not. A contended that this system discriminated unfairly against "non sector" vessels as compared with the regime in place for "sector" vessels. At first instance, it was held that such differences as existed between the two regimes were justified as fulfilling the objective of ensuring an even spread of fishing over the year. The "non sector" group had a high level of uptake against its quota which the judge at first instance considered outweighed the lack of flexibility involved in monthly catch limits. A sought permission to appeal and a reference to the ECJ, arguing that since "non sector" operators could not carry their unused entitlements forward, this adversely affected their catch record and also their future quota allocations. Further, that monthly restrictions made fishing trips uneconomic for many operators, and that the enforcement regime of fines and penalties was discriminatory compared to the regime operated by POs for their members.

Held, granting permission to appeal but dismissing the appeal (Evans, L.J. dissenting in part), that (1) whether a measure discriminated between producers contrary to the EC Treaty Art.34(3 (now, after amendment, Art.29(3) EC) was a question to be decided in the light of the objective behind the measure and its consistency with EU policy, according to the principle of proportionality, *Firma Albert Ruckdeschel & Co v. Hauptzollamt Hamburg-St Annen (C117/76)* [1977] E.C.R. 1795, [1978] C.L.Y. 1226 and *Mignini SpA v. Azienda di Stato per Gli Interventi sul Mercato Agricola (AIMA) (C256/90)* [1992] E.C.R. I-2651, [1992] C.L.Y. 4672 followed; (2) a reviewing court would interfere with the a decision only if it was not a legally available option. The decision's appropriateness was to be judged objectively, but the requisite degree of appreciation of the decision's proportionality by the decision maker would vary in the circumstances of each case, *R. v. Ministry of Agriculture, Fisheries and Food, ex p. First City Trading Ltd (1996)* [1997] 1 C.M.L.R. 250, [1997] C.L.Y. 2384 followed; (3) there was no evidence that the questioned system was the only way of ensuring an even spread of fishing for the "non sector" allocation. The trial judge had attached too much importance to the increased costs and inconvenience that a different system might engender. These considerations would not justify discrimination; (4) since there were two different systems of quota allocation, run by the POs in the case of the "sector" and by MAFF in the case of the "non-sector", and neither was obliged to conform to the practices of the other, the differences between them afforded no ground for complaint. All vessel owners were liable to prosecution if they breached the terms of their licences; (5) MAFF's decision to impose monthly limits on catches for the "non sector" group was not manifestly inappropriate, and (6) A's application was of dubious merit, since it arose following A's prosecution for an offence unrelated to catch limits, for which all fishermen were liable to prosecution.

R. v. MINISTRY OF AGRICULTURE, FISHERIES AND FOOD, *ex p.* ASTONQUEST LTD [2000] Eu. L.R. 371, Robert Walker, L.J., CA.

2641. Fishing – Community control measures

SEA FISHING (ENFORCEMENT OF COMMUNITY CONTROL MEASURES) ORDER 2000, SI 2000 51; made under the Fisheries Act 1981 s.30. In force: February 8, 2000; £3.50.

This Order revokes, and largely re-enacts, in providing for the enforcement of Council Regulation 2847/93 ([1993] OJ L261/1) establishing a control system applicable to the common fisheries policy in consequence of it having been amended by Council Regulation 2846/98 ([1998] OJ L358/5) and the creation of offences in respect of the Regulations, the provisions of the Sea Fishing

(Enforcement of Community Control Measures) Order 1994 (SI 1994 451). It also revokes the Sea Fishing (Enforcement of Community Control Measures) (Amendment) Order 1996 (SI 1996 2) insofar as it extends to England and Northern Ireland.

2642. Fishing – Community control measures – Wales

SEA FISHING (ENFORCEMENT OF COMMUNITY CONTROL MEASURES) (WALES) ORDER 2000, SI 2000 1075 (W.69); made under the Fisheries Act 1981 s.30. In force: April 1, 2000; £5.80.

This Order, which implements Council Regulation 2846/98 ([1998] OJ L358/5), revokes and replaces, with amendments, the Sea Fishing (Enforcement of Community Control Measures) Order 1994 (SI 1994 451) and the Sea Fishing (Enforcement of Community Control Measures) (Amendment) Order 1996 (SI 1996 2) insofar as they apply to Wales.

2643. Fishing – conservation – prohibition of fishing for lobsters and crawfish

LOBSTERS AND CRAWFISH (PROHIBITION OF FISHING AND LANDING) ORDER 2000, SI 2000 874; made under the Sea Fish (Conservation) Act 1967 s.5, s.6, s.15. In force: April 17, 2000; £1.50.

This Order prohibits fishing for, and landing of, lobsters and crawfish bearing a V notch, or mutilated in such a manner as to obscure a V notch, by both relevant British fishing boats and Scottish fishing boats and gives British sea-fishery officers further enforcement powers in relation to relevant British and Scottish fishing boats.

2644. Fishing – enforcement of Community quotas

SEA FISHING (ENFORCEMENT OF COMMUNITY QUOTA AND THIRD COUNTRY FISHING MEASURES) (AMENDMENT) ORDER 2000, SI 2000 2008; made under the Fisheries Act 1981 s.30. In force: September 1, 2000; £1.50.

This Order amends the Sea Fishing (Enforcement of Community Quotas and Third Country Fishing Measures) Order 2000 (SI 2000 827) by adding to Sch.1 a reference to Council Regulation 2742/1999 ([1999] OJ L341/1) Art.7, which prohibits fishing by European Community vessels in certain Norwegian and Icelandic waters.

2645. Fishing – enforcement of Community quotas

SEA FISHING (ENFORCEMENT OF COMMUNITY QUOTA AND THIRD COUNTRY MEASURES) ORDER 2000, SI 2000 827; made under the Fisheries Act 1981 s.30. In force: April 11, 2000; £2.50.

This Order provides for the enforcement of certain enforceable Community restrictions and other obligations relating to sea fishing by both Community and third country vessels set out in Council Regulation 2742/1999 ([1999] OJ L341/1), which fixes total allowable catches and Member States' quotas for 2000, lays down certain conditions under which they may be fished, authorises fishing by vessels of Norway and the Faroe Islands for specified descriptions of fish in certain specified areas within Member States' fishery limits in 2000 and imposes requirements concerning fishing quotas and authorised zones, methods of fishing, the holding of licences and observance of licence conditions, the keeping of log books, the making of reports and similar matters. It revokes the Sea Fishing (Enforcement of Community Quota Measures) Order 1999 (SI 1999 424) and the Third Country Fishing (Enforcement) Order 1999 (SI 1999 425) except in relation to Scotland and Wales.

2646. Fishing – enforcement of Community quotas – Wales

SEA FISHING (ENFORCEMENT OF COMMUNITY QUOTA AND THIRD COUNTRY FISHING MEASURES) (WALES) ORDER 2000, SI 2000 1096 (W.74); made under the Fisheries Act 1981 s.30. In force: April 11, 2000; £3.50.

This Order provides for the enforcement of certain enforceable Community restrictions and other obligations relating to sea fishing by both Community and third country vessels set out in Council Regulation 2742/1999 ([1999] OJ L341/1), which fixes total allowable catches and Member States' quotas for 2000, lays down certain conditions under which they may be fished, authorises fishing by vessels of Norway and the Faroe Islands for specified descriptions of fish in certain specified areas within Member States' fishery limits in 2000 and imposes requirements concerning fishing quotas and authorised zones, methods of fishing, the holding of licences and observance of licence conditions, the keeping of log books, the making of reports and similar matters. It revokes the Sea Fishing (Enforcement of Community Quota Measures) Order 1999 (SI 1999 424) and the Third Country Fishing (Enforcement) Order 1999 (SI 1999 425) insofar as they relate to Wales.

2647. Fishing – enforcement of restrictions – Irish sea

SEA FISHING (ENFORCEMENT OF MEASURES FOR THE RECOVERY OF THE STOCK OF COD) (IRISH SEA) ORDER 2000, SI 2000 435; made under the Fisheries Act 1981 s.30. In force: February 25, 2000; £2.00.

The Order makes provision for the enforcement of restrictions on the use of specified types of nets and fishing gear within a specified geographical area of the Irish Sea contained in Commission Regulation 304/2000 ([2000] OJ L35/10) Art.1 concerning the conservation of fishery resources through measures for recovery of the stock of cod in the Irish Sea.

2648. Fishing – enforcement of restrictions – Irish sea – Wales

SEA FISHING (ENFORCEMENT OF MEASURES FOR THE RECOVERY OF THE STOCK OF COD) (IRISH SEA) (WALES) ORDER 2000, SI 2000 976 (W.46); made under the Fisheries Act 1981 s.30. In force: March 18, 2000; £3.00.

This Order implements Commission Regulation 304/2000 ([2000] OJ L35/10) by providing for the enforcement of restrictions concerning the conservation of fishery resources through measures for the recovery of the stock of cod in that part of the Irish Sea (ICES Division VIIa) which lies within the territorial sea adjacent to Wales. It provides for the enforcement of the requirement in Art.4(4)(b) of Council Regulation 850/98 ([1998] OJ L125/1), for the conservation of fishery resources through technical measures for the protection of juveniles of marine organisms, relating to the percentage composition of catches of target species taken by different ranges of mesh sizes. In addition, it confers powers of enforcement on British sea-fishery officers in relation to fishing boats and on land and in relation to the seizure of fish and fishing gear as well as on other officers in relation to nets and fishing gear.

2649. Fishing – North East Atlantic control measures

SEA FISHING (NORTH-EAST ATLANTIC CONTROL MEASURES) ORDER 2000, SI 2000 1843; made under the Fisheries Act 1981 s.30. In force: July 24, 2000; £3.00.

This Order provides for the enforcement of restrictions and obligations contained in Council Regulation 2791/99 ([1999] OJ L337/1), for laying down certain control measures applicable in the area covered by the Convention on future multilateral cooperation in the North-East Atlantic fisheries.

2650. Fishing – oil and chemical pollution – emergency prohibitions

See FOOD. §2676

2651. Fishing vessels – control of satellite based vessel monitoring systems

SEA FISHING (ENFORCEMENT OF COMMUNITY SATELLITE MONITORING MEASURES) ORDER 2000, SI 2000 181; made under the Fisheries Act 1981 s.30. In force: February 21, 2000; £2.00.

This Order provides for enforcement of Art.3 and Art.28c of Council Regulation 2847/93 ([1993] OJ L261/1) establishing a control system applicable to the common fisheries policy and Commission Regulation 1489/97 ([1997] OJ L202/18) laying down detailed rules for the application of Council Regulation 2847/93 as regards satellite-based vessel monitoring systems. It creates offences in respect of breaches of the provisions referred to in Art.4 of this Order.

2652. Fishing vessels – control of satellite based vessel monitoring systems – Wales

SEA FISHING (ENFORCEMENT OF COMMUNITY SATELLITE MONITORING MEASURES) (WALES) ORDER 2000, SI 2000 1078 (W.71); made under the Fisheries Act 1981 s.30. In force: April 7, 2000; £3.00.

This Order provides for the enforcement of Council Regulation 2847/93 ([1993] OJ L261/1) Art.3 and Art.28c establishing a control system applicable to the common fisheries policy, within the territorial sea adjacent to Wales, and Commission Regulation 1489/97 ([1997] OJ L202/18) laying down detailed rules for the application of Council Regulation 2847/93 as regards satellite-based vessel monitoring systems. It creates offences in respect of breaches of the provisions referred to in Art.4 of this Order.

2653. Sea Fishing Grants (Charges) Act 2000 (c.18)

This Act makes provision to ensure the validity of charges made in the administration of certain grant schemes relating to sea fishing.

This Act received Royal Assent on July 28, 2000 and comes into force on July 28, 2000.

2654. Publications

Long, Ronan; Curran, Peter – Enforcing the Common Fisheries Policy. Hardback: £89.50. ISBN 0-85238-261-8. Blackwell Science (UK).

FOOD

2655. Agricultural produce – coffee and chicory extracts – labelling requirements

COFFEE EXTRACTS AND CHICORY EXTRACTS (ENGLAND) REGULATIONS 2000, SI 2000 3323; made under the Food Safety Act 1990 s.16, s.17, s.26, s.48. In force: January 15, 2001; £2.00.

These Regulations, which implement Directive 1999/4 ([1999] OJ L66/26) of the European Parliament and the Council relating to coffee extracts and chicory extracts, revoke and replace the Coffee and Coffee Products Regulations 1978 (SI 1978 1420). They prescribe definitions and reserved descriptions for coffee extracts and chicory extracts, provide for the Regulations to apply to coffee extracts and chicory extracts ready for delivery to the ultimate consumer or to a catering establishment, restrict the sale of foods labelled with a reserved description, require reserved descriptions and specified declarations to be applied to designated products, and prescribe the manner of marking or labelling to be employed.

2656. Animal products – diseases and disorders – food safety

FRESH MEAT (BEEF CONTROLS) (NO.2) (AMENDMENT) (ENGLAND) REGULATIONS 2000, SI 2000 3378; made under the Food Safety Act 1990 s.16, s.26, s.48. In force: January 1, 2001; £1.50.

These Regulations, which amend the Fresh Meat (Beef Controls) (No.2) Regulations 1996 (SI 1996 2097) in so far as they extend to England, provide for the enforcement of Art.2 of Commission Regulation 2777/2000 ([2000] OJ L321/47) adopting exceptional support measures for the beef market. That Article, applicable until June 30, 2001 at the latest, provides that meat from bovine animals aged more than 30 months and slaughtered in the Community after January 1, 2001 can only be released for human consumption or for export if tested negatively for bovine spongiform encephalopathy by an approved rapid test as referred to in Commission Decision 98/272 ([1998] OJ L122/59).

2657. Animal products – diseases and disorders – specified risk material

SPECIFIED RISK MATERIAL (AMENDMENT) (ENGLAND) ORDER 2000, SI 2000 2726; made under the Animal Health Act 1981 s.1, s.10, s.11, s.29, s.35, s.76, s.83, Sch.2. In force: October 25, 2000; £1.75.

This Order, which amends the Specified Risk Material Order 1997 (SI 1997 2964) insofar as it extends to England, gives effect to Art.3.1 of Commission Decision 2000/418 ([2000] OJ L158/76) regulating the use of material presenting risks as regards transmissible spongiform encephalopathies. It brings the definition of "specified risk material" (SRM) into line with the definition contained in the Decision, extends the categories of premises to which SRM must be sent if it is to be imported, and requires food and feedingstuffs containing SRM to be accompanied by a certificate where they are imported from a third country.

2658. Animal products – diseases and disorders – specified risk material

SPECIFIED RISK MATERIAL (AMENDMENT) (ENGLAND) REGULATIONS 2000, SI 2000 2672; made under the Food Safety Act 1990 s.16, s.17, s.19, s.26, s.48, Sch.1 para.2, Sch.1 para.3, Sch.1 para.5, Sch.1 para.6. In force: October 1, 2000; £1.75.

These Regulations, which amend the Specified Risk Material Regulations 1997 (SI 1997 2965), give effect in part to Art.3.1 of Commission Decision 2000/418 ([2000] OJ L158/76) regulating the use of material presenting risks as regards transmissible spongiform encephalopathies, which requires Member States to ensure that certain material from cattle, sheep and goats is removed and destroyed in accordance with Annex I to the Decision. In particular, the definition of "specified risk material" is brought into line with the definition contained in the Decision.

2659. Animal products – diseases and disorders – specified risk material

SPECIFIED RISK MATERIAL (AMENDMENT) (ENGLAND) (NO.2) REGULATIONS 2000, SI 2000 3381; made under the Food Safety Act 1990 s.16, s.17, s.19, s.26, s.48, Sch.1 para.2, Sch.1 para.3, Sch.1 para.5, Sch.1 para.6. In force: January 1, 2001; £1.75.

These Regulations, which make a further amendment to the Specified Risk Material Regulations 1997 (SI 1997 2965) in so far as they extend to England, give effect to Commission Decision 2000/418 ([2000] OJ L158/76) regulating the use of material presenting risks as regards transmissible spongiform encephalopathies by inserting a revised definition of specified risk material and bringing the definition of "specified bovine material" in Reg.4(1) of that instrument into line with the revised definition of specified risk material.

2660. Animal products – diseases and disorders – specified risk material – Wales

SPECIFIED RISK MATERIAL (AMENDMENT) (WALES) (NO.2) REGULATIONS 2000, SI 2000 3387 (W.224); made under the European Communities Act 1972 s.2; and the Food Safety Act 1990 s.16, s.17, s.19, s.26, s.48, Sch.1 para.2, Sch.1 para.3, Sch.1 para.5, Sch.1 para.6. In force: January 1, 2001; £2.00.

The Specified Risk Material Regulations 1997 (SI 1997 2965) and the Specified Risk Material Order 1997 (SI 1997 2964) define certain material from bovine animals, sheep and goats as Specified Risk Material and place restrictions on the use of such material for human consumption. These Regulations implement, in relation to Wales, European Commission Decision 2000/418/EC which amends Decision 2000/418 ([2000] OJ L158/76) regulating the use of material presenting risks as regards transmissible spongiform encephalopathies by extending the definition of Specified Risk Material to include the entire intestine of bovine animals.

2661. Drinking water – quality – undertakings by water companies

See WATER INDUSTRY. §5376

2662. Food composition – baby foods – cereal based foods

PROCESSED CEREAL-BASED FOODS AND BABY FOODS FOR INFANTS AND YOUNG CHILDREN (AMENDMENT) (ENGLAND) REGULATIONS 2000, SI 2000 1510; made under the Food Safety Act 1990 s.16, s.17, s.26, s.48. In force: July 1, 2002; £1.00.

These Regulations amend the Processed Cereal-based Foods and Baby Foods for Infants and Young Children Regulations 1997 (SI 1997 2042) in relation to England, in implementation of Commission Directive 1999/39 ([1999] OJ L124/8) amending Directive 96/5 on processed cereal-based foods and baby foods for infants and young children. They extend the prohibitions on manufacture and sale in the 1997 Regulations to food of that nature containing individual pesticide residues above a level of 0.01 mg/kg, measured when ready for use or when reconstituted according to the manufacturer's instructions and bring the reference to the 1996 Directive up to date.

2663. Food composition – children – infant formula

INFANT FORMULA AND FOLLOW-ON FORMULA (AMENDMENT) (ENGLAND) REGULATIONS 2000, SI 2000 1509; made under the Food Safety Act 1990 s.16, s.17, s.26, s.48. In force: July 1, 2002; £1.00.

These Regulations amend the Infant Formula and Follow-on Formula Regulations 1995 (SI 1995 77), in relation to England, in implementation of Commission Directive 1999/50 ([1999] OJ L139/29) amending Commission Directive 91/321 ([1991] OJ L175/35) on infant formulae and follow-on formulae. They extend the prohibitions in the 1995 Regulations on sale, or export to third countries, to food of that nature containing individual pesticide residues above a level of 0.01 mg/kg, measured when ready for use or when reconstituted according to the manufacturer's instructions and make consequential amendments.

2664. Food composition – sweeteners – Council Directive

Commission Directive 2000/51 of July 26, 2000 amending Directive 95/31 laying down specific criteria of purity concerning sweeteners for use in foodstuffs. [2000] OJ L198/41.

2665. Food hygiene – dairy products – inspection charges – Wales

DAIRY PRODUCTS (HYGIENE) (CHARGES) (AMENDMENT) (WALES) REGULATIONS 2000, SI 2000 1738 (W.121); made under the Food Safety Act 1990 s.45, s.48. In force: May 20, 2000; £1.50.

These Regulations, which amend the Dairy Products (Hygiene) (Charges) Regulations 1995 (SI 1995 1122) in relation to Wales, remove liability for charges payable by producers of milk from registered holdings in respect of dairy farm visits carried out for the purpose of ascertaining whether the provisions of the Dairy

Products (Hygiene) Regulations 1995 (SI 1995 1086 as amended) except in respect of visits for the purpose of taking samples of drinking milk which is raw cows' milk for analysis and examination to check compliance with provisions in those Regulations relating to microbiological criteria.

2666. Food hygiene – dairy products – inspections – charges

DAIRY PRODUCTS (HYGIENE) (CHARGES) (AMENDMENT) (ENGLAND) REGULATIONS 2000, SI 2000 1209; made under the Food Safety Act 1990 s.45, s.48. In force: May 10, 2000; £1.50.

These Regulations amend the Dairy Products (Hygiene) (Charges) Regulations 1995 (SI 1995 1122) under which charges are payable by producers of milk from registered holdings in respect of dairy farm visits carried out for the purpose of ascertaining whether provisions of the Dairy Products (Hygiene) Regulations 1995 (SI 1995 1086 as amended by SI 1995 1763, SI 1996 1499, SI 1996 1699, SI 1997 1729, SI 1998 2424 and SI 2000 656) are being met. They remove liability to such charges, except in respect of visits for the purpose of taking samples of drinking milk which is raw cows' milk for analysis and examination to check compliance with provisions relating to microbiological criteria. The charge in that case remains at £63.

2667. Food hygiene – meat products

MEAT PRODUCTS (HYGIENE) (AMENDMENT) (ENGLAND) REGULATIONS 2000, SI 2000 790; made under the European Communities Act 1972 s.2; and the Food Safety Act 1990 s.16, s.17, s.26, s.48, s.49, Sch.1 para.5, Sch.1 para.6. In force: Reg.3: March 31, 2000; remainder: March 30, 2000; £1.50.

These Regulations amend the Meat Products (Hygiene) Regulations 1994 (SI 1994 3082); the Meat Products (Hygiene) (Amendment) Regulations 1999 (SI 1999 683); and the Products of Animal Origin (Import and Export) Regulations 1996 (SI 1996 3124) to permit a third method of preparation for meat-based prepared meals from March 31, 2000.

2668. Food hygiene – meat products – Wales

MEAT PRODUCTS (HYGIENE) (AMENDMENT) (WALES) REGULATIONS 2000, SI 2000 1885 (W.131); made under the European Communities Act 1972 s.2; and the Food Safety Act 1990 s.16, s.17, s.26, s.45, s.48, s.49, Sch.1 para.5, Sch.1 para.6. In force: July 31, 2000; £1.75.

These Regulations amend, insofar as they apply to Wales, the Meat Products (Hygiene) Regulations 1994 (SI 1994 3082 as amended) and the Products of Animal Origin (Import and Export) Regulations 1996 (SI 1996 3124) by permitting a third method of preparation for meat based prepared meals with effect from July 31, 2000.

2669. Food safety – additives – colours

COLOURS IN FOOD (AMENDMENT) (ENGLAND) REGULATIONS 2000, SI 2000 481; made under the Food Safety Act 1990 s.6, s.16, s.17, s.26, s.48, Sch.1 para.1. In force: June 30, 2000; £1.50.

These Regulations amend the Colours in Food Regulations 1995 (SI 1995 3124) by bringing up to date a reference to Commission Directive 95/45 ([1995] OJ L226/1) laying down specific criteria concerning colours for use in foodstuffs, so as to cover its amendment by Commission Directive 1999/75 ([1999] OJ L206/19) which changed the specification for "E160a(i) Mixed Carotenes".

2670. **Food safety – additives – colours – Wales**

COLOURS IN FOOD (AMENDMENT) (WALES) REGULATIONS 2000, SI 2000 1799 (W.124); made under the Food Safety Act 1990 s.6, s.16, s.17, s.26, s.48, Sch.1 para.1. In force: July 8, 2000; £1.50.

These Regulations amend the Colours in Food Regulations 1995 (SI 1995 3124), in relation to Wales, by bringing up to date a reference to Commission Directive 95/45 ([1995] OJ L226/1) laying down specific criteria concerning colours for use in foodstuffs in consequence of its amendment by Commission Directive 1999/75 ([1999] OJ L206/19) which changed the specification for "E160a(i) Mixed Carotenes".

2671. **Food safety – animal feedingstuffs – control of contaminated feedingstuffs from Belgium – emergency controls**

See AGRICULTURE. §151
See AGRICULTURE. §146

2672. **Food safety – animal feedingstuffs – control of contaminated feedingstuffs from Belgium**

See AGRICULTURE. §152

2673. **Food safety – animal products – control of contaminated products from Belgium – emergency controls**

See AGRICULTURE. §147

2674. **Food safety – beef – labelling – enforcement of schemes**

BEEF LABELLING (ENFORCEMENT) (ENGLAND) REGULATIONS 2000, SI 2000 3047; made under the European Communities Act 1972 s.2. In force: January 1, 2001; £2.00.

These Regulations, which revoke and replace the Beef Labelling (Enforcement) Regulations 1998 (SI 1998 616) in so far as they apply in England, provide for the enforcement of the compulsory and voluntary beef labelling schemes established by European Parliament and Council Regulation 1760/2000 ([2000] OJ L204/1) establishing a system for the identification and registration of bovine animals and regarding the labelling of beef and beef products, Commission Regulation 1825/2000 ([2000] OJ L216/8) laying down detailed rules for the application of the 2000 Regulation, and Commission Regulation 1141/97 ([1997] OJ L165/7) laying down detailed rules for the implementation of Council Regulation 820/97 as regards the labelling of beef and beef products.

2675. **Food safety – cocoa and chocolate products – Council Directive**

European Parliament and Council Directive 2000/36 of June 23, 2000 relating to cocoa and chocolate products intended for human consumption. [2000] OJ L197/19.

2676. **Food safety – emergency prohibitions – fish – oil and chemical pollution**

FOOD PROTECTION (EMERGENCY PROHIBITIONS) (OIL AND CHEMICAL POLLUTION OF FISH) (NO.2) ORDER 1993 (REVOCATION) (ENGLAND, WALES AND NORTHERN IRELAND) ORDER 2000, SI 2000 1314; made under the Scotland Act 1998 s.104, s.112, s.115, Sch.7 para.1, Sch.7 para.2. In force: May 17, 2000; £1.00.

This Order revokes the Food Protection (Emergency Prohibitions) (Oil and Chemical Pollution of Fish) (No.2) Order 1993 (SI 1993 143), insofar as it extends to England, Wales and Northern Ireland, to remove the remaining prohibitions in respect of Mussels and Norway lobsters in relation to a designated area of sea.

2677. Food safety – food hygiene – duplicitous informations – due diligence – breach of hygiene regulations

[Food Safety Act 1990; Fresh Meat (Hygiene and Inspection) Regulations 1995 (SI 1995 539) Sch.7.]

H was the proprietor of a meat processing business and the occupier of cutting premises licensed pursuant to the provisions of the Food Safety Act 1990 and the Fresh Meat (Hygiene and Inspection) Regulations 1995. Inspectors who visited the premises found four food preparation areas to be unhygienic and H was charged with offences contrary to the Act and the Regulations. Following his conviction by the magistrates and the dismissal of his appeal by the Crown Court, H appealed by way of case stated, contending, amongst other things, that (1) in respect of breaches of Sch.7 to the Regulations, there was no criminal sanction available, merely administrative action; (2) the informations laid were duplicitous, and (3) the court had not dealt correctly with his defence of due diligence.

Held, dismissing the appeal, that (1) a breach of Sch.7 amounted to a breach of the Regulations giving rise to criminal liability; (2) the informations were not duplicitous. The prosecution had been correct to include all aspects of the uncleanliness of the four separate food preparation areas in the informations charged as this exposed H to one conviction under each information charged rather than four, *Carrington Carr Ltd v. Leicestershire CC* [1994] 158 J.P. 570, [1994] C.L.Y. 946 followed, and (3) the court had applied the correct test in respect of the defence of due diligence albeit that only brief reasons for rejecting the defence had been given.

HOLMES (T/A BR&M HOLMES) v. MINISTRY OF AGRICULTURE, FISHERIES AND FOOD [2000] E.H.L.R. 369, Morison, J., QBD.

2678. Food safety – food sales – mobile hot-dog stand – meaning of "carrying on the business"

[Food Safety Act 1990 s.53.]

C sold hot dog sausages from a mobile trolley and was convicted of offences under the food safety legislation. To be found guilty of the offences charged a defendant had to be "the proprietor of a food business". "Proprietor" was defined in the Food Safety Act 1990 s.53 as "the person by whom that business is carried on". On appeal, it was submitted that the evidence showed only that the appellant was conducting commercial operations in relation to food. A conclusion that he was the proprietor of a food business could only be drawn if there was material on which the justices could discount the possibility that he was not an employee or agent of another person.

Held, allowing the appeal, that in the absence of any previous authority, the words "carrying on the business" had to be given their ordinary and natural meaning. The preparation and selling of food was not of itself sufficient to be treated as "carrying on the business". Although it was not necessary to prove ownership those words had to be taken to involve some entrepreneurial role, namely the taking of risk with a view to profit. Employees would not fall within that definition; franchisees might, depending on the circumstances of the case. If it had been Parliament's intention to fasten mere employees with criminal responsibility that could have been made clear in the Act or the subordinate regulations. The prosecution had failed to show that the appellant was anything more than a salesman and the submission of "no case" had been wrongly rejected by the justices.

CURRI v. WESTMINSTER CITY COUNCIL [2000] E.H.L.R. 16, Ognall, J., QBD.

2679. Food safety – Food Standards Agency

FOOD STANDARDS ACT 1999 (TRANSITIONAL AND CONSEQUENTIAL PROVISIONS AND SAVINGS) (ENGLAND AND WALES) REGULATIONS 2000,

SI 2000 656; made under the Food Standards Act 1999 s.42. In force: April 1, 2000; £4.00.

These Regulations make transitional and consequential provisions and savings in preparation for, in connection with or in consequence of the coming into force of provisions of the Food Standards Act 1999 and the operation of enactments repealed or amended by provisions of that Act. They transfer functions to the Food Standards Agency under legislation relating to food safety, consumer protection and animal feed and provide for continuity in relation to transferred functions.

2680. Food safety – genetically modified organisms – labelling

GENETICALLY MODIFIED AND NOVEL FOODS (LABELLING) (ENGLAND) REGULATIONS 2000, SI 2000 768; made under the Food Safety Act 1990 s.6, s.16, s.17, s.18, s.26, s.48. In force: April 10, 2000; £2.50.

These Regulations make continued provision for the enforcement of Council Regulation 1139/98 ([1998] OJ L159/4) concerning the compulsory indication on the labelling of certain foodstuffs produced from genetically modified organisms and the labelling requirements in Council Regulation 258/97 ([1997] OJ L43/1) Art.8(1) concerning novel foods and novel food ingredients. They also make provision for the enforcement of Commission Regulation 49/2000 ([2000] OJ L6/13) and Commission Regulation 50/2000 ([2000] OJ L6/15) on the labelling of foodstuffs and food ingredients containing additives and flavourings that have been genetically modified or have been produced from genetically modified organisms.

2681. Food safety – genetically modified organisms – labelling – Wales

GENETICALLY MODIFIED AND NOVEL FOODS (LABELLING) (WALES) REGULATIONS 2000, SI 2000 1925 (W.134); made under the Food Safety Act 1990 s.6, s.16, s.17, s.18, s.26, s.48. In force: July 25, 2000; £3.00.

These Regulations provide for, in relation to Wales, the enforcement of Council Regulation 1139/98 ([1998] OJ L159/4) concerning the compulsory indication, on the labelling of certain foodstuffs produced from genetically modified organisms, of particulars other than those provided for in Council Directive 79/112, Commission Regulation 50/2000 ([2000] OJ L6/15) on the labelling of foodstuffs and food ingredients containing additives and flavouring that have been genetically modified or have been produced from genetically modified organisms, and the labelling requirements in Art.8(1) of Council Regulation 258/97 ([1997] OJ L43/1) concerning novel foods and novel food ingredients. In addition, they amend the Food Labelling Regulations 1996 (SI 1996 1499) and the Novel Foods and Novel Food Ingredients Regulations 1997 (SI 1997 1335), insofar as they apply to Wales, and incorporate specified provisions of the Food Safety Act 1990.

2682. Food safety – inspections – charges – repackaging centres

MEAT (HYGIENE AND INSPECTION) (CHARGES) (AMENDMENT) (ENGLAND) REGULATIONS 2000, SI 2000 224; made under the Food Safety Act 1990 s.17, s.45, s.48. In force: March 1, 2000; £1.00.

These Regulations amend the Meat (Hygiene and Inspection) (Charges) Regulations 1998 (SI 1998 2095) in their application to England by permitting charges to be made for the carrying out of health inspections at re-packaging centres as defined in the Fresh Meat (Hygiene and Inspection) Regulations 1995 (SI 1995 539). They also enable the Minister to withdraw inspection services where, despite a court order requiring him to pay the inspection charges for which he is liable under the 1998 Regulations, the occupier of licensed premises fails to comply with the order.

2683. Food safety – irradiation of food and food ingredients – labelling

FOOD IRRADIATION PROVISIONS (ENGLAND) REGULATIONS 2000, SI 2000 2254; made under the Food Safety Act 1990 s.16, s.17, s.18, s.19, s.26, s.45, s.48, Sch.1 para.1, Sch.1 para.4. In force: September 20, 2000; £2.50.

These Regulations amend, insofar as they extend to England, the Food (Control of Irradiation) Regulations 1990 (SI 1990 2490 as amended) and the Food Labelling Regulations 1996 (SI 1996 1499 as amended), by giving effect to European Parliament and Council Directive 1999/2 ([1999] OJ L66/16) on the approximation of the laws of the Member States concerning foods and food ingredients treated with ionising radiation and European Parliament and Council Directive 1999/3 ([1999] OJ L66/24) on the establishment of a Community list of foods and food ingredients treated with ionising radiation.

2684. Food safety – meat and meat products – disease control

MEAT (DISEASE CONTROL) (ENGLAND) REGULATIONS 2000, SI 2000 2215; made under the European Communities Act 1972 s.2; and the Food Safety Act 1990 s.16, s.17, s.19, s.26, s.45, s.48, s.49, Sch.1 para.5, Sch.1 para.6, Sch.1 para.7. In force: August 16, 2000; £2.00.

These Regulations, which extend to England only, give effect in part to the provisions of Council Directive 72/461 ([1972] OJ Spec Ed L302/3) on health problems affecting intra-Community trade in fresh meat, Council Directive 77/99 as amended by Council Directive 92/5 ([1992] OJ L57/1) on health problems affecting the production and marketing of meat products and certain other products of animal origin, Council Directive 80/215 ([1980] OJ L47/4) on animal health problems affecting intra-Community trade in meat products, Council Directive 91/494 ([1991] OJ L268/35) on animal health conditions governing intra-Community trade in and imports from third countries of fresh poultry meat, and Council Directive 94/65 ([1994] OJ L368/10) laying down the requirements for the production and placing on the market of minced meat and meat preparations. They make certain amendments to the Meat Products (Hygiene) Regulations 1994 (SI 1994 3082), the Fresh Meat (Hygiene and Inspection) Regulations 1995 (SI 1995 539), the Minced Meat and Meat Preparations (Hygiene) Regulations 1995 (SI 1995 3205), the Poultry Meat, Farmed Game Bird Meat and Rabbit Meat (Hygiene and Inspection) Regulations 1995 (SI 1995 540) and the Products of Animal Origin (Import and Export) Regulations 1996 (SI 1996 3124).

2685. Food safety – meat and meat products – disease control – Wales

MEAT (DISEASE CONTROL) (WALES) REGULATIONS 2000, SI 2000 2257 (W.150); made under the European Communities Act 1972 s.2; and the Food Safety Act 1990 s.16, s.17, s.19, s.26, s.45, s.48, s.49, Sch.1 para.5, Sch.1 para.6, Sch.1 para.7. In force: August 23, 2000; £2.50.

These Regulations, which extend to Wales only, give effect in part to the provisions of Council Directive 72/461 ([1972] OJ Spec Ed L302/3) on health problems affecting intra Community trade in fresh meat, Council Directive 77/99 ([1977] OJ L26/85) as amended by Council Directive 92/5 ([1992] OJ L57/1) on health problems affecting the production and marketing of meat products and certain other products of animal origin, Council Directive 80/215 ([1980] OJ L47/4) on animal health problems affecting intra Community trade in meat products, Council Directive 91/494 ([1991] OJ L268/35) on animal health conditions governing intra Community trade in and imports from third countries of fresh poultry meat, and Council Directive 94/65 ([1994] OJ L368/10) laying down the requirements for the production and placing on the market of minced meat and meat preparations. They make certain amendments to the Meat Products (Hygiene) Regulations 1994 (SI 1994 3082), the Fresh Meat (Hygiene and Inspection) Regulations 1995 (SI 1995 539), the Minced Meat and Meat Preparations (Hygiene) Regulations 1995 (SI 1995 3205), the Poultry Meat, Farmed Game Bird Meat and Rabbit Meat (Hygiene and Inspection)

Regulations 1995 (SI 1995 540) and the Products of Animal Origin (Import and Export) Regulations 1996 (SI 1996 3124).

2686. Food safety – meat products – enforcement

MEAT (ENHANCED ENFORCEMENT POWERS) (ENGLAND) REGULATIONS 2000, SI 2000 225; made under the European Communities Act 1972 s.2; and the Food Safety Act 1990 s.16, s.17, s.19, s.26, s.37, s.48, Sch.1 para.5, Sch.1 para.6, Sch.1 para.7. In force: March 1, 2000; £4.00.

These Regulations amend the Fresh Meat (Hygiene and Inspection) Regulations 1995 (SI 1995 539), the Poultry Meat, Farmed Game Bird and Rabbit Meat (Hygiene and Inspection) Regulations 1995 (SI 1995 540), the Meat Products (Hygiene) Regulations 1994 (SI 1994 3082), the Minced Meat and Meat Preparations (Hygiene) Regulations 1995 (SI 1995 3205), the Meat Hygiene Appeals Tribunal (Procedure) Regulations 1992 (SI 1992 2921), and the Products of Animal Origin (Import and Export) Regulations 1996 (SI 1996 3124), by providing enhanced powers of enforcement in relation to those Regulations; imposing new obligations on persons engaged in activities which would otherwise be exempt, and imposing revised provisions relating to licensing and approval of meat product premises.

2687. Food safety – medical food

MEDICAL FOOD (ENGLAND) REGULATIONS 2000, SI 2000 845; made under the Food Safety Act 1990 s.6, s.17, s.26, s.48. In force: November 1, 2001; £1.50.

These Regulations implement Commission Directive 1999/21 ([1999] OJ L91/29) on dietary foods for special medical purposes requiring Member States to ensure that such food may only be marketed if it complies with the Directive, and laying down requirements for formulation, composition and instructions for use of such food, and for its naming and labelling. They set out enforcement responsibilities, offences and penalties and application of provisions of the Food Safety Act 1990.

2688. Food safety – medical food – Wales

MEDICAL FOOD (WALES) REGULATIONS 2000, SI 2000 1866 (W.125); made under the Food Safety Act 1990 s.6, s.17, s.26, s.48. In force: November 1, 2001; £2.00.

These Regulations implement in Wales Commission Directive 1999/21 ([1999] OJ L91/29) on dietary foods for special medical purposes by prohibiting the sale of such food unless it is marketed in accordance with the requirements of the Directive relating to the formulation, composition, instructions for use of the food, and its naming and labelling. They set out enforcement responsibilities, offences, penalties and the application of provisions of the Food Safety Act 1990.

2689. Food safety – packaging – plastics

PLASTIC MATERIALS AND ARTICLES IN CONTACT WITH FOOD (AMENDMENT) (ENGLAND) REGULATIONS 2000, SI 2000 3162; made under the Food Safety Act 1990 s.16, s.17, s.26, s.48. In force: December 31, 2000; £2.50.

These Regulations which amend, for England, the Plastic Materials and Articles in Contact with Food Regulations 1998 (SI 1998 1376) implement Commission Directive 1999/91 ([1999] OJ L310/41) amending Directive 90/128 relating to plastic materials and articles intended to come into contact with foodstuffs. They update, restrict and specify the monomers and additives which can be used in the manufacture of plastic materials and articles intended to come into contact with food and, in particular, specify the maximum permitted quantity of the substance in the finished material or article. In addition, they bring products obtained by bacterial fermentation within the scope of the 1998 Regulations and impose restrictions and specifications for such products.

2690. Food safety – tetrachloroethylene in olive oil

TETRACHLOROETHYLENE IN OLIVE OIL (REVOCATION) REGULATIONS 2000, SI 2000 960; made under the Food Safety Act 1990 s.17, s.48. In force: May 1, 2000; £1.00.

These Regulations revoke the Tetrachloroethylene in Olive Oil Regulations 1989 (SI 1989 910), which provided for the enforcement of Commission Regulation 1860/88 ([1988] OJ L166/16) Art.1 on the establishment of special marketing standards for olive oil and which set a limit for tetrachloroethylene.

2691. Food Standards Act 1999 (c.28) – Commencement No.1 Order

FOOD STANDARDS ACT 1999 (COMMENCEMENT NO.1) ORDER 2000, SI 2000 92 (C.2); made under the Food Standards Act 1999 s.43. Commencement details: bringing into force various provisions of the Act on January 11, 2000; £1.00.

This Order brings into force, on January 11, 2000, the Food Standards Act 1999 s.1 (1), s.2, s.3(1) (2) (3), s.36(2), s.41,s.42 and Sch.1. It also brings into force, for certain purposes, s.3(4) (5) (6), s.5(1), s.5(4), s.36(1) Sch.2 para.1, para.5 and para.6. These provisions between them provide for the constitution of, and for particular appointments to, the Food Standards Agency, the establishment of advisory committees for Scotland and Wales and the making of transfer schemes and transitional regulations.

2692. Food Standards Act 1999 (c.28) – Commencement No.2 Order

FOOD STANDARDS ACT 1999 (COMMENCEMENT NO.2) ORDER 2000, SI 2000 1066 (C.31); made under the Food Standards Act 1999 s.43. Commencement details: bringing into force various provisions of the Act on April 1, 2000; £1.00.

This Order brings the Food Standards Act 1999 into force on April 1, 2000, in so far as it is not already in force.

2693. Imports – emergency controls – peanuts from Egypt

FOOD (PEANUTS FROM EGYPT) (EMERGENCY CONTROL) (ENGLAND AND WALES) ORDER 2000, SI 2000 375; made under the Food Safety Act 1990 s.6, s.13, s.48. In force: February 23, 2000; £1.50.

This Order replaces the Food (Peanuts from Egypt) (Emergency Control) Order 1999 (SI 1999 1800) which prohibited the import of peanuts from Egypt. It permits such importation in accordance with Commission Decision 2000/49 ([2000] OJ L19/46) Art.1 which imposes special conditions on the import of peanuts and certain products derived from peanuts originating in or consigned from Egypt.

2694. Schools – school meals – nutritional standards

See EDUCATION. §1937

2695. Publications

Painter, Anthony A. – Butterworths Food Law. 2nd Ed. Paperback: £50.00. ISBN 0-406-89548-1. Butterworths.

GOVERNMENT ADMINISTRATION

2696. Appropriation Act 2000 (c.9)

This Act applies a sum out of the Consolidated Fund to the service of the year ending on March 31, 2001 and appropriates the supplies granted in this session of

Parliament. In addition, it repeals certain Consolidated Fund and Appropriation Acts.

This Act received Royal Assent on July 20, 2000 and comes into force on July 20, 2000.

2697. **Consolidated Fund Act 2000 (c.3)**

This Act applies certain sums out of the Consolidated Fund to the service of the years ending on March 31, 1999, 2000 and 2001.

This Act received Royal Assent on March 21, 2000 and comes into force on March 21, 2000.

2698. **Consolidated Fund (No.2) Act 2000 (c.45)**

An Act to apply certain sums out of the Consolidated Fund to the service of the year ending on March 31, 2001.

This Act received Royal Assent on December 21, 2000.

2699. **Contracting out – petroleum royalty payments**

CONTRACTING OUT (FUNCTIONS IN RELATION TO PETROLEUM ROYALTY PAYMENTS) ORDER 2000, SI 2000 353; made under the Deregulation and Contracting Out Act 1994 s.69, s.77. In force: February 15, 2000; £1.00.

This Order provides that certain functions relating to the payment or repayment of petroleum royalty conferred on the Secretary of State by or under the Petroleum Act 1998 may be exercised by any person whom the Secretary of State may authorise to do so.

2700. **Development Commission – dissolution**

DEVELOPMENT COMMISSION (DISSOLUTION) ORDER 2000, SI 2000 1505; made under the Regional Development Agencies Act 1998 s.35. In force: June 8, 2000; £1.50.

This Order dissolves the Development Commission on July 1, 2000; transfers some property to the Secretary of State and any remaining functions, property, rights and liabilities to the Countryside Agency; and applies the Superannuation Act 1972 to certain employees or former employees of the Development Commission and the Rural Community Councils with pension rights under the Development Commission (Staff) Superannuation Scheme 1984, to enable them to join the Principal Civil Service Pension Scheme.

2701. **Government Resources and Accounts Act 2000 (c.20)**

This Act makes provision about government resources and accounts. In particular, it provides for financial assistance for a body established to participate in public-private partnerships.

This Act received Royal Assent on July 28, 2000.

2702. **Government Resources and Accounts Act 2000 (c.20) – Commencement No.1 and Transitional Provision Order**

GOVERNMENT RESOURCES AND ACCOUNTS ACT 2000 (COMMENCEMENT NO.1 AND TRANSITIONAL PROVISION) ORDER 2000, SI 2000 3349 (C.111); made under the Government Resources and Accounts Act 2000 s.30. Commencement details: bringing into force various provisions of the Act on December 22, 2000 and April 1, 2001; £1.75.

This Order brings into force most of the remaining provisions of the Government Resources and Accounts Act 2000 which did not come into force in the passing of the Act.

2703. Ministerial responsibility – transfer of functions – agriculture and fisheries

TRANSFER OF FUNCTIONS (AGRICULTURE AND FISHERIES) ORDER 2000, SI 2000 1812; made under the Ministers of the Crown Act 1975 s.1. In force: August 15, 2000; £2.00.

This Order transfers the roles of the Secretary of State for Scotland, the Secretary of State for Wales and the Secretary of State in the exercise of certain functions relating to agriculture and fisheries to the Minister of Agriculture, Fisheries and Food. Its purpose is to transfer functions which are in practice exercised by the Secretary of State for Scotland or the Secretary of State for Wales and which have become unnecessary following the devolution of functions to the Scottish Parliament and Executive and to the National Assembly for Wales.

2704. Ministerial responsibility – transfer of functions – computers and telecommunications

TRANSFER OF FUNCTIONS (MINISTER FOR THE CIVIL SERVICE AND TREASURY) ORDER 2000, SI 2000 250; made under the Ministers of the Crown Act 1975 s.1. In force: April 1, 2000; £1.50.

This Order provides that functions with respect to the centralised procurement or provision of goods, services and facilities in the fields of computers and telecommunications which are exercisable by the Minister for the Civil Service may also be exercised by the Treasury. It transfers to the Treasury rights and liabilities in connection with those functions.

2705. Ministers – designated powers

EUROPEAN COMMUNITIES (DESIGNATION) (NO.2) ORDER 2000, SI 2000 1813; made under the European Communities Act 1972 s.2. In force: August 14, 2000; £1.50.

This Order designates certain authorities which may exercise the power to make regulations conferred by the European Communities Act 1972 s.2(2) and specifies the matters in relation to which that power may be exercised.

2706. Ministers – designated powers

EUROPEAN COMMUNITIES (DESIGNATION) (NO.3) ORDER 2000, SI 2000 2812; made under the European Communities Act 1972 s.2; and the Government of Wales Act 1998 s.29. In force: November 13, 2000; £1.75.

This Order, which amends the European Communities (Designation) Order 1972 (SI 1972 1811), designates authorities which may exercise the power to make regulations conferred by the European Communities Act 1972 s.2(2) and specifies the matters in relation to which that power may be exercised.

2707. Public authorities – accounts – information

WHOLE OF GOVERNMENT ACCOUNTS (DESIGNATION OF BODIES) ORDER 2000, SI 2000 3357; made under the Government Resources and Accounts Act 2000 s.10. In force: April 1, 2001; £2.00.

This Order designates bodies for the purposes of Government Resources and Accounts Act 2000 s.10, for the financial year ending with March 31, 2002. The Treasury intends the "whole of government" accounts to be prepared for that year under s.9 of the Act should relate in part to the bodies designated by this Order, and the designation enables the Treasury to require those bodies to provide financial information in relation to that year.

2708. Publications

Cheeseman, Henry R. – Legal and Regulatory Environment. 2nd Ed. Contemporary Perspectives in Business. Hardback: £39.99. ISBN 0-13-012954-2. Prentice Hall.

HEALTH

2709. Chiropractors Act 1994 (c.17) – Commencement No.4 Order

CHIROPRACTORS ACT 1994 (COMMENCEMENT NO.4) ORDER 2000, SI 2000 2388 (C.65); made under the Chiropractors Act 1994 s.44. Commencement details: bringing into force various provisions of the Act on September 7, 2000; £2.00.

This Order brings into force various provisions of the Chiropractors Act 1994 relating to the General Chiropractic Council's duty to develop, promote and regulate the profession; the Council's functions; statutory committees and their role in respect of professional conduct, fitness to practise and connected appeals; and the appointment of legal and medical assessors.

2710. Clinical negligence – abortion – false representation by GP on ethical grounds

See NEGLIGENCE: Barr v. Matthews. §4189

2711. Community health councils – primary care trusts

COMMUNITY HEALTH COUNCILS (AMENDMENT) REGULATIONS 2000, SI 2000 657; made under the National Health Service Act 1977 s.17, s.126, Sch.7 para.2, Sch.7 para.3. In force: April 1, 2000; £1.50.

These Regulations amend the Community Health Councils Regulations 1996 (SI 1996 640) to make provision in relation to primary care trusts. They provide that a chairman or member of a primary care trust and a person dismissed from the employment of a relevant primary care trust are disqualified from membership of a community health council; that health authorities must consult a council on proposals which a primary care trust in their area may have under consideration for substantial variations or developments in the health service in the council's district; that primary care trusts must provide information to councils about the planning and operation of health services in their area and hold annual meetings with councils; and that councils may inspect premises controlled by primary care trusts.

2712. Community health councils – terms of office – Wales

COMMUNITY HEALTH COUNCILS AMENDMENT (WALES) REGULATIONS 2000, SI 2000 479 (W.20); made under the National Health Service Act 1977 s.126, s.128, Sch.7 para.2. In force: March 1, 2000; £1.50.

These Regulations amend the Community Health Councils Regulations 1996 (SI 1996 640) by providing that in the event of the terms of office of every member of a Council terminating on the same date, a situation which will arise in the case of all Councils in Wales on March 31, 2000, the terms of office of members appointed to Councils in consequence of that event shall be settled as if they were on first appointment upon the establishment of a new council.

2713. Dentists – professional conduct – appeals – time limits – power to allow appeal out of time if appeal had substantial merits

[Dentists Act 1984 s.29.]

B, a dentist, applied by way of notice of motion to the Judicial Committee of the Privy Council seeking permission to lodge an appeal out of time. B had been found guilty of serious professional misconduct by the professional conduct committee of the General Dental Council on December 8, 1999. The committee had directed that B should be suspended from the register of dentists for one year. B did not lodge a petition of appeal until April 11, 2000.

Held, dismissing the application, that the Dentists Act 1984 s.29 provided a right of appeal within 28 days of service of notification of the decision of the professional standards committee, but there was no power to extend the time limit for lodging appeals, though the Board could, in exercising its inherent jurisdiction, allow an appeal out of time where it was in the interests of justice to do so and if the case had substantial merits. However, this was not justified in the instant case as B's appeal had no substantial merits.

BAINTON v. GENERAL DENTAL COUNCIL *The Times*, October 17, 2000, Lord Hutton, PC.

2714. Dentists – professional conduct – suspension for driving offences disproportionate

See ADMINISTRATION OF JUSTICE: Dad v. General Dental Council. §38

2715. Doctors – disciplinary procedures – communication between medical officer and patient – categorisation of personal conduct or professional conduct – reasonableness of decision

C, a doctor employed by CHCS, carried out a cervical smear test on P. P later complained to CHCS that C had not introduced herself, or asked about P's concerns, or given P an opportunity to discuss the findings. CHCS categorised the complaint as one involving personal conduct and, after an internal investigatory meeting, issued C with a first written warning of misconduct. C sought a declaration that the warning was invalid as the wrong procedure had been adopted and the complaint should have been treated as one of professional conduct. The disciplinary procedure applicable to complaints of professional conduct, unlike that pertaining to personal conduct, involved a hearing before a panel of independent members. C contended that communication with a patient was a matter of professional judgment and a complaint about that judgment was for a professional, not a manager, to decide.

Held, refusing the application, that the issue of categorisation fell to CHCS to be decided and its decision, being within a range of reasonable responses open to it to make, would not be disturbed. There was a duty incumbent on CHCS to act in good faith in exercising their discretion and to give full consideration to the question at issue. In the instant case, the complaint was not about C's professional competence, but that she was uncommunicative, contrary to CHCS's standard of behaviour for all staff. The complaint had been properly categorised, although the distinction between the two types of complaint would often be difficult, and could overlap.

CHATTERJEE v. CITY AND HACKNEY COMMUNITY SERVICES NHS TRUST (1999) 49 B.M.L.R. 55, Lightman, J., Ch D.

2716. Doctors – hours of employment – Working Time Directive – scope of protection – European Community

[Council Directive 89/391 on the introduction of measures to encourage improvements in the safety and health of workers at work; Council Directive 93/104 concerning certain aspects of the organisation of working time Art.2(4), Art.16(2), Art.17, Art.18.]

SIMAP, the union representing the interests of primary care doctors in the region of Valencia, Spain, brought proceedings against the Ministry of Health for the region on the basis that, as the regional legislation on primary care doctors did not provide for any limit on the doctors' working time, it was in breach of Council Directive 89/391 on health and safety and the Working Time Directive 93/104. The Spanish court referred a series of questions to the European Court of Justice.

Held, giving a reference, that (1) the activity of doctors in primary health care teams fell within the scope of both directives. It was clear from the objects of Directive 89/391 that its scope was broad and that any exceptions should be interpreted restrictively, and doctors in primary care did not fall within the scope of the exceptions. Nor did they fall within the exceptions provided under the Working Time Directive; (2) it was possible, under Art.17 of the Working Time Directive, for Member States to derogate from its main principles (on maximum hours of work and rest periods) provided that, even in the absence of implementing measures, national law complied with the conditions laid down in this Article; (3) time spent "on call", when doctors were required to be at the health centre, fell under the definition of "working time" and where appropriate as overtime, within the meaning of the Working Time Directive; (4) doctors in primary care who were on call at night could not be defined as "night workers" under Art.2(4). Their work, however, constituted "shift work" for the purposes of the directive; (5) in the absence of national provisions implementing Art.16(2) or adopting any of the derogations contained in Article 17 of the directive, those provisions had direct effect, and (6) whilst it was possible under Art.18 for both sides of industry to derogate by private agreement from the provisions on the duration of working time, agreement could not derive from the terms of a collective agreement, a worker had to agree individually to longer working hours.

SINDICATO DE MEDICOS DE ASISTENCIA PUBLICA (SIMAP) v. CONSELLERIA DE SANIDAD Y CONSUMO DE LA GENERALIDAD VALENCIANA (C303/98) [2000] I.R.L.R. 845, GC Rodriguez Iglesias (President), ECJ.

2717. Doctors – professional conduct – General Medical Council – complaints procedure – compliance with Human Rights Act 1998 – need for public hearing of complaints

[Medical Act 1983; Human Rights Act 1998; General Medical Council Preliminary Proceedings Committee and Professional Conduct Committee (Procedure) Rules Order of Council 1988 (SI 1988 2255).]

T applied for judicial review of a decision of the General Medical Council (GMC) not to allow him to proceed further with his complaint against a doctor for serious professional misconduct. The decision not to allow T's complaint to progress beyond the preliminary filtering stage had been taken on two occasions by the screener. It was argued that the filtering process had lacked transparency. The complaints procedure was governed by the Medical Act 1983 and the General Medical Council Preliminary Proceedings Committee and Professional Conduct Committee (Procedure) Rules Order of Council 1988. It was submitted that the principle underlying those rules was that a complaint to the GMC, in the absence of any strong reasons to the contrary, would be publicly investigated by the professional conduct committee. Furthermore, it was argued that the role of the screener did not include investigating the substantive issues of a case in any detail.

Held, granting the application, that the two decisions not to allow the complaint to proceed would be quashed and the case remitted for reconsideration. It was important for the GMC to bear in mind that their complainants had a legitimate expectation that their complaints would be publicly investigated by the professional conduct committee, unless there were strong reasons to the contrary. Moreover, it was important to ensure that justice was seen to be done, particularly if the registered practitioner continued to practice. Medical complaints should be heard publicly and it was recognised by the GMC that there was a need for transparency to achieve compliance with the Human Rights Act 1998. The screener might conclude that a case should not proceed further because, for example, it did not amount to a complaint in law or because the matters complained of did not constitute a serious professional misconduct. However, it was not the function of the screener to look at the substantive issues of the complaint, such as the prospects of the complaint succeeding, in detail or to investigate the fairness of a complaint being allowed to continue. The role of the screener was limited to acting as preliminary filter. Any doubts should be resolved in favour of allowing the complaint to proceed, particularly where the practitioner concerned continued to practise.

R. v. GENERAL MEDICAL COUNCIL, *ex p.* TOTH [2000] 1 W.L.R. 2209, Lightman, J., QBD.

2718. **Doctors – professional conduct – General Medical Council – misconduct – extent of requirement to give reasons for determination**

[General Medical Council Health Committee (Procedure) Rules Order of Council 1987 (SI 1987 2174).]

S, a general practitioner, appealed against a finding of the Professional Conduct Committee of the GMC that he had been guilty of serious professional misconduct. S submitted that the reasons given by the Committee for its finding were inadequate and that reasons should have been given for the Committee's finding against him on questions of fact.

Held, dismissing the appeal, that under the General Medical Council Health Committee (Procedure) Rules Order of Council 1987 the Committee was not required to give reasons for its finding but current practice dictated that à brief explanation on the finding as to whether or not a practitioner was guilty of serious professional misconduct, should be given, *Libman v. General Medical Council* [1972] A.C. 217, [1972] C.L.Y. 2838 disapproved and *Rai v. General Medical Council* (Unreported, May 14, 1984) considered. However, because the Committee was composed of medical practitioners and lay members, with legal advice only given on points of law, and with no means of voicing dissent, it was not expected that it should provide detailed reasons for its findings. A general explanation for its finding regarding serious professional misconduct and the penalty imposed was sufficient in most cases. The Committee's decision was always going to depend on inferences which it made from agreed facts and on its assessment of S's credibility. S only needed to know the decision of the Committee in order to decide what to do next and accordingly he had not suffered prejudice.

SELVANATHAN v. GENERAL MEDICAL COUNCIL [2001] Lloyd's Rep. Med. 1, Lord Hope of Craighead, PC.

2719. **Doctors – professional conduct – sexual intercourse with former patient not misconduct – opportunity to comment on advice given by legal assessor**

[General Medical Council (Legal Assessors) Rules 1980 (SI 1980 941) r.4.]

N, a doctor, was charged with 13 heads of professional misconduct, six of which involved allegations of sexual misconduct and dishonesty, and were held to have been proven. N appealed against one of the heads of sexual misconduct, arguing that (1) the allegation that he had sexual intercourse at his surgery, without more, was irrelevant to the issue of professional misconduct, and (2) the transcript of the private deliberations of the professional conduct committee, PCC, should be disclosed to him, because he had been excluded whilst the legal assessor gave his advice to the PCC, and although he was informed, upon re admission what advice had been given, pursuant to the General Medical Council (Legal Assessors) Rules 1980 r.4, he had been denied the right to make representations, which was a breach of the rules of natural justice.

Held, allowing the appeal in part, that (1) the alleged sexual intercourse committed with a former patient had no impact on N's professional conduct as doctor, because the professional relationship once existing between them, had come to an end, and (2) the purpose of the duty imposed on the legal assessor under r.4 to inform all the parties of the advice given to the PCC, was to promote fairness, so that any comments could be made and considered by PCC prior to a decision being announced. It was not a mere formality, and practice should therefore be altered to ensure that parties were informed of their right to comment on any advice given by the legal assessor, and to have any errors corrected. Nevertheless, in the instant case it was clear that the advice given contained no material defect, which called for correction, and the matter was to be remitted to the PCC for reconsideration as to whether N's conduct as a whole justified erasure of his name from the register of medical practitioners.

NWABUEZE v. GENERAL MEDICAL COUNCIL [2000] 1 W.L.R. 1760, Lord Hope of Craighead, PC.

2720. Drugs – drug addiction – European Monitoring Centre – Council Regulation

Council Regulation 2220/2000 of 28 September 2000 amending Regulation 302/93 on the establishment of a European Monitoring Centre for Drugs and Drug Addiction. [2000] OJ L253/1.

2721. Equipment – in vitro diagnostic medical devices

IN VITRO DIAGNOSTIC MEDICAL DEVICES REGULATIONS 2000, SI 2000 1315; made under the European Communities Act 1972 s.2; the Finance Act 1973 s.56; and the Consumer Protection Act 1987 s.11, s.27. In force: June 7, 2000; £4.00.

These Regulations implement Council Directive 98/79 ([1998] OJ L331/1) on in vitro diagnostic medical devices. They provide that devices placed on the market, put in to service or supplied must comply with the relevant essential requirements, as defined by reference to the essential requirements specified in Annex I of the Directive. They require devices to bear a CE marking which meets the requirements of the Directive.

2722. Food safety – medical food – Wales

See FOOD. §2688

2723. Food safety – medical food

See FOOD. §2687

2724. General Medical Council – committees – professional conduct

GENERAL MEDICAL COUNCIL (FITNESS TO PRACTISE COMMITTEES) RULES ORDER OF COUNCIL 2000, SI 2000 2051; made under the Medical Act 1983 Sch.1 para.24. In force: August 3, 2000; £2.50.

The Rules approved by this Order of Council, which amends the General Medical Council (Constitution of Fitness to Practise Committees) Rules 1996 (SI 1996 2125), the General Medical Council Preliminary Proceedings Committee and Professional Conduct Committee (Procedure) Rules 1988 (SI 1988 2255), the General Medical Council Health Committee (Procedure) Rules 1987 (SI 1987 2174) and the General Medical Council (Professional Performance) Rules 1997 (SI 1997 1529), provide for the reference of cases to the new Interim Orders Committee from the various parts of the existing fitness to practise procedures. They also revise and clarify the procedures for the investigation of complaints against doctors relating to convictions or conduct and make certain other amendments to the procedures and constitution of the fitness to practise committees of the General Medical Council consequential on provisions contained in the Medical Act 1983 (Amendment) Order 2000 (SI 2000 1803).

2725. General Medical Council – committees – professional conduct

GENERAL MEDICAL COUNCIL (THE PROFESSIONAL CONDUCT COMMITTEE, THE GENERAL HEALTH COMMITTEE AND THE COMMITTEE ON PROFESSIONAL PERFORMANCE) (AMENDMENT) RULES ORDER OF COUNCIL 2000, SI 2000 2034; made under the Medical Act 1983 Sch.4 para.1. In force: July 1, 2000; £3.00.

The Rules approved by this Order of Council set out the procedures to be followed by the General Medical Council's Professional Conduct Committee, Health Committee and Committee on Professional Performance when considering applications for restoration to the Register of Medical Practitioners following voluntary erasure from the Register. In addition, the rules modify, in a number of respects, the rules of these committees that apply to other types of hearing conducted by the committees.

2726. **General Medical Council – General Medical Council disciplinary procedures – admissibility of illegally obtained evidence**

See EVIDENCE: Idenburg v. General Medical Council. §303

2727. **General Medical Council – Interim Orders Committee – constitution**

GENERAL MEDICAL COUNCIL (CONSTITUTION OF INTERIM ORDERS COMMITTEE) RULES ORDER OF COUNCIL 2000, SI 2000 2052; made under the Medical Act 1983 Sch.1 para.24. In force: August 3, 2000; £1.50.

The Rules approved by this Order of Council establish and regulate the constitution of the Interim Orders Committee, a new statutory committee of the General Medical Council provided for in the Medical Act 1983 (Amendment) Order 2000 (SI 2000 1803).

2728. **General Medical Council – Interim Orders Committee – disciplinary procedures**

GENERAL MEDICAL COUNCIL (INTERIM ORDERS COMMITTEE) (TRANSITIONAL PROVISIONS) RULES ORDER OF COUNCIL 2000, SI 2000 2054; made under the Medical Act 1983 Sch.4 para.1. In force: August 3, 2000; £1.50.

The Rules approved by this Order of Council give effect to powers provided for in the Medical Act 1983 (Amendment) Order 2000 (SI 2000 1803) to make rules in respect of cases where, on the date the Order comes into force, proceedings in respect of interim suspension or interim conditional registration have commenced before, but no order has been made by, the Preliminary Proceedings Committee or where such an order is in force following a decision by that committee. The Rules provide that a decision as to whether an interim suspension order or an order for interim conditional registration should be made or, where such an order is already in force, a decision as to whether it should be renewed or revoked, shall be made by the Interim Orders Committee.

2729. **General Medical Council – Interim Orders Committee – disciplinary procedures**

MEDICAL ACT 1983 (AMENDMENT) ORDER 2000, SI 2000 1803; made under the National Health Service Act 1977 s.126; and the Health Act 1999 s.60. In force: August 3, 2000; £2.50.

This Order amends the Medical Act 1983 by providing for a new statutory committee of the General Medical Council to be called the Interim Orders Committee. It provides for powers for persons authorised by the GMC to require disclosure of information that would assist them in the carrying out of their functions in respect of fitness to practise or professional conduct; obliges the committees of the GMC to notify specified persons when formal proceedings are initiated against a practitioner in respect of his fitness to practise or professional conduct; provides that a practitioner's name may be erased from the register, or his registration may be suspended or made subject to conditions, if he is convicted of a criminal offence in the British Islands or abroad; provides for a right of appeal to the Judicial Committee of the Privy Council; increases the period of time that a person who has been erased from the register must wait before being able to apply for restoration from ten months to five years; and defines the circumstances in which the Interim Orders Committee may make an order providing for a practitioner's registration to be suspended or to be made subject to conditions on an interim basis.

2730. General Medical Council – Interim Orders Committee – procedure

GENERAL MEDICAL COUNCIL (INTERIM ORDERS COMMITTEE) (PROCEDURE) RULES ORDER OF COUNCIL 2000, SI 2000 2053; made under the Medical Act 1983 Sch.4 para.1. In force: August 3, 2000; £2.00.

The Rules approved by this Order of Council give effect to provisions brought into force by the Medical Act 1983 (Amendment) Order 2000 (SI 2000 1803). They set out the procedure to be followed by the Interim Orders Committee when making an order that the registration of a practitioner be subject to conditions or be suspended where the Interim Orders Committee are satisfied that this is necessary for the protection of members of the public or is otherwise in the public interest or the interests of the practitioner.

2731. General Medical Council – legal assessors

GENERAL MEDICAL COUNCIL (LEGAL ASSESSORS) (AMENDMENT) RULES 2000, SI 2000 1881; made under the Medical Act 1983 s.43, Sch.4 para.7. In force: August 16, 2000; £1.00.

These Rules provide for the General Medical Council (Legal Assessors) Rules 1980 (SI 1980 941), which regulate the functions of legal assessors appointed by the General Medical Council to advise certain committees on questions of law arising in proceedings before them, to apply in the same way to the new Interim Orders Committee, created by the Medical Act 1993 (Amendment) Order 2000 (SI 2000 1803).

2732. General Medical Council – register of medical practitioners

GENERAL MEDICAL COUNCIL (VOLUNTARY ERASURE AND RESTORATION) REGULATIONS ORDER OF COUNCIL 2000, SI 2000 2033; made under the Medical Act 1983 s.31A, s.32. In force: July 1, 2000; £2.00.

The Regulations approved by this Order of Council give effect to the provisions brought into force by the Medical (Professional Performance) Act 1995 (Commencement No.4) Order 2000 (SI 2000 1344) relating to the powers of the General Medical Council to consider applications for voluntary erasure from the Register of Medical Practitioners and subsequent applications for restoration to the Register. They enable the Registrar of the GMC to refuse application for voluntary erasure in certain circumstances and set out circumstances in which applications for restoration may be referred to one of the GMC's statutory committees.

2733. General Medical Council – registration fees

GENERAL MEDICAL COUNCIL (REGISTRATION (FEES) (AMENDMENT) NO.2 REGULATIONS) ORDER OF COUNCIL 2000, SI 2000 3194; made under the Medical Act 1983 s.32. In force: December 4, 2000; £1.75.

The Regulations approved by this Order of Council amend Reg.4(2) of the Medical Practitioners Registration (Fees) Regulations 1985 (approved by SI 1986 149) to provide for the payment of a fee for provisional registration by doctors registered under the Medical Act 1983 s.15A, inserted by the Medical Act 1983 (Provisional Registration) Regulations 2000 (SI 2000 3041).

2734. General Medical Council – registration fees

GENERAL MEDICAL COUNCIL (REGISTRATION (FEES) (AMENDMENT) REGULATIONS) ORDER OF COUNCIL 2000, SI 2000 2141; made under the Medical Act 1983 s.32. In force: January 1, 2001 in accordance with Sch. para.1 (1); £1.50.

The Regulations approved by this Order of Council amend the fees payable to the General Medical Council by medical practitioners in respect of retention in, or restoration to, the register. The General Medical Council (Registration (Fees) (Amendment) Regulations) Order of Council 1999 (SI 1999 3189) is revoked.

2735. Health Act 1999 (c.8) – Commencement No.2 Order – Wales

HEALTH ACT 1999 (COMMENCEMENT NO.2) (WALES) ORDER 2000, SI 2000 1026 (C.26; W.62); made under the Health Act 1999 s.63, s.66. Commencement details: bringing into force various provisions of the 1999 Act on April 1, 2000; £2.00.

This Order brings into force, in relation to Wales, certain provisions of the Health Act 1999 which provide for the abolition of GP fund holding, allow for amendment of representation on Local Dental and Medical Committees, and make consequential amendments to National Health Service Legislation.

2736. Health Act 1999 (c.8) – Commencement No.3 Order – Wales

HEALTH ACT 1999 (COMMENCEMENT NO.3) (WALES) ORDER 2000, SI 2000 2991 (W.191; C.92); made under the Health Act 1999 s.63, s.66, s.67. Commencement details: bringing into force various provisions of the Act on December 1, 2000 and January 1, 2001; £2.50.

This Order brings into force further provisions of the Health Act 1999 in relation to Wales which provide for partnership between NHS bodies and Local Authorities, including payments between NHS bodies and Local Authorities and arrangements between them. In addition, it makes provision for the commencement of repeals relating to Joint Consultative Committees and of the Health Service Joint Consultative Committees (Access to Information) Act 1986.

2737. Health Act 1999 (c.8) – Commencement No.8 Order

HEALTH ACT 1999 (COMMENCEMENT NO.8) ORDER 2000, SI 2000 779 (C.17); made under the Health Act 1999 s.67. Commencement details: bringing into force various provisions of the Act on March 15, 2000; £2.00.

This Order brings into force provisions of the Health Act 1999 relating to the regulation of health care and associated professions, including the amendment of legislation relating to such professions, by means of Orders in Council.

2738. Health Act 1999 (c.8) – Commencement No.9 Order

HEALTH ACT 1999 (COMMENCEMENT NO.9) ORDER 2000, SI 2000 1041 (C.28); made under the Health Act 1999 s.67. Commencement details: bringing into force various provisions of the Act on April 1, 2000; £2.00.

This Order brings into force on April 1, 2000 further provisions of the Health Act 1999. In particular it brings into force, in relation to Wales, s.9 and s.21 of the Act and, in relation to England and Wales, various repeals in Sch.5 to the Act.

2739. Health authorities – change of name

COUNTY DURHAM HEALTH AUTHORITY (CHANGE OF NAME) ORDER 2000, SI 2000 1241; made under the National Health Service Act 1977 s.8, s.126. In force: June 1, 2000; £1.00.

This Order, which makes a consequential amendment to the Health Authorities (England) Establishment Order 1996 (SI 1996 624), changes the name of County Durham HA to County Durham and Darlington HA.

2740. Health authorities – change of name

EAST RIDING HEALTH AUTHORITY (CHANGE OF NAME) ORDER 2000, SI 2000 1240; made under the National Health Service Act 1977 s.8, s.126. In force: June 1, 2000; £1.00.

This Order, which makes a consequential amendment to the Health Authorities (England) Establishment Order 1996 (SI 1996 624), changes the name of East Riding HA to East Riding and Hull HA.

2741. Health authorities – functions and administration arrangements – Wales

NATIONAL HEALTH SERVICE (FUNCTIONS OF HEALTH AUTHORITIES AND ADMINISTRATION ARRANGEMENTS) (WALES) AMENDMENT REGULATIONS 2000, SI 2000 1035 (W.66); made under the National Health Service Act 1977 s.16D, s.17, s.18, s.126. In force: April 1, 2000; £1.50.

These Regulations amend the National Health Service (Functions of Health Authorities and Administration Arrangements) Regulations 1996 (SI 1996 708) by providing for certain health authorities in Wales to exercise the National Assembly's function of providing hospital facilities pursuant to the National Health Service Act 1977 s.4. The relevant services are in relation to persons who are liable to be detained under the Mental Health Act 1983 and who are considered to require treatment under conditions of high security on account of their dangerous, violent or criminal propensities.

2742. Health authorities – health care – standards

SPECIAL HEALTH AUTHORITIES (DUTY OF QUALITY) REGULATIONS 2000, SI 2000 660; made under the National Health Service Act 1977 s.126; and the Health Act 1999 s.18. In force: April 1, 2000; £1.00.

These Regulations extend the duty in the Health Act 1999 s.18, to put and keep in place arrangements for the purpose of monitoring and improving the quality of health care which an NHS body provides to individuals, to the National Blood Authority and to the Ashworth, Broadmoor and Rampton Hospital Authorities.

2743. Health authorities – Health Education Authority – abolition

HEALTH EDUCATION AUTHORITY (ABOLITION) ORDER 2000, SI 2000 604; made under the National Health Service Act 1977 s.11, s.126. In force: April 1, 2000; £1.50.

This Order abolishes, on April 1, 2000, the Health Education Authority, a special health authority established under the National Health Service Act 1977 s.11 by the Health Education Authority (Establishment and Constitution) Order 1987 (SI 1987 6). It makes provisions for the transfer of officers, property, rights and liabilities of the Authority and for the winding-up of its affairs.

2744. Health authorities – membership and functions – Ashworth, Broadmoor and Rampton Hospital Authorities

ASHWORTH, BROADMOOR AND RAMPTON HOSPITAL AUTHORITIES (FUNCTIONS AND MEMBERSHIP) AMENDMENT REGULATIONS 2000, SI 2000 2435; made under the National Health Service Act 1977 s.126, Sch.5 para.12. In force: October 1, 2000; £1.00.

These Regulations amend the Ashworth, Broadmoor and Rampton Hospital Authorities (Functions and Membership) Regulations 1996 (SI 1996 489) to provide that, during the period between the establishment date of an NHS trust and its operational date, the chairman or a non executive director of the trust may hold office as the chairman or a non officer member of the Ashworth Hospital Authority, the Broadmoor Hospital Authority or the Rampton Hospital Authority.

2745. Health authorities – membership and procedure

HEALTH AUTHORITIES (MEMBERSHIP AND PROCEDURE) AMENDMENT REGULATIONS 2000, SI 2000 696; made under the National Health Service Act 1977 s.126, Sch.5 para.12. In force: April 1, 2000; £1.50.

These Regulations amend the Health Authorities (Membership and Procedure) Regulations 1996 (SI 1996 707) to take account of the establishment of primary care trusts and to provide that the chairman and members of the Health Development Agency are not disqualified for appointment as the chairman or a member of a health authority. They provide that the chairman and members of a primary care trust are disqualified for appointment as the chairman or a member of the National Health Service Litigation Authority.

2746. Health authorities – National Clinical Assessment Authority – establishment and constitution

NATIONAL CLINICAL ASSESSMENT AUTHORITY (ESTABLISHMENT AND CONSTITUTION) ORDER 2000, SI 2000 2961; made under the National Health Service Act 1977 s.11, Sch.5 para.9. In force: November 27, 2000; £1.50.

This Order provides for the establishment and constitution of a special health authority, to be known as the National Clinical Assessment Authority, to exercise such functions in connection with the assessment of the performance and conduct of doctors and dentists engaged in the health service and such other functions as the Secretary of State may direct.

2747. Health authorities – National Clinical Assessment Authority – membership and procedure

NATIONAL CLINICAL ASSESSMENT AUTHORITY REGULATIONS 2000, SI 2000 2962; made under the National Health Service Act 1977 s.126, Sch.5 para.12, Sch.5 para.16. In force: November 27, 2000; £2.00.

These Regulations make provision concerning the membership and procedure of the National Clinical Assessment Authority which is a Special Health Authority established under the National Health Service Act 1977 by the National Clinical Assessment Authority (Establishment and Constitution) Order 2000 (SI 2000 2961). In particular, they provide for the appointment and tenure of office of the chairman and members of the Authority, disqualification for appointment, and termination of office.

2748. Health authorities – National Health Service Logistics Authority

NATIONAL HEALTH SERVICE SUPPLIES AUTHORITY (ESTABLISHMENT AND CONSTITUTION) AMENDMENT ORDER 2000, SI 2000 603; made under the National Health Service Act 1977 s.11, s.126. In force: April 1, 2000; £1.00.

This Order changes the name of the National Health Service Supplies Authority, a special health authority established under the National Health Authority Act 1977 s.11, to the National Health Service Logistics Authority.

2749. Health authorities – prescribing incentives

NATIONAL HEALTH SERVICE (FUNCTIONS OF HEALTH AUTHORITIES) (PRESCRIBING INCENTIVE SCHEMES) AMENDMENT REGULATIONS 2000, SI 2000 661; made under the National Health Service Act 1977 s.16, s.126. In force: April 1, 2000; £1.50.

These Regulations amend the National Health Service (Functions of Health Authorities) (Prescribing Incentive Schemes) Regulations 1998 (SI 1998 632), which confer a function on health authorities to establish and operate prescribing incentive schemes, by removing the reference to fund-holding practices in the definition of "practice" and adding a definition of "primary care group".

2750. Health authorities – primary care trusts – prescribed functions

NATIONAL HEALTH SERVICE (PAYMENTS BY LOCAL AUTHORITIES TO NHS BODIES) (PRESCRIBED FUNCTIONS) REGULATIONS 2000, SI 2000 618; made under the National Health Service Act 1977 s.28BB, s.126. In force: April 1, 2000; £1.50.

These Regulations prescribe certain functions of health authorities and primary care trusts for the purposes of the National Health Service Act 1977 s.28BB which allows local authorities to make payments to those NHS bodies towards expenditure incurred by them in connection with the performance of any of the prescribed functions.

2751. Health authorities – psychiatric services

NATIONAL HEALTH SERVICE (FUNCTIONS OF HEALTH AUTHORITIES AND ADMINISTRATION ARRANGEMENTS) AMENDMENT REGULATIONS 2000, SI 2000 267; made under the National Health Service Act 1977 s.16D, s.17, s.18, s.126. In force: April 1, 2000; £1.00.

These Regulations amend the National Health Service (Functions of Health Authorities and Administration Arrangements) Regulations 1996 (SI 1996 708) by making provision for Health Authorities to exercise the Secretary of State's function of providing high security psychiatric services but only by making NHS contracts with Ashworth, Broadmoor or Rampton Hospital Authority or an NHS trust approved by the Secretary of State for the purpose of providing such services.

2752. Health authorities – United Kingdom Transplant

UNITED KINGDOM TRANSPLANT SUPPORT SERVICE AUTHORITY (ESTABLISHMENT AND CONSTITUTION) AMENDMENT ORDER 2000, SI 2000 1621; made under the National Health Service Act 1977 s.11, s.126. In force: July 12, 2000; £1.00.

This Order changes the name of the United Kingdom Transplant Support Service Authority, a special health authority established under the National Health Service Act 1977 s.11, to United Kingdom Transplant. In addition, it provides for an increase in the number of members of the Authority.

2753. Health authorities – wrong health authority – acting in relation to practitioners

HEALTH AUTHORITIES ACT 1995 (RECTIFICATION OF TRANSITIONAL ARRANGEMENTS) ORDER 2000, SI 2000 179; made under the Health Act 1999 s.44, s.63. In force: February 21, 2000; £2.50.

This Order amends the Health Authorities Act 1995 (Transitional Provisions) Order 1996 (SI 1996 709) so as to rectify certain defects in that Order with retrospective effect. The effect is that where one health authority acted in relation to practitioners providing services under the National Health Service Act 1977 Part II where another health authority should have acted, the proper health authority will be treated as though it had been the acting one.

2754. Health Service Commissioners (Amendment) Act 2000 (c.28)

This Act amends the Health Service Commissioners Act 1993.

This Act received Royal Assent on November 23, 2000 and comes into force on February 23, 2001.

2755. Immunisation – personal injury – compensation

VACCINE DAMAGE PAYMENTS ACT 1979 STATUTORY SUM ORDER 2000, SI 2000 1983; made under the Vaccine Damage Payments Act 1979 s.1. In force: July 22, 2000; £1.00.

This Order increases from £40,000 to £100,000 the sum which is payable under the Vaccine Damage Payments Act 1979 s.1 (1) when the Secretary of State is satisfied that a person in respect of whom a claim for payment is made on or after the date of this Order coming into force is, or was immediately before his death, severely disabled as a result of vaccination against any disease to which that Act applies. The Vaccine Damage Payments Act 1979 Statutory Sum Order 1998 (SI 1988 1587) is revoked.

2756. Medical examinations – professional conduct – late disclosure of material evidence to general practitioner accused of misconduct

R, a general practitioner, appealed against a finding of the Professional Conduct Committee of the General Medical Council that he had been guilty of serious professional misconduct. Patient A alleged that R had conducted an inappropriate breast examination during a consultation for the contraceptive pill. Patient B alleged that R had performed an inappropriate breast examination and kissed her during a consultation for depression. On the morning of the hearing before the Professional Conduct Committee, counsel for the Committee provided R and his representatives with a copy of a diary entry made by patient B in which the consultation with R had been noted as being at 3.40 pm. The Committee at first instance found R guilty of serious professional misconduct in relation to both incidents. On appeal, R contended that (1) late disclosure of the diary entry had resulted in injustice since R had not had the opportunity to adduce evidence concerning his surgery hours. R maintained, supported by the evidence of two former receptionists, that his afternoon surgery commenced at 4.30 pm and that the alleged consultation had never taken place. R further contended that it was surgery practice to mark in patients' notes details of their forthcoming consultations and that no such entry had been made for the consultation which B had alleged had occurred, and (2) performance of a breast examination during a consultation for the contraceptive pill was standard medical practice and whilst R may have omitted to obtain A's specific consent to the procedure he had not been guilty of any improper behaviour.

Held, allowing the appeal, that (1) the diary entry was highly relevant to the allegations made and should have been disclosed to R and his representatives long before the hearing before the Committee, *R. v. Maguire (Anne Rita)* [1992] Q.B. 936, [1992] C.L.Y. 812 and *R. v. Ward (Judith Theresa)* [1993] 1 W.L.R. 619, [1993] C.L.Y. 723 applied. The verdict of the Committee was therefore unsafe so far as patient B was concerned, and (2) the allegations made in respect of patient A were different to those made in respect of patient B. There could have been no possible justification for a breast examination in a consultation for depression but that was not necessarily true of a consultation for the contraceptive pill. The possibility existed that the Committee may have been influenced by the evidence and their conclusions in relation to patient B when considering the allegations made by patient A and concluded that R was conducting breast examinations for the purposes of sexual gratification. In those circumstances the finding in relation to patient A was also unsafe.

RAJAN v. GENERAL MEDICAL COUNCIL [2000] Lloyd's Rep. Med. 153, Lord Hutton, PC.

2757. Medical profession – chiropractors – appeals

JUDICIAL COMMITTEE (CHIROPRACTORS RULES) ORDER 2000, SI 2000 2822; made under the Chiropractors Act 1994 s.10, s.31. In force: November 10, 2000; £1.75.

This Order provides for the rules governing procedure for appeals to Her Majesty in Council under the Chiropractors Act 1994.

2758. Medical profession – chiropractors – General Chiropractic Council – appeals procedure

GENERAL CHIROPRACTIC COUNCIL (APPEALS AGAINST DECISIONS OF THE REGISTRAR) RULES ORDER 2000, SI 2000 2265; made under the Chiropractors Act 1994 s.29, s.35. In force: June 23, 2000; £2.00.

This Order approves rules made by the General Chiropractic Council which make provision in respect of procedure for appeals to that Council from decisions of the Registrar as to whether a chiropractor should be on the register and if so whether as fully, conditionally or provisionally registered.

2759. **Medical profession – chiropractors – General Chiropractic Council – appeals procedure**

GENERAL CHIROPRACTIC COUNCIL (HEALTH APPEAL TRIBUNAL) RULES ORDER 2000, SI 2000 3214; made under the Chiropractors Act 1994 s.30, s.35. In force: December 18, 2000; £2.00.

This Order approves Rules made by the General Chiropractic Council which provide for the procedure to be followed by appeal tribunals dealing with appeals from decisions of its Health Committee.

2760. **Medical profession – chiropractors – General Chiropractic Council – health committee**

GENERAL CHIROPRACTIC COUNCIL (HEALTH COMMITTEE) RULES ORDER OF COUNCIL 2000, SI 2000 3291; made under the Chiropractors Act 1994 s.26, s.35, Sch.1 para.21. In force: December 11, 2000; £2.50.

This Order approves Rules made by the General Chiropractic Council which provide for the procedure to be followed by the Health Committee in considering allegations that a chiropractor's ability to practise is impaired because of his physical or mental condition and in dealing with existing conditions of practice and suspension orders.

2761. **Medical profession – chiropractors – General Chiropractic Council – Investigating Committee**

GENERAL CHIROPRATIC COUNCIL (INVESTIGATING COMMITTEE) RULES ORDER OF COUNCIL 2000, SI 2000 2916; made under the Chiroprators Act 1994 s.10, s.20, s.35, Sch.1 para.21. In force: November 10, 2000; £1.75.

This Order of Council approves Rules made by the General Chiropractic Council which provide for the procedure to be followed by the Investigating Committee in connection with an allegation that an entry on the register has been fraudulently procured or incorrectly made and in considering allegations made against a chiropractor as to his conduct or competence.

2762. **Medical profession – chiropractors – General Chiropractic Council – legal assessors**

GENERAL CHIROPRACTIC COUNCIL (FUNCTIONS OF LEGAL ASSESSORS) RULES ORDER 2000, SI 2000 2865; made under the Chiropractors Act 1994 s.26, s.27, s.29, Sch.1 para.21. In force: October 12, 2000; £1.75.

This Order approves rules made by the General Chiropractic Council which confer additional functions on the legal assessors appointed by the Council under the Chiropractors Act 1994 s.27 and contain provisions relating to the procedures by which the assessors give advice in proceedings attended by the parties.

2763. **Medical profession – chiropractors – General Chiropractic Council – medical assessors**

GENERAL CHIROPRACTIC COUNCIL (FUNCTIONS OF MEDICAL ASSESSORS) RULES ORDER 2000, SI 2000 2866; made under the Chiropractors Act 1994 s.26, s.28, s.29, Sch.1 para.21. In force: October 12, 2000; £1.75.

This Order approves Rules made by the General Chiropractic Council which confer additional functions on medical assessors appointed by the Council under the Chiropractors Act 1994 s.28 and contain provisions relating to the procedure by which the assessors give advice in proceedings attended by the parties.

2764. Medical profession – chiropractors – General Chiropractic Council – professional conduct

GENERAL CHIROPRACTIC COUNCIL (PROFESSIONAL CONDUCT COMMITTEE) RULES ORDER OF COUNCIL 2000, SI 2000 3290; made under the Chiropractors Act 1994 s.26, s.35, Sch.1 para.21. In force: December 11, 2000; £2.50.

This Order approves Rules made by the General Chiropractic Council which provide for the procedure to be followed by the Professional Conduct Committee in considering allegations as to a chiropractor's conduct or competence and in dealing with existing conditions of practice and suspension orders.

2765. Medical profession – doctors – choice of medical practitioner – Wales

NATIONAL HEALTH SERVICE (CHOICE OF MEDICAL PRACTITIONER) AMENDMENT (WALES) REGULATIONS 2000, SI 2000 1708 (W.115); made under the National Health Service Act 1977 s.28F, s.126. In force: July 1, 2000; £1.50.

These Regulations amend the National Health Service (Choice of Medical Practitioner) Regulations 1998 (SI 1998 668), relating to the right of persons to choose the doctor from whom they wish to receive primary medical services, by giving effect in Wales to the textual amendments of the 1998 Regulations made by the National Health Service (Choice of Medical Practitioner) Amendment Regulations 1999 (SI 1999 3179).

2766. Medical profession – doctors – foreign nationals – registration

MEDICAL ACT 1983 (PROVISIONAL REGISTRATION) REGULATIONS 2000, SI 2000 3041; made under the European Communities Act 1972 s.2. In force: December 4, 2000; £1.75.

These Regulations amend the Medical Act 1983 by inserting s.15A to extend provisional registration to EEA nationals who have obtained their medical degree in an EEA state other than the UK, but have yet to complete the period of clinical experience.

2767. Medical profession – doctors – pre-registration house officers – conditions of residence

MEDICAL ACT 1983 (APPROVED MEDICAL PRACTICES AND CONDITIONS OF RESIDENCE) AND NATIONAL HEALTH SERVICE (GENERAL MEDICAL SERVICES) (AMENDMENT) REGULATIONS 2000, SI 2000 3040; made under the National Health Service Act 1977 s.29, s.126; and the Medical Act 1983 s.11. In force: December 4, 2000; £1.75.

These Regulations amend the Medical Act 1983 (Approved Medical Practices and Conditions of Residence) and National Health Service (General Medical Services) (Amendment) Regulations 1998 (SI 1998 1664) to extend the definition of a pre-registration house officer to a person employed under the Medical Act 1983 s.15A, which was inserted by the Medical Act 1983 (Provisional Registration) Regulations 2000 (SI 2000 3041).

2768. Medical profession – nurses and health visitors – training

NURSES, MIDWIVES AND HEALTH VISITORS (TRAINING) AMENDMENT RULES APPROVAL ORDER 2000, SI 2000 2554; made under the Nurses, Midwives and Health Visitors Act 1997 s.19. In force: August 31, 2000; £2.00.

The Rules approved by this Order amend the Rules approved by the Nurses, Midwives and Health Visitors Rules Approval Order 1983 (SI 1983 873) to provide for the introduction of a new form, and a more flexible structure, of training to prepare student nurses for entry to Parts 12 to 15 of the register. The new provisions will apply to some courses which begin in September 2000 and will in due course replace the current training provisions. In addition, they amend the training provisions on health visitors to allow for more flexibility in the arranging of periods of attendance on a course and to add to the categories of nurse who may be admitted to training as a health visitor.

2769. **Medical profession – osteopaths – appeals**

JUDICIAL COMMITTEE (OSTEOPATHS RULES) ORDER 2000, SI 2000 251; made under the Osteopaths Act 1993 s.10, s.31. In force: March 8, 2000; £1.50.

This Order contains the Rules governing procedure for all appeals to Her Majesty in Council under the Osteopaths Act 1993.

2770. **Medical profession – osteopaths – conduct – General Osteopathic Council – Professional Conduct Committee**

GENERAL OSTEOPATHIC COUNCIL (PROFESSIONAL CONDUCT COMMITTEE) (PROCEDURE) RULES ORDER OF COUNCIL 2000, SI 2000 241; made under the Osteopaths Act 1993 s.26. In force: March 8, 2000; £3.00.

This Order of Council approves Rules made by the General Osteopathic Council prescribing the procedure to be followed by the Council's Professional Conduct Committee in cases where a question has been raised as to whether an osteopath registered under the Osteopaths Act 1993 may have been guilty either of conduct which falls short of the standard required of a registered osteopath or of professional incompetence, or may have been convicted in the UK of a criminal offence.

2771. **Medical profession – osteopaths – fitness to practise – General Osteopathic Council – Health Committee**

GENERAL OSTEOPATHIC COUNCIL (HEALTH COMMITTEE) (PROCEDURE) RULES ORDER OF COUNCIL 2000, SI 2000 242; made under the Osteopaths Act 1993 s.26, s.27, s.28, s.35, Sch.para.21. In force: March 8, 2000; £3.00.

This Order of Council approves Rules made by the General Osteopathic Council prescribing the procedure to be followed by the Health Committee of the Council in respect of cases where an osteopath's fitness to practise is called into question on grounds of a physical or mental condition.

2772. **Medical profession – osteopaths – General Osteopathic Council – appeals**

GENERAL OSTEOPATHIC COUNCIL (HEALTH COMMITTEE) (APPEALS) RULES ORDER OF COUNCIL 2000, SI 2000 243; made under the Osteopaths Act 1993 s.30, s.35. In force: March 8, 2000; £2.00.

This Order of Council approves rules made by the General Osteopathic Council specifying the procedure to be followed by tribunals set up to hear appeals from decisions of the Health Committee of the Council.

2773. **Medical profession – osteopaths – General Osteopathic Council – recognition of qualifications**

GENERAL OSTEOPATHIC COUNCIL (RECOGNITION OF QUALIFICATIONS) RULES ORDER OF COUNCIL 2000, SI 2000 1281; made under the Osteopaths Act 3; the Osteopaths Act 14; and the Osteopaths Act 1993 s.36. In force: May 9, 2000; £1.50.

This Order approves Rules made by the General Osteopathic Council requiring the Education Committee of the Council to publish a statement indicating matters which will be taken into account by the Committee when advising whether or not to recognise a qualification for the purposes of the Osteopaths Act 1993 and providing for a person with a qualification in osteopathy obtained outside the UK, not holding a recognised qualification, but who satisfies the Registrar of the Council that he has reached the required standard of proficiency, to be treated as having a recognised qualification.

2774. Medical profession – osteopaths – General Osteopathic Council – registration

GENERAL OSTEOPATHIC COUNCIL (APPLICATION FOR REGISTRATION AND FEES) RULES ORDER OF COUNCIL 2000, SI 2000 1038; made under the Osteopaths Act 1993 s.36. In force: May 9, 2000; £3.00.

This Order approves Rules made by the General Osteopathic Council prescribing the procedure for applying for registration as a registered osteopath after the end of the transitional period and specifying the various fees to be charged after the end of that period for making, retaining and restoring an entry in the register of osteopaths.

2775. Medical profession – osteopaths – General Osteopathic Council – registration

GENERAL OSTEOPATHIC COUNCIL (RESTORATION TO THE REGISTER OF CONDITIONALLY REGISTERED OSTEOPATHS) RULES ORDER OF COUNCIL 2000, SI 2000 1037; made under the Osteopaths Act 1993 s.36. In force: May 9, 2000; £1.50.

This Order approves Rules made by the General Osteopathic Council prescribing the procedure to be followed by the Professional Conduct Committee of the Council in respect of applications for restoration to the register by conditionally registered osteopaths who have had their entry in the register removed as a result of an order under the Osteopaths Act 1993 s.22(4)(d), and for restoration as a fully registered osteopath.

2776. Medical profession – supplementary professions – registration

PROFESSIONS SUPPLEMENTARY TO MEDICINE (REGISTRATION) (AMENDMENT) RULES ORDER OF COUNCIL 2000, SI 2000 3182; made under the Professions Supplementary to Medicine Act 1960 s.2. In force: December 1, 2000; £1.75.

The Rules approved by this Order of Council, which amend the Professions Supplementary to Medicine (Registration Rules) Order of Council 1962 (SI 1962 1765), increase, by amounts ranging from approximately 29 per cent to approximately 42 per cent, the registration, retention and restoration fees payable to the Boards established under the Professions Supplementary to Medicine Act 1960.

2777. Medical treatment – contractual liability – statutory duty – nature of relationship between doctor and patient

[National Health Service Act 1977; National Health Service (General Medical Services) Regulations 1992 (SI 1992 635).]

H, a general medical practice, applied to strike out amendments to particulars of claim filed on behalf of a patient, R. R alleged that she had been assured by doctors at H on two separate occasions that she was not pregnant and that the results of a urine pregnancy test had been negative. R maintained that as a result of these assurances she did not discover that she was in fact pregnant until it was too late for her to undergo a termination of a type acceptable to her. R instituted proceedings alleging medical negligence against the surgery but following the decision in *McFarlane v. Tayside Health Board* [1999] 3 W.L.R. 1301, [2000] C.L.Y. 6162 cited, sought to re-amend her claim to plead a breach of duty in contract. H applied to strike out the re-amendments, contending that (1) there was no contract subsisting between an NHS doctor and patient in view of the absence of consideration and the lack of intention to create legal relations; (2) such a view was supported by authoritative textbook authors, the Pearson Report 1978 from the Law Commission and by analogy with precedent in associated areas of law. R maintained that consideration could be established from the fact that the mere act of joining a doctor's NHS list increased a doctor's remuneration.

Held, granting the application and striking out the re-amendments, that the arrangement between doctor and patient was based upon statutory obligation rather than contract. Once the patient had elected to join the doctor's list there was no freedom to bargain as to the extent or nature of the care to be provided since the obligations of the doctor were extensively set out in the National Health Services Act 1977 and the National Health Service (General Medical Services) Regulations 1992. The fact that either party was entitled to terminate the relationship did not point towards the existence of a contract. Patients and doctors were free to enter into a contractual relationship but in doing so the patient would become a private patient, in which event the doctor's obligation would be to exercise reasonable skill and care. The argument that merely by joining the doctor's list, the patient was contributing consideration and had thereby suffered a detriment was fallacious, since the fact that the patient was only permitted to join a single list was merely an incidental aspect of the statutory scheme, *Pfizer Corp v. Ministry of Health* [1965] A.C. 512, [1965] C.L.Y. 2940 applied.

REYNOLDS v. HEALTH FIRST MEDICAL GROUP [2000] Lloyd's Rep. Med. 240, Simmons, J., CC (Hitchin).

2778. **Medical treatment – foreign nationals – trust's discretion to require deposit before treatment**

[National Health Service (Charges to Overseas Visitors) Regulations 1989 (SI 1989 306) Reg.2.]

R, a Nigerian national, who had travelled to the UK to undergo a kidney transplant to be funded by his father's employer, had been permitted to stay in the UK for six months as an overseas visitor pending the operation which was then postponed as a result of R's illness. R required ongoing non-emergency dialysis treatment, for which R's father's employer indicated it was not prepared to pay, although it was prepared to pay for the same treatment in Nigeria. H decided to discontinue the non-emergency dialysis unless payment or a guarantee of payment was made in advance. R appealed against the refusal of his application for judicial review (*The Times*, July 27, 2000) of H's decision. R contended that (1) he was no longer an overseas visitor for the purposes of the National Health Service (Charges to Overseas Visitors) Regulations 1989 Reg.2 by virtue of his stay in hospital, which had exceeded his original period of leave to enter, and therefore he was not required to pay for treatment; (2) H was not entitled to seek undertakings or payments in advance, and (3) in the alternative, if H was entitled to seek advance payment, it had a discretion as to whether it should do so and, in R's case, had failed to exercise that discretion.

Held, dismissing the appeal, that (1) R was an overseas visitor for the purposes of Reg.2 as the purpose of R's stay in the United Kingdom had not changed, *R. v. Barnet LBC, ex p. Shah (Nilish)* [1983] 2 A.C. 309, [1983] C.L.Y. 1157 considered; (2) H was therefore required to charge for the treatment and had an implied discretion under the Regulations to seek payment in advance or a guarantee of payment, and (3) the evidence showed that H had exercised its discretion and that it had done so rationally.

R. v. HAMMERSMITH HOSPITALS NHS TRUST, *ex p.* REFFELL C/2000/0025, Waller, L.J., CA.

2779. **Medical treatment – learning difficulties sterilisation – contraceptive alternative – patient's best interest predominent**

The mother of SL, a female aged 29 who had been born with severe learning difficulties, was concerned about the possibility of SL becoming pregnant when she moved into a local authority home and applied for a declaration that SL could be lawfully sterilised or given a partial hysterectomy despite her inability to consent. The judge held that both contraception or surgery were lawful options and had left the decision to SL's mother. The Official Solicitor appealed against the declaration, contending that the judge (1) had wrongly rejected unanimous medical opinion that the insertion of an intra uterine coil was a more appropriate procedure on the principal of primum non nocere, and (2) had misapplied the test in *Bolam v. Friern Hospital Management Committee* [1957] 1 W.L.R. 582, [1957] C.L.Y.

2431, employing it as a conclusive test rather than considering the patient's best interest.

Held, allowing the appeal, that (1) the judge had erred as the expert evidence had been unanimously in favour of intra uterine contraception as a less invasive procedure notwithstanding that it would require repeated intervention, and (2) once the *Bolam* test had been satisfied, it became irrelevant compared with the consideration of what was in the best interests of the patient. That was a judicial decision involving far broader considerations than the medical options and which could not be determined as a range of options. The correct decision was that the insertion of the intra uterine device was in the best interests of SL as it was the least invasive option, was not irreversible, and left room for surgical procedures if it were ineffective. Furthermore, it acknowledged the possibility that subsequent medical advances might provide alternative options.

S (ADULT PATIENT: STERILISATION: PATIENT'S BEST INTERESTS), *Re; sub nom.* SL (ADULT PATIENT) (STERILISATION), RE; SL v. SL; SL (ADULT PATIENT) (MEDICAL TREATMENT), *Re* [2001] Fam. 15, Dame Elizabeth Butler-Sloss (President), CA.

2780. Medical treatment – learning disabilities – sexually aware male with Down's syndrome – operation not in best interests at present time

A, aged 28, had Down's syndrome and was on the borderline of significant and severe impairment of intelligence. He was cared for by his mother, M, who supervised him. M was concerned that when, given her ill health, A moved into local authority care he might have a sexual relationship and be unable to understand the possible consequences. M applied as his next friend for a declaration that a vasectomy was in his best interests. The judge found that, whilst A was sexually aware and active, he did not understand the link between intercourse and pregnancy, but refused the declaration on the basis that the effect on A would be minimal. M appealed.

Held, dismissing the appeal, that male sterilisation on non therapeutic grounds could only be carried out if in the best interests of the patient, taking into account not just medical but emotional and all welfare issues. Neither the fact of the birth nor the disapproval of his conduct was likely to impinge on a mentally incapacitated man to a significant degree other than in exceptional circumstances. It was clear that whilst M cared for him, A would be subject to continued close supervision. The degree of supervision exercised over A when attending a day centre was not dependent on his fertility and inappropriate behaviour was curtailed by the supervisors as it was a public place and this would continue even if A had the operation, *F v. West Berkshire HA* [1990] 2 A.C. 1, [1989] C.L.Y. 3044 considered. A fresh application could be made if, on A's moving into local authority care, his freedom was restricted because of fears that he would have a sexual relationship with another resident. However, in such circumstances, it would be most likely that the female concerned would be subject to extra supervision, as opposed to A.

A (MENTAL PATIENT: STERILISATION), *Re; sub nom.* A (MEDICAL TREATMENT: MALE STERILISATION), RE; R-B (A PATIENT) v. OFFICIAL SOLICITOR; RB (MALE PATIENT: STERILISATION), *Re* [2000] 1 F.L.R. 549, Dame Butler Sloss, CA.

2781. Medical treatment – learning disabilities – sterilisation – Down's syndrome patient suffering from heavy and painful menstruation – total cessation by hysterectomy in patient's best interests

Z, aged 19, suffered from Down's syndrome. Her periods were heavy, irregular and painful, the regularity only being improved by taking oral contraception. She also experienced personal hygiene difficulties during menstruation, which were extremely unpleasant and embarrassing for her. Z was starting to live independently of her family, and a move to a residential unit was anticipated. Z had a boyfriend, and her mother, M, recognising that a sexual relationship was probable, sought a declaration that it was in Z's best interests to undergo a laparoscopic subtotal hysterectomy. The Official Solicitor opposed a major surgical procedure and argued for the fitting of an IUD as a means of reducing the bleeding and length of Z's periods. Four experts gave conflicting opinions as to the appropriate treatment.

Held, granting the declaration, that whilst the experts were to be listened to with respect, the decision was one for the court, and it was in Z's best interests to have a complete cessation of her periods and complete protection from pregnancy. Her periods brought her nothing but pain and discomfort, and furthermore, pregnancy, child birth and the removal of the child would be a catastrophe, as would the psychological and emotional consequences of an abortion.

ZM AND OS (STERILISATION: PATIENT'S BEST INTERESTS), *Re*; *sub nom*. Z (MEDICAL TREATMENT: HYSTERECTOMY), *Re* [2000] 1 F.L.R. 523, Bennett, J., Fam Div.

2782. **Medical treatment – termination – kidney patient also suffering from dementia – patient denied of treatment – New Zealand**

[Bill of Rights Act 1990 (New Zealand) s.8.]

W suffered from a potentially fatal kidney disease and required dialysis until a kidney transplant could be arranged. He also suffered from dementia and was unable to cooperate with the treatment. The health authority, acting within guidelines, refused a transplant and ceased dialysis. His representatives, whose application for judicial review of the health authority's decision had been unsuccessful, appealed arguing that W had been refused life saving treatment in breach of the requirement of good medical practice and of his constitutional right not to be deprived of life save as provided for within the principles of natural justice.

Held, dismissing the appeal, that the decision to discontinue dialysis and refuse a transplant had been reached after consultation with appropriately qualified experts and in accordance with guidelines developed by a recognised committee comprising well qualified legal and medical persons. Even though there had been some disagreement among the experts, the judgment of those with personal knowledge of W's case could not be faulted. Consultation with an ethical body was not necessary since no ethical questions were raised, nor was the consent of W's family required since long term dialysis was clinically inappropriate. W had not been deprived of life nor had there been a refusal to provide him with the necessaries of life so that there was no need to determine whether there had been a breach of the Bill of Rights Act 1990 (New Zealand) s.8.

SHORTLAND v. NORTHLAND HEALTH LTD (1999) 50 B.M.L.R. 255, Richardson, P, CA (NZ).

2783. **Medical (Professional Performance) Act 1995 (c.51) – Commencement No.4 Order**

MEDICAL (PROFESSIONAL PERFORMANCE) ACT 1995 (COMMENCEMENT NO.4) ORDER 2000, SI 2000 1344 (C.40); made under the Medical (Professional Performance) Act 1995 s.6. Commencement details: bringing into force various provisions of the Act on May 18, 2000; £1.50.

This Order brings into force the remaining provisions of the Medical (Professional Performance) Act 1995, which amends the Medical Act 1983, the National Health Service Act 1977, the National Health Service (Scotland) Act 1978 and the Health and Personal Social Services (Northern Ireland) Order 1972 (SI 1972 1265).

2784. **Medicines – fees**

MEDICINES FOR HUMAN USE AND MEDICAL DEVICES (FEES AND MISCELLANEOUS AMENDMENTS) REGULATIONS 2000, SI 2000 592; made under the Medicines Act 1971 s.1; the European Communities Act 1972 s.2; and the Finance Act 1973 s.56. In force: April 1, 2000; £2.00.

These Regulations amend the Medicines (Homoeopathic Medicinal Products for Human Use) Regulations 1994 (SI 1994 105) by increasing the amounts of the capital fees payable for applications for certificates of registration and for variations of certificates of registration and the amount of the periodic fee payable by holders of certificates of registration by an overall average of 14 per cent; the Medical Devices (Consultation Requirements) (Fees) Regulations 1995 (SI 1995 449) by increasing the amounts of all the fees specified in those Regulations by an overall average of 14 per cent; and the Medicines (Products for Human Use - Fees) Regulations 1995 (SI 1995 1116) by limiting the occasions when a higher rate periodic fee is payable in connection with the holding of a marketing authorisation in respect of a new active substance, a limited use drug or a derivative of such a substance or drug.

2785. Medicines – fees – marketing authorisations

MEDICINES (PRODUCTS FOR HUMAN USE -FEES) AMENDMENT REGULATIONS 2000, SI 2000 3031; made under the European Communities Act 1972 s.2. In force: December 1, 2000; £2.00.

These Regulations amend the Medicines (Products for Human Use -Fees) Regulations 1995 (SI 1995 1116), which provide for the fees payable relating to marketing authorisations, licences and certificates in respect of medicines for human use. They provide for new definitions and make provision relating to the setting of new capital fees for assistance in obtaining marketing authorisations in other countries that are contracting parties to the Agreement on the European Economic Area. In addition, they provide for the time at which capital fees are to be paid, set out the different amounts for the new fees and allow for small companies to delay payment of part of the fee in prescribed circumstances.

2786. Medicines – general sale list

MEDICINES (PRODUCTS OTHER THAN VETERINARY DRUGS) (GENERAL SALE LIST) AMENDMENT ORDER 2000, SI 2000 1092; made under the Medicines Act 1968 s.51, s.129. In force: May 10, 2000; £1.50.

This Order amends the Medicines (Products Other Than Veterinary Drugs) (General Sale List) Order 1984 (SI 1984 769), which specifies classes of medicinal products which can with reasonable safety be sold or supplied otherwise than by or under the supervision of a pharmacist, by inserting an entry for mepyramine maleate for products of maximum strength 2.0 per cent for the symptomatic relief of insect stings and bites and nettle stings in adults and in children aged two and over.

2787. Medicines – general sale list

MEDICINES (PRODUCTS OTHER THAN VETERINARY DRUGS) (GENERAL SALE LIST) AMENDMENT (NO.2) ORDER 2000, SI 2000 2526; made under the Medicines Act 1968 s.51, s.129. In force: October 4, 2000; £1.50.

This Order amends the Medicines (Products Other Than Veterinary Drugs) (General Sale List) Order 1984 (SI 1984 769), which specifies classes of medicinal products which can with reasonable safety be sold or supplied otherwise than by or under the supervision of a pharmacist, by inserting an entry for famotidine for tablets of maximum strength 10 mg, for use for the short-term symptomatic relief of heartburn, indigestion, acid indigestion and hyperacidity, with a maximum dose of 10 mg and a maximum daily dose of 20 mg, and entries for alpha-pinene and heparinoid for products of maximum strength 1.0 per cent for the relief of bruises, sprains and soft tissue injuries in adults and in children aged 6 years and over.

2788. Medicines – general sale list

MEDICINES (SALE OR SUPPLY) (MISCELLANEOUS PROVISIONS) AMENDMENT REGULATIONS 2000, SI 2000 1070; made under the Medicines Act 1968 s.53, s.129. In force: May 10, 2000; £1.50.

These Regulations amend the Medicines (Sale or Supply) (Miscellaneous Provisions) Regulations 1980 (SI 1980 1923) to provide that medicinal products containing mepyramine maleate and which are on the general sale list may be sold or supplied from outlets other than registered pharmacies only in separate and individual containers or packages containing not more than 20 grams of the product.

2789. Medicines – general sale list

MEDICINES (SALE OR SUPPLY) (MISCELLANEOUS PROVISIONS) AMENDMENT (NO.3) REGULATIONS 2000, SI 2000 2494; made under the Medicines Act 1968 s.53, s.129. In force: October 4, 2000; £1.50.

These Regulations amend the Medicines (Sale or Supply) (Miscellaneous Provisions) Regulations 1980 (SI 1980 1923) by providing that medicinal products containing bisacodyl and which are on a general sale list may have the maximum pack size increased; that medicinal products containing famotidine and which are on a general sale list may be sold or supplied from outlets other than registered pharmacies but only in separate and individual containers or packages containing not more than 12 tablets; and medicinal products containing heparinoid and which are on a general sale list may be sold or supplied from outlets other than registered pharmacies in separate and individual containers or packages containing not more than 20 grams of the product.

2790. Medicines – general sale list – exemptions

MEDICINES (PHARMACY AND GENERAL SALE-EXEMPTION) AMENDMENT ORDER 2000, SI 2000 1919; made under the Medicines Act 1968 s.57, s.129. In force: August 9, 2000; £2.00.

This Order amends the Medicines (Pharmacy and General Sale -Exemption) Order 1980 (SI 1980 1924) and provides for exemptions from the Medicines Act 1968 s.52 and s.53 for the supply of a medicinal product for human use by a specified national health body, where the product is supplied for the purpose of being administered in accordance with the patient specific directions of a doctor or dentist, or is supplied by a designated health professional belonging to a specified class for the purpose of being administered in accordance with a Patient Group Direction, and for the supply by a designated health professional, who assists a doctor or a dentist in providing NHS services, where the product is supplied for the purpose of being administered in accordance with a Patient Group Direction and certain conditions are fulfilled.

2791. Medicines – general sale list – wholesale dealings

MEDICINES (SALE OR SUPPLY) (MISCELLANEOUS PROVISIONS) AMENDMENT (NO.2) REGULATIONS 2000, SI 2000 1918; made under the Medicines Act 1968 s.61, s.129. In force: August 9, 2000; £1.50.

These Regulations amend the Medicines (Sale or Supply) (Miscellaneous Provisions) Regulations 1980 (SI 1980 1923) Sch.1 by inserting a reference to additional classes of person to whom prescription only medicines and pharmacy medicines may be sold by way of wholesale dealing.

2792. Medicines – marketing authorisations

MEDICINES FOR HUMAN USE (MARKETING AUTHORISATIONS ETC.) AMENDMENT REGULATIONS 2000, SI 2000 292; made under the European

Communities Act 1972 s.2. In force: Reg.4(2): March 1, 2001; remainder: March 1, 2000; £2.00.

These Regulations amend the Medicines for Human Use (Marketing Authorisations Etc.) Regulations 1994 (SI 1994 3144) by changing the definition of "the relevant Community provisions", to take account of amendments made by Commission Directive 1999/82 ([1999] OJ L243/7) and Commission Directive 1999/83 ([1999] OJ L243/9). They contain a new statutory procedure for determinations by the licensing authority as to whether or not a product is a "relevant medicinal product". They make a minor amendment to the special warnings which must be included on the packaging of medicinal products containing paracetamol on the general sale list.

2793. Medicines – prescription only

PRESCRIPTION ONLY MEDICINES (HUMAN USE) AMENDMENT (NO.2) ORDER 2000, SI 2000 2899; made under the Medicines Act 1968 s.58, s.129. In force: November 16, 2000; £1.75.

This Order, which amends the Prescription Only Medicines (Human Use) Order 1997 (SI 1997 1830), provides for certain new exemptions from the restrictions in the Medicines Act 1968 s.58(2).

2794. Medicines – prescription only – classes

PRESCRIPTION ONLY MEDICINES (HUMAN USE) AMENDMENT ORDER 2000, SI 2000 1917; made under the Medicines Act 1968 s.58, s.129. In force: August 9, 2000; £2.50.

This Order amends the Prescription Only Medicines (Human Use) Order 1997 (SI 1997 1830) by providing for certain new exemptions from the restrictions in the Medicines Act 1968 s.58(2), including an exemption for the supply or administration of a prescription only medicine by a specified national health service body in accordance with the patient specific directions of a doctor or dentist, or a Patient Group Direction. In addition, it provides for similar exemptions in relation to a designated health professional who assists a doctor or dentist in providing NHS services and a person lawfully conducting a rental pharmacy business under an arrangement with a national health service body.

2795. Medicines – prescription only – exemption

PRESCRIPTION ONLY MEDICINES (HUMAN USE) AMENDMENT (NO.3) ORDER 2000, SI 2000 3231; made under the Medicines Act 1968 s.58, s.129. In force: January 1, 2001; £1.50.

This Order, which amends the Prescription Only Medicines (Human Use) Order 1997 (SI 1997 1830) Sch.1, provides that medicinal products consisting of or containing Levonorgestrel may be sold or supplied otherwise than as a prescription only medicine provided that they are at a maximum strength of 0.75 mg and are sold or supplied exclusively for use as an emergency contraceptive in women aged 16 years and over.

2796. Medicines – products – Commission Directive

Commission Directive 2000/38 of June 5, 2000 amending Chapter Va (Pharmacovigilance) of Council Directive 75/319 on the approximation of provisions laid down by law, regulation or administrative action relating to medicinal products. [2000] OJ L139/28.

2797. Medicines – prohibitions – Aristolochia – Mu Tong – Fangji

MEDICINES (ARISTOLOCHIA AND MU TONG ETC.) (TEMPORARY PROHIBITION) ORDER 2000, SI 2000 1368; made under the Medicines Act 1968 s.62, s.129. In force: June 16, 2000; £1.50.

This Order, which revokes the Medicines (Aristolochia) (Temporary Prohibition) Order 1999 (SI 1999 2889), prohibits the sale, supply and importation of any medicinal product for human use which consists of or contains a plant belonging to a species of the genus Aristolochia, or extracts from such a plant, or is presented as consisting of or containing Mu Tong or Fangji or extracts from such a plant. The prohibitions are subject to three exceptions, firstly, where the sale and supply is to, or the importation is made by or on behalf of, a person exercising functions in relation to the enforcement of food or medicines legislation, secondly in the case of the prohibition on importation, where the products are imported from a Member State and finally, where the products are the subject of a product licence, marketing authorisation or homeopathic certificate of registration.

2798. National Health Service – clinical negligence – indemnity scheme

NATIONAL HEALTH SERVICE (CLINICAL NEGLIGENCE SCHEME) AMENDMENT REGULATIONS 2000, SI 2000 2341; made under the National Health Service Act 1977 s.126; and the National Health Service and Community Care Act 1990 s.21. In force: September 27, 2000; £1.50.

These Regulations amend the National Health Service (Clinical Negligence Scheme) Regulations 1996 (SI 1996 251), which established a Scheme whereby NHS trusts and certain other bodies providing NHS services may make provision for meeting liabilities to third parties in connection with personal injury arising out of negligence in the carrying out of their functions in England. They provide for primary care trusts to be eligible to participate in the Scheme; amend the requirements as to the timing for applications for membership and admission; and make consequential amendments regarding the timing of notices sent to members with respect to contributions and payments.

2799. National Health Service – clinical negligence scheme – liabilities to third parties

NATIONAL HEALTH SERVICE (LIABILITIES TO THIRD PARTIES SCHEME) AMENDMENT REGULATIONS 2000, SI 2000 2385; made under the National Health Service Act 1977 s.126; and the National Health Service and Community Care Act 1990 s.21. In force: September 27, 2000; £1.50.

These Regulations amend the National Health Service (Liabilities to Third Parties Scheme) Regulations 1999 (SI 1999 873) which established a Scheme whereby NHS trusts and certain other bodies providing NHS services may make provision for meeting liabilities to third parties in connection with loss, damage or injury arising out of the carrying out of the bodies' functions in England other than liabilities to which the National Health Service (Clinical Negligence Scheme) Regulations 1996 (SI 1996 251) and the National Health Service (Existing Liabilities Scheme) Regulations 1996 (SI 1996 686) apply, or expenses to which the National Health Service (Property Expenses Scheme) Regulations 1999 (SI 1999 874) apply. In particular, they provide for primary care trusts to be eligible to participate in the Scheme, amend the timing for applications for membership and admission to the Scheme, and make consequential amendments to the timing of notices sent to members in relation to contributions and payments under the Scheme.

2800. National Health Service – Commission for Health Improvement – functions

COMMISSION FOR HEALTH IMPROVEMENT (FUNCTIONS) AMENDMENT REGULATIONS 2000, SI 2000 797; made under the National Health Service Act 1977 s.126; and the Health Act 1999 s.20, s.23. In force: April 1, 2000; £1.00.

These Regulations amend the Commission for Health Improvement (Functions) Regulations 2000 (SI 2000 662) to correct errors in the cross references to other provisions of those regulations in Reg.20(5) and Reg.22.

2801. National Health Service – Commission for Health Improvement – functions

COMMISSION FOR HEALTH IMPROVEMENT (FUNCTIONS) REGULATIONS 2000, SI 2000 662; made under the National Health Service Act 1977 s.17, s.126; and the Health Act 1999 s.20, s.23. In force: April 1, 2000; £3.00.

These Regulations make provision in relation to the functions of the Commission for Health Improvement established under the Health Act 1999 s.19. They set out the functions of the Commission to be exercised in addition to those specified in the 1999 Act and make provision in relation to the exercise of the Commission's functions in England.

2802. National Health Service – Commission for Health Improvement – functions – Wales

COMMISSION FOR HEALTH IMPROVEMENT (FUNCTIONS) (WALES) REGULATIONS 2000, SI 2000 1015 (W.57); made under the National Health Service Act 1977 s.17, s.126; and the Health Act 1999 s.20, s.23. In force: April 1, 2000; £3.50.

These Regulations make provision in relation to the exercise in Wales of the functions of the Commission for Health Improvement established under the Health Act 1999 s.19. In particular, they provide for the preparation of the Commission's annual work programme; the provision by the Commission of advice of information with respect to clinical governance arrangements to the National Assembly for Wales and health service bodies; the conduct of local reviews of such arrangements and follow up reports and action relating to those reviews; reports following national service reviews of particular types of health care; and the conduct of investigations into the management, provision or quality of health care for which National Health Service bodies have responsibility.

2803. National Health Service – damage to property – reimbursement scheme – eligibility

NATIONAL HEALTH SERVICE (PROPERTY EXPENSES SCHEME) AMENDMENT REGULATIONS 2000, SI 2000 2342; made under the National Health Service Act 1977 s.126; and the National Health Service and Community Care Act 1990 s.21. In force: September 27, 2000; £1.50.

These Regulations amend the National Health Service (Property Expenses Scheme) Regulations 1999 (SI 1999 874) which established a Scheme whereby NHS trusts and certain other bodies providing NHS services may make provision for claiming reimbursement for certain expenses arising from any loss of or damage to their property. They provide for primary care trusts to be eligible to participate in the Scheme; amend the requirements as to the timing for applications for membership and admission; and make consequential amendments regarding the timing of notices sent to members with respect to contributions and payments.

2804. National Health Service – dental services

NATIONAL HEALTH SERVICE (GENERAL DENTAL SERVICES) AMENDMENT REGULATIONS 2000, SI 2000 2459; made under the National Health Service Act 1977 s.15, s.35, s.36, s.37, s.126. In force: Reg.5: November 13, 2000 (in part); remainder: October 3, 2000; £1.50.

These Regulations amend the National Health Service (General Dental Services) Regulations 1992 (SI 1992 661) which regulate the terms on which general dental services are provided under the National Health Service Act 1977. They provide that dentists' remuneration under Determination V of the Statement of Dental Remuneration is to be paid by the Dental Practice Board rather than health authorities; amend the circumstances in which records must be produced for inspection; and insert a new requirement for a dentist to ask to see evidence in support of a patient's claim that he is entitled to exemption from, or remission of, dental charges and to record his claim for remuneration when he does not see such evidence. In addition, they require the dentist to complete a form and obtain a signature from the patient when he makes a claim for remuneration following his recall to his practice for an emergency outside usual practice hours and insert a requirement for separate claim forms to be completed for treatment given by assistants.

2805. National Health Service – dental services – Wales

NATIONAL HEALTH SERVICE (GENERAL DENTAL SERVICES) AMENDMENT (WALES) REGULATIONS 2000, SI 2000 3118 (W.197); made under the National Health Service Act 1977 s.15, s.35, s.36, s.126. In force: Reg.4: January 1, 2001; remainder: December 1, 2000; £2.00.

These Regulations, which amend the National Health Service (General Dental Services) Regulations 1992 (SI 1992 661), provide for a dentist's obligations in respect of forms and records, the circumstances in which records must be produced for inspection, a new requirement for a dentist to ask to see evidence in support of a claim that a patient is entitled to exemption from, or remission of, dental charges and to record on the dentist's claim for remuneration for the treatment provided to such a patient when such evidence has not been seen, and a new requirement so that a dentist is required to complete a form when he or she makes a claim for remuneration following being recalled to the dental practice in order to provide a patient with treatment for an emergency outside the usual practice hours. The dentist is also obliged to obtain on the said form the signature of the patient, or a person responsible for the patient, that he or she has been recalled to treat.

2806. National Health Service – dental treatment – maximum charge

NATIONAL HEALTH SERVICE (DENTAL CHARGES) AMENDMENT REGULATIONS 2000, SI 2000 596; made under the National Health Service Act 1977 s.79A, Sch.12 para.3. In force: April 1, 2000; £1.00.

These Regulations, which amend the National Health Service (Dental Charges) Regulations 1989 (SI 1989 394), increase from £348 to £354 the maximum charge payable by the patient for dental treatment and appliances where the contract or arrangement leading to the provision of such treatment or appliances is made on or after April 1, 2000.

2807. National Health Service – dental treatment – maximum charge – Wales

NATIONAL HEALTH SERVICE (DENTAL CHARGES) AMENDMENT (WALES) REGULATIONS 2000, SI 2000 977 (W.47); made under the National Health Service Act 1977 s.79A, Sch.12 para.3. In force: April 1, 2000; £1.50.

These Regulations amend the National Health Service (Dental Charges) Regulations 1989 (SI 1989 394) to increase from £348 to £354 the maximum charge payable by the patient for dental treatment or appliances, where the contract or arrangement leading to the provision of such treatment or appliances is made on or after April 1, 2000. In addition, the National Health Service (Dental Charges) Amendment Regulations 1999 (SI 1999 544) are revoked.

2808. National Health Service – doctors – removal from medical lists on conviction of criminal offences – Wales

NATIONAL HEALTH SERVICE (GENERAL MEDICAL SERVICES) AMENDMENT (WALES) REGULATIONS 2000, SI 2000 1707 (W.114); made under the National

Health Service Act 1977 s.29; the National Health Service Act 1977 Act 29B; and the National Health Service Act 1977 Act s.126. In force: July 1, 2000; £2.00.

These Regulations amend the National Health Service (General Medical Services) Regulations 1992 (SI 1992 635) which regulate the terms on which doctors provide general medical services under the National Health Service Act 1977. In particular, they require a health authority to remove the name of any doctor convicted of murder or convicted of a criminal offence and sentenced to at least six months' imprisonment from its medical list; impose a requirement on a doctor applying to a health authority for nomination or approval for a practice vacancy to make a declaration as to whether he has been convicted of any criminal offence, been bound over or cautioned, or is the subject at present of criminal proceedings, and whether he is or has been the subject of any disciplinary proceedings by his professional body or regulatory body, whether in the UK or elsewhere; provide that a health authority shall not approve a doctor if they consider him unsuitable having considered the declaration; and that the details of the declaration must be included in the information provided by a health authority when making a reference to the Medical Practices Committee.

2809. National Health Service – drugs and appliances – fees

NATIONAL HEALTH SERVICE (CHARGES FOR DRUGS AND APPLIANCES) AMENDMENT REGULATIONS 2000, SI 2000 2393; made under the National Health Service Act 1977 s.77, s.83, s.126. In force: October 1, 2000; £1.00.

These Regulations, which amend the National Health Service (Charges for Drugs and Appliances) Regulations 2000 (SI 2000 620), change the requirements placed on doctors in relation to charges recovered for drugs and appliances supplied under the National Health Service Act 1977. They make provision for doctors to retain any charges they are required to make under the Regulations for the provision of pharmaceutical services and for any such charges to be set off against any sums payable to them by a Health Authority in respect of the provision of general medical services or personal medical services.

2810. National Health Service – drugs and appliances – fees – recovery of charges

NATIONAL HEALTH SERVICE (CHARGES FOR DRUGS AND APPLIANCES) AMENDMENT REGULATIONS 2000, SI 2000 122; made under the National Health Service Act 1977 s.77, s.126. In force: February 14, 2000; £1.50.

These Regulations further amend the National Health Service (Charges for Drugs and Appliances) Regulations 1989 (SI 1989 419) which provide for the making and recovery of charges for drugs and appliances supplied by doctors, and chemists providing pharmaceutical services, and by Health Authorities and NHS trusts to out-patients to make provision in relation to the recovery of charges for drugs and appliances supplied to patients attending Walk-in-Centres.

2811. National Health Service – drugs and appliances – fees – recovery of charges

NATIONAL HEALTH SERVICE (CHARGES FOR DRUGS AND APPLIANCES) AMENDMENT (NO.2) REGULATIONS 2000, SI 2000 3189; made under the National Health Service Act 1977 s.77, s.83, s.126. In force: December 11, 2000; £1.75.

These Regulations amend the National Health Service (Charges for Drugs and Appliances) Regulations 2000 (SI 2000 620) by providing for the making and recovery of charges for drugs and appliances supplied under the National Health Act 1977 when they are supplied in accordance with Patient Group Directions.

2812. **National Health Service – drugs and appliances – fees – recovery of charges**

NATIONAL HEALTH SERVICE (CHARGES FOR DRUGS AND APPLIANCES) REGULATIONS 2000, SI 2000 620; made under the National Health Service Act 1977 s.77, s.83, s.83A, s.126, Sch.12 para.1. In force: April 1, 2000; £3.00.

These Regulations, which revoke and replace the National Health Service (Charges for Drugs and Appliances) Regulations 1989 (SI 1989 419), provide for the making and recovery of charges for drugs and appliances supplied by doctors and chemists providing pharmaceutical services, by health authorities, NHS trusts and primary care trusts and at walk-in centres. They increase the charges by approximately 2 per cent and include provision in relation to primary care trusts.

2813. **National Health Service – drugs and appliances – fees – Wales**

NATIONAL HEALTH SERVICE (CHARGES FOR DRUGS AND APPLIANCES) AMENDMENT (WALES) REGULATIONS 2000, SI 2000 1422 (W.102); made under the National Health Service Act 1977 s.77, s.126. In force: April 1, 2000; £2.00.

These Regulations amend the National Health Service (Charges for Drugs and Appliances) Regulations 1989 (SI 1989 419) which provide for the making and recovery of charges for drugs and appliances supplied by doctors and chemists providing pharmaceutical services, and by Health Authorities and National Health Service Trusts to outpatients. They increase certain charges for prescriptions, elastic stockings and tights, and hair wigs.

2814. **National Health Service – drugs and appliances – reimbursement**

NATIONAL HEALTH SERVICE TRUSTS AND PRIMARY CARE TRUSTS (PHARMACEUTICAL SERVICES REMUNERATION -SPECIAL ARRANGEMENT) ORDER 2000, SI 2000 595; made under the National Health Service Act 1977 s.103, s.126. In force: April 1, 2000; £1.00.

This Order obliges NHS trusts and primary care trusts to reimburse health authorities for the cost of drugs, medicines or listed appliances which have been ordered by a doctor or a dentist in pursuance of the functions of an NHS trust or a primary care trust for dispensing in the community.

2815. **National Health Service – fund holding practices – transfer of assets – Wales**

HEALTH ACT 1999 (FUND-HOLDING PRACTICES) (TRANSFER OF ASSETS, SAVINGS, RIGHTS AND LIABILITIES AND TRANSITIONAL PROVISIONS) (WALES) ORDER 2000, SI 2000 999 (W.56); made under the Health Act 1999 s.63. In force: April 1, 2000; £3.50.

This Order makes transitional provisions in connection with the abolition, by the Health Act 1999 s.1, of the system of general practitioner fund holding in Wales. In particular, it provides for the transfer of assets, rights and liabilities connected with the fund holding to the relevant health authority of the former fund holding practice and for the use by the health authority of those assets in meeting liabilities transferred to it and those retained by the former members of the fund holding practice.

2816. **National Health Service – general medical services – allowances for training doctors**

NATIONAL HEALTH SERVICE (GENERAL MEDICAL SERVICES) AMENDMENT (NO.2) REGULATIONS 2000, SI 2000 601; made under the National Health Service Act 1977 s.29, s.126. In force: April 1, 2000; £1.00.

These Regulations amend the National Health Service (General Medical Services) Regulations 1992 (SI 1992 635) Reg.34(2) by removing the reference to allowances for training doctors from the matters for which provision shall be made in a determination under that regulation. Health authorities are now to make payments in respect of allowances for training doctors in accordance with the directions to health authorities concerning GP Registrars.

2817. National Health Service – general medical services – allowances for training doctors – Wales

NATIONAL HEALTH SERVICE (GENERAL MEDICAL SERVICES) AMENDMENT (NO.2) (WALES) REGULATIONS 2000, SI 2000 1992 (W.144); made under the National Health Service Act 1977 Act s.29, s.126. In force: August 1, 2000; £1.50.

These Regulations amend the National Health Service (General Medical Services) Regulations 1992 (SI 1992 635), which regulate the terms on which general medical services are provided under the National Health Service Act 1977. In particular, they provide for a health authority to make payments, in accordance with the rates and conditions determined by the National Assembly, to doctors who provide general medical services in its area in respect of allowances for training doctors in accordance with the directions to health authorities concerning GP Registrars.

2818. National Health Service – general medical services – doctors – maintenance of medical records

NATIONAL HEALTH SERVICE (GENERAL MEDICAL SERVICES) AMENDMENT (NO.4) REGULATIONS 2000, SI 2000 2383; made under the National Health Service Act 1977 s.29, s.126. In force: October 1, 2000; £1.50.

These Regulations amend the National Health Service (General Medical Services) Regulations 1992 (SI 1992 635) Sch.2 to enable doctors to keep medical records relating to their patients either on paper or on computer or both. Where a doctor wishes to keep records either wholly or partly on computer, he must first obtain the health authority's consent, and where a doctor is required to send copies of his records to the health authority, he may only provide them other in written form where the health authority has consented.

2819. National Health Service – general medical services – doctors – prescription of drugs

NATIONAL HEALTH SERVICE (GENERAL MEDICAL SERVICES) AMENDMENT (NO.3) REGULATIONS 2000, SI 2000 1645; made under the National Health Service Act 1977 s.29, s.126. In force: August 1, 2000; £1.00.

These Regulations amend the National Health Service (General Medical Services) Regulations 1992 (SI 1992 635), which regulate the terms on which doctors provide general medical services under the National Health Service Act 1977, by adding the drug Propecia (finasteride 1 mg) to the list in Sch.10 to the 1992 Regulations, which lists drugs and other substances which may not be prescribed for supply in the course of pharmaceutical services under the 1977 Act.

2820. National Health Service – general medical services – doctors – removal from medical lists on conviction of criminal offences

NATIONAL HEALTH SERVICE (GENERAL MEDICAL SERVICES) AMENDMENT REGULATIONS 2000, SI 2000 220; made under the National Health Service Act 1977 s.29, s.29B, s.126. In force: February 4, 2000; £1.50.

These Regulations amend the National Health Service (General Medical Services) Regulations 1992 (SI 1992 635) by requiring a health authority to remove the name of any doctor convicted of murder or convicted of a criminal offence and sentenced to at least six months' imprisonment from its medical list. They impose a requirement on a doctor applying for nomination or approval for a practice vacancy to declare whether he has been convicted of any criminal offence, been bound over or cautioned, or is the subject at present of criminal proceedings, and whether he is or has been the subject of any disciplinary proceedings by his professional or regulatory body.

2821. National Health Service – general medical services – prescription of drugs – Wales

NATIONAL HEALTH SERVICE (GENERAL MEDICAL SERVICES) AMENDMENT (NO.3) (WALES) REGULATIONS 2000, SI 2000 1887 (W.133); made under the National Health Service Act 1977 s.29, s.126. In force: August 1, 2000; £1.50.

These Regulations amend the National Health Service (General Medical Services) Regulations 1992 (SI 1992 635), which regulate the terms on which General Medical Services are provided under the National Health Service Act 1977, by adding the drug Finasteride 1 mg (Propecia) to the list in Sch.10 to the 1992 Regulations, which lists drugs and other substances which may not be prescribed for supply in the course of pharmaceutical services under the 1977 Act.

2822. National Health Service – injury benefits – primary care trusts

NATIONAL HEALTH SERVICE (INJURY BENEFITS) AMENDMENT REGULATIONS 2000, SI 2000 606; made under the Superannuation Act 1972 s.10, Sch.3. In force: April 1, 2000; £1.50.

These Regulations amend the National Health Service (Injury Benefits) Regulations 1995 (SI 1995 866), which provide for the payment of injury benefits to or in respect of any person engaged in the National Health Service whose earning ability is reduced, or who dies, as a result of an injury suffered in the course of his or her duties, by including provision for persons employed by primary care trusts and by changing the definitions of "dental pilot scheme employee" and "medical pilot scheme employee" to make clear that individuals who are employed by corporate bodies are included within those expressions.

2823. National Health Service – medical treatment – foreign nationals

NATIONAL HEALTH SERVICE (CHARGES TO OVERSEAS VISITORS) AMENDMENT (NO.2) REGULATIONS 2000, SI 2000 909; made under the National Health Service Act 1977 s.121, s.126. In force: March 31, 2000; £1.00.

This Order corrects an omission from the National Health Service (Charges to Overseas Visitors) Amendment Regulations 2000 (SI 2000 602) to provide a coming into force date for those Regulations.

2824. National Health Service – medical treatment – foreign nationals – primary care trusts

NATIONAL HEALTH SERVICE (CHARGES TO OVERSEAS VISITORS) AMENDMENT REGULATIONS 2000, SI 2000 602; made under the National Health Service Act 1977 s.121, s.126. In force: April 1, 2000; £1.00.

These Regulations amend the National Health Service (Charges to Overseas Visitors) Regulations 1989 (SI 1989 306) to reflect the establishment of primary care trusts and to remove Hong Kong from Sch.2 which sets out countries or territories in respect of which the UK Government has entered into a reciprocal agreement.

2825. National Health Service – medicines – price control scheme – appeals against determinations

HEALTH SERVICE MEDICINES (PRICE CONTROL APPEALS) AMENDMENT REGULATIONS 2000, SI 2000 870; made under the Health Act 1999 s.37. In force: April 17, 2000; £1.00.

These Regulations correct errors in the Health Service Medicines (Price Control Appeals) Regulations 2000 (SI 2000 124) by substituting references to the "enforcement decision" for references to the "disputed action"; correcting a cross reference in Reg.27(4); and substituting Reg.30(4) to correct the layout and to provide a reference to the Civil Procedure Rules 1998 (SI 1998 3132).

2826. National Health Service – medicines – price control scheme – appeals against determinations

HEALTH SERVICE MEDICINES (PRICE CONTROL APPEALS) REGULATIONS 2000, SI 2000 124; made under the Health Act 1999 s.37. In force: February 14, 2000; £3.00.

These Regulations make provision in relation to appeals against determinations made under the National Health Service price control scheme set out in the Health Service Medicines (Control of Prices of Branded Medicines) Regulations 2000 (SI 2000 123). They provide for the manner in which, and the time within which, such an appeal may be made, and the procedure to be followed where such an appeal is made.

2827. National Health Service – medicines – price regulation

HEALTH SERVICE MEDICINES (CONTROL OF PRICES OF BRANDED MEDICINES) REGULATIONS 2000, SI 2000 123; made under the National Health Service Act 1977 s.126; and the Health Act 1999 s.34, s.36, s.37, s.38. In force: February 14, 2000; £2.00.

These Regulations control the price of branded medicines sold for National Health Service purposes. They apply only to medicines in respect of which marketing authorisations have been granted that are supplied by companies which are not scheme members within the meaning of the Health Act 1999 s.33(4). The maximum price for such medicines is based on the "initial price" as defined by the Department of Health.

2828. National Health Service – medicines – price regulation

HEALTH SERVICE MEDICINES (CONTROL OF PRICES OF SPECIFIED GENERIC MEDICINES) REGULATIONS 2000, SI 2000 1763; made under the National Health Service Act 1977 s.126; and the Health Act 1999 s.34, s.36, s.37, s.38. In force: August 3, 2000; £2.

These Regulations make provision to control the price of certain generic medicines which are sold for the purposes of the National Health Services in England and Wales, Scotland and Northern Ireland. They apply only to the medicines specified in the list of controlled prices which is published on the web site at the address http://www.doh.gov.uk/generics. Printed copies of the list are available from the Department of Health, Room 130, Richmond House, 79 Whitehall, London SW1A 2NS. In addition, they apply only to medicines in respect of which marketing authorisations have been granted.

2829. National Health Service – partnership arrangements – funding – Wales

NATIONAL HEALTH SERVICE BODIES AND LOCAL AUTHORITIES PARTNERSHIP ARRANGEMENTS (WALES) REGULATIONS 2000, SI 2000 2993 (W.193); made under the National Health Service Act 1977 s.126; and the Health Act 1999 s.31. In force: December 1, 2000; £2.50.

These Regulations make provision for certain National Health Service bodies and local authorities to enter into arrangements for the exercise of specified functions. They prescribe the conditions which must be satisfied before partnership arrangements may be entered into, the NHS functions and the health-related local authority functions which may be the subject of partnership arrangements and provide for the establishment of a fund made up of contributions from the partners out of which payments may be made towards expenditure incurred in the exercise of their functions, for the exercise by National Health Service bodies of local authority functions and for the exercise by local authorities of National Health Service functions; and require the partners to set out the terms of the arrangements in writing.

2830. **National Health Service – pharmaceutical services – prescriptions – nurses**

NATIONAL HEALTH SERVICE (PHARMACEUTICAL SERVICES) AMENDMENT REGULATIONS 2000, SI 2000 121; made under the National Health Service Act 1977 s.41, s.42, s.126. In force: February 14, 2000; £1.00.

These Regulations amend the National Health Service (Pharmaceutical Services) Regulations 1992 (SI 1992 662) to add suitably qualified nurses working in Walk-in Centres to the categories of nurse who may prescribe under the National Health Service in England.

2831. **National Health Service – pharmaceutical services – primary care trusts**

NATIONAL HEALTH SERVICE (PHARMACEUTICAL SERVICES) AMENDMENT (NO.2) REGULATIONS 2000, SI 2000 593; made under the National Health Service Act 1977 s.41, s.42. In force: April 1, 2000; £1.00.

These Regulations amend the National Health Service (Pharmaceutical Services) Regulations 1992 (SI 1992 662) to take account of the role which may be played by primary care trusts and local authorities in the provision of primary health care in consequence of changes made by the Health Act 1999. They take account of the fact that primary care trusts may issue prescription forms and that both primary care trusts and local authorities may employ nurses who are able to prescribe under the NHS.

2832. **National Health Service – primary care trusts – exercise of functions**

PRIMARY CARE TRUSTS (FUNCTIONS) (ENGLAND) REGULATIONS 2000, SI 2000 695; made under the National Health Service Act 1977 s.17, s.17A, s.18, s.126. In force: April 1, 2000; £3.00.

These Regulations make provision for functions of health authorities to be exercised by primary care trusts and place certain restrictions on the exercise of those functions by primary care trusts.

2833. **National Health Service – primary care trusts – psychiatric services**

HEALTH ACT 1999 (SUPPLEMENTARY, CONSEQUENTIAL ETC. PROVISIONS) ORDER 2000, SI 2000 90; made under the National Health Service Act 1977 s.126; and the Health Act 1999 s.63. In force: Art.3(2): April 1, 2000; remainder: February 8, 2000; £3.00.

This Order makes amendments to certain enactments consequential upon provisions of the Health Act 1999 concerning Primary Care Trusts and high security psychiatric services.

2834. **National Health Service – primary care trusts – psychiatric services**

HEALTH ACT 1999 (SUPPLEMENTARY, CONSEQUENTIAL ETC. PROVISIONS) (NO.2) ORDER 2000, SI 2000 694; made under the National Health Service Act 1977 s.126; and the Health Act 1999 s.63. In force: April 1, 2000; £1.50.

This Order makes amendments to certain enactments consequential upon provisions of the Health Act 1999 concerning primary care trusts and high security psychiatric services.

2835. **National Health Service – prohibited professions**

NATIONAL HEALTH SERVICE (PROFESSIONS SUPPLEMENTARY TO MEDICINE) AMENDMENT REGULATIONS 2000, SI 2000 523; made under the National Health Service Act 1977 Sch.5 para.10. In force: April 1, 2000; £1.00.

These Regulations amend the National Health Service (Professions Supplementary to Medicine) Regulations 1974 (SI 1974 494) by adding prosthetists, orthodontists and arts therapists to the list of professions whose employment by health authorities and special health authorities is prohibited for the purposes of providing services under the National Health Service.

2836. National Health Service – travelling expenses – remission of charges

NATIONAL HEALTH SERVICE (TRAVELLING EXPENSES AND REMISSION OF CHARGES) AMENDMENT REGULATIONS 2000, SI 2000 621; made under the National Health Service Act 1977 s.83A, s.126, s.128. In force: April 1, 2000; £1.50.

These Regulations amend the National Health Service (Travelling Expenses and Remission of Charges) Regulations 1988 (SI 1988 551) to provide for the payment of travelling expenses to asylum-seekers and their dependants; to provide for the payment of travelling expenses incurred in attending establishments managed by primary care trusts; and to make amendments with regard to payments to persons resident in the Isles of Scilly.

2837. National Health Service – travelling expenses – remission of charges

NATIONAL HEALTH SERVICE (TRAVELLING EXPENSES AND REMISSION OF CHARGES) AMENDMENT (NO.2) REGULATIONS 2000, SI 2000 837; made under the National Health Service Act 1977 s.83A, s.126, s.128. In force: March 31, 2000; £1.00.

These Regulations correct an omission from the National Health Service (Travelling Expenses and Remission of Charges) Amendment Regulations 2000 (SI 2000 621).

2838. National Health Service – travelling expenses – remission of dental charges

NATIONAL HEALTH SERVICE (TRAVELLING EXPENSES AND REMISSION OF CHARGES) AMENDMENT (NO.3) REGULATIONS 2000, SI 2000 2870; made under the National Health Service Act 1977 s.83A, s.126, s.128. In force: November 13, 2000; £1.75.

These Regulations amend the National Health Service (Travelling Expenses and Remission of Charges) Regulations 1988 (SI 1988 551) to provide for the remission of dental charges to be determined by reference to the claimant's circumstances either at the time the arrangements for treatment are made or at the time the charge for treatment is made; for remission to apply in respect of the course of treatment concerned; and, in relation to claims for repayment of relevant charges or travelling expenses, that the claimant's resources and requirements are to be calculated by reference to the date when the charges and expenses were paid in full.

2839. National Health Service Litigation Authority – membership

NATIONAL HEALTH SERVICE LITIGATION AUTHORITY (AMENDMENT) REGULATIONS 2000, SI 2000 2433; made under the National Health Service Act 1977 s.126, Sch.5 para.12. In force: October 1, 2000; £1.00.

These Regulations amend the National Health Service Litigation Authority Regulations 1995 (SI 1995 2801) to provide that a non executive director of an NHS trust may hold office as the chairman or a non officer member of the National Health Service Litigation Authority.

2840. NHS trusts – appointment of trustees

NATIONAL HEALTH SERVICE TRUST (TRUST FUNDS: APPOINTMENT OF TRUSTEES) ORDER 2000, SI 2000 212; made under the National Health Service and Community Care Act 1990 s.11. In force: February 4, 2000; £1.00.

This Order provides for the appointment of trustees for the Central Sheffield University Hospitals NHS Trust; the Community Health Sheffield NHS Trust; the Guy's and St Thomas' NHS Trust; the Hammersmith Hospitals NHS Trust; the King's Healthcare NHS Trust; the Leeds Teaching Hospitals NHS Trust; the Northern General Hospital NHS Trust; the Royal Free Hampstead NHS Trust; the Sheffield Children's Hospital NHS Trust; the United Bristol Healthcare NHS Trust and the University College London Hospitals NHS Trust.

2841. NHS trusts – appointment of trustees

NATIONAL HEALTH SERVICE TRUSTS (TRUST FUNDS: APPOINTMENT OF TRUSTEES) AMENDMENT ORDER 2000, SI 2000 3116; made under the National Health Service and Community Care Act 1990 s.11. In force: Art.2(b): April 1, 2001; remainder: November 29, 2000; £1.50.

This Order amends the National Health Service Trusts (Trust Funds: Appointment of Trustees) Order 2000 (SI 2000 212) by adding six NHS trusts to the list of trusts for which the Secretary of State is to appoint trustees and by removing the name of two NHS trusts which are being dissolved. Under the National Health Service and Community Care Act 1990 s.11 (1) such trustees have power to accept, hold and administer trust property for the purposes of the NHS trust for which they are appointed or for any other purpose relating to the NHS.

2842. NHS trusts – change of name – King's Healthcare

KING'S HEALTHCARE NATIONAL HEALTH SERVICE TRUST (CHANGE OF NAME) ORDER 2000, SI 2000 2389; made under the National Health Service Act 1977 s.126; and the National Health Service and Community Care Act 1990 s.5. In force: September 15, 2000; £1.00.

This Order, which amends the King's Healthcare National Health Service Trust (Establishment) Order 1991 (SI 1991 2362), changes the name of the King's Healthcare National Health Service Trust to the King's College Hospital National Health Service Trust, and makes consequential amendments to that Order and transitional provisions.

2843. NHS trusts – community care – closure of centre used by voluntary groups – extent of statutory duty

[National Health Service Act 1977 s.3, s.22; National Health Service and Community Care Act 1990 s.47.]

B applied for permission to seek judicial review of a decision by BMH to close a centre leased to WCC, a local authority, and used by 18 voluntary groups as a resource centre for mentally and physically handicapped persons. The closure decision was taken on financial grounds, with WCC opposed to closure but not undertaking the necessary individual assessments of the centre's users so as to provide continuity of care.

Held, refusing the application, that the centre had not been used by BMH to deliver NHS services and it was not unlawful to close it and sell the building for economic reasons. This was so even if BMH, WCC and the local health authority had failed to ensure that services would be provided elsewhere. Duties under the National Health Service Act 1977 s.3 and s.22 were "target duties", *R. v. Secretary of State for Social Services, ex p. Hincks* (1979) 123 S.J. 436, [1979] C.L.Y. 1839 considered, and their extent was unclear in the instant case. BMH had not ceased to provide a service, so that the closure decision itself could not be challenged by way of judicial review. Although WCC had not assessed the centre's users' needs on an individual basis, as required under the National Health Service and Community Care Act 1990 s.47 in time for the closure date, it could not be said that it was in breach of its duty under s.47 of the 1990 Act and it was actively collaborating with the health authority to ensure alternative provision for the users, *R. v. Secretary of State for the Environment, ex p. Ward* [1984] 1 W.L.R. 834, [1984] C.L.Y. 3438 applied.

R. v. BATH MENTAL HEALTHCARE NHS TRUST, *ex p.* BECK (2000) 3 C.C.L. Rep. 5, Owen, J., QBD.

2844. NHS trusts – dissolution – Andover District Community Health Care

ANDOVER DISTRICT COMMUNITY HEALTH CARE NATIONAL HEALTH SERVICE TRUST (DISSOLUTION) ORDER 2000, SI 2000 847; made under the

National Health Service 1977 s.126; and the National Health Service and Community Care Act 1990 s.5, Sch.2 para.29. In force: April 1, 2000; £1.00.

This Order provides for the dissolution on April 1, 2000 of the Andover District Community Health Care National Health Service Trust. The Andover District Community Health Care National Health Service Trust (Establishment) Order 1992 (SI 1992 2505) is revoked.

2845. NHS trusts – dissolution – BHB Community Health Care, Forest Healthcare, Havering Hospitals and Redbridge Health Care

BHB COMMUNITY HEALTH CARE, THE FOREST HEALTHCARE, THE HAVERING HOSPITALS AND THE REDBRIDGE HEALTH CARE NATIONAL HEALTH SERVICE TRUSTS (DISSOLUTION) ORDER 2000, SI 2000 1416; made under the National Health Service Act 1977 s.126; and the National Health Service and Community Care Act 1990 s.5, Sch.2 para.29. In force: April 1, 2001; £1.00.

This Order provides for the dissolution of the BHB Community Health Care, Forest Healthcare, Havering Hospitals, and Redbridge Health Care National Health Service Trusts. The BHB Community Health Care Trust (Establishment) Order 1992 (SI 1992 2515), the Forest Healthcare National Health Service Trust (Establishment) Order 1991 (SI 1991 2348), the Havering Hospitals National Health Service Trust (Establishment) Order 1992 (SI 1992 2512) and the Redbridge Health Care National Health Service Trust (Establishment) Order 1992 (SI 1992 2517) are revoked.

2846. NHS trusts – dissolution – Doncaster Royal Infirmary and Montagu Hospital and the Bassetlaw Hospital and Community Services

DONCASTER ROYAL INFIRMARY AND MONTAGU HOSPITAL AND THE BASSETLAW HOSPITAL AND COMMUNITY SERVICES NATIONAL HEALTH SERVICE TRUSTS (DISSOLUTION) ORDER 2000, SI 2000 3124; made under the National Health Service Act 1977 s.126; and the National Health Service and Community Care Act 1990 s.5, Sch.2 para.29. In force: April 1, 2001; £1.50.

This Order dissolves the Doncaster Royal Infirmary and Montagu Hospital National Health Service Trust and the Bassetlaw Hospital and Community Services National Health Service Trust on April 1, 2001. The Doncaster Royal Infirmary and Montagu Hospital National Health Service Trust (Establishment) Order 1990 (SI 1990 2411) and the Bassetlaw Hospital and Community Services National Health Service Trust (Establishment) Order 1991 (SI 1991 2326) are revoked.

2847. NHS trusts – dissolution – East Hertfordshire – North Hertfordshire

EAST HERTFORDSHIRE AND NORTH HERTFORDSHIRE NATIONAL HEALTH SERVICE TRUSTS (DISSOLUTION) ORDER 2000, SI 2000 536; made under the National Health Service Act 1977 s.126; and the National Health Service and Community Care Act 1990 s.5. In force: April 1, 2000; £1.00.

This Order, which provides for the dissolution of the East Hertfordshire National Health Service Trust and the North Hertfordshire National Health Service Trust, revokes the East Hertfordshire National Health Service Trust (Establishment) Order 1991 (SI 1991 2343) and the North Hertfordshire National Health Service Trust (Establishment) Order 1990 (SI 1990 2430).

2848. NHS trusts – dissolution – Grantham and District – Lincoln and Louth – Pilgrim Health

GRANTHAM AND DISTRICT HOSPITAL, THE LINCOLN AND LOUTH AND THE PILGRIM HEALTH NATIONAL HEALTH SERVICE TRUSTS (DISSOLUTION) ORDER 2000, SI 2000 411; made under the National Health Service Act 1977 s.126; and the National Health Service and Community Care Act 1990 s.5, Sch.2 para.29. In force: April 1, 2000; £1.00.

This Order on April 1, 2000 provides for the dissolution of the Grantham and District Hospital National Health Service Trust, the Lincoln and Louth National Health Service Trust and the Pilgrim Health National Health Service Trust. The Grantham and District Hospital National Health Service Trust (Establishment) Order 1994 (SI 1994 3175), the Lincoln Hospitals National Health Service Trust (Establishment) Order 1993 (SI 1993 2560) and the Pilgrim Health National Health Service Trust (Establishment) Order 1993 (SI 1993 2567) are revoked.

2849. NHS trusts – dissolution – Herefordshire Community Health

HEREFORDSHIRE COMMUNITY HEALTH NATIONAL HEALTH SERVICE TRUST (DISSOLUTION) ORDER 2000, SI 2000 1749; made under the National Health Service Act 1977 s.126; and the National Health Service and Community Care Act 1990 s.5, Sch.2 para.29. In force: October 1, 2000; £1.00.

This Order, which revokes the Herefordshire Community Health National Health Service Trust (Establishment) Order 1991 (SI 1991 2358), provides for the dissolution on October 1, 2000 of the Herefordshire Community Health National Health Service Trust.

2850. NHS trusts – dissolution – Kent and Sussex Weald – Mid Kent Healthcare

KENT AND SUSSEX WEALD AND THE MID KENT NATIONAL HEALTH SERVICE TRUSTS (DISSOLUTION) ORDER 2000, SI 2000 238; made under the National Health Service Act 1977 s.126; and the National Health Service and Community Care Act 1990 s.5, Sch.2 para.29. In force: April 1, 2000; £1.00.

This Order provides for the dissolution on April 1, 2000 of the Kent and Sussex Weald and Mid Kent Healthcare National Health Service Trusts. The Kent and Sussex Weald National Health Service Trust (Establishment) Order 1994 (SI 1994 163) and the Mid Kent Healthcare National Health Services Trust (Establishment) Order 1992 (SI 1992 2531) are revoked.

2851. NHS trusts – dissolution – Milton Keynes Community Health

MILTON KEYNES COMMUNITY HEALTH NATIONAL HEALTH SERVICE TRUST (DISSOLUTION) ORDER 2000, SI 2000 2662; made under the National Health Service Act 1977 s.126; and the National Health Service and Community Care Act 1990 s.5, Sch.2 para.29. In force: October 1, 2000; £1.50.

This Order, which revokes the Milton Keynes Community Health National Health Service Trust (Establishment) Order 1991 (SI 1991 2371), provides for the dissolution of the Milton Keynes Community Health National Health Service Trust.

2852. NHS trusts – dissolution – Mount Vernon and Watford Hospitals – St. Albans and Hemel Hempstead

MOUNT VERNON AND WATFORD HOSPITALS AND ST. ALBANS AND HEMEL HEMPSTEAD NATIONAL HEALTH SERVICE TRUSTS (DISSOLUTION) ORDER 2000, SI 2000 733; made under the National Health Service Act 1977 s.126; and the National Health Service and Community Care Act 1990 s.5, Sch.2 para.29. In force: April 1, 2000; £1.00.

This Order provides for the dissolution on April 1, 2000 of the Mount Vernon and Watford Hospitals and the St. Albans and Hemel Hempstead NHS Trusts. The Mount Vernon and Watford Hospitals National Health Service Trust (Establishment) Order 1994 (SI 1994 852) and the St. Albans and Hemel Hempstead National Health Service Trust (Establishment) Order 1994 (SI 1994 177) are revoked.

2853. NHS trusts – dissolution – Phoenix

PHOENIX NATIONAL HEALTH SERVICE TRUST (DISSOLUTION) ORDER 2000, SI 2000 846; made under the National Health Service 1977 s.126; and the National Health Service and Community Care Act 1990 s.5, Sch.2 para.29. In force: April 1, 2000; £1.00.

This Order dissolves the Phoenix National Health Service Trust on April 1, 2000. The Phoenix National Health Service Trust (Establishment) Order 1991 (SI 1991 2385) is revoked.

2854. NHS trusts – dissolution – Southend Community Care – Thameside Community Healthcare

SOUTHEND COMMUNITY CARE SERVICES AND THE THAMESIDE COMMUNITY HEALTHCARE NATIONAL HEALTH SERVICE TRUSTS (DISSOLUTION) ORDER 2000, SI 2000 407; made under the National Health Service Act 1977 s.126; and the National Health Service and Community Care Act 1990 s.5. In force: April 1, 2000; £1.00.

This Order provides for the dissolution on April 1, 2000, of the Southend Community Care Services National Health Service Trust and the Thameside Community Healthcare National Health Service Trust. The Southend Community Care Services National Health Service Trust (Establishment) Order 1991 (SI 1991 2405) and the Thameside Community Healthcare National Health Service Trust (Establishment) Order 1992 (SI 1992 2513) are revoked.

2855. NHS trusts – dissolution – Stockport Acute Services – Stockport Healthcare

STOCKPORT ACUTE SERVICES AND THE STOCKPORT HEALTHCARE NATIONAL HEALTH SERVICE TRUSTS (DISSOLUTION) ORDER 2000, SI 2000 841; made under the National Health Service Act 1977 s.126; and the National Health Service and Community Care Act 1990 s.5, Sch.2 para.29. In force: April 1, 2000; £1.00.

This Order provides for the dissolution on April 1, 2000 of the Stockport Acute Services and the Stockport Healthcare National Health Service Trusts. The Stockport Acute Services National Health Service Trust (Establishment) Order 1993 (SI 1993 2622) and the Stockport Healthcare National Health Service Trust (Establishment) Order 1993 (SI 1993 2628) are revoked.

2856. NHS trusts – establishment – Aylesbury Vale Community Healthcare

AYLESBURY VALE COMMUNITY HEALTHCARE NATIONAL HEALTH SERVICE TRUST (ESTABLISHMENT) AMENDMENT ORDER 2000, SI 2000 2663; made under the National Health Service Act 1977 s.126; and the National Health Service and Community Care Act 1990 s.5. In force: October 1, 2000; £1.50.

This Order amends the Aylesbury Vale Community Healthcare National Health Service Trust (Establishment) Order 1991 (SI 1991 2321) by substituting a new Art.3, which makes provision relating to the nature and functions of the trust.

2857. NHS trusts – establishment – Barking, Havering and Redbridge Hospitals

BARKING, HAVERING AND REDBRIDGE HOSPITALS NATIONAL HEALTH SERVICE TRUST (ESTABLISHMENT) ORDER 2000, SI 2000 1413; made under the National Health Service and Community Care Act 1990 s.5, Sch.2 para.1, Sch.2 para.3. In force: June 5, 2000; £1.50.

This Order establishes the Barking, Havering and Redbridge Hospitals National Health Service Trust provided for in the National Health Service and Community Care Act 1990 s.5. It provides for the functions of the trust and the number of executive and non-executive directors. In addition, it specifies the operational date and the accounting date of the trust and makes provision for assistance to the trust by the Barking & Havering HA before its operational date.

2858. NHS trusts – establishment – Birmingham Specialist Community Health

BIRMINGHAM SPECIALIST COMMUNITY HEALTH NATIONAL HEALTH SERVICE TRUST (ESTABLISHMENT) AMENDMENT ORDER 2000, SI 2000 2044; made under the National Health Service Act 1977 s.126; and the National Health Service and Community Care Act 1990 s.5. In force: August 7, 2000; £1.00.

This Order amends the constitution of the Birmingham Specialist Community Health National Health Service Trust, an NHS trust established by the Birmingham Specialist Community Health National Health Service Trust (Establishment) Order 1999 (SI 1999 3467), by increasing the number of non-executive directors from 5 to 6.

2859. NHS trusts – establishment – Blackpool, Wyre and Flyde Community Health Services

BLACKPOOL, WYRE AND FLYDE COMMUNITY HEALTH SERVICES NATIONAL HEALTH SERVICE TRUST (ESTABLISHMENT) AMENDMENT ORDER 2000, SI 2000 993; made under the National Health Service Act 1977 s.126; and the National Health Service and Community Care Act 1990 s.5. In force: April 5, 2000; £1.00.

This Order amends the Blackpool, Wyre and Fylde Community Health Services National Health Service Trust (Establishment) Order 1993 (SI 1993 2597), which established the Blackpool, Wyre and Fylde Community Health Services National Health Service Trust, to confer on it the purposes of providing goods, hospital accommodation and services and community health services at or from Wesham Park Hospital, Rossall Hospital, the site at Kincraig Road and at or from any associated hospitals, establishments and facilities.

2860. NHS trusts – establishment – Bro Morgannwg

BRO MORGANNWG NATIONAL HEALTH SERVICE TRUST (ESTABLISHMENT) AMENDMENT ORDER 2000, SI 2000 1076 (W.70); made under the National Health Service Act 1977 s.126; and the National Health Service and Community Care Act 1990 s.5, Sch.2 para.1, Sch.2 para.3. In force: April 7, 2000; £1.50.

This Order amends the Bro Morgannwg National Health Service Trust (Establishment) Order 1998 (SI 1998 3319), which established the Bro Morgannwg National Health Service Trust, to confer on it the purposes of providing goods and services, including hospital facilities and community health services, at or from specified hospitals. It makes provision in relation to the transfer of all services from Neath General Hospital and its closure and the provision of such services to be provided at a new hospital at Baglan Way, Port Talbot.

2861. NHS trusts – establishment – Doncaster and Bassetlaw Hospitals

DONCASTER AND BASSETLAW HOSPITALS NATIONAL HEALTH SERVICE TRUST (ESTABLISHMENT) ORDER 2000, SI 2000 3125; made under the National Health Service and Community Care Act 1990 s.5, Sch.2 para.1, Sch.2 para.3, Sch.2 para.4, Sch.2 para.5. In force: December 4, 2000; £1.50.

This Order, which establishes the Doncaster and Bassetlaw Hospitals National Health Service Trust, provides for the functions of the trust and the number of executive and non executive directors. It specifies the operational date, the accounting date of the trust and the trust's limited functions before the operational date. In addition, it specifies the trust's liabilities which will be discharged by the Doncaster Health Authority if incurred between the establishment date and the operational date.

2862. NHS trusts – establishment – East and North Hertfordshire

EAST AND NORTH HERTFORDSHIRE NATIONAL HEALTH SERVICE TRUST (ESTABLISHMENT) ORDER 2000, SI 2000 535; made under the National

Health Service and Community Care Act 1990 s.5, Sch.2 para.1, Sch.2 para.3, Sch.2 para.4, Sch.2 para.5. In force: March 13, 2000; £1.50.

This Order establishes the East and North Hertfordshire National Health Service Trust, provides for the functions of the trust and the number of executive and non-executive directors, specifies the operational and accounting dates, details the trust's limited functions before the operational date and sets out the trust's liabilities which will be discharged by the East and North Hertfordshire HA if incurred between the establishment date and the operational date of the trust.

2863. NHS trusts – establishment – East Gloucestershire

EAST GLOUCESTERSHIRE NATIONAL HEALTH SERVICE TRUST (ESTABLISHMENT) AMENDMENT ORDER 2000, SI 2000 2741; made under the National Health Service Act 1977 s.126; and the National Health Service and Community Care Act 1990 s.5. In force: October 14, 2000; £1.50.

This Order amends the East Gloucestershire National Health Service Trust (Establishment) Order 1990 (SI 1990 2412) by substituting a new address for the Trust's headquarters premises.

2864. NHS trusts – establishment – East London and the City Mental Health

EAST LONDON AND THE CITY MENTAL HEALTH NATIONAL HEALTH SERVICE TRUST (ESTABLISHMENT) AMENDMENT ORDER 2000, SI 2000 1669; made under the National Health Service Act 1977 s.126; and the National Health Service and Community Care Act 1990 s.5. In force: June 30, 2000; £1.00.

This Order amends the East London and The City Mental Health National Health Service Trust (Establishment) Order 2000 (SI 2000 522), which established the East London and the City Mental Health National Health Service Trust, by inserting a new Art.4A to provide that the trust is to be regarded as having a significant teaching commitment.

2865. NHS trusts – establishment – East London and the City Mental Health

EAST LONDON AND THE CITY MENTAL HEALTH NATIONAL HEALTH SERVICE TRUST (ESTABLISHMENT) ORDER 2000, SI 2000 522; made under the National Health Service and Community Care Act 1990 s.5, Sch.2 para.1, Sch.2 para.3, Sch.2 para.4, Sch.2 para.5. In force: March 3, 2000; £1.50.

This Order establishes the East London and the City National Health Service Trust, provides for the functions of the trust, the number of executive and non-executive directors, specifies the operational date and accounting date of the trust, sets out the trust's limited functions before the operational date and details the trust's liabilities which will be discharged by the East London and the City HA if incurred between the establishment date and the operational date of the trust.

2866. NHS trusts – establishment – Maidstone and Tunbridge Wells

MAIDSTONE AND TUNBRIDGE WELLS NATIONAL HEALTH SERVICE TRUST (ESTABLISHMENT) ORDER 2000, SI 2000 237; made under the National Health Service and Community Care Act 1990 s.5, Sch.2 para.1, Sch.2 para.3, Sch.2 para.4, Sch.2 para.5. In force: February 14, 2000; £1.50.

This Order establishes the Maidstone and Tunbridge Wells National Health Service Trust, provides for the functions of the trust and the number of executive and non executive directors, specifies the operational and accounting dates of the trust, the trust's limited functions before the operational date and the trust's liabilities.

2867. NHS trusts – establishment – Mid-Sussex

MID-SUSSEX NATIONAL HEALTH SERVICE TRUST (ESTABLISHMENT) AMENDMENT ORDER 2000, SI 2000 1362; made under the National Health

Service Act 1977 s.126; and the National Health Service and Community Care Act 1990 s.5. In force: May 26, 2000; £1.00.

This Order amends the Mid-Sussex National Health Service Trust (Establishment) Order 1994 (SI 1994 165), which established the Mid-Sussex National Health Service Trust, to correct the details of the Stead Resource Centre site, described defectively in the Mid-Sussex National Health Service Trust (Establishment) Amendment Order (SI 1999 199).

2868. **NHS trusts – establishment – North East London Mental Health**

NORTH EAST LONDON MENTAL HEALTH NATIONAL HEALTH SERVICE TRUST (ESTABLISHMENT) ORDER 2000, SI 2000 1415; made under the National Health Service and Community Care Act 1990 s.5, Sch.2 para.1, Sch.2 para.3. In force: June 5, 2000; £1.50.

This Order establishes the North East London Mental Health National Health Service Trust, provided for in the National Health Service and Community Care Act 1990 s.5. It provides for the functions of the trust and the number of executive and non-executive directors. In addition, it specifies the operational date and the accounting date of the trust and makes provision for assistance to the trust by the Redbridge and Waltham Forest HA before its operational date.

2869. **NHS trusts – establishment – Northern Lincolnshire and Goole Hospitals**

NORTHERN LINCOLNSHIRE AND GOOLE HOSPITALS NATIONAL HEALTH SERVICE TRUST (ESTABLISHMENT) ORDER 2000, SI 2000 2885; made under the National Health Service and Community Care Act 1990 s.5, Sch.2 para.1, Sch.2 para.3, Sch.2 para.4, Sch.2 para.5. In force: October 31, 2000; £1.75.

This Order establishes the Northern Lincolnshire and Goole Hospitals National Health Service Trust, provides for the functions of the trust, the number of executive and non-executive directors, specifies the operational date and accounting date of the trust, sets out the trust's limited functions before the operational date and details the trust's liabilities which will be discharged by the South Humber Health Authority if incurred between the establishment date and the operational date of the trust.

2870. **NHS trusts – establishment – Nottinghamshire Healthcare**

NOTTINGHAMSHIRE HEALTHCARE NATIONAL HEALTH SERVICE TRUST (ESTABLISHMENT) ORDER 2000, SI 2000 2908; made under the National Health Service and Community Care Act 1990 s.5, Sch.2 para.1, Sch.2 para.3, Sch.2 para.4, Sch.2 para.5. In force: November 6, 2000; £1.75.

This Order, which establishes the Nottinghamshire Healthcare National Health Service Trust as an NHS trust provided for in the National Health Service and Community Care Act 1990 s.5, provides for the functions of the trust and the number of executive and non executive directors. In addition, it specifies the operational date, the accounting date of the trust, the trust's limited functions before the operational date and that the trust's liabilities will be discharged by the North Nottinghamshire Health Authority if incurred between the establishment date and the operational date.

2871. **NHS trusts – establishment – Oxford Radcliffe Hospitals**

OXFORD RADCLIFFE HOSPITALS NATIONAL HEALTH SERVICE TRUST (ESTABLISHMENT) AMENDMENT ORDER 2000, SI 2000 961; made under the National Health Service Act 1977 s.126; and the National Health Service and Community Care Act 1990 s.5. In force: April 11, 2000; £1.00.

This Order amends the constitution of the Oxford Radcliffe Hospitals National Health Service Trust by increasing the number of non-executive directors from five to six.

2872. NHS trusts – establishment – Sheffield Teaching Hospitals

SHEFFIELD TEACHING HOSPITALS NATIONAL HEALTH SERVICE TRUST (ESTABLISHMENT) ORDER 2000, SI 2000 2909; made under the National Health Service and Community Care Act 1990 s.5, Sch.2 para.1, Sch.2 para.3, Sch.2 para.4, Sch.2 para.5. In force: October 31, 2000; £1.50.

This Order, which establishes the Sheffield Teaching Hospitals National Health Service Trust as an NHS trust provided for in the National Health Service and Community Care Act 1990 s.5, provides for the functions of the trust and the number of executive and non-executive directors. In addition, it specifies the operational date and the accounting date of the trust and the trust's limited functions before the operational date. It also specifies the trust's liabilities which will be discharged by the Sheffield Health Authority if incurred between the establishment date and the operational date.

2873. NHS trusts – establishment – South Essex Mental Health and Community Care

SOUTH ESSEX MENTAL HEALTH AND COMMUNITY CARE NATIONAL HEALTH SERVICE TRUST (ESTABLISHMENT) ORDER 2000, SI 2000 406; made under the National Health Service and Community Care Act 1990 s.5, Sch.2 para.1, Sch.2 para.3, Sch.2 para.4, Sch.2 para.5. In force: February 28, 2000; £1.50.

This Order establishes the South Essex Mental Health and Community Care National Health Service Trust, provides for the functions of the trust, the number of executive and non-executive directors, specifies the operational date and the accounting date of the trust, the trust's limited functions before the operational date and the trust's liabilities.

2874. NHS trusts – establishment – Stockport

STOCKPORT NATIONAL HEALTH SERVICE TRUST (ESTABLISHMENT) ORDER 2000, SI 2000 842; made under the National Health Service and Community Care Act 1990 s.5, Sch.2 para.1, Sch.2 para.3, Sch.2 para.4, Sch.2 para.5. In force: April 1, 2000; £1.50.

This Order establishes the Stockport National Health Service Trust, provides for the functions of the trust and the number of executive and non-executive directors and specifies the operational date and the accounting date of the trust.

2875. NHS trusts – establishment – United Lincolnshire Hospitals

UNITED LINCOLNSHIRE HOSPITALS NATIONAL HEALTH SERVICE TRUST (ESTABLISHMENT) ORDER 2000, SI 2000 410; made under the National Health Service Community Care Act 1990 s.5, Sch.2 para.1, Sch.2 para.3. In force: February 28, 2000; £1.00.

This Order establishes the United Lincolnshire Hospitals National Health Service Trust, provides for the functions of the trust both before and after its operational date and the number of executive and non-executive directors. It specifies the operational date and the accounting date of the trust and makes provision for assistance to the trust by Lincolnshire HA before its operational date.

2876. NHS trusts – establishment – West Hertfordshire Hospitals

WEST HERTFORDSHIRE HOSPITALS NATIONAL HEALTH SERVICE TRUST (ESTABLISHMENT) ORDER 2000, SI 2000 732; made under the National Health Service and Community Care Act 1990 s.5, Sch.2 para.1, Sch.2 para.3, Sch.2 para.4, Sch.2 para.5. In force: March 23, 2000; £1.50.

This Order establishes the West Hertfordshire Hospitals National Health Service Trust, provides for the functions of the trust and the number of executive and non-executive directors. It specifies the operational date and the accounting date of the trust, the trust's limited functions before the operational date and the trust's liabilities which will be discharged by the West Hertfordshire HA if incurred between the establishment date and the operational date of the trust.

2877. NHS trusts – establishment – West London Mental Health

WEST LONDON MENTAL HEALTH NATIONAL HEALTH SERVICE TRUST (ESTABLISHMENT) ORDER 2000, SI 2000 2562; made under the National Health Service and Community Care Act 1990 s.5, Sch.2 para.1, Sch.2 para.3, Sch.2 para.4, Sch.2 para.5. In force: October 1, 2000; £1.50.

This Order, which establishes the West London Mental Health National Health Service Trust, provides for the functions of the trust and the number of executive and non executive directors and specifies the operational date, the accounting date of the trust and the trust's limited functions before the operational date. In addition, it specifies the trust's liabilities which will be discharged by the Broadmoor Hospital Authority if incurred between the establishment date and the operational date.

2878. NHS trusts – establishment – West Suffolk Hospitals

WEST SUFFOLK HOSPITALS NATIONAL HEALTH SERVICE TRUST (ESTABLISHMENT) AMENDMENT ORDER 2000, SI 2000 2387; made under the National Health Service Act 1977 s.126; and the National Health Service and Community Care Act 1990 s.5. In force: September 13, 2000; £1.00.

This Order, which amends the West Suffolk Hospitals National Health Service Trust (Establishment) Order 1992 (SI 1992 2565), inserts a new Art.4A to provide that the trust is to be regarded as having a significant teaching commitment and that one of the non executive directors shall be appointed from the University of Cambridge.

2879. NHS trusts – establishment – West Yorkshire Metropolitan Ambulance Service

WEST YORKSHIRE METROPOLITAN AMBULANCE SERVICE NATIONAL HEALTH SERVICE TRUST (ESTABLISHMENT) AMENDMENT ORDER 2000, SI 2000 2312; made under the National Health Service Act 1977 Act s.126; and the National Health Service and Community Care Act 1990 s.5. In force: September 8, 2000; £1.00.

This Order amends the establishment order of the West Yorkshire Metropolitan Ambulance Service National Health Service Trust by increasing the number of non-executive directors and executive directors from 3 to 4 in each case.

2880. NHS trusts – establishment – Whipps Cross Hospital

WHIPPS CROSS HOSPITAL NATIONAL HEALTH SERVICE TRUST (ESTABLISHMENT) ORDER 2000, SI 2000 1414; made under the National Health Service and Community Care Act 1990 s.5, Sch.2 para.1, Sch.2 para.3. In force: June 5, 2000; £1.00.

This Order establishes the Whipps Cross Hospital National Health Service Trust, provided for in the National Health Service and Community Care Act 1990 s.5. It provides for the functions of the trust and the number of executive and non-executive directors. In addition, it specifies the operational date and the accounting date of the trust and makes provision for assistance to the trust by the Redbridge and Waltham Forest HA before its operational date.

2881. NHS trusts – establishment and change of name – Walsgrave Hospitals

WALSGRAVE HOSPITALS NATIONAL HEALTH SERVICE TRUST CHANGE OF NAME AND (ESTABLISHMENT) AMENDMENT ORDER 2000, SI 2000 2886; made under the National Health Service Act 1977 s.126; and the National Health Service and Community Care Act 1990 s.5. In force: October 30, 2000; £1.75.

This Order, which amends the Walsgrave Hospitals National Health Service Trust (Establishment) Order 1993 (SI 1993 811), changes the name of the trust to the

University Hospitals Coventry and Warwickshire National Health Service Trust and provides for recognition of the trust as having a significant teaching commitment and for one of its non-executive directors to be appointed from the University of Warwick.

2882. NHS trusts – local authorities – partnership arrangements

NHS BODIES AND LOCAL AUTHORITIES PARTNERSHIP ARRANGEMENTS REGULATIONS 2000, SI 2000 617; made under the National Health Service Act 1977 s.126; and the Health Act 1999 s.31. In force: April 1, 2000; £2.00.

These Regulations make provision for certain NHS bodies and local authorities to enter into partnership arrangements for the exercise of specified functions. They define the nature of partnership arrangements; provide for the establishment of a fund made up of contributions from the partners out of which payments may be made towards expenditure incurred in the exercise of their functions; and provide for the exercise by NHS bodies of local authority functions and for the exercise by local authorities of NHS functions.

2883. NHS trusts – membership and procedure

NATIONAL HEALTH SERVICE TRUSTS (MEMBERSHIP AND PROCEDURE) AMENDMENT (ENGLAND) REGULATIONS 2000, SI 2000 2434; made under the National Health Service Act 1977 s.126; and the National Health Service and Community Care Act 1990 s.5. In force: October 1, 2000; £1.50.

These Regulations amend, in respect of England, the National Health Service Trusts (Membership and Procedure) Regulations 1990 (SI 1990 2024), which make provision in connection with the membership and procedure of NHS trusts established under the National Health Service and Community Care Act 1990 Part I. In particular, they provide that if an NHS trust provides high security psychiatric services and other mental health services the maximum number of NHS trust directors, excluding the chairman, shall be 14 and the maximum number of executive directors shall be seven; in these circumstances the executive directors of the NHS trust shall include a chief officer with responsibility for high security psychiatric services; the chairmen and non officer members of certain special health authorities may be appointed as non executive directors of NHS trusts; and a chairman or a non officer member of the Ashworth, Broadmoor or Rampton Hospital Authorities may be appointed as a non executive director of an NHS trust during that trust's preparatory period.

2884. NHS trusts – originating capital

NATIONAL HEALTH SERVICE TRUSTS (ORIGINATING CAPITAL) ORDER 2000, SI 2000 607; made under the National Health Service and Community Care Act 1990 s.9. In force: March 31, 2000; £1.50.

This Order determines the amount of the originating capital provided for in the National Health Service and Community Care Act 1990 s.9 in relation to NHS trusts established in the year beginning April 1, 1999.

2885. NHS trusts – originating capital – Wales

NATIONAL HEALTH SERVICE TRUSTS (ORIGINATING CAPITAL) (WALES) ORDER 2000, SI 2000 1142 (W.80); made under the National Health Service and Community Care Act 1990 s.9. In force: March 31, 2000; £2.00.

This Order determines the amount of the originating capital, provided for in the National Health Service and Community Care Act 1990 s.9, of certain NHS trusts established under that Act.

2886. NHS trusts – transfer of assets – Avon and Western Wiltshire Mental Health Care

AVON AND WESTERN WILTSHIRE MENTAL HEALTH CARE NATIONAL HEALTH SERVICE TRUST (TRANSFER OF TRUST PROPERTY) ORDER 2000, SI 2000 658; made under the National Health Service Act 1977 s.92. In force: April 7, 2000; £1.00.

This Order provides for the transfer of trust property from the North Bristol National Health Service Trust to the Avon and Western Wiltshire Mental Health Care National Health Service Trust.

2887. NHS trusts – transfer of assets – Central Sheffield University Hospitals, Community Health Sheffield, Northern General Hospital and Sheffield Children's Hospital

SHEFFIELD HEALTH AUTHORITY (TRANSFERS OF TRUST PROPERTY) ORDER 2000, SI 2000 609; made under the National Health Service Act 1977 s.92, s.126. In force: April 1, 2000; £1.00.

This Order provides for the transfer of trust property, and any rights and liabilities arising from that property, from the Sheffield HA to the Central Sheffield University Hospitals National Health Service Trust, the Community Health Sheffield National Health Service Trust, the Northern General Hospital National Health Service Trust and the Sheffield Children's Hospital National Health Service Trust.

2888. NHS trusts – transfer of assets – Central Sheffield University Hospitals, Community Health Sheffield, Northern General Hospital and Sheffield Children's Hospital

SPECIAL TRUSTEES FOR THE FORMER UNITED SHEFFIELD HOSPITALS (TRANSFER OF TRUST PROPERTY) ORDER 2000, SI 2000 608; made under the National Health Service Act 1977 s.92, s.126. In force: April 1, 2000; £1.00.

This Order transfers to the trustees for the Central Sheffield University Hospitals, the Community Health Sheffield, the Northern General Hospital, and the Sheffield Children's Hospital National Health Service Trusts trust property held by the Special Trustees for the Former United Sheffield Hospitals.

2889. NHS trusts – transfer of assets – Guy's and St Thomas'

SPECIAL TRUSTEES FOR GUY'S HOSPITAL AND THE SPECIAL TRUSTEES FOR ST THOMAS' HOSPITAL (TRANSFERS OF TRUST PROPERTY) ORDER 2000, SI 2000 614; made under the National Health Service Act 1977 s.92, s.126. In force: April 1, 2000; £1.00.

This Order provides for the transfer of trust property, and any rights and liabilities arising from that property, from the Special Trustees for Guy's Hospital and the Special Trustees for St Thomas' Hospital, to the trustees for the Guy's and St Thomas' National Health Service Trust.

2890. NHS trusts – transfer of assets – Hammersmith Hospitals

HAMMERSMITH HOSPITALS NATIONAL HEALTH SERVICE TRUST (TRANSFER OF TRUST PROPERTY) ORDER 2000, SI 2000 861; made under the National Health Act 1977 s.126; and the National Health Service and Community Care Act 1990 s.11. In force: April 1, 2000; £1.00.

This Order transfers trust property from the Hammersmith Hospitals National Health Service Trust to the trustees established for that trust under the National Health Service and Community Care Act 1990 s.11 (1).

2891. NHS trusts – transfer of assets – Hammersmith Hospitals

SPECIAL TRUSTEES FOR THE HAMMERSMITH AND ACTON HOSPITALS, THE SPECIAL TRUSTEES FOR THE CHARING CROSS AND WEST LONDON HOSPITALS AND THE SPECIAL TRUSTEES FOR THE QUEEN CHARLOTTE'S

AND CHELSEA HOSPITAL (TRANSFERS OF TRUST PROPERTY) ORDER 2000, SI 2000 613; made under the National Health Service Act 1977 s.92, s.126. In force: April 1, 2000; £1.00.

This Order provides for the transfer of trust property, and any rights and liabilities arising from that property, from the Special Trustees for the Hammersmith and Acton Hospitals, the Special Trustees for the Charing Cross and West London Hospitals and the Special Trustees for the Queen Charlotte's and Chelsea Hospital, to the trustees for the Hammersmith Hospitals National Health Service Trust.

2892. NHS trusts – transfer of assets – Leeds Teaching Hospitals

LEEDS TEACHING HOSPITALS NATIONAL HEALTH SERVICE TRUST (TRANSFER OF TRUST PROPERTY) ORDER 2000, SI 2000 859; made under the National Health Act 1977 s.126; and the National Health Service and Community Care Act 1990 s.11. In force: April 1, 2000; £1.00.

This Order transfers trust property from the Leeds Teaching Hospitals National Health Service Trust to the trustees established for that trust under the National Health Service and Community Care Act 1990 s.11 (1).

2893. NHS trusts – transfer of assets – Leeds Teaching Hospitals

SPECIAL TRUSTEES FOR THE GENERAL INFIRMARY AT LEEDS AND THE LEEDS ST JAMES'S UNIVERSITY HOSPITAL SPECIAL TRUSTEES (TRANSFERS OF TRUST PROPERTY) ORDER 2000, SI 2000 612; made under the National Health Service Act 1977 s.92, s.126. In force: April 1, 2000; £1.00.

This Order provides for the transfer of trust property, and any rights and liabilities arising from that property, from the Special Trustees of the General Infirmary at Leeds and the Leeds St James's University Hospital Special Trustees, to the trustees for the Leeds Teaching Hospitals National Health Service Trust.

2894. NHS trusts – transfer of assets – Royal Free Hampstead

SPECIAL TRUSTEES FOR THE ROYAL THROAT, NOSE & EAR HOSPITAL AND THE SPECIAL TRUSTEES FOR THE ROYAL FREE HOSPITAL (TRANSFERS OF TRUST PROPERTY) ORDER 2000, SI 2000 610; made under the National Health Service Act 1977 s.92, s.126. In force: April 1, 2000; £1.00.

This Order provides for the transfer of trust property, and any rights and liabilities arising from that property, from the Special Trustees for the Royal Throat, Nose & Ear Hospital and the Special Trustees for the Royal Free Hospital to the trustees for the Royal Free Hampstead National Health Service Trust.

2895. NHS trusts – transfer of assets – United Bristol Healthcare

AVON HEALTH AUTHORITY (TRANSFER OF TRUST PROPERTY) ORDER 2000, SI 2000 616; made under the National Health Service Act 1977 s.92, s.126. In force: April 1, 2000; £1.00.

This Order transfers to the trustees for the United Bristol Healthcare National Health Service Trust trust property held by Avon HA.

2896. NHS trusts – transfer of assets – United Bristol Healthcare

SPECIAL TRUSTEES FOR THE UNITED BRISTOL HOSPITALS (TRANSFERS OF TRUST PROPERTY) ORDER 2000, SI 2000 615; made under the National Health Service Act 1977 s.92, s.126. In force: April 1, 2000; £1.00.

This Order provides for the transfer of trust property, and any rights and liabilities arising from that property, from the Special Trustees for the United Bristol Hospitals to the trustees for the United Bristol Healthcare National Health Service Trust.

2897. NHS trusts – transfer of assets – University College London

UNIVERSITY COLLEGE LONDON HOSPITALS NATIONAL HEALTH SERVICE TRUST (TRANSFER OF TRUST PROPERTY) ORDER 2000, SI 2000 860; made under the National Health Act 1977 s.126; and the National Health Service and Community Care Act 1990 s.11. In force: April 1, 2000; £1.00.

This Order transfers trust property from the University College London Hospitals National Health Service Trust to the trustees established for that trust under the National Health Service and Community Care Act 1990 s.11 (1).

2898. NHS trusts – transfer of assets – University College London Hospitals

SPECIAL TRUSTEES FOR THE UNIVERSITY COLLEGE LONDON HOSPITALS AND THE SPECIAL TRUSTEES FOR THE MIDDLESEX HOSPITAL (TRANSFERS OF TRUST PROPERTY) ORDER 2000, SI 2000 611; made under the National Health Service Act 1977 s.92, s.126. In force: April 1, 2000; £1.00.

This Order provides for the transfer of trust property, and any rights and liabilities arising from that property, from the Special Trustees for the University College London Hospitals and the Special Trustees for the Middlesex Hospital, to the trustees for the University College London Hospitals National Health Service Trust.

2899. Opticians – fees and payments

NATIONAL HEALTH SERVICE (OPTICAL CHARGES AND PAYMENTS) AMENDMENT REGULATIONS 2000, SI 2000 594; made under the National Health Service Act 1977 s.78, s.126, Sch.12 para.2, Sch.12 para.2A. In force: April 1, 2000; £1.50.

These Regulations amend the National Health Service (Optical Charges and Payments) Regulations 1997 (SI 1997 818), by increasing the redemption value of a voucher issued towards the cost of replacement of a single contact lens, increasing the maximum contribution by way of a voucher to the cost of repair of a frame and increasing the value of vouchers issued towards the costs of the supply and replacement of glasses, contact lenses and special categories of appliance.

2900. Opticians – fees and payments

NATIONAL HEALTH SERVICE (OPTICAL CHARGES AND PAYMENTS) AMENDMENT (NO.2) REGULATIONS 2000, SI 2000 3029; made under the National Health Service Act 1977 s.78, s.126, Sch.para.2A. In force: December 1, 2000; £1.50.

These Regulations amend the National Health Service (Optical Charges and Payments) Regulations 1997 (SI 1997 818) which provide for payments to be made by means of a voucher system in respect of costs incurred by certain categories of persons in connection with sight tests and the supply, replacement and repair of optical appliances. They amend the definition of "NHS sight test fee" to reflect the values of the two levels of fees for such tests payable to ophthalmic medical practitioners and opticians.

2901. Opticians – fees and payments – Wales

NATIONAL HEALTH SERVICE (OPTICAL CHARGES AND PAYMENTS) AMENDMENT (NO.2) (WALES) REGULATIONS 2000, SI 2000 3119 (W.198); made under the National Health Service Act 1977 s.126, Sch.2A para.12. In force: December 1, 2000; £1.75.

These Regulations amend the National Health Service (Optical Charges and Payments) Regulations 1997 (SI 1997 818), which provide for a scheme of payments to be made by Health Authorities and National Health Service Trusts, by means of a voucher system, towards the costs incurred by certain categories of person in connection with sight tests and the supply, replacement and repair of optical appliances. These Regulations amend the definition of "NHS sight test fee" to reflect the values of the two levels of fee for National Health Service sight tests payable to ophthalmic medical practitioners and opticians at the time these regulations come into force.

2902. Opticians – fees and payments – Wales

NATIONAL HEALTH SERVICE (OPTICAL CHARGES AND PAYMENTS) AMENDMENT (WALES) REGULATIONS 2000, SI 2000 978 (W.48); made under the National Health Service Act 1977 s.126, Sch.12 para.2A. In force: April 1, 2000; £2.00.

The National Health Service (Optical Charges and Payments) Regulations 1997 (SI 1997 818) provide for a scheme of voucher payments to be made by health authorities and NHS trusts towards costs incurred by certain persons in connection with sight tests and obtaining optical appliances. These Regulations amend the definition of "NHS sight test fee" to reflect the values of the two levels of fees payable for sight tests and include people aged 16 to 18 and in full time education in the categories of patient who may be eligible for assistance with the costs of sight tests. They increase the redemption value of a voucher issued towards the cost of replacement of a single contact lens, the maximum contribution by way of a voucher to the cost of repair of a frame and the value of vouchers issued towards the costs of the supply and replacement of glasses, contact lenses and special categories of appliance.

2903. Osteopaths Act 1993 (c.21) – Commencement No.5 Order

OSTEOPATHS ACT 1993 (COMMENCEMENT NO. 5) ORDER 2000, SI 2000 217 (C.6); made under the Osteopaths Act 1993 s.42. Commencement details: bringing into force various provisions of the Act on March 8, 2000; £1.50.

This Order brings into force on March 8, 2000 the remaining provisions, with certain exceptions, of the Osteopaths Act 1993. The provisions not being commenced by the Order relate to offences committed by persons describing themselves as osteopaths or in similar ways without being registered with the General Osteopathic Council, GOsC, and provisions relating to the election and appointment of the Chairman and members of the GOsC after the end of the relevant transitional periods defined in the Act.

2904. Osteopaths Act 1993 (c.21) – Commencement No.6 Order

OSTEOPATHS ACT 1993 (COMMENCEMENT NO.6 AND TRANSITIONAL PROVISION) ORDER 2000, SI 2000 1065 (C.30); made under the Osteopaths Act 1993 s.42. Commencement details: bringing into force various provisions of the Act on May 9, 2000.; £2.00.

This Order brings into force on May 9, 2000, the Osteopaths Act 1993 s.7(3), s.32(1) and s.32(3) relating to offences committed by persons describing themselves as osteopaths or in similar ways without being registered with the General Osteopathic Council.

2905. Pharmaceutical industry – registration of premises – fees

MEDICINES (PHARMACIES) (APPLICATIONS FOR REGISTRATION AND FEES) AMENDMENT REGULATIONS 2000, SI 2000 3235; made under the Medicines Act 1968 s.75, s.76, s.129. In force: January 1, 2001; £1.75.

These Regulations amend the Medicines (Pharmacies) (Applications for Registration and Fees) Regulations 1973 (SI 1973 1822) by increasing the fees for registration of premises at which a retail pharmacy business is carried on from £139 to £143 where the premises are in Great Britain and from £75 to £77 where the premises are in Northern Ireland, by increasing subsequent annual fees and by increasing the penalty for failure to pay retention fees. The Medicines (Pharmacies) (Applications for Registration and Fees) Amendment Regulations 1999 (SI 1999 3295) are revoked.

2906. Pharmacists – examinations – legitimacy of restricting number of resits

[Pharmacy Act 1954 s.3(4)(a).]

M, a qualified pharmacist in Pakistan, sought to be registered as a pharmacist in the United Kingdom. He failed the registration examination three times, and was told that he could not resit the exam again as more than three attempts were prohibited by bylaw 29, made by RPS under its Royal Charter first granted in 1843. M brought an application for judicial review, arguing that bylaw 29 was unlawful as either (1) RPS had no power to make it under either the Royal Charter nor under the Pharmacy Act 1954; (2) it was in restraint of trade, or (3) it was irrational.

Held, refusing the application, that (1) s.3(4)(a) of the Act empowered RPS to make bylaws establishing "periods of time" in relation to examinations. As registration examinations were only held twice a year and other bylaws legitimately prevented the examination being taken after a certain period following pre registration study, bylaw 29 was effectively doing no more than setting up an overall maximum time limit for the taking of the exam, and was therefore within RPS's powers under the Act; (2) it was a justifiable restraint of trade and served to protect the public and maintain the integrity of the profession, *Pharmaceutical Society of Great Britain v. Dickson* [1970] A.C. 403, [1968] C.L.Y. 3880 applied, and (3) bylaw 29 was created in response to an enquiry into the practice and training of pharmacists, and was aimed at ensuring that only those with the appropriate level of knowledge should be allowed to practice. It therefore had a legitimate aim, was put into practice sensitively and could not be said to be irrational.

R. v. ROYAL PHARMACEUTICAL SOCIETY OF GREAT BRITAIN, *ex p.* MAHMOOD [2001] U.K.C.L.R. 148, Holman, J., QBD.

2907. Pharmacists – relocation – relocation of services within neighbourhood – sufficiency of provision

[National Health Service (Pharmaceutical Services) Regulations 1992 (SI 1992 662) Reg.4.]

ACS applied to FHSAA to relocate the premises from which it operated its pharmaceutical business. The application was made under the National Health Service (Pharmaceutical Services) Regulations 1992 Reg.4(2)(b)(ii), being an application to change premises from which pharmaceutical services were provided to others in the same locality. Paragraph 7 of the application form stated that it was to be completed by all applicants except for those changing within the same neighbourhood. S applied under Reg.4(2)(a) for new premises to be included on the FHSAA's pharmaceutical list in the same neighbourhood. In accordance with its statutory obligations to ensure that there were sufficient pharmaceutical services within any particular neighbourhood, FHSAA rejected S's application, on the grounds that there were already sufficient services within the neighbourhood in question. ACS's application was granted, and S applied for judicial review of both decisions on the grounds that ACS's application had been made in the wrong form and that FHSAA had been wrong to reject S's application. The argument pertaining to ACS was based on Reg.4(3)(a), which provided that an application must be granted by the FHSAA where the applicant intended to change within the neighbourhood, the premises from which he provided pharmaceutical services. It was contended that since ACS were providing the same services within the same neighbourhood the change was a "minor relocation" and that accordingly the form had not been completed correctly.

Held, refusing the applications, that ACS had made an application for relocation under Reg.4(2)(b)(ii) and there was nothing in the Regulations to prevent it from having taken that course. The FHSAA was required to consider whether the change was a "minor relocation", and if it was, then the Reg.4(3) procedure had to be followed. In the instant case, there was no suggestion that the change was a "minor relocation" and, accordingly, ACS had completed the form correctly and the proper procedure had been followed. The contention that the FHSAA did not have sufficient evidence before it that ACS's new premises, which were linked to a new doctor's surgery that had not yet opened, would not actually commence operations was without merit. Even if ACS's new premises were not opened that would not have assisted S because its own application had been rejected on the basis that there were sufficient chemists in the relevant neighbourhood.

R. v. FAMILY HEALTH SERVICES APPEAL AUTHORITY, *ex p.* SAFEWAY STORES PLC [1999] J.P.L. 1133, Collins, J., QBD.

2908. **Pharmacy – medicines – parallel imports – marketing authorisation for new version of product – revocation of authorisation for previous version – European Community**

[EC Treaty Art.36 (now, after amendment, Art.30 EC); Council Directive 65/65 on proprietary medicinal products.]

M, a member of a group of pharmaceutical companies, obtained marketing authorisations issued by the Medicines Control Agency, the MCA, in compliance with Council Directive 65/65 for a medicinal product called Zimovane (generic name zopiclone). It appointed R as its agent to manufacture and market that product. After some years, R developed a new version of Zimovane containing the same active ingredients as the old product but different inert substances (excipients) and was said to be more beneficial to public health. The MCA varied the necessary authorisations, so allowing R to market the new version in the UK, and subsequently revoked the authorisations under which the old version had been marketed. R thereafter marketed only the new version in the UK, although it continued to market the old version in other member states. Prior to the aforementioned revocation, parallel import licences for the old version had been granted and the MCA decided to treat those licences as still valid. M and R sought judicial review of the MCA's decisions claiming that, in the absence of any subsisting marketing authorisations of the old version in the UK, imports of that version into the UK were not parallel imports, so it was contrary to UK legislation and Community law to treat them as such. The MCA contended that, had it treated the two versions of Zimovane as different products and required the parallel importers of the old version to apply for marketing authorisations under the Directive, it would have created an unjustifiable restriction on imports contrary to EC Treaty Art.36 (now, after amendment Art.30 EC). The matter was referred to the ECJ, where R also claimed that the particular benefit to public health provided by the new version would not be achieved if the old version was present on the UK market.

Held, that where it was sought to import a medicinal product (Product A) from one Member State into a second Member State, it was permissible for the person seeking to do so to obtain a parallel import licence in that Member State without meeting all the requirements of the directive if (1) Product A was the subject of a marketing authorisation granted in the first Member State and was the subject of such an authorisation which had ceased to have effect in the second Member State; (2) Product B was the subject of a marketing authorisation granted in the second Member State but not of one granted in the first Member State where both medicinal products had the same active ingredients and therapeutic effect, but did not use the same excipients and were manufactured by different processes, provided that the competent authority in the second Member State was able to verify that Product A complied with the necessary quality requirements and could ensure pharmacovigilance; (3) the authorisations referred to in (2) were granted to different members of the same group of companies and the manufacturers of both products were also members of that group, and (4) companies within the same group as the holder of the authorisation for Product A which had ceased to have effect in the second Member State continued to manufacture and market Product A in other Member States. The competent authority was not required to take into consideration the fact that Product B was developed and introduced in order to provide a particular benefit to public health which Product A did not provide or that that particular public health benefit might not be achieved if both products were on the market in the second Member State at the same time.

R. v. MEDICINES CONTROL AGENCY, *ex p.* RHONE POULENC RORER LTD (C94/98); *sub nom.* R. v. LICENSING AUTHORITY ESTABLISHED BY THE MEDICINES ACT 1968 (REPRESENTED BY MEDICINES CONTROL AGENCY), *ex p.* RHONE POULENC RORER LTD (C94/98) [2000] All E.R. (EC) 46, GC Rodriguez Iglesias (President), ECJ.

2909. Prescriptions – breach of confidence – disclosure of prescriptions void of personal details – information sold to pharmaceutical company – no risk to privacy

S appealed against the refusal ([1999] 4 All E. R. 185, [1999] C.L.Y. 2845) to grant a declaration that a Department of Health document was made in error. The policy document advised that the practice of general practitioners and pharmacists selling anonymous prescription details was a breach of confidence.

Held, allowing the appeal, that the law was concerned to protect the right to privacy but that had not been breached because all the patient's personal details had been expunged. The patient had no property rights to the prescription or the information contained therein.

R. v. DEPARTMENT OF HEALTH, *ex p.* SOURCE INFORMATICS LTD (NO.1) [2001] Q.B. 424, Simon Brown, L.J., CA.

2910. Primary care trusts

PRIMARY CARE TRUSTS (MEMBERSHIP, PROCEDURE AND ADMINISTRATION ARRANGEMENTS) REGULATIONS 2000, SI 2000 89; made under the National Health Service Act 1977 s.16B, s.126, Sch.5A para.5. In force: February 8, 2000; £3.00.

These Regulations, which make provision concerning the membership and procedure of Primary Care Trusts in England, include provisions relating to the number of members, conditions of membership and tenure of office of members, the termination of tenure of office, disqualifications, the vice-chairman, the appointment of committees and sub-committees, and meetings and proceedings, including disability for taking part in proceedings on account of pecuniary interest. They also provide for the arrangements which may be made by Primary Care Trusts for their functions to be exercised jointly with other bodies, or by their committees, sub-committees or officers, or by other Primary Care Trusts or Special Health Authorities.

2911. Primary care trusts – establishment – Airedale

AIREDALE PRIMARY CARE TRUST (ESTABLISHMENT) ORDER 2000, SI 2000 1942; made under the National Health Service Act 1977 s.16A, s.126, Sch.5A para.1, Sch.5A para.2. In force: July 26, 2000; £1.50.

This Order, which establishes the Airedale Primary Care Trust as provided for under the National Health Service Act 1977 s.16A, specifies the area for which the trust is established, its operational date and limitations on the exercise of its functions during its preparatory period. In addition, it makes provision for the membership of the trust and for assistance to the trust during its preparatory period.

2912. Primary care trusts – establishment – Bexley

BEXLEY PRIMARY CARE TRUST (ESTABLISHMENT) ORDER 2000, SI 2000 1962; made under the National Health Service Act 1977 s.16A, s.126, Sch.5A para.1, Sch.5A para.2. In force: July 28, 2000; £1.50.

This Order, which establishes the Bexley Primary Care Trust as provided for under the National Health Service Act 1977 s.16A, specifies the area for which the trust is established, its operational date and limitations on the exercise of its functions during its preparatory period. In addition, it makes provision for the membership of the trust and for assistance to the trust during its preparatory period.

2913. Primary care trusts – establishment – Birmingham North East

BIRMINGHAM NORTH EAST PRIMARY CARE TRUST (ESTABLISHMENT) ORDER 2000, SI 2000 2338; made under the National Health Service Act 1977 s.16A, s.126, Sch.5A para.1, Sch.5A para.2. In force: September 11, 2000; £1.50.

This Order, which establishes the Birmingham North East Primary Care Trust, as provided for under the National Health Service Act 1977 s.16A, specifies the area for which the trust is established, its operational date and limitations on the exercise of its functions during its preparatory period. In addition, it makes provision for the membership of the trust and for assistance to the trust during its preparatory period.

2914. Primary care trusts – establishment – Blackburn with Darwen

BLACKBURN WITH DARWEN PRIMARY CARE TRUST (ESTABLISHMENT) ORDER 2000, SI 2000 1167; made under the National Health Service Act 1977 s.16A, s.126, Sch.5A para.1, Sch.5A para.2. In force: May 1, 2000; £1.50.

This Order establishes the Blackburn with Darwen Primary Care Trust, specifies the area for which the trust is established, its operational date and limitations on the exercise of its functions during its preparatory period. It provides for the membership of the trust, for assistance to the trust during its preparatory period and contains a restriction on the exercise of functions by the trust.

2915. Primary care trusts – establishment – Bournemouth

BOURNEMOUTH PRIMARY CARE TRUST (ESTABLISHMENT) ORDER 2000, SI 2000 2155; made under the National Health Service Act 1977 s.16A, s.126, Sch.5A para.1, Sch.5A para.2. In force: August 14, 2000; £1.50.

This Order, which establishes the Bournemouth Primary Care Trust as provided for under the National Health Service Act 1977 s.16A, specifies the area for which the trust is established, its operational date and limitations on the exercise of its functions during its preparatory period. In addition, it makes provision for the membership of the trust and for assistance to the trust during its preparatory period.

2916. Primary care trusts – establishment – Bradford City

BRADFORD CITY PRIMARY CARE TRUST (ESTABLISHMENT) ORDER 2000, SI 2000 1945; made under the National Health Service Act 1977 s.16A, s.126, Sch.5A para.1, Sch.5A para.2. In force: July 26, 2000; £1.50.

This Order, which establishes the Bradford City Primary Care Trust as provided for under the National Health Service Act 1977 s.16A, specifies the area for which the trust is established, its operational date and limitations on the exercise of its functions during its preparatory period. In addition, it makes provision for the membership of the trust and for assistance to the trust during its preparatory period.

2917. Primary care trusts – establishment – Bradford South and West

BRADFORD SOUTH AND WEST PRIMARY CARE TRUST (ESTABLISHMENT) ORDER 2000, SI 2000 1943; made under the National Health Service Act 1977 s.16A, s.126, Sch.5A para.1, Sch.5A para.2. In force: July 26, 2000; £1.50.

This Order, which establishes the Bradford South and West Primary Care Trust as provided for under the National Health Service Act 1977 s.16A, specifies the area for which the trust is established, its operational date and limitations on the exercise of its functions during its preparatory period. In addition, it makes provision for the membership of the trust and for assistance to the trust during its preparatory period.

2918. Primary care trusts – establishment – Carrick

CARRICK PRIMARY CARE TRUST (ESTABLISHMENT) ORDER 2000, SI 2000 2158; made under the National Health Service Act 1977 s.16A, s.126, Sch.5A para.1, Sch.5A para.2. In force: August 14, 2000; £1.50.

This Order, which establishes the Carrick Primary Care Trust, as provided for under the National Health Service Act 1977 s.16A, specifies the area for which the trust is established, its operational date and limitations on the exercise of its functions during its preparatory period. In addition, it makes provision for the membership of the trust and for assistance to the trust during its preparatory period.

2919. Primary care trusts – establishment – Central Derby

CENTRAL DERBY PRIMARY CARE TRUST (ESTABLISHMENT) ORDER 2000, SI 2000 218; made under the National Health Service Act 1977 s.16A, s.126, Sch.5A para.1, Sch.5A para.2. In force: February 11, 2000; £1.50.

This Order establishes the Central Derby Primary Care Trust, specifies the area for which the trust is established, specifies its operational date and limitations on the exercise of its functions during its preparatory period, makes provision for the membership of the trust and provides for assistance to the trust during its preparatory period. It also contains a restriction on the exercise of functions by the trust.

2920. Primary care trusts – establishment – Central Manchester

CENTRAL MANCHESTER PRIMARY CARE TRUST (ESTABLISHMENT) ORDER 2000, SI 2000 1965; made under the National Health Service Act 1977 s.16A, s.126, Sch.5A para.1, Sch.5A para.2. In force: July 31, 2000; £1.50.

This Order, which establishes the Central Manchester Primary Care Trust as provided for under the National Health Service Act 1977 s.16A, specifies the area for which the trust is established, its operational date and limitations on the exercise of its functions during its preparatory period. In addition, it makes provision for the membership of the trust and for assistance to the trust during its preparatory period.

2921. Primary care trusts – establishment – Dartford, Gravesham and Swanley

DARTFORD, GRAVESHAM AND SWANLEY PRIMARY CARE TRUST (ESTABLISHMENT) ORDER 2000, SI 2000 2043; made under the National Health Service Act 1977 s.16A, s.126, Sch.5A para.1, Sch.5A para.2. In force: August 7, 2000; £1.50.

This Order, which establishes the Dartford, Gravesham and Swanley Primary Care Trust, as provided for under the National Health Service Act 1977 s.16A, specifies the area for which the trust is established, its operational date and limitations on the exercise of its functions during its preparatory period. In addition, it makes provision for the membership of the trust and for assistance to the trust during its preparatory period.

2922. Primary care trusts – establishment – Daventry and South Northamptonshire

DAVENTRY AND SOUTH NORTHAMPTONSHIRE PRIMARY CARE TRUST (ESTABLISHMENT) ORDER 2000, SI 2000 211; made under the National Health Service Act 1977 s.16A, s.126, Sch.5A para.1, Sch.5A para.2. In force: February 11, 2000; £1.50.

This Order establishes the Daventry and South Northamptonshire Primary Care Trust, specifies the area for which the trust is established, specifies its operational date and limitations on the exercise of its functions during its preparatory period, makes provision for the membership of the trust and provides for assistance to the trust during its preparatory period. It also contains a restriction on the exercise of functions by the trust.

2923. Primary care trusts – establishment – Doncaster

DONCASTER CENTRAL PRIMARY CARE TRUST (ESTABLISHMENT) ORDER 2000, SI 2000 1961; made under the National Health Service Act 1977 s.16A, s.126, Sch.5A para.1, Sch.5A para.2. In force: July 31, 2000; £1.50.

This Order, which establishes the Doncaster Central Primary Care Trust as provided for under the National Health Service Act 1977 s.16A, specifies the area for which the trust is established, its operational date and limitations on the exercise of its functions during its preparatory period. In addition, it makes provision for the membership of the trust and for assistance to the trust during its preparatory period.

2924. Primary care trusts – establishment – Epping Forest

EPPING FOREST PRIMARY CARE TRUST (ESTABLISHMENT) ORDER 2000, SI 2000 287; made under the National Health Service Act 1977 s.16A, s.126, Sch.5A para.1, Sch.5A para.2. In force: February 17, 2000; £1.50.

This Order establishes the Epping Forest Primary Care Trust, specifies the area for which the trust is established, its operational date and limitations on the exercise of its functions during its preparatory period. It makes provision for the membership of the trust and for assistance to the trust during its preparatory period and contains a restriction on the exercise of functions by the trust.

2925. Primary care trusts – establishment – Fenland

FENLAND PRIMARY CARE TRUST (ESTABLISHMENT) ORDER 2000, SI 2000 286; made under the National Health Service Act 1977 s.16A, s.126, Sch.5A para.1, Sch.5A para.2. In force: February 17, 2000; £1.50.

This Order establishes the Fenland Bay Primary Care Trust, specifies the area for which the trust is established, its operational date and limitations on the exercise of its functions during its preparatory period. It makes provision for the membership of the trust and for assistance to the trust during its preparatory period and contains a restriction on the exercise of functions by the trust.

2926. Primary care trusts – establishment – Greater Yardley

GREATER YARDLEY PRIMARY CARE TRUST (ESTABLISHMENT) ORDER 2000, SI 2000 2339; made under the National Health Service Act 1977 s.16A, s.126, Sch.5A para.1, Sch.5A para.2. In force: September 11, 2000; £1.50.

This Order establishes the Greater Yardley Primary Care Trust, as provided for under the National Health Service Act 1977 s.16A, specifies the area for which the trust is established, its operational date and limitations on the exercise of its functions during its preparatory period. In addition, it makes provision for the membership of the trust and for assistance to the trust during its preparatory period.

2927. Primary care trusts – establishment – Harlow

HARLOW PRIMARY CARE TRUST (ESTABLISHMENT) ORDER 2000, SI 2000 2820; made under the National Health Service Act 1977 s.16A, s.126, Sch.5A para.1, Sch.5A para.2. In force: October 21, 2000; £1.75.

This Order establishes the Harlow Primary Care Trust, as provided for under the National Health Service Act 1977 s.16A, specifies the area for which the trust is established, its operational date and limitations on the exercise of its functions during its preparatory period. In addition, it makes provision for the membership of the trust and for assistance to the trust during its preparatory period.

2928. Primary care trusts – establishment – Herefordshire

HEREFORDSHIRE PRIMARY CARE TRUST (ESTABLISHMENT) AMENDMENT ORDER 2000, SI 2000 2553; made under the National Health Service Act 1977 s.16A, s.126. In force: October 2, 2000; £1.00.

This Order amends the Herefordshire Primary Care Trust (Establishment) Order 2000 (SI 2000 1748) by removing the restriction in Art.8 of the Order whereby, in the exercise of functions, the trust shall not provide services directly to patients, other than community health services.

2929. Primary care trusts – establishment – Herefordshire

HEREFORDSHIRE PRIMARY CARE TRUST (ESTABLISHMENT) ORDER 2000, SI 2000 1748; made under the National Health Service Act 1977 s.16A, s.126, Sch.5A para.1, Sch.5A para.2. In force: July 14, 2000; £1.50.

This Order establishes the Herefordshire Primary Care Trust, specifies the area for which the trust is established, its operational date and limitations on the exercise of its functions during its preparatory period. It provides for the membership of the trust, for assistance to the trust during its preparatory period and contains a restriction on the exercise of functions by the trust.

2930. Primary care trusts – establishment – Hertsmere

HERTSMERE PRIMARY CARE TRUST (ESTABLISHMENT) ORDER 2000, SI 2000 1384; made under the National Health Service Act 1977 s.16A, s.126, Sch.5A para.1, Sch.5A para.2. In force: May 29, 2000; £1.50.

This Order establishes the Hertsmere Primary Care Trust, specifies the area for which the trust is established, its operational date and limitations on the exercise of its functions during its preparatory period. It provides for the membership of the trust, for assistance to the trust during its preparatory period and contains a restriction on the exercise of functions by the trust.

2931. Primary care trusts – establishment – Hillingdon

HILLINGDON PRIMARY CARE TRUST (ESTABLISHMENT) ORDER 2000, SI 2000 209; made under the National Health Service Act 1977 s.16A, s.126, Sch.5A para.1, Sch.5A para.2. In force: February 11, 2000; £1.50.

This Order establishes the Hillingdon Primary Care Trust, specifies the area for which the trust is established, specifies its operational date and limitations on the exercise of its functions during its preparatory period, makes provision for the membership of the trust and provides for assistance to the trust during its preparatory period. It also contains a restriction on the exercise of functions by the trust.

2932. Primary care trusts – establishment – Isle of Wight

ISLE OF WIGHT PRIMARY CARE TRUST (ESTABLISHMENT) ORDER 2000, SI 2000 2982; made under the National Health Service Act 1977 s.16A, s.126, Sch.5A para.1, Sch.5A para.2. In force: November 13, 2000; £1.75.

This Order, which establishes the Isle of Wight Primary Care Trust as provided for under the National Health Service Act 1977 s.16A, specifies the area for which the trust is established, its operational date and limitations on the exercise of its functions during its preparatory period. In addition, it makes provision for the membership of the trust and for assistance to the trust during its preparatory period.

2933. Primary care trusts – establishment – Mansfield

MANSFIELD DISTRICT PRIMARY CARE TRUST (ESTABLISHMENT) ORDER 2000, SI 2000 226; made under the National Health Service Act 1977 s.16A, s.126, Sch.5A para.1, Sch.5A para.2. In force: February 11, 2000; £1.50.

This Order establishes the Mansfield District Primary Care Trust, specifies the area for which the trust is established, specifies its operational date and limitations on the exercise of its functions during its preparatory period, makes provision for the membership of the trust and for assistance to the trust during its preparatory period, and contains a restriction on the exercise of functions by the trust.

2934. Primary care trusts – establishment – Milton Keynes

MILTON KEYNES PRIMARY CARE TRUST (ESTABLISHMENT) ORDER 2000, SI 2000 2015; made under the National Health Service Act 1977 s.16A, s.126, Sch.5A para.1, Sch.5A para.2. In force: August 4, 2000; £1.50.

This Order, which establishes the Milton Keynes Primary Care Trust, as provided for under the National Health Service Act 1977 s.16A, specifies the area for which the trust is established, its operational date and limitations on the exercise of its functions during its preparatory period. In addition, it makes provision for the membership of the trust and for assistance to the trust during its preparatory period.

2935. Primary care trusts – establishment – Morecambe Bay

MORECAMBE BAY PRIMARY CARE TRUST (ESTABLISHMENT) ORDER 2000, SI 2000 2392; made under the National Health Service Act 1977 s.16A, s.126, Sch.5A para.1, Sch.5A para.2. In force: September 15, 2000; £1.50.

This Order establishes the Morecambe Bay Primary Care Trust, specifies the area for which the trust is established, specifies its operational date and limitations on the exercise of its functions during its preparatory period, makes provision for the membership of the trust and provides for assistance to the trust during its preparatory period.

2936. Primary care trusts – establishment – Nelson and West Merton

NELSON AND WEST MERTON PRIMARY CARE TRUST (ESTABLISHMENT) ORDER 2000, SI 2000 254; made under the National Health Service Act 1977 s.16A, s.126, Sch.5A para.1, Sch.5A para.2. In force: February 16, 2000; £1.50.

This Order establishes the Nelson and West Merton Primary Care Trust, specifies the area for which the trust is established, its operational date and limitations on the exercise of its functions during its preparatory period. It makes provision for the membership of the trust and for assistance to the trust during its preparatory period and contains a restriction on the exercise of functions by the trust.

2937. Primary care trusts – establishment – Newark and Sherwood

NEWARK AND SHERWOOD PRIMARY CARE TRUST (ESTABLISHMENT) ORDER 2000, SI 2000 223; made under the National Health Service Act 1977 s.16A, s.126, Sch.5A para.1, Sch.5A para.2. In force: February 11, 2000; £1.50.

This Order establishes the Newark and Sherwood Primary Care Trust, specifies the area for which the trust is established, specifies its operational date and limitations on the exercise of its functions during its preparatory period, makes provision for the membership of the trust and for assistance to the trust during its preparatory period, and contains a restriction on the exercise of functions by the trust.

2938. Primary care trusts – establishment – North Bradford

NORTH BRADFORD PRIMARY CARE TRUST (ESTABLISHMENT) ORDER 2000, SI 2000 1944; made under the National Health Service Act 1977 s.16A, s.126, Sch.5A para.1, Sch.5A para.2. In force: July 26, 2000; £1.50.

This Order, which establishes the North Bradford Primary Care Trust as provided for under the National Health Service Act 1977 s.16A, specifies the area for which the trust is established, its operational date and limitations on the exercise of its functions during its preparatory period. In addition, it makes provision for the membership of the trust and for assistance to the trust during its preparatory period.

2939. Primary care trusts – establishment – North Dorset

NORTH DORSET PRIMARY CARE TRUST (ESTABLISHMENT) ORDER 2000, SI 2000 2157; made under the National Health Service Act 1977 s.16A, s.126, Sch.5A para.1, Sch.5A para.2. In force: August 14, 2000; £1.50.

This Order, which establishes the North Dorset Primary Care Trust, as provided for under the National Health Service Act 1977 s.16A, specifies the area for which the trust is established, its operational date and limitations on the exercise of its functions during its preparatory period. In addition, it makes provision for the membership of the trust and for assistance to the trust during its preparatory period.

2940. Primary care trusts – establishment – North East Lincolnshire

NORTH EAST LINCOLNSHIRE PRIMARY CARE TRUST (ESTABLISHMENT) ORDER 2000, SI 2000 219; made under the National Health Service Act 1977 s.16A, s.126, Sch.5A para.1, Sch.5A para.2. In force: February 11, 2000; £1.50.

This Order establishes the North East Lincolnshire Primary Care Trust, specifies the area for which the trust is established, specifies its operational date and limitations on the exercise of its functions during its preparatory period, makes provision for the membership of the trust and provides for assistance to the trust during its preparatory period. It also contains a restriction on the exercise of functions by the trust.

2941. Primary care trusts – establishment – North Hampshire

NORTH HAMPSHIRE PRIMARY CARE TRUST (ESTABLISHMENT) ORDER 2000, SI 2000 2547; made under the National Health Service Act 1977 s.16A, s.126, Sch.5A para.1, Sch.5A para.2. In force: October 1, 2000; £1.50.

This Order establishes the North Hampshire Primary Care Trust as provided for under the National Health Service Act 1977 s.16A. It specifies the area for which the trust is established, its operational date and limitations on the exercise of its functions during its preparatory period. In addition, it makes provision for the membership of the trust and for assistance to the trust during its preparatory period.

2942. Primary care trusts – establishment – North Manchester

NORTH MANCHESTER PRIMARY CARE TRUST (ESTABLISHMENT) ORDER 2000, SI 2000 1964; made under the National Health Service Act 1977 s.16A, s.126, Sch.5A para.1, Sch.5A para.2. In force: July 31, 2000; £1.50.

This Order, which establishes the North Manchester Primary Care Trust as provided for under the National Health Service Act 1977 s.16A, specifies the area for which the trust is established, its operational date and limitations on the exercise of its functions during its preparatory period. In addition, it makes provision for the membership of the trust and for assistance to the trust during its preparatory period.

2943. Primary care trusts – establishment – North Peterborough

NORTH PETERBOROUGH PRIMARY CARE TRUST (ESTABLISHMENT) AMENDMENT ORDER 2000, SI 2000 877; made under the National Health Service Act 1977 s.16A, s.126, Sch.5A para.1, Sch.5A para.2. In force: April 4, 2000; £1.00.

This Order amends the North Peterborough Primary Care Trust (Establishment) Order 2000 (SI 2000 283) to add areas omitted in error from that Order.

2944. Primary care trusts – establishment – North Peterborough

NORTH PETERBOROUGH PRIMARY CARE TRUST (ESTABLISHMENT) ORDER 2000, SI 2000 283; made under the National Health Service Act 1977 s.16A, s.126, Sch.5A para.1, Sch.5A para.2. In force: February 17, 2000; £1.50.

This Order establishes the North Peterborough Primary Care Trust, specifies the area for which the trust is established, its operational date and limitations on the exercise of its functions during its preparatory period. It makes provision for the membership of the trust and for assistance to the trust during its preparatory period and contains a restriction on the exercise of functions by the trust.

2945. Primary care trusts – establishment – North Stoke

NORTH STOKE PRIMARY CARE TRUST (ESTABLISHMENT) ORDER 2000, SI 2000 2014; made under the National Health Service Act 1977 s.16A, s.126, Sch.5A para.1, Sch.5A para.2. In force: August 4, 2000; £1.50.

This Order, which establishes the North Stoke Primary Care Trust, as provided for under the National Health Service Act 1977 s.16A, specifies the area for which the trust is established, its operational date and limitations on the exercise of its functions during its preparatory period. In addition, it makes provision for the membership of the trust and for assistance to the trust during its preparatory period.

2946. Primary care trusts – establishment – Poole Bay

POOLE BAY PRIMARY CARE TRUST (ESTABLISHMENT) ORDER 2000, SI 2000 255; made under the National Health Service Act 1977 s.16A, s.126, Sch.5A para.1, Sch.5A para.2. In force: February 16, 2000; £1.50.

This Order establishes the Poole Bay Primary Care Trust, specifies the area for which the trust is established, its operational date and limitations on the exercise of its functions during its preparatory period. It makes provision for the membership of the trust and for assistance to the trust during its preparatory period and contains a restriction on the exercise of functions by the trust.

2947. Primary care trusts – establishment – Poole Central and North

POOLE CENTRAL AND NORTH PRIMARY CARE TRUST (ESTABLISHMENT) ORDER 2000, SI 2000 256; made under the National Health Service Act 1977 s.16A, s.126, Sch.5A para.1, Sch.5A para.2. In force: February 16, 2000; £1.50.

This Order establishes the Poole Central and North Primary Care Trust, specifies the area for which the trust is established, its operational date and limitations on the exercise of its functions during its preparatory period. It makes provision for the membership of the trust and for assistance to the trust during its preparatory period and contains a restriction on the exercise of functions by the trust.

2948. Primary care trusts – establishment – South Hams and West Devon

SOUTH HAMS AND WEST DEVON PRIMARY CARE TRUST (ESTABLISHMENT) ORDER 2000, SI 2000 2156; made under the National Health Service Act 1977 s.16A, s.126, Sch.5A para.1, Sch.5A para.2. In force: August 14, 2000; £1.50.

This Order, which establishes the South Hams and West Devon Primary Care Trust as provided for under the National Health Service Act 1977 s.16A, specifies the area for which the trust is established, its operational date and limitations on the exercise of its functions during its preparatory period. In addition, it makes provision for the membership of the trust and for assistance to the trust during its preparatory period.

2949. Primary care trusts – establishment – South Manchester

SOUTH MANCHESTER PRIMARY CARE TRUST (ESTABLISHMENT) AMENDMENT ORDER 2000, SI 2000 2576; made under the National Health Service Act 1977 s.16A, s.126. In force: October 1, 2000; £1.00.

This Order amends the South Manchester Primary Care Trust (Establishment) Order 2000 (SI 2000 210) by removing the restriction in Art.8 concerning the provision of services directly to patients and by adding another electoral ward to the area for which the primary care trust is established.

2950. Primary care trusts – establishment – South Manchester

SOUTH MANCHESTER PRIMARY CARE TRUST (ESTABLISHMENT) ORDER 2000, SI 2000 210; made under the National Health Service Act 1977 s.16A, s.126, Sch.5A para.1, Sch.5A para.2. In force: February 11, 2000; £1.50.

This Order establishes the South Manchester Primary Care Trust, specifies the area for which the trust is established, specifies its operational date and limitations on the exercise of its functions during its preparatory period, makes provision for the membership of the trust and provides for assistance to the trust during its preparatory period. It also contains a restriction on the exercise of functions by the trust.

2951. Primary care trusts – establishment – South Peterborough

SOUTH PETERBOROUGH PRIMARY CARE TRUST (ESTABLISHMENT) AMENDMENT ORDER 2000, SI 2000 876; made under the National Health Service Act 1977 s.16A, s.126, Sch.5A para.1, Sch.5A para.2. In force: April 4, 2000; £1.00.

This Order amends the South Peterborough Primary Care Trust (Establishment) Order 2000 (SI 2000 284) to add areas omitted in error from that Order.

2952. Primary care trusts – establishment – South Peterborough

SOUTH PETERBOROUGH PRIMARY CARE TRUST (ESTABLISHMENT) ORDER 2000, SI 2000 284; made under the National Health Service Act 1977 s.16A, s.126, Sch.5A para.1, Sch.5A para.2. In force: February 17, 2000; £1.50.

This Order establishes the South Peterborough Primary Care Trust, specifies the area for which the trust is established, its operational date and limitations on the exercise of its functions during its preparatory period. It makes provision for the membership of the trust and for assistance to the trust during its preparatory period and contains a restriction on the exercise of functions by the trust.

2953. Primary care trusts – establishment – Southampton East

SOUTHAMPTON EAST HEALTHCARE PRIMARY CARE TRUST (ESTABLISHMENT) ORDER 2000, SI 2000 257; made under the National Health Service Act 1977 s.16A, s.126, Sch.5A para.1, Sch.5A para.2. In force: February 16, 2000; £1.50.

This Order establishes the Southampton East Healthcare Primary Care Trust, specifies the area for which the trust is established, its operational date and limitations on the exercise of its functions during its preparatory period. It makes provision for the membership of the trust and for assistance to the trust during its preparatory period and contains a restriction on the exercise of functions by the trust.

2954. Primary care trusts – establishment – Southend on Sea

SOUTHEND ON SEA PRIMARY CARE TRUST (ESTABLISHMENT) ORDER 2000, SI 2000 307; made under the National Health Service Act 1977 s.16A, s.126, Sch.5A para.1, Sch.5A para.2. In force: February 18, 2000; £1.50.

This Order establishes the Southend on Sea Primary Care Trust, specifies the area for which the trust is established, its operational date and limitations on the exercise of its functions during its preparatory period. It also makes provision for the membership of the trust and for assistance to the trust during its preparatory period. It also contains a restriction on the exercise of functions by the trust.

2955. Primary care trusts – establishment – Sunderland West

SUNDERLAND WEST PRIMARY CARE TRUST (ESTABLISHMENT) ORDER 2000, SI 2000 2042; made under the National Health Service Act 1977 s.16A, s.126, Sch.5A para.1, Sch.5A para.2. In force: August 7, 2000; £1.50.

This Order, which establishes the Sunderland West Primary Care Trust, as provided for under the National Health Service Act 1977 s.16A, specifies the area for which the trust is established, its operational date and limitations on the exercise of its functions during its preparatory period. In addition, it makes provision for the membership of the trust and for assistance to the trust during its preparatory period. It also contains a restriction on the exercise of functions by the trust.

2956. Primary care trusts – establishment – Tendring

TENDRING PRIMARY CARE TRUST (ESTABLISHMENT) ORDER 2000, SI 2000 285; made under the National Health Service Act 1977 s.16A, s.126, Sch.5A para.1, Sch.5A para.2. In force: February 17, 2000; £1.50.

This Order establishes the Tendring Primary Care Trust, specifies the area for which the trust is established, its operational date and limitations on the exercise of its functions during its preparatory period. It makes provision for the membership of the trust and for assistance to the trust during its preparatory period and contains a restriction on the exercise of functions by the trust.

2957. Primary care trusts – establishment – Torbay

TORBAY PRIMARY CARE TRUST (ESTABLISHMENT) ORDER 2000, SI 2000 2154; made under the National Health Service Act 1977 s.16A, s.126, Sch.5A para.1, Sch.5A para.2. In force: August 14, 2000; £1.50.

This Order, which establishes the Torbay Primary Care Trust as provided for under the National Health Service Act 1977 s.16A, specifies the area for which the trust is established, its operational date and limitations on the exercise of its functions during its preparatory period. In addition, it makes provision for the membership of the trust, assistance to the trust during its preparatory period and a restriction on the exercise of functions by the trust.

2958. Primary care trusts – establishment – Trafford South

TRAFFORD SOUTH PRIMARY CARE TRUST (ESTABLISHMENT) ORDER 2000, SI 2000 1168; made under the National Health Service Act 1977 s.16A, s.126, Sch.5A para.1, Sch.5A para.2. In force: May 1, 2000; £1.50.

This Order establishes the Trafford South Primary Care Trust, specifies the area for which the trust is established, its operational date and limitations on the exercise of its functions during its preparatory period. It provides for the membership of the trust, for assistance to the trust during its preparatory period and contains a restriction on the exercise of functions by the trust.

2959. Primary care trusts – establishment – West Norfolk

WEST NORFOLK PRIMARY CARE TRUST (ESTABLISHMENT) ORDER 2000, SI 2000 1718; made under the National Health Service Act 1977 s.16A, s.126, Sch.5A para.1, Sch.5A para.2. In force: July 7, 2000; £1.50.

This Order establishes the West Norfolk Primary Care Trust and specifies the area for which the trust is established, its operational date and limitations on the exercise of its functions during its preparatory period. It provides for the membership of the trust, for assistance to the trust during its preparatory period and contains a restriction on the exercise of functions by the trust.

2960. Radiation – medical exposure – health protection

IONISING RADIATION (MEDICAL EXPOSURE) REGULATIONS 2000, SI 2000 1059; made under the European Communities Act 1972 s.2. In force: Reg.4 (1) (2): May 13, 2000; remainder: January 1, 2000; £3.00.

These Regulations, together with the Ionising Radiations Regulations 1999 (SI 1999 3232), partially implement Council Directive 97/43 ([1997] OJ L180/22) laying down basic measures for the health protection of individuals against dangers of ionising radiation in relation to medical exposure. They impose duties on those responsible for administering ionising radiation to protect persons undergoing medical exposure whether as part of their own medical diagnosis or treatment or as part of occupational health surveillance, health screening or voluntary participation in research or medico legal procedures.

2961. Surgical procedures – right to life – children's welfare – separation of conjoined twins

See HUMAN RIGHTS: A (Children) (Conjoined Twins: Medical Treatment) (No.1), *Re.* §3246

2962. Wardship – medical treatment – termination – withdrawal of artificial nutrition resulting in death permitted – right to life implied right to die naturally

[Irish Constitution Art.40.3.1, Art.40.3.2.]

The ward had suffered severe brain damage during the course of routine surgery 23 years ago, when aged 22. She was completely dependent on others. She had been fed through a naso gastric tube which she had dislodged many times and then, as from 1992, through a gastrostomy tube. She appeared to recognise certain people, follow them with her eyes and, possibly, react to noise. In March 1995 her family applied for an order that the artificial nutrition and hydration be withdrawn, arguing that it was the prerogative of her family to determine whether the life supporting artificial feeding should be maintained or withdrawn. The High Court granted the application on the grounds that the patient was virtually a PVS victim, that her condition would not improve, that she would not want to continue in her present state if she had expressed any views on the subject, and that in the absence of such views her family was entitled to determine what her best interests were from the standpoint of a good, prudent and loving parent. The Attorney General and the institution caring for the ward appealed against the decision on the grounds that (1) the judge had failed to take into account the Irish Constitution Art.40.3.1, which guaranteed the personal rights of the citizen and Art.40.3.2, which protected the life, person, good name and property rights of every citizen; (2) the best interests test applied more properly to terminally ill patients rather than those who were chronically ill, and (3) the judge had erred in holding that artificially feeding the patient constituted medical treatment.

Held, dismissing the appeal (Egan, J. dissenting), that the invocation of wardship proceedings meant that the court was required to determine all issues pertaining to the ward under its parens patriae jurisdiction. The court could have regard to the wishes of the family but was not bound by them. The question for the court was not whether life should be terminated but whether, under the law and constitution, artificial feeding and antibiotic treatment should be withdrawn with death resulting shortly thereafter. The nature of the right to life, which was guaranteed by the Constitution, imposed a strong presumption in favour of taking all steps to preserve it, save in exceptional circumstances. However, since the process of dying was a necessary part of life, the right to life implied a right also to die naturally rather than have life prolonged by artificial means. It did not include a right to terminate life prematurely. The right to bodily integrity, privacy and self determination implied a right to refuse medical treatment, notwithstanding that death would result. The provision of nutrition through a gastrostomy tube was intrusive and did not amount to medical treatment; it could not be regarded as normal even though it had lasted for a long time. Since the withdrawal of nutrition would result in the ward's death, she had to be regarded as terminally ill. The ward was entitled to have her constitutional rights respected and defended even though she was incapable of exercising any independent judgment. The manner in which those rights should be exercised was a matter for the court, which would take into account the views of the family, whose decision had been taken after consultation with medical, legal and theological advisers. The judge had taken into account the proper interests of the ward from the point of view of a prudent, loving and good parent in deciding that artificial nutrition should be withdrawn with the result that she was permitted to die. The cause of death would be the injuries sustained in 1972. Each case was special and to be determined on its own particular facts.

WARD OF COURT (WITHHOLDING MEDICAL TREATMENT), *Re* (1999) 50 B.M.L.R. 140, Hamilton, C.J., Sup Ct (Irl).

2963. Publications

Coombes; Hendrick – Law and Ethics in Health Care. Paperback: £17.50. ISBN 0-7487-3321-3. Stanley Thornes.

Davison, Judith Ann – Legal and Ethical Considerations for Dental Hygienists and Assistants. Paperback: £19.95. ISBN 1-55664-422-1. Mosby.

Francis, Robert; Johnston, Christopher – Medical Treatment Decisions and the Law. Paperback: £47.50. ISBN 0-406-90490-1. Butterworths Law.

Freeman, Michael; Lewis, Andrew – Law and Medicine. Current Legal Issues, Vol 3. Hardback: £70.00. ISBN 0-19-829918-4. Oxford University Press.

Gunning, Jennifer – Assisted Conception: Research, Ethics and Law. Hardback: £50.00. ISBN 0-7546-2149-9. Ashgate Publishing Limited.

Hare, John; Greenaway, Heather – Obstetrics for Lawyers. Medico-legal Practitioner. Hardback: £39.95. ISBN 1-85941-598-9. Cavendish Publishing Ltd.

Holburn, Colin; Solon, Mark; Bond, Catherine; Burn, Suzanne – Healthcare Professionals As Witnesses to the Court. Hardback: £24.50. ISBN 1-900151-22-7. Greenwich Medical Media.

Kennedy, Ian; Grubb, Andrew – Medical Law-text with Materials. 3rd Ed. Paperback: £38.00. ISBN 0-406-90325-5. Butterworths.

Peacock, Nicolas; Foster, Charles – Clinical Confidentiality. Hardback: £45.00. ISBN 1-87124-151-0. Monitor Press.

Richards, Margaret – Community Care for Older People. 2nd Ed. Paperback: £40.00. ISBN 0-85308-468-8. Jordans.

Tweedale, Geoffrey – Magic Mineral to Killer Dust: Turner & Newall and the Asbestos Hazard. Hardback: £40.00. ISBN 0-19-829690-8. Oxford University Press.

HEALTH AND SAFETY AT WORK

2964. Chemicals – occupational exposure limit – Commission Directive

Commission Directive 2000/39 of June 8, 2000 establishing a first list of indicative occupational exposure limit values in implementation of Council Directive 98/24 on the protection of the health and safety of workers from the risks related to chemical agents at work. [2000] OJ L142/47.

2965. Construction industry – design regulations

CONSTRUCTION (DESIGN AND MANAGEMENT) (AMENDMENT) REGULATIONS 2000, SI 2000 2380; made under the Health and Safety at Work etc. Act 1974 s.15. In force: October 2, 2000; £1.50.

These Regulations amend the Construction (Design and Management) Regulations 1994 (SI 1994 3140) by substituting a new definition of "designer";

providing that any reference to a person preparing a design shall include a reference to his employee or other person under his control preparing it for him; and providing that the requirement on designers in Reg.13(1) does not apply to an employer who supplies his employee to a designer.

2966. Construction industry – vicarious liability of danger – application of design regulations – personal injuries

[Health and Safety at Work etc. Act 1974 s.33(1)(c); Construction (Design and Management) Regulations 1994 (SI 1994 3140) Reg.2(2)(b)(iv), Reg.13(2)(a).]

A workman was fatally injured when a conveyor, which was part of the plant PW had contracted to install at Port Talbot Steel Works fell and crushed him. PW had contracted F to provide construction drawings of its design and to manufacture it, and F had contracted the manufacture to U. Due to faulty drawings, the latching devices of the conveyor did not incorporate a locking or securing pin, the absence of which caused the accident. PW was convicted for contravention of the Construction (Design and Management) Regulations 1994 Reg.13(2)(a), contrary to the Health and Safety at Work etc. Act 1974 s.33(1)(c) and fined £60,000. PW appealed.

Held, allowing the appeal, that the case did not fall within the Regulations as those applied only to a designer who "prepares a design" which PW had not. To own, to arrange to have prepared, or to approve a design was not enough. Further there could be no finding of vicarious liability as, under the meaning of Reg.2(2)(b)(iv), PW had not arranged for a party under his control to prepare a design. The fact that he had not objected to F arranging for U to prepare the design was insufficient to establish such a finding.

R. v. PAUL WURTH SA [2000] I.C.R. 860, Pill, L.J., CA (Crim Div).

2967. Employers liability – accidents – floors – slippery surface – strict liability

[Workplace (Health, Safety and Welfare) Regulations 1992 (SI 1992 3004) Reg.12.]

D, who was employed by G as a customer service agent, slipped on vinyl floor tiles in G's warehouse suffering serious comminuted fractures to her right hip and leg. D contended that the floor was slippery and this evidence was supported by the ambulance paramedics who attended to take her to hospital. There was no allegation that there was any water or anything transient on the surface to cause the slip. G's managers gave evidence that no one else had ever slipped on the floor, many other employees walked over the floor each day and that on the day of the accident the floor was not slippery when tested by the manager herself. Two expert engineers inspected the floor and tested its coefficient of friction 12 to 18 months after the accident, both concluding that the floor was suitable when dry. D's expert advised that the slip resistance of the floor was satisfactory in general, although it was variable across the floor and in patches it was below the BS recommended standard of 0.40. G's expert asserted that no patches were below standard. The experts agreed that poor cleaning technique could reduce the floor's slip resistance but there was little direct evidence of any particular failure in that cleaning regime.

Held, giving judgment for the claimant, that (1) the Workplace (Health, Safety and Welfare) Regulations 1992 Reg.12(1) and Reg.12(2) imposed strict liability on the employer. This was to be contrasted with Reg.12(3) which imposed a qualified duty where there was water or oil or some other slippery substance on the floor for which the employer only had to exercise such case as was reasonably practicable, and (2) the floor was slippery and caused the fall, accepting D's evidence and that of D's expert. Hence the employers were liable under the strict provision of the Regulations. It was not necessary to prove fault on the defendant's part for liability to follow.

DRAGE v. GRASSROOTS LTD, September 5, 2000, Judge Viljoen, CC (Watford). [*Ex rel.* Andrew Ritchie, Barrister, 9 Gough Square, London].

2968. Employers liability – fatal accidents – obvious forseeable and continuing risk

[Health and Safety at Work Act 1974.]

R, a company, had pleaded guilty before a magistrates' court to failing to discharge its duty to ensure the health, safety and welfare at work of all its employees, contrary to the Health and Safety at Work Act 1974. R was committed to the Crown Court for sentence. A 19 year old trainee who was working at the premises of the company fell through a suspended ceiling at one of the units, a distance of about 9 feet, and died from head injuries which he received. The deceased had apparently climbed on to the ceilings which were not designed to be load-bearing in order to remove some piping. He had not been told of the dangers which would arise if he went on to the ceilings. R was ordered to pay a fine of £60,000 and £9,273 prosecution costs.

Held, dismissing the appeal, that the fault of the company was in failing to realise that employees might have to obtain access to the ceiling areas over offices in order to place on them items for storage, forgetting that those areas were not weight-bearing. That was a risk that was obvious, foreseeable and continuing. It was serious in that if there should be a fall through the ceiling to the floor below, death was distinctly possible. Where death resulted from a criminal act, that was an aggravating feature of the offence. The penalty should reflect public disquiet at the unnecessary loss of life and the concern that penalties in some similar cases had been too low. The sentencer had taken into account the company's prompt admission of responsibility reflected in the plea of guilty, the company's good safety record and the fact that steps had been taken promptly to remedy the deficiency. The Court had had regard to the accounts of the company. They showed that the company could well afford both fine and costs. The objective of the prosecution of health and safety offences in the workplace was to achieve a safe environment for those who worked there and for other members of the public who might be affected. A fine needed to be large enough to bring the message home, where the defendant was a company, not only to those who managed it but also to its shareholders. The fine had therefore been fixed at the right level. *R. v. F Howe & Son (Engineers) Ltd* [1999] 2 All E.R. 249, [1998] C.L.Y. 2839 considered.

R. v. RIMAC LTD [2000] 1 Cr. App. R. (S.) 468, Brian Smedley, J., CA (Crim Div).

2969. Employers liability – hearing impairment – requisite date of knowledge of noise induced deafness

K, a bus driver, claimed damages against S for noise-induced hearing loss, allegedly caused by his having driven a Leyland double decker bus, PD3, with a large diesel engine in proximity to the drivers compartment, over a period of up to six hours during the relevant periods. K contended that the relevant date that S should have had requisite knowledge of the dangers of noise induced deafness was 1962, when "Noise and the Worker" was published by the Ministry of Labour. S contended that this document related only to factories and, in any event, there was nothing within it that should have put them on notice of potential deafness problems for drivers of PD3's.

Held, giving judgment for S, that there was no evidence of complaints in the possession of S at the time the 1962 document was published which would have prompted them to consider that its bus drivers in general, or bus drivers of PD3's in particular, were being exposed to potentially damaging levels of sound. S's requisite knowledge could therefore not pre-date the 1972 codes.

KILL v. SUSSEX COASTLINE BUSES LTD, January 28, 2000, Judge Rudd, CC (Southampton). [*Ex rel.* DLA & Partners, Solicitors, Fountain Precinct, Balm Green, Sheffield].

2970. Employers liability – nurse hit by trolley – applicability of Manual Handling Operations Regulations 1992

[Manual Handling Operations Regulations 1992 (SI 1992 2793) Reg.4(1) (b).]

P was employed as a nurse in the accident and emergency department when a patient collapsed in the waiting area and was placed on a hospital trolley. P was standing by the right side of the trolley towards the foot, but was not actually holding or pulling it. Another nurse, A, pulled the trolley from the front and towards the left, so that the rear of the trolley swung to the right and struck P thereby causing him a back injury. P claimed damages for negligence and for breach of statutory duty, namely the Manual Handling Operations Regulations 1992 Reg.4(1)(b)(i) and Reg.4(1)(b)(ii). N contended that the Regulations were inapplicable because the duty imposed by them on an employer was owed only to an employee who was carrying out an operation in respect of injuries which he or she may suffer whilst doing so, and in the instant case they could not be invoked by P because the manual handling operation was being carried out by A and not P.

Held, giving judgment for N, that (1) the Regulations were applicable. They should not be read in the restricted sense for which N contended, as to do so would, in the instant case, involve treating what was in reality a single operation as though it consisted of artificially distinct component parts, namely getting the patient on to the floor, lifting him on to the trolley, moving the trolley. Further, each nurse would be regarded as being involved for the purposes of the Regulations only at those moments when he or she was physically active in handling the load; (2) N was not in breach of Reg.4(1)(b)(i) and Reg.4(1)(b)(ii). A suitable and sufficient risk assessment would not have recognised the risk of injury to one nurse from the pulling of a trolley by another, nor would steps to reduce the risk have involved giving instructions which should have led A to pull the trolley forward rather than to the left or to tell the other nurses that she was about to move, *Koonjul v. Thameslink Healthcare Services* [2000] P.I.Q.R. P123, [2000] C.L.Y. 2983 applied.

POSTLE v. NORFOLK AND NORWICH NHS HEALTHCARE TRUST, September 19, 2000, Judge Langan Q.C., CC (Norwich). [*Ex rel.* Nicholas Yell, Barrister, No.1 Sergeants' Inn, Fleet Street, London].

2971. Employers liability – police officers – training – removal of protester single handedly

[Manual Handling Operations Regulations 1992 (SI 1992 2793); Council Directive 90/269 on the minimum health and safety requirements for the manual handling of loads.]

P, a police officer, claimed damages for injuries sustained when he attempted to move a person who was taking part in a peaceful protest at a power station. All officers at the site had been instructed by the senior officer to physically remove any protesters sitting in the road. As the protesters outnumbered the officers, P attempted to remove the sitting protester on his own and in so doing injured his back. P contended that CC was in breach of Council Directive 90/269, as implemented by the Manual Handling Operations Regulations 1992, and liable in negligence in relation to the instruction given and the lack of training.

Held, giving judgment for P, that Directive 90/269 applied to CC as an emanation of the State. The provisions of the Directive were directly effective even though CC did not employ the officers. The Directive was intended to have a wide effect and to apply in favour of all kinds of workers who were effectively controlled when on duty and acting under the instruction of other senior workers. There was a breach of the Directive in that P was allowed to lift on his own, or more specifically not instructed to lift only with a fellow officer, and had not received any training about lifting in such circumstances. There was also a breach of the common law duty of care in respect of training and instruction.

PECK v. CHIEF CONSTABLE OF AVON AND SOMERSET, May 18, 1999, Recorder Harrop, CC (Bristol). [*Ex rel.* Russell Jones & Walker, Solicitors, 15 Clare Street, Bristol].

2972. Equipment – employers duties – absolute duty to ensure efficient state of work equipment

[Provision and Use of Work Equipment Regulations 1992 (SI 1992 2932) Reg.6.]

C, a production operator, was employed by VM when he sustained a painful soft tissue jolting injury to his lower back. At that time he was operating a work handler and pneumatic work equipment which was being used to manoeuvre a strut into position, which expelled air and suddenly dropped. C was pulled forward and downwards and he thereby sustained injury. C brought proceedings against VM for damages and liability was denied throughout. C contended that VM were in breach of the Provision and Use of Work Equipment Regulations 1992 Reg.6, that it negligently failed to ensure that the work handler was maintained in an efficient state, in efficient working order and in good repair and further that VM had failed to provide C with safe plant and equipment. C contended that Reg. 6 imposed an absolute duty on VM, *Stark v. Post Office The Times*, March 29, 2000, [2000] C.L.Y. 2973 cited.

Held, giving judgment for C, that Reg. 6(i) imposed an absolute obligation on employers to ensure that work equipment was maintained in an efficient state, in efficient working order and in good repair. Arguments raised by VM on the issue of "reasonableness" of their system of inspection or maintenance were found to be irrelevant.

CADGER v. VAUXHALL MOTORS LTD, March 28, 2000, Judge Rylands, CC (Central London). [*Ex rel.* Rowley Ashworth Solicitors, 247 The Broadway, Wimbledon, London].

2973. Equipment – employers duties – absolute duty to maintain in working order – stricter approach than under EC law

[Provision and Use of Work Equipment Regulations 1992 (SI 1992 2932) Reg.6(1); Council Directive 89/655 concerning the minimum safety and health requirements for the use of work equipment by workers at work.]

S, a postman, was injured when the stirrup on the front brake of his delivery bicycle broke. S's claim for damages for personal injuries was dismissed and S appealed, contending that there was an absolute obligation on the employer under the Provision and Use of Work Equipment Regulations 1992 Reg.6(1) to ensure the safe and efficient operation of all equipment. Moreover, it was argued that Council Directive 89/655 was concerned to set a minimum standard and did not prevent member states from putting in place more stringent requirements.

Held, allowing the appeal, that Reg.6(1) imposed an absolute obligation and as the bicycle was not in an efficient working order when the brake broke, the post office was in breach of its absolute duty under the Regulations. The Directive set a minimum standard in terms of the duty of employers to ensure the health and safety of workers but Member States were free to adopt a stricter approach.

STARK v. POST OFFICE [2000] I.C.R. 1013, Waller, L.J., CA.

2974. Equipment – pressure systems

PRESSURE SYSTEMS SAFETY REGULATIONS 2000, SI 2000 128; made under the Health and Safety at Work etc. Act 1974 s.15, s.47, s.82, Sch.3 para.1, Sch.3 para.14, Sch.3 para.15, Sch.3 para.16. In force: February 21, 2000; £3.00.

These Regulations revoke and re-enact, with amendments, the Pressure Systems and Transportable Gas Containers Regulations 1989 (SI 1989 2169) which imposed safety requirements with respect to pressure systems which are used or intended to be used at work. They also imposed safety requirements to prevent certain vessels from becoming pressurised. Changes made by these Regulations include the modification and extension of provisions for sending, keeping and passing on in electronic form reports of examinations.

2975. Genetically modified organisms – contained use – health, safety and environmental protection

GENETICALLY MODIFIED ORGANISMS (CONTAINED USE) REGULATIONS 2000, SI 2000 2831; made under the European Communities Act 1972 s.2; and the Health and Safety at Work etc. Act 1974 s.15, s.43, s.52, s.82, Sch.3 para.1, Sch.3 para.4, Sch.3 para.5, Sch.3 para.6, Sch.3 para.8, Sch.3 para.9, Sch.3 para.11, Sch.3 para.13, Sch.3 para.14, Sch.3 para.15, Sch.3 para.16, Sch.3 para.20. In force: November 15, 2000; £6.50.

These Regulations, which implement, as respects Great Britain, Council Directive 90/219 ([1990] OJ L117/1) on the contained use of genetically modified micro organisms as amended by Commission Directive 94/51 ([1994] OJ L297/29) and Council Directive 98/81 ([1998] OJ L330/13), aim to protect persons and the environment from risks arising from activities involving the contained use of genetically modified micro organisms and genetically modified organisms which are not micro organisms. In particular, they provide that any activity involving genetic modification of micro organisms, or organisms other than micro organisms, is prohibited unless the person intending to undertake the activity in question has ensured that an assessment of the risks created by that activity to human health and the environment has been carried out; a person who carries out such an assessment must establish a safety committee to advise him; and no person shall use premises for the first time for the purpose of undertaking an activity involving genetic modification unless he has notified the competent authority. The Genetically Modified Organisms (Contained Use) Regulations 1992 (SI 1992 3217 as amended) are revoked and replaced.

2976. Hazardous substances – batteries and accumulators

BATTERIES AND ACCUMULATORS (CONTAINING DANGEROUS SUBSTANCES) (AMENDMENT) REGULATIONS 2000, SI 2000 3097; made under the European Communities Act 1972 s.2. In force: December 18, 2000; £1.75.

These Regulations implement Commission Directive 98/101 ([1999] OJ L1/1) which amends Council Directive 91/157 ([1991] OJ L78/38) on batteries and accumulators containing certain dangerous substances. They amend the Batteries and Accumulators (Containing Dangerous Substances) Regulations 1994 (SI 1994 232) to apply to batteries and accumulators put on the market as from January 1, 1999, containing more than 0.0005 per cent of mercury by weight and batteries and accumulators put on the market as from September 18, 1992, containing more than 25mg of mercury per cell, except alkaline manganese batteries, more than 0.025 per cent of cadmium by weight, more than 0.4 per cent of lead by weight and alkaline manganese batteries containing more than 0.025 per cent of mercury by weight.

2977. Hazardous substances – controls – Council Directive

European Parliament and Council Directive 2000/54 of September 18, 2000 on the protection of workers from risks related to exposure to biological agents at work (seventh individual directive within the meaning of Art.16(1) of Directive 89/391). [2000] OJ L262/21.

2978. Health and Safety Executive – fees

HEALTH AND SAFETY (FEES) REGULATIONS 2000, SI 2000 2482; made under the European Communities Act 1972 s.2; and the Health and Safety at Work etc. Act 1974 s.43, s.82. In force: October 10, 2000; £4.50.

These Regulations revoke and replace the Health and Safety (Fees) Regulations 1999 (SI 1999 645 as amended). They fix or determine the fees payable by an applicant to the Health and Safety Executive in respect of miscellaneous applications, including an approval under mines and quarries legislation, approval of certain respiratory protective equipment, and approvals in respect of explosives, dangerous substances, agriculture and freight legislation. In addition, they fix or determine the fees payable by specified persons in the offshore, rail and gas industries for the performance by the Executive of the functions specified in those provisions; update the fees to be paid in respect of medical examinations and surveillance by an employment medical adviser which are required under certain of the relevant statutory provisions; and update maximum fees which may be charged under the Explosives Act 1875, the Petroleum (Consolidation) Act 1928 and the Petroleum (Transfer of Licences) Act 1936.

2979. Occupational health – clothes – changing facilities for male and female employees – categorisation of uniform as "special clothing"

[Health and Safety at Work Act 1974 s.21; Workplace (Health, Safety and Welfare) Regulations 1992 (SI 1992 3004) Reg.24.]

F, an Environmental Health Officer, served a notice on PO under the Health and Safety at Work Act 1974 s.21 in relation to one of its delivery offices. The notice required works to be carried out to provide separate changing facilities for male and female employees. The notice was upheld by an employment tribunal, and PO appealed, arguing that the uniform did not constitute "special clothing" within the Workplace (Health, Safety and Welfare) Regulations 1992 Reg.24 as it was worn to and from work by some employees, and that separate facilities were available as women could change in the women's toilets.

Held, dismissing the appeal, that the tribunal had not erred and their decision was not *Wednesbury* unreasonable. They were entitled to find that the fact that employees were required to wear uniforms at work and could choose to wear them to or from work did not put the uniform outside the definition within Reg.24. They were equally entitled to find that the need for privacy dictated that women employees should be allowed facilities which did not require them to undress in front of other women, and that the current facilities were therefore unsuitable.

POST OFFICE v. FOOTITT [2000] I.R.L.R. 243, Ognall, J., QBD.

2980. Occupational health – diseases and disorders – asthma – criteria for identifying occupational cause

B, a theatre nurse who suffered from asthma, sought damages from her employer, NMH on the basis that her asthma, which she developed in 1995, was caused by exposure at work to a substance known as Glutaraldehyde or Cidex. The issues were (1) whether B was exposed to a risk of injury from the Cidex fumes, and (2) whether the cause of her asthma was occupational or constitutional. B's symptoms had worsened, until she eventually retired on health grounds. NMH resisted B's claim on the grounds that there had been a time lapse of 20 years between her exposure to Cidex and the onset of her symptoms, and that late onset asthma, triggered by an upper respiratory tract infection, was a more likely explanation for the condition.

Held, finding in favour of B, that she had satisfied all the criteria for a diagnosis of occupational disease, in that (1) she had been exposed to a sensitising agent; (2) her condition had improved when away from work; (3) there had been prompt recurrence on re exposure, and (4) there was a time lag between the start of exposure and the onset of symptoms. There was no clear evidence that B had suffered from a chest infection in March 1995, hence NMH's submission remained unsupported, and B had therefore established her case on a balance of probabilities.

BROBBEY v. NORTH MANCHESTER HEALTHCARE NHS TRUST, March 22, 2000, Judge Holman, CC (Manchester). [*Ex rel.* Thompsons Solicitors, Acresfield, 8 Exchange Street, Manchester].

2981. Risk assessment – accidents – duty to provide guidance under Manual Handling Regulations

[Manual Handling Regulations 1992 (SI 1992 2793) Reg.4(1)(b).]

S, an experienced production fitter, instituted a claim for damages against his employer, DM, following a crush injury to his right hand. The injury had been caused by the unexpectedly heavy weight of a roller as S stripped down a newly delivered conveyer. The court at first instance held that S had been engaged in the assessment process required by the Manual Handling Regulations 1992 Reg.4(1)(b)(i) and that in consequence the obligation upon DM, as employer, to provide guidance under Reg.4(1)(b)(iii) did not arise. S appealed, contending that (1) he had not been engaged in an assessment process, and (2) the fact that an employer had been in breach of its obligation to carry out an assessment should not enable it to escape liability for a failure to provide guidance under Reg.4(1)(b)(iii) despite the apparent absence of any culpability under Reg.4(1)(b)(i). DM maintained that the obligation to provide guidance would only arise if an assessment under Reg.4(1)(b)(i) would identify a risk of injury.

Held, allowing the appeal, that (1) S had not been engaged in the statutory assessment process but rather in urgent maintenance. In circumstances where an employer was in breach of its obligation to carry out the statutory assessment procedure, the fact that he was in breach of that obligation could not be prayed in aid if, as a result of that failure, it omitted to provide the guidance required by Reg.4(1)(b)(iii). The Regulations did not impose three discrete duties but should be read conjunctively, and (2) a detailed assessment might have involved obtaining manufacturer's manuals and specifications to highlight potential problems with the machinery and if there had been insufficient information then caution should have resulted in a presumption that the roller might be unduly heavy and such concern should have been communicated to S under Reg.4(1)(b)(iii), *Hawkes v. Southwark LBC* (Unreported, February 20, 1998) distinguished.

SWAIN v. DENSO MARSTON LTD [2000] I.C.R. 1079, Robert Walker, L.J., CA.

2982. Risk assessment – hospitals – failure to assess risk and individual capabilities – breach of Manual Handling Operations Regulations 1992

[Manual Handling Operations Regulations 1992 (SI 1992 2793) Reg.4.]

W, a midwife of 28 years' experience, was in 1994 required by WHHA to work in the delivery suite in the local hospital. This work involved heavy manual handling of patients. W had a long history of back complaints and a small disc prolapse in her lower spine. WHHA did not send W to their occupational health department to assess her fitness for the work in delivery suite despite being told expressly by W of her back problems. The manual handling work in the delivery suite aggravated Ws lower back problem and increased the disc prolapse such that she had to have surgery within one year and was retired on grounds of ill health in November 1996.

Held, finding in favour of W, that (1) the Manual Handling Operations Regulations 1992 applied to W's work as a midwife in the delivery suit in the hospital; (2) WHHA failed to carry out a risk assessment in accordance with Reg.4(1) of the 1992 Regulations; (3) WHHA failed to carry out an assessment of W's individual capabilities in accordance with Reg.4(1); (4) WHHA was therefore in breach of their statutory duties and also negligent; (5) the work accelerated W's back condition by two years, and (6) W was not contributorily negligent.

WELLS v. WEST HERTFORDSHIRE HA, April 5, 2000, N Baker Q.C., QBD. [*Ex rel.* Andrew Ritchie, Barrister, 9 Gough Square, London].

2983. Risk assessment – residential care – back injury – no duty to assess each individual task

[Manual Handling Operations Regulations 1992 (SI 1992 2793) Reg.4(1).]

K, a 47 year old care assistant employed in a residential home for children with learning difficulties, sustained a back injury as she bent to pull a low wooden bed from against the wall. K commenced proceedings against her employers, THS, and the court at first instance dismissed the claim on the basis that the task resulted in no significant risk of injury for the purposes of the Manual Handling Operations Regulations 1992 Reg.4(1). K appealed, contending that there should not have been a presumption that the task would have been carried out in a normal manner and there was no requirement that the risk of injury should be significant

Held, dismissing the appeal, that whilst nothing more than a real risk was required to bring a particular case within the scope of Reg.4, it was nevertheless also necessary to consider the background against which the incident had taken place and assess the alleged obligation in its real context. In the instant case, the judge had been entitled to take into account the fact that this was a small residential home with a small number of staff and that K was an experienced staff member who had been carrying out similar tasks for very many years. Further, the court had been entitled to take into account the fact that K had received prior training in bending and lifting techniques. The imposition of a duty to assess each task and provide guidance as to how those tasks were to be carried out in circumstances where innumerable everyday domestic tasks were involved would be impracticable. In the circumstances there was no breach of statutory duty and in any event K would have been held 100 per cent contributorily negligent.

KOONJUL v. THAMESLINK HEALTHCARE SERVICES [2000] P.I.Q.R. P123, Hale, L.J., CA.

2984. Work related upper limb disorders – employers liability – medical evidence of physical origin of symptoms

A and four other claimants were employed by MB as part time encoders, which required fast keyboard inputting of numerical data, with an average keying speed of 12,700 key depressions per hour. There was a great pressure on the employees to maintain this work rate such that time spent away from the machine was closely monitored, there was a no talking rule and two hourly breaks had been reduced from 15 minutes to 10. All five experienced pain in their necks, arms and hands and brought claims for damages, supported by expert evidence, on the grounds that they had sustained work related upper limb disorders. The claims succeeded at first instance and MB appealed, contending that the judge had erred in deciding that the case was either physical or psychogenic in origin, before going on to consider the likelihood that it was the latter, without first being satisfied on the balance of probability as to the acceptability of A's experts' evidence.

Held, dismissing the appeal, regarding the issue of burden of proof, the judge was presented with two alternative explanations for what were accepted to be work related injuries experienced by A. The judge had correctly stated that the burden of proof remained on A throughout to establish on the balance of probabilities that her condition was physical. In practice, given the state of medical knowledge concerning the pathology of such conditions, A was required to show that the physical explanation for her condition was more probable than the psychogenic one. Being faced with two alternative explanations, the judge had to consider the plausibility of both of them and the order in which he did so was immaterial. On finding that the psychogenic case was unconvincing, it was a matter of simple common sense that the physical explanation was the more probable, *Rhesa Shipping Co SA v. Edmunds (Herbert David) (The Popi M)* [1985] 1 W.L.R. 948, [1985] C.L.Y. 3207 distinguished. In arriving at this decision, the judge was quite entitled to prefer the evidence of A's medical experts to those called by MB. Furthermore, the judge was right to use his common sense, and remind himself that, simply because a precise pathological explanation could not be given for the condition, it did not necessarily mean that the condition was psychosomatic. The facts showed that several reliable witnesses, including the claimants, had all described similar work related symptoms, and none of those witnesses displayed symptoms showing that they were vulnerable to a psychogenic illness. The findings were made against a background of general knowledge that a poorly organised work regime, such as that operated by MB, could have given rise to A's symptoms.

The judge had accurately summarised the medical evidence and given his assessments of the witnesses, he had been entitled to reject MB's criticisms of that evidence and in the circumstances it would have been surprising had he not done so, given the strength of A's case.

ALEXANDER v. MIDLAND BANK PLC; LANCASTER v. MIDLAND BANK PLC; MULHOLLAND v. MIDLAND BANK PLC; OSLER v. MIDLAND BANK PLC; ROLFE v. MIDLAND BANK PLC [2000] I.C.R. 464, Stuart-Smith, L.J., CA.

2985. Publications

Alli, Benjamin – Fundamental Principles of Occupational Health and Safety. Paperback: £9.95. ISBN 92-2-110869-4. International Labour Office/ ILO/ International Labour Organisation.

Barrett, Brenda; Howells, Richard – Cases and Materials on Occupational Health and Safety Law. 2nd Ed. Paperback: £24.95. ISBN 1-85941-560-1. Cavendish Publishing Ltd.

Bentley – Safety Management and Risk Assessment for the Chemical Industry. Spiral/comb bound: £495.00. ISBN 1-85978-478-X. Informa Chemical Intelligence.

Cox, Robin; Edwards, Felicity; Palmer, Keith – Fitness for Work: the Medical Aspects. 3rd Ed. Paperback: £37.50. ISBN 0-19-263043-1. Oxford University Press.

Tolley's Health and Safety At Work Handbook 2001. Paperback: £67.00. ISBN 0-7545-0741-6. Tolley Publishing.

HIGHWAY CONTROL

2986. Bridges – foot and cycle bridges – Norwich

COUNTY COUNCIL OF NORFOLK (CONSTRUCTION OF CANNON WHARF FOOT/CYCLE BRIDGE, NORWICH) SCHEME 2000 CONFIRMATION INSTRUMENT 2000, SI 2000 2746; made under the Highways Act 1980 s.106. In force: in accordance with Art.1; £2.00.

This Instrument confirms the County Council of Norfolk (Construction of Cannon Wharf Foot/Cycle Bridge, Norwich) Scheme 2000 with modifications.

2987. Bridges – foot and cycle bridges – Norwich

COUNTY COUNCIL OF NORFOLK (CONSTRUCTION OF OLD BARGE YARD FOOT/CYCLE BRIDGE, NORWICH) SCHEME 2000 CONFIRMATION INSTRUMENT 2000, SI 2000 2745; made under the Highways Act 1980 s.106. In force: in accordance with Art.1; £2.00.

This Instrument confirms the County Council of Norfolk (Construction of Old Barge Yard Foot/Cycle Bridge, Norwich) Scheme 2000 with modifications.

2988. Bridges – Mayrose Bridge

ESSEX COUNTY COUNCIL (MAYROSE BRIDGE) SCHEME 1999 CONFIRMATION INSTRUMENT 2000, SI 2000 2707; made under the Highways Act 1980 s.106. In force: in accordance with Art.1; £2.00.

This Instrument confirms the Essex County Council (Mayrose Bridge) Scheme 1999 without modifications.

2989. Bridges – River Tees

BOROUGH COUNCIL OF STOCKTON-ON-TEES (RIVER TEES BRIDGE) SCHEME 2000 CONFIRMATION INSTRUMENT 2000, SI 2000 1921; made under the Highways Act 1980 s.106. In force: In accordance with Art.1; £2.50.

This Instrument confirms the Scheme set out in the Schedule, which authorises the Borough Council of Stockton-on-Tees to construct a bridge over the navigable waters of the River Tees.

2990. Bridges – tolls – Severn bridges

SEVERN BRIDGES TOLLS ORDER 2000, SI 2000 3256; made under the Severn Bridges Act 1992 s.9. In force: January 1, 2001; £1.50.

This Order, which revokes the Severn Bridges (Tolls) Order 1999 (SI 1999 3252), fixes the tolls payable for use of the Severn Bridge and the Second Severn Crossing during the year 2001.

2991. Disabled persons – motor vehicles – badges – Wales

DISABLED PERSONS (BADGES FOR MOTOR VEHICLES) (WALES) REGULATIONS 2000, SI 2000 1786 (W.123); made under the Chronically Sick and Disabled Persons Act 1970 s.21. In force: July 1, 2000; £7.10.

These Regulations, which revoke, in relation to Wales, the Disabled Persons (Badges for Motor Vehicles) Regulations 1982 (SI 1982 1740), introduce a system of blue badges for disabled people from Wales that will be valid across the EU to replace the current orange badge system. They prescribe the persons entitled to a badge, give local authorities the right to issue a badge to an institution, specify the maximum fee that a local authority can charge and make provision for the issue of replacement badges.

2992. Disabled persons – traffic orders – exemptions

LOCAL AUTHORITIES' TRAFFIC ORDERS (EXEMPTIONS FOR DISABLED PERSONS) (ENGLAND) REGULATIONS 2000, SI 2000 683; made under the Road Traffic Regulation Act 1984 Sch.9 para.23. In force: April 1, 2000; £1.50.

These Regulations, which replace the Local Authorities' Traffic Orders (Exemptions for Disabled Persons) (England and Wales) Regulations 1986 (SI 1986 178), require that orders made by local authorities which prohibit vehicles from waiting on roads marked by yellow lines or which prohibit the waiting of vehicles in roads or in street parking places include an exemption from waiting prohibitions in certain circumstances and from charges and time-limits at places where vehicles may park or wait in respect of vehicles displaying a disabled person's badge.

2993. Disabled persons – traffic orders – exemptions – Wales

LOCAL AUTHORITIES' TRAFFIC ORDERS (EXEMPTIONS FOR DISABLED PERSONS) (WALES) REGULATIONS 2000, SI 2000 1785 (W.122); made under the Road Traffic Regulation Act 1984 Sch.9 para.23. In force: July 5, 2000; £2.00.

These Regulations introduce a system of blue badges for disabled people from Wales that will be valid across the EU to replace the current orange badge system. They revoke Local Authorities' Traffic Orders (Exemptions for Disabled Persons) (England and Wales) Regulations 1986 (SI 1986 178), which specified the exemptions in favour of disabled people that it would be necessary for local authorities to include in orders regarding parking prohibitions and limits and the charges that could be imposed, and specify the relevant orders and the way in which the exemptions will affect them.

2994. Footpaths – Oxfordshire CC (Buscot Footbridge) Scheme

OXFORDSHIRE COUNTY COUNCIL (BUSCOT FOOTBRIDGE) SCHEME 1999 CONFIRMATION INSTRUMENT 2000, SI 2000 298; made under the Highways Act 1980 s.106. In force: in accordance with Art.1; £3.00.

This Scheme confirms, with modifications, the Oxfordshire CC (Buscot Footbridge) Scheme 1999.

2995. Local authorities – icy pavement – duty to maintain pathway

See NEGLIGENCE: Shedden v. Sheffield City Council. §4245

2996. Local authorities powers and duties – litter clearance – transfer of responsibility

HIGHWAY LITTER CLEARANCE AND CLEANING (TRANSFER OF RESPONSIBILITY) (A13 TRUNK ROAD) ORDER 2000, SI 2000 1508; made under the Environmental Protection Act 1990 s.86. In force: July 2, 2000; £1.50.

This Order transfers from certain local authorities to the Secretary of State, responsibility for the discharge of the duties imposed by the Environmental Protection Act 1990 s.89 in respect of specified parts of the A13 trunk road.

2997. Motor vehicles – hire agreements – owner liability – road traffic offences

ROAD TRAFFIC (OWNER LIABILITY) REGULATIONS 2000, SI 2000 2546; made under the Road Traffic Offenders Act 1988 s.84. In force: October 16, 2000; £3.50.

These Regulations, which revoke the Road Traffic (Owner Liability) Regulations 1975 (SI 1975 324) and the Road Traffic (Owner Liability) (Scotland) Regulations 1975 (SI 1975 706), prescribe forms for use in connection with the Road Traffic Offenders Act 1988 s.62 to s.68 and Sch.4 and stipulate the particulars which must be contained in vehicle hiring agreements in order to attract the provisions of s.66 of the Act.

2998. Motorways – connecting roads – M62

M62 MOTORWAY (NEW JUNCTION 8 AND WIDENING JUNCTION 8 TO 9) CONNECTING ROADS SCHEME 2000, SI 2000 2; made under the Highways Act 1980 s.16, s.17, s.19. In force: January 27, 2000; £1.00.

This Scheme authorises the provision of special roads, which are specified connecting roads at Junction 8 and 9 of the M62, and provides for those roads to be trunk roads.

2999. Motorways – M1 – connecting roads

M1-A1 LINK (BELLE ISLE TO BRAMHAM CROSSROADS SECTION AND CONNECTING ROADS) SCHEME 1994 (VARIATION) (NO.2) SCHEME 2000, SI 2000 1137; made under the Highways Act 1980 s.16, s.17, s.19, s.106, s.108, s.326. In force: May 26, 2000; £1.00.

This Scheme varies provisions of the M1-A1 Link (Belle Isle to Bramham Crossroads Section and Connecting Roads) Scheme 1994 (SI 1994 1020) as varied by the M1-A1 Link (Belle Isle to Bramham Crossorads Section and Connecting Roads) Scheme 1994 (Variation) Scheme 1995 (SI 1995 426).

3000. Motorways – speed limits – M1

M1 MOTORWAY (JUNCTION 15) (SPEED LIMIT) REGULATIONS 2000, SI 2000 1800; made under the Road Traffic Regulation Act 1984 s.17. In force: August 8, 2000; £1.00.

These Regulations impose a speed limit of 40 miles per hour on a length of the northbound entry slip road linking the A508 with the northbound carriageway of the M1 motorway, at Junction 15 in the county of Northampton. The length affected runs from the junction of the slip road with the A508 for a distance of 30 metres northward.

3001. Motorways – speed limits – M1 and M62

M62 AND M1 MOTORWAYS (LOFTHOUSE LINK ROADS) (SPEED LIMIT) REGULATIONS 2000, SI 2000 1565; made under the Road Traffic Regulations Act 1984 s.17. In force: July 12, 2000; £1.00.

These Regulations impose a speed limit of 50 miles per hour on specified link roads at junction 29 of the M62 Motorway and at junction 42 of the M1 Motorway.

3002. Motorways – speed limits – M11

M11 MOTORWAY (JUNCTIONS 5-4, REDBRIDGE) (SPEED LIMIT) REGULATIONS 2000, SI 2000 854; made under the Road Traffic Regulation Act 1984 s.17. In force: April 25, 2000; £1.50.

These Regulations impose a speed limit of 50 mph on a length of the M11 Motorway in the London Borough of Redbridge.

3003. Motorways – speed limits – M61

M61 MOTORWAY (KEARSLEY SPUR) (SPEED LIMIT) REGULATIONS 2000, SI 2000 1593; made under the Road Traffic Regulation Act 1984 s.17. In force: July 17, 2000; £1.00.

These Regulations, which revoke and replace the M61 Motorway (Kearsley Spur) (Speed Limit) Regulations 1999 (SI 1999 2359), impose a speed limit of 50 miles per hour on part of the Kearsley Spur of the M61 Motorway and a slip road from that spur.

3004. Motorways – speed limits – M65

M65 MOTORWAY (JUNCTION 1A) (SPEED LIMIT) REGULATIONS 2000, SI 2000 2705; made under the Road Traffic Regulation Act 1984 s.17. In force: October 30, 2000; £1.50.

These Regulations impose a 50 mph speed limit on a section of the westbound exit slip road of the M65 at Junction 1A, between a point 200.1 metres west of the centreline of the A49 Wigan Road and a point 440.7 metres west of the centreline of the A49 Wigan Road.

3005. Motorways – speed limits – M621

M621 MOTORWAY (SPEED LIMIT) REGULATIONS 2000, SI 2000 1811; made under the Road Traffic Regulation Act 1984 s.17. In force: August 11, 2000; £2.00.

These Regulations, which revoke and replace the Motorways Traffic (M621 Motorway) (Speed Limit) Regulations 1983 (SI 1983 1280) and the Motorways Traffic (Leeds South East Urban Motorway) (Speed Limit) Regulations 1973 (SI 1973 846), impose revised speed limits on the slip roads to, and specified lengths of, the M621 motorway at Leeds to take account of improvements and realignments.

3006. Parking – controlled parking zones – vehicular crossings – relevant considerations for request under Highways Act 1980

[Highways Act 1980 s.184(5), s.184(11).]

E, a resident and property owner in the borough of Kensington and Chelsea, applied for judicial review of the local authority, R's, refusal to grant his request under the Highways Act 1980 s.184(11) to construct a vehicle crossing over the footpath outside his house which was within an area that had been designated as a Controlled Parking Zone, CPZ. E submitted that (1) it was unlawful for R to take into account the impact of a vehicle crossing on the CPZ as the only factors that should be considered were those detailed in s.184(5), and (2) that R's decision that the provision of a vehicular crossing would have an adverse effect on the CPZ was unreasonable in the *Wednesbury* sense, as the provision of a crossing would enable him to park his car off the road, thus freeing on road parking for the use of other residents.

Held, refusing the application, that (1) R had been entitled in deciding whether to grant the request under s.184(11) to consider the impact upon the CPZ and was not restricted to only those considerations laid out in s.184(5). Such a conclusion was consistent with both the wording and legislative history of the provision, and (2) the decision was not unreasonable or irrational given that construction of the crossing would result in the loss of on road parking space which could not be compensated for by the fact that E was now parking off road.

R. v. KENSINGTON AND CHELSEA RLBC, *ex p.* EMINIAN *The Times*, August 17, 2000, Maurice Kay, J., QBD.

3007. Parking – Greenwich Park

GREENWICH PARK (VEHICLE PARKING) REGULATIONS 2000, SI 2000 934; made under the Parks Regulation (Amendment) Act 1926 s.2; and the Road Traffic Regulation Act 1984 s.62. In force: April 3, 2000; £1.50.

These Regulations introduce a "pay and display" charging scheme for vehicle parking in Greenwich Park.

3008. Parking – special parking areas – Ashford

ROAD TRAFFIC (PERMITTED PARKING AREA AND SPECIAL PARKING AREA) (COUNTY OF KENT) (BOROUGH OF ASHFORD) ORDER 2000, SI 2000 2430; made under the Road Traffic Act 1991 Sch.3 para.1, para.2, para.3. In force: October 2, 2000; £2.00.

This Order designates the Borough of Ashford, excluding the M20 Motorway, together with its on and off slip roads, for the whole of its length in the borough, a section of the A2070 and a section of the A2042, as both a permitted parking area and a special parking area in accordance with the Road Traffic Act 1991 Sch.3. In addition, it applies with modifications various provisions of Part II of that Act to the designated area and modifies the Road Traffic Regulation Act 1984 in relation to the designated area.

3009. Parking – special parking areas – Bedford

ROAD TRAFFIC (PERMITTED PARKING AREA AND SPECIAL PARKING AREA) (COUNTY OF BEDFORDSHIRE) (BOROUGH OF BEDFORD) ORDER 2000, SI 2000 2871; made under the Road Traffic Act 1991 Sch.3 para.1, para.2, para.3. In force: November 13, 2000; £2.50.

This Order designates a part of the borough of Bedford as both a permitted parking area and a special parking area in accordance with the Road Traffic Act 1991 Sch.3. In addition, it applies with modifications various provisions of Part II of the 1991 Act to the designated area and modifies the Road Traffic Regulation Act 1984 in relation to the designated area.

3010. Parking – special parking areas – Bolton

ROAD TRAFFIC (PERMITTED PARKING AREA AND SPECIAL PARKING AREA) (METROPOLITAN BOROUGH OF BOLTON) ORDER 2000, SI 2000 2169; made under the Road Traffic Act 1991 Sch.3 para.1, para.2, para.3. In force: September 4, 2000; £2.00.

This Order designates the Metropolitan Borough of Bolton, excluding the section of the A666 trunk road, together with its on and off slip roads, from its junction with the M61 Motorway to its junction with Topway/St. George's Road, as both a permitted parking area and a special parking area in accordance with the Road Traffic Act 1991 Sch.3. It also applies with modifications various provisions of

Part II of that Act to the designated area and modifies the Road Traffic Regulation Act 1984 in relation to the designated area.

3011. Parking – special parking areas – Bristol

ROAD TRAFFIC (PERMITTED PARKING AREA AND SPECIAL PARKING AREA) (CITY OF BRISTOL) ORDER 2000, SI 2000 699; made under the Road Traffic Act 1991 Sch.3 para.1, para.2, para.3. In force: April 1, 2000; £2.00.

This Order designates the County of the City of Bristol as both a permitted parking area and a special parking area in accordance with the Road Traffic Act 1991 Sch.3. It also applies various provisions of Part II of that Act to the designated area and modifies the Road Traffic Regulation Act 1984 in relation to the designated area.

3012. Parking – special parking areas – Reading

ROAD TRAFFIC (PERMITTED PARKING AREA AND SPECIAL PARKING AREA) (BOROUGH OF READING) ORDER 2000, SI 2000 1719; made under the Road Traffic Act 1991 Sch.3 para.1, para.2, para.3. In force: October 30, 2000; £2.00.

This Order designates the Borough of Reading, excluding those parts of the M4 Motorway and its slip roads situated within the borough, as both a permitted parking area and a special parking area in accordance with the Road Traffic Act 1991 Sch.3. It applies with modifications various provisions of Part II of that Act to the designated area and modifies the Road Traffic Regulation Act 1984 in relation to the designated area.

3013. Parking – special parking areas – Sandwell

ROAD TRAFFIC (PERMITTED PARKING AREA AND SPECIAL PARKING AREA) (METROPOLITAN BOROUGH OF SANDWELL) ORDER 2000, SI 2000 791; made under the Road Traffic Act 1991 Sch.3 para.1, para.2, para.3. In force: April 10, 2000; £2.00.

This Order designates the Metropolitan Borough of Sandwell as both a permitted parking area and a special parking area in accordance with the Road Traffic Act 1991 Sch.3. It also applies various provisions of Part II of that Act to the designated area and modifies the Road Traffic Regulation Act 1984 in relation to the designated area.

3014. Parking – special parking areas – Sefton

ROAD TRAFFIC (PERMITTED PARKING AREA AND SPECIAL PARKING AREA) (METROPOLITAN BOROUGH OF SEFTON) ORDER 2000, SI 2000 8; made under the Road Traffic Act 1991 Sch.3 para.1, para.2. In force: February 1, 2000; £2.00.

This Order designates the Metropolitan Borough of Sefton, with the exception of specified lengths of road, as both a permitted parking area and a special parking area in accordance with the Road Traffic Act 1991 Sch.3. It also applies with modifications various provisions of Part II of that Act to the designated area and modifies the Road Traffic Regulation Act 1984 in relation to the designated area.

3015. Parking – special parking areas – Shepway

ROAD TRAFFIC (PERMITTED PARKING AREA AND SPECIAL PARKING AREA) (COUNTY OF KENT) (DISTRICT OF SHEPWAY) ORDER 2000, SI 2000 722; made under the Road Traffic Act 1991 Sch.3 para.1, para.2, para.3. In force: April 3, 2000; £2.00.

This Order designates the District of Shepway as both a permitted parking area and a special parking area in accordance with the Road Traffic Act 1991 Sch.3. It applies various provisions of Part II of that Act to the designated area and modifies the Road Traffic Regulation Act 1984 in relation to the designated area.

3016. Parking – special parking areas – Tonbridge and Malling

ROAD TRAFFIC (PERMITTED PARKING AREA AND SPECIAL PARKING AREA) (COUNTY OF KENT) (BOROUGH OF TONBRIDGE AND MALLING) ORDER 2000, SI 2000 2120; made under the Road Traffic Act 1991 Sch.3 para.1, para.2, para.3. In force: September 1, 2000; £2.00.

This Order designates the Borough of Tonbridge and Malling, excluding the M2 Motorway, the M20 Motorway, the M26 Motorway and the A21 trunk road, together with their on and off slip roads, for the whole of their lengths in the Borough, as both a permitted parking area and a special parking area in accordance with the Road Traffic Act 1991 Sch.3. In addition, it applies with modifications various provisions of Part II of that Act to the designated area and modifies the Road Traffic Regulation Act 1984 in relation to the designated area.

3017. Parking – special parking areas – Trafford

ROAD TRAFFIC (PERMITTED PARKING AREA AND SPECIAL PARKING AREA) (METROPOLITAN BOROUGH OF TRAFFORD) ORDER 2000, SI 2000 3317; made under the Road Traffic Act 1991 Sch.3 para.1, para.2, para.3. In force: January 15, 2001; £2.00.

This Order designates the Metropolitan Borough of Trafford, excluding certain lengths of roads, as both a permitted parking area and a special parking area in accordance with the Road Traffic Act 1991 Sch.3. In addition, it applies with modifications various provisions of Part II of that Act to the designated area and modifies the Road Traffic Regulations Act 1984 in relation to the designated area.

3018. Parking – special parking areas – York

ROAD TRAFFIC (PERMITTED PARKING AREA AND SPECIAL PARKING AREA) (DISTRICT OF YORK) ORDER 2000, SI 2000 2534; made under the Road Traffic Act 1991 Sch.3 para.1, para.2, para.3. In force: October 8, 2000; £2.00.

This Order designates the district of York, excluding that part of the A64 trunk road situated within the district, together with most of its on and off slip roads, and the A1237 road, as both a permitted parking area and a special parking area in accordance with the Road Traffic Act 1991 Sch.3. In addition, it applies with modifications various provisions of Part II of that Act to the designated area and modifies the Road Traffic Regulation Act 1984 in relation to the designated area.

3019. Road safety – traffic calming measures – consultation requirements

HIGHWAYS (TRAFFIC CALMING) (AMENDMENT) REGULATIONS 2000, SI 2000 1511; made under the Highways Act 1980 s.90GA. In force: July 3, 2000; £1.00.

The Greater London Authority Act 1999 s.269 amends the Highways Act 1980 s.90G, so as to confer on local highway authorities in Greater London the power to construct traffic calming works if they fall within s.90GA. These Regulations amend the Highways (Traffic Calming) Regulations 1999 (SI 1999 1026) to prescribe requirements as to consultation and publicity with which a local highway authority must comply if works are to fall within s.90GA.

3020. Road Traffic Reduction Act 1997 (c.54) – Commencement Order – England and Wales

ROAD TRAFFIC REDUCTION ACT 1997 (COMMENCEMENT) (ENGLAND AND WALES) ORDER 2000, SI 2000 735 (C.15); made under the Road Traffic Reduction Act 1997 s.4. Commencement details: bringing into force various provisions of the Act on March 10, 2000; £1.00.

This Order brings the Road Traffic Reduction Act 1997 into force on March 10, 2000.

3021. Road works – funding

STREET WORKS (SHARING OF COSTS OF WORKS) (ENGLAND) REGULATIONS 2000, SI 2000 3314; made under the New Roads and Street Works Act 1991 s.85, s.104. In force: January 15, 2001; £2.00.

These Regulations, which replace and revoke the Street Works (Sharing of Costs of Works) Regulations 1992 (SI 1992 1690) as respects England, change the undertaker's share of the costs of diversionary works in the case of certain major transport works to 7.5 per cent. rather than 18 per cent.

3022. Roads – GLA roads

GLA ROADS (CONTINUITY OF ORDERS ETC.) ORDER 2000, SI 2000 2615; made under the Greater London Authority Act 1999 s.405, s.406. In force: October 18, 2000; £1.75.

This Order provides for orders of specified types relating to non motorway trunk roads in Greater London to have effect as if they referred to Transport for London in place of the Secretary of State and for the transfer of associated property, rights and liabilities. In addition, it puts Transport for London in the same position as the Secretary of State under the Town and Country Planning Act 1990 with regard to the carrying out of development in pursuance of such orders.

3023. Roads – GLA roads

GLA ROADS (SUPPLEMENTARY PROVISIONS) ORDER 2000, SI 2000 1064; made under the Greater London Authority Act 1999 s.405, s.406. In force: May 5, 2000; £1.00.

This Order provides that the Highways Act 1980 s.14A is to have effect so that roads in Greater London which are not highways and which were built by an urban development corporation may be designated by the Secretary of State as GLA roads and will become highways maintainable at the public expense.

3024. Roads – GLA roads – designation

GLA ROADS DESIGNATION ORDER 2000, SI 2000 1117; made under the Highways Act 1980 s.14A. In force: May 22, 2000; £3.00.

This Order designates certain highways as GLA roads for which Transport for London will be the highway authority with effect from July 3, 2000.

3025. Roads – GLA roads – designation

GLA ROADS DESIGNATION (AMENDMENT) ORDER 2000, SI 2000 1230; made under the Highways Act 1980 s.14A. In force: June 9, 2000; £1.00.

This Order amends the GLA Roads Designation Order 2000 (SI 2000 1117) which designates specified roads as GLA roads for which Transport for London will be the highway authority with effect from July 3, 2000. It makes three additions to the list of designated GLA roads.

3026. Roads – GLA side roads – Barking and Dagenham

GLA SIDE ROADS (LONDON BOROUGH OF BARKING AND DAGENHAM) DESIGNATION ORDER 2000, SI 2000 1256; made under the Road Traffic Regulation Act 1984 s.124A. In force: June 19, 2000; £1.50.

This Order designates specified roads in the London Borough of Barking and Dagenham as GLA side roads for which Transport for London will be the traffic authority with effect from July 3, 2000.

3027. Roads – GLA side roads – Barnet

GLA SIDE ROADS (LONDON BOROUGH OF BARNET) DESIGNATION ORDER 2000, SI 2000 1257; made under the Road Traffic Regulation Act 1984 s.124A. In force: June 19, 2000; £2.00.

This Order designates specified roads in the London Borough of Barnet as GLA side roads for which Transport for London will be the traffic authority with effect from July 3, 2000.

3028. Roads – GLA side roads – Bexley

GLA SIDE ROADS (LONDON BOROUGH OF BEXLEY) DESIGNATION ORDER 2000, SI 2000 1258; made under the Road Traffic Regulation Act 1984 s.124A. In force: June 19, 2000; £1.00.

This Order designates specified roads in the London Borough of Bexley as GLA side roads for which Transport for London will be the traffic authority with effect from July 3, 2000.

3029. Roads – GLA side roads – Brent

GLA SIDE ROADS (LONDON BOROUGH OF BRENT) DESIGNATION ORDER 2000, SI 2000 1259; made under the Road Traffic Regulation Act 1984 s.124A. In force: June 19, 2000; £1.50.

This Order designates specified roads in the London Borough of Brent as GLA side roads for which Transport for London will be the traffic authority with effect from July 3, 2000.

3030. Roads – GLA side roads – Bromley

GLA SIDE ROADS (LONDON BOROUGH OF BROMLEY) DESIGNATION ORDER 2000, SI 2000 1260; made under the Road Traffic Regulation Act 1984 s.124A. In force: June 19, 2000; £2.00.

This Order designates specified roads in the London Borough of Bromley as GLA side roads for which Transport for London will be the traffic authority with effect from July 3, 2000.

3031. Roads – GLA side roads – Camden

GLA SIDE ROADS (LONDON BOROUGH OF CAMDEN) DESIGNATION ORDER 2000, SI 2000 1261; made under the Road Traffic Regulation Act 1984 s.124A. In force: June 19, 2000; £2.00.

This Order designates specified roads in the London Borough of Camden as GLA side roads for which Transport for London will be the traffic authority with effect from July 3, 2000.

3032. Roads – GLA side roads – City of London

GLA SIDE ROADS (CITY OF LONDON) DESIGNATION ORDER 2000, SI 2000 1262; made under the Road Traffic Regulation Act 1984 s.124A. In force: June 19, 2000; £1.50.

This Order designates specified roads in the City of London as GLA side roads for which Transport for London will be the traffic authority with effect from July 3, 2000.

3033. Roads – GLA side roads – City of Westminster

GLA SIDE ROADS (CITY OF WESTMINSTER) DESIGNATION ORDER 2000, SI 2000 1379; made under the Road Traffic Regulation Act 1984 s.124A. In force: June 19, 2000; £3.00.

This Order designates specified roads in the City of Westminster as GLA side roads for which Transport for London will be the traffic authority with effect from July 3, 2000.

3034. Roads – GLA side roads – classification

ROAD TRAFFIC REGULATION ACT 1984 (GLA SIDE ROADS AMENDMENT) ORDER 2000, SI 2000 2237; made under the Road Traffic Regulation Act 1984 s.124A. In force: October 1, 2000; £1.50.

This Order amends the Road Traffic Regulation Act 1984. In particular, it inserts a new s.124B, which specifies the procedure whereby a road may become or cease to be a GLA side road, and s.124C, which provides for the giving of certificates as evidence that a road is or is not a GLA side road and for the keeping of records of the roads which are GLA side roads.

3035. Roads – GLA side roads – Croyden

GLA SIDE ROADS (LONDON BOROUGH OF CROYDON) DESIGNATION ORDER 2000, SI 2000 1263; made under the Road Traffic Regulation Act 1984 s.124A. In force: June 19, 2000; £3.00.

This Order designates specified roads in the London Borough of Croydon as GLA side roads for which Transport for London will be the traffic authority with effect from July 3, 2000.

3036. Roads – GLA side roads – Ealing

GLA SIDE ROADS (LONDON BOROUGH OF EALING) DESIGNATION ORDER 2000, SI 2000 1286; made under the Road Traffic Regulation Act 1984 s.124A. In force: June 19, 2000; £2.00.

This Order designates specified roads in the London Borough of Ealing as GLA side roads for which Transport for London will be the traffic authority with effect from July 3, 2000.

3037. Roads – GLA side roads – Enfield

GLA SIDE ROADS (LONDON BOROUGH OF ENFIELD) DESIGNATION ORDER 2000, SI 2000 1287; made under the Road Traffic Regulation Act 1984 s.124A. In force: June 19, 2000; £2.00.

This Order designates specified roads in the London Borough of Enfield as GLA side roads for which Transport for London will be the traffic authority with effect from July 3, 2000.

3038. Roads – GLA side roads – Greenwich

GLA SIDE ROADS (LONDON BOROUGH OF GREENWICH) DESIGNATION ORDER 2000, SI 2000 1288; made under the Road Traffic Regulation Act 1984 s.124A. In force: June 19, 2000; £2.50.

This Order designates specified roads in the London Borough of Greenwich as GLA side roads for which Transport for London will be the traffic authority with effect from July 3, 2000.

3039. Roads – GLA side roads – Hackney

GLA SIDE ROADS (LONDON BOROUGH OF HACKNEY) DESIGNATION ORDER 2000, SI 2000 1289; made under the Road Traffic Regulation Act 1984 s.124A. In force: June 19, 2000; £3.00.

This Order designates specified roads in the London Borough of Hackney as GLA side roads for which Transport for London will be the traffic authority with effect from July 3, 2000.

3040. Roads – GLA side roads – Hammersmith and Fulham

GLA SIDE ROADS (LONDON BOROUGH OF HAMMERSMITH AND FULHAM) DESIGNATION ORDER 2000, SI 2000 1290; made under the Road Traffic Regulation Act 1984 s.124A. In force: June 19, 2000; £1.50.

This Order designates specified roads in the London Borough of Hammersmith and Fulham as GLA side roads for which Transport for London will be the traffic authority with effect from July 3, 2000.

3041. Roads – GLA side roads – Haringey

GLA SIDE ROADS (LONDON BOROUGH OF HARINGEY) DESIGNATION ORDER 2000, SI 2000 1291; made under the Road Traffic Regulation Act 1984 s.124A. In force: June 19, 2000; £2.50.

This Order designates specified roads in the London Borough of Haringey as GLA side roads for which Transport for London will be the traffic authority with effect from July 3, 2000.

3042. Roads – GLA side roads – Havering

GLA SIDE ROADS (LONDON BOROUGH OF HAVERING) DESIGNATION ORDER 2000, SI 2000 1292; made under the Road Traffic Regulation Act 1984 s.124A. In force: June 19, 2000; £2.00.

This Order designates specified roads in the London Borough of Havering as GLA side roads for which Transport for London will be the traffic authority with effect from July 3, 2000.

3043. Roads – GLA side roads – Hillingdon

GLA SIDE ROADS (LONDON BOROUGH OF HILLINGDON) DESIGNATION ORDER 2000, SI 2000 1293; made under the Road Traffic Regulation Act 1984 s.124A. In force: June 19, 2000; £1.50.

This Order designates specified roads in the London Borough of Hillingdon as GLA side roads for which Transport for London will be the traffic authority with effect from July 3, 2000.

3044. Roads – GLA side roads – Hounslow

GLA SIDE ROADS (LONDON BOROUGH OF HOUNSLOW) DESIGNATION ORDER 2000, SI 2000 1307; made under the Road Traffic Regulation 1984 s.124A. In force: June 19, 2000; £3.00.

This Order designates specified roads in the London Borough of Hounslow as GLA side roads for which Transport for London will be the traffic authority with effect from July 3, 2000.

3045. Roads – GLA side roads – Islington

GLA SIDE ROADS (LONDON BOROUGH OF ISLINGTON) DESIGNATION ORDER 2000, SI 2000 1371; made under the Road Traffic Regulation Act 1984 s.124A. In force: June 19, 2000; £3.00.

This Order designates specified roads in the London Borough of Islington as GLA side roads for which Transport for London will be the traffic authority with effect from July 3, 2000.

3046. Roads – GLA side roads – Kensington and Chelsea

GLA SIDE ROADS (ROYAL BOROUGH OF KENSINGTON AND CHELSEA) DESIGNATION ORDER 2000, SI 2000 1308; made under the Road Traffic Regulation 1984 s.124A. In force: June 19, 2000; £2.50.

This Order designates specified roads in the Royal Borough of Kensington and Chelsea as GLA side roads for which Transport for London will be the traffic authority with effect from July 3, 2000.

3047. Roads – GLA side roads – Kingston upon Thames

GLA SIDE ROADS (ROYAL BOROUGH OF KINGSTON UPON THAMES) DESIGNATION ORDER 2000, SI 2000 1309; made under the Road Traffic Regulation 1984 s.124A. In force: June 19, 2000; £1.50.

This Order designates specified roads in the Royal Borough of Kingston upon Thames as GLA side roads for which Transport for London will be the traffic authority with effect from July 3, 2000.

3048. Roads – GLA side roads – Lambeth

GLA SIDE ROADS (LONDON BOROUGH OF LAMBETH) DESIGNATION ORDER 2000, SI 2000 1312; made under the Road Traffic Regulation 1984 s.124A. In force: June 19, 2000; £3.50.

This Order designates specified roads in the London Borough of Lambeth as GLA side roads for which Transport for London will be the traffic authority with effect from July 3, 2000.

3049. Roads – GLA side roads – Lewisham

GLA SIDE ROADS (LONDON BOROUGH OF LEWISHAM) DESIGNATION ORDER 2000, SI 2000 1310; made under the Road Traffic Regulation 1984 s.124A. In force: June 19, 2000; £3.00.

This Order designates specified roads in the London Borough of Lewisham as GLA side roads for which Transport for London will be the traffic authority with effect from July 3, 2000.

3050. Roads – GLA side roads – Merton

GLA SIDE ROADS (LONDON BOROUGH OF MERTON) DESIGNATION ORDER 2000, SI 2000 1313; made under the Road Traffic Regulation 1984 s.124A. In force: June 19, 2000; £2.00.

This Order designates specified roads in the London Borough of Merton as GLA side roads for which Transport for London will be the traffic authority with effect from July 3, 2000.

3051. Roads – GLA side roads – Newham

GLA SIDE ROADS (LONDON BOROUGH OF NEWHAM) DESIGNATION ORDER 2000, SI 2000 1311; made under the Road Traffic Regulation 1984 s.124A. In force: June 19, 2000; £1.50.

This Order designates specified roads in the London Borough of Newham as GLA side roads for which Transport for London will be the traffic authority with effect from July 3, 2000.

3052. Roads – GLA side roads – Redbridge

GLA SIDE ROADS (LONDON BOROUGH OF REDBRIDGE) DESIGNATION ORDER 2000, SI 2000 1372; made under the Road Traffic Regulation Act 1984 s.124A. In force: June 19, 2000; £2.00.

This Order designates specified roads in the London Borough of Redbridge as GLA side roads for which Transport for London will be the traffic authority with effect from July 3, 2000.

3053. Roads – GLA side roads – Richmond upon Thames

GLA SIDE ROADS (LONDON BOROUGH OF RICHMOND UPON THAMES) DESIGNATION ORDER 2000, SI 2000 1373; made under the Road Traffic Regulation Act 1984 s.124A. In force: June 19, 2000; £2.50.

This Order designates specified roads in the London Borough of Richmond upon Thames as GLA side roads for which Transport for London will be the traffic authority with effect from July 3, 2000.

3054. Roads – GLA side roads – Southwark

GLA SIDE ROADS (LONDON BOROUGH OF SOUTHWARK) DESIGNATION ORDER 2000, SI 2000 1374; made under the Road Traffic Regulation Act 1984 s.124A. In force: June 19, 2000; £3.00.

This Order designates specified roads in the London Borough of Southwark as GLA side roads for which Transport for London will be the traffic authority with effect from July 3, 2000.

3055. Roads – GLA side roads – Sutton

GLA SIDE ROADS (LONDON BOROUGH OF SUTTON) DESIGNATION ORDER 2000, SI 2000 1375; made under the Road Traffic Regulation Act 1984 s.124A. In force: June 19, 2000; £3.00.

This Order designates specified roads in the London Borough of Sutton as GLA side roads for which Transport for London will be the traffic authority with effect from July 3, 2000.

3056. Roads – GLA side roads – Tower Hamlets

GLA SIDE ROADS (LONDON BOROUGH OF TOWER HAMLETS) DESIGNATION ORDER 2000, SI 2000 1376; made under the Road Traffic Regulation Act 1984 s.124A. In force: June 19, 2000; £3.00.

This Order designates specified roads in the London Borough of Tower Hamlets as GLA side roads for which Transport for London will be the traffic authority with effect from July 3, 2000.

3057. Roads – GLA side roads – Waltham Forest

GLA SIDE ROADS (LONDON BOROUGH OF WALTHAM FOREST) DESIGNATION ORDER 2000, SI 2000 1377; made under the Road Traffic Regulation Act 1984 s.124A. In force: June 19, 2000; £1.50.

This Order designates specified roads in the London Borough of Waltham Forest as GLA side roads for which Transport for London will be the traffic authority with effect from July 3, 2000.

3058. Roads – GLA side roads – Wandsworth

GLA SIDE ROADS (LONDON BOROUGH OF WANDSWORTH) DESIGNATION ORDER 2000, SI 2000 1378; made under the Road Traffic Regulation Act 1984 s.124A. In force: June 19, 2000; £4.00.

This Order designates specified roads in the London Borough of Wandsworth as GLA side roads for which Transport for London will be the traffic authority with effect from July 3, 2000.

3059. Roads – hazard on pavement – contributory negligence – local authority's system of inspection

See NEGLIGENCE: Rowe v. Herman (Quantum). §4243

3060. Roads – local authorities – duty to maintain – extent of duty

See NEGLIGENCE: Goodes v. East Sussex CC. §4237

3061. Roads – road signs – obscured road markings – local authority statutory duty to maintain

[Highways Act 1980 s.41; Road Traffic Regulations Act 1984.]

After emerging from the junction of a minor road to cross a major road, C collided with a vehicle driven by M. Both roads were one way, going south to north on the minor road and west to east on the major road. Originally a conventional double broken white line lay across the mouth of the junction and a triangle was marked on the road surface before the junction and on the right, and left before that "no left turn" signs with a warning triangle on poles were situated. There was no specific "give way" sign mounted on a pole beside the road. C approached the junction without realising he had to give way, claiming the road markings were obscured and other signage was inadequate. As a result, C crossed the junction without braking and slowing down and a collision occurred. There was no evidence that either driver was speeding. C brought an action against EFDC and ECC claiming that they were in breach of the Highways Act 1980 s.41 by failing to maintain road signs, to maintain the road surface, to warn of a priority junction, and to erect give way signs. Alternatively the claim was brought in negligence.

Held, dismissing the claim, that although the road markings across the mouth of the junction had been to all intents and purposes completely obliterated and the warning triangle on the road surface had become degraded, the local authority was not in breach of a statutory duty. Considering the Road Traffic Regulations Act 1984, the local authority had a power but not a duty to place signs by the road and there was no duty for the local authority to place signs on the road, thus no case on breach of statutory duty. Furthermore, the absence of signs and or maintenance of markings was not causative of the accident.

CHESTNUTT v. MARTIN, January 12, 1999, Judge Rose, CC (Central London). [*Ex rel.* AE Wyeth & Co Solicitors, Bridge House, High Street, Dartford, Kent].

3062. Roads – special roads scheme – combined cycle path and footway

CRIBBS CAUSEWAY -EASTON-IN-GORDANO SPECIAL ROADS SCHEME 1964 (VARIATION) SCHEME 2000, SI 2000 2847; made under the Highways Act 1980 s.16, s.17, s.19. In force: December 18, 2000; £1.50.

This Scheme varies the Cribbs Causeway -Easton-in-Gordano Special Roads Scheme 1964 (SI 1964 309) by removing the existing footway over the Avonmouth Bridge and providing for the existing cycle track to become a combined cycle track and footway.

3063. Roads – statutory duty – local authorities – inadequate system of inspection

See NEGLIGENCE: Dingley v. Bromley LBC. §4244

3064. Roads – title to land – dedication of land to the public – agreement between previous landowner and local council amounted to acceptance by public of dedication

[Land Registration Act 1925 s.70(1) (a).]

The Secretary of State sought a declaration that an area of land registered in the name of BL had been dedicated to the public. The land had been subject to an agreement in 1964 between a previous landowner and the local council by which it had been allocated for highway widening work. The highway widening work was subsequently not carried out.

Held, granting the declaration, that whereas actual use by the public usually substantiated the acceptance of dedication, the agreement between the previous landowner and local council had amounted to an acceptance by the public of dedication. A highway authority was viewed under current legislation as a representative of the public and consequently was provided with the ability, in instances of express dedication, through a written agreement with a landowner to accept the dedication on behalf of the public. Accordingly the surface of the land vested in the highway authority and subsequently, on its transformation into a road, with the Secretary of State. In the instant case, the Secretary of State had an overriding interest over the surface of the land pursuant to the Land Registration Act 1925 s.70(1) (a). It followed that BL upon becoming registered proprietor of the land did not deprive the Secretary of State of his title to the land.

SECRETARY OF STATE FOR THE ENVIRONMENT, TRANSPORT AND THE REGIONS v. BAYLIS (GLOUCESTER) LTD; BAYLIS (GLOUCESTER) LTD v. BENNETT CONSTRUCTION (UK) LTD; *sub nom.* BENNETT CONSTRUCTION

(UK) LTD v. BAYLIS (GLOUCESTER) LTD (2000) 80 P. & C.R. 324, Kim Lewison Q.C., Ch D.

3065. Trunk roads – bus lanes – A4

A4 TRUNK ROAD (BATH ROAD, HILLINGDON) (BUS LANE) ORDER 2000, SI 2000 981; made under the Road Traffic Regulation Act 1984 s.6. In force: April 10, 2000; £1.00.

This Order places a general prohibition on the presence of vehicles in a designated bus lane.

3066. Trunk roads – classification – A30

A30 TRUNK ROAD (HONITON TO EXETER IMPROVEMENT) (DETRUNKING) (NO.2) ORDER 2000, SI 2000 2660; made under the Highways Act 1980 s.10, s.12. In force: October 25, 2000; £1.75.

This Order provides that a prescribed length of the A30 trunk road shall cease to be a trunk road.

3067. Trunk roads – classification – A40

A40 TRUNK ROAD (PARK ROYAL SLIP ROADS) ORDER 2000, SI 2000 38; made under the Highways Act 1980 s.10. In force: March 6, 2000; £1.00.

This Order authorises the Secretary of State to construct new roads along prescribed routes which will become trunk roads as from the date when this Order comes into force.

3068. Trunk roads – classification – A43

A43 TRUNK ROAD (M40 TO B4031 IMPROVEMENT) ORDER 2000, SI 2000 1354; made under the Highways Act 1980 s.10, s.41. In force: June 9, 2000; £1.50.

This Order provides for newly constructed roads to be classified as trunk roads.

3069. Trunk roads – classification – A43

A43 TRUNK ROAD (M40 TO B4031 IMPROVEMENT) (DETRUNKING) ORDER 2000, SI 2000 1355; made under the Highways Act 1980 s.10. In force: June 9, 2000; £1.00.

This Order provides that a prescribed length of the A43 trunk road shall cease to be a trunk road.

3070. Trunk roads – classification – A43

A43 TRUNK ROAD (M40 TO B4031 IMPROVEMENT -ARDLEY INTERCHANGE) ORDER 2000, SI 2000 1353; made under the Highways Act 1980 s.10, s.41. In force: June 9, 2000; £1.00.

This Order provides for newly constructed roads to be classified as trunk roads.

3071. Trunk roads – classification – A43

A43 TRUNK ROAD (M40 TO B4031 IMPROVEMENT -ARDLEY INTERCHANGE) (TRUNKING) ORDER 2000, SI 2000 1350; made under the Highways Act 1980 s.10. In force: June 9, 2000; £1.00.

This Order provides for specified lengths of the A43 and B430 to be classified as trunk roads.

3072. Trunk roads – classification – A43

A43 TRUNK ROAD (M40 TO B4031 IMPROVEMENT-ARDLEY INTERCHANGE SLIP ROADS) ORDER 2000, SI 2000 1351; made under the Highways Act 1980 s.10, s.41. In force: June 9, 2000; £1.50.

The Order provides for new slip roads connecting the M40 with a new roundabout to be classified as trunk roads.

3073. Trunk roads – classification – A43

A43 TRUNK ROAD (M40 TO B4031 IMPROVEMENT SLIP ROADS) ORDER 2000, SI 2000 1352; made under the Highways Act 1980 s.10, s.41. In force: June 9, 2000; £1.50.

This Order provides for a new main road and slip roads to be classified as trunk roads.

3074. Trunk roads – classification – A63

A63 TRUNK ROAD (SELBY ROAD JUNCTION) ORDER 1994 (VARIATION) ORDER 2000, SI 2000 1138; made under the Highways Act 1980 s.10, s.41. In force: May 26, 2000; £1.00.

This Order varies provisions of the A63 Trunk Road (Selby Road Junction) Order 1994 (SI 1994 1024).

3075. Trunk roads – classification – A66 – slip roads

A66 TRUNK ROAD (SADBERGE GRADE SEPARATED JUNCTION, SLIP ROAD) ORDER 2000, SI 2000 2649; made under the Highways Act 1980 s.10, s.41. In force: October 18, 2000; £1.75.

This Order reclassifies the prescribed slip road as a trunk road and makes provision in relation to the maintenance of the road.

3076. Trunk roads – classification – A249

A249 TRUNK ROAD (BOBBING JUNCTION) (DETRUNKING) ORDER 2000, SI 2000 943; made under the Highways Act 1980 s.10, s.12. In force: May 15, 2000; £1.00.

This Order re classifies a specified length of the A249 trunk road as a classified road.

3077. Trunk roads – classification – A249

A249 TRUNK ROAD (IWADE BYPASS TO NEATSCOURT ROUNDABOUT AND BRIDGE) ORDER 2000, SI 2000 2695; made under the Highways Act 1980 s.10, s.41, s.106. In force: October 19, 2000; £1.75.

This Order provides for a new highway to be classified as a trunk road and makes provision for the maintenance of that road.

3078. Trunk roads – classification – A249

A249 TRUNK ROAD (IWADE BYPASS TO QUEENBOROUGH IMPROVEMENT) (DETRUNKING) ORDER 2000, SI 2000 2694; made under the Highways Act 1980 s.10, s.12. In force: October 19, 2000; £1.50.

This Order provides that specified lengths of the A249 trunk road shall cease to be a trunk road.

3079. Trunk roads – classification – A421

A421 TRUNK ROAD (MARSH LEYS IMPROVEMENT) (DETRUNKING) ORDER 2000, SI 2000 1073; made under the Highways Act 1980 s.10, s.12. In force: May 19, 2000; £1.00.

This Order reclassifies a specified length of trunk road as a principal road.

3080. Trunk roads – classification – A421

A421 TRUNK ROAD (MARSH LEYS IMPROVEMENT) (TRUNKING) ORDER 2000, SI 2000 1074; made under the Highways Act 1980 s.10. In force: May 19, 2000; £1.00.

This Order provides for a length of the A421 to be classified as a trunk road.

3081. Trunk roads – classification – A458

A458 TRUNK ROAD (SHELTON TRAFFIC LIGHTS TO CHURNCOTE ROUNDABOUT) (DETRUNKING) ORDER 2000, SI 2000 1320; made under the Highways Act 1980 s.10, s.12. In force: June 5, 2000; £1.00.

This Order reclassifies a specified length of the A458 trunk road as a principal road.

3082. Trunk roads – classification – A494 – Wales

DOLGELLAU TO SOUTH OF BIRKENHEAD TRUNK ROAD (A494) (IMPROVEMENT AT TAFARN Y GELYN) ORDER 2000, SI 2000 1283 (W.98); made under the Highways Act 1980 s.10. In force: May 25, 2000; £1.50.

This Order provides for a new road to be classified as a trunk road.

3083. Trunk roads – classification – A3015

A30 TRUNK ROAD (HONITON TO EXETER IMPROVEMENT) (TRUNKING OF PART OF A3015) ORDER 2000, SI 2000 2661; made under the Highways Act 1980 s.10. In force: October 25, 2000; £1.50.

This Order provides that a prescribed length of the A3015 shall be classified as a trunk road.

3084. Trunk roads – classification – A4777 – Wales

ST CLEARS-PEMBROKE DOCK TRUNK ROAD (A477) (SAGESTON-REDBERTH BYPASS) ORDER 2000, SI 2000 1172 (W.95); made under the Highways Act 1980 s.10, s.12. In force: May 17, 2000; £1.50.

This Order classifies a new road as a trunk road and provides that a certain length of road shall cease to be a trunk road once the new trunk road is open for through traffic.

3085. Trunk roads – classification – M1-A1

M1-A1 LINK (A63 TRUNK ROAD ELONGATED JUNCTION) (CONNECTING ROADS) SCHEME 2000, SI 2000 1136; made under the Highways Act 1980 s.16, s.17, s.19. In force: May 26, 2000; £1.00.

This Scheme enables the Secretary of State to authorise certain roads for the exclusive use of traffic of Classes I and II set out in the Highways Act 1980 Sch.4. Those roads will become trunk roads on the date this Order comes into force.

3086. Trunk roads – prescribed routes – A406

A406 TRUNK ROAD (HANGER LANE AND WOODVILLE GARDENS, EALING) (PROHIBITION OF RIGHT TURN) ORDER 2000, SI 2000 1796; made under the Road Traffic Regulation Act 1984 s.6. In force: July 1, 2000; £1.00.

This Order provides that no person shall cause or permit any vehicle having entered Hanger Lane from Woodville Gardens to proceed in any direction other than northwards.

3087. Trunk roads – red routes – A13

A13 TRUNK ROAD (TOWER HAMLETS) RED ROUTE TRAFFIC ORDER 2000, SI 2000 1647; made under the Road Traffic Regulation Act 1984 s.6. In force: June 26, 2000; £2.50.

This Order places a general prohibition on stopping in a designated area during restricted hours.

3088. Trunk roads – red routes – A3220

A3220 TRUNK ROAD (HAMMERSMITH & FULHAM) RED ROUTE (CLEARWAY) TRAFFIC ORDER 2000, SI 2000 1643; made under the Road Traffic Regulation Act 1984 s.6. In force: June 30, 2000; £2.00.

This Order provides that no person shall cause any vehicle to stop at any time in the trunk road red route clearway.

3089. Trunk roads – red routes – bus lanes – A1

A1 TRUNK ROAD (ISLINGTON) RED ROUTE (BUS PRIORITY) EXPERIMENTAL TRAFFIC ORDER 2000, SI 2000 247; made under the Road Traffic Regulation Act 1984 s.9, s.10. In force: February 21, 2000; £2.00.

This Order places a general prohibition on the presence of vehicles in designated bus lanes during restricted hours.

3090. Trunk roads – red routes – bus lanes – A1

A1 TRUNK ROAD (ISLINGTON) RED ROUTE (BUS PRIORITY) TRAFFIC ORDER 1999 EXPERIMENTAL VARIATION ORDER 2000, SI 2000 830; made under the Road Traffic Regulation Act 1984 s.9, s.10. In force: March 31, 2000; £1.00.

This Order varies provisions of the A1 Trunk Road (Islington) Red Route (Bus Priority) Traffic Order 1999 (SI 1999 1476).

3091. Trunk roads – red routes – bus lanes – A205

A205 TRUNK ROAD (LEWISHAM) RED ROUTE (BUS PRIORITY) TRAFFIC ORDER 2000, SI 2000 530; made under the Road Traffic Regulation Act 1984 s.6. In force: March 13, 2000; £2.00.

This Order places a prohibition on the presence of vehicles in designated bus lanes during restricted hours.

3092. Trunk roads – red routes – prescribed routes – A4

A4 TRUNK ROAD (GREAT WEST ROAD AND BOSTON MANOR ROAD, HOUNSLOW) (PROHIBITION OF TRAFFIC MOVEMENTS) ORDER 2000, SI 2000 872; made under the Road Traffic Regulation Act 1984 s.6. In force: March 20, 2000; £1.00.

This Order prescribes the direction of traffic flow along part of the A4.

3093. Trunk roads – red routes – prescribed routes – A4

A4 TRUNK ROAD (GREAT WEST ROAD AND BOSTON PARK ROAD, HOUNSLOW) (PROHIBITION OF TRAFFIC MOVEMENTS) ORDER 2000, SI 2000 871; made under the Road Traffic Regulation Act 1984 s.6. In force: March 20, 2000; £1.00.

This Order prescribes the direction of traffic flow along part of the A4.

3094. Trunk roads – red routes – prescribed routes – A4

A4 TRUNK ROAD (GREAT WEST ROAD AND RIVERBANK WAY, HOUNSLOW) (PRESCRIBED ROUTES) ORDER 2000, SI 2000 873; made under the Road Traffic Regulation Act 1984 s.6. In force: March 20, 2000; £1.00.

This Order prescribes the direction of traffic flow along part of the A4.

3095. Trunk roads – red routes – prescribed routes – A406

A406 TRUNK ROAD (GUNNERSBURY AVENUE, HOUNSLOW) RED ROUTE (PRESCRIBED ROUTE) TRAFFIC ORDER 2000, SI 2000 529; made under the Road Traffic Regulation Act 1984 s.6. In force: March 17, 2000; £1.00.

This Order prescribes the direction of traffic flow along part of the A406.

3096. Trunk roads – red routes – revocation – A23

A23 TRUNK ROAD (CROYDON) RED ROUTE (PROHIBITED TURNS) (NO.3) EXPERIMENTAL TRAFFIC ORDER 1998 REVOCATION ORDER 2000, SI 2000 246; made under the Road Traffic Regulation Act 1984 s.9, s.10. In force: February 22, 2000; £1.00.

This Order revokes the A23 Trunk Road (Croydon) Red Route (Prohibited Turns) (No.3) Experimental Traffic Order 1998 (SI 1988 2242).

3097. Trunk roads – red routes – stopping prohibition – A10

A10 TRUNK ROAD (HARINGEY) RED ROUTE TRAFFIC ORDER 2000, SI 2000 408; made under the Road Traffic Regulation Act 1984 s.6. In force: March 13, 2000; £2.00.

This Order places a general prohibition on stopping in a designated area during restricted hours.

3098. Trunk roads – red routes – stopping prohibition – A40

A40 TRUNK ROAD (HAMMERSMITH & FULHAM, KENSINGTON & CHELSEA AND WESTMINSTER) RED ROUTE (CLEARWAY) TRAFFIC ORDER 2000, SI 2000 1644; made under the Road Traffic Regulation Act 1984 s.6. In force: June 30, 2000; £2.00.

This Order provides that no person shall cause any vehicle to stop at any time in the trunk road red route clearway.

3099. Trunk roads – red routes – stopping prohibition – A501

A501 TRUNK ROAD (WESTMINSTER) RED ROUTE (CLEARWAY) TRAFFIC ORDER 2000, SI 2000 1642; made under the Road Traffic Regulation Act 1984 s.6. In force: June 30, 2000; £2.00.

This Order provides that no person shall cause any vehicle to stop at any time in the trunk road red route clearway.

3100. Trunk roads – red routes – stopping prohibitions – A205

A205 TRUNK ROAD (LEWISHAM) RED ROUTE TRAFFIC ORDER 2000, SI 2000 1285; made under the Road Traffic Regulation Act 1984 s.6. In force: May 17, 2000; £3.00.

This Order places a general prohibition on stopping in the trunk road red route during restricted hours subject to miscellaneous exemptions.

3101. Trunk roads – red routes – variation – A1

A1 TRUNK ROAD (BARNET) RED ROUTE (CLEARWAY) TRAFFIC ORDER 1996 VARIATION ORDER 2000, SI 2000 2118; made under the Road Traffic Regulation Act 1984 s.6. In force: June 30, 2000; £1.00.

This Order, which revokes the A1 Trunk Road (Barnet) Red Route (Clearway) Traffic Order 1996 Experimental Variation Order 1999 (SI 1999 997), varies the provisions of the A1 Trunk Road (Barnet) Red Route (Clearway) Traffic Order 1996 (SI 1996 819) and amendment slip.

3102. Trunk roads – red routes – variation – A4

A4 TRUNK ROAD (HILLINGDON) RED ROUTE (CLEARWAY) TRAFFIC ORDER 1996 VARIATION ORDER 2000, SI 2000 554; made under the Road Traffic Regulation Act 1984 s.6. In force: March 24, 2000; £1.00.

This Order varies provisions of the A4 Trunk Road (Hillingdon) Red Route (Clearway) Traffic Order 1996 (SI 1996 1163).

3103. Trunk roads – red routes – variation – A4

A4 TRUNK ROAD (HILLINGDON AND HOUNSLOW) RED ROUTE TRAFFIC ORDER 1997 VARIATION ORDER 2000, SI 2000 778; made under the Road Traffic Regulation Act 1984 s.6. In force: March 31, 2000; £1.00.

This Order varies certain provisions of the A4 Trunk Road (Hillingdon and Hounslow) Red Route Traffic Order 1997 (SI 1997 1507).

3104. Trunk roads – red routes – variation – A10

A10 TRUNK ROAD (HARINGEY) RED ROUTE EXPERIMENTAL TRAFFIC ORDER 1999 EXPERIMENTAL VARIATION ORDER 2000, SI 2000 1162; made under the Road Traffic Regulation Act 1984 s.9. In force: May 4, 2000; £1.50.

This Order amends the A10 Trunk Road (Haringey) Red Route Experimental Traffic Order 1999 (SI 1999 2635).

3105. Trunk roads – red routes – variation – A41

A41 TRUNK ROAD (BARNET) RED ROUTE (NO.2) TRAFFIC ORDER 1997 VARIATION ORDER 2000, SI 2000 1405; made under the Road Traffic Regulation Act 1984 s.6. In force: May 30, 2000; £1.00.

This Order varies the provisions of the A41 Trunk Road (Barnet) Red Route (No.2) Traffic Order 1997 (SI 1997 1210).

3106. Trunk roads – red routes – variation – A205

A205 TRUNK ROAD (GREENWICH) RED ROUTE TRAFFIC ORDER 1998 VARIATION ORDER 2000, SI 2000 777; made under the Road Traffic Regulation Act 1984 s.6. In force: April 4, 2000; £1.00.

This Order varies provisions of the A205 Trunk Road (Greenwich) Red Route Traffic Order 1998 (SI 1998 382).

3107. Trunk roads – red routes – variation – A205

A205 TRUNK ROAD (LEWISHAM) RED ROUTE TRAFFIC ORDER 1998 VARIATION ORDER 2000, SI 2000 769; made under the Road Traffic Regulation Act 1984 s.6. In force: April 3, 2000; £1.00.

This Order varies provisions of the A205 Trunk Road (Lewisham) Red Route Traffic Order 1998 (SI 1998 1835).

3108. Trunk roads – red routes – variation – A205

A205 TRUNK ROAD (LEWISHAM) RED ROUTE TRAFFIC ORDER 1999 VARIATION ORDER 2000, SI 2000 1238; made under the Road Traffic Regulation Act 1984 s.6. In force: May 15, 2000; £1.00.

This Order varies the provisions of the A205 Trunk Road (Lewisham) Red Route Traffic Order 1999 (SI 1999 81).

3109. Trunk roads – red routes – variation – A205

A205 TRUNK ROAD (SOUTHWARK) RED ROUTE TRAFFIC ORDER 1999 VARIATION ORDER 2000, SI 2000 1237; made under the Road Traffic Regulation Act 1984 s.6. In force: May 15, 2000; £1.00.

This Order varies the provisions of the A205 Trunk Road (Southwark) Red Route Traffic Order 1999 (SI 1999 1805).

3110. Trunk roads – red routes – variation – A316

A316 TRUNK ROAD (RICHMOND) RED ROUTE TRAFFIC ORDER 1997 VARIATION ORDER 2000, SI 2000 1141; made under the Traffic Regulation Act 1984 s.6. In force: May 10, 2000; £1.00.

This Order varies provisions of the A316 Trunk Road (Richmond) Red Route Traffic Order 1997 (SI 1997 1824).

3111. Trunk roads – red routes – variation – A501

A501 TRUNK ROAD (CAMDEN, ISLINGTON AND WESTMINSTER) RED ROUTE TRAFFIC ORDER 1997 VARIATION ORDER 2000, SI 2000 1566; made under the Road Traffic Regulation Act 1984 s.6. In force: June 19, 2000; £1.00.

This Order varies the A501 Trunk Road (Camden, Islington and Westminster) Red Route Traffic Order 1997 (SI 1997 2002).

3112. Trunk roads – slip roads – classification – A249

A249 TRUNK ROAD (IWADE BYPASS TO QUEENBOROUGH IMPROVEMENT) (SLIP ROADS) ORDER 2000, SI 2000 2696; made under the Highways Act 1980 s.10, s.41. In force: October 19, 2000; £1.50.

This Order provides for newly constructed slip roads to be classified as trunk roads.

3113. Trunk roads – speed limits – A316

A316 TRUNK ROAD (HANWORTH ROAD, COUNTRY WAY AND GREAT CHERTSEY ROAD, HOUNSLOW AND SPELTHORNE) (SPEED LIMITS) ORDER 2000, SI 2000 1671; made under the Road Traffic Regulation Act 1984 s.84, Sch.9 Part IV. In force: May 30, 2000; £1.00.

This Order imposes speed limits of 40 mph and 50 mph on specified lengths of road.

3114. Trunk roads – U turns – A4

A4 TRUNK ROAD (BATH ROAD, HILLINGDON) (PROHIBITION OF U-TURNS) ORDER 2000, SI 2000 980; made under the Road Traffic Regulation Act 1984 s.6. In force: April 10, 2000; £1.00.

This Order prohibits "U" turns in a designated area of the A4.

HOUSING

3115. Disabled persons – children – failure to address practical problems – council assessment Wednesbury unreasonable

C, a nine year old partially sighted boy also suffering from dyspraxia, severe asthma, incontinence and dyslexia, appealed against the refusal of his application for judicial review of the decision of ELBC to reject his application for rehousing. C lived with his mother and brother in a two-bedroomed local authority owned flat where he was obliged to share his mother's bed, partly owing to space constraints but also owing to his particular disabilities. C contended that the assessment process had been fundamentally flawed and that the decision of ELBC was *Wednesbury* unreasonable.

Held, allowing the appeal that ELBC had failed to address important practical problems faced by C when considering his application for rehousing and therefore the decision was *Wednesbury* unreasonable, *Secretary of State for Education and Science v. Tameside MBC* [1977] A.C. 1014, [1976] C.L.Y. 829 applied.

R. v. EALING LBC, *ex p.* C (A MINOR) (2000) 3 C.C.L. Rep. 122, Judge, L.J., CA.

3116. Grants – housing relocation grants – forms – Wales

RELOCATION GRANTS (FORMS OF APPLICATION) (AMENDMENT) (WALES) REGULATIONS 2000, SI 2000 1710 (W.116); made under the Housing Grants, Construction and Regeneration Act 1996 s.132, s.146. In force: July 4, 2000; £2.00.

These Regulations amend the Relocation Grants (Form of Application) Regulations 1997 (SI 1997 2847) and the Relocation Grants (Form of Application) (Welsh Form of Application) Regulations 1999 (SI 1999 2315) by modifying the Forms set out in the respective Schedules.

3117. Grants – housing renewal grants – forms

HOUSING RENEWAL GRANTS (PRESCRIBED FORM AND PARTICULARS) (AMENDMENT) (ENGLAND) REGULATIONS 2000, SI 2000 538; made under the Housing Grants, Construction and Regeneration Act 1996 s.2, s.101, s.146. In force: April 3, 2000; £2.00.

These Regulations amend the Form set out in the Housing Renewal Grants (Prescribed Form and Particulars) Regulations 1996 (SI 1996 2891) to be used by owner-occupiers and tenants when applying for housing renewal grants under the Housing Grants, Construction and Regeneration Act 1996 Ch.I Part I.

3118. Grants – housing renewal grants – forms – Wales

HOUSING RENEWAL GRANTS (PRESCRIBED FORM AND PARTICULARS AND WELSH FORM AND PARTICULARS) (AMENDMENT) (WALES) REGULATIONS 2000, SI 2000 1735 (W.119); made under the Housing Grants, Construction and Regeneration Act 1996 s.2, s.146. In force: In accordance with Reg.1; £2.00.

These Regulations amend the forms, set out in the Housing Renewal Grants (Prescribed Form and Particulars) Regulations 1996 (SI 1996 2891) and the Housing Renewal Grants (Welsh Form and Particulars) Regulations 1998 (SI 1998 1113), to be used by owner occupiers and tenants when applying for housing renewal grants under the Housing Grants, Construction and Regeneration Act 1996 Part 1 Ch.1 in consequence of amendments made to the Housing Renewal Grants Regulations 1996 (SI 1996 2890).

3119. Grants – housing renewal grants – means test

HOUSING RENEWAL GRANTS (AMENDMENT) (ENGLAND) REGULATIONS 2000, SI 2000 531; made under the Housing Grants, Construction and Regeneration Act 1996 s.3, s.30, s.31, s.146. In force: April 3, 2000; £2.50.

These Regulations amend the Housing Renewal Grants Regulations 1996 (SI 1996 2890) which set out the means test for determining the amount of renovation grant and disabled facilities grant which may be paid by local housing authorities to owner-occupier and tenant applicants under the Housing Grants, Construction and Regeneration Act 1996 Ch.I Part I. Most of the amendments are consequential on changes to the Housing Benefit (General) Regulations 1987 (SI 1987 1971).

3120. Grants – housing renewal grants – means test

HOUSING RENEWAL GRANTS (AMENDMENT NO.2) (ENGLAND) REGULATIONS 2000, SI 2000 910; made under the Housing Grants, Construction and Regeneration Act 1996 s.30, s.146. In force: April 3, 2000; £1.00.

These Regulations amend the Housing Renewal Grants Regulations 1996 (SI 1996 2890), which set out the means test for determining the amount of renovation grant, disabled facilities grant and common parts grant payable by local housing authorities to owner-occupiers or tenant applicants under the Housing Grants, Construction and Regeneration Act 1996, by increasing the applicable amount which is to be deducted from an applicant's financial resources as part of the means test. The Regulations amend the Housing Renewal Grants (Amendment) (England) Regulations 2000 (SI 2000 531) by revoking the provisions relating to housing allowance.

3121. Grants – housing renewal grants – means test – Wales

HOUSING RENEWAL GRANTS (AMENDMENT) (WALES) REGULATIONS 2000, SI 2000 973 (W.43); made under the Housing Grants, Construction and Regeneration Act 1996 s.3, s.30, s.31, s.146. In force: April 3, 2000; £1.50.

The Housing Renewal Grants Regulations 1996 (SI 1996 2890) set out the means test for determining the amount of renovation grant and disabled facilities grant which may be paid by local housing authorities to owner-occupier and tenant applicants under the Housing Grants, Construction and Regeneration Act 1996 Part I, Ch.1. These Regulations make applicable to Wales, in relation to grant applications made on or after April 3, 2000, certain provisions of the Housing Renewal Grants (Amendment) (England) Regulations 2000 (SI 2000 531) and the Housing Renewal Grants (Amendment No.2) (England) Regulations 2000 (SI 2000 910), which amended the 1996 Regulations.

3122. Grants – housing renovation grants

HOUSING GRANTS (ADDITIONAL PURPOSES) (ENGLAND) ORDER 2000, SI 2000 1492; made under the Housing Grants, Construction and Regeneration Act 1996 s.12, s.17, s.27, s.146. In force: July 4, 2000; £1.50.

This Order provides that the improvement of energy efficiency shall be an additional purpose for which a grant under the Housing Grants, Construction and Regeneration Act 1996 s.12 (renovation grants), s.17 (common parts grants) and s.27 (HMO grants) may be given.

3123. Grants – relocation grants – forms

RELOCATION GRANTS (FORM OF APPLICATION) (AMENDMENT) (ENGLAND) REGULATIONS 2000, SI 2000 720; made under the Housing Grants, Construction and Regeneration Act 1996 s.132, s.146. In force: April 3, 2000; £1.50.

These Regulations amend the form set out in the Schedule to the Relocation Grants (Form of Application) Regulations 1997 (SI 1997 2847), to be used for an application for relocation grant payable under the Housing Grants, Construction and Regeneration Act 1996 s.131 to s.140.

3124. Grants – renovation grants – failure to disclose income – material facts at date of submission – discretionary power to demand repayment

[Housing Grants, Construction and Regeneration Act 1996 s.42(2).]

In 1993 W, an owner occupier, made an application for a renovation grant from N to repair her property. In September 1996, following an inspection of the property, she filled in forms giving details of her income. At that time she was not working and was in receipt of benefits and, although she had lodgers, they had only recently arrived and were not paying rent as their application to N for housing benefit was still pending. In December 1996 both applications were granted, the lodgers' housing benefit being backdated to August 1996. In July 1997, N withdrew W's grant on the ground that she had failed to disclose the income from the lodgers, and demanded repayment of the sums already paid. W applied for judicial review of that decision.

Held, allowing the application, that N's decision was wrong in law. W's renovation grant application was made on the date the application was submitted. At that time she had no income from her lodgers and therefore her application was accurate and complete and there was no failure to disclose. Under the Housing Grants, Construction and Regeneration Act 1996 s.42(2) N had a discretion to demand repayment of a grant. By taking the stance that repayment was mandatory following a failure to disclose, N had unlawfully fettered its discretion. Further, N had failed to consider whether the alleged failure to disclose was material.

R. v. NEWHAM LBC, *ex p.* WATTS (2000) 32 H.L.R. 255, Ognall, J., QBD.

3125. Grants – renovation grants – obligation to approve grant applications where works required pursuant to notices served under Housing Act 1985

[Housing Act 1985 s.189, s.190; Local Government and Housing Act 1989 Part VIII s.102, s.113.]

GI, the owner of a number of properties, applied to GLBC for renovation grants following the service of notices requiring repairs under the Housing Act 1985 s.189 and s.190. The applications were refused by GLBC on the basis that GI had failed to provide two estimates for the repairs as required by the Local Government and Housing Act 1989 s.102, and further that one application had been received after the works had been completed. GI sought judicial review of the refusal, contending that, by virtue of s.113 of the 1989 Act, GLBC was obliged to approve the applications where notices had been served under s.189 and s.190 of the Act. The application was successful and GLBC appealed, contending that there had been no valid "application" for the purposes of s.113 if s.102 and the accompanying regulations were not complied with. GLBC maintained that the requirement for estimates enabled it to assess the reasonableness of the sum claimed and that if applicants were entitled to claim grant monies after the works had been completed it would have lost all opportunity to assess the standard and worth of the work. GLBC further contended that in s.113 the phrase "is necessary" was used implying that the works in question were yet to be carried out.

Held, dismissing the appeal, that attention had to be paid to the clear intention in s.113 of the Act to render approval of certain grant applications mandatory. By virtue of s.102(2)(b) a discretion was conferred upon the local authority to dispense with the requirement for estimates and therefore the argument that any application not accompanied by an estimate was invalid could not be supported. That discretion to dispense with estimates was elevated into an obligation where a mandatory grant was concerned. The use of the present tense in s.113 was a recognition that notices had been served under the 1985 Act and did not affect the time period in which an application could be submitted.

R. v. GREENWICH LBC, *ex p.* GLEN INTERNATIONAL LTD [2000] E.H.L.R. 382, Pill, L.J., CA.

3126. Grants – renovation grants – renovation of kitchen in multiple occupancy dwelling – categorisation of property – imposition of condition relating to kitchen location – intention to gain funding outside statutory guidelines

[Housing Act 1985 s.190, s.352.]

S owned a large property occupied by himself and his son and up to seven lodgers, the latter having separate rooms but sharing a bathroom and one kitchen with the rest of the household. S applied for a renovation grant from CBC to carry out works including fitting a new kitchen. CBC agreed to the grant but stipulated that, as the property was a "Category A" house in multiple occupation, the kitchen had to be within one floor of the rooms it was to serve, and therefore S's plan to site the extra kitchen in the basement was unacceptable. S contended that the accommodation constituted "self catering lodgings" not bedsits. CBC served notices on S to carry out works and repairs under the Housing Act1985 s.352 and s.190. S's appeal against the notices was dismissed on the basis that CBC's categorisation of the property was correct and that the notices were valid. S appealed.

Held, dismissing the appeal, that the judge was right to find that CBC's categorisation was correct, and S's attempt to hide the true nature of the accommodation by the use of the obscure and non statutory term "self catering lodgings" was ineffective. The judge had dealt with the question of reasonableness as part of his examination of the issue of categorisation. S had accepted that improved kitchen facilities were necessary and therefore it was required to make a choice between CBC's plan, which was within its guidelines and eligible for funding, and S's plan which was not. The judge's finding on the validity of the notices showed that he had taken account of the fact that only the first choice was reasonable. The underlying aim of S's appeal was to induce CBC to award funding outside their guidelines, which was outside the court's jurisdiction as it amounted to an appeal against the funding allocation.

STAFFORD v. CHARNWOOD BC [1999] E.H.L.R. 438, Potter, L.J., CA.

3127. Grants – renovation grants – time limits – revocation of grant – work not completed within time limits

[Housing Act1985 s.189(1); Local Government and Housing Act1989 s.134(2), Part VIII.]

TP sought judicial review of N's decision to cancel an improvement grant for carrying out repair works to TP's property. The property was subject to a notice under the Housing Act 1985 s.189(1), requiring TP to make repairs on the ground that it was unfit for human habitation. TP obtained the grant under the Local Government and Housing Act 1989 Part VIII, conditional upon the works being completed by an approved contractor within 12 months of the making of the award. A supplementary grant was made in January 1997 and TP asserted that the 12 month time period had been extended to January 1998 as a result. Further, TP stated that it obtained oral agreement to a change of contractors which it confirmed in writing. No reply was received from N, however, and the authority denied agreeing to the change. TP sought an extension to February 1998 when the works were completed. In March 1998, N informed TP that the grant had been cancelled on the basis that the works had not been completed on time and that an unapproved contractor had been used.

Held, refusing the application, that a decision to revoke a grant under s.134(2) of the 1989 Act was not limited to exceptional circumstances. The legislation linked the award of a grant to the 12 month time limit for completion of the work, with a discretionary power to extend. Taking into account the fact that the works had not been completed within 12 months of the supplementary grant, the decision to cancel the grant was not unreasonable.

R. v. NEWHAM LBC, *ex p.* TRENDGROVE PROPERTIES LTD (2000) 32 H.L.R. 424, Dyson, J., QBD.

3128. Homelessness – accommodation – accommodation offer lapsed following application for review – policy unlawful

[Housing Act 1996 s.193(5).]

B was offered housing by RBKC as a homeless person, but, in line with RBKC's policy, the offer lapsed when he applied for it to be reviewed. The review upheld the original offer and RBKC contended that it had fulfilled its duties under the Housing Act1996. B sought judicial review of the decision, contending that RBKC could not satisfy itself that the offer was suitable as required by s.193(5) of the 1996 Act until it had paid due regard to the representations made in support of the review application. B maintained that, as a result, it was only after the review that RBKC could reach a decision on suitability, and therefore could not lawfully be discharged from its duties until the review was complete. RKBC contended that keeping the offer open until the review process had been completed was not a statutory requirement, and would result in vacant accommodation in an area where local authority housing was already in extremely short supply.

Held, allowing the application, that there was nothing in the relevant legislation to prevent B from accepting the offer and asking for a review. RBKC would then have been obliged to keep the accommodation available until after the review was completed. Although that could cause administrative difficulties, RBKC was obliged to reflect that procedure in its policy, and its omission rendered the policy unlawful. Consequently, RBKC had not discharged its duty to B under the 1996 Act. The action had been properly brought by way of judicial review rather than as an appeal arising from the review, as it did not relate to the legality of the review procedure itself, but rather to B's rights prior to the review.

R. v. KENSINGTON AND CHELSEA RLBC, *ex p.* BYFIELD; R. v. KENSINGTON AND CHELSEA RLBC, *ex p.* ROUASS (1999) 31 H.L.R. 913, Moses, J., QBD.

3129. **Homelessness – accommodation – date for determining local connection was date of decision or review – interim accommodation pending review could constitute normal residence when establishing local connection**

[Housing Act 1996 s.188, s.198(2), s.199(3), s.202.]

S, a homeless person, applied to ELBC, a local housing authority, for priority accommodation. ELBC referred the duty to provide accommodation to another local housing authority, WCC, as the referring authority under the Housing Act 1996 s.198(2), on the basis that S had no local connection with ELBC. This decision was quashed on appeal by S, who had moved from WCC's area and begun living with his family in interim accommodation in ELBC's area by the time of the decision letter and ELBC appealed. The judge below had found that ELBC had failed to consider that S had a connection with the borough by the date of the decision letter and ELBC contended that the interim accommodation provided could not contribute towards a local connection. M appealed in similar circumstances against HFLBC's decision that he had no local connection with HFLBC, but instead had a local connection with ELBC.

Held, dismissing ELBC's appeal and allowing M's appeal, that (1) the material date for determining whether a homeless person had a local connection was the date of the initial decision, or where the case was under review, the date the local housing authority reviewed its decision, and (2) interim accommodation could constitute normal residence of an applicant's own choice pursuant to s.199(3) therefore establishing a local connection with a local housing authority's area. In determining a local connection it was necessary to consider family associations and any other special circumstances, for example, if M's and S's circumstances changed, such as by obtaining employment in the borough, or by ceasing to be in priority need. Reviews under s.202 had to be based on all the relevant facts and those would have to be considered afresh to determine if a local connection had been established.

EALING LBC v. SURDONJA; MOHAMED v. HAMMERSMITH AND FULHAM LBC; *sub nom*. SURDONJA v. EALING LBC; MOHAMMED v. HAMMERSMITH AND FULHAM LBC [2001] Q.B. 97, Henry, L.J., CA.

3130. **Homelessness – accommodation – offer of permanent accommodation refused – locus standi of daughter of family to reapply**

[Housing Act 1996 Part VII s.193(7).]

H, a 20 year old Somalian who had been living in temporary accommodation with her mother and five brothers, sought judicial review of the local authority's refusal to consider her rehousing application pursuant to the Housing Act 1996 Part VII. H's widowed mother had been offered permanent four-bedroom accommodation for herself and her six children, which she had refused on the basis of its unsuitability. H contended that, as she had played no part in her mother's refusal of the accommodation, she was entitled to apply in her own right for the rehousing of the family. The local authority maintained that the four-bedroom accommodation previously offered was in accordance with current housing policy for families of that size, and having made a reasonable offer of permanent accommodation, it had satisfied its obligations under s.193(7) of the 1996 Act. Consequently, since there had been no change of circumstance it had been entitled to refuse to consider H's application.

Held, refusing the application, that the local authority had fulfilled its obligations to the household under the Act and, barring any change in circumstances, H had no standing to replace her mother as an applicant for family accommodation regardless of the fact that she had not been a party to her mother's rejection of the accommodation offered, *R. v. North Devon DC, ex p. Lewis* [1981] 1 W.L.R. 328, [1981] C.L.Y. 1302 distinguished.

R. v. CAMDEN LBC, *ex p.* HERSI *The Times*, October 11, 2000, Brooke, L.J., CA.

3131. Homelessness – accommodation – temporary accommodation – suitability – duty of local authority to assess needs

[Housing Act 1985 Part III; Housing Act 1996 Part VI, Part VII.]

S, a mother of five who had particular medical needs, was a homeless person to whom LLBC, her local authority, had owed a full housing duty under the Housing Act 1985 Part III for a period of six years. During that period, S had been compelled to move between eight temporary places of residence. On one occasion she had been released from hospital after giving birth to find that her room had been relet. On another she had been evicted from her home owing to repossession proceedings commenced against the head lessee. S applied for judicial review of LLBC's failure to provide her with accommodation which she regarded as suitable. Relying on the provisions of the Housing Act 1996 Part VII which laid down a regime for the homeless superseding Part III of the 1985 Act, S argued that accommodation would only be suitable if available for at least two years from the date when it was first secured, and that LLBC could only discharge its duty by granting her a secure tenancy of suitable accommodation. This could be achieved by virtue of the allocation scheme established by Part VI of the 1996 Act under which points were allocated to qualifying persons according to their circumstances and needs. S contended that no points had been awarded in respect of her current unsatisfactory housing conditions, which were unsuited to her medical needs, and that she should have been granted discretionary points to take into account LLBC's maladministration over a period of six years. In October 1998, four months after S had been granted leave to apply for judicial review, LLBC decided that S's existing accommodation was suitable. In March 1999, LLBC visited and assessed S's property. Shortly thereafter LLBC ascertained from S's landlord that the landlord's lease would not expire until January 2001 at the earliest. S argued that LLBC had an obligation to carry out an assessment of her property needs before accommodation was viewed to see whether it fulfilled those needs.

Held, refusing the application, that although S had been very poorly treated by LLBC, LLBC was currently complying with its duties under Part III of the 1985 Act and Part VI of the 1996 Act. It had taken reasonable steps, albeit belatedly, to satisfy itself in March 1999 that S's property would be available for a suitable period of time. The provisions of Part VII of the 1996 Act were independent of those contained in Part III of the 1985 Act and therefore there was no basis for contending that accommodation would only be suitable under Part III of the 1985 Act if available for a full two years. LLBC was not required to carry out an assessment of S's property needs before considering the suitability of the accommodation in which she was presently residing. LLBC had acted lawfully and reasonably in deciding to award points only for the medical priority which had resulted from S's housing conditions. It was not appropriate to award points separately for the housing conditions which caused S's medical priority. Furthermore, LLBC's decision to decline to award discretionary points to S was justified; S's interests had been adequately protected by the awarding of points for the length of time she had been on the waiting list.

R. v. LAMBETH LBC, *ex p.* TOUHEY; *sub nom.* R. v. LAMBETH LBC, *ex p.* SHAKES (2000) 32 H.L.R. 707, Richards, J., QBD.

3132. Homelessness – accommodation – temporary accommodation in seaside resorts – unreasonable to ignore families' educational and employment requirements

[Housing Act 1988 s.188.]

NLBC purported to discharge its duty under the Housing Act 1988 s.188 to provide suitable temporary accommodation for homeless people by securing bed and breakfast accommodation at seaside resorts. S and other homeless people in receipt of housing benefit applied for judicial review of the decision, contending that the policy of securing accommodation at such a distance from London failed to take into account the effect it would have on their children's education and on the employment of family members. In response, NLBC argued that it could neither afford nor find accommodation for S locally, or even in London, and that its policy was to refrain from accommodating people out of London only if there was a "serious risk to life or health" and the effect on education or employment was irrelevant.

Held, allowing the application, that NLBC was clearly *Wednesbury* unreasonable not to have considered the effect of location on the education of the children and on the employment of family members. Although NLBC could rightly take into account financial and housing resource constraints, there was a minimum below which "suitable accommodation" could not be allowed to fall. That minimum was to be defined in terms of the needs of the family, taking into account such matters as the effect of location on education and employment. NLBC's policy was too narrowly defined in that it settled criteria in advance that prevented a proper consideration of whether the accommodation out of its area was suitable for the needs of individual applicants and their family members.

R. (ON THE APPLICATION OF SACUPIMA) v. NEWHAM LBC; *sub nom.* R. v. NEWHAM LBC, *ex p.* SACUPIMA (2001) 33 H.L.R. 1, Dyson, J., QBD.

3133. Homelessness – appeals – right of appeal – failure to appeal in time – judicial review not available as alternative where right of appeal not exercised

[Housing Act 1996 s.204.]

O's application to BLBC as a homeless person was refused and she was informed of her right to appeal within 21 days under the Housing Act 1996 s.204. O did not appeal, partly because she did not believe that there was any point in doing so. After the time limit had expired, O applied for permission to move for judicial review of BLBC's refusal.

Held, dismissing the application, that O had been aware of an alternative remedy. She had chosen not to exercise that remedy and there were no exceptional circumstances warranting departure from the requirement that all other remedies had to be exhausted before judicial review would be available.

R. v. BRENT LBC, *ex p.* O'CONNOR (1999) 31 H.L.R. 923, Tucker, J., QBD.

3134. Homelessness – delay – duty of local housing authority under Housing Act 1996 s.193 not subject to time limit

[Housing Act 1996 s.193.]

A, a couple with three children, applied to SLBC to be rehoused on the basis that they were statutorily homeless. They were all living in one bedroom accommodation. SLBC accepted in May 1997 that it had a duty to rehouse A under the Housing Act 1996 s.193. In August 1997 SLBC wrote to A, informing them that they would be rehoused in accordance with SLBC's policy within six months. There were difficulties in finding four bedroom accommodation in SLBC's area, therefore A agreed that three bedroom accommodation possibly outside their preferred areas would be acceptable. SLBC made two offers of three bedroom accommodation in May and June 1998. Each was rejected, and SLBC accepted that the properties were unsuitable. A third offer was also rejected in December 1998, which SLBC again accepted was unsuitable, however, by this time, A had already obtained leave to seek judicial review of

SLBC's failure to find suitable accommodation. At the time of the hearing, the suitability of a fourth offer was under review by SLBC.

Held, refusing the application, that there was no time limit under which a local authority must carry out its obligations under s.193. It was clear from the facts that SLBC had been attempting to house A and that the delay was due to a lack of suitable housing stock. On the facts, there was no foundation in A's contention that SLBC did not intend to carry out its s.193 duty.

R. v. SOUTHWARK LBC, *ex p.* ANDERSON (2000) 32 H.L.R. 96, Moses, J., QBD.

3135. **Homelessness – housing policy unlawful – local authority failed to give consideration to factors which might give homeless applicant priority**

[Housing Act 1996 s.167(2), Part VI.]

A and his family were homeless and WCC accepted that it was under a duty to provide permanent accommodation under the Housing Act 1996 Part VI. A sought judicial review of WCC's failure to provide accommodation, arguing that, having accepted that the family was homeless, WCC was under a duty to consider certain other factors, including, inter alia, health and welfare issues, listed in s.167(2)(a) to (f) of the Act. WCC argued that, once it had accepted an obligation under Part IV of the Act, it was entitled to allocate priority according to the date it had accepted the applicant as homeless, without reference to any other factors.

Held, allowing the application, that WCC had failed to give a proper consideration to the categories of need listed in s.167(2). The needs specified therein were not separate, but cumulative, so that an applicant could be covered by more than one category. WCC had acted unlawfully by refusing to give any thought to other factors once it had decided that A was homeless.

R. v. WESTMINSTER CITY COUNCIL, *ex p.* AL-KHORSAN (2001) 33 H.L.R. 6, Latham, J., QBD.

3136. **Homelessness – immigrants – accommodation**

PERSONS SUBJECT TO IMMIGRATION CONTROL (HOUSING AUTHORITY ACCOMMODATION AND HOMELESSNESS) ORDER 2000, SI 2000 706; made under the Asylum and Immigration Act 1996 s.118, s.119, s.166. In force: April 3, 2000; £2.50.

This Order revokes all extant Orders made under the Asylum and Immigration Act 1996 s.9 and specifies classes of persons subject to immigration control for the purposes of s.118, which requires a housing authority to secure that a tenancy of or licence to occupy housing accommodation is not granted to a person subject to immigration control unless he is of a specified class, and s.119, which provides that a person who is subject to immigration control is not eligible for accommodation or homelessness assistance in Scotland or Northern Ireland unless he is of a specified class.

3137. **Homelessness – immigrants – local authority housing and assistance**

HOMELESSNESS (ENGLAND) REGULATIONS 2000, SI 2000 701; made under the Housing Act 1996 s.185, s.194, s.198, s.215. In force: April 3, 2000; £2.00.

These Regulations, which revoke and re-enact with changes the Homelessness Regulations 1996 (SI 1996 2754), prescribe classes of persons subject to immigration control who are eligible for housing assistance under the Housing Act 1996 Part VII and prescribe periods for notices and applications for the purposes of that Part. The class of persons subject to immigration control, who are eligible for housing assistance because they are nationals of states which are signatories to the European Convention on Social and Medical Assistance or the European Social Charter, has been amended.

3138. Homelessness – immigrants – local authority housing and assistance – Wales

HOMELESSNESS (WALES) REGULATIONS 2000, SI 2000 1079 (W.72); made under the Housing Act 1996 s.185, s.194, s.198. In force: April 1, 2000.

These Regulations, which revoke the Homelessness Regulations 1996 (SI 1996 2754 as amended), provide for the Homelessness (England) Regulations 2000 (SI 2000 701) to have effect in Wales. Those Regulations prescribe classes of persons subject to immigration control who are eligible for housing assistance under the Housing Act 1996 Part VII and prescribe periods for notices and applications for the purposes of that Part.

3139. Homelessness – intentional homelessness – decision making process – local authority's failure to disclose reasons for decision

R had the tenancy of a flat from BLBC. A suspended possession order had been made by which R was required to pay off her rent arrears in weekly instalments. R went to Jamaica in 1994 to care for her sick mother, who subsequently died. R had left the flat in the care of her two sons who did not keep up the arrears repayments, and the flat was repossessed by BLBC in March 1996. R returned to the UK in August 1997 and presented herself as homeless. R was interviewed by BLBC and they wrote in her file that she had told them that she had been aware of the repossession before she returned to the UK, although R later informed them that she had not been aware of it until her arrival in the UK. R's application was refused on the ground that she had made herself intentionally homeless by leaving her accommodation in Jamaica. On review, the decision was upheld, but at no time did BLBC specifically refer to R's purported admission in relation to the time of her knowledge of the repossession. R's appeal to the county court was dismissed and she appealed to the Court of Appeal.

Held, allowing the appeal and quashing the decision, that given that they were aware that there was a potential dispute in relation to the time of R's knowledge of the repossession, BLBC had acted unfairly in failing to disclose that they had relied on R's purported admission in reaching their decision, as R had thereby been denied the opportunity of bringing evidence to refute it.

ROBINSON v. BRENT LBC (1999) 31 H.L.R. 1015, Hutchison, L.J., CA.

3140. Homelessness – intentional homelessness – issue of affordability irrelevant to application for homelessness assistance

[Housing Act 1996 s.177; Homelessness (Suitability of Accommodation) Order 1996 (SI 1996 3204).]

W presented herself to LLBC as homeless, claiming that she had left her previous accommodation as a result of harassment from her landlady, rent arrears and her belief that she was not entitled to remain at the property following the expiry of the contractual term of her assured shorthold tenancy. LLBC decided that she was intentionally homeless. The decision, which was made on the same day as the application, was based on one interview and limited supplementary inquiries. No inquiries were made as to her ability to afford that accommodation. W appealed against LLBC's decision.

Held, dismissing the appeal, that it was necessary under the Housing Act 1996 s.177 and the Homelessness (Suitability of Accommodation) Order 1996 for an authority to consider an applicant's ability to afford accommodation only if it was relevant to the application for homelessness assistance. The question of affordability was not relevant to W's application: although she had told LLBC that she was in arrears, she had said that that was owing to delays in the processing of her housing benefit claim, which had not been finally determined at that time. It was not, therefore, possible for LLBC to inquire into whether she could or could not have afforded the rent, as she did not know how much housing benefit she was entitled to. Furthermore, her claim that she had left because she did not know that she was entitled to remain until her landlord had obtained a possession order was a mistake of law and not fact and did not make her actions non-deliberate. On the basis of its inquiries, LLBC had been entitled to find that she was intentionally homeless.

WATSON v. LAMBETH LBC, December 7, 1999, Judge Compstone, CC (Wandsworth). [*Ex rel.* David Carter, Barrister, Arden Chambers, 27 John Street, London].

3141. Homelessness – intentional homelessness – local authority empowered to reconsider application for housing and reject on different grounds

[Housing Act 1996 s.183, s.184(3), s.193(2), s.202, s.204.]

B was threatened with homelessness following the non payment of rent. At that time the court had ordered that she be reunited with her children following their temporary placements with foster parents. Following B's application to CBC under the Housing Act 1996 s.183, she was informed that, whilst she was threatened with homelessness and eligible for assistance, CBC was under no duty under s.184(3) to provide accommodation as she was not in priority need and her children were not residing with her. A reconsideration of CBC's decision was confirmed. B appealed to the county court under s.204 of the Act, and during the proceedings CBC issued a supplementary decision, stating that whilst B had priority need, in that her children were expected to be living with her, CBC had no duty to rehouse her as she had become homeless intentionally. Following legal advice B pursued her appeal, contending that the latter decision was *Wednesbury* unreasonable as CBC had erred by reinforcing its original decision on different grounds not notified to B as stipulated under s.184(3). The judge found for B, ruling that there was a duty to rehouse her under s.193(2), and CBC appealed.

Held, allowing the appeal, that CBC had correctly based its decision upon the satisfaction of priority need and intentionality under the 1996 Act. Whilst it had not erred by revisiting the earlier decision, the question for the court was whether B's circumstances, when looked at as a whole, justified any relief in public law. CBC's latter decision was the one in issue, and whilst different grounds had been employed to reach its conclusion, they were not flawed and had to be considered. The order was set aside, pending B's request for a review, under s.202, of CBC's earlier decision.

CRAWLEY BC v. B (2000) 32 H.L.R. 636, Buxton, L.J., CA.

3142. Homelessness – intentional homelessness – prisoners – commission of offence constituted deliberate act notwithstanding subsequent house move

[Housing Act 1996 s.191(1).]

M, who had been evicted from council accommodation on the grounds of nuisance, subsequently held a six month assured tenancy in private rented accommodation. Following sentence for a number of offences committed during the period of her council tenancy, M was informed by the probation service that housing benefit would not be paid to her landlord during her sentence and as a result she lost the tenancy. M was notified by SCC that she was considered to be intentionally homeless under the Housing Act 1996 s.191(1) on the basis that her criminal activities had constituted "deliberate" actions, the consequence of which was her homelessness. M appealed and, whilst conceding that under a literal reading of s.191(1) she was intentionally homeless, argued that the offences should have been viewed only in relation to their consequences upon her council tenancy which was in effect when they were committed and should have no bearing upon her private tenancy.

Held, dismissing the appeal, that there were no practical or policy grounds for discounting M's criminal actions while at a previous property which had later resulted in the loss a subsisting tenancy as "deliberate" actions under s.191(1). It followed that M, in committing the offences, had made herself intentionally homeless.

MINCHIN v. SHEFFIELD CITY COUNCIL *The Times*, April 26, 2000, Henry, L.J., CA.

3143. Homelessness – intentional homelessness – review procedures – involvement of original decision maker

[Housing Act 1996 Part VII, s.202, s.204; Allocation of Housing and Homelessness (Review Procedures) Regulations 1999 (SI 1999 71).]

B applied to be rehoused on the basis that she was homeless under the Housing Act 1996 Part VII. FBC's homelessness officer decided that she was not in priority need because she was not vulnerable. B applied for a review of the decision under s.202 of the Act. The reviewing officer decided that she was not in priority need, and that she was intentionally homeless. B appealed to the county court under s.204 of the Act. During the course of disclosure and the exchange of evidence, B discovered that the original homelessness officer had assisted the reviewing officer during the course of the review. The assistance included writing and receiving letters, assisting with further enquiries and attending with the reviewing officer at a further interview with B. The judge gave B permission to raise the involvement of the original homelessness officer during the review as an additional ground of appeal, and dealt with this ground as a preliminary issue. B relied on the Allocation of Housing and Homelessness (Review Procedures) Regulations 1999.

Held, dismissing the appeal, that the 1999 Regulations only required that the decision on review was made by a senior officer who had not been involved in the original decision, they did not prevent the original decision-maker from assisting the reviewing officer to carry out routine work in the course of the review. It would be prohibitively expensive and inappropriate for small local housing authorities to construct "chinese walls" within their housing departments. The answers obtained in the instant case would not have been different had a different officer made the enquiries.

BUTLER v. FAREHAM BC, June 26, 2000, Judge Thompson, CC (Southampton). [*Ex rel.* Robert Duddridge, Barrister, 2 Gray's Inn Square Chambers, London].

3144. Homelessness – intentional homelessness – voluntary departure from country of birth – request for local authority accommodation – facts for consideration

P, an Indian national, lived with her parents-in-law following her husband's death before moving with her two daughters to England where she obtained employment and stayed in temporary accommodation with friends. P approached the local housing authority, MLBC, on the basis that she had been given notice to quit and was therefore threatened with homelessness. It was found at first instance that P was intentionally homeless on the basis that she had voluntarily left her accommodation in India and had come to the UK to avoid payment of an Indian residence tax and to better her children's education. P appealed, submitting written representations to the effect that, amongst other reasons, she had suffered emotional abuse from her father-in-law as a consequence of which life in India had become intolerable. MLBC maintained its original stance on reviewing P's case, referring to P's description of the abuse, but not mentioning her summary in which she stated that life had become intolerable. P appealed, contending that (1) the written representations raised a new factual issue which any reasonable authority would have investigated further, and (2) P had left India in ignorance of a relevant fact, namely whether she would obtain settled housing within a reasonable time of her arrival in the UK.

Held, dismissing the appeal, that MLBC was entitled to take account of P's written representations and rely on the contents of the paragraph detailing the abuse rather than the description applied in the summarising paragraph. MLBC had thus satisfied the test, *R. v. Kensington and Chelsea RLBC, ex p. Bayani* (1990) 22 H.L.R. 406, [1991] C.L.Y. 1897 applied. Further, P had not investigated whether she would be likely to find settled housing within a reasonable time of arrival, nor did she have any specific housing in mind. Those circumstances amounted to no more than an expectation or aspiration, *R. v.*

Westminster City Council, ex p. Obeid (1997) 29 H.L.R. 389, [1996] C.L.Y. 3050 considered..

PERIERA v. MERTON LBC, June 26, 2000, Recorder Cooper, MCLC. [*Ex rel.* Wayne Beglan, Barrister, 2-3 Gray's Inn Square, London].

3145. Homelessness – personal property – damages for burglary – no duty to provide protection unless real likelihood of harm

[Housing Act 1985 s.70; Housing Act 1996 s.211.]

D appealed against the dismissal of her claim (Unreported, October 22, 1998) against SLBC for damages suffered as a result of a burglary at her council flat. D had complained to the council of harassment from a neighbour which culminated in an assault which left her in need of hospital treatment. Shortly afterwards D applied to the council for alternative accommodation on the basis that she was unintentionally homeless and also advised the council that her property was likely to be at risk from burglary if the flat was not made secure. SLBC admitted a duty to house existed under the Housing Act 1985 s.70 (subsequently the Housing Act 1996 s.211) but denied that they owed any duty to D to protect her property.

Held, dismissing the appeal, that local authority owed no duty to protect the property of persons who were homeless, unless the authority had reason to believe there was a real likelihood of harm to the property and no suitable alternative arrangements had been made. It was not sufficient for the local authority to have reason to believe that the person was homeless or threatened with homelessness.

DEADMAN v. SOUTHWARK LBC *The Times*, August 31, 2000, Ward, L.J., CA.

3146. Homelessness – possession orders – secure tenancy obtained by fraud – discretion to consider future application on homelessness grounds

LBC sought a possession order for a flat held on a secure tenancy by A. A had obtained the tenancy by misrepresenting to LBC that she was homeless, whereas she already had a tenancy with another local housing authority. LBC's application succeeded at first instance and A appealed, contending that the order was futile because taking possession of the flat would cause her to be homeless and consequently would raise an identical obligation in LBC to rehouse her.

Held, dismissing the appeal, that although it was accepted that A would be made homeless if the order was granted, it was not for the court to fetter LBC's discretion, or to exercise it instead of LBC, in relation to any further application A might make to be housed on grounds of homelessness.

LEWISHAM LBC v. AKINSOLA (2000) 32 H.L.R. 414, Sedley, L.J., CA.

3147. Homelessness – possession orders – threatened homelessness – local authority's duty to act prior to eviction

[Housing Act 1996 s.175(1)(c), s.184, s.195.]

A possession order was granted in favour of the landlord in respect of the house K occupied. K applied for housing assistance for herself and her extended family based on the threat of homelessness. NLBC deferred taking action to accommodate the family, informing them to stay in the house until the bailiffs evicted them. When K was evicted the council offered unsuitable temporary accommodation in Great Yarmouth. K's request that the family should be housed together was refused. K applied for judicial review of NLBC's decision to provide accommodation which was unsuitable and only when eviction had occurred, thereby failing to fulfil their statutory duty under the Housing Act 1996 s.195.

Held, allowing the application, that (1) in the period between the order for possession and K's actual eviction, she was not classed as homeless under s.175(1)(c) of the Act, *R. v. Newham LBC, ex p. Sacupima The Times*, January 12, 2000, [2000] C.L.Y. 3132 disapproved, but rather as threatened with homelessness. Accordingly NLBC had erred in failing to take steps immediately under s.184 of the Act to determine whether K was eligible for assistance and, in priority need and whether a duty was owed to her under s.195 of the Act, and (2) NLBC had acted unreasonably in not seeking to house K with her family.

R. v. NEWHAM LBC, *ex p.* KHAN (2001) 33 H.L.R. 29, Collins, J., QBD.

3148. Homelessness – priority needs – change in circumstances – no power to revoke earlier lawful decision

[Housing Act 1996 s.193(2), s.202(1)(b).]

S applied to BLBC for housing at a time when his son was living with him. BLBC informed him that it had an obligation under the Housing Act 1996 s.193(2) to assist him with housing provision for a period of two years as he had a priority need. Shortly after that decision, S's son went to live with his mother and S's solicitors informed BLBC of the change in circumstances. BLBC subsequently informed S that it was unable to provide him with further housing assistance as he was no longer in priority need. S applied for a judicial review of that decision. BLBC contended that relief should be refused on the grounds that the proper procedure was for S to seek review of the decision under s.202(1)(b) of the Act.

Held, granting the application, that BLBC was not empowered to revoke its earlier lawful decision concerning its obligation to provide accommodation. The original decision remained lawful because the change in circumstances occurred after that decision had been made, *Crawley BC v. B The Times,* March 28, 2000, [2000] C.L.Y. 3141, distinguished, *R. v. Lambeth LBC, ex p. Miah* (1995) 27 H.L.R. 21, [1996] C.L.Y. 3075, approved. A code setting out the circumstances in which a local housing authority ceased to be duty bound to provide accommodation was provided under s.163(6) of the Act, but it did not embrace applicants who no longer had priority need. Notwithstanding the uncertainty over the appropriate review procedure, the High Court maintained a residual jurisdiction which it exercised in favour of S.

R. v. BRENT LBC, *ex p.* SADIQ; *sub nom.* BRENT LBC v. SADIQ *The Times,* July 27, 2000, Moses, J., QBD.

3149. Homelessness – priority needs – judicial review – local authority's refusal to exercise discretionary powers to provide accommodation pending determination of appeal

[Housing Act 1996 s.189, s.202, s.204.]

W, the father of two children, C, was in receipt of income support and child benefit payments on their behalf. The children's mother was being treated for drug addiction and C spent a large part of their time with their father, who was living in temporary accommodation which was inadequate for their needs. W applied to the local housing authority, TH, on the basis that he was homeless and in priority need pursuant to the Housing Act 1996 s.189. At the same time, he applied for a residence order in respect of C. An interim joint residence order was made, under which C stayed with their father for five nights each fortnight. TH decided on the basis of this order that W did not qualify for priority accommodation and declined to exercise its power under s.204(4) of the 1996 Act in W's favour. W asked for a review under s.202 of the Act and also asked for an extension of W's permission to remain in the temporary accommodation which he had been allocated pending the final outcome of his application to the Family Proceedings Court. TH advised W of his right of appeal under s.204 of the Act but declined to exercise its power under s.204(4) to accommodate W pending determination of the appeal. W sought permission to apply for judicial review of TH's decision.

Held, granting permission to apply for judicial review, that (1) s.204(4) conferred a broad discretion on a local housing authority and only exceptionally would a decision not to exercise that discretion be amenable to judicial review, *R. v. Brighton and Hove BC, ex p. Nacion* (1999) 31 H.L.R. 1095, [1999] C.L.Y. 3043 considered. The correct procedure would normally be to seek an expedited hearing of the appeal, to avoid the making of applications under s.202 or appeals under s.204 without merit; but in the instant case there were practical difficulties in obtaining an expedited hearing of the full appeal; (2) W's circumstances were exceptional in that he had been the primary carer for C for the previous two years; (3) it was arguable that there had been errors in law in the decision making process, namely in the interpretation of the wording of s.189 to determine the extent of residence in a situation where there was joint residence, and (4) there was an issue of procedural impropriety on the s.202 review. Overall, there was sufficient evidence to conclude that TH might not have adequately addressed the matters which they ought to have taken into account in considering the exercise of its powers under s.204(4).

WILLIAMS v. TOWER HAMLETS LBC, April 27, 2000, Peter Gibson, L.J., CA. [*Ex rel.* Jon Holbrook, Barrister, 2 Garden Court, Middle Temple, London].

3150. Housing benefit – rent officers – functions

RENT OFFICERS (HOUSING BENEFIT FUNCTIONS) (AMENDMENT) ORDER 2000, SI 2000 1; made under the Housing Act 1996 s.122. In force: April 3, 2000; £2.00.

This Order amends the Rent Officers (Housing Benefit Functions) Order 1997 (SI 1997 1984) which confers functions on rent officers, in connection with housing benefit and rent allowance subsidy, and requires them to make determinations and redeterminations in respect of tenancies and licences of dwellings.

3151. Housing policy – allocation of housing

ALLOCATION OF HOUSING (ENGLAND) REGULATIONS 2000, SI 2000 702; made under the Housing Act 1996 s.160, s.161, s.162, s.163, s.215. In force: April 3, 2000; £2.00.

These Regulations, which revoke and re-enact with changes the Allocation of Housing Regulations 1996 (SI 1996 2753), make provision for cases where allocations of housing accommodation by local housing authorities are not subject to the Housing Act 1996 Part VI and prescribe classes of persons who qualify to be allocated housing under that Part. The class of persons subject to immigration control, who are eligible for housing assistance because they are nationals of states which are signatories to the European Convention on Social and Medical Assistance or the European Social Charter, has been amended.

3152. Housing policy – ill health – transfer on basis of medical needs – failure to accord priority to multiple cases in same household

Tenants of T applying for transfers on the basis of medical needs were awarded points by T's medical officer, with priority given to those holding higher numbers of points. However, there was no means of awarding extra points in cases where more than one person had medical needs in a given household. U sought judicial review of T's decision, refusing his transfer request. Three of his children were anaemic and one also suffered from leukaemia and he contended that it was irrational not to take account of the cumulative effect in cases of multiple medical need.

Held, allowing the application and granting a declaration, that a household containing more than one person with medical needs had to be considered as being in greater need than a household with only one person with an equivalent need. A rational allocations policy ought properly to allow for such a contingency. Accordingly, T's policy was unlawful, *R. v. Lambeth LBC, ex p. Ashley* (1997) 29 H.L.R. 385, [1997] C.L.Y. 2698 and *R. v. Islington LBC, ex p. Reilly* (1999) 31 H.L.R. 651, [1998] C.L.Y. 3032 applied. Further, there was no evidence that the discretion to grant priority to certain applications had ever been deployed in cases of multiple medical need.

R. v. TOWER HAMLETS LBC, *ex p.* UDDIN; R. v. TOWER HAMLETS LBC, *ex p.* CURTIS; R. v. TOWER HAMLETS LBC, *ex p.* TAHID (2000) 32 H.L.R. 391, Keene, J., QBD.

3153. Local authorities – discretionary loans – interest rate

HOUSING (SERVICE CHARGE LOANS) (AMENDMENT) (ENGLAND) REGULATIONS 2000, SI 2000 1963; made under the Housing Act 1985 s.450A, s.450B, s.450C. In force: August 14, 2000; £1.00.

These Regulations amend, in relation to local authorities which are housing authorities, the Housing (Service Charge Loans) Regulations 1992 (SI 1992 1708), which give tenants a right to a loan in respect of service charges for repairs where the lease was granted under the Housing Act 1995 Part V and the landlord is a housing authority. They disapply the Housing Act 1985 Sch.16 as regards the rate of interest for discretionary loans and, as a consequence, the rate of interest payable on such loans shall be such a reasonable rate as may be determined by the local authority making the loan.

3154. Local authority housing – allocation – Wales

ALLOCATION OF HOUSING (WALES) REGULATIONS 2000, SI 2000 1080 (W.73); made under the Housing Act 1996 s.160, s.161, s.162, s.163. In force: April 1, 2000; £2.00.

These Regulations provide for certain provisions of the Allocation of Housing (England) Regulations 2000 (SI 2000 702), prescribing cases, classes, information and requirements for the purposes of the Housing Act 1996 s.160, s.161, s.162 and s.163 respectively, to have effect in Wales and revoke, in relation to Wales, the Allocation of Housing Regulations 1996 (SI 1996 2753 as amended).

3155. Local authority housing – duty to house immigrants – Wales

PERSONS SUBJECT TO IMMIGRATION CONTROL (HOUSING AUTHORITY ACCOMMODATION) (WALES) ORDER 2000, SI 2000 1036 (W.67); made under the Immigration and Asylum Act 1999 s.118, s.166. In force: April 1, 2000; £1.50.

The Immigration and Asylum Act 1999 s.118 requires a housing authority, so far as practicable, to secure that a tenancy of, or a licence to occupy, housing accommodation provided under the Housing Act 1985 Part II is not granted to a person subject to immigration control unless that person is of a specified class, or the licence to occupy such accommodation is granted in accordance with arrangements made under s.95 of the 1999 Act. This Order provides for the classes of persons which are specified for the purposes of s.118 in relation to England by the Persons Subject to Immigration Control (Housing Authority Accommodation and Homelessness) Order 2000 (SI 2000 706) to be specified for such purposes in relation to Wales.

3156. Possession orders – nuisance – secure tenancies – nuisance and annoyance caused by child of household – grounds for possession

[Housing Act 1985 s.83, Sch.2 Ground 2.]

B, a secure tenant under the Housing Act 1985, appealed an order dismissing her appeal against a suspended possession order made against her. PCC, the local authority, had sought a possession order against B under Sch.2 Ground 2 of the 1985 Act. The particulars of the grounds set out in the s.83 notice served on B included allegations that B had "allowed" her two teenage grandsons to act in a manner that had caused nuisance and annoyance to other residents. A possession order was made and suspended for 22 months on compliance with the terms of the tenancy agreement. B appealed, contending that (1) the ground relied upon by PCC required that some fault on her part be established; (2) PCC had not satisfactorily particularised the ground relied upon by incorrectly stating that she had "allowed" her grandsons to behave the way they had, and (3) the order and the period of suspension were unreasonable.

Held, dismissing the appeal, that (1) Sch.2 Ground 2 unambiguously required no fault, or even knowledge, on the part of the tenant to be established; (2) B had allowed the acts committed by her grandsons, as she had failed to control them over a considerable period of time, and (3) the imposition of a suspended order and the period of suspension had been reasonable in all the circumstances, *Kensington and Chelsea RLBC v. Simmonds* [1996] 3 F.C.R. 246, [1996] C.L.Y. 3767 followed.

BRYANT v. PORTSMOUTH CITY COUNCIL; *sub nom.* PORTSMOUTH CITY COUNCIL v. BRYANT [2000] E.H.L.R. 287, Simon Brown, L.J., CA.

3157. Possession orders – rent arrears – order granted on basis of rent arrears – local authority seeking to rely on allegations of nuisance as ground for possession

B was the tenant of a flat, which she had rented from H since 1981. In September 1997, H obtained a suspended possession order against B on the basis of rent arrears of £1,718.47, which B was to pay at the rate of £2.50 per week. Owing to problems with housing benefit, B breached the suspended possession order and in August 1999 H applied for a warrant of possession on the basis of arrears amounting to £2,106.36. B applied to suspend the possession warrant and H produced in evidence a witness statement from its housing officer exhibiting police and witness statements in relation to a number of offences committed by B's sons for which they had received custodial sentences. By October 1999, as a result of further housing benefit payments, B's arrears had reduced to £1,756.20. At the hearing, the judge refused B's application to adjourn the proceedings to enable her to obtain representation and dismissed her application to suspend the warrant on the basis that (1) there was no outstanding housing benefit; (2) B was £170.48 behind with the payments due under the order, and (3) the offences relating to antisocial behaviour by her sons had been taken into account. B appealed against this decision and made an alternative application to suspend the warrant on the basis of fresh information, namely that she was due a further payment of housing benefit which would reduce her arrears to £1090.53, so that she would have paid more than she was liable to pay under the suspended possession order. H opposed the application on the basis that arrears were still in existence and that it had grounds for possession in relation to nuisance which should be taken into account, *Islington LBC v. Reeves* (Unreported, November 19, 1996), [1997] C.L.Y. 2715 cited. B contended that the warrant should be set aside on the basis of the rent history and the possession order varied to postpone the date of possession, which would resurrect B's tenancy and allow H to bring proceedings for breach of the tenancy agreement if it so wished. B argued that the allegations in relation to antisocial behaviour should be given little or no weight, as they were not admitted, had not been tested and/or were unrelated to the tenancy, *Cumming v. Danson* [1942] 2 All E.R. 653 cited.

Held, allowing the appeal, that any allegations of antisocial behaviour should be dealt with in separate proceedings and the appeal was allowed purely on the basis of the rent situation. The date of possession was postponed to 28 days after the hearing date with the possession order suspended for so long as B continued to pay her current rent plus £2.50 of the arrears of £1,090.53.

HAMMERSMITH & FULHAM LBC v. BROWN, November 2, 1999, Judge Bevington, CC (Willesden). [*Ex rel.* Beatrice Prevatt, Barrister, 2 Garden Court, Middle Temple, London].

3158. Right to buy – approved lending institutions – Wales

HOUSING (RIGHT TO BUY) (PRIORITY OF CHARGES) (WALES) ORDER 2000, SI 2000 349 (W.7); made under the Housing Act 1985 s.156. In force: January 20, 2000; £1.50.

This Order specifies three bodies as approved lending institutions for the purposes of the Housing Act 1985 s.36 and s.156 and the Housing Act 1996 s.12.

3159. Right to buy – rate of discount

HOUSING (RIGHT TO ACQUIRE) (DISCOUNT) ORDER 2000, SI 2000 1622; made under the Housing Act 1996 s.17. In force: July 17, 2000; £2.00.

This Order, which revokes the Housing (Right to Acquire) (Discount) Order 1999 (SI 1999 1135 as amended), specifies for local authority areas in England the amount of discount for the purposes of the Housing Act 1996 s.17 that is available to tenants of registered social landlords who have a right to acquire their homes. The amount of the discount varies according to the area in which the dwelling is situated. In addition, it limits the maximum discount a tenant may receive to 50 per cent of the market value of the dwelling.

3160. Publications

Challen, Lydia – Unauthorised and Temporary Occupiers: Law and Practice in the Management of Social Housing. Arden's Housing Library. Paperback: £16.95. ISBN 1-898001-50-2. Lemos & Crane.

Dymond, Andrew – Houses in Multiple Occupation: Law and Practice in the Management of Social Housing. Arden's Housing Library. Paperback: £16.95. ISBN 1-898001-16-2. Lemos & Crane.

Henderson, Josephine – Children and Housing. Arden's Housing Library. Paperback: £17.95. ISBN 1-898001-20-0. Lemos & Crane.

Housing Law Reports: Vol 31, 1999. Hardback: £265.00. ISBN 0-421-69700-8. Sweet & Maxwell.

Hughes, David; Lowe, Stuart – Public Sector Housing Law. 3rd Ed. Paperback: £24.95. ISBN 0-406-98301-1. Butterworths.

Journal of Housing Law. Hardback: £75.00. ISBN 0-421-69770-9. Sweet & Maxwell.

Kilpatrick, Alyson – Discrimination in Housing. Arden's Housing Library. Paperback: £16.95. ISBN 1-898001-34-0. Lemos & Crane.

Pawson, Hal; Mullins, David; McGrath, Siobhan – Allocating Social Housing: Law and Practice in the Management of Social Housing. Arden's Housing Library. Paperback: £16.95. ISBN 1-898001-53-7. Lemos & Crane.

Stanesby, Anne – Mental Disability and Social Housing: Law and Practice in the Management of Social Housing. Arden's Housing Library. Paperback: £16.95. ISBN 1-898001-39-1. Lemos & Crane.

HUMAN RIGHTS

3161. Abortion – legal rights – status of foetus – constitution interpreted on strictly legal basis – South Africa

[Constitution of the Republic of South Africa Act 1996; Termination of Pregnancy Act 1996 (South Africa).]

The Christian Lawyers Association applied to strike down the choice of Termination of Pregnancy Act 1996 (South Africa) which permitted abortion at any stage after conception prior to the birth of a child. They contended that it conflicted with the Constitution of the Republic of South Africa 1996 s.11, guaranteeing the right to life. The Minister of Health noted an exception to the action on the ground that it disclosed no cause of action. It was argued that a foetus had no rights under the Constitution, that the Constitution permitted the termination of pregnancy in certain circumstances, and that the Constitution protected the right of women to have abortions. The Association sought to adduce expert evidence on the nature and commencement of life in order to establish the rights of a foetus. It was also argued that evidence of the legislative history and circumstances prevailing at the time of the passing of the Constitution were admissible in order to arrive at its correct interpretation. The Minister of Health responded that such evidence was not permissible as an aid to the construction of a statute.

Held, refusing the application, that the central question was whether "everyone" or "every person" as written in the Constitution applied to an unborn child. That question had to be determined, not with reference to medical, scientific, religious or philosophical evidence on the nature and development of human life but with reference to the proper legal interpretation of s.11 of the Constitution. While at common law the status of a foetus was uncertain, it was clear that in comparable jurisdictions, a foetus only gained rights if it was subsequently born alive. Moreover s.12(2) of the Constitution guaranteed an individual's right to autonomy over her body and reproductive issues, which right was not qualified by the state in order to protect the foetus, although the circumstances in which abortion was permitted were circumscribed by the state as permitted by s.36 of the Constitution. The rights of a child were protected by s.28, which did not extend those rights to a foetus since "child" was defined by its age and age commenced at birth. There were also sound policy reasons for not according a foetus the same rights as other persons since to do so would place a blanket prohibition on abortion. If the state had intended to grant rights to a foetus, it would have done so in clear and unequivocal terms. Evidence of the surrounding circumstances was not admissible when interpreting a constitutional or legislative provision, save where a judicial enquiry had preceded the passing of a statute with a view to ascertaining its mischief and where the evidence had to be unambiguous, not in dispute and clearly relevant in understanding the meaning of a particular statutory provision.

CHRISTIAN LAWYERS ASSOCIATION OF SOUTH AFRICA v. MINISTER OF HEALTH (1999) 50 B.M.L.R. 241, McCreath, J., Prov Div (SA).

3162. **Admissibility – confessions – psychiatric report protected statement – linked statements – interpretation of legislation – Canada**

[Canadian Charter of Rights and Freedoms 1982 s.7; Criminal Code RSC 1985 s.672.21 (3) (f).]

G was charged with an offence following a confession to police that he had sexually abused his cousin. During a psychiatric assessment ordered by the court, he made another self incriminating statement in response to a question about his statement to the police. The psychiatric report was a "protected statement" which could only be admitted as evidence with the consent of the accused, or where the credibility of the accused was at issue due to inconsistencies in the version of events. G was assessed as fit to stand trial, despite the concern that he appeared to lack understanding as to the implications of his confessions. At the trial the judge held in a voir dire that G's statement to the police was inadmissible because of the findings of the psychiatric assessment. G denied the charges and was cross examined in relation to the statement made to the psychiatrist, in accordance with the Criminal Code RSC 1985 s.672.21 (3) (f), which allowed such cross examination in order to test credibility. G was convicted, largely because of the inconsistencies between his oral evidence and his statement to the psychiatrist. The Court of Appeal overturned the conviction and ordered a new trial on the ground that the statements were linked and, as the one to the police had been ruled inadmissible, so should the one to the psychiatrist. The Crown appealed to the Supreme Court, contending that the use of the protected statement was authorised by the code when the accused's credibility was in issue, and by not objecting to the cross examination, the defence had waived its right to have the statement excluded.

Held, dismissing the appeal, that the common law rule that a statement which was linked to a confession which was ruled inadmissible could not be put in evidence even to test credibility was enshrined in the Canadian Charter of Rights and Freedoms 1982 s.7. The obligations under the Charter effectively governed the court's discretionary power to exclude evidence where the prejudice suffered was likely to outweigh any probative value. In accordance with the presumption that statutory provisions were valid, and as there was nothing to suggest that Parliament had intended to override the common law rule, s.672.21 (3) (f) had to be construed as complying with it. Here, the statement to the psychiatrist had stemmed from the earlier statement to the police and was therefore inadmissible. Further, that by failing to object to the cross examination, the defence had not waived its rights, since silence, or a mere lack of objection, could not constitute a lawful waiver.

R. v. G (B) 7 B.H.R.C. 97, Bastarache, J., Sup Ct (Can).

3163. Admissibility – statements – road traffic accidents – conversation – inadmissible to prevent abuse of power by police officers

[British Colombia MotorVehicleAct RSBC1979 s.61; Canadian Charter of Rights and Freedoms 1982 s.7.]

W was involved in a road traffic accident which resulted in a man's death. She reported the accident to the police the following day, and was visited by a police officer who talked to her about the accident and told her of her right to remain silent. The officer told her that although she did not have to make a written statement, she could be required to make an accident statement under the British Colombia Motor Vehicle Act RSBC 1979 s.61, but that the latter could not be used against her in criminal proceedings. W was charged with failing to stop at the scene of an accident, and the Crown sought to put in evidence W's conversation with the officer. W claimed that the information she had given had been in connection with her duty under the Act and that its disclosure would be in violation of her right not to incriminate herself under the Canadian Charter of Rights and Freedoms 1982 s.7. The judge refused to allow admission of the conversation. The Crown's appeal to the Court of Appeal was dismissed and it appealed to the Supreme Court.

Held, dismissing the appeal, that there had to be a balance between the prevention of abuse of power by the state in relying on what might be unreliable confessions, and the proper use of compelled statements to promote highway safety. Protection from self incrimination was relevant in respect to the Act in that (1) the role of a police officer in obtaining information from a driver about an accident was in potential conflict with his additional role as the provider of information about the driver's rights under the Charter; (2) the perceived authority of the police officer could put pressure on the driver and lead to unreliable statements being made, and (3) allowing the admission of accident statements in criminal proceedings could place an incentive on officers to push for information. An accident statement would not be admissible where a driver was able to show that she had made the statement in the honest and reasonable belief that it was her legal duty to do so. W had shown this in the instant case, and therefore the evidence of the conversation with the police was inadmissible.

R. v. WHITE (JOANN) 7 B.H.R.C. 120, Iacobucci, J., Sup Ct (Can).

3164. Asylum seekers – third counties – recognition by Germany of inhuman treatment by non state agents

[Asylum and Immigration Act 1996 s.2; European Convention on Human Rights 1950 Art.3, Art.13; Convention Determining the State Responsible for Examining Applications for Asylum Lodged in One of the EC Member States 1990; Aliens Act 1990 s.53 (6) (Germany).]

T, a Sri Lankan Tamil, had been refused asylum in Germany and his appeal to an administrative court there had been dismissed. He claimed asylum in the UK. The Secretary of State rejected the claim and certified the case under the Asylum and Immigration Act 1996 s.2, ordering his removal to Germany, which acknowledged responsibility for his claim under the Dublin Convention 1990. T's application for judicial review was refused by the Court of Appeal and he complained to the European Court of Human Rights, arguing that, as Germany would return him to Sri Lanka, the UK was in breach of the European Convention on Human Rights 1950 Art.3 and Art.13.

Held, refusing the application, that the prohibition against torture and inhuman treatment under Art.3 was of such fundamental importance that the UK could not derogate its responsibility to investigate by relying on the provisions of the Dublin Convention. Therefore, it was necessary to examine whether the UK was in breach of Art.3. Although T could make a fresh asylum application in Germany, his previous application and the doubts as to his credibility would be taken into account, and Germany did not generally recognise non state agents of persecution. However, asylum seekers, including Tamils, faced with non state persecution had been given protection by Germany under the Aliens Act 1990 s.53(6), and that, although Germany set rigorous standards for asylum seekers, the threshold was not unreasonably high so that T's asylum application would be given due consideration by Germany and the UK was not in breach of Art.3. Judicial review by the UK courts was an effective remedy in terms of Art.13, so there was no merit in that part of T's application.

TI v. UNITED KINGDOM [2000] I.N.L.R. 211, J-P Costa (President), ECHR.

3165. **Bail – criminal record – automatic denial of bail pending trial constituted violation**

[Criminal Justice and Public Order Act 1994 s.25; Crime and Disorder Act 1998 s.56; European Convention on Human Rights 1950 Art.5, Art.13, Art.14, Art.41.]

C had been convicted of manslaughter and released in 1988. He was convicted of attempted rape and assault occasioning actual bodily harm in 1997, but following his arrest, and pending trial, no application for bail was made in view of the Criminal Justice and Public Order Act 1994 s.25 and in the light of his previous conviction. The 1994 Act was amended by the Crime and Disorder Act 1998 s.56, which granted a consideration of bail if exceptional circumstances were justified. C applied to the European Commission on Human Rights contending that the automatic refusal of bail violated the European Convention on Human Rights 1950 Art.5.(3) and Art.5.(5), both alone and in conjunction with Art.13 and Art.14. The Commission opined that Art.5.(3) and Art.5.(5) had been violated, but that there had been no violation of Art.13 and that it was unnecessary to consider Art.14. The case was referred to the European Court of Human Rights.

Held, granting the application, that there had been a violation of Art.5.(3) and Art.5.(5). In accepting the UK Government's recognition of a violation, the court was empowered to grant compensation under Art.41 and C was awarded £1,000 for non pecuniary damage and £15,250 costs. As C had not pursued his complaint concerning Art.13, the Court made no further examination. In addition, whilst C's complaint embracing Art.14 concerned alleged discriminatory practice, no further considerations were made in the light of the Government's concession.

CABALLERO v. UNITED KINGDOM (2000) 30 E.H.R.R. 643, L Wildhaber (President), ECHR.

3166. **Bankruptcy – trustees in bankruptcy – interference with correspondence – no justification for breaching legal professional privilege**

[Insolvency Act 1986 s.371; European Convention on Human Rights 1950 Art.8, Art.8.(2).]

F, a bankrupt, was serving a four year prison sentence for corruption offences. Three years after his conviction, a redirection order was made under the Insolvency Act 1986 s.371 to the effect that all postal packets addressed to F would be redirected to his trustee in bankruptcy for a period of three months. The correspondence that was redirected during this period included letters from F's legal advisers in connection with receivership proceedings and an application to the ECHR. F contended before the ECHR that his right to respect for his correspondence under the European Convention on Human Rights 1950 Art.8 had been breached since there was no justification for the trustee in bankruptcy to read, copy and file correspondence from his legal advisers and moreover the interference with his mail had continued beyond the expiry of the redirection order. The UK government did not dispute that there had been an interference but contended that it was justified under Art.8.2 as being necessary for the protection of the rights and freedoms of others, since the trustee's aim was to locate and secure assets for the benefit of F's creditors.

Held, granting the application, that there had been a breach of Art.8 since the interference with F's mail after the expiry of the redirection order was not "in accordance with the law" as required by Art.8. Prior to the expiry of the order a legal basis for the interference existed, since the trustee's application for a redirection order was foreseeable and his access to correspondence was restricted to particular items which might assist him in securing funds for creditors, which was a legitimate aim. However, notwithstanding the pursuit of a legitimate aim and the existence of a legal basis, interference with correspondence between F and his legal advisers was not a proportionate measure to adopt and even with regard to the UK's margin of appreciation such interference could not be justified as it was not in keeping with the principle of professional legal privilege and confidentiality, *Campbell v. United Kingdom (A/233A)* (1993) 15 E.H.R.R. 137, [1993] C.L.Y. 2155 considered. Accordingly, the interference could not be justified on the grounds of being "necessary in a democratic society" within the meaning of Art.8.(2). The fact that the trustee in bankruptcy was also the court appointed receiver was a further compelling reason for forwarding, unread, correspondence from F's legal advisers.

FOXLEY v. UNITED KINGDOM 8 B.H.R.C. 571, J-P Costa (President), ECHR.

3167. Care proceedings – medical reports – disclosure of expert evidence – parent's right against self incrimination

[European Convention on Human Rights 1950 Art.6, Art.8.]

Care proceedings were instigated when it was suspected that a mother, M, a heroin addict, had deliberately allowed her child, L, to swallow methadone. M obtained an expert report from a consultant clinical pathologist who took the view that L had not been given methadone before, but did not believe M's explanation for the incident in question. A request by the police for disclosure of the report was granted by the judge at first instance ([1995] 2 F.C.R.12), a decision ultimately upheld by the House of Lords ([1997] A.C.16, [1996] C.L.Y. 502) but no action was taken against M because of lack of evidence. M complained that her right to a fair trial under the European Convention on Human Rights 1950 Art.6 had been violated. She argued that disclosure of the report breached her right against self incrimination, and that the nature of the care proceedings was unfair, as in order to put her case properly she ran the risk of self incrimination.

Held, refusing the application that all parties in care proceedings were equally affected by the disclosure rules and M could have adduced other evidence to counter that of the expert and therefore she had not been prevented from putting her case. The right not to incriminate oneself related to an accused's right to exercise free will to remain silent, and did not include evidence from third parties, particularly where, as in instant case, the expert had not interviewed M directly. Compulsory disclosure of expert evidence did not equate with putting pressure on an accused to make admissions. Whilst L's interests had taken precedence, M had been able to put her case properly, and therefore Art.8(2) had been satisfied.

L (A CHILD) v. UNITED KINGDOM (DISCLOSURE OF EXPERT EVIDENCE); *sub nom.* L v. UNITED KINGDOM [2000] 2 F.L.R. 322, J-P Costa (President), ECHR.

3168. Child abduction – Israel – jurisdiction of Beth Din

See FAMILY LAW: S (Abduction: Intolerable Situation: Beth Din), *Re.* §2448

3169. Child protection – duty of care – failure of local authority to prevent ill treatment – liability in negligence

[European Convention on Human Rights 1950 Art.3, Art.6, Art.13.]

The claimants, five children from the same family, brought proceedings for damages against the local authority, B, alleging negligence and breach of statutory duty arising from a failure to protect their welfare when children. The claimants had suffered neglect over a long period of time and it was alleged that B had failed properly to protect them, causing psychological damage. B's application to strike out the claim as disclosing no cause of action succeeded at first instance ([1993] 2 F.L.R. 575). The Court of Appeal dismissed the claimants' appeal ([1994] 2 W.L.R. 554, [1994] C.L.Y. 4296) as did the House of Lords ([1995] 2 A.C. 633, [1995] C.L.Y. 3452), which held that B had immunity from suit in respect of actions brought against it concerning the discharge of its duties relating to the welfare of children. The claimants complained that their rights under the European Convention on Human Rights 1950 Art.3 had been violated. They argued that B's failure to protect them from abuse and neglect meant that the state had failed to protect its most vulnerable citizens from inhuman treatment or degrading punishment. Further, that the decision in the House of Lords denied them their only remedy and prevented the facts of the case from being investigated, as required under Art.13. They also asserted that they had been denied the right to a fair hearing under Art.6. The Commission conducted a preliminary assessment of the case and its merits.

Held, granting the application, that the case was admissible. The case contained complex issues of fact and law that need to be determined after examination of the merits of the application in its entirety.

KL v. UNITED KINGDOM [2000] F.C.R. 274, Trechsel (President), Eur Comm HR.

3170.   **Child protection – duty of care – failure of local authority to prevent ill treatment – liability in negligence**

[European Convention on Human Rights 1950 Art.3, Art.6.]

Issues arose as to the potential liability of a local authority, BCC, in relation to the condition of four siblings born between 1982 and 1988. The conditions in which they were living were first referred to BCC in 1988, but no order was sought until 1993. At the outset, BCC had failed to appoint a case worker for the children. In the intervening time, the police had had occasion to visit the property and notified BCC of its appalling condition. Neighbours and school teachers similarly notified BCC as to their concerns from 1988 onwards. A case worker was not appointed to the family until December 1989. In 1990, it was reported to BCC that the children were frequently locked outside, neighbours reported hearing screaming from the building and it was discovered that the children were bruised and had smeared their own excrement on the windows of their bedrooms, as well as defecating in their rooms, and that they were prevented from leaving their rooms. Following their parent's divorce in 1992, the mother insisted that the children be taken into care and that they were at risk of assault by her. In October 1992, a guardian ad litem was appointed and the current proceedings were commenced in 1993. It was contended that BCC had breached its duty of care and/or its statutory duty in that it ought to have acted more rapidly and effectively to prevent the children suffering psychological injury. The House of Lords rejected any liability in respect of BCC ([1995] 2 A.C. 633). Proceedings were therefore brought before the European Commission of Human Rights.

Held, that there had been a breach of the European Convention on Human Rights 1950 Art.3 because BCC knew of the children's plight and that they were at risk of continuing maltreatment and neglect. BCC had an obligation to take effective and practical steps to safeguard the children. Although BCC could not be required to prevent all instances of abuse, it failed to take the necessary steps to end the ill treatment, given the known deterioration in the children's circumstances. Further, there had been a breach of Art.6 in that the children's access to a court had been limited by the decision of the House of Lords in holding that there was no duty of care owed by BCC or its agents, *Osman v. United Kingdom* [1999] 1 F.L.R. 193, [1998] C.L.Y. 3102 considered. Whilst it could be a legitimate aim to exclude a defendant from a negligence action, it was disproportionate to do so in the instant case as no consideration had been given to either the degree of damage suffered or the nature of the negligence concerned.

Z v. UNITED KINGDOM [2000] 2 F.C.R. 245, Trechsel (President), Eur Comm HR.

3171. Custodial sentences – time limits – continued detention in psychiatric institution after expiry of committal order due to procedural error – violation of European Convention on Human Rights 1950 Art.5(1)

[European Convention on Human Rights 1950 Art.5(1).]

E was convicted of manslaughter in June 1990 and a custodial sentence of five years was imposed in addition to an order committing E to a psychiatric institution. In view of E's disturbed mental state, he was committed for a two year period beginning in July 1991. The usual procedure was that such a placement would not commence until the detainee became eligible for early release, which in E's case was February 1993. In May 1993, the public prosecutor requested a one year extension of the placement. This was done in accordance with the relevant provisions of the Dutch criminal procedure code, which required the request to be lodged with the court registry at least one month before the current period expired. A copy of the request was sent to E and he was informed of his right to be represented by counsel at the judicial examination of the request. However, the request was placed in the court archives by mistake and was only uncovered following queries raised three months later by E, who was concerned that he had heard no more about the extension. At the examination of the request for an extension, E argued that the request should be declared inadmissible due to the procedural failure. The court rejected E's arguments and extended his placement for a further year, holding that, while the procedural failure would in principle invalidate the request, E's case contained special circumstances justifying a departure from that principle. These included the fact that E was not prejudiced by the failure to lodge the request. No appeal lay against the decision of the Regional Court and E applied to the Commission in October 1993, alleging that the extension of his placement in the circumstances amounted to an unlawful deprivation of his liberty, contrary to the European Convention on Human Rights 1950 Art.5(1).

Held, granting the application, that (1) the preliminary objection concerning an alleged failure to exhaust domestic remedies would be dismissed. Theoretically, E had the option of instituting summary civil proceedings to test the legality of his detention, however he was entitled to have assumed that the request had been lodged in time and could not therefore be criticised for not using the summary procedure, and (2) although Art.5(1) was primarily concerned with compliance with the substantive and procedural aspects of the relevant rules of national law, it also required that detention did not deprive persons of their liberty in an arbitrary manner. In the instant case, it was not in dispute that the procedural rules concerning the request for a placement extension had been respected. While the legality of the extension order was in accordance with previous domestic case law, this was not decisive of the question as to whether there had been a violation of Art.5(1). The delay of two months in lodging the request at the court registry was substantial, and the fact that it was E's own actions that set the judicial proceedings in motion revealed a lack of adequate safeguards to ensure his release would not be unreasonably delayed, *Winterwerp v. Netherlands (A/33)* (1979-80) 2 E.H.R.R. 387, [1981] C.L.Y. 1089 distinguished and *Johnson v. United Kingdom* (1999) 27 E.H.R.R. 296, [1998] C.L.Y. 3898 applied. The court had failed to take into account E's interests in securing his liberty, since by that time he was eligible for early release. While there was a countervailing public interest in protection against further violent assaults, that interest could not be relied upon as justification for E's continued unlawful detention for two and a half months in circumstances where various public authorities were aware that E's placement had expired and there was a failure to take any steps to check whether the request for extension had been received at the court registry.

ERKALO v. NETHERLANDS (1999) 28 E.H.R.R. 509, R Bernhardt (President), ECHR.

3172. **Death penalty – due process – inhuman or degrading treatment – domestic law did not incorporate international law procedures – constitutional rights not violated – Bahamas**

[American Convention on Human Rights 1969; Constitution of the Bahamas Art.16, Art.17(1).]

H and M were convicted of murder and sentenced to death by a Bahamian court. They lodged petitions with the Inter American Commission of Human Rights, a body under the Organisation of American States, of which the Bahamas was a member. Although the Bahamas was not a party to the American Convention on Human Rights 1969 the Commission had the power to consider applications made to it and to give non binding recommendations. The government wrote to the Commission, stating that it considered 18 months a reasonable time in which to allow the Commission to deal with the petitions, after the expiry of which, the dates for executions were fixed. However, a stay of execution was granted since H and M had also brought constitutional motions in the Bahamas, on the basis that execution would be a violation of their right to life under the Constitution of the Bahamas Art.16, since their petitions to the Commission were still pending and to order execution would be contrary to the due process of law. Further, that if carried out, the executions would be inhuman or degrading treatment or punishment contravening Art.17(1) of the Constitution, in view of the pre trial delay and the prison conditions under which they had been kept. The motions were dismissed at first instance and again on appeal to the Court of Appeal of the Commonwealth of the Bahamas. H and M appealed to the Privy Council.

Held, dismissing the appeal (Lord Steyn and Lord Cooke dissenting on the issue of conditions of incarceration), that the right to petition the Commission and its powers to make recommendations were founded in international law in the Constitution of the Organisation of American States, under which the Commission received its powers. However, the treaty was not incorporated into the domestic law of the Bahamas and therefore the domestic courts lacked jurisdiction to construe or apply its provisions. There was no legitimate expectation that the government would wait for more than a reasonable time before ordering the sentences to be carried out, *Fisher v. Minister of Public Safety and Immigration (No.2)* [1999] 2 W.L.R. 349, [1998] C.L.Y. 3067 applied. The principle of carrying out the sentences, having regard to the due process of law, was implied into Art.16 of the Constitution, but that did not mean that the domestic law could incorporate international law procedures, *Thomas v. Baptiste* [1999] 3 W.L.R. 249, [1999] C.L.Y. 758 distinguished. On the second point, it would be rare for a pre trial delay or prison conditions to be regarded as additional punishment amounting to inhuman or degrading treatment. There was no connection between the death sentence and the manner in which the prisoners were detained and the court had correctly found that the prison conditions did not exceed reasonable standards of decency, given the financial and security considerations. The pre trial delay and the conditions under which the prisoners were kept were not matters that were connected to the imposition of the death sentence and thus Art.17(1) had not been violated.

HIGGS v. MINISTER OF NATIONAL SECURITY [2000] 2 A.C. 228, Lord Hoffmann, PC.

3173. **Death penalty – prisoners rights – protection afforded by International Covenant on Civil and Political Rights 1966 Optional Protocol – Trinidad and Tobago**

[International Covenant on Civil and Political Rights 1966 Optional Protocol.]

K was convicted of murder. The Court of Appeal allowed his appeal against conviction and ordered a retrial at which he was convicted and sentenced to death. The Court of Appeal refused leave to appeal, and K's petition to the Judicial Committee of the Privy Council was dismissed. K petitioned the Human Rights Committee under the International Covenant on Civil and Political Rights 1966 Optional Protocol, alleging several violations of the Covenant in relation to procedural delays, inhuman treatment and K's right to a fair hearing. TT submitted that, since K was a prisoner under sentence of death, the Committee was not competent to consider the matter, as TT had made a reservation on its reaccession to the Optional Protocol under which it did not recognise the Committee's competence in relation to any matters concerning prisoners under sentence of death.

Held, granting the petition that the reservation was an attempt to prevent the Committee exercising its jurisdiction under the Covenant in relation to a defined class of persons. This meant that prisoners such as K were effectively being marked down as deserving a lesser standard of protection than the rest of society, which was incompatible with the objectives of the Covenant and the Optional Protocol.

KENNEDY v. TRINIDAD AND TOBAGO 8 B.H.R.C. 230, Judge not applicable, UN Human Rights Committee.

3174. Deportation – right to family life – sexual offences against children – proportionality of deportation

See IMMIGRATION: B v. Secretary of State for the Home Department (Deportation: Proportionality). §3345

3175. Detention – judicial review – expeditious review of lawfulness of detention – domestic law remedy ineffective – Malta

[European Convention on Human Rights 1950 Art.5, Art.41.]

TW brought a complaint that his rights under the European Convention on Human Rights 1950 Art.5(3) had been violated as, having been detained, he was not brought promptly before a judge capable of ordering his release. Further, that there was a violation of his right to a habeas corpus remedy under Art.5(4) to obtain a review of the lawfulness of his detention expeditiously under Maltese law. The Government of Malta, M, argued that a right of review existed under domestic law and that TW had failed to rely on it.

Held, granting the application, that in order to comply with the aim of Art.5(3), which was to ensure against arbitrary and unreasonable detention, the domestic remedy had to be an automatic and prompt investigation of the merits of the detention. Timeliness could not be broadly interpreted, but in this case the fact that TW was brought before a judge the day after his arrest satisfied the condition that judicial control needed to be prompt. However, this did not ensure compliance with Art.5(3) because the magistrate had no power to order TW's release. Furthermore, the review of the merits of detention was not exercised by the magistrate who heard TW in person. In the instant case the domestic remedy pleaded, whilst going wider than the requirements of Art.5(3), had to be applied for and was not automatic. It had not been shown that the remedy was capable of successfully challenging the underlying reasons for a detention. M's objection was therefore not made out, the remedy did not satisfy Art.5(3) and TW's rights under Art.5(3) had been violated, and therefore justified an award for non-pecuniary damages to TW under Art.41. Article 5(4) was not considered.

TW v. MALTA; AQUILINA v. MALTA (2000) 29 E.H.R.R. 185, L Wildhaber (President), ECHR.

3176. Detention – mental hospitals – mental impairment leading to repeated aggression and violence – preventive detention did not infringe right to liberty under ECHR Art.5(1) – Norway

[European Convention on Human Rights 1950 Art.5; Penal Code (Norway) Art.39; Code of Criminal Procedure (Norway) Art.171.]

E suffered serious brain damage as a result of a car accident in 1965. Psychiatric assessments concluded that E was not mentally ill but was suffering from an underdeveloped and permanently impaired mental capacity. From 1967 onwards, E exhibited violent and aggressive tendencies, and was incarcerated for periods of preventive detention following convictions for assault and threatening behaviour. The Penal Code (Norway) Art.39(1)(e) authorised detention in a mental hospital as a security measure where a person under a mental incapacity had committed a punishable act where their condition gave rise to a danger of repetition and the Code of Criminal Procedure (Norway) Art.171 provided for detention on remand pending an extension of security measures under Art.39. In September 1984, E was sentenced to 120 days' detention with security measures authorised for a maximum five year period. E's appeal was dismissed and during his detention he assaulted staff and social workers on several occasions. A psychiatric report in June 1989 stated that E's mental state had not changed since 1965 and the prison board requested in October 1989 that the security measures due to expire in February 1991 be extended. This request was upheld by the court, which found that the requirements of Art.171 of the Criminal Code were fulfilled. E's appeal against this decision was dismissed and his complaint that his detention from February to May 1990 infringed his right to liberty under the European Convention on Human Rights 1950 Art.5(1) was upheld by the Commission.

Held, refusing the application, that (1) while the link between the initial conviction and the extension of preventive detention might reduce over time, if such an extension was decided upon by a court within the period of the maximum authorised detention under Art.39(1) of the Penal Code it would comply with Art.5(1)(a) of the Convention. In the instant case, having particular regard to E's continued violent behaviour, the likelihood of his re-offending and the probability of prolonged detention under Art.39, his detention from February to May 1990 was directly linked to the 1984 conviction and therefore was within the scope of Art.5(1)(a), and (2) E's detention was also justified under Art.5(1)(c), on the grounds that detention was reasonably necessary to prevent further offending. On the facts, there were substantial grounds for believing that E would commit further offences, and he had actually done so after May 1990. Although Art.5(1)(c) would not justify continued detention on a mere suspicion that similar offences could be committed, this did not include a situation where the purposes of detention was to determine whether further detention was necessary on security grounds. In the instant case, detention was justified, given E's impaired mental state and propensity for violence, pending the outcome of the prosecution's request for a short period of further detention under Art.39(1), so that E could be brought before the court.

ERIKSEN v. NORWAY (2000) 29 E.H.R.R. 328, Judge Bernhardt (President), ECHR.

3177. **Disability discrimination – employment – pre-existing medical condition – interpretation of "handicap" – Quebec**

[Charter of Human Rights and Freedoms (Quebec) s.10.]

M and H were denied employment and T was dismissed on the ground of pre-existing medical conditions, although the conditions did not affect the performance of their duties. They complained of discrimination on the basis of handicap contrary to the Charter of Human Rights and Freedoms (Quebec) s.10. The Court of Appeal held in favour of complainants and CM appealed as to the meaning of "handicap" in s.10.

Held, dismissing the appeals, that (1) "handicap" in s.10 included both ailments and the perception of such conditions; (2) guidelines on interpretation would be more appropriate than an exhaustive definition of handicap. These allowed for the development of concepts by judicial interpretation in line with biomedical and other factors. However, human dignity and equality rights were to be emphasised over and above a strictly medical or biological approach. Courts must also consider the context in which the alleged discrimination occurred, and (3) in most cases, where the existence of a handicap was proven, the burden would be on the applicant to establish (a) different treatment; (b) that it was based on a s.10 ground, and (c) that the different treatment had impaired their human rights.

CITY OF MONTREAL v. COMMISSION DES DROITS DE LA PERSONNE ET DES DROITS DE LA JEUNESSE DU QUEBEC; CITY OF BOISBRIAND v. COMMISSION

DES DROITS DE LA PERSONNE ET DES DROITS DE LA JEUNESSE DU QUEBEC 8 B.H.R.C. 476, L'Heureux-Dube, J., Sup Ct (Can).

3178. Disability Discrimination Act 1995 (c.50) – Commencement No.7 Order

DISABILITY DISCRIMINATION ACT 1995 (COMMENCEMENT NO.7) ORDER 2000, SI 2000 1969 (C.50); made under the Disability Discrimination Act 1995 s.70. Commencement details: bringing into force various provisions of the Act on August 30, 2000; £2.00.

This Order brings into force the Disability Discrimination Act 1995 ss.40-45 and the remainder of s.48. These provisions empower the Secretary of State to make public service vehicles accessibility regulations to ensure that disabled persons may get on to and off regulated public service vehicles in safety and without unreasonable difficulty; provide that a regulated public service vehicle shall not be used on a road unless a vehicle examiner has issued an accessibility certificate that such provisions of any regulations as are made are satisfied in respect of the vehicle; empowers the Secretary of State to authorise the road use of a regulated public service vehicle of a specified class or description and prescribe fees in respect of applications for, or grants of, approvals and certificates, for copies of such certificates and for reviews and appeals.

3179. Disability Discrimination Act 1995 (c.50) – Commencement No.8 Order

DISABILITY DISCRIMINATION ACT 1995 (COMMENCEMENT NO.8) ORDER 2000, SI 2000 2989 (C.91); made under the Disability Discrimination Act 1995 s.70. Commencement details: bringing into force various provisions of the Act on December 1, 2000 and March 31, 2001; £2.00.

This Order brings into force, in relation to England and Wales, the Disability Discrimination Act 1995 s.37, which imposes a duty on taxi drivers to carry in their taxis a guide dog, hearing dog or other prescribed category of dog when it accompanies the hirer and provides for a taxi driver to be exempted from that duty on medical grounds if a certificate of exemption has been issued to him by a licensing authority, and s.38, which provides for a right of appeal against the refusal of a licensing authority to issue a certificate of exemption.

3180. Disability Rights Commission – formal investigations – time limits

DISABILITY RIGHTS COMMISSION (TIME LIMITS) REGULATIONS 2000, SI 2000 879; made under the Disability Rights Commission Act 1999 s.12, s.13, Sch.3 para.15, Sch.3 para.16, Sch.3 para.17, Sch.3 para.18, Sch.3 para.26. In force: April 25, 2000; £1.50.

These Regulations supplement the Disability Rights Commission Act 1999 Sch.3 Part I by making provision for time limits in relation to the conduct of formal investigations by the Disability Rights Commission and prescribing the periods at the end of which action plans become final under Sch.3 Part III to the Act.

3181. Disability Rights Commission Act 1999 (c.17) – Commencement No.2 Order

DISABILITY RIGHTS COMMISSION ACT 1999 (COMMENCEMENT NO.2 AND TRANSITIONAL PROVISION) ORDER 2000, SI 2000 880 (C.21); made under the Disability Rights Commission Act 1999 s.16. Commencement details: bringing into force various provisions of the Act on March 23, 2000 and April 25, 2000; £1.50.

This Order brings certain provisions of the Disability Rights Commission Act 1999 into force on March 23, 2000 and April 25, 2000. The provisions brought into force on March 23, 2000 confer power on the Secretary of State to make regulations in connection with the conduct of formal investigations or the procedure for issuing non-discrimination notices and to prescribe the periods at the end of which an action plan becomes final. The provisions brought into force on April 25, 2000 relate to the abolition of the National Disability Council, the powers and duties of the Disability Rights Commission, the procedure for amending the

Disability Discrimination Act 1995 s.7(1) and consequential amendments and repeals.

3182. Eviction – landlord and tenant – enforcement proceedings – system of staggered evictions and priority of police enforcement – excessive burden on landlord

[European Convention on Human Rights 1950 Protocol 1 Art.1; European Convention on Human Rights 1950 Protocol 1 Art.6(1).]

From 1983, T was the subject of lawful applications and orders that he quit his leased apartment following the expiry of the lease. IS, and its predecessor, as owner, made 11 attempts to recover possession between 1988 and 1996, after the bailiff had made several unsuccessful similar attempts. A statutory scheme was introduced to alleviate the housing shortage, whereby police assistance was provided to enforce eviction orders. The cases were dealt with in order of priority. IS was not entitled to assistance because its case was not deemed a priority. IS complained to the European Commission of Human Rights that the lack of police assistance under the scheme violated its right to peaceful enjoyment of property under the European Convention on Human Rights 1950 Protocol 1 Art. 1, and of its rights to access to a tribunal and to a hearing within a reasonable time under Protocol 1 Art.6(1). The Commission was of the view that both Art.1 and Art.6(1) had been contravened and referred the case to the European Court of Human Rights.

Held, that there was a violation of both Art.1 and Art.6(1). In principle a system of temporary suspension or staggering of evictions could be within the margin of appreciation permitted to states in balancing the demands of the general interest against interference with the right to property. However, there had to be safeguards against arbitrary or unforeseeable impact on landlords' property rights. The practical effect of the scheme was that non urgent orders were never being enforced due to the volume of applications. The system imposed an excessive burden on IS and did not balance the protection of right of property with the requirements of general interest. The right to a court established by Art.6 also required that the enforcement of judicial orders could not be unduly delayed. A stay of execution pending resolution of public order problems might be within a state's margin of appreciation, but this scheme effectively deprived IS of its right to have its dispute with T decided by a court, which violated Art.6(1).

IMMOBILIARE SAFFI v. ITALY (2000) 30 E.H.R.R. 756, L Wildhaber (President), ECHR.

3183. Eviction – residential tenancies – government tenant – exclusion from statutory protection – discrimination could not be objectively justified – Cyprus

[Rent Control Law 1983 (Cyprus); European Convention on Human Rights 1950 Art.8, Art.14.]

L, a retired civil servant who had rented his home from C, the Cypriot government, for 20 years, was ordered to quit, and was denied the statutory protection of the Rent Control Law 1983 (Cyprus), on the basis that his property had been allocated to him by an administrative order because of his position in the civil service and that he did not occupy the property under a tenancy agreement recognised by the relevant statutory provisions. He complained to the Commission that he had been the subject of unlawful discrimination as a government tenant, contrary to the European Convention on Human Rights 1950 Art.8 and Art.14. He contended that, if he had been a private individual renting property to the government, the government would enjoy statutory protection, and likewise tenants of private persons were also afforded greater protection. Further, that the lease he had originally signed contained many features, which were all typical of a tenancy agreement. C contended that L's situation was not analogous to that of a private tenant renting from a private landlord, since the property in question was government owned and any transactions involving that property had to take account of the public interest. To afford L protection from eviction was not in the public interest. The Commission gave a unanimous decision in L's favour and referred the case to the European Court of Human Rights.

Held, that there was a violation of Art.14 in conjunction with Art.8, as a difference in treatment was discriminatory if it did not pursue a legitimate aim and there was no reasonable or objective justification for excluding L from the protection afforded to private tenants. The tenancy agreement which was made by C in a private capacity, did not suggest that the property was let to L in his capacity as a civil servant, and was silent as to the consequences of L's retirement. Consequently, L was the victim of unfair discrimination in the exercise of his right to respect for his home.

LARKOS v. CYPRUS (2000) 30 E.H.R.R. 597, L Wildhaber (President), ECHR.

3184. **Freedom of expression – armed forces – statutory ban on trade union membership by members of South African Defence Forces – breach of constitutional right – South Africa**

[DefenceAct1957 (South Africa) s.126B; Constitution of the Republic of South Africa 1996 s.23, s.36.]

SAND claimed that the Defence Act 1957 s.126B, which prohibited members of the armed forces from taking part in an act of public protest or joining a trade union, violated the right to freedom of expression and trade union membership conferred under the Constitution of the Republic of South Africa 1996.

Held, granting the application, that (1) although the very wide definition of acts of public protest in s.126B(2) was a restriction on the right to freedom of expression permitted under s.36 of the Constitution, the restriction was only allowed where it was reasonable and justifiable. The effect of the Act, however, was to require soldiers to separate themselves artificially from, and have no voice in, the legitimate everyday concerns of society. That was a serious infringement of their rights which was not justified by the need for a politically neutral defence force, and (2) as soldiers were arguably in the position of employees in relation to the defence force, and the International Labour Organisation defined them as "workers", they qualified for the constitutional right of trade union membership. The Act's absolute prohibition on such membership was an infringement of that right that outweighed the state's reasonable need for a managed and regulated defence force.

SOUTH AFRICAN NATIONAL DEFENCE UNION v. MINISTER OF DEFENCE 6 B.H.R.C. 574, O'Regan, J., Const Ct (SA).

3185. **Freedom of expression – binding over – hunt saboteurs rights violated – order not "legally prescribed" as required by European Convention on Human Rights Art. 10**

[European Convention on Human Rights 1950 Art.5(1), Art.10(2).]

Two hunt saboteurs whose appeals against binding over orders and payment orders of £100 were dismissed, applied to the European Court of Human Rights, complaining that their rights to freedom of expression, as guaranteed under the European Convention on Human Rights Art.10, had been violated. H contended that the description of his behaviour as being contra bonos mores was so broadly defined that it failed to comply with the requirement in Art.10(2) that any interference with freedom of expression must be "prescribed by law".

Held, granting the application, that the order by which the applicants were bound over was not legally prescribed as required under Art.10(2). Any interference with the freedom of expression necessitated the utmost scrutiny, *Steel v. United Kingdom* (1999) 28 E.H.R.R. 603, [1998] C.L.Y. 3068 distinguished on the grounds that, although "lawfulness" under Art.5(1) was seen as similar to the requirement that interference be "prescribed by law", the applicants in *Steel* had breached the peace unlike the applicants in the instant case. The court disagreed with the UK Government that the definition of behaviour contra bonos mores as "wrong rather than right in the judgment of the majority of contemporary fellow citizens" contained an objective element equivalent to conduct "likely to cause annoyance". It simply meant conduct expressed to be wrong in the opinion of a majority of citizens.

HASHMAN v. UNITED KINGDOM (2000) 30 E.H.R.R. 241, L Wildhaber (President), ECHR.

3186. Freedom of expression – flags – statutory provisions criminalising desecration of national and regional flags – justifiable interference – Hong Kong

[National Flag and National Emblem Ordinance (Hong Kong) s.7; Regional Flag and Regional Emblem Ordinance (Hong Kong) s.7; Basic Law (Hong Kong) Art.39; International Covenant on Civil and Political Rights 1966 Art.19.]

N and L were charged with desecrating the national and regional flags during a non violent demonstration, for which they were charged with offences under the National Flag and National Emblem Ordinance s.7 and the Regional Flag and Regional Emblem Ordinance s.7. N and L argued that the charges breached their right to freedom of expression under the International Covenant on Civil and Political Rights 1966 Art.19, which applied to Hong Kong by virtue of the Basic Law Art.39. Further, that the anti desecration provisions were ultra vires the powers of the HK legislature, as they were not required for public order purposes. N and L were convicted at first instance, but they succeeded on appeal to the Court of Appeal (6 B.H.R.C. 591) and HK appealed.

Held, allowing the appeal, that freedom of expression was a fundamental freedom guaranteed by the Basic Law, subject to clearly defined restrictions on public order grounds, as permitted under Art.19(3) of the Covenant. Further, protection of the flags played a key role in implementing the "one country, two systems" principal. The Ordinances' restrictions were not wide, as they did not interfere with the freedom of expression by other means. As such the Ordinances were a justifiable restriction on freedom of expression that occupied a place on the limit of constitutionally permitted control.

HONG KONG SPECIAL ADMINISTRATIVE REGION v. NG KUNG SIU 8 B.H.R.C. 244, Li, C.J., CFA (HK).

3187. Freedom of expression – imprisonment – article condemning government activities – disproportionate penalty – Turkey

[European Convention on Human Rights 1950 Art.10; Criminal Code (Turkey) Art.312.]

C, a Turkish trade union leader, wrote an article condemning the Turkish government for its treatment of the Kurdish people in south eastern Turkey. C was convicted of an offence of inciting hatred under the Criminal Code Art.312 for which he was sentenced to 20 months' imprisonment and fined TKL100,000. C complained that the prosecution and sentence breached his right to freedom of expression under the European Convention on Human Rights 1950 Art.10.

Held, granting the application, that there had been an interference with C's right to freedom of expression. C's prosecution was "prescribed by law" under Art.10(2) in that the Criminal Code served the legitimate aim of preventing incitement to violence and hatred in a volatile area of the country. However, the second limb of Art.10(2), "necessary in a democratic society", was of narrow application since freedom of expression was a fundamental right which, in order to be meaningful, had to include criticism of the state and its actions. The article was a political rallying call bordering on the extreme, but it did not expressly condone or encourage violence. Whilst the Turkish government had legitimate concerns about terrorist activities, other ways of reacting to the article could have been used before resorting to the criminal law. The penalty imposed on C was out of proportion to the mischief it was aimed at and therefore the interference with C's freedom of expression exceeded the measures necessary in a democratic society.

CEYLAN v. TURKEY (2000) 30 E.H.R.R. 73, Judge Wildhaber (President), ECHR.

3188. Freedom of expression – journalists – conviction for criminal libel – subject matter of articles in public interest – Romania

[European Convention on Human Rights 1950 Art.10; Criminal Code (Romania) Art.206.]

In 1994 D, a journalist, was convicted of criminal libel under the Criminal Code (Romania) Art.206 in relation to articles he had written about G, the chief executive of a state owned company, and R, a senator. He was fined and banned from working as a journalist. His appeal was unsuccessful, although the ban was lifted, and he continued to publish similar articles. In 1995, D claimed that the convictions violated his right to freedom of expression under the European Convention on Human Rights 1950 Art.10. D died in March 1998, shortly before the case was referred to the European Court of Human Rights. His convictions were quashed by the Romanian Supreme Court of Justice in May 1998, and Romania argued that D's claim should not continue as the quashing of the convictions constituted an acceptance that Art.10 had been violated, for which D's widow could claim compensation.

Held, granting the application, that quashing the convictions did not constitute acknowledgement of a violation of Art.10 as it had been done on the basis of D's death. Reparation was not automatic as D's widow would have to commence fresh proceedings, and therefore she was entitled to continue with the instant application. Romania accepted that the convictions interfered with D's right to freedom of expression, since the effective exercise of such freedoms by a journalist in a democratic society had to be broad enough to accommodate aspects that could appear to be inflammatory. The articles were of significant public interest as they related to matters concerning the administration of state owned assets and they had not impinged on the private life of G or R to any great extent. Therefore, although the interference with the freedom of expression was provided for under domestic law, D's conviction and sentence constituted a disproportionate interference with his freedom of expression unnecessary in a democratic society.

DALBAN v. ROMANIA 8 B.H.R.C. 91, Wildhaber (President), ECHR.

3189. Freedom of expression – judiciary – re-appointment refused due to statements expressed in academic lecture – unjustifiable interference – Liechtenstein

[European Convention on Human Rights 1950 Art.10, Art.13.]

Whilst W was a member of the Liechtenstein government a dispute arose between the government and the Prince. The dispute was resolved and W was appointed President of the Administrative Court by the Prince. W subsequently stated in an academic lecture, reported in the media, that the Constitutional Court could intervene in a dispute between the Prince and parliament. The Prince wrote to W stating that he believed W's views made him unfit to hold public office and that he would not be re-appointed at the end of his fixed term in office. When parliament later recommended W for re-appointment the Prince refused his approval. W complained that the Prince's actions violated his right to freedom of expression under the European Convention on Human Rights 1950 Art.10 and further that he had been deprived of an effective remedy in Liechtenstein in violation of Art.13.

Held, granting the application, that although civil service appointments did not come within the Convention, civil servants already holding office could claim its protection. The Prince's indication, albeit in a private letter, that he intended to penalise W for expressing his views was an interference with W's freedom of expression as the Prince was acting in his capacity as an organ of the state, and the letter would have had the effect of discouraging W from expressing similar views in the future. W was not acting improperly in taking part in academic debate on the issue of constitutional powers, and the Prince had not cited circumstances going to W's ability to fulfil his role as President of the Administrative Court. Therefore the interference was not justifiable in terms of the protections necessary in a democratic society so that there had been a breach of Art.10. As the only remedy available to W was against parliament, not the Prince, there had also been a breach of Art.13.

WILLE v. LIECHTENSTEIN (2000) 30 E.H.R.R. 558, E Palm (President), ECHR.

3190. **Freedom of expression – newspapers – seal hunters defamed in publication – public interest justification – Norway**

[European Convention on Human Rights 1950 Art.10.]

A Norwegian newspaper, BT, was found guilty of defamation when it published extracts from a government inspector's report accusing seal hunters of inhumane practices. The article formed part of BT's ongoing series on the seal hunting industry, but the government claimed the report was largely untrue. BT's appeal to the Supreme Court was dismissed and it complained to the ECHR, alleging a violation of its freedom of expression under the European Convention on Human Rights 1950 Art.10.

Held, granting the application, that the press played a vital role in a democratic society by disseminating matters of public importance. However, Art.10 did not give unlimited protection as the press were required to carry out their role in good faith within the bounds of established journalistic ethics, and a state could intervene if it perceived a justifiable social need to do so. BT had published the report in order to further a legitimate debate, during which different viewpoints had been put, on preserving the future of the seal hunting industry, and did not intend to malign the individual hunters involved. The need to protect the reputation of those hunters was therefore not a pressing social need sufficient to outweigh the public's right to the debate.

BLADET TROMSO v. NORWAY (2000) 29 E.H.R.R. 125, Wildhaber (President), ECHR.

3191. **Freedom of expression – picketing – union members leafleting store customers – statutory restriction on secondary picketing did not include leafleting – Canada**

[Canadian Charter of Rights and Freedoms 1982 s.1, s.2(b); Labour Relations Code SBC 1992 s.1 (1), s.65, s.67.]

KM operated 11 retail stores in British Columbia. UF was the union certified to represent employees at two stores, which were regarded under Canadian labour law as "primary employers". KM's other stores were regarded as secondary sites. During 1992, UF was in dispute with KM over the treatment of employees at the two primary employer stores and its members handed out leaflets at secondary stores urging customers to shop elsewhere. The information in the leaflets was factual and not defamatory, and there was no evidence of verbal or physical intimidation. KM obtained an order from the predecessor of the Industrial Relations Board, restraining the leafleting, on the grounds that it constituted unlawful picketing at a secondary site, contrary to the predecessor of the Labour Relations Code 1992. Section 1 (1) of the Code defined picketing as attending at a place of business to persuade people not to enter. UF argued unsuccessfully that the definition was unconstitutional because it infringed the right to freedom of expression in the Canadian Charter of Rights and Freedoms 1982 s.2(b), and as such should be interpreted as excluding consumer leafleting. On a reconsideration, the Board held that, while picketing had a broad definition, most forms of consumer leafleting were contiguous with picketing and could be restricted. UF's application for judicial review was dismissed at first instance and by the British Columbia Court of Appeal. On further appeal to the Canadian Supreme Court, KM conceded that s.1, s.65 and s.67 infringed s.2(b) of the Charter, but contended that such infringements were justified under s.1 of the Charter.

Held, allowing the appeal, that (1) leafleting was an effective and economical means of providing information and conducting rational persuasion. Freedom of expression was important for employees generally, and especially so for vulnerable individuals such as workers in the retail sector. Section 1 (1) of the Code defined picketing in very broad terms and it followed that s.1, s.65 and s.67 of the Code restricted leafleting in a way that infringed UF's freedom of expression; (2) there was a clear distinction between conventional picketing and consumer leafleting, *RWDSU v. Dolphin Delivery Ltd* [1986] 2 S.C.R. 573 distinguished. The former acting as a barrier or a signal not to cross, and its effectiveness in an industrial dispute was founded on its coercive effects on fellow workers. Consumer leafleting, by contrast, was based on rational discourse and persuasion, issues which lay at the heart of freedom of expression. The motivation of leafleting was irrelevant; it was the effects of the actions that had to be considered, *RJR-MacDonald Inc v. Attorney General of Canada* [1995] 3 S.C.R. 199 applied. Leafleting might be viewed as picketing where, for example, it was done in an intimidatory manner, but that was not so in the instant case, and (3) the right to freedom of expression was not impaired by the Code to the minimum extent possible. While some deference should be shown to the legislature in a complex field such as industrial relations, the courts still had to determine whether the balance struck was within acceptable limits, *RJR-MacDonald Inc* applied. In the instant case, the deferential approach was inappropriate because the relevant restriction was not designed to protect a vulnerable group in society. It could not be accepted that the mere presence of UF members would threaten KM's customers. Having regard to the fundamental importance of the leafleting for the workers and its social value, the blanket restriction imposed by s.1, s.65 and s.67 of the Code was too broad and could not be justified as the minimum impairment necessary to achieve the legislative objectives.

UNITED FOOD & COMMERCIAL WORKERS LOCAL 1518 v. KMART CANADA LTD 7 B.H.R.C. 384, Lamer, C.J., Sup Ct (Can).

3192. Freedom of expression – police – constitutional bar on political activity – restriction justified given past association with ruling party – Hungry

[European Convention on Human Rights 1950 Art.10, Art.11; Constitution of Hungary Art.40/B (4).]

A police officer, R, brought a complaint that the Constitution of Hungary Art.40/B (4), which prohibited the police and army from joining a political party or carrying out any political activity, violated the rights of freedom of expression and freedom of association in the European Convention on Human Rights 1950 Art.10 and Art.11.

Held, refusing the application, that there had been no violation, that given Hungary's recent history as a one party state with which the army and police force were openly aligned, it was important for the state now to ensure that the police were seen to be politically separate from the governing party. Article 40/B (4) was not an unreasonable or sweeping provision, and therefore justifiably outweighed the rights of the individual in the instant case.

REKVENYI v. HUNGARY (2000) 30 E.H.R.R. 519, L Wildhaber (President), ECHR.

3193. Freedom of expression – press – news review carrying interview with PKK leader – article not capable of inciting violence – role of press in democratic society – Turkey

[European Convention on Human Rights 1950 Art.6 (1), Art.10.]

S and O, respectively the major shareholder and editor of a weekly Turkish political review, were convicted by a security court of disseminating propaganda against the indivisibility of the state, following publication of an interview with a PKK leader and a joint declaration issued by four left wing groups. Both S and O were found guilty, O being sentenced to six months' imprisonment and fined TL 150M while S was fined TL 120M. Their appeals to the court of cassation were dismissed and their sentences confirmed. S and O applied to the Commission, complaining that their convictions constituted an infringement of their right to freedom of expression under the European Convention on Human Rights 1950 Art.10. They also complained that they had not had a fair trial contrary to Art.6 (1).

Held, granting the applications, that (1) while the convictions and sentences were accepted to be violations of the right to freedom of expression as guaranteed by Art.10, the infringements were prescribed by law and pursued the legitimate aims of protecting national security, territorial integrity and the prevention of crime. However, the convictions and sentences were disproportionate to those aims in that they exceeded what was necessary in a democratic society under Art.10(2). Proportionality had to be considered against the background of the case as a whole, particularly in view of the role of the press in a political democracy and its duty to disseminate information and ideas. Article 10(2) did not provide a wide scope for restrictions on political speech on matters of public interest, and it was essential that government acts or omissions were subjected to close public scrutiny. It was proper for governments to act where remarks incited violence against an individual or group, but much would depend on the facts of each case, including the prevention of terrorism in the case of Turkey. In the instant case, the PKK leader's interview did not, taken as a whole, reveal an incitement to violence or hatred. In imposing the convictions and the sentences the security court had had insufficient regard to the public's right to know of the newsworthy views expressed by the PKK leader, and there had been a violation of Art.10, and (2) there had also been a violation of Art.6(1), in that S and O had well founded and objectively justified fears about the impartiality of the composition of the security court, which included a regular army officer. As had been held previously, aspects of the status of military judges in such courts, including their continued membership of the army, and the consequent control which that institution had over their appointment, made their impartiality questionable, *Incal v. Turkey* 4 B.H.R.C. 476, [1998] C.L.Y. 3093 and *Ciraklar v. Turkey* [1998] H.R.C.D. 955 followed.

SUREK v. TURKEY 7 B.H.R.C. 339, L Wildhaber (President), ECHR.

3194. Freedom of Information Act 2000 (c.36)

This Act makes provision for the disclosure of information held by public authorities or by persons providing services for them and amends the Data Protection Act 1998 and the Public Records Act 1958.

This Act received Royal Assent on November 30, 2000.

3195. Freedom of religion – Members of Parliament – requirement to swear oath with religious content

[European Convention on Human Rights 1950 Art.9.]

B, elected to the Parliament of the Republic of San Marino, did not wish to take the standard oath, requiring him to swear on the Holy Gospels, and swore allegiance in writing without a religious reference. The Secretariat of the Parliament held that the oath was invalid. B then took the standard oath but complained to the EHCR that his right to freedom of religion and conscience under the European Convention on Human Rights 1950 Art.9 had been violated.

Held, allowing the application, that Art.9 was one of the fundamental rights in a democratic society. San Marino's laws generally protected that right, but the oath of allegiance was in violation of it since it prevented those elected to a Parliament intended to represent a cross section of society from holding office unless they committed themselves to a specific religious belief.

BUSCARINI v. SAN MARINO (2000) 30 E.H.R.R. 208, L Wildhaber (President), ECHR.

3196. Human Rights Act 1998 (c.42) – Commencement No.2 Order

HUMAN RIGHTS ACT 1998 (COMMENCEMENT NO.2) ORDER 2000, SI 2000 1851 (C.47); made under the Human Rights Act 1998 s.22. Commencement details: bringing into force various provisions of the Act on October 2, 2000; £1.00.

This Order provides that the remaining provisions of the Human Rights Act 1998, giving effect to the European Convention on Human Rights 1950, shall come into force on October 2, 2000.

3197. Ill treatment – investigations – police beatings – detention in custody – lack of effective investigation – right to trial within reasonable time – Bulgaria

[European Convention on Human Rights 1950 Art.3, Art.5, Art.6, Art.13, Art.25.]

In September 1992, A, then aged 14, was arrested by an off-duty policeman and taken to a nearby bus station. Further officers were called. A's parents who worked at the bus station remonstrated for his release. Following the arrival of two other policemen a dispute ensued during which A and his parents alleged they were subjected to beatings and detained. Subsequent to their release without charge they obtained medical certificates stating that A had injuries consistent with beating by truncheons. In October 1992 A's mother filed a complaint about A's beating and asked for the officers to be prosecuted, which was not carried out. A subsequent request for prosecution to the Regional Military Prosecution Office (RMPO) was refused as was an appeal to the General MPO who regarded the medical certificates as evidence of blows administered as a result of A's disobedience to police orders. Several years later, A spent two years in custody following charges of robbery, of which he was subsequently convicted. A's mother had made numerous requests for his release whilst he was in custody, all of which were refused, on the basis of the seriousness of the charges and risk of A's reoffending. A applied to the Commission, complaining of breaches of the European Convention on Human Rights 1950 Art.3, Art.6(1) and Art.13 in relation to his alleged previous ill treatment by police. That application was declared admissible. The Commission expressed the opinion that there had been a violation of Art.13 as regards police beating and violations of Art.5(3), Art.5(4) and Art.25 as regards subsequent events. The remainder of the application was dismissed.

Held, granting the application in part, that (1) there was enough circumstantial evidence to raise a reasonable suspicion that the injuries, following the alleged police beatings which were sufficiently serious to amount to "ill treatment" within the meaning of Art.3, may have been caused by the police, and the State was therefore required to carry out an effective investigation into the allegations. The investigation actually carried out was inadequate and accordingly there had been a violation of Art.3. The GMPO and RMPO investigations were likewise cursory and inadequate; (2) the lack of an effective investigation into A's allegations coupled with the lack of effective access for A to the investigatory authorities meant that there had also been a breach of Art.13; (3) as regards events from July 1995, there had been a violation of A's right to be "brought promptly before a judge or other officer authorised by law to exercise judicial power" under Art.5(3). A's application for release was not brought before a judge until he had been detained for three months, which was insufficiently "prompt" for these purposes. A was not heard in person by any of the prosecutors who considered his release applications and in any event they were not sufficiently independent or impartial to satisfy Art.5(3); (4) A's pre-trial detention period of two years was excessive. It followed that there had been a violation of his right to "a trial within a reasonable time" under Art.5(3); (5) the failure of Bulgarian law to allow A to challenge the legality of his detention more than once and even then to have held the hearing in camera meant that there had been a violation of A's right under Art.5(4) to take proceedings to determine the lawfulness of his detention, and (6) the questioning of A' parents by the State authorities and the resulting sworn declaration "amounted to improper pressure in hindrance of the right of individual petition", contrary to Art.25(1).

ASSENOV v. BULGARIA (1999) 28 E.H.R.R. 652, R Bernhardt (President), ECHR.

3198. Juvenile offenders – right to fair trial – murder conviction – conduct of trial – right to fair trial breached

[European Convention on Human Rights 1950 Art.3, Art.5, Art.6.]

The applicants, T and V, were convicted of murder committed when they were aged 10. The trial took place when the applicants were 11. The applicants brought an action in the European Court of Human Rights, arguing that their fundamental rights as enshrined in the European Convention on Human Rights 1950 Art.3, Art.5 and Art.6 had been breached by the way that the trial had been conducted and by their general treatment.

Held, granting the applications in part, that Art.6 had been breached by the way that the trial had been conducted. Although the Crown Court in which the case had been heard had been modified to take into account the age of the applicants, the degree of formality and ritual must have seemed oppressive to T and V. The layout of the court had been such that the applicants had been in full view of the media and public. Considering the intense attention the case attracted, it was impossible to conclude that the applicants could have consulted with their lawyers free of any inhibition. Nevertheless, it could not be said that the applicants had been subjected to degrading treatment contrary to Art.3 by virtue of their age. The selection of 10 for the age of criminal responsibility was not significantly lower than the age of responsibility elsewhere in Europe. Nor could it be said that a sentence with a punitive element amounted to degrading treatment. However, Art.6, which guaranteed a fair hearing before an impartial tribunal, was breached when the Home Secretary, as part of the executive, had fixed the tariff. Furthermore, as the tariff fixed by the Home Secretary had been quashed by the House of Lords and no new tariff had been set, there was no opportunity to review the case by the Parole Board in breach of Art.5.

T v. UNITED KINGDOM; V v. UNITED KINGDOM [2000] 2 All E.R. 1024 (Note), L Wildhaber (President), ECHR.

3199. Legal aid – international organisations – UN Human Rights Committee – New Zealand

[Legal Services Act 1991 (New Zealand) s.19(1); Treaty of Waitangi (Fisheries Claims) Settlement Act 1992; International Covenant on Civil and Political Rights 1966 First Optional Protocol.]

T and 19 others submitted a communication to the United Nations Human Rights Committee, HRC, complaining that by the enactment of the Treaty of Waitangi (Fisheries Claims) Settlement Act 1992, the New Zealand Government had denied their right freely to pursue their economic and cultural development. The communication claimed that the alleged infringement breached their civil and political rights under the International Covenant on Civil and Political Rights 1966 First Optional Protocol to which New Zealand had acceded. In order to pursue her claim T applied to WDLSC for legal aid under the Legal Services Act 1991 (New Zealand) s.19(1)(e), which set out a residual category of courts and tribunals for which legal aid was available. Section 19(1)(e)(v) made provision for the availability of legal aid in proceedings before "any administrative tribunal or judicial authority", in cases where legal representation was required and in its absence the applicant would suffer substantial hardship. WDLSC rejected T's application for legal aid, on the basis that there was no jurisdiction under the 1991 Act to grant legal aid for proceedings outside New Zealand. The High Court declared that this decision was unlawful but this judgment was reversed on appeal by the New Zealand Court of Appeal (3 B.H.R.C. 1). On T's appeal to the Privy Council, it was accepted that the Government was under no international obligation to make legal aid available for proceedings before the HRC, and accordingly the sole question for determination was whether the HRC was a "judicial authority" within the meaning of s.19(1)(e)(v) of the Act of 1991.

Held, dismissing the appeal, that the words "any...judicial authority" could not be read literally and, since they did not include any judicial authority anywhere in the world, a limitation had to be placed on their scope. The limitation was that the judicial authority in question must have some relevant connection with New Zealand and the New Zealand legal system. While legal aid would not be restricted to proceedings wholly within New Zealand, it would not extend to bodies not forming part of that legal system. All the courts and tribunals designated by s.19(1) of the 1991 Act were part of that system and exercised a coercive jurisdiction within it. The HRC, by contrast, was not part of any state's legal system but was established by international convention, and its jurisdiction over states was consensual. While New Zealand might be said to have conferred jurisdiction on the HRC by submitting to its adjudicative jurisdiction, the HRC did not thereby exercise New Zealand's own sovereign jurisdiction. The source of its jurisdiction, therefore, distinguished the HRC from the other courts and tribunals listed in s.19(1). It followed that the HRC was not a "judicial authority" for the purposes of s.19(1) and New Zealand legal aid was not available for proceedings before it.

TANGIORA v. WELLINGTON DISTRICT LEGAL SERVICES COMMITTEE [2000] 1 W.L.R. 240, Lord Millett, PC.

3200. Local authorities – race discrimination – meaning of provision of "goods, facilities or services" for purpose of Race Relations Act 1976

[Race Relations Act 1976 s.20; Children Act 1989 s.105.]

C argued in proceedings before the employment tribunal that his former employer, NLBC, had been guilty of racial discrimination under the Race Relations Act 1976 s.20 by refusing to permit a black child in its care to go on holiday with a white family. The tribunal held that decisions taken by a local authority in respect of children in its care fell outside the scope of s.20. C appealed. NLBC argued that, since the child was the subject of a care order, it had parental responsibility for the child and therefore could not provide "goods, facilities or services" to the child under s.20 with the result that the 1976 Act did not apply.

Held, allowing the appeal, that for the purpose of s.20 a local authority provided goods, facilities and services for children looked after by that authority, *Applin v. Race Relations Board* [1975] A.C. 259, [1974] C.L.Y. 19 applied. Such a conclusion was supported by the normal meaning of the words "goods, facilities or services", the purpose of the 1976 Act, and the definition of "service" in the Children Act 1989 s.105. Since the 1989 Act made no distinction between children in care, being children for whom a local authority had parental responsibility, and children accommodated by an authority, it would not be appropriate to draw such a distinction for the purpose of the applicability of s.20.

CONWELL v. NEWHAM LBC; *sub nom.* NEWHAM LBC v. CONWELL [2000] 1 W.L.R. 1, Charles, J., EAT.

3201. Prisoners rights – death penalty – exercise of prerogative of mercy – petition to international human rights organisations – fairness – Jamaica

[Constitution of Jamaica s.13, s.91.]

L and others, who had been sentenced to death upon conviction for murder in Jamaica, appealed against a decision to dismiss their applications for constitutional redress and for a stay of execution pending the recommendations of the United Nations Commission on Human Rights, UNCHR, and the Inter American Commission on Human Rights, IACHR. They contended that (1) they were entitled, on their petitions for mercy, to have access to the information that had been placed before the Jamaican Privy Council, pursuant to the Constitution of Jamaica s.91 and to make representations thereupon, and (2) they had a right to a stay of execution until both UNCHR and IACHR had reported on their petitions and then to present the same to the Privy Council for consideration in respect of the exercise of the prerogative of mercy. The Attorney General cross appealed, arguing that the court had been wrong to determine that instructions given by the Governor

General of Jamaica, laying down a timetable for applications to human rights organisations, were unlawful.

Held, allowing the appeal and dismissing the cross appeal (Lord Hoffmann dissenting), that (1) whilst the merits of a decision to grant or not to grant a petition of mercy could not be reviewed by the court, the fairness of procedures followed in reaching that decision could be subject to scrutiny. L and the others should have been given notice of the date on which their petitions were to be heard by the Privy Council, access to all relevant documents and an opportunity to make representations, such facility being tantamount to a judicial review procedure, *De Freitas v. Benny* [1976] A.C. 239, [1975] C.L.Y. 239 and *Reckley v. Minister of Public Safety and Immigration (No.2)* [1996] A.C. 527, [1996] C.L.Y. 1117 not followed, and (2) reports of international human rights organisations should also have been taken into account by the court when considering the exercise of its prerogative power and the requirements of natural justice. L had been entitled by virtue of s.13 of the Constitution to complete the petitions to UNCHR and IACHR prior to the application for mercy, but in future only a petition to the IACHR would be permitted. Accordingly, both the time limits imposed by the Governor General for the conduct of such petitions, and execution without consideration of the IACHR reports were unlawful, *Pratt v. Attorney General of Jamaica* [1994] 2 A.C. 1, [1994] C.L.Y. 491 considered and *Thomas v. Baptiste* [2000] 2 A.C. 1, [1999] C.L.Y. 758 applied.

LEWIS (NEVILLE) v. ATTORNEY GENERAL OF JAMAICA; TAYLOR (PATRICK) v. ATTORNEY GENERAL OF JAMAICA; McLEOD (ANTHONY) v. ATTORNEY GENERAL OF JAMAICA; BROWN (CHRISTOPHER) v. ATTORNEY GENERAL OF JAMAICA [2000] 3 W.L.R. 1785, Lord Slynn of Hadley, PC.

3202. **Prisoners rights – meals – restriction of access to food serving area – absolute right to provision of adequate food**

[European Convention on Human Rights 1950 Art.3; Prison Rules 1999 (SI 1999 728) r.24.]

R, a serving prisoner, challenged the prison governor's policy that prisoners within the segregation unit who, in protest, refused to wear prison clothing would be barred from collecting their daily three meal entitlement from the servery but be provided with one meal a day brought to their cell by prison staff. The prison governor justified the policy on the ground, inter alia, that to give in to the prisoners protests would undermine discipline and control within the prison. R sought a declaration that those prisoners affected by the policy were entitled to have all three meals brought to their cell, contending that the right to the provision of food was absolute and that no restriction or limitation could be placed upon it. In the alternative, R submitted that no restriction which constituted an interference with the fundamental human rights of a prisoner, in particular the right under the European Convention on Human Rights 1950 Art.3, could be imposed.

Held, granting the application in part, that (1) the prison governor's policy was unlawful and a potential breach of Art.3 of the Convention. The prison governor could lay down restrictions regulating a prisoner's access to food provided that policy satisfied an obligation to provide adequate food meeting the nutritional needs of the prisoner pursuant to the Prison Rules 1999 r.24. The right to the provision of adequate food could not be withdrawn as a punishment or sanction. In the instant case, the requirement for inmates within the segregation unit to wear prison clothes when visiting the servery had been legitimately justified on the grounds of good order and discipline, *McFeeley v. United Kingdom (8317/78)* (1981) 3 E.H.R.R. 161 applied. However, the failure of a prisoner to adhere to the requirement to wear prison clothes did not remove from the prison governor his obligation under r.24 to provide food to that prisoner, or reduce the fundamental right of that prisoner to adequate food. The policy had been introduced in an ad hoc manner and contained no provision to safeguard the prisoners health. The obvious alternative open to the prison governor had been the provision of adequate food to the prisoner in his cell, and (2) R was entitled to be provided with such food as was adequate under the provisions of r.24, rather than a guarantee of three meals a day. It followed that the declaration sought would not be granted.

R. v. GOVERNOR OF FRANKLAND PRISON, *ex p.* RUSSELL (RIGHT TO MEALS) [2000] 1 W.L.R. 2027, Lightman, J., QBD.

3203. Property rights – business tenancies – lease of open air cinema – eviction of leaseholder – exhaustion of domestic remedies

[European Convention on Human Rights 1950 Art.13, Protocol 1 Art.1.]

In 1978, I leased an open air cinema in Greece. The land on which it was built had been the subject of a dispute as to ownership between the private landowners and the State since 1953. An eviction order was made against I in 1989, and although it was later quashed, the local authority refused to give up possession. I complained, claiming breach of his rights to peaceful enjoyment of his possessions and to an effective remedy under the European Convention on Human Rights 1950 Art.13 and Protocol 1 Art.1. The Greek Government argued that I had not exhausted all available domestic remedies.

Held, granting the application, that I had exhausted available domestic remedies in making his application for the eviction order to be quashed. No other remedies would have succeeded, given the local authority's refusal to comply. The business of the cinema and its goodwill were assets capable of protection under Protocol 1 Art.1. The fact that I was being prevented from using those assets amounted to an interference with the principle of peaceful enjoyment of property, which, since the quashing of the eviction order, had no legal justification and was therefore in violation of Protocol 1 Art.1. Article 13 had also been violated as the remedy invoked by I had clearly not been effective since it had been ignored by both the Minister of Finance and the local authority.

IATRIDIS v. GREECE (2000) 30 E.H.R.R. 97, E Palm (President), ECHR.

3204. Property rights – hunting – small landowners – automatic transfer of hunting rights to association – discrimination – breach of freedom of conscience and peaceful enjoyment of possessions – France

[European Convention on Human Rights 1950 Art 11; European Convention on Human Rights 1950 Protocol 1 Art.1.]

C, a French landowner opposed to hunting on ethical grounds, was required under French national law to join an approved hunters' association, ACCA, resulting in the automatic transfer of hunting rights over his land to it. Only owners of land in excess of a certain area could object and C's land was smaller than that required. C complained to the European Commission of Human Rights that, inter alia, the law violated his rights to freedom of conscience and association and peaceful enjoyment of possession guaranteed by the European Convention on Human Rights 1950 Art.11 and Protocol 1 Art.1. C also complained of discrimination based on property, contrary to Art.14. The Commission, expressing opinion in C's favour, referred the complaint to the European Court of Human Rights.

Held, that (1) there was a breach of Protocol 1 Art.1, as although the aim of improving the technical organisation of hunting was in the general interest of the community, an automatic transfer of an individual's hunting rights in a way which was incompatible with their beliefs, was disproportionate to that aim and did not fairly balance the rights of the individual against the requirements of the general interest; (2) there was a breach of Protocol 1 Art.1 taken in conjunction with Art.14. A difference in treatment was discriminatory for the purposes of Art.14 if it did not pursue a legitimate aim or the means employed was disproportionate to the aim sought. The difference in treatment between large and small landowners could not be justified in the public interest, since the sole criterion was nothing more than the area of their land. There was discrimination in only allowing large landowners to use their land according to their conscience, and (3) there was a breach of Art.11, since to force a person to join an association contrary to his own beliefs and to surrender his land to a use of which he disapproved went beyond what was necessary to protect the

democratic participation in hunting, which, in any event, was not a Convention right.
CHASSAGNOU v. FRANCE (2000) 29 E.H.R.R. 615, L Wildhaber (President), ECHR.

3205. Race discrimination – gypsies – local authority – police not liable for aiding and abetting

[Race Relations Act 1976 s.20, s.21, s.33(1).]
The mother of S, a Romany gypsy, arranged to hire a local authority building for S's wedding. Responding to information relating to two gypsy weddings, from which 1500 guests were expected at one and disorder was expected at the other, two police officers informed the authority that they were anticipating a tenfold increase in the numbers attending S's wedding, that they feared disorder and that S's family was "well known" to them. The authority imposed extra conditions on the hire and S and her mother brought a claim for breach of contract against the authority. The claim was successful and the authority was also held to have breached the Race Relations Act 1976 s.20 and s.21. However, a further claim against the two police officers under s.33(1) was dismissed on the basis that they had not been party to the decision. S appealed, contending that the decision that the police were not guilty of aiding and abetting the authority was flawed.
Held, dismissing the appeal, that a secondary liability could not exist without knowledge that the primary party was treating or intending to treat someone less favourably on racial grounds. In the instant case, although the police information had been a contributory factor in the authority's decision to change the conditions, there was no evidence that the officers had known that the authority would act in a discriminatory manner.
HALLAM v. AVERY; *sub nom.* SMITH v. CHELTENHAM BC [2000] 1 W.L.R. 966, Judge, L.J., CA.

3206. Race Relations (Amendment) Act 2000 (c.34)

This Act extends further the application of the Race Relations Act 1976 to the police and other public authorities and to amend the exemption under that Act for acts done for the purpose of safeguarding national security.
This Act received Royal Assent on November 30, 2000.

3207. Regulation of Investigatory Powers Act 2000 (c.23)

This Act makes provision in relation to the interception of communications, the acquisition and disclosure of data relating to communications, the carrying out of surveillance, the use of covert human intelligence sources and the acquisition of the means by which electronic data protected by encryption or passwords may be decrypted or accessed. In addition, it provides for Commissioners and a tribunal with functions and jurisdiction in relation to those matters, to entries on and interferences with property or with wireless telegraphy and to the carrying out of their functions by the Security Service, the Secret Intelligence Service and the Government Communications Headquarters.
This Act received Royal Assent on July 28, 2000.

3208. Regulation of Investigatory Powers Act 2000 (c.23) – Commencement No.1 Order

REGULATION OF INVESTIGATORY POWERS ACT 2000 (COMMENCEMENT NO.1 AND TRANSITIONAL PROVISIONS) ORDER 2000, SI 2000 2543 (C.71); made under the Regulation of Investigatory Powers Act 2000 s.83, s.78. Commencement details: bringing into force various provisions of the Act on September 25, 2000, October 2, 2000 and October 24, 2000; £1.50.
This Order brings into force certain provisions of the Regulation of Investigatory Powers Act 2000 which regulate surveillance and the use of covert human

intelligence sources, relate to the interception of communications, and establish judicial commissioners to oversee the use of the powers conferred by the Act and a tribunal to consider complaints and cases brought under the Human Rights Act 1998 s.7(1)(a). In addition, it brings into operation provisions relating to interception by the controller of a private telecommunication system.

3209. **Right to fair trial – appeals – appeal inadmissible when lodged by convicted person who had not complied with arrest warrant – disproportionate sanction for non compliance**

[European Convention on Human Rights 1950 Art.6(1).]

O appealed on points of law against his conviction for laundering the proceeds of drug trafficking. The Court of Cassation found that O's appeal was inadmissible, because he had not complied with a warrant for his arrest, and therefore could not lodge an appeal through a legal representative on a point of law. O brought an application challenging the refusal, on the ground that it was a violation of his right to a fair trial under the European Convention on Human Rights 1950 Art.6(1).

Held, granting the application, that an individual's right of access to a court could be restricted but only in ways that were in proportion to the legitimate objective sought to be achieved and did not impinge on the fundamental right itself. O had not sought to evade arrest and had attended court when his attendance had been mandatory. The fact that O was required to surrender his liberty before he could have the right to question the legitimacy of the decision imposing that deprivation tested was out of proportion and weighed unfairly against O, to the extent that his right to a fair trial had been violated, *Poitrimol v. France (A/277-A)* (1994) 18 E.H.R.R. 130, [1994] C.L.Y. 2404 followed.

OMAR v. FRANCE; GUERIN v. FRANCE (2000) 29 E.H.R.R. 210, R Bernhardt (President), ECHR.

3210. **Right to fair trial – care proceedings – children – lack of oral hearing breached right to fair trial**

[European Convention on Human Rights 1950 Art.6(1), Art.8, Art.13.]

The authorities had implemented an open care regime in respect of the family's first child, P, for several years but, shortly after the birth of the second child, S, the mother, M, became mentally ill and both P and S were placed in care on a provisional basis. There was a suspicion that P had been sexually abused, although psychiatric observations did not reveal any evidence of this. However, a decision was then made to place P and S in care on the grounds that M and the father, F, could not provide adequate care and protection. The parents' appeal against this decision was dismissed without an oral hearing and the authorities refused access to M, F and the grandparents on the basis of their opposition to fostering. F and the paternal grandfather, G, complained that the decision to take P and S into care, and related procedures, were in breach of the European Convention on Human Rights 1950 Art.6(1), Art.8 and Art.13.

Held, dismissing the complaints regarding breaches of Art.8 and Art.13 but upholding that with regard to Art.6(1), that taking P and S into care had been justified because of the suspected sexual abuse. Where open care had been unsuccessful, full-time care should normally be only a temporary measure and a fair balance had to be observed between the family's rights and those of the child. Although it was a drastic measure to restrict access with F and G, this was reasonable given the sexual abuse allegations. However, the failure to conduct an oral hearing at some stage in the proceedings breached Art.6(1).

L v. FINLAND [2000] 2 F.L.R. 118, G Ress (President), ECHR.

3211. Right to fair trial – children – residence application – proceedings to be heard in open court – exhaustion of domestic remedies

[Family Proceedings Rules 1991 (SI 1991 1247); European Convention on Human Rights 1950 Art.6.]

F, the father of child B, separated from B's mother, M, shortly after B's birth in 1993. A residence order was made in M's favour, but F continued to make applications for residence and contact over a period of years. In 1996, having allegedly been told that M's new partner was violent, F applied for his pending residence application to be heard in open court. This was refused by the county court and upheld by the Court of Appeal ([1999] 2 F.L.R. 145, [1999] C.L.Y. 9), which held, in reliance upon *P-B (A Minor) (Child Cases: Hearings in Open Court), Re* [1997] 1 All E.R. 58, [1996] C.L.Y. 612, that the Family Proceedings Rules 1991 required family cases to be heard in chambers, with a discretion to sit in open court only where appropriate, which did not apply to the instant case. F complained to the European Court of Human Rights, arguing that there had been a violation of his right to a fair and public hearing under the European Convention on Human Rights 1950 Art.6. The UK government contended that it was in the interests of children and their families that hearings should be in private and that the application was not admissible as F had not exhausted domestic remedies because he could have asked again for a public hearing.

Held, granting the application, that as the Court of Appeal had dismissed F's appeal against the refusal to allow a public hearing a fresh application by F was unlikely to succeed so that he had exhausted his available domestic remedies, *Padovani v. Italy (A/257 B)* (Unreported) considered. The application raised serious issues of fact and law that required a consideration of the full merits of the case.

B v. UNITED KINGDOM (HEARING IN PRIVATE) (36337/97) [2000] 2 F.C.R. 97, J-P Costa (President), ECHR.

3212. Right to fair trial – compensation – infection with HIV from blood transfusion – lack of clarity in procedure under statutory scheme

[European Convention on Human Rights 1950 Art.6(1).]

FE was infected with HIV from a blood transfusion, and brought a civil action seeking compensation for the damage sustained. When his claim was dismissed, FE appealed to an appellate court. While that claim was pending, FE submitted a compensation claim to a national fund. In accepting the compensation offered, FE made it clear that his financial circumstances forced his acceptance, but that he reserved the right to bring proceedings against any liable third party. The appeal proceedings continued and his compensation claim was upheld on October 6, 1994. On June 6, 1997 the Court of Cassation quashed and annulled that judgment. FE relied on the European Convention on Human Rights 1950 Art.6(1) to contend that he had not had effective access to the civil courts in order to assert his right to compensation. Further, that the length of proceedings in the Court of Cassation, lasting two years and three months, had been unreasonable.

Held, granting the application, that the degree of access to a court had to be sufficient in terms of Art.6(1). For that right to be effective, an individual must have a clear opportunity to challenge an act that interfered with his rights. FE's understanding of the system was to be assessed at the time he accepted the fund's offer. At that time, the procedure was neither sufficiently clear nor protected by adequate safeguards to prevent a misunderstanding as to the available remedies and any restrictions arising due to their simultaneous application. Therefore Art.6(1) had been breached. The reasonableness of the length of proceedings had to be assessed in the light of the circumstances of the case. In particular, its complexity and the conduct of the parties. On the facts, FE was not responsible for any delay, but there had been considerable delay on the part of the authorities. FE's condition made expedition a matter of crucial importance. Although complex, the underlying facts of his case had been known to the Court of Cassation for several years. Accordingly, the proceedings did not satisfy the reasonable time requirement, such that Art.6(1) had also been breached in this regard, *Bellet v. France* (Unreported, December 4, 1995) considered.

FE v. FRANCE (2000) 29 E.H.R.R. 591, Thor Vilhjalmsson (President), ECHR.

3213. Right to fair trial – courts martial – appropriate level of compensation

See ARMED FORCES: McDaid v. United Kingdom. §258

3214. Right to fair trial – courts martial – pre trial detention – commanding officer not independent

[European Convention on Human Rights 1950 Art.5.]

J, a soldier, had completed a sentence but continued to be detained thereafter on the basis of suspected involvement in further offences. During that period of detention, J was brought before his commanding officer, CO, where a charge sheet was read to him. J was eventually released from detention, but was finally sentenced to imprisonment after pleading guilty at a court martial. J applied to the European Court of Human Rights, arguing that his pre-trial detention had been unlawful because the hearing before his CO could not be regarded as impartial and unbiased and, therefore, his detention was in breach of the European Convention on Human Rights 1950 Art.5.3. Furthermore, J argued that the failure to provide an enforceable right to compensation violated Art.5.5.

Held, granting the application, that there had been a failure to protect J's right to liberty and security of the person in breach of Art.5.3 and Art.5.5. The hearing before J's CO did not fulfil the requirement to hold a hearing because the CO, who would play a central role in the prosecution of the case and was responsible for discipline, could not be regarded as independent and unbiased, *Hood v. United Kingdom* (2000) 29 E.H.R.R. 365, [1999] C.L.Y. 3090 applied. Moreover, there had been a breach of Art.5.5 in that J did not have an enforceable right to compensation.

JORDAN v. UNITED KINGDOM (30280/96) (2001) 31 E.H.R.R. 6, J-P Costa (President), ECHR.

3215. Right to fair trial – courts martial – role of convening officer incompatible with independence and impartiality

[Air Forces Act 1955; European Convention on Human Rights 1950 Art.6(1).]

M and G, whilst serving in the Royal Air Force, were tried and convicted of a criminal offence by district courts martial pursuant to the Air Force Act 1955. M and G contended that they did not receive a fair or public hearing by an independent and impartial tribunal in violation of the European Convention on Human Rights 1950 Art.6(1).

Held, granting the application, that the convening officer of the courts martial had a central role in organising the prosecution and therefore the courts martial were not independent and impartial within the meaning of Art.6(1) of the Convention, *Findlay v. United Kingdom* (1997) 24 E.H.R.R. 221, [1997] C.L.Y. 2807 followed.

MOORE v. UNITED KINGDOM; GORDON v. UNITED KINGDOM (2000) 29 E.H.R.R. 728, Judge Costa (President), ECHR.

3216. Right to fair trial – delay – right to hear within reasonable time – delay between original sentence and Attorney General's Reference

[Criminal Justice Act 1988 s.36; European Convention on Human Rights 1950 Art.6.1.]

H was convicted in February 1995 of conspiracy to defraud and four counts of theft in relation to the take over of a company. He was sentenced to community service and ordered to pay compensation and costs. In March 1995 H launched an appeal against his conviction and in April of the same year the Attorney General made a reference to the Court of Appeal, seeking a review of the sentence under the

Criminal Justice Act 1988 s.36. H's appeal against conviction was dismissed in March 1997 and the Attorney General's reference was subsequently allowed in the same month with the result that a sentence of 20 months' imprisonment was imposed (*The Times*, April 10, 1997, [1997] C.L.Y. 1547). H applied to the European Court of Human Rights contending that the period of over two years that had elapsed between his original sentence and the later sentence following the Attorney General's reference constituted a delay contrary to the requirement under the European Convention on Human Rights 1950 Art.6.1 to hold a hearing "within a reasonable time".

Held, granting the application (Judge Cabral Barreto dissenting), that the proceedings had not taken place within a reasonable time and accordingly there had been a breach of Art.6.1. Although the fact that the Attorney General's reference, H's appeal and the appeals of his co-defendants, were running at the same time meant that the case was more complex than normal, the issues had been fully heard at first instance and were readily available for inspection. Moreover, the judgment in the Attorney General's reference had been short and gave no indication that the court had regarded the case as singularly complex. No case had been made to justify the length of the delay. There had been no judicial activity with regard to the case for the majority of the period of delay.

HOWARTH v. UNITED KINGDOM 9 B.H.R.C. 253, G Ress (President), ECHR.

3217. Right to fair trial – directors disqualification proceedings – character evidence refused

See COMPANY LAW: DC v. United Kingdom. §667

3218. Right to fair trial – directors disqualification proceedings

See COMPANY LAW: WGS v. United Kingdom. §666

3219. Right to fair trial – disclosure – public interest immunity – judge must assess whether non disclosure strictly necessary

[European Convention on Human Rights 1950 Art.6.]

During criminal proceedings involving R and four others, which related to various serious offences, relevant evidence was withheld from the defence by the prosecution on the basis of public interest immunity. The trial judge had not been notified of the decision to withhold evidence and played no part in assessing whether it was strictly necessary to do so. R applied to the European Court of Human Rights, alleging a breach of the European Convention on Human Rights 1950 Art.6, on the basis that the fundamental nature of a trial was adversarial and both sides must have the opportunity to comment on the observations filed and evidence adduced by the other.

Held, granting the applications, that there had been breaches of Art.6 since, although the right to disclosure of all relevant evidence was not an absolute right, the discretion must be exercised by the trial judge who was in a position to assess the evidence in the light of any arguments presented by the defence or new issues arising from the proceedings. There would be cases in which evidence could be withheld on the grounds of national security, the need to protect witnesses, or to maintain the secrecy of police investigative methods, but when exercising those restrictions the fundamental rights of the accused had to be weighed against the decision not to disclose. Furthermore, procedures for non disclosure had to include safeguards to ensure that the interests of the accused were not infringed. In the instant case, the trial judge had not been informed of the Crown's decision to withhold evidence and the Court of Appeal could only assess the evidence on transcript records and counsel's submissions, without the benefit of witness testimony or a full understanding of the issues in the case, *Edwards v. United Kingdom (A/247B)* (1993) 15 E.H.R.R. 417, [1993] C.L.Y. 2125 distinguished. In the other three cases changes in the law meant that the Crown had had to make an application to the judge on the issue of non disclosure and the defence had full summarised information regarding the evidence. That constituted the procedural safeguard necessary to protect the rights of the accused.

ROWE v. UNITED KINGDOM; JASPER v. UNITED KINGDOM; FITT v. UNITED KINGDOM (2000) 30 E.H.R.R. 1, L Wildhaber (President), ECHR.

3220. Right to fair trial – doctors – demotion – length of judicial review proceedings – dispute did not concern a civil right thus outside scope of Art.6(1)

[European Convention on Human Rights 1950 Art.6(1).]

A, a doctor employed at a local medical centre, was assigned to a staff category lower than that to which she considered she was entitled. A lodged an application for judicial review of the decision with the Sicilian regional administrative court. Following a period of nearly seven years during which proceedings remained pending A applied to the Commission complaining that the delay in the proceedings violated her right to have her civil rights determined by a tribunal within a "reasonable time" as provided by the European Convention on Human Rights 1950 Art.6(1). The Commission initially declared her application admissible on the basis that the dispute concerned "civil rights and obligations" under the ECHR since an economic interest was involved and expressed the view by a majority that there had been a violation of Art.6(1). However, the Italian Government submitted that Art.6(1) did not apply to A's case because her dispute concerned her employment in the public service and was not a civil right protected under the remit of the ECHR.

Held, refusing the application, that there was a well recognised and basic distinction in the laws of many Member States between civil servants and employees governed by private law. That distinction had resulted in rulings by the Court that "disputes relating to the recruitment, careers and termination of service of civil servants are as a general rule outside the scope of Art.6(1)", *Massa v. Italy (A/265-B)* (1994) 18 E.H.R.R. 266, [1995] C.L.Y. 2629 applied. In the instant case A's dispute clearly related to her recruitment and her career and as such did not concern a "civil right" within the meaning of Art.6(1).

ARGENTO v. ITALY (1999) 28 E.H.R.R. 719, R Bernhardt (President), ECHR.

3221. Right to fair trial – imprisonment for non payment of community charge – failure to provide legal aid

[European Convention on Human Rights 1950 Art.5, Art.6.]

P and the other applicants, O, were committed to prison by separate magistrates courts for failing to pay the community charge on the basis of wilful or culpable neglect. They had not been represented as there was no provision for legal aid at that time. All had been released on bail pending judicial review of the justices' decisions, which had been quashed as a result. They each complained that their rights to liberty and a fair trial under the European Convention on Human Rights 1950 Art.5 and Art.6 had been breached.

Held, granting the applications in part, that in assessing whether there had been a breach of Art.5 it was necessary to determine whether the justices actions had been ultra vires. The fact that the justices had not taken account of changes in P's circumstances and had not looked at alternatives to imprisonment for O had not been outside the justices' jurisdiction to the extent of rendering the decisions unlawful and therefore in breach of Art.5 on the ground of arbitrariness. The sanction of imprisonment served the legitimate aim of securing payment of the community charge and was therefore justifiable. There had, however, been a breach of Art.6 in the failure to provide legal aid, as this was required given the threat to liberty and the complexity of the cases, *Benham v. United Kingdom* (1996) 22 E.H.R.R. 293, [1996] C.L.Y. 3155 followed.

PERKS v. UNITED KINGDOM (2000) 30 E.H.R.R. 33, J-P Costa (President), ECHR.

3222. Right to fair trial – leave to remain – asylum seeker bringing action in malicious prosecution

See IMMIGRATION: R. v. Chief Immigration Officer, *ex p.* Quaquah. §3290

3223. Right to fair trial – legal advice – denial of access to legal representation – psychological coercion leading to self incrimination

[Prevention of Terrorism Act 1984 s.12; European Convention on Human Rights 1950 Art.6, Art.14.]

M was arrested under the Prevention of Terrorism Act 1984 s.12 in connection with a bomb attack in Northern Ireland. He was subjected to intense questioning for a period of 48 hours during which time he was denied access to legal advice despite having requested it and kept in isolation. At the sixth interview he admitted to being involved in the attack and signed a lengthy confession statement. The following day he was allowed access to a solicitor. M subsequently applied to the ECHR contending that his right to a fair trial under the European Convention on Human Rights 1950 Art.6 had been infringed owing to the denial of access to legal advice and the austere conditions in which he had been questioned, which amounted to psychological coercion and had led to his self incrimination.

Held, granting the application, that (1) Art.6 had been breached since the right to a fair trial also included conditions prevailing before the case was sent for trial where the fairness of the trial was likely to be seriously prejudiced. Access to legal advice was a minimum requirement under the Convention, *Imbrioscia v. Switzerland (A/275)* (1994) 17 E.H.R.R. 441, [1994] C.L.Y. 2407 applied. The conditions under which M had been questioned were intended to be psychologically coercive and designed to break down his resolve to remain silent throughout the interviews. To counteract the intimidating atmosphere M should have been given access to legal advice at an early stage. It made no difference that the court drew no adverse inferences from M's silence, since the denial of access to legal advice in the circumstances could not be justified, notwithstanding the fact that the confession had been obtained voluntarily and the applicant had not been ill treated, and (2) suspects arrested and questioned in England were entitled to access to legal advice immediately, which was not discriminatory and did not amount to a breach of Art.14 since it was the geographical location of the place of arrest which led to the differences in treatment and it was permissible for legislation to take account of regional differences.

MAGEE v. UNITED KINGDOM 8 B.H.R.C. 646, J-P Costa (President), ECHR.

3224. Right to fair trial – legal aid – absence of civil legal aid scheme – Guernsey

[Theft (Bailiwick of Guernsey) Law 1983 s.18(1)(b); Protection of Investors (Bailiwick of Guernsey) Law 1987 s.38(2)(b); European Convention on Human Rights 1950 Art.6, Art.13.]

F was charged with offences under the Theft (Bailiwick of Guernsey) Law 1983 s.18(1)(b) and the Protection of Investors (Bailiwick of Guernsey) Law 1987 s.38(2)(b). Following his release on bail, F applied for legal aid in connection with the pending criminal proceedings and various civil actions that had been brought against him. Since his release he had been living on welfare benefits and temporary low paid jobs, but he was referred to an advocate who agreed to represent him on a private client basis. F claimed that he was not informed that he would be unable to recover costs in the event of his acquittal. At trial, F was acquitted on the theft charges but remanded on the charge under the 1987 Act. F's advocate decided on an appropriate fee, as was customary practice in Guernsey, and sought recovery from F. The charge was later dropped, and F applied for legal aid to pursue an action of unlawful imprisonment against the police, which was refused on the basis that legal aid was not available for civil proceedings and there was no free legal aid scheme for criminal proceedings so that the advocate was entitled to make a charge if it was considered that F had sufficient means. F applied to the European Commission on Human Rights, complaining that the absence of a legal aid scheme was in breach of the European Convention on

Human Rights 1950 Art.6 and Art.13 in that he had been denied the right to a fair trial because he was unable to commence civil proceedings. Before the hearing, however, F and the Government reached a settlement on terms.

Held, refusing the application and accepting the terms of the settlement, that there had been a breach of Art.6 but there was no separate issue under Art.13. The Government had agreed to establish a civil legal aid system to comply with Guernsey's obligations under the Convention to come into force during 2000. The Guernsey Bar Council had been approached to offer suggestions as to what form the scheme should take and the Government also undertook to pay F compensation of £6000 and to cover his costs in bringing the application.

FAULKNER v. UNITED KINGDOM *The Times*, January 11, 2000, J-P Costa (President), ECHR.

3225. Right to fair trial – legal representation – company director seeking to represent company – constitutionality of practice rule requiring companies be legally represented – Zimbabwe

[Constitution of Zimbabwe s.18.]

P, the managing director of L, sought rescission of a judgment obtained by Z against L, P and P's wife. Z objected to P's wish to represent both himself and L, arguing that the court's rule of practice that companies had to be legally represented prevented it. The question of whether the practice rule violated the right to a fair hearing under the Constitution of Zimbabwe s.18 was referred to the Supreme Court by Z.

Held, that the rule that a company could only be represented by a legal practitioner was well established in many jurisdictions and could only be challenged if to enforce the rule might infringe a constitutional right of access to the courts. Under s.18 every "person" is entitled to the protection of the law. The parties agreed that "person" for the purposes of s.18 included both natural persons and artificial legal persons. Where a director of a company had such standing within the company as to be tantamount to the company's "alter ego", the practice rule's prohibition on that director being able to speak for the company would be a violation of the company's rights under s.18 as a legal "person". The practice rule would still be valid in the case of those connected to a company who could not be said to be its alter ego. If P could therefore show that he had the requisite standing within L then he should not be prevented from appearing on its behalf.

LEES IMPORT AND EXPORT (PVT) LTD v. ZIMBABWE BANKING CORP LTD 7 B.H.R.C. 647, Gubbay, C.J., Sup Ct (Zim).

3226. Right to fair trial – legal representation – constitutional right of parents in custody hearings – Canada

[Canadian Charter of Rights and Freedoms 1982 s.7, s.24(1).]

MHCS was granted temporary custody of G's children at a hearing at which G was not represented because of lack of funds. G's application for legal aid for the full hearing was refused as the scheme did not extend to cases brought by MHCS. G brought a motion requiring MHCS to ensure that she was legally represented and claiming that her right to a fair trial under the Canadian Charter of Rights and Freedoms 1982 s.7 had been violated. The judge declined to make a decision on the motion prior to the hearing date. At the hearing G was represented by counsel acting pro bono and the case was fully contested, resulting in the children being returned to G's care. G's motion was ultimately dismissed, as was her appeal to the Court of Appeal. G appealed to the Supreme Court.

Held, allowing the appeal, that the case raised for the first time the issue whether impoverished parents had a constitutional right to state-funded representation when a government sought to take custody of their children. Although the substantive issue in the case had been resolved, it was open to the court to adjudicate on the moot point of G's motion as it had been raised in an adversarial context. This raised a question of general importance that warranted clarification by the court and was not outside the court's institutional role.

Section 7 guaranteed every parent the right to a fair hearing in cases instigated by the state to obtain custody of their children. The protection of that right might in certain cases such as the instant case require the government to provide state-funded representation. In the instant case, the seriousness of the interests at stake, the complexity of the proceedings and G's capacity to understand and participate in the proceedings required that G be represented at the hearing. MHCS had therefore had a duty to fund G's representation at the hearing in order to avoid an infringement of s.7 and the judge should have availed herself of the court's power under s.24(1) to order compliance with that duty.

G v. MINISTER OF HEALTH AND COMMUNITY SERVICES 7 B.H.R.C. 615, Lamer, C.J., Sup Ct (Can).

3227. Right to fair trial – planning appeals – dismissal by Guernsey Royal Court Bailiff – Bailiff previously involved with legislative proceedings directly concerning planning application

[European Convention of Human Rights 1950 Art.6(1).]

M had appealed against a decision made by the Guernsey Island's Development Committee, refusing permission to permit residential use of his land. The appeal was dismissed. The Guernsey Royal Court Bailiff had previously sat in a non judicial capacity as President of the States of Deliberation, Guernsey's legislative body, when the draft development plan, which was directly applicable to M's land, was adopted. M applied to the European Commission of Human Rights in 1995, and in 1998 the Commission opined that there had been a violation of the European Convention of Human Rights 1950 Art.6(1) and referred the matter to the European Court of Human Rights.

Held, granting the application, that whilst it was not suggested that the Bailiff had been subjectively biased when he had considered M's planning appeal in 1995, the concepts of independence and objective impartiality were relevant, *Findlay v. United Kingdom* (1997) 24 E.H.R.R. 221, [1997] C.L.Y. 2807 considered. The question was whether the Bailiff possessed the required independence or objective impartiality required by the Convention. His direct involvement in the passage of legislation relevant to M's planning application cast doubt upon his judicial impartiality and independence, *De Haan v. Netherlands* (1998) 26 E.H.R.R. 417, [1998] C.L.Y. 3127 approved. M thus had legitimate reasons for assuming that the Bailiff's decision may have been influenced by his previous involvement in the legislative process, in breach of Art.6(1).

MCGONNELL v. UNITED KINGDOM (2000) 30 E.H.R.R. 289, J-P Costa (President), ECHR.

3228. Right to fair trial – presumption of innocence – access to legal advice denied – adverse inferences drawn by right to silence – compulsory forensic evidence

[Prevention of Terrorism (Temporary Provisions) Act 1989 s.14(1)(b); Criminal Evidence (Northern Ireland) Order 1988 (SI 1988 1987 (NI.20)) Art.3, Art.5; European Convention on Human Rights 1950 Art 6.1; European Convention on Human Rights 1950 Art 6.2; European Convention on Human Rights 1950 Art 6.3(c).]

A, who had been detained under the Prevention of Terrorism (Temporary Provisions) Act 1989 s.14(1)(b) in connection with a double murder, was denied access to a solicitor for 24 hours during the initial stages of his interrogation. He had been informed prior to the interrogation that under the Criminal Evidence (Northern Ireland) Order 1988 Art.3 and Art.5 he was not obliged to answer any questions, but failure to do so might result in adverse inferences being drawn from his silence. A did not respond to any questions throughout the interrogation. A testified in court to his whereabouts on the day of the murders and offered alternative explanations for the forensic evidence against him. The trial judge sitting alone drew adverse inferences from A's silence throughout his interrogation and convicted A of the double murder. The Court of Appeal reviewed the inferences drawn by the trial judge from A's silence and upheld the conviction on the basis that the inferences were only one element of the judge's reasoning. A complained to the European Court of Human Rights that there had been a violation of his right to a fair trial under the European Convention on Human Rights 1950. A contended that the denial of access to legal assistance for the first 24 hours of his interrogation violated Art. 6.1 of the Convention both separately and in conjunction with Art.6.3(3) and that the strong adverse inferences drawn by the trial judge from A's silence throughout his interrogation contravened his right to be presumed innocent under Art.6.2.

Held, granting the application in part, that (1) there had been a violation of Art.6.3(c) in conjunction with Art.6.1 as fairness required A to have access to legal assistance before being questioned. A's continued silence after obtaining such legal assistance had not legitimised the authorities' negligence in failing to provide such an important right. Domestic provisions in the Criminal Evidence (Northern Ireland) Order 1988 ensured that access to a solicitor was paramount and should be respected. There had, however, been no violation of Art.6.1 or Art.6.2, given that the right to silence was not an absolute right as the judge must consider (a) any extenuating circumstances of the case where inferences might be drawn; (b) their weight in the national courts, and (c) any evidence of compulsion, *Murray v. United Kingdom (Right to Silence)* (1996) 22 E.H.R.R. 29, [1996] C.L.Y. 1516 applied, and (2) the trial judge's decision to draw strong adverse inferences from A's silence was not the only or even the main element in convicting A, although (a) A could have been expected to answer the questions especially when he was questioned a second time in the presence of his legal adviser; (b) the compelling forensic evidence produced by the prosecution required A to produce an explanation, and (c) A had never contended that his silence had been based upon legal advice but only that he did not cooperate with the RUC as a matter of policy.

AVERILL v. UNITED KINGDOM 8 B.H.R.C. 430, J-P Costa (President), ECHR.

3229. **Right to fair trial – presumption of innocence – evidential burden of proof on defendant to provide special defence – no breach of human rights**

[Homicide Act 1957 s.2(2); Misuse of Drugs Act 1971 s.5(4), s.28; Human Rights Act 1998; European Convention on Human Rights 1950 Art.6(2).]

L appealed against a conviction for possession of a Class A drug with intent to supply. A and J appealed against their convictions for murder. The main point at issue was whether various statutory provisions offering benefits to defendants who could prove certain facts were compatible with the Human Rights Act 1998. It was argued that the Homicide Act 1957 s.2(2) and the Misuse of Drugs Act 1971 s.5(4) and s.28, which provided a defence to a charge of murder and possession of drugs respectively and placed a persuasive burden on a defendant to prove his case on a balance of probabilities, were in conflict with the presumption of innocence guaranteed under the European Convention on Human Rights 1950 Art.6(2). It was submitted that the general burden of proof should remain with the prosecution. In the cases of A and J, the jury had rejected the defence that the defendants should be found guilty of manslaughter by virtue of diminished responsibility. The onus had been on the defendants to prove that they were suffering from diminished responsibility under s.2 of the 1957 Act. Similarly, the effect of s.5(4) and s.28 of the 1971 Act was to offer mitigation to a defendant who could show that he was unaware of the contents of the container of which he was in possession. It was contended that the 1998 Act required that the statutory provisions should be interpreted in a manner that made them compatible with the Convention.

Held, dismissing the appeals, that the provisions of the 1957 and 1971 Acts, did not breach Art.6(2). The principle that the burden of proof should rest with the prosecution was fundamental at common law. Nevertheless, it could be displaced by Parliament where clear words were used to that effect. The Convention was an instrument for the protection of fundamental freedoms and it should be interpreted purposively so as to strike a balance between the rights of individuals and the rights of society in general, *Salabiaku v. France (A/141-A)*

(1991) 13 E.H.R.R. 379 applied. Moreover, the defendants were not being required to prove an essential element of the offence, rather they were being given the opportunity to establish a special defence. With reference to the cases of A and J, it could not be said that the alternative offence of manslaughter had become an essential element of the offence of murder. The purpose of s.2 of the 1957 Act was to offer defendants a benefit where they could be found guilty of a lesser offence than murder. The same was the case with s.5(4) and s.28 of the 1971 Act. Defendants could avoid liability by proving that they were unaware of the contents of a container. The statutory provisions did not have the effect of creating additional ingredients to the offence of possession of drugs with intent to supply. There was a clear social objective in curtailing the spread of drugs and those sections were well balanced and proportionate and accordingly did not breach Art.6(2).

R. v. LAMBERT (STEVEN); R. v. ALI (MUDASSIR MOHAMMED); R. v. JORDAN (SHIRLEY) [2001] 2 W.L.R. 211, Lord Woolf of Barnes, L.C.J., CA (Crim Div).

3230. **Right to fair trial – public inquiries – legal aid – discretion as to costs in human rights cases**

[Human Rights Act 1998 s.22(4); European Convention on Human Rights 1950 Art.6(1).]

C, a local resident, sought permission to apply for judicial review of a decision of the Secretary of State not to order legal assistance at a public enquiry for him and other residents to oppose the construction of additional inter London train links. C contended that (1) the public inquiry would involve a breach of his right to a fair hearing under the European Convention on Human Rights 1950 Art.6(1) and the Human Rights Act 1998. C maintained that because of the complex issues involved and the fact that legal aid was not available, there would be an "inequality of arms" in the representation of the opposing parties before the inquiry, and (2) if the challenge were unsuccessful, C should not be obliged to pay the costs of the application since to follow the normal practice as to costs could deter other potential objectors from seeking to enforce their human rights. R maintained that (1) C could not seek to rely upon legislation which was not yet in force, *R. v. DPP, ex p. Kebilene* [1999] 3 W.L.R. 175 cited, and (2) the denial of legal aid could only ever constitute a breach of Art.6(1) in an exceptional case. The public inquiry procedure was relatively informal and conducive to lay participation and there were other bodies whose views on the project coincided with those of C and who would be presenting detailed expert evidence before the inquiry and would therefore ensure that all relevant matters were raised. The court should resist the application that there be no order for costs, R submitted, on the basis that there had been no breach of C's human rights and the application had been brought prior to the relevant legislation becoming law.

Held, refusing the application, that (1) in the period prior to commencement of the 1998 Act it was possible to invoke a Convention right by virtue of s.22(4) of the 1998 Act which was now in force in relation to proceedings commenced by a public body, but although the Act could be used as a "shield" in those circumstances, it could not be used as a "sword". Even if that were not the case, C's submissions were based upon the lack of legal aid and would not have succeeded given the fact that there was provision in place for such funding and C's application had been considered and rejected. Furthermore, the involvement of other bodies in the proceedings would ensure that all issues were thoroughly explored and the information presented by C revealed a competent approach that would ensure that C's case was properly advanced before the inquiry, and (2) it would not be just or reasonable to oblige C to pay the costs of the application having taken into account the general approach to human rights cases argued for by C. It was observed that such a decision should not be taken as a general precedent. Each case would fall to be decided upon its particular merits.

R. v. SECRETARY OF STATE FOR THE ENVIRONMENT, TRANSPORT AND THE REGIONS, *ex p.* CHALLENGER [2001] Env. L.R. 12, Harrison, J., QBD.

3231. Right to fair trial – racism – complaint by juror of racial remarks indicating potential race bias – collective letter refuting allegations insufficient to remove doubt as to impartiality

[European Convention on Human Rights 1950 Art.6.1.]

S, an Asian, was convicted of conspiracy to defraud. The trial had been adjourned following a complaint by a juror of racist comments from two other jury members. The following day the judge received two letters, one of which contained an apology from a jury member as to his conduct and an assurance of non racial bias, and the other a collective letter from the jury refuting all allegations of racial bias. The judge subsequently redirected the jury but chose not to discharge them. S appealed to the Court of Appeal contending, inter alia, that the judge upon receipt of the juror's complaint should have discharged the jury as there had been a real danger of bias. The Court of Appeal held that the judge had not erred in failing to discharge the jury, given the collective letter refuting the allegations and the letter of apology from one of the jurors probably responsible for the remarks. S applied to the European Court of Human Rights complaining that he had not been tried before an impartial tribunal contrary to the European Convention on Human Rights 1950 Art.6.1.

Held, granting the application, that (1) the trial judge had not been in a position, having established that racist comments had been made by at least one jury member, to inquire into the nature of the comments. Accordingly the court had failed to establish from a subjective position that the jury had not been impartial; (2) there was some doubt as to the credibility of the collective letter considering that it had been signed by the jury member who had first raised fears as to racial bias. Furthermore, the letter which had been the product of a impromptu response represented a collective position of persons with different motives for denying race bias and accordingly could not be viewed as reliable as it was natural that upon accusation a person would deny racial bias, and (3) notwithstanding that the jury could not be presumed to be biased, the decision of the judge to redirect the jury rather than to dismiss it could not be said to remove doubt as to impartiality, *Gregory v. United Kingdom* (1998) 25 E.H.R.R. 577, [1997] C.L.Y. 2802 distinguished. The judge had both been informed of a serious allegation and received an indirect admission that racist remarks had been made. The judge had not, given the importance of removing doubts concerning impartiality, acted with sufficient stealth. It had not been adequate merely to accept the collective letter as ground that the jury had purged themselves of any prejudices they might have had.

SANDER v. UNITED KINGDOM 8 B.H.R.C. 279, J-P Costa (President), ECHR.

3232. Right to fair trial – right to family life – domestic structure for enforcement of contact orders

[European Convention on Human Rights 1950 Art.6(1), Art.8.]

A father brought a complaint before the European Court of Human Rights alleging that his rights to family life under the European Convention on Human Rights 1950 Art.8 had been violated as a result of the failure of the English and Scottish courts to enforce contact orders. This complaint was based on the mother's persistent non compliance with contact orders which had culminated in her leaving England and moving to Scotland. The father alleged that it was left to him to take the initiative in locating his former partner and his children. The High Court had taken action to locate the mother and children, had ordered Government agencies to divulge any information as to their whereabouts, and had invited the Official Solicitor to act as guardian ad litem. The father commenced enforcement procedures in Scotland. The Court of Session failed to make orders immediately, preferring instead to commence its own investigation of many of the issues. The father also alleged that the proceedings, at three years, were overly long and in breach of Art.6(1).

Held, refusing the application, that there was no absolute obligation of national authorities to ensure contact with non-custodial parents after divorce. The key question was whether the authorities had taken all necessary steps to facilitate contact within the special circumstances of each case. In the instant case, it was apparent that there was no fundamental defect in the structure available to enforce the father's rights. It was necessary within that structure that the welfare of the children and the interests of other parties were also taken into account sufficiently. The difficulties of enforcement in the instant case had resulted from the unilateral acts of the mother in relocating jurisdiction with the children. On these facts the courts had taken all reasonable steps and struck a balance between the competing rights of the parties, *Hokkanen v. Finland (A/299-A)* [1996] 1 F.L.R. 289, [1995] C.L.Y. 2660 applied. Further, the courts had been required to consider carefully their treatment of the mother and therefore had not exceeded a "reasonable time" in the overall length of proceedings. Accordingly, there had not been a violation of either Art.6(1) or Art.8.

G v. UNITED KINGDOM (CHILDREN: RIGHT OF CONTACT) (32346/96) [2001] 1 F.L.R. 153, J-P Costa (President), ECHR.

3233. Right to fair trial – right to silence – conversation in police cell between accused and undercover officer – information not actively elicited – Canada

[Canadian Charter of Rights and Freedoms 1982 s.7.]

L was arrested when he sold cocaine to an undercover police officer, J. The subterfuge continued so that it appeared that J had also been arrested, and he was placed in a cell with L. L struck up a conversation with J during which L made admissions. The admissions were excluded at L's trial as being in violation of L's right to silence under the Canadian Charter of Rights and Freedoms 1982 s.7 and L was acquitted. The Crown successfully appealed and a retrial was ordered, but L appealed to the Supreme Court on the question of his s.7 rights.

Held, dismissing the appeal by majority decision, that the right to silence related to a suspect's freedom to choose whether or not to make statements to the authorities. The use of undercover officers would only be in violation of this right where interrogation techniques were used to actively elicit information from a suspect. It was not necessary to establish that there was an atmosphere of oppression in order to prove a violation of the right to silence. What was crucial was the nature of the exchange and the nature of the relationship between an accused and the undercover officer. Although J had kept up the pretence, he had not built up a relationship of trust with L and his engagement in the conversation, which had been started by L, was not in any way manipulative and did not amount to interrogation.

LIEW v. R. 7 B.H.R.C. 708, Lamer, C.J., Sup Ct (Can).

3234. Right to fair trial – self incrimination – use of DTI interview transcripts by prosecution – violation of right against self incrimination

[European Convention on Human Rights 1950 Art.6.1.]

The applicants claimed an infringement of the European Convention on Human Rights 1950 Art.6.1 in that statements which they had been required by law to give to DTI inspectors, following allegations of criminal activity in their involvement in the acquisition of the Distillers company by Guinness, had been used by the prosecution at trial. The principal submissions were that there had been a breach of the right against self incrimination which, together with the prosecution's refusal to disclose documents to the defence and their collusion with the DPP and other institutions, had frustrated their right to a fair trial.

Held, granting the application in part, that the prosecution's use of the DTI interview transcripts had amounted to a violation of the right not to incriminate oneself, with the result that Art.6.1 had been breached in that respect, *Saunders v. United Kingdom* [1998] 1 B.C.L.C. 362, [1997] C.L.Y. 2816 followed. The remaining submissions, however, were not in violation of Art.6.1 and were thus rejected.

IJL v. UNITED KINGDOM; GMR v. UNITED KINGDOM; AKP v. UNITED KINGDOM 9 B.H.R.C. 222, J-P Costa (President), ECHR.

3235. Right to fair trial – speeding – road traffic offences – no appeal from automatic deduction of penalty points – France

[European Convention on Human Rights 1950 Art.6(1).]

M, a French citizen, was fined in June 1993 for exceeding the speed limit. Having elected to stand trial rather than pay the fines, he appeared in the Versailles Police Court in October 1993. M was found guilty, fined 1,500 FF, and disqualified from driving for 15 days with four penalty points out of a possible 12 deducted from his licence. The Police Court held that, since the relevant provisions of the Criminal Code did not apply to the deduction of points, the deduction was not a secondary criminal sanction triggered by a conviction and, accordingly, the legality of those provisions could not be considered by the criminal courts. M appealed, contending that the fact that the law did not provide for judicial review of a decision to deduct penalty points breached the European Convention on Human Rights 1950 Art.6(1). The appeal was dismissed and the court held, inter alia, that the deduction of penalty points was an administrative sanction. Further, that the legality of the imposition of that administrative sanction must be capable of being reviewed, but that at present the criminal courts lacked jurisdiction to do so. M appealed to the Court of Cassation, which dismissed his appeal in January 1995. In November 1994, M applied to the Commission, complaining that the systematic deduction of points without a right of appeal constituted a violation of the right of access to a tribunal under Art.6(1) and the Commission expressed the opinion by a majority that Art.6(1) was applicable but that it had not been breached.

Held, refusing the application, that Art.6(1) was applicable because the sanction of automatic deduction was a "criminal charge" within the meaning of Art.6(1). The concept of a "criminal charge" under Art.6(1) was autonomous in nature and not bound by the classification of the relevant sanction in domestic law, *Engel v. Netherlands (No.1) (A/22)* (1979-80) 1 E.H.R.R. 647 applied. Regarding the severity of the measure, it was relevant that if sufficient points were deducted a driver's licence would become invalid. The sanction was similar to a secondary penalty and the fact that Parliament and the courts had classified it as "administrative" could not alter its criminal nature. There had been no violation of M's right of access to a tribunal in relation to the sanction since the criminal conviction was by itself a review sufficient to satisfy the requirements of Art.6(1). It was not necessary to have a separate and additional judicial review of the automatic deduction of points from M's licence. Since M had elected not to pay the fine and to stand trial, he was given the opportunity to challenge the elements of the speeding offence forming the basis for the deduction of points. M was able to protest his innocence and submit all relevant factual and legal arguments before the Police Court and the Court of Appeal, both of which satisfied the requirements of a "tribunal" under Art.6(1). Since the offence led to the deduction of only four of a possible 12 points, the sanction was not disproportionate to the aims pursued as it did not lead immediately to disqualification and M could regain his points by not committing further offences within three years, or by attending a special training course.

MALIGE v. FRANCE (1999) 28 E.H.R.R. 578, R Bernhardt (President), ECHR.

3236. Right to fair trial – stay of execution – Convention rights subject to domestic laws – non appellate jurisdiction of ECHR

[Human Rights Act 1998 Sch.1 Part I Art.2(1)(a); European Convention on Human Rights 1950 Art.6(1).]

L was granted a warrant for possession in respect of residential premises. E sought a stay of execution pending the outcome of her application before the ECHR that she had been denied the right to a fair trial by an independent and impartial tribunal, contrary to the European Convention on Human Rights 1950 Art.6(1). E had previously applied for the deputy judge who was dealing with the possession proceedings to disqualify himself since he was a partner in a solicitors' firm involved in bankruptcy proceedings concerning E's husband. That application had been dismissed, (*The Times*, May 18, 1999, [1999] C.L.Y. 3796) and the decision upheld on appeal, ([2000] 2 W.L.R. 870, [1999] C.L.Y. 38). E contended that there were reasonable doubts about the judge's impartiality. It was submitted that the stay should be granted because if the complaint before the ECHR proved to be successful, the judgment of the deputy judge would be rendered unlawful.

Held, refusing the application, that a stay was not appropriate as the outcome of the case before the ECHR would not lead to an alteration in the law having direct consequences for those involved in the domestic proceedings, *Sparks v. Harland* [1997] 1 W.L.R. 143, [1996] C.L.Y. 838 distinguished. E's rights in relation to the property had been determined by the domestic courts and the ECHR was not to be treated as a further court of appeal. Although English courts would soon be bound to take into account ECHR decisions in view of the Human Rights Act 1998 Sch.1 Part I Art.2(1)(a), the rights defined under the Convention were expressly declared to be subject to the conditions provided for by domestic law as decided upon by domestic courts. Notwithstanding a favourable outcome for E in respect of her application before the ECHR, the lawfulness of executing the possession order would remain unaffected, although she would, if successful, be entitled to claim damages from the UK government.

LOCABAIL (UK) LTD v. WALDORF INVESTMENT CORP (NO.4) [2000] H.R.L.R. 623, Evans-Lombe, J., Ch D.

3237. **Right to fair trial – time limits – application to court out of time – strict application of procedural rules infringed right of access to court – Spain**

[European Convention on Human Rights 1950 Arts.6(1).]

P applied to the national court to have a settlement agreement relating to a dispute between herself and a neighbour declared void following the neighbour's non-compliance with the agreement due to his not being the owner of the property concerned. P had previously applied for enforcement of the agreement and the dismissal of that application was served on her at her home in Madrid. P had lodged her resposicion application with the court in Madrid but was informed that it should have been lodged with the court of first instance in Aoiz. P sent her application to the court in Aoiz, but it was declared inadmissible as being lodged outside the time limit of three days from the date of service. P applied to the Commission, complaining that the strict application of the procedural time limits had resulted in her being deprived of the opportunity of defending her legitimate interests in the courts, in violation of the European Convention on Human Rights 1950 Art.6(1). In October 1997 the Commission expressed the unanimous opinion that there had been a violation of Art.6(1).

Held, granting the application, that (1) while the right of access to a court was not absolute and the contracting States enjoyed a margin of appreciation in the limits placed on that right, those limitations could not be such as to result in the very essence of a person's right of access being impaired. Rules concerning time limits for lodging appeals were designed to ensure the proper administration of justice and compliance with the principle of legal certainty, however the application of those rules must not prevent litigants from using available remedies. In the instant case, P posted her resposicion application within the three day time limit and in the circumstances could not be accused of acting negligently in view of the short time limit and the need to state grounds for the application. To have required P to travel from her home in Madrid to the court of first instance was unreasonable, particularly in view of the fact that domestic Spanish legislation permitted courts to use the post in order to serve judicial process. The particularly strict application of the time limit in the instant case deprived P of her right to a court and there had accordingly been a violation of Art.6(1); (2) the judgment itself constituted sufficient just satisfaction for P's non-pecuniary damage, and (3) the sum of PST1,000,000, together with interest at 7.5 per cent per annum, would be awarded for costs and expenses.

PEREZ DE RADA CAVANILLES v. SPAIN (2000) 29 E.H.R.R. 109, R Bernhardt (President), ECHR.

3238. Right to family life – adoption – freeing order dispensing with mother's consent – adequacy of remedies

[European Convention on Human Rights 1950 Art.8, Art.13.]

S, the mother of A, who was born in March 1991, had a history of alcoholism. In June 1992, A was placed on the "at risk" register as the result of S being discovered drunk on a hospital floor. A had already been placed in local authority care by her father in August 1991. She had been placed with foster parents and was the subject of a series of interim care orders between September 1992 and May 1993. The local authority pursued a policy of rehabilitation during that time. Having spent time in psychiatric care for her alcoholism, S suffered a severe relapse in June 1993. In September 1993, the local authority decided to change its policy and opted for adoption instead. S had been in a clinic at the time of the meeting and was unable to attend. The court concurred with the local authority decision in an order made in October 1994, dispensing with the need for S's agreement to adoption. S complained to the European Court of Human Rights, contending that the effect of the court and local authority decisions contravened her rights under the European Convention on Human Rights Art.8 and Art.13, respectively, in that the failure to consult with her had led to the final court order and that the local authority's actions had been beyond the supervision of the court.

Held, refusing the application, that (1) it was necessary to consider whether or not the reasons adduced for the decision were sufficient for the purposes of Art.8(2). The margin of appreciation differed depending on the circumstances in issue. While local authorities enjoyed a wide margin when determining the necessity of taking a child into care, further restriction of parental rights and access was subject to closer control; (2) it had not been shown that the decision making process had been unfair, or that S had been insufficiently involved as a means of protecting her parental interests. Expert evidence showed that it would have been unsafe to return A to S while she continued drinking. Furthermore, the court had decided that to continue with the temporary placement would have been to A's detriment, and (3) S's right to apply for the care order to be discharged or to appeal against the freeing order amounted to adequate remedies for the purposes of Art.13.

SCOTT v. UNITED KINGDOM [2000] 1 F.L.R. 958, J-P Costa (President), ECHR.

3239. Right to family life – child protection – sexual abuse investigation – local authority failing to disclose video evidence

[Child Care Act 1980; European Convention on Human Rights 1950 Art.6, Art.8, Art.13.]

T lived with her daughter K in NLBC's area and the authority owed duties to K under the Child Care Act 1980. NLBC suspected that K had been sexually abused and in a video interview K disclosed that she had been sexually abused by a man of the same first name as T's boyfriend, but denied that he had been the abuser, stating that the abuser had been removed from the house. NLBC, in the person of a social worker and a psychologist, informed T of the allegations and subsequently formed the view that T would be unable to protect K. NLBC therefore obtained a place of safety order in relation to K and T applied for K to be made a ward of court. T's solicitors gained sight of the video interview a year later and discovered the denial of responsibility on the part of the current boyfriend. The wardship was discharged and K returned to live with T, who brought an action alleging breach of duty and vicarious liability in negligence against NLBC. These claims were struck out on appeal to the House of Lords ([1995] 2 A.C. 633), on the basis that no cause of action was disclosed against NLBC and that the psychologist and social worker had not assumed any professional duty of care in favour of KM. The decision also included assertions that a general duty of care was inconsistent with a statutory child protection scheme and that the powers of the Commissioner for Local Administration provided adequate redress in such situations. T obtained a reference to the European Commission on Human Rights.

Held, that (1) the delay in providing the video evidence amounted to a breach of the European Convention on Human Rights Art.8. As a result, T had not been provided with a fair or adequate opportunity to participate in the decision making procedures following K's removal. The manner in which the issue was dealt with demonstrated a lack of respect for T's and K's family life; (2) there was no breach of Art.6 in refusing to find a general common law duty of care nor in finding that the statute did not disclose any liability in damages. However, there had been a breach of Art.6 in that NLBC had failed to prevent K suffering preventable and foreseeable damage. K's access to a court had been limited by the decision of the House of Lords in holding that there was no duty of care in negligence owed by NLBC or its agents, *Osman v. United Kingdom* [1999] 1 F.L.R. 193, [1998] C.L.Y. 3102 considered, and (3) there had been a breach of Art.13 in respect of the wardship powers of the High Court because T had not been appraised of the significance of the video evidence. T should have been given an opportunity to apply for compensation for the psychiatric illness which had resulted from the facts of this case. Furthermore, the powers of the Commissioner for Local Administration did not amount to an effective remedy, as the Commissioner could only make recommendations.

TP v. UNITED KINGDOM (2000) 2 L.G.L.R. 181, Judge not applicable, Eur Comm HR.

3240. **Right to family life – deportation – offender returned to Morocco on completion of sentence for drug offences**

[European Convention on Human Rights 1950 Art.8.]

E, a Moroccan national, had lived in France since 1974. In 1989 he was convicted of drug trafficking and an order was made permanently excluding him from France at the end of his six year prison sentence. He appealed unsuccessfully in 1993 against the exclusion order, arguing that it should be rescinded as he was by then cohabiting with a French woman with whom he had a child. The order was enforced and E returned to Morocco. In 1994, E complained that the enforcement of the order was a violation of his right to family life under the European Convention on Human Rights 1950 Art.8.

Held, refusing the application, that E had a family life in France, within the meaning of Art.8, by virtue of the fact that he had lived there since he was seven and had close family members in that country. His relationship with the mother of his child was not relevant, however, as it post dated the enforcement of the order. The state's interference with the right was in accordance with the law of France. The fact that the conviction was for a serious offence, that E had committed further offences following his release from prison and that he still had ties with Morocco and had not taken French citizenship were all circumstances which weighed in favour of a finding that the interference occasioned by the order was necessary in a democratic society and pursued a legitimate aim.

EL BOUJAIDI v. FRANCE (2000) 30 E.H.R.R. 223, R Bernhardt (President), ECHR.

3241. **Right to family life – mental health – care orders made in respect of children of schizophrenic mother**

[European Convention on Human Rights Art.8.]

K, a mother, was a schizophrenic and had undergone compulsory hospital treatment for her condition. Her daughter, D, lived with her former partner, but her son, S, lived with K and her present partner, T, by whom K was expecting a third child. S was placed in short term residential care as a means of supporting the family because he was exhibiting behavioural problems. After the birth of the third child, J, an emergency care order was obtained preventing K from having unsupervised contact with J and both J and S were placed in care with restricted contact with K and T, although it was recognised that T could take care of the children. K and T complained that these actions were in breach of the European Convention on Human Rights 1950 Art.8.

Held, granting the application, that the care orders in the instant case were beyond the wide margin for assessing the necessity of taking a child into care. It was unjustified to remove J from K when she was in good health. The children were already in a safe environment where they were not at risk from K's mental health problems. The authorities had also breached the parents' rights by failing to consider reunification as an option, despite medical evidence that K would not always be unable to care for her children.

K v. FINLAND (25702/94) [2000] 2 F.L.R. 79, G Ress (President), ECHR.

3242. Right to family life – prisoners rights – child visits – validity of restrictions

[Mental Health Act 1983 s.37, s.41; Sex Offenders Act 1997 Sch.1; European Convention on Human Rights 1950 Art.8.]

ML, who had been convicted of murder, was sentenced to life imprisonment but subsequently moved to a high security hospital pursuant to the Mental Health Act 1983 ss.37 and 41. Visits by ML's nephews were not permitted until a risk assessment had been carried out. ML applied for judicial review of Health Circular HSC1999/160, which restricted visits by children to high security patients who had been convicted of murder, manslaughter or an offence listed in the Sex Offenders Act 1997 Sch.1, unless a limited category of relationship existed. The categories of permitted relationship included those where the patient was the parent or relative of the child; relative encompassing uncles and aunts. ML argued that (1) the Circular interfered with the right to family life as safeguarded by the European Convention on Human Rights 1950 Art.8, and (2) it was illogical to group those convicted of murder with sexual offenders.

Held, refusing the application, that (1) restrictions on child visits to patients at high security hospitals who had committed murder, manslaughter or sexual offences, were wholly justified and compatible with Art.8. It could not be argued that restricting visits to a limited category of relationship was irrational. No category of child was entirely excluded from visiting, as it was always possible to have recourse to the courts for a contact order, and (2) the fact that ML had been put in the same category as sexual offenders made no difference, since the nephews and nieces by whom he wished to be visited already fell within the permitted class of visitors. In any case, it was not obvious that the relationship between uncles and aunts and nieces and nephews necessarily fell within the meaning of family life under Art.8. Family life was a flexible concept and depended on the facts of each case. The purpose of the Circular was protect children and, in that regard, it was well balanced.

R. (ON THE APPLICATION OF L) v. SECRETARY OF STATE FOR HEALTH; *sub nom.* R. v. SECRETARY OF STATE FOR HEALTH, *ex p.* L (M) [2001] 1 F.L.R. 406, Scott Baker, J., QBD.

3243. Right to family life – prisoners rights – request by prisoner for right to artificially inseminate wife – justifiable interference

[Human Rights Act 1998 Sch.1 Part I Art.12.]

M, a prisoner serving a life sentence for murder, sought judicial review of the Secretary of State's refusal of his request for permission for his wife to be artificially inseminated with his sperm. M contended that (1) since prisoners retained all civil rights other than those removed expressly or by necessary implication, his right to found a family under the Human Rights Act 1998 Sch.1 Part I Art.12 necessarily implied a right to have a child by means of artificial insemination. M submitted that, given that it was not necessary to remove such a right for the preservation of prison security, order or discipline, the Secretary of State's refusal of his request amounted to a breach Art.12, and (2) the basis for refusing M's request had been flawed since the Secretary of State had wrongly concerned himself with the stability of M's marriage and the potential problems faced by a child whose father was incarcerated. M maintained that such considerations were no concern of the Secretary of State and rendered his decision irrational.

Held, refusing the application, that (1) the right to found a family did not mean that an individual was guaranteed the right at all times to conceive children, *X v. United Kingdom* (1975) 2 D. & R. 105 and *X v. Switzerland* (1978) 12 D. & R. 241 applied. M was accordingly not seeking to exercise a right but instead seeking to obtain a benefit to which he was not otherwise entitled, namely the facility to provide a semen sample for the purposes of artificial insemination, and (2) the public interest considerations cited by the Secretary of State and in particular the need to preserve public confidence in the criminal justice system would have amounted to a sufficiently "pressing need" to justify interference had any right to conceive a child by artificial insemination existed and therefore the decision could not be categorised as irrational.

R. v. SECRETARY OF STATE FOR THE HOME DEPARTMENT, *ex p.* MELLOR [2000] 2 F.L.R. 951, Forbes, J., QBD.

3244. Right to liberty – prisoners rights – discretionary life imprisonment – Parole Board reviews – period between reviews

See PENOLOGY: Oldham v. United Kingdom. §4322

3245. Right to liberty and security – childrens rights – secure accommodation order – compatibility

[Children Act 1989 s.25; Human Rights Act 1998 Sch.1 Part I Art.5.]

K, a child who had been subject to a series of secure accommodation orders made pursuant to the Children Act 1989 s.25, appealed against the latest of those orders, arguing that s.25 was not compatible with his right to liberty under the Human Rights Act 1998 Sch.1 Part I Art.5.

Held, dismissing the appeal, that while a secure accommodation order amounted to a deprivation of the liberty of a child, it was not incompatible with Art.5 since Art.5(1)(d) rendered permissible the detention of a child "by lawful order for the purpose of educational supervision". The local authority had a statutory obligation to provide K with education at the secure unit where he was detained. Furthermore, "educational supervision" was to be interpreted widely so as to encompass many aspects of the exercise by a local authority of parental rights over a child, *Koniarska v. United Kingdom (Decision on Admissibility)* (Unreported, October 12, 2000) applied.

K (A CHILD) (SECURE ACCOMMODATION ORDER: RIGHT TO LIBERTY), *Re*; *sub nom.* W BC v. DK; W BC v. AK [2001] 2 W.L.R. 1141, Dame Elizabeth Butler-Sloss (President), CA.

3246. Right to life – childrens welfare – separation of conjoined twins – inevitable death of child

The parents of six week old Siamese twins, M and J, appealed against a ruling granting medical staff authority to proceed with an elective surgical separation. M had severe brain abnormalities, no lung tissue and no properly functioning heart. The blood supply keeping M alive emanated from J who was in all other essential respects functioning and developing normally. The judge at first instance held that the operation would be in the interests of both children on the basis that for J it afforded a good chance of a normal and independent life and that for M it offered relief from a potentially painful few months of life as J grew more active. It was further held that the operation was lawful since the withdrawal of J's blood supply from M was comparable with the situation where a doctor lawfully withheld nourishment from a patient, *Airedale NHS Trust v. Bland* [1993] A.C. 789, [1993] C.L.Y. 2712 cited. In their appeal the parents contended that the judge had erred in his conclusions that the operation was both in the interest of each child and lawful.

Held, dismissing the appeal, that (1) while the wishes of the parents were entitled to great respect, the court was obliged to determine the issue on the basis that the welfare of the children was paramount, *B (A Minor) (Wardship: Medical Treatment), Re* [1981] 1 W.L.R. 1421, [1981] C.L.Y. 1790 referred to and *B (A Minor) (Wardship: Sterilisation), Re* [1988] A.C. 199, [1987] C.L.Y. 2533 applied; (2) the operation was clearly in the best interests of J since it would offer her the prospect of an independent existence and normal life expectancy, as opposed to almost certain death within a few months due to heart failure if she remained joined to M. The judge had, however, erred in his conclusion that M's life was of no value to her and that the operation, involving her certain death, was in her best interest. Each human life had an equal value and the issue for determination was not whether M's interest was best served by discontinuing treatment to prolong her life, but whether it was best served by active invasion of her bodily integrity, when the inevitable consequence of that was death. That would take away her inherent right to life; hence it could not be beneficial to her, *Bland* distinguished. Having concluded that the operation was in the interests of one child but not the other the court was obliged to conduct a balancing exercise to ascertain the least detrimental course of action, *Birmingham City Council v. H (No.3)* [1994] 2 A.C. 212, [1994] C.L.Y. 3180 considered. Having conducted such an exercise, the balance fell decisively in J's favour since M's death was inevitable within a short time and therefore the operation would be permitted, and (3) the operation would not constitute murder since the three components of the doctrine of necessity were satisfied, namely that (a) the act was required to avoid inevitable and irreparable evil; (b) no more would be done than was reasonably necessary for the purpose to be achieved, and (c) the evil to be inflicted was not disproportionate to the evil avoided, *R. v. Dudley and Stephens* (1884) L.R. 14 Q.B.D. 273 and *Airedale* considered.

A (CHILDREN) (CONJOINED TWINS: MEDICAL TREATMENT) (NO.1), *Re*; *sub nom.* A (CHILDREN) (CONJOINED TWINS: SURGICAL SEPARATION), *Re* [2001] Fam. 147, Ward, L.J., CA.

3247. **Right to life – medical treatment – child suffering from serious disabilities – interests of patient paramount**

[Human Rights Act 1998 Sch.1 Part I Art.2, Art.3.]

An NHS Trust sought a declaration that should a 19 month old child suffer future respiratory or cardiac failure or arrest they would have leave to administer a level of treatment that excluded resuscitation through artificial ventilation, but provided full palliative care which would allow the child to die peacefully and with dignity. Since birth, the child had suffered from a number of serious disabilities, notably an irreversible and worsening lung disease which resulted in a very short life expectation. The child had recovered from previous hospitalisation and was residing at home. The Trust submitted, with the support of a strong body of medical opinion, that given the child's poor state of health and prognosis it was in his best interests not to undergo resuscitation. The declaration was required, the Trust maintained, due to the fact that a decision relating to the provision of artificial ventilation might be required as a matter of urgency in the future. The child's parents opposed the application on the ground that it was premature.

Held, granting the declaration, that full palliative treatment was in the bests interests of the child and would allow him to die with dignity. The interests of a patient must be considered above all other views, even those of the parents, when deciding whether any medical treatment should be given or withheld. The body of medical opinion, in the instant case, was of the clear view that artificial ventilation would be an intrusive and painful process and would fail to offer any lasting benefit to the child. Provided that the suggested form of care was in the best interests of a child such a decision could not be said to contravene the Human Rights Act 1998 Sch.1 Part I Art.2 and Art.3.

NATIONAL HEALTH SERVICE TRUST v. D [2000] 2 F.L.R. 677, Cazalet, J., Fam Div.

3248. **Right to private life – archives – erroneous information held by intelligence services – failure to provide redress**

[European Convention on Human Rights 1950 Art.6, Art.8, Art.13.]

R applied to the Romanian court to suppress what he alleged was untrue information held about him by the state intelligence service, RIS. The information stated that R had been a subversive during the communist regime and prevented R from receiving enhanced pension rights. It was held at first instance that, although the information was false, the court had no jurisdiction to intervene. R appealed unsuccessfully and then complained to the European Commission on Human Rights, alleging breaches of the European Convention of Human Rights 1950 Art.6, Art.8 and Art.13. RIS then acknowledged that the information was false. R applied again to the appellate court, which quashed its previous decision. It declared the information to be false, but refused to award damages. The Commission found a breach of Art.8 and Art.13 and referred R's case to the European Court of Human Rights.

Held, granting the application, that the existence of secret information could violate Art.34 without R alleging it actually applied to him. Further, a decision favourable to R did not end his victim status if the authorities did not acknowledge the Convention breach or award damages. The national court's failure to rule on R's claim for damages and costs underlined this deficiency, *Klass v. Germany (A/28)* (1979-80) 2 E.H.R.R. 214, [1980] C.L.Y. 1388, *Amuur v. France* (1996) 22 E.H.R.R. 533, [1997] C.L.Y. 2766 and *Dalban v. Romania* 8 B.H.R.C. 91, [2000] C.L.Y. 3188 considered. There had been a breach of Art.8 as private life included both business and professional activities and public information covered a person's private life if stored in state files. This was especially so with information pertaining to the distant past, *Leander v. Sweden (A/116)* (1987) 9 E.H.R.R. 433, [1987] C.L.Y. 1919, *Niemietz v. Germany (A/251B)* (1993) 16 E.H.R.R. 97, [1993] C.L.Y. 2157, *Halford v. United Kingdom* [1997] I.R.L.R. 471, [1997] C.L.Y. 2795 considered. Intelligence activities had to be subject to legal safeguards and adequate supervision to comply with Art.8 and these were absent in R's case. Further, the failure to provide an effective domestic remedy violated Art.13, *Klass* considered, and the failure of the appellate court to award damages breached R's right to a fair trial under Art.6(1).

ROTARU v. ROMANIA 8 B.H.R.C. 449, L Wildhaber (President), ECHR.

3249. Right to private life – bugging – police surveillance – violation of rights

[Police and Criminal Evidence Act 1984 s.78; European Convention on Human Rights 1950 Art.6, Art.8, Art.13.]

K, a British citizen was sentenced to three years' imprisonment for the supply of drugs as a result of improperly obtained evidence from a secret listening device set up by the police in a private house without the knowledge of the occupants. K appealed against his conviction unsuccessfully to the Court of Appeal and the House of Lords. The House of Lords held that there was no right to privacy in English law, and highlighted the absence of statutory control of police surveillance. K applied to the ECHR complaining that (1) his right to privacy under the European Convention on Human Rights 1950 Art.8 had been interfered with and that interference was not "in accordance with the law" under Art.8.2 of the Convention; (2) there had been a violation of his right to a fair trial under Art.6, given that the only evidence used in the case had been obtained unlawfully, and (3) he had been denied an effective remedy in relation to his complaints which breached his right under Art.13 to an effective remedy under domestic law.

Held, that there had been a violation of Art.8 and Art.13 of the Convention. K's right to respect for private and family life had been violated and the interference was found not to be "in accordance with the law" as the phrase required compliance with domestic law. The national rules were unclear being set out only in the non statutory Home Office Guidelines and therefore the domestic law at the material time did not give protection against interference with an individual's rights. It was not the ECHR's role to determine whether the evidence was admissible and it found that the secretly taped evidence did not render the proceedings wholly unfair, as the domestic courts could have used their discretionary powers to exclude the evidence under the Police and Criminal Evidence Act 1984 s.78. The criminal proceedings did not provide a suitable remedy or protection from abuse, as the only body to which he could complain about the police surveillance was the Police Complaints Authority (PCA). The

ECHR found such an investigation would be insufficiently impartial and therefore Art.13 was also breached, *Govell v. UK* (Unreported, January 14, 1998) applied.

KHAN v. UNITED KINGDOM 8 B.H.R.C. 310, J-P Costa (President), ECHR.

3250. **Right to private life – employment – child protection – challenge to Consultancy Service Index – status of Convention rights in domestic context**

[European Convention on Human Rights 1950 Art.8.]

W sought judicial review of a decision to include his name in the Consultancy Service Index maintained by the Secretary of State for Health. The index contained the names and employment details of individuals where concerns existed as to their suitability for work with children. W submitted that whilst it had been established that the Secretary of State possessed the attributes of a natural person and that in exercising his discretion to create and maintain such a list he had acted lawfully, nevertheless the exercise of such discretion could be rendered unlawful if it did not comply with the European Convention on Human Rights 1950 Art.8.

Held, refusing the application, that Convention rights, pending the coming into force of the Human Rights Act 1998, were effective only in so far as they served to cast light upon the operation of domestic legislation already in existence. None of the authorities cited by W gave any credence to the submission that Art.8 had been afforded substantive legal status, *R. v. Chief Constable of North Wales, ex p. AB* [1999] Q.B. 396, [1998] C.L.Y. 4290 and *R. v. Secretary of State for Health, ex p. C* [2000] 1 F.L.R. 627, [2000] C.L.Y. 2212 applied.

R. v. WORCESTER CC, *ex p.* W (S); *sub nom.* R. v. WORCESTER CC, *ex p.* SW [2000] 3 F.C.R. 174, Newman, J., QBD.

3251. **Right to private life – homosexuality – group sexual activity – statutory provision violated privacy**

[Sexual Offences Act 1956 s.13; Sexual Offences Act 1967 s.1 (2) (a); European Convention on Human Rights 1950 Art.8.]

A, a homosexual, complained to the European Court of Human Rights that his conviction for gross indecency, relating to the commission of consensual, non-violent sexual acts with four other men which was depicted in a videotape seized from his home, infringed the European Convention on Human Rights 1950 Art.8. Although the acts took place in private, A was convicted under the Sexual Offences Act 1956 s.13 which made it an offence for a man to "commit an act of gross indecency with another man", whether in private or in public. A had not been convicted in relation to the making or distribution of the tapes. Although the Sexual Offences Act 1967 had decriminalised private homosexual acts between consenting adults, s.1 (2) (a) of the 1967 Act retained the prohibition on such acts where more than two men were present or taking part. A asserted that his conviction amounted to a violation of his right to a private life and was contrary to Art.8. A further contended that there were no corresponding statutory provisions regulating private acts between consenting homosexual women nor an equivalent provision for heterosexuals. The UK government argued that the activities fell outside the scope of Art.8, relying on *Laskey v. United Kingdom* (1997) 24 E.H.R.R. 39, [1997] C.L.Y. 2794 cited, and the fact that a number of people were involved and that the acts were recorded on videotape.

Held, granting the application and awarding damages of almost £21,000 and costs and expenses, that there had been a violation of Art.8. The existence of legislation prohibiting consensual sexual activity between adult males imposed unnecessary restrictions on private life in a democratic society. Whilst state interference might be justified in certain circumstances including the protection of morals or health, the activities had involved only a limited number of friends and it was unlikely that anyone else would have become aware of them. Moreover, although the acts were recorded on videotape, A had expressed a strong desire to remain anonymous and it was unlikely that he would have allowed the video to be publicly available. The acts were, therefore, purely private. As there were no public health issues to be considered, no interference with the right to engage in such activities was justified.

ADT v. UNITED KINGDOM [2000] 2 F.L.R. 697, J-P Costa (President), ECHR.

3252. Right to private life – telephone tapping – order failing to detail nature of suspected offences or duration of tap – Spain

[European Convention on Human Rights 1950 Art.8.]

VC, a Spanish citizen, worked for W as deputy head of personnel. He had previously had a relationship with M, a fellow employee. During 1984 and 1985, M received insulting and threatening anonymous phone calls and filed a complaint with an investigating judge in November 1984. The judge ordered that her telephone be tapped for a month, as provided for by the Constitution of Spain Art.18(3). During that period, a number of suspect calls were made from a telephone on W's premises to which only five persons, including VC, had access. The judge made an order for the further tapping of M's telephone in May 1985. In November 1985 the judge made an order under Art.18(3) of the Constitution for the tapping of VC's private telephone lines for one month. The monitoring showed that several calls had been made from them to M, but the caller could not be identified. In February 1986 VC was charged with making grave insults and threats following a search of his home and office for which he was sentenced to four months' imprisonment and ordered to pay fines and compensation. The court found that neither the monitoring nor the searches had been decisive in establishing VC's guilt. VC's appeal to the Supreme Court was dismissed and his appeal to the Constitutional Court on the grounds that his right to confidentiality in making telephone calls, as provided by Art.18(3), had been violated, was also dismissed. His complaint to the Commission of a violation of his right to respect for his private life and correspondence, contrary to the European Convention on Human Rights 1950 Art.8, was upheld in April 1997 by a majority.

Held, granting the application, that the monitoring of telephone conversations constituted an interference with the right to respect for private life and correspondence in breach of Art.8(2), unless it was carried out in accordance with a legal provision capable of protecting against arbitrary interference by the state with the rights guaranteed, *Malone v. United Kingdom (A/82)* (1985) 7 E.H.R.R. 14 applied. Further, the relevant provisions of domestic law must be both accessible and their consequences foreseeable, in that the conditions and circumstances in which the state was empowered to take secret measures such as telephone monitoring were clearly indicated, *Kruslin v. France (A/176-B)* (1990) 12 E.H.R.R. 547, [1990] C.L.Y. 2558 and *Halford v. United Kingdom* [1997] I.R.L.R. 471, [1997] C.L.Y. 2795 applied. In particular, the avoidance of abuse demanded certain minimum safeguards, including the conditions regarding the definition of categories of persons liable to have their telephones tapped, and the nature of offences that could give rise to such an order. In the instant case, the order permitting the monitoring of VC's private line omitted a statement detailing either of these requirements as well as failing to stipulate the duration of the tapping.

VALENZUELA CONTRERAS v. SPAIN (1999) 28 E.H.R.R. 483, R Bernhardt (President), ECHR.

3253. Sex discrimination – fire services – female firefighters – aerobic test setting standards of fitness not achievable by females – Canada

[British Columbia Human Rights Code 1996 s.13.]

M was dismissed after four years as a firefighter when she failed an aerobic test introduced by her employers, BC. Her union, BCGSEU, brought an action claiming that she had been discriminated against on the grounds of sex in contravention of the British Columbia Human Rights Code 1996 s.13(1) as women tended to have a lower aerobic capability than men. The arbitrator found for M, but on appeal, BC's defence that the discrimination was an occupational necessity and therefore permitted under s.13(4) was successful. M appealed to the Supreme Court.

Held, allowing the appeal, that BC had shown partial compliance with the requirements of s.13(4) in that the discriminatory test was logically linked to the need for firefighters to have high standards of fitness given the physically demanding nature of their job, and the test was introduced in good faith. However BC had not shown that passing the test was a bona fide occupational requirement and that BC would suffer undue hardship if the test was prohibited.

BRITISH COLUMBIA GOVERNMENT & SERVICE EMPLOYEES UNION v. BRITISH COLUMBIA 7 B.H.R.C. 437, McLachlin, J., Sup Ct (Can).

3254. Sex discrimination – homosexuality – financial provision on breakdown of relationship – exclusion of homosexual couples from legislative protection – Canada

[Canadian Charter of Rights and Freedoms 1982 s.1, s.15; Family Law Act RSO 1990 s.29.]

M and H, both women, lived together in a stable relationship for five years, in a house owned by H. Their joint business ran into financial difficulties, which caused problems in their relationship, and M left. She brought an application for spousal support under the Family Law Act RSO 1990 and for a declaration that s.29 of the Act discriminated against same-sex couples as they were not included in the definition of "spouse" which applied to unmarried heterosexual couples. The judge found that s.29 did contravene the right to equal protection by the law in the Canadian Charter of Rights and Freedoms 1982 s.15, and this was upheld by the Court of Appeal. The Attorney General appealed to the Supreme Court on the grounds that the discrimination was justified by s.1 of the Charter. H and M subsequently settled the issues between them.

Held, dismissing the appeal, that the 1990 Act did violate s.15 in that it discriminated against same-sex couples, who were already at a disadvantage in society. The purpose of the legislation was, to enable fair resolution of financial issues following the breakdown of an interdependent relationship and did not require the exclusion of same-sex partners. The infringement of s.15 was not a reasonable limit which could be demonstrably justified in a free and democratic society under s.1 of the Charter. The exclusion denied same-sex partners a fundamental right and gave the impression that such relationships were of lower status than heterosexual relationships, which could only have a detrimental effect on the human dignity of those in same-sex relationships.

ATTORNEY GENERAL FOR ONTARIO v. M 7 B.H.R.C. 489, Cory, J., Sup Ct (Can).

3255. Surveillance – authorisation by public authorities

REGULATION OF INVESTIGATORY POWERS (PRESCRIPTION OF OFFICES, RANKS, AND POSITIONS) ORDER 2000, SI 2000 2417; made under the Regulation of Investigatory Powers Act 2000 s.30, s.78. In force: September 25, 2000; £2.00.

This Order prescribes offices, ranks and positions for the purposes of the Regulation of Investigatory Powers Act 2000 s.30(1), under which individuals holding such offices, ranks or positions are designated persons for the purposes of granting authorisations under s.28 and s.29 of the Act.

3256. Surveillance – authorisations – notification to Surveillance Commissioner

REGULATION OF INVESTIGATORY POWERS (NOTIFICATION OF AUTHORISATIONS ETC.) ORDER 2000, SI 2000 2563; made under the Regulation of Investigatory Powers Act 2000 s.35. In force: September 25, 2000; £1.50.

This Order specifies the matters which must be notified to an ordinary Surveillance Commissioner when a person grants, renews or cancels a police or customs authorisation for the carrying out of intrusive surveillance under the Regulation of Investigatory Powers Act 2000 Part II.

3257. Surveillance – covert human intelligence sources – authorisations – cancellation

REGULATION OF INVESTIGATORY POWERS (CANCELLATION OF AUTHORISATION) REGULATIONS 2000, SI 2000 2794; made under the Regulation of Investigatory Powers Act 2000 s.45. In force: November 6, 2000; £1.50.

The Regulation of Investigatory Powers Act 2000 s.45 imposes a duty on a number of persons to cancel authorisations under Part II of the Act, provided certain conditions are met. These Regulations address the case where the duty falls on a person who is no longer available to perform it by providing for the duty to fall instead on the person who has taken over most of that person's responsibilities and providing a power to appoint a person for this specific purpose.

3258. Surveillance – covert human intelligence sources – authorisations – juveniles

REGULATION OF INVESTIGATORY POWERS (JUVENILES) ORDER 2000, SI 2000 2793; made under the Regulation of Investigatory Powers Act 2000 s.29, s.43. In force: November 6, 2000; £1.50.

The Regulation of Investigatory Powers Act 2000 s.29 allows authorisations to be granted for the use or conduct of covert human intelligence sources. This Order contains special provisions for the cases of covert human intelligence sources who are under eighteen.

3259. Surveillance – covert human intelligence sources – authorisations – source records

REGULATION OF INVESTIGATORY POWERS (SOURCE RECORDS) ORDER 2000, SI 2000 2725; made under the Regulation of Investigatory Powers Act 2000 s.29. In force: November 11, 2000; £1.50.

The Regulation of Investigatory Powers Act 2000 s.29(2)(c) provides that a person may not grant an authorisation for the conduct or use of a covert human intelligence source unless he believes that arrangements exist that satisfy the requirements of s.29(5), which include the requirement that the arrangements must be adequate to ensure that the records relating to the source contain particulars of certain matters. These Regulations specify those matters.

3260. Torture – police officers – physical and mental assaults in police custody – effective remedy implied a thorough and diligent investigation – sufficient gravity of suffering

[European Convention on Human Rights 1950 Art.3, Art.6.]

In November 1991, S was held in custody for four days in connection with a police investigation into a drug ring. At a pre trial hearing on drug related charges, S complained that he had been physically abused during his detention, including being beaten, urinated on and dragged by the hair. The judge ordered a forensic medical investigation, which reported that injuries suffered by S had occurred during a period of time that matched S's detention period. In February 1993, following his conviction on the drug charges, S lodged a criminal complaint against the police for assault occasioning bodily harm, including damage to his eyesight, and rape. At an identification parade S picked out four police officers. The case was transferred between various courts, and towards the end of 1998 the officers were convicted. However, in July 1999 the Court of Appeal allowed an appeal by the officers in relation to the rape charge on the grounds of insufficient evidence. S made a complaint to the European Commission of Human Rights, alleging that the actions of the police officers had been in violation of the European Convention on Human Rights 1950 Art.3, the guarantee against torture, and that the length of the proceedings had violated Art.6(1), right to a fair trial within a reasonable time. The French government objected to the case being brought before the ECHR on the grounds that S had not exhausted the available domestic remedy since S could claim damages from the police as a civil party joining the criminal action against the police. The government argued that this was an effective remedy. The Commission held unanimously that there had been such violations, and referred the matter to the European Court of Human Rights.

Held, that there could be no departure from Art.3 even in the demanding situation of tackling serious crime. As the protection of human rights had come to achieve greater prominence, acts that were formally seen as "inhuman and degrading" were becoming classifiable as torture, particularly when inflicted on those in custody. Although S's claim of rape was not made out, there was medical evidence to support his allegations of physical assault, which had been particularly reprehensible in their cruelty, their prolonged extent and the feelings of fear and inferiority which they had been calculated to cause in S. The assaults therefore constituted torture within the meaning of Art.3. In relation to Art.6(1), the fact that the proceedings had been brought in connection with allegations that came within Art.3 placed an onus on the court to investigate the matter properly and identify and deal with those responsible. The case was not legally complex and the courts were at least in part to blame for the huge delay, therefore S had been denied a fair trial within a reasonable time, nor had he been able to avail himself of an effective remedy through the domestic proceedings.

SELMOUNI v. FRANCE (2000) 29 E.H.R.R. 403, L Wildhaber (President), ECHR.

3261. Trespass – notice – protest at New Zealand Parliament – validity of notice by Speaker to leave the ground

[Trespass Act 1980 (New Zealand) s.3(1); Bill of Rights Act 1990 (New Zealand).]

B was among a group of 300 students protesting in the grounds of the New Zealand Parliament building. Initially their protest was authorised by the Speaker of the House of Representatives, but after an hour a member of his staff decided the protest should end. The protesters were informed by a member of the group and a police officer and warned that they would be arrested for trespass if they did not leave. Seventy five protesters were arrested under the Trespass Act 1980 s.3(1) but the case against them was dismissed after a preliminary hearing. The police appealed by way of case stated, requesting a determination as to whether (1) the Speaker had exercised his powers as occupier in accordance with the Bill of Rights Act 1990; (2) those powers could only be exercised where protesters were acting in an unlawful or disorderly fashion, and (3) in what circumstances a warning from the Speaker under s.3 would be invalid.

Held, permanently staying the prosecutions, that the Speaker, as the person elected by the House of Representatives to control use of the grounds, was authorised to exercise the rights of an occupier and to give warnings in relation to trespass; (1) although the 1990 Act did not apply to private activities, the Speaker was bound by it as he was carrying out a public role in his capacity as occupier; (2) the Speaker had to carry out that role reasonably, which would depend on all the facts of the case and not just on the protesters' behaviour, and (3) a warning by a person authorised to revoke the permission to be on the land was valid, provided those warned knew and understood that they had to leave, the actual means of communication being immaterial.

POLICE (NEW ZEALAND) v. BEGGS 8 B.H.R.C. 116, Gendall, J., HC (NZ).

3262. Tribunals – Investigatory Powers Tribunal – rules

INVESTIGATORY POWERS TRIBUNAL RULES 2000, SI 2000 2665; made under the Regulation of Investigatory Powers Act 2000 s.69. In force: October 2, 2000; £2.00.

These Rules, which are for the Tribunal established under the Regulation of Investigatory Powers Act 2000 Part IV, govern the jurisdiction described in s.65(2)(a) and (b) of the Act. They make provision in relation to cases brought under the Human Rights Act 1998 s.7(1)(a) for which the Tribunal is the appropriate tribunal and complaints for which the Tribunal is the appropriate forum.

3263. Unmarried fathers – parental responsibility – child abduction
See FAMILY LAW: B v. United Kingdom. §2453

3264. Publications
Addo, Michael K. – Freedom of Expression and the Criticism of Judges: a Comparative Study of European Legal Standards. Hardback: £55.00. ISBN 0-7546-2129-4. Ashgate Publishing Limited.

Alston, Philip – Promoting Human Rights Through Bills of Rights: Comparative Perspectives. Hardback: £55.00. ISBN 0-19-825822-4. Clarendon Press.

Austin, R.C.; Bonner, David; Whitty, Noel – Legal Protection of Civil Liberties. Paperback: £26.95. ISBN 0-406-55511-7. Butterworths Law.

Beatson, Jack; Cripps, Yvonne – Freedom of Expression and Freedom of Information. Hardback: £35.00. ISBN 0-19-826839-4. Oxford University Press.

Beyani, Chaloka – Human Rights Standards and the Movement of People Within States. Oxford Monographs in International Law. Hardback: £45.00. ISBN 0-19-826821-1. Oxford University Press.

Blackburn, Robert – European Convention on Human Rights: the Impact of the European Convention on Human Rights in the Legal and Political Systems of Member States. Hardback: £50.00. ISBN 0-7201-2229-5. Mansell.

Clayton, Richard; Tomlinson, Hugh; George, Carol – Law of Human Rights. Hardback: £145.00. ISBN 0-19-826223-X. Oxford University Press.

De Mello, Rambert – Human Rights Act 1998: a Practitioner's Guide. Paperback: £19.95. ISBN 0-85308-502-1. Jordans.

Donson, Fiona – Legal Intimidation. Paperback: £16.95. ISBN 1-85343-504-X. Free Association Books.

Doyle, Brian – Disability Discrimination. 3rd Ed. Paperback: £39.00. ISBN 0-85308-568-4. Family Law.

Edge, Peter; Harvey, Graham – Law and Religion in Contemporary Society: Communities, Individualism and the State. Hardback: £45.00. ISBN 0-7546-1306-2. Ashgate Publishing Limited.

Ewing, Keith; Gearty, Conor Anthony – Struggle for Civil Liberties: Political Freedom and the Rule of Law in Britain, 1914-1945. Hardback: £50.00. ISBN 0-19-825665-5. Clarendon Press.

Falk, Richard A. – Human Rights Horizons. Hardback: £45.00. ISBN 0-415-92512-6. Paperback: £14.99. ISBN 0-415-92513-4. Routledge, an imprint of Taylor & Francis Books Ltd.

Harris, David; O'Boyle, Michael – Cases and Materials on the European Convention on Human Rights. Paperback: £21.95. ISBN 0-406-90328-X. Butterworths.

Harris, D.J.; O'Boyle, M.; Warbrick, C. – Law of the European Convention on Human Rights. 2nd Ed. Paperback: £28.95. ISBN 0-406-90594-0. Butterworths.

Human Rights Bill: the Debate in Parliament. The Justice Series: Putting Rights Into Practice. Paperback: £15.00. ISBN 1-84113-098-2. Hart Publishing.

Hunt, Murray; Singh, Rabinder – Practitioner's Guide to the Impact of the Human Rights Act 1998. Paperback: £22.00. ISBN 1-901362-49-3. Hart Publishing.

Jones, Richard; Gnanapala, Welhengama; Jones, Richard – Ethnic Minorities and the Law. GEMS No 5. Paperback: £18.95. ISBN 1-85856-138-8. Trentham Books.

Koh, Harold Hongju; Slye, Ronald C. – Deliberative Democracy and Human Rights. Hardback: £26.00. ISBN 0-300-07583-9. Paperback: £12.95. ISBN 0-300-08167-7. Yale University Press.

Lord Lester of Herne Hill; Pannick, David – Human Rights Law and Practice Supplement: Supplement. Paperback: £30.00. ISBN 0-406-93231-X. Butterworths Law.

Moore, Nina M. – Governing Race: Policy, Process and the Politics of Race. Hardback: £48.95. ISBN 0-275-96761-1. Praeger Publishers.

Murray, Rachel – African Commission on Human and Peoples' Rights and International Law. Hardback: £30.00. ISBN 1-84113-122-9. Hart Publishing.

O'Donovan, Katherine; Rubin, Gerry R. – Human Rights and Legal History: Essays in Honour of Brian Simpson. Hardback: £40.00. ISBN 0-19-826496-8. Oxford University Press.

Peck, Lib; Cooper, Jonathan; Owers, Anne – Human Rights Bill: the Debate in Parliament. The Justice Series: Putting Rights Into Practice. Paperback: £15.00. ISBN 1-84113-098-2. Hart Publishing.

Robertson, Geoffrey – Crimes Against Humanity: the Struggle for Global Justice. Paperback (B format): £8.99. ISBN 0-14-025029-8. Penguin Books.

Scott, Craig – Torture As Tort: Comparative Perspective on the Development of Transnational Human Rights Litigation. Hardback: £35.00. ISBN 1-84113-060-5. Hart Publishing.

Steiner, Henry; Alston, Philip – International Human Rights in Context. 2nd Ed. Hardback: £60.00. ISBN 0-19-829848-X. Oxford University Press Inc, USA.

Supperstone, Michael; Pitt-Payne, Timothy – Guide to the Freedom of Information Act 2000. Paperback: £35.00. ISBN 0-406-93145-3. Butterworths Law.

Thierstein, Joel; Kamalipour, Yahya R. – Religion, Law, and Freedom: a Global Perspective. Hardback: £48.95. ISBN 0-275-96452-3. Praeger Publishers.

Wadham, John; Mountfield, Helen – Blackstone's Guide to the Human Rights Act 1998. 2nd Ed. Hardback: £21.95. ISBN 1-84174-173-6. Blackstone Press.

Wheeler, Nicholas J. – Saving Strangers: Humanitarian Intervention in International Society. Hardback: £30.00. ISBN 0-19-829621-5. Oxford University Press.